# CONTEMPORARY

# DESIGNERS

**CONTEMPORARY ARTS SERIES**

Contemporary Architects

Contemporary Artists

Contemporary Designers

Contemporary Fashion

Contemporary Masterworks

Contemporary Photographers

# CONTEMPORARY
# DESIGNERS

THIRD EDITION

Editor:
Sara Pendergast

Advisers:
Arnold Aronson, Howard Cohen
Carainn Childers Davies, Mary W. Davis
Kenji Ekuan, Nancye Green
Kathryn Hiesinger, Edmund Hubbard
Dr. Angela Schönberger, Robert Schwartz

## ST. JAMES PRESS
AN IMPRINT OF GALE

Detroit • New York • Toronto • London

Sara Pendergast, *Editor*
Tom Pendergast, *Lead Copyeditor*
Anne Boyd, Jonna Buell, Montgomery Buell, Richard Kimball, Tim Seul, and Jill Winski, *Copyeditors*
Nancy E. Boffa-Generelli, Daniela Cavallero, Michael Martin, and Tim Seul, *Translators*


ST. JAMES PRESS STAFF

David Collins, *Project Coordinator*
Laura Standley Berger, Peg Bessette, Joann Cerrito, Nicolet V. Elert, Miranda H. Ferrara,
Janice Jorgensen, Margaret Mazurkiewicz, Michael J. Tyrkus, *Contributing Editors*
Peter M. Gareffa, *Managing Editor, St. James Press*

Mary Beth Trimper, *Production Director*
Shanna Heilveil, *Production Assistant*

Cynthia Baldwin, *Art Director*
C. J. Jonik, *Desktop Publisher*
Pamela A. Hayes, *Photography Coordinator*
Randy Bassett, *Image Database Supervisor*
Mikal Ansari, Robert Duncan, *Imaging Specialists*

Victoria B. Cariappa, *Research Manager*
Jennifer Lund, *Research Specialist*
Julia C. Daniel, *Research Associate*

∞™ The paper used in this publication meets the minimum
requirements of American National Standard for Information Sciences—
Permanence Paper for Printed Library Materials, ANSI Z39.48-1984.

A CIP record is available from the British Library
ISBN 1-55862-184-9

Printed in the United States of America
Published simultaneously in the United Kingdom

St. James Press is an imprint of Gale

Cover photograph—Don Chadwick: *Aeron Chair*, (with Bill Stumpf) for Herman Miller, 1995, courtesy of the designer

10 9 8 7 6 5 4 3 2

# CONTENTS

Editor's Note                                    *page* vii

Advisers and Contributors                              ix

List of Entrants                                      xiii

ENTRIES A-Z                                             1

Nationality Index                                    945

Design Field Index                                   955

Notes on Advisers and Contributors                   971

# EDITOR'S NOTE

This book was compiled based on the need for detailed information about the background, work, and philosophies of important contemporary designers. While the book focuses on living designers, it also includes some deceased designers whose work continues to influence current design activity. The advisory board compiled a comprehensive list of international designers for inclusion, and the designers were chosen for inclusion based on the quality of the information uncovered through research and mailings that were made to all living designers on the list. Because in some cases much of the information needed to come directly from the designers themselves, the list of designers in the third edition is by no means complete and should not be taken as inclusive. There are many more qualified and important designers who could have been included and whose work influences current design activity. *Contemporary Designers* is thus a sampling of the best the design world has to offer and as such gives an overall view of the trends and dialogue of design.

## Entry Format

Entries in *Contemporary Designers* provide in-depth biographical, bibliographical, and critical information. The format of each entry is designed for ease of use—by students, teachers, scholars, librarians, curators, and the general public. Though the format may seem quite standardized, the entries themselves can be idiosyncratic. In an effort to impart the richest information we allowed for partial information to be published so that readers could be given leads to interesting and rare information about the designers. In addition, we allowed for easily recognizable differences in spellings to maintain the original voice and style of the designer and the critical essayists. *Contemporary Designers* entries are arranged as follows:

> **Born:** includes name if different, place, and date.
> **Education:** includes school, degree, and year.
> **Military Service:** includes branch of service, years, and rank upon departure.
> **Family:** includes marriage(s) and children.
> **Career:** includes position, firm, place, year(s), in chronological order. If the designer has a primary and secondary career, the primary career is listed first.
> **Member:** includes professional, civic, and other affiliations.
> **Exhibitions:** includes name, place, and date of exhibition.
> **Collections:** lists name and place of museum.
> **Honors:** lists name, awarding body, and date of award.
> **Address(es):** lists address of designer or contact person.
> **Died:** includes place and date of death.

> **Works:** includes a chronological list of the designer's important and representative works.

> **Publications:** includes two lists; one of publications *by* the designer and another of publications *on* the designer.

In addition to this standardized information, most of the entries also include the following:

> **Designer Comment:** Many of the designers included their thoughts on their work or the design world in general.

> **Critical Essay:** Signed critical essays, written by a diverse group of scholars, librarians, free-lance writers and consultants on design, and fellow designers, discuss the distinguishing characteristics of the designers' work. The approach taken with each essay varies, but the emphasis is on that which makes the designer's work important to his/her own field of design or to the design world in general.

**Representative Photograph of Work:** Designers were asked to select a photograph or illustration of a representative work.

## Indexes

In addition to the alphabetically arranged List of Entrants two indexes provide users easy access to individual entries:

**Nationality Index:** Alphabetically lists featured designers according to country of origin, lengthy residence, and/or country of citizenship.

**Design Field Index:** Alphabetically lists featured designers according to the fields of design in which they practice.

## Comments

While the objective of this book is to supply detailed biographical, bibliographical, and critical information on almost 690 designers, the aggregate of the information should not be overlooked. Though few will read every page of *Contemporary Designers,* the pages hold a diverse and lively dialogue about the trends in and across design fields: the designers' and critical essayists' opinions can give the reader a sense of the different approaches taken in different fields of design as well as the many commonalities in thinking about the future of design. While many readers will use this book to look up one designer at a time, curious readers are urged to take a bit longer and use the Nationality and Design Field indexes to read about the differences and similarities of these designers' backgrounds and approaches to their work. To get a sense of the dialogue in the book you may want to read Knud Holscher, Shuya Kaneko (GK Graphics), Vico Magistretti, Tucker Viemeister, and George Yabu's comments and Peter Blake, Kristina Goodrich, Jeremy Myerson, and Delbert Unruh's essays, which are particularly interesting.

## Acknowledgments

The editor gratefully acknowledges the members of the advisory board for their generous expertise, valuable suggestions and assistance, and general collaboration; Tom Pendergast for his diligent efforts to organize the sometimes sparse and incomplete information, his technical assistance, and his enthusiastic support throughout this project; Dave Collins for his advice and support; Félix Beltràn and Burton Kramer for their generous help in locating some designers; Vivianna Bülow-Hübe for her tireless efforts with her fax machine; Kristina Goodrich for her support and assistance in locating some designers; Richard Martin for his research assistance with fashion designers; Margaret Chamberlain for her advice regarding photograph copyrights; Yoko Koike for her valuable assistance; and all the designers without whose time and efforts much of this book would not have been possible. Though all of these people contributed to that which is valuable in this book, any errors or omissions are entirely the responsibility of the editor.

## Suggestions Are Welcome

The editor hopes that you find *Contemporary Designers* a useful reference tool and welcomes comments and suggestions. Please send comments to: The Editor, *Contemporary Designers,* St. James Press, 835 Penobscot Building, Detroit, MI 48226.

# ADVISERS

Arnold Aronson
Howard Cohen
Carainn Childers Davies
Mary W. Davis
Kenji Ekuan

Nancye Green
Kathryn Hiesinger
Edmund Hubbard
Angela Schönberger
Robert Schwartz

# CONTRIBUTORS

Mariane Aav
Sandra Michels Adams
James M. Alexander
Arnold Aronson
Andrea Arsenault
Clive Ashwin
Carl Auböck
Christopher Matthew Bakkila
John Barnicoat
James Beck
Reed Benhamou
Robert Blaich
Peter Blake
Charlotte Blauensteiner
Sarah Bodine
Brian Boigon
Szymon Bojko
Monica Boman
Nina Bremer
Jarka M. Burian
Frances Butler
Elizabeth Douthitt Byrne
Paul Caffrey
Ralph Caplan
Ken Carls
Peter Carlsen
Noel Carrington
Stefano Casciani
Barbara Cavaliere
Hazel Clark
Howard E. Cohen
Mildred Constantine
Hazel Conway
Anthony J. Coulson
Elizabeth Crawford
Catherine L. Currier
Helena Dahlback Lutteman
Tom David

Haig David-West
Carainn Childers Davies
Mary W. Davis
Toni Del Renzo
Diana De Marly
Florence D'Emilia
Friedrich Dieckmann
M. Droste
Michael Dunas
Kenji Ekuan
Carla Enbom
Lloyd C. Engelbrecht
Peter J. Exley
Alison Fitzgerald
Jorge Frascara
Arnold Friendmann
Norman Gambill
Madge Garland
Larry Gaudet
Kenneth Gaulin
Krisitna Goodrich
Rachel Gotlieb
Al Gowan
Grant Greapentrog
Nancye Green
Gertrud Gustafsson
Shukuro Habara
John Halas
Ulf Hård af Segerstad
Richard Hayhurst
Steven Heller
Kathryn B. Hiesinger
John E. Hirsch
Augustine Hope
Nancy House
Edmund Hubbard
D. Ichiyama
Alaboigoni Inko-Dokubo

Lee Jacobson
Jan Jennings
David Johnson
Toshihiro Katayama
Joel Katz
Deirdre Kerr
Robin Kinross
Sheila Klos
Harold Koda
Burton Kramer
Marjorie Kriebel
William Victor Kriebel
Paul Kunkel
Wolfgang Lange
Michael Large
Edith Cortland Lee
Julius Lengert
Maud Lindgren
Herbert Lindinger
Lennart Lindkvist
Ake Livstedt
Gunilla Lundahl
Floyd W. Martin
Richard Martin
Leena Maunula
Catherine McDermott
Anne McLean
Phillip B. Meggs
Gloria Menard
Russell Merzdorf
Lois Irene Miklas
Tom Mikotowicz
Elena Millie
Karen Moon
Jeremy Myerson
Eckhard Neumann
Kristina Paatero
Philip Pacey
Juhani Pallasmaa
Tapio Periainen
Ingeborg Pietzsch
Henry Pisciotta
André Pozner
Arthur J. Pulos

Roger Remington
Richard V. Riddell
Alan Rosenberg
Virginia Rose
Patricia A. Russac
Douglas A. Russell
Joseph Rykwert
Kunio Sano
Jan Sawka
Pamela Scheinman
Helmut Schmid
Angela Schönberger
Robert T. Schwartz
Lydia Ferrabee Sharman
Paul Shaw
Harlan Sifford
Carin Sjölander
Gillion Skellenger
Michael Robert Soluri
Jukka Sorjo-Smeds
Herbert Spencer
Mafalda Spencer
Raymond Spilman
Gordon Steele
Jerry Steimle
Ivar Stranger
Zenobiusz Strzelecki
Barbara Sudick
Masaaki Tanaka
Benjamin de Brie Taylor
Jacques Toussaint
Teal Ann Triggs
Maria Tulokas
Camilo Umaña
Delbert Unruh
G. Votolato
George Walsh
Hiroshi Watanabe
David W. Weiss
Dag Widman
Danuta Wróblewska
Richard Saul Wurman
Liz Wylie
Barbara Young

CONTEMPORARY
# DESIGNERS

# LIST OF ENTRANTS

Alvar Aalto
Eero Aarnio
Ken Adam
Adolfo
Mehemed Fehmy Agha
Agnes B.
Lis Ahlmann
Tom Ahlström
Otl Aicher
Anni Albers
Franco Albini
Walter Albini
Theoni Aldredge
Alan Aldridge
Walter Heinz Allner
Emilio Ambasz
Junichi Arai
Bruce Archer
Giorgio Armani
Boris Aronson
Paul Rodney Arthur
Laura Ashley
Brian Asquith
Associated Space Design
Sergio Asti
Carl Auböck
Gae Aulenti
Kiyoshi Awazu
Åke Axelsson

Lida Baday
Cristobal Balenciaga
Bogusław Balicki
Douglas Cameron Ball
Walter Ballmer
Pierre Balmain
Scott Barrie
Carlo Bartoli
James Basevi
Basile
Saul Bass
John Bates
Hans Theodor Baumann
Edward Bawden
Howard Bay
Herbert Bayer
Geoffrey Beene
Melchiorre Bega
Mario Bellini
Félix Beltrán
Maria Benktzon

Ward Bennett
Prince Sigvard Bernadotte
Lucian Bernhard
Harry Bertoia
Betanova
Laura Biagiotti
Michael Bierut
Max Bill
Joseph Binder
Acton Bjørn
Karin Björquist
Misha Black
Robert I. Blaich
Karl Oskar Blase
Bill Blass
Cini Boeri
Antonio Boggeri
Marc Bohan
Jonas Bohlin
Rodolfo Bonetto
Gui Bonsiepe
John Box
Robert Boyle
Bruno Bozzetto
Peter Bradford
Marianne Brandt
Pieter Brattinga
Marcel Breuer
Brioni
Alexey Brodovitch
Robert Brunner
Erik Bruun
Rut Bryk
Torun Vivianna Bülow-Hübe
Aaron Burns
Stephen Burrows
Will Burtin
John Bury
Rido Busse
Frances Butler

Jean Cacharel
Henry Thomas Cadbury-Brown
Max Caflisch
Pierre Cardin
Jean Carlu
Eugenio Carmi
Ben Carré
Edward Carrick
David Carson

Matthew Carter
Hugh Casson
Anna Castelli Ferrieri
Achille Castiglioni
Livio Castiglioni
Pier Giacomo Castiglioni
Pierluigi Cerri
Don Chadwick
Chamberlin Powell and Bon
Gabrielle Chanel
Pierre Charbonnier
Ivan Chermayeff
Serge Chermayeff
Chermayeff & Geismar
Paolo Chessa
Seymour Chwast
Roman Cieslewicz
Paul Colin
David Colley
Susan Collier/Sarah Campbell
Joe Colombo
Giulio Confalonieri
Sybil Connolly
Terence Conran
David Consuegra
Muriel Cooper
Paul Costelloe
André Courrèges
Morison S. Cousins
Lucien Coutaud
Enrico Coveri
Jonathan Crinion
Theo Crosby
Wim Crouwel
Donna Cummings
Gunnar Cyrén

Louis Danziger
Haig David-West
Lucienne Day
Richard Day
Robin Day
Tom Deacon
Jean D'Eaubonne
Jean-Charles de Castelbajac
Jan de Fouw
Hubert de Givenchy
Rudolph de Harak
Oscar de la Renta
Sonia Delaunay
Jean-Claude de Luca
Michele De Lucchi
Willy Maks De Majo
Donald Deskey
Ingrid Dessau
Niels Diffrient
Jay Doblin
Danilo Donati
Rinaldo Donzelli
Louis Dorfsman

Henry Dreyfuss
Raoul Pène du Bois
Duffy-Eley-Giffone-Worthington
Joseph D'Urso
Karl Duschek
Roman Duszek

Charles Eames
Ray Eames
Tom Eckersley
Tias Eckhoff
Heinz Edelmann
Hans Ehrich
Hermann Eidenbenz
Kenji Ekuan
Perry Ellis
Emigre
Environetics Group
Hans Erni
Erté
Vuokko Eskolin-Nurmesniemi
Hartmut Esslinger

Age Faith-Ell
Abdelkader Farrah
Gene Federico
Fendi
Perry Ferguson
Gianfranco Ferré
Edward Fields
Jochen Finke
Elio Fiorucci
Tazeena Firth
Richard Fischer
Louis Fishauf
Jules Fisher
Willy Fleckhaus
Allan Robb Fleming
Alan Fletcher
John Fluevog
Jean-Michel Folon
Colin Forbes
Gregory Fossella
Peter Fox
Kaj Franck
André François
Gina Fratini
Gianfranco Frattini
Achim Freyer
Friedrich Friedl
Arnold Friedmann
Sven Fristedt
frogdesign Inc.
A. G. Fronzoni
Anthony Froshaug
Adrian Frutiger
S. Neil Fujita
Shigeo Fukuda
Richard Buckminster Fuller

James Fulton
Margaret Furse
Roger Furse

James Galanos
Abram Games
James Gardner
Kenneth Garland
Jean-Paul Gaultier
Frank Gehry
Thomas H. Geismar
Steff Geissbuhler
Rudi Gernreich
Robert Gersin
Karl Gerstner
Piero Gherardi
Dante Giacosa
Bill Gibb
Arthur Gibney
Claude Gidman
Bob Gill
Alexander Girard
Giorgetto Giugiaro
GK Graphics
Milton Glaser
Albrecht Zeppo Graf Goertz
Ernö Goldfinger
Guillermo Gonzalez Ruiz
Mordecai Gorelik
Mieczyslaw Górowski
Gottschalk and Ash
Kenneth Grange
Grapus
Michael Graves
Eileen Gray
Milner Gray
J. Malcolm Grear
Vittorio Gregotti
April Greiman
Madame Grès
Franco Grignani
Anton Grot
Maija Grotell
Jerzy Gurawski
GVO Inc.

Halston
Denis Handy
William J. Hannon
Rolf Harder
Cathy Hardwick
Elisabet Hasselberg-Olsson
Ashley Havinden
Yoshio Hayakawa
Edith Head
Hein Heckroth
Desmond Heeley
Simo Heikkila
Pieter Hein
Dale Hennesy

F. H. K. Henrion
Jocelyn Herbert
Robert Heritage
Erik Herlow
Helena Hernmarck
Karl-Ernst Herrmann
David Hicks
Ernst and Ursula Hiestand
Hans Hillmann
Hubert Hilscher
George Him
Hipgnosis
Catherine Hipp
Gerald P. Hirshberg
Hans Peter Hoch
Armin Hofmann
Paul Hogan
Erik Höglund
James Holland
Hans Hollein
Knud Holscher
Harry Horner
Ann Hould-Ward
Max Huber
Johan Huldt
Allen Hurlburt
Ulrica Hydman-Vallien

Takenobu Igarashi
Giancarlo Iliprandi
ISD
Fujiwo Ishimoto
Robert Israel
Alec Issigonis
Shima Ito

Sally Jacobs
Arne Jacobsen
George Jenkins
Wolfgang Joop
Finn Juhl
Sven-Eric Juhlin
Dora Jung

Norma Kamali
Yusaku Kamekura
Tadeusz Kantor
Herbert W. Kapitzki
Albert Kapr
Donna Karan/Louis Dell'Olio
Toshihiro Katayama
Diti Katona
Mitsuo Katsui
György Kemény
Kenzo
Gyorgy Kepes
Kerr Keller Design Inc.
Leo Kerz
Emmanuelle Khanh
Chip Kidd

Günther Kieser
Kazuo Kimura
Jock Kinneir
Mark-Lee Kirk
Poul Kjaerholm
Anne Klein
Calvin Klein
Werner Klemke
Andrzej Klimowski
Vincent G. Kling
Florence Klotz
Peter Kneebone
Florence Knoll
Iwataro Koike
Ralph Koltai
Henning Koppel
Vincent Korda
Markku Kosonen
Burton Kramer
Boris Kroll
Yrjo Kukkapuro
Irma Kukkasjärvi
Mervyn Kurlansky

Karl Lagerfeld
Thomas Lamb
Pino Lancetti
Walter Landor
Ted Lapidus
Ugo La Pietra
Jean Larcher
Anya Larkin
Jack Lenor Larsen
Ralph Lauren
Maija Lavonen
Michael Lax
Bernard Leach
Eugene Lee
Ming Cho Lee
Harold Eliot Leeds
Jan Lenica
Krzysztof Lenk
Dennis Lennon
Alain Le Quernec
Olaf Leu
Herbert Leupin
Boris Leven
Michael Levine
Jan Le Witt
Börge Lindau
Bo Lindekrantz
Vicke Lindstrand
Ross Littell
Raymond Loewy
Ian Logan
George Lois
William Ivey Long
Santo Loquasto
Peter Lord
Eugene Lourié

Herbert Lubalin
Gerald Luss
Hans-Rudolf Lutz
Emanuele Luzzati

Ronald L. MacNeil
Vico Magistretti
Erik Magnussen
Mainbocher
Tomas Maldonado
Carl Malmsten
Leonard Manasseh
Mariuccia Mandelli
Karl Mang
Angelo Mangiarotti
Michael Manwaring
Giovanni Mardersteig
Enzo Mari
Javier Mariscal
Marian Marshall
Marshall Cummings & Associates
Noel Martin
Enid Marx
John Massey
Robert Massin
Tom Matano
Bruno Mathsson
Minoru Matsuba
Takaaki Matsumoto
Herbert Matter
Holger Matthies
Bruce Douglas Mau
Ingo Maurer
Almir Mavignier
Katherine McCoy
Michael McCoy
Mary McFadden
Richard Alan Meier
David Mellor
Perttu Mentula
Marjatta Metsovaara
Grethe Meyer
Francis Meynell
Jo Mielziner
Ludwig Mies van der Rohe
James Miho
Tomoko Miho
Masa Minagawa
Marcello Minale
Wilfried Minks
Ottavio Missoni
Rosita Missoni
Issey Miyake
Jan Młodozeniec
Børge Mogensen
Tanya Moiseiwitsch
Carlo Mollino
Bruno Monguzzi
Rune Monö
Claude Montana

Gene Moore
Hanae Mori
Alex Moulton
Olivier Mourgue
Jozef Mroszczak
Marcin Mroszczak
Thierry Mugler
Jean Muir
Rolf Felix Müller
Josef Müller-Brockmann
Bruno Munari
Tharon Musser
Martti Mykkanen

Kazumasa Nagai
Makoto Nakamura
John Napier
George Nelson
Louis Nelson
Hans Neuburg
Alexander Neumeister
Barbro Nilsson
Takeshi Nishizawa
Bob Noorda
Norman Norell
Eliot Noyes
Antti Nurmesniemi

Timothy O'Brien
Gearóid O'Conchubhair
Siegfried Odermatt
Donald Oenslager
Herbert Ohl
Tomoji Okada
Todd Oldham
Ott + Stein

Sven Palmqvist
Verner Panton
Victor Papanek
Ico Parisi
Art Paul
Andrzej Pawloski
Gustavo Pedroza
Pentagram Design
Sigurd Persson
Signe Persson-Melin
Gaetano Pesce
Francesco + Aldo Piccaluga, Inc.
Cipe Pineles
Pininfarina
Giovanni Pintori
Markku Piri
Warren Platner
William Lansing Plumb
Walter Plunkett
Gianni Polidori
Edward Pond
Jean-Pierre Ponnelle
Gio Ponti

Ferdinand Porsche
Porsche Design
Anthony Powell
Antoine Predock
Benno Premsela
James Prestini
Emilio Pucci
Arthur J. Pulos
Ritva Puotila
Andrée Putman

Mary Quant

Peter Raacke
Paco Rabanne
Gunter Rambow
Dieter Rams
Paul Rand
Jorgen Rasmussen
John Reid
Zandra Rhodes
Deane Richardson
Jens Risom
Carrie Robbins
M. Clark Robertson
Terrence Harold Robsjohn-Gibbings
Ernst Roch
Kevin Roche
Alberto Rosselli
Ann Roth
Martyn Rowlands
Emil Ruder
Cinzia Ruggeri
Gordon Russell
Erkki Ruuhinen
Sonia Rykiel

Bruno Sacco
Horst Sagert
Yves Saint Laurent
Kiyoshi Sakashita
John F. Saladino
Juhani Salovaara
Roberto Sambonet
Willem Sandberg
Jil Sander
Giorgio Sant'Angelo
Richard Sapper
Timo Sarpaneva
Jan Sawka
Carlo Scarpa
Tobia Scarpa
Mario Scheichenbauer
Hans Schleger
Douglas W. Schmidt
Hans Schmoller
Paul Schuitema
Herbert H. Schultes
Leokadia Serafinowicz
Raul Shakespear

Ronald Shakespear
Ronaldus Shamask
Irene Sharaff
Adele Simpson
Jack Martin Smith
Oliver Smith
Jerome Snyder
Yuri Soloviev
Luciano Soprani
Johnny Sørensen
Ettore Sottsass Jr.
Space Design Group
Basil Spence
Spencer Francey Peters
Herbert Spencer
Jurgen Spohn
Klaus Staeck
Anton Stankowski
Philippe Starck
Franciszek Starowieyski
Henry Steiner
Magnus Stephensen
Robert A. M. Stern
Brooks Stevens
Richard Stevens
Reynolds Stone
Giotto Stoppino
Studio Per
William Stumpf
Kohei Sugiura
Yoichi Sumita
Inez Svensson
Josef Svoboda
Waldemar Swierzy
Richard Sylbert
Jozef Szajna

TAC Interior Architecture and Graphic Communication
Roger Tallon
Tan Guidicelli
Ikko Tanaka
Masaaki Tanaka
Ilmari Tapiovaara
Brian Tattersfield
Dean Tavoularis
John J. Telnack
Rouben Ter-Arutunian
Eduardo Terrazas
Armando Testa
Chantal Thomass
Bradbury Thompson
Rud Thygesen
Stanley Tigerman
Rosmarie Tissi
Oiva Toikka
Henryk Tomaszewski
Carl Toms
Alexandre Trauner
Philip Treacy
Pauline Trigére

Gero Troike
Niklaus Troxler
George Tscherny
Jan Tschichold
George Tsypin
Alan Tye

Ximena Ulibarri
Emanuel Ungaro
Maciej Urbaniec
Leon Urbański

Valentino
Bertil Vallien
Jan Vančura
Koos van den Akker
John Vassos
Robert Charles Venturi
Gianni Versace
Jean Pierre Viau
Tucker Viemeister
Nelson Vigneault
Lella Vignelli
Massimo Vignelli
Madeleine Vionnet
Karl von Appen
Sohrab Vossoughi
Pekka Vuori
Ladislav Vychodil

Wilhelm Wagenfeld
Robin Wagner
Don Wallance
Tony Walton
Hermann Warm
Tokuji Watanabe
Jon Wealleans
Björn Weckström
Hans J. Wegner
Wolfgang Weingart
John Weitz
Robert Welch
Lyle Wheeler
Albert Whitlock
Zofia Wierchowicz
Bruno K. Wiese
Tapio Wirkkala
Henry Wolf
Ann Wolff
Lewis Woudhuysen
Russel Wright
Richard Saul Wurman
Lance Wyman

George Yabu
Kansai Yamamoto
Yohji Yamamoto
Sori Yanagi
Chris Yaneff
Jay Yang

Shoei Yoh
Tadanori Yokoo

Gianfranco Zaccai
Marco Zanuso
Hermann Zapf
Franco Zeffirelli
Eva Zeisel
Reinhart Zimmermann
Patricia Zipprodt
Piet Zwart

## AALTO, Alvar

Finnish architect, exhibition, furniture, and glassware designer

**Born:** Hugo Alvar Henrik Aalto in Kuortane, near Jyvaskyla, 3 February 1898. **Education:** Studied architecture, under Armas Lindgren, at the Technical University of Helsinki, Dip. Arch., 1921. **Military Service:** Served in the Finnish Army, 1939. **Family:** Married the architect Aino Marsio in 1924 (died, 1949); children: Johanna and Hamilkar; married the architect Elissa Makiniemi in 1952. **Career:** Worked as an exhibition designer, Göteborg, Tampere, and Turku, 1921-22; architect from 1923, and furniture designer from 1925, establishing office in Jyvaskyla, 1923-27, in Turku, 1927-33, and in Helsinki, from 1933; in partnership with Aino Aalto, 1924-49, and with Elissa Aalto, 1952-76; established experimental plywood workshop with Otto Korhonen, Turku, 1929, and Artek furniture design company with Aino Aalto and Harry and Mairea Gullichsen, Helsinki, 1935. Professor of Architecture, Massachusetts Institute of Technology, Cambridge, 1946-48. President of the Academy of Finland, 1963-68. **Member:** Honorary Royal Designer for Industry, Royal Society of Arts, London, 1947; senior fellow, Royal College of Art, London, 1950; honorary fellow, American Institute of Architects, 1958; fellow, World Academy of Arts and Sciences, Israel, 1963. Honorary member: Royal Institute of British Architects, 1937; American Academy of Arts and Sciences, 1957; Södra Sveriges Byggnadstekniska Samfund, Stockholm, 1957; Association of Finnish Architects, 1958; Accademia di Belle Arti, Venice, 1958; Norske Arkitekterns Landsforbund, Oslo, 1959; Västmanlands Dala Nation, Uppsala, 1965; Colegio de Arquitetos, Peru; Bund Deutscher Architekten, Germany, 1966; Engineering Society of Finland, 1966; American Academy of Arts and Letters, 1968; Akademie der Bildenden Künste, Vienna, 1975; Royal Scottish Academy, 1975. **Exhibitions:** Museum of Modern Art, New York, 1938; Kunstgewerbemuseum, Zurich, 1948 (with Aino Aalto); Gewerbemuseum, Basel, 1957 (with Mies van der Rohe); Keski-Suomen Museum, Jyvaskyla, 1962; Akademie der Künste, Berlin, 1963; Kunsthaus, Zurich, 1964; Palazzo Strozzi, Florence, 1965; Ateneum, Helsinki, 1967; Moderna Museet, Stockholm, 1969; Finlandia Hall, Helsinki, 1978 (toured); Museum Folkwang, Essen, 1979; Museum of Modern Art, New York, 1984 (toured). **Honors:** First prizes in Finnish and European architectural competitions, 1923, 1927, 1928, 1936, 1938, 1948, 1950, 1951, 1952, 1953, 1955, 1958, 1959, 1967; Royal Gold Medal, Royal Institute of British Architects, 1957; Sonning-priset, Denmark, 1962; Gold Medal, American Institute of Architects, 1963; Gold Cube, Svenska Arkitekters Riksforbund, Sweden, 1963; Gold Sash, Sociedad de Arquitetos, Mexico, 1963; Gold Medal, City of Florence, 1965; Palme d'Or du Mérite de l'Europe, 1966; City of Helsinki Prize, 1966; Thomas Jefferson Medal, University of Virginia, 1967; Litteris et Artibus Award, Sweden, 1969; Gold Medal Academie d'Architecture, Paris, 1972; Topiola Medal, 1975; National Arts Foundation Award, Liechtenstein, 1975. Honorary Doctorates: Princeton University, New Jersey, 1947; Technical University, Helsinki, 1949; Norges Tekniske Hojskole, Trondheim, 1960; Eidgenossiche Technische Hochschule, Zurich, 1963; Columbia University, New York, 1964; Politecnico, Milan, 1964; Technische Hochschule, Vienna, 1965; University of Jyvaskyla, 1969. Chevalier of the Légion d'Honneur, France, 1939; Kommendors Korset av Danebrog, Denmark, 1957; Grand Cross of the Lion of Finland, 1965; Grande Ufficiale al Merito, Italy, 1966; Grand Croix de l'Ordre du Faucon, Iceland, 1972. **Died:** Helsinki, 11 May 1976.

### Works

*Industrial Art* exhibition layouts, Tampere, 1922.
*7th Centenary Exhibition* layouts, Turku, 1929.
*Linked Chair 611* stackable chair in birch and plywood, for Jyvaskyla Civil Guards House, 1929-30.
*Armchair 15* stackable upholstered chair in birch and plywood, 1929-30.
Convertible upholstered sofa with metal frame, for Wohnbedarf AG, Zurich, 1930.
*Armchair 31* scroll chair in laminated birch and plywood with cantilever sides, for Paimio Sanatorium, 1931-32.
*Savoy* vase in green bottle glass, for Karhula, 1936.
*Tea Trolley 900* with laminated sides and wicker or basketwork top, 1936-37.
*Armchair 39* with laminated cantilever supports and wicker seat, 1936-37.
Forestry Pavilion, at the *Agricultural Exhibition,* Lapua, 1938.
Finnish Pavilion at the *World's Fair,* New York, 1938-39.
*Aalto-kukka* vases and dishes in clear glass, for Riihimaki, 1939.
*Artek Exhibition* pavilion, Hedemora, Sweden, 1945.
*Armchair 406* with laminated Supports, for Villa Mairea, 1946-47.
*Chair 612* with solid wood Y-leg supports, 1946-47.
*Armchair 45* with laminated armrest structure and webbing or rattan seat and back, 1946-47.
*Stool X66* in ash veneer with three X-legs, 1954.
*Stool X601* in ash with four fan-shaped X-legs, 1954.
Finnish Pavilion, at the *Biennale,* Venice, 1956.
X-leg armchair in birch with upholstered seat and back, for the National Pensions Institute, 1956.

(for a complete list of Aalto's buildings and architectural projects, see *Contemporary Architects*)

### Publications

**By AALTO: books**—*An Experimental Town,* Cambridge, Massachusetts, 1940; *Postwar Reconstruction,* New York, 1941; *Alvar*

**Alvar Aalto, *Scroll Chair*, for Artek, 1934. Photo: Cincinnati Art Museum**

*Aalto Synopsis* edited by Bernard Hoesli, Basel and Stuttgart, 1970; *Alvar Aalto: Sketches* edited by Göran Schildt, Helsinki, 1972, London and Cambridge, Massachusetts, 1978.

**On AALTO: books**—*Alvar Aalto: Architecture and Furniture,* exhibition catalogue, New York, 1938; *Alvar Aalto* by Giorgio Labo, Milan, 1948; *Alvar Aalto and Finnish Architecture* by E. and C. Neuenschwander, London and New York, 1954; *Alvar Aalto* by Frederick Gutheim, London and New York, 1960, Milan, 1963; *Alvar Aalto* by Göran Schildt and Leonardo Mosso, Jyvaskyla, 1962; *Alvar Aalto 1922-62* edited by Karl Fleig, Zurich, London, and New York, 1963; *L'Opera di Alvar Aalto,* exhibition catalogue by Leonardo Mossor, Florence, 1965; *Alvar Aalto* by Yukio Futagawa and others, Tokyo, 1968, London, 1970; *Alvar Aalto vol. II: 1963-70* edited by Karl Fleig, London, 1971; *Alvar Aalto,* adaptation of previous books by Karl Fleig, London, 1975, Zurich, 1979; *Alvar Aalto* by Carlo Cresti, Florence, 1975; *Architecture by Alvar Aalto,* Helsinki, no. 1, from 1976; *Alvar Aalto: A Bibliography* by William C. Miller, Monticello, Illinois, 1976, as *Alvar Aalto: An Annotated Bibliography,* Monticello, Illinois,

1984; *Alvar Aalto and the International Style* by P. D. Pearson, London and New York, 1978; *Architectural Monographs 4: Alvar Aalto* by Steven Groak, Liisa Heihonen and Demetri Porphyrios, London, 1978; *Alvar Aalto 1898-1976,* exhibition catalogue by Aarno Ruusuvuori, Helsinki, 1978; *Alvar Aalto* edited by Göran Schildt, London and Cambridge, Massachusetts, 1978; *Alvar Aalto—The Inner Process,* lecture paper by Malcolm Quantrill, London, 1978; *Alvar Aalto* by David Dunster, New York, 1979; *Alvar Aalto: das architektonische Werk,* exhibition catalogue edited by Zdenek Felix, Essen, 1979; *Alvar Aalto: tutto il design* by Luciano Rubino, Rome, 1980; *Alvar Aalto: Designer and Architect,* Monticello, Illinois, 1980; *Alvar Aalto versus the Modern Movement,* edited by Kirmo Mikkola, Helsinki, 1981; *Alvar Aalto als Designer* by Werner Blaser, Stuttgart, 1982; *Studies on Alvar Aalto* by Demetri Porphyrios, London, 1982; *Det vita bordet* by Göran Schildt, Stockholm, 1982, as *Alvar Aalto: The Early Years,* New York, 1984; *Alvar Aalto: A Critical Study* by Malcolm Quantrill, London, 1983.

*   *   *

Although a sense of personal expression permeates Alvar Aalto's work, in fact he developed close creative partnerships with both his first and second wives, who, like him, were trained as architects. After marrying for the first time in 1924 to Aino Marsio (1894-1949), they worked so closely together that it is impossible to identify their separate roles in their joint projects, or even to be certain which were joint projects and which were not. The historian and theorist Siegfried Giedion, who knew them both well, once wrote that Alvar was "restless, effervescent, incalculable," while "Aino was thorough, persevering, and contained." He added, "Sometimes it is a good thing when a volcano is encircled by a quietly flowing stream."

Aalto progressed from an early classicism, influenced by neo-classical buildings in Northern Europe as well as by the late Renaissance and early Baroque architecture of Italy, to mature work which was not at all revivalist, but which benefitted from the possibilities suggested by traditional expression and materials as well as from the new expressive and technical means revealed to him by his association with the architects of the Congrès Internationaux d'architecture Moderne. A similar progression can be seen in his furniture, which became more daring and original after his association with C.I.A.M.

Aalto's earliest furniture designs were based on traditional models derived from the eighteenth century or the early nineteenth century. There was also a resemblance to some of the furniture produced by the English Arts and Crafts movement. Only a tendency to make his designs simpler than comparable pieces gave a hint of Aalto's future mastery of furniture design. It is probable that his first contacts with experimental furniture were the bent-plywood chairs produced in Tallin, Estonia, by Luterma. This firm had once been headed by Christian Luther, whose late-nineteenth-century experiments with case-in bonding techniques and hot plate presses had led to a line of mass produced chairs with bent-plywood, one-piece back-and-seat units. These units, still marketed in the 1920s, had stimulated Aalto's imagination at just about the time he became interested in the C.I.A.M. (He joined the group in 1928 and attended its annual meeting in Frankfurt in 1929.) While there was some direct influence on Aalto from C.I.A.M. designers, such as Marcel Breuer, who developed a cantilever chair, the ability of Breuer and others in the group to create a sense of excitement about experimental furniture was more important.

The first product of Aalto's interest in plywood was a stacking chair, which had traditional, solid, wood legs, placed outside the limits of the seat to permit stacking; the seat was of formed plywood mounted on traditional seat rails. The chair was patented in 1929 and went into production that year in a factory in Turku, Finland, where the Aaltos maintained their office at that time. They worked closely with the factory manager, Otto Korhonen, in producing this chair. Another 1929 design for Korhonen's factory was a chair with a one-piece, bent-plywood seat-and-back unit mounted on a cantilevered, tubular-steel base. Its seat-and-back unit closely resembled one of Luther's units. In variation, portions of the L-shaped, curving plane of the back-and-seat unit were cut and folded forward to form arms, thus also providing greater strength because of the resulting multi-planar curve. At about the same time, the Aaltos initiated experiments which were more in the nature of sculpture than design; these were aimed at exploring some of the possibilities of bending and laminating strips of veneer and thin, wood rods.

Little of Aalto's furniture was conceived for his specific buildings, but his plans for interiors often included pieces of his furniture which had been put into production. However, some of Aalto's furniture, including some of the best known, was designed for individual buildings and later put into production for general sale. Examples are the furniture for the tuberculosis sanitorium at Paimio, Finland and for the municipal library at Viipuri (now Vyborg in the Soviet Union).

Aalto was awarded the contract for the design of the sanitorium at Paimio, along with its furnishings and equipment, in 1929, as the result of a competition. As it was constructed and outfitted from 1930 to 1933, he took special care with details. For example, the lighting fixtures were located for the benefit of reclining persons, and the plumbing was designed to minimize noise when it was used. The all-plywood scroll chair, conceived for this sanitorium, avoided metal parts so that it would be less noisy when moved, while its open structure and lack of upholstery aided in maintaining sanitary conditions. It consists of a bent-plywood back-and-seat unit, curving under the front and behind the back. Each end of this scroll-form unit is supported by stretchers which are attached to supports in the form of laminated-wood loops, which serve as armrests, and which are also joined by a stretcher in the rear.

For the library commission at Viipuri, also awarded as the result of a competition, Aalto took similar pains. The competition entry was submitted in 1927, the results were announced the following year, and in 1929 Aalto completed his revised plans. Subsequently, the site was changed, and the redesign of the building for the new site was not completed until 1933; construction and furnishing were completed in 1935. The main reading room was enlivened by dramatic changes of floor levels and was illuminated by roof-lights (developed earlier by Aalto) which employed cylindrical openings in the roof. These openings were deep enough to prevent direct sunlight from entering, and reflections off the sides provided diffused natural light. Lighting fixtures were placed above these roof-lights so that artificial light was diffused as well. The long, narrow lecture-discussion hall on the ground story had an undulating wooden ceiling, formed of slats of wood and designed for acoustic effect. Aalto's experiments with plywood furniture had led to this ceiling, and the integration of wood into buildings designed and constructed according to modern ideas and methods was to become a hallmark of Aalto's practice.

The furniture for the library included lounge chairs which were developed from the Paimio scroll chair. There was also a related series of stackable, wood, three-legged stools and four-legged chairs and tables with circular tops and seats. They rested on hook-shaped supports of birch, which had been formed by precision-sawing them at one end into thin leaves separated by grooves. Thin pieces of wood were then glued into the grooves. Until the glue set, the supports could be easily bent, but when attached to the undersides of the stools, tables, and chairs, they resulted in furniture that was nearly indestructible. Moreover, the cost was low. Although the library was severely damaged in World War II, excellent vintage photographs record its appearance.

International recognition began to come to the Aaltos in 1933 when they showed their furniture in a London exhibition set up by the *Architectural Review* and at the *Triennale* in Milan. Also in that year they moved their office to Helsinki. Here in the Finnish capital they were introduced to Harry and Mairea Gullichsen, with whom they formed the Artek Company to manufacture and distribute their furniture. (Some production continued simultaneously at Korhonen's factory.) Aino Aalto became supervisor of production, and sales increased greatly in Great Britain and other European countries as well as the United States, where their furniture was featured at an exhibition in the Museum of Modern Art in 1938.

The best-known of Aalto's exhibition designs was the Finnish Pavilion at the New York World's Fair in 1939, a joint commission with Aino. Its most striking feature was the exhibition court, highlighted by a dramatic, undulating wood screen, cantilevered out over a ground-level exhibition of Finnish products. The wood screen had three registers of splayed ribs on which photographs of Finnish scenes were mounted. Aalto returned to New York in 1940 to revise the exhibition to reflect changes wrought by the first Russo-Finnish War.

The Artek firm was revived after World War II, and Aalto's last two bursts of activity as a furniture designer occurred in 1947 and 1954-56. In 1947, he developed the "Y" leg, essentially a further development of the supports for his library tables and chairs at Viipuri. The "Y" leg was formed from two joined pieces of solid wood bent at the knees to diverge at right angles. The bend was accomplished in a manner similar to that used for the library furniture, except that a pattern of thin leaves projected beyond the bend; into these, horizontal members of solid wood, also precision-sawed at the ends into thin leaves, could be dovetailed and glued into position. Thus, a frame was provided for stool or table, and a chair variation allowed supports for the back to be integrated into two of the legs. In the mid 1950s, Aalto developed five-part uprights splayed at the top into a fan shape, thus permitting greater integration of vertical and horizontal members than was possible with the "Y" support.

In 1949, Aalto won a competition for the design of the village center of Säynätsalo, which was to become one of his finest and best-known achievements. That same year, Aino Aalto died. During the next two years, construction at Säynätsalo took place, supervised by a young architect, Elissa Mäkiniemi, who became Aalto's second wife in 1952. They, too, developed a close creative partnership, working together on architectural and planning commissions, and she supervised the production of her husband's furniture at Artek.

The architects and designers of the C.I.A.M. were strongly influenced by the Utopian social ideas current in Europe during the 1920s. Nevertheless, their International style work and that of their followers has often been criticized as rigid and lifeless. Whether that is a fair assessment or not, it is clear that nowhere were the humanistic intentions of the C.I.A.M. group more readily apparent than in Aalto's work and in the high regard its members had for his work. Aalto's particular achievement is that he maintained his roots in Finland and in the Baltic region while absorbing international influences and working with new technological means.

—Lloyd C. Engelbrecht

# AARNIO, Eero

Finnish industrial and interior designer

**Born:** Helsinki, 21 July 1932. **Education:** Institute of Industrial Arts, Helsinki, Diploma, 1957. **Career:** Freelance interior and industrial designer, specializing in chair design, Helsinki, since 1962; also photographer and graphic artist. **Exhibitions:** *Rattan Stools,* Asko Company, Helsinki, 1961; *7 x 7 Arkitekter,* Stockholm, 1964; Milan Triennale, 1964; *Fibreglass Furniture,* Asko Company, Helsinki, 1968 (travelled to Stockholm); *eurodomus,* Milan, 1970; *Modern Chairs 1918-1970,* Whitechapel Art Gallery, London, 1970; *Plastic as Plastic,* Museum of Modern Art, New York, 1970; *Design in Finland,* Asko Company, Cologne, 1979; *Scandinavian Modern Design 1880-1980,* Cooper-Hewitt Museum, New York,

1982; *Design Since 1945,* Philadelphia Museum of Art, 1983. **Collections:** Suomen Taideteollisuusmuseo, Helsinki; Louisiana Museum, Humlebaek; Stedelijk Museum, Amsterdam; Musee d'Art Moderne, Paris; Victoria and Albert Museum, London; Museum of Decorative Arts, Prague; Israel Museum, Jerusalem. **Honors:** First Prize Trade Mark Competition, Helsinki, 1958; First Prize, Scandinavian Street Furniture Competition, Stockholm, 1965; First Prize, International Furniture Competition, Cantu, 1965; International Design Award, American Institute of Interior Designers, 1968. **Address:** Riipakoivuntie 24, 02130 Espoo 13, Finland.

## Works

Logotype symbol, for Valmety steel factory, Helsinki, 1958.
*Appletree* chair, 1959.
*Jattujakkare* stool in wicker, 1961.
*Tomato* chair, for Asko, 1964.
*Mushroom* chair and stool in wicker, 1965.
*Thunderball* (also called *Bomb or Globe*) chair in upholstered fibreglass and metal, for Asko, 1965-66.
*Bubble* chair, for Asko, 1967.
*Pastilli* (also called *Gyro* or *Rock n'Roll*) chair in fibreglass, for Asko, 1968.

## Publications

**On AARNIO: books**—*Modern Furniture* by Ella Moody, London, 1966; *The Modern Chair, 1850 to Today* by Gilbert Frey, London and Niederteufen, 1970; *Modern Chairs 1918-1970,* exhibition catalogue with text by Carol Hogben, Dennis Young and others, London, 1970; *New Design in Wood* by Donald J. Willcox, New York and London, 1970; *The Modern Chair: Classics in Production* by Clement Meadmore, London, 1974; *Scandinavian Design: Objects of a Life Style* by Eileene Harrison Beer, New York and Toronto, 1975; *Modern Furniture* by John F. Pile, New York and Toronto, 1979; *Twentieth-Century Furniture* by Philippe Garner, London, 1980; *The Form and Substance of Finnish Furniture* by Riitta Miestamo, Lahti, 1981; *Neue Moebel 1950-1982,* edited by Klaus-Jürgen Sembach, Stuttgart, 1982, as *Contemporary Furniture,* New York, 1982; *Design Since 1945* edited by Kathryn Hiesinger and George Marcus, Philadelphia and London, 1983; *The Conran Directory of Design* edited by Stephen Bayley, London, 1985.

\*     \*     \*

Finnish design since the National Romantic movement of the early 1900s has retained throughout its development close links with the country's native materials and traditions. Aalto's classic furniture of the 1930s, for example, despite its exploitation of wood bending and laminating technology, is still firmly rooted in the centuries-old tradition of the Finnish farmhouse. Eero Aarnio started from this same tradition. One of his first works, the *Jattujakkare* wicker work stool, is a simple, straightforward adaption for multiple production of handcraft work, and the *Appletree* chair of the 1950s is a direct modern interpretation of the wooden chairs made by local craftsmen for centuries.

But Aarnio goes further. "Design," he says, "means constant renewal, realignment, growth." In support of this principle, he experimented in the 1960s with furniture in plastics and, in tune with the iconoclastic mood of the time, designed a series of chairs whose exotic names—*Tomato, Pastilli, Bubble, Thunderball*—underline their complete departure from traditional forms of seating. In these, he achieved visual excitement, practicality, and comfort with a logical and economic use of his material. He has now gone yet further: "The materials of the year 2000 are wood, metal, and plastics, upholstered with foam plastic and covered with fabric, leather, and artificial materials." In pursuance of this idea, he has evolved a system whereby the components of a chair—legs, seat, arms and back—become modules that may be manipulated by computer, with the use of natural and artificial materials for structure and finish. Therefore, a vast range of variations becomes available.

Aarnio is always ahead of his time. Although perhaps the most international of Finnish designers of furniture, he is nevertheless intensely individual. Not a follower of any school, but conceivably the founder of one, he nevertheless acknowledges his place as a link in a constantly evolving chain. Although Finnish at heart, he sees his country and its products objectively, within a wider, international context. He acknowledges without reservation the importance of the individual, and he sees how modern technology can serve the individual's way of life. "The personal approach of the past and the robot manufacture of the future clasp hands." Everyone can have the chair, say, that he wants. We have come full circle. "Industrial production will be so completely mastered that we can forget it," he predicts.

—Gordon Steele

# ADAM, Ken
British film designer

**Born:** Klaus Adam, in Berlin, Germany, 5 February 1921; emigrated to Britain in 1934, naturalized. **Education:** Educated at Le College Francais, Berlin, Craigend Park School, Edinburgh, and St. Paul's School, London; studied at Bartlett School of Architecture, University of London, 1937-39; articled in architectural firm C. W. Glover and Partners, London, 1939-40. **Military Service:** Served in the Pioneer Corps, 1940, and as fighter pilot in the Royal Air Force, 1941-46, Flight Lieutenant. **Family:** Married Maria-Letizia Moanro in 1952. **Career:** Joined film industry as a draughtsman, 1947; art director, from 1948, and production designer, from 1959. Freelance architectural and interior designer, London, from 1953; lecturer in the United States, United Kingdom, and New Zealand, from 1979; jury member, Cannes Film Festival, 1980. **Member:** Academy of Motion Picture Arts and Sciences; American Film Institute; United Scenic Artists, Local 829, New York; Art Directors Guild, Local 876, Los Angeles; European Academy for Film and Television; R.A.C., Great Britain; British Film Designers Guild. **Exhibitions:** *Ken Adam Retrospective,* Quimper, France, 1985; *Dr. Strangelove Design,* Smithsonian Institute, Washington, D.C., 1986-88; *Bond Designs,* Museum of Modern Art, New York, 1987; *Ken Adam: Masterworks of Film Design,* Deutsches Museum, Munich, 1994; *Production Design: Ken Adam,* toured Germany, 1994. **Collections:** American Museum of the Moving Image, Astoria, New York; Spoleto Museum, Italy; Cinemathèque, Paris. **Honors:** American Academy Award nominations, 1956, 1978, 1994, and Award for Best Art Direction, for *Barry Lyndon,* 1976, and for *The Madness of King George,* 1995; Best Art Direction, *The Trials of Oscar Wilde,* Moscow Film Festival, 1961; British Academy Award for Best Art Direction, for *Dr. Strangelove,* 1964, and for *The Ipcress File,* 1965, and nominations, 1965, 1973, 1975, 1978; Best Production Award for *Pennies from Heaven,* New York Film Critics, 1981; Best Technical Achievement of the Year, ALFS-London Film Critics Circle, 1993; honorary doctorate, Royal College of Art, London, 1995. **Address:** 34 Montpelier Street, London SW7 1HD, England.

## Works

Adams and Harvey exhibition stand, at Olympia, London, 1953.
Harlequin espresso bar, Oxford, 1953.
Cul de Sac espresso bar, London, 1956.
The Gondola espresso bar, Richmond, Surrey, 1956.
Mike Todd's "First Night" party, London Festival Gardens, 1957.
K.R.S. offices and boardroom, Dean Street, London, 1958.
House and apartment conversions, London, from 1958.
*La Fanciulla del West* opera production, Royal Opera House, London, 1977 and 1982.
Film art designs as draughtsman include—*This Was a Woman* (Whelan), 1947; *The Brass Monkey* (Freeland), 1948; *Third Time Lucky* (Parry), 1948; *The Queen of Spades* (Dickerson), 1948.
Film art designs as assistant art director include—*Obsession* (Dmytryk), 1948; *Your Witness* (Montgomery), 1950; *Captain Horation Hornblower* (Walsh), 1949; *The Intruder* (Hamilton), 1953; *Star of India* (Lubin), 1953; *Helen of Troy* (Wise and Walsh), 1953.
Film art designs as associate art director include—*The Crimson Pirate* (Siodmack), 1951; *The Master of Ballantrae* (Keighley), 1953.
Film art designs as art director include—*The Devil's Pass* (Conyers), 1953; *Soho Incident* (Sewell), 1955; *Around the World in Eighty Days* (Anderson), 1957; *Child in the House* (Enfield), 1956; *Gideon's Day* (Ford), 1957; *Ten Seconds to Hell* (Aldrich), 1958; *Beyond This Place* (Cardiff), 1959.
Film production designs include—*Night of the Demon* (Tournier), 1957; *Battle of the V.1* (Sewell), 1957; *The Angry Hills* (Cardiff), 1958; *The Rough and the Smooth* (Siodmack), 1959; *In the Nick* (Hughs), 1959; *Let's Get Married* (Scott), 1959; *The Trials of Oscar Wilde* (Hughs), 1960; *Sodom and Gomorrah* (Aldrich), 1960-61; *Dr. No* (Young), 1961-62; *In the Cool of the Day* (Stevens), 1962; *Dr. Strangelove* (Kubrick), 1962-63; *Woman of Straw* (Deardon), 1963; *Goldfinger* (Hamilton), 1963-64; *The Ipcress File* (Furie), 1964; *Thunderball* (Young), 1964-65; *Funeral in Berlin* (Hamilton), 1965; *You Only Live Twice* (Gilbert), 1966; *Chitty Chitty Bang Bang* (Hughs), 1967; *Goodbye Mr. Chips* (Ross), 1969; *The Owl and the Pussycat* (Ross), 1970; *Diamonds Are Forever* (Hamilton), 1971; *Sleuth* (Mankiewicz), 1972; *The Last of Sheila* (Ross), 1972; *Barry Lyndon* (Kubrick), 1973-74; *Salon Kitty* (Brass), 1975; *The Seven-Per-Cent Solution* (Ross), 1975; *The Spy Who Loved Me* (Gilbert), 1976; *Moonraker* (Gilbert), 1978; *Pennies from Heaven* (Ross), 1980-81; *King David* (Beresford), 1983-84; *Agnes of God* (Jewison), 1984-85; *Crimes of the Heart* (Beresford), 1986; *The Deceivers* (Meyer), 1987; *Dead Bang* (Frankenheimer), 1988; *Freshman* (Bergman), 1989; *Company Business* (Meyer), 1989-90; *The Doctor* (Haines), 1990-91; *Undercover Blues* (Ross), 1992; *The Addam's Family Values* (Sonnenfeld), 1992-93; *Boys on the Side* (Hytner), 1994; *Bogus* (Jewison), 1995.
Opera designs include—*La Fancuilla Del West,* Royal Opera House, Covent Garden, 1977, 1978, 1982, Charleston, 1985, and Spoleto, Italy, 1985.

## Publications

**By ADAM: articles**—"Designing Sets for Action" in *Films and Filming* (London), August 1956; interviews in *Esquire* (London), March 1967; *Screen International* (London), 12 February 1977; *Elle* (Paris), 3 January 1977; *Positif* (Paris), March 1977; *Vogue* (London), 15 April 1977; *Cinema* (Paris), January 1978; *Film Comment* (New York), January/February 1982.

**On ADAM: books**—*Dictionary of Film Makers* by Georges Sadoul, Paris, 1965, Los Angeles, 1972; *Le Dècor des Film* by Leon Barsacq, Paris, 1970, as *Caligari's Cabinet and Other Grand Illusions* Boston, 1976; *Hollywood, England* by Alex Walker, London, 1974; *Kubrick* by Michel Ciment, London, 1983; *The Film Encyclopedia* by Ephraim Katz, New York and London, 1979; *Film Architecture* by Peter Garr, Graz, 1986; **articles**—"Three Designers" by R. Hudson in *Sight and Sound* (London), Winter 1964/65; "20 Leading Film Designers" by B. Pattison in the *International Film Guide 1968* edited by Peter Cowie, London 1967; "Adam on Colour" in *Ideal Home* (London), December 1968; "Ken Adam on *Sleuth*" in *Ideal Home,* August 1973; "Le Meiller Ennemi de James Bond" in *Vogue/Hommes* (Paris), October 1978; *National Film Theatre* (London), October/November 1979; "Production Designer Takes on the Girl from the Golden West" in *Theatre Crafts,* November 1985; "On *Crimes of the Heart*" in *Architectural Digest,* December 1986; "Cinema Design: Ken Adam" by Anna Kyhreotis in *The Times* (London), 5 November 1990; "Ken Adam: Dialogue on Film" in *American Film* (Los Angeles), February 1991; "Ken Adam 45 Years of Film" in *Library of Congress* (Washington, D.C.), 15 July 1991; "One Weird Household in Search of a New Look" in *New York Times,* 6 June 1993.

*       *       *

Few have contributed more to the success of the British postwar cinema than Ken Adam. His credits as a designer, stage, and artistic director on feature films seem hardly credible, since it is difficult to conceive that any single designer could ever create so many major productions with such diverse disciplines and styles—ranging from the large-scale and expensive James Bond pictures like *Moonraker* to intimate and comparatively modest ones like *Queen of Spades.* The number of top name directors with whom Adam has collaborated proves him to be one of the most sought-after production designers in the Western hemisphere.

What makes Ken Adam's contribution so vital is his widely based talent and capabilities on so many essential levels. As a trained architect, he understands space and construction. His spirited sketches already contain an understanding of these and other problems that usually become evident only after the set design has finally been constructed. Technically, he is fully competent; he knows the filmic value of different materials from metal to plastic, from hard to soft materials. He has a highly inventive imagination, as shown by the plethora of astounding gadgets in his Bond pictures. His thinking is instinctively large-scale, and one can sense the tradition of the masters of early German expressionist and abstract styles of the 1920s in much of his work. He understands film timing, continuity, and movement, which is why he is able to work with the most talented directors. He is also keenly aware of the distinctions between fantasy and reality, using realism as a starting point, a departure to take the audience toward a world of visual fantasy to which film is so eminently suitable. Here, he is able to

expand his own inherent skills to enlarge on life. He is also practical, an attitude producers appreciate. He can adapt his work to budgets big or small by understanding the objectives and circumstances of a production. These values have made Ken Adam, for nearly fifty years, one of the most successful production designers on both sides of the Atlantic.

—John Halas

# ADOLFO
## American fashion designer

**Born:** Adolfo F. Sardiña in Cardenas, Matanzas, Cuba, 15 February 1933; emigrated to the United States, 1951, naturalized, 1958. **Education:** St. Ignacious de Loyola Jesuit School, Havana, B.A., 1950. **Military Service:** Served 3 years in the Cuban Army. **Career:** Apprentice, Cristobal Balenciaga hat salon, Paris, 1950-52; apprentice millinery designer, Bergdorf Goodman, New York, 1953-54; designer, Emme millinery shop, New York, 1954-62. Owner and head designer, Adolfo Inc., New York, from 1962; designer, Adolfo Menswear Inc., and Adolfo Scarves Inc., New York, from 1978; established fragrance line for Frances Denny, New York, 1979. **Member:** Member of the Council, Fashion Designers of America, 1962. **Honors:** Coty Award, 1955, for hats, and 1969, for costume; Neiman Marcus Award, 1956. **Exhibition:** *Fashion: An Anthology by Cecil Beaton,* Victoria and Albert Museum, London, 1971. **Collections:** Metropolitan Museum of Art, New York; Smithsonian Institution, Washington, D.C.; Dallas Museum of Fine Arts; Los Angeles County Museum of Art. **Address:** 60 East 42nd Street, Suite #1138, New York, New York 10165, U.S.A.

## Publications

**On ADOLFO: books**—*Fashion: An Anthology by Cecil Beaton,* exhibition catalogue, compiled by Madeleine Ginsburg, London, 1971; *With Tongue in Chic* by Ernestine Carter, London, 1974; *The World of Fashion: People, Places, Resources,* edited by Eleanor Lambert, New York, 1976; *The Changing World of Fashion: 1900 to the Present* by Ernestine Carter, London, 1977; *McDowell's Directory of Twentieth Century Fashion* by Colin McDowell, London, 1984, *The Encyclopaedia of Fashion from 1840 to the 1980s* by Georgina O'Hara, London, 1986.

*

To make clothes that are long-lasting and with subtle changes from season to season—this is my philosophy.

—Adolfo

*       *       *

Of the two designers who directly shaped his approach, Chanel and Balenciaga, Chanel affected Adolfo more. Her type of classic suit was a regular feature of Adolfo's collections throughout the 1970s, and his 1976 collection was Chanel down to the two-tone shoes. Among the models were a striped cardigan and blouse with a

**Adolfo: wool-blend suit, 1995**

plain skirt and a navy knit suit with a white silk crepe blouse, combinations that spoke the essence of Chanel. Future First Lady Nancy Reagan bought both outfits. During the subsequent presidential election campaign, Mrs. Reagan gave Adolfo front-page publicity, saying that she took his clothes on the campaign because they travelled well and remained impeccable. Between them, Adolfo and Mrs. Reagan aimed at a trim look, somewhat in the tradition of Main-bocher and the Duchess of Windsor, for they recognized that an important lady is most satisfied with the designer who can create the image she considers appropriate for her station in life. A little daring is permissible, as in Adolfo's off-one-shoulder evening gown which Mrs. Reagan wore as First Lady Elect, but the exposure was modest and most of the chest was covered. The fact that Adolfo does not strive for originality and sensation is greatly to his advantage when dressing the head of state's consort, whose clothes must have dignity and taste. In addition, Adolfo keeps himself in the background and is not a self-publicist to the extent that his chief American rival Halston is. At any court, the appointed purveyors are expected not to exploit their privilege.

Adolfo is an excellent example of the creator of good-quality clothes achieving a very successful career without gimmickry. He presents variations on established themes, not new ideas which seek to overthrow existing norms. As a conservative designer, his clothes accord fully with the regime for which he works. He gave Mrs. Reagan a conservative look, which expressed her political stance. Any time that a designer becomes associated with a particular government, he or she becomes responsible for part of the image of that regime, as has been seen time and time again, with Rose

Bertin and Queen Marie Antoinette, Leroy and Empress Josephine, Charles Frederick Worth and Empress Eugènie, and Edward Molyneux and the Duchess of Kent. Such a position very few couturiers can hope to attain, and on Adolfo's shoulders rests the responsibility of designing an image that will seem elegant in future history books; he fulfills this charge by following the established principles of his teachers.

—Diana de Marly

## AGHA, Mehemed Fehmy

American photographer, art director, graphic, and typography designer

**Born:** Of Turkish parents in Nicolaieff, Ukraine, 11 March 1896; emigrated to the United States in 1929, naturalized, 1936. **Education:** Studied at the Emperor Alexander Technical School, Nicolaieff, 1909-13; studied economics, Polytechnic Institute of Emperor Peter the Great, Petrograd, Russia, 1914-18; studied political science, Ecole Nationale des Langues Orientales Vivantes, Paris, Dip., 1923. **Career:** Studio chief, Dorland Advertising Agency, Paris, 1924-27; chief assistant and layout artist, *Vogue* magazine (German edition), Berlin, 1927-29; Art Director, Condé Nast Publications, working on *Vogue, Vanity Fair,* and *House and Garden,* New York, 1929-42; freelance design consultant and art director, establishing M. F. Agha design studio, New York, 1943-70 (worked principally for *Better Homes and Gardens, Seventeen, McCall's, Newsweek,* Saks Fifth Avenue, Bloomingdale's, Leo Burnett, Hart Schaffner and Marx, and Franklin Simon). **Member:** Founder-member, National Society of Art Directors, New York; advisory board, Cooper Union, New York; Institute of Graphic Arts, New York (honorary); president, Art Directors Club of New York, 1934-35; president, American Institute of Graphic Arts, New York, 1943-45, 1954-55. **Honors:** American Institute of Graphic Arts Medal, 1957; Art Directors Club of New York Hall of Fame Award, 1972. **Died:** Malvern, Pennsylvania, 27 May 1978.

### Publications

**By AGHA: articles**—"A Word on European Photography" in *Pictorial Photography in America* (New York), no. 5, 1929; "Surrealism or the Purple Cow" in *Vogue* (New York), November 1936; "Whistler's Hippopotamus: A Japing Dialogue on Photography, New and Old" in *Vogue* (New York), March 1937; "Woman's Place Is in the Dark Room" in *Vogue* (New York), October 1938: "George Melies: Movie Pioneer Fantasist" in *Vogue* (New York), March 1939; "Raphaels Without Hands" in *Vogue* (New York), June 1941; "Horseless Photography" in *Harper's Bazaar* (New York), November 1944; "Fashion Photography Today" in *Photography* (New York), Fall 1947; "Creative Rebellion Under Five Dollars" in *Architecture and Engineering* (New York), March 1948; "Remarks on Modern Decorative Design" in *Design* (London), March 1948.

**On AGHA: books**—*In Vogue: Sixty Years of Celebrities and Fashion* by Georgina Howell, London, 1975, 1978; *The Man Who Was Vogue* by Caroline Seebohm, New York, 1982; *Encyclopaedia of Fashion from 1840 to the 1980s* by Georgina O'Hara, London,

1986; **articles**—"Agha's American Decade" in *PM* (New York), no. 8, 1939; "Young Turk" in *Time,* 16 October 1939; "Mehemed Fehmy Agha" by J. Morrow in *Communication Arts* (Palo Alto), no. 4, 1972; "Art Directors Club of New York: 51st Annual Hall of Fame" in *Graphis* (Zurich), no. 163, 1972; "Profile: M. F. Agha" in *Upper and Lower Case* (New York), December 1978; "M. F. Agha" by S. Bodine and M. Dunas in *AIGA Journal* (New York), no. 3, 1985.

*     *     *

An astute and learned man who spoke five languages fluently and conversed in many more visually, Dr. Mehemed Fehmy Agha pioneered the profession of art direction in the United States. Born of Turkish parents in the Russian Ukraine at the turn of the century, Agha, who received his doctorate in Political Science (thus the term of address), started his career in Paris as a studio chief for the Dorland Advertising Agency. Due to his strong artistic and photographic work, he was sent to Berlin as chief assistant and layout man for the new German *Vogue.* Although this magazine was short-lived, Agha's skills were noticed by publisher Condé Nast, who offered him the job of redesigning the American magazine *Vogue.*

Upon his arrival in New York early in 1929, Agha took over not only the design of *Vogue* but also that of *Vanity Fair* and *House & Garden.* He applied his first-hand knowledge of Russian and European avant-garde art and design, as well as innovative magazines such as *Verve, Arts et Metiers Graphiques, Gebrauchsgraphik,* and *Novyi Lef,* to the visual needs of a modern American fashion magazine.

Avant-garde design ideas flooded Agha's treatment of *Vanity Fair.* He employed the asymmetric page layout already exploited by artistic movements such as De Stijl and Dada to add visual dynamism, lower-case letters to rejuvenate headlines and captions, and typecase dingbats to add visual shifts, reminiscent of El Lissitzky's layouts for Mayakovsky's poetry. He treated page layouts afresh as spreads rather than single entities, extending the format and developing a new visual orientation—a design idea that was concurrently employed by Alexey Brodovitch at *Harper's Bazaar.* (The first double-page spread appeared in the May, 1930 issue of *Vanity Fair,* with a photograph taken by Edward Steichen.)

In typography, Agha abolished the affected italic in favor of the more legible roman in titles, stretched out letter spacing, and flushed the type lines to the page margins. He substituted heavy black for decorative rules and eliminated clutter in illustrations and ornaments. Paralleling the theories of International Style architecture, the structural bones of typography were geometrically arranged within the taut skin of the page, providing a clean, spacious context for editorial content: the "less is more" mentality applied to layout.

At *Vogue,* Agha installed an in-house photography studio which incorporated a system of dramatic lighting that could emphasize shadows and stark, planar shafts of light, a translation of chiaroscuro to photography. To encourage his staff to think in terms of snapshots rather than portraits, he introduced extraneous props, such as a stepladder or planks of woods. In the studio shots of the early 1930s, subjects became noticeably more animated, gestural, and expressionistic. In layout, Agha eliminated border on the photographs and instituted bleeds while often radically cropping the images to show details of a face or silhouetted parts of the body.

Agha also introduced shots taken outside the studio, such as landscapes and cityscapes, to the pages of *Vanity Fair.* Aerial photographs of traffic taken from atop the newly constructed Chrysler Building or stark constructivist homages to the George Washington Bridge provided constant reminders of the machine age that he felt modern readers of a stylish magazine should appreciate.

Agha made an important contribution in securing a place for fine artists and art photographers in the popular world of magazine publishing. He invited the now-famous photographers George Hoynignen-Huene and Horst to work for the Condé Nast publications, as well as working with established photographers such as Cecil Beaton, Edward Weston, Berenice Abbott, and Steichen. He reproduced drawings by Picasso, Modigliani, George Kolbe, and Louis Lozowick, occasionally cajoling them into doing something original for the magazines. Cipe Pineles, who worked under Agha in the early 1930s, remembered: "Though the subject may have been fashion, the idea was that great artists could be given the freedom and challenge to work on its presentation."

Dr. Agha laid the groundwork for a new level of design participation in the popular magazine. The art director arose with the need to forge a "cultural commodity" in tune with the changing tastes of a sensitized and consumptive American public during the 1920s. His orchestration of design elements and editorial interpretation created an unprecedented empathy with the audience of his age. After Agha, the art director became an indispensable ingredient in popular magazine publishing.

—Sarah Bodine

# AGNÈS B. (Agnès Claret de Fleurieu)
French fashion designer

**Born:** Agnès Troublé in Versailles, 26 November 1941. **Family:** Married Christian Bourgeois in 1960; children: Etienne, Nicolas, Ariane, and Aurore; married Jean Rene Claret de Fleurieu in 1979; daughter: Iris. **Career:** Worked as junior editor, *Elle* magazine, Paris, 1964; designer with the Jacobsons, for Dorothée Bis, Paris, 1965-66; freelance designer, working for Limitex, Pierre d'Alby, and V de V, Paris, 1966-75; established own fashion design shop in Les Halles, Paris, 1975; first American boutique in SoHo, New York, 1980; opened men's and children's boutique Agnès B. Enfant, Paris, 1981; opened Agnès B. "Lolita" boutique for teenagers, and La Galerie du Jour art gallery/bookshop, Paris, 1984; skincare and cosmetics range, and maternity collection, 1987; fragrances include *Le B,* 1987, *Le petit b.b.,* 1990, and *Courant d'air,* 1992; has opened 86 shops, 35 in Europe, 7 in the United States, 44 in Asia (40 in Japan), and one in Australia. **Collections:** Musée des Arts de la Mode, Paris; Musée du Louvre, Paris. **Honors:** Order of Merit for Export, Paris. **Address:** 194 rue de Rivoli, 75001 Paris, France.

## Publications

**On AGNÈS B.: books**—*25 Ans de Marie-Claire de 1954 a 1979,* compiled by Francoise Mohrt, Paris, 1979; *The Encyclopaedia of Fashion from 1840 to the 1980s* by Georgina O'Hara, London, 1986; *Dictionnaire de la Mode au Xxe siecle* by Bruno Remaury, 1994; **articles**—"Succès par Excellence" by R. Voight in *Passion* (Paris), March 1983; "How to Live Straight from the Heart" by

Kathleen Jonah in *Self,* October 1983; "Agnès B. from A to Z" by Christopher Petkanas in *Women's Wear Daily* (New York), 22 April 1985; "A Certain Style: Agnès B." by Ingrid Bleichroeder in *Vogue* (London), January 1986; "Agnès B." in *Cosmopolitan* (London), September 1987; "Agnès B.: Chez les Soviets" by Philippe Tretlack in *Elle* (Paris), 26 October 1987; "Agnès B. Good" in the *Daily News Record* (New York), 2 May 1988; "French Dressers" by Debbie Bucket in *Clothes Show* (London), March 1989; "A Design Plan for No Seasons" by Roger Tredre in *The Independent* (London), 16 November 1989.

*

"I try to design clothes you can wear for a long time because they are not too much in fashion, so they don't go out of fashion quickly."

—Agnès B.

*      *      *

Agnés B. is a French sportswear designer who has catapulted herself to fame by challenging the need for fashion in clothing design. She denies the tenet that clothes must be stylized, highly detailed, and ephemeral in order to catch the public imagination. Her ascent began in the mid 1970s when, after only a few years in the fashion business, first as a junior editor at *Elle* magazine and then briefly as an assistant to Dorothée Bis, she opened her own boutique in a converted butcher shop in Les Halles to sell recut and redyed French workers' uniforms, black leather blazers, and T-shirts in striped rugby fabric. Her reputation grew as one of the first young French clothing designers to sell fashion to those who did not want to look too fashionable. In fact, her clothes, while identifiably French in no-nonsense cut, simple, subdued colors (often black), and casual mood, have an undated quality that keeps them current. The wrinkling common to natural materials, the "already worn" look that characterized the hippie ethos was translated by Agnés B. into a timeless chic—common sense with a flair.

In the age of name identification and personal marketing, Agnés B. is as well-respected for her business sense as she is for her easy clothing designs. The spontaneous, childlike hand with which she quickly fashioned the logo for her stores belies a sophisticated business savvy. Retaining her own independent boutiques rather than being swallowed up in larger department stores, she astutely perceived that the un-design of her clothes was too "fragile," that they would blend in with the other, trendier lines and be lost. She has opened 86 shops around the world, including a number in Paris, London, Tokyo, and two in New York City.

Her understated formula to design for real people (men and children as well as women) extends to her shows, which she calls "working sessions," where professional models are rarely used, and to her stores, in which casual and friendly salespeople mix their own antique or mod clothes with her separates. All the stores exude the same comfortable look, with pale wooden floors, white walls and the occasional decorative tile. The flimsy curtain that separates the display area from the communal dressing rooms is an implication of the marginal distinction between Agnès B. clothes and what everyone else is wearing.

Agnès B. strikes a commercial and creative balance—a radical chic. "I have no desire to dress an elite," she states. "It's all a game.

**Agnès B.**

I work as if I were still in my grandmother's attic, dressing up. Clothes aren't everything. When they become too important, when they hide the person wearing them, then I don't like them. Clothes should make you feel happy, relaxed and ready to tackle other problems."

—Sarah Bodine

# AHLMANN, Lis

Danish textile designer

**Born:** Mathilde Elisabeth Ahlmann, in Aarhus, 13 April 1894. **Education:** Studied painting under Harald Giersing. **Career:** Ceramics painter, Herman A. Kahlers workshop, Naestved, 1917-21; apprentice textile weaver, in the Gerda Henning workshop, Copenhagen, 1922-29; freelance textile designer, working with Kaare Klint, Mogens Koch, and Borge Mogensen, and establishing her own workshop in Copenhagen, from 1930; design consultant to C. Olesen Textiles and Cotil Textiles, Copenhagen. **Exhibitions:** Milan

Triennale, from 1957; *Formes Scandinaves,* Musée des Arts Decoratifs, Paris, 1958; *Ler, trae og vaev,* Danske Kunstindustrimuseet, Copenhagen, 1959 (with B. Mogensen and A. Fischer); *Nordisk Industridesign,* Kunstindustrimuseet, Oslo, 1976; *Design Since 1945,* Philadelphia Museum of Art, 1983. **Collections:** Danske Kunstindustrimuseet, Copenhagen. **Honors:** Tagea Brandt Prize, Copenhagen, 1948; Eckersberg Medal, Copenhagen, 1964; Cotil Prize, Copenhagen, 1974; C. F. Hansen Medal, 1978. **Died:** Copenhagen, 15 January 1979.

**Publications**

**On AHLMANN: books**—*Modern Danish Textiles* by Bent Salicath and Arne Karlsen, Copenhagen, 1959; *Made in Denmark* by Arne Karlsen and Anker Tiedemann, Copenhagen, 1960; *A Treasury of Scandinavian Design* edited by Erik Zahle, New York, 1961; *New Design in Weaving* by Donald J. Willcox, New York and London, 1970; *Lis Ahlmann: Tekstiler* by Thomas Mogensen, Copenhagen, 1974; *Danish Design* edited by Svend Erik Moller, Copenhagen, 1974; *Scandinavian Design: Objects of a Life Style* by Eileene Harrison Beer, New York, 1975; *Design Since 1945,* edited by Kathryn Hiesinger and George Marcus, Philadelphia and London, 1983.

# AHLSTRÖM, Tom (Erik Torbjörn)

Swedish industrial and product designer

**Born:** Of Swedish parents in Helsinki, Finland, 30 May 1943. **Education:** Studied metalwork, National College of Art, Craft and Design (Konstfackskolan), Stockholm, 1964-68; apprentice designer, Ogle design office, London, 1967. **Family:** Married Gun Dahlberg in 1988; daughter: Amanda. **Career:** Founder-director, with Hans Ehrich, A & E Design AB, Stockholm, from 1968, and Interdesign AB, Stockholm, from 1982, designing for Gustavsberg, Jordan, Arjo, Anza, Fagerhults, RFSU, ASEA, Colgate, Norwesco, Yamagiwa, Cederroth, PLM, Zanotta, and others. **Exhibitions:** *From Idea to Finished Product,* Form Design Center, Malmo, 1977 (travelled to Stockholm); *Contemporary Swedish Design,* Nationalmuseum, Stockholm, 1983 (toured); *Faces of Swedish Design,* Cranbrook Academy of Art, Bloomfield Hills, Michigan, 1988 (toured); *From Revolution to New Expressions 1968-1988,* Nationalmuseum, Stockholm, 1989; *The Movement of Form,* Liljevalchs Art Gallery, Stockholm, 1995. **Collections:** Nationalmuseum, Stockholm; Tekniska Museet, Stockholm; Röhsska Konstslöjdmuseet, Göteborg; Design Museum, London. **Honors:** Swedish State Award to Artists, 1971, 1972; Industrial Designer of the Year Award, 1987; 12-time recipient of the Excellent Swedish Design award. **Address:** A & E Design AB, Tulegatan 19 G, VI, S-113 53 Stockholm, Sweden.

**Works** (with Hans Ehrich)

Paintbrushes, for Anza, 1968.
Shower trolley and roll-in bath system, for Arjo Hospital Equipment, 1969.

*Bam-Bam* plastic stacking chairs, for Arjo Hospital Equipment, 1970.
*Dikken* plastic outdoor sofa, for Lammhults, 1970.
Queue ticket dispenser and number indicator, for Turn-O-Matic, 1974.
*Pilot* lift and transport chair, for Arjo Hospital Equipment, 1975.
*1230* dishwashing brush, for Jordan, 1975.
*Lucifer* desk lamp, for Fagerhults Belysning, 1975/76.
*Lift-Ride Chair,* for Arjo Hospital Equipment, 1980.
*Mobil* shower and toilet wheelchair, for RFSU Rehab, 1980.
*Stella Polaris* floor lamp, for Yamagiwa, 1983.
Paint scrapers and putty knives, for Anza, 1984/85.
*Giro* desk lamp, for Fagerhults Belysning, 1987.
*Rufus* shower and bathroom aids for the disabled, for RFSU Rehab 1987.
*Orbit* floor lamp, for Ateljé Lyktan, 1988.
*F1* table lamp, for Belysia, 1989.
Returnable plastic milk bottle, for Arla, 1992.
*Stockholm* folding stool, for Zanotta, 1994.

**Publications**

**On AHLSTRÖM/EHRICH: books**—*Design in Sweden* by Lennart Lindkvist, Stockholm, 1972; *Design* by Jocelyn de Noblet, Paris, 1974, *Contemporary Swedish Design,* exhibition catalogue by Monica Boman, Lennart Lindkvist, and others, Stockholm, 1983, *Industry Is Sweden* edited by Gullers Pictorial Inc., Stockholm, 1985; *Den Svenska Formen* by Monica Boman and others, Stockholm, 1985, *The Conran Directory of Design* edited by Stephen Bayley, London, 1985; *Sweden in Fact 1987* edited by Gustaf Olivecrona, Stockholm, 1986, *Design Art,* West Berlin, 1988; *International Design Yearbook 1988/89* edited by Arata Isozaki, London, 1988; *Faces of Swedish Design,* exhibition catalogue edited by Monica Boman, Stockholm, 1988; *Industrial Design, European Masters* edited by Francisco Asensio Cerver, Barcelona, 1991; *Industrial Design Review* edited by Action Group, Milano, 1995; **articles**—*Form* (Stockholm), no. 3, 1970; *Domus* (Milan), no. 489, 1970; *Domus,* no. 505, 1971; *Abitare* (Milan), no. 105, 1972, *Form* (Stockholm), no. 1, 1975; *Domus,* no. 555, 1976; *Japan interior Design* (Tokyo), no. 261, 1980; *Domus,* no. 614, 1981.

*See* EHRICH, Hans

\*

We seek an optimal balance between aesthetics, function, and the market.

—Tom Ahlström and Hans Ehrich

\*     \*     \*

Since 1982 A & E Design has been located on Tulegatan in downtown Stockholm. You enter through an unrevealing archway to find yourself in the midst of a craftsmen's quarter, full of studios, printing shops, and small factories. With two stories and a roof garden at their disposal, Hans and Tom were able to plan their own, customized interior, comprising a drawing office and a large, exceptionally well-equipped model workshop for producing every conceivable kind of model and prototype. This workshop is something of a

**Tom Ahlström: Returnable Milk Bottle designed in collaboration with Hans Ehrich for Arla, 1992**

nerve center for A & E, and the secret of many of Tom's and Hans's successes. Patient modelling is A & E's specialty. Their meticulous working models are constructed fullscale from the very outset, in order to penetrate technical and ergonomic functions.

The first thing one sees on entering the studio is a big showcase containing all the well-known products. Bright red, which has become something of a signature for A & E, dominates everything. Red plastic products with an unmistakable design, for instance. But one is easily deceived. Many of the products on display are handmade presentation models or prototypes, meticulously fabricated in wood and then perfectly painted with a plastic-like surface. Here are all the products which have made the A & E design team well known far beyond the borders of Sweden: dish-washing brushes, paint brushes and painter's equipment, queuing systems, light fittings, implements for the handicapped, and bathing and transport equipment for the disabled.

When the presentation models are tested and ready, exquisite boxes are made for each item. This reminds me of the Japanese stoneware masters who pack their materials in beautiful wooden boxes. Whenever Tom and Hans present a new model you are always fully convinced that this is the ultimate solution both to technical problems and to problems of design. And yet, after a few more years, they contrive to improve their product. The dish-washing brush for Jordan, for example, has undergone several successive improvements.

Hans and Tom specialized in using plastic at an early stage. Their very first assignment, for paint brushes, led them to acquire a specialist's knowledge of plastics. Few other people have succeeded in treating plastic with such a degree of awareness, devising a formal language which seems appropriate to the material.

Hans and Tom have spent much of their time designing aids and implements for the disabled. Their painstaking working methods and their frequently ingenious technical solutions have resulted in many fine products in this connection—among other things, a folding, locking armrest for toilets used by the disabled, extension handles for persons who cannot grip properly, and a lift-and-ride chair for transporting patients to the shower.

In the 1990s, A & E Design has managed to broaden the number of clients and worked with international manufacturers, creating, for example, a range of desk top products for a German company. In 1995 they invented and designed a new light folding museum stool, manufactured in Italy for the National Swedish Art Museum in Stockholm.

Most of A & E's products are admirably presented in fact sheets describing how they work. "Background," "Aims," "Research," and "The Design Process" are headings which make the whole thing look so simple and self-evident. Behind all this, however, there may be years of designing effort. Tom and Hans often develop product ideas on their own initiative. They devote at least 15-20 percent of their working hours to developing projects of their own.

What are the distinguishing qualities of A & E as designers? They attempt the following answer: "To a great extent our products are characterized by a strict geometrical formal language. We will have nothing whatsoever to do with imitation materials or décors, or other effects which do nothing to improve the functional properties of the product." Their motto has been: "We seek an optional balance between aesthetics, function, and the market."

Many Swedish industrial designers would genuinely endorse these aims, but it is abundantly clear that A & E have a formal language of their own, and one which I find highly distinctive. We see little here of what is commonly associated with "Scandinavian Design." Their

mentors, especially when they started, were unmistakably Italian. Hans Ehrich himself mentions Joe Colombo, and they have always been on close terms with Milan and the journal *Domus.* Few Swedish industrial designers have reaped so much attention from the international design magazines, but then few of their contemporaries have worked as hard as Hans and Tom to cultivate international contacts or to keep abreast of design developments in the world at large.

—Lennart Lindkvist

# AICHER, Otl

German graphic designer

**Born:** Otto Aicher, in Ulm, 13 May 1922. **Education:** Studied at the Akademie der Bildenden Künste, Munich, 1946-47. **Family:** Married Inge Scholl in 1952; children: Eva, Florian, Julian, and Manuel. **Career:** Freelance graphic designer, establishing studio in Ulm, from 1948; designed for the Ulm Volkshochschule, Ulm Stadtmuseum, BMW, Clima, Lufthansa, Erco, König Pilsner, Westdeutsche Landesbank, and others. Co-founder and developer, 1949-54, lecturer, 1954-65, Rektoratskollegium member, 1956-59, and Vice-Chancellor, 1962-64, Hochschule für Gestaltung, Ulm; visiting lecturer, Yale University, New Haven, Connecticut, 1958. **Exhibitions:** Yale University, New Haven, Connecticut, 1959; Museu de Arte Moderna, Rio de Janeiro, 1959; *Entschlüsselte Landschaften,* Paedagogische Hochschule, Weingarten, 1976; *Design Since 1945,* Philadelphia Museum of Art, 1983. **Collections:** Museum of Modern Art, New York; Museu de Arte Moderna, Rio de Janeiro. **Honors:** Prize of Honour, Milan Triennale, 1954; Best German Poster Prize, 1955; First Prize, European Typography Competition, Innsbruck, 1958. **Address:** Rotis 12, 7970 Leutkirch 1, Germany.

**Works**

Posters, for the Volkhochschule, Ulm, 1946-62.

Typographic layouts, for the *Allgemeine Sonntagszeitung* newspaper, Dusseldorf, 1956.

Total graphic design, for *Stuttgarter Gardinen* magazine, 1959.

Corporate identity graphics, for Firma Clima, Innsbruck and Vienna, 1960.

Colour coordination system, for the elevated railway, Hamburg, 1961.

Corporate identity graphics, for Lufthansa Airlines, 1962-64.

Corporate identity graphics, for the Westdeutsche Landesbank, Düsseldorf, 1964-75.

Signage system, for Frankfurt airport, 1967-70.

Total graphics system, for the 20th Olympic Games, Munich, 1972.

Corporate identity graphics, for Bayrische Ruchversicherung, Munich, 1972-75.

Graphic design of *PR* magazine, for BMW, Munich, from 1975.

Corporate identity graphics, for König Pilsner, Duisburg, 1975-76.

Total graphics system, for Erco, Ludenscheid, 1975-77.

Corporate identity graphics, for Sutex Textil Cooperative Society, Sindelfingen, 1977-78.

Colour coordination, architectural design, and orientation, for Krupp Hospital, Essen, 1978-79.

**Publications**

**By AICHER: books**—*Kritik am Auto,* Munich, 1984.

**On AICHER: books**—*Die neue Grafik/The New Graphic Art* by Karl Gerstner and Markus Kutter, Teufen and London, 1959; *Who's Who in Graphic Art* edited by Walter Amstutz, Zurich, 1962, Dubendorf, 1982; *Design Coordination and Corporate Image* by F. H. K. Henrion and Alan Parkin, London and New York, 1967; *Monografie des Plakats: Entwicklung, Stil, Design* by Herbert Schindler, Munich, 1972; *The Language of Graphics* by Edward Booth-Clibborn and Daniele Baroni, London, 1980; *Design Since 1945* edited by Kathryn Hiesinger and George Marcus, Philadelphia and London, 1983; *The Conran Directory of Design* edited by Stephen Bayley, London, 1985.

\*     \*     \*

German graphic designer Otl Aicher communicates each idea in a disciplined, organized, and readable style. It is a style he developed early in his career and subtly refined through experience.

Associated with the Hochschule für Gestaltung at Ulm, Aicher was a lecturer in visual communication. He was influenced by Max Bill, who served as director. Bill, a former student of the Bauhaus, brought with him the esthetic of functionalism which included regular geometric forms, simple silhouettes, flat finishes, and no extraneous ornament. The Hochschule für Gestaltung was the New Bauhaus. After Bill left in 1957, Aicher became co-director. While at the Hochschule für Gestaltung, among their projects, Aicher collaborated with Hans Gugelot on the design and display of products for Braun. The design was geometric, simple, without extraneous ornament and represented the successful expression of the esthetic of functionalism. Clarity of form and construction is evident in the work Aicher did for the Volkshochschule in Ulm. In a series of street posters, the designs go through a geometric mutation or evolution based on flat, simple, large forms which inform the public with a minimum of words. The message was designed to be absorbed by the passing public, rather than read in detail.

Aicher developed the graphic program for the XX Olympics held in Munich in 1972. The entire design program was coordinated by logo, typography, and specified colors, used on standard paper sizes, following specific rules of type and space distribution grids. Working within these design parameters, posters utilizing new photographic technology, street signs, program covers, informational maps, and pictographic symbols for the individual sporting events were created. Not only did the design team headed by Aicher work on the graphic designs, they developed all visual expressions of the games, including uniforms and interior decoration of the buildings. By working within this set of design limitations, the result was a clear, coherent, easily understood means of communication usable by the international audience.

Because of his success with the Olympic signage Aicher was hired to develop a system of pictograms for ERCO Leuchten. He created culturally neutral signs, understood by people of differing educational backgrounds, that communicated the necessary information. These were not illustrations, but signs. Aicher created designs for the town of Isny in Allgau, West Germany, to be used on posters and tourist literature. The flat black and white pictographs move beyond geometric forms based on a grid system to incorporate more pictorial images representing the town, its mountains, industry, and seasons. In all, Aicher maintained the elements of clarity and concise communication.

Illustrations for the book *Wilhelm von Occam, the Risk of Thinking Modern,* though less geometric, retain the flat forms seen in Aicher's earlier work. Soft colors are utilized, as the images move across the panels, telling the story. The shapes are simple, flat, and devoid of extraneous ornamentation.

Clarity of form and concise communication based on flat, geometric forms and spaces, are adjectives used to describe Aicher's work. His style evolved slowly, becoming less rigid. Elements of the esthetic of functionalism are evident in all of his work. He does not seek to be exciting, dramatic or unique. He does not seek a new language of communication. He does not seek to be so innovative that the message is lost. Yet Aicher's work does communicate an idea, directly and simply.

—Nancy House

# ALBERS, Anni
American graphic artist and textile designer

**Born:** Anni Fleischmann in Berlin, Germany, 1899; emigrated to the United States, 1933, naturalized, 1937. **Education:** Studied art, under Martin Brandenburg, Berlin, 1916-19; Kunstgewerbeschule, Hamburg, 1919-20; Bauhaus, in Weimar and Dessau, 1922-29, graduated 1929. **Family:** Married painter Josef Albers in 1925 (died, 1976). **Career:** Instructor and acting director, Bauhaus weaving workshop, Dessau and Berlin, Germany, 1930-33; assistant professor, Black Mountain College, North Carolina, 1933-49; Independent artist and designer, New Haven, Connecticut, from 1950. **Exhibitions:** Museum of Modern Art, New York, 1949 (toured); Wadsworth Atheneum, Hartford, Connecticut, 1953 (with Joseph Albers); Honolulu Academy of Arts, 1954; Currier Gallery of Art, Manchester, New Hampshire, 1956 (with Mary Callery and Sue Fuller); Massachusetts Institute of Technology, Cambridge, 1959; Carnegie Institute, Pittsburgh, 1959; Baltimore Museum of Art, 1959; Yale University Art Gallery, New Haven, Connecticut, 1959; Colorado Springs Fine Arts Center, Colorado, 1959; Contemporary Arts Museum, Houston, 1960; University of Bridgeport, Connecticut, 1971; Pollock Gallery, Toronto, 1973; Kunstmuseum, Düsseldorf, 1975; Bauhaus-Archiv, West Berlin, 1975; Brooklyn Museum, New York, 1977, Monmouth Museum, New Jersey, 1979; University of Hartford, Connecticut, 1979; Mattatuck Museum, Waterbury, Connecticut, 1979; *Anni Albers,* Galerie Denise Rene, Paris, 1984; *The Woven and Graphic Art of Anni Albers,* National Museum of American Art, Smithsonian Institution, 1985 (travelling); *Anni Albers: Prints,* Mary Ryan Gallery, New York, 1989; *Anni and Josef Albers,* Villa Stuck, Munich, 1989; *Anni Albers and Gunta Stolzl,* Museum of Modern Art, New York, 1990. **Collections:** Museum of Modern Art, New York; Metropolitan Museum of Art, New York; Brooklyn Museum, New York; Busch-Reisinger Museum, Harvard University, Cambridge, Massachusetts; Wadsworth Atheneum, Hartford, Connecticut; Yale University Art Gallery, New Haven, Connecticut; National Gallery, Washington, D.C.; St. Louis Art Museum; Fort Worth Art Museum, Texas; Art Gallery of Ontario, Toronto; Kunstmuseum, Dusseldorf; Israel

Anni Albers: *Partition* woven fabric, c. 1949

Museum, Jerusalem. **Honors:** Craftsmanship Medal, American Institute of Architects, 1961; Tamarind Lithography Workshop Fellowship, Los Angeles, 1964; Decorative Arts Book Award, 1965; Outstanding Achievement Award, Women's Caucus for Art, New Orleans, 1980; Gold Medal, American Craft Council, 1981; honorary doctorates from Maryland Institute College of Art, Baltimore, 1972, York University, Toronto, 1973, Philadelphia College of Art, 1976, University of Hartford, Connecticut, 1979, Rhode Island School of Design, Providence, 1990, Royal College of Art, London, 1990; elected to Connecticut Women's Hall of Fame, 1994. **Died:** Orange, Connecticut, 9 May, 1994.

**Publications**

**By ALBERS: books**—*On Designing,* New Haven, Connecticut, 1959, Middletown, Connecticut, 1962; *On Weaving,* Middletown, Connecticut, 1965, London, 1966 and 1974; **articles**—"Weaving" in *Junge Menschen,* edited by Walter Hammer, Hamburg 1924, Walluf 1979; "Work with Material" in *Black Mountain Bulletin* (North Carolina), no. 5, 1937; "Weaving at the Bauhaus" in *Bauhaus 1919-28,* edited by Herbert Bayer and others, New York,

1938, Boston, 1959; "Handweaving Today" in *Weaver* (Concord), January/February 1941; "Designing" in *Craft Horizons* (New York), May 1943; "We Need Crafts" in *Design* (Columbus), December 1944; "Constructing Textiles" in *Design,* April 1946; "Design—Anonymous and Timeless" in *Magazine of Art* (New York), February 1947; "Weaving" in *Art and Architecture* (Los Angeles), February 1949; "The Pliable Plane" in *Perspecta* (New Haven), 1957; "On the Designing of Textiles" in *American Fabrics* (New York), Summer 1960; "Conversation with Anni Albers" in *Craft Horizons,* July/August 1965.

**On ALBERS: books**—*Tapis et Tissus* by Sonia Delaunay, Paris, c. 1926; *Josef and Anni Albers: Paintings, Tapestries and Woven Textiles,* exhibition catalogue, Hartford, Connecticut, 1953; *Anni Albers: Pictorial Weavings,* exhibition catalogue, Cambridge, Massachusetts, 1959; *Artists at Work* by Bernard Chaet, Cambridge, 1960; *Anni Albers,* exhibition catalogue, Dusseldorf, 1975; *Anni Albers,* exhibition catalogue by Gene Baro, Brooklyn, 1977; *Americans from Germany* by Gerard Wilk, New York, 1977; *The Art Fabric: Mainstream* by Mildred Constantine and Jack Lenor Larsen, New York, 1981; *The Woven and Graphic Art of Anni Albers,* exhibition catalogue, with essays by Nicholas Weber, Richard Field, and Mary Jane Jacob, Washington, DC, 1985; *The Bauhaus Weaving Workshop: Source and Influence for American Textiles,* exhibition catalogue by Sonja Flavin and Sigrid Weltge, Philadelphia, 1987; *Women's Work: Textile Art from the Bauhaus* by Sigrid Weltge, San Francisco, 1993.

*

Design is often regarded as the form imposed on the material by the designer. But if we, as designers, cooperate with the material, treat it democratically, you might say, we will reach a less subjective solution to this problem of form and therefore a more inclusive and permanent one. The less we, as designers, exhibit in our work our personal traits, our likes and dislikes, our peculiarities and idiosyncrasies, in short, our individuality, the more balanced the form we arrive at will be. It is better that the material speaks than that we speak ourselves. The design that shouts "I am a product of Mr. X" is a bad design. As consumers, we are not interested in Mr. X but in his product, which we want to be our servant and not his personal ambassador. Now, if we sit at our desk designing, we cannot avoid exhibiting ourselves for we are excluding the material as our co-worker, as the directive force in our planning.

The good designer is the anonymous designer, so I believe, the one who does not stand in the way of the material; who sends his products on their way to a useful life without an ambitious appearance. A useful object should perform its duty without much ado. The tablecloth that calls "Here I am, look at me," is invading the privacy of the consumer. The curtains that cry "We are beautiful, your attention please," but whisper "though not very practical, we will need much of your time to keep us in shape," are badly designed. The unknown designer or designers of our sheets or of our light bulbs performed their task well. Their products are complete in their unpretentious form.

The more we avoid standing in the way of the material and in the way of tools and machines the better chance there is that our work will not be dated, will not bear the stamp of too limited a period of time and be old-fashioned some day instead of antique. The imprint of a time is unavoidable. It will occur without our purposely fashioning it. And it will outlast fashions only if it embodies lasting, together with transitory, qualities. (Reprinted from "Design: Anonymous and Timeless" (1947) in *On Designing*, 1959.)

—Anni Albers

\*       \*       \*

Anni Albers' abstract, grid-structured textile designs were based on the belief that high standards and philosophical underpinnings are necessary for modern crafts to become aesthetically satisfying works of art. She advocated the importance of the designer maintaining a direct experience of the medium, cooperating with and working through the material to attain a holistic design which focuses on the forms' inherent qualities.

In an approach which was new to her craft, Albers emphasized the thread as the beginning and the end in textile-making. Working through the weaving process, she believed, not imposing self on it and not letting oneself become influenced by the judgments of others, the maker who faced the work with an open mind and let the imagination take hold could attain a unified whole which is both ordered and mysterious. In Albers' view, the individual craftsman should carry through the design from beginning to end in order to avoid the fragmentation which results from division of work as practiced in industry. Albers encouraged the introduction of such practices to American textile production so that more people could be exposed to higher artistic standards of work.

Albers' textile designs, along with her writings and teachings on the history and practice of weaving and on the theoretical approach to design, exerted a deep influence on the generation of American weavers who matured during the decades of the 1930s to the 1960s. She also had a prominent effect on the American textile industry of the same period. Her influence can also be seen in some abstract paintings of her day, notably the delicate grid pictures of such artists as the American abstractionist Agnes Martin.

—Barbara Cavaliere

# ALBINI, Franco

Italian architect, exhibition and furniture designer

**Born:** Robbiate, Como, 17 October 1905. **Education:** Studied architecture at the Politecnico, Milan, Dip. Arch., 1929. **Family:** Married; son: Marco. **Career:** Architect and designer, Milan, from 1930; joined by partners Franca Helg, 1952, Antonio Piva, 1962, and Marco Albini, 1965; designed numerous exhibitions in Italy, especially the Milan Triennale, from 1936, and furniture for Rinascente, Brionvega, BBB Bonacina, Poggi Sirrah, Knoll International, and others, from 1940. Lecturer, American-Italian Commission of Cultural Exchange, Rome, 1954-63; professor of Architectural Composition, Politecnico, Milan, 1963-77. **Member:** UNESCO Commission for the Renewal of the Museums of the United Arab Republic, 1968-69; CIAM Congres Internationaux d'Architecture Moderne; Accademia di San Luca; Italian Institute of Town Planning; Scientific Institute of the Italian National Research Centre of Museography. **Exhibitions:** *Italian Contemporary Art, Design and Architecture,* Stockholm and Helsinki, 1953; *Ten Italian Architects,* Los Angeles, 1967; *28/78 Architettura,* Milan,

1979; *Design and design,* Milan and Venice, 1979, *Franco Albini: Architettura per un Museo,* Galleria Nazionale d'Arte Moderna, Rome, 1980. **Honors:** First Prize, Main Hall Competition, Milan Triennale, 1954; Compasso d'Oro Award, Milan, 1955, 1958, 1964; Olivetti National Architecture Medal, Milan, 1957; IN/ARCH Award, Milan, 1963, 1965; Biscione d'Oro Award, Milan, 1971; First Prize, Municipal Theatre Competition, Vicenza, 1971; Honorary Royal Designer for Industry, Royal Society of Arts, London, 1971; Honorary Fellow, American Institute of Architects. **Died:** Milan, 1 November 1977.

## Works

Lacquered wood furniture at the Milan Trade Fair, for the Dassi Company, 1932.
*Dwelling Exhibition* layouts, at the Milan Triennale, 1936.
Tensile structure suspended bookshelves in glass and brass cable, 1940.
*Criteria for the Modern Home* exhibition layouts, at the Milan Triennale, 1940.
*Home Furnishings* exhibition layouts, at the Palazzo dell'Arte al Parco, Milan, 1946.
Desk with metal frame and glass top, for Knoll International, 1950.
Armchair with upholstered movable seat and back, for La Rinascente, 1950.
Easy chair in rattan, for BBB Bonacina, 1951.
Folding wooden dining table, for La Rinascente, 1951.
*Italian Contemporary Art, Design and Architecture* exhibition layouts, in Stockholm and Helsinki, 1953.
Folding table in wood with woollen cloth cover, for Carlo Poggi, 1954-55.
*Luisa* upholstered armchair with wood frame for Carlo Poggi, 1955.
Councilman Chair, for the Council of Genoa, 1955.
*Premio La Rinascente/Compasso d'Oro* exhibition layouts, at the *World's Fair,* New York, 1956.
*Tre Pezzi* chair in tubular steel and foam rubber, for Carlo Poggi, 1959.
*International Glass and Steel Exhibition* layouts, at the Triennale, Milan, 1960.
*Why Steel* pavilion at the Milan Trade Fair, for Italsider, 1968.
*The School of Leonardo* exhibition layouts, Palazzo Reale, Milan, 1973.

(for a complete list of Albini's buildings and architectural projects, see *Contemporary Architects*)

## Publications

**On ALBINI: books**—*Forme Nuove in Italia* by Agnoldomenico Pica, Milan and Rome, 1957; *Public Interiors* by Misha Black, London, 1960; *Design for Modern Living* by Gerd and Ursula Hatje, Munich and Zurich, 1961, London, 1962; *Franco Albini* by Giulio Carlo Argan, Milan, 1962; *Il Design in Italia 1945-1972* by Paolo Fossati, Turin, 1972; *Tubular Steel Furniture* edited by Barbie Campbell-Cole and Tim Benton, London, 1979; *Franco Albini 1930-1970* by Franca Helg, Cesare De Seta, and Marcello Fagiolo, Florence, 1979, 1981, London, 1981; *Atlante del Design Italiano 1940/1980* by Alfonso Grassi and Anty Pansera, Milan, 1980; *Franco Albini: Architettura per un Museo,* exhibition catalogue, Rome, 1980;

*The Conran Directory of Design,* edited by Stephen Bayley, London, 1985.

*       *       *

Franco Albini was one of a talented group of architects, designers, and critics who emerged in Milan during the 1930s and who did so much to give Italian design its dominant characteristics and its international reputation. Compared to many of his fellows, of his own and successive generations, he was remarkably sparing with opinions in print, and the few occasions when he made such contributions were largely due to strong persuasion by others. This is not to say, however, that he was not aware of theoretical problems and their bearing upon his practice, which stemmed from a critical appreciation of the aims of Italian Rationalism, corrected by an understanding of the Bauhaus and of Russian avant-garde architecture and design.

His methods were rigorous but sufficiently flexible to lead him ever to invention rather than to any conventional resolution of so-called problems. His work thus always acquired a stylishness beyond any notions of forms arising from function, for he recognized that the designer's intervention modified, if not transformed, both function and form, through its structural proposals which constituted a sort of renewal of the object and of the meaning of its function.

Even the 1940 "suspension bookshelves" show this process of "resemantisation" through the structure Albini adopted. Utterly unlike any previous book storage, with which only the level planes have any similarity (and even that was minimised by making them of plate glass), the structure also proposed a new function for itself; it acted as a room-divider, of the sort destined to become a cliche of interior decoration through the 1950s and 1960s. The structure itself, of carefully shaped, complex members of wood and brass and steel cables both for suspending the shelves and as stays to the wooden members, recalls not only suspension bridges but sailing ship architecture. This is true, also, of much of Albini's earlier work and, in the case of spiral staircases, it persisted throughout his career, as can be seen in the Villa Neufer, Ispra (1940); in the Palazzo Rosso, Genoa (1952-61); in a staircase of reinforced concrete, marble, and wood, Parma (1950); and one of steel and white marble, Genoa (1970).

Perhaps another aspect of Albini's methods was his respect for materials and forms; this did not, however, appear to him as a constraint demanding slavish imitation. The cane-and-rush chairs of the 1950s are elegant examples of this sensitivity, while the remarkable room at the Palazzo Bianco for introductory, temporary, and largely documentary exhibitions is a particularly rich exploitation of structural and material promptings. Elsewhere in this museum, the flooring is in white marble, punctuated by little slate squares set diagonally; the lighting, mainly by cold, cathode tube; the walls, pale; the atmosphere, airy. This room reverses the floor pattern, the walls are dark, and the lighting falls in strong spots. The supports for the displays derive their module from the floor pattern.

—Toni del Renzio

# ALBINI, Walter

Italian fashion designer

**Born:** Born Gualtiero Albini in Busto Arsizio, near Milan, 9 March 1941. **Education:** Studied fashion and costume design, Istituto

Statale di Belle Arti e Moda, Turin. **Career:** Sketch artist and illustrator, working for Italian publications *Novita* and *Corriere Lombardo* and as apprentice to a fashion house, Paris, 1961-64; freelance fashion designer, Milan, 1964-1983; established Walter Albini Fashion House, designing for firms including Krizia, Billy Ballo, Basile, Callaghan, Escargots, Mister Fox, Diamantis, Trell, Mario Ferari, Lanerossi, Kriziamaglia, Montedoro, and Princess Luciana; launched ready-to-wear collection, 1978; established branches of Walter Albini Fashions in London, Rome, and Venice. **Died:** Milan, 31 May 1983.

## Publications

On ALBINI: books—*In Vogue: Sixty Years of Celebrities and Fashion from British Vogue* by Georgina Howell, London, 1975, 1978, New York, 1976; *Magic Names of Fashion* by Ernestine Carter, Englewood Cliffs, New Jersey and London, 1980; *McDowell's Directory of Twentieth Century Fashion* by Colin McDowell, London, 1984; *The Encyclopaedia of Fashion from 1840 to the 1980s* by Georgina O'Hara, London, 1986; **articles**—"Walter Albini" in *The Sunday Times* (London), 15 October 1972; "Walter Albini: Italian RTW Designer, Is Dead" in *Women's Wear Daily* (New York), 3 June 1983.

*       *       *

Walter Albini began his formal association with the fashion world by insisting that he be admitted to study at a fashion school in Turin, despite it being an all-girls school. For three years he lived in school rooms with walls covered with copies of drawings by Erte and pages from *La Gazette du Bon Ton,* both of which influenced him strongly.

Respected as a perfectionist, Albini created exciting clothing which was influenced by his admiration for the style of the glamorous actresses of the 1930s and 1940s, an attachment that dated back to the endless afternoons when he and his mother sat through the films of such stars as Greta Garbo, Marlene Dietrich, and Audrey Hepburn. He considered this to be the last revolutionary time of change in style, and his great devotion to Coco Chanel stemmed from the fact that she was one of those revolutionaries. He paid homage to her in the Walter Albini High Fashion show in Rome in 1975.

Through the 1960s Albini's motto, "dare to die," led him to take risks in designing sportswear collections with specific allusions to yachting and sailor uniforms for Chanel, the Duchess of Windsor, and the British Air Force. For Krizia, he designed long pleated crepe skirts and cardigans with sequins, for Billy Ballo he concentrated on drawings for fabrics, and for Cadette he created black cotton dresses with white cuffs. Later came successes for Basile, Misterfox, Sportfox, Callaghan, and Escargot.

Albini was always truthful to his belief in the need for mystery in women, and he continually observed the ways they expressed themselves in sitting, moving, and standing. Each of his early dresses and following sportswear lines was known for fantasy and pure femininity, but all were notable, too, for the quality of the natural fibers, the fine tailoring, and the attention to details in construction.

—Gillion Skellenger

# ALDREDGE, Theoni

American stage and film costume designer

**Born:** Theoni Vachliotis in Athens, Greece, 22 August 1932. **Education:** Studied at the American School, Athens, until 1948; studied at Goodman Memorial Theatre School, Chicago, 1949-52. **Family:** Married the actor Thomas E. Aldredge in 1953. **Career:** Independent costume designer, in Chicago, 1950-57, and in New York, from 1958; worked for the Goodman Theatre, Chicago, 1951-53, the Studebaker Theatre, Chicago, 1956-57, and the New York Shakespeare Festival, from 1962; has designed costumes for numerous Broadway and off-Broadway plays, ballets, operas, television specials, and films. **Honors:** Academy Award, Hollywood, 1975; Theatre World Award, 1976; British Motion Picture Academy Award, 1976; Obie Award, *Village Voice,* New York, 1976; Antoinette Perry (Tony) Award, 1977. **Address:** 240 East 27th Street, Apt. 12G, New York, New York 10016, U.S.A.

## Works

Stage costume designs include—*The Distaff Side,* Goodman Theatre, Chicago, 1950; *The Immoralist,* Studebaker Theatre, Chicago, 1956; *Much Ado About Nothing,* Studebaker Theatre, 1957; *A View from the Bridge,* Studebaker Theatre, 1957; *Lysistrata,* Studebaker Theatre, 1957; *The Guardsman,* Studebaker Theatre, 1957; *Heloise,* Gate Theatre, New York, 1958; *The Golden Six,* York Playhouse, New York, 1958; *Sweet Bird of Youth,* Martin Beck Theatre, New York, 1959; *The Geranium Hat,* Orpheum Theatre, New York, 1959; *The Nervous Set,* Henry Miller's Theatre, New York, 1959; *Silent Night, Lonely Night,* Morosco Theatre, New York, 1959; *A Distant Bell,* Eugene O'Neill Theatre, New York, 1960; *The Best Man,* Morosco Theatre, 1960; *Measure for Measure,* New York Shakespeare Festival, 1960; *Hedda Gabler,* Fourth Street Theatre, New York, 1960; *Mary, Mary,* Helen Hayes Theatre, New York, 1961; *Under Milk Wood,* Circle in the Square, New York, 1961; *Ghosts,* Fourth Street Theatre, 1961; *I Can Get It For You Wholesale,* Shubert Theatre, New York, 1962; *King Lear,* New York Shakespeare Festival, 1962; *Who's Afraid of Virginia Woolf?,* Billy Rose Theatre, 1962; *Strange Interlude,* Hudson Theatre, New York, 1963; *Antony and Cleopatra,* New York Shakespeare Festival, 1963; *The Trojan Women,* Circle in the Square, 1963; *The Three Sisters,* Morosco Theatre, 1964; *Hamlet,* New York Shakespeare Festival, 1964.

Film costume designs include—*Girl of the Night,* 1960; *You're a Big Boy Now,* 1967; *No Way to Treat a Lady,* 1968; *Up Tight,* 1968; *Last Summer,* 1969; *I Never Sang for my Father,* 1969; *Promise at Dawn,* 1970; *The Great Gatsby,* 1974; *Network,* 1976; *Semi-Tough,* 1977; *The Cheap Detective,* 1978; *The Fury,* 1978; *Eyes of Laura Mars,* 1978; *The Champ,* 1979; *The Rose,* 1979.

## Publications

**On ALDREDGE: books**—*The Biographical Encyclopaedia and Who's Who of the American Theatre* edited by Walter Rigdon, New York, 1966; *Who's Who in the Theatre* edited by Ian Herbert, London, 1982; **articles**—"Network Designer Theoni Aldredge" by E. L. Gross in *Vogue* (New York), August 1978; "Theater's Top Twofer is Tom and Theoni Aldredge: He Emotes, She Keeps Broadway in Stitches" by K. McMurran in *People Weekly* (Chicago), 29 June 1981; "Architectural Digest Visits: Theoni V. Aldredge" by Peter Carlsen in *Architectural Digest* (Los Angeles), December 1982.

\* \* \*

Theoni Aldredge appeared upon the design scene in New York at that moment when both detailed realism and a lush and spectacular romanticism in costume design were being replaced by costumes that were more closely integrated with direction, actor-movement, and the subtext of the drama. Aldredge seemed to have an innate sense of how to design costumes that were not just character clothes but integral visual support for the underlying soul of the play. From Tennessee Williams' *Sweet Bird of Youth* early in her career to the now-famous *Chorus Line,* through many Shakespearean productions and a host of major and minor Broadway scripts, the one thing that characterized Aldredge's costumes was visual projection of the inner life of the play and its action. The many production designs for Shakespeare-in-the-Park undoubtedly solidified this costume sensitivity, since Shakespeare's plays, when performed on an open stage, demand much from the costumes in the way of information, mood, subtext, and stage action. Possibly Aldredge's Greek heritage with its mystic, mythic sense of what underlies even the simplest tales and stories also strengthened her sense of the underlying appropriateness of each of her designs.

She has also undoubtedly been influenced by much of what went on in the art world of the 1960s and 1970s, although never in a direct way. Her work reflected the prevailing interest in texture, in physicality, and in presenting several visual ideas simultaneously, but these were never obvious nor presented so as to step forward from the production. Thus, Aldredge has been less the innovator than a subtle mirror for her times, reflecting in her costumes the visual moods and attitudes of our day within the essentially visual world of the drama.

—Douglas A. Russell

# ALDRIDGE, Alan

British illustrator, poster, book, and graphic designer

**Born:** Aylesbury, Buckinghamshire, in 1943. **Education:** Attended Romford Technical College, Essex. **Family:** Married; children: Miles and Saffron. **Career:** Worked various jobs, including, insurance clerk, barrow-boy, repertory actor, London, 1960-63; freelance designer and illustrator, London, since 1963; designed for The Great American Disaster Restaurant, Jonathan Cape publishers, Penguin Books, Macdonald publishers, *Melody Maker, Mirror Magazine, Daily Telegraph, Esquire,* and others. **Exhibitions:** Galerie Priebut, Amsterdam, 1967; *European Illustrators,* New York, 1968; *12 Illustrators,* Galerie Germain, Paris, 1969; Seibu Gallery, Tokyo, 1970; Galerie Bijenkorf, Amsterdam, 1971; Institute of Contemporary Arts, London, 1973; *The Contemporary Illustrator's Art,* The Minories, Colchester, 1978. **Honors:** Children's Book of the Year Award, London, 1974; Silver Medals, Designers and Art Directors Association, London, Scotsman International Awards, London. **Addresses:** c/o Jean-Howard-Spink, 5 Rosenau Road. London SW11, 4QN, England.

## Works

*The Penguin Book of Comics* book design, for Penguin Books, 1967.

*Doctor Robert* in *The Beatles Illustrated Lyrics book,* Macdonald, 1969.

*Being for the Benefit of Mr. Kite* in *The Beatles Illustrated Lyrics,* Macdonald 1969.

*What Goes On* in *The Beatles Illustrated Lyrics,* Macdonald, 1969.

*A Great Place for Hamburgers* poster, for the Great American Disaster Restaurant, London, 1970.

*I'm Happy Just to Dance with You* in *The Beatles Illustrated Lyrics 2,* Macdonald, 1971.

*Across the Universe* in *The Beatles Illustrated Lyrics 2,* Macdonald, 1971.

*The Ship's Cat* book design, for Jonathan Cape, 1977.

*Lion's Cavalcade* book design, for Jonathan Cape, 1980.

*Phantasia of Dockland, Rockland and Dodos* book design, for Jonathan Cape, 1981.

## Publications

**By ALDRIDGE: books**—*The Penguin Book of Comics,* editor, with George Perry, London, 1967, 1971, 1975; *The Beatles Illustrated Lyrics,* London, 1969: *Ann in the Moon,* with text by D. Francis, London, 1970; *The Beatles Illustrated Lyrics 2,* London, 1971; *The Butterfly Ball and the Grasshopper's Feast,* with poems by William Plomer and notes by Richard Fitter, London, 1973; *Bernie Taupin: The One Who Writes the Words for Elton John,* editor, with Mike Dempsey, London, 1976; *The Adventures and Brave Deeds of the Ship's Cat on the Spanish Maine,* with Harry Willock, text by Richard Adams, London 1977; *The Peacock Party,* with Harry Willock, poems by George F. Ryder, London 1979; *The Lion's Cavalcade,* with Harry Willock, poems by Ted Walker, London, 1980; *Phantasia of Dockland, Rockland and Dodos,* with Harry Willock, London, 1981.

**On ALDRIDGE: books**—*Graphic Design Britain,* edited by Frederick Lambert, London, 1967; *The Poster: An Illustrated History from 1860* by Harold F. Hutchison, London and Toronto, 1968; *Graphic Design Britain 70,* edited by Frederick Lambert, London and New York, 1970; *Alan Aldridge: An Exhibition of Illustrations 1968-1973,* exhibition folder, London, 1973; Graphis Record Covers, edited by Walter Herdeg, Zürich, 1974; *The Contemporary Illustrator's Art: Six Artists and Their Books for Children,* exhibition folder, with introduction by Alasdair Dunlop, Colchester, 1978; *Album Cover Album: The Book of Record Covers,* edited by Storm Thorgerson and Roger Dean, Limpsfield, Surrey 1979; *The Language of Graphics* by Edward Booth-Clibborn and Daniele Baroni, London, 1980.

\*     \*     \*

Alan Aldridge's success undoubtedly lies in his natural skill in inventing grotesque compositions which have great popular appeal. The combination of a talent that everyone can recognize, together with his ability to produce endless inventions, have ensured him a place in his generation. Not only has he provided many outstanding illustrations for children's books, but it might well be said that all his works are visual fairy tales and that they belong to the fantasies of every age group. In much the same way as the lyrics of the Beatles's songs have a place in everyone's personal experience, so Aldridge's strange designs give tangible forms to universal fantasies. His imagery takes its place in the psychedelic dreams of the 1960s, and there is a strong element of hallucination in his visions of insects and grotesque monsters. Many of his paintings have an illusion of roundness and solidity as though to give added weight to an ephemeral vision. Aldridge has also given additional dimensions to the human form, as in his poster for the film *Chelsea Girls* by Andy Warhol or in the actual body-painting in his illustration of "Sexy Sadie" from *The Beatles Illustrated Lyrics 2,* which he also edited. Although very much a product of his time, he has drawn on the past so frequently that his work, which is full of quotations, takes on a timeless quality. For example, his work sometimes recalls the exaggerations of Tenniel's drawings for Lewis Carroll's poem "Jabberwocky." Even further away in time, Giuseppe Archimboldo's grotesque heads composed of vegetables find a parallel in Aldridge's illustration to "Dr. Robert" in the *Beatles Lyrics.* Certainly, the bizarre carvings of the Gothic cathedrals's anonymous stonemasons also lie behind the visions of this inventive artist. The exaggerated features of the part-human, part-mythical beasts of the medieval gargoyles find modern descendants in his powerfully grimacing figures.

In spite of the sculptural references in his work—and many of the images are based on three-dimensional models—the finished work is firmly related to the small scale of illustration on a printed page. While its concept can often be monumental, the actual image is often as detailed as that of a miniature. As in the universal images that Hieronymus Bosch contained in a single panel, so within the covers of a book one can travel through an immense world of fantasy in Aldridge's illustrations, as for example to the verses of William Plomer in *The Butterfly Ball and the Grasshopper's Feast* (1973).

—John Barnicoat

# ALLNER, Walter Heinz

American painter and graphic designer

**Born:** Dessau, Germany, 2 January 1909; emigrated to the United States, 1949, naturalized, 1957. **Education:** Studied under Josef Albers, Vasily Kandinsky, Paul Klee and Joost Schmidt, at the Bauhaus, Dessau, 1927-30. **Family:** Married Colette Vasselon, 8 March 1938 (divorced, 1951); children: Michel; married Jane Booth Pope, 4 April 1954; children: Peter. **Career:** Apprentice designer, Gesellschafts-und Wirtschafts-museum, Vienna, 1929; assistant to the typographer and designer Piet Zwart, in Wassenaar, Netherlands, 1930; assistant to poster artist Jean Carlu, Paris, 1932-33; partner and art director, Omnium Graphique design firm, and art director of Formes Editions d'Art Graphique et Photographique publishers, Paris, 1933-36; Paris editor, *Graphis* magazine, Zurich, 1945-48; co-director, Editions Paralleles, Paris, 1948-51; founder-editor, *International Poster Annual,* for Zollikofer publishers, St. Gallen, 1948-52; independent graphic designer and consultant, New York, from 1949; staff member, 1951-62, art director, 1962-74, *Fortune* magazine; correspondent, *Signes* magazine, Paris, 1990-92; contributing editor, *Design Journal,* Seoul, Korea, 1990-92. Professor, Parsons School of Design, New York, 1974-86; visiting critic, Yale University School of Art, New Haven, Connecticut,

1972, 1974, and Ecole Supérieure d'Arts Graphiques, Paris, 1979, 1982, 1985; visiting lecturer, Swinburne Institute of Technology, in Melbourne, Adelaide, and Sydney, Australia, 1983. **Member:** Alliance Graphique Internationale (United States President, 1972; International President, 1974); Comite de Parrainage, Ecole Supérieure d'Arts Graphiques, Paris, 1985. **Exhibitions:** *Bauhausler in Amerika,* Bauhaus-Archiv, Darmstadt, 1969 (with Josef Albers and Fritz Goro); Musée d'Art Ancien, Brussels, 1974; Gallery Estel, Tokyo, 1974; *Bauhausler in Amerika,* Bauhaus Museum für Gestaltung, West Berlin, 1976; Hemisphere Club Gallery, New York, 1976; Cooper-Hewitt Museum, New York, 1976; Kunstbibliothek der Staatlichen Museen, West Berlin, 1980; Bauhaus Dessau, Germany, 1989. **Collections:** Museum of Modern Art, New York; Cooper-Hewitt Museum, New York; Bauhaus Museum für Gestaltung, West Berlin; Deutsches Plakatmuseum, Essen; Israel Museum, Jerusalem. **Honors:** Chicago Art Directors Club Award, 1952, 1960; Art Directors Club of New York Award, 1956, 1958, 1960. **Addresses:** 110 Riverside Drive, New York, New York 10024, U.S.A.; Box 167, Truro, Massachusetts 02666, U.S.A.

## Works

Magazine cover designs include—Time and Life Building "500" cover design, for *Fortune,* July 1964; computer-generated "500" cover design, for *Fortune,* July 1965; 35th anniversary "Wheel" collage cover design, for *Fortune,* February 1965; light-generated cover design, for *Fortune,* June 1968; "500" consumer products collage cover design, for *Fortune,* May 1972. Allner designed 79 covers for *Fortune* between 1951 and 1973.

## Publications

**By ALLNER: books**—*International Poster Annual,* St. Gallen, 1948-52; *A.M. Cassandre: Peintre d'Affiches,* St. Gallen, 1948; (editor) *Posters: Fifty Artists and Designers,* New York, 1952.

**On ALLNER: books**—*Die Neue Graphik/The New Graphic Design* by Karl Gerstner and Markus Kutter, Teufen and London, 1959; *Monografie des Plakats* by Herbert Schindler, Munich, 1972; *Who's Who in Graphic Art,* edited by Walter Amstutz, Dubendorf, 1982; *Inside Time Inc.* by Julia Lieblich and others, New York, 1986; **articles**—"Computer Graphics at *Fortune*" by J. Lahr in *Print* (New York), November/December 1966; "Covers of *Fortune* Magazine" in *Idea* (Tokyo), no. 89, 1968; "Walter Allner in Tokyo" by S. Fukuda in *Idea* (Tokyo), no. 129, 1975; "Walter Allner" by R. Newman in *Design in Australia* (Sydney), February 1984; "Walter Allner" by Massimo Dradi in *Lineagrafica* (Milano), 1984.

*       *       *

Walter Allner's imagination, artistic know-how, and creativity have produced inspired graphics, logos, magazine covers, car cards, and one-to 24-sheet posters. In his own words, "The contribution of the individual—the artist, the designer—in graphic originality, excellence, inventiveness and even audacity alone ... stimulates interest and establishes the bond between the advertiser and the public.... In all my work, whether it concerns a poster, a magazine cover or any other design—I try to be concise."

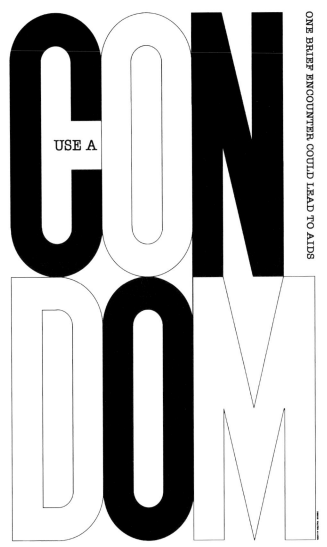

Walter Allner: *Use a Condom* poster, 1988

In this precise and concise way, Allner follows the principles he learned while at the Bauhaus in Dessau. He reveals the essence of each assignment clearly and simply, often using forceful graphic symbols. The message of text is always brief and to the point. His forms tend toward the abstract, with clear line and geometric shape enhanced by solid areas of pure color. In each instance, the design is unmistakable, and at once recognizable, as being a symbol of the product under consideration.

Before coming to the United States in 1949 Allner was already a noted painter, designer, and poster authority. While in Paris, he had assisted the posterist Jean Carlu and had worked with A. M. Cassandre. He had started his own design firm, Omnium Graphique, and was the art director for Formes, Editions d'Art Graphiques et Photographique.

Allner, along with others, has been credited with continuing the work of the Bauhaus in America. The spirit of functional design, which was so forcefully practiced there, can be seen particularly in the covers he created for *Fortune*. These covers demonstrate the range of possibilities in such an artistic medium. Allner believed every cover should be "something of a surprise." For one, he specified a program for a computer to design the cover. For the 35th anniversary issue, he designed a fold-out, using mangled cans to create an assemblage. Shortly after this was published, Allner received recognition for this work and was honored with an invitation to participate in the United States Information Agency's exhibit at the Berlin Industries Fair.

In the early 1980s, Allner was commissioned to design the inauguration poster for the new Bauhaus-Museum in West Berlin. Concurrently, a major exhibition of his editorial graphics and poster designs was held at the Kunstbibliothek of the Staatliche Museum in Berlin. His poster for this exhibition is a large, off-center "A", created out of the negative space of the white paper and defined by three colors: brown, green, and blue. The type in gray ink runs across the bar of the "A". A perfect example of his philosophy, created simply, directly, imaginatively, and concisely, the poster is logically symbolic of the product: Allner.

—Elena Millie

# AMBASZ, Emilio

Argentinean architect, industrial, graphic, and exhibition designer

**Born:** Resistencia, Chaco, 13 June 1943. **Education:** Studied architecture, Princeton University, New Jersey, MFA, 1966. **Career:** Curator of design, Museum of Modern Art, New York, 1970-75; freelance designer, establishing architectural practice, in New York, and industrial design office, in Bologna, Italy, from 1976; founder-president, Emilio Ambasz and Associates and Emilio Ambasz Design Group, New York, since 1981. Chief design consultant, for Cummins Engine Company, Columbus, Indiana, from 1981. Assistant professor of architecture, 1966-67, and Philip Freneau Professor, 1967-69, Princeton University, New Jersey; visiting professor, Hochschule für Gestaltung, Ulm, 1967. **Member:** Co-founder, 1967, and fellow, 1970-72, Institute for Architecture and Urban Studies, New York; president, Architectural League, New York, 1981-85. **Exhibitions:** Max Protech Gallery, New York, 1980; Leo Castelli Gallery, New York, 1980, 1983; Centro Domus, Milan, 1983; MAD Centro de Diseno/Galeria Ynguanzo, Madrid, 1984; Halle Sud, Geneva, 1987; Museum of Modern Art, New York, 1989; La Jolla Museum of Art, California, 1989 (toured). **Collections:** Museum of Modern Art, New York. **Honors:** Print Casebooks Certificate of Excellence, 1966, 1974; American Institute of Graphic Arts Award, 1973, 1976; Prix Jean de la Fontaine, 1975; *Progressive Architecture* Award, 1976, 1980, 1987; Resources Council Award, New York, 1977; International Business Designers Gold Award, 1977; Smau Prize, 1979; U.S. National Design Award, 1980; Designers Choice Award, 1981; Compasso d'Oro Award, Milan, 1981; Annual Interiors Award, 1981; Industrial Design Excellence Award, 1982, 1983; Merit Award, Art Directors Club of New York, 1983. **Address:** Emilio Ambasz and Associates, 636 Broadway, New York, New York 10012, U.S.A.

## Works

Arrow graphics poster, for Geigy, 1966.
*Italy: The New Domestic Landscape* exhibition design, for the Museum of Modern Art, New York, 1972.

*The Chairs of Charles R. Mackintosh* exhibition design, for the Museum of Modern Art, New York, 1974.
Center for Applied Computer Research and Programming, Las Promesas, Mexico, 1975.
Grand Rapids Art Museum, Michigan, 1975.
*The Taxi Project: Realistic Solutions for Today* exhibition design, for the Museum of Modern Art, New York, 1976.
*Vertebra* seating system, for Open Ark, 1977.
Banque Lambert interiors, in Milan, Lausanne, and New York, 1979-83.
Museum of American Folk Art, New York, 1980.
*Dorsal* seating system, for Open Ark, 1981.
Spotlights, for Logotec, 1981.
*Mimar* architecture magazine design, from 1981.
Lucile Halsell conservatory, for San Antonio Botanical Gardens, Texas, 1982.
*Oseris* lighting system, for Erco Leuchten, 1983.
Car showroom, for Mercedes Benz, New Jersey, 1985.
Obihiro department store, Hokkaido, Japan, 1988-91.

## Publications

**By AMBASZ: books**—*Italy: The New Domestic Landscape,* exhibition catalogue, New York, 1972; *Walter Pichler: Projects,* exhibition catalogue, New York, 1975; *The Architecture of Luis Barragan,* exhibition catalogue, New York, 1976; *The Taxi Project: Realistic Solutions for Today,* exhibition catalogue, New York, 1976; *Architecture 1,* exhibition catalogue, New York, 1977; *Il Disegno Oggi In Italia tra Produzione, Consumo e Qualcos'altro,* Rome, 1982; *Emilio Ambasz,* Milan, 1984; (editor) *The 1986 Design Zoo,* New York, 1986.

**On AMBASZ: books**—*The Print Casebooks: The Best in Posters* by Martin Fox, Washington, D.C., 1975; *Emilio Ambasz* by Marina Waisman, Buenos Aires, 1977; *Furniture by Architects,* exhibition catalogue, Cambridge, Massachusetts, 1981; *Emilio Ambasz: 10 Anni di Architettura, Grafica e Design,* exhibition poster with text by Fulvio Irace, Milan, 1983; *Concepts of Urban Design* by David Gosling and Barry Maitland, New York, 1984; *Emilio Ambasz 1984: Arquitectura, Diseno Grafico e Industrial,* exhibition catalogue, Madrid, 1984; *Twentieth Century Style and Design* by Stephen Bayley, Philippe Garner, and Deyan Sudjic, London and New York, 1986; *Emilio Ambasz,* exhibition catalogue edited by Giordano Tironi, Geneva, 1988; *Emilio Ambasz: The Poetics of the Pragmatic,* with text by Mario Bellini, Alesandro Mendini, Michael Sorkin, and Ettore Sottsass, New York, 1989.

*

I am an object maker, whether of graphic designs, products, or buildings. As for my attitude toward problem-solving in design, I can distinguish two features. First, I try, not always successfully, to go beyond the problem at hand. Second, since I am so lazy I always look around to see whether there is not something already existent which I may re-utilize.

Since I feel slightly guilty for having betrayed our forefathers' blind trust in progress and their belief in new products as the healers of mankind's problems, I have felt compelled to develop a little philosophical theory to justify such behaviors. It goes, more or less as follows: Europe's eternal quest remains Utopia, the myth of the end. America's returning myth is Arcadia, the eternal beginning. While the traditional vision of Arcadia is that of a humanistic garden, America's Arcadia has turned into a manmade nature, a forest of artificial trees and of mental shadows.

Like the first chair-maker who used the wood of surrounding trees, so now are some of America's designers beginning to use objects and processes (and sometimes, the memories) surrounding them. But, since no more trees remain, just chairs, they have to be careful that their creations are either capable of returning to their previous state, or of being re-utilized, lest they find themselves the gardeners of a manmade desert. The designer, that old thaumaturgus of the eternal gesture, must now learn both how to celebrate the ritual of the beginning and how to design for the ceremony of the end.

The principle underlying such notions of order is the concept of open-ended systems, where the possibilities for changing patterns of relationships remain always open, but where each of the component elements maintains its irreducible identity.

The methodological principle guiding my work is the search for basic principles and prototypical or pilot solutions which can first be formulated into a general method and then applied to solve specific problems.

A notion of design in dynamic consonance with a man-made nature in a constant state of becoming involves specialized tasks: first, *empirical,* to construct a cartography of the products and production techniques which populate the man-made garden; second, *normative,* to develop a program of individual needs and desires in the context of a larger program of social necessities, in order to guide the utilization of the empirical cartography; and third, *synthetic,* to give form to new structures which will allow man to reconcile his fears and desires within the limitations imposed by the empirical realm and the pressure of the normative domain. I believe that the designer's real task begins once functional and behavioral needs have been satisfied. We create objects not only because we hope to satisfy the pragmatic needs of man, but mainly because we need to satisfy the demands of our passions and imagination. It is not hunger, but love and fear, and sometimes wonder, which make us create. The poetic principle is the basis of our creating objects. The designer's milieu may have changed, but the task, I believe, remains the same: to give poetic form to the pragmatic.

—Emilio Ambasz

\*     \*     \*

Emilio Ambasz is one of the handful of interdisciplinary practitioners in the last half century to make contributions to industrial, exhibit, graphic, and architectural design.

Born in Argentina and trained in the United States, Ambasz is nevertheless linked with the current vanguard of Italian design. As curator of design at New York's Museum of Modern Art, he organized *Italy: The New Domestic Landscape* (1972), which first exposed the conceptual backbone of Italy's rebirth in consumer markets after World War II. As a polemic, and one that circumscribes Ambasz's own design efforts, the show demonstrated the shifting emphasis from the discrete, autonomous object to objects that function as part of a total environment, claiming for design roots in sociology, politics, and anthropology.

Ambasz established his reputation in industrial design with the *Vertebra* chair (1976), the first automatic, articulated office chair in

the world. *Vertebra* represented a new important re-statement of the role of ergonomics in modern seating. Rather than manipulating controls and levers to adjust the configuration of the chair, the user senses the chair as a dynamic organism as it responds automatically to the body's motions. The shift in Ambasz's approach is one from man's willful dominance over his environment to a more congenial, natural appreciation of his own physical condition in cooperation with the environment.

This same environmental consideration informs Ambasz's architectural projects. Rendered as visionary landscapes of mytho-poetic proportions, many of his projects remain unbuilt, promising a future rather than a present, where technological man finds a reconciliation with his rural past. With Luis Barragan as his closest influence, Ambasz pushes the idea of the machine in the garden to surrealist conclusions. His sites are often dotted with technological monuments that resemble neolithic menhirs, cartographic markers that are modern celestial notations of architectural mythology. The program, however, is visually concentrated underground, or in-ground, where the open-ended configuration of spaces and social patterns derives as much from the natural formation of the site as it does from man's appreciation of it. In an almost primitive reductionism, roofs dissolve into open sky, while containing walls are either transparent when above ground or bounded as excavated runs; in either case, the artifice of the architect's facade is denied. What is left is the rhythm of utility and psyche that is Ambasz's ritual goal.

Ambasz maintains a belief in the technological necessity of this romantic idealism. His most notable project to date, the San Antonio Botanical Garden Conservatory (1982), is a theater of virtuoso engineering. The truncated glass pyramids that signal its emergence above ground seem to be homages to the Crystal Palace, that temple of 19th-century technology, ironically constructed to accommodate full-grown trees among the exhibits. Functioning as a presentation of nature, Ambasz's conservatory offers downward views, upward views, as well a normative views, as foliage seem to emerge from underground or descend from the landscape. A sunken court with a natural pool at its center is surrounded by arcades with recessed viewing chambers acting as natural dioramas imbedded in cavernous rock. Access is provided underground through a bunker portal, from above via ramps that slice into the earth like natural fissures, or from a processional staircase that creates the effect of entering a Greek amphitheater.

Ambasz's intentions of giving poetic form to the pragmatic are evident in the dilemma he recognizes: "Europe's eternal quest remains Utopia, the myth of the end. America's returning myth is Arcadia, the eternal beginning. While the traditional vision of Arcadia is that of humanistic garden, America's Arcadia has turned into a manmade nature, a forest of artificial trees and of mental shadows."

—Sarah Bodine

# ARAI, Junichi

Japanese textile designer

**Born:** Kiryu City, Gunma Prefecture, 13 March 1932. **Education:** Trained in weaving at his father's textile factory, Kiryu, 1950-55; also studied at the Theatre Art Institute, Tokyo, 1953. **Family:** Married Riko Tanagawa in 1958; children: Motoni and Mari. **Career: Independent textile designer, Tokyo, from 1955; developed new metallic yarn techniques, 1955-66; worked with fashion designers Comme des Garcons, Issey Miyake, Rei Kawakubo, Shin Hosokawa, Yoshiki Hishinuma, and others, from 1970; created computer-designed woven fabrics, from 1979; founder, Anthology textile design and production studio, Tokyo, 1979, and Arai Creation System textile production company, Tokyo, 1987; opened Nuno fabrics shop, in Roppongi, Tokyo, 1984. Advisor to the Yuki Tsumugi Producers Association, Japanese Ministry of Trade and Industry, and the International Wool Secretariat, from 1987, and to several textile mills in Japan, from 1989. Also formed Tomodachi Zapoppet theatre group, Kiryu, 1950. **Exhibitions:** Gen Gallery, Tokyo, 1983; Nichifutsu Gallery, Kyoto, 1984; Sagacho Exhibition Space, Tokyo, 1984; Shimin Gallery, Sapporo, 1985; Takashimaya Store, Osaka, 1985; *Fabrics for the 80s,* Rhode Island School of Design, Providence, 1985; Axis Gallery, Tokyo, 1986; Apita Studio, Nagoya, 1986; Daimaru Store, Fukuoka, 1986; *Textile Convergence '88,* Chicago, 1988; La-Porte Hall, Kobe, 1989; *Hand and Technology: Textiles by Junichi Arai 1992,* Yurakucho Asashi Gallery, Asashi, Japan; Pacific Art Center, Los Angeles, 1993. **Collections:** Fashion Institute of Technology, New York; Cooper-Hewitt Museum, New York; Rhode Island School of Design Museum, Providence; Victoria and Albert Museum, London. **Honors:** Recognition Award, Japanese Association for the Welfare of the Blind, 1977; Special Prize, Mainchi Fashion Awards, Tokyo, 1983; Honorary Royal Designer for Industry, Royal Society of Arts, London, 1987. **Address:** K.K. Arai Creation System, 301 Esyc Heights, 5-16-8 Roppongi, Minato-ku, Tokyo, Japan.

## Works

*Bubble Blocks/103* bubble-structure fabric, for Rei Kawakubo, 1981.
*Cast Concrete/52* multiple-weave structure fabric, for Rei Kawakubo, 1981.
*Diagonal Fukure/106* bubble fabric with diagonal pattern, for Rei Kawakubo, 1982 (with Timney and Fowler).
*Split Rope/40* fabric with split warps and wefts for Issey Miyake, 1982.
*Nuno Me Gara* computer-designed patterned fabric, for Nuno, 1983.
*Big Hole/86* thick wool fabric with big holes, for Reiko Kawakubo, 1983.
*Organdie/139* puckered organdie fabric, for Nuno/Shin Hosokawa, 1983.
*Fringe/22* random cotton fringe on plain weave, for Issey Miyake, 1983.
*Warp Dye Marble/107* warp dye technique fabric, for Nuno/Hanae Mori, 1984 with Timney and Fowler.
*Big Check/36* transparent fabric of 4 thread types, for Yoshiki Hishinuma, 1984.
*Basket Weave Big Pockets/54* basket-texture fabric with large soft pucker, for Nuno, 1984.
*Spider Web/63* web-knit fabric, for Nuno/Koshino Hiroko, 1984 (with Riko Arai).
*Peach Fuzz/59* fluffy-surfaced fabric, for Osamu Maeda, 1985.
*Bell/28* thick wool fabric with pucker, for Shin Hosokawa, 1986.
*Big Sheep/29* thick wool fabric with big fringe, for Issey Miyake, 1986.
*Titanium Poison/32* double-sided thick wool/titanium lane pucker fabric, for Issey Miyake, 1986.
*Four-Layered Woven Magic* double-sided 4-layer patterned weaved fabric, for Nuno, 1988.

## Publications

**By ARAI: articles**—"Nuno Choryu" in *Ginka Bunka Shuppan* (Tokyo), no. 63, 1985.

**On ARAI: books**—*Fabrics for the 80s,* exhibition catalogue with text by Maria Tulokas, Providence, 1985; *International Design Yearbook 1987/88* edited by Philippe Starck, London, 1987; *International Design Yearbook 1988/89* edited by Arata Isozaki, London, 1988; *Ideas in Weaving* by Ann Sutton and Diane Saheenan, Loveland, Colorado, and London, 1989; *Hand and Technology: Textiles by Junichi Arai 1992,* exhibition catalogue by Junichi Arai and others, Asashi, Japan, 1992; **articles**—"Textile for the Eighties" by Tulokas in *Textilforum* (Hannover), September 1985; "Fabric About Fabric: Junichi Arai's Computer Creates a Textile for the 80s" by D. Cannarella in *Threads* (Newtown, Connecticut), November 1985; "Man of Cloth" by P. Popham in *Blueprint* (London), December 1987/January 1988; "Junichi Arai" by S. Anderson Hay in *Handbook for the Museum of Art, Rhode Island School of Design,* Providence 1989; "Textiles by Junichi Arai, 1979-1988" by M. Tulokas in *Textilforum* (Hannover), June 1989; "Junichi Arai" in the *New York Times,* 16 April 1990; "Arai Arrives" by Heather Smith MacIsaac in *HG* (New York), August 1990; "Junichi Arai and Reiko Sudo" in *Design Journal,* No. 42, 1991; "Junichi Arai's Creations Provoke, Mystify" by David Livingston in *The Globe and Mail* (Toronto), 16 January 1992; "Dream Weavers" by Naomi R. Pollock in *Metropolis,* September 1992; "A Fabric that Is Light, in Both Senses" by Elaine Louie in the *New York Times,* 25 March 1993.

*

From ancient times to the present day, mankind has been deeply concerned with fabric, from the cloth we are wrapped in at birth to the cloth we are wrapped in at death. If people were naked they would be like animals. By wearing fabric, we become aware of the changing weather and of sensations on the skin; we also derive feelings of joy and sadness from our clothing. Fabric clothes not only the body but also the spirit. Clothes are the proud emblem that connects us to God, and the weaver is the standard-bearer. Weavers were the standard-bearers for both the Renaissance and the Industrial Revolution.

Thus, the present technological world began with the relationship of people to fabric. And if we can properly understand both the advantages and pitfalls of new technology, we can start to make truly contemporary fabric. When things are made which look only backwards, to the supposedly golden past, they are the products of the nostalgia of weak people. Making a contemporary weave is like planting a seed into a new, uncultivated field. When the seed sprouts the resulting fabric is a fruit which communicates with all our senses and makes us rejoice. Newly conceived fabrics change our consciousness, change our spirit and so can change future society. This, therefore, is the mission of the weaver today: to pose the challenge of a new human revolution. Weaver, you are carrying the responsibility of beauty. What will you do if you cannot say, "This is a weaver's honour"?

A poet cannot write a poem if he has no words. In the same way, a contemporary weaver cannot create cloth without ideas. We cannot fulfill the needs of people today by mere nostalgia. We must understand the desires of the modern spirit so that we can create a truly appropriate contemporary fabric. Creating an image is the first step in making a work of art. But image alone cannot produce fabric; we need much more basic information in order to start to create: fibre, colour and twist of thread, weave structure, set and possible effect of finishing. We cannot start to create without our experience being applied to this information. But selecting from the possibilities offered by this information is essentially an ability of the soul. Fine contemporary cloths are the result of the human spirit and new technology working hand in hand.

We are asked about the ability of our soul to make such selections. The most enjoyable part of a weaver's task is transforming an idea into cloth. If a poet has only a limited amount of inspiration, he flounders: similarly, weavers must do more thinking and develop their ideas. Fortunately, the contemporary weaver has much new technology at his disposal, but this is also his greatest misfortune. He is confused and afraid of the tool that is the computer. This can only lead into a labyrinth with no exit.

How do we create ideas? How do we become inspired and cultivate the wasteland? The answer lies in the ability of the spirit to create and to nurture.

—Junichi Arai

\* \* \*

Master of traditional textile methods as well as a pioneer of modern technology, Junichi Arai has expanded the field of fabric design through his exploration of structure and materials. Arai's technical skill, unbridled imagination, and ability to achieve new and surprising effects in the interlacings of yarns—varying from wool and silk to plastic and other synthetic fibres—displays both his virtuosity and authority in textile design. When applied to fashion, the fluid fabrics seem to be made expressly for the body, allowing it to create its own form.

Arai's work was brought to public prominence by the Japanese avant-garde fashion movement, led by Rei Kawakubo and Issey Miyake in the 1970s and early 1980s. He collaborated with fashion designers, producing textiles that emphasized irregular texture and a handmade look with reference to tribal cultures. Working closely with mill owners and skilled technicians in his native town of Kiryu, traditionally a centre for the textile industry, Junichi Arai became influential not only in creating this new look in fabric but also in the redesign of highly technical machinery that had originally been developed to produce flawlessly uniform fabric. The computer, which the advanced textile industry had earlier adopted for design and weaving processes, became Arai's indispensable tool. Not only could the computer speed up the adaptation of a design for the loom, it enabled him to conceive structures whose complexity would be almost impossible to draft by hand.

With the computer, according to Arai, drafting the designs of his own multilayered fabrics—where patterns change from one side to another (with equal interest on both sides)—takes only a fraction of the time it would take by conventional means. The fabric *Nuno me Gara (Fabric about Fabric)* is a perfect example of his working process. Arai discovers an image he wishes to integrate into a fabric, then records it with a copying machine and produces a design that interlocks with itself to form a continuous pattern in repetition. The design is scanned by a computer to translate it into a double weave structure where two layers interchange in the black and white configurations of the design. Arai applies this pattern to a variety of special fabrics. In one, he uses overspun cotton yarn that curls back on itself when relaxed after the weaving process,

making the fabric denser and richer with stretch. Not only do Arai's fabrics show his remarkable facility for thinking three-dimensionally in terms of woven structures, but they also demonstrate his ability to envision the end results through many phases of a mechanical and indirect process. Arai's early experience with intricate and technically complex kimono fabrics most likely contributed to his prowess.

The relatively small textile mills of Kiryu with their modern technology have offered Junichi Arai ideal working conditions. Small scale production allows flexibility, experimentation at the loom, and finished samples within hours of the idea conception. In response to the needs of designers, manufacturers have developed a new range of yarns from natural and man-made fibres, making it possible for the weaving industry to achieve new effects. Texture, an important part of Arai's work, is accomplished with structure and, more often, with materials.

Arai has continued to design and produce fabrics for fashion designers as well as for his store in Tøkyo. In 1987, he concentrated his production with a newly-formed company, K. K. Arai Creation System. He has also expressed interest in designing interior fabrics.

While Arai's work expands the aesthetic and functional potential of fabric, it also carries with it the maker's inherent artistic vision. The distinction of the work lies in the directness of expression, his ability to convey experiences from the strength of his individuality. A variety of ingredients make up this character. Strongly organic surfaces of fabric, light reflected from synthetic material (at times juxtaposed with an organic texture), tactile quality, and black-and-white patterns with occasional organic colour bring a timeless quality to the work. Despite Arai's pioneering in textile technology, he remains firmly rooted in the human vision of his work.

—Maria Tulokas

# ARCHER, (Leonard) Bruce
British industrial designer

**Born:** London, 22 November 1922. **Education:** Henry Thornton School, Clapham, London, 1932-37; studied at the University of London, 1938-39; mechanical engineering, Northampton Polytechnic (now City University), London, 1945-50. **Military Service:** Served in the Scots Guards, British Army, 1941-44. **Family:** Married Joan Henrietta Allen in 1950; one daughter. **Career:** Worked in various industries as an engineering designer, 1946-50; design and management researcher, 1950-53; freelance design and management consultant, London, 1953-57. Lecturer, then Senior Lecturer in Industrial Design Engineering, Central School of Arts and Crafts, London, 1957-60; guest professor, Hochschule fur Gestaltung, Ulm, 1960-61; research fellow, 1961-71, and Professor of Industrial Design, from 1972, Royal College of Art, London; also visiting lecturer at several colleges and design institutions throughout the world, since 1956. **Member:** Science Policy Foundation, London, and Design Council, London, since 1972; Institute of Mechanical Engineers; Institute of Engineering Designers; Associates, Chartered Institute of Designers, London. **Honors:** National Prize, Institute of Engineering Designers, 1951; Kaufmann International Design Research Award, New York, 1964; Commander, Order of the British Empire, 1976. **Address:** 43 Avenue Road, London N6 5DF, England.

## Publications

**By ARCHER: books and papers**—*Training of the Industrial Designer,* Paris, 1963; *A Systematic Method for Designers,* London, 1964; *Design and the Community,* Vienna, 1965; *Architects Restructuring their Problems,* Cranbrook, Michigan, 1966; *Exploiting Instrument Development,* Eastbourne, 1966, 1970; *Design Methods in Architecture,* Portsmouth, 1967; *Structure of Design Processes,* Springfield, Virginia, 1968, Tokyo, 1970, Paris, 1971; *Technological Innovation and the Growth of the Economy,* Poconos, New York, 1970; *Design for Production,* Glasgow, 1970; *The Predicament of Man,* London, 1971; *Technological Innovation—A Methodology,* Frimley, Surrey, 1971; *Design Awareness and Planned Creativity in Industry,* Ottawa and London, 1974.

**On ARCHER: books**—*Industrial Design and the Community* by Ken Baynes, London, 1967; *All Things Bright and Beautiful: Design in Britain 1880 to Today* by Fiona MacCarthy, London, 1972; *Industrial Design* by John Heskett, London, 1980; *Design by Choice* by Reyner Banham, London, 1981; *The Conran Directory of Design* edited by Stephen Bayley, London, 1985; *Electrical Appliances* by Penny Sparke, London, 1987.

\*   \*   \*

Professor Bruce Archer's early career as a designer and teacher needs to be seen in the context of the growing enthusiasm for rigorous, systematic design methods, as voiced by J. Christopher Jones (*Design Methods: Seeds of Human Futures,* 1970) and the Design Research Society in Britain through the 1960s. It was hoped that if all the minute decisions involved in creating a design were recorded, it would be possible to build up a complete picture of the design process that would be explicable at all points. More recently, Archer has been advocating a position that goes beyond this extreme to the ethical concerns and intuitive elements of "planned creatively." "Good design is holistic design, in which all the functional, cultural, social and economic interests of all those who are directly or indirectly touched by it are enriched as much, or impoverished as little, as human ingenuity can contrive," he has written.

Through his teaching at the Royal College of Art and many international seminars and papers, he has stressed the vital role of design planning and organization in industrial management and company development. Increasingly, this has led him into the more general problems of "design awareness" and the place of design in education as a whole. Following a two-year research programme, "Design in General Education," funded by the Ministry of Education, he has argued that designing is a skill comparable to numeracy and literacy. He has proposed that design should be treated as an academic discipline separate from the humanities and the sciences with a focus on Design technology or "the study of the phenomena to be taken into account within the area of design application." He sees the following: "1. Design praxiology—the study of design techniques, skills and judgment applied in a given area. 2. Design language—the study of the vocabulary, syntax and media for recording, devising, assessing and expressing design ideas in a given area. 3. Design taxonomy—the study of the classification of design phenomena. 4. Design metrology—the study of the measurement of design phenomena, with special emphasis on the means for ordering or comparing non-quantifiable phenomena. 5. Design axiology—the study of goodness or value in design phenomena, with special regard to the relations between technical, economic, moral and aes-

thetic values. 6. Design philosophy—the study of the language of discourse on moral principles in design. 7. Design epistemology—the study of the nature and validity of ways of knowing, believing and feeling in design. 8. Design history—a study of what is the case, and how things came to be the way they are, in the design area. 9. Design pedagogy—the study of principles and practice of education in the design area."

Although the precise structure may be the subject of long dispute, his proposal may prove to be his most important contribution to design education.

—Anthony J. Coulson

# ARMANI, Giorgio
Italian fashion designer

**Born:** Piacenza, July, 1934. **Education:** Studied medicine, University of Bologna, 1952-53; also studied photography. **Military Service:** Italian Army, 1953-54. **Career:** Stylist, menswear buyer, for La Rinascente department store chain, Milan, 1954-60; worked for Hitman menswear manufacturer of the Cerrutti group in Milan, 1960-70; freelance designer, working with Sergio Galeoti to establish company manufacturing for Italian clothing factories, from 1970; created first collection under Giorgio Armani label, 1974; expanded design range to include womenswear, 1975; Giorgio Armani USA company formed, 1980; introduced sportswear range, and Emporio Armani shops selling younger collection in London, 1989; Armani Exchange boutiques launched in the United States, 1991; launched fragrances, *Armani le Parfum,* 1982, *Armani Eau pour Homme,* 1984, and *Gio,* 1992. Also film costume designer, for *American Gigolo, Thief,* and *48 Hours.* **Exhibitions:** *Intimate Architecture: Contemporary Clothing Design,* Massachusetts Institute of Technology, Cambridge, 1982; *Giorgio Armani: Images of Man,* Fashion Institute of Technology, New York, 1990-91 (travelled to Tokyo, Paris, London); retrospective, *Armani: 1972-92,* Palazzo Pitti, Florence, 1992. **Collections:** Costume Institute, University of Parma (sketches). **Honors:** Neiman Marcus Award, 1979; Cutty Sark Award, 1980, 1981, 1984; Manstyle Award, *Gentleman's Quarterly,* 1982; Grand'Ufficiale dell'Ordine al Merito Award, Italy, 1982; Gold Medal from Municipality of Piacenza, 1983; Council of Fashion Designers of America International Designer Award, 1983, 1987; L'Occhio d'Oro Award, 1984, 1986, 1987, 1988, 1994; Cutty Sark Men's Fashion Award, 1985; Bath Museum of Costume Dress of the Year Award, 1986; named Gran Cavaliere della Republica, Italy, 1987; Lifetime Achievement Award, 1987; Christobal Balenciaga Award, 1988; Media Key Award, 1988; Woolmark Award, 1989, 1992; Senken Award, 1989; Fiorino d'Oro award, Florence, 1992; Golden Effie Award, United States, 1993; Aguja de Oro Award, Spain, 1993; Academia del Profumo Award, Italy, 1993. Honorary Doctorate from the Royal College of Art, 1991. **Address:** Via Borgonuovo 21, 20122 Milan, Italy.

## Publications

**On ARMANI: books**—*The Changing World of Fashion: 1900 to the Present* by Ernestine Carter, London, 1977; *I Mass-Moda: Fatti e Personaggi dell' Italian Look/The Who's Who of Italian Fashion* by Adriana Mulassano, Florence, 1979; *Armani* by Richard deCombray, Milan, 1982; *The Collector's Book of Twentieth Century Fashion* by Frances Kennett, London and New York, 1983; *McDowell's Directory of Twentieth Century Fashion* by Colin McDowell, London, 1984; *The Conran Directory of Design* edited by Stephen Bayley, London, 1985; *The Encyclopaedia of Fashion from 1840 to the 1980s* by Georgina O'Hara, London, 1986; *Design Source Book* by Penny Sparke and others, London, 1986; *W, The Designing Life* edited by Lois Perschetz, New York, 1987; *International Design Yearbook 1988/89* edited by Arata Isozaki, London, 1988; *The Fashion Conspiracy* by Nicholas Coleridge, London, 1988; *Sultans of Style: 30 Years of Fashion and Passion 1960-1990* by Georgina Howell, London, 1990; *Giorgio Armani: Images of Man* by Richard Martin and Harold Koda, New York, 1990; **articles**—"Giorgio Armani's Fine Italian Hand" by Rita Hamilton in *Esquire* (New York), 22 May 1979; Cover story, in *Time,* May 1982; "La moda diventa arte" by Giampaolo Barbieri in *Amica* (Milan), December 1982; "Architectural Digest Visits Giorgio Armani" by E. Teston in *Architectural Digest* (Los Angeles), May 1983; "Armani: Success, Tailor Made" in *Vogue* (New York), August 1984; "Il nuovo studio di progettazione di Armani" in *Vogue* (Milan), September 1984; "Giorgio Armani: A Man for All Seasons" by Sarah Mower in *Woman's Journal* (London), April 1986; "A Cut Above" by Judith Thurman in *Connoisseur* (New York), August 1986; "Giorgio Armani: Il progetto dell'abito 1988" by Marco Romanelli in *Domus* (Milan), January 1988; "The Armani Mystique" by Ben Brantley in *Vanity Fair* (New York), June 1988; "The Emperor of New Clothes" by Bill Brantley in *The Daily Telegraph Weekend Magazine* (London), 17 December 1988; "Emperor Armani" by Sarah Mower in *Vogue* (London), January 1989; "The Emporio of Style" by Paul Keers in *GQ* (London), February/March 1989; "The Emporio Strikes Back" by Kevin Kostner in *Sky* (London), March 1989; "Giorgio Armani" by Carinthia West in *Marie Claire* (London), April 1989; "Giorgia Armani" by Eddie Lee Cohen in *Interior Design* (New York), April 1989; "Eagle's Spread" by Nick Jones in *Building Design* (London), 28 April 1989; "Alluring Armani" by Janine Furness in Interior Design (London), May 1989; "Giorgio Armani" in *Axis* (Tokyo), Summer 1989; "Emporio Armani" by Eddie Lee Cohen in *Interior Design* (New York), September 1989; "Armani's Island" by Sally Brampton in *Elle Decoration* (London), Autumn 1989; "The Genius of Georgio Armani" by Brenda Polan in *Options* (London), December 1989; "'What Is Man!'—The Image of Male Style of J. C. Leyendecker and Giorgio Armani" by Richard Martin in *Textile and Text,* 13 January 1990; "Armani: The Man Who Fell to Earth" by Georgina Howell in *The Sunday Times Magazine* (London), 18 February 1990; "La storia di Giorgio Armani" by Lucienne Mardore in *Marie Claire* (Paris), May 1990; "Giorgio Armani: This Is the Real Me" by Gisella Borioli in *Donna* (Milan), October 1990; "Sizing Up Giorgio Armani" by Ruth LaFerla in the *New York Times Magazine,* 21 October 1990; "The King of Classic: Armani" in *Elle* (New York), March 1991; "Giorgio Armani" by Anthea Gerrie in *Clothes Show* (London), June 1991; "To Give and to Take Away" by James Michaels in *Forbes* (New York), 28 October 1991; "The Armani Edge" by Ted Friend in *Vogue* (New York), March 1992; "Armani on Armani" in the *Daily News Record* (New York), 25 June 1992; "Armani's True Confessions" by Kevin Doyle in *Women's Wear Daily* (New York), 25 June 1992; "Giorgio Armani" by Lauren Hutton in *Interview* (New York), April 1993; "Giorgio Armani" in *Playboy,* May 1993; "Numero Uno: Giorgio Armani, the World's Most Successful Designer, Still Isn't Satisfied" by Sara Gay Forden

in *Women's Wear Daily,* 26 October 1994; "Lunch with Mr. Armani, Tea with Mr. Versace, Dinner with Mr. Valentino" by Stephen Schiff in *The New Yorker,* 7 November 1994; "Armani's Off-the-Rack Mozart" by Suzy Menkes in the *International Herald Tribune* (Paris), 17 January 1995; "According to Armani" by Sara Gay Forden in *Daily News Record* (New York), 19 January 1995; "World Class Armani Show Wraps Up Italian Season" by Suzy Menkes in the *International Herald Tribune,* 11-12 March 1995; "Armani and Ferré: A Study in Contrast" by Amy M. Spindler in the *New York Times,* 11 March 1995.

*

I do not design for a tall person or a short person, ugly or beautiful, jet-set or middle class. I aim at a client who dresses from individual choice, not imposed fashion, and not simply because something was designed by Armani. One must make one's own every eclectic and very subjective definition of style. A suit may now be a jacket with a pair of subtly contrasting sports trousers worn with a printed shirt and a zip-front vest. There should be no dictates, no rules.

My ideas come from unimportant things, from a book, a film, from talking to my staff, or from watching how people behave and live. I cannot allow myself the luxury of waiting for the "moment of inspiration." I design clothes that can be produced at a certain cost, that can be sold and worn.

—Giorgio Armani

*      *      *

Since he began designing clothing in 1974 Giorgio Armani has become one of the most influential European fashion designers. In a reverse of the usual progression from women's to men's clothing, Armani began with men's suiting and accessories. He brought into fashion the tiny, rounded shirt collar which was an important move to slim down proportions, and he created a soft, easy-to-wear alternative to the mode prevalent in the 1960s; notable in this new approach were longer proportions and a precise cut to show a man's body without restricting free movement. The most distinguishing feature of Armani's designs is the flawless tailoring, done with an attention to detail possible only by hand. He modified the inner structure of the jacket by not adhering the lining to the fabric's underside, a strategy which resulted in a free-flowing fall fundamental to the Armani style. He sloped the shoulders, dropped lapels, employed the lightweight fabrics which he often layers according to texture, color, and pattern. He frequently uses shimmering colors; his hooded sweatshirts, for example, were called "the jelly beans" because of their bright hues, and his linen suit has an iridescent cast. In addition to his famous alternatives to men's suiting, Armani has also offered his unique versions of leisure wear. His loosely draped, leather/bomber jacket and big-brimmed fedora over baggy slacks recalls the *Raiders of the Lost Ark* sensibility, modified into an up-to-date tone. Another relaxed outfit consisted of a velour sweatshirt paired with classic, white duck pants.

In a move perhaps even more innovative than his designs for men, Armani has translated men's basic classic clothing into a look for women which highlights the relaxed, revisionist, refined flair for which he is so well known. Big, flat-rimmed hats top loosely draped jackets, in gold silk lamé and wickerwork wool for dress and in subtle tones and stripes for business. These may be accompanied by long, freeflowing shirts or puffy, gaucho pants with classic,

25

low-heeled boots. The look is definitely feminine, sensuous, and emancipating in its practicality and comfort. Like his men's clothing, it too encourages diverse combinations to create for the wearer a feeling of self which is not totally dictated by designer regimes.

Armani has taken the basics of the "everyman's" wardrobe and given them possibilities for new varieties, open-ended and in tune with the freedom desired by the client who wants style without structure. His is a fashion revolution as prominent as that of Yves Saint Laurent or Pierre Cardin, less wildly severe or flamboyant than their approaches, more subtle yet emphatic and timeless. In a way very different from the methods of Elio Fiorucci, Armani has changed the bohemian into the fashionable, reshaping clothes from the ordinary world with a touch of the thrift shop but no hint of the cheap or gaudy. It seems totally appropriate that Armani's influence is both pervasive and subtle, felt by a young adult sector which is both professionally tuned in and relaxed in undogmatic independence. That influence extends to many who do not even know his name.

—Barbara Cavaliere

# ARONSON, Boris

American painter, sculptor and stage designer

**Born:** Kiev, Russia, 15 October 1898; emigrated to the United States in 1923, naturalized, 1930. **Education:** Studied at the State Art School, Kiev, Dip., 1916; worked under Alexandra Exter, School of the Theatre, Kiev; trained with Ilya Mashkov, School of Modern Painting, Moscow; studied etching and allied arts under Hermann Struck, Berlin, 1922. **Family:** Married Lisa Jalowetz, 1945; children: Marc-Henry. **Career:** Co-founder, Museum of Modern Art, Kiev, 1917; artist with the Culture League, Kiev, 1918; government artist and designer, making decorations and posters for street festivals and pageants, in Kiev and Moscow, 1918; principal technical and research assistant to Alexandra Exter, School of the Theatre, Kiev, 1919; freelance stage designer, in Moscow, 1919-22, and in New York, 1923-77; commissioned to design synagogue interiors and decors, in Washington, D.C., and Sands Point, New York, 1959. **Member:** German Artists' Association (Berlin), Moscow Artists' Association. **Exhibitions:** Anderson Galleries, New York, 1927; Odeon Theatre, Paris, 1928; *Painting With Light,* Museum of Modern Art, New York, 1947; Storm King Art Center, Mountainville, New York, 1963; Wright/Hepburn/Webster Gallery, New York, 1963; Vincent Astor Gallery, New York Public Library, 1981. **Collections:** Museum of Modern Art, New York; Museum of the City of New York; Library of the Performing Arts, Lincoln Center, New York; Theatre Collection, Harvard University. **Honors:** Guggenheim Fellowship, New York, 1950; Antoinette Perry (Tony) Awards, 1951, 1967, 1969, 1971, 1972, 1976; Ford Foundation Grant, 1962; Joseph Maharam Foundation Awards, 1965, 1967, 1970, 1971, 1976; Creative Arts Award, Brandeis University, 1969. **Died:** Nyack, New York, 16 November 1980.

## Works

Stage designs include—*Romeo and Juliet,* Kamerny Theatre, Moscow, 1919; settings for the Yiddish Kamerny Theatre, Moscow, 1922; *Day and Night,* Unser Theatre, Bronx, New York, 1924;

*Final Balance,* Unser Theatre, 1925; *Bronx Express,* Schildkraut Theatre, Bronx, 1925; *Tenth Commandment,* Yiddish Art Theatre, Bronx, 1926; *Tragedy of Nothing,* Irving Place Theatre, New York, 1927; *Angels on Earth,* Yiddish Art Theatre, 1929; *Jim Cooperkop,* Princess Theatre, New York, 1930; *Walk a Little Faster,* Schubert-Majestic Theatre, New York, 1932; *Small Miracle,* John Golden Theatre, New York, 1934; *Battleship Gertie,* Lyceum Theatre, New York, 1935; *Paradise Lost,* Longacre Theatre, New York, 1935; *Western Waters,* Hudson Theatre, New York, 1937; *The Merchant of Yonkers,* Guild Theatre, New York, 1938; *The Gentle People,* Belasco Theatre, New York, 1939; *Cabin in the Sky,* Martin Beck Theatre, New York, 1940; *The Night Before Christmas,* Morosco Theatre, New York, 1941; *The Snow Maiden,* Metropolitan Opera, New York, 1942; *The Red Poppy,* Music Hall, Cleveland, 1943; *Pictures at an Exhibition,* Metropolitan Opera, 1944; *The Desert Song,* Philharmonic Auditorium, Los Angeles, 1945; *Sweet Bye and Bye,* Shubert Theatre, New Haven, 1946; *The Changeling,* Project Theatre, New York, 1947; *Love Life,* 46th Street Theatre, New York, 1948; *Detective Story,* Hudson Theatre, New York, 1949; *Season in the Sun,* Cort Theatre, New York, 1950; *Country Girl,* Lyceum Theatre, 1950; *The Rose Tattoo,* Martin Beck Theatre, 1951; *Ballade,* New York City Center, 1952; *The Crucible,* Martin Beck Theatre, 1953; *The Master Builder,* Phoenix Theatre, New York, 1955; *Orpheus Descending,* Martin Beck Theatre, 1957; *The Firstborn,* Coronet Theatre, New York, 1958; *Coriolanus,* Shakespeare Memorial Theatre, Stratford-upon-Avon, 1959; *Do Re Mi,* St. James Theatre, New York, 1960; *Judith,* Her Majesty's Theatre, London, 1962; *Fiddler on the Roof,* Imperial Theatre, New York, 1964; *Cabaret,* Broadhurst Theatre, New York, 1966; *Mourning Becomes Electra,* Metropolitan Opera, 1967; *Zorba,* Imperial Theatre, 1968; *Company,* Alvin Theatre, New York, 1970; *Follies,* Winter Garden, New York, 1971; *A Little Night Music,* Sam S. Shubert Theatre, New York, 1973; *Pacific Overtures,* Winter Garden, 1976; *The Nutcracker,* Kennedy Center, Washington, D.C., 1976, and for CBS Television, 1977.

## Publications

**By ARONSON: books**—*Marc Chagall,* Berlin, 1923; *Contemporary Jewish Graphic Art,* Berlin, 1924; (illustrator) *Theatre in Life* by Evreinoff, New York, 1929.

**On ARONSON: books**—*Boris Aronson et l'Art du Theatre* by Waldemar George, Paris, 1928; *Boris Aronson: Recent Paintings,* exhibition catalogue by Marcel E. Landgren, New York, 1938; *Boris Aronson,* exhibition catalogue by Cecil Allen, Philadelphia, 1938, *Boris Aronson: From His Theatre Work,* exhibition catalogue with texts by Harold Clurman and others, New York 1981.

\*     \*     \*

In a tribute, the late director Harold Clurman said, "I know of no designer since (Robert Edmond) Jones who more unequivocally deserves the title of master visual artist of the stage than Boris Aronson." As early as 1926, Kenneth MacGowan referred to Aronson's work in the *New York Times* as "futuristic." Born in Kiev in 1898, Aronson studied art and stage design with Alexandra Exter, Tairov's leading designer and an exponent of radical stage design. From this exposure to the Russian experimental school

**Boris Aronson: model of setting for *Pacific Overtures***

(circa World War I), he began to formulate his theories of stage design: the set should permit varied movement, each scene should contain the mood of the whole play, and through the fusion of color and form, the setting should be beautiful in its own right. He would add, however, that a set is only complete when the actors move through it.

After brief stays in Berlin and Paris, he came to America to ply his craft with the Yiddish Art Theater and the Unser Theater, where he designed sets and costumes. While creating costumes for *A Chassidic Dance,* he said that it was necessary to examine the rhythm of the dancer, then to turn it into scenic construction. Design, to Aronson, dealt with the relationship of the actor to his environment. This inward approach, through the performer, marked most of his work. His early designs, however, reflected the Russian constructivism of his training. These influences can easily be seen in the sets for *Tenth Commandment,* in which he represented Hell as inside a human skull, or in *Little House in the Woods,* which takes place inside a house with walls and a roof that open up in full view of the audience.

For the Broadway stage, his work was equally inventive. *Walk a Little Faster* featured curtains, one of which was shaped like an iris lens, one that unzipped from top to bottom, and another which covered the performers' bodies except their dancing feet. *Do Re Mi*'s curtain of juke boxes evoked a cathedral's stained glass effect.

Aronson stated that his settings stemmed from either a "documentary," researched approach or from his imagination. The productions that he did with Harold Clurman during his Group Theater days, *Awake and Sing* and *Paradise Lost,* for example, showed the naturalistic, poor dwellings of the Depression era, while many of his other shows, such as Archibald MacLeish's *J. B.,* with its starry circus tent, explored the reaches of his and the audience's imagination.

He often stated that the theater is a collective art, and nowhere was this more evident than in his relationship with Harold Prince toward the latter years of his career. Aronson's Yiddish Art Theater experience came full circle with Prince's production of *Fiddler On the Roof* and his Berlin days, as well, with *Cabaret.* Prince brought out the pure versatility of his designer as evidenced by *Zorba*'s monochromatic settings and *Company*'s steel, plexiglas, and projections, which contrasted with the pastoral color of *A Little Night Music, Follies' "Loveland,"* and the Japanese-print style of *Pacific Overtures.*

Aronson was a technical innovator who, by employing projected scenery in *Battleship Gertie* (1935) and in Eugene Loring's ballet *The Great American Goof* (1940), became one of the first exponents of its use. In 1947, the Museum of Modern Art featured his projected scenery for the stage in a show called *Painting With Light.* He used modern materials to solve design problems, such as in deciding to build a giant mirror for *Cabaret* (in which the audience was to see itself) out of lightweight mylar instead of the usual weighty, and thus dangerous, glass. He even took advantage of new technology to aid the design process, as is illustrated by his use of a color copying machine to work out the pattern designs on the model of *Pacific Overtures.*

His work in ballet and opera, especially Mikhail Baryshnikov's *Nutcracker* and the Metropolitan Opera's *Mourning Becomes Electra,* proved that he was a well-rounded designer. Aronson's design of two synagogue interiors, writing of two books, and successful career as a painter and sculptor who had many one-person shows further distinguished him as one of the few leading figures in twentieth-century scene design.

—Tom Mikotowicz

# ARTHUR, Paul Rodney

Canadian signage and graphic designer

**Born:** Liverpool, England, 20 December 1924. **Education:** Studied at Upper Canada College and University College, University of Toronto, Ontario, Canada, BA, 1948. **Career:** Assistant editor, *Graphis* magazine, Zürich, 1951-56; founder, Paul Arthur + Associates (PA+A), Ottawa, Ontario, 1956-74; co-founder, Newton Frank Arthur Inc., Canada, 1974; founder and principal of design consulting firm, Paul Arthur VisuCom Limited (PAVL), Toronto, from 1974; designed signage and identity programs for large national and provincial institutions throughout Canada and the United States, including Canada Post Corporation, SaskPower, and the United States Postal Service. Editor, *Canadian Art* magazine, 1962-1967; director of publications, National Gallery of Canada, Ottawa, 1962-67; lecturer on design at institutions throughout the United States and Canada. **Member:** Founding member, Society for Environmental Graphic Design, 1973; Royal Canadian Academy of Arts; National Academy of Sciences, Washington, D.C.; chair, Canadian Standards Association Technical Committee CAN3-Z321 for Signs and Symbols in the Workplace; chair, Task Force on Design Issues of Exit Signs. **Honors:** Confederation of Canada Medal, 1967; Centennial Award, 1967; fellow, Society for Environmental Graphic Design, 1988; Order of Canada, 1994. **Address:** 10 Price Street, Toronto M4W 1Z4, Canada.

## Works

Signage programs for Winnipeg and Edmonton airports, for the Department of Transport, Canada, 1962.
Signage program, for *Expo '67,* Montreal, 1964-1967.
Graphic design for 12 university campuses, for State University Construction Fund, New York, c. 1965-1975.
Development of Picto'graficSystems©, a resource of coordinated graphic symbols, from 1967.
Travel information system, for the state of Vermont, 1968.
Identity program, for Stelco Inc., 1970.
Travel information system, for the state of Oregon, 1973.
Identity program, for the Province of Saskatchewan, Canada, 1974 (with Newton Frank Arthur Inc.).
Identity program, for Canada Post, 1989.

## Publications

**By ARTHUR: books**—*Campus Graphics: State of the Art,* New York, 1970; *Orientation and Wayfinding in Public Buildings,* Ottawa, 1988; (with Romedi Passini) *1-2-3 Evaluation and Design Guide to Wayfinding,* Ottawa, 1990; (with Passini) *Wayfinding: People, Signs, and Architecture,* New York, 1992; (with Robert Dewar) *Pictographs and Graphic Symbolism* (forthcoming).

\*

"Graphic design is the business of making or choosing marks and arranging them on a surface...." This nonsense, from a recently published English work on the subject, likens the design function to painting or even to doodling. Inappropriate as it surely is as a definition, it nonetheless accords with many practitioners' ideas about what it is that they do all day.

Manipulating marks in two-dimensional space, while a reasonable description of a technique that is involved in the day-to-day practice of graphic design, is nothing more than that: a technique or mechanical skill. But to say that it represents what graphic design *is,* is just too much of a simplification.

For one thing, as a definition, it ignores the idea that graphic design should have anything so mundane as a "function." The organizers of the Walker Art Center's 1989 exhibition, *Graphic Design in America,* got it a lot better when they described graphic design as a "visual language." And Adrian Moles, quoted early on in the catalog to the show, splendidly describes the function of the designer as being "to increase the legibility of the world." But even this definition does not satisfy if one believes that this form of design is in any way connected with problem solving.

Problem solving has nothing to do with elaborate compositions comprising photos, drawings, and layers of color, laid down over text matter, not as an aid to understanding but because it is considered the thing to do. These are to be seen every day in the pages of our national magazines. They are not designed to be read; they are designed to be viewed for what they really are: works of art in their own right. (From a chapter in the forthcoming *Pictographs and Graphic Symbolism.*)

—Paul Arthur and Robert Dewar

\*      \*      \*

The design and systematic use of visual communication has become increasingly significant as society becomes more mobile and multicultural. Paul Arthur believes that, as visual information is now so important, graphics can improve the quality of our lives by making information easier to find, understand, and use. His long and distinguished career has encompassed key developments in the growth of visual communications for identification and orientation.

One major development has been the adoption of identity design programs by corporations and governments, responding to the need for clarity and consistency made urgent by increasing institutional size and societal change. Canadian designers have an outstanding record in creating visual identities, and Arthur's major projects in the field include Stelco (1970), the Province of Saskatchewan (1974) and Canada Post (1989).

The second important development for Arthur's career has been the increasing complexity of the built environment and the public's corresponding need for visual help in finding their way around. His extensive contributions to the theory and practice of creating visual systems for orientation were more widely recognized abroad than at home until 1994, when he became the first communications designer to receive the Order of Canada (presented to Canadians "whose contributions enrich the lives of their contemporaries"). His achievement was cited as follows:

"A pioneer in the use of symbolic pictures in signage, he has made the built environment more accessible through the development of a new discipline in wayfinding. He was the co-author of Canada's national standard for signs and symbols in the workplace and is an international leader in his chosen art, dedicated to building 'readable' communications through graphic designs."

Arthur was one of the first to insist that design must be effective in answering the needs of a vast and varied audience, and that it must be seen as part of an interdisciplinary system, integrated with other aspects of communication and spatial planning. He invented the term "signage" in 1962, while working on programs for the Winnipeg and Edmonton Airports for the Canadian Department of Transport. Since then, he has undertaken many programs in the United States, notably for university campuses and the U.S. Post Office, and in Canada. He has also founded Picto'graficSystems©, a uniquely comprehensive system of pictographs for worldwide use under license.

Arthur's first large-scale use of pictographs was at Expo '67 in Montreal. It is over sixty years since Otto Neurath first described the need for "... a world language, or a helping picture language" in *International Picture Language,* but Arthur's objective distinction between successful communication and the designer's concern with style is still unusual. With a refreshing lack of designer's ego he has described how his own male and female washroom door signs at Expo were far less effective than the "hideously cute and vulgar" efforts of a local sign company.

Keenly aware that environmental graphic design must become a profession with clearly identifiable skills and expertise, in 1973 Arthur became a founding member of the Society for Environmental Graphic Design (SEGD) in Cambridge, Massachusetts, with six American designers. Arthur has written of the situation prior to the founding of the group, when he was working for the New York State University Construction Fund (SUCF). A well-known architect had expressed confusion: "We don't know what you know, what standards you have, where and in what you were trained, and therefore ... how seriously we should take you". Arthur was subsequently awarded a contract by SUCF to develop the ground-breaking document, *Campus Graphics: State of the Art,* in 1970.

Arthur's literary career has paralleled his design activities, and includes stints as assistant editor of *Graphis* magazine and later, editor of *Canadian Art.* He has since written several of the basic reference texts for print production and environmental graphics, including two standard manuals for Public Works Canada: *Orientation and Wayfinding in Public Buildings* (1988) and, with Romedi Passini, *1-2-3 Evaluation and Design Guide to Wayfinding* (1990).

The term "wayfinding," defined as spatial problem solving, marks a realization that information design must be user-centered. Arthur's book, *Wayfinding: People, Signs and Architecture* (1992, co-authored with Passini) develops the theme by analyzing how people orient themselves, and emphasizes the need for graphic designers and spatial planners to work together. Arthur and Passini define the processes involved in wayfinding as: decision making (planning action), decision execution (transforming the plan into action), and information processing (perceiving and understanding). As with the effective presentation of any kind of information, the audience

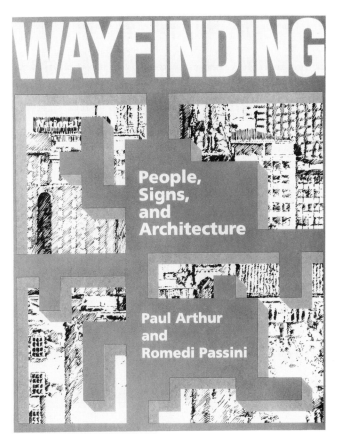

**Paul Arthur: cover of** *Wayfinding,* **forthcoming book on pictographs (with Romedi Passini)**

is actively involved: "The only way to approach wayfinding issues intelligently is for architects and designers to pay attention to how people perceive and understand the environment, how they situate themselves in space, and how they use information in the decision-making and decision-executing processes."

Arthur is systematically laying the groundwork for a comprehensive understanding of wayfinding (including issues such as bilingualism and the use of pictographs and arrows) in terms of legibility and readability. This is the kind of research and logical, interdisciplinary synthesis which is unusual in graphic design, where theory and practice rarely come together. In addition to his continuing design practice, Arthur is currently completing two more books about his field, *Effective Environmental Communication Design* and *Pictographs and Graphic Symbolism.*

—Michael Large

# ASHLEY, Laura
British textile, clothing, and product designer

**Born:** Laura Mountney in Dowlais, Glamorgan, Wales, 1925. **Education:** Educated at schools in London and Glamorgan; mainly self-taught in design, from 1953. **Family:** Married Bernard Albert Ashley, 1949; children: Jane, David, Nick, and Emma. **Career:**

Founder and partner, with Bernard Ashley, of Ashley-Mountney Limited printed textile company, 1954-68, renamed Laura Ashley Limited, 1968-1985; opened more than 100 retail shops in England, France, Germany, Austria, the United States, and throughout the world, 1967-1985; range expanded from scarves, smocks, dresses, and aprons to include home furnishing textiles, wallpapers, tiles, and perfumes. **Awards:** Queen's Award for Export Achievement, London, 1977. **Died:** Coventry, Warwickshire, 17 September 1985.

### Publications

**By ASHLEY: books**—*The Laura Ashley Book of Home Decorating* edited by Elizabeth Dickson and Margaret Colver, London, 1982, New York, 1984.

**On ASHLEY: books**—*A History of Fashion* by J. Anderson Black and Madge Garland, London, 1975, 1980; *The World of Fashion: People, Places, Resources* by Eleanor Lambert, New York and London, 1976; *Magic Names of Fashion* by Ernestine Carter, London, 1980; *British Design Since 1880: A Visual History* by Fiona MacCarthy, London, 1982; *The Collector's Book of Twentieth Century Fashion* by Frances Kennett, London and New York, 1983; *McDowell's Directory of Twentieth Century Fashion* by Colin McDowell, London, 1984; *The Encyclopaedia of Fashion from 1840 to the 1980s* by Georgina O'Hara, London, 1986.

*     *     *

Admittedly more an adapter than a designer, the Welsh wonderwoman of country cottage prints was the inspiration of millions. Laura Ashley's simplicity of pattern and design combined with a romantic nature inspired many to walk into a lifestyle where clothing was emotionally appealing, whimsical, and fun, yet practical, where home furnishings were traditional and frilly, yet comfortable and liveable. A love of nature dictated her style, as her designs were floral, soft, and organic, but much of her inspiration actually came from museum libraries, antique fabric pieces, old books, and the work of the pre-Raphaelite William Morris.

The Laura Ashley business covers textiles, fashion, and home furnishings. With a goal of becoming one of the best textile printers in the world, the company owns two textile plants with the capacity to bleach, print, and dye more than a million meters per week. The company's product line includes a line of country collage Victorian prints and a collection of distinct English Drawing Room prints to augment the seemingly endless possible mixtures of beautiful fabric combinations.

While the 1930s revival was dictating a sexy look in fashion, Ashley's clothing emerged fresh as spring air. The lovely garments brought a naivete to all who wore them, for in Ashley's world innocence and nature were synonymous. Expanding on this perception, Ashley designed wall coverings, furnishing fabrics (which take the company back to its origin in 1950s London), linens, bedding, and numerous other items from dishes to personal paraphernalia. Ashley even designed perfumes to extend the essence of nature.

Laura Ashley lives on in the imagination, standing in the countryside in a soft, romantic, country dress billowing in the gentle winds. As she picks flowers and concentrates on the color combinations encompassing her, we wonder how she would use them in her next collection. Ashley's ideas, descending from William Morris,

must bring all of us to feel a nostalgia for medieval art and pre-industrial values and to desire to get back to nature. In an increasingly computerized world, it's calming to know that Ashley saved a bit of nature for us all to enjoy. We must admire her sensitivity to style, her love of harmony, her respect for the past, and her ability to bring all these things to the production of a totally contemporary environment.

—Andrea Arsenault

# ASQUITH, Brian (Anthony)

British silversmith and industrial and product designer

**Born:** Sheffield, Yorkshire, 23 February 1930. **Education:** Studied at Sheffield College of Art, 1942-47; studied sculpture, under Frank Dobson and John Skeaping, at the Royal College of Art, London, ARCA, 1951. **Military Service:** Served in the Royal Army Education Corps, Colchester, 1953-55, Sergeant Instructor. **Family:** Married Barbara T. L. Tonge in 1949; children: Nicholas, Jeremy, and Patrick. **Career:** Partner, with David Mellor, metalware and product design workshop and office, Sheffield, 1955-60; established own design office, Sheffield, 1960-63, and Youlgreave, Derbyshire, from 1963; has designed for Redfyre, Spear and Jackson, British Airways, L.B. Plastics, Worshipful Company of Goldsmiths, International Tennis Federation, the Post Office, Baxi Heating, Renold Engineering, the Royal Family, and others. **Member:** Liveryman of The Goldsmiths Company; Society of Industrial Artists and Designers (fellow, 1965); Royal Society of Art (fellow); Chartered Society of Designers (fellow); Crafts Council. **Exhibitions:** *Hand and Machine,* Design Centre, London, 1965; *British Goldsmiths,* Lincoln Centre, New York, 1968; *British Modern Crafts Art Exhibition,* Tokyo, Japan, 1970; *Brian Asquith Silver,* St. Michaels Gallery, Derby Cathedral, 1973 (travelled); *Loot,* Goldsmiths Hall, London, 1974, 1975, 1976; *Silver from Derbyshire,* Foyles Gallery, London, 1977; *Lichfield Commission,* Victoria & Albert Museum, London, 1991; *International Gift Show,* San Francisco, 1993; *20th Century Silver,* Crafts Council, London, 1993; *Silver Trust National Collection,* Garrard and Co., London, 1994; *Silver Trust New York Exhibition,* Christie's, New York, 1995. **Collections:** Victoria and Albert Museum, London; Worshipful Company of Goldsmiths, London-Sheffield City Museum; Silver Trust Downing Street Collection of Silver, London. **Honors:** Silver Medal, Milan Triennale, 1965; six Design Council Awards. **Address:** Turret House, Youlgreave, Derbyshire DE45 1WL, England.

### Works

Font, in Birdseye marble, St. Mary's Church, South Ruislip, 1959.
*Elements Fire/Steel* sculpture, for National Westminster Bank, 1965.
Tea Set, for Goldsmiths Company, London, 1966.
Centrepiece, given by the British government to Mauritius to celebrate its independence, 1966.
Personal gifts for His Royal Highness, the Prince of Wales Investiture, 1969.
Bowra Tray, for Wadham College, Oxford, 1970.
Larmor Plate, for St. Johns College, Cambridge, 1970.
Regalia for Ribble Valley Borough Council, 1974.

World and Junior World Champions tennis trophies, for the International Tennis Federation, 1979-95.

Energy Conservation Trophies, for Post Office, London, 1981.

Chalice, paten, ciborium, and wine flagon, for Winchester Cathedral, 1982.

Chairmans Trophy for Innovation, for Grand Metropolitan PLC, London, 1984.

Sterling silver cutlery, for Goldsmiths Company, London, 1987.

Goblets, for Glaxo PLC, London, 1992.

Christopher Dresser collection, for Alessi S.p.a., Italy, 1992.

Coffee sets, for No. 10 Downing Street, London, 1993.

Company gifts, for Ove Arup Partnership, 1994.

Ceremonial mace, for Bolton Institute, 1994.

BAFTA Film Scholarship Award, for the Post Office, London, 1995.

Vase for Her Majesty the Queen, for Glaxo-Wellcome, London, 1995.

**Publications**

**On ASQUITH: books**—*Modern Silver Throughout the World 1880-1967* by Graham Hughes, London and Toronto, 1967; *All Things Bright and Beautiful: Design in Britain 1830 to Today* by Fiona MacCarthy, London, 1972; *Modern Design in Metal* by Richard Stewart, London, 1979; *The Contemporary Decorative Arts from 1940 to the Present Day* by Philippe Garner, London, 1980; *History of Silver* by Claude Blair, New York, 1995; **articles**—"Profile of a Designer" in *Stainless Magazine,* 1977; *Crafts,* November/December 1991; "Sources of Inspiration" by Marc Burden, *Crafts,* September/October 1993; "British Lifestyle Modern Design: Brian Asquith" in *British Embassy,* 1994.

\*

My prime consideration in all designs is to communicate the idea in simple, direct terms. I try to humanize the concept, to give balance and permanence to the object-form, which should be visually colourful and alive, and to communicate quality and precision. The design should be appropriate to the market for which it is intended, be economical to produce, reflect the age, and above all, be a statement about our future hopes. I am interested in forms and shapes that have timeless qualities and in solutions that involve exact geometry. On looking at an object, I try to analyze its meaning to the eventual universal user and its logic, to bring out only areas of importance, and to subdue other nonessential parts. The ultimate is to balance form, colour, and use, so that an uplifting experience is associated with the object or design. New technology brings forth limitless possibilities, but the criteria of planned obsolescence will be neutralized by world resources, both natural and economic. Designs will need to be timeless, simple statements that relate to their use, their material surroundings, and people.

—Brian Asquith

\*     \*     \*

Brian Asquith studied sculpture at Sheffield College of Art and the Royal College of Art. Sculptor Richard Bedford, the Keeper of Sculpture at the Victoria and Albert Museum, told him "I come from Devon so I use marble, you come from Sheffield so sculpt in

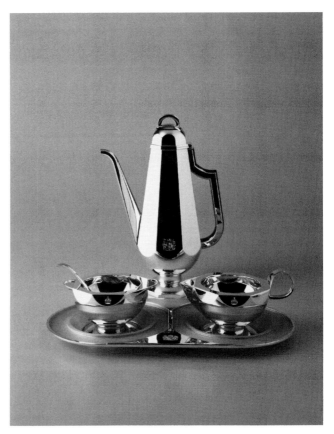

**Brian Asquith: Silver and gilt coffee set, part of The Silver Trust National Collection for use at No. 10 Downing Street, London. Photo by Mike Williams, courtesy of Brian Asquith**

steel." This Asquith did, notably with his monumental stainless steel and bronze sculpture for national Westminster Bank in Sheffield.

Asquith joined David Mellor in 1955 and opened on his own in 1960. In 1963, he moved out of Sheffield to the village of Youlgreave where he set up in the coach house of Turret House. In 1968, Asquith started making his silverware, applying an industrial approach with some basic components; the smooth, circular sections and the cast ribbed sections could be used in a variety of items. He has been very successful with silver, making a set of water jugs for Salford University, a silver centrepiece as a gift from the British government to Mauritius, a range of silver and gold boxes commissioned for the Prince of Wales' Investiture as personal gifts, a silver centrepiece presented by the Goldsmiths' Company to the City of Sheffield, a pair of silver wine coasters for the Officers' Mess of the Welsh Guards, a set of silver candlesticks presented by Darlington Corporation to Princess Anne, the ciborium, chalice, and alms plate for Derby Cathedral, and the chalice, paten, and ciborium for the nine hundredth anniversary of Winchester Cathedral in 1979. Asquith silver has also been ordered for sporting trophies, the Hamilton Formula Ford trophy, the Welsh squash trophy at Lancaster University, the World Tennis Championship trophies presented to Bjorn Borg and Chris Evert Lloyd in Paris (1981), and four cups for Davis Cup Zonal Competitions. For the Queen Mother's Eightieth birthday he was commissioned by the Victoria Cross and George Cross Associations to create a sundial of marble and bronze.

The bulk of the firm's business is with industrial work, machine tools, and domestic gas heating, but he keeps the craft work price down by using the stock components for the silverware in the industrial way. Asquith likes the contrast of shining plain silver with the textured sections deeply grooved like tree bark. He uses symbolism in some of his official commissions. The mayor's chain for the Ribble Valley Council (1974) has green agates to represent the countryside linked by wedges to represent the River Ribble. As the council is in Yorkshire the mayoress's chain bears the rose of York and Lancaster in gold. He loves stainless steel for its finish and toughness and for the contrast he can achieve with it, as in his stainless steel cross for St. Augustine's, Nottingham, in which sharp lines contrast with the Victorian tracery. While he has had to diversify for practical reasons, Asquith is at base a sculptor interested in textures and an innovator in giving the silver craft industrial methods.

—Diana de Marly

# ASSOCIATED SPACE DESIGN

American corporate planning and interior design firm

Founded as the interior design department of Finch, Alexander, Barnes, Rothschild, and Pashal architectural firm; incorporated as a separate firm, Associated Space Design, in 1963. Offices in Atlanta, Georgia, and Tampa, Florida. Officers: chairman, Cecil Alexander; president, William Pulgram; general manager and senior designer, Leonard Harding. Clients and projects include office spaces, corporate headquarters, churches, restaurants, and clubs, for Coca-Cola, Gulf States Paper Corporation, Neiman-Marcus stores, Island Creek Coal Company, McDonald Corporation, and others. **Address:** 100 Peachtree Street N.W., Atlanta, Georgia 30303, U.S.A.

## Publications

**On ASSOCIATED SPACE DESIGN: books—**_Interior Design: An Introduction to Architectural Interiors_ by Arnold Friedmann, John Pile, and Forrest Wilson, New York and Amsterdam, 1970, 1976; **articles—**in _Interiors_ (New York), August 1969, September 1970, January 1971, December 1973, August 1974, January 1976; _Domus_ (Milan), October 1973; _Contract Interiors_ (New York), March 1978; _Interior Design_ (New York), January 1982.

\*     \*     \*

With its main office in Atlanta and a branch in Tampa, Florida, Associated Space Design, one of the largest interior design firms in the country, is most likely the leading firm in the South. Founded in 1963, the firm had previously existed as an interior design department within an architectural firm for five years. Its president and chief executive officer, William T. Pulgram, has not only built up a first-rate interior design firm but has contributed enormously as a designer and leader in the field to many national causes. He is one of the most respected designers, and his activities with various governmental bodies, the American Institute of Architects, and a number of other civic and public groups have immeasurably advanced the recognition of the field of interior design.

Associated Space Design offers complete design services, including product and graphic design. The firm's clients include many leading corporations, banks, public institutions, and a number of governmental agencies. Known as a progressive and forward-looking firm since its inception, the firm won national attention for its McDonald Corporation in Oakbrook, Illinois in 1970. The open-office scheme for that project included the spaces for the top executives. The project also contained a highly publicized "think tank" and meditation room for those executives who needed to get away from their everyday work environment. In connection with the McDonald job, Associated Space Design developed a handsome and sophisticated line of systems furniture, which was subsequently marketed by a furniture manufacturer.

The success of the firm is partially due to the fact that it does not approach clients and projects with preconceived ideas. Pulgram stated in a recent interview that the firm does not have a marketing staff and that "we don't even have a decent brochure." He added, "We are involved more on a personal level." Most of the firm's new work is obtained by referral, which is about the highest compliment a firm of this size can receive. There are about forty members in the firm; some were trained as architects, including Pulgram, and some as interior designers, including vice-president Richard Stonis. One cannot ascribe a specific style to Associated Space Design; although the majority of its projects are work environments, it is remarkable to see the creative variety achieved among them.

—Arnold Friedmann

# ASTI, Sergio

Italian architect, exhibition, and industrial designer

**Born:** Milan, 25 May 1926. **Education:** Studied art and architecture, Politecnico, Milan, 1947-53. **Family:** Married Mariangela Erba in 1956; children: Marco, Paolo, Andrea, and Nicola. **Career:** Freelance architect and designer, Milan, from 1953; consultant to Ignis-Philips, 1956-67, ITT Europe, 1967, Ariston, 1968, Jabik wallpapers, 1975, Lange Italia sports goods, 1975-77, Lodi Gav, 1976-77, Corning France (Pyrex), 1978-81, and Alfa Romeo, 1981-82. Assistant instructor in interior design, 1953-58, and member of examination degree committee, 1989-1991, Politecnico, Milan; guest instructor in industrial design and furnishing, at Shizuoka Experimental Institute Japan, 1962, and at the National Institute for Industrial Research, Lisbon, 1966; visiting instructor in planning and design, State Art Institute, Venice, 1968-69; also visiting lecturer on design at professional institutes throughout Italy, Belgium, China and Japan, from 1962. Management committee member, from 1956, exhibition and competition committee member, 1995, Associazione Disegno Industriale, Milan; Italian correspondent, _Japan Interior Design_ magazine, Tokyo, from 1968; overseas associate, Spazio Institute, Tokyo, 1990. **Member:** Association des Amis D'Angkor. **Exhibitions:** Galleria Quattrifolio, Milan, 1967; Design Research, New York, 1970; Georg Jensen Inc., New York, 1972; Centro Cedit, Milan, 1975; Matsuya Design Gallery, Tokyo, 1981; Kyoto International Craft Center, Japan, 1983; Musée des Arts Décoratifs, Montreal, 1990, 1992; Salon International du Meuble, Paris, 1990; New York International Gift Fair, New York, 1991; International Glassware Show, Tokyo, 1992; Castello Sforzesco, Milan, 1992; Galleria D'Arte Moderna, Gallarate, 1993; Milan Triennale, 1995.

Sergio Asti: *NUVOLA* porcelain tableware, produced by Richard-Ginori, Milan, 1994

**Collections:** Museum of Modern Art, New York; Victoria and Albert Museum, London; Kyoto International Craft Center, Japan. **Honors:** Compasso d'Oro Awards, Milan, 1955, 1956, 1959, 1962, 1970; Gold and Silver Medals, Milan Triennale, 1957; MACEF Prize, Milan, 1972; Industrial Design Award, *BIO 5,* Ljubljana, 1973; World Crafts Council Prize, Toronto, 1974; Furniture Prize, Hannover, 1980; Honour Award, Institut d'Esthetique Industrielle, Paris, 1982; Board of Trade and Industry Prize, Tokyo, 1983; Honour Award, *BIO 10,* 1984, *BIO 11,* 1986, and *BIO 14,* 1994; 5 Stelle Award, Adi-Technhotel, Genova, 1992. **Address:** Via Bernardino Luini 12, 20123 Milano, Italy.

**Works**

Marano shoe shop interiors, Milan, 1955.
Kitchen units, for Boffi, 1956.
Tizianella apartment block, Milan, 1958.
Exhibition display, for Pirelli, in Teheran, 1958, 1969.
Charlie Max nightclub interiors, Milan, 1963.
FIAT showroom interiors, Milan, 1964.
Villa Brienno, Lake Como, 1967.
Fitzgerald nightclub interiors, Milan, 1967-68.
La Rinascente store interiors, Milan, 1969.

Crystal glassware, for Arnolfo di Cambio, 1969-83.
Colour television set, for Brionvega, 1973.
Stainless steel tableware, for I.C.M., 1975-83.
Car dashboard, for Alfa Romeo, 1981-82.
Stainless steel tableware, for Hiromori of Tokyo, 1981-82.
*Main Street Uno* wall lamp, for Eleusi, 1982-83.
*Alice* glassware collection, for Salviati, 1984.
*Alice* marble dining-table, for Up and Up, 1986.
Lamps, for Salviati, Murano, 1988-90.
Lamps, for Raak, Amsterdam, 1988-90.
Door handles, for Oshima, Tokyo, 1988-91.
Car steering wheels, for Diahatsu, Osaka, 1988-91.
Porcelain table set, for Richard-Ginori, Milano, 1988-94.
Ceramic objects, for Anthologie Quartett Bad, Essen, 1989.
Lamps, for Candle, Milano, 1989-90.
*Progetto Casa* ceramic tile design and consulting, for Ceramiche Ragno, Modena, 1989-91.
Marble furnishing, for Up & Up, Massa, 1990-91.
Lamps, for Salviati, Murano, 1990-92.
Lamps, for Soc. Coop. Artieri Alabastro, Volterra, 1991.
*Neos* electric wall clocks, for Lorenz, Milano, 1991, 1994.
Steel, wood, and porcelain table objects, for ICM, Lumezzane, 1992.
Marble objects, for Up & Up, Massa, 1992, 1994.

Design and consulting for furnishing accessories, for T. J. C. International Forum, Osaka, 1992.
Silver objects, for Miracoli, Milano, 1993.
Silver objects, for De Vecchi, Milano, 1993-94.
Glasses and glass table objects, for Nason & Moretti, Murano, 1994-95.

## Publications

**On ASTI: books**—*Forme nuove in Italia* by Agnoldomenico Pica, Milan and Rome, 1957; *Architettura ultima* by Pica, Milan, 1959; *International Modern Glass* by Geoffrey Beard, London, 1976; *Atlante del design italiano 1940/1980* by A. Grassi and A. Pansera, Milan, 1980; *Il disegno del prodotto industriale* by Vittorio Gregotti, Milan, 1982; *The World of Sergio Asti,* exhibition catalogue with texts by Vittorio Gregotti and Ettore Sottsass, Kyoto, 1983; *International Design Yearbook 1988/89,* edited by Arata Isozaki, London, 1988; *Italian Design 1870 to the Present* by P. Sparke, London, 1988; *Quality through Industrial Design* by A. Cannetta and S. Varadarajan, New Delhi, 1992; *Il Design Italiano,* 1992; *Storia del Disegno Industriale Italiano* by A. Pansera, 1993; *Dizionario del Design Italiano* by A. Pansera, 1995.

\*

I think it is always very difficult to speak of one's own work: to explain the "whys and wherefores," describe the "paths followed."

Our work, as designers, differs from others in that it does not require words, explanations or, worse still, justifications, but rather expresses itself by means of images, colors, and materials. It takes its cue from reason and rigor and constant self-criticism, but also from intuition, sensations created by surfaces and emotions that spring from seeing and touching (and also from using). It also takes its cue from the allegory of representation and symbols and from metaphor and allusion (not illusion). Not to mention from memory and from dreams of what we were and what we would have liked to have been. It is centered around new expressive adventures, new aesthetic experiences, ancient and sometimes mysterious paths, memories of ancient forms and techniques, the memory also of what has barely and inadvertently touched us (and yet has left an indelible mark).

It is centered around the ineffability of sentiments, passions, and emotions. That is why I think it is difficult for me to say something about my work. All of us have at our disposal an alphabet and, later, once adult, a wholly personal vocabulary which changes continually. While the alphabet is a freely-provided objective and mechanical instrument, our vocabulary reflects our world, our anxieties, and our labors. And the price to be paid is always very, very high. The space for the imagination, or for the imaginary, the space for all that is not a codified and immutable stereotype, is large or infinite, as the case may be. It is a space which is an integral part of our vocabulary. In fact, this space lays down the guidelines for it.

Our vocabulary, which is also our way of being, is, therefore, difficult to reduce to an unidirectional interpretation or to a geometrical univocality, but must instead be understood and deciphered as one would with a code.

And so, what explanation, in detail, can I give of my work? What can I say? Perhaps it is more reasonable that others should "interpret" and "decipher" and indeed more reasonable too, that these objects should go their way without backing or support, just as

they are: scintillating and joyful, because they are conceived and made not only to satisfy our physical needs but also to bring joy, to arouse emotions, to be looked at and touched and desired, and to be remembered for a long time. Like a beautiful woman. And so be it.

—Sergio Asti

# AUBÖCK, Carl

Austrian architect, clothing, and industrial designer

**Born:** Vienna, 6 January 1925. **Education:** Attended the Neustiftgasse High School, Vienna, graduated 1942; studied architecture, Technische Universität, Vienna, Dip. Ing., 1949; pursued postgraduate studies at the Massachusetts Institute of Technology, Cambridge, 1952. **Military Service:** Served in the Alpine Division of the German Army, 1942-43, Private. **Family:** Married Justine Krunes; children: Carl and Maria. **Career:** Freelance architect and designer, Vienna, since 1955; has designed for Ultra, Tyrolia, Wiesner-Hager, Schuhfabrik Koflach, Rosenthal, Radio Kock, Team 7, Firma Sowitsch, Ostovics, Philips, Tiroler Glashütte, Grabner, Firma Krotz, and others. Assistant lecturer, under Professor Merinsky, Institut für Baukunst und Ingenieurwesen, Technische Universität, Vienna, 1950-55; professor of architecture and design, Hochschule für Angewandte Kunst, Vienna, from 1969. **Member:** President, ICSID International Council of Societies of Industrial Design, 1973-76; president of the College of Delegates, Union Internationale des Architectes, 1982; president, Austrian Institute of Design, 1983. **Exhibitions:** Knoll International, Frankfurt, 1962; Design Centre, Brussels, 1968; Österreichische Werkstätten, Vienna, 1980; *Design Since 1945,* Philadelphia Museum of Art, 1983. **Collections:** Museum für Angewandte Künste, Vienna; Museum of Modern Art, New York. **Honors:** Gold Medal and Diploma of Honour, Brussels World's Fair, 1958; Silver Medal, Milan Triennale, 1961; Federal Design Awards and Awards of Honour, Austrian Ministry of Trade, 1962, 1964, 1966; Gold Medal, Liubliana Design Biennale, 1964; Austrian Coat of Arms Award, Austrian Ministry of Industry, Trade, and Commerce, 1975; International Design Award, Tokyo, 1978. Honorary fellow, American Institute of Architects, 1971, Instituto Tecnico Politico National de Diseno, Universidad de Guadalajara, Mexico, 1981, Kansas City Art Institute, Missouri, 1982, Bulgarian Architects Association, 1983. **Address:** Bernardgasse 21, 1070 Vienna, Austria.

## Works

*Amboss 2060* steel cutlery, for Neuzeughammer Ambosswerk, 1957.
*Amboss 2080* steel cutlery, for Neuzeughammer Ambosswerk, 1961.
*Burg* glassware, for Tiroler Glashütte Claus J. Riedel AG, 1961.
Electric food warmer, for Ultra, 1961.
*Tyrolia, Tyrolia Rocket,* and *Super Rocket* safety bindings, for Tyrolia, 1962-68.
*Neopan* research microscope, for C. Reichert Optische Werk, 1963.
School furniture and stacking chairs, for Wiesner-Hagner, 1963-65.
Construction/furniture programme, for Firma Grabner, 1964.
*MC* polyspray machine, for Firma Coudenhove, 1966.
Ski-boots in plastic, for Schuhfabrik Koflach, 1969.
Package design, for Radio Kock, 1975.

Enamel tableware, for Firma Riesswerke, 1975.
*Culinar* range of tableware and accessories in ceramic, cast iron, glass, wood, and textile, for Firma Ostovics, from 1979.
Furnishing fabrics, for Atelier Kindermann, 1981.
Tennis rackets, for Top Hit, 1982.
Floor and table lamps, for Philips, 1983.
Wall and freestanding electric clocks, for Firma Ostovics, 1983.
(Auböck has also designed numerous private houses, apartments, and public and industrial buildings throughout Europe and the United States, from 1952.)

**Publications**

**By AUBÖCK: articles**—in *MD Moebel Interior Design* (Stuttgart), no. 7, 1961, no. 11, 1982; *Ski Welt* (Solothurn), November 1971; *Brigitte* (Hamburg), December 1971; *Mosaik* (Zurich), March 1972; *Austria Today* (Vienna), nos. 3-4, 1975; *Werbung und Marktwirtschaft* (Vienna), June 1979; *Form und Zweck* (West Berlin), no. 5, 1981.

**On AUBÖCK: books**—*Mobili Tipo* by Robert Aloi, Milan, 1956; *Mercati e Negozi* by Robert Aloi, Milan, 1959; *International Shop Design* by Karl Kasper, Stuttgart and London, 1967; *Design* by Jocelyn de Noblet, Paris, 1974; *Contemporary Furniture* edited by Klaus-Jürgen Sembach, Stuttgart and New York, 1982; *Design Since 1945* edited by Kathryn Hiesinger and George Marcus, Philadelphia and London, 1983; *International Design Yearbook 1987/88* edited by Philippe Starck, London, 1987.

*

In the process of trying to increase and intensify the industrial potential of a country or a region, and to achieve a better socio-economic balance, long-range success without a growing element of planning for the future seems hard to imagine. Things simply have to be planned—designed—before they can be produced, and the capability, the know-how, and the professional qualities of the designer will, to a great extent, influence the success or failure of industrial production in the future. Therefore, the future of industrial design, and with it the socio-economic scene in a country (good or bad), will be the direct result of the planning efforts of today, and it will be up to the decision makers and their sense of responsibility to provide the choice and, indeed, a future for the community that will add to the quality of life. This will be true not only for highly industrialized countries but certainly even more so for the developing areas in the world. My own work as an architect and designer over the last thirty years has clearly shown a growing interest in the wider aspects and interrelations of the planning disciplines. The ideas expressed in this statement are intended to exemplify the interlocking aspects of evolution, both in architecture and industrial design, as an ongoing process rather than a series of accomplishments.

Although conducted as an international practice based in Vienna, my work inevitably reflects its Austrian background in the sense that there is a recognizable continuity with the twentieth-century tradition of architecture and design in Vienna, as established by pioneers and protagonists such as Otto Wagner, Adolf Loos, Josef Hoffmann, Oskar Sternad, Josef Frank, and others in the first half of the century. The intention of this statement is to explain the concern for quality in the planning as well as in the execution of buildings, products, and the general environment as they contribute to an increased quality of life in the complex context of the second half of the twentieth century.

Although I am equipped with specialized qualifications, my attitude as a problem-solver is that of a generalist able to deal with the problems on hand by inventing one's own working method and approach, rather than that of a specialist with a narrowed-down range of activities. The intentions and achievements in my work should therefore be considered as examples in a vital process of developing the creative potential of somebody who never was, nor in all probability ever will be, very much bound by the limits of professional or academic categories.

—Carl Auböck

*     *     *

Presented here as a designer, Carl Auböck is also an architect, entrepreneur, and university teacher. He himself sees no contradiction in these activities as they are all concerned with man's environment, and any separation of these activities seems to him an impoverishment. The description of designer is perhaps the most appropriate to Auböck because in its broadest sense it best expresses the unity of interest and action, of plan and execution.

His works in all their variety (buildings for groups or individuals, major planning or design of furniture, tableware, and sports articles) always bear his personal "handwriting," not in their appearance but rather in his approach to the problem, for example in the selection of materials, understood and put in the service of a function.

His direct relationships to materials is understandable against the background of his personal development in his father's workshop where bronze casting was carried out and where it was quite natural for the son to learn a craft along with his academic education. Craftsmanship is still necessary today in creating all the objects in metal, wood, leather, and horn which are produced to the design of Carl Auböck in the workshop of an old Biedermeier house in Vienna. This natural tradition is particularly important in Austria where tradition is often misunderstood because it does not rest on formal qualities but is defined as the promotion of quality in any work. The appointment of Carl Auböck as leader of a master class in metal design at the "University" for applied arts was a logical consequence, as was the fact that the students attending learn more than metalwork. Meanwhile, the master class is also called "Product design-metal."

While Carl Auböck's work is deeply rooted in Austrian culture with all its layers of art, literature, and history, it is not bound by frontiers. Postgraduate studies in the USA, a good knowledge of languages, and his personal curiosity have taken his activities far beyond Austria. It is perhaps indicative that he has built and furnished a cultural institute for the country abroad; his design work for international firms, his function as president of ICSID, and his lectures and publications abroad are also typical of him. As a consequence, he is much travelled and has the knowledge resulting from collaboration with and respect for alien mentalities. It is therefore understandable that Carl Auböck has worked out a "design policy" and long term concepts not only for Austria but also for other countries such as Brazil and Indonesia, and that he is frequently called into consultation by international organizations like UNIDO.

Carl Auböck cannot be fitted into any group or "direction," yet, or just for that reason, his works are contemporary. They are as new as possible in terms of materials, technology, and purpose; in their design and expression they are timeless. They do not deny their geographical and intellectual origins but they leave open every possibility for development in the future.

—Charlotte Blauensteiner

# AULENTI, Gae(tana)

Italian architect and interior, stage, exhibition, and industrial designer

**Born:** Palazzolo della Stella, Udine, 4 December 1927. **Education:** Studied at the Faculty of Architecture, Politecnico, Milan, Dip. Arch., 1954. **Career:** Freelance designer and architect in private practice, Milan, from 1954; has designed interiors for Fiat, Banca Commerciale Italiana, Pirelli, Olivetti, Knoll International, and products for Poltronova, Candle, Ideal Standard, Louis Vuitton, Artemide, and others. Assistant instructor in architectural composition, Faculty of Architecture, Venice, 1960-62, and Politecnico, Milan, 1964-67; collaborator in figurative research, with Luca Ronconi, Laboratorio di Progettazione Teatrale, Prato, Florence, 1976-79; also visiting lecturer at congresses and professional institutes, in Europe and North America, from 1967. Member, Movimento Studi per l'Architettura, Milan, 1955-61; editorial staff member, *Casabella Continuita* magazine, Milan, 1955-65; vice-president, Associazione per il Disegno Industriale, Milan, 1966; directive board member, *Lotus International* magazine, Milan, from 1974; executive board member, Milan Triennale, 1977-80. **Exhibitions:** *Aspetti dell'Arte Contemporanea,* I'Aquila, Italy, 1963; *Gae Aulenti,* Gimbels Department Store, New York, 1967; *Italian Design,* Hallmark Gallery, New York, 1968; *Italy: The New Domestic Landscape,* Museum of Modern Art, New York, 1972; *Gae Aulenti,* Padiglione d'Arte Contemporanea, Milan, 1979; *Le Affinite Elettive,* Milan Triennale, 1985; *10 Proposte per Milano,* Milan Triennale, 1985. **Honors:** Grand International Prize, Milan Triennial, 1964; honorary member, American Society of Interior Designers 1967; Ubi Prize for Stage Design, Milan, 1980; Architecture Medal, Académie d'Architecture, Paris, 1983; Josef Hoffmann Prize, Hochschule für Angewandte Kunst, Vienna, 1984; Chevalier de la Légion d'Honneur, France, 1987; Commandeur, Ordre des Arts et Lettres, France, 1987; Honorary Dean of Architecture, Merchandise Mart of Chicago, 1988; Accademico Nazionale, Accademia di San Luca, Rome, 1988. **Address:** Piazza San Marco 4, 20121 Milan, Italy.

## Works

*Sgarsul* rocking chair, for Poltronova, 1962.
*April* chair and stool, for Zanotta, 1964.
Italian Pavilion layout, XII Milan Triennial, 1964.
*Pipistrello* lamp, for Martinelli Luce, 1965.
Olivetti showroom interiors, in Paris, 1966, and Buenos Aires, 1967.
*Rimorchiatore* lamp, for Candle, 1967.
Knoll International showroom interiors, in Boston and New York, 1969.
Fiat showroom interiors, in Turin and Brussels, 1970.
Sanitary fittings, for Richard Ginori, 1973.
*Otto A* handles, for Fusital, 1977.

*Parola* lamps, for Fontana Arte, 1980.
Universal drafting device and drawing board, for Zucor and Bieffe, 1980.
Tea service, for Rossi Arcandi, 1980.
*Jumbo* table, for Knoll International, 1985.
Bench in marble, for Ultima Edizione, 1987.
Sanitary fittings, for Ideal Standard, 1988.
Watch, pen, pencil, and fountain pen, for Louis Vuitton, 1988.

(for a chronological list of Aulenti's buildings and architectural projects, see *Contemporary Architects*)

## Publications

**By AULENTI: books**—(with others) *Un Nuova Scuola di Base,* Milan, 1973; (with Franco Quadri and Luca Ronconi) *Il Laboratorio di Prato,* Milan, 1981; (with others) *Il Quartetto della Maledizione,* Milan, 1985; (with others) *Progetto Bicocca,* Milan, 1986.

**On AULENTI: books**—*Design Italia '70* by Davide Mosconi, Milan, 1970; *Design Process Olivetti 1908-1978* by Nathan H. Shapira, Los Angeles, 1979; *Gae Aulenti,* exhibition catalogue by Vittorio Gregotti, Emilio Battisti, and Franco Quadri, Milan, 1979; *Interior Views* by Erica Brown, London, 1980; *Knoll Design* by Eric Larrabee and Massimo Vignelli, New York, 1981; *Gae Aulenti e il Museo d'Orsay,* Milan, 1987; *International Design Yearbook 1988/89* edited by Arata Isozaki, London, 1988.

\*   \*   \*

One of Italy's few women architects, Gae Aulenti is a multi-faceted designer, teacher, and theoretician. She is a member of that second wave of postwar Italian designers who, stimulated and promoted by *Casabella* and *Domus* magazines, rejected the industry-oriented functionalism of the previous generation in favor of a more far-reaching experimental approach to the problems of design. She has produced a large body of work in such diverse fields as urban planning, scenic design, landscape architecture, furniture, and other consumer products but her international reputation rests primarily on her accomplishments as an interior designer. Her radical style is unremittingly modernist though she rejects, along with many of her contemporaries, the philosophical pretensions of the modern movement. Basic to this rejection is the rather poignant realization that the International Style is no longer experimental or avant garde. Aulenti's work reveals a desire to invest the by now traditional modern style with a humanistic dimension, with aspects of humor, mystery, ambiguity, and allusion that it has always lacked.

In her best-known interiors, whether private dwellings such as the Agnelli apartment in Milan (where a flock of sheep by French sculptor-designer Francas-Xavier Lilian are "pastured" in a hallway), or showrooms for Alleviate, Fiat, or Knoll from Buenos Aires to Boston, Aulenti has materialized the desire for a metaphysical dimension. Running through these works are features suggesting that the interior be viewed as a microcosmic landscape, a kind of interior "city." She has taken a formal, architectural approach to constructing domestic space as though it were urban space. She shapes and animates this space with purposely intrusive forms and protuberances, angled ceilings, and carpeted platforms, which become the symbolic "buildings" of her city scape, so that the interior becomes a background to "the daily scene" of living. She says, "Any man-made object, whether monument or hovel, cannot but allude to its relationship with the city, the place where [all] human conditions are found."

For Aulenti, the space should stand on its own and not need furniture to be defined. "It doesn't interest me to embellish walls that remain bare and useless and without meaning until the furniture and paintings arrive. What does matter to me is . . . to define a structure that in itself is . . . complete [so] that when you enter such empty surroundings they seem perfectly filled." Aulenti's environments, self-contained as they are, in fact, sometimes fight the furnishings that are brought in; this can be a serious liability for furniture showrooms in particular. Yet, the uniqueness of conception, the originality of the underlying motive, imbues each space with evidence of a complex sensibility at work behind the scene. The surfaces, frequently lacquered white and reflective, radiate an intellectual glow that reassures the inhabitant of the space and justifies its existence.

—Kenneth Gaulin

# AWAZU, Kiyoshi

Japanese graphic, stage, film and environmental designer

**Born:** Tokyo, 19 February 1929. **Education:** Studied at Hosei University, Tokyo, 1946-47. **Family:** Married Yaeko Shibuya in 1955; children: Miho and Ken. **Career:** Freelance designer, from 1955; organized *Persona* exhibit, Tokyo, 1965; art director, *Expo 70,* Osaka, 1970, and *Great Japan Exhibition,* Royal Academy, London, 1982; producer, *World Exposition of Science and Technology,* Tsukuba, 1982-83; director, National Anthropology Museum, Osaka, 1980-83. Associate professor of design, Musashino Art University, Tokyo, 1964-70; professor of design, Kyoto Junior College of Art, since 1980; directed, produced, participated in, and mediated at numerous exhibitions and design conferences. **Member:** Alliance Graphique International; Japan Graphic Designers Association. **Exhibitions:** *Japan Advertising Artists' Club Exhibition,* Matsuzakaya Department Store, Tokyo, 1955; *Future City,* Seibu Department Store, Tokyo, 1962; *From Spaces to Environments,* Matsuya Department Store, Tokyo, 1966; *Trends in Modern Art,* National Museum of Contemporary Arts, Kyoto, 1968; *Graphic Image 74,* Matsuya Department Store, Tokyo, 1974, and Watari Gallery, Tokyo and Nagoya, 1974; *Intergrafik Ausstellung,* Berlin, 1976; *3 Sections of Graphism,* Sao Paulo Biennale, 1977; *Traces and Memories: Prints by Kiyoshi Awazu,* Art Front Gallery, Tokyo, 1981; *Kiyoshi Awazu One Man Show-printed Works,* Earlham St. Gallery, London, 1981; *Kiyoshi Awazu,* La Forret Museum, Tokyo, 1984; *Kiyoshi Awazu Drawing,* Inax Gallery, Tokyo, 1984; (with F. Maki) *Tokyo, Form and Spirit,* Minneapolis Walker Art Center, 1986; *Kiyoshi Awazu Artist and Designer,* Ube, Japan, 1991; *Kiyoshi Awazu Exhibition and Workshop,* 43rd International Design Conference in Aspen, Colorado, 1993. **Collections:** Museum of Modern Art, New York; Stedelijik Museum, Netherlands; Poster Museum, Paris; Zürich Craft Museum, Switzerland; Zacela Art Gallery, Warsaw; Kawasaki City Museum, Japan; Toyama Kenrits Museum, Japan. **Honors:** Grand Prize, Japan Advertising Artists' Club, 1956; Film Poster Prize, Paris, 1958; Silver Medal, Milan Triennale, 1962; Mainichi Industrial Design Prize, Tokyo, 1966; Kisaku Ito Film Prize, Tokyo, 1969; Silver Medal and Special Award,

Warsaw Poster Biennale, 1970; Book Design Award, Japanese Ministry of Trade and Industry, 1973; Grand Prize, Leipzig Book Fair, 1974; Prize, Berlin International Graphic Contest, 1976; Nihon Academy Film Design Award, Tokyo, 1980; Special Prize, International Poster Biennial Exhibit, Warsaw, 1982; Purple Ribbon Medal, 1990. **Address:** 1-5-24 Minami ikuta, Tama-ku, Kawasaki City, 214 Kanagawa, Japan.

## Works

Iron gate, for the Izumo shrine, Izumo-shi, 1962.
*Persona Exhibit* design and layouts, Tokyo, 1965.
Playground, for Expo 70, Osaka, 1967-70.
*Inugami* stage design, for the Tenjo Sajiki theatre group, 1969.
*Akyu Gaiden* stage design, for the Bungakuza theatre group, 1969.
*Tokyo Three-Penny Operetta* stage designs, for the Geinoza, 1976.
*Great Japan Exhibition* design and layouts, Royal Academy of Art, London, 1982.
*World Exposition of Science and Technology* design and layouts, Tsukuba, 1982-83.
*Gaudi* exhibition design and layouts, Tokyo and Okinawa, 1978.
*Japanese governmental theme pavilion,* (including color scheme for entire exhibit), for Science Expo, 1985.
Eight murals, for Oyashirazu Pier Park, part of Hokuriku Highway System, 1988.
*Gigantic Sea Turtle, Million* sculpture, for Oyashirazu Pier Park, part of Hokuriku Highway System, 1989.
*Shonen no Umi* sculpted monument, for Oumi-Cho Junior High School, Japan, 1989.
*Save the Sea* poster, for the Foundation for Global Peace and Environment, Inc., 1993.
Film designs include—*Shinjo Ten no Amijima,* 1969; *Himiko,* 1974; *Denen ni Shisu,* 1975; *Hanaregoze Orin,* 1977, *Gaudi,* 1977 *Yashaga-ike,* 1980.
Book illustrations include—*Remi is still alive* by I. Hiramo, Tokyo, 1958.

## Publications

**By AWAZU: books**—(editor with Kohei Sugiura and Shomei Tomatsu) *Hiroshima/Nagasaki Document,* Tokyo, 1961; *The Discovery of Design,* Tokyo, 1964; *What Can Design Do?,* Tokyo, 1969; *Scrapbook of Kiyoshi Awazu's Designs,* Tokyo, 1970; *Talks on Design,* Tokyo, 1974; *The Thinking Eye,* Tokyo, 1975; *The Works of Kiyoshi Awazu,* 3 vols., Tokyo, 1978; *Gaudi Sanka,* Tokyo, 1981; *Design Junyu,* Tokyo, 1982; *The Works of Kiyoshi Awazu 1949-1989,* Tokyo, 1989.

**On AWAZU: books**—*Films and TV Graphics* edited by Walter Herdeg, Zürich, 1967; *Modern Graphics* by Keith Murgatroyd, London, 1969; *Monografie des Plakats: Entwicklung, Stil, Design* by Herbert Schindler, Munich, 1972; *Archigraphia: Architectural and Environmental Graphics* edited by Walter Herdeg, Zürich, 1978; *Who's Who in Graphic Art* edited by Walter Amstutz, Zürich, 1982, *Japanese Design* by Penny Sparke, London, 1987; *Awazu,* exhibition catalogue, Ube, 1991; *Kiyoshi Awazu* edited by Ikko Tanaka, Tokyo, 1994.

*

**Kiyoshi Awazu:** *The E,* 1992

Graphic design should be dedicated to human existence because it enriches life and makes it more beautiful. I have been mainly concerned with cultural themes—exhibitions, theater, cinema, and architecture—in my works, which are contributed to society rather than to commercialism. I firmly believe that graphic design should not only be used for commercial purposes but also for our daily life. Also, I believe that graphic design represents our ethnic backgrounds, history, and traditions. Needless to say, contemporary design has to make use of international methods. On the other hand, we still have to search for our own national identity in graphic design.

—Kiyoshi Awazu

\*   \*   \*

Kiyoshi Awazu's early poster "Give Back the Sea," which won first prize in the Japanese Advertising Artists Club 1956 exhibition, revealed the passion that he thereafter set out to make the basis of his design. Awazu's theme has been to continue to produce

works, created by means of his own strong intentions, while questioning the methods of expression in design.

In 1961, along with Kohei Sugiura and Shomei Tomatsu, he edited and produced the book *Hiroshima-Nagasaki Document,* which exemplifies the human conscience that wells up unavoidably in an individual in society where one is powerless to do anything alone, even though there may be a high level of scientific technique. Aware of nonrational and unconscious desires, he believes that even in fields such as science and mathematics, people are guided by their emotions. His work is motivated by the conviction that the expression of the passion of a single individual can shed a sacred light on modern, increasingly barren society.

Awazu's studio, built as an addition to his house ten years ago by the architect Hiroshi Hara, and fast becoming a well-known example of recent Japanese architecture, in itself speaks of Awazu's discernment and profound erudition. What particularly fascinates me among his numerous writings is an article on those who have influenced him, from Ben Shahn to Herbert Bayer and Antonio Gaudi, among others. In each case, Awazu has allowed them to pass through his sensibilities, analyzed them, and articulated their work through his own. It is as if they have all come together in fold upon fold, like the ripples created by many stones being thrown at once onto the surface of a lake, then been carefully considered, expanded, and given expression.

—Shukuro Habara

# AXELSSON, Åke

Swedish furniture and interior designer

**Born:** Visby, 1932. **Education:** Studied cabinetmaking, City Industrial Training School, Visby, 1958-59, and interior design, School of Arts, Crafts and Design, Stockholm, 1959-62. **Career:** Worked in an architectural office, Stockholm, 1960-62; independent interior and furnishing designer, establishing own office in Stockholm, from 1962, and workshop in Vaxholm, from 1970. Instructor in interior and furniture design, School of Arts, Crafts and Design, Stockholm, 1970-79. **Exhibitions**: Hantverket Gallery, Stockholm, 1968; *Ararat,* Moderna Museet, Stockholm, 1976; *Contemporary Swedish Design,* Nationalmuseum, Stockholm, 1983 (toured); *Faces of Swedish Design,* IBM Gallery, New York, 1988 (toured). **Address:** Galleri Stolen, Tyska Brunnsplan I-3, 111 29 Stockholm, Sweden.

## Works

*S 21 7* stackable beech chair with leather upholstery, for Gärsnäs AB, 1963.
*S 233* red beech armchair with leather upholstery, for Gärsnäs AB, 1967.
*Vaxholmaren* beech and leather armchair, for Gärsnäs AB, 1978.
Scandinavian stackable armchair, for Gemla Möbler AB, 1982.
*Kalmarsund I* knock-down chair in steamed beech, for Gemla Möbler AB, 1983.
*SAR* stackable lacquered red beech armchair with leather seat, for Gärsnäs AB, 1984.
Journalism House interiors, Stockholm, 1985.
*Classic Greek* teak and rope chair with linen cushion, for Skandia Insurance Company, Stockholm, 1986.

## Publications

**On AXELSSON: books**—*Form och Tradition i Sverige* edited by Birgitta Walz, Stockholm, 1982; *Contemporary Swedish Design,* exhibition catalogue by Monica Boman, Lennart Lindkvist and others, Stockholm, 1983; *Den Svenska Formen* by Monica Boman and others, Stockholm, 1985; *Made in Sweden: Art, Handicrafts, Design* by Anja Notini, London, 1987; *Faces of Swedish Design,* exhibition catalogue edited by Monica Boman, Stockholm, 1988.

\* \* \*

Chairs hang in bunches from the ceiling of Åke Axelsson's studio in the little town of Vaxholm. It is a peculiar collection, scarcely like any other Swedish furniture designer's. High up fly the ideas and prototypes—the inspiration. On the floor are the completed projects.

Åke Axelsson designs and handcrafts furniture, and is an interior designer. He is also a student of the history of the craft of furniture making. He claims he is driven by curiosity, a compulsion to test new solutions, but also respect for craftsmanship, the need to retain an open-minded relationship with tradition. He speaks of learning from history, seeking the common factor in different cultures in order to begin again from the beginning and peel away the inessential.

Åke believes in the future of utilitarian handicraft. Handcrafted furniture has so far been done mostly by exclusive loners. But Åke feels that it does not need to be like that. He has proven that handcrafted furniture is perfectly feasible, and a very attractive alternative to the mass-produced furniture of today. When the units become bigger and bigger, and production more and more rational, the products become impoverished: technology and the forces of distribution take over. "We need small-scale manufacture with limited resources," performed by people directly for other people, says Åke.

For a few years in the 1970s, together with an assistant, Åke Axelsson accomplished one of his dreams—starting small-scale production of simple handcrafted chairs, reasonable in price, and developed in close contact with the user.

In 1970 Åke Axelsson became a teacher at the National College of Art and Design in Stockholm. To teach others, one must teach oneself. Åke knew about the handicraft of today, but not that of history. He worked his way back to the earliest types of chairs in our civilization, those of ancient Egypt and Greece.

Hitherto they had been defined in the terms of the art historian, but Åke looked at them with the eyes of a craftsman. He wanted to see how these chairs actually worked beneath the veneer of antiquity, how they were constructed and how they had come to be designed as they were.

He did this by reconstructing the chairs themselves as full-scale models—a kind of basic research in which hand and brain together revived the knowledge of vanished eras.

He found a highly developed, refined technique, the result of a long process of historical evolution. He was impressed by the way in which people derived the utmost possible return from their material, and by the interaction between the structure and the weight of the person sitting on it. He has transferred this experience into his own handmade chairs.

Åke Axelsson has had many commissions over the years. In the 1960s he was involved in the renovation of the Operakallaren restaurant in Stockholm, under the direction of Peter Celsing. In this lavishly rich, dramatic nineteenth century setting, he learned how restoration could be combined with innovation. In the 1980s Sweden's Parliament Building in Stockholm was one of his major commissions. In Australia, the Parliament Building in Canberra was inaugurated in 1988 with 2,400 seats, all designed by Åke Axelsson. The furniture is produced by Gärsnäs but manufactured on licence in Australia.

His interior design projects have generated several chairs which have entered mass production. But Åke's great desire has been to immerse himself in unique furniture—the type that does not have to defer to a predetermined environment. He has made experimental furniture so bold that no manufacturer has yet dared to produce it: lightweight, steel strip constructions with seats and backs of beech slats—simple, clearly outlined designs, with spring and elasticity which shape themselves according to the movement of the body.

But at the same time Åke Axelsson continues to make new industrial chairs—among others, a knock-down chair for Gemla which was highly economical to produce. The same leg design can be used for three different models. But the essentials of craftsmanship are still there, and the source of inspiration was the old brewery chair. Tradition, rational production and craftsmanship do not have to be mutually exclusive.

At the same time he is experimenting to endow the purely industrial product with an artistic dimension. On the floor of his studio at the moment stands an extremely rudimentary chair with a seat and back of plywood boards. The parts can be put together like a Meccano construction, and the boards can be freely chosen from a color system devised by the concretist painter and color theorist K. G. Nilsson, who has also designed a decor of colored triangles to be printed on them.

The tension between craft and industrial design, art and mass production, furniture and space, is ever present in Åke Axelsson's work. Hitherto this has been a fruitful tension, resembling a magnetic field in which particles of ideas are constantly in motion, forming new patterns.

The dialogue between space and the chair is necessary, says Åke. It would be wrong to lose contact with the environment in which furniture is used.

—Monica Boman

# BADAY, Lida

Canadian fashion designer

**Born:** Hamilton, Ontario, 31 July 1957. **Education:** Graduated from Ryerson Polytechnical Institute, Toronto, 1979. **Family:** Married Mario Zuliani. **Career:** Pattern maker, Becker Fashion; designer, Kira Fashion and Miller Group; founder and designer, Lida Baday Ltd., Toronto, from 1987; collections available in specialty boutiques in Canada, the United States, and Europe; clients include Deborah Norville of *Inside Edition,* Jeanne Beker of *Fashion Television,* Bridget Fonda, Stefanie Powers, and Contess Serena Balfour; designs featured in films *Mrs. Winterbourne* (1996), *Copycat* (1996), and *Degree of Guilt* (NBC-TV). **Honors:** Fil D'Argent for Canada, Maison du Lin, Paris, 1990; Designer of the Year Award, City of Toronto, 1992; Buyer's Designer of the Year Award for Excellence in Canadian Fashion Design, Vidal Sassoon International, 1996. **Addresses:** (office) Lida Baday Ltd., 70 Claremont Street, Studio 200, Toronto, Ontario M6J 2M5, Canada; (showroom) Lida Baday Inc., 550 Seventh Avenue, New York, New York 10018, U.S.A.

## Publications

On BADAY: articles—*Marie Claire* (London), November 1995; *Mirabella* (New York), May/June 1996; features in Canadian fashion magazines *Flare, Toronto Life Fashion, Images,* and *Canadian Living.*

\*       \*       \*

Lida Baday is one of Canada's preeminent fashion designers. Her women's wear collections are characterized by simplicity of form, a minimum of decoration, and excellence in construction. She relies on fabric and cut to make her quiet, elegant statements, employing color and pattern in limited quantities.

Born in Hamilton, Ontario, a steel town in Canada's industrial heartland, Baday grew up watching and working with her mother, a custom dressmaker. Following her mother through fabric stores and notions shops, and acting as her mannequin, Baday developed a keen understanding of fit and fabric. She went on to study fashion at Ryerson Polytechnical Institute, which offers one of Canada's leading fashion design programs. After graduating in 1979, Baday worked for a number of dress manufacturers in Toronto, working her way up through the ranks. By 1987, she had established her own label with The Miller Group. Though the financial instability of the company enabled her to produce only one line, she credits the experience with teaching her about the business of fashion and with providing her with invaluable contacts.

By the end of 1987, Lida Baday had launched her own company and label. Her business has expanded slowly but steadily ever since. Starting from small specialty stores in Toronto, she has moved into Holt Renfrew, Canada's most exclusive department store chain. After showing at New York's Fashion Coterie for a few years, she opened a showroom on Seventh Avenue in 1994. The move paid off, landing her accounts with Sak's Fifth Avenue, Bergdorf Goodman, and Neiman Marcus.

Baday favors solid colors in muted shades. Dabs of saturated color in the collection are used for maximum impact; the sheath dress, a long, fluid sheath of silk, sleeveless and slit high on the thigh, comes in black, sand, or a luscious coral. The sheath dress is a classic in her collections, along with a t-shirt style dress and a princess-seamed knit jumper. Tailored favorites include short-cropped jackets and long shaped cutaway jackets.

Baday's style can be compared to the designs of Donna Karan, as both designers take their inspiration from a fabric and emphasize the body. However, Karan's tight jersey separates are womanly where Baday's draped jersey dresses are feminine. Both are sexy, but Baday's are unconsciously sexy.

In 1990, Baday won international recognition when she was awarded the Fil d'Argent for Canada in Paris from the Maison du Lin, the promotional arm of the Linen Commission of France. The McCall Pattern Company, an American company that makes patterns for home sewers, selected two outfits from her fall 1992 collection to be included in its pattern catalog, a first for a Canadian designer.

A shy designer, Baday is an anomaly in the ever-changing, flashy world of fashion. She consistently offers simplicity, impeccable fit and finishing, and quality fabrics.

—Elizabeth Crawford

# BALENCIAGA, Cristobal

Spanish fashion designer

**Born:** Guetaria, near San Sebastian, 21 January 1895. **Education:** Studied needlework and dressmaking with his mother in Guetaria, until 1910. **Career:** Established tailoring business, with sponsorship of the Marquesa de Casa Torres, San Sebastian, 1915-21; founded Eisa fashion house, Barcelona, 1922-31, and Madrid, 1932-37; director, Maison Balenciaga fashion house, on Avenue George V, Paris, 1937-40, 1945-68. Designed film costumes for *The Empty Star,* 1962. **Exhibitions:** *Fashion: An Anthology,* Victoria and Albert Museum, London, 1971; *The World of Balenciaga,* Metropolitan Museum of Art, New York, 1973. **Honors:** Chevalier de la Légion d'Honneur, France; Commander, L'Ordre d'Isabelle-la-Catholique. **Died:** Javea, Spain, 23 March 1972.

**Publications**

On BALENCIAGA: books—*Always in Vogue* by Edna Woolman Chase and Ilka Chase, London, 1954; *Kings of Fashion* by Anny Latour Stuttgart, 1956, London, 1958; *The Wheels of Fashion* by Phyllis Lee Levin, New York, 1965; *The Fashionable Savages* by John Fairchild, New York, 1965; *The Fashion Makers* by Leonard Halliday, London, 1966; *Fashion: An Anthology* by Cecil Beaton, exhibition catalogue compiled by Madeleine Ginsburg, London, 1971; *Paris Fashion: The Great Designers and Their Creations* edited by Ruth Lynam, London, 1972; *The World of Balenciaga,* exhibition catalogue with texts by Diana Vreeland and others, New York, 1973, *In Vogue: Sixty Years of Celebrities and Fashion* edited by Georgina Howell, London, 1975, 1978, New York, 1976; *The History of Haute Couture 1850-1950* by Diana de Marly, London, 1980; *Magic Names of Fashion* by Ernestine Carter, London, 1980; *McDowell's Directory of Twentieth Century Fashion* by Colin McDowell, London, 1984; *The Conran Directory of Design* edited by Stephen Bayley, London, 1985; *The Encyclopaedia of Fashion from 1840 to the 1980s* by Georgina O'Hara, London, 1986.

\*      \*      \*

Cristobal Balenciaga was a master couturier whose perfected skills and Spanish heritage resulted in abstract sculpture in silk and wool, wearable monuments to feminine dignity and elegance. His seamstress-mother taught him to cut and sew skillfully. As a young teenager, he so impressed the Marquesa Casa de Torres that she financed his first trip to Paris and also his first tailoring shop. Later, as a buyer for a Spanish store, he traveled often to Paris to purchase couture clothes. In the 1920s, this experience culminated in the opening of the first of two Spanish couture establishments, both named Eisa.

The Spanish Civil War hastened his move to Paris, where in 1937 Spanish friends backed the opening of the couture house bearing his name. The fashion press was hesitant to accept this newcomer to French couture, but Balenciaga found an immediate and lifelong champion in *Harper's Bazaar* editor Carmel Snow. During the late 1930s, the pages of *Bazaar* featured Balenciaga designs such as his Infanta gown of dramatic black and white silk, its padded hips and exaggerated sleeves achieving a popular, romantic silhouette.

Balenciaga's was one of the few Paris couture houses permitted to remain open during the German occupation. During this time he created lavishly embellished matador jackets worn with black evening gowns. He showed, too, closely molded bodices and bouffant skirts which would achieve their most popular expression in Christian Dior's New Look of 1947.

Balenciaga was the first couturier to experiment, as early as 1946, with prophetic, semi-fitted silhouettes. He initiated a gradual evolution towards minimal shaping. His lace chemise dress with dropped waistline was atypical for 1951. It looked ahead to the popularization of unfitted dresses in the late 1950s, notably the famous "sack" dress.

After Dior's death in 1957, Balenciaga was regarded as the world's foremost couturier. Always an innovator of silhouettes, in this period he designed idiosyncratic evening gowns that were aesthetic and technical masterworks. He cut and draped stiff, lightweight silk gazar into abstract volumes which hovered about the wearer and floated majestically as she moved. His released sheaths of flowered taffeta undulated from knee-length hems in front to buoyant, curved trains in back. These pure inventions in silk were likened by fashion writers to banked clouds, giant flowers, and gliding swans.

For day wear, Balenciaga tailored textured woolens into loose and supple suits and coats featuring flattering, round-mounted collars and shortened sleeves. These garments were prized for their easy fit, which concealed imperfections of the mature figure, and for their understated elegance, which assured their wearers fashion longevity. Moreover, Balenciaga's grandly dignified creations respected the social position of his privileged clientele, which included royalty, aristocracy, socialites, and film actresses. Indeed, exclusivity was the tone of the entire Balenciaga operation. He and his disciplined staff worked in near-total privacy, shunning publicity and admitting to their showings only a carefully-screened elite. Accordingly, Balenciaga's gowns were among the world's most expensive.

Though Balenciaga's silhouettes were widely copied, mass-manufactured versions could offer only generalizations of his subtle construction, for his apparently simple shapes were realized only through painstaking precision. Noteworthy was his design for a coat made with only one seam, including collar and sleeves. Balenciaga himself cut, draped, and refined his toiles until they met his impossibly high standards. He insisted that these skills be mastered by his assistants, who included Andre Courrèges and Emanuel Ungaro. Hubert de Givenchy was another Balenciaga disciple and a close friend who has maintained devotion to the couture.

While Balenciaga's influence on world fashion was greatest during the late 1950s, his inventions continued into the 1960s, expressing social transitions then occurring. His youthful, patterned tights and knee-boots were couture firsts in 1962, but he also continued to create austerely formal wedding gowns. By this time, sensing the demise of the privileged society which had patronized him, Balenciaga announced his retirement and closed his house in 1968. It was no longer economically feasible to dress the dwindling number of women who could afford his perfection. Socially, such conspicuous consumption had become unacceptable, and high fashion had become unfashionable. Elegant traditions seemed out of place in a world dominated by rebellious youth. Significantly, Balenciaga came out of retirement briefly in 1972 to create a white satin princess gown for the wedding of Generalissimo Franco's granddaughter.

A year after his death in 1972, a major exhibition of Balenciaga's designs at the Metropolitan Museum of Art provoked new critical appreciation of his work. In the years since, Balenciaga has been lauded as a sculptor in fabric, perhaps the last great couture tradition. As a couturier and as a person, Balenciaga ventured into the realm of pure creativity without denying human grace and dignity.

—Sandra Michels Adams

# BALICKI, Bogusław

Polish painter, poster, and graphic designer

Born: Czortkow, 25 June 1937. Education: Studied painting and design, College of Fine Arts, Łódź, 1957-62. Family: Married Ewa Stanislawska in 1973; children: Jakub. Career: Independent painter and designer, Łódź, 1964-67; partner, with Stanislaw Labecki, in Balicki and Labecki design studio, Łódź, 1967-75; freelance graphic designer, working principally for the Łódź Office of Art Exhibitions and the Muzeum Sztuki, Łódź, from 1975. Assistant Professor, under Stanislaw Fijalkowski, 1963-70, and Associate Professor, from 1976, College of Fine Arts, Łódź. Exhibitions: *Polish Poster Biennale,* Katowice, 1970, 1972, 1973, 1975, 1977, 1979,

Bogusław Balicki: exhibition poster for the work of Krzysztofa Dydo, 1985

1983, 1985, 1987, 1989, 1995; *International Poster Biennale,* Warsaw, 1970, 1972, 1974, 1976, 1980, 1984, 1986, 1988, 1990, 1994; *Polnische Plakate Heute,* Wilhelm-Lehmbruck Museum, Duisburg, 1971; *Best Poster Exhibition,* Warsaw, 1974, 1975; *l'Art de l'Affiche en Pologne,* Musée d'Art Moderne de la Ville, Paris, 1974; *Balicki and Labecki,* Gallery of Contemporary Art, Łódź, 1975; *The Polish Poster,* Kamakura Museum of Modern Art, 1975 (toured); *Balicki and Labecki,* Gallery of Contemporary Art, Warsaw, 1975; *The Polish Poster,* Kilkenny Castle, Ireland, 1976; *Poster Biennale,* Lahti Finland, 1977, 1979, 1981, 1983, 1987; *International Poster Exhibition,* Listowel, Ireland, 1978, 1980; *First International Poster Triennale,* Toyama, Japan, 1985; *Colorado International Invitational Poster Exhibition,* Colorado State University, Fort Collins, 1987; *100th Anniversary of Polish Poster Art,* Kraków, 1993. **Collections:** National Museum, Warsaw; National Museum, Poznan; National Museum, Wroclaw; Muzeum Sztuki, Łódź; Kamakura Museum of Modern Art, Japan; Lahti Museum, Finland; Musée de l'Affiche, Paris; Israel Museum, Jerusalem; Museum of Modern Art, Toyama, Japan; Krannert Museum, University of Illinois, Champaign-Urbana, Illinois, U.S.A.; Colorado State University, Fort Collins, U.S.A. **Honors:** Painting Award, Łódź, 1966; First Prize, *Eksperyment 66,* Lublin, 1967; Union of Polish Artists Medal, Łódź, 1968, 1969; Poster Medal, Union of Polish Artists, Przemysl, 1972; Silver Medal, Katowice Poster Biennale, 1973; Poster of the Month Award, Warsaw, 1973, 1974; Teaching Achievement Award, Polish Ministry of Culture, 1979; Second Prize, Ministry of Culture, 1979; First Prize, Ministry of Culture, 1991. **Address:** Art Studio 3, Inowrocławska Street 9/163, 91 020 Łódź, Poland.

**Works**

*Alain Jacquet* exhibition poster for the Muzeum Sztuki, Łódź, 1969.
*Aiko Miyawaki* exhibition poster for the Muzeum Sztuki, Łódź, 1970.
*Collection of 20th Century Art in the Łódź Fine Arts Museum* exhibition poster for the Muzeum Sztuki, Łódź, 1971.
*Japanese Graphics* exhibition poster for the Muzeum Sztuki, Łódź, 1973.
*Pieter Brattinga* exhibition poster for the Muzeum Sztuki, Łódź, 1974.
*Dydo* exhibition poster for the Office of Art Exhibition, Łódź, 1985.
*Srebro* exhibition poster for the Office of Art Exhibition, Łódź, 1985.
*Cieślewicz* exhibition poster for the Office of Art Exhibition, Łódź, 1986.
*Otreba* exhibition poster for the Office of Art Exhibition, Łódź, 1988.
*15 graveurs de la Communaute francaise de Belgique* exhibition poster for the Office of Art Exhibition, Łódź, 1989.

## Publications

**On BALICKI: books**—*Balicki and Labecki,* exhibition catalogue with foreword by Janina Filjakowska, Łódź , 1975; *Graphis Poster 76* edited by Walter Herdeg, Zürich, 1976; *Plakat Polski/The Polish Poster 1970-1978,* with introduction by Zdzislaw Scubert, Warsaw, 1979; *Czy to juz historia? 20 Years of GPD and ZPAP in Łódź,* exhibition catalogue with foreword by Michael Kuna, Łódź, 1980; *Polska Grafika Współczesna* by Danuta Wróblewska, Warsaw, 1983; *100th Anniversary of Polish Poster Art* by Szymon Bojko, Kraków, 1993; **articles**—*Novum Gebrauchsgraphik,* no. 1, 1981, no. 12, 1984.

*      *      *

Bogusław Balicki's artistic career is connected with Łódź, a center of light industry which was called before the war the "Polish Manchester," a term comprehensible to anyone who knows the cultural geography of Poland. This city, which survived the war by luck, preserved not only its buildings but also the character of an industrial center of the end of the nineteenth century. Like American cities, its topography consists of a geometric pattern of streets intersecting at right angles. Accented with factory chimneys, its landscape comprises rows of monotonous, red brick apartment houses, as well as the roar of spindles and machines. So, it was not incidental that this city was the seat of Polish constructivism, which stressed the new, attractive qualities of the machine epoch, deriving from the logic of construction, organization, function, and economy.

Here also was introduced the concept of a functional print, partly influenced by Jan Tschichold and formulated at the beginning of 1930s by Wladyslaw Strzeminski. While still a student in the Łódź School of Design, Balicki was influenced, through the intermediary of Professor S. Fijalkowski, by Strzeminski's theory of seeing, unism. This theory rejected the "pathos of dramatic outbursts" on behalf of the picture where all parts are organically connected, as in nature. Strzeminski was convinced that form in art should be derived from machinery techniques and that the geometrization of form would secure the objectivism and precision of illustration. The axiom of geometrism corresponding to the mood of that time has preserved its intellectual and artistic reasons for half a century since it was introduced into the constructivistic model of art. These reasons appealed to the imagination of the young, promising painter and graphic artist, and these principles of geometric order guided Balicki in his formulation of a visual code that could be applied in poster graphics as the transmitter of maximally objectivized, "machine-sembling" information. The co-author of this conception was Stanislaw Labecki, a graduate of the same school and also an admirer of Strzeminski's theory.

In the second half of the 1960s, the two of them formed a team and started to design posters and typography according to abstract conventions. Thus, their approach was totally different from that of the world-known "Polish poster school." However, the Balicki-Labecki team introduced some valuable concepts with regard to the structural layer of the picture. This included the exchangeability of elements of flat geometric forms with sharply contoured edges, as if reduced to a limited number of combinations of shapes. Designing resembled an engineer's work by such functions as adding deleting, multiplying, setting, contracting, or expanding-on the axis of symmetry, on the diagonal, centrally, or in dispersion, in combinations with patterns of check, mesh, square, and others. Lettering, being a part of that structure, was subjected to the same rigors of setting, with no departures regarding the arrangement of inscriptions, types and sizes of letters, spacing accentuation, and interlineation. The authors were inspired to develop this "cool" mode of designing when working for the Łódź Arts Museum, which favored the traditions of constructivism and insisted on a homogeneous form for its printed material. As a result, the Balicki-Labecki team developed a system of identification which encompassed catalogues, posters invitations, ideograms, and logograms. It was one of the first such systems ever used by a museum.

The separation of the team in 1975 did not cause any changes in Balicki's graphic and typographic work. His posters, made for exhibits and museums in Łódź, are still based on the same repertoire of arrangements.

—Szymon Bojko

# BALL, Douglas Cameron
Canadian industrial designer

**Born:** Peterborough, Ontario, 9 August 1935. **Education:** Diploma in Industrial Design, Ontario College of Art, Toronto, Ontario. **Career:** Principal, Douglas Ball Inc., Lac des Deux Montagnes, Quebec, from 1964; design director, Sunar furniture manufacturing company, Waterloo, Ontario, 1978-1990. **Member:** Royal Canadian Academy of Arts; International Member, Industrial Designers Society of America. **Exhibitions:** *Seduced and Abandoned: Modern Furniture Designers in Canada,* Art Gallery at Harbourfront, Toronto, 1986; *The Creative Spark '86,* John B. Aird Gallery, Toronto, 1986; *Art in Everyday Life: Observations on Contemporary Canadian Design,* The Power Plant, Toronto, 1988; *Canada—Designs for Business,* Canadian Embassy, Tokyo, 1992; *GOOD DESIGN Exhibition,* Chicago Athenaeum, Museum of Architecture and Design, 1995. **Collections:** Design Museum, London; The Chicago Athenaeum, Museum of Architecture and Design. **Honors:** MacLean Traveling Scholarship, 1958; Diploma di Collaborazione, Quattordicesima Triennale di Milano, Italy, 1968; Prix D'Excellence, 1970, 1971; Grand Prix D'Excellence, 1971; Design in Steel Citation for Excellence in Design, American Iron and Steel Institute, 1971; Award of Merit, Art Directors Club of Toronto, Canada, 1972; Award for Outstanding Design, Interior Designers of Canada, 1977; Product Design Award, American Society of Interior Designers, 1978; IBD/Contract Product Design Award, 1978 (four gold, one silver), 1979 (one gold), 1990, 1994; Citation, 1980, Special Award in Innovation, Research and Development, 1982, and Award of Merit, 1984, Design Canada Awards; fellow, Association of Canadian Industrial Designers, Quebec. **Address:** Douglas Ball Inc., 178 Senneville Road, Senneville, Quebec H9X 3L2, Canada.

## Works

*1200 Series Seating,* for Sunshine Office Equipment, 1962.
*S System* steel desk system for adapting to changing workplace needs, for Sunar, 1969.
*Uniwall System* lateral file system, for Sunar, 1969.
Curb-climbing wheelchair concept, designed for increased traction and stability, 1976.
Children's wheelchair concept, 1978.
*Race System* beam system for the office, for Sunar, 1978.
*Ballet* folding table for training room applications, for VECTA, 1990.
*Activity Products,* for Steelcase North America, 1992.

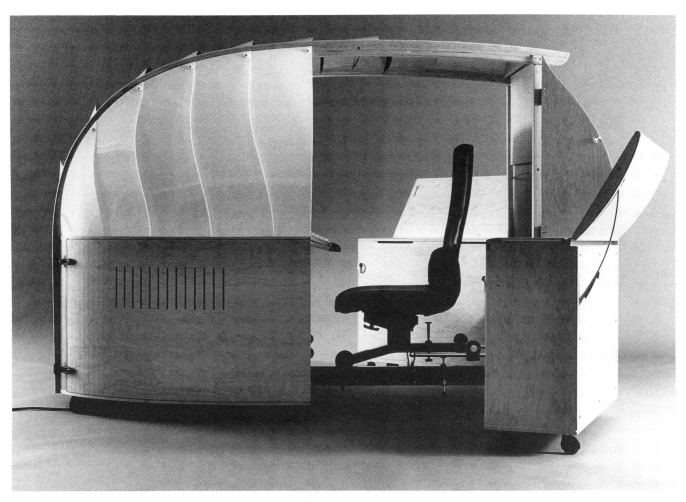

Douglas Ball: *Clipper* **CS-1 capsule type workstation for computer users, for New Space Inc., 1994**

*Clipper CS-1* capsule type workstation for computer users, for New Space Inc., 1994.

**Publications**

**On BALL: books**—*The New Furniture: Trends + Traditions* by Peter Donner, London, 1987; *Art in Everyday Life: Observations on Contemporary Canadian Design* by Peter Day and Linda Lewis, Toronto, 1988; *SIGHT LINES: Looking at Architecture and Design in Canada* by Adele Freedman, Toronto, 1990; **articles**—"Comfort While You Wait" by Lydia Ferrabee in *Design* (London), December 1963; *Contract Interiors* (New York), September 1978; "Eine Firma mit Mehreren Gesichtern" by Lydia Ferrabee in *MD* (Germany), April 1980; "Office Furniture that Hangs Off a Beam" by Lydia Ferrabee in *Design* (London), March 1980; "Canada's Compact Wheelchair just Climbs and Climbs" by Lydia Ferrabee in *Design* (London), July 1980; "Mobiler Durch Technik" by Lydia Ferrabee in *MD* (Germany), April 1981; *Interiors* (New York), June 1983, May 1990, April 1994; "Having a Ball" by Angi Bates in *Interiors* (New York), September 1990; *Architecture* (New York), October 1990; *Metropolis* (New York), July/August 1991; *Wired*, August 1994; *The Architectural Review* (London), April 1995.

*

If the idea of design had never existed then it is quite possible that I would have attempted to invent it. One has to be almost this naive in order to move forward. In my terms the word design has never meant simply the creation of another good looking product, but the creation of something that will work better.

Design is invention of the highest order.

Design is the art of looking at the same thing that everyone else is looking at but seeing something different.

Design is the art of being able to tear apart something you feel is good, and discovering that it can be put back in a more appropriate and interesting manner.

Design is the stubborn refusal to accept the idea that the human mind is incapable of solving problems. It is the belief that there is always a solution. We have just not found it ... yet.

Design is like a giant children's sand box that is there for the human mind to play in.

Design is like a mischievous child that does not always heed the rules set by others.

Design is very much like child's play.

Design is a state of mind.

—Douglas Ball

*   *   *

Douglas Ball has, since 1964, maintained his own consultant design office, Douglas Ball Inc., complete with model and prototype shop, on the shores of Lac des Deux Montagnes near Montreal, Canada. From this location, well removed from the acknowledged centers of design activity, he has designed and developed systems of office furniture which have had a major international impact. Because of the depth with which he considers a problem and the quality of his solutions, his products have remained unsurpassed on the market for decades and have changed people's attitudes and expectations.

Ball may take a number of years to complete a project. In recognition of the strain this can put on a company, he usually works solely on a royalty basis, taking the risk and reaping the rewards his designs provide. Their success has given him the freedom to refuse projects that do not provide him with the opportunity for the full investigation that he considers essential and to take on projects that he considers need to be addressed. Ball loves designing and claims he would have to do it even if it did not provide his livelihood. As a child he designed and made the toys he could not have or find, so he has always associated designing with play.

For most of his career, Douglas Ball has worked as a design consultant for Sunar, a manufacturing company near Waterloo, Ontario. This close relationship enabled him to become familiar with the needs and facilities of the company, but to maintain the detachment he considers necessary in order to originate new ideas and directions. When he began working for Sunar, the company was making a wide variety of metal products, including prams, roller skates, and office equipment. Decisions about what would be produced were made in-house and often involved the modification of American designs made at a lower cost for the Canadian market, a very Canadian approach at that time. Ball persuaded the company management of the value of originating designs of a higher quality than those currently available and therefore having the potential for an international market.

First, Douglas Ball designed an innovative line of general office wood furniture of a high standard of design and manufacturing quality and at a cost appropriate to market standards. The wood line was followed by a comprehensive line of metal office furniture, storage units, chairs, and a panel system which was the first to have integrated acoustic panels. Each new design system was integrated with the earlier ones. The quality and design value of these products quickly developed into an insiders' network of appreciative support in Canada and the United States.

It was this quality of design and manufacture that convinced Robert Cadwallader, past president of Knoll International, in combination with the American company, Hauserman, to purchase Sunar in 1978. Under the direction of Cadwallader and the group of well known design consultants he assembled, and with Douglas Ball as the Design Director, Sunar became a leading, internationally recognised manufacturer of office furniture. But it was always the furniture systems that Ball had designed before the company was bought by Hauserman that provided the the major portion of the sales. This included Race System, developed by Ball over a seven year period in the small sketch books he always has with him when he travels.

Neither furniture nor panel system, the Race System represented a completely new concept in office landscape design. The design incorporates a waist-high beam which contains the extensive wiring network which has become part of all office interiors. The work station components—tables, desks, lights, storage units, panels—are hung from the beam in a way that manages to create a space which is both open and contained. When it was launched in 1978, this unique system caused a great stir in the market place and has not been matched since. Many large companies in Canada, the United States, and Europe installed this product due to its simplicity and ease of use and the quality of its detailing.

When Sunar was liquidated in 1990, Douglas Ball was free to work for other companies for the first time since he started his design practice. Recently, he has undertaken furniture projects for VECTA, Atelier International, and Steelcase, and a flight simulator helmet for the Canadian company C.A.E. In the mid 1980s, Ball was teaching himself to use the Alias three-dimensional modelling system when he found that, after a few hours at the computer, he had severe eye strain and a pain in the neck. The thought of more of this discomfort led him to consider every aspect of the way one sits and works at the computer. His solution is now marketed as the Clipper. It is a capsule in which all aspects of the relationship between computer and user can be individually adjusted for comfort and convenience. Light is perfectly diffused and everything from your storage needs to your favourite sound system and CD-ROMs are at hand in this flexible mini-environment. It can be open for interaction or closed for total solitude. It has been well covered in the press and Ball has received requests from the Vitra Museum in Germany, the Design Museum in London, and the Athenaeum Museum in Chicago to have the Clipper in their permanent collections.

Years ago, Douglas Ball set up a small room next to his office. It was a quiet space inspired by the simplicity of the traditional Japanese interiors he admired. Outside views were excluded. The room was lit with soft, natural daylight diffused through a screen and a paper globe ceiling light. He had no telephone in the room and brought in only pen and paper for sketching. It was here that he achieved the creative and conceptual phases of his projects, a process that was not possible in the distracting clutter of things that needed his attention in his main office. It was his appreciation for the effectiveness of this space that influenced Douglas Ball in his design for the Clipper. Now the Clipper provides Ball with a place to withdraw and focus, the requirement so essential for his creative process, and he no longer uses the Japanese room.

—Lydia Ferrabee Sharman

# BALLMER, Walter
Swiss graphic, packaging, exhibition, and display designer

**Born:** Liestal, 22 July 1923; emigrated to Italy in 1947. **Education:** Studied under Hermann Eidenbez, at the Kunstgewerbeschule, Basel, 1940-44. **Career:** Worked for C. J. Bucher Verlag printers and publishers, Lucerne, 1945-47; graphic designer, Studio Boggeri, Milan, 1947-48; freelance graphic designer, working for Pirelli, Geigy, Olivetti, Montecatini, La Roche, and others, Milan, 1948-56; staff designer of graphics, packaging, and displays, Olivetti, Milan, 1956-81; founder-director, Unidesign graphics studio, working for Agusta, Hoffman La Roche, Valentino, Weber, Wertheim, and others, Milan, from 1981. **Member:** Arbeitsgemeinschaft Schweizer Graphiker, 1958; Associazione per il Disegno Industriale, 1963; Alliance Graphique Internationale, 1970. **Exhibitions:** *Forme et Recherche,* Paris, 1970; *Graphisme Design Suisse,* Paris, 1971; *107 Grafici dell'AGI,* Castello Sforzesco, Milan, 1974; Galleria Sincron, Brescia,

1974; Galleria A, Parma, 1974; Galleria Zen, Milan, 1975; Centro del Portello, Genoa, 1978; retrospective, Kantonmuseum Baselland, Liestal, 1989; Galerie Fischer, Lucerne, 1990; *Arte e spazio nella prospettiva degli,* Edizione Biennale d'Arte Contemporanea, San Martino of Lipari, Italy, 1990; Galleria Radice, Lissone, 1992; *La Sindrome di Leonardo,* Palazzina di Caccia di Stupinigi and Barcelona, Spain, 1994-95. **Collections:** National Museum, Warsaw. **Honors:** Compasso d'Oro Award, Milan, 1954; Merit Award, National Swiss Exposition, Lausanne, 1964, 1971; Gold Medal, Bio 5, Liubliana, 1973. **Address:** Unidesign, via Revere 16, 20123 Milan, Italy.

## Works

Olivetti Spazio showroom interiors, Milan, 1959.
*Stile Olivetti* touring exhibition layouts in Switzerland, Germany and Sweden, 1961.
*Wert und Haben* display at the Swiss National Exposition, Lausanne, 1964.
*Olivetti Innovates* touring exhibition layouts, in Greece, Africa and the Far East, 1965.
Logo and corporate identity program, for Olivetti, Milan, 1970.
Logo, for Wertheim stores, Barcelona, 1973.
*Graphis Packaging 3* cover design, Zürich, 1977.
Trade mark and corporate identity program for Valentino couture, Rome, 1978.
Trade mark and corporate identity program, for Weber carburettors, Bologna, 1978.
*Graphis* no. 204 magazine cover design, Zürich, 1980.
International publicity campaign, for Olivetti ET201 and ET221 typewriters, Milan, 1980.
75th Anniversary book design, for Agusta Helicopters, Milan, 1982.
Logo and corporate identity program, for Sestrieres holiday centre, Milan and Turin, 1983.
Annual report, for ERG Benzine Company, Genoa, 1987.
Annual report, for Hoffman La Roche, Basel, 1988.
Annual report, for Zurigo Assicurazioni, Zürich, 1988.
*Walter Ballmer: un designer tra arte e grafica* exhibition layouts, Liestal, 1989.
Logo, for La Roche, 1989.
Annual report, for VITA insurance company, Switzerland, 1989.
Booklets and logo, for Istud, 1990.
Corporate identity and publication design, for Eurograph-Nascor, 1990.
Trademark and image, for STG Swiss Trust Company, 1990.
Cover designs for pocket dictionaries, for La Roche, 1990.
Brochure, corporate identity, and advertisements, for La Roche, 1991.
*Quadro di insieme delle attività Istud 1992* brochure design, for Istud, 1991.
Trademark and corporate identity program, for SPA Research and SPA Education, Sistemi Pubblica Amministrazione, 1992.
Trademark and brochure, for PGA Strategia e Organizzazione consulting company, 1992.
Corporate identity program and trademark, for Brichetto 1873, 1992.
*A Commitment to Health* cover design, for La Roche, 1992.
Trademark and corporate identity, for SARAS Raffinerie Sarde, 1993.
Corporate identity program and graphic guidelines, for Hoffmann La Roche, 1993.

Walter Ballmer: Trademark for Saras Spa Raffinerie Sarde

Advertisements, for SARAS Raffinerie Sarde, 1994, 1995.
Monograph design, for 30th anniversary of the Moratti family and company, 1994.
*Roche in Europe, Towards the Year 2000* brochure design, for La Roche, 1994.
Symbol, for *Alleanza Grafici Internazionale* convention, AGI Italia, 1995.

## Publications

**By BALLMER: articles**—statement in *Art and Graphics* edited by Willy Rotzler, Zürich, 1983; "Come s'inventa la 'firma' di un 'Azienda" in *Sole—24 ore* (Milan), 8 January 1984; "Walter Ballmer ratselhafte Bildersprache" in *High Quality* (Heidelberg), no. 5, 1985; text in *Walter Ballmer: un designer tra arte e grafica,* brochure, Milan, 1989.

**On BALLMER: books**—*Die neue Grafik/The New Graphic Design* by Markus Kutter and Karl Gerstner, Teufen and London, 1959; *Design Coordination and Corporate Image* by F. H. K. Henrion, London, 1967; *Signet Signal Symbol* by Waltr Diethelm, Zürich, 1970; *107 Grafici dell'AGI,* exhibition catalogue with texts by Renzo Zorzi and Franco Grignani, Venice, 1974; *Who's Who in Graphic Art* edited by Walter Amstutz, Dubendorf, 1982; *World Trademarks and Logotypes* edited by Takenobu Igrashi, Tokyo, 1983; *Design Process—Olivetti 1908-1983,* Milan, 1984; *Posters by Members of the Alliance Graphique Internationale* edited by

Rudolph de Harak, New York, 1986; *Alle radici della comunicazione visiva in Italia* by Heinz Waibl, Como, 1988; *AGI Annals 1952-1987* edited by F. H. K. Henrion, Tokyo, 1989; *Fotoplakate* edited by Joseph Muller-Brockmann and Karl Wobmann, Stuttgart, 1989; *First Choice* edited by Ken Cato, Tokyo, 1989; **articles**—*High Quality* (Germany), no. 14, 1989.

# BALMAIN, Pierre (Alexandre Claudius)

French fashion designer

**Born:** Saint-Jean-de-Maurienne, Savoie, 18 May 1914. **Education:** Educated in Saint-Jean-de-Maurienne, 1920-25, and at the Lycée National, Chambéry, 1925-33; studied architecture, Ecole Nationale Supérieure des Beaux-Arts, Paris, 1933-34. **Military Service:** Served in the French Air Force, in Bron and Paris, 1936-38; Pioneer Corps of the French Army, in Saint-Jean-de-Maurienne, 1939-40. **Career:** Freelance fashion sketch artist, working for designer Robert Piguet, Paris, 1934; sketch artist and assistant designer, studio of Edward Molyneaux, Paris, 1934-38; designer, studio of Lucien Lelong, Paris, 1939 and 1941-45; founder-director, Maison Balmain fashion house, on the rue Francois Premier, Paris, 1945-82, Balmain Fashions, New York, 1951-55, and Caracas, 1954; Director General, Pierre Balmain S.A., Paris, 1977-82. Also stage and film costume designer from 1950. **Exhibitions:** *Fashion: An Anthology,* Victoria and Albert Museum, London, 1971. **Honors:** Knight of the Order of Dannebrog, Copenhagen, 1963; Cavaliere Ufficiale del Merito Italiano, Rome, 1966; Officier de la Légion d'Honneur, Paris, 1978; Vermilion Medal, City of Paris. **Died:** Paris, 29 June 1982.

## Works

Film costume designs include—*Night Without Stars,* 1951; *Betrayed,* 1954; *The Deep Blue Sea,* 1955; *Foreign Intrigue,* 1956; *The Happy Road,* 1956; *Fire Down Below,* 1957; *The Reluctant Debutante,* 1958; *Mr. Topaz,* 1961; *Tender is the Night,* 1961; *The Roman Spring of Mrs. Stone,* 1961; *Time Bomb,* 1961; *The Happy Thieves,* 1961; *The Millionairess,* 1961; *Two Weeks in Another Town,* 1962; *Come Fly With Me,* 1963; *In the Cool of the Day,* 1963; *Adorable Julia,* 1964; *Joy House,* 1964; *Arriverderci Baby (Drop Dead Darling),* 1966; *Mozambique,* 1966; *Topaz,* 1969.

## Publications

**By BALMAIN: books**—*My Years and Seasons,* London, 1964, New York, 1965.

**On BALMAIN: books**—*Dressmakers of France* by Mary Brooks Picken and Dora Louise Miller, New York, 1956; *Kings of Fashion* by Anny Latour, Stuttgart, 1956, London, 1958; *The Fashion Makers* by Leonard Halliday, London, 1966; *Fashion: An Anthology by Cecil Beaton,* exhibition catalogue compiled by Adeleine Ginsburg, London, 1971; *Paris Fashion: The Great Designers and Their Creations* edited by Ruth Lynam, London, 1972; *Costume Design in the Movies* by Elizabeth Leese, Bembridge, 1976; *The World of Fashion: People, Places, Resources* by Eleanor Lambert, New York and London, 1976; *The History of Haute Couture 1850-1950* by

Diana de Marly, London, 1980; *McDowell's Directory of Twentieth Century Fashion* by Colin McDowell, London, 1984; *The Encyclopaedia of Fashion from 1840 to the 1980s* by Georgina O'Hara, London, 1986.

\*     \*     \*

Pierre Balmain was a very successful designer for ladies. Captain Edward Molyneux taught him that no lady should look too fashionable. It was bad form to be avant-garde. A lady dressed with taste, not vulgar ostentation. The fashion press might give the impression that the most sensational designers were the most successful, but a discreet house might outlive the lot of them.

In 1934, when Balmain was accepted by Molyneux, the press was full of Elsa Schiaparelli's shocks, but Balmain as a Frenchman chose to study under a British courtier because royalty and the aristocracy dressed at Maison Molyneux.

The Captain's beautiful but unsensational clothes were regarded as the essence of good taste and were perfect for high society. Balmain learned that sophisticated elegance meant restraint. He applied this lesson in his own house and, consequently, inherited the same sort of clientele that Molyneux had had, starting in 1964 with the clothes for the marriage of Viscount Edman to Miss Carcano, leading on to the wardrobe for Thai Queen Sirikit's state visits to Europe and the United States, and then to the Wedding Dress for Princess Irene of the Netherlands on her Marriage to Prince Charles de Bourbon de Parme.

Balmain did not seek to be the first to raise the hemline or drop it. He would wait, like his teacher, to see whether the new length was lasting or was simply a flash in the pan. Only if it began to be accepted would Balmain adjust his hemlines accordingly. This conservative approach suited a conservative clientele who did not want to be rushed into a new look every year. The gradual approach was the correct one, for it avoided any rash mistakes. When Balmain was involved in designing for the stage and cinema, it was only for characters who were ladies. He dressed Katharine Hepburn in a stage production of Shaw's *The Millionaires* and, in film, Jennifer Jones in *Tender is the Night,* Kay Kendall in *The Reluctant Debutante,* and Vivien Leigh in *The Roman Spring of Mrs. Stone.*

Thus, Balmain was not a leader of fashion. He endorsed new trends but did not start them. Experimentation was for young designers as they floundered about to find their style and make an impact. A senior house kept away from the throng, and today there are still courtiers with this careful approach—Givenchy in Paris and Hardy Amies in London. The school of restrained dress design continues.

—Diana de Marly

# BARRIE, Scott

American fashion designer

**Born:** Philadelphia, 16 January 1946. **Education:** Studied applied arts, at Philadelphia Museum College of Art, and fashion design, at Mayer School of Fashion. **Career:** Designer, at Allen Cole boutique, 1966-69; founder-partner, with Robbie Wolfe, of Barrie Sports, 1969; business expanded to include Barrie menswear, and Barrie Plus, from 1974; also designed loungewear for Barad, and furs for

Barlan; designed dresses for S.E.L., mid 1980s; formed Scott Barrie Italy S.r.l., in partnership with Kinshido Company, Ltd., of Japan, 1983; designer, Milan D'Or division, for Kinshido, 1983-91; designer, signature line for Kinshido, 1983-91; freelance designer, Krizia, Milan, 1986-88. Designer of stage and film costumes and accessories, including work for the film *Blood,* 1972, and the Joffrey Ballet production *Deuce Coup,* 1973. **Died:** Alessandria, Italy, 8 June 1993.

## Publications

**On BARRIE: books**—*The World of Fashion: People, Places, Resources* by Eleanor Lambert, New York and London, 1976; *The Fashion Makers* by Bernardine Morris, New York, 1978; *Fairchild's Who's Who in Fashion* edited by Anne Stegemeyer, New York, 1980; *Fashion 2001* by Lucille Khornak, London, 1982; *McDowell's Directory of Twentieth Century Fashion* by Colin McDowell, London, 1984; *New York Fashion: The Evolution of American Style* by Caroline Milbank Rennolds, New York, 1989; **articles**—"Scott Barrie: Back and Renewed" by Constance C. R. White in *Women's Wear Daily* (New York), 20 November 1989; "Scott Barrie Dies at 52; Made Mark on S.A. in 70s" by Constance C. R. White in *Women's Wear Daily,* 10 June 1993; "Scott Barrie is Dead; Designer, 52, Made Jersey Matte Dresses" by Ann-Marie Schiro in the *New York Times,* 11 June 1993; "Fashion Designer Scott Barrie Dies" in *Jet* (Chicago), 28 June 1993.

*        *        *

The Art Deco style dominated Scott Barrie's imagination and lifestyle, for he lived with an Art Deco decor in his flat and had been using jersey, that fabric associated with the 1920s and 1930s, since 1966 as his preferred textile for clothes. His grandmother's career dressing such singers as Dinah Washington and Sarah Vaughan conditioned Barrie. He himself dressed the film *Blood* (1972) and the ballet *Deuce Coup* (1973) and was commissioned, most appropriately, to dress Bessie Smith herself.

He admitted in 1974 that his collection was pure 1930s, with its evening pyjamas, Vionnet cowl necklines, little hats, day dresses falling below the calf, and, of course, flowing jersey evening gowns. This preoccupation with 1930s glamour manifested itself in 1975 with a summer collection devoted exclusively to evening wear, with slinky black frocks, the blouson look, and inevitably jersey, for Barrie declared he was a designer of soft, feminine clothes. He had to admit that his fondness for slender fluidity did not suit all women, but his ideal woman was very much the cinematic one of his favourite period. However, as that lady could be improved by retouching her film negatives or by being photographed through silk screens, her look was not really possible, in all its essence, outside the studio. Barrie was a designer of dreams.

Barrie designed loungewear for Barad, furs for Barlan, accessories for his own Barrie Plus and his menswear range. Barrie was happiest doing glamour, so the lounge or evening dress inspired him most, and he was not known for innovative daywear. If television decided to do a soap opera set in the 1930s, Barrie would have been in his element designing the wardrobe.

—Diana de Marly

# BARTOLI, Carlo
Italian architect and industrial designer

**Born:** Milan, 28 June 1931. **Education:** Studied architecture at the Politecnico, Milan, Dip.Arch., 1957. **Family:** Married Albertina Amadeo in 1960; children: Anna and Paolo. **Career:** Established own office for architecture, furniture, and industrial design, in Milan, 1959-81, and in Monza, near Milan, from 1981; consultant to Arflex, Con and Con, Arclinea, Confalonieri UCG, Kartell, Oscam, Rossi di Albizzate, Colombo Design, Segis, Varenna, Ycami, Tisettanta, and others. Instructor, Advanced Industrial Design Course, Florence, 1967-70, and Rome, 1988-90. Instructor, Milan Polytechnic. **Exhibitions:** Milan Triennale, 1968; *Plastic as Plastic,* Museum of Contemporary Crafts, New York, 1968; Biennale of Industrial Design, Ljubljana, 1968; *The Modern Chair 1918-1970,* Whitechapel Art Gallery, London, 1970; *Design and Plastic,* Museum of Decorative Arts, Prague, 1972; *Italian Office Design,* Kyoto, 1979 (traveled to Hong Kong); *Italienisches Möbel Design 1950-1980,* Milan, 1981 (traveled to Cologne); *From Spoon to City: 100 Designers,* at the Milan Triennale, 1983; *Kartell 1949-1983: Products for the Present,* Noviglio, 1983; *Kitchens in the Shop Window,* Milan, 1988; *Forum Design 89,* Milan, 1989; *XVI Compasso D'Oro,* Milano, 1991; *Top Ten Prize—Promosedia 1991,* Manzano, 1991; *XIII Biennal of Industrial Design,* Ljubljana, 1992. **Collections:** Museum of Modern Art, New York; Architectural Museum, Ljubljana. **Address:** via Grigna 2, 20052 Monza (Milano), Italy.

## Works

*Gaia* fiberglass armchair, for Arflex, 1967.
*Set 1* office furniture, for Oscam, 1972.
*Chair 4875* in polypropylene, for Kartell, 1974.
*Blop* sofa, for Rossi di Albizzate, 1975.
*Knock Down* kitchen, for Arclinea, 1980.
*Flap* chair, for Arclinea, 1980.
*Bingo* wardrobe, for Confalonieri, 1984.
*Slang* shelf bracket, for Confalonieri, 1984.
*Atlante* table legs, for Confalonieri, 1985.
*Programma Coba* handrail, for Confalonieri, 1985.
*Roll* armchair and divan, for Rossi di Albizzate, 1986.
*Odeon* furniture range, for Arclinea, 1987 (with Giulio Ripamonti).
*Mix* unit bookshelves, for Tisettanta, 1987.
*Giunto* furniture range, for Confalonieri, 1987.
*Carol* chair and small armchair, for Matteo Grassi, 1987.
*Agora* office furniture, for Nobili Arredamenti, 1987.
*Junior* divan, for Rossi di Albizzate, 1987.
*Connly* divan, for Matteo Grassi, 1988.
*Sophia* chair, for Bonaldo, 1988.
*Cubic* and *Club* sofas, for Rossi di Albizzate, 1989.
*Major* glass table, for Remadesio, 1990.
*Novenovanta* chair, for Rossi di Albizzate, 1990.
*Lola* chair, for Accademia, 1990.
*Volo* sofa and armchair, for Rossi di Albizzate, 1991.
*Aqua* bathroom furniture system, for Merati, 1991.
*Zeppelin* relax armchair, for Rossi di Albizzate, 1992.
*Tacta* and *Mixa* handles, for Colombo Design, 1992.
*Gali'* chair, for Ycami, 1992.
*Metron* office leather furniture system, *Vela* chair, and *Dedalo* table for Matteo Grassi, 1993.

**Carlo Bartoli:** *Breeze* **armchair manufactured by Segis, 1995**

*Flesso* big handle, *Trio* clothes holder, *Luna* and *Onda* bathroom
   accessories, for Colombo Design, 1993.
*Mali', Bali',* and *Hole'* chairs, for Ycami, 1993.
*Zed* sofas, for Rossi di Albizzate, 1993.
*Moon* outdoor lamp, for Ing. Castaldi, 1994.
*Calice* floor lamp, for Antonangeli, 1994.
*Box* furniture system, for Bonacina Italia, 1994.
*Breeze* armchair, for Segis, 1995.
*Frog* chair, for Ycami, 1995.
*Icaro* kitchen, for Varenna, 1995.
*Tube* and *Shelly* sofas, for Rossi di Albizzate, 1995.

## Publications

**By BARTOLI: articles**—"Quale sara l'avvenire della plastica" in
*Corriere della Sera* (Milan), 20 February 1971; "Incontro con Carlo
Bartoli" in *Casa* (Milan), September 1980; "Allora questo Italian
Style?" in *Modo* (Milan), May 1981; "I designer degli anni 80" in
*Brava-Casa* (Milan), May 1982; "Carlo Bartoli, prodotti non
emergenti" in *Gap Casa* (Milan), March/April 1983 "I protagonisti
dell'arredo/ufficio" in *Ufficio Stile* (Milan), May 1985; "La cucina
oggi e domani" in *l 'Ambiente Cucina* (Milan), January/February
1986; "Incontro con Carlo Bartoli" in *Casa e Giardino* (Milan),
April 1988; "Magnificenza ed efficienza del nuovo centro di
Colonia" in *Folia di Acer* (Milan), September/October 1988.

**On BARTOLI: books**—*The Modern Chair 1918-1970,* exhibition
catalogue with texts by Carol Hogben and others, London, 1970;
*Atlante del Design Italiano* by Alfonso Grassi and Anty Pansera,
Milan, 1980; *Contemporary Furniture* by Klaus-Jürgen Sembach,
Stuttgart and New York, 1982; *Dal progetto al prodotto: plastiche
e design* by A. Morello and A. Castelli Ferrieri, Milan, 1984; *Made
in Italy* by L. Massoni, Milan, 1986; *Italian Industrial Design* by F.
Shimizu and M. Thun, Tokyo, 1987; *I Progettisti Italiani: Carlo
Bartoli* by Flavio Conti, Milan, 1988; **articles**—"Carlo Bartoli—Il
prodotto? Un progetto infinito ..." in *Design Diffusion News*
(Milano), January-February 1993; "L'equilibrio della forma" in *Il
Bagno Oggi e Domani* (Milano), September 1994.

\*

Objects destined for widespread use have to become part of the
users' daily view in a non-aggressive and non-prevaricating way.
While the introduction of new materials and technologies in a field
for which they had not been previously employed can justify violent breaks with the expressive tradition, when the use of the same
materials and technologies is consolidated and applied to objects
destined to enter every house, the project language must necessarily be "non-emerging." This does not mean that one should make
the expression banal; rather, one should strive for a proper balance,
transferring to the product what is valued in the culture and respecting the human dignity of tradition.

In the Italian language "design" has the rough translation of
"designo," which has more than one meaning: besides indicating the
graphic representation of an idea, it also means intention, plan for
doing something. Therefore each human intervention on the environment is preceded by a "designo," which means by the programmatic intention that precedes an operative choice—I feel design
acts in this sense. We, architects or designers, make these choices in
a more conscious way than other people do, but, after all, not in a
very different way. As a matter of fact, by nature man is made to
intervene upon things that surround him.

—Carlo Bartoli

\*     \*     \*

Carlo Bartoli isn't just Italian; he is Milanese. He was born when
Terragni completed his rationalist masterpiece, the Fascio House in
Como. In 1957, he graduated in architecture. In Northern Italy, this
was the most interesting period of architecture and design since
World War II.

Following the war, Italian architecture and design were bitten
with reconstruction enthusiasm and yet burdened with the legacy
they inherited from the Functionalists. From these circumstances
there emerged a new group less idealistic and more concrete. They
didn't consider space and society as abstract entities, as did the
Functionalists. This new group was capable of reflecting on the art
of architecture, as well as bringing effective solutions to these two
fields.

Ponti, Parisi, Gardella, Caccia Dominioni, all were very active
during the Italian reconstruction. They relaunched architecture and
design as a new challenge. As often had happened with great masters such as Aalto, Mies van der Rohe, and Le Corbusier, they were
forced to design furniture that rendered liveable their new architecture.

Bartoli dedicated his attention to interiors. His approach was
more removed from form and color than that of Ponti. Ponti was an
excellent planner of architectonic structures, but his interiors were

perhaps a bit excessively decorated. Bartoli carries out his designs according to an approach that is less stylistic and more technical. Technics alone cannot bring complete solutions, although during the High-Tech period there were examples where technical solutions performed the duty of resolving on their own or almost on their own the function of furniture.

Bartoli uses technical solutions in an intelligent way, discreetly offered within the object almost as a bonus to the buyer. His products perform all their functions without irritating the user. Bartoli habitually visits the factories and workshops where his designs are realized. While he chooses to remain far removed from the cycles of society, he is always present at his studio. His design competence is derived from the fact he is always revising his techniques. He designs his objects based on their intended use. His knowledge and techniques are applied to this thorough acquaintance with materials; that way they can be worked and then manufactured into a product. He never cuts short his design component, such as aesthetics or function, but considers all components to be integral to the final product. Without a doubt, these qualities are what place Bartoli among the most highly rated designers.

The fact that people quite ignorant of the latest styles and trends can relate to his products affirms that his designs are not meant only for the museums. Bartoli has never been touched by the rages of his profession; he has never fallen into the trap of the exhibitionist syndrome, nor of being a slave to the latest fads or crazes in design.

Many of Bartoli's objects, furniture or door handles, couches or bathroom accessories, have silently entered our homes. They are quality designed objects of everyday use that are durable: technically and stylistically. His objects never seem out-of-date; they are modern classics. Having entered our homes, these objects, much more than any written treatise could, give a true sense to the word design.

—Jacques Toussaint

# BASEVI, James
American film art director and special effects designer

**Born:** Plymouth, England, in 1890; emigrated to Canada, then to the United States, c. 1924. **Education:** Studied architecture. **Military Service:** Served in the British Army druing World War I, Colonel. **Career:** Worked as a draftsman, then as special effects director, Metro-Goldwyn-Mayer film company, Hollywood, California, 1924-36; special effects director, 1937-39, art director, 1939-43, and supervising art director, 1943-44, 20th Century-Fox film company, Hollywood; head of the art department, Vanguard Films, Hollywood, 1945. **Honors:** Academy Award, for *The Song of Bernadette,* 1943.

## Works

Film designs include—*Soul Mates,* 1925; *Fine Clothes,* 1925; *The Circle,* 1925; *The Big Parade,* 1925; *Confessions of a Queen,* 1925; *The Tower of Lies,* 1925; *Bardelys The Magnificent,* 1926; *Dance Madness,* 1926; *Love's Blindness,* 1926; *The Temptress,* 1926; *The Mysterious Island,* 1929; *History Is Made at Night,* 1937; *Dead End,* 1937; *The Hurricane,* 1937; *The Cowboy and the Lady,* 1938; *The Adventures of Marco Polo,* 1938; *Blockade,* 1938; *Raffles,* 1939; *Wuthering Heights,* 1939; *The Real Glory,* 1939; *The Long Voyage Home,* 1940; *The Westerner,* 1940; *Tobacco Road,* 1941; *A Yank in the R.A.B.,* 1941; *The Black Swan,* 1942; *Moontide,* 1942; *Thunder Birds,* 1942; *China Girl,* 1942; *Son of Fury,* 1942; *Bomber's Moon,* 1943; *Claudia,* 1943; *The Dancing Masters,* 1943; *Guadalcanal Diary,* 1943; *The Gang's All Here,* 1943; *Happy Land,* 1943; *Heaven Can Wait,* 1943; *Hello, Frisco, Hello,* 1943; *Holy Matrimony,* 1943; *Jitterbugs,* 1943; *The Moon Is Down,* 1943; *The Ox-Bow Incident,* 1943; *Paris After Dark,* 1943; *The Song of Bernadette,* 1943; *Stormy Weather,* 1943; *Sweet Rosie O'Grady,* 1943; *They Came to Blow Up America,* 1943; *Wintertime,* 1943; *Lifeboat,* 1944; *Bermuda Mystery,* 1944; *Buffalo Bill,* 1944; *The Eve of St. Mark,* 1944; *Four Jills in a Jeep,* 1944; *Greenwich Village,* 1944; *Home in Indiana,* 1944; *Jane Eyre,* 1944; *In the Meantime, Darling,* 1944; *Ladies of Washington,* 1944; *The Keys of the Kingdom,* 1944; *The Lodger,* 1944; *Pin-Up Girl,* 1944; *The Purple Heart,* 1944; *Roger Touhy, Gangster,* 1944; *The Sullivans,* 1944; *Tampico,* 1944; *Wilson,* 1944; *Spellbound,* 1945; *Claudia and David,* 1946; *The Dark Corner,* 1946; *Duel in the Sun,* 1946; *My Darling Clementine,* 1946; *Home, Sweet Homicide,* 1946; *It Shouldn't Happen to a Dog,* 1946; *Johnny Comes Flying Home,* 1946; *Somewhere in the Night,* 1946; *Strange Triangle,* 1946; *Margie,* 1946; *13 Rue Madeleine,* 1946; *If I'm Lucky,* 1946; *The Brasher Doubloon,* 1947; *Captain from Castile,* 1947; *The Homestretch,* 1947; *Carnival in Costa Rica,* 1947; *The Late George Apley,* 1947; *The Shocking Miss Pilgrim,* 1947; *Boomerang,* 1947; *Thunder in the Valley,* 1947; *Fort Apache,* 1948; *Three Godfathers,* 1948; *Mighty Joe Young,* 1949; *She Wore a Yellow Ribbon,* 1949; *To Please a Lady,* 1950; *Wagonmaster,* 1950; *Across the Wide Missouri,* 1950; *Night into Morning,* 1951; *The People Against O'Hara,* 1951; *Just This Once,* 1951; *My Man and I,* 1952; *Battle Circus,* 1953; *Island in the Sky,* 1953; *East of Eden,* 1954; *The Searchers,* 1956.

## Publications

**On BASEVI: books**—*Ragionamenti sulla Scenografia* by B. Bandini and G. Viazzi, Milan, 1945; *Filmlexicon degli Autore e delle Opere* edited by Michel Lacalamita, and others, Rome, 1958-67; *Hollywood in the Thirties* by John Baxter London and New York, 1968; *Le Decor de Film* by Leon Barsacq, Paris, 1970, as *Caligari's Cabinet and Other Grand Illusions,* Boston, 1976; *The International Film Encyclopedia* by Ephraim Katz, London and New York, 1980; *International Dictionary of Films and Filmmakers,* London and Chicago, 1985, 1991.

*       *       *

During Hollywood's Golden Age, James Basevi was one of the most successful and innovative set designers and special-effects men in the employ of the major studios. He worked with many of the greatest directors of his time including William Wyler, William Wellman, John Ford, and Elia Kazan. Both in collaboration with other leading designers and on his own, Basevi created some of the most memorable visual images in American film history.

Within a short time after his arrival in Hollywood around 1924, Basevi was an assistant to the highly influential Cedric Gibbons, working on silent classics such as *The Big Parade* (1925). Among numerous consultancies and collaborations, Basevi's work with Richard Day is particularly notable. Their films together include *Bardelys the Magnificent* (1926), *Hurricane* (1937), and *The Captain from Castile* (1947). During the 1930s, Basevi proved to be one of the greatest masters of special effects. In 1935, as head of MGM's special effects department, he collaborated with Arnold Gillespie on the effects for the lengthy and memorable earthquake sequence in *San Francisco*. This was, at that time, the most ambitious and technically exacting recreation of a natural catastrophe ever attempted; and even with the passage of many years, it remains extremely convincing. For John Ford's *Hurricane,* a 1937 vehicle for Dorothy Lamour, Basevi devised a 600-foot miniature set representing a tropical island village which was to be deluged by a gigantic tidal wave. The wave effect was produced by releasing many thousands of gallons of water onto the model in a controlled manner through tall, specially designed and constructed channels. The result is one of the most believable storms ever filmed using studio miniatures.

As art director at Twentieth Century Fox Studios from 1939 to 1944 and later as head of the art department at Vanguard Films and in subsequent freelance work, Basevi demonstrated a special skill in creating highly atmospheric images of the Old West. His sets for John Ford's *My Darling Clementine* (1946) and *She Wore a Yellow Ribbon* (1949) display the visual conventions of the Western genre at their most refined and persuasive.

—Gregory Votolato

# BASILE

Italian fashion design company

Founded as Gianfranco Basile men's tailors, Milan, 1951; taken over by FTM menswear manufacturers with Aldo Ferrante as manager-director, 1969; autonomous company Basile S.p.A. established in Milan, 1976; opened boutiques on Via della Spiga, Milan, in Bergdorf Goodman's, New York, on the Via Borgogna, Rome, and others. Launched jacket and trouser production, 1969, and the Basile suit for women, 1970; collections Basile, Misterfox, Sportfox Callaghan, and Escargot, designed by Waiter Albini, 1971-73; has also produced collections by designers Muriel Grateau and Luciano Soprani. **Exhibitions:** *Italian Re-Evolution,* La Jolla Museum of Art, California, 1982. **Address:** Viale Jenner 51, 20159 Milan, Italy.

**Publications**

On BASILE: books—*The World of Fashion: People, Places, Resources* by Eleanor Lambert, New York and London, 1976; *Il Tessuto Moderno: Disegno, Moda, Architettura* by Giovanni and Rosalia Fanelli, Florence, 1976; *I Mass Moda: Fatti e Personaggi dell'Italian Look/The Who's Who of Italian Fashion* by Adriana Mulassano and Alfa Castaldi, Florence, 1979; *Who's Who in Fashion* edited by Karl Strute and Theodor Doelken, Zurich, 1982; *Italian Re-Evolution: Design in Italian Society in the Eighties,* exhibition catalogue edited by Piero Sartogo, La Jolla, 1982; *McDowell's Directory of Twentieth Century Fashion* by Colin McDowell, London, 1984; *The Encyclopaedia of Fashion from 1840 to the 1980s* by Georgina O'Hara, London, 1986.

\*   \*   \*

It was Italian fashion designer Aldo Ferrante who was instrumental in propelling the fashion house called Basile into a position of worldwide acclaim. In 1949, Ferrante had begun by designing an inventive line of men's neckwear. He had previously been a corset salesman, and he subsequently worked with textiles. Next, he worked as sales agent for Krizia and Missoni. It is Krizia's Marriuccia Mandelli who is credited with having given Ferrante his real start in the business of fashion design. In 1969, Ferrante was concentrating on menswear with a characteristically tweedy and wide-shouldered approach that soon became influential in his later designs for women, as in his 1978 low-keyed, tweed jacket, which is pepped up by shiny blue and red silk tweeds woven into the fabric. Ferrante's typical evening wear is by comparison more flamboyant and feminine, done in softly clinging, embroidered silks of bold colors.

By the mid 1970s, Basile had achieved key status in the influential sphere of Milanese fashion under the ownership of FTM, a partnership including Ferrante, Monti, and Tositi. FTM had been created in 1967, operating as a production organization for knitwear by well-known designers such as Cerruti, Albini, and Missoni.

In 1980-81, with Gigi Monti at the forefront of the highly successful Basile business, the collection continued to stress its characteristic blend of fine tailoring, classic lines, and high quality, along with fresh and new contemporary details. Slim pants, tunics, waistcoats, and long jackets work together to produce the soft, layered effect preferred by Basile as well as by a number of other designers active in the Milanese fashion front of the period. The collection included a group of softly curved, romantic silhouettes with jackets shorter than previously, shoulders curved, and waists fitted. It also showed fashions with a minimum of details, using plain necklines, natural shoulders, and low waists.

The house of Basile has recently been well represented by the fashions of Luciano Soprani, whose distinctive designs fall into the highly touted recent trends of the Milanese scene. Soprani's work for Basile includes his 1982 light wool, black tuxedo jacket with black silk short pants and his 1983 collection of subdued sportswear and tailored clothing including ensembles for men incorporating the Basile square-ended tie and a wonderful (and characteristic) twist on the classic duffel coat with exaggerated shoulders and lots of flowing, black wool. In its brief but impressive history, Basile has made a considerable contribution to contemporary Italian fashion created with the Milanese touch for classic quality and an earthy, very modern flair.

—Barbara Cavaliere

# BASS, Saul

American graphic designer

**Born:** New York City, 8 May 1920. **Education:** Studied under Howard Trafton, at the Art Students League, New York, 1936-39, under Gyorgy Kepes, at Brooklyn College, New York, 1944-45. **Family:** Married Elaine Makatura in 1961; children: Jennifer and Jeffrey. **Career:** Freelance designer, New York, 1936-46; founder and president, Saul Bass and Associates, Los Angeles, 1946-78, and Saul Bass/Herb Yager and Associates, Los Angeles, since 1978; designed for United Airlines, Alcoa, American Telephone and Telegraph, Rockwell International, Warner Communications, Dixie Paper Products, Lawry's Foods, Exxon/Esso, Minolta, and others;

also filmmaker and film title designer, from 1954. **Member:** Executive Board Member, International Design Conference, Aspen, Colorado; Sundance Film Institute, Utah. **Exhibitions:** film retrospectives—Rotterdam Film Festival, 1981; Cinematheque Francaise, Paris, 1982; Zagreb Film Festival, Yugoslavia, 1984. **Collections:** Museum of Modern Art, New York; Library of Congress, Washington, D.C.; Stedelijk Museum, Amsterdam; Prague Museum, Czechoslovakia. **Honors:** Art Director of the Year Award, National Society of Art Directors, 1957; Artistic Design Award, Museu de Arte Moderno, Rio de Janeiro, 1959; Philadelphia Museum of Art Award, 1960; Gold Hugo Award, Chicago Film Festival, 1964; Academy Award, 1969; Gold Medal, Moscow Film Festival, 1970; Silver Design Medal, Tokyo, 1971; Hall of Fame Award, Art Directors Club of New York, 1978. Honorary Doctorates: Philadelphia College of Art; Los Angeles Art Center College of Design. Honorary Royal Designer for Industry, Royal Society of Arts, London, 1964; Honorary Fellow, Bezalel Academy, Jerusalem, 1984. **Address:** 7039 Sunset Boulevard, Los Angeles, California 90028, U.S.A.

## Works

Rose-and-flame motif and advertising campaign of film *Carmen Jones,* for Otto Preminger, 1954.

Title sequences and posters of film *Man With the Golden Arm,* for Otto Preminger, 1955.

Title and shower sequences of film *Psycho,* for Alfred Hitchcock, 1960.

Stalking cat title sequences of film *Walk on the Wild Side,* for Edward Dmytryk, 1962.

Car race sequences of film *Grand Prix,* for John Frankenheimer, 1966.

Logotype symbol, for the U. S . Government White House Council for Energy Efficiency, 1981.

Art and Industry commemorative postage stamp, for the U.S. Post Office, 1983.

Architectural design of gasoline station network, for Exxon/Esso, 1983.

Posters and graphics, for the Los Angeles Olympics, 1984.

Films (as director)—*The Searching Eye,* 1964; *From Here to There,* 1964; *Why Man Creates,* 1968; *Phase IV,* 1974; *Notes on the Popular Arts,* 1978; *The Solar Film,* 1980; *Quest,* 1984.

## Publications

**By BASS: articles**—in *Graphis* (Zurich), no. 89, 1960; *Cinema* (Beverly Hills), Fall 1968; *Film Dope* (London), August 1973; *American Cinematographer* (Hollywood), March 1977; *Banc-Titre* (Paris), April 1984.

**On BASS: books**—*The Silent Salesman* by James Pilditch, London, 1961; *Saul Bass* by G. Nelson, New York, 1967; *An International Survey of Packaging* by Wim Crouwel and Kurt Weidemann, London, 1968; *Design in America* by Ralph Caplan, New York, 1969; *The Corporate Search for Visual Identity* by Ben Rosen, New York and London, 1970; *Who's Who in Graphic Art* edited by Walter Amstutz, Dubendorf, 1982; *The Conran Directory of Design* edited by Stephen Bayley, London, 1985; *International Dictionary of Films and Filmmakers,* London and Chicago, 1985, 1991; *The Ameri-*

*can Design Adventure 1940-1975* by Arthur J. Pulos, London and Cambridge, Massachusetts, 1988.

\*       \*       \*

Saul Bass belongs to the generation of American designers—including Paul Rand, Bradbury Thompson, and Alvin Lustig—who emerged during and after World War II to establish an American approach to modern graphic design. Strong, elemental visual properties characterize Bass's designs, which have been successful in two-dimensional graphics that are static, frozen moments; in kinetic visual communications that exist in time and space (these include animated graphics and a full-length motion picture); and in three-dimensional works including packaging and exhibition design. Particular to Bass's genius is an ability to arrive at an uncomplicated and immediate expression of the essence of the subject. This simple graphic configuration is then extended into a whole range of communication needs. Bass's motion picture projects also pioneered the visual unity of all graphic materials associated with a film: logo, titling, advertising, theatre poster, etc. His film logotypes frequently feature an elementary, symbolic image that captures the theme of the film, as did the jagged, angular arm of the Otto Preminger film, *The Man with the Golden Arm.* This pictographic arm conveys the drug addiction theme as it jabs downward, contorted and painful, into a rectangle of slablike bars. In the film titles, abstract bars move in staccato rhythm to jazz music, as they form and reform patterns on the screen. These are joined by typography listing the film credits. Finally, the bars metamorphose into the pictographic arm. A milestone in graphic design, these film titles demonstrated that an abstract language of form and rhythm could become a powerful and expressive tool for visual communication, and that two-dimensional graphics could be successfully translated into kinetic form. Equally innovative was the consistency of all publicity and titling material produced for this motion picture.

Bass achieves surprising unity as he integrates image and letterforms in motion-picture graphics and corporate identification work. Just as the heavy, blocky, stencil letters of the film title *Exodus* amplify the form and message of the raised arms, so are Alcoa's virtues emphasized by the geometric perfection of its trademark, tempered by subtle, curved corners, and the smooth, curved transitions in the letter-forms of the word "Alcoa".

Bass proved that the insights and visual interests of the graphic designer could be translated into the motion-picture media. This was remarkably demonstrated by his film commissioned by Kaiser Aluminum, *Why Man Creates,* which received an Academy Award. Each segment in the film uses a different cinematic style and technique to express its content. In the particularly notable opening portion "The Edifice" gives a history of man's major ideas and inventions by a scrolling animation that portrays man's accomplishments as a colossal structure that builds upon itself.

—Philip B. Meggs

# BATES, John
British fashion designer

**Born:** Ponteland, Northumberland, in 1935. **Education:** Educated in Newcastle-upon-Tyne. **Military Service:** Served in the British

Army, 1953-55. **Career:** Worked as a trainee journalist and office assistant, London, 1951-52; sketch artist, Herbert Siddon design house, Chelsea, London, 1956-58; freelance fashion sketch artist and designer, selling to wholesale firms, London, 1959-63; partner-designer, in Jean Varon wholesale fashion house, London, 1964-80; founder-director, Capricorn fashion company, for the John Bates label, London, from 1981; designer, for Cojana wholesale fashions, London, from 1983. Also costume designer, for *The Avengers* television series in the 1960s. **Exhibition:** *Fashion: An Anthology,* Victoria and Albert Museum, London, 1971. **Collection:** Museum of Costume, Bath, Avon. **Honors:** Dress of the Year Award, Fashion Critics Association, London, 1965. **Address:** c/o Cojana Limited, 18 Great Marlborough Street, London Wl, England.

**Publications**

On BATES: books—*Fashion: An Anthology by Cecil Beaton,* exhibition catalogue compiled by Madeleine Ginsburg, London, 1971; *With Tongue in Chic* by Ernestine Carter, London, 1974; *Fairchild's Dictionary of Fashion* edited by Charlotte Calasibetta, New York, 1975; *The World of Fashion: People, Places, Resources* by Eleanor Lambert, London and New York, 1976; *Fashion in the 60s* by Barbara Bernard, London and New York, 1978; *The Guinness Guide to 20th Century Fashion* edited by David Bond, Enfield, 1981; *McDowell's Directory of Twentieth Century Fashion* by Colin McDowell, London, 1984; *The Encyclopaedia of Fashion from 1840 to the 1980s* by Georgina O'Hara, London, 1986.

\*     \*     \*

John Bates states very firmly that the foundation of good design is balanced proportion and quality of construction. In view of the arrival of the financial depression in the 1970s, he argues that designers must avoid extraordinary fantasies and concentrate on durable clothes that can be worn time and time again. His success is due precisely to this attitude, for his safe clothes in good style at moderate prices bring the customers to the door. This temperate approach, so typical of British couturiers, can be traced back to the Puritan Revolution which stressed plain chapels, as opposed to gaudy Catholic churches. This stress on simplicity and modesty, which has marked British clothes ever since, does not mean that a dress by Bates is dull. He may stamp a black dress in pleated silk with yellow or red features, but the shape will be simple; the line, uncluttered; and the colour, controlled. In 1982, he showed an evening jacket and skirt in red and white Ascher silk, the jacket had a frilled front and cuffs, but the skirt was kept absolutely plain. This self-discipline, this avoidance of excess even when being romantic, is the basis of Bates's approach.

Appreciating that women come in different shapes and sizes, he designs for all women of all ages and types, not only for the young and slender seen in fashion magazines. He creates for the fat and the thin, and many of his dresses are available with or without belts; full enough for the plump, they can be pulled in for the slim. Thus, his black dress with a while sailor collar could be worn loose like a smock or belted to form a bloused top. Such dresses are a principal feature of Bates's collections, and they guarantee a faithful clientele.

Common sense and an appreciation of the real world have made Bates a greatly appreciated designer, for he respects women and does not try to subject them to grotesque distortions. This, too, is

very much in the British tradition, and if some foreign correspondents have complained that British designers lack colourful vibrations, it is precisely because Bates and his compatriots design for real people and not for Parisian circus freaks. The Puritan avoidance of excess has created a school of design in Britain. The line has flowed from Worth to Creed and Redfern to Molyneux to Cavanagh and Hardy Amies, and now Jean Muir and Bates pass the tradition to the rising generation.

—Diana de Marly

# BAUMANN, Hans Theodor

German industrial designer

**Born:** Basel, Switzerland, 27 October 1924. **Education:** Studied painting, sculpture and design in Dresden, until 1945; painting, graphics, glasswork and interior design, at the Kunstgewerbeschule, Basel, 1946-50. **Family:** Married Luise Luz in 1947; daughters: Luise, Christine and Sabine. **Career:** Worked with Egon Eiermann on stained glass for the Pforzheimer Kirche and the Gedächtniskirche, West Berlin, 1953; freelance designer, establishing Baumann Design Studio, Schopfheim, from 1955; director, Baumann Product Design, Basel, since 1971; also established design studio in Gaillan en Medoc, France. Professor, Hochschule der Künste, West Berlin, since 1983. **Member:** Founder-member, 1959, president, 1959-61, business manager, 1964-68, and member of honour, from 1979, Verband Deutscher Industrie-Designer; founded chair for teaching of ceramics, National Institute of Design, Ahmedabad, 1970. **Exhibitions:** Milan Triennale, 1954, 1956, 1960; World's Fair Brussels, 1958; *Glas, Neue Sammlung,* Munich, 1959; *Design in Germany Today,* Smithsonian Institution, Washington, D.C., 1960 (toured); *H. Th. Baumann: Arbeiten,* Institut fur neue technischen Form, Darmstadt, 1961; *Concorso Ceramica,* Faenza, Italy, 1964, 1966, 1967, 1968, 1970, 1971, 1974, 1975, 1976; *Made in Germany,* Deutscher Werkbund, Munich, 1970; *Funf Jahre Gute Form,* Deutsches Museum, Munich, 1970; *Die Gute Industrieform,* at the Hannover Fair, 1974, 1976, 1977; *Deutscher Designertag: Design und Designer,* Karlsruhe, 1977; *New Glass,* Corning Museum, New York, 1979; *H. Th. Baumann: Design,* Kunstgewerbemuseum, Cologne, 1979 (traveled to Vienna); Museum of Applied Art, Belgrade, 1981; Galerie L, Hamburg, 1981; Museum of Applied Art, Zagreb, 1981; *Design Since 1945,* Philadelphia Museum of Art, 1983. **Collections:** Kunstgewerbemuseum, Hamburg; Kunstgewerbemuseum, Cologne; Kunstgewerbemuseum, West Berlin; Kestner-Gesellschaft, Hannover; Neue Sammlung, Munich; Coburg Glasmuseum, Stuttgart; Landesmuseum, Karlsruhe; Museum of Modern Glass, Valencia. **Honors:** Sculpture and glass prizes, World's Fair, Brussels, 1958; Honour Award, Liubliana Biennale, 1966; Premio Internazionale, Vicenza, 1966; *Daily Mail* Blue Ribbon Award, London, 1966; Wirtschaftsministeriums Bundespreis, West Germany, 1969, 1973; Porcelain Competition Prize, Tokyo, 1973; International Design Prize, Spanish Government, 1975; Coburg Glaspreis, Germany, 1977; Gold Medal, Zagreb International Fair, 1979. **Addresses:** Schutzmattstrasse 44, 4051 Basel, Switzerland; Frieseneggerweg 7, 7860 Schopfheim, West Germany.

## Works

Designs include porcelain for Staatliche Porzellanmanufaktur, Berlin; Rosenthal AG, Selb, West Germany; Schönwald, Arzberg; Hutschenreuther, Selb, West Germany; Tirschenreuth, glass for Glashutte Waldsassen Glashutte Gral, Dürnau; Glashütte Rheinkristall, Leichlingen; Thomas, Selb, West Germany; Rosenthal, Selb, West Germany; Daum, Nancy, France; Glashütte Sussmuth, Immenhausen; ceramics for Staatliche Majolika; Manufaktur, Karlsruhe; metal for Rosenthal, Selb, West Germany; Gebr. Deyhle, SchwäbischGmund, West Germany; Gebr. Hepp, Pforzheim, West Germany; plastics for Benzing, Ehingen, Vitra, Weil/Rhein; wood products for Design Continens, Schwarzwälder Holzwaren, Bernau, East Germany; lamps for Vitra, Weili Rhein; Trischmann, Stuttgart; Stölzle, Vienna; furniture for Sedus/Stoll, Waldshut; Domus, Schwaikheim; Walter Knoll, Herrenberg; Schwarzwälder Holzwaren, Bernau, East Germany; Holz Henkel, Göttingen, West Germany; Vitra, Weil/Rhein; Wilde und Spieth, Esslingen, West Germany; textiles for Irisette, Zell-Schönau; Contens Design, Schopfheim, West Germany; Erbe, Erlangen, West Germany; stained glass and wall-hangings.

## Publications

On BAUMANN: books—*Gestaltete Industrieform in Deutschland,* Dusseldorf, 1954; *Die Gute Industrieform,* exhibition catalogue with texts by Hans Eckstein and Robert Gutmann, Hamburg, 1955; *H. Th. Baumann: Arbeiten aus einem Werkstudio,* exhibition catalogue with text by Mia Seeger, Darmstadt, 1961; *Praxis der Porzellanmalerei* by Martin Mield and Rudolf Lanschke, Munich, 1965; *Made in Germany: Produktform Industrial Design,* exhibition catalogue, Munich, 1970; *New Glass: An International Survey,* exhibition catalogue, Corning, New York, 1979; *H. Th. Baumann: Design,* exhibition catalogue with introduction by Hans Mayr, Cologne, 1979; *Neue Moebel 1950-1982/ Contemporary Furniture* edited by Klaus-Jurgen Sembach, Stuttgart and London, 1982; *Design Since 1945* edited by Kathryn Hiesinger and George Marcus, Philadelphia and London, 1983.

*

All things that we shape or design are the result of human activity. They find their proper place within the bounds of their environments. The importance of a design does not spring from the formulas of mathematical calculation—it is solely the result of the ability of the human being to add to or take away. It is possible to bring weight, material, purpose, and function into such a relationship with one another that the object which results is beautiful. The path which leads to that beautiful thing doesn't matter—it can be known or unknown. What is important to recognize, however, is where it leads.

—H. Th. Baumann

# BAWDEN, Edward

British painter, printmaker, illustrator, book, mural, textile, and advertising designer

**Born:** Braintree, Essex, 10 March 1903. **Education:** Braintree High School, 1910-13, and Friends School, Saffron Walden, Essex, 1913-19; studied at the School of Art, Cambridge, 1919-21; Royal College of Art, London, 1922-25. **Military Service:** Served as official war artist, British Army, in the Middle East, 1940-45. **Family:** Married potter Charlotte Epton, 1932 (died, 1970); children: Joanna and Richard. **Career:** Freelance illustrator and designer, London, 1925-32, Great Bardfield, 1932-70, and Saffron Walden, from 1970; designed for Curwen Press, Chatto and Windus, Faber and Faber, Penguin Books, Nonesuch Press, Lion and Unicorn Press, *Architectural Review, Burlington Magazine, Signature, House and Garden, The Listener,* Cole and Sons, Imperial Airways, London Transport, Modern Textiles, Shell-Mex and British Petroleum, Twinings Teas, and others. Instructor in illustration, Goldsmith's College and Royal College of Art, London, from 1930, and Royal Academy Schools, London, 1963-70; visiting instructor, Banff School of Fine Arts, Alberta, Canada, 1949-50; Trustee, Tate Gallery, London, 1951-58. **Exhibitions:** Zwemmer Gallery, London, 1934, 1963; Leicester Galleries, London, 1938, 1949, 1952; Fine Art Society, London, 1968, 1975, 1978, 1979; Minories Gallery, Colchester, 1973 (toured); Fitzwilliam Museum, Cambridge, 1978. **Collections:** Tate Gallery, London; Victoria and Albert Museum, London; National Gallery of South Australia, Adelaide; Art Gallery of Ontario, Toronto. **Honors:** Commander, Order of the British Empire, 1946; Associate, 1947, and Academician, 1956, Royal Academy of Art, London; Royal Designer for Industry, Royal Society of Arts, London, 1949; Giles Bequest Print Prize, London, 1958; Silver Medal, Society of Industrial Artists and Designers, London, 1964; honorary doctorate, Royal College of Art, London, 1970, and University of Essex, 1974. **Died:** Saffron Walden, Essex, 21 November 1989.

## Works

Wallpaper designs, for Curwen Modern Textiles, 1926-39.
*The Life and Adventures of Peter Wilkins* (R. Paltock) book design, for J. M. Dent, 1928.
*Adam and Evelyn at Kew or Revolt in the Gardens* (R. Herring) book design, for Elkin Mathews and Marrot, 1930.
Posters, promotional leaflets, and flight maps, for Imperial Airways, 1930s.
*East Coasting* (D. Leigh) book design, for London and North Eastern Railway, 1931.
*Kynoch Press Note Book 1935* book design, for Kynoch Press, 1934.
Posters, advertisements, and booklet covers, for London Transport Passenger Board, 1935-55.
*The Weekend Book* (F. and V. Meynell) book design, for Nonesuch Press, 1939.
*The Voyages of Lemuel Gulliver* (J. Swift) book design, for The Folio Society, 1948.
*Life in an English Village* (E. Bawden and N. Carrington) book design, for Penguin Books, 1949.
*The Sundour Diary and Notebook 1953* book design, for Morton Sundour Fabrics, 1952.
*How Animals Move* (J. Gray) book design, for Cambridge University Press, 1953, and Penguin Books, 1959.
*The Histories of Herodotus of Halicarnassus* book design, for the Limited Editions Club, 1958.
Postcards and Christmas cards, for Blackwell's Booksellers, 1973-77.

## Publications

By BAWDEN: books—*Life in an English Village,* with introductions by Noel Carrington, London, 1949; *Take the Broom,* London, 1952; *The Sundour Diary and Notebook 1953,* Carlisle, 1952; *Hold

*Fast by Your Teeth,* London, 1963; *A Book of Cuts by Edward Bawden,* with text by Ruari McLean, London, 1979.

**By BAWDEN: books**—*Water Colour Drawings by Edward Bawden,* exhibition catalogue, London, 1933; *The Art of the Book* by Bernard H. Newdigate, London, 1938; *British Textile Designers Today* by H. G. Hayes Marshall, Leigh-on-Sea, 1939; *Edward Bawden* by J. M. Richards, London, 1946; *Edward Bawden* by Robert Harling, London, 1950; *Design in British Industry: A Mid-Century Survey* by Michael Farr, Cambridge, 1955; *Modern Book Design* by Ruari McLean, London, 1958; *London Transport Posters* by Harold Hutchins, London, 1963 *Magazine Design* by Ruari McLean, London and New York, 1969; *The World of Edward Bawden,* exhibition catalogue with texts by M. Chase and D. P. Bliss, London, 1973; *Industrial Design in Britain* by Noel Carrington, London, 1976 *Artists at Curwen* by Pat Gilmour, London, 1977; *Edward Bawden: A 75th Birthday Exhibition,* catalogue by Carel Weight, London, 1978; *Edward Bawden* by Douglas Percy Bliss, London, 1980; *British Art and Design 1900-1960,* exhibition catalogue with introduction by Carol Hogben, London, 1983, *Eye for Industry: Royal Designers for Industry 1936-1986,* exhibition catalogue by Fiona MacCarthy and Patrick Nuttgens, London, 1986.

*     *     *

From an early stage, Edward Bawden created an unmistakably individual style, range of techniques, and broad humour. As his biographer Douglas Percy Bliss has noted, "Bawden had his own way of seeing things. It was daft and original. Anyone could tell a Bawden..." Even though his work often seems far removed from any contemporary fashion, it nevertheless frequently seems modern and of the moment in its direct simplicity and crisp line. On the one hand, there is in his work the miniaturist's refinement of detail and technique, whilst on the other, there is the impressive ability to reduce complex forms to bold shapes and sprightly lines without needing theatrical effects of light and shade. Throughout, there is a strong interest in texture and pattern that shows itself most forcibly in the larger murals, such as the ingenious screen designed for the Lion and the Unicorn pavilion of the 1951 Festival of Britain.

As many of his illustrations and designs concentrate on well-known and often humorous aspects of British character and tradition, Bawden has been a popular choice to decorate British pavilions at international exhibitions, to brighten public places in colleges and large companies with murals, and, with posters and leaflets, to promote travel to the various parts of England.

He illustrated a very wide range of books, from Thomas More's *Utopia* (1970) to *Buttercups and Daisies* by Compton Mackenzie (1931), but he never concentrated on any particular author's work. The vitality of his illustrations comes from the graceful interplay of equally stressed shapes, not from exaggeration or caricature. This facility with pattern and balance of detail, which can be traced back to his early work on borders and printing decoration for Harold Curwen, is often used with great effect in his more occasional work designing wallpapers, menus, small advertisements, leaflets, and even pottery decoration.

Although it is difficult to trace direct influences, his virtuosity and range of skills clearly recall the great illustrators of the nineteenth century, and he has done much to revive and revitalise many of their techniques for the present century by his example of patient and industrious craftsmanship.

—Anthony J. Coulson

# BAY, Howard
American stage and film designer

**Born:** Centralia, Washington, 3 May 1912. **Education:** Studied at the University of Washington, Seattle, 1928; Chappell School of Art, Denver, Colorado, 1928-29; University of Colorado, Boulder, 1929; Marshall College, Huntington, West Virginia 1929-30; Carnegie Institute of Technology, Pittsburgh, 1930-31; Westminster College, New Wilmington, Pennsylvania, 1931-32; also studied in Europe, 1939. **Family:** Married Ruth Jonas in 1932 (died, 1978); children: Ellen and Timothy. **Career:** Freelance set and lighting designer for Broadway plays, operas, touring companies and film companies, from 1933; designer, working for the WPA project, at the Federal Theatre New York, 1936-39; designed operas for the National Orchestral Association, 1940; art director, Universal-International Pictures, 1946-48; also freelance producer and director for touring companies and art director for television productions. Instructor, University of Michigan, Ann Arbor, 1941; guest lecturer, Purdue University, West Lafayette, IN, 1962; instructor, Circle-in-the-Square Theatre School, New York, 1962-63; Andrew Mellon Guest Director, Carnegie Institute of Technology, Pittsburgh, 1963; lecturer, University of Oregon, Eugene, 1963; instructor, director, and professor of Theatre Arts, 1965-82, Alan King Professor and Chairman of the Theatre Department, 1966-69, Brandeis University, Waltham, MA; visiting professor, Yale University Drama School, New Haven, Connecticut, 1966-67; instructor, Cooper-Hewitt Museum, New York, 1976. **Member:** President, United Scenic Artists, New York, 1940-46 and 1952-53; National Advisory Board Member, International Theatre Institute, 1980-83. **Exhibitions:** New Gallery, New York, 1955; American Theatre Association, New York, 1968 (toured); Astor Gallery, Lincoln Center, New York, 1970. **Honors:** Guggenheim Fellowship, New York, 1939, 1940; New York Drama Critics Poll Award, *Variety* magazine, 1942; Donaldson Award, 1944, 1945; Antoinette Perry (Tony) Awards, 1960, 1966; Mahram Award, 1966. **Died:** New York City, 21 November 1986.

**Works**

Stage designs include—*Chalk Dust,* Experimental Theatre, New York, 1936; *Power,* Ritz Theatre, New York, 1937; *Native Ground,* Venice Theatre, New York, 1937; *One Third of a Nation,* Adelphi Theatre, New York, 1938; *Trojan Incident,* St. James Theatre, New York, 1938; *Sunup to Sundown,* Hudson Theatre, New York, 1938; *Life and Death of an American,* Maxine Elliott's Theatre, New York 1939; *The Little Foxes,* National Theatre, New York, 1939; *Morning Star,* Longacre Theatre, New York, 1940; *Brooklyn USA,* Forrest Theatre, New York, 1941; *Johnny 2 x 4,* Longacre Theatre, 1942; *The Moon Is Down,* Martin Beck Theatre, New York, 1942; *The Eve of St. Mark,* Cort Theatre, New York, 1942; *Something for the Boys,* Alvin Theatre, New York, 1943; *The Merry Widow,* Majestic Theatre, New York, 1943; *Carmen Jones,* Broadway Theatre, New York, 1943; *Follow the Girls,* Century Theatre, New York, 1944; *Ten Little Indians,* Broadhurst Theatre, New York, 1944; *Catherine Was Great,* Shubert Theatre, New York, 1944; *The Visitor,* Henry Miller's Theatre, New York, 1944; *Up in Central Park,* Century Theatre, 1945; *Show Boat,* Ziegfeld Theatre, New York, 1946; *The Big Knife,* National Theatre, 1949; *Come Back Little Sheba,* Booth Theatre, New York, 1950; *Two on the Aisle,* Mark Hellinger Theatre, New York, 1951; *The Shrike,* Cort Theatre, 1952; *Les Noces,*

Brandeis University, 1952; *The Desperate Hours,* Ethel Barrymore Theatre, New York, 1955; *A Very Special Baby,* Playhouse Theatre, New York, 1956; *Jolly Anna,* Philharmonic Auditorium, Los Angeles, 1959; *Toys in the Attic,* Hudson Theatre, 1960; *Milk and Honey,* Martin Beck Theatre, 1961; *Carmen,* San Francisco Opera, 1961; *Isle of Children,* Cort Theatre, 1962; *My Mother, My Father and Me,* Plymouth Theatre, New York, 1963; *Never Live Over a Pretzel Factory,* Eugene O'Neill Theatre, New York, 1964; *Natalya Petrovna,* New York City Opera, 1964; *Man of La Mancha,* ANTA Theatre, New York, 1965; *Knickerbocker Holiday,* Curran Theatre, San Francisco, 1971; *Volpone,* Asolo Theatre, Sarasota, Florida, 1977; *Oedipus,* Florida State University, Tallahassee, 1979; *The Speckled Band,* Missouri Repertory Company, Kansas City, 1983.

Film designs include—*The Exile,* 1947; *Up in Central Park,* 1948; *Go, Man, Go,* 1955; *Mr. Broadway* (television series), 1965; *A Midsummer Night's Dream,* 1966: *The Pueblo Incident,* 1973.

**Publications**

By BAY: book—*Stage Design,* New York, 1974

On BAY: books—*The Biographical Encyclopaedia and Who's Who of the American Theatre* edited by Walter Rigdon, New York, 1966; *Contemporary Stage Design* edited by Elizabeth Burdick, Peggy Hansen, and Brenda Zanger, Middletown, CT, 1974.

*

Dramatic design is somewhere between a craft and an art. The graphic sketch is not an end in itself but a promise of the finished product—an intention of just how the visual arm will complement the script, the music, the acting, and the direction of a given theatrical event and progress as the drama unfolds. That is why—with the exception of Picasso who adapted to the demands of the stage—the giants of modern art were poor scenic artists. Their self-contained constructions didn't mix with the round actors and dancers. The looser pictorialists fared better behind the footlights: Dufy, Cocteau, Berard, Tchelichev, Steinberg, Rauschenberg, Hockney, et al.

To serve the variety of dramatic fare, a designer must not polish a single style. The demands of dramaturgy are too assorted to be squeezed into a rigid, painterly manner. Incidentally, watercolor best captures the luminosity of a stage picture under lights. Immersion in research of time and place conditions the designer to think and draw, and then to create a relevant scenic environment.

Naturally, dramatic design is a plastic effort— we deal in three dimensions, and a model may be more appropriate than a rendering. Other hands execute our work, so our directions must be precise— working drawings are a large part of our labors.

Film art direction is a very realistic medium and everything must be measured by the human scale. The problem is to impregnate the naturalistic material with the emotional tenor of the scene.

Dramatic design is automatically a popular art form, partly because actors are not abstractions.

—Howard Bay (1984)

*   *   *

As with many designers, early influences seem to have made a great impression on Howard Bay's subsequent career, and thus the aims of his early work with the Federal Theatre—where beauty and style were secondary to the presentation of ideas, information, characters, and story—seems to have infused all the best work of his mature years. Though he admired the work of Robert Edmond Jones, who was the dean of American designers in the late 1920s and early 1930s, his eminently practical personality did not suit him to follow the older man's moody, symbolist, poetic style. What he did learn from Jones was the directness and simplicity that one could achieve through massive research followed by painstaking refinement.

Even though he became noted for his charming, nostalgic, painterly musicals during the late 1940s and early 1950s, it was eventually his innate pragmatism, realism, and practicality in solving design problems that made him a distinctive American designer with much to offer to students at Brandeis and to audiences of the American theatre. As an example of this practical brilliance, one should examine what he accomplished with his most famous design, that for *The Man of La Mancha.* He needed a prison entrance that was dramatic, that immediately set the feeling of a prison, that gave a long entrance, and that seemed to appear from nowhere. He satisfied this set of requirements with an unusual drawbridge lowered into the center of the action from the darkness at the upper back of the stage—for an effect that made persons from the outside world seem as if they came from another planet. It was a brilliant artistic solution that stemmed from the practical and realistic approach that Bay had always taken with his design assignments.

Except for his connection with the Federal Theatre, Bay was not a political or social commentator in his work, nor did he present vanguard artistic ideas. On the other hand, he was always fully contemporary in his work and receptive to new technology and new aesthetic concepts when they proved useful in the solution of particular design problems.

—Douglas A. Russell

# BAYER, Herbert

American photographer, architect, interior, graphic and product designer

**Born:** Haag, Austria, 5 April 1900; emigrated to the United States, 1938, naturalized, 1944. **Education:** Apprentice in architecture and decorative arts under Georg Schmidthammer, Linz, Austria, 1919; graphic design and typography assistant to Emanuel Margold, Darmstadt, Austria, 1920; studied mural painting and design with Vasily Kandinsky at the Staatliche Bauhaus, Weimar, Austria, 1921-23. **Military Service:** Served in the 14th Infantry Regiment, Austrian Army, 1917-18. **Family:** Married Irene Hecht in 1925 (divorced); children: Julia; married Joella Haweis Levy in 1944. **Career:** Young Master of Typography and Graphic Design, Staaliche Bauhaus, Dessau, 1925-28; director, Dorland Studio of Design, Berlin, 1925-38; art director, *Vogue* magazine, Berlin, 1928-30; freelance photographer, contributing to the *Die Line* and other magazines, Berlin, 1930-36; painter, photographer, graphic designer, and exhibition architect, New York, 1938-45; director, Dorland International, New York, 1945; consultant designer, 1945-56, and chairman of the Department of Design, 1956-65, Container Corporation of America, Chicago; consultant and architect, Aspen Institute of Humanistic Studies, Aspen, Colorado, 1964-85; art and design consultant, Atlantic Richfield Company, Los Angeles, 1966-85. **Exhibitions:** Kunstverein, Linz, 1929; Staatliche Bauhaus, Dessau, 1931; Kunstverein, Salzburg, 1936; Black Mountain College, North Carolina, 1939; Yale University, New Haven, Connecticut, 1940; North Texas State Teachers College, Denton, 1943; Brown University, Providence, Rhode Island, 1947 (retrospective, toured); Cleveland Institute of Art, 1952; Aspen Institute for Humanistic Studies, 1955, 1964; Germanisches Nationalmuseum, Nuremberg, 1956 (retrospective; toured); Fort Worth Art Museum, Texas, 1958 (toured); Städtische Kunsthalle, Düsseldorf, 1960; Museum am Ostwall, Dortmund, 1960; Bauhaus Archiv, Darmstadt, 1961; Städtisches Kunstmuseum, Duisburg, 1962; Neue Galerie, Linz, 1963, 1976, 1980; University of New Hampshire, Durham, 1966; Philadelphia Art Alliance, 1967; University of California at Santa Barbara, 1969; Hudson River Museum, Yonkers, New York, 1969; Centre Culturel Allemand, Paris, 1971; Oesterreichisches Museum fur Angewandte Kunst, Vienna, 1971; Landesbildstelle, Hamburg, 1973 (toured); Saarland Museum, Saarbrucken, 1973; Denver Art Museum, Colorado, 1973, 1980; Deutscher Ring, Hamburg, 1974 (retrospective; toured); Dartmouth College, Hanover, New Hampshire, 1977 (toured); Centre Georges Pompidou, Paris, 1981; Bauhaus Archiv, West Berlin, 1982 (toured); Museum für Gestaltung, West Berlin, 1986; Kiusthaus, Zug, 1987; Oberösterreichisches Landesmuseum, Linz, 1987. **Collections:** Denver Art Museum, Colorado; Museum of Modern Art, New York; San Francisco Museum of Modern Art; Neue Galerie der Stadt, Linz; Museum Folkwang, Essen; Bauhaus Archiv, West Berlin. **Honors:** First Prize, *Foreign Advertising Photography* exhibition, New York, 1931; City of Salzburg Medal, 1936; Gold Medal, Art Directors Club of Denver, 1957; Gold Medal, Art Directors Club of Philadelphia, 1961; Trustees Award, Aspen Institute for Humanistic Studies, Colorado, 1965; Ambassador's Award for Excellence, London, 1968; Kulturpreis for Photography, Cologne, 1969; Gold Medal, American Institute of Graphic Arts, 1970; Adalbert Stifter Prize, Linz, 1971; honorary member, Alliance Graphique Internationale, 1975; honorary fellow, Royal Academy of Fine Art, The Hague, 1975; Austrian Cross of Honour, 1978. Fellow, American Academy of Arts and Sciences, 1979; honorary doctorates from Technische Hochschule, Graz, 1973, Philadelphia College of Art, 1974, and Art Center College of Design, Pasadena, 1979. **Died:** Montecito, California, 30 September 1985.

## Works

*Universal* typeface, 1925.
*Elementare Buchtechnik* displays, at the *Pressa Ausstellung,* Cologne, 1928.
Deutscher Werkbund displays, at the *Exposition de la Societé des Artistes Décorateurs,* Paris, 1930.
Exhibition layouts, Building Workers Union, Berlin, 1931.
*Das Wunder des Lebens* exhibition catalogue and poster, Berlin, 1935.
*Gesunde Kost—Gesunde Menschen* advertisement, for Chlorodont Toothpaste, 1937.
*Gas und Wasser Ausstellung* exhibition layouts, for Junkers Industries, Leipzig, 1937.
*Bauhaus 1919-1928* exhibition layouts and catalogue, for the Museum of Modern Art, New York, 1938.

*Road to Victory* exhibition layouts, for the Museum of Modern Art, New York, 1942.
Series of press advertisements, for Cohama Neckties, 1943-45.
*Modern Art in Advertising* exhibition layouts at the Art Institute of Chicago, for the Container Corporation of America, 1945.
Office interiors, for the Title Insurance and Trust Company, Chicago, 1948.
Series of press advertisements, for Noreen Hair Color Rinse, 1953.
Seminar Building and Health Center, for Aspen Institute for Humanistic Studies, Colorado, 1953-55.
Paper mills and factory plants in California, Alabama, Washington, Illinois, Texas, Oklahoma and West Germany, for the Container Corporation of America, 1955-57.
Aspen Meadows Hotel complex, for Aspen Institute for Humanistic Studies Colorado 1964.
*50 Jahre Bauhaus* exhibition layouts, catalogue, and posters, for the Württembergischer Kunstverein, Stuttgart, 1968.
ARCO Towers and Plaza, for the Atlantic Richfield Company, Los Angeles, 1972-73.

(for information on Bayer's activity as a fine artist and as a photographer, see *Contemporary Artists* and *Contemporary Photographers*)

## Publications

**By BAYER: books**—*Fotomontagen* (portfolio of 11 photomontages), Berlin, 1932; *Fotoplastiken* (portfolio of 10 photographs), Berlin, 1937; (with Ise and Walter Gropius) *Bauhaus 1919-1928,* New York, 1938, 1959, 1975; *Seven Convolutions,* Colorado Springs, 1948; *World Geo-Graphic Atlas,* Aspen, Colorado, 1953; *Book of Drawings,* Chicago, 1961; *Eight Monochrome Suite,* Los Angeles, 1965; *Herbert Bayer: Paintings,* Chicago, 1965; *Herbert Bayer: Painter/Designer/Architect,* New York, Ravensburg, West Germany, London, and Tokyo, 1967; *Herbert Bayer,* with introduction by Dieter Honisch, Stuttgart, 1968.

**On BAYER: books**—*The Way Beyond Art: The Work of Herbert Bayer* by Alexander Dorner, New York, 1947; *Seven Designers Look at Trademark Design* edited by Egbert Jacobson, Chicago, 1952; *Fotoauge Herbert Bayer,* exhibition catalogue edited by Jan Tschichold, Munich, 1967; *Herbert Bayer,* exhibition catalogue with text by Ludwig Grote, London, 1968; *Two Visions of Space: Herbert Bayer and Ingeborg ten Haeff,* exhibition catalogue with introduction by Carl Black Jr., New York, 1969; *Herbert Bayer: A Total Concept,* exhibition catalogue with introduction by Karl Otto Bach, Denver, 1973; *Herbert Bayer: Das Druckgrafische Werk bis 1971* by Hans Wingler and Peter Hahn, West Berlin, 1974; *Herbert Bayer: Neue Werk und Projekte,* exhibition catalogue by Ida Rodriguez Prampolini, Zurich, 1974; *Herbert Bayer: un concepto total* by Prampolini, Mexico City, 1975; *Herbert Bayer: Beispiele aus dem Gesamtwerk 1919-1974,* exhibition catalogue with introduction by Peter Baum, Linz, 1979; *Herbert Bayer: From Type to Landscape,* exhibition catalogue by Jan van der Marck, New York, 1977; *Herbert Bayer: Photographic Works,* exhibition catalogue with text by Leland Rice and Beaumont Newhall, Los Angeles, 1977; *Herbert Bayer: Das Künstlerisches Werk 1918-1938,* exhibition catalogue, West Berlin, 1982; *Herbert Bayer: The Complete Work* by Arthur A. Cohen, Cambridge, Massachusetts, 1984; *Herbert Bayer and Modernist Design in America* by Gwen F. Chanzit, Ann Arbor, 1987.

\*    \*    \*

We may count Herbert Bayer as one of the few artists whose whole life's work was decisively influenced by the Bauhaus. This is confirmed in the universality of his artistic creation and his basic stylistic attitude through all the decades of this activity. He drew on the whole range of environmental design for his work. Bayer's first typographical works, produced at the Bauhaus in the early 1920s, still show the influence of "elementary typography," such as Lissitzky's, but he soon advanced beyond this, developing his own typographical style which became typical of the Dessau Bauhaus graphic image under Gropius. In the introduction of DIN norms, lower case script, and the inclusion of photography, Bayer's work set standards and acted as a direction pointer. As head of the Dessau Bauhaus print shop he was able to put his ideas into practice; among the many innovations he introduced into his teaching was the inclusion of advertising. In 1927 Bayer left the Bauhaus to work independently. He was active as painter and photographer, and his photo-sculptures and photo-montages, especially the photomontage self portrait of 1932, are well known.

Beginning in 1929, Bayer helped craft the image of the most modern family journal, *Die Line,* designing not only the print but also innumerable title pages. During his ten year association with the Dorland advertising agency he introduced the images of surrealism to advertising through the use of photography, retouch, and montage, decisively influencing the advertising style of the 1930s and becoming one of that decade's leading graphic designers.

Bayer's collaboration on exhibition design also acted as a direction pointer. The Paris exhibition of the "German Section" for the German Labour Union in 1930 is one of the summits in exhibition design. The principles were further developed for the first Bauhaus exhibition at the Museum of Modern Art in New York in 1938.

After his emigration to the United States in 1938 Bayer extended his field of work. He fought against the American advertising business, which to him was excessively oriented towards the "hard sell". From 1946 he was active as an architect in Aspen, Colorado. Until well into the 1960s he created a series of buildings for the Aspen Institute for Humanistic Studies which combine harmoniously with the mountain landscape. In 1955, Bayer created large sculptural designs—a marble garden and a grass wall formed from the landscape—for the Institute.

In his paintings, Bayer was occupied in the broadest sense with form and colour relationship. His post-1960s paintings can be seen as constant variations within the constructivist painting tradition after 1945. Bayer designed large series of advertisements and information sheets for the Container Corporation of America and for General Electric which demonstrate his talent for the visualization of complex facts. In 1957-58 Bayer designed a world atlas which is constructed on entirely new principles.

—Magdalena Droste

# BEENE, Geoffrey

American fashion designer

**Born:** Haynesville, Louisiana, 30 August 1927. **Education:** Studied medicine, Tulane University, New Orleans, 1943-46; University of Southern California, Los Angeles, 1946; Traphagen School of Fashion, New York, 1947-48; L'Ecole de la Chambre Syndicale de la Couture, and Académie Julien, Paris, 1948. **Career:** Display assistant, I. Magnin store, Los Angeles, 1946; apprentice tailor, Paris, 1948-50; assistant to Mildred O'Quinn, Samuel Winston Harmay, and other Seventh Avenue fashion houses, New York, 1951-54; designer, for Teal Traina, New York, 1954-63; founder-director, Geoffrey Beene Inc. fashion house, New York, from 1963; introduced first menswear collection, 1969, beenebag sportswear collection, 1971, men's fragrances *Grey Flannel,* 1975, and *Bowling Green,* 1987. **Exhibitions:** *Geoffrey Beene: 25 Years of Discovery,* Los Angeles, 1988; Western Reserve Historical Society, Cleveland, Ohio, 1988; National Academy of Design, New York, 1988; Musashino Museum, Tokyo, 1988; *Geoffrey Beene Unbound,* Museum at the Fashion Institute of Technology, New York, 1994. **Collections:** Metropolitan Museum of Art, New York; Los Angeles County Museum of Art; Chicago Historical Society; Western Reserve Historical Society, Cleveland, Ohio; Lyndon Baines Johnson Library, Austin, Texas. **Honors:** Coty Award, New York, 1964, 1966, 1968, 1974, 1975, 1977, 1981, 1982; Cotton Council Award, 1964, 1969, Neiman-Marcus Award, 1965; Ethel Traphagen Award, New York, 1966; Designer of the Year Award, 1986, 1987, and Special Award, 1988, Council of Fashion Designers of America. **Address:** Geoffrey Beene Inc., 550 Seventh Avenue, New York, New York 10018-3295, U.S.A.

## Publications

**On BEENE: books**—*Fashion: Dress in the Twentieth Century* by Prudence Glynn, London, 1978; *The Fashion Makers* by Bernardine Morris, New York, 1978; *Fashion: The Inside Story* by Barbaralee Diamondstein, New York, 1985; *Couture: The Great Designers* by Caroline Rennolds Milbank, New York, 1985; *The Encyclopaedia of Fashion from 1840 to the 1980s* by Georgina O'Hara, London, 1986; *Geoffrey Beene: The First Twenty-Five Years,* exhibition catalogue with text by Marylou Luther, Tokyo, 1988; *Geoffrey Beene Unbound,* exhibition catalogue edited by J. Abbott Miller, with texts by Grace Mirabella and Franz Kafka, New York, 1994; *Geoffrey Beene* by Brenda Cullerton, New York, 1995; **articles**—"It's a Beene" by J. Bowles in *Vogue* (New York), January 1977; "American in Paris: Beene's Private Showing" by B. Morris in the *New York Times,* 9 April 1978; "Architectural Digest Visits Geoffrey Beene" by P. Carlsen in *Architectural Digest* (Los Angeles), September 1979; "Paradise Found: Geoffrey Beene's Long Island Retreat" in *Architectural Digest* (Los Angeles), February 1984; "Designer Profile: 1988 Marks 25th Year in American Fashion for Geoffrey Beene" by K. Monget in *New York Apparel News,* May 1987; "American Beauty: The World of Geoffrey Beene" by P. Morrisroe in *New York,* 30 May 1988; "Beene: Innovative and, Yes, Intellectual" by Amy M. Spindler in *New York Times* (New York), 8 April 1995; "A Crisis in Confidence: Reinventing the American Dream" by Suzy Menkes in *International Herald Tribune* (Paris), 11 April 1995; "The Pearl of Oyster Bay" by Amy Fine Collins in *Harper's Bazaar* (New York), October 1995; "Beene's Homage to Mondrian" by Amy M. Spindler in *New York Times,* 4 November 1995; "Defining the Modern Look Without Frills" by Suzy Menkes in *International Herald Tribune* (Paris), 7 November 1995; "Beene There" by Laura Jacobs in *New Republic* (New York), 20 November 1995.

\*     \*     \*

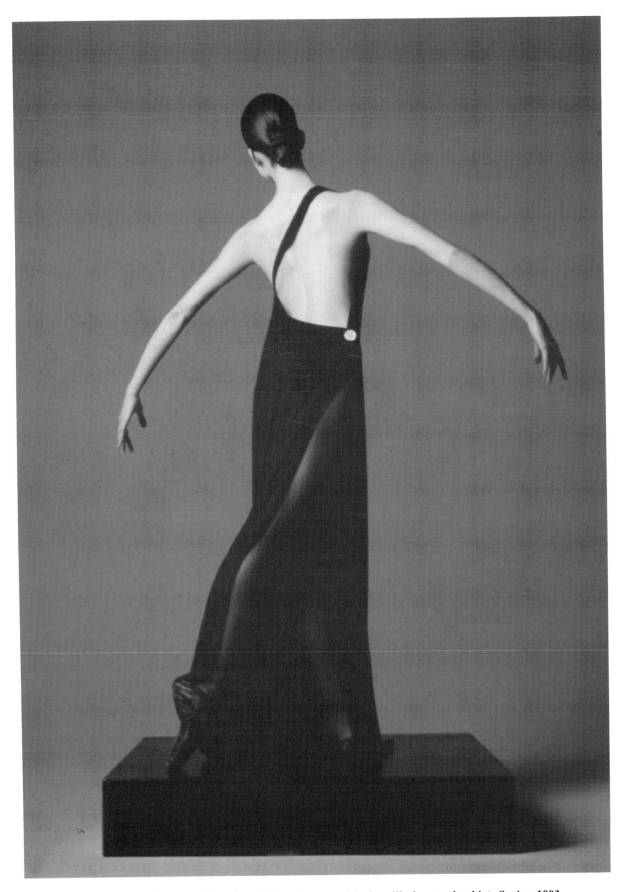

**Geoffrey Beene: One-shoulder toga dress in black wool crepe with chantilly lace underskirt, Spring 1993.**
**Photo: William Laxton**

The most important style to come from Geoffrey Beene was his relaxed look in 1977, when he stressed easy, pull-on clothes, as in his pullover shirt dress. He also expressed this look in several types of trouser-suit for women—the town suit with a short navy jacket, his white silk evening trouser suit, and his most relaxed version, the softly full pyjama suit worn with a long mackintosh. The following year, he made the pyjama his major theme in plain fabrics for day and in silks for evening. The easy look was also shown in short-sleeved shirtdresses with full skirts and in his sweater coat, which was a giant polo-necked jumper to the knee. All this was regarded as his most original contribution to fashion—presenting a casual wearability, an informal ease of attire.

Americans dubbed him the creator of liberated clothes for women, as his billowing frocks and unstructured suits did not impose any unnatural forms on them; these clothes could be moved in with ease, which could not be said for many of the ideas coming from Paris. These were clothes for working mothers who need clothes they can forget about once they are on. That they do not get in the way was a major attraction for the ordinary woman and a departure from the theatrical and sexist versions of women too often promoted in contemporary Paris, invariably by male designers exercising their own fantasies. However, Beene has matured enough to appreciate what life is really like for most women, and so he provides them with clothes that do not imprison or impede.

The American press has termed his clothes the essence of simplicity, but he cannot avoid some decorative touches, such as bejewelled girdles, double belts, and clustered necklaces—touches which to British eyes spoil the line. Nevertheless, Beene has made an important innovation in conventional clothes, one which, added to Norma Kamali's adaptation of sports clothes, creates the most original American statement in today's fashion—the relaxed and informal look.

—Diana de Marly

# BEGA, Melchiorre

Italian architect, interior, and furniture designer

**Born:** Crevalcore, Bologna, 20 July 1898. **Education:** Studied architecture, Istituto di Belle Arti, Bologna, Dip. Arch., 1922. **Military Service:** Served as an artillery lieutenant, Italian Army, 1914-18. **Family:** Married Maddalena Galimberti in 1931 (died, 1976); children: Maria, Paola, Anna, and Vittorio. **Career:** Freelance architect and designer, establishing own studio in Bologna, 1920-34, and in Milan, 1935-69; founded Bega Architetti Associati, Milan, 1969-76; concentrated on interior and furniture design, from 1950. Co-director with Carlo Pagani, 1941-42, and director, 1943-44, *Domus* magazine, Milan. President, Accademia di Belle Arti, Bologna, 1950-61. **Exhibitions:** Milan Triennale, 1933, 1940, 1951; *28/78 Architettura,* Palazzo delle Stelline, Milan, 1979; *Europäische Keramik seit 1950,* Museum für Kunst und Gewerbe, Hamburg, 1979 (traveled to Düsseldorf); City Hall, Bologna, 1984. **Honors:** Academician, National Academy of San Luca, Rome, 1963; Gold Medal for Education, Culture and Art, Rome, 1968; Gold Medal and Merit Award, Province of Bologna, 1968; Honorary Academician, Clementina Academy, Bologna, 1969; INARCH Design Prize, Rome, 1970; **Died:** Milan, 26 February 1976.

## Works

Albergo degli Ambasciatori interiors, Rome, 1926.
Savoia Hotel interiors, Florence, 1931.
*Savoia* yacht interiors, for the Royal Family of Italy, 1932.
*Conte di Savoia* Atlantic liner interiors, 1935.
Uaddan Casino and Theatre interiors, Tripoli, 1936.
Birreria Forst bar interiors, Milan, 1949.
Galtrusco fabric shop interiors, Milan, 1950.
Motta Bar interiors, Milan, 1955.
La Residenza administration centre, for the Milan Fair, 1958.
Galfa headquarters building, Milan, 1959.
Office suite, for the Ridotto dei Cineconvegni, Milan, 1960.
Shops interiors, for Perugina, New York, 1962.
Office interiors in Hamburg and Berlin, for Axel Springer, 1962-66.
Motta Grill restaurants on the Autostrada del Sole and Autostrada La Serenissima, Italy, 1967.
Palace of Congress interiors, Algiers, 1968.
*Anita M* oil-tanker cabin interiors, 1969.
Office building in Milan, for *Selezione/Reader's Digest,* 1970.
IRI Pavilion at the *Italian Produce* exhibition, for the IRI/Finsider Group, Beijing, 1973.

## Publications

**On BEGA: books**—*Melchiorre Bega architetto* by Giorgio Ramponi, Milan, 1931; *Melchiorre Bega: Architettura,* Milan, 1937; *Negozi d' Oggi* by Roberto Aloi, Milan, 1950; *Mobili Tipo by Roberto Aloi,* Milan, 1956; *Forme Nuove in Italia* by Agnoldomenico Pica, Milan and Rome, 1957; *Mercati e Negozi* by Roberto Aloi, Milan, 1959; *Public Interiors* by Misha Black, London, 1960; *Catalogo Bolaffi dell'Architettura Italiana 1963-1966* edited by Pier Carlo Santini and Giuseppe Luigi Marini, Turin, 1966; *Forme Nuove nell'Arredamento Italiano* edited by Paolo Portoghesi and Marino Marini, Rome, 1978; *Melchiorre Bega, Architetto* by Stefano Zironi, Milan, 1983.

\* \* \*

Coming from a family of Bolognese shop and interior fitters with some famous commissions to their credit, Melchiorre Bega brought this unique experience to bear upon his architectural training. It was natural that he should turn to shop and bar interior design in that period of change and expansion that followed on the Liberation. Even so, those early designs, which sought to use the refined means that Italian craftsmanship afforded, were extremely accomplished. He made use of the whole range of ceramics—such as tiles for both floors and walls, with rich glazes and many high-relief panels—and set these off against elegant metal fittings. However, this dazzling surface was supported by a rational structure arising from a serious analysis of the purpose the spaces were to serve.

This latter aspect of his gifts is best seen in the Galfa Skyscraper, which derives its name from the two streets forming the corner on which it stands. A tall, curtain-walled block, its finely wrought details on regular grid elevations are subtly accented by the discreet use of colour. The adroit planning of the floors manages access, lifts, stairs, and services in a way that is both logical and pleasant.

Perhaps the senior administration block for the Milan Fair, La Residenza, shows Bega's talents at full stretch. Again, the elegant geometry of the exteriors encloses very subtle planning of interior spaces, each skillfully attuned to its particular purposes which are also reflected in the carefully considered furnishings and fittings. This is especially noticeable in those areas that serve several functions without showing any sign of compromise. The spaces appear to adapt without undue forcing, and the fittings and furnishings seem to serve only that particular function. Again the colors are discreet, but being quite positive, they underline the disposition of the spaces.

The Ridotto dei Cineconvegni, though in actual forms quite different from La Residenza which preceded it by a couple of years, nevertheless is the result of the same design considerations, the same logical development from the requirements and integration of different functions and purposes within a unitary block. Some of the specialized demands could be met only by purpose-built accommodation, but against these fixtures, the rest of the space is allowed maximum flexibility to meet the different uses. Again, furniture, fittings, and color elegantly announce unity in diversity.

—Toni del Renzio

# BELLINI, Mario

Italian industrial designer

**Born:** Milan, 1 February 1935. **Education:** Studied architecture at the Politecnico, Milan, Dip. Arch., 1959. **Family:** Married Giovanna Agrati in 1960; children: Elena, Chiara, Claudio, and Marco. **Career:** Director of Design, La Rinascente department stores, Milan, 1961-63; partner, with Marco Romano, in architectural design studio, Milan, 1963-73; established Studio Bellini architecture and industrial design office, Milan, from 1973; has designed for Artemide, B & B Italia, Brionvega, Olivetti, Cassina, Flos Lancia, Marcatre, Yamaha, and others; chief industrial design consultant for office equipment, Olivetti, Milan, from 1963; research and design consultant, Renault cars, from 1978. Director of *Album* monograph yearbook, for Electra Publishers, Milan, since 1979; editor-in-chief, *Domus* magazine, Milan, since 1986. Professor of Design, Istituto Superiore di Disegno Industriale, Venice, 1962-65; visiting lecturer, Unione Costruttori Italiani Macchine Utensili, Cinisello Balsamo, 1971, Universita Internazionale dell'Arte, Florence, 1973, 1976, National Hoger Instituut, Antwerp, 1977, Royal College of Art, London, 1978, University of California at Los Angeles, 1979, and Hochschule fur Angewandte Kunst, Vienna, 1982-83. **Member:** Architects' Association of Milan, 1964; Gestione case per Lavoratori architectural section, Milan, 1967; vice-president, ADI Associazione per Disegno Industriale, Milan, 1969-71; founder-member, Environmedia, Milan, since 1973; Scientific Council Member, Milan Triennale design section, since 1979. **Exhibitions:** *The Modern Chair 1918-1970,* Whitechapel Art Gallery, London, 1970; *Italy: The New Domestic Landscape,* Museum of Modern Art, New York, 1972; *Design Process Olivetti 1908-1978,* University of California at Los Angeles, 1979; *Design and design,* Palazzo delle Stelline, Milan, 1979 (traveled to Venice); *Culture and Technology of Italian Furniture 1950-1980,* Stadtmuseum, Cologne, 1980; *Italian Re-Evolution,* La Jolla Museum of Art, California, 1982; *Design Since 1945,* Philadelphia Museum of Art, 1983; *Mario Bellini: Designer,* Museum of Modern Art, New York, 1987; *Architects Inside: From Mies to*

*Memphis,* International Design Center, New York, 1988. **Collections:** Studi e Archivio della Comunicazione, Parma; Museum of Modern Art, New York; Philadelphia Museum of Art; Musee des Arts Decoratifs, Montreal. **Honors:** Compasso d'Oro award, Milan, 1962, 1964, 1970, 1979, 1981; Gold Medal, Liubliana Industrial Design Biennale, 1968; Bolaffi Design Prize, Turin, 1973; SMAU Prize, Milan, 1978; ADIFAD Delta de Oro Award, Barcelona, 1977, 1979; INARCH Prize, Rome, 1979. **Address:** Corso Venezia 11, 20121 Milan, Italy.

## Works

*Programma* 101 microcomputer, for Olivetti, 1965.
*Amanta, Bambole* chairs and *Quattro Gatti* tables, for B B Italia, 1966-72.
TVC 250 computer terminal, for Olivetti, 1967.
*Totem* radio and record player in lacquered wood housing, for Brionvega, 1971.
*Logos* 50/60 series of calculators, for Olivetti, 1973.
*Divisumma* 18 calculator, for Olivetti, 1973.
The *Office World* furniture, for Marcatre, 1974.
*Area* 50 table lamps in porcelain and plastic, for Artemide, 1975.
TC *800* cassette deck in ABS plastic, for Yamaha, 1975-77.
*Logos 40* and *Logos 80* series of electronic calculators, for Olivetti, 1976.
*Cab* chair in steel and leather, for Cassina, 1977.
*TES 401* word processor equipment, for Olivetti, 1977.
*Monitor* television set, for Brionvega, 1977.
*ET101* electronic typewriter, for Olivetti, 1978-79.
Showroom in Tokyo, for Interdecor, 1981.
*Praxis* portable electric typewriter, for Olivetti, 1981.

## Publications

**By BELLINI: articles**—in *Gran Bazaar* (Milan), December 1979; *Abitare* (Milan), September 1980; *Corriere della Sera* (Milan), September 1980; *Album* (Milan), November 1981, September 1983; *Le Grandi Automobili* (Milan), Fall 1982.

**On BELLINI: books**— *Il Disegno Industriale e la sua Estetica* by Gillo Dorfles, Bologna, 1963; *Design Italiano: I Mobili* by Enrichetta Ritter, Milan and Rome, 1968; *The Modern Chair 1918-1970,* exhibition catalogue with texts by Carol Hogben and others, London, 1970; *Design in Italia 1945-1972* by Paolo Fossati, Turin, 1972; *The Modern Chair: Classics in Production* by Clement Meadmore, London, 1974; *Atlante del Design Italiano 1940-1980* by Alfonso Grassi and Anty Pansera, Milan, 1980; *Contemporary Furniture* edited by Klaus-Jurgen Sembach, Stuttgart and London, 1982; *An Industry for Design: The Research, Design and Corporate Image of B & B Italia* edited by Mario Mastropietro, Milan, 1982, 1986; *Design Since 1945* edited by Kathryn Hiesinger and George Marcus, Philadelphia and London, 1983; *Design Process Olivetti 1908-1983,* with text by Renzo Zorzi, Milan, 1983; *Mario Bellini: Designer,* exhibition catalogue edited by Susan Weiley, New York, 1987; *Design in Italy: 1870 to the Present* by Penny Sparke, London and New York, 1988.

*

The idea of a discipline that deals with the physical environment for the purpose of improving man's habitat, by changing spatial structures, services, facilities and products, is only a relatively recent one. It is almost sixty years since Walter Gropius had the intuition that later led him to state: "The term 'design' encompasses in general the whole orbit of our surroundings and of man's handiwork, from ordinary hold goods to the complex planning of an entire city."

Yet, half a century after the closing of the Bauhaus, the nineteenth-century, academic classification of disciplines still prevails. Architecture has remained a second-class activity useful for decorating its own empty spaces, and civil and transport engineering, a tightly enclosed field of applicational science and technology. All the while, the designing of machines and consumer products is treated as a world unto itself; it stubbornly clings to the mythical connotations of mass production, industrial manufacturing processes, and project methodology, with a now conspicuously outdated propaedeutic and Messianic streak.

Now, if this fragmentation may be justified within a narrow professional scope for reasons to do with operative skills, it is much less acceptable in schools, in their structures and curricula, where it nevertheless remains habitual. Witness the inviolate engineering and architectural schools, some of which may occasionally introduce a supplementary industrial design course in order to be abreast of progress. Witness the schools of industrial design proper, secluded within their reassuring methodological boundaries, which may at times be enriched to the point of providing some rudiments of architecture. And again, the many—too many—industrial design schools that germinated during modernization in academies or art schools, but which are often suffocated in a context inconsistent with their aims.

To complicate matters further, for us aspiring environment-designers (in Gropius' sense of the term) or heirs—even despite ourselves—to the modern movement, the unifying process is by no means under way. Indeed, the very ideological premises, the functionalistic doctrine and ensuing positivistic faith in a reassuring project methodology, upon which we wishfully thought we could establish a combined design discipline, now appear increasingly disputable and inadequate since the renewed enthusiasm of the early postwar years. It was in this prospect that I found myself, having been trained as an architect, starting out as a machine and consumer goods designer on the one hand, and as a chair and interior products designer on the other, while progressively and deliberately giving up architectural work.

Through research and practice, I had to explore branches of design that were different from my architectural background, as well as from one another—in my opinion, a calculating machine and a chair are further apart than a chair and a church. In an effort not to lose my identity, this led me to the constant quest for a common base which I have come to regard as intersecting these parallel activities, in a wider dimension that also now includes the notion of architecture, which I have taken up again with renewed interest. This dimension, aside from its value to me personally, could constitute a fresh contribution to the still open debate on the cultural unity of all design . . .

An effective improvement in the quality of our environment may be obtained from the reunification of design standards. However, it is my firm belief that such reunification can be accomplished only by superseding the compartmentalization of sectors and moving instead towards a more anthropocentric view of man's environment, at least as far as disciplinary and didactic, or cultural, aspects are concerned. (Excerpted from a speech made at the International Design Conference, Aspen, Colorado, June 1981.)

—Mario Bellini

*    *    *

On a recent (1989) trip, I had the chance to visit the Château Dufresne (Musée des Arts Decoratifs de Montréal). I was surprised and delighted to find an old "friend," *Chiara,* a not quite-five-foot high, twenty-five year old, cylindrical light sculpture formed from a sheet of mirror-finished stainless steel, developed by Mario Bellini in 1964. It is part of the museum's permanent collection of modern design. It has always been one of my favorite designs, if for no other reason than, in looking at it, one asks: "It is *so simple,* why didn't I think of that?" Evoking the image of a futuristic nun, the design could only have been made as a result of countless studies in folding paper cutouts. It would not seem possible to create such a form on a drafting board, regardless of the talent of its creator, and thus it truly expresses one aspect of that person.

Although trained as an architect, Mario Bellini is probably best known for his furniture and industrial design products. He apparently prefers working as a "sculptor"—using a series of models, including full-size prototypes—to design, experiment with, and develop his concepts. Tactile surfaces and materials, providing direct physical contact between the designer and the product, help to insure a positive and comforting reaction on the part of the eventual user.

Bellini has developed a playful attitude toward the workplace in many of his industrial designs. In 1972 for Olivetti, he and some associates developed the *Divisumma 18* Electronic Printing Calculator, a small, bright-yellow object, barely two inches high, with a continuous flexible, rubber-skinned keyboard. The skin is to protect the machine from dust, but it serves the design function of "feel," with the articulated buttons (keys) resembling nipples. It is almost impossible not to want to touch it.

Bellini produced other designs, for Olivetti and Yamaha (stereo equipment), that in triangular form and strong graphic communication also tempted the viewer to want to touch and play with them. He has taken a very similar attitude toward his furniture designs, especially chairs which he finds are both difficult and fascinating objects.

The *Amanta* series (1966) represents his early experiments with fiber glass reinforced polyester. A shell, with turned-up edges to snare fabric-covered cushions, was carefully studied to allow for anatomical demands within the limitations of the material. Elasticity of form, to accommodate the movement of the user, was attained by a deep slit in the back which lends a certain distinction to the resultant design.

One of his best known designs, the 932 series (1967), destroys all previous notions of furniture as a "structural" object. Here there is no evidence of structure save for blocks of polyurethane foam (stiffness was achieved by inserting a plywood cartilage within the foam) covered in rich leather and cinched around the "waist" with a leather belt. It could be assembled in a variety of sizes. There are no legs, no feet—none are necessary. Like a fashion designer, Bellini has thus "dressed" the foam and offered it as an irresistible haven, harkening back to Le Corbusier's *Grand Comfort,* but without the metal.

*Le Bambole* [The Dolls] (1972) continued the idea of the apparently structureless, overstuffed chair, using different density foams, now "dressed" in fabric, to generate a form suitable enough to, again, entice you to use it. It was produced in a variety of sizes and shapes. The advertising campaign that introduced it—featuring a bare-topped, female model in various poses—expressed the strength and flexibility of the seemingly nonstructured form, while enticing the viewer with the slogan: "Dolls that go ... on dolls that stay." The viewer soon realized that, although visually attracted to the model, they were really looking at the furniture—the model was subordinate—unlike similar instances of fashion photography where the model/clothing is, rightfully, paramount.

In 1976, again like a fashion designer, Bellini's CAB totally "dressed" a simple, welded steel frame in leather. Joint stitches were exposed for a demonstration of quality and feel, and the legs were treated with boot-like zippers. Originally a dining chair, it has been developed into an arm chair (1979) and sofa (1982). The almost planer-like quality of the CAB design was further developed in *Break,* a dining chair which again conceals its construction and is held together by zippers.

Bellini has recently directed his attention to lighting, interior fittings, and tableware items. His furniture designs in the 1980s seem to be taking on a more monumental, architectural form. This may be a parallel with the fact that he has had some architectural commissions in recent years. Whether or not this will conflict with his previous notions that when one sits one should not be aware of the structure of the seat but be supported with a sense of elasticity and comfort, remains to be seen. I have no doubt, in either case, that one will want to sit and will be very comfortable in doing so.

—William Victor Kriebel

# BELTRÁN, Félix (Juan Alberto)

Cuban graphic designer

**Born:** Havana, 23 June 1938. **Education:** Studied advertising design and layout, under Ivan Chermayeff, Bob Gill, and George Tscherny, School of the Visual Arts, New York, Dip., 1960; studied painting, American Art School, New York, Dip., 1962; studied life drawing, New School for Social Research, New York, 1962, and Círculo de Bellas Artes, Madrid, 1965-66; studied printmaking, Pratt Graphic Center, New York, 1962; studied philosophy, Centro Nacional de Investigaciones Científicas, Havana, 1978-80. **Family:** Married Lassie Sobera in 1963; children: Milena. **Career:** Associate art director, American Publishing Company, New York, 1959-62; associate art director, Cypress Books Company, New York, 1960-62; designer, Editorial Nacional de Cuba, Havana, 1962-63; art director, Ministerio de la Construcción, Havana, 1963-65; chief of promotion, *Exposicuba* exhibition, Havana, 1966-67; chief of design team, Comisión de Orientación Revolucionaria, Havana, 1967-77; president of the fine arts section, UNEAC Unión de Escritores y Artistas de Cuba, Havana, 1977-81; Cuban president, UNESCO International Association of Art, in Havana, 1979-82; director, Félix Beltrán + Asociados, Mexico City, from 1982. Professor, Escuela de Instructores de Arte, Havana, 1963-65, Escuela National de Diseño Industrial, Havana, 1964-65, Escuela Nacional de Arte, Havana, 1969, in the School of Journalism, 1967-73, and the School of Architecture, 1972-76, at the Universidad de la Habana, Havana, Curso Nacional de Cuadros, Havana, 1973-81, in the Faculty of Plastic Arts, at the Instituto Superior de Arte, Ha-

vana, 1976-81, and at the Universidad Autónoma Metropolitana and Escuela Nacional de Diseño, Mexico City, from 1982; course coordinator, División de Ciencias y Artes para el Diseño, Universidad Autónoma Metropolitana, and Escuela Nacional de Diseño, Mexico City, from 1982; curator, Galería Artis, Universidad Autónoma Metropolitana, from 1993, and Archivo de Diseño Gráfico Internacional, Universidad Autónoma Metropolitana, from 1993. Editorial board member, *Artes* magazine; foreign translation editor, *Step by Step Graphics* magazine, Milwaukee; advisory board member, *Tipográfica* magazine, Buenos Aires, American Biographical Institute, Raliegh, N.C., and International Biographical Center, Cambridge; international advisor, Conferencia Internacional de Diseño Grafico, Acapulco. **Member:** Comité Nacional Mexicano of the Association Internationale des Arts Plastiques, Paris; International Creators Organization; Art Directors Club, New York; Type Directors Club, New York; University and College Designers Association; Graphic Design Education Association; Association Typographique Internationale; Professors League International; International Council of Graphic Design Associations; Design History Society. **Exhibitions:** Galería UNEAC, Havana, 1967, 1971; Dum Kultury, Prague, 1969; Museo Nacional, Havana, 1971; Museo Provincial, Camagüey, 1971; Galería Rampa, Havana, 1971; Casa de la Cultura, San Antonio, 1971; Galería Elisava, Barcelona, 1971; Hochschule für Grafik und Buchkunst, Leipzig, 1971; Konstfachskolan, Stockholm, 1971; Galería de Cultura, Havana, 1972, 1974; Biblioteca Municipal, Guanabacoa, 1972; Graphicpack, Barcelona, 1972; Academia de Bellas Artes, Sadabell, Spain, 1972; Ravenbourne Gallery, Kent, 1972; Galería CENIC, Havana, 1973; Biblioteca Municipal, Guantanamo, 1973; Galería de Cultura, Matanzas, 1973; Galería L, Havana, 1973; Galería de Cultura, Pinar del Rio, 1973; Galería de Arte, San Cristobal, 1973; Galería de Arte, Bauta, 1973; Casa de la Juventud, Havana, 1973; Astilleros Marítimos, Casablanca, 1973; Center of Creation, Riga, 1973; Rousski Gallery, Sofia, 1973, 1977; Klub Zwiaskow Tworozych, Vroclav, 1973; Nairobi University, 1973; Bolton Gallery, Lancashire, 1973; Galerie SUPS, Praha, 1973; Fachhochschule, Darmstadt, 1973; Galería del Central, Havana, 1974; Salón JUCEPLAN, Havana, 1974; LMV Gallery, Riga, 1974; Sala Ocre, Caracas, 1974; Virginia Commonwealth University, Virginia, 1974; Biblioteca Municipal, Havana, 1974, 1975; Galería Dodecaedro, Havana, 1975; Galería La Polilla, Havana, 1975; Galerie Manes, Praha, 1975; Galería EDA, Mexico City, 1975; Galería Amelia Pelaez, Havana, 1976; Galería UAEM, Mexico City, 1976; Biblioteca Comunale, Milan, 1976; Laval University, Quebec, 1979; Galerie Tatran, Bratislava, 1979; Galería Azul, Guadalajara, 1985; Galerie Bunker, Frankfurt-Main, 1987; Art Poster Gallery, Dürkheim, 1988; Galería Trazo, Mexico City, 1990, 1991; Galería Frida Kahlo, Mexico City, 1990; Galería Atil, Mexico City, 1992; Galería Santos Balmori, Mexico City, 1993; Galería La Torre, Mexico City, 1993; Galería Códice, Mexico City, 1993; Galería Artis, Mexico City, 1993, 1995; Galería Sol y Sombra, Mexico City, 1995. **Collections:** Beltrán's works are held in more than 60 national and international museums. **Honors:** American Institute of Graphic Arts Awards, New York, 1961; Communication Arts Award, Palo Alto, 1962; Annual Type Directors Award, New York, 1962; Typomundus Awards, Stuttgart, 1969; Salón Nacional de Carteles Award, Havana, 1969, 1970, 1971, 1972; Leipzig Book Design Award, 1971; Brno Graphics Biennale Award, 1972; World Symbol and Trademarks Award, Milan, 1974; Cinema Poster Award, Cannes, 1974; Order of the Trabajadores de Cuba, 1975; Concurso 13 de Marzo Award, Havana, 1975, 1977, 1978; International Letterhead Design Awards, Kentucky, 1977; Order of the Union de Periodistas de Cuba, 1978; Olympic Poster Award, Moscow, 1980; Listowel Print Biennale Award, Ireland, 1980; Creativity Awards, New York, 1980-84, 1986-89; Accademici D'Italia con Medaglia D'Oro, Parma, 1980; Ministerio de Cultura Medal, Havana, 1981; Artistic Merit Medal, Washington, D.C., 1982; Gold Medal for Artistic Merit, Washington, D.C., 1982; Diploma di Maestro di Pittura Honoris Causa Award, Salsomaggiore, 1982; Académico de Honor Extranjero Award, Mexico City, 1984; Commemorative Medal of Honor and Hall of Fame Award, Raliegh, 1985; Fulbright Award, Washington, D.C., 1986; Golden Flame Award, Washington, D.C., 1986; World Fellowship Award, Raliegh, 1987; Biennial Competition of International Logos and Trademarks Award, Washington, D.C., 1990, 1992, 1995; Alfred Nobel Medal, Missouri, 1991; International Man of the Year Award, Cambridge, 1992. **Address:** Apartado Postal M-10733, México 06000 DF, México.

## Works

*The Sign Shows Where Danger Is* traffic safety poster, Cuba, 1969.
*Return Used Oil—It's Re-usable* public information poster, Cuba, 1970.
OEA logotype of the campaign to dismantle the Organization of American States, for the Comision de Orientacion Revolucionario, 1973.
*Ciril,* Latin America's first cyrillic typeface, Havana, 1974.

## Publications

**By BELTRÁN: books**—*Desde el Diseño,* Havana, 1970; *Letragrafía,* Havana, 1973; *Acerca del Diseño,* Havana, 1974; (With Ramón Cabrera) *Artes Plásticas,* Havana, 1981; *Diccionario de Diseño Gráfico,* Mexico City, 1996; **articles**—contributor to magazines including *Bohemia* (Havana), *El Mundo* (Havana), *La Gaceta* (Havana), *Propaganda* (Havana), *Revolucion y Cultura* (Havana), *Union* (Havana), *Arquitectura* (Mexico City), *Dominical* (Bogotá), *Bildende Kunst* (Berlin), *Semanario Cultural* (Cali), *Marka* (Lima), *Punto Grafico* (Valencia), *Casabella* (Milan), *Diseño* (Havana), *Plural* (Mexico City), *Visual Propaganda* (Sofia), *Bellas Artes* (Mexico City), *Art & Artists* (New York), *Sonntag* (Berlin), *Boceto* (Guadalajara), *Artes Plásticas* (Mexico City), *Artes* (Mexico City), and *La Iguana y el Nahual* (Mexico City).

**On BELTRÁN: books**—*Símbolos, Símbolos y mas Símbolos* by Servando Gonzales, Havana, 1970; *Who's Who in Graphic Art* edited by Walter Amstutz, Zürich, 1982; *Los Símbolos de Félix Beltrán* by Ramón Cabrera, Havana 1983; selected **articles**—in *Idea* (Tokyo), June 1962, January 1967, May 1970, July 1971; *Gebrauchsgraphik* (Munich), June 1963, September 1971, May 1977; *Neue Werbung* (Berlin), August 1975; *Diseño* (Mexico City), June 1983; *Print* (New York), April 1984; *Proa* (Bogotá), March 1986; *Plural* (Mexico City), April 1987, May 1990; *Novedades* (Mexico City), March 1990; *Tipográfica* (Buenos Aires), June 1990; *Punto* (Mexico City), September 1990; *El Universal* (Mexico City), September 1991; *Idea* (Tokyo), May 1993; *El Sol* (Mexico City), July 1993; *Organo Informativo* (Mexico City), October 1993; *El Financiero* (Mexico City), November 1993.

*

**Félix Beltrán: Cuban Red Cross Films Section trademark for Cruz Roja, Havana, 1980**

In the history of man-created images two main types are evident: arbitrary and equivalent images. Arbitrary images do not represent the content directly, but rather substitute an appearance arbitrarily, as in the case of writing, whereas equivalent images more or less correspond to the appearance of the content.

As contents become more complex and diverse in their parts, it is more difficult to find completely equivalent images. That is why symbols, as indirect reflections, play a decisive role in evoking what is most striking in the contents of an entity.

At present, there is a certain tendency to create images which, though simple and attractive, diverge from their essential goal of reflecting an entity. This is partly due to an overestimation of the creative act as an end in itself rather than as a means. This conflict stems essentially from the divergence between emotionalism and functionalism in the field of design. Functionalism is not a style—it does not eliminate imaginative possibilities; on the contrary, it channels them according to needs and conditions. Creation constitutes a decisive step toward the achievement of adequate images which should reflect that essence. Besides the images themselves, such qualities as size, position, and color determine effectiveness. Size can reflect content and is relative in relation to context. Position within the context also has communicative implications; this is also true of color, which is an inseparable property of images.

With time, visual images are learned, and they become rooted in the public mind, which responds to the messages, and thus the cycle is completed. Images are grasped by means of the perceptive act, which can be defined as the reflection of the qualities and parts of images directly acting upon the sensory organs. Sensation is a rather frequent partial level of perception. Sensation is also the reflection of isolated and striking qualities of the images, but what is striking does not always agree with what is fundamental. Perception is rendered complete with the public's previous experiences. A single phenomenon may be interpreted in different ways. This is vitally important so that images may be rendered as unambiguous as possible. This aspect is one of the main problems the designer has to face—cultural, social and even biological questions impinge on it. Despite the recent progress of science, enough objective data for the making of decisions in this sense are not always available. The search for images is to a great extent subject to the designer's relative deductive capacity.

—Félix Beltrán

\* \* \*

Félix Beltrán came to New York as a student in 1956, as that city was becoming the art capital of the world. Not content with a single source of influence, he graduated from the School of Visual Arts in advertising design, earned an additional diploma in easel painting at another school, and attended classes at the Art Students League, the New School for Social Research, and the Pratt Graphic Center. His particular mentors were Will Barnet, Ivan Chermayeff, Bob Gill, and George Tscherny. During the same period, he worked as an art director for two publishers. After an additional year of study in Madrid, he returned to Cuba, just prior to the revolution. Whether intentionally or accidentally, he has always been in the place where history was being made.

Beltrán has been the major influence on Cuban design standards in pedagogy and professional practice, and he has organized many unusual exhibitions. The blockade of goods into Cuba has required that visual messages for many public programs from films to health and agriculture be produced with readily available materials. Often the paper is made from rice, and there is little variety in inks and virtually no modern typography. Combining these handicaps with his commitment to socialism, Beltran has helped to create a unique socialist style with color, typography, power, and a total absence of heavy-limbed workers. He has also reconciled the conflict between what he calls "emotionalism and functionalism" in his own work—the difference between art and design.

He considers his greatest contributions to be introducing the first basic design course in Cuba in 1964, his first one-man show of trademarks in Cuba in 1967, the publication in 1970 of his book, *Desde el Diseño,* the first on Cuban graphic design, the creation of the first Cyrillic typeface produced in Latin America, and the organization of the first Exhibition of Latin American Trademarks with the participation of seven countries.

In 1982 Beltrán relocated to Mexico, founding the office of Felix Beltrán and Associates. There he is extremely influential in design education as the course coordinator of the Division of Graphic Design at the Universidad Autonóma Metropolitana in Mexico City as well as course advisor to the National School of Design, the National Institute of Fine Arts, and the Center for Advanced Communication. In 1993 Beltrán founded Galería Artis in Mexico City, Latin America's first gallery of graphic design, and established Latin America's first "Archive of International Graphic Design." Beltrán has written four books and many articles for national and international publications. He has received over 120 awards and an honorary Doctorate from the International University Foundation in Delaware.

Beltrán is active as a designer, painter, educator, and energetic organizer of design-oriented events, both national and international. His warm, energetic personality and international background play an important role in the current and future developments of the graphic design profession in Latin America.

—Al Gowan, updated by Burton Kramer

# BENKTZON, Maria

Swedish industrial designer

**Born:** Marie-Louise In Nyköping, 17 June 1946. **Education:** Studied textile design, National College of Art and Design, Stockholm, 1965-69. **Family:** Married Erling Ericsson in 1980; children: Emeli and Isak. **Career:** Freelance design consultant, Stockholm, 1969-72; partner, Ergonomi Design Gruppen AB, Bromma, from 1973; has collaborated with designer Sven-Eric Juhlin, from 1972, specializing in assistive technology and universal design. Visiting speaker and lecturer at numerous design congresses and professional institutes, throughout Europe and North America, from 1974. Board member, National College of Art, Craft and Design, Stockholm, from 1994. **Exhibitions:** *A Society Open to All,* Kharkov, U.S.S.R., 1977 (toured the Soviet Union, Poland, and Czechoslovakia); *Swedish Craft and Design,* Victoria and Albert Museum, London, 1980; *Scandinavian Modern Design 1880-1980,* Cooper-Hewitt Museum, New York, 1982; *Contemporary Swedish Design,* Nationalmuseum, Stockholm, 1983 (toured Scandinavia); *Design Since 1945,* Philadelphia Museum of Art, 1983; *International Design Exhibition,* Osaka, Japan, 1985; *Design in Sweden Now,* 1985-86 (toured Canada and Australia); *New Design for Old,* Boilerhouse, Victoria and Albert Museum, London, 1986; *Scandinavian Design: A Way of Life,* Toyama Museum of Modern Art, Japan, 1987; *Faces of Swedish Design,* IBM Gallery, New York, 1988 (toured the United States); *Designs for Independent Living,* Museum of Modern Art, New York, 1988 (toured the United States); *Design Art,* Internationales Design Zentrum, Berlin, 1988; *Suecia Forma y Diseno,* Montevideo, Uruguay, 1990 (toured South America); *Design Sweden,* Bombay, India, 1991 (toured India); *Vackrare vardagsvara,* Warszawa, Poland, 1992 (toured eastern Europe). **Collections:** Museum of Modern Art, New York; Nationalmuseum, Stockholm; Design Museum, London. **Honors:** First International Design Award, Japan Design Foundation, 1983 (with Sven-Eric Juhlin); Marianne och Sigvard Bernadottes Konstnärsfond, 1983; International Design Competition Prize, Japan Design Foundation, 1984 (with Sven-Eric Juhlin and Håkan Bergkvist); Bruno Mathsson Prize, Sweden, 1984; Swedish Design Excellence Award, 1988, and prize, 1991; named Professor by Swedish government, 1993; IKEA Award 1995. **Address:** Ergonomi Design Gruppen AB, Box 140 21, Missionsvägen 24, S-161 14 Bromma, Sweden.

## Works

Training toys and interiors, for Eugeniahemmet-Karolinska sjukhuset handicapped children's ward, 1969.

Adaptive designs for thalidomide children, 1970.

Handles and Grips project, for Swedish Institute for the Handicapped, 1973.

Kitchen knife and cutting-board, for AB Gustavsberg, 1974.

Pots and pans project, for STU Swedish National Board for Technical Development, 1977.

Eating and drinking implements project, for Folksam Research Foundation/STU Swedish National Board for Technical Development, produced by RFSU Rehab, 1980.

*Clothing and Disability* book, for STU Swedish National Board for Technical Development, 1980.

**Maria Benktzon: Feeding utensil for multihandicapped children, for STU Swedish National Board for Technical Development, produced by RFSU Rehab, 1989. Photo: Mike Stott, Ergonomi Design AB**

Gripping tongs project, for STU Swedish National Board for Technical Development, 1985.

*Fix* food preparation board, for STU Swedish National Board for Technical Development, produced by RFSU Rehab, 1985.

Cane for arthritics, for STU Swedish National Board for Technical Development, produced by RFSU Rehab, 1987.

Coffee- and teapot, for SAS Scandinavian Airlines System, 1988.

Knife for quadriplegics, for STU Swedish National Board for Technical Development, produced by RFSU Rehab, 1989.

Elbow crutch, for STU Swedish National Board for Technical Development, produced by Etac, 1989.

Eating and drinking implements for multihandicapped children, for Swedish Institute for the Handicapped, produced by RFSU Rehab, 1989.

Serving tray for the SAS airline, 1991.

Toothbrushes for people with limited hand-arm function, for the Swedish Handicap Institute, 1993.

Juice jug for the SAS airline, 1994.

Design and development of tools and equipment for personal hygiene, for RFSU Rehab, 1995.

Packaging design, for Pharmacia, 1995.

Design of hand-tools, for Tupperware, 1995.

## Publications

By BENKTZON: **books**—*Kläder och handikapp/ Clothing and Disability,* Stockholm, 1980; **articles**—(with Sven-Eric Juhlin) "Redskap för händer" in *Form* (Stockholm), no. 10, 1973; (with Sven-Eric Juhlin) "What Can Design Contribute to the Human Society of the Near Future?" in *Design Quarterly* (Tokyo), no. 2, 1984; "Ur behoven föds ideerna" in *Form* (Stockholm), no. 8, 1987; "Estetik och Funktion," *Designjournalen,* vol. 2, no. 1, 1995.

On BENKTZON: **books**—*Konsthantverk, Konstindustri, Design 1875-1975* by Dag Widman, Stockholm, 1975; *Design Since 1945* edited by Kathryn Hiesinger and George Marcus, Philadelphia and London, 1983; *Contemporary Swedish Design,* exhibition catalogue by Monica Boman, Lennart Lindkvist, and others, Stockholm, 1983; *Design Source Book* by Penny Sparke and others, London, 1986; *New Design for Old,* London, 1986; *Faces of Swedish Design,* exhibition catalogue edited by Monica Boman, Stockholm, 1988; *Design Art,* exhibition catalogue, West Berlin, 1988; **articles**—"Världmästare i hjälpmedel för handikappade" in *Svenska Dagbladet* (Stockholm), 7 October 1983; "Designing for the Disabled" in the *Irish Times* (Dublin), 11 April 1989.

Essentially, we feel in Ergonomi Design Gruppen that the industrial designer can make a contribution in almost any area that involves industrially manufactured products. We think it is vital to work in areas where there are unsolved problems, or where the solutions that exist do not satisfy the demands that the user is entitled to make. We think it is important to develop everyday products and environments for a "broader average"—including those who are elderly or disabled.

We believe in a collaborative approach to product development as a basis for creativity, aesthetics, and intuition. To achieve meaningful results, we feel that it is essential to involve the end user in the design process. The functional requirements of the user determines which design constraints must be met in the final product or environment. To design for a "broader average" means taking the disabled into consideration in the design of products, machines and environments.

Ergonomi Design Gruppen has had much experience designing products for people with disabilities. Our philosophy is to create products and environments which individuals can use equally whether they have a disability or not. The aim is to increase the independence of individuals through Universal design and the availability of well designed assistive devices. Ergonomi Design Gruppen have demonstrated that by applying this approach it is possible to design for a broader range of users, including the special needs of specific groups within the population, and resulting in products which offer a combination of performance, functionality, and aesthetic appeal.

—Maria Benktzon/Sven-Eric Juhlin

\*   \*   \*

When EDG was founded in 1979, the firm moved into a huge 19th-century gingerbread house in Traneberg, just outside Stockholm, which had previously housed a missionary institute. About half of the building's 1,350 square meters of floor space is used for model workshops. The former chapel contains large printing presses and full-scale agricultural machines.

The group develops products and equipment for different work environments in health care, care of the disabled, energy, and transportation. They receive commissions from industry, but what distinguishes the group more than anything is that many of its research and development projects are financed by institutions and government authorities. A method has been developed which integrates the know-how and opinions of the users into the product development phase. The existing work situation is systematically surveyed and measured. Then three-dimensional mock-ups are built in full scale for evaluation and simulation of the work process. The working method of the group is illustrated here by Maria Benktzon and Sven-Eric Juhlin, who have collaborated for over 15 years—all the time specializing in equipment for the handicapped.

To most people, the team of Maria Benktzon and Sven-Eric Juhlin is synonymous with Swedish design for the disabled. They are pioneers in this field and their studies are among the few projects in Sweden which really deserve the title of design research. Maria and Sven-Eric have created a methodology of design which has been an inspiration to many other designers outside of Sweden as well. Maria Benktzon and Sven-Eric Juhlin began working together in 1972 on a research project entitled "Handles/Grips," under the aegis of the Swedish Institute for the Handicapped. Their task was to study the need for technical aids for people suffering from impaired muscular strength and mobility, mainly as a result of rheu-

matoid arthritis. The aim was, if possible, to design products which could be used by everybody instead of constructing special aids in the form of accessories for standard products.

The survey concentrated on grips and handles. Comprehensive studies were undertaken in the homes of disabled persons, and among other things, tests were performed on various types of handles in order to discover which type required the least strength. The results were also discussed with medical experts and provided the starting point for the development of two new products. One of these was a kitchen knife with an extra wide blade, good balance, and a new type of handle for maximum utilization of the hand's strength—a classic example of Swedish design for the disabled.

As a direct sequel to the "Handles/Grips" project, Maria and Sven-Eric embarked a few years later on a new project aimed at developing products for eating and drinking. It resulted in a research report and several interesting new products. These included two items of cutlery, a transparent plastic drinking glass which had a high stem and weighed very little, a beaker comprising a glass and a holder, and a plate with a raised rim.

Both projects are based on the same working methods. A survey of physical resources and needs is followed by an analysis of functional requirements. The next stage is to prepare sketches and work out models which are tested in the homes of a number of experimental subjects. Maria and Sven-Eric take pains to stress that just fingering or looking at a product is not enough. Real-life testing is the only possible way of achieving a meaningful evaluation and useful results.

This approach has been made possible by research grants from government authorities, institutions, and foundations. Equally indispensable, however, has been the interest taken by the designers in methodically penetrating problems, and compiling and analyzing facts on which to base their design of new products. A more recent project is a support cane for people with arthritis. In collaboration with a doctor, a physiotherapist, and a number of patients, they took inventory of what was lacking in ordinary canes. They discovered that canes which took the weight off the weak leg also increased the load on the arms and hands. Many people who start using a cane find they develop pain in their wrists and shoulders because the cane's support surface against the palm of the hand is too small. The next stage was to design test canes to see how the handle could best fit into the hand.

The result was an entirely new cane, in which the handle is a hand-sculpture which organically follows the irregular shape of the palm and thus provides broader support than other canes. The handle is attached to the cane by an articulated joint which can be set at an exact angle suited to the individual. The shaft of the cane is based at the rear of the handle so that it will not be in the way of the fingers.

A large and important portion of Maria's and Sven-Eric's time has been spent in spreading their experience and their knowledge. For several years, Sven-Eric was a tutor in design methods and ergonomics at the National College of Art and Design. Together they have lectured on ergonomics at the Gothenburg School of Arts and Crafts. They have also been much in demand as lecturers in other countries, in conjunction with international conferences dealing with design and the disabled. Their approach to problems of design is constantly reaching new groups and winning new converts.

The former missionary institute is sending out missionaries of a new kind, to spread the word about Swedish design at its best.

—Lennart Lindkvist

# BENNETT, Ward

American sculptor, furniture, interior, fashion, jewelry, textile, and advertising designer

___

**Born:** New York City, 17 November 1917. **Education:** Studied at the Porto Romano School of Art, Florence, 1937; Academie de la Grande Chaumiere, and with the sculptor Constantin Brancusi, Paris, 1937-38; painting, under Hans Hofmann, in New York, 1943; apprentice, in the studio of architect Le Corbusier, Paris, 1948-50. **Military Service:** Served in the United States Army, 1940-43. **Career:** Worked in the fashion industry, for Chin Chin Crepe, Saks Fifth Avenue, and Joe Junior, in New York, 1930-33; freelance sketch artist, for American fashion buyers, in Paris, 1937-38; window dresser, for I. Magnin stores, in Los Angeles and San Francisco, 1939-40; clothing designer and window dresser, for Hattie Carnegie, New York, 1943-45; freelance jewelry designer, Mexico, 1945-46; interior designer, working in Europe and New York, 1947-50; independent designer, New York, from 1950; has designed for Lehigh Furniture, Chase Manhattan Bank, Gensler Company, Skidmore Owings and Merrill, Tiffany and Company, Brickel Associates, Supreme Cutlery, and others. Visiting Professor, Yale University, New Haven, Connecticut, 1962-63; instructor, 1969-71, and Associate Professor from 1971, Pratt Institute, Brooklyn, New York. **Exhibitions:** *Annual Exhibition of Painting and Sculpture,* Whitney Museum, New York, 1944; Riverside Museum, New York, 1944; Baldwin-Kingrey Gallery, Chicago, 1945; Museum of Modern Art, New York, 1945; *High Style: 20th Century American Design,* Whitney Museum, New York, 1985. **Collection:** Museum of Modern Art, New York. **Address:** 1 West 72nd Street, New York, New York 10023, U.S.A.

## Works

Penthouse interiors in New York, for Harry Jason, 1947.
*1148/58* Mobius range of office furniture, for Brickel Associates, 1970.
*University Chair,* for the L.B. Johnson Library at the University of Texas, produced by Brickel Associates, 1971.
*Sage* mohair fabric, for Brickel Associates, 1975.
*Sufi* wool viscose fabric, for Brickel Associates, 1975.
*Metro* stainless steel cutlery, for Supreme Cutlery, 1977-78.
*Cader* wool broadcloth fabric, for Brickel Associates, 1978.
*University 1550* armchair in kiln-dried ash, for Brickel Associates, 1978.
*Ankara* mohair fabric, for Brickel Associates, 1979.
*Trylon* stainless steel cutlery, for Supreme Cutlery, 1980.
*Hollandaise* cotton velvet fabric, for Brickel Associates, 1980.
*Helex* stainless steel cutlery, for Supreme Cutlery, 1981.
*Pentimento* wool twill fabric, for Brickel Associates, 1981.

## Publications

**By BENNETT: articles**—in *Interiors* (New York), October 1952, November 1965, January 1977; *Interior Design* (New York), September 1972.

**On BENNETT: books**—*Design for Modern Living* by Gerd and Ursula Hatje, Munich and Zurich, 1961; *Interior Design: An Introduction to Architectural Interiors* by Arnold Friedmann, John F. Pile and Forrest Wilson, New York and Amsterdam, 1970, 1976; *Modern Furniture* by John F. Pile, New York and Toronto, 1979;

*Interior Views* by Erica Brown, London, 1980; *The Conran Directory of Design* edited by Stephen Bayley, London, 1985; *High Style: 20th Century American Design,* exhibition catalogue by David Gebhard, Esther McCoy and others, New York, 1985.

*       *       *

Ward Bennett's life is a design testimony in itself, to a mode of living not often encountered, especially not today, when more compartmentalized patterns dominate the expectations of most individuals. His life has been one of continued exploration of all the possibilities for finding life interesting. In the pursuit of that interest, he has produced a wide range of useful, comfortable, and expressive products, from jewelry to buildings, from window decoration to interior design. In all of the varied products of his imagination, his guiding design principle is attention to the structure of space, both to the line that by bounding it makes space visible and to the way in which space extends outward from the person who inhabits it, shaping the range of his actions. Thus, his furniture while designed for comfort is made up of the minimum skeleton of elements necessary to hold the body with the requisite level of support. These chairs are generally visible as lines in space, rather than as bulky objects filling space. (Those furnishings that are solid, covered objects still present a fine edge, as, for example, the curve at the top of the Alexandra chair; this invigorates their surrounding space with the delicate tension of their own proportions.)

Bennett designs interiors that emphasize both freedom and the shape of the space. His spaces are carefully lit, to allow the orchestration of walls and planes into sequences of expansiveness then constraint, of open spaces then charged by the unexpected detail, such as an edge or corner which projects into visibility and which invites curiosity, or a dark wall cut by a wide door which frames a brilliant garden. He has learned from many sources that the sense of intrigue is the central joy of being human and that this interest is stimulated by the presence of the unusual, accompanied by the sense of personal time and space in which to pursue its contemplation.

All of his projects center on the pleasures of detail and incorporate fine craftsmanship, in woods or textiles with variegated coloration or mottled papers from Japan, in a juxtaposition of rough and smooth, shiny and soft that, by extension, allows him to incorporate into one room the products of heavy industry with the drawings of Paul Klee. While he is known as the originator of the high-tech interior style, those who followed his original esthetic have not managed to retain the quality of collage that made his most simplified spaces memorable and capable of being the site of creative contemplation. Ultimately, Bennett's knowledge of the components of interest for his own life has been translated into his designs for other people.

—Frances Butler

# BERNADOTTE, Prince Sigvard (Oscar Fredrik)

Swedish industrial designer

___

**Born:** Count Of Wisborg, in Stockholm, 7 June 1907. **Education:** Studied at the University of Uppsala, 1926-29, BA, 1929; Academy of Fine Arts, Stockholm, 1929-31; Staatschule für Angewandte Kunst, Munich, 1931. **Military Service:** Served in the Swedish Army, 1929, Lieutenant. **Family:** Married Marianne Lindberg (second wife) in 1961; son: Michael. **Career:** Freelance designer of silverware, textiles, bookbindings, glass, and porcelain, in Stockholm, from 1929; partner, with Acton Bjorn, in Bernadotte and Bjorn industrial design studio, Copenhagen and Stockholm, 1949-64; independent designer, as Bernadotte Design, Stockholm, since 1964. **Member:** President, International Council of Societies of Industrial Design, 1961-63. **Exhibitions:** *Die Gute Industrieform,* Kunstverein, Hamburg, 1955; *Nordisk Industridesign,* Kunstindustrimuseet, Oslo, 1976; Georg Jensen, Copenhagen, 1980; *Scandinavian Modern Design 1880-1980,* Cooper-Hewitt Museum, New York, 1982. **Collections:** Moderna Museet, Stockholm; Metropolitan Museum of Art, New York. **Honors:** Gold Medal, 1952, and Silver Medal, 1955, Milan Triennale. **Address:** Villagatan 10, 114 32 Stockholm, Sweden.

**Publications**

By BERNADOTTE: books—*Industrial Design: Modern Industriell Formgivning,* Goteborg, 1953; *Heads or Tails,* Stockholm, 1975.

On BERNADOTTE: books—*Konsthantverk och Hemslöjd i Sverige 1930-1940* edited by Åke H. Huldt, Mattis Horlén and Heribert Seitz, Göteborg, 1941; *Fifty Years of Silver in the Georg Jensen Tradition* by Edgar Kauffmann, Jr., Erik Lassen and Christian Reventlow, Copenhagen, 1956; *Svensk Form* edited by Åke H. Huldt and Åke Stavenlow, Stockholm, 1961; *Design in Sweden* edited by Lennart Lindkvist, Stockholm, 1972; *Scandinavian Design: Objects of a Life Style* by Eileene Harrison Beer, New York and Toronto, 1975; *Scandinavian Modern Design 1880-1980* edited by David Revere McFadden, New York, 1982.

*       *       *

One of the pioneers who helped to establish the industrial design profession in Europe, Swedish designer Prince Sigvard Bernadotte has enriched the lives of many individuals with a broad range of products designed for everyday use. For Bernadotte, good design is as necessary as food and drink. To him, the designer is someone who, through talent, education, inspiration, and hard work, creates something that is pleasing to the eye and easy on the hand. His products are not just ornamental objects that stand on a shelf or a table to be admired; instead, they are designed to have a purpose and to be used.

When Bernadotte began working for Georg Jensen in Copenhagen, the prevailing school of design was much the style of "grapes and flowers." His first efforts in silver, as a result, were an absolute revolution. Leaving out all the bulges and decorations, Bernadotte let the inherent beauty of the metal emerge. One of his most important pieces is the silver coffee service owned by the Metropolitan Museum of Art. The beautiful proportion and tasteful spacing of the ornament enhance the verticality both in form and detail, without interrupting the quiet simplicity of the design.

Bernadotte was also interested in the effects of color on an object, but because color did not enter into the design of silver, he turned to textiles. His inspiration for the blended colors and beautiful gradation of tones in his handwoven, wool rugs was the Swedish landscape. For Bernadotte, using colors was like painting. The lyri-

cal quality of his simple designs depended on the blending of rich reds, silver-greys, and moss greens. By designing rugs, Bernadotte not only had the opportunity to demonstrate the effects of colors when placed next to one another but also was able to work in two dimensions instead of three.

The final and all-embracing widening of his career was the beginning of his own industrial design company. His knowledge of materials and production methods was a valuable asset in helping him to understand new ways of manufacturing. Bernadotte was able to make the difficult journey from artisanship to mass production, first designing in silver, then textiles, and finally for industry.

—Patricia A. Russac

# BERNHARD, Lucian

American painter, illustrator, interior, type, and graphic designer

**Born:** Emil Kahn, in Stuttgart, Germany, 15 March 1883; emigrated to the United States, 1923, subsequently naturalized. **Education:** Studied painting at Akademie der Kunst Munich, but mainly self-taught in design, from 1905. **Career:** Worked as a freelance graphic designer, adopting pseudonym Lucian Bernhard, in Berlin, from 1905; designer, under E. Growald, at Hollerbaum und Schmidt printers, Berlin; also freelance type designer for Bauer of Frankfurt, Berthold of Berlin, Flinsch of Frankfurt, and American Type Founders of New Jersey; co-founder, with Hans Sachs, of *Der Plakat* (later titled *Gebrauchsgraphik*) magazine, Berlin, 1909; artistic leader, German Handicrafts Workshops, Berlin; co-founder, with Rockwell Kent, Paul Poiret and Bruno Paul, of Contempora graphic and interior design firm, New York. Professor of Advertising and Poster Design, Akademie der Kunst, Berlin, 1920-23; instructor, New York University, and Art Students League, New York. **Member:** Deutscher Werkbund; American Institute of Graphic Arts; New York Society of Illustrators. **Exhibitions:** Deutsches Museum, The Hague, 1913; *Three Rooms Designed in the Contemporary Spirit,* Rochester Memorial Art Gallery, New York, 1950 (with P. Poiret and B. Paul); *The 20th-Century Poster,* Walker Art Center, Minneapolis, 1984; *The Machine Age in America 1918-1941,* Brooklyn Museum, New York, 1986. **Died:** New York City, 29 May 1972.

**Works**

*Stiller-Schuh* posters, for Stiller shoes, 1908, 1912.
*Kaffee Hag* poster, for Hag coffee, 1909.
Typewriter poster, for the Adler Factory, 1909.
*Bernhard-Antiqua* typeface, for Bauer/Flinsch, 1911.
*Bernhard-Schmuck* typeface, for Bauer, 1911.
Automobile poster, for Audi, 1912.
*Bernhard-Fraktur* typeface, for Bauer, 1913.
Spark plugs poster, for Bosch, 1915.
Manoli cigarettes poster, 1915.
*Flinsch-Privat* typeface, for Flinsch, 1920.
*Bernhard-Schonschrift* typeface, for Bauer, 1924.
*Bernhard Roman* typeface, for Bauer, 1925.
*Kursiv* typeface, for Bauer, 1925.
*Bernhard-Handschrift* typeface, for Bauer, 1928.

*Lucian* typeface, for Bauer, 1928.
*Fashion* typeface, for American Typefounders, 1929.
*Gothic* typeface, for American Typefounders, 1929-31.
*Negro* typeface, for Bauer, 1931.
*Bernhard-Buchschrift* typeface, for Bauer, 1933.
*Tango* typeface, for American Typefounders, 1933.

**Publications**

**By BERNHARD: articles—**"What's Wrong with the American Poster?" in *PM* (New York), 1936.

**On BERNHARD: books—***Lucian Bernhard,* exhibition catalogue by F. Plietzsch, The Hague, 1913; *Art Deco Posters* by Nina Weinstock, Bansel, 1967; *The Poster: An Illustrated History from 1860* by Harold F. Hutchison, London and Toronto, 1968; *History of the Poster* by Josef and Shizuko Muller Brockman, Zurich, 1971; *Second World War Posters* edited by Joseph Darracott and Belinda Loftus, London, 1972; *The Thames and Hudson Manual of Typography* by Ruari McLean, London, 1980; *The 20th-Century Poster: Design of the Avant-Garde* by Dawn Ades, New York, 1984; *The Machine Age in America 1918-41,* exhibition catalogue by Richard Guy Wilson and Dianne H. Pilgrim, New York, 1986.

\*     \*     \*

Lucian Bernhard originally gained fame as a poster designer in Germany at the turn of the century. Influenced by art nouveau posters, especially the work of the Beggarstaff Brothers (James Pryde and William Nicholson), Bernhard's early designs, such as those for Manoli cigarettes and Stiller shoes, were noteworthy for their simple product images dramatically silhouetted against pale, monochrome backgrounds. These designs, beginning with one for Priester matches, employed bold roman letterforms instead of the more traditional Fraktur ones. The motifs were reduced to essentials and often outlined in thick, black strokes to match the bold letterforms. During these years, Bernhard helped launch *Das Plakat* to promote poster design, including his own esthetic of the "poster-object." His success as a poster designer culminated in an appointment as a teacher of poster design at the Royal Art Institute in Berlin.

His subsequent poster work exhibited a strikingly different style, yet was equally influential. During World War I, his posters reintroduced Fraktur letterforms, often used in a large outlined manner, and relied almost exclusively on slogans rather than objects for their content. Their design echoed medieval German woodcuts. The subtle colors of the prewar posters were replaced with bright, bold colors. The final stage in his evolution as a poster designer opened when Roy Latham invited him to work in the United States, where he eventually settled. Bernhard's American work, starting with his advertising for Rem cough syrup in 1926, was distinguished by a preference for red, white, and blue as the sole colors.

Bernhard used his success as a poster designer as a jumping-off point to design type, packaging, fashions, and furniture. For the Bauer typefoundry in Germany, he designed Bernhard Antiqua (1911), Bernhard Fraktur (1913), Bernhard Roman (1925), Bernhard Cursive (1925), and Bernhard Brush Script (date unknown). The first two were derived from his poster lettering of the period. In the United States, for the American Typefounders, he designed several faces, of which the best known are Bernhard Fashion (1929), Bernhard Gothic (1929-1931), and Bernhard Tango (1933). These

latter typefaces constitute his strongest American legacy. By 1930, he had become disenchanted with the increased emphasis on specialization in design and had turned his attention to sculpture and painting.

—Paul Shaw

# BERTOIA, Harry
American sculptor, architectural, furniture, jewelry, and graphic designer

**Born:** San Lorenzo, Udine, Italy, 10 March 1915; emigrated to the United States in 1930. **Education:** Studied at Cass Technical High School, Detroit, 1932-36; Society of Arts and Crafts, Detroit, 1936; Cranbrook Academy of Art, Bloomfield Hills, Michigan, 1937-39. **Family:** Married Brigitta Valentiner in 1943; children: Mara, Val, and Celia. **Career:** Instructor and founder of metal workshop, Cranbrook Academy of Art, Bloomfield Hills, Michigan, 1939-43; worked with Charles Eames in molded plywood division of Evans Products Company, Venice, California, 1943-46; graphics designer, at Point Loma Naval Electronics Laboratory, 1947-49; established own art and design studio, with support from Knoll International, in Bally, Pennsylvania, from 1950. **Exhibitions:** Karl Nierendorf Gallery, New York, 1940, 1943, 1947; Museum of Non-Objective Art, New York, 1943; Smithsonian Institution, Washington, D.C., 1943 (toured); Knoll International, New York, 1951; Fairweather-Hardin Gallery, Chicago, 1956, 1961, 1968, 1975; Staempfli Gallery, New York, 1959, 1961, 1963, 1968, 1970, 1976, 1978, 1981; Knoll International, Paris, 1964; Knoll International, Amsterdam, 1968; Knoll International, Zurich, 1968; K. B. Gallery, Oslo, 1972, 1975; Wadsworth Atheneum, Hartford, Connecticut, 1974; Art Institute of Chicago, 1975; Allentown Art Museum, Pennsylvania, 1975, 1986; Robert Kidd Associates, Birmingham, Alabama, 1982; Lancaster Community College, Pennsylvania, 1982; Benjamin Mangel Gallery, Philadelphia, 1983; Michigan State University, East Lansing, 1987. **Collections:** Museum of Modern Art, New York; Albright Knox Art Gallery, Buffalo, New York; Massachusetts Institute of Technology, Cambridge; Philadelphia Museum of Art; San Francisco Museum of Modern Art. **Honors:** Fine Arts Medal, 1955, Craftsmanship Medal, 1956, Pennsylvania Chapter Fine Arts Medal, 1963, and Gold Medal, 1973, American Institute of Architects; Graham Foundation Grant, New York, 1957. Honorary Doctorate, Muhlenberg College, Allentown, Pennsylvania, 1971. **Died:** 6 November 1978.

**Works**

*420* and *421 (the Bertoia Chair)* series of chairs in steel rod with wire-formed seats, for Knoll, 1951-52.
*423* lounge chair in steel rod with wire-formed seat, for Knoll, 1952.
*424* stool in steel rod with wire-formed seat, for Knoll, 1952.
*427P* chair in metal with plastic seat shell, for Knoll, 1955.

**Publications**

**On BERTOIA: books—***An Exhibition for Modern Living,* catalogue edited by A. H. Girard and W. D. Laurie, Jr., Detroit, 1949;

*Mobili Tipo* by Robert Aloi, Milan, 1956; *Stahlmoebel* by Gustav Hassnepflug, Dusseldorf, 1960; *Harry Bertoia, Sculptor* by June Kompass Nelson, Detroit, 1970; *The Modern Chair 1918-1970,* exhibition catalogue with text by Carol Hogben and others, London, 1970; *Harry Bertoia: An Exhibition of His Sculpture and Graphics,* catalogue by Beverly H. Twitchell, Allentown, 1975; *Knoll Design* by Eric Larrabee and Massimo Vignelli, New York, 1981; *Neue Moebel 1950-1982/Contemporary Furniture* edited by Klaus-Jürgen Sembach, Stuttgart and London, 1982; *Design Since 1945* edited by Kathryn Hiesinger and George Marcus, Philadelphia and London, 1983; *High Style: 20th Century American Design,* exhibition catalogue by David Gebhard, Esther McCoy and others, New York, 1985; *Design Source Book* by Penny Sparke and others, London, 1986; *The American Design Adventure 1940-1975* by Arthur J. Pulos, London and Cambridge, Massachusetts, 1988.

\*     \*     \*

Harry Bertoia worked alongside Charles Eames at Evans Products in Venice, California, during the war years, at first utilizing the newly developed plywood techniques in the manufacture of splints and the like for the military medical services. Later, they moved on to use this technology for furniture, such as the chairs to which Eames gave his name. Bertoia spent another three years at graphic design in the Point Loma Naval Electronics Laboratory before setting up a studio in Pennsylvania with the support of Knoll International, which gave him an exhibition in 1951 and launched the chair that bears his name the following year. After that, he had to his credit a string of commissions, largely for sculpture, exhibitions on an international scale, and a film dealing with his sculpture.

The chairs Bertoia designed for Knoll International were closely linked to his sculptural thinking, to lightness and airiness, and the development away from heavy objects bearing hard upon the ground. All of the chairs followed certain basic principles and methods. They are made of a shaped, wire lattice supported by a refined, metal frame which, though consistent in conception, varies somewhat in the bending of the metal and its attachment to the latticework, which can be wholly or partially covered with minimal upholstery, or not. The frame consists of one piece of metal bent to make a front support and side legs linked by runners on the floor, welded to the other supporting elements. The structure is wonderfully clear and articulated, underscored by the transparency of the latticework.

Throughout the 1950s and 1960s, these chairs were part of the iconographic expression of modernity, almost cult objects, though a great many people daily sat on them happily. Though they show clear parallels with the sculpture, they were and still are extremely practical and elegant seats, which is what they were designed to be.

—Toni del Renzio

# BETANOVA

American exhibition, display, and graphic designer

**Born:** Elizabeth Lydia Csintalan, in Bratislava, Czechoslovakia, 5 June 1954; emigrated to the United States in 1969, naturalized, 1974. **Education:** Attended Ridgefield Park High School, New Jersey, 1969-72; studied art and languages, New York University, BA, 1975. **Family:** Married the designer Haig David-West in 1974;

children: Alzo, Hegulka, and Gizelka. **Career:** Designer and director of Haig-Betanova design and publishing firm, Port Harcourt, Nigeria, since 1975; has designed for the Port Harcourt Arts Council, Port Harcourt Contemporary Arts Gallery, Komsky Enterprises, WI-Verlag, Seiyefa Publishers, and others. Instructor in visual education and display, 1976, and gallery manager, 1977-79, Arts Council, Port Harcourt; program coordinator, Artgroup, Port Harcourt, 1979-80; lecturer in creative arts, College of Education, Port Harcourt, from 1980. **Exhibitions:** *Eight Contemporary Rivers State Artists,* Contemporary Arts Gallery, Port Harcourt, 1977; Gong Gallery, Lagos, 1979. **Collections:** Gong Gallery, Lagos; Patricia Ellah Collection, Port Harcourt. **Honors:** Raymond Miller Fencing Championship Award, New York University, 1973; Junior Olympic Fencing Honor Award, Los Angeles, 1973. **Address:** Haig-Betanova, P.O. Box 4289, 24A Ellah Place, Trans-Amadi, Port Harcourt, Nigeria.

## Works

Visual Arts Office interiors, for the Port Harcourt Arts Council, 1975.
Contemporary Arts Gallery exterior design, for the Port Harcourt Arts Council, 1976.
*Traditional Woven Fabrics* exhibition layouts, for the Port Harcourt Arts Council, 1977.
Souvenir Shop interiors, for the Port Harcourt Arts Council, 1977.
Coordinated visual identity system, for Komsky Enterprises, Lagos, 1978.
*Akifpo Masks* exhibition layouts, for the Port Harcourt Arts Council, 1978.
*African Spirits* series of greeting cards, for WI-Verlag, Düsseldorf, 1979.
*Krieg macht blutige Hände* poster, for WI-Verlag, Düsseldorf, 1980.
*Francis and Patricia 25* total environment exteriors in Port Harcourt, for Senator Francis Ellah, 1981.
*Poetry Trilogy* book covers, for Seiyefa Publishers, Port Harcourt, 1982.

## Publications

**By BETANOVA: books**—*Careers in Art,* Port Harcourt, 1979; **articles**—"Graphic Design of the City of Port Harcourt" in *Dialogue on Graphic Design Problems in Africa* edited by Haig David-West, London, 1983.

**On BETANOVA: books**—*Arts Council Information,* booklet, Port Harcourt, 1977; **articles**—"Evolving a New Lyricism" by S. Agiobu-Kemar in the *Daily Times* (Lagos), March 1979; "African Symbolic Design at Play" by F. Balogun in *The Punch* (Lagos), March 1979.

\*

What I have tried to do since my arrival in Africa is to translate the vitality of material vernacular structure into new functional form under controlled circumstances, such as modern interiors, without losing the essential character of the culture. I think that the work I did for the *Akifpo Masks* exhibition (1978) may be considered a major contribution of my career in exhibit and display design.

In a culture where even the most spacious natural environments sometimes tend to be crowded, a new orientation to space needs to be learned. Such a culture progresses from the vernacular level of growth to a technological one within the framework of international currents that no society can deliberately neglect. I think that I am contributing to the introduction of the new orientation in Nigeria. The teaching methodology that I employ at the College of Education (Faculty of Primary Education—Creative Arts Section) seeks to translate craft into design and is aimed at preparing future creative arts teachers for the task before them—that of contributing towards cultural growth.

An imaginative use of space is vital for meaningful interpersonal relationships in our contemporary world. As modern living standards steadily replace traditional standards, deliberate effort must be made to discourage an erasure of traditional tendencies which ultimately differentiate one culture from the other. This is perhaps most important to the younger countries of the world (such as Nigeria) which tend to be on the consuming end of standards prescribed by the technological explosion of our generation. What could be done is to introduce change gradually without altering the essential structure of vernacular design content. I believe that the manner in which people arrange their environments reflects on the manner in which they organize their lives, and that in turn reflects on the manner in which they respond to political and social responsibilities. Therefore, in my designs, I try to show examples of how environments can be re-ordered to reflect the basic vernacular philosophies of art and design in unity with the excitement and worries of contemporary civilization.

—Betanova

\*     \*     \*

Arriving in Nigeria in 1974, Betanova brought with her background, mixing Slovak lyricism with New World excitement, the romantic aura of her native Bratislava with the electronic tempo of New York City, and the socialist ideological system with the capitalist one. Perhaps this interesting background has enabled her to operate at ease in Nigeria, which, like most Third World countries, demonstrates an admixture of all the elements of her background, and to introduce a new dimension to exhibit and display design in this country, thereby placing her among the innovative contemporary designers of our times.

In 1975, she began collecting examples of indigenous Nigerian art and crafts—from wood carvings to thorn carvings, from bead work to masquerade embellishments, and from shellwork to fish traps. Her art-and-crafts collecting was punctuated by discussions with old people in village settlements. Examining her collection in conjunction with these discussions, she noted that the naive, geometric formalism of vernacular art and design was fundamentally perceived first on a functional level, then in terms of visual appeal. She also noted that the formal "fear of space" in vernacular design reflected "togetherness" in social behavior. Further inquiry led her to conclude that in contemporary circumstances, freedom of mobility, which suggested "nonfear of space," was tolerable as a function of a new "fear" introduced by the technological age as evidenced by mechanics and automation.

These findings have greatly influenced Betanova's work in exhibit and display design, for, while retaining the general tempo of vernacular lyricism in indigenous art and design, she introduces the element of space-time as a functional mobility factor. Her environ-

ments are therefore a dialectical blend of tradition and contemporaneity; of naive "togetherness" and "togetherness" unmitigated by space-time control. Tangibly, this blend has introduced a new design format and a new functional excitement to the Nigerian contemporary experience. A most vivid example of this was her 1978 design for the *Afikpo Masks* exhibition in Port Harcourt's contemporary arts gallery; there, her innovative exhibition stands blended with the lyrical naive abstraction of vernacular wood carvings.

Besides interesting work in exhibit and display design, she has also produced outstanding work in graphic design and painting. Her paintings—notably the *Mat Motif* and *Mask Form* series which were exhibited in 1979 at the Gong Gallery in Lagos—are a direct offshoot from her research into vernacular lyricism, and, according to Sereba Agiobu-Kemar, art critic of Lagos, they pointed toward a new lyricism in Nigerian art. As a creative arts lecturer at Port Harcourt's College of Education, she lays emphasis on basic understanding of geometry with a blend of vernacular formal arrangements in solving design problems. This teaching strategy may create a new and more effective generation of art and design teachers in Nigeria.

In a society in which the socio-political temperament is still in formative stages, Betanova's work in exhibit and display design—which increasingly influences the way in which people perceive art and design generally and organize their lives and their environments specifically—may become increasingly useful in this process of development.

—Haig David-West

# BIAGIOTTI, Laura
Italian fashion designer

**Born:** Rome, 4 August 1943. **Education:** Studied literature, Rome, 1960-62. **Family:** Married; daughter: Lavinia. **Career:** Worked with her mother, Delia Biagiotti, in the family ready-to-wear fashion export firm, Rome, 1962-65; partner and designer, with Gianni Cigna, in clothing firm, designing for Schuberth, Barocco, Cappucci, Heinz Riva, Litrico, and others, in Rome, 1965-72; founder-designer, Laura Biagiotti Fashions, Rome, from 1972; took over MacPherson knitwear firm, Pisa, 1974; established headquarters at the castle of Marco Simone, Guidonia, 1980; created Portrait collection, 1981, Laurapiu collection, 1984, and Biagiotti Uomo collection, 1987, for Lebole Moda ready-to-wear clothing group; launched perfumes *Laura,* 1982, *Night,* 1986, *Roma,* 1988, and *Venezia,* 1992; signed licensing agreement for Biagiotti shops in China, 1993; opened LB shop in Beijing, China, Bangkok, Thailand, 1994, and in Moscow, Russia, 1994. **Honors:** Golden Lion Award, Venice, 1985; Commendatore Award, Republic of Italy, 1987; Marco Polo Award for high achievement in diffusing Italian style worldwide, 1993; Frenio Fragene for fashion achievements, 1994. **Address:** Biagiotti Export S.p.A., via Palombarese Km, 17.300, 00012 Guidonia, Rome, Italy.

**Works**

Handbags and luggage range, for Copel, 1978.
Sunglasses, for Safilo Group, 1980.

Perfumes and cosmetics, for Eurocos, 1981.
Shoes, for Colette, 1982.
Scarves, for Isa, 1983.
Ceramics and tiles, for Tagina, 1983.
Laurapiu women's clothing collection, for Lebole Moda, 1984.
Household linens collection, for Eliolona, 1984.
MacPherson's Diffusion collection of pullovers, 1985.
Furniture, for Corsini, 1985.
Linea Junior children's sports and leisure wear, for Italiangriffe, 1986.
Jeans collection, for I.T.S.A., 1986.
Costume jewellery, for Enny Bijoux, 1986.
Tights, for Levante, 1986.
Knitwear, for Ghinea, 1987.
Menswear collection, for Lebole Moda, 1987.
Ties, for Guarisco, 1987.
Hair accessories, for Santa Monica, 1988.
Leather wear, for Sicons, 1988.
Beach wear, for Karibe, 1988.
Ladies' lingerie, for Magnolia, 1988.
Bear's Bazaar young ladies' clothing, for Fim, 1988.

## Publications

On BIAGIOTTI: books—*I Mass-Moda: fatti e personaggi dell'Italian Look/The Who's Who of Italian Fashion,* with text by Adriana Mulassano, photos by Alfa Castaldi, Florence, 1979; *Who's Who in Fashion* edited by Karl Strute and Theodor Doelken, Zurich, 1982; *McDowell's Directory of Twentieth Century Fashion* by Colin McDowell, London, 1984; *The Encyclopaedia of Fashion from 1840 to the 1980s* by Georgina O'Hara, London, 1986; *Women of Fashion* by Valerie Steele, New York, 1991; articles—"Laura Biagiotti, Stylish et Italienne" by Massimo Gargia in *Vogue* (Paris), August 1978; "Women Designers" by Daniela Petroff in the *International Herald Tribune,* 3-4 October 1981; "Laura Biagiotti: Bianco per tutte le mode" in *Vogue* (Milan), October 1984; "The House of Biagiotti" in *House and Garden,* December 1986; "I cashmere ricamati di Laura Biagiotti" in *Donna* (Milan), October 1987; "Laura Biagiotti: I piaceri naturali" in *Donna,* February 1988; "Laura Biagiotti" in *Moda Italia* (Milan), 1988; "Couture's Grand Ladies" by Suzy Menkes in *Illustrated London News* (London), Spring 1990; "Biagiotti's U.S. Invasion" by Heidi Lender in *Women's Wear Daily* (New York), 12 February 1992; "Laura Biagiotti's China Syndrome" by Glynis Costin in *Women's Wear Daily* (New York), 21 May 1993; Cover story, in *Fashion,* September 1994.

* * *

At Guidonia, in the Roman countryside, ready-to-wear designer Laura Biagiotti fell in love with an eleventh-century castle she passed on her daily drive to and from her factory. When the castle, which was once inhabited by a Vatican cardinal and most recently by a family of farmers who had whitewashed the fifteenth-century frescos, came up for sale, Biagiotti and her business manager Gianni Cigna agreed that to purchase it would be a wise investment. Today, the sixty-nine room Castello di Marco Simone serves as factory, showroom, and offices as well as residence for Biagiotti, her daughter Lavinia, and a housekeeper.

Biagiotti had planned one day to be an archaeologist, but as her mother Delia, a Roman couturiere, tired of business demands, Laura interrupted her studies to turn her attention to fashion. Since then, living in her romantic factory/castle, she has successfully joined her love of antiquity with her professed virtues of discipline and hard work in order to succeed as a contemporary businesswoman.

When the time comes to develop a new line, Biagiotti reveals a mania for research. She studies fabrics—in particular, natural fibers—which are often combined with custom patterns and distinctive top-stitching. The work of Laura Biagiotti Exports has never been known to be shocking, but always feminine, luxurious, and finely constructed. The designer is an innovater in the form and construction of cashmere dresses which require minimal attention to sizing, as well as cardigans, sweaters, and recently, jogging outfits. Her particular preference for white was visible in a recent collection of New England lattice-work linen dresses.

Since her "outsider" showings in Florence in 1972, she presents semiannual, two-hundred-piece collections, which are always expected to emphasize high quality, sumptuousness, and femininity. Her 1983 cashmere dresses resemble long, easy sweaters; frequently, they display frilled or scarf necklines, cross-over bib detailing, or oversized, knitted cables. To cover all she takes the softest of cashmere blankets and creates capes or beehive jackets with trellis-top stitching. In 1983, she also introduced rainproof satin and an amusing leopard-skin pattern printed on cotton satin. The voluminous silhouette of the "bambola" or doll dress has become one of her classics, which she varies with detailing and fantasy-patterns.

Subsequently fifteen forms were developed into more than one hundred items of clothing to create Portrait by Laura Biagiotti, her line made for large production and distribution. As she developed Portrait, she combined her admiration of Matisse cut-outs and colors with inspiration drawn from flower photographs by Irving Penn to design a collection with classic lines in natural fibers.

In her 1990 spring/summer collection, Biagiotti offered basic pieces in the core colors of red, white, and navy, to be built upon or worn alone. With this collection, Biagiotti foresaw the 1990s emphasis on simple, fundamentals which could be adapted according to the taste of the wearer. Biagiotti's philosophy is that clothing should not "dress up" but enhance; her designs, she says, are "for when you want to be yourself."

—Gillian Skellenger

# BIERUT, Michael
American graphic designer

Born: Cleveland, Ohio, 29 August 1957. Education: Studied architecture and art, College of Design, University of Cincinnati, B.S., 1980. Career: Graphic designer, becoming vice president for graphic design, Vignelli Associates, New York, 1980-1990; partner, Pentagram Design, New York, from 1990. Lecturer and visiting professor, State University of New York at Purchase, Cooper Union, and Yale University School of Art. Contributing editor, *ID* magazine. Member: President, New York Chapter, 1987-89, and national board member, from 1995, American Institute of Graphic Arts; Alliance Graphique Internationale, from 1989. Collections: Museum of Modern Art, New York; Metropolitan Museum of Art, New York; Library of Congress, Washington D.C.; Musée des Arts Décoratifs, Montreal; Die Neue Sammlung, Munich. Address: Pentagram Design, 204 Fifth Avenue, New York, New York 10010.

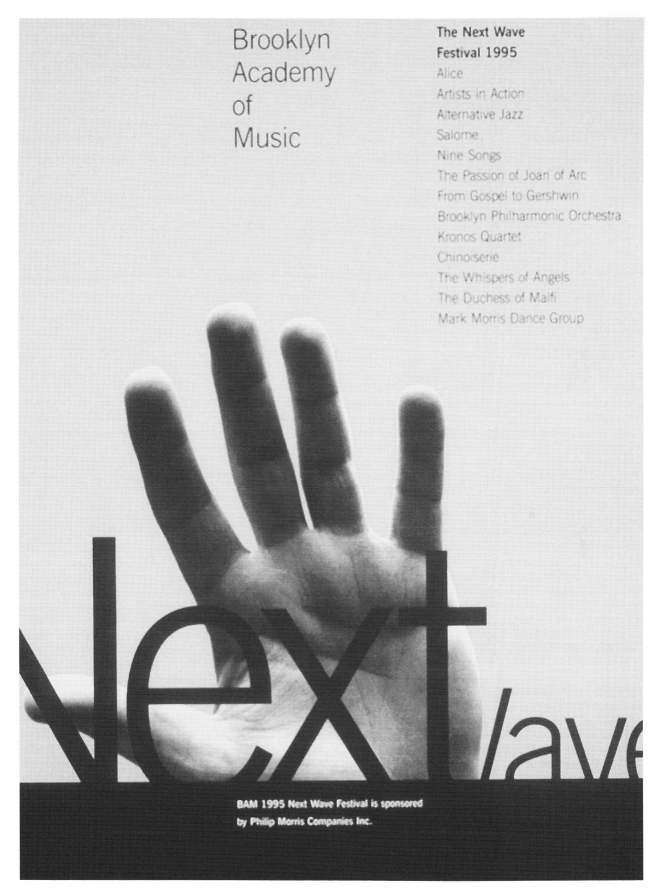

**Michael Bierut: poster for the Next Wave Festival, Brooklyn Academy of Music, 1995**

## Works

Posters, for the Architectural League of New York, 1982-1990.

Identity and print promotion, for the International Design Center, New York, 1985-1989.

Identity and catalogs, for Peter Joseph Gallery, New York, from 1990.

Identity, magazines, and brochures, for Mohawk Paper Mills, Cohoes, New York, from 1991.

Identity, for The Good Diner restaurant, New York, 1992.

Identity and architectural graphics, for Celebration, Florida, a new town by Disney Development Company, 1994.

Format, for *Interiors* magazine, 1995.

Identity and architectural graphics, for Minnesota Children's Museum, St. Paul, Minnesota, 1995.

Identity and print promotion, for the Brooklyn Academy of Music, New York, 1995.

## Publications

**By BIERUT: books**—(co-editor) *Graphic Design: New York,* New York, 1992; (co-editor) *Graphic Design: America,* New York, 1993; (co-editor) *Looking Closer: Critical Writings on Graphic Design,* New York, 1994.

**On BIERUT: articles**—*High Quality* (Heidelberg), no. 17, 1990; *Design Exchange* (Hong Kong), no. 10, 1994.

\*    \*    \*

Some designers are easily pigeonholed as identity specialists, book designers, product packagers, or poster makers. Some are decorators, others conceptualizers. Michael Bierut defies categorization. Since leaving his position as Vice President of Graphic Design at Vignelli Associates in 1990 to become a partner of Pentagram Design/New York, he has mastered all these disciplines, and more. While his work does not have a particular identifiable style, it has a distinct sensibility rooted in wit and humor.

Bierut is a proponent of "the big idea" or sophisticated visual statement. Take one of his masterpieces of simplicity, the quintessential graphic pun for the logo for the Fashion Center Business improvement District, a button with the holes inside forming an "F." Likewise, his comic mark for The Good Diner, an inexpensive restaurant in New York, is a crude rendering of a common coffee cup crowned with a halo. For both solutions Bierut borrows from, and transforms, the vernacular into a memorable icon imbued with a distinct character. Similarly, a special Fathers Day shopping bag for Brookstone, a men's clothing store, combines the universal sign for "no," a circle with a perpendicular slash, with the universal gift for dad, a tie; this is a wry commentary on one of the timeworn clichés of this commercial holiday.

Although taught in a Modern manner, Bierut is not a slave to one or another design doctrine. His total understanding of Modern form allows him to break the rules as he sees fit. And fitness knows no bounds. In fact, his wit leans towards the Post-Modern as a satiric commentary on tired design conventions. Such is the case with the signage for the Minnesota Children's Museum, which includes as its central graphic device photographs of hands signaling different floors and directions. Consistent with the logic of this motif the bathroom signs are photographs of cards bearing the universal (Department of Transportation) sign symbols of a boy and girl held by a hand.

The hand is also one of the visual anchors for the Brooklyn Academy of Music's Next Wave Festival promotion materials, a series of posters, programs, and announcements for a well known avant garde showcase that are tied together through controlled anarchy and a deliberate scheme. Without resorting to predictable and fashionable typographic tricks, Bierut provides a contemporaneous allure through fragmentation of the visual elements. Bits and pieces of common and uncommon images are woven between color bands and cropped letter forms in the print approximation of animation. The critical mass or fusion of these disparate elements results in a striking overall identity.

Bierut plays with these and other forms as a child plays with toys, ambitiously, obsessively, and lovingly. His posters for The Parallax Theatre are doodles with purpose. The images for the cautionary play, "Fool For Love," reprise old diagrams instructing how to apply bandages to private body parts; the poster for the ribald love story, "Marie and Bruce," is a sketch of buttocks with an emerging cupid shooting its arrow. Both are relatively quiet in a graphic sense, but pack a conceptual wallop. Just as playfully Bierut uses lettering to unlock the hidden child in himself and his audience. The chapter openers for American Photography, an annual of photographic excellence, are rendered in an updated reprise of the Palmer Method. His own crude scrawl for the 7th Annual Book Fair To Help The Homeless is a respite from the strict conventions associated with book design. And the poster for the American Center for Design 100 Show reveals the roots of Bierut's keen fascination in the childlike; for here he reproduces a handwritten composition on the characteristics of "Good Design" by his then eight year old daughter.

As practiced by Bierut, good design is clear communication executed with economy, passion, and humor. His designs are conversation points or openings for the audience to interact with that thing or idea being communicated. Taken as a whole Bierut's work may not have a singular visual style, but the very strength of his visual and verbal ideas mitigate the need for that.

—Steven Heller

# BILL, Max
Swiss painter, sculptor, and architect and stage, exhibition, and industrial designer

**Born:** Winterthur, 22 December 1908. **Education:** Trained as a silversmith, Kunstgewerbeschule, Zürich, 1924-27; studied art, Staatliche Bauhaus, Dessau, 1927-29. **Military Service:** Served in the Swiss Army, 1939-45. **Family:** Married Binia Spoerri in 1931 (died 1988); married Angela Thomas in 1991; children: Johann, Jakob. **Career:** Independent artist, architect, and exhibition designer, from 1929, and industrial designer, from 1944, working with the Abstraction-Creation group, Paris, 1932-36, Allianz, Zürich, 1937, CIAM Congrès Internationaux d'Architecture Moderne, 1938, UAM-Union des Artistes Modernes, Paris, 1949, and Deutscher Werkbund, 1956. Lecturer, Kunstgewerbeschule, Zürich, 1944-45; co-founder and rector, Hochschule für Gestaltung, Ulm, 1951-56; professor of environmental design, State Institute of Fine Arts, Hamburg 1967-74; president, Bauhaus Archives Society, Berlin, 1985. National Councillor, Swiss Parliament, 1967-71. **Member:** Schweizerische Werkbund (Central Board), 1952-62; Communal Council Member, City of Zürich, 1961; Swiss Federal Art Commission Board, 1961-69; Geschwister-Scholl Foundation, Ulm, 1964; Superior Council Member, Creation Esthetique Industrielle Paris, 1971-73. **Exhibitions:** Kunstmuseum, Basel, 1949; Museu de Arte Moderno, Sao Paulo, 1950; Ulmer Museum, Ulm, 1956 (toured); Helmhaus, Zürich, 1957; Städtisches Museum, Leverkusen, 1959; Staatsgalerie, Stuttgart, 1960; Kunstmuseum, Winterthur 1960; Kunsthalle, Bern, 1968; Kunstverein, Dusseldorf, 1968; Kunsthaus, Zürich, 1968; Gemeentemuseum, The Hague, 1968; Kunsthalle, Nuremberg, 1968; Arts Club, Chicago, 1969; Centre National d'Art Contemporain, Paris, 1969; San Francisco Museum of Art, 1970; Musée Rath, Geneva, 1972; Kunstmuseum, Aarhus, 1972; Albright-Knox Art Gallery, Buffalo, New York, 1974 (toured); San Francisco Art Institute; Museum für Kunst und Gewerbe, Hamburg, 1976 (toured); Akademie der Künste, West Berlin, 1976; University of Parma, Italy, 1977; Museo de Bellas Artes, Caracas, 1979; Mucsarnok Art Gallery, Budapest, 1986; National Gallery, Belgrade, 1987; Kunsthalle, Frankfurt, 1987; *Internationalen Grafik-Biennale,* Llubljana, 1991; *Raumplastik— Berlin Dankt Frankreich,* Berlin, 1994. **Collections:** Kunstmuseum, Winterthur; Kunsthaus, Zürich; Musée d'Art et d'Histoire, Geneva; Galleria Nazionale d'Arte Moderna, Rome; Centre Georges Pompidou, Paris; Wilhelm Lehmbruck Museum, Duisburg; Art Institute of Chicago; Museum of Modern Art, New York. **Honors:** Grand Prize, Milan Triennale, 1936, 1951, 1954; Kandinsky Prize, 1949; Sculpture Prize, Bienal of São Paulo, 1951; Gold Medal, Verucchio, 1966; City of Zürich Art Prize, 1968; Misha Black Medal, Society of Industrial Artists and American Institute of Architects, 1964; Extraordinary Member, Akademie der Kunste, West Berlin, 1972; Honorary Member, Royal Flemish Academy of Science, Literature and Art, 1973; Culture Prize, Winterthur, 1979; Great Cross of Merit, Federal Republic of Germany, 1979; honorary doctorate, Stuttgart University, 1979; Imperial Medal, City of Goslar, West Germany, 1982; Misha Black Medal, Society of Industrial Artists and Designers, London, 1982; crowned Knight of the Belgian Crown, 1982; Commandeur de L'Ordre des Arts and des Lettres, France, 1985; Frank J. Malina Leonardo Prize, International Society for the Arts, Sciences, and Technology, 1987; Premio Marconi per Arte e Scienza, Bologna, 1988; Piepenbrock Prize for Sculpture, Osnabrueck, West Germany, 1990; honorary award, 1991, and Grand Prize, 1993, International Graphics Biennial, Llubljana; Grand Prize, Chevalier de la Légion d'Honneur, 1993; Imperial Prize, Japan, 1993; honorary doctorate, Swiss Technical College, Zürich, 1994. **Died:** Berlin, 9 December 1994.

## Works

Swiss Pavilion design, at the Milan Triennale, 1936, 1951.
Swiss Pavilion design, at the *Worlds Fair,* New York, 1938.
City Building and National Planning display, at the *Swiss National Exhibition,* Zürich, 1939.
Three-legged table, for Wohnbedarf AG, Zürich, 1949-50.
Chair with wood frame and molded plywood seating unit, for Horgen-Glarus, 1950.
*The Unknown Present* exhibition layouts, at Globus Department Stores, in Basel, St. Gallen, Chur, and Aarau, 1957.
Fountain courtyard design, at the *International Hydraulic Engineering Exhibition,* West Berlin, 1961.
*Oedipus* stage designs, at the Municipal Theatre, Ulm, 1963.
*Bilden und Gestalten* displays, at the *Swiss National Exhibition,* Lausanne, 1964.

*Zurcher Kunstler* annual exhibition layouts, Zürich, 1968-70.
*Pavillion Sculpture,* Zürich, 1983.
*Continuity* sculpture, Frankfurt-am-Main, West Germany, 1986.
*Berlin Thanks France* plastic art exhibition design, Berlin, 1994.

(for a complete list of Bill's buildings and architectural projects, see *Contemporary Architects;* for his activity as a painter and sculptor, see *Contemporary Artists*)

## Publications

**By BILL: books**—*Quinze Variations sur même théme,* Paris, 1938; (editor) *Le Corbusier: Oeuvre Complete,* vol. 3, Zürich, 1939, London, 1964; *5 Konstruktionen & 5 Kompositionen,* Zürich, 1941; *10 Original Lithos,* Zürich, 1941; *X & X,* Zürich, 1942; *Leo Luppi: 10 Kompositionen,* Zürich, 1943; (with others) *Konkrete Kunst,* exhibition catalogue, Basel, 1944; (with others) *Hans Arp: 11 Configurations,* with others, Zürich, 1945; *Wiederaufbau,* Zürich, 1945; *Wassily Kandinsky: 10 Farbige Reproduktionen,* Basel, 1949; *Robert Maillart: Brucken und Konstruktionen,* Zürich, 1949, New York, 1969; *Moderne Schweizer Architektur 1925-45,* Basel, 1950; (editor) *Wassily Kandinsky,* Paris, 1951; *Form: A Balance Sheet of Mid-20th Century Trends in Design,* Basel, 1952; (editor) *Über das Geistige in der Kunst,* Bern, 1952; *Mies van der Rohe,* Milan, 1955; (editor) *Essays über Kunst und Kunstler,* Stuttgart, 1955, Bern, 1963; *Die gute Form,* Winterthur, 1957; (editor) *Punkt und Linie zu Flache,* Bern, 1959; (with Bruno Munari) *Enzo Mari,* Milan, 1959; (with Rene Wehrli and Margit Staber) *Konkrete Kunst: 50 Jallre Entwicklung,* exhibition catalogue, Zürich, 1960; *7 Scarions,* Genoa, 1967; *Zürcher Künstler,* exhibition catalogue, Zürich, 1968; *11 x 4,* Zürich, 1970; *Jahresgabe 1972,* Bern, 1972; *System mit funf vierfarbigen Zentren,* St. Gallen, 1972; *8 = (2 x 4/4) = 8,* Neuchâtel, 1974; *16 Constellations,* Paris, 1974; *7 Twins,* Neuchâtel, 1977; **articles**—"The Bauhaus Idea: From Weimar to Ulm" in *Architects' Year Book,* vol. 5, London, 1953.

**On BILL: books**—*Max Bill* by Tomas Maldonado, Buenos Aires, 1955; *Die Gute Industrieform,* exhibition catalogue by Hans Eckstein and Robert Gutmann, Hamburg, 1955; *Max Bill* by Max Bense and others, Teufen, 1958; *Moderne Deutsche Industrieform* by Heinz Spielmann, Hamburg, 1962; *Who's Who in Graphic Art* edited by Walter Amstutz, Zürich, 1962; *Max Bill* by Margit Staber, St. Gallen, 1971; *Max Bill* by Eduard Huttinger, Zürich, 1977; *Design Since 1945* edited by Kathryn Hiesinger and George Marcus, Philadelphia and London, 1983; *The Conran Directory of Design* edited by Stephen Bayley, London 1985.

\*     \*     \*

For Max Bill, geometry was the foremost foundation for form, geometry made visual as the mutual relationships of rhythmic elements on a surface or in space. Bill's work concentrated on showing the possibilities for endless variation within this philosophical and structural model, to which he adhered rigidly as symbolic of universal order and collective freedom. His choice of anti-illusionistic, mathematical/scientific form was not based on an "art-for-art's sake" mentality, but rather was viewed by Bill as the systemic basis capable of conveying high ideals which all can share and comprehend through their experience of all the arts. His faith in geometry as communicator of order and unity also allowed for the element of the indecipherable, a mysticism inherent in the very nature of the forms.

Bill's multi-media oeuvre demonstrates his position in history as a faithful and productive second-generation practitioner of Bauhaus philosophy and practice. From his earliest to his latest work as painter, sculptor, architect, industrial designer, and writer, Bill transmitted a direct kinship with his mentors, Josef Albers, László Moholy-Nagy, Piet Mondrian, Paul Klee, and Walter Gropius, among others. Consider his design for Ulm's Hochschule für Gestaltung buildings, which equate so closely with the earlier work of Gropius at the Bauhaus. The "no frills" simplicity of his door handle, electric plugs, and medical lamp, no differently than the strict, geometrical structures of his paintings, sculpture, and architecture, all pay homage to the ongoing viability of the Bauhaus spirit of pro-technological experimentation. Bill's was not the work of the innovator. His contribution to art and design was as a follower of an already established idea and visualization, and he remained tightly within the tradition and its systems while searching out possible variables which are direct extensions of the pre-established ideas and approaches.

The anti-individualist philosophy underlying Bill's work resulted in an output which stayed very close in both look and conception to that of his artist-teachers at the Bauhaus. He located some variables which are subtly realized and which never relax in their affirmation of the exclusive principles on which they are based. As painter and sculptor, Bill made a limited contribution, laudable for its tenacity of belief, yet too often openly dependent on the constructivist, neo-Plasticist tradition he inherited. There is greater feeling of success in Bill's industrial designs; their impersonal feeling, formal simplicity, use of industrial materials, and crisp sleekness speak of a period mode which found pertinence for its infusion of high art ideas into popular culture with wide distribution. Bill once stated that at the Bauhaus he found clarity, confirmation of his own views. There can be little doubt of his commitment to a tradition which is among the most fruitful of its time. Yet that tradition, like all others, yearns and needs to be broken, to be used conceptually as a route into future directions for the following generations, not to be adopted or co-opted in a literal fashion. The originators of the Bauhaus proclaimed a postpast view, one in which new discoveries in technology and science are adapted to art and design with an attitude of adventurous experimentation. Such an adventure is considerably watered down by a second-generation vantage point.

—Barbara Cavaliere

# BINDER, Joseph

American painter, typographer, and graphic designer

**Born:** Vienna, Austria, 3 March 1898; emigrated to the United States in 1935, naturalized, 1944. **Education:** Studied painting, under Berthold Loffler, at the Kunstgewerbeschule, Vienna, 1922-26; Staatspreis, 1926. **Military Service:** Served in the Austrian Army, 1916-18. **Family:** Married Carla Neuschil in 1925. **Career:** Apprenticed to lithographer Robert Scheffler, Vienna, 1912-16; freelance designer, establishing Joseph Binder Graphic Studio, in Vienna, 1924-35, and in New York, 1936-72; designed for Zuntz Kaffee Import, Juiius Meinl, Milchgenossenschaft, the American Red Cross, United Airlines, United Nations, *American Graphics,*

*Fortune, Graphis,* and others; art director and designer, United States Navy Department, Washington, D.C., 1948-58. Visiting lecturer, School of the Art Institute of Chicago; Society of Typographic Arts, Chicago; Minneapolis School of Art; Chouinard School of Art, Los Angeles; Teachers College, Columbia University, New York; Pratt Institute, Brooklyn, New York. **Member:** National Poster Campaign Committee Member, *Fortune* magazine, New York, 1942. **Exhibitions:** Austrian Werkbund, Vienna, 1935; Architectural League, New York, 1937; Academy of Art, Vienna, 1963; Rose Fried Gallery, New York, 1965, 1967, 1969; Austrian Institute, New York, 1966; Bucknell University, Lewisburg, Pennsylvania, 1967; Austrian Museum of Art and Industry, Vienna, 1972. **Collections:** Cornell University, Ithaca, New York; Metropolitan Museum of Art, New York; Museum of Modern Art, New York; Neuberger Museum, Purchase, New York; Library of Congress, Washington, D.C.; Smithsonian Institution, Washington, D.C.; Austrian Museum of Applied Arts, Vienna. **Honors:** Vertex Bulbs Poster Prize, Vienna, 1915; Vienna Music and Theatre Poster Prize, 1924; Baron C. Collier Medal, 1939, Annual Award Medal, 1944, and Certificate of Merit, 1956, Art Directors Club of New York; New York World's Fair Poster Prize, 1939; National Defense Department Poster Prize, Museum of Modern Art, New York, 1941; Direct Mail Certificate of Merit, New York, 1948; American Red Cross Poster Prize, 1952; Outdoor Advertising Award, Art Directors Club of Chicago, 1953; United States Navy Department Poster Prize, 1956; City of Vienna Medal of Honour, 1969. Honorary Professor, Austrian Ministry of Education, 1952; Honorary Member, BOEG Society of Graphic Designers, Vienna, 1952. **Died:** Vienna 26 June 1972.

## Works

*Meinl Kaffee* poster, for Julius Meinl AG, Vienna, 1923.
*Musik und Theulerfest* poster, for the Buro des Festes, Vienna, 1924.
*Meilch Tee* poster, for Julius Meinl AG, Vienna, 1925.
*Milch gibt* Kraft poster, for the Milchgenossenschaft, Vienna, 1928.
*Asko 1931* poster, for the Asko Zweite Arbeiter-Olympiade, Vienna, 1931.
*Zunzt Kaffee* poster, for Zuntz Kaffec Import, Munich, 1932.
Tank Tracks cover, for *Fortune* magazine, New York, 1938.
*A & P Iced Coffee* series of advertisements, for Paris and Pearl Advertising Agency, New York, 1939.
*Buy American Art* poster, for *Fortune* National Poster Campaign Committee, New York, 1942.
Skyscraper cover, for *Graphis* magazine, Zurich, no. 32, 1948.
*Pax* United Nations posters, for the Museum of Modern Art competition, New York, 1948.
*Answer the Call* poster, for the American Red Cross, 1952.
*The Most Important Wheels in America* poster, for the Association of American Railroads, Washington, D.C., 1952.
*Join the New Era* poster, for the United States Navy Department, Washington, D.C., 1955.

## Publications

**By BINDER: book**—*Colour in Advertising,* London, 1934; book designed—*Internationale Buchkunst Ausstellung,* exhibition catalogue, Leipzig, 1927.

**On BINDER: books**—*Die neue Graf k/The New Graphic Design* by Karl Gerstner and Markus Kutter, Teufen and London, 1959; *The Poster: An Illustrated History from 1860* by Harold F. Hutchinson, London and Toronto, 1968; *Joseph Binder, New York: Non-Objective Art,* exhibition catalogue with introduction by Wilhelm Mrazek, Vienna, 1972; *Joseph Binder: An Artist and a Lifestyle* by Carla Binder, Vienna, 1976; *Advertising: Reflections of a Century* by Bryan Holme, London, 1982.

\* \* \*

Joseph Binder belongs to the generation of graphic designers, including A. M. Cassandre and E. McKnight Kauffer, that brought the vitality and design qualities of modern art to the European poster. Binder's posters are based on close and careful observation of the world, but these observations are translated into a graphic language of great visual impact and energy. This is achieved through simplification that Binder learned from early modern European design and painting.

During his Vienna period, Binder applied several influences to pictorial poster design. From the Wiener Werkstatte, he learned simplified composition and the use of geometric patterns as design elements. Cubism's planar reduction of figurative subjects, constructivism's diagonal movements, and the asymmetrical balance of de Stijl were other important influences.

Figures and objects in his work are simplified into basic forms, consistent with Cezanne's precept that all objects in nature are based on the elemental geometric forms of cone, cube, and sphere. Binder expressed dimension by placing two flat planes of color side by side to represent light and shadow on the subject. To strengthen the graphic quality of objects in his posters, Binder rejected traditional perspective drawing in preference for orthogonal or parallel perspective construction.

Binder favored the presentation of symbolic persons or objects placed against a simple background of flat or modulated color. His posters are generally organized with strong horizontal, vertical, or diagonal construction lines.

During the 1930s, American design was markedly affected by immigrants from Europe. Due to his early arrival and the more pictorial and accessible nature of his work (as compared to the more formal and geometric work of constructivist and Bauhaus designers who came to America), Binder had an important early impact upon the development of modernist graphic design in America. After coming to the United States, Binder used the airbrush to execute his poster designs. This introduced the refined modulated form and color that are characteristic of pictorial graphic design from the 1930s and 1940s.

—Philip B. Meggs

# BJØRN, Acton
Danish industrial designer

**Born:** Copenhagen, 23 September 1910. **Education:** Technical High School, Copenhagen, 1926-30; Royal Academy of Fine Arts, Copenhagen, 1931-32. **Family:** Married Maureen Egeland in 1950; children: Juliane, Thomas and Andreas. **Career:** Freelance designer, Copenhagen, from 1949; partner, with Prince Sigvard Bernadotte,

in Bernadotte and Bjørn industrial design firm, with offices in Stockholm and Copenhagen, from 1950; also independent designer, establishing Acton Bjorns Tegnestue ApS, Copenhagen, from 1966. **Exhibitions:** *Design Since 1945,* Philadelphia Museum of Art, 1983; *Industrial Design in Focus,* Kunstindustrimuseum, Copenhagen, 1989. **Honors:** American Society of Industrial Designers Award, 1958; Eurostar Award, 1963, 1968; World Star Award, 1970; Dunhill Prize, London, 1980; ID Classics Prize, Danish Design Council, 1985. **Address:** Toldbodgade 89, 1253 Copenhagen, Denmark.

**Works**

Kitchen utensils, for Rosti, from 1955.
Office machinery, for Facit, from 1958.
Kitchen utensils, for Morsoe, from 1960.
Glassware, for Nordfalk, from 1960.
Radiator thermostats, for Danfoss, from 1963.
Glassware, for Vega, from 1965.
Transformer stations in Denmark, for Siemens, from 1972.
Bathroom equipment and fixtures, for Dansk Pressalit, from 1973.
Carpets, from EGE-Taepper, from 1979.

**Publications**

**On BJØRN: books**—*Dansk Møbelkunst* by Viggo Sten Moller and Sven Erik Møller, Copenhagen, 1951; *Packaging: An International Survey of Package Design* edited by Walter Herdeg, Zurich, 1959; *Svensk Form/Forma Sueca* edited by Ake Stavenlow and Ake H. Huldt, Stockholm, 1961; *A Treasury of Scandinavian Design* edited by Erik Zahlc, New York, 1961; *Konsten i Sverige: Konsthantverk, Konstindustri, Design 1875-1975* by Dag Widman, Stockholm, 1975; *Industrial Design* by John Heskett, London, 1980; *Design Since 1945* edited by Kathryn Hiesinger and George Marcus, Philadelphia and London, 1983.

# BJÖRQUIST, Karin
Swedish ceramics designer

**Born:** Säffle, 2 January 1927. **Education:** Studied at the National School of Art, Craft and Design, Stockholm, 1945-50. **Family:** Married Lennart Lindkvist in 1954; children: Jonas and Sara. **Career:** Assistant designer to Wilhelm Kåge, 1950-60, chief designer, 1960-80, and artistic director, 1980-89, Gustavsberg Porcelain Factory, Stockholm; freelance designer, for Rörstrand-Hackman AB, from 1989. Professor, named by Swedish Government, from 1992. **Exhibitions:** Milan Triennale, 1954; *H55,* Helsingborg, 1955; Nordiska Kompaniet, Stockholm, 1956, *Nordisk Keramik 1,* Lunds Konsthall, Sweden, 1961; Malmö Museum, Sweden, 1961; Georg Jensen Inc., New York, 1964; *Hantverkets 60-tal,* Nationalmuseum, Stockholm, 1968; *Gustavsberg 150 år,* Nationalmuseum, 1975; *Svensk Form: Swedish Craft and Design,* Victoria and Albert Museum, London, 1980 (toured); *Contemporary Swedish Design,* Nationalmuseum, 1982 (toured); *Scandinavian Modern Design 1880-1980,* Cooper-Hewitt Museum, New York, 1982 (toured); *Design in Sweden Now,* toured Canada and Australia, 1985-87; *The*

**Karin Björquist:** *Nobel* **dinner service for Rörstrand-Hackman AB, 1991. Photo by Pelle Bergström, Stockholm, courtesy of Karin Björquist-Lindkvist**

*Lunning Prize,* Nationalmuseum, 1986; *Scandinavian Design: A Way of Life,* Seibu Museum of Art, Tokyo, 1987 (toured); *Faces of Swedish Design,* IBM Gallery, New York, 1988 (toured); *Scandinavian Ceramics and Glass,* Victoria and Albert Museum, London, 1989. **Collections:** Nationalmuseum, Stockholm; Röhsska Konstslöjdmuseet, Göteborg; Malmö Museum; Museum of Applied Art, Copenhagen; Museum of Applied Art, Trondheim; Ceramic Center, Gustavsberg, Sweden; Victoria and Albert Museum, London; Museum of Applied Art, Vienna; Museum of Modern Art, New York; Cooper-Hewitt Museum, New York. **Honors:** Gold Medal, Milan Triennale, 1954; Svensk Form/Good Form Prize, Stockholm, 1961; Lunning Prize, 1963; Gregor Paulsson Statuette, Stockholm, 1973; Prince Eugen Medal for Outstanding Artistic Work, 1982; *Vi* Magazine Design Prize, Stockholm, 1986; Design Excellence Award, Swedish Society of Crafts and Design, 1986, 1992. **Address:** Johannesgatan 26, 111 38 Stockholm, Sweden.

## Works

*Everyday* tableware, for Gustavsberg, 1957.
Ceramic murals, for Nacka Hospital, Sweden, 1962.
Ceramic murals, for the Mariatorget underground station, Stockholm, 1963.
Ceramic murals, for SKS offices, Göteborg, Sweden, 1966.
Ceramic fountains, for the municipality of Valbo, Sweden, 1967.
*Octagon* tableware, for Gustavsberg, 1968.
Ceramic murals, for Löwenströmska Hospital, Göteborg, Sweden, 1968.
Ceramic mural, for the *Arbetet* newspaper offices, Malmö, Sweden, 1968.
Ceramic mural, for Österåker prison, Sweden, 1970.
Ceramic murals and fountains, for Östrabo School, Uddevalla, Sweden, 1970.
Ceramic mural, for the *Aftonbladet* newspaper offices, Göteborg, Sweden, 1970.
Ceramic stove, for the Swedish Embassy, Moscow, 1970.
Ceramic stove, for the Swedish Embassy, Paris, 1973.
BT stoneware, for Gustavsberg, 1973-82.
*Octavius* stoneware, for Gustavsberg, 1974.
Ceramic mural, for the Sveriges Riksbank, Stockholm, 1975-76.
BV bone chinaware, for Gustavsberg, 1978.
BV stoneware, for Gustavsberg, 1979.
BA *Stockholm* bone chinaware, for Gustavsberg, 1987.
Ceramic murals for the Sturebadet public baths, Stockholm, 1988.
*Nobel* service in bone china, designed for the Nobel Banquet for Rörstrand-Hackman AB, 1991.
Damask tablecloths for an official gift to King Carl XVI Gustav on the 20th anniversary of his coronation, 1992.
Tableware in bone china, for the Royal Palace, Stockholm, 1993-96.

## Publications

**On BJÖRQUIST: books**—*Svensk Form/Forma Sueca* by Åke Stavenow and Åke H. Huldt, Stockholm, 1961; *Karin Björquist of Gustavsberg,* booklet edited by Georg Jensen Inc., New York, 1965; *Design in Sweden* edited by Lennart Lindkvist, Stockholm, 1972, 1977, *Scandinavian Design: Objects of a Life Style* by Eileene Harrison Beer, New York, 1975; *Konsthantvek, Konstindustri, Design 1875-1975* by Dag Widman, Stockholm, 1975; *Keramik* by

Ulf Härd af Segerstad, Stockholm, 1976; *Scandinavian Modern Design 1880-1980* edited by David Revere McFadden, New York, 1982; *Contemporary Swedish Design,* exhibition catalogue by Monica Boman, Lennart Lindkvist, and others, Stockholm, 1982; *Serviser från Gustavsberg* by Inga Arnö-Berg, Stockholm, 1985; *The Lunning Prize,* exhibition catalogue edited by Helena Dahlbäck Lutteman and Marianne Uggla, Stockholm, 1986; *Made in Sweden: Art, Handicrafts, Design* by Anja Notini, London, 1987; *Faces of Swedish Design,* exhibition catalogue edited by Monica Boman, Stockholm, 1988; *Karin Björquist Formgivare* by Arthur Hald-Hedwig Hedqvist, Stockholm.

\*

Since the world today is so full of products, it is important that designers create meaningful articles. Above all, it is important to accept the age one lives in, to be neither nostalgic nor hypnotized by passing fashions.

—Karin Björquist

\*   \*   \*

In principle Karin Björquist works in only one field: ceramics. And she prefers working for mass production. Karin had already opted for industry when she graduated: "I wanted the anonymous."

Some prototypes of her "Everyday" service were presented at the Helsingborg exhibition H55 in 1955. This service had everything one could ask for. "Everyday" is pure and practical, yet nonetheless friendly and human. Since then, Karin Björquist has produced many variants of her excellent base products. Her services usually tend to be white. The decorations she has occasionally added are simple and discrete, especially for services. Superimposing a fish on something sky blue or patterned does not fit in with Karin's philosophy. Her ceramic output is simple and self-evident. In a way it is eternally youthful. But the fact is that she is acquiring the status of the great classicists, though she wears the mantle lightly. With more than 30 years' good and prominent output behind her, she cannot help becoming something of a historical figure. Don't make any mistake: with her working methods, she is more up-to-date than most others.

Karin Björquist is not afraid of simplicity. But she combines it with a purity and practicality which are poles apart from the dryness and dogmatism that functionalism can sometimes lapse into. Hers is not a clinical purity but a simplicity full of affection and feeling. Moreover, she has passed through a process of development, today emphasizing things which she did not use to. It is partly due to her sterling contribution that baseware has become more of a self-evident phenomenon. Now there are other things to be brought out—our perpetual need of a feast for the eye, for example. She herself says that one becomes less dogmatic with advancing age. But this change is also connected with the attainment of ambitions, added to the realization that beauty is one of the essentials of life.

Who can lay a table with such inspiration as Karin? Who can make such wonderful floral arrangements? Generous bunches of the driest straws or overwhelmingly magnificent lilies and roses help us to understand how fine her jardinieres and pots are. When Karin lays the table for a meal, she naturally uses her own service, but she likes to add items by kindred spirits in her arrangements or collages. Gunnar Wennerberg's hepatica decorations from the turn of the century fit well into her world. So do pictures of English gardens, in which the correct flowers thrive together with beautiful stones and shells. And, of course, the ceramics of Wilhelm Kåge.

Karin inherited Kåge's studio at Gustavsberg. He was her great predecessor, active from 1917 until his death in 1960. He introduced "Argenta"—silver ornamentation on a green background. In 1987 Karin took up this special technique in her own way: silver strips on large dishes with folded brims, on the edges of spouts, and as a silver accentuation on the feet of shell-shaped vessels. Karin's color scale is black, white, or pale tints with silver or gold. Kåge can be discerned in the background as a source of inspiration. The strict forms of the Empire style which so well suit the late 1980s may also be in the background. Or is it only Karin Björquist?

There is a great deal of responsibility involved in producing new things when so many exist already. But this does not lead her to refrain from new production. Everything has to be properly thought out. And, of course, the production of a new service nowadays is an immense undertaking. It may take years. The task is not only to devise an attractive new form, or to combine saleable parts into a whole: the starting point is the existence of a need.

It is quite an experience listening to Karin's deliberations about new restaurant tableware. Strength and stackability are fairly obvious requirements, but there is also the need for light weight—to save the backs of the waiting staff—refinements of manufacturing technique, and the overall appearance of the finished product. This is how classics are made.

In 1986 Karin Björquist's new bone china service was given the award for Excellent Swedish Design by the Swedish Society of Crafts and Design. The jury said that "the service skillfully utilizes the possibilities of bone china for combining strength with thinness and elegance. The design is pure and universal, and carries the decoration well. The functions are well tested. This service may become a classic."

It is an elegant service for formal use, with sparse decoration in black and gold by Jonas Lindkvist or her own celadon green brim accentuated by thin gold edges. Even such a representative of simplicity and basic function as Karin Björquist can be seen in the 1980s as showy and retrospective. Because what is the celadon decoration "Paris" if not a look at the 1930s, the decade of *art déco*? Karin knows she has done right in creating a formal service. The need is there—she feels this herself—so why should we accept anything less than the very best?

—Helena Dahlbäck Lutteman


# BLACK, Misha

British architect, exhibition, and industrial designer

**Born:** Baku, Azerbaydzhan, Russia, 16 October 1910; emigrated to Britain in 1912, subsequently naturalized. **Education:** Studied at Central School of Arts and Crafts, London, but mainly self-taught in design, from 1929. **Family:** Married Helen Lilian Evans in 1935 (divorced, 1952); children: Jacob and Julia; married Edna Joan Fairbrother in 1955; children: Oliver. **Career:** Architect and designer, in London, from 1929; partner, Industrial Design Partnership, 1933-39; principal exhibition architect, Ministry of Information, 1940-45; founder-partner, with Milner Gray Design Research Unit, 1945-77; partner, in Black, Bayes and Gibson architects,

1963-77; design consultant to the Gas, Light and Coke Company, Kardomah Limited, Tea Bureau, Festival of Britain, British Overseas Airways Corporation, British Railways Board, Beagle Aircraft, London Transport, South Wales Switchgear Limited, Vickers Limited, Hong Kong Rapid Transit Railways, and others. Professor of Industrial Design, 1959-75, Emeritus, 1975-77, Royal College of Art, London. **Member:** Chairman, Artists International Association, London, 1934-40; council member, 1938-52 and 1956-57, and president, 1954-56, Society of Industrial Artists and Designers, London; advisory council member, Society of Education in Art, London, 1942-59, and Institute of Contemporary Arts, London, 1951-67; national council member, 1952-54, and president, 1974-76, Design and Industries Association, London; member, Council of Industrial Design, London, 1955-64; executive board member, 1957-65, president, 1959-61, and Education Commission Chairman, 1965-69, ICSID, International Council of Societies of Industrial Design; vice-president, Modular Society, London, 1965-77; advisory council member, Science Museum, London, 1966-77; trustee, 1968-77, and Conservation Committee Chairman, 1974-77, British Museum, London; member, 1969-77, and chairman, 1973-77, Culture Advisory Committee, United Kingdom Commission for UNESCO; council member, Polytechnic of Newcastle-upon-Tyne, 1969-73; Engineering Design Advisory Committee Member, Design Council, London, 1971-74; Scientific Advisory Committee Member, Experimental Cartography Unit (NERC), London, 1973-75; Master of the Faculty of Royal Designers for Industry, Royal Society of Arts, London, 1973-75; Engineering Section President, British Association for the Advancement of Science, London, 1974; National Theatre Advisory Committee Member, London, 1974-76. **Honors:** Fellow, 1945, and Gold Medal, 1965, Society of Industrial Artists, London; Officer, Order of the British Empire, 1945; Designer for Industry, Royal Society of Arts, London, 1957; Fellow, Royal College of Art, London, 1960; Companion of the Institute of Mechanical Engineers, London, 1969; Knight Bachelor, 1972; Fellow, Faculty of Architects and Surveyors, London, 1974. Honorary Doctorates: Royal College of Art London, 1968; University of Bradford, 1974. **Died:** London, 11 August 1977.


**Works**

Pavilion at the Spanish-American Exhibition in Seville, for Rio-Tinto, 1929.

Kardomah Coffee bars in London and Manchester, for the Liverpool and China Tea Company Limited, 1936-50.

Peace Pavilion interiors, at the International Exposition, Paris, 1937.

Interiors of the United Kingdom Steel, Coal, Shipbuilding, and Public Welfare Halls, at the Empire Exhibition, Glasgow, 1938.

British Pavilion Public Welfare and Maritime Halls, at the World's Fair, New York, 1939.

*The Birth of an Egg-Cup* display, at the *Britain Can Make It* exhibition, Victoria and Albert Museum, London, 1946.

Regatta Restaurant and Dome of Discovery displays, at the Festival of Britain, London, 1948-51.

*Darkness into Daylight exhibition* layouts, Science Museum, London, 1948.

United Kingdom Pavilion, at the Rhodes Centenary Exhibition, Bulawayo, Southern Rhodesia, 1953.

Public rooms interiors on the liner *Oriana,* for Pacific and Orient Shipping Company, 1957-60.

Ontario Government Pavilion at *Expo 67,* Montreal, 1966-67.

Charles Clore Pavilion mammal house at London Zoo, for the Zoological Society, 1967.

Synagogue interiors on the liner *Queen Elizabeth 2,* for Cunard Shipping, 1969.

## Publications

**By BLACK: books**—(with others) *Physical Planning,* London, 1945; (with others) *The Practice of Design,* London, 1946; (editor) *Exhibition Design,* London, 1950; (editor) *Public Interiors: An International Survey,* London, 1960; *The Architect's Anguish,* Leicester, 1962; (with others) *Group Practice of Design,* London, 1967; (editor) *Industrial Design—An International Survey,* London and Paris, 1967; *The Misha Black Australian Papers* edited by Trevor Wilson, Sydney, 1970; *Papers on Design: Selected Writings* edited by A. Blake, Oxford, 1983.

**On BLACK: books**—*Modern Furniture* by E. Nelson Exton and Frederic H. Littman, London, 1936; *Design in British Industry: A Mid-Century Survey* by Michael Farr, Cambridge, 1955; *Window Display 2* edited by Walter Herdeg, Zurich, 1961; *Modern Graphics* by Keith Murgatroyd, London, 1969; *The Aspen Papers: Twenty Years of Design Theory* edited by Reyner Banham, London, 1974; *A Tonic to the Nation: The Festival of Britain 1951* by Mary Banham and Bevis Hillier, London, 1976; *Industrial Design* by John Heskett, London, 1980; *Misha Black* by Avril Blake, London, 1984; *The Conran Directory of Design* edited by Stephen Bayley, London, 1985; *Eye for Industry: Royal Designers for Industry 1936-1986,* exhibition catalogue by Fiona MacCarthy and Patrick Nuttgens, London, 1986; *Design Source Book* by Penny Sparke and others, London, 1986.

\*   \*   \*

Fluent and highly articulate, Misha Black favoured radical but pragmatic solutions to design problems. "The difference between an arrogant, conscious aesthetic and a conscientious searching for the most elegant solution is fundamental to my argument," he said. Black was the champion of many causes, from the prewar, left-wing Artists International Association to the most august, postwar International Council of Societies of Industrial Design. He relished the challenge of exhibition design, with its opportunity to express complex ideas in fresh and straightforward ways, its problems of coordinating a team of different skills, its pressures of limited time and resources, and its chance to present temporary, showcase solutions to a number of design problems. In his hands, a deceptively simple exhibition on the making of an eggcup (at the *Britain Can Make It* exhibition of 1946) became a revealing object-lesson on the problems confronting the designer of a simple, mass-produced object and on the necessary stages of industrial production.

This ability to design with simplicity and ingenuity but not extravagance made him a popular choice with cost-conscious organisations wishing to improve their corporate images and public places. His prewar designs, ranging from radios to the highly regarded Kardomah cafes, had already established a reputation for elegant combination of simple elements. Many of the larger projects that followed owed much to his ability to coordinate and enthuse designers and clients. His long association with Milner Gray before and after the Industrial Design Partnership (founded in the 1930s as

the first multi-skill design partnership) and through the privations of wartime exhibition work laid the foundations for the highly innovative and successful postwar Design Research Unit, which they led. As well as building up a large portfolio of architectural work, interior design commissions, and consultancies with large organisations, such as British Rail, he became passionately involved with his later role as a teacher at the Royal College of Art. There he was very important in developing contacts with industry and industrial research. This helped to change the basic training of many future industrial designers. Within his own profession and on public advisory bodies, he was much in demand for his skills as a chairman; he possessed the knack of extracting the essence of ideas, the ability to control unruly meetings with humour and purpose, and a talent for drawing together the threads of an argument and translating discussion into positive action.

—Anthony J. Coulson

# BLAICH, Robert I(an)

American design director

**Born:** Syracuse, New York, 25 February 1930. **Education:** Studied architecture, Syracuse University, New York, BFA, 1952. **Family:** Married Janet Streithof in 1953; children: Robert, David, and James. **Career:** Designer, 1953-60, manager of Special Products Division, 1960-68, vice president, Corporate Design and Communications, 1968-79, Herman Miller Inc., Zeeland, Michigan; also managing director, Herman Miller AG, Basle, Switzerland, 1969-70; founder/president, Connectives Inc., communications and design consultants, Grand Rapids, Michigan, 1979-80; senior managing director of Corporate Design, Philips Electronics N.V., Eindhoven, Netherlands, 1980-92; founder/president, Blaich Associates, Design Management Consultants, Aspen, Colorado, from 1992; clients have included Philips Electronics N.V., China External Trade Council, Taiwan, Texas Instruments, Philip Morris, Abbott Laboratories, Hewlett Packard, and Steelcase. Board or panel member, National Endowment for the Arts, Washington, D.C., 1968-78, Michigan Council for the Arts, 1976-78, Cranbrook Academy of Art, Bloomfield Hills, Michigan, 1976-78, London Business School, from 1982, Formica Corporation, 1984-86, Art Center College of Design, Vevey, Switzerland, from 1984, Design Management Institute, Boston, 1987-91, Institute of Design, Illinois Institute of Technology, Chicago, from 1989, American Center for Design, 1989-94, International Design Education Foundation, from 1990, International Design Conference, Aspen, from 1991, Finnish Design Management Institute; trustee, Kendall School of Design, Grand Rapids, Michigan, 1970-75, Grand Rapids Art Museum, Michigan, 1970-80, and American Federation of Arts, New York, 1975-80; chairman, Design Michigan Program, 1977-78; vice president, 1983, and president, 1987, International Council of Societies of Industrial Design (ICSID); visiting lecturer and speaker, at numerous universities, congresses, and professional institutes, in Europe and the United States, from 1980; professor of design leadership, University of Art and Design, Helsinki, from 1990. **Member:** Industrial Designers Society of America, 1967; American Society of Interior Designers, 1975; American Institute of Graphic Arts, 1978; Kring Industriele Ontwerpers, Netherlands, 1981. **Exhibitions:** *Design in Michigan 1967/1977,* Cranbrook Academy of Art, Bloomfield

Hills, Michigan, 1978 (toured); *New Design for Old,* Boilerhouse/Victoria and Albert Museum, London, 1986; *Natural Design,* Boilerhouse/Victoria and Albert Museum, London, 1986; *Natural Design,* Museum Boymans-van Beuningen, Rotterdam, 1987; *Mondo Materialis: Exploration and Celebration into Research and Materials,* Cooper-Hewitt Museum, 1990 (toured); *The Philips Collection,* Centre Georges Pompidou, Paris, and Vitra Museum, Weil am Rhein, Germany, 1991; *The Art of Design,* Marquette University, Milwaukee, Wisconsin, 1993. **Collections:** Museum of Modern Art, New York; Die Neue Sammlung, München; Design Museum, London; Boubourg, Paris. **Honors:** Governor's Recognition Award, Michigan, 1977; commendation, 4th Federal Assembly, Washington, D.C., 1978; fellow, Industrial Designers Society of America, 1981; fellow, Royal Society of Arts, London, 1982; President's Trophy, International Council of Graphic Design Associations (ICOGRADA), 1983; *Time* magazine Man of the Year Award, 1984; Worldesign Medal, IDSA, 1990; honorary doctorate, Syracuse University, New York, 1990; fellow, Society of Designers in South Africa, 1990; Design 100 Award, *Metropolitan Home* magazine, 1990; Ambassador, Kring Industriele Ontwerpers, Netherlands, 1991; knighted officer in the Order of Oranje Nassau by Queen Beatrix of the Netherlands, 1991; fellow, Design Institute of Australia, 1994. **Address:** Blaich Associates, 319 North Fourth Street, Aspen, Colorado 81611, U.S.A.

**Works** (as director of design):

All Charles Eames products, for Herman Miller, 1960-78.
All George Nelson products, for Herman Miller, 1960-78.
All Alexander Girard textiles, for Herman Miller, 1960-78.
Action Office System, for Herman Miller, 1964-78.
Chadwick Seating, for Herman Miller, 1971.
Ergon Seating, for Herman Miller, 1972.
Wilkes Seating, for Herman Miller, 1972.
Burdick Office System, for Herman Miller, 1979.
All products, systems, packaging and graphics, for N. V. Philips, 1980-92.

**Publications**

**By BLAICH: books**—(with Janet Blaich) *Product Design and Corporate Strategy,* New York, 1992; *New and Notable Product Design II,* Rockport, Massachusetts, 1995; **articles**—"Design: The Best of '83" in *Time* (New York), January 1984; "Design as a Corporate Strategy" in *Design Talks* edited by Peter Gorb, London, 1988; "Corporate Industrial Design" in *Interieur 8* (conference booklet), Brussels, 1988; numerous articles in *ICSID News* (Helsinki), 1988-89; "Design—A Personal Account" in *Design Issues* (Cambridge, Massachusetts), Spring 1989; "Philips Is Not Guilty of Design Imperialism" in *Designweek* (London), 26 May 1989.

**On BLAICH: books**—*The Design of Herman Miller* by Ralph Caplan, New York, 1976; *Design in Michigan 1967/1977* by Katherine McCoy, Detroit, 1978; *Industrial Design* by John Heskett, New York, 1980; *New Design for Old,* exhibition catalogue with texts by Helen Hamlyn, Eric Midwinter, and others, London, 1986; *The Design Dimension: Product Strategy and the Challenge of Global Marketing* by Christopher Lorenz, Oxford and New York, 1986; *Holland in Vorm: Dutch Design, 1945-1987* ed-ited by Gert Staal and Hester Wolters, Amsterdam, 1987; *Philips: A Study of Corporate Management Design* by John Heskett, London, 1989; *World Design: Nationalism and Globalism in Design* by Hugh Aldersey-Williams, New York, 1992; **articles**—in *The Wall Street Journal* (New York), 13 January 1988; *Designweek* (London), 21 April 1989.

*

In his book *Nelson Design,* the late architect and designer George Nelson said, "The designer is the latest of the human resources available to business in its eternal struggle to remain successfully competitive. Design is seen as a legitimate and effective tool for business and industry."

The premise that design has an important strategic role to play in business management is one that is still relatively unexplored by most businesses and underutilized by all but a few companies worldwide. Perhaps some of the problem begins with failure to make a connection between design and innovation. Indeed, there seem to be differing opinions about what constitutes innovation.

Christopher Lorenz, management editor of *The Financial Times,* states: "Good product design includes ease of manufacture, marketability, maintenance, reliable performance, and cost effectiveness to both producer and user. Of course it includes a well-designed exterior ... most often referred to as 'styling.'" Too often design and styling have been seen as synonymous. Actually, styling traditionally has represented a much more limited set of activities in the final phase in a sequential development process, after all the important decisions have already been made.

However, the Japanese gave a new interpretation to the concept of styling in their success with consumer electronics. They did not invent the technologies. These came from the United States and Europe. But the Japanese were innovative in their application of design, which in this case was styling, and in their marketing. The difference had to do with the process. The Japanese integrated the design activity into the whole process of market strategy and product development at the initial stages. In this sense, styling was innovative.

I can best analyze the design management process by telling you something about my own experiences. Although educated as an architect, I gravitated towards industrial design and communications design and have developed experience in design management over a 40 year period. I was associated with Herman Miller for 27 years and with Philips for 12. Even though what I was doing during the 40 year period was design management, it has only been recently—about the past ten years—that design management has been defined as an activity. Design management is a relatively new element in design professionalism, growing out of the recognition of increasingly sophisticated interaction with other areas of corporate planning and implementation. Successful innovations are essentially impossible today without an interrelationship between engineering, marketing, manufacturing, and design. Design management establishes the possibility that a company has a design program instead of an informal activity.

As the managing director of Philips Corporate Design (PCD), it was my responsibility to ensure that design was an integral part of the company's strategy and policy. PCD was and is responsible for the design, graphics, and packaging of all Philips' products for consumer electronics, domestic appliances, personal care, lighting, telecommunications, data systems, medical systems, and scientific and industrial equipment. Our goal was to produce the highest quality designs of which we were capable.

**Robert Blaich: "Philips Collection," designed to celebrate Philips Electronics N.V. centenary in 1991**

To accomplish this the design management process involved not only ensuring that PCD achieved its goal of producing high-quality designs, but that the design value added to the product was seamlessly and efficiently integrated into the entire design-to-market process so that the corporate goal of producing top-quality products could be achieved. Thus, the design management process is very largely about managing to achieve quality results. The design attributes of a product constitute a value that is quickly observable to consumers.

I believe that the product is the most important statement a company can make about its image—it is the image.

—Robert I. Blaich

\*     \*     \*

In the best possible sense, Robert Ian Blaich represents the transformation of a competent design manager into a corporate design director with a broadened perspective of the global importance of design and a personal conviction of a designer's social and cultural responsibilities.

In 1952, after receiving a BFA degree from Syracuse University in Syracuse, New York, he accepted a position in New York city where he became familiar with show-casing and marketing aspects of furniture. From there he joined Herman Miller Company of Zeeland, Michigan, manufacturers of modern furniture, that was expanding into products and product systems for institutional and office environments. The company appointed him in 1960 to manage its Special Products Division for new product development for educational and institutional fields. He worked directly with consultant designers such as Robert Propst, George Nelson, Charles

Eames, and Alexander Girard to develop and bring to market new furniture systems for storage and seating for schools, libraries, and business offices.

In 1968 Blaich became Vice President of Design and Development for Herman Miller and was given responsibility for long range product planning and development. In this position, Blaich searched for and developed new designers for the company's products and its facilities, from administration and manufacturing to offices and showrooms of the corporation in the United States and abroad. After 1976 his responsibility expanded to include Corporate Design and Communications related to the image and presentation of Herman Miller to its various publics. Between 1969 and 1970 he also served as Managing Director of Herman Miller A.G. at Basle, Switzerland, developing new design resources and introducing new products and systems into European markets.

On the public service side of his career, by the mid 1970s Robert Blaich was active in Washington as a member of selection panels reviewing applicants for grants from the National Endowment for the Arts. Over the period of celebration of the nation's Bicentennial in 1976, Federal Design Assemblies were held in Washington to focus the attention of elected officials and career employees of the government on design as an indispensable element in the quality and image of the federal government in the eyes of the public at home and abroad. An outcome of this was that Blaich initiated a similar program, Design Michigan, in his home state to increase an awareness of the designed environment among government and business people as well as the general public.

Robert Blaich elected to leave his position with Herman Miller in 1979 in order to establish Connectives, Inc., an independent organization offering consulting services in corporate communications, publishing, graphics, product design, interiors, and marketing. This move as well as his public service and the range of his experience with Herman Miller brought him to the attention of the Philips

Company of the Netherlands, which was seeking for a new director to reorganize its design activities on a global basis. The result was an offer from Philips that was too challenging to pass up.

In 1980, Robert Blaich became Director of Design for the Philips Company in charge of product and packaging design for all of the company's product divisions. In this capacity he was instrumental in restructuring the design programs to facilitate the design and development of products on a global scale, thus anticipating the entire company's shift to a global strategy. In order to implement this program, Blaich organized design workshops and seminars that brought outside consultants into a working and communicating relationship with internal designers and technicians of the design center on such subjects as youth markets, user interface, product semantics, and communications in product design. Another program of the Center invited internationally recognized speakers to share their special expertise.

Blaich organized the Professional Harmonization Program in 1986, which brought all of the Philips professional products for Telecommunications and Data systems, Test and Measurement, and Medical Systems under a professional house style that integrated all related products. This program was awarded the 1st prize for Ergonomics at *Ergodesign 86* in Montreaux, Switzerland. In addition to this award, the Philips Company received over 250 prizes under Blaich's leadership.

In 1992, Blaich left Philips to found his own design strategy and management consulting firm, Blaich Associates, in Aspen, Colorado. His new position has allowed him time to write several books, including *Product Design and Corporate Strategy* and *New and Notable Product Design II*. In the former, Blaich attempts to account for the increased attention paid to design by corporations worldwide. "Designers, educators, and business leaders have the design challenge in their midst now," he writes. "Some companies are well on their way to mastering design management. Those who haven't will either learn or fall behind in their competitive advantage. It should be sufficient warning that the Japanese government declared 1989 the Year of Design. The hour for mastering the management of design ... is already late."

—Arthur J. Pulos

# BLASE, Karl Oskar

German book, advertising, display, packaging, and typographic designer

**Born:** Cologne, 24 March 1925. **Education:** Studied design, Staatliche Werkkunstschule, Wuppertal, 1945-49. **Military Service:** Served in the German Army, 1944-45. **Family:** Married Margarete Speckenbach in 1952; sons: Christoph, Boris, and Benjamin. **Career:** Worked as design assistant, Jupp Ernst Studio, Wuppertal, 1949-50; founder/partner, with Felix Muller, of Muller-Blase Studio, Wuppertal, 1950-52; director, Amerika-Haus graphics studio, in Frankfurt, 1952-54, and in Bonn, 1954-58; also freelance designer, in Bonn, 1954-58, and in Kassel, from 1958; worked for *Form* magazine, 1957-60, Hessische Metallwerke, 1958-74, Atlas Film Distributors, 1959-66, Igus textile company, from 1963, Kassel *Documenta* exhibitions, from 1964, and Kassel Staatstheater, 1966-78; Art Consultant to the German Postal Ser-

vice, 1988. Founder-Member, Novum Gesellschaft für Neue Graphik, Frankfurt, 1959. Professor of Applied Arts, Kunstakademie, Kassel, from 1958. **Member:** Deutscher Werkbund, Cologne, 1952; Alliance Graphique Internationale, 1964. **Exhibitions:** Museum Schloss Morsbroich, Leverkusen, 1952; Kunstsammlungen, Bonn, 1958, 1969; Landesmuseum, Oldenburg, 1965; Kunstverein, Kassel, 1967, 1984, 1986; Kunstverein, Bonn, 1974; Haus am Lutzowplatz, West Berlin, 1981; Kunstverein, Offenbach, 1983; Galerie Circulus, Bonn, 1984; Kunsthaus am Museum, Cologne, 1986; Gesellschaft für Kunst und Gestaltung, Bonn, 1987; Mönchehaus Museum, Goslar, 1987; *Graphik-Design Karl Oskar Blase,* Galerie für Industrie-Design, Lippstadt, 1989; *Graphik-Design Karl Oskar Blase,* Gesellschaft für Kunst und Gestaltung, Bonn, 1990; *Karl Oskar Blase Zeichnungen,* Staatliche Museen Kassel, Kassel, 1992; *Karl Oskar Blase Grafik-Design 1949-1995,* Kasseler Kunstverein, Kassel, and Deutsches Plakatmuseum, Essen, 1995. **Collections:** Städtische Kunstsammlungen, Bonn; Städtisches Museum, Leverkusen; Staatliche Museen Kassel, Kassel; Landesmuseum, Oldenburg; Staatliche Museum, West Berlin; Neue Sammlung, Munich; Deutsches Plakatmuseum, Essen; Stedelijk Museum, Amsterdam; University of California, Berkeley. **Honors:** Best German Poster Prize, 1956, 1957, 1958, 1961, 1965, 1966, 1976, 1980; Gold Medal, Milan Triennale, 1957; First Prize, Fédération Internationale de la Presse Périodique, Rome, 1965. **Address:** Kuhbergstrasse 47, D-34131 Kassel, Germany.

## Works

Exhibition posters, for Amerika-Haus, in Frankfurt and Bonn, 1953-58.

55 postal stamp designs, for the Deutsche Bundespost, Bonn, 1955-88.

*Form* magazine design, for Westdeutscher Verlag, Opladen, 1957-68.

Logotype, packaging, and poster design, for Hessische Metallwerke, Schwalmstadt, 1958-74.

Display stand at the Düsseldorf Kunststoffmesse, for Bayer Farbenfabriken, Leverkusen, 1959.

Film posters, for Atlas Filmverleih, Duisburg, 1959-66.

German displays at the Turin International Exposition, for the Bundesarbeitsministerium, Bonn, 1961.

Corporate design, for Igus textile firm, Bergisch-Gladbach, 1963-89.

*Graphic Design—Documenta III* exhibition layouts, for the Documenta Organization, Kassel, 1964.

Theatre posters, for the Staatstheater, Kassel, 1966-78.

*Documenta 4* poster and catalogue, for the Documenta Organization, Kassel, 1968.

*Baumpate—Grün ist Leben* action/demonstration designs, for the cities of Berlin and Kassel, 1976-81.

*Documenta 6* poster and catalogue, for the Documenta Organization, Kassel, 1977.

*Documenta 8* visual images, for the Documenta Organization, Kassel, 1987.

Corporate design, for Stadtsparkasse Kassel, Kassel, from 1987.

Corporate design, for the Kasseler Musiktage, Kassel, 1988-89.

Corporate design, for Kultursommer Nordhessen, Kassel, 1989.

Corporate design, for EAM Energie-Aktiengessellschaft Mitteldeutschland, Kassel, from 1991.

## Publications

**By BLASE: books**—*Bodies and Stripes Variations, Karl Oskar Blase,* Kassel, 1966; *Arnold Bode zum 75. Geburstag,* Kassel, 1975; *Bonner Politiker-Porträts,* Kassel, 1979; *Karl Oskar Blase, Briefmarken-Design,* Cuxhagen, 1981; *Torso als Prinzip,* Kassel, 1982; *Karl Oskar Blase, Texte über Kunst und Visuelle Kommunikation,* Münich, 1991.

**On BLASE: books**—*Who's Who in Graphic Art* edited by Walter Amstutz, Zürich, 1962, Dubendorf, 1982; *German Advertising Art* edited by Eberhard Holscher, Münich, 1967; *Karl Oskar Blase,* exhibition catalogue with text by Alfred Nemeczek, Kassel, 1967; *Karl Oskar Blase,* exhibition catalogue with text by Rolf-Gunter Dienst, Wuppertal, 1968; *Monographie des Plakats* by Herbert Schindler, Stuttgart, 1978; *AGI Posters 1961-1985* edited by Rudolph de Harak, New York, 1986; *Karl Oskar Blase, Zeichnungen von 1964-1967 und 1989-1991,* exhibition catalogue with text by Ulrich Schmidt and Manfred Schneckenburger, Kassel, 1992; *Karl Oskar Blase Grafik-Design von 1949 bis 1995,* exhibition catalogue with text by Walfried Pohl and Frieder Mellinghoff, Köln, 1995.

*

"Doing graphic design" and "painting pictures"; I have always looked at these two apparently dissimilar kinds of art as a single activity, as a unity. The informative aim of a poster for example certainly demands more dependence and more restriction in relation to the desire for freedom of design, but it also provokes a clear, possibly distinct expression. But it is also the "art of the art" to work out what verbal language only imperfectly achieves, and there is the opportunity of working up subjective experiences which one can assume will be perceived by many as new information.

However obvious this formulated unity of graphic design and "free" art may appear, in professional reality it often comes up against a deep-rooted opposition. Keeping them separate is particularly cultivated in the German culture lobby. And for many artists of such a divided art, the decision in favor of a perhaps one-track stylistic form as a necessary prerequisite in the recipe for success sets in at an early stage, frequently even during studies.

As both these categories have to some extent had a dual influence on my work, my stylistic intention remains free from overly doctrinaire limitations. Yet in constructive compositions, I use the available artistic possibilities and media. I use illustrative drawing and systematic typography, painting and photography, according to the desired effect. Looking back on my work, I find in spite of the multiplicity an always recognizable structural concept and a constructive artistic element.

There remains my theoretical interest in aesthetic questions which expresses itself in a collection of smaller and larger statements. Problems of visual communication, of modern art, of our contemporary aesthetic, and of social and political relations are their subjects. In my recent pictures, I also include theoretical matters: "upheaval/radical change pictures" are on the one hand recognizable as text and lay-out pictures, but also as trivial images from books and newspapers or simply as pictures.

—Karl Oskar Blase

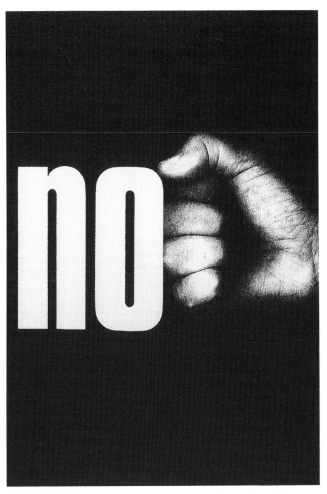

**Karl Oscar Blase: poster against violence for AGI, 1995**

In the 1950s and 1960s, Karl Oskar Blase was among the important graphic talents in Germany—especially in poster design. In 1956, his poster "American Primitive" received the Bund Deutscher Graphiker prize for best poster of the year, followed in subsequent years by many further distinctions.

Formal versatility and great sensitivity apply in all areas of his extensive work: stamp design, packaging, and exhibition design. Blase's works can never be arranged in a narrow order, just as he largely evades categories of period style. Clarity of expression is combined with great graphic talent. The penetrating effect of his works results mainly from an equilibrium between text and image. They are in harmony, enhance each other mutually, and are immediately understandable. The function of the visual image can, however, be taken over by a graphic symbol—as, for example, in the poster for the 1961 Turin Labour Exhibition. His packaging for Peter Raacke's Mono cutlery, designed in 1968, has still lost nothing of its clear, simple beauty. For *Documenta 4* in 1968, Blase developed a logo based on a design which could also serve as a signpost, indicator board, or entrance ticket. In this way, this great international art exhibition, taking place every four years, received an optical image sufficient to its exhibitors and distinguished by a great visual significance.

Blase draws on many ideas for his graphic works from his paintings. In his work as teacher at the Kassel Academy, he continues the tradition of the "Kassel School" which, in postwar Germany, developed into a centre of gravity for modern poster design.

—Magdalena Droste

# BLASS, Bill
American fashion designer

**Born:** William Ralph Blass, in Fort Wayne, Indiana, 22 June 1922. **Education:** Attended Fort Wayne High School, 1936-39; studied fashion design, Parsons School of Design, New York, 1939. **Military Service:** Served in the United States Army, 1941-44, Sergeant. **Career:** Sketch artist, David Crystal Sportwear, New York, 1940-41; designer, Anna Miller and Company Limited, New York, 1945; designer, 1959-70, and vice-president, 1961-70, of Maurice Rentner Limited, New York; owner-director, Bill Blass Limited (took over Rentner Limited), from 1970; licensed products include menswear, women's sportswear, Vogue Patterns, candies, furs, swimwear, jeans, bedlinens, towels, shoes, loungewear, perfumes, and an automobile. **Collections:** Metropolitan Museum of Art, New York; Indianapolis Museum of Art, Indiana; Phoenix Museum of Art, Arizona. **Honors:** American Fashion Critics (Winnie) Award, 1961, 1963, 1970, Menswear Award, 1968, Fashion Hall of Fame Award, 1970, and Special Citations, 1971, 1982, 1983, Coty, New York; Gold Coast Fashion Award, Chicago, 1965; Cotton Council Award, New York, 1965; Neiman-Marcus Award, 1969; Print Council Award, 1971; Martha Award, New York, 1974; honorary doctorate, Rhode Island School of Design, Providence, 1977; Ayres Look Award, 1978; *Gentleman's Quarterly* Manstyle Award, New York, 1979; Cutty Sark Hall of Fame Award, New York, 1979. **Address:** 550 Seventh Avenue, New York, New York 10018, U.S.A.

## Publications

**On BLASS: books**—*The Fashionable Savages* by John Fairchild, New York, 1965; *With Tongue in Chic* by Ernestine Carter, London, 1974; *Fashion: The Changing Shape of Fashion Through the Years* by Jane Dorner, London, 1974; *20th Century Fashion: A Scrapbook 1900 to Today* by Ernestine Carter, London, 1975; *A History of Fashion* by J. Anderson Black and Madge Garland, London, 1975, 1980; *The Changing World of Fashion: 1900 to the Present* by Ernestine Carter, London, 1977; *The Contemporary Decorative Arts from 1940 to the Present Day* by Philippe Garner, London, 1980; *McDowell's Directory of Twentieth Century Fashion* by Colin McDowell, London, 1984; *The Encyclopaedia of Fashion from 1840 to the 1980s* by Georgina O'Hara, London, 1986.

*     *     *

American fashion designer Bill Blass learned his craft and developed his approach in New York's garment district, where he made his way from sketch artist in 1940 to owner of Bill Blass Limited in 1970. His work concentrates on ready-to-wear outfitting for an elegant and worldly social class and cultivated for the Seventh Avenue scene, which had always made clothing for mass-market consumers. Blass's approach includes the interaction of the designer with his clientele; he furthered the role of the fashion designer as a

socially desirable friend and guest, practicing his idea that one must see how the rich live in order to make the proper clothing for them. His designs for women's evening wear are, as a result, extremely glamorous and filled with feminine touches such as ruffles and laces. His sportswear division, Blassport, produces a classic, tweedy look for women and men alike, using men's fabrics for both, maintaining a coordinated packaging from top to bottom.

Blass has been the recipient of numerous awards, including one for his overall excellence in many fields. He has made a name for himself in a wide variety of items and was one of the first fashion designers to do sheets and towels. With Hubert de Givenchy and Emilio Pucci, Blass worked on interiors for the Lincoln Continental's Mark IV and Mark V. Blass has noted, "In the seventies, the designer became a brand name. His name on products gave them validity. This helps establish design standards and, on the whole, is a good thing, providing it is not abused." Along with an ever-growing list of designers such as Piere Cardin, Gucci, Fiorucci, Sassoon, Calvin Klein, and so on, Blass has become a trademark, a name to be sported almost regardless of what it appears on. As his statement goes, that practice could be good if not abused.

Blass's clothes show many influences, perhaps a few too many to put his clothes in the class of true originals. His inventiveness has been more in the field of the designer's role and, most important, in the role of ready-to-wear's possibilities for upward mobility. He stands out almost more for his celebrity stature than for his particular designs, which basically alter previous and concurrent fashions invented by others. Blass is, after all, not someone who will be revered as an intellect or artist of the highest stature, yet he has developed a place among the gentry who want a classic look with room for glamour, while avoiding anything too new or too different.

—Barbara Cavaliere

# BOERI, Cini
Italian architect, furniture, and product designer

**Born:** Cini Mariani, in Milan, 19 June 1924. **Education:** Studied architecture at the Politecnico, Milan, Dip.Arch., 1951. **Family:** Married A. Boeri in 1949 (divorced, 1969); children: Sandro, Stefano, and Tito. **Career:** Director of interior design and furnishings, studio of Marco Zanuso, Milan, 1952-63; freelance architect and industrial designer, from 1963; clients include Arflex, Arnolfo di Cambio, Artemide, Fiam, Fusital, ICF, Knoll International, Rosenthal, Interflex, Venini, and others. Visiting Professor in Architecture, Industrial, and Interior Design, Politecnico, Milan, 1980-83; also guest lecturer at universities in Spain, Brazil, and the United States. **Member:** Associazione per il Disegno Industriale (ADI), Milan. **Exhibitions:** Milan Triennale, 1965, 1968, 1973, 1986; *Italy: The New Domestic Landscape,* Museum of Modern Art, New York, 1972; *Knoll au Musée,* Musée des Arts Décoratifs, Paris, 1972; *Design in Plastic,* Museum of Decorative Arts, Prague, 1972; *Desenho Industrial Italiano,* Porto Alegre, Brazil, 1975 (toured); *Design and design,* Palazzo delle Stelline, Milan, 1979 (travelled to Venice); *Cini Boeri,* Galerie Hans Schmuller, Bonn, 1980; *Italienische Moebel,* Kölnisches Stadtmuseum, Cologne, 1981; *Italian Re-Evolution,* La Jolla Museum of Art, California, 1982; *Design Since 1945,* Philadelphia Museum of Art, 1983; *Italian Design,* Sogetsu Kaikan Palace, Tokyo, 1984; *16 Italian Women*

Cini Boeri: *Serie di tavoli Shadows,* for ICF, 1983

*Designers,* Takashimaya Stores, Tokyo, 1985. **Collections:** Museum of Modern Art, New York. **Honors:** Compasso d'Oro Award, Milan, 1970; Roscoe Award, New York, 1978, 1985; *Design 85* Award, Stuttgart, 1985. **Addresses:** Piazza S, Ambrogio 14-20123, Milano, Italy; (agent) Zarmanian, Corso Concordia 16-20129, Milano, Italy.

## Works

*Cube storage* containers in wood and plastic, for Arflex, 1967.
*Partner* suitcases in ABS plastic and aluminum, for Franzi, 1967.
*Lamp 602 and Lamp 1098* in PVC and metal, for Arteluce, 1968.
*Lunar* table with steel base and wood/crystal top, for Knoll, 1970.
*Gradual* sofa system with triangular junction table, for Knoll, 1970.
*Serpentone* flexible sofa in polyurethane foam, for Arflex, 1971.
*Strips* armchair, sofa and bed collection, for Arflex, 1972.
*Abat-Jour* lamp with stone base and perspex opaline shade, for Tronconi, 1978.
*Strips 79* relaxer armchair with quilted cover, for Arflex, 1979.
*Folio* hinged panel dining-chair, for Rosenthal, 1980.
*Otto B* series of door handles and window pulls, for Fusital, 1980.
*Rever* symmetric round-edged door with rubber gasket trim, for Tre Piu, 1981.

*Prisma* collection of office furniture, for Rosenthal, 1981.
*Chiara* suspension and table lamps in blown glass, for Venini, 1984.
*Voyeur* free-standing room screen in sandblasted glass, for Fiam, 1987.
*Ghost* single-piece easy chair in crystal sheet, for Fiam, 1987 (with Tomu Katayanagi).
*Feltro* and *Lucia* lamps, for Venini, 1988.
*Ypsilon* contract furniture, for Rosenthal, 1988.
*Sette B* door handles, for Fusital, 1988.
*Palo Alto* coffee table, for Arflex, 1988.
*Amado* sofa, for Arflex, 1989.
*Service* small tables, for Arflex, 1989.
*Raggio/Di/Luna* bed, for Interflex, 1990.
*Touche* bathroom accessories, for Fusital, 1990.
*Butterfly* door handles, for Value Colombo, 1991.
*Forever* sofa, for Arflex, 1993.
*B94* and *Armida* door handles, for Fusital, 1993.
Spectacles, for Rodenstok, 1994.
Boeri's architectural and interior design work comprises numerous villas, family houses, and public buildings in Italy, as well as showrooms for: Franzi in Rome, 1965; Mosel in Bilbao, 1974; Knoll International in Los Angeles, Stuttgart, and Paris, 1975, in Milan, 1984, in Foligno, 1985, and in New York, 1989; Arflex in Milan, 1977, and in Tokyo, 1981; Abati in Perugia, 1980; Venini in Frankfurt, 1988, and in Venice, 1989.

## Publications

**By BOERI: books**—*Le Dimensioni Umane dell' Abitazoine,* Milan, 1980; *Cini Boeri: Quaderni di lavoro/Workbook,* Milan, 1982.

**On BOERI: books**—*Design Italiano: I Mobili* edited by Enrichetta Ritter, Milan and Rome, 1968; *Italy: The New Domestic Landscape* edited by Emilio Ambasz, New York and Florence, 1972; *Atlante del Design Italiano 1940-1980* by Alfonso Grassi and Anty Pansera, Milan, 1980; *Knoll Design* by Eric Larrabee and Massimo Vignelli, New York and London, 1981; *International Design Yearbook 1988/89* edited by Arata Isozaki, London, 1988; **articles**—"Milanese Woman Architect Specialized in Deco" by J. Rosenthal in *Christian Science Monitor* (Boston), 8 August 1969; "People in Design" by J. R. Guilfoyle in *Industrial Design* (New York), November 1972; "Cini Boeri: Design Activity in Architecture and Furniture" in *Japan Interior Design* (Tokyo), April 1980; "Design Community in Italy: Cini Boeri," special issue of *Idea* (Tokyo), April 1980; "Cini Boeri: Vent'anni di progetti" in *Corriere della Sera* (Milan), 12 June 1984; "Cini Boeri" in *Casa e Giardino* (Milan), November 1987.

*

The word "Design" has a very wide meaning. It refers to the planning of something. However in present day language the term "Design" is used indiscriminately to describe projects which have very little in common with each other: an architectural plan, a fabric or dress design, or the creation of a work of art. The difference I am inclined to emphasize, between my own training and professional experience and that of one who designs goods or clothing, is no less important when it is considered that my work has mostly been concentrated in the field of furnishing items rather than in architectural planning. I feel, therefore, it is important to underline that the industrial birth of many furnishing articles is, in my opinion, linked to Interior Decorating Schemes.

Fifteen years ago, product design occurred in a relatively orthodox context; we were dealing with a piece of furniture or a utensil. The design procedure was: identify the function required, research and enrich this function, identify the most suitable materials for the article, suggest a cost-effective mass production method. Then, as a logical consequence, study and project a clear image of the article so that the use of the product was immediately obvious to the consumer. This was the procedure before 1972.

My impression is that the operation involves two persons, the designer and the producer. As time passed, the latter prevailed on the former, due to the different quantities of economic "power" each possessed, and the articles were designed for industrial profit only. This profit would be acceptable, in my opinion, if the product remained innovative, economically coherent with its use, and easily recognizable as a result of mass production. The tendency today, however, is to launch new shapes, bizarre fashions, and expensive trends, substituting an educational operation which should improve the quality of man's life and allow distribution of current specific privileges to a wider range of classes with an unjustified quest for a Griffe.

—Cini Boeri

# BOGGERI, Antonio

Italian photographer, art director, and graphic designer

**Born:** Pavia, 8 April 1900. **Education:** Studied violin at the Conservatorio di Musica, Milan, 1919-22; mainly self-taught in photography and design, from 1924. **Military Service:** Served in the Italian Army School for Officers, 1917-18. **Family:** Married Lidia Giampiccoli in 1937; children: Anna. **Career:** Director, Alfieri e Lacroix printing firm, Milan, 1924-32; founder-director, Studio Boggeri design firm, working with designers Walter Ballmer, Xanti Schawinsky, Max Huber, Aldo Calabresi, Bruno Monguzzi, Ezio Bonini, and others, in Milan, from 1933; has designed for Società Nazionale Gasometri, Olivetti, Kardex, Franchi, Marxer, Roche, Glaxo, Richard-Ginori Dalmine, Pirelli, and others. **Exhibitions:** Milan Triennale, 1951, 1957, 1981; Galleria del Levante, Milan, 1980; *La Sperimentazione Fotografica Italia 1930-1980,* Galleria d'Arte Moderna, Bologna, 1983. **Honors:** Grand Prize, 1951, and Gold Medal, 1957, Milan Triennale; Vita di Pubblicitario, Federazione Italiana di Pubblicità, Milan, 1967; Member of Honour, Art Directors Club of Milan, 1970. **Address:** Via Soetti 19, 16038 Santa Margherita Ligure, Genoa, Italy.

**Works** (from Studio Boggeri)

*L'Uovo di Colombo* brochure, for Studio Boggeri, 1933 (A. Boggeri).
*L'Ete sur Mer* poster, for Societa Italia di Navigazinone, 1933 (X. Schawinsky).
Cover, for *Campo Grafico* magazine, December 1934 (Boggeri and Rossi).
Poster, for *Esposizione Aeronautica Italiana,* Milan, 1934 (Schawinsky).
*Illy Caffe poster,* for Società Hausbrandt, 1934 (Schawinsky).
Publicity posters, for Rodina, 1937 (Boggeri).
*Gas* poster, for Società Nazionale Gasometri, 1939 (F. Depero).
Office furniture catalogue, for Kardex, 1940 (R. Muratore).
*Vitaplex* brochure, for Glaxo, 1946 (C . Vivarelli).
Logotype trademark, for Isis waterproof fabrics, 1948 (Boggeri).
*Becozym* brochure, for Roche, 1950 (E. Bonini).
*Bili Complessi* brochures and packaging, for Marxer, 1956 (R. Martinelli).
*Redoxon Effervescente* brochures and packaging, for Roche, 1959 (A. Calabresi).
*Eupradyn* brochures and packaging, for Roche, 1961 (Calabresi).
*Guanti Satinati* advertisement, for Pirelli, 1962 (B. Monguzzi).

## Publications

**By BOGGERI: books**—*Mostra fotografica di Franco Grignani,* exhibition catalogue, Milan, 1958; *Mostra di manifesti stranieri,* exhibition catalogue, Milan, 1968; **articles**—in *Natura* (Milan), 1930, 1931; *Campo Grafico* (Milan), no. 12, 1934; *La pubblicità d' Italia* (Milan), nos. 5-6, 1937, nos. 50-54, 1939; *Graphis* (Zurich), no. 18, 1948, no. 209, 1980; *Linea Grafica* (Milan), 1948, 1949, 1969, 1974; *Typographica* (London), no. 2, 1960; *Incontri* (Milan), nos. 1-3, 1966; *Due Dimensioni* (Milan), no. 8/9, 1973; *Rassegna* (Milan), no. 6, 1981.

**On BOGGERI: books**—*Die neue Grafik/The New Graphic Design* by Karl Gerstner and Markus Kutter, Teufen and London,

1959; *Lo Studio Boggeri 1933-1973* edited by Paolo Fossati, Milan, 1974; *Storia e Cronaca della Triennale* by Anty Pansera, Milan, 1978; *Lo Studio Boggeri 1933-1981* edited by Bruno Monguzzi, Milan, 1981; *La Sperimentazione Fotografica in Italia 1930-1980,* exhibition catalogue with text by Carlo Gentili, Bologna, 1983.

\*

I worked for eight years with Alfieri and Lacroix, an important graphic arts firm famous for the accurate quality of its production. There I was able to follow closely the techniques of composing and printing, the processes of photoengraving and reproduction, and I acquired the knowledge that I was later to find so extremely important. That was when I had the idea of the future Studio and of the kind of services it would provide.

I realized that, in the end, the object of the typographical firm consisted primarily of the precise technical carrying out of the requirements of a demanding clientele in accordance with the precepts of established craft procedures, with no consciousness of any new relationship between object and graphic form. In contrast to the extreme conservatism of the printers, the work of the *maîtres d'affiche* had an extraordinary, imaginative liveliness, for they were masters of a complete, creative independence clearly pictorial in origin. The area of their free exercises, projects not strictly subject to any particular task, had no place in the Studio's research, which explains why we concerned ourselves with them so seldom.

For me, "graphics" meant the acquisition not merely of a different language, but of a language opposite to the repertoire accumulated on the untouchable remains of classical typography. It was something that had to reckon with the new demands of communication through the picture, whose visuality was far removed from the traditional visuality of reading: to say little with the introduction of the photograph into the page.

—Antonio Boggeri

# BOHAN, Marc (Roger Maurice Louis)
French fashion designer

**Born:** Paris, 22 August 1926. **Education:** The Lycée Lakanal, Sceaux, until 1944. **Family:** Married Dominique Gaborit in 1950 (died, 1962); married Huguette Rinjonneu (died); daughter: Marie-Anne. **Career:** Worked as assistant designer in Robert Piguet fashion house, Paris, 1945-49, and for Edward Molyneux, Paris, 1949-51; also briefly designed in the salon of Madeleine de Rauch, Paris, 1952; opened own fashion salon, producing one collection, Paris, 1953; head designer of haute couture, Jean Patou fashion house, Paris, 1954-58; creator of London collections, under Yves Saint-Laurent, at Christian Dior fashion house, Paris, 1958-59; dress and furs designer, for Revillon fashion house, Paris, 1960; art director and chief designer, Christian Dior S.A., Paris, 1960-89; fashion director for Norman Hartnell, London, 1990-92; also freelance stage and film costume designer. **Honors:** *Sports Illustrated* Designer of the Year Award, New York, 1963; Schiffli Lace and Embroidery Institute Award, 1963. Chevalier of the Legion d'Honneur, France, and of the Ordre de Saint Charles, Monaco.

**Works**

Stewardess uniforms, for Air France, 1962.
Roman Catholic habits, for the Daughters of Charity of Saint Vincent, 1964.
Film costume designs include—*Phedre,* 1961; *Topkapi,* 1963; *Arabesque,* 1966; *The Countess from Hong Kong,* 1966; *Secret Ceremony,* 1968; *L'Ours et la Foupee,* 1970; *The Lady in the Car with the Glasses and the Gun,* 1970; *Le Beau Monstre,* 1971; *Rude Journée pour la Reine,* 1974; *Verdict,* 1974; *L'Ironie du Sort,* 1974; *La Race des Seigneurs,* 1974; *L'Aggression,* 1975; *Le Chat et la Souris,* 1975; *Cassandra Crossing,* 1975; *Le Dernier Amant Romantique,* 1977; *Tour Feu—Tout Flammé,* 1981; *The Moon in the Gutter,* 1982.
Stage designs include—*Apres la Chute,* Theatre du Gymnase, 1963; *Le Cheval Evanoui,* Theatre du Gymnase, 1966, 1974; *Madame Princesse,* Theatre du Gymnase, 1966; *Fleur de Cactus,* Theatres des Bouffes Parisiens, 1966; *Le Misanthrope,* Theatre de l'Oeuvre, 1967; *40 Carats,* Theatre de la Madeleine, 1967; *L'Ascension du General Fritz,* Theatre des Ambassadeurs, 1967; *Les Yeux Creves,* Theatre du Gymnase, 1968; *Le Vision Voyageur,* Theatre du Gymnase, 1969; *Le Canard a l'Orange,* Theatre du Gymnase, 1970; *Du Cote de Chez l'Autre,* Theatre de la Madeleine, 1971; *Jean de la Lune,* Theatre du Palais Royal, 1972; *Ne Coupez pas mes Arbres,* Theatre du Gymnase, 1973; *Chat,* Theatre du Gymnase, 1973; *La Polka,* Theatre du Gymnase, 1974; *Cher Menteur,* Theatre du Gymnase, 1974; *Arret ton Cinema,* Theatre du Gymnase, 1977.

**Publications**

On BOHAN: books—*The Fashionable Savages* by John Fairchild, New York, 1965; *A View of Fashion* by Alison Adburgham, London, 1966; *With Tongue in Chic* by Ernestine Carter, London, 1974; *In Fashion: Dress in the Twentieth Century* by Prudence Glynn, London, 1978; *The Fashionable Mind: Reflections on Fashion 1970-1981* by Kennedy Fraser, New York, 1981; *Who's Who in Fashion* edited by Karl Strute and Theodor Doelken, Zurich, 1982; *McDowell's Directory of Fashion* by Colin McDowell, London, 1984; *The Encyclopaedia of Fashion from 1840 to the 1980s* by Georgina O'Hara, London, 1986; **articles**—"The Perfectionists" by Polly Devlin in *Vogue* (London), September 1974; "A Celebrated Stylist: Marc Bohan Commemorates 25 Years at Christian Dior" by Caroline Kellett in *Vogue* (London), June 1983; "Marc Bohan: j'aime vivre dans l'ambre" by Rosy Verdier in *L'Officiel* (Paris), August 1986; "A Dior Original" in *The Observer Magazine* (London), 29 March 1987; "Bohan: The Power Behind Dior" by Pat McColl in *Harper's Bazaar* (New York), September 1987; "Bohan Speaks Out: 27 Years of Fashion" by Debra Michals in *Women's Wear Daily* (New York), 12 November 1987; "Bye-bye Bohan" in *Time* (New York), 22 May 1989; "Hartnell's New Marc" by Jane Mulvagh in *Illustrated London News,* No. 1098, 1990; "Marc Bohan: New Heart to Hartnell" by Karen Wheeler in *DR: The Fashion Business* (London), 7 July 1990; "Hartnell's Silverman: Building on Bohan" by Arthur Friedman in Women's Wear Daily (New York), 18 September 1990; "New Look for the Royals" by Paula Reed in the *Sunday Times Magazine* (London), 27 January 1991; "Making His Marc" by Lisa Armstrong in *Vogue* (London), February 1991; "Designing for the Young at Hartnell" by Elizabeth Grice in the *Sunday Express Magazine* (London), 17 February 1991; "Hartnell

Goes High Street" by Liz Smith in *The Times* (London), 21 January 1992; "House of Hartnell" by Jeffrey Miller in *Interview* (New York), January 1991; "Bohan Talks with Hartnell on Early End to His Career" by James Fallon in *Women's Wear Daily* (New York), 16 September 1992.

*     *     *

By taking on the mantle of Dior, Marc Bohan committed himself to perfection of cut, finish, and appearance. For 29 years (1960-89), he continued the tradition, begun by Christian Dior, of producing classic, often luxurious, always finely made clothes for individual customers. His early career at Robert Piguet, as assistant to Captain Molyneux, and at Patou gave him a good grounding. Piguet's advice to him, to design clothes which would tempt women, provided him with a working motto. By doing so, he has played an important part in helping couture to survive in the face of the growing importance of ready-to-wear. He offers his clients what they want, rather than following every new change of style.

While perpetuating the essence of couture through delicate workmanship, superb cut, and extravagant embroidery, his designs have always been faithful to the times in which they were created. As early as 1961, his slim look acknowledged that finances were more restrained than in the past and that women were leading more active lifestyles. While remaining aware of modern life, Bohan has shown many and varied influences in recent years. The narrow, mid calf-length coats with epaulettes, worn with boots and slanted berets in 1966, were nicknamed his "Tin Soldier" look. The following year saw the introduction of safari-style suits and dress pants derived from African art and totem motifs. In classic couture tradition, fabrics and colour are both prime factors in Bohan's work. The Gigi suit, for instance, relied for its pretty, romantic effect on softly draping black velvet and wool. Even in the more tailored suits, the attention to detail signifies that they are part of the long-established heritage of haute couture. Gathered Pierrot collars have adorned velvet, taffeta, and satin capes; frilled white chiffon Bertha collars have similarly topped fitted, black velvet dresses.

In 1990, Bohan became fashion director for Norman Hartnell in London. At Hartnell, Bohan combined the classic with the contemporary and was able to attract a younger clientele to an established couture name. His 1991 creations include simple, elegant black sheath dresses and brightly colored scoop-necked dresses with full, short skirts, reminiscent of the bubble dresses he created for Dior in the late 1970s.

The recession of the early 1990s, which caused decreased interest in couture and closed several of the smaller fashion houses, put an end to Bohan's career at Hartnell. Bohan's creations, his innovative suits and elegant eveningwear, maintain their appeal.

—Hazel Clark

# BOHLIN, Jonas

Swedish architect, furniture, interior, and stage designer

**Born:** Stockholm, 10 February 1953. **Education:** Studied construction engineering, Aso Technical College, Sweden, 1970-74; interior architecture, National College of Art and Design (Konstfackskolan), Stockholm, 1976-81. **Career:** Freelance designer, working mainly with the Kallemo Furniture Company, in Stockholm from 1981.

Co-founder, Mobile art and design gallery, Stockholm, 1985-87. **Exhibitions:** *Labyrintformeln,* National College of Art and Design, Stockholm, 1981; *Provokationer,* Kulturhuset, Stockholm, 1982; *Utmarkt Svensk Form,* Galleri Heland, Stockholm, 1983; *New Swedish Furniture,* ASF-Gallery, New York, 1985; *Material Pleasure,* Queens Museum, New York, 1985; *Nordisk Mobeldesign,* Form/Design Center, Malmo, 1986; *Scandinavian Design: A Way of Life,* Toyama Museum of Modern Art, Japan, 1987 (toured Japan); *Asplund/Bohlin/Kandell,* Svensk Tenn, Stockholm, 1988; *Georg Jensen Prisen,* Illums Bolighus, Copenhagen, 1988; *Trois Generations: Asplund/Kandell/Bohlin,* Swedish Cultural Centre, Paris, 1989. **Collections:** Nationalmuseum, Stockholm; Röhsska Konstslöjdmuseet, Göteborg; Jonkopings Lans Museum, Sweden; Visby Konsthall, Sweden; Malmö Konstmuseer Sweden; Kunstindustrimuseet, Copenhagen. **Honors:** National College of Art and Design Stipend, Stockholm, 1981; Stipend, 1981, and Award of Honour, 1983, Föreningen Svensk Form, Stockholm; Swedish State Cultural Stipend, 1984; Estrid Eriksson Foundation Stipend, Stockholm, 1985; Swedish Artist's Stipend, 1986; Georg Jensen Prize, Copenhagen, 1988. **Address:** Jonas Bohlin Arkitektkontor AB, Nybrogatan 25, 114 39 Stockholm, Sweden.

### Works

*Concrete* chair in birch and steel, for Kallemo, 1980.
*Concrete* chair in concrete and steel, for Kallemo, 1981 (limited edition).
*Concrete* table in birch and steel, for Kallemo, 1982.
*Concave* couch in leather, canvas, beech and steel, for Kallemo, 1983.
*Concrete* table in concrete, glass and steel, for Kallemo, 1984.
*Zink* wall-shelf in birch, for Kallemo, 1984.
*Zink* floor-shelf in birch, concrete and steel, for Kallemo, 1984.
*Point* chair in leather and steel, for Kallemo 1985.
*Contact* table in birch and steel, for Kallemo, 1985.
*Espresso* wall-lamp in pine and porcelain, for Kallemo, 1987.
*Double Espresso* floor-lamp in aluminum, steel, and porcelain, for Kallemo, 1987.
*Nonting* couch in leather, canvas, and steel, for Kallemo, 1987.
*Slottsbacken* cupboard in oak, glass, and steel, for Kallemo, 1987 (limited edition).
*Kabin* wall-cupboard in parchment and ashwood, for Svenska Arkitekt Forbundet, 1987 (limited edition).
*Magasin* magazine rack in birch, for Kallemo, 1988.
*Triptyk* table in birch and steel, for Kallemo, 1988.

### Publications

**On BOHLIN: books**—*Den Svenska Formen* by Monica Boman and others, Stockholm, 1981; *International Design Yearbook 1985/1986* edited by Robert A. M. Stern, London, 1985; *Made in Sweden: Art, Handicrafts, Design* by Anja Notini, London, 1987; *International Design Yearbook 1987/1988* edited by Philippe Starck, London, 1987; *High Touch: The New Materialism in Design* by Robert Janjigian, London, 1987; *International Design Yearbook 1988/1989* edited by Arata Isozaki, London, 1988; **articles**—"Jonas Bohlin" by C. Christiansson in *Sweden in Fact* (Stockholm), 1987; "Jonas Bohlin: Between Two Different States" by G. Lundahl in *Scandinavian Review* (Stockholm), no. 2., 1989.

*

My work, my furniture, is an expression of my need and desire to channel my energy. My friend Sven Lundh, who is also the manufacturer of my furniture, once said: "Jonas Bohlin wants to create a subtle balance between abstract shapes for meditative purposes. The few elements keep precisely to the rules which give harmony and equilibrium, and a revelation of the exact (which we find outside ourselves) and the universal (which we find in ourselves)." This is a formulation which still pleases me greatly. I myself have difficulty in formulating my work through words and opinions. Furniture is a language in itself.

—Jonas Bohlin

\*   \*   \*

Jonas Bohlin has been the centre of many storms. He made his debut with an armchair of concrete and iron tubing. The new impertinent chair was equally uncomfortable, with echoes of Picasso's handlebars and the Readymades of Duchamp. The champions of comfort raged. A challenge to the public is a tall cupboard with double doors. It is made from softly polished rusty steel, bowed and joined like ship's plates and fastened with heavy brass bolts. When the doors are opened, a fragile, elegantly finished interior with glass shelves is revealed. The cupboard was originally named *Mutter.* Maybe it suggested Mother Earth with her ravaged exterior and her vulnerability. One day, however, the name was changed to *Slottsbacken:* a bus stop in Stockholm and a pretentious beer crate. "What is 'nice'? What is beautiful?," it whispers. And the fact that Jonas has signed and numbered the cupboard—just as he did with the concrete chair—is a constant minor provocation. Beauty contained in ugliness, ugliness in beauty, excites Jonas. It is in contrasts that discoveries are made, he says.

Another contribution to the 1989 Stockholm Furniture Fair was a table of undisputed beauty with elegant lines and personality. It is called *Triptyk.* The three parts consist of two iron pedestals cast in one piece with medium-sized tabletops. Each iron top may be surrounded by a somewhat larger ring of massive wood, which covers up the self-consciously moulded decorative letters that spell out "Jonas Bohlin." The assertive capitals are reminiscent of those found on a cannon or a wood stove. The third part consists of a long massive plank for the two stands. The wood is untreated. "Won't you get wine stains?", someone asks. To Jonas, furniture is serious business. It is about life, about working out your experiences.

Jonas Bohlin was born in Stockholm in 1953. He attended the College of Fine Arts from 1976 to 1981, but before that he had studied to become a construction engineer. Those were active and busy years as part of an intensive group. His concrete chair made its debut at the senior show, as part of an installation highlighting the juxtaposition of different materials. At that time, stage craft was Jonas's main interest. Now it is furniture.

The concrete chair immediately found a manufacturer, Sven Lundh at the Kallemo Furniture Company, who, with an unerring instinct for new things, has sought out the most talented and startling designers. Jonas Bohlin and John Kandell are his superstars. The collaboration between Sven Lundh and Jonas Bohlin is very important. Lundh's assessments of Jonas' ideas are on-the-mark: he supports or criticizes them, launching them enthusiastically and with personal commitment. "I wait until I have a good idea. Then I turn it over to Kallemo. I make furniture for him, and I have just enough ideas for one company."

In addition, Jonas works with interior design—offices, private dwellings and, quite recently, a restaurant. His resume also lists a couple of exhibitions. His office is in a converted mid-town factory. He is surrounded by designers and architects of different kinds but also by a printing shop and a candy factory. Sometimes the proximity invites collaboration, but usually Jonas is a loner in his work. "I don't fit in an architect's office," he says.

During the period 1985-87 a lot of time was taken up by a gallery, *Mobile.* Jonas started it together with three like-minded friends from various fields. They bought a windowless space next to the entrance of a parking garage. They painted it black and equipped it with dramatic lighting. The idea was to provide exhibition space for radical artists and designers. In between, the space would be available for rent to companies which would receive help in exhibiting their products. This would pay the rent. In addition, "ordinary people" with design ideas were to be offered exhibition space. The idea did not catch on either with the establishment or among radicals. However, there was time for a couple of exciting exhibitions before the adventure was over after two years. *Mobile* became part of history.

Jonas put on his most beautiful and expressive exhibit for the furniture fair in February 1989. Because of the Georg Jensen Prize, he was honoured with two podiums in the large entrance hall. One of the two white circles was taken up by birch and steel predecessors to the concrete chair, painted blue and black. They were arranged haphazardly with a shiny brown string instrument leaning against each one as if an orchestra had just left. Puzzling and beautiful, they left a strong impression on the viewer. The other podium housed a larger selection of Jonas' furniture production, among them the shelf system *Zink* zigzagging upwards on a diagonal. There were also the magazine rack, *Magasin,* a board with slots for newspapers. *Nonting,* a couch, was stood on end. It is reminiscent of a steam roller, and should always be in motion. Upended, its precise geometry became the main message. *Kabin,* a wall cupboard, is a delicate little collector's item for the members of the Architects' Association. A neat little row of shelves of smoothly sanded ash is wrapped in a sheet of cardboard leather which may be tied shut by two cotton ribbons. A lamp, *Espresso,* an introduced bowl, balanced on a rustic console, throws light at the ceiling. The floor version is a doubled espresso. It feels good to do something tacky, too. "Too many neat and elegant things are made today. We seem to have settled comfortably on our duffs. Time to venture out and make discoveries: to overthrow the law of gravity."

Success has come to Jonas in unanticipated measure, but then, he has long been in the habit of working seven days a week. He says the Georg Jensen Prize took him by surprise. Jonas Bohlin is an exception in the world of Swedish furniture. The prize was a recognition of his excellence and willingness to break the rules. It is to be hoped that his success will prepare the way for an even younger generation trying to find a profile for its own time.

—Gunilla Lundahl

# BONETTO, Rodolfo

Italian furniture, product, and industrial designer

**Born:** Milan, 18 September 1929. **Education:** Liceo, Milan, until 1947. **Family:** Married Evy Musmanno in 1959; son: Marco. **Ca-**

reer: Design consultant, for Pininfarina and other car body firms, Milan, 1951-58; founder-director, Bonetto Design SRL, for Autovox, Voxson, Elscint, Fiamm, Fiat, IPM, Lancia, Nordica, Novotecnica, Schick, Selenia, Sweda, Veglia Borletti, Zanussi, and others, in Milan, since 1958. Lecturer in Product Design, Hochschule fur Gestaltung, Ulm, 1961-65; instructor in Industrial Design, 1971-87. **Member:** Istituto Superiore Disegno Industriale, Rome, 1974-89; executive board member, 1963-69, executive board president, 1971-73, and president, 1979-82, ADI Associazione Disegno Industriale, Milan; executive council member, Creation Esthetique Industrielle, Paris, 1971; executive board member, 1971-73, vice-president, 1973-75, president, 1981, and member of the senate, 1988, ICSID (International Council of Societies of Industrial Design). **Exhibitions:** *Design and Design,* Palazzo delle Stelline, Milan, 1979 (traveled to Venice); *Design Process: Olivetti 1908 1978,* University of California, Los Angeles, 1979; *Italian Re-Evolution,* La Jolla Museum of Art, California, 1982; *Design Since 1945,* Philadelphia Museum of Art, 1983, Italia 2000, Moscow, 1988. **Collections:** Museum of Modern Art, New York; Philadelphia Museum of Art. **Honors:** Compasso d'Oro Award, Milan, 1964, 1967, 1970, 1976, 1979, 1981. **Address:** Bonetto Design SRL, Ripa di Porta Ticinese 55, 20143 Milan, Italy.

### Works

*Iveco* car instruments, for Veglia Borletti, 1970.
*LM and VP80* elevators, for Stigler-Otis, 1975.
*Supermirafiori 131* car interiors, for Fiat, 1975.
*Mostro* radio, for Voxson, 1978.
*Picchio* one-piece table telephone, for Sime, 1980.
*L20* cash register, for Sweda, 1986.
*Inspector 820* measuring machine, for Olivetti OCN, 1987.
*Ala* halogen table lamp, for Guzzini, 1987.
*Rotor 2* public telephone, for IPM, 1987.
*Tipo* car interiors, for Fiat, 1988.
*Excel 2400* music console, for Elscint, 1988.
*TB2* microchip process machine, for Tegal-Motorola New Enterprises, 1988.
*Premium Top* maintenance-free car battery, for Fiamm, 1989.
*Cross 6E* geared motor for sliding gates, for Novotecnica, 1989.

### Publications

**By BONETTO: articles**—"Rodolfo Bonetto" in *Design Quarterly* (Tokyo), no. 2, 1982; "Waking Up: facing the objects of the day", with A. Rossari, in *Italian Re-Evolution,* exhibition catalogue, La Jolla, 1982.

**On BONETTO: books**—*Italy: The New Domestic Landscape* edited by Emilio Ambasz, New York and Florence, 1972; *Design e forme nuove nell'arredamento italiano* edited by Paolo Portoghesi and Marino Marini, Rome, 1978; *Design Process: Olivetti 1908-1978,* exhibition catalogue, Los Angeles, 1979; *Atlante del design Italiano 1940-1980* by Alfonso Grassi and Anty Pansera, Milan, 1980; *Design Since 1945* edited by Kathryn Hiesinger and George Marcus, Philadelphia and London, 1983; *The Conran Directory of Design* edited by Stephen Bayley, London, 1985; *International Design Yearbook 1987/88* edited by Philippe Starck, London, 1987.

*       *       *

Rodolfo Bonetto represents in Italy the figure of the designer who works in the modern tradition, resolving functional problems of great complexity by applying a strict design methodology based on a technical and scientific approach to the creation of form.

In fact, he owes his cultural development largely to the Hochschule fur Gestaltung at Ulm, to which he was appointed while still very young to teach product design, from 1961 to 1965; the efforts made in that school to unite science and creativity and the powerful influence there of the psychological, ergonomic, social, economic, mathematical, and technological disciplines are all elements found now in Bonetto's own professional practice and in his various productions. This development and his first experiments in the field of automobile design allowed Bonetto always to take on projects of high technological and practical complexity, with the related problems of large-scale mass production; working in the field of machine tools and measuring instruments, for instance, he has been able to find a formal answer to the evolution of the technology, not only that "external" to the object in its production but also that which is "internal." In his designs, in fact, Bonetto has lived through the whole period of the change-over from the electro-mechanical operation of plants to the electronic. He always creates products that are less forms imposed on the machinery than they are complex systems, which tend to be anonymous in form, but in which the design is principally decided by consideration of the point at which machine and operator meet, something on which Bonetto's design work has largely concentrated, with important results.

Bonetto seems to be averse to intellectual classification and has always preferred to work in the professional field rather than the critical. This practical activity, however, is always accompanied by an active presence in situations which, at an international level, afford opportunities for publicity and discussion on the subject of industrial design. Besides teaching in the school at Ulm, Bonetto has for many years been a lecturer and member of the Scientific and Educational Committee at Rome's Istituto Superiore Disegno Industriale, the only national school of design at university level in Italy. There he has conducted on an experimental level research on the defining of new design methodologies. The subject matter of his work and the experience acquired on an international level by his professional activity are publicized by a constant presence at enterprises for the promotion of design, in particular in the Italian Association for Industrial Design, in which he has promoted meetings between the different forces operating in the field of design, and in the International Council of Societies of Industrial Design, for which he has addressed conferences and meetings all over the world and for which he promoted the organization of the Thirteenth World Congress at Milan.

Through this activity Bonetto has become an outstanding figure, designer and propagandist, making an indirect critical contribution to the evolution of design with his professional practice and promoting the discussion and enhancement of the study of design directly by his educational activities.

—Stefano Casciani

# BONSIEPE, Gui (Georg)
German product designer

**Born:** Glucksburg, 23 March 1934. **Education:** Studied classical languages, Karlsgymnasium, Stuttgart, until 1949; graphics and architecture, Akademie der Schönen Künste and Technische Universität, Munich, 1954-55; design theory, under Tomas Maldonado, Hochschule für Gestaltung, Ulm, Dip., 1959. **Family:** Married Jovita Alicia Hemmingsen in 1966; children: Jovita, Santiago, and Juan. **Career:** Freelance industrial designer, in Ulm 1959-68, in Santiago de Chile, 1968-74, in Buenos Aires, 1974-84, and in Brasilia, from 1981; industrial design consultant, International Labor Organization, Santiago, 1968-71; divisional head, INTEC Comite de Investigaciones Technologias, Santiago, 1971-73; divisional chief, Instituto Nacional de Tecnologia Industrial, Buenos Aires, 1974-76; partner and technical director of Studio MM/B Diseno (Mendes Mosquera/Bonsiepe/Kumcher), Buenos Aires, 1975-81; consultant, National Council for Scientific and Technological Development, Brasilia, from 1981. Assistant instructor, 1960-64, and Professor, 1965-68, Hochschule für Gestaltung Ulm, Guest Professor of Engineering, Catholic University, Santiago, 1971-72; head of product development workshop, Universidad Federal de Santa Catarina, Florianapolis, Brazil, from 1982. Consultant, UNIDO United Nations Industrial Development Organization, 1973-74, 1979, UNESCO, 1973, 1982, and OECD Organization for Economic Cooperation and Development, 1977, 1978. Editor, *Ulm* magazine, 1964-68, *INTEC* magazine, Santiago, 1971-73, and design section of *Summa* magazine, Buenos Aires, 1979-81. Vice-President, ICSID International Council of Societies of Industrial Design, 1973-75. **Member:** Vereinigung Deutscher Industrie-Designer, 1967. **Honors:** Berlin Senate Award for Design Methodology, 1967; ACELCO Prize, Buenos Aires, 1977; Harvesting Machine Competition Prize, Development Bank of Misiones, 1979. **Address:** Conselho Nacional de Desenvolvimento Cientifico e Tecnologico, CNPQ SDI/CDI, C.P. 11 1142, 70750 Brasilia, D.F., Brazil.

## Publications

**By BONSIEPE: books**—*Design im Ubergang zum Sozialismus,* Hamburg, 1974; *Diseno Industrial: Artefacto y Proyecto,* Madrid, 1975, as *Diseno Industrial, Tecnologia y Dependencia,* Mexico City, 1978; *Teoria e Pratica del Disegno Industriale,* Milan, 1975, Barcelona, 1978; *A'tecnologia da tecnologia,* Sao Paulo, 1983, as *Periferia del Diseno,* Barcelona, 1984; **articles**—in *Ulm* (Ulm), no. 10/11, 1964, no. 12/13, 1965, no. 19/20, 1967; *Contribuciones Tecnicas* (Buenos Aires), no. 3, 1966; *La Gazeta de Cuba* (Havana), no. 78, 1969; *Form und Zweck* (Berlin), no. 2, 1976, nos. 1 and 2, 1979.

**On BONSIEPE: books**—*Die Geschichte des Design in Deutschland* by Gert Selle, Cologne, 1978; *Industrial Design* by John Heskett, London, 1980; *An Introduction to Design and Culture in the Twentieth Century* by Penny Sparke, London, 1986.

*

I consider the term "design" rather misleading as long as it is not accompanied by a specifier: Design for whom? In which context? In a Eurocentric frame of reference, one might be seduced into suggesting a universally valid definition of design, but there is no concept applicable to both of the two profoundly different situations in the Centre and in the Periphery.

The universe of the Centre is one-eyed, often even blind to the realities beyond itself. Of course, the design scene is dominated by the output from the Centre, which defines product types and physiognomies that the industrial system spits out in ever-increasing rhythms. Much of that output touches the fringe of a pathology of consumption and can be interpreted as a symptom of the desire to discover small areas of need not yet occupied by material artifacts. The Centre also produces the theoretical output. After all, experiences with industrial design started in industrialized countries. Compared with that situation, the design scene in the Periphery is almost non-existent, trying desperately to find its own ways because the design solutions it needs are not available elsewhere and so must be invented here. Thus, I sustain the thesis that we have today two kinds of design: the design developed in and for the Centre and the design we hope is developing in and for the Periphery, matching local needs with local resources (materials, know-how, machinery).

The two design worlds have rather little in common. The circle of design maturation in the Centre is complete. The responsibilities of the professional are well-established, educational programmes are consolidated, design events fill design publications, and design centres go on in their daily routine. We may expect more perfection in the vertical direction—digging deeper in a well-marked field. But the designer's "universe of intervention" seems to me to be finite.

Controversies have arisen as to the validity of the modern movement, functionalism, and design rationalism, the death notices of which we find in almost every opportunity given to those who consider themselves beyond modernism. (I would rather think that we face a new type of pre-modernism.) In the end, these discussions seem to be simple attempts to put into brackets the social dimension of design under the cover of arguments about form and style. Passionate discussions of *stilemi* are the counterpart to political conservatism; "retro" in design corresponds to the "retro" in the social quality of the society in which we live.

Style is not a design priority in the Periphery. The question of design in the Periphery is linked to the problem of technological dependence (and, by implication, financial dependence). I came to interpret industrial design as technological variable. Design and technology go beyond product esthetics. They touch the nerve centre of the quality of the material culture—with proper characteristics, not simply of form, but of structure as well. The role of design in the Periphery is emancipatory, helping to get rid of domination. There are temptations to fall into the trap of technological primitivism (after all, rattan is technologically a rather limited material), though some priests of the new simplicity would have us do so. But much of the Centre's criticism of technology is essentially romantic because it is not ready to renounce the advantages modern technology offers. There is also the trap of "good design"—a cultural export of dubious value in the Periphery. The material culture of the Periphery has to be created; it cannot be found in the past. I doubt, for instance, that the study of pre-Colombian art can orient the Latin American designer in the design of a water tap or a metal-bending machine.

I favor an anti-narcissistic posture similar to Brecht's recommendation to the actor: not to confuse his personality with the role of the character he represents. Products produced by mass-production methods for everyday use are too important to serve as billboards for individuality. In designing a product, there are many more people involved than those labeled "designers." Design is the result of teamwork, and we use the designer's name mainly as a practical shorthand.

At present, I am interested in the zone of transition between (mechanical) engineering and industrial design. Some colleagues consider design as a kind of mini-architecture or sub-discipline of engineering—with esthetics added. I don't share these reductionist views. Architecture differs from design in its variable space and scale, whereas engineering differs in its approach to artifacts. Industrial design is user-centered and concerned with the efficiency of needs in a way that parallels the interest in physical efficiency prevalent in traditional "hard" disciplines. Industrial design is linked to the interface between product and user. Of course, interfaces imply an esthetic dimension (understood as a non-normative concept), and this dimension cannot be added or subtracted at will from a product. Esthetics are intrinsically interwoven with the manner in which we experience products; recognizing that, however, does declare it the dominating factor in design.

We handle esthetic aspects through nondiscursive codes which are unfortunately heavily underrepresented in our educational system. It is hardly understood how we acquire these codes and become proficient in their use. That is one of the most conspicuous shortcomings of design methodology as we know it today.

One scenario of the future of our profession presents the designer of tomorrow as a professional heavily relying on computers. But I wonder whether this view isn't overstating the influence of a tool on the quality of design solutions. Like radical phraseology, tools can be quite conservative. Car design continues as conservative as ever in spite of computer-aided design. We may reach destinations faster, but not necessarily new destinations. Tomás Maldonado once described the designer as a troublemaker. I agree with that; it is the essence of design.

—Gui Bonsiepe

# BOX, John
British film designer

**Born:** London, 27 January 1920. **Education:** Attended schools in Ceylon; studied architecture, Barlett School of Architecture, University of London. **Military Service:** British Army, 1939-45. **Career:** Film draftsman for London Films, Denham Studios, Buckinghamshire, 1947-49; assistant art director to Alex Vetchinsky and Carmen Dillon, 1950-53; art director, working on the films of Terence Young, Franklin Schaffner, Mark Robson, Carol Reed, Richard Quine, David Lean, John Cromwell, Fred Zinnemann, and others, from 1953. **Honors:** Academy Award, 1962, 1965, 1968, 1971; British Academy Award, 1967, 1974, 1975; Moscow Film Festival Award, 1968. **Addresses:** c/o William Morris Agency, 147 Wardour Street, London Wl; 28 Scarsdale Villas, London W8 6PR, England.

## Works

Film designs include—*The Million Pound Note* (Neame), 1953; *The Black Knight* (Garnett), 1954; *A Prize of Gold* (Robson), 1955; *Cockleshell Heroes* (Ferrer), 1956; *The Gamma People* (Gilling), 1956; *Zarak* (Young), 1957; *Fire Down Below* (Parrish), 1957; *How to Murder a Rich Uncle* (Patrick and Varnel), 1958; *High Flight* (Gilling), 1958; *No Time to Die* (Young), 1958; *The Inn of the Sixth Happiness* (Robson), 1958; *Our Man in Havana* (Reed), 1959; *Two-Way Street* (Day), 1960; *The World of Suzie Wong* (Quine), 1961; *Lawrence of Arabia* (Lean), 1962; *Of Human*

*Bondage* (Hughes), 1964; *The Wild Affair* (Krish), 1965; *A Man for All Seasons* (Zinnemann), 1966; *Oliver* (Reed), 1968; *The Looking Glass War* (Pierson), 1970; *Nicholas and Alexandria* (Schaffner), 1971; Travels with my Aunt (Cukor), 1972; *The Great Gatsby* (Clayton), 1974; *Rollerball* (Jewison), 1975; *Sorcerer* (Friedkin), 1977; *The Keep* (Mann), 1983; *A Passage to India* (Lean), 1984.

## Publications

**By BOX: articles**—interview in *Film Review* (London), January, 1975; *Cinematograph* (Paris), February, 1982.

**On BOX: books**—*Le Decor de Film* by Leon Barsacq, Paris, 1970, as *Caligari's Cabinet and other Grand Illusions,* Boston, 1976; *The International Film Encyclopedia* by Ephraim Katz, London, 1980; *The International Dictionary of Films and Filmmakers,* London and Chicago, 1987, 1991.

\*      \*      \*

John Box's designs are evidence that selection, care, and craftsmanship can make motion pictures artistic, even when apparent realism is the overall visual style desired by a director. For *Doctor Zhivago* (1965), for example, not only was Russia created in Spain, it was done so in a way that emphasized the color red at key points in the film. In that film, too, is the haunting image of the icy villa at the edge of the steppes. This image not only fulfills the need for a setting described in the script, but also suggests a doomed way of life.

Box works in the tradition of the big costume pictures of the 1930s, and, to go further back, in the tradition of nineteenth- and early twentieth-century paintings and illustrations of historical or exotic locations, carefully researched, yet artfully presented. One such nineteenth-century example is the set of illustrations of London districts by Gustave Doré. These were in fact used by Box in designing *Oliver!* (1968) in which he maintained a program of simplified forms and selected colors suitable for the artificial quality of a musical with production numbers. The artificial qualities are more subtly integrated into most of Box's films, as seen in two examples that convincingly show illusions of past times, the sixteenth-century England of *A Man for All Seasons* (1966) and early twentieth-century America of *The Great Gatsby* (1974). Box's sweeping and grand treatment of the past has influenced more recent epic films, such as *Reds* (1981) and *Gandhi* (1982). Perhaps Box's major contribution to motion picture design has been in maintaining artistic qualities associated with earlier periods of art and film without sacrificing the versimilitude of particular historical periods.

—Floyd W. Martin

# BOYLE, Robert
American film designer

**Born:** Los Angeles, California, in 1910. **Education:** University of Southern California, Los Angeles, B. Arch., 1933. **Military Service:** United States Army Signal Corps, 1942-45. **Career:** Worked for several architectural firms, then as a film extra, sketch artist, and draughtsman, at Paramount Studios, Hollywood, California; assistant art director, under Wiard Ihnen, at Universal Studios, Hollywood, from 1933-36; art director, at Universal Studios, 1936-42, at RKO Studios, 1946-47, and again at Universal Studios, from 1947; worked with directors Alfred Hitchcock, Bud Boetticher, Norman Jewison, Richard Brooks, Ernest Lehman, Douglas Sirk, and others. **Address:** 6904 Los Tilos Road, Los Angeles, California 90028, U.S.A.

### Works

Film designs include—*Saboteur* (Hitchcock), 1942; *Flesh and Fantasy* (Duvivier), 1943; *Shadow of a Doubt* (Hitchcock), 1943; *Good Morning, Judge* (Yarbrough), 1943; *South of Tahiti* (Waggoner), 1943; *Nocturne* (Marin), 1946; *They Won't Believe Me* (Pichel), 1947; *Ride the Pink Horse* (Montgomery), 1947; *Another Part of the Forest* (Gordon), 1948; *An Act of Murder* (Gordon), 1948; *For the Love of Mary* (de Cordova), 1948; *The Gal Who Took the West* (de Cordova), 1949; *Abandoned* (Newman), 1949; *Buccaneer's Girl* (de Cordova), 1950; *Louisa* (Hall), 1950; *The Milkman* (Barton), 1950; *Sierra* (Grenen), 1950; *Mystery Submarine* (Sirk), 1950; *Iron Man* (Pevney), 1951; *Mark of the Renegade* (Fregonese), 1951; *The Lady Pays Off* (Sirk), 1951; *Weekend with Father* (Sirk), 1951; *Bronco Buster* (Boetticher), 1952; *Lost in Alaska* (Yarbrough), 1952; *Yankee Buccaneer* (de Cordova), 1952; *Back at the Front* (Sherman), 1952; *Girls in the Night* (Arnold), 1953; *The Beast from 20,000 Fathoms* (Laurie), 1953; *Gunsmoke* (Juran), 1953; *Abbott and Costello Go to Mars* (Lamont), 1953; *Ma and Pa Kettle on Vacation* (Lamont), 1953; *It Came from Outer Space* (Arnold), 1953; *East of Sumatra* (Boetticher), 1953; *Ma and Pa Kettle at Home* (Lamont), 1954; *Johnny Dark* (Sherman), 1954; *Ride Clear of Diablo* (Hibbs), 1954; *Chief Crazy Horse* (Sherman), 1955; *Kiss of Fire* (Newman), 1955; *The Private War of Major Benson* (Hopper), 1955; *Lady Godiva* (Lubin), 1955; *Running Wild* (La Cava), 1955; *Never Say Goodbye* (Hopper), 1956; *A Day of Fury* (Jones), 1956; *Congo Crossing* (Pevney), 1956; *The Night Runner* (Biberman), 1957; *The Brothers Rico* (Karlson), 1957; *Operation Mad Ball* (Quine), 1957; *Buchanan Rides Alone* (Boetticher), 1958; *Wild Heritage* (Haas), 1958; *The Crimson Kimono* (Fuller), 1959; *North by Northwest* (Hitchcock), 1959; *Cape Fear* (Lee Thompson), 1962; *The Birds* (Hitchcock), 1963; *The Thrill of It All* (Jewison), 1963; *Marnie* (Hitchcock), 1964; *Do Not Disturb* (Levy), 1965; *The Reward* (Bourguignon), 1965; *The Russians Are Coming, the Russians Are Coming* (Jewison), 1966; *Fitzwilly* (Delbert Mann), 1967; *In Cold Blood* (Brooks), 1967; *How to Succeed in Business Without Really Trying* (Swift), 1967; *The Thomas Crown Affair* (Jewison), 1968; *Gaily, Gaily* (Jewison), 1969; *The Landlord* (Ashby), 1970; *Fiddler on the Roof* (Jewison), 1971; *Portnoy's Complaint* (Lehman), 1972; *Mame* (Saks), 1974; *Bite the Bullet* (Brooks), 1975; *Leadbelly* (Parks), 1976; *Winter Kills* (Richter), 1978.

### Publications

By BOYLE: articles—in *America* (New York), 19 November 1960, 2 February 1974; *Film Comment* (New York), May/June 1978; *Cahiers du Cinema* (Paris), June 1982.

On BOYLE: books—*Le Decor de Film* by Leon Barsacq, Paris, 1970, as *Caligari's Cabinet and Other Grand Illusions,* Boston, 1976; *The International Film Encyclopedia* by Ephraim Katz, London, 1980; *The International Dictionary of Films and Filmmakers,* London and Chicago, 1987, 1991.

*   *   *

Art director Robert Boyle collaborated with director Alfred Hitchcock in five films in which the suspense and heightened emotional response to the narrative is greatly due to the design elements. Two examples from Boyle's and Hitchcock's work show how their total control of the imagery established convincing illusions heightened by viewpoints impossible to achieve on location. In *North by Northwest,* much of the Mount Rushmore sequence was filmed on a stage, using rear projections to create the illusion that it was filmed in South Dakota. Boyle first made stills of the actual site, and from these then made detailed portions of the carvings in the studio. In *The Birds* there is a sequence, seen from a bird's eye view, showing the center of the town of Bodega Bay, where a man is attacked by birds as he is using a gas pump. He drops the pump and gasoline spreads to where another man, getting out of a car, lights a cigar and throws down the match, thereby starting a fire. Simultaneously the heroine, in a phone booth, is attacked by birds. In comments published in 1978, Boyle explained that the only real objects in the fire scene were the phone booth, one car, gasoline, and fire. All the rest—including a matte painted by Albert Whitlock, a shot of birds attacking, and miniature smoke—was an illusion. This short sequence is an important one in the film and its construction underscores the importance Boyle placed on absolute control of the image. This is also seen in his use of mattes simply to change the coloring of a sky to set a particular mood.

The apparent realism of Boyle's images is typical of Hollywood films of the 1950s and 1960s, when actual locations were more frequently used, or designed sets were made to be detailed illusions of real places. However, the care and selection that undergirds this apparent realism is suggestive of the methods of earlier film designers, who were very aware of the effect certain colors, shapes, or viewpoints can have on an audience.

—Floyd W. Martin

# BOZZETTO, Bruno
Italian advertising and animation film designer

**Born:** Milan, 3 March 1938. **Education:** Studied the classics, law, and geology, in Milan; also studied animation under John Halas, 1959-60. **Career:** Freelance animated film designer, Milan, 1958-59; founder-director, Bruno Bozzetto Film advertising and entertainment film company, Milan, from 1959. President, European Association of Animated Film, 1988. **Honors:** International Critics Award for *Alpha Omega,* Annecy, 1962; Special Jury Award for *I Due Castelli,* Tours, 1963; First Place award for *Il Signor Rossi compra l'automobile,* Cannes Film Festival, 1968; Best Animated Film award for *Il Signor Rossi al safari fotografico,* Tampere Film Festival, Finland, 1973; Gold Plaque for *Allegro non troppo,* International Film Festival, Chicago, 1976; Bronze Statuette for *La Piscina,* Tampere Film Festival, 1977; Jury Prize for *La Piscina,*

**Bruno Bozzetto: still from the film *Grasshoppers*, 1990**

1978, and Diploma of Honour, 1979, MIFED Film Festival, Milan; Prix du Public, Chamrousse, France, 1978; Grand Prix Golden Kuker for *Allegro non troppo,* First World Animated Film Festival, Varna, Bulgaria, 1979; Blue Ribbon for *Baby Story,* Los Angeles Film Festival, 1979; Gold Medal for *Quark,* Marburg Film Festival, Germany, 1982; Annual Annie Award, ASIFA, Hollywood, 1982; Fantoche Award for *Sigmund,* Hiroshima, 1985; Special Award for *Baeus,* Treviso, 1988; Silver Ribbon for *Cavellette,* Rome Film Festival, 1990; Oscar Nomination for *Grasshoppers,* Hollywood, 1991; "Pino Zac" Award to Bruno Bozzetto's career, Forte Dei Marmi, 1991; Premio di Qualità for *Under the Chinese Restaurant,* Italian Ministry, 1991; Prix de l'Humour for *Il Ciclista,* St. Gervais Mont Blanc, 1993; Audience Trophy, Premio Immagine Italia, 1993; and many others. **Address:** Bruno Bozzetto Film, via Melchiorre Gioia, 55-20124 Milano, Italy.

## Works

Animated and live-action films include—*Tapum, la storia delle armi,* 1958; *La storia delle invenzioni,* 1959; *Un Oscar per il Signor Rossi,* 1960; *Alpha Omega,* 1961; *I due castelli,* 1963; *Il Signor Rossi va a sciare,* 1963; *Il Signor Rossi al mare,* 1964; *West and Soda,* 1965; *Il Signor Rossi compra l'automobile,* 1966; *Una vita in scatola,* 1967; *L'Uomo e il suo mondo,* 1967; *Vip mio fratello superuomo,* 1968; *Ego,* 1969; *Il Signor Rossi al camping,* 1970; *Sottaceti,* 1971; *Oppio per oppio,* 1972; *Il Signor Rossi al safari fotografico,* 1972; *Opera,* 1973; *La Cabina,* 1973; *Self Service,* 1914; *Il Signor Rossi a Venezia,* 1974; *Gli sport del Signor Rossi,* 1975; *La piscina,* 1976; *Il Signor Rossi cerca la felicita,* 1976; *Allegro non troppo,* 1976; *I sogni del Signor Rossi,* 1977; *Le vacanze del Signor Rossi,* 1977; *Striptease,* 1977; *Baby Story,* 1978; *Happy Birthday,* 1979; *Giallo automatico,* 1980; *Sandwich,* 1980 *Ma comefanno afarli cosi belli?,* 1980; *Lilliputput* (13 films), 1980; *Homo Technologicus* (7 films), 1981; *Quark*

(series of 45 films), 1981-88; *Tennis Club,* 1982; *Sporting,* 1982; *Homo Technologicus* (8 films), 1982; *La Pillola,* 1983; *Sigmund,* 1983; *Nel centro del mirino,* 1983; *Milano Zero,* 1983; *Homo Technologicus* (6 films), 1983; *Moa Moa,* 1984; *Sandwich* (12 films), 1984; *Homo Technologicus* (8 films), 1984; *Eldorado,* 1985; *Homo Technologicus* (5 films), 1985; *Spider,* 1986; *Quark Economia* (13 films), 1986; *Baeus,* 1987; *Sotto il Ristorante Cinese,* 1987; *MiniQuark* (29 films), 1988; *Mister Tao,* 1988; *Grasshoppers,* 1990; *Big Bang,* 1990; *Dancing,* 1991; *Ski Love,* 1991; six spots for W.W.F., 1992; *Tulilem,* 1992; *Maleducazione in Montagna,* 1993; *Benvenuti a Cinema 5. Vi Aspettavamo,* 1993; five spots for W.W.F., 1993; *Drop,* 1993; *Help?,* 1995.

## Publications

**By BOZZETTO: articles**—interview in *Cinema International* (London), no. 16, 1967; *Filmblatter* (Berlin), 2 February 1968; *Banc-Titre* (Paris), October 1982.

**On BOZZETTO: books**—*Film and TV Graphics* edited by Walter Herdeg, with texts by John Halas and Robert Delpire, Zurich, 1967; *Bruno Bozzetto:Animazione primo amore* by G. Bendazzi, Milan, 1972; *Full Length Animated Feature Films* by Bruno Edera, London and New York, 1977.

\*　　\*　　\*

Bruno Bozzetto's first period of schooling consisted of classical studies and some years at university devoted to law and geology, but since entering animation and design at the age of seventeen, he has succeeded in a field which was primarily dominated by the Hollywood-based studios, such as those of Walt Disney, Hanna Barbera, and, more recently, Filmation and Ralph Bakshi.

Bozzetto's main attributes are his consistency of output and his inimitable style of grotesque, highly individual caricature. He can define with simple outlines the true essence of a personality which is instantly recognizable and commands interest. As a film cartoonist, he is able to expand a character with the right behaviour patterns and to create a complementary personality in depth. One of his stock characters, Il Signor Rossi, who appeared in numerous short cartoons from 1963 onwards and in three of his feature-length films, became the symbol of the Italian "little man"; resourceful, determined, greedy, and vain, he charmingly puts his family interests above all others.

Bozzetto's rare asset is his ability to coordinate and control story continuity, characterization of personalities, development of story, complementary sound effects and music (which underline the behavior of his figures), humor (which never steps out of context of the subject), and ideas (which are within the bounds of the technical flexibility of animation) to achieve the final effect. His sharp, European wit differs from the American (which is more physical), inasmuch as he comments satirically on human shortcomings, such as greed and stupidity. Nevertheless, his humor is light, it never swings over into preaching, it remains within the limits of traditional Italian comedy.

His large output, which includes several series for television and six full-length animated feature films, reached a peak with *Allegro non troppo* in 1976. A parody on a grand symphony concert, it plays on the unexpected happenings which could occur during such a concert. The film combines pleasing graphic design, close relationships between choreography of movement and music, and a degree of visual progression which few animated films have achieved so far. His recent productions include his first full-length live-action film *Under the Chinese Restaurant* (1987). Several of his shorter films, such as *Alpha Omega, Opera, Ego, Baeus,* and *Self Service,* all classic cautionary tales for our time, exemplify his integration of graphic design, story telling, and European humor. In 1988, he produced his longest television series to date, *MiniQuark,* consisting of 29 thirty-minute episodes. In 1988 Bruno Bozzetto also became president of the European Association of Animation Film.

—John Halas

# BRADFORD, Peter

American graphic designer

**Born:** Boston, Massachusetts, 24 May 1935. **Education:** Rhode Island School of Design, B.F.A., 1957. **Career:** Designer, I. M. Pei Architects, New York, 1957; designer, *Architectural Forum* magazine, New York, 1958-60; art director, *Industrial Design* magazine, New York, 1960-63; art director, CBS Inc., New York, 1963-65; principal, Peter Bradford and Associates design firm, New York, from 1963; owner, Wingspan Inc. educational software firm, Boston, Massachusetts, from 1984; owner, Cement Boat Company publishing firm, New York, from 1992. Board of directors, Documents of American Design; advisor, *Visible Language Quarterly*; advisor, Silver Mountain Foundation. **Member:** Alliance Graphique Internationale. **Exhibitions:** Numerous exhibitions with the Society of Publication Designers, from 1960, the New York Art Directors Club, from 1962, the American Institute of Graphic Arts, from 1963, and the Type Directors Club, from 1965. **Collections:** Library of Congress, Washington, D.C.; Cooper-Hewitt Museum, New York. **Honors:** Jesse H. Neal Medal, Society of Publication Designers, 1960; Silver Medal, New York Art Directors Club, 1976; National Magazine Award, Columbia University, 1977, 1978; numerous Design Merit Awards. **Address:** (agent) John F. Thornton, The Spieler Agency, 154 West 57 Street, New York, New York 10019, U.S.A.; (office) Cement Boat Company, 928 Broadway, Room 709, New York, New York 10010, U.S.A.

## Works

Five-year publications program, for Urban America Inc., 1964-69.
*View from the Bottom* documentary film on social welfare, 1968.
Publications program, for Ford Foundation, 1968-1972.
Monographs on master photography, including *Paul Strand* and *Edward Weston,* for Aperture Inc., New York, 1968-93.
Publications, for the American Institute of Architects, 1970-75.
Publication design, for *Play and Playgrounds,* 1972.
Publication design of *Callahan,* edited by John Szarkowski, for Aperture Inc. and the Museum of Modern Art, New York, 1976.
International advertising program, for Hitachi, Japan, 1978.
Text books and supporting documentation design, for *Ginn Basal Reading Program,* Xerox Corporation, 1980.
Publication design, for *Curriculum Dictionary,* 1988.
Packaging for reference program, for Random House, 1990-95.

*Cosmic Comics* (visual language for knowledge representations in encyclopedias), 1992.
Animated messages, for Emmy Awards broadcast, 1994.

## Publications

**By BRADFORD: books**—(editor and designer) *Chair: The Current State of the Art, with the Who, the Why, and the What of It,* New York, 1978; (and editor) *True Blue and the Figures of Speech,* 1993; (editor and designer) *Information Architects* by Richard Saul Wurman, Zürich, 1996; (editor and designer) *Jackie Tales,* forthcoming; (and designer) *The Furniture of Nicos Zographos,* forthcoming.

**On BRADFORD: articles**—*Print* (New York), September 1958; *Communication Arts* (Palo Alto), vol. 13, no. 4, 1971.

\*     \*     \*

Peter the paradox.
Peter the curious.
Peter the designer, Peter the anti-designer.
Peter the conundrum, Peter the stubborn.
Peter the great!
His desire for his truth makes him appear stubborn. His search for clarity rightfully makes him seem curious. His typography and bold illustrative talent make him the designer. The designer in him sometimes seems at odds with his passion for understanding and his stubbornness for the truth.

Peter is a great designer. A great graphic designer and the best of the information architects. He is as much at home as an explorer of the right word to the family of words as he is in investigating the concomitant visual image that embraces these words.

One can imagine that Peter works in the largest and the greatest of the five-star chef's saucepans, boiling down data to find the essence of meaning; pumping it back up again to envision it and form an explanation of his vision and unique vantage point. Whether its a dictionary or the biological sciences, a surgical procedure or statistics, the meaning of plate tectonics or the obsession of what a dictionary is, Peter explores like no other graphic designer.

His work is at the leading edge of understanding and it represents perhaps better than all others the braiding of word, picture, word image, number, and numerics.

Peter describes his attitude and clarifies what I call smart/stubborn in his own words:

Beneath the work, beneath the methods, beneath it all, I am trying to maintain an ethic that has nothing to do with design. It is a black and white, right and wrong kind of thing that, Lord knows, leads me into all kinds of trouble. But, the intractability (stubbornness you call it) is also the source from which I draw my determination to do things well. I think. I can only hope that others, as they watch me work, appreciate the obsession as professional, not personal.

His projects range from the analysis of Cliff Notes to his curriculum dictionary, from the organization of families of words by magnitude to the first clear diagram of the understanding of a calorie.

Peter calls this *explaining.* Explaining is a disarmingly powerful word, as is the word conversation—words that we use casually like, "let me explain something" or, "in a recent conversation," and yet, both have in them enormously deep hidden meanings and struc-

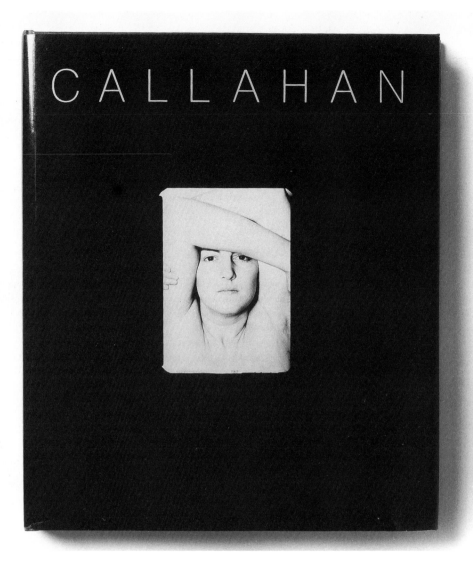

**Peter Bradford: Cover design, *Callahan*, Master Photography by Harry Callahan, Aperture Edition with Museum of Modern Art, New York**

ture. To explain something is not a trivial exercise and the structure of conversation is what makes us human.

I don't doubt that whales talk to each other in the ocean, but I'll bet they don't swim around and have wonderful conversations with each other; I just don't think it happens. I don't believe it happens between any animal species except man and it is from conversation you can easily fantasize the beginnings of all the great discoveries of all mankind.

It is their conversation and the subsequent explanations that various religious figures had with their flock from which the Koran and the various Bibles and even the Book of the Dead emerged. Conversation between priests who didn't know they were prophets, prophets who didn't know they were philosophers, and philosophers who didn't know they were teachers.

So, the word *explain* is at the essence of understanding. In fact, the yin/yang of understanding are curiosity/explanation and that's Peter Bradford.

—Richard Saul Wurman

# BRANDT, Marianne
German painter, collagist, and industrial designer

**Born:** Marianne Liebe, in Chemnitz (now Karl-Marx-Stadt), 1 October 1893. **Education:** Studied painting and sculpture, under Fritz Mackensen, Robert Wiese, and Richard Engelmann, at the Kunsthochschule, Weimar, 1911-14; metalwork, under Làszlò Moholy-Nagy and Wilhelm Wagenfeld, at the Staatliche Bauhaus, Weimar, 1923-25. **Family:** Married the Norwegian painter Erik Brandt in 1919 (separated). **Career:** Independent painter, living in Norway and France, 1919-22; metalware product and industrial designer, in Weimar and Paris, 1924-27, in Dessau and Berlin, 1927-29, and in Gotha, 1929-33; independent painter, tapestry and product designer, in Chemnitz, 1933-49, in Dresden, 1949-51, and in East Berlin, 1951-54; design assistant, in the office of Walter Gropius, working on the Dammerstock housing development, Berlin, 1929; head of design office, Ruppelwerk AG metalware factory, Gotha, 1929-33. Instructor, 1927-28, and head of metal workshops, Staatliche Bauhaus, Dessau; instructor in wood, metal and ceramics workshops, Hochschule der Bildenden Künste, Dresden, 1949-51, and at the Institut für Industrie-Formgestaltung, East Berlin, 1951-54. Retired to Karl-Marx-Stadt, 1954-76, and to Kirchberg, 1976-83. **Exhibitions:** *Moderne Formgestaltung,* Staatliche Galerie, Dresden, 1967; *50 Jahre Bauhaus,* Württembergischer Kunstverein, Stuttgart, 1968; *Die Zwanziger Jahre,* Kunstgewerbemuseum, Zurich, 1973; *Bauhaus 2,* Galerie am Sachsenplatz, Leipzig, 1977; *Tendenzen der Zwanziger Jahre,* Nationalgalerie, West Berlin, 1977; *Drei Künstler aus dem Bauhaus,* Kupferstichkabinett, Dresden, 1978; *Revolution und Realismus,* Nationalgalerie, East Berlin, 1978. **Collections:** Wissenschaftlich-kulturelles Zentrum Bauhaus, Dessau; Kupferstichkabinett, Dresden; Bauhaus-Archiv, Berlin. **Died:** Kirchberg, German Democratic Republic, 18 June 1983.

## Works

Spherical teapot in bronze, silver, and ebony, 1923-24.
Ashtray with tilting top, in bronze and silver alloy, 1924.
Hemi-spherical teapot in bronze, silver, and ebony, 1924.
Six-piece coffee and tea service in silver, 1924.
Four-piece tea set in brass, silver and ebony, 1924.
Adjustable pendant lamp in aluminum, 1926 (with Hans Przyembel).
Four-piece hotel tea service in nickel silver, 1926.
*Kandem* night table lamp in lacquered steel, 1928.
(Most of Brandt's Bauhaus period designs were produced by Korting und Matthiesson of Leipzig, 1927-32, and lighting appliances were reeditioned by Tecnolumen of Bremen, 1980).

## Publications

**On BRANDT: books**—*Bauhausbuch nr. 7: Neue Arbeiten der Bauhauswerkstatten,* Munich, 1925; *Bauhaus Weimar 1919-1924: Werkstattarbeiten* by Walther Scheidig, Leipzig, 1966; as *Crafts of the Weimar Bauhaus 1919-1924,* London, 1967; *The Bauhaus* by Hans and Maria Wingler, Cambridge, Massachusetts, 1968; *Bauhaus and Bauhaus People* edited by Eckhard Neumann, New York and London, 1970; *Goldsmiths and Silversmiths* by Hugh Honour, London, 1971; *Tendenzen der Zwanziger Jahre,* exhibition catalogue by Dieter Honisch, Eberhard Roters, and others, West Berlin, 1977; *Marianne Brandt, Hajo Rose, Kurt Schmidt: Drei Künstler aus dem Bauhaus,* exhibition catalogue with introduction by Werner Schmidt, Dresden, 1978; *Die Geschichte des Designs in Deutschland von 1870 bis Heute* by Gert Selle, Cologne, 1978; *In Good Shape: Style in Industrial Products 1900 to 1960* by Stephen Bayley, London, 1979; *Design Source Book* by Penny Sparke and others, London, 1986.

*       *       *

Perhaps most widely known for her early silver and bronze service vessels, Marianne Brandt deserves to be remembered also for her contribution to modern lamp and lighting fixture design. Her work directly reflects the evolution of Bauhaus philosophy from the arts-and-crafts bias of the Weimar period (1919-25) to the concern for industrial designs and technology of the Dessau period (1925-32). During the Weimar years, Brandt was a successful pupil of Christian Dell, and after 1925 she was influenced by Làszlò

Moholy-Nagy, who was deeply interested in the phenomenon of light, both aesthetically and practically.

During the early Bauhaus years, the theme "form follows function" had frequently been treated as an intellectual idea rather than as a guiding principle to successful design. Some of Brandt's early craft-oriented work, such as her 1924 tea service reflects this puristic thinking, which resulted in vessels composed of her favorite design forms—sphere, hemisphere, and cylinder—treated as geometric units without integrational considerations. This led at times to awkward results visually, structurally, and functionally, as is exemplified by the teapot of her 1924 service.

From 1925, when Moholy-Nagy took complete charge of the metal workshop, the Bauhaus developed a new relationship with industry; silver and bronze were set aside in favor of industrial metals, such as nickel-plated brass and aluminum. Even though she had designed lamps as early as 1924, Brandt's work underwent a change in direction at this time, as she ceased designing for appearance or the modern look, and became involved with solving problems related to consumer use. Henceforth, her design effort was put to producing prototypes for mass production.

In 1925, Brandt designed a movable wall fixture with adjustable reflector and a simple wall fixture composed of a frosted-glass cylinder mounted on a metal base. Also concerned with area lighting, she designed a lighting fixture for walls or low ceilings which consisted of a shallow, opaque-glass shield mounted in a simple, metal frame. In the following year, she devised an ensemble for shaving or makeup composed of a dull aluminum reflector lit by an electric bulb placed behind a mirror, as well as a lamp with a rise-and-fall cable, pull handle, and aluminum shade. One of her most successful designs, a small, metal-shaded bedside lamp set on a flexible stem for adjustability, was manufactured by Korting and Matthiesson in Leipzig in 1927. By this time, the modern lamp was in wide use in Germany and Switzerland, as is evidenced by the fact that between 1928 and 1932, Korting and Mathiesson made approximately 50,000 lamps based on prototypes of Bauhaus metal workshop students and staff. After 1925, Brandt continued to design serving vessels, although none of these were truly innovative or aimed at solving particular user-problems, such as her lamp and lighting-fixture design were.

—Barbara Young

# BRATTINGA, Pieter (Dirk)
Dutch graphic and exhibition designer

**Born:** Hilversum, 31 January 1931. **Education:** International Quaker School, Castle Eerde, Ommen, 1946-49. **Military Service:** Served in the Dutch Corps of Engineers, training with the British Army on the Rhine and the United States Army in Europe, 1950-52, First Lieutenant. **Family:** Married Wilhelmina Kooy in 1951 (divorced, 1971); married Annette Aeneae Venema in 1975; children: Rento, Anne-Suzanne, and Maartje. **Career:** Director of Design, Steendrukkerij de Jong and Company, Hilversum, 1951-74; Senior Partner, Form Mediation International art and design consultants, Amsterdam, from 1964; Managing Director, Mercis bv., Amsterdam, 1971-96. Professor and Chairman, Visual Communications Department, Pratt Institute, Brooklyn, New York, 1960-64; Visiting Professor, Technical Institute, Eindhoven, 1980-82. Secretary-general,

Pieter Brattinga: *The Man behind the Design for the Dutch Post Office* exhibition poster, 1960

ICOGRADA International Council of Graphic Design Associations, 1966-70; president, Art Directors Club of the Netherlands, 1968-71, and Netherlands Art Foundation, 1969-75; secretary-general, Alliance Graphique Internationale, 1991-95. **Exhibitions:** Southern Illinois University, Carbondale, 1961; Lodz Museum of Modern Art, Poland, 1974; Otto Nagel Haus, East Berlin, 1976; Kroller-Muller Museum, Otterlo, 1980. **Collections:** Stedelijk Museum, Amsterdam Kunstgewerbemuseum, Zurich; Wilanowa Palace, Warsaw; Museum of Modern Art, New York; Library of Congress, Washington, D.C.; Musashimo Art Museum, Tokyo. **Honors:** Grand Prix, *International Survey of Exhibition Design,* at the Brno Biennale, 1968. **Address:** Prinsengracht 628, 1017 KT Amsterdam, Netherlands.

## Works

Series of exhibition announcements and posters, for Steendrukkerij de Jong, 1958-72.
Typographic calendar, for Steendrukkerij de Jong, 1962.
Exhibition announcements and posters, for the Rijksmuseum Kroller-Muller, Otterlo, from 1965.

Postage stamps, for the Netherlands Post Office, from 1969.
*10 Europa 9* annual book design, for Grafisch Nederland, 1972.
*Sandberg: A Documentary* book design, for Kosmos, 1975.
*De Stijl* exhibition design, for the Rijksmuseum Kroller-Muller, Otterlo, 1982.
*The Graphic Image of Britain 1900-1970* chart supplement, for Idea Publishers, Tokyo, 1985.
*Kroller-Muller* book design, for Johan Enschede en Zonen, 1988.

## Publications

**By BRATTINGA: books**—*Industrial Design in the Netherlands,* Minneapolis, 1964; *Elements of Consideration for the Training of the Visual Communication Designer,* Warsaw, 1966; *Artypo: Kunst gemaakt met behulp van grafisch technieken,* Eindhoven, 1967; (with Dick Dooijes) *A History of the Dutch Poster 1890-1960* Amsterdam, 1968; *De Toekomst van de Grafische Industrie in Nederland,* Amsterdam, 1972; *50 Plakate, neun Hollandische Graphiker,* Munich, 1972; *A Portrait of Sandberg,* Amsterdam, 1972; *The Visual Rhythm of the Newspaper,* Amsterdam, 1974; (with Ad Petersen) *Sandberg: A Documentary,* Amsterdam, 1975; *Influences on Dutch Graphic Design 1900-1945,* Burgenstock, 1987.

**On BRATTINGA: books**—*The First International Poster Biennale,* with introduction by Jozef Mroszczak, Warsaw, 1968; *European Designers,* Tokyo, 1970; *History of the Poster* by Josef and Shizuko Muller-Brockman, Zurich, 1971; *Who's Who in Graphic Art* edited by Walter Amstutz, Dubendorf, 1982; *45-80: Typografisch Nederland* by C. Jongejans, Nijmegen, 1984; *Posters* by D. Adams, Minneapolis, 1984; *The Activities of Pieter Brattinga: Portrait of an Era* by G. Waldmann, Tokyo, 1989.

*

The facet which is most important to the visual communication designer is his thinking. He must have a flexible and well-organized mind to enable him to: 1) distinguish the real truth in a blurred and colored presentation; 2) abstract its essential points; 3) translate these points, in their order of importance, into a coherent solution—it is quite possible, in fact, that if he is able to make a very clear summarized statement about his commission, he will have solved his problem.

The visual communication designer must have a knowledge of related fields, as well as of the major developments in science, art, and philosophy. Only if he has the ability to select those items of information from which he can draw his own conclusions will he be the right person to give form to communication between people. Unlike the fine artist, most concerned with expressing his own inner feelings, the visual communication designer is primarily an intermediary in the communication of ideas. His education, therefore, must enable him to understand the language of scientists, artists, and officials, so that he can translate their thoughts and ideas into visual terms.

Specialization is one of the aspects of the visual communication field. Whereas the commercial artist of the 1920s was his own illustrator, letterer, and typographer, the designer of today usually occupies himself with only one segment of a project or, while functioning as an art director, he must be able to engage and coordinate the services of other specialists for specific tasks. The designer of today very rarely makes an end product. His sketch, script, or layout, unlike the autographic production of the fine artist, is only a plan for technical realization. He must develop his plan, therefore, within the limitations of a specific technical process.

—Pieter Brattinga

\*     \*     \*

The son of the owner of a printing press, Pieter Brattinga at an early age was made design director of a printing firm, where he became known for the non-commercial Quadrat Prints, first published in 1955 and featuring the work of many different designers. As they were of particularly high quality, the prints thus publicized the skill of the firm. In drawing attention to the quality of the work, Brattinga used the opportunity to further avant-garde ideas that would otherwise not have received such publicity. In addition, Brattinga has designed a number of exhibitions for such museums as the Stedelijk in Amsterdam and the Kroller-Muller in Otterlo. It is significant that his concern in this context is as much for the feelings of the audience as for the professional care of the objects: he is a natural propagandist. He has also had considerable experience as a teacher and writer on education and has produced significant statements on the program for training designers. These insist on the all-around development of the student, as well as the acquisition of skills.

Brattinga's particular influence, however, derives from his special expertise in typography and graphic design. Examples of his important work include his posters for the work of Mies van der Rohe (1959), for the Netherlands Post Office (1960), and for the Nippon Design Center (1963); their quite different concepts are linked by a high standard of typographical design. His characteristic approach lies in the clear presentation of an idea, usually using typographical elements, which often form a pattern as well as convey a message, as they did when he spread a large, single typeface across an entire wall in the Stedelijk Museum to produce a mural developing from left to right into a series of endless permutations. One was reminded of the tradition established by Hendrik Werkman.

In spite of the skills demonstrated by Brattinga as a designer, he has demonstrated also an ability to handle committees and organizations and to act as a force in spreading good design internationally. His reputation rests on the combination of these factors but first of all, on the respect owed to him as a professional designer.

—John Barnicoat

# BREUER, Marcel (Lajos)

American architect, interior, and industrial designer

**Born:** Pecs, Hungary, 22 May 1902; emigrated to the United States in 1937, naturalized, 1944. **Education:** Studied at the Allami Foreaiskola, Pecs, 1912-20; and at the Bauhaus, Weimar, 1920-24. **Family:** Married Martha Erps in 1926; married Constance Crocker Leighton in 1940; children: Thomas and Francesca. **Career:** Freelance architect, planner, and designer, in Dessau, 1925-28, in Berlin, 1928-31, and in London, 1935-36; founder and principal, Marcel Breuer and Associates, Cambridge, Massachusetts, 1937-46, and in New York, from 1946. Master of the Bauhaus, in Weimar,

1924, and in Dessau, 1925-28; associate professor, Harvard University School of Design, Cambridge, Massachusetts, 1937-46. **Member:** Honorary member, Association of Argentine Architects, 1946, and Association of Architects of Colombia, 1947; National Council of Architectural Registration Boards, 1947; Fellow, American Institute of Architects; member, National Institute of Arts and Letters. **Exhibitions:** *Exposition Werkbund,* Grand Palais, Paris, 1930; *Bauausstellung,* Berlin, 1931; *Bauhaus 1919-1928,* Museum of Modern Art, New York, 1938; *Marcel Breuer: Architect,* Museum of Modern Art, New York, 1949; *Marcel Breuer,* Metropolitan Museum of Art, New York, 1972; *Marcel Breuer: Architectures,* Musee du Louvre, Paris, 1973; Bauhaus Archives, West Berlin, 1974; Museum of Modern Art, New York, 1981 (retrospective). **Honors:** First Prize, International Aluminum Competition, 1930, 1933; Medal of Honor, 1965, Gold Medal, 1968, Award of Excellence, 1970, and Honor Awards, 1970, 1972, 1973, American Institute of Architects; New York State Council on the Arts Award, 1967; Bard Award, City Club of New York, 1968; Thomas Jefferson, Medal University of Virginia, 1968; Metropolitan Washington Board of Trade Award, 1969; Gold Medal, French Academy of Architecture, 1976. Honorary Doctorates: Pratt Institute, Brooklyn, New York, 1950; University of Budapest, 1957; University of Notre Dame, Indiana, 1968; Harvard University, 1970. **Died:** New York City, 1 July 1981.

## Works

*Wassily* collapsible easy chair in tubular steel and leather, 1926, produced by Gavina.
*Laccio* coffee table in tubular steel with wood or laminate top, 1925-26, produced by Knoll International and Thonet.
*B4* club armchair in tubular steel and canvas for Standard-Moebel, 1926.
*B6* side chair in tubular steel and wood, for Standard-Moebel, 1926-27.
*B32* (Cesca) cantilever side chair in tubular steel, wood and canework, 1928, produced by Thonet and Gavina.
*S286* desk in tubular steel and wood, 1928, produced by Thonet.
Reclining lounge chair in aluminum, for Tubecraft Limited, 1935.
Long upholstered chair in laminated wood, for Isokon, 1935.
Nesting tables in plywood, for Isokon, 1936.
Stacking chair in plywood, for Isokon, 1936.
Stacking chair in plywood and cane with rubber mounts, for the Museum of Modern Art Low-Cost Furniture Competition, 1945-48.
*New Canaan* desk, 1951, produced by Gavina.

(for a complete list of Breuer's buildings and architectural projects, see *Contemporary Architects*)

## Publications

**By BREUER: books**—*Sun and Shadow: The Philosophy of an Architect* edited by Peter Blake, New York and London, 1956; *Marcel Breuer: Buildings and Projects 1921-62,* Stuttgart and New York, 1962.

**On BREUER: books**—*The New Interior Decoration* by Dorothy Todd and Raymond Mortimer, London, 1929; *Modern Furniture* by E. Nelson Exton and Fredric H. Littman, London, 1936; *Marcel Breuer and the American Tradition in Architecture* by Henry Russell Hitchcock, Cambridge, Massachusetts, 1938; *Marcel Breuer: Architect and Designer* by Peter Blake, New York, 1949; *Marcel Breuer: Disegno Industriale e Architettura* by Giulio Carlo Argan, Milan, 1957; *Marcel Breuer 1921- 1962* by Cranston Jones, London, 1962; *Marcel Breuer: New Buildings and Projects* by Tician Papachristou, New York, 1970; *Marcel Breuer,* exhibition catalogue by Hans Wingler, West Berlin, 1975; *GA 5: Marcel Breuer—Koerfer House Tessin, Switzerland; Stillman House III, Litchfield, Connecticut,* with text by Stanley Abercrombie, Tokyo, 1977; *Tubular Steel Furniture* by Barbie Campbell-Cole and Tim Benton, London, 1979; *Marcel Breuer: Furniture and Interiors* by Christopher Wilk, New York, 1981.

*       *       *

Marcel Breuer's furniture designs so bespeak the philosophy of the Bauhaus that it is difficult to separate the two. His furniture designs were intended to become part of the architectural environment, not to perform as virtuoso, separate entities. Moreover, like other architecture of the modern movement, it intends to solve problems posed within the society it will serve. Breuer proceeded by searching for the fundamental design problem, then solving it in innovative ways. He thereby sometimes substantively changed for society the very concept on which he was working. He did not merely modify another style, nor even intend to create a new style. This approach to design is evident in both his tubular metal chairs (Wassily and Cesca), for instance, and in his modular storage units. His free-standing storage pieces, usually of wood, divide space and indicate changes of use while his wall-hung units define perimeters.

Breuer's aim was always to reach a broad market whose life would be bettered by his furniture designs, which were all conceived to be industrially produced, easily shipped, and economical. As space in modern low-cost dwellings was limited, the occupant, Breuer felt, must be relieved of clutter, both visual and actual. Tubular metal furniture, light in weight, relatively indestructible, and transparent, was his solution. Breuer chairs moved easily into every room and could be used in a variety of circumstances.

In 1926, a mock film strip with six "frames" by Breuer was published in the *Bauhaus Journal*. The first five frames each contain a date and a Breuer chair, while the sixth shows a sitter floating in a void. The caption explains: "Bauhaus movie lasting five years. Author: Life demanding its rights. Operator: Marcel Breuer who recognizes these rights better and better every year: In the end we will sit on air cushions."

Influences upon Breuer, apart from ideological coincidences between Bauhaus philosophy and his own, are easy to see. Earliest is that of de Stijl and Rietveld. At first (1921-24), he borrowed Rietveld materials—boards and plywood. But even in these early designs, Breuer added consideration of the occupant, using upholstery for comfort. Breuer thought of himself as the humanist of modern design.

Never admitted by Breuer is the apparent influence from Le Corbusier (for instance, his furnishing in the Pavillon de l'Esprit Nouveau). Here, Le Corbusier chose Thonet chairs and designed space-dividing cabinets. These may account for Breuer's storage units used to define space and, in part, for his intensified effort to create a chair which, like the Thonets, would not interrupt the flow of space. Nevertheless, his solution, the Wassily, is revolutionary, not imitative.

Influences emanating from Breuer are legion. Imitators and adaptors of his tubular designs appeared immediately. More important, significant designers found tubular metal useful for their own designs once Breuer's work was seen. Among those influenced by Breuer in this way were Mart Stam in Holland, Mies van der Rohe in Germany, Le Corbusier in France, and Aalto in Finland.

During the 1960s, revival of interest in tubular metal designs from the 1920s and 1930s led Breuer to contract licenses to manufacture his furniture. The Cesca Chair became enormously popular, outstripping all other revived designs. Breuer-licensed models are available now only to the wealthiest clients, but cheap imitations appear all over. Although Breuer deplored the poor workmanship in these, he rejoiced that the Cesca could reach the public he always hoped to serve.

—Nina Bremer

# BRIONI
Italian Fashion design firm

**Founded** by tailor Nazareno Fonticolo and entrepreneur Gaetano Savini in via Barberini, Rome, 1945. First men's tailored clothing show, Palazzo Pitti, Florence, 1952; launched accessory line, 1952; first men's runway show in New York, 1954; first show in Britain, 1959; established manufacturing company, Brioni Roman Style, Penne, Italy, 1960; launched neckwear collection, 1979; established tailoring school, Penne factory, 1980; opened first American freestanding Brioni store, Park Avenue, New York, 1982; company acquired Burini of Bergamo, 1991, and controlling interest in Sforza of Bologna leather goods creator, 1994. **Awards:** *Esquire* (magazine) Award for valued contribution to menswear, New York, 1959; International Fashion Council Award, 1962. **Address:** via Barberini 79-81, Rome, Italy.

### Publications

**On BRIONI: books**—*Esquire's Encyclopedia of 20th Century Men's Fashion* by O. E. Schoeffler and William Gale, New York, 1973; *Brioni: Fifty Years of Style* by Cristina Giorcetti and others, Florence, 1995.

*       *       *

In 1945, just as Italy was beginning its post-War renaissance, Nazareno Fonticolo and Gaetano Savini began to pursue an age-old ideal of handwork in refined men's tailoring. Their shop offered a complete, coherent styling for the man who bought their tailored apparel. The name Brioni was appropriated from a resort island off Trieste where elite society had frolicked in the 1930s. The motif of the island and brand was polo, one of the popular recreations, in a manner that anticipated Ralph Lauren's use of the same sport to betoken good times and leisure-class style. The Brioni shop was stocked with distinctive clothing exclusive to the shop and its lifestyle marketing. Tailoring began to adumbrate the "continental look" of the 1950s and such accessories as soft shoes—as opposed to heavy-soled English shoes and robust shoes of wartime—appropriate to the gentle tailored dress of a resort sensibility. Whether intentionally or simply under the impulse to simulate relaxed apparel, Brioni's tailoring moved away from the edifice-like principles of Italian traditional tailoring to create a new, modern silhouette. Slim silhouettes were being emphasized in the early 1950s, colors were not merely the grays and blue of cities, but the azures and brights of resort wear, and interfacing and other construction were more and more pliant. The Italian soft suit for younger men was created at Brioni. It was codified as Brioni's style when the entrepreneur Giovanbattista Giorgini invited Brioni to show along with his Sala Bianca women's shows in Florence, the first time that menswear was presented along with the elegant new womenswear. If tailoring was no longer as rigid, if the silhouette narrowed waist, hips, and trousers, then Brioni menswear had the effect of complementing the dressmaking and stylish sensibility of new Italian post-War women's design leading toward sportswear in the finest fabrics.

By 1955, the Brioni exploration of the fabric and color resources of the new Continental look was in full swing with silk suits and pink shirts for men, a sartorial revolution or fad that hit America with pink shirts in 1956-57. Brioni's styling and marketing was inexorably modern: soft Brioni suits were especially recommended for pre-Jet-Age air travel in their comfort and adaptability to world climates. The modern man would not settle for the stiffness of a stolid gray flannel when the most masculine and modern men from Clark Gable, Kirk Douglas, and John Wayne were going to Brioni for custom-made suits in the 1950s. The 1957 Hess Collection, launched at Hess's in Allentown, Pennsylvania, brought a painterly palette to silk jackets inspired by Italian painters, including Veronese, Giorgione, Titian, and Caravaggio. Brioni was dauntless in attributing aesthetic culture to the otherwise pragmatic and fixed ideas of menswear. Brioni was the high-end alternative to Savile Row, affording tailored clothing a life of leisure and a lightness of being to which the stuffy English tailors could not concede.

Gay Talese, in his interview in *Brioni: Fifty Years of Style,* described the Brioni style in an single word, "timeless." That description suits the streamlined silhouette and tactile materials of Brioni, but Brioni is also sensitive to style change as well. In the 1950s and 1960s, its runway shows and innovative marketing were startling harbingers of the Peacock Revolution of 1968-74. In the late 1950s, Brioni tried out cardigan-style collarless "maharajah" jackets in advance of Cardin, created elongated Edwardian jackets and dandy gestures before Carnaby Street, and offered leisure suits in velvet before polyester spoiled the leisure-suit option for decades. In the 1970s, Brioni was profoundly sensitive to cultural diversity, creating African-inspired shirt-jacket ensembles, Nehru-like suits, and collarless styles inspired by the Middle East. In its modernist consistency and conviction, Brioni was fearlessly confident, even unafraid to challenge Savile Row in runway shows in London in the 1960s and in the audacity to dress Pierce Brosnan as James Bond in the 1995 film *Goldeneye* in defiance of British tailoring traditions. In America, where Brioni was first carried in 1952 by B. Altman in New York, even as conservative journalists and retailers questioned the masculinity of soft and colorful menswear and boastfully claimed that American men were too big in frame and muscle for this tailoring, Brioni persisted with inventive fashion shows and encroachments of its new style in bright tuxedo jackets, silk suits, and relaxed clothing. Brioni never compromised its quality: it produces no secondary or diffusion line, preferring instead to serve only the prestigious and appreciative clientele that knows a suit with handmade details and choice fabrics luxurious in hand and fit.

Brioni has set a fundamental test of masculinity and luxury. Whether custom-made or ready-to-wear, a Brioni suit is an exercise in opulence and discriminating fit. Whereas more recent Italian menswear, most notably Giorgio Armani's, has successfully expanded the audience for quality menswear, Brioni is the menswear equivalent to women's haute couture. Armani's objective is style; Brioni's intent is the perfect suit replete with as much handwork as possible. No steps are eliminated if they might possibly enhance the quality and life of a suit. Brioni constructs softly, but builds suits to last for decades both in style and in construction. Such richness in technique is not incompatible with masculinity. As Talese argues, "What we still can do is to show our masculinity in how we dress. The attitude of the Italian man is never to be ashamed, but to be proud of who he is. In Brioni clothing, there is this particular sense of pride in masculinity built right into the design." In Brioni's case, clothing does, in some degree, make the man, not ostentatiously, but in the self-confidence often denied to men, ever since the nineteenth century Great Male Renunciation in dress. Brioni has established and steadfastly affirmed a minimalist, modern male style.

—Richard Martin

# BRODOVITCH, Alexey
## American photographer and graphic designer

**Born:** Ogolitchi, Russia, in 1898; emigrated to the United States in 1930, subsequently naturalized. **Education:** Studied at Gymnase Tenichev, 1914-15, and the Corps des Pages Military Academy, Saint Petersburg, 1915. **Military Service:** Served in the 12th Archtirsky Hussars, in Rumania, Austria, and Russia, 1916-18, Captain. **Family:** Married Nina Brodovitch in 1920 (died, 1959); children: Nikita. **Career:** Worked as a house-painter, stage scenery artist, furnishing, book, and poster designer, etc., in Paris, 1920-26; graphic designer, Maximilien Vox advertising agency, Paris, 1926-28; art director, Trois Quartiers department store, Paris, 1928; freelance book illustrator, working for Paris and London publishers, in Paris, 1928-30; designer, N. W. Ayer advertising agency, Philadelphia and New York, 1931-38; art director, under editor Carmel Snow, *Harper's Bazaar* magazine, New York, 1934-58; art director, Saks Fifth Avenue department store, New York, 1939-41; consultant, American Red Cross, United States Treasury Department, Office of Government Reports, and United Services Organization, 1941; art director, I. Miller and Sons, New York, 1941-43; art director and art editor, with Frank Zachery, of *Portfolio* magazine, New York, 1949-51; consultant, *Art in America* magazine, New York, 1965. Founder, Le Cercle designers Association, Paris, 1929-30, and Design Engineers designers' association, Philadelphia, 1932-34. Director, Advertising Arts Department, Philadelphia Museum School of Industrial Art (now Philadelphia College of Art), 1930-38; instructor in design, Donnelly Publishers, Chicago, 1939; visiting lecturer in design, at Cooper Union, New York University, and Pratt Institute, New York, 1940; instructor, Brodovitch Design Laboratory, New School for Social Research, New York, 1941-49, 1964 (at the Richard Avedon photo studio, 1947-49, 1964); instructor, Print Club of Philadelphia, 1946-48; visiting critic, Yale University, New Haven, Connecticut, 1955; instructor, School of Visual Arts, New York, 1964-65, and Corcoran Gallery, Washington, D.C., 1965; also held design classes at the

Avedon studio, New York, 1966. Retired to Oppede-les-Vieux, 1967-69, and to Le Thor, France, 1969-71. **Exhibitions:** Librairie Povolotski, Paris, 1928 (with A. Alexieff); *Advertising Designs,* Ayer Gallery, Philadelphia, 1931; Crillon Gallery, Philadelphia, 1933; Cosmopolitan Club, Philadelphia, 1933; Altman Department Store, Philadelphia, 1936; New Poster Show, Franklin Institute, Philadelphia, 1937; *Design for the Machine,* Philadelphia Museum of Art, 1937; Education Pavilion at the World's Fair, New York, 1939; *Alexey Brodovitch and His Influence,* Philadelphia College of Art, 1972 (traveled to Montreal); *Hommage a Alexey Brodovitch,* Grand Palais, Paris, 1982. **Collections:** Philadelphia College of Art; Fashion Institute of Technology, New York. **Honors:** First Prize, Bal Banal Poster Competition, Paris, 1924; 5 medals, *Exposition Internationale des Arts Decoratifs,* Paris, 1925; Book of the Year Award, American Institute of Graphic Arts, 1945; Robert Leavitt Award, American Society of Magazine Photographers, 1954; Hall of Fame Award, Art Directors Club of New York, 1972; D.F.A., Philadelphia College of Art, 1972. **Died:** Le Thor, France, 15 April 1971.

## Works

Book illustrations and designs include—*Monsieur de Bougrelon,* by Jean Lorrain, Paris, 1928; *Contes Fantastiques,* by Fyodor Dostoievsky, Paris, 1928; *A Brief History of Moscovia,* by John Milton, London, 1929; *Ballet,* with text by Edwin Denby, New York, 1945; *Paris by Day,* by André Kertész, New York, 1945; *Paris,* by Fritz Henle and Eliott Paul, New York, 1947; *Sun and Shadow,* by Marcel Breuer, edited by Peter Blake, New York, 1956; *Observations,* by Truman Capote, with photographs by Richard Avedon, New York and Lucerne, 1959; *Saloon Society,* by Bill Manville and David Attie, New York, 1960; *The World of Carmel Snow,* by Carmel Snow and Marie-Louise Aswell, New York, 1962; *Calder,* by P. Guerrero and H. H. Arnason, New York, 1966.

## Publications

**On BRODOVITCH: books**—*Advertising Directions* edited by Edward M. Gottschall and Arthur Hawkins, New York, 1959; *Buchgestaltung* by Albert Kapr, Dresden, 1963; *Alexey Brodovitch and His Influence,* exhibition catalogue by George Bunker, Philadelphia, 1972; *Alexey Brodovitch, His Work, His Influence,* thesis by Karim H. Sednaoui, Derby, 1974; *The Language of Graphics* by Edward Booth-Clibborn and Daniele Baroni, London, 1980; *Contemporary Photographers,* London and Chicago, 1982, 1988; *Brodovitch* by Andy Grundberg, New York and London, 1989.

\*       \*       \*

Alexey Brodovitch's impact upon editorial design, particularly magazine art direction, was phenomenal. The revolution that he brought to this area of graphic design was based not upon a philosophy or style but upon his perception and sensitivity. Brodovitch's intuitive vision, keen understanding of photography, and unerring sense of balance and visual flow marked his art direction of *Harper's Bazaar* for a quarter of a century. His unexpected cropping of photographs, use of white space as a design element, and classical purity of typographic layout permeated American graphic design

during his lifetime and continued to be a major influence after his death. During the 1930s, Brodovitch exposed Americans to the European avant-garde by commissioning art and photography from leading European artists and photographers, including A. M. Cassandre, Salvador Dali, Henri Cartier-Bresson, and the American expatriate Man Ray.

Brodovitch shaped our understanding and perception of photography as editorial communication. The manner in which he cropped photographs, juxtaposed them, and related a photograph's compositions and tones to the accompanying typography were his hallmarks, which since have been absorbed and assimilated by other designers. Photographer Irving Penn has observed, "All photographers are, whether they know it or not, students of Brodovitch." As a teacher, Brodovitch influenced a generation of designers and photographers at his Design Laboratory, which began with informal classes held in his home, then moved to the New School of Social Research. From the ranks of his students emerged leaders in visual communications, including photographers Penn, Richard Avedon, Art Kane, and Hiro; editorial art directors Otto Storch, Henry Woli, and Sam Antiput; and advertising designers Bog Gage, Helmut Krone, and Steve Frankfurt.

There is an almost oriental simplicity about many of Brodovitch's layouts. He was able to convey the essence of the subject with an economy rarely found in graphic design. Thus, it seems appropriate that his influence has not taken the form of stylistic mannerisms. Rather, Brodovitch stimulated the perceptual understanding and intuitive problem-solving of an entire generation of graphic designers.

—Philip B. Meggs

# BRUNNER, Robert
American industrial designer

**Born:** San Jose, California, 23 April 1958. **Education:** Studied industrial design, San Jose State University, B.S., 1981. **Family:** Married Carrie; children: Vanessa, Emily, and Luke. **Career:** Associate engineer, Electromagnetic Systems Laboratories, Sunnyvale, California, late 1970s; project manager, GVO Inc., Palo Alto, California, until 1983; founder/principal, Interform product design consultancy, Menlo Park, California, 1983-84; founder/principal, Lunar Design Inc. product design firm, Palo Alto, 1984-89; manager of industrial design, becoming senior director of industrial design, Apple Computer, Inc., Cupertino, California, 1989-96; founded Apple IDg (internal design group), Apple Computer, Inc.; partner, San Francisco office of Pentagram Design, from 1996. Jury member, IDEA Awards, Industrial Designers Society of America, from 1985, and consumer products awards, *ID* magazine's annual design review, from 1990. **Member:** Industrial Designers Society of America. **Exhibitions:** Museum of Modern Art, San Francisco, 1995. **Collections:** Museum of Modern Art, New York. **Honors:** Award, Society of the Plastics Industry, 1982; twelve IDEA Awards, Industrial Designers Society of America/*Business Week,* 1984-95; Awards, 1987, 1988, 1989, 1991, 1992, 1993, 1994, 1995, and Best of Category Award, 1994, *International Design* magazine; Top Ten Award, Industrie Forum competition, 1992, 1993, 1995; SMAU Prize, Italy, 1992, 1994, 1995; Chrysler Innovation in Design Award, 1993; Good Design Award, Chicago Athenaeum, 1995. **Address:** 19056 Montara Drive, Los Gatos, California 95030, U.S.A.

## Works

*Synovex* hormone implanter for cattle, for Syntex Agribusiness, 1981.
Personal computer, for Fortune Systems, 1982.
*Mindset* personal computer, for Mindset, 1983.
*Droidworks* video editing station, for Lucasfilm, Ltd., 1985.
*Opus 2* display terminal, for E-mu Systems, 1985.
Computing Densitometer, for Molecular Dynamics, 1987.
*Aquarius* concept, for Apple Computer, 1987.
*Q-Ball* 3D input device, for Apple Computer, 1987.
Visual design language, for 3-Com Corporation, 1988.
*E III* keyboard/synthesizer, for E-mu Systems, 1988.
*Apple IIsi,* for Apple Computer, 1988.
*Rapport* disk drive system, for Kennect Technology, 1988.
Sprinkler controller systems, for Toro, 1988.
*Macintosh LC* personal computer, for Apple Computer, 1989.
*Boom Box* study, for Apple Computer, 1989.
*Maspar* parallel computing systems, for Maspar, 1989.
Fluid analysis system, for Abbot Laboratories, 1989.
*Jaguar* concept, for Apple Computer, 1990.
*Paradigm* concept, for Apple Computer, 1990.
*PowerBook 100* series of laptop computers, for Apple Computer, 1991.
*PowerBook Duo* series of laptop computers, for Apple Computer, 1992.
*Apple AudioVision* display system, for Apple Computer, 1992.
*Newton MessagePad* personal digital assistant, for Apple Computer, 1993.
*Espresso* corporate design language, for Apple Computer, 1994.
*Pomona* concept, for Apple Computer, 1995.

## Publications

**By BRUNNER: articles**—in *Innovation* (McLean, Virginia), 1984, 1989.

**On BRUNNER: books**—*Product Design 2,* New York, 1987; *Product Design 3,* New York, 1988; *New American Design: Products for a Post-Industrial Age* by Hugh Aldersey-Williams, New York, 1988; *Design in Plastics* by Douglas Cleminshaw, New York, 1990.

*

My fascination has always been with objects. Large or small, we are surrounded by objects, influenced by them, controlling them, being held captive by them. This fascination ultimately led to my pursuit of industrial design as an occupation. The discovery that there was a profession responsible for the creation of mass produced objects was unbelievable.

In school there was an emphasis on creativity that I took to heart. I found myself pushing to always find more ideas, to do more sketches, to look at the problem from a different perspective. I also discovered my love for the craft of design, the thrill of a perfect execution, the satisfaction in creating something others took pleasure in experiencing.

It was never an overt intention of mine to focus on technology-based products. That was more an artifact of where I am, where I grew up. My father was a mechanical engineer who developed hard

disk drive technology for IBM. We always had mechanical components from these drives in our garage. It just seemed for me the appropriate medium to work in and where the work was.

After landing my first job, I discovered that there was a magic in high technology that the physical design should support and needed to support. The pace of development was breathtaking. Every product was doing something never done before. There was immense pride in the device from the people developing the idea. Everyone was on a mission to do the greatest thing ever done. It was heaven for a designer.

I've always been driven towards achieving elegance in my work. Whether the object was a toy or an industrial device, my design vocabulary has always consisted of visually simple elements. Early in my work this tended to be a modernist approach, but over time I've discovered that the idea extends beyond a rigid set of rules and has come to include a variety of shapes, both primitive and complex, with the final objective of a long-lasting beauty, appropriate to the device at hand.

I have observed that designers tend to be a narcissistic bunch, often complaining about the lack of appreciation of their work. I think I've avoided this by always believing it was my job to understand and learn to communicate with business, rather than it being their responsibility to come to my level. I also have always believed that you can do great art that achieves business objectives. You simply need to know what is on your "palette." You can create art from anything, as long as you understand the medium.

Today I find myself more than ever fascinated with objects, especially with how they fit into peoples' lives and within the context of the business world. A product should excite, satisfy, be useful, and have an inherent character that the user can identify with and take pride and pleasure in. This is what excites me.

—Robert Brunner

\* \* \*

Any portrait of Bob Brunner should begin with the physical and economic landscape of Silicon Valley, south of San Francisco, where Brunner was born, educated, and has spent his entire professional life. Dotted with more high-tech firms per square mile than anywhere in the world, the Valley is an ideal place for someone with a sure sense of aesthetics, driving ambition, and a sincere belief that industrial design can improve individual lives by making technology more available, understandable, usable, and fun.

Rooted in the late-phase modernism taught at San Jose State in the 1970s and practiced at design firms such as GVO, Brunner helped revive what could have become a tired and discredited style by infusing simple, almost reductive forms with a spark of life that was totally unexpected for someone so young. For example, while still in school, working part-time at GVO, Brunner gave a simple spring-loaded bovine hormone injector for Synovex (1980) the kind of expression and refinement that Mario Bellini would lavish on an Olivetti product. By enhancing the injector's gun-like form and enlarging and streamlining the handle and trigger (to accommodate gloves when using the product), he came away with something that would be more at home on the set of *Star Wars* than in a dairyman's barn. For *Mindset* (1981), his simple slab-like computer design featured oversized concave recesses on the front, not only to show users where to insert removable media, but to encourage them to do so, making it one of the first PCs with aesthetically interesting, user-centered design. Though Mindset eventually folded, Brunner's

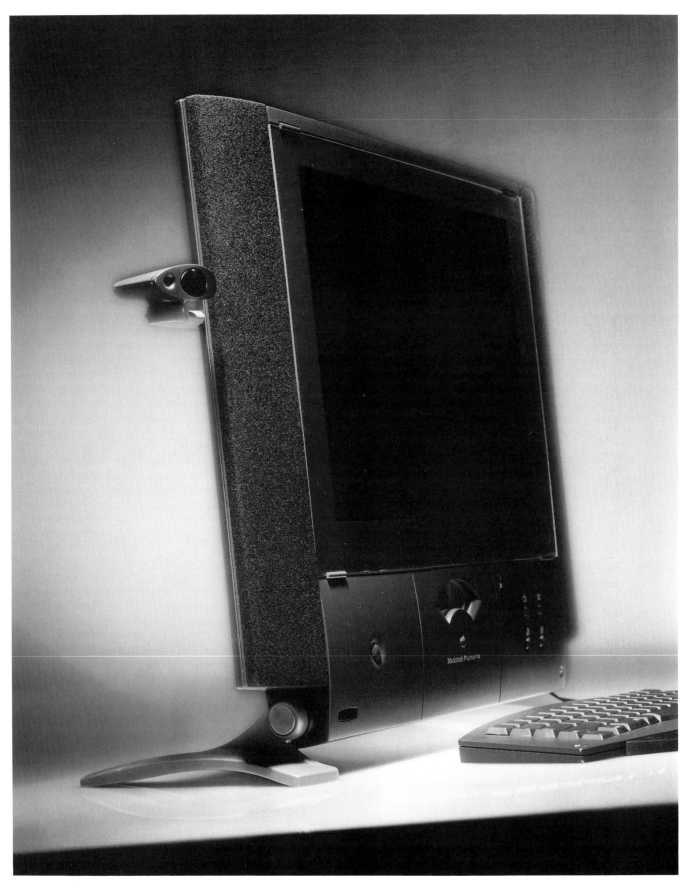

Robert Brunner: *POMONA* concept computer for Apple, 1995. Photo: Rick English design wound up at the Museum of Modern Art, after which Brunner and two colleagues from GVO formed Lunar Design, based in Palo Alto.

While at Lunar, Brunner continually refined his approach to form, combining simplicity and purposefulness with an occasional bold stroke. "I would start with a clean, almost primitive form," says Brunner, "then throw in a funny angle, add a funky color to one detail to make it pop out, or exaggerate the scale of one element as a way of throwing the design slightly off balance. Since all of our designs are technology-based, a modernist foundation is almost a given. The challenge is to add a sense of personality or drama without affecting the product's function or performance."

Unlike designers who establish a formula or develop a storehouse of ideas that they slowly use up, Brunner's mental process is simple and effective. With each new product, he imagines the simplest, most elegant form that the underlying technology will support. Then he studies the users' wants and needs, how they live and what purpose the product will serve—an act of mental modelling that results in an initial shape, which he sketches dozens of times to locate details and ensure that he hasn't overlooked an idea that is just one sketch away.

The speed of his work can be breathtaking. One colleague recalls working with Brunner on a concept for Apple Computer called *H2O* (1987). "I remember we started the project one afternoon, then I got sick and went home. When I came back the next morning, the design was finished."

Brunner's philosophy found its fullest expression at Apple Computer, where his flat pizza-box *Macintosh LC* design (1989) introduced a new generation of low-cost PCs. With its cuddly personality and upward tilt to the front, the *LC* reminded users of a friendly desktop pet. As director of the Apple Industrial Design Group (IDg), Brunner's influence extended to every aspect of the company's design. For the first *PowerBook* series (1990), he managed a multi-disciplinary effort that reshaped the modern laptop computer. For the in-house design effort called *Jaguar,* he synthesized his work with that of others to develop the *Espresso* design language, which has been used in nearly every Apple product since 1992. Apple's *Duo* system arose from an in-house Brunner investigation exploring how computers could be made extremely portable, yet connectable into powerful desktop systems, a project that adds research to his list of skills. He also recruited the most talented group of designers of any U.S. corporation, giving Apple IDg the kind of structure and identity that Braun developed under Dieter Rams.

Working in a corporate environment, Brunner knows the value of risk-taking as well as restraint. One of his favorite mottos is "Ask forgiveness, but not permission." "By the time you develop consensus within a corporation to support a new idea," says Brunner, "the idea is no longer valid. So when pursuing new concepts, I place my bet carefully, then go for it. If it blows up in my face, I ask forgiveness. But I never ask for permission to try." A recent idea based on this principle is the *Pomona* investigation, a program to develop computers tailored specifically for the home. The exotic yet restrained design of Brunner's next-generation concept, with its slim form factor, integrated CD-ROM, large active-matrix screen, and skilled use of wood veneer, metal, and leather, forces us to rethink the term "home computer."

Now a partner and director of industrial design at Pentagram, Brunner will help define the next era of industrial design as surely as he has the last.

—Paul Kunkel

# BRUUN, (Rolf) Erik

Finnish graphic, exhibition, and corporate designer

**Born:** Viipuri, 7 April 1926. **Education:** Studied graphic design, Institute of Industrial Arts, Helsinki, 1944-49. **Family:** Married the artist Sinikka Kinnunen in 1964; children: Jan-Erik, Peter, Daniel, Vega, and Sebastian. **Career:** Worked in an exhibition and display design studio, Helsinki, 1949-50; freelance graphic designer, working principally for Annonscentral AB, Helsinki, 1950-53; established own poster, graphics, and corporate design studio, working for Finncell, Finnish Wood Pulp Industry, Frederika Publishing Company, Kymmene-Stromberg Corporation, Tikkurila Oy, Union Bank of Finland, and others, in Helsinki, from 1953. Instructor in poster design, Commercial Graphic Designers' School, Helsinki, 1956-64. **Member:** Chairman, Union of Commercial Graphic Designers, Finland, 1958-59; board member, Ornamo Association of Finnish Designers, 1961-65. **Exhibitions:** *Erik Bruun: Posters,* Ministry of Foreign Affairs exhibition, toured Europe and the United States, from 1978; also in shows in Copenhagen, 1955, 1987, Weimar and West Berlin, 1965, Helsinki, 1967, 1981, 1985, Tel Aviv, 1973, Goteborg, 1977, 1987, Peking, 1981, and Tallinn, 1989. **Collections:** Poster Museum, Warsaw; Stedelijk Museum, Amsterdam. **Honors:** Best Poster of the Year Award, 1953, 1955, 1957, 1958; Finnish State Industrial Design Award, 1974; Björn Landstrom Award, Helsinki, 1989; Honorary Professor, Helsinki, 1989. **Address:** Suomenlinna 24 D, 00190 Helsinki, Finland.

## Works

*Destination North Finland* poster, 1957.
*Helsinki, the Capital of Finland* poster, 1962.
*Sea Eagle* poster, 1962.
*Turku Abo* poster, 1964.
Statistics reports, for Finncell, from 1964.
*Kymi-Kymmene International* house magazine, or Kymenne-Stromberg Corporation, 1976-85.
Posters and publications, for Savonlinna Opera Festival, from 1976.
Book designs, for Books from Finland, from 1976.
Kemira Paints graphic design, for Tikkurila Oy, from 1982.
New Finnish banknotes, for Finlands Bank, 1984-86 (with others).
*Kalevala* poster series, 1985 (with poet Lassi Nummi).
*Save Our Bears* poster, 1986.
Graphics, for Metsa-Serla, from 1986.
Graphics, for Union Bank of Finland, 1987.

## Publications

**By BRUUN: books**—*What We Have Here: Finnish Impressions,* Helsinki, 1973; (with Timo Sarpaneva) *100 Years of Finnish Industrial Design,* Helsinki, 1975; (with Sara Popovits) *Kaija and Heikki Siren,* Helsinki, 1976; *Face Finland: Finnish Impressions,* Helsinki, 1986.

**On BRUUN: books**—*Finland Creates* edited by Jack Fields and David Moore, Jyvaskyla, 1977; *Who's Who in Graphic Art* edited by Walter Amstutz, Zurich, 1982; *Erik Bruun: Finland,* with texts by Tapio Periainen and others, Espoo, 1987; **articles**—in *Form Function Finland* (Helsinki), no. 4, 1985; *Welcome to Finland,* Helsinki, 1987; *Graphics World* (Maidstone), May/June 1988.

# BRYK, Rut

Finnish ceramics designer

**Born:** Stockholm, Sweden, 18 October 1916. **Education:** Studied graphics, Central School of Industrial Art, Helsinki, 1936-39. **Family:** Married designer Tapio Wirkkala in 1945 (died, 1985), children: Sami and Maaria. **Career:** Ceramics designer, Arabia factory, Helsinki, since 1942; also designed woven textiles, for Finlaysson Forssa factory, Tampere, 1960-70, and ceramic ware decorations for Rosenthal AG Design Studio, Selb, West Germany, from 1960. **Exhibitions:** Gallery exhibitions, in Helsinki, 1949, 1953, 1962, 1968, 1970, 1985; Kunstnernes Hus, Oslo 1952; Smithsonian Institution, Washington D.C., 1956 (with Tapio Wirkkala, toured); Georg Jensen Inc., New York, 1964; Malmo Museum, Sweden, 1965; Stedelijk Museum, Amsterdam, 1970; Amos Anderson Art Museum, Helsinki, 1986; Rovaniemi Art Museum, Finland, 1987. **Collections:** Museum of Applied Arts, Helsinki; City Art Museum, Helsinki; Sara Hilden Art Museum, Tampere; Nationalmuseum, Stockholm; Rohsska Konstslojdmuseet, Goteborg; Nordenfjeldske Kunstindustrimuseum, Trondheim; Stedelijk Museum, Amsterdam; Kunstgewerbemuseum, Zürich; Bayerische Landesgewerbeanstalt, Nuremberg; Landesmuseum fur Kultur und Kulturgeschichte, Oldenburg; Museo Internazionale delle Ceramiche, Faenza, Italy, Ceramics Museum Vallauris, France; Victoria and Albert Museum, London; Everson Museum, Syracuse, New York; University of Calgary, Alberta. **Honors:** Grand Prix, 1951, and Diploma of Honour, 1954, Milan Triennale; International Ceramics Prize, Everson Museum, Syracuse, New York, 1958; A.I.D. International Design Award, New York, 1960, 1962; Domus Golden Obelisk Award, Milan, 1963; Premio Ravenna, Faenza, 1967; Grand Prix, Vallauris, 1972; State Award for Craft and Design, Helsinki, 1974; Exempla Prize, Munich, 1977; City of Helsinki Medal, 1978; Cultural Prize of the Year, Finnish Church, Helsinki, 1987. Pro Finlandia Medal, Helsinki, 1968, Commander, Ordre des Arts et des Lettres, France, 1980; Order of the Finnish White Rose, Helsinki, 1982; Doctor Honoris Causa, University of Helsinki, 1994. **Address:** Itäranta 24, Tapiola, 02110 Espoo, Finland.

## Works

*Banquet Table* wall relief, for Rosenthal AG, Selb, 1960. Fireplace, for the Bank of Finland, Helsinki, 1962.
*Thunder Clouds* wall relief, for *M/S Finlandia,* 1967.
*Gethsemane* wall relief, for Sipoo Burial Chapel, Finland, 1971.
*Blue Clouds* two-piece wall relief, for *M/S Viking,* 1973.
*Summer Rain* wall relief, for Turku Internal Hospital, Finland, 1973.
*Blue Spring* wall relief, for the Bahlsen Factory Hannover, 1974.
*City in the Sun* wall relief, for the City Hall, Helsinki, 1976.
*City by the Water* wall relief, for Volvo Head Office, Vantaa, 1982.
*The Tree* wall relief, for the Bank of Finland, Helsinki, 1982.
*Spring Comes to the North* wall relief, for the Finnish Embassy, New Delhi, 1985.
*JÄÄVIRTA/Ice Flow* seven-panel, undulating wall sculpture, for official residence of the President of Finland, 1988-1991.

## Publications

**On BRYK: books—***Rut Bryk,* exhibition catalogue with text by Lisa Licitra Ponti, Amsterdam, 1970; *Finnish Design 1875-1975* by Timo Sarpaneva, Erik Bruun, and Erik Kruskopf, Helsinki, 1975; *Nordenfjeldske Kunstindustrimuseum 1946-1979* by Jan Lauritz Opstad, Trondheim, 1980; *Scandinavian Modern Design 1880-1980* edited by David Revere McFadden, New York, 1982; *Finnish Vision,* with texts by Pekka Suhonen and others, Helsinki, 1983; *Rut Bryk,* exhibition catalogue with text by Juhani Pallasmaa, Helsinki, 1986; **articles—**"Rut Bryk" by S. Kallio-Visapaa in *Graphis* (Zürich), no. 35, 1951; "Painter Adopts Ceramic Medium" by A. Toikka-Karvonen in *Craft Horizons* (New York), October 1953; "Fifteen Contemporary Finnish Designers" in *Design Quarterly* (Tokyo), no. 37, 1957; "Pair of Designing Finns" by R. Moss in *Horizon* (New York), July 1963; "Ice Flow" by Ullamaria Pallasmaa in *Form Function* (Finland), March 1991.

\*      \*      \*

Rut Bryk has become so known for her abstract glazed tile reliefs that the other side of her personality and production, the earlier colourful tales in ceramics, has faded into the background. Seldom is an artist's work so clearly divisible into two style periods as Rut Bryk's. Her ceramic reveries and tile compositions form a kind of inverse symmetry.

Whereas her earlier works began with a pictorial theme in which colour was paramount, later works are built around abstract composition, shallow relief and the sensitive interplay of light and shade. If the works in her first period were a kind of ceramic painting, then those in the second come nearer to sculpture. Whereas her pictorial miniatures invited viewers to hear intimate stories whispered close at hand, the newer works reach out into space—the picturesque has been transformed into the architectonic.

In spite of this external dualism, the artist's work tells of an exceptionally single-minded journey towards extreme sensitiveness in expression and mastery of method towards the landscape of tranquillity in which all condenses into nothingness, as in Eastern art and mystic thought, and finally there is always the oneness one colour, time stood still, silence. Rut Bryk's artistic development is so logical it is like the humble fulfillment of a predestined pattern.

Rut Bryk was trained as a graphic artist, but like so many other designers of her generation, including her husband Tapio Wirkkala, she has worked more outside her vocation than within. In the years before and immediately after World War II, designing was considered more an attitude to life than a profession, and out of this idealism emerged the unique enthusiasm and strength of Finnish applied art during those decades. In recalling the architectonic features of Rut's works, it is not surprising to learn that she originally intended on becoming an architect and had even passed the entrance exam before her instinct drew her in the direction of the applied arts.

In addition to ceramic art—into which she came by accident following an invitation from Kurt Ekholm in 1942 to experiment with ceramics at the Arabia Factory—Rut Bryk has made linoprint textiles, church textiles, ryijy rugs, and designed woven fabrics for industrial production. Her career in textiles also began by chance when a colleague told her that the Vaasa Cotton Company was looking for a textile designer. Her refined *Seita* series from the 1960s is one of the classics of Finnish textile art, and there is reason

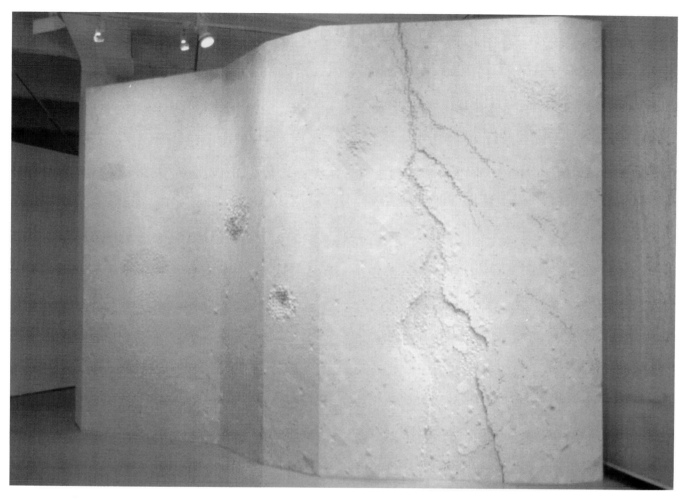

**Rut Bryk:** *JÄÄVIRTA/Ice Flow* **seven-panel, undulating wall sculpture, for official residence of the President of Finland, 1988-1991**

to hope that the best from her ten years of fabric designing will again be produced. The very timelessness of their elegant colour combinations can never wilt like fashions.

She designed some exquisitely tasteful patterns for the porcelain objects made by Tapio Wirkkala for the Rosenthal Factory. The decoration of an object is a kind of architectonic art in miniature— it may no more violate the shape of an object than a work of art fixed to the wall may ruin a room. In the Rosenthal series of artists, Rut Bryk appears alongside such illustrious names as Salvador Dali and Victor Vasarely. Philip Rosenthal, who commissioned the first monumental work now located in the studio of the Rosenthal Factory, suggested that the theme should be the company's products. These ordinary household objects the artist metamorphosized into the dishes and drinks, fruits and flowers on a table set for some fantastic banquet.

Colour is an essential motif of Rut Bryk's work. The luxuriance of colour and sense of depth have been achieved through successive layers of different coloured glazes. It is difficult to believe that these powerful and superbly balanced colours were created "blindly" from almost colourless glazing powders. The final colour appears only in the firing process, and so coloration depends on a skillful blend of imagination, memory, and experience. The artist can draw on some two hundred numbered, different coloured glazes developed in Arabia's laboratory. These she refers to by number as easily as a painter talks of "Lemon Yellow" or "Louis XV Green"— just as Vincent Van Gogh did in his letters to his brother. So "72 B" is a pine green, and "M 6" a dangerous and now forbidden uranium colour, an intense reddish orange that the artist used in many of her earlier works. A carefully kept book from decades past records the colours of her works in a series of numbers and letters, mysterious to an outsider.

All in all, Rut Bryk's output is an impressive example of work demanding unbelievable industry and patience on the odyssey towards supreme simplicity and clarity. Her works are masterpieces of patience. Each square block unit with its recesses, protrusions, and patterns is made individually. The surface patterns are scratched or pressed with an incredible variety of makeshift tools, ranging from nails and sticks to pan scrapers. Afterwards, each block receives its colour and glaze. Only then, when each single piece has been precast by hand, can the assembly begin. The whole work, which can measure up to 3 by 5 metres, is composed of thousands and thousands of carefully measured and completed blocks—just like a building. For reasons of transportation and assembly it is necessary to divide the work into parts, and the work of concealing the seams within the divisions of the mosaic surface demands great accuracy. When, after painstaking alterations and repairs, the work has found its final configuration, the cells of the mosaic may be fixed to the base board and finally jointed.

Only a friend who has experienced Rut's patience and perseverance, be it over a conversation or the detail of a meal, can understand the silent concentration and unyielding strength concealed in her frail figure.

—Juhani Pallasmaa (from *Journey to Landscapes of Tranquillity,*
exhibition catalogue, Helsinki, 1986)

# BÜLOW-HÜBE, Torun Vivianna
Swedish silversmith, ceramic, glass, and jewellery designer

**Born:** Malmö, 4 December 1927. **Education:** Studied at the National College of Art, Craft and Design (Konstfackskolan), Stockholm, 1948-51. **Family:** Married in 1946 (divorced) and in 1951 (divorced); four children. **Career:** Silversmith, Konstfackskolan, 1945-50; freelance designer, establishing own workshop in Stockholm, 1948-56, in Paris, then Biot, France, 1956-68, in Wolfburg and Wendhausen, Germany, 1968-78, and in Jakarta, Indonesia, from 1978; design consultant for a charitable organization, Jakarta, from 1978; has designed for Christofle, Orrefors, Glashütte Lohnberg, Hutschenreuther, Georg Jensen, Royal Copenhagen, and Dansk International. **Member:** Slojdforeningens Facksektion, Stockholm, 1951; Societé des Artistes Décorateurs, Paris, 1962; Gesellschaft der Goldschmiedekunst, Hamburg, 1970. **Exhibitions:** Galerie Blanche, Stockholm, 1951; Nordiska Kompaniet, Stockholm, 1951, 1961; Cercle d'Arts, Paris, 1952; Galerie du Siecle, Paris, 1954-68; Triennial di Milano, Milan, 1954, 1960; Musée Picasso, Antibes, 1958; National Museum, Stockholm, 1959; Stedlijke Museum, Amsterdam, 1960; Goldsmiths' Hall, Victorian & Albert Museum, London, 1961; *Torun of Biot,* Georg Jensen Inc., New York, 1963, 1964; World Exhibition, Seattle, 1962; La Petite Galerie, Rio de Janeiro, 1963; *Silverlek,* Hantverket, Stockholm, 1964; Georg Jensen, Copenhagen, 1969; Georg Jensen, Düsseldorf, 1970; *Danish Craft Industry,* Polytechnic Museum, Moscow, 1970; Georg Jensen, Stockholm, 1971; Georg Jensen, Tokyo, Sidney, and Melbourne, 1972; *TORUN, 25 Years a Silversmith,* La Boutique Danoise/Georg Jensen, Paris, 1973; *Georg Jensen Silversmiths 75th Jubilee Exhibition,* Museum of Decorative Art, Copenhagen, 1979-80; *4 X Torun,* NK, Stockholm, 1981; Malmö Museum, Sweden, 1981 (retrospective); National Museum, Stockholm, 1983; La Maison de Suède, Paris, 1983; *Torun: 40 Years of Jewelry,* Georg Jensen, Stockholm 1987 (retrospective; world tour, 1987-90); Sillegården, Värmland, Sweden, 1990 (retrospective); *What Modern Was: Design 1935-1965,* IBM Building, New York, 1991-1995 (toured); *Ten Danish Women in the Arts,* Museum of Women in the Arts, Washington, D.C., 1991 (toured); Konsthallen, Växjö, Sweden, 1992; *Les Bijoux de Torun,* Musée des Arts Décoratifs, Louvre, Paris, 1992-93; *Beyond Time—Themes by Torun,* Georg Jensen, Copenhagen, Paris, Hamburg, Taipei, Singapore, and London, 1992-95; *Torun,* Electrum Gallery, London, 1995. **Collections:** National Museum, Stockholm; Musée Picasso, Antibes; Malmö Museum, Sweden; Röhsska Museet, Gothenburg; Museum of Decorative Art, Copenhagen; Museum of Decorative Art, Bergen; Brighton Museum, England; Museum of Decorative Art, Oslo; Juleum, Helmstedt, Germany; Musée des Arts Décoratifs, Louvre, Paris; Worshipful Company of Goldsmiths, London; Cooper-Hewitt Museum, New York; Museum of Modern Art, New York. **Honors:** Silver Medal, 1954, and Gold Medal, 1960, Milan Triennale; Lunning Prize, 1960; Swedish State Grant, 1965; named Distinguished Silversmith by the Society for Contemporary Swedish Silver, Stockholm, 1983; Prince Eugen Medal, bestowed by King Car XVI of Sweden for outstanding artistic achievement, 1992. **Addresses:** Wisma Subud 17, Jalan Fatmawati 52, Jakarta 12430, Indonesia; (summers) 39 Valley Road North, Brome, Quebec J0E 1K0, Canada.

## Works

Rigid circular necklace in silver with stone pendant, 1948.
Moebius strip bracelet in silver, 1954.
Asymmetrical spiral necklace/sculpture in silver, 1954.
Collar and cuff circlet in silver, 1959.
Coffee service in silver, for Georg Jensen, 1960.
Figure-of-Eight glass spectacles, 1963.
Coffer-boxes in silver 1963.
Wristwatches in stainless steel, for Georg Jensen, 1969.
*Torun Silverplate* cutlery in stainless silver, for Dansk International, 1985.
Spiral movement earrings in silver, for Georg Jensen, 1987.

## Publications

**On BÜLOW-HÜBE: books—***Contemporary Swedish Design: A Survey in Pictures* by Arthur Hald and Sven Erik Skawonius, Stockholm, 1951; *Svensk Form/Forma Sueca* by Ake Stavenlow and Ake H. Huldt, Stockholm, 1961; *Modern Jewelry: An International Survey 1890-1964* by Graham Hughes, London, 1963, 1964; *Modern Silver Throughout the World 1880-1967* by Graham Hughes, London and Toronto, 1967; *Design in Sweden* by Lennart Lindkvist, Stockholm, 1972; *Scandinavian Design: Objects of a Life Style* by Eileene Harrison Beer, New York, 1975; *Modern Design in Metal* by Richard Stewart, London, 1979; *Scandinavian Modern Design 1880-1980* edited by David Revere McFadden, New York, 1982; *Den Svenska Formen* by Monica Boman and others, Stockholm, 1985; *Twentieth Century Jewelry* by Barbara Cartlidge, New York, 1985; *The Lunning Prize,* exhibition catalogue edited by Helena Dahlback Lutteman and Marianne Uggla, Stockholm, 1986; *TORUN: Conversations with Vivianna Torun Bülow-Hübe* by Ann Westin, London, 1993.

*

A piece of jewellery should be like a caress
Not capture you, but follow your every movement
and accompany you through life
That's why it should be timeless
it should reflect your uniqueness regardless of your age—
be it 17 or 87 ...

—Torun Vivianna Bülow-Hübe

*     *     *

Torun Vivianna Bülow-Hübe is a Scandinavian with an international air but her roots are in Sweden. She trained at the State School of Arts, Crafts, and Design and worked in Stockholm from 1948 to 1956, piecing together the uniqueness that made her into an international designer of jewelry and silver.

**Torun Vivianna Bülow-Hübe:** *The Open Watch* **in steel, 1962/1967. Courtesy of Georg Jensen Silversmiths**

The simple neck rings with pebbles and fossils suspended on a tongue belong to her first period, as do the superb mounts for pieces of flashed glass by Edward Hald. A broad, smooth bracelet to balance the shimmering glass, or a simple silver loop by which a glass drop dangles from the ear, are examples of her congenial settings for these starry amulets.

On a beach in France Torun Bülow-Hübe found pebbles that fascinated her because they were beautiful without being costly. She used them for ornaments in the true sense of the word: lovely, enticing, pleasurable, without also being an investment. "A simple silver coil that highlights the line of a neck is more beautiful than all the diamonds in the world." Then, without recognizing him, she had a fairytale meeting with Picasso on the beach where she was picking pebbles. He was fascinated and in 1958 she had an exhibition at the Picasso museum in Antibes. She had then spent two years in France and moved to Biot.

In Biot she built up a workshop with five assistants and stayed there until 1968. In an inspiring atmosphere, reverberating with the intensity of jazz, her work became increasingly sculptural. The mobile necklace was conceived here, floating freely about its own axis, wrought in one piece. This was the birthplace of rings that are pieces of sculpture, forms in their own right, made to be worn on a finger. It was here that she started to work with shifted forms—paper models were rotated on a disc so that the play of the form was revealed, corrected and fashioned into a supreme cigarette case

(a typical example of shifted design), a coffee service, or liqueur cups, with a gentle sheen in the smooth metal surface.

This was followed by a period as a designer for Georg Jensen and others. The sculptural wristwatches are outstanding but still no more than a small part of her output as a designer.

Torun Bülow-Hübe is now known as Vivianna and lives in Djarkarta, Indonesia. Just as she once used glass amulets, fossils, and pebbles in Europe, so she now works with mother of pearl horn, mystical stones, and shells in her new country. With complete simplicity—"The little smile that radiates from a thing."

—Helena Dahlback Lutteman

# BURNS, Aaron

American graphic and type designer

**Born:** Passaic, New Jersey, 25 May 1922. **Education:** Passaic High School, New Jersey, graduated 1940; studied at Newark Evening School of Fine and Industrial Arts, New Jersey, 1941-43; United States Armed Forces Institute, Brigham Young University, Provo, Utah, 1945. **Military Service:** Served in the United States Army, in Panama and Ecuador, 1943-46, Technical Sergeant. **Family:**

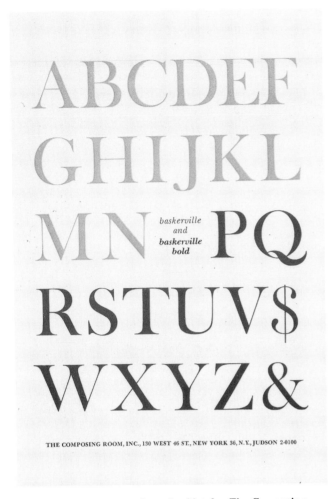

**Aaron Burns: Type specimen booklet for The Composing Room, New York, 1953**

Married Florence Browner in 1952; children: Laurie and Andrew. **Career:** Apprentice graphic designer, Alexander Ross Design Studio, New York, 1946-48; assistant graphic designer to Herb Lubalin, Sudler and Hennessy, New York, 1948; senior art director, Monogram Art Studio, New York, 1948-49; director of design and typography, Empire State Craftsmen (Rapid Typographers), New York, 1949-52, and The Composing Room, New York, 1952-60; president and creative director, Graphic Arts Typographers, New York, 1960-62; president, Aaron Burns and Company, a division of Rapid Typographers, New York, 1963-67; senior vice-president and creative director, 1967-69, and computer photosetting consultant, 1971-77, TypoGraphic Communications, New York; founder, with Herb Lubalin, and president, Lubalin, Burns and Company, New York, 1970-91, International Typeface Corporation, New York, 1970-91, and Design Processing International, New York, 1976-91. Editorial director, *Upper and Lower Case* magazine, New York, 1973-78. Instructor in advanced and experimental typographic design, Pratt Institute, Brooklyn, New York, 1955-60. Educational chairman, Type Directors Club of New York, 1956; founder, International Center for the Typographic Arts, New York, 1960; United States delegate, 1960-64, and board member, 1976-83, Association Typographique Internationale, Paris and Geneva; board member, American Institute of Graphic Arts, New York, 1963-66, 1978-81. **Member:** New York Type Directors Club; Art Directors Club of

New York; American Institute of Graphic Arts; Association Typographique Internationale. **Honors:** Hall of Fame Award, Art Directors Club of New York, 1983; named honorary lifetime vice president, Association Typographique Internationale, 1985; awarded medal for typographic excellence, New York Type Directors Club, 1985. **Died:** New York, 16 July 1991.

**Publications**

**By BURNS: books—***Typography,* New York, 1961; **articles—** "William Sandberg: Explorations in Typography" in *Print* (New York), January 1969.

**On BURNS: articles—**"Typography 1978" in *Print* (New York), May 1968; "The New York of Herb Lubalin and Aaron Burns" by H. Hara in *Graphic Design* (Tokyo), September 1971; "Aaron Burns" in *Art Directors Club Annual,* New York 1983; obituary, *New York Times,* July 1991.

*       *       *

An excellent and precise typographer, Aaron Burns was best known for co-founding and administering the International Typeface Corporation (ITC) and its publication, *Upper and Lower Case* (*U&lc*). His establishment of ITC and *U&lc* supported the field of typographic design by rewarding type designers through copyrights and royalties for their (previously unprotected) typeface designs and publishing typographic articles and type face specimens nationally. *U&lc*'s tabloid format made available, for the first time in the history of American graphic design, a publication that was affordable and easily accessible to designers and students. For some years, *U&lc* was the only source of international, socially relevant competitions to graphic design students. During his long career Aaron Burns encouraged and nurtured the design of new type faces and, through the International Typeface Corporation, saw to it that the best of these were copyrighted, produced, and disseminated.

I first met Aaron Burns at Carbondale, Illinois in 1959 when he addressed an audience of young designers who were convinced they had the power to change the world. He challenged us to care about fine typography and craft despite our idealism, tight deadlines, and often unfeeling clients. That lecture and the superb examples he showed that day continue to influence me.

As his New York Times obituary stated so well, "In many ways, Aaron Burns was a dreamer. He dreamed of an environment in which typefaces and their designers were free from unethical practices. He dreamed of a world where everyone could communicate efficiently, and beautifully, with type." His persistent, committed efforts in the typographic industry, before his death of an AIDS-related illness contracted during open heart surgery, helped to move us toward his dreams.

—Al Gowan

# BURROWS, Stephen (Gerald)

American fashion designer

**Born:** Newark, New Jersey, 15 September 1942. **Education:** Studied at the Philadelphia Museum College of Art, 1961-62; Fashion

Institute of Technology, New York, 1964-66. **Career:** Designer, at Weber Originals, New York, 1966-67; founder-proprietor, with Roz Rubenstein, of "O" fashion boutique, New York, 1968; designer-in-residence, at Henri Bendel, New York, 1969-73; founder-director of Burrows Inc., New York, 1973; worked with Pat Tennant, at Henri Bendel, New York, 1977-82, 1993; returned to ready-to-wear design, 1989, and to custom design, 1990; designed knitwear line for Tony Lambert Co., 1991. **Exhibitions:** Versailles Palace, 1973. **Honors:** Coty Winnie Award, 1973, 1977, and special award, 1974; Council of American Fashion Critics Award, New York, 1975; Crystal Ball Award, Knitted Textile Association, New York, 1975. **Address:** 550 Seventh Avenue, New York, New York 10013, U.S.A.

### Publications

On BURROWS: books—*The Fashion Makers* by Bernadine Morris and Barbara Walz, New York, 1978; *Fairchild's Who's Who in Fashion* edited by Ann Stegemeyer, New York, 1980; *McDowell's Directory of Twentieth Century Fashion* by Colin McDowell, London, 1984; *The Encyclopaedia of Fashion from 1840 to the 1980s* by Georgina O'Hara, London, 1986; *New York Fashion: The Evolution of American Style* by Caroline Milbank Rennolds, New York, 1989; articles—"The Look of Fashions for the Seventies—In Colours that Can Dazzle" by Bernadine Morris in the *New York Times,* 12 August 1970; "Designer Has Last Laugh on His Critics" by Ricki Fulman in the *New York Daily News,* 4 October 1971; "Burrows: I Am Growing More" by Elsa Klensch in *Women's Wear Daily* (New York), 6 April 1972; "The Story of Stephen Burrows" by M. R. Carter in *Mademoiselle* (New York), March 1975; "Burrows is Back" by J. Butler in the *New York Times Magazine,* 5 June 1977; "Stephen Burrows, Sportswear Designer" by Anne-Marie Schiro in the *New York Times,* 3 September 1989; "Color and Curves from Burrows" by Bernadine Morris in the *New York Times,* 9 January 1990; "The Rebirth of New York Culture" by Bernadine Morris in the *New York Times,* 1 May 1990; "The Return of an American Original" by Bernadine Morris in the *New York Times,* 10 August 1993.

*          *          *

"I make colorful adult toys because I think fashion should have a sense of humor, and I want people to be happy in my clothes," says Stephen Burrows, who is something of an innocent in his approach to business. After a time at Bendel's, he spent three-and-one-half years working for a mass-market manufacturer but found it stultifying, as the employer was afraid of new ideas and would use only cheap, artificial fabrics. In 1977, Burrows went back to Bendel's, where he could design as he pleased and could leave the difficulty of converting his ideas for the mass market to others. Thus, Burrows is the sort of designer who has to be shielded from the world if he is to create anything, and not one of those who can work in the midst of a crowd.

Influenced by the 1930s, he made his name with body-clinging dresses in jersey or velour. In 1975, his wrap-over summer evening gown in jersey was a best-seller. Beach gowns, leisure gowns, and informal evening gowns were full of 1930s fluidity. His 1977 collection showed better feeling for cut, with the bias, zigzag seams, and shirring all prominent. He also showed a reversible look in T-shirts and blousons which were one colour on one side and multi-colour on the other. By 1979, he was making the asymmetrical neckline his signature, as in a T-shirt with the shoulder straps set aslant. He took the traditional, Scottish tweed jacket and gave it asymmetrical lapels.

He maintains that he gets his greatest inspiration from the American craze for sports and athletics, so he wants to give his clothes some of the ease and enjoyment found in sportswear. The year 1980 saw him adopting the London Romantics' look in a white silk crepe de chine tunic with a deep collar and cuffs of lace to wear with narrow, olive satin trousers. Burrows, an adaptor of existing styles, gives them his own look with a modification or two, a policy that has paid off for designers before him. Comfortable clothes can achieve a comfortable turn-over.

Burrows enjoyed immense success in the 1970s, and since then his popularity in the fashion world has been sporadic, but his sensibility of design has remained consistent. Throughout the 1980s he designed custom-made clothing, juxtaposing the strongest colors, and in 1993 he returned to Henri Bendel to design eveningwear.

—Diana de Marly

# BURTIN, Will
American typographic, exhibition, and graphic designer

**Born:** Cologne, Germany, 27 January 1903; emigrated to the United States, 1938, naturalized, 1943. **Education:** Studied at Werkschulen in Cologne, 1927-30. **Family:** Married Hilda Munk in 1932 (died, 1960); daughter: Carol; married the graphic designer Cipe Pineles in 1961; stepson: Thomas Golden. **Career:** Worked as a typographic apprentice, Cologne, 1931-38; freelance graphic designer, New York, 1938-43; worked for the United States Army Air Force, 1943-44, and for the Office of Strategic Services, 1944-45; art director, *Fortune* magazine, New York, 1945-49; freelance exhibition and graphic designer, establishing own studio, and working for the Federal Works Administration, Eastman Kodak, Upjohn and Company, Union Carbide, the United States Government, and others, in New York, from 1949; design director and consultant, Upjohn Company, Kalamazoo, Michigan, 1950. Professor of design and chairman of the department of visual communications, Pratt Institute, Brooklyn, New York, from 1959. Program chairman, International Design Conference, Aspen, Colorado, 1955-56; chairman, First World Seminar on Typography, Silvermine, Connecticut, 1958. **Member:** American Institute of Graphic Arts; New York Art Directors Club; Society of Typographic Arts, Chicago, Typographic Designers of Canada; Alliance Graphique Internationale. **Exhibitions:** A-D Gallery New York, 1949; Art Directors Club of Chicago, 1949. **Honors:** New York Art Directors Club Medals, 1941, 1955, 1958; Detroit Art Directors Club Medal, 1953; Gold Medal, American Medical Association, 1958; Gold Medal, American Institute of Graphic Arts, 1971; awards from the Alliance Graphique Internationale, American Society of Industrial Designers, and New York Type Directors Club. **Died:** New York City, 18 January 1972.

### Works

*Kristallspiegelglas* promotional brochure, for a plate glass company, 1932.
WPA Pavilion at the New York World's Fair, for the Federal Works Agency, 1939.

*Scope* magazine design, for Upjohn Company, 1952-58.
*The Cell* exhibition layouts, for Upjohn Company, 1958.
*The Brain* exhibition layouts, for Upjohn Company, 1960.
*DNA* exhibition layouts, for Upjohn Company, 1962.
Exhibition displays at the New York World's Fair, for Eastman Kodak, 1964.
*The Atom in Action* exhibition layouts, for Union Carbide Company, 1964.

## Publications

**By BURTIN: books**—*Seven Designers Look at Trademark Designs* edited by Egbert Jacobson, Chicago, 1952; **articles**—in *Graphis* (Zurich), no. 27, 1949, September 1959, November 1962, no. 148, 1970; *Print* (New York), July 1955, January 1960, January 1964; *Design* (London), October 1963.

**On BURTIN: books**—*Posters: 50 Artists and Designers* edited by W. H. Allner, New York, 1952; *Advertising Directions* edited by Edward M. Gottschall and Arthur Hawkins, New York, 1959; *Die neue Grafik/The New Graphic Design* by Karl Gerstner and Markus Kuttner, Teufen and London, 1959; *Who's Who in Graphic Design* edited by Walter Amstutz, Zurich, 1962; *Design in America* edited by Ralph Caplan, New York, 1969; *Graphic Design for the Computer Age* by Edward A. Hamilton, New York, 1970; *Monografie des Plakats* by Herbert Schindler, Munich, 1972; *A History of Graphic Design* by Philip B. Meggs, New York and London, 1983; *The American Design Adventure 1940-1975* by Arthur J. Pulos, London and Cambridge, Massachusetts, 1988.

*       *       *

Will Burtin believed that science and the scientific method should be applied to all areas of human social and personal life, including art. Science allows people to "see the workings of nature, makes transparent the solid, and gives substance to the invisible." As a graphic and exhibition designer, Burtin sought to become the "communicator, link, interpreter, and inspirer" who is able to make scientific knowledge comprehensible. Burtin visualized that which was known but could not be seen, as he interpreted cell structures, molecular construction, and natural processes graphically. The "hand" of the designer was often unseen in Burtin's work, for he often used such techniques as photomontage, models, cutaway views, geometric diagrams, photographic blowups of microscopic forms, and overprinting as graphic devices to interpret and convey information.

The linking of science and art was expressed in his 1948 exhibition, *Integration—A New Discipline in Design.* It presented the four major realities upon which visual communications should be based: the reality of man, as measure and measurer; the reality of light, color, and texture; the reality of space, motion, and time; and the reality of science.

Soon after Burtin left *Fortune* in 1949 to concentrate on his growing design consultations and commissions, the Upjohn Company asked him to analyze its communications for the development of an unmistakable character which would project a cohesive image for the company. The most ambitious of Burtin's projects for Upjohn was the 1958 cell exhibit. Developed from indistinct microphotographs and consultations with scientists, this twenty-four-foot-diameter model of one-half of a human blood cell (enlarged

approximately one million times) was made to be entered by the viewer, for the purpose of observing and understanding the minute structures that make up the fundamental units of life. Moving, pulsating lights glowing within the model interpreted elemental life processes.

—Philip B. Meggs

# BURY, John
British stage designer

**Born:** Aberystwyth, Wales, 27 January 1925. **Education:** Attended the Cathedral School, Hereford, 1935-40; studied chemistry, University College, London, 1941-42. **Military Service:** Served in the Fleet Air Arm, Royal Navy, 1942-46. **Family:** Married Margaret Leila Greenwood in 1947 (divorced, 1962); married Elizabeth Rebecca Blackborrow Duffield in 1966; children: Adam, Abigail, and Matthew. **Career:** Actor and resident designer, Joan Littlewood's Theatre Workshop, Stratford, East London, 1946-63; associate designer, 1963-73, and head of design, 1965-68, Royal Shakespeare Company, London; associate director and head of design, National Theatre, London, 1973-85; also freelance designer for the commercial theatre, from 1964; worked for the Royal Opera House, London; Glyndebourne Festival Opera, England; Metropolitan Opera, New York; Santa Fe Opera, New Mexico; Los Angeles Opera; San Francisco Opera; and the Chicago Opera. **Member:** Drama Panel, 1960-68 and 1975-77, and chairman of the Designers' Working Group, 1962-78, Arts Council, London; chairman, Society of British Theatre Designers, London, 1975-85; scenographic committee, Organisation Internationale des Scenographs, Techniciens, et Architects du Théâtre, from 1990. **Honors:** Fellow, Royal Society of Arts, London, 1970; Gold Medal, Theatre Quadriennale, Prague, 1975, 1979; Officer, Order of the British Empire, 1979; Two Antoinette Perry (Tony) Awards, New York, 1981. **Address:** Burleigh House, Burleigh, Glouchester GL5 2PQ, England.

## Works

Stage designs include—*A Taste of Honey,* Theatre Workshop, Stratford, 1958; *Fings Ain't What They Used T'Be,* Theatre Workshop, 1959; *Oh—What A Lovely War,* Theatre Workshop, 1963; *The Wars of the Roses (Henry VI, parts 1, 2, and 3, Richard III),* Royal Shakespeare Company, London, 1963; *The Quatrecentennial History Cycle (Richard II to Richard III),* Royal Shakespeare Company, 1964; *Hamlet,* Royal Shakespeare Company, 1965; *Macbeth,* Royal Shakespeare Company, 1967; *Hamlet,* Shiki Company, Tokyo, 1969; *Calisto,* Glyndebourne Festival Opera, Sussex, 1970; *Tristan und Isolde,* Royal Opera House, London, 1971; *A Doll's House,* for Claire Bloom, New York, 1971; *Hedda Gabler,* for Claire Bloom, New York, 1971; *Phedre,* Shiki Company, 1973; *The Mozart Cycle (Figaro; Don Giovanni; Cosi fan Tutte),* Glyndebourne Festival Opera, 1973-75; *The Tempest,* National Theatre, London, 1974; *Tamburlane the Great,* National Theatre, 1976; *Amadeus,* National Theatre, 1979; *Amadeus,* Broadhurst Theatre, New York, 1979; *Boris Gudenov,* Australian Opera Company, 1980; *Macbetto,* Metropolitan Opera, New York, 1982; *The Bartered Bride,* English National Opera, London, 1985; *Romeo and Juliet,* Shiki Company, 1987; *Salome,* Royal Opera House, London, 1988; *Cosi fan Tutte,* Los Angeles Opera, 1988.

## Publications

**By BURY: articles**—"John Bury OBE" in *The Designer* (London), March 1979.

**On BURY: books**—*Who's Who in the Theatre* edited by Ian Herbert, London, 1977; **articles**—"Contemporary British Scenography" by J. Burian, in *Theatre Design and Technology* (Charlottesville), Spring and Fall, 1983.

\*     \*     \*

John Bury is perhaps the outstanding British example of a successful scenographer with no formal training in art, theatre design, or even architecture. His early work, for Joan Littlewood's Theatre Workshop, was characterized by improvisational ingenuity in the face of minimal budgets and by functionalism rather than artful design. He became known for assembling authentic raw materials and elements for the construction of sets.

Actually, Bury's chief interest was originally in lighting, which depends on the sets—especially their textured surfaces—for its maximum effect. Unlike almost all British designers, Bury continued to light his own sets until the pressures of his many administrative duties forced him to concentrate on sets and sometimes costumes.

For the *Wars of the Roses* productions, he provided a scenography that radically departed from the prevailingly romantic, decorative designs of the 1950s at Stratford-upon-Avon. It was harsher, more realistic, spare. Its powerful imagery and expressiveness were based on his use of a dominant material, steel, which covered the floor, segments of wall, and even some furniture, but was most evident in two huge periaktoi constructions that could rotate as well as move along curved tracks.

Bury was also involved in the development of a lighter, more abstract "box" approach to staging Shakespeare for the Royal Shakespeare Company. A basic box with a standard rake was used as a stage within the stage for a whole season of plays, providing permanent masking and an esthetically neutral environment.

Bury refers to his approach as selective, abstract realism. He is not attracted to fantasy, romanticism, or devices such as masks. Because the human actor is for him the basic measure, Bury rarely introduces marked distortion into his sets. Although he disclaims conscious artistry in his work, many of his productions reveal a fine sense of form and style, as was evident in the recurrent form of a Celtic brooch in the scenes of *Tristan and Isolde* (Covent Garden, 1971), the mirrored floor and reflective screen suspended above it for Pinter's *The Silence* (National Theatre, 1969), the stylized decor based on flown and projected scenery for *Amadeus* (London, 1979; New York, 1980), the pastiche of Victorian drop and wing settings for Verdi's *Macbeth* (Metropolitan Opera, 1982). Bury departed from the National Theatre in 1986, his last production there being Peter Shaffer's *Yonodab.* Since then he has worked closely with Peter Hall on opera productions in North America *(Salome, Figaro, Cosi fan Tutte),* as well as with other directors in England, Scotland, and Israel.

—Jarka M. Burian

# BUSSE, Rido
German industrial designer

**Born:** Wiesbaden, 14 August 1934. **Education:** Studied design, Hochschule für Gestaltung, Ulm, 1953-56. **Career:** Founder-director, Busse Design, Ulm, from 1959; has designed electronics and machinery for the West German Railways, Klocker-Moeller, Osram, Pelikan, Sennheiser, Siemens, Soehnle, Stihl und Vaillant, and others. **Member:** Central Council, VDID Verband Deutscher Industrie Designer. **Collections:** Museum of Modern Art, New York. **Address:** Robert-Bosch-Strasse 10, 7915 Elchingen, West Germany.

## Publications

**By BUSSE: books**—(editor) *Der gewerbliche Rechtsschütz als Monopolinstrument der Unternehmensfuhrung,* Ulm, 1985; **articles**—in *Absatzwirtschaft* (Düsseldorf), October 1977; *Frankfurter Allgemeine Zeitung* (Frankfurt), April 1978, August 1982; *Harvardmanager* (Hamburg), March 1979; *Verband Deutscher Industrie-Designer* (Düsseldorf), 1980; *Nurnberger Bund* (Essen), 1981; *Der Erfolgsberater* (Bonn), October 1983; *Form* (Leverkusen), 1983.

**On BUSSE: books**—*Il Disegno Industriale e la sua Estetica* by Gillo Dorfles, Bologna, 1963; *Fewerblicher Rechtsschutz* by A. Danner, Ulm, 1984; **articles**—in *Handelsblatt* (Düsseldorf), August 1977; *Wirtschaftswoche* (Dusseldorf), May 1980; *Technische Rundschau* (Bern), May 1982; *Zeitmagazin* (Hambuog), November 1982; *Maschine und Werrkzeug* (Coburg), July 1983; *Industriemagazin* (Munich), August 1983; *Scala* (Bonn), November 1983.

\*

I am the owner of Busse Design Ulm GmbH, founded in 1959. We now have 52 collaborators, and at our disposal an efficient establishment for mechanical engineering, precision engineering, electro-mechanics and electronics. With our own tooling as well as model and prototype workshops, Busse Design Ulm carries out complete developments up to readiness for fabrication. The enterprise annually awards the "Plagiarius," a negative distinction (booby prize) for imitators. Every three years we give the Busse Longlife Design Award as a prize for products which remain on the market for a long time. I am also active as expert consultant, competition juror, publicist, and member of the presidency of the Association of German Industrial Designers (VDID).

—Rido Busse

# BUTLER, Frances
American textile, graphic, and garden designer

**Born:** Frances Marie Clark, in St. Louis, Missouri, 28 November 1940. **Education:** Attended the American High School, Beirut, Lebanon, and Berkeley High School, California; studied history and design, University of California, Berkeley, BA, 1959, MA, 1966;

studied history, Stanford University, California, MA, 1964. **Family:** Married Jonathan Butler in 1964 (died, 1974). **Career:** Owner and fabric designer, Goodstuffs Handprinted Fabrics, Emeryville, California, 1972-79; owner and publisher, Poltroon Press, Oakland, California, from 1975. Instructor in typography, University of California at Berkeley 1966-69; professor of book design, University of California at Davis, from 1970; artist-in-residence, Visual Studies Workshop, Rochester, New York, 1984, San Francisco Center for Interdisciplinary and Experimental Studies, 1985, School of the Art Institute of Chicago, 1986-87, and Banff Centre for the Arts, Alberta, 1987. **Exhibitions:** *Pop Fabrics,* Victoria and Albert Museum, London, 1972; *Anatomy in Fabric,* Los Angeles County Museum of Art, 1973; *Art for Wearing,* San Francisco Museum of Modern Art, 1979; *Frances Butler: Retrospective Show,* University of California, Davis, 1982; *American Bookworks in Print,* USIA travelling exhibition, 1984-86; *Typo-Graphisme,* Centre Georges Pompidou, Paris, 1985; *Forwarding the Book in California,* Victoria and Albert Museum, London, 1988. **Collections:** Museum of Modern Art, New York; New York Public Library; Cooper-Hewitt Museum, New York; Los Angeles County Museum of Art; Victoria and Albert Museum, London; British Museum, London; Stedelijk Museum, Amsterdam. **Honors:** National Endowment for the Arts Grant, Washington, D.C., 1973, 1975, 1977, 1981. **Address:** 950 57th Street, Oakland, California, 94608, U.S.A.

## Works

*Cooked Goose Graphics* poster, for the University of California, Davis, 1970.
*Acute Angle, Try Using It* poster, for the University of California, Davis, 1971.
*Beat in the Jungle* printed cotton fabric, for Goodstuffs Handprinted Fabrics, 1971.
*Japanese Posters* silkscreen poster, for the University of California, Davis, 1971.
*In the Yellow River* printed cotton fabric, for Goodstuffs Handprinted Fabrics, 1972.
*Nippon Moon Landing* printed cotton fabric, for Goodstuffs Handprinted Fabrics, 1973.
*There's No Place to Rest Your Eyes* silkscreen poster, for Goodstuffs Handprinted Fabrics, 1973.
*Worried Man* printed cotton fabric, for Goodstuffs Handprinted Fabrics, 1974.
*Confracti Mundi Rudera* book design, for Poltroon Press, 1975 (with Alastair Johnston).
*Logbook* (T. Raworth) book design, for Poltroon Press, 1976.
*New Dryads (Are Ready for Your Call)* book design, for Poltroon Press, 1979.
*Shadow Gardens* garden layout, for the Butler residence, Berkeley, California, 1980-89.
*Career Options* book design, for Poltroon Press, 1985.
*Various Light* garden layout at Seattle University Hospital, for the Washington project for the Arts, 1986-89.
*Water Table* cement and tile mosaic sculpture, for San Francisco Art Institute, 1989.
Mosaic installation, for Mendelsohn House, San Francisco, 1989.

## Publications

**By BUTLER: books**—*Confracti Mundi Rudera* (with text by Alastair M. Johnston), Berkeley, 1975; *Colored Reading: The Graphic Art of Frances Butler,* Berkeley, 1979; *New Dryads* (with

text by Alastair M. Johnston), Berkeley, 1981; *Occult Psychogenic Misfeance,* Berkeley, 1981; *Light and Heavy Light: Contemporary Shadow Use in the Visual Arts,* Berkeley and Davis, 1985; *Career Options: A Catalog of Screens,* Rochester, New York, 1985; *Territorial Inventions,* Oakland, 1988; **articles**—in *Journal of the Society of Typographic Arts* (Chicago), January 1981, May 1989; *Arts and Architecture* (Los Angeles), Spring 1983; *Design Issues* (Chicago), no. 1, 1984; *Design Book Review,* 1986, Fall 1987; *Fine Print* (San Francisco), January 1985; *American Craft* (New York), February/March 1985; *Places* (Cambridge, Massachusetts), Summer 1984, September 1987; *Via* (Philadelphia), September 1989.

**On BUTLER: books**—*Craftsman Life Style: The Gentle Revolution* by O. Emery and T. Andersen, Pasadena, 1978; *Design on Fabric* by Meda Parker Johnston and Clen Kaufman, New York, 1981; *Typo-Graphisme: l'Image des Mots,* exhibition catalogue, Paris, 1985; *Women in Design: A Contemporary View* by Liz McQuiston, London, 1988; **articles**—in *Fiberarts* (Albuquerque), October, 1978; *Idea* (Tokyo), November, 1980; *Studio International* (London), no. 195, 1982; *Process Architecture* (Tokyo), Fall, 1985.

*

My interests for many years centered on the observation of human activity of the most quiet and ordinary kinds, and the incorporation of these observations into printed graphics on a wide variety of surfaces, most often fabric and paper. I opened a press so that I could publish books incorporating the kind of illustrations that I felt would expand the available range of expressive human gesture from the stereotyped to the idiosyncratic.

I then moved to the study of visual forms used, not to record experience, but to generate new ideas, visual tools to think with. I concentrated on the study of shadow as an old, multifarious, and continually changing formal image with which to define presence and power in the material and spiritual worlds. Writing articles and a catalog on the subject encouraged my development of a shadow garden in which I exploited some of the folklore of shadow, and shadow as a creative subject extended to the development of shadow plays and giant shadow puppets made to perform them.

Later my interests shifted from observation of and recreation of expressions of the already known, whether it be experiences, prejudices, or fears, to exploration of human cognitive tactics, and to both the material and the immaterial aids used to encourage and to support learning and thinking. I am especially interested in the ways devised by immigrants to learn how to understand and use their new culture, and the ways in which they both keep and modify their old cultures. My emphasis has been on the ways in which arrangement of both work and leisure spaces are structured by people to express their views of the world and how they fit into it. Immigrant gardens, produced by groups ranging from the Portuguese to the Southeast Asians, being quite different from the English vernacular garden which dominates the popular media, make the cognitive tactics of gardening startlingly visible. And, as usual, while writing on this subject (articles and a book, *Contemporary Vernacular Gardens,* with photographer Travis Amos) I am producing garden designs influenced by these immigrant gardens. Presently I am working on mosaics in the pictorial and ornamental traditions of the Mediterranean for gardens and some public buildings.

—Frances Butler

* * *

A prolific and versatile designer, Frances Butler is also an artist, scholar, educator, and writer on design. She has received wide recognition for her work in a number of media: fabric and textile design, managing her own textile design company; graphic design, typography and book design, managing her own small press with partner Alastair Johnston; and more recently, garden design, practicing alone and with others. In addition, her writing on design is well-received by a wide audience which ranges from practicing designers to art and social/cultural historians.

Butler's unusual combination of practical and theoretical knowledge and skill in design evolved from her education in both history and design. Her teaching and research, as well as extensive travels and a wide range of intellectual interests, also provide her with an appropriate and supportive base for this duality. Her flaunting of the usual pattern of success in design—selection of one aspect of design and sticking to it—has not been a detriment to her career. Rather, unconventionality and experimentation are a vital and integral part of her work which have contributed to her unique style in both design and writing about design.

Readily apparent in her teaching of design, Butler's philosophy is to combine the understanding of creativity and the processes of design with the critical and analytical approaches of design theory to expand the usually narrowly defined field of design.

Recurring themes in her work are sequential movement, time, and order in space; light and shadow; complex, overlapping layers of pattern; and an underlying humanistic concern. Human and animal figures almost always play a role in each piece. Despite the often whimsical and highly personal nature of her work, a deeper, intellectual content is communicated through literary, musical, or historical allusions and symbolism from the Orient and the West.

Butler's textile designs, bold and innovative, were sold internationally, most often as wall hangings or art, in single panels or yardage. "Beast in the Jungle" (1971), based on the Henry James novel, uses decorative, repetitive patterns to effectively create a sense of tension in the depiction of two tigers, one barely discernible, stealthily approaching a tea party. In her own words, "In the Yellow River" (1972) is a decorative, repeated image of "an Oxford educated (Chinese) princess (who) still winds up in a maze of packaging near the isle of Deshima and Mao-Tse-tung in the current, moving continuously."

Incorporating many of the same themes and patterns from her textile work into her graphic design, Butler created a structure for the organization of her work in direct contrast to the popular Swiss grid approach. She uses borders, but varies their relationship to the image and the page, breaking images through the borders, overlapping them, inserting text on the images, using text as borders. She also emphasizes size and relationship of images to one another and to the page, frequently as she has stated, ". . . grouping small images into large shapes to lead the viewer through the sequential reading of all the little goodies that make up the whole story. I wanted to create an experience that was 'just like at the movies,' where one sees the entire screen constantly while refocusing on subtle gestures." Color and experimentation with color are other characteristics of her work, and her revival of the nearly obsolete and labor-intensive pochoir technique brings an unusual richness to the palette of her printed work.

Her early studies in history led her to medieval manuscripts, which spurred an interest in calligraphy, then typography, and later book design and printing. Book design allowed her to experiment further with the themes of sequential movement and continuing patterns and images through the turning of the pages. "Confracti Mundi Rudera" (1975), the first book produced by her Poltroon Press, uses parallel interacting texts, one visual, one verbal. "Career Options, a Catalog of Screens Including the Gesture of Outward" (1985) is a beautifully crafted book full of surprises, like pop-up folded figures and a pocket of postcard-like images related to the images in the book itself. Mostly black and white, the pages are composed of photographic images of cut-out figures, some acrobatic, all casting strong shadows. Brief texts give light-hearted and poetic, but sound, advice about the jobs represented by each screen. Many of the images depicted have been used previously in her other work.

Butler has worked on her own private garden since 1980, constantly changing both the plantings and sculptural elements in it. Again emphasizing shadow and light, color, and the interplay of the visual and the verbal, her gardens are filled with many of the images and themes of her other work: order, movement, time, borders, sequence, and pattern. Trellises with large letters or words cast moving shadows across whimsically tiled plant beds, and light and color flow through cut-out screens and open-work tables. She incorporates her knowledge of history and literature into the words and quotes tiled into mosaic planters and borders. Influenced by the sophisticated poetry gardens and the naive and eccentric gardens she has researched, her gardens are delightful and ever-changing. From her book *Career Options* she sums up what a garden should be: "Once the possibilities are surveyed, make a garden or a stage. Now there is the possibility of entrance and exit and fragments of action can become stories."

Butler has also experimented with photography and photoprint collages, etchings, sculpture, furniture making, and mosaics, incorporating many of the themes and images from her graphic work into these forms. Frances Butler's work is eclectic, idiosyncratic, and impossible to categorize, but intriguing, analytical, humorous, delightful, and intelligent.

—Elizabeth Douthitt Byrne

# CACHAREL, Jean

French fashion designer

**Born:** Jean Louis Henri Bousquet, in Nimes, 30 March 1932. **Education:** École Téchnique, Nîmes, 1951-54. **Family:** Married Dominique Sarrut in 1956; children: Guillaume and Jessica. **Career:** Cutter and stylist, for Jean Jourdan, Paris, 1955-57; founder and director, Société Jean Cacharel ready-to-wear fashions, Paris, from 1964; worked with designer Corinne Sarrut, specializing in separates, dresses, shirts, sweaters, trousers and ties, from 1966; added children's line, early 1970s; launched perfume and jeans lines, 1978; added men's line, 1994; fragrances include *Anais Anais,* 1978, *Loulou,* 1987, *Cacherel pour Homme,* 1991, *Eden,* 1994; introduced cosmetics line, 1991. **Honors:** Export Trade Oscar, Paris, 1969. **Address:** 3 Rue du Colisee, 30931 Nimes, France.

## Publications

On CACHAREL: books—*Paris Fashion: The Great Designers and Their Creations* by Ruth Lynam, London, 1972; *The World of Fashion: People, Places, Resources* by Eleanor Lambert, New York and London, 1976; *In Fashion: Dress in the Twentieth Century* by Prudence Glynn, London, 1978; *Mode im 20. Jahrhundert* by Ingrid Loschek, Munich, 1978; *25 Ans de Marie-Claire de 1954 a 1979,* compiled by Francoise Mohrt, Paris, 1979; *Fairchild's Who's Who in Fashion* edited by Ann Stegemeyer, New York, 1980; *Who's Who in Fashion* edited by Karl Strute and Theodor Doelken, Zurich, 1982; *McDowell's Directory of Twentieth Century Fashion* by Colin McDowell, London, 1984; *The Encyclopedia of Fashion from 1840 to the 1980s* by Georgina O'Hara, London, 1986; articles—"Cacherel's Rag Trade Riches" by Jose Manser in *Design* (London), October 1969.

*       *       *

A May 1975 full-page advertisement for Higbee's [Ohio] Department Store in *Vogue* announces: "Cacharel Collectors ... gather 'round. See the new Cacharel collections of soft summer skirts, exquisite shirts and crisp blazers...." By 1975, innumerable women were gathering Cacharel clothing as virtual collectibles, a sure sign of artistic good taste and modern sensibility. The pieces—separates conjured out of sportswear, but often dressy enough for dinner—were adaptable, fluid styles, rich in pattern, well-made, and dependable, both socially secure and aesthetically charming. The same woman—imagining herself individualistic, gentle, sensible, and purposeful—who might have also bought Kenzo was collecting Cacharel for its youthful sense of sportswear separates and irreproachable quality along with a quiet aestheticism. Like Kenzo, Cacharel (Louis Henri Bousquet) was a clothing vagabond in the

first era of the Jet Age, appropriating paisley wools, Liberty prints, bold African prints, ethnic shirts, English tradition, and countless fashion basics from around the world to a yet discreet style of impeccable wardrobe-builders for cosmopolitan women (and later for men as well). Disestablishment hippies had led the way to a style that was soigné and sophisticated, yet supple and casual. A 1961 trip the designer took to St. Thomas, Puerto Rico, and Guadaloupe had brought back vibrant bermuda shorts and printed shirts from the Caribbean. These souvenirs became inspirations for culottes and body-clinging shirts for women as standards in the Cacharel collections.

The Cacharel collection was invariably built from fundamentals. Soft shirts mediated between being men's shirts (Cacharel's first business) and blouses in their suppleness; these shirts were basic, yet capable of ethnic variation, collars embroidered or unadorned that differed from Peter Pan demureness to long points, prints large and small, and sleeves tucked or wildly enlarged. Dresses, never the focus of the collection, tended to minimal construction, often with tucking or pleating, with a flattering indefiniteness of size that would eventually become the hallmark of Laura Ashley. It is always hard to pinpoint Cacharel geographically: it has an English prettiness and sometimes even a daintiness, but it is based in American sportswear separates and pragmatism, yet it is also French in its supple dressmaking and detailing, and always responsive to eclectic global fashion ideas.

In fact, Cacharel was such a merchandising phenomenon of the 1970s that it was widely copied for its innocent and decorous sportswear look. Moreover, Cacharel defined its client in influential advertising not only for the apparel, but also for the successful fragrances, including *Anais Anais,* launched in 1978. Romantic, suffused images by photographer Sara Moon have become icons of Cacharel woman, a little pre-Raphaelite, a little Eve, and very much a modern, no-nonsense woman of ready-to-wear basics. It is not surprising that the 1994 fragrance was called *Eden,* continuing the Cacharel signification of the innocent.

If Cacharel betokens innocence, its marketing has always been canny. Woman seeking wearable clothes that would not readily become dated have used the romanticism of Cacharel as wardrobe basics, annually collecting more skirts and blouses and blazers to assemble a likeable, harmonious style in no fear of being trendy or aggressive. In the 1980s, Cacharel could also enter the work wardrobe of modern women, especially those wanting to express an artistic inclination. Cacharel has also shown a strength in clothing for all seasons, not only because of the possibility of layered sweaters and blazers, but because of Cacharel's admired light wools, silks, and cottons, adaptable year-round in most climates. Menswear was first introduced in the 1970s and revived in the 1990s, stressing the same combining elements of traditional sweaters and shirts that could transfer from recreational clothing to casual, well-dressed style. Cacharel defines what is generally described as contemporary designer sportswear, a stylish modern practicality.

Cacharel takes its name from a wild duck in the romantic Camargue region of the South of France. The euphonious sound of the word and the images of a nonchalant modern style, touched by romantic longings and feel-good textiles, have for some thirty years represented products worthy of being collected.

—Richard Martin

# CADBURY-BROWN, Henry Thomas

British architect, interior, and exhibition designer

**Born:** London, 20 May 1913. **Education:** Westminster School, London, until 1930; studied at the Architectural Association School, London, 1931-35, Dip., 1935. **Military Service:** The Royal Artillery, British Army, 1939-45, Major. **Family:** Married Elizabeth Romeyn in 1953. **Career:** Worked in the office of architect Erno Goldfinger, London, 1936-37; in private architectural and design practice, London, 1937-39; and with partner John F. Metcalfe from 1945; in H. T. Cadbury-Brown Partnership, from 1962; also with Eric Lyons Cunningham Partnership, 1977. Instructor, Architectural Association School, London, 1946-49, and Royal College of Art, London, 1952-61; visiting critic, Harvard University School of Architecture, Cambridge, Massachusetts, 1956; Professor of Architecture, Royal Academy, London, 1958. **Member:** Royal Institute of British Architects, 1951-53; committee member from 1953, and President, 1959-60, Architectural Association, London; British committee member, Union Internationale des Architectes, 1951-54. **Honors:** London Architecture Bronze Medal, 1963; Fellow, Royal Institute of British Architects; Honorary Fellow, Royal College of Art, London; Officer, Order of the British Empire, 1967; Associate, 1971, and Academician, 1975, Royal Academy of Art, London. **Address:** 18 Fentiman Road, London SW8.

## Works

Exhibition displays at the *Design in Industry* exhibition, Olympia, London, 1938.
*Origins of the People* pavilion at the *Festival of Britain,* London, 1951.
Royal Pavilion at the *Royal Norfolk Agricultural Show,* 1952.
Chance Glass displays at the *Building Exhibition,* London, 1953.
National Farmers Union pavilion at the *Royal Agricultural Society Annual Show,* 1955.
Portland Library and Art Gallery interiors, Nottingham University, 1955.
Conference room interiors, Time-Life Building, London, 1956.
Directors dining-room interiors, Shell Centre, London, 1961.
Kurt Geiger shoe shop interiors in Bond Street and Sloane Street, London, 1965, 1969.
Royal Lancaster Hotel banquet room interiors, London, 1966.
Monk and Dunstone office interiors, Bristol, 1972.
Buildings and architectural works include:
British Railways offices, London, 1937-39.
School and housing, Harlow New Town, Essex, 1953-54.
Honrsey Lane School, London, 1955.
Housing, Hatfield, Hertfordshire, 1959.
Shops and housing, Basildon New Town, Essex, 1960.

Royal College of Art buildings, London, 1962-63.
Birmingham University halls of residence, 1964.
Civic Centre, Gravesend, Kent, 1968.
Ashburnham School, Chelsea, London, 1973.
World's End complex, Chelsea, London, 1977.

## Publications

**By CADBURY-BROWN: articles**—"Ludwig Mies van der Rohe" in the *Architectural Association Journal* (London), July/August 1959.

**On CADBURY-BROWN: articles**—"The Wrong Decision: Project for the New Royal College of Art Building" in *Architectural Review* (London), July 1973; "Crosland Sets Important Listed Building Precedent" in *Architects' Journal* (London), 26 November 1975; "V & A: History and Future Development" by Johnny Grey in *Architectural Design* (London), no. 7/8, 1977; "It's a Blue Ribbon Scheme" in *Building Design* (London), 5 June 1981.

\*     \*     \*

H. T. Cadbury-Brown, although personally modest to the point of reticence, has developed an authoritative architectural personality that few of his collaborators have been able to resist. There is an impression, however, that this personality was somewhat frustrated by Casson and Gooden (and maybe by the Senate of the Royal College of Art as well) in the Kensington Gore buildings where other decorative schemes were imposed (as, for instance, in the Senior Common Room). One has only to contrast this with the student refectory area as Cadbury-Brown left it or with the Gulbenkian Hall interior (where he was helped by Elizabeth Cadbury-Brown) to realize what was lost elsewhere in the building. The two residence halls at Birmingham University, commenced in 1963, also bear witness to his strength, and the commendation they received emphasises how much Cadbury-Brown contributed to gain the Gold Medal awarded to the Royal College of Art buildings.

Cadbury-Brown's work is invested with an eloquent geometry, largely polygonal, which provides all the decoration it requires. In this respect, his work relates more to Mackintosh and to the Horta of the Palais du Peuple than to the usual masters of the International Style. In some ways, the World's End complex of dwellings, offices, school, children's home, and shops—designed in collaboration with the Lyons and Cunningham partnership but owing much in its polygonal effects to Cadbury-Brown—recalls no other building so much as Mackintosh's Glasgow School of Art (which it in no way resembles, however).

Along with many other British architects of the time, following the breakthrough of the Festival of Britain on London's South Bank, Cadbury-Brown undertook a number of civic commissions for educational buildings. The list is impressive as much for the quality of the individual buildings as for their number—a primary school in West Bromwich, the RCA buildings in Kensington Gore, two residence halls, at Birmingham University, the sixth-form accommodation for Felixstowe College, the lecture theatre block for Essex University, as well as student housing there—all designed within the space of nine or ten years.

Before coming to the design of the World's End development, Cadbury-Brown had already designed the Taistock Crescent scheme for the same municipality. This had made ingenious use of the site to pack in some 132 dwellings along with a social services unit. He learned much from the experience, which underlay his obvious contributions to the World's End site. He has also produced distinguished buildings for the Gravesend and Cranbrook Councils.

—Toni del Renzio

# CAFLISCH, Max

Swiss book, typographic, and lettering designer

**Born:** Switzerland, 25 October 1916. **Education:** Studied typography, as an apprentice compositor, at the Studer-Schläpfer printing works, Horgen, and at the Kunstgewerbeschule, Zürich, 1932-36. **Family:** Married Aline Lüthi in 1943; children: Regula and Ulrich. **Career:** Typographer, under Jan Tschichold and Imre Reiner, at the Benno Schwabe and Birkhäuser printing works, Basel, 1938-40; typographer, then art director, Benteli AG publishers and printers, Bern-Bümpliz, 1941-62; freelance designer and typographic consultant, from 1944, for Swiss, German, English, and American publishers and firms. Advisor in type design and typographic consultant, IBM World Trade, New York, 1962-66, Bauer Type Foundry, Frankfurt, 1965-66, Hell of Kiel, 1972-89, and Adobe Systems Inc., Mountain View, California, 1990-92. Lecturer and instructor in typography, Allgemeine Gewerbeschule, Basel, 1940-41, Kunstgewerbeschule, Zurich, 1962-81, Technikerschule der Graphischen Industrie, Zürich, 1973-78. Contributor to *Schweizer Graphische Mitteilungen,* St. Gallen, 1938-40, *Typographische Monatsblätter/Swiss Typographic Magazine,* St. Gallen and Zürich, from 1939, *Revue Suisse de l'Imprimerie,* Lausanne, 1950, 1953, *Atlantis,* Zürich, 1954, *Schweizerisches Gutenbergmuseum,* Bern, 1956, 1960-62, *Der Schweizer Buchhandel,* Zürich, 1960-61, 1985, *Graphische Revue Oesterreichs,* Vienna, 1962, *Book Design and Production,* London, 1962, *Magyar Grafika,* Budapest, 1965, *Bogvennen,* Copenhagen, 1965, *Librarium,* Zürich, 1968, 1983, *Monotype Recorder,* London, 1968, 1987, *Schweizerische Lehrerzeitung,* Bern, 1969, *Litera,* Warszawa, 1978, *Imprimatur,* Frankfurt, 1980, *Fine Print,* San Francisco, 1983, *Philobiblon,* Stuttgart, 1987, *Officina,* Basel, 1988, 1995, *Font & Function,* Mountain View, California, 1992, *Helvetische Typographia,* Bern, 1994, *Form,* Frankfurt, 1994, *Typoscope,* New York, 1995. **Member:** Bund Deutscher Buchkünstler, Frankfurt; Association Typographique Internationale; Double Crown Club, London. **Exhibitions:** Stiftung Buchkunst, Frankfurt, 1968; Fachhochschule, Hamburg, 1968; Stadtbücherei Wilhelmspalais, Stuttgart, 1968; Gutenbergmuseum, Bern, 1969; Centro del bel Libro, Ascona, 1981; Universiteits-Bibliothek, Amsterdam, 1983; St. Kathrinen, St. Gallen, 1989; Deutsche Bibliothek, Frankfurt, 1992; Staatliche Akademie der Bildenden Künste, Stuttgart, 1992. **Collections:** Schweizerische Landesbibliothek, Bern; Stiftung Buchkunst, Frankfurt; Deutsche Bücherei, Leipzig; Klingspor-Museum, Offenbach; New York Public Library. **Honors:** Two Gold Medals, 1965, and Golden Letter Award, 1970, Leipzig International Book Fair; Preis der Schweizer Buchhandels, 1985; and more than 100 book awards in Switzerland and Germany. **Address:** In der Halden 12, CH-8603 Schwerzenbach, Switzerland.

## Works

*Chorfenster und Altäre des Berner Münsters* (Hans R. Hahnloser) book design, for Verlag Benteli, Bern-Bümpliz, 1950.
*Gedichte vom Mittelalter bis zur Neuzeit* book design, for Staatlicher Lehrmittelverlag, Bern, 1953.
*Columna* typeface, for Bauer, Frankfurt, 1955.
*Handbuch der Schweizerischen Volkswirtschaft* 2-volume book design, for Benteli-Verlag, Bern, 1955.
*Conrad Ferdinand Meyer: Samtliche Werke* book design, for Benteli-Verlag, Bern, 1958-70.
*Elégies et Sonnets de Lovize Labé Lionnoize* book design, for Alain Berlincourt, Bern, 1961.
*The Magic Mountain* (Thomas Mann) 2-volume book design, with engravings by Felix Hoffmann, for Limited Editions Club, New York, 1962.
*Der abenteuerliche Simplicius Simplicissimus* (Hans Jakob Christoph von Grimmelshausen) book design, with etchings by Max Hunziker, for Flamberg-Verlag, Zurich, 1964.
*Das Hohe Lied* book design, with woodcuts by Felix Hoffmann, for Flamberg-Verlag, Zurich, 1964.
*The Discourses of Epictetus* book design, for Limited Editions Club, New York, 1966.
*Der Psalter* book design, with illustrations by Max Hunziker, for Württembergische Bibelanstalt, Stuttgart, 1966.
*Die Bibel* (Hausbibel) book design, for Württembergische Bibelanstalt, Stuttgart, 1967.
*Die Bibel* (Perlbibel) book design, for Württembergische Bibelanstalt, Stuttgart, 1967.
*Die Bibel* (altar and chancel bible) design, for Württembergische Bibelanstalt, Stuttgart, 1968.
*Atlas de mycologie médicale* book design, for Editions Hans Huber, Bern, 1974.
*Digiset-Schriften der Firma Meier et Cie AG* catalogue design, for Meier et Cie, Schaffhausen, 1982.
*Heinrich Bullinger: Werke* book design, for Theologischer Verlag, Zurich, 1983.
*Catalogue of Typefaces* catalogue design, for Dr.-Ing. Rudolf Hell GmbH, Kiel, 1983.
*Mengensatz-Schriftprobe der Firma Typopress* book design, for Typopress, Zurich, 1983.
*Wilhelm Meisters Lehrjahre* (Johann Wolfgang Goethe) 2-volume book design, with illustrations by Felix Hoffmann, for Verlag Mirio Romano, Kilchberg, 1983.
*Johannes Gessners Pariser Tagebuch 1727* book design, for Hans Huber Verlag, Bern, 1985.
*Max Caflisch: Typographia practica* book design, for Maximilian-Gesellschaft, Hamburg, 1988.
*Romeo und Julia auf dem Dorfe* (Gottfried Keller) book design, with illustrations by Karl Walser, for Verlag Mirio Romano, Kilchberg, 1989.
*Gesunde Köoperhaltung im Alltag* (Dr. Alois Brügger) book design, for Verlag Dr. A. Brügger, Zürich, 1990.
*Caflisch Script* type design, for Adobe Systems Inc., Mountain View, California, 1993.
*Albrecht von Haller in Göttingen* (Urs Boschung) book design, for Verlag Hans Huber, Bern, 1994.
*Gesangbuch der Evangelisch-reformierten Kirchen der deutschsprachigen Schweiz* book design, Zürich, 1995.

## Publications

**By CAFLISCH: books**—(with others) *The Art of the Book,* London, 1951; *Die Antiqua und Kursiv des Buchhändlers, Verlegers, Schriftgießers und Druckers John Bell,* Bern, 1957; *William Morris, der Erneuer der Buchkunst,* Bern, 1959; *Kleines Spiel mit Ornamenten,* Bern, 1965; (with others) *Schätze der Typographie: Gebrochene Schriften,* Frankfurt, 1968; (with others) *Oldrich Menhart,* Hamburg, 1968; (with others) *Almanach 1969* and *1976,* Köln, 1968, 1975; *Fakten zur Schriftgeschichte,* Bern, 1972; *Schrift und Papier,* Grellingen, 1973; (with others) *J. T./Johannes Tzschichold/Iwan Tschichold/Jan Tschichold,* München, 1976; *Typographie braucht Schrift/Typography Needs Type/Typographie a besoin des caractères,* Kiel, 1978; (with others) *Fraktur Gotisch Schwabacher zeitlos schön,* Hildesheim, 1982; (with others) *HPW/ Hans Peter Willberg,* Verona, 1993; *Das schriftkünstlerische Werk von Eric Gill,* Basel, 1995; *Die Druckschriften, Schmuckserien und Vignetten von F. H. Ernst Schneidler* (in press).

**On CAFLISCH: books**—*Modern Lettering and Calligraphy,* edited by Rathbone Holme and Kathleen M. Frost, London and New York, 1954; *Manuale Typographicum* by Hermann Zapf, Frankfurt, 1954, 1968, New York, 1968, Cambridge, Massachusetts, and London, 1970; *A Book of Type and Design* by Oldrich Hlavsa, New York, 1960; *Who's Who in Graphic Art,* edited by Walter Amstutz, Zürich, 1962, 2nd edition, Dübendorf, 1982; *Buchgestaltung* by Albert Kapr, Dresden, 1963; *Calligraphy Today* by Heather Child, London, 1963, 1976; *Lettering Today: A Survey and Reference Book* edited by John Brinkley, London, 1964; *Letter Forms: 110 Complete Alphabets* edited by Frederick Lambert, London, 1964, New York, 1972; *A Manual of Decorated Typefaces* by R. S. Hutchings, London and New York, 1965; *Kürschners Graphiker Handbuch* edited by Charlotte Fergg-Frowein, West Berlin, 1967; *The Art of Written Forms: The Theory and Practice of Calligraphy* by Donald M. Anderson, New York, 1969; *Schriftkunst* by Albert Kapr, Dresden, 1971; *Architectural Signing and Graphics* by John Follis and Dave Hammer New York and London, 1979; *The Thames and Hudson Manual of Typography* by Ruari McLean, London, 1980; *Max Caflisch: Typographica practica,* Hamburg, 1988; *Max Caflisch zum fünfundsiebzigsten,* Stuttgart, 1992; *Book Design in Switzerland* by Jost Hochuli, Zürich, 1993; *Caflisch Script,* Mountain View, California, 1993.

*

Script and form have a decisive influence on the understanding of a text, and therefore on the legibility of a printed work. The activity of the typographer takes place in obscurity. It is true that his hand may be detected in the printed work but it should not intrude upon the reader. It is the typographer's prime task to serve the readers of every age and to produce printed matter which is as comfortable as possible. The more natural typography appears the more the typographer's work can be regarded as successful. In this sense, each typographical task is for me a constantly new challenge.

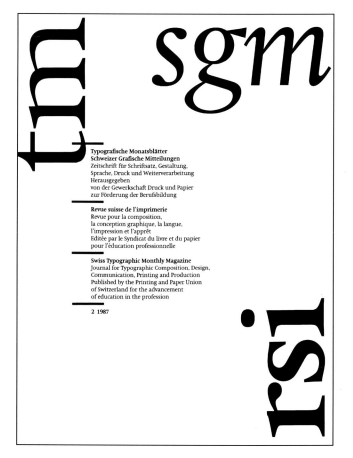

Max Caflisch: cover for *Typographische Monatsblätter*

In the late 1980s and early 1990s production and methods for making well designed printed matter have changed, but the demands of good typography (or graphic design) still are the same:

—the choice of a format according to the needs of the text and related ease of handling;

—the choice of an appropriate typeface and size which guarantees easy reading;

—a perfect typesetting technique;

—a practical and attractive design;

—an optimum reproduction quality of type and illustrations;

—paper and printing ink suited to the printing methods;

—appropriate printing and processing methods.

This quality level should be the aim of designers and printers.

—Max Caflisch

\*     \*     \*

Max Caflisch's work in book design shows mastery of all aspects of the task: the arrangement and setting of text (with meticulous attention to fine details of spacing and of editorial decision), the choice of paper and other materials, the design of binding and jacket. These skills can be attributed in part to his training as a compositor, as well as to his subsequent design education, and then to his years as an in-house designer with the printer and publisher Benteli A G. Caflisch is a notable product of the Swiss system of typographic training, which marries the instruction of technical printer's skills to a full education in design. But if Caflisch's work is an exemplary product of Swiss typographic culture, it nevertheless has little connection with the school of modernist graphic design and typography that, during the 1950s and 1960s, made "Swiss" typography famous as a dogmatic style.

Caflisch has designed generally within the assumptions of "classical" or "traditional" typography. He worked under Jan Tschichold in the late 1930s, just at the point when Tschichold was adopting a "traditional" typography, and he has sometimes been seen as having stayed in the shadow of Tschichold's influence. But though Caflisch's early work (at least as reproduced) does in some respects recall Tschichold's manner, the more important point is that both were working within the same large tradition. Caflisch's published statements make clear his conception of a broad and almost eternal historical sequence, in which his and much other work stands; the contribution of any individual is seen as subservient to this larger phenomenon, and the designer deviates from it at the risk of mere self-expression and disregard for the text and the reader. This doctrine is outlined in Stanley Morison's *First Principles of Typography*, a German-language edition of which Caflisch has translated and designed. The range of Caflisch's typographic skills and interests further recalls Tschichold—especially his lettering and calligraphy but also his published work on the history of the subject—though he has not shown the polemical urge that characterized Tschichold's career. During the heyday of modernist "Swiss typography", he continued his work untroubled by any wish to attack heresies. However, this description of Caflisch's work is not a final one. In his later work (particularly in display typography), there are signs of a loosening of approach, away from any rigid application of "classical" solutions and towards arrangements that find their own, less symmetrical form.

—Robin Kinross

# CARDIN, Pierre

French fashion designer

**Born:** Of French parents, in San Andrea da Barbara, Italy, 2 July 1922. **Education:** Educated in Saint-Etienne, France; studied architecture, Saint-Etienne. **Career:** Worked as an accountant, then as a tailor's cutter, Paris; designer, for Paquin fashion house and for Schiaparelli, Paris, 1945-46; head of workrooms, Christian Dior fashion house, Paris, 1946-50; founder-director, Pierre Cardin fashion house, Paris, from 1950; first ready-to-wear collections, 1959; also film costume designer, from 1946. Founder-director, Theatres des Ambassadeurs-Cardin (now Espace Cardin complex), Paris, from 1970; chairman, Maxim's Restaurant, Paris, from 1981. **Exhibitions:** *Fashion: An Anthology,* Victoria and Albert Museum, London, 1971; Victoria and Albert Museum, London, 1991; Musée des Beaux Arts, Montreal, 1991; Musée National de la Estampa, Mexico, 1993; Brazil, 1994. **Honors:** Gold Thimble Award, Paris, 1977, 1979, 1982; Chevalier de la Légion d'Honneur, France, 1983; Fashion Oscar, Paris, 1985; Prize of the Foundation for Garment and Apparel Advancement, Tokyo, 1988; Grand Officer, Order of Merit, Italy, 1988; Honorary Ambassador to UNESCO, 1991; Officier de la Légion d'Honneur, 1991; Décoration de l'Ordre du Trésor Sacré au Japon, 1991; Académicien des Beaux Arts, 1992. **Address:** 59 Faubourg Saint Honoré, 75008 Paris, France.

## Works

Film costume designs include—*La Belle et la Bete* (Cocteau), 1946; *A New Kind of Love* (Shavelson), 1963; *The VIPs* (Asquith), 1963; *Eva* (Hakim), 1964; *The Yellow Rolls-Royce* (Asquith), 1965; *Mata Hari Agent H-21* (Lepicier), 1967; *A Dandy in Aspic* (Mann), 1968 *The Immortal Story* (Rozan), 1969; *You Only Love Once* (Sanders), 1969; *Little Fauss and Big Halsy* (Ruddy), 1970.

## Publications

**On CARDIN: books**—*Dressmakers of France* by Mary Brooks Picken and Dora Loues Miller, New York, 1956; *The Beautiful People* by Marilyn Bender, New York, 1967; *Fashion: An Anthology by Cecil Beaton,* exhibition catalogue compiled by Madeleine Ginsburg London, 1971; *Paris Fashion: The Great Designers and Their Creations,* edited by Ruth Lynam, London, 1972; *The World of Fashion: People, Places, Resources* by Eleanor Lambert, London and New York, 1976; *Magic Names of Fashion* by Ernestine Carter, London, 1980; *McDowell's Directory of Twentieth Century Fashion* by Colin McDowell, London, 1984; *The Conran Directory of Design,* edited by Stephen Bayley, London, 1985; *The Encyclopaedia of Fashion from 1840 to the 1980s* by Georgina O'Hara, London, 1986.

\*     \*     \*

Intellectual, avant-garde, prolific Parisian fashion designer Pierre Cardin has built a worldwide fashion empire which has achieved continuous success from the late 1950s through the present in both couture and ready-to-wear fashions and a wide variety of accessories and goods. His earliest innovations in women's clothes include the chemise, mini-dress, and cartridge-pleated wools with scalloped

# pierre cardin

**Pierre Cardin: Fashion sketch, 1995**

edges. He also fashioned coats with draped hemlines and loose back panels. Cardin is credited with launching the Space Age theme in women's fashion; this included such experimental clothing as the short, stark tunic and smock worn over tights and boots, unisex astronaut suits, the batwing jumpsuit, vinyls with hard helmets and goggles, and metal body jewelry. He made wise use of man-made materials in his pursuit of this approach. Soon after he commenced his work for women, Cardin added clothes for men. He is considered the top designer to accomplish influential work for both sexes and was the first designer from Paris to sell ready-to-wear to department stores.

After World War II, Cardin had done costume designs based on the sketches of Christian Bérard for the film *La Belle et la Bete* by Jean Cocteau. He also was well acquainted with the cultural milieu of the period and had studied architecture. It is not, therefore, surprising that he would, in 1970, expand into the fields of art and entertainment. He redesigned a 1930s Paris nightclub called Les Ambassadeurs, turning it into a complex which includes a restaurant, cinema for experimental art, concert hall, art gallery, and meeting rooms, and called it Espace Cardin. Besides designing costumes for movies, Cardin himself has acted in a film with the famous star Jeanne Moreau.

All over the world, Cardin controls boutiques which have arrangements to sell his merchandise exclusively. This includes, of course, his renowned clothes for women, his characteristic men's suits with tight contours of cut and line, always precisely tailored, and the children's clothes he began making in the late 1960s. But the Cardin label can also be seen on jewelry, shoes, leather goods, toiletries such as aerosol deodorant and after-shave lotion, wigs, towels, sheets, luggage, candy, furniture, and even wine. He was one of the first designers to put his name on such a wide assortment of things, at the beginning of a trend which is currently pervasive in the area of ready-to-wear fashions from later designers. Aptly called the *fauve* (wild one) of post-World War II Paris designers, Cardin will be best remembered as a major creator of clothes for the Space Age, apparel to be found in science fiction films but not yet popularized in your local town or city on earth.

—Barbara Cavaliere

## CARLU, Jean (Georges Leon)
French illustrator, display, and graphic designer

**Born:** Bonniers-sur-Seine, 3 May 1900. **Education:** College de Saint-Germain-en-Laye; studied architecture, Ecole Nationale Supérieure des Beaux-Arts, Paris. **Family:** Married Marcelle Dorval in 1943. **Career:** Freelance and contract designer, mainly in Paris, from 1917; worked for B. Sirven printers, Toulouse, 1919-20; Avenir Publicité agency, Paris, 1921-23; W. S. Crawford agency, London, 1929-31; France Libre organization and American Office of War Information, 1940-45; Agence de Plas advertising, Paris, 1949-52; Larousse publishers, Paris, 1952-72; Publicité Vanypeco agency, Brussels, 1953-72; and Affiche S.A., Brussels, from 1958; also designed graphics and illustrations for the periodicals *La Lumière, La République, What's New, Flair, The Times,* and others. **Member:** International President, Alliance Graphique Internationale, Paris, 1945-46; President, Syndicat Nationale des Graphistes Publicitaires, Paris. **Exhibitions:** *Exposition des Arts Decoratifs,* Paris, 1925; *Exposition Union des Artistes Modernes,* Musée du Louvre, Paris, 1931; *Exposition Internationale Paris,* 1937; *France Comes Back,* New York, 1946; *France Comes to You* (toured United States), 1947; *Second World War Posters,* Imperial War Museum, London, 1972; *Jean Carlu,* Musée de l'Affiche, Paris, 1980; *The Twentieth Century Poster,* Walker Art Center, Minneapolis, 1984. **Collections:** Bibliotheque Nationale, Paris; Gewerbemuseum, Basel, Deutsches Plakat-Museum, Essen. **Honors:** Gold Medal, Art Directors Club of New York, 1941; Honorary Fellow, Royal College of Art, London; Officier de la Legion d'Honneur, France; Officier des Arts et des Lettrés, France. **Address:** Villa Les Cypres, Route de Saint-Blaise, Castagniers, 06670 Saint-Martin-du-Var, France.

### Works

*Automobiles Talbot* poster, for Avenir Publicite, 1923.
*Waterman-Jif* posters, for Avenir Publicite, 1923.
*Monsavon* poster, for Monsavon Soap, 1925.
*Eclairages-Machineries* and *Feu du Ciel* posters, for Theatre Pigalle, Paris, 1929.
*4 Routes to the Continent* poster, for London and North-Eastern Railways/Crawford Agency, 1930.
Railway signals poster, for Disques Odeon, Paris, 1930.

*L'Atlantide* (Pabst) film poster, Paris, 1932.
Cuisine Electrique poster, Paris, 1934-35.
*L'Optimiste* posters, for Cinzano, 1937-38.
*America's Answer—Production* poster, for the Office of Emergency Management, 1941.
*Entre le Marteau et l'Enclume* poster, for the Commisariat de l'Information, 1944.
Poster series, for Pan American Airways, 1947-48.
*L'Eau qui fait Pschitt. . . Perrier* poster, for Agence De Plas, 1949.
*Shell X100 Motor Oil* posters, for Agence De Plas, 1950.
Poster series, for Air France, 1957-59.
*Philips Auto-Radio* poster, for Publicite Vanypeco, 1958.

## Publications

**By CARLU: articles**—in *Arts et Metiers Graphiques* (Paris), no. 7, 1928; *Vendre* (Paris), March 1930; *L'Affiche* (Paris), May 1934; *Le Miroir du Monde* (Paris), 21 March 1936; *World's Press News* (London), 25 June 1936.

**On CARLU: books**—*Exposition de l'Affiche en Couleur, de Cheret a nos Jours,* exhibition catalogue, Paris, 1939; *The Story of Modern Applied Art* by Rudolph Rosenthal and Helena Ratzka, New York, 1948; *Die neue Grafik/The New Graphic Design* by Karl Gerstner and Markus Kutter, Teufen and London, 1959; *Who's Who in Graphic Art* edited by Walter Amstutz, Zurich, 1962; *History of the Poster* by Josef and Shizuko Muller-Brockmann, Zurich, 1971; *Retrospective Jean Carlu,* exhibition catalogue with texts by Alain Weill and Genevieve Gaëtan-Picon, Paris, 1980; *Advertising: Reflections of a Century* by Bryan Holme, London, 1982; *The Twentieth-Century Poster: Design of the Avant-Garde* by Dawn Ades, New York, 1984; *Typographic Design: Form and Communication* by Rob Carter, Ben Day, and Philip Meggs, New York, 1985.

*       *       *

Perhaps Jean Carlu's original study of architecture gave him his lasting interest in making monumental images, in sometimes experimenting with combinations of different media, and in the use of material such as aluminum and mosaic in his work. Certainly, many of his images have the power to make effective mural art. His famous design "Cuisine electrique" (1935) was made of patterned aluminum, aluminum sheet, beaten copper sheet, polished copper, mosaic, and luminous neon tubing. The image behind this mixed media was of a simple, formalised figure, as used by many cartoonists, but made possible by the visual languages of the cubists. The multiple textures used were given cohesion by a strong unifying design which was always Carlu's strength. There was also an intellectual rigour in his work, although he often introduced an element of humour into his designs. Without this element, his works might have become simply heroic.

His work is in any case as vital as that of many of his contemporaries working in other countries with political posters and murals. But Carlu worked as many of his French contemporaries did, with a more gentle, acceptable form of expression. However, an example of the possibilities of his strength as a political muralist is the poster that he designed in the United States in 1945: "America's Answer—Production." The title of the poster is displayed across the work. Beyond this, a large, gloved hand grasps a wrench which is fastened around the first "o" of the word "production," as though it were a nut. In this way, the typography literally links with the message. This ingenious and sophisticated simplification typifies Carlu's work.

His designs, although suitable for large-scale interpretation, were still effective on the printed page. His skillful use of typography, which was always successfully integrated with his imagery, looks immaculate on the page of a magazine. It is a tribute to his design skills that such an image could operate on any scale while still maintaining its vitality. He supplied illustrations for *Le Bourgeois Marie* by C. Villier as well as for giant billboards in the United States.

—John Barnicoat

# CARMI, Eugenio

Italian painter, sculptor, graphic, and industrial designer

**Born:** Genoa, 17 February 1920. **Education:** Studied painting with Barabino, Genoa, 1934-35; studied chemistry at the Eigenössische Politechnische Hochschule, Zürich, Dip.Ing.Chem., 1944; studied with sculptor Guido Galletti, Genoa, 1946; studied painting, in the studio of artist Felice Casorati, Turin, 1947-48. **Family:** Married Maria Vittoria Vices Vinci in 1950; children: Francesca, Antonia, Stefano, and Valentina. **Career:** Freelance artist and designer, in Genoa, 1950-65, and in Milan, from 1970; art director, Italsider's Cornigliano steelworks, Genoa, 1956-64. Founding member, Gruppo Cooperativo di Bocadasse, and Galleria del Deposito, Genoa, 1963-70. Instructor in visual art, Art Academy, Macerata, 1972-73, and Academy of Ravenna, 1976-79; also visiting lecturer at colleges in the United States, from 1965. **Member:** Alliance Graphique Internationale; correspondent member, Experiments in Art and Technology. **Exhibitions:** Milan Triennale, 1951; *Arte grafica e pubblicitaria,* Interclub, Genoa, 1953; *Design in Print,* Edinburgh, 1955; Galleria Numero, Florence, 1957, 1958, 1963; Galleria Danese, Milan, 1958; Museum of Modern Art, Zagreb, 1964; 23rd Venice Biennale, Venice, 1966; *Superland,* Bordeaux, France, 1967; Galeria Universitaria, Mexico City, 1967; *Cybernetic Serendipity,* London, 1968; Musée d'Art Moderne, Paris, 1971; Muzeum Sztuki, Lodz, 1971; Semiotics Conference, Milan, 1974; Palazzo dei Diamanti, Ferrara 1975; Centro Comunale di Cultura, Valenza, 1979; *La section d'Or o della Restaurazione,* Ravenna, 1979; Italian Cultural Institute, New York, 1980; Palazzo della Commenda, Genoa, 1982; Andome Wohndesign, Zürich, 1984; Italian Cultural Institute, Zagreb, 1985; Galleria Ponte Pietra, Verona, 1987, Atlantic Hotel Kempinski, Hamburg, 1988; Galerie Meissner, Hamburg, 1988; Galleria Editalia, Rome, 1989; Antological Show, Milan, 1990; Centro Studi Italiani, Zürich, 1990; Museo Italo Americano, San Francisco, California, 1991; Studio Reggiani, Milan, 1991; Royal Palace, Budapest, 1992; Talbot Rice Gallery, Edinburgh, 1992. **Collections:** Galleria Nazionale d'Arte Moderna, Rome; Muzeum Sztuki, Lodz; Victoria and Albert Museum, London; Museum of Modern Art, New York. **Honors:** First Prize, Milan Poster Triennale, 1957; Fourth Prize, International Biennale of Graphics, Cracow, 1970; First Prize, International Graphic Arts Triennale, Wroclaw, 1974. **Address:** Corso di Porta Vigentina 6, 20122 Milan, Italy.

## Works

*Corporate identity programme,* for Italsider, 1958-64.

Cover for *Immagine di una fabbrica/Image of a Factory,* for Cornigliano steelworks, 1959.

Enamel paintings on steel, for Leonardo da Vinci ship, 1960.

*The Bomb and the General* book design, for Bompiani, 1966, and Seckerand Warburg, 1988 (with Umberto Eco).

*The Three Astronauts* book design, for Bompiani, 1966, and Seckerand Warburg, 1988 (with Umberto Eco).

Paintings on canvas, for Edizioni Schwarz, 1969.

Experimental colour television programmes, for RAI, 1973-74.

Room decorations and flowerbed designs, for Rende nursery school, Calabria, 1980.

*Specchi di Carmi* mirrors, for Acerbis International, 1982-83.

Carpets, for Sisal Collezioni, 1987-88.

*Gli ebani di Carmi* mirrors, for Acerbis International, 1990.

## Publications

**By CARMI: books**—(with Cathy Berberian and Umberto Eco) *Stripsody,* Rome and Houston, 1966; (with Umberto Eco) *La Bomba e il Generale,* Milan, 1966, London, 1988; (with Umberto Eco) *I Tre Cosmonauti,* Milan, 1966, London, 1988; (with Umberto Eco) *Gli Gnomi di Gnù,* Milan, 1992, Paris, 1992; **articles**—"Dio artista" in *Res Publica,* Milan, 1980.

**On CARMI: books**—*Eugenio Carmi,* exhibition catalogue with text by Vera Horvat-Pintaric, Zagreb, 1964; *Eugenio Carmi: Chromosynclasma,* with text by Michelangelo Antonioni, Milan, 1971; *Apropos d'Eugenio Carmi,* exhibition catalogue by Pierre Restany, Paris, 1971; *Eugenio Carmi—una pittura di paesaggio?* by Umberto Eco, Milan, 1973; *Carmi,* with texts by Carmine Benincasa, Umberto Eco, and others, Milan, 1982, *Gli Specchi di Carmi,* trade catalogue with texts by Alessandro Mendini and Daniele Baroni, Bergamo, 1983; *Eugenio Carmi,* exhibition catalogue by Luciano Caramel, Milan, 1990; *Eugenio Carmi,* exhibition catalogue by Duncan MacMillan, Edinburgh, 1992.

\*

1. *Exodus 25:* "And the Lord spake unto Moses saying. . . that they bring me an offering: of every man that giveth it willingly with his heart, ye shall take my offering. And this is the offering which ye shall take of them; gold and silver, and brass. And blue, and purple, and scarlet, and fine linen, and goat's hair; and rams' skins dyed red, and badgers' skins, and shittim wood. Oil for the light, spices for anointing oil, and for sweet incense. Onyx stones, and stones to be set in the ephod, and in the breastplate. And let them make a sanctuary; that I may dwell among them. According to all that I shew thee, after the pattern of the tabernacle and the pattern of all the instruments thereof, and even so shall ye make it. And they shall make an ark of shittim wood: two cubits and a half shall be the length thereof, and a cubit and half the height thereof. And thou shalt overlay it with pure gold, within and without shalt thou overlay it, and shalt make upon it a crown of gold round about. And thou shalt cast four rings of gold for it, and put them in the four corners thereof; and two rings shall in the one side of it, and two rings in the other side of it. And thou shalt make staves of shittim wood, and overlay them with gold. And thou shalt put the staves

into the rings of the sides of the ark, that the ark may be borne with them. The staves shall be in the rings of the ark: they shall not be taken from it. And thou shalt put into the ark the testimony which I shall give thee." There follows a detailed description of models for the mercy seat of pure gold, of the table in shittim wood, of the gold candlestick, of the tabernacle of fine twined blue, purple, and scarlet, of cunning work with cherubims upon it.

2. God therefore is an artist and an architect. Probably he knew the earliest aesthetic manifestations of men, when they drew animals on cave rocks, and must have asked himself the old question: why produce aesthetic activity by using up energy needed for the primary business of survival?

3. A careful reading of the project which God the artist proposes to Moses supplies us with an original answer. While, almost bored, he reminds him of the codes of human behaviour, in ten points, he takes a lingering pleasure in giving Moses a graphic description rich with practical details (colours, measurements, materials) of his design for objects that he wants. The Ark must be in shittim wood and covered in pure gold, the linen for the tabernacle shall be of blue, purple, and scarlet; the candlestick shall be in beaten gold; the table, too, shall be of shittim wood covered in gold and with a golden crown and a border of a hand's breadth around it.

4. Thou shalt not kill, nor steal, nor covet they neighbour's wife. These are *negative* commands hastily pronounced. Blue, purple, scarlet, pure gold, a crown and shittim wood are the attributes of a reality to be invented; *positive* desires expressed with an enjoyment taken in the abundance of constructive details, gentle and consolatory images (linen cloths, crowns), and emotive stimuli (purple, scarlet). Desires.

5. And therefore: negative and positive.

6. The Negative. "Thou shalt NOT kill, NOT commit adultery, NOT steal, NOT bear false witness against thy neighbour, NOT covet thy neighbour's house, NOT covet thy neighbour's wife, NOR his manservant, NOR his maidservant, NOR his ox, NOR his ass NOR anything that is thy neighbour's" *(Exodus 20).* For the spectacle of the negative, God the artist constructs a dramatic stage set: a mass audiovisual piece with a great author, a consummate producer, and an audience overcome by the emotions of a rising state. "And it came to pass on the third day in the morning, that there were thunders and lightnings, and a thick cloud upon the mount, and the voice of the trumpet exceeding loud, so that all the people that was in the camp trembled" *(Exodus 19).* God knows human nature. And he confronts the people with his own behaviour. It is a people of peasants and servants, who make little use of their minds (as today). For this small part of their minds to work, they require the law of God. Desire belongs to the few. The law works on the negative.

7. The positive. God is intellectual, he is a nonconformist, an aesthete. He desperately seeks that minority which moves the other part of its mind. When Moses comes before him, he speaks to him and gives him a desperate warning: "Go down, charge the people, lest they break through unto the Lord to gaze, and many of them perish" *(Exodus 19).* Desperately, he knows that they would not understand. He knows that Moses alone, by using his mind, can live by art. And, abandoned to the total use of his being, he talks art to him. He imparts his wishes to him, supplies him with images and asks him for forms and colours. His speech grows tender, transformed into a longing for poetry; nature at last releases aesthetic energy. Do theft or adultery still mean anything in the moment of creative inebriation? By now it is the

positive, the emission of an energy that will never run out; it is art, the project. "And thou shalt speak unto all that are wise hearted, whom I have filled with the spirit of wisdom, that they may make Aaron's garments to consecrate him that he may minister unto me in the priest's office. And these are the garments which they shall make; a breastplate and an ephod, and a robe and a broidered coat, a mitre, and a girdle: and they shall make holy garments for Aaron thy brother, and his sons, that he may minister unto me in the priest's office. And they shall take gold, and blue, and purple, and scarlet, and fine linen. And they shall make the ephod of gold, of blue and of purple, of scarlet, and fine twined linen, with cunning work. It shall have two shoulder pieces thereof joined at the two edges thereof; and so it shall be joined together" *(Exodus 28).* End of metaphor.

8. Moses, like Giotto or Galileo or Bach, is certainly an extraordinary man who lives with the fantastic and dramatic contradiction of being an intelligent man and of feeling his mind "move." He goes up into Mount Sinai and imagines he is God. And invents. And he sees his people waiting for the law. But immediately afterwards he abandons himself to imagination and sees, or rather perceives, invents, raiments of marvellous colours, tables constructed in every minute detail with precious materials. He pursues happiness which only the vision of an imaginary environment can bring him. He becomes a maker of images for a different use of the mind. And in his aesthetic ecstasy he forgets the law of the NO, letting himself be drawn by the invention of happy behaviour. Is this perhaps what the people are waiting for?

9. The people. The people do not know.

10. The mind. The complexity of the cerebral machine is beyond the perceptive possibilities of the mind itself. The keystone of its working is synapsis (multiple interconnection which puts neurons into reciprocal contact). "The number of synapses is estimated to be around sixteen million billions. This staggering network of interneuronal connections gives rise in its turn to an inconceivable figure of possible preferential and contemporary combinations of nerve impulses. These constitute the continuous main operative cerebral state from which emerges the various activities required by environmental situations as they arise. This unpronounceable figure is assumed to be equal to 1.5 followed by three billion zeros" (Luigi Valzelli, *L'Uomo e il rettile,* Turin, 1978). To print three billion zeros one would need five thousand books of three hundred pages each.

11. Art. Art is a desperate and happy attempt at the identification of man with himself, that is to say, with the great God. It is a continuous reading of this open book containing three billion zeros. Other gods oppose this long and doubtful reading, seducing the people with false desires with few zeros, granted with the certainty of ignorance. But art is ambiguous; it allows the error and the doubts, and with them love.

12. Love. Love is being.

13. Imaginary signals. They are circles. They are hope, Utopia, dreams. They are the project of a thousand colours for the great fine twined cloth.

14. The people. The people are still under the mount. They see the great cloud and hear the trumpets sound, while paranoia prevents them from opening their great book of zeros. Slaves of the great omni-electronic God, they see no colours and do not love. Indeed, not all women can meet Dante and be Beatrice.

15. Reply to God's questions. Man is such only when the production of aesthetic energy becomes a primary activity for survival. In its albeit very brief existence, the history of this world is the

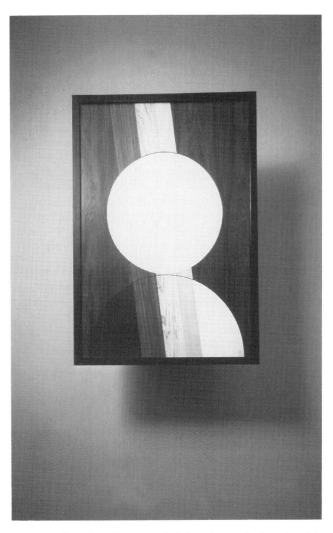

Eugenio Carmi: mirror and inlayed wood for Acerbis International, Seriat, Italy, 1990

history of the image of God the artist, that is to say, of creative man. And the rest is only a chronicle of the negative.

—Eugenio Carmi

*   *   *

The impressive list of exhibitions that Eugenio Carmi has to his credit bears witness to his prowess as an artist, but there has been an intimate connection between his painting and sculpture on the one hand and his designs on the other, as both call upon the same talents and creative resources. Carmi's work tends toward positive, geometric statements, sometimes of an almost abstract simplicity, but they are always much more complex than it at first seems. He is ever concerned to find an apt visual equivalent for quite intricate conceptual notions. These equivalents, however, are rarely reduced to isomorphism; instead, he achieves a subtle resonance out of primarily fairly simple forms in proximity. The richness of signifying is created, therefore, less by straightforward and simplistic denotation than by shapes that suggest a constantly renewed set of relations with the developing context,—that is, the full process of connotation.

It is obvious that Carmi's practice is directed by a theoretical concern for his materials and means, an approach which often sparks off quite interesting byproducts. He became fascinated by the effects of silkscreen printing upon tinplate, a process which he used for many different types of work. During his visits to the shops where this work was carried out, his eye, sharpened by his technical inquisitiveness and appreciation of a technological process, fed to his sensibility something of a shock of recognition upon seeing discarded sheets, out of register, overprinted or otherwise faulty, having served various purposes in setting the machines in motion. In their "Baroque" complexity and intricacy, these sheets were utterly unlike his usual work, yet he employed them as the material of an exhibition.

This ability to turn away from the expected and to prospect the unknown has been an important characteristic, not always leading to what might at first sight appear to be a stylistic volte-face, so much as bringing into his visual repertoire notions and ideas not normally thought to be expressible by those means. Neither in design nor painting, therefore, should his work be considered "abstract," since he is not concerned solely with forms and their relations but rather with the forms as a code, a perceptual code, and their relations which constitute the grammar or syntax appropriate to that code. Thus, his work is to be thought of as a scheme of figuration, geometric for the most part, able to comment upon the most complicated matters. The internal posters for Italsider are exciting examples of this approach, and their success is to be measured by the ease with which a bold typographical element can be inserted within the structure and complement it.

—Toni del Renzio

# CARRÉ, Ben

American art director and film designer

**Born:** Paris, France, in 1883; emigrated to the United States in 1912. **Education:** Studied scenic painting at the Académie Amable studios, Paris. **Career:** Scene painter at the Paris Opéra, Comédie Française, and other theatres, Paris, 1901-06; designer and scene painter, Pathé Gaumont film studios, Paris, 1906-12; designer, working mainly with director Maurice Tourneur, at Eclair Studios, Fort Lee, New Jersey, 1912-18; art director, again working with Tourneur, at several film studios, Hollywood, California, 1918-37; background designer and painter for Metro-Goldwyn-Mayer film studios, Hollywood, California, 1937-69; designed murals for General Motors pavilion at New York World's Fair, 1964; retired to concentrate on easel painting, Hollywood, 1969. **Exhibitions:** Film retrospectives—Telluride Film Festival, Colorado, 1977; Museum of Modern Art, New York, 1978. **Died:** Hollywood, California, 28 May 1978.

**Works**

Film designs include—*La Course aux Potirons* (Cohl), 1907; *Le Huguenot* (Feuillade), 1909; *La Mort de Mozart* (Feuillade), 1909; *Le Festin de Balthazar* (Feuillade), 1910; *Aux Lions les Chrètiens* (Feuillade), 1911; *The Dollar Mark* (Lund), 1914; *Mother* (Tourneur), 1914; *The Man of the Hour* (Tourneur), 1914; *The*

*Wishing Ring* (Tourneur), 1914; *The Pit* (Tourneur), 1914; *Alias Jimmy Valentine* (Tourneur), 1915; *Hearts in Exile* (Young), 1915; *The Boss* (Chautard), 1915; *The Ivory SnuffBox* (Tourneur), 1915; *A Butterfly on the Wheel* (Tourneur), 1915; *The Pawn of Fate* (Tourneur), 1915; *Camille* (Capellani), 1915; *A Girl's Folly* (Tourneur), 1916; *The Hand of Peril* (Tourneur), 1916; *The Closed Road* (Tourneur), 1916; *La Vie de Boheme* (Capellani), 1916; *The Rail Rider* (Tourneur), 1916; *The Velvet Paw* (Tourneur), 1916; *The Dark Silence* (Capellani), 1916; *The Deep Purple* (Young), 1916; *The Rack* (Chautard), 1916; *Trilby* (Tourneur), 1917; *The Cub* (Tourneur), 1917; *The Undying Flame* (Tourneur), 1917; *The Whip* (Tourneur), 1917; *The Law of the Land* (Tourneur), 1917; *Exile* (Tourneur), 1917; *Barbary Sheep* (Tourneur), 1917; *The Rise of Jenny Cushing* (Tourneur), 1917; *The Pride of the Clan* (Tourneur), 1917; *Poor Little Rich Girl* (Tourneur), 1917; *The Blue Bird* (Tourneur), 1918; *Rose of the World* (Tourneur), 1918; *Prunella* (Tourneur), 1918; *A Doll's House* (Tourneur), 1918; *Woman* (Tourneur), 1918; *Sporting Life* (Tourneur), 1918; *The White Heather* (Tourneur), 1919; *The Life Line* (Tourneur), 1919; *Victory* (Tourneur), 1919; *The Broken Butterfly* (Tourneur), 1919; *Stronger Than Death* (Bryant and Blache), 1920; *The River's End* (Neilan), 1920; *In Old Kentucky* (Neilan and Green), 1920; *Go and Get It* (Neilan and Symonds), 1920; *For the Soul of Rafael* (Garson), 1920; *My Lady's Garter* (Tourneur), 1920; *Treasure Island* (Tourneur), 1920; *Don't Ever Marry* (Neilan and Heerman), 1921; *Dinty* (Neilan and McDermott), 1921; *Man, Woman, and Marriage* (Holubar), 1921; *Custer's Last Stand* (Neilan), 1921; *The Wonderful Thing* (Brenon), 1921; *The Light in the Dark* (Brown), 1922; *When the Desert Calls* (Smallwood) 1922; *Queen of the Moulin Rouge* (Smallwood), 1922; *What Fools Men Are* (Terwilliger), 1922; *Wife in Name Only* (Terwilliger), 1923; *Thy Name is Woman* (Niblo), 1924; *The Goldfish* (Storm), 1924; *Cytherea* (Fitzmaurice), 1924; *Tarnish* (Fitzmaurice), 1924; *The Red Lily* (Fitzmaurice), 1924; *So This is Hollywood* (Green), 1924; *Lights of Old Broadway* (Bell), 1925; *The Phantom of the Opera* (Julian), 1925; *The Masked Bride* (Cabanne and von Sternberg), 1925; *Mare Nostrum* (Ingram), 1926; *La Boheme* (K. Vidor), 1926; *The Book* (Wellman), 1926, *Don Juan* (Crosland), 1926; *The Better 'ole* (Reisner), 1926; *My Official Wife* (Stein), 1926; *When a Man Loves* (Crosland), 1926; *The King of Kings* (DeMille), 1927; *Old San Francisco* (Crosland), 1927; *Soft Cushions* (Cline), 1927; *The Jazz Singer* (Crosland), 1927; *The Red Dance* (Walsh), 1928; *The River Pirate* (Howard), 1928; *The Air Circus* (Hawks and Seiler), 1928; *The Iron Mask* (Dwan), 1929; *The Woman from Hell* (Erickson), 1929; *The Valiant* (Howard), 1929; *The Cockeyed World* (Walsh), 1929; *Frozen Justice* (Dwan), 1929; *Hot for Paris* (Walsh), 1929; *City Girl* (Murnau), 1930; *River's End* (Curtiz), 1930; *Women of All Nations* (Walsh), 1931; *The Black Camel* (MacFadden), 1931; *Riders of the Purple Sage* (MacFadden), 1931; *Sailor's Luck* (Walsh), 1933; *Dante's Inferno* (Lachman), 1935; *A Night at the Opera* (Wood), 1935; *Let's Sing Again* (Neumann), 1936; *The Mine with the Iron Door* (Howard), 1936; *Great Guy* (Blystone), 1936; *23 1/2 Hours Leave* (Blystone), 1937; *The Wizard of Oz* (Le Roy), 1939; *Meet Me in St. Louis* (Freed), 1944; *An American in Paris* (Freed), 1951.

**Publications**

**By CARRÉ: articles**—interview in *Film Comment* (New York), May/June 1978.

On CARRÉ: books—*Le Décor de Film* by Leon Barsacq, Paris, 1970, revised and edited as *Caligari's Cabinet and Other Grand Illusions* by Elliott Stein, Boston, 1976; *American Silent Film* by William K. Everson, New York, 1978; *The Art of Hollywood* by John Hambley, London, 1979; *The International Dictionary of Films and Filmmakers,* London and Chicago, 1987, 1991.

\*    \*    \*

Ben Carré contributed to film design with his expertise in painting. Trained as a painter, he began his career producing elaborate theater backgrounds. This experience prepared him for the *trompe l'oeil* effects that early French filmmakers needed for their primitive productions; thus, he came to be employed by Pathé Gaumont Studio in 1901 to paint film scenery. There, Carré instituted the practice of painting the sets in color, even though they were photographed in black and white. Originally his purpose was to enliven the actors's performances. It was later realized that the range of colors actually photographed better.

Carré went to America in 1912 at the invitation of Eclair Studios. In 1914 he struck up a thirty-one film partnership with Maurice Tourneur. Their films were of two types. Some, such as the fairy tale, *The Bluebird* (1918), demanded a fantastic treatment, which was achieved with stylized sets, silhouetted backdrops, and special effects. Other films, such as *Trilby* (1917), the story of Bohemian Parisians, had an almost documentary look. For this film, Carré recreated the back streets of Paris in Greenwich Village and duplicated a Parisian art studio with a realism of the sort that influenced the work of director Erich von Stroheim.

Carré moved with Tourneur to Hollywood in 1918, and after 1920 he began working with other directors. One of his greatest creations from this period was the underground scene from *The Phantom of the Opera* (1925). Carré was called upon because of his knowledge of the Paris Opera House. Sketches of the watery caverns of the Phantom, however, came largely from Carré's imagination.

After the sound era began, Carré lost interest in art direction, in large part because the studio art departments became larger and more specialized, whereas Carré had been used to working alone. He may also have felt that sound drew emphasis away from the visual image. He worked at various studios designing parts of films for other art directors. For example, he did the glass paintings that gave the appearance of a raging fire in *Dante's Inferno* (1935).

Working as a background painter for MGM from 1937 to 1965, Carré created several memorable images: the shimmering Emerald City in *The Wizard of Oz* (1939), the large Victorian house in *Meet Me in St. Louis* (1944), and the pseudo-Impressionist background for the dream ballet in *An American in Paris* (1951). Carré's retreat to background painting at the end of his career demonstrates that he considered himself primarily a painter.

—Lois Miklas

# CARRICK, Edward

British illustrator, film, and stage designer

**Born:** Edward Anthony Craig, in London, 3 January 1905. **Education:** Studied art, photography and theatre history, in Italy, Ger-

many and France, 1917-26. **Family:** Married Mary Timewell in 1960; two children. **Career:** Photographer and sub-editor, *The Mask* magazine, London, 1926-28; art director, Welsh Pearson Film Company, London, from 1928; designer, for Basil Dean productions, for Associated Talking Pictures, London, 1931-35, and for Douglas Fairbanks Jr. productions, at Criterion Films, London, 1936-39; art director, Crown Film Unit, for the Ministry of Information, London, 1939-46; executive art director, Independent Producers (Rank Organization), London, 1947-49; art director, Ealing Films, London, from 1949; subsequently, freelance film and stage director, working for Hammer Films, Grand National Pictures, Independent Artists, Warwick Films, and others. Founder-resident, Grubb Group of modern artists, London, 1928-38; founder, AAT School of English Film, London, 1938; film critic, *International Film Review,* London, and contributor to *Architectural Review, Architectural Record, Theatre Notebook, Penrose Annual, La Tribuna,* and others. **Member:** Architectural Association, London; Society of Authors, London; Association of Cine Technicians, London; Society for Theatre Research, London. **Exhibitions:** St. Georges Gallery, London, 1927, 1928; Redfern Gallery, London, 1929, 1931, 1938. **Collections:** British Museum, London; Victoria and Albert Museum, London; Metropolitan Museum of Art, New York; Yale University, New Haven, Connecticut; University of Texas, Austin. **Honors:** Fellow, Royal Society of Arts, London. **Address:** Cutler's Orchard, Bledlow, Aylesbury Buckinghamshire HP17 9PA, England.

## Works

Film designs include—*Laburnum Grove* (Reed), 1936; *Jump for Glory* (Czinner and Garmes), 1937; *Target for Tonight* (Watt), 1941; *Western Approaches* (Jackson), 1944; *Captain Boycott* (Launder), 1947; *The Red Beret* (Young), 1953; *Bachelor of Hearts* (Riller), 1958; *Blind Date* (Losey), 1959; *Macbeth* (Schaefer), 1961; *Maniac* (Carreras), 1963; *Seaside Swingers* (Hill) 1964; *Hysteria* (Francis), 1965; *The Nanny* (Holt), 1965.

Stage designs include—*In Abraham's Bosom,* London, 1930; *Volpone,* Old Vic, London, 1932; *Queer Cattle,* Old Vic, 1932; *Macbeth,* Old Vic, 1932; *Cornelius,* London, 1932; *Night Must Fall,* London, 1935; *Autumn,* London, 1937; *Death on the Table,* London, 1938; *Last Train South,* London, 1938; *Henry V,* Old Vic, 1938; *Johnson Over Jordan,* London, 1939; *Macbeth,* Shakespeare Memorial Theatre, Stratford on Avon, 1948.

Books illustrated include—*Voyage to the Island of the Articoles* by André Maurois, London, 1928; *The Poems and Verse of John Keats* edited by John Middleton Murry, London, 1929; *The Review of Revues* edited by Charles B. Cochrane, London, 1930; *The Georgic of Virgil,* translated by R. D. Blackmore, London, 1931; *In Spring* by Edith Sitwell, London, 1931; *In Summer* by Edmund Blunden, London, 1931; *In Autumn* by Herbert Palmer, London, 1931; *In Winter* by W. H. Davies, London, 1931; *Above the River* by John Gawsworth, London, 1931; *Fifteen Poems, Three Friends* by John Gawsworth, London, 1931; *So Far So Glad* by E. Selsey, London, 1934; *The Life of Henry V* by William Shakespeare, London, 1939.

## Publications

By CARRICK: books—(Contributor) *Nothing or the Bookplate* edited by *Gordon Craig,* London, 1925; *Theatre Machines in Italy*

*1400-1800,* London, 1931; *The Theatre of Parma,* London, 1931; *Designing for Moving Pictures,* London, 1941, as *Designing for Films,* London, 1950; (compiler with Gerry Bradley) *Meet...the Common People,* London, 1942; *Art and Design in the British Film,* London, 1948; (contributor) *Oxford Companion to the Theatre,* London and New York, 1951; *Gordon Craig, The Story of His Life,* London, 1968; *Fabrizio Carini Motta, Trattato sopra la struttura de teatri,* Milan, 1971; *Baroque Theatre Construction,* Aylesbury, 1982.

**On CARRICK: books**—*La Scenografia nel Film* edited by Mario Verdone, Rome, 1956; *Who's Who in the Theatre, 12th edition* edited by John Parker, London, 1957, *Filmlexicon degli autore e delle opere,* 7 vols., edited by Michele Lacalamita, Fernaldo Di Giamatteo, and others, Rome, 1958-67; *Le Décor de Film* by Léon Barsacq, Paris, 1970, as *Caligari's Cabinet and Other Grand Illusions,* Boston, 1976.

*      *      *

Filmgoers and critics may rhapsodize about the stars, worship the writers, and idealize directors, yet they usually neglect the role of the film designer. Do audiences assume that characters wander into rooms fully formed, without the plan of a human hand determining these celluloid habitations? Edward Carrick crusaded against this image, striving to educate public and artist alike on the art of the motion picture.

Carrick's father, Gordon Craig, no doubt influenced this viewpoint, since he had named the art director as the unifying force behind theatrical productions. A prolific writer and innovative designer, Craig had revolutionized the English stage.

Carrick began by designing theatrical sets and costumes, as his father did, but motion pictures soon captured his attention. Carrick not only designed for films but published classic statements on the role of the film designer. He replaced his father's poetic tongue with a clear, nononsense language appropriate to the modern generation.

Carrick divided screen design into three types. The American or spectacular school derived from Italy. Heir to the tradition of pageantry, it was based on the traditional supposition that displays of wealth bring pleasure. The unreal dominated the German or Imaginist school, which came to be defined as Expressionistic. Carrick declared this to be the painter's turf, with artists achieving their effects through the power of suggestion. Carrick originated the Realist school with early westerns. Russians later adapted it for propaganda films. It succeeded in France where, Carrick claimed, the people have a natural appreciation for the everyday. World War II documentaries (in the making of which Carrick himself was a participant) stimulated its appearance in England. Carrick noted the Realists drew from architects and those interested in sociology, due to their "concrete" concerns.

Carrick believed that "a design for motion pictures should always be the background to an emotion...It is the mental state of the character that interests the audience and your background can help his." Carrick emphasized the importance of light sources, the quality of camera movement, and the differences between the film and theatre. He pragmatically analyzed studio structure and the positions of its artists. Carrick's fascination with special effects produced a virtual guidebook to the creation of screen images, illustrated with pictorial examples by much admired colleagues.

Carrick's filmography stands unimpressively next to the richly studded successes of his cohorts. However, as author and educator, Carrick reigns as the "Gordon Craig" of the cinema.

—Edith Cortland Lee

## CARSON, David
American graphic designer

**Born:** Palos Verdes, California, 1956. **Education:** Workshop, University of Arizona, Tucson; studied commercial art, San Diego State University and Oregon College of Commercial Art; workshop with Hans-Rudolf Lutz, Rapperswil, Switzerland. **Career:** Professional surfer, top ranking of eighth in the world, late 1970s; high school sociology teacher; intern, Surfer Publications, Los Angeles; part-time designer, *Transworld Skateboarding* magazine; designer and art director, *Musician* magazine, Massachusetts; designer, *Beach Culture* magazine, Los Angeles, from 1989; designer and art director, *Surfer* magazine; art director, *Ray Gun* magazine, 1992-1995; established David Carson Design (with Mike Jurkovac and Albert Watson), New York, from 1995; clients include Brooklyn Academy of Music, Nike, Kodak, Levis, Gannett Outdoor, Speak Magazine and the Magic Johnson Aids Foundation. Juror, AIGA sports graphics competition, 1996; board of directors, International Conference on Design Aspen, 1996.

### Publications

**By CARSON: books**—(with Lewis Blackwell) *The End of Print: The Graphic Design of David Carson* with introduction by David Byrne, London, 1995; **articles**—"Face to Face" with Neville Brody in *Creative Review* (U.K.), May 1994.

**On CARSON: articles**—"Riding the Wave" interview by Michael Chamberlain in *Creative Review* (U.K.), January 1992; "Two Art Directors and Their Cult(ure) Magazines" by Steven Heller in *Print* (New York), January/February 1992; "Magazine 2000" by Margaret Richardson and Joyce Rutter Kaye in *U&lc* (New York), Winter 1992; "David Carson" by Anna Griffiths in *Design Graphics* (Australia), October 1993; "United Artists" by Peter Hall in *Design Week* (supplement, U.K.), 27 May 1994; "Been There, Seen That, Doing It Tomorrow" by Rick Poynor in *Frieze* (U.K.), September/October 1994; "Designers' Choice" by Dan Foulkes in *Graphics International* (U.K.), October/November 1994; "Charles Spencer Anderson" by Colin Wood and Anna Griffiths in *Design World* (Australia), November 1994; "Surprise Us Please: Nike's Advertising Agency Gives Designers a Lot of Freedom" by Marc Vlemmings in *Items* (Netherlands), November 1994; "Thoughts on the New Typography" in *How* (Cincinnati, Ohio). January/February 1994; "Making Waves" by Michael Horsham in *Design Review* (U.K.), 1994; "Review: Turning the Tide on Type" by Lewis Blackwell in *Creative Review* (U.K.), February 1994; "Carson Splits with Ray Gun" in *Creative Review* (U.K.), 15 November 1995.

## CARTER, Matthew
British letterer and type designer

**Born:** London, 1937. **Career:** Cut punches by hand for metal types, Enschendé printing house type foundry, The Netherlands, 1955-57; free-lance designer of lettering and type, London, 1957-63; typographical advisor, supervising the manufacture of fonts for the Lumitype (Photon) photo typesetting machine, Crosfield Electronics, 1963-65; staff type designer, Merganthaler Linotype, New York, 1965-71; designs at Merganthaler Linotype included Snell Roundhand and Cascade scripts, Helvetica Compressed, a Hangul for the Korean language, Olympian for newspaper text, and the Video series of sanserif faces; freelance designer, London, 1971-1981; clients included Linotype, Pentagram Design, Victoria and Albert Museum; typographical adviser, Her Majesty's Stationery Office (the British government printer), 1980-1984; consultant, IBM Printer Planning Division, 1980-1981; co-founder, senior vice-president, and director, Bitstream Inc., digital typefoundry, Cambridge, 1981-1992; principal, Carter & Cone Type Inc., Cambridge, from 1992. Senior critic, graduate design school, Yale University. **Member:** Alliance Graphique Internationale; Chairman, Type Designers' Committee, and Board of Directors, Association Typographique Internationale. **Honors:** Elected, Royal Designer for Industry, London, 1982; elected, Society of Printers, Boston, 1985; Frederic W. Goudy Award, Rochester Institute of Technology, 1986; Honorary Doctorate of Fine Arts, Art Institute, Boston, 1992; Gold Award (Sophia typeface), Non-members category, Typodirectors Club, Tokyo, 1994; Middleton Award, American Center for Design, 1995. **Address:** Carter & Cone Type Inc., 2155 Massachusetts Avenue, Cambridge, MA 02140, U.S.A.

**Publications**

By CARTER: articles—"Olympian: A New Type for Newspapers" in *Interpress Grafik*, 1971(?); "How Typesetting Technology Affects Typeface Design" in *U&lc* (New York), 1977(?); "Galliard: A Modern Revival of the Types of Robert Granjon" in *Visible Language* (Cleveland, Ohio), Winter 1985; "The Type Revolution" edited by Jerome P. Frank in *Publisher's Weekly* (New York), 18 November 1988; "Aesthetics of the New Fonts" in *The Jeffe Report,* issue 31, December 1989; "Type Design Today" in *AIGA Journal of Graphic Design* (New York), vol. 6, no. 4, 1989; "Communicating Graphically" in *RSA Journal* (London), June 1990; "Bell Centennial" in *Evolution,* July 1990; "Aesthetics and the Future of Typography" in *The Jeffe Report,* issue 40, January 1991; "Theories of Letterform Construction: Part I" in *Printing History* vol. xiii, no. 2, 1991/ vol. xiv, no. 1, 1992; "Matthew Carter skriver själv om sitt typsnitt Galliard" in *Design Typografi Produktion,* April 1993; "The Future for Fonts" in *The Ampersand,* Spring 1993; "Close-up '93: The View from Tokyo TDC, 'My Work as a Type Designer'" in *Typodirection in Japan* (Tokyo), 1993.

On CARTER: books—*Twenty Years of the Frederic W. Goudy Award,* Rochester Institute of Technology, 1988; *Graphic Design in America: A Visual Language History,* Minneapolis, Minnesota, 1989; *Typographers on Type* edited by Ruari McLean, London, 1995; *Twentieth Century Type Designers,* New York and London, 1995; articles—"Virtuoso in the Making" by Ellic Howe in *The British Printer,* March 1959; "From Moxon to Carter" edited by Ellic Howe in *The New Mechanick Exercises,* no. 13, 1959; "London Airport Looks Up" in *Typographica 5,* June 1962; "On Type: Galliard" by Charles Bigelow in *Fine Print* (San Francisco), January 1979; "Type & Technology" in *Print* (New York), March/April 1981; "Typespec: Matthew Carter" by Dennis Mason in *Studio Magazine* (Rexdale, Ontario), August 1986; "Works in Progress: A Personal Type" by Alex Ward in *New York Times Magazine* (New York), 20 September 1987; "Galliard: Animated and Authoritative"

**☸ COLOPHON ☸**

M ANTINIA was designed by Matthew Carter and was digitized in Fontographer 3·5. This type specimen was set in QuarkXPress 3·1.

The keyboard positions given for characters on the center spread refer to System Seven on the Macintosh. On other platforms & under other systems they will vary.

MANTINIA is a trademark of Carter & Cone Type Inc. ITC GALLIARD is a registered trademark of International Typeface Corporation.

Copyright © 1993 Carter & Cone Type Inc. All rights reserved. Printed in USA.

Carter & Cone Type Inc.
2155 Massachusetts Ave, Cambridge MA 02140
*Telephone* 800 952–2129 *and* 617 576–0398
*Fax* 617 354–4146

**☸ MCMXCIII ☸**

Matthew Carter: Mantinia typeface specimen brochure, 1993

by Charles Bigelow in *Publish!* (New York), January 1988; "Art and the New Machines" by Jon Zonderman in *Yale* (Cambridge), March 1988; "An Existential Guide to Type" by Karrie Jacobs in *Metropolis* (New York), April 1988; "Matthew Carter: What a Type!" by Marjan and Gerard Unger in *Blad over Bladen,* no. 5, August 1988; "Talking Type" in *Publish!,* September 1988; "The Electronic Typefoundry" by Ed Cleary in *Studio Magazine,* November/December 1988; "Matthew Carter: Boston, 12/15/88" in "Graphic Designers and the Macintosh Computer" in *Emigre* (Berkeley, California), no. II, 1988; "Matthew Carter Confronts the Font Feeding Frenzy" edited by Louis Rossetto, *Language Technology,* no. 8, 1988; "Samtal om typografi" by Paul Frigyes in *Aktuell Grafisk Information,* no. 184, 1988; "Man of Letters" by Preston Gralla in *PC/Computing* (New York), January 1989; "Introducing Charter" by Clifford Burke in *Publish!,* January 1989; "Matthew Carter" by Dick Coyne in *Communication Arts* (Palo Alto, California), January/February 1989; "Five Making a Difference" in *NewsInc.,* July/August 1989; "Bistream's Bit-Mapped Course into Retail" by Jon Pepper in *Marketing Computers,* August 1989; "La Guerre des Polices aura-t-elle Lieu?" by Veronique Reynier in *Decision Informatique,* 18 September 1989; "Matthew Carter: A Champion of Good Typography" in *Lotus Magazine,* September 1989; "The Greening of BT" by Andrew Boag in *Graphics World* (Maidstone), September/October 1989; *"The Ampersand* interview with Matthew Carter" edited by Alastair Johnston and Frances Butler in *The Ampersand,* Autumn 1989; "Definitely My Type" by Wendy Richmond in *Scanlines,* Winter 1989;

"Bitstream Charter: Eine von Matthew Carter für Lichtsatz und Laserdruck gezeichnete Schrift" by Max Caflisch in *Typografische Monatsblätter* (Zürich), Heft 5, 1989; "Fonts for the '90s" by Toni and Daniel Will-Harris in *Ventura Professional!*, December 1989/January 1990; "Typography's New Priests" by Robin Kinross in *Eye* (London), January 1990; "Revolution in Type Make Headlines" by Randall Rothenberg in *New York Times* (New York), 23 July 1990; "Matthew Carter: Bell Centennial" in *Typographic*, Spring/Summer 1990, "Font Designer Typecast for Craft" by Quendrith Johnson in *Boston Business Journal* (Boston), 19 March 1990; "Type Design & Technology: An Interview with Matthew Carter" by Stuart Silverstone in *Aldus*, March/April 1990; "Character Assassination" by Nicholas Backlund in *I.D.* (New York), March/April 1990; "Fonts in Conflict" by Steve Hannaford in *Verbum* (San Diego, California), April 1990; "1991 Type Roundtable" by Pamela Pfiffner in *Publish!*, June 1991; "I'm Not a Believer in the Mystique" *Marlow RFD*, June 1991; "Let Typography Look Like Type" *Typographic*, Spring 1991; "Type Renaissance: A Primer on Digital Type" by Alex Brown in *MacWorld* (San Francisco, California), July 1991; "Mannen bakom Galliard, Bell och Charter" by Gunnar Von Sydow in *Apple News* (Fort Wayne, Indiana), January 1992; "Graphics" by Michael Rock in *I.D.*, May/June 1992; "Reverting to Type" by Roy Coxhead in *Printing World* (London), 12 August 1992; "Endlich wieder Schriften machen" by Albert Dommer in *Page*, November 1992; "Matthew Carter"s Scandinavian Galliard" by Gary Newman in *Mac Art & Design*, November 1992; "Reverting to Type" by John Stokdyk in *Designweek* (London), 20 November 1992; "The Typographic Niceties, Part I," by Will Powers in *Art Direction* (New York), December 1992; "Robert Granjons meisterhafte Kursiven" by Max Caflisch in *Typografische Monatsblätter*, Heft 2, 1992; "The Clever Type: Matthew Carter" by Michael Rock in *I.D.*, January/February 1993; "Matthew Carter" by Hiroko Sakomura in *Typographics*, March 1993; "The Undead" by Janet Waegel in *x-height*, Spring 1993; "Brunelleschi's Bargain" by Steven Sass in *Federal Reserve Bank of Boston Regional Review*, Fall 1993; "Opening the Floodgates: Digital Type Foundries on the Rise" by Gerald Lange in *Bookways* (Austin, Texas), October 1993; "Type Renaissance" by Greg Hofmann in *Step-by-Step Graphics*, November/December 1993; "Making Faces" by Will Powers in *Art Direction*, December 1993; "ITC Charter," in *U&lc*, Winter 1993; "Three New Faces" by Laurie Haycock Makela in *Design Quarterly* (Minneapolis), no. 158, Winter 1993; "Reputations: Matthew Carter" interview by Erik Spiekermann in *Eye*, vol. 3, no. II, 1993; "ITC Galliard, eine eindrucksvolle Schriftfamilie" by Max Caflisch in *Typografische Monatsblätter*, no. 1, 1993; "Baseline Reviews" in *Baseline 17*, March 1994; "Four Recently Released Fonts" by John D. Berry in *Aldus*, March/April 1994; "Type in Print" by Robert Bringhurst in *Print*, March/April 1994; "Digital Type Foundry for Typophiles: Carter & Cone Type Inc." by Gerald Lange in *Serif* (Kent, Ohio), Fall 1994; "Type in Print: Big Caslon CC" by Philip B. Meggs in *Print*, November/December 1994; "Matthew Carter vs Katsumi Asaba" in *Designers' Workshop*, 12 December 1994; "Die Titelschrift Mantinia" by Max Caflisch in *Typografische Monatsblätter*, Heft 4, 1994; "Matthew Carter" by Kathleen Tinkel in *Adobe Magazine*, March/April 1995; "Besta letrio ekki valio" by Þorsteinn Þorsteinsson in *DV* (Reykjavik), 15 July 1995; "Bespoke Type: The Subtle Art of Matthew Carter" by John Plunkett in *Wired*, August 1995; "Interview with Matthew Carter" in *Axis*, Winter 1995; "Æstetik og ny teknologi" by Henrik Holmegaard in *Digital Skrift*, 1995; "The Space Between the Letters" by Moira Cullen in *Eye*, Winter 1995; "Big Caslon" by Max Caflisch in *Typografische Monatsblätter*, Heft 4, 1995.

\*   \*   \*

Matthew Carter is best known for the design of ITC Galliard, a classical serif face whose exquisite details and proportions seem refreshing in the digital age, and also for Bell Centennial, a hardly noticeable sanserif face which has become the work horse for telephone books throughout America and has been adapted for those in the United Kingdom and other countries. Bell Centennial is a crisp sanserif in four weights, has a high character count and is readable in small sizes printed on inexpensive paper. Some critics liken Bell Centennial's contribution to clarity in this latter third of the twentieth century to the impact of Stanley Morrison's Times Roman, introduced through the London Times in 1932.

Matthew Carter has designed more than twenty typefaces, including Elephant (1992), Mantinia (1993), Sophia (1993), Big Caslon (1994), Skia (1994), nine Interchange Ziff screen fonts (1995), and Wiredbaum (for Wired, 1995). Each manifests his remarkable craftsmanship and sense of typographic color. His contributions to typography, as working designer, open-minded and generous critic (even toward interesting but barely legible type faces by relative novices), and energetic lecturer and teacher, places him as one of the world's most effective proponents of typographic excellence.

—Al Gowan

# CASSON, Hugh (Maxwell)

British architect, interior, exhibition, and stage designer

**Born:** London, 23 May 1910. **Education:** Studied at Eastbourne College, Sussex, 1924-27; St. John's College, Cambridge, MA 1931; Bartlett School of Architecture, University College, London, 1931-32; British School, Athens, 1933. **Military Service:** Camouflage officer, Air Ministry, London, 1940-44; technical officer, Ministry of Town and Country Planning, London, 1944-46. **Family:** Married the architect Margaret MacDonald Troup in 1938; children: Carola, Nicola, and Dinah. **Career:** In private practice as architect and designer, from 1933: with Christopher Nicholson, London, 1937-39; senior partner, Casson Conder Partnership, architects, London, from 1946. Director of Architecture, Festival of Britain, London, 1948-51; Professor of Environmental Design, 1953-75, and Provost, 1980-85, Royal College of Art, London; design consultant and committee member, Bath, Brighton, and Windsor Festivals, from the 1960s. **Member:** Royal Fine Art Commission, London, 1960-83; Royal Mint Advisory Committee, London, from 1972; trustee, British Museum (Natural History), London, from 1976; National Portrait Gallery, London, from 1976; Past President, Royal Academy of Art, London; Royal Institute of British Architects. **Exhibitions:** Annual one-person shows of paintings at the Workshop Gallery, London, and elsewhere; regular exhibitor at Royal Academy Summer Exhibitions, London. **Honors:** Fellow, Society of Industrial Artists and Designers, London, 1950; Royal Designer for Industry, 1951, and Master of the Faculty, 1969-71, Royal Society of Arts, London; Knight of the Order of the British Empire, 1952; Member of the Royal Danish Academy, 1954; Honorary Associate, American Institute of Architects, 1968; Royal

Academician, London, 1970; Knight Commander of the Royal Victorian Order, London, 1978; Italian Order of Merit, 1980; Companion of Honour, London, 1985. Honorary Doctorates: Royal College of Art, London, 1975; University of Birmingham, 1977. **Addresses:** (office) Casson Conder Partnership, 35 Thurloe Place, London SW7 2HJ; (home) 6 Hereford Mansions, Hereford Road, London W2 5BA, England.

## Works

(With Cassoll Conder Partnership):

British pavilion, Van Riebeck Festival Fair, Cape Town, 1952.
Arts faculty site, development plan, and 8 buildings, Cambridge University, 1952-82.
Queen Elizabeth II coronation street decorations, Westminster, London, 1953.
Royal apartments on *HMY Britannia,* 1953, 1983.
Royal apartments and guest suites at Windsor Castle, 1954-83.
King George V Memorial Hostel, London, 1960.
Public rooms and first class accommodations on S.S. *Canberra,* for P & O Orient Lines, 1961.
Hall of Residence at Worcester College, Oxford, 1962.
Elephant and Rhinoceros Pavilion at London Zoo, 1965.
Northwest Regional Headquarters Building in Manchester, for National Westminster Bank, 1970.
Science section displays in the British pavilion, *World's Fair,* Osaka, 1970.
Library at Badminton School, Bristol, 1974.
Study Centre at London Zoo, 1976.
Headquarters building, for W. H. Smith Ltd., London, 1976.
Royal apartments on the Royal Train, 1977.
Stage designs—*Alceste,* Glyndebourne Opera, Sussex, 1954; The Burning Boat, Royal Court Theatre, London, 1955; *Troilus and Cressida,* Royal Opera House, London, 1956; *The World of Paul Slickey,* Palace Theatre, London, 1959; *The Golden Touch,* Piccadilly Theatre, London, 1960; *Incoronazione di Poppea,* Glyndebourne Opera, Sussex, 1963-64; *La Fedelta Premiata,* Glyndebourne Opera, Sussex, 1979-80.

(for a complete list of buildings and architectural projects, see *Contemporary Architects)*

## Publications

**By CASSON: books**—*New Sights of London,* London, 1937; *Bombed Churches,* London, 1946; *Houses by the Millions: An Account of the Housing Achievement in the USA 1940-1945,* London, 1947; (with Anthony Chitty) *Houses: Permanence and Prefabrication,* London, 1947; *An Introduction to Victorian Architecture,* London, 1948; *Red Lacquer Days,* London, 1956; *The Unseeing Eye,* London, 1958; (editor) *Museums,* London, 1964; (editor) *Inscape: The Design of Interiors,* London, 1968; (with Joyce Grenfeli) *Nanny Says,* London, 1972; *Sketchbook,* London, 1975; *Diary,* London, 1981; *Hugh Casson's London,* London, 1983; *Hugh Casson's Oxford,* London, 1988.

**On CASSON: books**—*Design in British Industry: A Mid-Century Survey* by Michael Farr, Cambridge, 1955; *Public Interiors* by Misha Black, London, 1960; *Lettering Today* edited by John

Brinkley, London, 1964; *All Things Bright and Beautiful: Design in Britain 1830 to Today* by Fiona MacCarthy, London, 1972; *A Tonic to the Nation: The Festival of Britain 1951* edited by Mary Banham and Bevis Hillier, London, 1976; *Design By Choice* by Reyner Banham, London, 1981.

*

I have been in private practice since 1933, first with the late Christopher Nicholson and later with several partners under the name of Casson Conder Partnership. The work of the practice largely concentrated after the war in planning and building universities—Belfast, Birmingham, Cambridge, and Oxford—but has tended to specialise in "non-specialisation," winning principal, large commissions in open and limited competitions. We have consequently covered a wide range of architectural design, including commercial, industrial, and domestic buildings, landscapes, conservation, interior design, exhibitions, and product design.

I have personally been concerned as consultant on the conservation of Bath, Chichester, Winchester, and Salisbury, and the practice has won several awards for work in historically sensitive areas.

—Hugh Casson

*       *       *

It is not easy to give a balanced account about Sir Hugh Casson. There are so many of him. There is Hugh Casson the architect, the interior designer, the stage designer, the painter, the illustrator, the writer, the lecturer, the teacher, and, not last, the watercolour painter who excelled so brilliantly. Even such a list is far from complete. His contribution as a planner of universities and colleges has revealed his progressive, original mind, his ability to look forward with a clear vision towards the future. But it wasn't until his appointment as the president of the Royal Academy of Arts in 1976 that he revealed another dimension—as a supreme organiser capable of skillfully handling such an important assignment. It appears that each Casson was able to enrich the other as his activities expanded.

As the Director of Architecture for the Festival of Britain he brought originality and freshness into that profession; as a Committee member for the Bath, Windsor, and Brighton Festivals he opened up these communities to high quality arts; his development plans at Cambridge University's Arts Faculty site and those at Worcester College Hall in Oxford gave a lift to those sites, as well as in many other situations where he combined good architecture with excellent interior design updating these establishments to modern times. The Windsor Castle Royal Apartments and Prince Philip's Library in Buckingham Palace come into this category. These qualities have been utilised on a number of occasions not as permanent as the former, like the street decoration of the Queen's Coronation in 1953, and the British Pavilion design in the World Expo 1970 at Osaka. His stage performances include a number of productions in Glyndebourne, in the Royal Opera House, Covent Garden, London. One such stage design was *La Fedelta Premiata* for Glyndebourne in 1979/80.

His numerous books, mainly on architecture and visual appreciation, include some classics such as *Bombed Churches, The Unseeing Eye* and *Hugh Casson's London.* Another book on Oxford was published by Phaidon in 1988, a follow up to an illustrated book on Cambridge.

Sir Hugh Casson's contribution on so many levels of the arts, and to the cultural level of England, is without parallel. He has enriched the standard of each of these categories and especially during his presidency of the Royal Academy of Arts opened the doors of the establishment to the general public and democratised fine art making it accessible to the people.

—John Halas

# CASTELLI FERRIERI, Anna

Italian architect and furniture and industrial designer

**Born:** Anna Ferrieri, in Milan, 6 August 1920. **Education:** Studied at the University of Milan, Dip.Arch., 1943. **Family:** Married Giulio Castelli in 1943; children: Valerio and Maria. **Career:** Freelance architect, establishing office in Milan, from 1946; industrial designer, from 1965; designed for Apelli e Varesio, Arflex, Erpo International, Giorgetti Matrix, Kartell, Matteograssi, Nirvana, Oltolini, Sambonet, Seagram, Ycami, and others. Associated with architect Ignazio Gardella, 1959-73. Assistant Editor, *Costruzioni,* Milan, 1946-47; Italian correspondent, *Architectural Design* (London), in Milan, 1955-60. Guest professor, University of Milan, Faculty of Architecture 1984-86; professor, Domus Academy Postgraduate School of Design, Milan, from 1987; professor, RMIT Centre for Design, Melbourne, Australia, 1992; lecturer, Art Center College of Design, Pasadena, California, 1992. International President, United Nations Committee of Soroptimist International, 1973-75. **Member:** Founder-member, Movimento Studi per l'Architettura (MSA), Milan, 1945; Istituto Nazionale di Urbanistica (INU), from 1952; founder-member, from 1956, and President, 1969-71, Associazione Disegno Industriale (ADI), Milan. **Exhibitions:** *Design Italian Style,* Hallmark Gallery, New York, 1968; *Italy: The New Domestic Landscape,* Museum of Modern Art, New York, 1972; *Design and Design,* Palazzo delle Stelline, Milan, 1979 (travelled to Venice); *Italienisches Moebel Design,* Stadtmuseum, Cologne, 1980; *Dal Cucchiaio alla Città,* Milan Triennale, 1983; *Italian Women Designers,* Takashimaya Stores, Tokyo, 1985; *Anna Castelli Ferrieri per Kartell,* Galliano, Turin, 1985; *Anna Castelli Ferrieri at Gallery Modus,* Berlin, 1986; *Sedersi Kartell,* La Rinascente, Milan 1988; *Industrial Elegance,* Pacific Design Center, Los Angeles, 1992 (travelled to Denver and Chicago). **Collections:** Museum of Modern Art, New York; Stadtmuseum, Munich; Kunstindustrimuseet, Copenhagen; Israel Museum, Jerusalem; Design Museum, London; Sao Paulo Design Museum. **Honors:** Gold Medals, Milan Triennale, 1947 (two), 1950; Oscar Plast Award, London, 1968; Silver Medal Oesterreichisches Bauzentrum, Vienna, 1969; Gold Medal, Monza, 1972; MACEF Award Milan, 1972; Bundespreis Gute Form, West German Government, Bonn, 1973; SMAU Award, Milan, 1977; Product Design Award, Resources Council, New York, 1979, 1984; Premio Compasso d'Oro Awards, ADI, Milan, 1979, 1987; Design Award, American Societies of Industrial Design, Museum of Art, San Diego, 1981; Gold Medal, BIO9, Llubljana, 1982; Furniture Fair Design Award, Cologne, 1982, 1987; *Industrial Design* Magazine Annual Award, New York, 1983; Fine Furniture of the Year Award, Hamburg, 1984. **Address:** Corso di Porta Romana, 87/B 20122 Milan, Italy.

## Works

*Mostra del Mobile Singolo,* at Milan Triennale, 1947.
*Mostra dell'Abitazione,* at Milan Triennale, 1951.
Modular system kitchen furniture, for Oltolini, 1950.
Eight-story condominium at Via Marchiondi, Milan, 1951.
Four-story house at QT8 pilot neighborhood, for the Municipality of Milan, 1954.
Buildings at the INA CASA neighborhood, Milan and Cento (Ferrara), 1957-58.
Four-story office block in Milan, for Castelli Acciai, 1958.
Pilot residential neighborhood, with sponsorship of the National Committee for Building Productivity, Vicenza, 1959-61.
Two villas, Pineta di Arenzano, 1960-63.
Residence, Pineta di Arenzano, 1961.
*La Rotonda* apartments at Arenzano, for Cemadis, 1963.
Square stacking units in ABS plastic, for Kartell, 1967.
Canteen building at Podenzano, for Tecnitub, 1968.
Oval table in fiberglass, for Kartell, 1969.
Workshop and warehouse at Limbiate, Milan, for Castelli Acciai, 1970.
Five-story engineering offices at Arese, Milan, for Alfa Romeo, 1970-72.
Corporate headquarters buildings at Noviglio, Milan, for Kartell, 1973.
*Outline* wallpeg strip system in high-impact polystyrene, for Kartell, 1977.
Multi-use stools in four heights with expanded polyurethane seats, for Kartell, 1979.
Four-leg square table, injection molded in thermoplastic technopolymer, for Kartell, 1982.
Central-leg square table, injection molded in thermoplastic technopolymer, for Kartell, 1983.
*Esistere come donna* exhibition design, at the Milan Palazzo Reale, 1983.
Castek corporate offices, Milan, 1983-85.
Occasional tables in ABS plastic, for Kartell, 1985.
Stacking chair in injection-molded polypropylene, for Kartell, 1985.
*Silent Servant* valet/wardrobe in ABS plastic and steel, for Kartell, 1985.
Parish Center, Cesate, 1987.
*Stooble* stacking stool/table in injection molded polypropylene, for Kartell, 1987.
*Sedersi Kartell* exhibition, La Rinascente, Milan, 1988.
Armchair in injection-molded plastics, for Kartell, 1988.
*Narciso* tower, for Giorgetti Matrix, 1989.
*Segnale* sofas, for Arflex, 1990.
*Pyggy* chair, for Matteograssi, 1991.
*I Cirri* collection, for Sambonet, 1991.
*I Nomadi* collection, for Sambonet, 1991.
Restoration of an antique building with a Bramante cloister, Piazza S. Eustorgio, Milan, 1992.
*HannaH* cutlery service, for Sambonet, 1992.
*Lord* champagne trolley and *Partner* equipped with trays, for Seagram, 1992.
*Athena* and *Libra* single armchairs, for Erpo International, 1994.
*Contralto* table, for Ycami, 1994.

## Publications

**By CASTELLI FERRIERI: books**—(with Augusto Morello) *From Project to Product: Plastic and Design,* Milan, 1984, 1988; *The*

Anna Castelli Ferrieri: *HANNAH* cutlery service, for Sambonet, 1994

*Interfaces of Material,* Milan, 1991; **articles**— "Case prefabbricate inglesi" in *Construzioni* (Milan), no. 193, 1946; "L'avvio della ricostruzione" in *Casabella* (Milan), no. 440/441, 1978; "Progettare e comunicare" in *Interni Annual* (Milan), 1981; "Dal cucchiaia alla città, Milano Capitale del design" in *La Stampa* (Turin), October 1983; "Industrial Design: una mostra per capire" in *Habitat* (Milan), no. 1, 1985; "Dallo hard al soft il design italiano come sistema culturale" in *Nuovo* (Milan), no. 14, 1988; "Entropia e nuovo Umanesimo" in *Modo,* 1988; "Anni di piombo" in *Interni 400,* 1990; "Alchimia della materia" in *Neolite* (Milan), 1991.

**On CASTELLI FERRIERI: books**—*Italy: The New Domestic Landscape* edited by Emilio Ambasz, New York and Florence, 1972; *Design e Forme Nuove nell'Arredamento Italiano* edited by Paolo Portoghesi and Marino Marini, Rome, 1978; *Design and design,* exhibition catalogue with texts by Angelo Cortsei, Arthur Pulos, and others, Florence, 1979; *Italienisches Moebel Design,* exhibition catalogue with texts by Ignazio Gardella, Gillo Dorfles, and others, Cologne, 1980; *L'Alfa Romeo: Disegni e Progetti degli Uffici Alfa Romeo di Arese,* Milan, 1982; *L'oggetto e lo spazio* by Arturo dell'Acqua Bellavitis, Milan, 1987; *Paesaggio del Design Italiano*

*1972-1988* by Giampiero Bosoni, Milan, 1988; *Frauen im Design,* Stuttgart, 1989; *Annual of Furniture Designers,* Barcelona, 1989; *Anna Castelli Ferrieri* by Cristina Morozzi, Roma-Bari, 1993; **articles**—"Una donna e l'architettura" by Franco Menna, in *Casamica,* no. 22, 1982; "Rencontre avec Anna Castelli Ferrieri" in *Décors* (Bruxelles), 1986; "Anna Castelli, el diseno, mi pasion" by Ino Coll, in *Hogares,* no. 219, 1986; "Incontro con Anna Castelli Ferrieri" by Sonia Paolini Grianti, in *Casa e Giardino* (Milan), 1991; "Anna Castelli Ferrieri at Home" by Carol Souces King in *Empowered Spaces* (New York), 1993.

\*

The world has changed and calls for new projects. The quick spreading out of new sophisticated technologies that have changed the value of time and space can and must become a stimulus to turn limitations, especially the environmental ones, into new opportunities.

We shall go back to designing for people rather than for museums. We shall stop worrying about formal research, but instead about living better, designing what is missing in our everyday life, fair presences that may become familiar and will not uselessly encumber our already crowded physical world. We now are given the opportunity to link again with the tradition of the Modern Movement, giving life to a new "cultural functionality."

—Anna Castelli Ferrieri

\*    \*    \*

Dear Mrs. Ferrieri:
Slowly your objects entered my house's small universe. First a container, then a table. They seemed to fill a void, as if they were the pieces of a puzzle that were missing. Day after day, this unpretentious design that surrounds me began to find new initiates, a friend, a neigbor, a relative. Your objects, colored or not, are simple, tranquil, subtle but useful. I find them to be of our time, whereas those modern objects, the results of bravura that are the repertoire of museums, seem so far removed.

I bought a book in which your impressive life history is discussed. You have been dedicated to your profession and have received awards and recognition—it is not easy to create objects that are full of vitality but at the same time composed and not overpowering, mechanically reliable and pleasant to touch.

I am jubilant that a woman is creating this design and gaining recognition for it. To be fair, it is not as if architecture and design are lacking in examples of quality design created by women: Cini Boeri, Gae Aulenti, and the anticonformist Nanda Vigo, just to name a few talented female designers and architects. On the other hand, where is it possible to find another woman designer who considers everyday objects that are destined for everyone and not only for design fanatics?

Your forms are complete, mature, and spiritually gratifying, even if you use a material which is notoriously known for polluting, plastic. On this point, one must note that you are committed to moving away from the impasse and are trying to find new solutions for standardized production. In your collection there are containers made from recycled plastic. Using recycled materials is the way of the future, however, it is only the first response to the enormous refuse crisis. Unfortunately, modern man is still pushing consumerism and thus continues to generate untold amounts of waste.

The *Polvara* bookcase, another element of your collection, is beautiful and functional. For years it has followed me through all my house moves, whether to the seaside, the city, or the countryside where it rests today. These are the objects I need; however, I am not a slave of them.

In our busy cities the spirit of things has changed, and so, a new furniture system had to be invented. Objects that express our culture and the conscience of today's buyer. No more Eileen Greys museum house style, even though I do admire it. No more disposable products which are frustrating for their polluting effect and for the fact that it is impossible to feel any long-term affection for the object.

I wonder whether the things you thought about at the beginning of your career, when one is much more militant about creating pure design, have been realized. During these long years of work, have you remained disillusioned by the vulgar taste that continues to rage on? Was it an illusion to believe it was easy to inherit the Rationalists' dream and to develop a social role or did it run the risk of depersonalizing our homes, our offices, and our cities?

The fine sense of a designer and the practical side of a woman created these objects that I have become so familiar with and that populate my house. Please don't trouble yourself by answering my letter; instead continue to create new houses and things, those items for which we feel the need.

—Jacques Toussaint

# CASTIGLIONI, Achille
Italian architect, exhibition, and industrial designer

**Born:** Milan, 16 February 1918. **Education:** Studied architecture at the Politecnico, Milan, Dip. Arch., 1944. **Family:** Married Anna Maria Peraldo; married Irma Barni; children: Carlo, Monica, and Giovanna. **Career:** Freelance designer, Milan, from 1944, working with his brothers Livio Castiglioni, 1944-54, and Pier Giacomo Castiglioni, 1944-68; has designed for Aerotecnica Italiana, Alessi, Arnolfo di Cambio, Arteluce, BBB Bonacina, Bernini, Brionvega, Cassina, Cedit, Danese, Ferrania, Flos, Gavina, Gilardi, Ideal Standard, Kartell, Knoll, Lancia, Marcatre, Nova Radio, Palini, Petruzzi e Branca, Poretti, Siemens, Zanotta, Zari, and others; artistic consultant, Associazione Nazionale Industrie Elettroniche, 1949-80, RAI Radio Televisione Italiana, 1950-69, Internazionale Elettronica, 1977-80, Lanerossi furniture, 1978-80, and to the Comitato Elettronica Italiano and the Instituto Italiana del Marchio di Qualita; project chief, Illuminazione della Citta programme, Turin, 1982-83. Professor of industrial design and head of the faculty of architecture, 1969-77, head of interior design, 1977-78, professor extraordinary of industrial design, 1978-80, and ordinary professor of industrial design, 1980, Politecnico of Turin; external professor of design, Universita Internazionale dell'Arte, Florence, 1973; ordinary professor of design, Politecnico of Milan, from 1981. **Member:** Coordination committee member, 1947-64, scientific committee member, 1979-80, Milan Triennale; founder-member, 1956, directive committee member, 1963-64, exhibitions committee president and documentation committee member, 1965, and Compasso d'Oro jury member, 1970, ADI Associazione Disegno Industriale, Milan; directive committee member, Collegio degli Architetti, Milan, 1960-61; committee member, Centro Studi e Archivio dell Comunicazione, University of Parma, 1979-80. **Exhibitions:** *La Casa Abiata,* Palazzo Strozzi, Florence, 1965; *Oggetti per la Casa,* Centro Fly, Milan, 1966; *Fem Italienska Designer,* Stockholm, 1974; *Il Design dei Castiglioni,* Centro Masters, Lissone, 1978; *Art and Industry,* Victoria and Albert Museum, London, 1982; *Design Since 1945,* Philadelphia Museum of Art, 1983; *Achille Castiglioni: Form and Expression,* Paris, Milan, and London, 1985. **Collections:** Museum of Modern Art, New York; Victoria and Albert Museum, London; Staatliches Museum für Angewandte Kunst, Munich; Kunstgewerbemuseum, Zurich; Israel Museum, Jerusalem. **Honors:** Grand Prize, 1951, 1957, Gold and Silver Medals, 1957, 1960, 1963, Milan Triennale; Compasso d'Oro Awards, Milan, 1955, 1957, 1960, 1962, 1964, 1967, 1979, 1981; Architecture Prize, Bienal of Sao Paulo, 1957; Vis Securit Prize, Milan, 1957; First Prize, Reed and Barton Competition, 1960; European Design Prize, Seattle, 1961; Good Design Prize, New York, 1966, 1972; Graphic Prize, Brno, 1968; Gold Medal, Rimini, 1968; Siemens Telephone Competition Prize, Milan, 1977; Ikea Interiors Prize, Zurich, 1981. **Address:** Piazza Castello 27, 20121 Milan, Italy.

## Works

Hotel guestroom furniture range, for Zari, 1946.
*Tubino* lamp, 1951, produced by Flos, 1974.
*Luminator* lamp, 1955, produced by Gilardi and Arform, 1957.
*Cubo* armchair with polyfoam block upholstery, for Arflex, 1957.
*Mezzadro* stool in steel, 1957, produced by Zanotta, 1971.
*Sella* stool with bicycle seat, 1957, produced by Zanotta, 1983.
*Mariano* bookcase, produced by Brenna, 1958, produced by Gavina, 1961.
*KD51/Teli* lamp, produced by Kartell, 1959, produced by Flos, 1973.
*Lierna* chair, produced by Gavina, 1960, produced by Knoll International, 1969.
*Pitagora* espresso coffee machine, for Cimbali, 1961.
*Arco* lamp, produced by Flos, 1962.
*Giro* swivel armchair, for Gavina, 1962.
*Cyrius* television set, for Brionvega, 1964.
*RR126* stereo equipment unit, for Brionvera.
*Leonardo* work desk with glass or plastic laminate top, for Zanotta, 1968.
*Parentesi* floor-to-ceiling suspension lamp, for Flos, 1971.
*Ipotenusa* halogen desk lamp, for Flos, 1975.
*Bipbip* standard lamp, for Flos, 1977.
*Rosacamuna* folding chair, for Zanotta, 1983.

## Publications

**By CASTIGLIONI: books**—*Design e la sua Prospettive Disciplinari,* Milan, 1977; (with E. Battinelli and P. Ferrari) *Progetto e Produzione,* Linz, 1980.

**On CASTIGLIONI: books**—*Forme nuove in Italia* by Agnoldomenico Pica, Milan and Rome, 1957; *Disegno Industriale* by P. Tedeschi, Bologna, 1965; *Design Italiano: i mobili* by Enrichetta Ritter, Milan and Rome, 1968; *Il Design in Italia 1945-1972* by Paolo Fossati, Turin, 1972; *In Good Shape: Style in Industrial Products 1900 to 1960* by Stephen Bayley, London, 1979; *Atlante del Design Italiano 1940-1980* by Alfonso Grassi and Anty Pansera, Milan, 1980; *Il Disegno del Prodotto Industriale* by Vittorio Gregotti, Milan, 1982; *An Industry for Design: The Research, Design and Corporate Image of B & B Italia* by Mario Mastropietro, Milan, 1982, 1986; *Achille Castiglioni,* with text by Vittorio Gregotti and Paolo Ferrari, Paris and Milan, 1985; *Design in Italy: 1870 to the Present* by Penny Sparke, London and New York, 1988; *The Adventure of Design: Gavina* by Virgilio Vercelloni, New York, 1989.

*See* CASTIGLIONI, Pier Giacomo

\*

The need for a new and original approach in contemporary design is emerging more and more urgently. Such a new approach can be effected through design activity on two different levels. On the one hand, there is design for mass production, on the other, design for the production of a limited quantity.

In the first case, research faces the task of large-scale production and is broken off whenever the problems of constructional and commercial production do not arise. It goes without saying that the quality of the product will be closely connected with questions of use and of sales.

In the second case, however, research is carried out on all the problems and complexities. The product that results from it reflects the quality of the research and the standard of production, for the actual product may be regarded as a materialization of the standards of design.

—Achille Castiglioni

\*     \*     \*

Although trained as an architect, Achille Castiglioni is probably best known for his furniture and lighting designs (most in conjunction with his older brother, Pier Giacomo, with whom he collaborated from 1944 until the latter's death in 1968) and his exhibition work.

Since his brother's untimely death, Achille has continued to produce the fine-styled, highly imaginative designs for which they had become famous. Not limited to furniture or lighting, and continuing in their tradition of producing simple, obvious, and elegant design solutions, his bathroom fixtures for Ideal Standard (1971) demonstrated that such items could be both functional and well designed. In a similar fashion, his handsome flatware for Alessi (1982) brought his aesthetic integrity to the dining table in a comfortable, sculptural form, and was available in both silver and stainless steel. His oil and vinegar set (1984), for the same firm, again combined his technical expertise (the stainless steel lids opened as the glass containers were turned over) with his selective eye.

He has also designed a free-standing wine/drink cooler (a bent metal shaft which supports an ice bucket) which has been described as looking "faintly like an attentive but anorexic waiter." It bears a resemblance to a suspended, adjustable light, *Parentesi,* which he developed with Pio Manzu in 1970. Similarly, many of his recent lights take on other identities: *Gibigiana* (1981) looks more like a bird sculpture than a desk lamp, utilizing an angled mirror to reflect the light (housed in a flared, metal "skirt") downwards. He has combined metal and ceramics in an innovative floor lamp, *Bipbip* (1976), and in its recent companion piece, an uplight/wallwasher called *Bisbi.* One of his recent furniture favorites is *Basello* (1987), a tiered table which can be pivoted about a connecting point and set at different angles like a spiral "stairway," for which it is named *Milanese slang.*

Castiglioni, who has been honored seven times with the Compasso d'Oro, remains through his teaching and unerring design output a highly influential participant in the design world .

—William Victor Kriebel

## CASTIGLIONI, Livio

Italian architect and industrial designer

**Born:** Milan, 16 January 1911. **Education:** Studied architecture at the Politecnico, Milan, Dip. Arch., 1936. **Military Service:** Served in the Italian Army, 1940-44. **Family:** Married Xenia Bignami; married Giuseppina Ramponi; children: Giannino and Piero. **Career:** Freelance designer, Milan, 1936-79; worked with the architect Luigi Caccia Dominioni, 1938-40, with brother Pier Giacomo

Castiglioni, 1937-54, and brother Achille Castiglioni, 1944-54; design consultant to Phonola Radio, 1939-60, Brionvega, 1960-64, Osram Lamps, 1974-79, and Gulf International/Meridian Hotels, 1975-79; also designed for Artemide, ENI, Italsider, Montedison, Philips, RAI Radio Televisione Italiana, and others. **Member:** Founder-member, 1956, and president, 1959-60, ADI Associazione Disegno Industriale, Milan. **Exhibitions:** *Il Design dei Castiglioni,* Centro Masters, Lissone, 1978; *Culture and Technology of Italian Furniture,* Stadtmuseum, Cologne, 1980; *Design Since 1945,* Philadelphia Museum of Art, 1983. **Collections:** Museo della Scienza e della Tecnica, Milan; Museum of Modern Art, New York. **Honors:** Silver Medal, 1936, Golf Medal and Grand Prize, 1940, and Diploma, 1973, Milan Triennale; Gold Medal, Arts Convention, Rimini, 1968; Bolaffi Art Prize, Turin, 1974. **Died:** Milan, 1979.

### Publications

**By CASTIGLIONI: articles**—in *Domus* (Milan), no. 151, 1940, no. 196, 1944, no. 197, 1944, and no. 198, 1944; *Architecture d'Aujourd'hui* (Paris), no. 48, 1953; *Stile Industria* (Milan), no. 1, 1957.

**On CASTIGLIONI: books**—*Design e Forme Nuove nell'Arredamento Italiano* edited by Paolo Portoghesi and Marino Marini, Rome, 1978; *Plastics: Design and Materials* by Sylvia Katz, London, 1978; *Il Design Italiano degli Anni 50* edited by Centro Kappa, Milan, 1980; *Atlante del Design Italiano 1940-80* by Alfonso Grassi and Anty Pansera, Milan, 1980; *Il Disegno del Prodotto Industriale* by Vittorio Gregotti, Milan, 1982; *Il Disegno Industriale Italiano 1928-1981* by E. Fratelli, Milan, 1983; *Design Since 1945* edited by Kathryn Hiesinger and George Marcus, Philadelphia and London, 1983.

*   *   *

Livio Castiglioni was a retiring person whose collaboration was not always acknowledged, yet for many years his influence was pervasive. The flowing lines and harmonious detail of Castiglioni's radio sets for Phonola in 1939 and 1940 found echoes in the pressure beer dispenser designed for Splügen Brau in 1964 by his brothers, in some of the designs for radio and television sets by Marco Zanuso and Richard Sapper, in these same designers's Grillo telephone (1967), and in Mario Bellini's Logos 270 data processing machine for Olivetti (1970). None of these were cases of plagiarism; rather, they represent a cultural debt these designers owe to Livio Castiglioni.

Once the novelty of an object like the Phonola radio or the Boalum lamp ceases to be in the forefront of one's appreciation, they demonstrate the underlying preoccupation of Castiglioni's design practice: to achieve an object which is reduced to a unity in which no detail is obtrusive, however pleasing and attention-demanding the final form. In each case, the form created is certainly determined by its components, but these are harmonised into the whole, so that the final form is not the sum of these, nor could any of them be happily removed or separated.

Such is the case with Phonola radio, in which the components (the raised and angled perforated disk of the loudspeaker, the tuning dial, the ordered distribution of the button controls) achieve clear expression within a unified final design. Moreover, the intention that the radio might either sit on the table or hang on the wall was

allowed to play a predominant role in the manner in which the angles of the speaker and dial were set, in relation to each other, and to the base. The Boalum lamp is a ninety-centimeter, flexible, metal-and-plastic tube. That is all there is to it. Any number may be fitted together and slung about however one wishes; in tangled coils, in festoons, draped over furniture, heaped in a corner, or hung on the wall. Yet, one distinguishes, if not components, then the elements of which it is made—the metals stiffening and the translucent plastic skin.

—Toni del Renzio

## CASTIGLIONI, Pier Giacomo

Italian exhibition, interior, and furniture designer

**Born:** Milan, 22 April 1913. **Education:** Studied architecture at the Politecnico, Milan, Dip. Arch., 1937. **Family:** Married Maria Coduri de Cartosio; children: Giorgina. **Career:** Independent architect and designer, Milan, 1937-68; worked with the architect Luigi Caccia Dominioni, 1937-45, and with his brothers Livio Castiglioni, 1937-53, and Achille Castiglioni, 1944-68; also collaborated with the architect Carlo Pagani; design consultant to Associazione Nazionale Industrie Elettroniche, 1949-68; and RAI Radio Televisione Italiana, 1950-68; designed for Arteluce, Brionvega, Cassina, Ferrania, Gavina, Gilardi, Ginori, Kartell, Krupp, Leuci, Palini, Phonola, Rem, Zanotta, and others. Professor of Design, Politecnico of Milan, 1968. **Member:** Gruppo Domus, Milan, 1944-45; founder-member, Movimento Studi Architettura, Milan, 1945; board member, Architetti della Lombardia, 1949-51; founder-member, ADI Associazione Disegno Industriale, Milan, 1956; vice-president, Consiglio Regionale Lombardo degli Architetti, 1957-58. **Exhibitions:** *Colori e Forme nella Casa d'Oggi,* Villa Olmo, Como, 1952, 1954; *Italian Industrial Design,* Paris, 1957; *Contemporary Italian Design,* Tokyo, 1965; *P. G. Castiglioni: La Casa Abitata,* Palazzo Strozzi, Florence, 1965; *Oggetti per la Casa,* Centro Fly, Milan, 1966; *Originale und Plagiate,* Vienna, 1974; *11 Design dei Castiglioni,* Centro Masters, Lissone, 1978; *Culture and Technology of Italian Furniture,* Stadtmuseum, Cologne, 1980; *Design Since 1945,* Philadelphia Museum of Art, 1983. **Collections:** Museo della Scienza e della Tecnica, Milan; Kunstgewerbemuseum, Munich; Kunstgewerbemuseum, Zurich; Victoria and Albert Museum, London; Israel Museum, Jerusalem; Museum of Modern Art, New York. **Honors:** Grand Prize, 1951, 1954, Gold and Silver Medals, 1957, 1960, 1963, Milan Triennale; Compasso d'Oro Award, Milan, 1955, 1957, 1960, 1962, 1964, 1967; First Prize, Reed and Barton Competition, 1960; Graphics Prize, Brno, 1968; Gold Medal, Arts Convention, Rimini, 1968. **Died:** Milan, 27 November 1968.

### Works

*Cavalletto* table, produced by Gavina, 1955.
*KD51/Teli* lamp, produced by Kartell, 1959, and Flos, 1973.
*Sanluca* chair, produced by Gavina, 1960.
*Viscontea* lamp, produced by Gavina, 1960.
*Gatto* lamp, produced by Gavina, 1960.
*Taraxacum* lamp, produced by Gavina, 1960.
*Splugen Brau* table lamp, produced by Gavina, 1962.

*Toio* standard lamp, produced by Gavina, 1962.
*Arco* lamp, produced by Flos, 1962.
*Relemme* pendant lamp, produced by Flos, 1962.
*Taccia* lamp, produced by Flos, 1962.
*Black and White* glass pendant lamp, produced by Flos, 1965.
*Snoopy* table lamp, produced by Flos, 1967.

## Publications

**By CASTIGLIONI: books**—*Colori e Forme nella Casa di Oggi,* exhibition catalogue, Como, 1952.

**On CASTIGLIONI: books**—*Introduction to Design* by Arthur Drexler and Greta Daniel, New York, 1959; *Graphic Design in Advertising* by Pier Carlo Santini, Milan, 1962; *Disegno e Progettazione* by M. Petrignani, Bari, 1967; *Idee per la Casa/Modern Interiors* edited by Franco Magnani, Milan and London, 1969; *History of Modern Furniture* by Karl Mang, Stuttgart, 1978, London, 1979; *Atlante del Disegno Italiano 1940-1980* by Alfonso Grassi and Anty Pansera, Milan, 1980; *An Industry for Design: The Research, Design and Corporate Image of B & B Italia* edited by Mario Mastropietro, Milan, 1982, 1986; *Design Since 1945* edited by Kathryn Hiesinger and George Marcus, Philadelphia and London, 1983; *Design in Italy: 1870 to the Present* by Penny Sparke, London and New York, 1988; *The Adventure of Design: Gavina* by Virgilio Vercelloni, New York, 1989.

\*      \*      \*

In the early 1960s, I ordered an interior light for a bank project that I was working on. It arrived early at my office (the bank was not yet completed) and the rear truck doors were opened to reveal two cardboard boxes. Both were about a foot square in area, one about six feet high, the other only about eighteen inches high. The trucker braced himself to pick up the larger box. Lo and behold, it almost floated into the air. He returned for the little box, attempting to grip it under one arm. Alas, it would not move. This was my first physical introduction to the work of Pier Giacomo Castiglioni (and his younger brother, Achille). The boxes contained the parts of Arco: the taller, the stainless steel shaft/arm and spun aluminum shade; the smaller, a chamfer-cornered block of white Carrara marble, the base and "anchor" for the adjustable, cantilevered arm. (The lamp has been poorly copied ever since.) I assembled the lamp to check it, and fell in love with it. The design, materials, and detailing were exquisite.

Ten years earlier, the names of the Castiglioni brothers were only related to designs shown in handsome photos in *DOMUS* magazine. The Dino Gavina company, which had been producing Jeep hoods and railroad car upholstery, added a few pieces of furniture, including, in 1955, Pier Giacomo Castiglioni's Cavalletto (sawhorse). This was literally a table formed of a flat plane supported on two finely-made, wooden sawhorses. It was the start of a successful collaboration between designer and fabricator. In 1960, Gavina Spa was born with Carlo Scarpa as its president. Castiglioni, his brother Achille, Scarpa's son, Tobia, and a few others formed the nucleus of what would become one of the best known furniture producers in the country. The designs were aimed at mass production with careful attention to detail. The Castiglioni brothers' segmented chair, Sanluca, one of the company's first products, was praised by Carlo Scarpa as "an armchair for which a formalist like myself would gladly take credit."

It soon became apparent to Gavina that there were few lighting products then on the market which were compatible, either in quality or design, with the furniture he was producing. In 1962, in consort with another furniture manufacturer, Cesare Cassina, a new company, Flos, was born. However, Castiglioni had already started innovative experiments with both old and new materials. Rethinking a material developed for protecting vehicles transported on seagoing vessels—a plastic foam film that turned solid upon being sprayed with air—Viscontea, Gatto, and Taraxacum appeared (1960). The Castiglioni brothers' fabric lamp, Teli (1959), a classic design, was purportedly in answer to Gavina's desire to rid the warehouse of some leftover fabric! More designs, more innovations, more ingenuity, more experiments, more products: Splugen Brau (1961) effectively directed the light, projector-like, only on the table below and provided an architectural character for a Milan restaurant of the same name; Toio (1962) turned a low voltage lamp, pointed straight up, mounted in a chrome harness, into an art sculpture; Arco (1962), a floor lamp intended to light a table by hanging over it from the corner of a room; Relemme (1962), a counterbalanced, adjustable pendant lamp; Taccia (1962), a shimmering glass/metal table lamp; Black & White (1965), an opal glass pendant lamp; and Snoopy (1967), a jaunty little table lamp with a canted base and "hat," a stylized three-dimensional cartoon character.

About 1967, these designs started to be marketed in the U.S. Now the ingenuity, the quality of the materials, and the details could be appreciated at first hand. Regrettably, Pier Giacomo died the following year at the age of 55, a great loss to the design world. Fortunately, he has left us with a great legacy—his work—which we can continue to appreciate.

—William Victor Kriebel

# CERRI, Pierluigi

Italian architect and exhibition, graphic, book, interior, and industrial designer

**Born:** 1939. **Education:** Graduated from Polytechnic, Milan, B. Arch., 1969. **Career:** founder and partner, with Vittorio Gregotti and others, Gregotti Associati architects and designers, from 1974; image consultant, for Unifor, from 1982, Lingotto, from 1983 and Ferrari Auto, from 1989; art director, Biennale of Venice, 1976; editor, *Rassegna* magazine, from 1978, and *Casabella* magazine, 1982-1995; designed books, for Bompiani, 1973, Electa, 1976-1988, Einaudi, from 1981, Ubulibri, from 1981, and Bollati Boringhieri, 1987; art director, interactive CD-ROM series Encyclomedia (directed by Umberto Eco), from 1994. **Member:** Alliance Graphique Internationale. **Honors:** Award for good industrial design, Industrie Forum Design, Hannover, 1994; Compasso d'Oro, Associazione Disegno Industriale, 1995. **Address:** Gregotti Associati International, Via Bandello 20, 20123 Milan, Italy.

## Works

Graphic image, for Palazzo Grassi, Venice, 1984.
Visual identity, for Pitti Immagine, 1988.
Visual identity, for Italia 90 World Soccer Championship, 1990.

Pierluigi Cerri: installation of *Idea Ferrari* exhibition, Florence

Graphic image, for Kunst- und Ausstellungshalle der Bundesrepublik Deutschland, Bonn, 1992.

Interior design, for 55,000 ton ocean liners, "Costa Classica," 1988, "Costa Romantica," 1991, and "Costa Victoria," 1994.

Corporate identity, for Banca Popolare di Lodi, 1994

*Naòs* office system, for Unifor, 1994.

Graphic image, for Unifor, 1995.

Exhibition designs include—*Peter Behrens and AEG,* Internationale Design Zentrum, Berlin, 1978; *Carrozzeria Italiana,* Palazzo della Promotrice delle Belle Arti, Turin, 1978; *Identité Italienne,* Centre Georges Pompidou, Paris, 1981; *Alexander Calder,* Palazzo a Vela, Turin, 1983; *Italian Furniture Design,* Design Centrum, Stuttgart, Germany, and Sogetsu, Japan, 1983; *Venti Progetti per el futuro del Lingotto,* Lingotto, Turin, 1984; *Las Formas de la Industria,* Museo de Arte Contemporaneo, Madrid, 1987; *Marcel Duchamp: La Sposa e I Readymade,* Accademia di Brera, Milan, 1988; *The FIAT case,* Science Museum, London, 1988; *Arte Russa e Sovietica,* Lingotto, Turin, 1990; *L'Idea Ferrari,* Forte del Belvedere, Florence, 1990; *Civiltà dell Macchine,* Lingotto, Turin, 1990; *Erd-sicht,* KAH, Bonn, 1992; *Marcel Duchamp,* Palazzo Grassi, Venice, 1993; *I Goti,* Palazzo Reale, Milan, 1994; *L'Idea Ferrari,* Nationalgalerie, Berlin, 1994; *Jorden,* Moderna Museet, Stockholm, 1994.

**Publications**

By CERRI: books—*Vers une architecture,* editor, Milan, 1974; *Five Graphic Designers,* editor, Venice, 1976; *Pubblicità d'autore,* editor, Milan, 1983.

On CERRI: articles—"Gregotti Associati Communication Design" by Giovanni Anceschi in *Graphic Design* (Japan), September 1985; "The Plane Space Is not Enough Anymore: Pierluigi Cerri" by Paola Antonelli in *Graphis* (New York), July/August 1993.

# CHADWICK, Don
American furniture designer

**Born:** Los Angeles, California, in 1936. **Education:** Attended the University of California, Los Angeles, B.A., 1959. **Career:** Furniture designer, with studio in Santa Monica, California; consultant designer, Herman Miller Inc., Zeeland, Michigan, from 1974. Lecturer, Department of Design, University of California, Los Angeles, 1975-86, Art Center College of Design, Pasadena, California, 1976; graduate advisor, University of California, Los Angeles, and

Philadelphia College of Art and Design, from 1987. **Exhibitions:** *California Design 10* and *11,* Pasadena Museum of Art, 1968, 1971; *Contemporary Home Environs,* La Jolla Museum of Contemporary Art, California, 1973; *California Design 12,* Pacific Design Center, Los Angeles, 1976; *A Serious Chair,* Walker Art Center, Minneapolis, Minnesota, 1984; *High Styles: 20th Century American Design,* Whitney Museum, New York, 1985; *1935-1965: What Modern Was,* Los Angeles County Museum of Art, 1991; *Common Forms, High Art: Three Centuries of American Furniture,* Los Angeles County Museum of Art, 1995; *Mutant Materials in Contemporary Design,* Museum of Modern Art, New York, 1995. **Collections:** Museum of Modern Art, New York; San Francisco Museum of Modern Art, California; Denver Museum of Art, Colorado. **Honors:** Award for Design Excellence, 1970, 1971, 1973, 1974, Design of the Year, 1985, and Best of Category—Furniture, 1995, *ID Magazine;* First Place Award for Seating, 1974, Silver Award for Casegoods, 1980, and First Place Award for Seating, 1992, Institute for Business Designers; Governor's Award, Design Michigan, 1977; International Product Design Award, ASID, 1986; Design Innovations 95 Award, Design Zentrum, Germany, 1995. **Address:** Don Chadwick & Associates, Santa Monica, California, U.S.A.

## Works

*Chadwick* modular seating, for Herman Miller Inc., 1974.
*Equa* chair, for Herman Miller Inc., 1984 (with Bill Stumpf).
*Aeron* chair, for Herman Miller Inc., 1994 (with Bill Stumpf).

## Publications

**On CHADWICK: books**—*Design in Michigan 1967-1977* by Katherine McCoy, Detroit, 1978; *Modern Furniture* by John Pile, New York, 1979; *Innovative Furniture in America* by David Hanks, New York, 1981; *Dictionary of Furniture* by Charles Boyce, New York, 1985; *High Styles: 20th Century American Design,* exhibition catalogue by Lisa Phillips, New York, 1985; *Product Design 2* edited by Sandra Edwards, New York, 1987; *Elegant Solutions* by Owen Edwards, New York, 1989; *Mutant Materials in Contemporary Design,* exhibition catalogue by Paola Antonelli, New York, 1995; *New and Notable Product Design 2* edited by Robert Blaich, New York, 1995; **articles**—*Industrial Design* (New York), vol. 21, no. 10, 1974; "A Serious Chair" by Mildred Friedman in *Design Quarterly* (Cambridge, Massachusetts), no. 126, 1984; *International Design* (New York), vol. 32, no. 4, 1985; "Designs of the Decade" in *Time,* 1 January 1990; "Machine for Sitting" by Chee Pearlman in *I.D.,* vol. 41, no. 5, September/October 1994; *Blueprint,* no. 111, October 1994; *Abitare* (Milan), no. 333, October 1994; "Form+Function" by John Pierson in *Wall Street Journal,* 14 October 1994; *MD* (Uberspannt), February 1995; *I.D.,* July/August 1995; *Graphis* (Zürich), no. 299, September/October 1995; "Best New Products" in *Business Week,* 8 January 1996.

*

Born and raised in Los Angeles, I have been exposed to the likes and dislikes of this city for the past fifty eight years. This ever changing, diverse culture has always had the thirst for experiment—that "anything is possible" attitude. Whether it is developing an industry based on the moving image or creating the next generation of lightweight aerospace materials, this metropolis provides the fertile ground for innovation. In a city that has evolved around the automobile one cannot avoid this dominant form of transport and its pervasive effect on how we carry out our daily lives. The influences on a designer brought up in this diverse community are many and this is a place for the curious.

As a hands-on person, I have always been intrigued with the variety of materials and their respective properties and process capabilities. In my earlier, formative years the work of Michael Thonet, the Bauhaus, Alvar Aalto, and of course the plywood and fiberglass experiments of Charles and Ray Eames have had a profound influence on my approach to materials and their integral part of the process of design.

As a design problem the chair must demonstrate both structural and formal relationships that are in sympathy with the human body and its various postural modes. The chair has become a cultural symbol for how we interpret contemporary society at work and leisure. Right of wrong, the chair often represents society's attitudes to the material world and the built environment. The chair becomes the commemoration of ideas rooted in art and technology and for a designer like myself it represents a summation of thought and values at a particular point in time.

—Don Chadwick

*     *     *

My first contact with Don Chadwick was in the early 1970s when as the vice president of design for Herman Miller Inc. I was seeking new, younger designers to supplements Herman Miller's longtime consultant designs, George Nelson and Charles Eames.

I visited Don in his L.A. studio and was very impressed with both his design skills and his deep interest in new materials and processes. I could sense a match-up between his interests and Herman Miller's needs and capabilities. Shortly thereafter, I invited him to visit the Miller design and development center and factories in Zeeland, Michigan. This provided Don with a "look into the kitchen" to see what we were doing with a new "foam-in-place" technology that had been developed for a new range of Eames upholstered shell seating. We also reviewed the need for a new generation of public seating to complement that of Eames and Nelson.

Thus was born *Chadwick Modular Seating,* a system of square and pie-shaped seating units and tables that could be configured in a wide variety of straight or serpentine shapes. The new foam-in-place technology allowed for a very complex yet comfortable seating configuration that was not previously possible. The product was introduced in 1974 to a very receptive architect-specifier audience and was instantly successful. To his credit, this product has been in use in contract interiors worldwide for over 20 years and is still an important product in Herman Miller's program.

During this period we brought other designers into the Herman Miller team, including Danish designers Verner Panton, Poul Kjaerholm, and Jorgen Rasmussen, Swiss architect Fritz Haller, and Americans Robert Propst, Bruce Burdick, and Bill Stumpf. Herman Miller was going through the transition from the Nelson-Eames era to new and younger designers.

Recognizing that these designer relationships were often very fragile, I organized a series of idea workshops in places such as the Aspen International Design Conference. The consultant designers

**Don Chadwick:** *Aeron Chair*, **(with Bill Stumpf) for Herman Miller, 1995**

Don Chadwick, Bill Stumpf, and Bruce Burdick, along with communications consultants Ralph Caplan, John Massey, and internal design staff met for several days in what Burdick coined "The Fertile Ground" meetings. Indeed it was fertile ground which I believe spawned a long-term collaboration between Don Chadwick and Bill Stumpf and the subsequent design of the *Equa* and *Aeron* chair series. In my opinion Don, with his quiet thoughtfulness, brings an understated elegance to the designs which softens the high-tech approach inherent in these products.

In 1980 I joined Philips Electronics N.V. in the Netherlands as senior director of corporate design and I watched from a distance the results of the collaboration between Chadwick and Stumpf. The *Equa* chairs so impressed me that I refurnished our Design Center with them and was comfortably ensconced on them every day. In 1994, while researching designs for a new book, I was invited to preview the *Aeron* chair and was so impressed that as editor of the book *New and Notable Design 2* I featured it as an outstanding new product. This truly innovative seating solution recalls the chair innovations of Charles Eames, possible exceeding his superb contributions in its use of completely new materials and technologies. This quality of design innovation is something that attracted me and Herman Miller to Don Chadwick.

This then, closes the circle for me and my relationship to Don Chadwick, from finding a new talent in 1974 to celebrating his success in 1995. This is truly a "Fertile Ground" outcome.

—Robert Blaich

# CHAMBERLIN POWELL AND BON
British architectural, interior, and graphic design partnership

Established in London, 1952, by Peter Chamberlin (born 1919; died 1978), Geoffrey Powell (born 1920), and Christoph Bon (born 1921); additional partner, Frank Woods. Associate company: Chamberlin Powell and Bon (Barbican), London, established 1960; additional partner, Charles Greenburg. **Honors:** Bronze Medal, 1956, 1957, and Architecture Award, 1973, 1974, Royal Institute of British Architects; Ministry of Housing and Local Government Medal, 1965; Civic Trust Commendation, 1973; Concrete Society Award, London, 1983. **Address:** 1 Lamont Road Passage, Kings Road, London SW10 0HW, England.

## Works

Bousefield Primary School, South Kensington, London, 1957.
Shipley Salt Grammar School, Yorkshire, 1963.
Buildings and furnishings, for the University of Leeds, Yorkshire, 1963-75.
New Residential College, Cambridge University, 1966-67.
The Barbican Arts Centre and commercial development, London, 1966-82.
J. Sainsbury Shop, Folkestone, Kent, 1970.
General Electric Technical Marketing Centre, Warrington, Lancashire, 1974.
Napp Pharmaceutical Laboratories, Cambridge, 1981.

(for a complete list of Chamberlin Powell and Bon's buildings, see *Contemporary Architects*)

## Publications

**By CHAMBERLIN POWELL AND BON: reports**—*Residential Development within the Barbican Area* by Peter Chamberlin and others, London, 1956; *Barbican Redevelopment 1959* by Peter Chamberlin and others, London, 1959; *University of Leeds Development Plan,* Leeds, 1960; *Proposals for the redevelopment of central Weston-super-Mare* by Peter Chamberlin and others, London, 1961; *University of Leeds Development Plan Review 1963* by Peter Chamberlin and others, Leeds, 1963; *Barbican Arts Centre 1968,* London, 1968.

**On CHAMBERLIN POWELL AND BON: books**—*Public Interiors* by Misha Black, London, 1980; **articles**—in *Bauen und Wohnen* (Zurich), April 1974; *New Civil Engineer* (London), August 1975; *Progressive Architecture* (New York), July 1977; *Building Design* (London), November 1977, June 1981, September 1981; *Building* (London), 16 June 1978, 29 February 1980, 5 March 1982; *Architecture + Urbanism* (Tokyo), September 1979; *Design* (London), September 1981; *London Architect* (London), March 1982.

\* \* \*

Chamberlin Powell and Bon were engaged upon the finishing stages of their work on the Barbican when Chamberlin died. Inevitably, such a vast and complicated but unitary development, first projected in the 1950s, has aroused contradictory reactions. The largest redevelopment undertaken all of a piece in London, the finished complex remained true to the spirit of the original concept, even though it had changed somewhat in detail in response to the client's evolving understanding of their requirements; the finished building, particularly the Arts Centre, in a very few instances needed hurried adaptation at the eleventh hour. Much has been made of this by the scheme's detractors, often unfairly at the expense of the architects.

The scale of Barbican required a certain variety in the treatment of its space and in the relations of those spaces to the different functions they were to serve. This meant that the design activity at the level of detail, fittings, and furniture, in the public areas of the Arts Centre particularly, had to perform in two ways: it had to link architecturally distinct spaces with a visual coherence, and it had to be sufficiently varied to avoid confusion. The relations of the complex to its site and to its neighbours are such that even terms such as "ground floor" would have little meaning, so reference has had to be made to numbered levels. This has led to problems of orientation and direction which have been brilliantly solved at the design level, but there has remained a psychological inhibition among sections of the public; only continued practice in the use of the building may overcome this problem.

The scale, too, has meant that the office could not, on its own, have undertaken all the subsidiary design work, but it has clearly coordinated this work within its own overall vision. Again, this is especially true of the Arts Centre, where the successive stages of the client's maturing specifications of the Centre's roles led to modifications of original solutions. The various spaces are brought into order by a variety of means. Colour is used to define the concert hall conference area, and the theatre, foyers, library, cinema, and exhibition space relate to this and are linked by a spatial core articulated by flying staircases. These have been likened by many, to the Centre's detriment, to Piranesi's *Carceri,* though critics might with more justice and less malice have referred to some of this artist's architectural fantasies. This would have been even a reasonable aim, in view of the undoubted debt the Bank of England owed to Piranesi's architectural theories and suggestions.

—Toni del Renzio

# CHANEL, Gabrielle (Bonheur)

French fashion designer, nicknamed Coco Chanel

**Born:** Saumur, Auvergne, 19 August 1883. **Education:** Convent Orphanage, Aubazine, 1895-1900; Convent School, Moulins, 1900-02. **Career:** Clerk, Au Sans Pareil hosiery shop, Moulins, 1902-04; cafe-concert singer, with nickname "Coco," in Moulins and Vichy, 1905-08; established millinery business and fashion house with sponsorship of Arthur "Boy" Capel in Boulevard Malesherbes, Paris, 1909-10, Avenue Gabriel, then rue Cambon, Paris, 1910-40, 1954-71; established fashion shops in Deauville, 1913-15, and Biarritz, 1915-20; marketed *No. 5* perfume (by chemist Ernest Beaux) from 1920; introduced fragrances *No. 22,* 1922, *Gardénia,* 1925, *Bois des Iles,* 1926, and *Cuir de Russie,* 1927. Also stage costume designer, 1912-37; film costume designer, 1931-62. Lived in exile in Lausanne and Paris, 1945-53. **Exhibitions:** *Les Grands Couturiers Parisiens 1910-1939,* Musée du Costume, Paris, 1965; *Fashion: An Anthology,* Victoria and Albert Museum, London, 1971;

*The Tens, Twenties, Thirties,* Metropolitan Museum of Art, New York, 1977. **Honors:** Neiman-Marcus Award, New York, 1957; *Sunday Times* International Fashion Award, London, 1963. **Died:** Paris, 10 January 1971.

## Works

Stage costume designs include—*Bel Ami* (Nozière), Paris, 1912; *Antigone* (Cocteau), Paris, 1923; *Le Train Bleu* (Diaghilev), Paris, 1924; *Orpheus* (Cocteau), Paris, 1926; *Apollo Musagette* (Stravinsky/Balanchine), New York, 1929; *Oedipus Rex* (Cocteau), Paris, 1937.
Film costume designs include—*Tonight or Never* (Le Roy), 1931; *La Regle du Jeu* (Renoir), 1939; *Last Year at Marienbad* (Resnais), 1962.

## Publications

**On CHANEL: books**—*The Ways of Fashion* by M. D. C. Crawford, New York, 1948; *Dressmakers of France* by Mary Brooks Picken and Dora Loues Miller, New York, 1956; *Grands Couturiers Parisiens 1910-1939,* exhibition catalogue edited by Madeleine Delpierre and Henriette Vanier, Paris, 1965; *The Fashion Makers* by Leonard Halliday, London, 1966; *Coco,* stage musical by Alan Lerner, New York, 1969; *Fashion: An Anthology by Cecil Beaton,* exhibition catalogue compiled by Madeleine Ginsburg, London, 1971; *Chanel Solitaire* by Claude Baillen, Paris, 1971, London, 1973; *Coco Chanel: Her Life, Her Secrets* by Michael Haedrich, Boston and London, 1972; *L'Irreguliere* by Edmond Charles-Roux, Paris, 1974, published as *Chanel: Her Life, Her World,* New York, 1975, London, 1976; *L'Allure de Chanel* by Paul Morand, Paris, 1976; *Inventive Paris Clothes 1909-1939* by Diana Vreeland, with photos by Irving Penn, London and New York, 1977; *Chanel and Her World* by Edmond Charles-Roux, Paris, 1979, London, 1981; *Magic Names of Fashion* by Ernestine Carter, London, 1980; *McDowell's Directory of Twentieth Century Fashion* by Colin McDowell, London, 1984; *The Conran Directory of Design* edited by Stephen Bayley, London, 1985; *The Encyclopaedia of Fashion from 1840 to the 1980s* by Georgina O'Hara, London, 1986; *Mademoiselle Chanel* by François Baudot, published by Chanel, Paris, 1992; *Chanel: The Couturiere at Work* by Amy de la Haye, London, 1994.

\*      \*      \*

Even in her youth, Gabrielle Chanel was an original. She grew up during the ornate Belle Epoque but despised its fussy creations. She was a bit of a tomboy and the mistress of young men in the horsey set, where the way of life necessitated practical clothing. She did not hesitate to adopt masculine garments and, having started as a shop-girl, was not bothered about being a lady. Riding breeches, hacking jackets, men's sweaters, and matelot tunics all gave the freedom of movement that fashionable clothes for women did not. Chanel's great impact came from conveying this masculine freedom into feminine attire. Her fundamental rule was that clothes must be easy to wear, and she made sure they were by starting them on the body, not in an abstract drawings, as did male designers. She was wrong in thinking that no male had ever modelled fabrics on a woman because the founding father of French haute couture, Charles

**Gabrielle Chanel: evening dress, 1930. Photograph in modern setting by Karl Lagerfeld**

Frederick Worth, had done so, but he was long since in his grave. He had created the woman's suit with a mannish shirt back in 1869. In the 1920s Chanel translated this into the cardigan, shirt, and skirt ensemble which has been a classic combination ever since. Subsequently, she made the cardigan of tweed, and the Chanel suit was born; this outfit is probably still the most easily recognized couture creation in the world.

Having discovered these practical combinations, Chanel kept to them, and this consistency became an important feature of her house. She did not change her designs every year, and if one wished today to wear a Chanel jersey suit of 1929, the only alteration one would need to make would be to raise the jumper level from hip to waist. The Chanel suit has been copied by other designers in France and the United States for so long that it has become a standard. Moreover, with such simple clothes, Chanel showed older women how to remain young. The 1920s saw an enormous change from the rule that older women had to wear lace caps and black dresses. When she was in her fifties, dressed like a schoolgirl with a white blouse, navy suit, and a bow in her hair, Chanel rejuvenated a whole generation and pointed the way for its daughters.

—Diana de Marly

# CHARBONNIER, Pierre

French filmmaker, painter, stage and film designer

**Born:** Vienne, Isère, 24 August 1897. **Education:** Studied at the Collège de Vienne; studied painting at the Ecole des Beaux-Arts, Lyons, Ecole des Beaux-Arts, Paris, and Académie Ranson, Paris. **Family:** Married Annette Natanson in 1920 (divorced); children: Jean-Philippe; married Regina Centellas in 1950. **Career:** Independent painter and designer, working with architect Auguste Perret and others, Paris, 1921-28; publicity consultant, Centrales Electriques des Flandres, Ghent, from 1928; stage designer, working with Serge Diaghilev and others, Paris from 1928; filmmaker, collaborating with screenwriter Jean Aurenche, Paris, 1928-55; film designer from 1950. **Exhibitions:** Théâtre de l'Oeuvre, Paris, 1922; Galérie Percier, Paris, 1924; Galérie Zborovsky, Paris, 1926; Cercle Artistique, Ghent, 1928; Palais des Beaux-Arts, Brussels, 1933; Musée de Valence, France, 1939; Galérie Folklore, Lyons, 1939-57; Galérie Katia Granoff, Paris, 1951; Galérie Cahiers d'Art, Paris, 1956; Galérie Benador, Geneva, 1965; Galérie Albert Loeb, Paris, 1975. **Honors:** Chevalier de la Légion d'Honneur, France; Chevalier des Arts et des Lettres, France. **Died:** Paris, 2 July 1978.

## Works

Films—*Ode,* 1928; *Contact,* 1930; *Ce Soir a Huit Heures,* 1931; *Pirates du Rhône,* 1955; *Bracos de Sologne,* 1955; *La Fortune Enchantée* (animated film), 1955.
Film designs include—*Diary of a Country Priest* (Bresson), 1950; *A Condemned Man Escapes* (Bresson), 1956; *Pickpocket* (Bresson), 1959; *Les Mauvais Coups* (Leterrier), 1961; *The Trial of Joan of Arc* (Bresson), 1962; *Balthazar* (Bresson), 1966; *Une Femme Douce* (Bresson), 1969; *Four Nights of a Dreamer* (Bresson), 1971; *Lancelot of the Lake* (Bresson), 1974.

Books illustrated include—*Almanach de Cocagne,* Paris, 1922; *Atala* by Chateaubriand, Paris, 1925; *Les Noces Exemplaires de Mie Saucée* by A. Salmon, Paris, 1926; *Quatre Fascinantes* by Rene Char, Paris, 1951; *Le Fenêtre* by Francis Ponge, Paris, 1955.

## Publications

**On CHARBONNIER: books**—*Filmlexicon degii autore e delle opere* edited by Michel Lacalamita, Fernaldo Giametteo, and others, Rome, 1958; *Pierre Charbonnier; peintures de 1955 á 1965,* exhibition catalogue, with texts by René Char, Francis Ponge, and Jacques Prévert, Geneva, 1965; *Le Décor de Film* by Léon Barsacq, Paris, 1970, published as *Caligari's Cabinet and Other Grand Illusions: A History of Film Design* revised and edited by Elliott Stein, Boston, 1976.

# CHERMAYEFF, Ivan

American illustrator and architectural, graphic, and exhibition designer

**Born:** London, England, 6 June 1932; emigrated to the United States, 1939, naturalized, 1947. **Education:** Studied at Harvard University, Cambridge, Massachusetts, 1950-52; Institute of Design, Illinois Institute of Technology, Chicago, 1952-54 (Moholy-Nagy Scholarship); Yale University, New Haven, Connecticut, BFA, 1955 (Mohawk Paper Company Fellowship). **Family:** Married Sara Ann Duffy in 1956; children: Catherine, Alexandra, and Maro; married Jane Clark in 1978; children: Sam. **Career:** Assistant to designer Alvin Lustig, New York, 1955; assistant art director, Columbia Records, New York, 1956; founder and partner, Brownjohn, Chermayeff & Geismar Associates, New York, from 1960, and Cambridge Seven Associates, Cambridge, Massachusetts, from 1962. Design instructor, Brooklyn College, New York, 1956-57, and School of Visual Arts, New York, 1959-65. Board member, 1960-63, and president, 1963-64, American Institute of Graphic Arts; trustee, Museum of Modern Art, New York, from 1965; board member, 1967-78, and co-chairman, 1968, Aspen Design Conference, Colorado; vice-president, Yale Arts Association, 1970-74; committee member, Yale University Council on Art and Architecture, 1971; member, Board of Overseers, Harvard University Committee for Visual and Environmental Studies, 1972. Director, American Republic Insurance Company, New York, 1971-80. **Exhibitions:** *107 Grafici dell' AGI,* Casteloo Sforzesco, Milan, 1974; Addison Gallery of American Art, Andover, Massachusetts, 1984; Ingber Gallery, New York, 1987; Jamileh Weber Gallery, Zurich, 1988; Cooper Union, New York, 1989. **Honors:** Industrial Arts Medal, American Institute of Architects, 1967; Gold Medal, Philadelphia College of Art, 1971; Visual Environment Award, Fifth Avenue Association, New York, 1974; Fuess Award, Phillips Academy, Andover, Massachusetts, 1979; Gold Medal, American Institute of Graphic Arts, 1979; President's Fellowship, Rhode Island School of Design, Providence, 1981; Benjamin Franklin Fellowship, Royal Society of Arts, London. **Address:** Chermayeff & Geismar Associates, 15 East 26th Street, New York, NY 10010, U.S.A.

**Ivan Chermayeff:** *Jacob's Pillow* dance festival poster, 1993

## Works

Children's book illustrations include—*The Thinking Book* by Sandol Stoddard Warburg, New York, 1960; *Keep It Like A Secret* by Warburg, New York, 1961; *Blind Mice and Other Numbers,* New York, 1961; *The New Nutcracker Suite and Other Innocent Verses* by Ogden Nash, Boston, 1962; *Peter Pumpkin* by John Ott and Peter Coley, New York, 1963; *Ho for a Hat!* by William J. Smith, New York, 1964; (with Jane Clark Chermayeff) *First Words,* New York, 1989; (with Jane Clark Chermayeff) *First Shapes,* New York, 1991; *Furry Facts,* New York, 1994; *Fishy Facts,* New York, 1994; *Feathery Facts,* New York, 1995; *Scaly Facts,* New York, 1995; *The Hole Story,* New York, 1995.

## Publications

**By CHERMAYEFF: books**—*Observations on American Architecture,* with photographs by Elliott Erwitt, New York, 1972; (with Richard Wurman, Ralph Caplan, Peter Bradford, and Jane Clark) *The Design Necessity,* London and Cambridge, Massachusetts, 1973; *Chermayeff and Geismar Associates: Trademarks* New York, 1979; **articles**—*"How Designers See Themselves"* in *Print* (New York), January 1967.

*See* CHERMAYEFF & GEISMAR ASSOCIATES

# CHERMAYEFF, Serge

American architect, interior, exhibition, and furniture designer

**Born:** Grosby Dagestan Caucasus, Russia, 8 October 1900; sent to school in Britain in 1910, naturalized, 1928; emigrated to the United States in 1939, naturalized, 1946. **Education:** Studied privately in Moscow, until 1910; studied at Peterborough Lodge preparatory school, Hampstead, London, 1910-13, and Harrow School, Middlesex, 1914-17; studied art and architecture in Europe, 1922-25. **Family:** Married Barbara May in 1928; children: the graphic designer Ivan Chermayeff and the architect Peter Chermayeff. **Career:** Worked as a journalist for the Amalgamated Press, London, 1918-23; chief designer, for decorators E. Williams Ltd., London, 1924-27; director of the Modern Art Department, Waring and Gillow furnishers, London, 1928-29; in private architectural and design practice, London, 1930-39 (in partnership with Eric Mendelsohn, 1933-36), in San Francisco, 1940-41, and in New York, 1942-46. Professor of design, Brooklyn College, New York, 1942-46; president and director of the Institute of Design, Chicago, 1946-51; lecturer, Massachusetts Institute of Technology, Cambridge, 1952-62; professor of architecture, 1962-71, and professor emeritus, from 1971, Yale University, New Haven, Connecticut; Gropius Lecturer, Harvard University, Cambridge, Massachusetts, 1974; distinguished visiting professor, Ohio State University, Columbus, 1979. Consultant on planning, architecture, and industrial design, Museum of Modern Art, New York, 1942-47; consultant, Chicago Plan Commission, 1946-48. **Member:** Editorial board member, American Federation of Art, New York, 1942-47; founder, 1942, and executive council member, 1942-47, American Society of Planners and Architects. **Exhibitions:** First London Exhibition of Art, 1929; White City Exhibition, London, 1936; *Tomorrow's Small House,* Museum of Modern Art, New York, 1945; *The Chicago Plan,* City Hall, Chicago, 1949; *Thirties,* Hayward Gallery, London, 1979; *British Art and Design 1900-1960,* Victoria and Albert Museum, London, 1983. **Honors:** Gold Medal, Royal Canadian Institute of Architects, 1974; Architectural Education Award, Association of Schools of Architecture and American Institute of Architects, 1980; Misha Black Award, Society of Industrial Artists and Designers, London, 1980. Honorary Doctorates: Washington University, St. Louis, 1974; Ohio State University, Columbus, 1980. **Address:** Box 1472, Wellfleet, Massachusetts 02667, U.S.A.

## Works

*Modern Furnishings* exhibition layouts, Waring and Gillow, London, 1928.

Cambridge Theatre interiors, Seven Dials, London, 1930.

*S.S. Atlantique* ship interiors, 1931.

*R.P.7.* steel frame armchair, for PEL Limited, 1932.

*Bestlite* lamps, for Best and Lloyd, 1933.

*Ekco* bakelite radio cabinets, for E.K. Cole Limited, 1933-35.

*M-7* and *M-11* tubular steel frame armchairs, for Plan Limited, 1934.

De La Warr Pavilion, Bexhill-on-Sea, Sussex, 1935 (with Eric Mendelsohn).

W. and A. Gilbey office building, Camden Town, London, 1937.

Imperial Chemical Industries research laboratories, Blakely, Manchester, 1938.

*Design for Use* exhibition layouts, Museum of Modern Art, New York, 1944.

*The Chicago Plan* exhibition layouts, City Hall, Chicago, 1949.

British Railways office interiors, Rockefeller Center, New York, 1950.

Chermayeff House, New Haven, Connecticut, 1962.

(for a complete list of buildings and architectural projects, see *Contemporary Architects*)

## Publications

**By CHERMAYEFF: books and pamphlets**—*Color and its Application to Modern Building,* London, 1936; *Plan for A.R.P.—A Practical Policy,* London, 1939; *Report on the Future Development of Diamond K Ranch,* Cambridge, Massachusetts, 1955; *The Shape of Privacy,* Cambridge, Massachusetts, 1961; (with Christopher Alexander) *Community and Privacy,* New York, 1963; (with Alexander Tzonis) *Advanced Studies in Urban Environments,* New Haven, Connecticut, 1967; *Synopsis of Conclusions and Record of Progress: The Chermayeff Studio* edited by W. Mitchell, New Haven, Connecticut, 1969; (with Alexander Tzonis) *The Shape of Community,* New York, 1970; *Verse of Anger and Affection 1957-73,* Orleans, Massachusetts, 1973; *Design and the Public Good: Selected Writings 1930-1970,* Cambridge, Massachusetts, 1982.

**On CHERMAYEFF: books**—*Design in the Home* edited by Noel Carrington, London, 1933; *20th Century Houses* by Raymond McGrath, London, 1934; *The House: A Machine for Living In* by Anthony Bertram, London, 1935; *The Practical Idealists: 25 Years of Designing for Industry* by John and Avril Blake, London, 1969; *Projects and Theories of Serge Chermayeff* by Richard Plunz, Cambridge, Massachusetts, 1972; *PEL and Tubular Steel Furniture of* *the Thirties* by Tim Benton and others, London, 1977; *British Design Since 1880: A Visual History by Fiona MacCarthy,* London, 1982; *The American Design Adventure 1940-1975* by Arthur J. Pulos, Cambridge, Massachusetts, 1988.

* * *

In addition to his work as a designer, Serge Chermayeff was active as a fine artist, architect, planner, educator, and writer of prose and poetry. His design work includes interiors, theatre settings, displays and exhibitions, as well as designs for mass production of textiles, furniture, lighting fixtures, and radio cabinets.

It is in the breadth of his interests, and in his deep involvement with the human concerns underlying design, as well as in his innovative open-ended approach to the creative process, that Serge Chermayeff best displays the strong influence on him of leading figures from the first generation of European modernists. Born in 1900, and therefore a bit younger than the pioneers, Chermayeff extended their vision, through his own career, well into the latter part of the twentieth century. He was strongly influenced by such leading pioneer modernists as Eric Gill (during the early years of his work in England), Eric Mendelsohn (with whom Chermayeff practiced in England from 1933 to 1936), and Walter Gropius (founder of the German Bauhaus and a close friend during the years both lived in the United States).

A native of Grozny in the Caucasus, Chermayeff had little formal education in art and none in design or architecture. After private studies in Moscow, he was sent to England at age ten and enrolled at the Peterborough Lodge Preparatory School and the Royal Drawing Society. He completed his formal studies at the Harrow School. As a young man, much of his attention was devoted to painting and to ballroom dancing. The latter interest brought him to Buenos Aires in 1922, where he was a partner in a dance hall. In 1924 Chermayeff was hired by Ernest Williams Ltd., an interior decorating firm. In 1926 he designed stage sets for actor-director Gerald du Murier.

The London furnishing studio of Waring & Gillow hired Chermayeff to direct a Modern Art Studio and to create a suite of ten rooms for the 1928 Exhibition of Modern Art in Decorating and Furnishing. Chermayeff moved the firm away from its reliance on an eclectic historicism, working closely, he later recalled, with the firm's "group of elderly cabinet makers of great knowledge and skill" who, "to my surprise, welcomed the change from a tradition reaching back to the eighteenth century." He added, "they became enthusiastic collaborators. I never learned so much so fast ...." Other work for Waring & Gillow included a number of commercial and domestic interiors, as well as carpet designs manufactured by Wilton, and interiors on the French liner *l'Atlantique* designed in collaboration with Paul Follot in 1931.

Much of Chermayeff's early work could be described as "deco moderne," derived from the famed decorative arts exhibition held in Paris in 1925. In 1929 he came under the influence of Gill, who was his mentor for several years, and Chermayeff also developed close ties with a number of English artists, including Henry Moore, Ben Nicholson, and Barbara Hepworth. During his travels on the European continent for Waring & Gillow, he met leading figures of the Modern movement, including Eric Mendelsohn, then still living in Berlin. The result was an informal education in the creative process and in the social basis of art and design through which Chermayeff matured as a designer.

In 1930 Chermayeff renovated a house for himself and his wife, Barbara, as a study of what could be accomplished in new materials and furnishings. During the same year, he designed the interior, the lighting,

some of the sets, and the opening night program for the Cambridge Theatre in London. In 1931 he began collaboration on designs for a number of prototypes for mass-produced furniture for the London firms of Plan, Ltd., and PEL, Ltd., and the following year began designs for a number of studio interiors for the BBC, utilizing some of the PEL furniture. In 1933 he began designing molded thermoplastic, metal-trimmed *Ecko* radio cabinets for E. K. Cole; more than 140,000 of the most successful of these, "Model 74," were sold.

From 1933 to 1936 Chermayeff was in partnership with Mendelsohn. This was Chermayeff's real initiation into the practice of architecture. The most significant contribution of Chermayeff to the work of the partnership was the interior of the Entertainment Hall at Bexhill in 1935. Chermayeff's design origins were evident here; well-planned interior space proved to be a hallmark of his architectural work throughout his career.

Chermayeff emigrated with his family to the United States in 1940 and was appointed to Brooklyn College in 1942 as chair of the Art Department, which he soon renamed the Department of Design. His innovations at Brooklyn College included the first comprehensive attempt to implement a liberal arts design curriculum. He designed two exhibitions for the Museum of Modern Art in New York: *Design for Use* in 1944 and *Tomorrow's Small House* in 1945.

In 1947 Chermayeff left Brooklyn College and moved to Chicago as successor to Laszlo Moholy-Nagy as head of the Institute of Design, which had recently expanded in size due to the influx of returning war veterans. He retained many of Moholy's innovations, including a stress on the foundation course and on photography, but placed greater emphasis on architecture and environmental design, and he developed a successful graduate program. In 1949 he helped to bring the I.D. into the Illinois Institute of Technology, where it still operates. Most importantly, he managed to sustain the creative ferment which characterized the I.D. under Moholy. Gropius credited Chermayeff with achieving in Chicago, to a greater extent than elsewhere, the kind of education offered by the German Bauhaus.

In Chicago, Chermayeff began an intense period of activity as a painter, exhibiting widely in Chicago and elsewhere. From 1948 to 1955 he designed fabric patterns for L. Anton Maix of New York. In 1949 Robert Brownjohn of the I.D. faculty assisted Chermayeff in organizing an exhibition on planning in Chicago for the Chicago Planning Commission.

After leaving the Institute of Design in 1951, Chermayeff concentrated on his architectural practice and his writing, and he taught architecture at the Massachusetts Institute of Technology and Harvard and Yale universities. His architectural work continued to be inseparable from his concern with interiors, as is evident in his innovative schemes for alternatives to the detached suburban house and the urban highrise apartment.

—Lloyd C. Engelbrecht

# CHERMAYEFF & GEISMAR ASSOCIATES

American architectural, exhibition, graphic, and corporate design firm

Founded in New York, as Brownjohn, Chermayeff & Geismar Associates, 1956-59, and Chermayeff & Geismar Associates, from

1962. Current partners: Ivan Chermayeff, Thomas H. Geismar, John Grady, and Steff Geissbuhler, from 1962. Clients include Burlington Industries, Pan American World Airways, Best Products, Perkins-Elmer, New York University, Museum of Modern Art, United States Environmental Protection Agency, Smithsonian Institution, Mobil, Philip Morris, IBM, and others. **Honors:** First International Design Award, Japan Design Foundation, 1983. **Address:** 15 East 26th Street, New York, New York 10010, U.S.A.

## Works

Corporate identity program, for the Chase Manhattan Bank, 1959.
Corporate identity program, for the Mobil Corporation, 1962.
Corporate identity program, for the Xerox Corporation, 1965.
United States pavilion displays at *Expo 70,* Osaka, 1970.
Corporate identity program, for the Museum of Modern Art, New York, 1970.
Sculpture, for the Philip Morris Tower, 1972.
Mobil Masterpiece Theatre poster, for the Mobil Oil Corporation, from 1972.
*Red 9* sculpture at 9 West 57th Street, New York, for the Solow Building Corporation, 1974.
Exhibition displays at the JFK Library in Boston, for the Kennedy Family, 1980.
Corporate identity program, for Morgan Stanley and Company, 1982.
Corporate identity program, for Paine Weber, 1985.
PBS corporate identity program, for Public Broadcasting Systems, 1985.
Exhibition displays, for the Statue of Liberty Museum, 1985.
NBC symbol, for National Broadcasting Corporation, 1987.
Corporate identity program, for the Lincoln Center, New York, 1988.

## Publications

**On CHERMAYEFF & GEISMAR: books**—*Packaging: An International Survey of Package Design* edited by Walter Herdge, Zurich, 1959; *Typography* by Aaron Burns, New York, 1961; *Design Through Discovery* by Marjorie Elliott Bevlin, New York, 1963, 1977; *Design in America* edited by Ralph Caplan, New York, 1969; *Graphic Designers in the USA: 2* edited by Henri Hillebrand, London, 1971: *Packaging and Corporate Identity* edited by Idea Publishers, Tokyo, 1971; *107 Grafici dell' AGI,* exhibition catalogue with texts by Renzo Zorzi and Franco Grignani, Venice, 1974; *Chermayeff & Geismar Associates: Trademarks* by Ivan Chermayeff, New York, 1979; *Who's Who in Graphic Art* edited by Walter Amstutz, Dubendorf, 1982; *The Conran Directory of Design* edited by Stephen Bayley, London, 1985; *The American Design Adventure 1940-1975* by Arthur J. Pulos, Cambridge, Massachusetts, 1988.

*

The trademarks presented in this monograph have been developed by Chermayeff & Geismar Associates over a period of many years for a diverse range of clients. Large and small corporations, cultural institutions, government agencies, banks, stores, hotels, real estate developments, and even national celebrations are in-

cluded. Each has presented a special identification problem to be solved. Thus the designs take many forms—symbols, logotypes, acronyms, monograms—and encompass a variety of styles.

Many of the marks are part of large identification programs. This is only hinted at with the occasional illustration. But common to all is the underlying philosophy that design is partly a problem-solving procedure, and that appropriate trademarks cannot be developed until the client's identification problem has been clearly defined.

Therefore each design, while simple in form, is the culmination of a complex process we believe in. That process can be outlined as:
—listening objectively to the problem as described by the client;
—reviewing and evaluating that description against past performances and future intentions;
—defining an attitude or direction from which design development can begin;
—creating a series of design possibilities, continually sifting out the merely fashionable;
—presenting a proposed design by demonstrating its effectiveness within the context in which it will eventually appear;
—developing guidelines and specifications for implementation;
—helping to establish police protection against pressures, both external and internal, that tend to diminish effectiveness.

It should go without saying that the greatest effort is made to assure that each trademark design will be appropriate to the purpose of the business or institution it represents, and meaningful to the audiences it will be seen by.

Within these constraints, the final image should be succinct, memorable, and elegant in either conception or visualization, or if feasible, both. (*Excerpted from* Chermayeff & Geismar Associates: Trademarks.)

—Ivan Chermayeff and Tom Geismar

\*     \*     \*

Probably the most influential graphic designers in the United States, if not the world, the legendary principals Ivan Chermayeff and Thomas H. Geismar prefer to call their firm a "design office," since their work is so varied. Chermayeff and Geismar, both born in 1932 and graduates of Yale, where they met, brought with them broad aesthetic backgrounds and a vitality of interests, which supply a reservoir of new and old approaches to their commissions. Intellectual and aesthetic influences came not only from formal training, but also through personal connections as Chermayeff's father, noted architect Serge Chermayeff, and his friends, Marcel Breuer and Eliot Noyes, among others, were able to introduce an ever-widening circle of influence to the younger designers.

The basic philosophy upon which the firm operates is one which they have inherited from Bauhaus tradition: problem solving. Therefore, designs differ to suit different clients. Although they declare that they have no office style, their work has set standards for the period. Moreover, it evinces strong kinships with the visual arts, as is evident, for example, in some designs related to the architecture of Mies van der Rohe, the geometric abstractionist, and to minimal art, dada, and Pop art.

The Chermayeff and Geismar messages are not only clear but often multilayered, surprising, and evocative. Abstract logos by the firm are a case in point. A difficult problem was the Chase Manhattan Bank logo, which had to act as signature, convey a sense of reliability and security, express the essence of a bank, and suit all sorts of presentations from stationery to displays, matchbooks, and so forth. Their solution to the problem was a symbol that is made up of four wedges which enclose a square like guardian walls and that make reference to an ancient coin in the octagonal shape they form, thereby suggesting money, the real business of the bank. The abstract American Bicentennial logo used elements of the flag, with a central star surrounded by entwined stripes in red and white. It is clear to any American that the logo connotes patriotism, yet it is also pictorially akin to Jasper John's celebrated flag paintings and to the stripe paintings of other American artists.

The "supermarket principle" of collections of objects is used with a nod to Warhol and Johns, as well as other artists. The 1979 International Design Conference poster displaying a collection of baggage tags is one well-known example, but others vary greatly. For example, the 1974 poster for the National Park Service Museum of Immigration utilizes souvenir Statues of Liberty printed in many colors to suggest the diverse groups of immigrants the venerable Miss Liberty has greeted.

Recent designs from Chermayeff and Geismar show their continuing sensitivity to cultural changes. More loosely constructed, these tend to reveal the designer's process informally. A 1979 poster for the New York Art Expo purports to be the designer's working surface, yet conveys all sorts of information. As if mounted on a yellow background, the message appears to be on drawing paper attached by bits of tape. A felt-tipped pen forms the words "Art Expo, New York, 1979." Interspersed are notes in Chermayeff's handwriting, giving not only instructions but also references to various art styles, thus implying both associations of typeface in the finished product and the art styles which may be seen at the Expo. And to emphasize the message, place and dates of the event are printed in bold type on the "background" below.

Chermayeff and Geismar show no signs of falling out of tune with changing times. Since their philosophy is to accept the challenge of each new problem, rather than to be trendy or stylish, they remain among the leaders in design

—Nina Bremer

# CHESSA, Paolo (Antonio)

Italian architect, interior, and exhibition designer

**Born:** Milan, 24 February 1922. **Education:** Studied architecture in Milan, Dip. Arch., 1945. **Career:** Freelance architect and designer, Milan, from 1945; adviser on architecture to the Royal Afghan Government, Kabul, 1957-59. Editor, *Domus* magazine, Milan, 1945-47; also contributor to *Architectural Design, Bauen und Wohnen, Comunita, Interiors, Architecture d 'Aujourd'hui, The Architect, Architettura,* and *Nuestra Arquitectura,* from 1945. Instructor, architectural, interior, and furniture design, at the Politecnico of Milan. **Exhibitions:** *28/78 Architettura,* Palazzo delle Stelline, Milan, 1979. **Honors:** Grand Prize, Milan Triennale, 1947; First Prize, Teatro Carlo Felice competition, Genoa, 1949; First Prize, University of Bologna competition, 1950. **Address:** Via di Villa Basile 2/D, 65100 Pescara, Italy.

## Works

Armchair with metal frame and slung canvas seat, for J. G. Furniture, 1950.

Teatro Carlo Felice, Genoa, 1950-53.
Youth Hostel in the Park, Milan.
General Roca Hydro-Electric Centre, Rio Negro, Argentina.
Chiavari Housing Block, Genoa.
Carimate Residential Centre, Como.
Ethioplast Building, Addis Abbaba.
Westfalia Separator Company Headquarters, Milan.
Hitman Factory, Milan-Corsico.

## Publications

**On CHESSA: books**—*Stahlmöbel* by Gustav Hassenpflug, Düsseldorf, 1960; *Architettura moderna in Milano* by Agnoldomenico Pica, Milan, 1964; *Catalogo Bolaffi dell'architettura italiana 1963-1966* edited by Pier Carlo Santini and Guiseppe Luigi Marini, Turin, 1966; *Design e forme nuove nell'arredamento italiano* edited by Paolo Portoghesi and Marino Marini, Rome, 1978; *Storia e cronaca della Triennale by Anty Pansera,* Milan, 1978; *Modern Furniture* by John F. Pile, New York and Toronto, 1979; *28/78 Architettura,* exhibition catalogue, edited by Maria Grazia Mazzocchi Bonadonna, Milan, 1979; *Neue Mobel 1950-1982* edited by Klaus-Jurgen Sembach, Stuttgart, 1982, as *Contemporary Furniture: An International Review of Modern Furniture, 1950 to the Present,* New York and London, 1982; **articles**—"Il Carlo Felice de Genova" in *Domus* (Milan), no. 252, 1950; "Centro Idroelettrica in Patagonia" in *Domus* (Milan), no. 256, 1951.

\*       \*       \*

Paolo Chessa brought intelligence, sensitivity, and literacy to everything he tackled, and though he spent only two years as an editor at *Domus,* he carried on writing for architectural publications. In that magazine in 1956, he was able to present some of his observations on and experiences in the Sila, in southern Italy; this combined a critical account with acute perception of the historical, cultural, and practical dimensions of "the problem of the mezzogiorno." In 1961, in another magazine, he posed a social problem that an architect ought to be able to ameliorate in terms of its relation to the lifestyle of most Italians. At that time, thirty-five percent of dwellings in Milan were without individual sanitation, yet the average Italian, he argued, would rather have a Fiat to park under the noses of his neighbours, go to the tailor for a made-to-measure, hand-sewn suit, have a television set with umpteen controls, and so on. Though most of his work was tempered by such humane considerations, they were not allowed to have detrimental effect upon his design, which concentrated upon the best possible results from the most readily available materials. This was to be achieved by a system of planned interrelating units with exchangeable elements. The designs of the early 1950s were a step on the way to the high point of his 1955 kitchen furniture, which anticipated many ideas later taken up elsewhere.

His furniture designs, however, must be seen as only part of his activity, which remained very much concerned with architecture as far as it was possible to practise. He was in no sense utopian. He played a vital part in the development of Ligano, at the head of the Gulf of Venice and almost opposite Trieste. With the architect d'Olivo he produced the overall control plan, carefully siting the zones for development into the amenities for a resort and aiming to avoid haphazard building and other development damaging to the environment and the interests of the local population, who, on the contrary, were to benefit from the transformation. Chessa himself designed two interesting groups of holiday homes, both of which demonstrated the fine qualities of his architectural imagination and his concern for the quality of life. Planned as small communities, this fact was expressed in the aesthetic as well as social considerations of the schemes. An interesting interplay of curved brick walls, for instance, ensured privacy as well as collective services. The other group achieved similar ends by a circular arrangement of six rectangular dwellings somehow staggered and athwart the circle.

—Toni del Renzio

## CHWAST, Seymour

American illustrator and book and graphic designer

**Born:** New York, 18 August 1931. **Education:** Abraham Lincoln High School, Brooklyn, New York, graduated 1948; studied illustration and design, under Will Barnet and Antonio Frascosi, at Cooper Union, New York, Dip., 1951. **Family:** Married Jacqueline Weiner in 1953; children: Eve and Pamela. **Career:** Founder-partner, with Milton Glaser and Edward Sorel, 1954-82, and President, 1974-82, Push Pin Studios, New York; founder, with Milton Glaser and Reynold Rufhns, 1954, art director, 1955-81, and publisher-editor, 1974-81, *Push Pin Graphics* magazine, New York; founder and publisher, Push Pin Press, New York, 1976-81; director and president, The Pushpin Group Inc., New York, from 1982. Visiting lecturer, School of the Visual Arts, New York, 1972-74; visiting professor, Cooper Union, New York, from 1975. Vice-president, American Institute of Graphic Arts, New York, 1974-78. **Exhibitions:** *The Push Pin Style,* Musée des Arts Décoratifs, Paris, 1970; *A Century of American Illustration,* Brooklyn Museum, New York, 1973; *107 Grafici dell'AGI,* Castello Sforzesco, Milan, 1974; Galerie Delpire, Paris, 1975, 1981; Kunstgewerbemuseum, Zurich, 1981; Royal Palm Gallery, Palm Beach, Florida, 1983; Gutenberg Museum, Mainz, 1983; Jack Gallery, New York, 1987; Lustrare Gallery, New York, 1991; GGG Gallery, Tokyo, 1992; Recruit Gallery, Osaka, Japan, 1992; Giraffics Gallery, East Hampton, New York, 1992, 1993; Bradley Galleries, Milwaukee, Wisconsin, 1992; Hugh Hill Gallery, Kent, Connecticut, 1994; Pentagram Gallery, London, 1994; Green-On-Red Gallery, Dublin, 1994; Michael Kislinger Gallery, New York, 1994. **Collections:** Museum of Modern Art, New York; CooperHewitt Museum, New York; Library of Congress, Washington, D.C.; Gutenberg Museum, Mainz; Israel Museum, Jerusalem; Stadtmuseum, Munich; Suntory Art Museum, Osaka, Japan. **Honors:** Saint-Gaudens Medal, Cooper Union, New York, 1971; Hall of Fame Award, Art Directors Club of New York, 1983; Gold Medal, American Institute of Graphic Arts, 1986; honorary D.F.A., Parsons School of Design, 1992. **Address:** The Pushpin Group Inc., 215 Park Avenue South, New York, New York 10003, U.S.A.

## Works

*Nicholas Nickelby* poster, for Mobil Oil Corporation, 1983.
*I, Claudius* poster, for Mobil Oil Corporation, 1984.
*Rumpole of the Bailey* posters, for Mobil Oil Corporation, 1984-89.

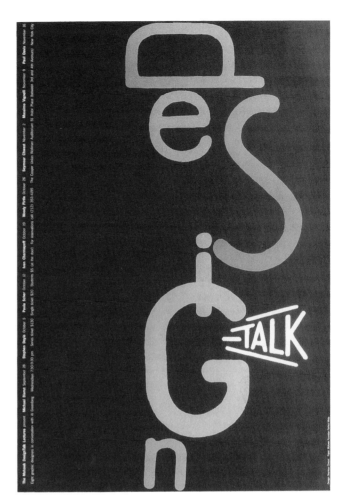

Seymour Chwast: design created to promote a design talk series at the Cooper Union School of Art, New York, 1994. Photo courtesy of S. Chwast, The Pushpin Group

*Forbes Fuels Your Drive* poster, for *Forbes* magazine, New York, 1986.
*War Is Madness* poster, New York, 1986.
*Design and Style* mixed media brochures, issues 1-5, for Mohawk Paper Mills Inc., 1986-89.
*Sam's Bar* woodcut book illustrations, for Doubleday Inc., 1987.
*Star Quality—Noel Coward* poster, for Mobil Oil Corporation, 1987.
*The Baseball Poster* poster, for Museum of the Borough of Brooklyn, 1987.
*The Charmer* poster, for Mobil Oil Corporation, 1989.
Books designed or illustrated include—*Sara's Granny and the Groodle,* New York, 1967; *Pancake King,* New York, 1970; *Still Another Alphabet Book,* New York, 1970; *Still Another Number Book,* New York, 1971, *Mother Goooose,* Boston 1971; *Still Another Children's Book,* New York, 1972, *Limerickricks* New York, 1973; *The House That Jack Built* New York, 1974; *Which One Is Different?,* New York, 1975, *Sweetheart Book and Others,* New York, 1975; *The Illustrated Cat,* New York, 1976; *Sleepy Ida,* New York, 1977; (co-editor) *The Literary Dog New York,* New York, 1983; *Happy Birthday Bach,* New York, 1985; *Just Enough Is Plenty,* New York, 1988; *Trylon and Perisphere,* New

York, 1989; *Harry's Bath,* New York, 1990; *The Alphabet Parade,* New York, 1992; *The Twelve Circus Rings,* New York, 1992; *Mathew Michael's Beastly Day* by D. Johnston, New York, 1992; *Paper Pets,* New York, 1993; *Bra Fashions by Stephanie,* New York, 1994.

## Publications

**By CHWAST: books**—*Graphic Style,* New York, 1988.

**On CHWAST: books**—*Packaging: An International Survey of Package Design* edited by Walter Herdeg, Zurich, 1959; *The Push Pin Style* by *Communication Arts* editors, with introduction by Jerome Snyder, Palo Alto, 1970; *Seymour Chwast* by T. Nishio, Tokyo, 1974; *107 Grafici dell'AGI,* exhibition catalogue with texts by Renzo Zorzi and Franco Grignani, Venice, 1974; *Seymour Chwast: The Left-Handed Designer* edited by Steven Heller, New York, 1985; *New American Design* by Hugh Aldersley-Williams, New York, 1988.

*

What motivates me is the challenge of converting information that has to be conveyed from one form to creative visual form. It is very important that my own graphic personality be imparted in whatever I do. While I am not particularly disposed to any style or type of image, I still follow the basic elements of design in my work. Good drawing is essential. Stylistic direction is dependent upon the concept. The concept is the content, while the style is the packaging. They are inseparable.

—Seymour Chwast

*     *     *

In a 1970 exhibition of the work of Push Pin Studios at the Musée des Arts Décoratifs in Paris, it was at once obvious that the group as a whole consisted of creative artists—painters and sculptors—working in the field of design. Notable among the group was the work of cofounder Seymour Chwast, whose own contribution consisted in the particular humor with which he made skillful use of the techniques of both painter and sculptor. The aim of Push Pin was to find an alternative to the established canon of design forms derived from Bauhaus and Swiss sources. By substituting for this freeranging license to choose any imagery from any period and to mix sophisticated designs and bad taste with quotations from the imagery of the great painters of the past, Push Pin provided a thoroughly eclectic program. It is to Chwast's credit that this magpie behavior with the acquisition of raw material was constructive and not merely tiresome. Basing their methods on the example of Picasso, who had established the worth of finding a solution from whatever comes to hand, instead of continuously searching for the absolute, Chwast and his associates brought this innovative technique into publicity. They also never forgot the debt which all public advertising owes to its popular origins, the broadsheet and the circus poster.

In the work of Chwast, humor plays a more significant part than in the sometimes whimsical or purely poetic notions of others in his group. Even his political posters carry a satirical message, as in the case of "End Bad Breath" or "War Is Good Business—Invest Your Son." Chwast's great contribution has been to bring back into publicity the vitality of the popular voice without degrading the sophisticated high

standards of professional design. In the brief history of the poster, there have been those masters, such as Cheret, Toulouse Lautrec, or Cassandre, who have set standards and lifted the role of the publicist to that of artist; but there have also always been those anonymous but spirited minor artists who have given the street its perennial vitality in the local commercial advertisement, as well as those amateurs who have energized public surfaces with graffiti. To bridge the gap between these extremes of high design and the vernacular requires the unusual technical skill and talent that Chwast has demonstrated. His great natural ability as an artist precedes his comments on and parodies of the language of publicity.

—John Barnicoat

# CIESLEWICZ, Roman

French cartoonist, illustrator, packaging, and graphic designer

**Born:** Lvov, Poland, 13 January 1930; emigrated to France in 1963, naturalized, 1971. **Career:** Worked at the Groszowice Cement Works, Opole, 1946-47; freelance graphic designer, working for WAG, WAF, RSW, Czytelnik and Iskry publishers, CWF Central Film Distributors, the Chamber of Foreign Commerce, and other government institutions, in Warsaw, 1955-63; designer of *Ty i Ja* magazine, Warsaw, 1959-63; freelance graphic designer in Paris, since 1963; chief layout artist, 1964-66, and art director, 1967-69, *Elle* magazine; graphic designer, *Vogue* magazine, 1966-67; art director, MAFIA (Maime, Arnodin, Fayolle, International Associes) publicity agency, 1969-72; designer of the magazines *Opus International,* 1967-69, *Kitsch,* 1970-71, *Musique en Jeu,* 1970-73, *CNAC-Archives,* 1971-74, *Kamikaze,* 1976, and *XX Siecle,* 1976; has also designed for the Centre National d'Art Contemporain, Féstival d'Automne, Centre Georges Pompidou, and the publishers Christian Bourgeois, G. Tschou, Julliard, J. J. Pauvert, Adam, Plon, Tolmer, and others. Professor, Ecole Nationale Supérieure des Arts Décoratifs, Paris, 1973-75, and Ecole Supérieure des Arts Graphiques, Paris, from 1975. **Exhibitions:** Goethe-Institut, Frankfurt, 1963; Club Synergie, Paris, 1964; Theâtre de la Cité, Villeurbanne, 1965; Muzeum Sztuki, Lodz, 1971; Musée des Arts Décoratifs, Paris, 1972; Stedelijk Museum, Amsterdam, 1973, 1978; Musée de l'Affiche, Vilanov, 1974; Centre Jean Prevost, Saint-Etienne-du-Rouvray, 1976; French Institute, Stockholm, 1977; Konsthall, Lund, 1978; Maison de la Culture, Grenoble, 1979, 1980; Teatr Narodowy, Legnica, 1980; Chelsea School of Art, London, 1981. **Collections:** Stedelijk Museum, Amsterdam; Moderna Museet, Stockholm; Musée des Arts Décoratifs, Paris; Museum Narodowe, Warsaw; Muzeum Sztuki, Lodz; Museum of Modern Art, New York. **Honors:** Trepkowski Prize, Poland, 1955; Grand Prix, Czech Cinema Posters Award, 1964; Grand Prize, Warsaw Poster Biennale, 1972: Special Cinema Poster Prize, Cannes, 1973; Grand Prix, Photomontage Biennale, Poland, 1979; Grand Prix, French Poster Awards, 1980. **Address:** c/o *Elle,* 100 rue Reaumur, 75002 Paris, France.

## Works

*Don Juan* (Mozart) poster, for the Warsaw Opera, 1961.
*Kanal* (Wajda) film poster, for Polski Film, Warsaw, 1967.

## Publications

On CIESLEWICZ: books—*L'Affiche Polonaise du Cinema* by Taydeusz Kowalski, Warsaw, 1957; *Polnische Plakatkunst* by Josef Mroszczak, Düsseldorf, 1962; *Roman Cieslewicz* by Alexander Wojciechowski, Warsaw, 1966; *History of the Poster* by Josef and Shizuko Muller-Brockman, Zurich, 1971; *Roman Cieslewicz: Wystawa foto-grafiki,* exhibition catalogue by Ursula Czartoryska, Lodz, 1971; *Roman Cieslewicz: Graphismes,* exhibition catalogue by Alain Jouffroy, Paris, 1972; *The Polish Poster 1970-1978,* with introduction by Zdzislaw Schubert, Warsaw, 1979; *Roman Cieslewicz: plakaty, fotomontaze* edited by Zdzislaw Schubert and Wanda Nelke, Poznan, 1981; *Roman Cieslewicz* by Margo Rouard-Snowman, Thames & Hudson, 1993.

*

In the profession which I practice, the pleasure of creating has always been the principal argument in its favour. For that reason, I cannot remember a single occasion on which my work has been conditioned by a client's demands at the expense of my own "research." I do not make a distinction between my so called "studio" work and graphic work said to be "commercial." I try, through my profession, to defer to the essential.

My work does not, in any case, need today's abundant and sophisticated techniques. For twenty years, all my work has been carried out on the basis of photographic montage and leaves my studio without any prior commercial agreement. Furthermore, my intervention as "visualist" has never occurred in relation to any object or action that I did not believe in. It is true that the number of my clients is limited and that I concentrate mainly on cultural themes. So, according to the stated principals—whether of Hieronymus Bosch, Capiello, Marcel Duchamp, or Rodchenko (and many others!)—which say that any image that doesn't shock is worth nothing, I try to carry on working.

—Roman Cieslewicz

\* \* \*

The posters and graphic designs of Roman Cieslewicz have undergone dramatic changes over the course of his career. During the initial phase of his career in his native Poland, Cieslewicz worked in the prevalent style of Polish poster design that was recognized as an important art form in Poland and acclaimed throughout Europe as an original, national contribution to graphic design. An important influence on Cieslewicz and other younger Polish graphic designers during this period was Henryk Tomaszewski, whose informally composed posters using colorful collage elements set the tone for the era.

After Cieslewicz settled in Paris, his posters began to move toward surreal juxtapositions of imagery. Cieslewicz used nineteenth-century engravings, Old Master art, and high-contrast photographs in assembling images for posters and illustrations. Greatly enlarged halftones became a signature element in his works, which produce a dual response. In addition to the image formed by the tonal values of the halftone, the viewer is also cognizant of the pattern of the enlarged halftone dots, which became concrete forms interacting with the surface of the paper upon which the image is printed.

During the 1970s, the imagery in Cieslewicz's posters became increasingly demonic, conveying a world without joy or hope. Un-settling distortions of the human form, including decapitated and cloned figures, gave morbid overtones to many of Cieslewicz's works of this period. A simple graphic device—joining two mirror-image photographs—takes on haunting overtones when the resulting configuration emerges as a cyclopean monster or as a massive authoritarian figure with a dwarfed pinhead. These poignant images evoke the despair of the Existentialist philosophers of Poland, which through much of its history, was subjugated by its larger and more powerful neighbors or subjected to dictatorial regimes.

—Philip B. Meggs

# COLIN, Paul (Hubert)

French painter, illustrator, stage, and graphic designer

Born: Nancy, 27 June 1892. Education: Studied at the Ecole Primaire Superieure, Nancy, the Ecole des Beaux-Arts, Nancy, and the Ecole des Beaux-Arts, Paris. Military Service: Served in the French Army, 1914-18. Family: Married Marcelie Minot (divorced); daughter: Paule. Career: Independent painter, Paris, 1920-25; freelance illustrator, poster, and stage decor designer, Paris, from 1925; worked for the Theatre des Champs-Elysees and others. Founder-director, Paul Colin School of Design, Paris. Member: Executive Council Member, Radiodiffusion-Television Francaise, Paris, 1959-64. Exhibitions: Musee de Arts Decoratifs, Paris, 1949; Maison de la Pensee Francaise, Paris, 1950; Galerie David-Drouant, Paris, 1953; Galerie Blanche, Stockholm, 1954; Galerie Creuze, Paris, 1955; Galerie de la Concorde, Paris, 1960; La Sorbonne, Paris, 1982. Honors: Croix de Guerre, 1918; Commandeur de la Legion d'Honneur, France. Died: Nogent-sur-Marne, near Paris, 18 June 1985.

## Works

Books illustrated—*La Maitresse Noire* by J. C. Roger; *Knock* by J. Romains; *Amies et Filles* by Paul Verlaine; *Nouvelles Theories du Docteur Knock, Scaron; Les Gloriales de Fauchon.*

## Publications

By COLIN: books—*La Croute,* Paris, 1957; *En Joue, Feu,* Paris, 1965.

On COLIN: books—*Paul Colin: Affischer—maquettes originales,* exhibition catalogue, Stockholm, 1954; *Who's Who in Graphic Art* edited by Walter Amstutz, Zurich, 1962; *Les Annees 25,* exhibition catalogue, by Francois Mathey, Paris, 1966; *Der Stil der Zwanziger* by Tina Volmerstein, Milan, 1966, Munich 1975; *The Poster: An Illustrated History from 1860* by Harold F. Hutchison, London and Toronto, 1968; *Paul Colin: maquettes d'affiches, peintures, dessins,* sales catalogue, Paris, 1969; *Geschichte des Plakates/Histoire de l'affichei History of the Poster* by Josef and Shizuko Muller-Brockmann, Zurich, 1971; *A Concise History of Posters* by John Barnicoat, London, 1972; *Monografie des Plakats: Entwicklung, Stil, Design* by Herbert Schindler, Munich, 1972; *The Language of Graphics* by Edward Booth-Clibborn and Daniel Baroni, London,

1980; *A History of Graphic Design* by Philip B. Meggs, New York and London, 1983.

\*    \*    \*

During his distinguished career in France, Paul Colin exhibited in the Salon d'Automne. However, his reputation was international, as he showed also in London, New York, Liege, Venice, Madrid, and Barcelona, where he gained the Premier Grand Prix. Colin signed more than five hundred posters and executed designs for the Opera, the Comedie Francaise, and the Theatre du Champs Elysees, among others. He also directed a world-famous school in Paris bearing his name.

In addition to his forceful poster designs for cabarets associated with Josephine Baker in the mid-1920s, Colin is remembered for posters such as "La Cavalier Elsa" (1925), "Jean Borlin" (1925), "Maya" (1927), "Lifar" (1934), "Line Viala" (1937), and "Musée d'Ethnographie Trocadere" (1938). His majestic tribute to the recovery of France from the Occupation in 1944 was his painting for the poster "Liberation" (1944). His major contribution to the poster generally was achieved through his ability to make a single forceful image with a distillation of many aspects brought together in a single statement—the essence of effective poster design.

—John Barnicoat

# COLLEY, (John) David

American photographer, typographic, and graphic designer

**Born:** Mayfield, Kentucky, 13 August 1940. **Education:** Studied at Columbia University, New York, 1962-64; studied at University of Illinois, Champaign-Urbana, 1966-69; studied at University of California, Santa Cruz, 1967; studied at Harvard University, Cambridge, Massachusetts, 1972; studied with the artist-musician John Cage, 1968-69, and with the photographer Ansel Adams, 1977. **Career:** Designer, Container Corporation of America, Chicago, 1972-73, Massachusetts Institute of Technology, Cambridge, 1975-76, and J. C. Penney Corporate Design Office, New York, 1978-79; graphic design and poster work, for Chicago Symphony, Museum of Contemporary Art, Chicago, and others, from 1969. Assistant professor, 1969-75, and associate professor, from 1979, University of Illinois, Champaign-Urbana; visiting lecturer, Massachusetts Institute of Technology, Cambridge, 1975-76, Ohio State University, Columbus, 1976-77, and Institute of Design, Illinois Institute of Technology, Chicago, 1977-78. **Member:** American Institute of Graphic Arts, New York; Society for Typographic Arts, Chicago. **Exhibitions:** Society for Typographic Arts, Chicago, 1968, 1970, 1974, 1980; *Vision and Expression,* International Museum of Photography, Rochester, New York, 1969; Murray State University, Kentucky, 1972; University of Illinois, Champaign-Urbana, 1973; Tyler School of Art, Temple University, Philadelphia, 1974; *Sailing at MIT,* Mead Paper Company, New York, 1977; *The New Typography,* Ryder Gallery, Chicago, 1978; *Four American Designers,* Amerika Haus, Munich, 1981 (toured Germany); *Posters,* Institute of Design, Illinois Institute of Technology, Chicago, 1983. **Collections:** Polaroid Collection, Cambridge, Massachusetts; Mead Paper Library of Ideas, New York; International Museum of Photography at George Eastman House, Roch-

ester, New York; Museum of Modern Art, New York; Smithsonian Institution, Washington, D.C.; Kennedy Center for Performing Arts, Washington, D.C.; Staatliches Museum für Angewandte Kunst, Munich; Musée National d'Art Moderne, Paris. **Honors:** Artist Grant, Polaroid Corporation, Cambridge, Massachusetts, 1970, 1972, 1980; Award of Excellence, United National International Children's Education Fund (UNICEF), New York, 1982. **Address:** 705 West Nevada Street, Urbana, Illinois 61801, U.S.A.

## Works

*Blessed Light: Shaker Architecture* book design, for University of Kentucky Press, 1970.
*Wednesday Night at the Lab* book design, for Harper and Row, 1971.
Poster, for the Joffrey Ballet, 1971.
*Technology Review* magazine design, for Massachusetts Institute of Technology, 1975.
*The New Earth Sciences* book design, for Massachusetts Institute of Technology, 1976.
Poster, for the American Library Association, 1976.
Visual identity program, for Edward Durell Stone Associates, 1978.
Visual identity program, for Boston Acoustics, 1979.
*Billy Budd* poster, for the Metropolitan Opera, New York, 1979.
*The Bartered Bride* poster, for the Metropolitan Opera, New York, 1979.
Visual identity program, for the Apt Corporation, 1980.
*The Educational Wastelands* book design, for University of Illinois Press, 1987.
*Marxism and the Interpretation of Culture* book design, for University of Illinois Press, 1989.
*Hall of the South American People* poster, for the American Museum of Natural History, 1989.

## Publications

**By COLLEY: books**—*A Was an Apple Pie,* Urbana, 1967; *Twelve Photographs,* Urbana, 1968; *Faulkner: A Photographic Representation,* Urbana, 1968; *Jardin des Tuileries: 12 Photographs 1984-1988,* Urbana, 1988; **articles**—"The Graphic Film" in *Novum Gebrauchsgraphik* (Munich), no. 45, 1974; "Twenty Years of Design in Chicago" in *Chicago Magazine,* November 1977; "Bill Bonnell: Designer, New York" in *Graphis* (Zurich), no. 224, 1983; "Graphic Design Education USA" in *Novum Gebrauchsgraphik* (Munich), no. 54, 1982; "Graphic Design: Undergraduate Education/Graduate Education" in *Journal of the Graphic Design Education Association,* no. 2, 1989.

**On COLLEY: books**—*Form and Expression* edited by Nathan Lyons, New York, 1969; *Typographic Design: Form and Communication* by Phillip Meggs, Ben Day, and Robert Carter, New York, 1985; *American Typographers* by Robert Carter, New York, 1988; *Type and Image* by Phillip Meggs, New York, 1988; **articles**—in *WFMT Guide* (Chicago), December, 1968; *Art in America* (New York), July/August 1969; *Parnassus* (New Haven) no. 2, 1980; *Novum Gebrauchsgraphik* (Munich), no. 52, 1981; *Art Direction* (New York), January 1981; *American Institute of Graphic Arts Journal of Graphic Design* (New York), January 1988.

\*

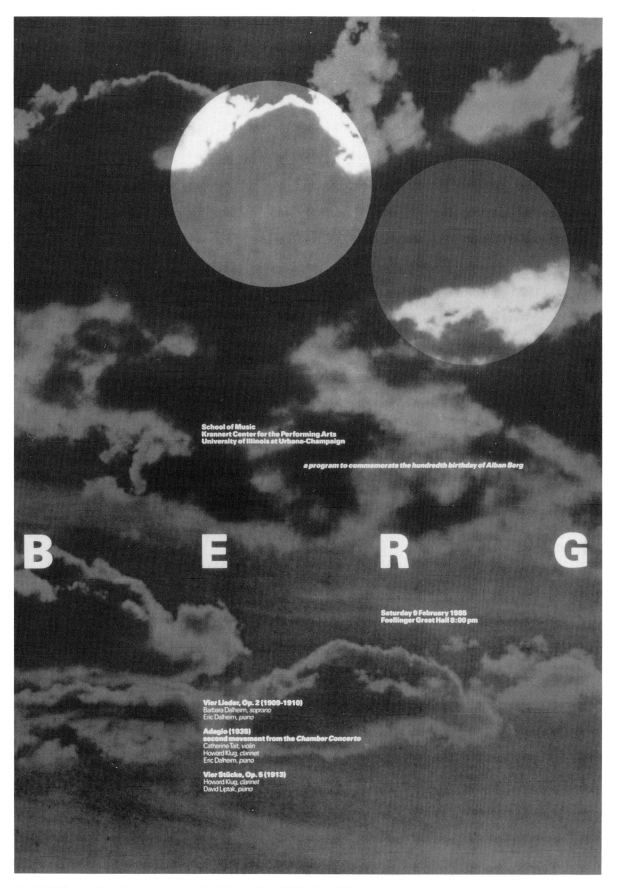

David Colley: *Alban Berg* poster for the University of Illinois, 1985

The primary problems that my work addresses are those related to educational and other cultural institutions. To this end, my design has directed itself most often toward the problem of complicated information which finds for itself a rather abstract or structural manifestation.

Most visual information can best be universally expressed as a distilled and refined sign of the content it represents, and it is to this manner of representation that I have most often turned in solving problems. I view graphic design as visual communication—the articulation of specific visual languages. And while my work may well articulate a specific visual language, that articulation must, by the definition of language, become an intelligible transformation of known sensations, structures, and forms. It is precisely the process of transformation which continues to hold my interest in visual communication. The changing and reforming of existing sensations and structures to create new forms seems not only a difficult task, but also one of magic, and, therefore, one which can never be completed or understood.

I see contemporary graphic design's task as addressing more and more what may well become known as information design, leaving the lesser tasks of visual communication to an automatic following or restating of the visual languages that have become part of the vernacular.

—David Colley

\*      \*      \*

The work of David Colley presents a unique blend of structure and objectivity, while deriving a sense of playfulness and beauty from within its structure. Deceptively simple, his designs extend the realm of visual language and typographic message by allowing the evolution of structure to come from its content.

Colley is proud to claim the formative experiments in the Bauhaus and the methodology of the Swiss school as major influences on his development as a designer. The work of Joseph Mueller-Brockman, in particular, enhanced his appreciation of clarity and beauty which are attainable in rational design. American designer Massino Vignelli inspired a sense of joy and elegance that can be found within the objectivity of design.

Colley considers the opportunities from institutions such as Container Corporation of America, Massachusetts Institute of Technology, and the J. C. Penney Company pivotal in his career, as these institutions were whole-heartedly dedicated to creating fine design. Each of these experiences helped him to develop his distinctive use of visual language. German-educated designer Dietmar Winkler particularly influenced Colley while at MIT, introducing him to a new level of typographic achievement.

In his philosophy toward his work, Colley states that a thorough understanding of any problem provides the means for the solution. He looks for visual metaphors that communicate a highly complex message through seemingly simple components and relationships. These metaphors are based on understood structures and structural laws which cross the line between verbal and visual communication. A poster design for an American music concert, for example, presents a slightly undulating title, indicative of flowing music or a fluttering flag. The interpretive colors of red, white, and blue enhance the meaning. Another example illustrating the highly expressive quality of Colley's approach is a poster created for the Joffrey Ballet. Three parallel lines of typography create a zig-zag shape similar to the contrapposto of classical Greek sculpture. Gradation

of type weight and size create a sense of choreographed motion and depth.

David Colley sets out to communicate new ideas by challenging the viewer to participate in his work. Going beyond the boundaries of everyday language, viewers must interact with what they know in order to understand what they do not.

—R. Merzdorf

# COLLIER, Susan/CAMPBELL, Sarah
British textile and furnishing designers

**Born:** (Collier) In London in 1938; (Campbell) in London, 1946. **Education:** (Collier) Studied catering and hotel management in London; (Campbell) Studied painting and graphics, Chelsea School of Art, London. **Career:** (Collier) Wardrobe assistant, then assistant costume designer to Peter Rice and Pat Albeck, London; staff textile designer, Liberty's store, London; freelance designer, working with Soieries Nouveautées, Jaeger, Habitat, Martes Fischbacher, Richard Allans, Rodier, Liberty Fabrics, and others; (Campbell) Freelance designer, concentrating on wallpapers and furnishing fabrics for Liberty's, Osborne and Little, and others. Sisters founded Collier Campbell Limited design firm, London. **Exhibitions:** *Liberty's 1875-1975,* Victoria and Albert Museum, London, 1975. **Address:** Collier Campbell Limited, 63 Old Town, London SW4, England.

**Publications**

**By COLLIER: articles**—in *Design* (London), July 1975; *The Designer* (London), July/August 1978.

**On COLLIER/CAMPBELL: books**—*Liberty's 1875-1975,* exhibition catalogue with text by R. Strong, B. Morris, V. Mendes, and others, London, 1975; *Liberty's: A Biography of a Shop* by Alison Adburgham, London, 1975; *The 1978 Fashion Guide* by Kaori O'Connor and Farrol Kahn, London, 1978; *The Conran Directory of Design* edited by Stephen Bayley, London, 1985; *International Design Yearbook 1987/88* edited by Philippe Starck, London, 1987; **articles**—in *Sunday Times Magazine* (London), 14 July 1974; *Design* (London), May, 1976; *The Designer* (London), July/August, 1983; *Design* (London), May, 1991; *House & Garden* April, 1991.

\*      \*      \*

Susan Collier thinks that textiles should be an inspiration in one's daily life and has successfully proved in the work of Collier/Campbell that this can be true. Observing the ugliness of fabrics sold in London stores encouraged Collier in her fresh, personal approach. When she joined Liberty's they were selling furnishing fabrics printed with staid designs from the 1950's. By setting herself the task of updating the patterns, she brought Liberty's furnishings into focus and gave them a reputation equal to that of their dress prints. The new floral look which she and her sister Sarah Campbell invented was inspired by a love of the English countryside, as is illustrated in their Cottage Garden range. At Liberty's, Collier's talents were nurtured and developed by the head of design production, Blair

Pride, who died an untimely death in 1973. It was he who made her realise that she and her sister would have greater opportunity to experiment with colour and design if they were working for themselves. When they established their own firm, they already had a reputation backed by a confidence in their own ability as designers and businesswomen.

While their skill as innovators with colour and design (as shown in their new collection *Six Views*) has put them in the forefront of British textile design, they have also proved that creative people can successfully run a business. It is rare that Collier/Campbell take their inspiration from an acknowledged source. With the exception of those evident in Bauhaus and the recent, Matisse-like print Cote d'Azure, few direct influences can be detected. Collier/Campbell are not confined by fashionable colours, but produce their collections in different, coordinating ranges. This said, they are best seen as painters who are intuitively in touch with the feeling of their times and practically aware of the means of production (chiefly rotary silkscreen). Collier/Campbell respect the discipline of having to use the limited colour range of a manufacturer such as Jaeger, who introduce only three new colours a season, but have confidence in their own instincts and experiments. Their ability in the fields of design, marketing, and manufacture is illustrated in the variety and vitality of their work, which has attracted clients such as the Swiss cloth manufacturer Fischbacher and the American Martex (bed linens), to which they sell designs under license. Collier/Campbell's love and understanding of colour and pattern has already put *Six Views* into consideration for the 1984 Design Council Awards.

—Hazel Clark

# COLOMBO, Joe

Italian architect, interior, furniture, exhibition and industrial designer

**Born:** Cesare Colombo in Milan, 1930. **Education:** Studied at the Accademia de Brera and the Politecnico, Milan, 1950-54. **Career:** Active as independent painter and sculptor, Milan, 1951-55; established his own industrial and commercial firm, Milan, 1955-62; freelance designer, establishing his own studio in Milan, 1962-71; designed for Arflex, Elco, Kartell, La Linea, O-Luce, La Rinascente, Alitalia, Bayer, and others. **Member:** Founder-member, Arte Concreta group of painters and sculptors, Milan, 1955. **Exhibitions:** Stedelijk Museum, Amsterdam, 1966; Design Research, New York, 1966; Musee des Arts Decoratifs, Paris, 1968; *Modern Chairs,* Whitechapel Art Gallery, London, 1970; *Italy: The New Domestic Landscape,* Museum of Modern Art, New York, 1972; *Design and design,* Palazzo delle Stelline, Milan, 1979; *Design Since 1945,* Philadelphia Museum of Art, 1983. **Honors:** IN/ARCH Award, National Institute of Architecture, Rome, 1963; Silver Medal, Milan Triennale, 1964, 1967; Compasso d'Oro Award, Milan, 1967; Association of Industrial Designers Award, New York, 1968. **Died:** Milan, 1971.

## Works

*Colombo* table lamp in brass and perspex, for O-Luce, 1962.
Portable mini-kitchen in wood and stainless steel, for Boffi, 1963.
*4801* easy chair in molded plywood, for Kartell, 1963.

Hotel Pontinental interiors, Sardinia, 1963.
*Elda 1005* swivel easy chair in plastic with leather upholstery, for Comfort, 1964.
Foldable container furniture, for Arflex, 1964-65.
*4868* stacking and linking chair in plastic, for Kartell, 1965.
*Supercomfort 1000* easy chair in bent plywood with leather cushions, for Comfort, 1966.
Flexible magnetic furniture system with plastic laminate finish, for La Rinascente, 1966-67.
*Triangular System* shelf/container units, for Elco, 1967.
*Poker twin-top* gaming and dining table in steel and plastic laminate, for Zanotta, 1967.
*Box 1* combined bedroom/study/living room furniture unit, for La Linea, 1967-68.
Display stand at the Turin Eurodomus exhibition, for the ADI Italian Association for Industrial Design, 1968.
*Square Plastic System* unit container furniture, for Elco, 1968-69.
*Additional System* seating in upholstered polyfoam segments, for Sormani, 1969.
*Living Center* furniture range in tubular steel with angular cushions, for Rosenthal, 1971.

## Publications

**By COLOMBO: books**—(with Sori Yanagi and others) *New Form Furniture: Japan,* Tokyo, 1970; **articles**—interview with A. Bellini in *MD Moebel Interior Design* (Leinfelden), January 1966.

**On COLOMBO: books**—*Il Disegno Industriale e la sua Estetica* by Gillo Dorfles, Bologna, 1963; *The Modern Chair: 1850 to Today* by Gilbert Frey, London and Niederteufen, 1970; *Modern Chairs 1918-1950,* exhibition catalogue by Carol Hofgben and others, London, 1970; *Italy: The New Domestic Landscape* edited by Emilio Ambasz, New York and Florence, 1972; *History of Modern Furniture* by Karl Mang, Stuttgart, 1978, London, 1979; *In Good Shape: Style in Industrial Products 1900-1960* by Stephen Bayley, London, 1979; *Atlante del Design Italiano 1940/1980* by Alfonso Grassi and Anty Pansera, Milan, 1980; *Design Since 1945* edited by Kathryn Hiesinger and George Marcus, Philadelphia and London, 1983; *The Conran Directory of Design* edited by Stephen Bayley, London, 1985; *Design Source Book* by Penny Sparke and others, London, 1986.

\* \* \*

One of the first industrial designers to achieve an international reputation, Colombo was trained as a painter and architect. A precocious student, he had his first building completed while he was still in architecture school. Although active and successful as an avant-garde painter (he was a member of the "Movimento Nucleare," a group of painters founded in 1951 by Enrico Baj and Sergio Dangelo), sculptor, and architect, he concentrated on product and furniture design from 1962 until his death in 1971. In this short period he produced many influential and internationally recognized works. His early focus on interior architecture led to his interest in furnishings and household objects, and later to research on efficient, modular, and mass-produced living units.

Bold and innovative, his designs were simple, flexible, brightly colored, functional, and appropriately futuristic for the times. Although Colombo claimed that his development process emphasized technical design and choice of materials so that his products could be inexpensively mass produced, his artistic eye was evident in the sculptural and well-proportioned qualities of his designs. Other characteristics of his work were variety and fine craftsmanship, the experimentation and use of new materials (injection-molded plastics, plastic laminates, and others), clearly articulated structure, and a systems approach that extended to the perception of living space as a whole.

Attempting to make good design accessible and acceptable to the masses, Colombo collaborated with industry and large department stores in Italy and other countries to produce furniture and household objects that would appeal to all tastes and budgets. In 1967, Gimbel's, then one of the largest department stores in the United States, held a Joe Colombo week, promoting some of his most popular works, including flexible storage cubes, numerous kinds of lamps, clocks, stemware, injection-molded plastic chairs with adjustable legs, and a variety of other seating. Exhibitions at Design/Research International in New York, the Stedelijk Museum in Amsterdam, and the Musee des Art Decoratifs in Paris also contributed to his widespread success. The New York Museum of Modern Art selected one of his arm chairs and his cubic, rolling mini kitchen for its permanent design collection. His work was influential and widely copied. He was the recipient of numerous awards, including 2 Compassi d'Oros and 2 International Design Awards from the U.S.A.

His application (with designer Ignazia Favata, one of the few designers with whom Colombo collaborated) of ecologically and ergonomically sound design principles to the problems of dwelling space resulted in a system of coordinated, flexible structures that created a dynamic, "total" living environment composed of four dwelling units: kitchen, cupboard, bed and privacy, and bathroom. Each was designed for maximum economy and flexibility in interior arrangement. Evolving through several variations, including the well-publicized "Visiona 69," a form of this futuristic, yet practical system was installed in his own home in Milan. In his attempt to create the perfect living space, Colombo increasingly concentrated on the utopian, humanistic needs of environmental design, emphasizing not only the relationships between city and dwelling, and green spaces and dwelling units, but also the relationship between man and the dwelling unit.

Some of his best known works were highly experimental, such as the Spider Lamp (1965), the first lamp to use the halogen bulb for interior lighting; the Elda Chair (1964), the first large armchair shell made entirely of fiberglass; and the Universale chair (1965), the first chair manufactured entirely of molded plastic.

Colombo was brilliant, dashing, iconoclastic, and charismatic. He developed almost a cult following from the 1960s until his death. Even though some of his pieces may appear dated to current sensibilities, his clear and logical solutions with tasteful appearance and reasonable prices have rarely been matched in the history of contemporary design.

—Elizabeth Douthitt Byrne

# CONFALONIERI, Giulio

Italian graphic and industrial designer

**Born:** Milan, 20 August 1936. **Education:** Studied political economy, Universita Bocconi, Milan; mainly self-taught in typography and design. **Career:** Independent painter, Milan, 1957-64; freelance designer, establishing own graphics studio in Milan, 1964-83; has designed publicity for Olivetti, Pirelli, Bassetti, Roche, Westinghouse, Total, Esso, Fulget, Mondadori, *PM* and *Domus* magazines, and products for Tecno, Boffi, Marcatre, Italsider, AGIP Petrols, and Ratti Silks. **Member:** Alliance Graphique Internationale; Associazione Disegno Industriale, Milan; American Institute of Graphic Arts, New York; Art Directors Club of New York; with Franco Grignani, Bruno Munari, Pino Tovaglia, and Silvio Coppola, the Gruppo di Ricerca Exhibition Design, Milan, 1969-78. **Exhibitions:** *Plastic Design Research,* Palazzo Reale, Milan, 1969; *Design 1970,* Musée d'Art Moderne, Paris, 1970; *Design 20. Jahrhundert,* Museum des 20. Jahrhundert, Vienna, 1972; *107 Grafici dell'AGI,* Castello Sforzesco, Milan, 1974. **Honors:** Graphic Award, 1957, and Gold Medal, 1969, Milan Triennale; Gold Medal for Book Design, Viareggio, 1959. **Address:** Via Lanzone 13, 20123 Milan, Italy.

## Publications

**By CONFALONIERI: books**—(with Ilio Negri) *Baldassare, Melchiorre, Gaspare,* Milan, 1956; (with Negri) *Racconti italiani,* Milan, 1958; (with Negri) *Primo catalogo dei caratteri de assa,* Milan, 1960; *Immagine di un libro,* Milan, 1965; *12 Finestre,* Milan 1965; *Towns,* Milan, 1978; *Graphic Adventure,* Milan, 1978.

**On CONFALONIERI: books**—*Who's Who in Graphic Art* edited by Walter Amstutz, Zurich, 1962, Dübendorf, 1982; *Monografie des Plakats* by Herbert Schindler, Munich, 1972; *Due Dimensioni* by Felice Nava, Milan, 1973; *107 Grafici dell'AGI,* exhibition catalogue with text by Franco Grignani and Renzo Zorzi, Venice, 1974; *Design e Forme Nuove nell'Arredamento Italiano* edited by Paolo Portoghesi and Mario Marini, Rome, 1978; *The Language of Graphics* by Edward Booth-Clibborn and Daniele Baroni, London, 1980.

\*       \*       \*

Giulio Confalonieri has tended to exploit somewhat stark contrasts: abrupt passages from black to white, juxtapositions of sharply differentiated colours or textures, powerful images and bold typography held in precarious equilibrium by generous white space. This way of working adds up to an individual use of the characteristics of Italian graphic design to which Confalonieri has, of course, very strongly contributed, along with Erberto Carboni, Max Huber, and Giovanni Pintori. However, his work for Cassina, especially, perhaps more nervy and gentler in its contrasts, has contributed as much to the style of that house as any of the designers of its furniture. Or, perhaps more precisely, he has helped to define and project that style, a subtle excitement urbanely contained.

A sophisticated taste informs all Confalonieri's work and thus controls his bold pattern making, which never gets out of hand and is never made simply for effect. Finely tuned statements in visual terms, however bold and contrasty, his patterns never seek to bludgeon the sensibility.

Not blunt instruments, then, but precision tools, each design—calculated in terms of client, purpose, and context—is elegantly appropriate. What will do for Cassina, what will do for Pirelli, and what, for Eurodomus, are highly differentiated, though, to be sure, his sophisticated and fastidious mark is always there. Whereas the work for Cassina creates patterns of an urbane lifestyle, that for

Pirelli, something of the ruggedness of the tyre as well as its suggestion of elegant motoring, the designs for Eurodomus somehow manage to express a quality of European furniture in creative rivalry and diversity.

It is obvious that intelligence guides hand and eye in this process of creative pattern-making but that intelligence is, in its turn, advised by a sophisticated sensibility. Though the patterns may almost be enjoyed purely aesthetically, that is not their purpose, and there is always something in their nature and in the nature of their components that halts any slide away from function. The patterns are not just vehicles but are themselves vital components of the message and are derived from it. That is to say, they are not arbitrary and imposed but result from an analysis of the complex interaction of the nature of client, brief, and cultural context, and none of these messages could be as well expressed without the particular pattern that has been created.

—Toni del Renzio

# CONNOLLY, Sybil

Irish fashion, textile, ceramics, glass, and interior designer

**Born:** Swansea, Wales, 1921. **Education:** Attended Convent of Mercy, Waterford; apprenticeship at Bradleys of Chepstow Place, London, 1938-40. **Career:** Clothing designer, 1940-43, and director, 1943-53, Richard Alan shop, Dublin, Ireland; showed first full collection, 1952; established own couture business, Sybil Connolly Ltd., Dublin, from 1953; showed first Winter collection, Dunsany Castle, County Meath, 1953; designed textiles, ceramics, and glass designer for clients including Brunschwig et Fils, Galway Crystal, Martex, Samuels and Tay, Schumacher, Sigma, Tiffany and Co., and others. Also writes on garden design and interior decoration. **Exhibitions:** International Fashion Review, Philadelphia Fashion Group, 1952; Palace Hotel, St. Moritz, 1956; Palazzo Grassi Fashion Fair, 1956; *The Pride of Ireland,* Bloomingdale's, New York, 1965, 1968. **Honors:** Honorary doctorate, National University of Ireland; honorary associate, National College of Art and Design, Dublin; honorary life member, Royal Dublin Society. **Address:** 71 Merrion Square, Dublin 2, Ireland.

### Publications

**By CONNOLLY: books**—(with Helen Dillon) *In an Irish Garden,* London, 1986; *In an Irish House,* London, 1988; *Irish Hands: The Tradition of Beautiful Crafts,* New York, 1994.

**On CONNOLLY: articles**—*Harper's Bazaar,* October 1953; *Vogue,* 15 March 1957; *House Beautiful,* Fall/Winter 1967; *House and Garden,* March 1990.

\*      \*      \*

Sybil Connolly is the first Irish fashion and textiles designer to have achieved international success. Trained in the world of haute couture fashion, she set out to combine the elegance, exquisite detailing, and perfectionism associated with couture fashion using essentially Irish textiles. She achieved early success and received international recognition in the 1950s, particularly in the United States. There her blend of feminine sophistication and the romanticism associated with the colors and textures of her clothes that were inspired by the Irish landscape were greatly appreciated. In the United States, she popularized the use of linen, a fabric particularly suited for use in warm climates. Her famous pleated linen dress was featured in *Time* magazine. This media success was greatly enhanced by her personal charm, which endeared her to an American audience and ensured some valuable commissions.

Connolly's use of native Irish textiles in her work has always been her greatest strength. In the 1950s she took a fresh approach to design, not by creating a new style or look, but by using traditional Irish linen and tweed. Damask linen had been widely used in the manufacture of table cloths and household goods but not in couture fashion. Connolly was responsible for a revival in Irish knitwear, linen lacemaking, hand-crocheted lace, and Carrickmacross lace. Her own high standards and eye for detail ensured a high quality of manufacture and craftsmanship.

Traditional Donegal tweeds were dyed into delicate pastel shades, an entirely new departure from traditional manufacture. Her collections were marketed using romantic Irish and neo-Georgian themes. This mixture of materials and themes helped to create an identity for Irish fashion both in Ireland, where her collections were made, and abroad.

Connolly has drawn on inspiration from the past for much of her ceramic and textile design, particularly from Irish design of the eighteenth century. She has designed china and table decorations for Tiffany that were inspired by Mrs. Delany's flower collages done in Dublin in the mid 1700s. Household textiles include floral chintzes for Brunschwig et Fils and bed linens for Martex inspired by flowers and fruit. Brunschwig et Fils printed the wallpaper and textiles she designed for the restored interiors at the Swiss Cottage, Cahir, County Tipperary, an exquisite cottage ornée designed in the 1820s by John Nash. There she reused the design of an architectural caprice that originally was printed on cotton by the firm of Robinson of Ball's Bridge, Dublin, in the 1770s. At Fort Belvedere, Windsor, she recreated an eighteenth century print room modelled on designs executed by Lady Louisa Conolly at Castletown, County Kildare, in the 1760s.

Since 1957 the couture house and showrooms of Sybil Connolly Limited have been situated in an eighteenth-century house in Merrion Square, Dublin, which is also the designer's home. Magnificently restored, the house is decorated with her own textiles, and the walls covered in her own pleated linen.

—Paul Caffrey

# CONRAN, Terence (Orby)

British architectural, interior, graphic, and industrial designer

**Born:** London, 4 October 1931. **Education:** Attended Bryanston School, Dorset, 1944-49; studied textile design, Central School of Arts and Crafts, London, 1949-50. **Family:** Married Shirley Ida Pearce in 1955 (divorced, 1962); children: Sebastian and Jasper; married Caroline Herbert in 1963; children: Tom, Sophie, and Edmund. **Career:** Textile designer for the Rayon Centre, London, 1950-51; interior designer, Dennis Lennon studio, London, 1951-52; freelance furniture designer, as Conran and Company, working for John Lewis Partnership, Edinburgh Weavers, Simpsons of

Piccadilly, and others, in London and Thetford, 1952-56; founder-proprietor, with Ian Storey, of Soup Kitchen restaurants, London, 1953-56; founder-director, with John Stephenson, 1956-71, and chairman, from 1971, Conran Design Group, London; founder-director, 1964-71, and chairman, from 1971, Habitat furnishing stores, in London, and subsequently throughout the world; joint-chairman, Ryman Conran Limited, London, 1968-71; managing director, Neal Street Restaurant, London, from 1972; chairman, Conran Stores, Inc., from 1977; chairman, Jasper Conran fashion company, London, from 1977; director, from 1979, and chairman, 1981-83, J. Hepworth and Son, London; chairman, Habitat Mothercare Limited, London, from 1982; director, Conran Roche architectural and city planning firm, London, from 1982; chairman, Conran Octopus publishing company, London, from 1983; chairman, Butlers Wharf Development, London, from 1984; director of Michelin House Development, London, from 1985; chairman of Bibendum Restaurant, from 1986; director of British Home Stores PLC and Savacentre Limited, London, from 1986. Founder-trustee, Conran Foundation for design and industry, from 1982, and the Design Museum, London, from 1989. **Member:** Royal Commission on Environmental Pollution, 1973-75; council member, Royal College of Art, London, 1978-81, and from 1986; advisory council member, 1979-83, and trustee, from 1984, Victoria and Albert Museum, London. **Honors:** Presidential Medal, 1968, 1975, and Bicentenary Medal, 1983, Royal Society of Arts, London; Society of Industrial Artists and Designers Medal, London, 1980; *Daily Telegraph*/Association for Business Sponsorship award, London, 1982; Knighthood, 1983; honorary fellow, Royal Institute of British Architects, 1984. **Address:** 196 Tottenham Court Road, London W1P 9LD, England.

## Publications

**By CONRAN: books**—*The House Book,* London, 1974; (with Maria Kroll) *The Vegetable Book,* London, 1976; *The Kitchen Book,* London, 1977; *The Bed and Bath Book,* London, 1978; (with Caroline Conran) *The Cook Book,* London, 1980; *The New House Book,* London, 1985; *The Conran Directory of Design* edited by Stephen Bayley, London, 1985; *Plants at Home,* London, 1986; *The Soft Furnishings Book,* London, 1986; *Terence Conran's France,* London, 1987.

**On CONRAN: books**—*Gute Moebel—Schoene Raume* edited by Mia Seeger, Stuttgart, 1953; *Public Interiors* by Misha Black, London, 1960; *Looking at Furniture* by Gordon Russell, London, 1964; *Design 1900-1960* edited by Thomas Faulkner, Newcastle, 1976; *Twentieth Century Furniture* by Philippe Garner, London, 1980; *The Entrepreneurs* by E. Hennessy, Newbury, 1980; *Neue Moebel 1950-1982/Contemporary Furniture* edited by Klaus-Jürgen, Stuttgart and London, 1982; *Conran and the Habitat Story* by Barty Phillips, London, 1984.

*

As creative retailers, our policy simply amounts to a belief that if reasonable and intelligent people are offered products for their home that are well made, well designed, work well, and are of decent quality at a price they can afford, then they will like and buy them.

—Terence Conran

\*     \*     \*

Terence Conran's belief in offering well designed products at reasonable prices has been proved correct many times over by a commercial empire now reaching from England to the United States and Japan. The Habitat range offers furniture to be used from bedrooms to kitchens, household linen, curtains, carpets, china, cutlery, casseroles, pots, glassware, lamps, spaghetti-makers, and plastic buckets. All the goods are simple in shape, and Conran sees the main influences on his style as the 1930s streamlined look and the plain, functional furniture found in servants' quarters before the war. One can also detect a strong influence from the United Kingdom's government-sponsored 1942 Utility scheme, which set out to offer plain but good-quality household and clothing products despite wartime shortages. With his acquisition of Mothercare in 1982, Conran entered the clothing area as well, planning to give mothers and children fashionable garments in addition to functional ones. The design of all these articles is handled by Conran Associates, the largest design organisation in Europe; it covers Habitat and Mothercare products, office products, and graphic design projects. Conran still likes to approve designs.

In the 1950s, before Habitat existed, modern design consisted of very expensive items from Sweden or Italy, while most shops stocked highly conservative furniture. Conran was able to break this pattern by producing an inexpensive range of modern furniture so that the young couple starting up could acquire a stylish home. With the expansion overseas, Conran has become an authority on national nuances. The English like bedroom furniture, but the French use little. English saucepans have lids, and the French ones do not. Mothercare found the same variations in national attitudes toward baby clothes. The bulk of Conran's creations do appeal over national borders, but an awareness of what will not transfer well is also essential, so that particular items can be designed for particular markets. A universal provider, Conran now has a design empire.

—Diana de Marly

# CONSUEGRA, David

Columbian illustrator and graphic designer

**Born:** Bucaramanga, 20 December 1939. **Education:** San Pedro Claver, Bucaramanga, until 1956; studied advertising design, School of Fine and Applied Arts, Boston University, B.F.A., 1961; studied graphic design, School of Art and Design, Yale University, M.F.A., 1963. **Career:** Independent graphic designer, from 1963; graphic designer, Museo de Arte Moderno, Bogotá, 1963-67; designer and editor, Bucaramanga, 1969-1975. Professor, Universidad de los Andes, Bogotá, 1963-68, 1983-84, 1985-88; professor, 1966-68, 1976-89, and professor emeritus, from 1989, Universidad Nacional, Bogotá; founder and professor, graphic design program, Universidad Tadeo Lozano, Columbia, 1967-68; visiting professor, Virginia Commonwealth University, Richmond, 1984-85; lecturer on design. **Member:** International Trademark Center, Ostende, Belgium. **Exhibitions:** *The Faces of Man,* Boston Commons, U.S.A., 1960; *Neoclásicos,* Galeria 25, Bogotá, 1965; *Carteles,* Casa de la Cultura, Bogotá, 1967; Bienal de Arte, Cali, 1971, 1973; II Biennial of Illustration, Bratislava, Czechoslovakia; I Expomarca Latinoamericana, Museo Nacional, Bogotá, 1981; International Book Exhibition, Leipzig, 1982; I Salón OP de Diseño Gráfico, Museo de Arte Moderno, Bogotá, 1983; World's Book Fair, Frankfurt, 1983;

*Art de l'Atelier et Art de la Rue,* Paris, 1984; retrospective, Museo de Arte, Universidad Nacional, Bogotá, 1988; *Consuegra,* Museo de Arte Moderno de Bucaramanga, 1989. **Honors:** I Prize, theater symbol, 1965; III Prize, poster design, UNESCO, 1976; I Prize, Colombia's graphic identification, 1991; I Prize, National Games identification, Bucaramanga, 1993. **Address:** Carrera 6 No. 75-11 Ap. 301, Apartado Aéreo 60093, Bogotá 2, Columbia.

## Works

Graphic identity, for Museo de Arte Moderno, Bogotá, 1963.
Graphic design, for *Nova* magazine, 1964-66.
Graphic identity, for Artesanías de Colombia, 1968.
Graphic identity, for INRAVISION, National Institute of Radio and Television, 1970, 1994.
Graphic design, for *Temas de Consulta* magazine, 1978-1982.
Graphic identity, for FEDEARROZ, National Rice Federation, 1979.
Graphic identity, for CROYDON S.A shoe manufacturing firm, 1980.
Graphic identity, for Facultad de Artes, Universidad Nacional, 1980.
Graphic design, for *Teoría & Práctica del Diseño Gráfico* magazine, 1982-86.
Graphic identity, for Fondo Ganadero de Santander (cattle breeders association), 1987.
Graphic identity, for Partido Liberal Colombiano political party, 1987.
Graphic identity, for ICOLLANTAS (Columbia's car tire industry), 1988.
Graphic identity, for the nation of Colombia, 1991.
Graphic identity, for XI Juegos Nacionales Departamentales (state games), 1993.
Exhibition catalogue design, for *Hermann Zapf,* Universidad Nacional de Columbia, 1994.

## Publications

**By CONSUEGRA: books—**(thesis) *On Trademarks,* New Haven, Connecticut, 1963; (for children) *Las 26 Letras,* Bogotá, 1964; *Ornamentación Calada en la Oríebrería Indígena Precolombina,* Bogotá, 1967; *Educacion Musical,* exhibition catalogue, Bucaramanga, 1971; *Graphica et Lettera,* Bucaramanga, 1975; *De Marcas y Simbolos,* Bucaramanga, 1976; (for children) *Máximas Mínimas,* Bogotá, 1981; (for children) *Poemario Vario,* Bogotá, 1981; (for children) *Una Vez Tres Veces,* 1983; (for children) *El Mundo de los Colores,* Bogotá, 1983; *25 Years of Graphic Synthesis: 1960-1986,* Bogotá, 1986; *ABC of World's Trademarks,* Bogotá, 1988; *En Busca del Cuadrado,* Bogotá, 1992.

**On CONSUEGRA: books—***Who's Who in Graphic Art* edited by Walter Amstutz, vol. 2, Zürich, 1982; *Trademarks of the World* by David Carter, vol. 3, New York, 1988; *Diseño Gráfico* by Enric Satué, Barcelona, 1988; *Consuegra,* exhibition catalogue, Museo de Arte Moderno de Bucaramanga, 1989; *Artistas Santanderesanos en la Década de 1960,* Banco de la República, 1991.

\*

Although design and graphic expression have been current in Colombia since pre-Columbian times, and although many outstand-

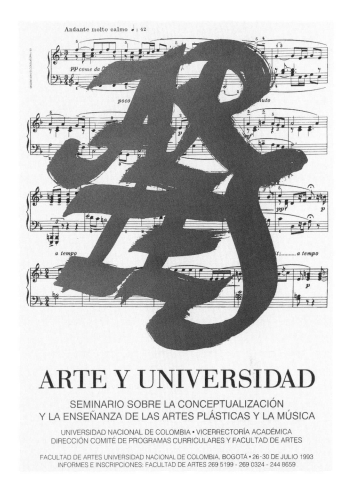

David Consuegra: seminar poster for the Art Department at the National University of Colombia, 1993. Photo: Jorge Gomez

ing artists—including Santiago Marínez Delgado, Sergio Trujillo Magnenat, Luis María Rendón, and Enrique Grau—have devoted their lives to designing posters, covers, and illustrations for books, magazines, and newspapers, graphic design did not develop into a clear concept until 1963. In that year I returned to Colombia, invited by the Universidad de Los Andes to set up the first program on graphic design in the country. Due to multiple causes this program was delayed until 1967, when I finally structured it at the Universidad Tadeo Lozano. Since then, I have been contributing as a program consultant to the development of various programs of graphic design and art education in Colombia, always with the intent of allowing concept, form, and communication to develop into a strong and legible identity. Today, although there is a group of good designers, there is not a trend or style that could be taken as representative of Colombia's graphic design as a whole. Their work reflects both their own personal approaches and the influence and education they have received abroad.

As far as I am concerned, graphic design is a blend of image synthesis and classical typography together with a clear conceptual management and a strong ingredient of organic character and poetic feeling. This is why my work makes wide use of calligraphy and hand drawn or cut letters. As a whole, my work can be divided into two main categories: corporate identity images and poster design. Within the first category, I have been able to blend Colombian graphic expression with a universal vocabulary of form and visual codes. Within the second, and thanks to the size of the media, I have been able to interrelate a personal handling of letter forms and color with a classical use of typography. Apart from these two types of expression, I have been much interested in children's books, not only as an illustrator but as a writer. It is my opinion that these two languages, within the context of the child's world, demand the best of the graphic designer's capacity.

—David Consuegra

*   *   *

On one hand, heterogeneity in design production is a constant factor that very often may hinder the identification of the designer's work; on the other hand, the designer's presence can become a landmark that, in the context of reiteration and perfectionism, will end up being identified as his own style. In some cases this so called "style" comes from an excess of originality, both in the use and selection of the materials; in other cases it is fundamentally the product of a moral and aesthetic attitude. This last combination is perhaps what best describes the work of designer David Consuegra.

With an M.F.A. in design from Yale University, Consuegra is part of that generation for whom creation was always solved through graphics, typography, and image—one of the goals of the 20th century. A generation that shared the emergence of pop, the underground culture, the beatnik literature, the improvement of the offset printing, the freedom of consciousness, peace, and sex, the Vietnam fiasco, and the inoperative scheme of government-power as the ruling formulae.

It is in this context that Consuegra, coming back to his home country, found new grounds to start designing in a restless city, where the genre of absurdity and the idyllic and flamboyant vision of Che Guevara went together with the needs of a cultural and manufacturing industry with the final purpose of creating a cultural identity and therefore an image of visual identification for its entities. From his very first posters, designed at the Universidad de Los Andes, and his first trademarks—especially that for the Museo de Arte Moderno—he defined with precision and with no trace of ambiguity the presence of a true artist. The Colombian scene then started to recognize the presence of design in its daily life.

But Consuegra goes further. Due to experience and disposition, his life is linked with a permanent search. He founded a magazine, *Nova*, in 1964, and a printing firm, Triblos, in 1973, and persisted in placing design as a right in daily life. Later on, he printed his own reports, *Temas de Consulta* (*Design Themes*) from 1978 to 1982, and *Teoría & Práctica del Diseño Gráfico* (*Theory & Practice of Graphic Design*), from 1982 to 1986, and finally published his own books *ABC de Marcas Mundiales* (*ABC of World's Trademarks*, 1986) and *En Busca del Cuadrado* (*In Search of the Square*, 1992).

Consuegra's work, already extensive, displays an excellence that rests on neatness. There is no element that shows formal carelessness, the presence of something unsolved, or the insolent speed of excess. On the contrary, a laborious conceptual work, a strictness of drawing, and a dedication above pressure and tiredness informs his creative work. And even further, the longed-for abyss of metaphysics. Because Consuegra, in his fight for formal pureness, has achieved a double effect: he has established a pattern of visual rigor in his work, and he has continued in his permanent search. Proof of the latter is his *Diccionario Enciclopédico de Diseño Gráfico* (*Graphic Design Encyclopedia Dictionary*), a work still in progress.

This is why to refer to David Consuegra as a mathematician of aesthetics is not gratuitous but is the only acceptable reply.

—Camilo Umaña

## COOPER, Muriel
American graphic and book designer

**Born:** Brookline, Massachusetts. **Education:** Ohio State University, Columbus; Massachusetts College of Art, Boston, BS, 1949; Southampton College summer sessions in experimental film, Hampshire, England; Massachusetts Institute of Technology summer sessions in computer graphics, Cambridge; Fulbright scholar in exhibition design, Milan, 1957-58. **Career:** Art director and designer, Massachusetts Institute of Technology Office of Publications (now Design Services), Cambridge, 1950-57; founder-director, Muriel Cooper Media Design, Cambridge, Massachusetts, from 1958, design director/media director, from 1967; special projects director, MIT Press, Cambridge, from 1967. Instructor, University of Maryland, College Park, Boston University, Simmons College, Boston, Museum School of Fine Arts, Boston, Massachusetts College of Art, Boston, and Massachusetts Institute of Technology Department of Architecture. Lecturer, director and professor of graphics, Visible Language Workshop, Massachusetts Institute of Technology. **Member:** Board of Trustees, Massachusetts College of Art, Boston, 1981-87; American Institute of Graphic Arts, New York, 1974-77; Alliance Graphique Internationale, Paris; Undergraduate Advisory Board, Department of Communications, Simmons College, Boston, from 1983. **Honors:** Silver Medal, Israel Book Biennale; Grand Prix d'Arles for book design; Distinguished Alumni Award, Massachusetts College of Art, 1983. **Address:** Visible Language Workshop, Media Laboratory, E15-443, 20 Ames Street, Cambridge, Massachusetts 02139, U.S.A.

**Works**

*Is Anyone Taking Notice?* (McCullin) book design for MIT Press, 1973.
Travelogue (Harbutt) book design, for MIT Press, 1973.

*   *   *

Muriel Cooper was inspired by the richness of the twenties—Gertrude Stein, Alfred Stieglitz, dadaism—and by Gyorgy Kepes during his early years at the Massachusetts Institute of Technology. She is convinced that an internal structure is necessary to produce anything of lasting value. Although her designs are sometimes described as "Swiss," she has been called a "method actress of design." Her attraction to books satisfies her need to design with time, as represented by the kinetic act of turning pages, yet enables her to create a lasting product.

Her practice, including print, photography, video, and three-dimensional work, has always been synthesized with media and technology. She has interwoven her professional activities with teaching and was, in the early 1990s, at the Massachusetts Institute of Technology, where she was a professor of graphics and director of the Visible Language Workshop.

If creativity is the ability to combine unlikely elements, then her unlikely combinations are evidenced in the people, equipment, and products of the Visible Language Workshop, where a concrete poem might be wrapped around a human figure or a gigantic image produced from a slide, altered, and recreated with jets of ink in Ron MacNeil's Architecture Machine. Her special summer sessions at the MIT/VLW, held since 1979, were the first computer-design workshops in the United States. The Visible Language Workshop produced ideas and images that would be impossible in a more conventional setting.

—Al Gowan

## COSTELLOE, Paul

Irish fashion designer

**Born:** Dublin, 27 June 1945. **Education:** Attended Blackrock College, Dublin; studied at the Ecole d'Chambre Syndicale de la Haute Couture, Paris, 1967-69. **Family:** Married Anne Cooper in 1981; children: Justin, Paul-Emmet, Gavin, Jessica, Robert, William, Nicholas. **Career:**

**Paul Costelloe: spring summer 1996**

Design assistant to Jacques Esterel, Paris, 1969-71; designer, Marks & Spencer, 1972; chief house designer, A Rinascente, Milan, 1972-74; designer, Anne Fogerty, New York, Pennaco, New York, and Trimfit, Philadelphia, 1974-79; co-founder, with Robert Eitel, Paul Costelloe International Ltd. design house, from 1979; first men's collection, 1981; introduced diffusion line, Dressage, 1989; introduced Studio Line, 1992; operated boutiques in Fenwicks of London, and Brown Thomas of Dublin; opened flagship store, 156 Brompton Road, London, 1994; launched Paul Costelloe retail franchises, 1994. **Member:** London Designers Collections, United Kingdom, 1980-93. **Honors:** Fil d'Or Award, International Linen Council, 1987, 1988, 1989; nominated British Designer of the Year, 1989; Designer of the Year, *Woman's Journal* magazine, 1990; Satzenbreau Designer of the Year, 1991. **Addresses:** (headquarters) Moygashel, Dungannon, Co. Tyrone, N. Ireland BT71 7PB; (showroom and marketing) 27 Cheval Place, London SW7 1EW; (overseas offices) Dymling Ryott Modeagentur, 117 60 Stockholm, Sweden; Bogstadvelen, 5a N-0355 Oslo, Norway.

### Publications

**On COSTELLOE: articles**—"Paul Costelloe—Designer Profile" in *Vogue* (London), November 1981; "A Bit O'Costelloe" by Richard Buckley in *DNR: The Magazine* (New York), August 1984; "The Tall Guy" by Jane Eastoe in *Fashion Weekly* (London), 3 August 1989; "A Profit in His Own Land" by Nicola Jeal in *Observer* (London), 17 September 1989; "Man of the Cloth" by Robert Burgess in *Country Living* (New York), May 1991.

## COURRÈGES, André

French fashion designer

**Born:** Pau, Pyrenées Atlantiques, 9 March 1923. **Education:** Studied engineering at the École des Ponts-et-Chaussées; apprenticed with Cristobal Balenciaga, Paris, 1948-59. **Family:** Married Jacqueline Barrière in 1966, daughter: Marie. **Career:** Independent fashion designer from 1959, founding Courrèges fashion house, Paris, 1961; first haute couture collection, 1965; Couture Future high priced ready-to-wear line introduced, 1969; perfume range, 1971; menswear line, 1973; bathrooms, cars, and windsurfing equipment, from 1980; Hyperbole line, 1980; produced collection with Jean-Charles de Castelbajac, spring-summer 1994 and 1995. **Exhibitions:** *Fashion: An Anthology,* Victoria and Albert Museum, London, 1971. **Collections:** Musée Carnavalet, Paris; Musée du Costume, Paris. **Honors:** Couture Award, London, 1964. **Address:** 40 rue François Premier, 75008 Paris, France.

### Publications

**On COURRÈGES: books**—*The Fashion Makers* by Leonard Halliday, London, 1966; *The Beautiful People* by Marylin Bender, New York, 1967; *Fashion: An Anthology* by Cecil Beaton, exhibition catalogue compiled by Madeleine Ginsburg, London, 1971; *Paris Fashion: The Great Designers and Their Creations* edited by Ruth Lynam, London, 1972; *In Vogue: Sixty Years of Celebrities and Fashion* by Georgina Howell, London, 1975, 1978, New York, 1976; *World of Fashion: People, Places, Resources* by Eleanor

Lambert, New York and London, 1976; *A History of Fashion* by J. Anderson Black and Madge Garland, London, 1975, 1980; *Magic Names of Fashion* by Ernestine Carter, London, 1980; *The History of Haute Couture 1850-1950* by Diana de Marly, London, 1980; *The Collector's Book of Twentieth Century Fashion* by Frances Kennet, London and New York, 1983; *McDowell's Directory of Twentieth Century Fashion* by Colin McDowell, London, 1984; *Couture: The Great Designers* by Caroline Milbank Rennolds, New York, 1985; *The Encyclopaedia of Fashion from 1840 to the 1980s* by Georgina O'Hara, London, 1986; *Design Source Book* by Penny Sparke and others, London, 1986; **articles**—"Courrèges" by Ann Ryan in Ruth Lynam's *Couture: An Illustrated History of the Great Paris Designers and Their Creations,* New York, 1972; "Courrèges" by David Wolfe in *International Textiles* (London), April 1990; "Up, Up and Hooray! Designer André Courrèges Celebrates 25 Years of Miniskirt Fame" by Karen Schneider in *People,* 9 July 1990; "Courrèges: Back to the Future" by Katherine Betts in *Women's Wear Daily* (New York), 22 January 1991; "Courrèges," special supplement of *L'Officiel* (Paris), 1994.

*

What will the future fashion trend be? Garments must be made in bright colors, youthful styles, and they must be easy to take care of, full of spirit, and dynamic. Clothes must be liberating—they must escape conventions.

The evolution of clothes toward the year 2000 will be distinguished by the use of new materials. Fabrics will be softer, and knits will be common because of their softness and their comfort—like second skins.

—André Courrèges

*    *    *

It took Courrèges only a short time to shake off the influence of his master, Balenciaga. In 1962, he began creating his own style, and during the next three years, he presented Paris with the shortest skirts around. His visionary image, rather than momentary fashion, showed an awareness of the need for greater freedom of movement. His approach was essentially that of a couturier, interested in cut and in making the most of the inherent qualities of his fabrics. Whether in the welted seams of his coats or the fit of his trousers, the cut was impeccable, the work of an architect.

Courrèges's predominant use of white enhanced the purity of his line. The palest blue, pink, strong green, red, or black were used sparingly, for emphasis. Like Mary Quant in England, he created a "little girl" look, consisting of short skirts, flat shoes, and little caps which epitomised the youthful exuberance of the 1960s. The popularity of the look meant that his work was widely copied. Crisp, geometric dresses were reproduced in soft double jersey; tiny, well-fitting baby caps became lumpy hand-knitted and crocheted bonnets. The mass-market succeeded in adapting Courrèges's ideas at such an alarming rate that he has turned from being a strictly couture designer to making a three-pronged attack on the world of fashion by dividing up his work into couture and two lines of ready-to-wear.

By 1967, the white moon-girls and the silver-sequined, space-age outfits had fallen from grace and Courrèges had begun to pay more attention to the body itself. Subsequently, he has experimented with knitted body coverings which create the effect of a second skin and give total freedom of movement. Courrèges's de-

signs generally did not fit in with the hippie, ethnic style so popular in the 1970s, but by 1990 he was again designing successfully, thanks in part to the 1960s revival which had begun to take place.

—Hazel Clark

# COUSINS, Morison S.
American industrial and product designer

**Born:** New York City, 10 April 1934. **Education:** Studied industrial design, Pratt Institute, New York, B.I.D., 1955. **Family:** Married Leonore Weiss (divorced 1978); children: Michele, Elizabeth. **Career:** Designer, International Harvester, Fort Wayne, Indiana, 1955-56, 1958-59; designer, Ira Schwartz, Inc., New York, 1960-62; founder and partner, Cousins Design, New York, 1963-90; director of design, Tupperware, Orlando, Florida, from 1990. Visiting professor, Istituto Superiore Industrie Artistiche, Rome, 1985, Ecole Nationale Superieure, Creation Industrielle (Les Atelier), Paris, 1986, and Rhode Island School of Design, Providence, 1986; lecturer on design at universities, museums, and conferences throughout the world. **Exhibitions:** The Smithsonian, Washington, D.C., 1963; Whitney Museum of American Art, New York, 1985; Hayden Gallery, Massachusetts Institute of Technology, Cambridge, 1984; Katonah Gallery, New York, 1984; Denver Art Museum, Denver, 1985; Metropolitan Museum of Art, New York, 1992; Design Museum, London, 1992. **Collections:** National Design Museum, The Smithsonian, New York; Museum of Modern Art, New York; Museum Boymans-van Beuningen, Rotterdam; Museum für Kunst and Gewerbe, Hamburg; Staatliches Museum für angewandte Kunst, Munich; Brooklyn Museum, New York; Metropolitan Museum of Art, New York; Victoria & Albert Museum, London; Philadelphia Museum of Art, Philadelphia; Musée des Arts Décoratifs de Montreal, Canada; Denver Museum of Art, Colorado; Virginia Museum of Fine Arts, Richmond; Carnegie Museum of Art, Pittsburgh. **Honors:** Design Awards, *Industrial Design* Magazine, 1965-1991; Rome Prize, The American Academy in Rome, 1984-85; Gold Award, Industrial Design Excellence Award, Industrial Designers Society of America, 1995. **Addresses:** (office) Tupperware, P.O. Box 2353, Orlando, Florida 32802, U.S.A.

**Works**

Product designs include: *Tensor* light meter, 1964; *Space Tel* telephone, for Atari, 1984; *Gillette Promax* hair dryer, for the Gillete Company, 1980; *Dynamic* car vacuum, for Dynamic Classics; *Gillette Curly Top* hair dryer, for Gillette; *Privecode* telephone access controller, for International Mobile Machines; *Maxim* convection oven, for Maxim; *Captain Kelly* fire extinguisher, for Gillette; *FuturePhone,* for Dictaphone, 1989; *Dixie* cup dispenser, for American Can Co.; *One Touch*® canisters and serving bowls, for Tupperware; *Zuppa a Noci* bowl, for Tupperware; *Thatsa*™ bowl, for Tupperware; *Wonderlier*® bowls, for Tupperware; *Bag Saver,* for Heller, Inc.; *Double Colander,* for Tupperware; *The Oracle,* for Tupperware; *On the Dot*™ timer, for Tupperware; *Sandwich Spreader,* for Tupperware, 1996.

*    *    *

Morison Cousins: Double colander, for Tupperware

Morison S. Cousins remembers the skepticism of his classmates when, as a design student at Pratt Institute, he declared his plans to make museum quality design accessible for the average person. Some thirty years later, the skeptics are believers. Nearly two dozen of his mass produced consumer products, bought by millions, have been acquired by museums for their design collections. The most recent products to be acquired by museums are his designs for Tupperware, which are characterized by pure geometric forms, subtle curves, elegant lines, simplicity, and sculptural elements.

Cousins always considered the geometric particularly appropriate to manufacturing. While living in Italy as the 1984 recipient of the Rome Prize from the American Academy (the second industrial designer ever to receive this honor from the 100-year-old Academy), he confirmed this tenet as he realized that pure geometric shapes produce the most aesthetically pleasing and timeless objects.

His precise and organized approach to form is steadied by an interest in the sculptural and a sensibility enamored of Brancusi's *Bird in Flight*. In his designs, geometric forms and sculptural elements converge, resulting in softness. The carefully proportioned rectangle of the *Tensor* light meter (1964), as well as the highly

organized design of the Atari *SpaceTel* telephone (1984), provide evidence of his extremely precise approach. His appreciation for the sculptural is present in early works such as a rendering of a percolator (1962) and the handles of Bonny flatware (1967). The juxtaposition of the geometric and the sculptural is beautifully exemplified in Dictaphone's *FuturePhone* (1989), a concept project. The strong geometric shapes of the work station and the grid-like approach to the arrangement of the controls is off-set by the handpiece's "crushed tube" form. This sculptural form came from a package Cousins designed and patented in 1968. The same shape appears again in the handle of *Sandwich Spreader,* a knife with flexible blade which will be released by Tupperware in the second half of 1996. The soft, elegant pared-down look of the *Gillette Promax* hair dryer's (1980) two crisp, perpendicular cylinders has made it a classic.

The Tupperware brand products Cousins has designed in the 1990s possess pure geometric shapes and sculptural elements. Tupperware's *On the Dot*™ kitchen timer is composed of simple forms in their purest state—cone, semi-circle, circle, and sphere. *Double Colander*'s base is a complete hemisphere with five arc-shaped legs; the sweeping, elegantly curved line of the cover contributes to its gracefulness. The bowls of the *Thatsa*™ bowl and

*Wonderlier®* bowl are hemispheres with the minimum cut off to create a steady base. *Thatsa™ Bowl's* sensuous quality derives from the bowl's full, rounded lip as it dips and broadens into an arc-shaped handle.

At times, charm camouflages the serious design considerations that create functional products. The user finds charm in the most utilitarian Tupperware *Bag Saver,* which brings a light-hearted mood and welcome order to the unruly collection of plastic bags people acquire when making purchases. It also invites a smile of recognition when people realize it looks like a happy face. *One Touch®* serving bowls, another Tupperware brand product, feature two double-arc handles that provide leverage for easy removal of the seals while adding charm. A trio of vegetable peelers he designed for Tupperware feature spritely cut-outs located near the handle's base, contributing a whimsical element.

Cousins believes that functional objects must be beautiful: "If it isn't lovely, it really doesn't function well."

—Florence D'Emilia

# COUTAUD, Lucien
French painter, mural, tapestry, and stage designer

**Born:** Meynes, Gard, 12 December 1904. **Education:** Studied at the Collège Saint-Stanislas, Nîmes, Ecole des Beaux-Arts, Nîmes, and the Ecole des Beaux-Arts, Paris. **Family:** Married Denise Bernollen in 1936. **Career:** Independent painter and stage designer, Paris, from 1928; worked with Charles Dullin's Atelier Théâtre, Paris, the Boboli Gardens, Florence, Italy, the Comèdie Francaise, Paris, and the Maggio Fiorentino, Florence; created three tapestries for the liner, *France,* and murals for the National Institute of Deaf-Mutes and the Palace of Discovery, Paris. Professor of etching, Ecole Nationale Superieure des Beaux-Arts, Paris, from 1964. **Member:** Founder-member of the Salon de Mai, Paris. **Exhibitions:** *Coutaud, Labisse, Couturier,* Musée Galliera, Paris, 1962; Musée d'Ingres, Montauban, France, 1969; also exhibited at Galerie Roux, Galerie Hentschel, Galerie Bonaparte, Galerie Maeght, David et Garnier, Sagotle Garrec, and Galerie Lucie Weill, all in Paris. **Collections:** Centre Georges Pompidou, Paris; Musee d'Art Moderne de la Ville, Paris. **Honors:** Grand Prix des Beaux-Arts de la Ville de Paris; Prix Daniel Wildenstein, Paris, 1971; Chevalier de la Légion d'Honneur, France; Officer des Arts et des Lettres, France. **Died:** Paris, June 1977.

## Publications

**By COUTAUD: books**—*J'aime le théâtre,* Lausanne, 1962.

**On COUTAUD: books**—*Décors de théâtre* by Raymond Cogniat, Paris, 1930; *La Tapisserie française* edited by P. Tisne, Paris, 1946; *Reflexions sur le théâtre* by Jean-Louis Barrault, Paris, 1949; *Les Cahiers d'Art-Documents, No. 32: Lucien Coutaud 1904* edited by Pierre Caillier, Geneva, 1956; *Cinq peintres et le théâtre* by Hélène Parmelin, Paris, 1956; *La Tapisserie* by Roger-Armand Weigert, Paris, 1956; *Catalogue raisonne de l'oeuvre gravé et lithographie de Lucien Coutaud* by Jean Adhémar, Geneva, 1960; *Coutaud, Labisse, Couturier,* exhibition catalogue, by Georges Charbonnier and others, Paris,

1962; *Lucien Coutaud* by Pierre Mazans, Geneva, 1964; *Coutaud: peintures, dessins et gravures,* exhibition catalogue, by Pierre Barbousse, Montauban, 1969; *The Decorative Thirties* by Martin Battersby, London, 1969, 1974, 1976.

# COVERI, Enrico
Italian fashion designer

**Born:** Prato, 26 February 1952. **Education:** Studied stage design, Accademia di Belle Arti, Florence, 1971-74. **Career:** Freelance fashion designer, working for Tycos, Touche, Acquarius, Lux Sports, Gentry, and Ilaria Knitwear, in Milan, 1972-79; established Enrico Coveri S.p.A. fashion firm, Milan, 1978, and Enrico Coveri France S.A.R.L., Paris, 1983; opened via San Pietro all'Orto boutique, Milan, 1981, and subsequent shops in Genoa, Viareggio, Piacenza, Paris, Saint Tropez, Beirut, and New York; launched perfumes *Paillettes,* 1982, *Dollars,* 1983, *Enrico Coveri pour Homme,* 1983, *Enrico Coveri pour Femme,* 1988, and *Firenze,* 1993; introduced home furnishing line, 1984; signed contract with Itochu, Ltd., to import to Japan, 1988; make-up line, *Coloratis-Sima,* introduced in 1989. **Exhibitions:** *Consequenze Impreviste,* Prato, 1982; *Italian Re-Evolution,* La Jolla Museum of Art, California, 1982; San Francisco Museum of Modern Art, 1982; Museum of Contemporary Art, Hartford, Connecticut, 1983; Musée d'Art Contemporain, Montréal, 1983; *Il Genio Antipatico,* Rome, 1984; Promotional Exhibition, Japan, 1985; Montreal Exhibition, Canada, 1987. **Honors:** World's Most Elegant Man Award, Paris, 1980; Uomo Europeo Award, Rome, 1982; Fil d'Or, Munich, 1982; Folklore e Turismo Prize, Prato, 1984; Pris Golden Medal, Paris, 1987; Ufficiale dell'Ordine della Republica, Rome, 1987; Italian Red Cross Gratitude Declaration, Pistoia, 1988; "Best Shop Windows" Prize, Firenze, 1989. **Died:** Florence, Italy, 6 December 1990.

## Publications

**On COVERI: books**—*I Mass-Moda: Falli e Personaggi dell 'Italian Look/The Who's Who of Italian Fashion,* with text by Adriana Mulassano, Florence, 1979; *Italian Re-Evolution: Design in Italian Society in the Eighties,* exhibition catalogue, edited by Piero Sartogo, La Jolla, 1982; *McDowell's Directory of Twentieth Century Fashion* by Colin McDowell, London, 1984; **articles**—in *Hommes Vogue* (Paris), March/April 1978; "Enrico Coveri: lo stilista del colore" by Luisa Baldacci in *Arbiter* (Milan), No. 2, 1982; *Il Tempo* (Milan), 17 September 1982; *Il Messagero* (Rome), 21 March 1983; "Enrico Coveri illustra il segreto della sua moda" in *La Nazione* (Florence), 14 June 1983; "Enrico Coveri: graffiti che corrono e ballano" in *Vogue* (Milan), January 1985; "Parigi: spot su Enrico Coveri. Enorme o incollato, la moda degli opposti" in *Vogue* (Milan), February 1985; "Enrico Coveri: nuovi schemi per il classico" in *L'Uomo Vogue* (Milan), July/August 1985; "Enrico Coveri" by Daniela Morera and Joe Dolce in *Interview* (New York), February 1986; "Enrico Coveri: uno stile all'inglese" in *Donna* (Milan), July/August 1987; "Enrico Coveri: righe, quadri, forme base..." in *Vogue* (Milan), January 1988; "Enrico Coveri Dies in Italy of Stroke" in *Women's Wear Daily* (New York), 10 December 1990.

\*    \*    \*

**Enrico Coveri: From autumn/winter collection, 1995**

"I go by instincts," said Enrico Coveri in 1979, "like puppies and children." A prodigy of young fashion, beginning with brilliant knitwear in the 1970s when so much attention was given to naive, creatively charged fashion, Coveri became an important force in young fashion and in retailing in the 1980s, but died in 1990 at the age of 38. If Coveri was so inexorably oriented to the young, a Pop sensibility, and exuberant fashion and so taken with intuition over the regimens of a fashion discipline, how could his collection be sustained in the 1990s? Coveri's fall-winter 1996-97 men's collection was newly named "Ricerche di Enrico Coveri," a line that brims with the youth and enthusiasm that was always the designer's forte. Strangely and a little ominously, even for a fall-winter collection, it tones down Coveri's history of fresh, brazen color. Posthumously, Coveri's company still projects the powerful imagery that seemed to be embodied only in the man and his era; Coveri has become abiding style, perennial youth, and illimitable day-glo brightness. Yet the sense of research or discovery remains for a design company that still values its role as the incubator of young ideas about simplified clothing. Never wholly persuasive in defining womenswear, the company has lately concentrated on the men's clothing that was always its aptitude.

Like many Italian designers of the post-War epoch, Coveri's first instinct was color in knits. His poor-boy sweaters and dazzling scarfs took the high color of popular culture, especially magazine reproductions, to the motives of youthful sportswear. There was no complication of the silhouette. At times, the Coveri look of the 1980s and 1990s could seem to be Benetton, so simple is its structure, but Coveri pushed color to luscious orange-crate oranges and zapped comic-book yellows. Further, knitwear encourages the natural Pop propensity to verbal expression in Coveri, borrowing sportswear's love of language and identifiers to use the Coveri name and logo in many designs from sweaters and scarfs through shirts and T-shirts. In fall-winter 1995-96, sweaters were graphically bold in high color.

Through the 1990s, the menswear of Enrico Coveri has taken on the palette of painting and vegetation, especially for the spring-summer collections, always the strength of Coveri in his lifetime. The Florence flagship boutique glows as a fruit basket of color. In spring-summer 1991, for example, linen blazers and light-weight coats were simple in cut, but aflame in color from bright reds through blue and turquoise. The spring-summer 1995 collection was indicative of the Coveri dilemma: some of the menswear tried to look grown-up and assume sophistication, but when it did, it looked like that of every other Italian designer of sophistication. Coveri fails to convince anyone that it holds Missoni's magic or Versace's sensuality. Rather, Coveri showed some pieces of what it does best: the touristic, Byblos-more-Byblos-than-Byblos kind of eternal sunlight, perpetual vacation-world that Coveri himself projected. There, the bold primaries and the over-the-top colors from the cabana begin to succeed. The company's 1996 recourse to the workshop should not be a signal to pretend to grow up and become academic. Rather, it should be a rejuvenation to the signature Coveri product, audacious, fresh, and colorful. Further, Coveri's progress parallels that of Moschino, which also attempts to sustain the designer's impish and idiosyncratic humor best only when it is as outrageously irreverent as its deceased founder was.

One prizes in Coveri clothing its utter lack of sophistication and its insistence on basics in color and graphic intensity. Coveri's legacy only falters when the collections of the 1990s seem to struggle to be tasteful and to try to grow up, a destiny that the designer never realized. What is a life's loss may, in fact, be the prize of the design that ought remain ever young.

—Richard Martin

# CRINION, Jonathan

Canadian industrial and furniture designer

**Born:** Liverpool, England, in 1953. **Education:** Studied industrial design, Carleton University, Ottawa; studied architecture, University of Toronto School of Architecture; studied product and systems design, Ontario College of Art, graduated 1980. **Career:** Designer, Kuyper Adamson Norton Ltd., Toronto, 1981; director of operations and design, Kuyper Adamson Norton Ltd., Vancouver, 1982-83; designer, Foster Associates, London, England, 1983; founder and principal, Crinion Associates Ltd., Toronto, from 1983; design consultant to Area, The Knoll Group, Teknion Furniture Systems Inc., Kiosk Mobilia, and others. Guest lecturer, Emily Carr College of Art and Design, Vancouver, 1983, Faculty of Architecture, Guelph University, Ontario, 1986, Ontario College of Art, Toronto, 1986-92, University of Toronto School of Architecture, 1992, and Technical University of Nova Scotia. **Member:** Board member, 1988, Association of Chartered Industrial Designers of Ontario, 1983-89; Chartered Society of Designers, London, England, from 1988. **Exhibitions:** *Creative Spark,* Royal Canadian Academy of Art, 1986 (toured Canada); *Canada Designs for Business,* Tokyo, 1992; *From Start to Furnish: Contemporary Furniture Design,* Genereux Grunwald Gallery, Toronto, 1993. **Collections:** Design Exchange, Toronto. **Honors:** Industrial Design Award, *ID* magazine, 1988, 1993; Virtu International Design Competition winner, 1989, 1991; Institute of Business Designers award, 1993; NeoCon Gold Awards, 1993, 1994; International Design Forty, *ID* magazine, 1994; Product Award, Association of Registered Interior Designers of Ontario, 1994. **Address:** Crinion Associates, 25A Morrow Avenue, Toronto, Ontario M6R 2H9, Canada.

## Works

*Universal Transaction Terminal,* for Esso Canada, 1985.
*Portable Transaction Terminal,* for Pinpoint Retail Systems Inc., 1986.
*Universal Transaction Terminal,* for Pinpoint Retail Systems Inc., 1986.
Outdoor credit authorization terminal, for Pinpoint Retail Systems Inc., 1986.
Inventory control terminal, for Pinpoint Retail Systems Inc., 1986.
*Gazelle Chair,* for Area, 1986.
*Aero* cafe table, for Area, 1988.
Under-cabinet task lamp, for Esmond Mfg. Inc., 1991.
Commercial composting system, for ECO Corporation, 1992.
*Teknion Banking* solution, Teknion Furniture Systems Inc., 1992.
Solid state HVAC panel, Teknion Furniture Systems Inc., 1992.
Color liquid crystal display with arm, Teknion Furniture Systems Inc., 1992.
Variable length office lighting, for Esmond Mfg. Inc., 1992.

Color and black and white LCD displays, for Teknion Furniture
  Systems Inc., 1993.
*Porky* CPU trolley, for Teknion Furniture Systems Inc., 1993.
*TeamBoard,* for Egan Visual, 1994.
*System 6 Enhancements* office furniture system, for The Knoll
  Group, 1994.
*Companion,* for The Knoll Group, 1994.
*Bebop* chair, for Kiosk Mobilia, 1995.

**Publications**

**By CRINION: articles**—"Tales of the Future Workplace" in *Insite*
(London), November 1993.

**On CRINION: books**—*Virtu 5,* exhibition catalogue, 1990; *Design and Technology,* Toronto, 1993; **articles**—"Terry Fox Plaza Competition" in *Vancouver Sun,* February 1983; "Terry Fox Plaza Competition" in *Canadian Architect* (Don Mills, Ontario), March 1983; "Terry Fox Plaza Competition" in *Architects Forum,* July 1983; "What You'll See Is All There Is: That Says it All" in *Globe and Mail* (Toronto), 7 June 1986; "Jonathan Crinion/Industrial Designers Ltd.: The Firm and Its Work" in *Azure,* December 1986; *ID Magazine Annual Review* (New York), July 1987, July 1988; "Keeping the Seat in Mind" in *Globe and Mail,* 7 May 1988; "Canada—On the Boarder Line" in *ID* (New York), May/June 1988; "Contemporary Furniture Shows Its Metal" in *Canadian Art* (Toronto), Winter 1989; *Azure,* December/January 1989/90; "Great Out of Doors" in *Homes,* May 1990; *Canadian Interiors,* October 1990; "Form and Content" in *Globe and Mail,* 5 March 1992; "The Unsung Heroes of Teknion" in *Contract* (New York), October/November 1992; "The Industrial Art of Jonathan Crinion" in *Contract,* October/November 1992; "The Teknion Technique" in *Azure,* November 1992; "Canadian Firm Wins Office Design Award" in *Financial Post* (Toronto), 21-23 November 1992; "Offices for a New Generation" in *Globe and Mail,* 7 January 1993; "Knows No Boundaries, Personalities Jonathan Crinion" in *Contract Design* (New York), October 1993; "Companion Wanted" in *Azure,* October 1993; "International Design Forty" in *ID* (New York), January/February 1994; "Knoll Targets Home-office Workers with Crinion's *Companion*" in *Globe and Mail,* 5 May 1994; "Team Player" in *Insite* (London), November 1994.

*       *       *

Toronto-based Jonathan Crinion is one of North America's leading industrial designers working in the office systems furniture market. In this thriving industry, Crinion has designed everything from panel-based office systems, to systems furniture specifically for banks, to products to work within these systems like mobile presentation boards.

Jonathan Crinion was born in Liverpool, England in 1953. He grew up in Ottawa, the capital of Canada, where his father was a vice-president of Canada Mortgage and Housing Corporation, the federal government agency responsible for stimulating the post-war housing market. Accompanying his father on visits to architectural studios, Crinion developed an early appreciation for design. He graduated from Toronto's Ontario College of Art in 1980. The systems approach to industrial design espoused in the school at this time made a strong impact on Crinion.

After graduation Crinion worked at Kuyper Adamson Norton Industrial Designers (KAN) in Toronto, Canada's leading multi-disciplinary design firm. KAN was the training ground for many Canadian industrial designers and for the next three years Crinion contributed to exhibition, furniture, and product design projects.

In 1983 Crinion opened his own design firm in Toronto. The *Gazelle* chair, created on speculation, became his first critically acclaimed work. Manufactured by the Ontario-based AREA Group in 1986, the design is inspired by Ernest Race's 1951 *Antelope* chair. Crinion adopted the *Antelope*'s curved metal arms, but used tubular metal instead of metal rod. Bending the sweeping curved arms required computerized equipment and reflected the new trend toward digital production. Crinion intended the *Gazelle* to compete with commonplace indoor/outdoor metal furniture and so far it has succeeded. Over 20,000 stacking *Gazelle* chairs have been sold throughout North America and the design remains in production.

In 1988, while on vacation in England, Crinion visited the "high tech" architectural firm of Sir Norman Foster. The office needed help with a furniture project for the Italian manufacturer Tecno and offered Crinion a job. In addition to helping refine the Nomos furniture system, Crinion contributed to the design of the firm's radical new office, with no private offices but one open room, and 200 people sharing just 13 row-length tables positioned towards a spectacular wall-to ceiling-view of the Thames. The result inspires Crinion to this day.

Since returning to Toronto in 1990, Crinion has become one of the leading designers of systems office furniture in North America. His clients have included Teknion, Egan Visual, and the Knoll Group. In 1992, Knoll commissioned Crinion to update its *System 6* office furniture. Crinion examined offices of leading edge designers and progressive corporations throughout North America. He concluded that the image of the typical worker sitting in an office cubicle amid a maze of panel-based furniture is giving way to a person sitting on a park bench with a laptop. Crinion's *System 6 Enhanced* offers greater flexibility for the emerging unstructured, impromptu office environment and has a wider variety of storage components, for everything from computer disks to a pair of shoes. Of particular note is the Knoll *Companion* storage unit, a cross between a grammar school desk and a Shaker cabinet on wheels. This desk height caddy has cleverly arranged drawers and cupboards for storing work-in-progress. Its mobility and small size also make it attractive to the expanding home office market.

In 1994, *International Design* magazine included Crinion in the International Design 40, its annual list of the top forty designers in the world. He is the first Canadian designer to receive this honor.

—Elizabeth Crawford and Rachel Gotlieb

# CROSBY, Theo

British architect and interior, exhibition, and industrial designer

**Born:** Mafeking, South Africa, 3 April 1925; settled in England, 1947. **Education:** Studied at the University of Witwatersrand, Johannesburg, B.Arch., 1947; attended Sir John Cass School, Central School of Art, and St. Martin's School of Art, all in London, 1947-56. **Military Service:** Served in the British Army in the 6th South Africa Armored Division, 1944-46, Signaller. **Family:** Married Anne Buchanan in 1960 (separated, 1977); children: Dido and Matthew. **Career:** Assistant architect, Fry, Drew, and Partners, then Fry, Drew, Drake, and Lasdun, London, 1947-52; technical editor, *Architectural Design* magazine, London, 1953-62; chief architect, Taylor Woodrow Euston Station project, London, 1962-64; founder-partner, with Alan Fletcher and Colin Forbes, of Crosby/Fletcher/Forbes, London, 1965-72, and with Fletcher, Forbes, Kenneth Grange, and Mervyn Kurlansky, of Pentagram Design, London and New York, 1972-94. Associate, Royal Institute of British Architects, 1944; fellow, Society of Industrial Design, 1963; associate, Royal Academy of Art, London, 1983. **Member:** Akademie der Künste, Berlin, 1978. **Exhibitions:** Institute of Contemporary Arts, London, 1960. **Honors:** Grand Prize, Milan Triennale, 1963; two Architectural Heritage Year Awards, 1973. **Died:** 14 September 1994.

## Works

*This Is Tomorrow* exhibition layouts, Whitechapel Art Gallery, London, 1956.
*The Architecture of Technology* exhibition layouts, for the International Union of Architects, London, 1961.
British section displays at the Milan Triennale, 1964.
Industry displays at the British pavilion, *Expo '67,* Montreal, 1967.
*The Lookout* observation lounge interiors on the *Queen Elizabeth II,* 1968.
Cape Universal Building Products display at the *International Building Exhibition,* Olympia, London, 1969.
Office interiors, for Rowe Rudd, Moorgate, London, 1969.
Office conversion and interiors, for Boase Massimi Pollitt advertising agency, Paddington, London, 1972, 1979.
*The Environment Game* exhibition layouts, Hayward Gallery, London, 1973.
Office interiors, for Geers Gross advertising agency, London, 1975, 1982.
*British Genius* exhibition layouts, Battersea Park, London, 1976.
Unilever House refurbishment and interiors, London, 1978-83.
Globe Theatre reconstruction and museum complex, South Bank, London, from 1982.
Headquarters building interiors, for Nederlandse Middelstande Bank, Amsterdam, 1984.
*Battle of Britain* monument, London, 1987.

(for a complete list of buildings and architectural projects, see *Contemporary Architects*)

## Publications

**By CROSBY: books**—*This Is Tomorrow,* exhibition catalogue, London, 1956; *Le Corbusier,* exhibition catalogue, London, 1959; (with Monica Pidgeon) *An Anthology of Houses,* London, 1960; *The Architecture of Technology, Designer,* London, 1961; *Architecture: City Sense,* London and New York, 1964; *The Necessary Monument,* London, 1969; (with Alan Fletcher and Colin Forbes) *A Sign Systems Manual,* London, 1970; (with Pentagram partners) *Pentagram: The Work of Five Designers,* London, 1972; *How to Play the Environment Game,* London, 1973; (with Pentagram partners) *Living with Design,* London, 1978; (with Pentagram partners) *Ideas on Design,* London, 1986; *Let's Build a Monument,* London, 1987; *The Battle of Britain Monument,* London, 1987.

**On CROSBY: books**—*Signs in Action* by James Sutton, London and New York, 1965; *European Designers: England, France, Italy* edited by Idea publishers, Tokyo, 1970; *History of the Poster* by Josef and Shizuko Muller-Brockmann, Zürich, 1971; *Design by Choice* by Reyner Banham, London, 1981.

\*

My work as a designer originates in a nine-year period as an editor of *Architectural Design* with Monica Pidgeon. I did the layouts, covers, and some writing—and learned a great deal about graphics, particularly from my friend Edward Wright.

The general basis of my work is collaborative in the sense that I see the designer's work as creating complex ensembles in which many other talents can be deployed. Diaghilev would be an exemplar.

I thus try to see all my tasks as an opportunity to extend the nature of a problem by involving the best people I know and by setting up the work in such a way as to make it easier for them to do good work. In most cases, this approach is rewarding and successful, and the client is often conspicuously well served.

In the general run of my practice, which consists of generally small-scale and complex interiors, I indulge in the design work myself. The task is often too small to involve someone else with dignity. These little tasks have developed into modest examples of furniture, stained glass, and other decorative works.

My main ambition is to re-engage the arts and crafts into the fabric of architecture, to make it as ordinary and integral a process as it used to be. This means relearning a great deal of architectural history, of the grammar of an ornament which has been discarded by the modern movement, and trying to make each task a practical demonstration.

—Theo Crosby

\*   \*   \*

The nine years Theo Crosby worked for the magazine *Architectural Design* introduced him to the British design establishment, and in 1956, he was appointed secretary and organiser of the influential exhibition *This is Tomorrow,* held at the Whitechapel Art Gallery. Working with more than thirty of Britain's most avant-garde architects, designers, and fine artists placed him firmly at the centre of new directions. This experience also initiated a successful exhibition-design career, which has included The British Section (with others) of the 1964 Milan Triennale, which was awarded a Gran Premio; the section of the British Industry Pavilion at *Expo '67,* for which he collaborated on films as well as the exhibition design; and the *British Genius* exhibition at Battersea Park for the Jubilee Year in 1978. In the mid-1960s, Crosby decided not to enter an architectural practice but to team up with graphic designers Alan Fletcher and Colin Forbes to form the nucleus of the group that became Pentagram in 1972. As a team, this firm of distinguished individualists have had an enormous impact on British design. Crosby took responsibility for such areas as exhibition, interior, and environmental design, which he carried out, like the other partners, with his own team of designers. Throughout his career, he stressed the importance of teamwork, seeing design as "the product of many inputs." Typical works include a shopping centre at Lewisham and the Arts Council book shop in London.

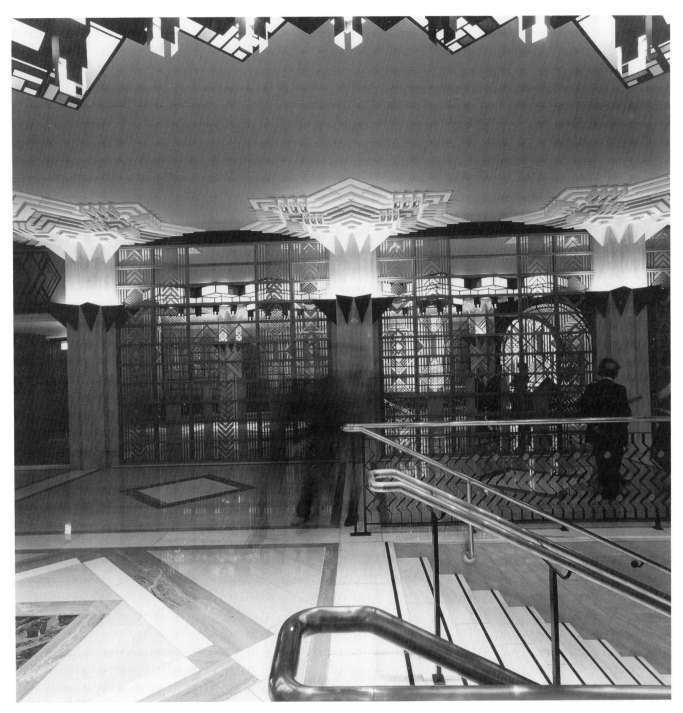

Theo Crosby: Unilever House interiors, Blackfriars, London, 1978-82

In the 1970s and 1980s, however, Crosby became the outspoken champion for decoration. Speaking at a seminar on art and architecture at the Institute of Contemporary Art in London, he talked about the important role the arts and crafts play in contemporary architecture and about his faith in the role of architectural history and its models, such as 19th-century books on the grammar of ornament. This rejection of the modernist ideology was also present in his work; the 1970s renovation of Nash House included decorative corbels, and he wrote on the need for a return to embellishment.

However, the project that brought these ideas to fruition was his work for Unilever in London. In the late 1970s Unilever decided to refurbish their 1939 head office rather than move out of the city, and they picked Crosby to design the scheme. Choosing to highlight and expand the Art Deco element with the large budget he had, Crosby designed carpets, Art Deco railings, diamond-shaped acrylic light fittings, and stylishly mirrored lifts. The tour-de-force main entrance with its blue-plaster ceilings topped with gold leaf and its white exotic columns opened in 1982 to acclaim in the design and architectural press, partly because the scale of the work was un-usual in Britain, but mainly because the ensemble was not a pas-tiche of the 1930s elements but an assembly of design motifs syn-thesized in a radically new way.

—Catherine McDermott

# CROUWEL, Wim (Willem Henrick)

Dutch exhibition, industrial, and graphic designer

**Born:** Groningen, 21 November 1928. **Education:** Groningen, un-til 1946; Akademie Minerva, Groningen, 1947-49; Institut voor Kunstnijverheidsonderwijs, Amsterdam, 1951-52. **Military Ser-vice:** Dutch Army, 1949-51. **Career:** Freelance designer, special-izing in exhibition design, Amsterdam, 1952-57; established design studio with architect Kho Liang le, Amsterdam, 1957-61; founded Wim Crouwel design studio, Amsterdam, 1961-63; founder and co-director, Total Design studio, Amsterdam, from 1963. Exhibitions and publications designer, for the Van Abbemuseum Eindhoven, 1955-63, and Stedelijk Museum, Amsterdam, from 1963. Instruc-tor, Koninklijke Akademie voor Kunst en Vormgeving, Den Bosch, 1954-57, and Institut voor Kunstnijverheidsonderwijs, Amsterdam, 1955-63; instructor in industrial design, Technical High School, Delft, from 1965. Graphics and design series editor, for Uitgeverij Lecturis, Eindhoven, 1974-79. Secretary General, ICOGRADA Inter-national Council of Graphic Design Associations, 1963-66. **Member:** Stichting Bond voor Kunst en Industrie Prijs, from 1974; Buitenlandse Tentoonstellingen CRM; President, Stichting Openbaar Kunstbezit, from 1977; Commission member, Museum Boymans-van Beuningen, Rotterdam, from 1980; President, Stichting Rietveld Schroderhuis, Utrecht, and the Stichting Van Doesburghuis, Paris, from 1980. **Exhi-bitions:** *20 Jaar Kalenders Drukkerij Van de Geer,* Printgallery Pieter Brattinga, Amsterdam, 1976; *Bladen en Spaties,* Printgallery Pieter Brattinga, Amsterdam, 1976; *Overzichtstentoonstelling,* Stedelijk Mu-seum, Amsterdam, 1979; *Overzichtstentoonstelling,* TNO, Apeldoorn, 1979. **Address:** Herengracht 567, 1017 CD Amsterdam, Netherlands.

## Publications

**By CROUWEL: books—***Nieuw Alfabet: een mogelijkheid voor de nieuwe ontwikkeling,* Hilversum, 1967; (with Kurt Weidemann) *An International Survey of Packaging,* London and Teufen, 1968; (with others) *3 x Trademarks,* Stuttgart, 1968; *Ontwerpen en drukken,* Amsterdam, 1974; **articles—**in *Drukkersweekblad* (Amsterdam), January 1958; *Forum* (Amsterdam), July 1961; *Print* (New York), no. 1, 1964; *Artscanada* (Toronto), June 1968; *Delta* (Amsterdam), no. 1, 1969; *Visible Language* (Cleveland), Summer 1974; *Holland Herald* (Amsterdam), December 1975; *TD-Publikatie* (Amsterdam), January 1977; *De Tijds* (Amsterdam), 13 July 1979.

**On CROUWEL: books—***Advertising Directions* by Edward M. Gottschall and Arthur Hawkins, New York, 1959; *Buchgestaltung* by Albert Kapr, Dresden, 1963; *An International Survey of Press Advertising* by Kurt Weidemann, Stuttgart and London, 1966; *Monografie des Plakats* by Herbert Schindler, Munich, 1972; *Wim Crouwel: Ontwerpen en Drukken* edited by Gerrit Jan Theimefonds,

Amsterdam, 1974; *Archigraphia: Architectural and Environmental Graphics* edited by Walter Herdeg, Zurich, 1978; *The Language of Graphics* by Edward Booth-Clibborn and Daniele Baroni, London, 1980.

\*      \*      \*

Wim Crouwel designs with the general public in mind. For more than three decades, he has imaginatively constructed esthetic solu-tions to design and communication problems encountered in mu-seum exhibitions and signage systems, in publications such as cata-logues and books, in letterforms and symbols, as well as in environ-mental displays. Crouwel believes that messages are relayed most effectively through plain and clear, yet creative, solutions. The unifying element running through all of Crouwel's work and in particular his widely circulated promotional posters, is his reliance on the geometry of a grid system.

In 1963, Crouwel was a founding partner in Total Design, the first Dutch design firm sufficiently large and diversified to take on comprehensive design projects in both public and private sectors. Almost simultaneously, he launched his influential design activities at the Stedelijk Museum in Amsterdam, thereby initiating a second long-term association with which his work has been particularly identified.

Before Total Design was formed, Crouwel worked in partner-ship with Kho Liang le, with whom he figured prominently in Pieter Brattinga's progressive gallery at de Jong lithographers in Hilversum. They redesigned the gallery space in 1958, and for the succession of exhibits that followed, they frequently contributed to the design of the exhibitions themselves.

In his 1967 publication *Nieuw Alfabet* [New Alphabet], Crouwel advocates a new type design aimed at the requirements of modern communication. He points out the efficiency and importance of updating type design to meet the demands of the computer age. The alphabet that he proposed "merely as an initial step" consists en-tirely of horizontal and vertical lines so that the letters may be clearly displayed on cathode ray tubes for the benefit of computer users and television viewers. Crouwel's ultimate goal is a simple and basic alphabet of universal application. He feels that mechani-cal reproduction will never match the perfection of which the hu-man eye is capable in producing legibility and esthetic feeling. He further suggests that our type design should reflect the current culture, which, of course, cannot be seen in its entirety today but may be sensed. It is unlikely, therefore, that one alphabet will satisfy our needs for any length of time. Crouwel goes so far as to suggest that a computer-language of pictograms might one day ful-fill our needs, for in principle his concern is with "communication symbols."

Crouwel has also focused his attention on package design—in effect, a three-dimensional means of communication. A year's work of critical analysis in collaboration with Kurt Weidemann produced the 1968 book *An International Survey of Packaging.* Here, the authors put forth their conception of the ideal package as one that comprises "a sound product, a new idea, a pleasing, functional, and easily-handled shape, and good graphics."

Crouwel consistently puts his many talents as designer, writer, thinker, and educator into his work as a communicator. He always demonstrates a knack for projecting information in the most ratio-nal and analytical of formats. The messages he sends are under-standable and meaningful, and they reach the audiences for which they are intended.

Crouwel has demonstrated that a market exists for clear, concise, and consistent design work, as may be demonstrated by his work for the Dutch government. Having worked with public agencies for several years, in 1967 he was appointed designer for the Dutch pavilion at the 1970 World's Fair in Osaka. Working with Eli Gros, he engineered an audio-visual display depicting Rotterdam's urban planning scheme through the year 2000. The pavilion might be seen as the "package" with which the Netherlands was presented for all to see and understand.

—Catherine L. Currier

# CUMMINGS, Donna
Canadian interior designer

**Born:** Uxbridge, Ontario, in 1945. **Education:** Studied interior design at the Ontario College of Art, graduated 1967. **Career:** Interior designer, Csagoly Miller Savage, Toronto, and Rice Brydone Ltd., Toronto; co-founder, Marshall Cummings & Associates, Toronto 1975. **Member:** Association of Registered Interior Designers of Ontario; Interior Designers of Canada; Toronto Board of Trade. **Address:** Marshall Cummings & Associates Ltd., 43 Davies Avenue, Toronto, Ontario M4M 2A9, Canada.

# CYRÉN, Gunnar (Carl)
Swedish silversmith and glass designer

**Born:** Gävle, 23 July 1931. **Education:** National College of Art, Craft and Design (Konstfackskolan), Stockholm, goldsmith diploma, 1951, silversmith diploma, 1956; apprenticed to silversmith Sven-Arne Gillgren, Stockholm, 1953-56; studied at Kolner Werkschule, Cologne, 1954. **Family:** Married Birgitta Backstrom in 1957; children: Marten, Henrik and Gustav. **Career:** Freelance designer, in Stockholm, 1956-59; designer, Orrefors Glassworks, Sweden, 1959-70, and from 1976; also freelance designer, for Dansk Design Ltd., New York, from 1970; established own silversmith's studio, Gävle, from 1975. Co-owner and director, Gallery Argentum, Stockholm, 1976-80, and Gallery Gamla Stan, Stockholm, 1981-86; owner-director, Gallery Gunnar Cyrén, Gävle, from 1986. **Exhibitions:** *Hantverkets, 60-tal,* Nationalmuseum, Stockholm, 1968; *Scandinavian Modern Design 1880-1980,* CooperHewitt Museum, New York, 1982; *Aktuell Svensk Form,* Ibsenhuset, Skien, 1982; *Design Since 1945,* Philadelphia Museum of Art, 1983; *Contemporary Swedish Design,* Nationalmuseum, Stockholm, 1983 (toured Sweden); *The Lunning Prize,* Nationalmuseum, Stockholm, 1986; *Faces of Swedish Design,* IBM Gallery, New York, 1988 (toured the United States). **Collections:** Nationalmuseum, Stockholm. **Honors:** Medal for Proficiency and Industry, Swedish Society of Industrial Design, 1956; Lunning Prize, 1966; Prince Eugen Medal, 1988; appointed Professor by Swedish Government, 1992. **Address:** Box 6101, 80006 Gävle, Sweden.

## Works

*Pop Glass* wine glasses with colored stems, for Orrefors, 1965.
Painted glass bowls, for Orrefors, 1967.
*Frescati* wine glasses, for Orrefors, 1968.
*Serpent* silver goblet, 1976.
*Helena* wine glasses, for Orrefors, 1977.
Collection of 24 silver boxes with crystal lids, 1982-83.
*Harmony* half crystal service, for Orrefors, 1983.
Collection of graal vases with figuring in crystal over- and underlay, for Orrefors, 1987.
Boat-shaped bowl in crystal, for Orrefors, 1987.
Symphony half crystal service, for Orrefors, 1987.
*Bird* bowl in silver with whaletooth and sapphire decoration, 1988.
Temples in crystal and silver, 1989.
Animals in bronze and silver, 1989.
Glasses and flatware, for the Nobel Prize banquet, 1991.
Medals, for the 5th IAAF World Championships in athletics, 1995.

## Publications

**On CYRÉN: books**—*Svensk Form/Forma Sueca* by Ake Stavenlow and Ake H. Huldt, Stockholm, 1961; *Scandinavian Design: Objects of a Life Style* by Eileene Harrison Beer, New York, 1975; *Form och Tradition i Svenge* edited by Birgitta Walz, Stockholm, 1982; *Scandinavian Modern Design 1880-1980* edited by David Revere McFadden, New York, 1982; *Design Since 1945* edited by Kathryn Hiesinger and George Marcus, Philadelphia and London, 1983; *Contemporary Swedish Design,* exhibition catalogue by Monica Boman, Lennart Lindkvist, and others, Stockholm, 1983; *Den Svenska Formen* by Monica Boman and others, Stockholm, 1985; *The Lunning Prize,* exhibition catalogue edited by Helena Dahlback Lütteman and Marianne Uggla, Stockholm, 1986; *Faces of Swedish Design,* exhibition catalogue edited by Monica Boman, Stockholm, 1988.

\*　　\*　　\*

When Gunnar Cyrén emerged from the National College of Art and Design in the mid 1950s the age of perfect craftsmanship was still in full swing. Soon, however, new winds began to blow. The only form accepted during the 1960s was the "rustic's rustic"—or at least that is how it seemed to Gunnar Cyrén. If you are something of a perfectionist, and enjoy working on a design until you've got everything right, it is not much fun living in a period when skill and precision are looked down on.

During the 1960s Gunnar Cyrén made a very firm imprint on the glassware produced at Orrefors. And in his own way he broke with traditions and prejudice. He produced cheerful enamelled decorations and created "Pop Glasses" with their opalescent bowls and colored stems. They are deliberately and confidently designed, with nothing left to chance. Everything he did was elegant in the positive sense of the term.

Gunnar Cyrén has never been interested in industry as a vehicle of personal expression and manifestation. He was unwilling to give excessively wide distribution to things which were highly personal. "You add something which nobody wants." He simply wishes "to be a designer for an industry." For him, this evidently means producing a good basic commodity which respects its purpose and perhaps endows the pieces with "correct" patterns. This may sound

**Gunnar Cyrén: *Bird* bowl in sterling silver with whaletooth and sapphire decoration, 1988**

functionalistic and tediously impersonal, but look at the *Frescati* wine glasses, based on some jubilee glasses he made in 1968. A couple of rounds on the bowl and he has produced a good basic commodity which respects its function. And yet they are highly personal, though in Cyrén's own way, without flamboyance.

Gunnar Cyrén has never compromised on workmanship. "True content is not improved by leaving anything unfinished," he says. So much for the ignorant and the slapdash. Chance and coincidence can sometimes produce very attractive results, but Gunnar Cyrén does not work that way. His approach is strictly intellectual, though his forms are never overloaded. It is simply that his personal mode of expression operates this way.

Gunnar Cyrén went in for silver in the mid 1970s. He studied metalworking at the National College of Art and Design, and was an apprentice silversmith. He started working with silver so as to experience complete independence. He was tired of merely adapting himself to other people's projects and making decisions together with others. An industrial designer has to defer to the market and the company's finances. Gunnar Cyrén's first silver was inspired by nature, though it was defiantly not natural-romantic. Its relationship to nature is highly disciplined and stylized; nature is hardly discernible and yet these pieces are manifestly inspired by pine cones, leaves, or writhing snakes. Birds and the occasional fish came next. The birds do not admit of zoological classification, though

they possibly belong to the "ale goose" family. Gunnar Cyrén discovered that he and the people carving the old birdlike wooden vessels for beer drinking had had the same problems with the transition from body to head and beak.

His production in the 1980s includes a series of austere, almost rectangular, boxes of silver with glass lids cut to an exact fit. When the lid takes the form of an open book, the spiritual subtlety of the box is accentuated. Cyrén's perfection makes the closed, architecturally constructed boxes into worthy bearers of expression. Function is a stage which was passed long ago. The final form seems self-evident, as if it could not have been made in any other way.

Gunnar Cyrén has a sense of the grandiose and magnificent. He is not reluctant to work with gold, but he always uses his own disciplined language. In the summer of 1987 an old Swedish castle, Gripsholm, celebrated its 450th anniversary. Cyrén was one of the silversmiths who were commissioned to produce an object from our time yet linked to the court and state silver tradition of old. His ceremonial staff is over a meter long, heavy and imposing, crowned by a naturalistically designed castle having a large green lawn of plexiglass. The language is the same that he uses for his enamelled glass. And it is an example of Gunnar Cyrén's extravagant style.

—Helena Dahlback Lutteman

# DANZIGER, Louis
American print and graphic designer

**Born:** New York City, 17 November 1923. **Education:** High school and Federal Art Project classes, New York, 1938-41; apprentice at a printing firm and a silk-screen printers, New York, 1938-39; studied graphics, under Alvin Lustig, Art Center College of Design, Los Angeles, 1947-48; studied magazine design, under Alexey Brodovitch, New School for Social Research, New York, 1948. **Military Service:** Served in the United States Army, 1942-45. **Family:** Married Dorothy Patricia Smith in 1954. **Career:** Worked as a stage designer for summer stock companies, New York, 1940-41; assistant to the art director, Delehanty Institute, New York, 1942; assistant art director, War Assets Administration, Los Angeles, 1946; designer, *Esquire* magazine, New York, 1948; freelance designer, establishing own office in Los Angeles, then Arcadia, California, from 1949. Design consultant, for The Dreyfus Agency, 1955-1970, Los Angeles County Museum of Art, 1958-80, Ponder & Best Inc. (Vivitar), 1959-1970, Nitto Advertising Agency, Tokyo, 1984-1986, and Federal Design Improvement Program, National Endowment for the Arts, Washington, D.C., 1975-1986, Olympic Games, Los Angeles, 1984; corporate design consultant, Atlantic Richfield Company, 1978-1985; also designed for the Container Corporation of America, Gelvatex, System Development Corporation, Clinton Laboratories, Champion Paper Company, and others. Instructor in advertising design, Art Center College of Design, Los Angeles, 1956-60, and from 1986, and Chouinard Art Institute, 1963-72; director of graphic design program, 1972-79, and senior faculty member, 1972-87, California Institute of the Arts, Valencia; visiting professor of visual and environmental studies Harvard University, Cambridge, Massachusetts, 1978-88; consultant, Osaka Communication Arts, Japan, and Tokyo Communication Arts, from 1986; visiting lecturer at universities throughout the world. Panelist, Design Arts Award Panel, National Endowment for the Arts, 1980-87. **Member:** Alliance Graphique Internationale; American Institute of Graphic Arts; Art Directors Club of Los Angeles; (honorary) American Center for Design. **Exhibitions:** Society of Typographic Arts, Chicago, 1955; works have been shown in exhibitions throughout the world. **Collections:** Museum of Modem Art, New York; Library of Congress, Washington, D.C.; Los Angeles County Museum of Art. **Honors:** Distinguished Achievement Award, Contemporary Art Council, Los Angeles, 1982; Distinguished Designer Award, National Endowment for the Arts, 1985; also received awards from New York Art Directors Club, Los Angeles Art Directors Club, Type Directors Club, American Institute of Graphic Arts, Western Association of Art Museums, and many others. **Address:** P.O. Box 660189, Arcadia, California 91066-0189, U.S.A.

## Works

Poster and announcements, for the International Design Conference, Aspen, Colorado, 1955.
*The Light Touch—Hard Sell* advertising campaign, for the Dreyfus Agency, 1956.
Logo, advertising, packaging, and design program, for Gelvatex Paint Company, 1956.
*Great Ideas of Western Man* advertisement, for the Container Corporation of America, 1958.
Logo, advertising, packaging, and design program, for Clinton Laboratories, 1958-63.
Advertising campaigns, for SDC Systems Development Company, 1960-63.
Packages advertisement, for the Container Corporation of America, 1961.
Vivitar packaging, brochures, and advertisements, for Ponder and Best, 1962-68.
*The New York School* exhibition catalogue and poster, for the Los Angeles County Museum of Art, 1965.
Kobena advertisements, for Ponder and Best, 1965.
*American Paintings from the Metropolitan Museum* exhibition catalogue and poster, for the Los Angeles County Museum of Art, 1966.
*Sculpture of the 60s* exhibition catalogue and poster, for the Los Angeles County Museum of Art, 1967.
Mamiya-Sekor packaging and advertisements, for Ponder and Best, 1967-69.
*Cerhard Marcks* exhibition catalogue, for the University of California at Los Angeles Art Gallery, 1969.
*Transparency, Reflection, Light, Space: 4 Artists* exhibition catalogue, for the University of California at Los Angeles Art Gallery, 1970.
*Art and Technology* exhibition catalogue, for the Los Angeles County Museum of Art, 1971.
*The Navajo Blanket* exhibition catalogue, for the Los Angeles County Museum of Art, 1972.
*The Russian Avant Garde* exhibition catalogue, for the Los Angeles County Museum of Art, 1980.
*Los Angeles in the 60s* exhibition catalogue, for the Los Angeles County Museum of Art, 1981.
Catalogue and poster, for the University of California at Los Angeles extension, 1990.

## Publications

**On DANZIGER: books**—*Packaging: An International Survey of Package Design* edited by Walter Herdeg, Zurich, 1959; *Exhibitions: An International Survey* edited by Klaus Frank, New York, 1961; *Who's Who in Graphic Art,* edited by Walter Amstutz, Zurich,

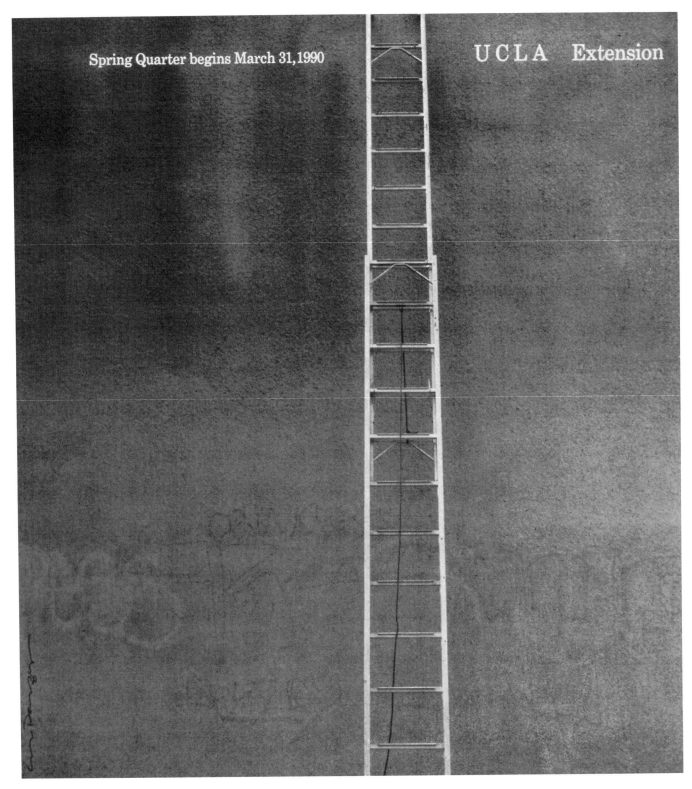

**Louis Danziger: UCLA Extension Catalog cover, 1990**

1962, Dubendorf, 1982; *An International Survey of Press Advertising* edited by Kurt Weidemann, Stuttgart and London, 1966; *Graphic Designers in the USA* edited by Henri Hillebrand, London 1971, New York 1972; *Who's Who in Graphic Art,* vol. 2, Dübendorf, 1982; **articles**—in *Graphis* (Zurich), no. 70, 1957, no. 191, 1978;

*Stile Industria* (Milan), no. 11, 1957; *Graphics Today* (New York), vol. 3, no. 1, 1978; *Print Magazine* (New York), vol. 44, no. 5, 1990.

\*

The problem of the graphic designer is quite different from that of the artist who deals essentially in private images. Because of the public nature of our work and because our commissions are generally problems of a specific nature, we find that we are continually trying to satisfy three distinctly different but not necessarily antagonistic judges. The three are the client, the audience, and one's self.

We must, if we accept a commission, use our skill and judgment to achieve our clients' objectives. As socially responsible people, we try to accomplish these aims in a positive way. We do this by performing some service for our audience. We provide information, entertainment, and aesthetic pleasure.

Most designers will, I believe, agree with the above. It is in the area of self-satisfaction that the methods and goals of designers vary. The concerns and approaches which provide satisfactions for me and direct the nature of my work are as follows:

I am concerned with finding an image which is visually strong and aesthetically gratifying, yet so pertinent to the idea that it becomes difficult to separate form from content.

There is a sense of achievement when one can solve a design problem in an elegant way (The word "elegant" is used here in the scientific sense, as the accomplishment of a great deal with a minimum of means.)

I am concerned with the production of work that demonstrates intelligence. There is continually a search for clarity and depth rather than cleverness.

Although I recognize that the work we do is essentially ephemeral, it is a source of satisfaction to produce work which avoids faddishness and looks fresh over a period of twenty years or longer.

The pressures imposed by the volume of work and the sheer magnitude of the clients move most successful designers more and more into the areas of direction and administration rather than the actual execution of work. For myself, I prefer to do less work and continue to remain more directly involved in its production. This involvement extends into photography. With but few exceptions, I produce all of the photographs seen in my work.

Designing is a source of much satisfaction and many frustrations, but I have always felt that it makes one useful and very special, and that, of course, provides the greatest satisfaction.

—Louis Danziger

*      *      *

In a 1978 article about Louis Danziger, the Swiss *Graphis* cited his answers to a series of questions. From this, we learn that Danziger's typographical instinct was formed from the annual *Gebrauchsgraphik,* which he used to look at in his youth, whereas to the question of who influenced him, he named Alvin Lustig and Alexey Brodovitch. Both pieces of information serve as keys to the understanding of this eminent American graphic designer's genealogy and way of thinking. In truth, several generations of graphic artists, typographers, poster designers, and, in general, lovers of print were raised on this German journal, which represented the highest graphic standard of the 1920s and 1930s. It was not only a source of information but a school of good taste. Something like a continuation of this informal education can be seen in his cooperation with Brodovitch in New York on the layout of the elite monthly *Esquire.*

Along with George Tscherny, Louis Dorfsman, Paul Rand, and perhaps a few other representatives of his generation, he has sound

historical erudition in the field of his discipline. This outlook on the evolution of graphic language in our century, deepened by his own experience, Danziger has for many years transmitted to students, and on this foundation, he has been able to develop in them a consciousness of the social, cultural, and artistic bases of visual mass-media. Not by accident does Danziger have in professional circles the reputation of a charismatic pedagogue.

Erudition, scientific interests, and synthesis of disparate elements into one visual, orderly whole: these characterize his works. To this, we must add a subtle feeling for the climate of a given design problem, for its stylistic framework, or just for its emotional context. An example is the catalogue for the exhibit *The Avant-Garde in Russia, 1910-1930: New Perspectives,* organized by the Los Angeles County Museum. The graphic and typographic concept of this nearly 300-page publication had to take into consideration the particular character of the exhibit, which reconstructed a closed epoch of art. The catalogue was to fulfill this same task, as well as a second, derivative goal: to express the general artistic tendency—in this case constructivist—of the documented exhibit by means of the language of typography. The designer, having at his disposal textual and iconographic material of varying derivation—without cohesion, from the point of view of graphic matter—manifested an important sensitivity for *Zeitgeist.* This is not something that can be learned; it does not belong to the technology of craft. We are dealing here with a work of great restraint and rational discipline, a work purely economical and in its own way elegant. The concept of elegance appears anyway, in Danziger's terminology, as "accomplishment with minimum means." If by elegance, we mean "aesthetic order," we will understand the essence of Danziger's style. This is exemplified in magazine advertisements for the Container Corporation of America, Clinton Laboratories, the Dreyfus Company, and in booklets for Champion Paper Company, as well as catalogues and posters for the Los Angeles County Museum of Art.

—Szymon Bojko

# DAVID-WEST, (Pryde) Haig

Nigerian graphic designer

**Born:** Port Harcourt, 18 June 1946. **Education:** Studied at Bali College, Republic of Cameroon, 1960-64; studied at Ahmadu Bello University, Zaria, Nigeria, BA, 1970; studied art and design, University of Wisconsin, Madison, MA, 1971; studied graphic design, under Henryk Tomaszewski and Jozef Mroszczak, Academy of Fine Arts, Warsaw, 1971-72; studied art education, under Jerome Hausman and David Ecker, New York University, PhD, 1975. **Family:** Married Elizabeth Lydia Csintalan (name changed to Betanova) in 1974; children: Alzo, Hegulka, and Gizelka. **Career:** Graphic designer, Nigerian Television, Lagos, 1966-69; art editor, Normedia Group, Lagos, 1967-69; freelance graphic designer, Port Harcourt, from 1970; consultant to Concert Managers of Wisconsin, 1970-71, Mountain Health Services of Georgia, 1973, Prince Street Center of New York, 1973-75, and JDR III Fund of New York, 1974. Chief executive, Arts Council of Port Harcourt, 1977-79. Instructor in graphic design, University of Georgia, Athens, 1972-73; lecturer in graphic design, University of Nigeria, Nsukka, 1975-76; head of fine and applied arts, College of Education, Port Harcourt, from 1981. **Member:** Executive board member, from 1980, vice president and Africa regional coordinator, from 1981, and convener/moderator of the Conference on Design Problems in Africa, 1982, ICOGRADA, International Council of Graphic Design Associations. **Exhibitions:** Arts Building, Zaria, 1969; United States Information Center, Kano, 1970; Government Hall, Port Harcourt, 1970; Black History Gallery, Madison, Wisconsin, 1971; Three Continents Gallery, Warsaw, 1972; Klub Kropka, Gliwice, 1972; Goethe Institut, Lagos, 1980. **Collections:** National Gallery and Museum of Modern Art, Lagos; National Gallery, Baghdad; Poster Museum, Warsaw; Lahti Art Museum, Finland. **Honors:** Bali College Graduation Award, Cameroun, 1964; International Labour Organization Stamp Design Prize, Lagos, 1969; Rivers State Award for International Studies, Nigeria, 1970; ICOGRADA/Polish Government Scholarship, 1970. **Address:** PMB 5047, Port Harcourt, Nigeria.

## Publications

**By DAVID-WEST: books**—*Russian Constructivist Art and Its Impact on Contemporary Poster Design,* PhD dissertation, New York University, 1976; *Haig David-West: Posters,* with foreword by Ronald Ruprecht, Port Harcourt, 1980; *New Visual Arts Programme,* Port Harcourt, 1981; (editor) *Dialogue on Graphic Design Problems in Africa,* London, 1983; **articles**—in *Corpscope* (Port Harcourt), no. 1, 1977; *Creative Communicator* (Chicago), no. 62, 1979; *Design Integration* (Helsinki), no. 1, 1982; *Symposium 82* (Brno), 1982.

**On DAVID-WEST: books**—*Modern Publicity* edited by Felix Gluck, London, 1978; *The Nucleus* edited by the Department of Culture, Lagos, 1982; **articles**—in *Projekt* (Warsaw), no. 131, 1978; *Graphis* (Zurich), no. 203, 1980; *UR* (London), no. 1, 1980; *The Nation* (Aba, Nigeria), no. 177, 1982.

*

All art forms are intended to communicate. They are created to "say" something to the viewer or audience. In this process the creator manipulates form to the point where satisfaction is reached. When the manipulation is individualistic, when the creator responds only to his or her "free" sensations regardless of social issues, the something which the work communicates or "says" tends to be limited to levels of consciousness that may not be tangibly functional to the cause of social progress. With the poster and other forms of committed graphic design, the manipulation process is guided by the creator's sense of social responsibility. The work must be tangibly functional; it must appeal to the conscience of society.

Typically, the poster demonstrates the use of two types of communication—namely the word-symbol and the picture-symbol, which must be organised in such a manner that a "quantum wholeness" and empathy are maintained. This suggests a dialectical situation in which a whole cannot be equated with the sum of X and Y sensations and reflexes, and in which the aesthetic experience where form fuses with moods, feelings, and emotions aroused by form remains at an equilibrium. Indeed there are posters which do not demonstrate the word-picture or semantic-iconographic dialogue; rather they rely completely on the picture or iconographic level of communication. This occurs when the word or semantic addition would appear to blur the message being communicated. Here again quantum wholeness is a significant factor.

Two groups of contemporary designers are immediately visible in the Nigerian experience. One group reduces itself to the level of disgusting subservience to the whims of its client, totally oblivious of its training and experience, thus edging toward creative prostitution. The other group elevates itself to the level of progressive and systematic educator or pedagogue, regarding design as a process during which an equation would be established between the old and the new—between vernacular culture and the main currents of world culture—while constantly guarding the elasticity of the equation, ensuring that a certain equilibrium is maintained. Critical to the world view of the latter is the concern to improve, by control processes, the general disposition of the non-literate stratum of society, while constantly ensuring that the literate stratum is not fed with banal material. It is this latter group that may be said to be addressing itself to the tangible problems of contemporary Nigeria.

In Europe's search for new artistic departures at the opening of the twentieth century, the primal geometry of masks from Africa had provided ready answers. In this search, which was essentially a feverish one, lay a restlessness that tended to becloud sound and systematic study. Hence, salient qualities of the art of the traditional African were slighted in favor of qualities that met with the immediate European expectation. Essentially, the mask was at no time regarded as a decorative device and was therefore not "art" to the traditional African. It was more of a ritualistic experience which in most instances was variegated with "calligraphic" forms reflective of the general social dispositions and world outlook of traditional man. In the vernacular culture of the African experience, therefore, it was this calligraphy that was intended as a language of visual communication. Herein lay the most positive evidence of a developed form of vernacular visual communication design in Africa thriving before the advent of modern forms of civilisation. In that culture which now appears to co-exist with technological changes, the visual representation of the beautiful maintained a plastic equilibrium with inter-personal and inter-group communication.

Colonialist administrative policies succeeded in creating generations of cultural invalids in Nigerian society. To a large extent, the performing arts—drama, dance, gymnastics, and others—were perceived by the colonialists as nothing more than dispositions developed for their entertainment. The intrinsic didactic content of these performances and their socialising tendency were disregarded. Our ancestors were encouraged to dance, sing, and perform for the enjoyment of the colonialist "spectator." Apparently, this tendency grew with our society; a lot of people still regard the performing arts as having only entertainment functions. There had been a systematic process of indoctrination through the generations.

Identifying the visual arts as a powerful medium for mobilising the masses of people, if encouraged along progressivist (and pluralist) growth lines, colonialist administrators infused an attitude of apathy toward this creative disposition among our people. Again, this apathy was transmitted to our time.

Perhaps the core of the controversy is found in the problem that grows out of the fact that subsequent formulators of our educational policies approached the matter of aesthetic inquiry with a cobweb attitude in which their view of global culture was astigmatic, thereby suggesting their inability to inculcate the idea that creative art and design are indeed fundamental to human growth and co-existence.

—Haig David-West

*     *     *

Haig David-West's work first came to national prominence fourteen years ago when, still an under-graduate at Ahmadu Bello University in the Northern Nigerian city of Zaria, he won all the prizes at the International Labour Organization postage stamp design contest organized by the Nigerian government. One year later, he made history again at the University by becoming the first student ever to graduate with first class honours in graphic design. He proceeded abroad for graduate study in the United States and Poland, where he was exposed to the social and political influences which were later to enable him to re-shape the direction of graphic design in Nigeria.

David-West's Polish experience seems to have been most significant for the development of his work. There he learned that graphic design, if seen in the context of the social sciences, could play a crucial role in mobilising people for action. While in Poland, he also came into contact with Marxism-Leninism as an aesthetic philosophy and felt the significant impact of the work of his Warsaw Academy teachers. These influences crystallized in his doctoral work at New York University, where he formulated his principle of "quantum wholeness"—the equilibrium of the conjunction of social responsibility and artistic form—while studying aesthetics under David Ecker.

In its practical application, quantum wholeness has taken the form in his work of an explosive, didactic iconography bathed in the indigenous Nigerian symbolism. This is most evident in the work that resulted from his investigation of vernacular calligraphy, as exemplified by such outstanding posters as *Regatta, Rex Lawson, Iria, Tam,* and *Tonjo Daye. Regatta,* which is a promotional poster for the regatta theatrical event, takes account of the fact that this occurrence, which epitomises creative activity in the Niger Delta, articulates the visual, kinetic, corporal, and linguistic expressions of the people simultaneously. The poster emphasises the rhythm of a choreography of silhouetted paddles in juxtaposition with vernacular calligraphic forms. Another indigenous symbol prominent in some of David-West's posters is derived from native hieroglyphics which make a concise political statement, decrying the continued cultural and ideological enslavement of African peoples and warning against the humiliation of neo-colonialist adventurism in Africa.

An evaluation of Haig David-West's work and philosophy cannot be complete without mentioning the role he has played in international design diplomacy. He has addressed a UNESCO conference and has convened an international conference in Africa in his capacity as ICOGRADA vice president and regional coordinator for Africa. His work in this area culminates in his call for committed and socially relevant graphic design, which will assist in consolidating national socio-cultural liberation struggles and ultimately serve as an anchor in international relations. In all he does, his central belief is that a designer operating in a third-world society cannot afford to be apolitical.

—Alaboigoni Inko-Dokubo

# DAY, Lucienne

British textile designer

**Born:** Lucienne Conradi, in Coulsdon, Surrey, 1 January 1917.
**Education:** Convent of Notre Dame de Sion Worthing, 1929-34;

studied at Croydon School of Art, London, 1934-37; Royal College of Art, London, ARCA. 1940. **Family:** Married the designer Robin Day in 1942; daughter: Paula. **Career:** Worked as a teacher, Beckenham School of Art, Kent, 1942-47; freelance designer, establishing studio in London, from 1948; has designed for Edinburgh Weavers, Heal's Fabrics, Wilton Royal Carpet Company, Cavendish Textiles, Tomkinson's Carpets, Thomas Somerset, John Lewis Rosenthal Porcelain, and others. Selection panel member, Duke of Edinburgh's Elegant Design Awards, 1960-63; jury member, Rosenthal Porcelain Studio-Line, 1960-68; council member Royal College of Art, London, 1963-68; textile consultants committee member, at Central School of Art, Croydon College of Art, and Kingston School of Art; president, Textile Society, from 1994. Created Royal Designer for Industry, 1963. **Exhibitions:** Prescote Gallery, Banbury, 1979; City Art Gallery, Edinburgh, 1980; Lyttelton Gallery, National Theatre, London, 1981; National Museums of Modern Art, Kyoto and Tokyo, Japan, 1982; Röhsska Konstslöjdmuseet, Göteborg, 1983; *British Art: New Directions,* New York, 1983; Oscar Woollens International, London, 1984; Footstool Gallery, St. John's Smith Square, London, 1986; National Theatre, London, 1991; John T. Worth Art Gallery, Manchester, 1993; Royal College of Art, London, 1993; Aberdeen Art Gallery, Scotland, 1994. **Collections:** Victoria and Albert Museum, London; Art Institute of Chicago; Cranbrook Museum, Bloomfield Hills, Michigan; Musée des Arts Décoratifs, Montreal; Kunstindustrimuseet, Trondheim; Röhsska Konstslöjdmuseet, Göteborg. **Honors:** Gold Medal 1951, and Grand Prize, 1954, Milan Triennale; First Award, American Institute of Decorators, 1952; fellow, Society of Industrial Artists and Designers, London, 1955; Design Council Awards, London, 1957, 1960, 1968; Gold Medal, California State Fair, 1959, 1960; first woman master, Royal Designer for Industry, 1987-1989; honorary doctor of design, Southampton University, 1995. **Address:** 49 Cheyne Walk, Chelsea, London SW3 5LP, England.

## Works

*Calyx* printed furnishing fabric, for Heal Fabrics Ltd., 1950.
*Elysian* printed furnishing fabric, for Edinburgh Weavers, 1950.
*Flotilla* printed furnishing fabric, for Heal Fabrics Ltd., 1951.
*Graphica* printed furnishing fabric, for Heal Fabrics Ltd., 1952.
*Ticker Tape* printed furnishing fabric, for Heal Fabrics Ltd., 1952.
*Florimel* printed furnishing fabric, for Edinburgh Weavers, 1952.
*Palisade* printed furnishing fabric, for British Celanese, 1952.
*Spectators* printed furnishing fabric, for Heal Fabrics Ltd., 1953.
*Linear* printed furnishing fabric, for Heal Fabrics Ltd., 1953.
*Travelogue* printed furnishing fabric, for British Celanese, 1953.
*Miscellany* printed furnishing fabric, for British Celanese, 1953.
*Acres* printed furnishing fabric, for Edinburgh Weavers, 1954.
*Fall* printed furnishing fabric, for Edinburgh Weavers, 1955.
*Tesserae* carpet, for Tomkinson's Carpets, 1957.
*Four Seasons* ceramic tableware, for Rosenthal China Ltd., 1958.
*Odyssey* ceramic tableware, for Rosenthal China Ltd., 1960.
Table linen range, for Thomas Somerset, 1967.
*Grey Line* ceramic tableware, for Rosenthal China Ltd., 1969.
*Tangrams* silk mosaic tapestries in the Commercial Union Building, London, for Shearman and Stirling, 1985.
*The Window* silk mosaic tapestry at the Queen Elizabeth Conference Centre, London, for Powell Moya and Partners, 1986.

Lucienne Day: *Three Daughters of Mexico* silk mosaic tapestries, 1992

*Aspects of the Sun* group of silk mosaic tapestries in the John Lewis Building, Kingston Surrey, for Ahrends Burton Koralek, 1989-90.

**Publications**

By DAY: articles—"Plain or Fancy" in *Daily Mail Ideal Home Book,* London, 1957.

On DAY: books—*British Textiles* by Frank Lewis, Leigh-on-Sea, 1951; *Design in British Industry: A Mid-Century Survey* by Michael Farr, Cambridge, 1955; *Printed Textiles* by Pat Albeck, London, 1969; *The Contemporary Decorative Arts from 1940 to the Present Day* by Philippe Garner, London, 1980; *Design Since 1945* edited by Kathryn Hiesinger and George Marcus, Philadelphia and London, 1983; *A Woman's Touch* by Isabelle Anscombe, London, 1984; *Lucienne Day: A Career in Design* by J. Harris, Manchester, 1993.

\*     \*     \*

In 1951, the Festival of Britain gave many young designers the opportunity to launch successful careers. Stimulated by a feeling of deep frustration with postwar austerity, change was in the air. Lucienne Day had married Robin Day soon after leaving the Royal College of Art, and for their work together on the Festival she designed her first major commission, the famous Calyx fabric. With its bold, spiky graphics and fresh, bright colour, it was an immedi-

ate success and did much to launch postwar, modern textile design in Britain. It was also the beginning of a successful twenty-one year partnership with Heal Fabrics Ltd., a London furniture store with a policy of promoting modern design. Through this relationship, Day developed as a skilled and sensitive pattern-maker with a respect for craft traditions and quality production inspired largely by the Scandinavian tradition.

Throughout her career, the textiles Day designed for Heal earned many international awards, including the gold medal at the ninth *Triennale di Milano* in 1951 and, three years later, the grand prize for another group of textiles: *Graphics, Spectator,* and *Linear.* She has also worked as a carpet designer; in 1957 *Tesserae,* for Tomkinsons, won the Design of the Year award, and more recently, she has produced the *Nova* range for Wilton Carpets. Nor is Day's work restricted to two dimensions: between 1957 and 1969, she designed china and dinner services for Rosenthal Porcelain; she has successfully collaborated with her husband on the interior of the BOAC passenger aircraft; she has consulted for John Lewis; and she has worked on design projects for department stores and super-markets.

In the 1980s her work changed direction somewhat, towards more craft-based production. Drawing on her experience as a colour consultant to industry, Day began to experiment with one-off wall hangings made up of small pieces of oriental plain or shot silk, sewn together by hand. She first showed this work in 1979; its success encouraged further exhibitions in Tokyo and a solo exhibition at the Röhsska Konstslöjd Museum in Göteborg, Sweden. Most of the pieces use a semi-abstract style, and many have been bought to complement formal architectural interiors.

—Catherine McDermott

# DAY, Richard

American art director and film designer

**Born:** Victoria, British Columbia, Canada, 9 May 1896; emigrated to the United States in 1918. **Military Service:** Served as model designer in the United States Marine Corps, 1942-45. **Family:** Married; 6 children. **Career:** Set decorator for film director Erich von Stroheim at MGM, Universal, Paramount, and United Artists studios, Hollywood, 1918-28; worked independently for Goldwyn and United Artists, Hollywood, 1928-38; art director, 1939-40, then supervising art director, 1940-42 and 1945-47, 20th Century-Fox, Hollywood; freelance designer for Goldwyn, RKO, United Artists, and Warner Brothers, from 1948. **Honors:** Academy Awards, 1935, 1936, 1941, 1942, 1951, 1954. **Died:** Hollywood, California, 23 May 1972.

**Works**

Film designs include—*Blind Husbands* (von Stroheim), 1918; *The Devil's Passkey* (von Stroheim), 1919; *Foolish Wives* (von Stroheim) 1922; *Merry Go Round* (Julian and von Stroheim), 1923; *Greed* (von Stroheim), 1925; *The Merry Widow* (von Stroheim), 1925; *Bright Lights* (Leonard), 1925; *The Only Thing* (Conway), 1925; *His Secretary* (Henley), 1925; *Beverley of Graustark* (Franklin), 1962; *Bardelys the Magnificent* (K. Vidor),

1926; *The Show* (Browning), 1927; *Mr. Wu* (Nigh), 1927; *Tillie the Toiler* (Henley), 1927; *The Unknown* (Browning), 1927; *Adam and Evil* (Leonard), 1927; *After Midnight* (Bell), 1927; *The Road to Romance* (Robertson), 1927; *Tea for Three* (Leonard), 1927; *The Student Prince in Old Heidelberg* (Franklin), 1927; *The Enemy* (Niblo), 1927; *The Divine Woman* (Sjostrom), 1928; *Wickedness Preferred* (Henley), 1928; *Rose Marie* (Hubbard), 1928; *The Big City* (Browning), 1928; *Circus Rookies* (Sedgwick), 1928; *Laugh, Clown, Laugh* (Brenon), 1928; *The Actress* (Franklin), 1928, *Forbidden Hours* (Beaumont), 1928; *Our Dancing Daughters* (Beaumont), 1928; *Excess Baggage* (Cruze), 1928; *While the City Sleeps* (Conway), 1928; *The Wedding March* (von Stroheim), 1928; *West of Zanzibar* (Browning), 1928; *The Bridge of San Luis Rey* (Brabin), 1929; *The Idle Rich* (W. deMille), 1929; *A Man's Man* (Cruze), 1929; *Wonder of Women* (Brown), 1929; *The Girl in the Show* (Selwyn), 1929; *The Unholy Night* (L. Barrymore), 1929; *The Hollywood Revue of 1929* (Reisner), 1929; *Wise Girls* (Hopper), 1929; *The Thirteenth Chair* (Browning), 1929; *The Kiss* (Feyder), 1929; *Their Own Desire* (Hopper), 1929; *Devil May Care* (Franklin), 1929; *Untamed* (Conway), 1929; *Gus Edwards' Song Revue* (Edwards), 1929; *Song Shop* (Lee), 1929; *Anna Christie* (Brown), 1930; *In Gay Madrid* (Leonard), 1930; *Whoopee* (Freeland), 1930; *Sins of the Children* (Wood), 1930; *Madame Satan* (C. deMille), 1930; *Le Spectre Vert* (Feyder), 1930; *The Devil to Pay* (Fitzmaurice), 1930; *The Front Page* (Milestone), 1931; *Indiscreet* (McCarey), 1931; *Street Scene* (K. Vidor), 1931; *The Unholy Garden* (Fitzmaurice), 1931; *Palmy Days* (Sutherland), 1931; *Arrowsmith* (Ford), 1931; *The Greeks Had a Word for It* (L. Sherman), 1932; *Rain* (Milestone), 1932; *Cynara* (K. Vidor), 1932; *The Kid from Spain* (McCarey), 1932; *Hallelujah I'm a Bum* (Milestone), 1933; *Secrets* (Borzage), 1933; *The Bowery* (Walsh), 1933; *The Masquerader* (Wallace), 1933; *Roman Scandals* (Tuttle), 1933; *Gallant Lady* (La Cava), 1933; *Moulin Rouge* (Lanfield), 1934; *Nana* (Arzner), 1934; *The Affairs of Cellini* (La Cava), 1934; *Born to Be Bad* (L. Sherman), 1934; *The House of Rothschild* (Werker), 1934; *The Last Gentleman* (Lanfield), 1934; *Bulldog Drummond Strikes Back* (Del Ruth), 1934; *Kid Millions* (Del Ruth), 1934; *Looking for Trouble* (Wellman), 1934; *We Live Again* (Mamoulian), 1934; *The Mighty Barnum* (W. Lang), 1934; *Folies Bergere* (Del Ruth), 1935; *Clive of India* (Boleslawski), 1935; *Cardinal Richelieu* (Lee), 1935; *The Call of the Wild* (Wellman), 1935; *The Dark Angel* (Franklin), 1935; *Barbary Coast* (Hawks), 1935; *Metropolitan* (Boleslawski), 1935; *Splendor* (Nugent), 1935; *Strike Me Pink* (Taurog), 1936; *These Three* (Wyler), 1936; *One Rainy Afternoon* (Lee), 1936; *Dodsworth* (Wyler), 1936; *The Gay Desperado* (Mamoulian), 1936; *Come and Get It* (Hawks and Wyler), 1936; *Beloved Enemy* (Potter), 1936; *Woman Chases Man* (Blystone), 1937; *Stella Dallas* (K. Vidor), 1937; *Dead End* (Wyler), 1937; *The Hurricane* (Ford), 1937; *The Goldwyn Follies* (Marshall), 1938; *The Cowboy and the Lady* (Potter), 1938; *The Adventures of Marco Polo* (Mayo), 1938; *Charlie Chan in Honolulu* (Humberstone), 1938; *The Little Princess* (W. Lang), 1939; *The Gorilla* (Dwan), 1939; *The Hound of the Baskervilles* (Lanfieldj), 1939; *The Return of the Cisco Kids* (Leeds), 1939; *Rose of Washington Square* (Raloff), 1939; *Young Mr. Lincoln* (Ford), 1939; *Frontier Marshal* (Dwan), 1939; *Quick Millions* (St. Clair), 1939; *The Adventures of Sherlock Holmes* (Werker), 1939; *Charlie Chan at Treasure Island* (Foster), 1939; *The Escape* (Cortez), 1939; *Hollywood Cavalcade* (Cummings), 1939; *Pack Up Your Troubles* (Humberstone), 1939; *Drums Along the Mohawk* (Ford), 1939;

*Day-Time Wife* (Ratoff), 1939; *City of Darkness* (Leeds), 1939; *Swanee River* (Lanfield), 1939; *The Honeymoon's Over* (Forde), 1939; *Everything Happens at Night* (Cummings), 1939; *City of Chance* (Cortcz), 1939; *Little Old New York* (H. King), 1940; *The Blue Bird* (W. Lang), 1940; *He Married His Wife* (Del Ruth), 1940; *The Grapes of Wrath* (Ford), 1940; *The Man Who Wouldn't Talk* (Burton), 1940; *Charlie Chan in Panama* (Foster), 1940; *Star Dust* (W. Lang), 1940; *Johnny Apollo* (Hathaway), 1940; *Shooting High* (Green), 1940; *I Was an Adventuress* (Ratoff), 1940; *Lillian Russell* (Cummings), 1940; *Girl in 313* (Cortez), 1940; *Earthbound* (Pichel), 1940; *Four Sons* (Mayo), 1940; *Manhattan Heartbeat* (Burton), 1940; *Maryland* (H. King), 1940; *The Man I Married* (Pichel), 1940; *Girl from Avenue A* (Brower), 1940; *The Return of Frank James* (F. Lang), 1940; *Pier 13* (Forde), 1940; *Young People* (Dwan), 1940; *Charlie Chan at the Wax Museum* (Shores), 1940; *Yesterday's Heroes* (Leeds), 1940; *The Gay Caballero* (Brower), 1940; *Down Argentine Way* (Cummings), 1940; *The Great Profile* (W. Lang), 1940; *The Mark of Zorro* (Mamoulian), 1940; *Street of Memories* (Traubc), 1940; *Tin Pan Alley* (W. Lang) 1940; *Youth Will Be Served* (Brower), 1940; *Murder Over New York* (Lachman), 1940; *Jennie* (Burton), 1940; *Chad Hanna* (H. King) 1940; *Hudson's Bay* (Pichel), 1940; *Michael Shayne, Private Detective* (Forde), 1940; *For Beauty's Sake* (Traube), 1941; *Remember the Day* (H. King), 1941; *Romance of the Rio Grande* (Leeds), 1941; *Western Union* (F. Lang), 1941; *Tobacco Road* (Ford), 1941; *That Night in Rio* (Cummings), 1941; *The Great American Broadcast* (Mayo), 1941; *Blood and Sand* (Mamoulian), 1941; *The Cowboy and the Blonde* (McCarey), 1941; *Man Hunt* (F. Lang), 1941; *A Very Young Lady* (Schuster), 1941; *Moon Over Miami* (W. Lang), 1941; *The Bride Wore Crutches* (Traube), 1941; *Accent on Love* (McCarey), 1941; *Dance Hali* (Pichel), 1941; *Dressed to Kill* (Forde), 1941; *Charley's Aunt* (Mayo), 1941; *Wild Geese Calling* (Brahm) 1941; *Private Nurse* (Burton), 1941; *Sun Valley Serenade* (Humberstone), 1941; *Belle Starr* (Cummings), 1941; *Charlie Chan in Rio* (Lachman), 1941; *We Go Fast* (McGann), 1941; *The Last of the Duanes* (Tinling), 1941; *Man at Large* (Forde), 1941; *A Yank in the RAF* (H. King), 1941; *Great Guns* (Banks), 1941; *Riders of the Purple Sage* (Tinling), 1941; *Weekend in Havana* (W. Lang), 1941; *Rise and Shine* (Dwan), 1941; *How Green Was My Valley* (Ford), 1941; *Swamp Water* (Renoir), 1941; *The Lone Star Ranger* (Tinling), 1942; *Son of Fury* (Cromwell), 1942; *Roxie Hart* (Wellman), 1942; *Song of the Islands* (W. Lang), 1942; *Rings on Her Fingers* (Mamoulian), 1942; *My Gal Sal* (Cummings), 1942; *The Man Who Wouldn't Die* (Leeds), 1942; *It Happened in Flatbush* (McCarey), 1942; *Whispering Ghosts* (Werker), 1942; *Moontide* (Mayo), 1942; *The Magnificent Dope* (W. Lang), 1942; *Through Different Eyes* (Loring), 1942; *The Postman Didn't Ring* (Schuster), 1942; *Ten Gentlemen From West Point* (Hathaway), 1942; *This Above All* (Litvak), 1942; *Footlight Serenade* (Ratoff), 1942; *A-Haunting We Will Go* (Werker), 1942; *Little Tokyo USA* (Brower), 1942; *Orchestra Wives* (Mayo), 1942; *The Loves of Edgar Allen Poe* (Lachman), 1942; *Berlin Correspondent* (Forde), 1942; *Careful, Soft Shoulders* (Garrett), 1942; *Just Off Broadway* (Leeds), 1942; *Iceland* (Humberstone), 1942; *Girl Trouble* (Schuster), 1942; *Manila Calling* (Leeds) 1942; *The Man in the Trunk* (St. Clair), 1942; *Tales of Manhattan* (Duvivicr), 1942; *Springtime in the Rockies* (Cummings), 1942; *That Other Woman* (McCarey), 1942; *The Ox-Bow Incident* (Wellman), 1942; *Thunder Birds* (Wellman), 1942; *China Girl* (Hathaway), 1942; *The Undying Monster* (Brahm), 1942; *Time to Kill* (Leeds), 1942; *The*

*Black Swan* (H. King), 1942; *Dr. Renault's Secret* (Lachman), 1942; *Quiet Please, Murder* (Larkin), 1942; *Life Begins at 8:30* (Pichel), 1942; *The Meanest Man in the World* (Lanfield), 1943; *Dixie Dugan* (Brower), 1943; *Immortal Sergeant* (Stahl), 1943; *He Hired the Boss* (Loring), 1943; *Chetniks* (L. King), 1943; *Margin for Error* (Preminger), 1943; *My Friend Flicka* (Schuster), 1943; *Tonight We Raid Calais* (Brahm), 1943; *Crash Dive* (Mayo), 1943; *Coney Island* (W. Lang), 1943; *Up in Arms* (Nugent), 1944; *The Razor's Edge* (Goulding), 1946; *Anna and the King of Siam* (Cromwell), 1946; *Boomerang* (Kazan), 1947; *Moss Rose* (Ratoff), 1947; *Miracle on 34th Street* (Seaton), 1947; *The Ghost and Mrs. Muir* (Mankiewicz), 1947; *Mother Wore Tights* (W. Lang), 1947; *I Wonder Who's Kissing Her Now* (Bacon), 1947; *Captain from Castile* (H. King), 1947; *Joan of Arc* (Fleming), 1948; *Force of Evil* (Polonsky), 1948; *My Foolish Heart* (Robson), 1949; *Our Very Own* (Miller), 1950; *Edge of Doom* (Robson), 1950; *Cry Danger* (Parrish), 1951; *Want You* (Robson), 1951; *A Streetcar Named Desire* (Kazan), 1951; *Hans Christian Andersen* (C. Vidor), 1952; *On the Waterfront* (Kazan), 1954; *Solomon and Sheba* (K. Vidor), 1959; *Exodus* (Preminger), 1960; *Something Wild* (Garfein), 1961; *Goodbye Charlie* (Minnelli), 1964; *Cheyenne Autumn* (Ford), 1964; *The Greatest Story Ever Told* (Stevens), 1965; *The Chase* (Penn), 1965; *The Happening* (Silverstein), 1966; *The Valley of the Dolls* (Robson), 1967; *The Sweet Ride* (Hart) 1967; *The Boston Strangler* (Fleischer), 1968; *Tora-Tora-Tora* (Fleischer), 1970; *Tribes* (Sargent), 1970.

**Publications**

**On DAY: books**—*The Mighty Barnum: A Screen Play,* with foreword by Gene Fowler, New York, 1934; *Filmlexicon degli Autore e delle Opere,* 7 vols., edited by Michele Lacalamita and others, Rome, 1958-67; *Hollywood in the Thirties* by John Baxter, London and New York, 1968; *Le Décor de Film* by Leon Barsac, Paris, 1970; *Caligari's Cabinet and Other Grand Illusions,* Boston, 1976; *The Art of Hollywood* edited by John Hambley, London, 1979.

*          *          *

Richard Day put to screen some of the seediest sets in Hollywood history. The constructions for *Dead End* (1937) so appalled producer Samuel Goldwyn that the mogul wondered why his money couldn't have been used to build a better slum! Despite his proclivity for suggesting human blight, Day equally eased into drawing room dramas and musical extravaganzas. What unities can be found in such versatility?

Day's film career began with his apprenticeship to director Erich von Stroheim, who was possessed by a violent forcefulness akin to the German expressionists. Attracted to fantasy and symbolism, in spirit he belonged with the German social realists such as George Grosz. Yet von Stroheim's meticulous attention to detail recalled the American realists (such as Thomas Eakins), with their fascination for everyday minutiae. Although Day absorbed these traditions, he equally shared the sensibilities of the American Regionalist school. His classically balanced urban scenes recalled Edward Hopper's works, serene even in their turmoil. His humble, rural environments interpreted the countryside with the same poignancy found in paintings by Thomas Hart Benton.

Day's films were lush with details. His expressions of poverty included every crack in the wall, thick coats of dust, peeling paint,

and the fading floral wallpaper of an out-of-date print. Stairways creaked, and laundry blocked the sky like a Piranesi prison. On the other hand, Day gilded grand staircases with elaborate ornamentation for the old-world wealthy. His swags of velvet drapery regally dressed richly veined marble colonnades. The "moderne chic" danced on floors of patent leather-black gleam. White multi-platform steps, kaleidoscopic mirrors, and Deco glass sculpture well served the slick set's "swells." Despite their apparent disparities, each style shared Day's love of the particular.

In the 1950s the "new breed" of actors and directors found Day's work well suited to their needs. Day could capture the brutal snap and underlying sensitivity dominating the works of such directors as Elia Kazan. As always, Day invested the commonplace with potent symbolism. His intensely ambient spaces suggested inner psychologies—a critical factor in artistic works of the time. However, despite Day's topicality, his modus operandi had barely changed since his collaborations with von Stroheim.

Day achieved richness through magnification of the specific. Amassing details, he combined visual intricacy with depth of content. As a result, his tragic visions spoke with the boldest tones. Day filled even his saddest images with a poetry that von Stroheim denied, thus giving his viewer a bittersweet sense of hope.

—Edith Cortland Lee

# DAY, Robin

British industrial, interior, and furniture designer

**Born:** High Wycombe, Buckinghamshire, 25 May 1915. **Education:** High Wycombe Art School, 1930-33; Royal College of Art, London, ARCA, 1939. **Family:** Married the designer Lucienne Conradi in 1942; daughter: Paula. **Career:** Freelance designer, London, from 1945; design consultant, Hille International furniture, from 1950; John Lewis Partnership, from 1962; Barbican Arts Centre, London, from 1968. Part-time instructor in design, Beckenham College of Art, Kent, 1940-47, and the Regent Polytechnic School of Architecture, London, 1948-50; Governor, London College of Furniture, 1974-80. **Exhibitions:** *Hille: 75 Years of British Furniture,* Victoria and Albert Museum, London, 1981; *Design Since 1945,* Philadelphia Museum of Art, 1983; *New Design for Old,* Victoria and Albert Museum, London, 1986. **Collections:** Museum of Modern Art, New York; Victoria and Albert Museum, London; Konstindustrimuseet, Trondheim; Nationalmuseum, Stockholm. **Honors:** Fellow, 1948, Design Medal, 1957, Society of Industrial Artists and Designers, London; First Prize (with Clive Latimer), International Furniture Design Competition, Museum of Modern Art, New York, 1949; Gold Medal, 1951, Silver Medal, 1954, Milan Triennale; two Design of the Year Awards, 1957, and Design Centre Awards, 1961, 1962, 1965, 1966, Council of Industrial Design, London; Royal Designer for Industry, Royal Society of Arts, London, 1959; officer, Order of the British Empire, 1983. **Address:** 49 Cheyne Walk, Chelsea, London SW3 5LP, England.

**Works**

*Hillestak* Chair, low-cost stacking chair in beech, for Hille, 1949.
Tip-up auditorium seating in steel, latex foam and uncut moquet, for the Royal Festival Hall, London, 1951.

British art and design displays, at the Milan Triennale, 1951.
Television and radio cabinets, for Pye Ltd., 1958.
Furniture, for Gatwick Airport, Sussex, 1960.
Chair range in injection-moulded polypropylene, for Hille, 1963.
Interiors of the Super VC10 and other passenger aircraft, for the
British Overseas Airways Corporation, 1963-74.
Seating, for the Barbican Arts Centre, Concert Hall and Theatre,
1980.
*Spectrum* seating in steel and polypropylene, for Hille, 1985.
*Stadium* seating in steel and polypropylene, for Hille, 1985.
Upholstered stacking chair in steel and formed ply, for Mines and
West, 1989.

## Publications

**On DAY: books**—*British Furniture Today* by Erno Goldfinger,
London, 1951; *The Adventure of British Furniture* by David Joel,
London, 1953, as *Furniture Design Set Free,* London, 1969; *Packaging: An International Survey of Package Design* edited by Walter
Herdeg, Zurich, 1959; *Public Interiors* by Misha Black, London,
1960; *Furniture in Britain Today* by Dennis and Barbara Young,
London, 1964; *Looking at Furniture* by Gordon Russell, London,
1964; *Industrial Design in Britain* by Noel Carrington, London,
1976; *Hille: 75 Years of British Furniture,* exhibition catalogue
by Sutherland Lyall, London, 1981; *Design Since 1945* edited
by Kathryn Hiesinger and George Marcus, Philadelphia and
London, 1983; *The Conran Directory of Design* edited by Stephen
Bayley, London, 1985; *New Design for Old,* exhibition catalogue
with texts by Helen Hamlyn, Eric Midwinter, and others, London, 1986.

\*

All man-made things and environments are designed in one
way or another. I believe that the quality of this design is important to the well-being of humanity. Designers have responsibilities other than the profit motive, and must be increasingly concerned with conservation and the sensible use of the planet's
resources.

I feel that all fields of design are interrelated and I personally
prefer to avoid over-specialisation by working in a number of design areas. I am less interested in fashion than in a synthesis of good
construction, good function, and aesthetics.

—Robin Day

\*   \*   \*

Though the early years of Robin Day's career were spent in
display and graphic design, his training and real interest lay in
furniture. It is in this field, especially in the development of injection-moulded plastic furniture, that Day made important innovative contributions. Of special interest throughout his career has
been mass production of low-cost units that put good design within
reach of the everyday householder.

Day was first brought to the attention of British furniture manufacturers in 1949 when he won first prize in a competition sponsored by the Museum of Modern Art in New York for a low-cost
storage unit. He shortly became a design consultant to the Hille
Company of London and in so doing, established one of the most

fruitful collaborative relationships of recent times in the British
design field. Sharing with Hille common interests in production of
low-cost furniture and in exploring new materials and technical
means, Day was placed in the ideal position of being able to carry
out research subsidized and encouraged by his employer.

In the early 1950s Day explored the potential of moulded
plywood using newly available plastic glues. This research resulted in the highly successful Hillestak chair which was, as its
name suggests, stackable, a feature then attracting much interest. However, despite the fact that the design looked simple, the
chair required assembly of twenty-two parts. Day further simplified the design of this inexpensive, stackable chair, and produced the Q Stak chair, which had a back and seat made of a
single piece of moulded plywood which bolted onto a metal legframe.

The liberating principle, which allowed for the seating shell and
the base to be separately considered and made of different materials, had been originally established in the mid 1950s by the American designer Charles Eames, who applied the idea first to his moulded plywood chairs and shortly thereafter to his moulded fiberglass
chairs. Soon, Hille acquired rights to produce the Eames chair made
of moulded, glass-reinforced plastic. Inspired by this chair, Day,
wanting to product a still lower-cost plastic chair, began his research into the properties of polypropylene, a cheap, durable, lightweight plastic invented in 1954 by the Italian Guilio Natta. By the
early 1960s Day had successfully developed a shell that could be
made of polypropylene and produced by means of injection moulding. This material and method reduced costs considerably over
fiberglass.

This versatile shell has been treated to a wide variety of uses (left
bare, padded with foam, and variously upholstered) and joined to
different kinds of bases (four legs and pedestal and swivel bases).
The shell has been used in mass seating arrangements both indoors
and outdoors, and it has been reduced in scale for child and youth
seating.

—Barbara Young

# DEACON, Tom
Canadian furniture designer

**Born:** Hamilton, Ontario, in 1956. **Education:** University of Toronto
School of Architecture, B.Arch., 1982. **Career:** Founder and designer, with Lee Jacobson, AREA Group furniture company,
Toronto, from 1984; consultant to Keilhauer Industries, Creative
Space, Design America, Bernhardt Furniture, and Nienkamper. **Exhibitions:** *Architects Inside,* International Design Centre, New York,
1988; *Art in Everyday Life,* Harbourfront Gallery, Toronto, 1988;
*Canada Designs for Business,* Canadian Embassy, Tokyo, 1992;
*Designed for Living: Furniture that Works,* Ontario Craft Council,
Toronto, 1995. **Collections:** Design Exchange, Toronto. **Honors:**
Graduation medal, Royal Architecture Institute of Canada, 1982;
Virtu International Design Competition winner, 1986, 1993, 1994;
honorable mention, *Progressive Architecture* Furniture Competition, 1987; Bronze Medal, Institute of Business Designers, 1991,
1993; NeoCon Silver Awards, 1993, 1994; honorable mention, *International Design* magazine, 1994; Product Award, Association of
Registered Interior Designers of Ontario, 1994.

## Works

*Spider* table, for AREA Group, 1984.
*Strala* lamp, for Portico, 1986 (with Scot Laughton).
*York* chair, for AREA Group, 1987.
*Deacon* side chairs, for Keilhauer Industries, 1989.
*Calais* side chairs, for Keilhauer Industries, 1990.
*Soho* lounge seating, for Keilhauer Industries, 1990.
*Elgin* lounge seating, for Keilhauer Industries, 1991.
*Vector* CD stand, for Creative Space Ltd., 1991.
*Simcoe* side chairs, for Keilhauer Industries, 1991.
*Franklin* side chair, for Keilhauer Industries, 1992.
*Truva* tables, for Prismatique, 1992.
*Cirrus* table, for Nienkamper, 1992.
*Studio* chair, for Bernhardt Furniture, 1993.
*Promenade* chair, for AREA Group, 1993.
*Danforth* executive seating, for Keilhauer Industries, 1993.
*Chatham* lounge seating, for Keilhauer Industries, 1994.

## Publications

**On DEACON: books**—*Art in Everyday Life,* exhibition catalogue by Peter Day and Linda Lewis, Toronto, 1988; **articles**—"Comment" in *Canadian Architect* (Don Mills, Ontario), August 1987; "Echoes of the Past, Visions for the Present" by Kurt Anderson in *Time,* 4 January 1988; "On the Borderline" by Annette Hanna in *ID* (New York), June 1988; *Vogue,* August 1988; "Everything but Kitchen Sink in Homegrown Design Show" by Christopher Hume in *Toronto Star,* 31 August 1988; "Tom Deacon" by David Lasker in *Canadian Interiors,* July/August 1989; "Q & A, Tom Deacon" in *Contract* (New York), August/September 1990; "The Deacon's Chair" in *Azure,* October 1990; *Canadian Interiors,* October 1990; *Globe and Mail* (Toronto), 24 November 1990; "Homegrown Furnishings" by Anne Bokma in *Financial Post* (Toronto), December 1990; "Deacon Beacon" in *Domino,* February 1991; "Seatings Supremo" by John Barber in *Globe and Mail,* 7 November 1991; "Sofa So Good" by John Barber in *Globe and Mail,* 27 August 1992; "Furniture Comeback" by John Barber in *Globe and Mail,* 29 October 1992; "Canadian by Design" by Brenda Dalglish in *Maclean's* (Toronto), 10 January 1994; "In the Driver's Seat" by Amy Milshtein in *Contract* (New York), March 1994; *ID Magazine Annual Design Review,* July/August 1994; "A Shaker for Moderns" in *Insite* (London), September 1994; "Art for Furniture's Sake" by Pamela Young in *Globe and Mail,* 22 June 1995.

*    *    *

Tom Deacon carved out a career specializing in the design of contract office furniture before he was 40 years old. He is significant for breaking down the cold feel of modern corporate contract seating and introducing a more humane and pluralistic approach. He favors natural wood materials over metal, and shows an appreciation for historical precedent.

Deacon graduated from the University of Toronto School of Architecture in 1982 but never practiced. Recognizing that it is almost impossible to design a building on speculation, he moved immediately into furniture design because it offers far greater concept-to-production control.

Just two years after graduating, he co-founded AREA Group, a furniture manufacturer in Toronto. AREA began by producing Le Corbusier's 1928 *Grand Confort* seating under license. With this hands-on manufacturing experience, the company soon expanded its repertoire to include the work of Deacon and other Canadian designers.

Deacon's first design for AREA to receive critical acclaim in Canada was the *York* chair. Launched in 1987, the bentwood tub chair with steel tube arms, although derivative of Philippe Starck's *Café Costa* chair, demonstrated Deacon's skillful ability to interpret the latest design trends.

In 1989 Deacon stepped back from the business of running AREA to spend more time designing. He currently designs on a freelance basis for major furniture manufacturers including Bernhardt Furniture, Nienkamper, and Keilhauer Industries.

One of Deacon's most successful freelance relationships has been with the Canadian contract seating manufacturer Keilhauer. In 1991 he designed the *Deacon,* his first chair for the young company, which helped to launch them both into the international arena. The *Deacon* was a turning point for the designer, reflecting his emerging ability to transform anonymous boardroom fixtures into warm, personal designs. It is his first all wood chair and reveals his interest in Shaker furniture. Made from Canadian maple, the armchair features rounded sweeping arms and a wide back with a single slat decorated by a circular cut out. Its low profile would become a common characteristic of all of Deacon's designs and suits the spacious boardroom environment for which it is intended. The *Deacon* chair won a gold award from the New York-based Institute of Business Design.

In 1994 Deacon entered the fast lane of adjustable swivel office chairs, where the Ferraris of the furniture world compete. Such ergonomically-tested, high-tech seating is typically made from molded plastic. In the *Danforth Series* for Keilhauer, Deacon introduced a wood frame and thereby brilliantly adapted ergonomic seating equipment into the typology of traditional furniture. Deacon drew his inspiration from the classic Boston rocker as exemplified in the *Danforth*'s rolled front seat and wooden scrolled armrests. Its swivel wood base also recalls the generic nineteenth-century all-wood desk chair.

Tom Deacon has done a great deal to put post-modern Canadian furniture design on the global map. He is the golden boy of Canadian design, choosing to remain in Toronto, but continually building a roster of international clients.

—Elizabeth Crawford and Rachel Gotlieb

# D'EAUBONNE, Jean (Adrien)
French painter and film designer

**Born:** Talence, Gironde, 8 March 1903. **Education:** Studied painting and sculpture under Antoine Bourdelle, Paris. **Career:** Painter and poster designer, Paris, until 1927; assistant film designer to Lazare Meerson and Jean Perrier, Paris, 1928-30; art director, working on the films of Marcel Carne, Jean Gremillon, Jean Cocteau, Max Ophuls, Maurice Gleizes, Jacques Feyder, Julien Duvivier, Vicente Minnelli, and others, Paris, 1930-39, 1946-71, and Hollywood, 1957-68. **Honors:** Venice Film Festival Prize, 1950; Punta del Este Film Festival Prize, 1950. **Died:** July 1970.

## Works

Film designs include—*Le Perroque Vert* (Milva), 1928; *Tarakanova* (Bernard), 1930; *Le Sang d 'un Poète* (Cocteau), 1930; *Le Defenseur* (Ryder), 1930; *La Ronde des Heures* (Ryder), 1930; *Azais* (Hervil), 1930; *Coup de Roulis* (de la Cour), 1931; *Le Juif Polonais* (Kemm), 1931; *Coquecigrole* (Berthomieu), 1931; *Pour un Sou d'Amour* (Gremillon), 1931; *Amour et Discipline* (Kemm), 1931; *Le Truc du Brésilien* (Cavalcanti), 1932; *Les Vignes du Seigneur* (Hervil), 1932; *L'Amour et al Veine* (Banks), 1932; *Mademoiselle Josette a Femme* (Berthomieu), 1933; *Mannequins* (Hervil), 1933; *Amede Clown* (Noe and Didier), 1933; *L'Ami Fritz* (de Baroncelli), 1933; *Coralieet Cie* (Cavalcanti), 1933; *La Femme Idéale* (Berthomieu), 1933; *Maitre Bolbec et son Mari* (Natanson), 1934; *Le Petit Jacques* (Roudes), 1934; *La Reine de Biarritz* (Toulout), 1934; *L'Aristo* (Berthomieu), 1934; *Le Clown Bux* (Natanson), 1935; *LesBeaux Jours* (M. Allegret), 1935; *Le Chant d'Amour* (Roudes), 1935; *Marie des Angoisses* (Bernheim), 1935; *Le Roman d'un Spahi* (Bernheim), 1936; *La Flamme* (Berthomieu), 1936; *Jenny* (Carne), 1936; *L'Amant de Madame Vidal* (Berthomieu), 1936; *Anne-Marie* (Bernard), 1936; *La Chaste Suzanne* (Berthomieu), 1937; *Police Mondaine* (Bernheim and Chamborantj), 1937; *L'Habit Vert* (Richebe), 1937; *Un Dejeuner de Soleil* (Cravenne), 1937; *Légions d'Honneur* (Gleize), 1937; *L'Homme sans Nom* (Vallee), 1937; *Les Gens du Voyage* (Feyder), 1938; *Le Train pour Venise* (Berthomieu), 1938; *Carrefour* (Bernhardt), 1938; *Trois Valses* (Berger), 1938; *Un de la Canebière* (Pujol), 1938; *Les Gangsters du Chateâu d'If* (Pujol), 1938; *Nuit de Decembre* (Bernhardt), 1939; *L'Enfer des Anges* (Christian-Jaque), 1939; *De Mayerling a Sarajevo* (Ophuls), 1939; *La Loi du Nord* (Feyder), 1942; *Une Femme Disparait* (Feyder), 1942; *Etoile sans Lumiere* (Blistene), 1945; *Macadam* (Blistene and Feyder), 1946; *La Foix aux Chimeres* (Chenal), 1946; *La Chartreuse de Parme* (Christian-Jaque), 1947; *Black Magic* (Ratoff), 1947; *L'Impasse des Deux Anges* (Tourneur), 1948; *Hans le Marin* (Villiers), 1948; *Le Paradis des Pilotes Perdus* (Lapmin), 1949; *Je n'Aime que Toi* (Montazel), 1949; *Pas de Week-end pour notre Amour* (Montazel), 1949; *Lady Paname* (Jeanson), 1949; *Orphée* (Cocteau), 1950; *La Ronde* (Ophuls), 1950; *La Dame Chez Maxim's* (Aboulker), 1950; *Ma Pomme* (Sauvajon), 1950; *Olivia* (Audry), 1950; *Nuits de Paris* (Baum), 1951; *Le Plaisir* (Ophuls), 1952; *Casque d'Or* (Becker), 1952; *Plaisirs de Paris* (Baum), 1952; *La Fête a Henriette* (Duvivier), 1952; *"Lysistrata"* episode of *Destinee* (Christian-Jaque), 1952; *Rue d'Estrapade* (Becker), 1953; *Jeunes Maries* (Grangier), 1953; *Le Mystère du Palace Hôtel* (Steckcl and Berna), 1953; *Madame de. . .* (Ophuls), 1953; *Cet Homme est Dangereux* (Sacha), 1953; *Julietta* (M. Allegret), 1953; *Touchez pas au Grisbi* (Grisbi), 1954; *Mam'zelle Nitouche* (Y. Allegret), 1954; *Scenes de Ménage* (Berthomieu), 1954; *Bonnes a Tuer* (Decoin), 1954; *Les Amants du Tage* (Vrrncuil), 1954; *Marianne de ma Jeunesse* (Duvivier), 1955; *Lola Montes* (Ophuls), 1955; *L'Affaire des Poisons* (Decoin), 1955; *Le Secret de Soeur Angèle* (Joannon), 1955; *Le long des Trottoirs* (Mo-guy), 1956; *Paris-Palace-Hôtel* (Verneuil), 1956; *L'Homme aux Cles d'Or* (Joannon), 1956; *Le Mariée est Trop Belle* (Gaspard-Huit), 1956; *BonsoirParis, Bonjourl'Amour* (Baum), 1956; *OSS 117n'est pas Mort* (Sacha), 1956; *Jusqu'au Dernier* (Billon), 1956; *Amère Victoire* (Ray), 1957; *Une Manche et la Belle* (Verneuil), 1957; *Quand la Femme s'en Mêle* (Y. Allcgrct), 1957; *Montparnasee 19* (Becker), 1957; *The Reluctant Debutant* (Minnelli), 1958; *Christine* (Gaspard-Huit), 1958; *Nina* (Boyer), 1958; *Ein Engel auf Erden* (Radvanyi), 1959; *Suspense au 2e Bureau* (de St.-Maurice), 1959; *Katja* (Siodmak), 1960; *Les Magiciennes* (Friedman), 1960; *Crack in the Mirror* (Fleischer), 1960; *The Big Gamble* (Fleischer), 1960; *Madame Sans-Gêne* (Christian-Jaque), 1961; *L'Affaire Nina B* (Siodmak), 1962; *Love is a Ball* (Swift), 1962; *Charade* (Donen), 1963; *Paris When it Sizzles* (Quine), 1964; *Le Repas des Fauves* (Christian-Jaque), 1964; *Lady L* (Ustinov), 1965; *Cartes sur Table* (Franco), 1965; *Galia* (Lautner), 1966; *Avec le Peau des Autres* (Deray), 1966; *Fleur d 'Oseille* (Lautner), 1967; *La Pacha* (Lauter), 1967; *Custer of the West* (Siodmak), 1968; *The Girl on a Motorcycle* (Cardiff), 1968; *Johnny Banco* (Y. Allegret), 1968; *Faut pas Prendre les Enfants du Bon Dieu pour des Canards Sauvages* (Audiard), 1968; *Une Veuve en Or* (Audiard), 1969; *Sur la Route de Salina* (Lautner), 1969; *Elle Boit pas, Elle Fume pas, Elle Drague pas, mais . . . Elle Cause* (Audiard), 1970; *Sappho* (Farrel), 1970; *Laisse Aller, c'est une Valse* (Lautner), 1970; *Le Cri du Cormorant le Soir, au-dessus des Jonques* (Audiard), 1970; *Le Drapeau Noir Flotte sur la Marmite* (Audiard), 1971.

## Publications

**On D'EAUBONNE: books**—*Dictionnaire des Cineastes* edited by Georges Sadoul, Paris, 1965, 1974; *Le Décor de Film* by Leon Barsacq, Paris, 1970; *Caligari's Cabinet and Other Grand Illusions,* Boston, 1976; *Screen Series: France* by Marcel Martin, London and New York, 1971; *The World Encyclopedia of Film* edited by Tim Cawkwell and John M. Smith, London, 1972; *The International Film Encyclopedia* by Ephraim Katz, London, 1980.

\* \* \*

Jean D'Eaubonne established his credentials as one of France's most talented art directors during his collaboration with Jean Cocteau on *Le Sang d'un poète.* His training as a sculptor and assistantship with Lazare Meerson perfectly suited Cocteau's concept of the film's surrealism. Reworking this style 20 years later in Cocteau's *Orphée* seemed to provide convenient bookends for the first half of D'Eaubonne's career. Yet neither film truly indicates his strengths or versatility.

Designing for many of France's important directors, such as Carne, Ophuls, Feyder, Becker, and Duvivier, D'Eaubonne excelled in extending Meerson's "poetic realism." In many ways similar to the visual strategies and thematic concerns of the German *Kammerspiel*, poetic realism employed sets to complement or advance a film's narrative and humanistic viewpoint. This allowed D'Eaubonne to design in many different fashions, depending on the need of each specific film. His elegant work in *Casque d'Or* borders on Impressionism while his few films in the United States, notably *Charade* and *Paris When it Sizzles,* suggest a development of poetic realism toward a rigid naturalism. His collaboration with Georges Annenkov and Christian Matras on Max Ophuls' last four films, *La Ronde, Le Plaisir, Madame de...,* and *Lola Montès,* yielded magnificent results. The sets, costumes, and cinematography combined perfectly to reveal a sensitivity to baroque detail in a variation of poetic realism best described as diffused Expressionism. The four began work on a film based on *The Marriage of Figaro,* but abandoned it after Ophuls's death.

Jean D'Eaubonne cannot be easily classified; his designs borrow from many schools and are applied upon narrative and thematic demand. His 40-year career bears testament to his range and skill.

—George Walsh

# de CASTELBAJAC, Jean-Charles

French fashion, interior, and furniture designer

**Born:** Of French parents, in Casablanca, Morocco, 28 November 1949. **Education:** Attended Catholic boarding schools in France, 1955-66; studied law, Faculté de Droit, Limoges, 1966-77. **Family:** Married Katherine Lee Chambers in 1979; sons: Guillaume and Louis. **Career:** Founder and designer, with his mother Jeanne-Blanche de Castelbajac, of Ko and Co ready-to-wear fashion company, Limoges, from 1968; also freelanced for Pierre d'Alby, Max Mara, Jesus Jeans, Etam, Gadgling, Julie Latour, Fusano, Amaraggi, Carel Shoes, Ellesse, Hilton, Levi-Strauss, Reynaud, and others, from 1968; director, Jean-Charles de Castelbajac fashion label, Paris, 1970, and Société Jean Charles de Castelbajac S.A.R.L., Paris, 1978; established boutiques in Paris, New York, and Tokyo, 1975-76. Also film and stage costume designer, notably for musicians Elton John, Talking Heads, and Rod Stewart, from 1976; interior and furniture designer, from 1979. **Member:** Didier Grumbach's Les Créateurs group of designers, Paris, 1974-77. **Exhibitions:** Centre Georges Pompidou, Paris, 1978; *Forum Design,* Linz, Austria, 1980; Laforet Museum, Belgium, 1984. **Collections:** Musée du Costume, Paris; Fashion Institute of Technology, New York. **Addresses:** 188 rue de Rivoli, 75001 Paris, France; 55 rue de Lisbonne, 75008 Paris, France.

### Works

Film costumes include—*Violette et Francois,* 1976; *Annie Hall,* 1977; *Who Killed My Husband?,* 1979; *Charlie's Angels,* television series, 1978-80.

### Publications

**On de CASTELBAJAC: books**—*The Changing World of Fashion* by Ernestine Carter, London, 1977; *Design ist unsichtbar* edited by Hellmuth Gsollpointer, Angela Hareiter, and others, Vienna, 1981; *Who's Who in Fashion* edited by Karl Strute and Theodor Doelken, Zurich, 1982; *Le Chic et la Mode* by Delbourg Delpais, Paris, 1982; *Flammarion Fashion Dictionary* by Jerome Deslanbre, Paris, 1983; *McDowell's Directory of Twentieth Century Fashion* by Colin McDowell, London, 1984; *The Encyclopaedia of Fashion from 1840 to the 1980s* by Georgina O'Hara, London, 1986; **articles**—"Un styliste bourrée d'idées: Jean-Charles de Castelbajac" in *Gap* (Paris), October 1975; "Jean-Charles de Castelbajac: French Revolutionary" in *GQ* (New York), April 1981.

\*

In 1974 I introduced into fashion the use of numerous materials originally destined for industry—materials like bandages, blankets, car upholstery, cheese cloth, linen sheeting, spinnaker nylon, cleaning fabric, etc. For daytime sport silhouette looks in 1975, I introduced a line of jogging wear, with quilted jackets, and created the quilted down coat now so famous in the U.S.A. I also made numerous coats and jackets from plaid and blanket materials. Subsequently I have worked with major artists on painted dresses (like a walking canvas), and have designed furniture.

My philosophy is based on timelessness, and my creative work—both in fashion and other fields of design—is informed by the same idea. I am never influenced by folk or ethnic styles, but by lifestyles and elegance. I consider my work akin to that of the painter, and my ideas come from observing nature and people going about their lives. I like working for different industries—in ceramics, automobiles, and furniture—because they are part of the puzzle which constitutes my style—a style of freedom.

—Jean-Charles de Castelbajac

\*   \*   \*

A man of passions, for form and function, for color, for comfort and protection—there lies the basis of this humanistic designer. Jean-Charles de Castelbajac began his obsession by cutting his first garment out of a blanket from boarding school. Because the material already existed, he was left to play with the form. Many times each year, he returns to this first gesture, cutting the cloth, so he remains close to its essence and function. This he must accomplish before thinking of embellishment, so a permanence results in his garments. They are never linked to fleeting moments or frivolity. De Castelbajac feels that above all a sentiment must be produced through color. Because of this, he has an affinity with painters, with whom he spends much time to strengthen his creative impulses.

A man of the future, he nevertheless does not make "futuristic" clothing. His designs fulfill the need for practical and unassuming fashion of maximum quality. Favoring soft natural colors, he also uses natural textures and fibers. Innovative but respectful of classics, de Castelbajac has been called a modern traditionalist. His fondness for architecture is apparent in the harmonious, architectonic shapes that flow through every collection. Since his imagination does not stop with garments, de Castelbajac has decided also to create other objects for the environment. Having a strong revulsion to prints on garments, he humorously solved the predicament by using large-scale motifs of Tom and Jerry or phrases from Nerval or Barbey d'Aurevilly inscribed on silk for very simple dresses. His clothing is identifiable by his manner of being true to himself—that is, being profoundly human and knowing something which is not only style.

—Andrea Arsenault

# DE FOUW, Jan

Dutch graphic and type designer

**Born:** The Hague, The Netherlands, 1929. **Education:** Studied commercial art at the Royal College of Art, The Hague. **Military Service:** Served in Dutch Army, 1949-51. **Career:** Freelance designer, KLM (Royal Dutch Airlines), 1947-49; freelance designer, Ireland, from 1951; art director, *Ireland of the Welcomes,* Irish Tourist Board bimonthly publication, 1952-1996; founding member, Graphic Studio, Dublin, 1962; founding member, Society of Designers in Ireland, 1972; director and chairman, Black Church Print Studio, Dublin, from 1980; lecturer in printmaking, typography, design history and layout, and design principles and practice, National College of Art, Dublin, from 1975; lecturer, College of Marketing and Design, Dublin, from 1988. **Exhibitions:** Triskel Arts Centre, Cork, 1982; *Irish Festival,* Milwaukee, 1986; *International Miniprint,* Hendricks Gallery, Dublin, 1987; Irish exchange exhibitions,

Beijing and Hangzhou, 1988; Art of the Irish Gallery, Boston, and Galerie Deux Tetes, Toronto, 1988; Crawford Municipal Gallery, Cork, 1989; *Phoenix,* Riverrun Gallery, Dublin, 1990; *European Large Format Printmaking,* Guiness Hop Store, Dublin, 1991. **Honors:** Packaging Design "Starpacks," 1963; Associateship of National College of Art and Design (honoris causa), Dublin, 1991; three time award winner, International Regional Magazine Association.

### Publications

**On DE FOUW: books—***Portfolio of Biographical Information on Studio Artists,* Black Church Print Studio, Dublin; *The Advertising Book* by Hugh Oram, Dublin, 1986; *Irish Mini Print,* exhibition catalogue, Dublin, 1989; *European Large Format Printmaking,* exhibition catalogue, Dublin, 1991; **articles—**"A Dutch Treat" by Jarlath Hayes in *Ireland of the Welcomes,* vol. 37, 1988.

\*     \*     \*

Dutch-born designer Jan de Fouw played an important role in the emergence of modern graphic design in Ireland during the postwar years. He came to Ireland in 1951, introducing the Bauhaus design principles he had absorbed as a student of commercial design in The Hague. A leading centre for modernist art and design, Holland was also renowned for its strong printing tradition and Dutch immigrants like de Fouw, Gus Melai, Piet Sluis, and Ries Hoek proved a decisive influence on the development of modern Irish advertising and graphic design.

Before coming to Ireland, de Fouw had worked as a designer for KLM (Royal Dutch Airlines), a company noted for its progressive approach to advertising. His first job in Ireland was as a freelance designer for the firm of Arks Advertising. At this stage, in the early 1950s, art education in Ireland did not address the realm of advertising in any specific way and de Fouw's professional approach and modern outlook proved exemplary, providing much needed stimulus for a generation of young Irish designers. He recalls that his first major commission was for a two-inch double column drawing of a steaming kettle for Arks for which he was paid £5.

In 1952, de Fouw embarked on a major undertaking as art director for the bimonthly periodical *Ireland of the Welcomes.* The periodical, which has a print run of 100,000 copies worldwide, serves as a celebration of Irish culture and heritage, with ninety percent of its subscribers residing in the United States. From the outset a consistently high standard of design has distinguished the publication. De Fouw cites magazine and book production as among his principle interests. He has worked for various Irish publishers including Gill and Macmillan, Mercier Press, Wolfhound Press, and Veritas, for whom he designed a book documenting the Papal visit to Ireland in 1979. Other related commissions include liaising with the Cultural Relations Committee of the Department of Foreign Affairs, and the Institute of Public Administration.

As an occasional lecturer of long standing association with Ireland's National College of Art and Design, Jan de Fouw has been responsible for directing the education of many of the country's latest designers. He is also well regarded as a guest lecturer at Dun Laoghaire School of Art and Design and the College of Marketing and Design, Dublin. His role in promoting awareness of graphic design in Ireland is reflected through his involvement with organizations such as the Black Church Print Studio in Dublin's artistic quarter, Temple Bar. The studio is a nonprofit organization operated by a group of established artists dedicated to promoting an increased understanding of the practice and principles of printmaking in Ireland. One of the company's chief concerns, detailed in promotional literature, is the advocation of "fine art printmaking as a valid means of artistic expression of equal importance to painting and sculpture. The studio's abiding concern is the encouragement of young artists, while encouraging all aesthetic and innovative approaches to the printmaking media." These initiatives are addressed through organized lectures, workshops, and demonstrations, in addition to national, European, and international exhibitions. To celebrate Dublin's year as European City of Culture in 1991, the studio organized a European Large Format Printmaking Exhibition, profiling the work of twelve European Union countries. Exhibitors included Uwe Bremer, Nino Longobardi, and de Fouw as one of over twenty Irish participants.

Many of de Fouw's own graphic works address the theme of man's relationship with nature and the elements, expressed primarily through the media of relief print and etching. For example, in a small work entitled *Metamorphosis* (1981), he uses the medium of etching on copper to produce a "portrait" which suggests man's affinity and oneness with nature. Twisting branches suggest a crop of human hair. The outline of a small fish echoes the almond oval of a human eye. A bird, its wings splayed in flight, evokes the outline of a dark bearded face. With characteristic versatility and flair, the artist has also provided a sensuous and personal insight into the etching process in a poem entitled *Artist's Proof,* which concludes as follows: "forgotten the long nights/of waiting, wrestling/for relenting result;/printed by hand on paper,/moist, soft, limited edition/ of a fleeting moment./ Numbered and dated or simply/signed A/P, artist's proof."

—Alison FitzGerald

# de GIVENCHY, Hubert (James Marcel Taffin)
French fashion designer

**Born:** Beauvais, 21 February 1927. **Education:** Studied at the Collège Felix-Faure, in Beauvais and Montalembert; studied at the Ecole National Supérieure des Beaux-Arts, Paris; studied at the Faculty of Law, University of Paris. **Career:** Worked in the fashion houses of Lucien Lelong, 1945-46, Robert Piquet, 1946-48, Jacques Fath, 1948-49, and Elsa Schiaparelli, 1949-51, all in Paris; established Givenchy fashion house in Parc Monceau, Paris, 1952-56, and Avenue George V, Paris, from 1956. President and director-general of Societé Givenchy-Couture and Societé des Parfums Givenchy, Paris, from 1954. Also film costume designer, from 1961. **Exhibitions:** *Fashion: An Anthology,* Victoria and Albert Museum, London, 1971. **Addresses:** 3 Avenue George V, 75008 Paris, France; 4 rue Fabert, 75007 Paris, France.

### Works

Film costume designs include—*Breakfast at Tiffany's* (Edwards), 1961; *Charade* (Donen), 1963; *The VIPs* (Asquith), 1963; *Paris*

*When It Sizzles* (Quine), 1964; *How to Steal a Million* (Wyler), 1966.

## Publications

**On GIVENCHY: books**—*Paris à la Mode* by Celia Bertin, Paris and London 1956; *Dressmakers of France* by Mary Brooks Picken and Dora Loues Miller, New York, 1956; *Kings of Fashion* by Anny Latour, Stuttgart, 1956, London, 1958; *The Fashionable Savages* by John Fairchild, New York, 1965; *The Fashion Makers* by Leonard Halliday, London, 1966; *Fashion: An Anthology by Cecil Beaton,* exhibition catalogue compiled by Madeleine Ginsburg, London, 1971; *In Vogue: Sixty Years of Celebrities and Fashion* by Georgina Howell, London, 1975, 1978, New York, 1976; *In Fashion: Dress in the Twentieth Century* by Prudence Glynn, London, 1978; *25 Ans de Marie-Claire de 1954 a 1979,* compiled by Francoise Mohrt, Paris, 1979; *The Guinness Guide to 20th Century Fashion* by David Bond, Enfield, 1981; *The Collector's Book of Twentieth Century Fashion* by Frances Kennet, London and New York, 1983; *McDowell's Directory of Twentieth Century Fashion* by Colin McDowell, London, 1984; *The Encyclopaedia of Fashion from 1840 to the 1980s* by Georgina O'Hara, London, 1986.

\*   \*   \*

Simple mix-and-match separates, which emphasize feminine curves; wide use of accessories such as scarves; blouses and jackets with widened shoulders and puffed sleeves; two-part evening gowns, with choice of either décolleté or plain jersey top; an almost exclusive limitation to black and white; the penchant for basic fabrics, especially cotton: these are some of the early characteristics which helped propel Parisian fashion designer Hubert de Givenchy into instant fame in the early 1950s. Givenchy's debut, accomplished on what was by Parisian couturier standards a shoestring budget, was quite a spectacular and imaginative display of women's fashions. Geared toward originality and affordability for the wearer, the designs accomplished these goals with simple fabrics and outfitting that encouraged interchangeability of parts. A comparison of two of Givenchy's 1952 outfits exemplifies the multiple possibilities he found in black and white. Consider first his wrap bathrobe coat of black net worn over a softly figure-hugging, strapless, floor length, white satin evening gown. Then consider his black alpaca skirt with high, stitched Flamenco waist teamed with a white cotton blouse that incorporates black and white Flamenco ruffles at the elbows of the wide sleeves. Accessories introduced at this time included a paper-lantern pleated babushka, a Garbo-like slouch hat, straw slippers with bandanna-knot toes, and a huge, multi-layered, white chiffon scarf bordered with navy-blue satin and worn knotted at the neck of his sleekly fitted, navy-blue gabardine suit.

Givenchy was only twenty-five in 1952 when he opened his own house in Paris, but he had learned both the practical and theoretical ends of his profession during eight years spent working with Jacques Fath, Robert Piquet, Lucien Lelong (where he took Dior's place), and Elsa Schiaparelli. Four years after the commencement of his own salon, Givenchy met the established "institution" of Parisian couture, Cristobal Balenciaga, and began a lifelong friendship which was an important influence on his ideas and approach to style. Critical opinion during the next years was mixed as to whether

Givenchy's resulting move away from the novel and toward a more cautious evolution led him into a kind of premature classicism or into a more timeless and conceptual approach, a steadily pursued course which in the long run would be to his lasting benefit. Following a basic cue from his prime mentor, Givenchy has expressed his beliefs in the nature of fashion design, seeing it as a discipline which should be a slow and steady evolution, dedicated to enhancing the meaning and movement of the human body, attentive to the needs of the changing times and concentrating also on the volume and proportions one puts on the body. He feels that fashion should allow adaption to personal style, resulting in an overall discreet mixture according to the individual's choices. During the 1960's, Givenchy was the choice of many notables such as Jacqueline Kennedy Onassis and Audrey Hepburn.

However, it is perhaps unfair to judge Givenchy on the basis of fame's currencies. His inventiveness and continuous striving to combine luxury with experiment, while not forgetting tradition, have earned him a prominent place among fashion designers of his time. It should not go unnoted that Givenchy the man—handsome, astute, patrician—is himself symbolic of the grand tradition of twentieth-century Parisian haute couture, which has generally waned with the current generation. Whether it is for his draped satin evening sheaths, his dresses embroidered with fruits, fish, or bamboo, his tiny tambourine hats over chiffon scarves, or the touches of fur on many costumes, Givenchy has left an indelible signature in the book of high fashion design.

—Barbara Cavaliere

# DE HARAK, Rudolph
American graphic designer

**Born:** Culver City, California, 10 April 1924. **Education:** Self-taught in design. **Career:** President, Rudolph de Harak and Associates, New York, from 1959. Instructor in design, Parsons School of Design, New York, and Pratt Institute, Brooklyn, New York, 1973-78; Frank Stanton Professor of Design, Cooper Union, New York, from 1979; also visiting professor, School of the Visual Arts, New York, 1962-63, Carnegie-Mellon University, Pittsburgh, 1966, Kent State University, Ohio, 1976, University of Missouri, Virginia Commonwealth University, and Minneapolis College of Art, 1977, Kutztown State College, 1978, and Yale University, 1979, 1980. **Member:** American Institute of Graphic Arts, 1957; Alliance Graphique Internationale, 1963. **Exhibitions:** American Institute of Graphic Arts, New York, 1964; Carnegie Mellon University, Pittsburgh, 1964. **Collections:** Museum of Modern Art, New York; Musée d'Art Moderne de la Ville, Paris; Museum für Angewandte Kunst, Vienna; Museum fur Kunst und Gewerbe, Hamburg; Stedelijk Museum, Amsterdam; National Museum, Warsaw; Israel Museum Jerusalem. **Honors:** American Institute of Graphic Arts awards, 1960, 1963, 1964, 1965, 1968, 1970, 1977, 1978, 1979, 1980; Communication Arts awards, Palo Alto, 1969, 1971, 1973; American Institute of Architects award, 1971; Type Directors Club awards, New York, 1976, 1977, 1980; Art Directors Club of New York awards, 1977, 1978, 1980; Brno Graphics Biennale prize, 1979. **Address:** 150 Fifth Avenue, New York, New York 10011, U.S.A.

## Publications

**By DE HARAK: books**—(editor) *Posters by Members of the Alliance Graphique Internationale,* New York, 1986.

**On DE HARAK: books**—*Graphic Designers in the U.S.A.* edited by Henri Hillebrand, London, 1971; *Archigraphia* by Walter Herdeg, Zurich, 1978; *Architectural Signing and Graphics* by John Follis and Dave Hammer, New York, 1979; *The Language of Graphics* by Edward Booth-Clibborn and Daniele Baroni, New York and London, 1980; *Who's Who in Graphic Art* edited by Walter Amstutz, Dubendorf, 1982; *Top Graphic Design* by F. H. K. Henrion, Zurich, 1983; *A History of Graphic Design* by Philip Meggs, New York, 1983.

*

To design is to create, organize, and use form in many situations and relationships. Its purpose is to visually communicate diverse categories of information in an increasingly complex environment.

Design is a problem-solving process. But for many of us, it is more than that. It is also a very personal process of searching for and developing new concepts that serve to clarify and extend ideas. Herein lies the creativity of design.

The climate within which the designer works is very complex, and, as in all creative fields, at times, painful and frustrating.

The designer's work must satisfy the tastes and opinions of the client and successfully reach the audience for which it is intended. Even though it should be self-rewarding, frequently, personal preferences have little meaning in the solving of design problems.

To accomplish his or her tasks, the designer must be thoroughly experienced—at once blessed with imagination, and, additionally, familiar with tools, techniques, and production methodologies.

Finally, it is critical that the designer work with a strong commitment, be articulate, have the ability to listen, have human concerns, and be alert to social needs.

—Rudolph de Harak

# DE LA RENTA, Oscar

Dominican fashion designer

**Born:** Santo Domingo, 22 July 1932. **Education:** Santo Domingo University; studied art, Academia de San Fernando, Madrid. **Family:** Married Françoise de Langlade in 1967 (died, 1983). **Career:** Staff designer under Cristobal Balenciaga, Eisa fashion house, Madrid; assistant designer to Antonio Castillo, at Lanvin-Castillo fashion house, Paris, 1961-63; designer, Elizabeth Arden couture and ready-to-wear range, New York, 1963-65; partner-designer, in Jane Derby Incorporated, New York, 1965-69; chief executive and Richton International board member, in Richton's Oscar de la Renta Couture, Oscar de la Renta II, Oscar de la Renta Furs, and Oscar de la Renta Jewelry, New York, 1969-73; director, Oscar de la Renta Limited, New York, from 1973; signature perfume introduced, 1977, followed by *Ruffles,* 1983, and *Volupté,* 1991; also owner of Oscar de la Renta specialty shop, Santo Domingo, from 1968; designer, couture collection for Balmain, from 1993. **Honors:** Coty American Fashion Critics' Winnie Award, New York, 1967, 1968; Neiman-Marcus Award, New York, 1968; Golden Tiberius Award, 1969; American Printed Fabrics Council Award, New York, 1971; Coty Hall of Fame Award, 1973; Fragrance Foundation Award, New York, 1978; Caballero of the Order of San Pablo Duarte, and Gran Commandante of the Order of Cristobal Colon, Dominican Republic, 1972. **Address:** 550 Seventh Avenue, New York, New York 10018, U.S.A.

## Publications

**On DE LA RENTA: books**—*Fairchild's Dictionary of Fashion* edited by Charlotte Calasibetta, New York, 1975; *The World of Fashion: People, Places, Resources* by Eleanor Lambert, London and New York, 1976; *The Fashion Makers* by Barbara Walz and Bernardine Morris, New York, 1978; *Fairchild's Who's Who in Fashion* edited by Anne Stegemeyer, New York, 1980; *The Collector's Book of Twentieth Century Fashion* by Frances Kennett, London and New York, 1983; *McDowell's Directory of Twentieth Century Fashion* by Colin McDowell, London, 1984; *Fashion: The Inside Story* by Barbaralee Diamonstein, New York, 1985; *Couture: The Great Designers* by Caroline Milbank Rennolds, New York, 1985; *The Encyclopaedia of Fashion from 1840 to the 1980s* by Georgina O'Hara, London, 1986; *W, The Designing Life* edited by Lois Perschetz, New York, 1987; *The Fashion Conspiracy* by Nicholas Coleridge, London, 1988; *New York Fashion: The Evolution of American Style* by Caroline Milbank Rennolds, New York, 1989; *Orientalism: Visions of the East in Western Dress,* exhibition catalogue by Richard Martin and Harold Koda, New York, 1994; **articles**—"Everybody's Oscar" in *Time* (New York), 10 November 1967; "The Business of Being Oscar" by S. Greenstein in *Vogue* (New York), May 1982; "How to Sniff Out the Right Kind of People" by Colin McDowell in *The Guardian* (London), 9 January 1986; "Mr. Peeper's Nights: The Magic Kingdom" in *New York,* 24 November 1986; "The Working Rich: The Real Slaves of New York" by Jesse Kornbluth in *New York,* 24 November 1986; "King of Ruffles" by Vicci Bentley in *Woman's Journal* (London), November 1987; "A Fitting with Oscar" by Michael Gross in *New York,* 18 April 1988; "The Snooty Dame at the Block Party" by Gerri Hirshey in the *New York Times Magazine,* 24 October 1993; "'Tasteful' Comes in Many Colors" by Anne-Marie Schiro in the *New York Times,* 4 November 1994; "Runway Report: My One and Only Hue: Oscar de la Renta" by Kathleen Beckett in the *New York Post,* 4 November 1994; "New York: Oscar de la Renta" in *Women's Wear Daily* (New York), 4 November 1994; "New York: Oscar de la Renta" in *Women's Wear Daily* (New York), 7 April 1995.

*     *     *

One of New York's most influential fashion designers, Oscar de la Renta was born in Santo Domingo of Spanish parents. His father, a successful insurance businessman, was disappointed when his only son failed to follow in his footsteps and instead went to Madrid to study painting. After his mother died, and his father refused to continue to pay for his artistic studies, de la Renta used his drawing skills to earn money, selling fashion sketches to magazines. Some of his sketches for original dress designs were seen by the American ambassador's wife, Mrs. John Lodge, who hired him to design a debutante gown for her daughter Beatrice. The young woman's appearance in the de la Renta dress on the cover of *Life* magazine in 1956 prompted him to abandon painting and obtain a position on the staff of Balenciaga's world-famous couture house in Madrid. Working with Balenciaga convinced de la Renta to become a fashion designer. In 1961, he went to Paris, and on the strength of his sketches and the boasts about his dressmaking skills, he was hired by Antonio Canovas del Castillo. Before he began this new position, de la Renta returned to Madrid to take an accelerated two-week dressmaking and designing course so he would be prepared to handle the new job at Lanvin-Castillo, where he specialized in tailoring.

In 1963, de la Renta came to New York as a designer of the Elizabeth Arden couture and ready-to-wear collection, which specialized in clothing for elegant, conservative, and wealthy women. Two years later, de la Renta bought into the Seventh Avenue design firm of Jane Derby, where he became designer and partner. After Derby's retirement and subsequent death, that firm evolved into Oscar de la Renta, Incorporated. No longer producing custom designs, the new firm maintained essentially the same clientele: women who purchased simple, elegant, and expensive designs with a custom-made look. He added to this look an unmistakably feminine and romantic quality, which has retained its appeal throughout his work. In 1969, his successful business was bought out by the fashion conglomerate Richton International, under which he served as chief executive of four divisions and also as a member of Richton's board of directors. However, in 1973, de la Renta bought back full control of his organization, which continues to be one of the most profitable and well-known fashion design firms in the world.

De la Renta's flair for lush color and sensuous fabrics is undoubtably the result of his love for art, especially abstract art, and his youthful ambition to be a painter. His training in the European couture houses of Balenciaga and Lanvin-Castillo taught him high standards of taste and quality and a sense of the dramatic. His work for Elizabeth Arden instilled in him an appreciation for casual elegance. The European elitism of haute couture led to his emphasis on designs for "beautiful people." Another influence on his work has been his love of things Far- and Near-Eastern, as evidenced in his gypsy look of the 1960s, and in the decorating of his own home. His late wife Françoise de Langlade, the former editor of French *Vogue,* helped him attract many of the rich, famous, and glamorous women who share the same luxurious lifestyle for which de la Renta designs.

De la Renta has had tremendous influence on the fashion world. In the 1960s, his Russian and gypsy lines initiated the widely popular ethnic look. The very next season, his introduction of the *belle époque* look was also extremely popular and influential worldwide. His use of boldly printed fabrics, lush colors, and see-through fabrics have also been pace-setting.

The innovations with which de la Renta is credited have been successful because of their novelty and beauty but also because of his expert sense of timing. His ability to introduce new lines at just the right time has contributed to the acceptance of his work. Among his major innovations was the introduction in 1966 of a moderately-priced, designer, ready-to-wear line, the Oscar de la Renta Boutique. Other designers followed when they saw its success. De la Renta was also the first American designer to become popular in both the United States and Europe and to cater his designs to the sophisticated woman over thirty. In 1968, he was among the first high-fashion designers of women's clothing to design menswear. In 1969, he was the first high-fashion designer in the United States in whose business enterprise, Richton International, the public could invest on the stock market. He was also among the first to establish a foothold in Japan, where de la Renta became a big name in fashion.

De la Renta's astute sense of business and design allows him to continue to design clothing that appeals to both the socialite and the working woman. His fashions have evolved from mostly lavish and expensive upper-class fashions to feminine yet practical clothing and accessories for today's active, professional woman. He is also aware that the socially elite are no longer the sole inspiration for fashions of the day. Women seek their own identities and styles. The working woman needs appropriate fashions for her career and her social life, and de la Renta's creations are attuned to these needs.

De la Renta's social conscience is indicated by his commitment to a Boy's Town type of home in Santo Domingo; for his charity there, he was presented the Dominican Republic's Grado Caballero de, Order of San Pablo Duarte, and the Grado Caballero de Commandante, Order of Cristobal Colon, in 1972.

De la Renta continues to design in New York today. His womenswear line, Signature, a couture line, Studio, a ready-to-wear line, and another line of suits and dresses, all confirm that the de la Renta name means top of the line elegance.

—Elizabeth Douthitt Byrne

# DELAUNAY, Sonia

Russian painter and stage, textile, and poster designer

**Born:** Sophie Stern, in Gradizhsk, Ukraine, 14 November 1885; adopted uncle's family name, Terk, in 1890. **Education:** St. Petersburg, until 1902; studied drawing and anatomy, Kunstakademie, Karlsruhe, 1903-04; studied painting, at the Academie de la Palette, Paris, 1905. **Family:** Married art critic Wilhelm Uhde in 1909 (divorced, 1910); married painter Robert Delaunay in 1910 (died, 1941), children: Charles. **Career:** Independent painter and graphic artist from 1905, stage designer from 1918, and textile designer from 1921; worked in Paris, 1905-10, 1921-39, 1944-79, in Nantes, 1910-12, in Spain and Portugal, 1914-20, in the Auvergne, 1940-41, and in Grasse, 1942-44. **Member:** Founder-member, with Robert Delaunay, Fredo Sides, Nelly Van Doesburg and others, of the Salon des Realites Nouvelles, Paris, 1939, and from 1946. **Exhibitions:** Nya Konstgalleriet, Stockholm, 1916; Galerie der Sturm, Berlin, 1920; Stedelijk Museum, Amsterdam, 1938; Städtisches Museum, Bielefeld, 1958; Musée des Beaux-Arts, Lyons, 1959; Galleria Civica d'Arte Moderna, Turin, 1960; Musée Rath, Geneva, 1964; Musée du Louvre, Paris, 1964; National Gallery of Canada, Ottawa, 1965; Musée des Arts Décoratifs, Paris, 1965; Musée National d'Art Moderne Paris, 1967, 1975, 1985; Maison de la Culture, Amiens, 1968; Museum Arkiv för Dekorativ Konst, Lund, 1968; Maison de la Culture, Rennes, 1969; Carnegie Institute, Pittsburgh, 1969; Musée des Beaux-Arts, Le Havre, 1969; National Gallery of Victoria, Melbourne, 1969 (toured); University of Texas, Houston, 1970; Musée de l'Impression sur Etoffes, Mulhouse, 1971; Fundacao Gulbenkian, Lisbon, 1972; Musée des Beaux-Arts, Nancy, 1972; Musée d'Art Moderne de la Ville, Paris, 1972 (travelled to Washington, D.C.), 1977; Musée des Beaux-Arts, La Rochelle, 1973; New York Cultural Center, 1973; Kunsthalle, Bielefeld, 1974; Musée de Grenoble, 1974; Internationaal Cultureel Centrum, Antwerp, 1975; National Museum of Modern Art, Tokyo, 1979; AlbrightKnox Art Gallery, Buffalo, New York, 1980; Art Institute of Chicago, 1981; House of Artists, Leningrad, 1986. **Collections:** Musée National d'Art Moderne, Paris; Musée des Arts Décoratifs, Paris; Centre de Documentation de Costume, Paris; Musée de l'Impression sur Etoffes, Mulhouse; Deutsches

Spielkarten Museum, Bielefeld; Stedelijk Museum, Amsterdam; Museum of Modern Art, New York; National Gallery of Canada, Ottawa. **Honors:** Gold Medal, Paris International Exposition, 1937; Grand Prix, International Women's Salon, Cannes, 1969; Grand Prix de la Ville de Paris, 1973; Stephan Lochner Medal, Cologne, 1974; Officier de la Légion d'Honneur, France, 1975. **Died:** Paris, 5 December 1979.

## Works

*Simultaneous Dress* body-painting garments, 1912-13.
*La Prose du Trans-Siberien et de la Petite Jehanne de France* book design, for Editions des Hommes Nouveaux, Paris, 1913 (with Blaise Cendrars).
*Chocolat posters,* for Chocolat Bensdorp, 1916-22.
*Cleopatra ballet* costumes, for Diaghilev's Ballets Russes, Paris, 1918.
*Le Coeur à Gaz* (T. Tzara) costumes, Theatre Michel, Paris, 1923.
*B12* car styling and decoration, for Citroen, 1925.
*Zig Zag* advertisement sculpture in neon, for Societé d'Electricité de France, 1936.
Mural panels in the Palais des Chemins de Fer and Palais de l'Air, at the Paris International Exposition, 1937 (with Robert Delaunay).
Exhibition stand at the Salon de l'Automobile, Paris, for Maison Berliet, 1957.
*Simultané* playing cards, 1959, produced by the Deutsches Spielkarten Museum, Bielefeld, 1964.
*Matra B530* sports car styling and decoration, 1967.
*International Women's Year* poster, for UNESCO, 1975.

## Publications

**By DELAUNAY: books—***L'Influence de la Peinture sur l'Art Vestimentaire* (lecture pamphlet), Paris, 1927; *Tapis et Tissus,* Paris, 1929; *Compositions, Couleurs, Ideés,* Paris, 1930; *Robes-Poemes,* Milan, 1969; *Alfabeto* edited by R. Marconi and G. Niccolai, Venice, 1970; *Nous Irons Jusqu'au Soleil,* Paris, 1978; *The New Art in Colour: The Writings of Robert and Sonia Delaunay* edited by Arthur Cohen, New York, 1978.

**On DELAUNAY: books—***New Interior Decoration* by Dorothy Todd and Raymond Mortimer, London, 1929; *Sonia Delaunay,* exhibition catalogue by Bernard Dorival, Paris, 1965; *Sonia Delaunay: tapis et oeuvres graphiques,* exhibition catalogue with text by Jacques Damase, Paris, 1970; *Sonia Delaunay: Rhythms and Colours* by Jacques Damase, Paris, 1971, London, 1972; *Robert et Sonia Delaunay a Portugal* by Fernando Pernes, Lisbon, 1972, *Sonia Delaunay: tapisseries,* exhibition catalogue with texts by Jacques Lassaigne and others, Paris, 1972; *Sonia Delaunay* by Arthur Cohen, New York, 1975; *La Rencontre: Sonia Delaunay—Tristan Tzara,* exhibition catalogue with texts by Jean Cassou and Jacques Damase, Paris, 1977; *Sonia Delaunay: noirs et blancs* by Germain Viatte, Paris, 1978; *Sonia Delaunay* by Bernard Dorival, Paris, 1980; *Sonia Delaunay: Art in Fashion* by Diana Vreeland and Elizabeth Morano, New York, 1986; *Sonia Delaunay: Magique Magicienne* by Dominique Desanti, Paris, 1988; *Sonia Delaunay: Fashion and Fabrics,* New York, 1991.

\*     \*     \*

Because she felt that abstract art allowed for a wider vision of man and nature and opened new areas of sensitivity and perception, Sonia Delaunay produced from her earliest works the now famous color rhythm series. Because she believed the essential premise that color was the basic element of the world, she used color to express emotion in all her work. The dynamism in her soft-edge geometric work allowed both of these—form and color, added to her response to movement and motion—to give essence and character to her concerns.

Hers was no naive understanding of geometry and its relation to color and motion; it was never mechanical, always more organic and thus presented a rhythmic action that served her purposes. She was equally concerned with the spectator's relationship to her work. She felt that there had to be a transformation process, so that the spectator became more than a mere recipient, a responsive viewer who could react to the motion, form, and color. Thus, she did not limit herself to painting, but painting influenced her other work: posters, illustrations, textiles, and even fashion design. This concern for all of the visual media was espoused as early as 1927 in her lecture at the Sorbonne on fashion design and the importance and contribution of painting to this universal area.

Delaunay was a truly self-contained woman. Working with men at a time when the work of women artists was little known and respected, it never occurred to her that her collaborative and individual work was on anything less than an equal footing with the men and women—people such as Robert Delaunay, Blaise Cendrars, Sophie Tauber-Arp, Jean Arp—with whom she related both in her work and in her personal life.

She was a tireless worker, employing not only her work but also her writings and lectures to project her point of view. It is only within the last few decades that the true importance and meaning of her life's work has gained the belated recognition of scholars and critics. And for other artists of our time, women and men, she remains a source of inspiration.

—Mildred Constantine

# DE LUCA, Jean-Claude

French fashion designer

**Born,** of French parents, in Barcelona, Spain, 13 October 1948. **Education:** Educated, Montcel private school and Lycée Jaccard, Lausanne; studied law, University of Milan. **Career:** Design assistant in Givenchy and Guy Laroche fashion houses, Paris, 1971-74; freelance designer, working with Dorothée Bis, Emanuel Ungaro, and others, Paris, 1974-76; founder-director, Jean-Claude de Luca fashion company, Paris, from 1976; first menswear collection, 1983. **Exhibitions:** *Design in Lace,* Musée Galliera, Paris, 1983. **Collections:** Musée de la Couture, Paris; Museum of Modern Art, New York. **Address:** 10 Avenue de l'Opéra, 7501 Paris, France.

## Publications

**On DE LUCA: books—***The 1978 Fashion Guide* by Kaori O'Connor and Farrol Kahn, London, 1978; *25 Ans de Marie-Claire* *de 1954 a 1979,* compiled by Francoise Mohrt, Paris, 1979; *Fairchild's Who's Who in Fashion,* edited by Ann Stegemeyer, New York, 1980; *Fashion 2001* by Lucille Khornak, London, 1982; *McDowell's Directory of Twentieth Century Fashion* by Colin McDowell, London, 1984; *The Encyclopaedia of Fashion from 1840 to the 1980s* by Georgina O'Hara, London, 1986.

\*

I design clothes for everyday wear, but luxurious clothes for the career woman who can afford to buy her own clothes. Clothes have to be like a visitor's card, a way of communicating with people—the clothes one wears being *you* and therefore translating one's character visually.

I try to keep in mind when designing a collection that clothes have to have a note of humour and poetry. The important thing is to remain curious about things at all levels. The mind has to be inquisitive and alert to new ideas, but foremost I believe in luxurious, natural fabrics used in new ways. My favorite colours are white and black, because they allow numerous possibilities to produce striking, classic, and stylish outfits. I believe in subtle changes of mood and ideas.

I am now very interested in painters as a motivation in my way of working—especially Goya: the colours, the forms, the construction—which goes hand in hand with my passion for the opera. My training in law studies has permitted me to use a certain meticulous and strict way of working—but it has not hindered progress by any means, only helped. I like active women who are sexy but not frivolous, who use their charm but not falsely: I like beautiful city girls, not feminine girls—and I design for these women. I design clothes for the really fulfilled woman, socially and career-wise, who knows how to get ahead. She has her head well sorted out and needs clothes that are stylish, luxurious, but comfortable and sporty, with a hint of humour and harmony of colours. I am a city person who loves the city life, the city's stimulus.

—Jean-Claude de Luca

\*     \*     \*

After spending over a year with Givenchy, Jean-Claude de Luca thought that the ready-to-wear world would be the best in which to work as the majority of women could not afford couture prices. He sold some designs to Dorothée Bis, and Ungaro commissioned a prêt-á-porter collection from him for 1974. After that, in 1976, de Luca opened on his own. He considers Paris a second-rate city, good only at fashion, with no theatre or ballet of note, but knows that fashion is important. "Clothes are your image," he insists, for clothes speak of group identity and social status, as well as fulfilling a fundamental physical necessity. De Luca likes best the basic garments—the waistcoat, jacket, and trousers—but he updates them by using contrasting fabrics, such as cotton and wool. He believes textiles will be increasingly important, in view of all the research going on to produce new types.

A graduate in law, de Luca can appreciate the needs of the professional woman, but one must query why he expects her to look like Superman. This was the theme of his 1978-79 collections, with shoulders built out like American football players', martial suits, officers' capes, metal buttons, and marching boots. Although this design approach contrasts strongly with his statement that he wants clothes to be practical and to fit daily activity, he repeated the mistake in 1980 with his Space Age look, which included brief tunics, tights, and again, boots. Does he really expect professional women to go to the office attired like Gestapo chiefs or Martians? Practical clothes are those which do not impede the wearer and do not leave her ill-covered in climatic extremes.

The root problem with male designers for women is that they do not wear the garments themselves. Wearing a brief tunic at a bus stop in rain or frost would be a good starting lesson, as would trying to type when loaded with enormous shoulders. Molyneux told Balmain and Dior that the first question to ask is whether the creation is wearable. There is still plenty of time for de Luca to study this approach, as he is still in his early stage, exercising his imagination. One hopes that he will sit down and work out what exactly women have to do and design clothes for that activity, which is mainly humdrum, not filled with romantic adventures at Waterloo or on other planets. It is the same lesson most young designers must learn, as they almost invariably start with fantasy.

—Diana de Marly

# DE LUCCHI, Michele

Italian industrial, interior, exhibition, and graphic designer

**Born:** Ferrara, 8 November 1951. **Education:** Liceo Scientifico Enrico Fermi, Padua, 1964-69; studied architecture, University of Florence, Dip. Arch., 1975. **Career:** Freelance designer, collaborating with designers Andrea Branzi, Gaetano Pesce, Ettore Sottsass Jr., the Superstudio group, and others, in Milan, from 1973; consultant to Centrokappa, Milan, 1978, and Olivetti Synthesis, from 1979. Founder-member, with Piero Brombin, Boris Premru and Valerio Tridenti, of Gruppo Cavart, Padua, 1973-76; founder, with Ettore Sottsass Jr., Barbara Radice, and others, of Memphis furniture design group, Milan, 1980. Professor of industrial design, Università Internazionale dell'Arte, Florence, 1976-77. **Exhibitions:** *Un'Idea per I Monti Ricchi,* Galleria Images 70, Abano Terme, 1973; *Esplorazione sul Territorio Corpo,* Galleria Stevens, Padua, 1975; *Laboratorio Indoor,* Studio Eremitani, Padua, 1976; *Il Design negli Anni '50,* Centrokappa, Milan, 1977; *Design Phenomène* Forum Design, Linz, 1980; *Una Generazione Post-Moderna,* Palazzo Bianco, Genoa, 1982; *Memphis,* Arc 74, Milan, 1982 (toured); *Ricerca per un Ambiente d'Ufficio Olivetti,* at the Milan Triennale, 1983; *Michele De Lucchi: A Friendly Image for the Electronic Age,* Amsterdam, 1985. **Addresses:** Via Cenisio 40, 20154 Milan, Italy; Via Vittoria Colonna 8, 20149 Milan, Italy.

## Works

*Il Design Italiano negli Anni '50* exhibition layouts, for Centrokappa, Milan, 1977.
*Sinerpica* and *La Spaziale* lamps, for Alchymia, 1978.
*Tarkin* chair, for Thema, 1978 (with M. Matzukase).
*Series 45* CR office furniture, for Olivetti Synthesis, 1980 (with Ettore Sottsass Jr.).
Via Giulini office and showroom interiors in Milan, for Olivetti Synthesis, 1980.
*Icarus* office furniture, for Olivetti Synthesis, 1981 (with Ettore Sottsass Jr.).

*Terrific* and *Fantastic* ceramic plates, for Abet Print, 1981.
*Kristall* table, for Memphis, 1981.
*Peter Pan* armchair, for Thalia, 1981.
Shop interiors in Milan, for Fiorucci, 1981 (with Ettore Sottsass Jr.).
*Gabbia* furniture system, for Alchymia, 1981.
*Fortune* trestle table, for Memphis, 1982.
*Vega* glass lamp, for Vitosi, 1982.
*Calcutta* marble coffee table, for Up & Up, 1982.
*Pool* armchair system, for Matau, 1982.
*Lido* divan, for Memphis, 1982.
*President* coffee table, for Memphis, 1983.
*Rotor, Roll* and *Round* lamps, for Bieffeplast, 1983.
*Cyclos* wall lamp, for Artemide, 1983.

## Publications

**By DE LUCCHI: books**—*Architetture Verticali,* Florence, 1968; (editor) *Solid: Un Nuova Collezione di Oggetti per la Casa,* Milan, 1987; **articles**—in *Parametro* (Faenza), June 1976; *Japan Interior Design* (Tokyo), December 1976; *Modo* (Milan), May 1979, January/ February 1980; *Space Design* (Tokyo), December 1979; *Donna* (Milan), April 1980, September 1980; *Casa Vogue* (Milan), September 1980; *Abitare* (Milan), November 1981; *Ufficio Stile* (Milan), June 1982; *Domus* (Milan), September 1982; *Nikkei Architecture* (Tokyo), February 1983; *Sumo* (Milan), March 1983; *Interni* (Milan), May 1983.

**On DE LUCCHI: books**—*Homo Trahens* by Grupo Cavart, Florence, 1976; *Dalla Citta la Cucchiaio* by Bruno Orlandoni, Turin, 1977; *Memphis: The New International Style* by Barbara Radice, Milan, 1981; *Design Process Olivetti 1908-83,* with text by Renzo Zorzi, Milan, 1983; *The Hot House: Italian New Wave Design* by Andrea Branzi, London, 1984; *Michele De Lucchi: A Friendly Image for Electronic Age,* exhibition catalogue, Amsterdam, 1985; *Memphis: Objects, Furniture and Patterns* by Richard Horn, New York, 1986; *Italian Design: 1870 to the Present* by Penny Sparke, London and New York, 1988.

*

The image of technology is different from actual technology, and there exist a lot of possibilities within the image of technology. We are living in an epoch of consumerism. Our way of communicating with each other is mass produced. We see it as sophisticated technology, for example, when the Japanese produce a stereo that is matte black and silver. We recognize it immediately as such because the "image" of sophisticated technology is matte black. Today we use more images, and the images we use are very sophisticated. People who work with images deal in a kind of iconology, a very sophisticated iconography. The ideal is to have a catalogue of iconography that exists today and to use this iconography to open up possibilities.

I chose objects that we have in our homes—objects that everybody uses, but no one would think to design—to explore the possibilities. We see a vacuum cleaner, but we don't think about the image of the vacuum cleaner. My feeling is that the vacuum cleaner is a mass-produced object that is also a means of communicating. It is possible to communicate an image with a vacuum cleaner—and even if it is only decorative, it will change the technology. As the

design of the shell changes, there will be changes on the inside. The designer creates the job. Technology fills the design. Decoration will change the way the object is perceived, the very nature of design. Not to just make a lamp but that this lamp will change the very idea of lamps. It's not that this lamp or this vacuum cleaner is the best lamp or best vacuum cleaner, or that this is the final lamp or vacuum cleaner, but that each will change the whole idea—a very little—of the way we conceive design.

I'm working on designing the idea of design. The traditional designer works with the manufacturer whose idea is to produce something that will become a bestseller. Then there are designers with a longer view. Ettore Sottsass was the first to say that when you design an object, you don't just design the object but also the environment in which the object will be put. And you also design the behavior of the people who will use the object. The idea was to open the possibilities of designing so that people could exercise their creativity, but we realize that most people need to have models. By seeing a model of change, the consumer is able to see possibilities of change.

—Michele De Lucchi

\*     \*     \*

Architect Michele De Lucchi became fairly famous at early age, mostly for his striking, architectural-like furniture and industrial designs. He is probably best known for his work done for Memphis (founded in 1980) and that done in collaboration with his friend and mentor, Ettore Sottsass.

De Lucchi uses bright colors and bold forms in his designs, in an attempt to foster different sensations or responses from the viewer/ user, which often appear more like a child's toys than "serious" furniture. Consider his prototypes for a vacuum cleaner and a hair dryer (1979), which look like multi-colored pull-toys; *Kristall* (1981), which has a bright yellow round table sprouting from a black and white diagonally-striped "box" supported on thin metal feet; *Lido* (1982), a multi-colored sofa, which appears to have been resurrected from a psychedelic bus or, perhaps, an amusement park; and *Peter Pan* (1981), a proposed tubular steel frame chair which can be dressed/undressed in upholstery of many patterns and colors. This playfulness is perhaps his greatest strength and, potentially, his greatest weakness—whether the eventual user will consider his work more than "fun" or an "object d'art" and really appreciate their value as usable items without all the stereotyped restrictions of the "real" world.

His work has often been called "ludicrous," to which De Lucchi replies: "...the word 'ludicrous' can certainly be used provided it refers to the demystification of a particular image of technology: the sort of technology that's remote, difficult, and inaccessible. After all, technology is really quite simple and banal, and is intended to help you." He elaborates: "...Design can push technology, because design can help technology to be understood...technology is only a factor which affects design...if a lower keyboard is required during the design of a computer, then a technological solution must be found."

De Lucchi sees that products, which may now be in fashion for five years, will soon be "in" for only one year. Replacement will come at a faster pace. He is a strong believer in consumerism, "the only factor which we can't eliminate and which assures the success of technology and industry." He does not treat it in the "political or social sense," but "in the context of fashion and consumption." He feels that "this is not decadence," but "a high level of sophistication concerning our relationship with the things around us."

In the 1990s, Michele De Lucchi has worked on a variety of projects for Olivetti and various producers of interior furniture and lighting.

—William Victor Kriebel

# DE MAJO, Willy Maks

British graphic and industrial designer

**Born:** Of Yugoslav nationality, in Vienna, Austria, 25 July 1917; emigrated to Britain in 1939; naturalized, 1947. **Education:** Studied at the Commercial Academy, Vienna; also attended classes on commercial art, under Professor Puchinger, Vienna Urania Polytechnic. **Military Service:** Served in Royal Yugoslav Air Force, attached to British Royal Air Force, 1941-43, in War Ministry, London, 1944, and Royal Air Force at SHAEF, in Africa, Middle East and Europe, 1945-46, Flight Lieutenant. **Family:** Married Veronica Mary Booker in 1941 (separated; died 1992); children: Monica, Francesca, and Sarina. **Career:** Freelance designer, in Belgrade, 1936-39, and in London, 1946-93; art director, Moda of Belgrade, 1938-39; design consultant to Miles-Martin (Biro) Pen Company, Sir Henry Lunn Limited, Miles Aircraft, British Overseas Airways, W. & A. Gilbey, Clayton Brothers, B.N.T. Limited U.K., Philips NV, Charles Letts and Company, John Millar and Sons (1884) Limited, Ti-Well Limited, and Micron CA of Caracas. Founder and president, ICOGRADA International Council of Graphic Design Associations, 1963; founder and chairman, ICOGRADA International Design Archive, 1991-1993. Guest speaker at numerous professional institutes and congresses. **Collections:** Victoria and Albert Museum, London; ICOGRADA Visual Archive, London and Reading, Berkshire. **Honors:** MBE, for service during World War II; Design Medal, Society of Industrial Artists and Designers (now Chartered Society of Designers), London, 1969; Commemorative Medal, ZPAP Association of Polish Artists and Designers, 1983. Honorary Member, GVN Graphic Designers Association, Netherlands, 1959, SAFT/SRF Swedish Advertising Association, 1965, CBG Belgian Chamber of Graphic Designers, 1966, and GDA Graphic Design Austria, 1988. **Died:** 17 October 1993.

## Works

Corporate identity programme, for Moda fashion store, Belgrade, 1938-39.
Interiors and gift products, for RAF Air Division Giftshop, Detmold, Germany, 1945-46.
Biro showroom interiors, displays, and packaging, for Miles-Martin Pen Company, London, 1946-52.
Cigarette lighter packaging, displays, and showroom interiors, for Ronson Products, 1948-63.
*Ulster Farm and Factory* exhibition layouts at the Festival of Britain, London, for the Government of Northern Ireland, 1950-51.
Fruit drinks and mineral water corporate identity programme and packaging, for Clayton Brothers, 1950-68.
Smirnoff Vodka and Perrier water promotional products and displays, for W. and A. Gilbey, 1950-66.

Exhibition displays at the Bulawayo Rhodes Centenary Exhibition, for the Schlesinger Organization of Johannesburg, 1953.
Corporate identity programme, interiors, and displays, for John Millar and Sons (1844) Limited, 1953.
Hand tools corporate identity programme and packaging, for Brades-Nash and Tyzack Industries, 1954-58.
Animated symbol, for ABC-TV television corporation, London, 1956-57.
Corporate identity programme, packaging, and displays, for Transparent Paper Limited, 1957-63.
Tricot jersey corporate identity programme, packaging and displays, for Ets. St. Joseph, Paris and Bordeaux, 1960-67.
*The BP Story* exhibition layout, for the Baden Powell Memorial Fund, 1961-62.
Design programme and displays at the National Advertising Exhibition in Olympia, London, for Adex Limited, 1962.
Carson's Chocolates gift packaging, for Carson Limited, 1965-66.
Corporate identity programme, packaging, display, and product design, for Charles Letts and Company, 1966-68.
Gift matches and presentation packs, for Neiman-Marcus, 1972.
Corporate identity programme, for Brentford Football Club, Middlesex, 1975 76.
Corporate identity programme, packaging, and product designs, for Ti-Well paper products.
Leather goods, for W. and A. Goold, 1984-86.

## Publications

**By DE MAJO: articles**—"Light and Structure" in *Print* (New York), July 1955; "Design for Prosperity versus Design for Posterity," *Design Quarterly* (Minneapolis), vol. 36, 1956; "Design of Gift Packs" in *Packaging* (Zurich), 1959; "Single Biggest Problem in the Design Field Today" in *Print* (New York), January 1961; "Conquering Export Markets Through Better Package Design" in International *Trade Forum* (Geneva), vol. 2, 1966; "One Man's Paper is Another Man's Problem" in *British Printer* (London), 28 March 1969; "Bibliography: Signs and Sign Systems" in *Print* (Washington, D.C.), November 1969; "Design '81 in Helsinki" in *Graphic Design* (Tokyo), December 1981; "Balloon Graphics" in *Graphic Design* (Tokyo), March 1982.

**On DE MAJO: books**—*Who's Who in Graphic Art* edited by Walter Amstutz, Zurich, 1962, Dübendorf, 1982; *All Things Bright and Beautiful* by Fiona MacCarthy, London, 1972; *A Tonic to the Nation* by Mary Banham, London, 1976; *Minerva at Fifty* by James Holland, London, 1980.

*

I was not exactly a great scholastic success at school, not being too keen on regimentation and discipline; my fertile mind seemed to get bored rather easily, resulting in my being a somewhat lazy student. However, once I was allowed to do my own thing, I quickly developed single-mindedness of purpose and perseverance which I have retained ever since. From an early age, I showed an interest in forms and colours, and I spent many hours sketching and developing ideas.

My father could not see much future in my becoming an "artist" and, as he had hoped that I would follow in his footsteps and eventually take over the successful export and import business

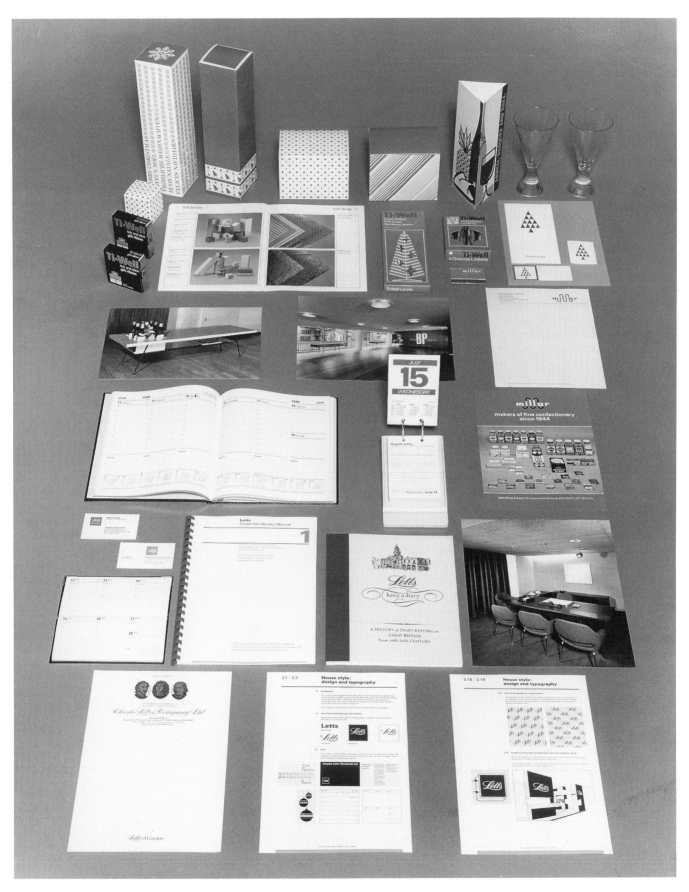

**W.M. de Majo: Corporate identity, packaging, and exhibit designs**

which he had built up, I was sent to the Commercial Academy in Vienna, where we lived at the time. Alas, I did not enjoy my business training. When around 1935 my father decided that the family should return to Belgrade, his native town, we agreed that I would work half the day for him as personal assistant and sales representative and the other half for myself as a commercial artist. It was a strenuous period, with many late evenings trying to do two jobs and not many design commissions. Even when one did get a job, it was badly paid. But I pressed on.

I sold my first poster to one of the local dress-material shops and my first commissions for advertisements followed from a small advertising agency. At the same time, every morning when I had to go out trying to sell my father's range of goods, mainly Czechoslovakian textiles, linoleum from Kirkcaldy, ties from Manchester and Italy, and various other goods, my heart sank. Although the products were all of good quality, their decorative designs were hideous. So I figured that the only way in which I could overcome my dilemma was to try to jump across the fence and become the person who creates the product. I reasoned that if a product were to be well designed, whoever manufactured it would enjoy doing his job. At the same time, the sales representative would be proud to sell it, and the end user happy to buy it. Little by little, I developed and implemented this theory and was lucky to find clients who believed in me and gave me opportunity and encouragement.

Thus, quite soon, aided by an inbred flair, and a considerable amount of cheek and courage, believing that almost nothing was impossible if one set one's mind to it, I succeeded in expanding my activities and experience. In early 1939, I had decided to emigrate, and the early war years found me in England where I did a number of unusual jobs, from being a lumberjack in Shropshire to joining the BBC Overseas Service as a news typist and broadcaster. From the end of 1941 until 1946, I served as an Officer and Pilot in the Royal Yugoslav Air Force, seeing war service in Africa, the Middle East and Europe, and was later transferred to the Royal Air Force. On my demobilization and after a brief, not very successful spell as an exporter, I got the chance of a lifetime, which I grabbed with both hands. I was offered the job of display designer for the Miles Martin Pen Company's new Biro showrooms. This was soon followed by my appointment as consultant designer to the company, as well as to Sir Henry Lunn and Miles Aircraft, and things have progressed ever since.

By the 1960s, I had been commissioned to design a great variety of items from a visiting card through stationery, publicity materials, products in paper, cardboard, leather, wood, glass, metal, plastics, and textiles to point-of-sales material, carpets, ties, and leather goods, liveries for transportation fleets, including vehicle bodies and the interior decoration scheme for a four-engined airliner. New challenges were designing the Baden-Powell museum exhibit and a number of extensive corporate identity programmes.

I have always been a great believer that integrated design plays an important part in any successful business, and by working over such a wide field, I feel that I can be more creative, bringing to the problem at hand a varied experience from different disciplines. The requirements for a successful designer are varied. They will consist, though not necessarily in this order, of some of the following:

An imaginative and quick mind

The ability to absorb information and details and a good memory.

A willingness to put in long hours, if necessary, and to try an unusual yet analytical approach.

A methodical mind, keen on attention to detail.

An ability to establish a clear and detailed design brief and to allow sufficient time for the job yet be able to work under pressure when required.

The ability to stay within budgets.

Above all, belief in what one is doing.

The designer must never lose his integrity even though he may have to make compromises on occasions. He needs to be a good salesman in order to put over his products and proposed solutions. He must be loyal to his client, yet remember the great moral responsibility he has as a designer; in many instances, he is the link between customer and manufacturer, and very often, the difference between success and failure of a job may rest in his hands. Sometimes, it is important that a designer should produce a solution which the client may have never dreamed he wanted or realised that he needed, in preference to just doing what the client may have asked for or thought that he required. Like a Queen's Counsellor, while he is not expected to know all the answers, he must know where to find them.

To me, good design, whether two-dimensional, like visual communication, publicity, or information design, or three-dimensional, like product design, is organic, something which grows and changes, develops and expands. No one part of it can be solved in a vacuum without a thorough understanding of the whole.

—W. M. de Majo

*      *      *

Among W. M. de Majo's many assets, four will assure his reputation. First was his organizational ability. Few would deny that the formation of ICOGRADA (the International Council of Graphic Design Associations) in 1963 was Willy de Majo's personal achievement. Without his patience, perseverance, and endless persuasion, the Council would not have come into being. Today, this Council has an important international voice in the world of design, representing as it does more than 40,000 graphic designers from some 30 countries. From 1963 to 1965, de Majo was the first president of ICOGRADA, and he held many other important posts, among them chairmanship of the first study group of the International Council of Societies of Industrial Design.

Second, one noted his enterprising and progressive outlook. Willy de Majo had the ability to absorb quickly a complex situation and come up with a practical solution to its problems. He was also able to project ahead and, based on his considerable experience, come up with answers to problems which, on the surface, may have seemed insoluble. These factors made him one of the significant catalysts and pioneers of the design profession. His work covered a spectrum of activity so wide that it would handicap most designers. However, de Majo made use of this breadth by cross-germinating one medium with another. At the same time, he gave attention to the full range of a client's concerns, from manufacturing to sales to consumer problems. These aspects were always seen in their relations and brought into focus.

Third was his professional competence, manifested by close attention to the minutest detail from the various stages of manufacture to the actual marketing. There was often visual and physical pleasure in the experience of holding an object, such as a book of matches or a diary, which had come through the stages of production supervised by de Majo. In all his work, there was a clarity and directness which were, of course, the prime elements of the end product.

Fourth, one remarked his abundant energy. His overall achievement, both in practising design and in international organization, is rare in the business of communication. One assumes that his energy derived from his colourful past in Vienna, Belgrade, and Paris. As his career progressed, de Majo became one of the most sought after speakers in the design world. After forty years of input, the design profession recognized his rich contribution with numerous awards from many countries.

—John Halas

# DESKEY, Donald
American interior, packaging, and industrial designer

**Born:** Blue Earth, Minnesota, 23 November 1894. **Education:** University of California, Berkeley, 1915-17; Art Institute of Chicago, 1918-19; California School of Fine Arts, San Francisco, 1919-20; Ecole de la Grande Chaumiere, Academie Colarossi, and Atelier Leger, all in Paris, 1920-22. **Military Service:** Served in the United States Army, 1917-18. **Family:** Married Mary Douthett in 1921 (divorced, 1946); children: Michael and Stephen; married Katharine Godfrey Brennan in 1952. **Career:** Freelance designer, from 1926; established Donald Deskey Associates, New York, 1935-75, opening branch offices in London, Frankfurt, Milan, Copenhagen, and Stockholm, in the 1950s and 1960s. Professor of Art, Juniata College, Huntingdon, Pennsylvania, 1922-24; Professor of Industrial Design, New York University, 1930-36; also lecturer at Massachusetts Institute of Technology, Harvard Business School, and other universities. **Exhibitions:** Metropolitan Museum of Art, New York, 1934; *The Machine Age in America 1918-1941,* Brooklyn Museum, New York, 1986. **Collections:** Metropolitan Museum of Art, New York; Art Institute of Chicago; Philadelphia Museum of Art; Yale University Gallery, New Haven, Connecticut; Virginia Museum of Fine Arts, Richmond; Cooper Hewitt Museum, New York. **Address:** 270 Island Creek Drive, St. John's Island, Vero Beach, Florida 32963, U.S.A.

## Works

Display windows, for Saks and Company, Fifth Avenue, New York, 1926-27.

Apartment interiors on Park Avenue, New Soda fountain, and beauty salon for Abraham and Straus, Brooklyn, 1928-30.

Apartment renovations on West 54th Street, New York, for Abby Aldrich Rockefeller, 1929-31.

Radio City Music Hall interiors, Rockefeller Center, New York, 1932.

Apartment interiors at Radio City Music Hall, New York, for Samuel L. (Roxy) Rothafel, 1932.

House interiors in Mount Kisco, New York, for Richard H. Mandel, 1933-35.

International Casino interiors at 1526 Broadway, New York, 1937.

Development of Weldtex board, for United States Plywood Corporation, 1940.

Design of all U.S. showrooms, for Bigelow Sanford Carpet Company, 1945-52.

Begins prefabricated housing, for Shelter Industries Incorporated, 1946.

Techniplan office furniture, for Globe-Wernicke Company, 1948-54.

Packaging designs, for Procter and Gamble, 1949-76.

Corporate identity program, for Sinclair Refining Company, 1954-56.

Marco Polo Club interiors at the Waldorf Astoria Hotel, New York, 1959.

Packaging and interiors, for Johnson and Johnson, 1959.

Wall Street Club interiors on Chase Manhattan Plaza, New York, 1960-62.

## Publications

**On DESKEY: books**—*The Story of Modern Applied Art* by Rudolph Rosenthal and Helena L. Ratzka, New York, 1948; *Packaging: An International Survey of Package Design* edited by Walter Herdeg, Zurich, 1959; *Design in America* by Ralph Caplan, New York, 1969; *The Decorative Thirties* by Martin Battersby, London, 1969, 1974, 1976; *The Streamlined Decade* by Donald J. Bush, New York, 1975; *80 Years of Ideas and Pleasure from House and Garden* edited by Mary Jane Pool and Caroline Seebohm, London, 1980; *Industrial Design* by John Heskett, London, 1980; *American Design Ethic* by Arthur J. Pulos, London and Cambridge, Massachusetts, 1983; *The Conran Directory of Design* edited by Stephen Bayley, London, 1985; *Design Source Book* by Penny Sparke and others, London, 1986; *The Machine Age in America 1918-1941* by Richard Guy Wilson and Dianne H. Pilgrim, New York, 1986; *Donald Deskey: Decorative Designs and Interiors* by David A. Hanks and Jennifer Toher, New York, 1987; *American Art Deco* by Alastair Duncan, New York, 1987; *The American Design Adventure 1940-1975* by Arthur J. Pulos, Cambridge, Massachusetts, 1988.

\* \* \*

Despite forty years of an active professional life which has encompassed nearly every phase of design, Donald Deskey is best known—indeed, one might say singularly known—for the furnishings and interiors he developed for Radio City Music Hall in 1931 and 1932. Readers of design history might even be excused for assuming that his contribution to the field consists solely of the private suite he created for the guiding spirit of that entertainment enterprise, "Roxy" Rothafel, since this environment, which used some of the most advanced materials of the day, is a staple in illustrated texts on the Art Deco period.

Deskey thus appears to have little accomplishment behind him, save for the one interior—although, admittedly, that interior is both a tour de force and a monument to the unabashedly exuberant 1930s. It is only with difficulty that we unearth references to his extensive work in graphics advertising, display exhibition, interior architecture, and product design. In his relative anonymity, however—which contrasts with the well-publicized careers of some of his early contemporaries such as Norman Bel Geddes and Raymond Loewy—he is the archetype of today's designers who are generally unknown even though their designs and concepts may have national impact.

He may also be said to be prototypical in that his career mirrors the development of design from applied art to profession. Prior to World War II, Deskey and other American artists blended the *arts décoratifs* of the Paris exposition of 1925 with the typographic inventions of the Bauhaus, and turned to illustration, graphic design, and advertising. The application of art to commerce that was advertising was soon extended to product design, and graphic artists were in great demand when merchants realized that esthetics would be profitable. Suddenly, Deskey and others like him were asked to turn their hand to windows, displays, exhibitions, costumes, products, and interior spaces. The best of them helped to transform merchandising practises and to create the Deco style characteristic of the 1930s.

World War II ended the society to which Deskey responded, and the post-war years were characterized by the faceless monoliths of the International Style. However, the pre-war decorative chutzpah, only partially civilized by a theatrical neo-classicism, has resurfaced as post-modernism. Deskey himself is not contributing to this revival, but his work lies as its roots, just as it lies at the roots of the design industry he helped create and to which he was a versatile contributor.

—Reed Benhamou

# DESSAU, Ingrid (Peterson)

Swedish textile designer

**Born:** Svalov, Malmö, 3 March 1923. **Education:** Studied at the National College of Art, Craft and Design, Stockholm, 1939-45. **Career:** Worked as a designer, for the Handcraft Society of Kristianstad County, Sweden, 1945-49; designer, Kasthallcarpet factory, Kinna, 1954-75, and for Kinnasand textile company, Kinna, 1970-84; freelance textile designer, working for Hitex, Kinnasand, and as a textile consultant, in Malmö, from 1984. **Exhibitions:** *Hantverkets, 60-tal,* Nationalmuseum, Stockholm, 1968; *The Lunning Prize,* Nationalmuseum, Stockholm, 1986; *Faces of Swedish Design,* IBM Gallery, New York, 1988 (toured). **Collections:** Nationalmuseum, Stockholm. **Honors:** Lunning Prize, 1955. **Address:** Sanekullävgen 40 F, 217 74 Malmö, Sweden.

## Works

*Zig Zag* double-weave cotton fabric, for Kinnasand, 1981.
Carpets and fabrics, for the Parliament Building, Stockholm, 1983.
*Joplin* linen-weave furniture fabric, for Kinnasand, 1985.
*Dixie* hand-knotted wool carpet, for Kinnasand, 1986.
*Basin Street* hand-woven high and low pile carpet, 1986.
*Blue Swell* hand-tufted carpet, for Hitex, 1987.

## Publications

**On DESSAU: books**—*Svensko Form/Forma Sueca* by Åke Stavenlow and Åke H. Huldt, Stockholm, 1961; *Scandinavian Design: Objects of a Life Style* by Eileene Harrison Beer, New York, 1975; *Den Svenska Formen* by Monica Boman and others, Stockholm, 1985; *The Lunning Prize,* exhibition catalogue edited by Helena Dahlback Lutteman and Marianne Uggla, Stockholm, 1986; *Faces of Swedish Design,* exhibition catalogue edited by Monica Boman, Stockholm, 1988.

\*

I prefer to work with carpets. They give a room an important base, and they can also serve as a decorative element. Carpets have a scale and architectural dimension which interests me. I have worked to a large extent with architects. My ultimate aim is trying to give vibrancy to what is simple.

—Ingrid Dessau

\*       \*       \*

Suddenly a pattern swarms densely with ... what? Fish. Fishbones swaying at an angle, fishbones of various sizes, pulsating and lively. Behind them you can imagine Ingrid Dessau's vigorous laughter. Normally, fishbones represent a strict weaving pattern, well under control, a given code. Here they have liberated themselves from the abstraction and swarm freely across the handwoven surface. Thus can a mature artist allow herself to play freely when she has her base in a superb sense of form. And thus can Ingrid Dessau bloom. She has devoted her life to examining the possibilities of weaving techniques, and transforming them into an infinite number of variations in simple, geometrical patterns. Abstract patterns which also resound to the joy and the confirmation of life, patterns which have made her both respected and loved.

The fishbone pattern is part of a collection of handwoven heavy pile carpets which the Swedish textile company Kinnasand has had woven in India.

"Now it's all coming out," says Ingrid Dessau, pleased with her new collection. Several years of intensive development work are now producing the best possible results. India has an unbelievable amount of know-how and fantastic traditions. But the will to do a perfect job lay fallow as long as purchasers asked only for the very cheapest carpets. In this case, the high standard of quality required has given a technical and artistic lift to both Kinnasand and the Indian weavers. In addition the carpets are woven under humane conditions. This was a condition set by Ingrid if she was to take on this task at all.

The first carpets had clean patterns with mirror images, friezes, and corners. They were soft as velvet and smooth. Their spare design and simplicity of color brought something new and refreshing to the traditional heavy pile carpets. And they have been highly successful.

They were as simple as possible and that was what was lacking at the time. They could fit in with a variety of settings. They were produced in strong, happy, normal colors.

The latest collection consists of carpets of twisted, double-threaded yarn, which gives a coarser and more grainy surface. These are dense, more individual, and with more detailed patterns. One is characterized by reliefs, another is more "avant garde," and yet another features the fishbones. There is a variety of coloring: dark plum, celadon, blue-gray, charcoal, gray-green, clear, dark purple, and dark red.

Ingrid Dessau prefers to work with carpets. They give a room its all-important base, and can also serve as a decoration. They have a scale and architectural dimension which suits Ingrid's temperament. For this reason she has worked to a large extent with architects—a much appreciated colleague who has made the fabrics for many interiors. Her major projects have included the textile program for the Swedish parliament building and Government House, which were renovated in the early 80s. Both were unusually advanced projects, both artistically and from the point of view of organization.

"I have more to do than I have time for," Ingrid says. She retired from Kinnasand in 1984 and has worked as a freelance since then. Her larger works have included the Indian carpets and handtufted carpets for Hitex. Collaboration with Hitex is important for her interior decoration assignments, and usually involves specially composed carpets. Usually such jobs have to be done quickly: the carpets come into the construction picture at a late stage, and then it's good to be able to do them in Sweden. The handtufted carpets also include much of the life and quality of a handwoven carpet.

Ingrid Dessau's interior fabrics for Kinnasand have so far offered the pleasure of an exquisite use of bindings in understandable geometrical patterns, series of variations in white on white, colorful double weaves and rhythmical humorous striping.

"I often begin with complicated patterns, but I peel them away bit by bit. What I make must fit in with a lot of other things."

Ingrid Dessau began her professional career at a famous handweaving factory and with the Swedish Handcraft Association, heavy with tradition. Her strong interest in the technical side gave her new forms of expression. She has since transferred her skill in hand weaving to industry, by testing the technical possibilities to their utmost.

"I am very particular," she admits.

But in the end it's a matter of diligence, discipline, a feeling for quality, and self-criticism based on a solid knowledge of the market. This is balanced by an imaginative flow of patterns which appear in a steady stream of sketches. The ultimate aim is to give vibrancy to what is simple.

—Gunilla Lundahl

# DIFFRIENT, Niels

American industrial and furniture designer

**Born:** Star, Mississippi, 6 September 1928. **Education:** Cass Technical High School, Detroit, 1943-46; Cranbrook Academy of Art, Bloomfield Hills, Michigan, BFA, 1953; attended Wayne State University, Detroit, 1951-52; Fulbright Fellowship in Design and Architecture, working with designer Marco Zanuso, Milan, 1954-55. **Family:** Married Lois Newell in 1952 (divorced, 1969); children: Scott, Julie, and Emily; married designer Helena Hernmarck in 1976. **Career:** Designer and modeler, at Eero Saarinen Associates, Bloomfield Hills, Michigan, 1948-53; staff designer, Walter B. Ford Associates, Detroit, 1953-54; designer and partner, Henry Dreyfuss Associates New York, 1955-81; founder-principal, Niels Diffrient Product Design, Ridgefield, Connecticut, from 1981; consultant to Ford Motor Company, Philips Corporation, Texas Instruments Inc., Amtrak National Railroad Corporation, and Howe Furniture Company. Assistant Professor-in-Residence, University of California at Los Angeles, 1960-69; visiting critic, School of Architecture, Yale University, 1990-1991. Board member, 1970, and vice-president, 1975, Industrial Design Society of America; advisory board member, Art Center College of Design, Pasadena, California, from 1972; board member, 1974-90, chairman, 1975, and treasurer, 1976, International Design Conference, Aspen, Colorado; advisory consultant, 1972, and policy panel member, 1980, National Endowment for the Arts, Washington, D.C.; president, International Design Education Foundation, 1976-92; editorial board member, *Industrial Design* magazine, New York, 1977-89; admission jury,

American Academy in Rome, 1978-90; advisory board, Corporate Design Foundation, from 1986; board of directors, American Center for Design, 1992-94. **Exhibitions:** *Niels Different: Knoll Seating,* Cranbrook Academy of Art Museum, Bloomfield Hills, 1980; *Design since 1945,* Philadelphia Museum of Art, 1983; *New Design for Old,* Boilerhouse/Victoria and Albert Museum, London, 1986; *World Design,* International Council of the Societies of Industrial Design, 1986; *Ceremonial Lights,* Israel Museum, Jerusalem, 1987; *Furniture as Object,* Aetna Institute/Gallery Jazz, New York, 1987; *397 Chairs,* Architectural League, New York, 1988. **Collections:** Cranbrook Academy of Art Museum, Bloomfield Hills; Philadelphia Museum of Art; Design Museum, London. **Honors:** First Medal in Design, Cranbrook Academy of Art, 1949, 1950, 1951; First Prize, Packard Automobile Design Competition, 1951; First Prize, Michigan Recreational Center, 1952; Compasso d'Oro Award, Milan, 1957; United States Government Award for Design for the Handicapped, 1970, 1974; fellow, Industrial Design Society of America, 1971; American Institute of Graphic Arts Award, 1972; DHL, Art Center College of Design, Pasadena, 1975; Design and Environment Award, 1976; Resource Council Award, New York, 1979, 1981; Institute of Business Designers Award, 1979, 1980, 1984, 1988, 1992; Designers Choice Award, *Industrial Design* magazine, New York, 1980, 1982, 1985, 1989; Design Excellence Award, Industrial Design Society of America, 1980, 1985, 1993; United States National Award for Transportation Design, 1981; *Time* magazine Best of 1982 Award, 1982; Honorary Royal Designer for Industry, Royal Society of Arts, London, 1987; Gold Medal, American Institute of Architects, 1989; Contemporary Design Award, Philadelphia Museum of Art, 1989; honorary member, American Center for Design, 1991, and Designers Institute of New Zealand, 1992; named to top 40 design innovators, *ID* magazine, 1993. **Address:** 879 North Salem Road, Ridgefield, Connecticut 06877, U.S.A.

## Works

Automated portable sewing machine in die-cast metal, for Borletti Company, 1956 (with Marco Zanuso).

High-voltage electricity pylons in steel, aluminum, and wood, for the Edison Electric Institute, 1964.

High-voltage sub-station in Covina, California, for the Southern California Edison Company, 1967.

Airplane interiors of the Boeing 747, 767, 727, 707, and Douglas DC-10, for American Airlines, 1968-80.

High capacity lift truck in steel plate and iron castings, for Hyster Company, 1972.

Pneumatic Hyway Vibrating Compactor heavy duty roller, for Hyster Company, 1974.

*Human Factors* information product in three volumes with graphic selector, for MIT Press, 1974, 1978.

Upholstered executive office chair in steel and aluminum casting, for Knoll International, 1978.

Task Seating series of upholstered office chairs with die-formed steel shell, for Knoll International, 1978.

8-passenger business jet interiors, for Gates Learjet Series 50, 1979.

Reclining upholstered office seating series in steel and aluminum, for Sunar Hauserman Company, 1982.

Reclining task chair and accessories in aluminum, steel and thermoformed plastic, for Sunar Hauserman Company, 1984.

Commercial table series, for Howe Furniture Company, 1989.

Training table system, for Howe Furniture Company, 1992.

## Publications

**By DIFFRIENT: books**—(editor) *Electrical Transmission Structures,* New York, 1965; (with Alvin R. Tilley and Jean C. Bardgajy) *Humanscale 1/2/3,* Cambridge, Massachusetts, 1974; *Design of Experience,* Minneapolis, 1975; (with Alvin R. Tilley and David Harman) *Humanscale 4/5/6,* Cambridge, 1981; (with others) *Humanscale 7/8/9,* Cambridge, 1981.

**On DIFFERENT: books**—*Design and Environment* by Ann Ferebee, New York, 1976; *Chair* by Peter Bradford and Barbara Prete, New York, 1978, *Niels Diffrient: Knoll Seating,* exhibition catalogue edited by Katherine McCoy, Birmingham, Michigan, 1980; *Knoll Design* by Eric Larrabee and Massimo Vignelli, New York, 1980; *The Conran Directory of Design* edited by Stephen Bayley, London, 1985; *The American Design Adventure 1940-1975* by Arthur J. Pulos, Cambridge, Massachusetts, and London, 1988; *Designing for Humanity,* London, 1991; *Encyclopedia of 20th Century Design,* London, 1993.

\*

My principal interest is in design for mass production—the products of daily use manufactured in quantity for large numbers of people. My goal is to achieve a combination of elegance and performance in mass-produced products to equal the fine products of the handcrafts. The constraints inherent in this pursuit are imposed by the separate demands of marketing, manufacturing, and engineering. In contrast to hand made products for which the designer is also the fabricator who transacts directly with the user and, most certainly, gets direct feedback on the product's performance, especially if it fails, those mass-produced products that are my goal must be achieved in the face of certain difficulties: someone else makes the products, they are sold to people you don't know, and you never gain sufficient information about how they work.

Designing is a practical art. In other words, it combines art and practicality. Art, as such, serves no practical purpose. To be successful at designing for practical use, the art as esthetics and amenity must be so inherent and natural in the performance of the product that it is not conceivable to have one without the other except at considerable sacrifice.

Objects that achieve this highly desirable state have been normally approached by one of two paths. The first has been going on for some time and springs from technical goals. Objects which are true to a clear function, such as boats and airplanes, are nearly always handsome. The other avenue is more recent and approaches the task from an aesthetic basis on the tacit assumption that the object that looks right will work right. Neither of these paths achieves

Niels Diffrient: *Jefferson* reclining task chair system for Sunar Hauserman, 1984

consistent success and rarely fulfills its potential. Most often the traditional goals of either extreme form the ultimate measure of accomplishment and override the concerns of the other.

The missing ingredient is a comprehensive measure of accomplishment. The technician is satisfied if the electro/mechanical performance is successful at a good price, and the aesthetic designer is satisfied if the product wins a design award. Neither result is complete, and the simple combination of the two would still leave something out. By better understanding the experience provided by the product, I believe it might be possible to surpass parochial professionalism and achieve designs that are less self conscious and more elegantly natural. All practical design includes performance, that is, how it functions in relation to the user—not just how the gears mesh or the electrons react, but whether it provides a positive experience, does its job, and possibly satisfies a deeper emotion. When the level of performance between product and person reaches an exquisite level of interaction, conceivably aesthetic in nature, then its appearance will be as natural as its technical elements; it will exceed the need for applied fashion but will at the same time create it.

—Niels Diffrient

\*　　\*　　\*

Niels Diffrient is an industrial designer whose professional accomplishments include aircraft interiors, construction equipment, high-voltage transmission towers, and sewing machines, but his reputation may rest ultimately on his designs for office seating. Previously well-known within his profession, he has achieved wider notoriety since the introduction of Knoll's Diffrient Seating (1979) and Sunar's Helena chair series (1982). These are technologically sophisticated office chairs engineered for high-volume production and featuring clearly articulated adjustment and control mechanisms. Conceptually, they exemplify Diffrient's thorough knowledge of mechanics and industrial processes: "Once you understand the tools, then you can design the parts."

Diffrient graduated from Cranbrook Academy in the generation following Charles Eames, Florence Knoll, and Eero Saarinen. He went to work for Saarinen in the late 1940s as model maker. It was here, while preparing Saarinen's first Knoll designs for production, that he became aware of the shortcomings of an industry that, paradoxically, utilized traditional handicraft technologies to produce modern furniture. From that experience, Diffrient became convinced that for good design to reach the widest possible audience it must be mass-produced. "To do something ... that will be produced by the most advanced techniques, and produced in the millions,... that is where the fascination (lies) for me," he has stated. His enthusiasm is tempered, however, by a concern for human factors.

Early in his career, he was exposed to the science of human engineering as a protege of Henry Dreyfuss, a pioneer in that field. Through collaboration with Dr. Janet Travell, who had treated President John F. Kennedy for back problems in the early 1960s, Diffrient has developed a keen, almost evangelical design philosophy which places human comfort above other design criteria. An unabashed functionalist even as the fashion grows to repudiate that thinking, he is nonetheless wary of some easy answers to be found in that approach. Of the Bauhaus pioneers, he says, "I don't think those folks cared whether the chair was comfortable... They were mainly interested in ... counter(ing) ... the Beaux-Arts tradition." Diffrient's own, frequently unusual, design solutions are the result of a mature

understanding of an object's intended function. His approach to problem-solving involves the constant reworking of existing solutions until, by one final refinement or inspirational leap, the design becomes uniquely his own—and perhaps uniquely useful.

—Kenneth Gaulin

## DOBLIN, Jay

American design planner and industrial designer

**Born:** New York City, 10 December 1920. **Education:** Studied industrial design, under Alexander Kostellow, Rowenna Reed, Donald Dohner and Gordon Lippincott, at the Pratt Institute, Brooklyn, New York, 1939-42. **Family:** Married Annette Woodward in 1949. **Career:** Designer of camouflage and other government projects, 1942-49; projects for Frigidaire, Shell Oil, Nabisco, Coca-Cola, Singer, British Petroleum, and others, at Raymond Loewy Associates, in New York and Chicago, 1950-55; co-founder, with Ralph Eckerstrom and others, and senior vice-president, of Unimark International design company, Chicago, 1964-72; freelance planning consultant, establishing Jay Doblin and Associates, Chicago, 1972-89; consultant to J. C. Penney, Standard Oil of Indiana, Borg-Warner, General Electric, Xerox Corporation, American Hospital Association, Beatrice Foods, and others. Director of the Industrial Design Evening School, Pratt Institute, Brooklyn, New York, 1948-52; professor and co-director, and adjunct professor of Design Theory of Technology, Chicago, 1955-69; professor, School of the Art Institute of Chicago, 1975-78; visiting professor, Graduate School for Business Studies, London, 1980. **Member:** Vice-president, 1956-57, president, 1957-58, board member, 1956-64 and 1977-80, and board chairman, 1958-59, Industrial Designers Society of America; design and education adviser, Japanese Ministry of International Trade and Industry, 1959; vice-president, ICSID International Council of Societies of Industrial Design, 1960-80; president, Industrial Design Educators Association, Chicago, 1963-64; board member, International Design Conference, Aspen, Colorado, 1963-67; advisory board member, *Industrial Design* magazine, New York, 1974, and Design Management Institute, New York, 1980. **Honors:** Honor Student Award, Pratt Institute, 1942; Fellow, 1959, Distinguished Design Program Award, 1974, and Personal Achievement Award, 1982, Industrial Designers Society of America; Kaufmann International Design Award, New York, 1964; Distinguished Alumnus Award, Pratt Institute, New York, 1973; Honorary Fellow, Society of Typographic Arts, Chicago, 1979; Royal Society of Arts, London, 1980. **Died:** Chicago, 11 May 1989.

### Publications

**By DOBLIN: books**—*Perspective: A New System for Designers,* New York, 1955; *100 Great Product Designs,* New York, 1969.

**On DOBLIN: books**—*Il Disegno Industriale e la sua Estetica* by Gillo Dorfles, Bologna, 1963; *Design in America* by Ralph Caplan, New York, 1969; *A History of Design from the Victorian Era to the Present* by Ann Ferebee, New York, 1970; *The Conran Directory of Design,* edited by Stephen Bayley, London, 1985; *An Introduction to Design and Culture in the Twentieth Century* by Penny

Spark, London, 1986; *The American Design Adventure 1940-1975* by Arthur J. Pulos, London and Cambridge, Massachusetts, 1988.

\*

I began as a hardgoods designer with Raymond Loewy in New York. It was during Loewy's most prolific years; he had a staff of more than 100 and many major accounts, including Pennsylvania Railroad, Studebaker, Coca-Cola, Frigidaire, Greyhound, and Singer. He gave me the opportunity to design dozens of major products. After ten years, Loewy made me head of their newly formed marketing group. We did full-scale redesigns of Shell, BP, Nabisco, etc. The experience changed me; I began to think of design as systems composed of integrated disciplines rather than products.

By 1955, after fifteen years, I had lost interest in commercial design for giant companies. I accepted the directorship of the Institute of Design at Illinois Institute of Technology. This school, founded by Moholy-Nagy, was being joined to Mies van der Rohe's School of Architecture in Mies's newly finished Crown Hall. This was a fresh challenge.

During the fourteen-year period at the Institute of Design, I went through two phases. In the beginning, I oriented the school and myself to do simple, clear uncommercial design. I felt that this was where design would go. It succeeded: the work was fresh and useful. But in the mid 1960s, it became clear that the computer would change design, so we changed the school's central emphasis to systems design methodology. It wasn't the machine itself but the disciplined algorithmic thinking that computer-assisted design required. This was an explosive revelation to me. I worked enthusiastically at this time for ten years at the school and at Unimark (a new design firm I co-founded with Ralph Eckerstrom and others in 1965).

By the mid 1970s, I changed again; I began doing large-scale corporate design planning. One, for J. C. Penney, co-ordinated 300 designers in eight design activities (products, packaging, interiors, exteriors, catalogues, advertising, internal communications, and displays). Later, I did similar assignments for Standard Oil, Xerox, American Hospital Association, Beatrice Foods, Borg-Warner, and others. This history may sound like a straight development from product design to systems of products to corporate design planning, with an increase of complexity at each stage. But paralleling this has been a deep interest in design theory. Now, no client has ever paid me for theory. They don't want it. In fact, they freeze when they're exposed to it. And yet, this is my central interest. My problem is that I'm not smart enough to solve the essential design-theory problems. And large scale corporate design planning involves business strategy and organization (which includes politics). Both of these are frustratingly difficult for me; my early background as a hardgoods designer does not support these. So, as someone once said, I've reached my level of incompetence at both theory and design planning. The decision for those who reach this point is to either go back to where they can operate competently or to keep at it and hope one's competence rises to meet the problems. I am confronted by this.

During my early and middle years, I wanted to be where I now am. But now that I'm here, I wonder why I did it when I was so happy and productive in the earlier stages. My present goal is to develop theories of design that will support the emergence of a profession from what is now a practice or trade. Compared to law, management, consulting, architecture, accounting, advertising, and even interior design, product and message design is a small, low-grade activity. The reason I am so interested in doing this is that

product design, the prime control of how industrial output should impact culture, ought to be respected and well supported.

—Jay Doblin (1984)

\*　　\*　　\*

Designer, planner, professor, and theorist, Jay Doblin was in the forefront of the industrial design profession after his graduation from the Pratt Institute in 1942. He was a practical designer, a planner, a visionary. He taught design, wrote about design, and proselytized about the mission of the designer.

Doblin began his career in the 1940s as a product designer for Raymond Loewy, one of the great practitioners, in his heyday. As executive designer, he worked on many product programs and took particular pride in having contributed to hit products like the Edison Voicewriter. Although a good draftsman and a practical designer, he seemed to have found new challenges in establishing and directing Loewy's marketing design group. Later, as vice-president of Unimark and as a consultant, he worked on design and product planning for large corporations, devising new and original techniques of analysis and problem-solving. His work for J.C. Penney earned the Industrial Design Society of America's 1974 Award for Distinguished Design Programs. He had come to be considered a multi-talented designer, able to analyze highly complex, interactive, business and design problems and to propose innovative and holistic solutions.

Always interested in education and possessing a natural flair for teaching, Doblin maintained a close connection with educational institutions throughout his professional career. At the Institute of Design, where, as Director, he was successor to László Moholy-Nagy and inheritor of the Bauhaus tradition, he brought a new focus to the industrial design program, emphasizing professional orientation and practice. His classroom experience and his love of theory undoubtedly contributed to the fresh and critical evaluations which Doblin brought to a variety of design problems. He lectured widely and wrote about design process, planning and evaluation. Doblin believed in speaking out on issues he considered to be important. Invariably, others listened.

—Benjamin deBrie Taylor

# DONATI, Danilo

Italian stage and film costume designer

**Born:** Luzzara, in 1926. **Education:** Studied art in Florence. **Career:** First stage designs for opera productions of Luchino Visconti, Rome 1955; film designer, working notably with directors Pier Pasolini and Federico Fellini, in Rome, from 1962; supervising art director, RAI television network, Rome. **Honors:** Academy Award and British Academy Award, 1968, 1976. **Address:** via Due Macelli 31, 00100 Rome, Italy.

## Works

Film costume designs include—*La Steppa* (Lattuada), 1962; *Rogopag* (Pasolini and others), 1962; *Il Vangelo Secondo Matteo* (Pasolini) 1964; *La Mandragola* (Lattuada), 1965; *El Grefo*

(Salce), 1966; *Uccellacci e Uccellini* (Pasolini), 1966; *The Taming of the Shrew* (Zeffirelli), 1966; Oedipo Re (Pasolini), 1967; *Romeo and Juliet* (Zeffirelli), 1968; *La Cintura di Castita* (Festa Campanile), 1968; *Porcile* (Pasolini), 1969; *Medea* (Pasolini), 1969; Satyricon (Fellini), 1969; *La Monaca di Monza* (E. Visconti), 1969; *I Clowns* (Fellini), 1970; *I Decameron* (Pasolini), 1971; *Roma* (Fellini), 1972; *I Racconti di Canterbury* (Pasolini), 1972; *Fratello Sole, Sorella Luna* (Zeffirelli), 1972; *Il Fiore delle Mille e Una Notte* (Pasolini), 1974; *Amarcord* (Fellini), 1974; *Salo, o le 120 Giornate di Sodoma* (Pasolini), 1975; *Caligula* (Brass), 1976; *Casanova* (Fellini), 1976; *Hurricane* (Troell), 1979; *Flash Gordon* (Hodges), 1980; *Ginger e Fred* (Fellini), 1985.

## Publications

On DONATI: books—*Le Decor de Film* by Leon Barsacq, Paris, 1970, as *Caligari's Cabinet and Other Grand Illusions,* Boston, 1976; *On the Set of "Fellini-Satyricon"* by Eileene Lanouette Hughes, New York, 1971; *The Classic Cinema* by Stanley J. Solomon, New York, 1973; *Pier Paolo Pasolini: Trilogia della Vita* edited by Giorgio Gattei, Bologna, 1975; *Luchino Visconti: Il Mio Teatro,* 2 vols., edited by C. D'Amico and R. Renzi, Bologna, 1979; *The International Dictionary of Films and Filmmakers,* London and Chicago, 1987, 1991.

\*   \*   \*

Danilo Donati has to his credit costume and set designs for an impressive list of memorable cinematic and theatrical productions, many of which depict great classics of opera, the Bible, Greek tragedy, and Shakespeare, as interpreted according to some of the most important contemporary film and stage directors of Italy. After his training in Florence as a muralist and fresco painter, Donati spent several years as supervising art director at RAI, Italy's national television network. During the 1960s, he realized some of his finest achievements in the designs he created for the movies of Pasolini, Fellini, and Zeffirelli. During the same period, he also did costumes for the stage, one of the most flamboyant examples being the work he did for *Festa italiana,* a spectacle and ball staged by Gino Landi, Italian choreographer of television spectaculars, and held at New York's Madison Square Garden in 1966. For the occasion, Donati dressed Roman charioteers, flag throwers, gladiators, medieval knights, and more; made wild, orange tarantella costumes; and came up with a resplendently somber, medieval scene in black-and-white for dancers who re-enacted the live chess game which is held every year in Marostica.

One of Donati's more recent projects consists of costumes and sets he created for Dino De Laurentis' adventure-fantasy movie, *Flash Gordon.* It took more than seven months to make the 600-plus original, futuristic costumes for the extravaganza, for which Donati also did massive sets that filled 250,000 square feet at three London studios. From the ancient to the futuristic, Donati's designs have covered the centuries, including contemporary costumes for movies such as Fellini's *Roma* (1972) and early Fascist-era outfittings for Fellini's highly acclaimed portrait of adolescence in the Italy of that time, *Amarcord* (1974).

It is Donati's flair for the lavish and historic which has earned him a serious and lasting position as designer. His five Oscar nominations (including two wins) alone serve as ample exemplar of the

central character of his contribution to the history of movie costume and set design. *La Mandragola* (1966), *The Gospel According to Saint Matthew* (1964), *The Taming of the Shrew* (1967), *Romeo and Juliet* (1968), *Casanova* (1976): the list reads like a who's who of outstanding contemporary Italian cinema. The work he has accomplished with Fellini alone is evidence enough of the high-caliber movies with which Donati has been associated. *Satyricon* (1969), *Roma* (1972), *Amarcord* (1974), *Casanova* (1976): this list of some of Fellini's finest achievements demonstrates Fellini's continued confidence in Donati's particular abilities, even as it suggests the breadth of the challenge Donati has faced in his field. It also brings to mind the general situation of the costume and set designer whose work can easily be overlooked in light of the fame of the filmmaker, while the contribution of the costume designer is too often taken for granted. Over his career, Donati's work has been well-researched historically, fittingly elaborate or simple, always attuned to the overall effect of the movie as a whole. And these are the signs which point to a knowledgeable and inventive designer for the entertainment media.

—Barbara Cavaliere

# DONZELLI, Rinaldo

Italian graphic, industrial, and corporate designer

Born: Mariano Comense, near Como, 12 September 1921. **Education:** Educated at the Scuola Secondaria di Avviamento Professionale, Como, 1932-35; mainly self-taught in design. **Military Service:** Served in the Italian Army, 1941-45. **Family:** Married Giuseppina Rosa Molteni in 1948; children: Mariapia, Anna, Silvia, Palo, Elena, Elisabetta, Giovanni, and Alberto. **Career:** Worked in a sawmill and a carpenter's shop, Como, 1936-38; independent portrait painter, Como, 1938-41; freelance designer, from 1945; design consultant, Motogilera motorcycle company, Arcore, Milan, 1950-64, and Motoguzzi motorcycle company, Mandello del Lario, Como, 1965-72. **Address:** Via Isonzo 87A, 22066 Mariano Comense (Como), Italy.

## Publications

By DONZELLI: books—(and illustrator) *Lavori in legno,* Milan, 1978; *Disegnare una persona,* Bologna, 1979.

On DONZELLI: books—*Design e forme nuove dell'arredamento italiano* edited by Paolo Portoghesi and Marino Marini, Rome, 1978; *Atlante del design italiano* by Alfonso Grassi and Anty Pansera, Milan, 1980; *Da cosa nascecosa* by Bruno Munari, Bari, Italy, 1981.

\*

Find the interesting—the useful—the true—immediately.
To be Donzelli
requires Rinaldo
to stay a young fellow.

—Rinaldo Donzelli

# DORFSMAN, Louis
American graphic designer

**Born:** The Bronx, New York, 25 April 1918. **Education:** Studied at Cooper Union, New York, BFA, 1939. **Military Service:** Served in the United States Army, 1943-46. **Family:** Married Ann Hysa in 1940; children: Elissa, Mitchell, and Neil. **Career:** Exhibit and display designer, for the New York World's Fair, 1939; director of training films for the United States Navy, 1940-43; joined Columbia Broadcasting System as a designer, New York, 1946; vice-president of advertising and sales promotion, CBS Radio, 1959-69; director of advertising and sales promotion, CBS Television Network, 1960-64; designed interiors, signage, and printed materials, for CBS building on 52nd Street, from 1962; director of design, 1964-68, and vice president of advertising and promotion, from 1968, CBS Inc., New York. Instructor, New York Workshop School of Design, and Cooper Union, New York. **Member:** Board Member, International Design Conference, Aspen, Colorado; trustee, Cooper Union, New York. **Exhibitions:** American Institute of Graphic Arts, New York; Cooper Union, New York; Washington University, St. Louis. **Collections:** Museum of Modern Art, New York; Metropolitan Museum of Art, New York. **Honors:** Special Citation, 1956, and Augustus St. Gaudens Medal, 1963, Cooper Union, New York; Gold Medal, Philadelphia Print Club, 1962; Gold Medal, American Institute of Graphic Arts, 1978; Hall of Fame Award, 1978, 13 Gold Medals, Art Directors Club of New York. **Address:** CBS Inc., 51 West 52nd Street, New York, New York 10019, U.S.A.

## Works

*Living Off the Main Line* newspaper advertisement, for CBS Radio, 1951.
*The Importance of Good Connections* magazine advertisement, for CBS Radio, 1954.
*Summertime Promotion Kit* brochure, for CBS Radio, 1955.
*Impact* magazine advertisement, for CBS Radio, 1957.
*CBS Preview 62* promotional packaging, for CBS Television, 1962.
*The Rocket's Red Glare...* magazine advertisement, for CBS Television, 1962.
*CBS Mid-Season Promotion* promotional packaging, for CBS Television, 1964.
*Daytime Program Promotion* promotional packaging, for CBS Television, 1963.
Typographic assemblage mural, for the CBS cafeteria, New York, 1963.
*What in the World's Going On Here?* newspaper advertisement, for CBS Television, 1966.
*Of Black America* newspaper advertisement, for CBS Television, 1968.

## Publications

**By DORFSMAN: books**—(with Tadanori Yokoo and Masataka Ogawa) *Push Pin Studios,* Tokyo, 1972; **articles**—in *Graphis* (Zurich), no. 141, 1969, no. 185, 1976; *Communication Arts* (Palo Alto), no. 4, 1972.

**On DORFSMAN: books**—*Die neue Grafik/The New Graphic Design* by Karl Gerstner and Markus Kutter, Teufen and London, 1959; *Advertising Directions* edited by Edward M. Gottschall and Arthur Hawkins, New York, 1959; *Typography* by Aaron Burns, New York, 1961; *Who's Who in Graphic Art* edited by Walter Amstutz, Zurich, 1962, Dubendorf, 1982; *An International Survey of Packaging* by Wim Crouwel and Kurt Weidemann, London, 1968; *The Corporate Search for Visual Identity* by Ben Rosen, New York and London, 1970; *Monografie des Plakats: Entwicklung, Stil, Design* by Herbert Schindler, Munich, 1972; *The Design Concept* by Allen Hurlburt, New York, 1981; *A History of Graphic Design* by Philip B. Meggs, London and New York, 1983; *The Conran Directory of Design* edited by Stephen Bayley, London, 1985.

*     *     *

The son of a sign painter, Louis Dorfsman was born and raised in the Bronx and graduated from Cooper Union in New York City. He began working at CBS in 1946, when he was hired directly by William Golden, creative director for the company. Dorfsman's early work centered around identifying and defining opportunities in selling advertising time on the CBS radio network, very much competing for the advertising dollar with CBS-TV. His early ads, such as "Busy Markets," evidenced an approach to problem-solving and visual fact not before seen in radio advertising.

Upon Golden's sudden death in 1959, Dorfsman was named to his position, from which, for the next decade, he produced high-quality tune-in ads, corporate brochures, entertainment packages for the new TV season, books, film, and animation, in all of which taste, craft, and humor more than suggested that a designer could have an aesthetic. With the support of William S. Paley, chairman and founder of CBS, and Dr. Frank Stanton, president of CBS through 1973, the art department under Dorfsman's direction flourished as an in-house operation.

His *Gastrotypographicalassemblage* was a major project designed and constructed in the mid-1960s in the new corporate office building for the employee cafeteria. Often collaborating with his lifelong friend, Herb Lubalin, Dorfsman created a mural that was as much an environmental installation as it was a typographic self-portrait of a man whose ease at arranging and designing type is joy and self-expression.

Dorfsman's animation concepts and narrative film interpretations advertising the network are visually stimulating and usually amusing. In one, announcing the beginning of a National Football League game, a television fan is watching a game from his easy chair when suddenly, a football shoots out of the television and is followed by the entire team rushing on the viewer. In another, he used two members of the Broadway mime group Mummenshantz to characterize "happy" and "sad" as a means of announcing the CBS afternoon playhouse.

A sense of classicism, often mixed with the spirit of child-like exploration, taste, and old-world craftsmanship characterize to this day the wide range and qualities of Dorfsman's work for CBS, as well as for the Dansk Company and the design conferences at Aspen. His exploration of alternative mediums to meet the evolving marketing needs and to shape the public perception of CBS has been virtually unique in twentieth-century design, for Dorfsman has worked for the same company for more than thirty years and consistently maintained quality by relying on personal wit, streetside sensitivity, and acute business skills, in addition to his artistic talents.

—Michael Robert Soluri

# DREYFUSS, Henry

American industrial and stage designer

**Born:** New York City, 2 March 1904. **Education:** Ethical Culture School, New York. **Family:** Married Doris Marks in 1930; children: John, Gail, and Ann. **Career:** Apprenticed to designer Norman Bel Geddes, New York, 1924; stage presentation designer for the Strand Motion Picture Theatre, New York, and guide for American Express in Europe, 1925-27; freelance stage designer for theatres in New York, 1927-30; established own industrial design office, New York, from 1929; designed for Bell Telephone Laboratories, General Electric, the 1939 New York World's Fair, New York Central Railroad, John Deere Company, Mergenthaler Linotype, Hoover, Eversharp, Royal Typewriters, Lockheed Aircraft, American Export Lines, Western Electric, *McCall's* magazine, and others. Professor of Engineering, California Institute of Technology, Pasadena, from 1952; visiting lecturer at Harvard University, Yale University, and Massachusetts Institute of Technology. **Member:** Board member, Ford Foundation Educational Facilities Laboratories, and the Performing Arts Council of Los Angeles Music Center; executive committee member, National Reading Council; trustee, California Institute of Technology, People to People, and Los Angeles County Art Museum. **Honors:** American Designers Institute Award, 1943; Gold Medal, Architectural League of New York, 1951, 1954; American Institute of Graphic Arts Award of Excellence, 1953; Philadelphia Museum College of Art Design Award, 1958, 1962; American Society of Industrial Designers Award, 1960; American Iron and Steel Institute Design Award, 1963, 1965; Ambassador Award for Achievement, London, 1965; National Association of Schools of Art Award, 1969; Jack A. Kraft Award, Human Factors Society, 1971; Benjamin Franklin Fellow, Royal Society of Arts, London; Fellow, Industrial Designers Society of America; Honorary Member, Telephone Pioneers of America. Honorary doctorates: Occidental College, Los Angeles, 1953; Pratt Institute, Brooklyn, New York, 1963; Otis Art Institute, Los Angeles, 1968. Order of the Orange Nassau, Netherlands, 1952. **Died:** Pasadena, California, 5 October 1972.

## Works

Upright vacuum cleaner, for Hoover, 1935.
*Mercury* diesel locomotive, for New York Central Railroad, 1936.
*300* combined handset desk telephone, for Bell Telephone Laboratories, 1937.
*Engine 5450* diesel locomotive, for New York Central Railroad, 1938.
*Twentieth Century Limited* train design, for New York Central Railroad, 1938.
*Democracity: The City of Tomorrow* exhibit, at the New York World's Fair, 1939.
*McCall's* magazine re-design, New York, 1940.
Embankment compacter and lift truck, for Hyster Company, 1950s.
*Constellation* and *Electra* passenger airplane interiors, for Lockheed, 1953.
*Touch-Tone Trimline* telephone, for Bell Telephone Laboratories, 1955.
*Injector* one-piece safety razor, for ASR Products Company, 1959.

## Publications

**By DREYFUSS: books**—*Industrial Design: A Pictorial Accounting,* New York, 1929, 1958; *Designing for People,* New York, 1955, 1967; *The Measure of Man: Human Factors in Design,* New York, 1960, 1967; *Henry Dreyfuss Symbol Source Book,* with Doris Marks Dreyfuss, New York, 1972; **articles**—in *The Enamelist* (Cleveland), November 1933; *House Beautiful* (London), November 1933; *Electrical Manufacturing* (New York), May 1934, February 1936, October 1937; *Architect and Engineer* (San Francisco), July 1936; *Art and Industry* (New York), September 1944; *Arts and Architecture* (San Francisco), September 1947; *American Fabrics* (New York), no. 38, 1956.

**On DREYFUSS: books**—*Art and the Machine* by Sheldon and Martha Cheney, New York, 1936; *Industrial Design: A Practical Guide* by Harold Van Doren, New York and London, 1940; *Design in British Industry: A Mid-Century Survey* by Michael Farr, Cambridge, 1955; *The Business of Product Design* by James Pilditch and Douglas Scott, London, 1965; *Design in America* by Ralph Caplan, New York, 1969; *The Streamlined Decade* by Donald J. Bush, New York, 1975; *Industrial Design* by John Heskett, London, 1980; *Design Since 1945* edited by Kathryn Hiesinger and George Marcus, London and Philadelphia, 1983; *The Machine Age in America 1918-1941* edited by Richard Guy Wilson and Dianne H. Pilgrim, New York, 1986; *The American Design Adventure 1940-1975* by Arthur J. Pulos, London and Cambridge, Massachusetts, 1988.

\*   \*   \*

Henry Dreyfuss, among the first of the great American industrial designers, was always concerned with his guiding vision—to make machines to fit people, thus making life more efficient and less irritating. His credo was, sharply stated, "that what we are working on is going to be ridden in, sat upon, looked at, talked into, activated, operated, or in some way used by people individually or en masse." He never shied away from the concept of beauty in the functional and was neither slave to the swings of art and taste nor to the modernistic styles of the times.

His early education at the Ethical Culture school produced in him concern for people and their environment. Later, he studied stage design with Norman Bel Geddes, and it is obvious that, although industrial design was not the theme of his studies, exposure to this seminal designer was a great influence in his life and in his future work.

It was through Dreyfuss's mediation as an industrial designer and his insistence on working with engineers that he made the aims of business coincide with the needs of people who used the products he designed. Not only did he serve clients as an industrial designer, but he also served as corporate advisor to Hallmark Cards, Polaroid, American Airlines, and American Telephone and Telegraph.

He was on the faculty of the Engineering Division of the California Institute of Technology for many years and lectured annually on industrial design to the students in Business Economics. On the Board, he persuaded his fellow Trustees to employ the best architects to design new buildings on the campus. As well, he was a leader in such civic organizations as the Center for the Performing Arts, the Music Center, the Los Angeles County Museum, Los Angeles Beautiful, and Pasadena Beautiful.

No evaluation would be complete without the mention of Doris Marks Dreyfuss, his wife, as many of his accomplishments belong to both of them. Their last and greatest collaborative work, the *Henry Dreyfuss Symbol Sourcebook,* an international dictionary of symbols, projects his belief that the eye can catch symbols faster and more easily than the mind can catch words. Mrs. Dreyfuss's contribution was her insistence upon absolute clarity of meaning with simplicity of expression. Thus, their book was aimed at the literate, the illiterate, at people of many different cultures, and at the high speed required in our technological world.

—Mildred Constantine

# DU BOIS, Raoul Pène (-Henri Charles)

American stage and film designer

**Born:** Staten Island, New York, 29 November 1914. **Education:** Studied at the Grand Central Art School, New York, but mainly self-taught in design. **Career:** Worked as assistant to designer Cleon Throckmorton, at the Christopher Morley Theatre, Hoboken, New Jersey, 1932-33; freelance muralist, fashion sketch artist and window display designer, New York, 1933-34; stage set and costume designer, from 1934: first designed for the Ziegfeld Follies production at the Shubert Theatre, New York, 1934, then for other musicals, revues, ballets and films; created costumes for performers Ethel Merman, Ginger Rogers, Dorothy Lamour, Paulette Goddard, Sonja Henie, Ed Wynn, and others; contract film designer, Paramount Studios, Hollywood, California, 1941-45. Independent painter, Paris, 1959-65. **Exhibitions:** Wright/Hepburn/Webster Gallery New York, 1968. **Honors:** Antoinette Perry Award, New York, 1953, 1971; Joseph Maharam Foundation Award, New York, 1971. **Member:** Member, United Scenic Artists, New York. **Died:** New York City in 1985.

## Works

Stage designs (Broadway, except as noted) include—*Life Begins at 8.40,* 1934; *Jumbo,* 1935; *Home and Beauty* (London), 1937; *The Two Bouquets,* 1938; *Leave It to Me,* 1938; *Du Barry Was a Lady,* 1939; *Too Many Girls,* 1939; *One for the Money,* 1939; *Two for the Show,* 1940; *Panama Hattie,* 1940; *Hold on to Your Hats,* 1940; *Liberty Jones,* 1941; *Carmen Jones,* 1943; *The Firebrand of Florence,* 1945; *Are You With It?,* 1945; *Heaven on Earth,* 1948; *Lend an Ear,* 1948; *Alive and Kicking,* 1950; *Call Me Madame,* 1950; *Make a Wish,* 1951; *New Faces of 1952,* 1952; *In Any Language,* 1952; *Wonderful Town,* 1953; *Maggie,* 1953; *Charley's Aunt,* 1953; *Mrs. Patterson,* 1954; *Carmen Jones,* 1956; *Bells Are Ringing,* 1956; *The Music Man,* 1957; *Gypsy,* 1959; *The Student Gypsy,* 1963; *PS I Love You,* 1964; *Royal Flush,* 1964; *Darling of the Day,* 1968; *Peter and the Wolf,* 1969; *Here and Now,* 1969; *Rondelay,* 1969; *No, No, Nanette,* 1971; *Rain,* 1972; *Irene,* 1973; *No, No, Nanette* (London), 1973; *Gypsy* (London), 1973; *Gypsy* (London), 1974; and *Doctor Jazz,* 1975. Film designs include—*Louisiana Purchase, Lady in the Dark, Dixie, Frenchman's Creek,* and *Kitty;* for the ballet—*Ghost Town,* for the Monte Carlo Ballet, and *Jeux,* for the New York City Ballet; for revues and spectacles- several editions of the Ziegfeld Follies;

*John Murray Anderson's Almanac,* 1953; Sonja Henie's ice show; Maurice Chevalier's New York show, 1963; and numerous Billy Rose entertainments, in New York, Texas, and Cleveland, including several versions of the Aquacade, the Diamond Horseshoe review, and *Let's Play Fair* (a cabaret-theatre revue) at Casa Manana, New York, 1938.

## Publications

**On DU BOIS: books**—*The Biographical Encyclopaedia and Who's Who of the American Theatre* edited by Walter Rigdon, New York, 1966; *Hollywood Costume Design* by David Chierichetti, New York and London, 1976; *Who's Who in the Theatre* edited by Ian Herben, London and Detroit, 1977; *The Oxford Companion to the American Theatre* edited by Gerald Bordman, New York, 1984.

\*    \*    \*

Raoul Pène du Bois was only a youth when he skyrocketed to fame as a costume and set designer for theatrical productions. He gained his widest acclaim for the long list of Broadway musicals on which he worked over the years, beginning with the world-renowned hit *Jumbo* (1935) and spanning the next four decades with works such as Rodgers and Hart's *Too Many Girls* (1939), Oscar Hammerstein's *Carmen Jones* (1943), Leonard Bernstein's *Wonderful Town* (1953) and *The Bells Are Ringing* (1956), and Jules Styne's *Gypsy* (1959).

During the 1930s, du Bois had a number of fertile collaborations with director-producer Billy Rose, whose showmanship du Bois matched with his flamboyant displays, such as his sparkling setting for Rose's Aquacade at the New York World's Fair. Here, for the curved stage, he created a backdrop composed of a row of pillars; at the finale of the show, ten fountains shot up between the pillars and a curtain of water stained with colored lights arose for a breathtaking effect. Fire blazed from each of the twelve urns above the colonnade and 200 performers paraded in costumes of saffron satin and gold kid. During the same period, du Bois also distinguished himself for his more classic and studied designs such as those for the ballet *Ghost Town* (1939) which he was commissioned to do by the Monte Carlo Ballet. Du Bois' lavish outfittings included women dressed with bustles, deep gathers, and feathered hats; gents garbed in elegant suitings and high hats; and a muscleman in stars-and-stripes tights—all historically authentic in the manner of apparel worn in a Nevada mining town of the 1870s and all slightly exaggerated to enhance the appropriate entertainment quality.

From 1941 to 1945, du Bois was under contract to Paramount studios in Hollywood, and, while he continued his work for the theatre, he also worked on movies such as *Dixie, Frenchman's Creek, Lady In the Dark,* and *Louisiana Purchase.* For the latter, du Bois captured the spirit of the story, using as few colors as he could for most scenes and going wild with colorful effects in the Mardi Gras and ballroom sequences.

Except for the period between 1959 and 1965, when du Bois lived in Paris and spent almost all of his time at easel painting, most of his energy in later years was dedicated to theater design. Outstanding among his numerous achievements was his 1971 production of *No, No, Nanette.* Du Bois spent the better part of two years designing costumes and sets which capture the look and feel of the mid-1920s with meticulous attention to every detail. Working out of old issues of *Harper's Bazaar* and *Vogue,* he came up with 270 costumes, each unique, including those for every member of the chorus. For her Charleston number, star Helen Gallagher wore a fitted, gray wool suit jacket bound in navy braid and a pleated skirt. The ensemble was completed with vest and matching, gray felt fedora. Her partner in the scene, Bobby Van, was outfitted with a gaily striped jacket and jaunty white pants and sport shoes. The look of the roaring twenties was also appropriately recreated in the stage sets, with arches as frames and side flats of scenery used in the authentic manner of the period.

Du Bois often discussed the principles which undergirded all of his work. He saw costumes for the theater as part of the set, working together with it to communicate a sense of exaggeration and suggestion—not retiring into the background but asserting themselves as a contribution equal to all other elements which compose the overall show. The main thing, as he said, is to "contribute entertainment," "produce a sort of unreal brilliance," because the theater is not suited for realism, morals, or message-making but geared to a more fanciful tone. Theatrical design is different, he has noted, from fashion design to be worn in real life; theater costumes are like "moving scenery" and the costume designer should be a "historian of taste." He also differentiated sharply between theater and movie designing, suggesting, for example, that theater sets are like framed pictures while in movies, they are a part of the action, most often using a real environment and not one that is contrived and constructed. Du Bois certainly put his theories into practice with a long-time commitment and also with a unique ability which earned him a prominent place in the annals of recent theater design.

—Barbara Cavaliere

# DUFFY-ELEY-GIFFONE-WORTHINGTON

British architectural, interior, and furniture design partnership

Founded by the New York design firm JFN Associates, in London, 1974. Founder Partners: Francis Duffy, Peter Eley, Luigi Giffone, and John Worthington; subsequently joined by partners: Colin Cave in 1977, John Francis in 1982, and Chris Byng-Maddock in 1982; DEGW Overseas, under managing director Luigi V. Mangano, founded in 1981. Clients include American Express, Banco Nacional de Mexico, Barclays Bank, British Nuclear Fuels, British Telecom, Eagle Star Insurance Group, Factory Mutual International, Hewlett Packard, IBM International, London Electricity Board, Port of London Authority, Royal Institute of British Architects, and the United Kingdom Atomic Energy Authority. **Address:** Porters North, 8 Crinan St., London N19SQ, England.

## Works

Office interiors, for American Express, London, 1973-74.
Graphics and sign systems, for IBM Netherlands, Amsterdam, 1975-76.
Office interiors, for BBDO Advertising Agency, London, 1978-79.
Office building, for the United Kingdom Atomic Energy Authority, Warrington, Lancashire, 1979.

Birch Wood Science Park, Warrington, Lancashire, 1979.
Warehouse interiors, for British Leyland/Unipart, Coventry, 1979-80.
Headquarters offices, for Factory Mutual International, London, 1979-81.
Offices, for the Digital Equipment Corporation, Evry, France, 1980-81.
Sales and accounts office interiors, for the Ryan Hotel, London, 1980-81.
Salesroom interiors, for Christie's, Amsterdam, 1980-81.
Office interiors and furniture, for the Leagas Delaney Partnership, London, 1981-82.
Fleetway House interiors, for Barclays Bank, London, 1982-83.

## Publications

**By DEGW: books**—*Planning Office Space,* London, 1979; *Industrial Rehabilitation,* London, 1980; *Information Technology and Office Design,* London, 1983.

**On DEGW: articles**—in *Building Refurbishment and Maintenance* (London), January/February 1980; *Domus* (Milan), September 1980; *Building Design* (London), 19 December 1980, 15 May 1981; *Design* (London), January 1981; *Building* (London), 19 June 1981; *Interior Design* (Morden), August 1981, December 1981, September 1982; *Techniques et Architecture* (Paris), June 1982.

*       *       *

Duffy says that many existing office buildings are becoming prematurely obsolete, as they were not designed to cope with computer technology. Offices are now being crowded with computer terminals, word processors, printers, graphic generators, and information distributors, with their miles of cable for which office blocks do not have the space. The problems of where to put the wiring and whether the office is to become a factory with workers glued to machines concern DEGW very closely. In 1982, the group was appointed to the Orbit Study established by the Department of Industry and British Telecom to tackle office research on buildings and information technology. The partner John Worthington sees that buildings will have to be designed to function more flexibly, instead of being erected for a specific process. He points out that buildings must now accommodate mixed functions because technology is changing all the time. More flexible leasing of property must also be organised, as firms expand or condense depending on their new equipment. The electrical engineer must work with the architect to resolve questions of placing power points and masses of cable.

The partnership puts great importance on labour relations in design. The problem with the British Leyland Unipart warehouse was that it had been designed as a vast shell, with little room for workers to make their own nooks, so DEGW broke the central buffet into three, making it possible for workers to have their own without walking all the way to the middle.

DEGW have produced three books, *Information Technology and Office Design, Planning Office Space,* and *Industrial Rehabilitation,* and in May 1983 they launched *Facilities,* a monthly digest for building administration managers with Duffy as editor-in-chief. The partners also are regular contributors to *The Architects' Journal.* Thus, they are in the forefront in explaining the new problems facing offices and in creating solutions to accommodate technological developments.

—Diana de Marly

# D'URSO, Joseph (Paul)

American architectural, interior, and industrial designer

**Born:** Newark, New Jersey, 8 April 1943. **Education:** West Side High School, Newark, 1958-61; studied interior design and architecture, Pratt Institute, Brooklyn, New York, BFA, 1965; Royal College of Art, London, 1966-67; Manchester College of Art and Design, England, MA, 1968. **Career:** Freelance designer, establishing D'Urso Design Inc., in New York, from 1968; has designed private residences, restaurants, art galleries, discotheques, showrooms, offices, and a range of furniture for Knoll International. **Exhibitions:** Museum of Modern Art, New York, 1968; Pratt Institute, Brooklyn, New York, 1968. **Honors:** American Institute of Interior Designers Award, 1965; Burlington Industries Designer of the Year Award, 1973; Stuttgart Fair Best in Show Award, 1982; Good Design Prize, Bonn, 1983. **Address:** P.O. Box 1154, Watermill, New York 11976, U.S.A.

## Publications

**By D'URSO: articles**—in *Manhattan Catalog* (New York), Summer 1979, November 1979, Fall 1980; *Skyline* (New York), April 1980.

**On D'URSO: books**—*Interior Design: The New Freedom* edited by Barbaralee Diamonstein, New York, 1982; *Joe d'Urso: Designer,* Minneapolis, 1983; *International Design Yearbook 1987/88* edited by Philippe Starck, London, 1987; **articles**—in *Interior Design* (New York), February 1976, February 1977, January 1979, August 1980, January 1981, March 1981, May 1983; *Progressive Architecture* (Stamford), September 1977; *Avenue* (New York), October 1977; *Skyline* (New York), October 1979; *Interiors* (Radnor), August 1980; *Architectural Record* (New York), December 1980; *Casa Vogue* (Milan), January 1981, February 1982; *Artnews* (New York), February 1981; *Metropolitan Home* (New York), June 1981; *Architectural Digest* (New York), August 1983.

*

As a designer, I am obviously interested in all aspects of the visual world from the largest scale to the smallest. There is, however, a special excitement for me in three-dimensional spaces on the human scale. By this I mean being in a space or walking in a series of spaces, as opposed to picking up an object, however beautiful.

I have often thought that perhaps it would be simpler to be an artist in the traditional sense—thereby eliminating the client—but no matter how much I am stimulated by great painting and sculpture, I am most stimulated and rewarded by manipulating three-dimensional space within a structural and functional framework.

My experiences in travelling widely, teaching, and researching great architectural works of the past have formed my sensibility and given me a full reserve to draw on in my work. This exposure is essential, but ultimately, I believe most in concentration and hard work. In today's working world full of distractions, I think concentration is the most elusive of all states of mind, and one must work extremely hard at preserving it.

My personal involvement with all of my projects and clients is intense and exhaustive, and I take full responsibility for the work. My feeling is that the best work is produced by a triangle consisting of the space or program involved at the apex, and the client and the designer focusing from the base corners toward the apex.

—Joseph D'Urso

*    *    *

A major talent, Joseph Paul D'Urso is one of the most important and influential designers in America. His international fame is based primarily upon his work in interior design, although he also has been highly acclaimed as a product designer through his development of a line of furniture for Knoll International. D'Urso's meteoric ascent to design stardom started with his 1968 exhibition at the Museum of Modern Art of the work he had done as a teaching fellow graduate student in Manchester, England. He was twenty-four at the time, and it is doubtful whether there are other interior designers of any age who have had one-person shows of their own at the Museum of Modern Art.

D'Urso has executed projects ranging from houses to apartments to lofts and other residences—all with a strongly personal style. He has also designed a number of commercial projects, including a highly acclaimed showroom for Calvin Klein's menswear and, most recently, the 60,000 square-foot "1" club in Hong Kong. Publications that have featured his work include the *New York Times* (many times) and just about every major design magazine, as well as many other books and magazines, and he has been honored with several awards.

D'Urso is a minimalist, yet his work is strongly architectural and always elegant in an understated way. He creates a three-dimensional work of art in a simple space with just a few elements. Although there is a definite look to his work, he is responsive to the needs of his clients, and he approaches design as a problem-solving activity.

—Arnold Friedmann

# DUSCHEK, Karl (Erich)

German graphic and corporate identity designer

**Born:** Braunschweig, 14 March 1947. **Education:** Studied graphic design, Staatliche Hochschule für Bildende Künste, Braunschweig, 1963-66, Dip., 1970. **Career:** Assistant lithography teacher, Staatliche Hochschule für Bildende Künste, Braunschweig, 1968-70; graphic designer, Atelier für Künstlerischen Steindruck, for Edition Pro Litho, Lausanne, 1970-72; freelance designer and partner, with Anton Stankowski, in Atelier Stankowski + Duschek graphic design firm, Stuttgart, from 1972; founded studio, Künstlergemeinschaft, Mettingerstraße, Esslingen, from 1992; has designed corporate image for the Deutsche Bank AG, Frankfurt, from 1974, and for Bayern Versicherung insurance company, Munich, 1975-80; city design, for the 11th Olympic Congress, Baden-Baden,

Karl Duschek: cover design for *eins und ... zwei und ...* **Journal for Art and Creation**, Stuttgart, 1993

1976-81; sign system image for the Messe-Fair, Frankfurt, from 1982. **Member:** Deutschen Werkbunds; Künstlergruppe Konstruktive Tendenzen; Gessellschaft für Kunst und Gestaltung, Bonn. **Exhibitions:** Galerie Beatrix Wilhelm, Leonberg/Stuttgart, 1978, 1983; Galerie Seestrasse, Rapperswil, 1980 (with A. Stankowski); Kunstverein, Ludwigsburg, 1980 (with H. Treiber); Ausstellungsraume Leitner, Stuttgart, 1982; Galerie Circulus, Bonn, 1985; Städtische Galerie, Stadt Ostfildern, 1986 (with A. Stankowski); Städtische Galerie, Leonberg/Stuttgart, 1987 (with A. Stankowski); Galerie im Burgenlandzentrum, Stuttgart, 1989 (with K. H. Franke and H. Kapitzki); Städtische Galerie Filderhalle, Leinfelden-Echterdingen, 1990 (with Hans Geipel); Städtische Galerie, Göppingen, 1991; E-Werk Freiburg Gallen für Kunst, 1992; Galerie der Kreissparkasse, Kirchheim unter Teck, 1992 (with Friedemann Hahn); Alpirsbacher Galerie, 1993 (with A. Stankowski); Gessellschaft für Kunst und Gestaltung, Bonn, 1993; Galerie Beatrix Wilhelm, Stuttgart, 1994 (with Hermann Glöckner and A. Stankowski). **Collections:** Staatsgalerie, Stuttgart; Deutsches Plakatmuseum, Essen. **Honors:** First International Farb-Design-Preis, Stuttgart, 1981; Design Plus Prize, Frankfurt, 1990; Art and Sport Trophy, International and National Olympic Committee, Frankfurt, 1991; Poster of the Year Award, Wien, 1993; Book Prize, Esslingen, 1994. **Address:** Bebelstrasse 121, 7000 Stuttgart 1, Germany.

## Works

Trademark logo, for Zehnder radiators, 1979.
Trademark logo, for Landesausstellung Niedersachsen, 1985.
Logo, for the Berchtesgaden bid for the 1992 Winter Olympics, 1985.
Trademark logo, for Bisterfeld und Weiss, 1985.
Signage system, for Design Tech Jürgen R. Schmid, 1986.

Adaptable logo system, for the Volkhochschules of Baden-Württemberg, 1986.
Logo, for the University of Stuttgart, 1987.

## Publications

**By DUSCHEK: books**—*Die Anzeige,* Stuttgart, 1976; **articles**—"Farbe im visuellen Erscheinungsbild" in *MD: Moebel Interior Design* (Stuttgart), November 1982; "Frankfurter zum Zauberkasten" in *Form* (Seeheim), January 1983.

**On DUSCHEK: books**—*Karl Duschek: System und Serie,* exhibition catalogue by Matthias Gotz and Friedrich Heckmanns, Leonberg and Aachen, 1982; *Kunst im Deutschen Südwesten von 1945 bis zur Gegenwart* by Günther Wirth, Stuttgart, 1982; *Braunschweiger Konstruktivisten,* exhibition catalogue by Peter Luft, Braunschweig, 1984; **articles**—in *Novum Gebrauchsgraphik* (Munich), no. 7, 1978; *Idea* (Tokyo), July 1982; *Kunstforum* (Mainz), January 1983; *Revue K* (Alfortville), no. 29, 1987; *Delfin* (Siegen), no. 11, 1988.

\*

1. The importance of thought and perception in design is oriented towards problems of time. Timeless design is quality.

2. Whether thought (logic) or perception (emotion) has more importance may be tested in the contemplation and evaluation of visual objects.

3. Important works contain inventions. These inventions appear frequently as effects. In this case, one has to decide whether these effects are mainly part of the project or whether they come to life by being seen.

4. Every work should reveal a particular aesthetic basis. In a qualified sense, an anti-aesthetic can also make its contribution.

5. Political or social problems are merely suggested by design means.

6. Innovative values need a meaningful or functional quality. Formal elements can act as a support.

7. Logic, geometry, and order are an important part of our thought and action.

8. Producing order has become a natural occurrence. Disorder in order can gain acceptance, but on the other hand, order in disorder, rarely.

9. Certain formal results are without tension in the visual statement; monochrome and total symmetry, for example.

10. The quality of a work is often not clear if the overall concept is not perceived.

11. Colours influence the emotions (sympathy value).

12. Colour harmonies work for the moment. Forms or groups of forms support the long-term effect.

13. Forms, especially groups of forms with connections to each other, act as an impetus to visual ideas.

14. Artistic thought should simply be to achieve. Formal quality in signs, symbols is necessary to concise art.

15. In the artistic sense, an ornament cannot be functional. Without the principle of order, the ornament is a way of expressing perception.

16. Purity can be accepted as a criterion of quality; for example, the preference for primary colours over mixed colours. In the academic teaching of design, a work is regarded as impure if, through pure technique, it is overworked (drawn to death, for example).

17. Computer graphics in the sphere of design, despite their roots in geometry and order, are far from convincing.

18. Serial design is largely involved with formal modules. Principles such as rows, groups, development variation, and others, are the basis of industrial production. The time factor, or the process for accomplishing a time phase, is more important compared to stylistic innovations. Serial solutions broaden the working of static individual objects.

19. The reduction of stylistic elements, even in schemes of thought, should lead to solutions which nevertheless fulfil their purpose.

20. Spatial effects in a sign/symbol form do not correspond to the basic principle of concise reduction.

21. Contours of a flat form contradict the unequivocal form.

22. Scientific experiences can only narrowly be turned to account in design work.

23. A qualitative judgment of design must be followed subjectively.

24. Quantitative examinations of design qualities, market research for example, debase design quality and inhibit innovations.

25. The earliest discussion of a problem or theme often leads to the opening up of a preconceived opinion.

26. It is, perhaps, not the maintenance of a consistent understanding but the meaningful analysis of experience that is important to development.

27. Spontaneous commitments can be just as important as spontaneous criticisms.

—Karl Duschek

# DUSZEK, Roman

Polish graphic designer

**Born:** Warsaw, 8 November 1935. **Education:** Studied graphic design, Academy of Fine Arts, Warsaw, M.A., 1959. **Family:** Married Maria Duszek in 1959; children: Eva and Marta. **Career:** Freelance graphic designer, from 1960; graphic designer, at Reklama advertising agency, Warsaw, 1960-62; graphic designer, with Lonsdale advertising agency, Paris, 1966-68; creative art director, Polish Technical School Publishers, Warsaw, 1969-73, Polish School and Educational Publishers, Warsaw, 1973-74, and KAW State Publishing Agency, Warsaw, 1976-78; visual communications consultant, Lot Polish Airlines, from 1980. Associate professor of Graphic Design, Academy of Fine Arts, Warsaw, 1978-84; visiting professor, School of Art and Design, University of Illinois, Urbana-Champaign, 1984-88; professor, Art and Design Department, Southwest Missouri State University, from 1988. **Member:** Executive Board Member, 1977-79, and Vice-President, 1979-83, International Council of Graphic Design Associations (ICOGRADA); Polish Artists and Designers Association (ZPAP), from 1990; Graphic Design Educators Association (GDEA), from 1990; International Trademark Center, Belgium, from 1994; Polish Ministry of Culture and Art; ZAIKS Association of Authors, Warsaw. **Collections:** National Museum, Warsaw. **Honors:** Award of Distinction, Ministry of Culture and Art, Warsaw, 1962, 1963, 1980; Gold Chestnut Award, Warsaw, 1964; Package Design Prize, Poznan, 1972; IBM Fellowship, International Design Conference, Aspen, Colorado, 1980; First Prize, International Council of Societies of Industrial Designers Kyoto Awards, Japan, 1983; Award of Excellence, American Corporate Identity, 1989; First Prize, American Craft Council's Logo Competition, 1993; Second Prize, Computer Art Biennial, Poland, 1995; Award of Excellence, Supon Design Group, New York, 1996. **Address:** 2730 S. Claremont Avenue, Springfield, Missouri 65804, U.S.A.

## Works

*La Vache Qui Rit* trademark symbol and packaging, for the Lonsdale Agency, Paris, 1967.

Corporate identity program and signage system, for the Intercontinental Hotel Victoria, Warsaw, 1976.

Corporate identity program, for LOT Polish Airlines, 1977 (with A. Zbrozek).

Identification logotype symbol, for Polish Television, 1978.

Identity program, for Polish Television News, 1979.

Visual information system and signage, for the Warsaw Subway, 1983 (with others).

Visual information system, for Memorial Hospital, Lodz, Poland, 1983.

Corporate identity program and publications system, for National Center for Supercomputing Applications, Urbana-Champaign, Illinois, 1988.

Corporate identity program and publications system, for Young-Shannon Gold Mines Ltd., Toronto, Canada, 1991.

Corporate identity program, for International Association for Humanitarian Research, 1992.

Corporate identity program, for Structured Biological Incorporated, Toronto, 1994.

Corporate identity program, for European Association of Poisons Centers and Clinical Toxicologists, 1996.

## Publications

**On DUSZEK: books**—*Trademarks and Symbols of the World* by J. Kuwayama, Japan, 1987, 1989; *American Corporate Identity 5,* New York, 1989; *Logo,* Belgium, 1995; **articles**—in *Zycie Warszawy* (Warsaw), 17 March 1976, 22 July 1977; *Reklama* (Warsaw), June 1976, January/March 1982; *Magazyn Rodzinny* (Warsaw), December 1972; *Projekt* (Poland), April 1978, June 1979; *Literatura* (Warsaw), no. 1, 1981; *Kaleidoscope* (Warsaw), 15 April 1982; *Kurier Polski* (Warsaw), 16 August 1983; *Architektura* (Poland), vol. 2, no. 418, 1984; *Design Issues* (Illinois), no. 2, 1985; *Grafik-Design* (Austria), March 1985; *Modus* (Warsaw), 1989.

*

If I had to describe my place as a designer or my ideological preferences, I would locate myself somewhere in between the "Polish Romantic" and Swiss "structured" schools of design. Structural thinking and a systematic layout, combined with a more subjective, spontaneous expression of graphic form, probably would be the most appropriate description of my preferences, but not necessarily my style. The design process and style should be individually adapted according to the problem to be solved. To me graphic design is the conscious and intuitive effort to impose meaningful order and a creative process leading to communication. Analysis of the message and selection of appropriate means for its transmission

**Roman Duszek:** *The Last Samurai: Hommage to Akiro Kurosawa,* 1996

lay down a ground for the design solution. This leads to a project in which form is inseparable from function.

—Roman Duszek

\*     \*     \*

Roman Duszek's way to designing started, as with most Polish designers, in fine arts. He might have become an artist and enjoyed the charms of aquatint, etching, lithography, woodcutting, or the noble art of drawing. Instead, he was attracted by the idea of harmonizing art with the material of the human environment. His education helped him develop a basic sensitivity of visual perception and an artistic consciousness. Such a humanistic background—without which there is no good, conscious creativity—turned out to be a priceless investment for Duszek and affected the whole body of his creative work. Incidentally, this is what the graduates of even the world-renowned schools of graphic design miss. To be a modern designer, it is not enough to display technical skills. More important is the ability to perceive the world through the prism of human nature, to understand the profound layers of the human psyche, which is the source of our common mythology, of reflexes, preferences, and fascinations.

Duszek acquired the knowledge of his new field initially through practice on a modest scale, while designing small forms of commercial graphics, such as flyers, labels, insets, and trademarks. Then he went on to three-dimensional graphics in the form of package design. In postwar Poland, with socialized, monopolized production, no competition, demand dominating supply, and product scarcity, a sophisticated form of package design was a luxury. Duszek was one of those who broke the inertia of the market and who, driven by professional ambitions, introduced their designs into mass production. For his total work on package design, he was granted the first award in the Polish Exhibit of Package design in Poznán.

The next step in his self-education was a longer, independent practice in Lonsdale, a Paris design agency. This work initiated him into all stages of this profession, including the industry-market-consumer system, as well as the rules and turmoils of free compe-

tition. He mastered the techniques of testing preferences. The problem of "how to do it" was not so difficult for him any longer as were the more complex questions regarding the selection of his concepts and of their esthetic values.

At that time, Paris was a good ground for intellectual growth. The world was shaken by conflicts in the midst of prosperity. In art, conceptualism and minimal art—trends appealing to the intellect and not to the emotions—were given preference. A keen observer captured the Parisian paradox: "Art was cold and life—hot." A similar situation pertained in the field of mass media. On the one hand, there was a wave of underground prints, graphically lax magazines for young people, "hot" cover designs for pop music records, neo-secession in lettering. On the other, the unquestionable authority of Swiss typography; Helvetica was almost a symbol of functional type—cool and ascetic. It seems that Duszek's esthetic disposition oscillated between representation and abstraction, between emotional and rational attitudes. Such preferences would dictate his style in the following years.

In the mid 1970s, some essential changes took place in his work. He won a competition (together with A. Zbrozek) for the system of identification for the Polish Airlines, LOT, and carried it out. In its scale and complexity, this work subdued everything he had done before. Moreover, it was one of the first examples of "corporate identity" applied in Poland. In the opinion of experts, the value of this project lay in a successful solution of the difficult problem of identification in the air and from the ground of the airline sign located on the fuselage. His second great success was his work on the interior decoration of the Warsaw Hotel Victoria. Thanks to this work, the image of the hotel was brought up to the international level. Another complex task was to prepare (together with A. Bojar) an informative system for the metro in Warsaw.

Trademarks and logotypes have become important forms of expression for Duszek. They form his language of communication with the external world. Many of them are in wide circulation, like the stamp for the National Fund of Health Protection and the main logotype of Polish Television.

—Szymon Bojko

# EAMES, Charles

American architect, filmmaker, interior, exhibition, and furniture designer

**Born:** St. Louis, Missouri, 17 June 1907. **Education:** Washington University School of Architecture, St. Louis, 1924-26. **Family:** Married Ray Kaiser in 1941; children (by previous marriage): Lucia. **Career:** Worked for Trueblood and Graf architectural firm, St. Louis, 1925-27; in private practice as architect and designer, St. Louis, 1930-36; Fellow, 1936, and Head of Experimental Design Department, 1937-40, Cranbrook Academy of Art, Bloomfield Hills, Michigan; worked in the art department of Metro-Goldwyn-Mayer film company, Los Angeles, 1941; began experimental plywood molding laboratory, with John Entenza, Gregory Ain, Margaret Harris, and Griswald Raetz, in Los Angeles, 1942-45; in design partnership with Ray Eames, in Los Angeles and Venice, California, 1944-78; formed Molded Plywood Division of Evans Products Company, Los Angeles, 1944; Consultant Designer, Herman Miller Inc., Los Angeles, from 1946. Lecturer, California Institute of Technology, Pasadena, 1953-56; Charles Eliot Norton Professor of Poetry, Harvard University, Cambridge, Massachusetts, 1970. **Member:** National Council on the Arts, 1970-78; American Academy of Arts and Sciences. **Exhibitions:** *Organic Design in Home Furnishings,* Museum of Modern Art, New York, 1941 (toured); *New Furniture Designed by Charles Eames,* Museum of Modern Art, New York, 1946; *An Exhibition for Modern Living,* Detroit Institute of Arts, 1949; *The Modern Chair 1918-1970,* Whitechapel Art Gallery, London, 1970; *Charles Eames,* Museum of Modern Art, New York, 1973; *One Hundred Modern Chairs,* National Gallery of Victoria, Melbourne, 1974; *Connections: The Work of Charles and Ray Eames,* University of California at Los Angeles, 1976; *Design in Michigan 1967/1977,* Cranbrook Academy of Art, Bloomfield Hills, Michigan, 1978 (toured); *Design Since 1945,* Philadelphia Museum of Art, 1983; *High Style: 20th Century American Design,* Whitney Museum, New York, 1985; *The Machine Age in America 1918-1941,* Brooklyn Museum, New York, 1986. **Collections:** Library of Congress, Washington, DC; Museum of Modern Art, New York; Philadelphia Museum of Art. **Honors:** Furniture Prize, Museum of Modern Art, New York, 1940; Industrial Designers Institute Award, 1951; Gold Model, 1954, Grand Prize, 1957, Milan Triennale; Kaufmann International Design Award, 1960; Honorary Royal Designer for Industry, Royal Society of Arts, London, 1960; Fellow, Royal College of Art, London, 1960; National Honor Award, 1964, Los Angeles Chapter Honor Award, 1967, Industrial Arts Medal, 1972, and Distinguished Service Award, 1974, American Institute of Architects; Design Medal, Society of Industrial Artists and Designers of Great Britain, 1967; Elsie de Wolfe Award, American Society of Interior Designers, 1975; Royal Gold Medal, Royal Institute of British Architects, 1979. Honorary doctorates: Kansas City Art Institute, 1955; California College of Arts and Crafts, 1962; Pratt Institute, Brooklyn, 1964; Washington University, St Louis, 1970; University of Cincinnati, 1978. **Died:** St. Louis, 21 August 1978.

## Works

Molded plywood chair, for the Museum of Modern Art *Organic Furniture* competition, 1940 (with Eero Saarinen).
Child's chair, for Evans Products Company, 1944.
Dining and side chairs in steel rod and molded walnut plywood with rubber mounts, for Herman Miller, 1946.
Chairs in steel rod and aluminum with molded plastic seats, for Herman Miller, 1949-53.
ESU 275 chest of drawers in steel and birch with walnut or birch top, for Herman Miller, 1950.
*Good Design Show* exhibition layouts, for the Museum of Modern Art, New York, 1950.
Storage units in steel and plastic-coated plywood, for Herman Miller, 1950.
Chair in wire rod with wire seat and removable cushion, for Herman Miller, 1951.
*Eames Storage Units/ESU* desk in steel with walnut or birch, for Herman Miller, 1952.
*670* and *671* swivel-base upholstered lounge chair and ottoman in aluminum and molded plywood, for Herman Miller, 1957.
Solar toy, for Alcoa Aluminum, 1957.
*675* lobby chair in cast aluminum with leather upholstery, for Herman Miller, 1960.
*La Fonda* chair in cast aluminum and fiberglass with polyfoam upholstery, for Herman Miller, 1960.
*Eames Contract Storage* cupboard/bed/study units in birch plywood, for Herman Miller, 1961.
*RE-204* sofa in aluminum with polyfoam and plastic upholstery, for Herman Miller, 1962,
*Tandem 2600* single/double row seating in aluminum and steel with plastic upholstery, for Herman Miller, 1962.
IBM exhibit design at the *World's Fair,* New York, for International Business Machines, 1964.
*Photograph and the City* exhibition layouts, for the Smithsonian Institution, Washington, D.C., 1968.
*Chaise ES106* (Soft Pad group) couch in aluminum with polyfoam and leather cushions, for Herman Miller, 1969.
*The World of Franklin and Jefferson* touring exhibition layouts, for the American Bicentennial Administration, 1975-76.

(for a list of Eames' buildings and architectural projects, see Contemporary Architects)

Films (with Ray Eames)—*Traveling Boy,* 1950; *Parade; or, Here they Come Down the Street,* 1952; *Blacktop,* 1952; *Bread,* 1953;

*Calligraphy,* 1953; *Communications Primers,* 1953; *Sofa Compact,* 1954; *Two Baroque Churches in Germany,* 1955; *House,* 1955; *Textiles and Ornamental Arts of India,* 1955; *Eames Lounge Chair,* 1956; *The Spirit of St. Louis* (aerial sequences only), 1956; *Day of the Dead,* 1957; *Tocatta for Toy Trains,* 1957; *Information Machine,* 1957; *Expanding Airport,* 1958; *Herman Miller at the Brussels Fair,* 1958; *De Gaulle Sketch,* 1959; *Glimpses of the U.S.A.,* 1959; *Jazz Chair,* 1960; *Introduction to Feedback,* 1960; *Fabulous Fifties* (sequences in CBS-TV Special), 1960; *IBM Mathematics Peep Show,* 1961; *Kaleidoscope,* 1961; *Kaleidoscope Shop,* 1961; *ECs,* 1962; *House of Science,* 1962; *Before the fair,* 1962; *The Good Years* (sequences in CBS-TV Special), 1962; *Think,* 1964; *Think* (revised version), 1965; *IBM at the Fair,* 1965; *Westinghouse ABC,* 1965; *The Smithsonian Institution,* 1965; *The Smithsonian Newsreel,* 1965; *Horizontes,* 1966; *Boeing: The Leading Edge,* 1966; *IBM Museum,* 1967; *A Computer Glossary,* 1967; *National Aquarium Presentation,* 1967; *Schuetz Machine,* 1967; *Lick Observatory,* 1968; *Photography and the City,* 1969; *Tops,* 1969; *The U.N. Information Center,* 1970; *Man's View of Himself,* 1970; *Memory,* 1970; *The Perry Expedition,* 1970.

**Publications**

**By EAMES: books**—*The Eames Report,* leaflet with Ray Eames, Los Angeles, 1958; *A Computer Perspective,* Cambridge, Massachusetts, 1973; *The World of Franklin and Jefferson,* exhibition catalogue, Los Angeles, 1976; **articles**—in *Arts and Architecture* (Los Angeles), September 1941, December 1941; *Interiors* (New York), November 1965; *Domus* (Milan), January 1970; *Architectural Forum* (New York), June 1971; *American Scholar* (Washington, DC), Summer 1971.

**On EAMES: books**—*Organic Design in Home Furnishing,* exhibition catalogue with text by Eliot Noyes, New York, 1941; *Prize Designs for Modern Furniture* by Edgar J. Kaufmann Jr., New York, 1950; *Shaping America's Products* by Don Wallance, New York, 1956; *The Modern Chair 1918-1970,* exhibition catalogue with texts by Carol Hogben and others, London, 1970; *Charles Eames,* exhibition catalogue by Arthur Drexler, New York, 1973; *Connections: The Work of Charles and Ray Eames,* exhibition catalogue by Ralph Caplan and Philip Morrison, Los Angeles, 1967; *Furniture Designed by Architects* by Marian Page, New York and London, 1980; *Ray and Charles Eames: il collettivo della fantasia* by Luciano Rubino, Rome, 1981; *The American Design Adventure 1940-1975* by Arthur J. Pulos, London and Cambridge, Massachusetts, 1988; *Eames Design: The Office of Charles and Ray Eames 1941-1978* by Ray Eames, with John and Marilyn Neuhart, London, 1989.

*       *       *

Charles Eames and Ray Kaiser first collaborated as designers in 1940, and after their marriage the following year, they worked so closely together that most of their work from 1941, until the death of Charles in 1978, is best considered a joint effort. Charles Eames studied architecture at Washington University, then stayed in St. Louis to work as an architect before Eliel Saarinen appointed him head of the Experimental Design Workshop at the Cranbrook Academy in Bloomfield Hills, Michigan, in 1937. At about the same

time, Eames joined the architectural office of Saarinen and his son, Eero. Ray Kaiser studied with the German-American artist Hans Hofmann in New York and Provincetown before enrolling at Cranbrook in 1940.

Charles Eames and Eero Saarinen entered the 1940 exhibition and competition *Organic Design in Home Furnishings* at the Museum of Modern Art in New York. They were assisted by Ray Kaiser in preparing their entries, which won first prizes in two categories. The winning designs included three plywood chairs molded into compound curves, made possible by using thin veneers laminated to layers of glue. It was expected that the winning designs would be put into production, but the entry of the United States into World War II prevented any immediate attempt to overcome production obstacles. Nevertheless, a few prototypes, produced at great expense, were part of an exhibition seen in New York, Cincinnati, and other cities in 1941 and 1942.

Shortly after their marriage, Charles and Ray Eames moved to southern California, where Charles designed sets for the MGM film studios, and they continued during the war years to experiment with plywood. Initially, they used their small apartment as a workshop, but later, with the help of some friends, they moved their workshop to a vacated bakery. In 1942, they began supplying leg splints to the United States Navy. These were made of molded plywood to provide maximum support and comfort to wounded persons. In 1943, their workshop became the southern California branch of the Detroit-based Evans Products Company and expanded into production of laminated glider parts and other items. Meanwhile, the experiments with molded-plywood chairs progressed, and when the war ended, the Evans Products Company was ready to put the first Eames chairs into production.

In 1946, the Museum of Modern Art presented *New Furniture Designed by Charles Eames,* an exhibition that included pieces manufactured by the Evans Products Company, as well as some experimental pieces that were never mass-produced. (As would be the case many times with their joint endeavors, the role of Ray Eames was not credited.) The chairs, designed for a variety of outdoor and indoor uses, attracted the most attention. Some of these were of all-plywood construction, while others were of plywood and metal. The seat and back units of the chairs were made of resin-impregnated plywood, bonded together at the time of molding into compound curves, and stained with brilliant dyes in shades of red, yellow, and blue, which penetrated the wood piles without blurring the natural grain. The parts of the chairs were attached to each other by means of rubber shock-mounts originally developed for engine mountings.

Because the 1946 Museum of Modern Art exhibition was very successful, the Evans Company decided to sell distribution rights for its Eames-designed products to the Herman Miller Furniture Company of Zeeland, Michigan, which had recently appointed George Nelson director of design. Two years later, when the Miller Company purchased production rights, a long association between the Eameses and Herman Miller began. The Eames studio was moved to a converted automobile repair-shop in Venice, California, where Charles and Ray Eames worked with a staff of assistants, usually numbering about twenty.

Two of the chairs designed by Charles and Ray Eames for Herman Miller have become so well known they are often simply called "Eames chairs." One of these is the 1946 dining chair of plywood shock-mounted onto slender steel rods, a variation on some of the chairs exhibited earlier that year. The other, put into production ten years later, is a leather-covered, plywood, lounge chair with a metal swivel base; it is accompanied by a related ottoman. The first Eames-designed chairs with one piece, molded-plastic, seat-and-back units were put into production by Herman Miller in 1950. Because of their light weight, simple lines, and low cost, a number of Eames-designed chairs were almost equally successful in home and office environments, and consequently millions of them have been sold. (In addition, millions of unauthorized copies made by other manufacturers have been sold.) The Eameses also designed a number of advertisements and showroom displays for Herman Miller, beginning in 1948.

In 1947, Charles and Ray Eames designed a house for themselves in Santa Monica, California. One of a group of "case study" houses with which Charles was involved under the sponsorship of the magazine *Arts and Architecture,* the house was first planned as a box-like structure, utilizing prefabricated parts intended for constructing factories, and was to be suspended between two steel trusses. Later, it was redesigned to utilize the already-delivered parts but to maximize the amount of enclosed volume. The result, with its mass-produced, steel column, window, and door elements, and its modular units of stucco and metal siding, is an open and light-flooded space. The straight lines and right angles of the interior are softened by displays of antique toys, plants, furniture, and fossils, so that the effect is more domestic than industrial. (Some of the Eames collection of antique toys, along with peep-shows, posters, and other items, is displayed in the converted automobile repair-shop studio.)

Among the earliest exhibition designs of the Eameses was a multi-screen slide presentation for the 1959 American National Exhibition in Moscow. Their grid-work of slides, which vividly depicted a cross section of the everyday lives of Americans, was well received by Soviet viewers. A series of exhibitions commissioned by the International Business Machines Corporation ranged from *Mathematica* at the California Museum of Science and Industry in Los Angeles in 1961 to A Computer Perspective for the IBM Exhibit Center in New York in 1971. For the latter, there was a related film and a book, *A Computer Perspective,* published in 1973. Another exhibition, *Franklin and Jefferson,* for the American Bicentennial was seen in Paris, Warsaw, and London and in several American cities in 1975-76.

The short films made by the Eameses range from the previously mentioned *A Computer Perspective* and other films, such as *Powers of Ten* (1968, new version 1977-78), that clearly and imaginatively explained complex mathematical and technical concepts, to whimsical films based on the Eames collection of toys; these included *Toccata for Toy Trains* (1957) with original music by Elmer Bernstein, and *Tops* (1969).

Charles and Ray Eames developed a close relationship with India from 1953 when they were invited to investigate its problems and opportunities related to design. *The Eames Report* of 1958 led to the establishment of the National Institute of Design at Amedabad in 1961. In 1964 the Eameses used the N.I.D. as a working base to set up a Jawarharlal Nehru memorial exhibition that opened in New York the following year and was later seen on four continents. Ray Eames last visited India in 1987 to confer the N.I.D.'s first Charles Eames Award.

As significant as the individual achievements of the Eameses are, it is nevertheless the cumulative power of their lives and their work which ultimately will be judged most important. They were not blinded by their success at meeting industrial demands or by the "classical" status some of their designs achieved. Rather, Charles and Ray Eames retained a clear sense of human needs and values.

One indication of this is their deep and long-standing attraction to objects embodying the incidental, the humorous, and the whimsical. An extensive Eames archive was established in 1985 at the Library of Congress in Washington, aided by a grant of $500,000 from International Business Machines. Included in the archive are letters, drawings, photographs and films.

—Lloyd C. Engelbrecht

# EAMES, Ray
American artist, film maker, exhibition, interior, and furniture designer

**Born:** Ray Kaiser, in Sacramento, California, in 1916. **Education:** May Friend Bennet School, Mill Brook, New York, 1931-33; studied painting, under Hans Hofmann, in New York and Provincetown, Massachusetts, 1933-39; Cranbrook Academy of Art, Bloomfield Hills, Michigan, 1940-41. **Family:** Married the architect and designer Charles Eames in 1941. **Career:** Freelance designer, in partnership with Charles Eames, 1940-78. **Member:** Founder Member, American Abstract Artists, New York, 1940. **Exhibitions:** *An Exhibition for Modern Living,* Detroit Institute of Arts, 1949; *The Modern Chair 1918-1970,* Whitechapel Art Gallery, London, 1970; *Connections: The Work of Charles and Ray Eames,* University of California at Los Angeles, 1976; *Design Since 1945,* Philadelphia Museum of Art, 1983. **Honors:** Kaufmann International Design Award, 1960; Elsie de Wolfe Award, American Society of Interior Designers, 1975. **Died:** Venice, California, 21 August 1988.

See EAMES, Charles

# ECKERSLEY, Tom
British graphic designer

**Born:** Newton-le-Willows, Lancashire, 30 September 1914. **Education:** Studied at Salford School of Art, Lancashire, 1930-34. **Military Service:** Served as a cartographer in the Royal Air Force, 1940-45. **Family:** Married Daisy Mudge in 1937 (divorced, 1965); Mary Kessell in 1966 (died, 1977); children: Anthony, Richard, and Paul. **Career:** Graphic designer, in partnership with Eric Lombers, London, 1934-40; also designed posters for the General Post Office, the Ministry of Information and National Service, and for the Royal Society for the Prevention of Accidents, London, 1940-45; freelance graphic designer, London, from 1945; has designed for London Transport, Shell Mex, British Broadcasting Corporation, Austin Reed, and others. Visiting lecturer in graphic design, Westminster School of Art, London, 1938-39; head of Graphic Design Department, London College of Printing, 1959-75. **Member:** Society of Typographic Designers, New York. **Exhibitions:** *Shell Posters,* Shell Mex House, London, 1938; *Eight British Designers,* National Museum, Stockholm, 1952; *Graphic Art from Britain,* American Institute of Graphic Arts, New York, 1956; *European Design,* University of California at Los Angeles, 1962; *107 Grafici dell'AGI,* Castello Sforzesco, Milan, 1974; *Homage to Tom Eckersley,* London College of Printing, Paperpoint Gallery, 1975;

*Tom Eckersley: Posters and Other Graphic Works,* Camden Arts Centre, London, 1980 (toured); Newscastle Gallery of Art, 1983; *Tom Eckersley Past and Present,* Dundee College of Art, Scotland, 1985; *Tom Eckersley: Retrospective,* Maidstone College of Art and Design, Kent, 1985; Oxford Polytechnic, 1986; *Eye for Industry: Royal Designers for Industry 1936-1986,* Victoria and Albert Museum, London, 1986. **Collections:** Imperial War Museum, London; Victoria and Albert Museum, London; Museum of Modern Art, New York; Australian National Gallery, Canberra. **Honors:** Heywood Medal, Salford School of Art, 1934; Order of the British Empire, 1948; fellow, Society of Artists and Designers, London, 1961; honorary fellow, Manchester College of Art and Design, 1961, and Humberside College of Higher Education, 1985; Royal Designer for Industry, Royal Society of Arts, London, 1963; Design Award, Slovak Union of Nature Protectors, 1988. **Address:** 53 Belsize Park, London NW3 4JL, England.

## Works

*His Action Station* poster, for the Post Office Savings Bank, 1942.
*Good Mornings Begin with Gillette* poster series, for Gillette Razor Company, 1948.
*Please Pack Parcels Carefully* poster series, for the General Post Office, 1954.
*Extension of the Piccadilly Line* poster, for London Transport, 1970.
*Keep an Eye on Valuables* poster, for the London College of Printing, 1974.
*Open Week* poster, for the London College of Printing, 1974.
*Long Hair is Dangerous* poster, for the London College of Printing, 1975.
*Help Lepra Fight Leprosy* poster, for LEPRA Medical Charity, 1975.
*Ceremonial London* poster, for London Transport, 1975.
Murals at Heathrow Airport underground station, for London Transport, 1977.
*Artists from London Art Schools 1953-83* Royal Academy exhibition poster, for the Inner London Education Authority, 1983.
Books illustrated include—*Animals on Parade* by E. A. Cabrelly, London, 1947; *Cat O' Nine Lives* by D. Eckersley, London, 1947.

## Publications

**On ECKERSLEY: books**—*Die Neue Grafik/The New Graphic Design* by Karl Gerstner and Markus Kutter, Teufen and London, 1959; *Graphic Design Britain* edited by Frederick Lambert, London, 1967; *107 Grafici dell'AGI,* exhibition catalogue with texts by Renzo Zorzi and Franco Grignani, Venice, 1974; *Tom Eckersley: Posters and Other Graphic Works,* exhibition catalogue with texts by Zuleika Dobson and George Him, London, 1980; *Top Graphic Design* by F. H. K. Henrion, Zurich, 1983; *Posters by Members of the Alliance Graphique Internationale* edited by Rudolph de Harak, New York, 1986; *World Graphic Design* edited by Kodansha Publishers, Tokyo, 1988; *The Poster* by Alan Weill, London, 1988.

\*

From 1934 until World War II, I worked in partnership with Eric Lombers under the signature Eckersley-Lombers. Since the end of the hostilities, I have worked on my own. My career has been divided equally between my work as a graphic designer and as a teacher. I have always found the two compatible and stimulating. I consider it vital that if you teach, you should also practice. In Europe and the United States, many leading designers and painters have given time to teaching, the Bauhaus being an outstanding example. My aim in my own work has always been to combine aesthetics and purpose in solving a graphic problem. I believe that in any civilized society this should be the aim in all areas of design.

The poster has always had immense appeal for me. The fact that it is mainly the work of one individual suits my temperament and approach to graphic work. I believe strongly in the individuality that most of the great designers have always brought to their work; while solving problems, they have always brought a personal identity to whatever they do.

—Tom Eckersley

\*    \*    \*

Tom Eckersley is arguably the foremost living British poster artist and, through his massive output and his long service in teaching, the most important single influence on the British poster in this century. The style of pictorial poster prevalant in Britain during his youth and training tended to be highly figurative, often featuring human incident and volumetrically rendered landscape. As a student, Eckersley was deeply impressed by a Manchester exhibition of poster design, which included examples by Cassandre, in turn heavily influenced by post-cubist painting in France. He was also much influenced by the exhibition of surrealist art held in London in 1936 and both these traditions, cubism and surrealism, are evident in his mature work.

His early poster designs, some of them undertaken in conjunction with Eric Lombers (with whom he had been a student), show a high degree of simplification and progressive abstraction of form, although they retain stippled half-tones loosely related to the depiction of volume. His mature designs reveal a highly intelligent process of simplification towards the concept of the "visual telegram", as Cassandre put it, in which everything superfluous is eliminated. They often include brilliant exploitation of visual pun and humour, a tendency which has a peculiar strength in the British graphic tradition. His approach to poster design was influential in overthrowing the reigning orthodoxy of strict segregation or stratification of the conventional ingredients of the poster: headline, image, copy. In Eckersley's work, they frequently become inextricably interwoven and interact upon one another in a subtle and complex manner.

His 1975 poster of Lepra, the British Leprosy Relief Appeal, may be taken as a paradigm of this approach. A world map showing the distribution of leprosy is laid over a simple profile of a negro child's head in such a way that the map may be read on one level as information and on another, possibly subliminally, as a metaphor for the destructive consequences of the disease.

In his early posters, he made extensive use of stencils combined with the brush stipple, a medium which reproduced well in lithography. Following the perfection of silkscreen techniques in the late 1960s he moved to that medium, attracted by its potential for powerful, hard-edge forms in brilliant colour. The recent expansion in the range and quality of coloured papers has permitted him to design by means of a papier collé technique, which has further reinforced the flat, schematic character of his imagery.

Eckersley has never adopted the fulsome and often over-loaded effects of full-colour photography, nor the ruthless exploitation of sex and violence so widespread in contemporary advertising. His persistence with a highly personal and idiosyncratic style of design, the origins of which can be so easily identified and dated, paradoxically still permits him to produce work which is fresh, vigorous, and novel, a welcome counterbalance to the strident hyperbole and the cult of the new which is so prevalent in contemporary publicity graphics.

—Clive Ashwin

# ECKHOFF, Tias

Norwegian ceramics, metalware and furniture designer

**Born:** Vestre Slidre, 25 June 1926. **Education:** Studied ceramics, National College of Crafts and Industrial Design, Oslo, Dip., 1949; also trained in the studio of Nathalie Krebs, Saxbo, Denmark, 1947-48. **Family:** Married Janicke Didrichsen in 1952; children: Eivind, Sigrid, and Sven. **Career:** Designer from 1949, art director, 1953-60, consultant from 1960, and board member from 1974, Porsgrund porcelain factory, Porsgrunn; also freelance designer, for Norsk Stalpress, Georg Jensen, Dansk Knivfabrik, Trio-Ving, Lundtofte Design, and others, in Oslo, from 1957. **Exhibitions:** Lunning Prize-winners, Georg Jensen Inc., New York, 1956; *Scandinavian Modern Design 1880-1980*, Cooper-Hewitt Museum, New York, 1982 (toured); *Design Since 1945*, Philadelphia Museum of Art, 1983; The Lunning Prize, Nationalmuseum, Stockholm, 1986. **Collections:** Museum of Modern Art, New York; Victoria and Albert Museum, London; Kunstmuseum Cologne; Landesgewerbemuseum, Stuttgart; Röhsska Konstslöjdmuseet, Göteborg; Danske Kunstindustrimuseum, Copenhagen; Nordenfjeldske Kunstindustrimuseum, Trodheim; Vestlandske Kunstindustrimuseum, Bergen; Kunstindustrimuseet, Oslo. **Honors:** Glassware Prize, Hadelands Competition, Oslo, 1951; Cutlery Prize, Georg Jensen Inter-Scandinavian Competition, Copenhagen, 1953; Statens Brugskunststipend, Oslo, 1953; Lunning Prize, 1953; Gold Medals, Milan Triennale, 1954, 1957, 1960; Gold Medal, Deutsche Handwerkmesse, Munich, 1961; Design Prize, Norwegian Export Council, 1961; *Norwegian 10* Prizes, Oslo, 1961, 1965, 1966, 1974, 1976; Good Design Prize for *Chaco* flatware cutlery, Norwegian Design Council, 1990; Classical Prize, *Maya* flatware, Norwegian Design Council, 1991. **Addresses:** (home) Lyder Sagensgate 6, 0358 Oslo 3, Norway; (office) Fastingsgate 6, 0358 Oslo 3, Norway.

## Works

*Det Riflete/The Fluted One* porcelain tableware, for Porsgrund, 1952.
*Cypress* flatware cutlery in sterling silver, for Georg Jensen, 1952.
*Glohane/Glowing Cock* ovenproof ware, for Porsgrund, 1955.
*Opus* flatware cutlery in stainless steel and plastic, for Dansk Knivfabrik, 1959.
*Maya* flatware cutlery in stainless steel, for Norsk Stalpress, 1961.

*Regent* porcelain tableware, for Porsgrund, 1961.
*Fuga* flatware cutlery in stainless steel, for Dansk Knivfabrik, 1962.
*Una* flatware cutlery in stainless steel, for Norsk Stalpress, 1973.
*Tiki* flatware cutlery in stainless steel, for Norsk Stalpress, 1974.
*Ana chair* in plastic and steel with wool upholstery, for Ana-Tomi, 1980.
*Tomi* chair in plastic and steel with wool upholstery, for Ana-Tomi, 1983.
*Chaco* flatware cutlery in stainless steel, for Norsk Stalpress, 1989.
Contract chairs and tables in laminated wood, for Smithco Line, Denmark.

## Publications

**By ECKHOFF: articles**—"Keramiske Materialer i husholdningen" in *Bonytt* (Oslo), no. 15, 1955; "Om smak og behag" in *Glassposten* (Oslo), no. 6 1962.

**On ECKHOFF: books**—*Industridesigneren Tias Eckhoff* by Alf Boe, Olso, 1965; *Porsgrunds Porcelaenfabrik 1885-1965* by Alf Boe, Oslo, 1965; *34 Skandinavske Designere* by Sven Erik Moller, Copenhagen, 1967; *Nordisk Kunsthandverk og Design* by Fredrik Willdhagen and others, Oslo, 1981; *Scandinavian Modern Design 1880-1980* edited by David Revere McFadden, New York, 1982; *Design Since 1945* edited by Kathryn Hiesinger and George Marcus, Philadelphia and London, 1983; *The Lunning Prize,* exhibition catalogue edited by Helena Dahlbä Lütteman and Marianne Uggla, Stockholm, 1986; *Norge i Form* by Fredrik Wildhagen, Oslo, 1988.

\*

My background as a designer is in the postwar Scandinavian design movement. This movement dictated that good design should combine function, aesthetics, economy and social awareness—an engaging and stimulating milieu in which to develop.

However, the most important factor for my subsequent work must have been the fact that I grew up on a farm where the sovereign craftsman of the district had a small cottage. He was able to make anything—from building a violin to repairing and reconstructing agricultural machinery. I spent a considerable part of my childhood in that cottage, where big new problems were solved with small and simple remedies.

And so I have strived in my work to approach tasks in a simple and practical way, and to preserve the tenets of good ergonomic and economical solutions applied to "beautiful articles for everyday use" (the 1950s slogan in Scandinavia), articles that will last for many years. Fortunately, most of my design products from the 1950s and 1960s are still in production and on sale.

—Tias Eckhoff

\*     \*     \*

Born in 1926, Tias Eckhoff is a prominent Norwegian designer whose career has developed from the postwar period to the present day. He was educated as a craftsman in the ceramics department of Oslo's National College of Arts and Crafts, where his refined linear draughtmanship was soon noticed.

Tias Eckhoff: *CHACO* stainless steel cutlery for Norsk Stålpress, 1989

In 1949, while still attending the National College, he was named as designer by the Porsgrund porcelain factory. His first table service in feldspar porcelain, *Det Riflede/The Fluted One* (1952), won a gold medal at the Milan Triennale of 1954. Stressing the material quality and purity of design, *The Fluted One* was the very essence of "Scandinavian Design." A complementary and contemporary work is *Glohane/Glowing Cock* (1955), a more rustic series of heatproof jugs and servers in bright monochrome colours produced by the sanitary division of the same factory when capacity was available. His undecorated coffee service, *Regent* (1961), has a supple linear grace that makes it an outstanding representative of Eckhoff's ceramic design.

After leaving his position as chief designer at the Porsgrund factory in 1960, Eckhoff established his own design in Oslo. As a freelance and consultant designer, he developed designs for different purposes: furniture, kitchen equipment, locking devices, armoured steel doors, etc. For the contract market, Eckhoff not only designed *Tomi* (1983), an easy and elegant chair in steel and plastic with upholstery in woven wool, but also its production machinery and equipment as well.

Cutlery is another field to which Eckhoff has dedicated himself. His first set, *Cypress* (1952), was produced in silver by Georg Jensen of Copenhagen. Later, he created a long series of designs for cutlery ranges in stainless steel. The set *Maya* (1961), produced by Norsk Stalpress of Bergen, won the Classical Prize from the Norwegian Design Council in 1991 and remained in production in the early 1990s. It represents a balanced conception between elongated and rounded forms. *Fuga* (1962), produced by Dansk Knivfabrik of Copenhagen, is another set characterized by a sophisticated sobriety which bears witness to a simplified process of manufacture. A recent addition to this field is *Chaco* (1989), also produced by Norsk Stalpress.

As a consultant designer, Eckhoff is associated with a long list of widely-differing firms. He has played a major role in the activities of Norwegian design organizations, was elected member of the American Institute of Interior Designers, and has won numerous gold medals and awards at home and abroad. The greater part of Eckhoff's commissioned work is for the consumer market. The excellence of his design rests on a sound basis of technical and ergonomic analysis. Still, his most compelling virtue as a designer is his exquisite line of draughtmanship.

—Ivar Stranger

# EDELMANN, Heinz

German animated film and graphic designer

**Born:** Of German parents, in Usti nad Labem, Czechoslovakia, 20 June 1934. **Education:** Studied art, at the Kunstakademie, Düsseldorf, 1953-58; mainly self-taught in design. **Family:** Married Anna Edelmann; children: Valentine. **Career:** Worked as an advertising agency copywriter, Düsseldorf, 1958-59; freelance graphic designer, working with Anna Edelmann, Düsseldorf, 1959-70, and in the Hague, from 1970; has designed for Atlas-Film Verlag, Ernst Klett Verlag, Gertraud Middlehauve Verlag, Hoechst, Sandoz, Der Deutsche Ring insurance company, Düsseldorfer Kammerspiele, Westdeutscher Rundunk, and others. Staff designer, with Willy Fleckhaus, of *Twen* magazine, Cologne and Munich. Instructor, Werklehrseminar, Düsseldorf, 1959-61, Werkkunstschule, Düsseldorf, 1961-63, the Werkkunstschule, Düsseldorf, 1961-63, the Free Academy and Royal Academy, The Hague, from 1971. **Exhibitions:** *107 Grafici dell'AGI* Castello Sforzesco, Milan, 1974. **Address:** Leuvensestraat 83, s-Gravenhage, Netherlands.

## Works

Book designs include—*The Once and Future King* by T. H. White; *The Last Unicorn* by Peter S. Beagle; *The Dream-Quest of Unknown Kadath* by H. P. Lovecraft; *Amadis von Gallien,* 2 vols.; *Die Goldene Kuppel des Comes Arbogastoder Lichtenberg in Hamburg* by Helmut Heissenbuttel; *Die Heiliger Drei Konige auf der Reise* by J. Rausch; *Die Prinzessin aus Elfenland* by Lord Dunsany; *Manuel Gassers Kochleverzeichnis: Die Kuche meine Tante Marie* by Manuel Gasser; *Unter dem Regemond* by Oscar Beni; *Uber die Engel* by Rafael Alberti; *Ökonomie des Arbeit,* 2 vols., by Gerhard Brinkmann; *Der Deutsche Werkbund 1907-1934* by Joan Campbell; *Bemerkungen* by Erwin Chargaff; *Waldstein* by Sven Delblanc; *Der Antike Staat* by Numa Denis and Fustel de Coulanges; *Die Versager* by Henning Grunwald; *Goethe and Cotta; Briefwechsel 1797-1832* edited by Dorothea Kuhn; *Textbucher 1-6* by Helmut Heissenbuttel; *Sturm* by Ernst Junger; *Rattus Rex* by Colin McLaren; *Verteidigung des Briefes* by Pedro Salinas; *Schulbuch-Schelte* by Gerd Stein; *Sprechmaschine Pechmarie* by Ralf Thenior; *Phonetik* by H. G. Tillmann and P. Mansell; *Handbuch der Kulturanthropologie* by Frank Robert Vivelo.

## Publications

**By EDELMANN: books**—(with introduction by Kurt Weidemann) *Die 51 schönsten Buchumschlage von Heinz Edelmann,* Stuttgart, 1982.

**On EDELMANN: books**—*Das Plakat* by Anton Sailer, Munich, 1965; *German Advertising Art* edited by Eberhard Holscher, Munich, 1967; *Book Jackets and Record Sleeves* edited by Kurt Weidemann, Stuttgart and London, 1969; *Monografie des Plakats: Entwicklung, Stil, Design* by Herbert Schindler, Munich, 1972; *107 Grafici dell'AGI,* exhibition catalogue with texts by Zenzo Zorzi and Franco Grignani, Venice, 1974; *Full Length Animated Feature Films* by Bruno Edera, London and New York, 1977; *Who's Who in Graphic Art* edited by Walter Amstutz, Dubendorf, 1982.

*       *       *

Heinz Edelmann combines in his work the spirit and fashion of his time, the traditions of the darker fantasies of Central Europe, and a formidable technical professionalism. At one time, he was a member of the editorial staff of the magazine *Twen,* a pace-setting phenomenon of its day. In addition, he absorbed much of the then-current imagery of Pop art. Later his work reflected the colourful fantasies of the psychedelic decorations of the 1960s. Edelmann has continuously developed his style but retained the intensity of his vision so that in spite of a wide range of expression his creative output is imprinted with his fundamentally powerful integrity.

Despite his inventiveness, important traditional elements appear in his work. For example, one can sometimes relate his work to the images of the macabre found in the woodcuts and drawings of medieval Germany. Likewise, he has used the imagery of popular prints of the nineteenth century. His work has frequently been used in children's books, and even among the well-known designs made for WDR, it is the posters for children's television programmes that one remembers most forcefully. The traditional themes of violence and cruelty presented in decorative terms so characteristic of the great literary classics for children are given a new currency through Edelmann's designs. His constant stylistic changes, which contain an erratic, often terrifying element, stay abreast of events in design and keep him ahead of his imitators. Never melodramatic, he frequently parodies himself, and his work is, at its basis, humorous.

Among his most recent designs are the eighteen posters made for the World Theatre Festival in Cologne in 1981. The designs, which consist of incongruous images, can be used in any context by over-printing text. It is to Edelmann's credit that he has the rare gift of producing images still capable of disturbing the sophisticated tastes of the 1980s. Publicity has relied on such methods now for decades, yet Edelmann's designs are fresh and original. A recent poster for Crazy Programmes on WDR children's television reveals his facility as a linear draughtsman and links the contemporary idioms of montage with the circus drawings of Toulouse-Lautrec.

—John Barnicoat

# EHRICH, Hans

Swedish industrial designer.

**Born:** Of Swedish and German parents, in Helsinki, Finland, 25 September 1942. **Education:** Studied metalwork and design, National College of Art, Craft and Design (Konstfackskolan), Stockholm, Sweden, 1962-68; apprentice designer, in Turin and Milan, 1965. **Career:** Founder-director, with Tom Ahlström, A & E Design AB, Stockholm, from 1968, and Interdesign AB, Stockholm, from 1982, designing for Gustavsberg, Jordan, Arjo, Anza, Fagerhults, RFSU, ASEA, Colgate, Norwesco, Yamagiwa, Cederroth, PLM, Zanotta, and others. **Exhibitions:** *From Idea to*

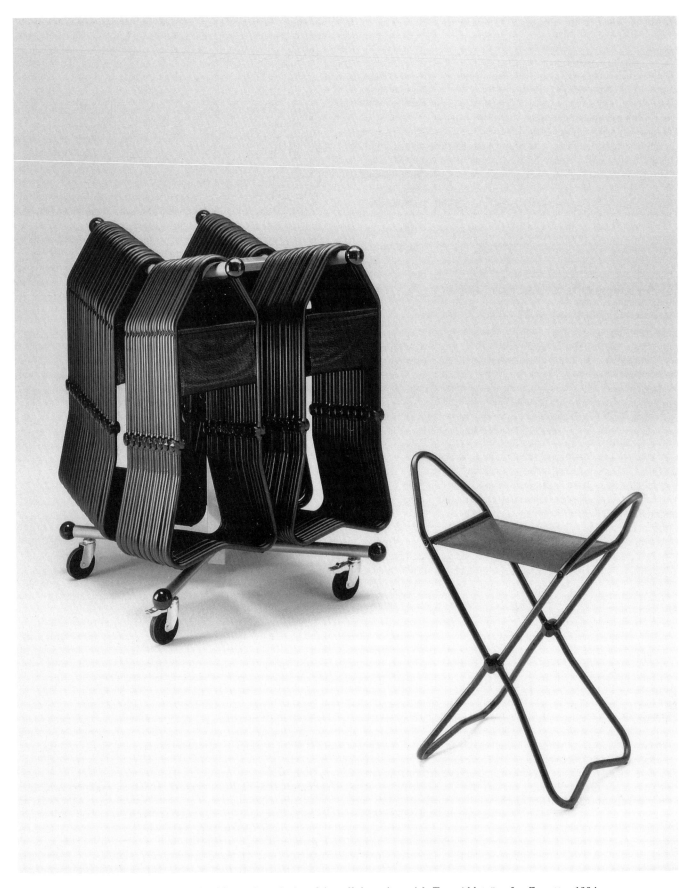

**Hans Ehrich:** *Stockholm* **folding stool with carriage designed in collaboration with Tom Ahlström for Zanotta, 1994**

*Finished Product,* Form Design Center, Malmo, 1977 (travelled to Stockholm); *Contemporary Swedish Design,* Nationalmuseum, Stockholm, 1983 (toured); *Faces of Swedish Design,* Cranbrook Academy of Art, Bloomfield Hills, Michigan, 1988 (toured); *From Revolution to New Expressions 1968-1988,* Nationalmuseum, Stockholm, 1989; *The Movement of Form,* Liljevalchs Art Gallery, Stockholm, 1995. **Collections:** Nationalmuseum, Stockholm; Tekniska Museet, Stockholm; Röhsska Konstslöjdmuseet, Göteborg; Design Museum, London. **Honors:** Swedish State Award to Artists, 1971, 1972; Industrial Designer of the Year Award, 1987; 12-time recipient of the Excellent Swedish Design award. **Address:** A & E Design AB, Tulegatan 19 G, VI, S-113 53 Stockholm, Sweden.

See AHLSTRÖM, Tom

# EIDENBENZ, Hermann
Swiss graphic, lettering, and typographic designer

**Born:** Of Swiss parents, Cannanore, India, 4 September 1902. **Education:** Studied graphics, under Ernst Keller, Kunstgewerbeschule, Zürich, 1919-23; apprentice, Orel Fussli printers, Zürich, 1921-22. **Military Service:** Served in the Swiss Army, 1940-45. **Family:** Married Lotte Christoffel in 1945; children: Florian, Thomas, Mathias, and Franziska. **Career:** Design assistant in Wilhelm Deffke's studio, Berlin, 1923-25, and in O. H. W. Hadank's studio, Berlin, 1925-26; founder-partner, with brothers Reinhold and Willy, of graphic design, photography, and advertising studio, Basel, 1923-53; designer and advertising consultant, Reemtsma cigarette manufacturers, Hamburg, 1955-67; freelance designer, Basel, from 1970. Instructor in lettering and graphic design, Kunstgewerbe und Handwerkschule, Magdeburg, 1926-32; instructor in graphic design, Werkkunstschule, Braunschweig, 1953-55. **Exhibitions:** Helmhaus, Zürich, 1940; Kunstgewerbemuseum, Zürich, 1959; Gewerbemuseum, Basel, 1979; Reinhold Brown Gallery, New York, 1980. **Collections:** Gewerbemuseum, Basel; Kunstgewerbemuseum, Zürich. **Died:** 25 February 1993.

## Works

Coat of arms, for the City of Basel, 1947.
*The Film: It's Economic, Social, and Artistic Problems* by Georg Schmidt and others, book layout design, London, 1948.
Coat of arms, for the City of Braunschweig, 1954, 1981.
Ten and twenty franc bank notes, for the Central Swiss Bank, 1956-80.
All West German bank notes, for the Deutsches Bundesbank, from 1964.
Coat of arms, for the City of Trier, 1982.

## Publications

**On EIDENBENZ: books**—*Packaging: An International Survey of Package Design* edited by Walter Herdeg, Zürich, 1959; *Die Neue*

Hermann Eidenbenz: poster for the Mustermesse, Basel

*Grafik/The New Graphic Design* by Karl Gerstner and Markus Kutter, Teufen and London, 1959; *Moderne Werbe- und Gebrauchs-Graphik* by Hans Neuburg, Ravensburg, 1960; *Who's Who in Graphic Art* edited by Walter Amstutz, Zürich, 1962, Dubendorf, 1982; *The Western Heritage of Type Design* by R. S. Hutchings, London and New York, 1965; *Schriftkunst* by Albert Kapr, Dresden, 1971; *History of the Poster* by Josef and Shizuko Muller-Brockmann, Zürich, 1971.

# EKUAN, Kenji
Japanese industrial designer

**Born:** Tokyo, 11 September 1929. **Education:** Educated at the College of Buddhism, Kyoto, and trained for the priesthood at Chioin Temple, 1947-49; studied design, National University of Fine Arts and Music, Tokyo, BA, 1955; studied industrial design, Art Center College of Design, Pasadena, 1956 (Japan External Trade Organization scholarship). **Military Service:** Served in the Japanese Navy, Cadet. **Career:** Founder-President, GK (Group Koike) Industrial Design Associates, Tokyo, and subsidiaries GK Sekkei,

GK Inc., GK Shop, GK Institute, Kyoto Design Center, and GK Design International (Los Angeles), from 1957. President, Kuwasawa Design School. **Member:** Board Member, from 1962, and president, 1970-72, Japan Industrial Designers Association; vice-president of the Executive Board, 1973-75, president, 1976-79, and senate member, from 1979, International Council of Societies of Industrial Design; member, Design Advisory Committee, Japanese Ministry of International Trade and Industry, from 1975; board member of the Japan Design Foundation, Japan Exhibition Association, Japan Livelihood Association, and Japan Society for Future Research; advisory committee member, Art Center College of Design, Pasadena, Japan Ergonomics Association, Hiroshima Metropolitan Museum of Modern Art, and Japan Computer Graphics Association; organizing committee member, Tokyo National Museum of Modern Art; international member, Industrial Designers Society of America; Mexican Academy of Design. **Exhibitions:** *Kenji Ekuan and His World,* Axis Gallery, Tokyo, 1982. **Honors:** First Prize, Nippon Telegraph and Telephone Competition, 1953; First Prize, 1955, 1958, and Grand Prix, 1974, 1977, Mainichi Industrial Design Competition; Kaufmann International Design Study Grant, New York, 1964; First Prize, Misawa Prefabricated Housing Competition, 1969; Japanese Ministry of International Trade and Industry Awards, 1972, 1975, 1977; ICSID Colin King Grand Prix, 1979; International Design Award, Japan Design Foundation, 1987. Honorary Royal Designer for Industry, Royal Society of Arts, London, 1974; honorary fellow, Industrial Design Institute of Australia, 1981; honorary member, ORNAMO Finnish Association of Designers, 1981; honorary doctorate, Art Center College of Design, Pasadena, 1981. **Address:** 2-19-16 Shimo-ochiai, Shinjuku-ku, Tokyo 161, Japan.

## Works

Motorcycles, snowmobiles, powerboat engines and golf carts, for Yamaha Motorcycle Company, from 1953.

Public telephone booth, for Nippon Telegram and Telephone Corporation, 1953.

Bicycles, for Maruishi Cycle Industrial Company, from 1955.

Soy sauce bottle and package design, for Kikkoman Shoyu Company, from 1958.

Office furniture, for Okamura, from 1961.

Opera glasses, binoculars and lens accessories, for Hoya Corporation, from 1963.

Systems kitchens and bathroom fittings, for Nas Stainless Company, from 1963.

Offset printing press and catalogues, for Komori Printing Machinery, from 1965.

World clock, program timers, exhibition displays and *Expo 70* official timer system, for Hattori Company (Seiko), from 1970.

Interiors, signage system and cash dispensers, for Fuji Bank, from 1973.

Kashima Jingu station plaza and environmental plan, for Kashima Cho Office, Tochigi Prefecture, 1975-83.

*Sunliner* and *Sunpoint* glass display systems, for Asahi Glass Company, 1979.

SLR ZE-X camera, for Mamiya Camera Company, 1981.

*Rumina 1460* sewing machine, for Singer Nikko, 1982.

Security alarm systems, for Secom Company, from 1982.

SV-250 community vehicle, for the Japan Small Vehicle Association, 1982.

## Publications

**By EKUAN: books**—*Dogu Ko,* Tokyo, 1967; *Industrial Design: The World of Dogu, its Origins, its Future,* Tokyo, 1971; *Design: The Relationship of Man and Technology,* Tokyo, 1972; *Ekuan: Dunhill Industrial Design Lecture Series 1973,* Sydney, 1975; *The History of Kitchen Utensils,* Tokyo, 1976; *Makunouchi Bento No Bigaku/The Aesthetics of the Makunouchi Box Lunch,* Tokyo, 1980; *The Philosophy of Tools,* Tokyo, 1980; *The World of GK: The Concept and Development of Industrial Design,* Tokyo, 1983; *Butsudan to Jidosha/The Buddhist Altar and the Automobile,* Tokyo, 1986.

**On EKUAN: books**—*The Conran Directory of Design* edited by Stephen Bayley, London, 1985; *Japanese Design* by Penny Sparke, London, 1987; **articles**—"Tokyo's Mister Less-Is-More" by S. Braidwood in *Design* (London), January 1981; "Design and Democracy" by J. Fair in *PHP* (Tokyo), September 1982; "Kenji Ekuan Muovailee Esineelle Sielun" in *Helsingin Sanomat* (Helsinki), 10 February 1987; "Kenji Ekuan: Industrial Designer" in *PHP* (Tokyo), November 1988.

*

My primary concern as an industrial designer is to simplify complex elements through design to create things which are easily appreciated and understood by the masses. The widespread diffusion of small cars, sophisticated cameras, and mini-calculators is essentially a democratization of high culture. Technology, by simplifying the operation of complex mechanisms and machineries, has made such products readily available to the masses. It is the designer's task to bring the fruits of civilization to people. He must strive to humanize technology and familiarize it to laymen. By creating a congenial man-machine interface, he can offer cultivated or cultural beauty. Through the power of design the two worlds of man and material things can be made to function together in harmony.

When the historical and cultural references of the design of a nation are, by means of mature techniques and technology, enlivened by products introduced to the world, material things can enrich man's life. When those products are globally appreciated, internationalization of a local culture is achieved. The "cultural connection" through design has been my lifelong pursuit.

I have a great fascination for the communicative quality of design as a tangible medium. Because design is blessed with the power to create a culture of living, serious thought must be given to designing products which can bring living comfort to people. While I am proud to be a designer, I am constantly reminded of the tremendous responsibility demanded by my profession as a creative mediator of man and the material world.

—Kenji Ekuan

*        *        *

"To seek the soul in material things" is one of the declared goals of GK (Groupe Koike)—the largest design office in the world. In 1953, under the guidance of Professor Iwatoro Koike, Kenji Ekuan and some other designers and architects formed a team, which developed into GK. Ekuan, who has been President since the group's founding, can in many ways be considered representative of the postwar generation of Japanese designers.

The wisdom of Ekuan—being not only a designer but also a Buddhist monk—and his determination "to keep the spiritual purity of a novice" has fundamentally influenced the development and growth of GK for over thirty years. It would probably lead too far to note all the details of GK's success story—winning many competitions as well as many prizes sponsored by the municipal governments of Tokyo and other major Japanese cities. The group, and Ekuan with it, gained recognition as a leading design practice by working with large industries like Yamaha and others, in Japan and internationally. Cooperation with famous Japanese architects, including Kenzo Tange, Kisho Kurokawa, and others, stimulated Ekuan's existing interest in urban and environmental matters. Active participation in important design events, such as the 1962 World Design Conference in Tokyo, the EXPO '70 in Osaka, the 1973 International Council of Societies of Industrial Design congress in Kyoto, and the 1983 International Design Festival in Osaka, has contributed to make Ekuan an internationally well-known design personality. This development crested with his election as President of the International Council of Societies of Industrial Design at its 1976 assembly in Brussels.

However, nothing could be further from the truth than to confuse Ekuan with the successful organization man that he sometimes might appear to be. It is his basically reflective and philosophical quality, incorporating the finest elements of Japanese culture and tradition, that leads him into a continuous, ongoing search for a Nirvana of beauty, satisfying infinite desires by seeking the soul beyond the material aspects of things that form the human environment.

An inborn sense of dignified respect for symbolic meaning as well as for methodology and a pronounced lack of satisfaction with achievements and success have—not surprisingly—contributed to make (and keep) Ekuan one of the most interesting figures in the world of design. He provides living proof that spirituality, talent, and future-oriented activity in this particular field can very well rely on the cherished background of one's culture, tradition, and symbolic values in a post-industrial future that—on the face of it—seems far from safe or certain.

—Carl Auböck

# ELLIS, Perry (Edwin)

American fashion designer

**Born:** Portsmouth, Virginia, 30 March 1940. **Education:** Studied business, College of William and Mary, Williamsburg, Virginia, BA, 1961; retailing studies, New York University, MA, 1963. **Career:** Buyer, Miller and Rhoads department store, Richmond, Virginia, 1963-67; design director, John Meyer, New York, 1968-74; sportswear designer, Vera Companies, New York, 1974-75; sportswear designer with own "Portfolio" label, Manhattan Industries, New York, 1975-78; independent designer, New York, 1978-86, established Perry Ellis Sportwear, 1978, and Perry Ellis Menswear, 1980; also designed furs, household textiles, toiletries, clothing and patterns for Levi Strauss, Greif, Martex, Visions Stern, *Vogue,* and others, from 1978. Established Perry Ellis fashion studies scholarship, with Marshall Field and Company, at the Art Institute of Chicago. **Honors:** Neiman Marcus Fashion Award, 1979; eight Coty American Fashion Critics Awards, and Coty Hall of Fame

Award, 1981; Council of Fashion Designers American Sportswear Award, 1981. **Died:** New York City, 30 May 1986.

## Publications

**On ELLIS: books**—*Fairchild's Who's Who in Fashion* edited by Ann Stegemeyer, New York, 1980; *McDowell's Directory of Twentieth Century Fashion* by Colin McDowell, London, 1984; *The Encyclopedia of Fashion from 1840 to the 1980s* by Georgina O'Hara, London, 1986.

*        *        *

Without a doubt, Perry Ellis was the most "charming" of his generation of American designers. The romance of the Victorian period is evident even in his most "serious" designs. He was preeminently a designer for the young, but there is nothing pejorative about this observation. On the contrary, Ellis's sensibilities, while simple on the surface, were actually shrewd and sophisticated. It would be wrong to dismiss his work as revivalistic, for it is actually a reexploration of simple, traditional clothes and their possibilities.

Starting with a simple linen dress, Ellis could, by carefully realigning and exaggerating the proportions, suggest infinite resources and artfulness. Which is why, although on the surface conservative, his designs never suggest revivalism. Instead they convey the past viewed through the prism of the late twentieth century, with all that the latter quarter has taught us about masculinity, femininity, and clothing as ritual, as seduction, as fantasy. The designer's predilection for the slightly "off" in the proportioning of his clothes is the closest he comes to a trademark. Ellis would, for example, give a tweed coat impossibly deep and full cuffs on the sleeve, or place the waist of a dress a couple of inches higher than it "should" be. Ellis stands out as a highly subtle modifier of our perceptions, but his base line was always the status quo.

It is this curious conservatism, which Ellis shared with the other leading American designers of his day, that makes America famous for clothes that are easy, functional, even elegant, but never wildly original or avant-garde. Why late twentieth-century American clothing has never matched its art or dance in originality poses a fascinating question for historians; in the meantime, what is pleasurable, particularly with regard to Ellis, is the mastery of the restatement and distillation of the main theme of American clothing.

—Peter Carlsen

# EMIGRE

American graphic design magazine and graphic and typography design firm

**Founded** in 1984 by Rudy VanderLans, Marc Susan, and Menno Meyjes as an experimental culture magazine, *Emigre Magazine,* published quarterly from 1988; principals since 1986 include VanderLans (**Born:** in The Hague, Holland, 10 October 1955. **Education:** Royal Academy of Fine Art, The Hague, B.A.; attended University of California, Berkeley.) and Zuzana Licko (**Born:** Bratislava, Slovakia, 2 October 1961. **Education:** University of California, Berkeley, B.A.); graphic design projects by Vanderlans conducted under the name Emigre Graphics, from 1984; typefaces by Licko conducted under the name Emigre Fonts, from 1985; Emigre Fonts releases about 30 fonts per year, from 1988; clients have included: American Center for Design, M-Works, Rykodisc, Imago Recording Company, Van Nostrand Reinhold, *Ray Gun* magazine, *Wired* magazine, Apple Computer Inc., *Psychology Today* magazine, *Esprit* magazine, Limn Furniture, Cairo Cinemafilms, Nike, *Details* magazine, Tokyo FM, Adobe Systems, *Publish* magazine, DeTienne Associates, San Francisco Artspace, *GlasHaus* magazine, *MacWeek* magazine, *MacWorld* magazine, *Mother Jones* magazine, University of California, Berkeley, Sam Davis Architects, *San Francisco Chronicle, Design Book Review;* VanderLans and Licko are frequent lecturers at conferences and universities throughout the United States, and in Canada and Europe. **Exhibitions:** *Pacific Wave: California Design,* Museo Fortuny, Venice, Italy, 1987; *Au Pied de la Lettre,* Port Autonome, Rouen, France, 1989; *Experimental Typography,* Design Museum, London, England, 1989; *Graphic Design in America: A Visual Language History,* Walker Art Center, Minneapolis, 1989; Design Museum London, England, 1990; *Touch Design America,* Parcway, Tokyo, Japan, 1991; *Typography Now,* Design Museum, London, England, 1992; Bradley University, Peoria, Illinois, 1993; Art Institute of Southern California, Laguna Beach, California, 1993; *Subjects & Objects,* Museum of Modern Art, San Francisco, California, 1995. **Collections:** Museum of Modern Art, San Francisco, California. **Honors:** Chrysler Award for Innovation in Design, 1994. **Address:** *Emigre,* 4475 D Street, Sacramento, California 95819, U.S.A.

### Publications

**By EMIGRE: books**—*Emigre (The Book): Graphic Design into the Digital Realm,* New York, 1993.

**On EMIGRE: books**—*Pacific Wave; California Graphic Design,* Magnus, 1987; *New American Design* by Hugh Aldersey-Williams, New York, 1988; *Experimental Typography* by Kimberly Elam, New York, 1990; *Click* by J. Ellen Gerken, New York, 1990; *Low Budget, High Quality* by Steven Heller and Anne Fink, New York, 1990; *Graphic Design in America: A Visual Language History,* Minneapolis, Minnesota, 1990; *Modern Magazine Design* by William Owen, New York, 1991; *A History of Graphic Design* by Philip B. Meggs, New York, 1992; *Typography Now: The New Wave* by Rick Poynor, London, 1992; *Designers on Mac* by Takenobu Igarashi, Tokyo, 1992; *20th Century Type* by Lewis Blackwell, London, 1992; *The Graphic Edge* by Rick Poynor, London, 1993; *Graphis Publication 1* edited by B. Martin Pederson, Zürich, 1994; *Graphis Typography 1* edited by B. Martin Pederson, Zürich, 1994; **articles**—"Surf's Up" in *Design Week* (England), 1987; "CultureTabs" in *ID* (New York), 1987; "Review" in *TYP* (Holland), 1988; "Bold Faces" in *Publish,* 1988; "US Design" in *Design* (London), 1988; "High Fashion Type" in *Language Technology* (Holland), 1988; "HotShots" in *Adweek* (New York), 1989; "Emigre Art" in *How,* 1989; "Design Works" in *Axis* (Japan), 1989; "Brave New (Mac) World" by Amy Fischel in *Ipso Facto,* 1990; "Two Colours, One Vision" by Mike Jones in *Design* (London), 1990; "Emigre" by Mike Daines in *Baseline* (England), 1990; "Say It Ain't So Joe" by Karrie Jacobs in *Metropolis* (New York), 1990; "New Directions in Products and Graphics" by Rick Poynor in *Blueprint* (London), 1990; "Emigre" in *Evolution* (Japan), 1990; "Deconstructing Typography" by Philip Meggs in *Step-By-Step,*

1990; "Font Pirates: A Personal View" in *How,* 1991; "New Types, New Faces" in *U&lc,* 1991; "Desk Talking Point" in *Tategumi Yokogumi* (Japan), 1991; "Emigre, Les Nouveaux Primitifs Du Graphic Design" in *Communication et Langages,* 1991; "DTP" in *Nikkei Design* (Japan), 1991; "Emigre" by Patrick Coyne in *Communication Arts* (Palo Alto), March/April 1992; "Fonts on the Fringe" by Poppy Evans in *Confetti,* March/April 1992; "Type-Image 1992" in *Designers' Workshop* (Japan), vol. 9, no. 56, 1992; "Kicking up a Little Dust" by Michael Dooley in *Print* (New York), September/October 1992; "Reputations" by Julia Thrift in *Eye* (London), vol. 2, no. 7, 1992; "The I.D. Forty" in *ID* (New York), January/February 1993; "The Next Wave" in *Portfolio* (Japan), No. 49, 1993; "Opening the Floodgates: Digital Typefoundries on the Rise" by Gerald Lange in *Bookways,* October 1993; "Emigre is Ten Years Old" by John Plunkett in *Wired,* November 1993; "Grunge Type" in *BAT,* January 1994; "Comments on the New Typography" by Kit Hinrichs in *How,* February 1994; "Trends" in *Axis,* Winter 1994; "Clip Art Fonts" in *Communication Arts* (Palo Alto), January/February 1994; "Emigre, For Example" by Paola Antonelli in *Abitare* (Milan), Number 327, March 1994; "Rolling with the Punches" by Anne Telford and Ruth Hagopian in *OnLine Design,* May 1994; "Emigre Comes of Age" by Michael Rock in *ID* (New York), May/June, 1994; "Emigre: The Mouse that Roared" by John Belknap in *Blueprint* (London), June 1994; "Graphic Design into the Digital Realm" in *Digital Output,* September 1995; "Emigre" by Rebecka Lindberg in *Cap&Design,* December 1995; "Type a la Modem" by Ken Coupland in *How,* February 1996.

\*     \*     \*

Emigre, the magazine and the type foundry, has had a universally acknowledged impact on graphic design and typography. Though radical and controversial in the early years, Emigre's stylistic influence has been seen in mainstream print and television graphics since the late 1980s. In addition to many innovative and widely used digital typefaces, Emigre has contributed to a greater expressive freedom and visual complexity in layouts, contrasting with the strict grids and grey, visual neutrality of the Swiss International Style. More significantly, Emigre has been at the center of debates about legibility, design philosophy, and the use of new technology.

*Emigre* was founded in 1984 by Rudi VanderLans, Marc Susan, and Menno Meyjes as a culture magazine for Dutch immigrants living in California; Susan and Meyjes left in 1986 and were replaced by Zuzan Licko. It soon developed a broader focus on international artists before starting to concentrate on graphic design in 1989. Both VanderLans and Licko are from Holland, a country noted for high standards in graphics. VanderLans had been trained in the rules of Swiss typography there, but learned the limits of such a rigid system while working for the *San Francisco Chronicle.* Licko, who he met in California, has a background in science, which may have contributed to the freshness of her approach to design and new technology. They are credited, along with a few other pioneers such as April Greiman, with bringing graphic design into the digital age.

In the same vein as radical art publications from the early years of this century, *Emigre* and its Dutch predecessors, such as *Hard Werken,* were produced by small collectives of mainly fine artists and writers, with no preconceptions about design, functionality, or legibility. One of the aims of VanderLans was to rebel against the dryness of the Swiss approach and to revisit the experimental richness of early Modernist groups such as Dada. He also had no money to produce *Emigre,* so he employed inexpensive, unconventional methods and materials. Prior to the introduction of the Mac, the visual effects of the magazine were achieved by using a typewriter and photocopies. Manual techniques such as collage and torn images were combined with free-form layout, layering of type and images, and dramatic scale contrasts.

The Mac was the ideal tool to pursue this approach. In the mideighties, Licko and VanderLans were intent on exploiting the possibilities, recognizing that this was a technological revolution calling for a complete reappraisal of visual tradition. VanderLans has since recalled that: "It was especially exciting to sit behind this machine right at the beginning, when no one else had really explored it yet. There were no visual standards and no existing language to copy or be inspired by."

The computer was both a creative catalyst and a revolutionary production tool in their work. VanderLans and Licko were able to earn the money for the early issues of *Emigre* by producing some of the earliest Mac illustrations in the mid 1980s, either for Apple or the new computer magazines. In their book, *Emigre (The Book): Graphic Design into the Digital Realm,* they have said of the first Mac: "We had already printed the first issue of *Emigre* magazine, but it was the Macintosh that made it economically possible to continue publishing. It also inspired us to design and manufacture original typefaces, an area previously dominated by only a few large type foundries."

Letterform design using computers produced bit-mapped fonts, the crudeness of which repelled some designers but was seen as an extraordinary opportunity by a small number of innovators such as Licko. In her first typefaces Licko was able to use the strict limitations of the early Mac to advantage, perhaps because she did not come from the traditional, calligraphic background normal for type designers. Her first three typefaces (Emperor, Oakland, and Emigre) used simple modular elements derived from the low-resolution characteristics of screen display and dot matrix printing. She defended the coarseness of the early faces as being an appropriate aesthetic for the medium, pointing out that "the digital concept of combining predetermined units as distinct elements to form a coherent image" has been common in mosaics, embroidery, and weaving throughout history.

By 1987 Licko was concentrating on typeface design and working for Adobe Systems, Inc., while VanderLans quit the *San Francisco Chronicle* that year to work for Emigre Graphics, and developed other magazine formats, for *GlasHaus* in 1987 and *Shift* magazine in 1988. Licko began to issue her typefaces on diskette in response to increasing requests from other designers. With the introduction of PostScript in 1985, it became possible to use curves, though she still showed restraint, keeping her faces simple (such as Modula, Citizen, and Triplex, 1985, and Matrix, 1986), sometimes creating new designs simply by smoothing out the stepped, bit-mapped profile of earlier ones. Though technological capability has since increased enormously, she believes that the geometric aesthetic of the Bauhaus and other early Modernist schools is more appropriate for the digital medium than the digitizing of calligraphic fonts, and has expressed regret that the Mac's presence in type design has not continued to develop a unique, expressive style.

Licko has acknowledged that some of her letterforms are difficult for some people to get used to, and both the type and layouts produced by Emigre have been attacked as illegible by senior designers schooled in the Swiss tradition. Licko's response has been that "you read best what you read most"; familiarity with new forms makes them seem more conventional and therefore under-

standable. Likewise, VanderLans has said that the rules are a beginning, not the "absolute truth."

The traditional aim of typography has been invisibility, that is, that the design should convey the message directly without drawing attention to itself. The resulting standardization, in the opinion of Licko and VanderLans, is not sufficiently flexible for all communications requirements. They share a concern with the design process rather than a preconceived vision of what the product should look like. In this they have been amongst the leaders of the first Mac-design generation.

—Michael Large

# ENVIRONETICS GROUP
American architectural and interior design firm

**Founded** as Michael Saphier Associates, in New York, 1937; incorporated as Saphier, Lerner, Schindler, 1958; became SLS Environetics, 1962, Environetics International, 1981, and, after merger with David Mandl Associates, Environetics Group, 1995. Principals include Martin Hertz, Richard Korchien, David Mandl, and Donald White; senior associates include John Totino, Connie Steuerwalt, and Zak Silapaswag. Offices in Los Angeles, Sydney, Mexico City, and London. **Addresses:** Environetics Group, 215 Park Avenue South, New York, New York 10003.

## Works

Sears Roebuck and Company interiors, Chicago, 1973.
United Technologies Corporation interiors, Hartford, Connecticut, 1978.
Swiss Bank Corporation interiors, at the World Trade Center, New York, 1979.
Federated Department Stores interiors, Cincinnati, Ohio, 1979.
William Collins Publishers interiors, Glasgow, 1979.
W. H. Smith bookshops interiors, London, 1980.
Hanes Corporation interiors, Winston-Salem, North Carolina, 1980.
American Can Company interiors, Stamford, Connecticut, 1981.
Federal Land Bank interiors, St. Paul, Minnesota, 1982.
Planning Research Corporation interiors, Washington, D.C., 1982.
Philips Petroleum interiors, London, 1983.
Bendix Corporation interiors, Rosslyn, Virginia, 1983.
John Paul Getty Museum interiors, Malibu, California, 1983.
DG Bank interiors, New York and London, 1983.

## Publications

**By ENVIRONETICS GROUP (Lawrence Lerner): articles**—in *Office Management* (Beckenham, Kent), July 1958; *The Office* (Stamford, Connecticut), July 1959, August 1960, July 1964; *The Executive* (London), November 1959; *Contract* (New York), July 1962, September 1964, April 1965, March 1966, May 1966, March 1979; *Interior Decorators News* (New York), August 1962, March 1963; *Journal of Property Management* (Chicago), May/June 1964; *The Steelcase Circle* (New York), December 1964; *Business Products* (Arlington, Virginia), January 1966; *Progressive Architecture* (New

York), November 1969; *Designers West* (Los Angeles), August 1973; *Management World* (Willow Grove, Pennsylvania), June 1975; *Realty* (New York), June 1979, July 1980; *Administrative Management* (Beckenham, Kent), January 1981; *Index Report* (New York), May 1982; *Words* (Willow Grove, Pennsylvania), September 1982.

\*

Environetics International, Inc. was the first interior architectural firm to organize its administrative management structure into a classic commercial enterprise. It was the first interior architectural professional service to merge with a major American industrial corporation (Litton Industries), all of whose stock was in the hands of the public. Environetics was also the first interior architectural firm to create a network of offices in major cities across the United States and ultimately around the world. The sequence was as follows: Cleveland, 1956; Los Angeles, 1958; Chicago, 1960; San Francisco, 1961; New Orleans, 1962; Boston, 1968; Houston, 1970; London, 1972; Washington, D.C., 1973; Tokyo, 1980; Minneapolis, 1980; Mexico City, 1981. The New Orleans, Minneapolis, Boston, and Houston offices were project-oriented and have been closed.

The company was years ahead of its time in its involvement in computer graphics as applied to architectural working drawings. As far as we know, it was the only company in the profession to have its own in-house software and hardware for the production of architectural working drawings as early as 1969. It was only in the late 1970s and early 1980s that other firms became involved in such state-of-the-art procedures.

In 1955, the Gulf Oil Corporation retained Environetics to plan the use of a projected building from the inside out. The architect was retained after our study was completed, and the size and shape of this building and its individual floors were determined by our study. Environetics has been known for this basic technique and philosophy. It was applied in 1969 to the creation of the world's largest commercial office building, the Sears Tower, which is 4.4 million square feet. All of the working drawings for the entire interior of the Sears Tower were produced on the Environetics MAN/MAC computer graphic system. In the years since 1973 when Sears occupied the Tower, the MAN/MAC system has been in continuous use in maintaining major changes in the occupancy of the building.

All of our clients are constrained by budgetary limitations. These limitations, however, do not restrict their need and desire to fulfill all of their functional and aesthetic requirements. We therefore consider it our task to produce an environment for them that permits their employees to work in stimulating, exciting, and beautiful surroundings while satisfying all the constraints of budget and time. In short, we feel that it is a designer's responsibility always to create an aesthetically pleasing environment regardless of functional and budgetary requirements.

—Lawrence Lerner (former Chairman and CEO, retired 1986)

\*        \*        \*

Environetics International was so closely identified with its chairman and president, Lawrence Lerner, that it is hard to separate the firm from Lerner, the designer. Whatever the firm's particular strength and orientation, it is due in some way to the talent and leadership of this chief executive officer. The firm was started by Michael Saphier, and it was Michael Saphier Associates that Lerner joined in 1948.

In 1958, he was made president of the company, and the name of the practice was changed to Saphier Lerner Schindler.

Environetics International is one of the world's leading firms in interior design and planning. It is also one of the largest, but throughout the past thirty years, the firm could have made its mark simply as an excellent and totally professional firm offering design services to corporate clients in a manner appropriate to any respected by commerce and industry. Until the early 1950s, interior design was not the serious profession that it is now. Lerner was one of the pioneers who made space planning and the design of business environments a highly respected specialty. The firm specialized in the design of office environments at a time when the concept was new, and others were still practicing interior design as decoration.

Under Lerner's leadership, the firm went beyond space planning and interior design to become the recognized expert in the office of the future and the techniques appropriate to that concept. While working on a design project for NASA in 1961, Lerner saw the computer technology used to interpret data supplied from satellites. This sparked the idea which started Environetics International on the road to establishing one of the first and most extensive computer-aided design facilities in architecture and interior design.

Lerner's mind was attuned to technology, and he was probably the most knowledgeable designer interfacing with computer technology for "high tech" offices in the 1970s. In 1971, he led a design team conducting a feasibility study for an off-shore airport for New York City. This widely acclaimed, imaginative project typifies the accomplishments of the firm and of Lerner the designer.

In 1986, Lerner retired from Environetics but continued to work as a consultant to the company. The Environetics Group, its name following a 1995 merger with David Mandl Associates, continues to be a leader in the field of computer-aided design. The entire staff is networked on Draw Base and Auto Cad, in addition to its own proprietary systems. Environetics major projects in the 1990s have included corporate relocation projects for U.S. Life Corporation, Saks Fifth Avenue, Broad, Inc., and Bank of America.

—Arnold Friedmann

# ERNI, Hans

Swiss painter, sculptor, illustrator, stage, mural, ceramic, and graphic designer

**Born:** Lucerne, 21 February 1909. **Education:** Volksschule, Lucerne, 1915-23; apprentice surveyor and architectural draughtsman, in Lucerne, 1924-27; studied at the Kunstgewerbeschule, Lucerne, 1927-28, Académie Julian, Paris, 1928-30, and under Heinrich Wölfflin, at the Vereinigte Staatschule für Freie und Angewandte Kunst, Berlin, 1929-30. **Military Service:** Served in the transport and camouflage units of the Swiss Army, 1940-45. **Family:** Married Doris Kessler in 1949. **Career:** Independent painter and designer, in Lucerne, London, and Berlin, 1930-39, and with studio in Lucerne, from 1945: first stage designs, 1946, postage stamp designs, 1949, and ceramic designs, 1950. **Member:** Founder-member, Allianz group of artists, Zurich, 1938. **Exhibitions:** Galerie

Schulthess, Basel, 1935; Kunst und Gewerbe museum, Winterthur, 1945; Kunstkring Rotterdam, 1946; Musée de i'Athenée, Geneva, 1948, 1957, 1961, 1969, 1974; Gutenberg Book Guild, Zurich, 1950; Main Street Gallery, Chicago, 1951, 1953, 1955, 1956, 1959, 1960, 1963, 1967, 1970; Librairie Paul Morihier, Paris, 1950, 1953; Zwemmer Gallery, London, 1956; Musee Royale, Brussels, 1958; Hammer Galleries, New York, 1959, 1964; Kunstverein, Mannheim, 1962; National Gallery of Victoria, Melbourne, 1964; Museum zur Allerheiligen, Schaffhausen, 1966; Musee Rath, Geneva, 1969; Kunstmuseum, Lucerne, 1971; Kulturzentrum Seedamm, Pfaffikon, 1976; German Nationalmuseum, Nuremberg, 1977; Hans-Erni-Museum, Lucerne, 1979. **Collection:** Hans-Erni-Museum, in the Swiss Transport Museum, Lucerne (opened 1979). **Honors:** Lucerne Mural Competition Prize, 1935; Rimini Biennale Prize, 1952; Gold Medal, Cannes Ceramics Exhibition, 1955; Warsaw Poster Biennale Prize, 1966. **Address:** Kreuzbuchstrasse, Meggen, Lucerne, Switzerland.

## Works

*Coffee* sgraffito mural, for Nestle Building, Vevey, 1959.

Mosaic, for the College Abbaye de Saint-Maurice, Valais, 1961.

*Day and Night* and *Towards Humanity* murals, for the Bankverein, Geneva, 1963.

Mosaic, for the SRG Swiss Radio and Television Building, Bern, 1964.

*Business Organization* mural, for the Lausanne Exposition, 1964.

*La Noce* mural, for the Hotel Intercontinental, Lausanne, 1965.

*The Valais* mural, for the Union des Banques Suisses, Sion, 1966.

*Sgraffito* mural, for the Swissair airlines headquarters, Zurich, 1967.

*Poseidon* mural, for the Municipal Swimming Pool, Lucerne, 1969.

*Four Elements* mural, for the Winterthur Insurance Company, Winterthur, 1970.

*Prometheus* metal mural, for the Municipal Electricity Board, Lucerne, 1972.

*Man and Progress* tapestry, for the Savings Bank of Geneva, 1974.

*Man in Flight* mural, for the International Civil Aviation Organization, Montreal, 1975.

*Penta Rhei* mural, for the Hans Erni Museum, Lucerne, 1984-86.

Books illustrated include—*Le Banquet* by Plato, Zürich, 1941; *Das Lied des Friedens* by Albius Tibullus, Basel, 1942; *Work Through the Centuries* by G. Canevascini, Zürich, 1943; *Olympiques* by Pindar, Lausanne, 1944; *Troy Tales from Ancient Greece* by Hans Bracher, Bern, 1948; *King Oedipus* by Sophocles, Lausanne, 1949; *Antigone* by Sophocles, Lausanne, 1950; *Daphnis and Chloe* by Longus, Lausanne, 1950; *Anthologie de la nouvelle francaise* by Marcel Raymond, Lausanne, 1950; *Histoires naturelles* by Jules Renard, Lausanne, 1953; *Fables* by La Fontaine, Lausanne, 1955; *Portrait of an Age,* London, 1957; *Verheissung des Menschen* by André Bonnard, Berlin, 1957; *Metamorphoses* by Ovid, New York and Verona, Italy, 1958; *The Golden Ass* by Apuleius, Zürich, 1960; *Homer's Odyssey,* New York, 1961; *The Trial and Death of Socrates* by Plato, New York and Verona, Italy, 1962; *Siddartha* by Hermann Hesse, Paris, 1963; *Candide* by Voltaire, Geneva, 1966; *Die Physiker* by Friedrich Durrenmatt, Lausanne, 1969; *The Queen of Sheba's Nightmare* by Bertrand Russell, Zürich, 1970; *Der Fall Sokrates* by W. W. Schutz, Zürich, 1970; *Song of Songs* by Robert Gravés, London, 1973; *Iliad* by Homer, New York, 1974; *Shakespeare l'ancien* by Victor Hugo, Lausanne, 1975.

## Publications

**By ERNI: books**—*Promesse del l'Homme,* with André Bonnard, Paris, 1953; *Liebesgedicht,* Lausanne, 1962; *Sketchbook 1,* Zürich, 1963; (editor) *The Aldus Encyclopaedia,* 10 vols., London, 1958-65; *Hans Erni* (portfolio), Zürich, 1969; *Sketchbook: Israel,* Zürich, 1971; *Sketchbook: India,* Zürich, 1973; *Erotidien,* Zürich, 1973; *Minuskeln,* Lucerne, 1975; *Hans Erni: Gedanken und Gedichte,* Frauenfeld, Switzerland, 1978.

**On ERNI: books**—*Hans Erni: ein Maler unserer Zeit* by Konrad Farner, Zurich, 1945; *Les Fresques de Hans Erni* by Jean Gabus, Neuchatel, 1955; *Hans Erni* by Claude Roy, Geneva, 1955; *Hans Erni* by P. F. Schneeberger, Geneva, 1961; *Peintures en Relief de Hans Erni* by Walter Ruegg, Geneva, 1963; *Hans Erni: Perspectives and Ideas on the Arts* by P. Carroll, Chicago, 1963; *Hans Erni* by Claude Roy, Lausanne, 1964; *Erni* by Manuel Gasser and Mondo Annoni, Geneva, 1969; *Catalogue Raisonné de l'Oeuvre Ltthographie et Gravé de Hans Erni,* 2 vols., edited by Peirre Cailler, Geneva, 1969, 1971; *Hans Erni* by Carl Burckhardt and Walter Ruegg, Lausanne, 1970; *Hans Erni: ein Weg zum Nächsten,* 5 vols., edited by Jean-Christophe Ammann, Lucerne, 1976; *Hans Erni: Das Malerische Werk* by Walter Ruegg, Frauenfeld, 1979; *Hans Erni: Das Zeichnerische Werk und Offentliche Arbeiten* by John Matheson, Frauenfeld, 1981.

*        *        *

Hans Erni is an artist, a designer who has blurred the lines between design art, commercial art, and fine art. His early training as an architectural draftsman gave him a respect for the neat line and the well-defined shape, as well as the clear eye of a naturalist. His contact with artists working in Paris in the late 1920s broadened his vision to abstraction, especially after he joined the Abstraction-Creation group. From these early experiences, he melded a style of graphic expression that included the direct appeal of realistic representation along with the broader scope of abstraction. To this, he added the psychological punch of surrealism. His graphic work was very popular during the 1950s in advertising, book design, and illustration. Characteristically, in this work, the human figure, often painted before a dark background is suspended in a fine-lined framework of symbolic importance. This same subject and style, easily acceptable, made his lithographs collectable both in the original and in reproduction.

Although his murals are of a more visible and enduring nature, his graphic works are better known and have been more influential. A twentieth-century artist, he nevertheless continues the nineteenth-century tradition of accommodation between graphic art and design, for he has found no conflict between the two. Because critics from both worlds have had difficulty assigning his work its artistic value, it has yet to receive a just critical reception. Erni's work has been consistently popular with both the commercial world and the general public, as he moves in and out and sometimes back in the mention of fine art critics, in the world of commercial awards, and in best-of-the-year publications. His multi-faceted style and interest in a gentle sensuality has influenced many illustrators, while his concern for subject content may have more influence on the non-commercial artist than is yet evident.

—Harland Sifford

# ERTÉ

French graphic artist, sculptor, illustrator, fashion, stage, and film designer

**Born:** Romain de Tirtoff, in St. Petersburg, Russia, 10 November 1892; emigrated to France in 1911, and subsequently naturalized. Adopted pseudonym Erté from his initials R.T. **Education:** Studied painting and drawing under Repine and Lossewsky at the Academy of Fine Arts, St. Petersburg, from 1906; Academie Julian, Paris, 1912. **Career:** Fashion artist for couturier Paul Poiret, Paris, 1912-13; stage costume designer, from 1913, for Théâtre de la Renaissance, Le Bataclan, Théâtre Femina, Folies Bergeres, Théâtre Sarah Bernhardt, Bal Tabarin, Opera Comique, Théâtre Palais du Chaillot, Bouffe Parisiens, Théâtre du Châlelet, Théâtre de la Madeleine, and Théâtre du Vieux Colombier, in Paris, for George White's Scandals and the Ziegfeld Follies, in New York, for the San Carlo Opera, in Naples, for the Teatro de Quattro Fontane, in Rome, and for the Saville Theatre, London; freelance illustrator, from 1915, for *Harper's Bazaar, Vogue, Cosmopolitan, Delineator, Femina, L'Illustration, Art et Industrie, Le Gaulois Artistique, La Gazette du Bon Ton, Plaisir de France, The London Sketch,* and *Illustrated London News*; freelance film costume designer, for William Randolph Hearst's Cosmopolitan Films, 1919, and contract costume designer, Metro-Goldwyn-Mayer film company, Hollywood, California, 1925. **Member:** Motion Picture and Television Costume Designers Guild, New York; Ordre de Mérite Cultural, France, 1972; officier de l'Ordre des Arts et des Lettres, France, 1976; chevalier de la Légion d'Honneur, France, 1985. **Exhibitions:** Madison Hotel, New York, 1925; Galerie Charpentier, Paris, 1926, 1929; Galerie du Studio, Brussels, 1927; Warren and Cox, New York, 1929; Waldorf Astoria Hotel, New York, 1935; Galerie Ror Volmar, Paris, 1964; Galerie la Motte, Paris, 1965; Galerie Jacques Perrin, Paris, 1966; Galleria Milano, Milan, 1966; Grosvenor Gallery, London, 1967; Galerie Lambert-Monet, Geneva, 1972; Electrum Gallery, London, 1975; Smithsonian Institution, Washington, D.C., 1979; Musee Boulogne-Billancourt, Paris, 1986. **Collections:** Metropolitan Museum of Art, New York; Museum of Modern Art, New York; Victoria and Albert Museum, London. **Died:** Paris, 21 April 1990.

## Works

Costume designs include—for Gaby Deslys, Paris, 1915; *Legendary Kings,* Theatre Femina, Paris, 1919; *Faust,* Chicago Opera Company, 1920; *Pélleas et Mélisande,* Metropolitan Opera, New York, 1927; *Casanova,* Scala Theater, Berlin, 1930; *Louis Xl,* Alhambra, Paris, 1933; *Joys of the Capitol,* Theatre de la Madeleine, Paris, 1936; *The Bottom of the Sea,* French Casino, New York, 1946; *Capriccio,* Opéra-Comique, Paris, 1957; *Castor et Pollux,* Theatre Antique de Fourvieres, Lyons, 1961; Zizi Jeanmaire costumes for *Zizi Je T'aime,* Casino de Paris, 1972.

Set and costume designs include—*Awakening the Past,* Alcazar Music Hall, Marseilles, 1923; *Rhapsody in Blue,* Radio City Music Hall, New York City, 1988.

Film designs for MGM include—*The Mystic,* 1925; *Bright Lights,* 1925; *Time, the Comedian,* 1925; *Dance Madness,* 1925; *La Boheme,* Paris, 1925.

Illustrated alphabet, completed 1967, published as lithographs, 1977.

*La Traviata* playing-cards, for Alfred Dunhill Limited, 1969.

Six designs of "De Luxe" cognac bottles, for Courvoisier, 1988.

## Publications

**By ERTÉ: books**—*Things I Remember: An Autobiography,* New York and London, 1975; *Designs by Erté: Fashion Drawings and Illustrations from Harper's Bazaar,* New York and London, 1976; *Erté Graphics: Five Complete Suites,* New York, 1978; *Erté,* London, 1978; *Erté's Theatrical Costumes in Full Color* edited by Salome Estorick, New York, 1979; *Erté's Costumes and Sets for Der Rosenkavalier,* New York, 1980; *Erté's Fashion Designs: 218 Illustrations from Harper's Bazaar 1918-1932,* New York and London, 1981; *Erté at Ninety: The Complete Graphics,* London, 1982; *Erté Sculpture,* London, 1986; *Erté at Ninety-Five: Graphics,* London, 1987; (illustrator) *Ermyntrude and Esmeralda* by Lytton Strachey, London, 1970.

**On ERTÉ: books**—*Romain de Tirtoff—Erté,* exhibition catalogue by Giuliana Veronesi, Milan, 1966; *Erté* by Charles Spencer, London, 1970; *Erté* by Roland Barthes, Parma, 1972, New York, 1975; *Illustrateurs des Modes et Manières en 1925,* exhibition catalogue with text by Marcel Astruc, Paris, 1972; *Romantic and Glamorous Hollywood Design,* exhibition catalogue by Diana Vreeland, New York, 1974; *Stage Design* by Donald Oenslager, New York, 1975; *Hollywood Costume Design* by David Chierichetti, London, 1976; *Designs by Erté* edited by Stella Blum, New York, 1977.

\*   \*   \*

Rather than using his own name when he came to Paris, Romain de Tirtoff called himself Erté (after the French pronunciation of his initials) to avoid offending his aristocratic Russian family who thought an artistic career undignified. Already inspired by the graphic style of Greek vase painting seen in the Hermitage in Leningrad and by the colours and detail of Indian and Persian miniatures, he arrived in a Paris attuned to Orientalism. The influence of Poiret and the Ballets Russes had created an atmosphere into which Erté was quickly absorbed.

His exotic fantasy-figures captured the mood of the moment. Using pen and Indian ink and later gouache, he visualised a stylised ideal of beauty which he based on Marie du Plessis, an eighteenth-century French courtesan. Elegant women were captured in motion, frozen in poses which best displayed their garments, their jewellery, their accessories, their furs. They are latter day fashion models springing from the imagination. With his contemporaries such as Iribe, Lepape, and Barbier, Erté created bold fashion illustrations which epitomised the mood of the 1920s. Always beyond the whims of fashion, Erté's work toward the end of his career, such as his designs for *Der Rosenkavalier,* revealed the same exquisite use of line and stark contrast that it had seventy years earlier.

His desire to create individual garments which relied on hand craftsmanship for their detailed perfection made them unsuitable for the mass market. By turning more to the theatre, he was able to continue as he wished. One stage set, titled "Gold," which he produced for the Ziegfeld Follies, required the use of six and a half miles of gold lame to create the desired impact.

A master of exotic fantasy, Erté was also an innovator who worked in many areas of design. He was one of the earliest designers in the twentieth century to create for total environments. His use of metal detailing on clothes, his fashion version of the caftan, and his one-shoulder and cut-out dresses of the 1920s all predated recent trends. Acknowledged as a highly skilled draughtsman, he was also a witty observer. His meeting of the fat and thin lady wearing the same dress show him making a comment on fashion, not just a document of it. The revival of Art Deco in the late 1960s drew new attention and acclaim to his work. This success inspired him to move into sculptural formes picturales, one of which inspired the candelabra appearing in *Der Rosenkavalier.*

—Hazel Clark

# ESKOLIN-NURMESNIEMI, Vuokko

Finnish product, exhibition, fashion, and textile designer

**Born:** Vuokko Hillevi Lilian Eskolin, in Helsinki, 12 February 1930. **Education:** Studied ceramics, Institute of Industrial Arts, Helsinki, 1948-52. **Family:** Married the designer Antti Nurmesniemi in 1953. **Career:** Ceramics designer, Wärtsilä-Arabia, Helsinki, 1952-53; chief fashion and printed textile designer, Printex-Marimekko, Helsinki, 1953-60; produced printed and woven textiles and rugs, Helsinki, 1960-62; founder-director, Vuokko Oy fashion and textile design company, Helsinki, 1964-88, and head designer of Oy Vuokko AB, Helsinki, from 1988. Designer of glass, for Wärtsilä Nuutajärvi Glass, Helsinki, of ryijy wall rugs, for Friends of Finnish Handicrafts, Helsinki, and of woven and printed fabrics, for Villayhtymä, Helsinki, Pausa of Germany, and Borås Väveri of Sweden, 1956-57; designer of exhibitions, for Nordiska Galleriet, Stockholm, Design Research, Boston, 1958, and the Milan Triennale, 1964; designer of clothing, for Villayhtymä, Helsinki, 1963-64. **Member:** Texo Association of Finnish Textile Designers; MTO Association of Finnish Fashion Designers. **Exhibitions:** Artek Gallery, Helsinki, 1957, 1964; Artek Gallery, Stockholm, 1958; Bonniers, New York, 1966; Nordic House, Reykjavik, 1976; University of Texas, Arlington, 1976; Design Center, Tokyo, 1978; Form i Göteborg, 1979; *30 Years of Design,* Milan, 1980; Konstmuseet, Göteborg, 1980; Glyptotek Museum, Copenhagen, 1981; Malmö Museum, Sweden, 1983 (with husband, Antti Nurmesniemi); Historical Museum of Gothenburg, Sweden, 1984 (with Nurmesniemi); Design Center, Helsinki, 1985; Museu de Arte, Sao Paulo, 1988; National Design Festival, Osaka, Japan, 1991 (with Nurmesniemi); Ikaalinen Art Center, Finland, 1994; *Three Women, Three Life's Work,* Pyrri Galleria, Savonlinna City, 1995; *Classic Makers,* Design Forum Finland, Helsinki, 1995. **Collections:** Museum of Applied Arts, Helsinki; Museum of Industrial Design, Copenhagen; Malmö Museum, Sweden; Röhsska Konstslöjdmuseet, Göteborg; Royal Scottish Museum, Edinburgh; Victoria and Albert Museum, London, Metropolitan Museum of Art, New York; Musée de l'Impression sur Etoffes, Mulhouse, France. **Honors:** Gold Medal, 1957, and Grand Prix, 1964, Milan Triennale; City of Helsinki Bursary, 1958; Danish-American Lunning Prize, 1964; Pro Finlandia Medal, Helsinki, 1968, Finnish State Prize for Design, 1968; Ingrid Jespersen Foundation Prize, 1973; honorary member, Academia Mexicana de Diseno, Mexico City, 1981; Prince Eugen Medal, 1986; honorary Royal Designer for Industry, Royal Society of Arts, London, 1988; Japan Design Foundation Award, Osaka, 1991 (with Nurmesniemi). **Address:** Vuokko Nurmesniemi Oy, Hopeasalmentie 27, 00570 Helsinki, Finland.

## Works

Ceramic tableware, for Arabia, 1952.
Clothing and printed cotton fabrics, for Marimekko, 1953-60.
Glass bowls, vases and plates, for Wärtsilä Nuutajärvi, 1957.
Woven woollen household fabrics, for Villayhtymä, 1957.
Exhibition layouts, for Design Research of Boston, 1958.
Clothing, printed, and woven fabrics, for Vuokko Oy, 1964-88.
Ecclesiastical textiles, for Kaleva Church, Tampere, 1966.
Ecclesiastical textiles, for Kannelmaki Church, Helsinki, 1968.
Ecclesiastical textiles, for Lieto Church, Finland, 1972.

## Publications

**On ESKOLIN-NURMESNIEMI: books—***Finnish Design 1875-1975* by Erik Bruun, Timo Sarpaneva, and Erik Kruskopf, Helsinki, 1975; *Finland Creates* edited by Jack Fields and David Moore, Jyvaskyla, 1977; *One Hundred Great Finnish Designs* edited by Per Mollerup, Snekkersten, 1979; *Finnland Gestaltet,* exhibition catalogue by Tapio Periainen, Simo Heikkila, and others, Espoo, 1981; *Contemporary Textile Art: Scandinavia* by Charles S. Talley, Stockholm, 1982; *Scandinavian Modern Design 1880-1980* edited by David Revere McFadden, New York, 1982; *Design Since 1945* edited by Kathryn Hiesinger and George Marcus, Philadelphia and London, 1983; *Finnish Vision,* with texts by P. Suhonen, J. Lintinen, and others, Helsinki, 1983; *The Encyclopaedia of Fashion from 1840 to the 1980s* by Georgina O'Hara, London, 1986; *The Lunning Prize,* exhibition catalogue edited by Helena Dahlback Lutteman and Marianne Uggla, Stockholm, 1986; *Finnish Industrial Design* edited by Tua Pontasuo, Helsinki, 1987; *Encyclopedie de la Moda,* Paris, 1989; *Il Dizionaria Della Moda,* Bologna, 1990; *Images of Design, 1960-1990* by Juliana Balint, Tietopuu, 1991; **articles—**"Thirty Four Lunning Prizewinners" in *Mobilia* (Snekkersten), September 1967; "Some Call Them Purists" by M. Kaipanen in *Form Function Finland* (Helsinki), no. 2, 1981; "Prince Eugen Medal to Vuokko Nurmesniemi" in *Form Function Finland,* no. 1, 1987.

\*

By training, I am a ceramic artist, a craftsman. In practice, however, I have worked in the textile and garment field, using the many possibilities offered by modern technology. During my professional training to become a ceramic artist, I discovered my interest in clothing design. In the evenings, I began practising cutting clothes.

I have always wanted to experiment, to find and develop new things, to play. I try to look at design as an all-encompassing phenomenon: I cannot think of garments as simply pieces of clothing; I think of them as pieces of material, as expressions of colour, as complete entities that I have designed and combined myself.

I love my work which, during the last few years, has mainly been in the textile and garment field. But I have not forgotten the planning of exhibitions and the making of graphics wherever these have had a tangent on the presentation of my own production. I have tried to simplify my creations without forgetting the richness of life itself and its direct influence on my creations.

—Vuokko Eskolin-Nurmesniemi

\*        \*        \*

Vuokko Eskolin-Nurmesniemi: *VEISTOS* dress in viscose velvet, 1986. Photo Max Petrelius

Vuokko Eskolin-Nurmesniemi represents the ideological principles of design at their purest. She has an unusually sound and harmonious view of the world, which reflects directly on her designs.

Eskolin-Nurmesniemi has a scholarly and theoretically well-founded approach to her work which she has directed to a closely restricted social group. By ecological and humanistic means she has reached the mystic timeless forms. People keeping up with the times are still wearing dresses designed by her in the 1950s. Her great strength is the happy synergy of theory and fantasy, reason and emotion. As a clothes designer Eskolin-Nurmesniemi is a Constructivist, for whom the primary aim of design is simple structure, by which she is able to create uncomplicated everyday garments as well as dramatic effects of fest dresses.

She has had innovative insights, such as printing one colour partly on top of another, thus producing a third colour, which in the 1950s was to become Marimekko's trademark. Her deep research into the characteristic features of fabrics made of natural fibres and the use of this knowledge on the cut has resulted in garments that live and move with ease and beauty. Designing fabrics, models, and garments as a harmonious whole has made possible their free variation and combination. Experiments on seams—on dresses, skirts, trousers, coats, etc., and with one seam, two seams, three seams, etc.—form an interesting part of Eskolin-Nurmesniemi's product development. She has experimented as well with unprejudiced renovation and simplification of small structural and functional details: off with folds, adhesive bands to replace buttons, zips to speed up dressing, etc.

Eskolin-Nurmesniemi believes there is no fashion, just time. We follow our time, and time follows us. "In many ways I don't mind when others call me a purist. I think things must be functional, easy to wear and of high quality," she has said. "I've always said there are two sides to me: the very clean Vuokko and the fantasy Vuokko. I must say that I prefer the clean me. If you are too complicated no one understands you."

Eskolin-Nurmesniemi has been in many respects a pioneer in her field on its many essential levels: technically, socially, functionally, aesthetically, and ecologically. All of these are central dimensions of design and designer, and Eskolin-Nurmesniemi takes continual responsibility for them, officially as well as in her own design. She is significant for far more than clothes design, as her philosophy is the basic ideology of design.

—Tapio Periainen

# ESSLINGER, Hartmut

German industrial designer

**Born:** Beuren (now Simmersfield), 5 June 1944. **Education:** Studied electrical engineering, Technical University, Stuttgart; College of Design, Schwabisch Gmund, B.I.D. **Military Service:** German Federal Armed Forces (Bundeswehr), 1964-66, Lieutenant (technical services). **Career:** Founder/president, esslinger design, Mutlangen-Schwabisch Gmund, Germany, 1969; moved to Altensteig, Germany, 1970; moved to Campbell, California, U.S.A., 1982, and renamed frogdesign inc.; moved to Menlo Park, California, 1987, and to Sunnyvale, California, 1994. **Member:** Verband Deutscher Industrie Designer (VDID); German Industrial Designers; Association of Fine Artists, Baden-Württemberg; Industrial Designers Society of America (IDSA). **Exhibitions:** *Good Offices and Beyond,* Cooper-Hewitt Design Museum, New York; *New Design for Old,* Boilerhouse Museum, London, 1985; Philadelphia Design Forum, 1988; USSR Exhibition, 1990; Hamburg Exhibit, Museum für Kunst und Gewerbe, Hamburg, 1992; National Design Museum, Smithsonian Institute, New York, 1994; *Mutant Materials in Contemporary Design,* Museum of Modern Art, New York, 1995; *Good Design Exhibition,* Chicago Athenaeum, Chicago, 1996. **Collections:** Neue Sammlung, Munich, Germany; Museum of Modern Art, New York; Whitney Museum of Modern Art, New York; Museum of Modern Art, Philadelphia; Museum of Modern Art, San Francisco. **Honors:** Grafik Design Award, Germany, 1981; Design of the Year, *Time* Magazine, 1984; Award, Art Directors Club, Germany, 1988; Grand Prize G-Mark, MITI, Japan, 1990; First Prize, CEBIT Industrie-Form Hannover, 1991; IDSA/Industrial Design Excellence Award, 1991 (5), 1992 (7), 1993 (3), 1994 (2); Design Annual, *CA* magazine, 1992; and numerous other awards. **Address:** frogdesign inc., 1327 Chesapeake Terrace, Sunnyvale, California 94089, U.S.A.

## Works

TV and Stereo designs, including concept *51 K, C-TV homelab,* and *color 30/20 t.v.,* for WEGA, from 1971.

Dental instruments and equipment, including dentist workstation and physiochair, for Kaltenbach & Voight (KaVo), from 1971.

Bathroom fixtures and showers, for Hansgrohe, 1971-1985.

Office furniture, for König & Neurath, 1973.

Consumer electronics, including *C-TV* and *Trinitron* television line, for Sony, 1974-88.

Luggage and luxury goods, for Louis Vuitton, 1976-85.

Electronics, for Texas Instruments, 1977.

Personal computers, including *Snow White, II, IIc, IIgs, Macintosh SE,* and *Image Writer II,* for Apple, 1982-86.

Bathroom ceramics and systems, for Villeroy & Boch, 1984.

Computer accessories (*kidz mouse, track man I* and *II*), logo, and packaging, for Logitech, 1985.

Computer workstations, including *SPARC* station, for Sun Microsystems, 1986-91.

Optical industries, including camera, microscope, camera LiOM, for Olympus, 1986-92.

Consumer electronics, including feature phone, for Samsung, 1986-92.

*NeXT* cube and corporate identity, for NeXT computer, 1987-92.

Metalware, including serving tray, for Alessi, 1987-89.

Tableware, for Rosenthal, 1989.

Supercomputer, for nCube, 1989-91.

Telecommunications, including answering machine, for AT&T, 1990-93.

Computers and communications, for IBM, 1990.

Consumer electronics and corporate identity, for Zenith Data Systems, 1990.

Computers and communications, for Motorola, from 1990.

Computer peripherals and corporate identity, for Lunaris/Elecom, 1990.

*Memphis* multimedia systems, for MediaVision, 1992.

Personal computers and multimedia, for Packard Bell, from 1993.

Thermometers, for Thermoscan, 1994.

**Publications**

**On ESSLINGER: articles**—"The Successfrogs" in *Manager,* 1985; "frogdesign: The World According to Esslinger" in *Graphis* (Zürich), 1986; "Hartmut Esslinger: Be a frog!" in *FAZ Magazine,* 1987; "High-Tech dressed to kill" in *Newsweek* (New York), 1988; "The frog That Roared" by Phil Patton in *Connoisseur* (New York), 1990; "Rebel With a Cause" in *Business Week* (New York), 3 December 1990.

*See* frogdesign inc.

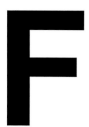

# FAITH-ELL, Age

Swedish textile designer

**Born:** Anna Margareta Faith-Ell, in Växjö, 9 July 1912. **Education:** Växjö Girls' School, Dip., 1930; studied art-embroidery and dressmaking, Saint Birgitta's School, Stockholm, 1930-31; studied weaving, at Johanna Brunsson's Weaving School, Stockholm, Dip., 1934; studied under E. J. Wimmer-Wisgrill, Hochschule für angewandte Kunst, Vienna, 1935; studied machine-woven textiles, Staatslehr und Versuchsanstalt fur Textilindustrie, Vienna, 1943. **Career:** Textile designer, with the Swedish Handicraft Society, in Malmö, Uppsala, Linköping, Stockholm, and Kalmar, 1936-42; textile designer and instructor, R. Atkinson/Irish Poplin House, Belfast, 1946-49; textile designer, AB Kinnasand, Kinna, 1955-56, and 1964-65, Eriksbergs Väveri AB, Kinna (for Nordiska Komapniet department store), 1960-61, AB Marks Jacquardväveri, Björketorp, 1961-63; also freelance designer, Växjö, from 1955; has designed for AB Stobo, 1956-58, Mab and Mya, 1957-60, AB Hagaplast, 1958-64, AB Tidstrands Yllefabriker, 1958-67, AB Kinnasand, 1960, 1970-71 and 1978, Arova of Switzerland, 1967-68. Instructor, Hochschule für Angewandte Kunst, Vienna, 1942-45; Higher Secondary School, Växjö, 1962-78. **Member:** Swedish Society of Industrial Design, 1935; Swedish Society of Artist-Craftsmen and Industrial Designers, 1963; American Institute of Interior Designers, 1963; specialist committee member, Swedish Society for Industrial Design, 1957-66. **Exhibitions:** *Our Home,* Röhsska Konstslöjdmuseet, Göteborg, 1938; *Scandinavian Decorative Arts,* Liljevalchs Konsthall, Stockholm, 1946; *Woven/Printed,* Neue Sammlung, Munich, 1959; *Drei Schweden,* Institut fur neue technische Form, Darmstadt, 1959 (with K. E. Ekselius and E. Hoglund; toured); *Woven This Spring,* Nordiska Kompaniet, Stockholm, 1960; *Blankets,* Nordiska Kompaniet, Stockholm, 1962; *Yard-Goods for Public Places,* Swedish Design Centre, Stockholm, 1966; *SID Design Prize,* Sverigehuset, Stockholm, 1974; *The Swedish Handicraft Association,* Liljevalchs Konsthall, Stockholm, 1982; *58 Swedish Industrial Designers,* Design Center, Stockholm and Malmö, 1986; *Excellent Swedish Design,* Design Center, Stockholm and Malmö, 1987; *Design/Form/Colour,* Kalmar Art Museum, Sweden, 1988. **Collections:** Nationalmuseum, Stockholm; Röhsska Konstslöjdmuseet, Göteborg; Kalmar Art Museum, Sweden; Neue Sammlung, Munich. **Honors:** Silver Medal, Stockholm Crafts Association, 1934; Andersson Fellowship, 1935; 6 textile competition prizes, 1937, and Peter Beijer Fellowship, 1942, Swedish Society for Industrial Design; Swedish Board of Commerce Fellowship, 1942; Swedish Handicraft Association Fellowship, 1942; Gold Medal, Milan Triennale, 1960; Association of Industrial Designers Award, New York, 1963; Växjö Lions Club Fellowship, 1965; Fellowships, 1967, 1968, and Artist's Stipend, 1977, Swedish Artists' Fellowship Committee; Pattern Competition Prize, Sellgrens Vaveri/Norwegian Association for Applied Art, 1976; City of Växjö Cultural Prize, 1984; Excellent Swedish Design Award, 1987. **Address:** Kungsvagen 54, 352 33 Växjö, Sweden.

## Works

*Ribbon* curtain fabric in linen and cotton, for Eriksbergs Väveri, 1960.
*Jungfrulin* curtain fabric in linen and cotton, for Marks Jacquardväveri, 1961.
*Bjornfloka* curtain fabric in cotton, for Marks Jacquardväveri, 1961.
*Baldersbra* curtain fabric in cotton, for Marks Jacquardväveri, 1961.
*Knippfryle* curtain fabric in cotton, for Marks Jacquardväveri, 1961.
*Sjösala* curtain fabric in cotton, for AB Kinnasand, 1963.
*Malin* curtain fabric in linen and cotton, for AB Kinnasand, 1963.
*Vävruta* curtain fabric in cotton, for AB Kinnasand, 1963.
*Lotta* curtain fabric in cotton, for AB Kinnasand, 1976.
*Onyx* curtain fabric in cotton, for AB Kinnasand, 1987.
*Opal* curtain fabric in cotton, for AB Kinnasand, 1987.
*Grafit* curtain fabric in cotton, for AB Kinnasand, 1987.
*Klitter* curtain fabric in cotton, linen and polyester, for AB Kinnasand, 1987.
*Safir* curtain fabric in polyester, for AB Kinnasand, 1987.
*Noja* curtain fabric in cotton, for AB Kinnasand, 1988.
*Rigg* curtain fabric in polyester, for AB Kinnasand, 1988.

## Publications

**By FAITH-ELL: articles**—"Interview mit Age Faith-Ell" in *Moebel Interior Design* (Stuttgart), July 1966.

**On FAITH-ELL: books**—*Konsthantverk och Hemslöjd i Sverige 1930-1940* edited by Ake H. Huldt, Mattis Horlen, and Heribert Seitz, Göteborg, 1941; *Svensk Heminredning* by Lilly Arrhenius, Stockholm, 1957; *Scandinavian Design* by Ulf Hård af Segerstad, Stockholm and London, 1961; *A Treasury of Scandinavian Design* edited by Erik Zahle, New York, 1961; *Modern Svensk Textilkonst* by Ulf Hård af Segerstad, Stockholm, 1963; *Tio Textilkonstnarer* by Gerd Reimers, Falun, 1965; *Decorative Art in Modern Interiors* by Ella Moody, London, 1969; *New Design in Weaving* by D. J. Willcox, New York and London, 1971; *Design in Sweden* edited by Lennart Lindkvist, Stockholm, 1972; *Konsten i Sverige: Konsthantverk, Konstindustri, Design 1875-1975* by Dag Widman, Stockholm, 1975.

\*

It has been my good fortune to have been born and raised in an optimal environment. My father was not only a furniture and house architect, but also a revolutionary force in the pedagogics of drawing and school handicraft. Renowned both in Sweden and internationally for his pioneering ideas within this important field, he had strong convictions and was often described as a fiery spirit. Like all pioneers, he had his opponents. Naturally, my father's activity has had great impact on the development of the creative force in my own life. He was absolutely my best teacher. Even in my youth, however, he made me realize that an existence as an artist is no bed of roses. Despite this, I trained to become a designer.

After completing my training, I was employed as a designer by the Swedish Handicraft Society, which is represented in every municipality, and worked in several cities. It was my task to renew collections, but often I was met by resistance. I enjoyed my work, as I felt that I had been given an important assignment, but at that time, the Society did not pay its designers well, and our names were seldom advertised. As to the period I spent within this institution, I would like to quote from the chapter about me in Gerd Reimer's book, *Tio Textilkonstnärer:*

> At first, however, it was the Swedish Handicraft Society that benefited from her work. This was in the 1930s, when the range of colours was boring and drab, and she had to go through a difficult struggle to force through light and airy colours.
>
> Quite a number of the carpets and curtains that the Swedish Handicraft Society delivered to private and public collections during these ten years would have borne Age Faith-Ell's name if, at that time, it had been the custom to sign such utility goods. This wasn't the case, and much of the handicraft of the 1930s has therefore faded into anonymity. Among the things that Faith-Ell designed at this time were carpets, curtains, and draperies. This collection has been important for her development as an industrial designer, and as such, she has never lost contact with the tradition that the years within handicraft conveyed.

Tired of moving from one small Swedish town to another, I gladly accepted an offer to work as a teacher at the Hochschule fur angewandte Kunst in Vienna, where I previously had been a student. Austria was occupied, there was a war going on, and we worked under difficult conditions, with daily bombing attacks and lack of material and food. Despite this, my period as a teacher at this school was the happiest in my life. Unfortunately, the war situation forced me to leave the school and Austria after three years.

Following a few years as a designer and instructor at R. Atkinson/ Irish Poplin House in Belfast, I returned to Sweden in the early 1950s to take care of my mother, since my father had suddenly passed away. I arrived at the right time. Sweden's rapid recovery from the war brought with it a need for high-quality interior decoration because new theatres, schools, and hotels were being built. Designers were hired—not the least, textile designers—who were now tied to industry, and numerous talented individuals were finally recognized. For many of us, it was the golden era, the period when "Swedish modern" became a concept outside the borders of Sweden. There is a reason that the 1950s are referred to as "the decade of textiles" here in Sweden: I dare say that Swedish textile design more or less set the fashion throughout the world at that time.

However, my debut as an industrial designer occurred in Germany. The Institut fur neue technische Form in Darmstadt asked me to have an exhibition there, after having seen my design collection. The success of this exhibition resulted in the Nordiska Kompaniet immediately asking me to have an individual exhibition in Stockholm. The management made arrangements with a factory to manufacture my collection of textiles, and naturally, Nordiska retained sole rights to this production. All of a sudden all doors had opened for me. I had achieved the peak of my career, perhaps also of my life. I was forty-eight years old.

At the end of the 1960s, our luck turned. There was a crisis in the textile industry. Many factories were closed, and many designers lost their jobs. I went back to my work as a teacher, this time unfortunately not at an art school, but at a secondary school, where I worked until I retired.

I would like to end my narrative with a few more words from *Tio Textilkonstnärer:*

> Age Faith-Ell is one of our most versatile textile designers—an uneasy spirit who can never settle down anywhere, it is said by someone who wants to be cruel.
>
> An untiring experimenter who constantly wants to try new roads, says another, more respectful voice.
>
> What is the truth? Perhaps it lies somewhere in between because it is clear that Age Faith-Ell, who undoubtedly can include a long list of company names in her curriculum vitae, is a restless, searching spirit. At the same time, however, her work is more whole than that of many others because in it, one can trace a development, a logical growth, which becomes more and more convincing for each new exhibition, each new collection. Furthermore, she is one of the Swedish industrial designers who is most renowned abroad. She has attained many international awards and participated in numerous exhibitions, both individual and collective.
>
> It may be a fact that the picture of Age Faith-Ell is many-coloured, with respect to the kind and number of assignments she has had, but if one looks at the picture as a whole, her activity becomes more homogeneous. She knows her style and does not diverge from it—her work is not least about devotion to a set purpose.

—Age Faith-Ell

# FARRAH, Abdelkader

Algerian stage designer

**Born:** Ksar-El-Boukhari, 28 March 1926. **Education:** Self-taught in painting and design. **Career:** Freelance designer, from 1953; head of design, Comedie de l'Est, Strasbourg, 1955-61; associate designer, Royal Shakespeare Company, Stratford-upon-Avon, 1962-65; head of design, Royal Lyceum Company, Edinburgh, 1965-66; Royal Shakespeare Company, working in Stratford-upon-Avon and London, from 1969. Head of Design Course, Ecole d'Art Dramatique, Strasbourg, 1955-61; National Theatre School of Canada, Montreal, 1968-69. **Exhibitions:** Prague Quadriennale, 1979; Maison Internationale du Theatre, Paris, 1982; *Contemporary British Theatre Design,* London, 1983. **Collections:** Victoria and Albert Museum, London. **Honors:** Meilleur Spectacle de l'Annee award, Paris, 1959, 1972; *Plays and Players* magazine award, London, 1971; Society of West End Theatres Award, London, 1976, 1977. **Address:** Royal Shakespeare Company, Barbican Theatre, Barbican, London EC2Y 8BQ, England.

## Works

Stage designs include—*Samson and Dalila,* Nederlandsche Opera, Amsterdam, 1953; *Caucasian Chalk Circle* and *Mann ist Mann,* Comedie Saint-Etienne, 1955-59; *Mayor of Zalemea,* Comédie de l'Est, Strasbourg; *Prometheus Bound,* Comédie de l'Est, 1958; *Andromaque,* Comédie de l'Est, 1959; *Don Giovanni,* Opéra de Strasbourg, 1959; *Oedipus Rex,* Sadler's Wells Opera, London, 1960; *The Cherry Orchard,* Royal Shakespeare Company, 1961; *King Lear,* De Haagsche Comedie, The Hague, 1964; *Three Sisters,* English Stage Company, London, 1965; *Carmen,* Welsh National Opera, Cardiff, 1965; *The Birds,* Royal Lyceum Company, Edinburgh, 1966; *The Dragon,* English Stage Company, London, 1966; *Galileo Galilei,* Royal Lyceum Company, 1967; *Doctor Faustus,* Royal Shakespeare Company, 1968; *Oh, Calcutta,* Somerford Productions, London, 1970; *The Balcony,* Royal Shakespeare Company, 1971; *Richard III,* Comédie Francaise, Paris, 1972; *Enrico IV,* Sol Hurok Concert Inc., New York, 1973; *Henry IV,* parts 1 and 2, Royal Shakespeare Company, 1975; *Henry V,* Royal Shakespeare Company, 1975; *Othello,* Paris Opera, 1976; *Troilus and Cressida,* Burgtheater, Vienna, 1977; *Coriolanus,* Royal Shakespeare Company, 1977; *As You Like It,* Burgtheater, Vienna, 1979; *Parsifal,* Royal Opera House, London, 1979; *Women Beware Women,* Teatro Stabile, Genoa, 1981; *Julius Caesar,* Royal Shakespeare Company, 1983; *Red Noses,* Royal Shakespeare Company, 1985; *The Danton Affair,* Royal Shakespeare Company, 1986; *Romeo and Juliet,* Royal Shakespeare Company, 1989.

## Publications

**By FARRAH: book**—*The Rebec Player,* London, 1955; **articles**—interview in *Plays and Players* (London), November 1982.

**On FARRAH: books**—*Stage Design Throughout the World Since 1950* edited by René Hainaux, Brussels, 1964; *Stage Design Throughout the World Since 1960* edited by René Hainaux, Brussels, 1973; *Lights of Western Theatre* by Alfred Farag, Cairo, 1989.

*

I was brought up in a non-European environment; East and West are two complementary realities in my own experience.

For more than 30 years, I have worked on plays, occasionally on operas, ballets, musicals, reviews, and some popular celebrations.

A designer helps to state that special way of addressing an audience—his work should not be isolated from the general context. The challenge is to reconcile opposites and find out how far one can go without tilting the balance. Objectivity to one person may become subjectivity to the next.

I have been involved with assignments concerned with the following ideas: respect of the classics or their rejection, escapist entertainment or didactic reassessment of political struggle, naturalistic narrative, cult of aesthetics or their demystification; slow exploration process when and if allowed by time, finances, and belief, rigour and ritual on a "bare stage", disintegration of traditional space by mixing audience and action.

One wave follows the other, and today's avant-garde becomes the corroded cliche of tomorrow. Each design movement reaches a point of crisis and temporary death and is reincarnated later under a new guise. To some, it becomes a revelation, to others it is a rediscovery—I respect a designer who can achieve the right metaphor about a piece.

The needs create the means, and the design alphabet is impressive, bearing in mind stylistic suitability and economics: scenic painting; hard, soft, or pneumatic architecture; timber textiles; metals; plastics; reflective surfaces; engineering allowing dynamics of all kinds: lights, projections, laser and audio-visual technology—without forgetting the body and voice of the performer.

To conclude, my views about contemporary design are without a clear-cut conclusion, for the theatre, and designers, will still go on, subjected to that never-ending pendulum swing.

—Abdelkader Farrah

*      *      *

Despite Abdelkader Farrah's background in painting, his scenography is distinguished as much by an architectonic and theatrical shaping of space on stage as by a painter's talent for bold design and color in costumes and properties. A Farrah set may occasionally be lean and unobtrusive, almost Brechtian, but it is never anonymous or expressionless. As he has stated, he imitates nature in its inner dynamic rather than its epidermic look.

Explicitly theatrical scenography was evident in Genet's *The Balcony* (Royal Shakespeare Company, 1971), in which a complex series of kinetic panels and boxes, all mirrored, created chambers of illusion in a brothel. A legacy of his association with Michel Saint Denis is Farrah's fascination with masks. The 1963 *Tempest* included half-masks of the conspirators' own features, and the 1968 Royal Shakespeare Company *Doctor Faustus* masked the Seven Deadly Sins. For *Richard III* (Royal Shakespeare Company, 1970), Farrah elaborated the helmets of warriors into enlarged, bust-like masks of heraldic beasts to signify allegiance to opposing armies.

A primarily architectonic approach was evident in *Coriolanus* (Royal Shakespeare Company, 1977), the set consisting almost entirely of large, metallic, mobile blocks with steeply slanted tops; these functioned as walls, gates and battlements. *Henry V* (Royal Shakespeare Company, 1975) was equally stark and architectonic but included a few striking elements of colorful spectacle. The stage was stripped to its brick walls, which were then painted white. The bare floor contained a platform with a mild rake, encompassed by galleries, bridges, and lighting instruments that were completely exposed. Suspended above the stage was a huge, dull-colored canvas sack, the inner surface of which was richly emblazoned with appliqued heraldic motifs and emblems. Depending on whether the canvas material was suspended or released, it could represent the nobility of France or, when lowered to the floor, the muddy battleground of France. (Farrah had been inspired by circus tents.) Moreover, part of the floor was laterally hinged, and thus, one whole section of it could lift up to form a steep, dangerous surface to be scaled during the battle scenes.

Similar techniques of variously inclining planes were evident in Royal Shakespeare Company productions of *Richard II* and *As You Like It*. In each, the opening scene occurred on a relatively shallow forestage backed by a wall. For the subsequent scenes, the wall was lowered backward to form the rear part of the stage floor. An added, gracefully expressive element in *As You Like It* were trunks of trees that curved up from the floor to a vertical position to suggest stylized waves or some exotic stringed instrument. Together with other natural and folk motifs, they created an effect that was warmer, softer, and more humane than Farrah sets that convey a certain hard-edged, aggressive boldness.

—Jarka M. Burian

# FEDERICO, Gene

American graphic designer

**Born:** New York City, 6 February 1918. **Education:** Studied under Leon Friend, at Abraham Lincoln High School, New York, until 1936, under Tom Benrimo, at Pratt Institute, New York, 1937-38, and under Howard Trafton and Herbert Bayer, at the Art Students League, New York, 1939-41. **Military Service:** Served in the United States Army, 1941-45. **Family:** Married Helen Federico in 1942; daughters: Lisa and Gina. **Career:** Advertising art director in New York from 1938; art director, Abbott Kimball Company, 1938-40, and 1945-46; associate art director, *Fortune* magazine, 1946-47; art director, Grey Advertising, 1949-51, and Doyle Dane Bernbach, 1951-54; vice president and art director, Douglas D. Simon advertising agency, 1954-59; vice-president and group head, Benton and Bowles agency, 1959-65; vice-president and creative director, Warwick and Legler, 1965-66; executive vice-president and creative director of Lord, Geller, Federico, Einstein agency, from 1966. **Honors:** Gold Medal, 1959, 1981, Hall of Fame Award, 1980, Art Directors Club of New York; Silver Medal, Art Directors Club of Philadelphia. **Address:** 655 Madison Avenue, New York, New York 10021, U.S.A.

## Publications

**On FEDERICO: books—***Posters: 50 Artists and Designers* edited by W. H. Allner, New York, 1952; *Who's Who in Graphic Art* edited by Walter Amstutz, Dubendorf, 1982; **articles—**in *Communication Arts* (Palo Alto), no. 3, 1972; *Idea* (Tokyo), May 1973.

*

If an ad isn't seen, it can't be read. And if it isn't seen and read, it won't be believed, and it won't be acted upon. So I begin with the problem of visibility, of working to strip away the nonessentials so that the effect is concentrated and the message stands out in the environment of the medium. Print's more challenging. For a simple reason. It's easier to flip a page than a channel.

—Gene Federico

*     *     *

Graphic designer Gene Federico has worked for more than forty years in advertising. Quick to state that he is a craftsman, not an artist, he seeks to give the client a voice, rather than to project his own "personality" on his designs. However, Federico has consistently aimed to make "elegant" solutions to marketing problems; by this he means "beautiful simplicity, directness and efficacy," qualities that relate his work to precedents by A. M. Cassandre and Paul Rand. Avoiding the "trendy" or merely stylish, he hopes that over years his basic solutions to clients' requests will be effective.

Each ad he designs must stand out from the welter of others, must be easily understood and read. At the same time, Federico has attempted to avoid becoming set in a mode; he tries to keep up with what he sees in the social climate and then to apply this within his own philosophy.

Clients who have used his designs over many years include IBM, Hennesy cognac, and Napier, a manufacturer of costume jewelry. The ads designed by this major design partner of the firm Lord, Geller, Federico, and Einstein exhibit a tough-minded similarity which mark them as Federico's. For example, an ad done for IBM's electric typewriter in the early 1960s breaks rules of advertising practice yet is one of his most successful. Federico entirely omitted the headline, allowing a centrally located photograph of the typewriter with its prominent IBM logos to state the subject immediately and succinctly. Above the typewriter appears the symbol of Aldus Manutius, the early sixteenth century Venetian printer, while below the typewriter, rather more copy than is usual is presented in easily readable and classic form to establish a base for the two photographed images and explain the advantages of the new IBM typewriter in light of the history of writing. The background shades from dark blue across the top behind the pale, plaster-cast symbol to medium blue behind the silver typewriter and palest blue behind the copy below. The ad works most effectively to establish the cerebral worth of the typewriter in historical terms.

Federico's clients are for the most part advertising agencies, which must then appeal to the seller of product or service, but occasionally the client comes directly to him, as was the case with the Killington ski resort just after it had installed its snow-making system. Federico's assignment was to convince his audience to send for booklets about the resort in order to plan vacations well in advance of the season. For this advertisement, Federico headlined "Killington" in light blue upon a dark blue background of the two-tone page. The background gradually lightens as it descends, until it is virtually white on the bottom third of the page. The whole page is sprinkled with white circles, suggesting artificial snowflakes; these are densest on the darkest blue, become sparser in the middle, and vanish in the field of white "snow" at the bottom. Copy and coupon are set against the white. Headline, text, and coupon are easily readable, and the pictorial image confirms the text. This advertisement succeeded in drawing a high rate of response in coupon return.

—Nina Bremer

# FENDI

Italian fashion design firm

Established as a small leather and fur workshop by Adèle Casagrande (died, 1978), in Rome, 1918; name changed to Fendi on Adèle's marriage to Edoardo Fendi in 1925. **Career:** Fendi offices, workshops, and fur studio established in the Via Borgognona, Rome, 1964. Principals include the five daughters of Adèle and Edoardo Fendi: Paola (born 1931) and her husband Ciro Saracino; Anna (born 1933); Franca (born 1935) and her husband Luigi Formilli; Carla (born 1937) and her husband Candido Speroni; and Alda (born 1940). The firm designs and makes leather and fur clothing and accessories, a ready-to-wear line, as well as knitwear and beachwear; designer Karl Lagerfeld has been chief fur design consultant since 1967. **Exhibitions:** *Art-Fashion-Design,* Prato Museum, Italy, 1982. **Collections:** Metropolitan Museum of Art, New York; Art Institute of Chicago. **Address:** Via Borgognona 7, 00187 Rome, Italy.

## Publications

**On FENDI: books**—*I Grandi Personaggi della Moda* by Maria Vittoria Alfonsi, Verona, 1974; *The Fashion Makers* by Bernadine Morris, New York, 1978; *I Mass-Moda: Fatti e Peronaggi dell'Italian Look* by Adriana Mulassano, Florence, 1979; *Moda e Modi* by Adriana Mulassano, Milan, 1980; *Pelle a Pelle* by Prudence Glynn, Rome, 1982; *McDowell's Directory of Twentieth Century Fashion* by Colin McDowell, London, 1984; *The Encyclopaedia of Fashion from 1840 to the 1980s* by Georgina O'Hara, London, 1986.

*

Speaking about Fendi furs means speaking about new techniques, about sophisticated research in workmanship, about traditional skins used in an unusual way, and about pelts considered "poor" until yesterday and now revalued through creativity and man's skill.

Therefore, the name "Fendi" is a synonym for leader in fur research. But Fendi also means anticipation of shapes, perception of new colours, lightness, softness, and inventiveness which unpredictably transforms leather, renewing a fashion concept which seemed unchangeable some years ago.

The evolution of Fendi furs is an escalation towards perfection, new colours, and a uniqueness which has always respected the basic principle of discretion. Fendi furs are styled by Karl Lagerfeld.

—Fendi

\*     \*     \*

Walking along various streets around via Borgognona in Rome, you would no doubt notice the prestigious name of Fendi at several boutique entrances. These are accessory and ready-to-wear stores and the glamorous fur salon at no. 39. The salon is office and showroom to the Fendi sisters and their families involved in management, sales, and design. Paola is the technical expert, as she develops new tanning methods, discovers new materials, and invents new stitching techniques. Unique to Fendi furs are unusual combinations, often brightly dyed, with unconventional detailing including dramatic openings, slashes, pleating, ruffling, and appliqué. Anna works as a designer, while Franca works with customer relations. Carla acts as coordinator of the firm, and Alda is sales director. Each one is respectful of the others, and all are particularly reverent in their appraisal of the work. Joined by their husbands and children and close relatives, the clan works very smoothly to introduce each year several collections combining high-fashion furs, ready-to-wear, mass-produced items, and leather accessories. The firm serves eighty sales outlets in the Italian market and others also in America, Canada, Germany, and Switzerland. On Fifth Avenue in New York, Bergdorf Goodman opened a leather-goods boutique repeating the facade of the main store in Rome. Here, one sees the Fendi handbags, immediately recognizable by their trademark of a stamped or printed, repeated double-F motif.

During the fall/winter season of 1982, the firm introduced evocations of a romantic Russian past with voluminous, layered coats,

accessorized with flower-shaped brooches and necklaces in fur and leather. That particular year, skins were also joined together to form flower patterns, and fur ruffles were used as detailing. Modeled were Tibetan lamb coats, weasel, marmoridea, fitch, Russian squirrel, beaver, fisher, mink, and lynx. Pants and sweaters were suggested for day, and pants, skirts, and blouses, for evening, with a fur greatcoat in loden green to cover all. Among the other fabrics used were velveteen, flannel, embroidered taffetta, cashmere, alpaca, and shetland in loden, black, and coffee.

A year later, in 1983, the shape created was a wide look, which now included constructed shoulders. The furs were shown with soft blousing and dolman or set-in sleeves. The poncho-coat, with long, puffed fur, was matched with sheared pelts flattening in the front and back. Very long fur scarves with tasseled fringe were added. Fur inserts were seen, as were tissue-thin suede and irregular, zigzag stitching for accents. High-waisted sweaters in striped and geometric jacquards were shown, as well as skirts worn like a second skin and flannel doubled with cashmere. Colors were dusty pastels, copper, lead, and pewter. New additions to exotic fur combinations were marbled suede, stained suede, and shearling printed in flowered tapestry or ritual and mask designs. Always to be noted are the beautiful fabrics, as well as accessories manufactured to their own design from such companies as Garolini for shoes, Colony for belts, and Portolano for gloves. The Fendi firm is a clan that continues to be a credit to the founder, spiritual leader and until 1978, head of the family, Adèle Casagrande Fendi.

—Gillion Skellenger

# FERGUSON, Perry (Field)
American film designer

**Born:** Fort Worth, Texas, 12 November 1901. **Family:** Married; son: Perry. **Career:** Art director, 1935-41, and supervising art director, 1941-53, at RKO Studios, Hollywood, California; also worked on films for United Artists, Columbia, Universal and Metro-Goldwyn-Mayer, from 1949; collaborated with designers Van Nest Polglase and George Jenkins.

## Works

Film designs include—*Hooray for Love* (W. Lang), 1935; *Winterset* (Santell), 1936; *Bringing Up Baby* (Hawks), 1938; *Gunga Din* (Stevens), 1939; *The Story of Vernon and Irene Castle* (Potter), 1939; *The Swiss Family Robinson* (Ludwig), 1940; *Citizen Kane* (Welles), 1941; *Ball of Fire* (Hawks), 1942; *They Got Me Covered* (D. Butler), 1943; *North Star* (Milestone), 1943; *Up in Arms* (E. Nugent), 1944; *Casanova Brown* (S. Wood), 1944; *Belle of the Yukon* (Seiter), 1945; *The Kid from Brooklyn* (McLeod), 1946; *The Stranger* (Welles), 1946; *Song of the South* (H. Foster), 1946; *The Best Years of Our Lives* (Wyler), 1946; *The Secret Life of Walter Mitty* (McLeod), 1947; *Desert Fury* (L. Allen), 1947; *The Bishop's Wife* (Koster), 1947; *A Song Is Born* (Hawks), 1948; *Rope* (Hitchcock), 1948; *Without Honor* (Pichel), 1950; *711 Ocean Drive* (J. Newman), 1950; *Sound of Fury* (Endfield), 1950; *The Groom Wore Spurs* (Whorf), 1951; *Queen for a Day* (Lubin), 1951; *The Lady Says No* (Howe), 1951; *The*

*Big Sky* (Hawks), 1952; *Main Street to Broadway* (Garnett), 1953; *The Shaggy D.A.* (Stevenson), 1976; *Herbie Goes to Monte Carlo* (McEveety), 1977.

## Publications

**On FERGUSON: books**—*Filmlexicon degli Autori e delle Opere,* supplement, edited by Michele Lacalamita and others, Rome, 1973; *Le Decor de Film* by Leon Barsacq, Paris, 1970, as *Caligari's Cabinet and Other Grand Illusions,* Boston, 1976.

\*     \*     \*

Perry Ferguson's art direction told stories through style and space. *Ball of Fire* (1942), for example, contrasted a professor's nineteenth-century lodgings (an antiquity enclosed by dusty walls of books and surrounded by a garden like that of a medieval cloister) with New York nightlife (studded with spacious, slick, and fashionable supper clubs). At the same time, Ferguson used circular spaces to complement the ensemble acting and to emphasize Sugarpuss O'Shay as the storyline's pivot.

The artistic credit for Ferguson's greatest achievement, *Citizen Kane* (1941), has not always been properly assigned. On the film, Van Nest Polglase received the art direction credit, with Ferguson named as associate. Moreover director Orson Welles put his own strong visual stamp on this film as on all of his productions. However, both Welles and photographer Greg Toland have emphasized Ferguson's role as art director, thus validating his rightful acclaim.

*Kane's* visual complexity spans volumes of analysis. Perhaps most memorable was Xanadu: a creation of extensive research (including a study of the Hearst mansion) culminating in a tasteless hodge-podge of styles. This frantically electric building symbolized Kane's obsession to possess. Xanadu also captured multiple psychological spaces. For instance, the vacuous, over-sized palace with dwarfing fireplace, high ceilings, and cold, polished floor provided a striking image of loneliness for the bored, idle Susan it engulfed. Her bedroom, suggesting the *horror-vacuui* of a child's mind, interpreted her as a toy trapped in Kane's demonic doll house. She eventually left the claustrophobic atmosphere, but Kane, framed ad infinitum by his own mirrored reflection, would be trapped forever in this ego-prison of his own making.

Styles changed like points of view in this film. Kane grew up with a Currier and Ives childhood, a Beaux-Arts adolescence, an expressionistic adulthood, and a surrealist senility—or were these merely perceptions of his narrators? The film is notable for spatial changes (enhanced by Toland's creative photography): closed, open, horizontally narrow, vertically narrow, dominating characters, overwhelmed by characters, disorienting. Such diverse spaces are the basis of the film's formal design, as well as agents of expression.

Ferguson's enhancement of the narrative in *The Best Years of Our Lives* (1946; in collaboration with George Jenkins) opens with a crowded room of faceless GI's. Eventually, the camera targets on our protagonists, cramped together on the plane ride home. The banker returns to his comfortable, but efficient, high-priced apartment (acknowledging an affluence devoid of ostentation). The local boy enters a homecoming straight out of a Norman Rockwell illustration, with sentimental front porches and shady trees iconographic of small-town folksiness. The ex-soda jerk cum war hero, confused in his father's crowded trailer, out of place in his floozy wife's bachelorette apartment, has no real home. He returns to a womb-like airplane cockpit to relive the pains of the war. Through these sets, Ferguson illustrated the differences and universalities of former GI's returning to once familiar worlds as strangers and each searching for a space to call his own.

—Edith Cortland Lee

# FERRÉ, Gianfranco

Italian fashion designer

**Born:** Legnano, in 1944. **Education:** Studied architecture, Politecnico, Milan. **Career:** Freelance jewellery and fashion accessory designer, Milan, 1969-73; fashion designer, Baila Company, Milan, 1974-78; launched Gianfranco Ferré fashion label, Milan, in 1978; first women's collection, 1978; first menswear collection, 1982; launched perfumes and accessories lines, 1984; first haute couture collection, 1986; furs collection, 1987; introduced Ferréjeans, 1989; introduced fragrance for women, *Ferré by Ferré,* 1991; introduced household linens collection, 1992; artistic director, Christian Dior fashion house, Paris, from 1989. **Exhibitions:** *Italian Re-Evolution,* La Jolla Museum of Contemporary Art, California, 1982 (travelled to Hartford, Connecticut); *Intimate Architecture: Contemporary Clothing Design,* Massachusetts Institute of Technology, Cambridge, 1982; *Design Italian Society in the Eighties,* La Jolla Museum of Contemporary Art, 1982; *Creators of Italian Fashion 1920/1980,* Daimaru Museum, Osaka, 1983 (travelled to Tokyo); *The Unpleasant Genius: Creativity and Technology of Italian Fashion 1951/1983,* Sala Congressi del Galoppatoio di Villa Borghese, Rome, 1984; *Moda Italia,* Pier 88, New York, 1988; *Tartan,* Fashion Institute of Technology, New York, 1988; *Momenti del design italiano nell'industria e nella moda,* Seoul, 1990; *Japonism in Fashion,* National Museum of Modern Art, 1994. **Honors:** Tiberio d'Oro Award, 1976; Best Stylist of the Year Award by *Asahi Shimbun* and *Women's Wear Daily,* 1983; Modepreis for women's fashions, Monaco, 1985; Cutty Sark Men's Fashion Award, New York, 1985; Medal of Civic Merit, Milan, 1985; named Commendatore dell'Ordine al Merito della Repubblica Italiana, 1986; De d'Or prize for first haute couture collection for Dior, 1989; named "Milanese of the Year" by the Famiglia Menaghina, 1989; I Grandi Protagonisti prize from the Italian Furs Association, 1990; Lorenzo il Magnifico award from the Medicean Academy, Florence, 1990; Occhio d'Oro prize, 1983, 1983/84, 1985, 1986/87, 1987/88, 1989; Il Fiorino d'Oro Award, 1991; Pitti Immagine Uomo Award, 1993. **Address:** Via della Spiga 19/A, 20121 Milan, Italy.

## Publications

**By FERRÉ: articles**—"Le ragioni del sentimento" in *L'Uomo Vogue* (Milan), October 1987.

**On FERRÉ: books**—*I Mass-Moda Fatti e personaggi dell'Italian Look/The Who's Who of the Italian Fashion,* with text by Adriana Mulassano and photos by Alfa Castaldi, Florence, 1979; *Italian Re-Evolution,* exhibition catalogue edited by Piero Sartogo, La Jolla, 1982; *Leaders in Fashion: I grandi personaggi della moda* by Maria-Vittoria Alfonsi, Bologna, 1983; *The Italian Look Reflected,* with text by Silvia Giacomoni and photos by Alfa Castaldi, Milan,

1984; *The Unpleasant Genius,* exhibition catalogue edited by Pia Soli, Milan, 1984; *McDowell's Directory of Twentieth Century Fashion* by Colin McDowell, London, 1984; *The Encyclopaedia of Fashion from 1840 to the 1980s* by Georgina O'Hare, London, 1986; *W, The Designing Life* edited by Lois Perschetz, New York, 1987; *La moda italiana* by various authors, Milan, 1987; *Moda Italia,* exhibition catalogue edited by Bonizza Giordani Argani, Milan, 1988; *Sultans of Style: Thirty Years of Fashion and Passion* 1960-90 by Georgina Howell, London, 1990; *In Vogue* by Georgina Howell, London, 1992; "Bello & Brutto: Lo Stile Secondo Ferré" by Maria Vittoria Carloni in *Panorama,* June 1994; **articles—**"New Architects of Fashion" in the *New York Times Magazine,* 16 August 1981; "The New Architectural Approach to Fashion" in *Vogue* (New York), June 1982; "Gianfranco Ferré: Expanding His Research" in *Women's Wear Daily* (New York), 5 April 1986; "Gianfranco Ferré: Uniformi d'eccezione" in *Vogue* (Milan), July/August 1987; "Roma alta moda: Gianfranco Ferré" in *Vogue* (Milan), September 1987; "Architect of New Classics" by Liz Smith in *The Times* (London), 8 December 1987; "Gianfranco Ferré: Da alla donna forma e slancio" in *Vogue* (Milan), January 1988; "Who'll Pay the Ferré Man?" in *W* (London), 28 January 1988; Ferré's Blueprint for Men's Wear Is Surprisingly Realistic" in the *Daily News Record* (New York), 12 April 1988; "Fashion by Ferré" in the *New York Times,* 19 July 1988; "Gianfranco Ferré Is the Nonconformist" by Georgina Howell in *Vogue* (New York), July 1988; "Ferre and Gigli, Architects of Modern Style" in *Elle* (London), October 1988; "Sinnliches Tuch" in *Der Spiegel,* 23 January 1989; "Gianfranco Ferré" in *Donna* (Milan), March 1989; "Un Italien cousu Dior" by Fabian Gastellier in *Elle* (Paris), 29 May 1989; "The Italian Connection" by Suzy Menkes in the *Sunday Express Magazine* (London), 11 June 1989; "Ferré's Debut at Dior: Much Too Serious" in *Women's Wear Daily* (New York), 25 July 1989; "My Fair Ferré" by Liz Smith in *The Times* (London), 25 July 1989; "Back to the Future" in the *Sunday Times* (London), 30 July 1989; "Gianfranco Ferré" by Françoise Baudet in *Vogue* (Paris), August 1989; "Du nouveau dans la mode" by Lucienne Mardore in *Marie Claire* (Paris), September 1989; "Ferré Strikes Gold" by Suzy Menkes in *Illustrated London News* (London), Autumn 1989; "Dior for Ever" in *Elle* (New York), October 1989; "O Dior mio!" by Margit J. Mayer in Vogue (Munich), October 1989; "Ferré in Focus" by Paul Kleers in *GQ* (London), March 1990; "Thinking Big" by Marina Mattioni in *Donna* (Milan), March 1990; "Ferré's a Jolly Good Fellow" by Peter Mayle in *GQ,* September 1990; "Gianfranco Ferré: I Am a Mix of Sensitivity and Concreteness" by Gisella Boriou in *Donna* (Milan), November 1990; "Dior Sees Red" in *Elle* (New York), December 1990; "Gianfranco Ferré" in *Current Biography,* July 1991; "Frankly Ferré" by Sara Gay Forden in the *Daily News Record,* 21 June 1993; "The Babar of Milan" by Jane E. Dickson in *The Independent Magazine,* October 1993; "Le Donne di Ferré" by Natalia Aspesi in *Il Venerdi' di Repubblica,* April 1994; "La Parole est Dior" in *Vogue Paris,* May 1994; "New-look Dior Fails to Suit Nineties Woman" by Tamsin Blanchard in *The Independent* (London), 11 October 1994; "Armani and Ferré: A Study in Contrast" in the *New York Times,* 11 March 1995; "The Gilda'd Age" by Ruth La Ferla in *Elle* (New York), June 1995.

\*     \*     \*

Gianfranco Ferré has always been faintly uncomfortable with the idea of fashion as a relentlessly changeable phenomenon. He has always claimed that his clothes—even when he was most involved with abstraction, as in his early women's collections—were meant for "real people," by implication, people who were concerned with style, rather than fashion. While this has become a common-enough claim in an era in which it has become fashionable in itself to decry the idea of being in fashion, Ferré is obviously sincere in his determination to create a serene, even classical point of view, which varies only subtly from season to season.

At the core of the designer's sensibility there is a finely-tuned concern for simplicity. His architectural training is often cited as the root of his exceptionally sober and economical sense of cut, and it is a training which shows in his own environment, in his own style of dressing, and which is indeed the epitome of his fashion esthetic. On this foundation, Ferré has evolved a style which uses traditional fabrics and deceptively conventional tailoring to suggest the mobility and necessary condensed qualities inherent in modern life. To look at a Ferré dress fleetingly is almost like looking at a sketch, a quick impression of line and color. In this sense, he rather resembles his contemporary, Karl Lagerfeld, who has a similar ability to suggest the timeless and whose work on closer inspection reveals vast subtleties. Unlike Lagerfeld, however, Ferré is far less concerned with the sympathetic reinterpretation of the past and more with the intimate relationship between the wearer and the garment.

Another of the designer's hallmarks is his bold use of primary colors, juxtaposed with gray, black, or green. These bright, almost industrial hues—tractor yellow, fire truck red—add an additional energy to Ferré's work, suggesting the bright world of the laboratory or the flash of skyscrapers glimpsed from a highway.

Ferré became the artistic designer for Dior in 1989; his assignment was to remake Dior's image for the 1990s. Instead of building on Dior's romantic and flirtatious style of the past, Ferré created an austere and refined collection using mostly black and white, but including evening dresses in deep, rich colors with sweeping trains.

Ferré is known for the confidence and elegance of his creations, which are powerfully feminine or masculine. The crisp white shirt is one of his hallmarks, and red is his signature color in the collections bearing his name, but he has expanded as a designer to include a variety of customers. Ferré feels that he has enhanced the meaning of the words "made in Italy."

—Peter Carlsen

# FIELDS, Edward
American textile designer

**Born:** New York City, 1913. **Military Service:** Served in the United States Merchant Marine, until 1941. **Family:** Married Eleanor Fields in 1935. **Career:** Performer in Fields Brothers' song-and-dance team at the Ziegfeld Follies, New York, 1922; worked at various jobs in New York, until 1935; opened own rug showroom, New York, 1935; acquired "magic needle" prototype and began manufacturing own large-scale, high fashion rugs and carpets, from 1941; with his brother Eliot Fields established Edward Fields Inc. carpet manufacturing firm, Flushing, New York, from 1950 (the firm continues at 232 East 59th Street, New York); clients include the White House, American Airlines, and others. **Member:** Board Member, Fashion Institute of Technology, New York; honorary fellow, American Society of Interior Designers, 1978. **Died:** Clearwater, Florida, 17 April 1979.

## Publications

**By FIELDS: articles**—interview in *Interiors* (New York), November, 1978.

**On FIELDS: articles**—in *Interiors* (New York), July 1956, January 1972, June 1979; *Interior Design* (New York), September 1967, February 1971, May 1979; *Residential Interiors* (Radnor), January 1977; *Architectural Digest* (Los Angeles), August 1982.

\*   \*   \*

The day after his marriage in 1935, Edward Fields opened his business as a carpet representative in the New York showroom of Hampton Shops, a fashionable decorating firm. His wholesale carpet and rug business flourished, but he became dissatisfied with the lines he was able to offer. In 1941 he acquired the model for a rug-making machine with a special needle from Joseph Blumfeld, a Viennese rug-maker. This device evolved into Fields's "magic needle" machine, resembling a miniature handgun, which enabled him to start making his own rugs in 1942-43.

During the 1930s and 1940s, the carpet industry was aggressively and successfully promoting wall-to-wall broadloom as a universal solution to floor covering requirements, but after World War II, furniture began to be arranged in a more organized fashion, so that with increasing frequency, the rug became the central design element. Moreover, the new vogue for radiant heating in floors mandated the need for rugs which did not cover the entire floor surface. Thus, when Fields established his own business in 1950, with more distinctive rug designs in mind, he decided that the firm's output would be custom work, produced entirely in the United States under his supervision and handcrafted with the highest standards from 100 percent wool yarn. Fields felt that a rug should not be the entire center of attention in a room but that it could be treated as a distinctive design element. He often referred to the floor as the room's "fifth wall."

During the 1950s and 1960s, he worked with a number of outstanding designers to produce significant rug designs, which were frequently viewed as a form of art. Marion V. Dorn, who had worked with Elsie de Wolfe and Syrie Maugham, designed rugs that were based on abstract South American motifs. These rugs differed from other contemporary designs in that they were derived from ethnic, rather than *moderne,* sources. Raymond Loewy, a close friend of Fields, encouraged him to produce rugs which would be in keeping with the avant-garde movement of the time. This resulted in a collaboration with William Raiser, an interior designer who had been associated with Loewy. A collection of contemporary rugs was generated, and Fields dubbed them "area rugs." The area rug concept was soon picked up by well known interior designers and architects, who brought their own designs to Fields for translation into rugs in custom sizes and colors for modern interiors.

In the 1960s, Fields employed Annie Sanders Bohlin, a Cranbrook graduate and Fulbright scholar, to design contemporary rugs for him in the free-form style so popular at the time. Darren Pierce, Percival Goodman, Joan Gerson, Chaim Gross, Van Day Truex, Robert Motherwell, and Helen Frankenthaler also designed for Fields's carpets.

Fields's rugs for the White House included a blue and gold oval rug, with motifs from each state, for the Diplomatic Reception Room and a floral-bordered carpet in the President's Oval Office. Fields designed the tapestry rugs which were used on the bulkheads of American Airlines' passenger fleet, and his firm wove the large, scenic tapestry for American's passenger terminal at the Dallas-Fort Worth airport.

He established two yearly awards for the Fashion Institute of Technology, where he served as a member of the board—the William G. Raiser Award for interior design and the Edward C. Fields Award for product design. His son, Jack Fields, president of Edward Fields, Inc., and his widow, Eleanor Fields, chairman of the board, today continue the strong tradition of excellence for which the company is known. The thousands of designs in the firm's collection now include rugs based on geometry, organic references, interpretations of historic designs, natural motifs, and *trompe l'oeil,* with a palette ranging from subtly textured monochromatic rugs to highly exuberant designs in brilliant colors with dramatic sculpturing.

—Grant Greapentrog

# FINKE, Jochen
German stage designer

**Born:** Glogau, Germany (now Glogow, Poland), 3 August 1941. **Education:** Educated in Grimma, until 1959; studied stage design, under Heinrich Kilger, Kunsthochschule, East Berlin, Dip., 1969; graduate studies, under Karl von Appen, Akademie der Kunste, East Berlin, 1969-71. **Married** Renee Hendrix in 1973; son: Jakob. **Career:** Worked as a gardener in Dresden, as stage decorator in Stralsund, as technical draughtsman in East Berlin, and several other jobs, 1960-64; first stage designs, Frankfurt on Oder, 1965; resident stage designer, Deutsches Theater, East Berlin, 1971-79; chief designer, Volksbühne, East Berlin, from 1980. Leading member of the stage design group, Verband Bildender Künstler, East Berlin, from 1975; vice-president of the DDR section, and member of International Scenography Commission, OISTAT Organization Internationale des Techniciens et Architects de Theatre, from 1982. Guest instructor, at the Fachschule für Gestaltung, East Berlin, from 1974, Kunsthochschule, East Berlin, 1977-79, Hochschule für Schauspielkunst, East Berlin, from 1980, and Theaterhochschule, Helsinki, 1985. **Exhibitions:** Galerie im Turm, East Berlin, 1979; Kleine Galerie Pankow, East Berlin, 1986; Kleine Galerie, Eberswalde, 1989. **Collections:** Kleist-Museum, Frankfurt on Oder; Goethe Nationalmuseum, Weimar; Gerhart Hauptmann Museum, Erkner. **Honors:** Goethe-Prize, 1986. **Address:** Parkstrasse 64, 1100 Berlin, Germany.

## Works

Stage designs include—*Kabale und Liebe,* Deutsches Theater, East Berlin, 1971; *Juno und der Pfau,* Deutsches Theater, 1972; *Torquato Tasso,* Deutsches Theater, 1975; *Ein Sommernachtstraum,* Hans Otto Theater, Potsdam, 1976; *Schwanensee,* Komische Oper, East Berlin, 1977; *Faust,* Mecklenburgisches Staatstheater, Schwerin, 1979; *Berlin Alexanderplatz,* Volksbühne, East Berlin, 1981; *Tinka,* Berliner Ensemble, East Berlin, 1982; *Die Niebelungen,* Staatsschauspiel, Dresden, 1984; *Mahagonny,* Teatro Sao Carlos, Lisbon, 1985; *Optimistische Tragödie,* Volksbühne, 1985; *Penthesilea,*

Staatsschauspiel, Dresden, 1986; *Der Meister und Margarita,* Volksbühne, 1987; *Warten auf Godot,* Volksbühne, 1988; *Romeo und Julia,* Teatro Aberto, Lisbon, 1988; *Hamlet,* Volksbühne, 1989.

## Publications

**By FINKE: articles**—"Der Spiel-Raum" in *Theater der Zeit* (East Berlin), October 1976; "Verwandlungen" in *Theater der Zeit,* April 1979; "Heinrich Kilger" in *Der Sonntag* (East Berlin), March 1982; "Bestandsaufnahmen" in *Theater der Zeit,* September 1983; "Mahagonny in Portugal" in *Podium* (East Berlin), January 1986; "Szenographie" in *Szenographie der Volksbühne,* East Berlin 1989.

**On FINKE: books**—*Stage Design Throughout the World 1970-1975* by René Hainaux and Nicole Leclercq, Brussels and London, 1976; *Buhnenbilder* by Friedrich Dieckmann, East Berlin, 1978; *Tasso 75* by Christoph Funke, East Berlin, 1978; *100 Jahre Deutsches Theater Berlin* by Michael Kuschnia, East Berlin, 1983; *Bild und Szene* by I. Pietzsch and others, East Berlin, 1988; *Wolfgang Engel inszeniert Penthesilea* by Michael Funke and Dieter Goerne, East Berlin, 1989.

\*

One cannot exhibit stage design. So one acquires a theatre ticket and attends the only possible stage design exhibition—the theatrical performance. The stage design does not exist without the actor, the singer, the dancer, and the spectator. These are the true producers of the stage design, that is, of that which can be experienced on the stage as a pictorial interpretation of reality.

Stage design is not static. During its short lifetime between the beginning and the end of a theatrical performance, it is subject to continual transformation. Existence on the stage is defined by the event. *(From a text accompanying a theatre design exhibition.)*

Each stage design comes to life in the process of adapting a dramatic work to the present time. If one is successful in shaping the stage as a visible expression of social or historic structures, the actor is given the opportunity in his concrete relation to his surroundings to represent the dramatic figure in its social determination. The space, in making possible and limiting the scene, becomes a lively theatrical means of expression. As a restraint on the presented events, it becomes an aestHetic system of the definition of our relationship to historical material. *(From "Der Spiel-Raum" in* Theater der Zeit.)

The classical definitions of stage design no longer apply. Concepts such as decor, illusion, and history hardly matter. In their place, we talk of space, movement, performance. Stage design statements are better understood as spatial statements. Without space, there is no movement; without movement, no scene. Stage design is now regarded as nothing other than the visual relation between figure and space. In consequence, the stage designer has become not only partner of the director but, even more, partner of the actors. By unequivocally concentrating on the scene in his work, the designer is forced deeper into the production process. The boundaries between stage design and production have become permeable. The actor stands once again at the heart of the theatre.

Like literature and the plastic arts, theatre has title to its existence only if it communicates something, if it says something about reality in a concrete social situation, if it formulates an attitude toward the world. Hence, the necessity for a continual expansion of rules and proven methods. Contemporary theatre is always experimental. And the search for new possibilities is the only form of artistic survival. *(From "Bestandsaufnahme" in* Theater der Zeit.)

—Jochen Finke

\*   \*   \*

In his work, the designer Jochen Finke, a pupil of Karl von Appen and Heinrich Kilger, is primarily interested in giving visual expression to spiritual problems. He feels particularly inspired by the romantic painter Caspar David Friedrich, and by the Surrealists de Chirico and Magritte. Finke renounces imitative and illustrative methods: he likes to bring new meaning to real objects by placing them in unfamiliar juxtapositions, producing a kind of irritation or alienation. The concrete objects on the stage (trees, water, fire, lamps, etc.), through their relationships to each other and to the actions of the players, express new connections which are revealed in prominent and significant ways. Materials are not just imitated—the objects on stage are genuine, concrete material. Finke works analytically: before he paints, he writes. The piece, its dramaturgy, its conceptual information, take prime place in the work process. He learned this methodical approach from his teacher Heinrich Kilger.

For this designer, space is a lively means of expression in the theatre. Spatial changes, disruption of perspectives, light—always in relation to the play of the actors—are consciously-used methods to make clear space/time relationships. Finke's stage designs are imbued with an acute rationalism and clarity. His first work for the Deutsches Theater in Berlin, the design for Schiller's *Intrigue and Love,* showed stage space and furniture in an even white. Areas of social difference (petit bourgeois and the court) were made meaningful through differing ceiling heights. A sort of passe-partout frame—decorated on its movable upper part with Schiller's writing—gave to the whole a strong, contoured form. The social problems were rendered by optical rhythm. In the design of Goethe's *Torquato Tasso,* Finke returned to the movable scenery of Goethe's time. The relationship of the interiors to nature outside gave particular significance to this production at the Deutsches Theatre. The more Tasso found himself prisoner at the court of Ferrara, the more the naturalistic elements were pushed back, until at the end of the play, with all the scenic devices removed, Tasso took the road to freedom in a clear light on an almost empty stage. The costumes, too, were derived from the original period of the piece. Finke considers the historic circumstances of the plot very precisely, consciously rejecting any contemporary interpretation.

In *Berlin Alexanderplatz* (based on Doblin's novel), which was premiered at the Berlin Volksbühne, the irritations of the large city to which the hero sees himself exposed were expressed in grey-blue steel constructions and scaffolding. These devices were movable, and so from time to time gave out on new vistas and spaces. A few birches hinted at landscape, almost crowded out by the image of the city. *Tinka,* a contemporary piece by the East German author Volker Braun, and performed in 1983 at the Berliner Ensemble, takes place in a large enterprise. Finke designed a space carousel with a deliberately sterile effect, which—when moved by the revolving stage—allowed the scenes to glide easily into one another. The cool high walls between each scenic space isolated people from one another. Finke's offerings are always to the point, concrete, and precise. In this, above all, lies their aesthetic effect.

—Ingeborg Pietzsch

# FIORUCCI, Elio
Italian fashion designer

**Born:** Milan, 10 June 1935. **Career:** Proprietor, Fiorucci shoe store, Milan, 1962-67 (opened by his father in the mid 1940s); founder and director, Fiorucci fashion shop, Galleria Passerella, Milan, selling clothes by Ossie Clark, Zandra Rhodes, and others, from 1967; began first wholesale and retail production of jeans, fashion accessories, and household items, 1970; founded Fiorucci S.p.A., Milan, 1974, and Fiorucci Inc., New York, 1976; opened major boutique-cultural centers in New York, 1976, in Boston and Los Angeles, 1978, and throughout Europe, the United States, Japan, and Southeast Asia, from 1978; signed licensing agreements with stores and manufacturers in Japan, 1983, Australia, Brazil, Chile, and New Zealand, 1992, Hong Kong, Hungary, and Turkey, 1993; sold Fiorucci trademark to Edwin Jeans, 1990, retaining identity and design responsibility; established worldwide design headquarters for the Fiorucci trademark as Sagittario S.R.L., 1991; launched Fiorucci collection of jeans, bags, jewelry, and watches in Europe, 1994. Founder, Technical Design School, Milan, 1977.

Contributor to *Donna* magazine, Milan. **Exhibitions:** *Italian Re-Evolution,* La Jolla Museum of Art, California, 1982; Centro Cultural Polifunzionale, Bra, 1995; *I Capi del Cuore: raccolta di capi Fiorucci dal 1967 ad oggi,* Istituto Europeo di Design, Milan, 1995; *Histoire du Jean du 18ème à nos jours,* Palais Galliera, Paris, 1995; *Diseno Italiano,* Museo de Bellas Artes, Santiago, Chile, 1996. **Address:** Fiorucci S.R.L., Galleria Passerella 2, 20122 Milan, Italy.

## Publications

**On FIORUCCI: books—***I Mass-Moda: Fatti e Personaggi dell'Italian Look* by Adriana Mulassano, Florence, 1979; *Italian Re-Evolution: Design in Italian Society in the Eighties,* exhibition catalogue edited by Piero Sartogo, La Jolla, 1982; *McDowell's Directory of Twentieth Century Fashion* by Colin McDowell, London, 1984; *The Conran Directory of Design* edited by Stephen Bayley, London, 1985; *The Encyclopaedia of Fashion from 1840 to the 1980s* by Georgina O'Hara, London, 1986; *Italian Design: 1870 to the Present* by Penny Sparke, London, 1988; *The Andy Warhol Diaries* edited by Pat Hackett, New York, 1989; *Fashions of a*

**Elio Fiorucci:** *Furry Handcuffs,* 1995

*Decade: The 1960s* by Yvonne Connikie, London, 1990; *Jeans* by Ugo Volli, Italy, 1991; *The Jeans Encyclopaedia* by Sportswear International, Germany, 1992; *Challenges of Plastic* by Half Moon, Milan, 1993; *Les Annees 70* by Anne Bony, Paris, 1994; **articles—**"Mr. Fiorucci: 20 Years of Global Pollution" by Terry Jones in *i-D* (London), September 1987; "Fiorucci: Going Places Again" by Roger Tredre in *Fashion Weekly* (London), 28 July 1988; "The Fall and Rise of the Fiorucci Phenomenon" by Bronwyn Cosgrave in *The European,* 3-9 December 1993; "Fiorucci Fever" by Angela Buttolph in *Elle U.K.,* October 1995.

\*

My handcuffs are a joyful object and a symbol of love, seduction, sensuality, and complicity. They are toys for couples; bracelets addressed to those fiancés who enjoy playing without taboos and who want to stay together all life long.

—Elio Fiorucci

\*     \*     \*

Elio Fiorucci is the guiding light for a fashionably naughty kitsch which has recently become trendy among chic youth and well-known personalities alike in both the United States and Europe and, in fact, the world around. He is vehemently opposed to haute couture, which he terms "pathetic," yet his outrageously flamboyant clothes and accessories have an inimitable style and attitude which has caught on and been copied both by fashionable stores and by the cheap wholesalers who supply street vendors with their "plastic" wares. Fiorucci's major innovation is turning ordinary apparel and accessories into flashy transformations for colorful fun; he offers an up-to-the-minute, high-tech look achieved by a mix-and-match choice left to the discretion of the individual customer. More of a wholesaler, promoter, and distributor than a fashion designer as such, he uses various designers for each class of item which bears his name.

The origins of Fiorucci's popularity lie in the pop culture scene of the mid 1960s, his first clothes being the Carnaby Street look of that period. He helped open the European and Japanese markets to acceptance of the new, and his influence can be seen as well in such nouveau chic areas of the United States as the East Village in New York and Los Angeles' New Wave scene. He is preferred by many celebrities, drawing admiration from clients such as Brooke Shields, John Travolta, Jackie Onassis, and even Princess Diana, to whom he sent a sweatshirt adorned with a jeweled crown for the royal wedding.

Fiorucci's famous stores in New York and Milan offer a "total atmosphere," with flashing strobe lights and new wavey/disco music blasting amidst the arrays of loudly colorful and patterned items, all bearing the Fiorucci label. His shoes and boots are his most longstanding trademark items, with patent-leather reds, yellows, blues, greens, and purples predominant, along with animal-skin or bright colored insets on black. The ordinary sweatshirt has never before been so varied and so "smart," going longer, becoming a dress, turning inside out, decorated with abstract patterns or worn with diversely shaped belts and scarves. There are variously emblazoned or solid-colored headbands, socks, gloves, sweatpants, jackets, book bags, looseleaf binders, note pads, magic markers, pencils, license plates, postcards, hats, purses, calendars, boxes, and so on, with fringes, zippers, holes, leopard skin designs, fake fur, or fishnet, all in plastic, metal, acrylic, netting, or some other new material. It's all Fiorucci's droll expression of the idea that the cheap, gaudy, and slightly kinky be worn as an emblem of "rebellion," a comment on the plastic society of the present.

For Fiorucci, who has been called the "Titan of Trash Flash," thrift-shop clothing and junkshop accessories can be re-arranged and made over into jazzy outfittings that are both affordable and stylish, and, perhaps most important, appealing to the trendy sets who are "in the know" and want to express themselves with an eyebrow-raising, fun-loving twist. His success over the past decade has been rather phenomenal, and it will be interesting to see if he can continue to capture the world's fashion eye in the future.

—Barbara Cavaliere

## FIRTH, Tazeena (Mary)

British stage and exhibition designer

**Born:** Southampton, Hampshire, 1 November 1935. **Education:** Educated at St. Mary's School, Wantage, Berkshire, 1943-50; Chatelard School, Les Avents, Switzerland, 1950-52. **Career:** Designer, for Theatre Royal, Windsor, Berkshire, 1954-57, for the English Stage Company, Royal Court Theatre, London, 1957-60, Royal Shakespeare Company, Stratford-upon-Avon, Warwickshire, 1966-74, and for the National Theatre, London, 1974-77; worked in collaboration with designer Timothy O'Brien, from 1961. **Exhibition:** *British Theatre Design '83-87,* Riverside Studios, London, 1988. **Collections:** Victoria and Albert Museum, London; Theatre Museum, Göteborg. **Honors:** Gold Medal, Prague Quadriennale, 1975. **Address:** 33 Lansdowne Gardens, London SW8 2EQ, England.

**Works**

Stage productions (with Timothy O'Brien) include—*The Bartered Bride,* Sadler's Wells Theatre, London, 1962; *Girl of the Golden West,* Sadler's Wells Theatre, 1962; *Next Time I'll Sing to You,* Arts Theatre, London, 1963; *Licence to Murder,* Vaudeville Theatre, London, 1963; *Luv,* Arts Theatre, 1963; *Poor Bitos,* Arts Theatre, 1963; *Hedda Gabler,* Arts Theatre, 1964; *Entertaining Mr. Sloane,* Arts Theatre, 1964; *A Scent of Flowers,* Duke of York's Theatre, London, 1964; *Poor Bitos,* Arts Theatre, New York, 1964; *Waiting for Godot,* Royal Court Theatre, London, 1964; *Tango,* Aldwych Theatre, London, 1966; *Days in the Trees,* Aldwych Theatre, 1966; *Staircase,* Aldwych Theatre, 1966; *All's Well That Ends Well,* Royal Shakespeare Company, Stratford-upon-Avon, 1967; *As You Like It,* Royal Shakespeare Company, Stratford-upon-Avon, 1967; *Romeo and Juliet,* Royal Shakespeare Company, Stratford-upon-Avon, 1967; *The Merry Wives of Windsor,* Royal Shakespeare Company, Stratford-upon-Avon, 1968; *Troilus and Cressida,* Royal Shakespeare Company, Stratford-upon-Avon, 1968; *The Latent Heterosexual,* Aldwych Theatre, 1968; *Pericles,* Royal Shakespeare Company, Stratford-upon-Avon, 1969; *Women Beware Women,* Royal Shakespeare Company, Stratford-upon-Avon, 1969; *Bartholomew Fair,* Aldwych Theatre, 1969; *Measure for Measure,* Royal Shakespeare Company, Stratford-upon-Avon, 1970; *The Knot*

*Garden,* Royal Opera House/Covent Garden, London, 1970; *The Merchant of Venice,* Royal Shakespeare Company, Stratford-upon-Avon, 1971; *Enemies,* Aldwych Theatre, 1971; *Man of Mode,* Aldwych Theatre, 1971; *La Cenerentola,* Municipal Theatre, Oslo, 1972; *Lower Depths,* Aldwych Theatre, 1972; *The Island of the Mighty,* Aldwych Theatre, London, 1972; *As You Like It,* Arts Theatre, Cambridge, 1972; *Richard II,* Royal Shakespeare Company, Stratford-upon-Avon, 1973; *Love's Labours Lost,* Royal Shakespeare Company, Stratford-upon-Avon, 1973; *Summer Folk,* Aldwych Theatre, 1974; *Pericles,* Comedie Francaise, Paris, 1974; *The Bassarids,* English National Opera, London, 1974; *Next of Kin,* National Theatre, London, 1974; *The Marrying of Ann Leete,* Aldwych Theatre, 1975; *The Bassarids,* Stadt Oper, Frankfurt, 1975; *John Gabriel Borkman,* National Theatre, London, 1975; *Peter Grimes,* Royal Opera House/Covent Garden, London, 1975; *Wozzeck,* Adelaide Festival, South Australia, 1976; *The Zykovs,* Aldwych Theatre, London, 1976; *The Force of Habit,* National Theatre, London, 1976; *Tales from the Vienna Woods,* National Theatre, London, 1977; *Bedroom Farce,* National Theatre, London, 1977; *Falstaff,* Berlin Opera, 1977; *The Cunning Little Vixen,* Stora Theatre, Göteborg, Sweden, 1978; *Evita,* Palace Theatre, London, 1978 (and productions worldwide); *A Midsummer Night's Dream,* Sydney Opera House, Australia, 1978; *The Rake's Progress,* Royal Opera House/Covent Garden, London, 1978; *Lulu,* Royal Opera House/Covent Garden, London, 1981; *A Doll's Life,* Mark Hellinger Theatre, New York, 1982; *Turandot,* Vienna State Opera, 1983; *Katerina Ismailova,* Göteborg, 1984; *La Traviata,* Umea, 1985; *The Trojan Women,* Göteborg, 1985; *Bluebeard's Castle,* Copenhagen, 1985; *Il Seraglio,* Göteborg, 1986; *The Magic Flute,* Umeå, 1987; *Rigoletto,* Umeå, 1987; *War and Peace,* Leningrad, 1991.

*See* O'BRIEN, Timothy

*

A theatre designer's job is to persuade people to think and feel certain things—it could be said, "to prevent them from thinking the wrong thing." It is important to remember that the audience does not have the advantage of having heard the discussions that lead up to a production; they are informed only by what they see and hear in front of them.

Beautiful sets and luxurious costumes, in themselves works of art, are no help unless they reinforce the dramatic intentions. The stage is a deceptive place where the genuine can seem false. The theatre has its own reality where tall poles covered with green carpet can communicate more to an audience than trees cut fresh from the forest. Beware the overly complex unless it looks simple, for the singer or actor is made in the human scale. These all-important humans should complete the design, not compete.

—Tazeena Firth

*     *     *

Precision and a search for an ideal visual image that lies between prosaic reality and conscious art or metaphor underlies all of the work of Timothy O'Brien and Tazeena Firth. A prime example was the scenography for Gorki's *Summerfolk* (Royal Shakespeare Company, 1974). Three walls and the floor were covered with a green wool carpet, which had a variety of subtle shades but no distinct pattern. Trees were represented by absolutely straight columns covered with the same carpet. A genuine feeling of external nature was evoked without a hint of naturalistic detail. A more metaphoric and abstract approach was found in Etheredge's *Man of Mode* (Royal Shakespeare Company, 1971), the chief element of which consisted of a series of polished, silvery spheres in different, neatly organized configurations; these marvelously conveyed both precision and playfulness, even as they helped re-describe the space for various scenes.

O'Brien sees his and Firth's works as having evolved toward greater expressiveness over the years. It has also become technically more complex. For the Michael Tippett opera *The Knot Garden* (Covent Garden, 1970), the set consisted of eleven miles of thick string forming a series of wings and a backdrop in several layers. High-powered projectors cast pointillistic photos of gardens onto the strings, filling the stage with an abstract impression of nature in which the characters stood out in the beams of tightly focussed spotlights. Kinetics contributed to scenes of psychological stress as two concentric arcs of steel rods on substage rails rode around in grooves in the field of projected images, thereby creating a visually disorienting effect.

The set for the musical *Evita* (London, 1978) was a culmination of increased expressiveness for which O'Brien and Firth drew upon both traditional scene painting and sophisticated technology. The scenographically crucial element was a very large projection screen that glided up and down stage at an oblique angle to receive projected images of photographs and documentary newsreels. Also present was a metal bridge construction that served as a ceremonial platform; as wide as the stage, it moved toward the audience from the rear of the stage for several crowd scenes. Framing the total stage picture were huge murals on the proscenium facade, and intensifying the visual effect of the action on stage were not only spotlights shining up through the stage floor but mirrors that lined the inner surfaces of the proscenium arch as well as the side walls of the stage.

—Jarka M. Burian

# FISCHER, Richard

German industrial and product designer

**Born:** Neumarkt, Oberpfalz, 30 October 1935. **Education:** Educated at Grundschule, 1940-45, and Gymnasium, 1946-51, in Neumarkt; studied mechanical engineering, Berufsschule, Neumarkt, 1952-55; studied product design, Hochschule für Gestaltung, Ulm, Dip., 1959. **Family:** Married Caecilia Ochsenkuhn in 1960; children: Katja and Angela. **Career:** Designer, for BASF chemical firm, Ludwigshafgen, 1959-60, and for Braun AG, Frankfurt, 1960-68; freelance designer, in Offenbach, from 1968; designed for Minox, Canton, Keiper, Demolux, Medium and Company, Coronet-Werke, and others. Instructor and Head of Product Design, Werkkunstschule, Offenbach, 1968-72; Professor of Product Design, Hochschule für Gestaltung, Offenbach, from 1972. **Member:** Verband Deutscher Industrie-Designer. **Honors:** Berliner Kunstpreis Junge Generation, 1965; Design Prize, Zentrum für Produktform, Vienna, 1976; Product Design Awards, Design Center, Stuttgart, 1980. **Address:** Lausitzerstrasse 11, 6050 Offenbach-Burgel, Germany.

## Works

*Sixtant S* mains/battery electric razors, for Braun AG, 1966.
*KM2* range of coffee grinders, blenders, peelers, and juice extractors, for Braun AG, 1966.
*35 EL* 24 x 36mm format camera with flashgun attachments, for Minox, 1975.
*Gamma 800* high-performance receiver, for Canton Elektronik, 1976.
*Dynavit* computer-training equipment, for Keiper, 1976, 1989.
*EC* 9 x 11mm format camera, for Minox, 1977.
*HC 100* home and car compact loudspeaker, for Canton Elektronik, 1977.
*City* flooring and kitchen cleaner, for Coronet Werke, 1983.
*EC-P* pre-amplifier, for Canton Elektronik, 1985.
Computerized calibration equipment for eye glasses and spectacles, for Eyemetrics-Computer Optik, 1987.
Epidiascope projector with integrated carrying case, for Medium and Company, 1988.

## Publications

**By FISCHER: articles**—"Zur Anzeichenfunktion" in *HfG: Bericht 5* (Offenbach), November 1975; "Anzeichenfunktionen" in *HfG: Fachbereich Produktgestaltung* (Offenbach), November 1978; "Formgebung—das Erzeugen einer Produktsprache" in *Konstruktion, Elemente, Methoden* (Leinfelden), October 1981.

**On FISCHER: books**—*1. Deutscher Designertag 1977, Karlsruhe: Design und Designer,* exhibition catalogue, Dusseldorf, 1977; *The Conran Directory of Design* edited by Stephen Bayley, London 1985.

*

The work of the designer, based on my twenty five years of practical experience, presents itself as follows: the designer comes into his own only if he is also a significant member of a team of specialists. In this team, he will be seen as the expert on the appearance of the object—that is, his task will be seen as attending to the object's physical perceptibility. The layman would say that the designer is responsible for the "appeal" of a product, the product's symbolic dimension.

His role, as described here, is in startling contradiction to the usual concept of the designer as coordinator. In my opinion, the designer has to understand and take into consideration a great many of the problems of other disciplines (technology, psychology, sociology, economics), for product appeal rests upon symbolic conversion of the substance of the above-named disciplines. Frequently, the designer will even be entrusted with the complete technical development of simple objects up to the construction of a model. The more areas he can take over from the whole spectrum of development, the more effective and smooth, as well as cost-effective, will be the overall development of a product. But, as these tasks vary from case to case, design becomes an "interdiscipline."

Because the chief task of a designer is to master product appeal, it follows that he must be able not only to interpret meanings which will be transmitted through the object but to realise the essence in his design of the product. By means of product appeal, the consumer can be informed how an object is constructed, how it func-

tions, how to handle it, and whether it is built to last. The consumer can also be reached by appeal to his psychosocial self-image.

Products not only fulfill practical functions but can be the bearers of social symbolism (for example, status symbols) and also of expectations such as warmth, comfort, etc. All this should be conscious, rather than intuitive, on the part of the professional designer: he should be able to articulate his intentions verbally in order to make these perceptions known to his other team colleagues in marketing, sales, development, and production.

—Richard Fischer

# FISHAUF, Louis
Canadian graphic designer

**Born:** Ulm, Germany, 10 July 1949. **Education:** Studied communication and design, Ontario College of Art, Toronto, graduated 1972. **Career:** Junior designer and production artist, Typsettra Ltd., Toronto, 1972-73; associate art director, *Chatelaine* magazine, 1973-77; art director, *The City* magazine, Toronto, 1977-79; art director, *City Woman* magazine, 1980-82; consulting art director, *Saturday Night* magazine, 1982-86; founding partner and creative director, Reactor Art & Design Ltd., Toronto, from 1982. Board of directors, Art Directors Club of Toronto, 1988-92; Graphic Design Advisory Committee, George Brown College, Toronto, 1991-92; board of directors, Worldwide Publishing Consortium, 1994; Technology Committee, CAPIC Digital, 1994-95. **Exhibitions:** *InSpirit '90,* AIGA, Birmingham, Alabama, 1990; *SIGGRAPH 91,* Las Vegas, Nevada, and Pratt Institute, New York, 1991; *30 Posters on the Environment and Technology,* United Nations Environmental Summit, Rio de Janeiro, 1992; *Touch Design U.S.A.,* Tokyo, Japan, 1992; *Digital Masters,* MacWorld Expo, San Francisco California, 1994; *Pixel Pushers,* Vancouver, British Columbia, 1994; *Poster & Computer,* Brno, Czechoslovakia, 1994. **Honors:** 26 Gold and 39 Silver Awards, Art Directors Club of Toronto; Five Gold and Two Silver Awards, National Magazine Awards; Five Awards of Excellence, Graphic Designers of Canada Best of the 80s; First Prize, 1989, and Third Prize, 1990, Anglo Oriental Carpet Design Competition; First Place, Graphic Design, Macintosh Masters Art Competition, 1990; Gold (4), Silver, and Bronze Medals, Special Judges' Award, 1991, and People's Choice Award, 1992, Canadian Computer Graphics Association (CCGA) Art and Design Awards; Les Usherwood Award, Art Directors Club of Toronto, 1991. **Address:** Reactor Art & Design Ltd., 51 Camden Street, Toronto, Ontario M5V 1V2, Canada.

## Works

Retail advertising and in-store promotional campaigns, for Bata footwear chain, 1985-90.
Poster/program/t-shirt graphic, for Toronto Film Festival, 1990.
Signature graphic, for the 1993 Macworld Expositions promotional campaign, 1993.
Cover illustrations for *Design Essentials,* 1992, and *Imaging Essentials,* 1993, for Adobe Press.
Packaging redesign for national beer brand, Molson Canadian Packaging, 1995.
Superheroes stamps, for Canada Post Corporation, 1995

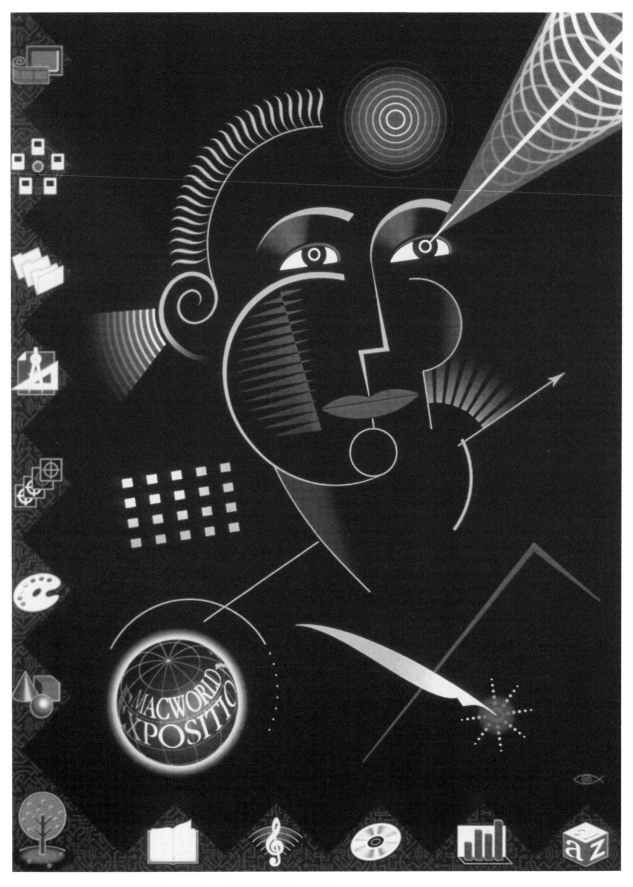

**Louis Fishauf: signature graphic for Macworld Expositions, 1993**

## Publications

**By FISHAUF: articles**—"A Promo Poster: Fun With Computers" in *Step by Step,* January 1990; "Posters" in *How* (United States), September/October 1991.

**On FISHAUF: books**—*Click!* by J. Ellen Gerken, New York, 1990; *Print Casebooks 9: The Best in Covers & Posters* edited by Teresa Reese, New York, 1991; *Directions 1991,* Toronto, 1991; *30 Posters on the Environment and Development* by Felipe Taborda, Rio de Janiero, Brazil, 1992; *Who's Who in Graphic Design* edited by Walter Amstutz, Dubendorf, 1992; *The Mac Design Bible,* Japan, 1993; **articles**—"Profile: Louis Fishauf" by Carol Stevens in *Print* (New York), November/December, 1983; "Reactor" in *Bàt* (France), 1986; "Five On Type" in *Applied Arts* (Canada), Fall 1986; "The Reactor Factor" by David Hayes in *Canadian Business* (Canada), July 1987; "Branching Out" by Mary Yeung in *How* (United States), March/April, 1988; "Reactor Art and Design" by Bruce Hager in *How Business Annual* (United States), 1989; "Reactor Art And Design" by Dennis Mason in *Studio* (Canada), January/February 1990; "The Electronic Canvas" by Celina Bell in *Applied Arts* (Canada), Winter 1990; "Computer Wizardry" by Gordon Graham in *Applied Arts* (Canada), Fall 1990; "Screen Test" by Matthew Rothenberg in *MacWeek* (Canada), 18 December 1990; "Type Set" By Gary Shilling in *EC&I* (Canada), January/February 1991; "Reactor" by Wolfgang Bergmeir in *Novum Gebrauchsgrafik* (Munich), 11 November 1991; "Digital Collage with Photoshop" by Simon Dumenco in *Step by Step Graphics* (United States), January/February 1992; "Poster Design: Adventures In The 4th Dimension" by Clay Andres in *Illustrator Illuminated* (United States), 1992; "Tips, Tricks, & Techniques for Adobe Photoshop" by Linnea Dayton and Jack Davis in *Photoshop Wow Book* (United States), 1993; "Louis Fishauf" by Michael Kaplin in *Communication Arts* (Palo Alto, California), July 1993; "Artist & Artwork: Louis Fishauf" in *MdN* (Japan), March/April 1994; "Portfolio: Louis Fishauf" in *Adobe Magazine* (United States), May/June 1994; "Digital Masters: Totally Digital In Toronto" by Danyll Wills in *IdN* (Hong Kong), July/August 1994.

*

I do not belong to any particular "school" or discipline of design. My work is (I hope) constantly evolving, and is heavily influenced by popular culture, media, and technology. It tends to be visceral rather than intellectual in approach, with an emphasis on bold graphics, primary colors, and direct communication.

I believe that the Digital Revolution has given today's graphic designers the tools to help define the visual syntax of the next millennium, and I look forward to the opportunities that will arise from the convergence of today's media streams into the digital realm.

—Louis Fishauf

\*   \*   \*

Louis Fishauf is a preeminent graphic designer working out of the city of Toronto. Fishauf is less an innovator and more a brilliant translator of new ideas and trends for the mass market. In particular, he has been a key player in transforming avant-garde post-modern—also known as new age—graphic arts into a popular style.

Since graduating from the Ontario College of Art in 1972, Fishauf has brought the post-modern aesthetic to magazine layouts, posters, book covers, T-shirts, advertising packaging, corporate communications, and even postage stamps.

Fishauf began popularizing post-modern eclecticism in the magazine industry. He served as art director for many leading Canadian periodicals, including *Chatelaine,* a Canadian woman's monthly, *T.O.,* a short-lived Toronto lifestyle magazine aimed at the yuppie market, and *Saturday Night,* Canada's oldest and most prestigious commentary magazine.

Versatile and prolific, Fishauf has a great talent for satisfying corporate clients. His designs strike the perfect balance between the anarchical off-beat and the legible mainstream. Typical of the post-modern sensibility, he employs a great variety of visual elements, including illustration, photography, color, texture, and typography, and arranges them into whimsical, anti-classical, flat collage compositions.

In 1982, Fishauf moved into advertising and packaging design when he co-founded Reactor Art & Design Limited, a Toronto-based graphic design agency. This firm provides graphic design and illustration services in Canada and the United States. Fishauf's most commercially recognized design at Reactor is his 1986 retail merchandising for the Toronto Blue Jays baseball team, which illustrates an abstracted linear heroic-realism. His naive pictorial rendition of the four seasons for the 1987 Bata Shoe company's advertising campaign is an award winning design.

Fishauf also is one of the first established graphic designers in North America to embrace the computer as a creative tool with successful results. Since he already utilized photomechanical reproduction methods, joining the digital revolution was easy for him. He began experimenting with the Apple Macintosh computer in 1986 and soon dropped the convention of thumb nail sketches in favor of creating directly on the computer. Software programs like Adobe Illustrator proved ideal, suiting his style of two-dimensional hard-edge layered graphics. Moreover, through the sheer speed of the computer, Fishauf currently is able to juggle the demanding role of Reactor's creative director, as well as designing his own projects.

Fishauf's facility with digital media has made him a favorite of the computer industry. Software companies frequently commission him to design samples using their programs. The purpose is twofold: as an experienced designer he evaluates industry's prototype products, while at the same time he demonstrates to the design community the ease of the new programs with his simple creations. His appropriation of Botticelli's painting *Birth of Venus,* in 1992, as a subject to promote Adobe Illustrator software program is a well known example. That year he also designed the packaging for the software company Alias Research Inc.'s graphic programs Sketch and Upfront.

In 1991 Fishauf won the prestigious Les Usherwood Lifetime Achievement Award sponsored by the Art Directors Club of Toronto.

—Rachel Gotlieb

# FISHER, Jules (Edward)
American stage lighting designer

**Born:** Norristown, Pennsylvania, 12 November 1937. **Education:** Studied at Pennsylvania State University, University Park, 1956;

Carnegie Institute of Technology, Pittsburgh, BFA, 1960. **Career:** Assistant stage manager and carpenter, Valley Forge Music Fair, Devon, Pennsylvania, 1955; assistant electrician, at the Shubert Theater, and Circle in the City, Philadelphia, 1956; worked in stock, then at the 74th Street, Theatre, New York, 1958-59; independent lighting designer, in New York, from 1959. President, Jules Fisher Associates theater consultants, working for Circle in the Square, New York, Deauville Star, Miami, Studio Theatre of Brooklyn Academy of Music, California Institute of Arts, Valencia, WJC-TV Channel 78, Jacksonville Public Television Studio, and C. W. Post College Concert Theatre at University of Greenville, New York, from 1963; president, Jules Fisher and Paul Marantz architectural and lighting design firm, designing for St. Louis Art Museum, Hubert Humphrey Metrodome in Minneapolis, Lake Placid Winter Olympic Stadium, Boston Museum of Fine Arts, New York Grand Hyatt Hotel, and others, from 1971; president, Jules Fisher Enterprises, New York, from 1973. **Honors:** Antoinette Perry (Tony) Award, 1973, 1974, 1978; Drama Desk Award, New York, 1981. **Address:** 126 Fifth Avenue, New York, New York 10011, U.S.A.

## Works

Production lighting designs include—(all New York) *All of the King's Men*, 1959; *West Side Story* (toured), 1960; *Riding Hood Revisited*, 1961; *Red Roses for Me*, 1961; *O Say Can You See*, 1962; *Porgy and Bess*, 1962; *Six Characters in Search of an Author*, 1963; *Spoon River Anthology*, 1963; *The Trojan Women*, 1963; *Enter Laughing*, 1963; *Don Giovanni*, 1963; *The Subject Was Roses*, 1964; *PS I Love You*, 1964; *Half a Sixpence*, 1965; *The Devils*, 1965; *Searjeant Musgrave's Dance*, 1966; *The Threepenny Opera*, 1966; *Little Murders*, 1967; *South Pacific*, 1967; *Iphigenia in Aulis*, 1967; *The Canterbury Tales*, 1968; *Hair*, 1968; *Butterflies are Free*, 1969; *Steambath*, 1970; *Soon*, 1971; *Hamlet*, 1971; *Lenny*, 1971; *Jesus Christ Superstar*, 1971; *Pippin*, 1972; *Mourning Becomes Electra*, 1972; *The Iceman Cometh*, 1973; *Uncle Vanya*, 1973; *Ulysses in Nighttown*, 1974; *Sergeant Pepper's Lonely Hearts Club Band on the Road*, 1974; *Dancin'*, 1978; *Beatlemania*, 1978; *Frankenstein*, 1980; *Rock and Roll: The First 5,000 Years*, 1982; *La Cage aux Folles*, 1983; *The Rink*, 1983; *Big Deal*, 1985; *Song and Dance*, 1986; *Rags*, 1987; *Elvis*, 1988; *Legs Diamond*, 1988.

## Publications

**On FISHER: books**—*The Art of Stage Lighting* by Frederick Bentham, London, 1968, 1980.

*

Lighting design has been my craft and profession for twenty five years. It continues to give me rewards as I strive to improve my work. The primary sense of satisfaction comes from witnessing my contribution to the elucidation of the drama by using light to make each moment within the drama better express the intentions of the playwright and the directors; aiding the actor in his performance by providing an environment, a motivation, and an atmosphere in the space he or she inhabits; and assisting the audience to see, through a command of the variables of the light that affect the eye and the brain. The joy in my work has been the process of attempting to fulfill these goals.

As to a future goal, I would hope that improvements in the technical propagation and control of light, paralleled by my own continuing growth and maturity as a craftsperson, will bring about the ability to infinitely mold and sculpt the lightspace to the greatest artistic end.

—Jules Fisher

*   *   *

Jules Fisher developed an attraction to lighting design as a youth. After some initial exposure to theatre in high school, Fisher became involved as a stage manager, carpenter, and assistant electrician in summer stock and local Philadelphia area theatres. His work on three New York musical touring productions that played in the Shubert in Philadelphia led to his becoming lighting designer for three productions at the Circle in the City Theatre there. By the time Fisher received his B.F.A. from the Carnegie Institute for Technology in 1960, he was already designing shows in New York at several Off-Broadway theatres. Unlike other young designers who go to New York City to build a career, Fisher never interned with a major lighting designer. Instead, he forged his training out of practical experience, working on production after production.

His first New York show was *All of the King's Men* (1959). It was during this early stage of his career that he developed the basic tenets of his approach to lighting design. Primarily, Fisher believes that a show "must move an audience emotionally," and he sees the role of the lighting designer as serving that purpose. According to Fisher, the lighting designer must work with a director from the beginning of the production process. The designer must create a plan that supports the whole production by enhancing the director's and playwright's intention. Fisher enjoys working with directors who can easily transmit their ideas to him. Among his favorite directors are the late Bob Fosse, Mike Nichols, and Tom O'Horgan.

Fisher's lighting designs for plays indicate his eclectic tastes. One of Fisher's earliest achievements and one of his favorites, *Spoon River Anthology* (1963), not only insured his continuing career, but also manifested his simple, economic approach to the craft of lighting. Working with Charles Aidman, who adapted the material and staged it, Fisher created lighting that illuminated the performers without calling attention to itself. The small cast performed a series of monologues on a stage that was sparsely decorated with four rough-hewn benches, a lectern, and two chairs, all of which was illuminated against a blue background. By using different combinations of light from the top, sides, back, and front, each monologue was uniquely lit to suit the material.

Fisher's subsequent lighting designs for such successful plays as *Enter Laughing* (1963), *Butterflies Are Free* (1969), *Mourning Becomes Electra* (1972), and *Uncle Vanya* (1973) revealed this same straightforward approach to his craft. In *Uncle Vanya*, directed by Mike Nichols at the Circle in the Square Theatre, Fisher's design "illuminated" not only the stage, but the story through subtle shifts in color and intensity. As the show progressed, these slight changes in lighting helped to create the moods and focus necessary to motivate the characters' ultimate realization of the inevitability of life passing. Fisher is very aware that "lighting is constantly in motion in a show," and he uses this kinetic capability to support the transformations that occur through the course of a production.

In contrast to his designs for the lighting of many successful plays, he was also involved with the rock musicals *Hair* (1968) and *Jesus Christ Superstar* (1971). These productions displayed a more sophisticated and provocative application of theatrical lighting. *Hair* incorporated one of the earliest uses on Broadway of lighting, with bold, deep, saturated colors that shifted and pulsated in time to the music. This is the same presentational technique that is used in rock and roll concerts, and unlike traditional lighting practice in which shifts are logically placed to coincide with the values in a scene. The lighting for *Jesus Christ Superstar* was equally daring. Heralded as a "masterpiece of engineering and design" by one critic, Fisher's design employed highly placed backlights which shone brilliantly on the heads and shoulders of the performers who walked on set designer Robin Wagner's steeply raked stage floor. In the London version, Fisher installed multi-colored fluorescent tube lights behind plexiglass panels in the raked floor which would flash and change, similar to those in discotheques. Subsequently, his interest in rock and roll show lighting led to his becoming production supervisor for the *Rolling Stones* tour of the United States in 1975.

Fisher believes in closely coordinating his work with that of the set designer. Working with Tony Walton, who designed the scenography for *Pippin* (1972), he created much more than a workable lighting design. From the opening musical number in *Pippin,* in which only the performer's white-gloved hands were visible against a black void, through the big, splashy production numbers, to the end of the show where only a work light on a bare stage was seen, Fisher's lighting insinuated itself in an organic manner and became more than mere illumination. In itself it was metaphorical, and integral to the scenic values of the production.

In *Pippin* and his other work for director Bob Fosse, Fisher showed his amazing ability to theatrically light dancers' moving bodies. In *Chicago* (1975), and *Dancin'* (1978), Fisher's talent for lighting the dancing form was duly noted by the critics. In the *New York Times* review for *Dancin',* Richard Eder stated that Fisher's lighting "is integrated into Mr. Fosses's precise and stylish rhythms." Ted Kalem, of *Time Magazine,* commented about the same show that "Fisher's lighting, like the hand of a master painter, seems to turn those same bodies into efflorescent still lifes even when they are in dynamic motion." Fisher has employed this same talent in musical shows that Fosse did not direct, such as *Ulysses in Nighttown* (1974), for which he won a Tony Award, and *La Cage Aux Folles* (1983). About the latter, Clive Barnes wrote in the *New York Post* that Fisher's lighting, "a flashy flash-load of light, provides the show with its special fashion."

Fisher keeps busy not only with lighting design, but with several other activities related to theatre. He has co-produced such shows as *Lenny* (1971), *Dancin'* (1978), *Rock and Roll, The First 5,000 Years* (1982), *The Rink* (1983), *Big Deal* (1985), and *Elvis* (1988), for which he co-designed the lights and acted as production supervisor/director. As a theatre building consultant, Fisher has worked on such major performance and entertainment spaces as the Brooklyn Academy of Music, Circle in the Square Theatre, and New York's Palladium Night Club. He is very aware of the dangers inherent in theatre design. He considers it a problem when architects do not consider that the function of a theatre is to provide people with an emotional experience. They may approach theatre design as merely an opportunity to make a "visual statement." Fisher counters this limited approach by affirming that "sometimes a good building for theatre is less dramatic architecturally."

Fisher strives to improve his craft as a designer. He does not want to develop a recognizable style, but wants each of his lighting designs to serve the needs of the various productions. Throughout his career, he has been attracted to the use of film in theatre, influenced by the Czech designer Josef Svoboda. *Beatlemania, Rock and Roll, The First 5,000 Years,* and *Elvis* have featured live actors and film projections to create what Fisher refers to as a "three-dimen-

sional experience on a two-dimensional plane." Very much concerned with the future of lighting technology, he believes that through developments in stage lighting the lighting designer will more effectively serve the artistic intentions of the playwright, director, performer, and ultimately, the audience.

—Tom Mikotowicz

# FLECKHAUS, Willy

German book, magazine, poster and graphic designer

**Born:** Velbert, 21 December 1925. **Family:** Married Ursula Thonnisen in 1951; four children. **Career:** Freelance graphic designer, working for Westdeutscher Rundfunk radio, Cologne municipal theatres, the Munich Olympics, and others; art director, *Twen* magazine, Cologne and Munich, 1959-70; art editor, Suhrkamp Verlag book publishers, Frankfurt; art director, *Frankfurter Allgemeine Zeitung* newspaper, Frankfurt. Professor, at University of Wuppertal, Gesamthochschule of the University of Essen, and the Folkwangschule, Essen; founder-director of the Tuscany Summer School. President, Art Directors Club of Germany, 1972-73. **Exhibitions:** Stadtmuseum, Munich, 1995. **Honors:** Culture Prize, Deutsche Gesellschaft fur Photography, Cologne; Gold Medal, Art Directors Club of Germany; Hall of Fame Award, Art Directors Club of New York, 1987. **Died:** 12 September, 1983.

## Works

Books designed (for Suhrkamp Verlag) include—*Der Schatten des Korpers des Kutches* (P. Weiss), 1960, *Stucke 1/11* (M. Frische), 1962; *Materialen zu Weiss' Marat/Sade,* 1967; *Holderlin: Ein Chronik in Text und Bild,* 1970; *Mein Gamili* (R. Wolf), 1971; *Der Kurze Brief zum Langen Abscheid* (P. Handke), 1972; *Grunverschlossene Botschaft* (H. Atmann), 1972; *Polaris,* 1973; *Philosophische Terminologie* (T. Adorno), 1973; *Herman Hesse: Leben und Werk im Bild,* 1973; *Kinder und Hausmachen* (Grimm), 1974; *Tartarin von Tarasca* (A. Daudet), 1974; *Die Grossen Detektive,* 1975; *Reineke Fuchs* (J. Goethe), 1975.

## Publications

**On FLECKHAUS: books**—*Magazine Design* by Ruari McLean, London and New York, 1969; *Graphis Record Covers* edited by Walter Herdeg, Zurich, 1974; *Der Marianbader Korb: Uber di Buchgestaltung im Suhrkamp Verlag* by Siegfried Unseld, Hamburg, 1976; **articles**— in *Graphis* (Zurich), May/June 1987; *Idea* (Tokyo), March 1988.

# FLEMING, Allan Robb

Canadian typographic, book, and graphic designer

**Born:** Toronto, 7 May 1929. **Education:** Studied advertising art, Western Technical School, Toronto, 1943-46. **Family:** Married Nancy Chisholm in 1951; children: Martha, Peter, and Susannah.

**Career:** Design assistant, T. Eaton Company, Toronto, 1946-49, Aiken McCracken advertising agency, 1949-51, and the Art and Design Service, 1951-53; freelance designer, London, 1953-54; designer, John Tait and Partners, London, 1954-55; freelance designer, Toronto, 1955-57; vice-president and creative director, Cooper and Beatty typographers, Toronto, 1957-62; art director, *Maclean's* magazine, Toronto, 1962-63; vice-president and creative chief, MacLaren Advertising Company, Toronto, 1963-68; chief designer, University of Toronto Press, 1968-77; associate, Burton Kramer Associates, Toronto, 1973-76, and Burns, Cooper, Donahue, Fleming and Company, Toronto, 1976-77. Instructor in typographic design, Ontario College of Art, Toronto, 1956-60 and 1977. **Exhibitions:** Gallery of Contemporary Art, Toronto, 1958; *Printing for Commerce,* American Institute of Graphic Arts, New York, 1959; Vancouver Art Gallery, 1976 (toured). **Died:** Toronto, 31 December 1977.

**Publications**

**On FLEMING: books**—*Packaging: An International Survey of Package Design,* edited by Walter Herdeg, Zurich, 1959; *Who's Who in Graphic Art* edited by Walter Amstutz, Zurich, 1962; **articles**—*Canadian Art* (Ottawa), November, 1959; *Industrial Design* (New York), July, 1961; *Domus* (Milan), June, 1962; *Vanguard* (Vancouver), September 1976; *Saturday Night* (Toronto), November 11, 1976; *The Canadian* (Toronto), August 6, 1977; *Graphis* (Zurich), no. 34., 1978.

\*    \*    \*

As an advertising designer, Allan Fleming left scraps of his philosophy behind in writings. Most of his ads, though, were ephemeral, and of his renowned presentations to clients, we also have no record. As a trademark and logo designer, however, he left a legacy that is still very much alive. His CN logo, for instance, has not become dated after almost twenty-five years of use. Its smooth, controlled shape, its feeling of unity, and its metaphorical suggestion of linked railway cars seen from the air, still work well. His 1965 logo for Ontario Hydro uses the "O" and "H" from the company name only as starting points. The letters are shaped and combined to form an electrical plug (with the stems of the "H" as its prongs). The letter forms tend to disappear so that the logo becomes a symbol in its own right, as was generally Fleming's method; he usually manipulated essential typographical elements to form a symbol, often involving a metaphor.

Fleming was primarily a book designer during the last ten years of his life. He produced many high-quality works, which earned him a reputation in the more erudite, esoteric strata of Canadian society. His work was highly effective. His 1962 redesign of *Maclean's* (a new national magazine), for example, caused its newsstand circulation to more than double.

Fleming's influence has not been so much a stylistic one as it has been an example to younger designers of professionalism and inventive originality. Often regarded as having helped graphic design in Canada to come of age, he helped to establish the field as a respected one in Canada during a time when illustration was popularly considered to be the only commercial "art." Perhaps his most notable public recognition came in the 1976 twenty-year retrospective exhibition of his work organized by the Vancouver Art Gallery and circulated to other provinces.

He was a unique designer, not adhering to any one approach or school. Some have credited him with creating a distinctively Canadian style in his work. This may be a specious tack, but certainly Fleming's fresh, resolved look in trademark and logo design did a great deal to inspire young designers and to elevate the quality of work in what now can be seen as Canada's formative years in design.

—Liz Wylie

# FLETCHER, Alan (Gerard)
British graphic, packaging, book, and typographic designer

**Born:** Of British parents, in Nairobi, Kenya, 27 September 1931. **Education:** Christ's Hospital School, Horsham, Sussex, 1941-48; Central School of Arts and Crafts, London, 1950-51; Royal College of Art, London, ARCA, 1956; Yale University, New Haven, Connecticut, MFA, 1957. **Family:** Married Paola Biagi in 1956; children: Raffaella. **Career:** Worked at Berlitz language school, Spain, 1952-53; assistant to typographer Herbert Spencer, London, 1956; designer, Container Corporation of America, Chicago, 1957, and *Fortune* magazine and Time-Life Inc., New York, 1957-59; consultant art director, Time-Life International, London, 1959-64; freelance designer, London, 1959-62; founder-partner, with Colin Forbes and Bob Gill, of Fletcher/Forbes/Gill design firm, London, 1962-65; founder-partner, with Theo Crosby and Colin Forbes, of Crosby/Fletcher/Forbes design firm, London, 1965-72; founder-partner, with Theo Crosby, Colin Forbes, Kenneth Grange, and Mervyn Kurlansky, of Pentagram Design partnership, London and New York, from 1972. President, Designers and Art Directors Association, London, 1973, and Alliance Graphique Internationale, Paris, 1982-84. Visiting Lecturer, Yale University, New Haven, Connecticut, 1979. **Exhibitions:** *Graphic Design: London Group,* London, 1960; *International Poster Biennale,* Warsaw, 1966; *107 Grafici dell'AGI,* Castello Sforzesco, Milan, 1974; *Eye for Industry,* Victoria and Albert Museum, London, 1986; *Pentagram's Portfolio,* ITC Center, New York, 1986. **Collections:** Stedelijk Museum, Amsterdam; Museum of Modern Art, New York. **Honors:** Federation of British Industries Fellowship, 1956; fellow, Society of Industrial Artists and Designers (now Chartered Society of Designers), 1964; Royal Designer for Industry, Royal Society of Arts, London, 1972; One Show Gold Award, New York, 1974; Gold Award, 1974, and President's Award, 1977, Designers and Art Directors Association, London; Medal, Society of Industrial Artists and Designers, London, 1982; senior fellow, Royal College of Art, London, 1989. **Address:** Pentagram Design, 11 Needham Road, London W11 2RP, England.

**Works**

Packaging, for the Container Corporation of America, Chicago, 1959.
Promotional graphics, for *Fortune* magazine, New York, 1959.
Promotional graphics (articulated symbol), for Pirelli, Milan, 1972.
Poster and calendars, for Olivetti, Milan, 1973.
Logotype and corporate identity, for Reuters international news agency, 1973.
Mural, for Kodak, Harrow, Middlesex, 1975.

Logotype and corporate identity, for the Commercial Bank of Kuwait, 1980.
Signage programme, for IBM Europe headquarters building, Paris, 1983.
Signage programme, for Lloyd's of London building, 1984.
Corporate identity, for Mandarin Oriental Hotel Group, Hong Kong, 1985.
Logotype and corporate identity, for Lloyd's of London, 1986.
Design consultancy programme, for OUN Corporation, Tokyo, 1987.
Symbol and signage programme, for the Victoria and Albert Museum, London, 1988.

## Publications

**By FLETCHER: books**—(with Colin Forbes and Bob Gill) *Graphic Design: Visual Comparisons,* London, 1963; *Was ich Sah,* Hamburg, 1967; (with Theo Crosby and Colin Forbes) *A Sign Systems Manual,* London, 1970; (with Germano Facetti) *Identity Kits: A Pictorial Survey of Visual Arts,* London, 1971; (with Pentagram partners) *Pentagram: The Work of Five Designers,* London, 1972; (editor, with Edward Booth Clibborn) *Design and Art Direction 74,* London, 1974; (with Pentagram partners) *Living By Design,* London, 1978; (with Pentagram partners) *Ideas on Design,* London, 1986.

**On FLETCHER: books**—*Who's Who in Graphic Art* edited by Walter Amstutz, Zurich, 1962, Dubendorf, 1982; *Signs in Action* by James Sutton, London and New York, 1965; *Graphic Design Britain* edited by Fredrick Lambert, London, 1967; *History of the Poster* by Josef and Shizuko Muller-Brockmann, Zurich, 1971; *107 Grafici dell'AGI,* exhibition catalogue with texts by Renzo Zorzi and Franco Grignani, Venice, 1974; *Top Graphic Design* edited by F. H. K. Henrion, Zurich, 1983; *The Conran Directory of Design* edited by Stephen Bayley, London, 1985; *Eye for Industry: Royal Designers for Industry 1936-1986,* exhibition catalogue by Fiona MacCarthy and Patrick Nuttgens, London, 1986.

*       *       *

In his work with Pentagram, Alan Fletcher demonstrated the value of the designer who is integrated into a total design practice. His enterprise in typography and in packaging, for example, brings together two aspects of design which in practice have to be closely related. The range of work handled by Pentagram spreads from letterheads to interior design, from product design to posters. The solutions arrived at by analysing the problems set by one commission are shared by the group and give an extra dimension to work of the organization as a whole.

Fletcher has brought to the group his own talent as a graphic designer but also his sense of the place for good design in society itself. For example, he is associated with a number of designs that are dependent on their location in the street to bring them to life. These include the long poster for Pirelli that stretched along the side of double-decker buses in London. Appearing just below the upper windows, it supplied the legs and feet of the actual passengers whose profiles appeared in the windows above, thereby creating a graphic joke that incorporated the daily lives of the people who became a living part of Fletcher's design.

In other ways, his designs have become a familiar part of the lives of Londoners and have brought to areas previously dominated by

the decorations of the untutored popular design—the cafe or shop—the sophistication and humour of a professional designer. The impeccable standards required of first-rate designers prompted many of their number in the 1950s and 1960s to treat their discipline lightly and turn away from purer aspects of refined design to bring their talents into the marketplace. Fletcher, unlike many of his contemporaries, has achieved this feat not by changing his style or employing the shock tactics of the surrealists but by maintaining clear design standards and giving his work enough social relevance that his design fits naturally into the surroundings of everyday life.

—John Barnicoat

# FLUEVOG, John

Canadian shoe designer

**Born:** Vancouver, British Columbia, 15 May 1948. **Education:** Graduated from Burnaby South High School, Vancouver. **Family:** Married to second wife, Ingrid; children: Jonathan, Adrian, Britta. **Career:** Shoemaker, Shepherd Shoes, Vancouver, 1969-70; partner, with Peter Fox, Fox and Fluevog Shoes, with stores in Vancouver, Victoria, and Edmonton, 1970-80; founder, John Fluevog Shoes, with stores in Vancouver, Toronto, Seattle, Boston, New York, from 1980. Sponsor, John Fluevog Shoe Contest, *Sassy* magazine, from c. 1993. **Addresses:** (headquarters) 852 Granville Street, Vancouver, British Columbia, Canada; 104 Prince St., New York, New York 10012, U.S.A.; 302 Newbury St., Boston, Massachusetts 02115, U.S.A.

## Publications

**On FLUEVOG: articles**—"Shoe Designer Succeeds by Creating Style with Sole" in *Portland Press Herald* (Oregon), 9 January 1991; "The Godfather of Sole" in *Western Living,* April 1992; "Prince of New York" in *Footwear News* (New York), 30 November 1992; "Anarchy Underfoot" in *Seattle Times* (Washington), 3 March 1993; "Sole Man" in *Flare,* November 1993; "A Really, Really Big Shoe" in *Saturday Night* (Toronto), March 1994.

*       *       *

A designer of outrageous men's and women's shoes, John Fluevog is best known for the splay-heeled platforms that have been made popular by pop singers Lady Miss Keir, Madonna, and Paula Abdul. His collections also feature an eclectic mix of styles, from high-heeled sneakers to wooden clogs.

Fluevog grew up behind his father's Luxury Freeze drive-in dairy bar in the 1960s, in Vancouver, Canada. While working at Sheppard Shoes selling conventional wingtips, Fluevog met Peter Fox, and in 1970 the two opened a shoe store in Vancouver's bohemian Gastown district. This funky shop virtually defined 1970s footwear; the wildly colored, over-the-knee platform boots for men designed by Fox and Fluevog placed them at the forefront of the more feminine or "unisex" trend in men's fashion. "We didn't know what we had back then," recalls Fluevog. "We had no idea that there were no other stores like that in the world—absolutely none!"

In 1980, Fluevog bought out Fox, who continued to make a different kind of shoe, and continued to run the Gastown store. By 1986, Fluevog had opened his first store under his own name in Seattle. Capitalizing on the burgeoning contemporary music scene in Seattle, Fluevog funked up the classic Doc Marten boot, adding color and extreme treads to appeal to the "grunge" crowd. "Grunge" was the pop music trend, personified by the band Nirvana, that attracted the world's attention to the Seattle music scene in 1990.

Fluevog's outrageous take on the 1970s platform shoe caught the attention of the avant-garde fashion world in 1990. Wearing Fluevog's orange patent leather platforms in one of her first music videos, Lady Miss Keir of the techno-pop group Deee-lite attracted as much attention for her shoes as for her music. Not to be left behind, established pop music celebrities Madonna and Paula Abdul quickly donned "Fluevogs."

Soon after, innovative fashion designer Anna Sui used Fluevog's platforms in her runway shows, even commissioning green-and-yellow checked sandals to be worn with a full-skirted mini-dress of the same fabric. In 1991, Fluevog sold 70,000 pairs of shoes, prompting *Entertainment Weekly* to name him one of the "sixteen style makers who dare push the envelope—the innovators who will change the face of fashion."

Fluevog's mail-order catalogue has made the Fluevog vision available beyond his retail stores. Started in the mid 1980s, this wacky piece of infotainment innocently combines marketing with philosophy and humor. Early editions were illustrated by Fluevog; later issues featured full-color photography. The subject matter ranges from a Sole Food Cookbook to a Sin Test which correlates customer loyalty with character. If you have a low Sin Score, Fluevog predicts, "Your life is in apple-pie order and you call your mother on a regular basis... Of course, you already own numerous pairs of Fluevogs and plan to buy many more at the earliest opportunity." Inversely, a high Sin Score indicates that "You are some scum. No, we don't want a hit of crack. Get your hand off my knee... You will never be Fluevog material. Be gone, vile cur, and never darken our doorstep again."

In contrast to the rebellious youth who are his customers, Fluevog is a church-going husband and a father of three. He tithes ten percent of his earnings to charity, answers all of his fan mail, and owns only one pair of shoes at a time. He admits that sometimes "I'm not very impressed by those kids wearing my shoes and maybe that's why I do my catalogues the way I do. I want to express some ethics, some moral guidelines. To let them know that there's more to my shoes—and more to life—than being cool."

—Elizabeth Crawford

# FOLON, Jean-Michel

Belgian cartoonist, painter, illustrator, stage, and graphic designer

**Born:** Uccle-Brussels, 1 March 1934. **Education:** Studied at the Ecole Supérieure d'Architecture de la Cambre, Brussels; mainly self-taught in painting and design. **Career:** Freelance painter and designer in Paris, from 1956; designed graphics for the magazines *Holiday, Fortune, Time, Graphis, New Yorker, L'Express,* and *Le Nouvel Observateur,* murals for the Brussels Metro and Waterloo Rail Station, London, as well as numerous graphics for books, stage,

and film. **Exhibitions:** Librairie Le Palimugre, Paris, 1966; Galerie de France, Paris, 1968; Lefebre Gallery, New York, 1969, 1972, 1978, 1980, 1982; Musée des Art Décoratifs, Paris, 1971; Palais de Beaux-Arts, Charleroi, Belgium, 1971; Arts Club of Chicago, 1972; Palais des Beaux Arts, Brussels, 1975; Deutsches Plakat-Museum, Essen, 1976; Museum Boymans van Beuningen, Rotterdam, 1976; Institute of Contemporary Arts, London, 1977, Musée d'Art Moderne, Liége, 1978; Centre d'Action Culturelle, Saint Brieuc, 1980; Musée de la Poste, Paris, 1982. **Honors:** Grand Prix, Triennale of Honour in Art, Italy, 1965; Art Directors Club of New York Award, 1966; Grand Prix, Bienal of Sao Paulo, 1973. **Address:** Burcy, 77890 Beaumont-du-Gatinais, France.

## Publications

**By FOLON: books**—*Le Message: Dessins de Folon,* Paris, 1967, 1974; *La Mort d'un Arbre,* Paris, 1974; *Les Ruins Circulaires,* portfolio with text by Jorge Luis Borges, Monte Carlo, 1974; *Lettres à Giorgio 1967-1975,* Geneva, 1976; *Affiches de Folon,* with text by Milton Glaser, Paris, New York and Milan, 1978; *Le Regard du temoin,* Paris, 1979; (with Milton Glaser) *The Conversation,* New York, 1983.

**On FOLON: books**—*Film and TV Graphics* edited by Walter Herdeg, Zurich, 1967; *Folon,* exhibition catalogue with text by Francois Mathey, New York, 1969; *Modern Graphics* by Keith Murgatroyd, London, 1969; *Graphic Designers in Europe-1* edited by Henri Hillebrand, London, 1971; *Jean-Michel Folon,* exhibition catalogue with text by Francois Mathey, Paris, 1971; *Monografie des Plakats: Entwicklung, Stil, Design* by Herbert Schindler, Munich, 1972; *Vue Imprenable* by Giorgio Soavi, Paris, 1974; *Folon,* exhibition catalogue with text by Andre Fermigier, Geneva, 1975; *Who's Who in Graphic Art* edited by Walter Amstutz, Dubendorf, 1982.

*       *       *

Jean-Michel Folon's great popularity has its source in the topicality of his vision. He is able—as few can—to express the taste and bitterness of our times in a concise and almost childishly simple manner. As a result of his ability to perceive the half-conceived ideas, worries, and goals by which people live, the speed with which these are transferred into the iconosphere, Folon's drawings rank as symbols of our Zeitgeist. The famous Japanese critic, Masaru Katsumie, called Folon a "peintre moraliste," while his philosophical stance suggests to him analogies of the French thinker "What do I know?."

His first trip to New York in 1967 left a strong imprint on the artist. Here he met the absurd heights of a city—Moloch, cut by cement canyons, a city in which instead of trees grow thickets of signposts, like walls of green in impassible tropical forests. A lonely, tortured, little man gives in to their hypnotic operations. Like the Biblical wife of Lot, he, too, transforms himself into a directional arrow, which grows out in every direction and forms a finely wrought arabesque, a jumble of lines obligatorily ending in the point of an arrow. Another critic, Dino Buzzati, says that the metropolises pictured in Folon's drawings are kingdoms of alienation where man is reduced to the status of a robot:

A nightmare? yes, definitely. But thanks to the heavens, an artist who does not translate the horrible alienation into despairing masks or moans of agony.... With an inexhaustible eruption of stylistic discoveries, qualitatively not inferior to Steinberg, Folon laughs at it or at least smiles at it, while transforming the nightmare into a stupefying, vertiginous, hallucinating, megalopolitan ballet.

Buzzati also emphasizes the poetry of Folon's imagination. Michel Ragon does the same thing in his book about urbanism of the future, *La Cité de l'an 2000,* which includes a series of the artist's drawings. One of them represents a monotonous panorama of uniform buildings, but at a certain spot there is an open window and in it, a flowerpot, from which a lonely little branch climbs into the distant space.

Folon studied architecture in Brussels, he dropped it for the craft of drawing, which he pursues with mastery. From the beginning of his career, he worked out a style of his own (some critics see in his work Paul Klee's influence), characterized by a simple designer's line. Ignoring the evolution of contemporary drawing, he does not change it. He began with little pictures, but with time, passed on to large formats, which he continues to execute precisely with pen or brush. Thanks to a transparent facture, the colorful, well-saturated surfaces create the impression of a light, ethereal material. Their open quality reduces the drawings' graphic hardness and softens their dramatic expression. In these luminous, colorful drawings/reflections, Folon dispels the contemporary electronic and computerized world.

—Szymon Bojko

# FORBES, Colin

British graphic and typographic designer

**Born:** London, 6 March 1928. **Education:** Educated at Sir Anthony Browne's School, Brentwood, Essex; studied graphic design, Central School of Arts and Crafts, London. **Family:** Married Wendy Schneider in 1967: 3 children. **Career:** Assistant to typographer Herbert Spencer, London, 1952; freelance designer, London, 1953-57; art director, Stuart Advertising agency, London, 1957-58; freelance designer, London, 1961-62; founder-partner, with Alan Fletcher and Bob Gill, of Fletcher/Forbes/Gill design firm, London, 1962-65, with Theo Crosby and Alan Fletcher, of Crosby/Fletcher/Forbes design firm, London, 1965-72, and with Theo Crosby, Alan Fletcher, Kenneth Grange and Mervyn Kurlansky, Pentagram Design partnership, London and New York, from 1972. Lecturer, 1953-57, and Head of Graphic Design, 1958-61, Central School of Arts and Crafts, London. International President, Alliance Graphique Internationale, 1976-79; Vice-President, American Institute of Graphic Arts, from 1981; Chairman, Stanford Design Forum, California, 1988. **Member:** Designers and Art Directors Association, London. **Exhibitions:** *International Poster Biennale,* Warsaw, 1966; *Kinetics,* Hayward Gallery, London, 1970; *107 Grafici dell'AGI,* Castello Sforzesco, Milan, 1974. **Address:** Pentagram Design, 212 Fifth Avenue, New York, 10010, U.S.A.

## Works

Conference signage, for the Zinc Development Association, 1966.
Posters, for Pirelli Tyres, 1966-69.

Campaign poster against museum admission charges, 1970.
Corporate identity programme, for Lucas Industries, 1972-76.
Re-design and consultancy, for *Interiors* magazine, New York, 1982-83.
Logotype, for Nissan, 1984.
Publications designs, for Drexel Burham Lambert, 1986.
Charitable contributions campaign, for IBM, 1987.
NFL catalogue, for USA National Football League, 1989.

## Publications

**By FORBES: books**—(with Alan Fletcher and Bob Gill) *Graphic Design: Visual Comparisons,* London, 1963; (with Alan Fletcher and Theo Crosby) *A Sign Systems Manual,* London, 1970; (co-author) *Creativity and Communication,* London, 1971; (with Pentagram partners) *Pentagram: The Work of Five Designers,* London, 1972; (co-author) *New Alphabets: A to Z,* London, 1973; (with Pentagram partners) *Living By Design,* London, 1978; (with Pentagram partners) *Ideas on Design,* London, 1986.

**On FORBES: books**—*Lettering Today: A Survey and Reference Book* edited by John Brinkley, London, 1964; *Signs in Action* by James Sutton, London and New York, 1965; *Graphic Design Britain* edited by Frederick Lambert, London, 1967; *History of the Poster* by Josef and Shizuko Muller-Brockmann, Zurich, 1971; *107 Graficidell'AGI,* exhibition catalogue with texts by Renzo Zorzi and Franco Grignani, Venice, 1974; *Who's Who in Graphic Art* edited by Walter Amstutz, Dubendorf, 1982.

*       *       *

The one constant in the work of British graphic designer Colin Forbes is the high quality of design. He believes a visual problem has an infinite variety of solutions, and that many are valid. Just as there are an infinite variety of design solutions, Forbes has used an infinite variety of styles in his work.

Working as a freelance designer in London, Forbes joined Alan Fletcher and Robert Gill in the firm Fletcher, Forbes, Gill in 1962. The firm became Crosby, Fletcher, Forbes in 1965 when architect Theo Crosby replaced Gill in the firm. This group helped define British design of the 1960s. It was not the clean, cool design of the Swiss, nor the expressionist work known in America, but was based on irony, wit, and humor. In 1972, the firm became known as Pentagram because additional designers joined the group, and they chose not to just add names to the list.

Forbes' specialty in the Pentagram design group is graphic and typography design, working on corporate identity programs, packaging, book design, and advertising art. Because the persuasive element of communication art responds to fashion and obsolescence, there is not one unified style or philosophy of design evident in Forbes' work. The design solution emerges from the requirements of the individual problem as determined by the client, the purpose, the longevity of the project, the audience, and the cost. Self-expression does not enter into Forbes' design solution. He practices the craft of design.

A change of wording and signatures on a petition being circulated among the populace became a memorable poster designed by Forbes against museum charges in Britain. Forbes used the male-female version of the number 6 as the logotype for the Pressure Die Casting Conference held in 1966. In 1983, Forbes chose a post-modern design as the graphic solution for Designer's Saturday, a showcase of ideas for members of the professional design community. He utilized a serif typeface with classic geometric elements employed in a three-dimensional manner, combining historical elements with contemporary design vocabulary. Pastel coloring was introduced in the printed materials.

Because of his current position as leader of the major design group, Pentagram, and his affiliation with professional design organizations, Forbes is instrumental in influencing current design trends. Throughout his career Forbes has incorporated new technologies and new design fashions into his work without developing a defined style. Forbes the designer is anonymous, while his work is known. He knows that there are a multiplicity of valid solutions to any design problem. Design is not just a business for Forbes, but a way of life.

—Nancy House

# FOSSELLA, Gregory

American industrial, interior, exhibition, and corporate designer

**Born:** Brockton, Massachusetts, 26 August 1933. **Education:** Studied at the Rhode Island School of Design, Providence, BFA, 1957. **Military Service:** Served in the United States Army, 1953, Corporal. **Family:** Married Janet Ostberg in 1963 (divorced); children: Craig, Dean, and Nicole. **Career:** Founder-President, Gregory Fossella Associates industrial design consultancy, Boston, from 1960; has designed for Acoustic Research, American Optical, Anchor Hocking, Armstrong, Black and Decker, Bristol-Meyers, Colgate-Palmolive, Corning, Data General, Exxon, Ford Motor Company, General Electric, General Motors, Hughes Aircraft, ProctorSilex, Sears Roebuck, Western Electric, Xerox, and others. **Member:** Board Member, 1957, and Trustee and College Council Member, from 1980, Rhode Island School of Design, Providence; Industrial Designers Society of America. **Honors:** Merit Award, 1965, and Award of Excellence, 1987, Industrial Designers Society of America; Industrial Design Annual Review Award, New York, 1965, 1968, 1969, 1970, 1972, 1973, 1975; Award of Excellence, 1968, 1970, Silver and Merit Awards, 1975, Art Directors Club of Boston; Merit Award, Art Directors Club of New York, 1968, 1973; United States Government Best in US Design Award, 1969; Communication Arts Award of Excellence, 1973; Packaging Design Award of Excellence, 1973, 1974; *Fortune* Magazine Best 25 Products Award, 1975; Governor's Award, Design Michigan, 1975; Francis Hatch Award, 1975, 1980; Print Casebook Design Excellence Award, 1979; Hardware Industry Merit Award, 1979; IDEA Prize, 1987. **Address:** 97 Main Street, Box 838, Osterville, Massachusetts 02655, U.S.A.

## Works

*MPD* gas pump, for Gilbarco, 1980.
Textile equipment, for Leesona, 1980.
Fishing reel, for Ryobi, 1980.
*S-Serve* incubators, for GCA, 1980.
*CNC Control,* for Cincinnati Milocron, 1981.

*X-15* pitchers, for Aladdin, 1981.
*400 Series* matrix printer and robotic systems, for General Electric, 1981.
*500D* helicopter, for Hughes Aircraft, 1981.
Detergent container, for Colgate, 1981.
*Magic Score* module and bowling center, for AMF, 1982.
Emergency response center, for Life Time Products, 1982.
Modular printer, for Dennison, 1982.
*Sprint CPU,* for Four Phase, 1982.
Executive terminal, for Exxon, 1983.
Pen set, for Sheaffer, 1983.
Fireplace insert, for AOC, 1983.
Oil container, for Penzoil, 1984.
Airline ticket printer, for Data Products, 1987.
Audio loudspeakers and component range, for Teledyne AR, 1987.

## Publications

**On FOSSELLA: books**—*The Book of American Trade Marks: 1* edited by David E. Carter, Ashland, 1972; **articles**—"Designers in Boston" in *Industrial Design* (New York), November 1971; "Business Helicopters: Fossella Styles for Corporate Identity" in *Rotor and Wing International* (Peoria), February 1981; "Gregory Fossella: Industrial Designer Par Excellence" in *Inflight Magazine* (Minneapolis), September/October 1981; "At Home with Top Designer Gregory Fossella" in *Boston Herald Celebrity Magazine,* 13 June 1983; "Logan Airport Signage System" in the *Boston Globe,* 17 April 1984.

\*    \*    \*

Described as a person with energy to spare, Gregory Fossella has earned the respect of his colleagues for his success in running an industrial design firm with frankness and honesty. As an active participant in the system of his company's designs, Fossella oversees the product division. His most efficient way of working is with his staff in this area. As a result his firm is effective in the marketplace. Fossella lets his clients know he is not going to make their job difficult. They are informed through formal presentations, at which Fossella encourages feedback. According to him, a company buys a design firm because it is buying a group of minds; therefore, he considers it vital to know how to work with people.

Whether Fossella is designing graphics packaging, or products for companies such as Brilliant Seafood or International Data Sciences, his designs do not assault the consumer's sensibilities. Conservative in taste, Fossella designs his products to sell by determining the best mix of function, appearance, material, quantity, and consumer preference. For example, his package for Clean Laundry Detergent was designed to convey a certain image. By combining the triangular configuration of the box, integrated handle, and package graphics with clouds, stylized flowers, or abstract soap suds, Fossella was able to communicate a clear and simple, or perhaps a "clean," message. To Fossella, when industrial designers put out a shingle, they had better be ready to solve the client's problem. Judging from the number of design awards he has received, and the broad range of areas in which he works, Fossella has indeed, been successful.

—Patricia A. Russac

# FOX, Peter

Canadian shoe designer

**Born** in London, 19 May 1933; emigrated to Canada, 1956. **Education:** Attended Bryanston School, Dorcet, Camberwell Art School, London, and Maidstone Art School, Kent; studied sculpture under Don Potter. **Family:** Married wife, Linda. **Career:** Shoe salesman, Harrod's department store, 1954-56; shoemaker, Sheppard Shoes, Vancouver, British Columbia, Canada, 1956-70; co-founder, with John Fluevog, Fox and Fluevog Shoes, with stores in Vancouver, Victoria, and Edmonton, 1970-80; co-founder, with wife Linda, of Peter Fox Shoes, SoHo, New York, from 1981. **Exhibitions:** *Right Foot Show,* San Francisco Airport Commission, California, 1987-88; *Fancy Feet: A Historic Collection of Ladies' Footwear,* Brooklyn Museum, New York, 1994. **Collections: Brooklyn Museum, New York. Address:** 55 Bloor Street West, Unit 108, Toronto, Ontario M5T 1W1, Canada.

## Works

Granny boot with Louis Heel, 1981.
Medieval look shoes, 1985.
Platform shoe, 1986.
Arts and Crafts shoes, 1990.
Adult Baby Shoe, 1993.

## Publications

**On FOX: books**—*Wedding Flowers* by Marie McBride-Mellinger, Bullfinch Press, 1992; *Dressing the Bride* by Larry Goldman, New York, 1993; **articles**—*Details* (New York), October 1986.

*

Good design requires an equal expression of function, beauty, and originality; however, good design for footwear must also heed the superior scheme of the human body.

—Peter Fox

*   *   *

The shoes designed by Peter Fox are inspired by footwear from historical periods as diverse as the Medieval times and the 1970s. His subtle twists on history have initiated many trends, but the Victorian and Edwardian styles are constants in his collection and have inspired his company's highly popular bridal collection.

Born into a "rag trade" family, Fox began his career in 1954 as a shoe salesman for Harrod's in London. Two years later, he emigrated to Canada to work for a traditional men's retailer in Vancouver, Sheppard Shoes. There he learned the craft of shoemaking from an old-time Italian shoemaker. After fourteen years with Sheppard, Fox left to open his own business with his children's former babysitter and Sheppard co-worker, John Fluevog. Their store in Vancouver's bohemian Gastown district virtually defined footwear in the 1970s. Their wildly coloured, over-the-knee platform boots for men placed them at the forefront of the more feminine or "unisex" trend in men's fashion.

After an amicable split with Fluevog in 1980, Fox opened a shoe shop in New York's SoHo district with his wife Linda. As equal partners under the label Peter Fox, Peter now designs the shape and form of their shoes, while Linda adds detail and chooses color. Classic Fox designs include the Victorian-inspired, lace-up "Granny boot" and the fan-throated pump with Louis XIV heel.

Often anticipating trends, Fox revived the 1970s platform sole in 1985. A pair of black patent leather platform sandals with wide straps at the toe, arch, and ankle appeared on the cover of the American popular culture magazine *Details* in October 1986. This was seven years before the widespread revival of the platform, led, ironically, by former partner John Fluevog. More recently, Fox's 1994 Adult Toddler styles, featuring flat pumps with round, wide toes, reminiscent of old-fashioned children's shoes, were imitated by urban youth market chain stores.

The theatricality, rich materials, and distinct styles of Fox's designs have attracted the attention of Hollywood and Broadway producers. Fox's footwear has appeared in the Hollywood films *Batman Returns, The Beverly Hillbillies,* and *The Butcher's Wife,* and in stage productions of *The Phantom of the Opera, Showboat,* and *The Secret Garden.*

Another of life's major productions, weddings, have become a showcase for the couple's work. Linda re-inscribes romantic Victorian and Edwardian-inspired themes into their designs through her use of white brocade, satin, and silk doupioni. Ornamented with lace, ribbons, and beadwork, the Louis XIV heel pumps and Toddler ballet slippers are in such high demand by brides-to-be that the Foxes have converted their SoHo men's footwear shop into a bridal boutique.

While they are trend-setting, Fox's styles should certainly not be called trendy. The craftsmanship of his shoes is exquisite, and shows great attention to detail. His innovations are subtle and classic, ensuring his sophisticated clientele many seasons of wear. Catering to an upscale market, Peter Fox Shoes has seven shops in four cities: New York, Santa Monica, Toronto, and Boston, as well as its own shoe boutique in the Kleinfeld Bridal store in Brooklyn, New York.

—Elizabeth Crawford

# FRANCK, Kaj

Finnish glass, ceramic, furniture, textile, and interior designer

**Born:** Viipuri, 9 November 1911. **Education:** Studied interior design, Institute of Industrial Arts, Helsinki, 1929-32. **Military Service:** Served in the Finnish Army, 1932-33, 1939-40, and 1941-44, Lieutenant. **Career:** Designer in Helsinki, working for Taito Oy, 1933, Riihimaki Glass, 1934, Oy Tema, 1934-37, Wollfabriken, 1937-39, Wärtsilä-Arabia, 1945-60, and Wärtsilä-Nuutajärvi glassworks, 1950-76; artistic director, Institute of Industrial Arts, Helsinki, 1960-67; art director, Silicab Group of the Oy Wärtsilä Corporation, Helsinki, 1967-73; occasional freelance designer after his retirement in 1976. Art Professor of the Finnish State, Helsinki, 1973-78; also visiting design lecturer in Tokyo, Munich, Jokkmokk, Tbilisi, Amsterdam, Dublin, Krakow, and London, 1960-81. **Exhibitions:** Milan Triennale, 1951, 1954, 1957, 1960, 1968; *Design in Scandinavia,* toured the United States and Canada, 1954-57; *Glass 1959,* Corning Glass Museum, New York, 1959; *Fins Glas,* Stedelijk

Museum, Amsterdam, 1972 (travelled to Dusseldorf); *100 Years of Finnish Crafts and Design,* Ateneum, Helsinki, 1975; *Metamorphoses Finlandaises,* Centre Georges Pompidou, Paris, 1978; *Finland: Nature, Design, Architecture,* toured the United States, 1981-83; *Scandinavian Modern Design 1880-1980,* Cooper-Hewitt Museum, New York, 1982; *Design Since 1945,* Philadelphia Museum of Art, 1983; *The Lunning Prize,* Nationalmuseum, Stockholm, 1986; *Scandinavia: Ceramics and Glass in the Twentieth Century,* Victoria and Albert Museum, London, 1989. **Collections:** Finlands Glassmuseum, Helsinki; Museum of Applied Arts, Helsinki; Nationalmuseum, Stockholm, Nordenfjeldske Kunstindustrimuseum, Trondheim; Kunstindustrimuseet, Copenhagen; Stedelijk Museum, Amsterdam; Kunstmuseum, D sseldorf; Victoria and Albert Museum, London; Corning Glass Museum, Corning, New York. **Honors:** Gold Medal, 1951, Honour Award, 1954, and Grand Prix, 1957, Milan Triennale; Lunning Prize, Copenhagen, 1955; Compasso d'Oro Award, Milan, 1957; Pro Finlandia Medal, Helsinki, 1957; Prince Eugen Medal, Stockholm, 1964, State Arts and Crafts Prize, Helsinki, 1977; Svenska Kulturfonden Honour Award, Stockholm, 1981; honorary doctorate, Royal College of Art, London, 1983. **Address:** Raunigrand 6, 00610 Helsinki 61, Finland.

## Works

*Kilta* earthenware kitchen and table service ranges, for Arabia, 1948-53.
*Polaris* earthenware table service, for Arabia, 1951.
Wärtsilä shop interiors, Helsinki, 1952.
Wärtsilä showroom interiors, Helsinki, 1961.
Walter Runeberg Museum interiors, Porvoo, 1961.
*Facet* glassware, for Nuutajärvi, 1962.
Amos Andersson Museum interiors, Helsinki, 1965.
*Prisma* glassware, for Nuutajärvi, 1967.
*Luna* glassware, for Nuutajärvi, 1972.
Railway car earthenware table service, for Arabia, 1975.
Nuutajärvi Glass Museum interiors, Nuutajärvi, 1978.
*Delfoi* glassware, for Nuutajärvi, 1978.
*Easy Day* plastic tableware and cutlery, for Sarvis, 1979.
*Teema* earthenware kitchen and table service ranges, for Arabia, 1979-81.

## Publications

**By FRANCK: books**—(editor, with others) *Ornamo 1950-1954: Finnish Decorative Art,* Helsinki, 1955.

**On FRANCK: books**—*Finnish Designers of Today* by Oili Maki, Helsinki, 1954; *The Beauty of Modern Glass* by R. Stenett-Willson, London and New York, 1958; *A Treasury of Scandinavian Design* edited by Erik Zahle, New York, 1961; *Finnisches Glas* by K. Niilonen, Helsinki, 1966; *34 Scandinavian Designers* by Svend Erik Møller, Copenhagen, 1967; *Fins Glas,* exhibition catalogue with text by H. Wakefield, Amsterdam, 1972; *Scandinavian Design: Objects of a Life Style* by Eileene Harrison Beer, New York, 1975; *One Hundred Great Finnish Designs* edited by Per Mollerup, Snekkersten, 1979; *Scandinavian Modern Design 1880-1980* edited by David McFadden, New York, 1982; *Design Since 1945* edited by Kathryn Hiesinger and George Marcus, Philadelphia and

London, 1983; *The Conran Directory of Design* edited by Stephen Bayley, London, 1985; *Twentieth Century Design: Glass* by Frederick Cooke, London, 1986; *Scandinavia: Ceramics and Glass in the Twentieth Century* by Jennifer Hawkins Opie, London 1989.

\*   \*   \*

Kaj Franck, one of Finland's most distinguished designers, was educated in Helsinki during the interwar period in which the country made a tremendous contribution to architecture and design, most notably through the work of Alvar Aalto. Franck learned the lessons of functional modernism well.

Unlike the other Scandinavian countries, Finland was not quite so obsessed with the social role of design. In the postwar period, the country developed a powerful and individual design image with a rather purist approach that can be best seen in the work of Franck and firms such as Marrimekko and Vuokko. Part of this success can be attributed to the importance given to design in the structure of the Finnish economy. Because production tended to concentrate around large firms, rather than small workshops, design in Finland has been given a great deal of support. In the mid 1930s, for example, Arabia was employing more than 1,000 workers, and in the period after the war, when it became one of Europe's largest ceramic manufacturers, it employed more than thirty designers. Of these, Franck was the most distinguished, and his work revolutionized modern standards of production for domestic ceramics.

Opposed to the idea of complete, uniform services, he offered the alternative of large numbers of practical and attractive pieces to complement each other. The *Kilta* range, familiar to a whole generation of Finns in their homes, cafes, and restaurants, is the best example of this approach. Another is a 1953 set of stacking preserve jars in pure cylindrical forms and bright, concordant colours. In 1957, Franck's set of vitreous enamel bowls for Wärtsilä won the Grand Prize at the Milan Triennale. Sophisticated, durable, light, stackable, like the other designs, they were intended to be mixed and matched. With their surfaces of pale and dark blue, red, yellow, green, and white, designs such as these show Franck's disciplined functionalism at its best.

Another aspect of Franck's design personality, one interested in playful humour and experimentation, is best expressed in his glass designs, which because of the nature of the material can ignore rational considerations. Franck has also followed a traditional Scandinavian pattern in that he has also produced, besides his industrial designs, a substantial body of craft objects, as for example, his glass *Nuuta* plate of 1965. In this area, however, his understanding of the potential of the material and his sense of pattern remain consistent with the design principles of his other work.

—Catherine McDermott

# FRANÇOIS, André
French illustrator and graphic designer

**Born:** André Farkas, in Timisoara, Rumania, 9 November 1915; emigrated to France in 1935, naturalized, 1938; adopted name François, 1939. **Education:** Studied at the School of Fine Arts, Budapest, 1932-34; studied privately with A. M. Cassandre, Paris, from 1935. **Family:** Married Margaret Edmunds in 1939; children:

Pierre and Catherine. **Career:** Freelance graphic designer, Paris, from 1935; commercial artist, working for Standard Oil, Olivetti, Perrier, Dutch Masters Cigars, and others, 1935-44; caricaturist and cartoonist, for *Vogue, Femina, Holiday, Punch, Tribune des Nations,* 1953-60, and for the *New Yorker* (designed more than 50 covers), from 1963; book illustrator from 1946 and author, mainly of children's books, from 1952; stage set and costume designer, working for Roland Petit, 1956, Peter Hall, 1958, Jean Babilee, 1959, Gene Kelly, 1960, and others; also independent painter and sculptor. **Member:** Alliance Graphique Internationale. **Exhibitions:** Galerie La Hune, Paris, 1955, Bianchini Gallery, New York, 1962; Galerie Delpire, Paris, 1965, 1973, 1981; Stedelijk Museum, Amsterdam, 1967; Wilhelm Busch Museum, Hannover, 1967; Musée des Arts Décoratifs, Paris, 1970; Galerie Melisa, Lausanne, 1971; Galerie Gurlitt, Munich, 1971; Arts Club of Chicago, 1975; Château des Papes, Avignon, 1977; Musée Saint Georges, Liege, 1977; Palais des Beaux-Arts, Brussels, 1977; Musée de Pontoise, 1979; Galerie Mecanorma, Paris, 1979; Galerie Bartsch-Chariau, Munich, 1981; Palais de Tokio, Paris, 1986 (retrospective); Musée-Chateau de Dieppe, 1989; Musée de Cherbourg, 1993; Bibliotheque Nationale, Paris, 1993; Mitsukoshi Museum, Tokyo, 1995. **Collections:** Musée des Arts Décoratifs, Paris; Wilhelm Busch Museum, Hannover; Musée des Beaux-Arts, Brussels; Stedelijk Museum, Amsterdam; Museum of Modern Art, New York. **Honors:** *New York Times* Children's Illustrated Book Award, 1952, 1956, 1958, 1970; Chevalier des Arts et des Lettres, France, 1957; Gold Medal, Warsaw Poster Biennale, 1972; Honorary Royal Designer for Industry, Royal Society of Arts, London, 1975; Honorary Doctorate, Royal College of Art, London, 1977; Prix Honoré Daumier, Paris, 1979; Grand Prix National des Arts Graphiques, Paris, 1980. **Address:** 16 Rue Robert Machy, 95810 Grisy-les-Platres, France.

## Works

Books illustrated include—*Jacques le fataliste* (Diderot), Paris, 1946; *William Waste* (J. Symonds), London, 1946; *L'Odyssée d'Ulysse* (J. Le Marchand), Paris, 1947, London, 1960; *Little Boy Brown* (I. Harris), Philadelphia, 1949; *The Magic Currant Bun* (J. Symonds), Philadelphia, 1952; *Lettres des Iles Baladar,* Paris, 1952; *Travellers Three* (J. Symonds), Philadelphia, 1953; *Beau Masque* (R. Vailland), Paris, 1954; *On vous l'a dit* (J. Anselme), Paris, 1955; *Contes drolatiques* (Balzac), Paris, 1957; *Roland* (N. Stephane), New York, 1958; *Ubu Roi* (A. Jarry), Paris, 1958; *Tom and Tabby* (J. Symonds), Paris, 1964; *Grodge-Cast and the Window Cleaner* (J. Symonds), New York, 1965; *Le meilleur des mondes* (A. Huxley), Paris, 1961; *Si tu t'imagines* (R. Queneau), Paris, 1979; *L'Arrache coeur* (B. Vian), Paris, 1981.

## Publications

**By François: books**—*Double Bedside Book,* London, 1952, as *The Tattooed Sailor and Other Cartoons from France,* New York, 1952; *Crocodile Tears,* London, 1955, Paris, 1956; *The Half Naked Knight,* New York and London, 1958; *Heikle Themen,* Zurich, 1959; *The Biting Eye of André François,* with preface by Ronald Searle, London, 1960; (with John Symonds) *Dapple Gray,* London, 1962; *The Penguin André François,* London, 1964; *You Are Ri-di-cu-lous,* New York, 1970; *Les Rhumes,* Paris, 1971; *Qui est le plus marrant?,* Paris, 1971; *Santoun,* Paris, 1972; *Toi et moi,* Paris, 1973; (with

**André François:** *L'Ascendant* **painting with collage, 1974**

Roger McGough) *Mr. Noselighter,* London, 1977; *André François: Graphics, Paintings, Sculpture and Stage Designs,* Paris, 1986, London and New York, 1987.

**On François: books**—*Posters: 50 Artists and Designers* edited by W. H. Allner, New York, 1952; *Window Display 2* edited by Walter Herdeg, Zurich, 1961; *Who's Who in Graphic Art* edited by Walter Amstutz, Zurich, 1962, Dubendorf, 1982; *The Poster: An Illustrated History from 1860* by Harold F. Hutchinson, London and Toronto, 1968; *107 Grafici dell'AGI,* exhibition catalogue with texts by Renzo Zorzi and Franco Grignani, Venice, 1974; *Illustrators of Children's Books 1967-1976* by L. Kingman, G. Allen Horgarth, and H. Quimby, Boston, 1978.

*

A millionaire was once asked: "Is it very expensive to run a yacht?" He replied: "If you have to ask, it means you can't."

So when I am asked whether it is possible to practice free art and commercial art side by side, my answer is: "No." If the inner drive is strong enough, the question simply does not arise. The attempt to demonstrate the influence of free art on commercial art—and vice versa—seems to me completely superfluous. Both are facts of life, and I can only express myself quite subjectively about their possible division.

In the life of every artist there comes a moment when he no longer feels the urge to jump through hoops or to occupy himself with the problems of others, with all the limitations and obligations that they involve. The artist develops his own rules, and he wants to jump through his own hoops and experience his personal problems on his own. The "commercial" artist's habit of reacting to every impulse from without—be it a telephone call or a written contract—is hard to eradicate. To express oneself and to obey only the impulse from within requires a long process of re-education. It is impossible to work for an advertiser in the morning and be a painter in the afternoon; a long period of continuity is necessary in both cases. Neither training nor technical knowledge divide the free artist from the commercial artist: only the nature of the work and the demands made on the imagination are decisive. The artist who devotes 80 percent of his time to painting is a painter, the artist who devotes 80 percent of his time to posters is a poster artist.

In commercial art an attempt is made to give form to an idea; free art, on the other hand, obtains its meaning in the course of the work and the form does not find its meaning until the work is completed. One activity starts with the idea and is brought into a form, while the other starts with the form and ultimately obtains its meaning.

Depending on my state of mind at the time, I could argue the opposite of the above with equal conviction. It can happen that I take on the adventure of a difficult task of applied graphics with great pleasure and am delighted by a satisfactory solution. It can also happen that I try to turn a serious commitment into a game and work out an illustration or a poster with playful enjoyment. My view is: Whatever I do, I am.

This does not alter the fact that navigation from one harbor to the other can be difficult and dangerous, that the facets of truth are many and contradictory—and liable to many changes between one shore and the other. (*Previously published* in Arts and Graphics, *Zurich 1983.*)

—André François

\*     \*     \*

To assess the accomplishments of André François, one must look back over the years and into almost all categories of design, illustration, painting, and sculpture. In this search a common denominator appears: the François humor—shy and subtle.

The design of sets for a modern ballet, while posing stringent requirements, still offers the opportunity for François to be François. This is true also when he addresses the demands of product advertising. Even in these situations, François always is able to create a warm and gentle spirit, which undoubtedly is beneficial as well as distinctive.

François has a penchant for perceptively exploring symbols and endowing inanimate objects with human features and characteristics. In his illustrations for magazine covers, and more recently in his paintings, François evokes a magical gift—possession of a bottomless trove of ideas for transforming parts of the human body—an eye, an ear, a foot—into new roles, in which they are sometimes disconnected and able to prance about independently. Although it appears that he has only to reach into the box, not so, says François. He works and re-works

persistently, sometimes not sure where his explorations will lead, not sure when he has arrived. How is it that the final piece can be so fresh, after constant struggle? It is, perhaps, that his work is so individual, such a personal expression, that it is, indeed visually surprising and fresh to anyone else.

He has said, himself, that materials and technique must be subordinate to the thought expressed. Some of his paintings employ pebbles affixed to his canvas. This suggests the plastic, sculptural element in François' work, but in his view, the pebbles are there not to provide three-dimensionality but to act as visual elements of the thought he is conveying.

No doubt the painter in François was there from the beginning, even though his early work was in applied fields. Still, his illustrations for covers of such magazines as *Punch* and the *New Yorker* can be seen as precursors of his present-day paintings. At least one of his old-broken-clockface paintings, a device which has grown to be a François cachet, also has appeared on the cover of the *New Yorker*.

In all, his has been a phenomenally productive career, one that has been as long as it has been successful. It has given him the opportunity to apply himself in many fields and bring to each his own, special sense of the humor in this life.

—Jerry Steimle

# FRATINI, Gina

British fashion designer

**Born:** Georgia Caroline Butler, of British parents, in Kobe, Japan, 22 September 1931. **Education:** Educated in Simla, India, until 1943; Hathrop Girls' School, Gloucestershire, 1944-46; studied fashion design, under Madge Garland, at the Royal College of Art, London, 1947-50. **Family:** Married Renato Fratini in 1960. **Career:** Assistant set and costume designer, Kathleen Dunham dance group, in London, Italy, and the United States, 1951-54; freelance costume and fashion designer, London, from 1954; established Gina Fratini Limited, London, from 1964; designed stage production costumes for *Side By Side By Sondheim,* and *Nymphs and Satire,* 1963; designed costumes for film *Stop The World: I Want to Get Off,* 1966. **Exhibitions:** *Fashion: An Anthology,* Victoria and Albert Museum, London, 1971. **Collections:** Victoria and Albert Museum, London; Bethnal Green Museum, London; Birmingham Museum of Art, Warwickshire; Bath Museum of Costume, Avon. **Address:** Gina Fratini Limited, 17 Wandle Road, London SW17 7DL, England.

**Publications**

On FRATINI: books—**Fashion: An Anthology by Cecil Beaton,** exhibition catalogue compiled by Madeleine Ginsburg, London, 1971; *A History of Fashion* by J. Anderson Black and Madge Garland, London, 1975, 1980; *The World of Fashion: People, Places, Resources* by Eleanor Lambert, New York and London, 1976; *The Magic Names of Fashion* by Ernestine Carter, London, 1980; *The Collector's Book of Twentieth Century Fashion* by Frances Kennet London and New York, 1983; *McDowell's Directory of Twentieth Century Fashion* by Colin McDowell, London, 1984; *The Encyclopedia of Fashion from 1840 to the 1980s* by Georgina O'Hara,

London, 1986; *The Fashion Conspiracy* by Nicholas Coleridge, London, 1988; *The History of Twentieth Century Fashion* by J. Mulvagh, London, 1988.

*     *     *

Gina Fratini, all British in spite of her name, was born in Japan, where her father was a government official. She spent her childhood in the Far East and received her first schooling in India. Later, she went to one of England's most famous girls' schools, Hathrop Castle in Gloucestershire. Then, she began at the recently founded School of Fashion Design at London's Royal College of Art, from which she graduated with honours. After college, she joined the Kathleen Dunham dance troupe and studied body movements, which later were to be of great assistance to her in designing clothes; her creations always move beautifully, and the natural graces of the body are never hampered by an ill-considered cut.

Fratini started dressmaking almost by chance. She had always made her own clothes, and one day an impecunious friend asked her for help in obtaining a ballgown for a very special occasion. She obliged, and her friend's dress was so much admired that several other friends wanted to know its origin. Fratini was besieged by requests and for several years continued to work alone, turning out fabulously pretty dresses all made by herself. One day, a friend in the fashion business implored her to make a small collection of a dozen models which he guaranteed he would show to an influential fashion editor. Fratini made the dresses, modelled them herself, and so excited the fashion editor that she arranged for them to be seen by the owner of one of London's most exclusive retail shops. "Madame" bought the lot, sold them immediately, and demanded repeats. Gina had no workroom, no assistants, no knowledge of the international wholesale fabric market, but somehow managed, and success followed success.

Now she sells only to the most exclusive "Madame" shops throughout England and to special departments in such stores as Harrods. Privately, she makes for all the "Royals," including the young duchesses of the Royal family. She has never deviated from her personal choice of a romantic and very feminine style, and it is not surprising that her favorable client is the romantically beautiful Princess of Wales.

—Madge Garland

# FRATTINI, Gianfranco

Italian architect and interior, exhibition, and industrial designer

**Born:** Padua, 15 May 1926. **Education:** Educated at the Liceo Classico, Milan, 1943-45; studied architecture, at the Politecnico, Milan, Dip., 1953. **Family:** Married Ingeborg Weber in 1957; children: Emanuela and Marco. **Career:** Worked as assistant designer, studio of Gio Ponti, Milan, 1951-53; freelance designer, establishing own studio in Milan, from 1953; has designed for Cassina, B. Bernini, Arteluce, Artemide, Molteni, Ricci, Fratelli Faver, Gio Caroli, Fantoni, Insa, Former, Ballato, and others. Exhibition Committee Member, 1958-59, Ethical Council Member, 1972-75, and Directive Committee Member, 1979-82, ADI Associazione Disegno Industriale, Milan; Building Commission Member, Portofino City Council, Genoa, from 1975; Administrative Councillor, Milan

Triennale, from 1983; State Examinations Commission Member, Faculty of Architecture, Politecnico of Milan, 1974-75. **Exhibitions:** *Contemporary Italian Architecture,* Malmo Museum, Sweden, 1968; *Domus Design,* Teheran, 1975; *Il Design Italiano negli Anni '50,* Centro Kappa, Milan, 1977; *Design and design,* Palazzo delle Stelline, Milan, 1979 (traveled to Venice); *Dal design all'habitat,* Bari, Italy, 1982; *Il Lavoro del Designer,* Trieste, 1983; *Dal cucchiaio alla città,* Palazzo Triennale, Milan, 1983; *Design Since 1945,* Philadelphia Museum of Art, 1983; *Disegnare il marmo,* Carrara, 1986; *Nouveaux Projets pour l'Habitat,* Paris, 1988. **Collections:** Museum of Modern Art, New York; Museum of Contemporary Art, Chicago; Museum of Applied Arts, Helsinki. **Honors:** Compasso d'Oro Awards, Milan, 1955, 1956, 1957, 1979, 1981, 1987; Gold Medal, 1957, Grand Prize, 1960, Silver Medal, 1973, Milan Triennale; Gold Medal, Mostra del Vimini, 1959; Plast Oscar Award, Milan, 1968; Award of Honour, Liubliana, 1973, 1981; MACEF Award, Milan, 1974; International Diamond Award, New York, 1976; Casa Amica Award, Milan, 1976; Furniture Award, Valencia, 1987. **Address:** Via Santa Anese 14, 20123 Milan, Italy.

## Works

*Model 849* armchair, for Cassina, 1957.
*Model 530* writing-desk, for G. B. Bernini, 1957.
*Model 804* secretaire-desk, for G. B. Bernini, 1964.
*Sesann* divan and armchair, for Cassina, 1970.
*Boalum* lamp, for Artemide, 1970.
*Larco* range of furniture, for Molteni, 1970.
*560 Series* range of furniture, for G. B. Bernini, 1971.
*Kioto* table, for Pier Luigi Ghianda, 1974.
*Nuela Series* range of furniture, for Lema, 1976.
*Megaron* lamp, for Artemide, 1979.
*Simbio* range of furniture, for Former, 1979.
*Model 45* beaker in handblown glass, for Progetti, 1980.
*Sesamo* roll-top writing-desk, for G. B. Bernini, 1983.
*Capri* square table in beech and leather, for Cassina, 1985.
*Caprile* upholstered seating in beech, for Cassina, 1985.
*Proust* adaptable worktable in ash, for Acerbis International, 1986.
*Proust* bookcase in lacquered ash, for Acerbis International, 1987.
*Acheo* standard lamp in steel and pyrex, for Artemide, 1988.

## Publications

**On FRATTINI: books**—*Mobili tipo* by Robert Aloi, Milan, 1956; *Design for Modern Living* by Gerd and Ursula Hatje, Munich and Zurich, 1961, London, 1962; *Forme e colore nell'arredamento moderno* by Giulio Peluzzi, Milan, 1967, as *The Modern Room,* London, 1967; *Design Italiano: i mobili* by Enrichetta Ritter, Milan and Rome, 1968; *Italian Look* by G. Bocca and others, Milan, 1972; *Design e Forme Nuove nell'Arredamento Italiano* edited by Paolo Portoghesi and Marino Marini, Rome, 1978; *Twentieth Century Furniture* by Philippe Garner, London, 1980; *Neue Moebel 1950-1982* edited by Klaus-Jurgen Sembach, Stuttgart, 1982, as *Contemporary Furniture,* New York, 1982; *Design Since 1945* edited by Kathryn Hiesinger and George Marcus, Philadelphia and London, 1983; *International Design Yearbook 1988/89* edited by Arata Isozaki, London, 1988.

*

There is an immediate contrast between the present day and the period when I began my career; in the 1950s, there was everything to do and much opportunity to carry out new ideas. New pieces of design often sprang from problems of interior architecture, since the choice of pieces available on the market at that time was limited, and pieces initially produced for a given setting were later appropriately modified and put into industrial production.

Today, however, the production of "so-called design" is exceptional. Very often, perfectly good pieces are scrapped because the continual launching of "novelties" on the market to make a quick profit makes the public so confused that they can no longer identify and distinguish the really good pieces. Today more than ever, it is essential to have a thorough knowledge of the material you are working with and to offer a consistent and fair product.

There is a lot of talk today about the postmodern movement, both in architecture and design. My own view is that it is a phenomenon that is bound to make its mark on the products of design, though on the whole, it seems to me that a symbiosis between industrial design and postmodernism can hardly be put forward. The problem of technological research seems to be deliberately ignored, and the prospects for series production, a basic element in order to talk of design, seem very remote; for these reasons, in my view—and also because of their prices—the products of postmodernism have more the qualities of objects of applied art.

I personally think of myself as a rationalist, and I believe in the validity of the double slogan of "form-function," even if during phases in the planning, the conformation of an object has to pass through a number of filters of an individual nature—the designer's cultural background, his sensibility, aesthetic sense, and mentality. If it were not so, even design problems could be solved by a mathematical formula, whereas, fortunately, even when we start from objective premises, our work leaves room for individual expression.

—Gianfranco Frattini

\*   \*   \*

G. F. Frattini's achievement was summed up by Gio Ponti as "*una bella funzionalita,*" meaning that his close attention to the practicalities of his brief was combined with an equally close attention to elegant design. No detail was overlooked. For instance, his elegant Stork Club in the centre of Milan served a house Scotch for which he designed the label on the bottle. This combination of elegance and functionalism has characterised all his work but has not excluded a certain toughness when, as in the case of the 1976 plastic crash helmet, this was a necessity. Similarly, for beyond its smart atmosphere designed by Frattini, the Ritrovo Saint Andrew's was an eminently workable interior that allowed the rapid and easy dispensation of drinks and snacks; everything seemed to happen in a relaxed and relaxing manner, due as much to the nature of the design as to the service personnel.

This is a clue to this designer's achievement—a delight in fine materials finely wrought for specific purposes and embracing an attention to the most mundane aspects of practicalities. In his social interiors as in individual products, they are designed not only to work their best but also to look their best and communicate their purposes. The first demountable armchair for Cassina in 1955 clearly announced its evident comfort as an easychair in which to lounge, but it made equally obvious the fact that it could easily be taken apart; both of these attributes were expressed in the elegance of the design which bespoke a characteristic, aesthetic economy of means.

Much of this same point of view could be seen in the marvelous, flexible, segmented tube of light that he designed with Livio Castiglioni for Artemide. This Boalum lamp could be coiled, knotted, tangled, stretched out, draped over other pieces of furniture. Its form resided in its minimal character. What are often separable structural members in a lighting fitting were brought together in one unique unprecedented object that achieves style in its very shapelessness and, at the same time, overcomes the limitations that conventional structures place upon flexibility of use and purpose. All of these contradictory demands have been resolved in a truly surprising simplicity whose title to pure functionalism needs no further mention while its elegance arises equally from the boldness of the proposal.

—Toni del Renzio

# FREYER, Achim

German painter, environmental artist and graphic, stage, costume, and animated film designer

**Born:** Berlin, 30 March 1934. **Education:** Studied at the Meisterschule für Graphik, East Berlin, 1951-55; stage design, in the studio of Bertolt Brecht, Akademie der Kunste, East Berlin, 1954-56. **Career:** Freelance painter, working in East Berlin, 1956-72, and as playwright, director, and painter, in West Berlin, from 1972: resident designer, Deutsches Theater, East Berlin, 1964-72; also created room performances and environments, East Berlin, 1965-68; stage designer of plays and operas in West Berlin, from 1972; established Freyer Ensemble, Berlin, 1991. Professor, Akademie der Kunste, Berlin, from 1976. **Exhibitions:** *Documenta 6,* Museum Fridericianum, Kassel, 1977; *Achim Freyer—Malerei, 1966-1983,* Orangerie of Charlottenburg Castle, Berlin (toured to Hamburg and Stuttgart), 1990; *Achim Freyer: Chaos und Stille,* City Galerie, Kornwestheim, 1992; *Neue Arbeiten,* Galerie Helmut Leger, Munich, 1992; *Taggespinste Nachtgesichte, Achim Freyer—Malerei, 1992-1994,* Akademie der Kunste, 1994; *Achim Freyer—Arbeiten zu Peer Gynt,* Galerie Graphics Arts Press, Berlin, 1994; *Achim Freyer—Malerei,* Exhibition Hall of the Federal Republic of Germany, Bonn, 1994; *Tristan und Isolde,* Theatre Royal de la Monnaic, Brussels, 1994. **Honors:** Award, Great Exhibition of Arts, Berlin, 1960; German Federal Cross of Merit (Bundesverdienstkreuz 1 Klasse), 1990. **Address:** Kadettenweg 53, 1000 Berlin 45 (West), Germany.

## Works

Stage and environmental designs include—*Zwangsraume, Bilder, Objekte,* West Berlin, 1973; *Monument des Heinrich von Kleist,* Staatstheater, Stuttgart, 1975; *Beethoven Innenraum-Landschaft,* Stadtisches Theater, Frankfurt, 1976; *Mauricio Kagel: Musiktheater,* Städtische Oper, Cologne, 1977; *Faust,* Staatstheater, Stuttgart, 1977; *Immanuel Kant,* Staatstheater, Stuttgart, 1978; *Iphigenie auf Tauris,* Bavarian State Opera, Munich, 1979; *Der Freischütz,* Staatstheater, Stuttgart, 1980; *Satyagraha,* Staatstheater, Stuttgart, 1981; *Die Zauberflote,* Vienna Festival, 1982, 1991; *Echnaton,* Staatstheater, Stuttgart, 1984; *The Messiah,* German Opera, Berlin, 1985; *Metamorphosen*

Achim Freyer: *Metamorphosen des Ovid oder Die Bewegung von den Rändern zur Mitte hin und umgekehrt,* Burgtheater, Wien, 1987. Photo: Matthias Horn

*des Ovid,* Burgtheater, Vienna, 1987; *Einstein on the Beach,* Staatstheater, Stuttgart, 1988; *Woyzeck,* Burgtheater, Vienna, 1989; *Phaeton,* Burgtheater, Vienna, 1991; *Alceste,* Berlin State Opera Unter den Linden, 1994, and Opera Bastille, Paris, 1994; *Turandot,* Gran Teatro La Fenice, Venice, 1994; *Persephone,* Gran Teatro La Fenice, Venice, 1994; *Tristan und Isolde,* Opera National de Munt la Monnaie, Brussels, 1994.

**Publications**

**By FREYER: articles**—"Aus einem Brief an R. R. Leipzig" in *Theater Heute,* 1979; "Zwischenraume" in *Theater Heute,* 1979; "Ales ist Raum" in *Daidalos* (Berlin), 1984; "Uber mein Theater" in *Phaeton,* exhibition catalogue, Burgtheater, Vienna, 1991.

**On FREYER: books**—*Stage Design Throughout the World 1970-1975* by René Hainaux and Nicole Leclercq, Brussels and London, 1976; *Documenta 6: Band 1,* exhibition catalogue with texts by Klaus Honnef and others, Kassel, 1977; *Das Theater der Siebziger Jahre: Kommentar, Kritik, Polemik* edited by Georg Hensel, Stuttgart, 1980; **articles**—"Meister der Illusion" by Gesa Engelschall in *Architektur und Wohnen,* 1990; "Achim Freyer: Finden, Was der Gedanke Nicht Sucht" by Ilske van Schweinitz in *Zyma,* November/December, 1990; "Abstraktion und Einfühlung: Über das Bildertheater des Achim Freyer" in *Theater der Zeit,* 1991; "Theater als Zeitlupe" by Friedrich Diekmann in *Theater der Zeit,* May/June 1993; "Farbe, Körper, Klang, Bewegung, Zeit" by Jürgen Beckelmann in *Vivace* (Berlin), January 1994.

*

Making the concealed visible,
Evincing richness in nothingness, in the void.
The stage is a reflection.
A reflection is a surface,
on which appears the image of an object,
not the object itself.
The image is a simulation.
It consists of symbols
which reveal, and therefore, explain true nature.
True Nature
unexpressed, unknown, undescribed, cannot
account for itself.
Theater, which attempts to depict true nature, an object, through the same object, or through the simulation of this object, compels the observer to visualize the object.

However, God says, "Do not picture in the mind what exists in heaven, nor what is on earth, or in the water under the earth."

The object is related to the mind not directly but through language.

The represented object exists only on the side of the self-reflecting object not on the side of the reflected object.

Pictures and languages enable the "reading" observer to realize the object.

It reflects itself, and thus, experiences itself, the world and God.

The reflection renders visible the concealed, and renders essential the immaterial; the emptiness, the void—is abundance.

—Achim Freyer

*     *     *

Achim Freyer once described himself as an artist who works in a number of media, the theater being just one of them. He first became involved in the theater in 1954 when Bertolt Brecht showed interest in puppets Freyer had made. After serving as assistant to Brecht and Karl von Appen, the resident designer at the Berliner Ensemble, Freyer left the theater for an extended period of time to work solely on painting and the graphic arts. By the mid 1960s, feeling pressured by the government in East Berlin to comply with the officially accepted style of art, he sought refuge in the company of others by working again in the theater. After several successes with directors Benno Besson and Ruth Berghaus, Freyer again ran afoul of the regime when he designed Goethe's *Clavigo* in an East German Pop-art manner. The production was banned, and shortly thereafter Freyer seized an opportunity to emigrate to West Germany.

After a few years of successful freelancing, Freyer settled in Stuttgart and did some of his best work designing for director Claus Peymann at the Staatstheater Stuttgart. For productions such as *Kaethchen von Heilbronn* he created what he called "monuments," visual compositions that reflected his personal reaction to the author. These pieces grew out of Freyer's long-standing interest in contemporary art and music, particularly in the work of Joseph Beuys, Robert Rauschenberg, Mauricio Kagel, Dieter Schnebel, and Philip Glass. He exhibited his monuments in the lobbies of theaters, offering audiences an opportunity to confront purely visual imagery inspired by the designer's encounter with the play. Gradually, the monuments moved out of the theater and into the art gallery, and in 1977 Freyer exhibited a monument, now called a *Raum,* at the Documenta 6 international art exhibition. This work, *Deutschland, ein Lebensraum,* was a conglomeration of associative images representing Freyer's reaction to contemporary German life.

In all its various guises, on stage, in the lobby, or in the gallery, Freyer's art is intensely personal. He considers his work a process of continuous self-exploration. Looking back at an earlier design, he once said, "That was important to me. That brought me further." On another occasion, asked to explain an earlier design for *Pélleas and Melisande,* he answered, "How can I possibly conceive today how I dreamed and worked at that time? The conception has become something else." Although fascinated by many plays and operas, Freyer has said he can design only for those works in which he finds his own themes, those being the conflict between isolation and communion and the conflict between the establishment of order by a state and the disruption of that order by the individual.

—Richard V. Riddell

# FRIEDL, Friedrich
German graphic and exhibition designer

**Born:** Of German parents, in Fulnek, Czechoslovakia, 7 September 1944. **Education:** Educated in Besigheim/Neckar, 1950-54; high school, Stuttgart, 1954-61; studied graphic design, Werkkunstschule, Darmstadt, Dip., 1972. **Family:** Married Regina Bardt in 1976 (divorced, 1987); children: Andreas and Christian. **Career:** Worked as an apprentice, then as typesetter, Stuttgart, 1961-66; freelance graphic designer, Darmstadt, from 1972; designed for the West Berlin Internationale Design Zentrum, Darmstadt Rat für Formgebung, Deutscher Werkbund, Letratset Deutschland, Galerie Hoss in Munich, Edition Hoffmann of Friedberg, Edition E of Munich, and the Darmstadt Fachbereich Gestaltung. Instructor in typography, basic design, and visual communications, at the Fachbereich Gestaltung of the Fachhochschule, Darmstadt, 1972-82; instructor in experimental design, Hochschule für Gestaltung, Offenbach, from 1980; professor of typography, Fachhochschule Hildesheim, 1982-83, and Hochschule für Gestaltung, Offenbach, from 1983. Co-editor, *Schriftwechsel* magazine of typography, Frankfurt, from 1982. **Exhibitions:** Print Gallery Pieter Brattinga, Amsterdam, 1976; Atelier Dawo, Dusseldorf, 1977; Marielies-Hess-Stiftung, Frankfurt, 1979; Leopold-Hoesch-Museum, Düren, 1981; Städtische Galerie, Bergisch-Gladbach, 1982; Leitner Ausstellungen, Stuttgart, 1984; Galerie Hoffmann, Friedberg, 1984; Kunstverein, Frankfurt, 1986; Wilhelm-Hack-Museum, Ludwigshafen, 1987; Karmeliterkloster, Frankfurt, 1994; Museum Ostdeutsche Galerie, Regensburg, 1996. **Collections:** Klingspor Museum, Offenbach-Deutsches Plakatmuseum Essen; Poster Museum, Warsaw; Stadt Frankfurt. **Honors:** Recipient Graphic-Design in Deutschland Prize, 1969, 1970, 1971, 1974, 1975, 1977; Warsaw Poster Biennale Prize, 1972, 1974, 1978; Essen Poster Triennale Prize, 1976, 1980. **Address:** Blumenstraße 4, 60318 Frankfurt, Germany.

**Publications**

**By FRIEDL: books**—*Das Gewöhnliche Design,* Cologne, 1979; *Exakte Zeichnungen,* Munich, 1981; *Thesen Über Typografie,* 3 vols., Eschborn, 1985-89; *Typografische Mitteilungen, Sonderheft Elementare Typografie,* Mainz, 1986; *Walter Dexel, Neue Reklame,* Düsseldorf, 1987; *Plakate für das Sparen,* Stuttgart, 1992; **articles**—in *Letratime* (Frankfurt), nos. 1, 2, 1978; *Schriftwechsel* (Frankfurt), nos. 1-6, 1982-83.

**On FRIEDL: books**—*Modern Publicity 1981* edited by Felix Gluck, London, 1980; *Friedrich Friedl: Exakte Gestaltung,* Frankfurt/Mainz, 1994.

*

In my design work, I do not try to appear intelligible to the largest possible number of people. Rather, I try to find a form that will do justice to the complicated content and complex connections.

I try to further boundaries in visual communication and not to repeat existing positions. For me, design is an ever new visual and intellectual experiment that has nothing to do with commercial graphics.

—Friedrich Friedl

*     *     *

As a young composer, Friedrich Friedl was influenced by the aesthetic philosophy of Max Bense. From beginnings in informal painting, which he developed along with his daily work in the compositor's workshop of a large printing firm in Stuttgart, there appeared in the 1960s his first structural picture compositions. Consisting of connecting lines, these did not end in systematic networks but were distinguished by a dynamic of form in detail and a repose of form overall.

The use of letters, numbers, and parts of sentences in his recent works gives his attractive collages a highly designed character. In alienating letters from their original function as bearers of information and changing them into variable elements of a concrete design concept, Friedl has created an individual pictography which has extended the accepted ideas of concrete art. His fine-art works are characterized by painterly values to which he has recently added lively colour.

Friedl designs posters and other means of communication for cultural clients with similar results. His chief medium in graphic design is typography. He uses text information also as a structural design element, and with this approach, he has achieved a new and innovative expression.

—Eckhard Neumann

# FRIEDMANN, Arnold

American interior designer

**Born:** Nuremberg, Germany, 12 May 1925; emigrated to the United States in 1947, naturalized, 1955. **Education:** Educated at high schools in Europe and Palestine; studied art, Brooklyn Museum of Art School, New York, 1947; studied interior design, Pratt Institute, Brooklyn, New York, B.F.A., 1953; studied art education and design, at Pratt Institute and New York University, M.S., 1960; studied environmental behavior and design, Union Graduate School, Cincinnati, Ohio, Ph.D., 1976. **Military Service:** Served in the British Army, 1943-46, Sergeant. **Family:** Married Susanne Kirsch in 1949; children: Daniel and Ronald. **Career:** Worked as a cabinet-maker and furniture designer, New York, 1947-49; freelance interior and furniture designer, establishing own office in New York, 1954-72; vice-president, Danco Design Associates, Northampton, Massachusetts, 1975-77; partner, Amherst Design Associates, Massachusetts, from 1980. Instructor, then professor of design, 1954-72, and chairman of interior and environmental design department, 1969-72, Pratt Institute, Brooklyn, New York; head of textiles, clothing, and environmental arts department, 1972-73, professor of design, director of the design program, graduate design program director, and adjunct professor of landscape architecture and regional planning, 1973-90, associate dean of humanities and arts, 1984-90, and professor emeritus, from 1990, University of Massachusetts, Amherst. Visiting professor/fellow, Southern Illinois University, 1964, Institute for Man and Environment at the University of Massachusetts, 1976-77, Glasgow School of Art, Scotland, 1983, and Royal Melbourne Institute of Technology, Australia, 1984. Editor, International Federation of Interior Architects *Education Newsletter,* from 1981; chairman, 1972-74, Standards Committee of the Foundation for Interior Design Education and Research; editorial committee member *Journal of Interior Design Education and Research,* from 1976. **Honors:** Design Project Fellowship, Na-

tional Endowment for the Arts, 1979; Distinguished Teacher Award, University of Massachusetts, 1980; Special Award, Interior Design Hall of Fame, 1994. Honorary Member, American Society of Interior Designers, 1979, and Design Institute of Australia, 1985. **Address:** 42 North Maple Street, Hadley, Massachusetts 021035, U.S.A.

## Works

Corporate offices and showroom in New York, for Henri Polak Diamond Corporation, 1974.
Cooperative residential apartment in New York, for Mr. Milton Gelfand, 1974.
House interiors in Mamaroneck, New York, for Mr. and Mrs. S. Singer, 1975.
Psychiatric practice offices in New York, for Dr. Harold Kaplan, 1976.
Factory workspaces and cafeterias in Greenfield, Massachusetts, for TRW-Greenfield Tap and Die Corporation, 1980.
YMCA Health Club in Greenfield, Massachusetts, for the Young Men's Christian Association, 1981.
Engineering firm office in Greenfield, Massachusetts, for Douglas G. Peterson and Associates, 1983.
National corporate headquarters in Holyoke, Massachusetts, for the American Pad and Paper Company, 1984.
Executive offices and library in Springfield, Massachusetts, for the Basketball Hall of Fame, 1984.
Admissions and waiting-room additions in Northampton, Massachusetts, for the Cooley Dickinson Hospital, 1985.
Medical offices in Springfield, Massachusetts, for Dr. Kenneth Frankel, 1987.
YMCA hotel guestrooms, lobby, and public facilities in Springfield, Massachusetts, for the Young Men's Christian Association, 1985-89.

## Publications

**By FRIEDMANN: books—***A Critical Study of Interior Design Education,* New York, 1968; (with John Pile and Forrest Wilson) *Interior Design: An Introduction to Architectural Interiors,* New York, 1970, 1982; *Course Outline: A Study Course for NSiD Qualifications Examination,* New York, 1973; *Commonsense Design,* New York, 1976; (with Craig Zimring and Ervin Zube) *Environmental Design Evaluation,* New York, 1978; (with William Rupp) *Construction Materials for Interior Design,* New York, 1989.

*

My primary professional interest and activity has been in education, although I am a designer before anything else. Design is a state of mind and a lifestyle as well as a profession. I have always tried to imbue students with that sense of mission which is very real to me. Perhaps more than the transmission of knowledge and the kindling of creativity, it has always mattered most to me to give students a strong sense of commitment to design and to design excellence.

I have devoted my professional life to design education at two institutions. I have tried to help with the shaping of first-rate programs or have initiated such programs to go beyond the confines of the schools with which I have been associated. I did so, recognizing

**Arnold Friedman: Interior of remodelled 1930 farm woodshed, Massachusetts, 1979**

the need to improve interior design education nationally and internationally. Through the publication of my *Critical Study* in 1968, I had the opportunity to become a moving force in the field of design education and in the professionalization of interior design. In that study, I proposed the accreditation of schools, as well as the accreditation of individual designers. Now that both concepts have been realized, they have measurably strengthened and enhanced the profession of interior design.

In my personal work, I have been more interested in the humanization of the work environment and the personalization of living spaces than in trying to develop a design style recognizable as mine. Through my work as a writer and academician, I have been concerned with the development of theoretical approaches to design—including interior design criticism and environmental/behavior research—and have written extensively on some of these subjects.

—Arnold Friedmann

\*       \*       \*

Arnold Friedmann's commitment to the "improved quality of life that good design can bring to an environment" is evident in his design commissions but finds its fullest expression in his dedica-

tion to design education. In seventeen years at Pratt Institute and more than twenty at the University of Massachusetts, Amherst, he has produced a legacy of designers who share his commitment and goal of excellence. Through personal example and close, one-to-one working relationships with his students, Friedmann has promoted the development of many mature designers.

His involvement with teaching has not been limited to the classroom; it encompasses the broadest implications of professionalism. In 1962, Friedmann helped to found the Interior Design Educators Council, which was organized to provide a forum for the improvement of interior design teaching. His report *A Critical Study of Interior Design Education,* produced for the curriculum research-committee of this organization in 1968, was the first comprehensive research on the topic. This study proposed two instruments essential to the profession: a formal program of accreditation of schools and a national examination for professionals. These proposals and Friedmann's unstinting help initiated today's accrediting agency, the Foundation of Interior Design Education and Research, and examining board, the National Council for Interior Design Qualifications. Friedmann has held major offices or chairmanships in each of these organizations, having been Standards Committee chairman of FIDER and board member and secretary of NCIDQ as well as secretary and president of the Interior Design Educators Council.

Friedmann's encouragement was also a factor in the merger of the American Institute of Interior Designers and the National Society of Interior Designers into the American Society of Interior Designers, which further united and strengthened the profession. As co-chairman of the Education Committee of the International Federation of Interior Architects and editor of the IFI *Education Newsletter,* he promotes high-quality education internationally as well as nationally. *Interior Design: An Introduction to Architectural Interiors,* which he co-authored, is one of the most concise and complete texts in the field.

Friedmann's concern with the quality of an environment, not just its design style, is reflected in his doctoral work in environmental psychology at Union Graduate School, his investigations of the effect of the environment on behavior patterns of the institutionalized mentally retarded, and his recent studies of fast food establishments, airports, and other public spaces. Consciousness about design in public and private spaces is fundamental to his research and teaching: "Our ordinary spaces are much more important than the kind pictured in an architectural or design magazine," he says.

—Marjorie Kriebel

# FRISTEDT, Sven

Swedish textile designer

**Born:** Stockholm, 29 November 1940. **Education:** Studied textiles at Anders Beckman School, Stockholm, 1957-59. **Career:** Fabric designer, Mab and Mya, Stockholm, 1959-61; designed clothing fabric patterns, for Katja of Sweden, Stockholm, 1961-1965; woven and printed textile designer, Borås Wäfveri, Sweden, from 1965; freelance designer, for Ikea, in Simrishamn, from 1970. **Exhibitions:** *Scandinavian Modern Design 1880-1980,* Cooper-Hewitt Museum, New York, 1982; *Faces of Swedish Design,* IBM Gallery, New York, 1988 (toured the United States). **Collections:** Nationalmuseum, Stockholm; Museum of Modern Art, New York. **Address:** Östergatan 4, 279 00 Simrishamn, Sweden.

## Works

*Orinen/Serpent* printed cotton fabric, 1972.
*Satin Cross* collection of printed fabrics, for Borås Wäfveri, 1983.
*Puzzle* cotton fabric, for Borås Wäfveri, 1986.
*Loppcirkus/Flea Circus* cotton fabric, for Borås Wäfveri, 1986.
*Pram* cotton fabric, for Borås Wäfveri, 1986.
*Glass and Concrete* collection of fabrics, 1986-87.
*Living It Up* collection of clothing and furnishing fabrics, 1987.

## Publications

**On FRISTEDT: books**—*Svensk Textilkonst/Swedish Textile Art* by Edna Martin and Beate Sydhoff, Stockholm, 1980; *Scandinavian Modern Design 1880-1980* edited by David Revere McFadden, New York, 1982; *Trycka Tyger* by Inez Svensson, Stockholm, 1984; *Den Svenska Formen* by Monica Boman and others, Stockholm, 1985; *Faces of Swedish Design,* exhibition catalogue edited by Monica Boman, Stockholm, 1988.

*        *        *

He's on his way to India when we meet in Stockholm. His eyes shine with curiosity and expectation. He is dressed in an elegant black-and-gray patterned shirt and trousers of cotton, sewn in his own patterns. Spiritually he is already on his journey: he has arrived in Stockholm from his house in southern Sweden in order to get ready for the trip.

He squirms a little, as though facing a challenge. It is exciting. Memories of his travels usually make a definite impression on his new collections.

Sven always talks luxuriantly and generously. For over 20 years his decorative desires to fill surfaces with symbols, flourishes, and colors have raised Swedish interior fabrics to bubbling heights. His patterns are grandly luxuriant or just the opposite: a surface of dense, arcane symbols in the form of prints or screens with the addition of the occasional dot of color.

Sven's first trip after completing his education was to Italy. His teacher, Göta Trägardh, had encouraged him and arranged financial support. That was in the early 1960s, and for Sven it provided an unbelievable kick, and inspiration from which he has luckily never recovered. All the fruits, vegetables, and flowers.... And his meeting with the American designer Ken Scott, who created rich patterns in fantastic color combinations.

Flying leaves, flowers, strawberries, melons, gooseberries, suns, sky, clouds, and gay stripes have flooded Sven's patterns in a never-ending stream. In the intervals he has "washed" his excesses of rich patterns clean with more strict geometrical exercises: large squares, broad stripes, narrow stripes.

His strict discipline is counterbalanced with the joy of color. One example is his *Glass and Concrete* collection which he created together with Vivianne Sjölin. Narrow and wide stripes in a flood of colors is also a recurring theme in many of his collections. *Puzzle* has become a bridge between the different languages of design.

In the 1960s it was not easy for young designers to sell patterns to the textile industry. Katja of Sweden opened the door for Sven by asking him to design patterns for her clothes. A few years later he came into contact with Borås Wäfveri after having an argument with one of the directors. "Why are your patterns so boring and cautious when the time is now ripe for bolder designs?" he asked— young and green, yet very sure of himself. "Go home and make some of those designs yourself," replied the manufacturer. "You won't find it so easy!"

He did and his patterns turned out to be a commercial success. Since then he has taken innumerable trips to the city of Borås in southwestern Sweden. Their collaboration has continued without interruption. For both the Swedish and international public, it has become a custom that new collections appear at regular intervals. Today his patterns comprise 25 percent of Borås' manufacture. He makes patterns for both domestic and public environments. IKEA usually orders a special collection, and it is not unusual to find his fabrics on Italian sofas at the furniture fair in Milan.

At the beginning of the 1980s he was in Japan. This made an impression on his *Living it Up* collection, which is one of his favorites—patterns which he both dresses in and surrounds himself with. At home in Simrishamn he entertains himself, his friends, and his neighbors with his fabric collages and arrangements. The washing line in the back garden allows the townspeople to keep up to date on the sheets, tablecloths, and other fabrics which Sven is currently working on. Everybody knows that his wash hanging on the line is aesthetically entertaining. You can look through the window of his studio, a former painting shop, and see him designing patterns and, when the mood is on him, painting pictures. The frames are always decorated: they present no obstacle to the flow of his imagination.

—Hedvig Hedqvist

# frogdesign Inc.

## American strategic design group

Founded by Hartmut Esslinger as esslinger design, Mutlangen-Schwabisch Gmund, Germany, 1969; moved to Altensteig, Germany, 1970; headquarters moved to Campbell, California, U.S.A., 1982, and renamed frogdesign inc.; moved to Menlo Park, California, 1987, and to Sunnyvale, California, 1994. Office philosophy: "Form Follows Emotion"; Sunnyvale, California office designed in concert with Michael McDonough Architect, New York. **Member:** Industrial Design Society of America; American Institute of Graphic Arts; Verband Deutscher Industrie Designer. **Collections:** The Boilerhouse, London; Neue Sammlung, Munich; Museum of Modern Art, New York; Museum of Modern Art, San Francisco; The Design Museum, London; Whitney Museum of Art, New York; Cooper Hewitt Museum, New York; Smithsonian Institution, Washington, D.C.; The Design Athenaeum, Chicago. **Address:** frogdesign inc., 1327 Chesapeake Terrace, Sunnyvale, California 94089, U.S.A.; frogdesign gmbh, Grenzweg 33, D-72213 Altensteig, Germany.

## Works

Office furniture, for Holzapfel, from 1970.
Dental instruments and equipment, for Kaltenbach & Voigt, from 1971.
Bathroom fixtures and showers, for Hansgrohe, 1971-85.
Office furniture, for Konig & Neurath, from 1973.
Consumer electronics, for Sony, 1974-88.
Luggage and luxury goods, for Louis Vuitton, 1976-85.
Electronics, for Texas Instruments, from 1977.
Bathtubs, for Kaldewei, 1977-85.
Electronics, for Apple Computer, 1981-86.
Instant cameras, for Polaroid, 1984-85.
Radio clock and radio watches, for Junghans, from 1984.
Bathroom ceramics, for Villeroy & Boch, from 1984.
Cameras, for Eastman Kodak, 1985-87.
Computer peripherals and graphic identity, for Logitech, from 1985.
Workstations, for Sun Microsystems, 1986-91.
Consumer electronics, for Matsushita/Panasonic, 1986-92.
Optical products, for Olympus, from 1986.
Electrical products, for General Electric, 1986-89.
Consumer electronics, for Samsung, 1986-92.
Computers, for NeXT, 1987-92.
Metalware, for Alessi, 1987-89.
Cookware, for Fissler, from 1987.
Tableware, for Rosenthal, from 1989.
Consumer electronics, for a/d/s/, 1989-92.
Supercomputers and graphic identity, for nCube, 1989-91.
Optical products, for Zeiss, from 1990.
Consumer electronics, for ReVox, 1990-93.
Communications products, for AT&T, 1990-93.

Computer products, Zenith Data Systems, from 1990-93.
Computer workstations and graphic identity, for Hyundai/Axil, from 1990.
Computers, for IBM, 1990-94.
Computer monitors, for Mag Innovision, from 1990.
Communications products and graphic identity, for Motorola, from 1990.
Electronic language products and graphic identities, for Langenscheidt, 1991-94.
Computers and graphic identities, for Elecom/Lunaris, from 1991.
Desktop products, for Shachihata, from 1991 (in collaboration with COATO and Dentsu).
Sanitary fixtures and graphic identity, for DAL, from 1992.
Telephones and graphic identity, for Genesis, 1992-93.
Watch packaging, for Swatch, 1992-94.
Computer products and graphic identities, for Media Vision, 1992-94.
Supercomputer, for Convex, 1992-94.
Virtual reality product, for David Sarnoff/Hasbro, 1993-94.
Personal computers, multimedia, and graphic identity, for Packard Bell, from 1993.
Graphic identity, for Network Appliance, from 1993.
Sporting goods, for Head, from 1993.
Personal computers and graphic identities, for Siemens Nixdorf, from 1994.
Personal computers and graphic identity, for Acer America, from 1995.

## Publications

**By frogdesign: books**—(annual) *RANA,* Sunnyvale, California, from 1994.

**On frogdesign: articles**—"The Successfrogs" in *Manager,* 1985; "Hartmut Esslinger: Be a frog!" in *FAZ Magazine,* 1987; *Graphis* (Zürich), March-April 1987, January-February 1994, March-April 1994, September-October 1994, November-December 1994, January-February 1995, May-June 1995, September-October 1995, November-December 1995; "The frog That Roared" by Phil Patton in *Connoisseur* (New York), 1990; *Design* (London), February 1990, June 1990; *Business Week,* 12 March 1990; *ART: das Kunstmagazin* (Germany), April 1991; *PC Magazine,* August 1991, August 1992; *Brandweek* (New York), 20 May 1996.

*See* ESSLINGER, Hartmut

*

frogdesign is an integrated strategic design agency. From its birth as an industrial design consultant more than 25 years ago, frogdesign has progressed to the point where it now forms brand identities through all manner of two- and three-dimensional media. Uniting industrial design with mechanical engineering and graphic design, this strategy has allowed frogdesign's clients to get to market faster and with greater efficacy.

Over the years, certain characteristics have proven to consistently emerge from frogdesign's studios. Projects typically embody provocation, deep concern for the user, and the use of bold, iconography-rich design languages created anew each time. Arguably more than any other design company, firm, or agency, frogdesign

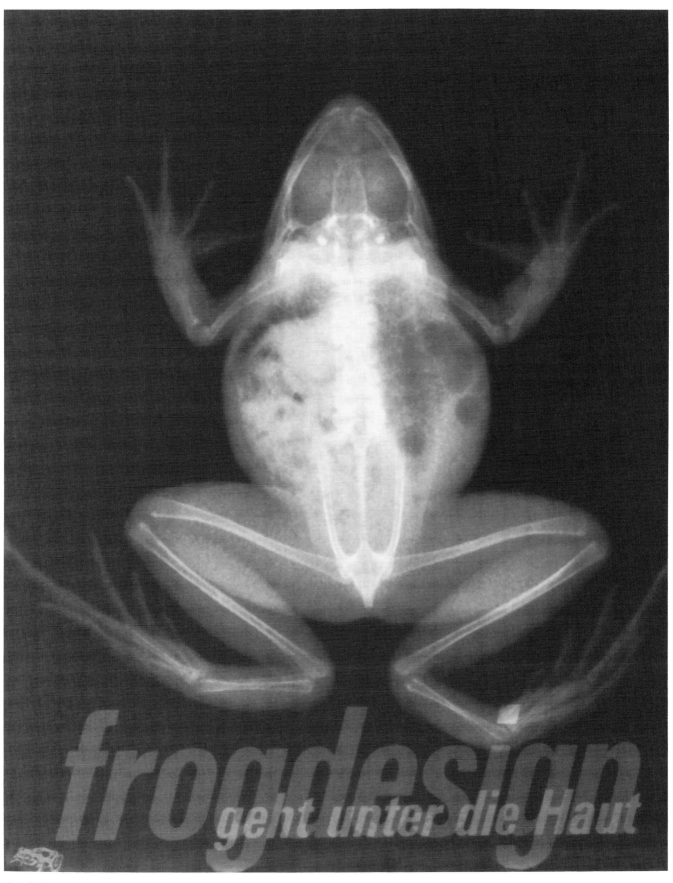

frogdesign

has pushed to expand the possibilities for success in its projects, and in doing so, has used its lean-and-mean horizontal structure to create wealth for its clients far disproportionate to the office's relatively small size.

frogdesign believes the 1950s were the Age of Production, the 1960s were the Age of R&D, the 1970s were the Age of Marketing, the 1980s were the Age of Finance, and the 1990s are the Age of Integration. This is why frogdesign's internal and external orientation has moved toward bringing areas of expertise together that have traditionally been kept apart. This is manifested in a number of our recent projects where frogdesign has worked collaboratively with architects, environmental designers, and textile designers from around the United States, with the goal being the creation of the most synergistic results.

During its entire lifespan, frogdesign has been leading the convergence between consumer electronics, computers, and communications technologies. In urging this convergence forward, frogdesign has constantly thought first and foremost of how the user of these products and services might benefit. Such empathy with the users of design has infused frogdesign's work from the very beginning, and when conjoined with a self-expressive streak that has combined color and complexly-curved forms, it has made for a powerful combination that consumers and clients alike have responded to.

A classic drive for progress has also driven frogdesign on, but it has generally been balanced by a deep belief in responsible production where manufacturing aims to be in concert with nature. Fundamentally, we at frogdesign engage in the production of objects and images. But most of all, we are engaged in the production of meaning and optimism.

—Steven Skov Holt, strategy manager, frogdesign

\*     \*     \*

Perhaps more has been written about frogdesign and its leader, Hartmut Esslinger, IDSA, than any other design firm in the past decade. Media attention peaked with a cover story in *Business Week* magazine in 1990, the first national magazine cover story on an industrial designer since Raymond Loewy made the cover of *Time* in 1947. But what some may see as a cult of personality is in fact an enduring, evolving, and remarkably successful international design firm whose team has embraced the essential philosophy of its founder and added to it in a continuous dedication to improvement, honesty, and integrity.

frogdesign's fundamental principle is to go beyond technological sophistication and aesthetics to define a product in terms of culture, emotion, and usefulness. To that end, it has devised the Integrated Strategic Design process, wherein its three groups—Corporate Design, Industrial Design, and Engineering—collaborate in a five phase development process. That process begins with brainstorming an understanding of the use environment, need, and opportunities, and ends with plant-site approval of all aspects of a product to ensure design integrity and quality. In between, the frog team researches, explores, refines, documents, and tests its way from blue-sky imaginings to tooling bids. It applies the latest in engineering and design technology to, as frog puts it, "... streamline the naturally iterative cycle of creation while providing design excellence." And it designs not only the product but the corporate identity and the packaging and merchandising, a holistic approach that ensures continuity of message and meaning to the user.

Among the characteristics frog has become famous for is its conviction that the key to a successful design program lies as much in the nature and character of the client as in the opportunity and the designer. "Nothing is more crucial to us than finding the right client," says Esslinger in *RANA*, the firm's new annual. "Like any partnership, mutual respect, high ethics, and a true need for each other are vital." And frog has done that very well over the years, amassing a client list that is the envy of many. Two things jump out about frog's list of clients: the high proportion of them that have been with frog for more than ten years; and the business successes each can boast of in that timeframe.

Ironically, one of frogdesign's shorter, albeit most celebrated, client relationships—Apple Computer, Inc.—produced its biggest impact. The seeds planted in that four-year relationship have, arguably, blossomed into a dramatic change in how we perceive computers and technology vis-a-vis the user. Through its design strategy for Apple, as embodied by the Macintosh and Apple IIc computers, frogdesign made a statement about usability, emotion, and the human element in technology that not only transformed thinking about computers and software but that may have helped to fuel thinking about the designer's responsibility to help people use technology, in areas as diverse as consumer electronics and medical instruments.

frog refers to the outcome of what it learned from that and other programs as the "Threshold of Usability," or TU, a hard to find place where "ease of use meets sufficient benefit." Among its most dramatic assertions regarding TU is that, in order to make a product usable, indeed useful, you may have to reduce the number of functions it performs, a risky business in today's technology-driven marketplace. frogdesign "distills" the truly useful functions from the merely usable by subscribing to the formula, "Form Follows Purpose." That is to say, if you have clarity of purpose, rather than availability of technology, as the guiding principle of a design program, you can distill technology down to its true value and enhance it to create a rich new product experience people will love to use. What greater goal could a design firm have?

—Kristina Goodrich

# FRONZONI, A(ngiolo) G(iuseppe)
Italian architect, interior, graphic, and product designer

**Born:** Pistoia, 5 March 1923. **Education:** Self-taught in design. **Family:** Married Marina Fra in 1947; children: Elena, Paola, and Camilla. **Career:** Freelance designer, working in Brescia, 1945-55, and in Milan, from 1956. Founder-director, *Punta* magazine, Brescia, 1947-65; editor and designer, *Casabella* magazine, Milan, 1965-67. Coordinator of global design research project, Collegio Regionale Lombardo degli Architetti, Milan, 1964-65; instructor in visual communications, Umanitaria di Milano, 1967-69, Istituto Statale d'Arte, Monza, from 1968, and Istituto Universitario Isia, Urbino, 1975-77; founder and coordinator, Istituto di Comunicazione Visiva, Milan, 1978-79. **Exhibitions:** Libreria Salto, Milan, 1963; London College of Printing, 1965; Instituto de Arte y Comunicacion Visual, Buenos Aires, 1966; Politecnico, Turin, 1969; Moravska Galerie, Brno, 1975. **Collections:** Bibliothèque Nationale, Paris; Musée des Arts Décoratifs, Paris; Kunstgewerbemuseum, Zürich; Stedelijk Museum, Amsterdam; Deutsches Plakatmuseum, Essen; Deutsches

Bücherei, Leipzig; Royal Ontario Museum, Toronto; Museum of Modern Art, New York. **Honors:** Zanotti Bianco Prize, Rome, 1978. **Address:** via Solferino 44, 20121 Milan, Italy.

## Works

Book designs include—*Bonalumi,* Milan, 1973; *Arte e Materie Plastiche,* Milan, 1975; *Acque di Sicilia,* Milan, 1977.

## Publications

**On FRONZONI: books—***A. G. Fronzoni,* exhibition catalogue by Umbro Apollonio, Turin, 1969; *A History of Visual Communication* by Josef Muller-Brockmann, Teufen, 1971; *Design e Forme Nuove nell'Arredamento Italiano* edited by Paolo Portoghesi and Marino Marini, Rome, 1978; *Atlante del Design Italiano 1940/1980* by Alfonso Grassi and Anty Pansera, Milan, 1980; *Grid Systems in Graphic Design* by Josef Muller-Brockmann, Teufen, 1981.

*

I began working as a designer in 1945, with the war just over and the reconstruction of Europe under way. It was a particularly stimulating period. I was determined to learn by doing. I believed that I could contribute through my work to the transformation of society, that I could help produce objects and facts of social meaning. I had faith in the progressive function of applied rationality.

I persevered with my work, acting in a design context of total spatiality conceived as an information system, in a search for the image of contemporary society, for a model for the use of that *Gesamtkunstwerk,* the city. An attitude derived from a personal, critical background led me to regard design as a protest and a transgression; to seek a design that could subject technical tools to cultural choices; not to satisfy the client's needs, but to eradicate them; to relentlessly avoid waste and redundance; and to cater to the necessities of the social community as the true client.

I have never given in, although one question remains open: whether the innovative autonomy of this work may not eventually turn out to be really an illusion.

In this situation, the designer's task is an arduous one. But this does not discourage me. Anyone who tries to play a civilised and progressive role is put to a hard test in any environment, especially if his job, as in the case of the designer, is always to put every environment to a hard test, and especially if his work consists in continuous designing, which is certainly for him intentionally to exist in the future.

Since 1967, when I added teaching to my activities, I have been increasingly conscious that the true task of the designer is that of an educator more than that of a technician. His real purpose is not to create a city but to educate people to build the city, conceived as a sensitive form of civilisation.

—A. G. Fronzoni

*   *   *

A. G. Fronzoni has always tended to refine his designs to a deceptive simplicity, eschewing more and more all unnecessary elements and emphasising the rectangular geometry that is gener-

ally apposite. Where it was appropriate, as in the 1964 furniture produced in series by Galli, this natural rectangularity was further accented by the choice of square-section, metal tubing, particularly successful for a chair and a bed frame, which were sparse but not Spartan. In many of these pieces, the airy framework of the supporting structure contrasted with the slab forms of seat or cupboard or drawer unit.

This same aesthetic informed the elegant pages he produced for *Casabella* when he was the editor and art director (1965 to 1967). The simple, logical, sensitively composed pages exploited the somewhat unusual format and held the bold, sans serif type to reasonable sizes, while page succeeded page in a carefully planned sequence, and feature was separated from feature by a subtle articulation of internal elements. Much the same could be said of the catalogues and invitation cards designed for the Galleria La Polena in Genoa during the latter years of the 1960s; they managed to achieve, within what in clumsier hands would have been a severely restrictive style, a quite distinct character. The same sort of character had been achieved in the gallery itself which he had designed in 1965 within an old building. Again, careful, minimal detail created an admirable background for the display of works of art. Perhaps the experience gained with this gallery stood him in good stead when he came to some of his later conversions of historical buildings to newer purposes, chiefly as galleries or museums.

In spite of or even because of his quietly uncompromising modernism, he showed a respect and understanding towards these ancient buildings, and his installations drew upon them in a formal dialogue of proportion. Influential here was Ernesto Rogers, who had been the editor of *Casabella* and had researched and set up a small but significant exhibit at the 1951 Triennale, *Architettura, misura d'uomo* [Architecture, the measure of man], which spanned the centuries and saw proportion and rationalism (this word, too, has a link with notions of *ratio,* measure) as civilising elements and as the means by which otherwise contrasting styles could be brought into fruitful formal dialogue. Whether from Rogers himself or from the Triennale exhibit, Fronzoni certainly learned the lesson and profited from it in the run of restoration work he undertook from the late 1960s into the 1980s.

—Toni del Renzio

# FROSHAUG, Anthony

British typographer and graphic designer

**Born:** London, 1920. **Education:** Studied drawing, book production, and engraving, Central School of Arts and Crafts, London, 1937-39; medicine, St. Mary's Hospital School, London, 1940-43; and architecture, Architectural Association School, London, 1967-69. **Career:** Freelance designer, 1941-84; typographer and exhibition designer, London, 1941-47; established own printing press and workshop, Cornwall, 1949-52 and 1953-57; designer in London, 1962-84, establishing own printing workshop, from 1971. Lecturer, 1948-49, senior lecturer in typography, 1952-53, and lecturer in graphic design, 1970-84, Central School of Art and Design, London; docent, Department of Visual Communications, Hochschule für Gestaltung, Ulm, 1957-60; guest professor, Technical University of Norway, Trondheim, 1960; tutor in graphic design, Royal College of Art, London, 1961-64; senior lecturer in graphic design,

Watford College of Technology, Hertfordshire, 1964-67; tutor in graphic design, Coventry College of Art and Design, Warwickshire, 1969-70. **Member:** Society of Industrial Artists and Designers, London, 1947. **Exhibition:** Watford College of Technology, Hertfordshire, 1965. **Collection:** St. Bride Printing Library, London. **Died:** London, 15 June 1984.

## Publications

**By FROSHAUG: books**—*Typographic Norms,* Birmingham and London, 1964; *Typography 1945-65,* Watford, 1965; **articles**—in *Ulm* (Ulm), April 1959; *Design* (London), October 1963; *Ark* (London), June 1964; *The Designer* (London), January 1967; *Typographic* (London), no. 7, 1975.

**On FROSHAUG: books**—*Design in Britain,* annuals edited by Peter Ray, London, 1947, 1951; *Art Without Boundaries 1950-1970* edited by Gerald Woods, Philip Thompson, and John Williams, London, 1972; *Typography: Design and Practice* by John Lewis, London, 1978.

*       *       *

Anthony Froshaug's typography took its first inspiration from the work of Jan Tschichold. After an initial phase of absorption (with more understanding than other contemporaries in Britain showed), Froshaug began to pursue an approach that was no more than latent in Tschichold's "new typography." Thus, the constraints in a task—the meanings and possible semantic structures of a text and the given elements of standard and optimal sizes of materials employed—come to dominate and determine final form, which is therefore correspondingly less subject to the designer's arbitrary will. This approach comes into its own with material more complex than simple prose: listed items, tabular matter, text integrated with pictorial or diagrammatic illustration. Yet, if Froshaug's work takes its bearings from constraints, it also has qualities of visual and physical distinction that can only be finally explained by positing some "feeling for form."

Although Froshaug showed a new approach, his work also had quite un-modern traits. The workshop experiment may have been forced by the difficulties of getting trade printers to follow unconventional instructions, but it was also a statement of allegiance with the earliest printers. His early practice of setting text unjustified had modern associations but also ancient ones—the work of the scribes. A further point of reference here is the work René Hague and Eric Gill did between 1931 and 1940; this was another un-private press that tried to do good, everyday work. The larger rationale for Froshaug's workshop was made explicit in Lewis Mumford's *Technics and Civilization,* as an acceptance of new technologies kept small-scale and knowable, directed towards human needs.

The workshop situation allows experiments not otherwise open to a designer, and Froshaug's work of that time has qualities of invention and play that are less evident later. His years at the Hochschule für Gestaltung in Ulm might be considered a factor in this development towards a sterner approach. It was natural that Froshaug should be attracted by the invitation to teach at this reformulation of the Bauhaus: it was small and limited in scale, politically radical, and approached its work with a seriousness not to be found in Britain. Here Froshaug began to apply his interest in mathematics to problems of design.

In later years, Froshaug's mathematical interests focussed on the uses of small computers. Again, as in his printing, there is a concern with the maximal use of very limited machines. Published results of this work have yet to surface.

—Robin Kinross

# FRUTIGER, Adrian
Swiss graphic, calligraphic, and typographic designer

**Born:** Interlaken, 24 May 1928. **Education:** Apprentice type-compositor, under Ernst Jordi and Walter Zerbe, at Otto Schaefli AG, Interlaken, 1944-48; studied illustration, engraving, and sculpture, under Walter Kaech and Alfred Willimann, at the Kunstgewerbeschule, Zürich, 1948-50. **Career:** Typeface designer, Deberny et Peignot printers and typefounders, Paris, from 1951; also freelance type and symbol designer, working for Sofratype, Lumitype, Monophoto, Bauer, D. Stempel, IBM, Mergenthaler-Linotype, Facom Tool Company, Brancher Printing Ink Company, Gaz de France/Électricité de France, Métro de Paris, Air France, British Petroleum, Ahmedabad Institute of Design, and others, from 1959; established own typography and advertising design studio, with Andre Gurtler and Bruno Pfaffli, in Paris, 1962, and in Arceuil, 1965; art director, Editions Hermann publishers, Paris, 1957-67; design consultant, IBM typewriter faces, from 1963; also architectural sculptor, from 1962. Instructor, Ecole Estienne, Paris, 1952-60, and Ecole Nationale Supérieure des Arts Décoratifs, Paris, 1954-68. **Exhibitions:** Mono-type House, London, 1964; Galerie Pierre Beres, Paris, 1968; Kunstgewerbeschule, Basel, 1970; Gewerbemuseum, Bern, 1973; Gutenberg Museum, Mainz, 1977; Könizer Galerie, Bern, 1988; Sitodruk Burski, Gdansk, 1988; International Club der Presse, Gdansk, 1989; Maison du Livre, Villeurbanne, France, 1994. **Honors:** Paul-Haupt-Preis, Bern, 1985; Gutenberg-Preis, Mainz, 1986; Type Directors Club of New York Medal, 1987; Frederic W. Gaudy Award, Rochester, New York, 1988; Jäggi-Preis, Basel, 1989; Grand Prix National, Paris, 1992. **Address:** Kunoweg 15, CH-3047 Bremgarten-Bern, Switzerland.

## Works

*Président* typeface, for Deberny et Peignot, 1952, adapted for D. Stempel AG, Frankfurt am Main, 1985.
*Phoebus* typeface, for Deberny et Peignot, 1953.
*Ondine* typeface, for Deberny et Peignot, 1953, adapted for D. Stempel AG, Frankfurt am Main, 1981.
*Meridien* text typeface, for Deberny et Peignot, 1954, adapted for D. Stempel AG, Frankfurt am Main, 1975.
*Univers* typeface family, for Deberny et Peignot, 1954-55, adapted for D. Stempel AG, Frankfurt am Main, 1969-84.
*Egyptienne* text typeface for Sofratype, for Deberny et Peignot, 1955-56, adapted as *Egyptienne F.* for D. Stempel AG, Frankfurt am Main, 1976.
*Concorde* text typeface for Sofratype, for Deberny et Peignot, 1959.
Alphabet, for Orly Airport, Paris, 1959.
Alphabet, for Électricité de France-Gaz de France, Paris, 1959.
*Opéra* text typeface for Sofratype, for Zeilensatz-Matrizen, Paris, 1961.

*Apollo* text typeface, for Monotype Corporation Ltd., 1962.

*Alpha-BP* typeface, for the British Petroleum Company, 1965.

*Serifa* typeface family, for Bauersche Giesserei, 1967, adapted for D. Stempel AG, 1976.

*OCR-B* Optical Character Recognition standard typeface, for the European Computer Manufacturers Association, 1968-73, adapted for D. Stempel AG, Frankfurt am Main, 1978.

*Dokumenta* typeface, for the Basler National-Zeitung, Basel, 1969.

Corporate identity program, for Réunion des Musées Nationaux, Paris, 1970.

*Roissy Alphabet,* for Aéroport Charles de Gaulle, Paris, 1970.

House typeface, for the Facom Tool Company, Paris, 1971.

*Iridium* typeface, for D. Stempel AG, 1972.

House typeface, for the Brancher printing ink company, Paris, 1972.

*Alphabet Métro* signage system, for the Parisien Métro, 1973.

*Frutiger* series typefaces for photocomposition, for D. Stempel AG, 1975-76.

*Glypha* condensed typeface series, for D. Stempel AG, 1978-79.

*Icone* typeface series, for D. Stempel AG, 1980.

*Breughel* typeface, for D. Stempel AG, 1981.

*Versailles* typeface, for D. Stempel AG, 1983.

*Linotype Centennial* typeface for photocomposition, for Linotype, 1984.

Corporate identity program, for Goethe Universität, Frankfurt, 1985.

Corporate identity program, for Westiform, Bern, 1986.

*Avenir* typeface for photocomposition, for D. Stempel AG, 1988.

*Westside* typeface, for D. Stempel AG, 1989.

*Vectora* typeface for photocomposition, for D. Stempel AG, 1991.

*Herculaneum* typeface, for D. Stempel AG, 1991.

*Rusticana* typeface, for D. Stempel AG, 1992.

*Pompejana* typeface, for D. Stempel AG, 1993.

Book illustrations include—*Genesis,* Paris, 1960; *Partages,* Paris, 1962; *Das Hohe Lied Solomos,* Zürich, 1966; *Im Anfang...,* Zürich, 1969; *La Cité de Dieu,* Paris, 1977; *Heinz Piontek: Eh der Wind umsprang,* Echzell, 1983; *Jonas,* Köniz, 1988.

## Publications

**By FRUTIGER: books**—*Die Kirchen am Thunersee,* booklet, Interlaken, 1948; *The Development of the Roman Alphabet,* Zürich, 1951; *Typographical Training for Technicians and Technical Training for Typographers,* booklet, Copenhagen, 1973; *Der Mensch und seine Zeichen,* 3 vols., Echzell and Frankfurt, 1978-80, Lausanne, 1983; *Type, Sign, and Symbol,* with texts by M. Besset, E. Ruder, and H. R. Schneebeli, Zürich, 1980; *Signs and Symbols,* New York, 1981; *Adrian Frutiger, son oeuvre typographique et ses ecrits,* Villeurbanne, France, 1994; **articles**—"Das Schriftbild: Kleid der Lesebotschaft" in *Deutscher Drucker,* no. 35, 1978; "Type, paper and man today" in *Typographische Monatsblätter,* June 1980; "Das Miterleben einer Wandlung" in *Gutenberg-Jahrbuch,* 1985; "L'histoire des Antiques" in *Typographische Monatsblätter,* January/February 1988; "Adrian Frutiger Himself" (interview) in *Der Druckspiegel,* no. 8, 1988; "Avenir: une nouvelle Antique constructiviste" in *Typographische Monatsblätter,* February 1989.

**On FRUTIGER: books**—*Who's Who in Graphic Art* edited by Walter Amstutz, Zürich, 1962, Dubendorf, 1982; *Graphismes by Frutiger* by John Dreyfus, London, 1964; *Letter Forms: 110 Complete Alphabets* edited by Frederick Lambert, London, 1964, New York, 1972; *Serifa: Die neue Schrift von Adrian Frutiger* by Emil Ruder, Frankfurt, 1967; *Serifa, Vorprobe* by Hermann Zapf, Frankfurt, 1967; *Adrian Frutiger: Ein Sternseminar* edited by the Graphisk Institut, Stockholm, 1968; *Schrift, Signet, Symbol: Formgebung in Schwarz und Weiss—Adrian Frutiger,* exhibition catalogue by Walter Zerbe, Bern, 1973; *Adrian Frutiger: Zeichen, Schriften, Symbole,* exhibition folder with text by Kurt Weidemann, Mainz, 1977; *The Thames and Hudson Manual of Typography* by Ruari McLean, London, 1980; *The Conran Directory of Design* edited by Stephen Bayley, London, 1985; *Typographic Design: Form and Communication* by Rob Carter, Ben Day, and Philip Meggs, New York, 1985; *Adrian Frutiger, Gutenbergpreisträger 1986* by Walter Greisner, Mainz, 1986; *Twentieth Century Type Designers* by Sebastian Carter, London, 1988; **articles**—"Typography, Technology and Adrian Frutiger" in *Graphics World,* September/October 1986; "Frutiger Looks to the Future" by Andrew Bluhm in *Graphic Repro,* December 1988; "Face to Face with Adrian Frutiger" by Carrie Blackford in *Hot Graphics,* no. 15, 1988; "The Hamlet of Types" by Robin Kinross in *Blueprint,* no. 54, 1989.

\*

The typographer can get involved in scientific and technical aspects, particularly with the new composing methods. He can also devote himself to artistic aspects, where he has to solve space problems—problems of a white page that he has to divide and make come alive. The typographer is the one who renders thoughts accessible to everybody, he is the intermediary between the one who thinks, the one who creates, and the one who receives. This is one of the most beautiful professions—and also one of the most difficult.

I became enraptured by the simplicity of the abstract sign, by the magic of these twenty-six letters which, by themselves, can encompass the entire world's thought. I feel, for instance, that the inside white spaces are more important than the outside contours of a letter. The letters of an alphabet are like the various elements of a house: the material of typography is the black, and it is the typographer's task, with the help of this black, to capture space, to create harmonious whites inside the letters as well as between them. A letter only exists in its relation to the others. In addition, the look of a page printed in a given typeface must be the same in all languages. This is where the problem of the frequency of letters arises.

In typography, as in other art forms, the "hand," the "stamp" of the one who creates the character is recognizable. Once the typographer has acquired the full knowledge of his profession and the skill of his hands corresponds to his sensitivity and logic, he can no longer escape from an aesthetic shaped by his temperament, his education, his cultural heritage, and the experiences of many years' work. It is only in retrospect that one realizes that one is the child of one's own epoch, that one submits to one's time. For instance, the style of *Univers* was in the air after the War. Although this is a bit of an exaggeration, I could almost say that it was anticipated, that there was a need for it to be created.

My way of thinking can be described as organized; everything has to pass through my head. To a degree, I lack spontaneity; my creative mechanism is always based on logic, on a text, on a development; it could well be that this renders my work more understandable than that of others, more communicable.

I believe that in a person's life, his area of specialization becomes more and more demanding and may result, in a certain way, in a loss of his freedom. For me, the retreat from this specialization is in the applied use of typography and letters. The studio is very important to me; without it I'd be in an ivory tower. I need contact with the concrete and the daily application of the materials I create, even if, as is obvious, I don't necessarily use my own type faces or the machines for which I am designing. It's different with the illustration of books. I relinquish the "alphanumeric skeleton" when expressing my personal philosophical or religious thought. It is true that I love this work also, but I would not be unhappy if I had nothing but the "alphanumeric skeleton": it is really so rich. And besides even in the realm of personal aesthetic expression, I'd never be an Artist with a capital "A."

I am of Germanic origin, since I was born in the German section of Switzerland, and have received a German-type scholastic and professional education; for this I am grateful. With the methods and knowledge acquired there, I have been able to do more constructive, rational, better-organized work. And, since I have also led a very active life in a Latin country, the two influences complement each other. The result is a combination of qualities which have undoubtedly contributed to the success of *Univers*—which is accepted just as favorably in the Latin countries as it is in the Germanic ones.

—Adrian Frutiger

*        *        *

When the historical importance of contemporary typographers is analyzed, Adrian Frutiger stands out as the designer who led the way in several essential directions. Beyond the usual four options, his *Univers* offers a set of new possibilities with its twenty-one variations based on slant, proportion, and weight. Unlike most sans-serif alphabets designed before 1954, *Univers* is based on a geometrical construction thoroughly corrected to meet visual and technological needs. For example, a high x-height reduces the excessive conspicuousness of capitals and increases readability in small sizes; slightly wider strokes in the capitals than in the lower cases help maintain a similar stroke-weight to letter-size relation; progressive thinning of the strokes as they meet helps maintain constant apparent width. These and many other details show Frutiger's fine sensitivity to typeface design.

His adaptation of *Univers* for the IBM composer placed in the market a new class of product between typesetting and typewriting, one that revolutionized the visual standards of low technology in typography. To compensate for the distortions occurring in phototypesetting, he introduced new details in type design for this medium. Re-evaluating the actual form of the strokes, their ends, and their encounters, he aimed at maintaining the desirable consistency already pursued through optical corrections in the design of the *Univers.*

Working with a grid three times finer than the one in use at the time and pushing available technology to its limits, he designed the Optical Character Recognition typeface Class B for the European Computer Manufacturers Association, thereby bringing computer typography back to meet the needs of the reader after a period of hardware-imposed design. His *Frutiger* series, excellent for signage, shows generous counters and more open ends (particularly in the lower cases a, c, e, and s, the upper cases C, G, and S, and the numerals 2, 3, 5, 6, and 9); these contribute to a greater distinctiveness for each character and move away from the Bauhaus concept of beauty based on consistency toward the concept of performance based on differentiation within a system.

Much as Claude Garamond opened new avenues to typeface design in 1544 by providing an appropriate response to the technology and the needs of the time, so Frutiger has responded to the needs of our century, with an equally deep understanding of technology and a comparable grace.

—Jorge Frascara

# FUJITA, S(adamitsu) Neil

American graphic designer

**Born:** Waimea, Kauai, Hawaii, 16 May 1921. **Education:** Studied at Chouinard Art Institute, Los Angeles, 1940-42, and 1947-49; Columbia University, New York, 1957-59. **Military Service:** Served in the United States Army, 442nd Infantry Regiment, in Italy and France, 1944-46, and with G-2 Intelligence, in Okinawa, 1946-47, Staff Sergeant. **Family:** Married Aiko Tamaki in 1949; children: Kenji, David, and Martin. **Career:** Art Director, at N. W. Ayer and Son, Philadelphia, 1953-54; director of design and packaging, Columbia Records, New York, 1954-60; freelance designer, New York, 1960-63; founder and president of Ruder, Finn, and Fujita, New York, 1963-77, and of S. Neil Fujita Design Incorporated and Wisteria Field Incorporated, New York, from 1977. Instructor, Philadelphia College of Art, 1953-54, Pratt Institute, Brooklyn, New York, 1960-62, The New School for Social Research, New York, 1969, and the Parsons School of Design, New York, from 1979. **Exhibitions:** Philadelphia Art Alliance, 1954; Atwater Kent Museum, Philadelphia, 1954; Los Angeles County Museum of Art, 1955; Virginia Museum of Fine Arts, Richmond, 1955; American Institute of Graphic Arts, New York, 1956; Santa Barbara Museum of Art, California, 1956. **Collections:** Atwater Kent Museum, Philadelphia. **Honors:** Gold Medal, Art Directors Club of New York, 1952, 1957, Art Directors Club of Chicago, 1953, and Art Directors Club of Philadelphia, 1953, 1954; Merit Award, Art Directors Club of New York, 1953, 1954, and Art Directors Club of Chicago, 1953; Excellence Award, American Institute of Graphic Arts, 1954, 1955, 1977, and Type Directors Club, New York, 1954, 1955, 1957; Service of Freedom Award, International Rescue Committee, 1970. **Address:** 415 Central Park West, New York, New York 10025, U.S.A.

## Publications

**By FUJITA: book**—*Aim for a Job in Graphic Art and Design,* New York, 1968, 1977; **articles**—in *Print* (New York), 1964, 1967, 1969; *Financial World* (New York), 26 June 1968; *Idea* (Tokyo), May 1970; *Public Relations Journal* (New York), October 1970; *Publishers Weekly* (New York), 10 April 1972; *Graphics USA* (New York), October 1974, January 1977.

**On FUJITA: book**—*Printing History* by Gordon Nearill, New York, 1979; *Album Covers* by Martina Schmitz, Munich, 1987.

*

The understanding of our purpose in life and work doesn't necessarily apply only to a designer or art director; it applies to everyone. Somehow I feel that the designer, like anyone working in the creative arts, should understand this purpose better. Perhaps I am inclined to think so because people in the creative field are constantly arranging and composing, or drawing things together to make their creativity work.

The designer, for example, graphically starts with a clear white surface. To this surface he brings originality and a purpose. I suggest this is totally irrelevant to what it takes to recognize clearly the complexities of human behavior and make what we have learned about human nature work for us.

Is the designer, who works with an uninterrupted clear white surface, unaware of the role he must also play as a performer on the surface of humanity? I hardly think so; I think the designer is well aware that he is first an individual, an integral part of the human race, who understands his role and function and is capable of meeting his responsibility as a human being.

The designer is certainly capable of reaching out for goals far greater and richer in human values than to be satisfied with the attainment of a mere visual creation. I think he is capable of grouping and unifying personalities and emotions in a composition of people and relationships. For this reason, improbable as it may seem, a designer who works with ideas, materials, personalities, and a surface could very well sit in the General Assembly at the United Nations and function effectively as a designer for a creative unit international in magnitude and diversity. I feel that merely replacing a flat surface with an arena of human dimensions is all it takes to put the designer on not too unfamiliar ground. On both surfaces there are varied shades of colors to work with as well as other related elements required to create harmonious composition.

But the truth is, many of us are still looking for answers and directions on the clear white, unobtrusive surface. We haven't bothered to look beyond the edge of our drawing pads. We haven't learned to bridge the gap between our purpose and function in life. Call this link a rapport—or better still, call this connecting span a translation between people. No matter how we look at it, this transmission between man and the world around him should be bridged, and the job requires, for lack of a better term, a super-engineer.

Human engineering covers a tremendously broad area—an area so big that many of us have failed miserably to understand it. This not only means understanding our purpose in life and work, but also covers the area of understanding others. It is here, I think, where we divide the men from the boys. It is here where we divide the executives from the executors. It is here we learn to give and take. It is also here, in one of the categories of the humanities, where we truly find the purpose of our craft and concepts.

To understand the immediate area of where we stand as designers or art directors, it is a good starting point to learn the meaning of our purpose in life and work. Like everyone, we must start from where we are.

The artist, for example, who paints, functions best when he excludes himself from his society in order to create, but ironically it is the same society that later recognizes his accomplishments. The designer, on the other hand, functions in reverse. He creates for the society he lives in and never excludes himself from it. He is like an actor who needs an audience to speak to with his graphic gesture and iconology. The painter who expresses and the designer who interprets do have one thing in common: they are both communicators. But they work from different approaches.

It is clear that the painter finds his audience after his work is completed, while the designer knows his audience before he starts.

This is, I believe, the general consensus. However, this theory doesn't always hold true because there are painters who paint for a specific audience and there are designers who like to take the role of a painter, neglecting their purpose as graphic communicators of a client's message. I think it is sad when a painter thinks commercially or when a designer thinks purely idealistically.

The respect I hold for both is too great to allow indifference of opinion to nullify their respective positions and functions as craftsmen. My respect for the painter is high because it takes guts and perseverance to paint. My respect for the designer is equally high because it takes guts and diplomacy to survive.

What separates one from the other professionally does not, however, remove them from a common denominator. They are both considered to be craftsmen. Of course, there are others, perhaps not in the creative arts, but nevertheless men who are equally devoted to their craft. There is the carpenter, the blacksmith, the plumber, the typographer, the engraver, the printer, and countless others who perform functions that exemplify an honest and practical definition of the performing craft. I place the role of the designer and painter, in part, in a similar category.

But when the designer removes himself from the category of the craftsman, it is like a plumber talking with verbosity about the esthetic qualities of his wrench, rather than tending to the leak in the pipe. Or, with equal absurdity, it is like the typographer talking about the beauty of a metallic alphabet giving metal to a word or sentence. This all means that designers shouldn't continue merely to talk about design; they should use it effectively, giving substance to their function and purpose.

It is the substance we put into our purpose in life and work that truly measures the depth of our function. As designers, we approach our duties and responsibilities not only with the understanding of ourselves, but also with the respect of others. And we go on performing our function as craftsmen, devoted to the values of accomplishment, not the volume of accolades. The reward we win will be the satisfaction of knowing that we have done our job as professionals, not tyros; as responsible artists responsible to man. (*Reprinted from "Human Engineering: A Neglected Design Tool" in* Print *[New York], 1969.*)

—S. Neil Fujita

# FUKUDA, Shigeo

Japanese graphic designer

**Born:** Tokyo, February 1932. **Education:** Studied at the National University of Arts and Music, Tokyo, 1952-56. **Family:** Married Shizuko Fukuda in 1961; daughter: Miran. **Career:** Freelance graphic designer, Tokyo, from 1960. Instructor, National University of Arts and Music, Tokyo, from 1980, and Yale University, New Haven, Connecticut, 1983. **Member:** Japan Graphic Designers Association; Japan Design Committee; Alliance Graphique Internationale. **Exhibitions:** Cosy Space, Tokyo, 1978; Seibu Department Store, Tokyo, 1978, 1979; Gallery Marronnier, Kyoto, 1978; Gallery Lukoan, Osaka, 1978; Matsuya Design Gallery, Tokyo, 1979; Nick Design Gallery, Fukuoka, 1979; Kokugeki Gallery, Asahikawa City, Hokkaido, 1979; Ikebukuro Parco Gallery, Tokyo, 1980; Space 21, Tokyo, 1980; Green Collections, Tokyo, 1980; Matsuda Rotary Club, Tokyo, 1980; Galery Tosenbo, Kyoto,

1981. **Collections:** Museum of Modern Art, New York; Walker Art Center, Minneapolis; Yale University, New Haven, Connecticut; University of Colorado, Boulder; Musée de l'Affiche, Paris; Modern Art Museum, Warsaw; Modern Art Museum, Brno. **Honors:** Brno Graphics Biennale Awards, 1966, 1970, 1974; Gold Medal, Warsaw Poster Biennale, 1972, 1976; 30th Anniversary Poster Competition Prize, Warsaw, 1975; Montreal Olympics Poster Prize, 1975. Honorary Royal Designer for Industry, Royal Society of Arts, London, 1986. **Address:** 3-34-25 Kamikitazawa, Setagaya-ku, Tokyo, Japan.

## Publications

**By FUKUDA: books**—*Toyo,* Tokyo, 1970; *Element of Idea,* Tokyo, 1977; *Forms of Shigeo Fukuda,* Tokyo, 1977; *Hyohonbako,* Tokyo, 1978; *Shigeo Fukuda,* Tokyo, 1979; *Visual Illusion,* Tokyo, 1982; *Posters of Shigeo Fukuda,* Tokyo, 1982; **articles**—in *Idea* (Tokyo), July 1971; *Graphic Design* (Tokyo), December 1971.

**On FUKUDA: books**—*Modern Graphics* by Keith Murgatroyd, London, 1969; *107 Grafici dell'AGI,* exhibition catalogue with texts by Renzo Zorzi and Franco Grignani, Venice, 1974; *Archigraphia: Architectural and Environmental Graphics* edited by Walter Herdeg, Zurich, 1978; *The 20th-Century Poster: Design of the Avant-Garde* by Dawn Ades, New York, 1984; *Eye for Industry: Royal Designers for Industry 1936-1986,* exhibition catalogue by Fiona MacCarthy and Patrick Nuttgens, London, 1986; *Japanese Design* by Penny Sparke, London, 1987.

*       *       *

Asked about Shigeo Fukuda, the graphic designer comments, "One of the greatest designers of our time," while a leading New York art dealer states, "Fukuda? Well, an outstanding sculptor," and an art scholar from Yale says, "What a thinker!" Amazingly, they all talk about the same person. When asked about his own opinion as to which part of his work is most important, Fukuda only smiles enigmatically.

The son of a family long known as toy manufacturers, Fukuda was almost destined to follow the tradition. And, so to say, in many respects he does. Especially, one sees in the enormous production of the last twenty years strong currents directly linked to two kinds of toys—a wood puzzle you can play with in many ways and the traditional Japanese *origami* folded-paper craft.

Fukuda's posters first achieved recognition on the international scene at the *Expo '70* in Osaka. Later, when the possibilities were bigger and the invitations from abroad followed, Fukuda grew in a more personal direction. Hundreds of his own *origami* paper constructions were followed by the posters for his own exhibitions of those paper marvels. They were more intimate, disciplined in a strange way, suggesting that indeed, less is better. In the early 1970s, the two-dimensional forms reached a peak of quality.

The "Environmental Pollution" series of black-and-white silkscreen prints was based on real objects Fukuda fashioned from wood, painted, and regularly exhibited. Combined with humorous paper cut-out models to make three variants, they transformed the character of Fukuda's activity from smart design to avant-garde art. The careful craftsmanship and logical design only reinforced the power of pure artistic imagination.

Another gigantic project followed. Fukuda was co-author of a very risky, almost kamikaze-like attempt to try the tired *Mona Lisa* portrait once more. His installation of 100 transformations of the famous subject was a masterpiece of a gamble of eastern mastery playing with a cult object of western civilization. The effect was striking in its universality.

Recently, Fukuda has concentrated more and more on three-dimensional forms. Using many media, he develops huge public spaces marked by his brisk wit and endless reserves of sophisticated humor. But the most important realization of freestanding objects are wood sculptures, quite large in scale, painted in plain but contrasting colors. They are the puzzles again—two-sided constructions bearing serious messages. From one angle, we see a pianist, from another, the violinist. But in others, the symbols are written on one side, portrayed visually on the other. Often these clash violently—as in real life, theory versus practice.

Viewed in larger numbers, they state Fukuda's philosophy: Nothing is real, every truth has many faces, the symbols don't work, bad is good—pure life indeed.

The artist breaks all barriers—as between design and fine art while he happily mixes his Japanese tradition with western meanings. With his witty humor and enormous energy, he hates to pose as the teacher of what is right in art; rather, he tries to puzzle us and gently force us to think. He plays with his toys, with their intellectual means, but he's deeply concerned about the state of our world. A smile with a little tear.

—Jan Sawka

# FULLER, Richard Buckminster

American architectural designer

**Born:** Milton, Massachusetts, 12 July 1895. **Education:** Milton Academy, 1904-13; Harvard University, Cambridge, Massachusetts, 1913-15; United States Naval Academy, Annapolis, Maryland, 1917. **Military:** Served in the United States Navy, 1917-19, Lieutenant. **Family:** Married Anne Hewlett in 1917; daughters: Alexandra (died) and Allegra. **Career:** Assistant export manager, Armour and Company, New York, 1919-21; national accounts sales manager, Kelly Springfield Truck Company, 1922; president, Stockade Building System, Chicago, 1922-27; founder and president, 4D Company, Chicago, 1927-32; founder, director, and chief engineer, Dymaxion Corporation, Bridgeport, Connecticut, 1932-36; assistant to the director of research and development, Phelps Dodge Corporation, New York, 1936-38; vice-president and chief engineer, Dymaxion Company, Delaware, 1940-50; chief mechanical engineer, United States Board of Economic Warfare, Washington, D.C., 1942-44; special assistant to the deputy director of the United States Foreign Economic Administration, Washington, D.C., 1944; chairman and chief engineer, Dymaxion Dwelling Machine Corporation, Wichita, Kansas, 1944-46; chairman, Fuller Research Foundation, Wichita, 1946-54; president, Geodesics, Forest Hills, New York, 1949-83, Synergetics, Raleigh, North Carolina, 1954-59, and Plydomes, Des Moines, Iowa, 1957-83; chairman, Tetrahelix Corporation, Hamilton, Ohio, 1959-83; senior partner, Fuller and Sadao, Long Island City, New York, 1979-83; chairman of the board, R.

Buckminster Fuller, Sadao and Zung Architects, Cleveland, Ohio, 1979-83; senior partner, Buckminster Fuller Associates, London, 1979-83. Charles Eliot Norton Professor of Poetry, Harvard University, 1962-63; Harvey Cushing Orator, American Association of Neuro-Surgeons, 1967; Nehru Lecturer, New Delhi, 1969; Hoyt Fellow, Yale University, New Haven, Connecticut, 1969; fellow, St. Peter's College, Oxford, 1970; research professor, 1959-68, university professor, 1968-75, distinguished service professor, 1972-75, and university professor emeritus, 1975 until his death in 1983, Southern Illinois University, Carbondale; world fellow in residence, Consortium of the University of Pennsylvania, Swarthmore College, Bryn Mawr College, and the University City Science Center, Philadelphia, and consultant to the Design Science Institute, Philadelphia, 1972 until his death in 1983; university professor emeritus, University of Pennsylvania, Philadelphia, 1974 until his death in 1983; tutor in design science, International Community College, Los Angeles, 1975; distinguished lecturer, College of Engineering, Villanova University, Pennsylvania, 1976; Distinguished Half Century Lecturer, University of Houston, 1977; Ezra Pound Lecturer, University of Idaho, Moscow, 1977; Grauer Lecturer, University of British Columbia, Vancouver, 1977; distinguished lecturer, University of Calgary, Alberta 1979; Adjunct Professor of Humanities, Texas Wesleyan University, Fort Worth, 1980; Regents Lecturer, University of California at Los Angeles, 1982. Consultant to Architects Team 3, Penang, Malaysia, 1974 until his death in 1983. Editor and publisher, *Shelter* magazine, Philadelphia, 1930-32; technical consultant on the staff of *Fortune* magazine, New York, 1938-40; editor-at-large, *World Magazine,* New York, 1972-75. **Member:** President, Triton Foundation, Cambridge, Massachusetts, 1967; international president, MENSA, Paris, 1975, and World Society for Ekistics, Athens, 1975; National Academy of Design; fellow, American Institute of Architects, and of the Building Research Institute of the National Academy of Sciences; life fellow, American Association for the Advancement of Science; National Institute of Arts and Letters; fellow, American Academy of Arts and Sciences; Mexican Institute of Architects; honorary member, Society of Venezuelan Architects, Israel Institute of Engineers and Architects, Zentralvereinigung der Architekten Österreichs, and Royal Society of Siamese Architects; Benjamin Franklin Fellow, Royal Society of Arts; honorary fellow, Royal Institute of British Architects. **Exhibitions:** Harvard University, Cambridge, Massachusetts, 1929; American Institute of Architects, Washington, D.C., 1930; World's Fair, Chicago, 1933; Museum of Modern Art, New York, 1937, 1940, 1943, 1959, 1968, 1977; United States Embassy, London, 1962; United States Geodesic Pavilion at *Expo '67,* Montreal, 1967; Spoleto Festival, Italy, 1967; Museum of Science and Industry, Chicago, 1973 (toured the United States and Canada); Cooper-Hewitt Museum, New York, 1976; Ronald Feldmann Fine Arts Gallery, New York, 1977 (2 shows); Philadelphia Museum of Art, 1977; Carl Solway Gallery, Cincinnati, 1977 (travelled to Carl Solway Gallery, New York); Protetch McIntosh Gallery, Washington, D.C., 1977; Dumont and Kenyon Associates, Van Wezel Performing Arts Center, Sarasota, Florida, 1978; Drawing Center, New York, 1979 (travelled to the Smithsonian Institution, Washington, D.C.); Getler-Pall Gallery, New York, 1981; Carl Solway Gallery, Cincinnati, 1981; DeCordova and Dana Museum, Lincoln, Massachusetts, 1982; Fendrick Gallery, Washington, D.C., 1982; Galerie Watari, Tokyo, 1982. **Collections:** Metropolitan Museum of Art, New York; Museum of Modern Art, New York; Museum of Fine Arts, Boston; Fogg Museum, Harvard University, Cambridge, Massachusetts; Philadelphia Museum of Art; Baltimore Museum

of Art; Art Institute of Chicago; Museum of Science and Industry, Chicago; Seattle Art Museum; Los Angeles County Museum of Art; Staatliche Museum, Berlin; Victoria and Albert Museum, London. **Honors:** Award of Merit, American Institute of Architects, New York Chapter, 1952; Grand Prize, *Triennale,* Milan, 1954, 1957; Award of Merit, United States Marine Corps, 1955; Gold Medal, National Architectural Society, 1958; Gold Medal American Institute of Architects, Philadelphia Chapter, 1960; Franklin P. Brown Medal, Franklin Institute, Philadelphia, 1962; Allied Professions Gold Medal, 1963, Architectural Design Award, 1968, and Gold Medal, 1970, American Institute of Architects; Plomado de Oro Award, Society of Mexican Architects, 1963; Delta Phi Delta Gold Key, 1964; Creative Achievement Award, Brandeis University, Waltham, Massachusetts, 1965; First Award of Excellence, Industrial Designers Society of America, 1966; Order of Lincoln Medal, Lincoln Academy, Illinois, 1967; Gold Medal for Architecture, National Institute of Arts and Letters, 1968; Royal Gold Medal for Architecture, Royal Institute of British Architects, London, 1968; Citation of Merit, United States Department of Housing and Urban Development, 1969; Citation of Excellence, National Institute of Steel Construction, 1969; Humanist of the Year Award, American Association of Humanists, 1969; McGraw-Hill Master Designer in Product Engineering Award, 1969; R. Buckminster Fuller Chair of Architecture established at the University of Detroit, 1970; Alpha Rho Chi Master Architect Life Award, 1970; President's Award, University of Detroit, 1971; Salmagundi Medal, Salmagundi Club, New York, 1971; Annual Award of Merit, Philadelphia Art Alliance, 1973; Honorary Citizenship Award, City of Philadelphia, 1973; Planetary Citizens Award, United Nations, 1975; honorary doctorates, North Carolina State University, Raleigh, 1954, University of Michigan, Ann Arbor, 1955, Washington University, St. Louis, 1957, Southern Illinois University, Carbondale, 1959, Rollins College, Winter Park, Florida, 1960, University of Colorado, Boulder, 1964, Clemson University, South Carolina, 1964, University of New Mexico, Albuquerque, 1964, Monmouth College, West Long Branch, New Jersey, 1965, California State Colleges, 1966, Long Island University, Greenvale, New York, 1966, California College of Arts and Crafts, Oakland, 1966, Clarkson College of Technology, Potsdam, New York, 1967, Dartmouth College, Hanover, New Hampshire, 1968, University of Rhode Island, Kingston, 1968, New England College, Henniker, New Hampshire, 1968, Ripon College, Wisconsin, 1968, Bates College, Lewiston, Maine, 1969, Boston College, 1969, University of Wisconsin, Madison, 1969, Brandeis University, Waltham, Massachusetts, 1970, Columbia College, Chicago, 1970, Park College, Parkville, Missouri, 1970, Minneapolis School of Art, 1970, Wilberforce University, Ohio, 1970, Southeastern Massachusetts University, North Dartmouth, 1971, University of Maine, Orono, 1972, Grinnell College, Iowa, 1972, Emerson College, Boston, 1972, Nasson College, Springvale, Maine, 1973, Rensselaer Polytechnic Institute, Troy, New York, 1973, Beaver College, Glenside, Pennsylvania, 1973, Pratt Institute, Brooklyn, New York, 1974, McGill University, Montreal, 1974, St. Joseph's College, Philadelphia, 1974, University of Pennsylvania, Philadelphia, 1974, University of Notre Dame, Indiana, 1974, Hobart and William Smith Colleges, Geneva, New York, 1975, Hahnemann Medical College and Hospital, 1978, International College, 1979, Southern Illinois University, Carbondale, 1979, Alaska Pacific University, Anchorage, 1979, Roosevelt University, Chicago, 1980, Georgian Court College, 1980, Newport University, 1980, Texas Wesleyan University, Fort Worth, 1981. **Died:** Los Angeles, 1 July 1983.

## Works

United States Air Force Early Warning System Domes, the Arctic, 1954.
United States Exhibition Pavilion, Sokolniki Park, Moscow, 1959.
Climatron botanical garden, St. Louis, 1960.
Cinerama Theatre, Hollywood, California, 1963.
United States Pavilion, *Expo 67,* Montreal, 1967.
Airplane Museum, Schipol Airport, Amsterdam, 1969.
Weather Radome, Mount Fuji, Japan, 1973.
Archaeological Site Dome, Ban Chiang, Thailand, 1979.
Fly's Eye Information Center, Los Angeles, 1981.
Spruce Goose Airplane Hanger, Long Beach, California, 1982.
Spaceship Earth Dome, Walt Disney World, Orlando, Florida, 1982.
Patents include—Stockade (building structure), 1927; Stockade (pneumatic forming process), 1927; 4D House, 1928; Dymaxion Car, 1937; Dymaxion Bath, 1940; Dymaxion Deployment Unit 1944; Dymaxion Airocean World, 1946; Fuller House, 1946; Geodesic Dome, 1954; Paperboard Frame, 1959; Plydome, 1959; Catenary, 1959; Octertruss, 1961; Tensegrity, 1962; Submarisle, 1963; Aspension, 1964; Monohex, 1965; Laminar Dome, 1965; Octa Spinner, 1965; Star Tensegrity, 1967; Rowing Device, 1970; Tensegrity Dome with Spaced Lesser Circles, 1973; (with Shoji Sadao) Geodesic Hexa Pent, 1974; Floating Breakwater, 1975; Non-symmetrical Tension-integrity Structures, 1975; Floating Breakwater, 1979.

## Publications

**By FULLER: books**—*The Time Lock,* privately printed, 1928, as *4D Time Lock,* Corrales, New Mexico, 1970; *Nine Chains to the Moon,* Philadelphia, 1938, London, 1973; *Designing a New Industry: A Composite of a Series of Talks,* Wichita, Kansas, 1945-46; *Earth, Inc.,* lecture, New York, 1947; *Design for Survival—Plus,* Ann Arbor, Michigan, 1949; *Untitled Epic Poem on the History of Industrialization,* Millerton, New York, 1962; *Education Automation: Freeing the Scholars to Return to Their Studies,* Carbondale, Illinois, 1962; *Ideas and Integrities: A Spontaneous Autobiographical Discourse* edited by Robert W. Marks, Englewood Cliffs, New Jersey, 1963; *No More Secondhand God, and Other Writings,* Carbondale, Illinois, 1963; *World Design Science Decade Documents,* 6 vols., Carbondale, Illinois, 1963-67; *Comprehensive Thinking* selected and edited by John McHale, Carbondale, Illinois, 1965; *What Am I Trying to Do?,* London, 1968; *Reprints and Selected Articles,* Belfast, Maine, 1969; *Operating Manual for Spaceship Earth,* Carbondale, Illinois, 1969; *Utopia or Oblivion: The Prospects for Humanity,* New York, 1969, London, 1970; *Fifty Years of Design, Science, Revolution and the World Game,* Carbondale, Illinois, 1969; *Planetary Planning,* New Delhi, India, 1969; (with others) *Approaching the Benign Environment,* University, Alabama, 1970; *The Buckminster Fuller Reader* edited by James Meller, London, 1970; (with Jerome Agel and Quentin Fiore) *I Seem to Be a Verb,* New York, 1970; *The World Game: Integrative Resource Civilization Planning Tool,* Carbondale, Illinois, 1971; *Old Man River: An Environmental Domed City,* St. Louis, Missouri, 1972; *Intuition,* New York, 1972; *Buckminster Fuller to Children of Earth,* New York, 1972; (with E. J. Applewhite) *Synergetics: Explorations in the Geometry of Thinking,* New York, 1975; *And It Came to Pass—Not to Stay,* New York, 1976; *Pound, Synergy, and the Great Design,* Moscow, Idaho, 1977; *Buckminster Fuller: An Autobio-*

*graphical Monologue/Scenario* edited by Robert Snyder, New York, 1977, 1980; *R. Buckminster Fuller on Education* edited by Peter H. Wagschal and Robert D. Kah, Amherst, Massachusetts, 1979; (with E. J. Applewhite) *Synergetics 2: Further Explorations in the Geometry of Thinking,* New York, 1979; *Critical Path,* New York, 1982; *Tetrascroll: Goldilocks and the Three Bears: A Cosmic Fairy Tale,* New York, 1982; *Grunch of Giants,* New York, 1982; *Inventions,* New York, 1983.

**On FULLER: books**—*The Dymaxion World of Buckminster Fuller* by Robert W. Marks, New York, 1959; *R. Buckminster Fuller* by John McHale, New York, 1962; *Wizard of the Dome: R. Buckminster Fuller, Designer for the Future* by Sidney Rosen, Boston, 1969; *Bucky: A Guided Tour of Buckminster Fuller* by Hugh Kenner, New York, 1973; *Mind's Eye of Buckminster Fuller* by Donald W. Robertson, New York, 1974; *Buckminster Fuller at Home in the Universe* by Alden Hatch, New York, 1974; *Cosmic Fishing: An Account of Writing Synergetics with Buckminster Fuller* by E. J. Applewhite, New York and London, 1977; *Pilot for Spaceship Earth* by Athena V. Lord, New York, 1978; *Robert Buckminster Fuller: uno spazio per la technologia* by Pier Angelo Cetica, Padua, Italy, 1979; *Buckminster Fuller: An Autobiographical Monologue/Scenario* by Robert Snyder, New York, 1980; *Richard Buckminster Fuller: A Bibliography* by Mary Vance, Monticello, Illinois, 1980; *Synergetic Stew: Explorations in Dymaxion Dining,* Philadelphia, 1982.

*     *     *

It was R. Buckminster Fuller's lifelong belief that humanity is capable of using the high technology it has invented to the positive end of gaining a physical and spiritual world view which would raise life above the barriers of entropy. His premise was based on what he called "dymaxion," an approach to design and ideals. Aimed at using fewer resources to achieve maximum output, this principle, he believed, could regenerate the forces of energy for the planet as a whole. In order to accomplish this goal, Fuller taught, outmoded conventions must be eliminated and the advances of the scientific and technological revolution of the twentieth century must be employed to raise humanity's standard of living.

Many of Fuller's designs were geared to create possibilities of greater mobility, an aim he felt to be highly necessary in attaining his ideals. In 1927, he designed the easily movable and totally self-contained Dymaxion House, a structure hung from a central core. Continuing his search for more inexpensive, resource-saving, and mobile structures, Fuller invented the Dymaxion Car in 1933. His most famous construct, the Geodesic Dome, created in 1947, further advanced the move toward less cost, weight, and material. Used widely by industry and the military during the 1950s, the Geodesic dome remains among the most outstanding design inventions of the late twentieth century.

Fuller was as famed a writer and speaker as he was a maker and thinker. The inspiring and gregarious lectures he gave around the world until his death left his audiences breathless and inspired with new hope for the positive uses of technology based on humanistic commitment without nostalgia or dependence on old traditions. Throughout his many books and articles, published over a period of fifty years, Fuller could always be counted on to raise controversy and to purvey insatiable inventiveness and optimism. In *Earth, Inc.* (1973), for example, he wrote passionately and convincingly of the need for a design-science revolution which, he noted, we now have all the resources to accomplish.

His was a revolution of education, of the commitment of world youth, and of the creative intelligence of all, working together for the common good. His many designs made practical his idealism, bringing the philosophy into reality.

The main influence on Fuller was his broad study of the history of science and mathematics, which he seems to have combined with the science-fiction genius of H. G. Wells. He can be likened to the renaissance man who combines broad-based studies to achieve vital artistic invention. Fuller's is also an extension of the beliefs and practices of the great Bauhaus architects and artists whose uses of modern technology for design constitute one of the greatest achievements of the early twentieth century. Fuller's impact has been especially felt by contemporary sculptors who base their monumental abstractions on architectural principles and use new materials to achieve an aura of great mass and weightlessness.

—Barbara Cavaliere

# FULTON, James (Franklin)

American industrial designer

**Born:** Cincinnati, Ohio, 13 April 1930. **Education:** Studied industrial design under Alexander Kostellow, Rowena Reed, and Eva Zeisel, at the Pratt Institute, Brooklyn, New York, 1948-51. **Family:** Married Mary Sherman Walbridge in 1953 (divorced, 1975); children: Martha, James, and Laurel. **Career:** Designer, at Towle Sterling company, Newburyport, Massachusetts, 1951, and at Owens-Corning Fiberglas Corporation, Toledo, Ohio, 1952-53; senior designer, Harley Earl Associates, Warren, Michigan, 1953-58; design director, then managing director, Compagnie de l'Esthetique Industrielle (C. E. I. Raymond Loewy), Paris, 1958-60; director of product design, transportation, and housing components, 1960-62, vice-president, 1962-64, and senior vice president, 1964-66, Loewy/Snaith design firm, New York; founder and president of Fulton + Partners planning and design consultants, New York, from 1966; director, Endt + Fulton Partners, Paris, from 1975. Founder and chairman, Design Publications Incorporated (including *Design Review, Industrial Design,* and others), New York, from 1977. Trustee, from 1968, executive committee member, from 1973, and chairman of the planning and development committee, from 1977, Pratt Institute, New York; art collection committee member, Owens-Corning Fiberglas Corporation, Toledo, Ohio, from 1968; founder and chairman, International E22 Class of racing yachts section, New York Yacht Club, from 1968; president, 1975-76, and chairman, 1977-78, Industrial Designers Society of America; trustee, Dime Savings Bank, New York, from 1982. **Honors:** Dean's Medal, Pratt Institute, 1951; Contemporary Achievement Award, Pratt Institute, 1967; Fellow, Industrial Designers Society of America, 1976. **Address:** Fulton + Partners, 330 West 42nd Street, New York, New York 10036. U.S.A.

## Works

Folding playpen in net and aluminum, for Trimble, 1957.
Corporate visual image, for British Petroleum, 1958-60.
Corporate visual imagery, for Trans World Airlines, 1960-63.
Pattern programme and corporate imagery, for Formica, 1960-65.

Modular FRP bathroom, for Owens-Corning Fiberglas, 1962-64.
Corporate symbol, for Shell Oil Company, 1964.
Agricultural tractor, for Allis Chalmers, 1972-74.
Open-office screening system, for Owens-Corning Fiberglas, 1976.
Construction equipment, for Koehring, 1976-80.
*Bantam 366* excavator cab, for Koehring, 1980.

## Publications

**By FULTON: articles—***Reinforced Plastics* (Connecticut), May 1964; *IDSA Journal* (New York), 1968, 1970; *Idea* (Tokyo), June 1974; *Yachting* (New York), October 1978.

*

Designers are in a unique position to assist industry in the constructive use of technology. The ability to recognize needs and their full implications is basic. An additional strength lies in the ability to maintain an objective point of view and to coordinate various talents in an effective and innovative way. We as designers can and should be the link between maker and user.

As designers, we must accept the responsibility for the practical utilization of resources and the humane use of technology in our projects. This demands a high degree of sensitivity, intelligence, and a broad understanding of the many disciplines which contribute to successful problem solving. We choose to practice design in the context of its impact on the total system, and proceed with the conviction that excellence is one quality which does not become obsolete. Our design responsibility begins with planning—the process of developing a detailed program of action. This essential first phase consists of analyzing the overall problem, identifying its design components, and defining objectives which are in harmony with user needs and the producer's technical capabilities. It is only when this effort is thorough that meaningful goals can be set, priorities established, and creative energy usefully directed. With this kind of background, we can proceed to explore and probe for concepts which hold the promise of a solution.

Comprehensive plans and the finest design ideas can be distorted when follow-through is inadequate. The complex matrix of design decisions which produces a solution requires the balancing of many considerations. When changes are needed as a project is carried into production, the designer is best qualified to choose which, among the available alternatives, will achieve the original intent.

The commitment to excellence in design is an attitude which motivates us in all of our professional activities. Our ideal is to be both responsive and responsible.

—James Fulton

# FURSE, Margaret

British stage and film costume designer

**Born:** Alice Margaret Watts, in London, 18 February 1911. **Education:** Educated at Miss Campbell's School, Hampstead, London, and in Versailles, France, 1921-27; studied costume design, under Jeanetta Cochrane, at Central School of Arts and Crafts, London, 1928-30. **Family:** Married the stage and film designer Roger Furse in 1936 (divorced, 1951); married the film critic Stephen Watts in 1952. **Career:** Stage designer, working with the Motley Group of designers, London, 1930-39; assistant stage designer under Roger Furse, at the Old Vic Theatre, London, 1940; film designer, working for British-Gaumont, the Rank Organization, Cineguild, Warner Brothers, Twentieth Century-Fox, Walt Disney, Joseph Levine, Hal Wallis Universal, and several independents, 1941-73. **Collection:** British Film Institute, London. **Honors:** British Film Academy Award, 1965; American Film Academy Award, 1969; American Television Academy Award, 1974. **Died:** London, 9 July 1974.

### Works

Film costume designs include—*Henry V* (Olivier), 1944; *Great Expectations* (Lean), 1946; *Blanche Fury* (Allegret), 1948; *The Prince and the Pauper* (Keighley), 1947; *Oliver Twist* (Lean), 1948; *The Passionate Friends* (Lean), 1948; *Madeleine* (Lean), 1949; *Night and the City* (Dassin), 1950; *No Highway* (Koster), 1951; *The House in the Square* (Baker), 1951; *Meet Me Tonight* (Pelissier), 1952; *The Crimson Pirate* (Siodmak), 1952; *The Master of Ballantrae* (Keighley), 1953; *The Million Pound Note* (Neame), 1954; *The Spanish Gardener* (Leacock), 1956; *The Inn of the Sixth Happiness* (Robson), 1958; *Kidnapped* (Stevenson), 1959; *Sons and Lovers* (Cardiff), 1960; *Greyfriar's Bobby* (Chaffey), 1960; *The Horsemasters* (Fairchild), 1961; *In Search of the Castaways* (Stevenson), 1961; *The Prince and the Pauper*, 1962; *Becket* (Glenville), 1964; *A Shot in the Dark* (Edwards), 1964; *Young Cassidy* (Cardiff), 1964; *Return from the Ashes* (Lee-Thompson), 1965; *The Trap* (Hayers), 1966; *Cast a Giant Shadow* (Shavelson), 1966; *Great Catherine* (Flemyng), 1968; *The Lion in Winter* (Harvey), 1968; *Sinful Davey* (Huston), 1968; *Anne of the Thousand Days* (Jarrott), 1969; *Scrooge* (Neame), 1970; *Mary Queen of Scots* (Jarrott), 1971; *Bequest to the Nation* (Jones), 1973; *A Delicate Balance* (Richardson), 1975.

### Publications

**On FURSE: books**—*Filmguide to Henry V*, Bloomington, Indiana, 1973; *Costume Design in the Movies* by Elizabeth Leese, Bembridge, 1976; *Hollywood Costume Design* by David Chierichetti, London, 1976.

*       *       *

Laurence Olivier's *Henry V* (1944) auspiciously introduced Margaret Furse's film career, since the entire concept of the movie presented great challenges. The story jumped several centuries. It also exploited a wide variety of regional, physical, and social types, so actors needed theatrical costumes, military uniforms, liturgical vestments, royal finery, peasant rags, and middle-class, everyday wear. The frequent crowd scenes demanded colorful diversity. Good and evil were to be differentiated through imagery. All this had to be done in the face of wartime restrictions. As easily as applying silver paint to crochetwork to serve as soldiers' chainmail, Furse, along with husband Roger, solved these problems.

For *Henry V*, costumes were based on miniature Elizabethan portraits and International Gothic illuminated manuscripts, but even for simple comedies, such as *The Million Pound Note* (1953), Furse

took no less care in research. In that film, characters seem to step from the pages of *Godey's Ladies Book*. Among these well-dressed matrons and self-consciously, finely tailored gentlemen, the innocent heroine stands apart. Moderately frilled in virginal white, full of spunk and vigor, she is seen by the audience, as by the hero, as visually apart from the crowd.

Crowning her excellence in British period costume, one of Furse's final films, *Mary Queen of Scots* (1971), transcends simple historical design. The film opens with Mary, youthful and naive, cavorting in an unencumbering white nightgown, which flows *a la* Isadora Duncan. Furse developed Mary's character primarily in soft pastels and pale golds, emphasizing Mary's pre-Raphaelite-like romanticism. In contrast, clear-headed Elizabeth wore the sharper hues. The foil of Elizabeth's increasing sartorial splendor through time culminates in her final confrontation with Mary. Furse fitted the English queen in a massive, explosively patterned gown, accessorized by an awesome hat, so that Elizabeth recalled the adamant image of her father, Henry VIII. In contrast, Mary dresses like a nun, drained of all color and earthly adornments. Styled with affectation in France, Mary had grown severe in Scotland. As she approaches her death, Furse shrouded her in black. With a final speech at the executioner's block, Mary boasts of her rebirth to a greater life in heaven and triumphantly reveals beneath her cloak a startling, bright red dress, more powerful in color than anything previously seen in the film. At the conclusion, Elizabeth, despite her temporal power and decorations, can conquer neither Mary's spirit nor visual impact.

Furse, the expert at historical costume, never served as its slave. She manipulated her references as metaphors, uniting the academic with the imaginative.

—Edith Cortland Lee

# FURSE, Roger (Kemble)

British painter, illustrator, stage, and film designer

**Born:** Ightham, Kent, 11 September 1903. **Education:** Educated at St. George's Choir School, Windsor, Berkshire, 1910-14; Eton School, Buckinghamshire, 1914-20; studied painting, Slade School of Fine Art, London, 1921-24, and in Paris, 1924-27. **Military:** Served in the Royal Navy, 1940-43. **Family:** Married Alice Margaret Watts in 1936 (divorced, 1951); married Ines Sylvia Perg in 1952. **Career:** Worked as a portrait painter and commercial artist in Paris, 1925-27, and in New York, 1927-31; stage designer, working for the Gate Theatre, Old Vic, Ambassadors Theatre, Vaudeville Theatre, Queen's Theatre, Strand Theatre, Westminster Theatre, Haymarket Theatre, Piccadilly Theatre, St. James's Theatre, Covent Garden Opera House, Sadler's Wells Opera, and Duke of York's Theatre, in London, and for the Stratford Shakespeare Memorial Theatre, Chichester Festival Theatre, and the Cambridge Festival Theatre, from 1931; art director, Perranporth Summer Theatre, Cornwall, 1936-38; film costume and set designer, in London and Hollywood, California, from 1943. **Exhibition:** Leicester Galleries, London, 1948. **Honors:** Academy Award, 1948; Royal Designer for Industry, Royal Society of Arts, London, 1949. **Died:** Corfu, Greece, 19 August 1972.

## Works

Film designs include—*Henry V* (Olivier), 1944; *The True Glory* (Reed/Kanin), 1945; *Odd Man Out* (Reed), 1946; *Hamlet* (Olivier), 1948; *Under Capricorn* (Hitchcock), 1949; *The Angel with the Trumpet* (Bushell), 1949; *Ivanhoe* (Thorpe), 1952; *Knights of the Round Table* (Thorpe), 1953; *Helen of Troy* (Wise), 1955; *Richard III* (Olivier), 1955; *The Prince and the Showgirl* (Olivier), 1956; *Saint Joan* (Preminger), 1957; *Bonjour Tristesse* (Preminger), 1957; *Spartacus* (Kubrick), 1960; *The Roman Spring of Mrs. Stone* (Quintero), 1961; *The Road to Hong Kong* (Panama), 1961.

## Publications

**By FURSE: articles**—in *Films and Filming* (London), April 1955, May 1955.

**On FURSE: books**—*Roger Furse: Exhibition of Designs for the Film Hamlet,* catalogue, London, 1948; *Film Today Books: Screen and Audience* edited by John E. Cross and Arnold Ketterbury, London, 1949; *Le Decor de Film* by Leon Barsacq, Paris, 1970, as *Caligari's Cabinet and Other Grand Illusions,* Boston, 1976; *Filmguide to Henry V,* Bloomington, Indiana, 1973; *Costume Design in the Movies* by Elizabeth Leese, Bembridge, 1976; *The International Film Encyclopedia* by Ephraim Katz, New York and London, 1980.

\*　　\*　　\*

Roger Furse produced many fine designs but none more glorious than those achieved in film with Laurence Olivier. Dismiss their final film collaboration, *The Prince and The Showgirl* (1956); these sets sparkle with studied grandeur, but they lack genius. For that, look to their settings of Shakespeare for the screen.

The communal effort of Olivier's production company (unofficial and, later, official as a short-lived theatrical venture called Laurence Olivier Productions, Ltd.) brought forth the Shakespearean series. *Henry V* (1944) credited Paul Sheriff (assisted by Carmen Dillon) as art director while Furse and his wife Margaret served as costume designers. Visually, they transported the spectator from the Elizabethan theatre to the pages of fifteenth-century illuminated manuscripts and back again. For Renaissance England, the Furses recreated elegant gentlemen and ragged braggarts with equal authenticity. For the era of King Henry, they drew an elegant France and noble England, a world both tragic and comic, evil and divine. The Furses painted red and gold against blue and silver, dividing allegiances with a colorful palette.

Assisted by Carmen Dillon, Roger Furse designed sets and costumes for *Hamlet* (1948). Though described by critics as mannered, theatrical, or expressionistic, the film was intended to contrast dramatically with the *Henry V* production. Olivier and Furse conceived *Hamlet* as a black-and-white etching to differentiate it from *Henry V's* colorfully painted pageantry. A range of tonal values punctuated by recurring shadows and mists accentuated the concept. Furse further echoed Prince Hamlet's moody loneliness with the castle's vast, empty spaces to achieve what he later described as Olivier's desire for "a dream-like cavernous place as the setting for a drama which is centered in the shadowy regions of the hero's mind." He indicated that he had used Norman arches, Byzantine-like wall paintings, and tapestries of an even later period as a setting for the action rather than as period documentation.

*Richard III* (1956) returned Olivier to technicolor, with Furse serving as costumer and art director. Stark, airy spaces served to highlight those few details that were retained. Emphasizing the crown motif and underlining the story with recurring Christian imagery, Furse contributed an unspoken reinterpretation of Shakespeare's play, even as he created visual unity.

Olivier planned on a fourth film project which, of course, included Furse on its staff. However, he could find no funding for *Macbeth* because potential backers doubted such a title's commercial success. As for the film's possible artistic strides, unfortunately, we shall never know.

—Edith Cortland Lee

# GALANOS, James
American fashion designer

**Born:** Philadelphia, Pennsylvania, 20 September 1924. **Education:** Studied art and drapery at Traphagen School of Fashion, New York, 1943. **Career:** Freelance fashion sketch artist for clothing manufacturer, New York, 1942-43; worked for designer Hattie Carnegie, New York, 1944; assistant to designer Jean Louis, Columbia Studios, Hollywood, California, 1946-47; apprentice designer, studio of Robert Piguet, Paris, 1947-48; designer, at Davidow, New York, 1949-50; established Galanos Originals fashion company, in Beverly Hills, from 1951, and in Los Angeles, from 1983; licenses include Galanos Furs, introduced 1984, and Parfums Galanos, 1980; also occasional film and stage costume designer, from 1967. **Exhibitions:** *Fashion: An Anthology,* Victoria and Albert Museum, London, 1971; *Galanos Retrospective, 1952-1974,* Costume Council of the Los Angeles County Museum of Art, 1975; *Galanos—25 Years,* Fashion Institute of Technology, New York, 1976. **Collections:** Metropolitan Museum of Art, New York; Philadelphia Museum of Art; Art Institute of Chicago; Denver Art Museum, Colorado; Dallas Museum of Fine Arts, Texas; Los Angeles County Museum of Art; Smithsonian Institution, Washington, D.C. **Honors:** Neiman Marcus Distinguished Service Award, 1954; Coty American Fashion Critics Winnie Award, 1954; Return Award, 1956; Hall of Fame Award, 1959; Costume Institute Award, Metropolitan Museum of Art, New York, 1954; International Achievement Fair Creativity Award, 1956; Filene Young Talent Award, Boston, 1958; Cotton Fashion Award, New York, 1958; Coty American Hall of Fame Award, 1959; *Sunday Times* International Fashion Award, London, 1965; Council of Fashion Designers of America Lifetime Achievement Award, 1985; Stanley Award, 1986. **Address:** 2254 South Sepulveda Drive, Los Angeles, California 90064, U.S.A.

## Publications

**On GALANOS: books**—*The Wheels of Fashion* by Phyllis Lee Levin, New York, 1965; *The Beautiful People* by Marylin Bender, New York, 1967; *Fashion: An Anthology* by Cecil Beaton, exhibition catalogue compiled by Madeleine Ginsburg, London, 1971; *In Fashion: Dress in the Twentieth Century* by Prudence Glynn, London, 1975; *The Fashion Makers* by Barbara Waltz and Bernadine Morris, New York, 1978; *Fairchild's Who's Who in Fashion* edited by Ann Stegemeyer, New York, 1980; *McDowell's Directory of Twentieth Century Fashion* by Colin McDowell, London, 1984; *Fashion: The Inside Story* by Barbaralee Diamonstein, New York, 1985; *Couture: The Great Designers* by Caroline Milbank Rennolds, New York, 1985; *The Encyclopaedia of Fashion from 1840 to the 1980s* by Georgina

O'Hara, London, 1986; *New York Fashion: The Evolution of American Style* by Caroline Milbank Rennolds, New York, 1989; **articles**—"Good as Gold Clothes" by Carrie Donovan in the *New York Times,* 23 November 1980; "A Certain Quality: Galanos" by Andre Leon Talley in *Vogue* (New York), April 1985; "The Loner" by Ariane and Michael Batterberry in *Connoisseur* (New York), May 1985; "James Galanos: Disciplined Elegance in the Hollywood Hills" by Caroline Milbank Rennolds in *Architectural Digest* (Los Angeles), September 1988; "By Galanos, the Simplest of Splendors" by Bernadine Morris in the *New York Times,* 27 February 1990; "A Galanos...Why Is It Worth It?" in *Harper's Bazaar* (New York), June 1991; "Galanos Has the Last Word for Fall" by Bernadine Morris in the *New York Times,* 24 August 1993.

*

Fashion is a living art form. It is the function of the designer to arrange harmoniously and artistically all the components of design, such as color, line, details, so that the garment becomes one with the human form.

—James Galanos

*     *     *

James Galanos is one of a handful of designers in the world today designing couture-quality clothes for a luxury clientele. Recipient of many fashion awards and owner of his Los Angeles design establishment for more than thirty years, he achieved success only after years of discouraging attempts to interest buyers in his highly individualized and necessarily expensive creations.

His designs are distinguished less by any consistency of style than by his adherence to couture standards learned while an apprentice to Robert Piguet in Paris in the late 1940s. He is known for his imaginative handling of distinctive, often boldly-patterned, European fabrics, which sometimes cost $50 a yard. After being cut individually, hand-basted, and sandwiched with layers of interlining, each garment is molded on a form and manipulated into shape with steam and pressing. Since darts are not used, the customer can have simple alterations done without time-consuming fittings. Hand-finishing and silk linings are so meticulous that Galanos garments have actually been modeled inside-out. Evening gowns are hand-embroidered and beaded. Each piece, handled by numerous skilled workers, takes as long as two weeks to make. This is why Galanos prices range in the thousands of dollars.

Before shipment to specialty stores, each garment is inspected by the designer, who sometimes attaches to it a note with suggestions for accessories. Personal attention is an important part of maintaining his diminishing clientele of the few women who appreciate Galanos quality and are able to pay for it. He travels with his collections to New York semi-annually and meets with his customers at showings across the country, consulting individually with regular clients who include film stars and international socialites.

Fashion writers in the 1950s considered Galanos avant-garde. In the 1960s, his subtly molded suits were paragons of constructed chic. By the 1970s, his clientele had matured and his designs became correspondingly conservative. But in the early 1980s, he once again offered fresh and youthful designs, such as multi-level suits with cropped trousers. Galanos attracted widespread publicity when Nancy Reagan, one of his long-time customers, became First Lady and had Galanos design her inaugural ballgown. Apart from his limited-distribution signature fragrance, the Galanos name is associated exclusively with his own designs.

After more than forty years in business, Galanos continues to challenge himself with the idea of the perfect design. He is not interested in imitating the current trends; he works in isolation and designs for an elite who appreciate his timeless durability and collect his designs like works of art.

—Sandra Michels Adams

# GAMES, Abram

British graphic designer

**Born:** London, 29 July 1914. **Education:** Educated at the Grocers Company School, London, 1925-30. **Military Service:** Served as infantryman, in the British Army, 1940-41; official War Office poster designer, 1941-46, Captain. **Family:** Married Marianne Salfield in 1945; children: Daniel, Sophie, and Naomi. **Career:** Freelance designer, working on posters, magazines, logos, advertisements, postage stamps, and corporate identity programmes, London, 1937-40, and from 1946; has designed for BBC Television, the 1951 Festival of Britain, London Transport, British Airways, Guinness, British Aluminium, and others; inventor of "Imagic" and "RLF" copying processes. Visiting Tutor, Royal College of Art, London, 1946-53. **Exhibitions:** Reklamførening, Stockholm, 1943; Palais des Beaux-Arts, Brussels, 1946; Bezalel Museum, Jerusalem 1950, 1963; Tel Aviv Museum, 1950; Ben Uri Gallery, London, 1952; *8 British Designers,* Nationalmuseum, Stockholm, 1952; Museu de Arte, Sao Paulo, 1954 (toured Brazil); *Design From Britain,* Florida State University, Tallahassee, 1956; Waldorf-Astoria, New York, 1960; Visual Arts Center, Chicago, 1961; *Second World War Posters,* Imperial War Museum London, 1972; *Eye for Industry,* Victoria and Albert Museum, London, 1986. **Collections:** Victoria and Albert Museum, London; Imperial War Museum, London; Stedelijk Museum, Amsterdam; Kunstgewerbermuseum, Zurich; Israel Museum, Jerusalem; Australian National Gallery, Canberra; Australian War Memorial Museum, Canberra; Museum of Modern Art, New York; Library of Congress, Washington, D.C.; Museum of Tolerance, Los Angeles. **Honors:** Prizes in international poster competitions, 1957-64; Officer, Order of the British Empire, 1957; Royal Designer for Industry, Royal Society of Arts, London, 1959; First Prize, International Philatelic Competition, Asiago, Italy, 1976; Design Medal, Society of Industrial Artists and Designers, London, 1960; Silver Medal, Royal Society of Arts, London, 1962; Hon. F., 1993, and Hon.

Abram Games: Emblem for the Uranium Institute, the International Industrial Association for Energy from Nuclear Fuel, 1994

D.Litt., 1994, Royal College of Art, London. **Address:** 41 The Vale, London NW11 8SE, England.

**Works**

Twenty-two posters for London Transport, 1937-75.
ATS Auxiliary Territorial Service poster, for the War Office, 1941.
Displaced Persons poster, for the Central British Fund, 1946.
Thirteen posters, for British Airways, 1947-59.
Emblem, for the 1951 Festival of Britain, 1948.
Magazine advertisements, for British Aluminium, 1948-53.
Eight posters, for the *Financial Times,* London, 1951-59.
Poster, for Osram Lamps, 1952.
Poster, for Guinness, 1956.
*Freedom from Hunger* poster, for FAO/United Nations, 1960.
Three posters, for *The Times,* London, 1960-62.
Emblem, for the Queen's Award to Industry, 1966.
Emblem, for the GKN Group, 1968.
Cover, for the *Encyclopaedia Judaica,* 1969.
Set of four postage stamps, for Jersey, Channel Islands, 1974.
Emblem, for the 1985 Festival of British Jewry, 1984.

## Publications

**By GAMES: books**—*Over My Shoulder,* London, 1960.

**On GAMES: books**—*Posters: 50 Artists and Designers* by Walter Allner, New York, 1952; *Design in British Industry: A Mid-Century Survey* by Michael Farr, Cambridge, 1955; *Die Neue Grafik/The New Graphic Design* by Karl Gerstner and Markus Kutter, Teufen and London, 1959; *Graphic Design Britain* edited by Frederick Lambert, London, 1967; *History of the Poster* by Josef and Shizuko Muller-Brockman, Zurich, 1971; *Air Powered,* New York, 1979; *Who's Who in Graphic Art* edited by Walter Amstutz, Dubendorf, 1982; *Advertising: Reflections of a Century* by Bryan Holme, London, 1982; *The Conran Directory of Design* edited by Stephen Bayley, London, 1984; *Design Source Book* by Penny Sparke and others, London, 1986; *Eye for Industry: Royal Designers for Industry 1936 1986,* exhibition catalogue by Fiona MacCarthy and Patrick Nuttgens, London, 1986; *Did Britain Make It?: British Design in Context 1946-86* edited by Penny Sparke, London, 1986; *Graphic Style* by Seymour Chwast and Steven Heller, New York, 1988; *Graphic Design* by Richard Hollis, London, 1994; *Persuading the People,* London, 1995; *A Smile in the Mind,* London, 1996.

\*

My personal philosophy on design can be summarised as: "maximum meaning-minimum means."

—Abram Games

\*   \*   \*

Abram Games was designing posters during the 1930s, but he achieved his reputation during World War II and the decades following. In many ways, he followed the inspired example of designers such as Edward McKnight Kauffer, Tom Purvis, and Fred Taylor in Britain, as he extended into the postwar years the new graphic arts language inspired by the avant-garde movements of the earlier part of the century.

Far from being merely an interpreter of the modern movement for the masses, Games proved to be a powerful propagandist and a forceful salesman. Using many of the devices of the surrealist, for example, he made sophisticated use of symbolism to express his message clearly and without compromise. His war posters advising against careless talk were designed to shock; and in this way, his imagery compares with that of his contemporaries in other countries where imagery had traditionally been more dramatic than in the lyrical designs used in Britain for public transport.

Games is very much the professional designer whose immaculate working methods are always evident in the absolute precision of his final image. He often starts with a sketch that contains the essence of his idea but which is also a creative mark. This eventually becomes a thoroughly rationalised design, from which all traces of the artist's rough indication have been polished away to reveal a clear-cut symbol easily grasped at first sight. Thus, Games the artist sublimates his own reactions and feelings about the subject and channels his skill into the final message required by his client.

For several decades, he produced hundreds of first-class posters at a time when competition was high. His designs for the emblem for the Festival of Britain in 1951 and for British Broadcasting Television both won him first prizes. In his own words, the de-

signer "has the great gift of the artist, the power of the propagandist, the technique and machinery of modern civilisation, printing presses, the cinema, radio and television."

—John Barnicoat

# GARDNER, (Leslie) James
British exhibition designer

**Born:** London, 29 December 1907. **Education:** Educated in London schools until 1922; mainly self-taught in design. **Military Service:** Served in the British Army, 1939-45, Chief Camouflage Officer. **Family:** Married Mary Williams in 1936 (died, 1965); sons: Brian and Neil. **Career:** Worked as a jewellery designer, for Cartier, London, 1924-31; independent designer, London, from 1947; designed exhibitions for the Council of Industrial Design, Central Office of Information, Board of Trade, Federation of British Industries, Pilkington Brothers, NV Philips, United Kingdom Atomic Energy Authority, Institute of Geological Sciences, Maryland Academy of Sciences, New York City Council, Cunard Steamship Company, Delta Queen Steamboat Company, and others. **Exhibitions:** *Eye for Industry,* Victoria and Albert Museum, London, 1986. **Collections:** Victoria and Albert Museum, London. **Honors:** Royal Designer for Industry, Royal Society of Arts, London, 1947; Commander, Order of the British Empire, 1959; Senior Fellow, Royal College of Art, London, 1987; Minerva Medal, Chartered Society of Designers, 1989. **Died:** March 1995.

## Works

*Britain Can Make It* exhibition at the Victoria and Albert Museum, London, for the Council of Industrial Design, 1946.
United Kingdom pavilion and exhibits at the Brussels World Fair, for the Central Office of Information, 1958.
British Trade Fair in New York, for the Board of Trade/Federation of British Industries, 1960.
Glass Museum at St. Helen's, Lancashire, for Pilkington Brothers, 1965.
Evoluon Technological Museum in Eindhoven, for NV Philips, 1966.
Above-water lines of the *Queen Elizabeth II,* for the Cunard Steamship Company, 1966.
*Britain Today* exhibit at *Expo 67,* Montreal, for the Central Office of Information, 1967.
*The Peaceful Uses of Atomic Energy* exhibition in Geneva, for the United Kingdom Atomic Energy Authority, 1971.
*The Story of the Earth* exhibition at the Geological Museum, London, for the Institute of Geological Sciences, 1972.
Maryland Science Centre in Baltimore, for the Maryland Academy of Sciences, 1974.
Museum of the Jewish Diaspora in Tel Aviv, for the Jewish Congress, 1978.
Shipping Museum in Copenhagen, for A. P. Moller, 1979.
Pavilion at *Expo 85,* Tsukuba, Japan, for the Asian Development Bank of Manila, 1985.
Design concept for Butterfly World, Fort Lauderdale, Florida, 1988.

James Gardner: "Cafe Street Scene, Berlin, Germany, c. 1932," 2/3rds scale reconstruction, Museum of Tolerance, Los Angeles. Photo copyright Jim Mendenhall, 1992, courtesy of the Simon Wiesenthal Center

National Museum of Natural Science, Taiwan, for the Taiwanese Government, 1988.

Tower of David Museum, Jerusalem, Israel, for the Jerusalem Foundation, 1989.

Museum of Tolerance, Los Angeles, California, for the Simon Wiesenthal Center, 1993.

The Nelson Gallery, London, for the National Maritime Museum, 1995 (with 3d Concepts).

**Publications**

**By GARDNER: books**—(with Caroline Heller) *Exhibition and Display,* London and New York, 1960; *Elephants in the Attic,* London, 1983.

**On GARDNER: books**—*Industrial Design in Britain* by Noel Carrington, London, 1976; *A Tonic to the Nation: The Festival of Britain 1951* edited by Mary Banham and Bevis Hillier, London, 1976, *Industrial Design* by John Heskett, London, 1980; *Design Source Book* by Penny Sparke and others, London, 1986; *Eye for Industry: Royal Designers for Industry 1936-1986,* exhibition catalogue by Fiona MacCarthy and Patrick Nuttgens, London, 1986;

*Did Britain Make It? British Design in Context 1946-86* edited by Penny Sparke, London, 1986.

\*

Designing is the facility to unravel the logic of a situation or problem, coupled with the ability to make mental models of possible answers, and motivated by the desire to initiate, not follow the orthodox pattern. Producing what one has designed is hard work; so why work on something that has already been done? I did not aim for any specialist branch of the profession. Things just happened to me, and whatever came, I had a go. A success, and other jobs followed. One is then competing with oneself, with what one did before. As a result, I have shown that within the correct designing facility, one need not specialise—I have designed matchbox covers (my smallest design) and the *Queen Elizabeth II* oceanliner (my largest).

In time, one gains experience right across the board, and know-how gathered for one task contributes (maybe with a new look) to another. When in doubt on a technical point, one can always ask the expert; the lesson here is to ask the top expert, someone who actually does it, not a technocrat with a university degree.

The real way to learn is to study a subject for a definite purpose; this programmes the mind on active, meaningful lines and stimulates one's adrenalin, as one must not fail if one is to survive. To learn a subject for, say, an examination, and not for "doing," is a waste of time and leads to mental imbalance, a mind full of facts and theories—aimed at nothing and so, redundant.

Most children are born with a designer's imagination and dexterity, but they lose it when they go to school, where the rewards and punishments are for "taped," ready-made mental programmes. A designer who hopes to be creative comes up against the problem that the majority of the people are conformists and fear the unorthodox, so most designers, from practice, end up doing the orthodox.

—James Gardner

# GARLAND, Kenneth (John)
British graphic designer

**Born:** Southampton, Hampshire, 19 February 1929. **Education:** Studied at the West of England Academy of Art, Bristol, 1947-48; studied under Paul Hogarth, Anthony Froshaug, Herbert Spencer, and Jesse Collins, at Central School of Arts and Crafts, London, National Diploma in Design, 1954. **Career:** Art editor, National Trade Press, London, 1954-56, and *Design* magazine, London 1956-62; founder-director, Ken Garland and Associates design consultants, London, from 1962. Visiting lecturer in graphics, Central School of Arts and Crafts, London, 1957-60; visiting tutor in graphics, Reading University, Berkshire, from 1971, and Royal College of Art, London, from 1977. **Exhibitions:** *Linescape, Lithoscape, Landscape,* University of Reading, 1987; *Ken Garland and Associates: Graphics, Toys and Games, Photography,* Dundee, 1989 (toured); *Harry Beck's Last Stand,* Reading, 1994 (toured). **Collections:** Victoria and Albert Museum, London. **Honors:** Gute Form Prize, West Germany, 1971. **Address:** Ken Garland and Associates, 71 Albert Street, London NW1 7LX, England.

## Works

Publicity programmes, for the Campaign for Nuclear Disarmament, 1962-66.
Book designs, for the Ministry of Technology London, 1962-67.
Corporate house style, for Barbour Index, 1962-73.
Corporate house style, for James Galt and Company, 1962-82.
Corporate house style, for Race Furniture, 1963-66.
Book designs, for the Cambridge University Press, 1973-75.
Book and catalogue designs, for the Arts Council of Great Britain, 1978-82.
Graphic style, for Derbyshire College of Higher Education, 1984-86.
Book designs, for Heinemann, 1985.
House style, for Keniston Housing Association, 1985-86.
Brochures, for Derwent Publications, 1986-89.
Brochures, annuals, books, and exhibition graphics, for National Museum of Science.
Book designs, for Jonathan Cape, 1990-1994.

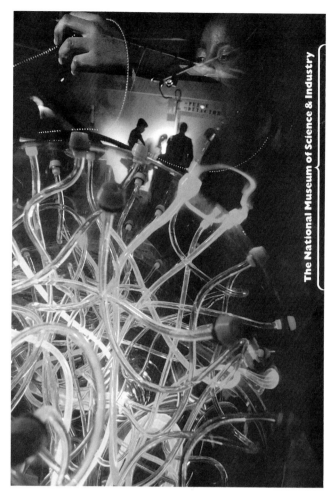

Ken Garland: Light pipes, Launch Pad, for The National Museum of Science & Industry, England. Photo by Phil Sayer, courtesy of Ken Garland

## Publications

**By GARLAND: books**—(with others) *Lettering Today,* London, 1964; *Graphics Handbook,* London and New York, 1966; *Graphics Glossary,* London, 1980; *Ken Garland and Associates: 20 Years of Work and Play 1962-1982,* London, 1982; *Graphics, Design, and Printing Terms: An International Dictionary,* London and New York, 1989; *Mr. Beck's Underground Map,* Harrow Weald, 1994.

**On GARLAND: books**—*Designers in Britain 5* edited by Herbert Spencer, London, 1957; *Left, Left, Left* by Peggy Duff, London, 1971; **articles**—in *Gebrauchsgraphik* (Munich), July 1960, April 1976; *Der Polygraph* (Frankfurt), no. 14, 1963; *Design* (London), July 1963; *The Designer* (London), April 1967, April 1983.

*

Every single day since I started work as a graphic designer in 1955, I have gone to my studio in the morning with the keenest sense of pleasure and anticipation. It has always delighted and intrigued me that my clients have been prepared to pay me for doing that which I enjoyed most: what splendid indulgence! What luck!

At the same time, paradoxically, I have to record an almost continuous sense of disappointment in the results of my work. Why could I not have done better? It was not, I believe, for want of trying, nor for the lack of sympathy and support from clients, and certainly not for lack of money, since I think that is rarely the determining factor in matters of design quality.

It may be that the paradox is insoluble—an occupational syndrome perhaps—but I would dearly love, some time in my working life, to produce one substantial piece of work which has been well conceived, well handled, well finished and well received; something of which I could feel unreservedly proud.

In the meantime, I look forward to getting to the studio tomorrow, regardless of the results.

—Ken Garland

\*       \*       \*

Ken Garland was of the generation of graphic designers emerging in post-1945 Britain who were the first to be fully aware of the work of the prewar Continental modernists and also to look towards the work of contemporaries in Europe and the United States. His article, "Structure and Substance" (*Penrose Annual,* 1960), provides a good summary of that moment in British graphic design.

As art editor of *Design* and since then as head of Ken Garland and Associates, his work has been notable for its fresh approaches. For example, he has integrated photography and drawn images as much as possible with text. (The British tradition of illustration had discouraged this.) There is also much care evident in the treatment of details, as also of textual niceties; diagrams are thought out from scratch and have considerable elegance as well as clarity. But the work is not smoothly elegant; the photography employed shows a realist, documentary tendency, rather than a pattern-making one. The "associates" in the practice (which has always stayed small) have made their own initiatives, and this has reduced the possibility of an overbearing style.

Social and political commitments are evident in Garland's work. Active in the Committee of 100 and the Campaign for Nuclear Disarmament, he designed posters, banners, and leaflets for CND in the 1960s. This work, done for love, to tight deadlines and on low budgets, has a consequent simplicity and directness. The manifesto "First Things First" that Garland wrote and himself published in January of 1964 (co-signed by twenty-one other designers and photographers) was a forthright statement of belief; it stood against the misapplication of graphic design (to high-pressure consumer advertising, in particular) and for socially useful work across the broadest range of tasks. The wish expressed by this statement was not "to take any of the fun out of life" but rather to reverse "priorities in favour of the more lasting forms of communication." Garland's best work has built pleasure into serviceable and useful graphic design.

Garland's written contributions have been of a piece with his practice. The *Graphics Handbook* and *Illustrated Graphics Glossary* are compilations of useful knowledge, but they widen the traditionally limited scope of such books. Among his articles, that on the design of the London Underground diagram (*Penrose Annual,* 1969) is still the best source of information and criticism on this subject.

—Robin Kinross

# GAULTIER, Jean-Paul

French fashion designer

**Born:** Arceuil, Valde-Marne, 24 April 1952. **Education:** École Communale, the College d'Enseignement, and at the Lycée d'Arceuil, until 1969; mainly self-taught in design. **Career:** Worked as a design assistant in the fashion houses of Pierre Cardin, Jacques Esterel and Jean Patou, Paris, 1970-74; designer of United States collections for Pierre Cardin, in Manila, Philippines, 1974-75; independent designer, for Majago and others, Paris, 1976-78; founder, Jean-Paul Gaultier S.A., Paris, from 1978; menswear line introduced, 1984; Junior Gaultier line introduced 1987; furniture line introduced, 1992; licenses include jewelry, from 1988, perfumes, from 1991, and jeans, from 1992; has designed costumes and videos for R. Chopinot, Rita Mitsuko, Yvette Horner, and others, from 1985. **Honors:** Best Designer Oscar Award, Paris, 1987; FiFi Award, Paris, 1994, 1995. **Address:** 30 Rue du Faubourg, Saint Antoine, 75012 Paris, France.

## Works

Costumes for the film *The Cook, The Thief, His Wife, and Her Lover* (Greenaway), 1989.

**Jean-Paul Gaultier: Man's suit with coordinated shirt and necktie, 1989**

Costumes for Madonna's *Blond Ambition World Tour,* 1991.
Costumes for the film *The City of Lost Children* (Caro), 1995.

## Publications

**By GAULTIER: books**—*A nous deux la mode,* Paris, 1990.

**On GAULTIER: books**—*McDowell's Directory of Twentieth Century Fashion* by Colin McDowell, London, 1984; *The Encyclopaedia of Fashion from 1840 to the 1980s* by Georgina O'Hara, London, 1986; **articles**—in *Sunday Times Magazine* (London), 14 October 1984; *Drapers Record* (London), 6 December 1986; "An Audience with Jean-Paul" in *Fashion Weekly* (London), 11 December 1986; "The Defiant Ones" by Deborah Drier in *Art in America* (New York), September 1987; *Elle* (London), November 1987; *Harrods Magazine* (London), Spring 1988; "Gaultier: Tongue in Chic" by Janvier Arroyuelo in *Vogue* (New York), August 1988; "Alaia e Gaultier, due stilisti a confronto" in *Vogue* (Milan), October 1988; "An Oxymoranic Jacket by Jean-Paul Gaultier" by Richard Martin in *Textile and Text,* 13 March 1990; "Gaultier" by John Duka in *Vogue* (New York), January 1989; "Gaultier, Comic Genius" by Sarah Mower in *Metropolitan Home,* February 1991; "The Maestro of Mayhem" by Georgina Howell in *Vogue* (New York), March 1991; "Jean-Paul Gaultier: Fashion's Main Man" by Jeff Yarbrough in *The Advocate* (USA), 17 November 1992; "Machismo in Trapunto: Jean-Paul Gaultier's 1991 Physique Sweater" by Richard Martin in *Textile and Text,* 14 March 1992; "Jean Paul the First" by Fay Weldon in *Tatler* (London), March 1995; "Four Who Have No Use for Trends" by Amy M. Spindler in the *New York Times,* 20 March 1995; "Show, Not Clothes, Becomes the Message" by Suzy Menkes in *International Herald Tribune* (Paris), 20 March 1995.

# GEHRY, Frank
American architect and furniture designer

**Born:** Toronto, Ontario, Canada, 28 February 1929; family moved to Los Angeles, California, 1947. **Education:** Studied architecture, University of Southern California, Los Angeles, B. Arch., 1954; Graduate School of Design, Harvard University, Cambridge, Massachusetts, 1956-57. **Military Service:** Served in the United States Army, 1955-56. **Family:** Married; children: Alejandro and Sami. **Career:** Worked for Victor Gruen Associates, Los Angeles, 1953-54 and 1958-61; planner and designer, Robert and Company architects, Atlanta, 1955-56; architectural designer and planner, Hideo Sasaki Associates, Boston, 1957; architectural designer, William Pereira and Luckman, Los Angeles, 1957-58; project designer and planner, André Remondet, Paris, 1961; principal, Frank O. Gehry and Associates, Los Angeles, from 1962. Assistant Professor, University of California at Los Angeles, 1977 and 1979; William Bishop Professor, 1979, and Charlotte Davenport Professor of Architecture, 1982, 1985, 1987, 1988, and 1989, Yale University, Cambridge, Massachusetts. **Exhibitions:** *International Design: New Attitudes, New Forms,* Contemporary Arts Museum, Houston, Texas, 1972; *45 Years of Architectural Design,* Musée des Arts Décoratifs, Paris, 1973; *Innovations: Contemporary Home Environs,* La Jolla Museum of Contemporary Art, California, 1974; *Drawings of American Architects,* Cooper-Hewitt Museum, New York, 1977; *Collaboration: Artists and Architects,* Architectural League, New York, 1981; *Window Room, Furniture,* Cooper Union, New York, 1981-82; *The New Buildings,* Institute of Contemporary Arts, London, 1983; *The Architecture of Frank Gehry,* Walker Arts Center, Minneapolis (toured the United States), 1986. **Honors:** Special Award, American Institute of Architects/*Sunset* magazine, 1975; Honor Award, 1975 (twice), 1976, and 1978, and Merit Award, 1975 and 1977, Southern California Chapter, American Institute of Architects; Honor Award, American Institute of Architects, 1977; Architectural Design Award 1981, and Special Merit Award, 1983, California Coastal Commission; California Chapter Honor Award, 1982; Los Angeles Chapter Honor Award, 1983 and 1984, American institute of Architects; Arnold W. Brunner Memorial Prize, American Academy and Institute of Arts and Letters, 1983; Pritzker Architecture Prize, 1989; Imperiale Award in Architecture, Japan Art Association, 1992; Wolf Prize, 1992. Fellow, American Institute of Architects, 1974, American Academy and Institute of Arts and Letters, 1987, and American Academy and Institute of Arts and Sciences, 1991; trustee, American Academy, Rome, 1989. **Address:** 1520-B Cloverfield Boulevard, Santa Monica, California 90404, U.S.A.

## Publications

**On GEHRY: books**—*12 California Architects* edited by N. Charles Slert and James R. Harter, Pomona, Los Angeles, 1978; *American Architecture Now* edited by Barbaralee Diamonstein, New York, 1980; *Gehry, Site, Tigerman: trois portraits de l'artiste en architecte* by Olivier Boissière, Paris, 1981; *Follies: Architecture for the Late-Twentieth-Century Landscape* by B. J. Archer and A. Vidler, New York, 1983; *Frank Gehry: Buildings and Projects* edited by Peter Arnell and Ted Bickford, New York, 1985; *The Architecture of Frank Gehry,* New York, 1986; *Frank O. Gehry: A Bibliography* by Sara Richardson, Monticello, Illinois, 1987; *Deconstructivist Architecture* by Philip Johnson and Mark Wigley, 1988; *Frank Gehry: Vitra Design Museum* by Olivier Boissière and Martin Filler, London, 1990; *Frank Gehry: New Bentwood Furniture Designs,* exhibition catalogue, Montreal Museum of Fine Arts, Montreal, 1992; *Schnabel House, Brentwood, California, 1990* by James Steele, London, 1993; *Frank O. Gehry: Individual Imagination and Cultural Conservation,* London and New York, 1995.

*       *       *

Frank Gehry's architecture and design constitute a consolidation of art and architecture in a seamless whole not known for centuries. In fact, Gehry produces the pertinently idiosyncratic buildings and products of a pre-industrial culture formulated at the end of the industrial epoch. His whimsy of personalized fishes, his ingenuity in ductile and agreeable furniture, and his architecture as sculpture have used modern design's technical skills to create a frisky pre-civilization of joy in the things that surround and enable modern life. Gehry presents an extraordinary oxymoron of being a feeling theorist. Philip Johnson and Mark Wigley in *Deconstructivist Architecture* refer to the Gehry House in the pastiche beach-frontier-L.A. town of Santa Monica, California, as "an extended essay on the convoluted relationship between the conflict within forms and the conflict between forms." Yet Gehry is also an architect-designer of raw instinct who can recognize the caress of cardboard edges in a chair or chaise as being like corduroy.

Mildred Friedman has said in *The Architecture of Frank Gehry,* "In his Los Angeles work, Gehry is always mindful of history and context without being archaistic." Yet in some sense, Gehry's wisdom of an architecture that defies modern architecture inexorably reverts to the pueblo, cave, and agora. His Loyola Law School (1984) is a new place for public policy as much as a cloister for a legal studies. Gehry's rambling *bricolage* aesthetic of warehouse abandonment is always wistful and old-fashioned, but so purposefully antediluvian as to suggest the future. He creates a raw architecture as opposed to the cooked technology of building.

At the same time, Gehry is an architect of distinct privacy and unconventional curiosity who prefers perturbed forms of beauty and the architect of some of the most brilliant public spaces of modern life, including museums he designed for Frederick Weissman Museum (1993) at the University of Minnesota, Minneapolis, and the ill-fated American Center in Paris (1994). In understanding personal dimensions and in accommodating collective delight, Gehry touches on both popular culture and the highest realms of architecture and design. The enchanting charm of Gehry's design verges on the theme park, in his case exalting California modernity, adhocism, and a love of the casual and vernacular.

In fact, some of Gehry's best works have been improvisations or accommodations, most notably The Temporary Contemporary (1983) designed for the Museum of Contemporary Art, Los Angeles. Initially opened as a space provisional on the completion of a more formal architectural site, The Temporary Contemporary proved to be so ingratiating and so useful that it became permanent, just as many of Gehry's works seem to be improvisations, but caught with jazz's ability to distill the concoction into a viable permanent structure. Gehry's *Easy Edges* cardboard furniture (1971-72) was originally intended for mass consumption, a happy Pop Art made for Matisse's model of art being like a comfortable armchair. Yet Gehry is keenly aware of construction and manufacturing: the lamination and construction of his *Easy Edges* furniture were a patented process and his buildings, for all their ramshackle sprawl and sense of homey dilapidation, depend upon an involved engineering to make bridges, cut-back roofs, skylights, veneers and sidings, pueblo-like extensions, and lighting internal and external work to a favorable effect. The first impression may be of a late-modern archeology into the principles and history of building, but the primitivism is enabled by awareness of contemporary technique. He is the Piranesi of our age, conceiving of freedom through architecture and design, imagining a fantasy constructed, and despising any imprisoning ideology or architecture.

Gehry finds creativity in decay or its semblance. At one point, he had planned to work with artist Gordon Matta-Clark on the De Menil house, New York (1978), allowing the artist to demolish the house and then giving himself the challenge to contravene the destruction. Gehry is a true contrarian: he works best adversarially, whether reversing decay or bringing high culture to the simple joys of the visual and comfortable culture of the poor and easy. His Rouse Company Headquarters, Columbia, Maryland (1974), is an implicit critique of the modern open-office landscape spread by Knoll. Gehry abhors uniformity and so configured a building plan that would work especially for the humanistic environment of the Rouse Company, but also as testament to Gehry's inexorable loathing for standardized, repeated forms.

Gehry evinces a keen spirit of collaboration. His exhibition installations with Senior Curator Stephanie Barron of the Los Angeles County Museum of Art have demonstrated an integrity of design, interpretation, and museum presentation. His works with artists Richard Serra and Claes Oldenburg have been at least as fruitful for the artists as for the specific collaborations themselves.

Gehry's bentwood furniture is indicative of the designer's intelligent and relaxed innovation. The *Cross Check* armchair (1989-91) remembers Thonet, enjoys a chair's innate bounce, demonstrates a virtuoso control over laminated maple, and suggests an extraordinarily modern way of living. Gehry remarked in *Frank Gehry: New Bentwood Furniture Designs,* "The material forms a single and continuous idea. What makes all this work and gives it extraordinary strength is the interwoven, basketlike character of the design. Now structure and material have freed bentwood furniture from its heaviness and rigidity." If structure and material yield freedom, it is only because they are governed by Gehry's genius to render design and architecture uninhibited and as free as beauty and building must have been at the very beginning of architecture and art. Informing this architecture of origins and of the future is Gehry's indomitable optimism, a *promesse de bonheur,* or promise of happiness as espoused by Thomas Mann, that makes Gehry's architecture and design so grandly and generously humanistic.

—Richard Martin

# GEISMAR, Thomas H.

American architectural, graphic, and exhibition designer

**Born:** Glen Ridge, New Jersey, 16 July 1932. **Education:** Studied at Brown University and Rhode Island School of Design, Providence, BFA, 1953; Yale University, New Haven, Connecticut, MFA, 1958. **Military Service:** Served in the United States Army, 1955-57. **Family:** Married Joan Hyams in 1958; children: Peter, Kathryn, and Pamela. **Career:** Founder-Partner, in Brownjohn, Chermayeff & Geismar Associates, New York, 1956-59, Chermayeff & Geismar Associates, New York, from 1960, Cambridge Seven Associates, Cambridge, Massachusetts, from 1962, and Mea Form, New York, from 1980. Carnegie Professor, Cooper Union, New York; Albert Dorne Visiting Professor, University of Bridgeport, Connecticut; former vice-president and director, American Institute of Graphic Arts. **Member:** Advisory Committee on Transport Signs and Symbols, United States Department of Transportation; Yale University Council for the School of Art. **Exhibition:** *107 Grafici dell'AGI,* Castello Sforzesco, Milan, 1974. **Honors:** Gold Medal, American Institute of Graphic Arts, 1979. **Address:** Chermayeff & Geismar Associates, 15 East 26th Street, New York, New York 10010, U.S.A.

*See* CHERMAYEFF & GEISMAR ASSOCIATES

# GEISSBUHLER, Steff

American graphic designer

**Born:** Stephan Geissbuhler, in Zofingen, Switzerland, 21 October 1942; naturalized U.S. citizen, 1988. **Education:** Studied graphic design, under Armin Hofmann, Emil Ruder, Walter Bodmer, and

Donald Brun, at the Allgemeine Gewerbeschule, Basel, Dip., 1964. **Family:** Married Sigrid Bovensiepen in 1966 (divorced, 1974); children: Marc and Christopher; married Elissa Beth Feuerman in 1983; children: Alexander and Benjamin. **Career:** Promotions designer, J. R. Geigy AG pharmaceutical and chemical corporation, Basel, 1964-67; associate and designer, Murphy/Levy/Wurman architectural and urban planning firm, Philadelphia, 1968-71; designer and member, GEE Group for Environmental Education, Philadelphia, 1968-73; consultant designer, George Nelson Inc., New York, 1969; freelance designer, New York, 1971-73; associate and designer, Anspach/Grossman/Portugal, New York, 1973-75; designer, 1975, associate, 1976, and partner, from 1979, Chermayeff & Geismar Inc., New York. Assistant Professor of Graphic Design, 1967-70, Associate Professor, 1970-73, Design Coordinator, 1971-73, and Chairman of the Graphic Design Department, 1973, Philadelphia College of Art. **Member:** National vice president, 1976-78, and New York chapter president, 1985-86, American Institute of Graphic Arts; Alliance Graphique Internationale; American Center for Design, Chicago; Poster Society, New York. **Exhibitions:** *Annual Exhibition of Applied Arts,* Bern, 1966, 1967; *Graphic Design Alumni Allgemeine Gewerbeschule,* Kunstgewerbemuseum, Basel, 1967 (toured); *Color Show,* Whitney Museum, New York, 1974 (toured); Beijing, China, 1995. **Collections:** Museum of Modern Art, New York; Kunstgewerbemuseum, Basel. **Honors:** Swiss National Prize for Applied Arts, Bern, 1966, 1967; United States Government Federal Design Achievement Award, 1988; and numerous awards from the American Institute of Graphic Arts, Type Directors Club, and Art Directors Clubs of New York and Los Angeles. **Addresses:** (office) c/o Chermayeff & Geismar Inc., 15 East 26th Street, New York, New York 10010, U.S.A; (home) 60 Hollywood Drive, Hastings-on-Hudson, New York 10706, U.S.A.

## Works

Product identification, posters, and promotional graphics, for J. R. Geigy corporation, Basel, 1964-67.

Corporate logotype, packaging, and promotional graphics, for the May Department Stores Company, from 1970.

*Book 7* and *Process of Choice* book series design, for the GEE Group for Environmental Education, published by MIT Press, 1973.

Illustrations for *The Process of Choice* by Alan Levy, Cambridge, Massachusetts, 1973.

Illustrations for *Our Man-Made Environment: Book 7,* Cambridge, Massachusetts, 1973.

*A Nation of Nations* exhibition poster, publications, signage and graphics, for the Museum of Natural History and Technology, Smithsonian Institution, Washington, D.C., 1976.

*Taking Things Apart and Putting Things Together* exhibition poster and graphics, for the American Chemical Society, 1976.

Corporate identity program, for Morgan Stanley investment bankers, 1977.

Graphic identification system, for the U. S. Environmental Protection Agency, 1977.

Corporate identity program, for the Union Pacific Corporation, from 1978.

Convention center logotype, symbol, and graphics program, for the Centro de Convenciones de Cartagena, Colombia, 1980.

Corporate identity program graphics, for Barneys New York, 1981.

25th Anniversary logotype, posters, and graphics, for the Alvin Ailey American Dance Theater, 1983.

Graphic identification program, for Charles Square multi-use real estate development, Cambridge, Massachusetts, 1983.

Corporate identity program, for Paine Webber investment bankers, 1984.

*Louisiana Journey* exhibit logotype and graphics at the New Orleans World's Fair, for the State of Louisiana, 1984.

Corporate identity program, for NBC National Broadcasting Company, 1985.

Corporate identity program, for Nashua office systems and supplies, 1986.

Peace poster, for the Shoshin Society, 1987.

*New York and the Arts: A Cultural Affair* series of nine posters, for the New York Department of Cultural Affairs, 1989.

Corporate identification systems and graphics for clients including—Merck, Telemundo, Univision, Time Warner, Artear, New York Public Library, New 42nd Street, Inc., New Victory Theater, New York, Dana Alliance for Brain Initiatives, New York, CARE International, Crane Business Papers, Hotel MIA, Miami, Conrad Hotels, and National Public Radio.

## Publications

**On GEISSBUHLER: books**—*Graphic Design Manual* by Armin Hofmann, Niederteufen, 1965; *Publicity and Graphic Design in the Chemical Industry* by Hans Neuburg, Zürich, 1967; *15 Graphiker* by Armin Hofmann, Basel, 1967; *Signs, Symbols and Signals* by Walter Diethelm, Zürich, 1976; *30 Years of Poster Art* by Armin Hofmann, Basel, 1982; *Who's Who in Graphic Art* edited by Walter Amstutz, Dubendorf, 1982; *A History of Graphic Design* by Philip B. Meggs, New York, 1983; *Low Budget High Quality Design* by Steven Heller, New York, 1990; *The Ultimate Portfolio* by Martha Metzdorf, Cincinnati, Ohio, 1991.

\*

Post Modern, New Wave, Swiss Punk, Pluralist, West Coast, Avant Garde, Deco. The recent development in graphic design has many labels, depending on your location, point of view, and/or attitude.

Rarely has a direction in design caused such emotional response. Designers whose philosophy of "form follows function" overrides everything are irritated and angry at this overemphasis on decor and sometimes purely visual esthetic treatment of information. Others brush it off as a fading fad and are disturbed at the fact that it doesn't go away and seems even to creep into their own work. To me, the rediscovered freedom in design is a very positive and exciting evolution.

Perhaps some of the clearest changes are to be found in typography. Jan Tschichold, Emil Ruder, Josef Müller-Brockmann, Max Bill, and others taught us to deal with verbal information in a disciplined, structured, organized, and readable fashion. We reduced the elements to the minimum necessary to achieve clarity and simplicity, which lead to strong and architectural solutions. We practiced the philosophy of "less is more." We straightened out the crooked pictures on the walls of commercial art. The Swiss did it especially well; to be orderly is our nature.

Wolfgang Weingart, after taking over Emil Ruder's teaching position for typography in Basel, brought with him a fresh, inquisitive

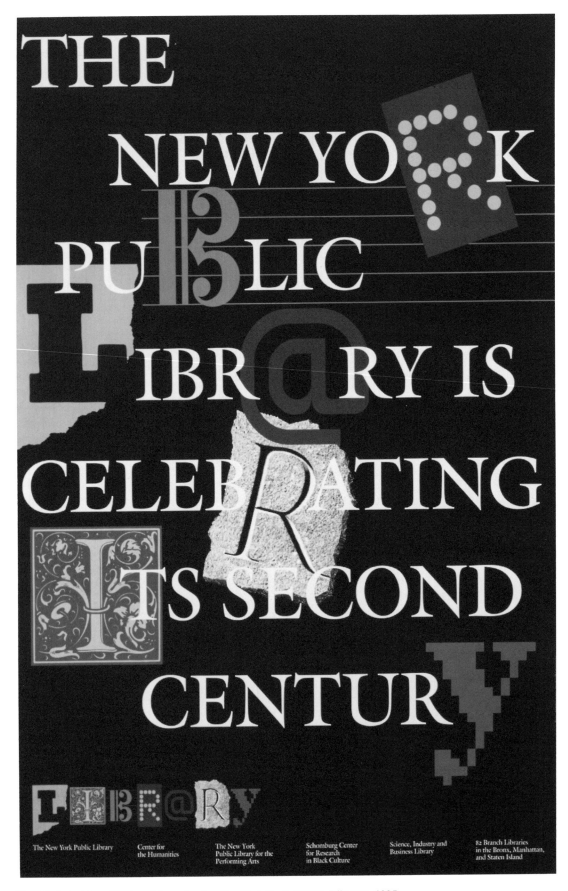

Steff Geissbuhler: Centennial poster for the New York Public Library, 1995

approach. Having, as a student, observed Ruder, he could not possibly tighten the system any further, but he started to build on this strong foundation, exploring, challenging, and expanding the design of verbal information. If Gutenberg could invent movable type, Weingart could teach it to dance. Typography became again a means of expression.

During a lecture tour through the United States, Weingart introduced and explained his philosophy at various schools, questioning the current state of the arts in typography. The audience's reaction was very mixed and caused turmoil, confusion, and outright rejection, but the seed had been sown and was welcomed by some as a necessary change.

None of this is really new. We need only to go back to the work of Stéphan Mallarmé, the Italian futurists, Dada, the Russian constructivists, El Lissitzky, and of course, the Bauhaus with Herbert Bayer, Moholy-Nagy, Piet Zwart, et al. What is different is the rediscovered freedom, the playfulness, and the inquisitive daring to try beyond the tested principles, to accept the beauty of an accident and the seemingly uncontrolled. In order to be truly free in the search for expression, readability is often ignored, sacrificing the information, but leading to unusually beautiful and intriguing solutions.

Although it is easier to find acceptance of this work with smaller clients or for more decorative applications, it seems to find its way into the more hardcore corporate world of annual reports, identity programs, and even (up until now untouchable) financial forms and documents.

Of course, as in other design directions, there are imitators using this kind of visual vocabulary as a surface style. I call this group the "New Wave Surfer Club," trying to ride the waves other people have created to the shores of a new era. The strong talents keep challenging the tested and successful recipes and keep searching for new expressions in solving old problems.

It is impossible to mention all the influences which led to this point. It is a cycle in the evolution of design to which art, architecture, photography, music, and fashion, all contribute and are, in turn, affected. *(By permission of Graphis Press, Zürich, Switzerland.)*

—Steff Geissbuhler

\*    \*    \*

Much of the design and many of the designers we see today get locked into a particular style of school, but the work of Steff Geissbuhler defies simple classifications. Instead, his work can best be defined by the nature of the design problems he has had to solve for a diversified list of clients.

For Geissbuhler, problem-solving means doing what is appropriate. Each new project brings a new set of parameters and, as the problems constantly change, so too must the solutions. Though his own feelings and ideas will indeed be part of the finished work, design for him is not merely a means of self-expression. Rather, graphic communication of the ideas and image of the client, with careful consideration of the audience, are of prime importance. Thus, the large variety of clients with whom Geissbuhler has had an opportunity to work explains the variety and diversity of his design. From his early work at Ciba to the work for the United States Government and large corporations as a partner at Chermayeff and Geismar, his diverse styles have still maintained a consistent quality. Bold, yet clean graphics and innovative integration of type and illustrative material are characteristic of his work.

Drawing has always been important to Geissbuhler, both as a means of self-expression and as a working tool for his design. This fundamental discipline, too often dismissed by designers today, was taught strictly and thoroughly in his native Switzerland. Though the training was rigorous, drawing has never restrained or confined his design because for him, drawing has never been a rigid practice. Even his early student work, seen by designers around the world in Armin Hofmann's *Graphic Design Manual,* was recognizably expressive. Though his drawing is controlled, its spontaneity has actually opened all the applications of graphics to him. Whether the final product is typographic, photographic, or illustrative, drawing is his conceptual and visual starting point and therefore remains integral to his work.

His desire and ability to adapt has made it possible for him to integrate his strict and disciplined European training with the American willingness to experiment, thereby forming a unique foundation from which to solve design problems. This blending, both of cultures and design ideology, is at the heart of his work and better represents his talent than any simple label.

—Barbara Sudick

# GERNREICH, Rudi
American fashion designer

**Born:** Vienna, Austria, 8 August 1922; emigrated to the United States in 1938, naturalized, 1943. **Education:** Studied at Los Angeles City College, 1938-41; Los Angeles Art Center School, 1941-42. **Career:** Fabrics salesman for Hoffman company and freelance clothing designer, Los Angeles and New York, 1948-51; designer, Walter Bass Incorporated, Beverly Hills, California, 1951-59; swimwear designer for Westwood Knitting Mills, Los Angeles, 1953-59; shoe designer for Genesco Corporation, 1958-60; also designed swimwear for Harmon Knitwear of Marinette, Wisconsin, and home furnishings for Knoll International, New York. Founder-president, GR Designs, 1960-64, and Rudi Gernreich Incorporated, Los Angeles from 1964. Dancer with the Lester Horton Dance Theatre troupe, 1942-48. **Member:** Montgomery Ward International Design Advisory Council from 1967. **Honors:** *Sports Illustrated* Designer of the Year Award, 1956; Wool Knit Association Creative Achievement Award, 1960; Coty American Fashion Critics' Special Award, 1960, Winnie Award, 1963, Return Award, 1966, and Hall of Fame Award, 1967; Neiman-Marcus American Fortnight Trophy, 1961; Sporting Look Award, 1963; *Sunday Times* International Special Award, London, 1965; Filene Design Award, Boston, 1966; Knitted Textile Association Crystal Ball Award, 1975. **Died:** New York, 21 April 1985.

## Publications

**By GERNREICH: articles**—interviews in *Forbes Magazine* (New York), 15 September 1970; *Holiday* (New York), June 1975.

**On GERNREICH: books**—*The Fashionable Savages* by John Fairchild, New York, 1965; *A View of Fashion* by Alison Adburgham, London, 1966; *In Vogue: Sixty Years of Celebrities and Fashion* by Georgina Howell, London, 1975, 1978, New York, 1976; *In Fash-*

*ion: Dress in the Twentieth Century* by Prudence Glynn, London, 1978; *The Collector's Book of Twentieth Century Fashion* by Frances Kennett, London and New York, 1983; *McDowell's Directory of Twentieth Century Fashion* by Colin McDowell, London, 1984; *The Encyclopedia of Fashion from 1840 to the 1980s* by Georgina O'Hara, London, 1986; *Design Source Book* by Penny Sparke and others, London, 1986.

*      *      *

Rudi Gernreich was a most important designer of women's clothing in the 1960s. The strong impact of his fashion statements was felt not only in the world of high fashion, where he first received attention, but in the clothing worn by all women and, indirectly, men as well.

He produced several startling innovations that received international acclaim. His work as a dancer and his delight as a swimmer led him to explore the advantages of knitted fabrics. He not only freed the bathing suit from its armored understructure but also, eventually, from one-half of its coverage, making fashion headlines with the topless swimsuit. This momentous design has not yet become a household necessity, but his other uses of knits have. These include the tanksuit, other unstructured swimwear, and the tank top, which has appeared in all guises from sportswear to the most formal wear. In addition, the minidress in many fabrics, knitted or otherwise, has been a constant of women's wardrobes, whether worn alone with long white boots, as Gernreich originally introduced it, or as an overblouse with skirts or slacks.

The casualness of the designs that Gernreich introduced in the 1960s, the easy care of most of the fabrics used, and a price range that would fit most budgets have had lasting effects on women's clothing. His designs did away with richness of detail with the qualities of daring color and lots of white, as well as simple cuts and straightforward one-statement styles. But at times richness of detail was replaced by the absurdity of his innovation, particularly in the cutouts. Always youthful, his clothing was designed for movement. At his best startling—the see-through blouse, the Swiss cheese swimsuit—and touched with humor, his ideas, with time, have come to belong to a society that finds the human body as acceptable as the clothes it wears.

Although his designs may not be seen on every street corner, there are few corners which are not affected by what was once thought to be his brashness. Gernreich's youthful clothes that revel in the beauty of the youthful body, especially its activity and movement, are a strong and lasting statement. The lack of acceptance of some of his fashion prophecies, such as the soft, flowing, unisex caftan for older persons, has little to do with either its esthetics or practicality.

—Harlan Sifford

# GERSIN, Robert (Peter)

American industrial and graphic designer

**Born:** Boston, Massachusetts, 12 April 1929. **Education:** Boston English High School, 1944-47; Massachusetts College of Art, Boston, BA, 1951; Cranbrook Academy of Art, Bloomfield Hills, Michigan, MA, 1952. **Military:** Served in the United States Navy Office

of Naval Research, Washington, D.C., 1952-56, Lieutenant Junior Grade. **Career:** Founder-president, Robert P. Gersin Associates design consultancy, New York, 1959-89. **Member:** Advisory board member, Alfred University, Alfred, New York, 1979-89; editorial board member, *Industrial Design* magazine, New York, 1975-88, and *Metropolis* magazine, New York, 1981-88. **Honors:** Numerous awards from the American Institute of Graphic Arts, American Institute of Interior Designers, *Industrial Design* magazine, Industrial Designers Society of America, New York Museum of American Crafts, New York Art Directors Club, Type Directors Club, and others. Honorary doctorate from Massachusetts College of Art, 1982. **Died:** New York City, 18 October 1989.

## Works

Exhibit and corporate identity program, for Avon Books, 1964-66.
Packaging, graphics, exhibits and corporate identity program, for the Xerox Corporation, 1968-80.
Graphics and interiors, for American Telephone and Telegraph, 1971.
Exhibition displays, for Houston Lighting and Power Company, 1972.
United States Pavilion exhibit at *Expo '75,* Okinawa, for the United States Information Agency, 1975.
Exhibit, for the Smithsonian Institution, Washington, D.C., 1975.
Exhibit, for NASA National Aeronautical and Space Administration, 1976.
Product design, for the Timex Corporation, 1976, 1978.
Graphics and packaging, for Myojo Foods.
Packaging, for Underberg GmbH, 1979.
Signage and graphics, for the City of Niagara Falls, New York, 1980.
Food packaging, for Bloomingdales, 1980-81.
Exhibits and packaging for Miles Pharmaceuticals, 1981.
Exhibition displays, for COMSAT Communications Satellite Corporation, 1982.
Quick Fix packaging and Answer Center interiors, for General Electric, 1982.
Packaging, for the Government of Jamaica, 1983-85.
Graphics and interiors, for the U.S. Shoe Corporation, 1983-89.
Graphics and interiors, for the Great Atlantic and Pacific Tea Company, 1984.
Corporate identity program, interiors, packaging, and graphics, for Sears Roebuck and Company, 1984-87.
Corporate identity program, for the United States General Accounting Office, 1985-87.

## Publications

**By GERSIN: articles**—"Designer's Case Study" in *Industrial Design* (New York), September 1962; "Design and Printing for Commerce" in *AIGA Journal* (New York), Summer 1968; "Packaging: What Lies Ahead" in *Industrial Design* (New York), April 1970; "On Design Values and Self-Analysis" in *Industrial Design* (New York), September/October 1975; (with L. Ferrabee) "Robert P. Gersin Associates," in *Idea* (Tokyo), no. 182, 1983; "Corporate Identity and the Latent Visual Memory" in *Directory of International Package Design* (Tokyo), 1985; "Shopping Bags Are Walking Billboards" in *Shopping Bag Design* (New York), 1987; "The

Arrogance of the Right Angle" in *High Quality Magazine* (Heidelberg), January 1988.

**On GERSIN: books**—*Modern Publicity,* annuals, New York, 1966, 1967, 1968, 1974, 1977, 1978, 1981; *50 Ads and 50 TV Commercials* by Helmut Krone, New York, 1971; *Developing a Corporate Identity* by Elinor Selame, New York, 1975; *Casebooks Packaging,* annuals, Washington, D.C., 1975, 1977, 1978, 1980, 1982; *International Trademark Design* by Peter Wildbur, London, 1979; *Packaging Design* by Stanley Sacharaw, New York, 1983; *American Design Classics* by Joan Wessel and Nada Westerman, New York, 1985; *World Graphic Design Now* by Katsuo Kimura and Shin Matsunaga, Tokyo, 1988; *Information Graphics* by Peter Wildbur, London and New York, 1989.

\*     \*     \*

For thirty years, Robert Gersin maintained a successful office in the heart of Manhattan where the struggle for conspicuous design excellence is probably at its most intense. While the first generation of professional industrial designers was characterized by flamboyant individuals carving out an identity for a struggling new profession, the second generation, to which Gersin belonged, works in quite a different context. He worked within an atmosphere in which the value of industrial design programs has become more generally recognized and the demand more widespread. New products are abundant, consumers are better educated and more selective, and a client's products and visual identity must be quickly established in highly competitive markets.

Three areas of Gersin's experience can be identified as having had the greatest influence on his work. His education, derived from the philosophy of the Bauhaus, gave him a respect for innovation, experimentation, the scientific approach, and the honest expression of materials, function, and purpose. His travels throughout the United States and abroad enabled him to observe and document many different cultural and regional approaches to design problems, and the social and commercial environment of the last twenty years led him to emphasize understanding the user's perceptions and needs and meeting these needs first rather than those of the designer or even the client. This pragmatic approach was largely responsible for the success of Gersin's projects, whether they were products, packaging, corporate identity programs, graphics, exhibits, or interiors.

Most of his projects combined several disciplines, as did the design of the United States Pavilion at *Expo '75* in Japan; the computer equipment, interiors, graphics, and signage for the Houston Lighting and Power Energy Control Center; and American Telephone and Telegraph's protoype retail program. User-research was integral to all of Gersin's projects. In the Quick Fix packaging program for General Electric, his company tested users' desires to repair their appliances and their misgivings about doing so, and then designed a packaging system using symbols, drawings, a simple text, and color-coding to enable users to find and replace parts easily.

Gersin's innovations included a dramatic 150-ton-capacity, circular, acrylic aquarium for the United States Pavilion at *Expo '75;* a durable microscope, produced for less than $1.50 for Xerox Learning Systems; a portable school planetarium with a dome using fiberglass technology from the sailcraft industry, which could be assembled by children using only a dime; and a new container for yogurt that doubled the shelf life of the product.

—Lydia Sharman

# GERSTNER, Karl

Swiss painter and lettering, typographic, and graphic designer

**Born:** Basel, 2 July 1930. **Education:** Educated in Basel, 1937-44; studied graphic design and typography, at the Allgemeine Gewerbeschule, Basel, 1945-46; apprentice designer in the Fritz Buhler advertising studio, Basel, 1946-49; influenced by Armin Hofmann, Emil Ruder, and Hans Finsler. **Military Service:** Served in the Swiss Army, 1946-47. **Family:** Married Inge Hoechberg in 1958; children: Muriel. **Career:** Freelance designer, working with Max Schmidt, for Geigy pharmaceutical company, Basel, 1949-53; freelance photographer and graphic designer, establishing Bureau Basel design studio, in Basel, 1953-59; founder-director, with copywriter Markus Kutter, of Gerstner + Kutter advertising agency, Basel, 1959-62, and with industrial designer Paul Gredinger, of GGK (Gerstner-Gredinger-Kutter) agency, Basel, 1962-70; established branches throughout the world. Retired from GGK to concentrate on painting, from 1970. Visiting lecturer, at San Francisco State College, Massachusetts Institute of Technology, University of Hawaii, University of California, Berkeley, and the Royal College of Art, London, from 1958. **Member:** Verband Schweizer Graphiker; Schweizerischer Werkbund. **Exhibitions:** Club Bel Etage, Zürich, 1957; Galerie Suzanne Bollag, Zürich, 1961; Galerie Denise Rene, Paris, 1962, 1967, 1969, 1974, 1982, 1986; Haus am Lutzowplatz, West Berlin, 1963, 1970; Galerie der Spiegel, Cologne, 1963, 1966, 1984; Staempfli Gallery, New York, 1965, 1967, 1985; Galerie Denise Rene/Hans Mayer, Düsseldorf, 1969, 1971, 1972, 1978, 1981, 1990; Museum of Modern Art, New York, 1973; Kunstmuseum, Düsseldorf, 1974; Kunstmuseum, Solothurn, 1978; Studio Bombelli, Cadaques, 1981; Galerie Appel und Fertsch, Frankfurt, 1986; *Karl Gerstner,* Museum für Gegenwartskunst, Basel, 1992 (toured); Galerie Littmann, Basel, 1992; Galerie am Lindenplatz, Liechtenstein, 1992; Galerie APC, Zürich, 1992; Von der Heydt-Museum, Wuppertal, 1993. **Collections:** Museum of Modern Art, New York; Tate Gallery, London; Kunstmuseum, Düsseldorf; Staatsgalerie, Stuttgart; Kunstmuseum, Solothurn. **Honors:** Gold Medal, Milan Triennale, 1957. **Address:** Mönchsbergerstrasse 10, CH-4024 Basel, Switzerland.

**Works**

Corporate identity programmes for British Overseas Airways Corporation, Burda, Ringier, Swissair and the Basel *National-Zeitung.*
Advertising and graphics for Citroen, Holzapfel Schwitter, Bech Electronic Center, Geigy, Philips, Volkswagen, IBM, Jaegermeister, Dow Chemicals, Boîte à Musique, Sinar Fachkamerabau, Keramikfabrik Felix Handschin, Intermobel, and others.

**Publications**

**By GERSTNER: books**—*Kalte Kunst?,* Teufen, 1957; (with Markus Kutter) *The New Graphic Design,* Teufen and London, 1959; (with Markus Kutter) *Gerstner + Kutter: Werbung-Gaphik-Publizitat,* Basel, 1959; (with Markus Kutter) *Gerstner + Kutter 1960,* Basel, 1961; *Designing Programmes,* Teufen and New York, 1963; *Mit dem Computer Kunst produzieren,* Zagreb, 1968; *Do-it-Yourself Kunst,* Cologne, 1970; *Compendium for Literates,* Teufen,

Karl Gerstner: subway poster for the Schwitters exhibition for the Centre Pompidon, Paris, 1994. Text reads: "Imagine the joy Kurt Schwitters would have had not only to be shown in Paris, but also to be advertised here."

1970, Cambridge, Massachusetts, 1972; *Typographisches Memorandum,* St. Gallen, 1972; *Think Program,* New York, 1973; *Andre Thomkins: Inspiration und Methode,* Hannover, 1974; *15 Variationen uber einen Satz von Max Bill,* Ulm, 1978; *Gute Kunst, schlechte Kunst,* Hamburg, 1981; *Kunst in der Demokratie—ein Utopie,* Frankfurt, 1981; *Der Wert der Kunst,* Basel, 1982; *Der Kunstler und die Mehrheit,* Frankfurt, 1986; *The Forms of Color,* Cambridge, Massachusetts, 1986; *Color Fractals,* Sindelfingen, 1988; *Vingt et un passages à travers le Rouge,* Genf, 1989; *Karl Gerstners Avant Garde Küche,* Teufen, 1990; *Ideenskizzen aus 40 Jahren Canon Farbkopien,* Genf, 1991; *Le Plat Plat,* Genf, 1992.

On GERSTNER: books—*Advertising Directions* edited by Edward M. Gottschall and Arthur Hawkins, New York, 1959; *Typography* by Aaron Burns, New York, 1961; *Design Coordination and Corporate Image* by F. H. K. Henrion and Alan Parkin, London and New York, 1967; *An International Survey of Packaging* by Wim Crouwel and Kurt Weidemann, London, 1968; *History of the Poster* by Josef and Shizuko Muller-Brockmann, Zürich, 1971; *Karl Gerstner: Color Sounds,* exhibition catalogue with interview by Wibke von Bonin, New York, 1975; *Karl Gerstner: Color Forms,* exhibition catalogue with text by Grace Glueck, Düsseldorf, 1981;

*The Spirit of Color: The Art of Karl Gerstner* edited by Henri Stierlin, Stuttgart, Paris, and Cambridge, Massachusetts, 1981; *Karl Gerstner's Private Pinakothek,* Solothurn, 1983; *Gerstner's Muhle,* Hamburg, 1985; *Le Prince des Couleurs* by Pierrette Fleutiaux, Geneva, 1987; *Ein Maß für das Unermeßliche* by Hans-Joachim Müller, Zürich, 1988; *Karl Gerstner,* exhibition catalogue edited by Vilém Flusser, Düsseldorf, 1990; *Karl Gerstner im Gespräch,* exhibition catalogue by Christine Breghan and Katerina Vatsella, Bremen, 1991; *Karl Gerstner,* exhibition catalogue with texts by Christian Baur, Christof Markwalder, Frank Oleski, and Alexander von Steiger, Basel, 1992.

\*

When I was twenty, I set up on my own—with the aim of putting into practice, to the best of my ability, the Bauhaus philosophy of the unity of culture. As a graphic designer, I thought to design things of everyday life like works of art; and as a picture-maker, I thought to design works of art like things of everyday life. Soon after, I established my own office. My objective was to realize my dream, i.e., to found a kind of Bauhaus—not as a school, but as a commercial agency for all kinds of creative tasks, from the visiting card to city planning. This agency, "Bureau Basel," was intended to bring together a team of designers, architects, photographers, sociologists, psychologists, writers, musicians, and so on. All of them were full of ideas and ready to resolve problems in interdisciplinary cooperation. But the dream remained a dream; the Bureau Basel never worked as it should have.

After that common experience, Markus Kutter and I decided to found a conventional advertising agency—with unconventional work, because neither of us understood anything about advertising. Thus, in 1959, Gerstner + Kutter was founded in Basel, and I concentrated my energy on building up this enterprise. As a consequence of our ignorance, we were obliged to develop our own ideas and principles, which turned out to be the basis of the future success of the agency.

About ten years later, when I was forty, I retired from the agency, for I had realized that the Bauhaus philosophy led to many contradictions. I also wanted to concentrate on what has always been close to my heart: doing nothing, having time, making pictures. What I didn't know at that time was that I was starting on another—rather unexpected—career; as a typographic designer for printed media. I conceived concepts for several monthly, weekly, and daily papers, and these tasks in the communication business gave me much satisfaction. As both a designer and a picture-maker, I have always accompanied my work with theoretical reflections and research, and I have written several articles and books exploring the efficiency of creative processes. This inquiry led to my summarizing formula, "Instead of solutions of problems, programs for solutions."

—Karl Gerstner

\*       \*       \*

Today, the process of writing has become increasingly complex, as it combines both science and art, which have spawned a variety of scientific branches as well as art forms. Typography is one of the remarkable results of this combination, and its scientific and artistic connections are still being debated.

In 1959, Karl Gerstner formed an advertising agency in Switzerland and began his investigations into typography, language, and writing. The results have included a series of publications—*Kalte Kunste?* (1957), *Designing Programmes* (1963), *Typographical Memorandum* (1972) and *Compendium for Literates* (1970)—and a 1973 exhibition at the Museum of Modern Art in New York; the latter, titled *Think Program,* included material based on these publications and reinforced his theories on systematizing (programming) the problem-solving process.

In all of these endeavors, typography was viewed as a scientific as well as artistic phenomenon. Gerstner classified typography by separating it into categories—for instance, typography as language, as image, as field, or as sequence. This enabled the reader to see how language and writing changed once they were transformed into type. For example, typography can transform language or writing into a visual idea. Words and sentences can be visually manipulated so that verbal meaning is enhanced. By a simple distortion of a letter or word, the viewer can be presented with a visual pun.

Gerstner further acknowledges that type alone is an inadequate form of communication. Visual materials such as photographs, drawings, and diagrams support the copy and can make possible its reduction. However, to the proverbial picture that's worth a thousand words, Gerstner retorts that "the text could not be replaced by a thousand pictures."

The subject of space and time is an important one in typography. How long it takes to speak a line or a paragraph is identical to the amount of space required to print it. Thus, a designer must consider spatial organization and type selection, just as a speaker is concerned with speech patterns and briefings. For the designer, the use of a highly developed grid can provide all the flexibility and freedom to arrange and organize typography and other visual material.

Finally, the limitation of space in typography can be solved and expanded by the use of a series of spaces or pages. This process involves the development of a sequence which can be a creative force in design, particularly book design. Though each page is new and different, a sense of similarity and uniformity is sought and maintained.

These summary observations culminated in the publication of Gerstner's *Compendium* in 1972. Though he no longer practices advertising, his outlook is sufficiently wide-ranging to afford him the luxury of pursuing varied forms of creativity. Since 1970, he has been applying these concepts to other art forms, particularly painting and constructions.

—D. Ichiyama

# GHERARDI, Piero

Italian stage and film designer

**Born:** Poppi, Arezzo, 20 November 1909. **Education:** Mainly self-taught in art and design. **Career:** Worked as an architect, in the 1930s, and as a film set dresser and furnisher, 1945-49, in Rome; art director, working on the films of Federico Fellini, Duilio Coletti, Mario Soldati, Mario Monicelli, Gianni Franciolini, Alberto Lattuada, King Vidor, Luigi Zampa, and others, in Rome, 1950-71; stage designer, working on productions in Italy, and for the National Theatre, London, from 1953. **Honors:** Academy Award, 1961, 1963; Gold Sash Award for Film Design, Italy, 1961, 1965, 1967. **Died:** Rome, 8 June 1971.

## Works

Film designs include—*Notte di Tempesta* (Franciolini), 1945; *Eugenia Grandet* (Soldati), 1946; *Daniele Cortis* (Soldati), 1946; *Amanti senza Amore* (Franciolini), 1947; *Senza Pieta* (Lattuada), 1948; *Proibito Rubare* (Comencini), 1948, *Fuga in Francia* (Soldati), 1948; *Campane a Martello* (Zampa), 1949; *Napoli Milionaria* (de Filippo), 1949; *Cinema d'Altri Tempi* (Steno), 1950; *Her Favourite Husband* (Soldati), 1950; *Romanzo d'Amore* (Coletti), 1950; *Camicie Rossi* (Alessandrini), 1950; *Sensualita* (Francassi), 1951; *Iolanda la Figlia del Corsaro Nero* (Soldati), 1951; *Anni Facili* (Zampa), 1953; *Proibito* (Monicelli), 1954; *Le Notti di Cabiria* (Fellini), 1956; *War and Peace* (K. Vidor); *Padri e Figli* (Monicelli), 1957; *La Grande Strada Azzurra* (Pontecorvo), 1957; *Il Medico e lo Stregone* (Monicelli), 1957; *Il Soliti Ignoti* (Monicelli), 1958; *La Dolce Vita* (Fellini), 1960; *Kapo* (Pontecorvo), 1960; *Risate di Gioia* (Monicelli), 1960; *Sotto Dieci Bandiere* (Coletti), 1960; *Crimen* (Camerini), 1960; *Il Gobbo* (Lizzani), 1960; *Il Carabiniere a Cavallo* (Lizzani), 1961; *Il Re di Poggioreala* (Coletti), 1961; "Renzo e Luciana" episode of *Boccaccio 70* (Monicelli), 1962; *Violenza Se Greta* (Moser), 1962;

*Otto e Mezzo/8 1/2* (Fellini), 1963; *La Ragazza di Bube* (Comencini), 1963; "Peccato nel Pomeriggio" episode of *Alta Infedelta* (Petri), 1964; "Fatebene Fratelli" episode of *Tre Notti d'Amore* (Comencini), 1964; "La Telefonata" and "Il Trattato di Eugenetica" episodes of *Le Bambole* (Risi and Comencini), 1964; *Giulietta degli Spiriti* (Fellini), 1965; *Madamigella de Maupin* (Bolognini), 1965; *L'Armata Brancaleone* (Monicelli), 1965; "Fata Armenia" episode of *Le Fate* (Monicelli), 1966; *Se Tutte le Donne del Mondo* (Levin and Maiuri), 1966; *Diabolik* (Bava), 1967; *The Appointment* (Lumet), 1969; *Queimada* (Pontecorvo), 1969; *Infanzia, Vocazione, e Prime Esperienze di Giacomo Casanova, Veneziano* (Comencini), 1969; *Brancaleone alle Corciate* (Monicelli), 1970; *Le Avventure di Pinocchio* (Comencini), 1971.

## Publications

By GHERARDI: articles—interview in *Sight and Sound* (London), Winter 1969-70.

On GHERARDI: books—*Federico Fellini's Juliet of the Spirits* edited by Tullio Kezich, New York, 1965; *Dizionario del Cinema Italiano 1945-1969* by Gianni Rondolino, Turin, 1969; *Le Decor de Film* by Leon Barsacq, Paris, 1970, as *Caligari's Cabinet and Other Grand Illusions,* Boston, 1976; *The International Film Encyclopedia* by Ephraim Katz, New York and London, 1980; *The International Dictionary of Films and Filmmakers,* London and Chicago, 1987, 1991.

\*   \*   \*

Piero Gherardi collaborated with Federico Fellini on his major films of the late 1950s and early 1960s. The styles of these films show an infusion of new artistic qualities into the established practices of Neorealist films of the late 1940s. In *La Dolce Vita, 8 1/2,* and *Juliet of the Spirits* there still was the use of some actual locations and some non-professional actors, characteristics of the Neorealist movement. But Gherardi and Fellini brought certain surrealistic images into their films, such as the opening of *La Dolce Vita,* in which a statue of Christ with outstretched arms is suspended from a helicopter. Though such a situation is plausible, the image is striking and memorable because it juxtaposes familiar objects with an unusual context.

The sets and costumes of *8 1/2* and *Juliet of the Spirits* established the dreamlike quality of the films. The spa in *8 1/2* is not a real location but a set, modeled not on an existing place but on the memories of one Gherardi had visited as a child. Similarly, the train station is the memory of one—all the viewer sees are a locomotive, a platform, and some steam. In *Juliet of the Spirits,* the conservative heroine's surroundings are mostly white, while the interiors of the house of her liberated friend Suzy are red, yellow, and violet. Juliet's house, an environment of purity, is contrasted to Suzy's, which has the atmosphere of circus and brothel. Gherardi considered a costume more than a mere covering for a character; it reveals that character and defines the personality. Likewise, his sets did more than give documentary information about a place. Gherardi often mixed the ordinary with the simplified or the surrealistic. In so doing, he emphasized the artificial quality of films and helped to focus attention on characters and situations whose components were as complex as the visual elements.

—Floyd W. Martin

# GIACOSA, Dante

Italian car designer

Born: Rome, 3 January 1905. Education: Educated at the Ginnasio and Liceo Classico, Alba, Piedmont, 1914-22; studied mechanical engineering, at the Politecnico, Turin, D.Ing., 1927. Military Service: Served in the Italian Army Apprentice Cadet School, 1927-28, and as an air force engineer, 1937. Family: Married Laura Gherzi Paruzza in 1936; daughter: Mariella. Career: Draughtsman, S.P.A. Motor Vehicle Company, Turin, 1928-30; worked for the Fiat Automobile Company, Turin, from 1930: in diesel engines engineering, 1930-32; foreman, aero engines engineering, 1932-33; passenger car engineering design chief, 1933-46; director of engineering for Fiat Motor Vehicle and Fiat Styling, 1946-55; principal director of Fiat Styling, 1955-65; member of Fiat Directive Committee, 1960-70; divisional manager of engineering and styling, 1965-70; consultant engineer to Fiat from his retirement in 1970. President, Societa Industriale Ricerche Automotoristiche research and development company, Turin, from 1974. Professor of engineering design, Turin University, 1947-67. President of the Commissione Unificazione Nazionale Autoviecoli, 1955-75, Associazione Tecnica Automobile, from 1965, and Federation Internationale des Societés d'Ingénieurs des Techniques de l'Automobile, 1968-69. Exhibitions: *Carrozeria Italiana,* Palazzina della Promotrice delle Belle Arti, Turin, 1978 (toured); *Design and design,* Palazzo delle Stelline, Milan, 1979 (travelled to Venice); *Gli Annitrenta,* Palazzo Reale, Milan, 1982; *Peggy Guggenheim Collection,* Solomon R. Guggenheim Foundation, New York, 1995. Collections: Museo dell'Automobile, Turin. Honors: Fellow, Society of Automobile Engineers, Pennsylvania, 1948; Order of Merit, Italian Republic, 1956; Order of Merit, Societé Francaise pour la Recherche et l'Invention, 1957; Compasso d'Oro Award, Milan, 1959; fellow, Institute of Mechanical Engineers, London, 1964; Gold Medal, Rimini Biennale, 1968; Colombiana Medal, Genoa, 1970; Gold Medal, Societé des Ingénieurs de l'Automobile, Paris, 1981; honorary doctorate, Pasadena Art School, California, 1981. Died: In Turin, 31 March, 1996.

## Works

Car designs include—Fiat *1100S,* 1933; Fiat *500 Topolino,* 1936; Fiat *1400,* 1950; Fiat *1100-103 Turbine,* 1953; Fiat *600,* 1955; Fiat *Nuova 500,* 1957; Fiat *1800,* 1959; Fiat *A109 Primula/Autobianchi,* 1964; Fiat *124 Coupe,* 1966; Fiat *128,* 1969; Fiat *A112/Autobianchi,* 1969; Fiat *127,* 1971.

## Publications

By GIACOSA: books—*Motori Endotermici,* Milan, 1938, 1984; *Forty Years of Design with Fiat,* Milan, 1981; (with Enzo Altorio) *La Fiat Nuova 500,* Teramo, Italy, 1993; articles—in *Royal Auto* (Brussels), January 1952; *Automobile* (Rome), Summer 1961; *Stile Industria* (Milan), no. 35, 1961; *Form und Technik* (Zurich), August 1961; *Pirelli* (Turin), no. 4, 1962, no. 6, 1965; *First Edition* (Milan), May 1963; *Style Auto* (Milan), December 1963; *Atti del Convegno* (Rome), Winter 1981, *Le Grandi Automobili* (Milan), no. 3, 1982; *Modo* (Milan), no. 55, 1982.

**Dante Giacosa:** *Fiat Nuova 500* **two-door salon, 1957-60**

**On GIACOSA: books**—*Fiat* by Michael Sedgwick, London, 1974; *The Library of Motoring: The Designers* by L. J. K. Setright, London, 1976; *A Source Book of Classic Cars* by G. N. Georgano, London, 1977; *Carrozeria Italiana: Cultura e Progetto,* exhibition catalogue edited by Anfelo Tito Anselmi, Milan, 1978; *Cars of the Thirties and Forties* by Michael Sedgwick, London and Göteborg, 1979 *Architeture delle Macchine,* Milan, 1982; *Italian Design: 1870 to the Present* by Penny Sparke, London, 1988; **articles**—"Dante Giacosa 40 Ans de Fiat" by Jean Bernardet, *Retrovisuer,* June 1995.

\*

A design is good when it produces a feeling of true balance between art and engineering. The technician can become a good designer only in an environment which inspires him with the idea that a high standard of functional value can be reached only if united with beauty of shape; one who can attain this vital balance between engineering and art will reach the summit in design.

To achieve his purpose, the industrial designer must work in close cooperation with a number of specialists and must, on occasion, coordinate the work of a number of different industries. Ultimately responsible for the work, he is both the leader and a part of a great organisation. He must have the mind of an architect, concerned with both technique and art, and his mode of expression must link technical and artistic language.

An elaborate graph made at any stage in the planning of a modern vehicle will express clarity, accuracy, geometrical exactitude, and constructional possibility, exactly as though it were an architectural plan. And it is with such a series of drawings that the designer produces ideas in graphic form first for himself and then for the other technical departments, the sales manager, the production manager, and the executive of every other branch concerned. The work of the designer will be more expressive or more technical in character, according to whether the artist or the technician predominates. But if he combines the technician and the artist equally within himself, his most expressive design will always have that technical touch to differentiate it from a similar design produced by the pure artist. It is for the technical design and not for the artist to number in detail the external and internal components required to create a whole; he cannot stop at the purely superficial aspect but is driven on towards the technical considerations and the functional purpose behind the design.

The designer-artist will succeed in harmonising functional value and visual appearance; smoothness of line in a vehicle will be accompanied by a comparable smoothness in running and the style of the body-work will be reflected in the behavior of the machine on the road. That is why I maintain that the automobile industry will achieve its best results when its working conditions allow for the training of designers who can combine technical knowledge with means of artistic expression.

Le Corbusier, in his much-discussed treatise on modern architecture, states, "Basing their work upon calculations, engineers employ geometric shapes which satisfy our eyes by their geometrical construction and our spirit by their mathematical expression; such achievement belongs to great art."

Le Corbusier, in my opinion was right; technique, which has introduced us to "rational" shapes and taught us the use for materials, makes it possible for us, in our closest approach to the field of art, to maintain that sincerity of expression which imbues a piece of work with the spirit of its time.

Today, scientific knowledge has reached the point where the man is capable of creating monuments that have no direct connection with nature but that nevertheless can express new ways of feeling, which can be one day objects of a new history of art. Such a history will deal with the story of engineering as though it were that of architecture, and it will describe the styles adopted, for instance, in the field of automobile design as though they were architectural, for the development of automobile design towards maturity has points of resemblance with the development of design in architecture. *(Excerpted from a paper presented in 1951 before a London conference organized by the Council of Industrial Design.)*

—Dante Giacosa

# GIBB, Bill

British fashion designer

**Born:** William Elphinstone Gibb in Fraserburgh, Scotland, 23 January 1943. **Education:** Went to school in Fraserburgh until 1960; studied at St. Martin's School of Art, London, Dip. AD., 1966; studied under Janey Ironside, Royal College of Art, London, Des. RCA., 1968. **Career:** Founder and partner, with others, of Alice Paul clothing boutique, London, 1967-69; freelance designer, working for Baccarat fashion house, London, 1969-72; founder-chairman, Bill Gibb Fashion Group, London, 1972-88; opened first shop in Bond Street, London, 1975. **Member:** Fellow, Society of Industrial Artists and Designers, London, 1975. **Exhibitions:** *British Design,* Musée du Louvre, Paris, 1971; *Fashion: An Anthology,* Victoria and Albert Museum, London, 1971; *Bill Gibb: 10 Years,* Albert Hall, London, 1977. **Collections:** Bath Museum, Avon; Leeds Museum, Yorkshire; Victoria and Albert Museum, London; Royal Ontario Museum, Toronto. **Honors:** *Vogue* Designer of the Year, 1970; ITV Best Fashion Show Award, London, 1979. **Died:** London, 3 January 1988.

**Publications**

**By GIBB: articles**—in *The Designer* (London), May 1981.

**On GIBB: books**—*Fashion: An Anthology by Cecil Beaton,* exhibition catalogue compiled by Madeleine Ginsburg, London, 1971; *In Vogue: Sixty Years of Celebrities and Fashion* edited by Georgina Howell, London, 1975, 1978, New York, 1976; *The Changing World of Fashion: 1900 to the Present* by Ernestine Carter, London, 1977;

*The Guinness Guide to 20th Century Fashion* by David Bond, Enfield, 1981; The *Collector's Book of Twentieth Century Fashion* by Frances Kennett, London and New York, 1983; *Sixty Years of Faces and Fashion* by Prudence Glynn, London, 1983; *McDowell's Directory of Twentieth Century Fashion* by Colin McDowell, London, 1984; *The Encyclopedia of Fashion from 1840 to the 1980s* by Georgina O'Hara, London, 1986; *Design Source Book* by Penny Sparke and others, London, 1986.

*

From the age of 12 there was no doubt in my mind that I wanted to pursue a career in fashion. It was an obsession. Arriving in London at the age of 19 from northeast Scotland, I strove for the top and achieved it within ten years. The motivation is inexplicable in the sense that I feel that I have been given a rare gift of talent to design beautiful clothes.

There is nothing comparable to the sheer joy and challenge of confronting a blank sheet of paper in order to create a collection. I discipline myself by deciding on a theme: for example, a collection based on a porcelain look, a Scottish theme, or a Byzantine influence (which I used for one of my most successful collections, Autumn/Winter 1975). From many rough sketches, I edit down to what I consider to be a complete, comprehensive, exciting, and desirable amount, around sixty to seventy outfits. I believe in coordinates that give women a choice and the enjoyment of putting together their own look in the Gibb style. The sensuality of women is important, and I believe my clothes achieve this for them.

I enjoy all aspects of design, and although I am better known for fantasy gowns, my feeling for knitwear is perhaps stronger because to me it is of the earth, more honest—probably being a Celt, the roots cannot be denied.

To travel is to glean knowledge, and I know this is essential in my quest for constant inspiration. I probably belong to the Romantic genre of designers, but I can appreciate and understand street fashion, probably again, because of its honesty.

Fashion designs today, I feel, no longer dictate "The Look." Since 1947 and "The New Look" created by Dior, women have become quite educated in their style of dress and what suits them in particular. I feel, rather than dictate. I create a mood which is taken up by those who like to wear my particular look.

Fashion, being so transient, has a message for everyone. Now, in the 1980s, fashion still seems to revolve around more awareness of the body which began in the 1970s when health foods and diets were high on the list of priorities—hence the current popularity of sportswear to coincide with the increasing number of people who exercise more and more to attain this eternal "spirit of youth" now dominating our society.

People will always be fascinated by clothes and fashion—they can be varied: frowned upon, unbearable, risque, dowdy, always exciting and moving, searching, and a force to be reckoned with.

—Bill Gibb (1984)

*       *       *

Once upon a time, there was a dream of synaesthesia and of picturesque unanimity about the visual world. Bill Gibb is the product and keeper of that 1960s dream and propagated its most extravagant enactment in fashion in the 1970s. At St. Martin's School and the Royal College of Art in London in the 1960s, developing in the wake of slightly older personalities from David Hockney to Zandra Rhodes and Ossie Clark and from the yeasty ferment of rock and King's Road London, Gibb took a rainbow of multicultural and multi-colored possibilities, creating clothing for a hedonistic scenic world as a stage. Frustratingly, perhaps Gibb could have achieved a commercial foothold—and the full cachet of 1960s style— if only he had started out a few years earlier. His first major order for a New York store was Henri Bendel: his work exemplified the Bendel's pursuit under Geraldine Stutz for distinctive, fluid, and expressive clothing for both day and evening. Like Giorgio di Sant' Angelo in the United States, he seized the drama of the rhapsodic 1960s and fashioned a kaleidoscope of swirling textiles and luxurious exoticisms to the quality standards of the 1970s. Further, like di Sant' Angelo, he did not live to see the work fully vindicated as the visionary fashion that it was.

In 1977, as his influence was waning, Gibb presented a characteristically unapologetic and unabashed retrospective at the Royal Albert Hall, London. Gibb convened the opulent textiles of Eastern exoticism, the sexy declaration of the body, the pastiche and print, and the grand sense of an ad hoc theatricalism that had been his motif for the years leading up to 1977. Designer Jean Muir, remembering Gibb in *Vogue* (London), claims "he had a wonderful, romantic Celtic quality, a rich imagination quite different from an Anglo-Saxon one." There were no brakes for Gibb's flamboyant, layered sense of decoration; he was a unrepentant and gifted romantic living in modern times.

First a free-lance designer with Baccarat in London from 1969-72— where he was remembered by Monty Black as "the greatest designer of his decade, who made the clothes of the hippies into clothes that people could wear"—and then on his own after 1972 with a retail shop opened in 1975, Gibb promoted a clothing of free, easy, and eclectic lifestyle. Caftans, luxury knitwear (which may have returned him to his Scottish origins), and rampant pattern created the cross between hippie reductivism and gypsy pattern proliferation that Gibb took into luxurious clothing. The extravagance of style had many adherents, but few clients could, by the later 1970s, carry off the boisterous wildness of his heavy wools, feathery laces, Kitsch appropriations from Carnaby Street, embroidery, and exotic perturbed paisleys, all in one outfit. His hooded capes, stylized appearances, and piles of jewelry and accessories made splendid editorial copy in a colorful time, but relatively few clients wanted the voluptuous hoard of ideas and pieces that Gibb assembled with such panache. In fact, few clients could live with the massing of elements (bright leggings and knits, gypsy skirts almost to the floor, slashed Elizabethan doublets, paisley shawls, glitter and jewels, etc.) that Gibb's effect required. The problem was that Gibb at his best required an act of faith and identification for the client, one who would be able to pile on clothing in a full ardor for Kitsch, complication, and surfeit.

In the same era, other designers from Saint Laurent through Zandra Rhodes would visit the possibilities of rich hippies and exotic costumery, but they would also create more conservative collections. Gibb believed unremittingly, even dogmatically, in fashion as a theatrical *Gesamtkunstwerk* rich in historical and global allusions and equally rich in pattern, accessories, and texture. Even as Gibb invokes memories and dreams of the Venetian Renaissance or the Middle East (though slightly through Sebastian Flyte's perspective), his art was seen in the pragmatic 1970s and 1980s as being too resplendent, a dazzle that seemed more clamorous rather than a mere register of the rich. Moreover, Gibb's style, in its excess, seemed too idiosyncratic, quirky, and un-serious to be taken seriously.

Gibb never compromised. In the 1980s, in reversed fortunes and in a brief collaboration with knitwear maker Kaffe Fassett, Gibb continued as the great decorator in a time that abjured decoration. He held fast to a fantasy about fashion that had briefly exploded into popularity and of which he was a perfect example of that moment of fashion idealism. To look at Gibb's colorful work today is to render the 1970s faraway and nostalgic, but also to perceive "swinging London" as an aesthetic utopia where intensely personal artistic freedom, such as Gibb's, was prized and flourished, if only fleetingly.

—Richard Martin

# GIBNEY, Arthur
Irish architect and interior designer

**Born:** Dublin, Ireland, 1932. **Education:** Studied craft design and painting at the National College of Art, Dublin, 1949-1953; studied architecture at the College of Technology, Bolton Street, diploma in architecture, 1952-57; writing Ph.D. thesis on historic building technology, Trinity College, University of Dublin. **Career:** Worked as an assistant to Michael Scott, Michael Scott and Associates, 1958-1961; co-founder, Stephenson Gibney and Associates, 1961; in partnership with architect Sam Stephenson, 1961-1975; founder, Arthur Gibney and Partners, from 1976. Extern examiner for the diploma in architecture, College of Technology, Bolton Street, 1970-75; extern examiner for the diploma in architecture, School of Architecture, University College, Dublin, 1979-81; consultant and adviser, Kilkenny Design Workshops. **Member:** President, 1974-75, Society of Designers in Ireland; extern examiner in craft design, 1979-81, and, board member, 1989-93, National College of Art and Design; An Comhairle Ealaíon (The Arts Council of Ireland), 1988-95; fellow, and president, 1989-90, Royal Institute of Architects of Ireland; International Heritage Jury of the European Community, 1990-92; Board of Governors, National Museum of Ireland, 1992-95; academician, and secretary, 1994-96, Royal Hibernian Academy of Arts. **Honors:** Taylor Scholarship for Art, Royal Dublin Society, 1953; Travel Scholarship, Royal Institute of Architects of Ireland, 1955; Architectural Association Prize, 1956; Harrington Award for the use of color in design, 1958; Triennial Gold Medal, Royal Institute of Architects of Ireland, 1978; Building of the Year Award, 1982; Europa Nostra Award, 1994. **Address:** Arthur Gibney and Partners, 20 Hartcourt Street, Dublin 2, Ireland.

## Works

Irish Pavilion, Montreal Expo, 1967.
*ROSC* exhibition design, for the National Museum of Ireland, 1967.
Electricity Supply Board Headquarters, Fitzwilliam Street, Dublin, 1969.
Irish Pavilion, Osaka Expo, 1970.
*ROSC Viking Age Art* exhibition design, for the Royal Dublin Society, 1971.
*Trinity College Silver* exhibition design, 1970.
Merrion Hall, Sandymount, Dublin, designed for the Irish Export Board, 1974.

Building and interiors, for the Irish Management Institute, Sandyford, County Dublin, 1978.

Interiors, for Restaurant Patrick Guilbaud, Dublin, 1981.

Community School, Leixlip, County Kildare, 1981-82.

Additions and glazed walkway, for Dublin City University, mid 1980s.

Delmas Bindery, Marsh's Library, Dublin, 1988.

Restoration of c. 1720 building and conversion of interiors to office use, Dr. Steevens' Hospital, Dublin, 1988-92.

Irish Pavilion, Seville Expo, 1992.

Restoration of the Colonnades and *Book of Kells* exhibition design, for Trinity College, University of Dublin, 1992-94.

Other architectural designs include—Irish Embassy, Riyadh, Saudi Arabia, and Dahran International Airport Hotel.

*     *     *

Arthur Gibney has practiced as an architect, interior, and exhibition designer since the early 1960s. Gibney first worked with Michael Scott, a committed modernist. Scott designed the Busáras (the Central Bus Station, Dublin, 1994-1952), one of the first postwar examples of the International Modern Style of Europe. The Busáras building and Scott's domination of Irish architecture in the 1950s and 1960s were the most influential factors in spreading the use of International Modernism in Ireland. During this period there was also an unprecedented expansion in industry; the Irish economy witnessed record growth and with it increasing demand for commercial office buildings in Dublin.

Imbued with his own interpretation of International Modernism, Gibney—in partnership with Sam Stephenson—was responsible for designing key office developments in the 1960s and 1970s. Stephenson Gibney and Associates' Electricity Supply Board Headquarters, Fitzwilliam Street, Dublin (1969) is an example of infill office development set within a Georgian terrace that was characteristic of many developments of the 1970s. The scheme respects the height, horizontal divisions, and vertical rhythm of the earlier houses and the facade was constructed of brick-colored pre-cast concrete panels. This type of development was enormously controversial, however, not because of the design of the building, which was award-winning, but for the destruction of the late eighteenth century houses that it replaced. Built during a period when Dublin's Georgian heritage was undervalued, this development became the test case in the battle between the conservationists and developers. The controversy marked the beginning of an increased awareness of urban preservation and encouraged the fledgling architectural conversation movement in Ireland.

Stephenson Gibney and Associates' Educational Building Society Offices, Westmoreland Street, Dublin, also respected the height and scale of the eighteenth century streetscape. The facade is entirely clad in reflective glass, which reflects the buildings opposite, traffic, and passersby. Significantly the ornate terra cotta Art Nouveau facade of an earlier building (by Frederick Jermyn, 1914) was retained to form a focal point for the entrance to the banking hall/office. This forms a contrast with the flat glass facades of the new building.

The Irish Management Institute building (1978) and Merrion Hall, designed for the Irish Export Board (1974) allowed Gibney greater freedom. Working in suburban locations free from the constraints of the city streetscape, Gibney created sophisticated office buildings with corporate America as a model. Merrion Hall is a freestanding construction with an exposed trabeated concrete struc-

ture. In strong contrast, behind this clearly articulated skeleton stands a clean and uniform curtain wall of reflective glass.

Exhibition design emerged as a specialty early in Gibney's career when he was commissioned to design glass display cases for the exhibition of antiquities at the *ROSC* exhibitions in 1967 and 1970. He went on to design the Irish Pavilions at the International Expositions at Montreal and Osaka.

One of Gibney's most important public commissions was Leixlip Community School, County Kildare (1981), which won the Building of the Year Award in 1982. The school buildings of red brick contrast dramatically with high-pitched slate roofs. The most inventive feature is the entrance in the form of a glazed atrium that links the diverse elements of the design.

At this time Gibney also designed his most delightful interior, that of the Restaurant Patrick Guilbaud, Dublin (1981). This purpose-built restaurant combines a large, ergonomically efficient kitchen with a spacious and elegant dining-room. The interiors are airy and well lit by natural light which falls from a system of concealed skylights high in the ceiling. The brilliant white walls of the restaurant are covered with an exceptional collection of paintings by Irish artists which form a perfect backdrop to this exquisite interior.

More recently, Arthur Gibney and Partners have been involved in restoration work on historic buildings at Trinity College, Dublin, and notably at Dr. Steeven's Hospital. The restoration and conversion of Dr. Steeven's into the administrative headquarters of the Eastern Health board was awarded a European Architectural Heritage Award by the European Community.

—Paul Caffrey

# GIDMAN, Claude

Canadian product and industrial designer

**Born:** Claresholm, Alberta, 1934. **Education:** Studied transportation design, Art Center College of Design, California, B.P.A. (Bachelor of Professional Art), 1960. **Career:** Designer, Ford Motor Co., London, England, 1960-65; designer, Robin Bush and Associates, Toronto, Ontario, Canada, 1965-67; founder and principal, Gidman Design Associates, Toronto, from 1967. Faculty, from 1967, chair of the industrial design department, from 1985, Ontario College of Art, Toronto; founder and director, Creative Design Research Unit, University of Toronto, from 1987. **Member:** Royal Canadian Academy of Arts; Association of Chartered Industrial Designers of Ontario; Industrial Designers Society of America; Human Factors and Ergonomics Society; Society of Automotive Engineers. **Exhibitions:** *Art in Every Day Life,* Harbourfront Gallery, Toronto, 1987; *Creative Spark,* Royal Canadian Academy of Art, 1986 (toured Canada); *International Touring Exhibition of Canadian Designers,* Royal Canadian Academy of Arts, toured Europe, 1995-97. **Honors:** Toronto Arts Award, Design and Architecture, 1987; Gold Medal, Canada Awards of Excellence, Industrial Design, 1985. **Address:** Gidman Design Associates, Box 283, 55 McCaul St., Toronto, Ontario, Canada.

## Works

Snowmobile designs, for Northway Snowmobiles, Pointe Claire, Quebec, 1971-1973.

*CLRV "Streetcar", Canadian Light Rail Vehicle,* for the Urban Transportation Development Corporation in conjunction with Toronto Transit Commission, 1974-1977.
*Motor Grader,* for Champion Road Machinery Ltd., Goderich, Ontario, from 1981.
*Orion II* bus, for Ontario Bus Industries, Mississauga, Ontario, 1982.
*Niagara People Mover,* for Ontario Bus Industries, 1983.
*Locomotive Control Console,* for General Motors Canada Ltd., Diesel Division, London, Ontario, 1983.
*Long Distance Train Design Study,* for VIA Rail Canada Inc., Montreal, 1983-1984.
*Double-Decker Railcar Design (Long Haul),* for VIA Rail Canada Inc., Montreal, 1984.
*"Signature"* line desk accessories, for Esselte Pendaflex Canada, Mississauga, 1987-1988.
*Ultra II* water purifiers, for Brita Canada, Mississauga, 1988.
*Theme Park Hi-Tech Simulators,* for SimEx Inc., Toronto, Vancouver, Japan, from 1989.
*Accessible Intercity Charter Coach,* for Transportation Development Corporation, Montreal, 1993.
*Accessible Intercity Coach Seating,* for Transportation Development Corporation, Montreal, 1995.

**Publications**

On GIDMAN: books—*Art in Every Day Life,* exhibition catalogue, by Linda Lewis and Peter Day, Toronto, 1987; **articles—**"Truck Driver's Office" in *Canadian Interior,* November 1970; "Urban Transit: The Designer's Role" in *Canada Design,* Office of Design, Department of Industry, Trade and Commerce, January 1975; "Face to Face: Claude Gidman Design Associates" in *Canada Design,* September 1975; "More Than Skin Deep" in *Challenges,* Summer 1989; "Succeeding by Design" in *Enroute,* January 1992.

\*   \*   \*

Claude Gidman is an industrial designer who excels in the field of transportation. Working in Canada, a country which has never successfully designed and manufactured its own automobile, this is no small thing. From small town Alberta to Los Angeles to London and back to Canada, Gidman has, nonetheless, managed to design all types and all aspects of vehicles, including airplane interiors, forklift cabs, and streetcars.

Claude Gidman was born in 1934 in a small town on the Canadian prairies. Like many boys of his generation, Gidman grew up dreaming of cars. In 1956, his dreams became a reality when he was accepted into the prestigious transportation design program at Art Center College of Design in California. Lack of finances, however, interrupted his studies, and he returned home to work for Canadian Car Company (now Hawker-Siddeley). Gidman persevered and graduated with honors from Art Center a year later in 1960.

Fresh out of college, Gidman went to work for Ford in Britain, working with an international team of designers at the time when Ford was developing some of the more contemporary designs that made the company number one in Europe. Based in Essex, Gidman was design studio manager of Advanced and then Production Interiors, having worked on successful tractor, car, and van designs in his first few years with Ford.

Gidman returned to Canada in 1965, enticed by the whirlwind of design activity generated in anticipation of the Montreal World's Fair, Expo '67. Gidman soon joined Robin Bush and Associates, one of the busiest design studios in Canada. The firm was responsible for the design and coordination of three Canadian pavilions, including "Man in the Community," one of the key theme pavilions.

After Expo, Gidman returned to transportation design and established his own consultancy. Today his client list includes almost every transportation development firm in Canada, including Bombardier, the Urban Transportation Department Development Corporation, Canadian Vickers, and Flyer Industries.

One of Gidman's most innovative works is the 1984 Orion II bus for Ontario Bus Industries. The challenge: to design a vehicle to allow passengers in wheelchairs as well as others passengers to enter directly from the road without having to climb steps. Instead of using the market standard, slow and conspicuous hydraulic chair lifts, the Orion II bus has a very low, flat floor and utilizes air bag suspension which supports the vehicle and allows it to be lowered almost to ground level. When the bus comes to a stop, the driver releases the air from the airbags and, in just a few seconds, the bus lowers, as if kneeling. With a quick switch of a button, a small, automatic ramp bridges the gap between the curb and the bus. The bus has been successfully integrated into public transportation systems around the world.

In 1967 Gidman joined the faculty of the Ontario College of Art in Toronto and has been active in design education ever since. He became chair of the industrial design department in 1985. He is also founder and director of the Creative Design Research Unit at the University of Toronto. Established in 1986, the program fosters interdisciplinary projects and cooperative activity between the university's engineering students and industrial design students from the art college.

Never a stylist, always a pragmatist, Gidman strives to meet the needs of all users: passengers, operators, service people, and the manufacturer. Gidman especially prides himself in addressing the needs of the driver. For example, with his upgrade of the Toronto Streetcar, he insisted on elevating the operator's seat. This single change enabled the seated driver not only to see better, but, now eye level with standing passengers, can better relate to them.

Gidman has won many awards throughout his career. Of particular note, he was the first industrial designer to win the Toronto Arts Award in 1987.

—Elizabeth Crawford and Rachel Gotlieb

# GILL, Bob

American graphic designer

**Born:** New York City, 17 January 1931. **Education:** Studied design, at Philadelphia Museum School of Art, 1948-51; studied painting, at Pennsylvania Academy of Fine Arts, Philadelphia, 1951; City College of New York, 1952, 1955. **Military Service:** Served in the United States Army, 1952-54. **Family:** Married Elizabeth Mills in 1967 (divorced, 1974). **Career:** Freelance designer and illustrator, New York, 1954-60; art director, at Charles Hobson advertising agency, London, 1960-62; partner, with Alan Fletcher and Colin Forbes, in Fletcher/Forbes/Gill design studio, London,

1962-67; freelance designer, illustrator, and filmmaker, in London, 1967-75, and in New York, from 1976; creator of documentaries and industrial films for clients including Olivetti, Pirelli, Singapore Airlines, Holiday Inn, and the Lincoln Center. Instructor, School of Visual Arts, New York, 1955-60, Pratt Institute, Brooklyn, New York, 1959, Central School of Art, London, 1967-69, Chelsea School of Art, London, 1969, Royal College of Art, London, 1970-75, Hornsey School of Art, London, 1972-74, and Parsons School of Design, New York, 1981. **Exhibitions:** School of Visual Arts, New York, 1959; American Institute of Graphic Arts, New York, 1966; Stedelijk Museum, Amsterdam, 1970. **Collections:** Museum of Modern Art, New York; Victoria and Albert Museum, London. **Honors:** Gold Medal, Art Directors Club of New York, 1954; Silver Medal, Design and Art Directors Association, London, 1968, 1970; numerous American Institute of Graphic Arts and Type Directors Club awards, New York. **Address:** 1200 Broadway, New York, New York 10001, U.S.A.

## Works

Books illustrated and designed include—*New York: Places and Pleasures* by Simon, 1957; (and author, with Alastair Reid) *The Millionaires,* 1959; (and author, with Reid) *A Balloon for a Blunderbus,* 1960; (and author) *A to Z,* 1961; (and author) *What Colour Is Your World?,* 1963; (and author, with Colin Fletcher and Alan Forbes) *The Present,* 1963; (and author) *The Green-Eyed Mouse and the Blue-Eyed Mouse,* 1965; (and author, with Botsford) *Parade,* 1967; (and author) *Bob Gill's Portfolio,* 1968; (and author) *I Keep Changing,* 1971; (and author) *Ups and Downs,* 1974; (and author) *Forget All the Rules You Ever Learned About Graphic Design,* 1981.

## Publications

**By GILL: books**—(with Alan Fletcher and Colin Forbes) *Graphic Design: Visual Comparisons,* London, 1963; (with John Lewis) *Illustration: Aspects and Directions,* London and New York, 1964; *Graphic Design Made Difficult,* New York, 1992.

**On GILL: books**—*The New Graphic Design* by Karl Gerstner and Markus Kutter, Teufen and London, 1959; *Graphic Design Britain* edited by Frederick Lambert, London, 1967; *Graphis Record Covers* edited by Walter Herdeg, Zurich, 1974; *The Language of Graphics* by Edward Booth-Clibborn and Daniele Baroni, London, 1980.

\*     \*     \*

Bob Gill is more an artist than anything, but he understands how to utilize his creativity, harness it to graphic purposes, and to feed purely "mechanical" typography with inspiration. This is shown very clearly in the many logotypes he has designed, as in the reversed capital "R" for Real Typographers (1953), and the lower-case "e" balanced on the top right of a capital "B" for Blond Educational Books (1963). His value as a graphic designer may depend on his understanding of when not to draw and how far to go with a drawing. The two covers, *Graphis* No. 119 and *Design* No.166, demonstrate this in exemplary fashion. The *Graphis* cover reproduces the postal wrapper of a packet sent to the editor; it includes stamps, labels, postmarks, and all the rest. The *Design* cover is a simple drawing of a black-and-white post for a traffic sign with, instead of such a sign, a rough square with the word "sign" written on it.

As the occasion has demanded, he can go much farther with the drawing. The record cover for George Harrison's *Wonderwall Music* (Apple Records, 1968), is really a charming painting in its own right. It does, of course, also summon a vivid impression of the music.

He also put his talent to good purpose in some of the packaging commissions he undertook. On the boxes of typing paper for Spicers (1961), stark-white, reverse lettering on red and blue ground gives the effect of torn paper. In 1967, for Pickerings, he devised packages for combinations of a can of filling and a packet of pastry mix sold together in one box; these reproduced the two on its faces as though the box were transparent.

Perhaps the distinctive quality that runs through Gill's work, in addition to the irrepressible wit and irony, is an ability to seize the essential in a memorably condensed image, as in the montage of torn photographs for the film *A Severed Head* (1968), for example, or the record cover for Troubadour Records of the Colin Bates Trio, a seeming photograph of a record with hole and label well off center. These imaginatively compressed images, however, are not always all that simple. For instance, Spicers Kingsbury paper was advertised by a rough little drawing in thick outline of one of those Swiss army knives opened up to show all the little gadgets and attachments for the many uses it could serve.

—Toni del Renzio

# GIRARD, Alexander (Hayden)

American architect and interior and industrial designer

**Born:** New York City, 24 May 1907. **Education:** Studied at the Architectural Association School, London, 1925-29; Royal School of Architecture, Rome, 1930-31; New York University, 1932-35. **Career:** Worked in several architectural offices, in Florence, Rome, London, Paris, and New York, 1929-32; independent architect and designer, establishing own architectural office in Florence, 1930, in New York, 1935-37, in Detroit, 1937-52, and in Santa Fe, New Mexico, from 1953; design director, textile division of Herman Miller Inc., Zeeland, Michigan, from 1952. Established Girard Foundation for collections of toys and folkcraft objects, Santa Fe, 1961 (donated to state of New Mexico, 1978); Girard Wing of Museum of International Folk Art, Santa Fe, opened 1982. **Exhibitions:** *International Exposition,* Barcelona, 1929; *Printed Textiles for the Home,* Museum of Modern Art, New York, 1947 (toured); *Textiles USA,* Museum of Modern Art, New York, 1956; *The Design Process at Herman Miller: Nelson, Eames, Girard, Probst,* Walker Art Center, Minneapolis, 1975 (toured). **Honors:** Gold Medal, Barcelona International Exposition, 1929; Museum of Modern Art Fabrics Prize, New York, 1946; League of New York Trailblazer Award, 1952; Medal of Honor, Architectural League, New York, 1962, 1965; Elsie de Wolfe Award, American Institute of Interior Designers, 1966; Allied Professions Medal, American Institute of Architects, 1966; *Institutions Magazine* Award, Chicago, 1967; Burlington House Award, Los Angeles, 1974; Gold Medal, Honor Fraternity of Tau Sigma Delta, San Antonio, 1980; Governor's Award, New Mexico, 1981. Honorary Royal Designer for Industry, Royal Society of Arts, London, 1965. **Address:** P.O. Box 2168, Santa Fe, New Mexico 87501, U.S.A.

## Works

Italian exhibit layouts, at the *International Exposition,* Barcelona, 1929.

Junior League shop interiors, Grosse Pointe, Michigan, 1936.

Office and plant interiors, for the Detrola Corporation, Detroit, 1943.

Office interiors, for the Ford Motor Company, Dearborn, Michigan, 1946.

*Design for Modern Use: Made in USA* travelling exhibition layouts, for the Museum of Modern Art, New York, 1950.

Fabrics and wallpaper ranges, for Herman Miller Inc., 1952.

*Michigan Bulletin* magazine redesign, for the American Institute of Architects, Detroit, 1953.

Furniture showroom interiors in Grand Rapids, Michigan, for Herman Miller Inc., 1953.

Glassware, ceramics, and leather goods design programme, for Georg Jensen Inc., New York, 1955.

Showroom interiors in San Francisco, for Herman Miller Inc., 1958.

Plant and office interiors, for the Cummins Engine Company, Columbus, Indiana, 1960-64.

Textiles shop interiors in New York, for Herman Miller Inc., 1961.

Administration Centre three-dimensional mural, for John Deere and Company, Moline, Illinois, 1964.

Corporate visual programme, for Braniff International Airline, Dallas, 1964.

*El Encanto de un Pueblo* exhibition pavilion and layouts, for *Hemisfair 68,* San Antonio, Texas, 1967.

Girard Group furniture range, for Herman Miller Inc., 1967.

*African Fabrics* exhibition layouts, for the Colorado Springs Fine Arts Center, Colorado, 1976.

*Multiple Visions* inaugural exhibition layouts, for the Girard Wing of the Museum of International Folk Art, Santa Fe, New Mexico, 1982.

## Publications

**By GIRARD: books**—*The Magic of a People/El Encanto de un Pueblo,* New York, 1968; film—(with Charles Eames) *Day of the Dead,* 1956.

**On GIRARD: books**—*House and Garden: The Modern Interior* edited by Robert Harling, London, 1964; *80 Years of Ideas and Pleasure from House and Garden* edited by Mary Jane Pool and Caroline Seebohm, London, 1980; *Knoll Design* by Eric Larrabee and Massimo Vignelli, New York, 1981; *The Conran Directory of Design* edited by Stephen Bayley, London, 1985; *The American Design Adventure 1940-1975* by Arthur J. Pulos, London and Cambridge, Massachusetts, 1988.

\*

Every new project presents some version of basic order. In it, the ingredients for the exercise of fantasy and magic may usually be found.

These ingredients, if discovered and used significantly, can give special individuality and identity to the project or the client, or better, both.

When the client joins in the search, the ideal conditions exist for the realization of the best solution to the project.

My greatest enjoyment and satisfaction in the solution of any project is uncovering the latent fantasy and magic in it and convincing my client to join me in this project.

—Alexander Girard

\*     \*     \*

It is impossible to think of Alexander Girard without considering his lifelong collecting of children's toys and folk art. Over 100,000 of these items now form the Girard Foundation Collection at the Museum of International Folk Art in Santa Fe, New Mexico.

As a designer and as a person, Girard is most often regarded as a humanist. From 1940 to 1960, when American design was mostly enslaved by machine technology and the rigors of the International Style, Girard respected both sources but distinguished himself by similarly valuing childlike joy and the richness of folk art and culture. With his respect for the overall view, his complete and completed designs resulted from a multi-faceted order of details, rich and rewarding. He was as concerned with the buttons on the waiters' coats as he was with the floor plans of the restaurants he designed.

Girard's eye has always seen beyond period style to that which is timeless, not because of its quaintness nor historic value only, but because of its intrinsic human quality that could be continuously used. His turn-of-the-century music hall transformed into the Herman Miller showroom in San Francisco showcases his design thinking. Here was no reconstruction of a music hall atmosphere as a background for displaying, in sharp contrast, the Miller collection but instead the bold openness of the architectural structure, strengthened with clear color and the sparkle of the brilliant, medallion-cut glass windows. He removed the original murky clutter to reveal not bare bones but a lively and enriched structure, a space, open, bright, and right, one that could be an integral part of a display of objects designed fifty years later.

His respect for contemporary technology is obvious in his textile design. He has always esteemed what the machine can produce in quantity and with ease. He has respected the quality of folds and flow that fabric can have and has enriched this surface with geometric and simple, abstracted design. These qualities are often evident in native fabrics, and he has produced outstanding exhibitions of fabrics both native and contemporary.

As a humanist, Girard sees the interrelatedness of human activity through both history and daily living. He gives rightful due to architectural soundness of structure and furnishes that structure with the wit and charm of a child's toy. His interiors are to be lived in, and they also display the lives lived within. The restaurants he designed and other public spaces he has created, while fulfilling the demands of their functions, have also enriched the eye with his carefully chosen and ordered world of visual pleasure. In a time when contemporary design has been most often formalized into an international sameness, Girard has maintained his richness of spirit, his wit, and his childlike wonder at all that the visual world has to offer. As a designer, he brings order to the chaos of wonder.

—Harlan Sifford

# GIUGIARO, Giorgetto

Italian industrial designer

**Born:** Garessio, Cuneo, 7 August 1938. **Education:** Studied fine art and technical drawing, Accademia di Belle Arti, Turin, 1953-55. **Family:** Married Maria Teresa Serra; children: Fabrizio and Laura. **Career:** Designer, under Dante Giacosa and Bruno Barbero, at Fiat Car Styling Center, Turin, 1955-59; head of Styling Department, under Nuccio Bertone, at Carrozzeria Bertone, Grugliasco, Turin, 1959-65; director of Styling and Project Center, Carrozzeria Ghia, Turin, 1965-68; founder and director, with Aldo Mantovani, of Italdesign car styling company (as Studi Industriali Realizzazione Prototipi SpA), Moncalieri, Turin, from 1968; established Italdesign industrial design division, from 1974; Giugiaro Design, the former industrial design division, became independent company, from 1981; designed cars for Alfa Romeo, Audi, BMW, Chrysler, DMC De Lorean, Fiat, Ford, General Motors, Hyundai, Isuzu, Jaguar, Karmann, Lamborghini, Lancia, Lotus, Maserati, Mazda, Renault, Saab, Skoda, Seat, Volkswagen, Volvo, and ZCZ, and products for Parker, Sony, Philips, 3M, Apple, Sanyo, Makita, Fiat Ferroviaria, JVC, Martini & Rossi, Imetec, Kodak, Shiseido, Interbrew, Johnson & Johnson, Dow Chemical, Alitalia, Head, and others. Management Committee member, Italian Industrial Design Association (ADI), from 1985; instructor, Faculty of Architecture, Turin, 1985. **Exhibitions:** *The Taxi Project,* Museum of Modern Art, New York, 1976; *Giugiaro: Car Designer,* Lijnbann Centrum, Rotterdam, 1981; *Carrozeria Italiana,* Pasadena Art Center, California, 1981; *The Italian Idea,* Aspen Design Center, Colorado, 1981; *Die Nutzlichen Kunste,* Messegelande am Funkturm, West Berlin, 1981; *Italian Re-Evolution,* La Jolla Museum of Contemporary Art, California, 1982; *Design Since 1945,* Philadelphia Museum of Art, 1983; *Giugiaro: Beyond Design,* Palazzo Barberini, Rome, 1983; *The Asahi Shimbun,* Kyoto Museum of Modern Art, 1989 (toured Japan); *The Direction of Design,* Museo dell'Automobile, Turin, 1990; *Giugiaro: la Syntèse des Formes,* Pantin Centre de l'Automobile, Paris, 1991. **Honors:** Silver Medal, British Society of Artists and Industrial Designers, London, 1980; Compasso d'Oro Award, Italian Industrial Design Association (ADI), Milan, 1984; honorary degree in design, Royal College of Art, London, 1984; Golden Steering Wheel, Bild am Sonntag, Springer, 1995. **Address:** Italdesign SpA, Via Achille Grandi 11, 10024 Moncalieri, Turin, Italy.

## Works

Automobile designs include—Gordon Keeble *GT,* 1960; Alfa Romeo *2000/2600 Sprint,* 1960; BMW *3200 CS,* 1961; ASA *1000 coupe,* 1961; Simca *1000/1200 Coupe,* 1962; Iso Rivolta *330/340 GT,* 1962; Alfa Romeo *Giulia GT,* 1963; Iso *Grifo,* 1963; Fiat *850 Spider,* 1965; Mazda *Luce 1500/1800,* 1965; Isuzu *117 coupe,* 1966; De Tomaso *Mangusta,* 1966; Maserati *Ghibli,* 1966; Fiat *Dino* coupe, 1967; Iso Rivolta *Fidia,* 1967; Maserati *Ghibli Spider,* 1968; Maserati *Bora,* 1971; Alfa Romeo *Alfasud,* 1971; Maserati *Merak,* 1972; Lotus *Esprit,* 1972; Volkswagen *Passat,* 1973; Volkswagen *Scirocco,* 1974; Volkswagen *Golf,* 1974; Alfa Romeo *Alfetta GT/GTV,* 1974; Hyundai *Pony,* 1974; Alfa Romeo *Alfasud Sprint,* 1976; Maserati *Quattroporte,* 1976; Audi *80,* 1978; BMW *M1,* 1978; Lancia *Delta,* 1979; Fiat *Panda,* 1980; De Lorean *DMC 12,* 1981; Isuzu *Piazza,* 1981; Lancia *Prisma,*

1982; Fiat *Uno,* 1983; Hyundai *Stellar,* 1983; Saab *9000,* 1984; Seat *Ibiza,* 1984; Isuzu *Gemini* coupe, 1984; Isuzu *Gemini/ Chevrolet Spectrum,* 1984; Lancia *Thema,* 1984; Hyundai *Excel,* 1985; Hyundai *Presto,* 1985; Fiat *Premio/Duna,* 1985; Seat *Malaga,* 1985; Fiat *Croma,* 1985; Renault *21,* 1986; Fiat *Duna Weekend,* 1986; Eagle *Premier,* 1987; ZCZ *Florida,* 1988; Jaguar *Kensington,* 1990; Bugatti *ID 90,* 1990; Nazca *M12,* 1991; Subaru *SVX,* 1991; Seat *Toledo,* 1991; Nazca *C2,* 1991; Lexus *GS 300* (Toyota *Aristo*), 1993; Seat *Ibiza,* 1993; Fiat *Punto,* 1993; Fiat *Punto Cabrio,* 1993; Seat *Cordoba,* 1993; Lamborghini *Calà,* 1995.

## Publications

**On GIUGIARO: books**—*The Library of Motoring: The Designers* by L. J. K. Setright, London, 1976; *Art and the Automobile* by D. B. Tubs, Guildford and London, 1978; *Atlante del Design Italiano 1940-1980* by Alfonso Grassi and Anty Pansera, Milan, 1980; *Giugiaro Design* by Bruno Alfieri, Milan, 1980; *Giugiaro and Ital Design* by Akira Fujimoro, Tokyo, 1981; *Giugiaro, Car Designer: 20 Years of Research of Form and Function in Car Design,* exhibition catalogue with text by Giuliano Molineri, Rotterdam, 1981; *Carrozzeria Italiana,* exhibition catalogue with text by Giuliano Molineri, Pasadena, 1981; *Design Since 1945* edited by Kathryn Hiesinger and George Marcus, Philadelphia and London, 1983; *The Conran Directory of Design,* edited by Stephen Bayley, London, 1985; *Italian Design: 1870 to the Present* by Penny Sparke, London, 1988; *Giugiaro Italdesign: How to Create a Car,* Milan, 1995.

\*

The car has dominated the industrial panorama of our century. It has mobilized economies, freed whole strata of society, become a status symbol. It has caused entire populations to migrate into new industrial areas; it has promoted research and a never-ending series of technological conquests; it has maximized individuality and speeded up personal and professional relationships; it has focused the dreams and the yearnings of generations of young people.

Today, we see that there is a price to pay for the triumph of the car that is on a collision course with the urban and indeed the general natural environment that has gone much too far in its consumption of our basic resources.

In this age of automation, robotics, computer-aided production, factories are turning out thousands of cars a day in Europe alone, cars that are destined to clog up our streets, our motorways, our public spaces.

Society—in the form of its public administration, national and supranational legislative authorities—has always reacted after the event to the problems caused by the car. There has never been any preventive planning, any broad program. The great national and international road networks were built years ago and are now undersized for present purposes: their lanes are as inadequate for the performance of today's car as they are the size of today's truck.

Our cities are bursting at the seams and the attempts to ban private cars from town centers or build huge parking lots, below or above ground, are an inadequate response.

In a country like Germany which has done better than most in adapting its structures to the automotive civilization, I might seem to be exaggerating, but if you look at Europe as a whole, I think most people would agree with me.

Europe's national governments and the representatives of European institutions have really got to set up a committee of independent experts to work out the specifications, particularly as regards to size, for the cars of the next century. That would provide the manufacturers with specific guidelines on which to base their projects.

The auto industry cannot be left to tackle the problem on its own; for one thing, the perceived interests of the industry do not always coincide with the good of the general community.

Given the aid of this back-up structure, any capable, experienced designer will be able to come up with a car design that solves the problem of its adaptability to the needs of our urban and general environment.

The fact is that the car is a bulky object and statistically is seen rarely to carry more than one person: a person who is not willingly going to sacrifice the advantages his car has to offer, especially in terms of individual freedom or movement compared to standard public transport. And the richer motorist, the luxury car buyer, does not have the right to occupy one and a half times the public space simply because he is prepared to pay the extra tax.

My own feeling is that it might be helpful to impose a length limit on private cars in general. I hope it won't shock you too much if I propose a maximum length of 4.50/4.60 meters. A car that length can still offer practicality and comfort and it can be ultra-reliable. One good example is the Volkswagen *Passat,* which offers two meters of living room (from brake pedal to rear seatback).

I do realize that it is a matter of some delicacy and might sound provocative to suggest such measurements in a country like Germany, that has shown such consummate ability in combining quality and safety with comfort and generous dimensions. Yet after their first predictable shock, the public has really taken to the new look of the compacts and especially the MPVs and has begun to appreciate the application of safety and luxury to taller passenger compartments with a revolutionary layout and seating that may be more vertical but remains ultra-comfortable.

This does not mean the disappearance of the luxury car. There is no reason why we should not be offered a choice between the compacts/MPVs and the Rolls Royces, and Jaguars, and Mercedes, in rather more compact size. There is, I feel sure, enough creative talent around to adapt to the new specifications.

Think for a moment of our town and city centers, our downtowns where there is an increasing battle for the available space. Our national and extranational legislators are going to have to confine these areas to rail-based and public transport vehicles. And they ought to be able to insist on the use of cars that are not privately owned, that are no more than 2.30/2.50 meters long, that are no more than ways of getting from point A to point B. Such vehicles could be driven by a hybrid or electric power unit and designed to carry 4-5 passengers including disabled people in wheelchairs. Users could gain access to them via a "Smart Card" then leave them to the next user so that they wouldn't be parked for hours taking up space. All it would require to keep this fleet in constant circulation would be the construction of huge parking areas in every town center.

I have been working on a project along these lines and have even built a prototype that I have called *Biga.* And why shouldn't there be similar specifications for taxis that would ensure adequate comfort, ease of access, room for luggage, and so on, but make them smaller and release them from the constraints they suffer from being private cars adapted for public transport use. I realize that this would all cost money, but here too human intelligence can surely find solutions and obtain satisfactory results.

To conclude, I believe that all human progress has depended on our ability to impose limitations on ourselves, to establish and to obey rules of civilized behavior.

So why shouldn't the car learn this lesson from history?

—Giorgetto Giugiaro (excerpted from a speech given on the occasion of the Golden Steering Wheel Award, at the Springer publishing house, Berlin, 1995)

\*    \*    \*

It was the work of Giorgetto Giugiaro as director of Bertone that first drew comments about the Italian combination of eye, hand, and brain. And to be sure, his work from the 1960s right up to the present time has always carried, almost as a hallmark, the stamp of intelligence, sensibility, and fine craftsmanship. Elegance has not been reserved for the outer bodywork alone but has shaped the interior, the seating, the instrument panel, the steering wheel, and other controls; all have been conceived as part of a whole design, meticulous and finely detailed, though on occasion the priorities shock Anglo-Saxon pragmatics. Giugiaro believes that an automobile should *fare una bella figura*—cut a fine figure—but that only a well-engineered vehicle can do it. The finer the car the finer the figure! Put another way, the dominant concept of design at Bertone and, subsequently, at Italdesign has been the general notion of an elegant box encompassing intelligently disposed components. Of course, the elegance of the box depends upon the particular use that is to be made of it, so none of the automobile bodies have appealed to fanciful streamlining and space-travel effects. Moreover, when aerodynamic considerations have influenced the shape of an automobile, there has never been any question of transferring that shape to some other product. Giugiaro's sewing machines for Necchi are not about to take off for outer space or even to dash along the highway at 100 miles an hour. The elegance of their lines stem from quite other and far more civilized considerations.

Italian design, as in this case exemplified by Giugiaro, has, in the main, been a search after the appropriate without settling for the banal and the unadventurous. While function is not to be ignored, it alone cannot ensure the success of a design, which must question that aesthetic assumptions built into definitions of function. Design has to be a cultural product, a part of the civilizing process; it arises not only to meet new functions but to meet new ways of functioning. In this, it fulfills in our time something analogous to the development of good manners in the past. It is in this way and from these cultural considerations that Giugiaro's elegant designs are to be seen as positive and innovating good taste, a conscious stand against "kitsch," "camp," and those substitutes for the positive exercise of eye, hand, and brain which are "metaphorical," such as "high-tech" (now some thirty years or more after its original appropriation), Art Deco, and other revivals.

—Toni del Renzio

# GK GRAPHICS

Japanese packaging, corporate identity, visual identity, signage, computer graphics, and editorial design firm

**Founded** as a section of GK Industrial Design Associates, Japan, 1957; incorporated as GK Graphics Incorporated in 1985; one of eleven subsidiaries of GK Design Group. President: Shuya Kaneko (**Born:** Tokyo, 1937. **Education:** graduated from Tokyo National University of Fine Art and Music. **Member:** President, Japan Package Design Association (JPDA); Package Design Council; jury and committee of Design Promotion Policy, Ministry of International Trade and Industry (MITI).) **Exhibitions:** *GK Graphics— Integration,* Shibuya Toho Life Insurance Building, 1980; *Graphics for Creating Everyday Living,* Tokyo Gas Ginza Pocket Park Gallery, 1985. **Honors:** Gold medal, Package Design in Japan, 1989, 1992; Grand Prize, Sign Design Association Award/Ministry Award of MITI, 1990; World Gold Star Award, 1992; Good Design Mark product, 1992; SDA Promotional Award, 1992. **Address:** 2-19-16 Shimo-ochiai, Shinjuku-ku, Tokyo, 161, Japan.

## Works

Image improvement plan, for Japan Horse Racing Association, 1987.
Coffee container, for Café no Bar, Mitsubishi Corporation, 1987.
Directory sign system, for East Japan Railway, 1989.
Logo design, for CO-OP Kobe (Consumers Co-operative), 1991.
Soy sauce dispenser, for Kikkoman Corporation, 1991.
Packaging design, for Lux bath products, 1992-94.
Visual identity program, for National Science Museum, Tokyo, 1994.
Packaging design, for Kirin Ice Beer, 1994.

## Publications

By GK GRAPHICS/KANEKO: books—*Industrial Design Handbook,* Shakaishiso-sha, Japan, 1961; *Industrial Design,* Kodansha, Japan, 1965; *Package Design: Even the Night and the Globe Are Packages,* Kashima-Shuppan-kai, Japan, 1989; *Process of Package Design—ABC and D,* Kirihara Shoten, Japan, 1991.

*

Trinity of Design

We can find many cases of creative work with the trinity as the canon in traditional Japanese culture. Take flower arrangement, for instance: the sky, the earth, and man are considered as the trinity. The trinity is derived from the harmony that is created among the three natural elements by a branch and flower. The flower then becomes alive in the natural order.

In Japanese painting, "sparse, dense, and irregular" are considered as the canon. It is said that a fine arrangement of the three brings visual variation and balance, spatial scale and depth, lapse of time, mental stimulation, and comfort.

"Approach, break, and climax" are taken as the canon of Japanese music. These elements dramatize the flow of sound and produce pure musical comfort by creating three kinds of flow in a piece of music.

The trinity applied to many other creative works, such as arts and crafts, are "truth, good, and beauty."

Any one of these trinities is relative concept. The level of each element cannot be judged by the quantitative approach of the left half of the brain. Achieving the highest level of the trinity requires an intuitive understanding that can be obtained only through intensive training.

Therefore, there is no manual of instruction or "how to" besides a sample and a commandment for practicing the trinity. The state of the trinity is achieved when a state of good balance is achieved. The good balance indicated requires a liberty of mind that sees far beyond the opposition and discrimination of new versus old, self versus others, or man-made versus nature. For these characteristics, we do not make truth, good, and beauty as absolute positions, respectively. A truth is relative to another truth and so are good and beauty. Creative work based on the trinity begins and ends with a creator's deep thoughts about the truth, good, and beauty that best fit his own objective. In addition, the end does not mean a completion, but is taken as a step in the preparation for the next deep thoughts about truth, good, and beauty.

The canonical trinity of "truth, good, and beauty" is profoundly submerged not only in creative work but also in the designing activities of daily life; it is as submerged as cultural DNA. The full course arrangement of Japanese cuisine provides a good example. Japanese formal cuisine is praised for the great varieties of table wares that are used. It is opposed to the formality of western style cuisine, in which the wares should conform to each other in style. Japanese table arrangement is free style, so to speak, with the pitfall that it may end up as chaos. So what rescues the arrangement from chaos? In part, it is the extent to which the host and chef can create a sense of "truth, good, and beauty" for the guest of the day. The host and chef employ their full knowledge of cooking, table wares, and arrangement of food on the plate according to the trinity. Another source of order is a sense of the season. In Japan, with its varying seasons, a sense of the season is an important theme in the Japanese life style. The table is set with wares having a pattern, form, color, material, and texture suited to reflect the delicate change of each season. In this context, an arrangement unmatched to the season shows poor sense and economy as well. Another source of order is the occasion. If it is a celebration of some happy event, the table is set with wares that have ornamental figures of "pine, bamboo and plum, crane and turtle, red, white and gold things" as symbols of happiness. In formal Japanese table setting, variety is balanced against chaos according to the invisible canon. The canon is a combination of a delicate sense, a feeling for the season, and a theme for the occasion. The canon must be recreated anew for every table.

"Truth, good, and beauty" still hold some value for design creation today as a canon that precedes technique. Nevertheless, it may be hard to understand if I leave the canon with these particular terminologies. I will describe them according to today's creative activities as follows:

Truth is function, and it is related to the application of established technology that has been developed based on natural science.

Good is a social existence. It relates itself to the quest for its reason for existence in humanity.

Beauty is a matter of mentality. It is related to the expression of pleasure felt by the five senses.

Our attempt to unify these elements of the trinity is called design. Even though a thing has truth, or function, it is ill fated if it lacks good and beauty. An object lacking beauty, though truth and good are there, may be just like a man who is dull and too square. An object may be just like a luring swindler, if it lacks good though it holds truth and beauty. However well a thing fulfills a social aspect or is good for man, if it lacks truth and beauty, it is just like a meddler forcefully applying his own good to others. Or it is just like a man or woman who is good looking but irresponsible and ill natured.

The virtue that design requires is not just about being convenient, right, beautiful, new, or overwhelming others. It is about a good balance that unifies the functional, social, and spiritual entities at their higher stage. The trinity of the canon "truth, good, and beauty" liberates design from naive comparison and competition, and puts it in the liberal world that is different from liberty in eternal hell. Design's existence is not such that it can be sustained by a fixed ideology. It is born through a sincere approach to each project, one by one. The traditional canons of "truth, good and beauty" provide an effective guide for creative work in this era of coexistence with all things.

—Shuya Kaneko, President, GK Graphics

# GLASER, Milton

American illustrator and graphic, exhibition, and interior designer

**Born:** New York City, 26 June 1929. **Education:** High School of Music and Art, New York, 1943-46; studied at Cooper Union, New York, graduated 1951; Accademia di Belle Arti, Bologna, 1952-53 (Fulbright scholarship). **Family:** Married Shirley Girton in 1957. **Career:** Founder, with Seymour Chwast and Edward Sorel, 1954, and President, 1954-74, Push Pin Studios, New York; President, Milton Glaser, Inc., New York, from 1974, responsible for redesigning the magazines *Paris Match, Cue, New West, L'Express, L'Europe, Jardin des Modes,* and *Esquire;* founding partner, with Walter Bernard, of the publication design firm WBMG, New York, from 1983, responsible for redesigning *L'Espresso* (Rome), *Alma* (Paris), Rizzoli's *Journal of Art, Magazine Week, The Washington Post, La Vanguardia* (Barcelona), *Manhattan, Inc., Family Circle, Adweek, U.S. News, New York Law Journal,* and *Lire.* Founder, with Reynold Ruffins and Seymour Chwast, 1955, and co-art director, 1955-74, *Push Pin Graphic* magazine, New York; founder, with Clayton Felker, president, and design director, *New York Magazine,* 1968-77; vice-president and design director, *Village Voice* magazine, New York, 1975-77. Lecturer, Pratt Institute, Brooklyn, New York, and School of Visual Arts, New York, from 1961. Board member, Cooper Union, School of Visual Arts, and Aspen Design Conference (president, 1990-91); former vice-president, American Institute of Graphic Arts, New York. **Exhibitions:** *The Push Pin Style,* Musée des Arts Décoratifs, Paris, 1970; Museum of Modern Art, New York, 1975; Portland Visual Arts Center, Oregon, 1975; Centre Georges Pompidou, Paris, 1977 (toured); Carl Solway Gallery, Cincinnati, 1980; Peabody Gallery, Harvard University, Cambridge, Massachusetts, 1981; Lincoln Center Gallery, 1981; Houghton Gallery, Cooper Union, New York, 1984; Vicenza Museum, 1989; *Giorgio Morandi/Milton Glaser,* Galleria Communale d'Arte Moderna, Bologna, 1989; Art Institute of Boston, 1995; poster retrospective, Ravello, Italy, 1995. **Collections:** Museum of Modern Art, New York; Israel Museum, Jerusalem; Chase Manhattan Bank, New York; National Archive, Smithsonian Institution, Washington, D.C. **Honors:** Society of Illustrators Gold Medal, 1979; St. Gaudens Medal, Cooper Union, New York, 1979; Hall of Fame Award, Art Directors Club of New York, 1979. Honorary doctorates from Minneapolis Institute of Arts, 1971, Moore College, Philadelphia, 1975, Philadelphia Museum School, 1979, School of the Visual Arts, New York, 1979, Queens College, CUNY, New York University at Buffalo, and Royal College of Art, London.

Milton Glaser: *Angels in America* logo, 1993

Honorary Fellow, Royal Society of Arts, London, 1979. **Address:** Milton Glaser Inc., 207 East 32nd Street, New York, New York 10016, U.S.A.

## Works

*Bob Dylan* album insert poster, for Columbia Records, 1966.
Product promotion poster series, for Olivetti S.p.A., from 1968.
*Signet Shakespeare* book series cover designs, for Signet Classics, 1968-72.
Childcraft Store interior, exterior, and merchandising design, for Childcraft Stores, New York, 1970.
600-foot mural, for the Federal Office Building, Indianapolis, Indiana, 1974.
World Trade Center observation deck and restaurants signage, exhibit, theme, and graphics system, for INHILCO/Port Authority of New York and New Jersey, 1975.
*I Love NY* tourism campaign symbol, for the New York State Department of Commerce, 1976.
Supermarket interiors, packaging, merchandising, and advertising programs, for The Grand Union Company, from 1978.
*Sesame Place* educational play park signage, theme, and graphics system, in Bucks County, Pennsylvania, for Children's Television Workshop, 1981-83.
Graphic design, theming, and signage, for Franklin Mills Mall, Philadelphia, 1986-89.
The Rainbow Room identity and graphics program, in the Rockefeller Center, New York, for the Rockefeller Management Corporation, 1987.
Queens College identity, graphics, and advertising program, New York, from 1987.
*World Cities and the Future of the Metropolis* exhibition, for the Triennale di Milano International Exhibition, Milan, 1987-88.

International AIDS symbol and poster, for the World Health Organization, 1987.

Exterior, interior, and graphic designs, for Trattoria dell'Arte restaurant, New York, 1988.

Conceptualization and interior design, for New York Unearthed museum, New York, 1990.

Exhibition design for tribute to Italian artist Piero della Francesca, for Pierro 500 Anni, 1991.

Logo, for the play *Angels in America,* by Tony Kushner, 1993.

Books illustrated include—*The Smallest Elephant in the World* by Alvin Tresselt, New York, 1960; *Cats and Bats and Things with Wings* by Conrad Aitken, New York, 1965, *Help, Help, The Gobolinks* by Gian Carlo Menotti, New York, 1970; *Fish in the Sky* by George Mendoza, New York, 1971; (with Seymour Chwast and Barry Zaid) *Rimes de la Mere Ole,* Boston, 1971; *The Illustrated Don Juan* by Isaac Asimov, New York, 1972.

**Publications**

**By GLASER: books**—(with Shirley Glaser) *If Apples Had Teeth,* New York, 1960; (with Jerome Snyder) *The Underground Gourmet,* New York, 1968, 1970; *Milton Glaser: Graphic Design* edited by Peter Mayer, New York and London, 1973; *The Milton Glaser Poster Book,* with introduction by Giorgio Soavi, New York, 1977.

**On GLASER: books**—*The Push Pin Style Book,* exhibition catalogue, Palo Alto, 1970; *History of the Poster* by Josef and Shizuko Muller-Brockmann, Zurich, 1971; *Graphic Designers in the USA: 3* edited by Henri Hillebrand, London, 1972; *Who's Who in Graphic Art* edited by Walter Amstutz, Dubendorf, 1982; *The Conran Directory of Design* edited by Stephen Bayley, London, 1985; *New American Design* by Hugh Aldersley-Williams, New York, 1988.

                                   *

The distinctions between fine and applied art are frequently blurred, particularly in the historical sense. I don't know how to characterize a Persian rug or an Islamic book illustration or an African ritual sculpture in terms of whether they are fine or applied art, although I know that a study of their form has influenced me. I would say that in my work, both fine and applied arts have been significant influences. In fact, all sorts of random visual material, artifacts, objects, printed ephemera, as well as the history of art itself, have been influential in my graphic work. Drawing has been essential to my work for many years as a tool for understanding visual occurrences and as a basic resource for experiencing form.

The vocabulary of form between professional graphic art on the one hand and fine art on the other share many conventions of structure, texture, scale, and color; what seems to be most significantly different is the fundamental intention that illuminates each form of activity. Fine art metaphysically transforms man. The commercial graphic arts convey information of a specific kind that motivates the viewer towards action.

                                   —Milton Glaser

                        *      *      *

Among international designers whose work came to fruition in the middle 1950s, Milton Glaser remains an outstanding figure.

Like many of the best of his contemporaries, he sought to replace the ascendancy of the formal qualities associated with the best design from Switzerland with a new, eclectic approach. Ideas could be borrowed from material past or present using in particular the devices of juxtaposition—already a method used by surrealists to jolt the imagination. His work is often witty but, unlike that of his associates, seldom comic. Always decorative, Glaser's work frequently contains a message and is not strictly commercial.

His great contribution at Push Pin Studios was to give currency in design to a process already established in painting and sculpture, particularly by Picasso: first a mastery of technical skill and then an imaginative use of quotation and parody. This eclectic use of images can be seen to parallel the proliferation in the middle-twentieth century of fast reproductive graphic processes available to everyone. As well as quotations from as far afield as the work of Piero di Cosimo, one finds in Glaser's work a complete assimilation of more recent art history, including such developments as art nouveau, Art Deco, dada, and surrealism. The passage of Pop and Op art have also been absorbed into his work. Glaser is the design counterpart to such artists as Johns, Rauschenberg, Oldenburg, and Lichtenstein, whose search through the archives of museum and daily life alike have produced a new language of expression. Glaser, for all his intelligence and sophistication, has not forgotten the grass roots of mass advertising, and among his impeccably professional designs appears suddenly the unpretentious popular quotation, perhaps from some anonymous sign-writer. In his own words: "My work has achieved its balance through the mixture of chance and professionalism."

                                   —John Barnicoat

# GOERTZ, Albrecht Zeppo Graf

German industrial designer

**Born:** Brunkensen/Alfeld, 1914; emigrated to the United States, 1936; returned to Germany after reunification, 1989. **Education:** Trained as a bank apprentice, Hamburg and London, before emigration to the United States; studied industrial design, Pratt Institute, New York, beginning in 1947. **Career:** Joined Raymond Loewy Design, 1947; joined Carl Otto Design, 1951; joined Norman Bel-Geddes Design and started own company, 1953; clients included Porsche, BMW, Hohner, Datsun Puma, Montblanc, Agfa, and Fuji. **Honors:** Many special honors, including an award from the Design Horizons Exhibition. **Address:** Goertz Industrial Design, Postfach, 31061 Brunkensen/Alfeld, Germany.

**Works**

*507 Roadster,* for BMW, 1954.
*240Z,* for Datsun.

                                   *

Visual Design is a small, but important part toward the success of a product.

For me the biggest reward was: to be able to give pleasure.

Design is an emotion and so far cannot be produced by a computer.

                                   —Albrecht Zeppo Graf Goertz

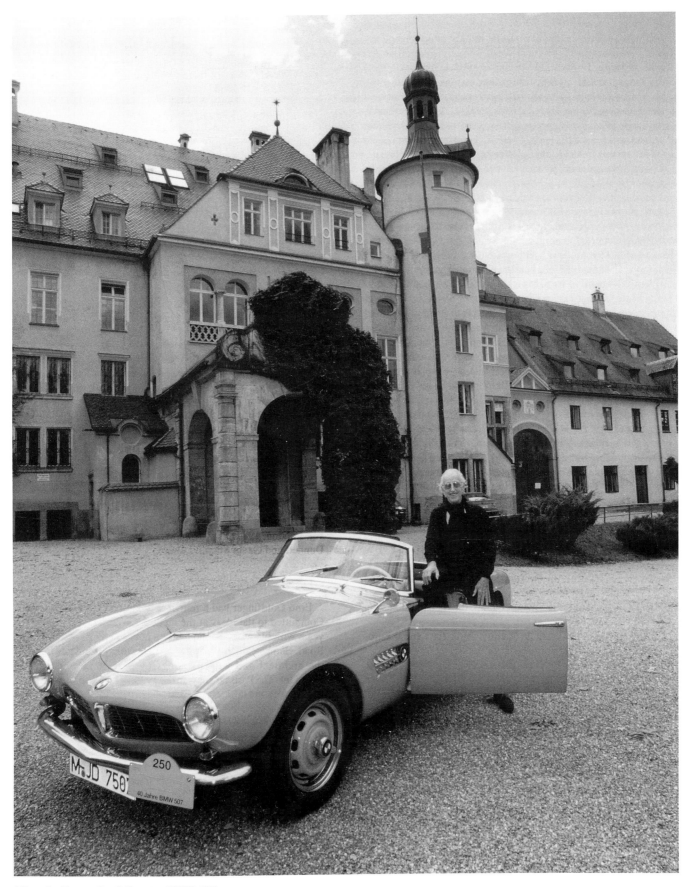

**Albrecht Zeppo Graf Goertz: BMW 507**

# GOLDFINGER, Ernö

British architect, interior, exhibition, and furniture designer

**Born:** Budapest, Hungary, 11 September 1902; emigrated to Britain, 1934, naturalized, 1945. **Education:** Gymnasium, Budapest, 1912-19; Le Rosay School, Gstaad, Switzerland, 1919-20; studied architecture, the Atelier Jaussely, Paris, 1922-23, Ecole des Beaux-Arts, Paris, 1923, the Atelier Auguste Perret, 1924, and the Ecole d'Urbanisme, Sorbonne, Paris, 1927-28. **Family:** Married Ursula Ruth Blackwell in 1933; children: Peter, Elisabeth and Michael. **Career:** Freelance architect and designer, in partnership with Andre Sive, Paris, 1924-29, in private practice, Paris, 1930-34, and in partnership with Gerald Flower, London, 1934-79. London correspondent, *l'Architecture d'Aujourd'hui* magazine, Paris, 1934-74; editor, *MARS News,* London, 1944-45. **Member:** Founder-member, CIAM Congres Internationaux d'Architecture Moderne, 1928-59, and of MARS Modern Architecture Research Society (British section of CIAM), 1935-60; Foreign Relations Committee Member, Royal Institute of British Architects, 1937-45; council member, Architects Registration Council, London, 1941-50; Architectural Association, London, 1960-63, 1965-68; Council of Industrial Design, London, 1961-65; the Royal Academy of Art, London, 1974; fellow, Royal Institute of British Architects, 1966, and Royal Society of Arts, London, 1968; associate, 1968, and academician, 1975, Royal Academy of Art, London; honorary member, Association of Hungarian Architects, 1969. **Exhibitions:** *CIAM Exhibition,* Athens, 1934; *Housing Exhibition,* Grand Palais, Paris, 1934 (travelled to London); *MARS Group Exhibition,* Burlington Gallery, London, 1938; *CIAM Exhibition,* Aix-en-Provence, 1952; *This Is Tomorrow,* Whitechapel Art Gallery, London, 1955; *UIA Sport Buildings Commission,* Moscow, 1968; *Thirties,* Hayward Gallery, London, 1979; *Works I: Ernö Goldfinger,* Architectural Association, London, 1983. **Collection:** Royal Institute of British Architects, London. **Died:** London, 15 November 1987.

## Works

Beauty salon interiors in Grafton Street, London, for Helena Rubinstein Beauty Salons, 1926.

Office interiors in Grafton Street, London, for Helena Rubinstein Beauty Salons, 1926.

Office interiors in rue Godot de Mauroy, Paris, for Central European Express, 1927.

Exhibition stand at the *British Industries Fair,* Olympia, London, for Alpina Limited, 1928.

Offices and apartment interiors in the rue de Varenne, Paris, for Suzanne Blum, 1930.

Stacking chairs in steel, for Entas, Paris, 1931.

Toy showroom in Endsleigh Street, London, for P. and M. Abbatt Company, 1933.

Kitchen fittings and furniture, for Easiwork, 1935.

Children's section of the British Pavilion, at the World's Fair, Paris, 1937.

Exhibition stand at the *British Industries Fair,* Olympia, London, for ICI, Imperial Chemical Industries, 1938.

Shop interiors in Shaftesbury Avenue, London, for S. Weiss, 1951.

Showroom interiors in Albemarle Street, London, for Taylor Woods, 1956.

*This Is Tomorrow* exhibition layouts, for the Whitechapel Art Gallery, London, 1956.

Office interiors in the Haymarket, London, for the French Government Tourist Office, 1958.

Hille House Offices and showrooms in Watford, Hertfordshire, for Hille and Company, 1960.

Office interiors in Piccadilly, London, for the French Government Tourist Office, 1963.

SNCF Travel Offices in the Champs Elysees, Paris, for the French Government Tourist Office, 1967.

(for a complete list of Goldfinger's buildings and architectural projects, see *Contemporary Architects*)

## Publications

**By GOLDFINGER: books**—(with E. J. Carter) *County of London Plan Explained,* London, 1945; *British Furniture Today,* London, 1951; **articles**—in *Pester Lloyd* (Budapest), 8 August 1925, 30 December 1925; *l'Architecture d'Aujourd'hui* (Paris), March 1934, July 1938, September 1950, February 1952, February/March 1960; *Architectural Review* (London), November 1941, December 1941, January 1942, May 1954; *The Architects' Journal* (London), April 1942, March 1943, October 1980; *Architect and Building News* (London), January 1943; *Das Werk* (Zurich), April 1947; *Architectural Design* (London), July 1954; *RIBA Journal* (London), September 1969; *Building Design* (London), 7 March 1975.

**On GOLDFINGER: books**—*Shops* by Brian and Norman Westwood, London, 1937; *Modern Houses in England* by F. R. S. Yorke, London, 1944; *British Achievement in Design* by Noel Carrington and Muriel Harris, London, 1946; *Gute Moebel/Schoene Raume* edited by Mia Seeger, Stuttgart, 1953; *Public Interiors* by Misha Black, London, 1960; *Ernö Goldfinger* by Mate Major, Budapest, 1970; *Industrial Design in Britain* by Noel Carrington, London, 1976; *Hille: 75 Years of British Furniture* by Sutherland Lyall, London, 1981; *Architects' Designs for Furniture* by Jill Lever, London, 1982; *Ernö Goldfinger: Works I* compiled by James Dunnett and Gavin Stamp, London, 1983.

\*       \*       \*

Ernö Goldfinger had a remarkably long and successful career. Committed to the ideas of the modern movement, he lived for 50 years with his wife and mother in a house he designed in Willow Road, Hampstead, in 1937; it was filled with furniture designed by the architect and with paintings by Max Ernst and Amédée Ozenfant. The Paris he knew in the 1920s left a deep impression on his attitudes and taste. He met and socialised with Ernst and Fernand Léger at the Café du Dôme and visited the 1925 Paris International Exposition with Adolf Loos who encouraged Goldfinger to visit London. There, in 1926, he designed the now-destroyed beauty salon for Helena Rubenstein in Grafton Street. Shopfronts in England were rather conventional at this time, largely, as Goldfinger recalls, done up in sage green paint or fake Queen Anne, like Fortnum and Mason's. In that context, his sparse, steel-and-glass design was a shock. Sage's, then the biggest shopfitters in London, was commissioned to do the work and felt so sorry for Goldfinger, assuming that his lack of decoration indicated an inability to draw, that they added some details. Nevertheless, the final design was admired, particularly by C. H. Reilly who printed a photograph in the *Architectural Review.*

Returning to Paris, Goldfinger worked on shop and apartment interiors, very modern in taste, usually with furniture to his own designs. But in the early 1930s, he came to England to build a practice. Some of the early commissions he obtained there included a toy shop and toy designs for P. A. Abbatt in Wimpole Street and unit furniture for the Canadian kitchen furniture manufacturer Easiwork. After the war, he designed exhibition kiosks for the 1951 Festival of Britain, then developed work as an exhibition designer, most notably for the famous 1956 *This is Tomorrow* exhibition, which showed the work of more than thirty of Britain's avant-garde artists, architects, and designers. He also continued to design furniture, most of which actually extended his architectural work. In 1951, he published a small book, *British Furniture Today,* which offers a good idea of his design philosophy and a number of rare photographs of his own work. The book particularly indicates that his design interests were in tune with those of the period, including interchangeable parts, unit furniture, small-scale pieces, new technology, and a concern for the growing awareness of ergonomics. Goldfinger quotes widely from the pioneer ergonomic study by Bengt Akerblom, *Standing and Sitting Posture* (1948), and many of his chairs explore ergonomic devices such as self-adjusting backs.

—Catherine McDermott

# GONZALEZ RUIZ, Guillermo

Argentinean architectural, exhibition, and graphic designer

**Born:** Cascomus, Buenos Aires Province, 18 March 1937. **Education:** Educated at the Colegio Nacional, Buenos Aires, until 1955; studied architecture and city planning under Gaston Breyer and Wladimiro Acosta at the University of Buenos Aires, Dip. Arch., 1965. **Family:** Married Maria Solanas in 1966 (divorced, 1980); children: Diego, Caroline, and Pablo. **Career:** Freelance designer, establishing first graphics studio with architect Mario Wainstein, in Buenos Aires, 1959-62; staff designer, 1962-64, and art director, 1967-68, at Agens Studio, Buenos Aires; designer, with Cicero Studio, Buenos Aires, 1968-69; partner, with Ronald Shakespear, of Ruiz and Shakespear design studio, Buenos Aires, 1969-73; freelance designer, with own graphic and architectural design studio, Buenos Aires, from 1973; director of design, Municipality of Buenos Aires, 1971-73. **Exhibitions:** Kunstmuseum, Cologne, 1968; Stedelijk Museum, Amsterdam, 1968; Applied Arts Biennale, Montevideo, 1969; Cali Graphics Biennale, Colombia, 1972; Brno Graphics Biennale, Czechoslovakia, 1973, 1975, 1977, 1979; Lapiz de Plata Awards Exhibition, Buenos Aires, 1982. **Collections:** Stedelijk Museum; Museo de la Ciudad de Mar del Plata, Argentina. **Honors:** National Poster Competition Prize, Buenos Aires, 1957, 1960, 1962, 1963; National Symbol and Logotype Competition Awards, Buenos Aires, 1966, 1967, 1971, 1973; Lapiz de Plata Prize, 1982. **Address:** Ricardo Rojas 401, piso 13°, 1001 Buenos Aires, Argentina.

## Works

Graphic identity programme, for the Banco de la Ciudad de Buenos Aires, 1970.
Sign system, for the city of San Juan, 1971.

Sign system, for the city of Buenos Aires, 1971-73.
Argentine regional offices sign system, for the Banco de Italie y Rio de la Plata, 1975-77.
Urban sign system, for Planta Aluar, Puerto Rico, 1976.
Airport buildings sign system and graphic identity, for Austral S.A., Buenos Aires, 1977-78.
Corporate identity programme, for Credibanco, Buenos Aires, 1978.
Corporate identity programme, for Carta Credencial, Buenos Aires, 1978.
Point-of-sales visual identity programme, for Vinilia Wallpapers, 1979.
Graphic sign system, for the Naval Hospital, Buenos Aires, 1980-81.
Plant and workshops sign systems, for Serenisima, Buenos Aires, 1983.

## Publications

**By GONZALEZ RUIZ: books**—*Sistema de Senales Urbanas de la Ciudad de Buenos Aires,* Buenos Aires, 1972; *Sistema de Identificacion Visual de la Municipalidad de la Ciudad de Buenos Aires,* Buenos Aires, 1972; *Sistema Tipo de Senalamiento Urbano y Edilicio,* Buenos Aires, 1975; **articles**—*Summa* (Buenos Aires), no. 1, 1963, no. 16, 1964, no. 28, 1965, no. 50, 1970; *Nuestra Arquitectura* (Buenos Aires), no. 42, 1973; *Graphic Design* (Tokyo), March 1980.

**On GONZALEZ RUIZ: books**—*Modern Publicity,* London, 1976, 1978; *Top Symbols and Trademarks of the World,* Milan, 1977, 1978; *Archigraphia: Architectural and Environmental Graphics* edited by Walter Herdeg, Zürich, 1978.

*

The beginning of my expressive and intellectual development acknowledges various influences.

1) My teachers of the School of Architecture (1957-65). My visual formation is essentially architectural. In school, I learned systematic thought. The rational structure of my thinking is the result of experience at the university, where I learned to think in terms of form and acquired my basic visual cultivation. My first brilliant teacher was titular professor of vision Gastón Breyer, who introduced me to the psychology of form, to Köler, to Kofka, to the *Gestalt* conception, and to the theory of color. In the architectural composition class of another beloved teacher, Wladimiro Acosta, now deceased, I learned to use my projectual mechanism, which I later transferred to graphic design. There, I essentially redeemed the humanist sense of design.

2) Publicity agencies (1962-67). There, I learned graphic work and the processes of composition, photoengraving, and printing. I began my apprenticeship at Agens (1962-64) and was at Agens again in 1967 as art director. Though this work was a valuable aid to my learning, I believe I was experiencing autodidactic growth at this stage. Because of the influences and experiences I have mentioned, I consider myself a graphic architect, and not a graphic designer and architect. This process of synthesis demanded a lot of effort for ten years (1960-70), and I got through it with the help of analytic therapy, not without first going through periods of anguish, confusion, frustration, and doubt. The second decade (1970-80) and the beginning of the third found me solid and sure of my convictions

(not vocational, because I've had a visual vocation since childhood. When I was nine years old I won a first place prize in drawing. I refer to those that channeled my career toward a particular area of graphic design, systematic design. That is to say, the systems of visual identification and of municipal and urban signage).

3) The Argentine architects (1963-70). The first of these, Carlos Mendez Mosquera, was my initial life-model. He belonged to the generation before mine and was skilled in the graphic-architectural areas that attracted me. Although he wasn't practicing design, he possessed a visual culture that was for me, at that time, undeveloped. I was acquainted with him at Agens in 1964, he gave me work at Cicero, and he financed Shakespear and me during the first months of our independent study (1968). He gave me an assistantship and exposed me to the journal he had just established—*Summa*—so that I could make my first notes about design. All these things he did in order to connect me with the outstanding architects both of the previous generation and of my own. I'm very grateful to Mendez Mosquera for the things he did for me between 1964 and 1968, and I'm grateful to all the architects who in the subsequent years made it possible for me to exercise my expression and enrich my learning.

4) Graphic designers (1960-70). The graphic designers who influenced my work in the first formative stage were Juan Carlos Distefano, Franco Grignani, Silvio Coppola, Josef Müller-Brockmann, Armin Hofmann, Alan Fletcher, Bob Gill, Heinz Edelman, and Saul Bass. They all possessed that balance of freedom and order, of intuition and rationalism that is so important in graphic expression.

5) My colleagues and collaborators (1969-73). Among the first, I want to mention Ronald Shakespear, with whom I spent two years at Agens and six as an associate in our common study. Gifted with a solid graphic vision, he is a strong defender of the idea-object as generator of all work. By working closely with him on many projects, I embraced the concept of synthesis and strength in graphism. Gabriel Ezcurra Náon, with whom I collaborated for ten years (1970-80), influenced me with his extreme perfectionism in graphic drawing and his silent and invaluable contribution to the final execution of the design and to the constant force in graphic work.

My work as a graphic architect displays particular traits and tendencies. (1) A structuralist conception of graphics, whether two- or three-dimensional. (2) The predominance of formal conceptions based on pure geometric forms. (3) The frequent use of point and line as generator of graphism. (4) The constant seeking for visual potential and synthesis (the tendency the Kepes calls optic scandal). (5) The frequent intention of the balance of form and function, product of a rationalist ideology that I maintain in spite of the new post-modernist aesthetic tendencies. Though these are the predominant characteristics of my work, they themselves don't imply a contribution. The distinctive characteristics, perhaps, should be looked for within the specific sign design project because it is through spatial and material graphics that I have been able to integrate the graphic and architectural components. Signage is, for me, the visual transcription of the circulatory structures of cities or buildings. Because of this, my ideas for signage systems are based on previous knowledge of the flow of vehicles, persons, and things, and on the spatial and constructive nature of the environment where the signage is to be.

I conceive of signage as part of municipal or urban equipment, and this approach induces me to always look for ideas linked to the spatial aspect of the signs. That is why there are structures of circular pipe sections in the project for Buenos Aires (to go along with the semaphore and luminaries of the city). For the same rea-

son, the signs of Aluar are of premolded concrete, and those of a commercial gallery are of crystal, due to the fact that its roof is transparent. The signs of the central market are trapezoidal, like the many doors of its pavilion. The signals of the San Isidro Hippodrome are rectangular with curved corners, because that is the predominant shape there, from the racetrack to the roof and columns. And, finally, the constructive system of the Pediatric Hospital is interchangeable, letter for letter, because the entire place has a kind of freedom and total interchangeability.

I sincerely believe that herein lies my most significant contribution—graphic-industrial design plans that revolve around the environment in which the objects are to be placed. To project any system of signage, before looking at the paper I look at the space. Because of this, in my trajectory I cannot differentiate the projects by their magnitude, scale, transcendence, or popularity. The approximately 50 systems I have developed are, independent of their degree of complexity, true expressions of the optic by which my plans are governed. Logically, those that stand out the most are "the big ones," but at times, those aren't exactly the ones that reflect that integrative conception to which I have referred. On the other hand, one project practically unknown, the signage for the Club Hípico in Uruguay, is a symbol for me of my governing ideas. It integrates a series of wood signs composed of horizontal slabs that connote jumping hurdles.

Another possible contribution of my work could be in the spatial, rather than planar, conception of the signs. That is what permitted me to come up with a proposal for Buenos Aires' street signs. It answers, with only four joined plaques, the most diverse questions about traffic, nomenclature, and numbering. I confess that even now, after 12 years, I continue seeing it as a good proposal. I believe that its massive and indiscriminate diffusion in all the cities of the country, and in Uruguay, Paraguay, and Chile is not accidental. Its surprisingly widespread use should surely not be attributed only to the commercial interest of the sign factories, but also to the fact that it resolves the urban street-sign problem. And the third possible contribution could lie in my firm belief in using a technological language that grows as a result of the use of national productive processes and materials, and not as a transference of external experiences to local industrial reality.

—Guillermo Gonzalez Ruiz

*     *     *

More than a designer of signage or of visual identities, Guillermo Ruiz is a designer of systems. He devises the macro-structures that establish order, categorize information, and integrate the systems' elements on the basis of sub-ordinations. In his signage system for the Argentinean Social Welfare housing programs, signs link highway access to apartments through five categories of information coded in clear steps. Sub-codes are used within some of those categories to meet different needs.

He designs as a city planner, understanding sign systems as the visual transcription of circulation patterns, where the elements appear as extensions of the architectural environment. Examples of this are the signage for Buenos Aires, for the Aluar aluminum plant, and for the San Isidro Racing Track, where the signage furniture in each case relates to the specific architectural characteristics of the environment.

The individual components of his systems are frequently adopted by other users, as was the signage for the city of Buenos Aires (that was massively, and often not too wisely, taken over by other cities). In this system, four metal plates attached to a tubular column display the name of the street, the range of address numbers of the corresponding blocks, and the direction of circulation for vehicles. Appropriate sizing and placing satisfy the needs of the drivers without obstructing pedestrian circulation or overloading the visual environment.

In the 1960s, Gonzalez Ruiz worked on graphic products in a variety of areas, including promotion for consumer products and for cultural activities, corporate identities, and film graphics (in Agens, possibly the most inventive advertising agency that ever existed in South America, in Cicero, and in his own studio with Shakespear). In this work, he showed a visual power reminiscent of Müller-Brockmann, Hofmann, Distefano, Coppola, or Bass, particularly in the poster, in the use of strong scale-contrast in typography, and in an expressive but structural use of form and figure-ground relationships. In the 1970s, he concentrated on visual identity programs and signage systems.

Simplicity of form, clarity of language, adjustment in the detail, and integration with the environment are characteristics of Gonzalez Ruiz's present design production, an excellent example of design that works without imposing itself distractingly between the message and the user.

—Jorge Frascara

# GORELIK, Mordecai

American playwright, stage, and film designer

**Born:** Shchedrin, Minsk Province, Russia, 25 August 1899; emigrated to the United States in 1905, naturalized, 1909. **Education:** Attended Boys' High School, Brooklyn, New York, until 1917; studied at the Pratt Institute, Brooklyn, New York, 1918-20; apprenticed at Neighborhood Playhouse and Provincetown Players, New York, 1920-22; studied stage design under Robert Edmond Jones, Norman Bel Geddes, and Serge Soudeikin, New York, 1920-30. **Military:** Served in the United States Student Army Corps, 1917, the Office of War Information, 1944, and as theatre consultant to the United States Military Government in Germany, 1949. **Family:** Married Frances Strauss in 1935 (died, 1966); children: Eugene and Linda; married Lorraine Kable in 1972. **Career:** Scene painter and technician with Provincetown Players, New York, 1920-21; freelance designer, New York, from 1924; sketch artist and film production designer, working for Metro-Goldwyn-Mayer, 20th Century-Fox, Republic, and RKO Pictures, Hollywood, from 1944. Instructor and designer, School of the Theatre, New York, 1921-22; American Academy of Dramatic Arts, New York, 1926-32; research professor in theatre, 1960-72, and professor emeritus from 1972, Southern Illinois University, Carbondale. Visiting lecturer, New School for Social Research, New York, 1940-41, Biarritz American University, France, 1945-46, New York University and University of Toledo, Ohio, 1956, University of Hawaii and University of Miami, 1958, Bard College, Annandaleon-Hudson, New York, 1959, Brigham Young University, Provo, Utah, 1961, California State University, Los Angeles, 1964, San Jose State University, California, 1965, Buffalo State College, New York, 1967, University of Massachusetts, Boston, 1972, University of Southern California, Los Angeles, 1975. Sponsor, ACTF Mordecai Gorelik

Award, 1981, American Theatre Association Fellowship, from 1982, Southern Illinois University Mordecai Gorelik Award, from 1983. **Member:** American Theatre Association; Speech Communication Association. **Exhibitions:** *International Theatre Scenic Exhibition,* London, 1925 (toured); Bourgeois Galleries, New York, 1926; *International Scenic Exhibition,* New York, 1927; Harvard Society, Cambridge, Massachusetts, 1932; Montclair Art Museum, New Jersey, 1932; Architectural League, New York, 1932; *International Theatre Arts Exhibition,* New York, 1934; Pratt Institute, Brooklyn, New York, 1936; McCord Theatre Museum, Dallas, Texas, 1936; *International Exhibition of Theatrical Art,* Vienna, 1936. **Collection:** Morris Library Special Collections, Southern Illinois University, Carbondale. **Honors:** Guggenheim Fellowship, New York, 1936, 1937; Rockefeller Foundation Grant, New York, 1946, 1950; Fulbright Fellowship, Washington, D.C., 1962; Theta Alpha Phi Award, 1971; United States Institute for Theatre Technology Award, 1981. **Died:** Sarasota, Florida, 7 March 1990.

## Works

Stage designs include (in New York unless otherwise indicated) — *King Hunger,* Players Club, Philadelphia, 1924; *Processional,* for the Theatre Guild, Garrick Theatre, 1925; *Last Love,* Schildkraut Theatre, Bronx, New York, 1926; *Nirvana,* Greenwich Village Theatre, 1926; *The Moon is a Gong,* Cherry Lane Theatre, 1926; *Loudspeaker,* 52nd Street Theatre, 1927; *The Final Balance,* Provincetown Playhouse, 1928; *God, Man and the Devil,* Yiddish Art Theatre, 1928; *Uncle Moses,* Yiddish Art Theatre, 1930; *1931,* Mansfield Theatre, 1931; *Success Story,* Maxine Elliott's Theatre, 1932; *Big Night,* Maxine Elliott's Theatre, 1933; *Little Ol' Boy,* Playhouse, 1933; *Men in White,* Broadhurst Theatre, 1933; *All Good Americans,* Henry Miller's Theatre, 1933; *Gentlewoman,* Cort Theatre, 1934; *Sailors of Cattaro,* Civic Repertory Theatre, 1934; *Mother,* Civic Repertory Theatre, 1935; *The Young Go First,* Park Theatre, 1935; *Golden Boy,* Belasco Theatre, 1937; *Tortilla Flat,* Henry Miller's Theatre, 1938; *Casey Jones,* Fulton Theatre, 1938; *Thunder Rock,* Mansfield Theatre, 1938; *Rocket to the Moon,* Belasco Theatre, 1939; *The Quiet City,* Belasco Theatre, 1939; *Night Music,* Broadhurst Theatre, 1940; *Walk Into My Parlor,* Sayville, New York, 1941; *Volpone,* Actors Laboratory Theatre, Los Angeles, 1944 (also costume designer; and at Biarritz American University, France, 1946; Rooftop Theatre, New York, 1957; Southern Illinois University, Carbondale, 1980, also director); *Doctor Knock,* Biarritz American University, France, 1945 (also director); *All My Sons,* Coronet Theatre, 1947; *Paul Thompson Forever,* Actors Laboratory Theatre, Los Angeles, 1947 (also author and director); *Desire under the Elms,* American National Theatre and Academy, 1952; *Danger, Men Working!,* Circle Workshop, Los Angeles, 1952 (also director); *Saint Joan,* Playhouse, Wilmington, Delaware, 1954 (toured the United States); *The Flowering Peach,* Belasco Theatre, 1954; *A Hatful of Rain,* Lyceum Theatre, 1955; *Born Yesterday,* University of Toledo, Ohio, 1956 (also director); *The Sin of Pat Muldoon,* Cort Theatre, 1954; *Plough and the Stars,* Barbizon Plaza Theatre, 1956 (also director); *Guests of the Nation,* Theatre Marquee, 1958; *A Distant Bell,* Eugene O'Neill Theatre, 1960; *The Dybbuk,* Brigham Young University, Provo, Utah, 1961 (also director; and at San Jose State College, California, 1956; Southern Illinois University, Carbondale, 1971); *The Annotated Hamlet,* Southern Illinois

315

University, Carbondale, 1961 (also director); *The House of Bernarda Alba,* Southern Illinois University, Carbondale, 1962 (also director); *Marseilles,* Southern Illinois University, Carbondale, 1963 (also director); *The Good Woman of Sechuan,* Southern Illinois University, Carbondale, 1964 (also director); *The Firebugs,* California State University, Los Angeles, 1964 (also translator and director; and at Southern Illinois University, Cardondale, 1965); *Rainbow Terrace,* Southern Illinois University, Carbondale, 1966 (also author and director; and at Ghost Ranch, New Mexico, 1983); *Andrus and the Image,* Kansas State University, Manhattan, 1977 (also author; and at East Central University, Ada, Oklahoma, 1979).

Films, as production designer, include—*Days of Glory,* 1944; *Our Street,* 1944 (not produced); *Salt to the Devil,* Plantagenet Films, London, 1949; *L'Ennemi Publique no. 1/The Most Wanted Man,* Cite Films, France, 1954; *None But the Lonely Heart,* 1955.

## Publications

By GORELIK: books—*New Theatres for Old,* New York, 1940, 1962, 1975, London, 1947; *Paul Thompson Forever* (one-act play), Boston, 1950; (translator) *Biedermann and the Firebugs* by Max Frisch, in *Masters of Modern Drama* edited by M. Block and Robert G. Shedd, New York, 1962, as *The Firebugs,* New York, 1963, 1980, reprinted in *Best Short Plays of the World Theatre* edited by Stanley Richards, New York, 1968, and in *Classics of Modern Thought: Vol. III; The Modern World,* New York, 1980; *The Big Day* (one-act play) in *Best Short Plays 1977* edited by Stanley Richards, New York, 1978; *Rainbow Terrace* (one-act play) in *Wrestling with God,* New Orleans, 1984; *Toward a Larger Theatre* (7 plays), privately printed, Smithtown, New York, 1984.

On GORELIK: articles—"The Work of Mordecai Gorelik" by Djuna Barnes in *Theatre Guild* (New York), February 1931; "Plough and the Stars" in *Variety* (Hollywood, California), 11 April 1956; "Dramatist Raps 'Absurd Trend'" by Barbara Huddard in the *Denver Post* (Colorado), 21 April 1965; "Theatre: The Search" by Leonard Radic in *The Age* (Melbourne, Australia), 3 October 1967.

\*     \*     \*

Unlike many of the other famous designers of his generation in the United States, Mordecai Gorelik was far more influenced by the ideas behind the development of new theatrical forms than by painting, decorating, or purely visual sources. From the beginning, he wanted his settings to speak to the audience's mind as well as its eye, and he was strongly attracted to plays of ideas that demanded a presentational style. Though he studied and apprenticed with Robert Edmond Jones, Norman Bel Geddes, and Serge Soudeikin, his personal style is closer to that of the Living Newspaper and Epic Theatre, and he has had a lifelong allegiance to Bertolt Brecht's production methods. This devotion to the presentational ideas behind a stage setting led him to shun beautiful, moody pictures in favor of sets that underlined and projected the message behind the action of a play. His sketches have never been beautiful works of art; they are idea-sketches that state the visual facts of a production very directly.

Though he made his early reputation in the 1930s when Jo Mielziner and Donald Oenslager were also becoming major design figures on Broadway, Gorelik did not participate in their impres-

sionistic symbolism or realism but reached ahead to the new presentational styles inherent in the theatre of ideas. Thus, even in his sixties, he could be an innovator, as he was when he brought to the United States his own adapted translation of a famous absurdist drama, *The Firebugs,* which he co-directed off-Broadway. His keen intellect made him an ideal teacher and writer, and he made many contributions to the development of younger designers through his book, articles, and his many faculty positions held throughout the United States. Thus, his contribution, like that of the fine artists from the years just before World War I until the beginning of the 1960s, has been in the area of intellectual abstraction, presenting the relativity of realities on stage. Probably the key source of his visual thinking, as with so many other artists of his persuasion, has been the college, and we are indebted to him for bringing us the ideas of Brecht and Piscator when they were still little-known theatrical names.

—Douglas A. Russell

# GÓROWSKI, Mieczyslaw
Polish graphic, poster, and industrial designer

**Born:** Milkowa, Novy Sacz, 4 February 1941. **Education:** Educated at Milkowa Primary School, and Tarnow Secondary School of Fine Arts, 1948-59; studied interior design, painting under Waclaw Taranczewski, and industrial design under Andrzej Pawlowski, at the Academy of Fine Arts, Kraków, MA, 1966. **Family:** Married Ewa Giza in 1969. **Career:** Freelance designer, Kraków, from 1969; worked with the Research Center of the Metal Products Industry, Kraków, 1969-78; has concentrated on theatre posters, from 1975. Assistant to Andrzej Pawlowski, 1966-69, lecturer in industrial design, 1971-81, independent lecturer, 1981-92, associate professor, from 1992, Academy of Fine Arts, Kraków; French government scholarship, Paris, 1979; invited professor, Université du Québec á Montréal, Canada, 1989-90, 1992-93; invited speaker, Tokyo and Fukuoka, Japan, 1990. **Member:** Polish Artists' Union, from 1966; Polish Ecological Club, from 1980. **Exhibitions:** *Polish Poster Biennale,* Katowice, 1969, 1973, 1975, 1977, 1979, 1981; *International Poster Biennale,* Warsaw, 1970, 1972, 1976, 1978, 1980; *Graphics and Posters from Kraków,* Cultureel Centrum, Venlo, 1975; Polish Academy of Science Centre, Paris, 1977; University Library, Caen, 1978; Poets' Club, Paris, 1978; *Designing for Children,* Warsaw, 1979; *Polish Graphics and Posters,* Kamakura Municipal Museum, Japan, 1980; Poster Gallery, Warsaw, 1980; *Kunstler aus Krakau '80,* Staatstheater, Darmstadt, 1980; Galerie Chabin, Paris, 1981, 1983-84, 1991, 1994-95; Galerija Schody, Kraków, 1981; University of Illinois, Urbana-Champaign, 1981; Castle of Breton Princes, Nantes, 1982; B.W.A. Gallery, Poznan, Poland, 1984; Pavillon du Verdurier, Limoges, France, 1985; Gallery Academy of Fine Arts, Kraków, Poland, 1988; Komm Gallery, Nürnberg, Germany, 1989; Creation Gallery, Tokyo and Fukuoka, Japan, 1990; Maison Des Arts, Laval, Canada, 1992; Maison de la Culture Mercier, Montréal, Canada, 1993; Palace of Fine Arts, Kraków, 1995. **Collections:** Academy of Fine Arts, Kraków; Poster Museum, Warsaw; Lahti Poster Museum, Finland; Kungliga Dramatiska Theatern, Stockholm; Musée de l'Affiche, Paris; Centre Georges Pompidou, Paris; Bibliotheque Forney, Paris; Museum

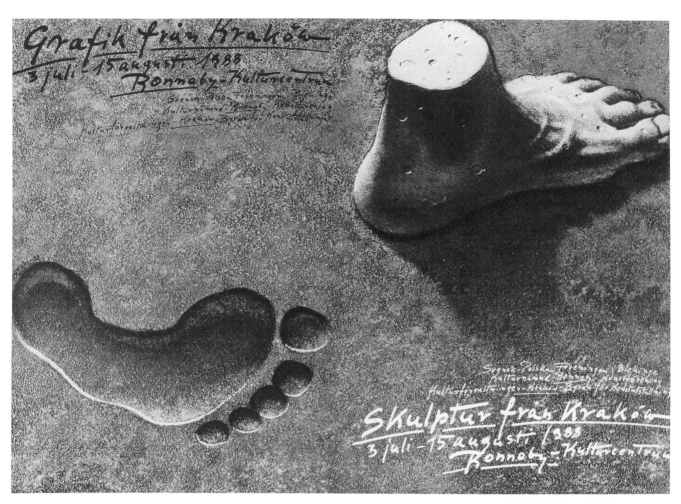

Mieczyslaw Górowski: poster, 1988

of Modern Art, New York; National Museum, Poznan; Israel Museum, Jerusalem; Musée des Arts Décoratifs, Montréal; Dansk Plakatmuseum, Aarhus. **Honors:** Kraków Poster Biennale Grand Prize, 1969; Kraków Folklore Poster Competition Prize, 1974, 1975; Publicity Award, Kraków, 1976; Poster of the Year Award, Kraków, 1976, 1977, 1979; Polish Ministry of Culture and Art Award, 1979; Katowice Poster Biennale Award, 1981 (2), 1987, 1989 (2); Poster Collectors Club Award, Poznan, 1983, 1989; First Prize (ex aequo), International Poster Exhibition, Colorado, 1983; Polish Prime Ministers Award for Design Creation for Children, Warsaw, 1984; Bronze medal, First International Poster Triennial, Toyama, 1985; honorary mention, Art Directors Club of New York, 1987; Tarnovian Voivode Award, Tarnow, 1988; First Prize, International Poster Biennial, Mexico, 1992; Tarnovian President Award, Tarnow, 1994; First Prize, bronze medal, and two awards, National Poster Competition, Kraków, 1995. **Address:** ul. Slomiana 4/23, 30-316 Kraków, Poland.

## Publications

**By GÓROWSKI: articles**—in *Wiadomosci IWP* (Warsaw), February/March 1977; *Gazeta Poludniowa* (Kraków), no. 257, 1980; *Form und Zweck* (Berlin), August 1980, February 1981.

**On GÓROWSKI: books**—*Interdesign '71 ICSID,* Minsk, 1971; *Grafiek en Poster uit Krakau,* exhibition catalogue, Venlo, 1975; *Polish Graphics and Posters,* exhibition catalogue, Kamakura, 1980, *Kunstler aus Krakau '80,* exhibition catalogue, Darmstadt, 1980; *M. Górowski's Posters* by Anna Szpor-Weglarska, Warsaw, 1980; *Polish Theatre Poster 1980-1985,* exhibition catalogue, Budapest, 1985; *Polish Poster,* Japan, 1988; *Exposition D'Affiches Polonaises,* exhibition catalogue, Angers, 1988; *The Modern Poster,* New York, 1988; *Recent Polish Poster,* exhibition catalogue, Australia, 1988; *Górowski* by Raymond Vezina, Montreal, 1992; *Who's Who in Graphic Design,* Zurich, 1994; *100: The Best Posters from Europe and the United States,* Tokyo, 1995; *The Four from Kraków,* exhibition catalogue with texts by Yusaku Kamekura and Janusz Krupinski, Kraków, 1995; *Masters of the Polish Poster,* Kraków, 1995; **articles**—"Mieczyslaw Górowski" by Krzysztof Dydo in *Projekt,* March 1988; *Creation* (Tokyo), no. 4, 1990; *Illustration* (Tokyo), no. 65, 1990; *Idea* (Tokyo), 240, 1993.

\*

I'm involved in poster making. This gives me a great satisfaction as this type of artistic activity has several advantages:

1. I am aware, even before making a poster, that my single picture will be copied in magnified size and in many copies.

2. Such a large number of copies could easily be delivered to many locations in the world.

3. Exhibiting my posters is easy to do: one roll of posters weighing around three kilos, sent by mail, is sufficient for a big exhibition.

4. If a roll of posters is lost, it's not a big deal; I have a lot of copies.

5. Usually I exhibit my posters in the largest "galleries": on streets and squares of towns where posters are located in their proper places. Not every art gallery has such a large number of visitors ...

... too bad for me, however, if my poster does not succeed (misjudged concept, poor quality of copy, etc.). Then I'd better avoid walking on the streets and squares ...

—Mieczyslaw Górowski

\*       \*       \*

Mieczyslaw Górowski made his debut with graphic works that he composed for local cultural events and festivals, works being more decorative than of informative value on a mass scale. However, he proved that his eye was not trained in vain in the visual communication workshop, where he had acquired skill in defining signs or ideograms. And certainly, he must have been also well acquainted with the psychology of perception, ergonomics, and anthropotechnics. He was aware that the task of a designer is different from that of an illustrator. Trained in methods of designing, in solving each problem through reasoning, analyzing the usefulness and the function of each single product—a machine or a print, a working environment or a living space—Górowski used methods of abstraction. He treated the poster, and rightly so, as an industrial product. Accordingly, he concentrated his attention on the language of message-semantics, syntactics, and pragmatics, exploring the relations between shape and meaning as well as between the graphic representation and the anticipated reaction of the recipient.

In order to avoid a narrative approach, he operated with a highly objective, abstract form, with an archetype of the concept, abstract though not totally free of its informative aspect. However, a sign, even when having the form of a segment of the rainbow, of a circle, or of an isolated letter, must convey some meaning, so that it is not reduced to a mere ornament. This is what Górowski always kept in mind, along with another design doctrine—reliance on the module system and, resulting from it, combinatory sets. Górowski's first posters to appear on the walls of Kraków were so designed that, without additional cost, they could be turned into a series of repeating pictures to intensify the perception. For instance, the poster "Peoples' Holiday" (1972) constituted a graphic rhythm formed with multiple, crisscrossing vertical lines, resembling furrows in the soil, and horizontal lines. He also sought humor, as in his poster "Days of Cracow" (1973) which presents the image of a legendary dragon in the form of a pull-apart toy. The trunk of the dragon, divided into segments and printed on separate sheets of paper, could be freely extended.

The convention of the poster as an impersonal symbol, with emotional tones reduced to minimum, satisfied Górowski only in the initial stage of his creative work. Since the mid 1970s the influence of constructivism, of geometric abstraction, and of Optical art has diminished in his work. Also, his designing has been less associated with posters. One critic described this new period as "a change from design to painting methods, from rationalism to romanticism." Suddenly, this artist became aware of the limitations of

the symbol system and of the monotony of its repertoire. He was not able to express himself in it well enough. He found himself as if enclosed in a corset of doctrine, and, in order to get out of it, he had to replace the abstraction with a representation, with pictorial form. This probably suited his visual temperament and his narrative imagination, which had been subdued and restrained so far. When he was offered the opportunity to collaborate with Kraków's J. Slowacki Theater, one of the oldest dramatic theaters in Poland, he decided to express himself in a different visual language, semantically and formally richer, while designing its posters and, later, those for other theaters.

In this city, where since the period of "Young Poland" (art nouveau), posters had traditionally been painted by great artists, such as Wyspiański, Frycz, Axentowicz, and Mehoffer, suddenly something fresh appeared. The originality of Górowski's visual language was contained in his meaningful, intriguing, artfully designed metaphors that often could be immediately and directly unravelled. The metaphor, though discreet in its expression, set forth commentary on the given drama or the opinion of the poster's author. At the same time, it emphasized the play and its moral message.

A task of this type required changes in formal means, in the technology of designing. Thus, his posters were given a new quality; the mood of the picture was created by the texture, with subtle variations of the structure: a wall, a piece of board or stone, a fabric, an eroded rock, flesh, rust, or feathers. Monochromatic textures in hushed tones of grey or brown instill a kind of atmosphere, a blanket from under which shapes and fragments of human body, objects, and accessories emerge. To achieve this, Górowski has used photography as an initial substance, which he transforms until he has obtained a uniform picture surface.

—Szymon Bojko

# GOTTSCHALK AND ASH INTERNATIONAL

International environmental, graphic, packaging, and corporate design group

**Founded** by Fritz Gottschalk (born 1937) and Stuart B. Ash (born 1942) in Montreal, 1966; established offices in Toronto, 1970, New York, 1978, and Zürich, 1979. Other principals have included Kenneth Carbone, Leslie Smolan, Peter Steiner, Michael Friedland, Tiit Telmet, Peter Adam, and Les Holloway. **Career:** The firm has provided corporate, environmental, graphic, packaging, and design management programmes for Alusuisse, American Stock Exchange, Anca Inc., Bank of Nova Scotia, Ciba-Geigy, Canadian Pacific Enterprises, Contraves AG, Government of Canada, GTE Corporation, Hudson's Bay Company, Maclean-Hunter Limited, Northern Telecom, Royal Bank of Canada, Syntex, and others. **Exhibitions:** Mead Library of Ideas, New York, 1967; National Gallery of Canada, Ottawa, 1969; Museum of Fine Arts, Montreal, 1970; Container Corporation of America, Chicago, 1975. **Addresses:** 2050 rue Mansfield, Montreal, Quebec H3A 1Z3, Canada; 322 King Street West, Toronto, Ontario M5V 1JA, Canada; 170 Fifth Avenue, New York, New York 10010, U.S.A.; Sonnhaldenstrasse 3, 8032 Zürich, Switzerland.

## Publications

**On GOTTSCHALK AND ASH: books**—*107 Grafici dell'AGI,* with text by Renzo Zorzi and Franco Grignani, Venice, 1974; *Who's Who in Graphic Art* edited by Walter Amstutz, Dubendorf, 1982; **articles**—*Graphis* (Zürich), no. 148, 1970; *Communication Arts* (Palo Alto), no. 1, 1973; *Typographische Monatsblatter* (St. Gallen), August/September 1974; *Idea* (Tokyo), January 1975, September 1978, January 1979.

*

Design is communication. Good design has the power to involve, inform, motivate, and sell. It translates emotion into images and creates lasting impressions. How an organization is perceived by all of its audiences depends greatly on the effectiveness of its comprehensive design program.

At Gottschalk and Ash International, we believe design must reflect the best basic qualities of each organization, product, or personality. It must speak to the public directly and clearly, yet with great imagination to attract and hold attention.

Because communication requirements are unique and aimed at specific audiences, we have assembled a uniquely broad range of design talents and management skills. Each of our offices provides complete design and project coordination services that include a thorough understanding of local markets as well as access to our international design network. Within each office are the resources to solve corporate identity programs, consumer packaging, environmental design programs, annual reports, and print communication.

At Gottschalk and Ash International, we consciously plan not to become unifaceted in any given area of design or with a specific client mix. We pride ourselves on our multidisciplinary approach to all areas of design, working with a diverse range of clients, both large and small, and covering a spectrum of cultural, institutional, and corporate organizations. The firm has a commitment to the design community, and many associates are involved in teaching, lecturing, and judging or working with design organizations, thus fostering the future of good design.

—Gottschalk and Ash International

\* \* \*

Gottschalk and Ash International was formed in Montreal in 1966 by Fritz Gottschalk, a Swiss-born designer, and Stuart Ash, a Canadian specializing in typography. The firm's constant, strong affiliation with Swiss design is evident not only stylistically in their flat, graphic, and precise forms, but also in their rigorous research methods, high level of integration within their programs, and carefully considered applications of their designs. Usually clear and readable, their work has a strong, immediate impact, yet is often lighthearted in tone. Their packaging for various pharmaceutical products made by Anca and Syntex, for example, uses flat shapes in highly saturated, bright colours and simple, clear letterforms to help remove the medicinal connotations of the products. Their logo designs are versatile, and accompanying manuals outline the various applications possible to the client. A symbol produced in 1981 for Maclean-Hunter, a large Canadian magazine publishing firm, can work alone in some applications or in conjunction with the company name in others. Two zigzag, opposing forces seem to merge as they meet within a two-colour rhomboid, producing a dynamic effect.

The work of Gottschalk and Ash is once rich, yet reductivist, and always contemporary in feeling. At times, though, their programs can be very anonymous in nature, with no human or personal feeling. For example, as designers of the insignia and logo for the Royal Bank of Canada, Gottschalk and Ash also did the interior signage for the Royal Bank Plaza, a downtown office complex built in Toronto in the late 1970s. Their use of Helvetica type throughout this project makes the information very clear but does not alleviate the impersonal, corporate feeling of the environment.

Some would see keeping strictly to a Swiss approach and style as limiting and monotonous, because a Swiss look is not appropriate for every client or situation. But since Gottschalk and Ash work so frequently for large companies and since their work embodies the best aspects of Swiss design—its clarity, unity, and integration of disparate factors, for example—their use of this kind of design seems legitimate. At its best, their work is masterful within the limits of the Swiss method.

—Liz Wylie

# GRANGE, Kenneth (Henry)

British industrial and product designer

**Born:** London, 17 July 1929. **Education:** Attended Sir John Cass School, and Wembley Hill Elementary School, London, 1936-44; studied at Willesden School of Arts and Crafts, London, 1944-47. **Military Service:** Served as a technical illustrator in the British Army Royal Engineers, 1947-48. **Career:** Worked as a design assistant, Arcon Chartered Architects, London, 1947; architectural assistant, Bronek Katz and Vaughan, London, 1949-50; designer, with Gordon Bowyer design firm, London, 1950-52, and with Jack Howe and Partners design firm, London, 1952-58; freelance industrial designer, establishing Kenneth Grange Design, London, 1958-71; founder-partner, with Theo Crosby, Alan Fletcher, Colin Forbes, and Mervyn Kurlansky, of Pentagram Design, London, from 1972; consultant design director to Wilkinson Sword Company, and to Thorn-EMI major domestic appliances division, 1982; designed for Reuters, Plessey, British Rail, Kodak, Kenwood Appliances, Ronson, Morphy Richards, Maruzen, Parker Pens, GEC, Platignum, and others. Industrial design advisor to the Design Council, London, 1979. Master of the Faculty of Royal Designers for Industry, London, 1985-87; President, Chartered Society of Designers, London, 1987-88; Chairman of the Design Business Association, 1993-95. **Exhibitions:** Boilerhouse/Victoria and Albert Museum, London, 1983; *Design Since 1945,* Philadelphia Museum of Art, 1983; *Eye for Industry,* Victoria and Albert Museum, London, 1986; *New Design for Old,* Boilerhouse/Victoria and Albert Museum, London, 1986; *The Product Designs of Kenneth Grange and Pentagram,* Tokyo, 1989; *'UK 90',* Tokyo, 1990. **Honors:** Ten *Design Council Awards,* London, 1959-81; fellow, Society of Industrial Artists and Designers (now Chartered Society of Designers), London, 1959; Duke of Edinburgh's Elegant Design Award, Council of Industrial Design, London, 1963; Royal Designer for Industry, Royal Society of Arts, London, 1969; Honorary Professor, Heriot-Watt University, Edinburgh, 1987. Honorary doctorates from Royal College of Art, London, 1985, and Department of Arts and Crafts, Heriot-

**Kenneth Grange:** *Protector Razor* **featuring twin blades wrapped with fine wires for Wilkinson Sword Ltd, 1992. Photo: Nick Turner**

Watt University, Edinburgh, 1986. **Address:** Pentagram Design, 11 Needham Road, London W11 2RP, England.

## Works

44A Camera, for Kodak, 1959.
Parking meter, for Venner, 1960.
Chef food mixer and more than 100 domestic appliances, for Kenwood, from 1960.
Milward Courier electric shaver, for Needle Industries, 1963.
Brownie Vecta Camera, for Kodak, 1964.
Window fittings, for Henry Hope and Sons, 1965-67.
Variset hat and coat systems, for A. J. Binns, 1965-70.
Classic Dry Irons, for Morphy Richards, 1966.
Mariner instruments, for Taylor Instruments, 1968.
Corporate symbol, typewriters, calculators, and sewing machines, for Maruzen, 1968-72.
Instamatic Camera, for Kodak, 1970.
High-speed train exterior, for British Rail, 1971-73.
Information terminals, for Reuters, 1975.
Pocket Instamatic Camera, for Kodak, 1975.
*Royale* razor, for Wilkinson Sword, 1977.
Alphatex sign system, for Wood & Wood, 1978.
Identity, name, container, pack, and logotype for *Tactics* men's cosmetics, for Shiseido, 1978.
Parker 25 fountain pen, for Parker Pens, 1979.
Hi-fi speakers, for B & W, from 1980.
Electronic parking meter, for GEC, 1982.
Accountant pen, for Platignum, 1983.
Kompakt Design razor, for Wilkinson Sword, 1988.
*Image* Sunglasses, for Polaroid, 1988.
X Stage KG bathroom, for INAX Corporation, 1989.
ShowerAge shower for the elderly, for Ideal Standard, 1989.
Townplan 2000, bus shelter, and street furniture, for More O'Ferrall/Adshel, 1990.
Child Safety Seat, for Takata Corporation, 1991.
Fan Heater, for Osaka Gas Corporation, 1991.
*Protector* razor, for Wilkinson Sword, 1992.
PDA 600 Pen Pad, for Amstrad, 1993.
Mondex Wallet, for National Westminster Bank, 1993.
*Silk Effects* razor, for Wilkinson Sword/Schick, 1994.

## Publications

**By GRANGE: books**—(co-author) *Pentagram: The Work of Five Designers,* London, 1972; (co-author) *Living By Design,* London and New York, 1978; *Kenneth Grange at the Boilerhouse: An Exhibition of British Product Design,* catalogue edited by Stephen Bayley and Jon Ward, London, 1983; (co-author) *The Compendium,* London, 1993.

**On GRANGE: books**—*The Business of Product Design* by James Pilditch and Douglas Scott, London, 1965; *Modern Design in Metal* by Richard Steward, London, 1979; *Design Since 1945* edited by Kathryn Hiesinger and George Marcus, Philadelphia and London, 1983; *The Conran Directory of Design* edited by Stephen Bayley, London, 1985, *Eye for Industry: Royal Designers for Industry 1936-1986,* exhibition catalogue by Fiona MacCarthy and Patrick Nuttgens, London, 1986; *New Design*

*for Old,* exhibition catalogue with texts by Helen Hamlyn, Eric Midwinter, and others, London, 1986.

\*      \*      \*

Kenneth Grange's concept of the designer's role is one of the most significant aspects of his work and influence. His convictions that product design should be an integral part of the manufacturing process, that the designer is primarily an innovator, and that his authority transcends any narrow specialism have in many cases led to his participation in redevelopment of existing products or creation of the image for a new artifact or technology. For instance, major redevelopment was carried out for the Frister and Rossman 804 sewing machine, for which setting back the main shaft to allow more space in front of the needle exemplifies Grange's fresh approach to component layout. Further, he realigned the ends, so that the machine can be upended and balanced on the handwheel, thus neatly resolving a longstanding servicing problem. For the Post Office's new Confravision studios, Grange created a continuous, L-shaped conference table with wings; it unifies the studio, provides camera-viewing space for document display, and restricts movement of the participants out of camera range.

Believing that design has social as well as economic function, Grange argues that his emphasis on the consumer's pleasure and satisfaction is an essential element of the designer's responsibility to the manufacturer. These views place Grange squarely within mainstream design thought of the 1960s and 1970s, but the outstanding success of his industrial design practice has lent considerable weight to his arguments and has reinforced the influence of the designer, and particularly the design consultant, in Britain and as far afield as Japan.

While Grange would be the first to deny that industrial design is simply styling, his work has a clearly recognizable visual identity established in the 1960s when the influence of the Italians and of West German companies such as Braun was strong. Close formal links with Italian design can be seen by comparing, for example, Grange's Variset cloakroom hanger system for A. J. Binns (1978) with the Sedia Poeta chair by Gigi Sabadin for Stilwood (both using flat, angular shapes with rounded corners) or again, the nose end of the High Speed Train with Cini Boeri's lamp model 2401 for Stilnovo of Milan. The High Speed Train, the Frister and Rossman 804, and Grange's prize-winning Courier shaver for Milward (1963) all demonstrate his preference for strong, sculptural forms which unify the design. Keeping control areas to a minimum, he uses moulded materials and flush surfaces to promote this effect.

—Karen Moon

# GRAPUS

French Graphic design group

**Founded** by Pierre Bernard (born 1942), Gérard Paris-Clavel (born 1943), and François Miehe (born 1942), in Paris, 1970. Principals have included Pierre Bernard, Gérard Paris-Clavel, Alexander Jordan (born 1947), and Jean-Paul Bacholle (born 1930). Grapus has designed graphics and posters for Secours Populaire Français, Amis de la Terre, Amitiés Franco-Vietnamiennes, Confédération General du Travail, French Communist Party, Renault-Cuincy, Front

Démocratique pour le Libération de la Palestine, Festivals of La Rochelle and Avignon, Centre Georges Pompidou, Musée des Arts Decoratifs, Théâtre de la Salamandre, Comédie Française, Radio Lorraine Coeur d' Acier, *La Vie Ouvrière, l'Humanité, La Nouvelle Critique, France Nouvelle,* Avant Garde, and others, from 1970. **Exhibitions:** Comité d'Entreprise de l'Aerospatiale; Chatillon-sous-Bagneux, 1978; Galerie Saluden, Quimper, 1979; *Grapus: l'Image Flottante,* Athens, 1981; Stedelijk Museum, Amsterdam, 1981; *A la Tienne, Estienne,* Ecole Estienne, Paris, 1981; Pecsi Galeria, Pecs, 1982; Dorttya Galeria, Budapest, 1982; Kunstgewerbemuseum, Zurich, 1982; Musée de l'Affiche, Paris, 1982; Forradalmi Museum, Szombathely, 1982; *100 Affiches de Grapus,* Salle de l'Aigalier, Martigues, 1983; Musée des Arts Decoratifs, Lausanne, 1983; Aspen Center of Visual Art, Colorado, 1983. **Collections:** Poster Museum, Vilanov; Museum of Decorative Arts, Prague; Galeria Moravia, Brno; Deutsches Plakatmuseum, Essen; Stedelijk Museum; Museum of Modern Art, New York; Bibliothèque Nationale, Paris; Musée de l'Affiche; Bibliothèque Fourney, Paris. **Honors:** Warsaw Poster Biennale Medals, 1978, 1980; Brno Graphics Biennale Medals and Prizes, 1978, 1980, 1982; Lahti Poster Biennale Awards, 1981, 1983; Colorado Poster Exhibition Prize, 1983. **Address:** 4 Allée Georges Braque, 93300 Aubervilliers, France.

### Publications

**On GRAPUS: books**—*Grapus,* exhibition catalogue with text by Alain Weill, Paris, 1982; *Images de la Révolte 1965-1975,* with text by Steef Davidson, Paris, 1982; *Top Graphic Design* by F. H. K. Henrion, Zurich, 1983; **articles**—*l'Humanité* (Paris), 11 April 1977; *ATAC Informations* (Paris), no. 96, 1978; *Novum Gebrauchsgraphik* (Munich), August 1979; *Projekt* (Warsaw), August 1979; *The Designer* (London), May 1980; *Idea* (Tokyo), May 1981; *Graphis* (Zurich), no. 213, 1981; *Révolution* (Paris), 30 April 1982; *International Herald Tribune* (Paris), 14 January 1983; *Werbung/Publicité* (Zurich), May 1983; *Direction* (London), March 1987; *Graphics World* (Maidstone), November 1987.

*

We know once and for all that images are not innocent. We want to show this each time we make one. We give people the opportunity to see the obvious manipulation, the mechanism which produced the emotion. We appeal to their capacity for recognition and to their past experience in order to better awaken their critical judgment. In the mass communication process, we refuse to consider the public as a mass of consumers or as a public opinion to be manipulated. We want to address everyone, each in *his* or *her* difference, as a "citizen to be moved." But, for this, producers of mass messages—our clients—have to be our accomplices. They must enter into this new and more difficult relationship. It is, thus, by a mutual effort that we can really see that graphic design, rather than simply reflecting power, can truly become an instrument that powers reflection.

—Grapus

*     *     *

Grapus began as an association of three French graphic designers, communists. They were not admen. They have always worked

collectively and signed their works as a group. Of the founder-members of the group, two have studied under the renowned Henryk Tomaszewski at Warsaw's Academy of Arts—and the group was fired with the endeavor to cultivate beautiful pictures to change the world, such as they had discovered in Poland. It is a rare thing in the design profession to exchange the well-marked-out future of an illusion-maker for the insecure one of a history-maker. After all, they could have had a good material life working on publicity for tuna fish in mayonnaise or for cars. But they opted for the risky business of fighting against unemployment and for freedom of expression.

As they saw it, the prevailing factor in the production of pictures in France was the promotion of merchandise, the signal-sender not responding to need, but creating it himself in order to conquer a new area of the market. The functional advertisement for a better commodity (one that corresponds better to its utilitarian purpose) had ceased to exist. One of their difficulties lay in the situation whereby the socio-cultural poster has the marginal status of a squatter. Very few of the unemployed have the means to pay for advertising space. And so, Grapus went for the most sympathetic of established client/sponsors they could find and produced all manner of materials for organizations such as Conféderation Générale du Travail, the French Communist Party, the journal *Avant-Garde,* and the Théâtre de la Salamandre. They aimed at a constancy of relationship, a continuum instead of just a brief fascination with no future. Their work has appeared in various formats, including small posters, stickers, stationery, flags, journals, and other economical programmes.

Today, Grapus is not just a group of politically committed artists or communist semiologists, but artist-communists who want to convey their message at once clearly and subjectively. Having produced more than 1,000 pictures committed to the social and cultural struggle, however, they are aware of a partial irresponsibility on the part of the genuine artist. They believe in Godard's axiom: "This is not a just picture, this is just a picture." Their works, they realize, are freely floating objects, like bottles cast into the sea—but they leave no one indifferent when they reach the opposite shore.

—George Walsh

# GRAVES, Michael

American architect and interior and furniture designer

**Born:** Indianapolis, Indiana, 9 July 1934. **Education:** University of Cincinnati, Ohio, B.S. (Architecture), 1958; Harvard University, Cambridge, Massachusetts, M.Arch., 1959; American Academy, Rome, 1960-62 (Brunner Fellowship). **Career:** Worked in the design office of George Nelson, New York, 1962-64; founder-principal, Michael Graves Architect architectural and design firm, Princeton, New Jersey, from 1964; founder of Graves Design Studio Store, Princeton, marketing Graves Design furniture, furnishings, and artifacts; furniture, furnishing, and lighting designs for Atelier International, Kron, Dunbar, Arkitektura, Baldinger, Alessi, The Markuse Corporation, Steuben, Moller, Gilbert International, Belvedere Studio, Vorwerk, Tajima, and others. Lecturer, 1962-63, assistant professor, 1963-67, associate professor, 1967-72, and Schirmer Professor of Architecture, from 1972, Princeton University, New Jersey; visiting fellow, Institute for Architecture and Urban Studies, New York, 1971-72; visiting professor, University of Texas, Austin, 1973-74, University of Houston, Texas, 1974, 1978, New School for Social Research, New York, 1975, and University of California at Los Angeles, 1977; architect-in-residence, American Academy, Rome, 1979. **Member:** American Academy and Institute of Arts and Letters. **Exhibitions:** *40 Under 40,* Architectural League, New York, 1966; *Architecture of Museums,* Museum of Modern Art, New York, 1968; *Five Architects,* Princeton University, New Jersey, 1974 (travelled to Austin, Texas); *The New York Five,* Art Net, London, 1975; *Michael Graves: Projects 1967-76,* Columbia University, New York, 1976; *Beyond the Modern Movement,* Harvard University, Cambridge, Massachusetts, 1977; *Trends in Contemporary Architecture,* New Gallery of Contemporary Art, Cleveland, Ohio, 1978; *Ornament in the Twentieth Century,* Cooper-Hewitt Museum, New York, 1978; *Michael Graves: Progetti 1977-81,* Rome, 1981; *Design Since 1945,* Philadelphia Museum of Art, 1983; *Intuition and the Block Print,* John Nichols Printmakers and Publishers, New York, 1984. **Honors:** Prix de Rome, American Academy, Rome, 1960; New Jersey Society of Architects Awards, 1967, 1973, 1974, 1975 (2), 1976 (2), 1977, 1978 (4), 1980 (4), 1981 (2), 1982, 1983 (3), 1984, 1985 (2), 1987 (6), 1988, 1989 (2), 1990 (3), 1991 (6), 1992 (3), 1994 (3), and Special Recognition Honor Award, 1982; *Progressive Architecture* Design Awards, 1970, 1976, 1977, 1978, 1979, 1980 (3), 1983, 1988, 1989 (2), and Furniture Design Awards, 1982, 1983; American Institute of Architects National Honor Awards, 1975, 1979, 1982, 1983, 1985, 1987 (2), 1990, 1992; Arnold W. Brunner Memorial Prize in Architecture, American Academy of Arts and Letters, 1980; Resources Council Commendations, 1980, 1982; Institute of Business Designers Awards, 1982 (2), 1990; Indiana Arts Award, 1983; Euster Award, Miami, Florida, 1983; Honored Artist, Young Women of the Arts, Atlanta, Georgia, 1985; Henry Hering Memorial Medal, Portland, Oregon, 1986; Gold Plate Award, American Academy of Achievement, 1986; I.D. (International Design) Awards, Consumer Products, 1989, 1990, and Furniture, honorable mention, 1989; Award of Excellence in Graphic Design, American Federation of Arts, 1990; New Jersey Business and Industry Association Award, 1990; Downtown New Jersey Excellence Award for Downtown Development, 1990; Walt Whitman Creative Arts Award, New Jersey, 1991. Honorary doctorates from University of Cincinnati, 1982, Boston University, 1984, Savannah College of Art, 1986, Rhode Island School of Design, 1990, New Jersey Institute of Technology, 1991, and Rutgers University, 1994; fellow, Society for the Arts, Religion and Culture. **Address:** 341 Nassau Street, Princeton, New Jersey 08540, U.S.A.

**Works**

Urban County Nature and Science Museum, Mountainside, New Jersey, 1967.
N.E.S.T. rehabilitation housing, Trenton, New Jersey, 1967-71.
Three murals in Transammonia Inc. offices, New York, 1974.
Mural in the School of Architecture, University of Texas, Austin, 1974.
Abrahams Dance Studio, Princeton, New Jersey, 1977.
Mural in the John Witherspoon School, Princeton, New Jersey, 1978.
Newark Museum Children's Museum, New Jersey, 1978.
Furniture showrooms and office in New York and Cleveland, for E.F. Hauserman Corporation, 1978.

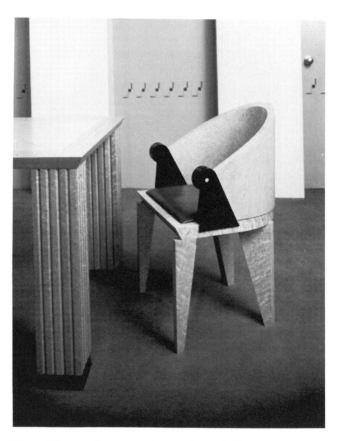

Michael Graves: *Sunar* armchair made of bird's eye maple and ebony, for Sunar Hauserman, 1982

The Portland Building, Portland, Oregon, 1980.
Humana Building, Louisville, Kentucky, 1982.
San Juan Capistrano Regional Library, California, 1983.
Riverbend Music Center, Cincinnati, Ohio, 1983.
Diane Von Furstenberg boutique, Fifth Avenue, New York, 1984.
Clos Pegase Winery and Residence, Napa Valley, California, 1984.
Columbus Circle Redevelopment, New York, 1985.
Whitney Museum of American Art, New York, 1985.
The Disney Company corporate headquarters, Burbank, California, 1986.
Historical Center for Industry and Labor, Youngstown, Ohio, 1986.
Walt Disney World Dolphin and World Swan hotels, Florida, 1987.
Yokohama Portside District Condominium Tower, Yokohama, Japan, 1987.
10 Peachtree Plaza office building, Atlanta, Georgia, 1988.
Hotel New York, for Euro Disneyland, France, 1989.
Indianapolis Art Center, Indianapolis, Indiana, 1990.
Fukuoka Hotel and Office project, Fukuoka, Japan, 1990.
*Birth of Democracy* exhibition, National Archives, Washington, D.C., 1991.
*Rome Reborn* exhibition, Library of Congress, Washington, D.C., 1992.
Pittsburgh Cultural Trust, Theater, and Office Building, Pittsburgh, Pennsylvania, 1992.
Federal Courthouse, Trenton, New Jersey, 1992.
Taiwan Pre-History Museum, Taipei, Taiwan, 1993.
International Finance Corporation headquarters, Washington, D.C., 1993.

Bayou Place Theater, Houston, Texas, 1993.
Saint Martin's College Library, Lacey, Washington, 1994.
Delaware River Port Authority office building, Camden, New Jersey, 1994.

(for a complete list of Graves' buildings and architectural projects, see *Contemporary Architects*)

## Publications

**By GRAVES: books**—*Michael Graves: Buildings and Projects 1966-81,* New York, 1982; *Michael Graves: Buildings and Projects 1982-1989,* New York, 1990; *Michael Graves: Buildings and Projects 1990-1994,* New York, 1995; **articles**—in *Journal of Architectural Education* (Washington, D.C.), September 1975, September 1978; *Architectural Design* (London), June 1977, March 1979; *AIA Journal* (Washington, D.C.), October 1978; *Artsmagazine* (New York), April 1980; *Architectural Record* (New York), June 1980; *Via* (Cambridge, Massachusetts), no. 4, 1980; *Architecture + Urbanism* (Tokyo), December 1982, December 1983; *Connaissance des Arts* (Paris), March 1984.

**On GRAVES: books**—*40 Under 40,* exhibition catalogue by Robert A. M. Stern, New York, 1966; *Five Architects: Eisenman, Graves, Gwaihmey, Hejduk, Meier* by Kenneth Frampton and Colin Rowe, New York, 1972; *New Directions in American Architecture* by Robert A. M. Stern, New York, 1977; *Trends in Contemporary Architecture,* exhibition catalogue edited by James N. Wood, Cleveland, Ohio, 1978; *Architectural Monographs 5: Michael Graves* by Alan Colquhoun and others, London, 1979; *Collaboration: Artists and Architects* by Barbaralee Diamonstein, New York, 1981; *Kings of Infinite Space: Frank Lloyd Wright and Michael Graves* by Charles Jencks, London and New York, 1983; *The Conran Directory of Design* edited by Stephen Bayley, London, 1985; *Twentieth Century Design: Furniture* by Penny Sparke, London, 1986; *Modern Furniture Classics* by Miriam Stimpson, London, 1987; *New American Design* by Hugh Aldersley-Williams, New York, 1988; *Michael Graves Design Monograph,* Berlin, 1994.

*       *       *

It is too soon to say whether the environments Michael Graves is now creating will permanently alter our stylistic direction or whether they will testify only to the eclecticism of the 1980s. What can be said is that Graves, first as an architect and then as a designer of interior spaces and furnishing, is a force to be reckoned with.

The visual references in his work—"analogies," as Graves calls them—are plain. The forms of Rome and the Renaissance appear often in witty translation whenever structure is, or appears to be, at issue. Furnishings borrow more directly from the stylized forms of the 1930s. However, one may wonder whether even Graves, daring as he seems to be, would have advanced so quickly to such bold combinations had not Robert Venturi plowed the intellectual ground in which Graves' postmodern seed now flourishes. But he probably would have arrived at the scenographic aesthetic which is evident in his showroom designs.

In the showroom environments, boundaries are finessed with trompe l'oeil painting and controlled vistas. The techniques can be traced to Rome or to the illusion of the stage. The result should exalt the product, but Graves does his architectural job too well.

Rather than gaining importance from their luminous surround, the mass-productions of sponsoring Sunar often seem anticlimactic afterthoughts. This schism between environment and furniture is said to have led Graves to design his own furnishings; and certainly the well-staged outlines of his neo-moderne pieces hold their own against the postmodern backdrop, even in a residential setting (as *Metropolitan Home* proved when it commissioned Graves to transform a boxy apartment). But creating furniture to enhance atmosphere, the architect's traditional means of self-protection, often leads to visually exciting, physically uncomfortable pieces (as Graves, like Frank Lloyd Wright before him, admits). It might be remembered that, historically, styles which have responded only to their own aesthetic have not survived outside the museum vignette.

—Reed Benhamou

## GRAY, Eileen

Irish architect, interior, furniture, and textile designer

**Born:** At Brownswood, Enniscorthy, County Wexford, 9 August 1879. **Education:** Studied drawing and painting, at Slade School of Fine Art, London, 1898-1902; lacquer work, in D. Charles furniture workshops, Soho, London, 1900-02; drawing, at Academie Julian and Academie Colarossi, Paris, 1902-05; lacquer work and cabinetmaking, with Sugawara, Paris, 1907-14. **Military Service:** Served as an ambulance driver, in the French Army, 1914-15. **Career:** Independent furniture and interior designer from 1908, textile designer from 1910, and architect from 1926, in Paris and southern France: proprietor, with Sugawara, of lacquer work and furniture studio, in London, 1915-17, and in Paris, 1917-22; director, Jean Desert shop and showrooms, Paris 1922-30; freelance designer, working mainly on architectural projects with Jean Badovici, in Roquebrune 1926, in Castellar 1939-45, and in Paris, 1945-76. **Exhibitions:** *Salon des Artistes Decorateurs,* Paris, 1913, 1922; *Exposition Internationale,* Paris, 1937; Royal Institute of British Architects, London, 1973; l'Annee 1925, Musee des Arts Decoratifs, Paris, 1976; Victoria and Albert Museum, London, 1979 (travelled to New York). **Honors:** Honorary Royal Designer for Industry, Royal Society of Arts, London, 1972; Fellow, Royal Institute of Irish Architects, Dublin, 1973. **Died:** Paris, 28 November 1976.

## Works

Suzanne Talbot apartment interiors and furnishings, Rue de Lota, Paris, 1919-22.
Monte Carlo Boudoir, 1923 (project).
Eileen Gray apartment interiors and furnishings, 21 Rue Bonaparte, Paris, 1925-28.
House for an engineer, 1926 (project).
E-1027 (Eileen Gray house) villa and furnishings, Roquebrune, Cap Martin, France, 1927-29 (with Jean Badovici).
Jean Badovici studio and apartment interiors rue Chateaubriand, Paris, 1930.
Tempe a Pailla (Eileen Gray house) villa and furnishings, Castellar, near Menton, France, 1932-34.
House for two sculptors, 1933 (project).
Tube house, 1937 (project).
Centre des Vacances, 1937 (exhibition project).

Eileen Gray apartment interiors and furnishings, St. Tropez, France, 1939 (destroyed, 1944).
Cultural and Social Centre, 1946-49 (project).

## Publications

**By GRAY: articles**—in *l'Architecture d'Aujourd'hui* (Paris), no. 1, 1930.

**On GRAY: books**—*Cli Elementi dell'Architettura Funzionale* by Alberto Sartoris, Milan, 1932; *Des Canons, des Munitions? Merci: Des Logis . . .* by Le Corbusier, Paris, 1938; *Eileen Gray: Designer 1879-1976,* exhibition catalogue by Stewart Johnson, London, 1979; *The Conran Directory of Design* edited by Stephen Bayley, London, 1985; *Twentieth Century Design: Furniture* by Penny Sparke, London, 1986; *Design Source Book* by Penny Sparke and others, London, 1986; *Modern Furniture Classics* by Miriam Stimpson, London, 1987.

*       *       *

It is for her originality and her fund of ideas that Eileen Gray is remembered, together with the fact that she was one of the few women working independently in the field of architecture and design in the interwar period. Her interest in lacquer work led her to settle in Paris (where she had been studying for five years) in 1970, and her furniture designs using this new technique were imaginative and exotic. For example, a dark green lacquer table (1914) had green silk cords with amber beads and tassles looped through the ends; it was supported on legs with stylised white lotus lilies at the top. Her first interior design commission (1919), for Suzanne Talbot, included the remarkable lacquer pirogue and a screen consisting of 450 thin, lacquer plaques textured with powdered stone. This was used to shorten a long, narrow space in a simple, unexpected way. Four years later, she designed a bedroom-boudoir for the 1923 Salon des Artistes Decorateurs. This featured pierced screens of lacquered plaques and clean-lined furniture. The effect of clarity of line and space was quite different from current French taste in interior design, and it was greeted with derision by the French press but attracted the attention of the de Stijl group. Some of her work had been exhibited in Amsterdam the previous year, and her 1922 table showed that they shared similar concerns. In June 1924, the Dutch art journal *Wendingen* devoted a complete issue to her work.

By this time, her work had come to the attention of members of the modern movement, such as Gropius, Kiesler, and Le Corbusier, and she was encouraged by them to turn to architecture. Her house at Roquebrune, E-1027 (1924-26), designed with Jan Badovici, an architect and editor of *L'Architecture Vivante,* showed close links with the International Style in its flat roof, ribbon windows, and pilotis. In its furniture, which used space economically, she explored cantilevering and the use of such materials as tubular metal, glass, and aluminum. This concern with the potential of new materials could also be seen in her fluid, painted, steel-rod chair with laced canvas seat (1930) and her free-form table of oak on a slender, steel-rod frame (1938). Both of these showed features that came to be emphasized in contemporary design in the 1950s, namely concern with organic form and with the interrelationship between forms.

—Hazel Conway

# GRAY, Milner (Connorton)

British industrial, exhibition, and graphic designer

**Born:** Blackheath, London, 8 October 1899. **Education:** Studied painting and design, Goldsmith's College of Art, London, 1916-17 and 1919-21. **Military Service:** Served in the British Army camouflage unit, 1917-19, Private. **Family:** Married Gnade Osborn-Pratt in 1934. **Career:** Founder and senior partner, Bassett-Gray Group of Artists and Writers multi-discipline design practice, London, 1922-35, re-named Industrial Design Partnership, 1935-40; principal exhibition designer and head of Exhibitions Branch, Ministry of Information, London, 1940-44; founder-partner, with Misha Black, from 1945, and senior consultant since 1980, Design Research Unit, London; consultant to Foley China, E. Brain and Company, Royal Staffordshire Pottery, A. J. Wilkinson and Company, and others. Principal, Sir John Cass College of Art, London, 1937-40; visiting lecturer, Goldsmith 's College of Art, London, 1932-40, Chelsea School of Art, London, 1934-37, Reimann School of Art and Design, London, 1937-39, and Royal College of Art, London, 1939-40. Founder-member, 1930, honorary secretary, 1932-40, vice-president, 1940-43, president, 1943-49 and 1966-67, fellow, 1945, and chairman of the Board of Trustees, 1963-88, Society of Industrial Artists (now Chartered Society of Designers), London; member, Council on Art and Design, London, 1944-46; board member, Hornsey College of Art and Design, London, 1949-56; advisor, BBC Schools Broadcasts, London, 1949-55; National Art Examination Committee member, Ministry of Education, London, 1949-52; advisory committee member, Royal Mint, London, 1952-88; master of the Faculty of Royal Designers for Industry, Royal Society of Arts, London, 1955-57; vice-president, 1955-57, and council member, 1959-65, Royal Society of Arts, London; formation committee member, ICSID International Council of Societies of Industrial Design, 1956; National Art Education Advisory Council member, 1959-69; council member, from 1959, and vice-president, 1981, Artists General Benevolent Institution, London; master of the Art Worker's Guild, London, 1963; Post Office Stamp Committee member, Council of Industrial Design (now Design Council), London, 1963-67; British president, Alliance Graphique Internationale, 1963-71. **Exhibitions:** *British Industrial Art,* Dorland Hall, London, 1933; *107 Grafici dell'AGI,* Castello Sforzesco, Milan, 1974; *Thirties,* Hayward Gallery, London, 1979; *Eye for Industry,* Victoria and Albert Museum, London, 1986. **Collections:** Victoria and Albert Museum, London. **Honors:** Royal designer for industry, Royal Society of Arts, London, 1938; Design Medal, Society of Industrial Artists and Designers, London, 1955; Diploma, Milan Triennale, 1957; Design Centre Award, London, 1957; Commander, Order of the British Empire, 1963; honorary fellow, 1963, senior fellow, 1971, and honorary doctorate, 1979, Royal College of Art, London; honorary design associate, Manchester College of Art and Design, 1965; Queen's Silver Jubilee Medal, London, 1977; fellow, Institute of Packaging, 1987. **Address:** Felix Hall, Kelvedon, Essex CO5 9DG, England.

## Works

London Building Centre symbol, poster, and advertising programme, 1932.
Kardomah Cafes murals and decorations, in London, Birmingham, and Manchester, 1936-40.

Milner Gray: Royal Coat of Arms for the Council of Industrial Design, London, 1951

Coal and Steel Halls murals of the United Kingdom pavilion, *Empire Exhibition,* Glasgow, 1938.

Section displays at *MARS Exhibition of Modern Architecture,* London, 1938.

*Design at Home* exhibition layouts, National Gallery, London, 1945.

Taxicab and cooking-stove designs, at *Britain Can Make It* exhibition, Victoria and Albert Museum, London, for the Council of Industrial Design, 1946.

Rolex symbol, house style, and package designs, for Rolex Watch Company, Geneva, 1946.

*Design at Work* exhibition layouts at the Royal Academy, London, for the Royal Society of Arts, 1948.

Corporate identity programme, for Austin Reed Limited, London, 1949-50.

*Festival of Britain* signage system, South Bank, London, 1949-51.

Milk bottle filling and capping machine, for UD Engineering Company, 1950.

Royal Coat-of-Arms engraved glass screen, at the Royal Festival Hall, London, 1951.

Pyrex oven-to-table glassware, for James Joblings Limited, 1955-65.

Corporate identity programme, for Watney Mann Group of breweries, 1956-70.

Armorial bearings, for the Central Electricity Generating Board, 1963.

Corporate design programme, for the British Railways Board, 1963-68.

Corporate identity programme, for the British Aluminium Company, 1967-72.

Armorial bearings and common seal, for the General Post Office, London, 1970.

Official emblem, for the Queen's Silver Jubilee, 1976-77.

## Publications

**By GRAY: books**—(with others) *The Practice of Design,* London 1946; *Package Design,* London and New York, 1955; (with Ronald Armstrong) *Lettering for Architects and Designers,* London, 1962, Tokyo, 1965.

**On GRAY: books**—*British Achievement in Design* edited by Noel Carrington and Muriel Harris, London, 1946; *Design in British Industry: A Mid-Century Survey* by Michael Farr, Cambridge, 1955; *Who's Who in Graphic Art* edited by Walter Amstutz, Zürich, 1962, Dubendorf, 1982; *An International Survey of Packaging* by Wim Crouwel and Kurt Weidemann, London, 1968; *107 Grafici dell'AGI,* exhibition catalogue with text by Renzo Zorzi and Franco Grignani, Venice, 1974; *Industrial Design in Britain* by Noel Carrington, London, 1976; *Milner Gray* by Avril Blake, London, 1986.

\*

To designers, I would just like to say that the work we most admire is often the simplest and the most obvious—of the kind that we all know we could have done, had we only thought of it. It is simple and inevitable because, the right question having been asked, there was no longer any difficulty in finding the right answer. As soon as we tackle a design problem, we ourselves become a part of the problem we aim to solve, bringing to its solution our own predilections, which may not coincide with those of the others associated with us in its solution. The solution will seldom be achieved by bulldozing our ideas over the other fellow, who is as identified with the problem as we are.

I believe that the designer's originative capacity derives from an inward urge to bring new forms into being. His creative contribution differs not in *quality* but in *kind* from that of other industrial workers—the factory manager who evolves a new production-line technique or the business executive who conceives a new sales system. The designer's originative capacity is not necessarily superior or fundamentally different; the difference lies in his application of it. This, which turns the tolerable into the beautiful, the merely functional into the highly desirable, makes him as valuable to industry as his scientific and executive colleagues.

Every design is, in a sense, an act of communication: a statement of a conviction about the nature and the functions of an article, a statement for which the designer accepts responsibility. The greater the intensity with which he appreciates and the integrity with which he expresses the whole truth about the product as he perceives it, the better his design. Integrity of expression comes from the integration of thought and action, integration of mind, eye and hand, of honest, disciplined work. The designer's social contribution and responsibility is to realize the true and total value to the ultimate users of the products he designs. *(Excerpted from a speech at the summary session of the International Design Conference in Aspen, Colorado, 18-24 June 1961)*

—Milner Gray

\*       \*       \*

In a very productive and successful career, Milner Gray has established a worldwide reputation for his immaculate draughtsmanship and his interest in lettering. Before World War II, he combined a busy career in practice with several important teaching posts. Later, he helped create many of the best-known symbols, packaging materials, and corporate liveries in Britain for large companies from brewers to pottery manufacturers. He is well known for his designs of badges, particularly for royalty. The official emblem for Queen Elizabeth II's Silver Jubilee is one example. These types of design show his respect for tradition and attention to detail, as well as a knack for identifying distinctive features that help to make the design feel contemporary and clear-cut.

Perhaps his greatest contribution to twentieth-century design has been what he has accomplished as a planner and organiser of people: drawing colleagues into the first viable professional society of designers in Britain, pulling together very different characters and talents to make effective wartime exhibitions, and creating and sustaining design practices—first the Bassen-Gray partnership, then the Industrial Design Partnership, and finally the first large, multi-skill group in Britain, the Design Research Unit. His ability to coordinate many different people, ideas, and interests laid the foundations for the detailed and memorable design schemes and programmes that the Design Research Unit has helped to devise for organisations with such different activities as British Rail, Wedgwood, Imperial Chemical Industries, and the brewers John Courage Ltd.

He is clear about his most positive achievement: "The only thing I have done that I think will stand up is the setting up of the S.I.A.D. (Society of Industrial Artists and Designers) in 1929-30." But he will probably be best remembered for his skillful and persistent advocacy of democratic principles in creating professional organisations, maintaining design practices, and working out design schemes with clients. "The committee should initiate the field of study, establish areas of research, and organise and programme the work of the design development team," he has said. In championing the committee system, he has laid great emphasis on the need for the designer to be a skilled communicator in both the boardroom and the factory. The designer must be able to argue the case but not assume that he is the only person with the correct solution.

—Anthony J. Coulson

# GREAR, J(ames) Malcolm

American graphic designer

**Born:** Mill Springs, Kentucky, 12 June 1931. **Education:** Studied at the Art Academy of Cincinnati, Ohio, 1955-58. **Military Service:** Served as an aviation metalsmith in the United States Navy, 1950-54. **Family:** Married Clarice Simpson in 1955; children: Jason, Joel, Amie, and Leah. **Career:** Founder and chief executive officer, Malcolm Grear Designers Inc., Providence, Rhode Island, from 1960; has designed corporate image programs, environmental graphics and packaging for medical facilities, museums, corporations, universities, government agencies, and communities. Lecturer in basic and graphic design, Art Center Association, Louisville, Kentucky, 1958-60, and Allen R. Hite Institute, University of Louisville, Kentucky, 1959-60; associate professor of Graphic Design, 1960-79, head of graphic design department, 1965-69, professor of graphic design, 1980-88, and Helen M. Danforth professor, from 1988, Rhode Island School of Design, Providence. **Member:** Member of the Graphic Design Review Panel for Federal Agencies, National Endowment for the Arts, 1973-78; executive com-

mittee member, Rhode Island Committee for the Humanities, American Institute of Graphic Arts, 1978-86. **Exhibitions:** *Communication by Design,* Institute of Contemporary Art, Boston, 1964 (toured); *Communication Graphics,* American Institute of Graphic Arts, New York, 1971, 1972, 1981; *International Annual of Poster Art,* Zürich, 1973; *Environmental Design: Signing and Graphics,* American Institute of Graphic Arts, New York, 1977; *Malcolm Grear Designers,* travelling studio exhibit, 1984-86. **Collections:** Cooper-Hewitt Museum, New York; Whitney Museum, New York. **Honors:** Annual Book of the Year Award, American Institute of Graphic Arts, 1968, 1970, 1971, 1974, 1977, 1979, 1981, 1985; Governor's Award, Rhode Island State Council on the Arts, 1969; *Print* magazine Poster of the Decade Award, 1971; Art Libraries Society Museum Publication Award, New York, 1976; New England Book Show Design Excellence Awards, 1976; Annual Design Award, Art Society of North America, 1977; Design Excellence Awards, 1979, Design Award, 1981, and Gold Medals, 1983, Art Directors Club of Boston; Typographic Excellence Awards, Type Directors Club, New York, 1980; Design Excellence Awards, Society of Typographic Arts, Chicago, 1980, 1982; Silver Medal, Leipzig Book Design Exhibition, 1982; John R. Frazier Award for Excellence in Teaching, 1986; American Federation of Arts Design Excellence Awards, 1987; Honorary Alumnus Award, Rhode Island School of Design, 1989. **Address:** 391-393 Eddy Street, Providence, Rhode Island 02903, U.S.A.

## Works

Exhibition design, for Merrimack Valley Textile Museum, Andover, Massachusetts, 1962.
*Biology* (H. Curtis) book design, for Worth Publishers, New York, 1969.
*Biochemistry* (A. Lehinger) book design, for Worth Publishers, New York, 1970.
Environmental graphics, for the Oakwood Comprehensive Training Center, Somerset, Kentucky, 1971.
Outpatient hospital signage and wall murals, for Boston City Hospital, 1971.
*Jean Miro: Magnetic Fields* exhibition catalogue design, for the Guggenheim Museum, New York, 1972.
*Places: Aaron Siskind Photographs* exhibition book design, for the Light Gallery, New York, 1976.
*Robert Motherwell and Black* exhibition catalogue design, for the William Beneton Museum of Art, University of Connecticut, 1976.
*Tall Ships '76* identity program and image application, 1976.
*Henri Matisse: Paper Cut-Outs* exhibition catalogue design, for the St. Louis Art Museum and Detroit Institute of Arts, 1977.
Total sign system, dedication book, and exhibit, for King Khalid City, Saudi Arabia, 1977-80.
*Planar Dimensions* exhibition catalogue design, for the Guggenheim Museum, New York, 1979.
Identity program, for the U.S. Department of Health and Human Services, 1980.
Sign system, for the Boston Museum of Fine Arts, 1980.
*Dale Chihuly: Glass* book design, for Dale Chihuly, 1982.
Series of library book designs, for the Scientific American Library, 1982-86.
Identity program, for the Presbyterian Church of the U.S.A., 1984.
*Earth Zero* poster commemorating the Hiroshima bombing, for The Shoshin Society Inc., 1986.

## Publications

**On GREAR: books**—*Trademarks USA* edited by the Society of Typographic Arts, Chicago, 1968; *Signet, Signal, Symbol* by Walter Diethelm, Zürich, 1970; *Book of American Trademarks* by David E. Carter, New York, 1972, 1973; *Trademark and Symbol* by Yasaburo Kuwayama, Tokyo, 1973; *Architectural Signing and Graphics* by John Foulis and David Hammer, New York, 1979; *Graphic Art for our Environment* by Takenobu Igarashi, Tokyo, 1980; *Visual Puns in Design* by Eli Kence, New York, 1982; *American Corporate Identity* by David E. Carter, New York, 1988; *Type and Image* by Philip B. Meggs, New York, 1988.

\*      \*      \*

Malcolm Grear works closely with his staff of designers to solve a variety of design problems by sharing creativity in a relaxed, familial atmosphere. Although the firm began as a two dimensional design studio, his expertise has grown to include space planning for hospitals and schools and designs for exhibitions and trade shows. In applying his talents to the more complex problems of environmental planning and architectural graphics programs, Grear goes beyond the traditional role of a graphic designer as one who arranges type and visual elements on a two-dimensional surface.

Grear's ability to bring graphic insight to what have been traditionally non-graphic problems is evident in his large-scale environmental projects, which are problems in use and communication. For Grear, it is a matter of figuring out how people relate to one another and then designing according to their needs. For the Oakwood Comprehensive Training Center, a state-run facility for emotionally disturbed children in Kentucky, Grear brought together the buildings and grounds by designing an environment with architectural graphics, sculptures, and movable animal cutouts. One of his most ambitious projects, however, was the space planning of the Westminster Center public mall in Providence, Rhode Island. In order to respect the vitality of the area and its architecture, Grear had the project enlarged by one block. In doing this, he avoided making an exhibit of a mall by effecting a response to the cross streets.

As others have noted, Grear brings to his work a strong commitment to moral principle. Just as an art poster or museum catalogue must respect the work of the artist involved, so must the architectural graphics and space planning respect the architecture with which it works. Whether the designs are his crisp, clean graphic symbols or his large-scale environmental projects, Grear brings to them the same enthusiasm for combining graphic qualities with the personal identities of his clients.

—Patricia A. Russac

# GREGOTTI, Vittorio

Italian architect and interior, exhibition, and industrial designer

**Born:** Novara, 10 August 1927. **Education:** Studied architecture, at the Politecnico, Milan, Dip.Arch., 1952. **Family:** Married Marina Mazza in 1975. **Career:** Partner, with Lodovico Meneghetti and Giotto Stoppino, in Architetti Associati, Novara, 1953-63, and Milan, 1964-68; established private architectural and design practice, Milan, 1968-74; established Gregotti Associati architects and designers, with Pierluigi Cerri and Hiromichi Matsui, Milan, from 1974; partners currently include Vittorio Gregotti, Pierluigi Cerri, and Augusto Cagnardi. Associate editor, with Ernesto N. Rogers, 1953-55, and editor-in-chief, from 1982, *Casabella* (Milan); chief editor, *Casabella-Continuita* (Milan), 1955-63; editor-in-chief, *Edilizia Moderna* monographs, Milan, 1963-65; architectural editor, *Il Verri* (Milan), 1963-65; co-editor, *Lotus* (Venice), from 1974; editor-in-chief, *Rassegna,* from 1979; architectural editor, *Panorama,* 1984-92; columnist, *Corriere della Sera,* from 1992. Professor of architectural composition, Politecnico, Milan, from 1964, and Istituto Universitario di Architettura, Venice, from 1978; also visiting professor, Harvard University, Princeton, Massachusetts Institute of Technology, and Cambridge University, and at universities in Tokyo, Buenos Aires, Sao Paulo, Lausanne, and Philadelphia. Consultant, Rinascente stores group, Milan, 1968-71; director of the visual art and architectural section, Venice Biennale, 1974-76. **Exhibitions:** *Milan Triennale,* from 1951; *28/78 Architettura,* Palazzo delle Stelline, Milan, 1979 (travelled to Venice); *Vittorio Gregotti: Progetti,* Palermo. 1981; *La Modernité,* Paris, 1982; *Il Mestiere di Architetto: Botta, Piano, Gregotti,* Ferrara, 1984; *Vittorio Gregotti,* Harvard University, Cambridge, Massachusetts, 1984; *The European Iceberg,* Art Gallery of Ontario, Toronto, 1985. **Honors:** Grand Prize, Milan Triennale, 1964; Compasso d'Oro Award, Milan, 1968; IACP Housing Development Prize, Palermo, 1970; University of Florence Design Prize, 1971; University of Calabria Design Prize, 1973. **Address:** Gregotti Associati, Via Bandello 20, 20123 Milan, Italy.

## Works

Exhibition pavilion, at the Marketing Fair, Novara, 1953.
Headquarters Building, for the Istituto di Credito, Novara, 1958-59.
Master plan, for the City of Novara, 1962-67.
Entrance pavilion, for the Milan Triennale, 1964 (with Peppo Brivio).
Cotton mill building, for Bossi, Novara, 1968.
Headquarters building, for the Instituto di Credito, Bra, 1968.
Two supermarkets, for La Rinascente, Milan, 1969.
Science department buildings, for the University of Palermo, 1972-84.
Offices and warehousing, for Gabel, Como, 1973-74.
New University of Calabria, Cosenza, 1973-75.
Music store, for Ricordi, Milan, 1974-75.
Office building, for Bossi, Novara, 1981-83.
Olympic Stadium, Barcelona, 1984.
Luigi Ferraris Stadium, Genoa, 1986.
Sports complex, Nimes, 1986.
Belèm Cultural Centre, Lisbon, 1986-1993.
Redevelopment of the former Pirelli Bicocca industrial area, Milan, 1986-1995.
Accademia Carrara Modern and Contemporary Art Gallery, Bergamo, 1987.
*Le Corbusier* exhibition, Center Georges Pompidou, Paris, 1987.
New Passengers Harbour, Venice, 1989.
Renovation of the Salle des Etats, Louvre, Paris, 1991.

(for a complete list of Gregotti's buildings and architectural projects, see *Contemporary Architects*)

## Publications

By GREGOTTI: books—*Il Territorio dell'Architettura,* Milan, 1966; *L'architettura dell'espressionismo,* Milan, 1967; *New Directions in Italian Architecture,* New York, 1968; *Il Disegno del Prodotto Industriale-Italia 1860-1980,* Milan, 1982; *Question di Architettura,* Turin, 1986; *Cinque Dialoghi Necessari,* Milan, 1990; *Dentro l'Architettura,* Turin, 1991; *La Citta Visible,* Turin, 1993; *Le Scarpe di Van Gogh,* Turin, 1994; articles—in *Casabella* (Milan), no. 216, 1957, no. 228, 1959, no. 229, 1959, no. 240, 1960, no. 254, 1961, September 1977, July 1978, January 1981, October 1982; *Edilizia Moderna* (Milan), no. 86, 1965; *L'Arte Moderna* (Milan), no. 91, 1967, no. 94, 1967; *L'Architecture d'Aujourd'hui* (Paris), September 1968; *Domus* (Milan), October 1973, May 1974, May 1981; *Parametro* (Bologna), June 1977; *Alfabeta* (Milan), June 1979; *Rassegna* (Milan), July 1981, September 1982; *Daidalos* (Berlin), June 1984.

On GREGOTTI: books—*Design Italiano: i mobili* by Enrichetta Ritter, Milan and Rome, 1968; *Design e Forme Nuove nell'Arredamento Italiano* edited by Paolo Portoghesi and Marino Marini, Rome, 1978; *Il Progetto per l'Universita delle Calabrie e Altre Architetture di Vittorio Gregotti,* Milan, 1979; *Moderno Postmoderno Millenario* edited by Andrea Branzi, Milan, 1980; *Vittorio Gregotti* by Manfredo Tafuri, Milan, 1982; *A History of Industrial Design* by Edward Lucie-Smith, Oxford, 1983; *The European Iceberg,* exhibition catalogue edited by Germano Celant, Milan, 1985; *The Conran Directory of Design* edited by Stephen Bayley, London, 1985; *Vittorio Gregotti* by Sergio Crotti, Bologna, 1986; *Italian Design 1870 to the Present* by Penny Sparke London, 1988; *Gregotti Associati 1973-1988* by Werner Oechslin, Milan, 1990; *Gregotti Associati* by Joseph Rykwert, Milan, 1995.

*   *   *

Perhaps more than most Milanese architects and designers, Vittorio Gregotti has maintained an intellectually valid common denominator to all his many and varied activities, as he has run through all the roles of architect, publicist, editor, critic, historian, designer, impresario, and, above all, apologist. His commitment to the so-called "Neo-Liberty," a "revival" of art nouveau, was particularly courageous, while the theoretical underpinning he sought demonstrated equally his forthright honesty and subtle articulation of the concept of historicism. His intellectual approach was characterized then, as it is now, by a sophisticated understanding that the two intellectual notions alike designated by the term "historicism," are somehow intertwined. Revivalism, the genuine attempt to recreate the style of previous practices, is doomed to failure, but at the same time, history is a key. The point for him was to pick up the possibilities from the presumed moment of deviation without losing the benefit of hindsight. Gregotti's return to art nouveau was a return to principles, and he attempted to proceed with those principles in the light of all that had happened meanwhile. His approach was not at all a rejection of the Italian twentieth-century experience but rather a critical revaluation of it, an attempt to reinvigorate it with a more precise historical perspective.

By 1964, his section of the Milan Triennale—the entrance pavilion (with Peppo Brivio)—showed the full cultural significance of his departure from any principles and his transcendence of the limitations revivalism might be thought to have imposed. In the light of his recent undertakings, it is clear that at no time did Gregotti

think to limit himself to historically prescribed models. There was nothing of the Gothic Revival spirit in his conception of Neo-Liberty, and none of his work shows any sign of slavish imitation, of pastiche. The creative vigor in all his work would have pushed him beyond such limitations even if pure revivalism had ever been his aim.

No discussion of Gregotti can ignore his undoubted achievement of a unity of theory and practice, however precarious, which informs all his work alike, including his most committed book to date, *Territorio dell'Architettura*; the Zen Housing Development, Cardillo, Palermo; the Community Centre at Gibelina in Sicily, which occupied him through the 1970s; the new university at Cosenza and new buildings for the University at Florence; and, of course, his many activities as an editor.

—Toni del Renzio

# GREIMAN, April

American graphic, environmental, and poster designer

Born: Rockville Center, New York, 22 March 1948. Education: Kansas City Art Institute, Missouri, BFA, 1970; studied under Armin Hofmann and Wolfgang Weingart, at the Allgemeine Kunstgewerbeschule, Basel, 1970-71. Career: Freelance graphic designer, working for The Architects Collaborative, Boston, Museum of Modern Art, New York, and Anspach/Grossman/Portugal, New York, 1971-75; established April Greiman Associates, Los Angeles, California, from 1976; design clients include A&M Records, Aldus Software, AND Interactive, Apple Computer, Benetton, CBS Broadcasting, Center for Creative Imaging, Citicorp Partners, Esprit, Fox Television, Knoll International, Lifetime Television, Limbex Corporation, Los Angeles Olympics, LUX Pictures, MCI Telecommunications, Museum of Contemporary Art (Los Angeles), Museum of Applied Arts (Vienna), Nicola Restaurant, Okamoto Corporation (Japan), Ove Arup Engineering, PacTel, Random House Publishing, ROTO Architects, Inc., Southern California Institute of Architecture, The Gap, Time/Life Corp., U.S. Postal Service, Warner Brothers, Xerox Corporation, and others. Assistant professor of design, Philadelphia College of Art, 1971-75; design instructor, Otis/Parsons Art Institute, Los Angeles, from 1982; director, Program in Visual Communications, California Institute of the Arts, from 1983. Jury member, AIGA Communications Graphics competition (chairperson), 1993, City of Berlin Graphic Identity Competition, 1993, and Netherlands Design Competition, 1995. Lecturer at universities and corporations around the world. Member: American Institute of Graphic Arts; Society of Typographic Arts. Exhibitions: Philadelphia College of Art, 1974; Meghan Williams Gallery, Los Angeles, 1978, University of California at Los Angeles, 1979; Tokyo Gallery, Japan, 1979; Rhode Island School of Design, Providence, 1979; *April Greiman/Michael Graves,* Northern Illinois University, DeKalb, 1982; *April Greiman/Jayme Odgers/Chris Garland,* Kent State University, Ohio, 1983; Kansas City Art Institute, Missouri, 1983. *The 20th Century Poster,* Walker Art Center, Minneapolis, 1985 (toured); *April Greiman, One Woman Show,* Reinhold/Brown Gallery, New York, 1986; *April Greiman: Large Scale Posters,* 1987 (toured); *Pacific Wave,* Fortuny Museum, Venice, 1987; *April Greiman,* Israel Museum, Jerusalem, 1989; *Design USA,* United States Information Agency, travelling

April Greiman: 19th Amendment commemorative stamp, issued August 1995

exhibit in U.S.S.R., 1989; *Computer Graphics—April Greiman,* Itoya Gallery, Ginza, Tokyo, 1991; *International Poster Exhibition,* Tel Aviv Museum of Art, 1993; *April Greiman Exhibition,* Arc en Rêve, Centre d'Architecture, Bordeaux, France, 1994. **Collections:** Cooper-Hewitt Museum, New York; Walker Art Center, Minneapolis; Pratt Institute, New York; Library of Congress, Washington, D.C.; Metropolitan Museum of Art, New York; Museum of Modern Art, New York; Smithsonian Institute, Washington, D.C.; Albright-Knox Gallery; Robert Kauthammer Collection; Stampa Gallery; R. T. Livingston Collection; Gemeentemuseum, The Hague; Swiss National Print Collection; Neiman Marcus; Nakahara-Takahashi Collection; Visual Studies Workshop. **Honors:** *Taxi Project* exhibition catalogue, 1976, and *Irvin Tepper* catalogue, 1983, named to 50 Best Books of the Year; Gold Medals, 1985-1989, and Vesta Award, 1985, Art Director's Club of Los Angeles; Hallmark Fellow, Aspen Design Conference, 1987; UNESCO International Poster Contest winner, 1987; Grand Prize, *MacWorld* magazine Macintosh Masters Art Contest, 1988; named to Women in Design's *Ten Years—Women in Design* list, 1988;

Look West Award, Fashion Group International, Los Angeles, 1989; Hall Chair Fellowship, Hallmark Corporation, Kansas City, Missouri, 1989; named to American Center for Design 100, 1989, 1990; AIGA Awards, 1990, 1991; Annual Design Review Award, *ID* magazine, 1992; named to "Ten Most Influential Designers of Today" list, *How* magazine, 1993; "Der Stiftung Buchkunst Pramiert" Best Books of the World, Frankfurt, 1994; Bronze Medal for *from the edge,* Southern California Institute of Architecture, 1994. **Address:** 620 Moulton Avenue, #211, Los Angeles, California 90031, U.S.A.

**Works**

Designed graphic materials, signage, and environmental works for *The Taxi Project* exhibition, Museum of Modern Art, New York, 1976.

"Los Altos Spirit Alive," for *Los Angeles Times Calendar Magazine,* 1979.

*Spacemats,* laminated, offset printed images created with photographer Jayme Odgers and sold at Albright Knox Museum, Fiorucci, Henri Bendel, Bloomingdales, and other outlets, 1979-1981.

Poster, for 1984 Olympic Games, Los Angeles, 1984.

*L.A. Map* cultural map/poster of Los Angeles, for *Metropolitan Home* magazine, 1989.

*Graphic Design in America* billboard and poster, for Walker Art Center, Minneapolis, 1989.

*Poet's Walk Project,* for Citicorp Plaza, 1989.

*19th Amendment* postage stamp design, for U.S. Postal Service, 1995.

Magazine covers include—*Art Direction,* July 1978; *WET,* July 1979, September 1979; *IDEA,* September 1983; *Progressive Architecture,* 1983; *Los Angeles Times Calendar Magazine,* December 1984; *PC World,* February 1987; *Interiors,* June 1987; *AIGA Graphic Design,* no. 8, 1987; *HOW,* November/December 1988, April 1994; *Publish!,* May 1989; *Var Business,* 1990; *Domus,* 1993; *Aldus Magazine,* June 1994; also designed graphics and layout for *Art Forum, IDEA, McCalls, Metropolitan Home, Sports Illustrated, Time,* and others.

Environmental and interior design clients include—Carlson/Reges residence; Cerritos Center for the Performing Arts; China Club, Los Angeles; Dorland Artist Colony; Douglas Frye, Attorney; Gemini Learning Center; Nicola Restaurant; and Sasson.

## Publications

**By GREIMAN: books**—*Hybrid Imagery: The Fusion of Technology and Graphic Design,* New York, 1990; *it's notwhataprilyouthinkitgreimanis,* exhibition catalogue, Zurich, 1994; **articles**—in *Artifacts at the End of a Decade,* exhibition catalogue by Steve Watson and Carol Huebner, New York, 1980; *Kansas City Institute Magazine* (Missouri), Fall 1982.

**On GREIMAN: books**—*The 20th-Century Poster: Design of the Avant-Garde* by Dawn Ades, New York 1984; *7 Graphic Designers,* Tokyo, 1985; *April Greiman: Large Scale Posters,* exhibition catalogue, North Carolina, 1987; *New American Design* by Hugh Aldersley-Williams, New York 1988; *Women in Design,* New York, 1988; *The Modern Poster,* Mew York, 1988; *Designers on Mac,* London, 1992; *International Women in Design,* New York, 1993; *International Poster Exhibition,* exhibition catalogue, Tel Aviv, 1993; *The 100 Show,* Chicago, New York, 1994; *Cutting Edge Typography,* New York, 1995; **articles**—in *Typographische Monatsblatter* (St. Gallen), January 1975; *Anan* (Tokyo), no. 267, 1980; *Print* (New York), January 1981; *Idea* (Tokyo), no. 167, 1981, Winter 1983; *Modo* (Milan), Spring 1982; *Studio International* (London), no. 995, 1982; *Graphis* (Zurich), March/April 1983; "Women Designer of America" in *IDEA,* special issue, 1988; "April Greiman: Riding a New Wave" in *Publish!,* February 1988; "Designer's Guide to a Computer Studio" in *Print,* May/June 1988; "April Greiman Update: Tile Design" in *MacWEEK,* 31 January 1989; "A Graphic Lesson in Popularity" in *Los Angeles Times,* 5 August 1990; "April Greiman Inc." in *Electronic Studio,* March/April 1990; "April Greiman" in *Studio,* March/April, 1990; "Graphic Design in America" in *Time,* March 1990; "April Greiman Interview" in *Emigre,* no. 14, 1990; "Queen of the Mac" in *Design Week,* November/December 1990; "Mixing Business and Pleasure" in *Los Angeles Times,* 17 April 1991.

\*　　\*　　\*

April Greiman is one of a small group of graphic designers who quickly adapted to the introduction of the first Macintosh computer in 1984, evolving an appropriate aesthetic for the revolutionary new tool. Though she was trained in the logical principles and disciplined visual organization of the International Style in Switzerland, Greiman was already leading the way towards the more intuitive and complex approach of Post Modernist, or New Wave, graphics even before the Mac.

There is more continuity in that transition than we might expect. Greiman, an American, received part of her education at the Allgemeine Kunstgewerbeschule in Basle, under Wolfgang Weingart. Weingart was the most internationally influential figure in the New Wave typography of the nineteen seventies. He began teaching at Basle in 1968, two years before Greiman arrived for graduate study, and passed on to his students his desire to revitalise the functional but standardised aesthetic of Swiss design. Weingart's work in the nineteen seventies used traditional techniques to achieve greater freedom of expression, revisiting the dynamic experiments of early Modernism found in the typographic collages of the Futurists and Dadaists. He introduced elements such as layered type and images, mixed type weights and sizes within words, enlarged textures and type reversed out of rectangular bars. These were to be developed by Greiman and combined with brilliant colour, geometric shapes and spatial depth, with impressive compositional virtuosity. Greiman has said that, "Design must seduce, shape, and perhaps more importantly, evoke emotional response."

She regards colour as the most influential aspect of her work in the eighties, and has attributed her colour sense to her move, in 1976, to California, where the landscape and the light were "incredibly inspiring." In Los Angeles she produced provocative work for several high-tech companies and in 1982 became head of the graphics department at the California Institute of the Arts. She worked closely with photographer Jayme Odgers and began to collect and utilise video images in her designs. The horizontal scan lines of video were combined with found papers, enlarged colour separations and colour photocopies (with the later addition of the pixel textures of the computer). She manipulated the scale of these, combining geometric shapes reduced in scale to textures, and textures enlarged to dramatic forms. Her work created a sense of visual depth, either by overlapping elements, as in the Wet magazine cover (1979) or by dramatic perspective, seen in her poster for the 1984 Los Angeles Olympics.

Greiman's work became increasingly complex and eclectic with her use of computers in the eighties. Opposed to the reductivist simplicity of the Swiss style, she has said in interviews that she prefers to add things ("Give them all they can handle"). The resulting collages show the influence of Surrealism and Russian Constructivism, though Greiman has said that her highly personal approach, centred on symbolic meaning rather than formalism, owes more to Carl Jung's Man and his Symbols. In a 1988 Blueprint interview with Dean Morris, she stated, "I'm always in the doghouse because people say I'm an artist not a designer...I am just interested in growing, and somehow my growth has always been involved with new tools."

Personal expression and new computer tools came together with great originality in several key examples of her work in this period. Her fold-out, self-portrait, poster collage for *Design Quarterly,* "Does it Make Sense?" (1986), was a complex "tour-de-force" using the MacDraw program and exploiting then-available technology to the limit. Greiman's fascination with image technologies is also seen in the Graphic Design in America billboard for the Walker

Art Center (1989) - the US flag is seen through the development of reproduction technologies, from wood engraving through offset lithography to photography and computer manipulation. Computers also allowed her to develop her continuing interest in surface textures, as seen in the sand, sky and water in the 1988 *AIGA Annual* cover.

Her designs for textiles, architectural ceramics and restaurants, in addition to graphics, have all been natural extensions of these recurring themes of texture and pattern (whether occurring naturally or as a product of technological processes) combined with brilliant, highly decorative colour and a concern with spatial perception.

Greiman has recounted being introduced to the Macintosh computer in a department store; she saw its significance immediately. In her book, *Hybrid Imagery* (1990) she describes digital technology as the converging of image technologies" into a common language, a single integrated creative environment." The title of her book refers to this integration of digital technologies with traditional techniques, a revolution that is transforming design and media. The breadth and interdisciplinarity of Greiman's approach to her work is ideally suited to the resulting freedom: "to feel lost is great", she says, and "nothing is ever finished."

In *Hybrid Imagery*, Eric Martin has said of digital language: "A word is a color is a sound is a movement. The new significant media are hybrids. The age of the specialist is being replaced by the age of the dedicated generalist." This is revitalising discourse about graphic design and transforming its professional practice. In interviews, Greiman has decried Swiss graphics as the language of big business, telling everyone what to do, while condemning the design press for being obsessed with "style wars." Such attitudes, expressions of traditional design concerns with control and superficial visual sophistication, are an inadequate foundation for serious discussion of the cultural complexity created by new tools and hybrid media. Interactivity, sound and motion are becoming increasingly important considerations for designers following pioneers like Greiman, as their orderly, print-based world of is being transformed into a multi-media, many-to-many communications environment.

—Michael Large

# GRÈS, Madame

French fashion designer

**Born:** Germain "Alix" Barton in Paris, 1903. **Education:** Studied painting and sculpture, Paris; apprenticed in Premet fashion house, Paris, 1931-33. **Family:** Married the painter Serge Czerefkov (divorced); daughter: Anne. **Career:** Established own dress pattern design and cutting business, under the name Alix Barton, in Rue Miromesnil, Paris; designer, then director, Maison Alix fashion house, in the Faubourg Saint-Honore, Paris, 1934-42; director, Grès Couture (after husband's pseudonym "Grès"), in the Rue de la Paix, Paris, from 1942; accessory line introduced, 1976; ready-to-wear line introduced, 1980; retired, 1988. Perfumes include: *Cabochard,* 1959, *Grès pour Homme,* 1965, *Qui Pro Quo,* 1976, *Eau de Grès,* 1980, *Alix,* 1981, *Grès Nonsieu,* 1982, and *Cabotine de Grès,* 1990. Also film costume designer in the 1930s. President, Chambre Syndicale de la Couture Parisienne, Paris, 1972. **Exhibitions:** *Fashion: An Anthology,* Victoria and Albert Museum, London, 1971; *The 10s, 20s, and 30s,* Metropolitan Museum of Art,

New York, 1974; *Franzosisches Kunslhandwerk Heute,* Overstolzenhaus, Cologne, 1981; *Madame Grès,* Metropolitan Museum of Art, New York, 1994. **Honors:** Chevalier de la Legion d'Honneur, France, 1947; Dé d'Or Award, 1976; New York University Creative Leadership in the Arts Award, 1978. **Died:** the South of France, 24 November 1993 (death not made public until December 1994).

**Publications**

**On GRÈS: books—***Paris Couturiers and Milliners* by Alice K. Perkins, New York, 1949; *Always in Vogue* by Edna Woolman Chase and Ilka Chase, London, 1954; *Dressmakers of France* by Mary Brooks Picken and Dora Loues Miller, New York, 1956; *Kings of Fashion* by Anny Latour, Stuttgart, 1956, London, 1958; *In My Fashion* by Bettina Ballard, London, 1960; *Fashion: An Anthology by Cecil Beaton,* exhibition catalogue compiled by Madeleine Ginsburg, London, 1971; *Couture: An Illustrated History of the Great Paris Designers and Their Creations* edited by Ruth Lynam, New York, 1972; *In Vogue: Sixty Years of Celebrities and Fashion* edited by Georgina Howell, London, 1975, 1978, New York, 1976; *The World of Fashion: People, Places, Resources* by Eleanor Lambert, New York, and London, 1976; *Inventive Paris Clothes 1909-1939* by Diana Vreeland, New York and London, 1977; *The History of Haute Couture 1850-1950* by Diana de Marly, London, 1980; *McDowell's Directory of Twentieth Century Fashion* by Colin McDowell, London, 1984; *Couture: The Great Designers* by Caroline Milbank Rennolds, New York, 1985; *The Encyclopaedia of Fashion from 1840 to the 1980s* by Georgina O'Hara, London, 1986; *Women of Fashion: Twentieth-Century Designers* by Valerie Steele, New York, 1991; Petit Précis de Mode: Collections du Musée de la Mode, Marseilles, 1992; *Madame Grès,* exhibition catalogue by Richard Martin and Harold Koda, New York, 1994; **articles—** "Grès Grey Eminence" in *Realities* (San José, California), July 1965; "Mme. Grès" in *Current Biography* (New York), January 1980; "Mme. Grès, Hélène de Paris" in *Jardin des Modes* (Paris), December/January 1980-81; "The Timeless Fashions of Madame Grès" by Pascale Villiers le Moy in *Connoisseur,* January 1985; "Lovely Grès" by Françoise Sciaky in *American Fabrics and Fashions* (New York), No. 128, 1983; "Mme. Grès for the People" in *Connoisseur,* January 1985; "How Madame Grès Sculpts with Fabric" by Arlene Cooper in *Threads* (Newtown, Connecticut), April/May 1987; "The Ionic Woman" in *Harper's Bazaar* (New York), September 1994; "Eminence Grès" by Eve Auchincloss in *Town & Country* (New York), September 1994; "Mme. Grès" by Silvana Bernasconi in *Vogue* (Italy), March 1994; "New York: Grès Gardens" in *Women's Wear Daily* (New York), 1 November 1994; "La Mort confisquée de Madame Grès" by Laurence Benaim in *Le Monde* (Paris), 13 December 1994; "The Strange, Secret Death of Madame Grès" by Godfrey Deeny in *Women's Wear Daily* (New York), 14 December 1994; "Surprising the Fashion World, to the Last" by Amy M. Spindler in the *New York Times,* 14 December 1994; "Grès Eminence" by Jane Mulvagh in *Vogue* (London), May 1995.

\*      \*      \*

The white salon with drawn shades seems to defy time and change. There is no blaring music, there are no gimmicks, nothing to detract from the clothes themselves. Madame Grès lived for her clothes and had no interest in herself. She conducted a love affair with fabric, knowing how each one fell and what each would or would not do. All her designs started on the body with the reality of the fabric on a moving form, not in abstract drawings. While she maintained a careful approach to mainstream fashion following a dominant line and despising extreme subfashions, her most famous range was composed of her changeless, Grecian evening dresses. Here, Grès was supreme, the most famous exponent of drapery. No matter what ornate fantasies other designers create, these classical gowns stand on Olympus, for as the Duchesse d'Orleans remarked, Grès seemed to design for Greek goddesses. The simplicity of these dresses comes as close to timelessness as any human being can achieve. Although they were a standard form, such was Grès's invention that each year produced new variations on the theme. They could be white or in two tones of blue or in contrasting black and cerise. After all, the ancient Greeks did colour their statues; the neo-Classical movement was wrong in thinking everything Greek had to be marble-white.

Grès grew up under Art Deco influence, and this streamlined simplicity conditioned her own approach. Her clothes were sculptural; her early ambition was to be a sculptor. Her shapes were pure because she was a technician. As precise as an engineer, late in her life she still did some sewing herself, and also manipulated the folds to produce that faultless fall of fabric. The purity of perfection was the only standard Grès allowed. Every museum with a costume collection would like to be given a Grès gown, for she was regarded as the greatest exponent of her art.

Grès, being the consummate artist as opposed to the couturière in step with the fashion of the day, shunned ready-to-wear for years until the 1980s, when she opened herself to its possibilities.

—Diana de Marly

# GRIGNANI, Franco

Italian painter, photographer, architect, graphic, and industrial designer

**Born:** Pieve Porto Morone, Pavia, 4 February 1908. **Education:** Educated at the Istituto Tecnico and Liceo Scientifico, Pavia, until 1926; studied architecture at the Politecnico, Turin, 1929-33. **Military Service:** Served in the Italian Army Artillery, 1939-43, Lieutenant. **Family:** Married Jeanne Michot in 1942; daughters: Daniela and Manuela. **Career:** Independent painter, photographer, and designer, Milan, from 1932; art director, *Belleza d'Italia* magazine, Milan, 1948-60, Alfieri e Lacroix printers, Milan, from 1952, and *Pubblicita in Italia* yearbook, Milan, 1956-82. Participated in the second Futurist movement, Milan, in the 1930s; founder-member, Gruppo Exhibition Design, Milan, 1969. Instructor in visual design, Nuova Accademia di Belle Arti, Milan, from 1979. Italian section president, Alliance Graphique Internationale, 1969-81. **Member:** Alliance Graphique Internationale; International Center of Typographic Art. **Exhibitions:** Galleria delle Tre Arti, Milan, 1934; Paris EXPO, 1937; Libreria Salto, Milan, 1958, 1960; Libreria Comunale, Milan, 1958; Normandy House STA Gallery, Chicago, 1960; Centro Culturale Pirelli, Milan, 1967; 500D Gallery, Chicago, 1970; Biennale di Venezia, Venice, 1972; Palazzo Reale, Milan, 1972; Museo Rotonda Besana, Milan, 1975; Museo de Bellas Artes, Caracas, 1977; Salone Comunale, Reggio Emilia, 1979; Galleria

Flaviana, Locarno, 1981; Lorenzelli Arte, Milan, 1981; Massalubrense come Arles, Naples, 1982; *Photo-graphica di Franco Grignani,* Palestra Civica, Pieve Porto Morone (Pavia), 1983; Galleria Quanta, Milan, 1984; Quentin Gallery, Perth, Australia, 1984; Galleria Il Salotto, Como, 1985; Galleria Koh·I.Noor, Milan, 1986; *Visual Design Exhibition,* Galleria Municipale di La Salle, Val d'Aosta, 1987; *La Realtà Ambigua, Mostra Documentaria 1928/ 1988,* Galleria Arte Struktura, Milan, 1988; Galleria Lorenzelli Arte, Milan, 1988; Museo di Arte Contemporanea, Genoa, 1990; Galleria Arte Struktura, Milan, 1991, 1995; *Il Futurismo a Milano tra le due guerre,* Palazzo Reale, 1992; *Bauhus e Razionalismo,* Galleria Fonte d'Abisso, Milan, 1994; Galleria EIDOS, Asti, 1994, 1995; *La sindrome di Leonardo,* Palazzina di caccia dello Juvara a Stupinigi, Turin, 1995; Graphic Design Galleria AIAP, Milan, 1995; Biennale di San Paulo, Brazil, 1995. **Collections:** Galleria Civica del Comune, Modena; Poster Museum, Warsaw; Stedelijk Museum, Amsterdam; Museum of Modern Art, New York; Victoria and Albert Museum, London. **Honors:** Grand Prize, 1951, Gold Medal, 1957, Milan Triennale; Gold Medal for Publicity and Advertising, Milan, 1954; Palma d'Oro, Italy, 1959; Il Ponte Group Silver Lion Award, Venice, 1962; honorary member, Society of Typographic Arts, Chicago, 1967; G. Puecher Gold Medal, Milan, 1974; Certified as Ambassador, 1993, and EURO Design Award, 1994, International Trademark Center; honorary member, American Center of Design, Chicago. **Address:** Via Bianca di Savoia 7, 20122 Milan, Italy.

## Works

Two gold necklaces, for Palazzo Strozzi, 1980.
Book design for *Samburu* (Kenia), for Edizione Moneta, Milan, 1980.
Publication and cover design, for *Pubblicita in Italia* annual, Milan, 1981, 1982.
Illustrated tables for *Simmetrie infrante nella scienza e nell'arte,* for Ediz. Clup, Milan, 1983.
Drawings for "Arte e Design" by Marchio Mulinetto in *Il Sole/24 Ore/24 Ore,* Milan, 1984.
Magazine design for *Interarte* no. 29, Bologna, 1987.
Book design for *The Dynamics of Ambiguity* (Giuseppe Caglioti), for Springer-Verlag, Germany, 1992.
Calendar, for A. T. Sistem, 1992.
*The Butterfly of Las Vegas* gold jewelry design, for the city of Arezzo, Italy, 1995.
Symbol for HOSPICE, 1995.

## Publications

**By GRIGNANI: books**—*107 Grafici dell'AGI,* exhibition catalogue with text by Renzo Zorzi, Venice, 1974; *Franco Grignani: Art and Graphics* edited by Willy Rotzler, Zürich, 1983; *Iperbolicità Comunicare le forme dell'eccesso e dell'assurdo,* Rome, 1986; *5 diagonali iperboliche: Franco Grignani,* exhibition catalogue, Milan, 1988; **articles**—in *Linea Grafica* (Milan), 1963, no. 3, 1970, no. 5, 1972, no. 1, 1973; *Graphis* (Zürich), no. 108, 1963; *Print* (New York), January/February 1964; *Soli* (Turin), no. 4, 1967; *Design* (Bergamo), no. 3, 1974; *IBM Review/Italy* (Milan), no. 4, 1976; *European Trademarks and Logotypes* (special issue of *IDEA* magazine, Tokyo), 1980-81; "Signs and Symbol" in *IDEA* (Tokyo), no. 223, 1990.

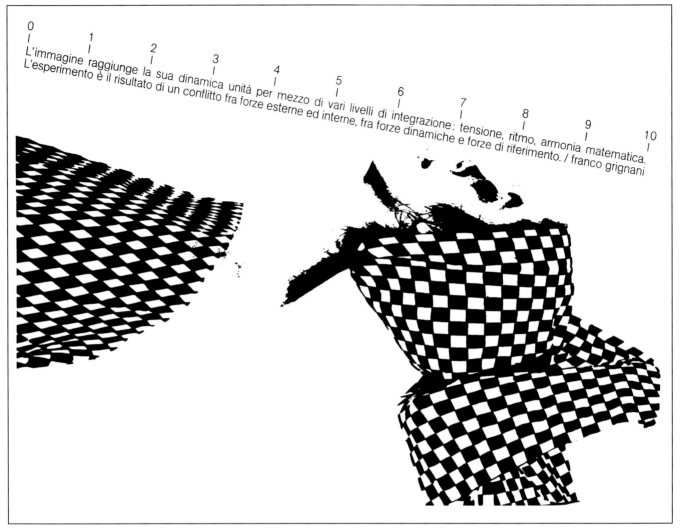

Franco Grignani: experimental poster of VISUAL DESIGN, 1983

On GRIGNANI: books—*Layout* by Raymond A. Ballinger, New York, 1956; *Die neue Grafik/The New Graphic Design* by Karl Gerstner and Markus Kutter, Teufen and London, 1959; *Who's Who in Graphic Art* edited by Walter Amstutz, Zürich, 1962, Dubendorf, 1982; *Franco Grignani* by Giulio Carlo Argan, Milan, 1967; *Franco Grignani: Graphic Designer in Europe,* Tokyo, 1971; *Franco Grignani: El Sentido de una Larga Busqueda* by Giulio Carlo Argan, Caracas, 1977; *Franco Grignani: Il Segno come Matrice* by Giuseppe Turroni, Milan, 1978; *Mostra Antologica di Franco Grignani,* exhibition catalogue by Bruno D'Amore and Giuseppe Berti, Reggio Emilia, 1979; *Typography Today: 65 Designers of the 20th Century* by *IDEA* magazine, Tokyo, 1980; *Contemporary Photographers,* Chicago and London, 1988; *World Graphic Design Now,* Tokyo, 1988; *20th Century Type* by Lewis Blackwell, London, 1992; *Logo World* edited by Paul Ibou, Belgium, 1994; *Franco Grignani: Linguaggio per un epoca a cura* by G. Schermi, Rome, 1994; *Arte e Scienza* by Barilli, Caglioti, Dorfles, and Fagone, Nuore, 1994; *Fotografia Italiana dal 1900 ad oggi* by Itale Zannier, Modena, 1995; *Franco Grignani: Progetti grafici e comunicazione visiva,* exhibition catalogue, Milan, 1995; *The 100 Best Posters of the World,* Tokyo, 1995; **articles**—"Fisica quantistica e Design con fenomenologie di Franco Grignani" in *Il Giornale* (Milan), 1982; "L'inimmaginabile" by Giuseppe Turroni in *Il Giornale* (Milan), 1983; "Quando il disordine serve ad informare. Citazioni sul lavoro di Franco Grignani" by Gillo Dorfles in *Corriere della Sera,* 1984; "Tra Scienza e Technologia" by Carmele Strano in *Il Sole/24 Ore* (Milan), 1985; "Franco Grignani: Un dialogo col colore che dura da sessant'anni" by Carlo Franza in *Il Giornale* (Milan), 1989; "I Grandi Fotografi" by Alberto Piovani in *Progresso Fotografico,* 1980; *IDEA* (Tokyo), no. 223, 1990; "Franco Grignani: Il Vero Immaginario" in *Il Sole/24 Ore* (Milan), 1995.

*

Given that all my activities, covering some decades, have been directed towards experiment and research in graphic communication, using technical knowledge and scientific methods for a broad investigation of visual phenomena, it is clear that what interested me was the existential problems of our technological civilization taken "to the physical limits of the human eye." From this basic starting point, I proceeded to a long and complex accumulation of optical-visual experiments, which revealed to me the importance of reality changed by tensions and distortions, a "skidding" of the pictures, overcoming the mental and visual inertia so as to break down concrete optics.

For these reasons, my graphic designs always have an aesthetic content, in order to give the viewer room for mental manoeuvre. And the graphic symbol, never inert and passive, acquires a decisiveness by breaking down the bastions of custom so as to constitute an aesthetic training for a social culture and an individual intellectual liberation.

Where there exists beauty there can be no wastage of the values; basing myself on this assertion, I seek in symbolical forms a vitality and an influence that makes the eye of the viewer a participant through a challenge to the surrounding world, in a time that creates certainties and can no longer be overtaken and overcome in imagination.

—Franco Grignani

# GROT, Anton

Polish-American film designer

**Born:** Antocz Frantiszek Groszewski, in Kelbasin, Poland, 18 January 1884; emigrated to the United States in 1909. **Education:** Studied illustration and design, at the School of Art, Krakow, and at the Technische Hochschule, Königsberg, Germany. **Career:** Set designer, for Sigmund Lubin Manufacturing Company, Philadelphia, 1913-17, for Blache, 1917-18, and for Pathe, in New Jersey, 1918-21; designed for directors Louis Gasnier, 1918-19, George B. Seitz, 1919-21, and George Fitzmaurice, 1920-22; designer for Fairbanks/Pickford films, for United Artists, Hollywood, 1922, and for Cecil B. DeMille films, Hollywood, 1922-27; art director, Warner Brothers Films, 1927-48; retired, to concentrate on painting, Los Angeles, 1948-74. **Collection:** University of California at Los Angeles. **Honors:** Special Academy Award, 1940. **Died:** Los Angeles, California, 21 March 1974.

## Works

Film designs include—*The Mouse and the Lion* (Brooks), 1913; *Arms and the Woman* (Fitzmaurice), 1916; *The Recoil* (Fitzmaurice), 1917; *The Iron Heart* (Fitzmaurice), 1917; *The Seven Pearls* (Mackenzie), 1917; *The Naulahka* (Fitzmaurice), 1918; *Sylvia of the Secret Service* (Fitzmaurice), 1918; *Bound and Gagged* (Seitz), 1919; *Pirate Gold* (Seitz), 1920; *Velvet Fingers* (Seitz), 1920; *Robin Hood* (Dwan), 1922; *Tess of the Storm Country* (Robertson), 1922; *Dorothy Vernon of Haddon Hall* (Neilan), 1924; *The Thief of Baghdad* (Walsh), 1924; *A Thief in Paradise* (Fitzmaurice), 1924; *Don Q, Son of Zorro* (Crisp), 1925; *The Road to Yesterday* (DeMille), 1925; *The Volga Boatman* (DeMille), 1926; *Silence* (Julian), 1926; *Young April* (Crisp), 1926; *White Gold* (Howard), 1927; *Vanity* (Crisp), 1927; *The Little Adventuress* (W. DeMille), 1927; *The Country Doctor* (Julian), 1927; *The King of Kings* (DeMille), 1927; *Stand and Deliver* (Crisp), 1928; *Hold 'em Yale* (E. Griffith), 1928; *The Blue Danube* (Sloane), 1928; *Walking Back* (Julian), 1928; *A Ship Comes In* (Howard), 1928, *The Godless Girl* (DeMille), 1928; *The Barker* (Fitzmaurice), 1928; *Show Girl* (Santell), 1928; *Noah's Ark* (Curtiz), 1928; *Why Be Good?* (Seiter), 1929; *Smiling Irish Eyes* (Seiter), 1929; *The Man and the Moment* (Fitzmaurice), 1929; *Her Private Life* (A. Korda), 1929; *Footlights and Fools* (Seiter), 1929; *Lilies of the Field* (A. Korda), 1930; *Playing Around* (LeRoy), 1930; *No, No, Nanette* (Badger), 1930; *A Notorious Affair* (Bacon), 1930; *Song of the Flame* (Crosland), 1930; *Bright Lights* (Curtiz), 1930; *Top Speed* (LeRoy), 1930; *Outward Bound* (Milton), 1930; *Little Caesar* (LeRoy), 1930; *Body and Soul* (Santell), 1931; *Svengali* (Mayo), 1931; *Heartbreak* (Werker), 1931; *Honour of the Family* (Bacon), 1931; *The Mad Genius* (Curtiz), 1931; *Surrender* (Howard), 1931; *One Way Passage* (Garnett), 1931; *Big City Blues* (LeRoy), 1931; *The Hatchet Man* (Wellman), 1932; *Alias the Doctor* (Curtiz), 1932; *Two Seconds* (LeRoy), 1932; *Doctor X* (Curtiz), 1932; *The Match King* (Bretherton/ Keighley), 1932; *Scarlet Dawn* (Dieterle), 1932; *Lawyer Man* (Dieterle), 1932; *20,000 Years in Sing Sing* (Curtiz), 1932; *Mystery of the Wax Museum* (Curtiz), 1933; *Grand Slam* (Dieterle), 1933; *The King's Vacation* (Adolfi), 1933; *Gold Diggers of 1933* (LeRoy), 1933; *Baby Face* (Green), 1933; *Ever in My Heart* (Mayo), 1933; *From Headquarters* (Dieterle), 1933; *Footlight Parade* (Bacon), 1933; *Son of a Sailor* (Bacon), 1933; *Easy to Love* (Keighley), 1933; *Mandalay* (Curtiz), 1934; *Gambling Lady* (Mayo), 1934; *Upperworld* (Del Ruth), 1934; *He Was Her Man* (Bacon), 1934; *Dr. Monica* (Keighley), 1934; *The Firebird* (Dieterle), 1934; *Side Streets* (Green), 1934; *British Agent* (Curtiz), 1934; *Six Day Bike Rider* (Bacon), 1934; *The Secret Bride* (Dieterle), 1934; *Gold Diggers of 1935* (Berkeley), 1934; *Red Hot Tires* (Lederman), 1935; *The Florentine Dagger* (Florey), 1935; *Travelling Saleslady* (Enright), 1935; *The Case of the Curious Bride* (Curtiz), 1935; *Stranded* (Borzage), 1935; *Broadway Gondolier* (Bacon), 1935; *Bright Lights* (Berkeley), 1935; *Dr. Socrates* (Dieterle), 1935; *A Midsummer Night's Dream* (Reinhardt/Dieterle), 1935; *Captain Blood* (Curtiz), 1935; *The Golden Arrow* (Green), 1936; *The White Angel* (Dieterle), 1936; *Anthony Adverse* (LeRoy), 1936; *Stolen Holiday* (Curtiz), 1936; *Sing Me a Love Song* (Enright), 1936; *The Life of Emile Zola* (Dieterle), 1937; *Tovarich* (Litvak), 1937; *Confession* (May), 1937; *The Great Garrick* (Whale), 1937; *Fools for Scandal* (LeRoy), 1938; *Hard to Get* (Enright), 1938; *They Made Me A Criminal* (Berkeley), 1939; *Juarez* (Dieterle), 1939; *The Private Lives of Elizabeth and Essex* (Curtiz), 1939; *The Sea Hawk* (Curtiz), 1940; *A Dispatch from Reuters* (Dieterle), 1940; *The Sea Wolf* (Curtiz), 1941; *Affectionately Yours* (Bacon), 1941; *Thank Your Lucky Stars* (Butler), 1943; *The Conspirators* (Negulesco), 1944; *Rhapsody in Blue* (Rapper), 1945; *Mildred Pierce* (Curtiz), 1945; *My Reputation* (Bernhardt), 1946; *One More Tomorrow* (Godfrey), 1946; *Never Say Goodbye* (Kern), 1946; *Deception* (Rapper), 1946; *Nora Prentiss* (V. Sherman), 1947; *The Two Mrs. Carrolls* (Godfrey), 1947; *Possessed* (Bernhardt), 1947; *The Unsuspected* (Curtiz), 1947; *Romance on the High Seas* (Curtiz), 1948; *June Bride* (Windust), 1948; *One Sunday Afternoon* (Walsh), 1948; *Backfire* (V. Sherman), 1948.

## Publications

**On GROT: books**—*Filmlexicon degli Autore delle Opere,* 7 vols., edited by Michele de La-calamita and others, Rome, 1958; *One Reel a Week* by Fred J. Balshofer and Arthur C. Miller, Berkeley, 1967; *Le Decor de Film* by Leon Barsacq, Paris, 1970, as *Caligari's*

*Cabinet and Other Grand Illusions,* Boston, 1976; *The Hollywood Exiles* by John Baxter, London, 1976; *The Warner Brothers Story* by Clive Hirschhorn, New York, 1979; *The International Dictionary of Films and Filmmakers,* Chicago and London, 1987, 1991.

\*     \*     \*

Anton Grot's special Academy Award in 1940 for his invention of a "ripple machine", which created weather and light effects on water, perhaps symbolizes his particular interest in the expressive qualities of light in motion pictures. Of all the major designers working in Hollywood in the 1930s, Grot was among those whose work was most strongly affected by European modernism in films and painting. The angular shadows and strong, light-and-dark contrast found in *Little Caesar,* for example, help to establish the underworld context of the film. In the pressbook for *Doctor X* (a Technicolor film), Grot explained how he used heavy construction, low arches, dark colors, and shadows to create a mood of mystery and melodrama: "We design a set that imitates as closely as possible a bird of prey about to swoop down upon its victim, trying to incorporate in the whole thing a sense of impending calamity, of overwhelming danger." Similar expressive qualities are found, particularly in scenes of danger or terror, in the melodramatic swashbucklers Grot designed, such as *Captain Blood* (1935), *The Private Lives of Elizabeth and Essex* (1939), and *The Sea Hawk* (1940). In his designs for "The Forgotten Man" production number in *The Gold Diggers of 1933,* Grot cast jagged shadows on the women who sing of their forgotten men, and in the finale of the song, he silhouetted unemployed veterans marching ceaselessly over a machine like a series of curved bridges. Using traditional and natural forms freely in *A Midsummer Night's Dream* (1935), Grot created such memorable images as the entrance of Oberon, king of the fairies, crowned with a spiky headdress, and wearing a sparkling black cloak that sweeps for many yards behind the horse on which he is riding.

Grot's use of stylistic qualities of twentieth-century European art no doubt derived in part from his Polish background, yet this interest parallels that of contemporary American painters such as John Marin, Charles Burchfield, and Georgia O'Keeffe. Just as the abstract qualities found in the paintings of these artists is crucial to the success of their works, so, too, Grot's film designs can be seen as combinations of realistic details built upon abstract formal qualities, particularly those of light and shadow.

—Floyd W. Martin

# GROTELL, Maija

American ceramics, glass, and product designer

**Born:** Helsinki, Finland, in 1899; emigrated to the United States, 1927. **Education:** Studied painting, sculpture, and design, at the Central School of Industrial Art, Helsinki, including graduate studies in ceramics. **Career:** Worked as a draughtsman and textile designer for the National Museum of Finland, Helsinki, until 1926; freelance ceramics and industrial designer, in New York and Michigan, 1927-73. Instructor in ceramics, Henry Street Crafts School, New York, 1929-38, and at the School of Ceramic Engineering, Rutgers University, New Brunswick, New Jersey, 1936-38; direc-

tor of the department of ceramics, Cranbrook Academy of Art, Bloomfield Hills, Michigan, 1938-67. **Exhibitions:** Museum of Contemporary Crafts, New York, 1963, 1968; Cranbrook Academy of Art, Bloomfield Hills, Michigan, 1967. **Collections:** Museum of Contemporary Crafts, New York; Metropolitan Museum of Art, New York; Detroit Institute of Arts, Michigan; Art Institute of Chicago; Cleveland Museum of Art, Ohio; Cranbrook Academy of Art, Bloomfield Hills, Michigan. **Honors:** International Exposition Award, Barcelona, 1929; Paris Salon Medal, 1937; Syracuse Museum Award, New York, 1936, 1946, 1949; Detroit Institute of Art Award, 1955; Charles F. Binns Medal, Alfred University, New York, 1961; Founders Medal, Cranbrook Academy of Art, 1964. **Died:** 1973.

## Publications

**On GROTELL: books**—*The Art of Interior Design* by Victoria Kloss Ball, New York, 1960; *Objects: USA* by Lee Nordness, London and New York, 1970; *Twentieth Century Design: Glass* by Frederick Cooke, London, 1986; **articles**—in *Craft Horizons* (New York), September 1968, November 1969, February 1974, February 1977.

\*     \*     \*

Maija Grotell's experimentation in ceramic surface decoration contributed to the creation of the modern American ceramic esthetic, which views clay as an expressive medium. In her constant experimentation with glaze effects, she rediscovered the beauty and subtlety of ancient Oriental glazes, such as copper red, gun metal, and ash, and found substitutions for toxic glaze ingredients, such as chrome and iron for uranium to produce bright oranges. During the 1940s and 1950s, when little information on glazes had been published (except for industrial use), Grotell and some of her peers, including Glen Lukens, Marguerite Wildenhain, and Gertrude and Otto Natzler, revolutionized the ceramic surface by experimenting with rough, textured effects, including bubble and crater glazes and deep, rich colors. Grotell further transformed the surface by making pronounced finger ridges during throwing and by applying sparse, glaze-resist patterns, which emphasized raw clay as a painterly field. For most of her career she concentrated on spherical and cylindrical vessel shapes—heavy, fluid volumes which formed the basis for decoration. Her work of this period was covered with geometric and organic motifs, which she used in abstract patterning of planes, lines, and angles compatible with the scale and proportions of the host vessel. This work achieved international recognition for its simplicity and presence, as well as its statement of the dynamic personality of its maker.

Grotell's teaching methods strongly influenced ceramic instruction in the United States. She rejected the prevailing structured approach of Arthur Baggs, Myrtle French, and others, championing instead the teaching of productive thought. Her own independent investigations into ceramic surfaces, textures, and patterns challenged the next generation of potters to push further the plastic value of the medium. The ceramics department which she created at Cranbrook Academy is considered one of the nation's finest, and many of her students went on to become noted ceramists, among them Toshiko Takaezu, John Glick, and Richard DeVore.

Grotell's work brought international recognition to the American artist potter; she is considered responsible for an important philosophic shift in the emphasis from pottery as functional household necessity to pottery as sculpture with esthetic merit.

—Sarah Bodine

# GURAWSKI, Jerzy

Polish architect and stage designer

**Born:** Lwow, 4 September 1935. **Education:** Educated at schools in Lwow, Katowice, and Bielsko, 1942-54; studied architecture, Technical University, Kraków, M.Arch., 1961. **Family:** Married Teresa Pankow in 1963; children: Wojtek and Bartek. **Career:** Architect of the Laboratory Theatre, in Opole and Wroclaw, 1961-70; designer in the State Architecture Offices, in Opole and Poznań, since 1962. Instructor in architecture, Technical University, Poznań, since 1974. Chairman of the Poznań Jury Council, from 1976, and Coordination Council Member, from 1980, SARP Association of Polish Architects. **Exhibitions:** *15th Anniversary of Polish Scenography,* Palace of Culture, Warsaw, 1962; *Quadriennale Scenografii,* Prague, 1971; *Moderne polsk scenografi,* Kunstindustrimuseet, Oslo, 1971; *Modern Polish Scenography,* Vienna, 1972; *Theatre of Nations,* Nancy, France, 1984. **Honors:** First Prize, Touring Theatre Competition, Association of Polish Architects, 1959; Gold Medal, *Quadriennale of Scenography,* Prague, 1971. **Address:** ul. Bonin 26/9, 60-658 Poznań, Poland.

## Works

Skansen Museum, Silesia, 1964-70.
City Library, Opole, 1970.
Mountain Resort Guest House, Glucholazy, 1970-75.
Nursery Building, Opole, 1972-77.
Roman Catholic Church and School, Glogow, 1980-89.
Hospital and Clinic, Poznań, 1981-85.
Roman Catholic Church, Leszno, 1981-89.
New University complex, Poznań, 1981-89.
Students' Hostel, Poznań, 1982-85.
Twin Tower Church, Zielona Gora, 1985.
Excavated Basilica Cathedral Church, Gorzow, 1987.
Hospice, Monastery and Workshop reconstruction, Glogow, 1987.
Museum and Educational Pavilion in the Botanical Gardens, Poznań, 1988.
Stage designs include—*Siakantula,* Theatre Laboratory, Opole/Kraków/Wroclaw, 1960; *Dziady,* Theatre Laboratory, Opole/Wroclaw, 1961; *Kordian,* Theatre Laboratory, Opole/Kraków, 1962; *Akropolis,* Theatre Laboratory, Opole, 1962; *Tragical History of Dr. Faustus,* Theatre Laboratory, Opole, 1963; *Principe Constante,* Theatre Laboratory, Opole, 1964; *Duke the Unbroken,* Theatre Art Research Institute, Wroclaw, 1965; *Bertha the Fat,* Juliusz Slowacki Theatre, Kraków, 1980; *Phaedra,* Second Wroclaw Studio, 1986.

## Publications

**By GURAWSKI: books**—(with others) *Design of the New University,* Poznań, 1978; **articles**—"On Ethnographic Parks Planning" in *Ethnographic Review* (Opole, Poland), no. 22-24, 1970; (with others) "About the Corridor," in *Architektura* (Warsaw) no. 393, 1979; (with others) "Designing of Medium-Sized City Centres," in *Miasto* (Warsaw), no. 4, 1979; "Marian Fikus and Jerzy Gurawski," interview in *Architektura* (Warsaw), no. 407, 1982; "Gurawski on Grotowski," interview with Monika Kuc, in *Kultura* (Warsaw), March 1988.

**On GURAWSKI: books**—*Polska plastyka teatralna* by Z. Strzelecki, Warsaw and New York, 1963; *Toward a Poor Theatre* by Jerzy Grotowski, Holstebro, Denmark, 1968; *Kierunki scenografii wspolczesnej* by Strzelecki, Kraków, 1970; *Scenic Revolutions of the 20th Century* by Denis Bablet, Paris, 1975, Warsaw, 1980; *Grotowski e jego Laboratorium* by Z. Osinski, Warsaw, 1980; *Wspolczesna scenografia polska* by Strzelecki, Warsaw, 1983; **articles**—"Scenographie nouvelle" by Jacques Polieri in *Aujourd'hui art et architecture* (Paris), no. 42-43, 1963; "Architect in the Theatre Laboratory" in *Dialog* (Warsaw), May 1984.

*

Theatre—Kraków, 1956-60—a breath of fresh air after Stalinism. Lively movement of the theatrical avant-garde inspired my interests in the variability of the scenic space. First, two theatre designs came into being—the "circular" theatre and "variable audience" theatre competition, the former of which was my diploma design. Then, in 1960, I met Jerzy Grotowski; confrontation of our views resulted in cooperation. The ten scenic spaces that I worked out for his stagings between 1960 and 1974 I regard as my most important professional achievements. The influence of Grotowski's unique personality on intensifying my search for the roots of form has proved essential—in the fields of both theatre and architectural design.

I have been looking for archetypes of form and its place in the time and culture of both region and nation. The direction of my research was the transposition into our time of those historical forms of which the meaning and function has been preserved, both in the "micro" and "macro" scale, from theatrical space, through the forming of architecture, to large-scale urban layouts.

Putting into effect the projects for two large Roman Catholic churches in cooperation with my partner Marian Fikus, I drew largely on the rich store of forms historically connected with sacral buildings, and I attempted to transpose them into modern times, so that the spatial object reveals a logical and hierarchical wholeness—symbolizing the continuity and, simultaneously, the changeability of Time.

—Jerzy Gurawski

*   *   *

The name of Jerzy Gurawski is linked to the theatrical conception of Jerzy Grotowski's Theatre 13 Rzedow in Opole and, later, the Laboratory in Wroclaw. An architect, in contrast to all other Polish scenographers, whose foundations are in painting or color, Gurawski is a builder of theatrical space; he organizes both the activity of the actor and the perception of the spectator.

Instead of decorations on a box-like stage, he creates functional constructions in the space of the whole theatre auditorium: territories of actors and territories of spectators in a mutual relationship, different each time, depending on the point of view of a particular staging. He rejects all illusionism (painted views, imitative decorations), employing only authentic material, primarily wood not camouflaged by any painting, and authentic accessories and props (costumes are always designed by Waldemar Krygier). One can perhaps see here a convergence with the interest in the plastic arts in *objets trouvés,* found objects which manifest a similar interest in the authentic. However, one can also find in Gurawski's work a certain element of metaphor in the preference of one territory of acting over another, one world over another. Above all, he continues and realizes twentieth-century dreams, as he turns back from the Italian stage and its illusionism of acting and decorations, its domination of drama, and replaces them with an integral theatrical creation.

The Theatre 13 Rzedow began its activity as an axial and box-like stage. Each spectacle is a step forward in the direction of conquering the total space of the theatre. In *Siakuntala,* the action extends into the audience's space. In *Dziady* (Forefather's Eve), there is no stage—rather the drama plays itself out in the center, among the spectators. In *Kordian,* the auditorium is filled with beds, as in some nightmarish hospital, and the beds are placed in tiers; the national hero's drama is situated in an insane asylum! The audience takes its seats on the beds next to the actors. *Doctor Faustus* takes place as if in a cloister refectory: the audience sits at two rows of table-podiums, thereby to participate in this gathering and confession. At the head on a high chair presides Faust in monk's robes. *Prince Constant* takes place as if in a dissecting room: in the center stands a table-podium, around which, behind a barrier, are seats for the spectators.

In none of these cases does the "architecture" imitate a hospital, a refectory, or a dissecting-room. Rather, the set is based on the fundamental schema of these places, while utilizing the location of the two theatrical groups: the acting and the perceiving (actors and spectators). But it does not shy away from theatricality and thus from the authenticity of the very place in which we find ourselves.

Gurawski cooperated with Grotowski in his "classic" period. He did not participate either in the early presentations, when Grotowski employed the Italian arrangement, nor in the late, when the spectacle form was discarded. The Theatre 13 Rzedow can be considered, from the spatial point of view, as a continuation of Warsaw's 1933 interwar Zoliborz Theatre, in which Szymon Syrkus, also an architect, created a uniform space—the action took place amidst the audience, while seats for the spectators were placed on podiums. In contrast to many monumental attempts, which were projected in the east and in the west but which were never realized, both of these theatres, though small audience institutions, were achieved. To a certain degree, they can be traced back to the theatrical conception preached by Adam Mickiewicz in his lesson XVI at the Collège de France in Paris, that is, to a conception of a Polish theatre.

—Zenobiusz Strzelecki

# GVO Inc.

American product-analysis, industrial design, and engineering firm

**Founded** in 1966; principal officers include: co-founder and chief executive officer, Noland Vogt (**Education:** studied mechanical engineering at the University of Nebraska, Art Center College of Design, Los Angeles, B.S. **Career:** Guest lecturer, Stanford University, San Jose State University, and University of California; chairman and treasurer, San Francisco chapter of the Industrial Designers Society of America (IDSA); chairman, Ethics Advisory Council, IDSA (national). **Member:** Industrial Designers Society of America; Association of Professional Design Firms (APDF); Product Development and Management Association (PDMA). **Honors:** Fellow, IDSA, 1995.); president, Steve Albert (**Education:** California College of the Arts, Oakland, B.S.); senior vice-president, Robert C. Hall, (**Education:** Studied mechanical engineering, Montana State University, B.S. **Career:** Founded GVO's mechanical engineering practice, 1979.); vice-president of Industrial Design, Jay Wilson (**Education:** Graduated, University of Kansas. **Career:** Guest lecturer, Stanford University and San Jose State University. **Member:** IDSA. **Honors:** Two "Kudos" awards, San Francisco chapter, IDSA.) vice-president of Analysis, Michael Barry, (**Education:** studied mechanical engineering, Stanford University School of Engineering, B.S., M.S. **Member:** Chairman, 1988-90, IDSA; Royal Society of Arts, London. **Honors:** Fellow, Royal Society of Arts, London.); clients include Alps, Alza, Apple Computer, Atari Corporation, BCC, Canon, Dionex, Digital Equipment Corporation, Endosonics, e-on, GridSystems, Hamilton Beach/Proctor Silex, Hewlett-Packard, Hyundai, IBM, Intel, Interactive Network, Johnson Controls, Maxiswitch, Matsushita, Metcal, Microradian, Multipoint Networks, PF. Magic, Samsung, Sega, Sharp Electronics, Solbourne, Sony, Texas Instruments, 3M, TelePad, Toray, Tosiba, Visioneer, Wedge Innovations, Wireless Access, and Zeos. **Address:** GVO Inc., 2370 Watson Court, Palo Alto, California 94303., U.S.A.

## Works

Synanthic Rumen Injector, for Syntex Agribusiness, 1982.
Growth Hormone Implanter, for Syntex Agribusiness, 1982.
*Metasys* climate control system, for Johnson Controls, Milwaukee, 1990.
Intraossius Injector for drug delivery, for Lifequest Medical, 1991.
*Paragon* super computer, for Intel, 1992.
*Smart Level* digital level, for Wedge Innovations, Inc., 1992.
*Paperport* scanner, for Visioneer, 1993.
*Glidepoint,* for Alps Electric, 1994.
Electric Vehicle Charging Station, for Electric Power Research Institute, 1994.

## Publications

**On GVO: articles**—"Green Also Stands for Caution" by James Braham in *Machine Design,* 12 February 1993; "Concurrent Engineering Comes of Age in Era of Global Competition" by Marty Weil in *Managing Automation,* August 1993; "Scanning System Lets Your PC Read the Paper" by Walter S. Mossberg in *Wall Street Journal,* 10 February 1994; "A Select Few Push the Edge of Design" by Caren D. Potter in *Computer Graphics World,* April 1994; "Testing the Water" by Bob St. Nice in *Sound & Image,* Spring 1994; "Information Technology: PF. Magic" in *Fortune,* 11 July 1994; "Small Scanner Clears the Water" by L. Stavnicky in *Designfax,* August 1994; "A Deeper Shade of Green" in *Industry Week,* 15 August 1994; "Review: BCC Avanti 425C" in *Laptop Buyer's Guide and Handbook,* vol. 11, no. 9.

\*

The world of design has changed, is changing more, and will continue to change in the future. Since designers are *agents of change* (creating new products, new ideas, new styles, etc.), they must recognize that change will occur in the way they approach product development. The days of isolation are over, and have been for quite some time. It is just that there are some practitioners that took longer than others to realize it. The technology tools that are being used will continue to progress and continue to reduce new product time to market.

The days of multi disciplinary groups and teams and new vocabularies are here. We will need a new dictionary or glossary of terms so that all the members of this process can understand each other—e.g.: "prototypes" mean different things to different people and even mean different things to people in differing industries. We are rapidly building a Tower of Babel. Product design is in the middle ground of the overall process. This middle ground consists of industrial designers, human factors specialists, interface designers, mechanical designers, and engineers. At the front end are researchers, product planners, market strategists, product definition people, cultural anthropologists, business managers, financial people and, yes, designers and engineers. At the other end are toolers, fabricators, manufacturers, etc.

Many products fail in the marketplace, not because they are poorly designed, but because they are the *wrong* product. Determining the right product requires the right process. Up front, early on, the customer or potential customer must be recognized, involved, listened to, and observed—really observed on what the individual does, not just what he or she says. Enter in the global influence and now the cultural differences and preferences must be factored into the product definition. *In many instances one size might not fit all.*

When we use the words, "customer," "consumer," or "user," we mean everyone that comes in contact with that product throughout its life cycle. These words include the people that manufacture and assemble the product, the people who order it, who place the package on the shelf, who buy it, who unpack it. They include the actual user or operator, the people who maintain and service the product, and even the people who recycle the product or its parts.

No longer can one discipline "throw their efforts or results over the wall" to the next discipline. All the disciplines must be aware and involved, to some extent, from definition to marketplace. The ideal situation is for the same researchers and definition people that started the cycle to follow-through when the produced product is in the marketplace: again questioning, observing, and beginning to define the next generation. And so the loop is complete and starts again.

There is no product if it is the wrong product.

There is no product if there is no market.

There is no product if it is unaffordable.

*There is no product if it is of poor quality and cannot be maintained.*

If there is no product, there are no revenues and therefore there is no company. The end!

—Noland Vogt

*   *   *

Founded 30 years ago as an industrial design firm, GVO made a pioneering decision in 1979 to include mechanical engineering capabilities. It was almost ten years before this concept caught on like

GVO Inc.: *Metasys control system, for Johnson Controls, Milwaukee, 1985-1989*

wildfire in the broader industrial design community, and by then GVO had moved on to expand its approach still further, embracing human interface design and the capability to rapidly create prototypes in house. It now provides turnkey product development, starting with the user research and concept development that underlies a successful product and carrying it through tooling to close collaboration with manufacturing.

Perhaps the most telling characteristic of this firm is its commitment to achieving success for its clients. It has a stellar track record in this regard, having won the Design of the Decade Award from the Industrial Designers Society of America for the market success of its Synanthic® Rumen Injector. Its most noteworthy success story is probably the Metasys family of building control systems, which it designed for Johnson Controls in the late 1980s. In the system's first year on the market, Johnson Controls grew from $300 million in sales to $500 million, making significant inroads into its competitor's market share.

A key component of that success was GVO's focus on understanding the user. To this end, it has worked in a consortium to develop several methodologies that help identify breakthrough product ideas by listening and observing the user. Going well-beyond market research, GVO now uses Contextual Inquiry (Research for Creative Breakthroughs) and Symbolic Modeling (Structuring Data into Insights) to find directions that minimize risk in that first five percent of a product's development, the point at which most of the product's cost is determined. GVO believes that, with these methods, it can base its ideas for new products on an informed understanding of how the users live, their frustrations and wishes. It uses these methods to give focus to an otherwise ambiguous and high-risk time, when the character of a product might otherwise be determined by intuition and a scramble to incorporate features.

GVO has made a tradition of leading its field, not only by pushing the edges of how the field's contribution is defined and executed, but by unstintingly sharing that knowledge with its peers. For example, it has encouraged its staff to share information (a less than common activity) through publishing and conference speaking. Its articles have described ways to effectively integrate the product development process and all its contributors; case studies on ecologically responsible design; and methods of evaluating how users will value a product. It has also demonstrated leadership by mentoring young designers as they establish new (and competing) firms and by volunteering extensively to support the nonprofit associations of its professional staff.

In a very fundamental way, this leadership has been inspired by firm founder Noland Vogt, its current Chair and Chief Executive Officer. His standards of ethical conduct have permeated Silicon Valley's industrial design community, through the many firms founded by designers he encouraged. The resulting atmosphere inspires excellence, and nowhere more so than at GVO itself. There Vogt's sense of professional ethics have inspired the "GVO Core Values," which the firm lives by. These values lead off with, "We believe that technical solutions must be combined with social understandings to align our clients' products and communications with customers and cultures." The statement values "the insight to challenge old knowledge, the humility to discover new knowledge, and the creativity and courage to reinvent" both the firm itself and its clients. Finally, the statement recognizes that "ultimately, it is individuals who contribute to the company and its clients." With values such as these, an aspiring industrial designer would have a worthwhile foundation on which to build a career of successful business relationships.

—Kristina Goodrich

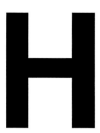

# HALSTON
American fashion designer

**Born:** Roy Halston Frowick, in Des Moines, Iowa, 23 April 1932. **Education:** Studied at Indiana University, Bloomington, and the School of the Art Institute of Chicago, until 1953. **Career:** Independent hat designer, Chicago, 1952-53; window dresser, Carson-Pirie-Scott department store, Chicago, 1954-57; designer and manager of the hats division, Lily Daché company, New York, 1958-59; designer for the millinery salon and for the clothing collections, Bergdorf Goodman, New York, 1959-68; founder and designer, Halston Limited fashion business, New York, 1962-73; with Henry Pollack Incorporated, established Halston International company for mass-marketing, New York, 1970; with Ben Shaw, founded Halston Originals ready-to-wear business, New York, 1972; Halston Limited renamed Halston Enterprises, a division of Norton Simon Incorporated, New York, 1973; Halston III fashion range initiated for J. C. Penney, 1983. **Honors:** Coty American Fashion Critics' Special Award, 1962, 1969, Winnie Award, 1971, Return Award, 1972, and Hall of Fame Award, 1974. **Died:** San Francisco, 27 March 1990.

## Publications

**By HALSTON: articles**—in *Harper's Bazaar* (New York), October 1977.

**On HALSTON: books**—*Fashion Merchandizing* by Mary D. Troxell, New York, 1971, 1976; *A History of Fashion* by J. Anderson Black and Madge Garland, London, 1975, 1980; *Quest for the Best* by Stanley Marcus, New York, 1979; *Fairchild's Who's Who in Fashion* edited by Ann Stegemeyer, New York, 1980; *The Collector's Book of Twentieth Century Fashion* by Frances Kennett, London and New York, 1983; *McDowell's Directory of Twentieth Century Fashion* by Colin McDowell, London, 1984; *The Encyclopedia of Fashion from 1840 to the 1980s* by Georgina O'Hara, London, 1986.

\*     \*     \*

In an interview in 1972, Halston listed his most admired predecessors as Balenciaga, Chanel, Givenchy, and Saint Laurent, and he condemned Britain for never having produced a major look. He followed this in 1974 by trying to revive the British miniskirt, the most famous look of the 1960s, and went on to claim that he was the creator of the uncluttered elegance he promoted, but that is something for which the British have been celebrated for generations. Maybe there was more British influence on Halston than he cared to admit. He had to cope with a degree of unpopularity in the

American press for which he left himself wide open by declaring himself the king of American fashion. Not surprisingly, the press then demanded to know what exactly he had done that was so outstanding. He could claim caftans for evening and hot pants, but what else was new? However, as can be seen with many other couturiers, outstanding originality is not important. There is a market for good quality and for conservative clothes, which Halston was well able to satisfy.

His policy was sensibly based on designing clothes for his customers' lifestyles, in which he participated by going to parties with his patrons, such as Liza Minelli, Marisa Berenson, and Elizabeth Taylor. In 1973, he stated, "Women want clothes that have a long life. They want fewer clothes and things to wear for several different seasons. And that goes right across the board. The richest women in the world are now very practical." This sensible approach was good business and, because couture houses remain durable by diversifying their interests, Halston embraced ready-to-wear Halston Originals, Halston furs, Halston luggage, Halston menswear, and the Halston fragrance line.

Halston could lack discipline. His 1980 "ruffle look" used them as collars, shoulder wings, skirts, and bustles and even to decorate bathing suits; this approach was hardly in the tradition of Chanel and Balenciaga. One cannot envisage Halston emulating Molyneux in selling one standard, three-quarter length coat for more than thirty years. Such absolute continuity was probably beyond him, as it is so British to retain a popular model in dresses (as in motor cars), such as the Mini, for decades, whereas the United States puts so much stress on novelty. However, American designers can survive this frenzy by following a conservative path, and Halston was of this band.

—Diana de Marly

# HANDY, Denis
Irish architect and interior designer

**Born:** Dublin, 7 June 1942. **Education:** The High School, Dublin; St. Columba's College, County Dublin; studied architecture, College of Technology, Bolton Street, Dublin, Dip.Arch., 1967. **Family:** Married Deirdre Maher in 1967; children: Janine, Melanie, and Kevin. **Career:** Contract work, London, 1967; worked in the offices of Stephenson Gibney and Associates, 1968; architect, Aer Rianta (Irish Airports Authority), 1969-72; worked with architect Edwin Squire, 1972-76; established private practice, 1976-79; partner, with Derek Ryan and Kenneth O'Brien, Ryan O'Brien Handy, Architects and Designers, from 1979; following the death of Derek Ryan and retirement of Kenneth O'Brien, partnership continued with Denis Handy and John V. McCarthy. **Member:** Founder member, member of the Development Committee, treasurer, 1987-88, and president, 1989, Society of Designers in Ireland; fellow, 1990, honorary treasurer, 1993-94, and member of competition juries and professional conduct committee, 1993-96, Royal Institute of Architects of Ireland; founder member, and treasurer, 1993-96, European Institute for Design and Disability; treasurer, 1989-93, president-elect, 1993-95, president, 1995-97, executive board, 1995-97, and committee member, 1997 Ireland Congress, International Federation of Interior Architects/Designers; Architects Registration Council of the United Kingdom of Great Britain and Northern Ireland; founder member, Institute for Design and Disability. **Honors:** First Premium, Bathroom Design Competition, 1966; First Premium, Hotel of the Future Design Competition, 1968; Building of the Year Award, *Plan* magazine, 1973; commendation, Royal Institute of Architects of Ireland; landscaping award, Ailt an Oir Methodist housing community project for older people. **Address:** Ryan O'Brien Handy, Architects and Designers, 6 Percy Place, Dublin 4, Ireland.

## Works

Airport seating, part of an integrated range of furniture designed for Aer Rianta, 1972.

Community housing for the elderly, Ailt an Oir, Glenageary, County Dublin, 1993.

Adaptation for multi-purpose use, for Holy Trinity Church, Rathmines, Dublin.

Interior architecture and office design, for Kodak, Cabinteely, County Dublin.

Office design, for Irish Bank of Commerce, Harcourt Centre, Dublin.

Office and interior design, for Anglo-Irish Bank, St. Stephens Green, Dublin.

Ericsson Systems Expertise, Adelphi Centre, Dun Laoghaire.

Interior and office design, for Korean Air Reservations Centre, Dawson Street, Dublin.

Interior architecture, for Glaxo, Grange Road, Dublin.

## Publications

**By HANDY: articles**—in *Interior Designers of the World,* Japan Interior Designers Association, 1995.

\*

The purpose of design lies above personal reputation and profit. Design will have no contribution to make if not founded on the needs of "all people" in a time of accelerating change and technological opportunities. Design may be the only means of relating future technology and environment to human needs.

The wonderful human mind is demonstrating a huge capacity to adapt and develop but genetically is almost static by comparison with the rate of technological advance. The mind and the body will be increasingly stressed by these rapid changes unless the priorities are corrected.

We are only beginning to think of what these needs are and how design could create the necessary supportive environment.

—Denis Handy

\* \* \*

The work of Denis Handy and his firm of architects and designers brings together three related areas of design, notably, environmental design, universal design, and interior architecture. His most important domestic housing project that includes these three factors is his community housing project for elderly people, Ailt an Oir, Glenageary, County Dublin. The project brief was to provide high quality residential accommodation for older people and this was to be done at a reasonable cost to the commissioning body, the Dublin Central Mission, a charity of the Methodist Church in Ireland.

Built on a 2.5 acre site, the scheme consists of forty single-story housing units suitable for independent living with the support of communal social facilities and health care. The individual units are grouped and arranged in wings with central glazed courtyards. These glazed areas are connected to a community building forming enclosed streets and pathways which are climate controlled but external in character. The houses were designed with safety and ease of access as a priority. Particular attention was given to providing the maximum amount of natural light and the sitting rooms open out to the extensively landscaped gardens.

Ryan O'Brien Handy have successfully adapted an historic church building for parish community use. The Holy Trinity Church, Rathmines, Dublin, was designed by the distinguished Irish architect John Semple in 1828 (opened in 1833). The church stands in a striking position in an island in the middle of the road. The church was enlarged in 1863 by adding aisle and transepts to the original building. Ryan O'Brien Handy's brief was to alter the interior to provide for multi-purpose use. The enlarged aisles and transepts of the church have been skillfully partitioned off and the church occupies the chancel and transepts. The nave is now the parish hall and the side aisles are divided into smaller meeting rooms. The partition walls are removable, which allows for maximum flexibility. None of these changes are visible on the exterior of the building. This creative solution to the ever increasing number of redundant church buildings is both sympathetic to the building's original purpose and a model of historic conservation.

—Paul Caffrey

# HANNON, William J.

American industrial designer

**Born:** Boston, Massachusetts, 11 November 1934. **Education:** Studied design, Massachusetts College of Art, B.F.A., 1956; attended Boston Architectural Center, 1957-58; studied public affairs, University of Massachusetts, Boston, M.S., 1982; doctoral candidate, University of Massachusetts, Amherst, from 1985. **Military Service:** U.S. Army Infantry, 1956-1957. **Career:** Staff designer, Morton Hollis Associates, Boston, 1957-58; director of design, The MacBick Company, Cambridge, Massachusetts, 1958-63; senior account designer, Williams Associates, Lynnfield, Massachusetts, 1963-65; president and chief executive officer, Corporate Design Consultants, Boston, 1965-1971; partner, Keohan & Hannon Associates, Milton Village, Massachusetts, 1985-1995; principal, HannonDesign, etc., Cohasset, Massachusetts, and New London, New Hampshire, from 1995. Associate professor and chair of Design Division (included departments of Graphic Design, Industrial Design, Architecture, Illustration, and Fashion), 1971-78,

**William Hannon: Symbol for Polyfiltronics, Inc.**

associate dean for Design and Media, 1978-79, acting vice president of Student Affairs, 1980-81, assistant to the president for External Affairs, 1980-81, vice president for External Affairs and Development, 1981-1985, and professor of design, from 1985, Massachusetts College of Art, Boston. Columnist, *Bay State Business World,* 1968-70; founder, Design Research Unit (a student non-profit design service), Massachusetts College of Art, 1972; editorial board, *DMI Journal,* 1980; founder, Massachusetts College of Art Foundation, 1981; founder, ProArts Consortium (a consortium of five degree-granting professional schools), 1983; organizer, first *Design Education and New Technologies* conference, Boston, 1983; advisor, Association of Independent Colleges of Art and Design, 1987; lecturer on design in the United States and Europe. **Member:** Founding member, Industrial Design Society of America; founder, 1976, and board member, from 1976, Design Management Institute (DMI). **Exhibitions:** Brooklyn Museum of Art, 1965; *American Trade Marks,* U.S. Department of Commerce European Exhibit, 1968; Third Biennale, Yugoslavia, 1968; Design USA, 1970; *Design In Boston,* 1980; Trademarks USA traveling exhibit; *Distinguished Alumni,* Massachusetts College of Art, 1991. **Honors:** Named to 100 Best Packaging Ideas, *Packaging Design* magazine, 1964; Certificate of Merit, Associated Industries of Massachusetts, 1965; Award, *Industrial Research* magazine, 1967, 1968; Award, *Product Engineering* magazine, 1968; Design in Steel Award, American Iron and Steel Institute, 1968, 1969; Walter Dorwin Teague Research Grant, Industrial Design Society of America, 1970; fellow, Center for Public Design, 1979; Certificate of Merit and Silver Medal, Art Directors Club of Boston, 1983, 1984, 1985; Walter Smith Distinguished Alumni Award, 1989; fellow, Royal

Society of Arts, London, 1990. **Address:** HannonDesign, etc., 79 Linden Drive, Cohasset, Massachusetts 02025, U.S.A.; 73 Bunker Road, New London, New Hampshire 03257, U.S.A.

## Works

Designs include—Polaroid *Big Shot* camera; prefabricated bath room, for Sheraton Hotels; cardiac output computer, for Abbot Labs; steam cooker, patient's station, and pharmacy storage, for Market Forge; surgical closure, urinary drainage system, drug distribution cart, linen truck, corporate identity, and packaging, for Macbick Company; EKG, for Becton Dickenson; intra aortic balloon pump, for Mansfield Scientific; package design, for Gillette; computer system, for Adage, Inc.; packaging, for Parker Brothers; packaging, for U.S. Plywood; symbols, for Information International Incorporated, Curtis Farms Supermarkets, Borowko Associates Architects, Polyfiltronics,Inc., Nartech Medical Group, The Macbick Company, S.A.Y Industries, and Franklin Industries.

## Publications

**By HANNON: articles**—"Industrial Design Considerations in Medical Instrumentation" in *Medical Instrumentation,* 1965; "Strategic Visual Management" in *Industry,* 1965; "The MacBick Program" in *Industrial Design* (New York), 1972; "Design Promotion Policy in Great Britain" in *DMI,* 1991; "Should the Federal Government Promote Design?" in *Design Management Journal,* 1993.

**On HANNON: articles**—*Industrial Design* (New York), August 1962.

*

Design is so ubiquitous and so ordinary an activity that it challenges our capacity to control it by caging it behind the bars of simplistic definitions. Everything, after all, that is not made by God or nature is designed by human beings.

Most of us—designers included—don't see the sea of objects and images we swim through every day. Often it is only when designed objects or images are shown to us out of context that we really take notice of them. It's in the shop window, the museum display, or the magazine article that these artifacts compel us to notice them. Or, unfortunately, when designers fail. The wisdom tooth pain of some television commercials, the infuriating complexity of controls, the shoddy, the shabby, and the crass are all too often the designer's progeny.

—Bill Hannon

*     *     *

William J. Hannon is best known as the founder of the Design Management Institute and as one of the few American design educators who has fought to make design's role sustainable and visible to business and government. His practice-based solutions to problems in education led to the establishment of professional review boards at Massachusetts College of Art in 1972 which still override class grades. While chairman, at a time when funding was scarce, he proposed and obtained open studio space so that five design disciplines (architecture, industrial design, graphic design, illustration, and fashion design) could work between and after classes and practice interdisciplinary design. This open studio plan persists to this day. In 1972 he established what is now America's oldest, continuously operating student design office, the Design Research Unit, with a board of directors made up of successful alumni who hold student officers accountable during twice annual meetings for profit and loss and a showing of projects.

Hannon planned the first Design Management Conference held on Nantucket in 1976 and focused the need for an ongoing institute to share, evaluate, and publish design management case studies. As a result, the Design Management Institute, of which William Hannon is still a board member, is presently a world wide design management organization. At critical times in their development William Hannon was able to invite a number of now important design organizations to share space at the Massachusetts College of Art, the Design Management Institute, Adaptive Environments (which led to handicap access legislation), The ProArts Consortium, The Boston Chapter of AIGA, and the Computer Arts Learning Center.

During his entire career, Hannon has continued to practice design as both an industrial designer and graphic designer, to speak out on controversial design issues, and to formulate thoughtful and innovative proposals for integrating design into everyday life. As one who understands design management, his principal contribution has been to establish organizations in such a way that they continue to be healthy and relevant decades later.

—Al Gowan

# HARDER, Rolf (Peter)

Canadian graphic designer

**Born:** Hamburg, Germany, 10 July 1929; emigrated to Canada in 1955, naturalized, 1973. **Education:** Educated at Christianeum High School, Hamburg, until 1948; studied at the Academy of Fine Arts (Landeskunstschule), Hamburg, 1948-52. **Family:** Married Maria-Inger Rumberg in 1958; children: Christoph and Vivian. **Career:** Designer, with Rolf Ruehle Werbung, Hamburg, 1952-55, and with Schneider Cardon Ltd., Montreal, 1955-56; Art Director, George Ferguson Associates, Montreal, 1956-57; visualizer, Lintas GmbH, Hamburg, 1957-59; established Rolf Harder Design, Montreal, 1959-65; co-founder and principal, with Ernst Roch, Design Collaborative Associates graphic design firm, Montreal, 1965-77; founder/director, Rolf Harder and Associates Inc. graphic design consultants, working for Hoffman-La Roche Limited, Alcan Aluminium Ltd., Consolidated Bathurst Inc., Canadian Pulp and Paper Association, Canada Post Corporation, Government of Canada, Bell Canada, Teleglobe Canada, IBM Canada, Grand Prix du Canada, and others., in Montreal, from 1977. Canadian group president, Alliance Graphique Internationale, from 1975; international advisory board member, *Typos* magazine, London, from 1979. Guest lecturer at colleges and professional institutions throughout Canada, from 1970. **Member:** Royal Canadian Academy of Arts, Alliance Graphique Internationale; American Institute of Graphic Arts; International Centre for Typographic Arts. **Exhibitions:** *AIGA Packaging,* American Institute of Graphic Arts, New York, 1960, 1961, 1964, 1965; *Annual Exhibition of Advertising and Editorial Arts,* Los Angeles, 1960, 1961, 1964, 1968, 1982; *Typomundus,* New

York, 1965, Munich, 1970; *Annual Exhibition,* Type Directors Club, New York, 1967, 1974, 1981; *Graphic Design by Rolf Harder and Ernst Roch,* Musee des Beaux-Arts, Montreal, 1970 (toured Canada, Germany, Yugoslavia, and the United States, 1970-74); Royal Canadian Academy of Arts, Toronto, 1970, 1971, 1980, 1987; Biennale of Graphic Design, Brno, 1970-96; Experimental Graphic Design section, Venice Biennale, 1973; *107 Graphic Designers of the AGI,* Castello Sforzesco, Milan, 1974 (travelled to Brussels, Toronto, Montreal, and Caracas); *Canadian Graphic Design,* Design Gallery, Tokyo, 1975; *100 Years of the Poster in Canada,* Art Gallery of Ontario, Toronto, 1979 (toured Canada); *Rolf Harder: Graphic Design,* Pointe-Claire Cultural Centre, Montreal, 1980; Royal Canadian Academy of Arts, 1980, 1987; *Jardin D'Images,* Blois, France, 1990; *Observatoire International Des Prisons,* toured France, 1993-95. **Collections:** Library of Congress, Washington, D.C.; University of New York College at Fredonia; Université du Québec à Montréal. **Honors:** First Prize, Canadian Association for Retarded Children Symbol Competition, 1964; Special Prize, Biennale of Graphic Design, Brno, 1970; Special Prize, International Poster Competition Moscow, 1987; Fellow, Society of Graphic Designers of Canada, 1985. **Address:** 273-A, Bord du lac, Pointe-Claire, Québec H9S 4L1, Canada.

**Works**

Visual identity program, for Hoffmann-La Roche Limited, 1959-77.

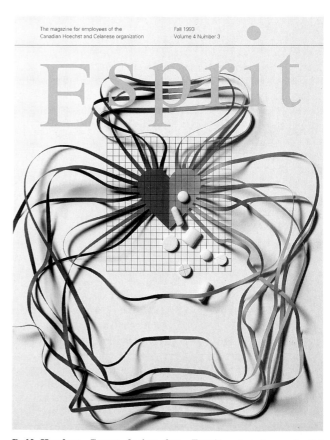

**Rolf Harder: Cover design for *Esprit* magazine, playful intrepretation of cardiovascular system illustrating feature article on clinical trials; client: Hoechst Celanese, 1993**

Visual identity program, for Canadian pavilion, XIV Milan Triennale, 1968.
Logo, for RoyFund Limited, 1969.
Logo, for Imasco Limited, 1970.
Logo, for Queenswear Limited, 1972.
Postage stamps, for Canada Post Corporation, from 1975.
New alphabet, for Northern Telecom, 1976-77.
Visual identity program, for Grand Prix du Canada, 1977.
Logo, for IBM Eastern Region Productivity Centre, 1978.
Logo, for International Design and Woodcraft, 1978.
Centennial logo, for Bell Canada, 1979.
Logo, for CompuDesign Inc., 1982.
Logo, for McMillan Bathurst Inc., 1983.
Visual identity program, for Maison Alcan, 1984.
Symbol and signage, for Protestant School Board of Greater Montreal, 1987-89.
Publications concept, for Transport Canada, 1988.
*Esprit* company magazine redesign, for Hoechst Celanese, 1993.

**Publications**

**By HARDER: books**—(co-publisher) *Pitseolak, Pictures Out Of My Life,* Montreal, 1971; (co-publisher) *Arts of the Eskimo: Prints,* Montreal, 1975; (author of introduction) *Who's Who in Graphic Arts* edited by Walter Amstutz, Zurich, 1982; (contributor) *World History of the Poster,* Paris, 1988.

**On HARDER: books**—*Optical Illusions and the Visual Arts* by Carraher Thurston, New York, 1966; *Graphic Design by Rolf Harder and Ernst Roch,* exhibition catalogue with texts by Hans Neuburg and Allan Harrison, Montreal, 1977; *International Trade Mark Design* by Peter Wildbur, London, 1979; *Who's Who in Graphic Arts* edited by Walter Amstutz, Zurich, 1982; *Letterheads* by Takenobu Igarashi, Tokyo, 1986; *World Trade Marks and Logotypes II* edited by Takenobu Igarashi, Tokyo, 1987; *World Graphic Design: Packages,* Tokyo, 1988; *World Graphic Design: Corporate Identity,* Tokyo, 1989; *Typographic Communications Today* by Edward M. Gottschall, Cambridge, Massachusetts, and London, 1989; *AGI Annals,* Zurich and Tokyo, 1989; *Thames & Hudson Encyclopedia of Graphic Design and Designers,* London, 1992; **articles**—in *Communication World* (San Francisco), April 1986; *Novum Gebrauchsgraphik* (Munich), October 1987; *Print* (New York), January/February 1990.

*

Let me begin by stating what, in my view, the graphic designer is *not*.

We are not artists who, in solitary struggle, produce a piece of art. Although "art" may be the result, our primary aim is to solve communication problems. Our attitude in approaching an assignment can be compared to that of the architect who, apart from very important aesthetic considerations, always has to keep the building's function in mind as he designs it. In other words, we are first of all pragmatists whose desire for self-expression must not interfere with a clear and unequivocal formulation of a given message.

Aesthetics, craftsmanship, a feeling for an understanding of form, colour and composition, are necessary prerequisites for the designer's work. Beyond this, there is still plenty of room for wit, imagination, intuition, and talent. But all this has to be tempered by a healthy amount of intellectual self-control which keeps questioning and reappraising the developing ideas. Contrary to the fine artist, who poses his own problems of concept and content, we graphic designers are given a problem which we have to analyze thoroughly. We have to formulate intellectually and visually the requirements in order to reach the desired objective, which is to communicate a specific message.

Another aspect of the designer's work: he contributes in many ways, some small, others more significant, towards the shaping of our environment; he exerts a certain influence on the thinking and behavior of his fellow men. Therefore, a sense of responsibility is necessary, if his endeavors are to go beyond the mere purpose of earning a living.

Alan Gussow, an American artist-environmentalist, said: "When our environment is degraded, we are degraded, since we are not distinct from our place—we are that place. The value of the individual tends to decrease along with that of the place."

If a designer's work is aesthetically satisfying, intellectually stimulating, imaginative, and at the same time concise and informative—in short, generally in harmony with our needs—he has made a positive contribution towards a more human environment.

—Rolf Harder

*     *     *

Rolf Harder has been a major force in Canadian graphic design since he opened his first studio in Montreal in 1959. German-born, Harder studied at the Hamburg Academy of Fine Arts before emigrating to Canada in the mid-fifties. At that time design in Canada was strongly influenced by the American approach to advertising and marketing illustration, known as "commercial art". With few exceptions, most efforts were, at best, mediocre. The international style which Harder helped pioneer and the standards of quality he espoused created a new awareness of aesthetics and form that changed the face of graphic design in his adopted country.

For Harder, the purpose of design is not to decorate, but to communicate. His strength as a designer nevertheless owes much to his talent as artist and illustrator. His inspired melding of colour, line, and typography is evident in his striking logos, book designs, and posters. The postage stamps he has designed for Canada Post are particularly fine examples of his functional, and sensitive, work.

Harder's contention that graphic design has a crucial social role to play was not familiar to the area in which he decided to specialize, industrial and institutional graphics. Acquiring government agencies and some of Canada's major corporations as clients, however, enabled him to spread the message. Granted, those clients may not have been altruistically moved in their choice of Harder as designer of their logos, visual identity programs, and prestigious publications, but their visual environment has nonetheless been enhanced by the chief selling feature of his work—finely-crafted, superbly functional design.

The visual clarity and pristine form that is Harder's trademark belies the depth and complexity of his approach to design development. A painstaking analysis of all aspects of the project is made before any design is begun. It is at this investigative stage that potential solutions to the design problem evolve and their possibilities are weighed. When the optimum resolution finally emerges, then the designer's imagination can take over and develop the graphics "package" that best suits the purpose. One admiring critic has described Harder's technique as "working from the inside out."

It is a technique based on logic. One that calls for systematic thinking and intellectual discipline. To be successful, it also requires a sense of adventure and a commitment to beauty. Harder's postage stamps are fine examples of discipline, artistic achievement. So are the creative packaging designs developed for his pharmaceutical clients.

Harder is a disciple of constructivism, although not in a dogmatic sense. In his work, form never takes precedence over function but he does enjoy experimenting with his designs, often in quite a playful way. Eventually it is how he balances organization of form with the aesthetic elements of the piece that sets his work apart. So too the vitality of his design that captures the viewer's attention and does exactly what Harder has set out to do: communicate. Says one colleague, "Harder consistently produces design solutions that are intellectually satisfying and emotionally pleasing."

Highly respected by colleagues and clients, Harder has been called a "designer's designer." The influence he has had both on the profession and on other designers' work is profound. National and international recognition has come with over 100 awards, exhibitions of his work around the world, and reviews of his designs in the leading professional publications. And after thirty years of imaginative and innovative design, Harder's work is as fresh and as stimulating as ever.

—Gloria Menard

# HARDWICK, Cathy

American fashion and interior designer

**Born:** Cathaline Kaesug Sun, in Seoul, Korea, in 1933; emigrated to the United States in 1952, naturalized, 1959. **Education:** Mainly self-taught in design. **Family:** Married Anthony Hardwick in 1966; four children. **Career:** Clothing designer, for Alvin Duskin, San Francisco, in the 1960s; freelance designer, establishing own boutique in San Francisco, 1968-74; sportswear designer, Pranx, New York; designer, Cathy Hardwick 'n' Friends, New York, 1972; president and designer, Cathy Hardwick Ltd., 1975-81, and Cathy Hardwick Design Studio, New York, from 1977; also sportswear designer for Sears Roebuck and Co., from 1990. **Honors:** Coty Special Award, New York, 1975. **Address:** 215 West 40th Street, New York, New York 10018, USA.

## Publications

**On HARDWICK: books—***The Changing World of Fashion: 1900 to the Present* by Ernestine Carter, London, 1977; *The Fashion Makers* by Bernadine Morris and Barbara Walz, New York, 1978; *Fairchild's Who's Who in Fashion* edited by Ann Stegemeyer, New York, 1980; *McDowell's Directory of Twentieth Century Fashion* by Colin McDowell, London, 1984; *The Encyclopaedia of Fashion from 1840 to the 1980s* by Georgina O'Hara, London, 1986; *New York Fashion: The Evolution of American Style* by Caroline Milbank Rennolds, New York, 1989; **articles—**"She's A Natural" by Joan O'Sullivan in *Living Today* (Wheaton, Illinois), 16 September 1977; "East Village with Seoul: A Hands on Approach to Fall" by Marge Colborn in the *Detroit News* (Michigan), 4 May 1986;

"Cathy Hardwick—Success with Style" by Elsa Klensch in *Vogue* (New York), June 1988.

\*

I make clothes to celebrate and enhance the woman's body— these are clothes for a very secure, happy person, who is successful in her life, and whose body and mind are in good shape, whatever her age. Of course, anyone can wear my clothes, since I think they are as ageless as my ideal woman.

—Cathy Hardwick

\*      \*      \*

Cathy Hardwick came into her own as one of a group of young, recognized American designers of relatively moderately priced ready-to-wear women's clothing soon after she arrived in New York from San Francisco and opened her own design studio in the early 1970s. The very next year, she launched her line of simple, fluid dresses, pants, jackets, and blouses, by opening her own manufacturing firm on Broadway.

A consistency runs throughout Hardwick's work. She likes simplicity and understatement and most often uses fine, natural fabrics, preferring cotton for summer and wool for winter. She is not what one might call a major innovator, but is rather a subtle stylist who adds her personal, innovative touches to the basic items of wardrobe, incorporating a certain panache into her very wearable and versatile creations. Exemplary of her uses of individualistic variations are her jumpsuits. In her spring 1975 version, loose, midcalf pants were slit to the thighs, topped with a narrow tank tied at the side, and the whole was enlivened by the multicolored stripes on the black, lightweight, cotton fabric. Hardwick's fall 1975 modification of the popular jumpsuit was of the drop-shoulder variety, with frilly ruffled shoulderline; its sensuous lines were enhanced by the choice of pale lavender rayon crepe de chine. Hardwick's penchant for the subtle touch of the exotic was also prominent in her 1976 jumpsuit of raspberry-colored crinkled cotton, strapless and harem-hemmed, light, fluid, and bare for easy yet sophisticated wear. She also often demonstrates her liking for chinoiserie, as in her 1975 wool and silk tunics and frog-closed jackets of quilted florals or embroidered silks. Hardwick again used frog closures in her spring 1994 collection on a series of light tops.

Another basic in Hardwick's output is the look of total coordination achieved through multiple mix-and-match possibilities. Take, for example, her 1975 knits, which included pullovers cut like T-shirts, soft mohair cardigans, and softly gathered or slim skirts, all dyed to match, along with a group of scarf-hats. Also outstanding were her 1978 pale blue silk "waterfall" neckline blouses with rounded collars and narrow wrists to go with navy silk pleated pants for Dessina.

Whether they are playclothes of terrycloth or crinkled cotton or holiday wear of wool challis or red velvet, Hardwick's creations always stress a basic simplicity with elegant feminine touches. They are geared for women of all ages who are looking for clean, solid feminity with a not-too-far-out flash of spirited arrogance.

—Barbara Cavaliere

# HASSELBERG-OLSSON, Elisabet
Swedish textile designer

**Born:** Elisabet Hasselberg, in Göteborg, 15 October 1932. **Education:** Self-taught in weaving and textile design, from 1960. **Family:** Married the architect John Olsson in 1956; children: Anna. **Career:** Concentrated on tapestry weaving, initially in Elsa Gullberg's workshop in Vaxholm, from 1964; established own workshop, Täby, 1966. **Exhibitions:** *Why a Brush?,* Hantverket Gallery, Stockholm, 1966; Finnish Design Center, Helsinki, 1969; Form Design Center, Malmö, 1969; Galleri Glaucus, Stockholm, 1971; *Expressions Textiles Nordiques,* Angers, France, 1973; *First World Crafts Exhibition,* Toronto, 1974; Sundsvalls Museum, Sweden, 1975; Södertälje Konsthall, Sweden, 1975; *Swedish Textile Art—Five Temperaments,* toured Cuba, Canada, and Mexico, 1976; *Tre Temperament i Väv,* Nationalmuseum, Stockholm, 1976; *Expressions Suédoise,* Brussels, 1977; Centre Culturel Suedois, Paris, 1978; *Scandinavian Crafts Exhibition,* Tokyo 1978; *Scandinavia Today,* toured the United States, 1982; *Contemporary Swedish Design,* Nationalmuseum, Stockholm, 1983; *Scandinavia Today,* toured Japan and the United States, 1987-88; Västerbottens Museum, Umeå, 1988 (travelled to Södertälje and Borås); retrospective, Waldemarsudde, Stockholm, 1993; *A New Century in European Design,* Japan, 1994-95. **Collections:** National museum, Stockholm; Malmö Museum, Sweden; Röhsska Könstslöjdmuseet, Göteborg. **Honors:** Prince Eugen medal, 1984. **Address:** Arrendevagen 23, 18338 Täby, Sweden.

## Works

*Stammar/Trunks* linen on cotton warp tapestry, 1964.
*Vision I* linen and art silk on linen warp tapestry, 1965.
*Inscription Vietnam* linen on linen warp tapestry, 1968.
*Till Havet II/To The Sea II* linen and art silk on linen warp tapestry, 1968.
*Hemmet/The Home* linen and art silk on linen warp tapestry, 1970.
*Vägen Hem/The Homeward Road* linen, art silk, and wool on linen warp tapestry, 1970.
*Förväntan/Expectation* linen on cotton warp tapestry, 1971.
*Molnet/The Cloud* linen on cotton warp tapestry, 1973.
*Kappan/The Coat* linen and art silk on cotton warp tapestry, 1973.
*Gryning/Dawn* linen and art silk on cotton warp tapestry, for Tibble Church, Taby, 1973.
*Aker/Farmland* linen on cotton warp tapestry, 1974.
*Elden/The Fire* linen and art silk on cotton warp tapestry, for the Kooperativa Forbundet, 1974.
*Trasmattan/The Rag-Carpet* linen on cotton warp tapestry, 1975.

Elisabet Hasselberg-Olsson: *Rooms beyond Room,* linen yarn, made in two parts, placed in the city hall of Stockholm, 1992. Photo by Anders Qwarnström, courtesy of Elisabet Hasselberg-Olsson

*Stranden/The Beach* linen and art silk on cotton warp tapestry, 1976.

*Oppen dorr/Open Door* linen on cotton warp tapestry, 1978.

*Fabrik/Factory* linen on cotton warp tapestry, 1980.

*Memory of a Landscape* linen, boucle, and wool on cotton warp tapestry, for the Swedish House of Parliament, Stockholm, 1982-83.

*Horn/Corner* linen on cotton warp tapestry, 1986.

*Spar/Tracks* linen on cotton warp tapestry, 1987.

*Stenar/Stones* linen on cotton warp tapestry, 1988.

*Stones II* linen on cotton warp tapestry, 1988.

*Archipelago Stockholm* linen on cotton warp tapestry, 1990.

*Beach* linen on cotton warp tapestry, 1990.

*Dawn* linen on cotton warp tapestry, 1990.

*Ground without Snow* linen on cotton warp tapestry, 1991.

*Rooms beyond Room* linen on cotton warp tapestry, 1992.

*Fields* linen on cotton warp tapestry, 1993.

*Swedish Landscape* linen on cotton warp tapestry in four parts and scene curtain, for ASTRA AB, Sweden, 1994.

*Path* linen on cotton warp tapestry, for Ersta Hospice, Stockholm, 1995.

**Publications**

**On HASSELBERG-OLSSON: books**—*Tre Temperament i Väv,* exhibition catalogue by Dag Widman, Helena Lutteman, and Katja Walden, Stockholm, 1976; *Svensk Textilkonst/ Swedish Textile Art* by Edna Martin and Beate Sydhoff, Stockholm, 1980; *Form och Tradition i Sverige* edited by Birgitta Walz, Stockholm, 1982; *Contemporary Swedish Design,* exhibition catalogue by Monica Boman, Lennart Lindkvist, and others, Stockholm, 1983; *Elisabet Hasselberg-Olsson: Memory of a Landscape,* exhibition catalogue with text by Gunilla Lundahl, Stockholm, 1984; *Den Svenska Formen* by Monica Boman and others, Stockholm, 1985; *Elisabet Hasselberg-Olsson: Bildvävar 1965-1988,* exhibition catalogue with texts by Elisabeth Rasch, Beate Sydhoff, and Per Drougge, Umeå, 1988; exhibition catalogue by Beate Sydhoff, Waldermarsudde, 1993.

\*

I seek to weave the light into my images. It is not the light of reality but the light of reminiscence. An empty room, a few stones on a beach, a scenery, can recreate within ourselves images of the once seen experience—the universal.

—Elisabet Hasselberg-Olsson

# HAVINDEN, Ashley (Eldrid)

British painter, typographer, textile, and graphic designer

**Born:** Rochester, Kent, 13 April 1903; also known as "Ashley." **Education:** Educated at Christ's Hospital School, Horsham, Sussex, 1912-20; studied drawing and design, Central School of Arts and Crafts, London, 1922-23; also private studies with the sculptor Henry Moore, Hampstead, London, 1933. **Military:** Served in the British Army camouflage unit, 1941-45, Captain. **Family:** Married Margaret Kirk Sangster in 1928; children: Michael and Venice.

**Career:** Trainee and designer, 1922-29, art director and board member, 1929-60, and vice-chairman, 1960-67, W. S. Crawford advertising agency, London; director, 1946-48, and chairman, 1948-67, Design International (Sir William Crawford and Partners) industrial design firm, London; freelance designer, with own studio in Hertingfordbury, Hertfordshire, 1967-73; designed for the Milk Marketing Board, General Post Office, London County Council, Central Office of Information, Simpson's of Piccadilly, KLM Royal Dutch Airlines, Morton Sundour Fabrics, Wilton Royal Carpet Factory, Edinburgh Weavers, Duncan Miller Interior Design, Chrysler Motors, Osram Lamps, Pretty Polly Stockings, and others. **Member:** Council member, 1946-47, and president, 1953, Society of Industrial Artists and Designers, London; governor, 1950-57, and chairman, 1955-56 and 1958-59, London College of Printing; president, Advertising Creative Circle, London, 1955, Double Crown Club, London, 1956, and Alliance Graphique Internationale, Paris, 1957-59; advisory committee member, 1958-65, and governor, 1965-67, Chelsea School of Art, London; governor, Central School of Arts and Crafts, London, 1959-67; master of the faculty of Royal Designers for Industry, Royal Society of Arts, London, 1967-69. **Exhibitions:** *Union des Artistes Modernes,* Paris, 1933; Lund Humphries Gallery, London, 1937; London Gallery, London, 1937; *Exposition Internationale,* Paris, 1937, Leicester Galleries, London, 1938; Alex Reid and Lefevre Galleries, London, 1939; *Golden Gate Exposition,* San Francisco, 1939; *Design at Work,* Royal Academy of Art, London, 1946; *Britain Can Make It,* Victoria and Albert Museum, London, 1946, Marlborough Fine Art, London, 1965; *Second World War Posters,* Imperial War Museum, London, 1972; *Thirties,* Hayward Gallery, London, 1979; *Eye for Industry,* Victoria and Albert Museum, London, 1986. **Honors:** Fellow, 1945, and Royal Designer for Industry, 1947, Royal Society of Arts, London; Fellow, Society of Industrial Artists and Designers, London, 1946; Honoured Member, Advertising Creative Circle, London, 1966; Fellow, Institute of Practitioners in Advertising, London, and Central Institute of Art and Design, London. Honorary Doctorate: Manchester University, 1961. Officer, Order of the British Empire, 1951. **Died:** Hertingfordbury, Hertfordshire, 31 May 1973.

**Publications**

**By HAVINDEN: books**—*Line Drawing for Reproduction,* London, 1933, 1941; *MARS Group of Modern Architects,* exhibition catalogue with text by John Summerson, London, 1938; *Advertising and the Artist,* with introduction by Stephen Tallens, London, 1956; *Advertising and the Motor-Car* edited by Michael Frostick, London, 1970.

**On HAVINDEN: books**—*British Textile Designers Today* by H. G. Hayes Marshall, Leigh on-Sea, 1939; *Packaging: An International Survey of Package Design* edited by Walter Herdeg, Zurich, 1959; *Who's Who in Graphic Art* edited by Walter Amstutz, Zurich, 1962; *The Poster: An Illustrated History from 1860* by Harold F. Hutchinson, London and Toronto, 1968; *Second World War Posters,* exhibition catalogue edited by Joseph Darracott and Belinda Loftus, London, 1972; *Industrial Design in Britain* by Noel Carrington, London, 1976; *Advertising: Reflections of a Century* by Bryan Holme, London, 1982; *Eye for Industry: Royal Designers for Industry 1936-1986,* exhibition catalogue by Fiona MacCarthy and Patrick Nuttgens, London, 1986.

\*      \*      \*

At the opening of Ashley Havinden's career, British graphic design was dominated by late Victorian and Edwardian conventions such as the prominent, obligatory use of tasteless company "nameblocks" in thick script, company slogans, and redundant figurative imagery. As a young designer, he met and fell under the charismatic influence of Stanley Morison, the great typographic designer then engaged with the systematic revival of classic typefaces for the Monotype Corporation. Partly in response to Morison's influence, Havinden produced a number of designs which were tastefully balanced, symmetrical, and typographically refined.

Although these early designs made progress toward simplification of pictorial imagery and a tauter relationship between text and image, Havinden later recognised the Morison influence as a blind alley. By the mid-1920s, he had become aware of the design innovations of the Bauhaus, the constructivists, and such figures as László Moholy-Nagy and Jan Tschichold. He visited Germany and eventually was to spend a year there absorbing the Continental influence on graphic design. The campaign for Chrysler cars dispensed with many of the conventions of the day and used instead dramatic, highly simplified imagery; a bold, sans-serif typeface; and a strong, constructive alignment in layout. The use of the Chrysler designs internationally necessitated cutting the letterform he designed for it as a typeface.

An important feature of Havinden's career is his intelligent openness to the influence of fine art and architecture. As a young man, he took lessons from the sculptor Henry Moore, and he continued to work and exhibit as a painter. He read and absorbed the foremost theorists of his day, including Tschichold, Gropius, and Le Corbusier, at the same time converting what they had to say into something which was uniquely his own. This, combined with a refined and discriminating taste, made him one of the leading figures in British graphic design for more than four decades.

Prominent in Havinden's early mature work is the machine aesthetic, with its bold, rectilinear letterforms and simple, hard-edge pictorial imagery. By the late 1930s, a more relaxed mood emerged, perhaps in reaction to the extremism of Continental design of the day. In his "Drink Milk Daily" poster of 1936, the text is still set on a diagonal, but the letterform has a pleasantly improvised chalk-and-blackboard look.

Havinden's postwar designs exhibit a wide variety of approaches and possibilities, ranging from the firmly constructed look of his work for the National Book League, to free, improvisatory motifs reminiscent of graffiti, as in his corporate image for Richard Shops. His designs for Pretty Polly stockings, which utilize a pastiche of rustic *lettres ornées,* are still currently in use and look as vivid and fresh as the day they were produced.

—Clive Ashwin

# HAYAKAWA, Yoshio

Japanese illustrator, display, book, and graphic designer

**Born:** Osaka, 13 February 1917. **Education:** Studied at the School of Osaka High School of Industrial Arts, Osaka, 1931-36. **Family:** Married Ume Chibata in 1949; children: Maku. **Career:** Display designer, Mitsukoshi Department Store, Osaka, 1937-38; advertising designer, Kintetsu Department Store, Tokyo, 1948-52; freelance graphic designer from 1952, establishing Yoshio Hayakawa Design

Office, Tokyo, from 1954; councilor, Art Directors Club of Tokyo, from 1980. Founder/member, DAS Society of Designers, Tokyo, 1956; co-founder, NIC Japan Illustrators Congress, 1969; planning committee member, *Expo* 70 exhibition, Osaka, 1970. Lecturer, University of Fine Arts, Kyoto, 1953-70; panelist, ICSID, Kyoto, 1973. **Member:** Alliance Graphique Internationale. **Exhibitions:** *Yoshio Hayakawa: Commercial Design,* Osaka, 1952; *Graphics 55,* Tokyo, 1955; *Japanese Posters,* toured Europe, 1979; *Modern Japanese Posters,* Toyama Museum of Art, Japan, 1982; *Yoshio Hayakawa: Women Original Paintings,* Tokyo, 1989. **Collections:** Museum of Modern Art, New York; Stedelijk Museum, Amsterdam; Neve Sammlung National Art Museum, Munich; Philadelphia Museum of Art, Philadelphia; Tochigi Prefectural Art Museum, Japan; Museum of Modern Art, Toyama, Japan; Kawasaki City Museum, Japan; Musashino Art University Library, Japan. **Honors:** Osaka Prefectural Art Award, Osaka, 1954; 1st Mainichi Industrial Design Prize, Tokyo, 1954; Tokyo Art Directors Club Medal, 1957, 1959; Ministry of International Trade and Industry Award, 13th Book Cover Contest, Tokyo, 1978; 12th Kodansha Culture Award for Book Design, Tokyo, 1981; Purple Ribbon, Japanese Government, Tokyo, 1982; 5th Yamana Prize, Tokyo, 1984; Class Order of the Sacred Treasure, Japanese Government, Tokyo, 1988. **Address:** Yoshio Hayakawa Design Office, 6-27-113, Akasaka 8 chome, Minato-ku, Tokyo 107, Japan.

## Publications

**By HAYAKAWA: books**—*The World of Yoshio Hayakawa* (collected essays), Tokyo, 1985; *Turezure Kankaku* (essays), Tokyo, 1986; *Yoshio Hayakawa* (essays), Tokyo, 1993; **articles**—in *Print* (New York), January 1967.

**On HAYAKAWA: books**—*Posters* by W. H. Allner, New York, 1952; **articles**—in *Graphis* (Zurich), no. 46, 1953, no. 55, March 1956.

*

It is clear that one function of graphic design is to communicate messages. I believe, however that it should not end up being just a technique and that it is important that we invite the world of graphic design, with its formative appeal consisting of color and shape, to inject elements of beauty into people's lives. Although my expression takes various forms depending on the purpose of the message, I strive for human warmth in all cases.

—Yoshio Hayakawa

\*			\*			\*

After completing his education at the School of Industrial Design in Osaka, Yoshio Hayakawa entered commercial design. His graphic design compositions are solid and unique works, the result of his individual style and the emotion one can sense in his illustration. He has had a great influence on Japanese graphic design, and there are many who follow his style.

His superlative temperament as an artist is based on solid ideas. At first glance, his work seems all to be in the same style, but each piece has something different about it and possesses an agreeability which serves to calm those who view his works. He on occasion

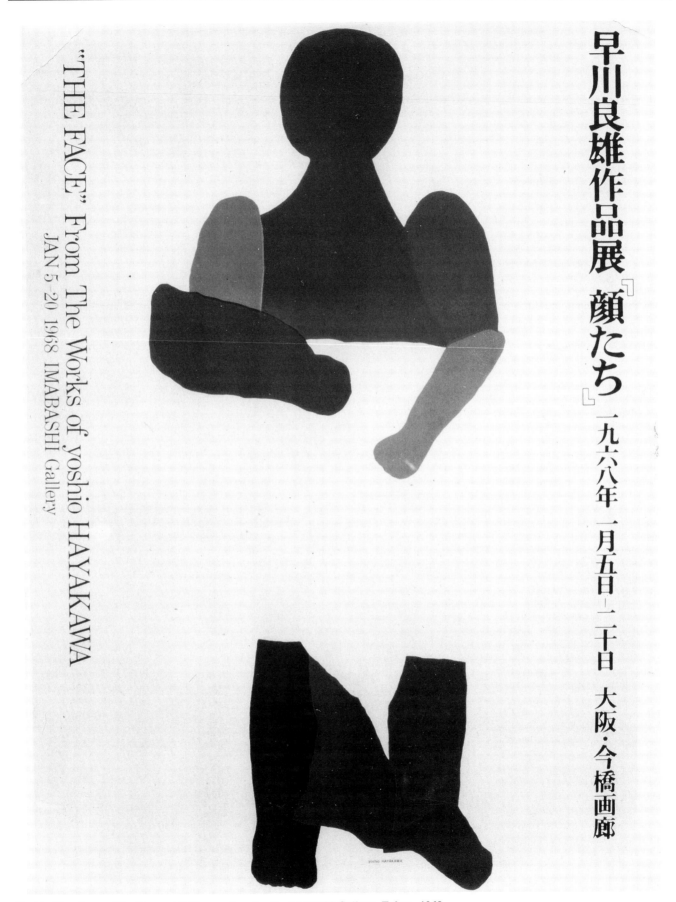

Yoshio Hayakawa: *The Face* exhibition poster, for the Imabashi Gallery, Tokyo, 1968

presents exhibits of his drawings and paintings; these always manifest his desire to progress in the creation of new work.

—Masaaki Tanaka

# HEAD, Edith

American film costume designer

**Born:** Edith Claire Posener in San Bernadino, California, 28 October 1897. **Education:** Educated in Redding and Los Angeles, California; studied at the University of California at Los Angeles, BA; Stanford University, California, MA; also attended classes at the Otis Art Institute and Chouinard Art School, Los Angeles. **Family:** Married Charles Head in 1923 (divorced, 1923); married the designer Wiard Ihnen in 1940 (died, 1979). **Career:** Instructor in French, Spanish, and art at Bishops School for Girls, La Jolla, and at Hollywood School for Girls, Los Angeles, 1923; sketch artist, 1924-27, assistant to Travis Banton, 1927-38, and head of design, 1938-66, Paramount Film Studios, Hollywood; chief costume designer, Universal Studios, Hollywood, 1967-81. Also designed uniforms for Pan American Airlines, the United States Coastguard, and United Nations tour guides. Lecturer, University of Southern California, 1949-51, 1973. Fashion editor, *Holiday* magazine, 1973. **Exhibitions:** *Romantic and Glamorous Hollywood Design*, Metropolitan Museum of Art, New York, 1974; *Hollywood Film Costume*, Whitworth Art Gallery, Manchester, 1977. **Honors:** Academy Awards, 1949, 1950, 1951, 1953, 1954, 1960, 1973; Film Designer of the Year Award, Mannequins Association, Los Angeles, 1962; Costume Designers Guild Award, 1967. **Died:** Los Angeles, California, 26 October 1981.

## Works

Film designs include—*Peter Pan*, 1924; *The Golden Bed*, 1925; *The Wanderer*, 1925; *Mantrap*, 1926; *Wings*, 1927; *The Saturday Night Kid*, 1929; *The Virginian*, 1929; *The Wolf Song*, 1929; *Along Came Youth*, 1930; *Only the Brave*, 1930; *The Santa Fe Trail*, 1930; *The Big Broadcast of 1932*, 1932; *Love Me Tonight*, 1932; *Undercover Man*, 1932; *She Done Him Wrong*, 1933; *Cradle Song*, 1933; *Hello Everybody*, 1933; *Sitting Pretty*, 1933; *Strictly Personal*, 1933; *Little Miss Marker*, 1934; *The Big Broadcast of 1936*, 1935; *Lives of a Bengal Lancer*, 1935; *Mississippi*, 1935; *Ruggles of Red Gap*, 1935; *Peter Ibbetson*, 1935; *Wings in the Dark*, 1935; *The Big Broadcast of 1937*, 1936; *The Jungle Princess*, 1936; *The Milky Way*, 1936; *Poppy*, 1936; *Woman*, 1936; *Trap*, 1936; *College Holiday*, 1936; *The Barrier*, 1937; *Blond Trouble*, 1937; *Blossoms on Broadway*, 1937; *Borderland*, 1937; *Bulldog Drummond Comes Back*, 1937; *Bulldog Drummond Escapes*, 1937; *Bulldog Drummond's Revenge*, 1937; *Clarence*, 1937; *The Crime Nobody Saw*, 1937; *A Doctor's Diary*, 1937; *Double or Nothing*, 1937; *Ebb Tide*, 1937; *Exclusive*, 1937; *Forlorn River*, 1937; *Girl from Scotland Yard*, 1937; *Murder Goes to College*, 1937; *The Great Gambini*, 1937; *Hideaway Girl*, 1937; *Hills of Old Wyoming*, 1937; *Hold 'Em Navy*, 1937; *Hotel Haywire*, 1937; *Her Husband Lies*, 1937; *Interns Can't Take Money*, 1937; *John Meade's Woman* (with Bridgehouse), 1937; *Last Train from Madrid*, 1937; *Let's Make a Million*, 1937; *Make Way for*

*Tomorrow*, 1937; *Midnight Madonna*, 1937; *Mind Your Own Business*, 1937; *Mountain Music*, 1937; *Souls at Sea*, 1937; *Night Club Scandal*, 1937; *A Night of Mystery*, 1937; *North of the Rio Grande*, 1937; *On Such a Night*, 1937; *Outcast*, 1937; *Partners in Crime*, 1937; *Partners of the Plains*, 1937; *She Asked for It*, 1937; *She's No Lady*, 1937; *Sophie Lang Goes West*, 1937; *Texas Trail*, 1937; *This Way Please*, 1937; *Thrill of a Lifetime*, 1937; *True Confession*, 1937; *Wild Money*, 1937; *Turn Off the Moon*, 1937; *Waikiki Wedding*, 1937; *Wells Fargo*, 1937; *Artists and Models Abroad*, 1938; *The Arkansas Traveler*, 1938; *Bar 20 Justice*, 1938; *Booloo*, 1938; *Born to the West*, 1938; *Bulldog Drummond in Africa*, 1938; *Bulldog Drummond's Peril*, 1938; *Campus Confessions*, 1938; *Coconut Grove*, 1938; *Professor Beware*, 1938; *Prison Farm*, 1938; *Pride of the West*, 1938; *Men with Wings*, 1938; *Love on Toast*, 1938; *Little Orphan Annie*, 1938; *King of Alcatraz*, 1938; *In Old Mexico*, 1938; *Illegal Traffic*, 1938; *Hunted Men*, 1938; *Her Jungle Love*, 1938; *Heart of Arizona*, 1938; *Give Me a Sailor*, 1938; *The Frontiersman*, 1938; *College Swing*, 1938; *Ride a Crooked Mile*, 1938; *Say It in French*, 1938; *Scandal Sheet*, 1938; *Sing You Sinners*, 1938; *Tropic Holiday*, 1938; *Touchdown, Army*, 1938; *Tom Sawyer Detective*, 1938; *Tip-off Girls*, 1938; *Thanks for the Memory*, 1938; *Sons of the Legion*, 1938; *Spawn of the North*, 1938; *Stolen Heaven*, 1938; *Arrest Bulldog Drummond*, 1939; *All Women Have Secrets*, 1939; *Honeymoon in Bali*, 1939; *Heritage of the Desert*, 1939; *Back Door to Heaven*, 1939; *Beau Geste*, 1939; *Boy Trouble*, 1939; *The Great Victor Herbert*, 1939; *Grand Jury Secrets*, 1939; *The Gracie Allen Murder Case*, 1939; *Disputed Passage*, 1939; *Disbarred*, 1939; *Death of a Champion*, 1939; *The Cat and the Canary*, 1939; *Cafe Society*, 1939; *Bulldog Drummond's Secret Police*, 1939; *Bulldog Drummond's Bride*, 1939; *Night Work*, 1939; *The Night of Nights*, 1939; *Hotel Imperial*, 1939; *I'm Missouri*, 1939; *Invitation to Happiness*, 1939; *Island of Lost Men*, 1939; *The Lady's from Kentucky*, 1939; *Law of the Pampas*, 1939; *The Light That Failed*, 1939; *The Llano Kid*, 1939; *The Magnificent Fraud*, 1939; *Man About Town*, 1939; *Million Dollar Legs*, 1939; *Never Say Die*, 1939; *$1,000 a Touchdown*, 1939; *Undercover Doctor*, 1939; *This Man Is News*, 1939; *Television Spy*, 1939; *Sudden Money*, 1939; *St. Louis Blues*, 1939; *Some Like It Hot*, 1939; *The Star Maker*, 1939; *Rulers of the Sea*, 1939; *Our Leading Citizen*, 1939; *Our Neighbors, the Carters*, 1939; *Paris Honeymoon*, 1939; *Persons in Hiding*, 1939; *What a Life*, 1939; *Unmarried*, 1939; *Zaza*, 1939; *Adventure in Diamonds*, 1940; *Buck Benny Rides Again*, 1940; *Cherokee Strip*, 1940; *Christmas in July*, 1940; *Comin' Round the Mountain*, 1940; *Dancing on a Dime*, 1940; *French Without Tears*, 1940; *Doctor Cyclops*, 1940; *Emergency Squad*, 1940; *The Farmer's Daughter*, 1940; *Geronimo*, 1940; *The Ghost Breakers*, 1940; *Rhythm on the River*, 1940; *Remember the Night*, 1940; *Rangers of Fortune*, 1940; *Queen of the Mod*, 1940; *Quarterback*, 1940; *A Parole Fixer*, 1940; *Opened by Mistake*, 1940; *A Night at Earl Carrols*, 1940; *Golden Gloves*, 1940; *The Great McGinty*, 1940; *I Want a Divorce*, 1940; *Love Thy Neighbor*, 1940; *Moon Over Burma*, 1940; *Mystery Sea Raider*, 1940; *Road to Singapore*, 1940; *Safari*, 1940; *Seventeen*, 1940; *The Show Down*, 1940; *Stagecoach War*, 1940; *Those Were the Days*, 1940; *Women Without Names*, 1940; *The Way of All Flesh*, 1940; *Untamed*, 1940; *Typhoon*, 1940; *Three Men from Texas*, 1940; *Aloma of the South Seas*, 1941; *Among the Living*, 1941; *Life with Henry*, 1941; *Las Vegas Nights*, 1941; *The Lady Eve*, 1941; *Kiss the Boys Goodbye*, 1941; *I Wanted Wings*, 1941; *Hold Back the Dawn*, 1941; *Bahama*

*Passage*, 1941; *Birth of the Blues*, 1941; *Buy Me That Town*, 1941; *Caught in the Draft*, 1941; *Doomed Caravan*, 1941; *Flying Blind*, 1941; *Forced Landing*, 1941; *Glamour Boy*, 1941; *Henry Aldrich for President*, 1941; *West Point Widow*, 1941; *World Premiere*, 1941; *You're the One*, 1941; *You Belong to Me*, 1941; *Ball of Fire*, 1941; *Skylark* (with Irene), 1941; *Kiss the Boys Goodbye*, 1941; *Sullivan's Travels*, 1941; *The Road to Zanzibar*, 1941; *Here Comes Mr. Jordan*, 1941; *There's Magic in Music*, 1941; *Virginia*, 1941; *Shepherd of the Hills*, 1941; *Reaching for the Sun*, 1941; *New York Town*, 1941; *One Night in Lisbon*, 1941; *The Gay Sisters (with Milo Anderson)*, 1942; *I Married a Witch*, 1942; *The Major and the Minor*, 1942; *The Road to Morocco*, 1942; *This Gun for Hire*, 1942; *Beyond the Blue Horizon*, 1942; *The Remarkable Andrew*, 1942; *The Fleet's In*, 1942; *Young and Willing*, 1942; *My Favourite Blond*, 1942; *Are Husbands Necessary?*, 1942; *Holiday Inn*, 1942; *The Glass Key*, 1942; *Star Spangled Rhythm*, 1942; *Lucky Jordan*, 1942; *Flesh and Fantasy* (with V. West), 1943; *True to Life*, 1943; *Lady of Burlesque* (with Natalie Visart), 1943; *Not Time for Love* (with Irene), 1943; *The Crystal Ball*, 1943; *China*, 1943; *Salute for Three*, 1943; *Five Graves to Cairo*, 1943; *Riding High*, 1943; *Let's Face It*, 1943; *Hostages*, 1943; *Tender Comrade* (with Renie), 1943; *And Now Tomorrow*, 1944; *Going My Way*, 1944; *Here Come the Waves*, 1944; *I Love a Soldier*, 1944; *I'll Be Seeing You*, 1944; *Our Hearts Were Young and Gay*, 1944; *The Uninvited*, 1944; *Standing Room Only*, 1944; *Lady in the Dark* (with Du Bois and Leisen), 1944; *Rainbow Island*, 1944; *Double Indemnity*, 1944; *Ministry of Fear*, 1944; *And the Angels Sing*, 1944; *Hour Before Dawn*, 1944; *The Affairs of Susan*, 1945; *The Bells of St. Mary's*, 1945; *Christmas in Connecticut* (with Milo Anderson), 1945; *Duffy's Tavern* (with Dodson), 1945; *Incendiary Blonde*, 1945; *The Lost Weekend*, 1945; *Love Letters*, 1945; *Masquerade, in Mexico*, 1945; *A Medal for Benny*, 1945; *Miss Susie Slagle's* (with Dodson), 1945; *Out of This World*, 1945; *The Road to Utopia*, 1945; *The Stork Club*, 1945; *The Blue Dahlia*, 1946; *My Reputation* (with Rhodes), 1946; *Notorious*, 1946; *The Strange Love of Martha Ivers*, 1946; *To Each His Own*, 1946; *The Virginian*, 1946; *The Well-Groomed Bride*, 1946; *Blue Skies* (with Waldo Angelo), 1946; *The Perfect Marriage*, 1946; *Cross My Heart*, 1946; *The Bride Wore Boots*, 1946; *California*, 1946; *The Road to Rio*, 1947; *The Two Mrs. Carrolls* (with Milo Anderson), 1947; *Welcome Stranger*, 1947; *My Favorite Brunette*, 1947; *Desert Fury*, 1947; *I Walk Alone*, 1947; *Where There's Life*, 1947; *Wild Harvest*, 1947; *Perils of Pauline*, 1947; *Variety Girl*, 1947; *Blaze of Noon*, 1947; *Ramrod*, 1947; *The Big Clock*, 1948; *The Emperor Waltz* (with Gile Steele), 1948; *A Foreign Affair*, 1948; *Miss Tatlock's Millions*, 1948; *The Night Has a Thousand Eyes*, 1948; *Rachel and the Stranger*, 1948; *Sorry Wrong Number*, 1948; *Arch of Triumph*, 1948; *Dream Girl*, 1948; *My Own True Love*, 1948; *Beyond Glory*, 1948; *Sainted Sisters*, 1948; *So Evil My Love*, 1948; *Isn't It Romantic*, 1948; *June Bride* (with Rhodes), 1948; *The Heiress* (with Gile Steele), 1949; *Red, Hot and Blue*, 1949; *Rope of Sand*, 1949; *My Friend Irma*, 1949; *The Great Lover*, 1949; *The Great Gatsby*, 1949; *Beyond the Forest*, 1949; *Copper Canyon* (with Gile Steele), 1950; *Mr. Music*, 1950; *My Foolish Heart* (with Wills), 1950; *My Friend Irma Goes West*, 1950; *Riding High*, 1950; *Samson and Delilah* (with Gile Steele, Jeakins Wakeling, and Elois Jenssen), 1950; *Sunset Boulevard*, 1950; *Paid in Full*, 1950; *September Affair*, 1950; *All about Eve* (with Charles LeMaire), 1950; *The Big Carnival*, 1951; *Branded*, 1951; *Detective Story*, 1951; *Here Comes the Groom*, 1951; *The*

*Lemon Drop Kid*, 1951; *Payment on Demand*, 1951; *A Place in the Sun*, 1951; *That's My Boy*, 1951; *Carrie*, 1952; *The Greatest Show on Earth* (with Jeakins and White), 1952; *Jumping Jacks*, 1952; *Just for You* (with Wood), 1952; *My Favorite Spy*, 1952; *Sailor Beware*, 1952; *Son of Paleface*, 1952; *Something to Live For*, 1952; *The Caddy*, 1953; *Come Back Little Sheba*, 1953; *Off Limits*, 1953; *Road to Bali*, 1953; *Roman Holiday*, 1953; *Sangaree*, 1953; *Scared Stiff*, 1953; *Shane*, 1953; *The Stooge*, 1953; *Red Garters* (with Wood), 1953; *The Stars Are Singing*, 1953;, *Elephant Walk*, 1954; *Here Come the Girls*, 1954; *Knock on Wood*, 1954; *Living It Up*, 1954; *Money from Home*, 1954; *The Naked Jungle*, 1954; *Rear Window*, 1954; *Sabrina*, 1954; *White Christmas*, 1954; *The Country Girl*, 1954; *About Mrs. Leslie*, 1954; *Artists and Models*, 1955; *The Bridges at Toko-Ri*, 1955; *The Desperate Hours*, 1955; *The Far Horizon*, 1955; *The Girl Rush*, 1955; *Hell's Island*, 1955; *Lucy Gallant*, 1955; *The Rose Tattoo*, 1955; *Run for Cover*, 1955; *The Seven Little Foys*, 1955; *Strategic Air Command*, 1955; *Three Ring Circus*, 1955; *To Catch A Thief*, 1955; *The Trouble with Harry*, 1955; *You're Never Too Young*, 1955; *Anything Goes*, 1956; *The Birds and the Bees*, 1956; *The Court Jester* (with Wood), 1956; *Hollywood or Bust*, 1956; *The Leather Saint*, 1956; *The Man Who Knew Too Much*, 1956; *The Mountain*, 1956; *The Proud and the Profane*, 1956; *Pardners*, 1956; *The Rainmaker*, 1956; *The Scarlet Hour*, 1956; *The Search for Bridey Murphey*, 1956; *The Rose Tattoo*, 1956; *The Ten Commandments*, 1956; *The Buster Keaton Story*, 1957; *Beau James*, 1957; *The Delicate Delinquent*, 1957; *The Devil's Hairpin*, 1957; *Fear Strikes Out*, 1957; *Funny Face* (with Hubert de Givenchy), 1957; *Gunfight at the O.K. Corral*, 1957; *Hear Me Good*, 1957; *The Joker Is Wild*, 1957; *Loving You*, 1957; *The Sad Sack*, 1957; *Short Cut to Hell*, 1957; *The Ten Commandments* (with Jeakins, Jester, John Jensen, and Arnold Friberg), 1957; *The Tin Star*, 1957; *Three Violent People*, 1957; *Wild is the Wind*, 1957; *As Young as We Are*, 1958; *The Buccaneer* (with Jester), 1958; *The Geisha Boy*, 1958; *Hot Spell*, 1958; *Houseboat*, 1958; *Splendour in the Grass*, 1958; *The Facts of Life*, 1960; *Pepe*, 1960; *A Pocketful of Miracles*, 1961; *David and Lisa*, 1962; *America, America*, 1963; *Ladybug, Ladybug*, 1963; *Fail Safe*, 1964; *Harvey Middleman*, 1965; *Fireman*, 1965; *The Pawnbroker*, 1965; *The Group*, 1966; *The Oscar* (also personal appearance), 1966; *Bye Bye Braverman*, 1968; *The Night They Raided Minsky's*, 1968; *The Subject Was Roses*, 1968; *The Swimmer*, 1968; *Alice's Restaurant*, 1969; *Sweet Charity*, 1969; *Butch Cassidy and the Sundance Kid*, 1969; *Topaz*, 1969; *Cotton Comes to Harlem*, 1970; *Airport*, 1970; *Myra Breckinridge*, 1970; *Sometimes a Great Notion*, 1971; *Hammersmith Is Out*, 1972; *Pete n' Tillie*, 1972; *A Doll's House*, 1973; *The Sting*, 1973; *The Taking of Pelham 123*, 1974; *Airport 1975*, 1974; *Serpico*, 1974; *Rooster Cogburn*, 1975; *The Man Who Would Be King*, 1975; *Gable and Lombard*, 1976; *W.C. Fields and Me*, 1976; *Family Plot*, 1976; *Airport 77*, 1977; *The Big Fix*, 1978; *Olly Olly Oxen Free*, 1978; *Sextette*, 1978; *The Last Married Couple in America*, 1979; *Dead Men Don't Wear Plaid*, 1982.

## Publications

**By HEAD: books**—(with Jane Kesner Ardmore) *The Dress Doctor*, Boston, 1959; (with Joe Hyams) *How to Dress for Success*, New York, 1967; (with Paddy Calistro) *Edith Head's Hollywood*, New York, 1983; **articles**—in *Silver Screen* (New York), September 1946, January 1948; *Hollywood Quarterly* (Los Angeles), October 1946; *Photoplay* (New York), October 1948; *Good Housekeeping* (New York), March 1959; *Holiday* (New York), January 1973, July 1973, September 1974, November 1974, January 1975, March 1975, September 1975, March 1976; *Inter/View* (New York), January 1974; *Take One* (Montreal), October 1976; *American Film* (Washington, D.C.), May 1978; *Cine Revue* (Paris), 19 April 1979.

**On HEAD: books**—*Fashion Is Our Business* by Beryl Williams, New York, 1945, London, 1947; *Hollywood Speaks: An Oral History* by Mike Steen, New York, 1974; *Romantic and Glamorous Hollywood Design,* exhibition catalogue by Diana Vreeland, New York, 1974; *Hollywood Costume* by Dale McConathy, New York, 1976; *Hollywood Costume Design* by David Chierichetti, London, 1976; *Hollywood Film Costume,* exhibition catalogue by Michael Regan, Manchester, 1977; *In a Glamorous Fashion: The Fabulous Years of Hollywood Costume Design* by W. Robert La Vine, Boston and London, 1981.

*       *       *

Fashion designer Edith Head is probably the most noted purveyor of Hollywood glamour during its heyday as the epitome of resplendent fashion extravaganza. Her approach to designing fashions and makeup for the stars of the movies was to create the total aura of the special characterization called for by each role. She achieved her aim by adapting her subject so that the viewers would be persuaded to believe the primary reality of the part over the real-life persona of the star. When she worked with Grace Kelly in three very different parts, with Bette Davis in *All About Eve,* or with Audrey Hepburn in *Roman Holiday,* she always considered unique, on-camera personality as primary, using what she has called a "cross between camouflage and magic" to dream up the hairstyle, complete outfitting, and type of makeup that would bring the character in that role to life most vividly.

During the period of Head's reign in Hollywood, the clothes a star wore were the real thing—expensive furs, jewels, hand-beaded gowns—lavishly gorgeous and stressing imaginative appeal over accuracy to ordinary daily lifestyles. While always allowing for the settings and times of the roles, Head also enveloped the actor or actress in a complete image, so as to build a mystique which contributed quite prominently to the total spell of the glamorous Hollywood myth of her time. She was successful in enchanting movie goers to anticipate the work of her fashion designs almost as much as they would the acting or the script. More than any other single designer for films, Head will always be remembered for clothes which started fashion rages that swept the country when one of her movies was released. She also gained further influence as a character and as a journalist in her own right, appearing often in her customary garb of heavily-framed glasses, basic suit, and severe bun hairdo on television and radio shows over the years and putting out a popular column of fashion commentary which was printed regularly in more than forty newspapers.

Head's basic tenets of design were geared to making people look both younger and thinner. She advocated using darker colors in what she called "the danger areas," the places where the figure is thicker, and she believed that heavier people should never wear tight clothing or choose shiny fabrics or bold patterns for the larger parts of their physiques. During most of her career, Head dressed women, but she also did some outstanding work for male stars, such as Paul Newman and Robert Redford in the 1973 movie, *The Sting.*

In her last years, as the high glamour of Hollywood declined in favor of a "real life" preference for jeans over jewels, Head designed uniforms for Pan American airline stewardesses and women in the Coast Guard. She also designed clothing to appear as Vogue Patterns for women to sew for themselves. But Head will always be synonymous with the era of Hollywood glamour as personified by Joan Crawford and Barbara Stanwyck.

—Barbara Cavaliere

# HECKROTH, Hein
German painter, stage, and film designer

**Born:** Giessen, 14 April 1901. **Education:** Educated at the Volksschule, Giessen, until 1914; studied book printing and typography, in Giessen, 1915-19; studied painting, under Ludwig Gies, at the Stadelsche Kunstinstitut, Frankfurt, 1920, and under Reinhold Ewal, at the Zeichnen-Akademie, Hanau, 1921. **Family:** Married the painter Ada Maier in 1924; daughter: Renate. **Career:** Independent painter and stage designer from 1921, film designer from 1939, and television designer from 1953, in Wiesbaden, 1921-23, Munich, 1924-26, Essen, 1927-33, Amsterdam, 1933, Paris, 1934, London, 1935-39 and 1941-54 (interned in Australia, 1940-41), and in Frankfurt, 1955-70. Stage designer, for the Kunstlertheater für Rhein und Main, Wiesbaden, 1921, and for choreographer Kurt Joos, in Munich and throughout Europe, 1924-35; art director, Municipal Theatres, in Essen, 1927-33, and in Frankfurt, 1956-70; also guest designer at theatres in Chemnitz, Cologne, Hagen, Düsseldorf, Munich, and Paris, 1927-33, and in London, Baltimore, Berlin, Frankfurt, and Milan, 1935-70. Art director, for Michael Powell and Emerica Pressburger's Archer Films, then for Rank, London, and Lion Films, working in London, Munich, and Hollywood, 1945-66. Head of stage design, Folkwangschule, Essen, 1929-33; professor of stage design, Akademie der Bildenden Künste, Dresden, 1932; instructor, Dartington Hall, South Devon, 1935-39. **Exhibitions:** Modern Art Gallery, London, 1943; Kunstverein, Frankfurt, 1970; Kunsthalle, Kassel, 1977. **Honors:** Kunstpreis der Rheinische Sezession, 1932; International Choreography Competition Prize, Paris, 1932; Academy Award, 1948. **Died:** Alkmaar, Netherlands, 6 July 1970.

## Works

Film designs include—*Caesar and Cleopatra* (Pascal), 1945; *A Matter of Life and Death* (Powell and Pressburger), 1946; *Black Narcissus* (Powell and Pressburger), 1947; *The Red Shoes* (Powell and Pressburger), 1948; *The Small Back Room* (Powell and Pressburger), 1948; *Gone to Earth* (Powell and Pressburger), 1950; *The Elusive Pimpernel* (Powell and Pressburger), 1950; *The Tales of Hoffmann* (Powell and Pressburger), 1951; *The Story of Gilbert and Sullivan* (Gilliat), 1953; *Ludwig II* (Kautner), 1954; *Oh... Rosalinda* (Powell and Pressburger), 1955; *The Sorcerer's Apprentice* (Powell), 1955; *The Battle of the River Plate* (Powell and Pressburger), 1956; *Robinson soll nicht sterben* (von Baky), 1957; *Die Dreigroschenoper* (Staudte), 1962; *Bluebeard's Castle* (Powell), 1964; *Torn Curtain* (Hitchcock), 1966.

## Publications

**By HECKROTH: booklet**—*Meine Arbeit als Buhnebilder, Filmarchitekt und Fernseedesigner,* Rotary Club address, Frankfurt, 1962; **articles**—in *Programmheft des Theaters der Stadt Munster* (Munster), no. 3, 1924, no. 5, 1924, no. 10, 1924; *Die Theater-Welt* (Frankfurt), no. 10, 1930; *Programm der Deutschen Oper am Rhein* (Düsseldorf), no. 2, 1957.

**On HECKROTH: books**—*Surrealist Paintings by Hein Heckroth,* exhibition folder with text by Herbert Read, London, 1943; *Art in Modern Ballet* by G. Arbert, New York, 1946; *Art and Design in the British Film* by Edward Carrick, London, 1948; *The Red Shoes Ballet: A Critical Study* by Monk Gibbon, London, 1948; *Hein Heckroth 1901-1970,* exhibition catalogue by Helmut Grosse and Ewald Rathke, Frankfurt, 1970; *Le Decor de Film* by Leon Barsacq, Paris, 1970, as *Caligari's Cabinet and Other Grand Illusions,* Boston, 1976; *Hein Heckroth 1901-1970,* exhibition catalogue by Erich Herzog and Karlheinz Gabler, Kassel, 1977; *The International Film Encyclopedia* by Ephraim Katz, New York and London, 1980.

\*   \*   \*

Hein Heckroth preserved his German cosmopolitanism in his years of exile, and it formed the cultural base from which his irony could inform his work. There was, thus, a considerable continuity to his work, though his consistency at no time inhibited his development or zest for experiment, which probably underlay *Sins,* enjoyed in its 1960 Frankfurt revival. It was said that his contribution had played an important part in that success, which came on the heels of his two films that also had successful showings in Germany.

Heckroth's freely brushed style of design might lead one to underestimate his meticulous attention to the details of production. However, at no time during his career did he have to revise his designs in the light of practical theatrical requirements. For his films, his foresight was even more striking, as they needed great, labyrinthine sets that could easily have been disastrous failures had he not had a grasp of the spaces they would use. In his designs, he also brilliantly overcame the shortcomings of the colour film process of that time by avoiding the difficult colours and awkward combinations.

In the light of his style of drawing and painting and in view of the somewhat loose terminology used about German art of the early years of the twentieth century, the label "expressionist" has sometimes been attached to his work. As far as this term is taken to mean merely avant-garde art of an alternative tendency to that associated with developments in Paris up to the war, then it probably is not misleading. However, as his association with Kurt Joos demonstrates, his work retained a strong intellectual content, while his sense of irony precluded indulgence in self-expression. Furthermore, his very method of working, although often initiated by sketches of a rudimentary nature, was one of elaboration from initial idea through to finished project, every detail and effect carefully calculated, and nothing left to chance.

Nowhere was this latter aspect of his work more evident than in the film *Red Shoes,* for which he not only had to design the sets and costumes but the angles from which the action would be shot. This, none of your splash-and-dash expressionism could have permitted. It is worth remembering that he told a wartime London audience that the calculation that went into *The Cabinet of Dr. Caligari,*

along with what he held to be its anti-nationalist message, removed that film from the taint of expressionism. How much more so must we understand that this was to apply as well to his own work for the cinema.

—Toni del Renzio

# HEELEY, Desmond

British stage designer

**Born:** West Bromwich, Staffordshire, 1 June 1931. **Education:** Educated at All Saints primary and secondary schools, West Bromwich, 1936-44; Ryland School of Art, West Bromwich, 1945. **Career:** Worked for the Birmingham Repertory Theatre Company, Warwickshire, 1945-47; wardrobe and property assistant, 1947-52, and designer, from 1955, Shakespeare Memorial (now Royal Shakespeare) Theatre Company, Stratford-on-Avon, Warwickshire; designer, for the Stratford Festival, Ontario, 1957-73, the Old Vic Theatre, London, from 1958, and for the Tyrone Guthrie Theatre, Minneapolis. Instructor, Central School of Arts and Crafts, London. Has also worked as a television drama designer. **Honors:** Two Tony Awards, New York, 1968. **Address:** c/o Metropolitan Opera, Lincoln Center, New York, New York 10023

## Works

Stage productions include—*Toad of Toad Hall,* Shakespeare Memorial Theatre, Stratford-on-Avon, 1948; *The Lark,* London, 1955; *Titus Andronicus,* Shakespeare Memorial Theatre, 1955; *Hamlet,* Shakespeare Memorial Theatre, 1956; *Titus Andronicus,* London, 1957; *Twelfth Night,* Old Vic, London, 1958; *Macbeth,* Old Vic, 1958; *Farewell, Farewell, Eugene,* London, 1959; *The Double Dealer,* Old Vic, 1959; *The Merchant of Venice,* Shakespeare Memorial Theatre, 1960; *Toad of Toad Hall,* London, 1960; *Much Ado About Nothing,* Shakespeare Memorial Theatre, 1961; *The Devils,* London, 1961; *Romeo and Juliet,* Shakespeare Memorial Theatre, 1961; *Oh, Dad, Poor Dad,* London, 1961; *Cyrano de Bergerac* (with Tanya Moiseiwitsch), Straford, 1963; *Misalliance,* London, 1963; *Divorce a la Carte,* London, 1963; *Gentle Jack,* London, 1963; *Hamlet,* Old Vic, 1963; *Carving a Statue,* London, 1964; *La Contessa,* London (and U.K. tour), 1965; *Rosencrantz and Guildenstern Are Dead,* Old Vic, 1969; *Norma,* Metropolitan Opera, 1970; *In Praise of Love,* London, 1973; *Cyrano,* New York, 1973; *The Matchmaker,* Tyrone Guthrie Theatre, Minneapolis, 1976; *Don Pasquale,* Metropolitan Opera, 1978; *Manon Lescaut,* Metropolitan Opera, 1980.

## Publications

**By HEELEY: books**—*The Life of Timon of Athens: Designs by Desmond Heeley,* with introduction by Paul Scofield, London, 1976.

**On HEELEY: books**—*Who's Who in the Theatre,* London, 1972, 1977; *Creative Canada,* vol. 1, Toronto and Buffalo, 1974; *Metro-*

*politan Opera Encyclopedia,* New York, 1987; *British Theatre Design* edited by John Goodwin, London, 1989.

\*　　\*　　\*

Though he began his career in theatre at the Birmingham Repertory Theatre, it was in the shops of the Memorial Theatre, Stratford-on-Avon, working on the spectacular and richly romantic productions of Shakespeare presented there in the late 1940s and early 1950s, that Desmond Heeley developed his love of surface textures under light. Since his first work was with stage properties, it is not surprising that his first costume designs for *Toad of Toad Hall,* first at Stratford and later in London, stressed the idea of costumes as expanded properties, particularly in the wonderful masks, headdresses, hands, and feet designed for this production.

From then on, in his many famous productions at Stratford and the Old Vic, his costume designs were always praised for their wonderful sense of movement, layered texture, subtle coloration, and great depth of surface. No matter what the production, the costumes always conjured up a world of lushness and complex richness that spoke with great force to the senses. All kinds of surface techniques were presented—from shredding, painting, and spattering, to layering one transparent or open-work surface over other glinting or opalescent textures. The historical sense of these costumes was always very fully developed, but the audience's sense of whatever historical period was being presented was always deepened and strengthened by the extra dimension of textures and tactile richness. His style could be said to be that of impressionistic symbolism, with the added sense of texture that has come to modern art through junk art, collage, action painting, and abstract expressionism. Thus, the overall effect was moodily and impressionistically romantic, but the direct perception of forms and surfaces was deeply physical.

Heeley's work has been seen at its best in Shakespeare and opera where the imagery and poetry of story and character are larger than life and operate upon an audience by making it expect an enhanced richness and depth of costume effect. Thus, Heeley's work never presents an audience with visual ideas and never relates to the real world of politics, values, or the environment, but always operates subliminally to give the spectator a colorful fantasy world. His particular influence upon younger Shakespearean designers has been in the area of surface techniques, including costume painting, the use of melted plastics, the outlining of braids and buttons, the highlighting and shadowing of costumes, and the development of laces and nets over other textures to give richness and surface complexity to a production.

—Douglas A. Russell

# HEIKKILA, Simo
Finnish interior, exhibition, and furniture designer

**Born:** Helsinki, 2 May 1943. **Education:** Studied at the Academy of Applied Arts, Helsinki, Dip., 1967. **Career:** Assistant designer, Marimekko textile company, Helsinki, 1967-70; freelance designer, establishing own studio in Helsinki, from 1971; has designed furniture for Asko, Avarte, Haimi, Nupponen, Tarzan, Uveka, Vivero/Economic, and others; collaborated with designer Yro Wiherheimo,

1972-80; has worked with experimental furniture designs, from 1981. Instructor, Institute of Technology, Helsinki, 1971-75, and University of Industrial Arts, Helsinki, since 1975. **Exhibitions:** *Finland Designs 2,* Museum of Applied Arts, Helsinki, 1981; *Finnland Gestaltet,* Museum für Kunst und Gewerbe, Hamburg, 1981 (toured); *Scandinavian Modern Design 1880-1980,* Cooper-Hewitt Museum, New York, 1982 (toured); *Finland: Nature, Design, Architecture,* Cranbrook Academy of Art, Bloomfield Hills, Michigan, 1982 (toured); *Simo Heikkila: Pieces of Wood,* Galleri Bronda, Helsinki, 1984; *Finse Vormgeving,* Van Reekummuseum, Apeldoorn, 1984; *Full-Scale Furniture,* Kluuvi Gallery, Helsinki, 1984; *New Chairs from Scandinavia,* Artek Gallery, Helsinki, 1984; *Simo Heikkila: Pezzi di Legno,* Galleria Carelia, Milan, 1985. **Collections:** Museum of Applied Arts, Helsinki; Kunstindustrimuseet, Oslo; Museum für Kunst und Gewerbe, Hamburg; Cooper-Hewitt Museum, New York; Victoria and Albert Museum, London. **Honors:** Asko Furniture Competition Prize, Helsinki, 1968; *Kaunis Koti* magazine award, 1969; Finnish Association of Designers Scholarship, 1976; ESPE Competition Prize, Helsinki, 1980; Abitare Prize, Milan, 1981; Three-Year Finnish State Scholarship, 1981; SIO Interior Architects Award, Helsinki, 1983, 1984; First Prize, Lahti Design Competition, 1985; Finnish State Award for Industrial Design, 1985. **Address:** Vilhovuorenkatu 1 B, 00500 Helsinki, Finland.

### Publications

**By HEIKKILA: books**—(with Tapio Periainen and others) *Finnland Gestaltet,* exhibition catalogue, Espoo, 1981.

**On HEIKKILA: books**—*Scandinavian Modern Design 1880-1980* edited by David Revere McFadden, New York, 1982; *Finnish Vision,* with texts by P. Suhonen, J. Lintinen, and others, Helsinki, 1983; *Finnish Industrial Design* by Tuula Pontasuo, Helsinki, 1987.

# HEIN, Pieter
German stage and costume designer

**Born:** Berlin, 14 October 1938. **Education:** Studied stage design under Willi Schmidt, at the Hochschule für Bildende Kunste, Berlin-Charlottenburg, 1956-61; postgraduate studies under Karl von Appen, at the Deutsche Akademie der Kunste, East Berlin, 1962-64. **Family:** Married (divorced); children: Hieronymus, Yvonne, and Claudia. **Career:** Freelance stage designer, working for the Städtische Bühnen, Quedlinburg, and Volksbühne am Luxemburgplatz, East Berlin, 1961-63; assistant to Karl von Appen, 1965-67, and designer, 1968-69, Berliner Ensemble, East Berlin; designer, Volksbühne am Luxemburgplatz, East Berlin, 1970-80; freelance set and costume designer, East Berlin, from 1980; has worked with directors Manfred Karge and Matthias Langhoff, 1968-74, and with Fritz Marquardt, from 1974. **Exhibitions:** Prague Quadriennale of Scenography, 1967, 1971, 1976; *Die Bühne als szenischer Raum,* Zurich, 1980; *Bild und Szene,* East Berlin, 1981; *IX Kunstausstellung der DDR,* Dresden, 1982. **Honors:** *Berliner Zeitung* Critics' Prize, East Berlin, 1969, 1977. **Address:** Elsa-Brandström-Strasse 38, 1100 Berlin, Germany.

## Works

Productions include—*Emilia Galotti,* Volksbühne, East Berlin, 1962; *Die Rundkopfe und die Spitzkopfe,* Landestheater, Halle, 1964; *In der Suche J. R Oppenheimer,* Berliner Ensemble, East Berlin, 1965; *Der Schuhu und die fliegende Prinzessin,* Student-Ensemble, Staatliche Schauspielhaus, East Berlin, 1967; *Die Gesichte der Simon Machard,* DDR Television, 1968; *Wald,* Volksbhüne, 1971; *Die Rauber,* Volksbühne, 1971; *Der Brotladen,* Théâtre de la Commune, Aubervilliers, 1972; *Othello,* Volksbühne, 1972; *Die Wildente,* Volksbühne, 1973; *Spektakel,* Volksbühne, 1974; *Der Menschenhasser,* Volksbühne, 1975; *Die Bauern,* Volksbühne, 1976; *Danton's Tod,* Institut für Schauspielregie BAT, East Berlin, 1977; *Emilia Galotti,* Burgtheater, Vienna, 1978; *Ein Puppenheim,* Burgtheater, Vienna, and Akademietheater, East Berlin, 1979; *Die Fledermaus,* Schauspielhaus, Bochum, 1980; *Der Bau,* Volksbühne, 1980; *Gräfin Mariza,* Theater Greifswald, 1981; *Lulu,* Staatstheater, Dresden, 1983; *Gespenster,* Kammerspiele des Deutschen Theaters, East Berlin, 1983.

## Publications

**On HEIN: books**—*Stage Design Throughout the World 1970-1975* by René Hainaux and Nicole Leclercq, Brussels and London, 1976; *Die Schauspieltheater der DDR und das Erbe 1970-1974* edited by Manfred Nossig, East Berlin, 1976; *Streifzuge: Aufsätze und Kritiken* by Friedrich Dieckmann, East Berlin and Weimar, 1977; *Bühnebilder der DDR: Arbeiten aus den Jahren 1971-1977* edited by Friedrich Dieckmann, East Berlin, 1978; *Theaterbilder* by Friedrich Dieckmann, East Berlin, 1979.

\*     \*     \*

The stage designer Pieter Hein, one of the most original talents in the East German theatre, was a master pupil of Professor Karl von Appen. His stage designs are clearly influenced in their intellectual and dramatic content (but not in their practical artistic execution) by his teacher and model. Their rationalism and clear structure allow for telling arrangements, the actor becoming a decisive interpreter between image and scenic process. With extreme economy of decorative elements, Hein achieves a practical functionalism of the scene and, at the same time, great aesthetic effect. Brecht's epic theatre, the early German painters (particularly Albrecht Altdorfer), and the nineteenth-century Romantic Caspar David Friedrich have all inspired this artist.

Hein sees the stage as space, as a dynamic element that can be quickly and easily transformed. Theatre is presented in its dramatic functionalism. Nothing figurative or imitative is allowed; rather, he finds spatial solutions of expressive simplicity. Colors frequently play a decisive role: a brilliant red for Shakespeare's *Othello;* a stark white for Schiller's *The Robbers;* white, too, for Heiner Müller's *Peasants;* and gray for Müller's production piece *The Building.*

The *Robbers,* produced at the Berlin Volksbühne in 1971, was a sensational success due, not in the least, to Hein's stage design. For the castle scenes, he built an easily adaptable, multilayered, synchronized decor from fabrics and scaffolding. The forest dwelling of the young, rebellious robbers was presented totally bare before a few white hangings on an almost empty stage—until the rich plunder covered it. The theme of the play—young people protesting anarchically against old, inherited hierarchies—came over clearly in the designer's presentation, which deliberately gave free play to the associative fantasies of the audience. At the end, the robbers crouched like enormous, dark birds in the white, burnt frame of the castle from which the fabrics had been torn.

Ibsen's *Wild Duck* presented in the first scene a gorgeous winter garden, richly furnished in the style of the period, and in due course, a stage crammed and overstuffed with lumber and torsos. In the background was to be seen a tableau vivante from which the characters stepped out, with a well calculated alternation of private and ceremonial behaviour. For Müller's *Peasants,* in a sequence from the early history of the German Democratic Republic, Hein designed an enormous, white stairway (which clearly called on expressionist precedents) on which figures and properties, historically exact and realistic, presented dramatic effects.

The frequent collaboration with the producers Manfred Karge and Manhias Langhoff, who were also previously active at the Berliner Ensemble and influenced by Brecht's epic theatre, substantially influenced Hein's work; from the effort of these producers to achieve a demonstrative method of acting aimed at alienation, Hein discovered those spatial solutions in which consciously exhibited theatricality and rationally developed action also find their place in stage design.

—Ineborg Pietzsch

# HENNESY, Dale
American painter and film designer

**Born:** Washington, D.C., 1926. **Education:** Studied painting and motion picture illustration, the School of Applied Arts, Glendale, California, 1948-50. **Career:** Sketch artist and illustrator, from 1952, chief sketch artist for art director John DeCuir, 1956-62, art director, 1963-81, 20th Century-Fox film studios, Hollywood. Also taught private classes in painting. **Honors:** Academy Award, 1966. **Died:** Los Angeles, California, in 1981.

## Works

Film designs include—*Under the Yum Yum Tree* (Swift), 1963; *Good Neighbor Sam* (Swift), 1964; *John Goldfarb Please Come Home* (Lee Thompson), 1965; *Fantastic Voyage* (Fleischer), 1966; *In like Flint* (Douglas), 1967; *Adam at 6AM* (Scheerer), 1970; *Cover Me, Babe* (Black), 1970; *The Christian Licorice Store* (Frawley), 1971; *Simon, King of the Witches,* 1971; *Dirty Harry* (Siegel), 1971; *Everything You Always Wanted to Know About Sex* (Allen), 1972; *A Time to Run* (Adamson), 1972; *Slither* (Zieff), 1973; *Battle for the Planet of the Apes* (Lee-Thompson), 1973; *Sleeper* (Allen), 1973; *Young Frankenstein* (Brooks), 1974; *Logan's Run* (Anderson), 1976; *King Kong* (Guillermin), 1976; *Dog Soldiers* (Reisz), 1978; *The Island* (Ritchie), 1980; *The Competition* (Oliansky), 1980; *Wholly Moses* (Weis), 1980; *Annie* (Huston), 1982.

## Publications

**On HENNESY: books**—*Le Decor de Film* by Leon Barsacq, Paris, 1970, as *Caligari's Cabinet and Other Grand Illusions,* Boston,

1976; *Special Effects* by Christopher Finch, New York, 1984; **articles**—in *American Cinematographe* (Paris), 1 January 1977; *Film Comment* (New York), May/June 1978.

# HENRION, F(rederick) H(enri) K(ay)
British graphic and industrial designer

**Born:** Nuremberg, Germany, 18 April 1914; emigrated to Britain, 1936, naturalized, 1946. **Education:** Attended the Melanchton Gymnasium, Nuremberg, 1924-33; trained as a textile designer, Paris, 1933-34; studied graphic design, École Paul Colin, Paris, 1934-36. **Military Service:** Served as exhibitions consultant, British Ministry of Information, and United States Office of War Information, 1940-45. **Family:** Married Daphne Hardy in 1947 (separated, 1970); children: Max, Paul, and Emma. **Career:** Independent designer from 1936; chief consultant designer, Sir William Crawford and Partners, London, 1946-47; art editor, *Contact* publication, London, 1947-48; art director, British Overseas Airways Corporation publications, 1949-51, and *Future* magazine, London, 1951; art editor, Bowater Papers, London, 1951-53; principal, Henrion Design Associates, 1951-73, HDA International, 1973-82, and Henrion, Ludlow, and Schmidt, London, from 1982; also design consultant to Blue Circle Cement, Braun AG, British Broadcasting Corporation, British Leyland, Coopers and Lybrand, KLM Royal Dutch Airlines, Volkswagen AG, Vorwerk AG, General Post Office, and others. Tutor in graphic design, 1948-50, and governor, 1957-61, Central School of Arts and Crafts, London; visiting lecturer, Royal College of Art, London, 1951-56; head of visual communications, 1976-79, and visiting lecturer in typography, 1979-83, London College of Printing; guest professor, Universidad Autonoma Metropolitana, Mexico City, 1982, Cooper Union, New York, 1984, and University of Essen, 1984-85. President, Society of Industrial Artists and Designers, London, 1960-62, Alliance Graphique Internationale, Paris, 1963-66, and ICOGRADA International Council of Graphic Design Associations, 1968-70; member, Council for Industrial Design, London, 1964-67; master of the faculty of Royal Designers for Industry, Royal Society of Arts, London, 1971-73. **Exhibitions:** *Henrion Design,* Institute of Contemporary Arts, London, 1960; *International Design Systems,* Intergraphic Gallery, Munich, 1971 (travelled to Darmstadt); *Corporate Design,* Design Centre, London, 1973, 1976; *Eye for Industry,* Victoria and Albert Museum, London, 1986. **Collections:** Imperial War Museum, London; Victoria and Albert Museum, London; Stedelijk Museum, Amsterdam; Museum für Kunst und Gewerbe, Hamburg; Museum of Modern Art, New York; Library of Congress, Washington, D.C. **Honors:** Order of the British Empire, 1951; Royal Designer for Industry, Royal Society of Arts, London, 1959; Japanese Institute of Packaging Award, 1969; Royal Society of Arts Duke of Edinburgh Award, London, 1971, 1973; Design and Art Direction Award, London, 1973; Brno Graphics Biennale Award, 1974; *Packaging* magazine Package of the Year award, New York, 1975; SIAD Design Medal, London, 1976; Senior Fellow, Royal College of Art, London, 1988. **Died:** London, 5 July 1990.

## Works

*Smoke Abatement* exhibition layouts, at Charing Cross Station, London, 1939.

*Dig for Victory* exhibition layouts, London Zoo, 1942.

Magazine covers, for *Harper's Bazaar,* New York, 1942-45.

Advertising campaign, for Harella Fashions, 1942-46.

*Design for Living* exhibition layouts, for the Army Bureau of Current Affairs, London, 1944 (with Herbert Read).

Electric sewing machine, for *Britain Can Make It* exhibition, Victoria and Albert Museum, London, 1946.

*Speedbird* magazine layouts and graphics, for British Overseas Airways Corporation, London, 1949-51.

Agriculture and Country Pavilions, at the Festival of Britain, South Bank, London, 1950-51.

*US and UK Laugh* exhibition layouts, at the London Tea Centre, 1953 (travelled to New York).

*Keep Britain Tidy* exhibition layouts, at the London Tea Centre, 1962.

British Pavilion exhibits, signs and graphics, at *Expo '67,* Montreal, 1967.

ICOGRADA posters, for the International Council of Graphic Design Associations, 1980-89.

Logotype symbol, for the National Theatre, London, 1983 (with Jan Dennis).

## Publications

**By HENRION: books**—(with Alan Parkin) *Design Coordination and Corporate Image,* London and New York, 1969; *Top Graphic Design,* Zürich, 1983; *AGI Annals 1989,* Tokyo, 1989; **articles**—in *Print* (New York), August 1956; *Art and Industry* (London), February 1957; *Design* (London), August 1959; *Design for Industry* (London), November 1959; *Industrial Design* (New York), August 1961; *Graphis* (Zürich), no. 129, 1967; *Print* (Washington, D.C.), November 1969.

**On HENRION: books**—*Who's Who in Graphic Art* edited by Walter Amstutz, Dubendorf, 1982; *The Conran Directory of Design* edited by Stephen Bayley, London, 1985; *An Introduction to Design and Culture in the Twentieth Century* by Penny Sparke, London, 1986; *Eye for Industry: Royal Designers for Industry 1936-1986,* exhibition catalogue by Fiona MacCarthy and Patrick Nuttgens, London, 1986; *Design Source Book* by Penny Sparke and others, London, 1986; **articles**—*Novum Gebrauchsgraphik,* 6-13 March 1989; *Print,* September/October 1990; *Design,* August 1990.

*

   In my fifty years of design practice, I have always believed that a designer's job is to adjust to new conditions and be ready to cope with them, ideally when they happen. Thus, although trained as a poster designer, I went into packaging, exhibition, and product design, and into advertising and TV design in the late 1950s, 1960s, and 1970s. I was one of the first to design corporate identity programmes in Europe and am now very interested and involved in computer-generated design. To some degree, my career has been the history and evolution of graphic design over the last fifty years and I hope it will continue to be so.

—F. H. K. Henrion

*       *       *

**F.H.K. Henrion:** *Metaphor and Ambiguity* **poster, for the International Council of Graphic Design Associations, 1989**

F. H. K. Henrion could measure up a situation from the periphery and trace it back to the central point of the argument with great speed. He was a lateral thinker, who could summarise clearly. Able also to detach himself from his own personal interest and viewpoint in order to see the interests of others, he could evaluate the consequences of an act in their entirety. These qualities, combined with intelligence and patience, account for Henrion's career as a successful designer for half a century. His clients included top advertising agencies, governments, and well-known corporations throughout Europe.

Henrion's work included exhibition design, typographical and sign systems, and industrial design. Although he was trained initially as a poster designer, he soon widened his interests to include packaging, exhibition and product design, and, from the mid-sixties, advertising and television design using computer and video techniques. One of the first to design corporate identity programmes in Europe, he integrated applied graphics over a wide field of uses: in transport, architecture, and symbols.

Henrion's style of design incorporates clear, crisp organisation which may be compared to the best of Swiss typography. His method functions on multiple levels; beyond the surface, there is always additional enriching meaning which is identifiable with the client's activities. Henrion's attention to detail was meticulous, and no matter what the end product—a brochure or a complex pavil-

ion—it was always well executed to the last detail, technically perfect. This designer's presentations to clients were exemplary, containing not only an understanding of the client's problems, but solutions which go beyond the client's expectations in practical terms and in spirit. Henrion's contribution to the new generation of designers has been considerable. Besides teaching at the Royal College of Art, the Central School of Art and Design, and the London School of Printing, he was a member of the National Council for Diplomas in Art and Design and of the National Advisory Council on Art Education. These and other similar posts gave him a chance to help revolutionise design education in Great Britain to such an extent that by the mid-1970s, Britain had become a leading nation in communication graphics and the quality of teaching, an example for other nations.

Henrion was both the chairman and programme organiser of the International Council of Graphic Design Associations Annual Student Seminar in London and the Alliance Graphique Internationale Student Seminar in Paris and New York, each attended by more than 1,000 students. He was also visiting professor at various universities in Europe and the United States.

—John Halas

## HERBERT, Jocelyn

British stage and film designer

**Born:** London, 22 February 1917. **Education:** Educated at Saint Paul's Girls School, London, until 1932; studied painting, Académie André L'Hôte, Paris, 1932-33; studied under Leon Underwood, Slade School of Fine Art, London, 1934-36; studied stage design, with Michael Saint Denis and George Devine, at the London Theatre Studio, 1936-37. **Education:** Married Anthony B. Lousada in 1937 (divorced, 1960). **Career:** Resident stage designer, English Stage Company, Royal Court Theatre, London, 1956-58; freelance designer, London, from 1958. **Exhibitions:** *Eye for Industry,* Victoria and Albert Museum, London, 1986; *British Theatre Design '83-'87,* Riverside Studios, London, 1988; retrospective, National Theatre, London, 1993 **Honors:** Associate, Royal College of Art, London, 1964; Royal Designer for Industry, Royal Society of Arts, London, 1971. **Address:** 45 Pottery Lane, London W11, England.

**Works**

Stage productions (for the Royal Court Theatre, London, unless specified) include—*The Chairs,* 1957; *Purgatory,* 1957; *The Sport of My Mad Mother,* 1958; *Krapps' Last Tape,* 1958; *Roots,* 1959; *Sergeant Musgrave's Dance,* 1959; *Chicken Soup with Barley,* 1960; *I'm Talking About Jerusalem,* 1960; *Trials by Logue: Antigone, The Trial of Cob and Leach,* 1960; *The Changeling,* 1961; *The Kitchen,* 1961; *Luther,* 1961; *Richard III,* Stratford-on-Avon, 1961; *A Midsummer Night's Dream,* 1962; *Chips With Everything,* 1962; *Happy Days,* 1962; *Skyvers,* 1963; *Exit the King,* 1963; *Baal,* Phoenix Theatre, London, 1963; *The Seagull,* Queen's Theatre, London, 1964; *Saint Joan of the Stockyards,* Queen's Theatre, 1964; *Inadmissible Evidence,* 1964; *Othello,* National Theatre at the Old Vic, London, 1964; *A Patriot for Me,* 1965; *Mother Courage,* National Theatre at the Old Vic, 1965; *The Lion and the Jewel,* 1966; *Ghosts,* Aldwych Theatre, 1967;

*Pygmalion,* His Majesty's Theatre, 1967; *Heartbreak House,* His Majesty's Theatre, London, 1967; *Tyger,* National Theatre, 1967; *Life Price,* 1969; *Three Months Gone,* 1970; *Home* (also in New York), 1970; *The Changing Room,* 1971; *Not I,* 1973; *Krapps' Last Tape,* 1973; *Savages,* 1973; *Cromwell,* 1973; *Beckett,* 1973; *End Game,* 1973; *Life Class,* 1974; *What the Butler Saw,* 1975; *Teeth-n-Smiles,* 1975; *Play and Other Plays,* 1976; *The Merchant of Venice,* New York, 1977; *Saratoga,* Aldwych Theatre, 1978; *Early Days,* National Theatre, 1980; *Galileo,* National Theatre, 1980; *The Orestia,* National Theatre, 1981; *Portage to San Cristobal of Adolph Hitler,* Mermaid Theatre, London, 1982; *The Devil and the Good Lord,* Lyric Hammersmith, London, 1984; *Gigi,* Lyric Shaftesbury, London, 1985; *J.J. Fahr, Phoenix* Theatre, London, 1987; *The March on Russia,* National Theatre, London, 1987; *Timon of Athens,* Leicester Haymarket, 1988; *The Trackers of Oxyrhynchus,* National Theatre, 1988; *Square Rounds,* National Theatre, 1992; *Stages,* National Theatre, 1992; *The Kaisers of Carnuntum,* Roman ruins of the arena in Carnuntum, Austria, 1995; *The Labourers of Herakles,* excavated site of the New Theatre of E.C.C.D., Delphi, Greece, 1995.
Opera stage designs include—*Orpheus and Eurydice,* Sadler's Wells Theatre, London, 1967; *The Force of Destiny,* Paris Opera, 1975; *The Abduction from the Seraglio,* Metropolitan Opera, New York, 1979; *Rise and Fall of the City of Mahagonny,* Metropolitan Opera, New York, 1979; *The Mask of Orpheus,* Coliseum, London, 1986.
Film designs include—*Tom Jones* (Richardson), 1961; *Isadora* (Reisz), 1968; *If...* (Anderson), 1969; *Hamlet* (Richardson), 1969; *Ned Kelly* (Richardson), 1970; *O' Lucky Man* (Anderson), 1973; *Hotel New Hampshire* (Richardson), 1984; *The Whales of August* (Anderson), 1987.

## Publications

**On HERBERT: books**—*Who's Who in the Theatre,* London, 1972, 1977; *Encyclopedia of World Theatre,* New York, 1973; *Eye for Industry: Royal Designers for Industry 1936-1986,* exhibition catalogue by Fiona MacCarthy and Patrick Nuttgens, London, 1986; *British Theatre Design '83-'87,* with texts by Timothy O'Brien and David Fingleton, London, 1988; *Jocelyn Herbert: A Theatre Workbook* edited by Cathy Courtney, London, 1993.

\*     \*     \*

Credited by Peter Brook with restoring a new simplicity and purity to the English theatre, Jocelyn Herbert exercises a scrupulous restraint regarding traditional stage decor and seeks a few key elements—usually realistically based, preferably of authentic materials—to capture the essence of a play or its specific scenes. She is attracted to minimal settings because she finds beauty in an empty stage with perhaps a single telling object on it. Both Herbert and the Royal Court Theatre as a whole openly acknowledged their debt to Bertolt Brecht in their work—not only in a concern with social, humanistic issues in the choice of plays, but also in their essentially austere, functional, quietly expressive mode of staging. Theatricality was present but never aggressively so, most often being subordinated to function and cleanness of form. In this, they augmented their initial commitment to the Copeau-Saint Denis model of discipline, economy, and grace, rather than departing from it.

Herbert's spare, realistically slanted work was especially evident in Royal Court productions such as John Arden's *Sergeant Musgrave's Dance* (1959), Arnold Wesker's *Chips with Everything*

(1962), and Brecht's *Baal* (1963), all of which employed a bare stage with cyclorama (sometimes with projections of painted murals) backing up relatively few, carefully selected and composed objects, usually lit by exposed instruments.

Her later work observed the same pattern but became larger in scale and more complex in operation. For Brecht's *Galileo* (1980), she stripped the stage to the bare walls but added a large, flown projection screen and a mobile platform to facilitate the flow of action and epic establishment of the story's context. For *The Orestia* (1981), she was able to draw upon her extensive work with masks in the Saint Denis school and strove for a balance of abstraction and character flavor. She also created a balance of ancient Greek and universal modern in the setting. In the middle of the stage rose a stark, metallic facade that echoed the huge, stageshop doors of the Olivier Theatre, thus establishing a striking unity between this contemporary theatre and the Greek setting. Offsetting the rectangular facade was a white circle for the chorus; such interplay of forms is a recurrent motif in her work. In all of Herbert's productions one is aware of a fine sense of spatial proportion and composition; her selectivity is never empty or bland.

—Jarka M. Burian

# HERITAGE, Robert

British furniture and product designer

**Born:** Birmingham, Warwickshire, 2 November 1927. **Education:** Studied at Birmingham College of Art, 1942-46; studied furniture design, Royal College of Art, London, 1948-51. **Family:** Married Dorothy Shaw in 1953; children: Paul, Rachel, and Michael. **Career:** Staff designer, at G. W. Evans furniture manufacturers, London, 1951-53; freelance designer, working with Dorothy Heritage, London, from 1953; founder-partner, with Harold Bartram, Ron Carter, George Cayford, and George Freeman, of Design Partners design studio, London, 1960-61; consultant to Archie Shine, Concord/Rotaflex, Elliott's, Race Furniture, Beaver and Tapley, Meurop, Green and Vardy, Eglin, Slumberland, Cintique, Program Furniture, and others. Instructor in design, Twickenham School of Art, London, 1953-55; professor of furniture design, Royal College of Art, London, 1974-85. **Exhibitions:** *Modern Chairs 1918-1970,* Whitechapel Art Gallery, London, 1970; *Design Since 1945,* Philadelphia Museum of Art, 1983; *Eye for Industry,* Victoria and Albert Museum, London, 1986. **Collections:** Museum of Modern Art, New York; Philadelphia Museum of Art; Victoria and Albert Museum, London; Museu de Arte Moderno, Rio de Janeiro. **Honors:** Honorary Designer, Royal College of Art, London, 1951; 13 Design Council Awards, London, 1958-1993; fellow, Chartered Society of Designers, London, 1960; Royal Designer for Industry, Royal Society of Arts, London, 1963; British Aluminium Award, London, 1966; Gute Form Prize, Bonn, 1972; Commander, Order of the British Empire, 1980. **Address:** 12 Jay Mews, Kensington Gore, London SW7 2EP, England.

## Works

*Heritage* wall storage units, for Archie Shine Limited, 1963.
Stainless steel cutlery, for Yote Manufacturing Company, 1963.

Robert Heritage: *Control Spot* for Concord Lighting, 1993. Courtesy of Concord Lighting

*Quartet* spotlight range, for Concord Lighting International, 1966.
*QE2* dining chair, for Race Furniture, 1969.
*Powerflood* halogen light fitting, for Concord Lighting International, 1971.
Master clock, for English Clock Systems, 1973.
*Superjet* bed lamp, for Concord Lighting International, 1979.
*Tipster* stacking and linking chair, for Race Furniture, 1980.
*Aspect* cellular ceiling system, for Interlight International, 1981.
*Articula* office chair range, for Antocks Lairn, 1981.
*Ambit* modular lighting system, for Tecnolyte, 1984.
Airport seating, for Eglin Furniture, 1993.
*Control Spot* lighting, for Concord Lighting, 1993.

**Publications**

**By HERITAGE: articles**—in *The Designer* (London), March 1972.

**On HERITAGE: books**—*The Adventure of British Furniture* by David Joel, London, 1953, as *Furniture Design Set Free,* London, 1969; *Furniture in Britain Today* by Dennis and Barbara Young, London, 1964; *Modern Chairs 1918-1970,* exhibition catalogue by Carol Hogben and others, London, 1970; *Modern Design in Metal* by Richard Stewart, London, 1979; *Twentieth Century Furniture*

*Design* by Philippe Garner, London, 1980; *Design Since 1945* edited by Kathryn Hiesinger and George Marcus, Philadelphia and London, 1983; *The Conran Directory of Design* edited by Stephen Bayley, London, 1985; *Eye for Industry: Royal Designers for Industry 1936-1986,* exhibition catalogue by Fiona MacCarthy and Patrick Nuttgens, London, 1986; *Twentieth Century Design: Furniture* by Penny Sparke, London, 1986.

# HERLOW, Erik

Danish architect and exhibition and industrial designer

**Born:** Helsingør, 5 January 1913. **Education:** Educated in Helsingør, until 1933; studied at the Royal School of Building, Copenhagen, 1933-36; Royal Academy of Fine Arts, Copenhagen, 1937-44. **Family:** Married Birgit Utzon Frank in 1946; children: Eva, Christian, and Camilla. **Career:** Architect and designer, Copenhagen, from 1942; consultant to A. Michelsen Metalworks, Copenhagen, 1942-49, Royal Danish Porcelain Factory, Copenhagen, from 1955, and Dart Industries, Europe and the United States, from 1968. Director of design instruction, Guldmedehøjskolen, Copenhagen, 1952-54; lecturer in industrial design, 1957-59, professor and director of industrial design courses, 1959-79, Royal Academy of Fine Arts, Copenhagen; visiting lecturer throughout Europe, the United States, and Japan. Scandinavian team consultant to the Association of Irish Industry and Applied Arts, Dublin, 1956; Committee Member, Danish National Bank Jubilee Fund, Copenhagen, 1968-75. **Member:** Member, Dansk Designerrad. **Exhibitions:** *An Exhibition for Modern Living,* Detroit Institute of Arts, 1949; Milan Triennale, from 1951; *Scandinavian Design,* 1954 (toured the United States); *Formes Scandinaves,* Musée des Arts Décoratifs, Paris, 1958; *Design Since 1945,* Philadelphia Museum of Art, 1983. **Collections:** Kunstindustrimuseet, Copenhagen; Röhsska Konstslöjdmuseet, Göteborg; Nationalmuseum, Stockholm; Kunstindustrimuseum, Bergen; Museum of Modern Art, New York; Victoria and Albert Museum, London. **Honors:** C. F. Hansen Prize, Copenhagen, 1948; Knud V. Engelhardt Memorial Grant, Copenhagen, 1949; Grand Prize, 1951, Gold Medal, 1954, 1957, and Silver Medal, 1954, 1960, Milan Triennale; Eckersberg Medal, Copenhagen, 1958; Life Stipend, Danish State Fund for the Endowment of the Arts, from 1980. **Address:** Erik Herlows Tegnestue, Gothersgade 143, 1123 Copenhagen K, Denmark.

## Works

Danish pavilion displays, at the Milan Triennale, 1951.
United States Embassy building, Copenhagen, 1952.
Coffee pot, for Dansk Aluminum Industri, 1952.
*Formes Scandinaves* exhibition layouts, for the Musée des Arts Décoratifs, Paris, 1958.
Museum of Forestry, Gavle, Sweden, 1961.
Dansk-Norsk Kvaelstoffabrik building, Grenaa, Denmark, 1961-63.
Shell Oil Refinery, Fredericia, Denmark, 1963-64.
Town Centre redevelopment, Albertslund, Denmark, 1963-67.
Research Centre, Vedbaek, Denmark, 1963-69.
Superflos factory and ancillary buildings, Vedbaek, Denmark, 1973-82.
Haldor Topsoe buildings, Ravnholm, Denmark, 1975-77.
*Airbus 300* interiors, for Scandinavian Airlines System, 1978-79.

## Publications

**By HERLOW: books**—*Good Things for Everyday Use,* Copenhagen, 1949; (with Ibi Trier-Morch) *Study Designs for Goldsmiths,* Copenhagen, 1952.

**On HERLOW: books**—*An Exhibition for Modern Living,* catalogue by A. H. Girard and W. D. Laurie, Detroit, 1949; *Modern Danish Silver* by Esbjorn Hiort, New York, London, and Copenhagen, 1954; *Made in Denmark* by Arne Karlsen and Anker Tiedemann, Copenhagen, 1960; *A Treasury of Scandinavian Design* by Erik Zahle, New York, 1961; *Scandinavian Design* by Ulf Hard af Segerstad, London and Stockholm, 1961; *Contemporary Danish Design* by Arne Karlsen, Bent Salicath, and Mogens Utzon-Frank, Copenhagen, 1966; *Dansk Kunstindustri 1900-1950* by Viggo Sten Moller, Copenhagen, 1970; *Danish Design* edited by Svend Erik Moller, Copenhagen, 1974; *Scandinavian Design: Objects of a Life Style* by Eileen Harrison Beer, New York and Toronto, 1975; *Design Since 1945* edited by Kathryn Hiesinger and George Marcus, London and Philadelphia, 1983;

*The Conran Directory of Design* edited by Stephen Bayley, London, 1985.

\*

My work as an industrial designer has, at all times, consisted of teamwork where a group works toward the development of products for and with industry. The main task of the designer is to influence the group work on the basis of a comprehensive view so that, at the earliest possible stage, it is possible to assess what the consequences of the development work for the enterprise, the consumer, and the society, will be. This implies that work should be performed methodically on the basis of a general knowledge and understanding, with the support of professional ability and artistic faculties. The general knowledge implies that the industrial designer is more freely placed as regards innovation in relation to the more unilateral and highly specialized members of the development group. The industrial designer will, in that situation, never be able to say "This is my creation." Rather, he can state, "This development work has been a success for us, for the benefit and pleasure of the producer, consumer/user, and society."

Therefore, the decisive factor is that the designer participates in the collaboration from the very beginning so that in all phases of development, the group can jointly evaluate the consequences of the work performed. By "consequences" I mean the financial and development results that the product development may have for the enterprise, both from a long-term and a short-term point of view. For the consumer, the consequence of the development work will be the satisfaction of a need in the best and finest way and not the establishment of an unnatural need. For society, the consequence must be assessed on the basis of the point of view that the satisfaction of a need will not have decisive or damaging effects on other justified needs and sectors. The physical design of a product reaches its optimal usefulness when there is an interrelation between economy, construction, material, function, aesthetics, ethics, and use.

—Erik Herløw

# HERNMARCK, Helena (Maria)
American weaver and tapestry designer

**Born:** Stockholm, Sweden, 22 April 1941; emigrated to the United States in 1975, naturalized, 1984. **Education:** Studied at Handarbetets Vanner Weaving School, Stockholm, 1958, and School of Art, Craft and Design (Konstfackskolan), Stockholm, 1959-63. **Family:** Married Jan Barynin in 1963 (divorced, 1967); married Michael Maconochie in 1971 (divorced, 1976); married Niels Diffrient in 1976. **Career:** Freelance professional tapestry designer working in Montreal, 1965-72, in London, 1972-73, in Blandford, Dorset, 1973-75, in New York City, 1975-80, and in Ridgefield, Connecticut, since 1980. Faculty and visiting critic, Rhode Island School of Design, Providence, 1993, 1995. **Exhibitions:** Quebec Architects Association, Montreal, 1965; Museum of Modern Art, 1973; Los Angeles County Museum of Art, 1974; Museum of Applied Art, Copenhagen 1977; Hiram Halle Memorial Library, Pound Ridge, New York, 1981; Birmingham Public Library, Alabama, 1986; Galleri Osterdahl, Stockholm, 1988, 1992; Greenwich Library, Connecticut, 1989; American Swedish Historical Museum,

Philadelphia, 1990; *Frontiers in Fiber: The Americans,* North Dakota Museum, 1988-90 (toured Asia); *State of the Art: Contemporary Fiber,* Loveland Museum, Loveland, Colorado, 1993; *Visions-Tapestry,* Minneapolis College of Art and Design, 1994; Brown/ Grotta Gallery, Wilton, Connecticut, 1994-95. **Collections:** Nationalmuseum Stockholm; Swedish State Council for the Arts, Stockholm; Röhsska Konstslöjdmuseet, Göteborg; National Gallery of Victoria, Melbourne; Museum of Modern Art, New York, Los Angeles County Museum of Art; Metropolitan Museum of Art, New York; Art Institute of Chicago; Minneapolis Institute of the Arts; Museum of Art, Rhode Island School of Design, Providence. **Honors:** Craftsmanship Medal, American Institute of Architects. **Address:** 879 North Salem Road, Ridgefield, Connecticut 06877, U.S.A.

## Works

*The Launching of the QE2* three tapestries, for Cunard Steamship Company, London, 1968.

*Newspapers* tapestry, for Swedenhouse, Stockholm, 1969 (relocated to National Museum).

*Rainforest* and *Vine Covered Maple* tapestries for Weyerhauser Company, Tacoma, Washington, 1970-71.

*Steel 1, 2* and *3* three tapestries, for Bethlehem Steel, Pennsylvania, 1973.

*Boston Harbor, Hancock Coat of Arms,* and *Sylt* tapestries, for John Hancock Mutual Life Insurance Company, Boston, 1973-75.

*Cloudscape* tapestry, for United Services Automobile Association, San Antonio, Texas, 1975.

*Sailing* tapestry, for Federal Reserve Bank, Boston, 1976.

*Journey* tapestry, for Aid Association for Lutherans, Appleton, Wisconsin, 1977.

*Poppies* and *Bluebonnets* tapestries, for Dallas Centre, Texas, 1978-79 (relocated to Anatol Hotel, Dallas).

*Wordscape* tapestry, for Stanford University Library, California, 1979.

*Family Feeling 1/2* two tapestries, for Johnson and Johnson, Skillman, New Jersey, 1981- 89.

*Six Flags of Texas* tapestry, for Texas Commerce Bank, Houston, 1981.

*Front Pages* tapestry, for Newsday, Melville New York, 1982.

*Oklahoma Suite* three tapestries, for Oklahoma First Tower, Oklahoma City, 1982.

*Blue Wash 1/2* two tapestries, for Pitney-Bowes Stamford, Connecticut, 1984.

*Divided Landscape* tapestry and carpet, for Kellogg's Company, Battle Creek, Michigan, 1986.

*Homage to Louis Sullivan* tapestry, for Fifield Development Corporation, Chicago, 1986.

*1909 Plan of Chicago* tapestry, for John Buck Company, Chicago, 1988.

*Up and Down* four tapestries, for Pepsicola, Somers, New York. 1989.

*Urn* tapestry, for One Ninety-one Peachtree Associates, Atlanta, Georgia, 1990.

*Beech Tree East* and *Beech Tree West* tapestries, for 450 Lexington Avenue Venture, New York, 1991.

*Springtime* and *Currency* tapestries, for NationsBank, Atlanta, Georgia, 1992.

*Tegelanbud,* for Posten AB, Stockholm, Sweden, 1994-95.

## Publications

**By HERNMARCK: articles**—"Helena Hernmarck: An Interview" in *Fiberarts* (Taos) March/April 1978; "A Letter to the Readers" in *International Tapestry Journal* (Portland, Oregon), Summer 1995.

**On HERNMARCK: books**—*Tree Temperament i Väv,* exhibition catalogue by Dag Widman, Helena Lutteman, and Katja Walden, Stockholm, 1976; *Swedish Textile Art* by Edna Martin and Beate Sydhoff, Stockholm, 1980; *Scandinavian Modern Design 1880-1980,* edited by David Revere McFadden, New York, 1982; *Craft Today: Poetry of the Physical* by Paul Smith, New York, 1986; *Helena Hernmarck,* exhibition catalogue with texts by Jack Lenor Larsen and Joan Barnum, Greenwich, Connecticut, 1989; *Tapestry* by Barty Philips, London, 1994; *Svenska Textilier 1890-1990,* Signum-Lund, 1994; *Tanken och Handen* edited by Gunilla Widengren, Stockholm, 1994; *Helena Hernmarck and Markku Kosonen,* exhibition catalogue, Wilton, Connecticut, 1994; **articles**—"Helena Barynina Hernmarck" in *Craft Horizons* (New York), March/April 1970; "Helena Hernmarck and the New Pointillism" by P. Blake in *Architecture Plus* (New York), April 1973; "Helena Hernmarck: Tapestry Designer" in *Interior Design* (New York), April 1977, "Photo Realism in a Mediaeval Medium" by A. Knight in *Horizon* (New York), December 1977; "The Artist and the Corporation: A Success Story" by M. Slavin in *Interiors* (New York), July 1981; "Painting Pictures with Fabric" by W. Von Eckhardt in *Time* (New York), 28 January 1985; "Dialogue with Architecture: Helena Hernmarck" by P. Scheinman in *American Craft* (New York), June/July 1988; "Made in America by Designing Duo" by Lyn Green-Rutanen in *FORM Function* (Finland), March 1988; "Weaver Scales Down Her Art for Show" by B. Liebenson in *New York Times,* 17 May 1989; "Swedish Roots Transplanted" by K. Wickman in *FORM Design Annual—Global Sweden* (Stockholm), 1989; "A Corporate Yarn" by M. Zelinsky in *Interiors,* April 1992; "Diffrient-Hernmarck" by Peter Blake in *Interior Design,* October 1994; "Helena Hernmarck Scales Down in Size Only" by Susan Tamulevich in *Fiberarts* (Asheville, North Carolina), Summer 1995.

\*

My design compositions fall loosely into four categories: photorealism; trompe l'oeil; watercolor designs; calligraphy and collage. Smaller pieces in residential scale tend to be more subtle and contemplative, whereas the corporate commissions, which are viewed in a hurried circumstance, are often large and startling. Landscapes and scenes from nature are used for their timelessness. Most of all, the image must be sympathetic to the architecture. I research for existing images, take photographs and use the color xerox machine. Lately, I'm experimenting with illusions of folded paper.

The goal is textile art, not production weaving. However, beyond tapestries, I also weave utilitarian textiles such as bedspreads, drapes, or upholstery fabrics. I enjoy threads and yarns, I like the way they carry color. So I choose this medium both for the material and the technique. I am a painter with yarn. Picture and fabric are created at once; the character of the cloth is part of the image. Photorealism is achieved by weaving the way that light and shadows fall on each form.

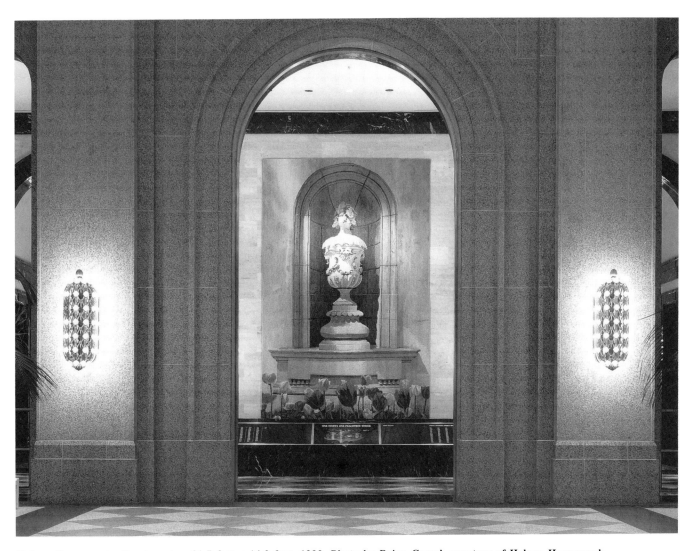

**Helena Hernmarck:** *Urn* **tapestry, 21.7 feet x 14.3 feet, 1990. Photo by Brian Gassel, courtesy of Helena Hernmarck**

From the structure of the weaving one gets a different impression, depending on whether it is seen from near or far. Observed from close up, each area is separated into layers, woven as tabby and pattern of blended yarns and colors. The image is defined by passing the bundle of pattern weft through the tabby—creating dots, dark areas against light, one surface under another to achieve translucent effects. Like Pointillism, this technique makes our eyes blend the colors and fill in the missing information. Colour mixes are adjusted constantly, and judged by looking through a reducing glass. Quality is achieved when workmanship, skill of execution, and finish look complete, with nothing superfluous. Then the image stands on its own as a woven textile. Additionally, weaving is time-consuming and, in translating the image, nothing of the fleeting moment must be lost. I work at the horizontal warp loom because it handles large work and gives me access to several harnesses and pedals. Choice of warp has bearing on the final look, even if the tapestries are weft faced. For weft, we assemble 500-600 colors of yarn for an average size tapestry of 10 feet by 15 feet, weighing a hundred pounds. It is important it hangs straight and stays flat, and carries its own weight. The largest tapestries are over 400 square feet, and take over nine months to complete. It is when I undertake these large-scale tapestries that assistants are a help, and almost seventy large pieces have been completed in the past thirty years.

—Helena Hernmarck

\*      \*      \*

Helena Hernmarck has achieved a distinctive contemporary style through her inventive fusion of photorealism and Swedish handweaving techniques. Her unique role has been in adapting the European workshop model to a modern corporate clientele, concentrating on large-scale photographic subjects, meticulously researched and rendered in luminous detail. Accessible and dramatic, her tapestries of striped flags billowing, newspaper pages, and wild flowers, among others, serve as vivid icons that enliven the corporate lobby or boardroom with a specific sense of place or history.

Hernmarck's reputation was enhanced by an early and continuous association with prominent U.S architectural firms, such as I.M Pei & Partners, and Skidmode, Owings & Merrill—the fruit of scheduled cross-country trips in 1967 and 1972 to present her portfolio while she resided and worked briefly in Canada and England. Through such influential architects, her work received immediate critical attention, beginning with the widespread publication of her two *Rainforest* commissions (1970-71) for the Weyerhauser Company of Tacoma, Washington, a decisive factor in the establishment of Hernmarck's studio in the Soho area of New York City in 1975.

In a climate sympathetic to Swedish design, and with the added prestige of a one-person exhibition at the Museum of Modern Art in New York in 1973, Hernmarck set out to build a career in an arena closed to most American craftsmen. With a single-minded enthusiasm and professional skill, she created tapestries for top corporations in the United States as well as in Europe and Australia. Her success can be measured not only by the durability of her works in situ—as compared with much fiber art that suffered disintegration or vandalism—but also by its acquisition for major permanent collections of twentieth-century design, including the double-sided *Mao/Yin Yang* (1971) by the Museum of Modern Art and *Glastonbury Tor* (1973) by the Metropolitan Museum of Art in 1987.

While the preference for custom spun and dyed Swedish wools and an uncompromising care in the weaving process are legacies of Hernmarck's training in Stockholm, her choice and interpretation of images account for her standing as an innovator. After moving to Ridgefield, Connecticut, in 1980, Hernmarck employed a greater variety of media for designing—striving always to respond freshly to each problem. *Blue Wash I and II* (1984), a pair of narrow vertical pieces for Pitney Bowes, of Stamford, Connecticut, provided a rare opportunity to experiment with abstraction, taken from a liquid watercolor design resembling a cascade. Hernmarck used a symmetrical geometric composition for the first time in a 1986 commission for the Fifield Corporation of Chicago, enlarging a ceiling pattern from the historic Stock Exchange Trading Room in her *Homage to Louis Sullivan.* By 1987, she felt ready to translate more personal images into a series of intimate exhibition pieces.

A resurgent interest in loom weaving, as fiber art returned to the wall in the 1980s, and notably in the coalescing of an international tapestry movement at a symposium organized in Melbourne, Australia in May 1988, at which Hernmarck was a keynote speaker, highlighted her importance in the evolution of contemporary tapestry. At the same time, a renewed emphasis on the role of the decorative arts in architectural design brings acclaim to Helena Hernmarck's pioneer work in corporate art.

—Pamela Scheinman

# HERRMANN, Karl-Ernst

German stage designer

**Born:** Berlin, in 1936. **Education:** Studied at the Meisterschule für Kunsthandwerk, West Berlin, 1953-57; studied stage design under Willi Schmidt, at the Hochschule für Bildende Künste, West Berlin, 1957-62. **Career:** Freelance stage designer, Ulm, 1962; designer, with Wilfried Minks, for the Stadttheater, Bremen, 1963-69; freelance designer, in Braunschweig, 1969-70; head of design, Schaubühne am Hallseschen Ufer, West Berlin, from 1970; guest designer, at the Hamburg Schauspielhaus, Hamburg Burgtheater, Munich Kammerspiele, and the Salzburg Festivals. **Address:** c/o Schaubühne am Lehniner Platz, Kurfurstendamm 153, 1000 Berlin 31, Germany.

## Works

Stage productions (at the Schaubühne, West Berlin, unless noted) include—*Jungle in the Cities,* Munich, 1968; *Die Mutter,* 1970; *Der Ritt uber den Bodensee,* 1971; *Peer Gynt,* 1971; *Das gerettete Venedig,* 1971; *Geschicheten aus dem Wiener Wald,* 1972; *Prinz Friedrich von Homburg,* 1972; *Optimistic Tragedy,* 1972; *Fegefeuer in Ingolstadt,* 1973; *Himmel und Erde,* Stuttgart, 1974; *Antiken Projekt: Ubungen für Schauspieler,* 1974; *Sommergäste,* Berlin, 1975; *Shakespeare's Memory,* 1976; *As You Like It,* 1977; *Gross und Klein,* 1978; *The Orestia,* 1980; *Kalldewey Farce,* 1981.

## Publications

**By HERRMANN: books**—(editor, with Ellen Hammer and Botho Strauss) *Peer Gynt: ein Schauspiel aus den neunzehnt Jahrunderts,* West Berlin, 1977.

**On HERRMANN: books**—*Stage Design Throughout the World 1970-1975* edited by René Hainaux and Nicole Leclercq, Brussels and London, 1976; *William Shakespeare: Wie es euch gefallt/As You Like It* by Northrop Frye, West Berlin, 1977; *Theater Lexikon* edited by Christoph Trilse, Klaus Hammer, and Rolf Kabel, West Berlin, 1978; *Das Theater der siebziger Jahre: Kommentar, Kritik, Polemik* edited by Georg Hensel, Stuttgart, 1980.

*       *       *

Karl-Ernst Herrmann's name is inextricably linked with director Peter Stein's because Herrmann has been Stein's principal designer at the Schaubühne, in West Berlin, since 1971. Herrmann first worked with Stein in 1968 on a production of Brecht's *Jungle in the Cities,* in Munich. This came at the end of Herrmann's tenure as the junior designer at the Bremen Stadttheater during the 1960s, a time of great excitement in Bremen when designer Wilfried Minks was creating daring and innovative theater. Emerging from Minks' shadow when he moved to the Schaubühne in 1971, Herrmann began filling neutral spaces with complete audience-stage environments.

His most famous works, in collaboration with directors Stein, Luc Bondy, and others, were created for the Schaubühne, first in the confines of an old lecture hall (e.g., *Peer Gynt,* 1971; *Optimistic Tragedy,* 1972; and *Summerfolk,* 1974). When the Schaubühne ensemble outgrew this hall, Herrmann designed more extravagant spaces in an old film studio in Spandau (e.g., *Shakespeare's Memory,* 1976; *As You Like it,* 1977; and *Gross und Klein,* 1978). Finally, in the late 1970s, the city of Berlin gave the by then world-renowned ensemble a permanent home in a renovated Erich Mendelsohn movie theater on Lehniner Platz. In this flexible space, outfitted with sophisticated technical machinery that can transform the interior into one, two, or three separate theaters with variable floors, Herrmann designed imaginative spaces for *The Oresteia* (1980), and *Kalldewey Farce* (1981), among others.

Throughout his work at the Schaubühne, Herrmann has demonstrated a strong regard for the importance of the actor and the text. Unlike other prominent German designers of the 1970s and 1980s who gave their designs independent expression apart from the text and actors, Herrmann's work always played a supportive role within the dramatic hierarchy. Thus, although he has stimulated others to use unconventional rooms for theater productions, Herrmann has always adhered to the traditional, conservative view of the function of stage design, seeing it as subordinate to, and supportive of, the dramatic action.

—Richard V. Riddell

# HICKS, David (Nightingale)

British interior and furnishings designer

**Born:** London, 25 March 1929. **Education:** Educated at Charterhouse School, London, until 1937; studied at the Central School of Arts and Crafts, London, 1938-42. **Military Service:** Served in the Royal Army Educational Corps., 1949-51, Sergeant. **Family:** Married Lady Pamela Mountbatten in 1960; children: Edwina, Ashley, and India. **Career:** Independent designer, London, from 1953; founder-principal, Hicks and Parr decorating firm, 1956-59, David Hicks Limited, from 1960, and David Hicks International Marketing Limited, with branch offices in Switzerland, France, Belgium, Germany, Pakistan, and Australia, from 1970. Designed interiors for Helena Rubinstein, the Prince of Wales, the QE2 liner, British Steel, Aeroflot airlines, the British Embassy in Washington, and others; also designer of clothing and fashion accessories for the Association of Japanese Manufacturers, from 1977, and womenswear collections, from 1982. Master, Worshipful Company of Salters, London, 1977-78. **Honors:** Design Council Award, London, 1970; Fellow, Royal Society of Arts, London. **Address:** 13 Albany, Piccadilly, London W1V 9RP, England.

## Publications

**By HICKS: books**—*David Hicks on Decoration,* London, 1966; *David Hicks on Living ... With Taste,* London, 1968; *David Hicks on Bathrooms,* London, 1970; *David Hicks on Decoration with Fabrics,* London, 1971, *David Hicks on Decoration: 5,* London, 1975; *David Hicks Book of Flower Arranging,* London, 1976; *David Hicks: Living with Design,* London, 1979; *David Hicks Garden Design,* London, 1982; *David Hicks Style and Design,* London, 1988.

**On HICKS: books**—*Interior Architecture and Decoration* by Alain Demachy, London, 1974; *Design Matters* by Bernat Klein, London, 1976; *The Contemporary Decorative Arts from 1940 to the Present Day* by Philippe Garner, London, 1980; *Environmental Interiors* by Mary Jo Weale and W. Bruce Weale, New York and London, 1982; *The Conran Directory of Design* edited by Stephen Bayley, London, 1985.

\*   \*   \*

David Hicks means tasteful interior decor to millions of people in the English-speaking world and elsewhere. He established his reputation among professionals as the result of prescience and became known to the general public as a celebrated tastemaker through successful marketing and especially through publishing.

In the late 1950s, when well-designed interiors were contemplative spaces, often rectilinear Miessian voids dotted with a few ovoid womb chairs, young Hicks introduced a somewhat kooky clutter. His admixture of odd antiques, boldly patterned surfaces, formal symmetry, and casual wit was spirited enough to be enjoyed as part of the Pop aesthetic of the sixties, but comfortable enough with the past to accommodate his well-bred clientele. In his early practice he was in partnership with an antique dealer while creating Op Art patterns for textile manufacturers.

This combination typified his acceptance of old and new vocabularies—anything that could be assembled to make statements of comfort and luxury. By the early 1970s, when the historicizing principles of Postmodernism had been articulated, Hicks was well-positioned as an established master of eclecticism.

He abandoned pattern-on-pattern schemes for texture-on-texture arrangements and muted his palette for the times, but his designs continued to be based upon pleasurable combinations of discrete elements that each maintain their individual attraction. His most comprehensive employment of this sort of historical appropriation was the Palladian Villa Verde in Portugal, where he was both architect and interior designer.

Running somewhat contrary to this dominant tendency toward pragmaticism are a few of the recurring elements of a signature style. Some of these are idiosyncratic. Hicks often pushes the bathtub toward the center of a room (not always a bathroom) and maintains a fascination for obelisks, not only as curios but as the shape for cupboards and night stands. Lighting sources are many and seem to be dispersed equally among the people and the objects inhabiting a room. Wall-washing uplights are a favorite. More fundamentally, his solution to a design problem is found more frequently in abundance than focus. For example, he has remarked in his *Living with Design* that "If you are going to have a table of photographs, you must have enough of them: the more you have, the more interesting the table will become." Although the result of this approach sometimes seems lavish and busy, it has the merit of sustaining hours of enjoyment rather than minutes. The style travels well. David Hicks shops have been established in Switzerland, France, Belgium, Germany, Japan, and Pakistan, and he has undertaken projects in many other countries.

David Hicks' most important legacy has been as tastemaker, a popularizer of trends in design—absorbing styles from design's avant-garde, inventing a few of his own, blending them into comfortable mixes of the trendy and the traditional for clients such as the Duchess of Abercon, then describing the principles underlying his design for the Duchess's bathroom, or his own country house, in his popular books for more modest homeowners. The several volumes he has published are stuffed with pictures of his work and salted with instructions and aphorisms intended to stimulate design awareness and good taste among the general populace.

Through these publications, he seems to be today's foremost designer-author-tastemaker, which is a role in our society with a rich and long history. Like the many writers who popularized the late-nineteenth-century "aesthetic" interior (Charles Eastlake, Mary Haweis, Rhoda and Agnes Garrett, Maria Dewing, Candace Wheeler, and others) his free-wheeling eclecticism translates easily into the ad hoc pragmaticism sought by do-it-yourself designers.

—Henry Pisciotta

# HIESTAND, Ernst and Ursula

Swiss graphic, exhibition, and interior designers

Ernst Hiestand: **Born:** in Zurich, 16 September 1935; Ursula Hiestand: **Born:** Zurich, 4 April 1936. **Education:** Both studied graphic design in Zurich and Paris, worked in a Zurich advertising agency, then traveled in the United States, Japan and Africa. **Career:** Established joint graphic design studio, in Zollikon, Zurich, from 1960. Ernst Hiestand: instructor in graphic design, Kunstgewerbeschule, Zurich; guest lecturer at numerous schools in

Switzerland. **Exhibition:** *107 Grafici dell'AGI,* Castello Sforzesco, Milan, 1974. **Address:** Chupliweg 6, 8702 Zollikon-Zurich, Switzerland.

### Publications

**On the HIESTANDS: books**—*An International Survey of Packaging* by Wim Crouwel and Kurt Weidemann, London, 1968; *Modern Graphics* by Keith Murgatroyd, London, 1969; *107 Grafici dell'AGI,* with texts by Renzo Zorzi and Franco Grignani, Venice, 1974; *Archigraphia: Architectural and Environmental Graphics* edited by Walter Herdeg, Zurich, 1978; *Who's Who in Graphic Art* edited by Walter Amstutz, Dubendorf, 1982.

# HILLMANN, Hans (Georg)

German illustrator, book, and graphic designer

**Born:** Nieder-Mois, Silesia (now Poland), 25 October 1925. **Education:** Studied at the Staatliche Schule für Handwerk und Kunst, Kassel, 1948-49; studied graphics under Hans Leistikow, at the Staatliche Werkakademie, Kassel, 1949-53. **Military Service:** Served in the German Army, 1943-45. **Career:** Freelance graphic designer, working in Kassel, 1953-56, and in Frankfurt, from 1956. Founder-member, Novum Gesellschaft für Neue Graphik group, Frankfurt, 1959. Professor of graphic art, Staatliche Hochschule für Bildende Künste, Kassel, from 1961. **Member:** Deutscher Werkbund; Alliance Graphique Internationale; Kunstbeirat der Deutschen Bundespost. **Exhibitions:** *German Posters of Today,* Baghdad and New Delhi, 1959-60; *80 Masters: 160 Posters,* Den Bosch, Netherlands, 1960; *Novumgraphik,* Hessisches Landesmuseum, Darmstadt, 1960; *Hans Hillmann,* Kunstverein, Kassel, 1962; *Filmplakate,* Die Neue Sammlung, Munich, 1965; Warsaw Poster Biennale, 1966, 1968, 1970, 1972, 1974; *Hans Hillmann,* National Museum, Poznan, 1973; *Hans Hillmann: Filmplakate,* Neuer Berliner Kunstverein, 1974; *Fliegenpapier,* Institut für Neue Technische Form, Darmstadt, 1982. **Collections:** Landesmuseum, Kassel; Stedelijk Museum, Amsterdam; Royal Ontario Museum, Toronto. **Honors:** Best German Poster of the Year Awards, 1958, 1959, 1960; Toulouse-Lautrec Prize, Paris, 1962; Warsaw Poster Biennale Medal, 1966; Cinema 16 Prize, Colombo, 1966. **Address:** Neuhofstrasse 37B, 6000 Frankfurt-am-Main, Germany.

### Works

Posters, for Neue Filmkunst distributors, 1953-74.
Illustrations, for *Twen* magazine, Frankfurt, 1961-63.
*Film* magazine design, Frankfurt, 1963-64.
Book designs, for Fischer Verlag, Frankfurt, 1967-1968.

### Publications

**By HILLMANN: books**—*Ich hab Geträumt ich war ein Hund der Träumt,* Frankfurt, 1970; *ABC—Geschichten,* Frankfurt, 1975; *Ich hab mir in der Besprechung ein Bild gemacht,* Obertshausen, 1976.

**On HILLMANN: books**—*Deutsche Illustratören der Gegenwart* by E. Holscher, Munich, 1959; *Who's Who in Graphic Art* edited by Walter Amstutz, Zurich, 1962, Dubendorf, 1982; *Graphic Designers in Europe: 2* edited by Henri Hillebrand, London, 1972; *107 Grafici dell'AGI,* with texts by Renzo Zorzi and Franco Grignani, Venice, 1974; *The Language of Graphics* by Edward Booth-Clibborn and Daniele Baroni, London, 1980; *A History of Graphic Design* by Philip B. Meggs, New York, 1983.

# HILSCHER, Hubert

Polish book, magazine, trademark, and graphic designer

**Born:** Warsaw, 14 October 1924. **Education:** Studied under T. Kulisiewicz, at the Academy of Fine Arts, Warsaw, 1949-55. **Career:** Freelance designer, working in Warsaw, from 1956; art director, *Projekt* magazine, Warsaw, from 1962. Chairman of the Warsaw Graphic Arts section, Polish Union of Artists, 1960-63; deputy chairman, Warsaw Poster Biennale Committee, 1965-76. **Exhibitions:** Vienna, 1964; Düsseldorf, 1968; Berlin, 1969; Bratislava, 1969; Prague, 1969; Budapest, 1969; Sofia, 1969; Szczecin, 1971; Royan, 1972. **Honors:** Commercial Art Award, Polish Ministry of Culture, 1962; Ljubliana Applied Art Biennale Award, 1964; Manifesto Turistico Award, Milan, 1967, 1970; Warsaw Poster of the Year Award, 1973, 1975, 1980; Mayor's Award, Brno Poster Biennale, 1974; Polish Book Publishers Society Award, 1980; Lahti Poster Biennale Medal, 1981; Polish Gold Cross of Merit, 1955; Polish Anniversary Medal, 1974; Order of Polonia Restituta, Warsaw, 1976. **Address:** ul. Flitrowa 23, m. 3, 02-057 Warsaw, Poland.

### Publications

**By HILSCHER: articles**—*Projekt* (Warsaw), no. 3, 1978.

**On HILSCHER: books**—*Polish Poster Art Today* by Szymon Bojko, Warsaw, 1972; *Contemporary Polish Posters* edited by Joseph S. Czestochowski, New York, 1979; *The Polish Poster 1970-1978,* with introduction by Zdzislaw Schubert, Warsaw, 1979.

*       *       *

"I do not consider myself an artist. I practice an artistic craft, and I do so as the result of a combination of circumstances.... I do my own job as a printer, a carpenter, or a clerk does his. This is how I earn my living." Yes, Hubert Hilscher told this to an interviewer a few years ago.

Though this statement by one of the most renowned Polish designers is spiced with irony, it sounds like a calamity in a country that loves her poster designers and locates them at the very top of an artistic ladder, above the painters, sculptors, and printers. This artist's attitude toward his own profession is very unusual, divergent from that of the majority of his colleagues, who espouse free-wheeling creativity and sometimes even personalize commissioned work too much. For them, the rule is "form over function." Hilscher, on the other hand, knows and applies the strict rules of design to each case—the work on the book must serve the subject, not dominate it. The care about clean composition, as well as great control over the placement and function of each letter, are strong points of Hilscher's work.

Besides being a careful and intelligent lay-out person for thousands of issues of various publications, including the leading Polish art magazine, *Projekt,* Hilscher is a brilliant poster designer. The majority of his posters are composed with abstract, linear, or geometrical forms. Often, if done for an architectural subject, they look almost three-dimensional. This reminds us that Hilscher studied building construction early in his career. Something lasts.

A leading series of posters—mostly abstract compositions, laboriously crafted, vibrating, and flying at the walls of the concert halls—are dedicated to various musical events. He is also known for posters commemorating exhibitions of architecture, industrial design, and sculpture. However, Hilscher's most popular designs, which sell worldwide, are the zoo posters. Aggressively colorful wild animals—tigers, lions, parrots, elephants—attack everybody's eye. They're funny and mad. One wonders why such a disciplined person as Hilscher bursts with such an avalanche of colors and shapes. Yet, if one makes a little study of them, one sees that all those Op art effects and strange collisions of red and green, yellow and blue, are not accidental. His lions are pure, striking objects achieved through the logical exercise of visual composition. This vibrating shape against the flat field of the basic, sharp color, is determined by masterful but simple planning.

Hilscher tries to focus on the real and important role of visual art in society. He is sure that public tastes, good and bad, are shaped by the visual information attacking the eye of everybody everywhere. His small, private battle we can compare with the famous ideas of the prewar Bauhaus. For both, the most important task of any designer is to create correct visual behavior against the existing jungle.

Hilscher is less provocative and egomaniacal than most of his Polish colleagues, but his calm, organized, and sometimes underestimated work on many publications and albums dedicated to Polish graphic art has helped to present this art in the best, cleanest, and most elegant way to the whole world. All of us poster artists of Poland owe something to this friendly and modest gentleman.

—Jan Sawka

# HIM, George

British illustrator, graphic, and exhibition designer

**Born:** Lodz, Poland, 4 August 1900; emigrated to Britain in 1937, naturalized. **Education:** Studied religious history at the Universities of Lodz, Warsaw, Berlin, and Bonn, Ph.D., 1924; studied graphic design at the Staatliche Akademie für Graphische Kunst und Buchgewerbe, Leipzig, 1924-28. **Family:** Married Shirley Elizabeth Rhodes. **Career:** Freelance designer in Germany, 1928-33; partner with Jan LeWitt in LeWitt-Him design practice in Warsaw, 1933-37, and in London, 1937-54; freelance designer in private practice, London, 1955-82: designed posters and graphics for the Ministry of Information, Home Office, General Post Office, Festival of Britain, Schweppes, Haus Neuerburg, De Bijenkorf stores, *The Observer,* and others; design consultant, El Al Israel Airlines, 1952-78. Senior Lecturer, Leicester Polytechnic, 1969-76. **Member:** Fellow, Society of Industrial Artists and Designers, London; Society of Typographical Designers, London; Royal Designer for Industry, Royal Society of Arts, London; Member, Alliance Graphique Internationale, Paris. **Exhibitions:** London, 1937; Jerusa-

lem and Tel Aviv, 1948; New York and Philadelphia, 1957; *Second World War Posters,* Imperial War Museum, London, 1972; London College of Printing, 1976; Ben Uri Gallery, London, 1978, 1981; *Eye for Industry,* Victoria and Albert Museum, London, 1986. **Died:** London, 4 April 1982.

## Publications

**By HIM: books**—(with Jan LeWitt) *Locomotive,* London, 1937; (with Jan LeWitt) *The Little Red Engine,* London, 1942; *Israel, The Story of a Nation,* London, 1958; *25 Years of Youth Aliyah,* London, 1959; (written by Max Beerbohm) *Zuleika Dobson,* London, 1960; (with S. Potter) *Squawky,* London, 1964; (with Leila Berg) *Folk Tales,* London, 1966; (with F. Herrmann) *Giant Alexander* books, London, 1964-75; *Little Nippers* edited by Leila Berg, London, 1973, 1974; (with Ann Thwaite) *The Day with the Duke,* London, 1972; *Ann and Ben,* London 1974; (with Jim Rogerson) *King Wilbur* books, London, 1976; *Don Quixote,* London, 1980.

**On HIM: books**—*Window Display 2* edited by Walter Herdeg, Zurich, 1961; *Who's Who in Graphic Art* edited by Walter Amstutz, Zurich, 1962, Dubendorf, 1982; *Graphic Design Britain* edited by Frederick Lambert, London, 1967; *Film and TV Graphics* edited by Walter Herdeg, Zurich, 1967; *An International Survey of Packaging* by Wim Crouwel and Kurt Weidemann, London, 1968; *Advertising: Reflections of a Century* by Bryan Holme, London, 1982; *Eye for Industry: Royal Designers for Industry 1936-1986,* exhibition catalogue by Fiona MacCarthy and Patrick Nuttgens, London, 1986.

*See* LE WITT, Jan

\*      \*      \*

To evaluate the design work of Jan LeWitt and George Him, one must consider three aspects of their careers: their joint achievements during their partnership from 1933 to 1954, Him's own work until his death in 1982, and Him's character as a man, a personality, and a philosopher.

Upon his departure from the partnership, LeWitt kept himself in the background and concentrated on abstract visual art. He had an urge to make up for lost time from his neglected love of painting freely, without the restraint imposed by a brief from a commercial client. Him adopted exactly the opposite policy: he recognized the challenge of a given problem, enjoyed analyzing it as a surgeon does over the operating table, solving it logically, step by step. Their partnership had come into being through their eccentric plan to walk around the world together, earning their keep by sketching. Instead, they established themselves in London where they collaborated on book covers and children's illustrations. How two characters with such opposing personalities stayed together for seventeen years is still puzzling. One can only assume that through contradiction, argument, and continual friction they found their mutual strength and achieved better and richer solutions than they would have individually. They made a joint impact with their wartime posters in Britain, especially the one persuading the public to walk; this consisted of the shoe-shaped "Shanks' Pony," head and tail emerging from each end of the shoe, and lettering wearing shoes. Also a classic was their "Vegetabull" character (a bull made up entirely of vegetables), intended to encourage the public to substitute vegetable dishes for meat.

One of the most imaginative advertising campaigns ever to appear in Britain was originated by Him and the humourist Stephen Potter for the soft drinks company Schweppes in the early 1960s. It was based on "Schweppshire," an imaginary county somewhere in England. Potter, the inventor of "gamesmanship" and "lifesmanship," and Him created an English scene out of such nonsense and eccentricity. Later, they followed this with "Europe in PerSchwepptive," making fun of the Englishman's prejudice against Europe. As with Him's other works, wit and inventiveness dominated both the story and the images for these series. Besides the playful pleasures of content and form, everything the most demanding client needed to convey was there. Him's work, to the end, showed him to be mentally alert, fertile in ideas, and original in concept.

Him was a true amalgam of Eastern and Western Europe. His studies of art and philosophy in German universities and his choice of British soil as a location in which to function mixed to create a uniquely interesting and fascinating personality. Having had the privilege of working with him for some twelve years on animated films, I benefitted from his logic and penetrating analytical approach to story-development in arriving at a final conclusion. His brain was continually brimming over with ideas, but he was always able to control them with self-discipline and consideration for the point of view of others. His craftsmanship and sense of colour were superb and his speed of execution, unusually fast, contributed substantially to the fact that everything he created came to life.

Apart from his work in Europe, Him did a great deal in Israel, including the designs for the exhibition at Masada. He also taught at the Academy of Art and Design in Tel Aviv.

—John Halas

# HIPGNOSIS

British Graphic design partnership

**Founded** by Storm Thorgerson (born 1944) and Aubrey Powell (born 1946), in London, 1969; joined by additional partner Peter Christopherson (born 1955), in 1974. **Career:** Designed record sleeves and publicity material for rock music artists including Pink Floyd, The Police, 10CC, Sad Café, Led Zeppelin, Genesis, The Alan Parsons Project, Wishbone Ash, Peter Gabriel, Paul McCartney, XTC, Bad company, UFO, and others; designed advertising and graphic materials for Polygram, GGK Agencies, Volvo cars, Talbot cars, Colman's mustard, Stella Artois lager, Kronenbourg lager, Rank Xerox, and others. **Address:** c/o Aubrey Powell Productions, Ilford House, 133 Oxford Street, London W1, England.

## Publications

**By HIPGNOSIS: books**—(as editor, with Roger Dean) *Album Cover Album,* Limpsfield, 1977; (as editor) *Wings Tour USA: Hands Across the Water,* Limpsfield, 1978; *The Photodesigns of Hipgnosis: The Goodbye Look,* with text by Thorgerson, London, 1982.

**On HIPGNOSIS: books**—*The Contemporary Decorative Arts from 1940 to the Present Day* by Philippe Garner, London, 1980;

*The Dictionary of Visual Language* by Philip Thompson and Peter Davenport, London, 1980, 1982; *Album Cover Album 2* edited by Dean and David Howells, New York, 1982.

\*   \*   \*

When the children of the 1960s rejected their parents' lifestyles, music communicated that rebellion. The relative affluence of the decade afforded personal stereos for many, as well as the ability to purchase numerous phonograph records. An industry responded, providing music that gave pleasure, escape, and status. In addition, record-jacket art and posters accompanied each hot disc with images as eloquent as the sounds they packaged.

Music stores became galleries of pop culture. Comic book drawings, superficial Indian mysticism, art nouveau nostalgia, scenes of pastoral innocence, and bits of benign decadence were strewn through the record bins. Many covers were designed to shock the middle class right out of its pedal pushers. Psychedelia filled eyes, ears, and minds, as brightly colored letterings seemed to melt off the cardboard. By the time Hipgnosis entered the picture, a style had been established.

Even the charming "Hipgnosis" alluded to contemporary pretenses (hypnosis—influence of the unconscious; hip—modern, with-it; gnosis—ancient wisdom, mystical). Its earliest commission, Pink Floyd's *Saucerful of Secrets,* was typical for 1968. Multiple cosmic images meshed in formless color, while the musicians drifted in an unperturbed bubble. But by the time Pink Floyd released *Ummagumma* the next year, Hipgnosis had dropped the cliché for the daring. Repetitions of the musicians in frames, with slight alterations, played mind games with the viewer. Subtle suggestions of psychological states, such as infinite regression and déjà vu, better suggested mind-expanding experiences than light-show theatrics.

In the 1970s, Hipgnosis developed those themes established by earlier artists. As surrealism had stimulated the visionaries of the 1960s, so it continued to capture the imaginations of youth. Part of this heritage included the use of pun and collage—both frequent on covers by Hipgnosis. Another surrealist convention—overtly offending the bourgeoisie—was not ignored. In fact, what could be called the sexual innocence of the "love children" degenerated into jaded obscenities, continual crotch shots, grapplings, and graspings. This was always, of course, within the cannons of good design. Like fine times on a summer day, absurdity ran rampant.

Hipgnosis created works to which the viewer was forced to react as images played on the mind. Brand X's *Unorthodox Behavior* (1976), with its eye peeking through a venetian blind, affirms the drug-crazed suburbanite's ambiguous paranoia (does he stare at us or do we invade his privacy?). Hipgnosis intruded on our fantasies with narratives like paperback novels or one-second movie scenarios. Viewers who paid the price could dream for free of film noire mysteries, science-fiction illusions, or travels to exotic locales—all illustrated by Hipgnosis—with each purchase of the latest electronic boogie.

In the 1980s, a drop in disposable income curtailed record sales. Budget cuts and fewer manufactured LP's may spell the end of sophisticated album art. All is transitory. Mind expansion and sensory awareness fade as fads, and the creativity of Hipgnosis falls out of fashion. But during the record industry's peak of influence, Hipgnosis tapped the consciousness of a decade.

—Edith Cortland Lee

# HIPP, Catherine

American fashion designer

**Born:** Dallas, Texas. **Education:** Educated in Little Rock, Arkansas; studied liberal arts, University of North Carolina, Chapel Hill, BA, in English. **Career:** Worked as piece goods buyer, for Gunne Sax, San Francisco; independent fashion designer, in San Francisco and New York, from 1975; founder-director, Catherine Hipp Ltd. knitwear house, from 1975; co-founded, with Jackie Hayman, and designer, Catherine Hipp fashion house, from 1981. **Address:** 110 West 40th Street, New York, New York 10018, U.S.A.

## Publications

**On HIPP: articles**—"Catherine Hipp" in *Women's Wear Daily* (New York), 14 November 1983.

*

When I was in second grade in Little Rock, Arkansas, we all had to write what we thought everyone else would grow up to be. Everyone agreed that I would move to New York and be editor of a fashion magazine.

I never had to make a decision about what I was going to do. I always knew I would design clothes. I started sewing on my mother's little black Singer when I was seven. When I was thirteen, I taught myself to make patterns. I'd sit on the floor and cut newspapers into geometric shapes—cones, triangles, parallelograms, rhombuses—and stick them together into patterns.

At the University of North Carolina at Chapel Hill, I was very hot in trig and math, although I majored in English and took enough art history and religion for each to be a major. It never occurred to me to go to fashion school. I went to college to learn. I really was a student. I still am.

After graduation, I chose to go to San Francisco, *not* New York, and got a nothing job with a big dress company. In two weeks, they made me piece goods buyer. I stayed two and a half years, but I was also designing my own clothes on the side and the boss didn't like that. So, I left and started my own business doing "techy" clothes in slick nylon cire. Bright red, yellow, blue. They sold.

On my first trip to Europe, I was driving through the Rhone Valley and suddenly knew I had to move to New York. One day I went. I cried for two years. It was such a shock. New York has all the support systems for a designer. Top models. Great photographers. Vast libraries. Famous stores. But San Francisco is airy, and New York seemed so dark. That was in 1975. The city is light and open to me now, but it took time.

I've experimented a great deal. Sometimes I've been ahead of the times. My first collection in New York, for instance, included skinny knits that looked like the ballet warm-up clothes that are popular today, and also sportswear evocative of clown suits with suspenders. Well, skinny knits weren't in yet. And women weren't ready for humorous sportswear. It was something of a disaster, but I learned more from it than I could have at any fashion school. I've also done collections all in one color and in one fabric. From them, I learned how to achieve a variety of shapes and treatments when working with one material.

In 1981, Jackie Hayman and I started a new business. Jackie had been vice-president of Ann Taylor and has an almost uncanny knowledge of the kind of clothes women need and want. Real women in this real world of ours. We've been making clothes for them ever since, and we've grown into an international company.

I don't like to say that we make tailored clothes because that sounds like gray flannel business suits. But the clothes *are* meticulously tailored. We insist on high-quality workmanship and fabrics. In fact, we have all our fabrics and colors made to order. For me, shape comes first. I never start with color or fabric. I used to design at the barre—I have a passion for ballet—to see how the body looks in motion. I don't have to do that any more. And I no longer cut out geometric forms. With experience has come an interesting dynamic. Now, I'm subconsciously aware of the abstract interaction of shapes and how to relate them to the reality of a woman's body. I see certain planes of the body as more beautiful than others, and I try to show them off in the clothes. The chest, shoulders, hips. In the end, it comes down to making women look good and feel good, to designing clothes that enhance the female form and the female persona.

—Catherine Hipp

*     *     *

There is a laconic elegance to the clothes that suggest something very American, very poised, in the sense of a Katharine Hepburn or a Carole Lombard. One senses that Catherine Hipp is dressing a woman who can fend for herself in the often far-fetched scenarios of American life. But there is more to her clothes than wit or a talent for pastiche. Although Hipp agrees that it is the 1930s and the 1940s which appeal to her most in terms of fashion, and specifically the easy, functional, professional working women's clothes of those times, it is not simply comfortable nostalgia that makes her clothes work. There is also a clear-eyed understanding of what fashion means and of the alchemy by which a dress, say, based on a period prototype, comes into its own contemporary context with the addition of a small detail or a subtlety of cut.

Hipp herself believes that the most important source of inspiration for designers today should be the space program. Along with every other designer, she has yet to find a way to resolve the "costume party" overtones inherent in the translation of a space suit into a wearable resolution of that contemporary paradigm, the jump-suit. She believes, however, that there is a causal link between the modest, almost naive dresses she so lovingly collected in local thrift shops as a child, and the bone-pure blueprints of functional human covering represented by what men and women wear on space shuttles. She realizes that in terms of what women want and need today, functionalism is a critical element but not the only one. Hipp's work, then, is a piquant mix of the outright nostalgic, the shrewdly modern, and the sophisticatedly *soignée*.

Like many other highly gifted designers, Hipp is self-taught. She started with the simplest of cuts and developed as she went along. Yet, unlike a Shamask, there is not a sense of reductionism in her work that is meant to evoke a rather complicated set of responses— to America, to fashion, to the role of women in clothes. The clothes are, in spite of their surface simplicity, intellectual in intent and aesthetically pleasing objects in themselves.

—Peter Carlsen

# HIRSHBERG, Gerald P.

American industrial designer

**Education:** Studied mechanical engineering, Ohio State University; studied industrial design, Cleveland Institute of Art, B.I.D. **Family:** Married Linda (a clinical psychologist); children: two sons. **Career:** chief designer, General Motors Corporation, 1965; chief designer, Buick, Pontiac Division design studios, General Motors Corp.; designer, Nissan Motor Co.; vice president, 1980-95, president, from 1995, Nissan Design International, Inc., San Diego, California; clients include Apple, Toshiba, Yonca Teknik Yatirim of Turkey, Polk Audio, and IVAC; responsible for the design of the Nissan *Infiniti J30, Altima, Quest Minivan,* and *Pathfinder.* Chair, Art Advisory Board, city of San Diego, 1982-89; Mayor's Growth Management Task Force, city of San Diego, 1984-88; Design Arts Panel, National Endowment for the Arts, Washington, D.C., 1990; chairman, 1991 IDEA Awards, *Business Week* and Industrial Designers Society of America; board of Advisors, Graduate School of Pacific and International Studies, University of California, San Diego; board of trustees, Cleveland Institute of Art; board of trustees, San Diego Museum of Contemporary Art; contributor to *Design* magazine, London; lecturer on design at universities and conferences throughout the world. **Honors:** Nissan's vehicles have won numerous awards from automotive and design award-granting bodies. **Address:** Nissan Design International Inc., 9800 Campus Point Drive, San Diego, California 92124, U.S.A.

## Publications

**By HIRSHBERG: books**—*Creativity* manuscript, to be published by Harper Collins, 1997.

*

The greatest joys of design reside for me in its power to synthesize. In a world stressing analysis, design provides a much-needed impetus for bringing together divergent disciplines, polarized points of view and even cultures. By fusing the useful with the expressive

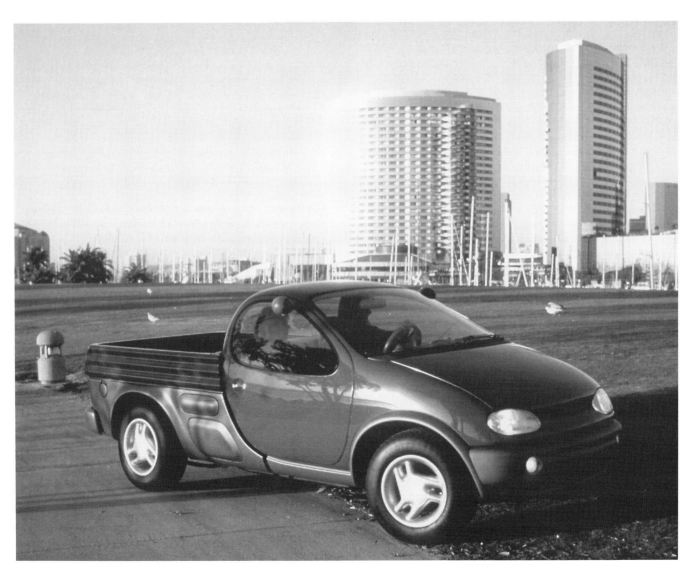

Gerald Hirshberg: *Gobi* concept car, Nissan Design

aspects of form, design endows the inanimate objects comprising the human-made environment with style, and at its highest level, with grace. It is an activity uniquely positioned to lead the way back to an integration of the rational with the aesthetic.

Design is also an activity I cherish for its wide-screen focus. To be a specialist in design is, by definition, to be a generalist. I treasure my little bit of knowledge about a great many things as it is precisely this diversity that provides food for the unexpected connections and leaps of characteristic creative thought.

—Gerald Hirshberg

\*　　\*　　\*

Musician, painter, engineer. Born both blessed and cursed with a passionate interest in so many different areas, Jerry Hirshberg chose the profession that defines itself as generalist in this day of the specialist: design.

Before making that choice, Jerry tried out a career in music, writing music, studying the clarinet, and leading a rock band that cut three records, opened for Frankie Avalon, Fabian, and Paul Anka and even hit the national charts with "Sparkling Blue." In the process, he had a lot of fun and made some extra money, but he found the music industry steeped in unpleasantness, no place for someone interested in the process of creation rather than its rewards. Today, he gives his broad interests room to breathe in his leisure hours, giving recitals on the clarinet, exhibiting his paintings, and contributing his time and insight to the design profession as well as to the broader community of San Diego.

In choosing industrial design, he found a medium replete with ambiguity, infinitely flexible and kept fresh only by a constant infusion of ideas and influences. "The strength of design is that it marries intuition and rationality, expressiveness and purpose," he explains. "Design is the most exquisite way for me to blur boundaries. I love to live in areas of overlap. There lies the potential for underived thinking, unexpected breakthroughs."

He accepted the position of vice president of design for Nissan Design International (NDI) because, in its bringing together of such different cultures, he saw the potential to unleash creativity. First of all there was the fundamental and obvious opportunity for creative energy fueled by the cultural differences inherent in a Japanese company opening a U.S. design office. Then he added spice by receiving Nissan's endorsement for NDI's designers to work as consultants, designing products for companies in other industries. Here was the influx of disparate information and ideas so essential to creativity.

And thus for 16 years he has tackled the strange business of managing a vortex of influences, using the chasm separating two cultures as a springboard for creativity. In the process, he has found a new truth: that culture is not a geographic issue alone, that cultures, their languages, icons, and *Weltanschauung,* also divide professions, and that these oft-ignored differences can create failure or success depending on how the tension is managed. "Creativity resides at the collision of multiple planes of thought. It can be very uncomfortable and scary."

He has thought a lot about creativity over the years. Enough to write a book about it, which will be published in 1997. In the book, Jerry uses his design experiences working in giant international companies to illustrate how creativity can turn business into an idea-making machine. "Efficiency, productivity, and the usual concerns of business are things machines and systems do well, yet they are directly enhanced by creativity. Yet creativity is the only thing people alone do. It's surely one of the great defining human characteristics."

In working to organize his thoughts for the book, Jerry has found himself aided in meeting the imperative of the new job he took in 1995: NDI's presidency. "The danger is to continue doing your old job. I have to find a new way to channel my creativity." The book also helps him understand and articulate the dynamics that have helped NDI achieve outstanding successes for almost two decades.

But it is not the awards and plaudits that Jerry considers most gratifying; it is the opportunity he has had to create an idea and a place, to explore what happens when you gather strong and diverse people and evolve a methodology and organization that is shaped by the needs and priorities of the creative process itself. To do that, he has had to subsume his ego. "I didn't want to be a 'star' designer with a group of apprentices who would do my bidding and polish my work. I wanted to help a group of strong designers find their voice. I believe a tone comes out of that, an NDI spirit, not an NDI style."

—Kristina Goodrich

# HOCH, Hans Peter
Swiss book, exhibition, and graphic designer

**Born:** Aarau, 26 June 1924. **Education:** Studied at the Höhere Fachschule für das Grafische Gewerbe Stuttgart, 1946; Arbeitsgemeinschaft Bildender Künstler, Bernstein, 1946-49; Akademie der Bildenden Künste, Stuttgart, 1949-51. **Family:** Married Margarethe Jerg in 1950; children: Christoph, Thomas, and Andreas. **Career:** Freelance designer, with own studio for communications, corporate, exhibition, signage, and graphic design, Stuttgart, from 1954. **Member:** Bund Deutscher Grafik Designer; Allianz Deutscher Grafik Designer; Alliance Graphique Internationale; Verband Bildender Künstler; Deutscher Werkbund. **Honors:** Best German Poster Prize, Stuttgart, 1963, 1965; Graphic Design in Deutschland Prize, 1971, 1974, 1978, 1981; Kieler Woche Prize, Kiel, 1973; Pro Plakat Poster Prize, 1976; Warsaw Poster Biennale Prizes, 1976; Für den Sport Postage Stamp Prize, 1979, 1980, 1986, 1987, 1989; Beautiful Book Prize, Germany, 1982; Leichtathletik Europameisterschaften Prize, Stuttgart, 1982; Berlin Kunstbibliothek Poster Prize, 1983; World Book Prize, Leipzig, 1983; Gedenkstätte Deutscher Widerstand Prize, Berlin, 1983. **Address:** Rechbergweg 8, 7066 Höhengehren, Germany.

**Works**

*Die Bibel: Gottes Wort im Wandel der Welt* exhibition layouts and catalogue, for the Rottenburg Diocese, Stuttgart, 1963.
*Bauhaus* exhibition layouts, poster, and graphics, for the Institut für Auslandsbeziehungen, Stuttgart, 1974.
Graphics and signage system, for the University of Tubingen, 1975.
*John Cranko: Ballett in Stuttgart* exhibition layouts, graphics, and poster, for the Institut für Auslandsbezieungen, Stuttgart, 1975.
*Kamerun: Konige Masken Feste* exhibition layouts, catalogue, and poster, for the Institut für Auslandsbeziehungen, Stuttgart, 1977.

*Fotografie im Wissenschaft und Technik* exhibition layouts and poster, for the Institut für Auslandsbeziehungen, Stuttgart, 1977.

*Für den Sport* postage stamps, for the German Ministry of Posts and Telecommunications, 1979-80.

*Entwicklung der Fotografie* catalogue series, for the Institut für Auslandsbeziehungen, Stuttgart, 1980-83.

*Leichtathletik Europameisterschaften Stuttgart 1986* logo, poster, and publicity graphics, for the Deutscher Leichtathletik Verband, 1982.

*Germans to America* series of 14 posters, for the Institut für Auslandsbeziehungen, Stuttgart, 1983.

*Kunst Landschaft Architektur* exhibition layouts, catalogue, and poster, for the Institut für Auslandsbeziehungen, Stuttgart, 1983.

## Publications

**On HOCH: books**—*European Designers: Germany, Holland, Switzerland* edited by Idea Publishers, Tokyo, 1970; *Who's Who in Graphic Art* edited by Walter Amstutz, Dubendorf, 1982; *Kunst und Design: Hans Peter Hoch,* Stuttgart, 1988.

*

Graphic design today can no longer be understood and judged by its previous meaning, for it is no longer simply an artistic, aesthetic activity, concerned just with form. Today, graphic design must incorporate the new demands of the fields of visual communication and extended information media.

We can separate graphic design into an artistic-emotional field and a functional-methodical one. Graphic design of the former sort strives for pleasant effects, and the work is valued according to its artistry. Graphic design of the latter type is concerned with the transmission of information visually, and its value depends on its success in doing so. Overall, we may say that the extensive range of graphic design today demands that the designer attempt to meet new requirements and conditions. This objective will require new methods of training.

—Hans Peter Hoch

# HOFMANN, Armin

Swiss sculptor, stage, and graphic designer

**Born:** Winterthur, 29 June 1920. **Education:** Studied at the School of Arts and Crafts, Zurich. **Family:** Married Dorothea Hofmann. **Career:** Freelance designer, working in Basel and Bern, from 1946. Instructor in graphic design, School of Arts and Crafts, Basel, 1947-55, and from 1957; visiting lecturer, Philadelphia Museum School of Art, 1955, Yale University, New Haven, Connecticut, 1955, Aspen International Design Conference, Colorado, 1956, and the National Design Institute, Ahmedabad, 1965. **Member:** Schweizerische Werkbund; Verband Schweizerischer Graphiker; Alliance Graphique Internationale. **Exhibitions:** *8 Swiss Graphic Artists,* 1957-58 (toured the United States); American Institute of Graphic Arts, New York, 1966; *107 Grafici dell'AGI,* Castello Sforzesco, Milan, 1974; *30 Jahre Plakat Kunst,* Gewerbemuseum, Basel, 1983; *The 20th-Century Poster,* Walker Art Center, Minne-

apolis, 1984; Swiss Institute, New York, 1986; *The Basel School of Design and Its Philosophy,* Moore College of Art, Philadelphia, 1986. **Collections:** Museum of Modern Art, New York. **Honors:** First Prize, Swiss National Exhibition, Lausanne, 1964. **Address:** Nadelberg 19, Bern, Switzerland.

## Publications

**By HOFMANN: books**—*Graphic Design Manual: Principles and Practice,* Teufen and London, 1965; **articles**—*Graphis* (Zurich), no. 146, 1969; *Design Quarterly* (Minneapolis), no. 130, 1985.

**On HOFMANN: books**—*The New Graphic Design* by Karl Gerstner and Markus Kutter, Teufen and London, 1959; *Who's Who in Graphic Art* edited by Walter Amstutz, Zurich, 1962, Dubendorf, 1982; *Film and TV Graphics* edited by Walter Herdeg, Zurich, 1967; *History of the Poster* by Josef and Shizuko Muller-Brockmann, Zurich, 1971; *107 Grafici dell'AGI,* exhibition catalogue with texts by Renzo Zorzi and Franco Grignani, Venice, 1974; *Archigraphia: Architectural and Environmental Graphics* edited by Walter Herdeg, Zurich, 1978; *A History of Graphic Design* by Philip B. Meggs, New York and London, 1983; *The 20th-Century Poster: Design of the Avant-Garde* by Dawn Ades, New York, 1984; *The Basel School of Design and Its Philosophy: The Armin Hofmann Years 1946-1986,* exhibition catalogue, Philadelphia, 1986.

*     *     *

Throughout this century, the poster has been a contemporary and viable communication medium. For the Swiss, it has become an enriching part of their culture and a source of international pride. For years, one of its major proponents has been Armin Hofmann. His creative use of word and image has produced scores of outstanding posters.

Because most of Hofmann's posters were commissioned by social and cultural organizations, experimentation and innovation seemed appropriate and were encouraged. His posters for the Kunsthalle in Basel display the ingenious and sensitive use of letter-forms. From the beginning, he decided to identify this series by utilizing letters, instead of art works, as a common denominator. This approach has produced posters that display his sensitivity and ability to manipulate letters, as well as the remarkable flexibility and elegance of the alphabet.

Another important aspect of Hofmann's posters is the dramatic and effective use of photography. With Swiss photographer Max Mathys, he produced an exquisite series for the city theatre in Basel. The distinguishing quality of these posters is the surreal nature of the compositions. Hands, ears, eyes, and faces are enlarged and juxtaposed to create startling and memorable images. One of the posters, for example, shows a series of hand gestures emerging from a solid black background. His posters dramatically express and symbolize the variety and energy of the theatre. Another promotes the performance of the play *Wilhelm Tell.* Here, in a truly elegant composition, a greatly enlarged apple is typographically penetrated by a clever arrangement of the name *Tell.* These examples demonstrate Hofmann's keen understanding of the formal and dynamic aspects of visual communication.

—D. Ichiyama

# HOGAN, Paul (Patrick)

Irish design management consultant

---

**Born:** Dublin, Ireland, 30 October 1934. **Education:** Studied under Professor Bernardus Romein, National College of Art, Dublin, 1953-56; studied at the School of Industrial Design, Royal Danish Academy of Fine Art, Copenhagen, 1963-64. **Family:** Married Virginia Connolly; children: three sons, one daughter. **Career:** Theatre set designer, Illisley McCabe Productions, Olympia Theatre, Dublin, 1957-58; textile designer, Galway Textile Printers, 1958-60; worked for Irish Packaging Institute, 1960-61; design manager, 1963-72, manager of design and consumer products department, 1973-75, director of the technical assistance programme, 1975-87, and chairman, 1986-1991, Córas Tráchtála (the Irish Export Board); clients included European Commission, the United Nations, and the World Bank; organized the first European Conference on Design for Disability, Dublin, 1989; Chairman, Institute for Design and Disability, from 1989 (reestablished as the European Institute for Design and Disability, 1992). Organizer and chairman, first UNIDO-sponsored meeting on Design and Exports from Developing Countries, 1973; established Trade Development Institute of Ireland, 1986; director, Rural Development International. **Member:** Board of Kilkenny Design Workshops; Gaelterra Éireann Handcrafts Committee; Council of the Irish Packaging Institute; Council of the Crafts Council of Ireland; Council of Design; Central Bank of Ireland Currency Design Committee; Advisory Committee of the Hugh Lane Municiple Gallery of Modern Art; Board of the International Council of Societies of Industrial Design; Design Committee of the Confederation of Irish Industry; founding member, Society of Designers in Ireland; Board of Building Construction Studies; National Council for Educational Awards. **Exhibitions:** (Organizer) *Tradition in Modern Japanese Productions,* Hugh Lane Municipal Gallery of Modern Art, Dublin; (organizer) *Jack Lenor Larsen Textiles* and *Chairs 1914-1964,* Trinity College, University of Dublin. **Honors:** Fellow of the Society of Industrial Artists and Designers; fellow of the Royal Society of Arts; honorary member of the Mexican Designers Association; IBM International fellow; fellow of the Chartered Society of Designers; Fellow of the Royal Society of Arts; founding-member and fellow of the Society of Designers in Ireland; IKEA Award, 1995. **Addresses:** (home) 44 Claremont Road, Sandymount, Dublin 4, Ireland; (contact) European Institute for Design and Disability, National College of Art and Design, 100 Thomas Street, Dublin 8, Ireland.

## Publications

**By HOGAN: books**—(editor) *Design in Ireland: Report of the Scandinavian Design Group in Ireland,* Dublin, 1962; *Report of the Killarney Industrial Design Education Conference,* Córas Tráchtála, Dublin, 1971.

**On HOGAN: books**—*Kilkenny Design: Twenty-One Years of Design in Ireland* by Nick Marchant and Jeremy Addis, Kilkenny and London, 1984; **articles**—John Turpin, "The Irish Design Reform Movement of the 1960s," *Design Issues,* vol. III, no. 1, Spring 1986.

\* \* \*

Paul Hogan has been at the center of the promotion of Irish design, the development of industrial design, and the reform of design education in Ireland since the 1960s. Through his work as Design Manager at Córas Tráchtála (the Irish Export Board), a government agency established for the improvement of design for industry, and more recently his involvement with the establishment of the European Institute for Design and Disability, Hogan has been one of the most influential figures in Irish design.

The Scandinavian Report of 1962, edited by Hogan and Córas Tráchtála, identified the problems facing industrial design in Ireland, namely, a general lack of design awareness in the country, inadequate higher education for designers in the art colleges and universities, and the absence of effective design managers. In response to the report Hogan organized a number of exhibitions of work by foreign designers in an attempt to promote design awareness in Ireland. He also instigated a scheme whereby designers from abroad spent time in Ireland working with industry.

Hogan established the Design Advisory Committee in 1969 to provide a forum for government, industry, and the design profession. The Committee set up a scholarship scheme which gave financial assistance to young designers who were sent abroad to work in industry. Hogan was responsible for organizing a conference on industrial design and design education in Killarney in 1970 which was a joint venture of Córas Tráchtála and the Department of Education. In 1971 he presented a report of the advisory group which examined industrial design education. Hogan presented the view that the education of artists and designers had little in common and that a new industrial design course should be established in a college of technology with the resources of a faculty of engineering. The first Irish industrial design degree course was eventually set up in the reformed National College of Art and Design as a joint course with the National Institute of Higher Education Limerick in 1976.

In 1975 Hogan was responsible for the establishment, direction, and financial management of the Technical Assistance Programme at Córas Tráchtála which provided consultancy services and training to developing countries. Building on Ireland's experience of an emerging design culture, Hogan carried out consultancy assignments in over 50 countries, including Bangladesh, Barbados, Cyprus, Greece, Grenada, Guyana, Honduras, India, Malawi, Mauritius, Malta, Morocco, Pakistan, Portugal, Sierra Leone, St. Lucia, St. Vincent, Sudan, Tanzania, Thailand, and Tunisia. He examined the effectiveness of the Pakistan Design Institute, and wrote reports on the development of policies for handicrafts training in Honduras and the design and marketing of wood products for Asian countries.

Hogan retired from active work with Córas Tráchtála in 1987 owing to the Multiple Sclerosis he had suffered for many years. But this did not deter him from the active promotion of design. "MS has given me a lifestyle which I would otherwise not have had, friends which I would otherwise not have made, and perhaps the beginning of wisdom," Hogan said. Hogan was the driving force behind the first European Conference on Design for Disability, and out of his initiative the European Institute for Design and Disability was established in 1992.

The philosophy underlying the work of the Institute was an extension of Hogan's views on design reform in Ireland: the promotion and importance of design of man-made objects with the additional proviso that the deficiencies in the design of products press heaviest on people with disabilities. Hogan sees design as the bridge between technology and the needs of people with disabilities.

"It is only in recent years that designers and manufacturers have come to realize that people with disabilities are consumers too with needs which must be factored into the development process. This 'designing for a broader average,' as Victor Papanek calls it, reflects both a greater social awareness and a commercial imperative to seek new niche markets. It also echoes the campaign to promote economic and social integration and an independent way of life for people with disabilities which has developed in Europe over the past decades," Hogan said.

The Institute acts a conduit for information on design and disability issues in liaison with the disabled, the designer, and industry. The work of the Institute takes place across Europe with conferences and meetings taking place in Lisbon, Milan, Paris, Dublin, and Barcelona.

—Paul Caffrey

# HÖGLUND, Erik (Sylvester)

Swedish sculptor and glass designer

**Born:** Karlskrona, 31 January 1932. **Education:** Studied at the National College of Art, Craft, and Design (Konstfackskolan), Stockholm, 1948-53. **Family:** Married Ingrid Callenberg in 1973; children: Anna, Erika, Albin, Eva-Maria, Ola, and Sara. **Career:** Designer, Kosta Boda Bruks AB glassworks, Boda, 1953-73; independent designer and sculptor, working in glass, bronze, wood, stone, and brick, Stockholm, from 1973. **Exhibitions:** Smålands Museum, Växjö, 1954; Blekinge Museum, Karlskrona, 1955; Kalmar Museum, Sweden, 1955; Lilla Galleriet, Stockholm, 1957; Illums Bolighus, Copenhagen, 1963; Georg Jensen Inc., New York, 1965; David Jones Gallery, Melbourne, 1965 (toured); Rosenthal, Zurich, 1966; *20 Years of Boda Glass,* Sverigchuset, Stockholm, 1973 (traveled to Gävle); Svensk Form, Malmo, 1974; Galleri Svenska Bilder, Stockholm, 1979; Heller Gallery, New York, 1982; Stadtmuseum, Düsseldorf, 1983; *30 År med Glas, Konst och Smide,* Smålands Museum, Växjö, 1984 (toured); Galerie Aix, Stockholm, 1988; Ronneby Kulturcentrum, Sweden, 1989; Finnish Glass Museum, Riihimaki, 1989. **Collections:** Nationalmuseum, Stockholm; Röhsska Konstslöjdmuseet, Göteborg; Konstmuseet Arkiv for Dekorativ Konst, Lund; Smålands Museum, Växjö; Blekinge Landsmuseum, Karlskrona; Landeschaftsmuseum, Darmstadt; Museum Bellerive, Zurich; Cooper-Hewitt Museum, New York; Corning Glass Museum, New York. **Honors:** Swedish Crafts Stipend, 1954; Swedish Royal Art Foundation Stipend, 1955; Lunning Prize, 1957. **Address:** Sigurd Rings Gata 7V, 12651 Hagersten, Stockholm, Sweden.

## Works

Vase in engraved crystal, for Boda, 1953.
Vases in bubbled glass, for Boda, 1954.
*Kanotister* bowl in engraved crystal, for Boda, 1954.
Drinking vessels in bubbled glass, for Boda, 1954.
Red glass jar with folded rim, for Boda, 1959.
Entrance gates in glass, copper, and brass, for Lorensberg Restaurant and Park Hotel, Göteborg, 1962.
Umbrella stand in forged iron and glass, 1963.

Decorative wall in crystal glass, for Ellagård School, Taby, 1964.
Jugs in bubbled glass, for Boda, 1965.
*Stone and Water* fountain and sculpture installation, for Sollentuna Centre, Stockholm, 1974-75.
*Snaps-Glass* wine-glasses, 1978-79.
Wall reliefs in brick, for the Sparbanken, Linköping, 1979-80.
*Circus* hanging sculptures in forged iron and glass, for the Government Building, Kristianstadt, 1980-81.

## Publications

**On HÖGLUND: books**—*Svensk Form/Forma Sueca* by Ake Stavenlow and Ake H. Huldt, Stockholm, 1961; *The Story of Boda and Erik Höglund* edited by Boda Glassworks, Boda, 1965; *Scandinavian Design: Objects of a Life Style* by Eileene Harrison Beer, New York, 1975; *Form och Tradition i Sverige* edited by Birgitta Walz, Stockholm, 1982; *Scandinavian Modern Design 1880-1980* edited by David Revere McFadden, New York, 1982; *Den Svenska Formen* by Monica Boman, Stockholm, 1985; *The Lunning Prize,* exhibition catalogue edited by Helena Dahlback Lutteman and Marianne Uggla, Stockholm, 1986; *Från Boda till New York: Konstnären Erik Höglund* by Gunnel Holmer, Stockholm, 1986; *Svenskt Glas 1915-]960,* exhibition catalogue with text by Helmut Ricke, Stockholm, 1987; *Mellan mörker och Ljus: Erik Höglunds 80-tal* by Björn Ranelid, Stockholm, 1988; *Erik Höglund under 40 Ar: Retrospektiv Utställning 1949-1989,* exhibition catalogue by Jan Torsten Ahlstrand, Ronneby, 1989.

*         *         *

Erik Höglund is something of an *enfant terrible.* In the 1950s he was one of those who punctured the myth that Scandinavian design is always clean-cut and refined. On leaving art school in 1953, at the age of twenty-one, he joined the Boda glass factory. With no previous experience and undaunted by the weight of tradition, he set to with a will. Slender, fragile designs and refined aesthetics were not for him. Solid, earthy forms were the thing right from the start.

His bottles and jugs in thick, clear glass were free and asymmetric, almost always with attached ornaments. Arms were made to project from the shoulders of a glass, the figure of a girl was pressed on, or he added a seal ornament as a sort of signature. A preference for coloured glass, somber grey or bright orange, appeared early on. To impart more life he soon used bubbly glass, which, strictly speaking, was a technical imperfection. His tobacco brown, green, grey, or red glass, completed in the glasshouse with an essentially free design, caused a sensation. Other pieces were engraved. Erik Höglund often did the work, which meant that he could express himself directly.

Many materials have caught his fancy besides glass—wood, clay, iron, and bronze. A turned wooden bed in the baroque spirit and wrought iron candelabra are notable items from the 1960s. He has devoted more and more time to monumental decorations, using glass, metal, and brick, and he has also sculpted in bronze.

Many designers and craftsmen see the material as their starting point. Not so for Erik Höglund, whose primary concern is free expression. He likes to try out his sculptural forms in different materials. One example is the head of a girl molded in glass or set in a brick wall. A lot of his work in the 1980s has been in brick, a hard, yellow type that he sculpts before firing and then combines with standard bricks.

Fragments set in high relief are composed into human figures in the manner of ancient Persian walls. The free fable-making and the search for new effects are reminiscent of his glass from the early 1950s.

—Helena Dahlback Lutteman

# HOLLAND, James

British graphic and industrial designer

**Born:** Gillingham, Kent, 19 September 1905. **Education:** Studied painting, Rochester School of Art, Kent, 1922-24; Royal College of Art, London, 1924-28. **Family:** Married Diana John in 1936 (divorced); married Jacqueline Arnall in 1953; children: Susan, Vivian, James, and Jane. **Career:** Art director, Lord and Thomas advertising agency, London, 1928-29; freelance painter and designer, London, 1929-40; art master, Beckenham Grammar School, Kent, 1940-42; exhibition designer, Ministry of Information, London, 1942-45; chief designer, Central Office of Information, London, 1945-48; joint chief designer, Festival of Britain, London, 1948-51; art director, Foote, Cone, and Belding advertising agency, London, 1951-53; associate design director, Erwin Wasey advertising agency, London, 1956-61. Co-founder, Artists International Association, London, 1933; education officer, Society of Industrial Artists and Designers, London, 1971-79. Head of visual communication, Birmingham Polytechnic, Warwickshire, 1963-71; visiting lecturer, Leicester Polytechnic, 1971-78. **Exhibitions:** *The Thirties,* Hayward Gallery, London, 1979. **Collections:** British Museum, London; Victoria and Albert Museum, London; Tate Gallery, London. **Honors:** Associate, Royal College of Art, London; Fellow, Society of Industrial Artists and Designers; Fellow, Royal Society of Arts, London; Order of the British Empire, 1951. **Address:** Romford Cottage, Romford Road, Pembury, Kent TN2 4BB, England.

## Publications

**By HOLLAND: books**—*Minerva at Fifty: The Jubilee History of the Society of Industrial Artists and Designers 1930-1980,* London, 1980.

**On HOLLAND: books**—*All Things Bright and Beautiful: Design in Britain 1830 to Today* by Fiona MacCarthy, London, 1972; *A Tonic to the Nation: Festival of Britain 1951* by Mary Banham and Bevis Hillier, London, 1975; *The Thirties: British Art and Design Before the War,* exhibition catalogue with texts by A. J. P. Taylor, Ian Jeffrey, and others, London, 1979; *AIA: The Story of the Artists International Association 1933-1953* by Lynda Morris and Robert Radford, Oxford, 1983.

*

Like many of my contemporaries (including Barnet Freedman and James Boswell), I trained at the Royal College of Art as a painter. I turned to design and illustration on leaving, initially to make a living, but later because I came to feel that graphic communication was a more significant social activity in the very disturbed world of the 1930s. With others, I helped to set up the Artists

International Association. During the war years, our experience on the social front was useful in the Ministry of Information, where I worked with Misha Black, Milner Gray, and others. From exhibitions to printed ephemera, my interest has been in graphic design as communication, and I am particularly concerned with the relation of word to image. I have always urged that this relation be considered important in the education of the young designer.

As moderator for the art colleges in the South West, from Bournemouth and Gloucester to Cornwall, I have become greatly involved in design education. Design education has never faced such difficult choices as are offered today, largely as a result of the technological explosion. I believe, however, and certainly hope that the "eternal verities" are still valid and may still point the way for the young designer bewildered by a variety of possible options. In the last resort, the graphic designer, bereft of all traditional tools, the media, and the products of modern technology, should still be able to convey his message by scratching the cave wall or drawing in the sand.

—James Holland

*   *   *

Throughout his career, James Holland has been involved in the institutional promotion of art and design. In the 1930s, he was a founder-member of the influential Artists International Association, as well as an art director for a major advertising agency. During the 1960s, his energies were increasingly channeled into advanced design education, as a teacher, head of a major design faculty, examiner, and, subsequently, as Education Officer of the Society of Industrial Artists and Designers, a position from which he retired in 1979.

Holland's work as a graphic designer responds sensitively to the nature of the task in hand and clearly exhibits his training and experience as a painter. His posters, often drawn broadly in four colors, are bold and dramatic in conception, with powerful chiaroscuro and contrasts of scale. Many of the subjects offered by his work for government ministries gave scope for strong, dramatic imagery, as was the case, for example, in his posters for exhibitions about the navy and life-saving at sea.

Although his book jackets are adjusted to the more intimate scale of the product, they are drawn freely and vigorously, in a lithographic manner, using three- or four-color line illustrations ingeniously. Some of his designs are straightforwardly figurative in conception, but the majority use degrees of abstraction, simplification, and overlay of juxtaposition of forms. Emphasizing movement, his line illustrations depend on an energetic, wiry line.

One of Holland's foremost preoccupations is the harmonious relation of text and image. This he achieves by means of discreetly selected type faces and, a forte of British graphic designers of his generation, a good command of hand lettering.

Holland's breadth of experience as a designer and art director, combined with his perceptive but relaxed demeanor as a person, have made him a teacher and educational adviser of considerable influence. His activities as Education Officer of the Society of Industrial Artists and Designers were of immense benefit not only to the growing national reputation of that body, but also to the numerous colleges, schools, and faculties of art and design with which it had connections.

—Clive Ashwin

# HOLLEIN, Hans

Austrian architect and interior, product, and exhibition designer

**Born:** Vienna, 30 March 1934. **Education:** Studied civil engineering, Bundesgewerbeschule, Vienna, 1949-53; studied architecture, Academy of Fine Arts, Vienna, Diploma, 1956; studied planning and architecture, Illinois Institute of Technology, Chicago, 1958-59; studied environmental design, University of California, Berkeley, M.Arch., 1960. **Career:** Worked in architectural offices in the United States, Australia, South America, Sweden, and Germany, 1960-64; in private architectural and design practice, Vienna, from 1964; design consultant to Herman Miller, American Optical Corporation, Franz Wittmann KG, Alessi, Memphis, Poltronova, Knoll International, Cleto Munari, and others, from 1966. Editor, *Bau* magazine, Vienna, 1965-70. Professor of architecture, Academy of Fine Arts, Dusseldorf, 1967-76; head of the Institute of Design, from 1976, and of the master class in architecture, from 1979, Academy of Applied Arts, Vienna; also visiting professor, Washington University, St. Louis, 1963-64 and 1966, Yale University, University of California, Los Angeles, and Ohio State University. Member, Austrian State Commission for the Venice Biennale, from 1978; member, Steering Committee of the Gallery of the State Opera, Vienna, 1982-85; member, Advisory Council "Kunst + Bau," Ministry of Education and Art, Vienna, from 1986; jury member on numerous competition juries and international award panels, from 1981. **Member:** Austrian Architects Association (vice-president); Austrian Chamber of Architects; Austrian Art Senate, from 1983; AKNW German Chamber of Architects; BDA League of German Architects; Club of Rome, Austrian Chapter, 1987; Commisió Internacional de Difusió de la Cultura Catalan, Barcelona, 1989; Royal Swedish Academy of Fine Arts. **Exhibitions:** *Hans Hollein/Walter Pichler,* Galerie Nächst St. Stephan, Vienna, 1963; Museum of Modern Art, New York, 1967; Musée d'Art Moderne, Paris, 1968; Lunds Konsthall, Sweden, 1968; *Hollein,* Feigen Gallery, Chicago, 1969; Städtisches Museum, Mönchengladbach, 1970, 1975, 1984; *Hans Hollein,* at the Venice Biennale, 1972; Museum Folkwang, Essen, 1972; *Umanesimo—Disumanesimo,* Palazzo Pali, Florence, 1980; Centre Georges Pompidou, Paris, 1986 (toured); Museum of the 20th Century, Vienna, 1987; Accademia delle Arti del Disegno, Florence, 1988; National Gallery, Berlin, 1988; Yurakucho Art Forum, Tokyo, 1989; Tsukashin Hall, Osaka, 1990; *Meuble/Immeuble,* Centre Georges Pompidou, Paris, 1993; *La Ville,* Centre Georges Pompidou, Paris, 1994; *Visiones Urbanas,* Barcelona, 1994; Historisches Museum der Stadt Wien, Vienna, 1995. **Collections:** Museum of Modern Art, New York; Albertina, Vienna; Museum of Modern Art, Vienna; Fondación Miró, Barcelona; Municipal Museum Abteiberg, Mönchengladbach, FRG; Deutsches Architekturmuesum, Frankfurt; Centre Georges Pompidou, Paris; Stedelijk Museum, Amsterdam; Metropolitan Museum of Art, New York; Musée Saint Pierre/Art Contemporain, Lyon; Art Institute of Chicago; Victoria and Albert Museum, London; National Museum of Art, Kyoto; Musée des Arts Décoratifs, Montreal, Quebec. **Honors:** Golden Fueger Medal, Vienna, 1954; State Award of the Academy of Art, Vienna, 1956; Reynolds Memorial Award, U.S.A., 1966, 1984; Clients Awards, Austrian Architects Association, 1967, 1968, 1976, 1979, 1984, 1989, 1990; Brno Biennale Committee Prize, 1968; Austrian State Award for Design, 1968, 1983; Bard Award, New York, 1970; Rosenthal Studio Prize, Frankfurt, 1973; City of Vienna Prize, 1974; *Industrial Design* Award of Excellence, New York, 1977; German Architecture Award, 1983; Grand Aus-

trian State Award for Fine Arts, 1983; *Sunday Times* Award, London, 1984; Pritzker Architecture Prize, 1985; Haas International Award, Berkeley, California, 1988; Prix Rhénan/Prix Soprema, Strasbourg, France, 1989; Chicago Architecture Award, 1990; Ehrenzeichen für Wissenschaft und Kunst, Vienna, 1990; Pilgrampreis, Austria, 1991; Award for superior standard of design, International Trademark Center and Interecho Press, Belgium, 1991; TypoGraphic Award, Society of Typographic Designers, London, 1992; Marble Architectural Award, Italy, 1993; Goldenes Ehrenzeichen um die Cerdienste um das Land Wien, Vienna, 1994. Honorary Fellow, American Institute of Architects, 1981; honorary chairman, R. M. Schindler Centennial, Los Angeles, 1987; honorary member, Royal Academy, The Hague, 1987; honorary fellow, Bezalel Academy of Arts and Design, Jerusalem, 1988; honorary fellow, Royal Institute of British Architects, 1993; and numerous awards in architectural competitions. **Address:** Argentinierstrasse 36, A-1040 Vienna, Austria.

## Works

Retti Candle Shop, Vienna, 1964-65.
CM Boutique, for Christa Metek, Vienna, 1966-67.
Richard Feigen art gallery, New York, 1967-69.
*Austriennale* exhibition layouts, at the 14th Milan Triennale, 1968.
*Death* exhibition layouts, for the Städtisches Museum, Mönchengladbach, 1970.
Exhibition layouts for EXPO 1970, Osaka, Japan, 1970.
Section N interior furnishings shop, Vienna, 1971-72.
*Paper* exhibition layouts, for the Austrian Design Centre, Vienna, 1972.
Schullin jewellery shop 1, Vienna, 1972-74.
Städtisches Museum Abteiberg, Mönchengladbach, 1972-82.
*MANtransFORMS* exhibition layouts, for the Cooper-Hewitt Museum, New York, 1974-76.
*Salon du Meuble* exhibition layout, for Wittmann-Austria, Paris, 1975.
Central office and three branch offices, for the Austrian Tourist Bureau, Vienna, 1976-79.
Museum of Glass and Ceramics, Tehran, 1977-78.
Alessi exhibit displays, at the Milan Triennale, 1979.
*Comedy of Seduction* stage design, Burgtheater, Vienna, 1979-80.
Public School of the City of Vienna, Köhlergasse, Vienna, 1979-90.
Beck department store, Munich, 1981.
Museum of Energy, Essen, 1981.
Schullin jewellery shop 2, Vienna, 1981-82.
*Ludwig Beck at Trump Tower* shop, New York, 1981-83.
National Museum of Egyptian Civilization, Cairo, 1983.
*Dream and Reality* exhibition layouts, for the Kunstlerhaus, Vienna, 1984.
*Le Affinità Elletive* exhibition layouts, at the Milan Triennale, Milan, 1985.
Haas Haus commercial building, Vienna, 1985-90.
*SCITEX Pavilion* layout, DRUPA, Dusseldorf, 1986.
Golfclub Schloß Ebreichsdorf, Ebreichsdorf, Austria, 1987-89.
Museum of Modern Art, Frankfurt, 1987-91.
Sign, for the Film Festival of Barcelona, Barcelona, 1988.
Banco Santander headquarters, Madrid, 1988-1993.
Erste Allgemeine Generali district headquarters with residential and business complex, Bregenz, Austria, 1988-93.

Archaeological Site, Michaelerplatz, Vienna, 1991-92.
*13 Austrian Positions* exhibition layouts at the Austrian Pavilion, Architecture Biennale Venice, Venice, 1991.
*Toccata* stage design, for the Ballet of the Opera House, Zurich, 1992.
Cultural District of the new capital of Lower Austria, St. Pölten, Austria, from 1992.
Study Donau-City, Vienna, 1993.
Architectural Visions for Europe, Düsseldorf, 1993-94.
European Centre of Volcanism, Auvergne, France, from 1994.
*Rosenkavalier* stage design, Finnish Opera, 1996.

(for a complete list of Hollein's buildings and architectural projects, see *Contemporary Architects*)

## Publications

**By HOLLEIN: books**—*GA 47: Otto Wagner,* edited by Y. Futagawa, Tokyo, 1978; *l'Ora di Ginnastica,* exhibition catalogue, Mönchengladbach, 1984; *Friedrich Achleitner: Schriften und Werk,* exhibition catalogue, Vienna, 1985.

**On HOLLEIN: books**—*Hans Hollein/Walter Pichler: Architektur,* exhibition catalogue by Joseph Esherick, Vienna, 1963; *Hans Hollein: Work and Behavior, Life and Death, Everyday Situations,* exhibition catalogue, Vienna, 1972; *Hans Hollein,* booklet by Christoph Makler, Aachen, 1978; *Architektur aus Österreich seit 1960* by Peter M. Bode and Gustav Peichl, Salzburg, 1980; *Hans Hollein: A Bibliography of Books and Articles* by Carol Cable, Monticello, 1983; *GA 8: Schullin Jewellery Shop, Vienna* edited by Yukio Futagawa, Tokyo, 1984; *Die Revision der Moderne: Postmoderne Architektur 1960-1980* by Heinrich Klotz, Munich, 1984, as *Post Modern Visions,* New York, 1984; *Hans Hollein: Works 1960-1988,* exhibition catalogue by Gianni Pettena, Milan, 1988.

*       *       *

Twenty-five years ago a number of unusual "architectural" projects were publicized. Called "Transformations" by their designer, Hans Hollein, they used photomontages to change the scale and surroundings of common or known objects: an aircraft carrier in the middle of a rolling landscape, a "high-rise building" which on closer view is clearly an oversized spark-plug, and a sleek, shiny skyscraper on Wall Street which turns out to be a radiator grille from a Rolls-Royce! Although these fantasies caused some stir in the art world, it was a tiny little shop in Vienna (1965) which brought instant fame to Hollein. Hailed in the architectural press for garnering the coveted Reynolds Metal Award for outstanding use of aluminum, Hollein earned a prize of $25,000, a considerable sum at the time, and said to be worth more than the shop's construction budget!

The Retti candleshop was the first of many successful designs that followed. Another tiny Vienna boutique, "CM" for Christa Metek (1966-67), utilized a storefront of aluminum, painted metal, and glass to provide a bull's-eye like sign/shop window/front door/air conditioner outlet all in a striking facade. The Richard Feigen Gallery (1967-69) turned the interior and facade of a New York brownstone into a sleek environment of shiny surfaces, bold curves, and visually connected multiple levels of exhibition space.

The "Austriennale" at the 14th Triennial in Milan (1968) featured a series of parallel corridors of varying lengths, enclosed at the ends by a row of identical doors. These individual environments offered a variety of physical and psychical experiences through artificial means, not the least of which was a pair of "Austrian (eye) Glasses," produced on the spot, which highlighted the exhibit and became a souvenir for the visitor.

Hollein moved into the 1970s with more projects, exhibition designs, shops, and competition entries. The "Section N" Showroom (1971) for furniture and objects in Vienna allowed a return to interconnecting volumes on several levels. His design for the Schullin Jewelry Store (1972) on the Graben in Vienna, as in "CM," again provided unusual expression for the air conditioner ventilation—a series of stainless steel/brass tubes piercing a fissure crack in the polished granite facade. Here again a tiny store is turned into an object almost as precious as the wares within.

Hollein's designs for the Munich Olympic Village Subway Entrance Area (1971-72), which won first place in a competition, became the guidelines for the entire village. The "Media Linien," an electrified tubular system on steel supports, allowed for the connection of various parts which adapted it to an almost endless variety of urban and climate conditions and displayed his interest in technology to the general public. Meanwhile, his nearby work for the Carl Friedrich von Siemens Foundation facilities brought his high style and attention to details to the semi-private business world.

Another competition produced what was his largest commission to date—the Municipal Museum Abteiberg Mönchengladbach, Germany (1972-82). Here the design, on a hillside overlooking the town, provides multiple level access to the building dug-in to the hill side to conceal its scale from the structures around it. The complex interior volumes are concealed from downhill by a series of undulating walls—stepped planters—climbing up to the "walk-on" roof which serves as a major access to the structure, which was home to Hollein's own exhibition "The Gymnasium Lesson" in 1984.

The Museum of Glass and Ceramics in Tehran (1977-78) gave rise to still more innovations in design and technology in the treatment and lighting of the custom designed display cases. Again, the polished materials of metal and glass strengthen the sense of value of the objects within, while indirect lighting plays off the ornate interior of the building which houses it.

Hollein's work for the Austrian Travel Service in the late 1970s, where simulated palm trees provide spatial articulation, as well as suggestions of exotic lands, and pseudo-Rolls-Royce radiator grilles become teller windows, started his excursion into the Post-Modernism of the period. The second Schullin Jewelry Store (1981-82) and the shop for Ludwig Beck at Trump Tower, New York City (1981-83) carry these excursions further, while his object/utensil/furniture designs for firms like Alessi, Munari, and Memphis transmute these ideas into a smaller, perhaps more palatable, scale.

Stage sets and exhibit designs flourished in the 1980s. Perhaps the most notable, "Dream and Reality: Vienna, 1870-1930" (1984-85), gave him the opportunity to transform the entire Kunstlerhaus into an informational and atmospheric consciousness of the period. Externally, one wing wall was painted in gold—the dream—while another was in gray—the reality. Internally, the grand staircase greeted the visitor with a parade of mannequins garbed as town burghers while it led one to a succession of rooms which conveyed the spirit of the Secession, Klimt, Loos, Otto Wagner, Mahler, Schonberg, Freud, and the political realities of Red Vienna and World

War I. Again the technological features of display and lighting design combined with Hollein's inherent and ingenious design sense.

—William Victor Kriebel

# HOLSCHER, Knud

Danish architect and industrial, product, and graphic designer

**Born:** Rødby, 6 May 1930. **Education:** Educated in Maribo, until 1949; studied architecture, Royal Academy of Fine Arts, Copenhagen, 1949-55, 1956-57. **Family:** Married Henny Meyland Rasmussen in 1958; children: Tine, Nils, and Rasmus. **Career:** Draughtsman, then associate, in the office of Arne Jacobsen, in Copenhagen, 1959-60, and in Oxford, 1960-64; partner with Alan Tye, in Holscher-Tye architects, Copenhagen, 1964-66; collaborated with the architect Svend Axelsson, from 1973; partner, 1966-95, and board member, from 1988, Krohn and Hartvig Rasmussen architects (later KHR AS architects), Copenhagen. Industrial and graphic designer, from 1963; founder-principal, Knud Holscher Industrial Design, Copenhagen, from 1995; design consultant to Blücher Metalvare, Bodilsen Furniture, Coloplast, Dampa, Dansk Pressalit, Design Funktion AB, ERCO Leuchten, Folsgaard Lamps, Fritz Hansen, George Jensen, Højgaard and Schultz, IFO Sanitar, Ifö Mörrum, Nordisk Solar, Norplan, OCLI, Øresund Link, Paustian, Perstorp, Pevo, Rosti, Royal Copenhagen, SaniScan, Stone Art, Thor Radiator, Toni Fittings, Tron-Pax ApS, and others. Assistant instructor, with E. Christian Sorensen, 1958-60 and 1964-68, and professor of architecture, 1968-1988, Royal Academy of Fine Arts, Copenhagen; visiting professor, Universities of Adelaide, Sydney, and Melbourne, Australia, 1986; professor, Design Institute, Royal Danish Academy of Art, 1994. **Member:** Association of Academic Architects; Council of Practicing Architects; Danish Design Council; Federation of Danish Architects; Industrial Designers Denmark. **Exhibitions:** *IDD Design Exhibit,* Nikolaj Plads, Copenhagen, 1972; *Danish Handicraft Products,* Sonderborg, 1973; *Nordisk Industriedesign,* Kunstindustrimuseet, Oslo, 1976; *Design Since 1945,* Philadelphia Museum of Art, 1983; Design Center, Stuttgart, 1986. **Honors:** British Design Award, London, 1964, 1966, 1970; British Aluminium Industry Prize, 1966; Guild of Architectural Ironmongers Prize, London, 1966, 1969; Theophilus Hansen Scholarship, Copenhagen, 1966; Eckersberg Medal, Royal Academy of Fine Arts, Copenhagen, 1970; IDD Danish Industrial Design Prize, 1975, 1977, 1978; Die Gute Industrieform Prize, Bonn, 1978, 1984; Traeprisen Award, Copenhagen, 1979; K. E. Engelhardt memorial grant, 1981; Scandinavian Lighting Fair Prize, Copenhagen, 1983; Hanover Fair Lighting Design Prize, 1983; Goed Industrieel Vorm Prize, Antwerp, 1987; Design Innovation Award, Essen, 1987; IG Design Prize, Copenhagen, 1987; Betonelementprisen Award, Copenhagen, 1989; Nykredit Prize, Seville, Spain, 1992; European Design Award, Denmark, 1992; Mies van der Rohe Award nomination, 1992, 1994; C. F. Hansen Medal, Royal Academy of Art, Denmark, 1993; Prize of Honour, Danish National Bank, 1993; Industrie Forum Design prize, Hannover, 1993; Auguste Perret Prize for Applied Technology in Architecture, 1993; Bundespreis Produkt Design, 1994; Highest Design Quality Award, Design Innovations '93, 1995; Aga Khan Award nomination, 1995; and numerous prizes in architectural competitions, from 1955. **Address:** Knud Holscher Industrial Design, Vermundsgade 40, 2100 Copenhagen, Denmark.

## Works

*Modric* series of fittings, for Allgood, Great Britain, 1962.
*Meridian One* and *Two* sanitary fittings, for Adamsez, Great Britain, 1962, 1965.
Office sign system, for Headway Syncronol, Great Britain, 1969.
Kitchen ware, for Georg Jensen, Denmark, 1974.
*D-Line* series of fittings, for Carl F. Petersen, Denmark, 1975-91.
SIB concrete beam system, for Højgaard & Schultz A/S, Denmark, 1977.
Container system, for Perstorp AB, Sweden, 1977.
Sanitary equipment, for Ifö Sanitär AB, Sweden, 1977.
Lamps, for H. Folsgaard Lighting, Denmark, 1977.
Radiator, for Thor Radiator, Denmark, 1977.
Air diffusors, for Riscanco A/S, Denmark, 1977-91.
Door system, for Pevo A/S, Denmark, 1978.
*Toni* series of tap fittings, for Toni A/S, Denmark, 1979.
Thermos, for Royal Copenhagen A/S, Denmark, 1983.
*Dampa* ceiling system, for Dampa A/S, Denmark, 1983.
*Theatre Chair,* for Fritz Hansen, 1983.
*Stringline* lighting range, for Nordisk Solar A/S, Denmark, 1985.
WC seats, for Pressalit A/S, Denmark, 1985.
Plast series *Club Manhattan,* for Stone Art, Belgium, 1985.
Bus stop standards, for Copenhagen Transport Co., Denmark, 1985.
Bus stop standards, for Decaux AFA, France, 1985.
Design manual, for the municipality of Herlev, Copenhagen, 1986.
Gas meter cabinet, for Metropolitan Natural Gas, Denmark, 1987.
Colostmi kit, for Coloplast A/S, Denmark, 1989.
Sanitary outlet, for Blücher Metalvare A/S, Denmark, 1989.
Storage system, for Nordplan A/S, 1989.
Post box, for Paustian A/S, Denmark, 1989.
*ILS 2000* light control, for Tronpax A/S, Denmark, 1989.
Stainless wash basins, for Ifö Mörrum AB, Sweden, 1989.
*io* office furniture, for Facit AB, Sweden, 1990.
Lamp system, for ERCO Leuchten GmbH, Germany, 1990.
Office furniture series, for Design Funktion AB, 1990.
Bathroom furniture, shower series, and *AQUA* lux series, for Ifö Sanitär AB, 1990.
Street furniture, for AFA JCDecaux A/S, Denmark, 1991.
Bathroom lamp series, for Ifö Electric AB, Sweden, 1994.
Uplight lamp system, for ERCO Leuchten, 1995.
System of guidelines for the blind, for Danish Designcenter, 1995.
Railway toilets, for EVAC AB, Sweden, 1995.
*Copenhagen 96* exhibition, for the National Bank, Denmark, 1996.
DSB Designkoncept, for DSB, Denmark, 1996.
Design program, for the Danish Museum of Decorative Art, 1996.
Major architectural works include—Odense University, Denmark, 1966-80; Jos University, Nigeria, 1977; Royal Danish Theatre, Copenhagen, 1978; Bahrain National Museum, 1981; Naestved Town Hall, Denmark, 1981; Copenhagen Airport, Kastrup, 1983; Unicon Beton Headquarters, Roskilde, 1989; Danish Pavilion at EXPO '92, Seville, Spain, 1992.

(for a complete list of Holscher's architectural projects please see *Contemporary Architects*)

## Publications

**By HOLSCHER: books**—(with others) *Culture in a Crisis Time,* Copenhagen, 1980.

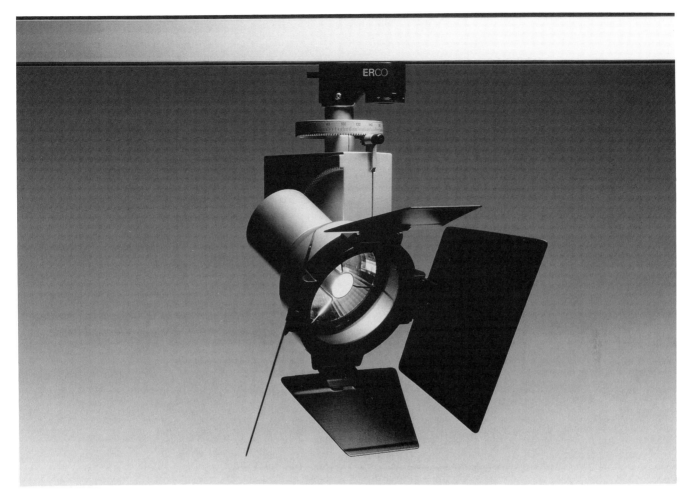

**Knud Holscher: Quinta/Erco halogen lighting, 1994**

**On HOLSCHER: books**—*Nordisk Industridesign,* exhibition catalogue by Lauritz Opstad and Alf Boe, Oslo, 1976; *Modern Design in Metal* by Richard Stewart, London, 1979; *Design Since 1945* edited by Kathryn Hiesinger and George Marcus, Philadelphia and London, 1983; *The Conran Directory of Design* edited by Stephen Bayley, London, 1985.

*

People talk about the rational, the causal principle as opposed to the irrational. Le Corbusier looked at this duality in the premises of architecture, he compared it to a river, of which one bank is the rational, the technical side, while the other is the humanist. You have to choose your bank of the river.

Architects express their ideas, their interpretation of a programme, in pictures: some make picturesque drawings, while others prefer to create ideas that tower over the landscape of architectonic manifestations like trees. These ideas are inspirational and may create standards for the general run of more ordinary architectural work.

Architects also work the opposite way; often they collect pictures to illustrate situations and environments, usually with the aid of the camera, all to help them in their efforts. These pictures sometimes illustrate very clearly all the problems involved, and they act as references.

One of the prettiest pictures I have is of the south coast of Holland. Showing a beach after snow, it is a composition showing how clumps of seaweed washed up on the sand have caught the snow, so that each clump of weed has pulled a little snowdrift after it.

At first it looks fine, very pretty, but after you look at it for a while, a marked, rational coherence becomes clear. Near the water the salt has melted the snow, so seaweed and wet sand are dominant; further up the beach the snow is firmer. The whole thing is clear, full of contrasts, very pretty, all rational and calculated. How hard it is to create such an attractive impression! We have to be continually revising, keeping an open mind. And where the snowscape so clearly balances the many sets of parameters against each other in its perfectly rational composition, we see the functional requirements that are so hard to harmonize in working out a project—technique, economy, and finally also the administrative burdens that make the creative process so much more difficult.

There are very few master builders who will listen to the aesthetic arguments; they prefer to stick strictly to the rational side in working out their programmes. Relatively few of us are thus alone in striving for a humanist interpretation of the rational and the presumptive.

The seashore is conceived in a single design, a single idea, and the eye can pass on to the conception of a wider landscape, in which the shore becomes a detail. This more comprehensive aesthetic experience is generally missing in architecture. Our world is badly off for creators of satisfactory environments, and yet we have classic examples of such complexes, which time has made easier to understand and to accept.

Our world is accelerating technocratically, everything is hurried, and, unfortunately, it is all commonplace. The creative process that used to take months is now all over in days. There is competition for swift solutions. The refinement that developed over a long period and found expression in traditional architecture is missing today. Hence, the few solutions that are outstanding. Hence also, perhaps, the poverty I mentioned earlier in the creation of complete environments; until one set of solutions has been tried out, there is no call for ordinary development to be revised.

The seashore strikes us as aesthetic, but it is not an artistic expression, and it was perhaps its rational coherence that made it comprehensible. A psychologist who has analyzed the process tells us that appreciation has certain associations; what happens, according to his analysis, is that we discover in the work an intention, an order, which has lain more or less hidden, and when we recognize it, it offsets the complexity of the work.

Architecture must contain a certain amount of fresh creation, of originality. Otherwise, its information content is reduced, and appreciation with it. Understanding depends on order and on certain known and accepted elements. However, too many familiar elements will transform the conception and it will be regarded as stylistic.

If the idea is too foreseeable, too familiar—if, that is, we say that a conception is stylistic—the idea withers away; thus, there is an implicit need in architecture for continual renewal. I will go so far as to say that the greatest renewal—by which I mean the lowest level of foreseeableness—calls for a maximum of simplicity, that is to say, a low level of complexity. It is just this conception we should be aiming for; it is what makes the strongest artistic impression.

The picture of the seashore was not a new creation; it was complex, very clearly in line with the psychologist's formula. The postulates of architecture are continually changing, so we must continually revise our own assumptions and causal relationships. Changing associations within society must be appropriately reflected in architecture.

Architecture must thus by nature be creative; if it is to be generally appropriate to its period, it must stand at a distance from what we know and recognize—that is true of questions of form but as I have mentioned, purely functional elements will also affect development.

Lack of political ability to solve our ecological problems in time has meant that within a decade we have moved from being a growth society to a society with inherited problems and different parameters for their solution. We are, thus, at the beginning of a new period, in which, among other things, the question of energy will have a great influence on planning and building and on our lifestyle.

As in the picture of the seashore, we have parameters for the solution of what is measurable, but up to now, we have had to give way to political-social relationships, which make a synthesis very much harder. The solution lies neither in the familiar round of nostalgic environment nor in pure, suntrap technocracy. The epitome, the synthesis alone will be acceptable. We must sail in the middle of the river, between the rational and the irrational banks. That is where we shall find a synthesis which will provide an answer to problems that are so complex that their formulation is found only in, and with, their solution.

—Knud Holscher

*      *      *

When the Danish Pavilion created a dynamic focal point at the 1992 Seville World Expo with its sail-like forms, it was a timely reminder to the design world that its Danish architect Knud Holscher was still capable of striking a chord with contemporary audiences.

Holscher is forever associated with the golden years of Scandinavian Modernism, which reached its peak in the 1950s and 1960s. He was after all, Arne Jacobsen's architectural associate on the St. Catherine's College project at Oxford. Jacobsen, a tough taskmaster, was undeniably a mentor. But while Holscher is happy to be a part of the classic tradition of Scandinavian Modern design, he points out that it is a living tradition and that he is "no-dyed-in-the-wool functionalist."

"The Danish pavilion is not just a functionalist building," he explains. "And if you look at my Quinta spotlights for Erco Lighting, there are lines which are not strictly needed but they are there as part of an expression to make the product better understood."

Like Arne Jacobsen himself, Holscher has successfully combined architecture and product design in his extensive career. The ribbing evocative of a sea shell on his Quinta spotlights, and wing-like reflectors on his Zenit uplighters, also for Erco, complement more mainstream architectural commissions such as the new extension at Copenhagen Airport, completed in 1986.

For 20 years Holscher was a professor in the architecture school at the Royal Academy of Arts in Denmark. But at the same time he was undertaking product design projects, such as tableware for Georg Jensen and architectural fittings for Carl F. Petersen, for whom his D-Line remains an international best-seller. "Younger designers may be more fashionable and ambitious, but my products increase in sales over a long time and clients tend to notice that kind of thing," says Holscher.

Both aspects of his work—buildings and artifacts—reveal how he has managed to remain relevant to today's audiences without sacrificing his design principles. His work reflects the virtues of clarity, honesty, simplicity, and precision which are essential to modern Danish design. It is a philosophy the writer Kim Dirckinck-Holmfeld has described as embodying "the poetry of moderation."

Indeed the idea of a "moderate Modernist" is especially well-suited to Holscher in area of office interiors, where he has sought to bring a more humanistic sense of form to highly technical lighting and furniture projects. His iO range of office desks, designed for Facit in 1991-92, conveys as essentially Scandinavian sense of human softness and roundness which has echoes of Alvar Aalto.

At 65, Knud Holscher is still making a major contribution. He recently left the large architectural practice Krohn & Hartvig Rasmussen to set up his own Copenhagen design office, and he is currently working on a wide range of projects. These include station designs for Copenhagen's S-train underground system, a new Danish road sign system, a range of sanitaryware for the Swedish company Ifoe, and lighting projects with Austrian lighting consultant Christian Barbenbach.

It is a heavy workload but Knud Holscher, empowered by the Modernist tradition which propels him forward, takes it all in his stride. "I enjoy my work too much to slow down," he stresses.

—Jeremy Myerson

# HORNER, Harry

American stage and film designer

**Born:** Holicz, Austria-Hungary, 24 July 1910; emigrated to the United States, 1935, naturalized, 1938. **Education:** Studied architecture, University of Vienna, 1929-34; studied stage design at Max Reinhardt's Seminary for Drama and Stage Direction, State Academy of the Theatre, Vienna, 1932-34; also studied costume design under Professor Roller, Vienna, 1934. **Military Service:** Served in the United States Army Air Force, 1942-44, Technical Sergeant. **Family:** Married Betty Pfaelzer in 1938 (died, 1950); married Joan Frankel in 1952; children: James, Christopher, and Antony. **Career:** Actor and designer, with Max Reinhardt's Repertory Company, Theater in der Josestadt, Vienna, and at Salzburg Summer Festivals, 1934-35, and with Reinhardt in the United States, 1935-36; freelance stage designer and director, from 1935, film designer, from 1940, and film director, mainly with 20th Century-Fox and United Artists, from 1951; founder, Enterprise Films of Canada, and Anglo Enterprise Films Limited, London, 1964. **Member:** Society of Motion Picture Directors; Canadian Directors Guild. **Exhibitions:** International Museum of Photography at George Eastman House, Rochester, New York, 1979. **Collections:** Lincoln Center, New York; George Eastman House, Rochester, New York; University of Illinois, Champaign. **Honors:** League of Nations Award, 1932; Academy Award, 1949, 1961; Los Angeles Critics Stage Design Award, 1970. **Died:** 5 December 1994.

## Works

Stage designs include (New York, unless noted)—*Victoria Regina,* for the Italian tour, 1935; *Eternal Road,* 1936; *The Magic Flute,* at the Salzburg Festival, 1937; *Ice Follies* (also director), Cleveland, 1937; *Night People,* 1938; *All the Living,* 1938; *Jeremiah,* 1939; *Family Portrait,* 1939; *Herod* (with Katharine Cornell), 1939; *Railroads on Parade,* at New York's World's Fair, 1939; *Orfeo,* Metropolitan Opera, 1939; *Il Travatore,* Metropolitan Opera, 1940; *Little Foxes,* 1941; *Lady in the Dark,* 1941; *Let's Face It* (musical), 1941; *Banjo Eyes* (musical), 1941; *Elektra,* San Francisco Opera, 1941; *Lily of the Valley,* 1942; *Heart of the City,* Star and Garter, 1942; *Kiss for Cinderella,* 1942; *Fidelio,* San Francisco Opera, 1942; *World of Christopher Blake,* 1942; *Winged Victory* (musical; also designed film version) and *You Bet Your life* (special service production for training camouflage units; also writer), for United States Army Air Force, 1943-45; *Me and Molly,* 1948; *Joy to the World,* 1948; *Turandot* (also director), San Francisco Opera, 1953; *Hazel Flagg* (musical), 1953; *The Portuguese Inn,* San Francisco Opera, 1955; *The Magic Flute* (also director), Metropolitan Opera, 1956; *Joan at the Stake,* San Francisco Opera, 1956; *Dialogue of the Carmelites* (also director), San Francisco Opera, 1957; *King David* (also director), world premiere at the Hollywood Bowl, 1958; *A Midsummer Night's Dream* (also director), at the Vancouver Music Festival, 1961; *The Magic Flute* (also director), at the Vancouver Music Festival, 1962; *Aida* (also director), for the opening of the Seattle Festival Opera House, 1963; *Idiot's Delight,* 1970.

Harry Horner: Set design for *Aida,* at the Seattle Festival Opera House, 1963

Film designs include—*Our Town* (Wood), 1940; *The Little Foxes* (Wyler), 1941; *Tarzan Triumphs* (Thiele), 1943; *Stage Door Canteen* (Borzage), 1943; *Winged Victory* (Cukor), 1944; *A Double Life* (Cukor), 1944; *The Heiress* (Wyler), 1949; *Tarzan and the Slave Girl* (Sholem), 1950; *Outrage* (Lupino), 1950; *Born Yesterday* (Cukor), 1950; *He Ran All the Way* (Berry), 1951; *Androcles and the Lion* (Erskine), 1952; *The Marrying Kind* (Cukor), 1952; *Separate Tables* (Delbert Mann), 1958; *The Wonderful Country* (Parrish), 1959; *The Hustler* (Rossen), 1961; *The Luck of Ginger Coffey* (Kershner), 1964; *They Shoot Horses, Don't They?* (Pollack), 1969; *Who Is Harry Kellerman and Why Is He Saying Those Terrible Things About Me?* (Grosbard), 1971; *Up the Sandbox* (Kershner), 1972; *The Blackbird* (Giler), 1975; *Harry and Walter Go To New York* (Rydell), 1976; *Audrey Rose* (Wise), 1977; *The River* (Hill), 1978; *Moment by Moment* (Wagner), 1978; *Strangers: The Story of a Mother and Daughter* (Katselas; for TV), 1979; *The Jazz Singer* (Fleischer and Furie), 1980.

Films directed include—*Red Planet Mars*, 1952; *Beware My Lovely*, 1952; *Vicki*, 1953; *New Faces*, 1953; *A Life in the Balance*, 1954; *Man from Del Rio*, 1956; *The Wild Party*, 1956.

## Publications

**By HORNER: articles**—in *Theatre Arts* (New York), November 1941, December 1947; *Hollywood Quarterly* (Los Angeles), Fall 1950; *American Film* (Washington, D.C.), February 1977; *Cinematographe* (Paris), February 1982.

**On HORNER: books**—*La Scenografia del Film* edited by Mario Verdone, Rome, 1956; *Scene Design for Stage and Screen* edited by Orvill Kurth Larson, East Lansing, 1961; *Le Decor de Film* by Leon Barsacq, Paris, 1970, as *Caligari's Cabinet and Other Grand Illusions,* Boston, 1976; *Filmmakers on Filmmaking* edited by Joseph McBride, Los Angeles, 1983; *The International Dictionary of Films and Filmmakers,* Chicago and London, 1987, 1991.

*

Just what is the art director's contribution to a play or film? The visual aspect of any dramatic work is an important part of the total effect. In a film, the dramatic effect lies in the camera movement, whereas the effect on the stage often lies in the movement of scenery to give the motion of the locale as part of the illusion. There is no question that the mood of a scene is strongly influenced by the scenic effect.

In a motion picture, camera movement can create the effect of a chase, a train ride, or even the movement of an army—in short, any effect and mood that is brought about by the movement of the camera itself. The stage, however, requires inventions in design in order to simulate motion. The stage might require the creation of devices such as turnable projections in order to move from one scene to another. In short, the designer of stage productions becomes a direct contributor to the creation and mood of a scene, and the audience is required to participate by substituting imagination for reality. In film, realism is expected. Even the trend toward space pictures requires fantasy to be realistic. One of the first modern designer-directors to do this was William Cameron Menzies.

Every imaginative production designer in film has his own favorite design subject. This means that we like to work on stories that

particularly appeal to us, that particularly move us more than other stories. Almost every motion picture I've designed falls into this category, and I found I was moved more by character development than by the plot itself. In other words, I look at a script and consider the character description seen by the writer and director to be the most important pre-condition of the design. For example, in the film version of *The Little Foxes,* Regina and the other characters moving around her became the focal elements of my design. The sets were designed to indicate Regina's greed and materialism. In *The Heiress,* the characters of Catherine and her father became the guides for architectural and artistic demands in the designs. The father's domineering personality, his daughter's shyness, which later turned into hatred, and her relationship with her lover became the focal points in my concept. The hotel in *Separate Tables* determined again my design by the characterizations of the people who frequented it. Even in a film which concentrated on action, such as *They Shoot Horses, Don't They?,* I tried to emphasize the conditions of the various people involved in the dance marathon.

In my interpretation, it is the character of the persons involved that determines the plot of the dramatic action, both on stage and in film, and that guides me in the execution of my designs.

—Harry Horner

\*     \*     \*

In his first film assignment, *Our Town* (1940), Harry Horner was personally introduced to the methods of production design by William Cameron Menzies himself. The young Horner had been assigned the film, but the producer wanted Menzies' experience and thus hired him as the production designer. Instead of redesigning the town, Menzies realized the value of Horner's meticulously researched program: Horner took small-scale views into the lives of the story's townspeople; this was stressed by using mostly closeups, and this microcosmic plan was supported by numerous props that became signs of characterization.

But director Sam Wood did not like Horner's unique plan, and so large sets (designed by Horner) were built. Though the original program was thwarted, Menzies maintained much of Horner's design. Nevertheless, visual unity was lost to the expanded scale; Horner's small details were made trite or were overpowered.

Ever since the film, it is significant that Horner has remained most interested in visual characterization. He has explained that he emotionally reacts to a script's characters. These very personal, intuitive, expressionistic responses are housed visually within stylistic and iconographic structures. Not only the major contributor to the visual style and iconography of most of his films, Horner also knew how to contrapuntally tie these structures to others, such as the literary/dramatic ones of plot, characterization, and performance.

To isolate Horner's contributions, the stylistic and iconographic elements of his films can be separated and appreciated. Stylistically, it is clear that Horner, like most major film designers, is not a strict realist but an eclectic realist. Horner's best production designs—*The Little Foxes, The Heiress, Born Yesterday, The Hustler, They Shoot Horses, Don't They?,* and *The Driver*—are eclectic; except for *Born Yesterday,* all use a mixture of realism and expressionism. Horner also used these two styles, in addition to surrealism, in his designs for *A Double Life, Up the Sandbox,* and *Who Is Harry Kellerman and Why Is He Saying All Those Terrible Things About Me?.* This film's eclecticism proves what postmodernist theory has lately rediscovered: that style's humanistic dimensions offers significant meanings in the contemporary world.

To prove Horner is not a realist but an eclectic realist, his floor plans for many film sets are *not* imitations of functional architectural space, even though to most people the room or building may appear to be real. For the illusion of reality, Horner uses highly crafted surface textures, appropriate patterns, and color, and these are also subject to his emotive responses so that they too fit within the design program. In scenes of tension or violence, for example, the floor plans tend toward polygonal forms that create angled walls. But with the "realistic" surfaces, such multi-planed walls, when photographed, will become a tense expressionist-realist environment for the performance.

Iconographically selected or designed objects, spaces, decor, and presentation on the screen are also hidden under these eclectic realist appearances. For example, in one of Horner's masterworks, *The Heiress* (1949), the meticulously researched, mid-nineteenth-century house of Dr. Sloper appears authentic, leading one to accuse Horner of a narrow historicism. But it was only an illusion. As Horner described it, the house was emotionally conceived as an elegant cage in which Catherine Sloper was psychologically interred. The floor plan was given many planes that compress the characters. Linear grids subtly appear in lattices, wallpaper, and in other details; they increase the sense of enclosure. To insure the emotional environment was correctly lit and photographed, Horner made continuity sketches with expressionistic, high-contrast lighting and extreme angles.

The sketches were discussed with Wyler and Leo Tover, the cameraman. Conversations about these drawings tightly integrated Horner's design program into the photography and performances. This film production from beginning to end met many of Horner's standards for a film's creative social aspect—the artistic family, headed by an esthetically sensitive director.

A spirit of collaboration between the specialized artists has existed in each film Horner has enjoyed working on, whether or not the film became a box-office success. Horner says that the films with incompatible production members usually become jobs unworthy of being called a production design.

—Norman Gambill

# HOULD-WARD, Ann

American costume designer

**Born:** Glasgow, Montana, 8 April 1954. **Education:** Mills College, B.A.; University Of Virginia, M.F.A.; studied at the Art Students League. **Career:** Worked alongside Patricia Zipprodt in the early 1980s; freelance costume designer. **Member:** United Scenic Artists Local no.829; League of Professional Theatre Women. **Exhibitions:** International Design Quadrennial, Prague, 1995; Animazing Gallery, New York, 1995. **Collections:** McNay Art Museum, San Antonio, Texas. **Honors:** Antoinette Perry (Tony) Award Nomination, 1984, 1988; Drama Desk Award Nomination, 1984, 1988; Maharam Award Winner, 1984, and Nomination, 1985; Helen Hayes Award Nomination, 1985; Denver Critics Circle Award, 1985; American Theatre Wing Design Nomination, 1987, 1994; Outer Critics Circle Award Nomination, 1988, 1994; Los Angeles Drama Critics Circle Award, 1989; Antoinette Perry (Tony) Award for *Beauty And The Beast,* 1994;

American Theatre Wing Design Award for *Beauty And The Beast,* 1994; Award, Prague Quadrenial, 1995; Ovation Award for *Beauty And The Beast,* Los Angeles, 1995. **Address:** 3001 Henry Hudson Pkwy., no.4-K, Riverdale, New York 10463, U.S.A.

## Works

Broadway costume designs include—*On The Waterfront* (Adrian Hall); *The Moliere Comedies* (Michael Langham); *Beauty And The Beast* (Rob Roth); *Merry Wives Of Windsor* (Dan Sullivan); *Timon Of Athens* (Michael Langham); *In The Summer House* (Joanne Akalaitis); *3 Men On A Horse* (Joe Tillinger); *St. Joan* (Michael Langham); *Falsettos* (James Lapine); *Into The Woods* (James Lapine); *Harrigan 'n Hart* (Joe Layton); *Sunday In The Park With George* (James Lapine).

Off-Broadway costume designs include—*Camping With Henry And Tom* (Paul Lazarus); *Personals* (Paul Lazarus); *Hyde In Hollywood* (Gerry Gutierrez), Playwrights Horizons; *Little Footsteps* (Gary Pearle), Playwrights Horizons; *Cymbeline* (Joanne Akalaitis), The Public Theatre; *Miami* (Gerry Gutierrez), Playwrights Horizons; *1,2,3,4,5* (Gerry Gutierrez), Manhattan Theatre Club; *Just So* (Julie Ann Boyd); *Emily* (Gerry Gutierrez), Manhattan Theatre Club; *Sunday In The Park With George* (James Lapine); *Romeo And Juliet* (Les Waters), The Public Theatre, Playwrights Horizons; *On The Verge* (Garland Wright), The Acting Company; *A Dancing Woman,* Jose Limon Dance Company; *Ten By Tennessee* (Michael Kahn), The Acting Company; *10 Little Indians,* Equity Library Theatre.

Other theatre costume designs include—*Beauty And The Beast* (Rob Roth), toured the United States, Japan, Austria, Canada, and Australia, 1994-1996; *Falsettos* (James Lapine), toured the United States; *Into The Woods* (James Lapine), Pace Theatrical, toured the United States; *Much Ado About Nothing* (Gerry Gutierrez), The Acting Company, toured the United States; *Five By Tennessee* (Michael Kahn), The Acting Company, toured the United States; *Timon of Athens* (Michael Langham), Stratford Festival, Stratford, Ontario; *Imaginary Cuckold/School for Husbands* (Michael Langham), Stratford Festival; (opera) *Don Giovanni* (Lou Gatterio), Santa Fe Opera.

Dance costume designs include—*El Baquine,* choreographed by Vicente Nebrada, Ballet Hispanico; *Nuevo Mundo,* choreographed by Graciella Danielle, Ballet Hispanico; *The World Waiting for a Sunrise,* White Oak Project; *American Gestures,* Lar Lubovitch Company; *Sinfonia Concertante,* Lar Lubovitch Company; *Stages,* choreographed by Graciella Danielle, Ballet Hispanico; *From Paris to Jupiter,* Lar Lubovitch Company.

Television and video costume designs include—*Into The Woods,* PBS (Great Performances); *Sunday In The Park With George,* PBS (Great Performances & Lorimar Home Video); *Hyde In Hollywood,* American Playhouse.

## Publications

**On HOULD-WARD: books**—*Costume Design* by Lynn Peckal, Backstage Books, 1993; *Costumes and Chemistry* by Sylvia Moss, 1995; *The Making of Beauty and the Beast* by Don Frantz, Round Table Press, 1995.

\*

I believe design works best from internal motivation. This does not always make it beautiful—it may make it humble, it may even make it ugly. But I think that tells the story in a way that lets the audience be a part of the plot and relate to the stage with an immediacy that allows the magic of story telling to come to the forefront in the theatre.

—Ann Hould-Ward

\*   \*   \*

Ann Hould-Ward came to the theatre comparatively late, already being in her late twenties when she began to assist Patricia Zipprodt. Zipprodt was one of the ground-breaking designers of the 1960s whose work with textured and painted fabrics changed the look of musicals and classical theatre in the United States. The work with Zipprodt led to their design collaboration on Stephen Sondheim's *Sunday in the Park with George,* one of the landmark productions of the 1980s, and this in turn led to a career that has blossomed over the years with shows such as *Into the Woods* and *Falsettos,* dance productions with Graciella Danielle and Lar Lubovitch, and most of the major regional theatres. She has won a Tony for *Beauty and the Beast* and numerous other awards and award nominations for her vast array of work.

Hould-Ward has, perhaps, the most beautiful rendering style of any contemporary costume designer and each rendering is not only a template for the costume shop but a frameable work of art. And from Zipprodt she has developed a sensibility for rich texture and a complex interweaving of color. This is often achieved through the overlayering of different kinds of fabric as well as painting and dyeing over the existing colors and patterns of the fabrics. Few if any contemporary designers equal her elaborate and exquisite tactile sensibility that almost leaps off the stage so the audience believes it can touch and feel the characters. In this regard she is in the tradition of Russian costume designer Alexandra Exter, who equated the weight and texture of fabrics with theatrical rhythms.

Hould-Ward has talked of the eyes "taking a journey" and has compared the act of seeing to that of touching; sight is a tactile sensation for Hould-Ward. She is a meticulous researcher as well as a meticulous designer—the energy of her designs come from a richness of detail and rigorous intelligence. Up close, her costumes sometimes have the quality of sculpture and could almost exist as free-standing works of art. Though such intricacy may not be seen directly by a theatre audience, it has a subconscious impact upon the viewer and plays a significant role in the understanding of character. Her work with ballet and modern dance requires a much greater simplicity and lightness to allow the dancers' movements. Hould-Ward achieves this while still using distinctive touches of fabric to obtain mood and texture in the design.

Though her recognition has come from rich, elegant, and stylish Broadway theatre, Hould-Ward has been able to span the worlds of commercialism and the avant-garde. She has worked with director Richard Foreman at the Guthrie Theatre and with iconoclastic director JoAnne Akalaitis on a controversial production of *Cymbeline* (with sets by George Tsypin) and *In the Summer House.* She is, in a sense, the prototypical designer of the 1990s in her ability to move gracefully among genres, performance styles, and sensibilities, all the while maintaining a distinctive look that is indisputably her own.

—Arnold Aronson

# HUBER, Max
Swiss typographic, industrial, display, and graphic designer

**Born:** Baar, Zurich, 5 June 1919. **Education:** Studied at the Kunstgewerbeschule, Zurich, 1935-38. **Career:** Assistant graphic designer in an advertising agency, Zurich, 1937-38; layout artist, for *Conzett* and *Huber* magazines, Zurich, 1938-40; designer and art director, Studio Boggeri, Milan, 1940; freelance designer, working mainly on exhibition designs, with Max Bill and Werner Bischof, in Zurich, 1942-46; art director, Artemis Verlag publishers, Zurich, 1943-46; freelance designer, working in Milan, from 1946; designed for La Rinascente stores, Edizioni Einaudi, Legler cotton mills, Automobile Club of Italy, RAI Radiotelevisione Italiana, Supermercatori Italiani, Birra Poretti, Olivetti, and others. **Exhibitions:** *Allianz,* Zurich, 1943; *Salon des Realités Nouvelles,* Paris, 1946; *Arte Astratta e Concreta,* Milan, 1947; Galleria Il Camino, Milan, 1948; Libreria Salto, Milan, 1950; *Purpose and Pleasure,* London, 1952; *Design and design,* Palazzo delle Stelline, Milan, 1979 (traveled to Venice); *Gli Annitrenta: Arte e Cultura in Italia,* Palazzo Reale, Milan, 1982. **Honors:** Gold Medal, Milan Triennale, 1954; Compasso d'Oro Award, Milan, 1954, 1960, 1964. **Address:** 6831 Sagno (Ticino), Switzerland.

### Publications

**On HUBER: books**—*Olivetti 1908-1958,* with texts by Adriano Olivetti, Libero Bigiaretti, and Franco Forlini, Turin, 1958; *The New Graphic Design* by Karl Gerstner and Markus Kutter, Teufen and London, 1959; *Moderne Werbe- und Gebrauchs-Grafik* by Hans Neuburg, Ravensburg, 1960; *Who's Who in Graphic Art* edited by Walter Amstutz, Zurich, 1962, Dubendorf, 1982; *History of the Poster* by Josef and Shizuko Muller-Brockmann, Zurich, 1971; *Design and Design,* exhibition catalogue with texts by Angelo Cortesi, Arthur Pulos, and others, Florence, 1979; *A History of Graphic Design* by Philip B. Meggs, New York and London, 1983; *Italian Design: 1870 to the Present* by Penny Sparke, London, 1988.

\*   \*   \*

Max Huber established himself in Milan soon after the end of the war and quickly became an influence, leading the way towards a creative use of typographical devices and means. Perhaps the most famous of his works in this respect was the logo and name-style for the Milan store, La Rinascente. Utterly stark and simple, it was an elegant combination of a modern face, italic, lower case "la" with a bold, sans serif "Rinascente," the two reduced to "l" and "R" for the logo, which appeared in a repeat pattern for paper bags and wrapping paper.

Another aspect of this strongly typographical approach to design was the label he designed for Frisia, a soft drink; simplified, sans serif capitals in different colours overlapped to make a distinctive but legible name-style. That was in 1958, the same year he designed the poster for the Bergamo Gran Premio for art films and films on art, and this, too, relied upon large sans serif capitals unusually placed together to form a striking pattern.

Again, this attachment to pattern-making with type added much to those exhibitions for which he was employed to take care of the graphics. Panels of sans serif type, for the most part, made positive contributions to the display and were not to be relegated to a discrete role of captioning the exhibits. This was particularly so at the *Triennale* in 1951; his collaboration in the section *La forma dell'utile* gave it a distinction it might well not otherwise have attained, while his work on the ENI stand at the 1955 Naples Petrol Exposition strikingly matched its structure.

In many ways, Huber might be thought of as having abandoned his Swiss origins, though occasionally there is a fleeting echo of Max Bill's graphic and exhibition design. Rather, he sought to build upon an Italian tendency that was initiated in the 1930s and that linked to the work of Giovanni Pintori, for example, and had been much the dominant style in the magazine *Campo grafico,* where the phrase *architettura del'libro,* the architecture of the book, had been coined to encapsulate the aesthetic of using type the way an architect of the modern and rationalist school uses the elements of building. Inevitably, this tendency was modified, both in Huber's own development and in the changing cultural climate since the end of Fascism, but it did provide a link and made possible Huber's career as well as his widespread and deep influence in Italy. His presence served to alert Italian graphic designers to possibilities still to be developed from their own immediate past and not to be dismissed as having been done under Fascism and therefore to be despised.

—Toni del Renzio

# HULDT, Johan (Gunnar Hampus)

Swedish furniture and industrial designer

**Born:** Stockholm, 1 January 1942. **Education:** Studied at Lidingö H. A. Laröverket, 1962; Military Naval College, Göteborg, 1963; Kalmar Naval College, 1963; studied industrial woodwork, Enskede Trade School, 1964; State School of Arts and Design, Stockholm, 1964-68; studied sociology, University of Stockholm, 1969. **Family:** Married Elisabeth Hintze in 1972; children: Mikael and Maria. **Career:** Founder, with Jan Dranger, of Innovator Design Studios, 1968, and Executive Manager of Innovator Design AB, Stockholm, from 1969; founder of Basic Design shop system, 1978, and Managing Director of Basic Design AB, Stockholm, 1983-89. Lecturer, Royal Swedish School of Design, Stockholm, 1975-78. Director, Swedish Furniture Research Institute, Stockholm, 1974-76; chairman, National Association of Swedish Interior Architects (S.I.R.), Stockholm, 1983-88. **Exhibitions:** Museu de Arte Moderna, Rio de Janeiro, 1972; Museu de Arte, Sao Paulo, 1973, 1980; Nationalmuseum, Stockholm, 1985, 1989. **Collections:** Nationalmuseum, Stockholm; Museum of Modern Art, New York; Museu de Arte, Sao Paulo; Museu de Arte Moderna, Rio de Janeiro. **Honors:** Scandinavian Chair of the Year Award, 1972-74; Gute Form Award, 1974. Honorary Collaborator, International Designers' School, Barcelona. **Address:** Innovator Design AB/Johan Huldt Design AB, Stora Skuggans Väg 9, 115 42 Stockholm, Sweden.

## Works

*Multoman* sofa, for Dux International, 1969.
*Tech Trolley* enamelled steel multipurpose trolley, for Möbelmontage, 1972.
*Stuns* upholstered lacquered steel armchair, for Möbelmontage, 1972.

*Woodstock* upholstered wooden armchair and sofa, for Möbelmontage, 1973.
*Balluff* sofa, for Möbelmontage, 1974.
*Vivaldi* folding chair, for Möbelmontage, 1975.
*Mari* upholstered wooden armchair and sofa, for Innovator Design, 1977.
*Columbi* table, for Akuma, 1978.
*Terminal* table, for Akuma, 1979.
*Butterfly* steel armchair, for Innovator Design, 1981.
*Slim* steel armchair, for Innovator Design, 1982.
*Flight* upholstered steel armchair, for Innovator Design, 1985.
*Galac Tech* steel chair, for Innovator Design, 1986.

## Publications

**On HULDT: books**—*Design in Sweden* by Katja Walden and others, Stockholm, 1972; *Konsthantverk, Konstindustri, Design 1875-1975* by Dag Widman, Stockholm, 1975; *Morgondagen Antikviteker* by Anders Neumüller, Stockholm, 1982; *The Conran Directory of Design* by Stephen Bayley and others, London, 1985; *The International Design Yearbook 1985/1986* edited by Robert A. M. Stern, London, 1985; *Den Svenska Formen* by Monica Boman and others, Stockholm, 1985.

\*       \*       \*

Johan Huldt began his professional design career in partnership with a classmate from the Stockholm High School of Design in 1968. For several years, he worked as a freelance designer for some of Sweden's most prominent furniture manufacturers. His reputation grew as his designs became more widely appreciated. Despite this, he still found it difficult to achieve his goals or to fulfil his design ideas as a freelancer—the selling of his own ideas and abilities required too much "design for the sake of design."

Brought up in a home where many famous Scandinavian designers were frequent guests and their works everyday objects, Huldt acquired a profound appreciation of quality in design. He found himself constantly objecting, however, to the fact that good design was so expensive; students and young people like himself were not consumers of good design. In his own work, he therefore dedicated himself to inexpensive design that stressed practical and functional properties.

During the 1970s, Huldt explored many different areas of design, such as the interiors of churches, sex-education shops, civil defence shelters and, of course, the more customary disciplines of graphic, textile, furniture and packaging design. His main activity, however, is furniture design—home furnishings for the young and young-in-spirit, people with "more taste than money." Early on, he formulated a comprehensive design concept to which he still remains true: he has to struggle to make the world "a little less ugly" for the many, rather than to design objects for people boasting a professional design taste. To accomplish these ideas, Huldt very soon left freelancing, joined a new partner, and went into the manufacture and retailing of furniture, thus controlling the entire chain from idea to ultimate consumer.

When asked to give his views on design, Huldt says: "Design work must be performed as a subtle balance between very precise human and functional demands, and an austere use of scarce raw materials—all in combination with harmony and beauty. Contemporary furniture design must therefore be based on the modern family in a new society, with its responsibility to nature and energy and an increased need for pleasure and beauty in a materialistic world. Real design work today includes many new fields that must be addressed by every conscientious designer. He has a great responsibility to research and formulate genuine human and social demands. He must also acquire a thorough knowledge of production and distribution techniques, as well as of economic systems and their effects. In my daily work, I find it equally important to consider the designer's view at all stages of a product's life, as well as other aspects of society not usually included in a designer's brief—thus involving problems other than those of shape or mere aesthetics. The task, then, is not only to create new possibilities, constructions and forms, but also to oppose those environmental objects that are produced without honest planning of shape and function. I believe it vital that today's designer should channel his ability to create good designs in terms of elegance and beauty, at the same time attending to the rigid technical and economic conditions which are the base for his work. He must therefore have confidence in himself, since the significance of this work will not be apparent in experimental dynamic shapes, as seen in the 1960s, nor in the scientific modular systems of the 1970s. The effect of his work may not even show in the final product, being instead an essential but unseen part of the process. Good design only differs in form from bad design through small but important details. This does not mean, however, that the end result will be less exciting than before, but we will have to educate ourselves to enjoy less dramatic expressions and to take pleasure in the importance of minor details."

Johan Huldt continues to create designs for his own company, Innovator, with manufacturing facilities in Sweden, Japan, Brazil, and Spain. His furniture is made in large editions and is to be found in more than 25 countries. He travels frequently to exchange ideas and keep in touch with the current international scene. It gives him satisfaction to see his furniture displayed in New York, Rio de Janeiro, Zurich, Paris, or London—and often more easily accessible there than in his native Sweden. With his very Scandinavian background, Huldt is deeply interested in a new "world culture"—as long as it is interpreted in a blue-jeans idea rather than in hamburgers.

—Maud Lindgren

# HURLBURT, Allen (Freeman)

American graphic designer

**Born:** Bridgeport, Connecticut, 24 October 1910. **Education:** Studied economics at the University of Pennsylvania, Philadelphia, B.S., 1932. **Family:** Married Regina Victoria Rowe in 1953; daughter: Susan. **Career:** Art Director, Bureau of Advertising, New York, 1937-43, and NBC National Broadcasting Company, New York, 1946-51; art director, 1952-67, editorial board member, 1953-72, director of design, 1968-72, and editorial adviser, 1970-72, *Look* magazine, New York; vice-president, 1962-72, and editorial adviser, 1970-72, Cowles Communications, New York. President, American Institute of Graphic Arts, New York, 1968-69. **Member:** Alliance Graphique Internationale; American Institute of Graphic Arts; Art Directors Club of New York; Fellow, Royal Society of Arts, London. **Exhibition:** Museum of Modern Art, New York, 1965. **Honors:** Gold Medal, Art Directors Club of New York, 1948, 1949, 1955, and 1961-70; Art Director of the Year

Award, National Society of Art Directors, 1965; Gold Medal, American Institute of Graphic Arts, 1973. **Died:** Sarasota, Florida, 30 June 1983.

## Publications

**By HURLBURT: books**—*Publication Design,* New York, 1971; *Layout: The Design of the Printed Page,* New York, 1977; *The Grid,* New York, 1978; *The Design Concept,* New York, 1981; *Photo/Graphic Design,* New York, 1983.

**On HURLBURT: books**—*The Stars* by Richard Schickel, New York, 1962; *The Language of Graphics* by Edward Booth-Clibborn and Daniele Baroni, London, 1980.

\*     \*     \*

Allen Hurlburt was open to all contemporary activity in the arts, architecture, literature, and the sciences. A bridge between the visual world and the public, his work in design raised the perception and altered the spectators' vision of verbal and visual material.

Through his own process of discovery and selectivity, he expanded the role and function of the magazine art director, bringing this discipline strongly and equally into the editorial pages of *Look* magazine, where, during his tenure as art director, he brightened the pages with illustrative material that reflected his broad knowledge and his spirit of investigation of the visual world. He had the rare ability to relate graphic originality to the requirements of journalism.

Concerned with typography and layout, he recognized the heritage of the past but was also responsive to the new technologies as he created his own standards and unified the appearance of the magazine, transforming it dramatically. Thus, he was a pioneer in art direction and possibly the most influential magazine art director of his day. Setting new standards, he gave the magazine not only a distinctive look but a visual identity which appealed to its audience.

Hurlburt never stopped studying and learning. His supportive interest in young designers and his ability to give of himself and his knowledge made him an excellent educator. With clarity of mind, he became the sounding board for precise shades of meaning in graphic design.

—Mildred Constantine

# HYDMAN-VALLIEN, Ulrica

Swedish painter, sculptor, glass, ceramics, and textile designer

**Born:** Ulrica Hydman, in Stockholm, 24 March 1938. **Education:** Studied at the National College of Art, Craft and Design, Stockholm, 1958-61; studied in the United States and Mexico, 1961-63. **Family:** Married designer and sculptor Bertil Vallien in 1963; children: Hampus and Markus. **Career:** Ceramics artist, establishing own studio in Eriksmala, from 1963; glass designer, Kosta Boda AB, Sweden, from 1972; ceramics designer, for Rörstrand AB, Lidköping, 1984-86; textile and wallpaper designer, for Kinnasand, Sweden and Germany, from 1990; carpet designer, for Drint, from 1990;

**Ulrica Hydman-Vallien:** *Nevada,* **glass blown into molds and handpainted, for Kosta Boda, Sweden, 1993**

chinaware designer, for Dukagruppen, from 1994; paper designer, for Paperproductdesign GmBh, Germany, from 1990; also freelance designer, working with Weil's, and others. Instructor, 1980-88, and member of International Council, from 1995, Pilchuk Glass School, Seattle, Washington; instructor, Bildwerk Frauenau, Germany, 1989. **Exhibitions:** *Adventure in Swedish Glass,* toured Australia, 1975; *Scandinavian Modern Design 1880-1980,* Cooper-Hewitt Museum, New York, 1982 (toured); Heller Gallery, New York, 1983; Museu de Arte Moderno, Sao Paulo, 1984, Essener Glasgalerie, West Germany, 1985; New Glass Gallery, New York, 1985; Sweden Center, Tokyo, 1986; Galleri Ikaros, Goteborg, 1987; Liljevalchs Konsthall, Stockholm, 1988; *Faces of Swedish Design,* IBM Gallery, New York, 1988 (toured); Heller Gallery, 1990; *New Glass in Europe,* Düsseldorf Kunstmuseum, 1990-91; Galleri Athén, Athens, Greece, 1990; Sanske Galleri, Zürich, 1991; Azabu Museum, Tokyo, 1992; Yokohama Museum of Art, Yokohoma, Japan, 1992; *New Art Form,* Chicago, 1993; Bellevue Art Museum, Bellevue, Washington, 1994; Taipei International Glassexhibition, Taiwan, 1995; and many other exhibitions. **Collections:** Nationalmuseum, Stockholm; Röhsska Konstslöjdmuseet, Goteborg; Kunstmuseum, Düsseldorf; Kunstsammlungen der Veste Coburg, Germany; Musée Décoratif des Arts, Paris; Corning Glass Museum, New York; Victoria and Albert Museum, London; National Museum of Modern Art, Tokyo; Hokkaido Museum of Modern Art; Powerhouse Museum, Sydney, Australia; Ebeltoft Glasmuseum, Denmark. **Honors:** Young Artist Award, Nationalmuseum, Stockholm, 1972; Major State Scholarship, Stockholm, 1973, 1974; Swedish National Artists

Award, 1980; Women in Design Prize, New York, 1983; Svensk Design first prize, National Museum, 1983; Excellent Swedish Form Award for glass, 1983, 1985, 1994, and for textiles, 1987; Swedish Artists Scholarship, 1983-87; Coburg Glaspreis Award, West Germany, 1985; Design Plus Competition award, Internationaler Frankfurter Messe Ambinete, Germany, 1992; **Address:** Åfors Glasbruk, Bromsväg 8, 361 94 Eriksmåla, Sweden.

## Works

*Tinto Mara* hand-blown coloured glassware, for Kosta Boda, 1972.
*Romantica* hand-blown painted glass tableware, for Kosta Boda, 1973.
*Butterfly* hand-blown painted glassware, for Kosta Boda, 1976.
*Pastell* hand-blown coloured glassware, for Kosta Boda, 1978.
*Poem* hand-blown painted glass tableware, for Kosta Boda, 1978.
*Paradise* hand-blown painted glassware, for Kosta Boda, 1985.
*Poem* hand-painted ceramic tableware, for Rörstrand, 1985.
*Cleopatra* clear glassware with snake decoration, for Kosta Boda, 1986.
*Open Minds* hand-painted blown vases and cups, for Kosta Boda, 1986.
*Caramba* hand-painted cotton fabric, for Weil's, 1986.
*Caramba* hand-painted blown glass vases and bowls, for Kosta Boda, 1987.

*Love* hand-painted blown glass vases and bowls, for Kosta Boda, 1988.

*Jade* blown glass vases and bowls, for Kosta Boda, 1988.

*Birdy* hand-painted glass vases and bowls, for Kosta Boda, 1989.

*Attention, Nightingale,* and *Happy Hour* textiles, for Kinnasand Textil, 1990-93.

*Tulipa* painted centrifuged and blown glass collection, for Kosta Boda, 1991.

*Somebody* painted glass, for Kosta Boda, 1992.

*Nevada* painted handblown glass collection, for Kosta Boda, 1993.

*Tulipa* and *Kiss* paper designs, for Kellerman Art Collection, 1993-94.

*Christmas* painted glass collection, for Kosta Boda, 1993-95.

## Publications

**On HYDMAN-VALLIEN: books**—*Modern Ceramics* by Geoffrey Beard, London, 1969; *Keramik* by Ulf Hard af Segerstad, Stockholm, 1976; *I Glasrike* by Bertil Palmqvist, Stockholm, 1979; *Glasboken: Historia, Teknik och Form* by Carl F. Hermelin and Elsebeth Welander, Boras, 1980; *Scandinavian Modern Design 1880-1980* edited by David Revere McFadden, New York, 1982; *Crystal Clear: New Glass from Sweden* by Helena Dahlbäck Lutteman, Uppsala, 1982; *Den Svenska Formen* by Monica Boman and others, Stockholm, 1985; *Made in Sweden: Art, Handicraft, Design* by Anja Notini, London, 1987; *Contemporary Glass* by Suzanne Franz, New York, 1989; *New Glass in Europe,* exhibition catalogue by Helmut Ricke, Dusseldorf, 1990; *Svenskt Glas* by Wahlström and Widstrand, 1991; *World Glass Now,* exhibition catalogue, Hokkaido, 1991; *Swedish Art in Glass 1900-1990* by Knutsson, 1991; *Glass and Love: Ulrica and Bertil Hydman-Vallien,* Stockholm, 1993; *Eight Visitors—Sixteen Friends,* exhibition catalogue, Stockholm, 1995; **articles**—"Bertil Vallien and Ulrica Hydman-Vallien: Designs for Art and Living" by K. Chambers in *New Work* (New York), no. 21/22, 1985; "Ulrica Hydman-Vallien" in Swedish Design *Annual,* Stockholm, 1987; "Bertil and Ulrica in the Kingdom of Glass" by Walter Lieberman in *Scandinavian Review,* spring-summer, 1991; "Hie Hexe von Åfors" in *Harpars Bazar* (Germany), March 1992.

\*

As a designer for Kosta Boda, I work closely with the craftsmen in the hot shop. I refuse to work with machines. My intention is to keep alive the old techniques and to add some new ones, and to find ways of extending the potential of the material.

As a designer and in production work, I like to put something of myself into everything—even in mass-production. In the "Artist's Collection" series, I can remain close to my own expression, as in painting. In the glass pieces *Open Minds* (1987) and *Birdy* (1989), I am able to make my personal mark, which is not always the most immediately acceptable to the public; I like to tease and challenge. The series *Cleopatra,* with a snake wound around the stems of hand-blown drinking glasses, are made for especially daring consumers. Although I have complete freedom in my artwork as a painter and sculptor, I want as much as possible to be true to myself in my design work, as well. By holding firmly to this principle, I have today gained acceptance for the idea in industrial design.

—Ulrica Hydman-Vallien

# IGARASHI, Takenobu

Japanese environmental, product, corporate, and graphic designer

**Born:** Takikawa City, Hokkaido, 4 March 1944. **Education:** Studied graphic design, Tama Art University, Tokyo, BA, 1968; University of California, Los Angeles, MA, 1969. **Family:** Married Fumiko Hashimoto in 1980; children: Tomoko and Shoko. **Career:** Independent designer from 1970, establishing Igarashi Studio, Tokyo, and Igarashi Inc., Los Angeles. Lecturer, 1975-76, and visiting professor, 1989, College of Fine Arts, University of California, Los Angeles; instructor, Department of Technology, Chiba University, 1979-83; professor and head of design, Tama Art University, Tokyo, from 1989. Board member, Japan Graphic Designers Association, Tokyo, 1985-95; executive committee member, Alliance Graphique Internationale, Zurich, 1985-91. **Exhibitions:** Fuji Gallery, Tokyo, 1972, 1975; *One Day, One Show,* Tokyo Designers Space, 1976; Print Gallery, Amsterdam, 1978; *One Week, One Show,* Tokyo Designers Space, 1979; Tokyo Designers Space Open Gallery, 1980; Parco Street Gallery, Tokyo, 1981; Matsuya Design Gallery, Tokyo, 1981; Reinhold Brown Gallery, New York, 1983; Mikimoto Hall, Ginza, Tokyo, 1983; Portfolio Center, Atlanta, 1984; Ginza Graphic Gallery, Tokyo, 1987; Macquarie Galleries, Sydney, 1987; Asahi Gallery, Tokyo, 1987; Gallery of Arts and Sciences, Keihan Department Store, Osaka, 1988; Von Oertzen Gallery, Frankfurt, 1988; Gallery 91, New York, 1990; IDCNY, New York, 1990; GOMA, Los Angeles, 1990; *East Looks West,* Deutsche Plakat Museum, Essen, 1993; *T-3 Collection Sculpture,* Tokyo, 1994; *Chaumont Poster Exhibit,* France, 1994; Museum of Modern Art, Ostend, Belgium, 1994; *50 Projects,* Fukuoka, Kanazawa, Tokyo, and Sapporo, Japan, 1995; Hosomi Gallery, Tokyo, 1995. **Collections:** Museum des 20. Jahrhunderts, Vienna; Kunstgewerbemuseum, Zurich; Museum of Modern Art, New York; Cooper-Hewitt Museum, New York; Art Center College of Design, Los Angeles; Library of Congress, Washington, D.C.; Toyama Museum of Modern Art, Japan; Haus Industrieform Essen, Germany; Denver Art Museum. **Honors:** Merit Award, 1976, 1978, and Bronze Prize, 1986, Warsaw Poster Biennale; Bronze Prize, Third Lahti Poster Biennale, Finland, 1979; Bronze Prize, Brno Graphics Biennale, 1980; Outstanding Public Signage Award, Japan Sign Design Association, 1980; Silver Prize, Warsaw Jazz Poster Salon, 1986; Gold and Bronze Prize, 1986, and Silver Prize, 1988, CS Design Award, Japan; Katsumie Masaru Design Award, Tokyo, 1989; Design Innovation Award, 1990; IF Award, Hannover, Germany, 1993; Governor's Award/Best Product Design, Hokkaido, 1995. **Addresses:** Igarashi Inc., 1775 Stone Canyon Rd., Los Angeles, California 90077, U.S.A.; Igarashi Studio, 6-6-22 Minami-Aoyama, Minato-ku, Tokyo 107, Japan.

## Works

*Expo '85* official poster, for the International Science and Technology Exposition Association, 1982.

Signage program, for the Mita and Hiyoshi campuses of Keio University, Tokyo, 1982, 1985.

Visual identity symbol, for the Kanazawa Institute of Technology, 1983.

Corporate identity program, for the Mitsui Bank Limited, 1984.

Poster calendar, for the Museum of Modern Art, New York, 1984-88.

*3* sculpture in stainless steel, for the Michael Peters Group, 1985.

Signage program, for the headquarters of the Honda Motor Company, Tokyo, 1985.

*Neocon 19* architecture and design convention poster, for the Merchandise Mart, Chicago, 1986.

Visual identity symbol, for the Suntory Classical Music Hall, Tokyo, 1986.

Corporate identity program, for Meiji Milk Products Company, 1986.

Africa Award for Leadership sculptural trophy in gold-plated aluminum, for the Hunger Project, 1987.

*Oun Collection* products and accessories range, for the Oun Corporation, from 1987.

*Fisso* desk accessories range, for the Fujii Company, 1988.

*Hyvalysti* gardening kit, for the Kai Corporation, 1988.

Zanders calendar, for Zanders Feinpapiere AG, 1988.

*Polaroid Impulse* poster, for the Polaroid Corporation, 1988.

Corporate identity program, for Suntory Limited, Tokyo, 1990.

Book design for *Designers on Mac* by Diane Burns, Tokyo, 1992.

Poster, for Morisawa & Co., Ltd., Tokyo, 1993.

Childrens furniture, for Cosine Ltd., Asahikawa, Japan, 1994.

Reading glasses, for Avanti Inc., Tokyo, 1995.

*Coiwa* clock, for Cosine Ltd., Asahikawa, 1995.

Poster for future office furniture design competition, for Inter Office Ltd., Tokyo, 1995.

Sculptures, for Asabu Juban Pocket Park, Tokyo, 1995.

Corporate identity program, for Tama Art University, Tokyo, 1995.

Cover design, for *WordPerfect* magazine, 1995.

## Publications

**By IGARASHI: books**—(editor) *Letterheads of the World,* Tokyo, 1977; *Graphic Design for Our Environment,* Tokyo, 1980; (editor) *World Trademarks and Logotypes,* Tokyo, 1983; (editor) *Letterheads: A Collection from Around the World,* Tokyo, 1986; (editor) *World Trademarks and Logotypes 2,* Tokyo, 1988.

**On IGARASHI: books**—*Igarashi Space Graphics* by Yoshiro Nakamura, Tokyo, 1983; *Seven,* Tokyo, 1985; *Igarashi Alphabets,*

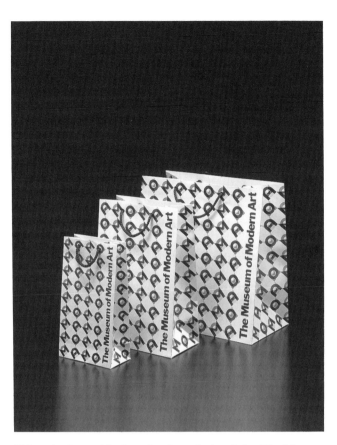

Takenobu Igarashi: shopping bags designed for The Museum of Modern Art, New York

Zurich, 1987; *Rock, Scissors, Paper,* Tokyo, 1992; *Igarashi Sculptures,* Tokyo, 1992; **articles**—"Man at His Best" in *Esquire* (New York), April 1991; "Takenobu Igarashi" in *Graphis,* January/February 1992; "Takenobu Igarashi" in *Mac Power* (Japanese edition), June 1995.

\*   \*   \*

As can be seen from his personal history, Takenobu Igarashi is one of the young generation who have grown up in the new Japanese world of design and studied in American universities. Igarashi's most distinctive contribution to design lies in his unique lettering and typography. In particular, he has successfully given three-dimensional expression to letters of the alphabet. At first glance, this work, which is decorative rather than functional, suggests the revival of Art Deco, but it is filled with a new sensibility. The manner in which he fashions the shape of each letter just as if he were constructing an edifice is of great appeal. Moreover, the delightfulness of shape and harmony of color are distinctive.

Igarashi also has a strong interest in graphic design in the environment, from supermarkets to public libraries, and has demonstrated substantial abilities in various types of visual communication design. He has done striking work in poster design, packaging, and editorial design.

—Masaaki Tanaka

# ILIPRANDI, Giancarlo
Italian industrial, type, and graphic designer

**Born:** Milan, 15 March 1925. **Education:** Educated at the Liceo Scientifico, Milan, until 1943; studied medicine, at the University of Milan, 1944-46; studied painting and stage design, at the Accademia di Brera, Milan, 1946-53; studied painting, at the Hochschule für Bildende Kunste, West Berlin, 1958; also attended seminars in American Studies, Salzburg, 1950. **Military Service:** Served in the Freedom Volunteer Corps, Italian Army, 1945, Adjutant-Major. **Family:** Married Lalla Aldrovandi in 1953 (separated, 1973; died, 1995); daughter: Viviana (died, 1995). **Career:** Worked as an independent painter and stage designer, Milan, 1945-55; freelance designer, Milan, from 1955; founder and principal, Iliprandi Associati, from 1993; designed for RAI Radiotelevisione Italiana, La Rinascente department stores, Standa department stores, Stanley Works, Arflex, Roche, Bassetti, Grancasa and Bossi shopping centers, Electa, Hunter Douglas, Montecatini, Edisport, Stilnovo, Olivetti, Pirelli, Honeywell ISI, RB Rossana, and others; art director of magazines *Scinautico,* 1960-64, *Sci,* 1965-70, *Popular Photography Italiana,* 1966-72, *Rivista RAI,* 1968-69, *Esquire and Derby,* 1977, *Interni,* 1979-82, *Arbiter,* 1980, *Il Diaframma,* 1980-82, and *Phototeca,* 1976-86. Founder and president, Art Directors Club of Milan, 1967-68, 1970-71; board member, 1971-73, 1985-88, 1991-92, and twice vice-president of ADI, Associazione Disegno Industriale, Milan; scientific didactic committee member, Istituto Superiore Industrie Artistiche, Urbino, 1974-84; scientific committee member, Centro Studie Archivio Comunicazione, Parma, from 1979; board member, from 1987, president, 1991-93, chairman of presidents forum, 1993-95, and chairman of the Friends of ICOGRADA, from 1995, ICOGRADA, International Council of Graphic Design Associations; chairman, Bureau of European Designers Associations, 1988-89; senior adviser, Bonetto Design Center, Monte Carlo, from 1994. Instructor, Societa Umanitaria, Milan, 1961-68, Scuola Superiore Pubblicita, Milan, 1965-73, and Istituto Europeo Design, Milan, 1982-85, 1989-95. **Exhibitions:** Saletta del Disegno, Milan, 1951; Galleria dell'Ariete, Milan, 1958; Libreria San Babila, Milan, 1959, 1961; Centro Internazionale della Grafica, Venice 1975; Galleria Il Diaframma, Milan, 1975; Galleria Il Libraio, Milan, 1978; Galleria Alzaia, Rome, 1987; Museo Civico, Caltagirone 1987; Maison Gerbollier, La Salle, 1990; Design Gallery, Milan, 1994. **Collections:** Wilanow Poster Museum, Poland; Museum of Modern Art, New York; Galleria d'Arte Moderna, Milan; Centro Studi e Archivio Comunicazione, Parma; ICOGRADA Library, Design Museum, London. **Honors:** International Award, Milan Triennale, 1964; Milan Art Directors Club Award, 1967; Typomundus 69 Merit Award, 1969; Design Award, Warsaw Poster Biennale, 1976; Compasso d'Oro Awards, Milan, 1979. **Address:** Via Vallazze 63, 20131 Milan, Italy.

### Works

Exhibition displays and pavilions, for RAI Radiotelevisione Italiana, 1955-65 (with A. and P. G. Castiglioni).
Displays, posters, and publicity graphics, for La Rinascente department stores, Milan, 1955-68.
Corporate image programme, displays, and graphics, for RB Rossana, Bergamo, 1960-91.

Corporate image programme and graphics, for Ankerfarm, Milan, 1964-74.

Corporate image programme and graphics, for Arflex, Milan, 1966-76.

*Forma, Dattilo,* and *Modulo* typefaces, for Nebiolo Typefoundry, Turin, 1967-78 (with others).

Displays and posters, for Standa department stores, Milan, 1968-72.

*Isola, Penisola, Arcipelago, Rossana Night,* and *Rossana Sole* kitchen units and furniture, for RB Rossana Cucine, Bergamo, 1969-72.

Corporate image programme, displays and graphics, for Stanley Works Italia, Como, 1974-79.

*131 Mirafiori* and *Ritmo Super* car instruments, for Fiat, 1978-81 (with Rodolfo Bonetto).

*Square, Round, Superegg,* and twenty other fonts for impact printers, for Honeywell Information Systems, 1981-86 (with Pesenti, Gandolfi, and Pizzigonij).

Graphic identity, posters, and catalogues, for the Gallerie Civiche Comune di Modena, from 1982.

Graphic identity and exhibition displays, for ADI Associazione Disegno Industriale, Milan, 1985-89.

Exterior and interior decor and displays, for Grancasa department stores, Milan, 1986-89.

Corporate identity programme and interior design, for Savinelli Smoking Pipes Industry, from 1983.

School books editorial design, for Elemond and Mondadori, from 1989.

**Publications**

**By ILIPRANDI: books**—*Linguaggio Grafico,* vols. 1-4, Milan, 1965-83; *Addio Liberty,* Varese, 1967; *Creativity Oggi,* Milan, 1971; *Storia della Comunicazione Visiva,* vols. 1-6, Urbino, 1977-83; *NY Inclusive Tour,* Naples, 1978; (with others) *Il Progetto Grafico,* Milan, 1981; (with others) *Visual Design,* Milan, 1984; (editor, with others) *Omnibook 2,* Milan, 1985; (editor, with others) *Omnibook 4,* Milan, 1988; *Un Progetto per Milano,* Milan, 1988; *Design Italiano,* Milan, 1988; *BEDA Dossier,* Milan, 1988; (editor) *Design Future Philosophy,* Singapore, 1992.

**On ILIPRANDI: books**—*An International Survey of Packaging* by Wim Crouwel and Kurt Weidemann, London, 1968; *Book Jackets and Record Sleeves* edited by Kurt Weidemann, Stuttgart and London, 1969; *Graphis Record Covers* edited by Walter Herdeg, Zurich, 1974; *Archigraphia: Architectural and Environmental Graphics* edited by Walter Herdeg, Zurich, 1978; *Il Linguaggio della Grafica* by Edward Booth Clibborn and Daniele Baroni, Mondadori, 1979; *Atlante del Design Italiano 1940-1980* by Alfonso Grassi and Anty Pansera, Milan, 1980; *Who's Who in Graphic Art* edited by Walter Amstutz, Dubendorf, 1982; *L'Italia del Design* by Alfonso Grassi and Anty Pansera Casale, 1986; *Alle Radici della Comunicazione Visiva Italiana* by Heinz Waibl, Como, 1988; *Il Dizionario del Grafico* edited by Giorgio Fioravanti Zanichelli, Bologna, 1993; **articles**—in *Rassegna Grafica,* May 1958; *Gebrauchsgraphik,* August 1959; *Pagina,* 1964-65; *Graphicus,* May 1969; *Idea* (Tokyo), 1970, 1974, 1980, 1983; *Design 1,* May 1973.

*

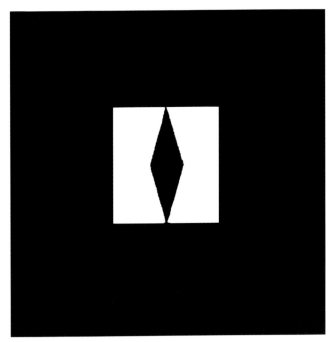

**Giancarlo Iliprandi: design for Bonetto Design Center, 1994**

I regard design as a creative activity aiming at the improvement of the quality of man's life. The design of visual communication is responsible not only for the matter it transmits through its own messages but also for the formal values that in any case represent a "consumerist" cultural heritage.

I believe that every designer ought to play his part—by active presence in associations, by participation in education, by contributing to professional reviews, by writing or editing books, as well as by the results of his own work—the affirmation of these principles: "better social quality of human life" and "moral responsibility of the productions of culture."

Experimental research and planning methodology seem only abstract theories of work, yet without a continual return to these basic principles, it is useless to hope for a practical, pragmatic meeting between form and function, between technical concepts and free creativity. That is, between cultures of "being" rather than of "having."

The culture of the designer, both what he absorbs and what he transmits, is a culture of doing, a continuous presence of gestures, words, shapes, signs, of writings, activities, commitment, discussion, of openings and closings. An active presence, then, in our case typically Italian, or rather, typically mid-European. (To be or to become?) Our bad habit of debating every problem started long before 1968 (as anyone knows who has read Plato or Cato, the censor) and will last longer, surviving "Le pouvoir à l'imagination" of the Maggio Francese at the main exhibition *Italy, The New Domestic Landscape* at the Museum of Modern Art in 1972 and even the great retrospective show organized by the municipality of Milan on the occasion of the 13th Congress of the International Council of Societies of Industrial Design under the name of *Visual Design 33-83, Fifty Years of Italian Production: A Jubilee.*

Italian design, whether associated with historic rationalism or functionalism or formalism or postmodernism or Memphis, or the fruit of an attachment to a tradition (but which tradition?), or generated by a reaction to the revolution (but which revolution?), will continue to live until the protagonists of it have learned to submit every problem to discussion. More central to the question, it is evident that Italian design will survive as long as it produces culture—as long, that is, as it succeeds in being occupied, even preoccupied, with improving the quality of life and in leaving no empty spaces from which consumerism can enter and begin the systematic destruction of our cultural heritage. The worst opportunism of all ages is ignorance.

—Giancarlo Iliprandi

# ISD (INTERIOR SPACE DESIGN)

American interior design firm

**Founded** as a subsidiary of Perkins and Will architectural firm, in Chicago and New York, 1960; independent corporation, from 1973. Chief executives have included Michael Pinto, J. Harrison Lassiter, Mel Hamilton, H. Davis Mayfield III, Jan Belson, Gary Lee, John Lijewski, Nancy Lindsay. **Collections:** Cooper-Hewitt Museum, New York. **Honors:** New York Art Directors Club Award of Merit, 1980; *Industrial Design* Designers Choice Award, New York, 1980; Illuminating Engineering Society Lumen Award, New York, 1980; *Interiors* Design Award, New York, 1982, 1983. **Addresses:** 305 East 46th Street, New York, New York 10017; 400 North State Street, Chicago, Illinois 60610; Two Shell Plaza, Houston, Texas 77002; 818 West 7th Street, Los Angeles, California 90017, U.S.A.

## Works

First National Bank interiors, Memphis, Tennessee, 1964.
City Hall interiors, Boston, Massachusetts, 1969.
Westinghouse Electric Corporation interiors, Monroeville, Pennsylvania, 1971.
Mercantile Exchange Building interiors, Chicago, 1972-74.
CBS Incorporated office interiors, Washington, D.C., 1976.
American Telephone and Telegraph office interiors, Basking Ridge, New Jersey, 1976-77, and Corporate Headquarters interiors, New York, 1983.
R. J. Reynolds World Headquarters interiors, Winston-Salem, North Carolina, 1978, and Plaza Tower interiors, 1981.
General Mills office interiors, Minneapolis, Minnesota, 1979.
Xerox Corporation Headquarters interiors, Stamford, Connecticut, 1979.
American Academy of Arts and Sciences interiors, Cambridge, Massachusetts, 1980.
British Petroleum office interiors, London, 1981.
PPG Industries Corporate Headquarters interiors, Pittsburgh, 1984.
Chemical Bank interiors, New York, 1988.
ARCO Oil and Gas interiors, Midland, Texas, 1988.
Walt Disney Corporation interiors, Burbank, California, 1989.

## Publications

**On ISD: articles**—*Architectural Record* (New York), May 1974; *American Bar Association Journal* (Chicago), April 1976; *Contract*

*Magazine* (New York), December 1976; *Buildings* (Cedar Rapids), October 1979; *Interior Design* (New York), November 1979, December 1981; *The Designer* (New York), November 1980; *Interiors* (New York), January 1983; *New York Post,* 17 February 1983; *Houston Chronicle,* 22 February 1983; *Dallas/Fort Worth Business,* 4 April 1983.

\* \* \*

A list of ISD's clients reads like an excerpt of the top corporations from the Fortune 500. The most talked-about building for which ISD has designed the interiors is Philip Johnson's AT&T tower in New York. ISD's rather spectacular and creative accomplishments for this building include the planning and design of millions of square feet of space. In this, the firm carried on the philosophy of design and traditions that had already made its work renowned, so that in its third decade of operation it had become one of the largest organizations of design professionals specializing in the design of interior spaces in the United States.

Some of ISD's most famous interiors include the First National Bank of Memphis, the Boston City Hall, the Academy of Arts and Sciences in Cambridge, Massachusetts, and the Xerox Corporation headquarters in Stamford, Connecticut—to name just a few. Although ISD offers technical services to meet the complex needs of planning and design, one of the firm's major interests in its work is art. ISD has long stressed the need for art in public places and has helped clients assemble major art collections. The firm has the ability to educate corporate clients to use works of art in their buildings and thus to enhance and enrich the quality of corporate environments. ISD is equally concerned with the research and development of office furniture and systems, and has a team that continuously monitors the development of new products.

The consistently high quality of ISD's work is due to the symbiotic combination of the firm's design principles and the inspired leadership of its executives. The many successful projects credited to the firm represent the team effort of a large design firm at its best.

—Arnold Friedmann

# ISHIMOTO, Fujiwo

Japanese textile and ceramic designer

**Born:** Ehime, 10 March 1941. **Education:** Studied graphic design, National University of Art, Tokyo, 1960-64. **Career:** Commercial artist, Ichida Company, Tokyo, 1964-70; designer, Decembre Oy, Helsinki, 1970-74; printed textile designer, Marimekko Oy, Helsinki, from 1974. **Member:** Ornamo, the Finnish Society of Applied Arts, from 1978. **Exhibitions:** *Designs for Madame Butterfly,* Helsinki, 1980, Seinäjoki, Finland, 1989, Ilmajoki, 1990; *Fujiwo Ishimoto + Marimekko,* Tokyo, 1982; *Textile Artist Fujiwo Ishimoto: Sources of Inspiration,* Helsinki and Jyväskylä, Finland, 1982; *The Great Bear Textiles,* Helsinki, 1984; *Fujiwo Ishimoto: Textile Designs,* Tokyo, 1988; *Fujiwo Ishimoto: Retrospective Fabric Exhibition,* Seinäjoki, 1989; *Keeping Company with Clay* ceramics exhibition, Helsinki, 1990; *Nocturnal Images* fabric exhibition, Helsinki, 1993, San Francisco, 1994. **Collections:** Museum of Applied Arts, Helsinki; Cooper-Hewitt Museum, New York; Röhsska Konstslöjdmuseet, Gothenburg; Montreal Museum of Decorative

**Fujiwo Ishimoto:** *Aatto* cotton fabric for Marimekko Oy, 1989. Courtesy of Merimekko Oy

Arts, Montreal. **Honors:** Roscoe Prize, U.S.A., 1983; honourable mention, Finland Designs Exhibition, 1983, 1989, 1993; State Industrial Arts Prize, Finland, 1993; Kaj Franck Design Prize, 1994. **Addresses:** Kauppiaankatu 13 E 25, 00160 Helsinki, Finland; (office) Marimekko Oy, Puusepänkatu 4, SF-00810 Helsinki, Finland.

### Works

*Sumo* brushstroke pattern fabric, for Marimekko Oy, 1977.
*Jama* brushstroke pattern fabric, for Marimekko Oy, 1977.
*Taiga* brushstroke pattern fabric, for Marimekko Oy, 1978.
*Seitseman/Seven Flowers* patterned fabric, for Marimekko Oy, 1978.
*Mattailla/Tussock* collection of earth-colour pattern fabrics, for Marimekko Oy, 1979.
*Tuulentupa/Castle of the Winds* collection of linear pattern fabrics, for Marimekko Oy, 1981.
*Ukkospilvi/Thunder Cloud* brushstroke pattern fabric, for Marimekko Oy, 1982.
*Nauru/Laughter* brushstroke pattern fabric, for Marimekko Oy, 1982.
*Kuiskaus/Whispering* brushstroke pattern fabric, for Marimekko Oy, 1982.
*Maisema/Landscape* collection of abstract pattern fabrics, for Marimekko Oy, 1983.
*Iso Karhu/Great Bear* collection of ikat-effect fabrics, for Marimekko Oy, 1984.
*Sinitaivas/Sky* collection of graduated pattern fabrics, for Marimekko Oy, 1986.
*Sydantalvi/Midwinter* collection of marble-effect fabrics, for Marimekko Oy, 1987.
*Aatto/Eve* watercolour technique fabric, for Marimekko Oy, 1989.
*Kesanto/Fallow* watercolour technique fabric, for Marimekko Oy, 1989.
*Leop/Rest* abstract linear pattern fabric, for Marimekko Oy, 1991.
*Ranta/Shore* abstract linear pattern fabric, for Marimekko Oy, 1992.
*Kesästä kesään/From Summer to Summer* series of four graphic fabrics depicting the course of life and nature, for Marimekko Oy, 1992.
*Yön kuvat/Nocturnal Images* collection of large-patterned, mystic fabric "paintings," for Marimekko Oy, 1993.
*Bambu/Bamboo* ceramic dish, for Arabia's Pro Arte collection, 1993.
*Huilu/Flute* wall vase, for Arabia's Pro Arte collection, 1993.
*Hamppu/Hemp* large patterned abstract fabric symbolizing growth, perseverance, and vitality, for Marimekko Oy, 1994.
*Aamurusko/Aurora* "birch branches glittering in the sun on a bright winter morning" fabric, for Marimekko Oy, 1995.

### Publications

**On ISHIMOTO: books**—*Design Since 1945* edited by Kathryn Hiesinger and George Marcus, Philadelphia and London, 1983; *International Design Yearbook 1985/1986* edited by Robert A. M. Stern, London, 1985; *Finnish Industrial Design* edited by Tua Pontasuo, Helsinki, 1987; *International Design Yearbook 1988/1989* edited by Aarata Isozaki, London, 1988; **articles**— "Marimekko Oy" in *Domus* (Milan), October 1979; "The Spirit of Things" by U. Pallasmaa in *Form Function Finland* (Helsinki), no. 3/4, 1981; "Castle of the Winds" by B. Obermaier in *Mobilia* (Snekkersten), no. 298, 1981; "Marimekko Exports Know-how" by M. Vuorimaa in *Form Function Finland* (Helsinki), no. 2, 1983;

"Design 87: Crosscurrents and Mutual Influences" by P. Gallo-Stenman in *Design in Finland* (Helsinki), 1987.

*

At the outset of designing a new collection, I work quite freely and spontaneously. My aim is to give expression to subjects that, at that very moment, interest me or are important to me. Finally, these personal ideas are communicated to other people, and it is time to see what kind of response my interests find. It is also essential that each new collection is up-to-date, fresh, and novel.

My foremost object is to design fabrics that are suitable for everyday use, fabrics that are not too "artistic". The fabrics can (or should) of course be of high aesthetic quality, but they also have to be appropriate for practical use. Here lies the basic difference between art and design. I do not generally design my fabrics for any particular application—the fabrics are sold by the yard, and they can be used for almost any purpose (curtains, tablecloths, bedlinen, clothes, and others). There is no "right" or "wrong" way of use.

Another important factor affecting the design process are the technical resources at hand. The design work has to be adjusted according to those printing methods that are available but, on the other hand, development of new techniques in collaboration with the manufacturer is one inspiring aspect of the work.

—Fujiwo Ishimoto

# ISRAEL, Robert
American set and costume designer

**Education:** Pratt Institute, New York, B.F.A., 1961; University of Michigan, M.F.A., 1963. **Career:** Stage set and costume designer, from 1966. Instructor, Minnesota School of Art, and the School of Visual Arts, New York City; assistant professor, Cooper Union, New York City; guest artist, North Carolina School of the Arts; professor, 1977-1989, Head of Design, 1986-1988, Head of Graduate Studies, 1987-88, University of California, San Diego; professor, University of California, Los Angeles, from 1989. **Exhibitions:** *Design for Opera, Costume Drawings for the Center Opera Company,* Walker Art Center, Minneapolis, 1967; *Paintings and Sculpture—Robert Israel and Joseph Zucker,* Dayton's Gallery 12, Minneapolis, 1969; *Concepts: Moveable Space,* Milwaukee Art Center, Milwaukee, 1969; *Robert Israel,* Whitney Museum of American Art, New York, 1969; *Readings: Jennifer Bartlett and Robert Israel,* Paula Cooper Gallery, New York, 1969; *Costumes and Costume Drawings,* Kornblee Gallery, New York, 1970; *Design for the Theatre,* Walker Art Center, Minneapolis, 1974; *Drawings of Six Artists,* Museum of Modern Art, New York, 1974; *Twentieth Century Theatre Design,* Museum of Modern Art, New York, 1974; *Costume Drawings,* Morris Gallery, Birmingham, Michigan, 1977; *Artists of the Theatre,* Philadelphia College of Art Gallery, 1977; *The Costume Drawings for Satyagraha,* Aspen Music Festival, Aspen, Colorado, 1980; Max Protetch Gallery, New York, 1982, 1984, 1986; *Artists and the Theater,* Museum of Modern Art, New York, toured 1982-83; *Contemporary Theater Design,* Museum of Modern Art, New York, 1982-83; *From Word To Image,* Robert Tobin Collection, Marion Koogler McNay Art Museum, San Antonio, Texas, 1984; Daniel Weinberg Gallery, Los Angeles,

1986; University of California, San Diego Art Gallery, March 1989. **Collections:** Levi Collection, San Francisco; Museum of Modern Art, New York. **Honors:** Rockefeller Foundation Grant, 1978; Guggenheim Fellowship, 1984; National Endowment for the Arts Grant, 1986; Joseph Maharam Foundation Award for collaborative design achievements, 1986; National Endowment for the Arts Grant, 1986-87; American Theater Wing Award for design, 1986; OBIE Award for set and costume design, 1987; American Theater Wing Award in design, 1987. **Addresses:** (home) 932 Hanley Ave., Los Angeles, California 90049, U.S.A.; (agent) Leigh Giroux, 575 Madison Avenue, New York, New York 10022, U.S.A.

## Works

Theatre set and costume designs include—*Good Soldier Schwiek,* Guthrie Theatre, Minnesota Opera Company, 1966; *The Minute Operas,* Guthrie Theatre, 1967; *Harpies,* Guthrie Theatre (world premiere), 1967; *Socrates,* Guthrie Theatre, 1967; *The Sorrows of Orpheus,* Guthrie Theatre, 1967; *Midsummer Night's Dream,* Guthrie Theatre, 1968; *Horspfal,* Guthrie Theatre (world premiere), 1969; *Punch and Judy,* Guthrie Theatre (world premiere), 1972; *Men At Play,* Foundation Maeght, St. Paul de Vence, France (world premiere), 1971; *Transformations,* Guthrie Theatre (world premiere), 1972; *The Good Soldier Schwiek,* National Opera of the Netherlands, 1974; *The Magic Flute,* Guthrie Theatre, 1975; *Eight Songs for a Mad King,* Walker Art Center, Minnesota Opera Company, 1975; (costumes only) *Seven Deadly Sins,* National Opera of Belgium, 1975; *Macbeth,* National Opera of the Netherlands, 1975; *The Kaiser of Atlantis,* National Opera of the Netherlands (world premiere), 1975, Festival of Two Worlds, Spoleto, Italy, 1976, National Opera of Belgium, Brussels, 1976, San Francisco Opera Company, San Francisco, California, 1977; *Love for Three Oranges,* National Opera of the Netherlands, 1976; *The Magic Flute,* Michigan Opera Theatre, Detroit, Michigan, 1976; *The Combat of Tancredi and Clorinda,* San Francisco Opera Company, 1977; *Savitri,* San Francisco Opera Company, 1977; *Transformations,* National Opera of the Netherlands, National Opera of Finland, Mexico City, 1977; *Lulu,* National Opera of the Netherlands, incomplete version, 1978, complete version, 1980; (design consultant) *Dead End Kids,* Public Theatre, New York, 1980; *Satyagraha,* Rotterdam, Amsterdam, Utrecht, the Hague (world premiere), 1980, Art Park and the Brooklyn Academy of Music, New York, 1981, Chicago Lyric Opera, 1987, Seattle Opera, 1988, San Francisco Opera, 1989; *Yellow Sound,* commissioned by the Guggenheim Museum, New York, performed in New York and Frankfurt, Germany, 1982; *The Turn of the Screw,* Santa Fe Opera, New Mexico, 1983; *Intelligent Systems,* Frankfort, Germany (world premiere), 1983; *Akhnaten,* Houston Grand Opera and the New York City Opera (American premiere), 1984; *Die Walkure,* Seattle Opera, 1985, 1986; *Das Rheingold,* Seattle Opera, 1986; *Siegfried,* Seattle Opera, 1986; *Gotterdammerung,* Seattle Opera, 1986; *Vienna: Lusthaus,* Martha Clarke & Music Theater Group, New York, St. Clement's Church, New York City, Public Theater, New York City, Eisenhower Theater at the Kennedy Center, Washington, D.C., 1986; *The Hunger Artist,* Lennox Music Group, New York City, 1987; *The Ring Cycle,* Seattle Opera, 1987; *The Fiery Angel,* Los Angeles Music Center Opera, Geneva Opera, English National Opera, 1987; *Miracolo D'Amore,* Spoleto Festival, Charlotte, and the Public Theatre, New York City, 1988; *Vienna: Lusthaus,*

Martha Clarke & Music Theater Group, Venice, Vienna, Madrid, Paris, 1988; *Mahagonny,* Angeles Music Center Opera and the Geneva Opera, Dorothy Chandler Pavilion, 1989; *The Fiery Angel,* Netherlands Opera, Amsterdam, 1990; *Don Giovanni,* Florence Opera, Maggio Musicale, 1990; *Endangered Species,* Next Wave Festival, Brooklyn Academy of Music, Majestic Theatre, 1990; *Katja Kabanova,* Metropolitan Opera, New York, 1991; *Don Giovanni,* Los Angeles Opera, Los Angeles Music Center, Dorothy Chandler Pavilion, 1991; *The Fiery Angel,* Opera de Paris, Bastille, 1991; *Aida,* Seattle Opera, 1992; *The Magic Flute,* joint production of the Glimmerglass Festival and the National Opera of Canada, 1992-93; *The Voyage,* Metropolitan Opera, New York, 1992; *Orphee,* joint production at the American Repertory Theatre, Harvard University, Cambridge, Massachusetts, and the Brooklyn Academy of Music, New Wave Festival, 1992-93; *Cosi Fan Tutti,* Glimmerglass Opera, 1993; *Schlemiel I,* American Repertory Theatre, Harvard University, Cambridge, Massachusetts, 1994; *Alice's Adventures Underground,* National Theatre, London, England, 1994; *The Fairy Queen,* English National Opera, London, England, 1995; *Aida,* Bavarian State Opera, Munich, Germany, 1996; *Wozzeck,* Metropolitan Opera, New York City, 1997; *Rienzi,* Vienna State Opera, 1997; *Tartuffe,* American Repertory Theater, Cambridge, Massachusetts (forthcoming); *Florencia on the Amazon,* Houston Grand Opera, Los Angeles Music Center Opera, Seattle Opera, National Opera, Washington, D.C. (forthcoming);

Set and costume designs, for *The Abduction from the Seraglio,* National Educational Television, 1970.

Permanent installation, commissioned by the Metropolitan Transit Authority, for subway station at the Lincoln Center, New York, 1996.

## Publications

**By ISRAEL: books**—(librettist with others; music by Philip Glass) *Satyagraha,* Dunvagen Music Publishers, 1984; **articles**—"A Designer's Perspective on the Opera, *Satyagraha"* in *EAR,* June/July 1980.

**On ISRAEL: books**—*American Set Design 2* by Ronn Smith, New York, 1991; *A Search for a Postmodern Theater* by John Louis DiGaetani, New York, 1991; **articles**—*Opera News* (New York), 19 December 1987; *Dance Magazine,* February 1992; *New York Times,* 13 September 1992, 11 October 1992; *Times Literary Supplement* (London), 30 October 1992; *Theatre Craft International,* November 1995.

*       *       *

Robert Israel is a set and costume designer, a teacher at the University of California, Los Angeles, and a philosopher whose love of language and conversation seems as great as his love of theatre and opera. This love of ideas, and his fascination with the spatial configuration of the stage, has made him an ideal collaborator for such visionary artists as Philip Glass, Jonathan Miller, and Martha Clarke on works including *Satyagraha, Akhnaten, Vienna: Lusthaus,* and *Miracolo D'Amore,* as well as David Gordon's production of *Schlemiel the First,* and opera productions with François Rochaix, David Pountney, and Andrei Serban. His work is shaped in part by his origins as a visual artist in New York City in the 1960s. Though the experimental theatre scene was quite active at

**Robert Israel: stage design for Richard Wagner's *Der Ring des Nibelungen* from *Die Walküre*, Seattle Opera, 1995. Photo: Matthew McVay**

this time, Israel was not involved—he was an active participant in the lively art world of the period.

Israel's design career began in opera—the largely domestic drama of the American theatre did not interest him. The image-rich productions of Europe and the political implications of that theatre, however, appealed to him strongly and shaped his development as a theatre artist. He has singled out Wolfgang Wagner's Bayreuth *Ring* as a pivotal event in modern design.

If the fantastic imagery and visual complexity of Israel's sets and costumes could be reduced to simple underlying themes, they would be the tension between illusion and reality (which he sees as an implicit metaphor for moral struggle), and the aggressive exploration of space. Israel loves to explore the illusionistic methods of earlier eras of theatre, but then to expose the illusions, rip away the facades, deconstruct the mechanisms by which spectators apprehend the theatre and make them think about the act of viewing and process of perception. Thus, his *Ring Cycle* at the Seattle Opera in the mid 1980s employed 19th-century painting techniques on flats—but the flats were precariously leaning against each other and fell, for instance, when Fafner strode through this "jerry-rigged" forest. For Martha Clarke's *The Hunger Artist* the stage floor was covered with dirt while her *Endangered Species,* which incorporated live animals (including an elephant), had a floor covered with grass and

wood chips. Many of his designs set distorted, neo-Expressionist rooms or iconic objects against Surrealist-like expanses of space creating a disconcerting sense of dislocation for the audience, what he has termed "anxiety" or "vibration."

Israel also objects to conventional sightlines—the idea that the whole audience must have an equal view of the stage. He likes the idea of multiple views and focus; the idea that what is true for one member of an audience may not be true for another. Such an approach turns the spectator into a participant in the theatrical event. So while most of Israel's work is designed for the decidedly proscenium theatre of opera, it comes from a sensibility of environmental theatre and sculpture and the direct engagement of the audience in a dialogue with the work of art.

—Arnold Aronson

# ISSIGONIS, Alec
British car designer

**Born:** Alexander Constantine Issigonis in Smyrna (now Izmir), Turkey, 18 November 1906; emigrated to Britain in 1922. **Educa-**

**tion:** Educated privately in Smyrna, until 1921; studied engineering, Battersea Polytechnic, London, 1924-27. **Career:** Worked in the Edward Gillett design office, London, 1928-33; draughtsman, Rootes Motors, Coventry, 1934-36; suspension engineer, then chief engineer, Morris Motors, Cowley, Oxfordshire, 1937-52; designer, Alvis Car Company, Gloucestershire, 1953-56; deputy engineering co-ordinator and chief engineer, 1957-61, technical director, 1961, director of research and development, 1961-72, and consultant in advanced design, 1972-88, British Motor Corporation, and subsequently British Leyland (Austin-Morris). **Exhibitions:** Institute of Contemporary Arts, London, 1970; *Eye for Industry,* Victoria and Albert Museum, London, 1986. **Honors:** Commander, Order of the British Empire, 1964; Royal Designer for Industry, 1964, Leverhulme Medal, 1966, and fellow, 1967, Royal Society of Arts, London: Knighthood, London, 1969. **Died:** Edgbaston, Birmingham, England, 2 October 1988.

## Works

Morris Minor saloon car, for Morris Motors, 1948.
Morris Mini Minor and Austin Seven car, for British Motor Corporation, 1957-59.
Morris 1100, for British Motor Corporation, 1962.
Austin 1800, for British Motor Corporation, 1967.

## Publications

**On ISSIGONIS: books**—*Transport Design* by Corin Hughes-Stanton, London and New York, 1967; *Automobile Design: Great Designers and Their Work* edited by Ronald Barker and Anthony Harding, Newton Abbot, 1970; *Issigonis,* exhibition catalogue, London, 1970; *The Library of Motoring: The Designers* by L. J. K. Setright, London, 1976; *Mini* by Bob Golding, London, 1979; *Design by Choice* by Reyner Banam, London, 1981; *The Conran Directory of Design* edited by Stephen Bayley, London, 1985; *Eye for Industry: Royal Designers for Industry 1936-1986,* exhibition catalogue by Fiona MacCarthy and Patrick Nuttgens, London, 1986.

*     *     *

Alec Issigonis was an engineer who thought little of car stylists, saying that if the engineering is right, the car will look right. In designing the Mini, which was very much one man's car and not the product of a committee, the basic problem he wanted to solve was how to create a small car without the transmission tunnel taking up such a slice of the limited interior. His solution of placing the engine sideways was highly original, and the nature of the car flowed from that arrangement, which was an engineering solution, not an artistic one.

Issigonis thought he was making the car for the working man, but the working man is a pretty conservative animal, and it was the smart set who snapped up the Mini and made it the "in" car of the 1960s. The Mini was cheeky, for it could nip into a parking place which a lordly Rolls Royce was maneuvering in vain to occupy. The young loved it. A Mini fan club grew up to organize rallies and races for standard and souped-up Minis. Other versions came from Issigonis and his team: the Mini estate car, the Mini van, the Mini pickup, the Mini beach car for warm climates, and the military model, Mini Moke. A Mini Cooper won the Monte Carlo rally in 1964. Peter Sellers ordered a special hatchback version, which is the ancestor of all today's hatchbacks. The Mini is so popular that many of its owners buy a second one when the first one has worn out. In 1983, Austin Morris stated that the Issigonis Mini was still one of their two best-selling models, so they were going to increase its production still further. Not bad for a car which celebrated its thirty-fifth birthday in August 1994 and whose sales have totalled well over five million.

The qualities which Issigonis built into his car are permanent ones: fuel economy, maneuverability, ease of parking in city conditions, and fast acceleration. There have been modifications over the years, of course, such as larger headlamps and a new front grille, but the Mini's basic qualities will not go out of date for some time to come, and the Mini is certain to enter the record books as one of the longest lasting vehicles in production.

—Diana de Marly

# ITO, Shima

Japanese product, industrial, and interior designer

**Born:** Kobe, 3 September 1937. **Education:** Studied art and design under Tsugiji Doi at Kyoto Technical University, BS, 1963; postgraduate studies in architecture, 1963-64. **Career:** designer of household electrical appliances for Matsushita Electric Works, in Hikone, Shiga Prefecture, 1964-74, and domestic products, in Osaka, from 1974; consultant, 1981-83, chief designer, 1983-85, and senior designer, from 1985, in the Kinki Business Department. Lecturer, Shiga Women's Junior College, Otsu, Shiga Prefecture, 1979. **Member:** Japan Industrial Designers' Association, 1973; Japan Home Economists in Business Council, 1980; Japan Illuminating Engineering Society, 1982. **Honors:** Machinery Design Prize, 1967; Matsushita President's Prize, 1974, 1979, 1982. **Address:** 11-16-2, Nishidemachi, Hyogo-ku, Kobe 652, Japan.

## Publications

**By ITO: books**—*A Thought from Lifestyle,* booklet edited by Matsushita Electric Works, Osaka, 1979; *Trend of Consumers Seen from the Show-Window,* booklet edited by Matsushita Electric Works, Osaka, 1983; **articles**—*Denko Gijutsu* (Osaka), April 1970, February 1976, June 1977, December 1980, January-May 1987; *Matsushita News* (Osaka), January 1978-September 1981.

*

In today's industrialized world, man cannot live without "things." Basically, the world of "things" does not change. The meaning and value of "things," however, vary according to the person and the time. Therefore, the timing and the target-audience are important production factors. "Things" cannot exist alone. They exist for a reason and are in a relationship with man and his environment. Therefore, things must be designed as elements of man's life.

The creation of things comes out of a frustration or dissatisfaction with life. The process of the production of things is the same as child-bearing and rearing. Just as in child care, full affection must be poured into the process.

What does society want now? What do people want to have at this very moment? For designers, it is indispensable to feel, with all of their senses, what the real needs are and to see accurately the essence of products from the users' standpoint. This basic attitude will not change even if the environment of producing things may change.

Ideology in design is, of course, important, but this alone does not produce things. The image of products must be given a concrete shape that is as simple and concise as possible. Superficially well designed products will soon disappear from the market. If products are made based on consumers' needs, they will be widely accepted and will sell well for a long period of time.

Perfect production is only an ideal. But, at the least, a product should have "something" in it, something like the attractive personality of a person. Design activity, however small it may be, can mobilize the people, the organization, and the management of business. Herein lies the mission and attractiveness of design.

The complexity and specialization that has come with the advancement of technology has, unfortunately, led to the homogeneity of design. We are now, however, moving from the age of mass-production toward the age of a small-quantity production of diversified designs. Thus, we are beginning to question the methodology, uniformity, and fixity of ideas.

A production system based on a vertical structure within the company and an efficiency-oriented way of thinking tends to restrict the horizon of designers. Therefore, they fail to see things from the viewpoint of human life. In order to get free from such a closed way of thinking, designers must develop a humane environment that is based on the spirit of service. Designers must stand between consumers and businesses, have flexible and broad hori-

zons, and create products from actual daily life. This is the work I endeavor to undertake.

—Shima Ito

\*      \*      \*

In conversation, Shima Ito often says, "As a woman, I think ..." She clearly identifies herself as a woman designer, tries to be a spokesperson for women consumers, and makes products from a woman's point of view. Although she works for a big producer of electrical appliances, she strives to make products based on what she observes in daily life rather than on a design policy that is led by survey data or theoretical writings. Potential needs become explicit in living daily life, and she considers this as the substance of product design. In her mind, producers and users are not in conflict with each other. Rather, both parties should cooperate to create a better life. She likens the relationship to that between a physician of a village and his patients. An able designer can integrate many factors, can see things in totality, and can reflect the above in production. Ito meets all of these qualifications.

Through her product design and consulting, she has made proposals to make better use of living space in Japanese houses. Looking straight at reality, she says, "The design of living space in Japan is still in a transition period. Originality in design may be found, but, in general, it is of a poor level. What the producer can do now is study and develop the basic function of the house and provide products in the form of prefabricated houses. In consideration of their total living environment, the lifestyles of users must be fully reflected in the design." Indeed, Japanese housing is complex. Traditional techniques, advanced technology, and Japanese and Western styles are all combined into a genuine expression of the culture. With her flexible thinking, however, Shima Ito will surely achieve great success.

—Kunio Sano

# JACOBS, Sally

British stage set and costume designer

**Born:** Sally Rich, in London, 5 November 1932. **Education:** Educated at Dalston County Grammar School, London, until 1946; studied at St. Martin's School of Art, London, 1946-47, and Central School of Arts and Crafts, London, 1957-60. **Family:** Married Alexander Jacobs in 1953 (died, 1979); children: Toby. **Career:** Worked as a production secretary and continuity assistant on British feature films, 1951-57; scene painter, with Colchester Repertory Theatre, Essex, 1960; freelance set and costume designer, working with Peter Brook for the Royal Shakespeare Company, London, 1960-67, for the Mark Taper Forum, Los Angeles, 1967-68, for the Manhattan Theatre Club and the Shakespeare Festival, New York, 1979-82, and for the English National Opera, Royal Opera House, and others, in London, from 1982. Lecturer, California Institute of the Arts, Los Angeles, 1970-71, University of California at Los Angeles, 1977, Actors and Directors Laboratory, New York, 1978-79, Theatre Arts Department of Stage Design, New York, 1979-82, Rutgers University, New Brunswick, New Jersey, 1980-82, and Central School of Art and Design, London, 1982-88. **Exhibitions:** Opera Design, National Theatre, London, 1986; *British Theatre Design '83-87*, Riverside Studios, London, 1988. **Honors:** *Plays and Players* Design Award, London, 1970; Drama Desk Best Design Award, New York, 1970; Obie Award, New York, 1980. **Address:** c/o Mrs. Emanuel Wax, A.C.T.A.C. Limited, 16 Cadogan Lane, London SW1, England.

## Works

Stage productions include—*Wildest Dreams* (musical), Cheltenham Everyman Theatre, 1960; *Five Plus One* (revue), Edinburgh Festival, 1961; *Women Beware Women* (sets only), Royal Shakespeare Company, Arts Theatre, London, 1962; *The Empire Builders,* Royal Shakespeare Company, Arts Theatre, London, 1962; *Nothing But the Best* (film; costumes only), 1963; *The Day of the Prince,* Royal Court Theatre, London, 1963; *Theatre of Cruelty* (experimental theatre), Royal Shakespeare Company, Lamda Theatre, London, 1964; *The Formation Dancers,* Arts Theatre, London, 1964 (moved to the Globe Theatre, London); *The Screens,* Royal Shakespeare Company, Donmar Theatre, London, 1964; *Marat/Sade,* Royal Shakespeare Company, Aldwych Theatre, London, 1964, adapted for the Martin Beck Theatre, New York, 1965, and film version by Peter Brook, 1966; *Love's Labour's Lost,* Royal Shakespeare Company, Stratford-upon-Avon, 1964; *Having a Wild Weekend* (film; costumes only), 1965; *Twelfth Night,* Royal Shakespeare Company, Stratford-upon-Avon, 1966; *Us,* Royal Shakespeare Company, Aldwych Theatre, London, 1966; *The Golden Fleece* and *Muzeeka,* Mark Taper

Forum, Los Angeles, 1968; *A Midsummer Night's Dream,* Royal Shakespeare Company, Stratford-upon-Avon, 1970, adapted for the Aldwych Theatre, London, 1970, Billy Rose Theatre, New York, 1970, American tour, 1970, and world tour, 1972; designed for Peter Brook's International Centre for Theatre Research tour of West Africa, 1973; *The Conference of the Birds,* Peter Brook's Centre in Paris, 1973 (toured the United States, including Teatro Campesino, San Juan Battista, California and Brooklyn Academy, New York); *Mahagonny Songplay* and *The Measures Taken,* Mark Taper Forum, Los Angeles, 1973; *Ajax,* Forum Lab, Los Angeles, 1974; *Of Mice and Men,* San Francisco Opera, 1974; *Savages,* Mark Taper Forum, Los Angeles, 1974; *Il Trovatore,* Houston Grand Opera, 1974; *Oedipus at Colonus* (also director), Forum Lab, Los Angeles, 1975; *Cross Country, Where She Shops, Ashes* (sets only) and *Three Sisters* (4 repertory plays), Mark Taper Forum, Los Angeles, 1976; *Meetings with Remarkable Men* (film; costumes only), 1976; *Ascent of Mount Fuji* (sets only), Hollywood Television Theatre, Los Angeles, 1977; *Much Ado about Nothing,* Los Angeles Shakespeare Festival, 1977; *Gethsemane Springs* (sets only), Mark Taper Forum, Los Angeles, 1977; *Black Angel,* Mark Taper Forum, Los Angeles, 1978; *Antony and Cleopatra,* Royal Shakespeare Company, Stratford-upon-Avon, 1978, adapted for the Aldwych Theatre, London, 1979; *Conference of the Birds* (revival), for Peter Brook's Centre, Paris, at the Avignon Festival, 1979 (toured Europe and the United States); *Ice,* Manhattan Theatre Club, New York, 1979; *End Game,* Manhattan Theatre Club, New York, 1980, adapted for the American Centre, Paris, 1980; *Selma* (sets only), Theatre for the New City, New York, 1981; *Three Acts of Recognition* (sets only), New York Shakespeare Festival, 1981; *Antigone,* New York Shakespeare Festival, 1982; *Die Fledermaus,* Opera de Paris, 1982-83; *The Relapse,* Lyric Theatre-Hammersmith, London, 1983; *Turandot,* Royal Opera House, London, and Los Angeles, 1984; *Fidelio,* Royal Opera House, London, 1986; *Turandot,* touring production, Korea and Japan, 1986; *Eugene Onegin,* English National Opera, London, 1989; *Last Tango on the North Circular* (also directed), Royal Opera House, London, 1989.

## Publications

**By JACOBS: articles**—in *Themes in Drama 2,* Cambridge, 1980.

**On JACOBS: books**—*British Theatre Design '83-87,* with texts by Timothy O'Brien and David Fingleton, London, 1988; *British Theatre Design* edited by John Goodwin, London, 1989.

*

I became a designer because I developed a passion for the theatre in the mid 1950s, when the Royal Court and the Theatre Royal

Stratford East produced a stream of plays with a burst of new energy which is now a part of theatre history. I decided to study theatre design and have been devoted to the theatre ever since.

When I started work with Peter Brook in 1964, I was introduced to a more international theatre for the first time. We read the *Tulane Drama Review Happenings* and Artaud's *Theatre of Cruelty*—and this was the beginning of one of the most important relationships in all of my theatre experience. With Brook, I learned to question everything and to invent a unique visual language for each piece we produced.

When I went to live in Los Angeles in 1967, I experienced the shock and excitement of a complete break with tradition and familiar cultural patterns, out of which came the *Midsummer Night's Dream* with Brook in 1970. Also during this time in Los Angeles, I learned how to use the thrust stage while designing several productions for Gordon Davidson at the Mark Taper Forum—another cornerstone of my design experience. Eventually, I spent some years in New York also, teaching and working with two directors whose work I have always admired, Joseph Chaikin and Richard Foreman. No rules can be imposed on the theatre, and it is only in retrospect that I can see that I have tended to concern myself more with the dynamics of space than with pictorialization and that the collaborative process has been, for me, a continual source of investigation and creative freedom.

—Sally Jacobs

\* \* \*

There is no question that the formative influence on the design work of Sally Jacobs was her close association with Peter Brook, who throughout the 1960s and early 1970s espoused a modified and updated version of Artaud's Theatre of Cruelty, in which all his productions worked strongly to gain a simple, physical, direct relationship with the audience. In *Marat/Sade,* Jacobs' plain, dirty, inmate uniforms, coupled with costume pieces from the period of the French Revolution, created such a vivid impression that the audience felt that it could smell the stench of the asylum. In *A Midsummer Night's Dream,* her simple, white, empty box set with catwalk and trapeze, along with colorful tunics and exercise pants with tie-dyed accents, created a feeling of physical exuberance and euphoria, as if the audience might be ready to soar into the air with the actors.

Thus, more than almost any other contemporary designer, Jacobs has been influenced by and has presented those aspects of the visual arts of the 1960s and 1970s which were the outgrowth of happenings, environmental art, process art, and sculptural tableaux. She has broken with period style in her costumes to express the essence of character- or play-mood, just as she has removed time and place in her settings in favor of an interesting space within which the actors can physically and visually tell their story. It is also true that the productions with which Jacobs has been connected have been for the most part socially and politically oriented toward antiestablishment values.

In general, Jacobs has been committed to presenting a collage of costumes and scenic pieces that are interesting as shapes, colors, and textures in themselves and that can be used by the director and the actors to tell the story in a most vivid and physically direct way without the interference of a great deal of factual and historic information.

—Douglas A. Russell

# JACOBSEN, Arne

Danish architect, interior, furniture, textile, and ceramics designer

**Born:** Copenhagen, 11 February 1902. **Education:** Studied architecture at the Royal Academy of Arts, Copenhagen, Dip. Arch., 1928. **Family:** Married; children: two sons. **Career:** Worked in the office of city architect Paul Holsoe, Copenhagen, 1927-30; in private architectural practice, Copenhagen, 1930-71; freelance furniture, textile, and ceramics designer, Copenhagen, 1943-71; designed for Graucob Textilen, August Millech, C. Olesen, A. Michelsen, Fritz Hansen, Louis Poulsen Company, and others. Professor of architecture, Royal Academy of Arts, Copenhagen, 1956-71. **Exhibitions:** Royal Institute of British Architects, London, 1959; McLellan Galleries, Glasgow, 1968; Ministry of Cultural Affairs, Copenhagen, 1971. **Honors:** Bellevue Seaside Development Prize, 1932; Eckersberg Medal, Copenhagen, 1936; Aarhus Town Hall Prize, 1937; Sollerod Town Hall Prize, 1939; Grand Prize, Sao Paulo Bienal, 1953. Honorary Doctorates: Oxford University, 1966; Strathclyde University, Glasgow, 1968. Honorary Corresponding Member, Royal Institute of British Architects; Honorary Fellow, American Institute of Architects. **Died:** Copenhagen, 24 March 1971.

**Works**

House of the Future, at the *Danish Building Exhibition,* Copenhagen, 1929 (with Fleming Lassen).
Bellevue Theatre and Gammel Bellevue Restaurant, Copenhagen, 1937.
*Dockleaves* printed fabric, for C. Olesen Company, 1942-43.
*Reed* printed fabric and wallcoverings, for C. Olesen Company, 1942-43.
Office interiors, for Poulsen and Company, Copenhagen, 1948.
Showroom and spares depot, for Massey-Harris, Copenhagen, 1952.
Stacking chair with 3 legs, for Fritz Hansen Company, 1952.
Desk, for the American-Scandinavian Foundation of New York, produced by Rudolf Rasmussen Company, 1952.
Ceiling lamp in opaline glass and brass, for Munkegaards School, produced by Louis Poulsen Company, 1955.
*3100 Chair,* for Fritz Hansen Company, 1955.
Stacking chair with 4 legs, for Fritz Hansen Company, 1957.
Cutlery in stainless steel, for A. Michelsen Company, 1957.
SAS Royal Hotel standard lamp in black varnished metal, produced by Louis Poulsen Company, 1957.
Chair in laminated wood, for Fritz Hansen Company, 1957.
*Egg* chair in upholstered plastic and steel, for Fritz Hansen Company, 1959.
*Swan* chair in steel and plastic with leather upholstery, for Fritz Hansen Company, 1959.
*Cylinda* range of tablewares, for Stelton Company, 1962.
Factories, for Novo Company, in Mainz and Charters, 1969-70.

(for complete list of Jacobsen's buildings and architectural projects, see *Contemporary Architects*)

**Publications**

**On JACOBSEN: books**—*Arkitekten Arne Jacobsen* by J. Pedersen, Copenhagen, 1954; *Danish Chairs* edited by Nanna and Jørgen

Ditzel, Copenhagen, 1954; *Modern Danish Furniture* by Esbjørn Hiort, Copenhagen, New York, and London, 1956; *Arne Jacobsen: Architecture, Applied Art,* exhibition catalogue by Poul Erik Shriver, London, 1959; *Modern Danish Textiles* edited by Bent Salicath and Arne Karlsen, Copenhagen, 1959; *Arne Jacobsen* by T. Faber, London, 1964; *Arne Jacobsen at the McLellan Galleries, Glasgow,* exhibition catalogue, Glasgow, 1968; *Arne Jacobsen* by Jørgen Kastholm, Copenhagen, 1968; *Arne Jacobsen: A Danish Architect* by Poul Erik Shriver, Copenhagen, 1972; *Arne Jacobsen* by Poul Erik Shriver and Ellen Waade, Copenhagen, 1976; *Arne Jacobsen: Opera Completa 1909-1971* by Luciano Rubino, Rome, 1980; *Modern Furniture Classics* by Miriam Stimpson, London, 1987.

\* \* \*

In all areas related to the arts, invention has become highly prized, and interpretation is frequently dismissed as of lesser value. And yet, inspired interpretation can equal or occasionally surpass an original, as Arne Jacobsen's work repeatedly proves. When we identify the sources of Jacobsen's classic chairs, *Egg* and *Swan,* we also identify his own creative abilities. *Egg* wraps its user in a protective shell of padded and upholstered fiberglass, while *Swan* takes its shape from the curved wing and neck of its drifting namesake. In both pieces, a minimal pedestal base allows curvilinear forms to float in space. Structurally and technologically, neither piece is original. One-piece bodies, developed by Eames and Saarinen, were widely used in America—although not, as yet, in Scandinavia—when Jacobsen incorporated them into his design vocabulary. The same can be said of the slender supports. Even the top line of *Egg* recalls the amoebic forms used by Finn Juhl in Denmark and, more especially, by Isamu Noguchi and Vladimir Kagan in the United States. Together, however, these borrowed elements are united by Jacobsen into forms that enlighten even as they explain, forms that establish him not only as a designer but as a sculptor of furniture.

Similar borrowings can be seen in the various versions of his molded-plywood, stacking chairs. Again, the material and approach come from Eames but the subtle changes of the contours—as well as the unexpected wit—of these mass produced designs come from Jacobsen alone. While he cannot be described as an originator, his power as an interpreter should lead us to realize the limitations of invention—unless it is potent enough to inspire others to internalize and surpass it.

—Reed Benhamou

# JENKINS, George

American stage and film designer

**Born:** Baltimore, Maryland, 19 November 1908. **Education:** Studied architecture, at the University of Pennsylvania, Philadelphia, 1929-31. **Family:** Married Phyllis Adams in 1955; children: Jane (by previous marriage), Alexandra (died). **Collections:** Billy Rose Collection, New York Public Library at Lincoln Center, New York; Theatre Collection, University of California at Los Angeles. **Career:** Worked as an interior designer and engineer, New York, 1932-36; assistant to stage designer Jo Mielziner, New York, 1937-41; freelance stage designer, New York, from 1942, and film and television designer from 1945; art director in charge of colour, CBS Co-

lumbia Broadcasting System, New York, 1953-54. Theatre consultant, University of Pennsylvania, Philadelphia, and professor of motion picture design, University of California at Los Angeles, from 1985. Theatre standards board member, American National Theatre Association, from 1954. **Honors:** Donaldson Award, New York, 1946; Academy Award, 1976. **Address:** 740 Kingman Avenue, Santa Monica, California 90402, U.S.A.

**Works**

Stage designs (New York, unless noted) include—*Early to Bed,* 1943; *Mexican Hayride,* 1944; *I Remember Mama,* 1944; *Dark of the Moon,* 1945; *Common Ground,* 1945; *Strange Fruit,* 1945; *Are You With It?,* 1945; *Lost in the Stars,* 1949; *Bell, Book, and Candle,* 1950; *Three Wishes for Jamie,* 1952; *Gently Does It,* 1953; *The Immoralist,* 1954; *The Bad Seed,* 1954; *Ankles Aweigh,* 1955; *The Desk Set,* 1955; *Too Late the Phalarope,* 1956; *The Happiest Millionaire,* 1956; *The Merry Widow,* 1957; *Rumple,* 1957; *Two for the Seesaw,* 1958; *Tall Story,* 1959; *The Miracle Worker,* 1959; *One More River,* 1960; *Critic's Choice,* 1960; *A Thousand Clowns,* 1962; *Jennie,* 1963; *Everybody Out, the Castle Is Sinking,* 1964; *Catch Me If You Can,* 1965; *Wait Until Dark* (also London), 1966; *The Student Prince* (San Francisco), 1966; *Night Watch,* 1972; *Sly Fox,* 1976.

Film designs include—*The Best Years of Our Lives* (Wyler), 1946; *The Secret Life of Walter Mitty* (McCloud), 1947; *The Bishop's Wife* (Koster), 1947; *A Song Is Born* (Hawks), 1948; *Enchantment* (Reis), 1948; *Little Women* (LeRoy) 1949; *Roseanna McCoy* (Reis), 1949; *At War with the Army* (Walker), 1950; *The San Francisco Story* (Parrish), 1952; *Monsoon* (Amateau), 1953; *The Miracle Worker* (Penn), 1962; *Mickey One* (Penn), 1965; *Up the Down Staircase* (Mulligan), 1967; *Wait Until Dark* (Young), 1967; *No Way to Treat a Lady* (Smight), 1968, *The Subject Was Roses* (Grosband), 1968; *Me, Natalie* (Coe), 1969; *The Angel Levine* (Kadar), 1970; *The Pursuit of Happiness* (Mulligan), 1971; *Klute* (Pakula), 1971; *1776* (Hunt), 1972; *The Paper Chase* (Bridges), 1973; *The Parallax View* (Pakula), 1974; *Funny Lady* (Ross), 1975; *Night Moves* (Penn), *All the President's Men* (Pakula), 1976; *Comes a Horseman* (Bridges), 1978; *The China Syndrome* (Bridges), 1978; *Starting Over* (Pakula), 1979; *Rollover* (Pakula), 1981; *The Postman Always Rings Twice* (Rafaelson), 1981; *Sophie's Choice* (Pakula), 1982; *The Dollmaker* (Petrie—for TV), 1984; *Orphans,* 1987; *See You in the Morning* (Pakula), 1989; *Presumed Innocent* (Pakula) 1990.

**Publications**

**By JENKINS: articles**—in *Film Comment* (New York), May 1978.

**On JENKINS: books**—*Le Décor de Film* by Leon Barsacq, Paris, 1970, as *Caligari's Cabinet and Other Grand Illusions,* Boston, 1976; *The International Film Encyclopedia* by Ephraim Katz, New York and London, 1980; *The International Dictionary of Films and Filmmakers,* Chicago and London, 1987, 1991.

\* \* \*

George Jenkins is a flexible designer who has worked for theater, film, and television. His first work was on the settings and lighting

George Jenkins: *The Miracle Worker*, International Company, 1960

of Broadway plays, and in 1946 he won an award for the intimate and homey sets of *I Remember Mama.*

Jenkins enjoyed designing for the stage because of the many points of view from which the audience sees the sets. His transition to film, however, was quite successful. He was brought to Hollywood in 1945 by Samuel Goldwyn to work for Goldwyn/RKO. The first film he designed (in collaboration with Perry Ferguson) was *The Best Years of Our Lives,* shot in deep focus by the cinematographer Gregg Toland and directed by William Wyler. The result of this happy collaboration is a beautiful film full of interesting long shots through doorways, windows, and mirrored rooms. Wyler conferred with Jenkins on the types of living quarters that would suit the characters.

Throughout his career, Jenkins has displayed a knack for creating environments that perfectly fit the scenario. Often, his designs are based on careful research. His background in theater seems to have made him extremely prop-conscious: he selects the right objects to suit the setting and the character. Jenkins designed a setting for *Little Women* (1949) copied from Louisa May Alcott's own childhood home. (Though the sets of the 1949 version of *Little Women* are based on Jenkins' drawings he received no screen credit because the production was transferred from David O. Selznick to MGM.) For the film *The Miracle Worker,* Jenkins sought out a setting that would closely resemble Helen Keller's actual home in Georgia. For *Klute,* Jenkins designed a highly individualistic apartment for the prostitute-heroine, Bree Daniels.

In the 1970s, Jenkins made two films with newspaper settings. *Parallax View* (1974) revolved around a small-town newspaper. To achieve a convincing newsroom, Jenkins visited many such news-paper offices and combined their characteristics. For his award-winning *All the President's Men,* Jenkins sketched and photographed the *Washington Post* newsroom. For the sake of accuracy, he even collected discards from the reporters to be spread on the desks in the film set.

—Lois Miklas

# JOOP, Wolfgang

German fashion designer

**Born:** Potsdam, 18 November 1944. **Family:** Married Karin Bernatzky; children: Henriette, Florentine. **Career:** Journalist, *Neue Mode*; freelance designer, Christian Aujard, Brecco, and others; showed first collection under own label, 1978; introduced *Joop!* ready-to-wear line, 1981; added menswear line, 1985; opened *Joop!* boutiques, Hamburg and Munich, 1986; introduced fragrances, 1987; added *Joop!* jeans, 1989; introduced ready-to-wear fur collection, 1990. **Address:** Harvestehuder Weg 22, 2000 Hamburg 13, Germany.

## Publications

**On JOOP: articles**—"Who Is First in the Market Sells" by Richard Morais in *Forbes,* 16 September 1991; "Talking Fashion" by

Belinda Morris in *FHM* (London), September 1993; *Avenue,* June-July 1993; *Vogue Australia,* February 1993; *The Village Voice* (New York), 9 March 1993; *Daily News Record,* 24 January 1994; *Women's Wear Daily* (New York), 22 February 1994; "New York Now" in *Women's Wear Daily* (New York), 31 October 1995; "American Visions Prevail" by Amy M. Spindler in *New York Times,* 31 October 1995; "Mizrahi, de la Renta, Kors Agree: It's Nice to Be a Rich Neo-Preppy!" in *New York Observer,* 13 November 1995.

*       *       *

Wolfgang Joop's fall-winter 1996-97 menswear collection included tweed suits that might have stepped off the Princeton campus, plaid pants shown with textural wind-breakers that would have been at ease on a golf course, and jeans dressing suitable for cowboys of the plains or mall. Joop is an implacably American-style designer. Despite being German. Despite having established his successful business in Europe before assailing America in 1992 with fragrance. Despite avowed personal affinities for Yohji Yamamoto, Rudi Gernreich, and Comme des Garcons. Despite telling Stacy Perman in *Women's Wear Daily,* "I am not a typical European or American designer. I want to be myself, carrying my own experience of life." Joop sees himself as an individual, but his fashion success has followed the models of American sportswear and marketing. Sexy men's underwear advertising, generally chaste womenswear, a supposedly nonchalant personal charisma, and high-profile fragrances are a Calvin Klein paradigm clearly influential for Joop.

Joop's disposition to place jeans at the core of his collections is reinforced by a rhetoric of democracy, decrying the style and economic excesses of the 1980s, claiming a desire to return to simpler times and simpler fashion and extolling the easy-going lifestyle. Further, it can hardly be a mere accident of real estate that Joop bought the Manhattan apartment vacated by Bill Blass. And Potsdam-born Joop knows New York intimately and shrewdly, telling Martine Trittoleno in *Avenue,* "In New York, beauty and the beast live together."

Marion von Adlerstein concludes a long assessment of Joop in *Vogue Australia* with the comment, "If a marketing mind were to create an image for a fashion designer in our times, it would be hard-pressed to top the reality of Joop. In a world of puffery and hyperbole, he's the genuine article." Joop's most convincing genuineness is his menswear. He has described himself as the ideal client for his own design and the menswear reflects this concentration upon himself. He described the man he dresses in *Daily News Record* in 1994 as "cosmopolitan, but there's a hint of country dirt on his shoes." Joop's demand for naturalism is beguiling and especially evident in his textural sportswear filled with corduroy, velvet, patterned and granular wools, and jeans. In tailored clothing, Joop tends to be a bit of a dandy. His fall-winter 1995-96 menswear collection, for example, seemed more artistic and etiolated; nothing to wear where you might get country dirt stuck to your shoes.

Yet not the menswear nor the womenswear nor even the *Joop! Kids* collection truly tells the story of Joop's design objectives. Rather, Joop is the aggregate of his important leather, accessories, shoes, jeans and men's bodywear (underwear, that is) collection, constituents of a large design ideal and a comprehensive view of the designer's role in modern life.

The keystone of the Joop collections is the jeans line, his first apparel launch in America. Indigo silk coat dresses for women fall in this category along with jeans basics in pants, shorts, shirts, and jackets in blue and black denim, white denim, and indigo silk and seersucker. Joop's womenswear can be seen as the mainstreaming of design first presented and refined by other designers, most notably in the 1990s collections of his countrywoman Jil Sander.

But Joop is the more complete designer, using fashion's complex imagery to create the sense of a young, sexy, and indifferent image that is personified by the designer but also transmitted in the range of no-nonsense, no-conspicuous-fashion products, including luxurious leather put into slouchy luggage and accessories and Joop's unusual breadth of jeanswear. Hilton Als has rightly called Joop in the *Village Voice,* "Germany's answer to Calvin Klein." Joop chafes at the comparison, invoking such avant-garde designers as Rei Kawakubo or Rudi Gernreich as his inspiration, but the designer's work is inexorably mainstream and ingratiating, neither one of which is a bad characterization for fashion. If Joop's image is hard to define beyond the big billboard of modern fashion promotion and the handsome, smiling blonde of his own appearance, Joop may be the quintessential designer in a nameless, ineffable, individualistic epoch at the end of the twentieth century.

—Richard Martin

## JUHL, Finn

Danish architect and industrial designer

**Born:** Copenhagen, 30 January 1912. **Education:** Sanct Jørgens Gymnasium, Copenhagen, until 1930; studied architecture under Kay Fisker at the Kunstakademiet, Copenhagen, 1930-34; mainly self-taught in industrial design. **Career:** Worked in the architectural office of Vilhelm Lauritzen, Copenhagen, 1934-45; freelance designer, establishing own office for exhibition and furniture design, Copenhagen, 1945-89; designed for Boex, France and Son, Baker Furniture, Georg Jensen, Bing and Grondahl, and others; consultant designer to General Electric, Louisville, Kentucky, 1954, and IBM Typewriters, New York, 1960. Head of the School of Interior Design, Copenhagen, 1944-55; guest professor, Institute of Design, Illinois Institute of Technology, Chicago, 1965. **Member:** Akademisk Arkitektforening, Copenhagen, 1940; Honorary Royal Designer for Industry, Royal Society of Arts, London, 1978. **Exhibitions:** Corcoran Gallery of Art, Washington, D.C., 1963; *I Grandi Designers,* Cantu, Italy, 1973; *Finn Juhl: Møbler og Andre Arbejder,* Kunstindustrimuseum, Copenhagen, 1982 (traveled to Oslo, Norway); *Scandinavian Modern Design 1880-1980,* Cooper-Hewitt Museum, New York, 1982; *Design Since 1945,* Philadelphia Museum of Art, 1983. **Collections:** Victoria and Albert Museum, London; Kunstindustrimuseum, Copenhagen; Museum of Modern Art, New York. **Honors:** Cabinetmakers Guild Annual Awards, Copenhagen, from 1937; Eckersberg Medal, Copenhagen, 1947; Diploma of Honour, 1954, and Gold Medals, 1954, 1957, Milan Triennale; Association of Industrial Designers Award, Chicago, 1954; Danish State Art Foundation Annual Stipend, 1971-89. **Died:** Copenhagen, 17 May 1989.

**Works**

Armchair in walnut with loose cushion, for Niels Vodder, 1945.
Shop and showrooms, for Bing and Grondahl, Copenhagen, 1946.

Finn Juhl: *Høvdingestol/chiefs* chair, 1949. Photo courtesy of the Danish Museum of Decorative Art

Sofa and matching armchair in mahogany with leather upholstery, for Niels Vodder, 1948.

*Egyptian* chair, for Niels Vodder, 1949.

*Good Design* exhibition layouts, for the Merchandise Mart, Chicago, and the Museum of Modern Art, New York, 1951.

Trustees Council Chamber interiors, for the United Nations building, New York, 1952.

Dining chair in beech with veneered seat and back, for Bovirke, 1953.

Easy chair in upholstered teak, for Niels Vodder, 1953.

Desk in teak and blue steel, for Bovirke, 1953.

*Danish Silver* exhibition layouts, for the Corcoran Gallery of Art, Washington, D.C., 1954.

Chair in teak with sprung upholstery, for France and Daverkosen, 1954.

European and Far East office interiors, and DC-8 airplane interiors, for Scandinavian Airlines System, from 1955.

*Formes Scandinaves* exhibition layouts, for the Musée du Louvre, Paris, 1958.

*The Arts of Denmark* exhibition layouts, for the Metropolitan Museum of Art, New York, 1960.

## Publications

**On JUHL: books**—*Dansk Møbelkunst* by Viggo Sten Moller and Svend Erik Moller, Copenhagen, 1951; *Danish Chairs* edited by Nanna and Jorgen Ditzel, Copenhagen, 1954; *Finn Juhl and Danish Furniture* pamphlet by Bent Salicath, Copenhagen, 1955; *Modern Danish Furniture* by Esbjorn Hiort, Copenhagen, New York, and London, 1956; *Modern Scandinavian Furniture* by Ulf Hård af Segerstad, Stockholm and London, 1963; *Danish Design* edited by Svend Erik Moller, Copenhagen, 1974; *En Kobenhavnsk Porcelaenfabriks Historie: Bing og Grondal 1853-1978* by Erik Lassen, Copenhagen, 1978; *Finn Juhl: Møbler og Andre Arbejder,* exhibition catalogue with text by Erik Lassen, Copenhagen, 1982; *Design Since 1945* edited by Kathryn Hiesinger and George Marcus, Philadelphia and London, 1983; *Modern Furniture Classics* by Miriam Stimpson, London, 1987.

*

During the depression in the early 1930s, the members of the Copenhagen Cabinetmakers' Guild were in bad straits. They had their excellent skill, their small workshops, hardly any showrooms, and no sales.

Prompted by the architect Tyge Hvass, they decided on a last great effort, consisting of an open invitation to a yearly competition of new designs, with very small awards, but with the splendid promise of producing at least one sample of each awarded design on the condition that the designer would arrange the presentation at the autumn-exhibitions at the Copenhagen Kunstindustrimuseum.

They were lucky to get Crown Prince Frederik and Crown Princess Ingrid as patrons, and they continued as such when they were King and Queen. Especially during the German Occupation, this combination of domestic design and royal patronage lead to a row of glorious events for the press, so that the designer of one chair might overnight be in the whole press with photographs of object and designer and the cabinetmaker hovering in the background.

The official School of Furniture at the Royal Academy was completely dominated by Professor Kaare Klint, who taught that the best furniture was the classical English or Chinese-inspired English. In many ways, it was an excellent school of furniture-making in traditional but functional design, although it lead to some inevitable epigonism and hardly any creativity. As I was not a student of Klint's, I had to play my David to his Goliath. Some of his surviving students are still disgusted with my audacity; for others, my efforts may have helped them to freedom. Were that the case, I would be happy.

My designs have been around so long that they cannot today appear rebellious, but so they were in an aesthetic sense, not in technique—after all, they were designed for my limited, hand made production to save the cabinetmakers' trade. Also, my displays were less realistic and tried to indicate that there was a connection between architecture, furniture, and other accessories and the contemporary free arts, just as there had been in former epochs, such as the Baroque, Empire, etc.

During World War II, few impulses came from abroad. We developed a kind of Danish design in almost all fields—silver, ceramics, glass, textiles, furniture. We worked as individualists but appeared after the war to the outer world as a homogenous group, which was an immense advantage for such a tiny country. At the same time, our being individualists made us more appealing to possible importers, as there was more to choose from. One success helped the other, so it was delightful being allowed to arrange the exhibitions abroad.

My furniture (also the latest designs for machine production) has often been called sculptural. Naturally it is three-dimensional, as is architecture, but I guess that it is more the continuation of one member into the other through a smooth joint and the varying, moulded sections of each member, plus the "readiness" to accept and support the sculptural human body with a great margin for movement, since sitting as well as sleeping involves a process of movements. I want my chairs to be comfortable. I also want them to be beautiful to look at, as we, in contrast to the Japanese, leave all our furniture "on stage," even when we need only one chair.

—Finn Juhl (1984)

*    *    *

Finn Juhl's work represents a high point in Scandinavian design during the 1950s, when America and Britain were influenced by the quality and strength of work coming from these countries. In the late 1940s the Danish furniture industry had been revitalized by a new generation of designers that included Juhl and Hans Wegner. The country had not suffered major devastation during the war and was therefore able to pick up quickly its long and rich design tradition, a tradition reinforced in the 1930s by the Copenhagen Cabinet Makers' Guild, which, under the inspired leadership of Kaare Klint, had become a major center for furniture design. It was Klint who had studied eighteenth-century English furniture for proportion and construction that could be adapted to a contemporary style, using the highest standards of craftsmanship. Klint's work and research made a deep impact on Juhl. If his work moved away from Klint's more functional orientation, the kind of furniture sculpture he developed, pushing wood as it did to the limits of its capacity, depended entirely on quality of craftsmanship for its success. The style he developed, with its curved contours, natural wood, and coarse-textured fabrics, captured the essence of 1950s design and was quickly adapted and imitated all over the Western world.

Juhl believed his design work to be closely allied to fine art, and his furniture often explored the borderlines between fine and applied art. He looked for inspiration to African primitive art and the work of abstract artists, such as Henry Moore and Barbara Hepworth. In the craft area, his work includes some famous wood bowls, usually in teak, showing the strong pattern of wood grain. In the 1950s, no avant garde interior was seen without one. During the 1950s and 1960s, Juhl played a part in promoting Scandinavian design worldwide. He organized and exhibited in shows such as *Formes Scandinaves* at the Louvre in 1958 and the *Milan Triennale.*

—Catherine McDermott

# JUHLIN, Sven-Eric

Swedish industrial designer

**Born:** Horndal, 6 May 1940. **Education:** Studied mechanical engineering, Katrineholm Technical School, 1958-61; studied sculpture and industrial design, National College of Art and Design, Stockholm, 1963-67. **Family:** Married Siv Larsson in 1964; children: Oskar and Pär. **Career:** Worked as a constructor, AB Electrolux, 1961-63; industrial designer, AB Gustavsberg, Sweden, 1967-76; partner, Ergonomi Design Gruppen, Bromma, from 1976; collaborating with designer Maria Benktzon, from 1972. Instructor in Ergonomics and Design Methods, National College of Art and Design, Stockholm, 1970-73; professor, Institute of Design, Umeå University, 1990-93; also visiting lecturer at congresses and professional institutes in Europe, Japan, and Canada, from 1983. Board Member, Swedish Society of Crafts and Design, Stockholm, 1970-76. **Exhibitions:** *A Society Open to All,* Kharkov, U.S.S.R., 1977 (toured the Soviet Union, Poland, and Czechoslovakia); *Swedish Craft and Design,* Victoria and Albert Museum, London, 1980; *Scandinavian Modern Design 1880-1980,* Cooper-Hewitt Museum, New York, 1982; *Contemporary Swedish Design,* Nationalmuseum, Stockholm, 1983 (toured Scandinavia); *Design Since 1945,* Philadelphia Museum of Art, 1983; *International Design Exhibition,* Osaka, Japan, 1985; *Design in Sweden Now,* 1985-86 (toured Canada and Australia); *New Design for Old,* Boilerhouse, Victoria and Albert Museum, London, 1986; *Scandinavian Design: A Way of Life,* Toyama Museum of Modern Art, Japan, 1987; *Faces of Swedish Design,* IBM Gallery, New York, 1988 (toured the United States); *Designs for Independent Living,* Museum of Modern Art, New York, 1988 (toured the United States); *Design Art,* Internationales Design Zentrum, Berlin, 1988; *Suecia Forma y Diseno,* Montevideo, Uruguay, 1990 (toured South America); *Design Sweden,* Bombay, India, 1991 (toured India); *Vackrare vardagsvara,* Warszawa, Poland, 1992 (toured eastern Europe). **Collections:** Museum of Modern Art, New York; Nationalmuseum, Stockholm; Design Museum, London. **Honors:** First International Design Award, Japan Design Foundation, 1983 (with Sven-Eric Juhlin); Marianne och Sigvard Bernadottes Konstnärsfond, 1983; International Design Competition Prize, Japan Design Foundation, 1984 (with Sven-Eric Juhlin and Håkan Bergkvist); Bruno Mathsson Prize, Sweden, 1984; Swedish Design Excellence Award, 1988, and prize, 1991. **Address:** Ergonomi Design Gruppen AB, Box 140 21, Missionsvägen 24, S-161 14 Bromma, Sweden.

## Works

Double-wall tablewares, for AB Gustavsberg, 1969.
Shopping basket, for AB Gustavsberg, 1970.
Gripping Tongs, for AB Gustavsberg, 1971.
Handles and Grips project, for Swedish Institute for the Handicapped, 1973.
*Linie* tableware set, for AB Gustavsberg, 1974.
Kitchen knife and cutting-board, for AB Gustavsberg, 1974.
Pots and pans project, for STU Swedish National Board for Technical Development, 1977.
Eating and drinking implements project, for Folksam Research Foundation/STU Swedish National Board for Technical Development, produced by RFSU Rehab, 1980.
Gripping tongs project, for STU Swedish National Board for Technical Development, 1985.
*Fix* food preparation board, for STU Swedish National Board for Technical Development, produced by RFSU Rehab, 1985.
Cane for arthritics, for STU Swedish National Board for Technical Development, produced by RFSU Rehab, 1987.
Coffee- and teapot, for SAS Scandinavian Airlines System, 1988.
Knife for quadriplegics, for STU Swedish National Board for Technical Development, produced by RFSU Rehab, 1989.
Eating and drinking implements for multihandicapped children, for Swedish Institute for the Handicapped, produced by RFSU Rehab, 1989.
Electric stapling tacker, for Isaberg Ab, 1991.
System PH 1500, for Isaberg AB, 1993.
Toothbrushes for people with limited hand-arm function, for the Swedish Handicap Institute, 1993.

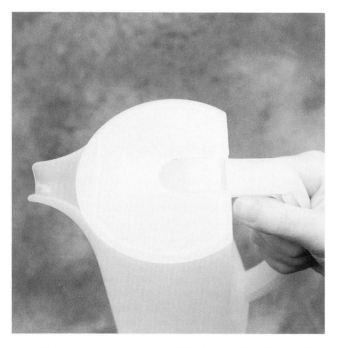

**Sven-Eric Juhlin: Juice jug for SAS airline, 1994. Photo: Mike Stott, Ergonomi Design AB**

Juice jug for the SAS airline, 1994.

Design and development of tools and equipment for personal hygiene, for RFSU Rehab, 1995.

Design of hand-tools, for Tupperware, 1995.

## Publications

**By JUHLIN: articles**—"Plast och miljö" in *Form* (Stockholm), no. 8, 1970; (with Maria Benktzon) "Redskap för händer" in *Form* (Stockholm), no. 10, 1973; (with Maria Benktzon) "What Can Design Contribute to the Human Society of the Near Future?" in *Design Quarterly* (Tokyo), no. 2, 1984.

**On JUHLIN: books**—*Konsthantverk, Konstindustri, Design 1875-1975* by Dag Widman, Stockholm, 1975; *Design Since 1945* edited by Kathryn Hiesinger and George Marcus, Philadelphia and London, 1983; *Contemporary Swedish Design,* exhibition catalogue by Monica Boman, Lennart Lindkvist, and others, Stockholm, 1983; *Design Source Book* by Penny Sparke and others, London, 1986; *New Design for Old,* London, 1986; *Faces of Swedish Design,* exhibition catalogue edited by Monica Boman, Stockholm, 1988; *Design Art,* exhibition catalogue, West Berlin, 1988; **articles**—"Världmästare i hjälpmedel för handikappade" in *Svenska Dagbladet* (Stockholm), 7 October 1983.

See BENKTZON, Maria

# JUNG, Dora (Elisabet)

Finnish textile designer

**Born:** Helsinki, 16 October 1906. **Education:** Studied textile design, Skola for Konstflit, Helsinki, 1932; study-travels in Scandinavia, 1934, England and France, 1937, 1950, and the United States, 1958. **Career:** Freelance textile designer, Helsinki, 1932-80; designed for the Tampella textile company and for churches and other public buildings. Instructor in design, Helsinki city schools, 1936-46. **Exhibitions:** Stockholm, 1948; Copenhagen, 1956; Helsinki, 1957, 1968, 1977; *D. Jung/K. Franck/B. Gardberg,* Göteborg, 1966; *Nordisk Industridesign,* Kunstindustrimuseet, Oslo, 1976; *Form und Struktur,* Österreichisches Museum für Angewandte Kunst, Vienna, 1980 (traveled to Nuremberg); *Scandinavian Modern Design 1880-1980,* Cooper Hewitt Museum, New York, 1982; *Design Since 1945,* Philadelphia Museum of Art, 1983. **Honors:** State Stipend for Design, Helsinki, 1934; Sverige Kulturforening Award, Stockholm, 1945, 1955; Grand Prize, Milan Triennale, 1951, 1954, 1959; Prince Eugene Medal, Stockholm, 1961; Cotil Prize, Copenhagen, 1962; Finnish State Design Prize, 1969; Svenska Folkskolans Vanner Culture Prize, Stockholm, 1970; Nordiska Craft and Design Prize, 1972; City of Helsinki Prize, 1972. Honorary Royal Academician, London, 1980. **Died:** Helsinki, 1980.

## Publications

**On JUNG: books**—*A Treasury of Scandinavian Design* edited by Erik Zahle, New York, 1961; *Modern Finnish Design* by Ulf Hard af Segerstad, London, 1969; *New Design in Weaving* by Donald J. Willcox, New York and London, 1970; *Finnish Design 1875-1975* by Timo Sarpaneva, Erik Bruun, and Erik Kruskopf, Helsinki, 1975; *Scandinavian Design: Objects of a Life Style* by Eileene Harrison Beer, New York and Toronto, 1975; *Scandinavian Modern Design 1880-1980* edited by David McFadden, New York, 1982; *Contemporary Textile Art: Scandinavia* by Charles S. Talley, Stockholm, 1982; *Design Since 1945* edited by Kathryn Hiesinger and George Marcus, Philadelphia and London, 1983; *The Conran Directory of Design* edited by Stephen Bayley, London, 1985.

## KAMALI, Norma

American fashion designer

**Born:** Norma Arraez, in New York City, in 1944. **Education:** Studied fashion illustration, at the Fashion Institute of Technology, New York, 1961-64. **Family:** Married Mohammed (Eddie) Houssein Kamali in 1967 (divorced, 1972). **Career:** Freelance fashion illustrator, New York, 1965-66; worked as an airlines reservation clerk, 1966-67; freelance fashion designer, and partner, with Eddie Kamali, in Kamali fashion imports and design shop on East 53rd Street, New York, 1968-74, and on Madison Avenue, New York, 1974-78; established OMO (On My Own) Norma Kamali store, and Norma Kamali Designs office, New York, from 1978; introduced ready-to-wear line, 1981; produced sportwear for Jones Apparel Group, 1981, children's sportswear for Empire Shield Company, 1982, Far East sportswear for Renown Incorporated of Japan, 1983, socks and tights for Camp Hosiery, 1983, headwear for Stetson hats, 1983, shoes, sneakers and bags for Vittorio Ricci, 1983-84, and belts for Raymon Ridless, 1985. **Exhibitions:** *Vanity Fair,* Metropolitan Museum of Art, New York, 1976. **Honors:** Coty American Fashion Critics' Award, 1981, Return Award, 1982, and Hall of Fame Award, 1983; Outstanding Designer Award, Council of Fashion Designers of America, 1983; Fashion Institute of Design and Merchandising Award, Los Angeles, 1984. **Address:** 11 West 56th Street, New York, New York 10019, U.S.A.

### Publications

**On KAMALI: books**—*Fairchild's Who's Who in Fashion* edited by Ann Stegemeyer, New York, 1980; *Fashion 2001* by Lucille Khornak, London, 1982; *The Collector's Book of Twentieth Century Fashion* by Frances Kennett, New York and London, 1983; *McDowell's Directory of Twentieth Century Fashion* by Colin McDowell, London, 1984; *The Encyclopaedia of Fashion from 1840 to the 1980s* by Georgina O'Hara, London, 1986.

\*   \*   \*

American-Lebanese Norma Kamali opened in New York in the 1960s, first with the help of her husband and, subsequently, on her own, calling her shop OMO (On My Own). She wanted ordinary women to be able to afford designer-quality clothes, although this was unusual in New York. As she said, "In Europe, fashion is treated as an art form. There's appreciation for the art rather than for the dollar. Here, it's big business with mass appeal. I am almost a displaced person in the fashion world here. Yet, it's worked. I'm earning a living and liking what I'm doing." When she launched her cheapest range in 1981 with nothing over $80, the queue of women was a mile long. She was

a pioneer in providing clothes to New Yorkers of a signature and a cut previously exclusive to salons.

Just as the nineteenth-century, English sportsman's blazer and grey flannels became fashionable wear from the 1920s, so Kamali has taken twentieth-century sportswear and turned that into street attire for women—now that looking sporty and healthy is no longer considered unfeminine. Taking old, military grey cotton fleece, she turned it into sweatshirts and jogging suits for the town. Through such designs, she has helped to alter the conservative attitude towards clothes found among Americans by encouraging individuality. So popular have her casual clothes become that she has been copied on an enormous scale by manufacturers in the United States and Europe. The quality of the fabric is not the same, nor the cut, but it is beyond the power of one designer to track down every imitation. Even the Parisian couturier Claude Montana has taken up Kamali's grey sweat shirts.

In addition to these loose garments, Kamali also creates a very slender range which she designs on the body. Her slinky gowns have the likes of Raquel Welch and Diana Ross after them, while her moulded swimsuits are considered daring in their sculptural sensuality. There is little doubt that Kamali is the most original designer in New York of the 1980s and 1990s. She displays the same total devotion to her work as other women couturieres, scorning the press and high society, for nothing must be allowed to interfere with the creation.

—Diana de Marly

## KAMEKURA, Yusaku

Japanese graphic designer

**Born:** Yoshidamachi, Nishi-Kambara, Niigata Prefecture, 6 April 1915. **Education:** Educated at Nippon University high school, Tokyo, 1928-33; studied constructivist theory under Renshichiro Kawakita, at the Institute of New Architecture and Industrial Arts, Tokyo, 1935-37. **Career:** Designer, 1937-40, and chief of the art department, 1940-60, Nippon Kobo (later re-named International Industrial Arts Information Company), Tokyo; co-founder and managing director, Nippon Design Center, Tokyo, 1960-62; freelance designer, establishing Kamekura Design Institute, Tokyo, from 1962; director, LD Yamagiwa Laboratory, Tokyo, from 1970; art director, *Nippon* magazine from 1937, and *Commerce Japan* magazine, from 1949; editor-in-chief, *Kaupapu* magazine, from 1939; editorial staff member, *Collection of Commercial Designs* series, for the Evening Star Company, Tokyo, from 1951, and *Outline of Design* series, for David Publishing, Tokyo, from 1954. Founder-member, Japan Advertising Art Club, Tokyo, 1951-70. **Exhibitions:** Chuokoron-sha Publishing House, Tokyo, 1953; Museum

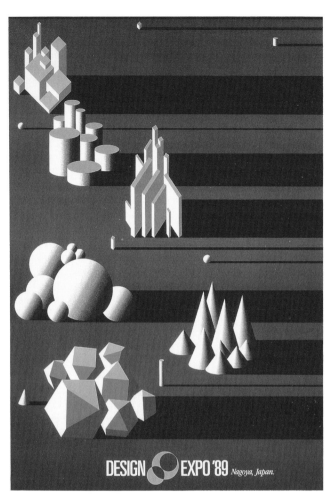

**Yusaku Kamekura: Official poster for *Design Expo '89*, Nagoya, 1987**

of Modern Art, Kamakura, 1953; *Graphic 55,* Tokyo, 1955 (travelled to Paris); *AGI International Exhibition,* Paris, 1955, London 1956, and Lausanne, 1957; Society of Typographic Arts, Chicago, 1956; *Kamekura: Retrospective Exhibition,* Tokyo, 1971; *Kamekura: Posters for Nikon,* Matsuya Department Store, Tokyo, 1982; *Designs by Yusaku Kamekura,* Matsuya Department Store, Tokyo, 1983; *Japon des Avant-Gardes,* Centre Georges Pompidou, Paris, 1986; *Works by Yusaku Kamekura,* Niigata, 1987, and Kirin Palace, Osaka, 1988; *Yusaku Kamekura Exhibition,* Tokyo and Osaka, 1994. **Collections:** Museum of Modern Art, New York; Stedelijk Museum, Amsterdam. **Honors:** Dentsu Advertising Award, 1955, 1956, 1961; Mainichi Design Award, 1955, 1957, 1963, 1994; Japan Advertising Club Award, 1956, 1963; Tokyo Art Directors Club Award, 1957, 1958, 1959, 1960, 1961, 1962, 1963, 1964, 1965, 1966, 1967, 1968, 1969, 1972, 1983; Grand Prize, Japanese Ministry of Education, 1961; Graphics Awards, Warsaw Poster Biennale, 1966, 1968, 1988; Kodansha Culture Prize, 1970; Brazilian Coffee Institute Poster Prize, 1970; Japan Sign Design Association Award, 1972, 1973, 1975, 1976, 1982; Japanese Ministry of Trade and Industry Prize, 1975, 1981; Brno Graphics Biennale Award, 1976, 1980, 1984; Gold Award of Merit, Japanese Red Cross Society, 1976; Asahi Prize, 1984; Lahti Poster Biennale Award, 1985; Japanese Order of the Sacred Treasure,

Tokyo, 1985; International Cultural Design Prize, Tokyo, 1986; International Graphic Design Prize, Yugoslavia, 1987; named Person of Cultural Merits, 1991; 6th International Design Award, Osaka, 1993; named to Hall of Fame, Art Directors Clubs of New York, Tokyo, 1994; honorary doctorate, Academy of Fine Arts, Warsaw, 1994. **Address:** Kamekura Design Office, Recruit Building, 8-4-17 Ginza, Chuo-ku, Tokyo 104, Japan.

**Works**

Poster series, for Nippon Kogaku, 1955.
*Peaceful Uses of Atomic Energy* poster, 1956.
Neon sign, for Meiji Confectionery Company, Tokyo, 1956.
Poster series, for Nikon Camera Company, from 1957.
Official poster, for the Tokyo Olympics, 1963.
Poster series, for Kokudokeikaju Ski Resort, 1969.
Signage and graphics, for the arcade of Matsuya Department Store, Tokyo, 1972.
*Performance Arts of Japan* poster, for the University of California at Los Angeles, 1981.
*Hiroshima Appeals '83* poster, 1983.
Cover design, for *Graphis,* no. 230, Zurich, 1984.
Logotype symbol, for Nippon Telephone and Telegraph Corporation, 1985.
Official poster of *Design Expo '89,* Nagoya, for the World Design Exposition Association, 1988.
*Europalia 89 Japan* poster, Belgium, 1989.
Poster for the *Bicenterary of the French Revolution,* France, 1990.
*Communication & Print* poster, 1991.
*I'm here* poster series, 1992-94.
*Mainichi Newspaper of Design* poster, 1993.

**Publications**

**By KAMEKURA: books**—(with others) *Graphic Design,* Tokyo, 1954, 1957; *Photo Design,* Tokyo, 1956; (editor) *Trademarks of the World,* Tokyo and New York, 1956; *Paul Rand,* Tokyo and New York, 1959; (editor) *Trademarks and Symbols of the World,* Tokyo and New York, 1965; (with Teiji Ito and Takeji Iwamiya) *Japanese Gardens,* Tokyo, 1971, New Haven, 1972; *Yusaku Kamekura: Graphic Works,* Tokyo and New York, 1971; *Takeoff/Landing,* compiler, Tokyo, 1972; (with Sofu Teshigahara and Ken Domon) *Three Men, Three Minds,* Tokyo, 1977; (editor) *The Minga of the Lee Dynasty,* Tokyo, 1982; *The Work of Yusaku Kamekura,* Tokyo, 1983; *Kyokusen to Chokusen no Uchu,* Tokyo, 1983; *Kamekura Yusaku no chokugenhiko,* Tokyo, 1991.

**On KAMEKURA: books**—*The New Graphic Design* by Karl Gerstner and Markus Kutter, Teufen and London, 1959; *Packaging: An International Survey of Package Design* edited by Walter Herdeg, Zurich, 1961; *Design Coordination and Corporate Image* by F. H. K. Henrion and Alan Parkin, London and New York, 1967; *An International Survey of Packaging* by Wim Crouwel and Kurt Weidemann, London, 1968; *History of the Poster* by Josef and Shizuko Muller-Brockmann, Zurich, 1971; *The Graphic Design of Yusaku Kamekura* by Masaru Katsumie, Tokyo and New York, 1973; *Who's Who in Graphic Art* edited by Walter Amstutz, Dubendorf, 1982; *A History of Graphic Design* by Philip B. Meggs, New York and London, 1983.

*       *       *

Yusaka Kamekura belongs to a generation which first introduced the Japanese graphic message to international circulation, placing it in the ranks of genuine art. The generation abounded in talents and outstanding individualities, such as Ikko Tanaka, Takashi Kono, Kazumasa Nagai, and Makoto Nakamura. It is to them that credit goes for the interesting and promising symbiosis of Eastern and Western culture in the visual mass media, to this day resulting in an intense exchange of material and intellectual goods. Though the coming together and interpenetration of the East and the West had its "prehistory" and latent stage, the process accelerated after World War II, a period in which graphic design performed the function of ambassador. It is no overstatement to say that, just as the Japanese woodcut ukyi-oe was the harbinger of a peculiar, different way of modelling the world to the Europeans at the close of the 19th century, the appearance of Kamekura's first works in the west in the late 1950s heralded the onset of an original school of graphic design. Graphic design, which had been the domain of the European spirit and the product of a long aesthetic evolution starting with Art Nouveau, had to accept the historical challenge.

Kamekura has certainly been the key figure in the competition going on before our eyes. Critics have pointed out the influence that Cassandre and the Bauhaus had on him at the outset of his career. Kamekura admits, with quite considerable pride, that this was really the case with him. This influence in turn reflects on his aesthetic leanings and priorities. At times, concepts originating in Esprit Nouveau, Purism, Constructivism, and Functionalism may also be identified in his work. This is probably the source of his evident disinclination for ornamental or disintegrated forms in favor of order based on unchanging, apparently natural canons of harmony. He is also consistent in discarding illusive spatiality on the plane and anecdotal interpretations of the subject, which precludes a banal illustrative approach. From the heritage of the post-Cubist avant-garde, Kamekura has assimilated certain techniques and formal devices, for instance the elaboration of the surface, masses, textures, and colour arrangements. His favorite lay-outs are based on crisp, compact forms, concentric or radial, or on full or open structures that may be reduced to geometric masses. He also finds delight in asymmetric compositions featuring diagonals, crossings, and kinetic transformations, in optical illusions quickening perception. In this, he is like a magician conjuring up fantastic beings. Like the Constructivists, Kamekura has reduced his palette to several basic colors, but his favorite colour is black.

The "European" quality of Kamekura's work remains in harmony with the Japanese roots of his vision and style. The Japanese quality is omnipresent in his posters, books, covers, and typography, and especially in his trademarks. His unforgettable, exquisitely beautiful signs and symbols (for example, *Expo '75*, 1972; *ICSID '73*, 1972, *Design Year 1973*, East-West Culture Communication Association, 1960) make one think of the old Japanese tradition of family crests. The linking factor of all his works is their linear quality, deeply rooted in old and contemporary Japanese art. We may speak of the wealth and culture of lines in his work: they are expressive, symbolic, and distinct. The lines themselves, as well as their complexes, bands, streams, and linear accents are orchestrated in an intricate way.

From my meetings with Kamekura in Tokyo and in Warsaw, where he was awarded the main prize at the International Poster Biennale in 1971, I remember the artist as one guided by ethical motives in his professional life. He has written: "No matter how much money I am offered, I will not do work that I am not convinced is right. This means that I refuse to do any work for political parties or religious groups, because I find that I usually cannot agree with their ideals and purposes.... I simply cannot get an inspiration to do work that does not seem worthwhile or of interest to me...."

—Szymon Bojko

# KANTOR, Tadeusz
Polish painter, graphic artist, and stage designer

**Born:** Wielopole, 16 March 1915. **Education:** Studied at the Academy of Fine Arts, Kraków, 1936-39. **Military Service:** Served in the Polish Resistance, directing underground theatre, Kraków, 1940-44. **Family:** Married Maria Stangret in 1962. **Career:** Stage designer, in Kraków, Warsaw, and throughout Poland, 1944-55; also independent painter and graphic artist, in Kraków and Warsaw, from 1948; founder and director, Cricot 2 Theatre, Kraków, from 1955. Nominated professor, Academy of Fine Arts, Kraków, 1949, 1968; visiting professor, Academy of Fine Arts, Hamburg, 1961. **Exhibitions:** Galerie Po Prostu, Warsaw, 1956; Galerie Krzystofory, Kraków, 1957, 1963, 1967, 1968; Muzeum Miejskie, Lublin, 1958; Kunsthalle, Dusseldorf, 1959; Galeria Foksal, Warsaw, 1965, 1967, 1968, 1970, 1971, 1973; Kunsthalle, Baden-Baden, 1966; Kunsthalle, Nuremberg, 1968; Musée des Arts Décoratifs, Lausanne, 1971; Henie-Onstad Kunstsenter, Oslo, 1971, 1976; Muzeum Sztuki, Lodz, 1975; Kulturhuset, Stockholm, 1975; Whitechapel Art Gallery, London, 1976; Riverside Studios, London, 1976, 1982. **Collections:** Muzeum Sztuki, Lodz. **Honors:** Painting Prize, Sao Paulo Bienal, 1969; Premio Roma Medal, Rome, 1969; Tadeusz Boy-Zelenski Theatre Prize, Warsaw, 1977; Mayor's Medal, Rome, 1978; Cyprian Norwid Art Critic's Prize, Warsaw, 1978; Goethe Foundation Rembrandt Prize, 1978; Mayor's Medal, Milan, 1979; Mayor's Medal, Florence, 1980; City of Gdansk Medal, 1980. **Addresses:** Theatre Cricot 2 (Cricoteca), Kanonisza Street 5, Kraków, Poland; Elblaska Street 6/11, Kraków, Poland.

## Works

Major productions and happenings include—*Sepia,* Galeria Krzystofory, Kraków, 1956; *The Cuttlefish,* Galeria Krzystofory, 1956; *In a Small House,* Galeria Krzystofory, 1961; *The Madman and the Nun,* Galeria Krzystofory, 1963; *Cricotage,* Galeria Foksal, Warsaw, 1965; *Line of Division,* Galeria S.H.S., Kraków, 1966; *The Waterhen,* Galeria Krzystofory, 1967; *Panoramic Seashore Happening,* Osieki, Baltic Seashore, 1967; *The Anatomy Lesson: After Rembrandt,* Kunsthalle, Nuremberg, 1968; *Conference with Rhinoceros,* Kunsthalle, Nuremberg, 1968; *The Cobblers,* Malakoff Theatre, Paris, 1972; *Lovelies and Dowdies,* Galeria Krzystofory, 1973; *The Dead Class,* Galeria Krzystofory, 1975; *Ou Sont les Neiges d'Antan,* Rome, 1978; *Wielopole, Wielopole,* Florence, 1980.

## Publications

**By KANTOR: books**—*Emballages,* Warsaw, 1976; *La Théâtre de la Morte,* Paris, 1978; *La Classa Morta,* with photos by Maurizio Buscarina, Milan, 1981; *Wielopole, Wielopole,* Milan, 1981.

**On KANTOR: books**—*Happening and Fluxus,* compiled by Hanns Sohm, Cologne, 1970; *Tadeusz Kantor: Emballages,* exhibition catalogue with texts by Wieslaw Borowski and Ryszard Stanislawski, Lodz, 1975; *Tadeusz Kantor: Emballages 1960-1976,* exhibition catalogue by Ryszard Stanislawski, London, 1976; *Contemporary Polish Theatre* by Witold Filler, Warsaw, 1977; *Tadeusz Kantor* by Wieslaw Borowski, Warsaw, 1982.

*       *       *

The Renaissance artist is almost a forbidden species in our time. Everyone narrows his activities in the hope of mastering some single act of creativity. But not Tadeusz Kantor.

For more than forty years, he has struggled at an amazingly wide range of the arts. Always a front-runner on untested ground, for many years he was misjudged and sometimes ridiculed.

This sketch must focus on Kantor's stage design, but it is impossible to separate this subject from the full panorama of Kantor's "life-theatre." Trained as a painter in the prewar Kraków Academy, but unable to practice his art, Kantor began experiments with the theatre—as he calls it, "closet-theatre"—in a mountain hide-out. After the war, despite Stalinist social-realism governing Polish art during the 1950s, Kantor maintained a rare position: he was one of a very few who never compromised his ideas. He tried some café theatre, he continued to paint. Having minimal contact with the world beyond the Iron Curtain and painting in his own style, to everyone's surprise he was nevertheless in tune with current European styles.

But his independence didn't pay well, even after 1956, when Poland opened herself to the West. Kantor was freer to experiment, but mere abstract painting was not his joy. The early 1960s brought a new series of paintings, dramatic compositions, partially ready-made. With objects incorporated, they suggested stage sets. Simultaneously, theatrical ideas flourished. A little, cavernous café in the old town of Kraków, the headquarters of the unofficial "Kraków Group" of painters (lead by Kantor, of course), served as a theatre. It had no stage and only a few rows of wood chairs for the public, but it was enough. Here, he first gave his attention to the works of the great Polish playwright Stanislaw Ignacy Witkiewicz, then an almost forgotten avant-garde figure from prewar Poland.

In the early 1970s, Kantor reached new frontiers. His adaptations of Witkiewicz's works, extremely personal as they were, limited his energy and self-realization. Now, for the first time, he created his own world, created all elements by himself. Only the music was not written by him but carefully selected and mixed to serve as Kantor's choice for Kantor's idea.

Two creations (*Dead Class,* 1975, and *Wielopole, Wielopole,* 1979) are truly masterpieces of Kantor's lifelong struggle. They put him at the very top of world theatrical achievements—past and present.

This sophisticated thinker, in touch with history, skillfully using the variety of actors' methods, this formidable director, "conducting" his team in every performance, this amazing creator of set, light, and music, recreates scenes from his life (our own as well) and forces us into deep reflection about our basic existence. The artist builds his performances with mixtures of touching scenes in which the atmosphere is tense with music, light, formidable actors playing with life-size puppets, and sometimes found objects—all these elements are carefully orchestrated to create the world according to Tadeusz Kantor.

His mastery is most obvious when he freezes moments that are fast, loud, and full of running people, dust, and the scream of old

Austrian military band music, so the spectator is struck by the beauty, strange and dramatic, of what seems to be an old photograph derived from a remote corner of everybody's mind. The antique, graying, sepia picture of man's fate, joy, and death, of the paranoia of switching borders, of religious ceremonies, of repeating holocausts, of births, weddings, sufferings—this picture of our ancestors and ourselves has an overwhelming effect. The whole spectacle in each case is built around a few painting-like scenes arranged carefully to the smallest detail, so that they call to mind the fading memory of childhood, the failure of our lives, Kantor's own autobiography—a Galician town with Poles and Jews, Catholic priests and rabbis, and armies, the rolling armies, every time a different color. Only soldiers remain the same—the father, the brothers, and you, too, maybe.

Kantor has achieved the dream of every theatrically oriented artist. He is able to catalyze all the aspects of visual spectacle into the very powerful and universal story of humanity. When you are watching his theatre, you are overwhelmed by his three-dimensional, live, monochromatic portraits of the human condition. They are as tragic and beautiful as the condition of all of us.

—Jan Sawka

# KAPITZKI, Herbert W.
## German graphic and industrial designer

**Born:** Danzig (now Gdansk, Poland), 24 February 1925. **Education:** Studied at the Hochschule für Bildende Kunste, Hamburg, 1946; Arbeitsgruppe für Bildende Künste, Bernstein, 1947-49; under Willi Baumeister, at the Akademie für Bildende Künste, Stuttgart, 1949-53. **Military Service:** Served in the German Army, 1940-43; prisoner of war, 1943-45. **Family:** Married Line Pinnow in 1980; children: Boris and Ivo. **Career:** Exhibition designer, for the Landesgewerbeamt Baden-Württemberg, Stuttgart, 1955-65; freelance designer, West Berlin, from 1965; layout and installation design coordinator, for the Historisches Museum, Frankfurt, 1970-74, and for Firma Schering AG, West Berlin, 1974-78. Docent, Hochschule für Gestaltung, Ulm, 1964-68; professor of visual communications, Hochschule der Künste, West Berlin, from 1970. **Exhibitions:** *Kunst in Baden-Württemberg,* Kunsthalle, Baden-Baden, 1962; *Design: Herbert W. Kapitzki,* Hochschule für Bildende Künste, Hamburg, 1965; Landesgewerbeamt Baden-Württemberg, Stuttgart, 1965; Kunstschule, Offenbach, 1965; National Museum, Helsinki, 1965; *107 Grafici dell'AGI,* Castello Sforzesco, Milan, 1974 (travelled to Venice); *Korper/Zeichen/Bilder,* Galerie Behr, Stuttgart, 1980; *Konstruktive Tendenzen, Prinzip Reihe,* Galerie unterm Turm, Stuttgart, 1987; Deutsches Plakatmuseum, Essen, 1988; Galerie im Burgenlandzentrum, Stuttgart, 1989; *Plakate,* Hochschule der Künste, West Berlin, 1989. **Collections:** Staatliche Museen, Stuttgart; Deutsches Plakatmuseum, Essen; Museum of Modern Art, New York. **Address:** Nymphenburger Strasse 11A, 1000 Berlin 62, Germany.

**Works**

*Dokumentation der Grafik* exhibition layouts, for the Landesgewerbeamt Baden-Württemberg, Stuttgart, 1961.

*Anton Stankowski* exhibition layouts, for the Landesgewerbeamt Baden-Württemberg, Stuttgart, 1962.
*Internationale Verpackungsaussellung* exhibition layouts, for the Landesgewerbeamt Baden-Württemberg, Stuttgart, 1965.
German pavilion layouts, at *Expo 67,* Montreal, 1967.
Installation layouts, for the Historisches Museum, Frankfurt, 1970-74.
Signage systems, for the Verband Deutscher Flughafen, West Berlin, 1972.
Building layouts and interiors, for Firma Schering AG, West Berlin, 1974-78.
Signage system, for the IDZ International Design Centre, West Berlin, 1976.
Signage system, for the Senat Building, West Berlin, 1980.
Signage and graphics, for the Ausstellungs Messe Kongress GmbH, West Berlin, 1988-89.
Signage and graphic identity, for Galerie und Edition Schlichtenmaier, Datzingen, 1989.

**Publications**

**By KAPITZKI: books**—*Programmiertes Gestalten,* Karlsruhe, 1980; *Proportionen,* West Berlin, 1981.

**On KAPITZKI: books**—*An International Survey of Press Advertising* by Kurt Weidemann, Stutgart and London, 1966; *German Advertising Art* edited by Eberhard Holscher, Munich, 1967; *Design with Type* by Carl Dair, London and Toronto, 1967; *Modern Graphics* by Keith Murgatroyd, London, 1969; *107 Grafici dell'AGI,* with texts by Renzo Zorzi and Franco Grignani, Venice, 1974; *Form und Kommunikation* by Walter Diethelm, Basel, 1977; *Visual Transformation* by Walter Diethelm, Basel, 1982; *Who's Who in Graphic Art* edited by Walter Amstutz, Dubendorf, 1982.

*

The design praxis that I have followed for three decades has always been determined by the realization that for every design project, a high degree of creativity to discover new relationships must be brought into play. Priority is given not to the arrangement of known elements but to the development of new areas of perception. From this point of view, a designer, whether he is active in the two- or in the three-dimensional field, must always examine his general design capabilities.

There is no doubt that in the long run this becomes increasingly difficult. In the visually experienced world of today, more and more pictures are produced and used. As the various broadcasting media in our technical world become increasingly complex, consumers demand more and more innovative visualizations. As a university teacher, I have become particularly aware in recent years that this also leads to other problems in society. It is clear that the greater the demands put on visual materials, the lower the creative (artistic-aesthetic) level tends to become. There are many reasons for this, among which ignorance of cultural responsibility of the people concerned, especially consumers, takes a prominent place. In most cases, design is treated purely as an economic factor. It is ignored that design is not only manipulation of form but also an expression of contents, even a manifestation of culture. However, our world of form and image is receiving more attention as a cultural factor than ever before.

In my own design, I try to develop images that appear rational on the basis of geometrically arranged factors but that nevertheless exhibit emotional levels of interpretation. The constructive design that develops from generative structures can provide many proportional relationships which can be employed for various semantic problems and which then can also be seen as harmonic aesthetic constellations.

—Herbert W. Kapitzki

\* \* \*

Herbert Kapitzki's most important contributions have been the development of information communication and the use of comprehensive planning principles in solving graphic design problems.

Early in his career, from 1956 to 1964, Kapitzki designed a series of posters and numerous exhibitions for the Stuttgart Trade and Industry Office. Here, he often innovated in the translation of the rational vocabulary of Op and programmed art into graphics. Later in the 1960s, his engagement at the Hochschule für Gestaltung in Ulm proved to be decisive to his further development in both the theoretical and practical spheres. During his tenure there, he developed the Baden-Baden South West Radio image, which demonstrated his strength in the design of a flexible yet constructive system. In 1969, the year after the Hochschule closed, he designed a new logotype for the Bund Deutscher Graphic Designer.

From the beginning of Kapitzki's teaching activity in Berlin in 1970, his emphasis has been on "visual research." He introduced video into the curriculum and extended the traditional framework of graphic design to embrace the field of visual communication. During these same years, outstanding projects included his re-design of the Frankfurt historical museum in 1971 and his comprehensive design scheme for Schering AG in Berlin. His achievement at the museum pointed the way for many others, which have since adopted his communication system. Conceiving of an exhibition as an "information-bank," he enriched it with audiovisual media. Placards and reproductions provided comprehensive information, and the individual areas were coded by colour and symbol. For Schering, he not only designed a communication system, but determined also the interior decor and graphic image of the firm.

—M. Droste

# KAPR, Albert
German book and type designer

**Born:** Stuttgart, 20 July 1918. **Education:** Appreticed as a compositor to Stahle und Friedel, Stuttgart, 1933-35, 1937-38; studied typography and book design under Ernst Schneidler, at the Akademie fur Bildende Künste, Stuttgart, 1938-40, 1945-48. **Military Service:** Served in the German Army, 1940-45. **Family:** Married Fanny Schmid in 1947, children: Johannes and Klaus. **Career:** Independent calligrapher, type, and book designer, from 1948; artistic director, Typoart typefoundry, Dresden, 1964-77. Assistant lecturer in typography, Technische Hochschule, Stuttgart, 1947-48; docent, Hochschule für Baukunst und Bildende Künste, Weimar, 1948-51; professor, 1951-56, head of the Institut für Buchkunst, 1951-78, and rector, 1959, 1966-73, Hochschule für Grafik und

**Albert Kapr: Book cover design for** *Schrift-und Buchkunst,* **1982**

Buchkunst, Leipzig. **Exhibitions:** *International Book Design Exhibition,* London 1957, Leipzig, 1959, 1965, 1971, 1977, 1982; *Wort und Werk,* Leipzig, 1968, 1977; Pushkin Museum, Moscow, 1976; National Museum, Prague, 1978. **Collections:** Deutsche Bucherei, Leipzig; Klingspor Museum, Offenbach. **Honors:** DDR Type Design Prize, Berlin, 1958; DDR National Prize, 1961; Gutenberg Prize, Leipzig, 1961; has also received more than 50 DDR Book of the Year Awards; honorary doctorate, Akademie für Bildende Künste, Stuttgart, 1974. **Died:** 31 March 1995.

**Works**

Faust-Antiqua typeface, for Typoart Foundry, Dresden, 1958.
Leipziger Antiqua typeface, for Typoart Foundry, Dresden, 1959.
*Faust I* and *Faust II* (Goethe) book designs, for Verlag der Kunst, Dresden, 1961.
Clarendon Neutra typeface, for Typoart Foundry, Dresden, 1965.
*Totentanz von Basel* (Grieshaber) book design, for Verlag der Kunst, Dresden, 1966.
Prillwitz-Antiqua typeface, for Typoart Foundry, Dresden, 1971.
*Marx-Engels Gesamtausgabe* book design, for Dietz Verlag, East Berlin, from 1972.
Garamond-Russisch typeface, for Typoart Foundry, Dresden, 1975.

**Publications**

**By KAPR: books (author and designer)**—*Deutsche Schriftkunst,* Dresden, 1955, 1965; *Johann Neudörffer: Der grosse Schreibmeister der deutschen Renaissance,* Leipzig, 1956: *Fundament zum rechten Schreiben,* Leipzig, 1958; *Buchgestaltung,* Dresden, 1963; *Schriftkunst: Geschichte, Anatomie und Schönheit der lateinischen Buchstaben,* Dresden, 1971, 1976, 1983; *Hundertundein Satze zur Buchgestaltung,* Leipzig, 1973, 1976; (with Hans Fischer) *Typoart-Typenkunst,* Leipzig, 1973; (with Walter Schiller) *Gestaltung und Funktion der Typografie,* Leipzig, 1977, 1980, 1983; *Johannes Gutenberg,* Leipzig, 1977; *Ästhetik der Schriftkunst,* Leipzig, 1979; *Buchkunst der Gegenwart: Thesen und Marginalien,* Leipzig, 1979; *Schrift-und Buchkunst,* Leipzig, 1982; *Stationen der Buchkunst,* Leipzig, 1984.

**On KAPR: books**—*Who's Who in Graphic Art,* edited by Walter Amstutz, Zurich, 1962, Dubendorf, 1982; *The Art of Written Forms* by Donald M. Anderson, New York, 1969; *Gebrauchsgraphik in der DDR* by Helmut Rademacher, Dresden, 1975; *Albert Kapr, Fraktur: Form und geschichte der gebrochenen schriften,* Mainz, 1993.

\*

Ever since my youth, I have felt myself drawn to type and book design. My first activity for the press consisted of an illegal pamphlet, which was directed against Hitler's war preparations.

I have Professor Ernst Schneidler—who headed the chair for typography and commercial art at the Akademie für Bildende Künste in Stuttgart—to thank for my artistic training.

During my more than thirty years of work in Leipzig, I have seen as my primary purpose to promote the good tradition of a center of publishing as well as to educate a particular breed of excellent book and type designer. The typeface, as an important element of every book, must even in its mature form become more highly developed for still better readability and expression of modern times. Computers, now used in the development of type and in type manufacture, must not be allowed to become dictators of the technocrats and media concerns. The new technological advances in the production of books and journals must be governed by the needs of mankind, as well as by aesthetic sensibilities, and so governed that the moral and social progress of the culture is not hindered, but rather, advanced. Books earn more material support than the bomb, and require more ingenuity than advertisements for consumer goods and merchandise. Books, as a form and symbol of human culture, its technical and aesthetic quality, must be defended and be kept alive by creativity and intelligence.

—Albert Kapr

# KARAN, Donna/DELL'OLIO, Louis
American fashion designers

Donna Karan: **Born:** Donna Faske in Forest Hills, New York, 2 October 1948. **Education:** Studied at Parsons School of Design, New York. **Family:** Married the menswear manufacturer Mark Karan; daughter: Gabrielle; married Stephen Weiss in 1977. **Career:** Assistant designer, Anne Klein and Company, and Addenda Company, New York, 1966-68; designer, 1968-71, associate designer, 1971-74, and director of design in association with Louis Dell'Olio, 1974-84, Anne Klein and Company, New York; launched Anne Klein II diffusion line, 1982. Designer, Donna Karan New York (DKNY), from 1985; added swimwear line, 1986; hosiery collection, 1987; DKNY bridge line, 1988; DKNY menswear collection, 1991; founded Donna Karan Beauty Company, fragrance and cosmetic division, New York, 1992; lingerie, and children's line, DKNY Kids, from 1992.

Louis Dell'Olio: **Born:** New York City, 23 July 1948. **Education:** Studied at Parsons School of Design, New York, 1966-69; Normal Norell Scholarship, 1968. **Career:** Assistant to designer Dominic Rompelio, at Teal Traina, New York, 1969-71; chief designer, for the Georgini division of Originals, New York, 1971-74; director of design in association with Donna Karan, at Anne Klein and Company, New York, from 1974. **Member:** Fashion Designers of America. **Honors:** Coty Awards, New York, 1977, 1981, 1984, 1985; Fashion Footwear Association of New York Award, 1988; Council of Fashion Designers of America Award, 1985, 1986, 1990, 1992; Woolmark Award, 1992. Honorary Degree, Bachelor of Fine Arts, Parsons School of Design, 1987. **Address:** 55O Seventh Avenue, New York, New York 10018, USA.

## Publications

On KARAN: books—*The World of Fashion: People, Places, Resources* by Eleanor Lambert, New York and London, 1976; *Cheap Chic Update* by Caterine Millinaire and Carol Troy, New York, 1978; *The Fashion Makers* by Bernadine Morris, New York, 1978; *Fairchild's Who's Who in Fashion* edited by Ann Stegemeyer, New York, 1980; *Fashion 2001* by Lucille Khornak, London, 1982; *The Collector's Book of Twentieth Century Fashion* by Frances Kennett, London and New York, 1983; *McDowell's Directory of Twentieth Century Fashion* by Colin McDowell, London, 1984; *Fashion: The Inside Story* by Barbaralee Diamonstein, New York, 1985; *The Encyclopedia of Fashion from 1840 to the 1980s* by Georgina Howell, London, 1986; *W, The Designing Life* edited by Lois Perschetz, New York, 1987; *The Fashion Conspiracy* by Nicholas Coleridge, London, 1988; *Women of Fashion: Twentieth-Century Designers* by Valerie Steele, New York, 1991; **articles**—"The Label Is Anne Klein, but the Name that Keeps It Going Is Donna Karan" by L. Wahlfert-Wihlborg in *People Weekly* (Chicago), 29 March 1982; "Cue: Designing Women—Donna Karan" in *Vogue* (London), September 1985; "The Making of New York Fashion" by Pedrix in *Connoisseur* (New York), February 1986; "How a Fashion Star Is Born" by Carrie Donovan in the *New York Times Magazine,* 4 May 1986; "Interview: Donna Karan" by Vivian Infantino in *Footwear News Magazine* (London), July 1986; "In Conversation: Donna Karan and Joan Burstein..." by Carolyn Gottfried in *Vogue* (London), October 1986; "Seventh Avenue Sweetheart" in *Fashion Weekly* (London), 5 May 1987; "Designing Women" by Liz Jobey in *Vogue* (London), July 1987; "Action Packed" by Ann Chubb in *Country Life* (London), 12 May 1988; "New Working Class" by Lisa Lebowitz and Patrick Pacheco in *Harper's Bazaar* (New York), March 1989; "Prima Donna" by Stephanie Mansfield in *Vogue* (New York), August 1989; "The New Queen of New York" by Jennet Conant in *Manhattan, inc.* (New York), October 1989; "Donna è Mobile" in *The Sunday Times Magazine* (London), 4

March 1990; "Donna Karan" by Ann Chubb in *Options* (London), August 1990; "Donna Karan" in *Current Biography* (New York), August 1990; "Designing Woman" by Katherine Weisman in *Forbes* (New York), 1 October 1990; "Donna Karan: USA Today" by Maggie Alderson in *Elle* (New York), October 1990; "Putting on the Style" by Georgina Howell in *The Sunday Times Magazine* (London), 7 April 1991; "Donna's Man" by Kimberly Cihlar in the *Daily News Record* (New York), 12 April 1991; "The Empress's New Clothes" by Randall Mesdon in *Esquire* (New York), September 1991; "Donna Karan: Talking Bridge" by Constance C. R. White in *Women's Wear Daily* (New York), 11 September 1991; "DKNY: A Home of Its Own" by Constance C. R. White in *Women's Wear Daily* (New York), 12 February 1992; "Karan Fashions a Fragrance" by Pete Born in *Women's Wear Daily* (New York), 1 May 1992; "Donna's Prime Time" by Georgina Howell in *Vogue* (New York), August 1992; "DKNY Kids the Real" by Adrienne Weinfeld-Berg in *Earnshaws,* October 1992; "Prima Donna" by June Ducas in *Women's Journal* (London), November 1992; "Queen D." by Sally Brampton in *Vogue* (London), December 1992; "Donna Inc." by Barbara Rudolph in *Time* (New York), 21 December 1992; "The Power Suit Chills Out" by Amy M. Spindler in the *New York Times,* 29 July 1993; "Partners at Odds, Donna Karan to Go Public" by Allen R. Myerson in the *New York Times,* 14 August 1993; "Piety on Parade: Fashion Seeks Inspiration" by Amy M. Spindler in the *New York Times,* 5 September 1993; "Donna Karan Crosses the Atlantic" by Bronwyn Cosgrave in *Élan* magazine of *The European* (London), 12-14 August 1994; "The Mega Mom-and-Pop Ship" by Arthur Lubow in *The New Yorker* (New York), 7 November 1994; "Slip-sliding to a Close: Donna Karan" by Kathleen Beckett in the *New York Post,* 5 November 1994; "Klein and Karan: Clothes that Do the Job" by Amy M. Spindler in the *New York Times,* 5 November 1994; "New York: Donna's Underworld" in *Women's Wear Daily* (New York), 7 November 1994; "Luxurious Armor by Karan, Klein, Mizrahi" by Amy M. Spindler in the *New York Times,* 8 April 1995; "Donna Krishna" in *Women's Wear Daily* (New York), 10 April 1995.

\*       \*       \*

The clothes created by Donna Karan and Louis Dell'Olio lasted not just for a season but for years. Like Anne Klein herself, with whom Karan was co-designer between 1971 and 1974, they did not believe in change for its own sake. While change is necessary, it occurs as a logical and gradual development in their work.

Karan and Dell'Olio succeeded in making Anne Klein one of the top names in American ready-to-wear, along with Calvin Klein, Ralph Lauren, and Perry Ellis, by creating clothes for real people. It is not only the lines themselves, but also the versatility of their collections and the quality of the fabrics, which give their garments a style that is more than mere short-lived fashion. Particularly concerned with fabrics for their own sake, they use them to provide the inspiration for the shape of a garment. By using soft suedes, crepe, and silks, they have transformed casual wear into something soft and sophisticated. The importance of the fabric is made evident by Takihyo's translations of them. Here, a different fabric can change the look, even though the style of Anne Klein still comes through.

Karan and Dell'Olio were in touch with their times but believed in quality and longevity in fashion. In 1982, after launching the diffusion line, Anne Klein II, Donna Karan decided to form her own company. In 1985 she launched the first Donna Karan collection.

**Donna Karan:** Neon pink wool velour short contour turtleneck jacket with black stretch wool twill short banded
contour skirt, Fall collection, 1994

New York City, with its frenetic pace and the vast and varied people it attracts, is a great inspiration to Karan. She believes clothing should be sensuous and fluid, easy to wear, and above all, flexible. Her designs are interchangeable; nothing is specifically day or evening, summer or winter. Karan believes that if one has the fundamentals underneath—bodysuits, unitards, black cashmere, bodywrap styles and stretch fabrics—these basics can be built upon in a variety of ways.

Karan sees designing as an extension of herself as a woman. Fashion, Karan says, should make easier the delicate balancing of roles—mother, wife, friend, businesswoman—required of most women in the 1990s. She believes clothing should simplify, not complicate, life.

—Hazel Clark

# KATAYAMA, Toshihiro

Japanese artist and environmental, exhibition, and graphic designer

**Born:** Osaka, 17 July 1928. **Education:** Self-taught in design. **Family:** Married Atsumi Fukui in 1960. **Career:** Freelance designer, 1952-60; designer, Nippon Design Center, Tokyo, 1960-1962, and, Geigy AG, Basel, 1963-66. Professor, 1966-1995, and director, 1990-1993, Carpenter Center for the Visual Arts, Harvard University, Cambridge, Massachusetts. **Exhibitions:** Herman Miller Showroom, Basel, 1965; Galerie ABC, Winterthur, 1965; Galerie Aktuell, Bern, 1965; Herman Miller Showroom, Zürich, 1966; American Institute of Graphic Arts, New York, 1968; Cooper and Beatty Gallery, Toronto, 1968, Gallery Plaza DIC, Tokyo, 1970; Harvard Graduate School of Design, Cambridge, Massachusetts, 1971; Brandeis University, Rose Art Museum, Waltham, Massachusetts, 1971; Kunstlerhaus, Vienna, 1977; Nantenshi Gallery, Tokyo, 1978, 1980, 1983, 1986, 1989; Sogetsu Kaikan, Tokyo, 1981; Clark Gallery, Lincoln, Massachusetts, 1982; Ginza Gallery, Tokyo, 1994; *Ritrospective,* Carpenter Center for the Visual Art, Harvard University, Cambridge, Massachusetts, 1995. **Collections:** Municipal Museum, Tokyo; Seibu Museum of Art, Tokyo; Municipal Museum, Toyama; Municipal Museum, Osaka; Rose Art Museum, Brandeis University, Waltham, Massachusetts; Fogg Art Museum, Harvard University, Cambridge, Massachusetts; Kunstlerhaus, Vienna; Staatsgalerie, Stuttgart; DeCordova and Dana Museum and Park, Lincoln, Massachusetts; Ohara Art Museum, Kurashiki; and others. **Addresses:** 16 Mystic Bank, Arlington, Massachusetts 02174, U.S. A.; 5-18-9 Inokashira, Mitaka-Shi, Tokyo 181, Japan.

## Works

Gund Hall banners, for Harvard Graduate School of Design, 1972.
*Star* mural and signage, for State Street Station, Boston subway, 1975.
*Josef Lluis Sert, Architect to the arts exhibition* design, for the Carpenter Center, Harvard University, 1978.
*Midnight* mural and environmental graphics, for Cronkhite Graduate Center, Radcliffe College, 1979.
Environmental graphics and signage at Alewife Station, for the Boston Subway, 1980 (with EMA Architects).

*Rainbow Elevator* graphics and marble Grand Floor, for the Shinjuku N.S. Building, Tokyo, 1982 (with Nikken Sekkei Architects).
*Homage to the Crystal* wall sculpture with stainless steel pipe, for the Akasaka Prince Hotel, Tokyo, 1983 (with Kenzo Tange and Urtec Architects).
Mural and large painting, for Taisho Marine and Fire Insurance Company, Tokyo, 1984 (with Nikken Seiki Architects).
*T* sculpture-sign, for Alewife Station, Boston subway, 1985 (with EMA Architects).
Plaza, restaurant, and fountain design, for the Toho Entertainment headquarters, Tokyo, 1987 (with Takenaka Construction Company).
*Le Corbusier* exhibition poster, for the Carpenter Center, Harvard University, 1987.
Theater curtains and tapestries, for Ohmiya Cultural Center, Saitama, 1988.
Stone sculpture and wall, for the Ohara Art Museum, Kurashiki, 1991.
Lobby landscape and sign, including granite wall, water fall, large steel sculpture, for Panasonic Information and Communication System Center, Tokyo, 1992.
Stone sculpture and wall reliefs, for Mitsui Marine and Fire Insurance Co., Chiba, 1994.
Public plaza floor and sculpture, Yokohama, 1995 (with Katayama's students).
Two wall reliefs using copper, for the J. T. Headquarters, Tokyo, 1995.
Calendar designs, for the Sezon Museum of Art, from 1977.

## Publications

**By KATAYAMA: books**—(with others) *Twelve Persons in Graphic Design Today,* Tokyo, 1968; (with Octavio Paz) *Visual Poetry: 3 Notations/Rotations,* New York, 1974; *Katayama's Students Work,* Musashino Art Uni, 1992.

**On KATAYAMA: books**—*Who's Who in Graphic Art,* edited by Walter Amstutz, Zürich, 1962, 1983, 1993; *Modern Graphics* by Keith Murgatroyd, London, 1969; *The Work of Toshi Katayama,* with texts by Kenzo Tange, Josef Lluis Sert, George Kepes, Josef Albers, Yusaka Kamekura, and others, Tokyo, 1980; *Toshi Katayama 30 Years of Paintings and Works in an Architectural Space,* with texts by Rudolf Arnheim, Shozo Baba, and others, Harvard University, Cambridge, Massachusetts, 1995.

*

There are no brushes or paints on my work desk. There is a scalpel. The rest are sharpened pencils and Kern drafting instruments. Instead of paints, I have at most eight different Coloraid papers. It would not be an exaggeration, therefore, to say that practically all my works have been produced with this Swiss surgical knife.

Actually, I do have brushes and paints. I put them, however, as far away as possible from my work desk, where I cannot find them. If they are not going to be used, they might as well be thrown away, but having them provides a feeling of security, much like having cold medicine on hand just in case, in fact there are occasions when I do use them, so I cannot throw them away. I keep them where I cannot see them to strengthen my will. I am afraid of having to have

417

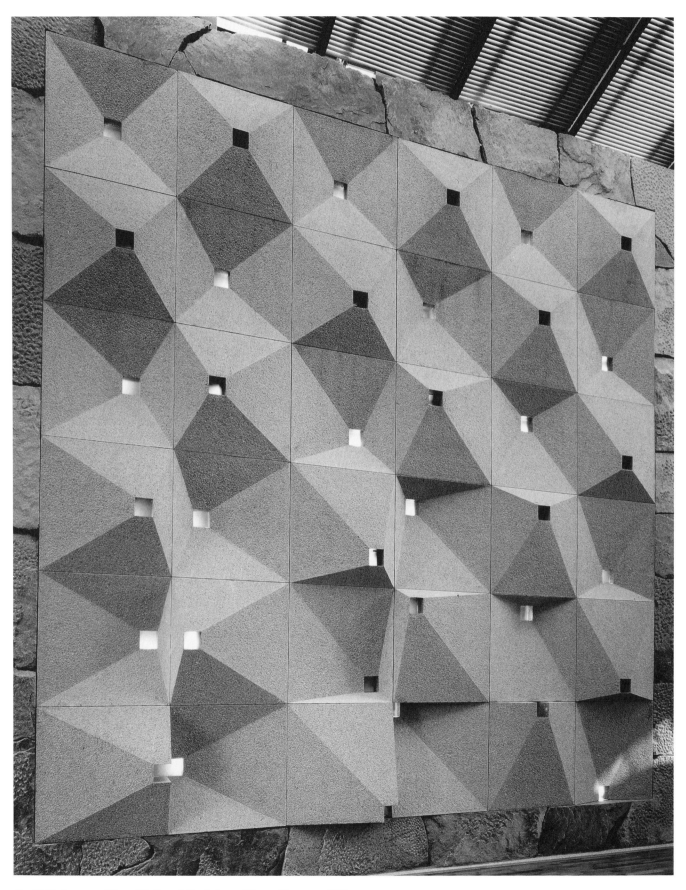

Toshi Katayama: Stone Wall and Sculpture, Ohara Museum, 1991

brushes and paints, a camera, countless books, and, on top of that, a number of collaborators to get work done. By not having brushes and paints and assistants—or rather, by not using them—I limit what I can do. By this I try to clarify what I am capable of doing and what my creative work, in a true sense, is.

Recently I have come to believe that there are two types of creative processes, the positive and the negative. In the positive process, a person will collect as much information and as many tools as he can and then work with numerous collaborators. I work, however, by a negative process. The more I seek a purity of approach, the deeper I enter this negative world. I have come to respect the artist with his singleminded devotion to his own world more than the designer accustomed to doing group work. Superficially, it is true that the more one limits oneself, the fewer opportunities there seem to be, when the will is weak, the greater this feeling is. One must be patient. When the work is not going smoothly, one must try to keep one's will strong. Luckily, fate handed me this knife.

I came upon the knife in the spring of 1963 in Basel, Switzerland, where I had been invited by Geigy AG and where I was to spend three years; in fact, it was on the day that I started work for Geigy. Designers put down their scalpels, which I had never seen or considered using in Japan, and shook hands with me. As I smiled, not being able to speak German or even English, my eyes were attracted strangely to the surgical knives. It was almost like being stabbed by them. In that moment I realized how the Swiss graphic designers, whom I had admired for a long time, were able to produce works of such quality and precision. From the knives I was able to intuit their source.

Men make tools, and tools may come to life depending on who uses them; tools accentuate a person's character. An artist ought to possess a tool he can call his own. If possible he should create it himself. Unless he creates his own tool or discovers a new material, it may be that no truly creative work is possible.

—Toshi Katayama

\*      \*      \*

In recent years, much of Toshi Katayama's impressive work has been done not in his capacity as a designer, but rather as an individual artist. His painting exhibitions, which occur almost yearly, evidence this, as do his architectural wall reliefs.

For Katayama, life and design activities in Switzerland may have been ascetic and constricting, for after he arrived in the United States, he came to incorporate into his works, a freehand line and accidental form, such as that which is achieved with the Japanese ink technique.

Thus, Katayama, who has expressed geometric form perceptively and meticulously, may be seen to be attempting a freer mode of expression. His problem henceforth will be the extent to which is able to bring clarity and perfection to these works.

—Shukuro Habara

# KATONA, Diti

Canadian graphic designer

**Born:** Toronto, Ontario, 3 May 1961. **Education:** York University, Toronto, B.F.A. **Family:** Married John Pylypczak. **Career:** Graphic designer, Taylor and Browning, Toronto, Reactor Art and Design, Toronto, and Jozsef Arendas, Budapest, Hungary; cofounder and principal, Concrete Design Communications, Toronto, from c. 1989; guest lecturer, 1992, and design faculty member, 1993-94, Ontario College of Art; design faculty member, York University, 1993; lecturer on design in the United States and Canada; frequent jury member for design awards. **Member:** American Institute of Graphic Arts; Advertising and Design Club of Canada; Graphic Designers of Canada. **Exhibitions:** *Canada Designs for Business,* toured Japan, 1992; *From Toronto,* Ville de Villeurbonne Maison du Livre, France, 1995. **Honors:** Award of Excellence, Phoenix Awards, Toronto, 1989, 1990, 1991, 1992; Silver Award, 1989, and awards, 1994, Typographers International Association, San Francisco; Gold Medal, 1989, 1990, and Silver Medal, 1990, Art Directors Club of Toronto; Silver Award, MerComm Show, New York, 1990; Award of Excellence, *Communication Arts* magazine, Palo Alto, California, 1990, 1991, 1993, 1995; Award of Excellence, American Institute of Graphic Arts, 1990, 1991, 1993, 1994; Merit Awards, Type Directors Club of New York, 1993, 1996; Black Book Award, 1993; Award of Excellence, International Trademarks and Logos III, Washington, D.C., 1993; Gold Medal, Silver Medal, and three Merit Awards, *Studio* magazine, 1993; *Graphis* Awards, Switzerland, 1994 (5), 1995 (6), 1996; Merit Award, 1995 (2), 1996 (3), and Silver Award, 1996, Society of Publication Designers, New York. **Address:** Concrete Design Communications Inc., 2 Silver Avenue, Main Floor, Toronto, Ontario M6R 3A2, Canada.

## Works

Annual reports, for Noranda, 1988-95.
*Secession* poster, for furniture company, Toronto, 1989.
Fashion brochures, for Zapata, 1989-94.
Identity, for Du Verre Specialty Housewares, Toronto, 1990.
Fashion brochures, for Lida Baday Ltd., from 1990.
Book cover for *Swing Era,* for Knopf Canada, 1993.
Identity, for the Design Exchange, Toronto, 1994.
Annual report, for YMCA, Toronto, 1995.

## Publications

**On KATONA: books**—*Graphic Design Solutions,* Albany, New York; *International Women in Design,* Washington, D.C., 1994; *International Typography,* New York, 1995; *Creativity for Graphic Designers,* New York, 1995; **articles**—*Financial Post* (London), May 1992; *Desktop Communications* (New York), May/June 1992; *Studio Magazine* (Toronto), July/August 1992; *Applied Arts* (Toronto), July/August 1992; *Communication Arts* (Palo Alto, California), March/April 1992; *Lineagrafica* (Milan), March 1993; *Applied Arts,* May/June/July 1994; *Graphics International* (London), April/May 1995.

\*

Concrete's philosophy:

1. Always use great pictures. People find them more interesting than great "design."

2. Always use either bodoni, garamond, bembo, centaur, franklin gothic, gill, futura, meta, or bell centennial. Use any other font with great caution.

**Diti Katona: Concrete Design Communications, Inc.: advertisement design, Secession Line by Wiesnerhager**

3. When in doubt, center.
4. Always remember—it's just litho.

—Diti Katona and John Pylypczak

\*     \*     \*

Diti Katona and John Pylpczak, the principals of Concrete Design Communications in Toronto, subvert the conventional wisdom that graphic designers belong to a somewhat precious subspecies of corporate propaganda specialist. They're more likely the standup comics of this business and, just possibly, they're also tribunes of common sense who, at all times, shoot straight from the hip.

"There's some truth to the idea that designers charge a lot of money to create pretty pictures and strange acronyms that come packaged with an entire book of jargon to justify their work," says Pylypczak, 35. "Charging the money's okay because there is an art in what we do. And it does the job. It's the jargon we can do without."

Katona, 34, is equally glib about the value of design because, in her view, there's far too much seriousness in what's essentially an ephemeral, wacky business. "Creating visual symbols, corporate identifiers, and design systems sometimes has little to do with enlightened aesthetics or sanity. It's often about the lunatic whim of clients and designers. Often both at the same time," she explains. "That may sound cynical. It isn't. It's the reality we've all come to know and love about the design world."

Another reality is that—glibness aside—Concrete Design Communications is arguably the preeminent graphic design agency in Canada. The design team of Katona and Pylypczak has probably created more award-winning annual reports, logo concepts, and print pieces than anybody else in Canada in recent years. They're recognized by juries in Toronto, New York, Los Angeles, Europe, and just about anywhere on the planet where international competitions are held and designers are smothered by self-congratulatory cliques.

Katona and Pylypczak met in 1985 when they were working at another agency. They went out on their own a few years later, about the time they got married. They settled on Concrete Design Communications as the company name because "using our own names would have made us sound like Eastern European immigration consultants," says Pylypczak. "Actually, we were in Italy and we saw a cement truck with a great-looking log for *Concrete Milano.* That was the extent of our thinking. Not some middlebrow artistic whim about the meanings of concrete—you know, as a design theory."

Over the years, Concrete Design has grown into a sizable hothouse of creativity that in the mid 1990s employs about ten people in a high-ceilinged studio in a building they own in Toronto's west end. The agency has won high-profile commissions from a who's who of the Canadian corporate elite: Northern Telecom, Noranda, American Barrick, CAE, and many others. Concrete Design has kept a hand in the flashier entrepreneurial netherworlds with its work for fashion designers, retailers, media companies, performing artists, and publishers. "It's important to cross-fertilize," says Katona. "Corporate budgets provide an opportunity to invest in the best photography, illustration, and production methods. But retail is what sells on the street. Being in both worlds keeps us sharp."

Katona was born and spent her early childhood in rural Ontario where her parents had emigrated after fleeing Hungary in the wake of the 1956 revolution. She graduated through various art programs at Toronto-area universities. Pylypczak was born in Toronto to parents of Ukrainian and German descent and he, too, is an art college graduate. "In the end, who really cares who we are?" asks Pylypczak. "It's far too early for anybody to even remotely care who our influences are. It's absurd the amount of self-adulation and navel-gazing foolishness that goes on."

Katona argues that the preoccupation with self-definition and neurotic yearning for corporate credibiity has led to the impoverished state of the design profession in North America. "How much have we evolved over the decades since design began to attract the attention of Bauhaus-obsessed industrialists? The short answer is: look at the skyscrapers, advertising campaigns, and billboards of the world. It's a landscape cluttered with circles, squares, and three-letter acronyms."

Adds Pylypczak on the subject of design clutter: "The growth in multimedia technologies and Internet websites will initally make it worse: more visual geniuses polluting the mental environment. Think of it this way. There's far too many of us competing for the visual doorway into the brain and there's not enough we can do to edit out the bad stuff. It's a development of evolutionary magnitude—the image or visual equivalent of the Black Plague. Where we go from here is anybody's guess. But in disaster, there's always opportunity."

Katona and Pylypczak believe the profession can be rehabilitated with a return to the spiritual roots of design. "Somehow, the term 'artist' has become a dirty word," says Katona. "Because we're trying to legitimize ourselves to those buying our services. We've become analytical and skilled at the art of proposal generation. We pitch business. We're problem solvers. What are we, for God's sake, accountants?"

Pylypczak says designers have to come clean and admit that an essential part of what they do is intuitive and emotional. "We design because of a need to express ourselves with pencils, pigments, paper, and pixels," he says. "We have an irrational but entirely human need to communicate. All the focus groups in the world won't change that."

—Larry Gaudet

# KATSUI, Mitsuo
Japanese graphic designer

**Born:** Tokyo, 6 September 1931. **Education:** Graduated, Department of Arts and Architectonics, College of Education, Tokyo University of Education, 1955; postgraduate work in design and photography, Tokyo University of Education, 1955-56. **Career:** Worked in Ajinomoto Company, Tokyo, 1956-1961; freelance graphic designer, establishing Katsui Design Office Inc., Tokyo, from 1961. Head professor, Musashino Art University, Tokyo; lecturer, Tsukuba University, Japan. **Member:** Tokyo Art Directors Club; Japanese Graphic Designers Association; Tokyo Designers Space; Alliance Graphique Internationale; Japan Inter-Design Forum. **Exhibitions:** *Fresh Eye,* Konishiroku Gallery, Japan, 1957; *Persona Exhibition,* Japan, 1966; *Art Poster Now,* Seibu, Tokyo, 1976; *Media Art Exhibition,* Seibu, Tokyo, 1977; *Poster of Japan in Twenty Years,* Netherlands, 1977; *Close Figure,* Gallery Watari, Tokyo, 1977; *Woodcut & Modern Times,* Ricker Museum, Tokyo, 1979; *Japan Style,* London, 1980; *Japanese Poster,* Mu-

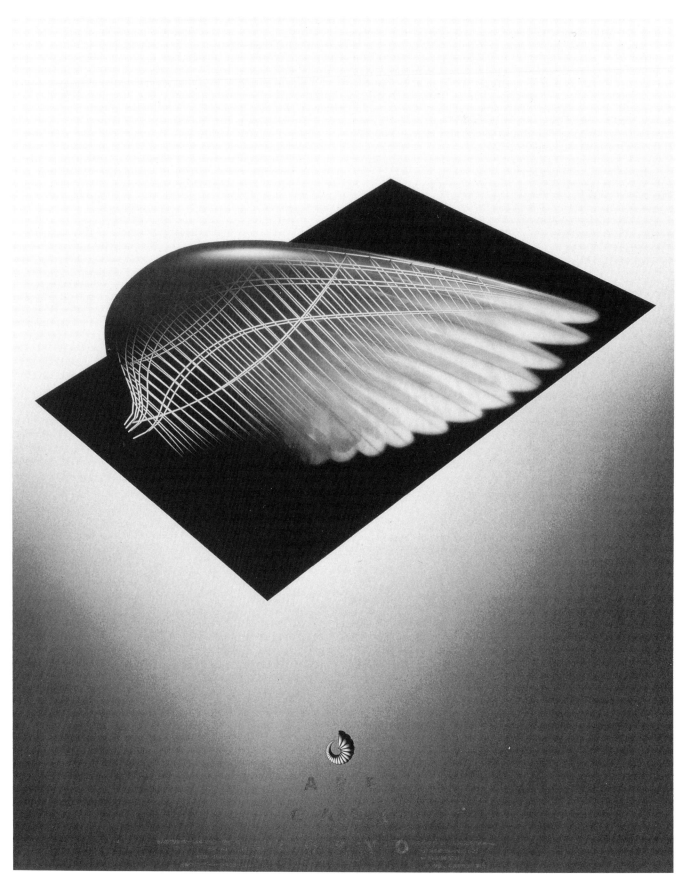

**Mitsuo Katsui:** *Ape Call From Tokyo*, 1992

seum of Modern Art, Toyama, Japan, 1982; *1/2,* Tokyo Designers Space, 1982; *Ape Call from Tokyo,* Tokyo Art Directors Club Gallery, New York, 1990; *Ape Call from Tokyo,* Doizaki Gallery, Los Angeles, 1991, Spiral Hall, Tokyo, 1992; *Design Marathon 1991-1995,* Tokyo Designers Space, 1991; *The Blessing of Light,* Ginza Graphic Gallery, Tokyo, 1993, DNP Duo Dojima Gallery, Osaka, 1993; *Katsui Mitsuo,* Brno, Czech Republic, 1994; *Elfin Light,* Hillside Forum, Tokyo, 1995. **Collections:** Museum of Modern Art, New York; Museum of Plastic Art, Zürich; Museum of Modern Art, Toyama, Japan; Kawasaki City Museum, Japan; Musashino Art University Library, Japan. **Honors:** 8th Japan Artists Club Award, Japan, 1958; The Mainichi Industrial Design Prize, Tokyo, 1965 and 1994; Silver Medal, Lettering Institute, 1969; Silver Medal, Typography Institution, Japan, 1971; 3rd Kodan-sha Publications Cultural Prize, Japan, 1972; Art Directors Club Members Award, Japan, 1972; Gold Medal, 1972, Bronze Medal, 1980, Silver Medal, 1988, Grand Prix, 1990, Biennale of Arts Graphiques, Brno, Czechoslovakia; Gold Medal and Silver Medal, Kalendarschau, West Germany, 1984; Bronze Medal, "The Most Beautiful Book" exhibition, East Germany, 1985; Gold Medal, Lahti Poster Biennale, Finland, 1987; Grand Prix, 1st Mexico Poster Biennale, 1991; Education Minister's Art Encouragement Prize of Art, Japan, 1993; Gold Prize, International Poster Biennale, Warsaw, 1994; Yamana Prize, Japan Advertising Club, 1994; Minister Prize of International Trade and Industry, Japan, 1994; Wittenborn Prize, The Art Librarians, U.S.A., 1995; Gold Prize, New York Art Directors Club, 1995; The Highest Standards of Excellence, Museum Publications Design Competition, U.S.A., 1995. **Address:** (Office) 3-48-9-B1F, Nishihara, Shibuya-ku, Tokyo, 151, Japan.

## Works

*Encyclopedia World Now 1-3* book design, for Kodan-sha Publishing Co., Ltd., 1972.
Art direction and official map, for *Expo '85,* Tsukuba, Japan, 1985.
Art direction and space design of *"Brain House,"* for pavilion of Kodan-sha Publishing Co. Ltd., Expo '85, 1985.
Symbol mark, for Expo '90, 1987.
*Hiroshima Appeals* poster, 1989.
*Ape Call from Tokyo* exhibition poster, 1990-92.
*The Blessing of Light* poster, 1993.
*Japanese Design: A Survey Since 1950* exhibition catalogue design, for Philadelphia Museum of Art, 1994.
*The 200th Anniversary of Sharaku* poster, 1995.

## Publications

**On KATSUI: books**—*The World's Graphic Design 6,* Tokyo; *Modern Design Dictionary,* Tokyo; *An Outline of Modern Graphic Design* (CD edition), Tokyo.

*

Through many years of experience with design work, I have gained much knowledge about the analog era. When looking at the digital era since the 1980s, it becomes clear that it is shorter in duration than the analog era and that software know-how used during the analog era is still effective, even today. It is my belief that our generation has a role to play in filling the gap in technology and

in taking over and making use of past developments. At present, the thing that I am most attracted to even more than printing or RGB, is "light" itself. As long as I can reach my audiences, I am willing to incorporate any kind of technology as a form of representation. While I am always interested in, and concerned with, new developments, I like a challenge and am therefore never disturbed by technology. This may be contradictory, but more than anything else I desire to be modest about techniques and technology. At this point, I will continue to think about the best uses of technology, always seeking the points of contact that humans hold in common with it, and will explore a little bit more about the two.

—Mitsuo Katsui

# KEMÉNY, György

Hungarian graphic designer

**Born:** Budapest, 25 May 1936. **Education:** Apprentice in the poster design studio of Pal Gabor, Budapest, 1954-55; studied painting and design, at the Hungarian Academy of Art, Budapest, 1956-61. **Career:** Freelance painter, environmental artist, and graphic designer, Budapest, from 1964; art director, *Interpress* magazine, Budapest, from 1975. **Exhibitions:** Feszek Artists' Club, Budapest, 1968; Club Bercsenyi, Budapest, 1971; Galleri Kirjavintii, Helsinki, 1971; Blue Chapel, Balatonboglar, 1975; Mucsarnok Exhibition Hall, Budapest, 1982; Little Gallery, Pecs, 1987; *The Best 66 Poster Designers of the World,* Paris, 1989. **Collections:** Hungarian National Gallery, Budapest; Museum Petofi, Budapest; Wilanow Poster Museum, Warsaw; Musée de l'Affiche, Paris. **Honors:** Silver Medal, Casalecchio di Reno Poster Competition, 1969, 1971; Warsaw International Poster Competition Prize, 1975; Toyama Poster Triennale Prize, 1985; New York Art Directors Club Merit Awards, 1987, 1988; Best Book Cover of 1994 Award, 1994. **Address:** Fodor utca 86, 1124 Budapest, Hungary.

## Works

*Marat/Sade* poster, for the National Theatre, Budapest, 1966.
*Pretty Girls, You Musn't Cry* film poster, for Mokep, 1971.
*Too Much Drink Is Poison* poster, for the National Alcoholism Prevention Committee, 1971.
*Dodeskaden* film poster, for Mokep, 1971.
*Bummm* record sleeve, for LGT Group, 1972.
*Football of Old Times* film poster, for Mokep, 1972.
*Seven Dutch Artists* exhibition poster, for the Mucsarnok Exhibition Hall, Budapest, 1977.
*Le Cinema Hongrois* exhibition layouts at the Centre Georges Pompidou, Paris, for Hungarofilm, 1979.
*Saint George and the Dragon* poster, for the National Theatre, Budapest, 1979.
*Studio 80* television special environment, for Miklos Jancso, 1980.
*Cabaret* film poster, for Mokep, 1980.
*Fiction and Objectivity* exhibition poster, for Galerie Budapest, 1981.
*Fact-Picture* exhibition layouts and poster, for the Mucsarnok Exhibition Hall, Budapest, 1981.

**György Kemény: trademark for the Budapest Zoo, 1995**

*101 Years of Hungarian Posters* exhibition layouts and poster, for
   the Mucsarnok Exhibition Hall, Budapest, 1986.
*Season of Monsters* film posters, for Mokep, 1987.
*Hanussen* film logo and poster, for Mokep and Hungarofilm, 1988.
*Mikyprint* logo, for a silkscreen firm, Budapest, 1988.
*World Graphic Design Now* poster, Tokyo, 1988.
*For Human Rights* poster, Paris, 1989.
*Graphis Poster '91* poster, Zürich, 1991.
*I.G.E.N. (Y.E.S.)* giant poster, for the Insurance Company of the
   Hungarian Sanitary, 1991.
Covers, for *Theatre* magazine, from 1991.
Logo, for Budapest Festival Ochestra, 1992.
Logo, for Budapest Art Expo, 1992.
Book covers for *The Stars of the Helikon Publisher* series, 1994.
*Graphis Design 94* poster, Zürich, 1994.
Logo, for Budapest Zoo, 1995.
*Graphis Design 95* poster, Zürich, 1995.

**Publications**

**On KEMÉNY: books**—*Muveszeti Kislexikon* edited by Edit Lajta,
Budapest, 1973; *Szora Birt Mutermek* by Janos Frank, Budapest,
1975; *Fiuk-Lanyok Konyve* by Judit Fekete, Budapest, 1976; **articles**—in *Graphis* (Zürich), no. 192, 1977; *Graphis Design* (Tokyo), December 1978; *Muveszet* (Budapest), April 1982, January
1986; *New Hungarian Quarterly* (Budapest), Summer 1983; *Creation* (Paris), February 1988.

\*

   In the first edition of this book I wrote very pessimistic sentences about the design situation and its future prospects. It was
reasonable at that time because economic recession was a characteristic phenomena all around the world, and the tension between two
world systems seemed about to culminate in a new, horrible world

war. With the exception of some examples, design and aestheticism played an unimportant and overshadowed role everywhere. If I think of the recent past I remember bitterly that the most brilliantly designed objects of that period were actually the American and West European fighter planes.

However, there were unexpected changes in the last years, such as the powerful economic development in numerous countries from Singapore to Turkey, the development of fantastic technologies to open up the world, and the movement of Eastern Europe and the Soviet Union out of deep political, economic, and intellectual crisis. The growing activity of designers and graphic artists could be seen again all over the world, now including Hungary, too. New commissions and claims appeared: up-to-date buildings, trendy dresses, or the very emblems of new firms are born not only in New York but also in Budapest, though weaker in numbers. Now satellites can broadcast even to Hungary the programs of different West European TV channels that contain aesthetic information just like the traditional mediums of cultural exchange: books, magazines, exhibitions. Our projects and designs can also be seen at other countries' exhibitions, in their books and magazines. I think that over and above politicians, scientists, engineers, it is the turn of us, designers—in the broadest sense of the word: artists—to come up to the requirements of the great challenge, to welcome worthily the new millennium. I can register again only the momentary situation: I am optimistic, I work.

—György Kemény

\* \* \*

In all György Kemény's graphic compositions, in his posters, bookjackets, illustrations, record covers, and other contributions to mass media, an attentive observer can discern the imprint of the time and place of their origin. Certainly, his design is different from what is customary in the developed countries of the West, not so much in the formal aspect of his design as in his approach to reality. By selecting certain means and forms of communication, this Hungarian designer reveals a broad scale of moods and emotions, such as violence, pain, anger, hope, and despair, as his way of reacting to certain phenomena and events. Showing his disdain for aestheticism, for a smooth, adorned picture of the world, he does not conceal his liking for certain models of mass or youth culture.

Under a thin layer of internationalism, it is easy to notice the national origin of Kemény's interests. He cannot and probably does not want to reject the burden of tradition because history, like geopolitics, is always present in this part of Europe. The quality of Kemény's design would be difficult to appreciate without regard for these conditions, restrictions, and suppressions, and so it is necessary to keep in mind the history and difficult experiences of the society and the individuals living in his country.

During the international poster competition organized in commemoration of the thirtieth anniversary of victory over fascism, Kemény shared the first prize. Presenting the story of his own World War II experience, when he faced evil and violence as a small boy, his poster shows two photographs taken from a family album; one depicts the face of nine-year-old György, and the second, György as a young man. Next to the pictures there is a typewritten text which is quoted here in full, as it is the most authentic testimony:

"I am György Kemény. I live in Budapest as a graphic designer. I work as everybody does. Thirty years ago, I was a Jewish boy of nine. My parents put me in an asylum to save my life. There, I was once shot at, but the bullet missed me. Next, I was taken to a mass execution at the river Danube, but an air raid dispersed my would-be murderers. When liberation came, I weighed 34 pounds. My mother still starts crying when remembering this. Today I live in Budapest. I am a graphic designer, and I work like everybody else."

There are very few similar examples of confession by means of the poster.

Although the author operates with a contemporary visual language and conventions that originated in conceptualism, yet he belongs among those Hungarian artists who in the past used mass prints as a tool of their individual personal expressions. This is a group of expressionists—Biró, Berény, Jeges, Pór, Uitz, as well as Kassak and Bortnyik. The participants in the big movement of Hungarian activism, they are the avant-garde, concentrated around the magazine *MA,* and associating themselves with new art in Europe, with Russian constructivism and Dutch neo-graphicism.

Kemény's preference for form, which is flat, two-dimensional, rough, and expressionistic, has its source in the national tradition. His drawing, often in pencil or in feather-pen, exposes the brutal and almost praises the ugliness and aggressiveness of things surrounding us.

Plainness and negligence in Kemény's work are used to challenge the consumer ideal. In this respect, he refers to the aesthetics of ugliness that was so popular in the period of the youth anti-culture, in the "underground" prints in England and the United States in the 1960s. These features are clearly evident in his record cover designs made for the Hungarian producers of "pop music" (Lokomotiv). At that time under the strong influence of American Pop art, Kemény tried to transplant it to Hungarian territory. He did so with grace and talent, but it was for him a temporary and superficial artistic adventure.

—Szymon Bojko

# KENZO
Japanese fashion designer

**Born:** Kenzo Takada, in Tokyo, 27 February 1939. **Career:** Designer for Sanai department store; pattern designer, *Soen* magazine, Tokyo, 1960-64; freelance fashion designer, Paris, from 1965; established Jungle Jap boutique, Paris, 1970; Rue Cherche Midi Boutique opened, 1972; Kenzo-Paris boutique opened, New York, 1983; menswear line created, 1983; boutiques opened in Paris, Aix en Provence, Bordeaux, Lille, Lyon, Saint-Tropez, Copenhagen, London, Milano, and Tokyo, 1984-85; menswear and womenswear lines, Kenzo Jeans, and junior line launched, 1986; boutiques opened in Rome, New York, 1987; childrenswear line, 1987; womenswear line, Kenzo City, launched 1988; boutiques opened in Brussels, 1989, and Stockholm, 1990; bath products line, Le Bain, launched 1990; boutiques opened in Hong Kong, 1990, Bangkok, 1991, and Singapore, 1991; Kenzo Maison line launched, 1992; Bambou line launched, 1994. Perfumes: *Kenzo,* 1988; Parfum d'Été, 1992. Also costume designer for opera, and film director. **Honors:** Soen Prize, 1960; Fashion Editors Club of Japan Prize, 1972; Bath Museum of Costume Dress of the Year Award, 1976, 1977; Chevalier de l'Ordre des Arts et des Lettres, 1984. **Address:** 54 rue Étienne Marcel, 75001 Paris, France.

## Publications

On KENZO: books—*A History of Fashion* by J. Anderson Black and Madge Garland, London 1975, 1980; *The Changing World of Fashion: 1900 to the Present* by Ernestine Carter, London, 1977; *In Fashion: Dress in the Twentieth Century* by Prudence Glynn, London, 1978; *The Guinness Guide to 20th Century Fashion* by David Bond, Enfield, 1981; *McDowell's Directory of Twentieth Century Fashion* by Colin McDowell, London, 1984; *The Conran Directory of Design* edited by Stephen Bayley, London, 1985; *Couture: The Great Designers* by Caroline Milbank Rennolds, New York, 1985; *The Encyclopaedia of Fashion from 1840 to the 1980s* by Georgina O'Hara, London, 1986; *Japanese Design* by Penny Sparke, London, 1987; *Kenzo* by Ginette Sainderichin, Paris, 1989; articles—"The JAP Designer" in *Newsweek* (New York), 1 May 1972; "Designer Does What He Likes—And It's Liked" by Bernadine Morris in the *New York Times,* 4 April 1973; "Lively Influence on Dull Paris Scene" in *The Times* (London), 1 September 1976; "Mini Redux" in *Newsweek* (New York), 8 November 1976; "Kenzo Grows Up" by Hebe Dorsey in the *New York Times Magazine,* 14 November 1976; "Kenzo: One Needs Folly to Work in Fashion" by André Leon Talley in *Women's Wear Daily* (New York), 17 February 1978; "Designer Becomes a Superstar: Kenzo Marches to Different Tunes; All of Them Are Hits" by Priscilla Tucker in the *New York Daily News,* 11 April 1978; "Kenzo Barges Up the Nile" by Marian McEvoy in *Women's Wear Daily* (New York), 20 October 1978; "Makers of Modern Fashion: Kenzo" by Maureen Cleave in *The Observer Magazine* (London), 14 December 1980; "L'oeil de Vogue: l'anniversaire de Kenzo" in *Vogue* (Paris), October 1985; "L'art d'être soi l-même" by Gerard-Julien Salvy in *Vogue* (Paris), February 1986; "Cap by Denny, So Why Buy Kenzo?" by Ann Boyd in *The Observer* (London), 8 January 1987; "Kenzo: creations tous azimuts" in *Profession Textile* (Paris), 5 February 1988; "Kenzo Back Home in Japan" by Gisella Boriolli in *Donna* (Milan), July/August 1989; "Kenzo Modern Folklore" in *Elle* (New York), September 1989; "Le pélerinage de Kenzo" in *Elle* (Paris), 5 September 1989.

*      *      *

When Kenzo arrived in Paris in 1965, haute couture dominated fashion. Shocked by the perfection of the work of couturiers such as Dior, Cardin, and Chanel, Kenzo found his inspiration in the young people in the streets; for them, he began to create exciting, wearable clothes. By aiming at the new, young market which had become so apparent in the late 1960s, Jap led the explosion of ready-to-wear as the major influence from Paris in the 1970s.

Kenzo's work is witty, lively, and unpredictable. While he has been responsible for many innovations, it is virtually impossible to predict what he is going to do next. Soft, white cottons were followed by bright, school-girl tunics, which gave way to sombre, natural-coloured tweeds. His inspiration, drawn from all over, has captured or even preempted the mood of the times. It was he who, in 1973, introduced the peasant folkloric types, which foreshadowed the "return to nature" later in the 1970s. His functional, survival clothing of 1974 predicted a move to days of harder economy. This ability to know what is right at the time, plus the spirit of adventure and a desire to cater to a wide, young market, made him a fashion leader.

Many influences are plainly apparent in Jap's collections. Russian peasants, Chinese coolies, tribal Africans, red Indians, swash-

buckling pirates, Buster Keaton, and Charlie Chaplin have all been reflected in his work, which never ceases to astonish. Kenzo became Minnie Mouse for his 40th birthday, and his menswear collection for spring/summer 1988 was a homage to Al Capone. But beneath these ephemeral, yet influential changes runs a powerful force—Japan. While his early sweaters and kimonos were clearly derivative, his uses of oversize and layers are more subtle appropriations of traditional roots. Kenzo's love of volume, as seen clearly in his balloon dresses, owes a great deal to Japanese costume, in which the shape of the body is of little concern. Likewise, this approach is also apparent when he uses five or six garments to create an outfit, often mixing colours and textures along the way. Colour and fabrics, which he designs himself, are his initial inspiration, and these wonderful textures and hues set a Jap original apart from a copy. Whilst price makes his typical customer the woman of thirty, his individual, light-hearted looks have been copied internationally for the young. Kenzo's collections have become less crazy than before but no less exciting. He is a master of the unpredictable; strong colours, bold shapes (seen in his sculpturally constructed, wrap dresses), embroidered tweeds, mixed plaids and stripes, frills, and layers all bear witness to this. Kenzo has shown that fashion as fun and fantasy can sell.

—Hazel Clark

# KEPES, Gyorgy

American painter, photographer, filmmaker, architect, and exhibition and graphic designer

**Born:** Selyp, Hungary, 4 October 1906, emigrated to the United States in 1937, naturalized, 1956. **Education:** Studied under Istvan Csok, at the Academy of Arts, Budapest, M.A., 1928. **Family:** Married Juliet Appleby in 1937; children: Juliet and Imre. **Career:** Independent painter and filmmaker, associating with the Munka Art Group, Budapest, 1929-30; freelance designer and teacher, working in Berlin, 1930-32, 1934-36, in London, 1936-37, in Chicago and New York, 1938-45, and in Cambridge, Massachusetts, from 1946; design consultant, to Travelers Insurance Company of Los Angeles, Container Corporation of America, Abbot Laboratories, *Fortune* magazine, and others, 1938-50. Head of the light and color department, New Bauhaus School (later Institute of Design), Chicago, 1938-43; professor of design, North Texas State College, Denton, and Brooklyn College, New York, 1943-45; professor of visual design, 1946-66, founder-director of the Center for Advanced Visual Studies, 1967-70, and Institute professor, 1970-74, Massachusetts Institute of Technology, Cambridge; also visiting lecturer and professor at colleges and universities throughout the United States, from 1939. **Exhibitions:** Katherine Kuh Gallery, Chicago, 1939; Art Institute of Chicago, 1944; Currier Gallery of Art, Manchester, New Hampshire, 1951; San Francisco Museum of Art, 1952, 1954; Cranbrook Academy of Art, Bloomfield Hills, Michigan, 1954; Stedelijk Museum, Amsterdam, 1955; Everson Museum of Art, Syracuse, New York, 1957; Dallas Museum of Fine Arts, 1957, 1959; Baltimore Museum of Art, 1959; Massachusetts Institute of Technology, Cambridge, 1959, 1978; Houston Museum of Fine Arts, 1959; Phoenix Art Museum, Arizona, 1966; Phillips Exeter Academy, New Hampshire, 1967; Museum of Science, Boston, 1973; Künstlerhaus, Vienna, 1976; Mucsarnok Exhibition Hall, Budapest, 1976; Bauhaus-Archiv, West Berlin, 1977; International Center of Photography, New York, 1984. **Collections:** Museum of Modern Art, New York; Rhode Island School of Design, Providence; Boston Museum of Fine Arts; Art Institute of Chicago; San Francisco Museum of Modern Art; Massachusetts Institute of Technology, Cambridge; National Museum of Fine Arts, Budapest; Bauhaus-Archiv, West Berlin. **Honors:** American Institute of Graphic Arts Typography Award, 1947; Guggenheim Fellowship, New York, 1960; Silver Medal, Architectural League of New York, 1961; American Institute of Architects Fine Arts Award, 1968; College Art Association of American Distinguished Teaching Award, 1982. Fellow, Rhode Island School of Design, and American Academy of Arts and Sciences; Academician, National Academy of Design; Member, Hall of Fame, Art Directors Club of New York; National Institute of Arts and Letters. **Address:** 90 Larchwood Drive, Cambridge, Massachusetts 02138, U.S.A.

## Publications

**By KEPES: books**—(with Gyorgy Dan) *Tul a Valon,* Budapest, 1925; *Language of Vision,* Chicago, 1944; *Graphic Forms: The Art as Related to the Book,* Cambridge, Massachusetts, 1949; *The New Landscape in Art and Science,* Chicago, 1956; (editor) *The Education of Vision,* New York, 1965; (editor) *Structure in Art and Science,* New York, 1965; (editor) *The Nature and Art of Motion,* New York, 1965; (with Bernard I. Cohen) *Light as a Creative Medium,* Cambridge, Massachusetts, 1965; (editor) *Module, Symmetry, Proportion, Rhythm,* New York, 1966; (editor) *Sign, Image, Symbol,* New York, 1966; (editor) *The Man-Made Object,* New York, 1966; *The Center for Advanced Visual Studies,* Cambridge, Massachusetts, 1967; (editor) *Arts of Environment,* New York, 1972; *El Arte y la Technologia,* Bogota, 1973; *Gyorgy Kepes Kialliasa,* with an introduction by Eva Korner, Budapest, 1976; *Portfolio of Photographs by Gyorgy Kepes,* with an introduction by Philip Hofer, Boston, 1977; *Gyorgy Kepes Irasai* edited by Ferenc Bodri, Budapest, 1978; *Gyorgy Kepes: The MIT Years 1945-1977,* with text by Judith Wechsler and Jan Van der Marck, Cambridge, Massachusetts, 1978; *Gyorgy Kepes: Lightgraphics,* with text by Anne Hoy, New York, 1984.

**On KEPES: books**—*Posters: 50 Artists and Designers* edited by W. H. Allner, New York, 1952; *Advertising Directions* edited by Edward M. Gottschall and Arthur Hawkins, New York, 1959; *Art as Design/Design as Art* by Sterling McIlhany, New York and London, 1970; *Gyorgy Kepes: Works in Review,* exhibition catalogue with texts by O. Piene, R. Arnheim, and others, Boston, 1973; *The Language of Graphics* by Edward Booth-Clibborn and Daniele Baroni, London, 1980; *A History of Graphic Design* by Philip B. Meggs, New York, 1983; *An Introduction to Design and Culture in the Twentieth Century* by Penny Sparke, London, 1986; *The American Design Adventure 1940-1975* by Arthur J. Pulos, London and Cambridge, Massachusetts, 1988.

\*    \*    \*

The importance of Gyorgy Kepes to design lies not only in his work as a designer, but in his teaching, in his leadership of interdisciplinary efforts, in his collaborative projects, and in his deep sense of the opportunities for serving human values through design. Work-

ing in Chicago from 1937 as a teacher and graphic designer, he had an electrifying impact because in his teaching and in his lively, innovative graphic designs, he explored the possibilities opened by recent developments in painting and photography as well as psychology. His exhibition designs explored ways of involving and educating the viewer, as was seen in his work on such diverse themes as *Close-up of Tintoretto* at the Art Institute of Chicago in 1942 and *Light as a Creative Medium.*

His projects for "civic art" move beyond individual experience to works on an epic scale, embodying a unified understanding. For instance, for an unrealized Boston Harbor project of 1964-65, Kepes designed a mile-long, luminous wall with programmed light modulations, interacting with mirrored buoys. These buoys recall a proposal Kepes made in Chicago during World War II, when he called for decoy lights floating in Lake Michigan to confuse pilots should there be an air attack.

Although Kepes had no direct connection with the German Bauhaus, he became part of the Bauhaus circle through his long associations with László Moholy-Nagy and Walter Gropius. Moreover, in his own work and in his teaching, Kepes recalls the Bauhaus masters by his experimental approach and by his interests in group effort and in links between design and architecture on the one hand and the arts and sciences on the other. Kepes' *Language of Vision,* a basic text in many schools for nearly forty years, has done more to spread Bauhaus educational methods than any other publication. Significantly, in 1982, Kepes received the annual "Distinguished Teaching of Art" award of the College Art Association.

*The New Landscape* and the earlier exhibition on the same theme constitute a bold attempt to expand the imagery familiar to designers and artists. The same kind of broad cooperation which Kepes elicited for that project also was required for the *Vision and Value* series, which includes individual volumes on such subjects as *The Education of Vision* (1965) and *Arts of the Environment* (1972). Such cooperation was also necessary at the Center for Advanced Visual Studies, which was set up as a workshop where interdisciplinary and cooperative projects are undertaken on a continuing basis.

Commissions for collaboration with architects include faceted glass windows for St. Mary's Cathedral in San Francisco (1965), done with Pietro Belluschi, Luigi Nervi, and A. McSweeney, and a programmed light mural based on night aerial views of cities for the KLM office in New York City (1959, no longer in place), with L. L. Rado. The KLM mural, like the Boston Harbor project, recalls Kepes' experiences during World War II, when he flew over Chicago at night as part of his research to formulate recommendations for protecting the city through the use of camouflage. Kepes has also collaborated with Walter Gropius, W. W. Wurster, Karl Loch, Welton Beckett, and other architects.

Throughout his career Kepes has also been active as an artist, from the paintings he made as a youth through photographs and multimedia compositions of the 1930s and 1940s to his later paintings, characterized by tones and textures which suggest aspects of the natural landscape.

The social role of design and the arts has been central to Kepes' thinking since his youth, when he read the works of John Ruskin and William Morris and also became aware of social injustices inflicted on Hungarian peasants. His convictions were reinforced through his association with Lajos Kassak and other artists allied with the Hungarian political left.

—Lloyd C. Engelbrecht

# KERR KELLER DESIGN INC.
Canadian industrial, furniture, and environmental design firm

**Founded** in Toronto, Canada, 1989; principals include Miles Keller (**Born:** in Calgary, 1959. **Education:** Graduated, University of Calgary, B.A.; University of British Columbia, Architecture; studied industrial design, Ontario College of Art.) and Helen Kerr (**Born:** Montreal, 1959. **Education:** studied Environmental Science, University of Waterloo; studied industrial design, Ontario College of Art.); clients have included Umbra, Corning, NEC, Keilhauer Industries, Kaufman Contract, Irwin Toys, Ottoman Empire, Pallazetti, Creative Space, Elika, Noradev, Brunswick, Sunnybrook Hospital, and Bank of Montreal. **Exhibitions:** *Virtu—Directions in Canadian Design,* toured Canada, Japan, Europe, 1988, 1989, 1990, 1992, 1993, 1995; *Beyond Reason,* Gallery 76, Toronto, 1988; *New Frontiers—Humanizing Technology,* Dallas, 1989; *Canada Designs for Business,* Japan, 1993; *Second Nature,* Design Exchange, Toronto, 1994; *Industrial Design Is ...,* Design Exchange, Toronto, 1995. **Honors:** *ID* Annual Design Review, 1988; Virtu 3, 1988; Virtu 4, 1989; Virtu 5, 1990; Virtu 6, 1992; Virtu 6 honorable mention, 1992; Design Arts Award, Ontario Arts Council, 1992; Design Arts Award, Ontario Arts Council, 1993; Virtu 7, 1993; Virtu 9, 1995. **Address:** Kerr Keller Design Inc., 1977 Queen Street East, Toronto, Canada M4L 1J1.

## Works

*Sail* halogen floor lamp, 1987.
*A26* floor lamp, 1988.
Dustpan and Brush, for Umbra, 1990.
Exhibit design, for Ministry of Community and Social Services, 1991.
*Aztec* and *Domino* wall mirrors, for Umbra, 1991.
Wood and glass bowls, for Umbra, 1991.
*Adelaide* wood mantle clock, for Umbra, 1991.
*Vitesse* desk series, for Umbra, 1991.
*Rocket* salt and pepper shakers/pepper mill/bowl, for Umbra, 1992.
*Saturn* coffee table, for Umbra, 1992.
*Pidet* fence neoprene doormat, for Umbra, 1992.
*Planet* wall clock, for Umbra, 1992.
*Rex* and *Lola* floor mirrors, for Umbra, 1992.
*Pagoda* wine rack, for Umbra, 1992.
*Bullrush* coatrack, for Umbra, 1992.
*Saturn* salad bowl and servers, for Umbra, 1992.
*Aaro* wood boxes, for Umbra, 1992.
*Dolfin* chair, for Ottoman Empire, 1992.
*Stilletto* table series, for Creative Space, 1992.
*Delta* CD and cassette storage rack, for Creative Space, 1992.
*Kensington* seating series, for Kaufman Furniture, 1992.
*Mosquito* sidechair, for Palazzetti, 1992.
Custom contract furniture (boardroom table, printer stands, coat closets, moveable panels), for Bank of Montreal Learning Institute, 1993.
*Sunrise* mantle clock, for Umbra, 1993.
*Nile* wall mirror, for Umbra, 1993.
*Ferro* bath accessories series, for Umbra, 1993.
*Porto* wall clock, for Umbra, 1993.
*Gateway* seating series, for Kaufman Furniture, 1993.
*Simcoe* pull-up chair, for Kaufman Furniture, 1993.

*Kestrel* sidechair, for Brunswick Manufacturing, 1993.
*Shift* conference/dining table, for Brunswick Manufacturing, 1993.
Picture frames, for Elika USA, 1993.
Side table, for BDI, USA, 1993.
Exhibit and graphic design, for various clients including Umbra, Brunswick, Sources GoGraphics, 1993.
*Pebble* soap dish, for Umbra, 1994.
*Trillium* glass dish, for Umbra, 1994.
Children's art cases, for Noradev, 1994.
Executive seating, for Kaufman Furniture, 1994.
Reconfigurable tabouret and table, for Egan Visual, 1994.
Travel toothbrush and razor, for Noradev, 1994.
Custom boardroom table, for Bank of Montreal, 1994.
*Chit Chat* chair, for Keilhauer, 1995.
Laptop computer case, for NEC, 1995.
*Talking Tables* sidetable series, for Nienkämper, 1995.
*Adept* and *Intrepid* contract executive seating, for Allseating, 1995.
Custom dining table, coffee table, sofa, nightstands, private commission, 1995.
Telebanking kiosks, for Bank of Montreal, 1995.
Step-on garbage can, for Umbra, 1995.
*Bolo* and *Sprout* candlesticks, for Umbra, 1995.
Bath hardware and accessories, for Umbra, 1995.
*Vibe* picture frame, for Umbra, 1995.
Halo, Wave, and Groove clocks, for Umbra, 1995.

## Publications

**By KERR KELLER: articles**—"Modernizing the 1950s Brunswick Chair" by Helen Kerr and Miles Keller in *Insite* (London), November 1993; "Newsreel" by Helen Kerr in *Insite* (London), November 1993.

**On KERR KELLER: books**—*Product Design 3* by Joe Dolce, New York, 1988; *Product Design 5,* New York, 1990; *International Design Yearbook,* London, 1991; *International Design Yearbook,* London, 1992; **articles**—*ID* Annual Design Review (New York), 1988; "Northern Lights, Shining Moments in Lamp Design" in *Homes,* March 1989; *Axis* (Japan), Summer 1990; "Canadian Design Is Coming of Age" by Christopher Hume in *Toronto Star* (Toronto), 23 October 1990; *Canadian Interiors* by Elizabeth Crinion, October 1990; "The Import of Exports" by Adele Freedman in *Globe and Mail* (Toronto), 24 November 1990; "Smooth Finish" by Anne Bokma in *Financial Post* (Toronto), December 1990; "Rays Pierce the Cloud" by John Barber in *Globe and Mail* (Toronto), 26 December 1991; "Best of the Basics" by Christopher Hume in *Toronto Star* (Toronto) 16 March 1991; "Success by Design" by Anne Kingston in *Financial Times of Canada* (Toronto), January 1992; "By Design; Contemporary Canadian Furniture Designers Make Their Mark" by Rise Levy in *Homes,* Summer 1992; "Taking a Stab at the Look of Cutlery" by John Barber in *Globe and Mail* (Toronto), 12 November 1992; *Newsweek* (New York), 7 December 1992; "Less Art, More Matter" by Rachel Rafelmen & David Lasker in *Globe and Mail* (Toronto), 23 March 1993; "Showcase" by Pamela Young in *Insite* (London), July 1995, September 1995; by Pamela Young in *Globe and Mail* (Toronto), Fashion and Design Supplement, November 1995.

*        *        *

The location of Helen Kerr and Miles Keller's industrial design office speaks volumes about their vision of product design. Above an art gallery on a bustling main street in a leafy Toronto neighborhood called The Beach, a reference to its proximity to the shores of Lake Ontario, their studio is very much part of the comings and goings of everyday urban life. Not surprisingly, the range of furniture and products that comes from this studio directly reflects and responds to the way that we really live and work in the world. Viewing the products from this team of designers it's as if the passing crowds are frequently invited up to test the products under development.

Kerr Keller's work demands to be held and touched. The forms, colors, and materials that they use are tactile, soft, and friendly. Their designs, whether at the scale of a soap dish or a chair, speak with a formal vocabulary that is soft-edged without being mushy. These are products that are worlds apart from the bulbous and bloated Jetson-like shapes found in so much current consumer products such as stereos and cars. While these products are some marketers' vision of the future, Kerr and Keller's forms are deeply rooted in an understanding and sensitivity to the way that products are manufactured and, more importantly, used. They respond to our hands, our eyes, and our bodies. Even in photographs, these are products that we can imagine sitting on, picking up, caressing, and using.

While stylish, these products are not self-consciously styled.

Kerr and Keller's forms are a result of a fascination with what materials can do within the context of what the purpose and use of the object is. A series of glass soap dishes have the look and feel of a small Brancusi sculpture sitting on the bathroom sink; their opaque texture and diffused colors make them always appear to be shrouded by steam. Pick them up and they are cool and sensuous to the touch.

Helen Kerr and Miles Keller's work has been significantly influenced by their education and training. Before studying industrial design, Keller studied architecture. Kerr's training was in environmental science. These paths to the field of product design provide the duo with an understanding of three factors that are constantly expressed in their work; an appreciation of the environments into which their products will ultimately reside, a firm grasp of the meaning of scale as it relates to consumer products, and a concern with developing products that are sensitive to environmental issues such as the selection materials and production processes. As an example of this last issue, Kerr and Keller's Vitesse series of desk accessories for Umbra are elegantly sculpted form plantation rubberwood.

Kerr and Keller are members of a generation of Canadian designers that have forged strong links with several small but aggressive Canadian manufacturers. The result is a series of ongoing collaborative relationships that have helped the firm gain a deeper understanding of the production, marketing, and financial factors that are increasingly critical in successful product development and design projects. And, increasingly, clients in both Canada and the United States such Corning, Sasaki, and Keilhauer are finding Kerr Keller's expertise and outlook refreshing and are utilizing the firm's services in product research and planning as well as design and production services. These relationships will no doubt mean more opportunities for Kerr Keller products to find their way into our willing hands.

—Lee Jacobson

# KERZ, Leo
German stage, film, exhibition, and graphic designer

**Born:** Berlin, 1 November 1912. **Education:** Studied at the Friedrich Ebert Oberrealschule, Berlin, BA, 1932; Academy of Arts and Sciences, Berlin, 1933; also studied design with Bertholt Brecht, Laszlo Moholy-Nagy, and Erwin Piscator, 1928-32, and with Traugot Mueller, 1930-33. **Career:** Stage and film designer from 1932; television designer from 1949; exhibition designer from 1955; worked for theatres in Berlin and Prague, 1932-37; founder, Pioneer Theatre, Johannesburg, 1937-42; art director, Pittsburgh Civic Light Opera Association, 1946-47, San Francisco Opera Association and New York City Opera Company, 1956; staff designer, CBS Television, New York, 1949-54. Lecturer, University of Witwatersrand, Johannesburg, 1938-39, and New School for Social Research, New York 1943-44; visiting professor, Montana State University, Bozeman, 1964. **Honors:** New York Music Critics Award, 1956; Outer Circle Award, 1961; United States Government Cultural Exchange Grant, 1963. **Died:** New York City, 1976.

## Works

Stage productions include—*The Threepenny Opera,* Pioneer Theatre, Johannesburg, 1938; *Miracle at Verdun,* Pioneer Theatre, 1939; *Golden Boy,* Pioneer Theatre, 1940; *The Cradle Will Rock,* Pioneer Theatre, 1941; *The Hairy Ape,* Pioneer Theatre, 1942; *The Rally of Hope,* Madison Square Garden, New York, 1946; *The Golden Doors,* Madison Square Garden, 1946; *Antony and Cleopatra,* Martin Beck Theatre, 1947; *A Long Way From Home,* Maxine Elliott's Theatre, New York, 1948; *Bravo Lyceum,* New York, 1948; *The Biggest Thief in Town,* Mansfield Theatre, New York, 1949; *The Gypsies Wore High Hats,* Cape Theatre, Dennis, Massachusetts, 1952; *The Victim,* President Theatre, New York, 1952; *The Sacred Flame,* President Theatre, 1952; *Troilus and Cressida,* San Francisco Opera, 1954; *Macbeth,* San Francisco Opera, 1954; *Aida,* San Francisco Opera, 1955; *Lohengrin,* San Francisco Opera, 1955; *Der Rosenkavalier,* San Francisco Opera, 1956; *Parsifal,* Metropolitan Opera, New York, 1956; *The Magic Flute,* Metropolitan Opera, 1956; *Landara,* Curtis Institute of Music Philadelphia, 1956; *Orpheus in the Underworld,* New York City Center, 1956; *Susannah,* New York City Center, 1956; *The Tempest,* New York City Center, 1956; *Clerambard,* Rooftop Theatre, New York, 1957; *Listen to the Mockingbird,* Colonial Theatre, Boston, 1958 (toured); *Moonbirds,* Cort Theatre, New York, 1959; *Rhinoceros,* Longacre Theatre, New York, 1961; *Der Stellvertreter,* Theater am Kurfurstendamm, Berlin, 1963.
Film designs include—*Extase* (Machaty), 1932; *Guilty Bystander* (Lerner), 1950; *Mr. Universe* (Lerner), 1951; *Teresa* (Zinnemann), 1951; *This is Cinerama,* 1952; *The Goddess* (Cromwell), 1958; *Middle of the Night* (Delbert Mann), 1959; *Odds Against Tomorrow* (Wise), 1959; *New York Confidential* (ABC Television), 1959; *In What America?* (television, for Esso World Theatre), 1964.

## Publications

**On KERZ: books**—*The Biographical Encyclopaedia and Who's Who of the American Theatre,* edited by Walter Rigdon, New York,

1966; *Le Decor de Film* by Leon Barsacq, Paris, 1970, as *Caligari's Cabinet and Other Grand Illusions,* Boston, 1976.

\* \* \*

When one goes to the core of Leo Kerz's work, it is clear that his early work with Irwin Piscator and Bertolt Brecht in Berlin continued to influence all his productions. He was always less interested in placing realism or romance on stage than in capturing several enlarged and enhanced historical shapes that could stand for an entire culture, or how an open stage defined by a number of large set pieces could give direction and movement to a play or an opera's action. In many ways, he was a transitional figure in stage design, using historic information from the romantic and symbolist past without stressing fuzzy mood and emotion. He was more interested in giving size, movement, character definition, and spatial clarity to the scene, while allowing a few broad images to carry the weight of the historical or emotional action of the play or opera. For example, in his first Broadway production, *Antony and Cleopatra,* he created a great bank of Egyptian columns across the stage; against and within these, he created the play's scenes with a minimal use of properties and accessories.

Following the lead of his teacher, Piscator, he also made great use of films and projections when they seemed appropriate, used a constructivist methodology to define space and give definition to actor movement, and made great use of texture as an integral and yet autonomous element in a stage setting. Thus, he combined the best of the past and present in the visual arts, using abstraction and spatial definition while still giving the audience a shorthand sense of place, time, and atmosphere. He also designed for industrial shows, pageants, and television and was a teacher at a number of United States schools and universities, where he spread the epic theatre theories of Piscator.

Though Kerz designed in all theatrical media, one can say that his major contribution to theatrical scene design was to solidify, modify, and spread the visual ideals of epic theatre.

—Douglas A. Russell

# KHANH, Emmanuelle

French fashion designer

**Born:** Renée Mezière, in Paris, 12 September 1937. **Family:** Married the designer Quasar Khanh (Manh Khanh Nguyen) in 1957; children: Othello and Atlantique-Venus. **Career:** Worked as a mannequin, for the fashion houses of Balenciaga and Givenchy, Paris, 1957-62; creator of collections for Belletete, Missoni, Dorothée Bis, Laura, Cacharel, Pierre d'Alby, Krizia, Max Mara, and Le Bistrot du Tricot, in Paris, 1962-69; founder-director, Emmanuelle Khanh fashion design company, Paris, from 1971, becoming Emmanuelle Khanh International, 1987; opened own boutiques, 1977. **Exhibitions:** *Antonio,* Images de Mode Musée des Arts et de la Mode, Paris, 1994; *Le Gant,* Couvent des Cordeliers, Paris, 1995. **Honors:** Arts and Letters Award, Ministre de la Culture, France, 1986. **Address:** Emmanuelle Khanh S.A., 45 Avenue Victor Hugo, 75116 Paris, France.

**Publications**

**On KHANH: books—**  *Fairchild's Dictionary of Fashion* edited by Charlotte Calasibetta, New York, 1975; *In Vogue: Sixty Years of Celebrities and Fashion* edited by Georgina Howell, London, 1975, 1978, New York, 1976; *A History of Fashion* by J. Anderson Black and Madge Garland, London, 1975, 1980; *The World of Fashion: People, Places, Resources* by Eleanor Lambert, New York and London, 1976; *In Fashion: Dress in the Twentieth Century* by Prudence Glynn, London, 1978; *Fairchild's Who's Who in Fashion* edited by Ann Stegemeyer, New York, 1980; *McDowell's Directory of Twentieth Century Fashion* by Colin McDowell, London, 1984; *The Encyclopaedia of Fashion from 1840 to the 1980s* by Georgina O'Hara, London, 1986; *Antonio 60-70-80: Images de Mode,* Paris, 1994; *Dictionnaire de la Mode du XXème Siècle,* Paris, 1994.

\*

Fashion bores me. Women inspire me. I am passionate about the subject. It is a way for a woman to participate in her time.

A style created with love ... reflects on the person wearing it.

I love the idea that women around the world wear a bit of myself and that I am a part of their memories, their universe.

—Emmanuelle Khanh
(From the preface, *Creatif de Choc* by Roger von Oech, Paris, 1991)

\* \* \*

**Emmanuelle Khanh: Blouse, summer 1993. Photo by M. Roulier, courtesy of Emmanuelle Khanh**

The look that Emmanuelle Khanh created in the 1960s can be placed between the styles being inspired by the new London designers and those of Parisian couturier such as Yves Saint Laurent. It was her beautifully produced youthful garments which foreshadowed the rise of ready-to-wear as a real threat, in the 1970s, to the dominance of haute couture. Skillful cutting, seaming, the use of innovative detail, such as the petal and "spaniel's ears" collars, and a preference for natural fabrics have continued to distinguish her personal style. Hers is a young, classical image which has ranged from updated versions of the trench coat and the two-piece suit to the jaunty "Jules and Jim" caps and knickerbockers of the early 1960s. By the late 1960s, she had made an impact well beyond Paris and had developed her range to include knitwear, ski-wear, and the light, natural underwear which was important for the young look.

Despite the range of her designs, Khanh has created a predominantly feminine style, which epitomizes her own relationship with clothes. The fact that she began her career in the fashion world as a model for such prominent houses as Balenciaga and Givenchy meant that she has been able, personally, to promote her new ideas, such as the show-topping shorts of 1971. The fact that she wears her own designs has led her to concentrate on comfort, freedom of movement, looseness, and the draping of fabric to produce individual yet essentially wearable garments.

Her individuality does not mean isolation, however, for she is also involved with cooperative design projects as part of a closely knit team. Quasar Khanh, her husband and business associate, is an interior designer who also designs Quasar menswear, while his sister Be Khanh is a textile fashion coordinator. A business partnership with her friend Aimer Bruno led to the organization of a firm which specialized in the use of Rumanian hand embroideries and then to the fashion firm Emmanuelle Khanh/-CINEC. This most recent use of hand embroidery on her dresses continues the emphasis on detail seen even in her earliest work.

As a female designer, Khanh works for an ideal of woman which she herself personifies. She has become a classic ready-to-wear designer whose attention to the specific, such as jewel-like effects by means of beading, marks her personal style.

—Hazel Clark

# KIDD, Chip

American book jacket, illustrator, and graphic designer

**Born:** Shillington, Pennsylvania, 1964. **Education:** Graduated in design, Pennsylvania State University. **Career:** Book designer, Alfred A. Knopf. **Address:** Alfred A. Knopf, Design Department, 201 East 50th Street, New York, New York 10022.

## Works

Book jacket design, *Grey is the Color of Hope* by Irina Ratushinskaya, for Knopf, 1989.
Book jacket design, *London Fields* by Martin Amis, for Harmony Books, 1989.
Book jacket design, *Nothing If Not Critical* by Robert Hughes, for Knopf, 1990.

Book jacket design, *In the Beginning* by Irina Ratushinskaya, for Knopf, 1990.
Book jacket design (with Carol Devine Carson), *Me: Stories of My Life* by Katharine Hepburn, for Knopf, 1991.
Book jacket design, *Typical American* by Gish Jen, for Houghton Mifflin, 1991.
Book jacket design, *Felix: The Twisted Tale of the World's Most Famous Cat* by John Canemaker, for Knopf, 1991.
Book jacket design, *Dreaming in Cuban* by Cristina Garcia, for Knopf, 1993.
Book jacket design, *Disclosure* by Michael Crichton, for Knopf, 1994.
Book jacket design, *Brazzaville Beach* by William Boyd, for William Morrow.
Book jacket design, *My Hard Decision* by Walter Kirk, for Knopf.
Book jacket design, *God's Phallus,* for Knopf
Book jacket design, *The Secret History* by Donna Tartt, for Knopf.
Book jacket design (photography by Anton Stankowski), *All You Who Sleep Tonight* by Vikram Seth, for Knopf.
Book jacket design, *Watching the Body Burn* by Thomas Glyn, for Knopf.
Book jacket design, *The Conscience of the Eye: The Design and Social Life of Cities* by Richard Sennett, for Knopf.
Book jacket design, *Darling* by William Tester, for Knopf.

## Publications

**By KIDD: articles**—"Viewpoint: Design Practice, Very Nice" in *Graphis* (New York), September/October 1993; "Run with the Dwarves and Win: Adventures in the Book Trade" in *Print* (New York), May/June 1995.

**On KIDD: articles**—"Mini-portfolio" by Paul Elie in *Print* (New York), September/October 1992.

# KIESER, Günther

German stage, exhibition, industrial, poster, and graphic designer

**Born:** Kronberg im Taunus, 24 March 1930. **Education:** Studied lithography and commercial design, at the Werkkunstschule, Offenbach am Main, 1947-50. **Career:** Freelance designer, with Hans Michel, in Michel + Kieser design studio, Offenbach 1951-63; established own design studio, in Frankfurt, from 1964; has designed posters for concerts, tours, and festivals. Instructor in lettering, College of Fine Arts, Frankfurt, from 1957; professor of communications design, Bergischen Universität, Wuppertal, 1981-92. **Member:** Alliance Graphique Internationale, Deutsche Werkbund; Berufsverband Bildenden Künstler, Münich. **Exhibitions:** Lincoln Center, New York, 1972; Internationales des Arts Graphiques, Chaumont, 1993; Museum für Kunst und Gewerbe, Hamburg, 1994. **Collections:** Museum of Modern Art, New York; Royal Ontario Museum, Toronto; Plakat-Museum, Essen; Museum für Kunsthandwerk, Frankfurt am Main. **Honors:** Best German Poster Award, 1956, 1957, 1958, 1959; Photokina Award, Cologne, 1958; New York Art Directors Club Award, 1966; Gold Medal, 1968, and Silver Medal, 1984, Warsaw Poster Biennale;

**Günther Kieser: poster for the 26th Jazz Festival, Frankfurt, Germany, 1995**

Toulouse Lautrec Gold Medal, Essen Poster Triennale, 1983; Grand Prix, Lodz Jazz Poster Salon, 1985; Gold Medal, Brno Poster Biennale, 1986; State Culture Prize, Essen, 1990; Litaßpreis, 1991. **Address:** Gunthers-burgallee 81, 6000 Frankfurt am Main 60, Germany.

## Works

*Dixieland Jubilee* poster, for Konzertbüro Lippmann, 1953.
*History of Jazz* poster, for Deutsche Jazz Föderation, 1954.
*Jazz Band Ball* poster, for Hot Club Frankfurt, 1955.
*Jazz Konzert Albert Nicholas* poster, for Konzertbüro Lippmann, 1956.
Posters for jazz, blues, and rock concerts and festivals, for Lippmann & Rau Concert Büro, 1962-85.
*American Folk Blues Festival* posters, for Lippmann & Rau Concert Büro, 1962, 1963, 1965, 1966, 1968, 1969, 1970, 1972, 1980, 1982.
*Jazz Jubilate Swingle Singers* poster, for Hessischer Rundfunk, 1963.
*Deutsches Jazz Festival Frankfurt* posters, for Lippmann & Rau and Hessischer Rundfunk, 1966, 1976, 1978, 1980, 1982, 1984, 1986, 1988, 1990, 1992, 1994, 1995.
*Berliner Jazz Tage* posters, for Konzertdirektion R. Schulte Barhenberg, 1968, 1969, 1970, 1972, 1973, 1975, 1977, 1978, 1979.
Posters, for Hessischer Rundfunk Hörfunk, from 1975.
*Kultur Kalendar* poster, for Hessischer Rundfunk, 1979.
*Doktor Faust* poster, 1980, and *Ballett Woche* poster, 1984, for Oper Frankfurt.
*Hilfe statt Gewalt* poster, for Deutscher Kinderschutzbund, 1980.
*Braun HiFi* poster, for Braun AG, 1980.
*Warum denn nicht Frieden?* poster, for Lippmann & Rau, 1982.
*Im Wandel der Zeiten, Richard Wagner, Heil'ge Hochzeit,* and *Anton Webern* posters, for Schauspiel Zyklus, Alte Oper Frankfurt, 1983.
*11.* and *12. Römerberg-Gespräche* posters, for Amt für Wissenschaft und Kunst, Frankfurt am Main, 1984, 1985.
*Jazz Fest Berlin* posters, for Berliner Festspiele, 1984, 1985, 1987, 1988, 1989, 1990, 1991, 1992, 1994.
*Musik & Schott* poster, for Musikverlag B. Schott's Söhne, Mainz, 1991.
*Ausstellung Oikos* poster, for Deutscher Werkbund, 1992.
*Goethe* poster, for Goethe-Institut, 1992.
*EXIL* poster, for Stadt Eisenach, 1994.

## Publications

**On KIESER: books**—*Who's Who in Graphic Art* edited by Walter Amstutz, Zürich, 1962, Dubendorf, 1982; *Illustration: Aspects and Directions* by Bob Gill and John Lewis, London, 1964; *The Poster: An Illustrated History from 1860* by Harold F. Hutchinson, London and Toronto, 1968; *Graphis Record Covers* edited by Walter Herdeg, Zürich, 1974; *Album Cover Album* edited by Storm Thorgerson and Roger, Limpsfield, 1979; *A History of Graphic Design* by Philip Meggs, New York, 1983; *The Art of Rock: Posters from Presley to Punk* by Paul D. Grushkin, New York, 1987; *The Modern Poster* by Stuart Wrede, New York, 1988; *First Choice: The Worlds Leading Graphic Designers Select the Best of All Their Work* by Ken

Cato, Tokyo, 1989; *Histoire(s), Image(s), Parol(s),* Paris, 1989; *Top Graphic Design* by F.H.K. Henrion, Zürich, 1989; *Wo der Buchstabe das Wort führt* by Kurt Weidemann, Germany, 1994; *bis Bennetton,* exhibition catalogue, Hamburg, 1994; *100 Posters: The Best from Europe and the United States* edited by Milton Glaser, Yusaku Kamekura, and Alain Weill, Tokyo, 1995; *Kieser, Plakate, Exchange,* Frankfurt am Main, 1995; **articles**—"Günther Kieser" by Kurt Weidemann in *Graphics,* no. 184, 1976/77; "Günther Kieser" by Rolf Müller and Günter Braus in *High Quality,* 1986; *Novum Gebrauchsgraphik* (Münich) no. 1, 1972, 1990.

# KIMURA, Kazuo

Japanese industrial designer

**Born:** Osaka, 24 July 1934. **Education:** Studied at Tokyo University of Arts, BFA, 1958. **Family:** Married Seiko Kimura; children: Mitsuhiro. **Career:** Chief designer, at Nissan Motor Company, Tokyo, 1958-72; freelance designer, Osaka, from 1972. Kyoto Conference Committee Member, 1972-74, and vice-president, from 1980, International Council of Societies of Industrial Design (ICSID); executive secretary, Japan Industrial Designers Association, from 1974; secretary general, Japan Design Foundation, from 1980. Contributor, *Industrial Design, Nikkei Architecture,* and *Design Age* magazines, Tokyo. **Address:** c/o Japan Design Foundation, Senba Center Building no. 4, 2-2 Senba Chuo, Higashi-ku, Osaka 541, Japan.

## Publications

**By KIMURA: books**—(editor) *ICSID 73: Official Report,* Tokyo, 1973.

**On KIMURA: books**—*The Language of Graphics* by Edward Booth-Clibborn and Daniele Baroni, London, 1980.

\*

Most of my recent work has been devoted, invisibly, to the promotion and development of industrial design in Japan because, in view of the development of our environment for better or worse, the role and responsibilities of industrial design seem extremely important. Therefore, I have endeavored to form organizations that promote design activities, to advance public relations at both the national and international levels, and to establish other professional activities with the help of the Japan Industrial Designers' association, in the hope that these may also relate to other fields of design.

—Kazuo Kimura

\*     \*     \*

The contemporary Japanese design movement, which was initiated in the early 1950s, can be said to have comprised three stages: study and experimentation; an autonomous period of growth; and the current internationalist stance. Among the many designers who guided this development—off stage, as it were—is Kazuo Kimura.

For fifteen years, Kimura was Chief Designer for Nissan Motors. But he then changed course, and since the early 1970s, he has been prominent in the administration of design organizations—to which he has made very substantial contributions. Kimura has great self-confidence as a designer, and he tries to promote his own philosophy of the value of the "hand-made"—but he is also a diplomat, a man held in great affection by his peers, and, essential to an administrator, he is always open-minded.

The conference of the International Council of Societies of Industrial Design, held in Kyoto in 1973, was the first such conference to take place outside of Europe or North America, and it was organized on a grand scale. The results of the conference provoked great discussion both in Japan and abroad; in fact, its theme of "mind/material" came to dominate design philosophies in the next decade. And it was Kimura who served as Secretary General of the organizing committee of the conference.

His career as a design administrator has evolved from that first success. He was appointed Executive Secretary of the Japan Industrial Designers Association, and he soon became the champion of industrial designers who suffered from the problems of low economic growth.

Then, in 1980, Kimura was appointed Secretary-General of the Japan Design Fundation, which was established under the auspices of the Ministry of International Trade and Industry, to actively organize various international programs. Thus, Kimura is responsible for providing opportunities for industrial designers in Japan and other countries to share information and exchange opinions; in effect, Japan, through the foundation, acts as a coordinator. In one sense, Japan, until now, has been a recipient of design information. From now on, however, it intends to be a disseminator as well—an active contributor to the world community of design. Kimura hopes that the Foundation's activities will provoke not only important symposia, but also new movements in design.

At about the same time, Kimura was also appointed Vice-President of ICSID; his position as an internationalist was confirmed. In both of these posts, Kimura continues to display his great competence and his abiding commitment to design.

—Kunio Sano

# KINNEIR, (Richard) Jock

British graphic designer

**Born:** Aldershot, Hampshire, 11 February 1917. **Education:** Studied at Chelsea School of Art, London, 1935-39. **Career:** Exhibition designer, Central Office of Information, London, c. 1945-50; designer, Design Research Unit, London, 1950-56; freelance graphic designer, Knightsbridge, from 1956; clients included Shell, Gatwick Airport, P & O, British Rail, British Airports Authority, and others. Part-time instructor, Chelsea School of Art, from 1956; head of graphic design, Royal College of Art, London, 1964-69; visiting lecturer, Aarhus School of Architecture, Denmark. **Member:** Alliance Graphique Internationale. **Exhibitions:** *107 Grafici dell'AGI*, Castello Sforzesco, Milan, 1974. **Honors:** Council of Industrial Design Award, London, 1967. **Died:** 23 August 1994.

## Publications

**By KINNEIR: books**—*Words and Buildings,* London, 1980; **articles**—in *Architectural Review* (London), May 1966, April 1978; *Arkitektur* (Copenhagen), no. 3, 1969; *The Designer* (London), November 1970; *Design and Art* (London), July 1983.

**On KINNEIR: books**—*Modern Graphics* by Keith Murgatroyd, London, 1969; *107 Grafici dell'AGI,* with texts by Renzo Zorzi and Franco Grignani, Venice, 1974; *Industrial Design in Britain* by Noel Carrington, London, 1976; *The Thames and Hudson Manual of Typography* by Ruari McLean, London, 1980; **articles**—"Fading Signature Tune" by Chris Ludlow in *Design Week* (London), 23 September 1994.

\*     \*     \*

One of the early jobs of Jock Kinneir's practice—a system of labelling for the P & O Company—exemplified on a small scale the character of his major contributions. The design of the system, of sets of elements to be assembled according to stated rules, emerged as the visual elements took the form of a coding system for information that was first analyzed and sorted. A set of labels was the outcome, but what had been designed, more fundamentally, was a system. So with signing systems such as those made for British Rail and the British Airports Authority: their success depended as much on the initial work of analysis and on the final work of formulating instructions for implementation as on the design of the particular visual elements employed. Another vital procedure was the testing and modifying of prototypes, as the signing systems were tested for legibility.

Kinneir's first alphabets—sanserif, upper-and lower-case—were not easily accepted, and a counter-proposal for his motorway signs—of a roman (seriffed) alphabet of capital letters only—was seriously entertained by some parties. One might now see the acceptance of the Kinneir letterforms and symbols as part of the belated arrival of the modern movement in Britain; these were also the years of the vogue for "Swiss," sanserif typography. But their place in the environment has proved more assured than an explanation on mere grounds of taste would allow.

The success of Kinneir's road signs in particular (the most complex of the various systems) lay in an avoidance of any unthinking formalism. And the system showed the benefits of considerable typographic sophistication, in such details as its use of brackets and indentation, as well as in forms of letters and numerals and (crucially) in spacing. The succession of the signing alphabets seemed to show a broad development, allowing for the clearly different functions of each. The Gatwick and also the road alphabets have what may seem oddities in certain characters. These disappeared in the rail alphabet, which is a more homogenous set of forms. The later alphabet, for the Tyne and Wear Metro, has slab serifs; it was developed by his partner, Margaret Calvert, as a typeface for printing (Monophoto Calvert).

That the signing systems designed by Kinneir's practice are now taken for granted by their users is one measure of the achievement. The work is ubiquitous and necessary. In all this, and in the manner in which the tasks have been tackled, this work represented a new level of maturity in British design.

—Robin Kinross

# KIRK, Mark-Lee

American film designer

**Career:** Designer, working mainly with supervising art director Richard Day, for 20th Century-Fox Film Studios, Hollywood, 1936-40; art director, with RKO Studios, Hollywood, 1940-44; and working with Lyle Wheeler, at 20th Century-Fox Studios, Hollywood, 1945-59. **Died.**

## Works

Films include—*Wake up and Live* (Lanfield), 1937; *Young Mr. Lincoln* (Ford), 1939; *Drums Along the Mohawk* (Ford), 1939; *The Grapes of Wrath* (Ford), 1940; *My Favorite Wife* (Kanin), 1940; *They Knew What They Wanted* (Kanin), 1940; *The Magnificent Ambersons* (Welles), 1942; *Journey Into Fear* (Foster and Welles), 1943; *I'll Be Seeing You* (Dieterle), 1944; *A Bell for Adano* (H. King) 1945; *A Royal Scandal* (Preminger), 1945; *Moss Rose* (Ratoff), 1947; *The Iron Curtain* (Wellmann), 1948; *The Prince of Foxes* (H. King), 1949; *Way of a Gaucho* (Tourneur), 1952; *Kangaroo* (Milestone), 1952; *White Witch Doctor* (Hathaway), 1953; *Prince Valiant* (Hathaway), 1954; *The Tall Men* (Walsh), 1955; *Prince of Players* (Dunne); *The Revolt of Mamie Stover* (Walsh), 1956; *Bus Stop* (Logan), 1956; *The Sun Also Rises* (H. King), 1957; *The Bravados* (H. King), 1958; *The Best of Everything* (Negulesco), 1959; *Compulsion* (Fleischer), 1959.

## Publications

**On KIRK: book**—*Le Décor de Film* by Leon Barsacq, Paris, 1970, as *Caligari's Cabinet and Other Grand Illusions,* Boston, 1976.

\*     \*     \*

Mark-Lee Kirk's reputation rested on his atmospheric period reconstructions. However, this wealth of well researched details transcended mere documentary display. Facts served as tools for revealing deeper insights into character and theme. For such philosophical art direction, one usually turned to Kirk's contemporary, Richard Day. Since the two collaborated on Kirk's earliest motion pictures, Day presumably influenced Kirk. However, Kirk alone served as art director on that masterpiece of "symbolic realism," *The Magnificent Ambersons* (1942).

The Amberson mansion, as designed by Kirk, played a more potent role than any member of the film's cast. With its genteel charm and ominous horror, it served at times as a sanctuary from reality, while in other instances it played the prison, trapping its owners in a gilded cage. As an intimidating baronial estate, the mansion's opulent decor encompassed Gothic, Victorian, and Edwardian styles, all emblems of the ruling class.

Neither Tara from the 1939 *Gone With the Wind* nor *Rebecca*'s Manderlay of 1940 rivaled Kirk's vision of the mansion. Only *Citizen Kane*'s Xanadu, from 1941, came close. The Amberson mansion surpassed its inhabitants in visual power. Isabel might be paralleled to the house, particularly with a zealous Freudian interpretation (with Eugene struggling to enter the doors and son George refusing to leave them), but her weak character undercuts the comparison.

As the audience first enters the mansion, it is swept (via camera), along with the other invited guests, from room to room, to marvel at the Ambersons' sparkling treasures. To enhance that sense of presence, Kirk added the illusion of all four walls, an impressive detail few films would bother including. This technical trick gave the mansion further structural credibility.

Kirk also built in the mansion an unusual staircase for interesting compositional and expressive effects. Characters hover over each other from banister to banister in sadistic domination. In another situation, the staircase provides a simile, as George and Lucy strolling on the upper levels echo the elder generation on the main floor.

Thematically, *The Magnificent Ambersons* considered the transitory nature of man's world. Kirk demonstrated this early in the picture by disrupting an idyllic, Currier-and-Ives snow scene with such vestiges of civilization as telephone wires. This image, more than correct historically, was prophetic. Later, as the small, midwestern town burst with urban blight, its clutter contrasted with the now empty, tomblike mansion.

Kirk created more than the documentation of days gone by. He drew beyond the backdrops of life's activities. Although few may recognize that a world exists outside its inhabitants and that this world influences us even as we assuredly alter it, Kirk's observations and interpretations of such environments added depth to his characters' cinematic surroundings.

—Edith Cortland Lee

# KJAERHOLM, Poul

Danish architect, furniture, and ceramic designer

**Born:** Øster Vra, 8 January 1929. **Education:** Studied design, at the Konsthantverkskolan, Copenhagen, 1949-52. **Family:** Married the architect Hanne Dam in 1953. **Career:** Freelance designer, working with Thorald Madsen, Fritz Hansen, E. Kold Christiansen companies, and others, in Copenhagen, 1953-80. Instructor, at the Konsthantverkskolan, Copenhagen, 1952-56; instructor, 1955-76, and professor, 1976-80, at the Kunstakademie, Copenhagen. **Exhibitions:** *Neue Forme aus Dänemark* (toured Germany), 1956-59; *Formes Scadinaves,* Paris, 1958; *The Arts of Denmark,* the United States, 1960-61; Stedelijk Museum, Amsterdam, 1966; *Les Assises du Siège Contemporain,* Musée des Arts Decoratifs, Paris, 1968; *Modern Chairs 1918-1970,* Whitechapel Art Gallery, London, 1970; *Classics,* Heal's Furniture Store, London, 1981; *Scandinavian Modern Design 1880-1980,* Cooper-Hewitt Museum, New York, 1982; *Design Since 1945,* Philadelphia Museum of Art, 1983; *The Lunning Prize,* Nationalmuseum, Stockholm, 1986. **Collections:** Kunstindustrimuseet, Copenhagen. **Honors:** Grand Prize, Milan Triennale, 1957, 1960; Danish Society of Applied Arts Annual Prize, 1957; Lunning Prize, Copenhagen, 1960; Knud V. Engelhardt Prize, Copenhagen, 1965; Brno Critics' Prize, 1968; Copenhagen Industrial Design Prize, 1973; Copenhagen Furniture Makers Association Prize, 1977. **Died:** Hillerod, Denmark, 18 April 1980.

## Works

Chair in chrome steel and linen, 1951, produced by E. Kold Christiansen, from 1957.

Coffee table in steel and marble, for E. Kold Christiansen, 1956.

Candle-holders in matt chromed steel, for E. Kold Christiansen, 1956.

Stackable tables in steel and acrylic, for E. Kold Christiansen, 1957.

Modular sectioned room-screen in pine, for E. Kold Christiansen, 1957.

*Number 24* chaise lounge in steel and wicker with leather neck-rest, for E. Kold Christiansen, 1958.

*Number 9* chair in chrome steel and glass fibre with leather upholstery, for E. Kold Christiansen, 1960.

*Model 91* folding stool in chrome steel and leather, for E. Kold Christiansen, 1961.

*Number 20* recliner chair in steel and leather, for E. Kold Christiansen, 1968.

Seating system and chairs, for the Louisiana Concert Hall, Humlebaek, 1973.

## Publications

**On KJAERHOLM: books**—*Danish Chairs* by Nanna and Jorgen Ditzel, Copenhagen, 1954; *Dansk Keramik* edited by Bredo L. Grandjean, David Westholm, and Arthur Hald, Stockholm, 1960; *Modern Scandinavian* Furniture by Ulf Hard af Segerstad, Copenhagen, 1963; *Contemporary Danish Design* edited by Arne Karlsen, Bent Salicath, and Mogens Utzon-Frank, Copenhagen, 1966; *34 Scandinavian Designers* by Svend Erik Moller, Copenhagen, 1967; *Modern Chairs 1918-1970,* exhibition catalogue by Carol Hogben and others, London, 1970; *The Modern Chair: Classics in Production* by Clement Meadmore, London, 1974; *Twentieth Century Furniture* by Philippe Garner, London, 1980; *Danish Design 1980* edited by Jens Bernsen and Per Mollerup, Copenhagen, 1980; *Scandinavian Modern Design 1880-1980* edited by David Revere McFadden, New York, 1982; *Contemporary Furniture* by Klaus-Jürgen Sembach, London, 1982; *Design Since 1945* edited by Kathryn Hiesinger and George Marcus, Philadelphia and London, 1983; *Mid-Century: Furniture of the 1950s* by Cara Greenberg, London, 1984; *Industrial Design: Unikate Serienerzeugnisse* by Hans Wichmann, Munich, 1985; *Design Source Book* by Penny Sparke, London, 1986; *Modern Furniture Classics* by Miriam Stimpson, London, 1987.

\*     \*     \*

Almost invariably, discussions of Poul Kjaerholm's work compare it to Mies van der Rohe's. Certainly, there are points of likeness in the approaches of these two architects. Both exhibit that elegance which can result only when all excess is banished. In their furniture, both favor flat, rather than tubular, steel frames, and they relied on the subtle stitching of leather upholstery to reinforce form.

But there are differences as well. Mies's work, however classic it has become, evinces a Germanic gravity that binds it to the floor. Kjaerholm's pieces, on the other hand, are more lightly tethered, their clearly articulated joints and imaginatively profiled frames implying an upward thrust. In Mies's famous Brno chair, for example, the cantilevered support promises a springing motion, but this is visibly denied by the uncompromising angle of seat and back. In contrast, the seductive sling of Kjaerholm's *Chair 20* (1968) works with the elasticity of its C-curved base even as it provides a visual complement.

Another illustration of their differences is the contrast between Mies's X-framed Barcelona stool and Kjaerholm's X-framed *Stool 91*. Both draw on a folding-furniture tradition which goes back to Egypt, if not beyond. In Mies's version, the supporting X is drawn with exquisite elegance and deception: the stool does not fold. *Stool 91* offers its own, equally elegant X, the quarter-turns of its frame shimmering in the light and introducing a sensation of movement. To this sensory impact is joined function: the stool folds. In historical terms, one might say that in these pieces the designers exemplify aspects of the Classic tradition—Kjaerholm exhibiting the honesty of Greece, Mies, the illusion of Rome.

Kjaerholm's use of the International Style's signature material, metal, sets him apart from the majority of his Scandinavian peers, most of whom remained committed to wood before the advent of the stylistic challenge of the Italians in the 1960s. Remaining as independent of the resulting move to plastics as he had been of traditional woodcraft, Kjaerholm continued his perfection of a machine esthetic. However, both the linear purity of his designs and his exploration of the subtleties to be drawn from his material enhance, rather than challenge, the comfort of the user. Kjaerholm's work meets the criteria of intellectual and structural honesty developed in the early years of the International Style and brings them into correspondence with the realities of the human experience.

—Reed Benhamou

# KLEIN, Anne

American fashion designer

**Born:** Hannah Golofsky, in Brooklyn, New York, 7 June 1923. **Education:** Studied art, at the Girl's Commercial High School, Brooklyn, until 1937; Traphagen School of Fashion, New York, 1937-38. **Family:** Married Ben Klein (divorced, 1958); married Matthew Rubinstein. **Career:** Worked as a designer, for Varden Petites, New York, 1938-40; designer of women's fashions, for Maurice Rentner, New York, 1940-47; founder and partner, with Ben Klein, of Junior Sophisticates fashion firm, New York, 1948-66; established Anne Klein Studio design and fashion consultancy firm, New York, 1965; founder, with Matthew Rubinstein, and president, of Anne Klein and Company, New York, 1968-74. Founder-member and trustee, Council of Fashion Designers of America. **Honors:** *Mademoiselle* Merit Award, New York, 1954; Coty American Fashion Critics Winnie Award, 1955, 1969, and Hall of Fame Award, 1971; Neiman-Marcus Award, New York, 1959, 1969; Lord and Taylor Award, New York, 1964; National Cotton Council Award, New York, 1965. **Died:** New York City, 19 March 1974.

## Publications

**On KLEIN: books**—*The Fashionable Savages* by John Fairchild, New York, 1965; *The World of Fashion: People, Places, Resources* by Eleanor Lambert, New York and London, 1976; *Birds of Paradise* by Rose Hartman, New York, 1980; *McDowell's Directory of Twentieth Century Fashion* by Colin McDowell, London, 1984; *The Encyclopedia of Fashion from 1840 to the 1980s* by Georgina O'Hara, London, 1986.

\*     \*     \*

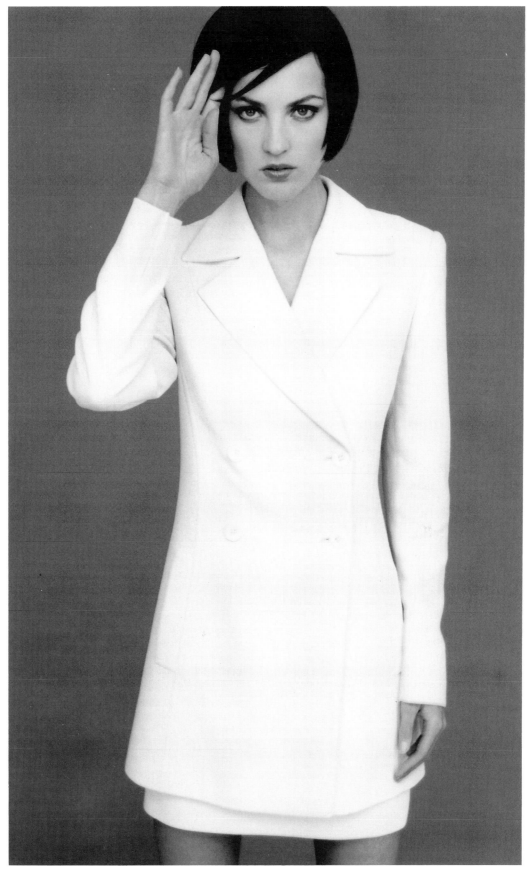

**Anne Klein (collection): double-breasted suit**

Anne Klein is as important an influence to the American look in women's clothes as Coco Chanel is to the French. "Breezy," "crystalline," "sharp," "fluid" are the words most often used to define her designs. She first worked out clothing designs for the shorter-figured woman and then did much to erase the all-too-fussy look of junior-sized clothing while at the same time not sacrificing its girlish quality. The Anne Klein look came to be a happy marriage of the advantages of sportswear with the sophistication of more formal attire. Her informal clothing, cut more sophisticatedly and enriched with well-chosen detail, never lost its active quality. Her formal wear is as relaxed as her casual wear (hooded jersey dresses for evening, as an example). The merchandizing of her clothing and related accessories that could be worn in variable combinations, presented in special Anne Klein Rooms in stores across the United States, made possible, and with ease, the complete look which has become somewhat of a standard. Her related separates—blazers, skirts, pants, sweaters—by a change of fabric, color, or detail have broken the barriers between casual and formal attire. Thus, through her, a number of fashion's dictates lost their sting.

In a comparatively short career, Klein made a definite impact on womenswear. At a time when the social role of women was changing dramatically, she provided clothes that were designed to complement these changes.

—Harlan Sifford

# KLEIN, Calvin (Richard)

American fashion designer

**Born:** The Bronx, New York, 19 November 1942. **Education:** Studied at the Fashion Institute of Technology, New York, 1959-62. **Family:** Married Jayne Centre in 1964 (divorced, 1974); daughter: Marci; married Kelly Rector in 1986. **Career:** Assistant designer, with Dan Millstein, New York, 1962-64; independent designer, New York, from 1964; formed Calvin Klein fashion company, in partnership with Barry Schwartz, New York, 1968; company reorganized, 1991. Fragrances include *Obsession,* 1985, *Eternity,* 1988, and *Escape,* 1991. Visiting critic, Parsons School of Design, New York, and Fashion Institute of Technology New York. **Member:** Council of Fashion Designers, New York. **Collections:** Museum of Modern Art, New York; Guggenheim Museum, New York; Whitney Museum, New York. **Honors:** Coty American Fashion Critics' Winnie Award, 1973, 1974, 1975; Hall of Fame Award, 1975; Bath Museum of Costume Dress of the Year Award, 1980; Council of Fashion Designers of America Award, 1993. **Address:** 205 West 39th Street, New York, New York 10018, U.S.A.

## Publications

**By KLEIN: articles**—in *Mademoiselle* (New York), September 1979.

**On KLEIN: books**—*Fashion Merchandizing* by Mary D. Troxell, New York, 1971, 1976; *The Changing World of Fashion: 1900 to the Present* by Ernestine Carter, London, 1977; *The Fashion Makers* by Bernadine Morris and Barbara Walz, New York, 1978; *Fairchild's Who's Who in Fashion* edited by Ann Stegemeyer, New

York, 1980; *Magic Names of Fashion* by Ernestine Carter, London, 1980; *The Collector's Book of Twentieth Century Fashion* by Frances Kennett, London and New York, 1983; *McDowell's Directory of Twentieth Century Fashion* by Colin McDowell, London, 1984; *The Conran Directory of Design* edited by Stephen Bayley, London, 1985; *The Encyclopedia of Fashion from 1840 to the 1980s* by Georgina O'Hara, London, 1986; *Design Source Book* by Penny Sparke and others, London, 1986; *W, The Designing Life* edited by Lois Perschetz, New York, 1987; *The Fashion Conspiracy* by Nicholas Coleridge, London, 1988; *New York Fashion: The Evolution of American Style* by Caroline Milbank Rennolds, New York, 1989; *Sultans of Style: 30 Years of Fashion and Passion 1960-1990* by Georgina Howell, London, 1990; *Obsession: The Lives and Times* of Calvin Klein by Steven Gaines and Sharon Churcher, New York, 1994; *The Designer Scam* by Colin McDowell, London, 1994; **articles**—"Stylish Calvinism" by Elizabeth Peer in *Newsweek,* 3 November 1975; "The Rag Trade to Riches Rise of Calvin Klein" by Erica Brown in *The Sunday Times Magazine* (London), 29 April 1980; "Calvin Klein" by Maureen Cleave in *The Observer* (London), 7 December 1980; "Calvin and the Family Firm" by Jonathan Alter and Ann Hughey in *Newsweek,* 12 December 1983; "Ragman" by Pamela Sherrid in *Forbes,* 15 February 1982; "Between Me and My Calvins" by Jeffrey A. Tractenberg in *Forbes,* 9 April 1984; "Calvin Klein Keeps It Smart and Simple" by Bernadine Morris in the *New York Times,* 1 May 1985; "In Step With Calvin Klein" by James Brady in *Parade Magazine* (New York), 26 October 1986; "The Secret of My Success" by Marion Hume in *Fashion Weekly* (London), 27 August 1987; "Drawing a Klein Line" by Sally Brampton in *Elle* (London), January 1988; "The Latest Calvin: From the Bronx to Eternity" by Michael Gross in *New York,* 8 August 1988; "A Star Is Reborn" by Maureen Orth in *Vogue,* September 1988; "Mr. Klein Comes Clean" by Georgina Howell in *The Sunday Times Magazine* (London), 10 September 1989; "Calvin Klein's Obsession" in *Cosmopolitan,* May 1991; "Calvin Klein's Bold Stategy in U.S., Europe" in *Women's Wear Daily,* 19 June 1991; "Nothing Between Success and Calvin" by Mandy Behbehani in the *San Francisco Examiner,* 30 January 1992; "Can Calvin Klein Escape" by Linda Grant in the *Los Angeles Times,* 23 February 1992; "I Don't Have Long-Term Plans. I Just Act Instinctively" by Pat Sloan in *Advertising Age,* 18 May 1992; "Calvin in Control" by Sarah Mower in *Harper's Bazaar,* 11 November 1992; "The Snooty Dame at the Block Party" by Gerri Hirshey in the *New York Times Magazine,* 24 October 1993; "Master of Ease" by Bernadine Morris in the *New York Times,* 6 February 1994; "Calvin Clean" by Sally Brampton in *Marie Claire* (London), August 1994; "Calvin's Clean Sweep" by Julia Reed in *Vogue* (New York), August 1994; "Slip-sliding to a Close: Calvin Klein" by Kathleen Beckett in the *New York Post,* 5 November 1994; "Klein and Karan: Clothes that Do the Job" by Amy M. Spindler in the *New York Times,* 5 November 1994; "New York: Calvin's Minimal Magnetism" in *Women's Wear Daily* (New York), 7 November 1994; "Luxurious Armor by Karan, Klein, Mizrahi" by Amy M. Spindler in the *New York Times,* 8 April 1995; "Calvin Cool Edge" in *Women's Wear Daily* (New York), 10 April 1995.

\*      \*      \*

Calvin Klein has created the "Classic American Look" in both men's and women's fashions and has had considerable success in bringing good design to the mass market. His unique approach has made him one of America's most influential designers. Many of his designs acknowledge American emphasis on physical fitness, as he has created clothes that fit the body in fabrics that "feel good against the skin." In the mid 1970s, Klein extended this emphasis by expanding his line to include make-up and skin care products, thus creating a total fashion approach.

When Klein began designing for women, he found that they no longer sought to assert liberation by wearing a pair of pants with a man-tailored jacket. Klein accommodated this shift by designing clothes that were more feminine. By 1978, the American woman had had enough of fashion gimmickery and over-designed clothes. She was interested, instead, in simple and comfortable styles, and Klein shifted his focus from soft blouses and gathered skirts to simple and tailored sportswear. The 1983 spring/summer collection, for example, succeeds in providing the American woman tailored suiting and an authoritative image without the loss of a feminine quality.

Klein is also important for bringing the look of designer clothes to the general market. The application of designer labels, instigated by Calvin Klein jeans, has flooded the mass clothing market from jeans to sheets and from infant clothing to high couture. Klein was responsible for bringing what only the rich could afford down to the masses, thereby opening the doors for other designers, such as Halston, who has designed for J. C. Penney, to participate in the mass clothing market.

Klein is one of a small group of designers who have shifted the focus away from Europe to develop sportswear into a distinctly American design classic. The Calvin Klein look, leaning toward informality and practicality, became the uniform of the 1970s and 1980s. European designers have looked at Klein and American merchandising techniques to learn about designing clothes for "the way we live."

Beginning with his 1980 television campaign which employed Brooke Shields as a jeans model, Klein has made an innovative and often bold contribution to advertising. This includes not only television but billboards and print media. Klein's campaigns have steadily extended the limits of what was previously "accepted" in advertising, addressing sexuality and, in the 1990s, gender; in 1994 Klein launched the first large-scale campaign for a shared gender fragrance, *CK One*.

—Teal Ann Triggs

## KLEMKE, Werner

German painter and illustrator and graphic and typographic designer

**Born:** Berlin, 12 March 1917. **Education:** Educated in Berlin; self-taught in design, from 1937. **Career:** Worked as animated cartoon draughtsman, Berlin 1935-39; freelance illustrator and graphic designer, in East Berlin, from 1945; designed books for publishers Siebholts, Ulenspiegel, Volk und Welt, Verlag Neues Leben, Verlag Volk und Wissen, Verlag Stichnote, Dietz Verlag, Verlag Rutten und Loening, Aufbau-Verlag, Verlag Tribune, and others; designed record sleeves, from 1952. Lecturer in book illustration, 1950-56, and professor of design and typography, from 1956, Hochschule für Bildende und Angewandte Kunste, Berlin-Weissensee. Permanent contributor, *Das Magazin* journal, East Berlin. Founder-member, Pirckheimer-Gesellschaft, Deutscher Künstlerbund, East Berlin,

1956. **Member:** DDR Akademie der Künste; Bund Deutscher Künstler; Alliance Graphique Internationale; USSR Academy of Fine Arts, (honorary). **Exhibitions:** Mexico City, 1956; Kleine Galerie, Hoyerswerda, 1977; Moscow, 1986; Leningrad, 1988. **Collections:** Nationalgalerie, East Berlin; Kupferstichkabinett, East Berlin; Kupferstichkabinett, Dresden. **Honors:** DDR Drawing Medal, Berlin, 1954, 1958, 1964; Children's Book Prize, DDR Ministry of Culture, 1957, 1962; Gutenberg Prize, Leipzig, 1962; DDR National Prize, 1962, 1969, 1977; Gold Award, Gesellschaft für Deutsche-Sowjetische Freundschaft, 1966; honorary citizen of Certaldo, Italy. **Address:** Tassostrasse 21, 1120 Berlin-Weissensee, Germany.

## Works

Books illustrated include—*Schelmufskis Reisebeschreibungen* by Charles Reuter, Munich, 1952, 1954; *Gargantua* by Rabelais, Munich, 1954; *Till Eulenspiegel,* East Berlin, 1955; *Leben und Abenteuer des Martin Chuzzlewit* by Charles Dickens, East Berlin, 1956; *Tagebuch aus China* by Bodo Uhse, East Berlin, 1956; *Das Rollwagenbuchlein* by J. Wickram, 1956; *Schule des Humors* by J. Hasek, East Berlin, 1957; *Decameron* by Boccaccio, 1958; *Betrugslexikon* by G. P. Honn, 1958; *Candide* by Voltaire, Munich, 1958; *Pont und Anna* by Arnold Zweig, East Berlin, 1962; *Die Berliner Antigone* by Rolf Hochhuth, Reinbek, 1964; *Hansel und Gretel* by Sarah Kirsche, Leipzig, 1972; *Die Schreckliche Pulver-Explosion zu Harburg* edited by Lukas Richter, East Berlin, 1973; *Im Mittelpunkt das Buch* by Horst Kunze, Leipzig, 1980.

## Publications

**By KLEMKE: books**—*Herbert Sandberg,* East Berlin, 1958.

**On KLEMKE: books**—*Who's Who in Graphic Art* edited by Walter Amstutz, Zurich, 1962; *Buchgestaltung* by Albert Kapr, Dresden, 1963; *Künstler der Gegenwart: Werner Klemke* by Bernhard Nowak, Dresden, 1963; *Deutsche Grafik* by Georg Piltz, Leipzig, Berlin, and Jena, 1968; *Werner Klemkes Gesammelte Werk* by Horst Kunze, Dresden, 1968, 1972, 1977; *Werner Klemke: Illustrationen und Plakate,* exhibition catalogue, Hoyerswerda, 1977; *Werner Klemke* by Jelena Marchenko, Moscow, 1986; *Werner Klemke* by Mikhail Liebman, Leningrad, 1988.

## KLIMOWSKI, Andrzej

British illustrator, film, stage, and graphic designer

**Born:** London, 1 July 1949. **Education:** Studied painting, at St. Martin's School of Art, London, Dip.AD., 1972; studied poster design and film animation, under Henryk Tomaszewski and Kazimierz Urbanski, at the Academy of Fine Arts, Warsaw, 1973-75. **Family:** Married Danusia Schejbal in 1974; children: Dominik and Natalia. **Career:** Freelance designer, in Warsaw, 1973-80, and in London, from 1980; designer, Film Polski, Warsaw, 1976-80; director, Semafor Short Film Studios, Lodz, 1980; art director, Artificial Eye Film Company, London, 1980-81; designer and art director, London Sinfonietta orchestra, 1986-87; designer for "Gustav Mahler and the 21st Century," Contemporary Music Foundation, Spoletto, 1991; designer and art director, Theatr Clwyd, 1992-95; designer and art director, Oberon Books, London, 1993-95; also designed for Polish television, *Szpilki* magazine, Warsaw's National Theatre, Teatr Wielki and Teatre Ateneum, Hamburg Deutsches Schauspielhaus, Wroclaw Contemporary Theatre, Royal Shakespeare Company, and others. Visiting Lecturer, Canterbury College of Art, Kent, 1981-89, West Surrey College of Art, Farnham, 1982-84, and Royal College of Art, London, from 1983; tutor in illustration and graphic design, Royal College of Art, 1990-95. **Exhibitions:** Contemporary Posters Gallery, Warsaw, 1978; Galeria Wielka, Poznan, 1980; Contemporary Theatre, Wroclaw, 1980; Galeria Grazyny Hase, Warsaw, 1981; South Hill Park Arts Centre, Bracknell, 1983; Vanessa Devereux Gallery, London, 1986, 1988; *The Depository,* David Hockney Gallery, Royal College of Art, London, 1995. **Collections:** National Museum, Warsaw; National Museum Poznan; Stedelijk Museum, Amsterdam; Library of Congress, Washington, D.C.; California Museum of Science and Technology, Los Angeles; Humberside University, Hull. **Honors:** *Hollywood Reporter* Key Art Award, 1977, 1978; Warsaw Film Poster Prize, 1978; Polish Poster Biennale Award, Katowice, 1981; *Campaign* Posters Silver Award, London, 1986; *Daily Telegraph Press* Advertisement Award, London 1988; fellow, Royal College of Art,

London, 1995; commended prize, National Arts Library Illustration Awards, 1995. **Addresses:** 105 Sutton Court, London W4 3EE, England; (work) Royal College of Art, Kensington Gore, London SW7 2EU, England.

## Publications

**By KLIMOWSKI: books**—(with Zbigniew Szydlo) *Montserrat 71,* London and Barcelona, 1971; *Klimowska/Klimowski,* exhibition catalogue, London, 1988; *The Depository* (novel without words), London and Boston, 1994; (with Andre Brighton) *Picasso for Beginners,* Cambridge, 1995; **films**—*19 bis, Dreamstrasse,* 1973; *Dead Shadow,* 1980; *Sonata,* 1983.

**On KLIMOWSKI: books**—*The Polish Poster 1970-1978,* with introduction by Zdzislaw Schubert, Warsaw, 1979; *Das Polnische Plakat,* West Berlin, 1980; *Who's Who in Graphic Art* edited by Walter Amstutz, Dubendorf, 1982, *A History of Graphic Design* by Philip B. Meggs, London and New York, 1983; **articles**—in *Studio Voice* (Tokyo), January 1991; *Eye* (London), vol. 14, no. 14, 1994; *Guardian,* 24 September 1994; *Times* (London), 13 October 1994.

\*

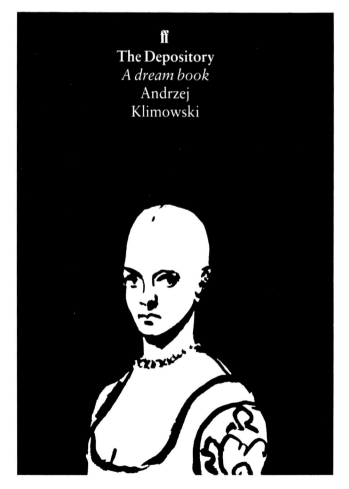

**Andrzej Klimowski: front cover design for** *DON CARLOS* **and wordless novel** *The Depository*

I have always been attracted to mass-media forms of communication, to everything that involves the creation of images for mass consumption. Contact with the streets is important, the pulse of city life. Yet this contact should be a warm one: I wish to maintain a human scale, just as when, in a letter to a friend or a loved one, I use the resources of the many possible metaphors, symbols, and signs that trigger human emotions as well as the intellect.

Of course, I realize that working through graphics I have to speak with a loud voice. Whispers and subtle reflections are futile—they cannot survive the fast and often aggressive momentum of urban life. Nevertheless, it is of vital importance to work to the human scale, embracing the very nature of man, and thus reflecting his weaknesses, fears, passions, his need for human contact, his anguish and solitude, his sense of humor, his vulnerability, etc.

I believe that, with the rapid advancement of technology, the sense of human scale is often lost. Figures and statistics become more important than people. This can prove disastrous in political life—something we are at present experiencing in the Western world. In this climate of monetarism and the worship of modern technology, where more and more decisions rely upon computers, there is an urgent need for individual voices which speak up for the individual.

The function of graphic artists and designers is similar to that of journalists. They are responsible for informing and educating a large public, using a language which is direct and unambiguous yet charged with strong beliefs and convictions. Paradoxical? Maybe—but needed in an atmosphere of anonymity, where most graphics can be reduced to mere packaging and empty decoration, perfect in technical execution but nothing beyond that. There are strong traditions in the not-too-distant past to turn to for inspiration: designers of the calibre of Cassandre, for example, whose laconic concepts were executed with tremendous flair. His posters sang out in the streets.

This flair and dynamism in execution accompanied by an intellectual poignancy is sadly missing in much of the graphic design work that we see today. Designers all too often look to fashion and popular trends, re-shaping their bag of graphic tricks accordingly. What is lacking is the weight, both intellectual and spiritual, to the visual messages that designers are communicating to the public.

I am very fortunate to be working for institutions and small publishers who allow and encourage me to send poetic signals to a large public. The book form is a very intimate one and when enhanced by good design and illustration works on the reader over a long period of time, shaping his or her ideas in a profound way.

We live in a time of very exciting technological changes and infinite possibilities in communication. Within this vast mosaic I find myself using materials and methods every more simple and traditional. I do not see this as a regression, rather a desire to strike directly at the heart of things.

—Andrzej Klimowski

\* \* \*

To put it frankly, almost every young graduate of the Warsaw Academy of Art dreams of going to the West—New York, Paris, London—and making it. Sure, why not London?

Andrzej Klimowski, born in London, the son of World War II emigrants, chose the opposite route. In the early 1970s, after graduating from art school in London, he left for Warsaw. His dream was simple—to go to the source and try himself in his dream discipline,

the poster. Certainly no place could be better (except Tokyo perhaps). After refining his skills in Henryk Tomaszewski's studio at the Warsaw Academy, Klimowski began his real struggle as a professional.

From the start, his works were different from the mainstream of the Polish school. He has developed a happy mixture of the photographic way of thinking prevailing in western Europe and the more painterly and romantic Polish style. In the early works of his Warsaw period, his style was somewhat inspired by Roman Cieslewicz, but soon, Klimowski distanced himself from that most prominent photocollagist. Since then, the photographic base has been preserved in his work. But the compositions look more like painting because of the color, softened black-and-white shapes, and extensive use of various filters and films. Titles and all additional texts were integrated into the overall compositions, never contrasting aggressively with the pictures.

The dominant area of Klimowski's activity in Poland was theatrical and movie posters. Some of them, such as a poster for Robert Altman's *Nashville,* are extremely accurate and dramatic, thanks to the artist's firsthand understanding of the West and its problems. On such occasions, his bi-cultural being pays off.

An important factor in Klimowski's work as a posterist is his private world of art, which, however, provides also many ideas for commercial work. He realizes himself best in a series of mostly silkscreen prints. Here, he creates his own little home-theatre, in which the heroine is usually his wife. As a model in specially created costumes, she plays a central role in Klimowski's "sets." Bursting with sexuality, sometimes posing as *la femme fatale,* she narrates the artist's story. The result is never overdone. The atmosphere of these delicate works of art is somewhat literary, following in the vein of England's great eighteenth- and nineteenth-century masters of graphic art. A happy mixture of delicate color and dark, mysterious compositions make them the best part of Klimowski's work today.

Back in London, Klimowski has taken off in a new struggle. He faces an uneasy future. His Polish achievements are much admired, but translating them into commercial commissions is not an easy task. Despite everything, I strongly believe this young artist will prevail. He is intelligent and flexible, has a decent intellectual capacity and energy. And he's home again. It's not too bad to have two built-in cultures and two homes in which to settle.

—Jan Sawka

# KLING, Vincent G(eorge)

American architect and interior designer

**Born:** East Orange, New Jersey, 9 May 1916. **Education:** Studied at Columbia University, New York, B.Arch., 1940; Massachusetts Institute of Technology, Cambridge, M.Arch., 1942. **Family:** Married Caperton Booth in 1942; children: Vincent and Robert. **Career:** Designer, with architects Skidmore, Owings, and Merrill, New York, 1943-46; in private architectural and design practice, Philadelphia, from 1946. **Member:** Architectural Advisory Panel member, United States General Services Administration; Philadelphia Citizens' City Planning Council; Chester County Airport Authority Board. **Exhibitions:** *47 Outstanding Examples of American Architecture,* Museum of Modern Art, New York, 1944. **Honors:**

National Honor Award, American Institute of Architects, 1954; Philadelphia Arts Festival Award, 1959; City of Quito Gold Medal, Ecuador, 1961; Samuel Finley Breese Morse Medal, National Academy of Design, 1968. Fellow, American Institute of Architects, 1960. **Address:** The Kling Partnership, 2301 Chestnut Street, Philadelphia, Pennsylvania 19103, U.S.A.

### Publications

**On KLING: book**—*Interior Spaces Designed by Architects* edited by Barclay F. Gordon, New York, 1974; **articles**—in *Pencil Points* (New York), May 1945; *Architectural Forum* (New York), March 1953, December 1958; *Architectural Record* (New York), December 1953, August 1959, October 1959, February 1963, April 1965; *AIA Journal* (Washington, D.C.), May 1957, June 1960; *Architectural Review* (London), December 1961; *Progressive Architecture* (New York), January 1962, November 1964, September 1966; *Interiors* (New York), February 1972.

*       *       *

Vincent G. Kling sees the architect as a "generalist by training and practice" who, to serve his clients fully, offers a comprehensive service. This breadth of vision enabled him to secure major commissions and be prominent in the "rebirth" of downtown Philadelphia in the late 1950s, when he designed the master plan, six buildings, and two plazas at Penn Center. He also designed other Philadelphia buildings, including the airport and the United States Mint.

While the office is known primarily as an architectural firm, Kling has always recognized interior design as integral to architecture: "What happens inside a building determines what happens outside." Thus, the firm was one of the first to establish an interior design department. Under the direction of Joseph Bobrowicz (1956-69), the department's responsibilities expanded from selection of colors and materials to total coordination of design and installation. Although not always the practical reality, the philosophical principle was that the interior staff should be part of the team from the beginning of the design process to assure that interior needs and organizational relationships would be an integral part of the total design. In the 1950s, Kling's office was a leader in the design of campus plans for corporate organizations. The Monsanto Company's national headquarters in St. Louis is an excellent illustration of total involvement of a number of disciplines, including interior design and landscape design. Simultaneity in development is most evident at Swarthmore College's Philip T. Sharples Dining Hall, where interior and exterior materials are one, and the internal volumes form the external shapes.

In keeping with Kling's generalist philosophy, the office was reorganized in 1971 as a multidisciplinary design partnership encompassing architecture, planning and landscape, interior design engineering, construction management, and computer services. Until reorganization, the interior design work had been carried out primarily in conjunction with architectural commissions, but the formation of Kling/Interior Design enabled the firm to compete for independent commissions, as well as work on buildings designed by Vincent G. Kling and Partners, the architectural division. Xerox's International Center for Training and Management Development in Leesburg, Virginia, is an example of a joint architecture and interior design commission. The differentiation of separate lounge spaces and coordinated color-coding are critical elements in personalizing

the six buildings which house 1000 persons for up to six weeks at a time. The American Telephone and Telegraph building in New Jersey offers a similar example of the successful coordination of the two divisions of the firm. The remodeling of Philadelphia's First Pennsylvania Bank executive offices into an exceptional, calm, thoroughly controlled sequence of expressively lighted spaces represents the work of Kling/Interior Design as an independent unit.

As an early and continued presence in the field of interior design, the department has trained many who are now principals in other interior design firms. Bobrowicz and Edward Semanko formed Semanko/Bobrowicz; Roland Gallimore became head of interior design at Geddes, Brecher, Qualla, Cunningham; Karen Daroff established Daroff Designs; Ralph Melick, Donald Kriebel, and Ann Sutphin each have offices; and Florinda Doelp was president of Interspace before returning to head Kling/Interior Design.

The Kling work could be labeled conservative; it certainly is not trendy. "High style is not our driver. We believe that the unique functional needs of each client should shape our design. Only by meeting these requirements can we fulfill our responsibilities to our clients." This response to owner and occupant of the 2,500 projects designed by the Kling offices and the straightforward quality of the work have brought many awards and repeat commissions from the corporate and institutional clients they serve.

—Marjorie Kriebel

# KLOTZ, Florence

American stage and film costume designer

**Born:** New York City, 28 October, 1920. **Education:** Studied at the Parsons School of Design, New York, 1940-41. **Career:** Freelance stage costume designer, New York, from 1951; film costume designer, in Germany, Austria, and the United States, from 1969. **Honors:** Antoinette Perry (Tony) Award, New York, 1971, 1973, 1976, 1985, 1993, 1994, 1995; Drama Desk Award, New York, 1971, 1976, 1978, 1989, 1993, 1994; Drama Critics' Circle Award, 1972; Fashion Award, 1975; Los Angeles Critics Circle Award, 1976, 1977; Academy Award nomination, 1977; Carbonell Award, 1981; Outer Critics Circle Award, 1989, 1995; TCI Award, 1994; Maharam Theatrical Design awards, American Theatre Wing. **Address:** 1050 Park Avenue, New York, New York 10028, U.S.A.

### Works

Stage costume designs include—(New York, unless noted) *Oklahoma!,* City Center Theatre, 1956; *South Pacific,* City Center Theatre, 1956; *Carousel,* City Center Theatre, 1956; *Annie, Get Your Gun,* City Center Theatre, 1956; *Superman,* 1960; *A Call on Kuprin,* Broadhurst Theatre, 1961; *Take Her, She's Mine,* Biltmore Theatre, 1961; *Never Too Late,* Playhouse Theatre, 1962; *On an Open Roof,* 1963; *Nobody Loves an Albatross,* Lyceum Theatre, 1963; *Everybody Out, the Castle is Sinking,* 1964; *One by One,* 1964; *The Owl and the Pussycat,* ANTA Theatre, 1964; *The Mating Dance,* Eugene O'Neill Theatre, 1965; *The Best Laid Plans,* Brooks Atkinson Theatre, 1966; *This Winter's Hobby,* 1966; *It's a Bird... It's a Plane... It's Superman,* Alvin Theatre, 1966; (also tour coordinator) *Golden Boy,* 1968;

*Norman, Is That You?* 1970; *Paris is Out,* Brooks Atkinson Theatre, 1970; *Follies,* Winter Garden Theatre, 1971; *A Little Night Music,* Shubert Theatre, 1973; *Sondheim: A Musical Tribute,* 1973; *Dreyfus in Rehearsal,* Ethel Barrymore Theatre, 1974; *Pacific Overtures,* 1976; *Legend,* 1976; *Side by Side by Sondheim,* 1977; *On the Twentieth Century,* 1978; *Ice Dancing,* 1979; *Harold and Maude,* 1980; *Little Foxes,* 1981; *Madam Butterfly,* Chicago Lyric Opera, 1982; *Dancin' in the Streets,* 1982; (with Peggy Lee) *Peg,* 1983; *Doll's Life,* 1983; *Grind,* 1985; *Jerry's Girls,* St. James Theatre, 1985-86; *Rags,* Mark Hellinger Theatre, 1986; *Roza,* Center Theatre Group, Mark Taper Forum, Los Angeles (travelled to New York), 1986-87; *City of Angels,* Virginia Theatre, 1989-90; *Kiss of the Spider Woman—The Musical,* Broadhurst Theatre, 1993; *Showboat,* 1994.
Film costume designs include—*Something for Everyone* (Prince), 1970; *A Little Night Music* (Prince), 1977; *Madame Butterfly,* 1989.
Television costume designs include—"Antique Epigraph" portion of "Fancy Free," *Great Performances,* PBS, 1986.

**Publications**

**On KLOTZ: books**—*Contemporary Stage Design USA* edited by Elizabeth Burdick, Peggy Hansen, and Brenda Zanger, Middletown, 1974; *Who's Who in the Theatre* edited by Ian Herbert, London and Detroit, 1977.

\*

Getting into any creative phase of the theatre is supposed to be terribly difficult—like aspiring to be a movie star. Yet, when I am asked whether I encountered any obstacles in entering my professional life and also about the difficulties for a woman to balance a private life and a profession, I have to confess. Actually, it has all been very easy. I became a costume designer mostly through sheer luck.

One day in 1941, I got a call from a friend to come "paint some materials" at Brooks Costume Company. In my ignorance, I didn't know that Brooks was, at that time, the most famous costume company in the theatre. I went, they gave me a paintbrush, and I was on my way.

The longer I was at Brooks, the more people I met. Soon I was accepted into the United Scenic Artists Union and began working as an assistant to some of the famous costume designers. I worked for and was greatly influenced by Lucinda Ballard, Miles White, and Irene Sharaff.

My first show as an assistant was the hauntingly beautiful *The King and I.* After that, I assisted on many musicals—*A Tree Grows in Brooklyn, Top Banana, Of Thee I Sing, Pal Joey, Pajama Game, Flower Drum Song, Juno, Carnival in Flanders, Jamaica, Pipe Dream, Mr. Wonderful, Wish You Were Here, Bells Are Ringing, The Music Man, The Sound of Music, Gay Life*—and plays—*Cat on a Hot Tin Roof, J.B., Kind Sir, Clearing in the Woods, Time Remembered.*

People began to know my work and ask for me. In the late 1950s I designed for the City Center such musicals as *Carousel, South Pacific,* and *Annie Get Your Gun.* In 1960, Harold Prince asked me to design *Take Her, She's Mine* and then many more plays for Broadway. My first musical was *Superman* (1966). My first movie was *Something for Everyone* (1969), made in Germany, with An-

Florence Klotz: Costume sketches for *Show Boat,* 1993

gela Lansbury. My first Tony Award was in 1971 for *Follies.* I also won the Drama Desk Award and Los Angeles Drama Critics Award for that show. Nothing I have done in my life will ever compare with the fear, stage fright, and nerves I suffered on having to walk up and appear *before* instead of *behind* the footlights. I went on to win several more Tonys, several Drama Desk Awards, and an Oscar nomination for the movie *A Little Night Music* with Elizabeth Taylor.

I still say success was made possible for me by a combination of luck, the adaptable skills I picked up, my basic artistic instincts, being in the right place (Brooks) at the right time, meeting and working for talented designers who helped me help myself while in their apprenticeship, and, finally, learning to go it alone. And I was fortunate in the people who believed in me and encouraged me.

—Florence Klotz

\*    \*    \*

In the years since her first Broadway design assignment, Florence Klotz has designed only about twenty-five productions on Broadway and a few films; she cannot be considered a prolific designer. From 1961 through 1970 she designed almost solely lightweight, contemporary-dress comedies. Although some of these were rather important plays of the time, their clothes could hardly be considered important design.

Klotz's career changed almost overnight when she was hired to design the costumes for Hal Prince's *Follies,* a complicated musical about a reunion of Ziegfeld Follies girls on the stage of a theatre in the process of being demolished. Each of them had come from a different era of the Ziegfeld Follies, and each was living a different sort of life. In addition, the action included flashbacks to each woman's day on the stage. Klotz's research was impeccable. Each character had her own rather moth-eaten look plus her glamorous recollection of herself. It was a sophisticated, intelligent, and glorious design.

*Follies,* the first of the collaborative works of Klotz with Prince and Stephen Sondheim, was followed by *A Little Night Music, Pacific Overtures, Side by Side by Sondheim,* and *On the Twentieth Century.* Each of the major Sondheim-Prince musicals had its distinctly different look, and thus they made very different demands on Klotz. Each required careful and specific research into complex worlds and Periods: *Follies* reflected fifty years of clothing; *A Little Night Music,* turn-of-the-century Sweden; *Pacific Overtures,* nineteenth-century Japan; and *On the Twentieth Century,* 1930s American Art Deco. For each, she developed a unique design concept: dresses out of trunks for aging showgirls and black-and-white recollections of glamour; ethereal, almost surrealistic, costumes for Swedish eccentrics in the country; multi-patterned, Americanized Kabuki; and softly colored, 1930s movie glamour. Each concept, as well as each costume, was done with great style and flair. With only a few concessions to quick changes and other theatrical requirements, Klotz maintains correct silhouette in her designs, although frequently they are as contemporary as they are period-style.

Klotz's costumes, mostly made by Barbara Matera Ltd. for these four productions, have shown a mastery of fabric and trim in color and cut. One of Klotz's favorite techniques for getting the right texture and color in garments (used in both *Follies* and *A Little Night Music*) is to layer repeatedly one color over another, and then to bead, trim, or decorate over the layers. As a result, the costume costs for these productions were astronomical.

—John E. Hirsch

# KNEEBONE, Peter (Jack George)

British illustrator, signage, and graphic designer

**Born:** Middlesbrough, England, 28 April 1923; resident in France from 1975. **Education:** Studied philosophy, politics, and languages, at University College, Oxford, 1942-43, 1946-48, MA, 1948. **Military Service:** Served as British Naval Liaison Officer, in Italy, and as Naval Broadcasting Representative, in Cairo, Royal Naval Volunteer Reserve, 1943-46, Lieutenant. **Family:** Married Catherine Shanks in 1958 (divorced, 1976); children: Anna, Jonathan, Sophie, and Lucy; married Françoise Jollant in 1976. **Career:** Assistant to the director of exhibitions, Festival of Britain, London, 1951; television producer, British Broadcasting Corporation, London, 1952-55; freelance designer, in Paris and London, 1952-90; illustrator for *News Chronicle, The Observer Sunday Times, Radio Times, New Scientist,* Central Office of Information, National Economic Development Office, Institute of Directors, Imperial Chemical Industries, Shell, British Broadcasting Corporation, and others, 1953-75; signage consultant, Philips Corporation, Netherlands, 1969-76, and Ministry of Industry, Paris, 1974-77; design consultant, National Fund for Research into Crippling Diseases, London, 1969-74, Salle Pleyel concert halls, Paris, 1980-81, Ministry of Research, Paris,

1981-88, Centre National d'Art Contemporain, Villa Arson, Nice, 1983, and Europrospective conference, Paris, 1986-87. Head of complementary studies, Kingston School of Art, Surrey, 1963-66; coordinator of postgraduate studies, Central School of Art and Design, London, 1967-74; visual communications coordinator, Ecole Nationale des Beaux-Arts, Nancy, 1980-89; also visiting tutor, University of Paris VII, 1978-81, and Parsons School of Design, Paris, 1981-88. **Member:** Secretary, 1963, secretary general, 1977-79, and president, 1979-81, ICOGRADA, International Council of Graphic Design Associations; fellow, Chartered Society of Designers, London; Society of Typographic designers, London. **Exhibitions:** *Funny Peculiar: Illustrations by Peter Kneebone,* Kilkenny, 1984; *Design Francais 1960-1980: Trois Decennies,* Centre Georges Pompidou, Paris, 1988 (toured). **Honors:** ICOGRADA President's Trophy, 1970; IBM Fellowship, Aspen Design Conference, Colorado, 1980. **Died:** Paris, 30 January 1990.

## Works

*Old Possum's Book of Practical Cats* television programme direction and illustration, for BBC Television, 1952.

*Look Before You Elope* book design and illustration, for Longmans, 1952.

Social commentary texts and illustrations, for *The Observer* newspaper, London 1955.

*Oiling the Wheels* book design and illustrations, for Shell, 1955-58.

Corporate identity and graphics, for the National Fund for Research into Crippling Diseases, London, 1955-75.

*Happy Families* typeface calendar, for the Monotype Corporation, London, 1963.

*English Pronunciation Illustrated* book design and illustrations, for the Cambridge University Press, 1965.

*Baby's Book* design and illustrations, for Charles Letts, 1971.

*Look Behind You* alphabet design and illustrations, for Associated Business Programmes, 1973.

*How to Interview* and *How to Be Interviewed* conceptual illustrations, for the British Institute of Management, 1975-80.

Sign system, for the *3rd Architectural Psychology Conference,* at the University of Strasbourg, 1976.

Corporate identity and graphics, for the Salle Pleyel concert halls, Paris, 1980-81.

CPE Centre visual identity and publications design, for the Ministry of Research, Paris, 1981-89.

Visual identity and graphics, for *Europrospective* conference, at the International Conference Centre, La Villette, Paris, 1987.

## Publications

**By KNEEBONE: books**—*Look Before You Elope,* London, 1952; *Sexes and Sevens,* London, 1953; *Oiling the Wheels,* London, 1957; (translator) *The Art of Afghanistan,* London, 1967; (co-author) *How to Interview,* London, 1975; *A Signature for Singapore,* Paris, 1979; (co-author) *How to Be Interviewed,* London, 1980; *Signaletique,* Paris, 1980; **articles**—in *Filmmaking in Schools and Colleges* (London), 1966; *ICOGRADA: The First Five Years* (London), 1968; *Print* (New York), special issue, March/April 1969, November/December 1969, March/April 1971; *The Designer* (London), September 1969, January 1970, May 1971, September 1971, March 1973; *Communication et Langages* (Paris), December 1969;

*Icographic* (London), no. 5, 1973, no. 8, 1974, no. 3, 1982; *British Travel News* (London), Summer 1974; *Neuf* (Brussels), March/April 1977; *Industrijsko Oblikovanje* (Belgrade), no. 35, 1977; *Design* (London), February 1979, March 1980, November 1983, July 1987, May 1988; *Graphic Design* (Tokyo), June 1985; *France Graphique* (Paris), August 1985; *Art Press* (Paris), January 1987; *Typographic* (London), August 1987.

**On KNEEBONE: books**—*Designers in Britain,* London, 1951-71; *Drawing for the Radio Times* by R. D. Usherwood, London, 1961; *Minerva at Fifty* by James Holland, London, 1980; *Trademarks and Symbols of the World,* Tokyo, 1987; *Trademarks Collection: Europe 1,* Tokyo, 1988; *Design Francais 1960-1980: Trois Decennies* by Margo Rouard and Françoise Jollant Kneebone, Paris, 1988, London, 1989.

*

I attempted to find apparently simple visual solutions to complex problems. "Apparently," because the aim of the simplicity is to make clear something that is not simple. This means a search not only for clarity but also for any answer that is satisfying because it works on more than a superficial level and that might be therefore more stimulating both for me and for the receiver/user of the message. In the case of my illustration design, this is usually done with some humour. Humour can make the message more immediate, more human. Wit can make it more memorable and, ideally, enhance design because I liked drawing and did the school posters. Not having a conventional professional training has kept me open-minded about my work and open-ended about its direction though not its spirit. It has also meant that I have been preoccupied with style and techniques as means rather than as ends. A great satisfaction comes from finding a fitting visual solution, one that communicates clearly, usefully, and, with luck, enjoyably and intellectually provocatively. This is why my greatest satisfaction lies in communicating concepts, ideas, and certain kinds of information. This is also why, apart from the illustration of concepts, I have been particularly interested in questions of visual identity, environmental communication, and information design.

Having been brought up with a combined English-French cultural background, and having studied languages, philosophy, and politics, has meant that I have been attracted by a wide range of problems and concerned with the nature of problems, with the asking of questions, with the relationship between verbal and visual communication (very important this), and with human needs. This is a necessary position because we design for others, and we should ask ourselves, with some humility, "What are the aptitudes and qualities that I have that can best be applied to what problems, to my satisfaction and to that of others?" I am unique and so is every problem. If I am not, then someone else could well be asked to solve it. If it is not, then a solution doubtless exists already. A sense of curiosity, an ability to make connections, a critical and self-critical faculty are essential attributes for a designer.

—Peter Kneebone

* * *

Peter Kneebone will be remembered as the originator of the idea for a representative, international, non-governmental organization for graphic design, the International Council of Graphic Design

Associations (ICOGRADA), founded in 1963 and dedicated to improving the practice of graphic design and to increasing the understanding and use of visual and graphic communications worldwide.

Kneebone was very interested in the use of drawing to explain verbal concepts and ideas, for an illustration can be remembered better than a lot of text. His style was full of detail in the 1950s, but after that he aimed for increasing simplicity and discarded the inessential. He liked the simple shape for its direct impact and employed humour to help get messages across, for he insisted that learning should be enjoyable. His training in philosophy, politics, and modern languages at Oxford taught him to be detached and analytical, and not tied to fashion in the way that some products of design colleges are. He wanted his drawings to encourage people to ask questions, rather than to assume that there is one doctrinal approach for everything.

As an educator himself, Kneebone was concerned with raising the standards of graphic design and with widening its ability to tackle a variety of communication problems. From this have come ICOGRADA's international student projects and the annual student design seminar in London, while the encouragement of innovation in graphic design has been established in the ICOGRADA-Phillips biennial award. Kneebone was very active in getting ICOGRADA recognised by UNESCO and by the council of Europe, and much involved in its activities. He saw his original concept blossom into a worldwide exchange of ideas and aims.

—Diana de Marly

# KNOLL, Florence

American architect and interior, furniture, and textile designer

**Born:** Florence Schust, in Saginaw, Michigan, 24 May 1917. **Education:** Studied Architecture under Eero Saarinen, at Kingswood School, and at Cranbrook Academy of Art, Bloomfield Hills, Michigan, 1932-39; Architectural Association, London, 1937-38; studied under Ludwig Mies van der Rohe, at the Illinois Institute of Technology, Chicago, B. Arch., 1941. **Family:** Married the manufacturer Hans Knoll in 1946 (died, 1955); married Harry Hood Bassett in 1958. **Career:** Worked for architect Wallace K. Harrison in New York, and for Walter Gropius and Marcel Breuer in Boston, 1941-43; founder-director, with Hans Knoll, of the Knoll Planning Unit furniture and textiles firm, New York, 1943-55; president, Knoll International New York, 1955-65; freelance designer, living in Florida and Vermont, from 1965. **Exhibitions:** *An Exhibition for Modern Living,* Museum of Modern Art, New York, 1949 (toured); *Die Gute Industrieform,* Kunstverein, Hamburg, 1955; *Knoll au Musée,* Musée des Arts Décoratifs, Paris, 1972; *A Modern Consciousness: D. J. DePree and Florence Knoll,* Smithsonian Institution, Washington, D.C., 1975; *Design in America: The Cranbrook Vision 1925-1950,* Detroit Institute of Art, 1983 (toured); *Design Since 1945,* Philadelphia Museum of Art, 1983. **Collections:** Museum of Modern Art, New York; Metropolitan Museum of Art, New York; Cranbrook Academy of Art, Bloomfield Hills, Michigan. **Honors:** Good Design Award, Museum of Modern Art, New York, 1950, 1951, 1952, 1953, 1954; American Institute of Decorators International Design Award, 1954, and Citation of Merit, 1957; New York Art Directors Club Merit Award, 1954, 1956; American Institute of Architects Gold Medal, 1961; American Institute of Interior Designers International Design Award, 1962, and Total Design Award, 1977; Illinois Institute of Technology Professional Achievement Award, 1969, and Hall of Fame Award, 1982; honorary D.F.A., Parsons School of Design, New York, 1979; honorary member, Industrial Designers Society of America, 1982; President's Fellow, Rhode Island School of Design, Providence, 1983. **Address:** Knoll Associates, 575 Madison Avenue, New York, New York 10022, U.S.A.

## Works

Chest in maplewood, for Knoll Planning Unit, 1947.
Stacking stool in steel and birchwood, for Knoll Planning Unit, 1947.
Cabinet in steel and rosewood veneer with marble top, for Knoll Planning Unit, 1950.
M. D. Anderson Cancer Research Hospital interiors, Houston, Texas, 1954.
CBS Columbia Broadcasting System headquarters interiors, New York, 1955.
Center for Advanced Study in Behavioral Sciences interiors, Palo Alto, California, 1955.
Southern Methodist University interiors, Dallas, Texas, 1956.
Refectory interiors, Rochester University, New York, 1956.
Dining and rest room interiors, Connecticut General Life Insurance Company, Hartford, 1957.
Oval table-desk in steel and teak veneer, for Knoll International, 1961.
Upholstered lounge chair in steel and hardwood with helical spring suspension, for Knoll International, 1962.

## Publications

**On KNOLL: books**—*An Exhibition for Modern Living,* exhibition catalogue edited by A. H. Girard and W. Laurie, New York and Detroit, 1949; *Die Gute Industrieform,* exhibition catalogue by Hans Eckstein and Robert Gutmann, Hamburg, 1955; *Public Interiors: An International Survey* by Misha Black, London, 1960; *World Furniture* edited by Helena Hayward, London, 1965, 1981; *The Modern Chair: 1850 to Today* by Gilbert Frey, London and Niederteufen, 1970; *Interior Design: An Introduction to Architectural Interiors* by Arnold Friedmann and others, New York and Amsterdam, 1970, 1976; *Knoll au Musée,* exhibition catalogue by Christine Rae, Paris, 1972; *A Modern Consciousness: D. J. DePree and Florence Knoll,* exhibition catalogue, Washington, D.C., 1975; *Twentieth Century Furniture* by Philippe Garner, London, 1980; *Knoll Design* by Eric Larrabee and Massimo Vignelli, New York, 1981; *Contemporary Furniture* edited by Klaus Jurgen Sembach, Stuttgart, London, and New York, 1982; *Design Since 1945* edited by Kathryn Hiesinger and George Marcus, Philadelphia and London, 1983; *Design Source Book* by Penny Sparke, London, 1986; *The American Design Adventure 1940-1975* by Arthur J. Pulos, London and Cambridge, Massachusetts, 1988.

*       *       *

Florence Knoll is an architect, interior space planner, and furniture designer. Her career is symbiotically linked with Knoll Interna-

tional, the furniture company founded by Hans Knoll, who later became her husband. The Knolls shared the conviction that a market could be created for innovative, high-quality, modern furniture. To promote their idea, they established the Knoll Planning Unit, which offered a unique package of original furniture and professional design services to a growing number of important corporate clients. Florence Knoll, as head of this service, is substantially responsible for the postwar acceptance of modern design by American business.

Knoll studied at Cranbrook Academy under the tutelage of Eero Saarinen, an admirer of Walter Gropius' Bauhaus movement. At Cranbrook, she discovered that everyone was interested in everything, from weaving, pottery, and furniture to architecture and city planning. Her studies continued in London at the Architectural Association and concluded with Ludwig Mies van der Rohe in Chicago.

She worked first for Wallace K. Harrison in New York and later for Gropius and Marcel Breuer in Boston. Her international training and her sympathy for the interdisciplinary approach produced in Knoll a firm, well-modulated esthetic which she brought to the Planning Unit. Her work on large-scale projects for clients such as Connecticut General Life Insurance and CBS conveys the self-assurance and sophistication which exemplified the best in postwar design in the United States and epitomizes the style of the 1950s.

In her planning, spaces interact in a relaxed but highly rational architectural integration. They are embellished with chastely elegant textiles and accented by vivid color contrasts and artful lighting. She designed much of the furniture her projects required and commissioned work from other designers such as Eero Saarinen, Mies van der Rohe, Harry Bertoia, Franco Albini, George Nakashima, and Isamu Noguchi, many of whom were friends or colleagues. Her own designs were frequently cited for awards, but she tended to think of them as relatively insignificant. "I designed the fill-in pieces that no one else was doing.... Eero and Bertoia did the stars.... I did it because I needed the piece of furniture for a job and it wasn't there."

Knoll's work with the Planning Unit and Knoll International's exceptional furniture products are now understood to have been responsible, in large measure, for initiating the modern corporate style of interior design which matured in the 1960s and, for a time, was referred to as "the Knoll look." *Architectural Forum* commented in 1957 that "... the Knoll interior is as much a symbol of modern architecture as Tiffany glass was a symbol of the architecture of the Art Nouveau."

—Kenneth Gaulin

# KOIKE, Iwataro

Japanese industrial designer

**Born:** Tokyo, 22 February 1913. **Education:** Studied under Sanzo Wada, Wajiro Kon, and Kitaro Kunii, at Tokyo University of Arts, Dip., 1935. **Family:** Married Taka Kinoshita in 1938; children: Natsuko, Taiso, and Yoko. **Career:** Design technician, working in Fukuoka City, 1935-39, and for the Industrial Arts Institute and Ministry of International Trade and Industry, in Sendai City, 1939-40; chief of Benbo Ceramics Workshops, Naha City, Okinawa, 1940-42; independent designer and theorist, Tokyo, from 1942. Lecturer, 1942-49, associate professor, 1949-65, and professor,

1965-79, at Tokyo University of Arts; founder, College of Urban Design, Tokyo; encouraged students Kenji Ekuan and Shinji Iwasaki and others as they formed GK industrial design firm (named after the initials for "Gruppe Koike," an informal salon of his students), from 1953. Director, Japan Industrial Designers Association, 1957, 1965-66; speaker at World Design Conference, Tokyo, 1960, and ICSID conference, Paris, 1963. **Exhibitions:** *Works of Iwataro Koike,* Tokyo University of Arts, 1979; *19 Designers: 30th Anniversary of the Japan Design Committee,* Matsuya Department Store, Tokyo, 1982. **Honors:** Ministry of International Trade and Industry Prize, Tokyo, 1939; honorary professor, Tokyo University of Arts, 1980; Kunii Industrial Art Award, 1985; Order of the Sacred Treasure, government of Japan, 1985. **Died:** 21 July 1992.

## Works

Record player, for GK, 1954.
Stacking ashtrays, for GK, 1955.
Whiskey bottle, for Ozeki Brewing Company, 1978.

## Publications

**By KOIKE: books**—*Basic Design: Composition and Formation,* Tokyo, 1956; *Arts,* Osaka, 1970; *Talk on Design: From Daily Life,* Tokyo, 1974, revised, 1985; **articles**—(with Shinji Iwasaki) "The Status of Product Design" in *Dezain no Kiseki (Tracks of Design)* edited by Japan Design Committee, Tokyo, 1977, 1985.

**On KOIKE: books**—*Japanese Design: A Survey Since 1950* by Kathryn B. Hiesinger and Felice Fischer, New York, 1994; **articles**—"Koike Iwataro" by Nagahama Masahiko in *Nikkei Design,* no. 22, April 1989.

*

I was born in 1913 in Tokyo, but my father, who was a furniture craftsman, moved to Shikoku Island in Kagawa Prefecture to be a teacher of wood-craft in an industrial arts school, so I grew up there. I, too, entered wood-carving at school—by my choice of course—but then I became rather interested in design, particularly in the form of bowls, dishes, and other tableware, because there was a ceramic workshop nearby.

In 1930, I proceeded to the Design Department of the Tokyo University of Arts. The design course then included commercial design, decorative design, and industrial arts; there were no specific majors. Japan at that time produced excellent decorative craftwork, but the design of useful things was slighted. I found this unfortunate and decided to enter the design field. Because there was no demand for industrial designers in the private sector, I was employed by Fukuoka Prefectural government on Kyushu Island as a technician for commerce and industry. In 1939, I was transferred to Sendai in Miyagi Prefecture, north of Tokyo, to work for the Ministry of International Trade and Industry, which was then promoting production of exportable merchandise. While I was working for these governmental agencies, I had time to learn about the actual situation of industrial design in Japan and in advanced countries. Later, I was assigned as chief of the Benbo Lacquerware workshop in Okinawa, where I studied design along with production and product control.

Iwataro Koike: *One Cup* for Ozeki Corporation

Design has been said to be a product of science and art, but I am of the opinion that the preeminent element of design is to be found in its ethics, based on the nature of society and humanity. If ethics is included as part of philosophy, then design is a product of philosophy, science, and art, and it is basically the affectionate heart which coordinates all these factors. In any case, the product should not be the advertising medium of the maker. Design is ideal when the designers' and makers' desire for self-manifestation is suppressed.

—Iwataro Koike

\* \* \*

Iwataro Koike was the preeminent teacher of design in Japan. He taught for almost forty years at the Tokyo University of Arts and wrote two secondary-school textbooks in which he described "beauty in daily life." And in his book *Talk on Design—From Daily Life,* he precisely clarified for his readers his concepts of design in easy-to-understand terms.

Koike said: "Design is synonymous with thinking; design starts from identifying a problem in one's own life." Everyone should have a "philosophy of life" a plan of how one will live his life, and this philosophy should inform one's view of life, means of livelihood, relation to society and nature, and the direction of one's desires. Design is a means of realizing these desires comprehensively and systematically—according to these aspects: science (truth); ethics (goodness); and aesthetics (beauty).

By "truth" Koike meant that the design would be useful, efficient, and economical; it would not be frivolous. One's effort must be a scientific approach to the truth of the natural world. By "goodness" he meant that the work will not be harmful or distressing to others. Design should strive to "make better" or "refine" the object. By "beauty" Koike meant that the design should strive to be pleasing, comfortable, and attractive; it should reveal the *quest* for beauty. Koike linked modern design to certain traditional Oriental values, and he made a conscious effort to instill elements of good design in the minds of his readers, who are, of course, also consumers.

For the Japanese people, with a culture stretching back over centuries, the coming of universal industrial civilization has been difficult. Even after 100 years of industrialization Japan has not yet managed to reconcile this new kind of civilization with her old culture. For a time, during the postwar period of rapid industrialization, "culture" was something of a catch phrase—but the reality of the time was the process from material paucity to material sufficiency. Koike's concern about current trends in design seemed to be based on his reflection that Japan had evolved into a society in which man must keep moving—running, almost; his apprehension was about the way of life of the people in such a society. He reiterated the question: "What is our true culture?" As he suggested that man in the modern age must be a person who inquires, he himself was determined to continue advocating the claims of humanity, whatever the pressures or criticisms to the contrary.

Into the late 1980s and early 1990s, Koike led a group of people devoted to "considering the colors of public amenities." One of their targets was the choice of color for the public buses of Tokyo, red and yellow. With public support, Koike succeeded in making the authorities change the color to a "soothing" green—proving that, even in Tokyo, there were still "human" beings.

—Kunio Sano

# KOLTAI, Ralph

British stage designer

**Born:** Berlin, Germany, 31 July 1924; emigrated to Britain in 1939, naturalized, 1947. **Education:** Waldschule Kaliski private school, Berlin, 1934-39; studied graphic design at Epsom School of Art, Surrey, 1942-44; studied stage design at the Central School of Arts and Crafts, London, 1948-51. **Military Service:** Served in the Royal Army Service Corps, at the International Military Tribunal, Nuremberg, 1945-46. **Family:** Married Annena Stubbs in 1956 (divorced, 1976). **Career:** Freelance stage designer, working mainly on operas, London, 1950-62; worked as a window display artist, London, 1951-53; associate designer, Royal Shakespeare Company, in London and Stratford-on-Avon, 1962-66 and from 1976; also designed for Sadler's Wells Company (now the English National Opera), Scottish Opera, Royal National Theatre, Chichester Festival Theatre, Royal Opera House/Covent Garden, London Opera

Club, Welsh National Opera, Ballet Rambert, Sydney Opera House, Nederlands Opera, Aalborg Teater, and others. Head of theatre design, 1965-73, and external assessor for diplomas in art and design, 1981-83, Central School of Art and Design, London. **Exhibitions:** McLaurin Art Gallery, Ayr, 1980; *British Theatre Design '83-87,* Riverside Studios, London, 1988. **Collections:** British Council, London; Arts Council of Great Britain, London; Victoria and Albert Museum, London; Robert Tobin Collection, McNay Museum of Art, San Antonio, Texas; University of Reading, Berkshire; Manchester University, Lancashire. **Honors:** London Drama Critics Awards, 1967 (2), 1981; Prague Quadriennale Gold Medal, 1975, 1979, 1983, and Silver Medal, 1987; Designer of the Year, Society of West End Theatre, London, 1978, 1984; Commander, Order of the British Empire, 1983; elected to The Royal Society of Arts, 1984. **Address:** London Management, 2-4 Noel Street, London W1V 3RB, England.

## Works

Stage productions include—*Two Brothers,* Ballet Rambert, 1958; *Carmen,* English National Opera, 1961; *Murder in the Cathedral,* English National Opera, 1962; *Conflicts,* Ballet Rambert, 1962; *The Caucasian Chalk Circle,* Royal Shakespeare Company, 1962; *Mahagonny,* English National Opera, 1963; *The Travellers,* Ballet Rambert, 1963; *The Representative,* Royal Shakespeare Company, 1963; *Dul de Sac,* Ballet Rambert, 1964; *The Birthday Party,* Royal Shakespeare Company, 1964; *Don Giovanni,* Scottish Opera, 1964; *Endgame,* Royal Shakespeare Company, 1964; *The Jew of Malta,* Royal Shakespeare Company, 1964; *Otello,* Scottish Opera, 1964, 1975; *The Merchant of Venice,* Royal Shakespeare Company, 1965; *Boris Godunov,* Scottish Opera, 1965; *Timon of Athens,* Royal Shakespeare Company, 1965; *The Rake's Progress,* Scottish Opera, 1967; *As You Like It,* National Theatre, 1967; *Little Murders,* Royal Shakespeare Company, 1967; *Soldiers,* Albery Theatre, London, 1968; *Back to Methuselah,* National Theatre, 1968; *The Tempest,* Chichester Festival Theatre, 1968; *Major Barbara,* Royal Shakespeare Company, 1970; *Elegy for Young Lovers,* Scottish Opera, 1970; *Wagner Ring Cycle,* English National Opera, 1970-73; *Taverner,* Royal Opera House, 1972; *Duke Bluebeard's Castle,* English National Opera, 1972; *Oedipus Rex,* Chichester Festival Theatre, 1974; *Billy,* Drury Lane Theatre, London, 1974; *Too True To Be Good,* Royal Shakespeare Company, 1975; *Old World/Wild Oats,* Royal Shakespeare Company, 1976; *The Cruel Garden,* Ballet Rambert, 1977; *State of Revolution,* National Theatre 1977; *Every Good Boy Deserves Favour,* Festival Hall and Mermaid Theatre, London, 1977; *The Seven Deadly Sins,* English National Opera, 1978; *Rosmersholm,* Haymarket Theatre, London, 1978; *The Ice Break,* Royal Opera House, 1978; *Brand,* National Theatre, 1978; *The Tempest,* Royal Shakespeare Company, 1978; *The Guardsman,* National Theatre, 1978; *Love's Labours Lost,* Royal Shakespeare Company, 1978; *Sons of Light,* Royal Shakespeare Company, 1978; *Hippolytus,* Royal Shakespeare Company, 1978; *Richard III,* National Theatre, 1979; *The Threepenny Opera,* Aalborg Teater, 1979; *Baal,* Royal Shakespeare Company, 1979; *The Wild Duck,* National Theatre, 1979; *Romeo and Juliet,* Royal Shakespeare Company, 1980; *Hamlet,* Royal Shakespeare Company, 1980; *The Love Girl and the Innocent,* Aalborg Teater, 1980; *Man and Superman,* National Theatre, 1981; *Terra Nova,* Aalborg Teater, 1981; *The*

Ralph Koltai: Model set for Zimmerman's *Die Soldaten,* at the Opera Lyon, 1982

*Love Girl and the Innocent,* Royal Shakespeare Company 1981; *The Carmelites,* Aalborg Teater, 1981; *Anna Karenina,* English National Opera, 1981; *Much Ado About Nothing,* Royal Shakespeare Company, 1982; *Moliere,* Royal Shakespeare Company, 1982; *Bugsy Malone,* Her Majesty's Theatre, London, 1983; *Cyrano de Bergerac,* Royal Shakespeare Company, 1983; *Custom of the County,* Royal Shakespeare Company, 1983; *Pack of Lies,* Lyric Theatre, London, 1983; *Les Soldats,* Opera de Lyons, 1983; *Mahagonny,* Aalborg Teater, 1984; *An Italian Girl in Algiers,* Opera de Geneve, 1984; *Troilus and Cressida,* Royal Shakespeare Company, 1986; *Othello,* Royal Shakespeare Company, 1986; *Tannhaeuser,* Opera de Geneve, 1986; *The Flying Dutchman,* Hong Kong Arts Festival, 1987; *Pacific Overtures,* English National Opera, 1988; *Carrie,* Royal Shakespeare Company, Stratford and New York, 1988; *They Shoot Horses, Don't They,* Royal Shakespeare Company, 1988; *Metropolis,* Piccadilly Theatre, London, 1989; (and director) *La Traviata,* Hong Kong Arts Festival, 1990; *E.A.R.W.I.G.,* Barbican Royal Shakespeare Company, 1990; *The Planets,* Royal Ballet, Covent Garden, 1990; *The Makropulos Case,* Norwegian Opera, 1991; *My Fair Lady,* Barry Weisler, New York (toured the United States), 1993; *Hair,* Old Vic, London, 1993; *La Traviata,* Stockholm Opera, 1993; *Otello,* Essen Opera, 1994; *Madam Butterfly,* Bunkamura, Tokyo, 1995.

**Publications**

**By KOLTAI: articles**—in *Design and Art Direction* (London), March 1983.

**On KOLTAI: books**—*Stage Design Throughout the World Since 1960* edited by René Hainaux and Yves Bonat, Brussels, 1972, London, 1973; *Who's Who in the Theatre* edited by Ian Herbert, London and Detroit, 1977; *British Theatre Design '83-87,* with texts by Timothy O'Brien and David Fingleton, London, 1988.

*

My work is very dependent on my development as an artist. I can't work like a painter, just pursuing one direction in a very single-minded way. I have a number of fascinations or directions. It might be kinetic art, it might be superhumanism, or Op art, or hard-edge painting or film. I'm very art motivated.

The primary consideration must always be honesty to the work. One must not be wilful, imposing personal visual notions in conflict with the author's essential message. Secondly, the actor must be the focus at all times. My object is to create an environment, an envelope with which the actor can identify, can relate to, and thereby help him/her to project the performance to maximum effect.

449

And what is best has to be best for that particular moment in time. The audience is conditioned to be on a particular wavelength, and you have to try to gauge that. Theatre is a progressive art form, and you can't have definitive productions. Maybe if you saw Peter Brook's *Midsummer Night's Dream* today, it wouldn't have the same effect. But in 1970, it was spot on right. I have sensed for the last couple of years that audiences are getting rather tired of the empty stage and spare decor and highly intellectualized productions. I think they actually want to see something for their money. I'm also bored with such productions. The minimalism with one chair in the middle of the stage has got rather tiresome. One could occasionally come back to it, but basically, at the moment, I'm inclined to be a little more exuberant, more colorful, more spectacular if you like. Not that I consciously think about being right for the moment in time. I'm hoping that I keep sufficiently abreast and alive to be automatically, subconsciously, intuitively in tune with the current mood.

I have problems turning a piece of work into an aesthetic object. I find it easier to create a piece of sculpture on which the actors perform than to create a mess which is a mess. My messes turn quite easily into being rather aesthetic messes. When I am aware that that is not what is required, I find it quite hard.

I think you have to be fiercely critical of yourself in order to produce anything that is worthwhile. It is quite easy to design a respectable show, but that would be a bore to me, and boredom is the greatest enemy. You don't get paid a lot of money in this business, so the only reason for doing it is the satisfaction of having explored a particular idea. There are some exciting moments—as when you are asked by a director you like and admire if you will do a particular play or opera. Then comes a period of calm, then a period of trauma when you don't seem able to solve the problem. And if it goes quite well, you are pleased for a moment. Maybe a day. Then you start on the next thing.

—Ralph Koltai

\*     \*     \*

Koltai refers explicitly to his art-oriented approach and to his intuitiveness, both of which are most evident in those productions that reveal a sculptor's eye for shape, mass, texture, and space, usually abstractly stylized rather than realistic. *Tännhauser* (Australia, 1973) had a smooth, raked floor unmarred except for two graceful segments that peeled up from its surface. The settings for Ibsen's *Brand* (National Theatre, 1978) and Ted Tally's *Terra Nova* (Denmark, 1981) represented landscapes of snow and ice: jagged sections of white plywood tilted up to suggest a cracking ice-field for *Brand,* while stainless steel on a gently curved base, echoed by the steel grill arching over part of the floor, captured the icescape of *Terra Nova.*

Fiberglass and plexiglas are typical of synthetic materials often employed by Koltai. Wagner's *Ring* (English National Opera, 1970-73) blended shimmering, splintery fiberglass with metallic, boulder-like spheres to create a fantasy landscape. Similarly striking effects were produced by panels of paint-sprayed and transparent plexiglas in *As You Like It* (National Theatre, 1976) and *Much Ado About Nothing* (Royal Shakespeare Company, 1982).

Koltai's sculptural scenography often blends with other techniques: for Brecht's *Baal* (Royal Shakespeare Company, 1979), he combined a rear wall in relief (created by protruding objects later to be used in the action) with projections that erased the effect of the relief surface during the scene changes; for Shaw's *Man and Superman* (National Theatre, 1981), a curving mirror formed the rear wall and reflected people and objects in the upstage part of the scene.

When the occasion demands, Koltai is able to be documentarily realistic, although that is not his natural heart, which inclines toward the metaphoric and imagistic. For Solzhenitsyn's *The Love Girl and the Innocent* (Royal Shakespeare Company, 1981), he constructed a barbed-wire freight yard including tracks, cars, and gantries with almost cinematic verisimilitude because the production concept demanded that approach.

Like Josef Svoboda, to whose work his own has been occasionally compared, Koltai demonstrates an ability to adapt contemporary technology to the needs of theatre art, as some of his most expressive scenography makes clear. Maxwell Davies' opera *Taverner* (Covent Garden, 1972) employed a large ring circumscribing a skeletal see-saw—capable of rotation and alternating vertical movement—to represent Renaissance science as well as the shifting fortunes of contending forces within the play. Shaw's *Back to Methuselah* (National Theatre, 1968), was more stylized and more consciously artistic. The creation of the universe and the earth was represented by a number of revolving travelling spheres in relation to a centrally suspended solar disk made luminous by lights concealed within its circumference.

Among his recent outstanding productions have been *Othello* (Royal Shakespeare Company, 1986), based on abstract configurations of fiber optics and transparent plastic—for which he was awarded a silver medal at the Prague Quadriennale; and the musical *Carrie* (Royal Shakespeare Company) in 1988. Koltai also extended his activities to include opera direction, with *The Flying Dutchman* (Hong Kong, 1987) and *La Traviata* (Hong Kong, 1990).

—Jarka M. Burian

## KOPPEL, Henning

Danish painter, sculptor, glass, ceramics, and metalware designer

**Born:** Ostenvold, Copenhagen, 8 May 1918. **Education:** Oregaards Gymnasium, Copenhagen, until 1934; Bizzie Hoyer School, Drawing, Copenhagen, 1935-36; studied sculpture under Einar Utzon Frank, Kunstakademie, Copenhagen, 1936-37, and under Malfrey, at the Academie Ranson, Paris, 1938. **Family:** Married Jytte Skouboe in 1941. **Career:** Independent painter, stone mason, and freelance jewelry designer, Svensk Tenn shop, Stockholm, 1942-45; contract silverware and jewelry designer, working with Harald Nielsen, Georg Jensen Solvsmedie, Copenhagen, from 1945; also freelance ceramics designer, working mainly for Bing and Gröndahl, Copenhagen, from 1961; glass designer, Holmgaards and Orrefors Glassworks, Sweden, from 1971. **Exhibitions:** Georg Jensen Inc., New York, 1966; *Scandinavian Modern Design 1880-1980,* Cooper-Hewitt Museum, New York, 1982; *Design Since 1945,* Philadelphia Museum of Art, 1983; *The Lunning Prize,* Nationalmuseum, Stockholm, 1986; *Scandinavia: Ceramics and Glass in the Twentieth Century,* Victoria and Albert Museum, London, 1989. **Honors:** Gold Medal, Milan Triennale, 1951, 1954, 1957; National Art Gallery Drawing Prize, Copenhagen, 1953; Lunning Prize, Copenhagen, 1953; International Design Award, New York, 1963; Golden Spoon Award, Munich, 1963; Diamonds International Award, New York,

1966; ID Design Prize, Copenhagen, 1966; Gold Medal for Design, Florence, 1967; Exempla Gold Medal, Munich, 1970. **Died:** Copenhagen, 27 June 1981.

## Works

Bracelet with silver links, for Georg Jensen, 1947.
Fish dish and cover in silver, for Georg Jensen, 1954.
Wine jug in silver, for Georg Jensen, 1955.
Bowl with pedestal feet in silver, for Georg Jensen, 1958.
Serving jug in silver, for Georg Jensen, 1959.
Jug in white porcelain, for Bing and Gröndahl, 1962.
*Koppel White* tableware range in white porcelain, for Bing and Gröndahl, 1963.
Jug in white porcelain, for Bing and Gröndahl, 1965.

## Publications

**On KOPPEL: books**—*Henning Koppel:Tegningen,* Copenhagen, 1938; *Modern Danish Silver* by Esbjrn Hiort, New York, London and Copenhagen, 1954; *Fifty Years of Silver in the Georg Jensen Tradition* by Edgar J. Kaufmann, Erik Lassen and C. Detlev Reventlow, Copenhagen, 1956; *Dansk Keramik* edited by Bredo L. Grandjean, David Westholm and Arthur Hald, Stockholm, 1960; *Modern Jewellery: An International Survey 1890-1964* by Graham Hughes, London, 1963, 1964; *Henning Koppel* by Viggo Sten Moller, Copenhagen, 1965; *34 Scandinavian Designers* by Svend Erik Moller, Copenhagen, 1967; *Danish Design* by Svend Erik Moller, Copenhagen, 1974; *International Modern Glass* by Geoffrey Beard, London, 1976; *En Kobenhavnsk Porcelaenfabriks Historie: Bing och Gröndahl 1853-1978* by Erik Lassen, Copenhagen, 1978; *Scandinavian Modern Design 1880-1980* edited by David Revere McFadden, New York, 1982; *Design Since 1945* edited by Kathryn Hiesinger and George Marcus, Philadelphia and London, 1983; *The Lunning Prize,* exhibition catalogue edited by Helena Dahlbäck Lutteman and Marianne Uggla, Stockholm, 1986; *Scandinavia: Ceramics and Glass in the Twentieth Century* by Jennifer Hawkins Opie, London, 1989.

\*   \*   \*

Henning Koppel began his professional career as a silversmith in the post-World War II period, when the axiom "form follows function" was seriously being challenged by a generation who sought to forge connections between art and craft. Their objective was greater expressive freedom within the constraints of the utilitarian form.

Koppel consciously worked silver as a sculptural medium, employed no surface decoration and concentrated entirely on producing pure, sensuous forms which invited the sense of touch. He was one of the leading figures, if not the most influential, in founding the new aesthetic which directed attention to the characteristics of silver, exploiting its reflective capacity and its high malleability.

His famous Fish Dish of 1954 has been displayed in museums around the world and is probably the best-known piece of modern Scandinavian metalwork. The hand grips formed at the ends of the cover were designed to suggest the mouth of a fish, and this theme, carried out in flowing, asymmetrical forms, characterized much of Koppel's subsequent work. The problems of covers, spouts, and handles led to integrational considerations which freed the utilitar-

ian vessel from strict symmetry and a central axis. His cutlery pattern *Caravel* (1957) was designed with top, back, and side views equally considered, thereby restoring this category of utensil to the realm of sculptural design from its more usual, rigid top view—or graphic—interpretation .

In 1965, for the ceramic company Bing and Gröndahl, Koppel designed the pattern *White Koppel,* which is completely devoid of decoration. *Blue Koppel* followed in 1975. In 1973 he designed the stainless steel cutlery pattern *New York.*

Koppel's work was a powerful source of inspiration to American smiths during the 1950s and 1960s when this craft was undergoing revitalization in the art departments of colleges and universities across the country. More than any other designer of his generation, Koppel succeeded in striking a harmony between the objectives of the artist and the capacities of the virtuoso craftsman.

—Barbara Young

# KORDA, Vincent
British painter and film designer

**Born:** Vincze Kellner, in Pusztaturpaszto, Hungary, in 1897; emigrated to Britain in 1932, naturalized, 1938. **Education:** Attended school in Turkey, Kecskemet, and Budapest, until 1909; studied at the College of Industrial Art, Budapest, 1910-12; apprentice in an architect's office, Budapest, 1910-12; studied painting and drawing under Belya Avanyi Grunwald, at Kecskemet art colony, 1912-15; studied painting in Vienna, Florence and Paris, 1919-25. **Military Service:** Served in the Hungarian Army, 1916-18. **Family:** Married the actress Gertrude Musgrove in 1933 (divorced, 1942); son: Michael. **Career:** Independent painter, Kecskemet, Nagbanya and Budapest, 1919-26, and Paris, 1927-32; film designer, working mainly for his brother, the producer-director Alexander Korda, Paris, 1929-32, and London and Hollywood, 1932-71; art director, London Films, Denham, Buckinghamshire, 1932-45, and British Lion Films, Shepperton, London, 1946-54. **Honors:** Academy Award, 1940. **Died:** London, 5 January 1979.

## Works

Film productions include—*Marius* (A. Korda), 1931; *Men of Tomorrow* (Sagan and A. Korda), 1932; *Wedding Rehearsal* (A. Korda), 1933; *The Private Life of Henry VIII* (A. Korda), 1933; *The Girl from Maxim's* (A. Korda), 1933; *Catherine the Great* (Czinner), 1934; *The Private Life of Don Juan* (A. Korda), 1934; *The Scarlet Pimpernel* (Young), 1935; *The Ghost Goes West* (Clair), 1935; *Sanders of the River* (Z. Korda), 1935; *Moscow Nights* (Asquith), 1935; *Things To Come* (Menzies), 1935; *The Man Who Could Work Miracles* (Mendes), 1936; *Rembrandt* (A. Korda), 1936; *Men Are Not Gods* (Reisch), 1936; *Elephant Boy* (Flaherty and Z. Korda), 1937; *I, Claudius* (von Sternberg—unfinished), 1937; *Action for Slander* (Whelan), 1937; *The Squeaker* (Howard), 1937; *Paradise for Two* (Freeland), 1937; *Over the Moon* (Freeland), 1937; *21 Days* (Dean), 1937; *The Drum* (Z. Korda), 1938; *The Challenge* (Rosmer), 1938; *Prison Without Bars* (Hurst), 1938; *Q Planes* (Whelan), 1939; *The Spy in Black* (Powell), 1939; *The Lion Has Wings* (Powell, Hurst and

Brunel), 1939; *The Conquest of the Air* (Z. Korda and others), 1940; *The Thief of Baghdad* (Berger, Powell and Whelan), 1940; *Old Bill and Son* (Dalrymple), 1940; *Major Barbara* (Pascal), 1941; *Lydia* (Duvivier), 1941; *That Hamilton Woman* (A. Korda), 1941; *To Be or Not to Be* (Lubitsch), 1942; *Jungle Book* (Z. Korda), 1942; *Perfect Strangers* (A. Korda), 1945; *An Ideal Husband* (A. Korda), 1947; *The Fallen Idol* (Reed), 1948; *Bonnie Prince Charlie* (Kimmins), 1948; *The Third Man* (Reed), 1949; *Miracolo a Milano* (De Sica), 1950; *Outcast of the Islands* (Reed), 1951; *Home at Seven* (Richardson), 1952; *The Sound Barrier* (Lean), 1952; *The Holly and the Ivy* (O'Ferrall), 1952; *Malaga* (Sale), 1954; *Summer Madness* (Lean), 1955; *The Deep Blue Sea* (Litvak), 1955; *Scent of Mystery* (Cardiff), 1960; *The Longest Day* (Annakin, Marton and Wicki), 1962; *The Yellow Rolls Royce* (Asquith), 1964; *Nicholas and Alexandra* (Schaffner), 1971.

## Publications

**By KORDA: articles**—in *Sight and Sound* (London), Spring 1934.

**On KORDA: books**—*Art and Design in the British Film* by Edward Carrick, London, 1948; *Alexander Korda* by Paul Tabori, London, 1959; *Le Decor de Film* by Leon Barsacq, Paris, 1970, as *Caligari's Cabinet and Other Grand Illusions,* Boston, 1976; *Alexander Korda* by Karol Kulik, New Rochelle, 1975; *The Hollywood Exiles* by John Baxter, London, 1976; *Charmed Lives* by Michael Korda, London, 1979; *The International Dictionary of Films and Filmmakers,* London and Chicago, 1987, 1991.

*       *       *

Vincent Korda, who took charge of the art department at Denham Film studios in the 1930s, brought to art direction there a quality far higher than that of the average designer in either theatre or film. His period as a painter in France made an imprint on both his personal set designs and those produced under his charge in the studio, while his strongly persuasive character and impatience dominated the work of those around him, from his fellow designers to the carpenters and decorators who carried out the finished sets.

The ideal situation in set design is a cooperative, integrated effort between the film director, the cameraman, and the designer. In many instances, the role of the latter has been considered unimportant, but Korda never allowed this to happen. If anything, his art direction, with its strong personality, dominated the production. On the other hand, he insisted on emphasising the director's ideas and the cameraman's artistic and technical potential. The end result was almost always satisfactory, well above average, and even when the film itself failed to gain acceptance, the set design received acclaim.

Such was the case with the film *Things to Come,* one of the first science fiction subjects brought to the screen by Denham Studios in 1936. The sets stunned with their functional, "Bauhaus" interiors and immensely distorted perspectives of exteriors. Korda pioneered the use of models for trick effects for this production, accentuating distances, and avoiding the flat, direct appearance of ordinary reality.

Possibly his most memorable designs were the sets for the film *Rembrandt,* also made in 1926. As a former painter, he found a remarkable sympathy with Rembrandt and succeeded in recreating the background and atmosphere of the subject. His knowledge of architecture, combined with his pictorial sense and attention to minute detail, as well as—for a change—the money lavished on his

production, resulted in one of the most satisfying achievements in the history of set design.

Korda's approach differed from Hollywood's. Instead of lavishing money on sets which did not reflect their cost on the screen, he spent little but made the sets look expensive. He strove frequently to save money and, with it, valuable time. He made his team work throughout the night on the production of *The Private Life of Henry VIII* (1933), reusing many props to turn a bedroom into a banquet hall ready for the cameras the following morning. The next night, he turned the same set back into a reception room. He even saved (as his son maintains) the nails and pasteboard structures to be used in another production. The success of this film included comments to the effect that no other film resembled such classic "Englishness" as *Henry VIII.*

He succeeded in applying his sense of period style in other films, including the unfinished *I Claudius* (1937), *That Hamilton Woman* (1941), and *The Thief of Baghdad* (1940), although the latter also demanded huge sets which proved to be almost beyond the technical resources of the British film industry at that time. In spite of his personal dislike for the style of the production, it won him an Oscar for art direction. Another production of great distinction was *The Drum* (1938), which once again gave proof of his unique sense of pictorial style, his talent for establishing the right atmosphere, and his technical perfection. Korda was one of the most imaginative art directors the medium of film has had.

—John Halas

# KOSONEN, Markku (Pekka)

Finnish craftsman

**Born:** Of Finnish parents, in Djupvik, Sweden, 22 January 1945. **Education:** Studied at the School of Handicrafts, Punkaharju, Finland, 1960-61; Institute of Applied Arts, Helsinki, 1964-68. **Family:** Married Tammi Outi in 1969; daughter: Emma. **Career:** Independent craftsman and designer, establishing own workshop, Helsinki, from 1968; full-time freelance artist, from 1985. Instructor, University of Industrial Arts, Helsinki, 1968-78; freelance critic and teacher, Helsinki, from 1975; planner, National Board of Vocational Education, Helsinki, 1979-85. Board Member, Ornamo Finnish Association of Designers, Helsinki, 1974-78 and from 1986. **Exhibitions:** *Five Finnish Artist Craftsmen,* Röhsska Konstslöjdmuseet, Göteborg, 1980; *Finland: Nature, Design, Architecture,* toured the United States, 1981; *Markku Kosonen/Kari Virtanen,* Galleria Artek, Helsinki, 1982; *Finnland Gestaltet,* Hamburg and Dusseldorf, 1983; *Design Finland,* Brighton, Sussex, 1987; *Markku Kosonen: Wood Objects,* Galleria Artek, Helsinki, 1987; *Scandinavian Design: A Way of Life,* Japan, 1987; *Markku Kosonen,* Konsthantverkana, Stockholm, 1988; *The Language of Wood,* American Craft Museum, New York, 1989; *Markku Kosonen: Easter,* Galleria 25, Helsinki, 1989; Galleria 25, Helsinki, 1989; *Nordic Form,* Malmö, Sweden, 1990; Galleria Lief, Los Angeles, 1990, 1993; Galleria Artek, Helsinki, 1990, 1992; Brown Grotta Gallery, Wilton, Connecticut, 1990-1995; EXPO Sevilla 92, Seville, Spain, 1992; *Design Finlandais,* Musée d'Art Moderne et d'Art Contemporain, Nice, France, 1995. **Collections:** Museum of Applied Arts, Helsinki; Röhsska Konstslöjdmuseet, Göteborg; Nationalmuseet, Stockholm; Kunstindustrimuseet, Oslo; Museum für Kunst und Gewerben, Hamburg; Museum für Kunsthandwerk, Frankfurt. **Honors:** Finn-

**Markku Kosonen: wooden memento boxes, 1990**

ish State Prize for Industrial Art, 1981; Three-Year Finnish State Artist's Grant, Finland, 1985-88; Artek Prize, 1991; Fifteen-Year State Artist's Grant, Finland, 1992-2008. **Address:** Luotsikatu 4 A 2, 00160 Helsinki, Finland.

## Works

Pestle and mortar in curly birch, 1975.
Workbench in birch, 1980.
Baskets in rush and willow, 1988.
Memento boxes and "craftsman's cabinet," 1990.
Willow basket, 1994.

## Publications

**On KOSONEN: articles**—"Av videung" by K. Wickman in *Form* (Stockholm), no. 5, 1988; "Only Brushwood?" by S. Parko in *Muoto* (Helsinki), no. 33, 1989.

\*

The life of a tree is in its seed, which carries in its flight the heritage of its species. After falling to the ground and taking root, it stays there all the time. A tree attains its full height during the lifespan of a human being. After that, it grows wiser—provided it is allowed to remain standing. The growth of a tree can be compared to that of a person. Such is its educational purpose. Since it is a renewable natural resource, a tree is an example of the eternal cycle of life. As a material it does not last forever. Wood "lives" even after death—by shrinking, swelling, or rotting. Time and insects eat it; it cracks and finally disintegrates. Wood is new to every era. In using it, one must consider what it is needed for, and what kind of ideals are to be interpreted from it.

The forests are our lungs and our souls: they give life to the entire Earth. A chill to the soul follows from the destruction of our forests. The forest has given such good cover and protection to we Finns that it has even isolated us. From trees we have derived energy for both warmth and food. We fend off physical cold with the help of a cell-structure insulating the heat of the wood. It surrounds the sphere of our life like the shell of a building. As protection from the changing weather and as a mediator on behalf of Nature, the tree teaches us the wisdom of an ecological way of life.

—Markku Kosonen

\*   \*   \*

There are 40 tree species growing in Finland. Of these, industry uses three: birch, spruce and pine. The rest can be left to artists and craftspeople.

453

Interior designer and craftsman Markku Kosonen has been working with wood for several years, using some of these 37 species left over by industry as his material. Birch, spruce and pine do not interest him because of their industrial character, but for example alder, apple, larch or willow offer somebody who can handle wood all kinds of fresh potential.

Markku Kosonen's wooden objects are mortars, chopping boards, dishes, baskets, boxes. For him, practical function is something he wants to stick to, although his 1987 exhibition at Artek in Helsinki also included some magnificent willow basket work, which was actually more like sculpture. "The willow is one of the visually most fascinating trees we have," says Markku Kosonen. "It constantly produces 'new' species. Each season of the year makes it look different. The colors of the trunks in the spring sun, ranging from yellow to dark brown, form a particularly beautiful sight."

The essential features of Markku Kosonen's work are his themes, developed out of the natural forms, the shapes, created using geometrical patterns with constant variation, and the beautifully finished treatment of the wood. When working with his hands, the artist has time to think and the thought gets conveyed to the object. The thought follows its own course, changing all the time, and the hand makes the next piece different, unique.

—Kristina Paatero

# KRAMER, Burton

Canadian graphic designer

**Born:** New York, 1932; attained Canadian citizenship, 1974. **Education:** Attended State University of New York, two years; studied visual design, Institute of Design, Illinois Institute of Technology, BS, 1954; Fulbright Scholar, Royal College of Art, London, 1955-1956; studied graphic design, Yale University, MFA, 1957. **Career:** Designer, Will Burtin Design Office, New York, 1957-59, and CIBA-Geigy, New York, 1959-61; design director, Halpern Advertising, Zürich, 1961-65, and Paul Arthur Associates, Toronto, 1965-66; director of corporate graphics, Clairtone Sound Corp. Ltd., 1966-67; president, Kramer Design Associates Limited, Toronto, from 1967. Instructor in Advanced Graphic Design, Typography, and Foundation Studies, Ontario College of Art, from 1978; lecturer, VIACOM, 1990, and 1st International Logo biennial, Belgium, 1994; visiting lecturer, York University, Sheridan College, and other U.S. colleges and universities. **Member:** President, 1972-74, and fellow, 1975, Society of Graphic Designers of Canada; Royal Canadian Academy of Arts, 1973; Alliance Graphique Internationale, from 1974. **Exhibitions:** Work exhibited throughout Canada, Switzerland, Japan, Czechoslovakia, Belgium, France, Italy, and the United States. **Collections:** Library of Congress, Washington, D.C.; Smithsonian Institute, Washington, D.C. **Honors:** Best Swiss Posters, Swiss Department of the Interior, 1964; ITCA Gold Medal for Radio Canada International Commemorative Canadian Postage Stamp; Gold Medal, Toronto Art Director's Club; medal, Leipzig Book Fair for *Art of Norval Morrisseau*; Awards of Excellence for corporate identity design programs, Canadian Department of Regional Expansion, 1985. **Address:** Kramer Design Associates Limited, 103 Dupont Street, Toronto M5R 1V4, Ontario, Canada.

**Works**

Corporate identity, advertising, packaging, and vehicles, for Clairtone Sound Corporation, 1966-67.

Graphics and signing, for EXPO '67, Montreal.

Corporate identity, publications, exhibits, advertising, vehicles, and signing, for Ontario Educational Communications Authority (Channel 19), 1967-69.

Corporate identity, for Canadian Broadcasting Corporation, SRC, Radio Canada International, 1974.

Wayfinding system, for Union Station, Toronto, 1984.

Signing, identity, and graphics, for CBC/SRC Broadcast Centre, 1984-92.

Identity, boutique design, signing, and graphics, for Canadian Museum of Contemporary Photography, 1986-92.

Identity, packaging, graphics, and advertising, for Zoomit Corporation International, from 1987.

Corporate identity and graphics, for Gemini Group, 1988.

Corporate identity, signing, and graphics, for North American Life Assurance, 1989-91.

Corporate identity, for National Research Council Canada, 1990.

Identity, signing and graphics for Canadian Pavilion, for EXPO '93, Taijon, Korea.

Corporate identity, signing and graphics, for The Municipality of Metropolitan Toronto, 1992-94.

Corporate identity, for CIBC, 1994.

**Publications**

**By KRAMER: books**—(introduction to Canadian section) *Top Trademarks and Symbols of the World,* Milan, 1973; (introduction) *Letterheads of the World,* Tokyo, 1977; **articles**—*IDEA* (Tokyo); *Print* (New York); *Studio* (Toronto); "It's Not a Bird, It's Not a Plane," *Applied Arts Quarterly* (Toronto), May 1987.

**On KRAMER: books**—*The Book of American Trademarks* by David Carter, New York, 1972, 1973; *Archigraphia: Architectural and Environmental Graphics,* Zürich, 1978; *International Trademark Design* by Peter Wildbur, London, 1979; *Visual Transformation,* Zürich, 1982; *Typographic Design: Form and Communication* by Rob Carter, Ben Day, and Philip Meggs, New York, 1985; *First Choice, World's Leading Graphic Designers...,* by Ken Cato, Tokyo, 1989; *Typographic Communications Today* by Edward M. Gottschall, Cambridge, 1989; *Typographic Eye; Graphic Design in Canada;* **articles**—"Burton Kramer Associates" in *IDEA* (Tokyo), vol. 22, no. 123, 1974; "Designers Notebook: Burton Kramer Associates Ltd." in *Canadian Interiors,* July 1975; "Graphic Magic for Mr. Everyday" by Adele Freedman in *Globe & Mail* (Toronto), 20 July 1985; "Graphic Design Education at the Ontario College of Art" in *IDEA* (Tokyo), no. 192, 1985; "Burton Kramer" by Winne Czulinski in *Studio,* February 1986; "Kramer" by Marjorie Harris in *Applied Arts Quarterly* (Toronto), vol. 3, no. 2, 1988; "If It Ain't Broke, Why Fix It?" by Adele Freedman in *Globe & Mail,* 7 November 1992; "Burton Kramer" in *IDEA* (Tokyo), No. 240, 1993; "Powerful Symbols" by Sally Ritchie in *Globe & Mail,* 31 August 1993.

*

Since my student days, first at the Institute of Design in Chicago, then later at Yale, it always seemed clear that the real

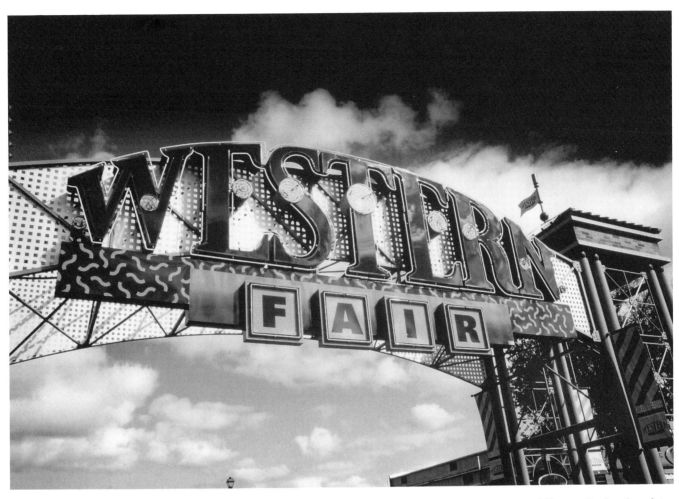

**Burton Kramer: Entrance structures and banners to** *Western Fair,* **London, Ontario, 1995. Photo courtesy of Kramer Design Associates Limited**

challenge for the designer involved participating in helping to make our world a "better" place than it would be without our efforts.

For this reason, the involvement of my office in environmental-architectural graphics and visual identity has grown over the years. This work has enabled us to really influence people, by making a long-term impact on their environment through a wide variety of graphics, signage, and, on occasion, public sculpture. The opportunity to create works that have some longevity, that do not rapidly become "waste paper," has been a satisfying experience, along with the opportunity to pass on some of this thinking to others, through teaching.

After talking recently with a fellow Yale graduate, one comment of his remained with me. "There were so few of us in those days." We did not realize! Today, the entire design landscape has altered. There are endless competitions, magazines, annuals, exhibits, conferences, and designers. More and more of all of these, particularly designers. Trained and untrained, self-taught or up-through-the-ranks. An enormous army to "fight the good fight." Visual sophistication and rational thought (the good guys) vs. the forces of visual illiteracy (the bad guys). But times have changed radically and it is more and more difficult to tell the good guys from the bad guys. In the ongoing struggle between

light and darkness, it is difficult to know who's winning. The results may not all be in for some time.

—Burton Kramer

\* \* \*

Burton Kramer designs logos. He also works in one. In 1988, having decided to move his offices, he purchased a narrow, three-storey brick house in downtown Toronto. Because it leaned to one side, Kramer's architect refaced the front of the building with corrugated aluminum, rounding the metal at the top so we know it's a false front. The door was relocated to one side, next to a rectangular piece of glass block which lights the reception area. The second-floor window, which looks like a bay pressed through a wringer, is off-center; the square window above is likewise asymmetrical. Frames are painted in different primary colors. Triangle, square, rectangle, curve, wedge. Red, blue, yellow, green. Kramer's line of business is well represented. So is the upbeat character of his graphic design, which he describes as "a resounding yes—for creativity, sunshine, silliness, sanity. Yes, yes, yes."

Kramer is best known for his bi-lingual symbol for the Canadian Broadcasting Corporation, introduced in 1974. The logo is based on the letter C, the only element shared by the corporation's English and French acronyms CBC and SRC. Wanting to convey a sense of broadcasting outwards—to all of Canada, and from Canada to the world—Kramer set C in the center and multiplied it in all directions to suggest a vibrant sphere, fading the colors at the circumference for a three-dimensional feeling.

In high-handed fashion, the corporation hired one of Kramer's competitors to "simplify" the logo in 1992, claiming it blurred when reduced in size to brand the corner of a television screen. Because the CBC owns the copyright, Kramer considered a lawsuit for infringement of moral rights instead. He didn't go ahead. Coarsened as well as simplified—the C is gone—the CBC medallion is still recognizable as Kramer's logo, a long-lived one at that.

Kramer is currently busier than he's ever been. Commissions run to signage, wayfinding systems, exhibition design, and publications, as well as corporate identity programs for public institutions and major banks. Increasingly, they call for large, free-standing architectural fixtures such as automated bank machines. To do the job right, Kramer's ten-strong staff now includes an industrial designer and an architect.

With in-house CAD systems, Kramer Design Associates will hire only computer-literate designers; Kramer's son Jeremy, now a creative partner in the firm, is one of them. Kramer Senior, the holdout of the bunch, nevertheless insists that "if we weren't so computerized, we'd probably be fifteen, not ten. We're doing things in days or hours that used to take weeks." The company has developed a sideline in computerized architectural renderings for local firms. Abetted by the computer, paper projects such as brochures and presentation folders tend to dynamic, multi-colored, multi-layered graphics that seem in constant motion.

Kramer isn't one to stand still, either. An outspoken enemy of the boring and banal, he turns to painting, sculpture, and furniture for inspiration. The exaggerations of Pop are an influence, as are cartoons and music videos. In the early eighties, Memphis, the Italian design movement led by Ettore Sottsass, made an impression. "I see a kind of playfulness, fun, and freedom," Kramer said at the time. "When I see a table with four legs all different, that does something to my sensibilities. It makes me rethink my position: 'What are they doing that adds to my understanding?'"

Kramer has taken to painting; his subject is color or "color moods," as he prefers. A couple of big canvases hang on his office walls; others await buyers at his next gallery exhibition. Unconventional, with an insistance on retaining a child-like sense of magic, Kramer insists on enjoying his creative work. In this way, he is able to give joy to others.

—Adele Freedman


# KROLL, Boris

American textile designer

**Born:** Buffalo, New York, 11 October 1913. **Education:** Apprenticed in family furniture manufacture business, New York, 1930-32; self-taught in design. **Military Service:** Served in the United States Army Corps of Engineers, in India, Burma, Philippines, and Japan, 1943-45. **Family:** Married Lynn Steyert in 1945; children: Geoffrey, Eric, and Lisa. **Career:** Freelance textile designer, from 1932, and manufacturer, New York, from 1938; founder, president, chief executive, and director of design, Cromwell Designs, 1938-61,

Boris Kroll Fabrics, from 1946, 220 East 51st Street Corporation, 1950-79, Boris Kroll Fabrics of Los Angeles, and Boris Kroll Prints, 1955-64, Boris Kroll Labs, and Boris Kroll Fabrics of Miami, 1957-64, Boris Kroll Fabrics of Illinois, 1959-64, Boris Kroll Jacquard Looms, from 1959, and BK Land Corporation, from 1968. President, Decorative Design Association, 1958; vice-president of the resources council, Association of Interior Designers, 1963; board member, Color Association of the United States, 1967; advisory committee member, SONA Handicrafts and Loom Export Corporation of India, 1967-70. **Exhibitions:** *Good Design,* Museum of Modern Art, New York, 1953; Seattle Art Museum, 1955; Detroit Institute of Arts, 1962, 1966; Victoria and Albert Museum, London, 1965; Purdue University, West Lafayette, Indiana, 1970; Georgia State University, Atlanta, 1970; Guild Hall of East Hampton, New York, 1977; Fashion Institute of Technology, New York, 1980. **Collections:** Detroit Institute of Arts; Victoria and Albert Museum. **Honors:** Museum of Modern Art Design Award, New York 1953; American Institute of Interior Designers Award, New York, 1967; *Industrial Design* Award, New York, 1970; American Society of Industrial Designers Award, 1976. Honorary doctorate, Philadelphia College of Textiles, 1971. **Address:** Boris Kroll Fabrics, 979 Third Avenue, New York, New York 10022, U.S.A.


**Publications**

**By KROLL: articles**—*Interiors* (New York), May/June 1968.

**On KROLL: books**—*Design Since 1945* edited by Kathryn Hiesinger and George Marcus, Philadelphia and London, 1983; **articles**—*New York World Telegram,* 7 October 1939; *American Fabrics* (New York), Fall 1958; *House Beautiful* (New York), November 1964; *Interiors,* January 1965, September 1969, January 1981, November 1981; *Seattle Times,* 17 April 1969; *San Francisco Chronicle,* 24 April 1969; *San Francisco Examiner,* 23 April 1969; *Atlanta Journal,* 21 April 1970; *Interior Design* (New York), February 1971, April 1982; *New York Times,* 16 January 1977.


\*


A creative fabric is the result of the calculated integration of color, fiber, weave, and design. Design in fabrics is the answer.

Even as the structural integrity of any architectural undertaking is intrinsic to its beauty, so is the quality of the infinite number of components which go into its interiors. As a manufacturer of fabrics for interiors, I am aware of my responsibility to that end. Durability must be considered. The selection of a particular fiber—wool, silk, linen, or nylon—does not necessarily guarantee long life for the fabric. What gives it resistance to wear is the fabric designer's engineering of construction, involving such factors as staple length, spinning system, how many turns are specified in the yarn in relation to the size of the yarn (heavy yarn needs fewer turns, finer yarn needs more turns), or, if the yarn is a plied yarn made up of two yarns each with specific turns, then plied with what specific number of turns in creating a final two-plied yarn ready for use in weaving, etc. For filling, less twist is used or what is known as a filling twist. It is a misconception by interior designers that the type of fiber or raw material necessarily means better-wearing fabric. This is simply not true. Durability is achieved by selecting and engineering yarns for warps. The number of ends per inch in the warp, the selection and combination of weaves, and the final determination of picks per inch are necessary factors in attaining the balance a fabric needs in order to affect the durability of the finished fabric. A heavy, bulky fabric is not necessarily long-wearing.

Superior resistance to the changes inevitably caused by exposure to sunlight, gas fading, crocking, water-spotting, and dry-cleaning is necessary in any contract fabric. Such superior resistance can only be achieved through the use of selected dyestuffs, chemicals, and expert dyeing techniques. Certain fibers must be dyed with certain types of dyes. Frequently, the fabric designer must compromise on the color desired in order to meet fastness standards. To achieve especially vibrant blues and greens and maintain a high degree of fastness to light, each fiber must be treated in an individual manner (i.e., linen—direct colors are used; cotton and rayon—direct and fiber reactive dyes; silk—directs and acids; wool—acid colors and modified reactives; orlon—poly disperse colors and basic colors). It is important to remember that within all these dyestuff categories, there are variations in the color fastness properties. A knowledgeable chemist and dyer will select and use only those that perform well. There are new and sophisticated machines to test the color fastness of dyes. Improper dyestuffs, or incorrect dyeing, may result in color that comes off when rubbed.

As in apparel fabrics, light and bright colors show the effects of soiling more rapidly than medium-value, neutral colors. Very dark colors frequently attract lint and show up dust particles more readily. The knowledgeable designer/specifier tries to avoid bright clear yellows and such color in areas that are subject to hard use. Design elements such as striae and multi-color effects will help reduce the visual effects of soiling. It is increasingly important that contract fabrics be engineered so that they can be cleaned with solvent drycleaning methods.

One of the biggest hazards a fabric must undergo is the stress and pull by the body which causes seam-slippage. I am constantly amazed at the fact that furniture designers are asked to design upholstered furniture which will hold snugly and securely to a petite feminine body and which at the same time will hold a lineman from a football team who may weigh 280 pounds. The problems can be avoided by proper engineering of fabrics, size of warp yarn, selection of size and type of filling, selection of weaves, both face and back weaves in relation to warp yarns, ends per inch, and picks per inch in order to avoid unravelling of both warp and yarn filling.

My life is dedicated to designing and manufacturing the highest quality fabrics for interiors. I can produce the kind of fabrics that I described above both for residential use and for use in public places because I have complete control over all phases of production. They are designed under my supervision in the design studio of Boris Kroll Fabrics. The yarn is spun to my specifications, the construction is determined, and experimental blankets are woven to find the most suitable yarns, weaves, wraps, fillings, etc. In addition, dyeing is accomplished in the dye laboratories of Boris Kroll Fabrics and, when everything is according to our specifications, it is woven in our own manufacturing center. My integrity of design can only be achieved because I have complete control over every phase of the manufacture of my fabrics.

—Boris Kroll

\*       \*       \*

As a result of his sensitivity as a designer, weaver, and colorist, combined with his technological knowledge, Boris Kroll is a world leader in the professional field of fabric design and production. In 1930, he started working in his brother's modern-furniture factory in New York. When, to his dismay, he discovered that the range of fabrics suitable for such furniture was extremely limited, he learned to weave on a hand loom and mastered the intricate Jacquard loom. In 1936, he began to produce custom fabrics from yarns he sometimes dyed in his own bathtub.

During the 1930s, he was particularly concerned with fabrics using silks and rayons, and his hand-woven fabrics were commissioned for many luxury liners, including the *S.S. America*. Following World War II, Kroll turned his attention to the use of nylon in fabrics for interiors. His unique handling of pattern and texture blossomed in the 1950s, particularly in his Caribbean and Mediterranean collections, which were marked by saturated colors and flamboyant designs. In the 1960s, he received enormous attention for his collection of hard-edged, geometric Jacquards, as well as for his fabrics which were woven or printed with organic motifs. He produced a series of limited-edition Jacquard tapestries, including Banners and Confetti, during the 1970s. His fabrics for the 1980s, including Jacquard weaves, have a more subtle, toned-down approach to design and coloration.

Kroll exercises great control over his designs, sometimes producing five or six hand-woven samples before approving the final production sample. Quality control has a high priority in his business. He has enormous enthusiasm for his profession and is constantly searching for new fabric designs and technological solutions. While his production is distinctive, the variety in his design, weave, texture, and color is enormous. He is intrigued by the triangle and has worked its angular, diagonal appeal into a number of fabrics with great success. This is particularly true with his Jacquards, when he builds on intricate geometries to generate an illusion of complexity and depth. Like a composer, he is a master at taking a design theme and transforming it with either bold or subtle variations sometimes through scale or color changes. For example, Bentley, a recent fabric with a subtle, zigzag linearity, is translated to Claridge, using lurex yarn in the figure for a change in fabric character. He delights in working with different scales, and is as intrigued with small block designs as he is with supergraphics with repeats of 48 inches or more. His color palette has included the shocking as well as the subtle, and he is particularly adept at using a variety of colored yarns to produce fabrics with an overall grayed tone.

He has also produced handsome contemporary handscreened velvets, such as Peregrine and Refractions, as well as distinctive modern sheers, often with delicate prints of tropical leaves or shells. His fabrics, such as Pampas, drawn from African or Latin American sources, reflect his interest in interpreting traditional forms for modern design solutions. This was especially true in his Shibui collection of 1963.

Kroll works in a wide vein, and his insistence on design quality and fabric performance have earned him his leadership in the industry.

—Grant Greapentrog

# KUKKAPURO, Yrjo

Finnish interior, exhibition, and furniture designer

**Born:** Viipuri, 6 April 1933. **Education:** Studied at Imatra Art School, 1951-52; Institute of Crafts and Design, Helsinki, 1954-58. **Family:** Married Irmeli Kukkapuro in 1956; children: Lisa. **Ca-**

reer: Freelance designer, establishing Studio Kukkapuro design firm, Helsinki, from 1959; designed interiors and exhibits for Marimekko, Scandinavian Airlines System (SAS), Rank Xerox, Finnish Design Center, Helsinki Ateneum Art Museum, and others, and furniture for Haimi, and others; Avarte Oy company set up to produce Kukkapuro furniture, Helsinki, from 1980. Instructor, Institute of Crafts and Design, Helsinki, 1963-69, and Department of Architecture, Helsinki Polytechnic, 1969-74; Professor, 1974-80, and Rector, 1978-80, University of Industrial Arts, Helsinki. Chairman, State Committee on Arts and Crafts; member, Central State Art Committee, Helsinki, from 1977. **Member:** SIO Interior Designers Association; Ornamo Finnish Association of Designers. **Exhibitions:** *Annual Design Exhibition,* Helsinki Art Hall, 1959; Milan Triennale, 1960, 1968; *Yrjo Kukkapuro: Furniture,* Finnish Design Centre, Helsinki, 1962; *75 Years of Finnish Design,* Liljevalchs Konsthall, Stockholm, 1963; *Art of Living,* Grand Palais, Paris, 1967; *The Modern Chair,* Victoria and Albert Museum, London, 1970; *100 Years of Finnish Design,* Ateneum Art Museum, Helsinki, 1975; *Metamorphoses Finlandaises,* Centre Georges Pompidou, Paris, 1978; *Form und Struktur,* Museum of Industrial Arts, Vienna, 1980; *Finnland Gestaltet,* Museum für Kunst und Gewerbe, Hamburg, 1981 (toured); *The Lunning Prize,* Nationalmuseum, Stockholm, 1986. **Collections:** Museum of Industrial Arts, Helsinki; Museum of Modern Art, New York; Victoria and Albert Museum, London. **Honors:** Kaunis Koti Bursary, Finnish Society of Crafts and Design, 1961; Grand Prize for Arts and Literature, City of Helsinki, 1963; Lunning Prize, 1966; Design Award, Republic of Finland, 1970; First Prize, Furniture of the Year Competition, Helsinki, 1972; Illum Prize, Copenhagen, 1977; First Prize, *New York* Magazine Chairs Competition, 1974; Gold Medal, Brno International Fair, 1981; Artek Prize, Helsinki, 1982; Pro Finlandia Medal, Helsinki, 1983; Institute of Business Designers Award, New York, 1984. **Address:** Alppitie 25, 02700 Kauniainen, Finland.

## Works

Shop interiors, for Marimekko, in Helsinki, 1963-65.
*Carousel 412* chair, 1965.
Finnish exhibit layouts, at the XIV Milan Triennale, 1968.
*Ars 69* exhibition layouts, for the Ateneum Art Museum, Helsinki, 1969.
Finnish displays, Scandinavian Furniture Fair, 1969, 1970, 1971.
New York air terminal, for SAS, 1971.
Rank Xerox head office interiors, Helsinki, 1972.
City Theatre interiors, Imatra, Finland, 1973.
City and main underground station interiors, Helsinki, 1973-77, and 1979-82.

## Publications

**By KUKKAPURO: books**—(with others) *New Form Furniture: Japan,* Tokyo, 1971.

**On KUKKAPURO: books**—*Scandinavian Design: Objects of a Life Style* by Eileene Harrison Beer, New York, 1975; *Finnish Design 1875-1975* by Timo Sarpaneva, Erik Bruun, and Erik Kruskopf, Helsinki, 1975; *One Hundred Great Finnish Designs* edited by Per Mollerup, Snekkersten, 1979; *Finnland Gestaltet,* exhibition cata-

logue by Tapio Periainen, Simo Heikkila, and others, Espoo, 1981; *Finnish Vision,* with texts by P. Suhonen, J. Lintinen, and others, Helsinki, 1983; *The Conran Directory of Design* edited by Stephen Bayley, London, 1985; *International Design Yearbook 1985/86* edited by Robert A. M. Stern, London, 1985; *The Lunning Prize,* exhibition catalogue edited by Helena Dahlbäck Lutteman and Marianne Uggla, Stockholm, 1986; *Finnish Industrial Design* edited by Tua Pontasuo, Helsinki, 1987; *International Design Yearbook 1988/89* edited by Arata Isozaki, London, 1988.

# KUKKASJÄRVI, Irma

Finnish textile designer

**Born:** Irma Anneli Hilska, in Helsinki, 8 February 1941. Studied handicrafts, 1962-63, and weaving, 1963-64, Helsinki Handicraft Teacher Training Institute; studied textiles, Institute of Applied Arts, Helsinki, 1964-68. **Family:** Married Kullervo Kukkasjärvi in 1966 (died, 1983); children: Sampo. **Career:** Freelance textile designer, working for industry, hotels and public buildings, in Helsinki, from 1968; designer for the Commonwealth Trust India Limited, London, from 1982. Designer of furnishing textiles, Uddebo Möbeltyg Väveri-Sweden, 1969-72, and Arola Oy, 1963-1976; designer of interior textiles, Texmads Oy, from 1976; designer of industrial interior textiles, Marimekko Oy, 1984-86; designer of industrial furniture, Tammervilla Oy, from 1986. Lecturer, University of Industrial Arts (later University of Art and Design), Helsinki, 1977-82; lecturer, University of Helsinki, 1977-78; professor, Department of Textile Art and Fashion Design, University of Art and Design, Helsinki, 1995. **Exhibitions:** *Towards Industry,* Talli-Skanno, Helsinki, 1968; *Experimental Nordic Textile,* toured Norway, Sweden and Denmark, 1970-71; Museum of Central Finland, Jyväskylä, 1972; *Expressions Textiles Nordiques,* Angers, France, 1973; *Finnish Textile Art,* Stockholm, 1974; 7th International Textile Biennale, Lausanne, 1975; *Tapisserie Vivante,* Palais de Congres, Paris, 1977; *Finnland Gestaltet,* Museum fur Kunst und Gewerbe, Hamburg, 1981 (toured Germany and Netherlands); *Five Finnish Textile Artists,* toured Scandinavia, 1982-83; *Irma Kukkasjärvi: Textiles,* Kluuvin Galleria, Helsinki, 1985; *Textile Artist Irma Kukkasjärvi,* Bronda Art Gallery, Helsinki, 1985; *Textiles in Space: Four Finnish Textile Artists,* Ontario Science Centre, Toronto, 1986 (traveled to Winnipeg and Montreal, 1987); *Art By Design: Reflections of Finland,* Katonah Gallery, New York, 1988; *Ryijy—Textiles Finlandais,* Glasgow, Paris, Canada, and United States, 1990-93; Design Forum, Helsinki, 1993; *From Dreams to Reality,* toured Baltic and Scandinavian countries, 1993-94; *Design Finlandais,* Musée d'Art Moderne, Nice, France, 1995. **Collections:** Museum of Applied Arts, Helsinki; Museum of Modern Art, Kyoto; Finnish House of Parliament, Helsinki; City Theatre, Lahti; City Theatre, Jyväskylä; Finnish Embassy, Canberra; City of Angers, France; Baghdad Conference Palace, Iraq; and numerous collections in Finland. **Honors:** Finnish State Award for Applied Arts, 1978; Product Design Award, American Society of Interior Designers, 1978; Silver Medal, International Textile Triennale, Lodz, 1978; State 3-year Grant for Artists, Finland, 1980; Textile Designer of the Year Award, Helsinki, 1984; Pro Finlandia Medal, Helsinki, 1985; Finnish Television Cultural Award, 1986; State 5-year Grant for Artists, Finland, 1987. **Address:** Vyökatu 9 B 12, 00160 Helsinki, Finland.

## Works

Carpets and rya relief, for Baghdad Conference Palace, Iraq, 1978.

Interior textiles and rya relief, for the Parliament House Annex, Helsinki, 1978-79.

Stage curtain, for the City Theatre, Jyväskylä, 1981-82.

Stage curtain and interior textiles, for the City Theatre, Lahti, 1983.

*Forum* collection of woven fabrics, for Marimekko, 1983-84.

Church textiles, for St. Mary's, Turku, 1984.

Furnishing fabrics, curtains and carpets, for Eka Group Headquarters, Helsinki, 1985.

Furnishing textiles, for Hämeenlinna Church, 1985-87.

Interior textiles, for Villa Johanna, Helsinki, 1986.

Auditorium carpet and textiles, for Amer Oy Headquarters, Helsinki, 1987.

Carpets, for Skop-Rahoitus, Vantaa, 1988.

Carpet, for Mec Rastor, Espoo, 1988.

Carpet, for Tuko Oy, Helsinki, 1989.

Carpets and handwoven blinds, for Partek Oy, Helsinki, 1989.

Furnishing textiles, for Iisalmi Cultural Centre, Iisalmi, 1989.

Stage curtain, for Tampere Congress and Concert Centre, Finland, 1989-90.

Furnishing textiles, for Mäntyniemi, official residence of the President of Finland, 1990-94.

## Publications:

**On KUKKASJÄRVI: books**—*Finnland Gestaltet,* exhibition catalogue by Tapio Periainen, Simo Heikkila, and others, Espoo, 1981; *Finnish Vision,* with texts by P. Suhonen, J. Lintinen, and others, Helsinki, 1983; *Textiles in Space: Four Finnish Textile Artists,* exhibition catalogue with text by Marianne Aav, Helsinki, 1986; *Art By Design: Reflections of Finland,* exhibition catalogue with texts by Tutta Runeberg and others, New York, 1988; *Soul in Design* by Tapio Periäinen, 1990; *Art in the Parliament House* by Liisa-Maria Hakala, 1994; *Diamond of the North: Mäntyniemi, the Presidential Residence* by Jorma Marttala, 1994; *Tango in Mäntyniemi* edited by Roger Connah; **articles**—"Famous Designer: Irma Kukkasjärvi" by C. Christiansson in *Contract,* no. 20, 1984; "Impressions of Irma" by M. L. Markkula in *Form Function Finland* (Helsinki), no. 1, 1987; "Textile Dualism: Function and Beauty" by Piia-Lii Toivola in *Form,* no. 1, 1992; "Textiles for the Presidential residence of Mäntyniemi" by Hanna Salakari in *Loimien Lomassa,* no. 1, 1994; films—*Irma Kukkasjärvi: Land of the Blue Flower,* Finnish television film by Kirsti Petäjäniemi, Helsinki, 1979; *Reflections of Light in the Arts* by Petäjäniemi, Helsinki, 1989.

\* \* \*

With respect to her manner of working, Irma Kukkasjärvi carries on the tradition created by Dora Jung. Her works unite designing interior fabrics and continuous cooperation with industry in the decorative textiles produced at her own textile atelier.

Kukkasjärvi graduated as a textile designer from the Institute of Applied Arts at the end of the 1960s, at a time when the importance of designing anonymous everyday objects was being stressed, and this factor is a source of the dualism which marks her work. She became interested in the traditional methods used to produce ryijy wall rugs when she was still a student, and she has undoubtedly

Irma Kukkäsjarvi: *Ice Cube* mini textile work in metal and cotton, 1994

developed into one of the leading ryijy designers in Finland. She has broken with established traditions of decorating ryijy rugs with different experiments involving both form and choice of material, as well as by using nap of various lengths in order to produce ryijy rugs with a relief effect.

Kukkasjärvi does not consider it possible to draw any clear line between decorative textiles and the textiles used for interior decorating. In public premises so-called purely decorative textiles, such as ryijy wall rugs, may, in addition to having aesthetic characteristics, also serve a functional purpose as noise abaters, and the whole created by well-designed interior textiles undoubtedly also provides a total artistic experience. The annex to the Finnish House of Parliament in Helsinki and the renovation of the older part of the building carried out during the late 1970s and early 1980s provided Kukkasjärvi with a large, unified interior to be decorated.

A splendid example of how the design of textiles for normal and decorative purposes can complete and enrich an architectural whole is provided by the main curtain Kukkasjärvi designed during 1981 and 1982 for the Jyväskylä City Theatre. The theatre is one of Alvar Aalto's creations, and the curtain was designed in close cooperation with the architect's office. Its simple vertical beam decorations continue the decorative elements used in the architecture, in addition to which they attempt in some manner to emphasize the impression created by the low space.

During 1983 and 1984 Kukkasjärvi designed a woven cotton collection of interior fabrics for Marimekko Oy which was given the name "Forum". In this collection the clear, timeless language of design was combined with the demands now made both on public premises and on the textiles used for home interior decorating.

—Marianne Aav

# KURLANSKY, Mervyn (Henry)

British graphic designer

**Born:** Johannesburg, South Africa, 3 March 1936; emigrated to Britain in 1958. **Education:** Educated at Highlands North High School, Johannesburg, until 1954; studied at Central School of Arts and Crafts, London, 1959-61. **Career:** Design assistant to Peter Wildbur, at BDMW Design Associates, London, 1960-61; freelance designer, London, 1961-62; graphics director, Planning Unit, Interiors International (Knoll International, UK), London, 1962-67; freelance designer, London, 1967-69; partner, with Theo Crosby, Alan Fletcher, and Colin Forbes, in Crosby/Fletcher/Forbes design studio, London, 1969-72; founder-partner, with Crosby, Fletcher, Forbes, and Kenneth Grange, in Pentagram Design partnership, London, 1972-93; design consultant, Mervyn Kurlansky Design, Copenhagen, from 1994. **Member:** Alliance Graphique Internationale; fellow, Chartered Society of Designers, London; Society of Typographic Designers, London; Royal Society for the Encouragement of Arts, Manufactures, and Commerce. **Exhibitions:** *107 Grafici dell'AGI,* Castello Sforzesco, Milan, 1974; *Forum Design,* Linz, Austria, 1980; *Libres d'Arhsta,* Spain, 1981; *Art and Design,* Plymouth College of Art, Devon, 1982; Reinhold Brown Gallery, New York, 1982; Israel Museum, Jerusalem, 1982; *Graphics UK,* Saint Martin's School of Art, London, 1982; Tyler School of Art, Philadelphia, 1983; *Pentagram Portfolio,* New York, 1986 (toured); Palevsky Design Pavilion, Israel Museum, Jerusalem, 1993. **Honors:** Design and Art Directors Association Silver Medal, London, 1972, 1973; Bronze Medal, Brno Graphics Biennale, 1978; Japanese Ministry of Trade and Industry Medal, 1978; Packaging Design Council Gold Medal, London, 1979; Gustav Klimt Prize, Vienna, 1995. **Addresses:** (office) Mervyn Kurlansky Design, Pilestraede 8, 1112 Copenhagen K, Denmark; (home) Hornbaekgaardsvej 2, 3100 Hornbaek, Denmark.

## Works

Promotional campaign graphics, for Interiors International, 1965.
Book cover designs, for Penguin Books Limited, 1967-69.
*Nobrium* promotional campaign, for Roche, 1970.
Coffee canister designs, for Lyons, 1972.
Music and catalogue cover designs, for Boosey and Hawkes, 1972-80.
Corporate identity, technical, and promotional graphics, for Reuters Limited, from 1972.
Promotional campaign and identity graphics, for Rotring UK, 1975.
*Tactics* men's cosmetics packaging, for Shiseido, 1977.
*Prestel* computer information service identity, for British Telecom, 1978.
*John Barr* whisky label and packaging, for John Walker and Sons, 1980.
Identity, signage, catalogue and poster designs, for the Museum of Modern Art, Oxford, 1987-93.
Identity, signage, and product designs for *Eureka!,* for the Museum for Children, 1987.
*Trendy* teenage body-care toiletries packaging, for Shiseido, 1988.
Signage design, for the British Library, London, 1992.
Identity, signage, and promotional design, for Danmarks Designskole, from 1993.
Identity and promotional campaign design, for Golden Days in Copenhagen cultural festival, from 1993.

Identity, signage, interior graphics, catalogues, and promotional material designs, for The Image Bank, from 1993.
Posters against Violence worldwide campaign, for the Gannett Outdoor Group, 1995.

## Publications

**By KURLANSKY: books**—(with Pentagram partners) *Pentagram: The Work of Five Designers,* London, 1972; (with Norman Mailer and Jon Naar) *Watching My Name Go By (The Faith of Graffiti),* London, 1973; (with Pentagram partners) *Living by Design,* London and New York, 1978; (with Pentagram partners) *Ideas on Design,* London and Boston, 1986; (with Pentagram partners) *Pentagram: The Compendium,* London, New York, and San Francisco, 1993; **articles**—*American Fashion and Fabrics* (New York), no. 127, 1982; *tipoGráfica* (Argentina), no. 20, 1983.

**On KURLANSKY: books**—*107 Grafici dell'AGI,* with texts by Renzo Zorzi and Franco Grignani, Venice, 1974; *The Conran Directory of Design,* edited by Stephen Bayley, London, 1985; **articles**—*Campaign* (London), July 1981; *Creative Review* (London), July 1982; *Typographic* (London), December 1982; *Jewish Chronicle* (London), June 1983; *Zoom* (Italy), no. 183, 1994; *Design Week* (London), 30 June 1995; *Blueprint* (London), October 1995.

*

Design serves for me a personal need to communicate. Earlier in my life, I tried to meet this need by making music and by painting. In music, I was quickly drawn to jazz, because of its immediate, expressive possibilities unfettered by the written score. In painting, my allegiances were futurist and abstract, with a strong attention to the industrial environment.

But neither of these avenues satisfied a second and equally powerful drive: to relate my creative work to the immediacy of everyday life. Design is inextricably bound up with the ordinary, living world. Its commercial basis, "art" and "life."

The teacher who influenced me most was a painter with an acute appreciation for visual language. I remember he compared looking at Malevich for the first time to hearing Japanese for the first time. You might "like" or "dislike" it, but until you had actually learned it, the new language would mean very little.

This sense of language informs my work in the way I use symbols, familiar images, even cliches—speaking to a particular audience in the visual vocabulary they already possess. I tend to prefer found objects to drawings, and like many of my contemporaries, I am completely eclectic in sources I use for both style and imagery.

I have an aversion to formulae and fixed styles, again like most present-day designers. In borrowing, I always alter the ideas I use—manipulating, recombining, and adding—in order to communicate something new. In fact, I believe that all ideas, including those yet to be seen, already exist: We gain access to them by learning to attend in the right way. So, in a sense, every work of art and design is a "found object."

Ours is the age of information. We have instantly available to us not only the images of our own time but also the wealth of the past, which is constantly growing as more of it is uncovered. Indeed, the past has become a present resource, and I draw on it without any sense of nostalgia. It is my nature to live in the present and to look

**Mervyn Kurlansky:** *Erase Violence* **poster, for The Gannett Outdoor Group, 1995**

forward to the future. I welcome the arrival of computer technology, for the richness of communication and new knowledge that it promises.

At the heart of good design is pleasure—the pleasure the designer takes in his work and the pleasure he creates for his audience. Of special importance to me is the "sudden, unexpected intellectual pleasure" of wit. The intellectual component here is essential, for I relish complex problems which can be expressed in a visual solution of surprising simplicity.

Politically, I believe in being alive to new possibilities rather than allying myself with one system of ideas in opposition to another.

As for my work, I have no "plans" for its future development. With each new job, I start again, holding my mind open to fresh discoveries—prepared to find, to create, and to communicate.

—Mervyn Kurlansky

\*     \*     \*

Graphic designer Mervyn Kurlansky is the epitome of the truly international consultant. His continent and culture-crossing career began when he left his native South Africa in 1958 at the age of 22 to study in Britain at the Central School of Arts and Crafts. As a London partner in the leading design practice Pentagram, he worked for multinational companies all over the world. In 1996 his creative journey isn't over: he is newly relocated to Copenhagen where he is forging a new post-Pentagram career at the heart of Scandinavian design.

A clue to Kurlansky's inquisitive and chameleon-like nature can be found in his extrovert behavior on his first voyage to England. A fancy dress party was held on board and Kurlansky recalls how he borrowed a sword from a fencing team among his fellow passengers and became a swashbuckling, bare-chested pirate. By being a 'man behind a mask' he was able to transform himself and do exceptional things—and Kurlansky has worn many masks in his long and distinguished career.

Perhaps the best-known 'mask' is the one he wore with pride for 21 years as a Pentagram partner. He had joined its forerunner, Crosby Fletcher Forbes, in 1969, having worked as a freelance designer in London and for Knoll International's design consultancy service. In 1972, Pentagram, the world's first design supergroup, was set up and Kurlansky became one of its best-known creative mainstays—responsible for enduring graphic design work for Reuters, Rank Xerox, ICI, Olivetti, L'Oreal, Shisido, Mazda, and the Museum of Modern Art, Oxford.

What drove Pentagram on to artistic heights was the often intense competition and withering criticism between the partners. Kurlansky knew he couldn't let his own side down and that his own peers would be his toughest critics. As he put it: "I knew I was joining a group with outstanding work and I knew that I would learn, but it was both challenging and daunting to join forces with the three heavyweights of the design industry. But after a while, a psychological shift takes place and you feel yourself to be a part of Pentagram and no longer worrying about not being part of your own smaller outfit."

Despite all the acclaim and the awards, Pentagram lost some of its allure for Kurlansky in the early 1990s. In 1994, he decided to leave the group and move to Copenhagen with his Danish wife, the graphic designer Karen Blincoe, who was returning to Denmark to become head of visual communication at the prestigious Danmarks Designkole. So began a new chapter in his career in a new land with an expressively democratic and green design culture.

This new setting has enabled Kurlansky to tap more overtly into the theme of social and environmental responsibility which has always been a part of his work. And he has continued to command international attention, working as a consultant art director and identity designer to the global Image Bank picture library, and even winning a worldwide competition to create a poster on the theme of stopping violence.

Kurlansky's solution, a memorable image of an eraser rubbing out large black pencil letters spelling VIOLENCE, reflects the simplicity, clarity, and power of so much of his work. His aversion to formulae and fixed styles is well-known; he prefers to create a visual language based on familiar symbols and found objects—and he has a huge personal collection of things and artifacts he collects which crop up regularly in his work.

Kurlansky's magpie sensibilities, his fondness for recycling found objects and his sense of economy in type and image are well suited to the traditions of Danish design. Major identity commissions from Danmarks Designkole and the Golden Days Copenhagen cultural festival are evidence of his acceptance in a new culture. Of all the masks Mervyn Kurlansky has worn, this one may be the most comfortable.

—Jeremy Myerson

# L

## LAGERFELD, Karl (Otto)
German fashion designer

**Born:** Hamburg, 10 September 1938. **Education:** In Paris, until 1955. **Career:** Worked as assistant to fashion designer Pierre Balmain, Paris, 1955-58; art director, Jean Patou fashion house, Paris, 1958-63; freelance fashion designer, working for Chloë, Krizia, Ballantyne, Timwear, Charles Jourdain, Valentino, Fendi, Cadette, Max Mara, and others, in Paris, from 1964; director of collections and ready-to-wear fashions, Chanel Haute Couture, Paris, from 1983; established Karl Lagerfeld ready-to-wear fashion house, Paris, and KL ready-to-wear in Germany, 1984; created fragrances *Lagerfeld,* for Elizabeth Arden 1975, *Chloë-Lagerfeld* for men, 1978, *KL* for women, 1983, and *KL* for men, 1984. Also film and stage costume designer and photographer. **Exhibitions:** *40 Years of Italian Fashion,* Trump Tower, New York, 1983; *Karl Lagerfeld: Fotografien,* Galerie Hans Mayer, Dusseldorf, 1989. **Honors:** Second Prize, International Wool Secretariat design contest, Paris, 1954; Neiman Marcus Award, 1980; Bath Museum of Costume Dress of the Year Award, 1981; Council of Fashion Designers of America Award, 1991; Fashion Footwear Association of New York Award, 1991. **Address:** 14 Boulevard de la Madeleine, 75008 Paris, France.

## Publications

**On LAGERFELD: books**—*Paris Fashion: Designers and Their Creations* edited by Ruth Lynam, London, 1972; *Fairchild's Who's Who in Fashion,* New York 1975, 1980; *A History of Fashion* by J. Anderson Black and Madge Garland, London, 1975, 1980; *The World of Fashion: People, Places, Resources* by Eleanor Lambert, New York and London, 1976; *In Fashion: Dress in the Twentieth Century* by Prudence Glynn, London, 1978; *French Style* by Suzanne Slesin and Stafford Cliff, New York and London, 1982; *The Collector's Book of Twentieth Century Fashion* by Frances Kennett, London and New York, 1983; *40 Years of Italian Fashion,* exhibition catalogue compiled by B. C. Aragno, Rome, 1983; *McDowell's Directory of Twentieth Century Fashion* by Colin McDowell, London, 1984; *The Conran Directory of Design* edited by Stephen Bayley, London, 1985; *Couture: The Great Designers* by Caroline Rennolds Milbank, New York, 1985; *The Encyclopaedia of Fashion from 1840 to the 1980s* by Georgina O'Hara, London, 1986; *Karl Lagerfeld: A Fashion Journal* by Anna Piaggi, London, 1986; *W, The Designing Life* edited by Lois Perschetz, New York, 1987; *The Fashion Conspiracy* by Nicholas Coleridge, London, 1988; *Sultans of Style: 30 Years of Fashion and Passion* 1960-1990, London, 1990; **articles**—"Karl's Classics" in *Women's Wear Daily* (New York), 11 April 1972; "How Karl Lagerfeld Changed Some Lives" by J. Buck in *Interview* (New York), March 1973; "In Focus—Karl Lagerfeld" in *International Textiles* (London), Winter

1974/75; "Great Designers of the World: Karl Lagerfeld" in *Vogue* (London), 1 March 1975; "Edna O'Brien Meets Karl Lagerfeld" in *Over 21* (London), February 1979; "The Man Who Takes Over from Chanel" by Suzy Menkes in *The Times* (London), 31 January 1983; "A Certain Style: Karl Lagerfeld" in *Vogue* (London), July 1984; "Karl Lagerfeld, the Devil of a Designer" by Jackie Moore in *Women's Journal* (London), April 1985; "Karl Lagerfeld: militaresco o sexy, semplicemente nero" in *Vogue* (Milan), October 1985; "Karl Lagerfeld: The Many Faceted Man" in *Vogue* (Paris), October 1985; "Baroque to His Bones" by G. Y. Dryansky in *Connoisseur,* December 1985; "Karl Lagerfeld, une collection de talents" by Colombe Pringle in *Elle* (Paris), 7 April 1986; "Playing Court to Kaiser Karl" by Pattie Barron in *Cosmopolitan* (London), October 1986; "A Diary of Dress" in *Du* (Zurich), No. 5, 1987; "Le film d'un film par Karl Lagerfeld" in *Vogue* (Paris), March 1987; "Shaping Up" by Peter S. Green in *Connoisseur,* October 1987; "A Life in the Day of Karl Lagerfeld" in *The Sunday Times Magazine* (London), 8 November 1987; "Karlsberg" by Rafaella Barker in *House & Garden* (New York), December 1987; "Lagerfeld Logs On: At 50, King Karl Makes a Foray into Men's Wear" by Alexander Lobrany in the *Daily News Record* (New York), 6 April 1988; "King Karl" by Danae Brook in the *Sunday Express Magazine* (London), 15 May 1988; "Karl Lagerfeld: Don't Talk to Me About Hemlines" in *Donna* (Milan), June 1988; "Pleins feux sur Jack Lang" by Philippe Jodidio in *Connaissance des Arts* (Paris), December 1988; "Petit Palais" by André Leon Talley in *Vogue* (New York), April 1989; "Royalist Leanings" by Georgina Howell in *Vogue* (New York), April 1989; "Karl Lagerfeld: A Burst of Genius" by Michele Ciavarella in *Maglieria Italiana* (Modena), April/June 1989; "At Home with Karl Lagerfeld" by Angela Levin in *You* magazine of the *Mail on Sunday* (London), 14 May 1989; "Reviving the Past" by Hamish Bowles in *Harpers & Queen* (London), September 1989; "A Lagerfeld Extravagance" in *The Independent* (London), 28 September 1989; "King Karl" by Karen Falconer in *Fashion Weekly* (London), 14 December 1989; "Of Shoes and Candlewax" by Leilah Farrah in *The Sunday Times* (London), 13 May 1990; "Kaiser Karl: The Darling Dictator" by Lawrence Mynott in *The Independent* (London), 24 May 1990; "He Came, He Drew, He Conquered" by Meredith Etherington-Smith in *Harpers & Queen* (London), September 1990; "The Designers Talk Passion, Whimsy and Picassos" in *ARTnews* (New York), September 1990; "Karl Lagerfeld" by Sarah Mower in *Vogue*(London), April 1991; "Karl Lagerfeld: Hartmarx's New European Connection" by Amy M. Spindler in the *Daily News Record* (New York), 30 May 1991; "The Chanel Obsession" by Jane Kramer in *Vogue* (New York), September 1991; "King Karl" by Margit Mayer in *Women's Wear Daily* (New York), 20 November 1991; "Kaiser Karl: Behind the Mask" by Maureen Orth in *Vanity Fair* (New York), February 1992; "The Kaiser's Empire" in *Women's Wear Daily* (New York), 2 June 1992; "The Last Emperor" by Anthony Lane in *The New Yorker,* 7 November 1994; "Chanel: Beauty without Gimmicks" by Suzy Menkes in the

*International Herald Tribune* (Paris), 25 January 1995; "Four Who Have No Use For Trends" by Amy M. Spindler in the *New York Times,* 20 March 1995; "Show, Not Clothes, Becomes the Message" by Suzy Menkes in the *International Herald Tribune* (Paris), 20 March 1995.

\* \* \*

A Hamburger who trained under Pierre Balmain and Jean Patou, Karl Lagerfeld has described himself as a romantic, full of nostalgia for the seventeenth and eighteenth centuries. "Clothes should put back what's missing in a woman's life. I want them to have the eighteenth-century countryside, the Elysian fields, the *douceur de vie,"* he stated. Lagerfeld wanted to recreate the paintings of Fragonard and Watteau by presenting modern women as shepherdesses. This is a very artificial concept of history, for the past was far from being Elysian to most women, and most flocks of sheep were watched over by shepherds, not girls. Lagerfeld revived so many historical looks that by April 1980 the *Sunday Times* was complaining that it was becoming boring and that he confused journalists and customers alike, for what was he mixing now, art nouveau and Art Deco? His clothes are a compound of the 1920s, 1930s, 1940s, 1950s and anything that went before. Skillfully made, they can be either in misty tones or in bright colour contrasts, such as black and yellow, but what is peculiarly Lagerfeld about them except the cut? He takes ideas from all sides, and his 1978 duster coat/dress had been featured in Sheridan Barnett's collection of 1974. This *omnium gatherum* approach is more theatrical entertainment than a serious attempt to contribute to mainstream fashion. Designers have always plundered the past, but it can be done more subtly than this.

In 1980, Lagerfeld stated, "The role of the designer is not to dictate length but to update," and proceeded to show no less than three hemlines, at mid-thigh mini, knee, and mid-calf lengths. However, trying to revive anything as recent as the mini could only fail, and it is the longer hemlines that have reached the High Street. It is clear that Lagerfeld has inherited some of the simplicity of line he received from Balmain after Molyneux, but lacking are that careful evolution and avoidance of dramatic change which those couturiers maintained as the fundamental principle of good design. What that requires is resolute self-discipline and a degree of modesty, but Lagerfeld is too fond of self-indulgence in fantasy. He lives surrounded by history in a château filled with state beds and wallpaper after Marie Antoinette frocks. One cannot imagine Lagerfeld feeling that the creation is more important than its creator, as do the best women designers. There are too many signs of the male ego at work.

Lagerfeld is so good at cut that really he does not need to strive for a sensational revival every season. He could produce the same classics every year, and they would still sell because of the beauty of the construction. Since 1983, Lagerfeld has shown with his work at Chanel that combining street style references with classic, traditional pieces gives the long-established fashion house a wider, younger appeal. Lagerfeld has combined his trademark wit with Chanel's familiar symbols—gilt buttons and chains, the traditional Chanel camellia—to produce a vibrant new look for the 1990s. He pairs black fishnet bodystockings and lace-up boots, for example, with leather jackets and flowing skirts, with the traditional Chanel camellia emblazoned across the breasts. He borrows from the New York club scene, bringing Chanel to the younger generation.

With his own label, KL, Lagerfeld is not as outrageous. Here he creates easy-to-wear jackets and sensuous body-hugging knitwear,

ensuring his longevity with a more classic approach. In 1993 he put an up-to-date twist on his work for Chloë in the 1970s. Models appeared wearing Afro wigs in different colors and flowing pastel chiffon highlighted with silk flowers. Although Lagerfeld has withstood criticism from the fashion press, his appeal to a new generation and his combination of ready-to-wear with the elegant cut of couture assures him a place in fashion history.

—Diana de Marly

## LAMB, Thomas

Canadian architect and furniture and industrial designer

**Born:** Orillia, Ontario. **Education:** Studied architecture, furniture, interior design, industrial, and graphic design, Ryerson Institute of Technology, B.I.D. **Career:** Designed and supervised construction of summer homes, C. E. Edmonds and Sons General Contractors and Builders, Keene Valley, New York, 1965; assisted in the development of the Radius Tension Drafting Board System, All Faux/Norman Wade Company, 1965; designer, Robin Bush and Associates, Toronto, 1966; director and product designer, Phase I Children's Retail Store, Toronto, 1967; architect of Chiropractic Clinic, Oakville, Ontario, 1967; designer of products, exhibits, graphics, and furniture, Design Collaborative, Toronto, c. 1967; founder, Thomas Lamb and Associates Ltd., Toronto, Ontario, from 1968; clients have included Stelco, Geonics, The Bunting Company, Paul Miller, Dimensions GT, Hughes Owens, Township of Mississauga, Ontario Department of Education, Metropolitan Toronto and Region Conservation Authority, Royal Bank of Canada, and others; design director, Plydesigns, 1980-1982; design director, Biltrite Nightingale Inc., 1984-86; designer, Nienkämper Furniture and Leather Goods, 1982-90; founder and designer, Future Enclosures T. M., patented concrete housing systems firm, from 1988; established Architectural Research Unlimited, a firm dedicated to searching for new technologies applied to personal enclosures, from 1989; design director, Steamer Furniture, Malaysia, from 1991; established U.B.U. bike company, Canada, from 1991. Design columnist, *Architecture Canada,* 1970; design competition juror, Nova Scotia Design Institute Awards, 1979, Montreal Museum of Decorative Art, 1986, and Nienkämper Chair Competition, 1990; lecturer on design and universities and conferences throughout the world. **Member:** Association of Canadian Industrial Designers; Royal Canadian Academy of Arts. **Exhibitions:** *The Mobile Community,* Museum of Modern Art, New York, 1973; *The Shape of Things Now,* toured Canada, 1975; *What Is Industrial Design,* Ontario Science Centre, 1978; *Wood,* Ontario Science Centre, 1979; Form & Function Gallery, Atlanta, Georgia, 1983; University of Toronto School of Architecture, 1985; Triennale Furniture Show, Milan, Italy, 1986; *The Creative Spark Toronto,* R.C.A. show, 1986; *Designed and Made in Ontario,* Lynnwood Art Center (toured Canada), 1988; *Art in Everyday Life, Aspects of Canadian Design 1967 to 87,* Power Plant, Toronto, 1988; *Prolific Impressions,* Formica Canada Opening, R.O.M. Culture Gallery, 1989; *Please be Seated,* I.F.I. re United Nations, *Decade for Cultural Development,* 1990. **Collections:** Museum of Modern Art, New York. **Honors:** EEDEE prize, Ontario Department of Industry and Tourism, 1967, 1968, 1972; Pavilion Architecture award, World's Fair, Osaka, 1970; Best showroom, American Association of Display Services, Chicago, 1971;

**Thomas Lamb:** *Steamer 2* **lounge chair, 1994**

Trillium Award, Government of Ontario, Canada, 1978, 1980; ROSCOE Award, Awards Resource Council Inc., New York, 1982-83, 1987; Gold Award, Institute of Business Designers, 1982-83; Three Nova Meuble award, Quebec, 1982; Design Canada Award, 1983; Two Office Furniture Design Awards, *Interior Design* Magazine, 1988; Best Booth Design Award, IIDEX Show, 1989; Association of Registered Interior Designers Ontario Award, IIDEX Show, 1990. **Address:** Thomas Lamb and Associates Design and Marketing Consultants, 31 Marietta St., Uxbridge, Ontario L0C 1K0, Canada.

**Works**

Trade exhibit, for Stelco, Home Show, Montreal and Toronto, 1969.

Stamped metal and tube lounge chairs, for The Bunting Company Inc., Philadelphia, Pennsylvania, 1969.

Vacuum formed production sports car, for Paul Miller, Dimensions GT, Cooksville, Ontario, 1969.

Patented drafting machine and drafting system, for Hughes Owens, Montreal, 1969.

Design of bus stop signage system, for Township of Mississauga, 1970.

I.D.A.P. program development for seating and component shelving system, for Curvply and Plydesign Wood Products, 1971.

Travelling exhibitions, for Art Gallery of Ontario, 1974-78.

Interpretive mobile amphitheatre, audio-visual presentation, and 3-dimensional self-supporting energy supply, interpretive exhibition buildings, and canoe display routes, for Division of Parks, Province of Ontario, Department of Natural Resources, 1975.

Signage, graphics, and design for *Arts and Artifacts* display and exhibit, for Toronto Public Library, 1976.

Audio-visual, graphics, booth concept, and design, for Ontario Government EEDEE booth, National Interior Design Show, 1976.

New building addition, renovation, and interpretation, for Ukrainian Cultural Centre, Toronto, 1976.

Travelling booth, for Ontario Ministry of Housing, Homexpo Show, Ottawa, Ontario, 1977.

Design and interpretation for the Kortright Centre for Conservation, Metropolitan Toronto and Region Conservation Authority, 1978.

Beds, mirrors, tables, and related accessories, for Baggots Brass Beds, 1978.

Steamer furniture, manufactured by Dubarry Furniture, 1978-90, and by Steamer Furniture Malaysia, from 1990.

*Artventure* movable wall system for art exhibit, for Royal Bank of Canada, 1980.

*Free Form Five* modular childrens furniture, for retail market, and school furniture, for the contract market, 1980.

Special surfaces of tables and bars, for Rosewood Ventures, 1981-82.

Public seating system, for Arcato Ltd. Canada, 1981-82.

Architectural design of summer home, for Mr. & Mrs. J. Foord, Lake Placid, New York, 1983-84.

Product design, photography, and graphic design, for Nienkämper Furniture and Leather Goods, 1982-90.

New corporate image, logo, showrooms, graphics, and products, for Biltrite Nightingale Inc., 1984-86.

Private residence, for John Mikula Stouffville, Ontario, 1988-89.

Development of Protozoa Housing System, 1988-89.

Development of Future Enclosures T.M. concrete housing systems, 1988-89.

## Publications

**By LAMB: articles**—"Coming Home by Way of Malaysia" in *International Contract* (Toronto), July 1992.

**On LAMB: articles**—"Look to the Future" in *Toronto Star,* 1972; *Industrial Design* (New York), April 1972; *Interiors* (New York), July 1972, October 1978, October 1990; *National Interior Design,* October 1972; *Montreal Star,* December 1972, May 1979; *Canadian Interiors* February 1973, January 1978, September 1983; *Toronto Sun* (Toronto), January 1974; *Canadian Architect* (Don Mills, Ontario), December 1974, January 1978; *Canada Design,* Office of Design, Industry, Trade, and Commerce, March 1975; *Abitare* (Milan), September 1978; *Macleans* (Toronto), 19 February 1979; *Globe and Mail* (Toronto), 1984, 14 May 1986, 11 June 1992, 29 October 1992; *Contract* (New York), January 1984; *Toronto Life* (Toronto), September 1985; "Hot Seats" by David Lasker in *Western Living,* April 1985; "A New Beginning for Canadian Design" *Macleans* (Toronto), 1985; "Sitting Pretty" by David Lasker in *City Woman,* Fall 1985; "A Modern Canadian Classic" in *Ontario Craft* (Toronto), Fall 1986; *Azure,* 1988; "The Man in the Hot Seat" in *Domino,* 1990.

\*

The overiding theme and process of my work is simplistic by nature. Create simple, workable, pleasing objects for people. You do this by extending and expanding the normal perimeters of a material, push the technology to its limits. If you have been one hundred percent honest in this search you will be assured that an original, unique, and visually exciting object will be created. The real secret, however, is to maintain an open, child-like mind during the process.

Unfortunately, the present reality is that humans are proliferating at an ever increasing rate and we will soon tip the natural balance of nature (a point of no return); thus we have somewhat lost control of our own destiny in our short sightedness as object makers and consumers. In our greed to expand and conquer we have unwittingly abandoned our evolutionary position in nature. I feel it is essential for our survival to relearn again the essence of the natural environmental vernacular. We should apply our newly learned technologies towards this impending threat; reminding ourselves that machines are merely the extensions of our hands and minds and there well be a natural limit to their long term constructive use. Thus less is still more.

—Thomas Lamb

\*     \*     \*

Thomas Lamb was one of Canada's foremost furniture designers in the 1970s and 1980s. In common with all Canadian designers, while most of his products reached the marketplace many did not.

Lamb began his design career in 1965 working for Al Faux, his mentor and teacher from Ryerson Polytechnic Institute. They developed the Norman Wade Radius Tension Drafting Board. This award-winning adjustable drafting table was still in production in 1995.

Lamb established his own studio in 1968. One of his first important clients was the Bunting Company in Philadelphia, a giant in the outdoor metal furniture industry. As is Lamb's custom, he created an innovative design ideally suited to Bunting's production capabilities. His prototype for a perforated stamped metal seat and backrest supported on a tubular metal crisscross frame gained wide critical acclaim. Unfortunately, the Bunting factory burned down during the race riots of the early 1970s and the fire destroyed the company moulds, including those by Lamb. However, according to Canadian furniture historian Virginia Wright, despite the short lifespan of the manufacturing of the seating, competitors copied Lamb's design and the seating continued to be influential in the North American garden furniture industry. In 1976, Lamb designed his most famous product, the Steamer lounge chair. In 1980, Lamb developed a range of bent plywood furniture for Plydesigns, including the cantilevered Roo stacking chair which equipped many Canadian schools and colleges.

In 1982, Lamb joined Nienkämper, a family company specializing in high-end leather office furniture. For eight years, he was responsible for product, graphic, and corporate design. Lamb contributed to Nienkämper's transformation from a supplier of contract furniture for the New York-based Knoll International to a leading manufacturer of Canadian design. His most notable products for Nienkämper include the 1987 modular architectonic Embassy table for the Canadian Chancery in Washington, and the 1982 neotraditional organic Sculpted chair.

The Museum of Modem Art inducted Lamb's Steamer lounge chair into its Study Collection in 1979—an honor bestowed on only a handful of Canadian products. The Steamer Collection was part of a renewal strategy in the late 1970s, sponsored by both the provincial and federal governments. Ironically, Canadian manufacturing has dealt a death blow to the design more than once. The Nova Scotia Design Institute and Design Canada commissioned Lamb to develop a new product for the Bass River Chair Company, one of Canada's oldest furniture manufacturers. Working with Bass River's old-fashioned steam bent wood technology, Lamb selected the classic Atlantic steamship deck chair for production. He simplified the design by bending the maple to a single radius and cutting each curved slat to one of three lengths. With these few pieces Lamb arranged a standard component system to make up a family of knock-down products including lounge and pull-up chair, ottoman, and table. The Steamer line was an instant success but the Nova Scotia company could not keep up with the demand. Two Ontario companies, DuBarry and Ambiant, in succession, took over the manufacturer of the collection. Both substituted moulded plywood for steamed solid wood. Both companies went bankrupt, Ambiant in 1990.

A cat has nine lives and so far the Steamer chair has four. In 1992, fed up with Canadian industry, Lamb set up shop in Malaysia to produce the Steamer Collection. This time he used solid steamed mabau teak and added new products to the repertoire. In 1995, Lamb's company was successfully exporting furniture worldwide.

Lamb is an individualist who avoids trends and prefers to find design solutions within the boundaries of function, material, and technological production. Revealing his common sense approach in *Canadian Design,* he declared, "I don't believe in market research. I think it's a corporate crutch. It usually only leads to styling change. Alexander Graham Bell didn't use it, he just invented the telephone." A further testament to his individuality, Lamb lives outside the Toronto design community, in the Ontario countryside. In his spare time, he is a triathlete and builds houses from his patented designs in the Adirondacks.

—Rachel Gotlieb

# LANCETTI, Pino

Italian fashion designer

**Born:** Giuseppe Lancetti, in Bastia Umbra, Perugia, 27 November 1932. **Education:** Studied fine arts at Bernardino di Betto Art Institute, Perugia, 1946-53; trained in fashion design with De Luca and Carosa, in Rome, 1956-61. **Career:** Worked as ceramics painter for Santarelli, in Gualdo Tadino, 1952; independent painter, Rome, 1954-56; freelance fashion designer, working for Simonetta and Fabiani, Rome, 1956-59; founder-director, of Lancetti Creazioni fashion house, Rome, from 1961; opened "Shop in Shop" boutiques in Osaka, 1979, Tokyo, 1980, Sapporo and Kobe, 1981, Fukuoka, 1982, Tokyo, Nagoya, and Kyoto, 1983, and Milan, 1983; designed kimono fabrics, for Ichida textile company, Tokyo, 1982. Also film costume designer, from 1962. Instructor in fashion design, Bernardino di Betto Art Institute, Perugia, 1968-72, and

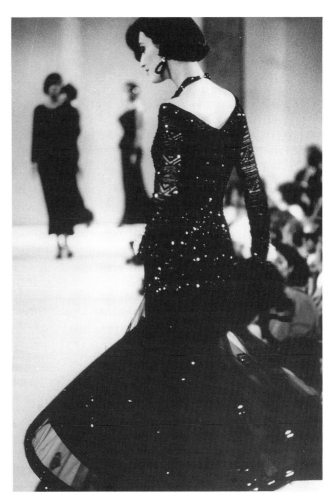

Pino Lancetti: High-fashion dress, 1983

Armando Diaz professional school, Rome, 1972-73. **Exhibitions:** *Il Disegno dell'Alta Moda Italiana dal 1940 al 1970,* National Institute of Graphic Arts, Rome, 1982 (toured); *Consequenze Impreviste,* Pretorio Palace, Prato, 1983; *Italian Fashion 1920-1980,* Daimaru Museum, Osaka, 1983 (toured); *40 Years of Italian Fashion,* Trump Tower, New York, 1983. **Honors:** *La Stampa* Premio Speciale, Florence, 1964; Tiberio d'Oro Award Capri, 1972; Cavaliere d'Onore, Rome, 1975. **Addresses:** Piazza di Spagna 93, 00187 Rome, Italy; Via Condotti 61, 00187 Rome, Italy; Via Bocca di Leone 25, 00187 Rome, Italy.

## Works

Film costumes include—*La Lebre e la Tartaruga,* 1962; *La Mia Signora,* 1964; *La Congiuntura,* 1964; *Three Bites of the Apple,* 1967; *La Lucertola dalla Pelle di Donna,* 1971; *La Luna,* 1979.

## Publications

**On LANCETTI: books**—*The World of Fashion: People, Places, Resources* by Eleanor Lambert, New York and London, 1976; *I Mass-Moda: Fatti e Personaggi dell'Italian Look/The Who's Who of Italian Fashion,* with text by Adriana Mulassano, Florence, 1979;

*Storie e Favole di Moda* by Nanda Calandri, Florence, 1982; *Il Disegno dell'Alta Moda Italiana dal 1940 al 1960,* exhibition catalogue by Bonizza Giordani Aragno, Rome, 1982; *Consequenze Impreviste,* exhibition catalogue by Rossana Bossaglia, Prato, 1983; *Italian Fashion 1920-1980,* exhibition catalogue by Bonizza Giordani Aragno, Tokyo, 1983; *40 Years of Italian Fashion,* exhibition catalogue compiled by Bonizza Giordani Aragno, Rome, 1983; *McDowell's Directory of Twentieth Century Fashion* by Colin McDowell, London, 1984; *The Encyclopaedia of Fashion from 1840 to the 1980s* by Georgina O'Hara, London, 1986.

*

Every fashion designer has a personal style, but he should always be aware of the socio-economic situation and evolution of life.

In my creative activity, I usually draw my attention to painting and costumes of other countries, in particular when I study my new collections. When the ideas are clear, I begin to draw by myself the fabrics that will be produced by the textile industries in northern Italy. The last phase of my work is to transform the fancy weave into a high fashion dress, maybe the most glamorous. My woman remains the "real woman," very feminine for the evening and inspired to a masculine gender for the day—but always with a womanly grace.

About my work I can tell that it is now developing in a double way: on one side, the high fashion collections, my passion, that remain for an elite and for my prestige; on the other side, a business programme in having licenses of many products, such as knitwear, furs, men's and women's perfume and make-up, bags and leather accessories, ties, umbrellas, shoes, bathing costumes, T-shirts, bed-linen, table-linen, ceramic tiles, scarves, optical frames, and leather clothes.

—Pino Lancetti

*   *   *

Lancetti can create great simplicity in crisply tailored coats and suits on the British model, but he cannot resist adorning them with embroidery, applique work, and panels. The 1930s are a strong influence on his daywear in particular. In 1973, he used not only 1930s motifs but also the look of the silent film vamp of the 1920s. His 1978 collection had Art Deco prints by D'Este and Etro, as in a blouson to hip level worn with a long fishtail skirt of distinctly 1930s style. He mixes 1930s pillbox hats with 1940s square shoulders on his wool suits.

Despite this historical influence, however, the biggest factor in Lancetti's style is brilliant colour in startling effects. He began the 1970s with white jackets contrasted with black skins adorned by large appliquéd flowers in white and red jackets teamed with white skirts splashed with large, black flowers. This look was still available in his ready-to-wear line at the end of the decade. His fascination with lurid brocades also demonstrates his interest in brilliant contrast; his very full-skirted evening dresses of the 1950s-type look like glittering cascades of silver and gold. His Balkan-Caucasian look of 1976-80 showed frocks in multi-coloured prints with broad sashes, accompanied by plenty of coin jewelry. In brilliant brocades, it featured harem trousers, off-the-shoulder blouses, turbans, and little jackets heavy with embroidered jewels, very Arabic in character, and no doubt created with the Gulf states market in

mind. In 1981, Lancetti decided on frills, and the brocades became even more elaborate. In contrast to all this extravaganza, in 1979-80, Lancetti showed quiet and simple tweed suits, which were very British; these proved that he is capable of restraint, which is usually overwhelmed by the brocade barrage.

Full of Latin flamboyance, Lancetti is a very theatrical designer whose clothes can only be for the very rich. A gown of gold and silver is not for every woman, and it cannot be copied for the mass market to the same brilliance. Lancetti is a good tailor, but in his clothing the construction disappears beneath the splendour. He creates for a world where every day is a gala, which is a long way from reality.

—Diana de Marly

# LANDOR, Walter (Joseph)

American corporate, environmental, industrial, and graphic designer

**Born:** Munich, Germany, 9 July 1913; emigrated to the United States, 1940. **Education:** Studied at the University of Munich, and University of London. **Family:** Married Jo Landor. **Career:** Founder-partner, Industrial Design Partnership, London, 1935-39; founder-president, then chairman, of Landor Associates design firm, San Francisco, from 1941; subsequently established regional offices in New York, Rome, Mexico City, Tokyo, and Singapore, and affiliate company, Communications Research Center, San Francisco. Associate professor, California College of Arts and Crafts, Oakland, 1940. **Member:** Package Designers Council, New York; Pratt Institute Creative Packaging Center, New York. **Honors:** Honorary doctorate, California College of Arts and Crafts, 1957. **Address:** Landor Associates, 1001 Front Street, San Francisco, California 94111, U.S.A.

## Works

Planning and design programmes for—Chase Manhattan Bank, New York; Bank of America, San Francisco; Landesgirokasse Bank, Stuttgart; Sanwa Bank, Tokyo; Banco Nacional de Mexico, Mexico City; Caja de Pensiones La Caixa, Barcelona; Wells Fargo Bank, San Francisco; Montedison S.p.A., Milan; Atlantic Richfield Company, Los Angeles; Industria Italiana Petroli, Genoa; Jardine Matheson Company, Hong Kong; General Tire and Rubber Company, Ohio; Mercedes Benz of America, New York; Nissan Motor Company, Tokyo; Fiat-Fabbrica Italiana Automobili, Turin; Scandinavian Airlines System, Stockholm; Alitalia Airlines, Rome; Singapore Airlines, Singapore; Thai International, Bangkok; Iberia Airlines, Madrid; US Air, Washington, D.C.; Westin Hotels, Seattle; Royal Viking Lines, Oslo; Raffles Hotel, Singapore; Las Hadas, Mexico; Italcable, Rome; American Telephone and Telegraph, New York; Sony Corporation, Tokyo; 20th Century-Fox, Los Angeles; Fuji Photo Company, Tokyo; General Electric Company, Connecticut; Safeway Stores, San Francisco; Magazzini Standa S.p.A., Milan; Delaize, Brussels; Isetan Department Stores, Tokyo; Cote d'Or, Belgium; Cospar Lancôme et Cie/Guy Laroche, Paris; Nestle Group, Germany; General Foods Corporation, New York; Pillsbury Company, Minnesota; H. J. Heinz

Company, Pennsylvania; Philip Morris International, New York; Seven-Up, Missouri; 3M Company, Minnesota; Levi Strauss, San Francisco; Coca-Cola Company, Georgia; Thomas J. Lipton, New Jersey.

## Publications

**On LANDOR: books**—*Package Design* by Milner Gray, London and New York, 1955; *Advertising Directions* edited by Edward M. Gottschall and Arthur Hawkins, New York, 1959; *Letter Design in the Graphic Arts* by Mortimer Leach, New York, 1960; *Design in America* by Ralph Caplan, New York, 1969; *Packaging and Corporate Identity* edited by Idea Publishers, Tokyo, 1971; *Archigraphia: Architectural and Environmental Graphics* edited by Walter Herdeg, Zurich, 1978; *The American Design Adventure 1940-1975* by Arthur J. Pulos, London and Cambridge, Massachusetts, 1988.

\* \* \*

In his ingenious blending of old and new architectural details, designer Walter Landor turned an old ferryboat in San Francisco into the floating offices of Landor Associates. For Landor, the beautiful, imaginative, and functional studio serves to stimulate the imaginations of his staff. A collection of old packages from around the world, which he uses as a reference source, is located on board, in his Museum of Packaging Antiques.

Landor has aligned his firm with a communications standpoint. As a result, he can provide a client company not only with a graphic identity, but also with a total, corporate image-building program. His design for a graphic "keystone," a bright, abstract device, suggestive of water and movement, for the Golden Gate Bridge Highway and Transportation District, was developed to help persuade the area's commuting population to accept the idea of public transportation. Landor emphasizes the importance of the color and design of these graphic symbols. They give companies new visual identifications to make their positions more effective in the marketplace.

Landor's approach to his design projects is research-oriented. By working with and reporting to the top management of his clients, he closely examines the problems and sets up the criteria to find solutions. For Allied Van Lines, which has as its primary communication medium the vehicle, Landor's design team was able to work out a symbol that simultaneously served as a "highway" and the letter "A." It was easily recognized as representing the company.

As one of the world's leading design firms, Landor Associates has offices located throughout Europe, the Far East, Africa, and Latin America, giving him a broad exposure to new kinds of problems. In repackaging Mexicali beer, Landor was faced with the problem of illiteracy. As a result, his design incorporated favorite Mexican emblems as a way of communicating to the people. This type of response to his foreign assignments demonstrates Landor's flexibility in developing successful solutions. Whether Landor is working for companies in the United States, or abroad, his strategy for designing communication methods, corporate image-building programs, and brand identities is based on a full understanding of the goals of his client companies.

—Patricia A. Russac

# LAPIDUS, Ted
French fashion designer

**Born:** Edmond Lapidus, in Paris, 23 June 1929. **Education:** Educated at the Lycée Saint-Charles, Marseille, the Lycée Berthollet, Annecy, and the Lycée Voltaire Paris, until 1945; studied medicine, at the University of Paris, Dip.Med., 1949; mainly self-taught in fashion design. **Family:** Married Ursula Mai in 1970, children: Olivier, Thomas, and Heloise. **Career:** Part-time freelance fashion designer, Paris, 1945-49; tailor, for the Club de Paris, 1950; founder-manager, 1951-70, and president, from 1970, Ted Lapidus Couture, Paris; administrator, Ted Lapidus International, from 1975. Instructor in clothing design, Industrial Arts College, Tokyo, 1961. **Member:** Chambre Syndicale de la Couture Parisienne. **Address:** 37 Avenue Pierre Premier de Serbie, 75008 Paris, France.

## Publications

**On LAPIDUS: books**—*Fairchild's Who's Who in Fashion,* New York, 1975, 1980; *A History of Fashion* by J. Anderson Black and Madge Garland, London, 1975, 1980; *The World of Fashion: People, Places, Resources* by Eleanor Lambert, New York and London, 1976; *McDowell's Directory of Twentieth Century Fashion* by Colin McDowell, London, 1984; *The Encyclopaedia of Fashion from 1840 to the 1980s* by Georgina O'Hara, London, 1986.

\* \* \*

Ted Lapidus was an evangelical advocate of ready-to-wear. He was an inborn futurist, conceiving of fashion as engineering, reaching fashion's clients in shops offering both men's fashions and women's wear, and extolling blue jeans, pantsuits, and other modern archetypes. He was the consummate tailor who subtly tailored menswear templates to the form of a woman's body, but he is also the creator of evocative, romantic blouses and gossamer gowns of the 1970s. Lapidus was a designer of acute contradictions. He was not, however, one who equivocated, but one who enthusiastically embraced the heterogeneity of post-War fashion. He made the obligatory gestures to the couture, but his heart was in the revolution of modern dress, bringing women and men together in "uni-sex" boutiques, sensibilities, and materials. His safari suit became the sign of a generation that took on fashion as a bold journey away from old and superannuated values to a new quest.

Less recognized and less commercial than Pierre Cardin, Lapidus was a fashion modern who reckoned with the new audiences for fashion and the new venues for fashion through retailing and licensing. Lapidus can be construed as one of the critical designers who, along with Cardin and Saint Laurent, made the transition into effective and democratic apparel even while exploring the possibilities of clothing of highest quality. In the 1960s and 1970s, Lapidus was making the defining signals of advanced fashion—mannish tailoring, ready-to-wear, boutiques, pantsuits, safari and the vernacular—earlier than, at the same time as, or later than other key designers, especially Cardin and Saint Laurent. He never held their impact in the couture and their clinch on the imagination, but he was part of the distinct and important fashion reassessment of late 1960s and 1970s. He was at flood-tide, either as the originator or as disseminator of the new fashion.

Lapidus was an earnest futurist, but he was also an indefatigable classicist. A quintessential Lapidus outfit is his fall 1976 gaucho outfit for a woman, an elegant full-sleeved blouse, velvet gaucho pants, and long velvet vest. All three elements could be used as separates, but they also fall back readily into the designer's jig-saw of modern style. Borrowed from the boys and appropriated from adventure, Lapidus's outfit signifies his courage is redefining fashion in every radical, imaginative way. In the same year, Lapidus' gray flannel "soft-suiting" for a woman gave the classic man's gray flannel to a woman's skirt and vest shown under a redingote of almost engineering simplicity and a cotton shirt with tie. Similarly, an editorial photograph by Helmut Newton in the fall-winter 1973 issue of *Elégance* shows Lapidus's audacity: male and female are attired in the same way in rakish short outercoats in black and white herringbone wool; both wear wool trousers. The most traditional menswear fabrics pervade Lapidus's clothes: Prince of Wales checks, flannel pants (often interestingly cut), wide-whale corduroy, knits in turtlenecks and caps and V-neck sweaters, and even women's shirts with self-ties are commonplace. Despite the matrix in menswear, Lapidus also made in the 1970s some romantic dresses and blouses, though a late 1970s pantsuit is a robo-reductivism, paring down the outfit to the Space Age efficiency. A photograph in *L'Officiel* (spring 1977) pairs a man in a Lapidus overcoat of severe cut with a woman in "a suggestive Ted Lapidus outfit in which shorts and latticed top are of suede." Whether safari or seduction, Lapidus knew the value of durable classics and the energy of their adaptive use.

Conceiving of clothing in his engineering mind in ways that he taught in France and Japan, Lapidus also conceived of an efficient and effective way of selling clothing for the modern era. His boutiques dotted France and the world; their modern spaces were cool and casual for the 1970s, an epitome of restrained modern taste; the boutiques welcomed men and women equally and dispensed with any fashion elitism. Late twentieth-century shopping in Europe, the Americas, and Japan is indebted to Lapidus: his sleek, businesslike boutiques beckoned to the future.

Though he was perhaps never the key designer of his time, Lapidus in the late 1960s and 1970s made the giant leap with a few foresighted colleagues to the new fashion. He deserves a greater place in history than is generally recognized today.

— Richard Martin

# LA PIETRA, Ugo

Italian architect and exhibition and furniture designer

**Born:** Milan, in 1938. **Education:** Studied architecture, at the Politecnico, Milan, 1957-61. **Career:** Independent artist and designer, Milan, from 1962; founder-member, with Lucia, Ferrari, Sordini, Verga, and Verni, of the Gruppo del Cenobio artist's group, Milan, 1963; organizer of numerous interdisciplinary exhibitions, in Milan, Brussels, Osaka, and other locations, from 1965. Instructor in architectural design, Politecnico, Milan, 1964-70. **Exhibitions:** Galleria Il Cenobio, Milan, 1963, 1967; Faculty of Architecture, Politecnico of Milan, 1964; Galleria Flaviana, Locarno, 1966, 1968, Galleria Cadario, Rome, 1967, 1969; Studio di Informazione Estetica, Turin, 1968; Galleria Toselli, Milan, 1970. **Collections:** Galleria Civica d'Arte Moderna, Turin; Museo Sperimentale d'Arte Contemporanea, Turin; American Crafts Museum, New York; Landesmuseum Joanneum, Graz. **Honors:** MPI

Study Scholarship, Milan, 1964, 1965; Premio Cesare da Sesto, Sesto Calende, 1968, Premio Castello Svevo, Termoli, 1970. **Address:** Via Garibaldi 50, 20121 Milan, Italy.

## Works

*Pretenziosa* armchair, for Busnelli, 1984.
*Agevole* sofa, for Busnelli, 1984.
*Flessuosa* sofa, for Busnelli, 1984.
*Anterevole* chairs, for Busnelli, 1985.
*AT-Tese* chair and table, for Busnelli, 1985.
*Incrocio* table and chair, for Busnelli, 1985.
*Articolata* chairs, Busnelli, 1986.

## Publications

**By LA PIETRA: books**—*La Ricerca Morfologica,* exhibition catalogue, Locarno, 1966; *Il Sistema Disequilibrante,* exhibition catalogue, Milan, 1970; *Recupero e Reinvenzione 1969-1976,* Milan, 1976; *La Riappropriazione dell'Ambiente,* Milan, 1977.

**On LA PIETRA: books**—*Ugo La Pietra,* exhibition catalogue by Germano Celant, Bergamo, 1967; *La Pietra,* exhibition catalogue by Tomasso Trini, Locarno, 1968; *Italy: The New Domestic Landscape* by Emilio Ambasz, New York and Florence, 1972; *Boutiquen, Shops und Schicke Laden* by Wolfgang Grub, Münich, 1974; *Living Spaces* edited by Franco Magnani, Milan, 1977; *Design e Forme Nuove nell'Arredamento Italiano* edited by Paolo Portoghesi and Marino Marini, Rome, 1978; *The Hot House: New Wave Italian Design* by Andrea Branzi, London, 1984; *Italian Design: 1870 to the Present* by Penny Sparke, London and New York, 1988.

# LARCHER, Jean

French calligrapher and graphic designer

**Born:** Rennes, 28 January 1947. **Education:** Educated at the Lycée Jacques Decourt, Saint-Denis, 1958-62; studied metal typography as an apprentice compositor and printing processes, at the Chambre de Commerce de Paris, 1962-65; self-taught student of Op Art and Cinetic painting under the influence of Victor Vasarely, 1966-76; also studied Spanish, from 1969. **Military Service:** Served in the French Army, in West Germany, 1966-67. **Career:** Worked as a graphic designer in numerous advertising agencies until 1973; freelance lettering artist and calligrapher, creating over 600 original logotypes for clients in advertising, publishing, press, television, recording, and other businesses, from 1973. Lecturer and guest artist, Chambre de Commerce de Paris, 1975-81, Ecole Supérieure de la Publicité, Paris, 1975-89, Ecole Nationale d'Art de Cergy-Pontoise, 1975, 1977, 1982-92, Escuela Superior de Arquitectura de Madrid, 1980, D.N.A.T. de Valence, 1985-95, Scriptorium de Toulouse, 1990-93, and more than twenty other fine art schools in France. **Member:** Society of Scribes Ltd.; Washington Calligraphers Guild; Friends of Calligraphy; Society of Scribes and Illuminators; Letter Exchange; Dal Segno alla Scrittura; Schweizerische Kalligraphische Gesselschaft; Schreib-Werkstatt Klingspor. **Exhibitions:** Galerie Paul Marquet, Paris, 1973; MJC de Colombes,

**Jean Larcher:** *I saw battle,* **original piece of calligraphy, for the SSI Exhibition "Celebration of Calligraphy," London, 1996**

France, 1973; Centre International de Séjour, Paris, 1974; Caravansérail, Kusadasi, Turkey, 1974; Galerie Sauvage-Moreau, Paris, 1976; Librairie La Hune, Paris, 1977; Victoria and Albert Museum, London, 1980; *Jean Larcher Calligraphe,* Bibliothèque Municipale, Rennes, France, 1986; Centre Georges Pompidou, Paris, 1987; *10 Calligraphes Exposent,* Toulouse, 1988; *Kalligraphia V,* San Francisco Public Library, 1988; *Dressing Words Old and New,* Paperpoint Gallery, London, 1989; Klingspor Museum, Offenbach, 1991; Biblioteca Comunale, Staranzano, 1992; *Calligraphies sur Pasteur,* Culture Passion, Morez, France, 1995; Crafts Council, London, 1995; *75th Meeting of the Society of Scribes and Illuminators, 1921-1996,* Lay Members Exhibition, London, 1996. **Collections:** Bibliothèque Nationale, Paris; Museo de Arte Contemporaneo, Madrid, Victoria and Albert Museum, London; Bibliothèque Forney, Paris; Bibliothèque des Arts-Graphiques, Paris; Newberry Library, Chicago; San Francisco Public Library; Klingspor Museum, Offenbach. **Address:** 16 Chemin des Bourgognes, 95000 Cergy, France.

## Works

*ABC/XYZ* solo exhibition poster, for Librairie La Hune, Paris, 1977.
Calligraphic catalog cover, for Letraset France, 1982.
Six calligraphic record sleeves, for Chant du Monde, Paris, 1983.
*Equilibre* sportswear manufacturer's logo, for the Brigitte Quakrat Agency, Paris, 1984.
Logo and masthead, for *Plaisir de la Maison* magazine, Paris, 1985.
Calligraphic New Year card, for fashion designer Emanuel Ungaro, 1986.
*Atelier Du* advertising agency logo, for J. P. Gauthier et Associes, Paris, 1986.
Logo and corporate identity, for fashion designer Paul Mercier, 1986.
*Quelques hommes qui on influencé l'Art Graphique* brochure, for Jombart, Kapp & Lahure Printers, Evreux, France, 1986.
Design and layout of phototypesetting catalog, for Ere Nouvelle, Paris, 1987.
*Bicentenaire de la Revolution Française 1789-1989* silkscreened calligraphic poster, self-published, Cergy, 1989.
*T comme Terre/Earth Day* silkscreened calligraphic print, self-published, Cergy, 1990.
New Year cards, signed and numbered, self-published, from 1991.
Calligraphy for brochure in six foreign languages, for AGF/Sophia, Paris, 1991.
Calligraphy for brochure in five foreign languages, for Baume & Mercier, Paris, 1995.
Design and layout of calligraphic book of poems, for VOIX D'ENCORE, Montélimar, France, 1995.
8 calligraphic postcards, self-published, Paris, 1980.
Logo and corporate identity, for Studio Guillaume Tell music recording studio, Paris, 1981.
*Pologne* exhibition logo, for the Banque d'Images pour la Pologne, Paris, 1982.

## Publications

**By LARCHER: books**—*Graphismes Cinétiques,* Paris, 1972; *Geometrical Designs and Optical Art,* New York, 1974; *Op Art Color-*

*ing Book,* New York, 1975; *Fantastic Alphabets,* New York, 1976; *The 3-Dimensional Alphabet Coloring Book,* New York, 1978; *Op Message Postcards,* New York, 1979; *Optical and Geometrical Allover Pattern,* New York, 1979; *News Announcements,* New York, 1981; *Calligraphies,* Paris, 1984; *Allover Patterns with Letter Forms,* New York, 1985; *Jean Larcher Calligraphe,* Rennes, 1986; **articles**—in *Communication et Langages* (Paris), no. 33, 1977, no. 36, 1977, no. 39, 1978, no. 40, 1978, no. 50, 1981, no. 54, 1982, no. 83, 1989, no. 84, 1990, no. 93, 1992, no. 94, 1992; *Campaña* (Madrid), no. 92, no. 101, 1978, no. 103, 1978, no. 120, 1978, no. 123, 1979; *Visible Language* (Cleveland), no. 2 1979; *B à T* (Paris), nos. 14-15, 1979; *Idea* (Tokyo), vol. 34, no. 196, 1986; *Arts et Métiers du Livre* (Paris) no. 140, 1986; *Calligraphy Review* (Norman), vol. 5, no. 2, 1987; *La Letra CEAC, Enciclopedia del Diseño* (Barcelona), no. 1, 1988; *Collector* (Paris), no. 1, 1990.

**On LARCHER: books**—*Pour une Semiologie de la Typographie* by Gerard Blanchard, Brussels, 1979; *Sixty Alphabets,* with introduction by G. Briem, London, 1986; *Trademarks Collection: Europe 1* by Yasaburo Kuwayama, Tokyo, 1988; *L'Histoire de l'Ecriture* by Armand Colin, Paris, 1990; *Calligraphy* by David Harris, England, 1991; **articles**—in *Print* (New York), no. 31, 1977; *Zoom* (Paris), no. 47, 1977; *Design Journal* (Seoul), no. 8, 1989; *Arte Grafika* (Belgium), no. 7, 1990; *Scriptores* (Netherlands), nos. 3/4, 1992.

\*

Since I left my typography school (the Paris Chamber of Commerce) in 1965, I have never ceased to be an enthusiast and, indeed, even much more than that. I have literally devoted my whole existence to my graphic activities (painting, typography, calligraphy, articles, exhibitions, conferences, etc.) My own curiosity, my interest in this profession, the passion for the written and printed word which continually motivates me have brought me quite far, for I have published eight books with Dover Editions in New York, and it is rather exceptional for a Frenchman to make a breakthrough in the United States.

I have not contented myself with doing and carrying out things only for myself; I have written numerous articles and continue to do so on designers throughout the world who seem interesting to me. I have organized nearly fifteen exhibitions in Paris (on typography, illustration, and design), with one at an international level on the phenomenon of letterheads—*Letterheads from the Four Corners of the World* in April of 1981—and I have myself actively taken part in some 140 exhibitions throughout the world, including fifteen solo exhibitions. My work, very eclectic at the start and now uniquely specialized in the field of calligraphy, shows well enough, I think, my personal development, an unceasing desire to progress, to improve myself, and to take part in an improvement in graphics in the widest sense of the word.

The first ten to twelve years of my work were quite hard, sometimes even very hard (including seven salaried years in various studios and advertising agencies.) Only for the last few years have my position, my research, my works been recognized in France, a country which unfortunately is not a graphic country and where typography and calligraphy are not taken into consideration—far from it. So everything remains to be done, but it is difficult, and the French are refractory in design and graphic matters. It is a question of education; our schools of design are of a very average level or even poor, and the results are felt much later in the profession and in the taste of the public, which is completely insensitive to graphics and very little interested in art in general.

For the present and future, I sincerely believe that faced with computers and with a certain abstraction in human relationships, if we still want to communicate in a natural and personal manner, graphics, illustration, photography, typography, calligraphy—everything that comes from the hand that is thought, realized, and carried out by a man or a woman—are very important. If we leave it to machines to carry out all these tasks in our place and are satisfied with watching, this is very dangerous. We must leave a large area to individual creation, to pleasure, to joy, to accident, to the imagination in all the fields of the visual arts, so that the professionals and the artists can express themselves instead of disappearing and so that the public in general may benefit in the environment in the broadest sense of the word. I decided to devote my life to the development of the aesthetics of printed matter so that my contemporaries may take part in it.

—Jean Larcher

*     *     *

All of Jean Larcher's graphic output is deeply imbued with a passion for lettering—lettering in an infinite profusion of forms, ranging from elegant copperplate flourishes to alphabets sculpted from Swiss cheese. Although trained in the canons of classical typography, Larcher disdains legibility, advocating imagination instead. His philosophy was articulated and dazzlingly illustrated in *Fantastic Alphabets* (1976), his third book for Dover Publications. In it he followed a "semantic approach to the letters, making use of specific themes," such as letters drawn in a variety of perspectives, letters created from objects, and letters inspired by Op Art. When properly conceived and executed, these letters are intended to function as "self-sufficient illustrations" of the messages they bear.

Larcher's concept of lettering as illustration is derived from several sources, most importantly the typographic work of Herbert Lubalin. Lubalin pioneered the notion of expressive typography with its emphasis on "wordgames" at the expense of readability. The other primary influence on Larcher's work in this realm has been Push Pin Studios. The various Pop art alphabets, such as Baby Teeth and Buffalo, created by Push Pin's Milton Glaser and Seymour Chwast during the 1960s, are the immediate predecessors of *Fantastic Alphabets.*

Larcher's other principal form of lettering is copperplate. Once again it was Lubalin, through the work of his associates (particularly Tony DiSpigna), who was the main contemporary influence on Larcher. Typeface designers and calligraphers like Hermann Zapf, Villu Toots, John Stevens, Werner Schneider, José Mendoza, and others also had a major influence on his work. Yet for Larcher, one of the few designers in France with a knowledge of calligraphy, the work of nineteenth-century Spanish writing master Ramón Sterling has been most important.

Both of Larcher's interests—in illustrative typography and in copperplate letterforms—are united by a common goal: to circumvent the increasing rationalization of "alphabetic codes" by new typesetting technologies. Larcher has insisted on the primacy of the artist's imagination and creativity in the design of letterforms for today and for the future.

—Paul Shaw

# LARKIN, Anya
American textile designer

**Born:** Ann Seymour Larkin, in Washington, D.C., 30 July 1945. **Education:** Studied at the Thomas School, Rowayton, Connecticut, Briarcliff College, and Silvermine College of Fine Arts, New Canaan, Connecticut, 1964-65. **Career:** Designer, Mary McFadden, Inc., New York, 1974-84; president and designer, Anya Larkin Limited textile design company, New York, from 1984; designed fashion and furnishing fabrics for Henri Bendel, Mary McFadden, and others. **Member:** Decorative Fabric Association. **Collections:** Textile Museum, Smithsonian Institution, Washington, D.C. **Address:** 39 West 28th Street, New York, New York 10001, U.S.A.

## Publications

**On LARKIN: articles**—*Fiberarts* (Ashville), January/February 1982.

*

A fabric design, like a painting, is no mere pattern sitting on the surface of the cloth. Rather, it has power and joy and is fascinating to the eye; it transforms the cloth into another dimension.

If the designer puts color together and combines unusual motifs to create action, the design is never flat or dead. It moves, it falls, it jumps if it has to, it twirls or is static and peaceful, or it is horizontal or vertical like a fresco, a frieze, or a woodblock. It has mystery and embodies the image of classical antiquity; it evokes memories and reminds you of something you can't quite put your finger on. It conjures up visions of other things (seen or felt)—imagery of the past. Its colors make your mouth water; they are pleasing to look at. It has life!

This design process is done best when it is done unconsciously, when it springs from the deep well of the subconscious—when it is not mapped out or planned, when there is no strategy or technique involved, only a moment of meditation before the creative process begins to happen, making a space for an action to take place. It is not an intellectual pursuit or exercise. It is only the art of tapping into the greater universal creative force.

—Anya Larkin

*     *     *

Anya Larkin began painting clothing for friends while working in the film industry in the early 1970s. Soon after, her napkins and painted suede jackets were being sold through Henri Bendel in Manhattan. She did not make a full commitment to the textile design business, however, until she began creating the fabrics for one of today's most successful American fashion designers, Mary McFadden. Since 1975, she has been producing all of McFadden's prints and stripes. As a result, her hand-painted silks, cottons, suedes, and challis have become quite recognizable.

Color is what Larkin's work is all about. Unable to find fabric suited to her own keen sense of color, she felt the need when quite young to create her own fabrics, using the colors she felt belonged together. She pairs color in unpredictable but wonderfully refreshing combinations. In the spirit of the *fauve* artists, her boldly stroked stripes and oversized prints remind one of a Kandinsky oil. Often, she will soften her palette a touch, working in more of an Impressionist mode, and she admits that Matisse is her greatest inspiration. "If you ever need a color, go to Matisse," she says. Her delicate pastels and bold brights are achieved through her own resist-wax method that is similar to batik. This technique, while very time-consuming, enables her to capture delicate, vivid hues.

In the past, she has dabbled in textile design for home furnishing. Now, she has decided to make this her main emphasis, while continuing to design dress fabric on the side. She will design a line of hand-woven textiles to be coordinated with her hand-painted ones. While she is adapting many of her fashion prints to fit the realm of home furnishing, all of her new creations are guaranteed to show the same fine quality and unique color sense as her previous work.

Why this change of focus? Larkin feels that the improving economy and the rage to own a home of one's own are being met with a revival in the home decorating industry. Consequently, people today will be investing in their homes. "Interior design just seems to be the proper direction in which to move for the moment," she states.

With her reputation firmly established as a textile designer, Larkin certainly can choose her area of concentration. Her success has shown that color is a very effective tool. Her combinations are exceptional; they are invigorating as well as comforting, and they undoubtedly move the spirit.

While the fashion and textile industries may determine the dominant color palette from one season to the next, it is the independent artist such as Larkin who provides an alternative to that palette as well as the impetus for subsequent color preferences. In this capacity, Larkin's sense of color will certainly endure as one of the most influential.

—Deirdre Kerr

# LARSEN, Jack (John) Lenor

American textile designer

**Born:** Seattle Washington, 5 August 1927. **Career:** Studied architecture and furnishing design, at the University of Washington, Seattle, BFA, 1950; Cranbrook Academy of Art, Bloomfield Hills, Michigan, MFA, 1951. **Career:** Freelance textile designer, in Seattle, 1949-50, and in New York, 1952-53; founder-president, 1953, design director, from 1953, and chairman of the board, from 1975, of Jack Lenor Larsen Incorporated, New York; established Larsen Design Studio, New York, 1958, and Jack Lenor Larsen International, in Zurich, Stuttgart and Paris, 1963; acquired Thaibok Fabrics, 1972; established Larsen Carpets, Larsen Leather Division, New York, 1973, and Larsen Furniture, New York, 1974. United States consultant, grass weaving projects of Taiwan and Vietnam, 1957-59; United States commissioner and design director, Milan Triennale, 1964. Co-director of fabric design, Philadelphia College of Art, 1960-63; artist-in-residence, Royal College of Art, London, 1975; member of the board of overseers, Parsons School of Design, New York, 1980; visiting committee member, Metropolitan Museum of Art, New York, from 1988. Vice-president, Architectural League of New York, 1966-67. **Exhibitions:** Portland, Oregon, 1949; M. H. de Young Memorial Museum, San Francisco, 1956; Stedelijk Museum, Amsterdam, 1968; Museum Bellerive, Zürich, 1970; Museum of Fine Arts, Boston, 1971; Smithsonian Institu-

tion, Washington, D.C.; Kunstindustrimuseet, Copenhagen, 1976; Fashion Institute of Technology, New York, 1978; Musée des Arts Décoratifs, Paris, 1981; *Jack Lenor Larsen Retrospective,* Deutsches Textilmuseum, Krefeld, Germany, 1995. **Collections:** Museum of Modern Art, New York; Metropolitan Museum of Art, New York; Cooper-Hewitt Museum, New York; Fashion Institute of Technology, New York; Philadelphia Museum of Art; Archives of American Art, Washington, D.C.; Art Institute of Chicago; Victoria and Albert Museum, London; Royal Scottish Museum, Edinburgh; Museum Bellerive, Zürich; Kunstindustrimuseet, Copenhagen; Musée d'Art Décoratif, Montreal; Stedelijk Museum, Amsterdam. **Honors:** Gold Medal, Milan Triennale, 1964; American Institute of Architects Gold Medal, 1968; Elsie de Wolfe Award, American Institute of Interior Designers, 1971; Tommy Award, American Print Designers, 1971; *House Beautiful* Pace Setter Award, 1973; fellow, American Society of Interior Designers, 1978, and American Crafts Council, 1978; Eliot Noyes Fellow, Aspen Design Conference, Colorado, 1978; honorary professor, University of Washington, Seattle, 1980; Honorary Royal Designer for Industry, Royal Society of Arts, London, 1983; IFDA Trailblazer Award, 1988; Edith Wharton Award for Excellence, Design & Art Society, 1989; Interior Product Designers Fellowship of Excellence Award, 1990; Dimmick Award, Color Marketing Group, 1992; Roscoe Award, *Interior Design* magazine, 1992; Founders Medal, Cranbrook Academy of Art, 1992. Honorary doctorates from Parsons School of Design, New York, 1981, Rhode Island School of Design, Providence, 1982, Philadelphia College of Art, 1982. **Address:** 41 East 11th Street, New York, New York 10003, U.S.A.

### Works

Draperies, for Lever House, New York, 1952.
Fine Arts Collection of sheets and towels, for J. P. Stevens, New York, 1965.
Art curtain, for Filene Center for the Performing Arts, Vienna, Virginia, 1971.
Fabric program, for Braniff International Airlines, 1972-78.
*Visiona IV* exhibition layouts, for Bayer AG, Frankfurt, 1974.
Silk hangings, for Sears Bank and Trust Company, Chicago, 1978.
Theatre curtain, for St. Charles Cultural Center, Illinois, 1978.
Dinnerware range in porcelain, for Dansk International Designs, 1980.
Upholstery collections, for Cassina and Vescom, 1981.

### Publications

**By LARSEN: books**—(with Azelea Thorpe) *Elements of Weaving,* New York, 1967; (with Mildred Constantine) *Beyond Craft: The Art Fabric,* New York, 1972; (with Jeanne Weeks) *Fabric for Interiors,* New York, 1975; (with A. Buhler) *Dyer's Art: Ikat, Batik, Plangi,* A. and G. Solyom, New York, 1977; (with Mildred Constantine) *The Art Fabric: Mainstream,* New York, 1981; (with Betty Freudenheim) *Interlace: On Plaiting and Related Techniques,* New York, 1984; *Material Wealth: Interior Fabrics for the 1990s,* London and New York, 1989; *The Tactile Vessel,* Cleveland, 1989.

**On LARSEN: books**—*Interior Design: An Introduction to Architectural Interiors* by Arnold Friedmann and others, New York and Amsterdam, 1970, 1976; *Objects: USA* by Lee Nordness, London, 1970; *Jack Lenor Larsen: 30 Years of Creative Textiles,* exhibition catalogue by Francois Mathey, Mildred Constantine, and others, Paris, 1981; *Design Since 1945* edited by Kathryn Hiesinger and George Marcus, Philadelphia and London, 1983; *The Conran Directory of Design* edited by Stephen Bayley, London, 1985; *High Style: 20th Century American Design* by David Gebhard, Esther McCoy, and others, New York, 1985; *Eye for Industry: Royal Designers for Industry 1936-1986,* exhibition catalogue by Fiona MacCarthy and Patrick Nuttgens, London, 1986; *The American Design Adventure 1940-1975* by Arthur J. Pulos, London and Cambridge, Massachusetts, 1988.

*

Larsen Design Studio's mentors—William Morris, Louis Tiffany, Mario Fortuny, the weavers of pre-Columbian Peru and Sassanian Persia—belong to other centuries. This gave them unfair advantages: they not only were there first, but with an aristocratic support system unavailable today. Like us they looked to evolving needs, created within new and old technologies, and sustained quality and style.

We started out as revolutionaries, wanting only to make brave new designs for a contemporary society. Today our mission is to maintain the great tradition for luxurious quality as a buffer against mass production. And, of course we are aware of the inheritance of all of history's art and technologies. These are riches not to be ignored.

Towards the future: The late Twentieth Century design challenge, for me, pivots on creating a civilized environment within the hostile indifference of mass culture. The challenge means a resolution of the present dilemma. Our society must make renewed efforts to allow for individual and rewarding expressions within our consumer culture.

We have not yet resolved design for an egalitarian republic. Do we have the courage to do so? Can we achieve the equivalent of the ready-to-wear revolution in the area of furnishings? This is of prime importance, since it contributes to our basic sense of shelter and security—and more: personal environment must support our need for identity.

As more of us spend more time indoors in an urban environment, as commercial communication becomes even more cunningly aggressive, as security becomes rarer, personal environment must provide more than small space inside locked doors.

We have learned that what matters is how we feel in a space and how we move within it. Art and the social sciences must work in tandem to achieve a keener understanding of the conditions that evoke these emotional responses. And we can very well look to theatre for inspiration, technology to orchestrate light, and color to evoke mood.

We now control climate and sound within space; why not as readily the visual elements? It is time for projected color and pattern to come into its own.

I believe that the revolution coming to architecture will center on designing from the inside out. The starting point will be not merely facade nor available structure (as it has been since the time of cavemen).

As it becomes possible for architect and client alike to afford the luxury and detail of residential commissions, the solution may be similar to that used in converted industrial lofts: residents will take blocks of open and undifferentiated space to divide, compose, and personalize according to need and ability. Such spaces can be multiple in purpose and, more importantly, multiple in mood.

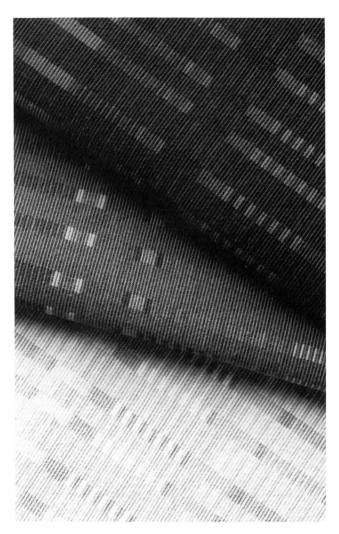

**Jack Lenor Larsen: "Bar None" fabric. Photo courtesy of Jack Lenor Larsen Incorporated**

Still, most of us will live and work in spaces without a sense of structure, materials, or architectural detail. In other words, shoe boxes, dull in themselves and undifferentiated one from another.

What distinguishes these spaces will be the contents within them. The furniture, to be sure, but mostly the fabric of floors, walls, windows, and furniture covers will be the means to achieving variation in scale and pattern, color and texture.

Wall fabrics will become increasingly important; they relieve monotony with their plays of pattern and texture and with tactile and visual softness. Depending on application, wall fabrics will dull noise from adjoining spaces and modulate sound within. We need a brave new vision and a new kind of environmental design team in which all of the design disciplines will contribute as a unit. Engineering and automation are but the means to realize the humanist message of social sciences. Poetic insight will remain basic to the exaltation of the individual. (Reprinted from *Jack Lenor Larsen: 30 ans de création textile/30 years of Creative Textiles,* Exhibition catalogue, Paris 1982.)

—Jack Lenor Larsen

*    *    *

Jack Lenor Larsen treats fabric as a singular presence in our lives and our environment. In his fabric for interiors, for industrial use, in art and in craft, he recognizes fabric as a tactile, visual, sensitive element in today's society. He is constantly aware of its relationship to people, to their bodies, and to the environment.

Beginning as a weaver, he produced as one of his earliest collections, *Andean,* which had been gestating since student days out of his admiration for pre-Columbian weaving. However in such works as *Conquistador,* an authentic wax batik on heavy upholstery velvet, he avoided imitation or reproduction of ancient design.

The name of Larsen stands worldwide for serious design, luxurious quality, and courageous variety stemming from his global view. His knowledge of past generations and cultures throughout the world takes him beyond the limits of his own tradition. Through his travels, he finds what he needs in materials and inspiration, and his respect for other cultures and their accomplishments perpetuates a craft tradition. His fantastic color sense has been influenced by Shibui shades of Japan, by the colors of his native northwest, by the subdued pastels of China and by the brilliance of Brazilian sunlight.

The fascination of his work also lies in his use of today's resources, whatever they are and wherever they happen to be. His respect is equal for natural and man-made materials. All of his fabric innovations reflect the environmental harmony which he makes a central aim of all his work.

—Mildred Constantine

# LAUREN, Ralph

American fashion designer

**Born:** Ralph Lifschitz, in the Bronx, New York, 14 October 1939. **Education:** Attended Yeshiva University; studied business science, City College of New York, 1958-61. **Military Service:** Served in the United States Army. **Family:** Married Ricky Low-Beer in 1965; children: Andrew, David, and Dylan. **Career:** Worked as a salesman, at Bloomingdales and Brooks Brothers, and as assistant buyer for Allied Stores, New York, 1962-65; New York representative, for Abe Rivetz necktie manufacturers, 1965-66; founder and designer, Polo Neckwear Division of Beau Brummel, New York, 1967; founder, with brother Jerry Lauren, designer, and chairman, Polo Fashions, New York, from 1968 (became Polo/Ralph Lauren Corp.); established Polo Menswear Company, 1968, Ralph Lauren Womenswear, 1971, Polo Leather Goods, 1979, Polo/Ralph Lauren Luggage, 1982; opened retail stores in the United States, Europe, and Japan, from 1971; launched fragrances *Polo* for men and *Lauren* for women, 1978, *Chaps* for men and *Tuxedo* for women, 1979, *Safari* for women, 1990, *Safari for Men,* 1992, *Polo Sport,* and others; launched childrens clothing lines, 1978; launched *Day, Night* and *Active* cosmetic lines for women, 1981; launched home collection, 1983; also designer of accessories, luggage, shoes, and myriad other items licensed to outside manufacturers. Also film costume designer for *The Great Gatsby* and *Annie Hall,* from 1974. **Exhibitions:** Denver Art Museum, Colorado. **Collections:** Fashion Institute of Technology, New York. **Honors:** Coty Award for menswear, 1970; Neiman-Marcus Distinguished Service Award, 1971; American Fashion Institute Award, New York, 1975; Council of Fashion Designers of America Award, 1981; Coty Hall of Fame

Award, New York, 1981. **Address:** Polo/Ralph Lauren, 650 Madison Avenue, New York, New York 10022, U.S.A.

## Publications

**On LAUREN: books**—*Fashion Merchandizing* by Mary D. Troxell, New York, 1971, 1976; *The Changing World of Fashion: 1900 to the Present* by Ernestine Carter, London and New York, 1977; *Fairchild's Who's Who in Fashion* edited by Ann Stegemeyer, New York, 1980; *Costume and Fashion* by James Laver, New York and Toronto, 1983; *McDowell's Directory of Twentieth Century Fashion* by Colin McDowell, London, 1984; *The Conran Directory of Design* edited by Stephen Bayley, London, 1985; *Fashion: The Inside Story* by Barbaralee Diamonstein, New York, 1985; *The Encyclopaedia of Fashion from 1840 to the 1980s* by Georgina O'Hara, London, 1986; *Design Source Book* by Penny Sparke and others, London, 1986; **articles**—"Ralph Lauren: Success American Style" by Jesse Kornbluth in *Vogue,* August 1982; "The Business of Being Ralph Lauren" by Fred Ferretti in *New York Times Magazine,* 18 September 1983; "High Style in Jamaica" by Steven M. L. Aronson in *House & Garden,* October 1984; "Selling a Dream of Elegance and the Good Life" by Stephen Koepp in *Time,* 1 September 1986; "Everybody's All-American" by Andre Leon Talley in *Vogue,* February 1992; "The American Dream" by Michael Gross in *New York,* 21-28 December 1992.

*

My clothing is anti-fashion. I design with the point of view that what I'm doing is for a person with a strong sense of style. I don't want anything I do to be this year's "hot look." I like things that will age—that will look better next year.

We all need different clothes for the different ways we live. We all go from office to dinner parties, from the city to the country, from the tennis court to the riding stable, and we all get actively involved in what we do. Even the wealthiest people take care of their own boats and horses and need clothing appropriate for all of these varied activities.

My inspiration comes from everything—from the books I read, the movies I see, the places I go. It comes from keeping my eyes open over the years, looking at photographs, seeing what appeals to me personally. I have always liked the look—the image—of certain people: Cary Grant, the Duke of Windsor, Anthony Eden, the look of the English aristocrat. It's the look too, of the Harvard and Yale men of past decades, and by extension, of their female counterparts at the prestigious women's schools.

I believe that fashion is a function of lifestyle. I believe in clothes that are natural to the way people live today—clothes that are as easy and nonchalant as a pair of jeans, that mix well, and that don't go out of style tomorrow. I want my clothes to become more personal and special as they are worn. I use only natural fabrics, avoid gimmicks, and concentrate on evolving and perfecting the classics. I strive for three things in the clothes I design: quality, simplicity, and longevity. The look I strive to achieve is antistyle—an untrendy, unpackaged individual look.

—Ralph Lauren

*    *    *

**Ralph Lauren: Black/cream houndstooth wool/cashmere ensemble, Fall collection, 1995**

Style, as opposed to fashion, is the major imperative underlying Ralph Lauren's work. Initially a designer of the high-quality ties which started the Polo label, Lauren soon directed his talents to menswear. Inspired by such notable dressers as the Duke of Windsor, Cary Grant, and Fred Astaire, he began to produce classic lines derivative of the elegant man-about-town or the country squire of a bygone age. A love of the fashions of the F. Scott Fitzgerald era led him to introduce wide neckties and bold shirt patterns. In 1974, he achieved world acclaim as the designer of the men's fashions in the film version of Fitzgerald's novel, *The Great Gatsby*. When he turned to women's wear, he applied the same qualities of timeless elegance to his designs. By using uniformly high-quality tweeds, by tailoring down men's trousers and jackets, and by producing shirts in finer cottons, Lauren created clothes for the active woman of the 1970s, as epitomized in the Annie Hall look. These classic, tailored garments have changed little since they were first introduced but continue to epitomize longlasting quality and style.

Another side of Ralph Lauren is seen in his Roughwear. Directly inspired by the tradition of America's past, this takes the form of long tweed or plaid skirts combined with colorful, hand-knitted, Fair Isle or sampler sweaters, tartan scarves, trilby hats, and lumberjack's wind cheaters and brushed cotton shirts. The origins are easy to trace, but the result is an updated, truly American style. Romantic touches of Edwardian and Victorian times occur in lace trimmed jabots and large collars delicately held together with aging cameo brooches. Shades of the classic English riding costume appear in his tailored tweed jackets. Lauren's contribution to fashion can perhaps be best summed up in the names which he gave to his cosmetics introduced in 1981—"Day," "Night," and "Active."

His skill and experience have enabled him to design for both men and women in all they do. As a native New Yorker, he has promoted a truly American casual style in his prairie look, whilst developing classic, uncluttered lines which have brought him international fame along with his colleagues Calvin Klein and Perry Ellis. For Ralph Lauren, fashion is something that lasts for more than one season. This timelessness, abetted by inspirations deep in the soil of America's past, distinguishes his work.

—Hazel Clark

# LAVONEN, Maija (Sisko)

Finnish textile designer

**Born:** Maija Luukela, in Ii, Oulun laani, 29 October 1931. **Education:** Studied at the University of Helsinki, 1953-55; Institute of Applied Arts, Helsinki, 1953-56; Free Art School, Helsinki, 1956-57. **Family:** Married Antti Ahti Lavonen in 1958 (died, 1970); children: Kuutti Johannes and Sussa Milona. **Career:** Worked as fashion designer, Katinette dress manufacturers, Helsinki, 1956-58; industrial designer, Muoti Tuote Oy, Helsinki, 1963; freelance industrial designer, working for Katinette dress manufacturers, Helsinki, 1963-65; founder-director and designer, Poppi Boutique fabrics shop, Helsinki, 1967-68; freelance textile artist and designer, from 1970; established own workshop in Helsinki, working for Forssa-Finlayson, 1970-74, Marimekko, 1971-76, Socota, 1972-74, OTK and SOK textile mills, 1972-76, Venilia Product and Griffine-Marechal wallpapers, 1972-77, Fiorete of Fino Mornasco, 1973-75, Rissanen Oy, 1973-77, Tampella, 1975, Almedahls, 1987;

concentrated on spatial art textiles for architecture, from 1978. Instructor in fashion design, Girls' Vocational School, in Kotka and Karhula, 1958-61; instructor in textile design, University of Industrial Arts, Helsinki, 1985-87, and from 1989. Board Member, State Committee for Applied Arts, Helsinki, 1974-76, and Museum of Applied Arts, Helsinki, 1979-85. **Exhibitions:** Kluuvin Galleria, Helsinki, 1970; Galleria Haimi, Helsinki, 1976; *Textiles Appliqués,* Musée Chateau d'Annecy, France, 1976; Waino Aaltonen Museum, Turku, 1978; Oulu Art Museum, Finland, 1978; Lapinlahti Art Centre, Finland, 1978; Hvittrask Cultural Centre, Finland, 1978; *Métamorphoses Finlandaises,* Centre Georges Pompidou, Paris, 1978; Galerie Artek, Helsinki, 1980, 1983; Galleria Sculptor, Helsinki, 1981; Kemi Art Museum, Finland, 1981; *Scandinavian Modern Design 1880-1980,* Cooper-Hewitt Museum, New York, 1982-83; *Fifth International Triennale of Tapestry,* Lodz, Poland, 1985; *For the Floor,* American Craft Museum II, New York, 1985; Maltinranta Art Centre, Tampere, 1986; Galleria Pelin, Helsinki, 1986; Museum für Kunsthandwerk, Frankfurt am Main, Germany, 1987; *New Form from Finland,* Royal Museum of Scotland, Edinburgh, 1988; Galleria 25, Helsinki, 1989; Art Center Pyynikinlinna, Tampere, 1992; Galleria Amer, Helsinki, 1993; *Design Finlandais,* Musée d'Art Moderne et d'Art Contemporain, Nice, France, 1995. **Collections:** Museum of Applied Arts, Helsinki; Röhsska Konstslöjdmuseet, Göteborg; Pori Art Museum, Finland; Kemi Art Museum, Finland; Union Bank of Finland, Helsinki; Sara Hilden Art Museum, Tampere, Finland; **Honors:** State Award for Industrial Design, Helsinki, 1981; 15-year State Grant for the Arts, 1982; Engel Prize, 1992; Pro Finlandia Medal, 1992. **Address:** Mariankatu 13 a A 7, 00170 Helsinki, Finland.

## Works

*Uudet tuulet/Fresh Winds* multi-part textile, for Suomen Puhallintehdas, Helsinki, 1978.
*Linjat/The Lines* three-part tapestry, for Valio, Jyväskylä, 1980.
*City of the Sea and Industry* two-part tapestry, for the City Theatre, Kemi, 1981.
*Luonto lahteena/Nature as a Source* two-part tapestry, for the Ministry of the Interior, Helsinki, 1982.
*Textile in Three Levels* tapestry, for the Finnish Parliament Building, Helsinki, 1982.
*Ps. 18:3* multi-part tapestry, for Malmi Church, Helsinki, 1982.
*Kalvikin ryijy* two-part ryijy rug, for Kalvik Villa, Bank of Finland, 1983.
*Karhumetsa/Bear Forest* two-part ryijy rug, for Pohjola Insurance Company, Helsinki, 1984.
*Haukivesi* three-level textile, for the City Library, Varkaus, 1985.
*Mutual Understanding* multi-art textile, for Hasselby Castle, Stockholm, 1985.
*Lahti* tapestry, for the City Hall Council Chamber, Lahti, 1986.
*Sininen kaari/Blue Vault* textile, for the Finnish Slot-Machine Association, Espoo, 1987.
*Double Beat* tapestry, for the Main Post Office, Helsinki, 1987.
Hand-embroidered church textiles, for St. Michael's Lutheran Church, Helsinki, 1987-88.
*Kivijalka/Corner Stone* ryijy rug, for Villa Haka, Helsinki, 1988.
*Kimmellys/Glimmer* tapestry, for the Savings Bank of Etela-Karjala, Lappeenranta, 1989.
*Blue Arch* tapestry, for the Bank of Finland, Helsinki, 1989.
*Forest* textile hanging, for the Kemi Company, Kemi, 1989.

**Maija Lavonen:** *Flygt*, **1992. Photo by Rauno Träskelin courtesy of Maija Lavonen**

*Water-Colour* linen, for the Institute of Technology, Espoo-Vantaa, Vantaa, 1990.

*Columns* linen, for the cafeteria of the Art Museum of the Ateneum, Helsinki, 1992.

*Tripartition* wool and linen architectural textile, for Veikkaus Oy, Vantaa, 1992.

*Good Tidings* linen and painted steel architectural textile, for the parish hall of Tikkakoski Church, Jyväskylä rural parish, Finland, 1994.

*Scala* wool architectural textile, for the Finnish National Opera, Helsinki, 1995.

## Publications

**By LAVONEN: articles—**"The Picture as a Door to an Era—A Code Image of our Times" in *Kulttuurivihkot* (Helsinki), no. 1, 1982; "Textiles of Kaarina Church" in *Arkkitehti* (Helsinki), no. 7, 1984; "As I Saw It: The Fading Glimmer" in *Helsingin Sanomat* (Helsinki), 12 August 1984; "Donna e progetto" in *Interni* (Milano), no. 352, 1985.

**On LAVONEN: books—***La Tapisserie—Art du XXème Siècle* by Madeleine Jarry, Fribourg, 1974; *Scandinavian Modern Design 1880-1980* edited by David Revere McFadden, New York, 1982; *Maija Lavonen,* seminar discourse by Leena Kaseva, University of Helsinki, 1983; *Form Finland* edited by Marianne Aav and Kaj Kalin, Helsinki, 1986;*Art By Design: Reflections of Finland,* exhibition catalogue by Barbro Kulvik and Antti Siltavuori, New York, 1988; **articles—**"Maija Lavonen—An Artisan" by H. Vehkaoja in *Anna* (Helsinki), no. 45, 1970; "Maija Brings Nature Inside" by L. Korhonen in *Me Naiset* (Helsinki), no. 30, 1981; "Maija Lavonen" by U. Pallasmaa in *Form Function Finland* (Helsinki), no. 3, 1982; "For the Floor" by N. Znamierowski in *American Craft* (New York), April/May 1985; "An Explorer in Textiles" by L. Maunula in *Helsingin Sanomat* (Helsinki), 15 May 1986; "Maija Lavonen's Art—A Dialogue of Metal and Textiles" by T. Runeberg in *Anna* (Helsinki), no. 11, 1989; "A Feeling of Handiwork in Everything" by Kari Alatalo in *Muoto* (Helsinki), no. 4, 1993; "Textiles Are Monuments of Their Time" by Liisa Aula in *Form Function Finland,* no. 4, 1993.

*

I am interested in public spaces, where we work and conduct our daily business: offices, city traffic, all the information surrounding us. I think it is ever more important to create alternatives, deviations from standardized universal design, relaxing places of rest and calming interiors.

In my own work, which today mostly consists of designing and making textiles for architecture, I aim at taking into consideration the forms and materials of the building while including my own personal vision. It is my belief that an independent work that is not too restrained gives an enlivening touch to a space. I believe in the power of simple geometric lines and rhythms. Textile in itself is forcible and impressive as a material; I want the material to breathe, to avoid heaviness. Sometimes I include a supplementary metal element in my works—as a feature that contrasts with and purifies the material feel of the textile.

I have also designed textiles for household use, but I believe that my work has greater significance in so-called public spaces or places of work. I would like to think that people might want to linger awhile near them, or simply receive an uplifting or calming touch while passing by. My designs are therefore a reaction to today's stressful life rhythm. I like to use very simple techniques in my spatial works. I want them to get across to people because of their general appearance and content rather than technical flourishes.

For reasons of tradition, textile art has a special position of its own in Finland. Textiles have always been used in Finnish homes for practical reasons alone, to fend off the cold. As building methods have changed, they are no longer needed in the same way. But now that textiles are becoming a part of architecture, I believe that the old functional tradition has largely helped to create a situation over the past twenty years where art textiles have become a relatively strong alternative to other visual arts. In Finland, unlike the rest of Europe, there is no tradition in tapestry: here, the ryijy rug has been the dominant textile. Tapestry in Finland is not set into one rigid pattern that continues to be imitated, but is very alive and open to variation. In Finland, the status of textiles has a firm basis.

My design work is based on feelings and observation of nature. I hope my works convey a suggestion of natural experience—perhaps of the bright light of noon, or the spatial experience of standing atop the crest of a rock. When I am at work choosing colors and materials, little things are important, such as the delicate hues and tints of colour. In taking natural observation as a starting point, I have wanted to bring to mind our right to experience nature, and stress the need to preserve it.

In addition to my latest spatial and public works, I have grown an increased interest in the 1990s in experimenting with silkprinting pigments on cotton in a very painterly way. It means that a large part of my latest production is very close to the abstract expressionist tradition and "support-surface" patterns. This has also brought me closer to personal, state-of-mind-rooted type of expression.

—Maija Lavonen

\*   \*   \*

Maija Lavonen's breakthrough to the front rank of Finnish textile artists happened in 1978 when she exhibited a group of works that lent new vitality and a new appearance to the ryijy-rug, which is so important in Finland. Lavonen's works, restrained yet full of feeling, transformed this classic of Nordic textile art in a propitious and balanced way. The transition from the tradition of the ryijy to the pictorial language of modern art had occurred without friction.

The transformation took place at a time when faith in the future of this warm woollen rug had almost been lost. For some time, artists had been having difficulty with getting a new hold of it. The economic depression affecting industry in the 1970s cast its shadow over much applied art, including textiles; crafts also, with their genuine but expensive natural materials, were going through a crisis. Public commissions for art textiles were rare.

Maija Lavonen abandoned her career as fashion designer and became an experimenter and innovator in art textiles in 1970, after the death of her painter husband. From the start, her work has carried the mark of a boundary breaking and experimental attitude while manifesting a firm belief in the functionalist rules of international modernism.

After her success with the ryijy, Lavonen began weaving linen into large, three-dimensional spatial works. With exhibitions of her work, she joined in the early 1980s topical debates concerning art in the civic environment, the role of ecology in the world of objects, and the human alternative offered by handicraft.

As a textile artist, Lavonen constantly refuses all extravagance in the use of her yarns. She regards them as basic materials to which one should be faithful while subjecting them to artistic control. She does not limit herself to yarns and threads alone, however. Being a lively discoverer, Lavonen has incorporated into her spatial works indigenous Lapp marble as well as international neon lighting. All her materials, including linen and silk fibers, she uses frugally in order not to squander the unique gifts of nature. Thus, even large works become light and airy, which aspect is further emphasized by the artist's preference for spare but fresh and always pure colors.

On the threshold of the 1990s, Lavonen returned to the heavier and more material idiom of the ryijy. In her ryijy-rugs or in any other works, Lavonen tells no stories, yet she is able to tap profound feelings of the Finnish people's close relationship with nature and its strongly contrasting seasons. One of the hidden themes of her works is in fact an interpretation of the effect of the seasons in her native district on the shores of the Gulf of Bothnia, where the sea sparkles with light in summer and lies leaden and foreboding in winter.

Maija Lavonen's modern textiles have evolved side by side with the liberation of architecture's formal language, and she has been able to realize many large-scale works in civic buildings. For her one-woman shows, she has always preferred to find a new gallery each time in order to be able to build a fresh, carefully considered, exemplary work of art. Lavonen has done pioneering work by reinstating textile art in the civic environment. In their restraint and equilibrium her works match well with contemporary Finnish architecture, which also bases its transformation on the more moderate traditions of modernism.

The role of the artist in applied arts in Finland includes diversification. Lavonen has designed fabrics for industrial manufacturers such as the Finnish firm of Marimekko as well as international companies. Church art, which holds an important position in Finland, has also provided work. A major commission is a large multipart spatial work in Kristian Gullichsen's Malmi church in a suburb of Helsinki. The central part of the tapestry is changed following changes of liturgical colors during the ecclesiastical year.

Teaching has also been a part of Lavonen's work. In addition to training students at the University of Industrial Arts, she has supervised the activity of municipal workshops in the northern Lapp town of Kemi. In 1982 she received the first 15-year state grant awarded to an artist of the applied arts.

—Leena Maunula

# LAX, Michael
American exhibition and industrial designer

**Born:** New York City, 8 November 1929. **Education:** Alfred University, New York, BFA, 1951; Fulbright study fellowship to Finland, 1953-54. **Career:** Freelance industrial designer, New York, from 1965; designed for American Cyanamid, Copco, Champion International, Eastern Airlines, Formica, Lightolier, Mikasa, Salton, N. A. Christensen, Coquet, Faveka, Artemide, Takatsuki Diecasting, Gullaskrufs Glasbruks, and others; also exhibit designs for the American Federation of Arts, Brooklyn Children's Museum, Ford Foundation, Metropolitan Museum of Art, Smithsonian Institution, and United States Information Agency. Lecturer, Pratt Institute, Brooklyn, New York, 1970-71, and Rhode Island School of Design Providence, 1975-76. **Member:** Industrial Designers Society of America; American Institute of Graphic Arts. **Exhibitions:** *Good Design,* Museum of Modern Art, New York, 1952; Museum of Modern Art, New York 1968; Nationalmuseum, Stockholm, 1975; Stedelijk Museum, Amsterdam, 1978; Musée des Arts Décoratifs, Paris, 1980; *Design Since 1945,* Philadelphia Museum of Art, 1983. **Honors:** Rome Prize Fellowship, 1977. **Address:** 124 East 65th Street, New York, New York 10021, U.S.A.

## Publications

On LAX: books—*Design in America* by Ralph Caplan, New York, 1969; *One Hundred Great Product Designs* by Jay Doblin, New York, 1970; *Environment Design of the World,* Tokyo, 1971; *Design Review Annual,* New York and London, 1978; *Design Since 1945* edited by Kathryn Hiesinger and George Marcus, Philadelphia and London, 1983.

# LEACH, Bernard (Howell)

British potter and ceramics designer

**Born:** Of British parents, in Hong Kong, 5 January 1887. **Education:** Attended schools in Hong Kong, Singapore and England, until 1902; studied drawing under Henry Tonks, at Slade School of Art, London, 1903-05; studied banking, at a commercial college, Manchester, 1906-08; studied etching, under Frank Brangwyn, at London School of Art, 1908-09; studied pottery, under Ogata Kenzan, in Tokyo and Korea, 1909-20. **Family:** Married Edith Muriel Hoyle in 1909; children: David, William, Edith, Ruth and Elizabeth; married Laurie Cookes in 1936; son: Maurice; married Jane Darnell in 1956. **Career:** Independent potter, working with Ogata Kenzan, in Tokyo and Korea, 1909-20; founder, with Shoji Hamada, and director of the Leach Pottery, St. Ives, Cornwall, 1920-79. Instructor in pottery, Dartington Hall, Devon, 1932, 1936; visiting lecturer in the United States and Japan, from 1950. **Exhibitions:** Cotswold Gallery, London, 1922; Beaux-Arts Gallery, London, 1931, 1933, 1952; Arts Council Gallery, London, 1961; Osaka Museum, Japan, 1961; Galerie de France, Paris, 1964; Crane Kalman Gallery, London, 1967; Victoria and Albert Museum, London, 1977. **Honors:** American Ceramic Society Binns Medal, 1950; World Crafts Council Award, Dublin, 1970; Japan Foundation Prize, 1974. Honorary doctorates: Manchester College of Art, 1960; University of Exeter, 1961. Commander, Order of the British Empire, 1962; Order of the Sacred Treasure, Japan, 1966; Freedom of the Borough of St. Ives, 1968; Companion of Honour, London, 1973. **Died:** St. Ives, Cornwall, 6 May 1979.

## Publications

By LEACH: books—*A Review 1909-1914,* Tokyo, 1914; *A Potter's Outlook* (pamphlet), London, 1928; *A Potter's Book,* London 1940, 1945, 1976, New York, 1948, 1967; *The Leach Pottery* (pamphlet), London, 1946; *A Potter's Portfolio: A Selection of Fine Pots,* London, 1951; *A Potter in Japan 1952-1954,* London, 1960, New York, 1967; *Kenzan and His Tradition: The Life and Times of Koetsu, Sotatsu, Korin and Kanzan,* London, 1966, New York, 1967; *A Potter's Work,* London, 1967, 1974, 1977; *The Unknown Craftsman: A Japanese Insight into Beauty,* editor, with Soetsu Yanagi, Tokyo and London, 1972; *Bernard Leach: Drawings Verse and Belief,* Bath, 1973; *Hamada, Potter,* Tokyo, New York and San Francisco, 1975, London, 1976; *A Potter's Challenge* edited by David Outerbridge, New York, 1975, London, 1976; *Beyond East and West: Memoirs, Portraits and Essays,* London, 1978.

On LEACH: books—*Design in the Home* edited by Noel Carrington, London, 1933; *The Work of the Modern Potter in England* by George Wingfield Digby, London, 1952; *Artist Potters in England* by Muriel Rose, London, 1955, 1970; *Bernard Leach: 50 Years a Potter,* exhibition catalogue by J. P. Hodin, London, 1961; *Bernard Leach* by Soetsu Yanagi, Tokyo, 1966; *Modern Ceramics* by Geoffrey Beard, London, 1969; *The Art of Bernard Leach* edited by Carol Hogben, London, 1977, 1978; *Contemporary International Ceramics* by Hildegaard Storr-Britz, Cologne, 1980; *The Conran Directory of Design* edited by Stephen Bayley, London, 1985.

\*   \*   \*

During his lifetime, Bernard Leach was called "the greatest living Western potter," ranking with Japanese masters Shoji Hamada, Kenkichi Tomimoto, and Kanjiro Kawai as one of the four supreme masters of clay in modern times. A painter and graphic artist, Leach was drawn by chance to pottery making while studying art in Japan in the early 1900s. Having participated in a party where Japanese raku vessels were being decorated and fired for use in the tea ceremony, Leach became fascinated with the application of ancient pottery techniques to contemporary needs. He studied raku under Ogata Kenzan VI, whose ancestors were potters in the raku tradition. Kenzan eventually gave Leach not only his glazing secrets but also bestowed on him the title Kenzan VII.

Upon his return to England in 1920, Leach established a studio in St. Ives, Cornwall with Shoji Hamada. Using local clay and glaze materials and firing with local wood, he sought to produce a truly contemporary British folk pottery. Leach's work, influenced by Mingei, or Japanese folk art, was in direct contrast to the shiny, hard, white translucency then fashionable in English ceramics. His one-of-a-kind pieces were based on traditional Chinese Sung Dynasty and Korean shapes and brush decoration. However, standard tableware produced at St. Ives largely adapted the British slipware tradition of jugs, beakers, sugar bowls, and creamers .

Leach is responsible for bringing handmade pottery back to British homes. During his lifetime, his studio at St. Ives was a mecca for pottery students and collectors alike. Apprentices from his studio, such as Warren MacKenzie and Byron Temple, have carried on the tradition of handmade affordable tableware in their own studios in the United States.

Leach's reputation as a potter is rivaled today by his reputation as a thinker and writer. His long friendship with writer and museum organizer Soetsu Yanagi fueled a fifty-year dialogue on the anonymous craftsman and beauty in art. Besides his 1940 *Potter's Book,* he wrote memoirs, *Beyond East and West,* and a variety of treatises and analyses of pots, pointing the way for future generations to understand the synthesis of Eastern and Western traditions. Once a Zen Buddhist, Leach ended his days as a devout member of the Baha'i faith.

In an age when mass production was a powerful influence, Bernard Leach advocated an appreciation of work by the human hand. He preached the virtues of innocence, modesty, and humility to a generation of Western students who listened and followed.

—Sarah Bodine

# LEE, Eugene

American stage, film, costume, and television designer

**Born:** 9 March 1939. **Education:** Studied at Carnegie Mellon University, Pittsburgh, and Yale University, New Haven, Connecticut. **Family:** Married designer Franne Newman; married Brooke Lutz in 1981; children: William and Edward. **Career:** Freelance designer, from 1965; worked for theatre companies in Philadelphia, New York, Washington, D.C., and Dallas; resident designer, Trinity Square Repertory Company, Providence, Rhode Island, from 1968; also designer of *Saturday Night Live* television programs, 1974-80. **Honors:** Drama Desk Award, New York, 1970; Antoinette Perry (Tony) Award, New York, 1974, 1979. **Address:** 31 Union Square West, New York, New York, 10003.

## Works

Stage productions include—*A Dream of Love,* Theater of Living Arts, Philadelphia, 1966; *Belch,* Theater of Living Arts, Philadelphia, 1966; *The Threepenny Opera,* Studio Arena Theater, Buffalo, 1967; *The Imaginary Invalid,* Studio Arena Theater, Buffalo, 1967; *HMS Pinafore,* Studio Arena Theater, Buffalo, 1967; *Enrico IV,* Studio Arena Theater, Buffalo, 1967; *A Delicate Balance,* Studio Arena Theater, Buffalo, 1968; *World War 2 1/2,* Martinique Theatre, New York, 1969; *Slave Ship,* Brooklyn Academy of Music, 1969; *The Recruiting Officer,* Theater of the Living Arts, Philadelphia, 1970; *Harry Noon and Night,* Theater of the Living Arts, Philadelphia, 1970; *Wilson in the Promised Land,* ANTA Playhouse, New York, 1970; *Alice in Wonderland,* Extension Theater, New York, 1970; *Saved,* Brooklyn Academy of Music, 1970; *Mother Courage,* Arena Stage Theatre, Washington, D.C., 1970; *Son of Man and the Family,* Rhode Island School of Design Theatre, 1970; *Taming of the Shrew,* Rhode Island School of Design Theatre, 1970; *Love for Love,* Rhode Island School of Design Theatre, 1971; *The Threepenny Opera,* Rhode Island School of Design Theatre, 1971; *Dude,* Broadway Theatre, New York, 1972; *Candide,* Brooklyn Academy of Music, 1973; *Gabrielle,* Studio Arena Theatre, Buffalo, 1974; *The Skin of Our Teeth,* Kennedy Center for the Performing Arts, Washington, D.C., 1975; *It's Me, Sylvia,* Playhouse Theatre II, New York, 1981; *Agnes of God,* Music Box Theatre, New York, 1982; *Some Men Need Help,* 47th Street Theatre, New York, 1982; *The Ballad of Soapy Smith,* New York Shakespeare Festival, 1984; *Misalliance,* Dallas Theater Center, 1984; *A Christmas Carol,* Dallas Theater Center, 1984, 1985; *The Normal Heart,* New York Shakespeare Festival, 1985; *Passion Play,* Dallas Theater Center, 1985; *The Three Sisters,* Dallas Theater Center, 1985; *You*

*Can't Take It With You,* Dallas Theater Center, 1985; *Good,* Dallas Theater Center, 1985; *The Skin of Our Teeth,* Dallas Theater Center, 1985; *The Marriage of Bette and Boo,* Dallas Theater Center, 1985; *The Glass Menagerie,* Dallas Theater Center, 1986; *The Tavern,* Dallas Theater Center, 1986; *The Ups and Downs of Theophilus Maitland,* Dallas Theater Center, 1986; *A Folk Tale,* Dallas Theater Center, 1986; *Kith and Kin,* Dallas Theater Center, 1986; *East Texas Hot Links,* Joseph Papp Public-Anspacher Theater, New York, 1993; *Show Boat,* North York Performing Arts Centre, Toronto, and Gershwin Theatre, New York, 1994. Stage productions at Trinity Square Theatre, Providence, include— *The Threepenny Opera,* 1967; *The Importance of Being Earnest,* 1967; *Year of the Locust,* 1968; *An Enemy of the People,* 1968; *Phaedra,* 1968; *Macbeth,* 1969; *The Homecoming,* 1969; *Billy Budd,* 1969; *Old Glory,* 1969; *Black/White,* 1969; *Wilson in the Promised Land,* 1969; *The Skin of Our Teeth,* 1970; *Lovecraft's Follies,* 1970; *You Can't Take It With You,* 1970; *Troilus and Cressida,* 1971; *Down by the River Where Waterlilies Are Disfigured Every Day,* 1971; *The Good and Bad Times of Cady Francis McCullum and Friends,* 1971; *Old Times,* 1972; *Royal Hunt of the Sun,* 1973; *Feasting with Panthers,* 1973; *Brother to Dragons,* 1973; *Ghost Dance,* 1973; *Aimee,* 1974; *Well Hung,* 1974; *A Man for All Seasons,* 1974; *Peer Gynt,* 1975; *Tom Jones,* 1975; *Seven Keys to Baldpate,* 1975; *El Grande de Coca-Cola,* 1980; *An Almost Perfect Person,* 1980; *Deathtrap,* 1980; *Arsenic and Old Lace,* 1980; *Betrayal,* 1980; *On Golden Pond,* 1980; *A Christmas Carol,* 1981, 1982, 1984, 1985; *The Iceman Cometh,* 1981; *Inherit the Wind,* 1981; *How I Got That Story,* 1981; *Whose Life Is It Anyway?,* 1981; *The Whales of August,* 1981; *Tintypes,* 1982; *The Crucifer of Blood,* 1982; *13 Rue de l'Amour,* 1982; *The Dresser,* 1982; *Translations,* 1982; *The Front Page,* 1983; *The Tempest,* 1983; *Pygmalion,* 1983; *The Web,* 1983; *Letters from Prison,* 1983; *Beyond Therapy,* 1984; *What the Butler Saw,* 1984; *Terra Nova,* 1984; *Passion Play,* 1984; *Tartuffe,* 1984; *Misalliance,* 1985; *And a Nightingale Sang,* 1985; *The Country Wife,* 1985; *Master Harold and the Boys,* 1985; *Present Laughter,* 1985; *The Marriage of Bette and Boo,* 1985; *Cat On a Hot Tin Roof,* 1985; *The Crucible,* 1986; *The Tavern,* 1986; *Life and Limb,* 1986; *Pasta,* 1986; *The Country Girl,* 1986; *Baby,* 1986; *Not By Bed Alone,* 1986. Film set designs include—*One Trick Pony,* 1980; *Easy Money,* 1982; *Mr. Mike's Mondo Video,* 1979; *Hammett,* 1982.

## Publications

**On LEE: books**—*The Cambridge Guide to World Theatre* edited by Martin Banham, Cambridge and New York, 1988; **articles**—in *Theatre Design and Technology* (Charlottesville), Summer 1982; *New York Times,* 23 January 1994; *Theatre* (New Haven), Winter 1982; *TCI,* 9 February 1994.

\*   \*   \*

Eugene Lee's large, provocative, audience-involving settings are generally unlike those of any other mainstream American designer today. Elements of his style, of course, have corollaries in other theatre artists, but there is no clear influence from any one source, no overriding similarity to any other designer. Totally unlike his contemporaries and classmates at Yale University, the wellspring of much contemporary stage design, he is closest in spirit to European theatricalists such as Luca Ronconi and Patrice Chereau. However, differences between European and American production styles, budgets, and repertoires preclude any extensive comparison. Lee admits to some influence from Peter Brook and Jerzy Grotowski—and indeed, his environmental designs began after seeing Grotowski's in Edinburgh—but the underlaying esthetics are different.

The key to Lee's style is his feeling that the audience should be involved, that the only significant relationship is between the actor and the audience, and that the entire space of the theatre—not only the stage—should be considered in relation to the demands of the play. As a result, each play is approached with no preconceptions as to the style, space, or scope of the setting.

In the late 1960s and early 1970s, when experimentation and iconoclasm were more readily accepted, Lee could take the ideas he had developed at Trinity Square and move them to the theatres on and off Broadway. For the production of Amiri Baraka's *Slaveship* (1969), the normal seating area of the Chelsea Theatre was platformed over, and the cramped hold of a slave ship was constructed in the center of the space. The audience, on wood benches, very close to the "slaves," was, in turn, surrounded by other acting platforms and spaces. The audience was thus enveloped by the production, which achieved a sense of claustrophobia and fear. The same principle, on a more elaborate scale, was employed for *Billy Budd* at Trinity Square earlier the same year to create the impression that the audience was within a nineteenth-century sailing ship. For *Alice in Wonderland* (1970), the audience entered through a three-and-a-half-foot door into a space covered by a parachute.

Lee's work at Trinity and elsewhere is typified by environmental design (or "atmospheric" as he calls it). Ramps jut into the auditorium, performance areas are scattered throughout the audience space, scenic elements dangle above the heads of the spectators. In general, there is an attempt to eliminate the proscenium and encompass the audience. His fondness for natural, non-traditional materials is not only to supply texture but to help in the creation of an aural environment as well. *Son of Man and the Family* (1970) for example, was set in a prison, and the sound of the actor/prisoners marching on the steel mesh catwalks of the set could frequently be heard.

With the production of *Candide* (1974), Lee and director Harold Prince hoped to signal the end of the proscenium on Broadway and to establish at least one, ongoing, flexible theatre space for commercial productions. *Sweeney Todd* (1979) was originally envisioned for the same space. But economics and an increasingly conservative trend among theatre-goers and producers defeated this idea. Lee continues to incorporate as many of his ideas as possible within the confines of commercial theatre or under-budgeted regional theatre, but he is unhappy with the current state of theatre and its lack of opportunities for experimentation. It is this, he feels, that has pushed him toward film and television.

—Arnold Aronson

# LEE, Ming Cho

Chinese-American painter and stage designer

**Born:** Shanghai, China, 3 October 1930; emigrated to the United States in 1949. **Education:** Educated at schools in Shanghai and Hong Kong until 1948; studied at Occidental College, Los Angeles, B.A., 1953; University of California, Los Angeles, 1953-54; also studied with watercolorist Kuo-Nyen. **Family:** Married Elizabeth Rapport in 1958. **Member:** Theatre Projects Committee, New York City Planning Commission; American Theatre Planning Board; United Scenic Artists, New York; California Watercolor Society. **Career:** Assistant designer to Jo Mielziner, New York, 1955-57; freelance designer, from 1958; worked with the Peabody Arts Theatre operatic company, Peabody Institute, Baltimore, 1959-63; art director and resident designer, San Francisco Opera, 1961-62; principal designer, New York Shakespeare Festival, 1962-73, Juilliard Opera Theatre, and American Opera Center of the Juilliard School of Music, New York, from 1964; also designed for ballet companies of Jose Limon, Martha Graham, Gerald Arpino, and Alvin Ailey; design consultant to the Performing Arts Center at the State University of New York, Purchase, the Cincinnati Music Hall, and the Patricia Corbett Pavilion of the University of Cincinnati School of Music. Instructor in set design, Yale University Drama School, New Haven, Connecticut, and the New York University Washington Square College. **Address:** 13 East 87th Street, New York, New York 10028, U.S.A.

## Works

Stage productions (New York unless noted) include—*The Crucible*, 1958; *Triad*, 1958; *The Infernal Machine*, 1958; *Mother Courage*, 1962, 1978; *King Lear*, 1962; *The Moon Besieged*, 1962; *Walk in Darkness*, 1963; *Conversations in the Dark*, 1963; *Slapstick Tragedy*, 1963; *Othello*, 1964; *Electra*, 1964; *Madame Butterfly*, 1965; *The Witch of Endor* (ballet), 1965; *A Time for Singing*, 1966; *Little Murders*, 1967; *Here's Where I Belong*, 1968; *Peer Gynt*, 1969; *Billy*, 1969; *La Strada*, 1969; *Gandhi*, 1970; *The Wars of the Roses (Henry VI, Parts I, II, III)*, 1970; *Our Town*, Washington, D.C. and tour of the Soviet Union, 1972; *Inherit the Wind*, Washington, D.C. and tour of the Soviet Union, 1972; *Myth of a Voyage* (ballet), 1973; *Two Gentlemen of Verona*, 1973; *The Glass Menagerie*, Minneapolis, 1975; *Boris Gudonov*, 1975; *The Sea Gull*, 1975; *All God's Children Got Wings*, 1975; *Colored Girls*, 1976; *Much Ado about Nothing*, 1976; *The Shadow Box*, 1977; *I Puritani*, 1977; *Lohengrin*, 1978; *K2*, 1983; *Khovanshchina*, 1985.

## Publications

**By LEE: articles**—"Designing Opera" in *Contemporary Stage Design* edited by Elizabeth B. Burdick, Peggy Hansen, and Brenda Zanger, Connecticut, 1975; in *Theater* (New Haven), Fall/Winter 1981; introduction to *American Set Dseign 2* edited by Ron Smith, New York, 1991.

**On LEE: books**—*The Biographical Encyclopaedia and Who's Who of the American Theatre* edited by Walter Rigdon, New York, 1966; *Stage Design* by Donald Oenslager, New York, 1975; *Who's Who in the Theatre* edited by Ian Herbert, London and Detroit, 1977; *The Cambridge Guide to World Theatre* edited by Martin Banham, Cambridge and New York, 1988; *Notable Asian Americans*, Detroit, 1995; **articles**—"The Twists, Turns, Trials, and Triumphs of a Theatrical Life" by Yu-mei Huang in *Free China Review*, January 1984; "Designers on Designing: Ming Cho Lee" by Patricia MacKay in *Theater Craft*, February 1984.

\*　　\*　　\*

Ming Cho Lee entered the world of professional design in the mid 1950s as an assistant to Jo Mielziner and, more briefly, to George Jenkins, Rouben Ter-Arutunian, and Boris Aronson. By the end of the decade, he was designing off-Broadway. His first production, *The Infernal Machine* (1958) at the Phoenix Theater, garnered favorable reviews which focused mainly on the decor and set his career in motion.

Early, Lee's preference in design tended toward the non-literal, with dance design being his favorite activity, followed closely by opera and Shakespeare. Now, he enjoys designing plays as well. Some of his critics accused him of a "too Brechtian" approach, but his emphasis on simplicity derived from an attempt to integrate the setting within the framework of the entire production. The sparseness was evident in Martha Graham's dance work *The Witch of Endor* because the designer chose to use only two thrones and a metal configuration. Equally spare for the New York Shakespeare Festival, his approach, however, suited the situation, since his ingenious simplicity triumphed over budget restraints. He sometimes designed one basic structure which might be used for three separate summer shows, thus saving the expense of additional scenery.

However, this type of multi-purpose setting was also effectively used (as for *The Shadow Box*) on Broadway, where budgets are not always a main concern. Lee's design of Brecht's *Mother Courage* (1978) prompted Mel Gussow of the *New York Times* to comment "Ming Cho Lee's set—an almost barren plane surmounted by Mother Courage's rustic wagon—is stark." Lee's intent was not to emphasize the setting, or to underplay its importance, but to blend it into the fabric of production so that the audience would experience what the designer refers to as "a total theatrical experience."

To his enjoyment, Lee's later career seems to be emphasizing more realistic, literal works, which he infuses with style. For *K2*, he reproduced a section of mountain, which actually replaced the stage, prompting Ted E. Kalem of *Time* to write, "Lee's awesome set is the playgoer's eye, restored to a 20/20 vision of the power, mystery, majesty and menace of undomesticated nature." Although realistic, Lee's *The Glass Menagerie* (in the words of the designer) "attempts to make connections between the verbal and the visual," resulting in an organic whole. He adds that this production was quite unlike the original that Jo Mielziner designed on Broadway.

His design process moves from the general to the specific. Reading the script only once, Lee keeps his mind open to interpretation until he meets the director. Although he has an initial, personal reaction to the play, Lee waits until he has conferred with the director to decide on matters such as the basic approach or the construction materials.

Brought up through the Broadway ranks by Mielziner, Lee, as a teacher at Yale's Drama School, now transmits his knowledge to future generations of designers. He feels an obligation to train his apprentices and pass along the crafts of his trade, while continuing to uphold a rigorous schedule of design activities.

—Tom Mikotowicz

# LEEDS, Harold Eliot

American architect and interior designer

**Born:** Meriden, Connecticut, 1 April 1919. **Education:** Studied at Harvard University, Cambridge, Massachusetts, BA, 1939; attended School of Architecture and Allied Arts, New York University, B.Arch., 1942. **Career:** Designer, working in New York, from 1942; draftsman, at Skidmore, Owings, and Merrill architectural firm; draftsman and designer, at Raymond Loewy Associates design firm; designer and director, at Donald Deskey Associates design firm, until 1946; founder and partner, of Warner/Leeds Associates, New York, 1947-55, and of Leeds Associates, New York, from 1955; freelance designer, in H. E. Leeds Design, New York, from 1970. Professor and chairman of the interior design department, Pratt Institute, Brooklyn, New York, 1959-69. **Address:** 64 Perry Street, New York, New York 10014, U.S.A.

## Works

Warner-Leeds design office interiors, New York, 1948.
Paris Theatre cinema interiors, New York, 1949.
Bonniers Bookstore interiors, New York, 1949.
Caribe Hilton Hotel interiors, San Juan, Puerto Rico, 1950.
Guest House interiors, St. Thomas, U.S. Virgin Islands, 1952.
Cerromar Beach Hotel, Dorado Beach, Puerto Rico, 1975-76.
Bedford Stuyvesant CABS Nursing Home interiors, Brooklyn, New York, 1976.

## Publications

**By LEEDS: articles**—*Interiors* (New York), November 1970.

**On LEEDS: books**—*Interior Design: An Introduction to Architectural Interiors* by Arnold Friedmann, John F. Pile, and Forrest Wilson, New York and Amsterdam, 1970, 1976; **articles**—*New Yorker*, 4 December 1948; *Architectural Forum* (New York), January 1949, March 1949, March 1950; *Interiors* (New York), August 1949, April 1950, January 1952, June 1969, November 1970, February 1976, December 1976; *Interior Design* (New York), July 1978.

*        *        *

Harold Leeds has made his strongest contribution to interior design as an educator. Under his chairmanship from 1959 to 1969, the Department of Interior Design at Pratt Institute in Brooklyn became the leading school in the field in the United States and most likely, the world. He assembled a group of experienced and dedicated faculty members, and he managed to attract the most talented students. The program he implemented there became the model for such courses throughout the United States. In 1970, upon completion of a sabbatical leave from Pratt, Leeds began to teach exclusively in the graduate interior design program, which had been initiated during his chairmanship. Perhaps the measure of Leeds' influence upon the world of design can best be expressed by the very large number of leading designers in many top positions, as principals of major design firms and as recipients of numerous awards. Many were his students during his administration or even during the years before that when he was a design critic at Pratt Institute for seven years.

Leeds is an enormously talented designer who produced a distinguished body of work prior to his teaching career and continues his professional work even now. After graduating from one of the finest architectural programs of the time, at New York University, he worked in several firms before establishing the Warner/Leeds partnership. Some of the most important projects done during that partnership were the Bonniers Shop and the Paris Theater in New York City, and the Caribe Hilton Hotel in Puerto Rico. Warner-Leeds was so far ahead of other firms in the accomplishment of excellent interior design work that the projects remained as important 20 years later as they had been at completion. Subsequently, Leeds established an active design firm under the name of Leeds Associates, which numbered offices, hotels, and colleges among its commissions.

Leeds is not interested in publicity, even though a number of his design projects have been published. Perhaps the public at large is not familiar with his work, yet he has been widely recognized, has served on many distinguished design juries, has been made a consultant to New York City's Transit Authority by the mayor, and has served as a design consultant and critic in several countries. If a poll were to be taken among designers and architects to name a truly great twentieth-century interior designer, chances are that Leeds would be one of the most frequently mentioned names.

—Arnold Friedmann

# LENICA, Jan

French filmmaker, stage, and graphic designer

**Born:** Poznan, Poland, 4 January 1928; emigrated to France in 1963, naturalized, 1981. **Education:** Studied at the Architectural High School, Warsaw, Ing. Arch., 1952. **Family:** Married Merja Alanen in 1969; children: Anneli and Maia. **Career:** Independent poster artist, working in Warsaw, 1950-58, and in Paris, from 1963; also animated film designer from 1957, and stage designer from 1972. Teaching assistant to Henryk Tomaszewski, at the Art Academy, Warsaw, 1954; professor, at the Kunstakademie Gesamthochschule, Kassel 1979-85; professor of graphic design, at the Hochschule der Künste, West Berlin, from 1986; artist in residence, Carpenter Center for the Visual Arts, Harvard University, Cambridge, Massachusetts, 1974. **Exhibitions:** Club of Young Artists, Warsaw, 1948; Filmmuseum, Copenhagen, 1966; Filmmuseum, Arnhem, 1967; Museum Villa Stuck, Munich, 1968; Poster Museum, Warsaw, 1968; Museum des 20. Jahrhunderts, Vienna, 1971; National Museum, Poznan, 1973; Harvard University, Cambridge, Massachusetts, 1973; Centre Georges Pompidou, Paris, 1980; Deutsches Plakatmuseum, Essen, 1980, 1983; Katholische Akademie, Hamburg, 1981; Kunstverein, Kassel, 1981; High School of Graphic Arts, Vienna, 1982; Modern Art Museum, Tampere, 1988; Polish Museum of America, 1990; Haus am Lützowplatz, Berlin, 1990; Museum für Kunst und Gewerbe, Hamburg, Germany, 1991. **Collections:** Poster Museum, Warsaw; National Museum, Poznan; Deutsches Plakatmuseum, Essen; Kunstgewerbemuseum, Zurich; Museum of Modern Art, New York; Library of Congress, Washington, D.C. **Honors:** Grand Film Prize, World's Fair, Brussels, 1958; Toulouse-Lautrec Prize, Paris, 1961; Warsaw Poster Biennale Prize, 1966; Max Ernst Award, Paris, 1966; City of Essen Prize, 1980; Jules Cheret Award, Paris, 1983; Alfred Jurzykowski Award, New York, 1987; Premio Grafico, Bologna, 1987; Art & Business Award, Grand Prix, 1991; best cultural poster, France, 1991. **Addresses:** 3 rue Saint Christophe, 75015 Paris, France; Passauerstrasse 34, 10789 Berlin, Germany.

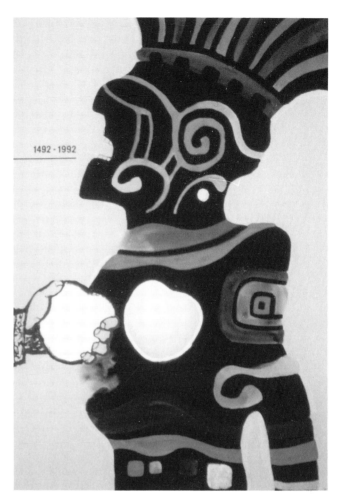

Jan Lenica: *1492-1992* poster commemorating discovery of America, 1992

## Works

Posters and graphic presentation, for Annecy International Animated Film Festival, 1983.
*1492-1992* poster commemorating the discovery of America, 1992.
Animated films include—*Strip-Tease,* 1957; *Once Upon a Time,* 1957; *Love Required,* 1957; *The House,* 1958; *Banner of Youth,* 1958; *Monsieur Tete,* 1959; *New Janko the Musician,* 1960; *Italia 61,* 1961; *Labyrinth,* 1962; *Rhinoceroses,* 1963; *A,* 1964; *Cul de Sac* (trailer for Polanski), 1964; *The Woman Flower,* 1965; *Weg zum Nachbarn,* 1966; *Adam 2,* 1969; *Still Life,* 1969; *Nature Morte,* 1970; *Fantorro, The Last Just Man,* 1972; *Landscape,* 1974; *King Ubu,* 1976; *Ubu and the Great Gidouille,* 1979.

## Publications

**By LENICA: books**—*Plakat Tadeusza Trepkowskiego,* Warsaw, 1958; (with A. Sauvy) *Population Explosion,* New York, 1962; *Monsieur Tête,* with text by Eugene Ionesco, Munich, 1970; *The Magic Bird,* Zurich, 1986; *Theo the Snowman,* Zurich, 1988; *Jan Lenica: Noir et Blanc,* Paris, 1988.

**On LENICA: books**—*Jan Lenica* by Zygmunt Kaluzynski, Warsaw, 1963; *Film and TV Graphics* edited by Walter Herdeg, Zurich,

1967; *History of the Poster* by Josef and Shizuko Muller-Brockmann, Zurich, 1971; *Polish Poster Art Today* by Szymon Bojko, Warsaw, 1972; *Full Length Animated Feature Films* by Bruno Edera, London and New York, 1977; *Jan Lenica* edited by Heinz-Jurgen Kristahn, West Berlin, 1981; *Who's Who in Graphic Art* edited by Walter Amstutz, Dubendorf, 1982; *A History of Graphic Design* by Philip B. Meggs, New York and London, 1983; *The International Dictionary of Films and Filmmakers,* Chicago and London, 1984, 1991; **articles**—"Jan Lenica: Philosopher with a Brush" by Frank Fox in *The World & I,* 1990; "Jan Lenica and Landscape" by Steve Weiner in *Film Quarterly* (New York), 1992.

*

I have always enjoyed working on the peripheries of art, at the edge of styles, penetrating the distant lands of the principal currents and those which are, as it were, more noble. I have amused myself in opposing the rules in force in the different disciplines, in associating apparently distant or entirely dissimilar elements, in blurring the edges between neighboring fields, in grafting more noble characteristics onto styles of "inferior rank"—in a word, I have enjoyed tacit diversion. Forms considered ordinary, scorned by those who work at more elevated levels, have always attracted me.

These remarks are perhaps surprising nowadays when there is general integration in the arts, emancipation in fields such as graphics, photography, and many others. But I remember the time when painters scorned graphics and when the name "graphic artist" had a disdainful aftertaste. Where are the snows of yesteryear? The doors of artistic salons wide open to graphics and those of the museum to the poster? Where nowadays is the dividing line between painting and graphics—and who today holds to "purity of style"?

During the 1950s, I was reproached for resorting, in the poster, to non-graphic techniques, supposedly incompatible with print technique, and for introducing particularly pictorial subjects—the portrait, for example. At present, there is no technique that the poster has not adopted or adapted to its own ends. The poster has freed itself from the utilitarian graphics which constrained it like a corset, it has released itself from prudish isolation, detached itself from its often servile functions to such a degree that even its definition has become unacceptable. The poster has returned to its roots, it has again become a picture—reproduced many times, a picture dealing with the "proposed subject."

I once believed that in the hands of an artist, the animated film could become an instrument with extraordinary possibilities. Film appeared to me as the most contemporary product, as an incomparable means of expression, as a vast and fertile field of activity. I did not see at the time the immense difficulties which face those who do not want to submit to the cinema's commercial system. The margin of creative liberty and of experiment which still existed recently—that is, in the short film—has almost entirely disappeared. No one needs it, there is no room for it in the cinema, and the festivals of shorts emit the melancholy of their past glory into a vacuum. As also in the socialist countries, it still has a raison d'etre in the United States, where the distribution network in the universities and lecture halls (in a way, cinematographic libraries) assure its diffusion and audiences for it.

The cinema continues its development in the show-business tradition. As an artistic product, which can demonstrate the character of an objet d'art in time and movement, the cinema has still not found either its patron or its destined collector. I see its only chance in the development of modern means of reproduction, in the popularity of cassettes and video discs which must soon appear on the market. They can radically change the situation and assure the cinema of the same popularity which literary and musical works enjoy.

—Jan Lenica

*    *    *

Jan Lenica's reputation rests on his artistic versatility. His contribution to poster design, book illustration, animated film, and stage design has caused him to emerge as one of the most significant practitioners in European graphic art. As a poster designer, animated filmmaker, and innovator in modern graphic techniques, Lenica demonstrates an unusual ability to interrelate the various media, thus enriching each of them.

In his posters, Lenica follows the highly respected tradition of Polish poster art but refreshes it. He has developed from realist representation to more and more subjective interpretation of themes as he has attempted to give poster art more freedom, more expressive power. At the same time, he recognizes that changes have taken place in the display of posters. Since he started designing, posters have lost their traditional location; they should now be planned for an intimate environment and for more subtle impact, as Lenica has done in his best posters, such as those for *Wozzeck, Faust, Othello,* and for the Olympic Games in Munich. Now, also, there are galleries and museums for poster design and many of his works are kept in fine art museums as examples of contemporary art.

Lenica maintains a similar approach to animated films. Using this entertaining form, he superimposes his own world, his own fantasies, his own fear, menace, and hallucinations in a surrealistic way to create a new, poetic, and fearful universe, a kind of graphics in motion. For him, animated film is a stepping stone toward visualizing his powerful imagination, as well as an admirable medium for the expression of an ideological view of man and society. To achieve these ends, Lenica uses various processes never before seen or tried in animation, such as hand-colored fragments of engravings, bold typographic layouts synchronized to music effects, and stylized graphic designs with thick outlines, as seen previously only in poster design, combined with simply choreographed motion. The result is a contemporary graphic impact which gives his films richness and a new look. It also opens up the world of subconscious vision where objects and subjects behave like automata in an electronic hell. Films such as *Monsieur Tête* (1959), *Labyrinth* (1962), *Rhinoceros* (1963), *A* (1964), *Adam II* (1969), and *Ubu* (1977), all of which have won numerous awards, are among the many that carry his message and help to widen the vocabulary of animated film.

—John Halas

# LENK, Krzysztof

Polish graphic designer and information architect

**Born:** Warsaw, 21 July 1936. **Education:** Studied at the Academy of Fine Arts Warsaw, 1954-57, and Krakow Academy of Fine Arts, Katowice, M.F.A., 1961. **Family:** Married Ewa Zembrzuska in 1963; children: Honorata and Jacek. **Career:** Graphic designer, in

Warsaw, 1958-82, and in Providence, Rhode Island, from 1982; design director, *Polish Machinery News* magazine, Warsaw, 1965-66; creative art director, AGPOL state advertising agency, Warsaw, 1966-68; art director and designer, *Jeune Afrique* magazine, Paris, 1968-69; design director, *Perspektywy* magazine, Warsaw, 1969-72, and *Polish Art Review* magazine, Warsaw, 1971-73; deputy chairman and art director, 1973-76, and consultant art director, 1976-82, of KAW Publishing House, Warsaw; design director, *Animafilm* magazine, Warsaw, 1978-82; also designed for SNIP, Paris, 1968; Erco Lighting Systems, Luedesheid, Germany, 1972-73; WIFON records and cassettes, 1977-82; Polski Fiat cars, 1978-80; *Solidarnosc* newspaper, 1981-82; partner, with Paul Kahn, and director of design, Dynamic Diagrams, Providence, Rhode Island, from 1990; clients have included Harvard University, Houghton Mifflin, IBM Corporation, Interleaf, Mead Data Central, Microsoft, Silicon Graphics, and Sun Microsystems. Assistant professor, 1973-76 and associate professor of graphic design, 1976-82, at the School of Design, Lodz; professor of graphic design, Rhode Island School of Design, Providence, from 1982; visiting professor, Ohio State University, Columbus, 1979, University of Illinois, Urbana, 1984, National Institute of Design, Ahmedabad, India, 1989, Ravensbourne College of Design and Communication, London, 1989, and University of Canterbury, Christchurch, New Zealand, 1992; also visiting lecturer at numerous colleges throughout Europe and the United States, from 1976. **Member:** American Institute of Graphic Artists, American Center for Design. **Collections:** National Poster Museum, Warsaw; National Museum, Poznan; Museum Folkwang, Essen. **Honors:** Excellence in Teaching Design Award, Polish Ministry of Culture, 1977, 1980; IBM Fellow, International Design Conference, Aspen, Colorado, 1983. **Addresses:** Department of Graphic Design, Rhode Island School of Design, 2 College Street, Providence, Rhode Island 02903, U.S.A.; Dynamic Diagrams Inc., 12 Bassett Street, Providence, Rhode Island 02903, U.S.A.

## Publications

**By LENK: articles**—in *International Biennale of Graphic Design Symposium* (Brno), 1976; *AIGA Journal* (New York), Summer 1988; *High Quality* (Heidelberg), 1991; *Visible Language* (Detroit), 1992; *Information Technology Quarterly* (Cambridge, Massachusetts), 1992.

**On LENK: books**—*Polish Poster Art Today* by Szymon Bojko, Warsaw, 1972; *Penrose Annual,* London, 1976; *Information Architects* by Richard Saul Wurman, Zürich, 1996; **articles**—in *Interpressgrafik* (Budapest), no. 1, 1975; *Projekt* (Warsaw), no. 5, 1976; *Literatura* (Warsaw), April 1978; *Solidarnosc* (Warsaw), November 1981; *Graphis* (Zürich), no. 238, 1985.

*

I am looking for emotional results using rather cool, logical tools.

—Krzysztof Lenk

*    *    *

The achievements of Krzysztof Lenk in design practice, thought and pedagogy pervade the field of visual communication. He is involved with models, processes, conditioning, and the technology of information—that is, communication which is motivated by logic. Lenk belongs to the generation of designers whose principles and philosophy—while rooted in the rationalism and functionalism of the first decades of the 20th century—were shaped by the advanced ideas of the 1960s and 1970s. It was at this time that new research disciplines arose in response to the changing needs of human communication.

Faced with the task of defining their orientation and preferences, designers looked to works by McLuhan, Barthes, Eco, Moles, Benze, Maldonado. There was a growing interest in Structuralism, Semiotics, Topology, Cultural Anthropology, Cognitive Sciences, as the means by which designers could reinforce their conscience. Design was identified with the humanistic ideas capable of opposing the threat of chaos in the world of visual civilization. This worldwide trend encompassed the most primordial iconosphere: sign codes, functional typography of mass media, and corporate identity systems. From a philosophical standpoint, it was a confirmation of Aristotelian logic, reason, and efficiency of a wisely organized world.

The Vietnam War and the youth rebellions in France and Germany in the late 1960s contradicted in the most dramatic way the idealistic image of a well organized and logically behaving society. Such was the state of design, roughly, when Lenk, having returned to Poland in 1969 from a two-year apprenticeship in Paris, began to manifest his own ideas and creative concepts. Lenk's experimental field was a weekly illustrated magazine for which he developed a modular structure based on a set of predesigned elements. The structure was very flexible and well coordinated with production and printing requirements. In Poland it was the first example of the modern approach to publication design. The weekly magazine demonstrated Lenk's design philosophy and skills and, like many of his other projects, proved to be much ahead of its time. It was his first life momentum, placing him within the ranks of the most competent designers.

In 1973 Lenk was appointed to the faculty at the School of Design in Lodz. As a teacher, Lenk together with a team of students initiated research and experimentation in the field of publication design. Studies in readability and legibility, and analyses of structures and systems newly applied in newspapers and periodicals, brought forth some genuine concepts for alternative magazines: the soccer fan's weekly served as a measure of reading absorption of thirty minutes; the prototype paper for commuters was designed to be read by people standing in crowded, shaking trains.

Since 1982 Krzysztof Lenk has been professor of Rhode Island School of Design, one of the most renowned design schools in the United States. His previous experience in advanced studies of visual communication enabled him to trace his own path among the challenges of the dominant trends of the 1980s. What were the evidently new features of that decade? In general, a true explosion of information. Pandora's Box has been opened and the entire world has been conquered by information, which penetrates all areas of life. Repercussions of this phenomenon reverberated through the design profession, redefining its philosophy and technology.

The appearance of the Macintosh computer in 1984 revolutionized the traditional process of design. For the first time, type became accessible to everyone. Newly developed software applications such as Adobe Photoshop and Illustrator made manipulation of images easy and the traditional boundaries separating photography, illustration, and typography became less rigid. The rapid expansion of the capacity of computer memory led to the creation of large database systems. As a result a new profession was born:

Information Design. Fortunately, the talents and achievements of the most prominent designers, including Richard S. Wurman, Peter Bradford, David Macaulay, soon elevated the new discipline to the degree of art in the classic, Hellenistic understanding of the Arte and Techne.

At the same time, Krzysztof concentrated on teaching this new field at Rhode Island School of Design. I must emphasize his openness to new ideas and ability to assimilate and adapt them to his personal philosophy and creative pedagogy. Explanatory design experiments, which began with diagrams and charts, evolved gradually into user interface design and kinetic typography for the computer screen. By 1985, his students' achievements were featured in *Graphis* (no. 238, 1985). Lenk's approach to pedagogy is based on the principle that shaping the mentality and the character of the young designer should be the goal of teaching. One cannot simply teach a student how to design, but one has to steer his thinking and teach him to ask questions and to be critical.

In 1990 Lenk, together with Paul Kahn, founded Dynamic Diagrams, Inc., Consultants in Visual Logic, a consulting company specializing in information design. A team of information designers and computer programmers develops interactive applications for clients from computer, publishing, and financial companies, as well as art and educational institutions. A variety of projects, ranging from CD-ROM publications and electronic prototypes, to user interface design and World Wide Web sites, has been developed for clients including IBM, Siemens Nixdorf, Silicon Graphics, and Harvard University. The high quality, innovative work of Dynamic Diagrams has been presented in many publications on diagrammatic and information design—most recently in Richard Saul Wurman's book, *Information Architects* (Graphis Press, 1996).

—Szymon Bojko

# LENNON, (John) Dennis

British architect and interior, furniture, and stage designer

**Born:** London, 23 June 1918. **Education:** Attended the Merchant Taylor's School, London, until 1935; studied architecture, at University College, London, 1936-39. **Military Service:** Served in the British Army Royal Engineers, in France, North Africa, and Italy, 1939-45 (prisoner of war in France, 1940; escaped), Military Cross, 1942. **Family:** Married Else Bull-Andersen in 1947; three children. **Career:** Assistant designer, in the architectural office of Maxwell Fry, London, 1946-48; director, Rayon Industry Design Centre, London, 1948-50; senior partner, Dennis Lennon and Partners architectural and design firm, London, from 1950; consultant architect, Royal Opera House Covent Garden, London. **Member:** Fellow, Royal Institute of British Architects; Chartered Society of Designers, London; Royal Society of Arts, London. **Honors:** Commander, Order of the British Empire, 1968. **Died.**

## Works

Rayon Design Centre interiors, London, 1948.
Desk in oak and formica laminate, for Dunn's of Bromley, 1950.
Sofas and chairs, for Scottish Furniture Manufacturers Ltd., 1951.

Thomas Cook and Sons office interiors, Berkeley Street, London, 1953.
London Steak Houses interiors, for J. Lyons, London, 1953-70.
Vono wholesale showrooms, Grosvenor Street, London, 1954.
Jaeger shops interiors in Oxford, Glasgow, Manchester, Bristol, and London, 1954-59.
Office furniture range, for Peter Jones Stores, London, 1957.
Hearing aid showroom and fitting center, for Ardente, London, 1958.
Bowater House showroom interiors, Knightsbridge, London, 1959.
Kayser Bondor boutique in Barker's Department Store, London, 1959.
White House restaurant and cocktail lounge interiors, Regent's Park, London, 1961.
L'Epee d'Or restaurant in the Cumberland Hotel, London, for J. Lyons, 1963.
Albany Hotel interiors, Glasgow, 1973.
Holiday Inn interiors, Swiss Cottage, London, 1974.
American Express Bank interiors in Moorgate, London, for Rothschild International, 1975.
Arts Club interiors, Dover Street, London, 1976.
Central dining hall interiors, for Harrow School, Middlesex, 1979.
Theatre Royal interiors, Bath, 1981.
Bank of Scotland interiors, Threadneedle Street, London, 1982.

## Publications

**On LENNON: books**—*British Furniture Today* by Erno Goldfinger, London, 1951; *Design in British Industry: A Mid-Century Survey* by Michael Farr, Cambridge, 1955; *Public Interiors: An International Survey* by Misha Black, London, 1960; *Hille: 75 Years of British Furniture,* exhibition catalogue by Sutherland Lyall, London, 1981.

\*   \*   \*

Dennis Lennon clearly announced a design personality from his first work to be known to the public, the Rayon Design Centre (1948), which was the conversion of a largish Georgian house in Mayfair, London. It is notable for the overall design plan meticulously pursued without any visible conflict with the equally meticulous respect for the existing building. Indeed, the two were brought together by the sensitive colouring of the plasterwork, which was in turn related to the colours used for the furniture and furnishings. These qualities continued to dominate Dennis Lennon and Partners, which, for most of its lifetime, remained small.

The thirty-seven London Steakhouses for J. Lyons (1953-1970), shopfronts and interiors, along with work for the hotels of that same company and for Grand Metropolitan Hotels, Trust House Hotels, Forte, and Metropolis Hotels Group, demonstrate the partnership's particular approach: an appreciation of the precise nature of the commission and a careful satisfaction of the requirements in painstaking attention to detail without giving any laboured effect whatsoever. In many cases, these even preserve the freshness of Lennon's original sketches.

Though the partnership produced a large number of interior designs, it was also responsible for some quite considerable architectural schemes, of which Plumtree Court in the City of London merits close examination for its consistency of design through plans, elevations, accommodation to the site, details, and fittings. The partnership's success is witnessed in the prestige office interiors for the Commercial Union, Sainsbury's, Vickers, Mercantile and General, Bank of America (the Dealers Room table is especially worthy of notice), and Rothschild Intercontinental.

It would be amiss not to comment upon the nature of some of these office interiors. Rothschild's is notable for a staircase, clad in stainless steel and linking three floors. The use of stainless steel for Sainsbury's also deserves mention, as do the revolving doors at the new entrance in Rennie Street, the two columns that distinguish the waiting area on the ground floor, and the handrails to the steps leading up to the reception and waiting areas. Of course, their various dining rooms for directors and for staff were all meticulously conceived and executed, as is the case in the staff dining room for Sainsbury's. Converted from a second basement cheese store, it was relined with London stock brick to give a forthright but welcoming air, underlined by the choice of furniture and subtly varied floor treatment, carpet, brick, and tiles.

The partners had a distinguished record in such conversions, which revealed in each case their appreciation of the qualities of the original building and a delicate bending of their repertoire of modern idiom to suit, without ever falling into eclecticism or mere revivalism. Their conversion of a medieval barn into a restaurant at Leeds Castle is an outstanding example.

—Toni del Renzio

# LE QUERNEC, Alain

French graphic designer

**Born:** Le Faouet, Morbihan, 15 November 1944. **Education:** Educated at the Lycée Dupuy de Lome, Lorient, until 1961; studied art, at the Lycée Claude Bernard, Paris, 1961-64, and graphic design under Henryk Tomaszewski, at the Academy of Fine Arts, Warsaw, 1972. **Military Service:** Served in the French Army, in Algeria, 1967-69. **Family:** Married Czeslawa Sykut in 1973; children: Paul, Mathieu, and Helene. **Career:** Freelance poster designer, working in Quimper, from 1972. Art teacher, at the Lycée Brizeux Quimper, from 1972. **Member:** Alliance Graphique Internationale, from 1990. **Exhibitions:** Press Club, Kalisz, 1972; Galerie du Steir, Quimper, 1973; Press Club Gallery, Warsaw, 1973; Musée des Jacobins, Morlaix, 1975, 1988; Galerie Gloux, Concarneau, 1978; Musée des Arts Decoratifs, Nantes, 1981; Stadtische Galerie, Erlangen 1984; Centre Culturel, Landerneau, 1986; Pecsi Galena, Pecs, 1986; Musée de la Publicité, Paris, 1987; Musée Departemental Breton, Quimper, 1987; Hochschule der Kunste, Offenbach, 1988; Deutsches Plakatmuseum, Essen, 1988; Palais des Congrès, Lorient, 1989; Musée La Cohue, Vannes, 1989; Bibliothèque Nationale, Paris, 1991; Museum of Modern Art, Tel-Aviv, Israel, 1992; Plakatmuseum am Niederhein, Emmerich, 1995; Centre de la gravure et de l'image imprimée, La Louviére, 1996. **Collections:** Museum of Modern Art, New York; Library of Congress, Washington, D.C.; National Poster Museum, Warsaw; Museum Narodowy, Poznan; Neue Sammlung, Munich; Deutsches Plakatmuseum, Essen; Plakatmuseum am Niederhein, Emmerich; Museum für Kunst und Gewerbe, Hamburg; Bibliotheque Forney, Paris; Musée de la Publicité, Paris; Bibliothèque Nationale, Paris; Australian National Gallery, Canberra; Israel Museum, Jerusalem.

**Honors:** Prize of Distinction, 1982, Bronze Medal, 1995, Mons Triennale, Belgium; Zycie Warszawie Prize, Warsaw, 1984; Lahti Poster Biennale Award, 1985, honorable mention, 1994; Poster Award of Honor, Paris 1986; ICOGRADA Prize, Warsaw Poster Biennale, 1988; Prix Honoré, Bibliothèque Nationale, Paris, 1988; Grand Prix de l'affiche culturelle, Paris, 1991; First Prize, Festival des Médias Locaux, Paris, 1992; Bronze Medal, Poster Biennale, Brno, 1992; Gold Medal, 1992, Silver Medal, 1994, Poster Biennale, Mexico; First Prize, Z Sculpture, New York, 1994; Master Eye Award, Trnava, 1994;. **Address:** Trogour Huella, 29180 Plogonnec, France.

## Publications

**By LE QUERNEC: articles**—in *Bon a Tirer* (Paris), no. 7, 1978, no. 14, 1978, no. 28, 1980, no. 57, 1983; *Novum Gebrauchsgraphik* (Munich), no. 5, 1988; "Henryk Tomaszewski" in *Idea* (Tokyo), no. 241, 1993; "The Choice of Le Quernec" in *Affiche,* no. 8; "In Memoriam Polish Poster" in *Bat,* no. 165.

**On LE QUERNEC: books**—*Sur les Murs de France* by Alain Gesgon, Paris, 1979; *Il Linguaggio della Grafica Politica* by Robert Philippe, Milan, 1981; *Alain Le Quernec: Affiches,* exhibition catalogue, Nantes, 1981; *Affiches* by Alain Gesgon, Paris, 1982; *Alain Le Quernec: Plakate,* exhibition catalogue, Erlangen, 1984; *L'Affiche dans le Monde* by Alain Weill, Paris, 1984; *Design Francais 1960-1990: Trois Decennies,* exhibition catalogue by Margot Rouard and Francoise Jollant Kneebone, Paris, 1988, London, 1990; **articles**— "Alain Le Quernec" in *Idea* (Tokyo), no. 218, 1990; "Alain Le Quernec's Students: L'Atelier d'Art Plastique" in *Idea,* no. 239, 1993.

*

Profession: Poster designer? The term is out of fashion. Graphic designer? The term is too technical. Artist? The term is too pretentious. Adman? No insults, please. I am not certain that a term exists to define this profession. I am not certain that the profession exists.

A self-taught poster producer since 1962, I spent a year (1972) in Warsaw, at the studio of Henryk Tomaszewski, whom I consider responsible, if not for my commitment to the practice of a particular graphic language, at least for the rigorous demands it implies. The Polish poster doesn't exist anymore as a street reality but the lesson of the Polish poster school, the most influential movement in world graphic design since the war, is for a poster producer to consider his rectangle of paper as a surface which is as free of constraints and conventions as the canvas is for a painter. This view of course must be accepted, if not demanded, by the person commissioning the poster. Although we may consider it regrettable that there does not really exist, in France today, a true demand or market for creative graphic design, which still remains an off-beat language, rarely accepted, encouraged, or honored, we should also ask whether this situation does not reflect the inability of creative designers to stimulate the awakening of such a desire amongst potential clients. In the meantime, we wait for a golden age...

—Alain Le Quernec

*     *     *

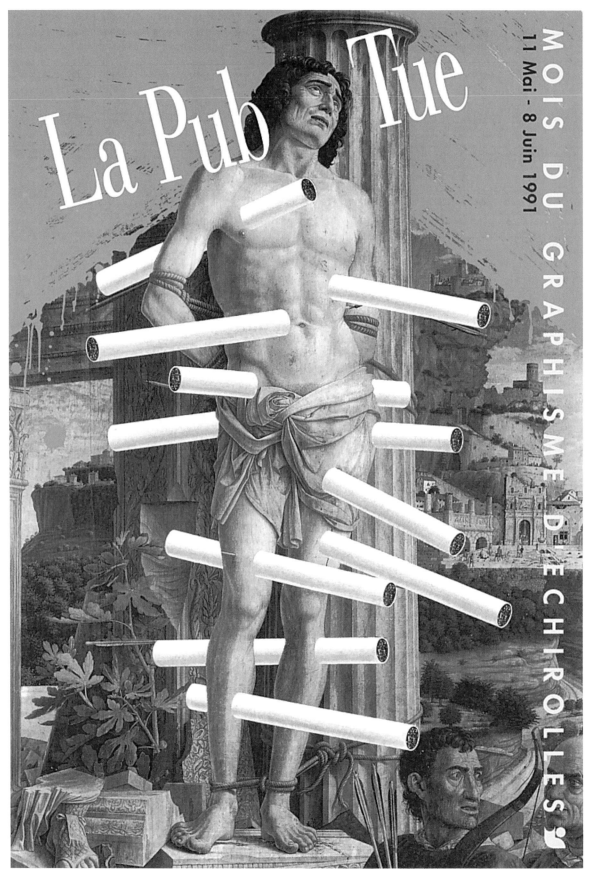

**Alain Le Quernec: design for the invitation to the second of the Mois du Graphisme d'Echirolles, 1991**

Brittany—a stony corner of France, with its roaring Atlantic and sturdy, individualistic people, a country within a country. The city of Quimper plays a prominent role in the entire region. Of course, it's not Paris, not LeHavre nor Lyon, but it has its cultural life, politics problems, and long tradition. And it has Alain Le Quernec.

After completing his education in Paris, this poster artist spent a year at the Warsaw Academy of Arts. Under Henryk Tomaszewski's eye, let us say that he didn't fool around. A big, burly man, he worked the way he looked, and early, he decided to master the skills of the poster in general, to learn how to approach every aspect rather than to concentrate on some narrow subject or visual style.

To the surprise of many friends, Le Quernec returned to Quimper, to his place, his sky and sea. With his Polish wife, he settled near the city and soon had established himself as the dominant posterist of the entire area. His poster-making activity reaches every aspect of life. From music concerts, art shows, and advertising to politics, the hand of Le Quernec is visible. Somewhat shockingly, sometimes political rivals from opposing parties collide on the same wall—their images both set by Le Quernec's hand.

Despite his overwhelming grip on local "poster affairs," Le Quernec manages to survive as a fresh, changing, intelligent force. He keeps an eye on the world art market, updates his own style, and aggressively advertises his own case elsewhere. You can find his works in major poster publications as well as in various competitions and biennales, from Lahti to Colorado. On the other hand, Le Quernec makes an important contribution to his own place and people. Popular in Quimper, this energetic person plays a central role in the artistic community of Brittany. Frequently, the best graphic artists from the wide world exhibit in Quimper, lured and befriended by Le Quernec, of course.

Working and living far away from the center of the country's cultural life makes a strong point against the old theory that "nothing happens outside Paris, London, or New York." Thanks to the happy combination of his energy, gift, ambition, and charm, he became a local master, joining the long tradition of cathedral builders, carpenters, sculptors, and painters that have formed the history and rich tradition of Brittany. But there is one important difference: through his activity, he links his distant Quimper with the world for the good of all involved.

—Jan Sawka

# LEU, Olaf

German graphic designer

**Born:** Chemnitz, Saxony (later Karl-Marx-Stadt, East Germany, then Chemnitz, Germany), 28 July 1936. **Education:** Educated at Volksschule and Gymnasium, 1942-51; apprenticed in a printing house, and studied typesetting at the Gewerbliche Berufsschule, Ravensburg and Ulm, 1951-54. **Family:** Married Eva Gutermann in 1977. **Career:** Type director, at Bauer Typefoundry, Frankfurt 1954-57; art director, Hanns W. Brose advertising agency, Frankfurt, 1957-59; freelance graphic designer, Wiesbaden, from 1960. Visiting lecturer and professor, London College of Printing, 1964, Manchester College of Art and Design, 1968, State University of Chile, 1975-77, St. Martin's School of Art, London, 1982-84, and Akademie der Bildenden Künste, Stuttgart, 1985-86; professor, Fachhochschule Rheinland-Pfalz, Mainz, from 1986. **Member:** Type Directors Club of New York; Art Directors Club of New York; German Designers Club. **Exhibitions:** Gewerbliche Berufsschule, Ulm, 1956; Akademie der Bildenden Künste, Karlsruhe, 1957; London College of Printing, 1964; Brighton College of Art and Design, Sussex, 1964; Haus am Lutzowplatz, West Berlin 1970; Museum der Stadt, Biberach an der Riss, 1971; Museum of Contemporary Arts, Santiago de Chile, 1976; Kulturamt der Stadt Wiesbaden, 1980; Bezalel Academy of Fine Arts, Jerusalem, 1981; International Typeface Corporation, New York, 1982; Akademie fur das Graphische Gewerbe, Munich, 1982; Wurttembergische Landesbibliothek, Stuttgart, 1985; Galerie von Oertzen, Frankfurt, 1985; Fachhochschule fur Gestaltung, Augsburg, 1986; German Poster Museum, Essen, 1990; University of South Australia, Adelaide, 1991; University of Canberra, Australia, 1991; Royal Melbourne Institute of Technology, Australia, 1991; Karmeliterkloster, Frankfurt am Main, 1992; Goethe Institute, Montevideo, Uruguay, and Buenos Aires, Cordoba, and Mendoza, Argentina, 1995. **Collections:** Museum of Modern Art, New York; International Typeface Corporation Center, New York; Cooper Union, New York; Deutsches Plakat Museum, Essen; Stiftung Preussischer Kulturbesitz, West Berlin; Museum für Gestaltung, Zürich. **Honors:** 58 Typographic Awards, Type Directors Club of New York, 1957-89; 50 International Calendar Awards, Stuttgart, 1969-89; Gold Medal, Philadelphia Art Directors Club, 1969; Silver Medal, Brno Graphic Biennale, 1970, 1982; New York Art Directors Club Award, 1974, 1975; Tokyo Calendar Awards, 1981, 1982, 1983. **Address:** Lanzstrasse 18, 65193 Wiesbaden, Germany.

## Works

Corporate design programme, for Gebruder Schmidt Druckfarben, Frankfurt, from 1960.
*Zeitloser Glanz* calendar, for Zanders Feinpapiere, Bergisch Gladbach, 1967.
*Zahlen aus aller Welt* calendar, for Roland Offsetmaschinenfabrik, Offenbach, 1970.
*Hans-Peter Haas druckt New York* calendar, for Hans-Peter Haas, Stuttgart, 1971.
*Old Games* calendar, for Roland Offsetmaschinenfabrik, Offenbach, 1975.
Corporate design programme, for Colonia Versicherung, Cologne, from 1981.
*The LinoType Show* promotion campaign, for LinoType AG, Eschborn, 1983.
*Still-Life* calendar, for Zanders Feinpapiere AG, Bergisch Gladbach, 1983.
*Ford Futura* calendar, for Ford Werke, Cologne, 1984.
*Porsche* calendar, for Porsche Sports Cars, 1985.
*Seh-Felder* calendar, for MAN-Roland Druckmaschinen AG, Offenbach, 1985.
*Feuer, Wasser, Luft und Erde* calendar, for Gebruder Schmidt Druckfarben, Frankfurt, 1988.
Corporate design programme, for the BHF-Bank, Frankfurt, from 1988.
*Pastorale* calendar, for Gebruder Schmidt Druckfarben, Frankfurt, 1989.

## Publications

**By LEU: books**—(with Wolfgang Schmittel) *Process Visual*, Zürich 1978; *Olaf Leu, Graphic Design Direction, 1955-1990,* edited by

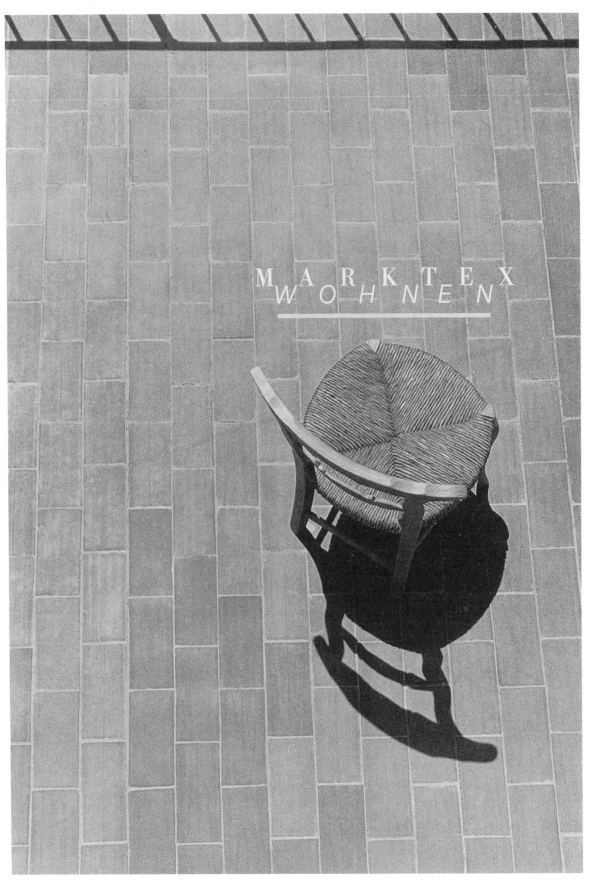

**Olaf Leu: "Living with Marktex" poster for Marktex Company, 1990**

H. Schmidt, Mainz, 1990; **articles**—in *Novum Gebrauchsgraphik* (Munich), no. 6, 1981, no. 12, 1981, no. 1, 1982, no. 3, 1982, no. 6, 1982, no. 9, 1982, no. 12, 1982, no. 10, 1983, no. 12, 1984, no. 9, 1985, no. 3, 1986, no. 10, 1987, no. 8, 1989; *Print* (New York), July/August 1981; *Offsetpraxis* (Stuttgart), no. 4, 1982, no. 9, 1982, no. 4, 1983, no. 10, 1983, no. 1, 1984, no. 4, 1984, no. 10, 1984, no. 10, 1985, no. 1, 1986, no. 4, 1987, no. 11, 1988; *Deutscher Drucker* (Stuttgart), no. 27, 1984, no. 33, 1986, no. 1, 1987, no. 3, 1988; *Der Polygraph* (Frankfurt), no. 8, 1986.

**On LEU: books**—*Modern Graphics* by Keith Murgatroyd, London, 1969, *Who's Who in Graphic Art* edited by Walter Amstutz, Dubendorf, 1982; **articles**—in *Novum Gebrauchsgraphik* (Munich), no. 11, 1956, no. 4, 1961, no. 6, 1963, no 12, 1971; *Print* (New York), May/June 1965, September/October 1982; *Graphis* (Zürich), no. 202, 1979, no. 253, 1988; *Deutscher Drucker* (Stuttgart), no. 16, 1985; *Der Polygraph* (Frankfurt), no. 24, 1986; *Novum Gebrauchsgraphik* (Munich), December 1987; *Grafik Design + Technik* (Munich), no. 2, 1988.

\*      \*      \*

Above all, a project must be fun. For me this pleasurable aspect inspires a great deal of enthusiasm, which then is manifest in the solution of the problem at hand. In order to pass this pleasure on to others, I try to surround a striking idea with a "joyful" quality, so as to produce a positive atmosphere.

I think that graphic design is meant to create an intelligent, humane order, but one which can include fashionable elements. For this reason, I have never sworn allegiance to any one direction in style or school of fashion. Therefore, all of my works which have appeared since 1956 express my own individuality even as they reflect the directions that taste was taking at the time of their origin. Because taste signifies change and activity, not stagnation, good graphic design is, indeed must be, fashionable. Just as our lives and environment undergo change, so must graphic design.

Every artistic statement reflects temperament, intelligence, experience, and age. These various components add up to the maturity and universality of a work. Although graphic design is an individualistic profession, since individuality itself is so rare, there is little truly individualistic design. Individuality is equally as rare in the client as in the graphic designer. The rare circumstance that they should happen to meet results in what observers call "good" graphic design.

The triad system makes for excellent graphic design:

1. It addresses the inner disposition of a company—its services, products, employees, and its leadership—economically, ecologically, and socially speaking.

2. It addresses the inner disposition of the commissioned designer.

3. It addresses the inner disposition of communication and its media.

For inner qualities determine outer appearance. Or, according to Johann Wolfgang Goethe, all that is on the inside is also on the outside.

—Olaf Leu

# LEUPIN, Herbert

Swiss painter, illustrator, advertising, and graphic designer

**Born:** Beinwil am See, 20 December 1916. **Education:** Educated at Realgymnasium, Basel, until 1931; studied graphics under Paul Kammuller and Theo Eble at the Allgemeine Gewerbeschule, Basel, 1932-35; apprenticed in the Hermann Eidenbenz design studio, Basel, 1932-35; studied poster design, at the Ecole Paul Colin, Paris, 1936-37. **Family:** Married in 1945; children: Tommy and Charly. **Career:** Graphic designer, in the Donald Brun studio, Basel, 1938; freelance designer, working in Basel, 1939-45, and in Augst, Baselland, from 1945; designed for Globi Verlag, Bata-Schuh AG, Roth-Handle Zigaretten, and others. **Member:** Alliance Graphique Internationale; Bund Grafischer Gestalter, Basel; Schweizerischer Werkbund. **Honors:** Foire de Paris Silver Medal, 1936; Schutzenfest Poster Prize, Lucerne, 1939; Poster of the Month Award, Munich and Vienna, 1952; Chicago Art Directors Club Medal, 1960; International Poster Prize, Toronto, 1961; Warsaw Poster Biennale Prize, 1968. **Address:** Augustinergasse 1-3, Basel, Switzerland.

## Works

Books designed include—*Bruder Grimm Marchen,* Zürich; *Hansel und Gretel,* Zürich; *Des tapfere Schneide Hein,* Zürich; *Hans im Gluck,* Zürich, 1944; *Tischlein deck dich!,* Zürich; *Schneewittchen und die sieben Zwerge,* Zürich, 1945; *Der gestiefelte Kater,* Zürich, 1946; *Der Wolf und die sieben junger Giesslein,* Zürich, 1947; *Dornroschen,* Zürich, 1948; *Frau Holle,* Zürich, 1949.

## Publications

**By LEUPIN: books**—*Herbert Leupin—Placards and Posters,* portfolio with text by Manuel Gasser, Zürich and Frankfurt, 1957, London, 1959.

**On LEUPIN: books**—*Posters: Fifty Artists and Designers* edited by W. H. Allner, New York, 1952; *Packaging: An International Survey of Package Design* edited by Walter Herdeg, Zürich, 1959; *The New Graphic Design* by Karl Gestner and Markus Kutter, Teufen and London, 1959; *Who's Who in Graphic Art* edited by Walter Amstutz, Zürich, 1962, Dubendorf, 1982; *Das Plakat* by Anton Sailer, Munich, 1965; *History of the Poster* by Josef and Shizuko Muller-Brockmann, Zürich, 1971; *Graphic Designers in Europe 2* edited by Henri Hillebrand, London, 1972; *The Language of Graphics* by Edward Booth-Clibborn and Daniele Baroni, London, 1980.

\*      \*      \*

For more than forty years, Herbert Leupin's posters have been injecting humor and novelty into the Swiss poster tradition. His simple and direct imagery is created with flat, cut-out forms. Copy is kept to an extreme minimum (just the name of the product or company), and colors are usually primaries. The playful arrangement of image, type, and color, however, betrays an understated elegance and sophistication, as in his ingenious posters for Eptinger mineral water. One shows an outline of a bottle and glass formed by white dots on a bright blue background. The product's white-and-red label and logotype, affixed to the bottle, become the focus of this deceptively simple composition, which conveys a clear message. Another shows a large caricature of a clown-like figure shaped into the capital letter "E" and holding a glass of mineral water. The only copy is the product's name displayed in an equally whimsical type style.

His circus posters are another outlet for his playfulness. One depicts a seal poised confidently on a ball. On each outstretched flipper is a fish and a series of colored balls, one on top of the other, spelling out the name of the circus. Again, the image is in broad areas of color, and copy is kept to a minimum. The sketch-like treatment, in an almost naive, child-like style adds tremendously to the vitality of the poster. Disarmingly simple, it has an impact reminiscent of Polish circus posters.

Leupin's work reflects a deep understanding of how and what communicates most thoroughly and effectively. His skillfully manipulated typography for the Suze beverage company poster, and the cartoon-like figure used in the Agfa photographic materials poster, both demonstrate a style which enhances and complements the products. To enjoy and appreciate Leupin's creations fully, one must view them in their outdoor setting, in competition with other advertisements, where their light-hearted visual statements provide a welcome contrast and are a joy to behold.

—Dennis Ichiyama

# LEVEN, Boris
American painter and film designer

**Born:** Moscow, Russia, 13 August 1908; emigrated to the United States in 1927, naturalized, 1938. **Education:** Studied architecture, at the University of Southern California, Los Angeles, B.Arch., 1932; Beaux-Arts Institute of Design, New York, 1932-33. **Military Service:** Served in the United States Army Air Force, 1942-45, Staff Sergeant. **Family:** Married Vera Gloushkoff in 1948. **Career:** Sketch artist and designer, for Paramount Pictures, 1933-35, and for Samuel Goldwyn Studios and David O. Selznick Productions, 1936, Hollywood, California; assistant art director, Major Pictures Corporation, Hollywood, 1936; art director, 20th Century Fox Studios, Hollywood, 1937-38, 1941-42, 1945-46, and Universal International Pictures, Hollywood, 1947-48; freelance art director and production designer, Los Angeles, 1939-41, and from 1948. **Member:** Society of Motion Picture and Television Art Directors. **Exhibitions:** Los Angeles County Museum of Art, 1952; Society of Motion Picture Art Directors, Los Angeles, 1963; *The Union Artist,* Los Angeles County Museum of Art, 1971; *The Art of Hollywood,* Victoria and Albert Museum, London, 1979; Hollywood Studio Gallery, California, 1980. **Honors:** Emerson Architecture Prize, New York, 1932; Beaux Arts Ball Prize, New York, 1932; American Institute of Steel Construction Prize, 1932; National Scarab Watercolor Prize, 1933; Art Direction Prize, American Institute of Decorators, 1947; *Photoplay* Magazine Award, 1956; Academy Award, 1961. **Died:** Los Angeles, California, 11 October 1986.

## Works

Film productions include—*Alexander's Ragtime Band* (H. King), 1938; *Just Around the Corner* (Cummings), 1938; *Second Chorus* (Potter), 1940; *The Shanghai Gesture* (von Sternberg), 1941; *Tales of Manhattan* (Duvivier), 1942; *Life Begins at 8:30* (Pichel), 1942; *Hello, Frisco, Hello* (Humberstone), 1943; *Doll Face* (Seiler), 1945; *Home Sweet Homicide* (Bacon), 1946; *Shock* (Werker), 1946; *The Shocking Miss Pilgrim* (Seaton), 1947; *I Wonder Who's Kissing Her Now* (Bacon), 1947; *The Senator Was Indiscreet* (Kaufman), 1947; *Mr. Peabody and the Mermaid*

(Pichel), 1948; *Criss Cross* (Siodmak), 1948; *The Lovable Cheat* (Oswald), 1949; *Search for Danger* (Bernhard), 1949; *House by the River* (F. Lang), 1949; *Woman on the Run* (Foster), 1950; *Quicksand* (Pichel), 1950; *Dakota Lil* (Selander), 1950; *Destination Murder* (Cahn), 1950; *Once a Thief* (W. Wilder), 1950; *The Second Woman* (Kern), 1951; *The Prowler* (Losey), 1951; *A Millionaire for Christie* (Marshall), 1951; *Two Dollar Better* (Cahn), 1951; *The Basketball Fix* (Feist), 1951; *Sudden Fear* (Miller), 1952; *Rose of Cimarron* (Keller), 1952; *The Star* (Heisler), 1953; *Invaders from Mars* (Menzies), 1953; *Donovan's Brain* (Feist), 1953; *The Long Wait* (Saville), 1954; *The Silver Chalice* (Saville), 1955; *Giant* (Stevens), 1956; *Courage of Black Beauty* (Schuster), 1957; *My Gun Is Quick* (White and Victor), 1957; *Zero Hour* (Bartlett), 1957; *Anatomy of a Murder* (Preminger), 1959; *Thunder in the Sun* (Rouse), 1959; *September Storm* (Haskin), 1960; *West Side Story* (Wise), 1961; *Two for the Seesaw* (Wise), 1962; *Strait-Jacket* (Castle), 1964; *The Sound of Music* (Wise), 1965; *The Sand Pebbles* (Wise), 1966; *Star* (Wise), 1968; *A Dream of Kings* (Daniel Mann), 1969; *The Andromeda Strain* (Wise), 1971; *Happy Birthday Wanda June* (Robson), 1971; *The New Centurions* (Fleischer), 1972; *Jonathan Livingston Seagull* (Bartlett), 1973; *Reflections of Murder* (Badham—for TV), 1974; *Shanks* (Castle), 1974; *Mandingo* (Fleischer), 1975; *New York, New York* (Scorcese), 1977; *The Last Waltz* (Scorcese), 1978; *Matilda* (Daniel Mann), 1978; *The King of Comedy* (Scorcese), 1983; *Fletch* (Ritchie), 1985; *The Color of Money,* 1986; *Wildcats,* 1986; *The Last Temptation of Christ,* 1986.

## Publications

**By LEVEN: articles**—in *Film Index* (Mosman Bay), no. 15, 1973; *Film Comment* (New York), May/June 1978.

**On LEVEN: books**—*Hollywood in the Forties* by Charles Higham and Joel Greenberg, New York, 1968; *Le Décor de Film* by Leon Barsacq, Paris, 1970, as *Caligari's Cabinet and Other Grand Illusions,* Boston, 1976; *The International Dictionary of Films and Filmmakers,* Chicago and London, 1987, 1991.

*

What interests me the most in designing a film is the final look! I try to visualize what this "look" will be during the early readings of the script.

I believe that the early feelings with regard to mood and style and textures are vitally important and should be the guiding force during the development of the design. I believe that the greatest contribution to the film on the part of the production designer is the creation of visual continuity, balance, and dramatic emphasis.

I believe that if a setting is well designed, one should be able, at a glance, to tell what it represents, what transpires in it, and who are its occupants.

In designing an individual setting, I constantly keep in mind the style of the entire film and how this setting relates to the whole.

I believe in utmost simplicity. Simplicity is the key to my thinking, and it is my only approach to creative work. In my life and relations with others, I have always tried to be as honest as I am with myself.

—Boris Leven

*        *        *

Boris Leven graduated from the architecture school at the University of Southern California during the Depression. With little prospect of work in architecture, following another year of study in New York, he took a job in Paramount's art department, which was run by Hans Dreier.

Leven was one of the few designers who benefited from the training of the strictly-run, big, Hollywood studio system, absorbed the eclecticism of styles prevalent in the 1930s and 1940s, survived the decline of the studios in the 1950s, and flourished as an independent designer since the mid 1950s. He cannot be associated with the independent realist designers of the post-World War II period, for his approach was more tied to the eclecticism of William Cameron Menzies, with whom he co-designed the 1953 *Invaders from Mars* (which Menzies also directed).

Leven's clear theory and method appear in a short definition of production design he wrote for a 1978 exhibition at the Museum of Modern Art. Like Harry Horner, who also acknowledges Menzies' influence, Leven stressed the twin components of research and the artistic or personal creative formulation of a design program.

As a designer, Leven mixed both actual locations and stylized or abstract sets within a film. He was very conscious of these juxtapositions, and to avoid "visual discrepancies," he made special studies of "textures, color and aging of each setting." His works also contain significant examples of expressive color programs. But most of all, Leven's designs revealed his architectural training in their masterful manipulations of planes and masses, whether in interior or exterior spaces or the integration of the two.

These architectonic sensibilities are found, for example, in *Giant* (1956, directed by George Stevens). The key set is the massive, Victorian mansion located on a vast, flat, Texas plain. Based in part on a painting by Edward Hopper, this imposing set is a visual character in its own right. Indeed, it gives the film a scale that the performers did not always bring to their roles. The great house helped to save the film and, as an imposing part of the production, gave the design program an overt but appropriate role. The mansion in *Giant* belongs to the film history of the house-as-character; this includes Tara from *Gone With the Wind*, designed by Lyle Wheeler and Menzies, and Dr. Sloper's house from *The Heiress*, designed by Horner. Leven's mansion is closer than Horner's to Menzies' idealization and grandeur, whereas Horner's more authentically conceived house leans toward the best aspects of the realist school.

In *West Side Story*, Leven joined the realistic and the expressionistic by juxtaposing actual New York locations with abstractly conceived sets, some painted with highly saturated, tension-filled colors. Similarly eclectic is the film's blends of Shakespeare and the contemporary, urban, ethnic poor; of opera and jazz; and of modern ballet and realistic performance. Despite these mixed treatments of plot, character, music, and dance, this film marked a high new standard for the film musical. Rarely have locations been so effectively married to song and dance, largely because the new realist school of designers have not explored the powers of eclecticism and do not understand how sets can relate to music or dance. Leven, who knew how to bring a set alive and give it character without overpowering the actors, believed that a set can be noticed in a film, that it should have strong expressive meaning even without the performers.

Because Leven's architectural sense of the plane and of pictorial surface were so basic to his work, his use of the wide-screen format is noteworthy. Superior are his interior and exterior spaces' sensitivity to the broad, horizontal format in *The Silver Chalice* (1954), *Giant, West Side Story, The Sound of Music,* and *New York, New York* (1977). This latter film depends upon an unusual eclecticism

in its boldly abstract sets, which are obviously painted and deliberately flat. While these make clear that Leven was not committed to authenticity, neither is his eclecticism arbitrary, for his first commitment was to overall structure.

—Norman Gambill

# LEVINE, Michael
Canadian stage designer

**Born:** Toronto, Ontario, Canada, 1960. **Education:** Attended the Ontario College of Art, Toronto 1977-78; studied set design, Central School of Art and Design, London, B.A.I., 1981. **Career:** Assistant designer, Glasgow Citizens' Theatre, 1981-83; freelance set designer, from 1983; clients include Canadian Opera Company, Toronto, Le Grand Théâtre de Genève, Geneva, Metropolitan Opera, New York, Royal National Theatre, London, and others. **Member:** Associated Designers of Canada. **Honors:** Two Dora Awards, 1986. **Address:** 360 Howland Avenue, Toronto, Ontario, Canada, M5R 3B9.

## Works

Stage designs include—*Tasso, The Impresario from Smyrna,* and *The Custom of the Country,* Glasgow Citizen's Theatre, 1981-83; *Strange Interlude,* Duke of Yorks Theatre, London, 1984; *The Skin of Our Teeth,* 1984, *Heartbreak House,* 1985, *The Women,* 1985, *Arms and the Man,* 1986, Shaw Festival, Niagara-on-the-Lake, Canada; *Mahogany Songs,* English National Opera, 1984; *Uncle Vanya,* Tarragon Theatre, 1985; *Hot House,* National Ballet of Canada, 1986; *Spring Awakening,* CentreStage, 1986; *Tectonic Plates,* du Maurier World Stage Festival, 1989; *Mephistofele,* Le Grand Théâtre de Genève, 1989; *Idomeneo,* 1987, *Wozzeck,* 1990, *Mario and the Magician,* 1992, and *Blue Beard's Castle/ Erwartung,* 1993, Canadian Opera Company; *A Midsummer Night's Dream,* National Theatre, London, 1992; *Cendrillon,* Welsh National Opera, 1993; *La Boheme,* De Vlaamse Theatre, Antwerp, 1993; *Light up the Sky,* Old Vic Theatre, London; *Don Giovanni,* Belfast Opera House; *Don Juan,* Actors Touring Company, Edinburgh Theatre Festival; *Rosencrantz & Guildenstern Are Dead,* Queens Theatre, Hornchurch, England; *Revenge Tragedy,* Royal Shakespeare Theatre.

## Publications

**On LEVINE: articles**—"Designer Gets Right Under Skin" in *Toronto Star,* 3 June 1984; "Theatrical Designer Is Reaping Rave Reviews" in *Toronto Star,* 17 February 1985; "Designing a Life in the Theatre" in *Globe and Mail* (Toronto), 27 April 1985; "Theatre's Boy Wonder Is Creating a Sensation" in *Toronto Star,* 20 April 1986; "Bright Lights by Design" in *Saturday Night* (Toronto), July 1986; "An Artist Sets the Stage" in *Maclean's* (Toronto), 6 April 1987; "*Tectonic Plates:* Bridging the Continental Drift" in *Canadian Theatre Review,* Summer 1988; *Opera Canada,* Fall 1988; *Canadian Art* (Toronto), Fall 1988; "Flexibility, Communication Theatre Designer's Main Tools" in *Globe and Mail* (Toronto), 25

January 1990; "Meet the Super Mario Team" in *Toronto Star,* 14 February 1992; "A Midsummer's Night's Dream" in *Theatre Record* (London), 1-14 July 1992; *Country Life* (London), 23 July 1992; *Globe and Mail* (Toronto), 22 July 1993; "The Theatrical Designs of Michael Levine" in *Insite* (Toronto), September 1993; "Bloody Hell in a Double-Bill" in *Globe and Mail* (Toronto), 28 January 1993;

\*   \*   \*

Michael Levine designs on a freelance basis for international opera houses, ballet, and theatre companies. Born in Toronto in 1960, Levine attended a progressive private high school and credits his art teacher for his early interest in painting. At the Ontario College of Art in 1977, Levine had his first experience with set designing while helping friends with their theatrical productions. He became so enamored with the process of marrying fine art with three-dimensional, large-scale construction that he transferred to the Central College of Art and Design in London to study theater design. Graduating with honors in 1981, Levine believes that learning both the art of reading a text and the art of collaboration were the most valuable skills that he developed over the course of his education.

After graduation, Levine joined his teacher Philip Prowse, director of design at the Glasgow Citizens' Theatre, as assistant designer. Between 1981-1983 Levine gained invaluable hands-on experience contributing to the experimental company's bi-weekly, shoe-string productions.

At the age of 24, Levine was dubbed a *wunderkind* for his 1984 design for Eugene O'Neill's *Strange Interlude,* starring Glenda Jackson. The production played in London and New York, garnering both Olivier and Tony nominations. With this feather in his cap, Levine returned to Toronto, which has become his home base. He designs for the Canadian Opera House, the Shaw Festival at Niagara-on-the Lake, and the Tarragon Theatre, as well as for leading international companies, including the Welsh Opera House, the English National Opera, De Vlaamese Theatre in Antwerp, the Old Vic Theatre in London, and the Vienna Opera House.

Levine develops his designs through extensive research, long discussions with the director, repeated listening to the score, and careful textual readings. After thousands of sketches and countless three-dimensional models, he reduces the story to what he conceives as its bare essence. Typically, Levine identifies and then exaggerates one critical aspect of the piece to emphasize and unify the conceptual interpretation. The resulting productions are always provocative, and often controversial.

In a 1986 production of Wedekind's *Spring Awakening* for Toronto's CentreStage, Levine heightened the story's theme of adolescent oppression: filling the stage with a gigantic school chalkboard covered in scrawls of mathematical equations and Latin conjugations.

As in all experimental work, sometimes Levine's conceptualizing backfires and obscures rather than enhances the story's meaning. A notorious case in point is Levine's 1992 collaboration with the renowned Quebecois director Robert Lepage on Shakespeare's *A Midsummer Night's Dream* for England's National Theatre. Intending to conjure up a Jungian archetypal nightmare, director and designer radically departed from the text and set the story in a mud pool rather than an enchanted wood. For many critics the concept

went too far: there were complaints that the slipping and sloshing of the mud wrestling actors drowned out Shakespeare's poetry.

Though Levine has outgrown the name of boy-wonder, he continues to thrive on probing and disturbing interpretations of texts. You will never find Levine designing for an Andrew Lloyd Webber production. He shuns Disney-like historical verisimilitude in favor of minimalist abstraction.

—Elizabeth Crawford and Rachel Gotlieb

# LE WITT, Jan

British painter, illustrator, stage, and graphic designer

**Born:** Czestochowa, Poland, 3 April 1907; emigrated to Britain in 1937, naturalized, 1947. **Education:** Educated in Czestochowa until 1942; mainly self taught in design, Warsaw, from 1927. **Family:** Married Alina Prusicka in 1939. **Career:** Freelance designer, Warsaw, 1927-33; partner with George Him, in Le Witt-Him design practice, in Warsaw, 1933-37, and in London, 1937-54; designed for Sadler's Wells Ballet, Murano Glassworks, the Festival of Britain, Ministry of Information, Home Office, General Post Office, and others; independent painter, London, from 1955; fellow, International PEN Club, London, 1978. **Member:** Alliance Graphique Internationale, Paris, 1948; executive council member, Societe Europeene de Culture, Venice, from 1961. **Exhibitions:** Society of Fine Arts, Warsaw, 1930; Lund Humphries, London, 1934; Zwemmer Gallery, London, 1947, 1953; Tate Gallery, London, 1950, 1952; Hanover Gallery, London, 1951; Galleria San Marco, Rome, 1952; AAA Gallery, New York, 1954; Galleria Apollinaire, Milan, 1957; Grosvenor Gallery, London, 1961; Musée d'Antibes, 1965; Narodni Museum, Warsaw, 1967; Galleria d'Arte, Venice, 1970; *Second World War Posters,* Imperial War Museum, London, 1972; Fitzwilliam Museum, Cambridge, 1989. **Collections:** Musée National d'Art Moderne, Paris; National Museum, Warsaw; Musée d'Antibes; Halifax Museum and Art Gallery, Yorkshire; British Council, London; Contemporary Art Society, London. **Honors:** Gold Medal, Vienna, 1948; Gold Medal, Milan Triennale, 1954; honorary member, Centro Internazionale dell'Arte del Vetro, Venice. **Address:** 10 Highfield Avenue, Cambridge CB4 2AL, England.

## Publications

**By LE WITT: books**—(with George Him) *Locomotive,* London, 1937; (with George Him) *The Little Red Engine,* London, 1942; *Vegetabull,* London and New York, 1956; *A Necklace for Andromeda,* London, 1976.

**On LE WITT: books**—*British Achievement in Design* edited by Noel Carrington and Muriel Harris, London, 1946; *Posters: 50 Artists and Designers* edited by W. H. Allner, New York, 1952; *Jan Le Witt,* with texts by Pierre Emanuel, Herbert Read, and others, London, 1971; *Second World War Posters,* exhibition catalogue by Joseph Darracott and Belinda Loftus, London, 1972; *The Language of Graphics* by Edward Booth-Clibborn and Daniele Baroni, London, 1980.

*See* HIM, George

# LINDAU, Börge

Swedish interior and furniture designer

**Born:** Åhus, in 1932. **Education:** Studied at the School of Arts and Crafts, Göteborg, 1957-61. **Career:** Worked in an architect's office, Helsingborg, 1961-63; freelance designer, establishing Lindau and Lindekrantz design firm, with Bo Lindekrantz, in Helsingborg, from 1964; has designed principally for Lammhults Mekaniska AB, from 1965. **Exhibitions:** *Scandinavian Modern Design 1880-1980,* Cooper-Hewitt Museum, New York, 1982 (toured); *Contemporary Swedish Design,* Nationalmuseum, Stockholm, 1983 (toured); *The Lunning Prize,* Nationalmuseum, Stockholm, 1985; *Faces of Swedish Design,* IBM Gallery, New York, 1988 (toured). **Honors:** Lunning Prize, 1969; SID Society of Swedish Industrial Designers Prize, 1975. **Address:** Box 100, 296 Åhus, Sweden.

**Works** (with Bo Lindekrantz):

*Opal* stackable hook-on armchair, for Lammhults, 1964.
*Ritz* stackable armchair, for Lammhults, 1965.
*Royal* stackable chair, for Lammhults, 1966.
*Joker* nursery furniture, for Lammhults, 1966.
*S-70* stackable chairs and stools in tubular steel, for Lammhults, 1967.
*Peking* stackable armchair, for Lammhults, 1970.
*Hacken* sectional sofa, for Lammhults, 1970.
City Library interiors, Norrkoping, 1971.
*Director's Chair* in steel and canvas, for Lammhults, 1971.
*X-75* collapsible tubular steel chairs and tables, for Lammhults, 1972.
*Morris* office chair, for Lammhults, 1977.
*Duet 8* easy chair, for Lammhults, 1977.
*Armchair 88* hook-on chair in tubular steel, for Lammhults, 1982.
*Solo* club armchairs, for Lammhults, 1983.
*Trio* stackable armchair, for Lammhults, 1985.
*Planka* chair in plywood and perforated metal, for Lammhults, 1985.

**Publications**

On **LINDAU/LINDEKRANTZ: books**—*Konthantverk, Kontindustri, Design 1875-1975* by Dag Widman, Stockholm, 1975; *Scandinavian Modern Design 1880-1980* edited by David Revere McFadden, New York, 1982; *Contemporary Swedish Design,* exhibition catalogue by Monica Boman, Lennart Lindkvist, and others, Stockholm, 1983; *Den Svenska Formen* by Monica Boman and others, Stockholm, 1985; *The Lunning Prize,* exhibition catalogue edited by Helena Dahlback Lutteman and Mariaane Uggla, Stockholm, 1986; *Faces of Swedish Design,* exhibition catalogue edited by Monica Boman, Stockholm, 1988.

*See* LINDEKRANTZ, Bo

\*    \*    \*

L&L plus L equals a long and faithful (but not long-winded) success story involving two designers and a manufacturer.

L&L are Börge Lindau and Bo Lindekrantz. They first met in the late 1950s at the Gothenburg School of Arts and Crafts. They were in the same class, and claim that they were drawn to each other because they felt so old. They happened to be five years older than their classmates. Afterwards they continued on to the same architect's office in Helsingborg and later set up on their own.

Two representatives from Lammhults, the third L, walked in one day and asked the two young designers if they could design a chair made of metal which would suit university students. The company was thinking of adding to its product range by manufacturing furniture.

Börge and Bo grandly proposed a condition: that they be allowed to design two chairs. These were the *Ritz* and *Royal* named after two rural cafés near the small town of Lammhult, in the province of the Småland. The chairs became classics, and after 20 years are still among the best-selling models in the collection. Since those initial successes, a unique collaboration has developed between the designers and the manufacturer.

The major breakthrough for Lammhults and the designers came at the end of the 1960s, with the *S-70* collection: Bauhaus-inspired chairs, tables, and clothes hangers of strong, painted tubes and corduroy garments in gay colors. The *S-70* furniture became popular for public environments which required modernity, youth, and a personal style.

But Börge and Bo also wanted to reach the public at home. The *X-75* series of folding chairs and tables offered flexible interior design. The chairs can be folded into a "bicycle rack" to be taken out according to need. The model itself appears to be as old as the hills; it existed in the days of the Pharaohs, but Börge and Bo further developed it by radically changing the folding mechanism. In the *X-75* you can sit comfortably and tuck your feet under the chair, in contrast to older versions. The *X-75* has been greatly appreciated in public milieus as well—including museums—both as a seat and as a display object. At the beginning of the 1980s, Börge and Bo separated. After working in the same premises for over 20 years, they thought they had had enough. So Börge moved back to his childhood town of Åhus and Bo remained in Helsingborg. Since then they have remained like two partners in a happily separated marriage—where the separation works. They have continued to develop more intensely than ever. There is a sort of creative ping-pong competition going on between L&L and L—Börge, Bo, and Lammhults. The finals take place at the factory.

Börge and Bo like to regard themselves as redesigners. Their models are often inspired by some well-known classic. What makes them exciting is that they produce not merely an improvement, but an addition which is fresh and innovative.

One example is the rebirth of the club chair—first in the sectional sofa *The Hedge* in the early 1970s and later in the *Solo* family, which includes both sofas and armchairs. In an elegant way they reveal their source, yet the new form and function are a refined addition for the benefit of the user.

Börge and Bo have devoted themselves to several interesting experiments in the furniture and design. There have been sculptures, flexible tabletops with varying heights, adaptable chairs, and *The Plank*—a seat and debating point in the discussion on ergonomics and materials. They have spent a lot of time thinking about how to be flexible with color and decoration, and how to give rational series production a new direction.

For Börge and Bo, there has also been the question of linking the human desire to recline and relax with the wish for an individual product.

Börge has also continued on his own with his *Blue Station*—a small collection of chairs, tables, and lamps, all having a laminated ring of birch as a common denominator. This is an experiment in carrying out a consistent theme using the greatest variety of approaches without sacrificing esthetic demands and technical construction.

Bo has returned to wood with renewed force. He continues to refine the tradition further.

—Hedvig Hedqvist

## LINDEKRANTZ, Bo
Swedish interior and furniture designer

**Born:** Kottenburg, in 1932. **Education:** Studied at the School of Arts and Crafts, Göteborg, 1957-61. **Career:** Worked in an architect's office, Helsingborg, 1961-63; freelance designer, establishing Lindau and Lindekrantz design firm, with Borge Lindau, in Helsingborg, from 1964; has designed principally for Lammhults Mekaniska AB, from 1965. **Exhibitions:** *Scandinavian Modern Design 1880-1980,* Cooper-Hewitt Museum, New York, 1982 (toured); *Contemporary Swedish Design,* Nationalmuseum, Stockholm, 1983 (toured); *The Lunning Prize,* Nationalmuseum, Stockholm, 1986; *Faces of Swedish Design,* IBM Gallery, New York, 1988 (toured). **Honors:** Lunning Prize, 1969; SID Society of Swedish Industrial Designers Prize, 1975. **Address:** Kullagatan 40, 252 20 Helsingborg, Sweden.

*See* LINDAU, Borge

## LINDSTRAND, Vicke (Viktor Emanuel)
Swedish glass and ceramics designer

**Born:** Göteborg, 27 November 1904. **Education:** Studied at the Svensk Slöjdforenings Skola, Goteborg, 1924-27; also study-travels in France and Italy, 1933-37. **Family:** Married Svea Kristina Frisch in 1929 (divorced, 1945); son: Ola; married Marianne Lilliesköld in 1946. **Career:** Worked as a cartoonist and illustrator, for *Handelstidningen* newspaper, Göteborg, 1922-28; designer, with Edward Hald and Simon Gate, at Orrefors Glassworks, Sweden, 1928-41; artistic director, at Ekebybruk ceramics factory, Uppsala Ekeby, 1942-50; design director, at Kosta Glassworks, Sweden, 1950-73; also designed glass sculptures from 1964. **Exhibitions:** Milan Triennale, 1933, 1951, 1957; Paris International Exposition, 1937, 1951; World's Fair, New York, 1939; *Orrefors 1917-42,* Nationalmuseum, Stockholm, 1942; *Scandinavia: Ceramics and Glass in the Twentieth Century,* Victoria and Albert Museum, London, 1989. **Collections:** Nationalmuseum, Stockholm; Röhsska Konstslöjdmuseet, Goteborg; Smålands Museum, Växjö; Konsthantverkmuseet, Oslo; Museum für Kunst und Gewerbe, Hamburg; Musée du Louvre, Paris; Metropolitan Museum of Art, New York; British Museum, London; Victoria and Albert Museum, London. **Honors:** International Design Prize, New York, 1963; Litteris et Artibus Award, Stockholm, 1976. **Died:** Åhus, Sweden, 7 May 1983.

### Works

*Samson and the Lion* engraved bowl in green glass, for Orrefors, 1929.
*See No Evil* painted and etched vase in clear glass, for Orrefors, 1930.
*Crowded Skies* engraved vase in clear glass, for Orrefors, 1930.
*Peach* jug and tumbler in clear glass, for Orrefors, 1933.
*The Diver* engraved vase in clear and black glass, for Orrefors, 1934.
*Nude and Fish* engraved vase in clear and black glass, for Orrefors, 1934.
*Trees in Mist* vase in clear, white and black glass, for Kosta, 1950.
Bowl in clear and brown glass, for Kosta, 1953.
Bowl in clear glass with blue and brown stripes, for Kosta, 1954.
Vase in cut and sandblasted clear glass, for Kosta, 1954.
*Laplander with Reindeer* object in green glass, for Kosta, 1960.

### Publications

**On LINDSTRAND: books**—*Modern Glass* by Guillaume Janneau, London and New York, 1931; *Orrefors 1917-1942,* exhibition catalogue edited by Elisa Hald-Steenberg, Stockholm, 1942; *Modernt Svenskt Glass* edited by Gregor Pauisson, Stockholm, 1943; *The Beauty of Modern Glass* by R. Stennett-Wilson, London and New York, 1958; *Forma Sueca* by Ake Stavenlow and Ake H. Huldt, Stockholm, 1961; *Design in Sweden* by Lennart Lindkvist, Stockholm, 1972; *Scandinavian Design: Objects of a Life Style* by Eileene Harrison Beer, New York and Toronto, 1975; *Legend i Glas* by Lars Thor, Stockholm, 1982; *Twentieth Century Design: Glass* by Frederick Cooke, London, 1986; *Scandinavia: Ceramics and Glass in the Twentieth Century* by Jennifer Hawkins Opie, London, 1989.

## LITTELL, Ross
American artist and furniture and textile designer

**Born:** Los Angeles, California, 1924. **Education:** Studied with Kaminski at Art Center College of Design, Los Angeles, 1942; studied with Alexander Kostellow and Rowena Reed at Pratt Institute, Brooklyn, B.I.D., 1949; studied in Milan, Italy, under Fulbright Scholarship, 1957-1958. **Family:** Married Inger Klingenberg in 1960 (divorced 1986). **Career:** Partner, with Bill Katavolos and Douglas Kelley, KLK Design, New York City, 1949-55; designed "The New Furniture" collection; designer, in Copenhagen, 1955-67, in Milan, 1971-95, and in California, from 1995. **Exhibitions:** *The New Furniture* collection, Milan Triennale, 1954; American Pavilion, Brussels Worlds Fair, 1958; "Luminars" exhibit, Herman Miller showroom, New York City, 1969; "Luminars" and paper art pieces, Denmark, 1978-83; white on white embossed/debossed pieces, Illums Bolighus, Copenhagen, 1984; *Design 1935-1965, What Modern Was,* Le Musée des Arts Décoratifs de Montreal, New York, 1991 (toured); experimental veneer intarsia works, OK Harris Gallery, New York City, 1993. **Collections:** Museum of Modern Art, New York; Metropolitan Museum of Art, New York; Stuttgart Design Center Collection; Atelier, Die Neue Sammlung, Staatliches Museum für Angewandte Kunst, Munich; Vitra Design Museum,

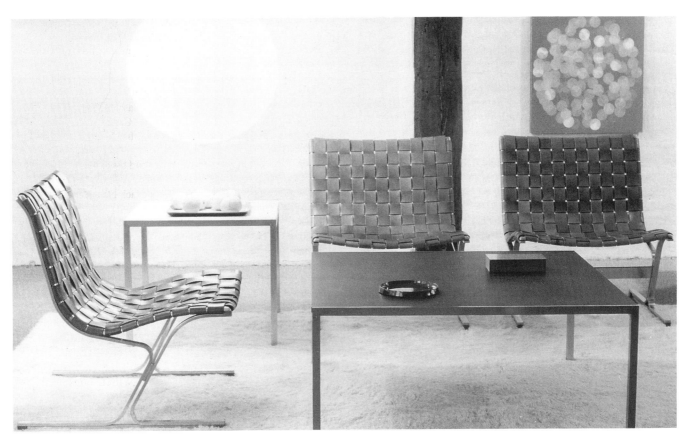

Ross Littell: Webbed leather seat and back low chair with chromed steel bar stock supports, and marble topped tables for I. C. F. De Padova, Milan, introduced in 1964

Weil am Rhein, Germany. **Honors:** First Prize, American Society of Interior Design, 1949, 1951, 1959; "Good Design" Award, Museum of Modern Art, New York, 1952; Illum's Prize, Illums Bolighus, 1966. **Address:** 1225 B East Cota Street, Santa Barbara, California 93103, U.S.A.

### Works

Furniture and showroom, for Laverne, New York City, 1949-55 (with KLK Design).
Textiles and wallpapers, for Laverne, 1949-55 (with KLK Design).
KLK furniture installation in lobby of the General Motors Technical Center, Warren, Michigan, 1956.
Textile print, for Anton Maix, New York City, 1956.
KLK Furniture installation in IBM showrooms, Los Angeles, 1957.
Textile prints, for Knoll International, New York City, 1957-59.
Textile prints and carpets, for Unika-Vaev, Copenhagen, 1960-65 (with Klingenberg).
Gift items, for Torben Ørskov (Form & Farve), Copenhagen, 1961.
Relief tiles, for Hasler Klinker, Copenhagen, 1963.
PLR chair and tables, for I.C.F. de Padova, Milan, 1964.
Textiles, for Kvadrat, Denmark, 1965-1980, and with Klingenberg from 1984.
Furniture, for Lorenzon, Udine, Italy, 1966.
Aluminum suspended dividers, for I.C.F. de Padova, Milan, 1968.
Corporate art, for Town Hall in Viborg, Denmark, 1972.

*Luar* table series, for I.C.F. de Padova, Milan, 1973.
Corporate art installations, for Mondadori building designed by Oscar Niemeyer, Milan, 1974.
Luminar commission, for the Sheik, Saudi Arabia, 1978.
Furniture, for Matteo Grassi, Mariano, Italy, 1984.
Furniture, for Atelier, Mariano, Italy, 1985.
Marble tables, for UP & UP, Massa, Italy, 1986.
Recycled paper gift items, for Arbos, Italy, 1993.

### Publications

**On LITTELL: books**—*Design 1935-1965, What Modern Was,* exhibition catalogue, New York, 1991; **articles**—*Living Architecture,* no. 8, 1988.

\*

In bridging the gap between design and art expression I've always tried to eliminate non-essentials. With regard to furniture, use materials with due respect for their inherent qualities, always stressing simplicity, that "less is more," going perhaps counter clockwise to current trends of "more is never enough." This was our KLK credo of the 1950s, including close partners Katavolos and Kelley, and like Eero Saarinen. We wanted to visually clean up the floor/scape with, in our case, our three-legged leather sling chair as part of "The New Furniture" Collection—embracing the use of combined noble materials, chrome steel, saddle leather, glass, and marble.

Yes, for me simplicity and elegance have been desired goals since the 1950s, goals which I strive to incorporate in both design and art expressions. Within the latter, "light" and its ever changing aspects have fascinated me as a medium available to all of us and encouraged the creation of art I named "Luminars."

—Ross Littell

*     *     *

From 1946 until 1949, when Ross Littell was attending the prestigious Pratt Institute, Mies van der Rohe, already 10 years in America, was constructing an impressive number of sky scrapers in Chicago. Hemingway had not yet written "The Old Man and the Sea," but Charles Eames had already begun his long collaboration with Herman Miller. Many European artists found refuge in America and had brought the basis of modern culture with them. In a few years things moved from the pomp of art-deco at Radio City Music hall by Raymond Head or William van Alen's Chrysler Building to an ascetic Bauhaus style with the drive-in Cantor restaurant in Indianapolis—a 50 meter wall of transparent glass suspended above the ground by gigantic steel beams.

At this point it was clear that it was time to turn the page and think of furniture in terms of these new spaces built with modern technology. In this direction Ross Littell's efforts have never been lacking. One could say that he has explored—by himself or with others—all the possibilities offered by such diverse materials as paper, ceramic, metal, leather, glass, cork, marble, and, above all, steel. Principles of light and refraction, translucency, illusion, and change were foremost in his thinking.

Each confrontation has brought forth objects of great simplicity, utility, and practicality and this is not chance. He simply knows how to observe. He observes things that no one else sees, a stone, the bark of a tree, the quality of light as it surrounds a subject. When he overcomes his timidity by offering you one of these wonders, there is no one else who can prepare such a gift in the pure Japanese tradition. Here we come to the complexity of his person. While living a monastic life, away from the world in his house with a thatched roof on the island of Aero in Denmark or set on the mountains over Lake Como reached by a steep path, he maintains strong work contacts and friendships throughout the world. He knows how to keep his distance, but at the same time he is the most affable work companion.

When he was 12 years old, living in Los Angeles above Silverlake across from the signature glass house and studio of Richard Neutra, there was an early awareness of what modern design stood for. Quite by chance the following year, a classmate, Gary Lovell, invited him to see his new house. This proved to be a renowned piece of architecture—the Lovell Health House in the Hollywood hills done by Richard Neutra a few years earlier. For Ross, this was an important milestone in his design development and dedication in the following years. In a photo probably taken before the Second World War one notes his elegant stride in New York City, moving surely on his way. In fact he found his way with an educated detachment, following a coherent and responsible way of life.

While his approach to his work is as complex as his vision of the world, his creations express simplicity and harmony. Where many designers have sought in vain to unite art and design, his insuperable *Luminar* tables made by ICF De Padova are stable and functional, covered with squares of stainless steel that form infinite designs due to their directionally brushed surface, like an optical

painting suspended above the ground; or his three legged sling chair of chrome and leather, designed with Kelley and Katavolos. His formations do not allow for extravagant gesture, provocation, or contradiction.

Littell moved undaunted through the postmodern epoch, coherent and steadfast. He resisted the highs and lows of trends that have influenced design. Just think of the exuberant 1950s and the extravagant biomorphic shapes of Vladimir Kagan and the years when George Nelson designed, with irony, the Marsh-Mellow sofa. In 1957, when Wright was finishing the Guggenheim Museum in New York, Ross left America and arrived in Ponti's Milan. Ponti had built the Pirelli building in 1954. In the euphoric climate that saw Zanuso, Frattini, Albini, Parisi working for the reconstruction and adapting to the growing industrial production, Ross Littell was also fascinated by Scandinavian furniture imported by only a few Italian companies. These pieces had the same qualities as his work: smooth, undramatic, classic forms, providing function with harmony.

Littell has sought these qualities with obstinacy, always looking for new solutions. It is useless to ask him to stop, to get his papers in order, or to ask for explanations of an old design—or worse—gather his pieces for a retrospective exhibit. He will say he doesn't have time or it isn't worth it; always modest, he avoids celebration.

—Jacques Touissant

# LOEWY, Raymond (Fernand)
American industrial designer

**Born:** Paris, France, 8 November 1893; emigrated to the United States in 1919, naturalized, 1938. **Education:** Attended University of Paris, 1910-12; Ecole de Lanneau, Paris, Dip. Ing., 1918. **Military Service:** Served in the French Army Corps of Engineers, as liaison officer with the American Expeditionary Force, 1914-18, Captain. **Family:** Married Jean Tomson in 1931 (divorced, 1945); married Viola Erickson in 1948; daughter: Laurence. **Career:** Freelance window display artist and fashion illustrator, working for *Vogue, Harper's Bazaar,* Macy's, Saks Fifth Avenue, and others, from 1919; industrial designer, establishing Raymond Loewy Associates, New York, from 1929; art director, Westinghouse Electric Company, 1929; also design consultant to Hupp Motor Company, Studebaker Motor Company, Coca-Cola, United Airlines, Shell Oil, Exxon Oil Company, International Business Machines, National Aeronautics and Space Administration, and others; established Compagnie de l'Esthétique Industrielle, Paris, 1952. **Member:** President, American Society of Industrial Designers, 1946, and French Chamber of Commerce of the United States, 1958; executive board member, Art Center College, Los Angeles; industrial design committee member, University of California, Los Angeles; vocational education board member, New York City Board of Education. **Exhibitions:** *An Exhibition for Modern Living,* Detroit Institute of Arts, 1949; *Le Design Francais,* Centre de Création Industrielle, Paris, 1971; *The Designs of Raymond Loewy,* Smithsonian Institution, Washington, D.C., 1975; *Raymond Loewy: Living in Space,* Sotheby's, London, 1981; *Design Since 1945,* Philadelphia Museum of Art, 1983; *The Machine Age in America,* Brooklyn Museum, New York, 1986. **Honors:** Interallied Medal, Croix de Guerre, and Grand Officier of the Legion d'Honneur, for military service in World War I; Gold Medal, Paris International

Exposition, 1937; Lord and Taylor Design Award, New York, 1938; Honorary Royal Designer for Industry, Royal Society of Arts, London, 1937; All-American Packaging Prize, Paris Exposition, 1939; *Sunday Times* 20th-Century Designer Award, London, 1969; Honorary Citizen of France, 1969; American Academy of Achievement Hall of Fame Award, 1978; American Society of Industrial Designers Distinguished Achievement Award, 1978; President's Award, France, 1980; ICSID Grand Prize, 1981. Honorary DFA: University of Cincinnati, 1956, Art Center College of Design, Los Angeles, 1970. Fellow, American Society of Interior Design, American Academy of Achievement, American Society of Industrial Designers. **Died:** Monte Carlo, 14 July 1986.

## Works

*Gestetner 466S* copying machine housing, for Gestetner Duplicating Machine Company, 1929.
*Hupmobile* streamlined car, for Hupp Motor Company, 1931-34.
*S-1* steam locomotive, for the Pennsylvania Railroad, 1933.
*Coldspot Super Six* refrigerator, for Sears, Roebuck and Company, 1934.
*International Harvester* "Farmall" tractor, for McCormick-Deering, 1940.
*Constellation* passenger aircraft interiors, for Lockheed, 1945.
*Scenicruiser* coach, for Greyhound Bus Company, 1946.
Streamlined radio receivers for Hallicrafter, 1947.
*Studebaker Starlight* coupe, for the Studebaker Motor Company, 1947.
Office interiors, for the Lever Brothers Building, New York, 1952.
*Studebaker Starliner* coupe, for the Studebaker Motor Company, 1953.
*2000* china coffee service, for Rosenthal Studio Line China, 1954.
*Studebaker Avanti* car, for the Studebaker Motor Company, 1961-62.
Logotype symbol, for the Exxon Oil Corporation, 1966.
Logotype symbol, for the Shell Oil Company, 1967.
*Skylab* interiors, for National Aeronautic and Space Administration, 1967-73.

## Publications

**By LOEWY: books**—*The Locomotive: Its Esthetics,* London, 1937; *Never Leave Well Enough Alone,* New York and Paris, 1951; *Industrial Design,* London and Woodstock, 1979.

**On LOEWY: books**—*Industrial Design: A Practical Guide* by Harold Van Doren, New York and London, 1940; *An Exhibition for Modern Living,* catalogue edited by A. H. Girard and W. D. Laurie, Detroit, 1949; *Packaging: An International Survey of Package Design,* edited by Walter Herdeg, Zurich, 1959; *L'Esthétique Industrielle* by Denis Huisman and Goerges Patrix, Paris, 1961; *An International Survey of Packaging* by Wim Crouwel and Kurt Weidemann, London, 1968; *Le Design Francais,* exhibition catalogue with introduction by Francois Mathey, Paris, 1971; *Streamline: Art and Design of the Forties* by Marc Arsenaux, San Francisco, 1975; *The Streamlined Decade* by Donald J. Bush, New York, 1975; *The Library of Motoring: The Designers* by L. J. K. Setright, London, 1976; *Twentieth Century Limited: Industrial Design in America 1925-1939* by Jeffrey L. Meikle, Philadelphia, 1979; *The Machine Age in America 1918-1941* by Richard Guy

Wilson and Dianne H. Pilgrim, New York, 1986; *New American Design* by Hugh Aldersley-Williams, New York, 1988; *The American Design Adventure 1940-1975* by Arthur J. Pulos, London and Cambridge, Massachusetts, 1988.

\*    \*    \*

To a degree unequaled by the names of any of the other founding fathers of industrial design, the name of Raymond Loewy radiates a charisma that has attracted public attention throughout the past half century. Loewy's flamboyant lifestyle included at various times country homes outside Paris, in southern France, Mexico, Long Island, and Palm Springs, as well as luxurious urban apartments in Manhattan and Paris. The worldwide image has been reinforced by his design offices not only in New York, Chicago, and Los Angeles, but also in London, Paris, San Juan, and São Paulo, among others.

This matter of image and style is important because—in combination with a keen business sense, a highly-developed imagination, and a rich design talent—it was an important element in generating a sense of excitement about, not only Raymond Loewy, but the new profession of industrial design itself.

Much has been written about the trial by fire the new profession underwent during the great Depression and how industrial design proved itself by demonstrating that in a shrinking market, the product "designed" by an industrial designer would win out over an otherwise similar and equal product. The office of Raymond Loewy provided more than its share of such demonstration cases—and did so with a flair that reflected credit on client, firm, and designer alike.

Loewy's design philosophy was not a deeply intellectual one. He summarized it with the acronym MAYA—most advanced, yet acceptable. The proliferation of clean, functional, and dynamic products that emerged from the Loewy offices throughout his long career provides testimony to his success in correctly making the prediction "most advanced, yet acceptable."

Examples of his designs that have become famous and that generated a public interest and acceptance far out of proportion to the company's relative size in the industry include: the 1947 *Studebaker Starlight* Coupe; the 1953 *Starliner Coupe*; the 1961 *Avanti*; the 1947 line of Hallicrafter radio receivers that conveyed a crisp precision far ahead of their time; the 1929 Gestetner duplicating machine; the 1934 Sears *Coldspot* refrigerator; and the S-I steam locomotive for the Pennsylvania Railroad. All were landmark designs that were extremely successful and influential in establishing higher design standards in their respective product areas.

It is difficult to measure precisely Loewy's impact on our contemporary environment, but it has certainly been a dynamic and significant one. His vitality and international influence were demonstrated by his being retained as a major industrial design consultant in the 1970s by the government of the Soviet Union—this as he entered his eighties!

—James M. Alexander

# LOGAN, Ian
British packaging and graphic designer

**Born:** Gloucester, 12 July 1939. **Education:** Studied art and design, at Bath Art School, Avon, 1952-55; studied textile design,

Ian Logan: Whittard of Chelsea coffee box designs, 1995. Courtesy of the Ian Logan Design Company

West of England College of Art, Bristol, 1959-61; Central School of Art and Design, London, NDD, 1964; studied at the Konstfackskolan, Stockholm, 1964-65. **Family:** Married Deborah Hugh-Jones in 1966 (divorced); children: Harriet and Barnaby. **Career:** Worked as a draughtsman for the Westinghouse Corporation, London, 1956-59; founder and principal, with other Central School graduates, of JRM Designs, London, 1966-70; founder/partner, of Ian Logan Associates, from 1968; president of Ian Logan Design Company, London, from 1972, and Ian Logan Wholesale-Export Company, London, 1975 (sold to French metal company, Massily, 1989); founder/partner, with Alan Colville, Ian Logan Group and International Graphics and Packaging group, London, from 1981; designed for the National Trust, Harrod's, Macy's, Boots, The Chemists, French Sugar Corporation, the Smithsonian Institution, Paraphernalia Alan Spiegelman, Fortnum & Mason, WH Smith, Whittard of Chelsea, Waitrose, OMK Furniture, Perrier, Buxton Mineral Water, and others; consultant, Woods of Windsor toiletries, from 1979, and Helenware Household Textiles, from 1982. Packaging juror, Royal College of Art London, 1982-83; chairman of the education committee, Design & Art Directors Association; governor, Guildhall University of London; visiting lecturer in textile design, Royal College of Art, London, and Hornsey College of Art, Middlesex. **Exhibitions:** Design Centre, London, 1981. **Collections:** Victoria and Albert Museum, London; Smithsonian Institution, Washington, D.C. **Honors:** *Observer* Design Award, London, 1978; fellow, Chartered Society of Designers, London, 1980; Silver nomination, UK Designers and Art Directors Association, 1995; Bronze Award, New York Festival, 1995. **Address:** 42 Charterhouse Square, London EC1M 6EU, England.

### Publications

**By LOGAN: books**—*Lost Glory,* London, 1976; (with Henry Nield) *Classy Chassy,* London, 1977; **articles**—*The Designer* (London), March 1981.

**On LOGAN: books**—*Design and Art Directors Annual,* London, 1980-83.

*

   Design in every visual aspect has always excited me, I suppose from when I was a small boy. Although I was trained as a textile designer, I very quickly realized that a textile was not very important on its own without an interior, and with the wrong interior and lighting effect, the textile furnishing would be stone dead.

I have always been excited by functional industrial design and layout, particularly that of military equipment, because it is usually designed for a function. The layout of fighter aircraft cockpits are a prime example of what I mean. The design of railway locomotives in America from the 1930s to the 1950s has also always influenced me, particularly the experiments in streamlining, some of which are totally stunning, e.g., the Rock Island Rockets of the 1950s. Also the displays of graphic images on American trains of this time show a freedom of style that, I think, has yet to be matched. Many, I believe, were designed by employees of the railway companies in competitions.

Early graphic images of airlines also stimulate me. I feel that any designer in any field should be totally aware of all things around him—from the latest space vehicle to the latest jacket designed by Giorgio Armani, from a drawing pen to the latest piece of furniture designed by Vico Magistretti.

—Ian Logan

\* \* \*

Ian Logan might be said to be a graphic designer who works in three as well as two dimensions. Images and colour, but images above all, are his stock in trade, and with a freedom characteristic of graphic designers, he regards humanity's creation and accumulation of an immense and endlessly various sign language, decade by decade, century by century, as being at his and our disposal. He sees a vast paintbox of images and styles which it would be wasteful not to use and to enjoy, but which cannot be used imaginatively without being extended and added to at the same time. A motif from Victorian times or the 1930s, for instance, reused today, at the very least finds itself transformed by its new context, quite apart from any transformation wrought upon it by the designer. What is wrong with "nostalgia" if nostalgia means, not vainly trying to escape into a past which has gone for ever, but enjoying and renewing what the past has bequeathed to us? This is the question with which Logan's artifacts rebuke the purist and the puritan.

Logan can get away with his joyful eclecticism because he specializes in the design of gifts and souvenirs, small things which would fail if they were not fun, and which would not be bought if they were not exquisitely tempting. A particular specialty, the manufacture of which he has helped to revive, is tinware—moneyboxes, biscuit tins, tea caddies, tin eggs, tin rulers—permanently useful, permanently decorative "packaging" which may come empty or with a first cargo of soap or sweets and which may itself be "packaged" in a distinctive point-of-sale display unit. Logan's products function dually: on the one hand to hold biscuits (or whatever), which they do splendidly, and on the other, to be enjoyed. Why should the concept of "functionalism" in design be tied to an unsmiling, humorless moral seriousness?

Logan is an important designer precisely because he has demonstrated that not only buildings and cars and furniture and washing machines can be well designed, but so also can the little things in our lives, if differently. He has moved into an area which other designers have chosen to ignore and which in consequence has been, and is, dominated by trash and he has shown that gifts and mementoes do not have to be outrageously expensive, or expensive at all, to be

desirable. In particular, his attitude toward the past—his refusal to see it either as something that has to be put away on its shelf and left to gather dust or a burden which must at all times weigh heavily upon us—has especially well equipped him to create souvenirs for museums and, for instance, for the National Trust in England, which has set high standards in this field with the assistance of Logan, among others.

—Philip Pacey

# LOIS, George (Harry)

American graphic designer

**Born:** The Bronx, New York, 26 June 1931. **Education:** Studied at the High School of Music and Art, New York, 1945-49; attended Pratt Institute, Brooklyn New York, 1949-50. **Military Service:** Served in the United States Army, in Korea, 1951-53, Private 1st Class. **Family:** Married Rosemary Lewandowski in 1951; children: Luke. **Career:** Designer, at Reba Sochis, 1951, and CBS-TV, New York, 1954-56; art director, at Sudler and Hennessey, 1956-57, and at Doyle Dane Bernbach, New York, 1958-59; executive vice-president and creative director, of Papert Koenig Lois, New York, 1960-67; chairman and creative director, of Lois Holland Callaway, New York, from 1967, then president of Creamer Lois, and chairman and creative director of Lois Pitts Gershon, New York. Columnist, *Art Direction* magazine, 1961-63, and *Adweek,* New York, 1980-82. President, Art Directors Club of New York, 1972-73. **Collections:** Museum of Modern Art, New York; Cooper-Hewitt Museum, New York. **Honors:** Alumni Award, High School of Music and Art, New York, and Pratt Institute, Brooklyn; Art Director of the Year Award, New York, 1963; Art Directors Hall of Fame Award, New York, 1978; Creative Hall of Fame Award, New York, 1984. Honorary DFA, Pratt Institute, Brooklyn, 1982. **Address:** Lois/GGK, 650 Fifth Avenue, New York, New York 10019, U.S.A.

## Publications

**By LOIS: books**—(with Bill Pitts) *George Be Careful,* New York, 1972; (with Bill Pitts) *The Art of Advertising,* New York, 1977; *The Dictionary of Visual Language,* New York, 1980; **articles**—*Photo/Design* (New York), August/September 1984; *Madison Avenue* (New York), November 1985; *Backstage* (New York), 12 October 1988.

**On LOIS: books**—*Advertising Directions* edited by Edward M. Gottschall and Arthur Hawkins, New York, 1959; *Typography* by Aaron Burns, New York, 1961; *The Language of Graphics* by Edward Booth-Clibborn and Daniele Baroni, London, 1980; *The Design Concept* by Allen Hurlburt, New York, 1981; *A History of Graphic Design* by Philip B. Meggs, New York, 1983; *Typographic Design: Form and Communication* by Rob Carter, Ben Day, and Meggs, New York, 1985.

\*

Any attempt to understand the art of advertising as a serious expression of a man's creative originality is usually overwhelmed by controversy over morality and ethics. We tend to equate art with virtue and commerce with sin. According to many critics who try to understand its massive impact on modern living, advertising is a twentieth-century love-potion; it arouses wants beyond means, it invites extreme consumption, and it conjures a material paradise as life's goal.

It is not easy to explain the complexity of the ethos that inspires my life of creating ideas for selling. Since I was a youngster in public school, I lived to draw, design, and rearrange things. I knew I was going to be an *artist.* When I went to a specialized high school—the High School of Music and Art—I could draw better, design better, sculpt better, paint better, and do better in history of art courses than anyone in the school. But my special fascination was with that art that was expected to persuade, to sell. Like no other art I was studying, it required a cause-and-effect connection, or it simply couldn't work.

In high school, I worshipped the paintings of Stuart Davis, with his floating words jammed between objects and images, but the spontaneity of a Cassandre poster seemed even more thrilling by the merging of words and images into a wholly new language. There were more hints of this new way of communicating in the work of Paul Rand, who struck out boldly during the 1940s by visualizing copy in an individualistic manner. At 16, I started to get more of a kick out of listening to Cassandre and Rand talk to me than I did from listening to Picasso, Léger, O'Keeffe, or Davis. I knew I was hooked.

From the role of artisan, craftsman, or designer, the art director of our media age has come a distance, and I hope I've played a part in shoving him into modern times. An art director must be a communicator, or he's simply someone who rearranges elements in a layout or design. An art director must be someone who treats words with the same reverence that he accords graphics because the verbal and visual elements of modern communication are as indivisible as words and music are in song. In retrospect, the pioneering of Paul Rand was an almost primeval advance, for he dealt, in the final analysis, with words and themes that were fragments of language related to him by copy-writers, rather than with fully integrated visual/verbal concepts.

Talking to people on a page or in a television commercial requires what I call "street talk." It has nothing to do with literature, other than using today's language. Art and words are merely tools for communicating. But all the tools in the world are meaningless without an essential idea—an artist, or advertising man, or doctor, or lawyer, or electrician, or factory worker, without an idea is unarmed. When the original idea springs out of a communicator's head and intuitions, the mystical and artful blending—or even juxtaposition—of concept, image, words, and art can lead to magic, where one and one can indeed be three.

I have had a lot of breaks in my life—including being raised in a hard-working Greek family and marrying the right woman—but three people recognized my talent and led me to what I do today. They are my public school art teacher, Miss Engle, my design teacher at Pratt Institute, Hershel Levit, and my first boss, Reba Sochis. After working for Reba Sochis and then for Bill Golden at CBS, I plunged into the mediocrity of the commercial world and got myself a reputation as the *enfant terrible* of advertising. I'm sure I deserved it, and I'm just as sure that without fighting for my work every second of my life, my work would be just as dull and uninspired as most of the so-called communications in the world—the bland leading the bland. To produce work I could be proud of, I've had to shove, push, cajole, persuade, wheedle, exaggerate, flatter,

manipulate, be obnoxious, occasionally lie, and always *sell.* And with all those lucky breaks of mother and father, teachers, wife and sons, and first jobs, I still believe a person decides his own fate, that he ordains what kind of work he wants to produce. He can decide that no client can make him run a bad ad! A client could kill and kill and kill what you think is right for him—the Abominable No-man—but he can't make you run bad work. (Your choice is to fight back with better work, or find better clients.)

Creative people in our business all speak of their "great ads" that remain on tissue paper in their dark file drawers. I say that you never did the job if you didn't sell it to the client. The accurate measure of a human being is what he actually gets done. In my life, I can't imagine any taste worse than the taste of sour grapes.

A work of art derives its identity from its visibility and from the response it evokes in others. I spend my spare moments drinking in that art created by generations of artists who have been the antennae of human sensibility—artists who understood that art of the past, but who broke with it according to the needs of their time. I see my own role as precisely that of an artist. But my kind of art has nothing to do with putting images on canvas. My concern is with creating images that catch people's eyes, penetrate their minds, warm their hearts, and cause them to act.

—George Lois

\*   \*   \*

Before he was 30, George Lois had created the first advertising agency headed by an art director. With his 15-hour-a-day energy, he invented advertising outrageous enough not to forget. Lois's humor in advertising, as evident in the work of more than 20 years as creative director of his agencies, is equally matched by an ability to simplify the message and sell the idea.

The notion that art directors could be successful businessmen was a revelation for the nature of the industry in the early 1960s as George and his associates startled the New York advertising community with a quality and visual brashness not before seen. But this advertising worked. Lois's accurate perception of the man-on-the-street within the American culture is a consistent element of his advertising fabric and strategy.

Visually recalling the spirit of film characters from his early childhood, Lois has often integrated the likes of Laurel and Hardy and the Marx brothers into television spot commercials in order to sell products through humor and appeal to the cinematic past. His humor, much like Lou Dorfsman's, is aimed at Everyman, while perhaps slightly chiding our culture and myths.

Whether in print ads or filmed spots for television, Lois's acuity for advertising is evident in an individuality of form and message, as seen in ideas ranging from caveman as businessman using a word processor, to Frankenstein combing a beautiful head of hair for a men's hair-spray. His use of celebrities and star athletes set a trend in American advertising, and particularly influential was the manner in which he developed graphic and conceptual ideas as the art director for the covers of *Esquire* for a decade. Often incorporating the photographic skills of Carl Fisher, realistic, often humorous ideas reflecting the nature and spirit of the times candidly challenged the consumer to buy the magazine. To Lois, it was nothing more than effective package design.

A strong belief that you have to love what you are doing, confidence in himself, and the desire to get things done and to sell characterize Lois personally as man and art director. His advertising energies are balanced by a supportive artist-painter wife and a collection of ancient and tribal masks, from the Pacific and elsewhere, considered to be one of the finest collections in New York.

—Michael Robert Soluri

# LONG, William Ivey
American costume designer

**Career:** Costume designer, Yale Repertory Theatre, New Haven, Connecticut, 1973-75, (and set designer) P.A.F. Playhouse, Huntington Station, New York, 1977-79, Arena Stage, Washington, D.C., 1978-79, American Repertory Theatre, Cambridge, Massachusetts, 1979, Goodman Theatre, Chicago, Illinois, 1981-82, Long Wharf Theatre, New Haven, 1983-84, and with the Paul Taylor Dance Company. **Honors:** Joseph Maharam Award, 1982; Antoinette Perry (Tony) Award, 1982, 1992, and nomination, 1989; Drama Desk Award, 1982, 1989, 1992; Obie Award for Outstanding Achievement, 1991; Outer Critics Circle Award, 1992; Dora Award, 1994; **Address:** 34 West 10th St., New York, New York 10011, U.S.A.

## Works

Stage costume design credits include—*The Wonderful O!,* Carolina Repertory Company, 1972; (and scenery) *Epiphanies,* University Theatre, Yale School of Drama, New Haven, Connecticut, 1971; *Mass,* Europe, 1973; (and scenery) *The Tempest,* North Carolina Dance Theatre, 1974; (and scenery) *Geography of a Horse Dreamer,* Yale Repertory Theatre, 1974; (and scenery) *An Evening with Dead Essex,* Yale Repertory Theatre, 1974; (and scenery) *Twelfth Night,* Yale School of Drama, 1974; *Idiots Karamazov,* Yale Repertory Theatre, 1974; (and scenery) *Scrontch,* Theatre at Noon/St. Peter's Church, New York, 1975; *Two Small Bodies* and *Earth-Worms,* Playwrights Horizons, New York, 1977; *The Killing of Yablonski,* P.A.F. Playhouse, Huntington Station, New York, 1978; (and scenery) *Hancock's Last Half Hour* and *The Gold Standard,* P.A.F. Playhouse, 1978; *Conjuring an Event,* American Place Theatre, New York, 1978; *The Vienna Notes,* Playwrights Horizons, 1979; *Jungle Coup,* Playwrights Horizons, 1979; *The Inspector General,* Circle in the Square, New York, 1979; *Altar Boys,* Theatre Four, New York, 1979; *The 1940's Radio Hour,* St. James Theatre, New York, 1979; *Gossip,* P.A.F. Playhouse, 1979; *Taming of the Shrew,* Wolftrap, Vienna, Virginia, 1979; *Postcard from Morocco,* Terrace Theatre, Kennedy Center, 1979; *The Impossible H.L. Mencken,* American Place Theatre, 1979, 1980; *Passione,* Playwrights Horizons, then Morosco Theatre, New York, 1980; *Johnny on a Spot,* Brooklyn Academy of Music, Brooklyn, New York, 1980; *True West,* New York Shakespeare Festival (NYSF), Public Theatre, New York, 1980; *Mass Appeal,* Manhattan Theatre Club, New York, 1980, then Booth Theatre, New York, 1981; *A Midsummer Night's Dream,* Alaska Repertory Theatre, Anchorage/Fairbanks, Alaska, 1981; *The Actor's Nightmare* and *Sister Mary Ignatius Explains It All for You* (double bill), Playwrights Horizons, 1981; *Hunting Scenes from Lower Bavaria,* Manhattan Theatre Club, 1981; *Twelve Dreams,* NYSF, Public Theatre, 1981; *The Front Page,* Goodman Theatre, New York, 1981; *Nine,* 46th Street Theatre,

New York, 1982; *Poor Little Lambs,* Theatre at St. Peter's Church, New York, 1982; *The Lady and the Clarinet,* Lucille Lortel Theatre, New York, 1983; *American Passion,* Joyce Theater, New York, 1983; *Equinox,* Paul Taylor Dance Company, 1983; *Not Quite Jerusalem,* Long Wharf Theatre, New Haven, 1983; *The Tap Dance Kid,* Broadhurst Theatre, New York, 1983, then Minskoff Theatre, New York, and toured the United States, 1984; *Play Memory,* Longacre Theatre, New York, 1984; *End of the World,* Music Box Theatre, New York, 1984; *Nine,* Opera House, Kennedy Center for the Performing Arts, Washington, D.C., and toured the United States, 1984; *Hey Ma ... Kaye Ballard,* Promenade Theatre, New York, 1984; *After the Fall,* Playhouse 91, New York, 1984; *Byzantium,* Paul Taylor Dance Company, 1984; *Roses,* Paul Taylor Dance Company, 1985; *A Broadway Baby,* Goodspeed Opera House, East Haddam, Connecticut, 1985; *The Marriage of Bette and Boo,* NYSF, Public Theatre, 1985; *One Man Band,* South Street Theatre, New York, 1985; *Dream Against Day,* Parsons Dance Company, 1985; *Threshold,* Parsons Dance Company, 1985; *Ballare,* Twyla Tharp, 1986; *Principia Scriptoriae,* Manhattan Theatre Club, 1986; *A Quiet Place* and *Trouble in Tahiti,* Vienna Staatsoper, Vienna, Austria, Houston Grand Opera, Texas, and Kennedy Center, New York, 1986; *Hamlet,* NYSF, Public Theatre, 1986; *Hamletmachine,* New York University, 1986; *Woyzek,* Welsh National Opera, 1986; *Smile,* Lunt-Fontanne Theatre, New York, 1986; *Sleight of Hand,* Cort Theatre, New York, 1987; *Laughing Wild,* Playwrights Horizons, 1987; *Kith and Kin,* Paul Taylor Dance Company, 1987; *Around the Corner,* Parsons Dance Company, 1987; *Linton,* Parsons Dance Company, 1987; *Scrutiny,* Parsons Dance Company, 1987; *Elysian Fields,* Parsons Dance Company, 1988; *Danbury Mix,* Paul Taylor Dance Company, 1988; *Barber Violin Concerto,* New York Ballet, 1988; *Wenceslas Square,* NYSF, Public Theatre, 1988; *Mail,* Music Box Theatre, 1988; *Italian American Reconciliation,* Manhattan Theatre Club, 1988; *Ask Me Again,* American Playhouse, 1988; *Together Again for the First Time,* Kaufman Theatre, 1989; *Lend Me a Tenor,* Royale Theatre, New York, 1989; *Eleemosynary,* Manhattan Theatre Club, 1989; *Welcome to the Club,* Music Box Theatre, 1989; *Carnival,* Cleveland Playhouse, Ohio, 1989; *Siegfried and Roy at The Mirage,* Mirage Hotel, Las Vegas, 1989; *Six Degrees of Separation,* Lincoln Center Theatre/Newhouse, 1990; *Abduction from the Seraglio,* San Francisco Opera, California, 1990; *Private Lives,* National Theatre, 1991; *Assassins,* Playwrights Horizons, 1991; *The Cutting Edge,* Toronto, Ontario, Canada, 1991; *The Homecoming,* Roundabout Theatre, 1991; *Crazy for You,* National Theatre/Shubert Theatre, 1992; *Guys and Dolls,* Martin-Beck Theatre, 1992; *Face Value,* Court Theatre, 1993; *DIFFA/A Demand Performance,* New York State Theatre, 1993; *Life with Mikey,* Toronto, 1993; *Laughter on the 23rd Floor,* Richard Rodgers Theatre, 1993; *Picnic,* Roundabout Theatre, 1994.

Television costume design credits include—*The 1985 Miss Universe Pageant,* CBS, 1985; *The 1988 Miss Universe Pageant,* CBS, 1988; *Miss Teen U.S.A.,* CBS, 1988; "Paul Taylor: Roses and Last Look," *Great Performances,* PBS, 1988; "Ask Me Again," *American Playhouse,* PBS, 1989..

Also designer of costumes for—The Pointer Sisters, Caesars Palace, Las Vegas, Nevada, 1986-89; Mick Jagger, Rolling Stones *Steel Wheels* tour, 1989; Patti LaBelle as the "Acid Queen" in *Tommy,* by The Who, 1989.

\*     \*     \*

**William Ivey Long: costumes for *Guys and Dolls*, 1992**

William Ivey Long designs with an elegance and theatricality that evokes a bygone era of theatre in which actors were expected to have a sense of sartorial style even in serious drama, and theatre audiences expected luxurious visual entertainment. Few contemporary costume designers equal Long's sheer theatricality, which itself seems to be an extension of his ebullient personality. His design credits range from the elegance of *Nine* and the flash and exuberant fun of *Crazy for You,* to the contemporary urban stylishness of *Six Degrees of Separation,* to the pure, unadulterated glitz and glamour of Las Vegas in *Siegfried and Roy,* to the surprising grittiness of *Picnic.* The latter, a 1994 revival of the 1953 William Inge play which is set in drab middle America, seems, at first, out of character for Long, but in a sense it provides an insight into his work: for all the stylishness and glamour, he is designing a character with tangible connections to the real world.

Long is fascinated with people and he seems to see the characters in a play as living individuals who are made understandable and accessible to an audience with his help. In the revival of *Guys and Dolls,* for instance, he noted that Tony Walton "created Runyonland, and I peopled it." He was not merely designing costumes but the inhabitants of a world. For Long, the quality of the people—the characters—is revealed to the audience through color, line, texture, draping, and light. In this context there is no such thing as an uninteresting character. That is why characters such as Madge or Flo from *Picnic* could possess theatricality in Long's design despite their lack of elegance. These characters may not have the flair of the showgirls in *Crazy for You* or the glamour of pop stars Mick Jagger, Patti LaBelle, or the Pointer Sisters—all of whom Long has costumed—but they have souls which can be expressively enhanced and even created by the subtleties of their dress in the context of a particular setting.

Just as Chekhov can write about bored characters who are anything but boring, Long can create "drab" characters who are visually astonishing. This derives, in part, from his meticulous attention to accessories. He has stated that hats and shoes are the most important costume elements. He is also concerned with every minute detail down to the amount of glitter or the number of buttons on a costume.

Long derives inspiration from the set designer's color schemes, from architectural details (the costumes for *Crazy for You* contain art deco and Pueblo motifs), and fashion. Though Long sees each characters as an individual, he is careful to create them as part of an ensemble in which each must fit with the other, as well as the decor, and the text. Looking at the collage boards of thumbnail sketches that Long creates as part of his process, one sees a rhythmic parade of color and forms that will translate into a powerful—if sometimes subliminal—shaping of audience perceptions.

—Arnold Aronson

# LOQUASTO, Santo

American stage and film designer

**Born:** Wilkes Barre, Pennsylvania, 26 July 1944. **Education:** Studied at King's College, Wilkes Barre, and at Yale University, New Haven, Connecticut, MFA, 1969. **Career:** Assistant, Williamstown Theatre Festival, Massachusetts, 1965-74; resident designer, Yale Repertory Theatre, New Haven Connecticut, 1969-72, and Kreeger Theatre, Arena Stage, Washington, D.C., from 1971; principal designer, New York Shakespeare Festival, and Twyla Tharp Dance

Foundation, New York, from 1971; designed for the Tyrone Guthrie Theatre, Minneapolis, the San Diego Opera, California, the Opera Society of Washington D.C., and the San Francisco Spring Opera. **Member:** United Scenic Artists. **Honors:** Drama Desk Award, New York, 1972, 1977; *Variety* New York Drama Critics Award, 1972; Antoinette Perry Award, New York, 1973, 1977, 1990; *Village Voice* Obie Award, New York, 1975; Joseph Maharam Award, New York, 1977. **Address:** c/o United Scenic Artists, 1540 Broadway, New York, New York 10036. U.S.A.

## Works

Stage productions include—*Push Comes to Shove and Other Dances,* American Ballet Theatre, New York, 1967; *Concerto,* American Ballet Theatre, 1967; *The Hostage,* Hartford Stage Company, Connecticut, 1968; *The Rose Tattoo,* Hartford Stage Company, 1968; *Tiny Alice,* Long Wharf Theatre, New Haven, Connecticut, 1968; *The Bacchae,* Yale Repertory Theatre, 1969; *The Waltz Invention,* Hartford Stage Company, 1969; *The Homecoming,* Hartford Stage Company, 1969; *The Farce of Scapin,* Hartford Stage Company, 1969; *Narrow Road to the Deep North,* Charles Playhouse, Boston, 1969; *Tartuffe,* Williamstown Theatre Festival, Massachusetts, 1969; *Hedda Gabler,* Williamstown Theatre Festival, 1969; *Rosencrantz and Guildenstern Are Dead,* Williamstown Theatre Festival, 1969; *The Skin of Our Teeth,* Long Wharf Theatre, 1970; *A Day in the Death of Joe Egg,* Hartford Stage Company, 1970; *Misalliance,* Hartford Stage Company, 1970; *The Trial of A. Lincoln,* Hartford Stage Company, 1970; *Anything Goes,* Hartford Stage Company, 1970; *Rosencrantz and Guildenstern Are Dead,* Hartford Stage Company, 1970; *Ring 'round the Moon,* Hartford Stage Company, 1970; *Three Philip Roth Stories,* Yale Repertory Theatre, 1970; *Cops and Horrors,* Yale Repertory Theatre, 1970; *The Revenger's Tragedy,* Yale Repertory Theatre, 1970; *The Story Theatre,* Yale Repertory Theatre, 1970; *The Unseen Hand,* Astor Place Theatre, New York, 1970; *Forensic and the Navigators,* Astor Place Theatre, 1970; *The Little Mahagonny,* Yale Repertory Theatre, 1971; *Sticks and Bones,* Public Theatre, New York, 1971; *The Seven Deadly Sins,* Yale Repertory Theatre, 1971; *A Gun Play,* Hartford Stage Company, 1971; *A Long Day's Journey into Night,* Hartford Stage Company, 1971; *Henry V,* Hartford Stage Company, 1971; *Wipe-Out Games,* Arena Stage, Washington, D.C., 1971; *Pantagleize,* Arena Stage, 1971; *The Sign in Sidney Brustein's Window,* Arena Stage, 1971; *Sticks and Bones,* John Golden Theatre, New York, 1972; *That Championship Season,* Public Theatre, 1972; *The House of Blue Leaves,* Arena Stage, 1972; *Uptight,* Arena Stage, 1972; *Old Times,* Mark Taper Forum, Los Angeles, 1972; *The Secret Affairs of Mildred Wild,* Ambassador Theatre, New York, 1972; *Sunset,* Chelsea Theatre Center, New York, 1972; *A Public Prosecutor Is Sick of It All,* Arena Stage, 1973; *Boom Boom Room,* Vivian Beaumont Theatre, New York, 1973; *La Dafne,* Spoleto Festival, Italy, 1973; *Siamese Connections,* Public Theatre, 1973; *The Orphan,* Public Theatre, 1973; *As You Like It,* Delacorte Theatre, New York, 1973; *King Lear,* Delacorte Theatre, 1973; *The Tempest,* Mitzi Newhouse Theatre, New York, 1974; *King Richard III,* Mitzi Newhouse Theatre, 1974; *Macbeth,* Mitzi Newhouse Theatre, 1974; *What the Wine Sellers Buy,* Vivian Beaumont Theatre, 1974; *Mert and Phil,* Vivian Beaumont Theatre, 1974; *The Dance of Death* Vivian Beaumont Theatre, 1974; *Pericles, Prince of Tyre,*

Delacorte Theatre, 1974; *The Merry Wives of Windsor,* Delacorte Theatre, 1974; *That Championship Season,* Garrick Theatre, London, 1974; *The Cherry Orchard,* Hartford Stage Company, 1974; *Sephardic Song,* American Ballet Theatre, 1974; *A Midsummer Night's Dream,* Mitzi Newhouse Theatre, 1975; *A Doll's House,* Vivian Beaumont Theatre, 1975; *Hamlet,* Vivian Beaumont Theatre, 1975; *The Comedy of Errors,* Delacorte Theatre, 1975; *Kennedy's Children* John Golden Theatre, New York, 1975; *Murderer Among Friends,* Biltmore Theatre, New York, 1975; *Legend,* Ethel Barrymore Theatre, New York, 1976; *Measure for Measure,* Delacorte Theatre, 1976; *The Glass Menagerie,* Hartford Stage Company, 1976, 1983; *Landscape of the Body,* Public Theatre, 1977; *Agamemnon,* Vivian Beaumont Theatre, 1977; *The Cherry Orchard,* Vivian Beaumont Theatre, 1977; *Miss Margarida's Way,* Ambassador Theatre, 1977; *Golda,* Morosco Theatre, New York, 1977; *American Buffalo,* Ethel Barrymore Theatre, 1977; *The Lower Depths,* Arena Stage, 1977; *Heartbreak House,* Arena Stage, 1977; *The Mighty Gents,* Ambassador Theatre, 1978; *Curse of the Starving Class,* Public Theatre, 1978; *Don Quixote,* American Ballet Theatre, 1978; *The Play's the Thing,* Brooklyn Academy of Music, 1978; *Ice Dancing,* Felt Forum, New York, 1978; *Stop the World—I Want to Get Off,* New York State Theatre, 1978; *King of Hearts,* Minskoff Theatre, New York, 1978; *Sarava,* Broadway Theatre, New York, 1979; *Bent,* New Apollo Theatre, New York, 1979; *The Goodbye People,* Belasco Theatre, New York, 1979; *Ramonda,* American Ballet Theatre, 1980; *The Member of the Wedding,* Hartford Stage Company, 1980; *The Suicide,* Academy Theatre, 1980; *The Floating Light Bulb,* Vivian Beaumont Theatre, 1981; *Field, Chair, and Mountain,* American Ballet Theatre, 1981; *Theme and Variations,* American Ballet Theatre, 1981; *A Midsummer Night's Dream,* Brooklyn Academy of Music, 1981; *Crossing Niagara,* Manhattan Theatre Club, New York, 1981; *Short Stories,* Los Angeles Music Center, 1981; *The Tempest,* Tyrone Guthrie Theatre, Minneapolis, 1982; *Happily Ever After,* Joffrey Ballet, New York, 1982; *Gardenia,* Manhattan Theatre Club, 1982; *The Wake of Jamey Foster,* Eugene O'Neill Theatre, New York, 1982; *Richard III,* Delacorte Theatre, 1983; *The Three Sisters,* Manhattan Theatre Club, 1983; *Little Malcolm and His Struggle Against the Eunuchs,* Yale Experimental Theatre, 1983; *Orgasmo Adulto Escapes from the Zoo,* Public Theatre, 1983; *America Kicks Up its Heels,* Playwrights Horizons, New York, 1983; *Uncle Vanya,* La Mama Annex Theatre, New York, 1983; *In Trousers,* Promenade Theatre, New York, 1985; *Virginia,* Public Theatre, 1985; *California Dog Fight,* Manhattan Theatre Club, 1985; *Singin' in the Rain,* Gershwin Theatre, New York, 1985; *Café Crown,* 1989; *Jake's Women,* 1992; *The Rose Tattoo,* Circle in the Square Theater, New York, 1995.

Film designs include—*Stop the World—I Want to Get off* (Saville), 1979; *Simon* (Brickman), 1980; *Stardust Memories* (Allen), 1980; *So Fine* (A. Bergman), 1981; *The Fan* (Bianchi), 1981; *A Midsummer Night's Sex Comedy* (Allen), 1982; *Zelig* (Allen), 1983; *Falling in Love* (Grosbard), 1984; *Desperately Seeking Susan* (Seidelman), 1985; *Radio Days* (Allen), 1986; *September* (Allen), 1987; *Bright Lights, Big City* (Bridges), 1988; *Big,* 1988; *Shadows and Fog* (Allen), 1992.

**Publications**

On LOQUASTO: articles—*Newsweek* (New York), March 1977; *People Weekly* (Chicago), 17 November 1980; *Theatre Design and Technology* (Charlottesville), Fall 1981; *Chicago Tribune,* 26 March 1995, 30 March 1995.

\*     \*     \*

Santo Loquasto is the logical heir to the tradition of American stage design that began with the simplification and abstraction of the New Stagecraft in the 1920s, and the uses of textural materials and emblematic design that grew popular under Boris Aronson Ming Cho Lee in the 1950s and 1960s. An overview of Loquasto's work reveals the use of rough wood, erosion cloth, metal tubing, and other textural and constructivist elements typical of the past few decades. In this, the influence of Lee is clearly evident, although Loquasto denies any intentional copying. His sets also display a strong use of vertical and horizontal lines in seeming opposition to the more common practice of asymmetry practiced by many designers.

A frequent Loquasto trademark in realistic sets is the use of "clutter." *American Buffalo* (1977), set in a junk shop, is the extreme example, but clutter occurs in many other designs as well. Loquasto states that it is not simply a thematic or decorative device but is there to break the stark, almost classic angularity of his sets. He uses texture to offset linearity. Loquasto considers himself a sculptural designer and, more than most other contemporary designers, he creates a strongly three-dimensional sense of space on the stage rather than a pictorial setting. This is a result of doing much of his work in arena and thrust spaces which, he says, force you to "push action forward and deal with space sculpturally."

Loquasto sees design as a unifying force in the production. The setting is the visual element that holds the production together through time. In fact, his sets have often helped to focus otherwise disjointed plays such as *Bent* (1982), or *Savara* (1978). Recently, like several other designers, he has begun to incorporate moving parts into his settings—not so much for spectacle, although this is important, as for their ability to alter and sculpt space fluidly. The moving back wall of *The Suicide* (1980), for instance, altered the space of the stage with both visual and psychological effect.

Loquasto has emerged as one of the best designers for the purpose of expressing subtleties of the play through setting, for creating and manipulating space and mood, and for deft use of color and texture. More than most designers, he is increasingly designing costumes as well as sets (something he has long done in ballet) to gain more visual control over the productions.

—Arnold Aronson

# LORD, Peter (John)

British architect and interior designer

**Born:** London, 1 September 1929. **Education:** Educated at Welwyn Garden City Grammer School, Hertfordshire, 1941-46; studied under Robert Furneaux Jordan, at the Architectural Association School, London, Dip.Arch., 1951. **Military Service:** Served in the British Army Royal Engineers, and in the Army Emergency Reserve, 1951-53. **Family:** Married Shirley Munday in 1956; children: Kathryn. **Career:** Architect and designer, with J. M. Austin-Smith architects, London, 1953-56; partner, 1956-80, and senior partner, from 1980, in Austin-Smith: Lord architects and designers, London. President, Chartered Society of Designers, London, 1969-70, and ICSID International Council of Societies of Industrial Design, 1985-87;

chairman, Association of Consultant Architects, London, 1989; associate, 1952, and fellow, 1959, Royal Institute of British Architects; member, 1956, and fellow, 1964, Chartered Society of Designers. **Honors:** Fellow, Royal Society of Arts, 1964; honorary member, Union des Designers en Belgique, 1974. **Address:** 10-12 Carlisle Street, London W1V 5RF, England.

## Works

Office and display warehouse interiors, for John Wright and Sons, London, 1956.

Shops, offices, and warehouses, for Heffers Booksellers and Heffers Stationers, Cambridge, from 1965.

Office, warehouse, and depot buildings, for IBM (UK) Limited, from 1969.

ABC Cinemas interiors, in Romford and Plymouth, 1970-71.

Office building and interiors, for Lloyds Bank, Oxford, 1972.

Headquarters office interiors, for the Central Electricity Generating Board, London, from 1980.

Manufacturing plant and office interiors, for Twentieth Century-Fox Video, Perivale, Middlesex, 1981.

Restaurants interiors, for Cranks Limited, from 1981.

Exhibit galleries and restaurant and cafeteria interiors, for the British Museum, London, from 1981.

Office interiors, for Twentieth Century-Fox, Soho Square, London, 1983.

## Publications

**By LORD: books**—*Materials Handling in Factories and Warehouses,* London, 1963; *The Concept of Professionalism in the Field of Design,* London, 1968; **articles**—in *The Designer* (London), September 1969, October 1969, October 1970, December 1970, October 1973; *Official Architect and Planning* (London), February 1970; *Management Today* (London), August 1972; *Interior Design* (London), October 1972, April 1973; *Housing Review* (London), August 1973; *Shopspec* (London), April 1982.

**On LORD: books**—*Architecture Guide to Cambridge and East Anglia Since 1970* by Charles McKean, London, 1982; **articles**—in *Official Architect and Planning* (London), April 1967; *Architectural Review* (London), May 1971; *Architects' Journal* (London), May 1982.

*

My training as an architect and practice as an architect/designer in all fields from urban planning and landscape through to project design and associated graphics underlines my personal philosophy that design must be a consistent thread within a total environment.

When distortions in emphasis occur through failure to analyse the problem or resolve conflicts—or just the plain inability of the designer—a solution cannot have an elegance that transcends the ordinary, a quality which is essential for me. I find pleasure in the design process, which for me more often than not starts before putting pencil to paper, and which is a synthesis of a building with its inhabitants, a product design with its user, and overall, a demonstration of harmony and purpose.

—Peter Lord

*   *   *

Since Peter Lord began to practice in 1953, his work has included interiors for the *Times* newspapers, Unilever, IBM (UK), London Weekend Television, Lloyds Bank, W. H. Smith, the Inn on the Park, British government Job Centres, the British Museum, Heffers of Cambridge, Dillons University Bookshop in London, and Hatchards of Piccadilly. In his presidential address to the Society of Industrial Artists and Designers in October 1969, Lord stated: "Even if we only defined design as the part of a creative process concerned with the visual and aesthetic aspect as an essential element in a comprehensive process, we must still recognise it as only part of a creative process. The emphasis which we and our clients—individual, corporate and governmental—place on this aspect will vary from year to year but it is our responsibility to see that this vital function is regarded from the outset as a criterion as important as utility and economy." Lord argued that the William Morris attempt to retreat from industrialisation was doomed to fail. Machines are here to stay, but there is no reason why industrial products cannot be well designed. He welcomed the institution of two A-level examination subjects in design as a major step in increasing the public understanding of design.

Lord regards himself as a pragmatist, not an idealist. Doing a good job within the brief allowed is what matters. The theoretical base must be sound, with a full understanding of cost-efficiency. Lord's style is one of functionalism which can be beautiful, not one of beautiful concepts devoid of practicality. The beauty must work. He does not want his interiors to be too fashionable, for that would date them too quickly; rather, he strives to attain a durable simplicity. This British reserve meshes very well with the Modern Movement, for it is the classic simplicity of Bauhaus designs that makes them still marketable sixty years later. Lord follows the same approach, aiming for a functional elegance that will remain efficient and useful for decades. For a theatre, the building and interior should not compete with the action on the stage, and the same applies to offices and shops. Lord is a modest designer who puts usability before any grandiose concepts, and that is why he is successful.

—Diana de Marly

# LOURIÉ, Eugene

American film designer

**Born:** Of French parents, in Kharkov, Russia, in 1905; emigrated to the United States in 1941. **Career:** Worked as an extra in Russian films, 1919; designed cinema publicity materials, in Istanbul, 1920; scenery painter and assistant to art director Lochakoff at Albatross Film Studios, Paris, 1921-23; freelance film designer and art director, in Paris, from 1923, and in Hollywood, California, from 1943; also stage set and costume designer, working for the Ballets Russes de Monte Carlo, the San Francisco Ballet, and others, from 1928; designed TV series *Kung Fu,* 1973-75.

## Works

Film designs include—*Le Brasier Ardent* (Mosjoukine), 1923; *Le Jouer d'Echecs* (Bernard), 1927; *Napoleon* (Gance), 1927; *Cagliostro* (Oswald), 1929; *Un Coupe de Telephone* (Lacombe), 1931; *Madame Bovary* (Renoir), 1933; *La Porteuse du Pain*

(Sti), 1934; *Jeanne* (Tourjansky), 1934; *Les Yeux Noirs* (Tourjansky), 1935; *Quand la Vie etait Belle* (Sti), 1935; *La Petite Sauvage* (de Limur), 1935; *Le Bebe de l'Escadrot* (Sti), 1935; *Crime et Chatiment* (Chenal), 1935; *Sous les Yeux d'Occident* (M. Allegret), 1936; *Baccara* (Mirandel), 1936; *Les Hommes Nouveaux* (L'Herbier), 1936; *Le Grand Refrain* (Siodmak), 1936; *Aventure à Paris* (M. Allegret), 1936; *Les Bas Fonds* (Renoir), 1936; *La Grande Illusion* (Renoir), 1937; *L'Alibi* (Chenal), 1937; *Le Messager* (Rouleau), 1937; *Nuit de Feu* (L'Herbier), 1937; *La Bête Humaine* (Renoir), 1938; *Ramuntcho* (Barberis), 1938; *L'Affaire Lafarge* (Chenal), 1938; *Werther* (Ophuls), 1938; *La Tragédie Impériale* (L'Herbier), 1938; *Le Paradis de Satan* (de Gandera), 1938; *Les Nouveaux Riches* (Berthomieu), 1938; *La Régle du Jeu* (Renoir), 1938; *Sans Lendemain* (Ophuls), 1939; *L'Or du Cristobal* (Becker), 1939; *Une Fausse Alerte* (de Baroncelli), 1940; *Air Pur* (Clair—unfinished), 1940; *Three Russian Girls* (Ozep), 1943; *This Land Is Mine* (Renoir), 1943; *Sahara* (Z. Korda), 1943; *The Impostor* (Duvivier), 1944; *In Society* (Yarbrough), 1944; *The House of Fear* (Neill), 1944; *Uncle Harry* (Siodmak), 1945; *The Southerner* (Renoir), 1945; *The Diary of a Chambermaid* (Renoir), 1946; *The Long Night* (Litvak), 1947; *The Song of Scheherazade* (Reisch), 1947; *A Woman's Vengeance* (Z. Korda), 1948; *The River* (Renoir), 1951; *The Adventures of Captain Fabian* (Marshall), 1951; *Limelight* (Chaplin), 1952; *The Diamond Queen* (Brahm), 1953; *The Beast from 20,000 Fathoms* (also director), 1953; *So This Is Paradise* (Quine), 1954; *Napoleon* (Guitry), 1954; *Si Paris nous etai Conte* (Guitry), 1955; *The Colossus of New York* (also director), 1957; *The Giant Behemoth* (also director), 1958; *Confessions of an Opium Eater* (Zugsmith), 1961; *Gorgo* (also director), 1961; *Back Street* (Miller), 1961; *Shock Corridor* (Fuller), 1962; *The Strangler* (Topper), 1962; *Flight from Ashiya* (Anderson), 1962; *That Touch of Mink* (Delbert Mann) 1962; *The Naked Kiss* (Fuller), 1963; *Bikini Paradise* (Tallas), 1964; *A Crack in the World* (Marton), 1965; *Battle of the Bulge* (Annakin), 1965; *Custer of the West* (Siodmak), 1966; *Krakatoa, East of Java* (Kowalski), 1969; *Royal Hunt of the Sun* (Lerner), 1969; *Eliza's Horoscope* (Sheppard), 1971; *What's the Matter with Helen?* (Harrington), 1972; *Burnt Offerings* (Curtiss), 1975; *An Enemy of the People* (Schaeffer), 1978; *Supertrain* (Curtiss), 1979; *Bronco Billy* (Eastwood), 1980; *Breathless* (McBride), 1983.

Television film designs include—*Death Takes a Holiday* (Butler), 1971; *The Delphi Bureau* (Wendkos), 1972; *Kung Fu* (Thorpe), 1972; *Haunts of the Very Rich* (Wendkos), 1972; *What Are Best Friends For?* (Sandrich), 1973; *Carola* (Lloyd), 1975; *Philemon* (Lloyd), 1975; *Time Travelers* (Singer), 1976; *Lacy and the Mississippi Queen* (Butler) 1978; *A Whale for the Killing* (Heffron), 1980; *Freebie and the Bean* (Auerback), 1980.

## Publications

**By LOURIÉ: books**—*My Work in Films,* New York, 1985; **articles**—in *Film Comment* (New York), May/June 1978; *American Film* (Washington, D.C.), January/February 1985.

**On LOURIÉ: books**—*Le Decor de Film* by Leon Barsacq, Paris, 1970, as *Caligari's Cabinet and Other Grand Illusions,* Boston, 1976; *Screen Series: France* by Marcel Martin, London and New York, 1971; *The International Dictionary of Films and Filmmakers,* Chicago and London, 1987, 1991; **articles**—in *Films and Filming*

(London), February 1960, December 1961; *Monthly Film Bulletin* (London), January 1972; *Film Comment* (New York), May/June 1978; *Film Dope* (London), February 1987.

*        *        *

By far, Eugene Lourié's best work was done with director Jean Renoir, who closely controlled all aspects of his films, including the visual. Perhaps Renoir's best known and well-liked film is *Grand Illusion,* about French soldiers held in a German prison. The prison, actually in a castle, shot at a combination of locations in Alsace, has a grimly realistic atmosphere. It contrasts with the light and airy atmosphere of the Swiss farm to which the prisoners flee. *The Human Beast,* based on a Zola novel, gives the impression of having been shot on location, but the railyard and railwaymen's homes were all created by Lourié. The dark, ramshackle buildings are an effective accompaniment for this tale of human depravity. Renoir's tendency to show many planes of depth within one camera shot is especially apparent in *The Rules of the Game.* Lourié's busy rooms and long hallways of the villa in which the socialities' verbal thrusts and foils take place provide excellent backgrounds for the camera's juxtapositions of characters.

Much of Lourié's work in the United States was done for mediocre productions, and he actually directed several typical science-fiction films. The first, *The Beast from 20,000 Fathoms,* had the most inventive effects. In the United States, he also had the opportunity to work with Renoir again. *The River,* shot on location in India, is noted for a brilliant use of color. To arrive at the desired color compositions, Lourié moved clumps of flowers and repainted trees in slightly different shades of green. It was not the last time a director would repaint natural scenery to achieve a special color effect; Michelangelo Antonioni did the same in 1964 for his famous film, *The Red Desert.*

Lourié discovered the essence of art direction in scouting a location for Renoir's rendition of a William Faulkner novel, *The Southerner,* for which he chose a California location that perfectly suited the story. He had found that the town in Texas where the story had actually taken place did not look at all right for the film. Lourié's simple conclusion could be considered an art director's credo: "The real truth is never as truthful as the invented truth."

—Lois Miklas

# LUBALIN, Herbert (Frederick)
American typographer and graphic designer

**Born:** New York City, 17 March 1918. **Education:** Studied at Cooper Union, New York, 1936-39. **Career:** Worked on New York World's Fair exhibits, for Display Counselors, New York, 1939; freelance book designer, New York, 1939-41; art director, Deutsch and Shea Advertising, New York, 1941-42, *Men's Wear* magazine Fairchild Publications, New York, 1942-43, Reis Advertising, New York, 1943-45; director, Herb Lubalin Incorporated design firm, New York, 1946-69; president, Lubalin Smith-Carnase design firm, New York, 1969-75, LSC & P Design Group, New York, 1976-78, and Herb Lubalin Associates design firm, New York, 1978; chairman, Lubalin Peckolick Associates, New York, 1980; also established subsidiary firms Lubalin Delpire, Paris, Lubalin Maxwell,

London, Good Book Publishing, New York, and Aki-Lubalin, Hawaii. Founder, with Aaron Burns, of Lubalin-Burns and Company, New York, 1970, International Typeface Corporation, New York, 1970, *Upper and Lower Case* typography magazine, New York, 1973, and Design Processing International, New York, 1976. Instructor, Cornell University, New York, and Syracuse University, New York; visiting professor, Cooper Union, New York. President and board member, Art Directors Club of New York; board member, American Institute of Graphic Arts international; president, Alliance Graphique Internationale. **Exhibitions:** Society of Typographic Arts, Chicago, 1957; American Institute of Graphic Arts, New York, 1958; Philadelphia School of Design, 1961; Gallery 303, New York, 1961. **Collections:** Museum of Modern Art, New York; Smithsonian Institution, Washington, D.C. **Honors:** Art Director of the Year Award, National Society of Art Directors, 1962; American Television Festival Cleo Award, 1963; Lotus Club Award, 1973; 3 Gold Medals, Advertising Club of New York; 9 Gold Medals, and Hall of Fame Award, 1977, Art Directors Club of New York; Cooper Union Alumnus of the Year Award, 1980; American Institute of Graphic Arts Medal, 1981. **Died:** New York 25 May 1981.

## Works

*Avant Garde Gothic* typeface, for the International Typeface Corporation, 1967.
*Serif Gothic* typeface, for the International Typeface Corporation, 1974.
*ITC Lubalin Graph* typeface, for the International Typeface Corporation, 1974.

## Publications

**By LUBALIN: book**—*Folio II,* New York, 1968; **articles**—in *Graphis*(Zurich), March 1959; *Print*(New York), January 1964, May/ June 1979; *Communication Arts* (Palo Alto), August/September 1969; *Form*(Cologne), no. 1, 1971.

**On LUBALIN: books**—*The New Graphic Design* by Karl Gerstner and Markus Kutter, Teufen and London, 1959; *Typography* by Aaron Burns, New York, 1961; *Who's Who in Graphic Art* edited by Walter Amstutz, Zurich, 1962, Dubendorf, 1982; *Graphic Designers in the USA: 1* edited by Henri Hillebrand, London, 1971; *The Language of Graphics* by Edward Booth-Clibborn and Daniele Baroni, London, 1980; *The Design Concept* by Allen Hurlburt, New York, 1981; *The Conran Directory of Design* edited by Stephen Bayley, London, 1985; *Typographic Design: Form and Communication* by Rob Carter, Ben Day and Philip Meggs, New York, 1985.

\*    \*    \*

One of the most influential American graphic designers, Herb Lubalin first achieved international acclaim during the 1950s for the originality of his typographic designs. Perhaps more than any other designer, Lubalin understood the design potential of phototypography, which during the 1960s, rapidly replaced hand-set metal type for display material and machine-set metal type for text matter. While metal type was constrained by limited sizes, fixed spacing between letters, and rigid geometric constraints, phototypography had the potential for large sizes, overlapping characters, distor-

tions, and extremely tight line-, word-, or letter-spacing. Lubalin demonstrated for designers throughout the world how the new capabilities of phototypography could be used for both impact and communication. In Lubalin's most innovative work, message and visual form are inseparably united. Examples of this are Lubalin's typograms, or brief, visual, typographic poems. For example, in the proposed logo for "Mother & Child," the ampersand cradles the word "Child" inside the "O" of the word "mother" to symbolize the mother-and-child relationship.

Lubalin's Avant Garde family of typefaces was inspired by the logo that he designed for *Avant Garde* magazine. A geometric, sans serif type, it features capital ligatures that tightly interlock into unique alphabetic configurations.

Because typeface designs cannot be copyrighted, piracy often seriously erodes royalty compensation for them. To combat this problem, in partnership with phototypography pioneer Edward Rondthaler and typographer Aaron Burns, Lubalin established the International Typeface Corporation in 1970 to provide royalties to typeface designers while licensing and making fonts available to all manufacturers of typesetting equipment. This event dramatically expanded the production of original type designs. ITC published a bimonthly journal, *U&lc (Upper and Lower Case),* to publicize and demonstrate its typeface designs. Designed by Lubalin, *U&lc* had a complex, dynamic layout style that became a major graphic design influence during the 1970s. ITC typeface designs favored a large x-height (height of the lower-case x) and short ascenders and descenders to allow a larger optical size in text settings.

—Philip B. Meggs

# LUSS, Gerald
American interior designer

**Born:** Gloversville, New York, 7 October 1926. **Education:** Studied at Rensselaer Polytechnic Institute, Troy, New York, 1945-48; Pratt Institute, Brooklyn, New York, BFA, 1948. **Family:** Married Ann Langhof in 1954 (died, 1975); children: Jan, Jil, Gay, and Jay; married Denise Feliziani in 1989; children: Jaclyn. **Career:** Director of design and executive vice-president, Designs for Business interior design firm, New York, 1948-65; founder-president and director of design, Luss/Kaplan and Associates, New York, 1965-87, and Gerald Luss and Associates, New York, from 1987. Visiting lecturer, Pratt Institute, Parsons School of Design, and Rhode Island School of Design. **Addresses:** 1060 Fifth Avenue, New York, New York 10128, U.S.A.; 100 Truesdale Drive, Croton on Hudson, New York 10520, U.S.A.

## Works

Interior designs include—corporate office, for Capital Centre, Landover, Maryland; corporate office, for AVX Incorporated, New York; education facility, for K-12 Cerebral Palsy Foundation of Brooklyn, New York; corporate office, for Corning Glass, New York; Coney Island leisure facility, Brooklyn, New York; national headquarters, for the Federal Aviation Administration, Washington, D.C., and regional offices in Atlanta, Oklahoma City and Los Angeles; FAA Air Route Traffic Control Centers, in Hawaii, Atlanta, and Miami; corporate headquarters, for Focus Technologies Incorporated, Washington, D.C.; offices, for Geers Gross Advertising, New York; Institute for Geriatric Care, for Long Island Jewish Hospital, New York; underground security and living facilities, for Iron Mountain Incorporated, Hudson, New York; offices, for Israel Discount Bank, New York; television broadcast facilities and office in Flint, Miami, Nashville, Norfolk, and Phoenix, for Knight-Ridder Incorporated; offices, for Maritime Overseas Corporation, New York; clubhouse and dining rooms, for Montauk Golf and Racquet Club, Long Island, New York; news bureaus in Atlanta, Boston, Los Angeles, New York, Washington, and Paris, for NBC National Broadcasting Company; country club and corporate offices, for Nevada Equities Incorporated, Las Vegas; ten-year expansion program, for North Shore University Hospital, Manhasset, Long Island, New York; United States Headquarters, for Polly Peck International, New York; corporate headquarters, for Post-Newsweek Stations Incorporated, Washington, D.C.; offices, for Sam Minskoff and Sons Incorporated, New York; offices, for South Nassau Medical Center, New York; offices and banking facilities, for Sumitomo Bank, New York; offices, for Time Incorporated, New York; offices and studios, for WDIV Television, Detroit; corporate offices for World Wide Volkswagen Corporation, New York; major residential developments in Bal Harbor, Bogota, Kings Point, Mexico City, Miami, New York, Palm Beach, and Washington, D.C.

**Publications**

**On LUSS: books**—*AIA Guide to New York* edited by Norval White and Ellen Willenski, New York, 1963; *Interiors Book of Offices,* New York and London, 1965; *Offices/Office Space,* New York, 1965; *Interior Design: An Introduction to Architectural Interiors* by Arnold Friedmann, John F. Pile, and Forrest Wilson, New York and Amsterdam, 1970, 1976.

*

I believe that the concept of order is to be most devoutly desired. In the quest for realization of such order, it is necessary that the function of every element—whether supportive or purely aesthetic—existing in any given environment be most clearly defined and in evidence in its purest state. To paraphrase, I believe that two lines should not be used if one line will enunciate as clearly. This concept does not eliminate the desirability or inevitability of any given design expression or historic period as, for example, the most beautiful of the Victorian era in which the simplest expression was achievable only with a multiplicity of profusion of many single lines still representative of the most direct expression of that area.

I have endeavored to achieve two goals in my work as a designer: 1) a redefinition of interior design as interior architecture, in which capacity the designer is responsible for and responsive to all elements realizing the total environment, rather than responsive only to cosmetic declarations; 2) the education of the client to the realistic necessity of the evolution of space on the basis of the final use of such space by its occupants, with the relegation of the design of the enveloping skin as simply the logical, final, creative step, rather than the reverse—in which the envelope-esthetics are conceived in a vacuum and the functional and esthetic environment is then forced to conform to this enclosure, which, in the vast majority of in-

stances, cannot realize the full potential or expression of functional and environmental prerequisites.

—Gerald Luss

*       *       *

Gerald Luss is the driving force and the creative spirit of the firm Luss/Kaplan and Associates. Before forming his present company, he had gone straight from Pratt Institute to Designs for Business, where he remained for seventeen years, bringing the firm to the forefront of American interior design and exerting an enormously strong influence upon design in the United States. Designs for Business was one of the largest and most highly respected firms during the 1950s and early 1960s. Under Luss's direction, the staff grew to more than 100 at peak periods, and just about every one of its major projects found its way into national design magazines. Luss was known as one of the stars in the field of contract design, and although he pioneered the team concept at Designs for Business, it was clearly his personal influence that determined the shape of every project. Some of the most important commissions included the huge Time-Life project, the Federal Aviation Agency, and the Internal Revenue Service.

Luss formed his own firm when he realized that a design firm can operate more efficiently when each job is assigned to a single designer, yet the high-quality work produced by Luss/Kaplan is very much controlled and influenced by Luss. Projects have included a number of health care facilities, large corporate offices, hotels, and governmental agencies. Since Luss/Kaplan does not engage in any promotional activities, all clients must find the firm on the basis of Luss's reputation.

Luss is a designer with a passion for order, clarity, and function. He insists upon making spaces work as background for their occupants. However, even though this Luss/Kaplan philosophy may consciously encourage understatement, each project turns out to be well-solved, innovative, and esthetically satisfying. Luss is a working prodigy who puts in incredibly long hours, yet he has found time to lecture at Pratt Institute, the Parsons School of Design, and the Rhode Island School of Design.

—Arnold Friedmann

# LUTZ, Hans-Rudolf
Swiss typographer and graphic designer

**Born:** Zürich, 14 January 1939. **Education:** Apprenticed as typesetter to Orell Füssli printers, Zürich, 1955-58; studied under Emil Ruder and Robert Büchler, at the Allgemeine Gewerbeschule, Basel, 1963. **Career:** Worked as a typesetter and printer, for Orell Füssli, Anton Schöb and Arthur Kümin, Zürich, 1959-60; freelance typesetter, typographer, and designer, Zürich, from 1961; leader of Expression Typographique group, at Studio Hollenstein, Paris, 1964-66; founder-publisher, of Lutz Verlag publications, Zürich, from 1966; co-founder and publisher, *Verlagsgenossenschaft,* Zürich, 1971-80; visual director of UnknownmiX multimedia performance group, Zürich, from 1983. Contributor, from 1966, and co-editor, from 1980, of *Typographische Monatsblatter,* St. Gallen. Instructor in design, Cours 19 Evening School, Paris, 1964-66; instructor in typography, Kunstgewerbeschule, Zürich, 1966-70; founder of typography department, and instructor in design, at the Schule für Gestaltung, Lucerne, from 1968; guest instructor, at F + F Schule für Experimentelle Gestaltung, Zürich, Schule für Gestaltung, Zürich, University of Alberta, Edmonton, Ohio State University, Columbus, and Rhode Island School of Design, Providence, from 1983. **Exhibitions:** *Hans-Rudolf Lutz: Exhibition on Typography,* Veranstalter stadt Frankfurt im Karmeliterkloster, 1991. **Address:** Lessingstrasse 11, 8002 Zürich, Switzerland.

### Works

*Zufall und Spiel* kinetic poster, for the Allgemeine Gewerbeschule, Basel, 1963.

*Univers* type program advertisement and poster series, for the Monotype Corporation, Bern, 1964.

*Die Varierung des Gleichen* series of cover designs, for *Typographische Monatsblatter,* St. Gallen, 1965.

*Communist Manifesto/Karl Marx* poster, for Ernst Gloor Typesetter, Zürich, 1968.

*ber die Russische Revolution/Rosa Luxemburg* poster, for Helvetische Typografia, Basel, 1971.

*Caractere Hollenstein* typeface specimen series, for Hollenstein Phototype, Paris, 1972.

*Kontinuierliche Stadtentwicklung* book design, for Birkhauser Verlag, Basel, 1975.

*Englersatz* poster series, for Englersatz, Zürich, 1976.

*Gestaltung ist Information* series of cover designs, for *Typographische Monatsblatter,* St. Gallen, 1977.

*My Edmonton Journal* book design, for Lutz Verlag, Zürich, 1977.

*CIAM: Congres International d'Architecture Moderne* book design, for Birkhäuser Verlag, Basel, 1979.

*UX, Loops, Mix 3, Snacks, Whaba, Dominadeq* record sleeves and labels, for UnknownmiX/Recrec Music, Zürich, from 1983.

Design work for the opera *Attinghausen,* for F.X. Nager, Zürich, 1983.

*Herzblut, Populäre Gestaltung in der Schweiz* exhibition poster, for the Museum fur Gestaltung, Zürich, 1987.

*Ausbildung in typografischer Gestaltung* book design, for Lutz Verlag, Zürich, 1987.

*Britische Sicht, Fotografie aus England* exhibition poster, for the Museum fur Gestaltung, Zürich, 1988.

UnknownmiX in Concert at the Fri-Son 40-minute video, for UX and Recrec Music, Zürich, 1989.

*Die Verpackung der Verpackung der Verpackung* book design, for Lutz Verlag, Zürich, 1989.

*Reading Cities* multimedia performance, with Mark Philipp and Heinz Nigg, Zürich, 1995.

### Publications

**By LUTZ: books**—*Grafik in Kuba,* Zürich, 1971; *Experiment F + 1; 1965-71,* Zürich, 1971; *Edmonton Journal,* Zürich, 1977; *1979: Eine Art Geschichte,* Zürich, 1980; *Bilderbuch 1: Menschen,* Zürich, 1986; *Bilderbuch 2: Geschichter,* Zürich, 1986; *Ausbildung in Typografischer Gestaltung,* Zürich, 1987; **articles**—"Typografie am Monitor" in *Passages,* no. 12, 1992; **audiovisuals**—*Grafiker auf der Strasse,* 1979; *A. Zerfall, Unordnung: B. Reproduction und Druck,* 1980; *Stadt für Tote: Stadt für Lebende,* 1980; *Uber die*

*fliessende Grenze zwischen verbalen und visuellen Information,* 1981.

**On LUTZ: books**—*Typography Today* by Helmut Schmid, Tokyo, 1980; *Typoundso,* Zürich, 1995; **articles**—in *Idée ... à Jour* (Basel), November 1988; *Der Alltag* (Zürich), February 1989; *Hochparterre* (Zürich), August 1990; *Der Druckspiegel,* April 1994.

\*

It's just typography, but I like it...

—Hans-Rudolf Lutz

## LUZZATI, Emanuele

Italian illustrator, filmmaker, stage, and graphic designer

**Born:** Genoa, 3 June 1921. **Education:** Studied at the Ecole des Beaux-Arts, Lausanne, 1940-45. **Career:** Freelance stage and graphic designer, in Genoa, from 1945, and animated film designer, from 1957. Professor of theatre design, Accademia di Arte Drammatica, Rome, 1967-82, and Centro Arti e Mestieri dello Spettacolo, Rome, 1982-83. **Member:** Alliance Graphique Internationale. **Exhibitions:** Venice Biennale, 1972; *107 Grafici dell'AGI,* Castello Sforzesco, Milan, 1974; *Il Sipario Magico,* Galera Nazionale, Milan, 1982 (toured); Genoa, 1984; Pontremoli, 1985; Israel Museum, Jerusalem, 1986; Galleria Nuages, Milan, 1987; Comune di Parma, 1987; Galleria Giulia, Rome, 1988; Casa del Mantegna, Mantova, 1988; Teatro Nazionale, Budapest, 1989. **Honors:** Ceramics Prize, Cannes, 1955; Bratislava Biennale Prize, 1967; Golden Rose Award, Albissola, 1970; Premio Andersen-Baia delle Favole, Sestrilevante, 1982; Ubu Award, Milan, 1982; Stage Production Prize, Verona and Milan, 1987. **Address:** Via Caffaro 12A, Apt. 7, 16125 Genoa, Italy.

### Works

Stage productions include—*Lea Lebowitz,* Teatro Nuovo, Milan, 1947; *Le Allegre Comari di Windsor,* Teatro dei Parchi, Nervi, 1949; *Peer Gynt,* Teatro d'Arte Italiano, 1950; *La Celestina,* Piccolo Teatro Eleonora Duse, Genoa, 1952; *La Diavolessa,* Teatro La Fenice, at the *Biennale,* Venice, 1952; *Il malato immaginario,* Piccolo Teatro Eleonora Duse, 1953; *Tieste,* Teatro d'Arte Italiano, 1953; *Mefistofele,* Maggio Musicale Fiorentino, 1953-54; *Colombe,* Piccolo Teatro Eleonora Duse, 1954; *Nabucco,* Maggio Musicale Fiorentino, 1955; *Volpone,* Piccolo Teatro Eleonora Duse, 1955; *Il figliol prodigo,* Maggio Musicale Fiorentino, 1957; *La Venere prigioniera,* Maggio Musicale Fiorentino, 1957; *Molto rumore per nulla,* Teatro Stabile, Trieste, 1957; *Renard,* Maggio Musicale Fiorentino, 1958; *Job,* Maggio Musicale Fiorentino, 1958; *Mavra,* Teatro Massimo, Palermo, 1959; *Il Cordovano,* Piccola Scala, Milan, 1959; *Giochi e favole per bambini: Girotondo, Gli abiti nuovi del re, Le lettere dell'alfabeto, Lo scoiattolo in gamba, Comica finale, La bambola malata, Ballettto, L'usignolo dell'imperatore,* and *Nardiello,* Teatro La Fenice, at the *Biennale,* Venice, 1960; *La Barraca,* Teatro del Lido, at the *Biennale,* Venice, 1960; *Santa Giovanna,* Teatro*

Mercadante, Naples, 1960; *La Cenerentola,* Teatro alla Scala, Milan, 1960; *Le Menage de Caroline,* La Borsa d'Arlecchino, Genoa, 1960; *Escurial,* La Borsa d'Arlecchino, 1960; *Il rinoceronte,* Teatro Mercadante, 1961; *Le rossignol,* Teatro San Carlo, Naples, 1961; *Per un Don Chisciotte,* Piccola Scala, 1961; *La bisbetica domata,* Teatro Romano, Verona, 1962; *Il figliuol prodigo,* Teatro alla Scala, 1962; *Andorra,* Teatro Manzoni, Milan, 1962; *Un uomo e un uomo,* Teatro Stabile, Trieste, 1963; *Vita di Edoardo II d'Inghilterra,* Compagnia dei Quattro, 1963; *Il bugiardo,* Teatro Stabile, Turin, 1963; *Il flauto magico,* at the Glyndebourne Festival, England, 1963; *Il re muore,* Teatro Stabile, Turin, 1963; *Chout, il buffone,* Teatro alla Scala, 1963; *Macbeth,* at the Glyndebourne Festival, 1964; *Tamburi nella notte,* Teatro Stabile, Bologna, 1964; *Il mandarino meraviglioso,* Maggio Musicale Fiorentino, 1964; *Cesare o Cleopatra,* Teatro Stabile, Turin, 1964; *La dannazione di Faust,* Teatro San Carlo, 1964; *L'Anconetana e Bilora,* Teatro Stabile, Turin, 1965; *Carmina Burana,* Chicago Lyric Opera, 1965; *L'heure espagnole,* Chicago Lyric Opera, 1965; *La luna,* Teatro Comunale dell'Opera, Genoa, 1965; *La gazza ladra,* Maggio Musicale Fiorentino, 1965; *La locandiera,* at the *Biennale,* Venice, 1965; *Prometeo incatenato,* Teatro Romano, Trieste, 1965; *Zip lap lip vap mam crep scap plip trip scrap e la grande Mam alle prese con la societa contemporanea,* at the *Biennale,* Venice, 1965; *Coppelia, Orfeo, and Danze Polostane,* Staatsoper, Vienna, 1966; *I dialoghi,* Teatro Stabile, Turin, 1965; *Come vi piace,* Teatro Romano, Verona, 1966; *Arlecchino,* Teatro Comunale, Bologna, 1967; *A Midsummer Night's Dream,* English Opera Group, London, 1967; *Don Giovanni,* at the Glyndebourne Festival, 1967; *Il mercante di Venezia,* Teatro Romano, Verona, 1967; *Le diavolerie,* at the Festival dei Mundi, Spoleto, 1967; *Le vedova scaltra,* Teatro La Fenice, at the *Biennale,* 1967; *I dialoghi,* Teatro Olimpico, Vicenza, 1968; *Rosencrantz e Guildenstern sono morti,* Compagnia dei Quattro, 1968; *Le mosche,* Teatro Olimpico, 1968; *Elettra,* Teatro Greco, Siracusa, 1968; *Le Fenicie,* Teatro Greco, Siracusa, 1968; *Il ratto dal serraglio,* at the Glyndebourne Festival, 1968; *Titus Andronicus,* Teatro Romano, Verona, 1968; *Le rossignol,* Chicago Lyric Opera, 1968; *Il prigioniero,* Teatro Comunale, Florence, 1969; *Cosi fan tutte,* at the Glyndebourne Festival, 1969; *Cosi fan tutte,* Bayerische Staatsoper, Munich, 1969; *El amor brujo,* Chicago Lyric Opera, 1969; *La Cenerentola,* Scottish Opera, Edinburgh, 1969; *La dame aux camelias o Festa per la beatificazione di Margherita Gautier, santa di 2° categoria,* at the *Biennale,* Venice, 1970; *La Moscheta,* Piccolo Teatro, 1970; *Il Turco in Italia,* at the Glyndebourne Festival, 1970; *Don Chrisciotte,* London Festival Ballet, 1970; *Elettra,* Teatro Greco, Siracusa, 1970; *Il signor Puntila e il suo servo Matti,* Teatro Stabile, Turin, 1970; *L'Italiana in Algeri,* Chicago Lyric Opera, 1970; *L'elisir d'amore,* Teatro alla Scala, 1970; *La Création du Monde,* Maggio Musicale Fiorentino, 1971; *Macbeth,* Teatro Romano, Verona, 1971; *La carriera di un libertino,* Teatro Regio, Turin, 1972; *Medea,* Teatro Greco, 1972; *Edipo Re,* Teatro Greco, 1972; *Sogno di una notte di mezza estate,* Gruppo della Rocca, 1972; *Peer Gynt,* Teatro Stabile, Turin, 1972; *Il mandarino meraviglioso,* Staatsoper, Vienna, 1972; *Elektra,* Teatro Massimo, 1973; *L'anima buona di Se-Zuan,* Teatro di Roma, 1973; *Petruska,* Staatsoper, Vienna, 1973; *Schweyk nella Il guerra mondiale,* Gruppo della Rocca, 1973; *La tarantella di Pulcinella,* Piccola Scala, 1974; *Divinas parablas,* Maggio Musicale Fiorentino, 1974; *Matilde di Shabran,* Teatro comunale dell'Opera, Genoa, 1974; *Il mercato di Malmantile,* Lincoln Center, New York, 1974; *O Cesare o nessuno!,* Teatro alla Pergola, Florence, 1974; *I due avari,* Teatro Comunale dell'Opera, Genoa, 1975; *Fuenteovejuna,* Teatro Stabile, Bolzano, 1975; *Il barbiere di Siviglia,* Teatro Comunale, Bologna, 1976; *Misura per misura,* Teatro di Roma, 1976; *Don Giovanni,* Teatro Comunale dell'Opera, Genoa, 1976; *La fantesca,* Teatro Stabile, Bolzano, 1976; *Le due giornate o Il portatore d'acqua,* Settimana Musicale Senese, 1976; *Gargantua Opera,* Teatro della Tosse, Genoa, 1977; *Volpone,* Teatro di Roma, 1977; *Leonzio e Lena,* Teatro Stabile, Bolzano, 1977; *Ubu incatenato,* Teatro della Tosse, 1977; *Il pipistrello,* Teatro Comunale dell'Opera, Genova, 1978; *L'Histoire du soldat,* Estate Romana all'Arancera, 1978; *Arlecchino,* Teatro Massimo, 1979; *Don Perlimplin,* Teatro Massimo, 1979; *La donna serpente,* Teatro Stabile, Genoa, 1979; *Le nozze di Figaro,* Teatro Comunale dell'Opera, Genoa, 1979; *I corvi,* Teatro della Tosse, Genoa, 1980; *Salome,* Teatro Comunale dell'Opera, Genoa, 1980; *L'Azzurro non si Misura con la Mente,* Gruppo della Rocca, 1980; *Il Cavalier della Rosa,* Teatro dell'Ater, Modena, 1983; *Facade,* Teatro all Scala, 1983; *Don Quixote,* Teatro di Roma, 1983; *Satiri,* Teatro della Tosse, Genoa, 1983; *Il Turco in Italia,* Festival of Pesaro, 1983; *Lo Stratagemma dei Bellimbusti,* Veneto Teatro, Padua, 1983; *L'Italiana in Algeri,* Teatro la Fenice, 1984; *Gargantua,* Teatro Regio, Turin, 1984; *Les Esprit,* Camus Festival, Angers, 1984; *Opera Buffa,* Teatro della Tosse, Genoa, 1984; *Pulcinella,* Ater Balletto, Reggio Emilia, 1985; *Piero d'Angera,* Teatro della Tosse, Genoa, 1985; *Il Barbiere di Siviglia,* Bergen Festival, 1985; *Pinocchio,* Teatro Opera of Genoa, 1985; *Armida,* Teatro la Fenice, 1985; *Sticus,* Teatro Greco, Se gesta, 1985; *Attila,* Teatro la Fenice, 1986; *Boîte à Joux Joux,* Teatro alla Scala, 1986; *Ballo in Maschera,* Staatsoper, Vienna, 1986; *Il Principe Felice,* Teatro alla Scala, 1987; *Pollicino,* Teatro Comunale, Florence, 1987; *Johnny Spieltauf,* Teatro Massimo, 1987; *La Piovana,* Teatro Romano, Verona, 1987; *La Coscienza di Zeno,* Compagnia Bosetti, Rome, 1987; *Hamlet,* Teatro dela Tosse, Genoa, 1987; *La Scuola delle Mogli,* Teatro di Genova, Genoa, 1988; *La Pace,* Teatro della Tosse, Genoa, 1988; *Le Tre Sorelle,* Haifa Theatre, 1988; *Oberon,* Opera Theatre of St. Louis, 1988; *La Scala di Seta,* Festival of Pesaro, 1988; *Lo Schiaccianoci,* Ater Balletto, Reggio Emilia, 1989; *La Mandragola,* National Theatre, Budapest, 1989.

Books written and illustrated include—*Viaggio alla città di Safed,* Rome, 1955; (with G. Rodari) *I paladini di Francia,* Milan, 1962; *La gazza ladra,* Milan, 1964; *Ali Babà e i quaranta ladroni,* Milan, 1968; *Ali Baba and the Forty Thieves,* New York, 1969; (adaptor) *Ronald and the Wizard Calico,* London, 1969; (adaptor) *The Magic Flute,* Oxford, 1971; *Il flauto magico,* Florence, 1979; *La tarantella di Pulcinella,* Milan, 1971; *Punch and the Magic Fish,* New York, 1972; (with T. Conte) *Dimbo recita,* Milan, 1974; *C'erano tre fratelli,* Milan, 1977; (with G. Davico Bonino) *Orlando in guerra,* Turin, 1979; *La Cenerentola di Rossini,* Milan, 1979.

Books illustrated include—*Calendario columbiano,* Genoa, 1953; *Chichibio e la gru* by Boccaccio, Rome, 1961; *Castello di carte* by Gianni Rodari, Milan, 1963; *Whistle, Mary, Whistle...* by Bill Martin Jr., New York, 1970; *L'uccelino Tic Tic* by E. Poi, Turin, 1972; *Il viaggio di Marco Polo* by D. Ziliotto, Turin, 1972; *The Travels of Marco Polo,* London, 1975; *Voglio comperare una tazza gialla con una ochetta blu* by I. Lepscky, Turin, 1974; *Il principe Granchio e altre fiabe italiane* edited by I. Calvino, Turin, 1974; *Italian Folk Tales,* London, 1975; *Il visconte dimezzato* by Calvino, Turin, 1975; *Dodici Cenerentole in cerca d'autore* by R. Cirio, Conegliano, Italy, 1976; *Walking and Talking with Yoav* by M. Sununit, Tel Aviv, 1976; *Gli uomini del libro* by G. Limentani, Milan, 1976; *Sundiata* by Ziliotto, Milan, 1980; *Il vizio del faraone* by Limentani, Turin, 1980; *I tre grassoni* by Tonino Conte, Rome, 1980; *Filastrocche lunghe e corte* by Rodari, Milan, 1981; *Oh che bel castello* by V. Savona, Milan, 1981; *La casa incantata* by F. Jesi, Milan, 1982; *Atalanta* by Rodari, Rome, 1982; *Belfagor arcidiavolo* by N. Macchiavelli, Genoa, 1982; *A Tiresia* by S. Guidro, Rome, 1983; *Il Libro dei Perche* by Rodari, Rome, 1984; *Filastrocche da Cantare* by Rodari, Milan, 1984; *Haggadah of Pessah,* Florence, 1983, New York, 1985; *Un Rabbi che Amava i Banchetti* by Enzo Bianchi, Milan, 1985; *Habitat per un'Idea* by Licia Odisio Genoa, 1985; *Le Avventure di Tonio l'Invisibile,* by Rodari, Rome, 1985; *Filastrocche per Tutto l'Anno* by Rodari, Rome, 1986; *Fiabe Lunghe un Sorriso* by Rodari, Rome, 1987; *I Sentieri della Notte* by Conte, Genoa, 1988; *Fiabe Scelte* by J. and W. Grimm, Milan, 1988; *The Monster of Jerusalem* by Meyr Shalev, Jerusalem, 1989.

Animated films (with Giulio Gianini, unless noted) include—*I due guerrieri,* 1957; *Pulcinella: Il gioco dell'oca,* 1959; *I paladini di Francia,* 1960; *Castello di carte* 1962; *La gazza ladra,* 1964; *L'Italiana in Algeri,* 1968; *Ali Baba,* 1970; *Il viaggio di Marco Polo,* 1971; *Pulcinella,* 1973; *Turandot,* 1974; *L'augellin belverde,* 1975; *Il flauto magico,* 1978; *I tre fratelli,* 1979; *La donna serpente,* 1979; *L'uccello di fuoco,* 1981; *Pulcinella e il pesce magico,* 1981; (with Jan Trmal) *La ragazza cigno,* 1980; (with Trmal) *La Palla d'Oro,* 1980; (with Trmal) *Il Libro,* 1984; (with Trmal) *Concerto per Gatti,* 1985.

## Publications

By LUZZATI: books—(with Conte) *Faccimo insieme teatro,* Turin, 1977; (editor, with Rodari) *Teatro Aperto '74,* Milan, 1978.

On LUZZATI: books—*The Italian Cinema* by Pierre Leprohon, Paris, 1986, London, 1972; *Gianni e Luzzati: Animazione per Due* by N. Ivaldi, Castellenza, 1971; *The Animated Film* by R. Stephenson, London and New York, 1973; *Emanuele Luzzati: Scenografie 1947-1975* by G. Davico Bonino, Turin, 1975; *Il Sipario Magico di Emanuele Luzzati* by S. Carandini and M. Fazio, Rome, 1980; *Pastelli, Pupazzi e Siparietti: Il Cinema di Gianini e Luzzati* by Sara Cortellazzo, Genoa, 1982; *Le Immagini di Emanuele Luzzati per La Tosse,* Genoa, 1984.

*

I had a very happy childhood. I liked making up stories, drawing, fooling around with scraps of paper, paints, and puppets. When I was seven, my little sister was born, providing the ideal audience for my puppet shows, my fairy tales, and pictures. My parents often took me to the theatre to see the "plays," which I unfailingly went home and reproduced with puppets and stage sets to the speechless delight of my little sister. This went on for a long while, except for five years when I had to flee to Switzerland to escape the racial laws (my family is Jewish) and where, in Lausanne, I attended a school of applied arts.

When I came back to Italy I did as a professional the same things I had done as a little boy. I threw myself into the theatre—so far I have designed costumes and sets for more than 300 productions. I told stories in various ways, as an illustrator and also as a writer. I've made up all sorts of characters in ceramics and concocted wall panels that tell of paladins and knights and old legends. And then with Giulio Gianini, film technician and cameraman, we started telling stories in the form of animated cartoons. They are, for me, probably the most complete form of narrations in which everything can be created from the beginning to the end, a story has to be made up, a script written, character and settings invented, music adapted— as I said, probably the most perfect to tell a story visually. I hasten to add, however, that all these different activities are interlinked and interrelated. Actually, I do nothing but tell the same stories over and over again. All that changes is the vehicle of expression.

The subjects are relatively few: from the "Paladins," those legendary knights we studied in school in the poetic texts of Ariosto and Tasso and then recast in a popular form in the traveling puppet shows of Italy (in particular, the Sicilian *"pupi"* or marionettes); to the characters of the commedia dell'arte, with a personal preference for Pulcinella, he too a sort of puppet in embryo who, with his shrewish wife and his dread of carabinieri, has delighted thousands of children in public parks; down to the more refined, but in Italy highly popular, characters of the opera stage, like Figaro or Papageno, or to those in the fables of Carlo Gozzi in which commedia dell'arte characters are mingled with Oriental heroes and heroines from *The Arabian Nights.*

If you come right down to it, I don't think I've ever strayed very far from these subjects, whether my stories were told in a panel of painted terracotta, or I brought them to life on a stage, or, animated by Gianini, they appeared on a movie screen, or lastly were set down forever on the pages of a printed book. Indeed, every book that I have written or illustrated has almost always appeared in the form of a stage work or an animated cartoon. Sometimes the book comes first, sometimes the animated cartoon, sometimes the stage work, but it is very rare that a given story with its characters and settings remains confined to only one of these three forms....

I don't know if I'm a painter, a story-teller or a theater-man, nor do I know if what I do is more or less valid artistically. But I do know that when a mother tells me: "To get my little boy to eat his soup, I always have to read him the Paladins of France," I have been useful for at least something in life. There's always a little child who, thanks to me, has eaten his soup or been lulled to sleep by the nursery rhymes of *Ali Baba.* And for me that's enough. (*Excerpted from an address to an illustrators' convention in Boston, 1981.*)

—Emanuele Luzzati

*     *     *

Emanuele Luzzati is rare in being able to pursue two careers at the same time. The first is as a stage designer for the opera, ballet, and theatre, and the second is as an animated film designer for the movies and television. His own style of design is successfully conveyed in his characters for animated film. They are light, humorous figures, easily identifiable, defined with bold lines. Their simple shapes allow them to be easily given movement, which is carried out by his partner Giulio Gianini (born in Rome, in 1927). Their cooperation in film animation dates to 1957 when Gianini began to animate Luzzati's figures and photograph them under the animation rostrum cameras, while Luzzati drew the characters, designed the backgrounds, and cooperated in the story development and the timing of the action. They chose the music together and fitted their pictures afterwards.

Among Luzzati's animated films with Gianini, possibly the best known are (feature length), *The Magic Flute, Ali Baba, The Pala-*

*dins, Turandot,* and *The Thieving Magpie.* The latter was chosen by a panel of specialists as one of the 15 most outstanding animated films of all time.

Luzzati's stage work has reached a dimension quite outstanding in the European theatre. He has designed more than 300 sets and costumes for La Scala in Milan, and for the operas in Rome, Naples, Venice, Florence, Vienna, Genoa, Munich, Lisbon, and Tel Aviv. Besides designing for the London Festival Ballet and the Glyndebourne Opera House, he has worked extensively in Chicago where, among other operas, he designed the sets for Rossini's *Italian Girl in Algiers.* The American public, like the European, responded to his style with delight.

Luzzati's approach is based on a colourful, decorative expression. With a strong sense of pictorial projection, he can manipulate his dress designs to unify all the visual elements on the stage. His sets light up with pictorial beauty and with an optimism that particularly helps some of the heavy operas.

Luzzati has also illustrated and written some of Europe's most popular children's books. He began his work as a ceramic artist some three decades ago at the Bianco Factory at Pozzo Garitta, and since that time he has produced art objects ranging from small, individual pieces to mural panels. In 1955, he received the first prize for ceramics at Cannes, and in 1970 he was awarded the Golden Rose at Albissola. He has created wall panels and tapestries for such transatlantic ships as the Leonardo da Vinci, the Michelangelo, and the Marco Polo. His graphic design work was represented in a show at the 1972 Venice *Biennale* in the experimental design section.

—John Halas

# MacNEIL, Ronald L.
American artist, researcher, and designer

**Born:** Wichita, Kansas, in 1942. **Education:** Studied physics at Rensselaer Polytechnic, 1960-63; studied art and design, Massachusetts Institute of Technology, B.S., 1971; Rhode Island School of Design, M.F.A., 1976. **Career:** Projectionist, NBC-TV, New York, 1963-65; apprenticeship with photographic artist Minor White, from 1973; co-founder and designer, from 1973, principal research associate, from 1984, Visible Language Workshop, Massachusetts Institute of Technology (M.I.T.), Cambridge. Instructor, 1968-77, author of photographics course, 1971, and assistant professor of graphic research, 1977-84, Department of Architecture/Visible Language Workshop, M.I.T; adjunct professor and visiting critic, Graduate Design Program, Massachusetts College of Art, Boston, from 1995; lecturer on art and design at universities and conferences throughout the world. **Exhibitions:** SIGGRAPH, 1983; Addison Gallery of American Art; M.I.T Creative Photography Gallery; Fogg Art Museum; Institute of Contemporary Art, Boston; Museum of Fine Arts, Boston; Rhode Island School of Design; Worcester Art Museum, Massachusetts; Institut fur Neue Technische Form, Darmstadt, Germany; Library of Congress, Washington, D.C.; New Orleans Contemporary Art Center, Louisiana. **Collections:** George Eastman House; Harvard University. **Honors:** Massachusetts Arts and Humanities Foundation Grant, Artist-in-Residence at the Visual Language Workshop (computer imaging), 1977. **Address:** Room E15-447, Visible Language Workshop, Massachusetts Institute of Technology, 20 Ames St., Cambridge, Massachusetts 02139, U.S.A.

## Works

Research for computer-aided printing for painting full size billboard images, resulting in a 20 x 25 foot, computer controlled, airbrush plotter, supported by national consortium of outdoor advertising companies, 1977-1983.
Research for micro-based interactive design and layout, supported by Hell GmbH, 1984-1989.
Research for intelligent personalized design tools for the naive user, supported by IBM, 1986-1989.
Research for constraint-based, case-based graphical programming tools, supported by Nynex and DARPA, 1989.
Research in novel approaches to Air Traffic Control displays, supported by Department of Transportation grant, 1992.
Research in novel approaches for Railroad Dispatch and Planning displays, supported by Department of Transportation grant, 1996.
Research in creating an experimental online design community, supported by Civiscape Grant, National Endowment for the Arts, 1996.

## Publications

**By MacNEIL: articles—**"TYRO: A Constraint-based Graphic Designer's Apprentice" in *IEEE VL Proceedings,* 1989; "TYRO: The Graphic Designer's Apprentice" in *IEEE Workshop on Visual Languages,* Rome, Italy, 1989; "Adaptive Perspectives: Case-based Reasoning with TYRO" in *IEEE VL Proceedings,* 1990; "Capturing Multimedia Design Knowledge Using TYRO, the Constraint Based Designer's Apprentice" in *SPIE/SPSE Proceedings,* 1991; *Technology Review,* October 1994.

**On MacNEIL: books—***The Media Lab: Inventing the Future at MIT* by Stewart Brand, Viking Press, 1987.

\* \* \*

Ronald MacNeil is best known for co-founding, along with Muriel Cooper, the Visible Language Workshop (VLW) at the Massachusetts Institute of Technology in 1973. His experience in science and art, at a time when the art-science fusion was usually paid mere lip service, helped establish the VLW as a credible research facility.

His *Airbrush Plotter* (1977-83) was the first large scale, full color computer-operated imaging system. As such, it captured the imagination of artists and advertisers alike. His careful and tough-minded mentoring of masters and doctoral research students in the Media Lab, as well his ability and willingness to extend his knowledge beyond M.I.T.'s walls, has carried on the tradition that Muriel Cooper built, but which was curtailed by her untimely death in 1994.

In the mid 1990s, under MacNeil's direction, the VLW was working on defining the future of electronic graphic design, changing what designers choose to make and devising new methods to do it. MacNeil sees the future moving toward meta-design, where designers build systems, or intelligent, dynamic object types which know how to communicate clearly in what has become an electronic sea of confusion.

—Al Gowan

# MAGISTRETTI, (Lodo) Vico
Italian architect and interior and industrial designer

**Born:** Milan, 6 October 1920. **Education:** Educated at the Liceo Parini, Milan, 1931-39; studied architecture, at the Politecnico, Milan, Dip. Arch., 1945. **Military Service:** Served in the Italian Army, 1942-43. **Career:** Freelance architect and designer, working in Milan, from 1946; designed for Artemide, Azucena, Cassina, Rosenthal Porzellanfabrik, Conran/Habitat, Knoll International, La

Rinascente, De Padova ICF, Montina Fratelli, O-Luce, Oca Brasil, Asko, Poggi, Carrara e Matta, Spalding, and others. Commission member, for the Milan Triennale, 1960, 1964, and for the Compasso d'Oro Awards, Milan, 1959, 1960. Visiting lecturer, Architectural School, Venice, 1962, Colegio de Arquitectura, Barcelona, 1962-67, and Royal College of Art, London, from 1980. **Member:** Accademia di San Luca, Rome, 1970. **Exhibitions:** Milan Triennale, 1948, 1951, 1954, 1960; Studio Marconi, Milan, 1971; *Knoll au Musée,* Musée des Arts Decoratifs, Paris, 1972; *One Hundred Modern Chairs,* National Gallery of Victoria, Melbourne, 1974; *Design e design,* Palazzo delle Stelline, Milan, 1973 (travelled to Venice); *Italian Re-Evolution,* La Jolla Museum of Art, California, 1982; *Design Since 1945,* Philadelphia Museum of Art, 1983; *New Design for Old,* Boilerhouse/Victoria and Albert Museum, London, 1986. **Collections:** Design Museum, London; Museum of Modern Art, New York. **Honors:** Grand Prize, 1948, 1954, and Gold Medal, 1954, Milan Triennale; Vis Prize, Milan, 1950; Compasso d'Oro Award, Milan, 1967, 1980; Honorary Fellow, Royal College of Art, London, 1983; Gold Medal, Society of Industrial Artists and Designers, London, 1985. **Address:** Via Conservatorio 20, 20121 Milan, Italy.

## Works

Torre Parco apartment building, Milan, 1956 (with Longoni).
Villa Arosio at Arenzano, near Genoa, 1959.
Marina Grande development at Arenzano, near Genoa, 1963.
*Demetrio* table in fiberglass and resin, for Artemide, 1964.
Cerruti department stores, in Paris, Tokyo, and Vienna, 1967-76.
*Stadio 80* table in fiberglass and resin, for Artemide, 1968.
*Selene* stacking chairs in fiberglass and resin, for Artemide, 1968-69.
New Town Hall, Cusano Milanino, Milan, 1969.
*Caori* table in black aluminum, for Knoll International, 1969.
Hotel and restaurant at Sarzana, near La Spezia, 1973.
*707 Fiandra* sofas and chairs, for Cassina, 1975.
*114 Nuvola Rossa* bookshelves, for Cassina, 1977.
High school at San Daniele del Friuli, near Udine, 1977.
*Maralunga* sofas and chairs, for Cassina, 1979.
Cutlery in stainless steel, for Cleto Munari, 1979-80.
*Kuta 250* table lamp, for O-Luce, 1980.
*Sinbad* seating range, for Cassina, 1981.
*Veranda* seating range, for Cassina, 1983.
*Idomeneo* lamp, for O-Luce, 1984.
*Planet* lamp, for Venini, 1986.

## Publications

**By MAGISTRETTI: articles**—*The Designer* (London), December 1982.

**On MAGISTRETTI: books**—*Mobili Tipo* by Robert Aloi, Milan, 1956; *Recent Italian Architecture* by Agnoldomenico Pica, Milan, 1959; *Public Interiors* by Misha Black, London, 1960; *The Modern Chair: 1850 to Today* by Gilbert Frey, London and Niederteufen, 1970; *History of Modern Furniture* by Karl Mang, Stuttgart, 1978, 1989, London, 1979; *Atlante del Design Italiano 1940/1980* by Alfonso Grassi and Anty Pansera, Milan, 1980; *Knoll Design* by Eric Larrabee and Massimo Vignelli, New York, 1981; *Design Since*

*1945* edited by Kathryn Hiesinger and George Marcus, Philadelphia and London, 1983; *Design Process Olivetti 1908-83,* with text by Renzo Zorzi, Milan, 1983; *Modern Furniture Classics* by Miriam Stimpson, London, 1987; *Italian Design: 1870 to the Present* by Penny Sparke, London and New York, 1988; *Italian Modern: A Design Heritage* by Giovanni Albera and Nicolas Monti, New York, 1989.

\*

Profound changes are taking place in every aspect of design—in the products, the methods of production, and the distribution of them. There are also changes in the words used. The famous "industrial design" no longer has the same mythical, liberating significance that it had in the 1960s.

We can, perhaps, now see that it hardly ever existed and that technology, the wicked fairy of industrial design, has not been the true protagonist of what it must already be time to call simply "Italian design." Technology is a means, never an end. You can make the finest design using the most complex of machinery to shape a brand new material, but you can also do it with pieces of wood if you use them in the right way.

Technology (the real technology of our times) has produced the Saturn rocket, not Italian design. Italian design was born and lives on as the result of a fortunate and quite casual meeting some 20 years ago between courageous small industries (craftsmen, almost) and designers.

After so great an interval of time, it is possible to say that, despite all the criticism and reserve on the ideological level, there is a positive result. A strong image, spread through the world, of Italian design and the birth—and I believe one can say this too without being ashamed of that naughty word—of an Italian "Style," translated into plans for certain objects which make their mark on a period and last in time. I think that an object of good design should last forever and should be an archetype of permanent validity, not an object of fashion. The production of "fashionable" articles (based on the 1930s, Art Deco, and various other revivals) is a fine way to kill the image of Italian design. We now have to design for a changed world which has no use for the provisional or the throw-away. It is a better-informed and more cultured world which wants, and can identify with, not the ridiculous expensive "status symbol," but much more simply, something that in a harder and more exhausting world is more authentic. This is the world which has emerged crippled from the "petrol war" and which can no longer afford the frivolities of the past but which will have an increasing need for a poetry of the authentic.

When recalling the antithesis that has emerged in recent years between the meaning of the words "design" and "styling," I think it is all worthwhile. Out of this contrast there has come the idea that styling was in some way inferior to design. Styling has always been thought of as useless decoration, superimposition, and superficial alteration. On the other hand, design meant the search for the essential, the unambiguous quality of the only form possible, as if it was wished to endow design with some ethical value and styling with an aestheticizing value, to the clear detriment of the latter. I believe that it should be possible to share such a judgment only after establishing that we are talking of two entirely different things, not necessarily opposed, but complementary.

I think that today, given the demands and the limitations that this western civilization has to face, the time has come to reach a definition, albeit synthetically and approximately, that can be stated thus: design does not need drawing, but styling does. What I mean by this is that an object of design could be described, even to the person who has to produce it, by spoken or written words. What materializes through the process is a precise function and, in particular, a special use of the materials which, as a matter of principle, leaves all aesthetic questions out of consideration because the object is to achieve a precise practical aim. Of course, that does not mean that a precise image cannot be produced that will reflect and express "aesthetic" qualities proper to the new methodology used in the conception of the object.

Styling, on the other hand, has to be expressed with the most exact drawings. This is not because it disregards function, but simply because it wraps that function in a cloak that essentially expressed qualities that are called "style" and that are decisive in making the quality of the object recognizable. Just think of the use of the world "styling" in the American motorcar industry, which perhaps coined the expression to justify superficial changes in each year's new model. The successive cars are identical in substance but slightly different in shape, that is to say in styling.

Once we make the distinction between design and styling, it should be possible to get rid of the negative premise of the word styling and to simply say that the two words have a different content. And their content is not in conflict with each other, but complementary in the creative definition of an object in which design and styling are two elements of which one or the other will prevail from time to time, thereby making it possible to define an object as an object of either design or styling. Nowadays, I believe that one will much less often come across an object in which design is prevalent than an object in which styling prevails.

Going back to my earlier example, I should say that the American motorcar is a typical object of styling alone. To make my point clear, I must add that such an object, simply because it is purely an object of styling, is a very negative example. On the application of design, styling to the needs of the contemporary world, and to future needs, I believe it is possible to express a choice by saying that today and tomorrow there will always be more need for design than for styling. That is to say, because we have to face a shortage of means available to us, we shall have to cope with an increasingly emphatic demand for simplification and essentiality where the useful life of the object is concerned.

Scarcity of materials and impossibility of maintenance will lead increasingly to the cutting out of a tendency of the past two decades to produce "throw-away" articles, made not to last but to be easily replaceable. We shall be dealing with a society growing at the same time poorer and more sophisticated. This society, accustomed to enjoying collective or scientific services of great sophistication, will learn that it can no longer rely on that sophistication and will want objects that look strong and simple, that need no maintenance or as little as possible, and that will never be quickly or economically replaced.

Design, understood in this way, will have to face these new and urgent demands. I believe that this situation will be beneficial because however attractive we may find the post-modernist slogan (a strictly pro-styling slogan) "less is a bore," we may well come to believe that Mies got it right in thinking that the best guarantee of durable quality lay in "less is more." Perhaps the time has come to say that first we thought that what was useful was beautiful, but now we know that what is beautiful is useful.

—Vico Magistretti

* * *

Sculptural forms with organic shapes, rounded edges, and understated structure predominate in all of Magistretti's designs. Whether executed in hard materials, such as plastic, wood, or metal, or such soft materials as wool, leather, or cotton, all designs have a fluid and developing quality. For example, in lounge seating the chair and sofa surfaces seem malleable.

The 928 (1962), the Maralunga (1973), the 707 Fiandra (1975), and the Sinbad (1982) groups typify Magistretti's innovations. They are marked by their sculptural form, imaginative use of fabric, design for comfort, and adaptability. Stylistically, these four seating groups range from the 928, an ample, traditional chair and sofa with a conservative treatment of materials, to Sinbad, his boldest attempt at sculptural form in lounge seating. Sinbad's fabric cover is loosely applied to the structure by means of Velcro and a system of hidden clips so that the sculptural drape of the fabric becomes the design statement. The colorful, rectangular, removable covers approximate the ease of throwing a blanket over a worn sofa, an idea with which Magistretti first experimented in the 707 Fiandra system. The Maralunga, 707 Fiandra, and Sinbad seating designs also express Magistretti's growing interest in comfort and adaptability. In all three designs single chairs and larger pieces have been structured to cushion the body in a gentle embrace. As for adaptability, the Maralunga's back cushion, in both the armchair and the sofa, can be raised by a concealed steel armature from a folded height to a high lounge position. In the 707 Fiandra series, large-scale seating components were designed to be ganged in a variety of configurations. Pieces in the Sinbad collection change upholstery to match environmental conditions—cotton for summer, brushed wool or thick leather for the winter. The ability to change fabrics also facilitates maintenance, another concept first introduced by means of zippered covers in the 707 Fiandra series.

Magistretti is a prolific and consistent designer who has concentrated on reinterpreting traditional lines and forms. Throughout the last 20 years, 95 percent of Magistretti's designs have remained in production, a testimony to his consistency and his philosophy of timeless design. According to Magistretti, "Good design has nothing to do with fashion. Good design has to last years."

—Jan Jennings

# MAGNUSSEN, Erik
Danish industrial designer

**Born:** Copenhagen, 31 March 1940. **Education:** Studied ceramics, School of Arts and Crafts (Kunsthandvaerkerskolan), Copenhagen, 1957-60. **Family:** Married Jonna Dreyer in 1982. **Career:** Furniture, ceramics, and glass designer, from 1960; ceramics designer for Bing and Grøndahl porcelain factory, Copenhagen, from 1962; designed for Stelton AS tablewares, Heilerup, from 1976, for Georg Jensen Silversmithy AS, Copenhagen, from 1978, and for Royal Copenhagen, Kevi, and others. Instructor, Royal Academy of Fine Arts, Copenhagen, 1970-73. **Exhibitions:** *Bing og Grøndahl 125 Ar,* Kunstindustrimuseet, Copenhagen, 1978; *Georg Jensen Silversmithy: 77 Artists, 75 Years,* Washington, D.C., 1980; *Scandinavian Modern Design 1880-1980,* Cooper-Hewitt Museum, New York, 1982; *Design Since 1945,* Philadelphia Museum of Art, 1983; *The Lunning Prize,* Nationalmuseum, Stockholm, 1986; *Erik*

**Erik Magnussen: Stainless steel flatware for A/S Stelton, 1995**

*Magnussen,* Munkeruphus-Dronningmoelle, 1993. **Collections:** Kunstindustrimuseet, Copenhagen; Statens Kunstfond, Copenhagen; Röhsska Konstslöjdmuseet, Göteborg; Victoria and Albert Museum, London. **Honors:** Lunning Prize, 1967; ID Prize, Danish Design Council, 1972, 1977, 1987, 1990; Furniture Prize, Copenhagen, 1975; Knud V. Engelhardt Memorial Fund award, 1977; Danish Designer of the Year Award, 1983. **Address:** 630 Strandvejen, DK-2930 Klampenborg, Denmark.

## Works

Teapot, for Bing & Grøndahl, 1961.
*Termo* tableware, for Bing and Grøndahl, 1965.
*Chair Z,* in steel and fabric, for Torben Orskov Company, 1968.
School furniture, for Kevi, 1969.
Carving set of stainless steel and POM-synthetic material, for Ørskov & Company, 1970.
*Hank* tableware, for Bing and Grøndahl, 1971.
Thermal Carafe, for Stelton AS, 1976.
*Porcelouis* porcelain lamps, for Louis Poulsen Bing and Grøndahl, 1983.
Bowls in steel and plastic, for Stelton AS, 1986.
Angle measurer, for Wernblad and Lokvig, 1988.
*Servizz* melamine tableware, for Rosti, 1988.
*201* cabin lamp, for Harlang and Dreyer, 1988.
*301* kerosene wall lamp in stainless steel, for Harlang and Dreyer, 1988.
*351* kerosene suspension lamp in stainless steel, for Stelton As, 1988.
Erik Magnussen Collection of tablewares, for Selangor Pewter of Malaysia, from 1988.
Chair and table, for Paustian, 1989.
Navigation instruments, for Shipmate, 1990-95.
*Park* chair, *EM* sofa, *Magnus* stacking chair and table, and *Pompidou* sitting furniture, for Paustian, 1990-95.
*Ring* wall/ceiling lamp, for Pandul, 1992.
*Click* table system, for Fritz Hansen, 1994.
Cutlery, for Stelton, 1995.

## Publications

**On MAGNUSSEN: books**—*Dansk Brugskunst og Design* edited by Landsføreningen DB+D, Copenhagen, 1972; *Dansk Design/ Danish Design* by Henrik Steen Moller, Copenhagen, 1975; *En Kobenhavnsk porcelaenfabriks historie: Bing og Grøndahl 1853-1978* by Erik Lassen, Copenhagen, 1978; *Bing og Grøndahl 125 År,* exhibition catalogue with introduction by Erik Clemmesen, Copenhagen, 1978; *Scandinavian Modern Design 1880-1980* edited by David Revere McFadden, New York, 1982; *Design Since 1945* edited by Kathryn Hiesinger and George Marcus, Philadelphia and London, 1983; *International Design Yearbook 1985/1986* edited by Robert A. M. Stern, London, 1985; *The Lunning Prize,* exhibition catalogue edited by Helena Dahlbäck Lutteman and Marianne Uggla, Stockholm, 1986; *Erik Magnussen* by Henrik Sten Moeller, Rhodos, 1990; **articles**—"Thirty-four Lunning Prizewinners" in *Mobilia* (Snekkersten), September 1967; "Erik Magnussen" by S. E. Moller in *Mobilia* (Snekkersten), July/August 1973; "The Magnussen/Stelton Bowls" in *DD Bulletin* (Copenhagen), March 1987.

# MAINBOCHER
American fashion and costume designer

**Born:** Main Rousseau Bocher, in Chicago, Illinois, 24 October 1890; adopted name Mainbocher in 1929. **Education:** Studied at the Lewis Institute, Chicago, from 1907; studied piano under Claire Osborn Reed, at Columbia School of Music, Chicago, 1907; studied design, at Chicago Academy of Fine Arts, 1908-09, and at the Arts Students League, New York, 1909-11; attended University of Chicago, 1911, and Königliche Kunstgewerbemuseum, Munich, 1911-12; also studied painting with E. A. Taylor, Paris, 1913-14, piano with Frank La Forge, New York, 1914, and opera under Henri Albers and Giulia Valda, New York, 1917-21. **Military Service:** Served in the American Ambulance Corps, and Intelligence Corps, Paris, 1917-18. **Career:** Worked part-time as a lithographer, New York, 1909-11; fashion sketch artist, for clothing manufacturer E. L. Mayer, New York, 1914-17; illustrator, *Harper's Bazaar,* in Paris, 1917-21; fashion correspondent, then editor, *Vogue* French edition, Paris, 1922-29; established Mainbocher fashion house, Paris, 1930-39, and Mainbocher Incorporated fashion firm, New York, 1939-71; also designed stage costumes, from 1932. **Exhibitions:** *Fashion: An Anthology,* Victoria and Albert Museum, London, 1971. **Collections:** New York Public Library. **Died:** New York City, 27 December 1976.

## Works

United States WAVE uniform, 1942.
American Girl Scout uniform, 1946.
American Red Cross uniform, 1948.
Nurses' uniforms, for Passavant Hospital, Chicago, 1949.
United States Marine Corps women's uniform, 1951.
Mary Martin's wardrobe for the television adaptation of *Born Yesterday,* NBC-TV, New York, 1956.
Stage costumes include (New York, unless noted)—*La Fleur des Pois,* Théâtre de la Michodière, Paris, 1932; for Peggy Wood and Leonora Corbett in *Blithe Spirit,* Morosco Theatre, 1941; for Katharine Cornell and Doris Dudley in pre-Broadway try-out of *Rose Burke,* Curran Theatre, San Francisco, 1942; for Mary Martin in *One Touch of Venus,* Imperial Theatre, 1943; for Ruth Chatterton in the pre-Broadway tryout of *A Lady Comes Home,* Nixon Theatre, Pittsburgh, 1943; for Ruth Gordon in *Over Twenty-One,* Music Box Theatre, 1944; for Betty Field in *Dream Girl,* Coronet Theatre, 1945; for Jean Arthur in the pre-Broadway tryout of *Born Yesterday,* Shubert Theatre, New Haven, Connecticut, 1945; for Tallulah Bankhead in *Private Lives,* Plymouth Theatre, 1948; for Ethel Merman in *Call Me Madam,* Imperial Theater, 1950; *The Prescott Proposals,* Broadhurst Theatre, 1950; *Point of No Return,* Alvin Theatre, 1951; (as consultant) *Wish You Were Here,* Imperial Theatre, 1952; for Rosalind Russell in *Wonderful Town,* Winter Garden Theatre, 1953; *Kind Sir,* Alvin Theatre, 1953; for Libby Holman in part one of *Blues, Ballads and Sin Songs,* Bijou Theatre, 1954; for Lynn Fontanne in *The Great Sebastians,* ANTA Theatre, 1956; for Mary Martin in *The Sound of Music,* Lunt-Fontanne Theatre, 1955; for Irene Worth in *Tiny Alice,* Billy Rose Theatre, 1964

## Publications

**On MAINBOCHER: books**—*Always in Vogue* by Edna and Ilka Chase, London, 1954; *Dressmakers of France* by Mary Brooks Picken and Dora Miller, New York, 1956: *The World in Vogue 1893-1963* edited by Bryan Holmes and others, New York and London, 1963; *Fashion: An Anthology by Cecil Beaton,* exhibition catalogue compiled by Madeleine Ginsburg, London, 1971; *American Fashion: The Life and Lines of Adrian, Mainbocher, McCardell, Norell, Trigere* edited by Sarah Tomerlin Lee, New York, 1975, London, 1976; *In Vogue: Sixty Years of Celebrities and Fashion* by Georgina Howell, London, 1975, 1978, New York, 1976; *Magic Names of Fashion* by Ernestine Carter, London, 1980; *Fairchild's Who's Who in Fashion* edited by Ann Stegemeyer, New York, 1980; *McDowell's Directory of Twentieth Century Fashion* by Colin McDowell, London, 1984; *The Encyclopaedia of Fashion from 1840 to the 1980s* by Georgina O'Hara, London, 1986.

\* \* \*

As editor of French *Vogue* from 1922 to 1929, Mainbocher simplified the layout, removed decorative borders, and started the editorial "Vogue's Eye View." Such simplification he carried over to his clothes design when he opened as a couturier in 1929. However, Mainbocher was very conservative in his view that fashion was only for ladies who were famous and aristocratic. He did not approve of Paul Poiret's oriental fantasies or Gabrielle Chanel's bold, unladylike, classless look, and he was unaware of Sonia Delaunay's textiles. To keep out copiers and tourists, he was the first designer to charge a caution, a pledge to buy, of visitors to his collections. He based his approach on those of two of the then-leading couturiers—the royal dressmaker Edward Molyneux's classic restraint and Madeleine Vionnet's fluid, bias-cut style— imitating their elimination of superfluous detail and their avoidance of gimmicks and dramatic changes. He was fond of simple contrasts, such as a white evening gown with a black printed train, a black dress with white cravat and gloves, a black evening gown with white piqué jacket, and a black dress with a red tie and red gloves. For evenings, trying to recreate the glamour of portraits by Winterhalter, Sargent, and Boldini, he used such historical items as overskirts and corsets. With his early training in opera, he liked to think of design as similar to music, with its variations on a theme, and he was not afraid to repeat ideas. He could have remained a quietly successful designer but for the arrival of fellow American, Wallis Simpson, who gave him worldwide publicity by ordering her wedding dress from Mainbocher when she espoused the Duke of Windsor. Her determination to be the best-groomed woman in high society gave Mainbocher enormous opportunity and impact.

In 1939, he had to flee back to the United States, but as the first Parisian couturier to base himself in New York, he received much attention. He demanded the same standards as a Parisian couture house, despised Seventh Avenue's rag trade, and until his retirement in 1971, refused to touch wholesale production, remaining always an exclusive couturier for the rich. In 1942, he designed the WAVES uniform for the United States Navy, and the Mainbocher suit, with more echoes of Chanel than he would acknowledge, became a fashion stalwart. His operatic background gave him a fascination with the theatre, and he dressed Leonora Corbett in *Blithe Spirit* (1941), Mary Martin in *One Touch of Venus* (1943) and *The Sound of Music* (1955), Ethel Merman in *Call Me Madam* (1950), Rosalind Russell in *Wonderful Town* (1953), Lynn Fontanne in *The*

*Great Sebastians* (1956), and Irene Worth in *Tiny Alice* (1964). Although Mainbocher was essentially a couturier on the pre-war model, he managed to continue operating in the very changeable post-war period.

—Diana de Marly

# MALDONADO, Tomas

Italian design theorist and industrial designer

**Born:** Buenos Aires, Argentina, 25 April 1922; emigrated to Italy in 1967, naturalized, 1976. **Education:** Studied at the Academia de Bellas Artes, Buenos Aires, 1938-43. **Career:** Independent painter, architectural, and industrial designer, in Buenos Aires, 1944-54; freelance designer, working on electronic, medical, optical, agricultural, and office products, in Ulm, 1954-66, and in Milan and Bologna, from 1967. Editor, *Nueva Vision* magazine, Buenos Aires, 1951; chief editor, *Casabella* magazine, Milan. Professor, 1954-66, and Rector, 1964-66, Hochschule für Gestaltung, Ulm; professor of environmental planning, University of Bologna, from 1967; visiting professor, Princeton University, New Jersey, 1967-70. Member, Arte Concreto-Invencion group of painters, Buenos Aires, 1945; executive committee president, ICSID International Council of Societies of Industrial Design, 1967-69. **Exhibitions:** Stedelijk Museum, Amsterdam, 1953; *6a. Biennale Internazionale della Grafica d'Arte,* Palazzo Strozzi, Florence, 1978. **Collections:** Stedelijk Museum, Amsterdam. **Addresses:** Via Manzoni 14, 20121 Milan, Italy; Via Zamboni 38, 40126 Bologna, Italy.

## Publications

**By MALDONADO: books**—*Max Bill,* Buenos Aires, 1955; *Tomas Maldonado: Buenos Aires—Montevideo,* Montevideo, 1964; (with Omar Calabrese) *Universita: La Sperimentazione Dipartimentale,* Florence, 1978.

**On MALDONADO: books**—*Il Disegno Industriale e la sua Estetica* by Gillo Dorfles, Bologna, 1963; *What Is a Designer?* by Norman Potter, London and New York, 1969, Reading, 1980; *The Aspen Papers: 20 Years of Design Theory* edited by Reyner Banham, London, 1974; *Die Geschichte des Design in Deutschland* by Gert Selle, Cologne, 1978; *Industrial Design* by John Heskett, London, 1980; *Moderno Postmoderno Millenario* edited by Andrea Branzi, Milan, 1980; *A History of Industrial Design* by Edward Lucie-Smith, Oxford, 1983; *The Conran Directory of Design* edited by Stephen Bayley, London, 1985; *Design Source Book* by Penny Sparke and others, London, 1986; *Italian Design: 1870 to the Present* by Penny Sparke, London, 1988.

\* \* \*

Although Tomas Maldonado has played a significant role in the burgeoning field of high-tech industrial design—computing equipment, typewriters, word processors, electro-medical and optical equipment—his enduring achievement is tied to the Hochschule für Gestaltung in Ulm, West Germany, where, as Professor and later Rector, he was the school's guiding force from 1954 to 1966.

As a design theorist and educator, Maldonado spearheaded a revolt in design thinking that became synonymous with the school at Ulm, one that set a course in opposition to esthetic taste and functional problem-solving as the fundamental criteria for successful practice.

The school at Ulm was established in 1951 (closed in 1968), under Max Bill as its first director, with the goal of rejuvenating Bauhaus ideals and thus reestablishing Germany as the center of design after the war. Upon Maldonado's arrival in the mid 1950s, from Argentina where he was a painter, designer, and editor, there was evidence of a radical shift in the educational philosophy at the school. Gone was the emphasis on form-building that marked the foundation of Bauhaus discipline in favor of an emphasis on the social sciences, mathematics, and semiology. Gone also were the Fine and Graphic Art Departments, replaced by studies in visual and verbal communication. The hierarchy of architecture as the mother of the arts was dismantled in favor of a more egalitarian enterprise that embraced every facet of the designed environment.

Maldonado was a tireless advocate of the changes wrought at Ulm, as he proselytized throughout the design community against the pervasive ideology of formalism. He believed that the growing complexity of design problems could not be solved by a reliance on intuition or historical research of prototypes but in developing more sophisticated analytical tools. What Maldonado offered was a systematic approach to design methodology—identified as "scientific operationalism"—that was more theory than prescription. Under his leadership, design at Ulm became allied with other social sciences in the study of human relationships that can be measured and tested in the communication of symbolic meanings.

Considering the technocratic overtones of this philosophy, there was an underlying humanism in the fulfillment of universal needs rather than idiosyncratic desires as the ultimate purpose of design. In this way, Ulm maintained a connection (in spirit) with its predecessor, the Bauhaus, and impelled a serious consideration of its experiments in the annals of design.

Currently, there is scant evidence of manufactured products that might attest to the success or failure of Maldonado's teachings. Maldonado himself had worked with German companies, most notably with Erbe of Tubingen, where he designed electronic surgical and radiation equipment that utilized concepts derived from mass-produced consumer goods. The best-known items that show the influence of Ulm, however, were the electrical appliances produced by Braun, a company that maintained a close relationship with the school during Maldonado's tenure. These appliances were the epitome of Ulm's rationalist approach to design. Appropriate in the extreme, they focused on user needs without the interference of style. They were not visually aggressive nor did they intrude upon the user's perception of function. The clarity of expression and the precise relationships of material, engineering, and form dissolved in attempts at a democratized solution to the human dependency upon tools.

—Sarah Bodine

# MALMSTEN, Carl (Per Hendrik)

Swedish interior, furniture, and textile designer

**Born:** Stockholm, 7 December 1888. **Education:** Educated at the Norra Realgymnasium, the Pahlmanns Handilsinstitut, and the hogskolan, Stockholm, until 1908; studied economics, in Lund, 1910; apprenticed in furniture workshops of Pelle Johnsons, Stockholm, 1910-12; studied handicrafts and architecture with Carl Bergten, Stockholm, 1912-15. **Military:** Served in the Royal Swedish Lifeguards, 1909-10. **Family:** Married Siv Munthe in 1917; children: Ulf, Kerstin, Egil, Vidar, and Torgils. **Career:** Freelance furniture and interior designer, in Stockholm, from 1916; established workshops at Tunnelgatan, 1916-19, at Arbetargatan, 1919-22, at Krukmakargatan, 1940-50, and at Renstiernagatan, 1950-73; director, Firma Carl Malmsten, Stockholm, 1933, and Carl Malmsten AB, Stockholm, 1944. Head of design, Naas Slojdseminarium, Stockholm, 1922-25, and Sigtuna Skolan, 1926-34; workshop founder, Oloffskolan, Stockholm, 1928-32; handicrafts instructor, at Svolvaer Bruksvaliarna and Hedemora, 1933-40, and at the Konstfackskolan, Stockholm, 1948; also instructor of summer courses, Viggbyholmsskolan, 1946-47, and Capellagarden School, 1958-72. **Member:** Founder of Malmstens Handicrafts Union, Stockholm, 1930, Nyckelbrodernas Forbundet Association, Stockholm, 1955, and of the Capellagardens Forbund, Stockholm, 1961. **Exhibitions:** Blanchs Konstsalong, Stockholm, 1917; *Jubilee Exhibition,* Göteborg, 1923; *Exposition des Arts Decoratifs,* Paris, 1925; *Jonsson-Malmsten-Munthe,* Liljevalchs Konsthall, Stockholm, 1928; *Swedish Arts and Crafts,* Dorland Gallery, London, 1930; *Malmsten/Måås-Fjetterström,* Konstslöjdmuseet, Göteborg, 1933, Liljevalchs Konsthall, Stockholm, 1934; *Swedish Exhibition,* Warsaw and Prague, 1938; New York World's Fair, 1939; *Nyttokonstnären,* Nationalmuseum, Stockholm, 1943; *Carl Malmsten: Retrospective,* Nationalmuseum, Stockholm, 1944; *Svenska Stolar,* Nationalmuseum, Stockholm, 1963; *Scandinavian Modern Design 1880-1980,* Cooper-Hewitt Museum, New York, 1982. **Collections:** Röhsska Konstslöjdmuseet, Göteborg; Nationalmuseum, Stockholm; Metropolitan Museum of Art, New York. **Honors:** Furniture Competition Prize, Stockholm, 1916; Grand Prize, Paris International Exposition, 1925; Litteris et Artibus Award, Stockholm, 1926; St. Erik and Prince Eugen Medals, Stockholm, 1945. **Died:** Stockholm, in 1972.

## Works

*Stadshusstolen* chairs, for Stockholm Town Hall, 1916.
*Konsert* armchair, for Stockholm Concert Hall, 1923.
*Jonas* upholstered armchair, for KV Larsson Eftr., 1938.
*Ingrid* chair, for P. Holsten, 1944.
*Widemar* writing chair, for Andoman-Padouk, 1944.
*Klyftan* cupboard, for AB Fanerkompaniet, 1946.
*Juni* chair, for L. and L. Cederlöf, 1949.
*Tidlösa* grandfather clock, for Bröderna Holm AB, 1953.
*Mittens Rike* cupboard, for Feuk and Wilson, 1964.
*Island* sewing cabinet, for Bröderna Holm AB, 1964.
*Sommar* cupboard, for Bröderna Holm AB, 1964.

**On MALMSTEN: books**—*Modern Decorative Arts of Sweden* by Erik Wettergren, Malmö and London, 1928; *Svenska Möbler* by Brynhof Hellner, Stockholm, 1947; *Carl Malmsten: Swedish Furniture* edited by Paul Artaria, Basel, 1954; *A Treasury of Scandinavian Design* edited by Erik Zahle, New York, 1961; *Carl Malmsten: Pionjar och Traditionsbevarare* by Ulf Hård af Segerstad, Stockholm, 1963; *Carl Malmsten hel och hallen* by Eric Wennerholm, Stockholm, 1969; *Design in Sweden,* edited by Lennart Lindkvist,

Stockholm, 1972; *Scandinavian Design: Objects of a Life Style* by Eileene Harrison Beer, New York and Toronto, 1975; *Twentieth Century Furniture* by Philippe Garner London, 1980; *Carl Malmstens Verkstadsskola 1930 1980* by P. O. Scote, S. Malmsten, and others, Stockholm, 1980; *Scandinavian Modern Design 1880-1980* edited by David Revere McFadden, New York, 1982; *The Conran Directory of Design* edited by Stephen Bayley, London, 1985; *Twentieth Century Design: Furniture* by Penny Sparke, London, 1986.

# MANASSEH, Leonard (Sulla)

British architect and environmental and interior designer

**Born:** London, 21 May 1916. **Education:** Studied at Cheltenham College, Gloucestershire, until 1935; studied at the Architectural Association School, London, Dip. Arch., 1940. **Military Service:** Served in the Royal Navy, 1943-46, Fleet Air Arm pilot. **Family:** Married in 1947 (divorced, 1956); children: two; married Sarah Delaforce in 1957; children: three. **Career:** Assistant architect, with C.R.E., North London, and Guy Morgan and Partners, London, 1941-43, and with Hertfordshire County Council, 1946-48; senior architect, Stevenage Development Corporation, Hertfordshire, 1948-50; in private architectural and design practice as Leonard Manasseh and Partners, in London and Bath, from 1950; with James Cubitt and Partners, established offices Cubitt, Manasseh, and Partners, in Singapore and Malaysia, 1953-54. Instructor, Kingston School of Art, Surrey, 1941-43, and Architectural Association School, London, 1941-43, 1951-59. Council Member, 1959-66, and president, 1964-65, Architectural Association, London; member, Council of Industrial Design, London, 1965-68; council member, 1968-70, 1976-82, and honorary secretary, 1979-81, Royal Institute of British Architects; Associate, 1976, and Academician, 1979, Royal Academy of Art, London; council member, National Trust, London, from 1977; member of the Ancient Monuments Board, London, 1978-84; president, Franco-British Union of Architects, 1978-79; board member, Chatham Historic Dockyard Trust, from 1984. **Member:** Royal West of England Academy, Bristol, 1972. **Honors:** *News Chronicle* Schools Competition Prize, London, 1938; Festival of Britain Restaurant Competition Prize, London, 1950; *Financial Times* Industrial Architecture Award, London, 1967; Ministry of Housing and Local Government Gold Medal, 1970; Royal Institute of British Architects Award, 1973; Structural Steel Design Award, London, 1974; National Heritage Award, London, 1974; *The Times*/Institute of Chartered Surveyors Conservation Award, London, 1975; European Architectural Heritage Year Award, 1975. Associate, 1941, and Fellow, 1964, Royal Institute of British Architects; Fellow, Chartered Society of Designers, London, 1965; Fellow, Royal Society of Arts, London, 1967; Officer, Order of the British Empire, 1982. **Addresses:** 6 Bacon's Lane, London N6 6BL; Leonard Manasseh and Partners, 58 Bloomsbury Street, London WC1, England.

## Works

Luxury restaurant, for the Festival of Britain, South Bank, London, 1950-51.
Manasseh house, Highgate, London, 1958-59.

Rutherford Secondary School in Marylebone, London, for the London County Council, 1960.
Furzedown Training College, London, for the London County Council, 1964-65.
National Motor Museum in Beaulieu, Hampshire, for Montagu Ventures Limited, 1971.
Master Builder Hotel extensions, Buckler's Hard, Hampshire, 1972.
Wellington Country Park in Heckfield, Hampshire, for Stratfield Saye Estates Management, 1975.
Manasseh house in Merindol, Provence, France, 1981.

## Publications

**By MANASSEH: books**—(with Roger Cunliffe) *Office Buildings,* London, 1962, Tokyo, 1964; (report, with E. U. Chesterton) *The Historic Core of King's Lynn,* London, 1964; *Snow-down Summit: A Report,* London, 1975; (report) *East-bourne Harbour Study,* London, 1976.

**On MANASSEH: books**—*Public Interiors: An International Survey* by Misha Black, London, 1960; *House and Garden: The Modern Interior* edited by Robert Harling, London, 1964; *The Practical Idealists: 25 Years of Designing for Industry* by Jon and Avril Blake, London, 1969.

\*       \*       \*

Manasseh became an associate of the Royal Institute of British Architects in 1941, but was obliged by the war to serve as a pilot in the Royal Naval Fleet Air Arm. From 1946 to 1948, he was an assistant architect at the Hertfordshire County Council and from 1948 to 1950, a senior architect at the Stevenage Development Corporation. Winning the Festival of Britain prize for a restaurant design encouraged him to open his own practice in 1950, and the partnership developed with work in housing and schooling such as the North Westminster School in London for the Westminster City Council.

An enormous brief arrived when Lord Montagu decided to rebuild and expand his motor museum, and the plan was agreed with by the Hampshire County Council in 1966. The client required the museum, an information centre, an administration block, a library, and a restaurant. Work began in 1970, and the complex was opened by the Duke of Kent two years later. The largest structure is the National Motor Museum, a vast square crossed by two diagonal transepts which provide top lighting and form the entrance canopies. To unify the complex, materials were limited to steel, blockwork, and glazing, the idea of a glass building in a park being inspired by such English precedents as Paxton's Crystal Palace and Decimus Burton's glasshouses at Kew Gardens. (Triangular glass roofs are, however, a regular feature of the firm's designs, as in the house for the film producer Richard Lester).

Impressed by the layout at Beaulieu, the Duke of Wellington asked Manasseh to design the information centre, restaurants, boating facilities, and museum at his new Wellington Country Park, Heckfield Hampshire. The west side of the park is for golf and riding, while the east side is organized into boating and fishing areas, nature trails, picnic sites, adventure areas for children, and a camping site. Manasseh based his designs on a six-meter structural grid to allow for future expansion, and pyramidal roofs dominate the buildings. He subscribes to Sir Henry Wotton's definition of architecture as

"Firmness, Commodity and Delight," and says that scale is all-important. He believes in modern architecture as honest form, not as self-expression. With Roger Cunliffe, he is author of *Office Buildings.*

—Diana de Marly

# MANDELLI, Mariuccia

Italian fashion designer

**Born:** Bergamo, Italy, in 1933. **Family:** Married Aldo Pinto. **Career:** Worked as a teacher, Milan, 1952-54; designer and founder with Flora Dolci, of Krizia fashion firm, Milan, from 1954; founded Kriziamaglia knitwear, 1966, and Kriziababy children's clothes, 1968; subsequently established Krizia boutiques, in Milan, Tokyo, London, New York, Detroit, Houston, and others. **Exhibitions:** *Italian Re Evolution,* La Jolla Museum of Art, California, 1982; *40 Years of Italian Fashion,* Trump Tower, New York, 1983. **Honors:** Fashion Press Award, Florence, 1964. **Address:** Via Agnelli 12, 20100 Milan, Italy.

**Publications**

ON MANDELLI: books—*A History of Fashion* by J. Anderson Black and Madge Garland, London 1975, 1980; *The World of Fashion: People, Places, Resources* by Eleanor Lambert, New York and London, 1976; *I Mass-Moda: Fatti e Personaggi dell'Italian Look* by Adrianna Mulassano, Florence, 1979; *Fairchild's Who's Who in Fashion* edited by Ann Stegemeyer, New York, 1980; *Who's Who in Fashion* edited by Karl Strute and Theodor Doelken, Zurich, 1982; *The Collector's Book of Twentieth Century Fashion* by Frances Kennett, London and New York, 1983; *40 Years of Italian Fashion,* exhibition catalogue compiled by B. G. Aragno, Rome, 1983; *McDowell's Directory of Twentieth Century Fashion* by Colin McDowell, London, 1984; *Design Source Book* by Penny Sparke and others, London, 1986; *The Encyclopedia of Fashion from 1840 to the 1980's* by Georgia O'Hara, London, 1986; **articles**—"Berets Are Off to Krizia" by Suzy Menkes in the *International Herald Tribune* (Paris), 7 March 1995; "La Beauté platonicienne de Krizia" by Gini Alhadeff in *Vogue* (Paris), April 1995; "A Roaring Forty" by Elizabetta Muritti in *Mondo Uomo* (Milan), May/June 1995.

*        *        *

The success of the Milanese boutique called Krizia, and, in fact, the prominence of Milanese fashion which has occurred during the 1980s and 1990s, are both largely due to the efforts of Krizia's founder and designer, Mariuccia Mandelli. Mandelli is one of the originators of the major contrast trend of Milan in which a simple, classic tailoring is punctuated with original and amusing accents to create a new face for stylish ready-to-wear fashion that is both eminently wearable and exuberantly youthful.

Among Krizia's early, important presentations was a showing at Orsini's on the invitation of Jean Rosenberg, vice-president of Bendel's. It was on this occasion that Mandelli was labeled "Crazy Krizia" by the fashion press for her combinations of simple shapes with madcap details. In 1976, Bergdorf Goodman featured stock by Krizia and other Milanese designers, providing the final step necessary for the Italians' rise to the forefront.

Representative of what has been called Krizia's "rough and sweet" look are Mandelli's 1977 outfittings consisting of nylon undershirts topped by matching rose-colored or dove-gray mohair bedjackets or cardigans in open-knit weaves and worn with dropped-waist ballerina skirts of scalloped lace. Mandelli's daywear tends toward the practical, she has, for example, put elastic waistbands on her skirts for comfortable ease of movement, and her 1982 group of sport suits of loose tweeds and checks are plain, loose, and stylized. Mandelli's uses of her signature "improbable contrasts," however, abound most openly in her evening clothes, such as the mixes of satin skirts with sporty Angora sweaters which appeared in 1978. In that same year, she also presented her preferred simple slip dress accompanied by characteristic touches of humourous flamboyance such as a long, feathered stole or quilted jacket of satin faced in a different shade of the same color.

Mandelli has often used jodhpur pants. One 1977 outfit consisted of loose, draping jodhpurs in silk charmeuse worn with a lacy, mohair camisole, the whole enlivened by the glowing berry colors she featured that year. Also among Mandelli's original fashion accomplishments is her development of what she named "harmonica pleats" which combine vertical and horizontal pleatings.

Outstanding among Mandelli's designs are her knits which include items such as her 1977 lacy, mushroom-colored, evening sweater teamed with double-scarf of silk taffeta and eyelet taffeta and jodhpur pants. In 1981, she showed subtly sophisticated shiny knits and white angoras bedecked with yokes of pearls. Often appearing on Mandelli's knitwear are her signature animal motifs. In 1978, there was a jacquard crepe blouse with the front view of a tiger on its front and rear-tiger-view on its back. In her 1980 collection, there were colorful knits featuring parrots and toucans; short knit dresses included a one-piece version sporting the front half of a leopard and a two-piece style revealing the leopard's rear half. Not limiting herself to knitwear, Mandelli also put highly colorful birds and parrots on that season's summer tote bags and shoulder purses. For 1984, it was the dalmation, sharing the scene with more streamlined suits and double-dresses such as a back-buttoned flare over a little bit longer slim skirt.

From the start, Krizia's Mariuccia Mandelli has continuously based her highly original designs on nervy eccentricity and wit which have earned her a prominent place in the recent Milanese force that has successfully nudged ready-to-wear fashion in a new direction.

—Barbara Cavaliere

# MANG, Karl

Austrian architect and interior, exhibition, and furniture designer

**Born:** Vienna, 5 October 1922. **Education:** Attended high school in Vienna, 1933-41; studied engineering, at the Technical University, Vienna, Dip.Ing., 1948; post-graduate studies, University of Rome, 1950-51. **Military Service:** Served in the German Army, 1941-45, Lieutenant. **Family:** Married the architect Eva von Frimmel in 1957; children: Bauxi, Carolina, and Hannerl. **Career:** Independent designer and architect, Vienna, from 1955; designed for Thonet, Morawa, Wienerberger, Austrian Ministry of Science, Vienna

**Karl Mang: Die Shaker exhibition layout for the Neue Sammlung, Munich, 1974**

Bundeskammer, Austrian Building Center, and others. Teaching assistant, Technical University, Vienna, 1948-54; instructor in furniture construction, Federal Trade School, Modling, 1954-59; lecturer, Academy of Applied Art, Vienna, 1963-72; guest professor, Staatliche Akademie der Bildenden Künste, Stuttgart, 1983; visiting professor, Universidad de Chile, Santiago, 1986. President, 1972-83, honorary president, from 1983, Österreichisches Institut fur Formgebung, Vienna; permanent member of the Denkmalbeirat, Vienna, from 1980. **Exhibitions:** Künstlerhaus, Vienna, 1964; Schloss Walchen, Austria, 1976; Ursulinenhof, Linz, 1978; Ingenieurkammer, Vienna, 1987. **Honors:** Communications Collaborative Certificate of Excellence, 1975; Chicago Book Clinic Award, 1975; titular professor, Vienna, 1977; Silver Medal of Honour, Vienna, 1981; and over 30 European architectural prizes. **Address:** Baumannstrasse 9, A-1030 Vienna, Austria.

## Works

*Das Werk Michael Thonets* travelling exhibition layouts, for the Austrian Center of Building, 1965.

*Wienerberger* variable pavilions in Graz, for Wienerberger, 1965, 1967.

*Creative Austria* travelling exhibition layouts, for the Bundeskammer, Vienna, 1970.

Thonet shops in Dusseldorf and Vienna, for Thonet, 1970-71.

Pocketbook shop, for Morawa, 1972.

*Die Shaker* travelling exhibition layouts, for the Neue Sammlung, Munich, 1974.

*Kommunaler Wohnbau in Wien* travelling exhibition layouts, for the City of Vienna, 1977.

*Österreichische Architektur in Zeichnungen 1860-1930* travelling exhibition layouts, for Austrian Ministry for Foreign Affairs, 1978-1987.

*Moderne Vergangenheit 1800-1900* travelling exhibition layouts, for Künstlerhaus, Vienna, 1981-82.

Vienna Imperial Treasury displays, for the Ministry of Science and Research, 1981-87; reconstruction and redesign, 1993-94.

Austrian Embassy interiors, Baghdad, for the Foreign Ministry, 1982.

Austrian Theatre Museum interiors, for the Ministry of Science and Research, from 1986.

Café Viennois interiors, for the Centre Georges Pompidou, Paris, 1986

*Industrie und Umweltschutz* fair pavilion, for Vienna Chamber of Commerce, 1989.

*Fashion Museum,* for City of Vienna, Schloß Hetzendorf, 1991.

*Das Rote Wien* exhibition, for Historisches Museum der Stadt Wien, Vienna, 1993.

Book shop, for Messrs. Morawa, Vienna, 1994-95.

**Publications**

By MANG: books—*Das Werk Michael Thonets,* exhibition catalogue, Vienna, 1965; *Die Shaker,* exhibition catalogue, with Wend Fischer, Munich, 1974; *Kommunaler Wohnbau in Wien, die Leistungen der zweiten Republik,* exhibition catalogue, Vienna, 1978; *Kommunaler Wohnbau in Wien 1923-1934,* exhibition catalogue, Vienna, 1978; *History of Modern Furniture,* Stuttgart, 1978, 1989, London, New York, and Tokyo, 1979, Rome, 1982; (with Eva Mang) *Viennese Architecture 1860-1930 in Drawings,* Stuttgart, New York, and London, 1979; *Neus Wohnen, Wiener Innenraumgestaltung 1918-1938,* exhibition catalogue, Vienna, 1980; *Moderne Verangenheit 1800-1900,* exhibition catalogue, Vienna, 1981; (with Eva Mang) *New Shops,* Stuttgart, 1981, New York, 1982; *Thonet Bugholzmöbel,* Vienna, 1982, 1985, Tokyo, 1985; (with Eva Mang) *Moebel unserer Zeit: Fibel fur die Einrichtung von Wohnungen,* Vienna, 1984; (with Peter Marchart) *Wohnen in der Stadt: Ideen fur Wien,* Vienna, 1988.

On MANG: books—*Mercati e Negozi* by Robert Aloi, Milan, 1959; *International Shop Design* by Karl Kaspar, Stuttgart and London, 1967; *Boutiquen, Shops und schicke Laden* by Wolfgang Grub, Munich, 1974; *Industrial Design* by Bernd Lobach, Munich, 1976; *Die Geschichte des Design in Deutschland von 1870 bis heute* by Gert Selle, Cologne, 1978; *Shop Design* by Ingrid Wenz-Gahler, Leinfelden, 1986.

*

Against the compulsion of consumer society to subject every product to rapid changes in fashion stands the desire of a small but continually growing number of people to escape from this pressure and to become actively involved in creating their own personal home environments. Yet a walk through any furniture fair, be it in Paris, Cologne, or Milan, should be enough to rob anyone of his illusions with respect to the true situation in the furniture market. It is safe to say that most furniture companies and retailers (not to mention most buyers) still prefer styles inspired by the past—prettily painted "peasant" furniture, for instance—perhaps as a way of compensating for the missing warmth in their daily lives. Rather than good contemporary designs, the stores offer fake Baroque, Spanish rustic, and the glib forms of a noncommittal Modern.

Good modern furniture has been granted only a very modest corner in our civilization, and the interiors of tomorrow will not come without some serious re-thinking in the field of city planning. What is needed in the face of our rapidly disappearing countryside is an industrialized program of housing, based on higher population density and offering apartments with open floor plans. The greatest possible variability and mobility for every individual are just as important as the chance to design and plan one's own surroundings—in a word, participation in the design of housing, under the guidance of trained architects and planners.

An urban environment conceived in this way, modest but well designed, will require furniture that is not sensational but useful, and above all flexible. It should be simple and human in form and designed for manufacture in large numbers at low prices. Furniture is basically always a child of its time, if only because the demands that people make on it change—and they often change several times even in the course of one lifetime. Nonetheless, this process should not be subject to the dictates of fashion alone. Then, too, many young people of today establish their households with very modest means. Having grown up in a rapidly shrinking world, they are accustomed to living in one apartment or city today and in another tomorrow. Rigid tradition has given way to a new, flexible style that, though it may express a greater social equality than ever before, is also characterized by an extremely individual view of interiors as personal environments. Light, versatile furniture makes it possible to furnish even today's tiny apartments in a pleasing way, even on a limited budget.

The variable furniture systems that have recently come on the market, often sold cash-and-carry to be assembled at home, are a good example of the kind of policy that is needed for the future. They provide an excellent means of supplementing, at a reasonable price, those single pieces which by reason of their aesthetic quality and their craftsmanship may still form the centre of gravity in any good contemporary interior.

Home furnishings of this type, if they are to be successful in the long run, will probably have to be accompanied by a program of consumer education. As long as most people's idea of formal quality swings back and forth between the poles of historicism and kitsch, a truly human and generally valid formal quality in home furnishings, as in architecture itself, will remain the dream of a few. There is reason to hope that a program of education in home furnishing, starting in the schools, might help people get over their status-consciousness and need for representation in choosing the objects they live with. If the mass media were to do their part, and if good, simple, modern furniture were made available at reasonable prices, then a change might truly come about. An architecture of quiet is going to have to follow the chaos of form and material of our consumer age, if we wish to continue existing reasonably with technology. Simple spaces for living, with clean well-designed furniture, will go far toward placing man in the center of his world again.

—Karl Mang

# MANGIAROTTI, Angelo

Italian architect and interior, exhibition, and industrial designer

**Born:** Milan, 26 February 1921. **Education:** Studied architecture, at the Politecnico Milan, Dip.Arch., 1948. **Career:** Architect and designer, in partnership with Bruno Morassutti, Milan, 1955-60; freelance designer and architect in private practice, Milan, from 1960; opened Mangiarotti & Associates office, Tokyo, 1989; design consultant to Porte Echappement Universel, La Chaux de Fonds, 1955-68, CGE of Milan, 1959, Alfa Romeo, Milan, 1960, and Electrolux, Stockholm, 1961; art director, Colle Cristallo di Val d'Elsa, Siena, from 1987. Visiting professor, Institute of Design, Illinois Institute of Technology, Chicago, 1953-54, University of Hawaii Honolulu, 1970, Ecole Polytéchnique Fédérale, Lausanne, 1975, University of Adelaide and South Australian Institute of Technology, Adelaide, 1976, University of Sao Paulo, 1978, and Politechnical University, Milan, 1990; lecturer, Istituto Superiore di Disegno Industriale, Venice 1963-64, and University of Florence, 1981-82. **Exhibitions:** *La Casa Abitata,* Florence, 1965; *Angelo Mangiarotti,* Zurich, 1966; *Angelo Mangiarotti,* Delft, 1966; *Ten Italian Architects,* Los Angeles, 1967; *Modern Chairs 1918-1970,* London, 1970; *Exposicion Internacional de la Vivienda,* Santiago de Chile, 1972; *Architettura 28/78,* Milan, 1978; *Design Since 1945,* Philadelphia, 1983; *Sammenhenger Angelo Mangiarotti,* Oslo, 1985;

*Poiesis: Alabastri di Angelo Mangiarotti* Milan, 1986; *Angelo Mangiarotti,* Genoa, 1988; *Poiesis: Sculture di Angelo Mangiarotti,* Milan, 1988; *Angelo Mangiarotti: La Seduzione della Materia,* Fortezza da Basso, Firenze, 1991; *Angelo Mangiarotti: Mostra sull'opera,* Politecnico di Milano, 1991; *Angelo Mangiarotti,* First Marble Symposium, Tokyo, 1993; *Matter's Tongue,* Chicago, 1995. **Honors:** Olimpiadi della Cultura Boy's Prize, Milan, 1952; Economic Development Center Prize, Trieste, 1953; Domus Formica Award, Milan, 1956; Gold Medal, Villa dell'Olmo, Como, 1957; Associazione Italiana Tecnico Economica del Cemento Award, 1962; In/Arch Lombardia Award, Milan, 1962; National Gulf of La Spezia Award, 1963; Associazione Italiana Prefabbricatori Award, 1972; Prix Europeen de la Construction Metallique, 1979; World Architecture Biennial Medal, Sofia, 1986; Targa Alcan Award, Milan, 1988; In/Arch Award special mention, 1990; Plus Prize, 1991; Special Award, Marble Architectural Awards, 1994; Compasso d'Oro for career, ADI, 1994. **Addresses:** Via Cesare da Sesto 15, 20123 Milan; Stradela Valmarana 2, 36100 Vicenza, Italy.

## Works

*Multi-Use* furniture system, for Poltronova, 1955 (with Bruno Morassutti).

*Secticon* series of mantle clocks, for Porte Echappement Universel, 1957 (with Morassutti).

Sewing machines, for Salmoiraghi, 1957 (with Morassutti).

Series of bronze vases, for Bernini, 1962.

*Cub8* furniture system, for Poltronova, 1967.

*In/Out* furniture system, for Knoll International, 1968.

Series of polyurethane armchairs and side chairs, for Zanotta, 1969.

*Eros* series of marble tables, for Skipper, 1971.

*De Nos* range of wood furniture, for Skipper, 1975.

*Incas* series of sandstone tables, for Skipper, 1978.

*Egina* wall and ceiling lamp, for Artemide, 1978.

*Asolo* series of granite tables, for Skipper, 1981.

*Primavera, Estate, Autunno,* and *Inverno* crystal vases, for Colle Cristalleria, 1981-89.

*Chicago* fibreglass chair, for Chicago, 1983.

*Clessidra* and *Sorella* glass lamps, for Skipper, 1985.

*Ice-Stopper* crystal glasses, for Colle Cristalleria, 1986.

*Anatis, Oinoche, Askos* and *Kyatos* crystal pitchers, for Colle Cristalleria, 1987.

Series of blown glass vases, for Vistosi, 1988.

*Techne* halogen lamp for Skipper, 1988.

*Casta* crystal centerpiece bowl, for Colle Cristalleria, 1988.

*Ebbro* glass, for Colle Cristalleria, 1990.

*Ergonomica* collection for the table, for Mepra, 1991.

Handles series, for Valli & Colombo, 1993.

Handles series, for Olivari, 1993.

(for a complete list of Mangiarotti's buildings and architectural projects, see *Contemporary Architects.*)

## Publications

**By MANGIAROTTI: books**—*In Nome dell'Architettura,* Milan, 1987; *Disegnare il Cristallo,* Milan, 1991; (contributor) *L'Atto Progettuale,* Milan, 1991; **articles**—in *Domus* (Milan), 1948-78; *Arts and Architecture* (Los Angeles) 1953-70; *L'Architecture d'Aujourd'hui* (Paris), 1953-73; *Casabella* (Milan), 1955-78; *L'Oeil* (Paris), 1956-72; *Architectural Forum* (New York), 1959-63; *Bauen und Wohnen* (Zurich), 1959-77; *Moebel Interior Design* (Stuttgart), 1960-75; *L'Industria Italiana del Cemento* (Rome), 1963-77; *Ottagono* (Milan), 1967-77; *Casa Vogue* (Milan), 1968-77; *Premiere* (Milan), 1987-88; *Design News* (Tokyo), 1984-88; "Architetture Techniche" in *Proporzione A,* no. 1, 1993; "Silver House: un sistema per abitare" in *Proporzione A,* no. 1, 1993.

**On MANGIAROTTI: books**—*Italian Contemporary Architecture,* London, 1952; *Mobili Tipo* by Robert Aloi, Milan, 1956; *Angelo Mangiarotti,* Tokyo, 1965; *Design Italiano: i mobili* by Enrichetta Ritter, Milan and Rome, 1968; *Introduzione al Disegno Industriale* by Gillo Dorfles, Turin, 1972; *History of Modern Furniture* by Karl Mang, Stuttgart, 1978, 1989, London, 1979; *Angelo Mangiarotti: Il Processo del Costruire* by Enrico D. Bona, Milan, 1980; *Il Design Italiano degli Anni '50* by Andrea Branzi and Michele De Lucchi, Milan, 1981; *Contemporary Furniture* by Klaus-Jürgen Sembach, Stuttgart and New York, 1982; *Furniture by Architects,* Tokyo, 1982; *Angelo Mangiarotti,* Zurich, 1985; *Bauten von Angelo Mangiarotti,* Stuttgart, 1985; *Mangiarotti* by Enrico D. Bona, Genoa, 1988; **articles**—"L'essenza costruttiva dei materiali lapidei" by Teruo Yokota in *Stones New Creative Magazine,* no. 1, 1994; "Experimente in Marmor" by Robert Stadler in *Naturstein,* no. 5, 1994.

\*

It is not easy to survey the contribution to design made by the development of human society; the difficulty is that the way of design is not clear. We can say that there was design before the industrial era and we can add that design is present in every civilization. But we have to make clear what we mean when we use the term "design" and establish what are the conditions which the concept of the design proposes.

The first condition is that the project serves for what it was conceived. The second one is that the object shows for what it serves and how it is to be used. Just beginning from these two basic conditions raises some doubt that design has made a positive contribution to human society.

In fact, there exist many examples, particularly in recent years, of objects designed which transgress these two basic conditions of design. It is clear that if this transgression should become the principal way of design, it will not be any thinkable positive contribution of design to society.

In this age it seems that most design tendencies suggest the replacement of the functional characteristics of the objects with "decorative significances." On the contrary, I think that it is necessary, for the survival of design itself, that we make up a vision of designing in which every object, every article, must be immediately legible through its materiality and that function must be respected.

Today the technical poorness and the imperfection of design are masked and introduced with the abundant use of decoration. But decoration cannot be used merely for itself because one must never deprive a structure of its significance related to the materials used and its functions.

The problem of design is always related to the possibility that materials and function will find expression. In this vision of which I speak, design can be placed alongside geometrics, mathematics, and biology and therefore creation is derivable from relations internal to the scientific community. Design cannot be placed—as the day's tendencies show—alongside painting, sculpture, literature, and poetry. One cannot perceive a statute of creation which is inseparable from the creator. On the contrary, design must try to give to an article the most possibly objective potential of reality.

It is possible to rely on the particular sensitivity of the designer for the materials or on his intuitive capacity to realize their possibility, but good design needs to start from a reality that has nothing to do with sensitivity and intuition. The necessary path to give form to amorphous matter begins from its nature and from its characteristics: it isn't possible to plan a vase in baked clay and then transfer it into glass. That would mean not to understand what is baked clay and what is glass. It would mean to misunderstand the whole culture behind ceramics. It would mean not to understand the basic condition of the project.

Faced with the impetus of contemporary society together with the rapid changes in economics, political, and social values, it would seem that the doctrinaire structure of the theories which have been formulated in the past as interpretation of reality are having to be reviewed and reformed at least in a different temporality in relation to the quicker ability to learn and absorb which distinguishes the individual in contemporary society. Thus it is impossible for a designer to begin his project from the object itself. Rather, he could

transcribe it coherent with his time, with the means, with the language, with the techniques and the materials that are at his disposal.

Of course, future design cannot repudiate tradition; every article, from a so-called "congenital cultural adherence," recalls antique forms. But it is not a question of using the past either as a fetish or as a model, but rather as a memory and as a structure. What is interesting about the past is its capacity to bring itself up-to-date in the present. In fact, what memory gives back to us is never a copy but the sense of relationship with the present. It is not the analogy between past and present which returns in the plan but its metaphor.

—Angelo Mangiarotti

\* \* \*

Angelo Mangiarotti has worked with various collaborators, often in fairly lasting partnerships, but his strong design personality seems to sweep his partners along his chosen path, in which certain forms and materials seem predominant, notably cones, truncated cones, and shapes generated from them to support tables. Besides the characteristic 1955-56 desk and the important 1963 tables, the

**Angelo Mangiarotti: "Ebbro" glasses, Colle Cristalleria, Colle Val d'Elsa, 1990**

M1 table of 1969 used these forms, this time in marble. Over several years after 1957, they also appeared in a series of table clocks for the Swiss firm Porte Echappement Universel.

It must not be supposed, however, that he is a designer who uses a single form in all his work. Mangiarotti constantly senses new formal possibilities, ad well as new uses of the forms he has employed in other situations, as can be seen, for example, in his apartment block at San Siro, Milan. Here, he used an ingenious arrangement of three cylinders that must have been thought out in three dimensions, although the coherence of the planning might suggest otherwise, and could have played a considerable role in the generation of the block. The general effect of the building, however, is so strikingly successful that the coherence must derive from the overall vision.

In the late 1950s in Milan, when a number of pioneer designers had virtually established the new shape of sewing machines, it took courage to accept such a commission and to stamp the design of the Salmoiraghi 44 with a character of its own, but this was exactly what Mangiarotti achieved. His sewing machine had a foursquare look, forthright but suitably refined with all corners and edges rounded. The final form was also admirably suited to the manufacturing process and assembly.

The storage and shelving units produced for Knoll International developed ideas with which he had first experimented a few years earlier in the Cub8 component wall-system and freestanding assemblies, for Poltronova. This design, which had also used extruded plastic and interlocking joints, in its turn departed from some of the aspects of an even earlier series of mass-produced bedroom units for Mascheroni, though in 1955 the clever use of trestle supports had seemed more interesting. These concerns were also to be seen in his research in the mid 1960s into a pre-fabrication building system, though the formal preoccupations changed with the changing situations.

It would be difficult to sum up Mangiarotti's qualities as a designer and even more so to attempt to characterise his work in other than somewhat general terms. To be sure, however, he always manifests concern for formal possibilities, for precise use of materials and finishes, and for immaculate detailing, as well as devotion to the most pleasing effect with the most rational use of manufacturing possibilities.

—Tonio del Renzio

# MANWARING, Michael

American graphic designer

**Born:** Palo Alto, California, 21 March 1942. **Education:** Studied under James Robertson, Gordon Ashby, and Barbara and Jack Stauffacher at the San Francisco Art Institute, BFA, 1964. **Family:** Married Dixie Wells in 1960; children: Elizabeth and Christopher. **Career:** Graphic designer, in the Gordon Ashby exhibition design studio, San Francisco, 1964, and in the Robertson/Montgomery graphic design studio, San Francisco, 1964-68; partner, in Reis and Manwaring graphic design studio, San Francisco, 1968-76; founder-president, The Office of Michael Manwaring, San Francisco, from 1976. Instructor in graphic design, California College of Arts and Crafts, Oakland, from 1976; visiting instructor in environmental graphic design, University of California, Berkeley, 1977. Co-founder, San Francisco chapter of the American Institute of Graphic Arts,

1982. **Collections:** Library of Congress, Washington, D.C. **Honors:** San Francisco Society of Communicating Arts Medal, 1972, 1974, 1980, 1981, 1982; *Architectural Record* interiors award, 1972; New York Art Directors Club Gold Medal, 1980; Typographers International Association Award, 1982. **Address:** 1005 Sansome Street, San Francisco, California 94111, U.S.A.

## Works

Graphic signage, for the Oakland/Alameida Coliseum, California, 1967.
Theme exhibit, for *Hemisfair '68,* San Antonio, Texas, 1968.
Bookstore graphics, for the San Francisco Museum of Modern Art, 1973.
Environmental graphics, for California Street Cooking School, San Francisco, 1973.
Showroom displays and interior graphics, for Patrick Carpet Mills, San Francisco, 1976.
Indian Basin Industrial Park graphic signage, San Francisco, 1977.
Graphic signage, for Oakville Grocery Company, San Francisco, 1980.
Centro Nuevo urban development graphics, Santiago de Chile, 1980.
Plaza Lyon urban development graphics, Santiago de Chile, 1981.
*AIASFLOO* exhibition graphics, for the American Institute of Architects, San Francisco, 1982.

## Publications

**On MANWARING: books**—*Letterheads of the World* by Yoshihisa Ishihara, Tokyo, 1977; *Print Casebooks: Environmental Graphics* by Susan Braybrooke, Baltimore, 1978, 1982; *Architectural Signing and Graphics* by John Follis and David Hammer, New York, 1979; *Graphic Design for Our Environment* by Takenobu Igarashi, Tokyo, 1980; *Print Casebook: Exhibition Design* by Susan Braybrooke, Baltimore, 1983; *New American Design* by Hugh Aldersley-Williams, New York, 1988; **articles**—*Novum Gebrauchsgraphik* (Munich), August 1991; *Graphis* (Zürich), November/December 1992.

*

Perhaps the most important factor regarding my design is that I am a native Californian. Our California graphic design source of influence is more Oriental than European. This gives our work intuitive, mystical, and sensual qualities, as contrasted with midwest or east coast design, which tends to be more literary, conceptual, and European.

I am for: a contextual approach to graphic design, elegance, richness, sensuality, appropriate ambiguity, and graphic design as cultural contribution. I am against: a dogmatic approach to graphic design, rigidity, pragmatism, international sign symbols, monoculture, and graphic design imitating art.

—Michael Manwaring

\* \* \*

Michael Manwaring was trained in the 1960s at the San Francisco Art Institute, a school which has long emphasized personal expression. Manwaring's work never partook of the sometimes funky naivete typical of student work there, but he did absorb the emphasis on personal symbolism and individual composition. Manwaring began his work as a graphic designer during the period of the primacy of the Swiss style, with its grid system for composition; reductivist repertoire of hard-edged, geometric shapes; brilliant, flat color; and very large type contrasting with the small. Therefore, his emphasis on texture (especially the delicate pencil shading of pointillist dots), his precise and touching detail, soft and unusual colors, and freedom from the grid in compositional placement, all made his work seem quietly revolutionary. In fact, over the ten years from 1972 to 1982, his style has so influenced the designers of northern California that at least half of them could be said to belong to his "school."

One of the crucial elements of his style, the exquisitely modulated tonal range of his drawings, has proved to be inimitable. His unique color repertory of grayed blues, roses, and greens and pale yellows, is distinctive, but even more influential has been his choice of scale of compositional elements. Instead of large, flat components, he has scattered white or colored-powder patterns of dots through both foreground and background areas. While no one has equalled Manwaring's finesse with grayed hues, the use of ornamental dot grids, and another of his innovations—the use of looping monoweight lines with split-font color gradations—have been widely copied.

Manwaring moved from compass-drawn shapes to a modified realism, featuring softly rounded curves. The edge, still an important component in his design, became variable, sometimes torn into letters or animal shapes from paper. In subject matter, too, his work is unique, especially in his sensitive rendering of flowers, flora in general, and small animals. All testify to his understanding of the pleasures of attending to detail in small things, often overlooked by the harried, brash, or blasé observer. Manwaring's emphasis on images of quiet contemplation are appropriate to his clients—who generally sell especially well-made clothing or delectable foodstuffs—but they are equally appreciated by a public eagerly looking for the gentle and humane in graphic design.

—Frances Butler

# MARDERSTEIG, Giovanni

Italian typographer, book, and typeface designer

**Born:** Weimar, Germany, 8 January 1892; emigrated to Italy in 1926. **Education:** Studied law, at the universities of Bonn, Vienna, Kiel and Jena, D. Jur., 1913. **Career:** Co-editor, with C. G. Heine, of *Genius* biannual, for Kurt Wolff Verlag, Munich, 1917-22; freelance typographer and book designer, from 1922; typographic and technical consultant, to William Collins and Sons publishers, London and Glasgow, 1934-35; founder-director, Officina Bodoni handpress in Montagnola, Switzerland, 1923-27, and in Verona, Italy, 1927-77; freelance type designer, from 1937; founder-director, Stamperia Valdonega typesetting and printing firm, Verona, 1947-77. **Member:** Society of Typographical Artists, London; Association Typographique Internationale. **Exhibitions:** Musée Lantin, Antwerp, 1954; Museum fur Kunst und Gewerbe, Hamburg, 1954; British Museum, London, 1954; Biblioteca Comunale, Verona, 1956; Staatliche Graphische Sammlung, Munich, 1958; Gutenberg Museum, Bern, 1963; Bibliotheque Royale, Brussels,

1965. **Honors:** First Prize, Gabriele D'Annunzio Competition, Rome, 1927; Order of the Grande Ufficiale, Rome; honorary member, Double Crown Club, London. **Died:** Verona, Italy, December 1977.

## Works

*A Socratic Dialogue by Plato* book design, for The Pleiad, Paris, 1926.
*Damianus Moyllus: Treatise on Classic Letter Design* book design, for the Pegasus Press, Paris, 1927.
*Zeno* typeface, 1936.
*Griffo* typeface, 1939.
*Paul Valery/C. Day Lewis: Le Cimetière Marin* book design, for Secker and Warburg, London, 1946.
*Dylan Thomas: 26 Poems* book design, for J. M. Dent, London, 1949.
*Dante* typeface, 1955.
*Pacioli* typeface, 1956.
*T S. Eliot: Four Quartets* book design, for Faber and Faber, London, 1960.
*T. S. Eliot: The Waste Land* book design, for Faber and Faber, London, 1961.

## Publications

**By MARDERSTEIG: books**—(editor) *Felice Feliciano Veronese: Alphabetum Romanum,* Verona, Italy, 1960; *Das Werkbuch der Officina Bodoni,* Wetzlar, West Germany, 1960; *The Remarkable Story of a Book Made in Padua in 1477,* translated by Hans Schmoller, London, 1967; *Ein Leben der Buchern gewidmet,* Mainz, 1968; *Manuale typografico di Giovanni B. Bodoni,* editor, Verona, Italy, 1968; *Libre del Officina Bodoni 1954-1968,* Verona, Italy, 1968; *Francesco Alunno di Ferrara,* Florence, 1970; *Liberale ritrovato nell'Esopo Veronese del 1479,* Verona, Italy, 1973.

**On MARDERSTEIG: books**—*L'Officina Bodoni: Biblioteca Civica di Verona 1923-62,* exhibition catalogue, Verona, 1962; *Buchgestaltung* by Albert Kapr, Dresden, 1963; *The Officina Bodoni 1923-62,* exhibition catalogue, Bern, 1963; *Officina Bodoni, Verona: Catalogue Raisonne 1923-1964* edited by Franco Riva and Luc Indestege, Verona, 1965; *Giovanni Mardersteig: An Account of His Work* by John Dreyfus, New York, 1966; *Ein beispielhaftes Lebenswerk: Laudatio auf Giovanni Mardersteig* by Rudolf Hafelstange, Mainz, 1968; *Officina Bodoni* by John S. Ryder, Pinner, 1972; *In Fair Verona,* edited by Nicholas Barber, Cambridge, 1972; *Giovanni Mardersteig, the Officina Bodoni: An Account of the Work of a Hand Press 1923-1977* by Hans Schmoller, Verona, 1980.

\*      \*      \*

Having been impressed as an adolescent in Weimar, Germany by the Kelmscott and Doves Press books, Giovanni Mardersteig as a young man worked for Kurt Wolff Verlag, the influential publisher of the German avant-garde. But the necessity of living in the more salutary climate of the Italian Alps (Mardersteig's lungs were fragile) propelled him into establishing his own press, the Officina Bodoni, in Montagnola in 1923 and then in Verona in 1927. In more than fifty years, he produced almost 200 books on a handpress, all scrupulously edited and designed, and from 1945 to 1977, larger editions of books printed by offset lithography at the Stamperia Valdonega.

Mardersteig's insistence on the highest standards of scholarship in his texts and, above all, on the most appropriate and the best-quality materials and meticulous workmanship constitutes the basis of one component of his reputation as a pre-eminent private publisher of the twentieth century. The other aspect of his work, famed in Italy and throughout Europe, was the simplicity of his typographic composition, recalling the spare perfection of the typography of his inspiration, the eighteenth-century master printer, Giambattista Bodoni, but not limited to imitation of any one format. Through this work, Mardersteig reactivated interest in Bodoni's design and Bodoni's types. (He was allowed to use Bodoni's matrices to cast types for the printing of Gabriele d'Annunzio's complete works, commissioned by the Italian Government.) His use of the sparkling Bodoni types, which called for princely generosity of format—wide leading, large type relative to the page, and lavish margins—continued the aesthetic introduced by T. J. Cobden-Sanderson and Emery Walker through their Doves Press and added an element of grandeur reflecting Italian book models. Eventually, he reset, from newly cast type, the monumental pages of Bodoni's *Manuale tipografico.*

However, Mardersteig also used other faces extensively and was responsible, working closely with the French punch-cutter Charles Malin, for the design of the typefaces Zeno, Griffo, Dante, and Pacioli Titling for his own use. All of these faces were based on the earliest roman types, cut in Italy 200 years before Bodoni, and they attest to the primacy of the Italian model—open, legible, elegant—in Mardersteig's imagination. In return for this Italian gift, Mardersteig renewed Italians' pride in their heritage, and his book design remains influential there, as is seen in the work of both small presses (such as that of Franco Maria Ricci) and large publishing houses. His design influence continues, too, in the Stamperia Valdonega, directed now by his son Martino Mardersteig.

—Frances Butler

# MARI, Enzo

Italian artist, illustrator, graphic, textile, furniture, and industrial designer

**Born:** Novara, 27 April 1932. **Education:** Studied classics and literature, Accademia di Brera, Milan, 1952-56; mainly self-taught in design from 1952. **Career:** Independent visual artist and researcher, from 1952, and freelance designer, Milan, from 1956; designed for Danese, Driade, Gabbianelli, Gavina, Artemide, Interflex, Alessi, Zanotta, and others; art director, for KPM, from 1993. Coordinator of Nuova Tendenza group of artists, Milan, 1963; Instructor, Umanitaria, Milan, 1963-66, Institute of Art, Rome, 1970, Centro Sperimentale di Cinematografia, Rome, 1971, Centro Studi di Comunicazione Visiva, University of Parma, 1972-84, Facoltà di Architettura, Politecnico, Milan, 1982, Accademia Belle Arti, Carrara, 1982-83, ISIA Firenze, 1984-86. **Exhibitions:** Galleria San Fedele, Milan, 1953; Studio B24, Milan, 1957; Galleria Danese, Milan, 1959, 1961, 1972, 1974; Muzej za Umjetnosti, Zagreb, 1962; Centro Arte Viva, Trieste, 1966; Stedelijk Museum, Amsterdam, 1966; Galleria del Naviglio, Milan, 1968; Musée des Arts Décoratifs, Paris, 1970; Museo di Castelvecchio, Verona, 1970;

Galleria Nazionale d'Arte Moderna, Rome, 1970; Galleria Milano, Milan, 1972, 1973, 1974; Galleria Uxa, Verona, 1974; CSAC Università di Parma, Palazzo Reale, Milan, 1984; Galleria Civica, San Marino, 1988; *Perchè una Mostra di falci?,* Galleria Danese, 1989; Mostra Itinerante Zanotta, Atene, Monaco, Barcelona, Baden-Baden, and Dusseldorf, 1993; *Enzo Mari per KPM,* International Design Zentrum, Berlin, 1994; *Ambiente 1995,* Francoforte, 1995. **Collections:** Museum of Modern Art, New York; Philadelphia Museum of Art; Denver Art Museum; Moderna Museet, Stockholm; Stedelijk Museum, Amsterdam; Museum für Kunst und Gewerbe, Hamburg; Galleria Nazionale d'Arte Moderna, Rome; Musée des Arts Décoratifs, Paris. **Honors:** Premio San Fedele, Milan, 1952, 1954; Premio Villa dell'Olmo, Como, 1957; Domus/Inox Prize, Milan, 1962; In/Arch Prize, Rome, 1963; Liubliana Graphics Biennale Prize, 1964, 1966; Premio Convegni di Rimini, 1965; Premio Michetti, Francavilla al Mare, 1967; Compasso d'Oro Award, Milan, 1967, 1979, 1986; Youth Book Prize, Bonn, 1971; International Design Center Prize, New York, 1987. **Address:** Piazzale Baracca 10, 20123 Milan, Italy.

## Works

*16 Animali* educational game in wood or plastic, for Danese, 1957.
*Putrelle* containers in welded sheet metal, for Danese, 1958.
*Paros* containers in marble, for Danese, 1960.
*Serie della Natura/Natural Fruit* serigraph print series, for Danese, 1960-72.
*Camicia* flower vases in aluminum and glass, for Danese, 1961.
*Celebes* wastebin, *Mascarene* umbrella stand, and *Kerguelen* hatstand in plastic, for Danese, 1962-68.
*Glifo* adjustable bookcase in plastic, for Gavina, 1967.
*Borneo* posacenere, for Danese, 1967.
*Serie Elementare* majolica ceramic tile system, for Gabbianelli, 1968.
*Vaso doppio,* for Danese, 1968.
*Java* contenitore in melamina, for Danese, 1969.
*Manca* cast-iron pot, for Le Creuset, 1970.
*Poltrona "sof-sof,"* for Driade, 1972.
*Day-Night* divan bed, for Driade, 1973.
*Samos* containers in handmade porcelain, for Danese, 1973.
*Frate, Fratello* and *Cugino* series of tables in crystal, cast iron, and wood, for Driade, 1974.
*Box* folding chair in plastic, for Anonima Castelli, 1975.
*Aggregato* lighting system, for Artemide, 1976.
*Tonietta* chair in cast aluminum, for Zanotta, 1985.
*Salina* desk accessories in pressed glass, for Danese, 1985.
*Opasis* tablewares in stainless steel, for Zani e Zani, 1986.
*Standard* carello, for Alessi, 1986.
*Paolina* chair in walnut, for Pozzi e Verga, 1986.
*Smith e Smith* kitchen tools and fittings in cast steel, for Zani e Zani, 1987.
*Resegone, Hot-Dog* and *Altino* series of tables in wood, for Lema, 1988.
*Toscolano* range of table cutlery in cast steel, for Zani e Zani, 1989.
*Tappeto Volante* couch, for Interflex, 1989.
*Copernico* pot, for Zani e Zani, 1990.
*Antiteledipendentitore,* 1992.
*Calvino* bath accessories, for Agape, 1992.
*Cartesio* couch, for Interflex, 1992.
*Marina* chairs, *Don Giovanni* table, and *Museo* appendiabiti, for Zanotta, 1992.

Enzo Mari: 719 Wunderkammer produced by Zanotta spa, 1994. Photo: Marco Angeretti

*Daniele* divan, for Zanotta, 1993.
*Manovella* fixture, for Fantini, 1993.
*Ecolo,* for Alessi, 1994.
*Wunderkammer, Novecento,* for Zanotta, 1994.

## Publications

**By MARI: books**—*La Funzione della Ricerca Estetica,* Milan, 1970; (with Iela Mari) *The Apple and the Butterfly,* London, 1970; *Falce e Martello,* Milan, 1973; *Proposta per un'Autoprogettazione,* Milan, 1974; (with Carla Vasio) *Romanzo Sorico,* Milan, 1975; *Ipotesi di Rifondazione del Progetto,* Milan, 1978; *Design e design,* Milan, 1979; *Dov' è l'Artigiano,* Florence, 1981; *Tre Piazze del Duomo,* Milan, 1984; *Perchè una mostra di Falci,* Milan, 1989.

**On MARI: books**—*Enzo Mari* by Max Bill and Bruno Munari, Milan, 1959; *Il Disegno Industriale e la sua Estetica* by Gillo Dorfles, Bologna, 1963; *Il Design in Italia 1945-1972* by Paolo Fossati, Turin, 1972; *Enzo Mari, Designer* by Renato Pedio, Bari, 1980;

*Contemporary Furniture* edited by Klaus-Jürgen Sembach, Stuttgart and New York, 1982; *Enzo Mari* by Arturo Carlo Quintavalle, Parma, 1983; *Italian Design: 1870 to the Present* by Penny Sparke, London and New York, 1988; *Enzo Mari: Modelli del Reale* by F. Leonetti, F. Menna, and R. Pedio, Milan, 1988; *Italian Modern: A Design Heritage* by Gianni Albera and Nicolas Monti, New York, 1989.

*   *   *

Like some of his product designs, Enzo Mari is an enigma. Following his studies at the Accademia di Brera, in 1952 he started his theoretical research into the psychology of vision, systems of perception, and the methodology of design. In the following years, he produced three-dimensional models of linear elements, planes, and other shapes. Mari soon discovered one reason that this esoteric work must be interrupted: he needed to produce some income, since he was not independently wealthy. There followed a series of product designs.

Probably the most notable are the objects and games that he conceived for the Italian firm Danese. The objects included vases, bowls, pen- and pencil-holders, and ashtrays, primarily in ABS and other plastics, in forms that could be easily mass-produced while still being beautiful to look at, tactile, and, of course, functional. Mari professed a "rational" design philosophy in which he defined "rational" as "elaborated or constructed in a way that corresponds exactly to the purpose or function."

Mari once contemplated the design of an ashtray for more than a year (while doing other things) before finally producing an extraordinarily handsome design that had one major drawback—its design was so carefully thought out and so inherently different from other designs that an uncomprehending public caused it to be unsuccessful in the marketplace. The project did, however, have a positive contribution to Mari's own lifestyle—by the end of the process he had abandoned his two-packs-a-day smoking habit!

Mari's games and game cards have usually been intended as communicative (instructional) instruments as well as tactile objects. *Il Gioco dell Favole/The Fable Game* was a series of twelve tablets slotted to interlock and portraying forty-five animals, the sun, moon, and others. These invited the user to "rediscover the pleasure of recognizing the symbols of his imagination," while inventing his own story as the cards were played. Some of the images (a sleeping bear, the head of a duck) were also enlarged into another form of object—a wall-hanging print—still another form of visual communication. Another series of cards provided a few lines—an idea upon which users could build by themselves, by actually drawing on the surface of the card.

Curiously, Mari, himself the designer of many beautiful objects, does not believe that the task of designing objects has any significance in today's society. He believes that the designer's role should be in the field of communication and, more important, that the designer should be politically active and responsive to the needs of contemporary society. It is not by accident that the pieces of *44 Valuations,* in spite of the curvy, irregular shapes, when assembled together produce a hammer and sickle—one symbol of social revolution. Recently, Mari's "objects" have grown into a variety of furniture designs for various manufacturers. All of them continue his "rational" approach.

—William Victor Kriebel

# MARISCAL, (Francisco) Javier (Errando)
Spanish fashion, textile, graphic, corporate, and industrial designer

**Born:** Valencia, 9 February 1950. **Education:** Educated in Valencia, until 1967; studied philosophy, at the Universidad de Valencia, 1967-70; studied graphic design, at the Escuela de Grafismo Elisava, Barcelona, 1971-73. **Military Service:** Served in the Spanish Army, 1974. **Career:** Worked as a gardener and handyman, in Ibiza, 1975-76; freelance designer, in Barcelona, from 1976; founded Estudio Mariscal, from 1989; has designed for Memphis furniture, BD Ediciones de Diseno, Marieta textiles, and others. **Exhibitions:** *Gran Hotel,* Galeria Mec-Mec, Barcelona, 1977; Sala Vinçon, Barcelona, 1979, 1981, 1982, 1986; Galeria Central, Madrid, 1980; Galeria Local, Madrid, 1980; Galeria Moriarty, Madrid, 1981, 1986, 1989, 1993; Galeria Fucares, Almagro, 1982; Galeria Temple, Valencia, 1983; Galeria Rene Metras, Barcelona, 1983; Espace Actuel, Paris, 1983; *100 Años con Mariscal,* La Lonja, Valencia, 1988; *Cent Anys a Barcelona,* Barco Mercante Puerto de Barcelona, 1989; Galeria Berini, Barcelona, 1989; Galeria Luis Adelantado, Valencia, 1990; *Monotypes,* Galeria Trama, Barcelona, 1991; retrospective, toured Japan, 1991; *Arco 94,* Galeria Trama, Barcelona, 1994; *El Señor Mundo,* Barcelona, 1994; *Mariscal a Paris,* Musée Galerie de la Seita, Paris, 1994; *Acuarinto Art,* Oldham Art Gallery, Manchester, 1994; *Paisajes,* Galerie Sen, Madrid, 1995; Galeria Trama, Barcelona, 1995. **Collections:** Philadelphia Museum of Art; Museum of Modern Art, New York; IVAM, Valencia; Aigües de Barcelona; Fundación La Caixa, Barcelona. **Address:** Estudio Mariscal, Pellaires 30-38, 08019 Barcelona, Spain.

**Works**

Textile collections, for Marieta, 1978-83.
*Duplex* bar stool, for BD Ediciones de Diseno, 1980.
*Bar-Cel-Ona* poster, for the City of Barcelona, 1980.
Duplex Bar interiors and furnishings, Barcelona, 1980.
*The Garriris* comic strip, for *El Vibora magazine,* 1980-82.
*Carnaval* poster, for the City of Barcelona, 1981.
*Hilton* food trolley, for Memphis, 1981.
*Arana* lamp, for BD Ediciones de Diseno, 1983 (with Pepe Cortes).
*Garraf* lamp, for BD Ediciones de Diseno, 1983 (with Pepe Cortes).
*Valencia* lamp, for BD Ediciones de Diseno, 1983 (with Pepe Cortes).
*Cobi,* mascot for 1992 Olympic Games in Barcelona, 1988.
Visual design for Mac World show, Barcelona, 1991.
Image design for Socialdemokraterna, the Swedish Social Democratic Party, Stockholm, 1993.
Bathroom tile, for Stonehouse, San Francisco, 1993.
Magazine cover, for *The New Yorker,* 1993.
Magazine covers, for *El Pais,* Spain, 1993, 1995.
Corporate design, for Frame Store, London, 1994.
Ceramics, for Rosenthal, Germany, 1994.
*El Señor Mundo* cartoon character for worldwide publishing, media, and merchandising project, Barcelona, 1994.
Magazine cover, for *Aldus,* 1995.
Furniture collection, for Moroso, 1995.
Album cover, packaging, and tour visuals, for singer Kiko Veneno, 1995.
Art clock tower for the 1996 Olympics in Atlanta, for Swatch, 1996.

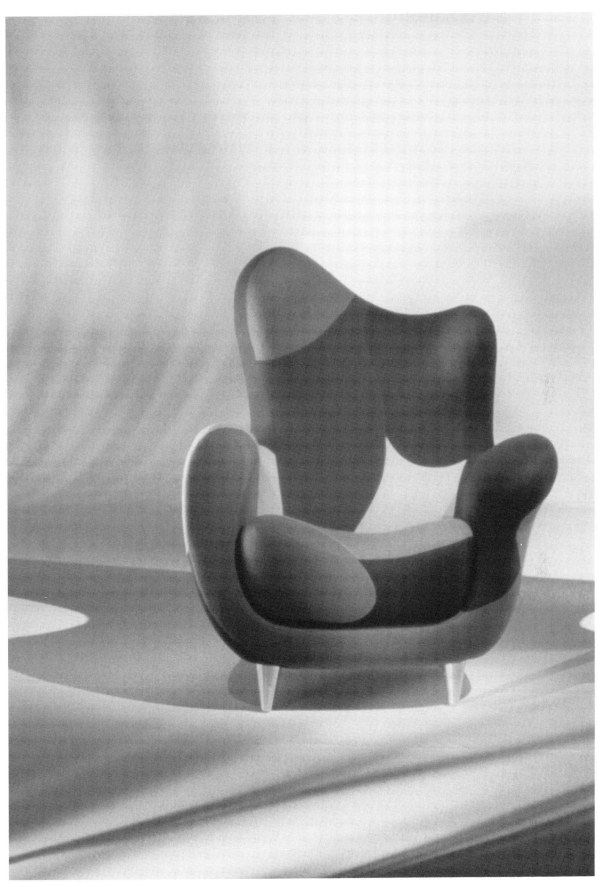

**Javier Mariscal: Alessandra chair. Photo copyright 1996, Artists Rights Society (ARS), New York/VEGAP, Madrid**

*Mondo Loco* animation project, based on *Los Garriris* comic strip, with Canal+, Spain, 1995.


## Publications

**By MARISCAL: books**—*ABC.DARI IL.LUSTRAT,* Barcelona, 1979; *Apuntes,* Barcelona, 1983; *Mariscal,* Paris, 1983.

**On MARISCAL: books**—*Memphis: The New International Style* edited by Barbara Radice, Milan, 1981; *Design Since 1945* edited by Kathryn Hiesinger and George Marcus, Philadelphia and London, 1983; *Design Source Book* by Penny Sparke and others, London, 1986; *De Diseño,* Barcelona, 1986; *Nouvelles Tendances,* with introduction by Francois Burkhardt, Paris, 1987; *International Design Yearbook 1988/89* edited by Arata Isozaki, London, 1988; *100 años,* Valencia, 1988; *Javier Mariscal: Designing the New Spain* by Emma Dent Coad, New York, 1991; *New Spanish Design* by Guy Julier, New York, 1991; **articles**—in *El Pais* (Madrid) 8 January 1978, 21 September 1978; *Ajoblanco* (Barcelona), March 1978; *Graphic Design* (Tokyo), no. 76, 1979; *New York Times,* 16 October 1980; *Casa Vogue* (Milan), August 1981; *Modo* (Milan), September 1981, December 1986; *Diagonal* (Barcelona), March 1982; *La Vanguardia* (Barcelona), 5 October 1982; *Bon a Tirer* (Paris), September 1985, January 1987; *Blueprint* (London), December/January 1986, June 1991, September 1993; *Form* (Stockholm), January 1987; *Design* (London), January 1988; *Design Review* (London), Summer 1991; *Progressive Architecture* (New York), September 1991; *Graphis* (Zürich), November-December 1991; "The World According to Mariscal" by Moira Cullen in *Communication Arts* (Palo Alto, California), January-February 1995.

\*

A designer is a person who plans objects for particular uses. The designs and objects that are interesting to me are those that have—in addition to and in spite of their usefulness—a special charm, something that makes them a little mysterious, magical, poetic, or simply pleasant. I love it when they're beautiful because the shapes, colors, and textures are in agreement with the internal philosophy of the object. This makes them aesthetically pleasing, natural, and harmonious.

—Javier Mariscal


# MARSHALL, Marian

Canadian interior designer

**Born:** Toronto in 1947. **Education:** Studied interior design at Ryerson Polytechnical Institute, graduated 1971. **Career:** Interior designer, A.D. Pollard and Associates, Toronto, and Rice Brydone Ltd., Toronto; co-founder and principal, Marshall Cummings & Associates, Toronto, from 1975. **Member:** Association of Registered Interior Designers of Ontario; Interior Designers of Canada; American Society of Interior Designers; board of management, Design Exchange; advisory and design co-ordinator, Ronald McDonald House; Toronto Board of Trade. **Honors:** Designer of the Year, Association of Registered Interior Designers of Canada, 1985.

**Address:** Marshall Cummings & Associates Ltd., 43 Davies Avenue, Toronto, Ontario M4M 2A9, Canada.


# MARSHALL CUMMINGS & ASSOCIATES

Canadian interior design firm

**Founded** in 1975 by Marian Marshall and Donna Cummings. **Exhibitions:** *Canada Designs for Business,* Tokyo, 1992. **Honors:** Six ARIDO (Association of Registered Interior Designers of Canada) Awards, 1984-92; Toronto Arts Award, 1988. **Address:** Marshall Cummings & Associates Ltd., 43 Davies Avenue, Toronto, Ontario M4M 2A9, Canada.


## Works

Interior design, for McDonald's headquarters and training facility, Toronto, 1985.
Interior design, for North American Life Centre marketing center, Toronto, 1985.
Interior design, for 16-20 North Audley Street office building, London, 1991.
Interior design, for CTV Headquarters, Toronto, 1995.
Other interior designs include—Canadian Imperial Bank of Commerce U.S. Headquarters, New York; Olympia & York executive offices, First Canadian Place, Toronto, and Canary Wharf, London; IBM showrooms, Toronto; and Aetna executive offices, Toronto.


## Publications

**On MARSHALL CUMMINGS & ASSOCIATES: articles**—"Marian Marshall: A Believer in Professionalism" in *Contract* (New York), January/February 1986; "Design Practice: Pressures to Prelease Open a New Market for the Design Professional" in *Interiors* (New York), July 1986; *Interiors* (New York), April 1988; "World Class: Marshall Cummings & Associates" in *Contract* (New York), July/August 1988; "Design for a Winning Partnership" in *The Financial Post* (Toronto), 8 May 1990.

\*   \*   \*

Marshall Cummings & Associates Ltd. is an interior design firm based in Toronto with clients across Canada and in New York and London. The firm specializes in large-scale corporate interiors.

Marshall Cummings & Associates was established by Marian Marshall and Donna Cummings in 1975. Marshall graduated from Ryerson Polytechnical Institute in 1971 and Cummings graduated from the Ontario College of Art in 1967. The pair met while working at Rice Brydone Inc. in Toronto. Ironically, Rice Brydone is now the firm's main Canadian competitor in the field of corporate interior design.

Marshall Cummings' corporate vision is "to effectively satisfy client-generated objectives through an innovative, efficient, and mutually rewarding process *while having fun."* Marian Marshall exemplifies this mandate with her keen business acumen and effusive personality. Marshall is the director of marketing, while the more reserved Cummings is director of administration and personnel.

The Toronto headquarters and training facilities of McDonald's Restaurants of Canada is a good example of Marshall Cummings ability to communicate a client's corporate vision through design. Designed by Marshall Cummings in 1985, the 105,000-square-foot project incorporated a 120-seat auditorium, two classrooms, a fitness center, film studio, cafeteria, computer facility, and offices. In keeping with McDonald's corporate philosophy of open communication and diminished hierarchy, the executive offices are not fully enclosed and are located on a middle floor accessible from above and below by a large spiral staircase. Each executive office was designed to reflect the individual's taste. The entire top floor is reserved for the staff lounge and cafeteria with access to a large wrap-around terrace. The palette throughout the building is peach and celadon green, enhancing fun furniture pieces like Michael Graves' Post-Modern club chair and Adam St. John's *McChair.* Architectural elements are playfully chunky, including oversized pillars and beams. The variety of spirited forms and colors is tied together by confetti-patterned carpeting throughout.

Another major client is Olympia & York, the Toronto-based development company. Marshall Cummings was responsible for the design of offices in Toronto, New York, and London. All three projects blended fine antiques and art work with contemporary furniture, resulting in light and elegant interiors with an air of tradition.

In the conservative field of corporate interiors Marshall Cummings & Associates have gained a reputation for well-planned, timeless spaces that are completed on time and budget.

—Elizabeth Crawford

# MARTIN, Noel

American exhibition and graphic designer

**Born:** Syracuse, Ohio, 19 April 1922. **Education:** Studied painting, drawing, and printmaking, at the Art Academy of Cincinnati, Ohio, 1939-41, 1945-47; self-taught in typography and design, from 1947. **Military Service:** Served in camouflage and information units, United States Army, 1942-45, Sergeant. **Family:** Married Coletta Ruchty in 1942; children: Dana and Reid. **Career:** Display and graphic designer, Cincinnati Art Museum, from 1947; freelance graphic designer and art director, working for the Mortgage Corporation of Detroit, Cincinnati Contemporary Arts Center, Abraham and Strauss, Standard Oil of New Jersey, *Atlantic Monthly, New Republic,* and others, in Cincinnati, from 1949; design consultant, Champion International, 1959-82, Xomor Corporation, from 1961, Federated Department Stores, 1962-83, and Hebrew Union College, from 1969. Assistant to the Director, Cincinnati Art Museum, 1947-55. Instructor, Cincinnati Art Academy, 1951-57; Adjunct Professor and Designer-in-Residence, University of Cincinnati, 1968-73. Advisory Board Member, Carnegie-Mellon University, Rhode Island School of Design, Cincinnati Symphony Orchestra, American Institute of Graphic Arts, and Aspen Design Conference. **Member:** Alliance Graphique Internationale; Interna-

tional Center of Typographic Arts. **Exhibitions:** *Four American Graphic Designers: Martin, Matter, Lionni, Shahn,* Museum of Modern Art, New York, 1954; Contemporary Arts Center, Cincinnati, 1954, 1971; Rhode Island School of Design, Providence, 1955; Society of Typographic Arts, Chicago, 1956; Cornell University, Ithaca, New York, 1956; American Institute of Graphic Arts, New York, 1958; Cooper and Beatty, Toronto, 1971. **Collections:** Museum of Modern Art, New York; Cincinnati Art Museum; Cincinnati Historical Society; Boston Museum of Fine Arts; Library of Congress, Washington, D.C.; Stedelijk Museum, Amsterdam. **Honors:** Art Directors Club Award, Philadelphia, 1957; Sachs Award, Cincinnati, 1973. **Address:** 6226 Robinson Road, Cincinnati, Ohio 45213, U.S.A.

## Publications

**By MARTIN: books**—(illustrator) *The Afternoon in Dismay* by P. Wild, Cincinnati, 1968; **articles**—"Tschichold's Position Today" in *Modern Graphic Design* (New York), Spring 1957; "Modern Art and Graphic Design" in *Printing Progress: A Mid-Century Report* (Cincinnati), 1959.

**On MARTIN: books**—*Who's Who in Graphic Art* edited by Walter Amstutz, Zürich, 1962, Dubendorf, 1982; **articles**—"Noel Martin: A Designer in the Midwest" by E. H. Dwight in *Print* (New York), October/November 1954.

\*     \*     \*

Noel Martin is known for the range of his work as a graphic designer which encompasses catalogs, brochures, books, posters, and advertisements for cultural, commercial, and industrial institutions, as well as for his exhibition designs. Martin is also an educator, in the broadest sense, because his work as a graphic designer made the Cincinnati area community aware of the expanded possibilities arising from new technical means and progressive concepts.

Born in a small river town in southeastern Ohio, Martin moved to Cincinnati as a young boy and spent the rest of his life there (except for military service). From 1939-1941 he studied at the Cincinnati Art Academy, where his teachers included the painter Ralston Crawford. He spent 39 months in the U.S. Army Air Force during World War II, assigned to camouflage and educational units, where he worked with fellow artists making drawings, models, and filmstrips. While on assignment in New York he became familiar with a wider range of modern art than he had been able to see in Cincinnati.

In 1945, Martin returned to his studies at the Cincinnati Art Academy, where he remained until 1947. While still a student, he began working in the nearby Cincinnati Art Museum. His duties included building display cases, mounting sculpture, and assisting in the installation of temporary exhibitions. Meanwhile, he continued his own work as a painter. He fell into the profession of graphic design by being asked to design some small printed pieces for the Museum. His interest in graphic design grew, in spite of what he later called his "art school snobbery." The Museum had its own print shop, and Martin spent a lot of time with the Museum printer, a skilled craftsperson, who taught him the basic mechanics of printing. Beyond this, Martin thinks of himself as a self-taught graphic designer. He asked a lot of questions, studied type books, and learned from some of his mistakes. He also began his lifelong practice of working very closely with the craftspersons who actually carry out his designs. And he studied the work of other graphic designers of the past and present.

Martin supplemented what could be learned locally and from publications by corresponding with other designers and meeting with designers who visited Cincinnati. In addition, he attended sessions of the International Design Conference at Aspen, Colorado.

From the beginning there was nothing parochial about Martin's designs. This is evident in the fact that he began to receive national recognition as early as 1954 when the Museum of Modern Art in New York included his work in its exhibition, *Four American Graphic Designers*. Later the same year he had his first one-person exhibition at the Contemporary Arts Center in Cincinnati. Other one-person exhibitions followed, including those at the Rhode Island School of Design in Providence, in 1955, the Society of Typographic Arts in Chicago, in 1956, and the American Institute of Graphic Arts in New York, in 1958.

From his base in the Cincinnati Art Museum, where he has designed most of the Museum's catalogs, posters, and brochures since 1947, Martin went on to become a designer for many leading cultural, commercial, and industrial institutions in Cincinnati and its surrounding communities. In doing so he expanded local awareness of the possibilities inherent in progressive concepts in graphic design and in advances in printing technology. Cincinnati had once been a leader in the fine arts and in ceramics. It had also been a leader in the printing arts, due to the lithographic firms which rose to prominence there during the nineteenth-century. But by the 1940s, Cincinnati had become a backwash and had generally remained unmoved by new developments in art and in graphic design.

The pioneering role in bringing new concepts in art and design to Cincinnati was taken by the Modern Art Society, founded in 1939 (and renamed the Contemporary Arts Center in 1954). The Modern Art Society is best known as co-organizer, with the Museum of Modern Art, of the 1941 exhibition *Organic Design in Home Furnishings,* and for staging, in 1946, the only one-person showing of the work of Laszlo Moholy-Nagy in the United States during his lifetime. The Modern Art Society also showed the work of Fred Lewy, an immigrant from Germany (via Spain), who did most of its early graphic design work and who was a pioneer in bringing the concepts of European Modernism to Cincinnati. Lewy, of course, and the Modern Art Society generally, were both strong influences on Martin. Thus, Martin may be said to have consolidated some of the influence the Modern Art Society had on the community, and to have extended and intensified it in the area of graphic design.

Another influence on Martin was his friend and collaborator, the late photographer George S. Rosenthal, who had studied with Moholy in Chicago.

Martin began working as a freelance designer in 1949, while continuing his work for the Cincinnati Art Museum, where he held the title of assistant to the director from 1947 to 1955. He taught at the Cincinnati Art Academy from 1951 to 1957, and was an adjunct professor at the University of Cincinnati from 1968 to 1973.

The range of Martin's work is due to his location in Cincinnati and to his pioneering role there. He has worked for cultural institutions such as the Cincinnati Symphony Orchestra, Contemporary Arts Center, and Hebrew Union College. In addition, he has worked for merchandisers such as Federated Department Stores, has provided graphic and exhibition designs for Xomor Corporation, an international valve company, since 1961, and has served as an advisor to Champion Papers from 1959 to 1980. Clients outside the

Cincinnati area have included the Museum of Modern Art, Alfred Knopf, *The Atlantic Monthly,* the *New Republic,* Abraham & Strauss, and Standard Oil of New Jersey. Martin has said that he will accept any kind of project, provided he is convinced that he will be allowed to do a good job.

Noel Martin maintains a small office, and usually has only one or two assistants at any given time. Most often these are his wife, Coletta, his son, Reid, or his daughter, Mrs. Dana Wolfe.

One of Martin's finest achievements, and one he looks back on with a great deal of pleasure, was, significantly, a project with a large dose of community education. This was a 1975-1976 exhibition at the Cincinnati Art Museum, *Change of Pace: Contemporary Furniture 1925-1975,* which he co-organized with Carol Macht, then the Museum's curator of decorative arts. In addition to designing the installation and the catalog, Martin designed a poster/mailer based on a photograph of a Marcel Breuer chair, printed in black on a brown ground, with lettering showing through from the bright white paper stock. The result conveys the basic information about the exhibition at a glance, but also allows the subtle image of the chair to emerge more slowly.

—Lloyd C. Engelbrecht

# MARX, Enid (Crystal Dorothy)

British illustrator and graphic and textile designer

**Born:** London, 20 October 1902. **Education:** Educated at Roedean School, Sussex, until 1919; studied at the Central School of Arts and Crafts, London, 1920-21, and at the Royal College of Art, London, 1922-25. **Career:** Apprentice technician and designer, in the Phyllis Barron and Dorothy Larcher textile studio, London, 1925-26; established own textile design and printing studio London, 1927-39; freelance graphic and textile designer, London, from 1939; textile consultant under Gordon Russell, Board of Trade Utility Furniture Advisory Committee, London, 1944-47; designed for London Transport, Whatajoy Luggage, Chatto and Windus publishers, Dunbar Hay Textiles, Penguin Books, Morton Sundour Fabrics, Aspinall Brothers, Combe, and others. Instructor in wood engraving, Ruskin School of Art, Oxford, 1931-33; design instructor, Bromley School of Art, Kent, 1935-39; head of dress, textiles, and ceramics, Croydon College of Art, London, 1965-70. **Exhibitions:** *Utility Furniture and Fashion 1941-51,* Geffrye Museum, London, 1974; *Thirties: British Art and Design Before War,* Hayward Gallery, London, 1979; *Enid Marx: Retrospective,* Camden Arts Centre, London, 1979; *The Maker's Eye,* Crafts Council Gallery London, 1981; *Design Since 1945,* Philadelphia Museum of Art, 1983; *Eye for Industry,* Victoria and Albert Museum, London, 1986; Sally Hunter Fine Art Gallery, 1990; Fine Art Society, Bond St., London, 1990; *London at War,* Imperial War Museum, London, 1995. **Collections:** Victoria and Albert Museum, London; Sheffield Art Gallery, Yorkshire; Bath Craft Study Centre, Bath; Scottish Arts Council Gallery, Glasgow; Musée des Arts Décoratifs, Paris; Museum of Fine Arts, Boston. **Honors:** Royal Designer for Industry, Royal Society of Arts, London, 1945; honorary fellow, 1982, and Senior Fellow, 1987, Royal College of Art, London; fellow, Chartered Society of Designers, London. **Address:** 39 Thornhill Road, Barnsbury Square, London N1 1JS, England.

## Publications

**By MARX: books**—(author, illustrator, and compiler, with Margaret Lambert) *When Victoria Began to Reign,* London, 1937; (illustrator) *A Childhood* by Francesca Allinson, London, 1937; (author and illustrator) *A Book of Nursery Rhymes,* compiler, London, 1938; (author and illustrator) *Bulgy the Barrage Balloon,* London, 1941; (author and illustrator) *Nelson the Kite of the King's Navy,* London, 1942; (author and illustrator) *The Little White Bear,* London, 1945; (author and illustrator) *Quiz,* London, 1945; (illustrator) *An Almanac* by Norman Douglas, London, 1945; (illustrator) *Tom Thumb,* London and New York, 1946; (illustrator) *A Book of Rigmaroles, or Jingle Rhymes,* London, 1946; (author and illustrator, with Margaret Lambert) *English Popular and Traditional Art,* London, 1946; (author and illustrator) *The Pigeon Ace,* London, 1946; (author and illustrator) *Menagerie Cut Out,* London, 1946; (author and illustrator, with Margaret Lambert) *English Popular and Traditional Art,* London, 1946, 1951; (author and illustrator) *Slithery Sam,* London, 1947; (author and illustrator) *Sam and Arry, or Thereby Hangs Two Tails,* London, 1972.

**On MARX: books**—*Design in the Home* edited by Noel Carrington, London, 1933; *British Textile Designers Today* by H. G. Hayes Marshall, Leigh-on-Sea, 1939; *British Textiles* by Frank Lewis, Leigh-on-Sea, 1951; *Design in British Industry: A Mid-Century Survey* by Michael Farr, Cambridge, 1955; *Utility Furniture and Fashion 1941-1951,* exhibition catalogue by Jeffery Daniels, John Vaizey, and others, London, 1974; *Enid Marx,* exhibition catalogue by Zuleika Dobson, Margaret Lambert, and others, London, 1979; *Design Since 1945* edited by Kathryn Hiesinger and George Marcus, Philadelphia and London, 1983; *The Conran Director of Design* edited by Stephen Bayley, London, 1985; *Eye for Industry: Royal Designers for Industry 1936-1986,* exhibition catalogue by Fiona McCarthy and Patrick Nuttgens, London, 1986.

\*

Enid Marx, 1938

Living through two world wars inevitably must influence the work of artists, for they, by definition, have a built-in responsiveness to the *Zeitgeist.* I therefore make no apologies for having worked in a variety of disciplines: printing, engraving, painting, and designing in many fields and often responding to unexpected and untried techniques. I started, however, as a painter and the desire to paint has persisted as a thread throughout a long working life, together with a basic interest in pattern and texture. For sixteen years I ran my own print workshop for furnishing textiles, interspersed with work for printers and publishers, mainly with pattern papers and book jackets.

I switched to design from weaving when I was invited by Christian Barmant to design some moquettes for seating for London Transport trains. This was one of the rare occasions when Christian Barmant, my client, gave me a perfect brief and his boss, Frank Pick, was prepared to back the designer's work throughout the manufacturing process. Pick's gift for captaining a team made London Transport, in the period he was in charge, an example of a successful enterprise which enjoyed world-wide respect.

In the 1930s I was invited to do some designs for post office stamps. In this case the brief filled two typed foolscap pages in such detail one felt that an outside designer was redundant. The only item omitted was provision for the designer and manufacturer to meet and cooperate, to my mind almost the most relevant necessity. I think our stamps are, or should be regarded as, our Queen and country's visiting card.

It was my good fortune that I shared living accommodations with a historian who was also interested in the upstairs/downstairs aspects of English life, so it came about that when we found any example of interest, I made a visual record and Margaret Lambert described its history. We produced four books together and wrote some articles for English and American papers.

I was exhibiting in London galleries and had a collection of hand-block printed textiles in the 1935 Paris World Fair, but all this came to an end with the outbreak of World War II. During the first winter of the blitz, on a drive through Regent's Park, I saw for the first time a "Bulgy" barrage balloon being launched by a team from the women's services at sunset, a lovely sight. I made drawings and later wrote a story which, to my surprise, was an instant success. This led me to write and illustrate three more children's stories plus some miniature children's booklets, printed on offcuts, as paper was in short supply.

Kenneth Clark formed the idea of getting artists to make records of war-torn Britain. I was one of the group of artists who were invited to participate in this scheme. What I had hoped for was to work with the camouflage team, adventurously led by James Gardener. Towards the end of the war when all commodities were in desperately short supply, the Board of Trade formed a committee to deal with furniture and I was invited by Gordon Russell to advise on the furnishing textiles. On finding that there were none and the only two fibres with which to weave were a fine Egyptian cotton and a condenser yarn, I settled down to produce about thirty designs. I found this very constricted brief an enjoyable challenge as a designer. The choice of colour range was not to my liking but I accepted that wider options would add to the burden of manpower and costing.

After the war ended the British Government sent teams of personnel to Germany to find out how the Germans set about training designers and I was invited to join one of these teams. A report on the findings, titled *Design Investigation in Selected Consumer Goods Industries 1947/48,* subsequently helped form many of the ideas of Robin Darwin when he became the Principal of the Royal College of Art and reshaped its entire philosophy and aims for its future students, alas no longer based on the development of visual sensitivity, knowledge, and respect for the arts as in the past but more related to commercial aspects. The demise of British industry is inducing art and industrial designers to migrate to other countries, whilst simultaneously many indigenous crafts of quality have ceased to exist.

Following the German tour, I joined another expedition to the Scandinavian countries, where I saw how excellently, in spite of the war, work of quality and innovation had been achieved. In 1952 a new set of postage stamps were to be issued for the coronation and I designed some of the stamps produced for that occasion. Since this time my life has been an incredible mixture of painting (alas, too little), teaching and lecturing, writing, and campaigning on art issues, with ever-increasing momentum.

—Enid Marx

\*    \*    \*

When the British Craft Council opened a lavish new gallery in London in 1981, celebrating the event with a major exhibition called *The Makers Eye* to which distinguished craftsmen were asked to contribute, it was no surprise that Enid Marx was included. For more than fifty years she has remained an indefatigable and highly respected maker. Originally trained as a painter, in 1925 she worked in the Hampstead craft workshop of weavers Phyllis Barron and Dorothy Larcher, who influenced her with their traditional methods of production—using, for example, vegetable and mineral dyes such a quercitron, madder red, and walnut. Marx believed in these production ethics throughout her life. "Craft," she wrote in 1982, "is for quality and not quirks." She did not, however, ignore or disapprove of industrial methods of production. In 1937, she produced small scale, abstract moquette patterns (which owed something of their inspiration to Paul Nash) for London tube train seats, and in 1941 she developed this work for the Utility scheme, where her style of limited colour ranges and small pattern repeats lent itself admirably to wartime constraints. She went on to design printed furnishing fabrics for the distinguished textile firm of Morton Sundour, set up by Alistair Morton. Her design achievement over this period was recognised by her election as Royal Designer for Industry in 1945.

After the war, publishers Chatto and Windus commissioned book covers and illustrations; the best known of her books is the whimsical and decorative *English Popular and Traditional Art,* written by herself and Margaret Lambert in 1946. Captivated by the exuberance and power of peasant art, as seen in corn dollies, inn signs,

and decorated barges, she drew heavily on these influences, and images from traditional English life gave her work great strength. Though in the postwar period her style remained rather static, it was always fresh and lively, as she turned her hand to stamp designs for the post office, to advertising posters for Shell and London Transport, and to teaching and lecturing, which won her the respect and admiration of a new generation.

—Catherine McDermott

# MASSEY, John (Vincent)
American painter and graphic designer

**Born:** Chicago, Illinois, 14 February 1931. **Education:** Studied at the University of Illinois, Urbana-Champaign, BFA, 1954. **Family:** Married Barbara Massey in 1971; children: Timothy, Stephanie, Scott, and Guy. **Career:** Freelance graphic designer, Chicago, from 1955; director of corporate design and communication, Container

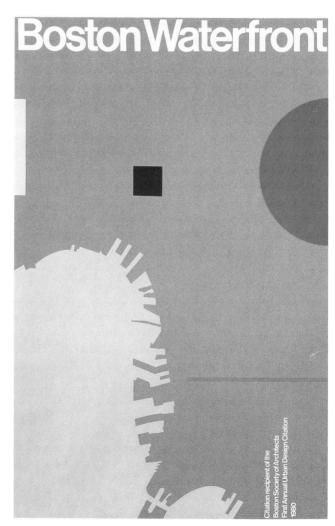

**John Massey: Boston Waterfront silkscreen poster, for the Boston Society of Architects, 1980**

Corporation of America, Chicago, 1957-83; founder-director, Center for Advanced Research in Design, Chicago, 1967-79; president, John Massey Incorporated design firm, Chicago, from 1983; has designed posters and graphics for the Field Museum of Natural History, Chicago Lakefront Adler Planetarium, Lincoln Park, and for the cities of Boston and San Francisco. Instructor in design, at the Institute of Design, Illinois Institute of Technology, Chicago. Advisory board member, Design Management Institute, Chicago. **Exhibitions:** Art Center College of Design, Pasadena, 1980; Rochester Institute of Technology, New York, 1981; University of Tennessee, Knoxville, 1982. **Collections:** Museum of Modern Art, New York. **Honors:** Art Director of the Year, National Society of Art Directors, 1967; Gold Medal, Art Directors Club of New York, 1979; honorary doctorate, Art Center College of Design, Pasadena, 1980; Gold Medal, Leipzig Book Fair, 1982; fellow, Rhode Island School of Design, Providence. **Address:** 2131 North Cleveland, Chicago, Illinois 60614, U.S.A.

**Publications**

**By MASSEY: books**—(editor) *Great Ideas of the Western World: Container Corporation of America,* Chicago, 1976.

**On MASSEY: books**—*Communication by Design: A Study in Corporate Identity* by James Pilditch, Maidenhead, 1970; *Who's Who in Graphic Art* edited by Walter Amstutz, Dubendorf, 1982; **articles**— in *Graphis* (Zurich), no. 135, 1968; *Industrial Design* (New York), November 1970; *Print* (New York), July/August 1971; *Projekt* (Warsaw), no. 5, 1974; *Communication Arts* (Palo Alto), March 1976; *Idea* (Tokyo), November 1978.

\*

The obligation of a designer is to create a vehicle to transfer a thought, concept, or idea from one mind to another. The concept to be transferred may range from a simple one to one of intricate complexity. As an example, a rather simple idea might be a poster to promote a theatre production. A more complex concept would be the transfer of the philosophy, products, and services of a multinational corporation from the corporation to the corporation's employees, customers, potential customers, media, shareholders, and local and national governmental agencies. In either case, it is the designer's responsibility to understand each problem as completely as possible and to develop a customized design solution accordingly.

Every solution must be relevant and to the point. It must be understood by the audiences for which it is intended, must have impact and recall through innovation, and must be void of extraneous or superficial elements.

If the designer is able to clarify thoughts and transmit them visually to the proper audiences, then the designer can provide a valuable communication service for the overall social and economic infrastructure.

—John Massey

\*    \*    \*

John Massey's appointment as Director of Communication at Container Corporation of America was important because it al-

lowed Massey to develop a visual identification program for the firm, one that would in the following years act as a model for other similar ones. These programs provided cohesive, visual identification and publication formats that reflected Massey's views on a "total environment." Massey applied the concept of corporate identification to the federal government in 1974 when he completed the first federal graphic standards manual for the Department of Labor; later, this was utilized as a model for other federal departments and agencies. The manual specified consistent publication formats, including sizes, typography, grid systems, papers, and colors. Massey had earlier developed for Atlantic Richfield (ARCO) a similar corporate system for which he had recognized the existing program and worked with marketing to develop new selling tools.

Massey's approach to creating unified programs extended to his designs for America's first civic cultural communication program, which consisted of posters and banners calling attention to areas and events in Chicago. The program was designed to convert areas such as the Chicago Civic Center Plaza from the "business environment of the day to a scene of festive aura in the evening." The simple posters and banners utilized abstract symbols and bold primary colors. Feeling that the business-industrial elite must embrace graphic design, Massey has stated, "They have a vital stake in improving the environment.... Conservation of human resources through the enrichment of man's surroundings is probably the most vital problem facing us today." His banners promote this view, as they provide visual excitement no less than information.

—Teal Ann Triggs

# MASSIN, Robert (Charles Joseph)
French graphic designer

**Born:** Boisvillette Eure-et-Loir, 13 October 1925. **Education:** Self-taught in design. **Family:** Married Huguette Hedouin in 1958; children: Laure and Julie. **Career:** Freelance graphic designer and art director, in Paris, from 1948; designer, Club Francais du Livre, 1948-52; art director, Club du Meilleur Livre, 1952-58, and Gallimard publishers, 1958-78; director, Hachette-Realités, 1979, and Hachette/Massin, 1980; editor, Editions Denoel, from 1981. **Exhibitions:** *Massin,* IMEC, 1990; *40 ans d'édition française, hommage à Massin,* Musée-Galerie de la Seita, Paris, 1989; *On a tous un Massin chez soi,* Centre Européen de la Jeune Création, Strasbourg, 1995. **Honors:** Prix des Graphistes, Paris, 1970. **Address:** 69 rue du Montparnasse, 75014 Paris, France.

**Works**

Book designs include—*Cent Mille Millards de Poèmes* by Raymond Queneau, Paris, 1961; *Exercises de style* by Queneau, Paris, 1963, 1979; *La Cantatrice chauve* by E. Ionesco, Paris, 1964, 1994, as *The Bald Soprano,* New York, 1965, and as *The Bald Prima-Donna,* London, 1966; *Conversation-Sinfonietta* by Jean Tardieu, Paris, 1966; *Délire à Deux* by E. Ionesco, Paris, 1966, 1994; *Le Chat et le Diable* by James Joyce, Paris, 1966; *The Tempest* by William Shakespeare, Paris, 1975; *Les Mariés de la Tour Eiffel* by Jean Cocteau, Paris, 1994; *Pierrot lunaire* by Arnold

Rencontre avec
Erik Orsenna.
Eric Fottorino
et Christophe Guillemin
à l'occasion de la parution
de leur livre *Besoin d'Afrique*
aux Editions Fayard.

Fnac Bordeaux
Fnac Grenoble
Fnac Librairie internationale
Fnac Metz
Fnac Montpellier
Fnac Orléans
Fnac Reims
Fnac Rennes
Fnac Strasbourg
Fnac Toulouse

**Massin: Afrique poster, for the fnac, 1992**

Schönberg, Montreal, 1995; *La Sonate ou les Trois Messieurs* by Jean Tardieu, Paris, forthcoming.

## Publications

**By MASSIN: books**—(preface) *Vignettes Français Fin de Siècle* edited by Deberny and Peignot, Paris, 1966; (with François Guiot, Maurice Pech and Marcel Viguier) *L'Amour la Ville,* Paris, 1968; *La Lettre et l'Image,* Paris, 1970, 1993, as *Letter and Image,* New York and London, 1970, as *Buchstabenbilder und Buchalphabete,* Ravensburg, West Germany, 1970, and as *La Lettera e l'Imagine,* Milan, 1995; (under pseudonym Claude Menuet) *Une Enfance Ordinaire* Paris, 1972; (under pseudonym Claude Menuet) *Le Pensionnaire* Paris, 1974; (under pseudonym Claude Menuet, with Gustave Aucouturier) *Album Dostoïevski,* Paris, 1975; *Les Cris de la Ville,* Paris and Munich, 1978; (with François Emile Zola) *Zola Photographe,* Paris, Munich, and Milan, 1979; *Les Célébrités de la Rue,* Paris, 1981; *Blasons Anatomiques du Corps Féminin,* Paris, 1982; *Contre-Blasons de la Beauté des Membres du Corps Humain,* Paris, 1982; *Le Branle des Voleurs* (novel), Paris, 1983; *Les Compagnons de la Marjolaine* (novel), Paris, 1985; (with Ségolène Le Men) *Alphabets,* Paris, 1986; *La Dernière Passion,* Paris, 1988; *Continuo: Fragments d'un Journal en Désordre,* Paris, 1988; *L'ABC du Métier,* Paris, 1989; *40 Ans d'Édition Française,* Paris, 1989; *La Cour des Miracles* (novel), Paris, 1991; *La Mise en Pages,* Paris, 1991; *Jouons avec les Chiffres,* Paris, 1993, as *Fun with Numbers,* New York, 1995; *Le Monde sens Dessus Dessous,* Paris, 1993; (with André Béguin) *Une Histoire des Images,* Paris, 1995; *La Grande Histoire du Livre,* Paris, forthcoming; *Le Piano des Couleurs,* Paris, forthcoming.

**On MASSIN: books**—*Massin et la Typographie Expressive* by Patrick Ferrey, Paris, 1967; *Design with Type* by Carl Dair, London and Toronto, 1967; *Massin et la typographie expressive* by Daniel Truong, Paris, 1968; *Art Without Boundaries 1950-1970* edited by Gerald Woods, Philip Thompson and John Williams, London, 1972; *The Language of Graphics* by Edward Booth-Clibborn and Daniel Baroni. London, 1980; *La Lettre et son image* by Emmanuël Souchiez, Paris, 1981; *Massinographie* by Valérie Rouzaud, Paris, 1993; *Graphic Design: A Concise History* by Richard Hollis, London, 1994; *Massin, Language Unleashed* by Richard Hollis, London, 1995; *Massin, au pied de la lettre* by Louis-René Béziers, Paris, 1995.

\*       \*       \*

In his book *Letter and Image,* Massin relates his role as graphic designer to that of stage director: translating and visually presenting the atmosphere, the movement, the speeches, and the silences, indicating time and space through the interplay of image and text.

While working with the Gallimard Press in Paris, Massin designed the graphics for Eugene Ionesco's play *La Cantatrice chauve (The Bald Soprano).* The characters in the play are represented by Henry Cohen's photographs from the Nicolas Bataille production. The words to be spoken by the characters are set in a wide variety of typefaces, depending on who is speaking and what is being said. By juxtaposing different typefaces on one page, Massin reiterates Ionesco's message that language has lost its ability to communicate.

Nevertheless, Massin's pages do communicate but through their overall design: the primary message is received at a glance, not word

by word. Whispers are shown in delicate, small letters: and shouts, in large, bold letters. Overlapping letters of various sizes, at disparate angles, indicate confrontations, boring passages become visually boring pages. Having rejected standard, horizontal line placement, Massin is free to place his words at any angle appropriate to illustrating the text. Space is likewise important. While some pages are busy with words, others are quiet and spare.

Among his other works, Massin created a "vocal calligram" as a tribute to Edith Piaf in *Evergreen Review.* The letterforms, printed on latex, are distorted to emulate the volume, range, and timbre of Piaf's voice.

Designing for a different purpose, Massin arranged the six voices in Jean Tardieu's *Conversation-Sinfonietta,* an approximation of dialogue set to music, according to the musical register. High voices are placed high on the page and set in slender, sans serif letterforms. Successively lower voices are lower on the page and are set in successively broader and heavier letterforms.

Massin did not attend art school, but learned his trade from his father, a sculptor and graphic designer. He also worked with Pierre Faucheux, a typographer associated with French avant-garde poets.

Influences on Massin's graphic work include Guillaume Apollinaire's *Calligrammes,* which are letterforms arranged in a design, and Stéphane Mallarmé's use of space in *Coup de dés (The Throw of the Dice).* Massin's work is also related to the Futurists' concept that writing and/or typography could become a concrete and expressive visual form.

Regardless of the topic of a work, Massin's primary concern has been to give visual reality to the literary content. He accomplished this through his innovative use of letters and letterforms, their selection and placement.

—Nancy House

# MATANO, Tom
Japanese automotive designer

**Born:** Nagasaki City, Japan, 7 October 1947. **Education:** Studied analysis engineering, Seikei University, Tokyo, Japan, 1966-70; studied transportation design, Art Center College of Design, California, U.S.A., B.S., 1974. **Career:** Assistant to the advertising director, Asahi Tsushin Co., Ltd. Tokyo, Japan, 1967-70; designer, Oldsmobile Studio, General Motors Design Staff, Warren, Michigan, U.S.A, 1974-76; freelance design project, Volvo AB, Sweden, 1975-76; consultant to Product Planning Group, Teijin Volvo Japan AB, Tokyo, Japan, 1975-76; assistant chief designer, General Motors Holden's Limited, Melbourne, Australia, 1976-82; assistant chief designer, BMW AG, Munich, Germany, 1982-83; chief designer, Product Planning and Research Division, Mazda North America Inc., Irvine, California, U.S.A. 1983-93; vice president, Design Division, 1991-93, executive vice president, Design Division, 1993-95, executive vice president, Western Operations, from 1995, Mazda R & D of North America, Inc., Irvine, California, U.S.A. Lecturer on advanced rendering techniques, Prahran College of Advanced Education, Melbourne, Australia, 1978-81; columnist, *Navi* (Automotive Magazine), Japan, 1985-89; member of Planning Committee, National Forum on Design, National Endow-

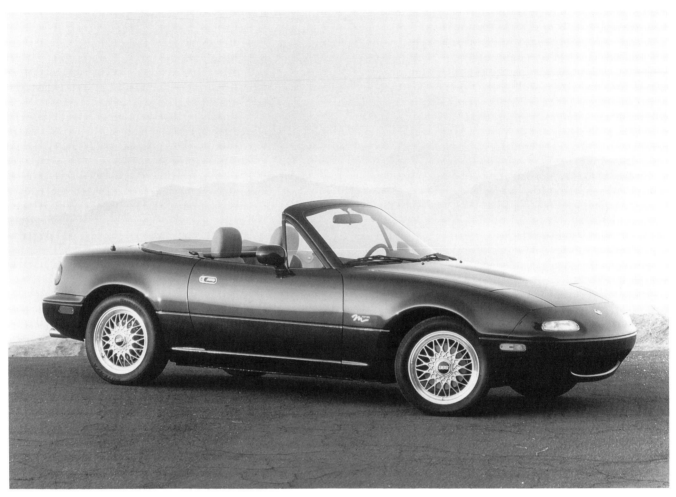

**Tom Matano: Miata M Edition, for Mazda, 1995**

ment for the Arts, 1994; frequent speaker on design at conferences and universities throughout the world. **Member:** Industrial Designers Society of America; board of trustees, WORLDesign Foundation, 1992. **Exhibitions:** *Second Nature,* Design Exchange, Toronto, Canada, 1994; *Mutant Materials in Contemporary Design,* Museum of Modern Art, New York, 1995. **Honors:** "Top 40 Design Innovator," *ID* magazine, 1993; selected as a "Trend Setter," *Los Angeles Times Sunday Magazine,* 1994; named to "Thinker: Design 100" list, *Metropolitan Homes* magazine, 1994; honorary committee member, Edsel B. Ford Design History Award, 1994. **Address:** 40 Choate, Irvine, California 92720, U.S.A.

### Works

1976 Oldsmobile Cutlass 4-4-2 Coupe, for General Motors, 1974.
1981 Commodore VH Series, for General Motors Holden's Ltd., 1978.
Initial design theme development for 1992 BMW 3 Series, for BMW, 1983.
Initial theme for 1988 Mazda MPV, for Mazda, 1984.
Initial theme for 1989 Mazda Miata, for Mazda, 1984.
Initial design theme for 1992 Mazda RX-7 and MX-6, for Mazda, 1988.
1994 Mazda B-Series Truck, for Mazda, 1990.

Initial design theme for 1995 Mazda Protege and Millenia, for Mazda, 1991.

### Publications

**By MATANO: articles**—*Car Styling,* vol. 351, no. 2, 1981; "Cultural Perception Differences" in *Innovation* (McLean, Virginia), Summer 1992; *IF,* 1993; *Innovation,* Spring/Summer 1995.

**On MATANO: articles**—"Heroes Column" in *Autocar & Motor* (England), February 1989; *BIL & MC* (Sweden), May 1989; *CAR* (England), April 1991; *Wheels* (Australia) June 1992; *Design World,* no. 28, 1994; *BIL Magazinet* (Denmark), August 1994; *American Way,* October 1994; "Cultural Traits Make Indelible Imprint on Car Design" in *The Sacramento Bee* (California), 1995.

*

The longer and deeper I work on design, the more I need to learn about Human Nature and the nature surrounding us.

When I design, I walk into the design and look out to see how the user views the object, instead of designing superficial surfaces. This technique enables me to add a depth in my design. I can make my design to communicate with the user's inner mind. The design of the Miata for example, communicates fun, happiness, cuddly, friendly, and so on. The RX-7 challenges and communicates that it is toned for taut driving and sheer driving fun.

The contents, purpose, and surfaces must match in order for the design to last. Visual weight distribution and manipulation of mass is key to functional yet attractive automobile design.

—Tom Matano

\*     \*     \*

Tom Matano, IDSA, has moved alot, first from school to school, four times within Tokyo itself, from private to public to private. His mother believed moving around was good for him, because it forced him to develop "survival" people skills and appreciate diversity. When he found it hard to focus on his engineering studies at Seikei University, escaping class as often as possible to work at odd jobs, she may have felt, for a time, that it hadn't worked. But, despite the disgrace to the family name, his mother agreed with his idea that he try his hand at design in the United States, and, once he found his way into Art Center, the trend of his life changed and the moving began to take on purpose.

Getting into Art Center College of Design in Pasadena, California, wasn't easy for an engineering student without language or drawing skills, but Tom knew he could beat anyone in the area of ideas. So he began with language classes and then went to drawing classes until he managed to gain acceptance at Art Center.

Then his mother's training began to pay off. Because wherever Tom moved and worked (from the United States to Japan to Australia to Germany and back to the States again), he brought with him a willingness to learn and understand different cultures. It wasn't easy. He has been hired for each position he has held in a foreign country as local personnel, meaning that there has been no special help provided for him in dealing with the mundane things in life like filing taxes. "When you live that way, do your taxes in a foreign country by yourself, you come to understand things about why people are the way they are. You understand why Germans won't work overtime. The extra money just goes in taxes!"

In fact, when he lived in Germany, people would often remark that he was just like an American, and of Americans they said, "You can hear an American before you see them." This puzzled Tom until, one day, he experienced it himself, hearing Americans around the corner of a building before he could see them. How could this be? Are Americans as boorish as the saying implies?

No, says Tom. The answer lies in how people live. Look at the size of the rooms in the average American's house. You have to yell to be heard from one room to the next in American houses, and TVs and stereos need to be louder to cross the distances. Since you don't live too close to others, you don't worry about disturbing the neighbors. "In America, you are conditioned over a matter of years to be louder," Tom explains. "But the Japanese and Germans are told to be quiet from the moment they are born, otherwise the neighbors will hear." The neighbors will especially hear in Germany because the windows are always open. Why? Because the Germans crave a close proximity with nature.

But why do these details matter to a designer of automobiles? In fact, his openness to truly understanding the different cultures, emotions, and psychology of people has imbued Tom's designs with a special quality. And that has provided Mazda with some very successful cars. "The more deeply into design I've gone, the more I have appreciated that you really have to understand people

in order to design well. The profession of design is really to learn about people, because what you do is design people's experience," Tom explains.

Tom feels that many designers work superficially, focusing on the exterior shape and texture, the surfaces of the objects. Even the interiors of such products as cars are sometimes treated superficially. To really design a product that optimizes the user's experience, you have to go inside the product, put yourself in the point of view of that object and think about how you could be better at what you do. "Say I'm designing a light switch," Tom suggests. "I try to think what it would be like to be a switch. How can I as a switch be arranged to make me more effortless to use?"

In part Tom is describing a depth of knowledge and understanding about things that approaches the intuitive. Such knowledge is beyond simulation by computers. He gives as an example the racing car engine that depends on getting one particular gear cut by hand. When a computer cuts it, it breaks every time. "The Austrian gear maker who handcrafts the gear understands the nature of the gear and the metal beyond what can be captured by strict data." It's why Olivetti's typewriter felt better to the fingertip than any of the others, even though at a glance they all looked the same. Its designers understood—in all its complexity—the angle and pressure transfer with which fingertips hit the keyboard.

The only road by which you can reach this level of understanding is to be open to change, to learning, to experience, to different ways of doing things. To respect those ways. Only then can a designer interpret change, culture, physiology, psychology, emotion, technology, and history into truly satisfying product experiences for people.

—Kristina Goodrich

# MATHSSON, Bruno

Swedish interior and furniture designer

**Born:** Värnamo, 13 January 1907. **Education:** Studied furniture-making with his father Karl Mathsson, in Värnamo, 1923-31. **Family:** Married Karin Margareta Sward in 1943. **Career:** Furniture designer, working mainly for Firma Karl Mathsson, Värnamo, from 1933. **Exhibitions:** Röhsska Konstslöjdmuseet, Göteborg, 1936; Svenska Stolar, National museum, Stockholm, 1963; *Nordisk Industridesign,* Kunstindustrimuseet, Oslo, 1976; *Kunsthandwerk und Industrieform,* Staatliche Kunstsammlungen, Dresden, 1976; *Scandinavian Modern Design 1880-1980,* Cooper-Hewitt Museum, New York, 1982; *Design Since 1945,* Philadelphia Museum of Art, 1983; *Faces of Swedish Design,* IBM Gallery, New York, 1988 (toured). **Collections:** Röhsska Konstslöjdmuseet, Göteborg; Museum of Industrial Arts, Prague; Konstindustrimuseet, Copenhagen; Museum of Modern Art, New York; Victoria and Albert Museum, London. **Honors:** Gregor Paulsson Medal, Stock Industry, Royal Society of Arts, London, 1978. **Died:** Värnamo, Sweden, 17 August 1988.

## Works

*Eva* workchair in laminated wood with leather upholstery, produced by Dux Moebel AB, 1934.

*Annika* coffee table in grained birch, produced by Dux Moebel AB, 1936.

*Pernilla* upholstered chair and chaise lounge with laminated beech frame, produced by Dux Moebel AB, 1944.

*Linda* table in birch with beech frame, produced by Dux Moebel AB, 1948.

*Glass House* (Bruno Mathsson residence), in Värnamo, Sweden, 1950.

*Superellipse* table, produced by Dux Moebel AB (with Piet Hein), 1964.

*Jetson* chair in steel with suspended leather seat, produced by Dux Moebel AB, 1966.

*Karin* chair in tubular steel with suspended canvas or leather seat, for Dux Moebel AB, 1969.

*Ulla* bed in tubular steel, for Dux Moebel AB, 1973.

*Mirja* conference chair in chrome tubular steel and padded leather upholstery, for Mathsson International AB, 1975.

*Sonja* sectional sofa in tubular steel with leather cushions, for Dux Moebel AB, 1976.

*Ingrid* chair, for Dux Moebel AB, 1976.

*Milton High* executive and conference swivel chair with padded leather upholstery, for Mathsson International AB, 1980.

*Kuggen* executive desk and conference table in beech veneer and chromed steel, for Mathsson International AB, 1983.

Computer workstation and desk with arm supports, for Mathsson International, 1983.

*Minister* upholstered swivel chair in tubular steel, for Mathsson International AB, 1987.


**Publications**

**On MATHSSON: books**—*Svenska Möbler* by Brynholf Hellner, Stockholm, 1947; *Contemporary Swedish Design: A Survey in Pictures* by Arthur Hald and Sven Erik Skawonius, Stockholm, 1951; *A Treasury of Scandinavian Design* edited by Erik Zahle, New York, 1961; *Svenska Stolar,* exhibition catalogue by Dag Widman, Åke Huldt and others, Stockholm, 1963; *Modern Scandinavian Furniture* by Ulf Hard af Segerstad, Copenhagen, 1963, London, 1964; *The Modern Chair: 1850 to Today* by Gilbert Frey, London and Niederteufen, 1970; *Design in Sweden* edited by Lennart Lindkvist, Stockholm, 1972; *Scandinavian Design: Objects of a Life Style* by Eileen Harrison Beer, New York and Toronto, 1975; *Contemporary Furniture* edited by Klaus-Jürgen Sembach, Stuttgart and London, 1982; *Mid-Century: Furniture of the 1950s* by Cara Greenberg, London, 1984; *Modern Furniture Classics* by Miriam Stimpson, London, 1987; *Faces of Swedish Design,* exhibition catalogue edited by Lennart Lindkvist and Monica Boman, Stockholm, 1988.

\*    \*    \*

With a self-confident and outgoing personality, Bruno Mathsson learned the craft of furniture design the hard way, as an apprentice in his father's carpentry workshop. It was, however, a background that gave him a thoroughly practical feeling for form and structure and a knowledge of wood. In the early 1930s, when Mathsson began to design furniture, the area was attracting a great deal of interest and debate in Sweden. Something of a battle had developed between modernists and followers of the Crafts movement. This split is best demonstrated by an incident at the famous 1930

Stockholm exhibition: Carl Malmsten, then Sweden's best-known furniture designer, refused to exhibit, in protest over Gunnar Asplund's steel-and-glass pavilion architecture. Allying himself with the new school, Mathsson began a series of experiments that culminated in a one-person show at the Röhsska Museum in Göteborg in 1936. The design principles he demonstrated there remained constant in his work for the next thirty years.

The immediate impression of a Mathsson chair is one of lightness, achieved with minimal structural parts and fabric support. The materials are unstained, bent beech with natural-coloured, canvas webbing or leather. The shapes, sculpturally moulded to fit the human body, reflect Mathsson's belief in function combined with maximum comfort. He has always based his designs on detailed anatomical studies, thus showing an early concern for ergonomic considerations. The result of this commitment to serious design principles was the evolution in the postwar period of an ergonomically sound range of seating furniture using laminated woods, usually beech or native woods. This furniture, because of its proportion, required little or no upholstery. In the general assessment of Scandinavian design, these have come to represent a standard of what can be produced with care, attention to detail, and a belief in form and function. This achievement was recognised by consistent backing from the Swedish government, which in the 1950s and 1960s featured Mathsson's work in the Swedish Consumers Association handbook *Mobelrad* (Furnishing Suggestions) and in exhibitions at home and abroad. Between 1945 and 1958, Mathsson's principles were extended into simple architectural projects, most notably summer vacation houses using the simplest possible construction of wood frames and concrete.

—Catherine McDermott


# MATSUBA, Minoru

Japanese industrial designer

**Born:** Osaka, 20 February 1929. **Education:** Studied at Osaka Prefectural Fuse Industrial School, 1942-48. **Family:** Married Toyoko Yamanishi in 1953; children: Yoko, Masakazu, and Yumi. **Career:** Display designer, for Nomural Design Company, Osaka, 1951-54; industrial designer, 1954-56, chief of radio design section, Osako Radio Plant, 1956-62, chief of the rotary machine design section, in Hokujo, 1962-66, chief of the wireless radio section, 1966-67, deputy director of the design department, 1967-70, director of the design department, 1970-82, and director of the design center, Gumma works, from 1982, all for the Sanyo Electric Company. Design committee deputy chairman, 1975, and chairman, 1976, Japan Electronic Industries Association; council member, Japan Machinery Design Center, from 1979. **Address:** 30-6 Kanamaya-cho, Ota-shi, Gumma Prefecture, Japan.


**Publications**

**On MATSUBA: books**—*Japan Design Annual,* Tokyo, 1965, 1966; *International Design Festival, Osaka,* Osaka, 1983.

\*

Before becoming an industrial designer, I dreamed of being an aircraft design engineer. Airplanes excited me as man's most intelligent product, filled with romantic and adventurous feeling. Unfortunately, I could not realize my dream because of Japan's defeat in the war, but the image of the airplane has never ceased to occupy my mind as a beautiful crystal of advanced technology and functional utility.

During this period, I read Raymond Loewy's *From Lipstick to Locomotive,* which showed me the way I should take. By adding an esthetic sense to already acquired aviation engineering and architectural engineering background, it would be possible to develop areas in which I could exhibit my ability. Wouldn't it be wonderful if I could share the fruits with users? With such an idea, I started collecting and reading books on industrial design.

In 1954, I took advantage of a chance which changed the course of my career from display design to industrial design. The Sanyo Electric Company, which started right after the war as a producer of electric appliances for the home, was looking for radio designers. Young and ambitious, I made the effort to sell myself (in spite of my ability), and fortunately, I was given a workroom in the radio factory.

The basic knowledge that I possessed in technical engineering was useful in order to integrate industrial design with technology. Our work went relatively smoothly because the role and the area of specialty of each staff member were identified. The technicians who thought that designers were artists were surprised when I submitted a structure plan along with a rendering. This experience made clear to me how important it is for designers to have a common means of communication with their partners on a job.

In the last thirty years, industrial designers have come to be indispensable to the production system, and the many new products developed have influenced the daily lives of people. Thus industrial designers are playing a significant part in creating a more comfortable and cozier life.

From its beginning with five designers, the design section of the Sanyo Electric Group has now expanded to exceed 300 designers who respond to diverse needs of consumers in electric appliances for the home. But the development of products can never be achieved by industrial designers alone. They must cooperate with those involved in research and analysis, graphics, photography, and other related areas.

In the 1980s a shift has taken place, along with the development of industry and economy, from an industrialized society to an information society, or in other words, from a materialistic value system to a quality-oriented one. The work of industrial designers should be reoriented from the production of things to the creation of lifestyle.

Although advanced technology today promotes the materialization of various functions of human life at a surprising speed, there is no guarantee that those products serve to create a happy life for people. Rather, they can lead to dehumanization. It is therefore important for designers to make use of the advanced technology as a means to a positive and desirable life.

Making proposals for more dynamic and higher-quality life and designing products to realize such a life are the tasks of designers. Humanity should not be forgotten as the basis of the designers' work.

—Minoru Matsuba

\*     \*     \*

Japan's reconstruction after World War II and its ensuing economic growth were both made possible by increased industrial production, the driving force of which was the "new technology." But a country such as Japan, with few natural resources, if it was to continue to develop, had to sell its products abroad—and Japan first recognized the usefulness of good industrial design when it came to the aid of the export effort. Forty years after the end of the war, the strategies have certainly worked: eighty percent of the population now claim to belong to the middle class. And now, with material prosperity achieved, the Japanese people have begun talking about "culture." Industrial design will therefore have a new role.

Until recently, because manufacturers were concerned about other matters, Japanese companies did not try to express a particular philosophy or design policy as many European and American corporations do. Rather, the catch phrase has been, "high-quality products at a cheap price." Now, too, designers in these companies are interested in "culture."

It is a theme that preoccupies Minoru Matsuba. He has worked for many years for the Tokyo Sanyo Electric Company, one of Japan's major producers of audio equipment and electrical appliances for the home. His career has gone through stages that, in a sense, reflect major concerns in design: how to make design recognized within a company; the search for method; the development of new techniques; the concentration and integration of design sections to enhance the influence of designers within a company; the expansion of good design through marketing; and, finally, the problem of culture, the response of a company to the changing consciousness of consumers. It would not be an exaggeration to say that such stages have been common to the careers of other Japanese industrial designers—yet much still depends on the individual designer. If Matsuba's career is typical, his work is of high quality, and his future is likely to be promising.

Matsuba is now most notable in his approach to the theme of the "fusion of civilization and culture." He says: "I recognize, as a premise, high technology: it can make people happier, more dynamic, more active, and richer. However, when I design things using the new technology, I would like to create not just individual, independent pieces but parts of an integrated lifestyle. We now make scenarios of different lifestyles—business executive, TV director, artist, school teacher, and others—and attempt to create products that integrate with that scenario. The designer can be the 'motivator' in such an enterprise."

Behind this apparently optimistic vision is Matsuba's belief that "just as the term 'consensus' became rooted in contemporary Japanese society, so the new age will create a new standard that cannot be measured by out-of-date concepts."

—Kunio Sano

# MATSUMOTO, Takaaki
Japanese graphic and product designer

**Born:** Kanazawa, 2 November 1954; emigrated to the United States in 1974. **Education:** Studied graphics at the Art Center College of Design, Los Angeles, BFA, 1980. **Family:** Married Julie Losch in 1989. **Career:** Designer, Gips and Balkind Associates, Inc., New York, 1980-82; art director, Knoll International, New York, 1982-87; founder/director, with Michael McGinn, of M Plus M Incorporated design firm, 1987-1994; founder/president, Matsumoto Incorporated, from 1994; designed for *Art in America, National Geographic,* Jack Lenor Larsen, Wacoal Interior Fabric, Sazaby Inc., Fashion Institute of Technology, Museum of Modern Art, Pratt Institute, Robert Isabell Inc., Steuben, Solomon R. Guggenheim Museum, Comme des Garçons, and others. Visiting lecturer, American Institute of Graphic Arts, New York, 1987, and University of Akron, Ohio, 1988. Artist-in-residence, Fabric Workshop and Museum, Philadelphia, 1995. Board of directors, International Design Network Foundation; board of trustees, Worldesign Foundation. **Exhibitions:** *Takaaki Matsumoto: Square Installation and Graphic Designs,* University of Akron, Ohio 1988; *Takaaki Matsumoto: Design Plus Square,* Fashion Institute of Technology, New York, 1989. **Collections:** Library of Congress, Washington, D.C.; Montreal Museum of Decorative Arts; Image for Peace, Montreal; Cooper-Hewitt Museum; Chicago Athenaeum; Berman Collection, New York. **Honors:** Silver Merit Award, Art Directors Club of New York, 1983, 1984, 1985, 1986, 1989, 1990, 1994, 1995; Award of Excellence, *Communication Arts* magazine, Palo Alto, 1983, 1985, 1986, 1987, 1992; Award of Excellence, American Institute of Graphic Arts, New York, 1983-95; Award of Excellence, *Graphis* magazine, Zurich, 1983, 1986, 1988, 1991, 1994, 1995; Merit Award, Type Directors Club, New York, 1983, 1986, 1987, 1988, 1989, 1990, 1995; Award of Excellence, *Industrial Design* magazine, New York, 1984, 1985, 1986, 1987; Merit Award, Art Directors Club of Los Angeles, 1985, 1986; Award of Excellence, Society of Typographic Arts, Chicago, 1985, 1986; Award of Excellence, *Print* magazine, New York, 1986; Award of Excellence, American Federation of Arts, San Francisco, 1988, 1989; Artist Grant, Art Matters Inc., New York, 1989; Award of Excellence, Lahti Poster Biennale, 1991; Merit Award, Siggraph 91, 1991; Certificate of Excellence, American Center for Design, 1991, 1992, 1995; and numerous other awards and certificates. **Address:** Matsumoto Incorporated, 17 Cornelia Street, New York, New York 10014, U.S.A.

## Works

*Making Paper* lithograph, for the American Craft Museum, New York, 1982.

*Design Message from Japan* exhibition catalogue, for Gallery 91, New York, 1983.

*Newsletter 84,* for Knoll International, 1984.

Catalogue, for Knoll International, 1984.

*Venturi* lithographed poster, for Knoll International, 1985.

Matsumoto Moving lithographed announcement, 1987.

*Uzuro* photo book, for Livro Porto Publishing, 1987.

Wristwatches, for Sointu USA, 1987.

Furniture catalogue, for Comme des Garçons, 1987.

*Square* lithographed poster, for the University of Akron, 1988.

Square installation, for the University of Akron, 1988, and the Fashion Institute of Technology, 1989.

Silkscreen series, for Serigrafia Ltd., 1989.

*Time Exposed* poster, for Hiroshi Sugimoto, 1991.

*Reorientations: Looking East* poster, for the Gallery at Takashimaya, 1993.

Identity, for Maharam, 1993.

*Rebecca Horn* poster, for the Solomon R. Guggenheim Museum, 1993.

*Roy Lichtenstein* poster, for the Solomon R. Guggenheim Museum, 1995.

*Neo-Dada* poster and invitation, for The Equitable Gallery, New York, 1995.

*Georg Baselitz* poster, for the Solomon R. Guggenheim Museum, 1995.

Annual catalogue, prospect catalogue, and advertisements, for Steuben, 1995.

## Publications

**On MATSUMOTO: articles—**"A Very Graphic Business" in *Metropolis* (New York), January 1985; "M Plus M Incorporated" in *Design Journal* (Tokyo), 1986; "Takaaki Matsumoto" in *Portfolio Design* (Tokyo), January 1986; "Takaaki Matsumoto" in *FP Design* (Tokyo), January 1987; "Discovery" in *Portfolio* (Tokyo), June/July 1987; "Square Installation" in *Sho-kukan Design* (Tokyo), April 1989; "How Does Your Plastic Grow?" in the *New York Times,* 13 April 1989; "M Plus M Incorporated" in *Graphic Design: New York* (New York), 1992; "Takaaki Matsumoto" in *Design Exchange: Hong Kong,* no. 10, 1993; "Matsumoto Incorporated" in *The Right Portfolio for the Right Job,* New York, 1994; "Takaaki Matsumoto" in *Tategumi Yokogumi Morisawa Quarterly* (Tokyo), 1995; "Takaaki Matsumoto: Selected Design Projects" in *Graphic Design Workshop,* Tokyo, 1995.

\*

The best way I know of to describe my ideas on design is to tell you a brief story which summarizes ever so simply and succinctly the way I approach my work. It goes something like this:

There was a blind boy in a hospital. One day, his doctor told him that his eyes would be cured. A week later, the boy's eye operation was completed and his doctor said, "I am going to take the bandages off your eyes tonight. It will be easier for you in the moonlight." Later that evening, the doctor guided the boy out into the night. Gently, he removed the bandages from the boy's eyes. The boy stared up at the perfect quarter moon and said to his doctor, "That is not the quarter moon I imagined. I imagined that a quarter moon would be shaped like a piece of pie."

—Takaaki Matsumoto

\*        \*        \*

Born into an art papermaking family from Kanazawa, a center of traditional Japanese arts, Takaaki Matsumoto brings to his fluency in the international design vocabulary a particularly Japanese concept of shibui—extraordinary refinement in the guise of apparent simplicity. In his graphic as well as his product designs, Matsumoto's signature is not the stridency of the bold stroke, but rather the harmony of the impeccably considered detail.

As the art director of Knoll International and as a co-founding partner in the design firm M Plus M, Matsumoto has created a body of graphics predicated on modernist intentions. But the essential utility and communicative functions of his designs are always cloaked in the accumulation of precise aesthetic judgements. Typically, Matsumoto's work mediates the reductive and the decorative, the elemental and the refined. His style of quiet but assertive elegance has successfully reflected the identities of such bastions of contemporary design and high culture as the American Craft Museum, the Museum of Modern Art, and *Art in America.*

**Takaaki Matsumoto: Square, 1988**

Matsumoto has suggested that he combines something of the formalism of the Bauhaus with a concept-oriented approach. He is both, and neither: his designs frequently evoke a Swiss classicism, but they avoid the rigidity of modernist ideology; his work is often imbued with a witty conceptual twist, but the humour is subtle and stops short of the populist. As a designer he is on high ground, but remains deliberately outside the ivory tower.

Much of Matsumoto's graphic work requires the active manipulation of his pieces for a full understanding of his concept. Closed or folded, his designs seem complete and readily apprehended, but this first comprehension is invariably partial. Only in the opening and unfolding of his work does one confront the fuller intentions of the piece. This transformative possibility extends to Matsumoto's product designs. The jagged Art Moderne hands of a watch become, at noon and midnight, the outline of the Empire State Building. On another, the markings of the watch face have been displaced to the crystal; the discrete units of time are enhanced by their own shifting shadows on the watch's blank face.

Given the terse gestures of his style, Matsumoto's choice of materials takes on significant aesthetic weight. Often surprisingly industrial, they are, however, always selected in faintly muted variation: corrugated plastic is given a translucent vinyl skin, aluminium sheeting a matte rather than polished finish, or black granite a dulled, almost porous, surface. The effect is at once strong and veiled. Matsumoto is a modernist with a poetic core that precludes the extreme resolutions of minimalism or functional brutalism.

Because Matsumoto enjoys the challenge of possibilities within defined limitations, he has been involved in an ongoing manipulation of the square in a series of graphics. By conforming to a rigid, formulistic use of modules, he has created his most distinctive work. Aided by a computer, his "Square" images have an astonishing freedom, affirming his contention that creativity is reliant less on limitless options than on simple but original perspectives.

—Harold Koda

# MATTER, Herbert

Swiss photographer and graphic designer

**Born:** Engelberg, in 1907; settled in the United States, 1936. **Education:** Studied painting in Geneva, 1925-27, and at the Academie Moderne, Paris, 1928-29. **Family:** Married Mercedes Matter; son: Alex. **Career:** Freelance designer and photographer, working with poster artist A. M. Cassandre, architect Le Corbusier, for Deberny et Peignot printing company, Paris, 1929-32, and for the Swiss National Tourist Board, Zurich, 1932-36; freelance photographer, working for *Harper's Bazaar, Vogue,* and others in New York, 1936-46; staff photographer, Condé Nast Publications, New York, 1946-57; freelance photographer and graphic designer, New York, 1956-84; design consultant, to Knoll International, 1946-66, New Haven Railroad, 1954-55, Guggenheim Museum and Houston Museum of Fine Arts, 1958-68, and New York Studio School, 1964-78. Professor of photography, Yale University, New Haven, Connecticut, 1952-82. **Exhibitions:** Pierre Matisse Gallery, New York, 1943 (toured); American Institute of Graphic Arts, New York, 1962; Yale University, New Haven, Connecticut, 1978; Kunsthaus, Zurich, 1978; Marlborough Gallery, New York, 1979. **Collections:** Kunstgewerbemuseum, Zurich; Musée des Arts Décoratifs, Paris; International Museum of Photography at George Eastman House, Rochester, New York. **Honors:** Honorary Royal Designer for Industry, Royal Society of Arts, London, 1982. **Died:** Southampton, New York, 8 May 1984.

**Publications**

**By MATTER: books**—*13 Photographs: Alberto Giacometti and Sculpture,* portfolio with Ives Stillman, New York, 1978; *Alberto Giacometti,* with text by Mercedes Matter, New York, 1987.

**ON MATTER: books**—*Die neue Fotografie in des Schweiz,* exhibition catalogue by Georg Schmidt and Peter Meyer, Zurich, 1932; *Herbert Matter: Photographs,* exhibition catalogue with text by James Johnson Sweeney, New York, 1943; *Advertising Directions* edited by Edward M. Gottschall and Arthur Hawkins, New York, 1959; *The New Graphic Design* by Markus Kutter and Karl Gertstner, Teufen and London, 1959; *History of the Poster* by Josef and Shizuko Muller-Brockmann, Zurich, 1971; *Herbert Matter: A Retrospective,* exhibition catalogue with text by Paul Rand, New Haven, 1978; *The Vogue Book of Fashion Photography* by Polly Devlin, London, 1979; *Knoll Design* by Eric Larrabee and Massimo Vignelli, New York, 1981; *Who's Who in Graphic Art* edited by Walter Amstutz, Dubendorf, 1982; *The 20th Century Poster: Design of the Avant-Garde* by Dawn Ades, New York, 1984; *Eye for Industry: Royal Designers for Industry 1936-1986,* exhibition catalogue by Fiona MacCarthy and Patrick Nuttgens, London, 1986; *New American Design* by Hugh Aldersley-Williams, New York, 1988; *Typographic Communications Today* by Edward M. Gottschall, New York, 1989; *American Typography Today* by Rob Caner, New York, 1989.

\*     \*     \*

For the past half century, Herbert Matter's photography and design have resulted in some of the period's most exciting and beguiling advertisements. Influenced early by Fernand Leger and Amedee Ozenfant at the Academie Moderne in Paris, he later worked with the architect Le Corbusier and the great French posterist A. M. Cassandre, both of whom deeply affected his work.

Matter is perhaps best known for his Swiss travel posters, which were created in the 1930s. Demonstrating his photographic vision and flair for the dramatic, these compositions rely particularly on scale and space. (All Swiss posters are uniform in size, approximately thirty-six by fifty-one inches.) The famous *Pontresina* poster with a huge, sunglassed head shows a bold contrast in scale and space between figure and ground. A diagonally-placed, larger-than-life head dominates the poster, while the background is a greatly reduced figure of a skier in a Swiss landscape. The type in the foreground "Pontresina," which occupies the entire width of the poster, is positioned on a slight incline. With the added impact of color, the total effect is highly active and dramatic.

Another classic example is a poster titled *All Roads Lead to Switzerland,* also done for the Swiss tourist office. As in the *Pontresina* poster, there are three distinct sections that form a coherent, overall composition. The base of the poster with the title leads immediately to the large, straight road penetrating the space and occupying seventy percent of it. It converges to a series of winding roadways which lead to the summit of the poster and the ever-present Alps.

For twenty years, from 1946-1966, Matter was design consultant to Knoll Associates where his innovative advertising designs became models that others emulated. Containing vestiges from his earlier posters in the play of forms, shapes, and space, the more abstract and playful Knoll advertisements exemplify the sophistication and sense of style that permeated all of Matter's work.

From 1952 to 1976, Matter was Professor of Photography at Yale University, where he trained a generation of graphic designers. In 1977, he completed photographing the works of Alberto Giacometti, and a decade later, the collection was published posthumously. Andrew Forge, then Dean of Yale School of Art, writes in the book's introduction, "Herbert Matter's photographs of Giacometti's sculptures are not only beautiful and moving in themselves, but very intelligent and totally convincing paraphrases of the sculptures as well."

—Dennis Ichiyama

# MATTHIES, Holger

German photographer and graphic designer

**Born:** Hamburg, 26 May 1940. **Education:** Trained in colour lithography, at Druckerei Baruth printing works, Hamburg, 1957-60; studied design, at the Werkkunstschule, Hamburg, 1961; studied graphics and design under Erwin Krubeck and Hans Michel, at the Hochschule für Bildende Kunste, Hamburg, 1962. **Family:** Married Gabriele Hoffmann in 1967. **Career:** Freelance graphic designer, with own studio, Hamburg, from 1965; has designed for the Hamburg Deutsches Schauspielhaus, Hamburg Thalia Theater, Berlin Schiller Theater, Münster Städtische Buhnen, Wuppertaler Bühnen, Kiel Stadttheater, Saarbrucken Saarländisches Staatstheater, Polydor International, Deutsche Grammophon, Teldec, Philips, Hamburg Museum für Kunst und Gewerbe, and others. Guest professor, 1970-72, and professor of communications design, from 1983, at the Fachhochschule für Gestaltung, Hamburg. **Exhibitions:** Städtische Bühnen, Dortmund, 1969; Fachhochschule für Gestaltung, Hamburg, 1970, 1978, 1985; Stedelijk Museum, Amsterdam, 1971; Stadttheater, Hildesheim, 1971; Theatre der Stadt, Schweinfurt, 1971; Stadtmuseum, Emmerich, 1972; Theater Baden-Baden, 1973; Bühnen der Landeshaupstadt Kiel, 1973; Museum für Kunst und Gewerbe, Hamburg, 1976; Musée de Marseille, 1976 (toured); Centre Culturel Allemand, Paris, 1980; Thalia Theater, Hamburg, 1980; Stadtmuseum, Oberhausen, 1981 (toured); Stadtmuseum, Lüneberg, 1982; Stadtmuseum, Kaltenkirchen, 1983; Museum of Bucharest, 1983; Colorado State University, 1983; Kunstindustrimuseum, Copenhagen, 1985; Art Poster Gallery, Lambsheim, 1986; Centre Culturel Allemand, Marseille, 1986 (toured); Theater der Stadt Gutersloh, 1989. **Collections:** Deutsches Plakatmuseum, Essen; Museum of Modern Art, New York; Colorado State University, Fort Collins; Museum für Kunst und Gewerbe, Hamburg. **Honors:** Brno Graphics Biennale Prize, 1970; Deutsches Plakatmuseum Gold Medal, Essen, 1976; Warsaw Poster Biennale Medal, 1980; Edwin-Scharff-Prize, Hamburg, 1981; Colorado Poster Exhibition Medal, 1981; Japan Graphic Designers Prize, 1982; Toulouse Lautrec Medal, Essen, 1984; New York Art Directors Club Merit Award, 1987. **Address:** Wrangelstrasse 13, 2000 Hamburg 20, Germany.

## Publications

**On MATTHIES: books—**_Book Jackets and Record Sleeves_ edited by Kurt Weidemann, Stuttgart and London, 1969; _Monografie des Plakats: Entwicklung, Stil, Design_ by Herbert Schindler, Munich, 1972; _Holger Matthies,_ exhibition catalogue with text by Axel von Saldern, Hamburg, 1976; _Who's Who in Graphic Art_ edited by Walter Amstutz, Dubendorf, 1982; _A History of Graphic Design_ by Philip B. Meggs, New York and London, 1983; _Les Années 60_ by Anne Bony, Paris, 1983.

\*

Designing posters is marvellous. Designing posters is agony.

The antagonism which lies in each relationship, which is performed with passion and obsession, which signifies heaven and hell, if one enters into it fully, will also on this branch line of "relationships" (shapes and surfaces) influence, change, sometimes destroy people.

I do not want to be overly solemn and maintain that this is a matter of life and death. Certainly not, but the silent scream of the empty surfaces produces echoes which will pursue you into your dreams.

The virginal quality of the untouched DIN format has a whiteness that makes mind and soul pale.

Splendour and misery are close neighbours. The muse whose kiss of enlightenment is so highly valued can also be a moody lady. She doesn't always kiss and certainly not everyone. First of all, the vertical or horizontal format is a challenge and enticement! The DIN as vertical format lies taut, disciplined, and essential before you. The horizontal format stretches out seductively and invitingly, offering you the full broadside. Now let's go!

Cut into it; that makes the viewer giddy. Photograph it in all poses; don't worry, she likes that. Spray it with colour, that cheers the spectator. Do not forget she has a public that can read. Inscribe it, fold it, divide it, tear it up, only don't do it awkwardly.

If you let everyone look at it, do not be mean; give this or that one a little, tender, loving touch.

Rough or smooth, stamped or varnished, matte or neon-bright, on ordinary or fine-art paper, it must hit you in the eye and explode in the head. At any price!

If it is ignored, the message is ignored, and you are ignored. That is the nightmare of the poster.

—Holger Matthies

\*    \*    \*

After World War II, it took a long time for the German poster to regain its strength. Two vital sources of inspiration were gone, as with a wind. The expressionistic ways personified in Kathe Kollwitz's political woodcuts directed at propaganda issues, as well as constructivist Bauhaus ideas, disappeared, smashed by Nazism.

Slowly, in the 1960s a new generation took charge, as the time of painful national confession, of terrible convulsion, was replaced by new voices, new ideas. Though almost mortally wounded, the culture began to regain its strength with new films, new literature, a theatre, and at last, the western part of this divided nation opened at her sources to new winds.

Especially in theatrical life, the harvest was very rich. Not surprisingly, posters for this institution were innovative and almost totally free of commercial restrictions. In some major cultural centers of West Germany, a few new masters began to emerge in the 1960s. Among the best of this group was the Hamburg-based artist Holger Matthies. More than thirty years later, he is not only still a leader in the German poster field, but he also counts on the international scene.

His great power rests on two important capacities. One is his brilliance in the technology of photography, printing, and the use of photomontage. The second is his enormous gift of mind, his happy marriage of a designer's eye for reduction and selection with a free-wheeling sense of surrealism and dadaism.

Sometimes metaphysical and demanding a certain intelligence of the viewer, his ideas are clearly realized technically. Carefully arranged ready-made objects play different roles from those they have served. His skilful touch of montage or collage doesn't show how they were rearranged; they state why the rearrangement took place. Subtle colors only add to the clarity. They don't shock. Rather, they slow your pace as if to say, "Think what we have to say to you." Matthies's theatrical posters reflect the playwright's message in an intelligent and intellectually well-developed way. These clients are fortunate to have him design their posters, for Matthies carefully mixes the sense of a play and the way a director stages it with our common understanding of the world and its culture. He demonstrates how good theatre can be served by the artist by exemplifying the sensible person who understands his role as an intermediary in the delicate balance of playwright, actor, director, and sometimes totally unaware public. Matthies tries not to play his own game, displaying mastery and technical tricks. Rather, he chooses a calm way of communicating between two worlds.

But when you see his work arranged together, you can enjoy the rich talent of a well-cultivated person with a strong, magical, surrealistic eye eagerly interpreting the marvels of the art of others—writers, musicians, actors. A true artist, he is the best example of regained cultural health in his native Germany.

—Jan Sawka

# MAU, Bruce Douglas

Canadian graphic designer

**Born:** Sudbury, Ontario, 25 October 1959. **Education:** Attended the Department of Communications and Design, Ontario College of Art, Toronto, 1978-80. **Career:** Designer, Fifty Fingers Inc., Toronto, 1980-82; designer, Pentagram Design, London, 1982-83; principal, Public Good Design and Communications Inc., Toronto, 1983-85; principal, Bruce Mau Design Inc., Toronto, from 1985; creative director, *I.D.* magazine, New York, 1991-93; editor, Swerve Editions, Toronto and New York, from 1991. Visiting instructor, Technical University of Nova Scotia, Faculty of Architecture, 1986, 1988; visiting critic, University of Toronto, 1988; Artist in Residence, Department of Fine Arts, California Institute of the Arts, 1989; visiting scholar, Getty Center for the History of Art and The Humanities, 1992; visiting Cullinan professor, Rice University, School of Architecture, 1996. **Member:** International Arts Advisory Council, Wexner Center for the Arts, Columbus, Ohio; The Power Plant Board of Directors, The Power Plant, Toronto; perma-

nent collection committee, Design Exchange, Toronto. **Exhibitions:** *Canada Designs for Business,* Tokyo, 1992; *Regeneration:A Series of Exhibitions,* sponsored by Ellis/Don Construction Ltd., Toronto, 1994; *S,M,L,XL in Progress: Rem Koolhaas and Bruce Mau,* Southern California Institute of Architecture, Los Angeles, 1994; *From Toronto, l'actualité du design graphique,* Villeurbanne, France, 1995. **Honors:** Alcuin Citation for excellence in book design, Canada, 1989, 1991; IOAAG Design Award, 1991; Annual 100 Show, American Center for Design, 1992, 1994; AIGA award, 1993; Publication Design Award, American Association of Museums, 1993; TDC 40, Type Directors Club Exhibition, 1993; Book Builders West Award, 1994; Cassie Award, Art Gallery of Ontario, 1995; Best of Category in graphics, *I.D.* magazine, 1996. **Address:** Bruce Mau Associates, 41 Dovercourt Rd., Toronto, Ontario M6J C32, Canada.

## Works

Graphic identity, for Zone Books, New York, 1985.
Graphic identity, for Walt Disney Concert Hall, Los Angeles, 1991.
Graphic identity, for Printed Matter Bookstore at Dia, New York, 1992.
Graphic identity, for Netherlands Architecture Institute, Rotterdam, 1993.
Graphic identity, for Andy Warhol Museum, Pittsburgh, 1993.
Graphic identity, for Ontario Arts Council, Toronto, 1993.
Graphic identity, for The Los Angeles Philharmonic, Los Angeles, 1994.
Advertising design, for the Barnes Exhibition, Toronto, 1994.
Advertising design, for The Wexner Center for Contemporary Art, Columbus, Ohio, 1994.
Exhibition design, for *Pop In Orbit: Design from the Space Age,* Toronto, 1995.
Exhibition and advertising design, for *The Oh! Canada Project,* for Art Gallery of Ontario, 1996.
Graphic identity, for Harbourfront Centre, Toronto, 1996.
Graphic identity, for Art Gallery of Ontario, Toronto, 1996.
Graphic identity, for The Wexner Center for Arts, Columbus, Ohio, 1996.
Advertising design, for Power Ten Campaign, Toronto, 1996.
Book design of *S, M, L, XL* by Rem Koolhaas, for Monacelli Press, New York, Milan, 1996.
Publication designs include—*ZONE 1/2: The Contemporary City* edited by Michel Feher and Sanford Kwinter, New York, 1986; *ZONE 3/4/5: Fragments for a History of the Human Body, Parts 1, 2, and 3* edited by Michel Feher with Ramona Nadaff and Nadia Tazi, New York, 1989; *ZONE 6: INCORPORATIONS* edited by Jonathan Crary and Sanford Kwinter, New York, 1992; *Frank Gehry: New Bentwood Furniture,* exhibition catalogue, Montreal, 1992; *The Invention of Pornography: Obscenity and the Origins of Modernity, 1500-1800* edited by Lynn Hunt, 1993; *The Society of the Spectacle* by Guy Debord, 1994.

## Publications

**By MAU: articles**—"Beyond Typography" in *The Lectures,* Rotterdam, 1992; *Insite* (Toronto), January 1996.

**On MAU: books**—*The Graphic Edge* by Rick Poyner, London, 1994; **articles**—"Zone Maps Life in the Big City" by Adele Freed-

**Bruce Mau: Pop in Orbit, 1995. Photo: Kevin Sugden**

man in *Globe and Mail* (Toronto), 31 May 1986; "La ville, zone érogène" by Pascaline Cuvelier in *Liberation,* 20 September 1986; "The Magazine Rack" by May Castleberry in *Afterimage,* March 1988; "Publisher Aims at the Intellect" by H. J. Kirchoff in *Globe and Mail* (Toronto), 13 April 1988; "On the Borderline" by Annetta Hanna in *I.D.* (New York), May/June 1988; "Producer as Author" by Rick Poynor in *Blueprint* (London), December 1989; "International Bruce Mau" by Freedman in *Canadian Art* (Toronto), Summer 1990; "The Mau Zone" by Howard Rombough in *Creative Review* (London), February 1992; "Notes on the Tendencies Exhibited through Free Time" by Burton Hamfelt and Mark Wasiuta in *Span* (Toronto), Spring 1992; "A Font of Innovation down to the Letter" by Freedman in *Globe and Mail* (Toronto), 5 June 1992; "Chairman Mau" by John Barber in *Globe and Mail* (Toronto), 18 June 1992; "Museum Quality" by Barber in *Globe and Mail* (Toronto), 3 September 1992; "Bruce Mau" by Will Novosedlik in *Studio Magazine* (Rexdale), September/October 1992; "Canadian Accent" by Claudia Neri in *Linea Graphica* (Milan), March 1993; "Toronto Graphic Designers Export Decidedly Different Styles" in *Financial Post* (Toronto), 10 September 1993; "The Producer as Author" by Novosedlik in *Eye* (London), Winter 1994; "Grafisch ontwerper Bruce Mau" by Corine Koole in *Eigenhuis & Interieur,* April 1994; "Maximal Mau" by Elizabeth Crinion in *Azure,* May/June 1994; "The Tall Order of Sizing Up a Very Large Book" by

Freedman in *Globe and Mail* (Toronto), 5 November 1994; "A Fascination for an Unstable Quality: Bruce Mau More than just a Designer" by Renny Ramakers in *Items* (Amsterdam), December 1994; "Plump Fiction" by John Shnier in *Canadian Architect* (Toronto), November 1995; "Buildings Born of Dreams and Demons" by Herbert Muschamp in *New York Times,* 7 January 1996; "Koolhaas in 2-D" by Brendan Gill in *New Yorker,* 12 February 1996; "Mr. Big Stuff" by Calvin Reid in *Publishers Weekly* (New York), 12 February 1996; "Hot Type" in *The Chronicle of Higher Education,* 16 February 1996; "Rem Koolhaas Sizes Up the Future" by Muschamp in *New York Times,* 3 March 1996; "Making a Splash" by Belinda Luscombe in *Time* (Toronto), 8 April 1996; "Going beyond Attention and Distraction" by Pamela Young in *Globe and Mail* (Toronto), 16 May 1996; "The Designer as Author" by Michael Rock in *Eye* (London), Spring 1996.

\*

Two principle issues animate my practice: formal innovation and content development. While the style has established the reputation of the practice, content is now becoming the focus of our work.

Our insistence on an editorial role in the projects in which we participate has been fundamental in shaping the direction of the aesthetic practice and in leading us toward the development of content. Our studio takes a more and more active role in any project that we undertake, collaborating to ensure the seamless realization of an innovative cultural product.

In fact we are now creating a separate business unit that will develop content independently. The new practice involves creating and inventing ideas and giving those ideas the most powerful and direct form. In business terms it means establishing partnerships with people and institutions that can provide the distribution we need. And it means developing the hybrid business relationships that will allow us to realize these new objects—whether they be books, exhibitions, websites, or films. What it really means is developing a content business with a form business inside it.

It has been the extraordinary scope and depth of the work with Zone, (six unique volumes of *Zone* address broad themes central to contemporary culture, 27 titles in a series of Zone Books explore philosophical and social issues) that has allowed me to develop a new, and increasingly supple understanding of form and content.

My collaboration with Rem Koolhaas on *S,M,L,XL* is the latest evidence of the rich possibilities that exist when design is defined as a true synthesis of content development and formal innovation.

The book consists of diagrams, revisions, story boards, cartoons, statistics, fairy tales, dreams, charts, marketing, manifestoes, essays, plans, sections, poems, scripts, chronologies, diaries, artworks, models, drawings, cinema, politics, dictionaries, sex, ambition, collage, montage, congestion, clarity, exhibitions, rants, complaints, tragedies, disasters, disappointments, and errors.

It's a book not so much about a particular office or architect, as it is about the state and fate of urbanism, architecture, design, and, even more generally, creative practice.

It's about what it takes to produce new work today. It's about the creative, spiritual, and intellectual resources extracted in the process of living this way. It's about the mix of enthusiasm and suspicion, steely nerves, brutal sophistication, and naive megalomania necessary in order to create post-industrial culture.

It's a book about how we can sustain a nervous hyper-connection to a supercharged global image machine without simply reproducing the most horrific parts of the milieu that we work in.

—Bruce Mau

\*      \*      \*

What is Bruce Mau?

You can kick Bruce Mau's work, or, it can be folded, peeled, burned, chewed, bent, photocopied, punctured, crushed, closed, opened, and thrown away. Under these and other circumstances, Bruce Mau's work keeps its deeply felt character. Certainly, under any adverse conditions a work can lose its substance. Yet I refer not to the possibility that Bruce Mau has superhuman powers (which protect his work), but a particular spatial talent for dense manifold ordering and synthetic use of organicist properties. Mau's work would melt into a molten puddle under extreme heat, but it's liquid state would most likely have been designed as part of its productive life. The Mau production model exists as a hybrid of farm, tea party, and Origami metaphors.

### Mau Farm

The modality of the agricultural farm is one based on time and the mobile system of the cultivated landscape. Mau's fields are rich and

simple in this metaphor. Not only does he "borrow" from the farmer the template of a living membrane as his working surface but also its properties of anamism. That is to say, Bruce Mau approaches his work as if it were alive. In the Bruce Mau studio, all forms of graphic behavior live.

### Mau Tea Party

Whereas the farm metaphor illustrates Mau's allusion to the organic life process, the Tea Party colors outside the lines of the "organic." An example can be found inside the celluloid illusion of life; the Mad Hatter's tea party (a scene from the Warner Brothers Studio animation version of Lewis Carol's book *Alice in Wonderland*). Watching the Hatter tear across a cacophony of forms from tea cups to swirling creamers and dancing spoons is like watching Bruce Mau pull his art direction seemlessly across the scopic theories of Bergson to the photographic enlargement of polyester golf pants! Borders between things are as arbitrary for Mau as they are in Alice in Wonderland. Here Mau and Mad Hatter are one and the same.

### Mau Origami

The 20th century philosopher Martin Heidegger often defined representation as one thing folding onto another (i.e. a picture of a thing and the "thing" itself). He called this concept "einfalt" or one-fold. Heidegger used his concept of the one-fold to dislodge the paradox of representation; the ability to see two things at once. For example, the simultaneous reading of a figure and ground. Heidegger's definition was perhaps physically illogical but pertinent to his thesis; that two names (i.e. figure and ground) could exist on the same pictorial plane. After all, what is Modern Art but the folding of the ground into the figure? Mau's one-fold is not only his signature tactic of image-compression, but also his overall pentiant for "folding" the organic and the illusory together (see the Zone anthology *Incorporations*). His talent then is in the art of folding these constituencies into a new kind of image origami. As Charles Mingus has said, "Good jazz drummers don't play where it is. They draw a picture away from the beat ... and tease the mind by not telling the audience what everyone knows—where one, two, three, and four are."

—Brian Boigon

## MAURER, Ingo

German lighting, industrial, and product designer

**Born:** On The Island of Reichenau, Lake Constance, Germany, in 1932. **Education:** Trained as a typographer in Germany and Switzerland; studied graphic design, 1954-58. **Career:** Freelance designer, New York and San Francisco, 1960-63, and Munich, 1963-66; founder, Design M studio, from 1966; design team has included Franz Ringelhan, Bernhard Dessecker, and Bernd Axel Kluge. **Exhibitions:** *Ingo Maurer Lumière aha SoSo,* Institute Français d'Architecture, Paris, 1986; *Design à la Villa Medici,* Rome, 1986; *Ingo Maurer: Lumière Hasard Réflexion,* Fondation Cartier pour l'Art Contemporain, Jouy-en-Josas, Paris, 1989; *Design ... ?? —*

*!! Lighting by Ingo Maurer and His Commandos,* State Museum of Ethnography of the People of the USSR, Leningrad, 1989; *Münchner Räume,* Stadtmuseum, Munich, 1991; *Ingo Maurer: Making Light,* Museum Villa Stuck, Munich, 1992; *Licht licht,* Stedelijk Museum, Amsterdam, 1993; *Identità e differenze. I racconti dell'abitare,* Milan Triennale, 1994; *die kunst und das schöne ding,* Neues Museum Weserburg, Bermen, 1995. **Collections:** Museum of Modern Art, New York. **Honors:** *Gute Form* Prize for *Dangler* lamp, German Federal Design Council, 1972; Chevalier des Arts et des Lettres, French Minister of Culture, 1986. **Address:** Ingo Maurer GmbH, Kaiserstrasse 47, 80801 Munich, Germany.

**Works**

*Bulb* lamp in chrome and glass, 1966.
*Bulb Clear* lamp in chrome and opaline glass, 1966.
*Spirale* lamp in chrome and opaline glass, 1967.
*ML 5B* lamp in acrylic and chrome, 1967.
*Tiffany* lamp in lead crystal, 1967.
*Light-Pole* lamp in chrome, 1967.
*No Fuss* lamp in chrome, 1969.
*Gulp* lamp in plain or varnished chrome, 1969.
*Big M* lamp in chrome, 1970.
*Ascher* lamp in anodized aluminum, 1970.
*Dangler* hanging lamp in polished or varnished aluminum, 1970.
*ML 181* floor lamp in chrome and opaline glass, 1970.
*Schreibtischlampe* lamp in polished or varnished chromium-plate, 1972.
*ML 40* lamp in chrome and plexiglass, 1973.
*Uchiwa I* fan lamp in bamboo and rice paper, 1973.
*Hana I* lamp in bamboo and rice paper, 1974.
*Nana Ju* lamp in bamboo and rice paper, 1975.
*Flischi* nickel-plated lamp, 1976.
*Galgen* lamps in lacquered iron with oval screens, 1977.
*Turm* lamp in net threaded paper, 1978.
*Tsching* glass-blown lamps, 1979.
*Savoie* lamp in white porcelain with silicone cable, 1979 (with Donato Savoie).
*Bulb Bulb* lamp in plastic, 1981.
*Bibibibi* standing lamps in porcelain, metal, and plastic, 1982.
Interior and exterior lights for a swimming pool and restaurant lighting, for Caprima, Dingolfing, Germany, 1983.
*Light Structure* lamp in glass and plastic, 1983 (with Peter Hamburger).
*Ilios* standing halogen lamp in metal and glass, 1983 (with Franz Ringelhan).
*Willydilly* lamp with adjustable plastic shade, 1983.
Design and lighting, for Garibaldi delicatessen and wine shop, Munich, 1984.
*YaYaHo* low-voltage halogen lighting system in ceramics, glass, plastic, metal, and porcelain, 1984.
*Fukuskú* lamp in metal and plastic, 1984.
Lighting, for La Giara restaurant, Sarzana, Italy, 1985.
*YaYaHo* lighting installation, for the exhibition *Lumières Je Pense à Vous,* Centre Georges Pompidou, Paris, 1985.
*Iló-Ilú* light fixture in metal, glass, and plastic, 1986 (with team).
Shop/showroom lighting installation, for bd ediciones, Madrid, Spain, 1986.
*Oh, Jack!* lamp in metal, glass, and plastic, 1986 (with Ringelhan).

*Little Black Nothing* lamp in metal, plastic, and glass, 1986 (with team).
Showroom lighting, for Sala Vinçon, Barcelona, Spain, 1986.
Suspended light object, for the Nick Havana night club, Barcelona, 1986.
*BaKaRú* low-voltage lighting installation in plastic and metal ceramics, 1986 (with team).
*Tijuca* and *Tijuca Wall* halogen lamps in metal and plastic, 1986 (with team).
Lighting, for the Blaue Ente restaurant, Zürich, Switzerland, 1987.
Lighting installation, for the exhibition *Design heute. Mass-Stäbe: Formgebung zwischen Industrie und Kunst-Stück,* Deutsches Architekturmuseum, in Frankfurt am Main, Germany, 1988.
Office lighting, for Driade, Piacenza, Italy, 1988.
Lighting for office/business rooms and restaurant, for Paustian, Copenhagen, Denmark, 1988.
Lighting with multi-functional ceiling construction of adjustable height, for City Hall, Coesfeld, Germany, 1988.
Lighting of plaza, elevators, and glass coupola, for Scala Shopping Centre, Copenhagen, 1989.
*One from the Heart* lamp in metal, plastic, and mirror, 1989.
*Don Quixote* halogen lamp in steel, aluminum, and flexible plastic, 1989 (with team).
*Eclipselipse* halogen lamp in metal, plastic, and glass, 1989 (with team).
Lighting of collections in the public treasury, for the Museum of Ethnography of the People of the USSR, Leningrad (St. Petersburg), Russia, 1990.
Light object in entrance hall, for Arbeitsamt, Augsburg, Germany, 1990.
Lighting concept and installation, for Hot Club jazz club, Perugia, Italy, 1990.
Lighting of dining hall, for Villa Eugenia, Livorno, Italy, 1990.
Lighting of foyer, boxes, and auditorium, for Teatro di Riuniti, Umbertide, Italy, 1990.
Lighting of presentation rooms in a landmark-protected villa, Lindau, Germany, 1990.
Showroom lighting, for See Spatial Environmental Elements, New York, 1990.
Lighting of winter-garden, for DG Bank, Frankfurt, Germany, 1991.
*001* lamp, 1991 (with team).
*Golden Nugget* electronic transformer-dimmer, 1991.
*Scooper* lamp in ultra-light aluminum, glass, and metal, 1991.
*It's Tatitime* lamp, 1991.
*Ontz* table in marble, maple-wood, and laminated Multiplex with steel legs, 1991.
*Hülot* lamp, 1991.
Exhibition lighting, for Musées Royaux des Beaux Arts, Brussels, Belgium, 191.
Lighting, for Grandage Golf Club, Kuguraku, Japan, 1991.
Lighting, for Comme des Garçons, Tokyo, 1991.
Lighting for conference room and Karaoke bar, Shirahama, Japan, 1991.
Lighting for nave and *Eternal Light,* for Heilig Blut Catholic Church, Munich, 1992.
Designing and lighting parts of the *Meeting Point,* for Airport Muc 2, Munich, 1992.
Lighting concept, for Garibaldi wine shop, Munich, 1992.
Showroom and office lighting, for Ambiente, Nagold, Germany, 1992.

Ingo Maurer: YaYaHo low-voltage lighting system, 1984. Photo: Christof Piepenstock

Lighting of glass-fronted staircase, for Berufsgenossenschaft Fahrzeuge, Munich, 1992.

Sales room lighting, for Eccel, Bolzano, Italy, 1992.

Light sculpture, for Archives du Monde du Travail, Roubaix, France, from 1992.

External and foyer lighting, and light objects for public piazza, for Performing Arts Center, Tel Aviv, Israel, 1994.

Special lighting installations, for the exhibition *Identità e differenze. I racconti dell'abitare,* Milan Triennale, 1994.

Stair case lighting, Leipzig, Germany, 1994.

*Hot Achille* halogen lamp in stainless steel, aluminum, and glass, for Ingo Maurer GmbH, 1994.

*Wandering Finger* halogen ceiling lamp in stainless steel, aluminum, and glass, for Ingo Maurer GmbH, 1994.

*One for the Recession* red halogen lamp in painted sheet steel, for Ingo Maurer GmbH, 1994.

*Los Minimalos Uno, Dos,* and *Tres* halogen lamps in stainless steel, spun steel, and aluminum, for Ingo Maurer GmbH, 1994.

Lighting concept, for Palais Grand Ducal, Luxembourg, from 1994.

Lighting object and illumination of building front, for Berufsgenossenschaft Fahrzeuge, Berlin, from 1994.

Lighting concept for Renaissance-era hall, for "Goldener Saal" at Major Hall, Augsburg, from 1994.

Lighting concept, for Center of Culture and Congress, Lucerne, Switzerland, from 1994 (with Jean Nouvel).

**Publications**

**On MAURER: books**—*International Design Yearbook 1986/87,* London, 1987; *Ingo Maurer: Making Light,* exhibition catalogue edited by Helmut Bauer, Munich and Tucson, Arizona, 1992; **articles**—*International Design,* July/August 1988; *Domus* (Milan), May 1990.

*                                *

What did we do with halogen lighting? We stripped it to its bones, respecting function and aesthetics, avoiding visual noise, adding formal expression, thus becoming birds, moons, flying somethings, on wires. Plagiarists have never understood what we did. Visual noise is what *they* make.

—Ingo Maurer

\* \* \*

Nobody has developed a combined vision of the aesthetic and the technical in lighting design quite like Ingo Maurer. For 30 years, ever since he first achieved prominence with his giant *Bulb Clear* lamp in 1966, based on the Pop Art of Jasper Johns, this German designer has constantly surprised and delighted his international audience with a succession of poetic, imaginative, and often whimsical innovations in light. As Vico Magistretti remarked of his work: "Ingo uses technology as a means of expressing a new sense of beauty."

The interesting thing about Maurer is that, unlike most lighting designers, who trained in theatre or architecture, he began his design career as a typographer and poster artist. "But I got fed up with people saying 'this should be green,' 'this should be more red,' 'this logo should be larger.'" *Bulb Clear* was his escape from the boredom and client tyranny of graphic design and he has never looked back.

He has also never wanted to repeat himself. His career has always been one of restlessly forging ahead in response to advances in light technology. He practically invented the entire genre of low-voltage wire lighting systems with his *YaYaHo* range in 1984, and a decade before he explored the lightness of Japanese design with his *Uchiwa* fan. If you visit his new light installations in the foyer areas at the new Tel Aviv Opera House and at the Louisiana Museum in Copenhagen, you will see that his genius is undimmed.

"I'm still searching for different ways to create lights," explains Maurer. "That's what keeps me going. To rest on your laurels and just do a lot of business with existing products would be too boring for words."

Ingo Maurer was born at Lake Constance in 1932, and has always lived and worked in Munich, where he set up his first company in 1967. "It's a nice town," he says. "It's slow and we don't get many visitors. There are no provocations but at least I can concentrate on my work." From this low-key base, Maurer has achieved enormous recognition. His company, Ingo Maurer, with around 50 staff, designs, makes, and sells lights without the aid of a retail showroom—but one is hardly needed to enhance his reputation.

Around 60 percent of Maurer's work is centered on one-off, large-scale project installations, such as the Tel Aviv foyer project. The other 40 percent comprises catalogue collections of wall and hanging lights, systems, table, and standard lamps. "When I started, I was interested in forms but now I'm more interested in the quality of light itself," he explains. "It gives me such a good feeling. You need to design lights with passion."

Ingo Maurer collaborates closely with Ron Arad, designer of the Tel Aviv foyer areas. They exhibit jointly every year at the Milan Fair and they share a mutual respect. "Some of Ingo's designs move dangerously close to kitsch but that's what makes him so interesting," says Arad. "Nothing is what it seems with Ingo. You look at a chandelier and you think it's a bonsai tree before you realize that light bulbs are growing on it."

Indeed a charming sense of wit and humor is an essential part of Maurer's vision. He believes in taking a playful approach and has a running joke in his lighting on the theme of the red kitsch throbbing heart; his latest version is entitled *One for the Recession.*

Too many lighting designers, argues Maurer, are over-serious and go over the top in terms of utilizing the technology available. He argues that maximum light effect should be achieved with minimal effort, but sees little evidence of restraint in lighting around him. "I don't mind architectural jewels being lit up," he says, "but large corporate offices on the way to the airport are lit like castles. It's crazy, it's fascist, and I don't like it." Fortunately, Maurer has himself become a beacon showing us more delicate and inventive ways with light.

—Jeremy Myerson

# MAVIGNIER, Almir (da Silva)

German painter and graphic designer

**Born:** Rio de Janeiro, Brazil, 1 May 1925; emigrated to West Germany in 1953. **Education:** Studied painting with an abstract art group in Brazil, from 1945; studied visual communications, at the Hochschule für Gestaltung, Ulm, 1953-58. **Family:** Married Sigrid Quarch in 1965; children: Delmar. **Career:** Freelance poster and graphics designer, with own studio, in Ulm, 1959-65, and in Hamburg, from 1965. Professor, Hochschule für Bildende Kunste, Hamburg, from 1965. **Exhibitions:** Pfälzische Landesgewerbeanstalt, Kaiserslautern, 1961; Ulmer Museum, Ulm, 1962; Casa do Brasil, Rome, 1962; Museu de Arte Moderna, Rio de Janeiro, 1962; *Mavignier/Kapitzki,* Library of Congress, Washington, D.C., 1965; Zacheta Museum, Warsaw, 1967; Kestner Gesellschaft, Hannover, 1968; Galerie Denise René-Hans Mayer, Düsseldorf, 1973; Kunstgewerbemuseum, Zürich, 1974; Die Neue Sammlung, Munich, 1975; Museu de Arte, Sao Paulo, 1977; Museum für Kunst und Gewerbe, Hamburg, 1981; Deutsches Plakatmuseum, Essen, 1982. **Collections:** Ulmer Museum; Kunstmuseum, Düsseldorf; Museum für Kunst und Gewerbe; Museum of Modern Art, New York; Museu de Arte Moderna, Sao Paulo. **Address:** Schöne Aussicht 35, 2000 Hamburg 76, Germany.

## Publications

**By MAVIGNIER: books**—*Permutationen,* exhibition pamphlet, Ulm, 1962; *Struktur in Rotation,* portfolio with serigraphs, Düsseldorf, 1980.

**On MAVIGNIER: books**—*Signals of Functional Poster Design* by Eckhard Neumann, Milan, 1963; *The Poster* by Harold F. Hutchinson, London and Toronto, 1968; *Deutsche Kunst: Eine Neue Generation* by Rolf-Gunter Dienst, Cologne, 1970; *History of the Poster* by Josef and Shizuko Müller-Brockmann, Zürich, 1971; *Deutsche Kunst der 60er Jahre* by Juliane Roh, Munich, 1971; *Almir Mavignier,* exhibition catalogue with text by Max Bense, Düsseldorf, 1973; *Almir Mavignier: Plakatretrospektiv,* exhibition catalogue, Hamburg, 1981.

\*

Like the actor, the poster designer must play different roles. If in so doing he only represents himself in order to achieve a particular "style," he is in danger of losing the interest of his audience. He must win public approval with form and metaphor, and he will discover his particular style by means of personal attitudes towards an aesthetic concept.

Like the actor, he works for an immediate audience, unlike the painter, whose audience is not necessarily directly influenced. The painter must await his audience and, more often than not, does not become closely acquainted with it.

The format of the poster changes with time. Toulouse-Lautrec would, for example, design his sketches differently today. Both the content of the message and the media of different times strongly affect the designer. For example, the modern billboard is suitable for communicating with the automobile driver. Rate of speed is also an important factor for the designer to consider—the faster the vehicle is travelling, the less time the driver has to concentrate on the billboard and, particularly, on its printed message. Basically, these things have to date influenced both the form and written content of the advertisement, and they will continue to do so. The advertisements for today's air passengers, for example, are futuristic.

—Almir Mavignier

\*   \*   \*

Almir Mavignier is, with equal intensity, both a painter and a graphic designer whose disciplined work leaves nothing to chance. His is a European rationale spiced with the Latin American magic of his native Brazil.

Trained in the Hochschule für Gestaltung in Ulm, Germany, he is a true disciple of Max Bill but was influenced as well by the color theories of the constructivists and Joseph Albers. This background imbued in him a demanding concern for logic with an emphasis on light and the interplay between surface and depth. He also recognizes the milestones in the development of abstract painting made by the pioneers Malevich, Mondrian, and Van Doesburg.

His work is almost hypnotic in effect, due to his optical experimentation with a variety of techniques and his visual play. Sometimes he uses overall geometric patterns and sometimes he clusters his design in the center of a page or canvas. Sometimes within a single work, he shifts from planar to three-dimensional effects to create dynamic illusions.

At first influenced by the Op art movement of the 1960s, he later became a more formalized exponent of the concrete art movement, but with a difference. This difference is manifest in his unorthodox (from the concrete art point of view) handling of color and use of a palette which is more exotic and less rigid. His color instrumentations are eye boggling. His work, therefore, flashes like signals, particularly in the posters, the perfect graphic medium for the effective broadcasting of documentation, information, and propaganda.

Although in his paintings and serigraphs his main aesthetic is close to the geometry of concrete art, in his posters he often uses photographs and other illustrative material. Even in these, there is an emphasis on light and the interplay between surface and depth. Often, a subtle, tactile quality is to be found, especially in the sea of polka dots made of three-dimensional colored points of paint. Although they adorn his work, they are not reduced to embellishments but placed to provide a tactile quality and to galvanize the eye. This stems from the degree of saturation of color tones and the position in which the dots are placed in relation to other tones.

Beyond the verbal information which it imparts, Mavignier's work has much to say to the spectator about *how* this information—an art for human experience—is stated. Indeed, this separates his work from the countless images with which we are surrounded.

—Milfred Constantine

# McCOY, Katherine

American industrial and graphic designer

**Born:** Decatur, Illinois, 12 October 1945. **Education:** Michigan State University, B.A., 1967. **Family:** Married Michael McCoy. **Career:** Designer, Unimark International, Detroit, 1967-68; senior designer, Chrysler Corporation Identity Office, Detroit, 1968-69; designer, Omnigraphics, Boston, 1969-70; designer, Designers and Partners, Detroit, 1970-71; partner, McCoy & McCoy, Detroit, from 1971; clients include Formica Corporation, Unisys, NV Philips, The Detroit Institute of Arts, and Cranbrook Educational Community. Co-chair, with Michael McCoy, Department of Design, Cranbrook Academy of Art, Bloomfield Hills, Michigan, 1971-95; Joyce Hall Distinguished Professorship, with Michael McCoy, Kansas City Art Institute, Missouri, 1987-88; faculty, Institute of Design, Illinois Institute of Technology, Chicago, from 1995. Vice-president, American Center for Design; secretary, American Design Education Foundation; advisory board, *Design Issues* magazine; contributing editor and editorial board member, *ID* magazine; Design Arts Policy Panel, National Endowment for the Arts; frequent lecturer on design and member of juried award panels. **Member:** Past president and fellow, Industrial Designers Society of America; Alliance Graphique Internationale; vice-president, American Institute of Graphic Arts. **Exhibitions:** *Cranbrook Design: The New Discourse,* toured New York and Tokyo, 1991; *Graphic Design in America: A Visual Language History,* Walker Art Center, Minneapolis; *L'Image des Mots,* Centre Georges Pompidou, Centre de Creation Industrielle, Paris; Cooper Hewitt Museum of Design, New York; Cranbrook Academy of Art Museum; International Design Conference at Aspen; Pacific Design Center; Design Museum, London; Museum of Modern Art, Rio de Janeiro, Brazil; Isreal Museum, Jerusalem; Cultural Palace, Riyadh, Kingdom of Saudi Arabia. **Honors:** Annual Design Review Awards, *ID* magazine, 1972-79; American Institute of Graphic Artists Award, 1972; Best of Packaging Award, Print Casebooks, 1976-79; "I" Award, *Interiors* magazine, 1980, 1986; IBM Fellow, International Design Conference at Aspen, 1982; Design Arts Research Grant, National Endowment for the Arts, 1986; Educator Award, Society of Typographic Arts, 1987; fellow, Industrial Designers Society of America. **Addresses:** Institute of Design, Illinois Institute of Technology, Chicago, Illinois 60616, U.S.A.; Box 2001, Buena Vista, Colorado 81211, U.S.A.

## Publications

**By McCOY: books**—(editor) *Projects & Processes,* Bloomfield Hills, Michigan, 1975; *Design in Michigan 1967-1977,* Detroit, Michigan, 1978; (editor) *New Media for Designers,* Washington,

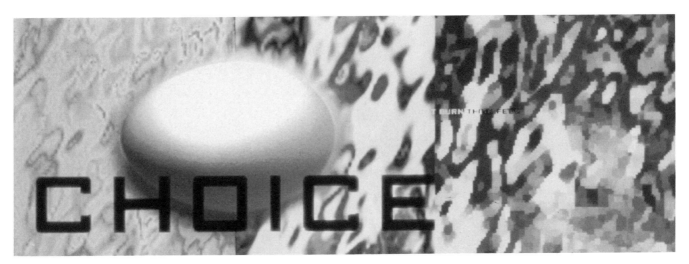

**Katherine McCoy: CHOICE, for Gilbert Paper, 1994**

D.C., 1984; **articles**—"Talking with Four Men Who Are Shaping Italian Design" in *ID* (New York), September/October 1981; (with Michael McCoy) "Good Partners: Theory and Practice at Cranbrook Academy of Art" in *Idea* (special Issue: Mid American Graphic Designers), 1982; "Reconstructing Dutch Graphics" in *ID* (New York), March/April 1984; "Industrial Design in the Post Industrial Age" in *Innovation* (McLean, Virginia), Fall 1984; "New Possibilities in the Teaching of Design" in *ICSID Design Milano,* Milano, 1984; "The Character of the Eighties" in *Design News* (Tokyo), no. 162-163, 1984; "Design in Japan: Two Viewpoints" in *Innovation: Design in the International Context* (McLean, Virginia), Spring 1985; "Foreward" in *Design in the Information Environment* edited by Patrick Whitney, New York, 1985; "Landscape of the Future: Speculations on the Post-industrial Age" in *Innovation,* Spring 1986; "A Revolution in Values" in *Innovation,* Spring 1986; (with David Frej) "Typography as Discourse" in *ID,* March/April 1988; "Is There Design After Graduate School?" in *AIGA Journal of Graphic Design* (New York), vol. 6, no. 3, 1988; (with Michael McCoy) "Introduction: Design in The Information Age" in *The New American Design* edited by Hugh Aldersey-Williams, New York, 1988; "Cutting Through the Aspen Conference" in *AIGA Journal of Graphic Design* (New York), vol. 6, no. 3, 1988; "Changing Values and the Role of Industrial Design in a Postindustrial Era" in *Design News* (Tokyo), no. 197, no. 198, 1988; "Graphic Design Education in Midstream" in *Statements,* Fall 1988; "Graphic Design: Sources of Meaning in Word & Image" in *Word & Image* (special issue), vol. 4, no. 1, 1988; "American Graphic Design Expression: The Evolution of American Typography" in *Design Quarterly* (Cambridge, Massachusetts) no. 149, 1990; "Digital Graphic Education" in *Statements,* Spring 1990; "Education in an Adolescent Profession" in *Graphic Design: World Views* edited by Jorge Frascara, Tokyo, 1990; "Why the Walker Show Is Excellent and Other Thoughts on Graphic Design History" in *Statements,* Fall 1990; "Professional Design Education: An Opinion and a Proposal" in *Design Issues* (Cambridge, Massachusetts), vol. VII, no. 1, 1990; (with Michael McCoy) "The New Discourse" in *Cranbrook Design: The New Discourse,* New York, 1990; "Rethinking Rational Functionalism" in *AIGA Journal of Graphic Design* (New York), vol. 9, no. 2, 1991;

"Another Take on Our Fiber Habit" in *Statements,* Spring 1991; "Ethics and Graphic Design: Educating a New Professional" in *Statements,* Winter 1991; "Education and Professionalism in Graphic Design" in *Choosing Design: How Business, Institutions, and Designers Shape the World We See* edited by Larsen, Quimby, and Marquardt, Minneapolis, Minnesota, 1991; "Establishing a Design Career" in *Graphic Design Career Guide 2* edited by James Craig, New York, 1992; "Digital Typography" in *How* (Cincinnati), March/April 1992; "Chairman's Essay" in *Fourteenth Annual American Center for Design 100 Show and Design Year in Review,* Chicago, 1992; films—(associate producer) *Future Wave: Japan Design,* television documentary, 1986.

**On McCOY: books**—*McCoy & McCoy Projects* by Roy Slade, Bloomfield Hills, Michigan, 1983; *Graphic Design Source Book* by Liz McQuiston and Barry Kifts, London, 1987; *Graphic Design In America: A Visual Language History,* exhibition catalogue, New York, 1989; *Cranbrook Design: The New Discourse,* New York, 1990; *Typography Now: The Next Wave* by Rick Poyner and Edward Booth-Clibborn, London, 1991; **articles**—"3 ... Days at Cranbrook" in *Emigre,* no. 19; "Products in the Eighties" in *Inform* (Virginia), vol. 1, no. 1,; "An Elementary Approach to a Broader Design Market" by J. Roger Guilfoyle in *Industrial Design* (New York), September/October 1975; "Design Michigan, An Aspect of Design Promotion in America" by Tadao Shimizu in *Industrial Design* (Tokyo), July 1978; "Global New Waves: Katherine + Michael McCoy" in *Graphic Design* (Tokyo), June 1979; *Idea* (special issue: Typography Today), edited by Helmut Schmid, 1980; "Plaza Sweet" by Margot Jacqz in *Interiors* (New York), January 1981; "Problem Solving in the Manmade Environment" in *Design News* (Tokyo), no. 124, 1981; "Katherine & Michael McCoy" in *Idea* (special issue: Mid American Graphic Designers), 1982; "Novum Education: Cranbrook Academy of Art" by Lanny Sommese in *Novum Gebrauchsgraphik* (Munich) February 1982; "Cranbrook Academy of Art" by Noboru Inouye in *Industrial Design* (Tokyo), January 1983; "Interiors Initiative: Hypermodern" by Maeve Slavin in *Interiors,* May 1983; "McCoy & McCoy" by Gijs Ockeleon and Erik-Jan Ruften in *KIO-Bulletin* (Amsterdam),

December 1983, December 1984; "College Poster Art" by Elena G. Millie in *Art Journal of the College Art Association,* Spring 1984; "Tooling Up" by Maeve Slavin in *Interiors,* September 1984; "Katherine McCoy" in *Design Perspectives* (McLean, Virginia), August/September, 1985; "The Real McCoys" by Gini Sikes in *Metropolis* (New York), March 1986; "Design School: Cranbrook Academy of Art" in *Axis Quarterly* (Tokyo), Spring 1987; "The Real McCoys" by William Owen in *Designers' Journal* (London), May 1988; "Machines Talk Back" by Ziva Freiman and David Staskoski in *Metropolitan Home* (New York), November 1988; "Katherine McCoy" in *Idea* (special issue: Women Designers of America), 1988; "USA: Katherine McCoy" by Liz McQuiston in *Women in Design: A Contemporary View,* New York, 1988; "Katherine McCoy" in *Ten Years,* Chicago, 1988; "Rocky Mountain High Style" by Mary Beth Jordan and David Staskowski in *Metropolitan Home* (New York), July 1989; "Katherine McCoy" by FHK Henrion in *AGI Annals* (Zürich), 1989; "Practicing What They Teach" in *Metropolitan Home,* April 1990; "Tradition and Vision" by Roy Slade in *Cranbrook Design: The New Discourse,* New York, 1990; "The Academy of Deconstructed Design" by Ellen Lupton in *Eye* (London), Spring 1991; "Katherine McCoy" by Chee Pearlman in *Electronic Exquisite Corpse,* Wisconsin, 1991; "Katherine McCoy" in *Macintosh Designers Network* (Tokyo), August 1992.

*     *     *

Katherine McCoy, FIDSA, design leader *extraordinaire.* As comfortable and influential in industrial design as in graphic design, Katherine has provided these professions with vision, intellect, and energy over a 20-year period. Whether her venue is a seminar, a design studio, a board room, or a journal, she has consistently pushed her peers and professional organizations to growth and new insights.

Why? Because she believes that the design associations are creating the dialogue and the atmosphere in which design can redefine itself and expand the ways it contributes. "Design is an evolving field, just born in the 20th century. I have a perpetual enthusiasm and interest to see where the design fields are going. I'm convinced that they must go—and are going—in important directions and that design organizations and their conferences, journals, and criticism are instrumental to that movement."

For an example of her catalytic influence simply look at her term on the boards of the Industrial Designers Society of America (IDSA), the American Institute of Graphic Arts (AIGA), and the American Center for Design (ACD). With her vision, leadership, and skill at motivating her colleagues, IDSA established its publications program, including the award-winning quarterly journal, *Innovation.* With her help, that journal went on to publish first on such influential topics as product semantics, design in the 21st century, multidisciplinary product development teams, usability testing, and ecological responsibility. As vice president of the AIGA, she helped develop its national chapter network and redefine its role as America's national graphic design organization. As president of ACD, she has led this organization to explore the growing impact of multimedia and interaction design as it generates a dynamic new territory between graphic and industrial design. And that only covers a handful of her contributions to three organizations.

In a sense, her volunteer leadership has been another avenue through which she could contribute to design education. "Holding

office in these organizations has helped me open another educational audience. These groups provide the opportunity to create forums that will get the stimulus of new ideas (education) out to the broader audience of professionals." Her position as co-chair of the Cranbrook Academy of Art's Design Department gave her the best forum of all for this purpose, of course, and she used it to prepare a generation of designers who can consider the broader implications and intellectual context of their work. Therein may lie her most lasting legacy.

The programs that she takes greatest pride in are exhibits, books, lectures, and articles that have pushed the design community's understanding of itself, its sources, and its responsibilities. For instance, her lecture in the late 1970s on "Modernism and Post-Modernism in Architecture and Graphic Design" helped bring to light the ways in which post-modern theory and its expression in architecture were influencing graphic design. When she curated the 1984 exhibit on contemporary Dutch graphic design, she exposed U.S. graphic designers for the first time to an important and fresh national movement that then proved extremely influential. Most recently, *Cranbrook Design: The New Discourse*, a book and exhibit she did with her husband, Michael, covers ten years of work by Cranbrook design students, alumni, and faculty. In it, the McCoys capture the sometimes controversial ideas explored by Cranbrook people between 1981 and 1991.

Katherine believes that this is a very interesting time to be involved in design. In today's global marketplace, she says that the "Age of Communication and Information" is creating new opportunities in an audience far more receptive to design's best contributions. "A lot of nondesigners may have usurped the lower levels of graphic design work due to desktop publishing, but the effect has been to upgrade the baseline of acceptable production values," she remarks. "And that has expanded the opportunities for graphic designers to contribute at the highest level to complex demands for visual communication." It has also opened a new world in need of design—interactive multimedia—and that world is changing so quickly there's no predicting where it will be in five years.

As electronics blur the distinction between two- and three-dimensional design and products become more about their information than about their form, Katherine recognizes that successful communication interaction will require designers to understand much more than typography and grid systems. It will require a willingness to learn and apply ideas from disciplines previously unconnected and independent.

One of the true intellectuals of the design field, Katherine McCoy's fascination with the relationship between abstract theories and professional practice has led her to seek ideas she can transform in application to improve the communicative outcome of graphic and industrial design. Many of the ideas she has examined over the past 15 years come from literary criticism and communication theory and their studies into the nature of meaning and its communication. By applying concepts about language—the nature of meaning, how language shapes and distorts meaning, how the receiver constructs meaning—to design, she has helped reshape the thinking behind graphic and industrial design. "In the 1970s, we were working with type and image as form, using it as self-expression for the designer," she explains. "In the 1980s and 1990s, we moved the focus to the audience. How does the audience construct meaning from the text and images we provide? We have recognized that the encoded meanings in the text and image and their relationship and how they interact with each other will be interpreted individually by each member of the audience."

Not everyone in design is comfortable with the experimentation and direction of her work. But that is precisely the point. Katherine believes that "Experimentation is essential in order to see the potential of an idea for professional practice. That's education's responsibility. We must push the limits of polemical proposals if the profession wants to find new pragmatic tools for practice. It is the most important role schools, especially graduate programs, can play."

Katherine now spends half of the year on practice and half of the year on education, half in the breathtaking nature of Colorado's Rockies and half in the dynamic city life of Chicago, at one of the nation's most well-respected design programs, Illinois Institute of Technology's Institute of Design. With this balance of practice and education, Katherine can push the design professions' intellectual content while she advances the state of information communication. It is a platform perfectly suited to her talents.

—Kristina Goodrich

# McCOY, Michael

American industrial designer

**Born:** Eaton Rapids, Michigan, 16 September 1944. **Education:** Michigan State University, B.A., 1966; Wayne State University, M.A., 1968. **Family:** Married Katherine McCoy. **Career:** Partner, McCoy & McCoy, Detroit, from 1971. Co-chair, with Katherine McCoy, Department of Design, Cranbrook Academy of Art, Bloomfield Hills, Michigan, 1971-95; Joyce Hall Distinguished Professorship, with Katherine McCoy, Kansas City Art Institute, Missouri, 1987-88; faculty, Institute of Design, Illinois Institute of Technology, Chicago, from 1995. **Member:** Industrial Designers Society of America (IDSA). **Exhibitions:** American Institute of Graphic Arts, New York, 1977-80; Pacific Design Center, Los Angeles, 1990; Cranbrook Academy of Art Museum, Bloomfield Hills, Michigan, 1991; United States Information Agency Exhibit, Museum of Modern Art, Rio de Janeiro, Brazil, National Museum of Fine Arts, Buenos Aires, Argentina, Israel Museum, Jerusalem, and the Cultural Palace, Riyadh, Saudi Arabia, 1991; Axis Building, Tokyo, 1991; British Design Museum, London, 1994; San Francisco Museum of Modern Art, California, 1995. **Collections:** National Design Museum, New York; San Francisco Museum of Modern Art, California; British Design Museum, London. **Honors:** Furniture Award, *Progressive Architecture,* 1980; *Interiors* magazine Award, 1985; European Ergodesign Award, 1986; Hannover Fair Prize, 1988; Second Prize, "Design The Future" Competition, Japan, 1989; Gold Medal, Industrial Designers Society of America, 1991; Best of Category, *ID* magazine, 1991; IBD Product Design Award, 1991. **Addresses:** Institute of Design, Illinois Institute of Technology, Chicago, Illinois 60616, U.S.A.; Box 2001, Buena Vista, Colorado 81211, U.S.A.

## Works

*Door* chair, for Arkitektura, 1984.
Litton Showroom, Merchandise Mart, Chicago, 1984.
*Colorado* seating, for Artifort, 1985.
Formica Showroom, Merchandise Mart, Chicago, 1987.

Electronic Office System, for Philips Electronics, 1987.
*Quadrio* seating, for Artifort, 1988.
*Bulldog* chair, for The Knoll Group, 1990 (with Fahnstrom/McCoy).
*Deskscape* desk accessories, for Steelcase Details 1991 (with Fahnstrom/McCoy).

## Publications

**By McCOY: books**—(with others) *Problem Solving in the Manmade Environment,* Detroit, 1975; **articles**—(with Katherine McCoy) "Good Partners: Theory and Practice at Cranbrook Academy of Art" in *Idea* (special Issue: Mid American Graphic Designers), 1982; "Defining a New Functionalism" in *Innovation: Semantics of Form* (McLean, Virginia), Spring 1984; "The Imagery of Business" in *The Los Angeles Times,* 31 May 1987; "Interpreting Technology Through Product Form" in *Industrial Design* (Tokyo), Summer 1987; "Point Counterpoint" interview by Annetta Hanna in *ID* (New York), September/October 1987; (with Katherine McCoy) "Introduction: Design in The Information Age" in *The New American Design* edited by Hugh Aldersey-Williams, New York, 1988; (with Lisa Krohn) "Beyond Beige: Interpretive Design for the Post-Industrial Age" in *Design Issues,* Spring 1989; "The Post-industrial Designer" in *Product Semantics 89,* Helsinki, 1989; "Concrete Dreams, Flesh and Glass" in *ID* (New York), November 1990; (with Katherine McCoy) "The New Discourse" in *Cranbrook Design: The New Discourse,* New York, 1990.

**On McCOY: books**—*McCoy & McCoy Projects* by Roy Slade, Bloomfield Hills, Michigan, 1983; Arthur C. Danto, *397 Chairs,* New York, 1988; **articles**—"An Elementary Approach to a Broader Design Market" by J. Roger Guilfoyle in *Industrial Design* (New York), September/October 1975; "Design Michigan: An Aspect of Design Promotion in America" by Tadao Shimizu in *Industrial Design 94* (Tokyo), July 1978; "Global New Waves: Katherine + Michael McCoy" in *Graphic Design* (Tokyo), June 1979; "Design Education USA: Cranbrook Academy of Art" by Ruth D'Arcy in *Designscape* (New Zealand), May 1980; "Plaza Sweet" by Margot Jacqz in *Interiors* (New York), January 1981; "Problem Solving in the Manmade Environment" in *Design News 124* (Tokyo), 1981; "Katherine & Michael McCoy" in *Idea* (special issue: Mid American Graphic Designers), 1982; "Top Teachers #2: Cranbrook Comes Back" by Daralice Boles in *Interiors* (New York), September 1982; "Cranbrook Academy of Art" by Noboru Inouye in *Industrial Design 121* (Tokyo), January 1983; "Interiors Initiative: Hypermodern" by Maeve Slavin in *Interiors* (New York), May 1983; "McCoy & McCoy" by Gijs Ockeleon and Erik-Jan Rutten in *KIO-Bulletin* (Amsterdam), March 1984, December 1984; "Tooling Up" by Maeve Slavin in *Interiors* (New York), September 1984; "Beyond Surface" by Nayana Currimbhoy in *Interiors* (New York), January 1986; "The Real McCoys" by Gini Sikes in *Metropolis* (New York), March 1986; "Design School: Cranbrook Academy of Art" in *Axis Quarterly* (Tokyo), Spring 1987; "The Real McCoys" by William Owen in *Designers' Journal* (London), May 1988; "Object Culture" by Hugh Aldersey-Williams in *Blueprint* (London), July/August 1988; "Machines Talk Back" by Ziva Freiman and David Staskoski in *Metropolitan Home* (New York), November 1988; "A Working Retreat That's User-Friendly" by Patricia Leigh Brown in *The New York Times,* 11 August 1988.

* * *

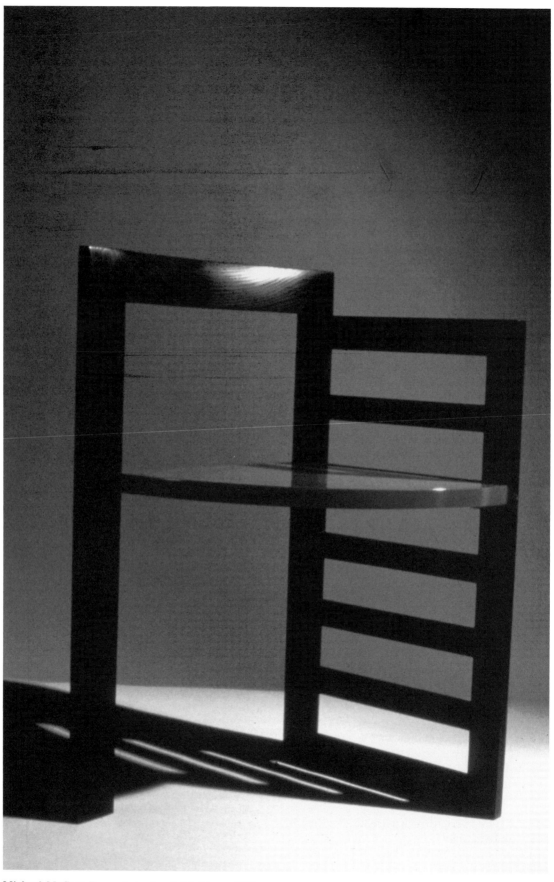

**Michael McCoy: Door chair, for Arkitektura, 1981**

America's Michael McCoy relishes the contradictions that are very much part of his work. Industrial designer, educator, and thinker, he makes constant bridges between theory and practice. Essentially his career can be defined by two objects, one of which he didn't actually design himself. On one hand, there is his *Bulldog* office chair which he designed in 1991 for Knoll International with his Chicago-based partner Dale Fahnstrom. This remains Knoll's best-selling chair today and reflects McCoy's ability to tap the corporate mainstream with a sensual and suggestive product.

On the other hand is a different object altogether: the *Phonebook* telephone answering machine of 1987, designed by Lisa Krohn, one of McCoy's postgraduate students at the Cranbrook Academy of Art near Detroit, Michigan. This award-winning design, giving an everyday electronic product the visual metaphor of a book with pages, reflects McCoy's importance as a teacher and generator of a new design language. The *Phonebook* effectively introduced the concept of "product semantics" to the wider world, showing that it is possible to "read" objects like text, through the use of symbols and visual metaphors.

Between 1971 and 1995, Michael McCoy was co-chair of Cranbrook's celebrated Design Department with his wife Katherine, the renowned graphic designer. In the 1980s, working closely with small groups of handpicked students, the McCoys began to develop the concept of "product semantics" by drawing on both their reading of French post-structuralist philosophy and the science of semantics and linguistic meaning.

As Cranbrook students burrowed an escape tunnel from the aesthetic prison of cool, anonymous Functionalism as a means of expressing function in products, large swathes of industry from car makers to computer companies breathed a deep sigh of relief. Apple, Sony, and Philips were among those industrial giants who collaborated with Cranbrook on a new generation of more expressive products. Michael McCoy became international news. It appeared that he had discovered the Holy Grail in design—a way out from the sterility of Modernism.

But his career has always been more about asking questions than proffering solutions and he has resolutely refused to allow a didactic design movement to grow up around him. "After you reject the utopian vision of early Modernism and deconstruct it, the last thing you do is build another utopian vision," says McCoy. "You put the parts back together, taking each idea ind assessing its worth. That means taking a pluralist view."

The McCoys' success at Cranbrook Academy of Art, with its impeccable Modernist credentials, its Saarinen-designed campus, and its accolade from *Time* magazine as "America's Bauhaus," was a long time coming. "It took us more than ten years to get an educational philosophy going," says Michael McCoy. "We were very young when we were appointed and we made a lot of mistakes." But when it happened, the reverberations stretched as far as Japan's car plants. Some commentators attribute the curvy lines of the Mazda Miata and its imitators to Cranbrook's innovative approach to form.

The McCoys met as design students at Michigan State University in the 1960s. Upon graduation, Michael worked briefly for a consulting firm designing mass transit systems, including the San Francisco, California, Bart system, and formed the design group McCoy & McCoy before he and his wife jointly took on the key Cranbrook educational challenge.

A quarter century later, his boyish enthusiasms are undimmed. At the end of the 1995 academic year, the McCoys left Cranbrook to teach in the design faculty at the Illinois Institute of Technology.

The new post provides an ideal opportunity to graft design theory and philosophy onto IIT's well-established scientific and analytical programs, says Michael McCoy. This is especially important in view of one of his key areas of interest: the humanizing of technology.

Essentially McCoy sees his consulting and education work as part of a single process of social and technological investigation. The fact that his Chicago design partner Dale Fahnstrom also teaches at IIT, and that his educational partner Katherine shares the McCoy & McCoy design studio, simply reinforces this sense of cultural continuum. Today McCoy divides his time between the Windy City and a home-cum-studio in Colorado, always thinking, always designing, never happier than when asking the questions. But plenty of design clients, including Steelcase, NEC, and Knoll, have been happy enough with his answers.

—Jeremy Myerson

# McFADDEN, Mary

American fashion designer

**Born:** New York City, 1 October 1938. **Education:** Studied at the École Lubec, and at the Sorbonne, Paris, 1955-57; Traphagen School of Design, New York, 1957-58; studied sociology, at Columbia University, New York, and at the New School for Social Research, New York, 1958-60. **Family:** Married Philip Harari in 1965 (divorced); married Frank McEwan in 1968 (divorced); married Kohle Yohannan in 1989 (divorced); daughter: Justine Harari. **Career:** Director of public relations, at Christian Dior, New York, 1962-64; merchandising editor, *Vogue* magazine, South Africa, 1964-65; travel and politics columnist, *Rand Daily Mail,* South Africa, 1965-68; founder, Vukutu sculpture workshop, Rhodesia 1968-70; also freelance editor, for *My Fair Lady,* Cape Town, and *Vogue,* Paris, 1968-70; special projects editor, American *Vogue,* New York, 1970; freelance fashion and jewelry designer, New York, from 1973; founder and C.E.O., Mary McFadden Incorporated New York, from 1976; home furnishings line introduced, 1978; lower priced line manufactured by Jack Mulqueen, from 1980; Mary McFadden Knitwear Company launched, 1981. Has designed for Henri Bendel, Jon Lakis Furs, Roscoe, Kirk-Brummel, Martex, and others. Director of the Fashion Group New York, 1981-82. **Member:** President and board member, Council of Fashion Designers of America, New York; design panel member, National Endowment for the Arts; advisory committee member, Steuben Glass, Kent State University, Cooper-Hewitt Museum, and Traphagen School. **Exhibitions:** *The Golden Eye,* Cooper-Hewitt Museum, New York, 1985; *A Passion for Fashion: The Mortimer Collection,* Wadsworth Atheneum, Hartford, Connecticut, 1993. **Honors:** Coty American Fashion Critics' Design Award, 1976, 1978, and Hall of Fame Award, 1979; Audemars Piquet Fashion Award, 1976; Rex Award, 1977; Moore College of Art Award, Philadelphia, 1977; Pennsylvania Governor's Award, 1977; Roscoe Award, 1978; Presidential Fellows Award, Rhode Island School of Design, 1979; Neiman Marcus Award of Excellence, 1979; American Printed Fabrics Council Tommy Award, 1991; Living Landmark Award for Excellency in Design, New York, 1994. DFA, Miami International Fine Arts

**Mary McFadden: The Noh Theatre Collection, Spring/Summer, 1996. Photo: Tom Haynes**

College, Florida, 1984. **Address:** 240 West 35th Street, New York, New York 10001, U.S.A.

## Publications

**By McFADDEN: articles**—in *Vogue* (New York), August 1970, October 1972, December 1977; *House and Garden* (New York), October 1978.

**On McFADDEN: books**—*The Fashion Makers* by Bernadine Morris and Barbara Walz, New York, 1978; *Fairchild's Who's Who in Fashion* edited by Ann Stegemeyer, New York, 1980; *McDowell's Directory of Twentieth Century Fashion* by Colin McDowell, London, 1984; *Fashion: The Inside Story* by Barbaralee Diamonstein, New York, 1985; *Couture: The Great Designers* by Caroline Rennolds Milbank, New York, 1985; *The Encyclopaedia of Fashion from 1840 to the 1980s* by Georgina O'Hara, London, 1986; *New York Fashion: The Evolution of American Style* by Caroline Rennolds Milbank, New York, 1989; **articles**—"Mary Had a Little

Dress" by Priscilla Tucker in the *New York Daily News,* 6 April 1980; "Mary McFadden: A New Type of Tycoon" by Bridget Foley in *New York Apparel News,* March 1983; "Mary McFadden" in *Current Biography* (New York), April 1983; "Beyond Fashion" by Diane Rafferty in *Connoisseur* (New York), October 1988; "Power Gives You an Aura, Say Mary McFadden" by Judith Thurman in *Mirabella* (New York), September 1989; "Mary, Mary, Quite Contrary: The Life and Loves of Mary McFadden" by Michael Gross in *New York,* 26 March 1990; "The Designers Talk Passion, Whimsy and Picassos" in *ARTnews* (New York), September 1990; "A Mary-Tale Romance" by Cathy Horyn in the *Washington Post,* 9 June 1991; "New York: Mary McFadden" in *Women's Wear Daily* (New York), 4 November 1994.

\*

The leitmotif that passes through my life is the adornment of a woman. My inspiration comes from ancient civilizations of the world. I have adapted symbols and religious signs from many civilizations for my decorative fabric designs. Bits of heraldry, calligraphic ornamentation, stylized leaves and clouds, mythical animals, and mosaics are ever present in my textiles and embroideries.

The Greek column is an ever present ghost in architecture and in my work. Classical Greek sculptors carved marble as if it were windswept cloth. For me, this is the ideal of beauty. Unique color, unusual color combinations, along with experimental fabric textures play the second most important part in my design concept. My clothes are constructed to look as if they were weightless shells on the human body. Simplicity and perfect proportion are the key elements.

—Mary McFadden

\*       \*       \*

The major ingredient in the high-fashion designs of Mary McFadden is a unique synthesis of the simple forms and proportions of Oriental, African, Greek, and other primitive civilizations with contemporary techniques of silkscreening and tie-dyeing. McFadden has revitalized the feel and flow of ancient robes and drapery by using new technology to achieve colors and prints of refinement and splendor.

Fabric is central to her designs. It may be Eastern silk or hand-painted, silk batik; it may be light and filmy, pleated or quilted, but the overall effect is always one of exotic sophistication, delicacy, and austerity, whether in a jumpsuit bound in ribbon with jacket of hand-painted suede or in a quilted jacket worn over a dress of abstract patterning. Taking their inspiration from the peasants' costumes of the Middle East, China, and Russia, McFadden's quilted coats and jackets with moleskin linings are stunningly cosmopolitan with their stitching running vertically for the thin look or outlined for a fuller sensation. Unintimidated by either the clinging jersey or the taffeta styles prominent when she began to work, McFadden practiced her preference for the lean, long tunic over pants or long skirt which became prevalent during the late 1970s. When she found that her unevenly hemmed tunic designs were being widely copied, she turned toward the creation of longer jackets over ankle-length skirts in combinations of rich colors and patterns based on various kinds of ancient and primitive abstract decorations and symbols.

At a time when costume jewelry was experiencing something of a downswing in popularity, McFadden began fashioning her own jewelry, suggestive of sculptural reliefs, beginning with gold-washed, abstract medallions, and she started making such accessories a central element of her overall style. The jewelry is plastic, modelled after antiquity like the clothing but always endowed with her flair for the contemporary. A medallion may be hung from a necklace of beads or coral, sometimes worn asymmetrically so that it hangs over one arm. Archaic symbols, leaf patterns, and the like abound on necklaces and bracelets; there are belt buckles like pre-Columbian idols which become integral ingredients in the total outfittings. Prints from McFadden's dresses have been adapted for wall paper and upholstery fabrics and for table coverings, and she added perfume to her repertoire in 1979.

McFadden's designs are often evocative of the past, but they never fail to look modern. She has maintained a constant aesthetic. Her designs are diverse enough to offer something for everyone. In the late 1980s, she experimented with bodices made of pleated strips which showed bare skin inbetween on gowns which clung in a smooth line to fit figures. She shortened her skirts to above the knee, and paired them with sequined tops. In spring 1992 she featured a bead-encrusted short dress with a beaded belt and a pleated sleeveless bodice. This was followed by her Japanese collection which included embroidered snakes and blossoms.

McFadden's fashions are closely related to the art she admires. As research for her work, she takes photographs of museum collections all around the world. She designs for a special, exclusive, and elite clientele, which sees her work as a wearable artform.

—Barbara Cavaliere

# MEIER, Richard Alan

American architect and industrial designer

**Born:** Newark, New Jersey, 12 October 1934. **Education:** Cornell University, Ithaca, New York, B. Arch., 1957. **Career:** Worked with Frank Grad and Sons, New Jersey, 1957, Davis Brody and Associates, New York, 1958-59, Skidmore, Owings, and Merrill, New York, 1959-60, and Marcel Breuer and Associates, New York, 1960-63; Principal, Richard Meier and Associates, Architects, New York, from 1963; office established in Pasadena, California, 1986. Adjunct instructor, 1963-66, assistant professor, 1966-69, and adjunct professor of architecture, 1969-73, Cooper Union, New York; visiting lecturer/critic, Princeton University, New Jersey, 1963, Syracuse University, New York, 1964, Pratt Institute, New York, 1965, Yale University, New Haven, Connecticut, 1967; resident architect, American Academy, Rome, 1973; William Henry Bishop Professor of Architecture, Yale University, 1975 and 1977; visiting professor, 1977, and Eliot Noyes visiting design critic, 1980-81, Harvard University, Cambridge, Massachusetts; chairman of the awards jury, American Institute of Architects, Philadelphia Chapter, 1972, American Academy in Rome, 1974, National AIA, 1975, Pennsylvania Society of Architects, 1975. **Exhibitions:** Knoll International, New York, 1978, and Tokyo, 1982; The High Museum of Art, Atlanta; Aichi Prefectural Museum, Nagoya, Japan, 1996. **Honors:** Excellence for House Design Award, 1964, 1968, 1969, and Award of Excellence for Design, 1977, *Architectural Record;*

Homes for Better Living First Honor Award, 1968, 1969, 1971, 1977, National Honor Award, 1969, 1971, 1974, 1976, 1977, Award of Merit, 1970, Low and Moderate Income Housing National Award, 1970, and Bartlett Award, 1977, American Institute of Architects; House Competition Prize, 1965, and Award for Outstanding Residential Design, 1968, AIA, New York Chapter; Honor Award, AIA, New England Regional Council, 1968; Honor Award, United States Department of Housing and Urban Development, 1970; Brunner Prize, National Institute of Arts and Letters, 1972; Bard Award, City Club of New York, 1973, 1977; Award of Honor, New York Society of Architects, 1973; fellow, American Institute of Architects, 1976; R. S. Reynolds Memorial Award, 1977; Architectural Award of Excellence, American Institute of Steel Construction, 1978; Pritzker Architecture Prize, Los Angeles, 1984; Best of Category, *I.D.* magazine, 1995. **Address:** 136 East 57th Street, New York, New York 10022; 371 Manford Way, Pasadena, California 91105.

## Works

Lacquered wood side chair, tables, and chaise-lounge, for Knoll International, from 1978.
Place settings, picture frames, and desk accessories, for Swid Powell, 1983-1996.
Glass bowls and vase, for Steuben, 1992.
Coordinated desks, tables, couches, work walls, and credenzas, for Stow Davis, 1995.
Limited edition Grand piano, for Ibach & Sohn, 1995-1996.

(for a complete list of architectural designs please see *Contemporary Architects*)

## Publications

**By MEIER: books**—*Recent American Synagogue Architecture,* exhibition catalogue, New York, 1963; *Richard Meier, Architect: Buildings and Projects 1966-1976,* New York, 1976; *Richard Meier: Drawings of Four Objects, A Post Card Book 1976,* New York, 1977; *Richard Meier, Architect: 1964-1984,* with introduction by Joseph Rykwert, New York, 1984; *Richard Meier Sculpture, 1992-1994,* New York, 1994; **articles**—"Planning for Jerusalem" in *Architectural Forum* (New York), April 1971; introduction to *Le Corbusier: Villa Savoye* edited by Yukio Futagawa, Tokyo, 1973; "Strategies: Eight Projects" in *Casabella* (Milan), May 1974; "Tre Recenti Progetti" in *Contospazio* (Bari, Italy), September 1975; "My Statement" in *Architecture + Urbanism* (Tokyo), April 1976; (with Arata Isozaki) "Dialogue" in *Architecture + Urbanism* (Tokyo), August 1976; "General Remarks" in *Japan Architect* (Tokyo), December 1976; "A Word from Richard Meier" and "Dialogue on Architecture" with Fumihiko Maki in *Space Design* (Tokyo), January 1978; "The Atheneum, New Harmony: in *Harvard Architecture Review* (Cambridge, Massachusetts), Spring 1981; "On the Spirit of Architecture" in *Architectural Digest* (Los Angeles), June 1981; "Remembering Breuer" in *Skyline* (New York), October 1981; "Atheneum, New Harmony, Indiana: Manchester Civic Center, New Hampshire" in *Cahiers de la Recherche Architecturale* (Roquevaire, France), no. 12, 1982; (with Myrielle Hammer) "Cross References: Frank Stella, Richard Meier" in *Techniques et Architecture* (Paris), February/March 1985; (with Thomas Phifer) "The Canal Plus Headquarters, Paris" in *Zodiac* (Milan), no. 4, 1990.

**On MEIER: books**—*Five Architects Eisenman/Graves/Gwathmey/Hejuk/Meier* by Kenneth Frampton and Colin Rowe, New York, 1972; *Richard Meier: Smith House and House in Old Westbury* by Yukio Futagawa, Tokyo, 1973; *Urban Design as Public Housing* by Jonathan Barnett, New York, 1974; *Richard Meier: Douglas House, Michigan* edited by Yukio Futagawa, Tokyo, 1975; *Five Architects, New York* by Manfredo Tafuri, Rome, 1976; *Judith Turner Photographs Five Architects,* with introduction by John Hejduk, London/New York, 1980; *Richard Meier: Matrix 58* exhibition catalogue, Hartford Connecticut, 1980; *Richard Meier: The Art of Architecture,* exhibition catalogue, Atlanta, Georgia, 1980; *GA 60: Richard Meier—The Atheneum, New Harmony, Indiana* by Paul Goldberger, edited by Yukio Futagawa, Tokyo, 1981; *Collaboration: Artists and Architects* by Barbaralee Diamondstein, New York, 1981; *Richard Meier: Buildings and Projects 1965-1981,* exhibition catalogue, Zürich, 1982; *Richard Meier, Architect: A Selected Bibliography* by Jamie Wright Coniglio, Monticello, Illinois, 1985; *Richard Meier: Architect 1985-1991* by Kenneth Frampton and Joseph Rykwert, New York, 1991; *Museum fur Kunsthandwerk: Richard Meier* by Michael Brawne, London, 1992; *Museum Builders* edited by James Steele, London and New York, 1994; **articles**—"The Very Personal Work of Richard Meier and Associates" by Joseph Rykwert in *Architectural Forum* (New York), March 1972; "Richard Meier: Public Space and Private Space" by Charles Hoyt in *Architectural Record* (New York), July 1973; "4 Projects by Richard Meier: Change and Consistency" by Charles Hoyt in *Architectural Record* (New York), March 1975; "Spatial Structure: Richard Meier" in special issue of *Architecture + Urbanism* (Tokyo), April 1976; "The Gospel According to Giedion and Gropius Is Under Attack" by Ada Louise Huxtable in *The New York Times,* 27 June 1976; "The Individual: Richard Meier" by Suzanne Stephens in *Progressive Architecture* (New York), May 1977; "White Existence Richard Meier 1961-77" special feature in *Space Design* (Tokyo), January 1978; "Architecture: Richard Meier" by Paul Goldberger in *Architectural Digest* (Los Angeles), September 1978; "Richard Meier: Master of Autonomous Architecture" in *AIT* (Stuttgart), no. 6, 1980; "Richard Meier: An American Architect" in *GA Document* (Tokyo), Summer 1980; "Richard Meier: Frankly Speaking" in *Interiors* (New York), October 1980; "Richard Meier: Two Projects in Context" in *Architectural Record* (New York), April 1981; "Richard Meier's New Furniture for Knoll" in *Architectural Record* (New York), November 1982; "Richard Meier Designs a New High for Atlanta" in *Interiors* (New York), October 1983; "Getty Museum Planned for LA" in *Architects' Journal* (London), 18 January 1984; "Meier's Triumph" in *Building Design* (London), 3 May 1984; "Affirming Modernism" in *Progressive Architecture* (New York), June 1984; "Eliel Saarinen, the Pei, now Meier" by Andrea O. Dean in *Architecture AIA* (New York), Octo-

**Richard Meier: office furniture, for Stow Davis, 1995**

ber 1985; "Frankfurt and Atlanta: Richard Meier as a Designer of Museums" by Peter Cannon-Brookes in *International Journal of Museum Management and Curatorship* (Oxford), March 1986; "Meier and the Modern Tradition" by Charles Jencks in *Architectural Design* (London), September/October 1988; "Richard Meier" in *World Architecture* (London), no. 3, 1989; "Richard Meier: The Getty Center" by Kurt W. Forster and other in *Architecture + Urbanism* (Tokyo) no. 11, supplement, November 1992; "Two European Buildings by Richard Meier" in *Casabella* (Milan), April 1993; *ID* (New York), July/August 1995.

\*

In my product designs, as in my architecture, I adhere to a modernist vocabulary, focusing on proportion, scale, and the manipulation of basic, strong geometry. Working on the design of furniture and objects for daily life, such as watches and tableware, I am conscious of participating in a tradition of designing for what might be considered a complete lifestyle, as have architects such as Hoffmann and Wright, or institutions such as the Bauhaus. In my case, the theoretical point of departure is consistently classical modernism.

—Richard Meier

\*   \*   \*

Richard Meier opened his office in 1963 and was one of five New York architects in the 1969 exhibit "Five Architects" later labeled as the "whites" in Tom Wolfe's book *From Bauhaus To Our House*. Meier's work is often distinguished, and occasionally criticized, for its consistency, often manifest via rigorous details and a palate that makes use of rectangular white panels. It is the spectacular pristine quality of buildings such as the Douglas House striding down a hillside to Lake Michigan (1973), the urban Giovannitti House in Pittsburgh, Pennsylvania (1979-83), and the Atheneum in New Harmony, Indiana (1979), with their elegantly proportioned façades, well-lit glazed natural interiors, gentle curves and slopes, and their dynamic interiors that has made Richard Meier one of America's most sought after architects for commissions of every building type.

Inspired by the classical architecture and planning of Karl Frederick Schinkel, the dynamic of Russian Constructivism, and the spaces of Frank Lloyd Wright, Meier's office has formulated successful designs for houses, schools, museums, factories, and office buildings, culminating in the commission for the Getty Center in Los Angeles. This 110 acre, $1 billion project (1984-1997) will combine a campus of six interlinked buildings (museum, Center for the History of Art and the Humanities, Institute, Trust building, auditorium, and restaurant) within a spectacular site, in Meier's words, "striving for an exquisite reciprocal relationship between built architecture and natural topography." Meier's approach to this, the largest single project of its type in the world, reflects his commitment to classicism and order. Rarely does any artist or designer achieve such a consistent portfolio over the length of a career, and Meier's shows little sign of deviation.

Beyond his architectural commissions, Meier is an accomplished painter and sculptor (he makes meticulous paper collages, often as studies for buildings) as well as a designer of household objects. His objects reflect his architecture and are executed in the tradition of "classical modernism"; his office resists the term "decorative arts",

reluctant to accept the classification, preferring instead the "minimalist" label. Meier is interested in smaller objects for the opportunity not just to design the buildings and their interiors but also the objects (and art) within them, in the tradition of architects such as Frank Lloyd Wright, Alvar Aalto, Josef Hoffmann, and Walter Gropius. Objects such as flatware, glassware, clocks, silver candlesticks, bowls, and picture frames are all geometric explorations with form, space, and light. In the case of these smaller more tactile objects (as opposed to more spatial buildings), Meier employs his ideas of form and geometry with the ergonomic necessity required to make objects truly functional as well as beautiful. In his textile designs for Design Tex, Meier also goes further in introducing color ranges beyond his normal white/gray palette to accommodate and celebrate his graphic textures within the weave of fabric.

Meier's lack of deviation from ideas spanning more than three decades are relevant as many designers strive for new fashions and trends. In such a light, with this obsessive attention to the design and craft of building and the integration of art and design into everyday life, one must surely advocate this approach.

—Peter Exley

## MELLOR, David
British industrial designer

**Born:** Sheffield, Yorkshire, 5 October 1930. **Education:** Studied at Sheffield College of Art, 1946-48; attended Royal College of Art, London, 1950-54; studied at British School, Rome, 1953-54. **Military Service:** Served in the British Army, 1948-49. **Family:** Married Fiona MacCarthy in 1966; children: Corin and Clare. **Career:** Silversmith, designer, manufacturer, and retailer, establishing David Mellor industrial design workshop, Sheffield, 1954; installed cutlery workshops in the historic Broom Hall, Sheffield, 1975, and in new factory at Hathersage, Derbyshire, 1988; opened shops in Sloane Square, London, 1969, Manchester, 1980, and Covent Garden, London 1981; design consultant to Walker and Hall, Abacus Municipal, Glacier Metal, Post Office, International Telephone and Telegraph, British Rail, James Neil Tools, and the Department of Environment. Chairman, Design Council Committee on Design Standards, 1981-83; National Advisory Board Member, Art and Design Working Group, from 1982; chairman, Crafts Council, London, 1982-1984. **Exhibitions:** Stedelijk Museum, Amsterdam, 1968; Welsh National Museum, Cardiff, 1972; *Design Since 1945,* Philadelphia Museum of Art, 1983; *New Design for Old,* Boilerhouse/Victoria and Albert Museum, London, 1986; *Eye for Industry,* Victoria and Albert Museum, 1986. **Collections:** Worshipful Company of Goldsmiths, London; Victoria and Albert Museum; Sheffield City Museum, Yorkshire; Museum of Modern Art, New York; Philadelphia Museum of Art. **Honors:** Royal College of Art Silver Medal, London 1953; Honorary Designer, 1954, and Honorary Fellow, 1966, Royal College of Art; Design Council Award, London, 1957, 1959, 1962, 1965, 1966, 1974, 1977; Royal Designer for Industry, Royal Society of Arts, London, 1962; Fellow, Chartered Society of Designers, 1964; Architectural Heritage Year Award, London, 1975; Honorary Fellow, Sheffield Polytechnic, 1979; Liveryman, Worshipful Company of Goldsmiths, 1981; Freeman, Cutlers' Company, London, 1981; Order of the British Empire, 1981; Royal Society of Arts Presidential Award, London, 1981;

Honorary D.Litt., Sheffield University, 1986; Chartered Society of Designers Medal, London, 1988. **Address:** Broom Hall, Broomhall Road, Sheffield S10 2DR, England.

## Works

Street lighting column, for Abacus Municipal, 1957.
*Pride* silverplate cutlery, for Walker and Hall, 1958 (now produced by David Mellor).
*Campden* stainless steel cutlery, for David Mellor, 1958.
Bus shelter system, for Abacus Municipal, 1960.
*Symbol* cutlery, for Walker and Hall, 1962.
*Embassy* sterling silver cutlery, for British Embassies, 1963.
*Thrift* basic stainless steel cutlery, for government canteens, 1965.
Road traffic signals, for the Department of the Environment, 1965-70.
Pillar box, for the General Post Office, 1968.
Automatic half-barrier crossing, for the Department of the Environment, 1969.
*Provençal* stainless steel cutlery, for David Mellor, 1973.
*Chinese* stainless steel cutlery, for David Mellor, 1975.
*Plane* stainless steel cutlery, for David Mellor, 1978.
*Flute* stainless steel cutlery, for David Mellor, 1983.
*Classic* stainless steel cutlery, for David Mellor, 1984.
*Hoffmann* stainless steel and silverplate cutlery, for David Mellor, 1985.
*Café* stainless steel cutlery, for David Mellor, 1985.
*Odeon* stainless steel cutlery, for David Mellor, 1986.
Cutlery range for the disabled, for the Hamlyn Foundation, 1987.
*Savoy* silverplate cutlery, for David Mellor, 1988.

## Publications

**By MELLOR: articles**—*The Guardian* (London), 11 October 1972; *The Designer* (London), November 1981.

**On MELLOR: books**—*Design in British Industry: A Mid-Century Survey* by Michael Farr, Cambridge, 1955; *Modern Silver Throughout the World 1880-1967* by Graham Hughes, London and Toronto, 1967; *Modern Design in Metal* by Richard Stewart, London, 1979; *Design Since 1945* edited by Kathryn Hiesinger and George Marcus, Philadelphia and London, 1983; *The Conran Directory of Design* edited by Stephen Bayley, London, 1985; *Eye for Industry: Royal Designers for Industry 1936-1986* by Fiona MacCarthy and Patrick Nuttgens, London, 1986; *New Design for Old,* exhibition catalogue by Helen Hamlyn, Eric Midwinter, and others, London, 1986; *International Design Yearbook 1987/88* edited by Philippe Starck, London, 1987.

*

Having trained as a silversmith, I tend to think of myself primarily as a maker. My work as an industrial designer, developing prototypes for quantity production, has been balanced by my work as a craftsman, making special one-off pieces of silver. My approach to design is still, to some extent, that of a craftsman. This is reflected in my involvement in directing all the detail and in making a design concept work from end to end.

In early 1970s, after long experience with the cutlery industry as a design consultant, I took the major step of beginning to manufac-

ture my own cutlery designs in my own factory. I acquired Broom Hall, a large historic building in central Sheffield, and gradually restored it to make purpose-design workshops and also to provide a living accommodation for myself and my family. It is part of my idea as a designer that work and leisure should merge almost imperceptibly and also that the same design standards should apply to industrial and domestic environments.

Expansion plans, however, made the premises at Broom Hall no longer viable. Therefore, in 1988 the cutlery factory moved out to a rural site at Hathersage in Derbyshire. The new building is circular, built on the site of a gas holder. It is constructed in natural stone with a lead roof, combining traditional materials with the most modern structural techniques. The workshops are highly mechanized, with some of the most modern equipment in the industry. Some of the machinery has been purpose-built—designed and made in our development workshop. Our principle has been to get away from traditional production procedures, with each worker doing a single operation, and to introduce a more flexible method of manufacturing whereby every cutler is gradually trained to use all of the machines.

Almost simultaneously with becoming a designer-manufacturer, I also became a designer-retailer, opening three shops successively—two in London and one in Manchester—which sell my own designs as well as many other designs which I have selected using the dual criteria of functional efficiency and visual quality. I feel strongly that the creative skill of choosing is an underrated aspect of designing.

For me, in all aspects of my activity—from the choice of our buildings and the selection of our office equipment, right down to the choice of the right rivets for my cutlery—aiming for the highest visual standards has been paramount, and perfecting this skill has been one of the main aims of my life as a designer.

—David Mellor

*       *       *

Trained as a silversmith, David Mellor has specialized in cutlery. Always concerned with industrial production, nonetheless in his early consultancy work, he completed various private and government commissions, including work for the Post Office, British Rail, and the Department of the Environment. In 1965, he was commissioned by the Ministry of Public Buildings and Works to design a contemporary pattern for both cutlery and hollowware to be used in British embassies, and in 1966, he was commissioned by the same agency to produce a low-cost pattern, Thrift, to be manufactured in volume and used in government institutions. Concurrently with his industrial design activities throughout the years, Mellor has designed and executed numerous private commissions, which include those for the Worshipful Company of Goldsmiths, the Cutlers' Company, Southwell Minister, Essex University, Darwin College, Cambridge, and others.

His most important innovations have been in the organizational methods he had devised in his own cutlery workshop at Broom Hall in Sheffield. Accomplishing this at a time when the Sheffield cutlery industry has been contracting, he has attempted to introduce a flexible method of manufacturing and avoid specialization. Each of his employees learns to perform all operations involved in the manufacture of his cutlery from start to finish. This has required a high degree of mechanization and investment in machines that are geared to perform specific operations required for each design. While the firm is still growing, Mellor sees the ultimate size of his work cell at about 30 employees, at which time some modifications would be required for his system of production.

The first David Mellor shop, opened in Sloane Square, London, in 1969, offered a comprehensive collection of equipment for cooking and eating, with a special emphasis on cutlery. This was followed by the David Mellor shop in Manchester (1980) and, more recently, by his second London shop in Convent Garden. His shops have given the designer scope to develop new products in special collections of pottery, woodware, basketware, and woven textiles. In these activities, Mellor acts as the entrepreneur who is able to promote individual craftsmen's work designed for volume production. Philosophically, Mellor sees this relationship of the craftsman to industry as being more realistic and economically feasible in the foreseeable future than the fine art/craftsman approach. He is perhaps the single figure in Britain who has been successful in combining the activities of craftsman and designer with those of the entrepreneur and businessman.

—Barbara Young

# MENTULA, Perttu

Finnish architect and interior, graphic, and industrial designer

**Born:** Lappeenranta, 5 March 1936. **Education:** Educated at Helsingin Kaksoisyhteislyseo high school, Helsinki, 1948-56; studied interior design, at the College of Industrial Arts, Helsinki, 1958-60. **Military Service:** Served in the Finnish Army Reserve Officers School, 1956-57. **Family:** Married Marika Tamme in 1983; children: Arttu, Atte, and Toomas. **Career:** Interior and product development designer, in the studios of Antti Nurmesniemi, Timo Sarpaneva, Toivo Korhonen, and Reino Lamminsoila, in Helsinki, 1958-60; freelance designer, with own studio, Helsinki, from 1960; director, Studio Perttu Mentula Oy, Helsinki, from 1977, and Design House Co., from 1985. Design consultant to Wärtsilä shipyards, Helsinki, 1964-66; design manager, Keriland Project, Kerimaki, from 1982; project chief for Arlandstad airport city scheme, from 1988. Professor of interior architecture, University of Gothenburg, from 1985; professor of product and environmental design, Helsinki University of Industrial Design, from 1985; visiting professor, University of Arts, Tallinn, Art Academy, Riga, Latvia, and Art Academy, Vilnius, Lithuania, from 1990. Board member, from 1968, and chairman of the assessment committee, 1970, 1978-80, Ornamo Federation of Industrial Arts, Helsinki; fine art commission member, Helsinki Festival, from 1974; chairman, SIO Interior Architects Society, Helsinki, 1978-80; arts commission and ideas group member, 1978, and vice-president, 1980-83, International Federation of Interior Designers; advisory committee member, Art Center College of Design/Europe, Switzerland, from 1985. **Member:** Helsinki Squash Rackets Association; Finnish Snooker Federation. **Exhibitions:** *Total Environment,* Finnish Design Centre, Helsinki 1966; *Textile Space,* PMK Showrooms, Helsinki, 1972; Uniform Project, Milan, 1975; *Wood and Textile,* Savonlinna Opera Festival, 1977; *Design by Perttu Mentula,* Copenhagen, 1977; *Scolt Lapp Culture,* Cathedral Crypt, Helsinki, 1978; *Finnish Design, Finlandia Hall,* Helsinki, 1980; *Starting Points and Visual Angles* (retrospective), Museum of Art, Lappeenranta Fortress, 1992. **Collections:** Museum of Industrial Design, Madrid; Museum of Applied Arts, Helsinki. **Honors:** Lighting Competi-

tion Prize, Helsinki, 1961; Export Furniture Competition Prizes, Helsinki, 1963; Silver Medal, Milan Triennale, 1964; Restaurant Furniture Competition Prize, Helsinki, 1966; Finnish travel and study grants, 1971, 1972, 1973, 1977, 1982-85; Tokyo Lighting Competition Awards, 1972; Scandinavian Environment and Furniture Prize, Copenhagen, 1973; Kerimaki Community Development Competition Prize, 1981; honorary Professor, Helsinki University of Industrial Design, 1981; honorary member, AIPI Italian Interior Architects Association, 1983; research grant, Finnish Dwelling Fair Fund, 1988; Skogster & Lehtinen Foundation Award, Helsinki, 1994. **Address:** Huvilakatu 8 A 2, 00150 Helsinki 15, Finland.

## Works

Wood furniture, for Varjosen Puunjalostus Oy, Uusikyla, 1960-63.
Kick sledge, for Velsa Oy, Kurikka, 1964.
Naval architecture, passenger liners, and icebreakers, for Wärtsila Shipyards, Helsinki, 1964-67.
*Interior Collection* printed fabrics, for Tampella Oy, Tampere, 1969-75.
*Ringside furniture* range, for Decembre Oy, 1969-79, and for Avitom Oy, 1979.
Uniform furniture range, for De Padova, Milan, 1973-74.
*Space Balk* office and exhibition systems, for Tampella Oy, Tampere, 1975.
Visitors' Building interiors, for Haka Building Company Obbnas, 1978.
*Edison de Lux* light fittings, for Airam Oy, 1981-83.
*Parkstreet* furnishing system, for Pohjoiskalotti Oy, Rovaniemi, 1983.
Playground constructions in wood, for Lappset Production, 1983-84.
Glass table collection, for Juvonen Glass Industries, 1989.
*Space Balk* system design, for Design House Co., 1990.
*Lighting Balk* system design, for Postipankki Oy, Helsinki, 1994.

## Publications

**By MENTULA: articles**—in *Architect* (Helsinki), no. 2, 1961, no. 6, 1964, no. 7, 1970, no. 8, 1970, no 6, 1972; *Launis Koti* (Helsinki), no. 5, 1963; *Engineer News* (Helsinki), no. 1, 1965; *Rank Xerox Magazine* (Helsinki), no. 1, 1972; *Abitare* (Milan), no. 10, 1972; *Ottagono* (Milan), no. 3, 1974; *Nyketekstiili* (Helsinki), no. 1, 1976; *Architect News* (Helsinki), no. 12, 1978; *Journal of Interior Design Education and Research* (New York), no. 1, 1979; *Muoto* (Helsinki), no. 1, 1980; *Finnish Furniture* (Helsinki), no . 1, 1981.

**On MENTULA: books**—*Modern Finnish Design* by Ulf Hard af Segerstad, New York, 1969; *New Design in Wood* by Donald J. Willcox, New York and London, 1970.

*

The relation between a product and the environment is changing.... The product is disengaging itself from the environment.

The sound product-environment concept that has always belonged to the substance of constructed and designed environmental culture has lost its meaning due to industrial and social development—to the turning from an industrial society to a educational, knowledge, and service society. An industrial product and a social product—man of today—have experienced the same fate.

**Perttu Mentula: Uniform furnishing elements. Produced by DePadova, Milan. Winner of the Scandinavian Furniture competition, 1974**

The thing, the product, was once a part of a harmonious integral, designed environment. In the same way man was a harmonious, integral part of society, family, community, the life environment—a village or a town.

Through social and educational development, man has become disconnected from the human environment—people's ties to traditional family community have loosened and man has become rootless and lonesome, especially in informational, educational, and service communities. Ties to the traditional have broken off and the development of design and education have partly caused this....

Year by year my attitudes to product and environment development have changed. Manysided and eager creativity at the beginning has now developed into critical consideration. My interest in constructed environment design has become more socially oriented and my interest in product development of public surroundings has grown in the course of the years.

On the other hand, self-criticism has more often arisen, along with a questioning of whether a product or an idea is necessary, whether a solution is practical or indispensable. As a 16-year-old year student of art and design staying at the Dominican Monastery of Rue de la Glacier in Paris I had the honour of meeting Pablo Picasso. He stimulated me to concentrate on something more useful and practical than becoming an artist, of which there were so many already. I learned a lesson from this conversation; already when young I learned to ask myself questions and to hesitate when things seemed to be self-evident.

It has been an interesting experience to develop from a schoolboy interested in art to an interior architect and a product and environment designer with professor's competence, to an international lecturer and leader of various projects. As the first interior designer to receive a marine architect's assignment at the Wärtsilä-Helsinki Shipyard in the 1960s I was able to create a new design field for interior architects which they now have ruled with great success for more than twenty years.

In my view the only way of developing our design image and profession is to gain experience without sacrificing creativity and to take a versatile attitude towards product and environment design.

—Perttu Mentula

\*   \*   \*

Perttu Mentula's design ideology originates from his native soil, from those vital impulses that contributed to the creation of the cultural ethos of "the country of a thousand lakes." The Finns, for generations and to a greater extent than their neighbors, have had an inherent respect for nature—wood, stone, sand, water, and air—for all that may be transformed with the artist's hands into objects that are economical, practical, and functionally harmonious with the natural environment. Because of their sober attitude toward life, the Finns have a higher appreciation for things that are lasting, reliable, and modest but noble in appearance than for those of sophisticated form. It seems as though every Finn bears within himself a germ of forms and appearances which fill the sphere of his imagination. As these forms exist in a collective imagination, in the community, they are not imposed from outside by a designer or producer, but they constitute a part of the Finn's world, such as a forest, rocks, the lake surface, or a loaf of bread. Perhaps deriving from the Protestantism of the North, the Finnish humbleness toward nature and alliance with it constitute a philosophical basis of sensible design. As a symbol of this philosophy, the sauna, like the tea ceremony in Japan, plays a cultural role. Although it is a physical treatment concerning human body and its fitness, at the same time it reaches the spheres of spiritual and metaphysical experience. A parallel tendency to unify practical with aesthetic elements, function with form, is characteristic of Finnish designers.

Mentula, like other Finns, has strongly emphasized the national factor in his designing. In his 1978 paper "The Role of Nationalism and Internationalism in Design," delivered at a conference in Washington, D.C., Mentula stated: "I am becoming ... convinced that the national factors and local environmental conditions constitute an extremely important part of design and the built-up environment. This is ... because I am concerned about deterioration in the quality of architecture and building and the lack of environmental values. I consider it important to be aware of the local environment, to know where we are and what the environmental realities are."

According to Mentula, the national and international factors do not oppose each other; on the contrary, they are considered to be different points of view which, when unified, lead the way to the universal. What has been brought from outside may be compared to the wind that contributes to the pollination of flowers. Such was the case in the architecture and design of Eero Saarinen and Alvar Aalto, who may serve as examples of designers that integrated local and international styles. In the same category, from among Mentula's works are a series of hanging chairs (1971-74), a sauna stool (1961), and some solutions in environmental design.

The portrait of Mentula's creative work would not be complete without emphasizing his indefatigable energy, which has been manifest in his numerous activities that were stimulating to designers, architects, and to those professions whose work has a formative influence on the environment.

Occasionally Mentula has an opportunity to show off his talents in organizing and programming teamwork. I had a chance to observe it while participating in an international creative workshop, organized with the aim of preparing a program, "Challenges of Kerimaki," for a small community, beautifully located among lakes and forests, away from the tourist trails. Mentula's enthusiasm for the idea of animating this region was so contagious that it encompassed everybody around, including some important economic officials. But perhaps the most important thing was that he demonstrated in practice his broad and progressive understanding of the concept of design.

—Szymon Bojko

# METSOVAARA, Marjatta

Finnish fashion and textile designer

**Born:** Åbo, 29 November 1927. **Education:** Studied textile design, at the Konstindustriella Läroverket, Helsinki, 1949; studied in the United States, 1961, 1964. **Family:** Married Kaj Erik Nyström in 1948; married Albert Van Havere in 1965; children: Kai, Katariina, Patrick, and Barbara. **Career:** Fashion designer, for Suomen Malto Oy, Helsinki, 1949-53; founder and chief designer, from 1954, and managing director, from 1957, of Metsovaara Oy textile firm, Helsinki; managing director, Marjatta Metsovaara Designs, Helsinki, from 1962; designed for Team Oy Finn-Flare, Oy Finnra AB, Oy Tampella AB, Villayhtyma Oy, NV Albert Van Havere of Belgium, Lusotufo of Portugal, Firth Carpets of England, and others. **Exhibitions:** Artek Showrooms, Helsinki, 1957; Konsthall, Helsinki, 1963, 1966, 1969; *Finnland Gestaltet,* Museum für Kunst und Gewerbe, Hamburg, 1981 (toured); *Design Since 1945,* Philadelphia Museum of Art, 1983. **Honors:** Gold Medal, Milan Triennale, 1960; Ornamo Silver Bowl Award, Helsinki, 1964; Signe d'Or Award, Brussels, 1968. **Address:** Puistokatu 3 A 4, 00140 Helsinki, Finland.

## Publications

On METSOVAARA: books—*Scandinavian Design* by Ulf Hård af Segerstad, Stockholm and London, 1961; *A Treasury of Scandinavian Design* edited by Erik Zahle, New York, 1961; *Modern Finnish Design* by Ulf Hård af Segerstad, London and New York, 1969; *New Design in Weaving* by Donald J. Willcox, New York and London, 1970; *Finnish Design: Facts and Fancy* by Willcox, New York, 1973; *Scandinavian Design: Objects of a Life Style* by Eileene Harrison Beer, New York and Toronto, 1975; *Finnland Gestaltet,* exhibition catalogue by Tapio Periainen, Simo Heikkila, and others, Espoo, 1981; *Design Since 1945* edited by Kathryn Hiesinger and George Marcus, Philadelphia and London, 1983.

\*    \*    \*

The long tradition of peasant weaving and rugmaking in Finland did not develop into formal textile design until Eeva Annttila became the country's first teacher of the subject in 1926. Marjatta Metsovaara was born in the following year. In her lifetime, work in textiles has grown to be one of the most important areas of Finnish design. Finland was the first European country to give women the vote. The majority of textile designers there today are women, and it is perhaps not too fanciful to perceive a link between a traditional women's craft and the sensitivity of contemporary designs.

Metsovaara's imagination is freshly fired with each new design by not only the technical means at her disposal, but also by the (to her) unlimited possibilities offered by the traditional materials of her craft and their combination with new and, in some cases, very unlikely alternatives. As early in her career as 1960, she made a curtain using polished copper strip and linen thread, with the fine linen thickened at intervals into patches of glowing colour reflected and enriched by the copper. Brightly coloured plastic strip or cable, metal wire or tape, even splinters of metal and wood, all find their way into her work. Her upholstery and clothing fabrics, carpets, blankets, shawls, and wall hangings incorporate every technique from flat weaves and pile fabrics, to embossed jacquards.

In cooperation with interior designers, some of Metsovaara's most striking and successful work has been as the designer of integrated fabrics for furnishings and floor and wall coverings. Perhaps the most striking, indeed startling, of these was the carpet used for both floor and walls of the night club in the Hesperia Hotel in Helsinki. The eight colours of its design included two with a phosphorescent glow in the club's special lighting.

Her work as a designer for printed textiles is secondary, but complementary, to her woven designs. These fabrics appear not only in Finland, but also worldwide. Her career is studded with successful exhibitions and international awards. When writing about her work, one cannot, as with most designers, concentrate on one or two major achievements. This is because her variety and originality, her adventurous use of all possible combinations of colour and texture, and her continually successful experiments have continued throughout her working life. Like many of her countrymen, she has constantly enlarged and enriched her national traditions.

—Gordon Steele

# MEYER, Grethe

Danish architect, ceramic, furniture, and industrial designer

**Born:** Svendborg, 8 April 1918. **Education:** Studied architecture, at the Royal Academy of Fine Arts, Copenhagen, until 1947. **Career:** Architect, working for the State Institute for Building Research, Copenhagen, 1955-60; freelance designer and architect, Horsholm, from 1960; designed for Kastrup Glassworks, Royal Copenhagen Porcelain, Georg Jensen, C. M. Madsen Furniture, and others. **Exhibitions:** *Nordisk Industridesign,* Kunstindustrimuseet, Oslo, 1976; *Design: The Problem Comes First,* Danish Design Centre, 1981-1992; *Scandinavian Modern Design 1880-1980,* Cooper-Hewitt Museum, New York, 1982; *Design Since 1945,* Philadelphia Museum of Art, 1983; *Scandinavia: Ceramics and Glass in the Twentieth Century,* Victoria and Albert Museum, London, 1989; *Denmark: Design for Living,* Danish Design Centre, 1989-90; *Innovation via Design,* Danish Design Centre, 1992; *Danish Design: Richness & Simplicity,* Danish Design Centre, 1992-94; *Design Pure, Purely Danish,* Danish Design Centre, 1993. **Honors:** Kajy Bojesen Grant, Copenhagen, 1960; Silver Medal, Faenza, 1965; Nordic Crafts Council Award, Copenhagen, 1973; ID Danish Industrial Design Award, 1976; Bindesbolle Award, Copenhagen, 1982. **Addresses:** Ved Stempedammen 23, 2970 Horsholm, Denmark; Danish Design Centre, HC Andersens Boulevard 18, DK-1553 København V, Denmark.

## Works

*Boligens Byggeskabe* storage units, for C. Danel and FDB Danish
    Consumers' Cooperative, 1952.
Table and chair set in beechwood, for C. Madsen A/S, 1957 (with
    Borge Mogensen).
*Stub og Stamme* glassware series, for Kastrup and Holmegaard Glassworks, 1959-60 (with Ibi Trier Morch).
*Blåkant/Blue Line* earthenware ceramic table range, for Royal
    Copenhagen Porcelain, 1964-65.
*Hvidpot* ceramic tablewares, for Royal Copenhagen Porcelain, 1971.
*Ildpot* ceramic tablewares, for Royal Copenhagen Porcelain, 1976.
*Rodtop* ceramic tablewares, for Royal Copenhagen Porcelain, 1981.
*Glas i Glas* glasswares, for Kastrup Glassworks, 1982.
*Picnic* porcelain tableware, for Royal Copenhagen Porcelain, 1982-83 (with Ole Kortzau).
*Ocean* vases, for Royal Copenhagen.
*Copenhagen* cutlery, for Royal Copenhagen.

Grethe Meyer: Copenhagen cutlery for Royal Copenhagen

## Publications

**On MEYER: books**—*Made in Denmark* by Arne Karlsen and Anker Tiedemann, Copenhagen, 1960; *Modern Scandinavian Furniture* by Ulf Hård af Segerstad, Copenhagen, 1963, London, 1964; *Contemporary Danish Design* edited by Arne Karlsen, Bent Salicath, and others, Copenhagen, 1966; *Danish Design* edited by Svend Erik Moller, Copenhagen, 1974; *Scandinavian Design: Objects of a Life Style* by Eileene Harrison Beer, New York and Toronto, 1975; *Danish Design 1980* edited by the Danish Design Foundation, Copenhagen, 1980; *Contemporary Furniture* edited by Klaus Jürgen Sembach, Stuttgart, London, and New York, 1982; *Scandinavian Modern Design 1880-1980* edited by David Revere McFadden, New York, 1982; *Design Since 1945* edited by Kathryn Hiesinger and George Marcus, Philadelphia and London, 1983; *Kongelig Dansk Porcelain 1884-1980* by Bredo L. Grandjean, Copenhagen, 1983; *Scandinavia: Ceramics and Glass in the Twentieth Century* by Jennifer Hawkins Opie, London, 1989; *Design: The Problem Comes First,* exhibition catalogue, Copenhagen, 1992; *Innovation via Design,* exhibition catalogue, Copenhagen, 1992; *Profession: Designer,* exhibition catalogue, Copenhagen.

*

One of my main theses when working with design is that the object should not rule the person. In all my work, I try to reach the point where the design is very simple and at the same time very complex. Let me give you an example. When I was given the task of designing a series of ovenware for the Royal Copenhagen Porcelain Factory, it began with a purely technical specification: the ovenware must be able to be transferred directly from the freezer to the oven without cracking. This resulted in the factory developing a new type of clay for stoneware. With this material in my hands, I designed a simple, sensible, and undecorated range of ovenware suitable for a wide range of purposes. Each unit was designed for typical portion sizes, in dimensions to fit into the racks of normal oven. They are good to handle and are easily stacked for storage. The more you use it, the more beautiful it becomes.

Whenever I design objects, I never think of market sales. I simply design things that I like myself and say, "This is my offer to the market." I cannot force people to use my things, and I could not dream of criticising those who prefer articles decorated with flowers and strawberries. I can only say that I think a particular design is right, then I try to make things that people can afford. I feel it is important to buy things that you really like and want. Instead of going out and buying a lot of bad quality items all at once, one should buy fewer items of better quality. Quality is the thread running through all my work.

—Grethe Meyer

# MEYNELL, Francis (Meredith Wilfrid)

British publisher, typographic, and book designer

**Born:** Palace Cate, London, 12 May 1891. **Education:** Attended Downside School, Bath, until 1909; studied at Trinity College, Dublin, 1909-11. **Family:** Married Hilda Saxe in 1914 (divorced); daughter: Cynthia; married Vera Mendel in 1923 (divorced); son: Benedict; married Alix Hester Kilroy in 1946. **Career:** Head of design, at Burns and Oates Catholic publishers, London 1911-13; freelance journalist, 1914-16, staff writer, 1916-18, and assistant editor and director, 1918-20, for the *Daily Herald* newspaper, London; founder-director, Pelican Press, London, 1916-18, 1921-22; editor, *The Communist* newspaper, London, 1921; founder-director, with David Garnett and Vera Mendel, of the Nonesuch Press, London, 1923-35, 1953-75 (press taken over by Limited Editions Club of New York, 1935-51); columnist, *News Chronicle* newspaper, London, 1934-35; advertising designer, for United Artists, Gaumont British Picture Corporation, Charles W. Hobson Limited, and others, 1935-39, and for the Ministry of Food, 1940-45; board member, Mather and Crowther advertising agency, London, 1935-60, and The Bodley Head publishers, London, 1960-75. Founder, Union of Democratic Control anti-war body, London, 1914, Non-Conscription Fellowship, London, 1915, Guild of the Pope's Peace, London, 1916, and Anglo Russian Democratic Alliance, London, 1917. Advisor on consumer needs, Board of Trade, London, 1940-45; alternate chairman of The Brains Trust, British Broadcasting Corporation, London, 1942-43. **Member:** Council of Industrial Design, London, 1944-48; advisory council member, Victoria and Albert Museum, London, 1945-48; director general, Cement and Concrete Association, London, 1946-58; advisory council member, The Royal Mint, London, 1954-70; president, Society of Typo-

graphic Designers, London, 1958-62; advisory council member, Royal Society of Arts, London, 1959-61; vice-president, Poetry Society, London, 1960-65. **Exhibitions:** First Editions Club, London, 1933; Wolverhampton Polytechnic, 1973; Cambridge University Library, 1973; Gainsborough House, Sudbury, 1974; Manchester Polytechnic, 1979. **Honors:** Royal Designer for Industry, Royal Society of Arts, London, 1945; Knighthood, London, 1946; D. Litt., University of Reading Berkshire, 1964. **Died:** London, 9 July 1975.

## Publications

**By MEYNELL: books**—*Typography,* London, 1923; (editor) *The Week-End Book,* London, 1923; (editor) *George Herbert: The Temple,* editor, London, 1927; (editor) *Bee-dome: Poems,* London, 1928; *The Typography of Newspaper Advertisements,* London, 1929; *The Nonesuch Century,* London, 1936; *Seventeen Poems,* London, 1945; *English Printed Books,* London, 1946; (editor) *The New Week-End Book,* London, 1955; *The Typography of Advertising,* London, 1960; *Poems and Pieces,* London, 1961; *By Heart,* London, 1965; *My Lives* (autobiography), London, 1971; (editor, with Herbert Simon) *Fleuron Anthology,* London and Toronto, 1973; **articles**—contributor of numerous writings on typography to *The Times, The Sunday Times, The Manchester Guardian, The Listener, Time and Tide, Encyclopedia Britannica,* and others.

**On MEYNELL: books**—*British Achievement in Design* edited by Noel Carrington and Muriel Harris, London, 1946; *Modern Book Design* by Ruari McLean, London, 1958; *The Typographic Book 1450-1935* by Stanley Morison and Kenneth Day, London, 1963; *Introduction to Typography* by Oliver Simon, London, 1964; *Industrial Design in Britain* by Noel Carrington, London, 1976; *Francis Meredith Wilfrid Meynell* by Alix Meynell, Burford, 1977; *Typography: Design and Practice* by John Lewis, London, 1978; *Sir Francis Meynell and the Nonesuch Press,* exhibition catalogue by Ian Rogerson, Manchester, 1979; *A History of the Nonesuch Press* by John Dreyfus, London, 1981; *Eye for Industry: Royal Designers for Industry 1936-1986* by Fiona MacCarthy and Patrick Nuttgens, London, 1986.

*       *       *

Francis Meredith Wilfrid Meynell justifiably titled his autobiography *My Lives,* for varied were his talents and activities—poet, editor, publisher, wit, advertising designer, games enthusiast, and civil servant. It is as a typographer and book designer, however, that he is best remembered. Meynell was born in 1891 into a family where literature was the common interest. His father, Wilfrid Meynell, was a distinguished journalist and editor. His mother, Alice, was a poet (at one time backed for the Laureate) and friend of Coventry Patmore, Meredith, and Browning. Both she and her husband were Catholic converts. Francis Thompson, whom they had rescued from destitution and established as a poet, was godfather to their youngest child, Francis.

As a Catholic, Francis was educated at Downside and Trinity College, Dublin. He entered the book trade in his father's Catholic publishing firm, Burns and Oates, in 1910. He and Stanley Morison worked together there on a handpress, the Romney Street Press, which Meynell had set up in his house. In 1916, Meynell founded the Pelican Press, where Morison also joined him. Its aim was to do for "jobbing printing" (catalogues, posters, press advertisements, etc.) what his hero Bruce Rogers, the great American typographer, had done for book design in America. He could boast that the Pelican always had in use some type held by no other printer.

Meynell was a socialist and a follower of George Lansbury, with whom he worked on the early *Daily Herald.* A conscientious objector in World War I, when called up by conscription, he suffered a self-imposed hunger and thirst strike and nearly died. Meynell retained his socialist faith throughout his life, but in 1923 he extricated himself from politics to renew his career as printer and publisher. The Nonesuch Press, which he founded in that year with the help of a small capital provided by Vera Mendel (who became his second wife) and with the literary advice of David Garnett, was not a private press on the model of William Morris's Kelmscott. He did maintain a small handpress, a compositor, and a wide range of typefaces for the experimental setting of title or sample pages, but his books were printed by firms with modern machinery, though every detail of type, paper, and binding were to his own fastidious design. The number printed for each edition was more than usual for works produced by private presses, sometimes four or five hundred, often into four figures, but they were almost always oversubscribed by the booksellers. Occasionally, Nonesuch issued an unlimited edition, such as *The Week-End Book,* which achieved bestseller status.

The choice of titles lay with the partners, aided by editors such as Geoffrey Keynes. They included neglected classics including the poems of John Donne and works of the Restoration playwrights, but of their publishing policy Meynell wrote, "We chose the books we wanted to have on our own shelves, and for those among collectors who also use books for reading."

Though Nonesuch was able to celebrate publication of its hundredth book within its first twelve years, it had not generated enough capital to weather the economic storm of the 1930s, and Meynell had to make over the press to George Macy in America while retaining the design of books printed in England in his own hands. In 1951, with the help of Max Reinhardt, he restarted Nonesuch in England and continued to run it till his death. Nonesuch Press was one of the most influential enterprises of the present century in the world of books: an enterprise small in itself and its staffing, but large in the number and quality of publications and in its effect on book production throughout the English-speaking world.

—Noel Carrington

# MIELZINER, Jo

American stage designer

**Born:** Paris, France, 19 March 1901. **Education:** The Ethical Culture School, New York, until 1917; studied at the National Academy of Design, New York, the Art Students League of New York, Pennsylvania Academy of Fine Arts, Philadelphia; also studied in Paris and Vienna, 1918-19. **Military Service:** Camouflage specialist in the United States Army Air Force, 1942-45. **Family:** Married Annie Laurie Witzel (divorced); married Maryana Mannes (divorced); married Jean Macintyre in 1938 (divorced); children: Michael, Neil, and Jennifer. **Career:** Actor and scene designer, Jessie Bonstelle Stock Company, Detroit, Michigan, 1921-22; actor, assistant manager, and apprentice designer under Lee Simonson,

at the Theatre Guild, New York, 1923; freelance stage designer, New York, from 1924; designed for the Lincoln Center Repertory Theatre, Los Angeles Music Center, Forum Theatre, University of Illinois Krannert Center, University of Michigan Theatre, American National Theatre and Academy, Washington Square Theatre, and others. **Member:** Chairman, American Theatre Planning Board; board member, United States Institute for Theatre Technology. **Exhibitions:** Lincoln Center, New York, 1966; Brandeis University, Waltham, Massachusetts, 1966; Coffee House Club of New York, 1966; Virginia Museum of Fine Arts, Richmond, 1967; International Exhibition Foundation touring exhibitions, 1968, 1969; Toneel Museum, Amsterdam, 1972; Amherst College, Massachusetts, 1973. **Honors:** Donaldson Awards, New York, 1945, 1947, 1950, 1952; Variety Critics Poll Award, New York, 1945, 1946, 1946, 1948, 1949, 1950, 1951, 1952, 1953; Academy Award, Los Angeles, 1955; New York Drama Critics Award, 1956; New England Theatre Conference Award, 1957; Charlotte Cushman Award, 1958; Ford Foundation Award, 1960; Lotus Club Award of Merit, 1961; Brandeis University Creative Arts Award, 1963; Maharam Awards, New York, 1970; Drama Desk Award, New York, 1970; American Theatre Association Award, 1975. DFA, Fordham University, 1947, University of Michigan, 1971; HHD, Otterbein College, 1967, University of Utah, 1972. Benjamin Franklin Fellow, Royal Society of Arts, London. **Died:** New York City, 15 March 1976.

## Works

Stage designs include (New York, unless noted)—*The Guardsman,* 1924; *Nerves,* 1924; *That Awful Mrs. Eaton,* 1924; *Mrs. Partridge Presents,* 1925; *First Flight,* 1925; *Caught,* 1925; *The Call of Life,* 1925; *The Enemy,* 1925; *Luck Sam McCarver,* 1925; *The Wild Duck,* 1925; *Little Eyolf,* 1926; *Masque of Venice,* 1926; *Unseen,* 1926; *Seed of the Brute,* 1926; *Pygmalion,* 1926; *Saturday's Children,* 1927; *Right You Are If You Think You Are,* 1927; *Mariners,* 1927; *The Second Man,* 1927; *Marquise,* 1927; *The Doctor's Dilemma,* 1927; *Fallen Angels,* 1927; *Cock Robin,* 1928; *The Grey Fox,* 1928; *The Jealous Moon,* 1928; *The Lady Lies,* 1928; *A Most Immoral Lady,* 1928; *Strange Interlude,* 1928; *The Sky Rocket,* 1928; *The Amorous Antic,* 1929; *Karl and Anna,* 1929; *Street Scene,* 1929; *Judas,* 1929; *Meet the Prince,* 1929; *Young Alexander,* 1929; *The First Little Show,* 1929; *Jenny,* 1929; *First Mortgage,* 1929; *Dread,* 1929; *Mrs. Cook's Tour,* 1929; *Uncle Vanya,* 1930; *Mr. Gilhooley,* 1930; *Solid South,* 1930; *Sweet and Low,* 1930; *The Second Little Show,* 1930; *The Barretts of Wimpole Street,* 1931; *Of Thee I Sing,* 1931; *I Love an Actress,* 1931; *Brief Moment,* 1931; *Anatol,* 1931; *The House Beautiful,* 1931; *Billy Rose's Crazy Quilt,* 1931; *The Third Little Show,* 1931; *Distant Drums,* 1931; *Gay Divorce,* 1932; *Never No More,* 1932; *Bloodstream,* 1932; *Bridal Wise,* 1932; *Biography,* 1932; *Emperor Jones* (opera), 1933; *Champagne Sea,* 1933; *A Divine Drudge,* 1933; *I Was Waiting for You,* 1933; *The Dark Tower,* 1933; *The Lake,* 1933; *By Your Leave,* 1934; *We Roll Along,* 1934; *Spring Song,* 1934; *Romeo and Juliet,* 1934; *Accent on Youth,* 1934; *The Pure in Heart,* 1934; *Merrymount* (opera), 1934; *Bird of Our Fathers* (tour), 1934; *It's You I Want,* 1935; *De Luxe,* 1935; *Panic,* 1935; *Winterset,* 1935; *Flowers of the Forest,* 1935; *Jubilee,* 1935; *Pride and Prejudice,* 1935; *A Room in Red and White,* 1935; *Co-Respondent Unknown,* 1935; *The Postman Always Rings Twice,* 1935; *Saint Joan,* 1935; *Daughters of Atreus,*

1935; *The Women*, 1935; *Ethan Frome*, 1936; *On Your Toes*, 1936; *St. Helena*, 1936; *Hamlet*, 1936; *The Wingless Victory*, 1936; *Hell Freezes Over*, 1936; *High Tor*, 1937; *The Star Wagon*, 1937; *Susan and God*, 1937; *Father Malacky's Miracle*, 1937; *Antony and Cleopatra*, 1938; *Barchester Towers*, 1937; *Your Obedient Husband*, 1938; *On Borrowed Time*, 1938; *Save Me the Waltz*, 1938; *Sing Out the News*, 1938; *Abe Lincoln in Illinois*, 1938; *Knickerbocker Holiday*, 1938; *I Married an Angel*, 1938; *The Boys from Syracuse*, 1938; *Mrs. O'Brien Entertains*, 1939; *Stars in Your Eyes*, 1939; *No Time for Comedy*, 1939; *Key Largo*, 1939; *Too Many Girls*, 1939; *Mornings at Seven*, 1939; *Christmas Eve*, 1939; *Two on an Island*, 1940; *Higher and Higher*, 1940; *The Little Dog Laughed* (toured), 1940; *Journey to Jerusalem*, 1940; *Pal Joey*, 1940; *Flight to the West*, 1940; *Mr. and Mrs. North*, 1941; *The Talley Method*, 1941; *Watch on the Rhine*, 1941; *The Wookey*, 1941; *Best Foot Forward*, 1941; *The Land is Bright*, 1941; *Candle in the Wind*, 1941; *The Seventh Trumpet*, 1941; *Solitaire*, 1942; *Pillar of Fire* (ballet), 1942; *By Jupiter*, 1942; *Foolish Notion*, 1945; *The Firebrand of Florence*, 1945; *Carousel*, 1945; *Hollywood Pinafore*, 1945; *Carib Song*, 1945; *Beggars Are Coming to Town*, 1945; *The Rugged Path*, 1945; *The Glass Menagerie*, 1945; *The Dream Girl*, 1945; *Jeb*, 1946; *Annie Get Your Gun*, 1946; *Windy City*, 1946; *Happy Birthday*, 1946; *Another Part of the Forest*, 1946; *The Big Two*, 1947; *The Street Scene*, 1947; *Finian's Rainbow*, 1947; *The Chocolate Soldier*, 1947; *Barefoot Boy with Cheek*, 1947; *Command Decision*, 1947; *Allegro*, 1947; *A Streetcar Named Desire* (London), 1947; *Mister Roberts*, 1948; *Shadow of the Wind* (ballet), 1948; *Sleepy Hollow*, 1948; *Summer and Smoke*, 1948; *Anne of the Thousand Days*, 1948; *Death of a Salesman*, 1949; *South Pacific*, 1949; *The Man*, 1950; *The Innocents*, 1950; *The Wisteria Trees*, 1950; *Burning Bright*, 1950; *Dance Me a Song*, 1950; *The Real McCoy*, 1950; *Guys and Dolls*, 1950; *The King and I*, 1951; *A Tree Grows in Brooklyn*, 1951; *Top Banana*, 1951; *Point of No Return*, 1951; *Flight into Egypt*, 1951; *Wish You Were Here*, 1952; *The Gambler*, 1952; *A Month of Sundays* (toured), 1952; *Picnic*, 1953; *Can-Can*, 1953; *Me and Juliet*, 1953; *Tea and Sympathy*, 1953; *Kind Sir*, 1953; *By the Beautiful Sea*, 1954; *All Summer Long*, 1954; *Fanny*, 1954; *Silk Stockings*, 1955; *Cat on a Hot Tin Roof*, 1955; *Island of Goats*, 1955; *Pipe Dream*, 1955; *The Lark*, 1955; *Middle of the Night*, 1956; *The Most Happy Fella*, 1956; (and producer) *Happy Hunting*, 1956; *Maiden Voyage*, 1957; *Miss Lonelyhearts*, 1957; *The Square Root of Wonderful*, 1957; *Look Homeward Angel*, 1957; *Oh Captain!*, 1958; *The Day the Money Stopped*, 1958; *Handful of Fire*, 1958; *The World of Suzie Wong*, 1958; *The Gazebo*, 1958; *Whoop-Up*, 1958; (lighting) *Rashomon*, 1959; *Sweet Bird of Youth*, 1959; *The Gang's All Here*, 1959; *The World of Suzie Wong* (London), 1959; *Gypsy*, 1959; *Silent Night, Lonely Night*, 1959; *There Was a Little Girl*, 1960; *The Best Man*, 1960; *Christine*, 1960; *Little Moon of Alban*, 1960; *Period of Adjustment*, 1960; *White Alice* (tour), 1960; *The Devil's Advocate*, 1961; *A Short Happy Life*, 1961; *Everybody Loves Opal*, 1961; *All American*, 1962; *Mr. President*, 1962; *The Milk Train Doesn't Stop Here Anymore*, 1963; *After the Fall*, 1964; *But For Whom Charlie*, 1964; *The Owl and the Pussycat*, 1964; *Danton's Death*, 1965; *The Playroom*, 1965; *Venus Is*, 1966; *Don't Drink the Water*, 1966; *My Sweet Charlie*, 1966; *The Paisley Convertible*, 1967; *That Summer...That Fall*, 1967; *Daphne in Cottage D*, 1967; *Mata Hari*, 1967; *The Prime of Miss Jean Brodie*, 1968; *I Never Sang For My Father*, 1968; *The Seven Descents of Myrtle*, 1968; *Slaughter on Tenth Avenue* (ballet), 1968; *Possibilities*,

1968; *Kingdom on Earth*, 1968; *1776*, 1969; *The Conjuror*, 1969; *Galileo*, 1969; *The Girls Upstairs*, 1969; *Child's Play*, 1970; *Georgy*, 1970; *Look to the Lillies*, 1970; *1776* (London), 1970; *Who Cares?* (ballet), 1970; *Child's Play* (London), 1971; (and lighting) *Father's Day*, 1971; *Love Me, Love My Children*, 1971; (and lighting) *Children! Children!*, 1972; (and lighting) *Voices*, 1972; (and lighting) *The Crucible*, 1972; (and lighting) *Out Cry*, 1974; (and lighting) *In Praise of Love*, 1974; (and lighting) *Miss Moffat*, (Philadelphia), 1974; *Don Giovanni* (opera), 1974.

## Publications

**By MIELZINER: books**—*Designing for the Theatre: A Memoir and Portfolio*, New York, 1965; *The Shapes of Our Theatre*, New York, 1970; (editor, with Edward F. Kook and Henry Hewes) *Theatre Check List: A Guide to the Planning and Construction of Proscenium and Open Stage Theatres*, Middletown, Connecticut, 1970.

**On MIELZINER: books**—*The Biographical Encyclopedia and Who Who's of the American Theatre* edited by Walter Rigdon, New York, 1966; *Contemporary Stage Design USA* edited by Elizabeth Burdick, Peggy Hansen, and Brenda Zanger, Middletown, 1974; *Stage Design: Four Centuries of Scenic Invention* by Donald Oenslager, New York, 1975; *The Cambridge Guide to World Theatre* edited by Martin Banham, Cambridge, 1988.

\*     \*     \*

In his memoir and portfolio *Designing for the Theatre*, Jo Mielziner states that he was born with an inherited gift for painting and drawing. His remarkable success as a designer of costumes, settings, and lighting supports this statement, but it is also true that Mielziner possessed remarkable taste, judgment, and imagination. All of these elements were seen in the theatre with his first productions in 1924, following his association with the great designers Joseph Urban, Lee Simonson, and Robert Edmond Jones. Urban and Jones helped Mielziner to learn the intricacies of what was then known as the New Stagecraft, a modern approach upon which he steadily built throughout his career.

Through trial and error, Mielziner eventually discovered the significant relationship between the setting and the actor which he soon espoused as a fundamental dictum of theatrical design. It is in this regard, as much as in the beauty and appropriateness of his designs, that Mielziner became an example for designers who have followed him. While seeing to the needs of the actor, Mielziner also demonstrated a frequently remarkable sensitivity to the play. Two of his most significant sets, for Maxwell Anderson's *Winterset* and for Arthur Miller's *Death of a Salesman*, differed radically from the author's original specifications. It was Mielziner's thorough and sensitive understanding of these plays which persuaded the authors to his point of view, to the benefit of both plays in their initial productions.

Lighting became a major interest for Mielziner early on, and he eventually designed lighting for all his settings. Unusually sensitive to light and color, he constantly experimented with colors and their combinations, spending long hours in a specially designed light laboratory in his studio. His interest led to the improvement of old lighting instruments and the invention of new devices through his close association with Edward F. Kook, a founder of Century Lighting Company. Despite Mielziner's strong advocacy of the need for a scene designer to light his own settings, this combination of skills remains rare.

Because so many of Mielziner's settings were associated with the greatest plays in American literature, he became a major influence on design throughout the United States. In the process, he raised the quality of American scene design to the position of superiority it maintains today.

—David W. Weiss

# MIES VAN DER ROHE, Ludwig

American architect, interior, and furniture designer

**Born:** Ludwig Mies in Aachen, Germany, 27 March 1886 (later adopted mother's name van der Rohe); emigrated to the United States, 1938; naturalized, 1944. **Education:** Educated at the Domschule, Aachen, 1897-1900; Aachen Trade School, 1900-02. **Military Service:** Served in the German Army, in the Engineer Corps, 1914-18. **Career:** Worked in his father's stonemason business, Aachen, 1900-02; draftsman, in a stucco decorating business, Aachen, 1903-04; worked briefly in office of an architect specializing in wood structures, Berlin, 1905; apprenticed to the architect and furniture designer Bruno Paul, Berlin, 1905-07; opened private architectural practice, Berlin, 1907-08; assistant, with Walter Gropius and Le Corbusier, in the office of Peter Behrens, Berlin, 1908-11; private practice, Berlin, 1911-14, 1919-37; private architectural practice, Chicago, from 1938; firm continues after his death as FCL Associates. Director of the Bauhaus, Dessau, 1930-32, and, Berlin, 1932 until it closed in 1933; director of architecture, Illinois Institute of Technology (formerly Armour Institute), Chicago, 1938-1959. Co-founder, *G* (Gestaltung) magazine, Berlin, 1921; director of architectural exhibits, Novembergruppe, Berlin, 1921-25; founder, Zehner Ring, Berlin, 1925; first vice-president, Deutscher Werkbund, Berlin, 1926-32, and director of the Werkbund exhibition *Weissenhofsiedlung,* Stuttgart, 1927, and the Werkbund section, "The Dwelling," Berlin Building Exhibition, 1931; president, CIAM (Congrès Internationaux d'Architecture Moderne). **Member:** Prussian Academy of Arts and Sciences, 1931; National Institute of Arts and Letters, 1963 **Exhibitions:** Museum of Modern Art, New York, 1947; Art Institute of Chicago, 1968 (toured the United States, Canada, and Europe); *A New City Square and Office Tower,* Royal Exchange, London, 1968; *Ludwig Mies van der Rohe: Furniture and Furniture Drawings,* Museum of Modern Art, New York, 1977; *Mies van der Rohe: Interior Spaces,* Arts Club of Chicago, 1982. **Honors:** Royal Gold Medal, Royal Institute of British Architects, 1959; Commander (with cross), German Order of Merit, 1959; Gold Medal, American Institute of Architects, 1960; Gold Medal of Honor, with Philip Johnson, Architectural League of New York, 1960; Fine Arts Prize, City of Berlin, 1961; United States Presidential Medal of Freedom, 1963; Gold Medal, Bund Deutscher Architekten, Germany, 1966; honrary doctorates from Institute of Technology, Karlsruhe, 1950, Institute of Technology, Braunschweig, Germany, 1955, University of North Carolina, Chapel Hill, 1956, Carnegie Institute of Technology, Pittsburgh, 1960, Wayne State University, Detroit, 1961, Northwestern University, Evanston, Illinois, 1963, and University of Illinois, Urbana-Champaign, 1964. **Died:** Chicago, 17 August 1969.

## Works

*MR* chair, 1927.
*Barcelona* chair, 1929.

## Publications

**By MIES VAN DER ROHE: books**—*Bauhaus,* Berlin, 1923, revised edition as *Der moderne Zweckbau,* Munich, 1926; *Industrielles Bauen,* Berlin, 1924; **articles**—"Hochhaus-projekt für Bahnhof Friedrichstrasse in Berlin" in *Frühlicht* (Berlin), January 1922; "Baukunst und Zeitwille" in *DER Querschnitt* (Berlin), April 1924; "Briefe an die Form" in *Die Form* (Berlin), January 1926; "Runschau: Zum neuen Jahrgang" in *Die Form,* February 1927; "Preface" and "Zu meinen Block" in *Weissenhofsiedlung,* Deutscher Werkbund exhibition catalogue, Stuttgart, 1927; "Werkbundaustellung: Die Wohnung Stuttgart: in *Die Form,* September 1927; "Zum Therma: Austellung: in *Die Form,* April 1928; "Über Kunstkritik" in *Die Kunstblatt* (Berlin), June 1930; "Frank Lloyd Wright: An Appreciation" in *College Art Journal* (New Haven, Connecticut), Autumn 1946; "Das Schöne is der Glanz des Wahren" in *Die Neue Zeitung,* Berlin, 1950; "Arbeitsthesch," "Über die Form in der Architektur," "Die Neue Zeit," and "Technik und Architektur" in *Programme und Manifeste zur Architektur des 20. Jahrhunderts,* Berlin, 1964; "Mies Speaks" in *Architectural Review* (New York), December 1968.

**On MIES VAN DER ROHE:** *Mies van der Rohe* by Philip Johnson, New York, 1947, 3rd edition, 1978; *Ludwig Mies van der Rohe* by Max Bill, Milan, 1955; *Mies van der Rohe* by Ludwig Hilberseimer, Chicago, 1956; *The Master Builders* by Peter Blake, New York, 1960; *Ludwig Mies van der Rohe* by Arthur Drexler, New York and London, 1960; *Theory and Design in the First Machine Age* by Reyner Banham, London, 1960; *Il Disegno Industriale e la Sua Estetica* by Gillo Dorfles, Bologna, 1963; *Mies van der Rohe: The Art of Structure* by Werner Blaser, New York, Stuttgart, and London, 1965; *Mies van der Rohe* by Martin Pawley, Tokyo, 1968, London, 1970; *Ludwig Mies van der Rohe Drawings in the Collection of the Museum of Modern Art* by Ludwig Glaeser, New York, 1969; *Mies van der Rohe at Work* by Peter Carter, London and New York, 1974; *Ludwig Mies van der Rohe* by Lorenzo Papi, Florence, 1975; *Mies van der Rohe: Barcelona 1929* by J. P. Bonta, Barcelona, 1975; *After Mies: Mies van der Rohe: Teaching and Principles* by Werner Blaser, New York, Basel, and Stuttgart, 1977; *History of Modern Furniture* by Karl Mang, Stuttgart, 1978, London, 1979; *Tubular Steel Furniture,* edited by Barbie Campbell-Cole and Tim Benton, London, 1979; *The Contemporary Decorative Arts from 1940 to the Present Day* by Philippe Garner, London, 1980; *Mies van der Rohe: Möbel und Interieurs,* Stuttgart, 1981; *Contemporary Classics: Furniture of the Masters* by Charles D. Gandy and Susan Zimmerman-Stidham, New York, 1981; *Mies van der Rohe, Continuing the Chicago School of Architecture* by Werner Blaser, Basel and Boston, 1981; *Mies van der Rohe, Furniture and Interiors* by Werner Blaser, Woodbury, New York, 1982; *Mies van der Rohe: Interior Spaces* by Franz Schulze, Chicago, 1982; *Mies van der Rohe* by David Spaeth, New York, 1985; *Mies van der Rohe: A Critical Biography* by Franz Schulze, Chicago, 1985; *Mies Reconsidered: His Career, Legacy, and Disciples,* Chicago, 1986; *Mies van der Rohe: Less Is More* by Werner Blaser, Zurich and New York, 1986; *Mies van der Rohe: Critical Essays,* Cambridge and

New York, 1989; *Architects of Fortune: Mies van der Rohe and the Third Reich* by Elaine Hochman, New York, 1990; *The Artless Word: Mies van der Rohe on the Building Art* by Fritz Neumeyer, Cambridge, 1991; *Mies van der Rohe: the Art of Structure* by Werner Blaser, New York, 1994; *Functionalist Design: An Ongoing History* by George Marcus, Munich, New York, 1995.

\*        \*        \*

Ludwig Mies van der Rohe, Germany's foremost modern architect, also was prominent in furniture design from the late 1920s until he came to the United States ten years later. His fame as designer rests on metal-supported furniture, such as the MR chair introduced at the Weissenhof Exposition in August 1927. Its most distinctive characteristics—tubular metal construction and cantilever design—were not revolutionary at that date. Marcel Breuer had introduced tubular metal furniture in 1926 to numerous visitors at the Dessau Bauhaus, and many of his designs were used in Weissenhof Exposition installations. Moreover, the idea of cantilevering a chair had been anticipated by Mart Stam, one of whose chairs was already installed at the same exposition months before the MR chair was ready. In turn, the Stam chair may have been dependent on Breuer's cantilevered Cesca chair, which did not actually appear until early in 1928, but which had been designed earlier. The other major source for the esthetics and purpose of the MR was Thonet's famous rocker (c. 1870). Both designers intended for their chairs to set the sitter in motion by a shift of his weight, while Mies's steel tubing serves the same visual purpose as Thonet's exuberant bentwood curves. Companion pieces in tubular metal included tables and stools from 1927 and lounge chairs, chaise-lounges, and other items from the ensuing years.

The Barcelona chair introduced, in 1929, a new group of flat-bar, metal-supported designs. These included a glass-topped, square table; cushioned ottomans; springy armed and armless Tugendhat chairs, cushioned like the Barcelona but cantilevered; and a new side chair, the Brno.

Mies left many drawings, some merely sketches, some surely meant for production, for both tubular and flat-bar designs. One of these, a tubular chaise, was realized for the 1977 exhibition *Mies van der Rohe: Furniture and Furniture Drawings* at the Museum of Modern Art in New York.

Before turning aside from designing furniture, Mies made several small, wood pieces; designed and sketched bent and laminated chairs; and, in 1935, took out a patent for resilient, runner-type wood supports for chairs which were never manufactured. In the United States early in the 1940s, drawings and sketches indicate that Mies was interested in molded shapes, for he produced sketches of conchoidal chairs, possibly in response to designs by Eames and Saarinen.

Mies's furniture designs are often thought of as the single most elegant contribution to design for the modern movement.

—Nina Bremer

# MIHO, James (Noboru)

American graphic designer

**Born:** Gridley, California, 20 November 1933. **Education:** Studied at Pasadena City College, California; Woodbury College, Los Ange-les, BS, 1952; studied painting under Lorser Feitelson, at the Art Center College of Design, Pasadena, BFA, 1957; studied video design, at Philadelphia Museum College, 1958; also attended Wayne State University, Detroit. **Military Service:** Served in the United States Army, in combat in Korea, 1950-51, M/Sergeant. **Family:** Married Tomoko Kawakami in 1956 (divorced, 1977); married Judith M. in 1978; stepdaughter: Jane. **Career:** Art director, at N. W. Ayer advertising agency, Philadelphia and Detroit, 1959-63; founder-partner, James Miho Incorporated design office, Los Angeles, 1964-65; creative director, Needham Harper and Steers, Chicago, 1965-67, and vice-president, Needham Harper and Steers, New York, 1967-69; freelance designer, working in New York, 1970-82, in Redding, Connecticut, 1982-88, and in Pasadena, California, from 1988; design consultant to Chrysler Corporation, 1957-60, Atlantic Richfield, 1970-72, Xerox Corporation, 1970-72, Denise Rene Gallery of New York, 1972, Danish Embassy, 1973-81. Advisor to the mayor's office, city of Los Angeles, 1989-94; advisor and designer, Japanese-American National Museum, 1990-93; advisor and designer, Museum of Contemporary Arts, Los Angeles, 1989-1994; design advisor, Pasadena Police Dept., 1993-95; education advisor to inner city high school, Pasadena, California, 1994. Lecturer in graphic design, Yale Graduate School, 1983-86; chairman of graphic and packaging design, Art Center College of Design, Pasadena, from

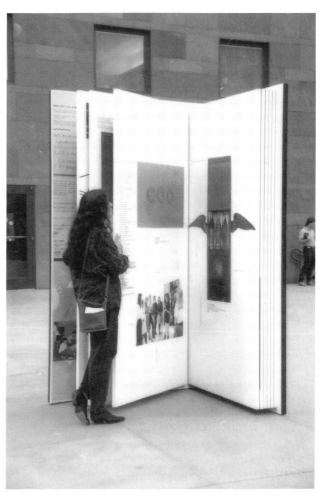

**James Miho: Giant book about art in Chinese, Korean, Japanese, Spanish, and English, at Museum of Contemporary Art, Los Angeles, 1994**

1988. Alumni Board Member, Art Center College of Design Pasadena, 1982-83. **Exhibitions:** Toppan Printing Company, Tokyo, 1973. **Collections:** Museum of Modern Art, New York; Library of Congress, Washington, D.C.; National Air and Space Museum, Smithsonian Institution, Washington, D.C.; Museu de Arte Moderno, Sao Paulo; Poster Museum, Warsaw. **Honors:** Gold Award, Cannes Film Festival, 1968, 1980; Advertising Campaign Award, Type Directors Club of New York, 1972; Industrial Film Award, Chicago Film Festival, 1981; and numerous New York, Cincinnati, Connecticut, Chicago, Philadelphia and Boston Art Directors Club awards. **Address:** 1200 Chateau Road, Pasadena, California 91105, U.S.A.

### Works

*Great Ideas of Western Man* poster series, for the Container Corporation of America, 1961-65.
*Imagination* poster series, for Champion International Paper Division, from 1965.
Design concept for *Real* and *Ideal* series on pollution, culture, education, and technology, for Atlantic Richfield Company, 1968-1973 (with Herbert Bayer).
Poster designs, for the National Air and Space Museum, Smithsonian Institution Washington, D.C., 1975-76.
*AIGA Annual* book designs, for the American Institute of Graphic Arts, New York, 1980-87.
Computer designs, for IBM Video Division, from 1982.
Book designs, for Connecticut Historical Society, from 1982.
*New American Paper Works* exhibition and catalogue design, for the Albright-Knox Art Gallery, Buffalo, New York, 1984.
*Fun and Games* promotional design, for Champion Papers, 1986.
*1640-1940: Furniture Design in New Mexico* book design, for the International Museum of Folk Art, Santa Fe, New Mexico, 1987.
*Behind the Mask in Mexico* book design, for the International Museum of Folk Art, 1988.
*Artists as Photographers* exhibition catalogue, for the Aldrich Museum of Contemporary Art, Ridgefield, Connecticut, 1988.
*Political Graphics in America* book design for the University of Hartford, Connecticut, 1988.
*Design USA in Russia* exhibition design, for United States Information Agency, 1989.
*Eileen Gray* poster, for Furniture of the Twentieth Century Incorporated, New York, 1989.
*Five Language Book,* for Museum of Contemporary·Art, Los Angeles, 1989-1994.
*Ban the Bomb* poster, for the Paris Group, 1994.

### Publications

**By MIHO: books—***Rock, Paper, Scissor,* Tokyo, 1992; **articles—**in *Communication Arts* (Palo Alto), 1970, 1973; *Lamp* (New York), 1970; *Print* (New York), September/October 1972; *Idea* (Tokyo), 1985.

**On MIHO: articles—**in *Communication Arts* (Palo Alto), April/May 1969; *Idea* (Tokyo), September 1970, December 1972; *Santa Fe Folk Art,* 1988; "Inner City Design" in *Los Angeles Times,* 1992.

It is time that designers not look to the top the mountain, but look to the valleys and forests where human life begins and lives. Conquering mountains does not solve the real issues. Exploring the rich abundance of life in the forests and preserving its variety is more important.

—James Miho

\*       \*       \*

In these days of inexorable technological change, it is important not to lose sight of the things that make us human. Corporations also must increasingly recognize their environmental and social responsibilities and accept obligations which cannot help but have a positive effect on their public image. To this end, James Miho has worked to turn business communication into progressive public information. His work is an expression of the wonder of nature and a celebration of human potential and imagination. He has helped a number of corporations and institutions not only to express their educational and aesthetic concerns, but also to establish their presences as socially responsible, creative organization.

In 1959, Miho took his first job out of school with the N.W. Ayer and Son agency, where he worked with Herbert Bayer on the "Great Ideas of Western Man" series for the Container Corporation of America. Bayer, who remains Miho's greatest influence, had already established a precedent of using artists such as Cassandre, Leger, Kepes, Matter, and Shahn to interpret the words and ideas of some of the world's greatest thinkers. Miho searched for new talent and brought, among others, Rauschenberg, Dine, Warhol, and Kane to the series.

Shortly after leaving Ayer, Miho was contacted by U.S. Plywood and Champion Paper. Inspired by Container Corporation's example, they had begun a promotion to show the creative use of their paper products. At his suggestion, a travel theme was established for these booklets. Since that time, Miho has literally traveled around the world producing the "Imagination" series for what is now Champion International. His approach to the series is evidence of Miho as an intelligent, responsible, and visually articulate person. Before he begins each piece, he reads and researches extensively. He then spends months at a time on location gathering information, working with local photographers and illustrators and formulating the idea for the final design. Though he works closely with writers on these projects, in the finished piece, the story that is told is primarily pictorial. For "Imagination XV" on Scandinavia, for example, struck by the idea of a Scandinavian smorgasbord, he used this concept in the booklet by showing a chronology of architectural styles with die cuts allowing old and new to be shown simultaneously. This work serves well the needs of his client by taking full advantage of creative work on paper. As many as thirty different production techniques may be used in a single booklet.

For a person who has explored our world so extensively, what new travels will the future bring? What new frontiers? Perhaps his personal interest in outer space is a clue.

—Barbara Sudick

# MIHO, Tomoko
American graphic designer

**Born:** Tomoko Kawakami, in Los Angeles, California, in 1933.
**Education:** Studied at Minneapolis College of Design, 1951; stud-

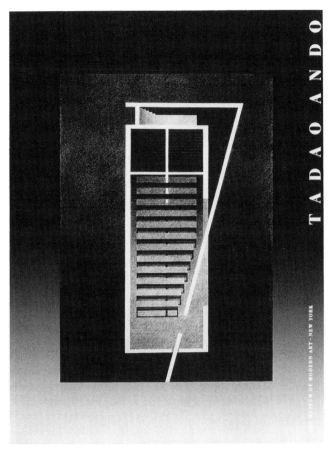

**Tomoko Miho: Book design for Japanese architect Tadao Ando, for The Museum of Modern Art, New York**

ied art and design under Mary Sheridan, Lorser Feitelson, Bernyce Polifka, and Gene Fleury, at the Art Center College of Design, Los Angeles, BA, 1956. **Family:** Married James Noboru Miho in 1956 (divorced, 1977). **Career:** Designer, 1960-63, and head of graphics department, 1963-64, George Nelson and Company, New York; founder-partner of Miho Design, Los Angeles, 1964-65; designer, Container Corporation's Center for Advanced Research in Design, Chicago, 1966-67, and design manager, Center for Advanced Research in Design, New York, 1967-74; partner, Miho Inc., New York, 1974-82; principal, Tomoko Miho Co., from 1982; has designed for Champion International Corporation, Herman Miller, Atlantic Richfield Company, Neiman-Marcus, Jack Lenor Larsen Inc., and others. **Member:** American Institute of Graphic Arts (board member, 1979-82); Alliance Graphique Internationale, from 1974; Society of Environmental Graphic Designers. **Exhibitions:** *Word and Image,* Museum of Modern Art, New York, 1968 (toured); *International Poster Biennale,* Warsaw, 1970; Toppan Printing Company, Tokyo, 1973; *Images of an Era,* Corcoran Gallery of Art, Washington, D.C., 1976 (toured); *AGI Posters,* Place Ville Marie, Montreal, 1982; *The Modern Poster,* Museum of Modern Art, New York, 1988; *AGI '88 Tokyo,* G7 Gallery and Ginza Graphic Gallery, Tokyo, 1988. **Collections:** Museum of Modern Art, New York; Library of Congress, Washington, D.C.; Museum für Gestaltung, Zürich; Die Neue Sammlung, Staatliches Museum für Angewandte Kunst, Münich. **Honors:** IBM Fellowship, International Design Conference, Aspen, 1979; Gold Medal, American Institute of Graphic Arts, 1993, 1995; awards from Art Directors

Club of New York, Advertising Club of New York, American Institute of Graphic Arts, Society of Typographic Arts, *Industrial Design* magazine, *Communication Arts* magazine, Art Directors Club of Los Angeles. **Address:** 1045 Fifth Avenue, New York, New York 10028, U.S.A

**Works**

Tower Suite and Hemisphere Club identity programs, for Restaurant Associates, New York, 1961.
Print materials, for Herman Miller, 1961-64, 1967-74.
Print materials, for Champion Papers, 1962, 1972-73.
ARCO corporate identity program, for the Atlantic Richfield Corporation, 1967-72.
Identity program and literature, for Omniplan Architects, 1970-92.
*Great Ideas of Western Man* exhibition poster, for the Container Corporation of America, New York, 1972.
Graphics and Gustafson award, for the National Council of Architectural Registration Boards, 1972-75.
Packaging program, for Neiman-Marcus, 1973-74.
Posters, for National Air and Space Museum, Smithsonian Institution, Washington, D.C., 1976 (with James Miho).
Catalogue and ad, for Jack Lenor Larsen, Inc., 1978.
Signage and graphics, for Andersen's Food Emporium, Hiroshima, 1978.
Graphic design for *The Jefferson Lecture in the Humanities,* for the National Endowment for the Humanities, 1979.
*Japan in Aspen* program book, International Design Conference, Aspen, 1979.
*Concentration* posters, for the Whitney Museum of American Art, New York, 1980.
United States pavilion banners and symbols, at the *Energy Expo,* Knoxville, Tennessee, 1982.
*Borrowed Landscape* poster, for the Herman Miller Ethospace System, 1984.
Environmental art, for Herman Miller showrooms in Los Angeles and New York City, 1984, and for International Design Center/ New York, Long Island City, 1987.
Graphic design, for the Isamu Noguchi Foundation, Inc., from 1984.
*The Isamu Noguchi Garden Museum* book design, for Harry N. Abrams, 1987.
Identity program, for Roberdeau Companies, Dallas, 1987.
Exterior and interior signage design, for the 546 Fifth Avenue office tower, New York, 1990.
Computer software packaging, for Abbott Systems, Inc., New York, 1990.
Stationery and cards, for the Willem de Kooning office, New York, 1990.
*Tadao Ando* exhibition catalogue/book design, for Museum of Modern Art, New York, 1991.
*Japanese Art: Personal Selections from the Mary and Jackson Burke Collection* book design, for the Morikami Museum, Florida, 1993.
Entrance signage design, for the 565 Fifth Avenue office tower, New York, 1993.
Exterior and interior signage design, for Neptune Orient Lines (NOL) Center, Jersey City, New Jersey, 1994.
Signage design projects, for Hellmuth, Obata & Kassabaum architects, and for Japan Airlines Co. Ltd., New York, 1994.
Signage design projects, for Amtrak at Pennsylvania Station, New York, 1995-96.

## Publications

**On MIHO: books—**_Word and Image,_ exhibition catalogue, New York, 1968; _Internationalen Plakatjarhbuch,_ Switzerland, 1968; _Signet, Signal, Symbol_ by Walter Diethelm, Zürich, 1970; _History of the Poster_ by Josef and Shizuko Müller-Brockmann, Zürich, 1971; _Images of an Era: The American Poster 1945-75,_ exhibition catalogue, London, 1975; _AGI: Alliance Graphique Internationale Posters_ edited by Rudolph de Harak, New York, 1986; _Letterheads: A Collection from Around the World_ by Takenobu Igarashi, Tokyo, 1986; _Planning and Design_ by Larry Klein, New York, 1986; _The Modern Poster,_ exhibition catalogue by Stuart Wrede, New York, 1988; _AGI Annals: Alliance Graphique Internationale 1952-87_ by F.H.K. Henrion, Switzerland, 1989; _First Choice_ edited by Ken Cato, Tokyo, 1989; _Graphics in the Third Dimension_ by Ken and Leigh Cato, Tokyo, 1992; _Graphic Design USA: 15,_ New York, 1994; **articles—**"Women in the Communication Arts" by Jerome Snyder in _Communication Arts_ (Palo Alto), vol. 13, no. 2, 1971; "James Miho and Tomoko Miho" in _Idea_ (Tokyo), no. 111, 1972-73; "Posters for New York City" in _Gebrauchsgraphik_ (Munich), April 1971; _Communication Arts,_ vol. 20, no. 4, 1978; "Tomoko Miho" in _High Quality_ (Heidelberg), no. 19, 1991.

*

My early formative experience was with George Nelson and Company, a wide-ranging, multi-discipline design office which did not confine itself to narrow boundaries. One continually tries to enlarge his or her vision in many areas. This cross-over orientation has led me into a broad range of projects. Working in a mix of two- and three-dimensional media is a continuing revelation that keeps stretching me, helping me to grow as a designer and a person.

To me, every project is an opportunity to learn. I devote as much time as possible to learning everything I can about it, building a solid foundation of understanding on which to base the design content and the concept that shapes it. Then I try to distill to the _essence_ of what needs to be defined and communicated. For me, paring to the _essence_ demands fierce attention to detail. My concern is for the perfect balance between form and content.

Defining that content and communicating it creatively is true for all media. The content is unlimited, so we must not limit ourselves, especially now, because today we are seeing an expanding range of new media, new contents. We have the opportunity to interface with these new venues and make a difference, as others have made a difference in the past.

In 1995, I had dinner with two AIGA Gold Medalists, Leo Lionni and Gene Federico, who continue to be an inspiration. Leo, now 85, is active and enthusiastic about his recent banner design for the Palio in Siena and illustrations for children's books.

I can think of no better proof than Leo that love for what we do is a sustaining force. And it is a vital force that can lead us in new directions as we cross over to complement other disciplines.

What good design brings to any discipline is clarity, harmony, and beauty.

—Tomoko Miho

*　　*　　*

It is about twenty five years ago that I heard the name of Tomoko from Mr. George Nelson. When I visited him at his New York studio for the first time, I had a chance to be shown works produced by the Graphic Division of his office. One of those was a voluminous catalogue for Herman Miller Co., a top furniture maker in America, where Mr. Charles Eames and Mr. Nelson himself used to work.

After three years of professional experience in Switzerland, I was confident that I had a fairly critical power of observation. Nevertheless, I was overwhelmed by the exquisite layout of the catalogue. I felt each page involved the designer's tremendous spiritual strength. Unconditionally I respected the author's patience. The author, I learned, was Tomoko. Ever since her name has been haunting my memory.

Her name deeply impressed me again while visiting Chicago. Mr. John Massey, who worked on graphic design for Container Corporation of America, showed me Tomoko's poster drawn for the City of Chicago. The poster is now among the art treasures at the Modern Arts Museum in New York. With modern architecture as its theme, Tomoko employed graphic technique, and successfully went beyond the object and created modern architecture with a difference. Her simple yet powerful drawing was so impressive I couldn't persuade myself that it was done by a female designer. The same designer demonstrated her incredibly meticulous skill in that enormous catalogue. The two different works enabled me to recognize her real capability.

Tomoko looks very nice in a dark dress. I've rarely seen her wear dresses of other colors. Dark is really becoming to her. Modest and reserved, Tomoko seems to be seeking proper words when she talks. She is a rare figure in the design world where there are many loquacious and frivolous people. She has the beauty Japanese women have nurtured for long years. Her highly refined works are unequivocally supported by this beauty.

—Toshi Katayama

# MINAGAWA, Masa
Japanese industrial designer

**Born:** Tokyo, 23 December 1917. **Education:** Studied under Takao Miyashita, at the Tokyo Higher Industrial Arts School (now Chiba University), 1936-40, Inumaru Prize, 1940. **Military Service:** Served in the Japanese Army, in Tokyo, 1942-45. **Family:** Married Akiko Kimura in 1946 (died, 1980), daughters: Hiromi and Yoshiko; married Masue Matsumoto in 1982. **Career:** Staff designer, at Toko Electric Company, Tokyo, 1940-54; freelance lighting and electrical appliance designer, establishing Masa Minagawa Design studio, Tokyo, from 1954. Professor, Kuwasawa Design Institute, Tokyo 1953-65; lecturer, Chiba University, Tokyo, 1957-63; dean of the industrial design department, Tokyo University of Arts and Design 1963-83. Founder-member, Japan Industrial Designers Association, Tokyo, from 1953; judge for the Mainichi Shimbun Industrial Design Competition, Tokyo, from 1962; organizing committee member of Design Year, from 1973; coordinating committee chairman, 1973, and design promotion council chairman, 1978-80, Ministry of International Trade and Industry, Tokyo. **Honors:** Blue Ribbon Medal, Japanese Government, 1978; awarded the Order of the Rising Sun, Gold and Silver Rays, Japanese Government, 1995. **Address:** 5-12-4 Kita Asagaya, Suginami-ku, Tokyo 166, Japan.

**Publications**

By MINAGAWA: books—*Lighting Practice of Japan,* vols. 1-6, Tokyo, 1957; *Design Collection: Metal and Non-Ferrous Metal,* 2 vols., Tokyo, 1965; *Sakana No Sokei,* Tokyo, 1994; **articles**—in *Industrial Design* (Tokyo), August 1983.

*

When I was about seventeen years old, I used to pass a river on my way to school. One day I saw two flowerpots on the boat of a family that lived on the water because the father was a water-transport worker. At that time, it occurred to me that those with little income too have a desire for beautiful things, and I thought even cheap tools, such as tea cups and chopsticks, should be easy to use and beautiful in shape. This was my motivation for entering Tokyo Higher Industrial Arts School.

In my philosophy of today, I believe in:

—products of good quality, of beautiful shape, of inexpensive price for wide use. Designers should be involved in basic layout and should endeavor to make easy-to-use products by pollution-free processes

—efforts to reduce production costs—for example, reduction of the number of parts and use of parts common to various products

—ease of assembly: for example, reduction of the number of screws

—ease and safety of handling

—beauty. The design should be as simple as possible and should make use of the natural flavor of materials

—Masa Minagawa

*    *    *

Masa Minagawa worked in the design department of Toko Electric Company from 1940 until 1954 and achieved prominence as one of the first noteworthy industrial designers of electrical appliances in Japan. He opened his own design firm in 1954, when there were few such independent design offices; he has continued to specialize in appliance as well as lighting systems design. Minagawa was also founding member of the Japan Industrial Designers Association and for twenty years (until his retirement in 1983) he was the Dean of the Industrial Design Department at Tokyo University of Arts and Design.

The Delta fan, designed by Minagawa in 1966, is typical of his work. He replaced the traditional, heavy, molded leg with light, chrome-plated iron pipe, and the fan is so designed that it can either stand on the floor or be hung on the wall. The light, fresh style creates a clear image of that kind of civilized life-style that Japanese industrial designers have tried to suggest to a public still suffering the "hangover" of postwar chaos. Minagawa's design has far-reaching effects: the Delta fan served as a prototype not only for later fans but also for other electrical appliances for the home.

In his work, Minagawa attempts to follow three rules:

1) A designer should be concerned with economy, with creating good products at cheap prices so that they can be available to the maximum number of consumers. Profit margins are not the responsibility of the designer.

2) A designer should strictly check whether his product is easy to handle, safe, and not a pollutant. These criteria are the designer's responsibility.

**Masa Minagawa: Delta electric fan, 1958**

3) A designer should not be concerned with just the external form of a product but should also be committed to the design of the basic layout of parts.

According to Minagawa, rational thinking can produce products that are universally useful. For example, his oil filter for cars was manufactured for sixteen years, and more than 160 million copies were produced.

Referring to the present environment for design, Minagawa says: "In order for better design to happen, good design must receive more recognition from the public." As for designers themselves, he advises: "Don't insist too much on yourself, your own personality; put yourself in an objective position when designing." His view, finally, is that the essence of design lies in honesty and sincerity, and his own products are obviously in conformity with that goal.

—Kunio Sano

# MINALE, Marcello

British graphic, interior, and industrial designer

**Born:** Of Italian parents, in Tripoli, Libya, 15 December 1938. **Education:** Studied at the Istituto Tecnico Naples, 1957-60. **Family:** Married Roberta M.; children: Marcello, Manlio, and Massimo. **Career:** Designer at the Taucker advertising agency, and art director of the Makkinointi Uierjuuri agency, Helsinki, 1960-62; design director, Young and Rubicam agency, London, 1962-64; founder-partner, with Brian Tattersfield, of Minale Tattersfield and Partners design firm, London, from 1964. President, Designers and Art Directors Association, London, 1982. **Exhibitions:** Design Centre, London, 1979; *Penguin Books,* Manchester Polytechnic, 1981; Museo d'Arte Contemporanea, Milan, 1983; Centro Cultural de la Villa de Madrid, Spain, 1985; Axis Gallery, Tokyo, 1988; Biennal, Mexico City, 1992. **Collections:** Poster Museum, Warsaw; Victoria and Albert Museum, London; Museum of Modern Art, New York. **Honors:** Silver Medals, 1972-82, and President's Award for outstanding contribution to British design, 1986, Design and Art Directors Association, London; Gold Medal, Art Directors Club of New York, 1977; fellow, Chartered Society of Designers, London. **Address:** Minale Tattersfield and Partners, The Courtyard, 37 Sheen Road, Richmond, Surrey TW9 1AJ, England.

**Works**

Corporate identity for Sydney Olympics 2000, 1992.
Corporate identity for Heathrow Express train, 1993.
Corporate identity for Eurostar Train, 1994.
Design of the Hammersmith Underground station, for London Transport, 1994.

**Publications**

**By MINALE: books**—(editor, with Brian Tattersfield) *Minale Tattersfield,* vols. 1-4, London, 1965-72; *Creatures Great and Small,* London, 1973; *The Black Pencil,* London, 1974; *The Tree That Could Fly,* London, 1976; *Tomo the Water Dragon,* London, 1977; *Minale Tattersfield Designers* edited by Edward Booth Clibborn, London, 1977; (editor) *Design: The World of Minale Tattersfield,* London, 1987; (editor) *The Leader of the Pack: How to Design Successful Packaging,* London, 1992; *How to Run an International Design Consultancy,* London, 1993; *The Image Maker,* London, 1995.

**On MINALE/TATTERSFIELD: books**—*Graphic Design Britain* edited by Frederick Lambert, London, 1967; *Modern Graphics* by Keith Murgatroyd, London, 1969; *European Designers: England, France, Italy* by Idea Publishers, Tokyo, 1970; *Minale Tattersfield Designers* by Idea Publishers, Tokyo, 1978; *Penguin Books: The Pictorial Cover 1960-1980,* exhibition catalogue by Evelyne Green, Manchester, 1981; *Who's Who in Graphic Art* edited by Walter Amstutz, Dubendorf, 1982; *Contemporary Furniture* edited by Klaus Jurgen Sembach, Stuttgart and New York, 1982; *Design Source Book* by Penny Sparke and others, London, 1986; *International Design Yearbook 1987/88* edited by Philippe Starck, London, 1987.

\*

These are my three basic principles of design:
1. Keep it simple even if it is complicated.
2. Think before designing instead of designing before thinking.
3. The duty of every designer is never to bore the audience.

—Marcello Minale

\*    \*    \*

**Marcello Minale: Poster for the 30th anniversary of Minale Tatterfield Designers, 1994**

The Minale Tattersfield corporate identity symbol is a soft black pencil scribble, a gentle poke at the cool Swiss formalism that constituted good graphics in the 1960s, but absolutely right for a company whose work is noted for its flair, originality, and wit. Marcello Minale and Brian Tattersfield met at Young and Rubicam in the early 1960s when New York-inspired ideas were transforming British advertising agencies. Frustrated with a lack of client contact, they set up a partnership, adopting the practical business lessons they had learned along with a fresh approach, a philosophy summed up by Minale as "expressing the maximum possible with the simplest means." With the reputation of being slightly crazy as well as avant-garde, they did at first find it hard to attract clients. A major breakthrough came with the commission to update Harrod's conventional, "establishment" image with a sortie into the swinging sixties boutique style. With new retailing methods, Pop art images, coffer bars, and subdued lighting, it caught the mood of the time perfectly.

In 1972, Minale and Tattersfield were appointed graphic design consultants to Milton Keynes, with a brief to help soften the hard qualities of new town architecture. Other commissions include De Beers offices, a new logo for the London furniture store Heal's, and work for a range of Italian clients, including Alitalia, Star, and Buitoni Perugina.

Sadly, because of financial cutbacks in 1979, some of their most brilliant work—especially the redesign of fifteen tube stations on

London Transport's Northern Line—was never executed. Since its pioneering work in the 1930s, London Transport has unfortunately declined, and Minale Tattersfield's strong and exciting visual identity would have done a great deal to revive a flagging image. What might have been is suggested by a full-scale mock-up of a ceiling vault for Oval Station and a Kings Cross subway decorated with the word "smile" in large, colourful letters.

Their design achievement has been recognised by a major retrospectives in London and Milan. Contemporary Alan Fletcher of Pentagram summed them up: "They represent to the world of graphics what Laurel and Hardy, Rodgers and Hammerstein, Romeo and Juliet, Gilbert and Sullivan, Young and Rubicam represent in their respective worlds."

—Catherine McDermott

# MINKS, Wilfried

Czechoslovak stage designer

**Born:** Binai, 21 February 1930. **Education:** Studied at the Meisterschule für Angewandte Kunst, Leipzig, 1950-54; studied stage design under Willy Schmidt at the Akademie der Bildende Künste, Berlin, 1955-57. **Career:** Assistant to Gerd Richter, at the Staatstheater, Stuttgart, 1957-58; resident designer, at the Stadttheater, Pforzheim, 1958-59, Städtische Bühnen, Ulm, 1959-62, and at the Stadttheater, Bremen, 1962-71; freelance designer and stage director, Frankfurt, from 1971. Professor, Hochschule für Bildende Künste, Hamburg, from 1970; board member, Schauspiel, Frankfurt, 1980-81. **Exhibitions:** *Die Neue Bühne,* Städtisches Museum, Leverkusen, 1967; Studio F, Ulm, 1967; Kunsthalle, Bremen, 1968. **Address:** c/o Schauspiel Frankfurt, Städtische Bühnen, 6000 Frankfurt 1, Germany.

## Works

Stage productions (Stadttheater, Bremen, unless noted) include—
*The Hostage,* 1964; *The Quare Fellow,* 1964; *Spring Awakening,* 1965; *Hamlet,* 1965; *Macbeth,* 1966; *The Robbers,* 1966; *War of the Roses,* 1967; *Tasso,* 1969; *The Tempest,* 1969; *Bremer Freiheit,* Concordia Cinema, Bremen, 1971.

## Publications

**On MINKS: books—***Die Neue Bühne,* exhibition catalogue, Leverkusen, 1967; *Die Bühne von Wilfried Minks,* exhibition catalogue, Bremen, 1968; *Stage Design Throughout the World Since 1960* edited by René Hainaux and Nicole Leclercq, Brussels, 1972, London, 1973; *Stage Design Throughout the World 1970-1975* edited by Hainaux and Leclercq, Brussels and London, 1976.

*        *        *

Wilfried Minks first invigorated German design through a return to bold realism in his designs for Peter Zadek's productions of Brendan Behan's plays in the early 1960s (*The Hostage, The Quare Fellow*). He was instrumental in shaking design out of a benign

formalism, represented most clearly to Minks by the work of Franz Mertz in the 1950s. Minks advocated a "tougher" design, one that used real materials and made reference to contemporary reality, either social or aesthetic.

By 1965, his work had developed in an eclectic direction, borrowing heavily from tendencies in the visual arts, especially Pop Art. For Zadek's production of Schiller's *The Robbers,* he blew up a painting by Roy Lichtenstein into a full stage backdrop and clothed the characters in comic strip costumes. For a production of *The Tempest* in 1969, he covered the entire stage floor with sand and erected a fluorescent rainbow over it. In creating works like these, Minks espoused a design that borrowed unabashedly from what were, in his mind, the more aggressive arts of contemporary painting and sculpture to make a visual comment and connection between the time in which the play was written and the contemporary world.

Gradually, Minks' designs gathered a strength of expression that rivaled the actor and playwright for attention. In 1970, he said that design "should have the self-sufficiency of landscapes." This tendency in German design, originated by Minks, was pushed to an extreme by later designers (Achim Freyer and Erich Wonder) who considered some of their designs independent visual statements, complete without actors. Minks was also instrumental in encouraging designers to seek out alternative spaces for their settings. For a production of Fassbinder's *Bremer Freiheit* in 1971, he transformed an old movie theater (the Concordia) into a complete audience-stage space. This design tendency was developed much further by Minks' colleague in Bremen, Karl-Ernst Herrmann, when he became the chief designer at the Schaubühne am Halleschen Ufer in Berlin.

Around 1972, Minks turned his attention away from design toward directing. By this time, his legacy could be seen throughout West Germany, where many of his former students, working in the major state theaters, were creating audacious stage designs that drew heavily on contemporary visual arts for inspiration. If Caspar Neher had shown how scene design could have a dramaturgical function, Minks made clear how it could make a purely visual comment on the text.

—Richard V. Riddell

# MISSONI, Ottavio

Italian fashion designer

**Born:** Ragusa, Yugoslavia, 11 February 1921. **Education:** Educated in Zara, Italy, until 1938, in Trieste, 1930-40, and in Milan, 1941-42. **Military Service:** Served in the Italian Army (prisoner of war, Egypt, 1942-46). **Family:** Married Rosita Jelmini in 1953; children: Vittorio, Luca, and Angela. **Career:** Designer and manufacturer of knitwear, from 1948; established knitwear factory, with Giorgio Oberweger, in Trieste, 1948-53; partner, with Rosita Missoni, in knitwear design and manufacturing firm, in Gallarate, Italy, 1953-68, and in Missoni S.p.A. workshop and factory, in Sumirago, Italy, from 1968; designed clothing and household fabrics for Biki, American Fieldcrest, Saporiti, T. e J. Vestor, and others. Launched *Missoni* women's perfume, 1981, and *Missoni Uomo* men's fragrance, 1983; designed costumes for the opera *Lucia di Lammermoor,* Teatro alla Scala, Milan, 1982, and for the ballet *Step into My Dream,* David Parsons Dance Company, New York; also creator of tapestries. **Exhibitions:** *Missoni and the Magic Machine,* Galleria del Naviglio, Venice, 1975; *Missoni Retrospective,* La Rotonda della Besana, Milan, 1978 (toured); *Italian Re-Evolution,* La Jolla Museum of Art, California, 1982; *Icontri Venezia,* Venice, 1982; *40 Years of Italian Fashion,* Trump Tower, New York, 1983; retrospective, Teatro della Pergola Annex, Florence, 1994. **Honors:** Neiman Marcus Award, 1973; Tommy Award, American Printed Fabrics Council, 1976; Gold Medal of Civic Merit, City of Milan, 1979; Fragrance Foundation Award, 1982; Pitti Immagine Prize, Florence, 1994. Athletic honors: Italian 400-meter champion, Milan, 1939; World Student Champion, Vienna, 1939; Olympic Games 400-meter finalist London, 1948. **Addresses:** Missoni S.p.A., Via Luigi Rossi, 21040 Sumirago, Varese, Italy; Missoni Press Office, Via T. Salvini 1, 20122 Milan, Italy.

## Publications

**On MISSONI: books—***20th Century Fashion: A Scrapbook* by Ernestine Carter, London, 1975; *Milano Fashion* edited by Isa Tutino Vercelloni, 1975; *In Vogue: Sixty Years of Celebrities and Fashion* by Georgina Howell, London, 1975, 1978, New York, 1976; *Missoni*

**Missoni: Autumn/winter collection, 1995/96. Photo: Tiziano Magni**

*and the Magic Machine,* exhibition catalogue by Guido Ballo, Venice, 1975; *In Fashion: Dress in the Twentieth Century* by Prudence Glynn, London, 1978; *I Mass Moda: Fatti e Personaggi dell'Italian Look* by Adriana Mulassano, Florence, 1979; *Italian Re-Evolution: Design in Italian Society in the Eighties,* exhibition catalogue edited by Piero Sartogo, La Jolla, 1982; *40 Years of Italian Fashion,* exhibition catalogue compiled by B. G. Aragno, Rome, 1983; *McDowell's Directory of Twentieth Century Fashion* by Colin McDowell, London, 1984; *The Conran Directory of Design* edited by Stephen Bayley, London, 1985; *Design Source Book* by Penny Sparke and others, London, 1986; *The Encyclopaedia of Fashion from 1840 to the 1980s* by Georgina O'Hara, London, 1986; *Italian Design: 1870 to the Present* by Penny Sparke, London, 1988; *Missonologia: The World of Missoni,* exhibition catalogue edited by Isa Tutino Vercelloni, Milan, 1994.

*See* MISSONI, Rosita

\*     \*     \*

Ottavio Missoni was born in Yugoslavia to a sea captain and a Dalmatian countess. While enjoying athletic triumph in England in 1948, he met Rosita Jelmini from Lombardy, then a student at Hampstead. At that time, he had already begun a small knitwear business in Trieste with partner Giorgio Oberweger. After the Missonis married, they began to develop women's knitwear in a small factory at Gallarate, outside Milan. Unfortunately for the sports world, after an injury, Tai (as Ottavio Missoni is known) retired from competition to devote all his time to experiments and to merchandizing the ready-to-wear line. He did admit, though, that in this field he would continue to compete: "The formula remains the same—an amazing pace, serious preparation, and a masterpiece in style."

Initially, while developing and refining knitting techniques by machine, the Missonis approached the problem of designing the patterns and colors with open minds. By concentrating on the material, they became famous for multicolored, brilliant hues, as well as muted, rich shades. Their garments are vehicles for these patterns, which they carry in simple, graceful lines. Their styles, introduced in collections twice a year, are classic and able to be worn at any age, during any season, and they can be beautifully mixed and matched (an innovative idea of theirs years ago).

About 1962 their famous flame-stitch pattern was introduced; variations included hard, soft, or curved lines in addition to the rainbow flame-stitch. In 1972, see-through net was introduced, to be followed by netted stripes in 1973, the zig-zag knit, as well as the shaded horizontal stripe and the wavy diagonal stripe. In 1975, the chenille knit was introduced, then printed on woolen shawls in 1976. The shaded herring-bone was created in soft colors, and the tartan-plaid knit followed in 1978.

As a guest, I was very impressed when the son, Vittorio Missoni, now in charge of production and sales, brother Luca, a pattern and color technician, and sister Angela, who creates accessories and organizes shows, hosted me and a group of fashion students. The entire family welcomed us into their modern factory and laboratories in the tranquil, wooded hills at Sumirago, north of Milan. Besides being thoroughly charmed, we were inspired. Typically, the Missoni family follows everything directly, overseeing 200 workers creating approximately 1,000 garments a day to supply fewer than 200 clients.

In his laboratory, Tai creates surrounded by stacks of samples, swatches, skeins, reels of wool and silk, paint pots, multitudes of colored felt-tip pens, and graph paper. Also at hand are a test-knitting machine and bits and pieces of fabrics collected from travels to serve as inspiration. In her workroom, Rosita concentrates on research influenced by her purchases at flea markets. She explained that their work is really their hobby. It expresses influences from travel, books, art, and music. They truly feel that they are not fashion creators but a private, happy family working together as artisans.

—Gillion Skellenger

## MISSONI, Rosita
Italian fashion designer

**Born:** Rosita Jelmini, in Golasecca, 20 November 1931. **Education:** Studied modern languages, at the Collegio Rosetum, Besozzo, 1948-51. **Family:** Married Ottavio Missoni in 1953; children: Vittorio, Luca, and Angela. **Career:** Worked as a design assistant in her parents' loungewear and furnishing fabrics factory, Vestor, 1950-53; partner, with Ottavio Missoni, in knitwear design and manufacturing workshop and factory, in Gallarate, 1953-68, and in Missoni S.p.A. knitwear design and manufacturing firm, in Sumirago from 1968; designed for Biki, American Fieldcrest, Saporiti, T. e J. Vestor, and others. Launched *Missoni* women's perfume, 1981, and *Missoni Uomo* men's fragrance, 1983. **Exhibitions:** *Missoni and the Magic Machine,* Galleria del Naviglio, Venice, 1975; *Missoni Retrospective,* La Rotonda della Besana, Milan, 1978 (toured); *Italian Re-Evolution,* La Jolla Museum of Art, California, 1982; *Icontri Venezia,* Venice, 1982; *40 Years of Italian Fashion,* Trump Tower, New York, 1983; retrospective, Teatro della Pergola Annex, Florence, 1994. **Honors:** Neiman Marcus Award, 1973; Tommy Award, American Printed Fabrics Council, 1976; Fragrance Foundation Award, 1982; International Design Award, New York, 1990; Pitti Immagine Prize, Florence, 1994. **Addresses:** Missoni S.p.A., Via Luigi Rossi, 21040 Sumirago, Varese, Italy; Missoni Press Office, Via T. Salvini 1, 20122 Milan, Italy.

### Publications

**On MISSONI: books**—*20th Century Fashion: A Scrapbook* by Ernestine Carter, London, 1975; *Milano Fashion* edited by Isa Tutino Vercelloni, 1975; *In Vogue: Sixty Years of Celebrities and Fashion* by Georgina Howell, London, 1975, 1978, New York, 1976; *Missoni and the Magic Machine,* exhibition catalogue by Guido Ballo, Venice, 1975; *In Fashion: Dress in the Twentieth Century* by Prudence Glynn, London, 1978; *I Mass Moda: Fatti e Personaggi dell'Italian Look* by Adriana Mulassano, Florence, 1979; *Italian Re-Evolution: Design in Italian Society in the Eighties,* exhibition catalogue edited by Piero Sartogo, La Jolla, 1982; *40 Years of Italian Fashion,* exhibition catalogue compiled by B. G. Aragno, Rome, 1983; *McDowell's Directory of Twentieth Century Fashion* by Colin McDowell, London, 1984; *The Conran Directory of Design* edited by Stephen Bayley, London, 1985; *Design Source Book* by Penny Sparke and others, London, 1986; *The Encyclopaedia of Fashion from 1840 to the 1980s* by Georgina O'Hara, London, 1986; *Italian Design: 1870 to the Present* by Penny Sparke, London, 1988; *Missonologia: The World of Missoni,* exhibition catalogue edited by Isa Tutino Vercelloni, Milan, 1994.

*See* MISSONI, Ottavio

\*

Our philosophy since we went into business has been that a piece of clothing should be like a work of art. It should not be bought for a special occasion or because it's in fashion, but because a woman likes it, finds it suits her needs, and feels she could wear it forever.

—Rosita Missoni

## MIYAKE, Issey
Japanese fashion designer

**Born:** Kazumaru Miyake, in Tokyo, 22 April 1939. **Education:** Studied at Tama Art University, Tokyo, 1959-63, and at La Chambre Syndicale de la Couture Parisienne, Paris, 1965. **Career:** Assistant to designer Guy Laroche, Paris, 1966-68, and to Hubert de Givenchy, Paris, 1968-69; designer, for Geoffrey Beene ready-to-wear fashion firm New York, 1969-70; freelance designer, establishing Miyake Design Studio, Tokyo, from 1970; also director of Issey Miyake International, Tokyo, Issey Miyake and Associates, Tokyo, Issey Miyake Europe, Paris, Issey Miyake USA, New York, and Issey Miyake On Limits, Tokyo. Lines include Issey Sport, Plantation, and Pleats Please; fragrances include *L'Eau de Missey,* 1993, and *L'Eau d'Issey pour Homme,* 1995. Also theater designer, from 1980. Executive adviser and planner, First Japan Culture Conference, Yokohama, 1980. **Exhibitions:** *Issey Miyake in the Museum,* Seibu Museum of Art, Tokyo, 1977; *Escape-Temps du Japon,* Musée des Arts Decoratifs, Paris, 1978; *Les Tissus Imprimés d'Issey Miyake,* Musée de l'Impression sur Étoffes, Mulhouse, 1979; *Intimate Architecture: Contemporary Clothing,* Massachusetts Institute of Technology, Cambridge, 1982; *Bodyworks,* international touring exhibition, 1983; *A New Wave in Fashion: Three Japanese Designers,* Phoenix Art Museum, Arizona, 1983; *À Un,* Musée des Arts Decoratifs, Paris, 1988; *Issey Miyake Pleats Please,* Touko Museum of Contemporary Art, Tokyo, 1990; *Twist,* Naoshima Contemporary Art Museum, 1992. **Collections:** Metropolitan Museum of Art, New York; Victoria and Albert Museum, London. **Honors:** Japan Fashion Editors Club Award, 1974; Mainichi Newspaper Fashion Award, Tokyo, 1976, 1984; Pratt Institute Design Excellence Award, New York, 1979; Council of Fashion Designers of America Award, 1983; Neiman Marcus Award, 1984; Officier de l'Ordre des Arts et Lettres, France, 1989; Hiroshima Art Prize, 1991; Chevalier de l'Ordre National de la Legion d'Honneur, Paris, 1993. Honorary Doctorate, Royal College of Art, London, 1993. **Address:** 1-23 Ohyamacho, Shibuyaku, Tokyo 151, Japan.

### Publications

**By MIYAKE: books**—*Issey Miyake, East Meets West* edited by Kazuko Koide and Ikko Tanaka, Tokyo, 1978; *Issey Miyake*

*Bodyworks* edited by Shozo Tsurumoto, Tokyo, 1983; *Issey Miyake and Miyake Design Studio 1970-1985,* Tokyo, 1985; *Issey Miyake PLEATS PLEASE,* Touko Museum of Contemporary Art and Miyake Design Studio, Tokyo, 1990.

**On MIYAKE: books**—*25 Ans de Marie-Claire de 1954 a 1979,* compiled by Françoise Mohrt, Paris, 1979; *Les Tissus Imprimés d'Issey Miyake,* exhibition catalogue by Yvonne Deslandres, Mulhouse, 1979; *Fashion 2001* by Lucille Kornak, London, 1982; *Intimate Architecture: Contemporary Clothing Design,* exhibition catalogue, Cambridge, Massachusetts, 1982; *A New Wave in Fashion: Three Japanese Designers,* exhibition catalogue, Phoenix, Arizona, 1983; *McDowell's Directory of Twentieth Century Fashion* by Colin McDowell, London, 1984; *New Fashion Japan* by Leonard Koren, Tokyo and New York, 1984; *The Conran Directory of Design* edited by Stephen Bayley, London, 1985; *Couture: The Great Designers* by Caroline Rennolds Milbank, New York, 1985; *Design Source Book* by Penny Sparke and others, London, 1986; *The Encyclopedia of Fashion from 1840 to the 1980s* by Georgina O'Hara, London, 1986; *Scenes from the Fashionable World* by Kennedy Fraser, New York, 1987; *Japanese Design* by Penny Sparke, London, 1987; *Issey Miyake: Photographs by Irving Penn* edited by Nicholas Calloway, Boston, 1988; *The Fashion Conspiracy* by Nicholas Coleridge, London, 1988; *Sultans of Style: 30 Years of Fashion and Passion 1960-1990* by Georgina Howell, London, 1990; *Ten Sen Men* edited by Miyake Design Studio, Tokyo, 1990; *Issey Miyake by Irving Penn 1991-1992* edited by Miyake Design Studio, Tokyo, 1992; *Issey Miyake by Irving Penn 1993-1995* edited by Miyake Design Studio, Tokyo, 1995; *Japanese Design: A Survey Since 1950* by Kathryn B. Hiesinger and Felice Fischer, 1995; **articles**—"Issey Miyake" by M. Bancou in *American Fabrics and Fashions* (Columbia, South Carolina), No. 106, Winter 1976; "Issey Miyake" by M. Takahashi in *Idea* (Concord, New Hampshire), No. 144, 1977; "Issey Miyake, Clothes Designer" in *Zoom* (New York/Milan), December/January 1978-79; "The Man Who Put Show in Fashion Shows" by J. Lewis in *Far East Economic Review* (Hong Kong), 22 January 1979; "Issey Miyake Revisted" by M. Bancou in *American Fabrics and Fashions* (Columbia, South Carolina), No. 115. Spring 1979; "Issey Miyake" in *The New Yorker,* 8 and 15 November 1982; "Issey Miyake" in *Art and Design* (London), March 1985; "The Emperor's New Clothes" by Peter Popham in *Blueprint* (London), March 1985; "Issey Miyake's *Bodyworks*" in *Domus* (Milan), May 1985; "Miyake's Marvelous But Issey Art" by Lesley White in *Cosmopolitan* (London), August 1985; "The Man Who's Changing Clothes" by Jay Cocks in *Time* (New York), 21 October 1985; "1970-1986: le phénomène Issey Miyake" in *Elle* (Paris), 3 February 1986; "Issey Miyake: Dateless Fashion" in *Art and Design* (London), October 1986; "Issey Miyake: le plus sculpteur des couturiers" by Gilles Neret in *Connaissance des Arts* (Paris), March 1987; "Zen and the Art of Fashion" by Sally Angel in *Blueprint* (London), October 1987; "Issey Miyake Is Changing the Way Men View Clothes" by Robert Knafo in *Connoisseur* (New York), March 1988; "Eye of the Artists: Issey Miyake" in *Vogue* (New York), October 1988; "Image of Second Skin" by Mark Holborn in *Artforum* (New York), November 1988; "Modern Master" by Sally Brampton in *Elle* (London), June 1989; "The Cubism of Issey Miyake" by Richard Martin in *Textile & Text* (New York), December 4, 1990; "Pleats Please" by Irving Penn and Ingrid Sischy in *Interview* (New York), September 1990; "Issey Miyake: Designer for the Millennium" by Mary Tilton in *Threads* (Newtown, Connecticut), June/

July 1991; "Issey Does It" by Michael Gross in *New York,* 22 July 1991; "Clothes that Grow on You" by Suzy Bucks in *The Independent on Sunday* (London), 3 July 1994; "Art or Vanity?: Fashion's Ambiguity" by Amy M. Spindler in the *New York Times,* 13 December 1994; "Photogenic, But Out of Focus" by Anne-Marie Schiro in the *New York Times,* 20 March 1995; "Show, Not Clothes, Becomes the Message" by Suzy Menkes in the *International Herald Tribune* (Paris), 20 March 1995.

\*     \*     \*

For Issey Miyake, the kimono is a perfect garment which epitomises the oriental concept of clothing. It is in the East that we find the roots of his designs which have proved a radical departure from the established Western traditions of haute couture. Miyake does not conform to the Western mode of tailoring garments to fit the body, but produces large, geometric shapes, unadorned with additional detail, which rely on the quality of the fabric for their effect.

Having studied the traditions of his craft, both in Japan and in Europe, he broke away to produce loose, free styles which were sympathetic to the freedom demanded from their clothes by young people in the 1970s. By concentrating on the space between body and clothes, he has experimented with the way fabric interacts with the human form. To this effect, he admits that his thinking was influenced by the work of Madeleine Vionnet, who employed the bias cut for her most famous garments, produced in the 1920s and 1930s. The result was that her dresses glided over the surface of the body, rather than clinging to the silhouette. In order to achieve a similar feeling, Miyake has been influenced by traditional japanese techniques which simplified cutting to a minimum and utilized the natural width of the fabric. The traditional influences do not stop there, for many of his garments have been adapted from time-honoured prototypes. The basic shape of the kimono, of course, underlies many of his forms. The *sashiko* labourers' garment and the uniforms worn for the martial arts such as Judo or Kendo have been adapted from their hand-sewn originals and recreated in industrially produced fabrics. The long, hooded *tanzen* lounging robe has become a loose wraparound coat. Even the dull, functional uniform of the Japanese student was updated, using bright, exciting prints, in 1973. Fabrics too look to tradition for their inspiration. This is the wellspring of his "folklore" or "countryside" stripe, his indigo dyed cottons, and his Balinese checked weaves.

While influences upon him are apparent, he uses them with great innovation which he hopes will stimulate the imagination of the wearer. His clothes do not have to be worn in a precisely defined manner, and by changing a belt or a manner of wrapping, they can be adapted by the individual. These large expanses of fabric are like canvases to which are applied the most stunning or subtle designs, influenced by both Eastern and Western cultures. In his first New York collection in 1970, Miyake featured prints influenced by Japanese tattoos but devoted to the memories of Jimi Hendrix, Janis Joplin, and Marilyn Monroe. Later, his design team produced the more obviously Eastern patterns—The Spinnaker in Indian Magic, Mantra and Tantra. The cooperative work between the Issey Miyake Design Studio and a Japanese dye printer led in 1977 to the invention of laser-beam printing to produce beautiful, geometric patterns of graduated colors.

Miyake's 1989-90 fall/winter pleated collection redefined the relationship between the human body and its movement, and in the 1990s Miyake seems committed irregularly pleated fabric, introducing entirely new ideas for dress. The boldly conceptual nature of these designs appeals to a forward-thinking, creative clientèle whose identity is based in energy and originality. Through his experiments with the new and revitalisation of the old, Miyake has shown us the importance of fabrics for the clothes of the future.

—Hazel Clark

# MŁODOZENIEC, Jan

Polish illustrator and graphic designer

**Born:** Warsaw, 8 November 1929. **Education:** Studied poster design under Henryk Tomaszewski, at the Academy of Fine Arts, Warsaw, Diploma, 1955. **Family:** Married Monika Ruszewska in 1953; children: Stanislaw and Piotr. **Career:** Poster designer and illustrator, working with the publishers Czytelnik, Iskry, WAG, KAW, PIW, Polfilm, and the magazine *Poland,* in Warsaw, from 1952. Contributor to *Miesiecznik Literacki* magazine, 1966-81, and *Film* magazine, 1973-77. **Member:** ZPAP (Zwiazek Polskich Artystow Plastykow, Warsaw); Alliance Graphique Internationale. **Exhibitions:** Kordegarda Gallery, Warsaw, 1962; Galerie in der Biberstrasse, Vienna, 1963; Vystavni sin Hollar, Prague, 1975; Galerie am Prater, Berlin, 1978; National Museum, Poznan, 1979; Polska Institute, Stockholm, 1981; Poster Museum, Wilanow, 1984; Maison Gerbolier, La Salle, Italy, 1985; BWA Gallery, Zakopane, 1986; Teatr Nowy Gallery, Warsaw, 1986; Polnisches Kulturzentrum, Leipzig, 1988; Librairie Polonaise, Paris, 1988; Galeria von Oertzen, Frankfurt, 1991; Deutches Plakat Museum, Essen, 1991; Creation Gallery G'8, Tokyo, 1991; Galeria Grafiki i Plakatu, Warsaw, 1992; Galeria Design, Wroclaw, 1993; Muzeum Xrawerego Dunikowskiego, Warsaw, 1994; Galerie Espace Ambuel, Sion, 1995; Galerie Bernauer 111, Berlin, 1995. **Collections:** Poster Museum, Wilanow; National Museum, Poznan; Deutsches Plakat Museum, Essen; Stedelijk Museum, Amsterdam; Kunstgewerbe Museum, Zurich; Bibliotheque Forney, Paris; Biblioteka Narodowa, Warsaw; Israel Museum, Jerusalem; Lahden Taidemuseo, Lahti, Finland; Dansk Plakatmuseum, Aarhus. **Honors:** Internationale Buchkunst Ausstellung Medal, Leipzig, 1965, 1971; The Best Poster of the Year Award, Warsaw, 1965, 1966, 1970, 1972, 1973, 1979, 1981, 1983, 1985, 1987, 1989; Gold Medal, 8th International Poster Biennale, Warsaw, 1980; First Prize, Lahti Poster Biennale, 1983. **Address:** ul. Naruszewicza 3 m. 7, 02627 Warsaw, Poland.

## Works

*Birth Certificate* film poster, for CWF, 1961.
*Slawomir Mrozek: Le Dindon* poster, for Teatr Dramatyczny, Warsaw, 1961.
*Paul Hindemith: Quatre Temperaments* poster, for the Warsaw Opera, 1962.
*Cyrk* (elephant) circus poster, for WAG, 1965.
*F. Durrenmatt: Meteor* poster, for Teatr Dramatyczny, Warsaw, 1966.
*Jean Genet: The Maids* poster, for Teatr Ateneum, Warsaw, 1967.
*Giancarlo Menotti: Konsul* poster, for Teatr Wielki, Warsaw, 1972.
*Cyrk* (dancing horse) circus poster, for KAW, 1972.
*Ruggiero Leoncavallo: I Pagliacci* poster, for the Wroclaw Opera, 1974.

Jan Młodozeniec: advertising poster, "Gallery Graphics and Posters," 1992

*Cromwell* film poster, for Polfilm, 1974.
*The Conformist* film poster, for Polfilm, 1974.
*Klute* film poster, for Polfilm, 1975.
*New York, New York* film poster, for Polfilm, 1979.
*Igor Stravinsky: l'Histoire d'un Soldat* poster, for Teatr Wielki, Warsaw, 1983.
*Zamosc Shakespeare Festival* poster, for BWA Zamosc, 1985.
*Molière: School for Wives* poster, for Teatr Polski, Szczecin, 1985.
*Spring Salon of Polish Poster* exhibition poster, for Poster Museum, Wilanow, 1990.
*Lahti 10th Poster Biennale* exhibition poster, for Lahden Taidemuseo, 1993.
*Stanislaw Wyspianski: Legenda* poster, for Teatr Studio, Warsaw, 1993.
*The Jurors 14th International Poster Biennale* exhibition poster, for Poster Museum, Wilanow, 1994.
*The Poster Gallery* promotion poster and logo, for Hoia 40, Warsaw, 1995.
*Radio France: Saison Musicale* poster, for Radio France, 1995.
Book illustrations include—*Perla/The Pearl* by John Steinbeck, Warsaw, 1956; *The Taming of the Shrew* by William Shakespeare, Warsaw, 1972, *The Stories of Cronopios and Famas* by Cortazar,

Warsaw, 1973; *Le Diable au Corps* by Radiguet, Warsaw, 1979; *L'École des Femmes* by Molière, Warsaw, 1983.

## Publications

**On MŁODOZENIEC: books—***Who's Who in Graphic Art* edited by Walter Amstutz, Zurich, 1962, 1994, Dubendorf, 1982; *The Polish Poster* by Jerzy Wasniewsky and Jozef Mroszczak, Warsaw, 1968, 1972; *Polish Poster Art Today* by Szymon Bojko, Warsaw and London, 1972; *Modern Polish Posters* by Janina Fijalkowska, Paris, 1974; *Contemporary Polish Posters* edited by Joseph S. Czestochowski, New York, 1979; *Jan Młodozeniec,* exhibition catalogue with text by Zdzislaw Schubert, Poznan, 1979; *Posters by Members of the Alliance Graphique Internationale* edited by Rudolph de Harak, New York, 1986; *Jan Młodozeniec,* exhibition catalogue with text by Edmund Lewandowski, Warsaw, 1986; *World Graphic Design 1: Posters* by Yusaku Kamekura and Ikko Tanaka, Tokyo, 1988; *The Thames & Hudson Encyclopedia of Graphic Design and Designers* by Alan and Isabella Livingston, London, 1992; *100th Anniversary of Polish Poster Art* edited by Krzystof Dydo, Krakow, 1993; **articles—**"The poster designer Jan Młodozeniec" by Alan le Quernec in *NOVUM Gebrauchsgraphik* (Munich), no. 9, 1984; "Jan Młodozeniec" by Ewa Kruswewska in *Graphis* (Zurich), no. 236, 1985; "Jan Młodozeniec" by Noboru Matsuura in *Creation* (Tokyo), no. 7, 1990; "100 Graphic Designers of the World" in *IDEA* (Tokyo), no. 240, 1993.

\*

Design is a line from Altamira, round the Greek vase, into Rembrandt's black, the circles of Vincent's sun, the sonorous color of posters is Jean Avril at the Moulin Rouge. It is Mucha, Steinlen, The Beggarstaff, Bernhard's shoe, Dada, Matisse, Colin, and the Salon Metro....

Posters and color are flowing through town. Flashes of art amidst the monotony of commerce are masterpieces by François, Fukuda, Chwast, and Tomaszewski.

Posters comprise ideas, color, layout, drawing and lettering, all closely knit and equally significant. The graphic designer, tailor, shoemaker ... all deal with subject matter, format, deadlines. The illustration is wife to the printed text, which is concise, equivocal and peripheral, with fantasy, synthesis and decoration in between.

Theater, poetry, cinema, music and painting are all worth promoting and recommending.

IDEA + COLOUR + LAYOUT + DRAWING + LETTERING = POSTER.

—Jan Młodozeniec

\*    \*    \*

If we want to understand the artist's way of thinking, it is important to note that Jan Młodozeniec is the son of a prominent Polish poet. A word, the power of writing, the beauty of a letter, its shape and weight—these particularly interest him. Yet, this leader in the Polish Poster School is also the master of drawing. His is simple, linear, realized with speed and energy mixed with accurate decisiveness.

Many of his early posters, in the 1950s, were large-scale drawings with lettering incorporated into the overall composition. Although very personal, they were always easily readable. At the same time, in his illustrations, Młodozeniec worked in almost an etcher's style, retaining the traditional Central European approach toward graphic art, as formulated in Munich and Vienna at the beginning of the century. The maze of lines, with heavy areas of black and white, produced a very expressionistic mood.

Slowly, his compositions, posters, private drawings, and illustrated books began to change. The artist reduced the illustrations to purely linear drawings, full of air and lightness. Despite this simplicity, they offer a nearly three-dimensional effect. His "purification" of the poster went even further. The role of details and ornament diminished, but the use of color became more extensive. The posters of the last fifteen years are built on a basis of black, linear compositions separating flat, deep colors. The effect is very powerful. Despite flatness, the colors fight aggressively, making the posters vibrate with energy.

This virtuoso at hand-lettering has developed his own style of integrating text with picture in his posters and has, as well, sometimes even successfully used his skills to make entire short books of poetry by hand. Some popular poetry books, priced at around fifty cents and printed by the hundreds of thousands, were "illuminated" by Młodozeniec in the fashion of medieval monks—but available for all.

Some critics have, at times, claimed that Młodozeniec was declining. They were wrong. The artist is developing his own distinctive style, his tides rising according to natural progress. He doesn't seek stardom. Calm, closed within himself, Młodozeniec lives in his own world of color, line, and ever-important words. He tries to improve, despite early success in the 1950s, knowing his abilities as well as his limitations and flaws, and he continues to master the good, eliminate the bad. This unusual self-discipline and enormous talent put him at the very top of the Polish graphic-art elite, then and now.

—Jan Sawka

# MOGENSEN, Børge (Vestergård)

Danish furniture and textile designer

**Born:** Aalborg, 13 April 1914. **Education:** Apprenticed to a cabinet maker in Aalborg, 1934-36; studied at the Konsthandvaerkskolan, Copenhagen, 1936-38; studied furniture design, under Kaare Klint, at the Royal Danish Academy of Arts, Copenhagen, 1938-41. **Family:** Married Alice Kluver Krohn in 1942. **Career:** Worked as an assistant to Mogens Koch, Kaare Klint, and other designers, in Copenhagen, 1938-42; furniture designer and head of the FDB Danish Consumers Cooperative, Copenhagen, 1942-50; freelance designer, Copenhagen, from 1950: design consultant, with Lis Ahlmann, to C. Olesen textile company, from 1953 designed for Soborgs Moebelfabrik, Fredericia Stolefabrik, Karl Andersson, Erhard Rasmussen, P. Lauritzen, Fritz Hansen, I. Christiansen, Jacob Kjaer, Ove Lander, L. Pontoppidan, Rudolf Rasmussens Snedkerier, Boligens Byggeskabe, and others. Assistant to Kaare Klint, 1945-47, and professor from 1947, at the Royal Danish Academy of Arts, Copenhagen. **Exhibitions:** Danish Cabinetworkers Guild exhibitions, Copenhagen, 1939-62; *Die*

*Gute Industrieform,* Kunstverein, Hamburg, 1955; *Two Centuries of Danish Design,* Victoria and Albert Museum, London, 1968 (toured); *Modern Chairs,* Whitechapel Art Gallery, London, 1970; *Børge Mogensen: Møbler/Lis Ahlmann: Tekstiler,* Kunstindustrimuseet, Copenhagen, 1974; *Nordisk Industridesign,* Konstindustrimuseet, Oslo, 1976; *Scandinavian Modern Design 1880-1980,* Cooper-Hewitt Museum, New York, 1982; *Design Since 1945,* Philadelphia Museum of Art, 1983; *Design au Danemark 1950-1987,* Château de Brion, Dordogne, 1987. **Collections:** Kunstindustrimuseet, Copenhagen; Statens Kunstfond, Copenhagen; Louisiana Museum, Humelbaek. **Honors:** Bissens Stipend, Copenhagen, 1945; Eckersberg Medal, Copenhagen, 1950; Silver Medal, Danish Trade Fair, Copenhagen, 1953; Cabinetmakers Guild Award of Honour, Copenhagen, 1958; Furniture Manufacturers Association Prize, Copenhagen, 1971; C. F. Hansen Medal, Copenhagen, 1972. Honorary Royal Designer for Industry, Royal Society of Arts, London, 1972. **Died:** Gentofte, 5 October 1972.

## Works

Drop-sided sofa in beech with woollen cushions, 1945, produced by Fritz Hansen from 1962.
Chair in natural beech with plaited hessian seat, for FDB Danish Consumers' Cooperative, 1947.
Chair in oak or oiled beechwood with woven cane seat, for FDB Danish Consumers' Cooperative, 1948.
Easy chair in oak with natural leather seat and back, for Erhard Rasmussen, 1950.
Table in oak with black slate top, for Erhard Rasmussen, 1951.
Adjustable tilting armchair in oak with stretched leather seat and back, for Erhard Rasmussen, 1955.
Dining chair in oak with woven cane seat, for P. Lauritzen, 1957.
*Cotil Collection* cotton drapery fabric, for C. Olesen, 1957 (with Lis Ahlmann).
*Spanish Chair* in natural oak with oxhide seat and back, for Fredericia Stolefabrik, 1958.
End-table and armchair with footstool in oak, for Fredericia Stolefabrik, 1960.
*Cotil Collection* rug, for C. Olesen, 1960 (with Lis Ahlmann).
*Asserbo 504* chair, for Karl Andersson, 1964.

## Publications

**On MOGENSEN: books—***Dansk Mobelkuns* by Viggo Sten Møller and Svend Erik Møller, Copenhagen, 1951; *Danish Chairs,* edited by Nanna and Jørgen Ditzel, Copenhagen, 1954; *Modern Danish Furniture* by Esbjørn Hiort, New York, London, and Stuttgart, 1956; *Modern Danish Textiles,* edited by Bent Salicath and Arne Karlsen, Copenhagen, 1959; *Modern Scandinavian Furniture* by Ulf Hård af Segerstad, Copenhagen, 1963, London, 1964; *Furniture Designed by Børge Mogensen* by Arne Karlsen, Copenhagen, 1968; *Modern Chairs 1918-1970,* exhibition catalogue with text by Carol Hogben and others, London, 1970; *Børge Mogensen: Møbler/Lis Ahlmann: Tekstiler,* exhibition catalogue, Copenhagen, 1974; *History of Modern Furniture* by Karl Mang, Stuttgart, 1978, London, 1979; *Scandinavian Modern Design 1880-1980* edited by David Revere McFadden, New York, 1982; *Twentieth Century Design: Furniture* by Penny Sparke, London, 1986; *Modern Furniture Classics* by Miriam Stimpson, London, 1987.

# MOISEIWITSCH, Tanya

British stage designer

**Born:** London, 3 December 1914. **Education:** Studied at the Central School of Arts and Crafts, London, 1928-32. **Family:** Married Felix Krish in 1942 (died). **Career:** Stage designer, working for repertory theatre, from 1934, and for the opera, from 1947; designed for the Abbey Theatre, Dublin, 1935-39, Q Theatre and Duchess Theatre, London, 1940, the Oxford Playhouse, 1941-44, the Old Vic Company in Liverpool and Bristol, 1944-46, New Theatre, London, 1945-46, Shakespeare Memorial Theatre, Stratford upon Avon, from 1949, Shakespeare Festival productions in Stratford, Ontario, from 1953, the National Theatre Company at the Old Vic, London, 1968-75, and others. Principal designer, Tyrone Guthrie Theatre, Minneapolis, from 1963; consultant designer, Crucible Theatre, Sheffield, 1971-73; associate director, Stratford Festival Stage, Ontario, from 1974. **Honors:** Honorary Doctorates: Birmingham University, 1964, University of Waterloo, Ontario, 1977, University of Toronto, Ontario, 1988; Commander, Order of the British Empire, 1976; Honorary Fellow, Ontario College of Art, Toronto, 1979; Diploma of Honour, Canadian Conference of Arts. **Address:** 17B St. Alban's Studios, St. Alban's Grove, London W8 5BT, England.

## Works

Stage productions include—*The Faithful,* Westminster Theatre, London, 1934; *Deuce of Jacks,* Abbey Theatre, Dublin, 1935; *The Golden Cuckoo,* Duchess Theatre, London, 1940; *Dr. Faustus,* Old Vic Company at Liverpool Playhouse, 1944; *John Gabriel Borkman,* Old Vic Company at Liverpool Playhouse, 1944; *The School for Scandal,* Old Vic Company at Liverpool Playhouse, 1945; *The Beaux Stratagem,* Old Vic Company at Theatre Royal, Bristol, 1945; *Twelfth Night,* Old Vic Company at Theatre Royal, Bristol, 1945; *Point Valaine,* Old Vic Company at Liverpool Playhouse, 1945; *Uncle Vanya,* Old Vic Company at the New Theatre, London, 1945; *The Critic,* Old Vic Company at the New Theatre, 1945; *Weep for the Cyclops,* Old Vic Company at Theatre Royal, Bristol, 1946; *Time of Your Life,* Lyric Theatre Hammersmith, London, 1946; *Cyrano de Bergerac,* Old Vic Company at the New Theatre, London, 1946; *Bless the Bride,* Adelphi Theatre, London, 1947; *Peter Grimes,* Royal Opera House/Covent Garden, London, 1947; *The Beggar's Opera,* English Opera Group, Aldeburgh, 1948; *Lady Rohesia,* Sadler's Wells Opera, London, 1948; *The Cherry Orchard,* Old Vic Company at the New Theatre, London, 1948; *Henry VIII,* Shakespeare Memorial Theatre, Stratford upon Avon, 1949; *Don Giovanni,* Sadler's Wells Opera, London, 1949; *A Month in the Country,* Old Vic Company at the New Theatre, London, 1949; *Treasure Hunt,* Apollo Theatre, London, 1949; *Captain Carvallo,* St. James's Theatre, London, 1950; *The Holly and the Ivy,* Duchess Theatre, London, 1950; *Home at Seven,* Wyndham's Theatre, London, 1950; *Romersholm,* Winter Garden Theatre, London, 1950; *Richard II,* Shakespeare Memorial Theatre, Stratford upon Avon, 1950; *The Passing Day,* Lyric Theatre Hammersmith, London, 1951; *A Midsummer Night's Dream,* Old Vic Theatre, London, 1951; *Henry IV,* parts I and 2, Shakespeare Memorial Theatre, Stratford upon Avon, 1951; *Henry V,* Shakespeare Memorial Theatre, Stratford upon Avon, 1951; *Othello,* Shakespeare Memorial Theatre, Stratford upon Avon, 1952; *Timon of Athens,* Old Vic Theatre, London, 1952; *The Deep Blue Sea,* Globe Theatre, London, 1952; *Julius Caesar,* Old Vic Theatre, London, 1953; *Henry VIII,* Old Vic Theatre, London, 1953; *The Matchmaker,* Theatre Royal, London, 1954; *Oedipus Rex,* Shakespeare Festival Stage, Stratford, Ontario, 1954; *A Life in the Sun,* Assembly Hall, Edinburgh, 1955; *The Cherry Orchard,* Piccolo Teatro, Milan, 1955; *Measure for Measure,* Shakespeare Memorial Theatre, Stratford upon Avon, 1956; *The Two Gentlemen of Verona,* Old Vic Theatre, London, 1957; *Much Ado About Nothing,* Shakespeare Memorial Theatre, Stratford upon Avon, 1958; *The Merchant of Venice,* Habimah Theatre, Tel Aviv, 1958; *Biederman and the Fire-raisers,* Habimah Theatre, Tel Aviv, 1958; *All's Well That Ends Well,* Shakespeare Memorial Theatre, Stratford upon Avon, 1959; *The Wrong Side of the Park,* Cambridge Theatre, London, 1960; *Ondine,* Royal Shakespeare Company at the Aldwych Theatre, London, 1961; *Coriolanus,* Shakespeare Festival Stage, Stratford, Ontario, 1961; *The Alchemist,* Old Vic Theatre, London, 1962; *Hamlet,* Tyrone Guthrie Theatre, Minneapolis, 1963; *The Miser,* Tyrone Guthrie Theatre, 1963; *The Three Sisters,* Tyrone Guthrie Theatre, 1963; *Saint Joan,* Tyrone Guthrie Theatre, 1964; *Volpone,* Tyrone Guthrie Theatre, 1964; *The Way of the World,* Tyrone Guthrie Theatre, 1965; *The Cherry Orchard,* Tyrone Guthrie Theatre, 1965; *As You Like It,* Tyrone Guthrie Theatre, 1966; *Skin of Our Teeth,* Tyrone Guthrie Theatre, 1966; *The House of Atreus,* Tyrone Guthrie Theatre, 1967; *Peter Grimes,* Metropolitan Opera, New York, 1967; *Volpone,* National Theatre Company at the Old Vic, 1968; *Uncle Vanya,* Tyrone Guthrie Theatre, 1969; *Cymbeline,* Shakespeare Festival Stage, Stratford, Ontario, 1970; *The Barber of Seville,* Brighton Festival, Sussex, 1971; *The Government Inspector,* Tyrone Guthrie Theatre, 1973; *The Misanthrope,* National Theatre Company at the Old Vic, 1973; *The Imaginary Invalid,* Shakespeare Festival Stage, Stratford, Ontario, 1974; *Phaedra Britannica,* National Theatre Company at the Old Vic, 1975; *The Voyage of Edgar Allan Poe,* Minnesota Opera Company, Minneapolis, 1976; *Rigoletto,* Metropolitan Opera, New York, 1977; *All's Well That Ends Well,* Shakespeare Festival Stage, Stratford, Ontario, 1977; *The Double Dealer,* National Theatre, London, 1978; *Red Roses for Me,* Abbey Theatre, Dublin, 1980; *La Traviata,* Metropolitan Opera, New York, 1981; *The Clandestine Marriage,* Compass Theatre Company at Albery Theatre, London, 1984 (toured); *The Government Inspector,* Festival Theatre, Stratford, Ontario, 1985.

## Publications

**On MOISEIWITSCH: books**—*Showcase* by Roy Newquist, New York, 1966; *The Biographical Encyclopaedia and Who's Who of the American Theatre* edited by Walter Rigdon, New York, 1966; *Stage Design Throughout the World 1970-1975* by René Hainaux and Nicole Leclercq, Brussels and London, 1976; *British Theatre Design* edited by John Goodwin, London, 1989.

*       *       *

Moiseiwitsch began her career at the Abbey Theatre in Dublin on a stage that demanded that less be more. She thus developed a sense of design in which—once she and the director had decided on the visual metaphor of the production—she was able to sweep

away the rich, multiple effects often intended by other designers in favor of a bold and very clear visual picture in both sets and costumes. Never allowing these supports for a play to interfere with or obscure the production, she learned to paint her visual effects with a large brush so that a larger-than-life world was created. When she was able to design her own theatre stage in consultation with Tyrone Guthrie, she created a bold thrust stage on which her costumes could be sculpted by light coming from widely divergent angles. If one were to think of a single phrase to describe her sense of the actor moving against a setting, it would be moving "sculpture in space." All Moiseiwitsch's settings are designed to create a spatial world for the actor, and all of her costumes are sculptures of fabric, trim, and color; they boldly present both the character of the actor and the world that he inhabits.

Because of the publicity given to *Oedipus Rex* and *The House of Atreus,* she also came to be known for the brilliance of her Greek masks, heightened and subtly exaggerated to give exactly the right expression that she and Guthrie had decided upon for the production. While an almost Victorian heavy-handedness and complexity in costume design has begun to be popular, it is instructive to look back at the best of Moiseiwitsch's work and see the basic simplicity and focus of her esthetic, even when she was designing rich, larger-than-life productions. She is a theatrical designer who has always worked for the essence of the play rather than surface display.

—Douglas A. Russell

# MOLLINO, Carlo

Italian architect, photographer, interior, exhibition, and industrial designer

---

**Born:** Turin, 6 May 1905. **Education:** Studied architecture at the University of Turin, 1927-31, Dip. Arch. 1931. **Career:** Architectural designer, working with his engineer father Mollino, Turin, 1928-31; freelance architect from 1931, exhibition and furniture designer from 1935, and car and aeronautical designer from 1954. Professor, Accademia di San Lucca, Turin, and Politecnico of Turin. **Exhibitions:** *Carlo Mollino: Aeronautica e Architettura,* at the Venice Biennale, 1978; *Architettura 28-78: Carlo Mollino,* Palazzo delle Stelline, Milan, 1979; *Omaggio a Mollino: Dal Designall'Habitat,* Fiera del Levante, Bari, 1982; *Carlo Mollino: Premier Designer des Années '50,* Galerie Denis Bosselet, Paris, 1984; *From Mackintosh to Mollino,* Barry Friedman Gallery, New York, 1985; *Carlo Mollino: Architettura, Mobili e Ambientazioni,* Spazio Trau, Turin, 1985; *Carlo Mollino: Cronaca,* Fulvio Ferrari Gallery, Turin, 1985; *Carlo Mollino: Primo Designer,* Southern California Institute of Architecture, Vico Morcote, Switzerland, 1985; Centre de Creation Industrielle, Paris, 1989. **Died:** Turin, in 1973.

## Works

Headquarter offices and interiors, for the Societa Ippica Torinese, Turin, 1937.
Furniture, for Lisa and Gio Ponti, Milan, 1940.
L'Elettrica shop interiors, Turin, 1941.

Radiogram, for Deaglio, Turin, 1941.
Furniture, for the San Giuseppe College, Turin, 1941.
Trademark logo, for Varda leather goods, 1944.
Offices and interiors, for Apelli e Varesio, Turin, 1945.
Offices and interiors, for Einaudi publishing house, Turin, 1945.
Lamp with counterweight, for P. Foa, Turin, 1947.
Furniture, for La Vigna Gallery, Florence, 1948.
Furniture, for the Underwood office, Turin, 1949.
Singer store interiors, Turin, 1950.
Offices and interiors, for the Lattes publishing house, Turin, 1951.
Exhibition stand at the Turin Motor Show, for AGIP-Supercortemaggiore, 1953.
Bar furnishings, for the Societa Lombardia Petroli, Turin, 1955.
Colour scheme of the De Havilland-Heron aircraft, 1956.
Cutlery range, for Reed and Barton, 1960.
Montanaro camera shop interiors, Turin, 1962.
Writing desk, pendulum clock and table sculpture, for Ada Minola, Turin, 1966.
Furnishings and interiors, for the Teatro Regio, Turin, 1970.

## Publications

**By MOLLINO: books**—*Completa y Veridica Historia de Picasso y el Cubismo,* Turin, 1945; *Il Messaggio della Camera Oscura,* Turin, 1945; (with F. Valdacchino) *Architettura, Arte e Tecnica,* Turin, 1947; *Il Linguaggio dell'Architettura: Il Volto della Citta,* Turin, 1949; *Introduzione al Discesismo,* Rome, 1951; (with G. Segni) *Istruzione ad Uso dei Candidati ed Asporanti alla Qualifica di Maestro Scelto,* Milan, 1953.

**On MOLLINO: books**—*Ritratti Ambientati di Carlo Mollino* by E. Scopinich, Milan, 1945; *Italy at Work: Her Renaissance in Design Today,* exhibition catalogue by Meyric Rogers, Rome, 1950; *Furniture for Modern Interiors* by Mario Dal Fabro, New York, 1954; *World Furniture* edited by Helena Hayward, London, 1965, 1981; *Carlo Mollino: Architecture as Autobiography* by G. Brino, Milan, 1979, London, 1987; *A Century of Chair Design* edited by Frank Russell, London, 1980; *Carlo Mollino: Premier Designer, Dernier Artisan des Années '50* by G. Brino, Turin and Paris, 1984; *Mid-Century: Furniture of the 1950s* by Cara Greenberg, London, 1984; *Carlo Mollino: Cronaca* by F. Ferrari, Turin, 1985; *Polaroid Carlo Mollino* by G. Arpino and D. Palazzoli, Turin, 1986; *Italian Design: 1870 to the Present* by Penny Sparke, London and New York, 1988; *Italian Modern: A Design Heritage* by Giovanni Albera and Nicolas Monti, New York, 1989; *L'Etrange Univers de l'Architecte Carlo Mollino,* Paris, 1989.

# MONGUZZI, Bruno

Swiss graphic and exhibition designer

**Born:** Mendrisio, Ticino, 21 August 1941. **Education:** Studied at the École des Arts Décoratifs, Geneva, St. Martin's School of Art, London, and the London College of Printing, 1956-61; Swiss Federal Diploma. **Family:** Married Anna Boggeri in 1969; children: Nicolas and Elisa. **Career:** Graphic designer, in the Studio Boggeri, Milan, 1961-63; freelance designer, working in Milan and London, 1963-65; designer, at Gagnon and Valkus studio, in New York and

Montreal, 1965-67; freelance designer, in Milan, from 1968; has collaborated on exhibition designs with Roberto Sambonet and Giancarlo Ortelli, in Milan, from 1972. Lecturer in typographic design and gestalt psychology, at the Cini Foundation, Venice, 1963-65; professor of typographic design and the psychology of perception, at the School of Applied arts, Lugano, from 1971; IBM Fellow, Aspen Design Conference, Colorado, 1981; visiting professor, Cooper Union, New York, 1982, 1987. **Member:** Alliance Graphique Internationale, Paris, 1979. **Exhibitions:** Museo de Arte, Sao Paulo, 1974; Artek Gallery, Helsinki, 1976; *Della Pazzia,* Galleria d'Arte, Milan, 1977; Casa del Mantegna, Mantua, 1978; Palazzo Bagatti Valsecchi, Milan, 1980; *Lo Studio Boggeri 1933-81,* at the Milan Triennale, 1981; *Il Progetto Grafico,* Milan, 1981; New York Public Library, Pound Ridge, 1982; *L'Italie d'Aujourd'hui,* Nice, 1985; *Bio 11,* Liubliana, 1986; *L'Image de la Lettre,* Centre Georges Pompidou, Paris, 1987; Art Directors Club, New York, 1987, 1989; XIII Brno Graphics Biennale, 1988. **Collections:** Centre Georges Pompidou; Stedelijk Museum, Amsterdam; Museum of Modem Art, New York. **Honors:** Prix Cailler, 1960; Bodoni Prize, 1971. **Address:** 6866 Meride, Switzerland.

## Works

*Processo per il Museo* exhibition design, for the Accademia di Brera, Milan, 1976.
*Della Pazzia* portfolio of drawings, for the Galleria d'Arte, Milan, 1977.
*Lo Studio Boggeri 1933-1981* exhibition catalogue design, for the Milan Triennale, 1981.
Signage, for the new Museo Cantonale d'Arte, Lugano, 1987.
*Il Ticino e i suoi Fotografi* exhibition poster, for the Museo Cantonale d'Arte, and the Kunsthaus, Zürich, 1987.
*Oskar Schlemmer/Igor Strawinsky: Les Noces* exhibition poster, for the Museo Cantonale d'Arte, 1988.
*Flavio Paolucci/Alberto Flammer* exhibition design, poster, and catalogues, for the Museo Cantonale d'Arte, 1988.
*Photographie aus der Sowjetunion* poster, for the Kunsthaus, 1989.

## Publications

**By MONGUZZI: books**—*Note per una Tipografia Informativa,* Venice, 1964; *Lo Studio Boggeri 1933-1981,* Milan, 1981; *Piet Zwart: The Typographical Work 1923-1933,* Milan, 1983.

**On MONGUZZI: books**—*Due Dimensioni,* Milan, 1964; *Who's Who in Graphic Art* edited by Walter Amstutz, Dubendorf, 1982; *Top Graphic Design* by F. H. K. Henrion, Zürich, 1983; *12 Grafici dell'AGI* edited by the Alliance Graphique Internationale, Milan, 1984; *Posters by Members of the Alliance Graphique Internationale* edited by Rudolph de Harak, New York, 1986; *Alle Radici della Comunicazione Visiva Italiana* by Heinz Waibl, Como, 1988; *Basic Typography: Design with Letters* by Rudi Ruegg, Zürich, 1989.

*

Perfection was not enough. What was to me the end, was to him the beginning. And I would walk back to the desk to look for the right mistake. One day he had explained to me the spider's web theory. Most Swiss design was only perfect, like the spider's web.

And useless. The web became useful only when injured by the entangled fly. It is there, with Antonio Boggeri, that the hunt began.

—Bruno Monguzzi

\*      \*      \*

That appropriate visual forms can arise only in response to the careful analysis of a problem is not an obscure idea in the late twentieth century; however, many lesser designers who purport to practice this concept, in actuality bow to the dictates of fashion and produce little more than stylistic affectation—rarely the answer to a client's needs. Bruno Monguzzi, however, conscientiously and successfully tailors solution to problem. He is as at home with three-dimensional design for exhibitions as he is with two-dimensional catalogues, posters, and printed ephemera. The entire scope of his work, though broad, reflects his careful consideration of each detail in relation to the desired communication. For example, in his poster "Di mano in mano, da uomo a uomo," the purpose of which was to request volunteers to aid the victims of the 1980 Irpinia earthquake, Monguzzi used a subtle gray rectangle surprinted over the main image to act as a soft veil, building a psychological distance between the viewer and the powerful, black image of the mourners. Such emotive power he achieved amid typographic elements interacting structurally with two squares and a rectangle which, in turn, overlap on a golden-section grid!

A rationalist by character, his Swiss training in the late 1950s introduced him to the typography of El Lissitzky and Piet Zwart, as well as the pioneers of the Swiss school. Later, his visual vocabulary was enriched, and the rigidity of Swiss formalism softened as a result of his associations with Italian design, most notably with Studio Boggeri, and with the early 1960s New York school of Herb Lubalin, Gene Federico, and Louis Dorfsman. These influences yielded a hybrid which is as logical in approach as the Swiss but, at the same time, is humanist.

By his own admission, Monguzzi is an outsider among his peers in the design field. He welcomes the role of intermediary in the process of public communication. In exercising this role, he insists on selecting appropriate tools to fulfill the criteria of a problem and generally operates intentionally outside the stifling confines of current trends. He gets right to the point—succinct communication. As Monguzzi himself says, "I find our society a bit noisy. I just would like to contribute a little silence."

—Ken Carls

# MONÖ, Rune (Gotthard)

Swedish industrial, graphic, and interior designer

**Born:** Helsingborg, 4 June 1920. **Education:** Educated at Karolinska Läroverket, Örebro, until 1937; Tekniska Gymnasiet, Örebro, 1938-41; mainly self-taught in industrial design, from 1941. **Family:** Married Irene Mary Gustavsson in 1943; children: Ralph and Elisabeth. **Career:** Engineering planner and draughtsman, SAAB Aeroplanaktiebolaget, Linköping, 1941-43; head of interior and graphic draughting studio, ABA/SAS Aktiebolaget Aerotransport/ Scandinavian Airlines System, Stockholm, 1943-49; freelance draughtsman and product designer, Täby, 1949-57; industrial design consultant, establishing firm AB Industridesign, Stockholm,

1957-64, and AB Rune Monö, Industridesign (now AB Rune Monö Design), Täby, from 1964; designed for LKB-Produkter, 1952-88, Alweg monorail company, 1954-57, Skagersviks Industrier, 1960-69, ICA-Forbundet, 1962-72, BT Bygg och Transportekonomi, 1965-73, Draco, 1972-79, Dynapac, 1973-80, Arcu Armaturindustri, 1978-86, Stiga, 1979-85, and others. Guest instructor, at the Konstfackskolan, Stockholm, the Högskolan for Design och Konsthantverk, Göteborg, and other schools in Sweden and Norway, from 1970. Co-founder, 1957, and president, 1957-61, Society of Swedish Industrial Designers; copyright panel member, 1976, and board member, 1979-85, Svensk Form Society of Crafts and Design, Stockholm. **Exhibitions:** *Hemmets redskap,* Östermans, Stockholm, 1958; *Svenska Industridesigner,* Nordiska Kompaniet, Stockholm, 1959; *Unga Nordiska Formgivare,* Röhsska Konstslöjdmuseet, Göteborg, 1962; *Swedish Industrial Design,* Design Centre, London, 1966; *Schwedische Form,* Design Center, Stuttgart, 1969; *Industridesign i Norden,* Kunstindustri Museet, Oslo, 1976; *Fran Revolution till nya uttryck,* Nationalmuseum, Stockholm, 1988. **Collections:** Nationalmuseum, Stockholm. **Honors:** First Prize, SAS Aircraft Emblem Competition, 1947; Svensk Form/God Form Award, Stockholm, 1961; Prize of Honour, Svensk Form, Stockholm, 1964; Gute Industrieform Award, West Germany, 1964; Best International Product Award, Toronto, 1984; Ütmarkt Svensk Form Award, Stockholm, 1985. **Address:** AB Rune Monö Design, Box 2023, 183 02 Täby, Sweden.

## Works

Aircraft logotypes, interior, and exterior designs, for SAS, 1945-64.

Logotypes and electronic medical instruments, for LKB-Produkter, 1952-88.

Monorail train and railway installation designs, for Alweg, 1954-57.

Grinding machine, for Ulvsunda Verkstader, 1958.

Petrol gauge, for Ljungmans Verkstader, 1959.

Intercommunications system, for Centrum Radio, Stockholm, 1960.

Stainless steel dishes, for Olofstrom, 1960-61.

Kitchen designs, for Skagersviks Industrier, 1960-69.

*Kalmar* lightweight car, for Swedish Post Office Administration, produced by Kalmar Verkstader, 1961.

Logotypes and corporate design programme, for ICA-Forbundet, 1962-72.

Television apparatus, for ITT Stockholm, 1963-65

Printing machine, for Grafiska Maskinaktiebolaget, 1964-67.

Elevating pallet trucks, for BT Bygg-och Transportekonomi, 1965-73.

Asthma inhalers, for Draco, 1972-79.

Trucks and roadwork machinery, for Dynapac, 1973-80.

Design function analysis system, for Sveriges Mekanförbund, 1974.

Clinical chemistry multi-purpose analysers, for Clinicon, 1978-79.

*Colorado* bathroom and kitchen sink mixers, for Arcu Armaturindustri, 1978-86.

Lawnmowers, for Stiga, 1979-85.

Packaging machines, for Norden Packaging Machinery, 1985-86.

## Publications

**By MONÖ: books**—(with others) *Mekanresukat 65024: Designarbete,* Stockholm, 1965; (with others) *Mekanresultat 71018: Modeller och modellarbete,* Stockholm, 1971; *Mekanresultat 74203: Analys och vardering av design funktioner,* Stockholm, 1974;

**Rune Monö: Ultramicrotome equipment, for LKB-Produkter, 1983**

*Produktdesign,* Lund, 1975; (with others) *Mekanresultat 76006: Maskiners anpassning till människan,* Stockholm, 1976; *Mekanresultat 76205: Maskinersforrn och gestalt,* Stockholm, 1976; *Närmare,* Stockholm, 1981; *Designutredning, report,* Stockholm, 1982; (with others) *Ting till synes,* Stockholm, 1985; *Njutningen av att akta tag,* Stockholm, 1988.

**On MONÖ: books**—*Forma Sueca* by Åke Stavenow and Åke H. Huldt, Göteborg, 1961; *Konsthantverk, Konstindustri, Design 1875-1975* by Dag Widman, Stockholm, 1975; *Den Svenska Formen* by Monica Boman and others, Stockholm, 1985; **articles**—"Firma for form" in *Industria* (Stockholm), no. 5, 1958; "Firma for produktveckling" in *Form* (Stockholm), no. 8, 1963; "God design och formgivning" in *Jern og Industrien* (Copenhagen), no. 7, 1972; "Designern far koll pa tyckandet" in *Industria* (Stockholm), June 1972; "Från patent till produkt" in *Forrn* (Stockholm), no. 8, 1983.

\*

Knowledge, imagination, and skill are essential to the industrial designer. The way he uses them differs according to who he is, the object concerned, the situation as well as current trends and ideas in society.

To me, professional rules and philosophies can be summed up in one particular concept. Having started my design career at a time when to fight against superficial "styling" seemed necessary, and

later trying to establish the profession in industry without locking it into doctrinaire functionalism, I see the word "honesty" as a guideline towards technique without dogmatism, an attractiveness without formalism.

It should be self-evident (but to some people it is not) that the purpose of industrial design lies outside the designer. It is hidden in the needs of human beings he will never know personally. He has to fulfil that purpose, making his way through a jungle of industrial technologies and economic conditions. He will succeed if he looks upon them as challenges rather than limitations. He has to leave prestige and the free artist's ideas of self expression behind, and be very clear about the specific role of his own profession.

The education of future industrial designers—trying to give them knowledge, imagination and skill—is still in its childhood, but is developing and growing. Their need for a comprehensive capacity is continuously increasing. Industrial design, however, can never be fully established as an integral part of product development until information about design practice and teaching in design management are incorporated into the education of future leaders in industry and commercial society. Industrial design has to be regarded as just as important as technology and marketing.

—Rune Monö

\*    \*    \*

When a special edition of a leading industrial journal was published in the autumn of 1988 with the title "Survival through Design," it went without saying that Rune Monö's name would be among the collaborators. Almost as obvious was the title of his article: "A little catechism for collaboration in design." Monö is not only one of Sweden's leading industrial designers, but is also one of the profession's idealists. As an idealist he is above all a champion of good work ethics.

Rune Monö's ideology is anchored in the idealistic post-war period, when a new and better world for all was to be built, and where an industrial designer would have a key role. He was strongly influenced by the objective philosophy that supported Scandinavian Design, which at this time was enjoying its greatest period. Monö wished to convey its concept of the good life in a beautiful home to a more pronounced engineering design.

During the less idealistic 1980s, Rune Monö adhered even closer to his original attitude that good design can only develop from a basis of good morale. As a veteran within the profession, he is assuredly conscious that successful activity demands great adaptiveness and willingness to compromise, but at the same time he rigorously maintains that there are principles that the good designer must never renounce. With this attitude Rune Monö has captured an undisputed position as one of the most honest of design's representatives, not only from the perspective of the patron, but also the customer.

This is not the place to give a detailed account of Rune Monö's design catechism. But its significance is: absolute honour. For instance you must never work with competing products. You should have a clear purpose and always work with clearly defined goals. In all areas you should give decipherable instructions and clear justifications. You should be prepared to collaborate with your patron during the entire length of the product's life. Regard others with appreciation and yourself with humour.

Rune Monö represents, both in theory and in practice, the classical attitude that aesthetics and ethics are inseparably bound with each other; that beauty and morals cannot be divided; that good industrial form is also honourable!

—Ulf Hård af Segerstad

# MONTANA, Claude

French fashion designer

**Born:** Paris, in 1949. **Career:** Freelance designer of fashion jewelry, in London, 1971-72; fashion designer, for MacDouglas leathers, Complice menswear, Ferrer y Sentis knitwear, and others, in Paris, from 1975; founded Claude Montana fashion company, with shops on the rue de Grenelle, Paris, 1977; launched *Montana Pour Femme* fragrance, 1986. **Address:** 31 rue de Grenelle, 75001 Paris, France.

**Publications**

**On MONTANA: books**—*Mode im 20. Jahrhundert* by Ingrid Loschek, Munich, 1978; *Fairchild's Who's Who in Fashion* edited by Ann Stegemeyer, New York, 1980; *The Collector's Book of Twentieth Century Fashion* by Frances Kennett, London and New York, 1983; *McDowell's Directory of Twentieth Century Fashion* by Colin McDowell, London, 1984; *Design Source Book* by Penny Sparke and others, London, 1986; *The Encyclopedia of Fashion from 1840 to the 1980s* by Georgina O'Hara, London, 1986.

\*   \*   \*

Claude Montana came to the field of fashion design rather offhandedly. In London and in need of money in 1971, he began making rhinestone-encrusted, papier-mâché jewelry which caught on, encouraging him to pursue his new-found direction. By 1974, Montana was freelancing, learning as he went along. The work he did for the French leather firm of MacDouglas was to form an important basis for his future, as Montana has continued to make wide use of leathers, especially a type called cuir de plongée, a spongy soft variety.

In 1977, Montana presented a leather line which included motorcycle hats and metal chains as well as honey-colored leather vests with long fringes. He was immediately accused of being "Nazi-like," a claim that was to wrap him in controversy and that unjustifiably ignored the dissimilarities of his creations to Nazi garb and also brushed aside his simultaneous showing of white cotton spencers with full trousers.

However, 1978 was another story. Montana's showing at Bergdorf Goodman was a smash success with its black, floor-length, leather dresses, sequined jeans, and concentration on the wide-shouldered look. His fall presentation included Montana's signature broad-shouldered jacket and narrow skirt, sailor costumes of white and navy linen with metallic tassels and middy collars, and characteristic jumpsuits which had big, big shoulders and puffed sleeves and which narrowed from the tight belt down. This time the press called Montana "strong, gutsy, refined, for women with an eye for quality."

The following year brought equally strong items and equally strong success. Among the most outstanding numbers were Montana's pantsuit of taupe herringbone linen with extended shoulders, worn with matching taffeta peplum blouse, and a group of futuristic sharp-shouldered jumpsuits, ultra-slick and svelte, worn with longish jackets with wing collars, high-heeled pumps, and wonderful, flat-brimmed hats, which had quarter-moons jutting out from one side and were intended to be worn at a jaunty angle. Montana favored this style of hat. He showed a wider-brimmed version with another 1979 outfit, a black and white, geometric faille jacket accompanied by silk brushstroke crepe de chine blouse, peplum, and silk skirt.

In the fall of 1980, Montana featured terry cloth in offerings such as a large bathrobe coat, worn with linen pants. Montana's silhouette seemed to be softening, with shoulders not so pronounced. His pantsuits of spring 1981 featured pleated trousers with slim, double-breasted jackets. In a marvelously fitted suit of 1982, Montana found a happy medium, maintaining the broad look softly fluid to the waist and moving down into a closely-fitted skirt. This black cotton outfit outlined in white also exemplified Montana's continual preference for this sharply contrasting color combination and, it should be added, pointed up his resemblance to the young Milanese designers who came to fame during the mid-1970s.

Montana's individualistic touch, however, continued to shine through in fall 1983 designs such as his flowing tunics, deeply draped across the chest and long, worn with white linen cropped pants, and his sensuous combination of big, loose, ribbed sweater with matching ribbed skirt sporting a slit to the top of the thigh.

—Barbara Cavaliere

# MOORE, (Charles) Gene

American photographer and display, exhibition, and stage designer

**Born:** Birmingham, Alabama, 10 June 1910. **Education:** Studied painting under Louise Cone, Birmingham, Alabama, (c. 1930-33); Academy of Fine Arts, Chicago, 1934-35; mainly self-taught in design, from 1936. **Career:** Worked in New York as delivery man, cafeteria bus boy, and as a waiter on a cruise ship to South America, 1935-36; display assistant, at I. Miller, 1936-38, and at Bergdorf Goodman store, New York, 1938-45; display manager Bonwit Teller store, New York, 1945-55; display manager and vice-president, Tiffany and Company, New York, 1955-1994; also freelance designer, from 1955, working for Clarence House, Seagram Building, Delmar Shoe Salon, Madison Avenue Bookstore, Bonwit Teller, American Museum of Natural History, Museum of Modern Art, Castelli Gallery, London, Old Vic Theatre Company, Paul Taylor Dancy Company, Lenox Square, Atlanta, and others. **Honors:** Lumen Award, Illuminating Engineering Society, New York, 1976; American Society of Interior Designers Award, 1988; New York Municipal Arts Society Award, 1989. **Address:** 16 East 52nd St., New York, New York, U.S.A.

## Publications

**By MOORE: books**—(with Jay Hyams) *My Time at Tiffany's,* New York, 1990.

**On MOORE: books**—*Window Display 2* edited by Walter Herdeg, Zurich, 1961; *Windows* by Michael Emory, Chicago, 1977; *The American Store Window* by Leonard Marcus, New York, 1978; *Windows at Tiffany's: The Art of Gene Moore* by Judith Goldman, New York, 1980; *Show Windows* by Barry James Wood, New York, 1982.

\*    \*    \*

About twenty-five years ago, I happened to see the windows at Tiffany and Company for the first time. They were a revelation to someone who had grown up in Buffalo and was used to seeing jewelry displayed on velvet-covered props with artificial flowers lurking in the background. Years later, I was informed that the magician behind the windows at Tiffany's is Gene Moore. He's been a hero of mine ever since.

Display, recently given the more important-sounding name of "visual merchandising," is one of those fields in which the output is short-lived and the designers, mainly anonymous. Nevertheless, among these previously most underpaid and underappreciated people in retailing, the talented ones are some of the most inventive, insightful, and unorthodox designers ever known. In this group, Moore is at the top. His work makes us think.

While Moore's work at Bonwit's and other New York stores was exceptionally fine, he is more clearly identified with Tiffany's, where for nearly forty years he generated ingenious displays in a series of windows so cramped that they would try any designer's patience. Tiffany's and Moore were made for each other. There was less snobbishness than one would expect from the best-known jewelry store in the world, and an unusually sensitive management allowed Moore to concentrate freely on producing beautiful windows to express the store's personality, rather than solely to sell merchandise.

Gene Moore: Fourth of July windows, Tiffany and Co., 1994. Fireworks jewelry by Tiffany with brass fireworks by artist Mark Davis

Because of its scale, jewelry is one of the most difficult items to display. Moore understands this in a way that few people do, partly because he scrupulously avoids the phony and the pretentious. He never talks down to us. Seeing beauty in both the common and the rare, he is as intrigued by a paper bag, a ball of twine, a mound of sand as by a ruby bracelet or gold watch. In his juxtaposition of the ordinary and the rare, each element in his display ornaments the other. Moore's connection with the human is something that moves behind the surface of his other displays and activates whatever memories, understanding, or humor may exist within the viewer. You don't just pass his works by. You stop, look, and think. His use of deliberate mistakes, his wit, and his lightheartedness reveal his world. Aware of music, dance, literature, science, and nature, he offers more than meets the eye. He can make a cultural or social comment through his displays without resorting to shock. He makes us smile, he makes us learn, he helps us to make peace with the world.

Moore's connection with the human also allows him to animate the inanimate. He has a strong feeling for spatial and scale considerations, and his sensitive use of lighting integrates spaces, objects, and emotions. Over the years, his work has become more spare, yet not arid, and he constantly returns to nature for inspiration, reminding us that the natural object must be considered as crucial and beautiful as the man-made artifact. To date, his skill and brilliance in visual merchandising have not been surpassed.

—Grant Greapentrog

# MORI, Hanae

Japanese textile, costume, and fashion designer

**Born:** Tokyo, 8 January 1926. **Education:** Studied literature, at Tokyo Christian Women's College, 1945-48. **Family:** Married to Kei Mori; children: Akira and Kei. **Career:** First atelier in Shinjuko, Tokyo, 1951; freelance fashion and film costume designer, designing for over 1,000 films, Tokyo, 1954-1961; established Hanae Mori fashion shop, in Shinjuku, Tokyo, 1955; first New York fashion show, 1965; showed in Monaco and Paris, 1975; haute couture collection and haute couture house established in Paris and member of Le Chambre Syndicale de la Haute Couture Parisienne, 1977; Hanae Mori International headquarters office and boutiques building established, in Omote-sando, Tokyo, 1978; Hanae Mori Boutique in Faubourg St. Honor, Paris, 1985; designer of costumes for La Scala, Milan; designer of costumes for Paris Opera Ballet, 1986; Hanae Mori Boutique launched, Monte Carlo, 1989. **Member:** La Chambre Syndicale de la Couture Parisienne, Paris, 1978; Japan Olympic Committee; chairman of Cultural Affairs Promotion Committee of Tokyo Chamber of Commerce and Industry, 1991. **Exhibitions:** *Avant-garde Japon,* Centre Pompidou, Paris, 1986; *Hanae Mori: 35 Years in Fashion,* Tokyo, 1989, Monte Carlo, 1990, and Paris, 1990; *Diana Vreeland: Immoderate Style,* Metropolitan Museum of Art, New York, 1993-94; *Japonism in Fashion,* Kyoto Costume Institute, 1994; *Japanese Design: A Survey Since 1950,* Philadelphia Museum of Art, 1994; *Orientalism,* Metropolitan Museum of Art, New York, 1994-95. **Honors:** Neiman-Marcus Award, 1973; Medaille d'Argent, City of Paris, 1978; The Symbol of Man Award, Minnesota Museum, 1978; Croix de Chevalier des Arts et Lettres, 1984; Purple Ribbon Decoration, Japan, 1988; Asahi Prize as pioneer of Japanese Fashion, 1988; named Chevalier de la Légion d'Honneur, 1989; Person of Cultural Merit, Japan, 1989. **Addresses:** 6-1, 3 Chome, Kita-Aoyama, Minato-ku, Tokyo, Japan; 17-19 Avenue Montaigne, 75008 Paris, France; 27 East 79th Street, New York, New York 10021, U.S.A.

## Publications

**By MORI: books**—*Designing for Tomorrow,* Tokyo, 1979; *A Glass Butterfly,* Tokyo, 1984; *Hanae Mori 1960-1989,* Tokyo, 1989; *Fashion—A Butterfly Crosses the Border,* Tokyo, 1993.

**On MORI: books**—*The World of Fashion: People, Places, Resources* by Eleanor Lambert, New York and London, 1976; *Quest for the Best* by Stanley Marcus, New York, 1979; *Fairchild's Who's Who in Fashion* edited by Ann Stegemeyer, New York, 1980; *McDowell's Directory of Twentieth Century Fashion* by Colin McDowell, London, 1984; *New Fashion Japan* by Leonard Koren, Tokyo, 1984; *The Conran Directory of Design* edited by Stephen Bayley, London, 1985; *The Encyclopaedia of Fashion from 1840 to the 1980s* by Georgina O'Hara, London, 1986; *Japanese Design* by Penny Sparke, London, 1987; *Chic Savages* by John Fairchild, New York, 1989; **articles**—"Hanae Mori: Legend in Her Own Time" in *American Fabrics and Fashions* (Columbia, South Carolina), Spring 1974; "Japan's Queen of Haute Couture" by Ron Whitehead in *Femina,* May 1979; "Hanae Mori" by Marianne Lohse in *Madame Figaro* (Paris), April 1987; "Hanae Mori première!" by Dorothée Lalanne in *Vogue* (Paris), March 1989; "Hanae Mori" by Laurence Beurdeley in *L'Officiel* (Paris), June 1989; "Hanae Mori:

Fashion that Fuses the East and West" by Suzy Menkes in the *International Herald Tribune* (Neuilly, France), June 1989; "Japan's Madame Couturier" by Elizabeth Bumiller in the *Washington Post,* February 1990; "Un souffle nouveau" by Philippe Davy in *L'Officiel* (Paris), February 1990; "Univers Hanae Mori: un empire au soleil levant" by Monique Davidson in *Joyce,* March/April 1991.

\*     \*     \*

Long before her work was known in the West, Hanae Mori had designed costumes for more than 1,000 Japanese movies. In order to satisfy the Japanese cultural traditions of dress, she solved the problem of creating appropriate costumes by using unusual colours to satisfy dramatic requirements. This work provided her with an introduction to the Japanese people and to the world of fashion. Since then, she has built up an international enterprise in partnership with her son and husband, a textile manufacturer who provided her with the initial impetus to design fabric.

While Mori produces Western styles, her textiles, which are woven, dyed, and printed specially, reveal her heritage. Her vivid colours and linear patterns are reminiscent of the work of Japan's Edo period. Recognising that everyone needs colour in their lives, she keeps her boldest and brightest tones for her evening wear. Stunning combinations, as seen in the violet, blue, green, yellow, and black striped creations from her 1979 Paris collection, bring to mind her earlier work for films. Her work reveals the excitement which colour and pattern bring to garment design. Floral and butterfly motifs—the Japanese symbols of femininity—occur frequently in her prints, and on occasion, she returns to adaptations of the traditional kimono shapes for the simple lines which best display her lively prints.

By successfully combining the influences of East and West, she proved herself worthy to show with the top Parisian couturiers. In the late 1970s, an evening outfit comprising a quilted satin jacket over a long, bias-cut dress with a halter neck in the same fabric evidenced both cultures. Likewise, in spring 1979, she showed asymmetrical hemlines and kimono jackets in the same collection as padded shoulders, bare shoulders, ruffles, and taffeta dresses. In a 1981 collection Mori balanced the leopard print of one silk dress with soft, flowing fabric. She also used bright, hot colours for dresses reminiscent of the kimono in cut. In her spring-summer 1989 collection she covered simple silk dresses with flowers in pastel colours on a black background and accentuated with short petal-pink jackets.

Mori has skillfully taken ideas from the East and the West in order to create classically elegant garments which have a wide appeal. In her ready-to-wear she has proved herself very aware of the practical needs of contemporary women. While her shapes are easy to wear, they are also elegant and feminine, and her fabrics provide an excitement that sets her garments apart.

—Hazel Clark

# MOULTON, Alex(ander Eric)

British vehicle engineer and designer

**Born:** Stratford-upon-Avon, Warwickshire, 9 April 1920. **Education:** Studied at Marlborough College, Wiltshire, 1933-37; King's

College, Cambridge, 1938-39, 1947-49, MA, 1949. **Career:** Worked in the engine research department, 1939-44, and as assistant to Sir Roy Fedden, 1940-42, Bristol Aeroplane Company, Bristol, Gloucestershire; works manager and technical research director, at George Spencer Moulton and Company family firm, Bradford-on-Avon, Wiltshire, 1945-56; founder chairman, 1956-67, and managing director, from 1967, Moulton Developments Limited design development engineers, Bradford-on-Avon; chairman and managing director, 1962-67, and director, from 1967, of Moulton Bicycles, Nottingham; director of Alex Moulton Limited, Bradford-on-Avon, and of Bicycle Consultants Limited, Nottingham, from 1967. Chairman of the Committee on Engineering Design Education, Design Council, London, 1975-76; Master of the Faculty of Royal Designers for Industry, Royal Society of Arts, London, 1982-83. **Exhibitions:** *Eye for Industry,* Victoria and Albert Museum, London, 1986. **Collections:** National Motor Museum, Beaulieu, Hampshire. **Honors:** Design Centre Award, London, 1964; Bidlake Memorial Cycling Award, London, 1964; Queen's Award to Industry, London, 1967; Royal Designer for Industry, Royal Society of Arts, London, 1968; Society of Industrial Artists and Designers Medal, London, 1976; Commander, Order of the British Empire, 1976; Clayton Prize, Crompton-Lanchester Medal, and Hawksley Medal, Institute of Mechanical Engineers, London, 1979; Fellow, Institute of Mechanical Engineers, 1980. Honorary doctorates: Royal College of Art, London, 1967; University of Bath, 1971. **Address:** The Hall, Bradford-on-Avon, Wiltshire BA15 1AJ, England.

## Works

Flexitor vehicle suspension, 1957.
Hydrolastic vehicle suspension, 1962.
Moulton compact pedal bicycle, 1962.
Moulton motor coach, 1968-70.
Hydragas vehicle suspension, 1973.
Alex Moulton pedal bicycle, 1983.

## Publications

**On MOULTON: books**—*Automobile Design: The Great Designers and Their Work* edited by Ronald Barker and Anthony Harding, Newton Abbot, 1970; *The Moulton Bicycle* by Tony Hadland, Reading, 1980; *Design By Choice* by Reyner Banham, London, 1981; *British Design Since 1880: A Visual History* by Fiona MacCarthy, London, 1982; *Eye for Industry: Royal Designers for Industry 1936-1986,* exhibition catalogue by Fiona MacCarthy and Patrick Nuttgens, London, 1986.

**Alex Moulton: AM2/Alex Moulton bicycle, 1983**

Olivier Mourgue: 1984 Sledge Seats

# MOURGUE, Olivier

French artist and industrial designer

**Born:** Paris, 15 April 1939. **Education:** Educated at the Lycée
Pasteur, Paris, 1946-54; studied interior design, at the Ecole Boulle,
Paris, Dip.Arch.Int., 1958; Ecole Nationale Supérieure des Arts
Décoratifs, Paris, Dip., 1960. **Military Service:** Served in the
French Army, 1960-62. **Family:** Married Christina Sanders in 1967
(divorced, 1980); children: Thomas and Mikael; married Anne Turlan
in 1981; children: Armel, Gaëtan, Maria. **Career:** Freelance designer, from 1959, establishing studio in the Rue Campagne-
Prèmiere, Paris, 1966-76, and in Kéralio, Brittany, from 1976;
worked with architectural designer Maurice Holland, at Nordiska
Kompaniet, Stockholm, 1960; interior designer, for Agence
d'Architecture Intérieure Gautier-Delaye, Paris, 1963; also designed
for Airborne, 1964-66, Atelier de Création du Mobilier National,
from 1966, Societé Pierre Charron, 1967, Societé Disderot, 1967,
Bayer fabrics, 1971, Societé Clairitex, 1972, Arconas Corporation,
and Mobilia; consultant, Renault automobile company, 1977-78,
1980. Professor, Ecole Nationale Supérieure des Arts Décoratifs,
Paris, 1969-72, and Institut d'Arts et Techniques de Bretagne
Occidentale, Ecole des Beaux-Arts, Brest, from 1976. **Exhibitions:**
*Expo 67,* Montreal, 1967; *Euro Design,* Nancy, 1969; *Eurodomus,*
Milan, 1970, 1972; *Expo 70,* Osaka, 1970; *Design Francais,* Musée

des Arts Décoratifs, Paris, 1971; *Portable World,* American Mu-
seum of Contemporary Crafts, New York, 1973; *S'Asseoir,* Musee
de Peintures et de Sculptures, Grenoble, 1974; *Design en France,*
Design Centre, Brussels, 1975; *Olivier Mourgue: Retrospective,*
Musée des Arts Décoratifs, Nantes, 1976; *On the Wings of the
Wind,* Saint Georges Chapel, Caen Château, France, 1982; *Design
Since 1945,* Philadelphia Museum of Art, 1983; *Twentieth Century
of Art,* Metropolitan Museum of Art, New York, 1987; *Design
Francais 1960-1990,* Centre Georges Pompidou, Paris, 1988
(toured); *Olivier Mourgue: Imaginary Gardens and Little The-
atres,* Sainsbury Centre for Visual Arts, University of East Anglia,
Norwich, England, 1992; *Le Design des Années Pop 1960-1973,*
Musée des Arts Décoratifs, Paris, 1995. **Collections:** Museum of
Modern Art, New York; Metropolitan Museum of Art, New York;
Musée des Arts Décoratifs, Paris. **Honors:** International Design
Award, New York, 1968; Eole 74 Prix d'Honneur, Paris, 1974;
Grand Prix National de la Creation Industrielle, Ministry of Cul-
ture, Paris, 1994. **Address:** Kéralio par Plouguiel, Côtex d'Armor
22 220, France.

## Works

*Joker* low-back armchair in chrome steel with leather upholstery,
  for Airborne, 1959-63.

*Djinn* chaise longue in tubular steel with jersey upholstery, for Airborne, 1964-65.

*Whist Dos à Dos* chair with metal frame and leather seat, for Airborne, 1964-65.

*Montreal* shell-structure armchair in polyester with loose cushions, for Airborne, 1966.

*Fleur* lamp series in chromed metal and aluminum, for Editions Pierre Disderot, 1967.

Trestle table in lacquered wood, for Editions Charron, 1967.

Cubic armchair with polyester shell and loose jersey cushions, for Airborne, 1968.

Furniture design for film *2001: A Space Odyssey* (Kubrick), 1968.

*Bouloum* chaise longue in polyester and jersey for the French pavilion at Expo 70, Osaka, 1968-70.

Five-pillar bookcase in natural wood with lacquered metal fixings, for Prisunic, 1969.

Mobile studios, with Land Rover in Italy, 1970, Saviem TP3 in Finland, Poland, Czechoslovakia, and Hungary, 1976, and Volkswagen in Denmark, Sweden, Finland, and Britain, 1986.

Design of *Fourre-tout/Junk Room* in canvas, for Clairitex, 1972.

*Games and Forest* ranges of textiles and carpets in synthetic fibres, for Bayer, 1972.

Hold-all storage systems (models A-D) in unbleached cotton, for Editions Clairitex, 1972.

*Rosita Hernandez* sofa in wood and fabric with mirrors and pompoms, for Editions Cedac-Minvielle, 1975-76.

Load-reduced version of Renault *4,* and design proposal for a basic vehicle for developing countries, for Renault automobile company, France, 1977.

*Little Theatres,* New York, 1984, and Helsinki, 1985.

Catalogue design, for Calder exhibition, La Roche Jaune, Brittany, 1986.

*Migrating Birds* animation of a covered public space measuring 200 square meters, Helsinki East, Finland, 1991.


## Publications

By MOURGUE: books—*Hexa For,* exhibition catalogue, Paris, 1975.

On MOURGUE: books—*The Modern Chair: 1850 to Today* by Gilbert Frey, London and Neiderteufen, 1970; *Portable World,* exhibition catalogue with texts by Paul J. Smith and Barbara Bullock, New York, 1973; *S'Asseoir,* exhibition catalogue by Maurice Besset, Grenoble, 1974; *Olivier Mourgue,* exhibition catalogue with text by P. R. Chaigneau, Nantes, 1976; *Contemporary Furniture* by Klaus-Jurgen Sembach, Stuttgart and London, 1982; *Designers' Workplaces* by Beverly Russell, New York, 1983; *Les Années 60* by Anne Bony, Paris, 1983; *Pentagram Papers No. 12: Olivier Mourgue's Little Theatre of Design* by Pentagram Design, New York, 1984; *Mid-Century: Furniture of the 1950s* by Cara Greenberg, London, 1984; *The Conran Directory of Design* edited by Stephen Bayley London, 1985; *Modern Furniture Classics* by Miriam Stimpson, London, 1987; *Design Francais 1960-1990: Trois Decennies,* exhibition catalogue by Margo Rouard and Françoise Jollant Kneebone, London, 1990; *Olivier Mourgue: Imaginary Gardens and Little Theatres,* exhibition catalogue with texts by Derek Gillman and Sir Norman Foster, Norwich, England, 1992; articles—"Water Colour Theatre" by Ullamaria Pallasmaa in *Form Function Finland,* no. 1, 1986.

*

*Preamble:* Fantasy, reveries, slowness. A sacred object. Emotion, a sense of plenitude, feeling. Play, the memory of distant lands. I find their echo in watercolours, in models, in little theatres, or in the light construction of scenery.

*Brittany, Côtes du Nord:* Near the sea where we live, near the students, near the trees, the dark blue-grey skies of winter, Brittany is a land of holy, intimate places that one must seek out: I think of the springs in the woods and fields, and of those enigmatic standing stones, the menhirs.

*Teaching and Research:* In a new system of teaching artistic problems watercolour plays an important role. The watercolour studio has become a kind of experimental laboratory with precise research goals. One must capture what is light, small, sacred, the precise detail, certain gestures... (Excerpted, with permission from the Sainsbury Centre for Visual Arts, from *Olivier Mourgue: Imaginary Gardens and Little Theatres* exhibition catalogue, 1992).

—Olivier Mourgue

\*   \*   \*

Like others on the Continent, but particularly like his compatriot Pierre Paulin, Olivier Mourgue manipulates the synthetic materials of the day to reawaken us to the sculptural and utilitarian possibilities of line. This is especially evident in the *Djinn* stool and chaise. Viewed from the side, as they are in advertisements, they appear first as line in space. Only later do we realize that these lines can also serve our needs for support and relaxation.

The *Djinn* chair, on the other hand, is always shown head on, so that we see it not only as a form but as a persona, a supposedly inanimate object with the jinni's ability to animate and deceive. These double meanings made it an appropriate choice to appear in *2001: A Space Odyssey.* Furthermore, we thought at the time that this was what the next century would be: clean, linear, artificially intelligent. (It is perhaps no coincidence that at the time Mourgue was designing his furniture for the future, another French designer, André Courrèges, was clothing charmingly dehumanized mannequins in space-boots and figure-skimming shifts beneath bubbles of hair like space helmets.)

Mourgue's work also looks backward, however. Structurally, its past lies in the metal tubing so frequently used by Breuer and Mart Stam (although there is little of their Bauhaus-inspired joy in material). Psychically, his furniture returns to that misty age when people lived surrounded by gods and assumed the existence of a spirit in every natural object. Both *Djinn* and *Bouloum* force us to recall that chairs are something we create in our own image; that they share our body parts of head, leg, arm, seat, foot, back; and that their forms can communicate spiritual and temporal power, as witness the bishop's chair and the sovereign's throne.

Mourgue's ability to combine myth, symbol, and esthetic and to express multiple meanings within a twentieth-century idiom has earned him a place in the pantheon of contemporary designers. One is left only to ask why such achievement now occurs so rarely in France, a country that once dominated furniture design and why the French capture of the spirit of the 1960s could not inspire a return to dominance.

—Reed Benhamou

# MROSZCZAK, Jozef

Polish illustrator, exhibition, and graphic designer

**Born:** Podhale, Nowy Targ, 11 May 1910. **Education:** Nowy Targ, until 1926; studied law, at the University of Krakow, 1927-28; studied design, under Bukowski and Uziembo, at the Academy of Fine Arts, Krakow, 1929-32; studied graphics and advertising, at the Kunstgewerbeschule, the Graphische Lehr-und-Versuchanstalt, and at a local commercial art school, Vienna, 1933-36. **Family:** Married; son: Marcin. **Career:** Freelance illustrator and designer from 1937, and exhibition designer from 1947, working in Katowice, 1937-40, 1945-53, in Nowy Targ, 1940-45, and in Warsaw, 1953-75; head of the graphic art department, WAG graphic art publishers, Warsaw, from 1953; co-founder and editorial board member, of *Projekt* magazine, Warsaw, 1956-75. Instructor, at the Commercial Secondary School, Katowice, 1937-38, the Giermynski Free School of Painting and Drawing, Katowice, 1938-40, and at the Secondary Commercial School, Nowy Targ, 1940-45; organizer and head of the applied graphic art department, Polish College of Art, Katowice, 1947-53; instructor, 1953-55, and professor, 1955-73, at the Academy of Arts, Warsaw. **Member:** Organizer of the Silesian section, Polish Union of Plastic Artists, 1945-46; Polish section chairman, ICOGRADA International Council of Graphic Design Associations; organizing committee chairman, Warsaw Poster Biennale; Dutch Union of Graphic Artists (honorary); Parma Academy of Fine Art; Alliance Graphique Internationale. **Exhibitions:** *Vier Polnische Plakat Künstler Deutsches Plakatmuseum,* Essen, 1971; *107 Grafici dell'AGI,* Castello Sforzesco, Milan, 1974. **Collections:** Poster Museum, Wilanow. **Honors:** Polish Government Graphic Art Prize, 1953; Warsaw National Poster Prize, 1953; Polish State Prize for Artistic Achievement, 1953, 1968; Leipzig Book Fair Gold Medal, 1965; Brno Poster Biennale Prize 1974. **Died:** Warsaw, 1975.

## Works

*King Solomon's Mines* (C. Bennett) film poster, for Polfilm, 1954.
*Die Blumen Volkspolens* poster, for the Polish national holiday, 1954.
*Aida* poster, for the State Opera, Warsaw, 1958.
*Boris Godunov* poster, for the State Opera, Warsaw, 1959.
*Bettelstudent* poster, for the Warsaw Operetta, 1961.
*Don Carlos* poster, for the State Opera, Warsaw, 1963.
*Word and Picture* exhibition poster, for the State Ethnographical Museum, Warsaw, 1967.
*The Icon in Poland* exhibition poster, for the Ethnographical Museum, Warsaw, 1967.
*Opening Exhibition* poster, for the Poster Museum, Wilanow, 1968.
*Cabal and Love* (Schiller) poster, for the Polish Theatre, Warsaw, 1969.
*Landscape After a Battle* (A. Wada) film poster, for Polfilm, 1970.

## Publications

**By MROSZCZAK: books**—*Polnische Plakatkunst,* Dusseldorf, 1966.

**On MROSZCZAK: books**—*Das Polnische Plakat,* Warsaw, 1952; *Who's Who in Graphic Art* edited by Walter Amstutz, Zurich, 1962;

*Buchgestaltung* by Albert Kapr, Dresden, 1963; *Das Plakat* by Anton Sailer, Munich, 1965; *Vier Polnische Plakatkunstler,* exhibition catalogue by H. Schardt, Essen, 1971; *Polish Poster Art Today* by Szymon Bojko, London, 1972; *Contemporary Polish Posters* edited by Joseph Czestochowski, New York, 1979; *The Polish Poster 1970-1978,* with introduction by Zdzislaw Schubert, Warsaw, 1979.

\*     \*     \*

If I had been asked to write about Jozef Mroszczak fifteen years ago, it would have been quite a difficult task. For years, he was regarded as one of two major "lions" of the Polish Poster School, sharing the position with Henryk Tomaszewski. It was the official cliche. Now that he is long ago gone, Mroszczak's position can be seen from a different angle.

As a designer, he was a very good one. No question about it. But it would be foolish to equate him with Tomaszewski, indisputably the master of his craft. Also, when pure craft, skill, and innovation are counted, quite a large group of younger colleagues outdid him. On this point, a little reflection: In many other countries, Mroszczak would have been number one as a posterist. But in Poland, the competition is greatest. The achievements, too.

Mroszczak himself was instrumental in creating this situation. It sounds paradoxical: Why would somebody build the competition against himself? But Mroszczak did, to such a point that years later, anybody was able to separate the pure designer from the great administrator and organizer. In the stormy, dark, late 1940s and early 1950s, Mroszczak persuaded the Communists that the poster must be the leading art form of the new regime. Of course, their goals differed greatly. Mroszczak had to fight for the quality of art, to save his discipline from the overwhelming Stalinization of cultural life. They, on the other hand, like the revolutionaries of 1918 in Moscow, sought a great tool of propaganda in the poster.

How Mroszczak managed to succeed, nobody will ever know. He keeps the whole truth to himself, forever. But we know that he engineered the Polish Poster School, Graphic-Agency, *Projekt* graphic-art magazine, the poster museum at Wilanow, near Warsaw, and—his biggest victory—Warsaw's *International Poster Biennale,* which took place for the first time in 1966. After a long, sneaky route, with double-goals and half-truths, the Polish poster achieved its global position. Not only did it dominate the domestic market as the premier art form, the poster museum was the first major one of its kind in the world, and the *Biennale* was established as the first such exhibition. It is still the most important.

Step by step, Mroszczak achieved all of this, with the help of many, but against many, too. He was a controversial figure all his life, overpraised by officials, underrated by society. But, years after his death, nobody can question his achievements. He was a first-rate designer, an excellent professor at the Academy, and the most crucial figure backing the rise and overwhelming success of his beloved child, the poster. Thank you, Jozef, for the job well done.

—Jan Sawka

# MROSZCZAK, Marcin (Jan)

Polish illustrator, photographer, stage, and graphic designer

**Born:** Katowice, 10 January 1950. **Education:** Studied graphics under Henryk Tomaszewski at the Academy of Fine Arts, Warsaw,

1968-73. **Family:** Married Maria Glinska in 1979; children: Mateusz. **Career:** Designer, Arte Graphica Silva agency, Parma, 1970, Pentagram Design studio, London, 1971, and Tel Design agency, The Hague, 1972; freelance designer, working with Andrzej Krauze, in Warsaw, 1971-75, and with photographer Tomasz Sikora, Warsaw, 1976-82; art director, Apport Infoplan agency (McCann-Erickson), Brussels, 1983-86; founder-partner, with Kris Lenaerts, of Corporate Images design studio, Brussels, from 1986; designed for the Warsaw National Theatre, Warsaw Theatre Powszechny, Łòdź Theatre Jaracza, and for films of Andrzej Wajda and Roman Polanski. Art Director, *Le Théâtre en Pologne* magazine, from 1972, and *Theatre* review, Warsaw, 1975-77. Instructor in graphic design, at the Academy of Fine Arts, Poznan, 1980, and the Académie Royale des Beaux-Arts, Ghent, from 1980. **Exhibitions:** Galeria Plakatu, Warsaw, 1978; BWA Gallery, Poznan, 1978; Author's Gallery, Amsterdam, 1979; Galeria On, Poznan, 1980; Galeria Wielka 19, Poznan, 1980. **Collections:** Museum of Contemporary Art, Lodz; Poster Museum, Warsaw; National Museum, Poznan; Stedelijk Museum, Amsterdam; Deutsches Plakatmuseum, Essen; Musée d'Art Moderne de la Ville, Paris. **Honors:** Katowice Poster Biennale Award, 1975, 1977; President's Medal, Warsaw Poster Biennale, 1978. **Address:** Corporate Images, Rue Faider 55, 1050 Brussels, Belgium.

## Publications

On MROSZCZAK: books—*Who's Who of European Designers: Belgium, Spain, Czechoslovakia, Poland* edited by Idea Publishers, Tokyo, 1972; *The Polish Poster 1970-1978,* with introduction by Zdzislaw Schubert, Warsaw, 1979; *Who's Who in Graphic Art* edited by Walter Amstutz, Dubendorf, 1982.

\*

I always work to order, which means that the problem to be solved is set by someone else. This already excludes any kind of universal theory, because the problem I face each time is very different. An interesting theatre poster and an advertising campaign which fulfills its role belong to two different worlds, though one and the other serve the same purpose—communication.

—Marcin Mroszczak

\* \* \*

It would be easy but unfair to state that Marcin Mroszczak has nothing to do with Jozef Mroszczak—maybe the name only. No, it is true that Marcin is the son of Jozef Mroszczak—one of the most important poster designers of postwar Poland and the main builder of the poster's fame and position. This acknowledgment will help us to understand the younger Mroszczak's ups and downs as an artist. Of course, to be the son of such a powerful figure in small Warsaw makes your life an instant success. And a nightmare, as well.

Growing up under his father's umbrella, Marcin had all ways, all doors, and all windows, wide open. He knew everybody important because almost everybody wanted to know his father. This privileged position, however, along with the older Mroszczak's sometimes blind desire to see his son become the leading poster artist, made his life quite difficult. He had to face friendships that were built on self-interest and that quickly disappeared when Marcin Mroszczak set up as a freelance designer of books, posters, magazines, record sleeves, and practically anything with a graphic arts application, in Warsaw in 1972. Best known for his work in the entertainment field, working on theatre and film posters, Mroszczak also began designing stage sets for the theatre. In collaboration with photographer Tomasz Sikora, he has designed and illustrated two yet to be published picture books: *Album* and Lewis Carroll's *Alice in Wonderland.* His skill at photographic montage and trompe-l'oeil imagery is best evidenced in his posters for the National Theatre, Warsaw, and the Jacaracza Theatre in Łòdź. He has also acted as art director of the magazines *Le Theatre en Pologne* and *Theatre Review* and, more recently, he moved to Belgium to act as art director for a branch of the prestigious McCann-Erickson advertising agency.

Marcin's connections and power had been "used," and the stiffening competition of his generation of artists did all they could to outdo the "Mroszczak-baby." Another obstacle was how to develop his own style. Like anyone else, he was criticized for copying, for borrowing, or simply for lacking his own style. Yesterday's friends, now turned major enemies, claimed it was their achievement but Marcin's signature.

Slowly, Mroszczak began to develop his own style. Knowing that drawing and painting are not his most formidable tools, he decided to use photography. When his technique had improved, he experimented with something which was not pure collage but not yet an object. Rather, these were pre-arranged situations, carefully staged, photographed, and afterward incorporated into poster compositions.

And, at this point, the real *Marcin* Mroszczak was born. Very theatrical, intelligent, and visually almost perfect posters appeared. The influence of theatre was obvious. Mroszczak likes film and theatre, and in the latter he feels at home. The atmosphere of theatre, its stage, set-design, and hundreds of requisites all enrich Mroszczak's mind. His constructions, or, better, his arrangements, are never heavy-handed. He organizes them intelligently, reserving for the public a delicate margin of interpretation of various allusions and the possibility of finding its own language of understanding. As time has passed, Mroszczak has developed his own image, style, and posture.

Now, people do not see him as the offspring of the old one—the past disappears and old wounds heal fast. Hard times of struggling alone, no longer the young lion with daddy's help, have crystallized the best from Mroszczak. Perhaps, as his father wished, he will one day be the best of the best.

—Jan Sawka

# MUGLER, Thierry
French fashion designer

**Born:** Strasbourg, Alsace, in 1946. **Education:** Lycée Fustel de Coulange, 1960-65; School of Fine Arts, Strasbourg, until 1966-67. **Career:** Ballet dancer with the Opéra du Rhin, Strasbourg, 1965-66; assistant clothing designer in the Gudule boutique, Paris, 1966-67; designer of fashion collections for André Peters, London, 1968-69; freelance designer, in Amsterdam and Paris, 1970-73; created *Café de Paris* fashion collection, Paris, 1973; founded Thierry

Mugler fashion firm, Paris, 1974, owner from 1986; also established Thierry Mugler Diffusion ready-to-wear company, with distribution in United States outlets including Saks Fifth Avenue, Bergdorf Goodman, Neiman-Marcus, Marshall Field, John Wanamaker, Bloomingdale's, and in Japan via Takashimaya department stores; opened boutiques on the Place des Victorias, and on Avenue Montaigne, Paris. Fragrances include *Angel,* 1992. Also professional photographer from 1967. **Address:** 130 rue du Faubourg Saint Honoré, 75008 Paris, France.

### Publications

**By MUGLER: books**—*Thierry Mugler, Photographer,* Paris and London, 1988.

**On MUGLER: books**—*Fashion and Anti-Fashion* by Ted Polhemus and Lynn Proctor, London, 1978; *25 Ans de Marie-Claire de 1954 a 1979,* compiled by Françoise Mohrt, Paris, 1979; *Fairchild's Who's Who in Fashion* edited by Anne Stegemeyer, New York, 1980; *Fashion 2001* by Lucille Khornak, London, 1982; *McDowell's Directory of Twentieth Century Fashion,* London, 1984, 1987; *The Encyclopaedia of Fashion from 1840 to the 1980s* by Georgina O'Hara, London, 1986; *Design Source Book* by Penny Sparke and others, London, 1986; *Fashion and Surrealism* by Richard Martin, New York, 1987; *Infra-Apparel* by Richard Martin and Harold Koda, New York, 1993; **articles**—"Thierry Mugler et Macbeth" by Dorothée LaLanne in *Vogue* (Paris), November 1985; "Thierry Mugler: l'homme qui aimait les légendes" by Martine Trittoleno in *L'Officiel* (Paris), November 1986; "Travelling Goddesses" by Nicoletta Gasperini in *Joyce* (Hong Kong), March 1988; "De la mode à la photo" by Frederique Mory in *Madame Figaro* (Paris), 2 July 1988; "Double objectif de Thierry Mugler" by Francois Baudot in *Elle* (Paris), 7 November 1988; "The Wild One" by Michael Gross in *New York Magazine,* 4 June 1990; "Mugler à Moscou" by Catherine Wrobel in France-Soir (Paris), 26 June 1990; "Mugler, Clarins Link for a Scent" in *Women's Wear Daily* (New York), 28 September 1990; "Thierry Mugler: l'art de se faire une griffe" by Nadège Forestier in *Le Figaro* (Paris), 6 October 1990; "Mugler" by Brenda Polan in *Elle* (Paris), December 1990; "How to Look Good in Thierry Mugler" by Ellen von Unwerth in *Interview* (New York), March 1991; "Fashion License: Clothing and the Car" by Richard Martin in *Textile and Text,* 13 April 1991; "Mugler's Monster Show" in *Elle* (New York), November 1991; "Thierry Mugler Talks Trends" by Jeff Yarbrough in *The Advocate* (USA), 21 April 1992; "Monsieur Mugler" by Amy M. Spindler in *Women's Wear Daily* (New York), 22 July 1992; "A Mature Mugler, Demeulemeester and Lang" by Amy M. Spindler in the *New York Times,* 18 March 1995; "The Paris Collections: The Ideas of March: Thierry Mugler" in *Women's Wear Daily* (New York), 17 March 1995; "Very Thierry" by Tina Gaudoin in *Elle* (London), April 1995.

*     *     *

Sharp, pointed, wide shoulders, sharply defined waistlines, tight, sensuously fitted skirts or pants, simple shapes and colors, no hint of the past or folksiness: these are the elements of costumes Thierry Mugler created for the 1980s. He likes the idea of the "uniform," so that everyone will look the same; it links people together, he says, both men and women. In the 1980s Mugler himself wore a broad-shouldered jumpsuit which suggests a cross between space cadet and race-driver. His silhouettes are not unrelated; note, for example, his 1979 dress with the exaggeratedly widened triangular shoulders and large, stiff, triangular hip-pockets with belt to match. Although his clothes are quite futuristic, they are never busy but simplified, incorporating a minimum of details.

Mugler spent two years of his youth as a classical ballet dancer, a brief career which, he believes, has been a primary source for his designs—first, for the architectural element, and second, for his emphasis on the shoulders to give a sense of height and grandeur to the figure. His showings are notoriously elaborate extravaganzas, like Kenzo's before him and also like those of his contemporaries Claude Montana and Jean-Claude de Luca. These tend to lend his clothes a far-out feeling, more science fiction-like than they seem in normal circumstances. Mugler's 1979 herringbone plaid pants suit, for example, with short jacket, padded shoulders, and buttoned pocket accents, is less wild when seen alone. Even his uses of accessories, such as his 1979 supervisor sunglasses, gladiator bracelets, and belts decorated with geometric shapes (triangles, diamonds) and pointed tips, come across more as contemporary classical than theatrical or elaborate.

A look at Mugler's designs from the early 1980s shows him remaining true to the fashions he created a decade earlier. His 1980 above-the-knee dress has a basic look, accented starkly by a sharply pointed waistband with two tails flowing down from the tie and matching triangular hemline; the accompanying shoes have similarly pointed insteps and wraparound, calf-height ties. In 1982, Mugler showed long, belted jackets with circle skirts and wide-legged pants in navy gabardine, an updating of a well-known classic look. His fall 1983 clothes for men included basic turtlenecks, thigh-length "car coat" jackets, slim pants, and "Perry Como" cardigans of mohair plush with ribbed-wool details, worn over simple, mock turtleneck sweaters, the emphasis being on loose, roomy, soft shoulders and sleeves.

In the early 1990s, Mugler made it apparent that his designs were meant for performance. He exhibited a love of glamour in his 1992 collection, which showed 1950s style at its most extravagant, updated for the 1990s. This penchant for the glamourous was also apparent in his 1988 book of photographs, *Thierry Mugler, Photographer,* which featured models in dramatic poses, dwarfed by grand and romantic backgrounds. Mugler choreographs his major shows like great Hollywood musicals, and has been known to show his collections in huge stadiums, giving the productions a rock concert feel. He has also designed the off-stage wardrobe for celebrities, including Madonna.

—Barbara Cavaliere

## MUIR, Jean (Elizabeth)
British fashion designer

**Born:** London, 1933. **Education:** Educated at Dame Harper School, Bedford, 1945-50. **Family:** Married Harry Leuckert in 1955. **Career:** Worked in a solicitor's office, London, 1951; salesgirl and fashion sketcher, Liberty's department store, London, 1952-55; designer, for Jacqmar, London, 1955, and for Jaeger dress and knitwear collections, London, 1956-63; founder-director, Jane and Jane fashion company, London, 1962-66; founder-partner, with

Harry Leuckert, and chief designer, of Jean Muir Limited, London, from 1966. **Exhibitions:** *Fashion: An Anthology,* Victoria and Albert Museum, London, 1971; *Eye for Industry,* Victoria and Albert Museum, 1986. **Collections:** Museum of Costume, Bath. **Honors:** British Fashion Writers Dress of the Year Award, 1964; Ambassador Achievement Year Award, 1965; Harper's Bazaar Trophy, 1965; Maison Blanche Rex International Fashion Award, New Orleans, 1967, 1968, 1974; Churchman's Fashion Designer of the Year Award, 1970; Neiman Marcus Award, 1973; Mayor's Citation Award, Philadelphia, 1977; British Fashion Industry Award, 1984; Federation Francaise du Prêt-à-Porter Feminin Award, 1985; Design Medal, Chartered Society of Designers, London, 1987. Honorary Doctorate, Royal College of Art, London, 1981. Royal Designer for Industry, Royal Society of Arts, London, 1972; Fellow, Chartered Society of Designers, London, 1978; Commander, Order of the British Empire, 1984. **Died:** London, 28 May 1995.

**Publications**

**By MUIR: books**—*Jean Muir,* London, 1981.

**On MUIR: books**—*The Fashion Makers* by Leonard Halliday, London, 1966; *Fashion: An Anthology by Cecil Beaton,* exhibition catalogue compiled by Madeleine Ginsburg, London, 1971; *In Vogue: Sixty Years of Celebrities and Fashion* by Georgina Howell, London, 1975, 1978, New York, 1976; *A History of Fashion* by J. Anderson Black and Madge Garland, London, 1975, 1980; *McDowell's Directory of Twentieth Century Fashion* by Colin McDowell, London, 1984, 1987; *The Encyclopedia of Fashion from 1840 to the 1980s* by Georgina O'Hara, London, 1986; *Eye for Industry: Royal Designers for Industry 1936-1986,* exhibition catalogue by Fiona MacCarthy and Patrick Nuttgens, London, 1986; *Design Source Book* by Penny Sparke and others, London, 1986; **articles**—*The Independent* (London), 2 June 1995; "The Prime of Miss Jean Muir" by Hamish Bowles in *Vogue* (New York), September 1995; "In London, Straining for Consistency" by Amy M. Spindler in *New York Times,* 24 October 1995.

\* \* \*

"Fashion is not Art, it is Industry. There are too many designers and not enough workers," says Jean Muir, who regards herself as a craftswoman before a designer. Glamorous ideas are worthless if one cannot turn them into a working pattern, and Muir is critical of colleges which turn out designers who cannot even cut and sew. The engineering is the basis of the art, and Muir insists on excellence in handwork as the foundation without which no fashion house can operate. Fashion is business, a production line, and Muir is now involved in ensuring that fashion students understand this.

Her approach to design is equally fundamental, for clothes must start on the body, not in abstract concepts. It is how the fabric flows on the human form which rules her talents, and she continues the approach of the greatest women couturières—Chanel, Grès, and Vionnet. Like them, she is fascinated by the fluidity of jersey on the female form, which produces a liquid sculpture echoing every movement. She is also fond of suede, and the same toile will be worked out and applied to both types of material to produce the different but related effects that characterize her collections. "I am a traditionalist with a sense of evolution, someone who loves evolving continuity. I prefer evolution or organic growth to revolution or

grand idealistic concepts," she states, thereby showing that she is also a representative of the British approach to design taught by Edward Molyneaux.

Obvious tricks, such as plunging necklines and skirts slit up to the hip, are vulgar. A reserved design can achieve a lasting quality and be infinitely more seductive in a subtle way. No Muir gown exposes a woman, but her soft lines are full of physical appeal. Customers will wear a Muir creation for years because its effect does not fade, and it is too well made to wear out. Carol Channing, Lauren Bacall, Elaine Stritch, and Glenda Jackson typify her clientele, who collect her clothes like treasures. Because Muir avoids major changes every year, her clothes rise above fashion to exist on that plateau with gowns by Grès. Such simplicity has a classical durability. They represent the modern movement at its very best.

—Diana de Marly

# MÜLLER, Rolf Felix

German illustrator, cartoonist, and graphic designer

**Born:** Lobenstein, 22 July 1932. **Education:** Educated at Grundschule, Lobenstein, 1939-47; apprentice lithographer, Gera, 1948-51; studied lettering and book design under Egon Pruggmayer, at the Hochschule für Grafik und Buchkunst, Leipzig, 1952-57. **Family:** Married MarieLuise Kahie in 1957; children: Thomas. **Career:** Freelance designer, in Gera, from 1957; has designed and illustrated books for Greifen Verlag, Insel Verlag, Eulenspiegel, Reclam, Union, Urania-Verlag, Kinderbuchverlag, and others. Instructor in poster and book design, 1985-87, lecturer in graphic design, 1987-93, and professor, from 1993, Hochschule für Grafik und Buchkunst, Leipzig. **Member:** Association of Fine Artists. **Exhibitions:** Haus des Lehrers, East Berlin, 1964; Schloss Heidecksburg, Rudolstadt, 1973; Sommerpalais, Greiz, 1973, 1982; Kleine Galerie, Unterwellenborn, 1974; Schauspielhaus, Karl-Marx-Stadt, 1975; Galerie Gucke, Bad Kostritz, 1976, 1981; Kunstgalerie, Gera, 1977; Studentenclub, Weimar, 1978; Kulturzentrum DDR, Warsaw, 1979; Kulturzentrum DDR, Budapest, 1980; Kreiskulturhaus, Meerane, 1981; Kunstsammlung, Cottbus, 1981; Galerie am Markt, Gera, 1981; der Kultur, Gera, 1982; Klubhaus Wema Union, Gera, 1984; Theater der Stadt, Rostow am Don, 1984; Kulturband-Galerie, Lobenstein, 1985; Galerie ans Steger, Zeulenroda, 1986; Kulturhaus Wilhelm Pieck, Schwarza, 1986; Staatliches Museum, Burgk, 1988. **Collections:** Museum für Deutsche Geschichte, East Berlin; Kunstbibliothek, East Berlin; Galerie Kunstsammlung, Kottbus; Mahrische Galerie, Brno; Museum Wilanow, Warsaw. **Honors:** Kunstpreis der Stadt Gera, 1959; Kunstpreis des Bezirkes Gera, 1964, 1970; Deutscher Turn und Sport Art Prize, 1972; Arts Prize, German Democratic Republic, 1973; GDR Medal of Merit, 1979; Special Award, Biennial Exhibition of Book Design, Brno, 1984; GDR National Prize, 1987; Honorary Award, International Poster Biennial, Lahti, 1987; named among the Best Posters of 1966-1989. **Address:** Oststrasse 8 07548 Gera, Germany.

**Works**

*Neunundneunzig Abenteuer* (Giacomo Casanova) book design, for Greifenverlag, Rudolstadt, 1958.

**Goldener Spatz '95**

Deutsches Kinder·Film & Fernseh·Festival
**in Gera vom 26. März – 1. April**

Rolf Felix Müller: Goldener Spatz festival poster, 1995

*Homo Sapiens* (Georg Christoph Lichtenberg) book design, for Eulenspiegel Verlag, Berlin, 1961.

*Seegang Satan Sansibar* (Hansgeorg Stengel) book design, for Eulenspiegel Verlag, Berlin, 1970.

*Tonca* (Hartmut Biewald) book design, for Der Kinderbuchverlag, Berlin, 1974.

*Die feine stenglische Art* (Hansgeorg Stengel) book design, for Eulenspiegel Verlag, Berlin, 1977.

*Leben ist Lernen* (Hans Lowe) book design, for Urania-Verlag, Leipzig, 1978.

*Gedichte und Epigramme* (Hansgeorg Stengel) book design, for Eulenspiegel Verlag, Berlin, 1981.

*Nadja, mein Liebling* (Lilo Hardel) book design, for Der Kinderbuchverlag, Berlin, 1982.

*Poesiealbum 186* (Hansgeorg Stengel) book design, for Verlag Neues Leben, Berlin, 1983.

*Pinocchios Abenteuer* (Carlo Collodi) book design for Verlag Philipp Reclam, Leipzig, 1986.

*Kleines Ratbuch fur Kinder* book design, for Der Kinderbuchverlag, Berlin, 1987.

*Kurzweil durch Mathe* (Johannes Lehmann) book design, for Urania-Verlag, Leipzig, 1988.

*Esel sei der Mensch* (Ernst Röhl) book design, for Entenspiegel Verlag, Berlin, 1995.

**Publications**

**On MÜLLER: books—***Gebrauchsgraphik in der DDR* by

Hellmuth Rademacher, Dresden, 1975; *Rolf F. Müller: Das Plakat als Kunstgegenstand,* exhibition catalogue, Rostock, 1980; *Plakate Rolf F. Müller,* exhibition catalogue with text by V. Waallenberg, Kottbus, 1980; *Who's Who in Graphic Art* edited by Walter Amstutz, Dubendorf, 1982; *Rolf Felix Müller: Arbeit fur das Buch,* exhibition catalogue with texts by Lothar Lang, Axel Bertram, and others, Burgk/Saale, 1988; *3X Grafik Design: Rolf Felix Müller,* exhibition catalogue by Museum für Angewandte Kunts, Gera, 1992.

\*

Next to book illustration, the theatre poster has a particular place in my work. If the poster is often described as the favorite child of commercial graphics, I consider cultural advertising and the art poster as one of the noblest and most enticing tasks I can think of. The theatre poster draws its charm not least from its relationship to its surroundings. It brings something meditative, a breath of poetry, into the everyday life of our towns, for the cultural atmosphere of a town is influenced by its billboards. Ideas and events are made visual in signs and images which challenge the thinking observer. It is here that the poster has its chance, along with its aesthetic and educational functions, to stimulate thoughtful attitudes.

—Rolf Felix Müller

# MÜLLER-BROCKMANN, Josef
Swiss graphic designer

**Born:** Josef Mario Müller, in Rapperswil, St. Gallen, 9 May 1914; adopted name Müller-Brockmann, 1942. **Education:** Studied architecture, design, and art history, at the Abendgymnasium Juventus, the ETH Eidgenossische Technische Hochschule, the University of Zürich, and at the Kunstgewerbeschule, Zürich. **Family:** Married Verena Brockmann in 1942 (died, 1964); children: Andreas; married Shizuko Yoshikawa in 1967. **Career:** Assistant designer to graphics and advertising consultant Walter Diggelmann, Zürich, 1934-36; freelance graphic and stage designer, in Zürich, from 1936; founder and co-editor, *Neue Grafik* magazine, Zürich, 1958-65; founder, Galerie 58 (later, Galerie Seestrasse), Rapperswil, 1965; design consultant, IBM Europe, in Paris, from 1966. Professor of graphic design, at the Kunstgewerbeschule, Zürich, 1956-59; guest lecturer, University of Arts, Osaka, from 1961, Hochschule für Gestaltung, Ulm, 1963, and Carlton University, Ottawa, 1972. President, Verband Schweizerische Graphiker, 1956-59; jury member, *Gute Form* committee, Bonn, from 1979. **Member:** Alliance Graphique Internationale, Paris. **Exhibitions:** Amerika Haus, Munich, 1952 (toured); Kongresshaus, Zürich, 1958; Institut für Auslandbezieungen, Stuttgart, 1958; Matsuya Department Store, Tokyo, 1961 (toured); Gewerbemuseum, Winterthur, 1963; AIGA Gallery, New York, 1967; BMW Pavilion, Munich, 1969; Feierabendhaus der Rosenthal, Selb 1971; Galerija Studenstskog Centra, Zagreb, 1973; Plakanda Gallery, Zürich, 1974; Osaka Art Center, Japan, 1975; Ryder Gallery, Chicago, 1977; Reinhold-Brown Gallery, New York, 1980; Engadiner Kollegium, St. Moritz, 1981; Plakat Galerie, Bern, 1982. **Collections:** Kunstgewerebemuseum, Zürich; Deutsches Plakatmuseum, Essen; Stedelijk Museum, Amsterdam; Gemeentemuseum, The Hague; Poster Museum, Warsaw; Museum of Modern Art, New York. **Address:** Enzianweg 4, 8048 Zürich, Switzerland.

## Publications

**By MÜLLER-BROCKMANN: books**—*Gestaltungsprobleme des Grafikers,* Teufen, 1961; *History of Visual Communication,* Teufen, 1971; (with Shizuko Müller-Brockmann) *History of the Poster,* Zürich, 1971; *Grid-System,* Teufen, 1981.

**On MÜLLER-BROCKMANN: books**—*Posters: 50 Artists and Designers* edited by W. H. Allner, New York, 1952; *The New Graphic Design* by Karl Gerstner and Markus Kutter, Teufen and London, 1959; *Modern Graphics* by Keith Murgatroyd, London, 1969; *Graphic Designers in Europe 1* edited by Henri Hillebrand, London, 1971; *Design* by Jocelyn de Noblet, Paris, 1974; *Who's Who in Graphic Art* edited by Walter Amstutz, Dubendorf, 1982; *Josef Müller-Brockmann: Typographie und Photographie in Konstruktiven Plakat,* exhibition catalogue by Willy Rotzler, Bern, 1982; *The 20th-Century Poster: Design of the Avant-Garde* by Dawn Ades, New York, 1984; *Typographic Design: Form and Communication* by Rob Carter, Ben Day, and Philip Meggs, New York, 1985.

\*

The use of the grid as an ordering system is the expression of a certain mental attitude inasmuch as it shows that the designer conceives his work in terms that are constructive and oriented to the future. This is the expression of a professional ethos: the designer's work should have the clearly intelligible, objective, functional, and aesthetic quality of mathematical thinking. His work should thus be a contribution to general culture and itself form part of it.

Constructive design which is capable of analysis and reproduction can influence and enhance the taste of a society and the way it conceives forms and colours. Design which is objective, committed to the common weal, well composed, and refined, constitutes the basis of democratic behaviour. Constructivist design means the conversion of design laws into practical solutions. Work done systematically and in accordance with strict formal principles makes those demands for directness, intelligibility, and the integration of all factors which are also vital in socio-political life.

Working with the grid system means submitting to laws of universal validity. The use of the grid system implies the will to systematize, to clarify; the will to penetrate to the essentials, to concentrate; the will to cultivate objectivity instead of subjectivity; the will to rationalize the creative and technical production processes; the will to integrate elements of colour, form, and material; the will to achieve architectural dominion over surface and space; the will to adopt a positive, forward-looking attitude; and the recognition of the importance of education and the effect of work devised in a constructive and creative spirit.

Every visual creative work is a manifestation of the character of the designer. It is a reflection of his knowledge, his ability, and his mentality. What is the purpose of the grid? The grid is used by the typographer, graphic designer, photographer, and exhibition designer for solving visual problems in two and three dimensions. The graphic designer and typographer use it for designing press advertisements, brochures, catalogues, books, periodicals, etc., and the exhibition designer, for conceiving his plan for exhibitions and show-window displays.

By arranging the surfaces and spaces in the form of a grid, the designer is favorably placed to dispose his texts, photographs, and diagrams in conformity with objective and functional criteria. The pictorial elements are reduced to a few formats of the same size. The size of the pictures is determined according to their importance for the subject. The reduction of the number of visual elements used and their incorporation in a grid system creates a sense of compact planning, intelligibility, and clarity and suggests orderliness of design. This orderliness lends added credibility to the information and induces confidence.

Information presented with clear and logically set out titles, subtitles, texts, illustrations, and captions will not only be read more quickly and easily, but the information will also be better understood and retained in the memory. This is a scientifically proved fact, and the designer should bear it constantly in mind. The grid can be successfully used for the corporate identities of firms. This includes all visual media of information from the visiting card to the exhibition stand, all printed forms for internal and external use, advertising matter, vehicles for goods and passenger transport, nameplates, lettering on buildings, etc.

—Josef Müller-Brockmann

\*     \*     \*

In order to appreciate the achievement of Josef Müller-Brockmann, it is necessary to set his clear, concise designs in the context of Swiss design generally. Although the Bauhaus moved from Germany to the United States, it may be said that the country that followed its achievements most closely was Müller-Brockmann's Switzerland. Two factors isolated this nation from the rest of the world at the time the designer was a young man. These were first, the economic depression which had originated in the United States and later, World War II, in which Switzerland remained neutral but became encircled. In this situation, with the help of the Swiss Ministry of the Interior, the design profession—and Müller-Brockmann—developed with a concentration on the precision long associated with Swiss craftsmanship.

This talented artist had exactly the skill and perception to provide a series of remarkable posters for the Zürich Tonhalle concerts just before 1960. As he explained, the posters, which were designed with strict formal elements, were intended as "the symbolic expression of the innate laws of music." Thus, for him, "thematic, dynamic, rhythmic, and metrical factors in music" have a corresponding form in the composition of the poster. In order to retain the economy and clarity he desired and yet provide the required information relating to the performances, all visual imagery based on the orchestra was dropped, and the essential musical element was conveyed solely in terms of typography. The resulting posters show lettering slanted diagonally in rhythmic intervals to produce images analogous to musical scores; equivalent to the disciplines of music, they are yet exciting visual experiences. Müller-Brockmann has also made a number of powerful posters for safety on the road. In these, he has combined the expressive typography demonstrated in the concert posters with dramatic photomontage imagery. Unlike the informationally oriented posters of the concert performances, these have the necessary single visual impact from which the entire message can be assimilated at a glance.

—John Barnicoat

# MUNARI, Bruno

Italian painter, sculptor, and photographer and exhibition, graphic, and industrial designer

---

**Born:** Milan, 24 October 1907. **Education:** Studied at the Technical Institute, Naples, 1924; self-taught in art and design. **Family:** Married Dilma Carnevali in 1934; children: Alberto. **Career:** Independent painter and sculptor, associating with Futurist groups, in Milan and Rome, from 1927; photographer and graphic designer, from 1932, and industrial designer, from 1948; designed for Danese, Olivetti, Pirelli, Mondadori, Einaudi, La Rinascente, Robots, IBM, Campari, Cinzano, and others. Professor, at the Scuola Politecnica di Design, Milan; visiting professor of design, at Harvard University, Cambridge, Massachusetts, 1970-71. **Exhibitions:** Galleria Tre Arti, Milan, 1933; Galleria Milano, Milan, 1934; Galleria Borromini, Milan, 1948; Galleria Cavallino, Venice, 1949; Galleria Elicottero, Milan, 1950; Museum of Modern Art, New York, 1954; Galleria Montenapoleone, Milan, 1958; Galleria Danese, Milan, 1959, 1961, 1963, 1965, 1968, 1980, 1981; Olivetti, Milan, 1962; Isetan, Tokyo, 1965; Galleria Obelisco, Rome, 1966; National Museum of Modern Art, Tokyo, 1966; Howard Wise Gallery, New York, 1966; Allgemeine Gewerbeschule, Basel, 1968; Galleria Sincron, Brescia, 1969, 1974, 1975, 1976, 1980, 1981, 1983; Galleria Uxa, Novara, 1970; Galleria San Fedele, Milan, 1971; Italian Cultural Institute, Copenhagen, 1972; Italian Cultural Institute, Stockholm, 1972; Galeria Cadaques Spain, 1975; Galleria Portello, Genoa, 1976; Galleria Mercato del Sale, Milan, 1976; Pinacoteca di Brera, Milan, 1977; University of Parma, 1979; Centro Culturale Olivetti, Ivera, 1980; Galleria Apollinaire, Milan, 1980. **Collections:** Galleria Nazionale d'Arte Moderna, Rome; Kaiser Wilhelm Museum, Krefeld; Museum of Modern Art, New York; Philadelphia Museum of Art. **Honors:** Gold Medal, Milan Triennale; Compasso d'Oro Award, Milan, 1954, 1955, 1979. **Address:** Via Vittoria Colonna 39, 20149 Milan, Italy.

## Works

*Zizi the Monkey* flexible toy, produced by Pigomma, 1953.
Ice bucket, produced by Tre A, 1955.
Cubic ashtray, produced by Danese, 1957.
*Cube* suspension lamp, produced by Danese, 1958.
Book designs, for Einaudi publishers, 1960s.
*X Hour* limited edition (50 examples) multiple, produced by Danese, 1963.
*Falkland* tubular lamp in aluminum and elastic knit, produced by Danese, 1964.
*Flexy* creative toy, produced by Danese, 1968.
*Lipari* ashtray in melamine and anodized aluminum, produced by Danese, 1971.
*Abitacolo* toy dwelling in steel, produced by Robots, 1971.
*Panarea* candlestick in stainless steel, produced by Danese, 1973.
*Datillo* lamp in plastic and iron, produced by Danese, 1978.
Hanging tensile bookshelf, produced by Robots, 1979.
Poster series, for Campari, from 1984.

## Publications

**By MUNARI: books—***I Libri Munari,* Milan, 1945; *Libro Illegibile,* Milan, 1949, New York, 1967; *The Lorry Driver,* London, 1953; *What I'd Like To Be,* London, 1953; *Nella notte buia,* Milan, 1956; *In the Dark of the Night,* New York, 1961; *Animals for Sale,* New York, 1957; *Who's There? Open the Door!,* New York, 1957; *Tic, Tac, Toc,* New York, 1957; *The Birthday Present,* New York, 1958; *The Elephant's Wish,* New York, 1959; *Jimmy Has Lost His Cap, Where Can It Be?,* New York, 1959; *Bruno Munari's ABC,* New York, 1960; *Alfabetiere secondo il metodo attivo,* Turin, 1960; *Il quadrato/The Square,* New York, 1960; *Discovery of the Square,* New York, 1963; *Vetrine, negozi italiani/Modern Design for Italian Shop-Windows,* Milan, 1961; *Good Design,* Milan and New York, 1963; *Supplemento al dizionario italiano/Supplement to the Italian Dictionary,* Milan and New York, 1963; *Bruno Munari's Zoo,* New York, 1963; *Il cerchio,* Milan, 1964; *Discovery of the Circle,* New York, 1965; *Arte come mestiere,* Bari, Italy, 1966; *Design as Art,* London, 1971; *Libro illeggibile NY 1,* New York, 1967; *Design e communicazione visive,* Bari, 1968; *Nella nebbia di Milano,* Milan, 1968; *Circus in the Mist,* New York, 1969; (editor) *Design italiano: Mobili,* Rome, 1968; (editor, with others) *Campo urbano: interventi estetici nella dimensione collettiva urbana,* Milan, 1969; *Artista e designer,* Rome, 1971; *Codice ovvio,* Turin, 1971; *Da lontano era un'isola,* Milan, 1971; *From Afar It Is An Island,* New York, 1972; *Cappuccetto verde,* Turin, 1972; *Cappuccetto giallo,* Turin, 1972; *Alfabetiere,* Turin, 1972; *Search for a Stone,* Milan and London, 1972; *A Flower with Love,* London, 1974; *12 Prelibri* (for children who do not know how to read), Milan, 1980; *Da cosa nasce cosa,* Bari, 1981; *Rose nell'insalata,* Turin, 1982; (editor, with G. Guiaro) *Made in Italia: Selezione dei Marchi Italiani,* Bologna, 1988.

**On MUNARI: books—***The New Graphic Design* by Karl Gerstner and Markus Kutter, Teufen and London, 1959; *Design Coordination and Corporate Image* by F. H. K. Henrion and Alan Parkin, London and New York, 1967; *Munari 71,* exhibition catalogue by Paolo Fossati and others, Milan, 1971; *Il Design in Italia 1945-1972* by Fossati, Turin, 1972; *Design e Forme Nuove nell'Arredamento Italiano* edited by Paolo Portoghesi and Marino Marini, Rome, 1978; *Bruno Munari,* exhibition catalogue by Giulio Carlo Argan and Alessandro Mendini, Parma, 1979; *Atlante del Design Italiano 1940/1980* by Alfonso Grassi and Anty Pansera, Milan, 1980; *L'Arte Anomala di Bruno Munari* by A. Tanchis, Bari, 1981; *Design Since 1945* edited by Kathryn Hiesinger and George Marcus, Philadelphia and London, 1983; *Bruno Munari: From Futurism to Post-Industrial Design* by Tanchis, London, 1987; *Italian Modern: A Design Heritage* by Giovanni Albera and Nicolas Monti, New York, 1989.

*     *     *

Bruno Munari began his career at the age of 19 in the engineering studio of an uncle in Milan. Although he quickly became involved in the Futurist movement, the experience in his uncle's studio was important because it convinced him that his artistic work should always be approached as a job rather than a stylistic undertaking, thereby eliminating financial dependence on an art market characterized by continuously changing tastes. Munari's work might be described as lacking any definable style. Over the course of nearly 70 years of making art he has experimented with, and been influenced by, a wide range of movements and individuals. But defining his own "style" is the essence of correctness of the design for the particular purpose. He believes that "if the form of an object turns out to be 'beautiful' it will be thanks to the logic of its construction, and to the precision of the solutions found for its various components. It is 'beautiful' because it is just right."

Munari participated in the Futurist exhibitions in Milan from 1927 to 1936. Few works from this period survive due to the perishable materials used for their construction, but his work showed a devotion to nature and an interest in the human figure which has been sustained throughout his career. His Futurist work led to experimentation with abstraction, but it was an abstraction free of formalist dogma. The *Useless Machines,* which he designed in the 1930s, developed out of his interest in the machine combined with his desire to create machines which were pacific, representing only themselves through their colors and the movement of forms. The idea for the *Useless Machines* arose from Munari's desire to free abstract forms from the painter's canvas and "let them share our surroundings with us, sensitive to the true atmosphere of reality..." Made of ordinary materials and mass producible, they were one of the earliest examples of kinetic sculpture.

Beginning in 1929, Munari worked as a graphic designer in a number of advertising studios, including Cassio's IPC where he pioneered the use of animated cartoons in Italian advertising. He also worked as a designer and illustrator for several magazines. In 1930 he opened a graphic design studio with Riccardo Ricas. His designs of the period show the influence of Enrico Prampolini, a Futurist, and Herbert Bayer. They often make reference to the human figure. His work in the 1930s and early 1940s ranged from painting to sculpture, photography (including photomontages and film), and set design, both for European and traditional N theatre. This range of experience with varied media no doubt facilitated his success in industrial design after World War II. In fact, Munari had worked in industrial design to a limited extent prior to the war, designing ceramic tiles, furniture (in which the pieces were painted in the style of his paintings), interior designs, and fabric designs.

One of Munari's greatest lifelong concerns has been communication, but not only visual communication. A prolific writer of essays, articles, poems, manifestoes, and books, he has strived to educate a broad audience, from children to adults, from artists to lay persons. Some of his writing, such as *Le Macchine di Munari* (1945) which contains imaginary machines like the "tail wagger for lazy dogs," displays an acute sense of humor in addition to didactic information.

In an effort to reconcile architecture, industrial design, and the visual arts, in 1948 Munari founded the Movimento Arte Concreta with Gillo Dorfles and Gianni Monnet. Their attempt to synthesize the arts was filled with disagreement and lasted only ten years, but during this time Munari worked on a series of paintings designed to challenge optical perceptions. His *Negative positives* were composed of non-objective shapes which alternately advance and recede, each capable of appearing to be either background or foreground. In the same way that his *Useless Machines* were an attempt to break with the ground, so too did the *Negative positives* attempt to break out of the confines of the plane of the painting.

This fascination with breaking the plane and with reducing a design to its simplest form can be seen in his industrial designs of the 1950s and 1960s. His designs for the *Tubular Falkland Lamp* of 1964 are the essence of simplicity. Made of knit fabric with aluminum rings of various sizes inserted to give them shape, the lamps break down easily into two dimensions when the rings are collapsed together. His candlesticks and ashtrays, produced by Danese in the 1970s, are exceedingly simple forms which are appealing precisely because of that simplicity. These and virtually all products which he designs are made of unadorned materials, often steel

or aluminum. They are so simple as to appear anonymous, in keeping with his belief that the objects are in fact incomplete until influenced by the owner's additions to the object or his placement of it with other objects. Munari has said, "It is always a question of clarity, of simplicity. There is much work to do that involves taking away, instead of adding. Taking away the superfluous in order to give exact information, instead of adding to and complicating the information." The imposition of the designer's style is seen by Munari as inappropriate because it is not essential to the function of the designed object. An excellent example is the *Abitacolo* of 1971. A multipurpose structure made of lightweight steel components assembled in a grid system, it is the ultimate living structure for a child, providing him with his own dwelling inside a dwelling. With components that may be rearranged at will, the *Abitacolo* incorporates into one structure bed, lamp, table, shelving, bins, and elements for hanging objects. It is essentially transparent, indestructible, completely devoid of any style. Its style becomes whatever the child makes it with his possessions.

In the 1940s Munari began to design and write for children, the artistic contribution for which he may be best known to the average person since, unlike his industrial designs, the work bears his name. Disturbed by the lack of educational books available to his son, he began writing and illustrating his own books and designing his own toys. Intended not just to amuse, but to improve the quality of a child's learning experience, his books and toys are, like his industrial designs, incomplete until the child interacts with them.

In the 1960s, convinced that children are less culturally conditioned and therefore show more potential for creativity than do adults, Munari shifted his focus largely to educating the young. He has travelled in Europe, Japan, and South America to conduct workshops with children. Anti-authoritarian in his approach to education, Munari's work with children in pre-schools, museum workshops, and elementary schools demonstrates his belief that experimentation with only limited direction is the key to the creative process.

—Sheila Klos

# MUSSER, Tharon

American stage lighting designer

**Born:** Roanoke, Virginia, 8 January 1925. **Education:** Studied at Berea College, Kentucky, BA, 1946; Yale University, New Haven, Connecticut, MFA, 1950. **Career:** Independent stage lighting designer, working in the United States and abroad, from 1949; staff designer, Center Theatre Group, Mark Taper Forum, Los Angeles, from 1970; advisor to the Chicago Auditorium, 1971, Los Angeles Shubert Theatre, 1971, and Dallas Music Hall, 1972; worked for Province Town Playhouse, Jose Limon Dance Company, Phoenix Theatre Company, American Theatre Festival Company, National Repertory Theatre Company, Boston Arts Festival, Dallas Civic Opera, Miami Opera Guild, Wolf Trap Foundation, and others. Lecturer, Yale University, New Haven, Connecticut, 1962, 1969, Bridgeport University, Connecticut, 1968, State University of New York, 1969, Bucknell University, Pennsylvania, 1973, Harvard University, Cambridge, Massachusetts, 1974-76. **Honors:** Los Angeles Drama Critics Circle Award, 1970, 1972, 1977, 1979; Antoinette Perry (Tony) Award, New York, 1971, 1975, 1981; Distinguished Alumnus Award, Berea College, Kentucky, 1973; United States Institute of Theatrical Technology Award, 1976;

Theatre Hall of Fame Award, New York, 1984. Honorary Doctorates: Berea College, Kentucky, 1979; Emerson College, Boston, 1980. **Address:** 21 Cornelia Street, New York, New York 10014, U.S.A.

## Works

Lighting designs include (in New York, unless specified)—*The Father,* 1949; *Naked,* 1950; *Lucky Sam McCarver,* 1950; *Long Day's Journey into Night,* 1956; *Shinbone Alley,* 1957; *Much Ado About Nothing,* Stratford, Connecticut, 1957; *Monique,* 1957; *The Makropoulos Secret,* 1957; *The Chairs,* 1958; *The Lesson,* 1958; *The Infernal Machine,* 1958; *The Firstborn,* New York and Tel Aviv, 1958; *The Entertainer,* 1958; *The Shadow of a Gunman,* 1958; *A Midsummer Night's Dream,* Stratford, Connecticut, 1958; *Murder in the Cathedral,* 1958; *JB,* 1958; *The Beaux' Stratagem,* 1959; *The Rivalry,* 1959; *Once upon a Mattress,* 1959; *Romeo and Juliet, A Midsummer Night's Dream,* and *The Merry Wives of Windsor,* all Stratford, Connecticut, 1959; *The Great God Brown,* 1959; *Only in America,* 1959; *Five Finger Exercise,* 1959; *Peer Gynt,* 1960; *The Long Dream,* 1960; *The Tumbler,* 1960; *Twelfth Night, The Tempest,* and *Antony and Cleopatra,* all Stratford, Connecticut, 1960; *As You Like It* and *Macbeth,* both Stratford, Connecticut, 1961; *The Garden of Sweets,* 1961; *The Turn of the Screw, Anatol,* and *Elizabeth the Queen,* all at the American Theatre Festival, Boston, 1961; *Advise and Consent,* on tour, 1961; *Mary Stuart* and *Elizabeth the Queen,* both National Repertory Theatre tours, 1961; *The Skin of Our Teeth, The Glass Menagerie,* and *The Miracle Worker,* all American Repertory Company State Department-sponsored tours, 1961; *Giants, Sons of Giants,* 1962; *Calculated Risk,* 1962; *Nowhere to Go But Up,* 1962; *HMS Pinafore* and *Androcles and the Lion,* both at the American Theatre Festival, Boston, 1962; *Andorra,* 1963; *Mother Courage and Her Children,* 1963; *King Lear, The Comedy of Errors,* and *Henry V,* all Stratford, Connecticut, 1963; *Here's Love,* 1963; *Marathon '33,* 1963; *Ring Round the Moon, The Seagull,* and *The Crucible,* all National Repertory Theatre tours, 1963; *Any Wednesday,* 1964; *Much Ado About Nothing, Richard III,* and *Hamlet,* all Stratford, Connecticut, 1964; *Golden Boy,* 1964; *Alfie,* 1964; *Hedda Gabler,* 1964; *Liliom,* 1964; *She Stoops to Conquer,* National Repertory Theatre tour, 1964; *Kelly,* 1965; *All in Good Time,* 1965; *Flora,* 1965; *The Red Menace,* 1965; *Coriolanus, Romeo and Juliet, The Taming of the Shrew,* and *King Lear,* all Stratford, Connecticut, 1965; *Mais Oui,* Beirut, 1965; *Minor Miracle,* 1965; *Rivals, The Madwoman of Chaillot,* and *The Trojan Women,* all National Repertory Theatre tours, 1965; *Malcolm,* 1966; *The Great Indoors,* 1966; *The Lion in Winter,* 1966; *Mame,* 1966; *Twelfth Night, Falstaff, Julius Caesar,* and *Murder in the Cathedral,* all Stratford, Connecticut, 1966; *A Delicate Balance,* 1966; *Tonight at 8:30, A Touch of the Poet,* and *The Imaginary Invalid,* all National Repertory Theatre tours, 1966; *Hallelujah, Baby!,* 1967; *A Midsummer Night's Dream, Antigone,* and *The Merchant of Venice,* all Stratford, Connecticut, 1967; *The Birthday Party,* 1967; *After the Rain,* 1967; *The Promise,* 1967; *Everything in the Garden,* 1967; *John Brown's Body* and *The Comedy of Errors,* both National Repertory Theatre tours, 1967; *House of Flowers,* 1968; *Catch My Soul,* Los Angeles, 1968; *Golden Boy,* Palladium, London, 1968; *As You Like It* and *Androcles and the Lion,* both Stratford, Connecticut, 1968; *The Lovers,* 1968; *Maggie Flynn,* 1968; *The Fig Leaves Are*

*Falling,* 1969; *The Gingham Dog,* 1969; *Spofford,* on tour, 1969; *Mame,* Drury Lane, London, 1969; *Fedora,* Dallas Civic Opera, 1969; *Blood Red Roses,* 1970; *Applause,* 1970; *The Boy Friend,* 1970; *The Dream on Monkey Mountain* and *Rose Bloom,* both Los Angeles, 1970; *The Merry Widow, Madama Butterfly, Il Tabarro,* and *Carmina Burana,* all Dallas Civic Opera, 1970; *L.A. under Siege,* 1970; *The Trial of the Catonsville Nine,* Los Angeles, 1970; *Follies,* 1971; *The Trial of the Catonsville Nine,* 1971; *Who Wants to Be the Lone Ranger,* Los Angeles, 1971; *On the Town,* 1971; *The Prisoner of Second Avenue,* 1971; *Major Barbara,* Los Angeles, 1971; *Fidelio,* Dallas Civic Opera, 1971; *Night Watch,* 1972; *The Creation of the World and Other Business,* 1972; *The Great God Brown* 1972; *Don Juan,* 1972; *The Sunshine Boys,* 1972; *Old Times,* Los Angeles, 1972; *The Dream on Donkey Mountain,* Munich, 1972; *Applause,* Her Majesty's Theatre, London, 1972; *A Little Night Music,* 1973; *Forget Me Not Lane,* Los Angeles, 1973; *Sondheim: A Musical Tribute,* 1973; *The Orphan,* 1973; *The Good Doctor,* 1973; *Andrea Chenier,* Dallas Civic Opera, 1973; *Candide,* 1974; *Saint Joan* and *The Last Charlatan,* both Los Angeles, 1974; *God's Favorite,* 1974; *Mack and Mabel,* 1974; *Good News,* 1974; *The Pearl Fishers,* Miami Opera Guild, 1974; *Lucrezia Borgia,* 1974; *Mignon,* Dallas Civic Opera, 1974; *The Wiz,* 1975; *Same Time, Next Year,* 1975; *A Chorus Line,* 1975; *Me and Bessie,* 1975; *Tales of Hoffman,* Dallas Civic Opera, 1975; *The Flying Dutchman,* Miami Opera Guild, 1975; *Pacific Overtures,* 1976; *Otello,* Miami Opera Guild, 1976; *1600 Pennsylvania Avenue,* 1976; *California Suite,* 1976; *A Chorus Line,* London, 1976; *Hooray USA!,* Miami Bicentennial Pageant, 1976; *Romeo and Juliet,* London Ballet Festival, 1977; *Doktor Faust,* Wolf Trap Foundation, Vienna, Virginia, 1977; *Chapter Two,* 1977; *The Act,* 1977; *Tribute,* 1978; *Ballroom,* 1978; *They're Playing Our Song,* London, 1979; *Terra Nova,* 1979; *Romantic Comedy,* 1979; *Whose Life Is It, Anyway?,* 1979; *1940s Radio Hour,* 1979; *Last Licks,* 1979; *The Roast,* 1980; *Children of A Lesser God,* 1980; *I Ought to Be in Pictures,* 1980; *42nd Street,* 1980; *Dreamgirls,* 1981; *Children of a Lesser God,* London, 1981; *Fools,* 1981; *Moony Shapiro's Songbook,* 1981; *Hoagy, Bix and Wolfgang,* Los Angeles, 1981; *Tales of Hollywood,* Los Angeles, 1982; *Special Occasions,* 1982; *Merlin,* 1983; *Brighton Beach Memoirs,* 1983; *Private Lives,* 1983; *The Real Thing,* 1984; *Open Admissions,* 1984; *Biloxi Blues,* 1985; *Odd Couple,* 1985; *Jerry's Girls,* 1985; *Broadway Bound,* 1986; *A Month of Sundays,* 1987; *Teddy and Alice,* 1987; *Rumors,* 1988; *Ziegfeld,* Paladium, London, 1988; *Dutch Landscape,* Los Angeles, 1989.

## Publications

**On MUSSER: books**—*The Biographical Encyclopaedia and Who's Who of the American Theatre* edited by Walter Rigdon, New York, 1966; *Contemporary Theatre, Film and Television 2,* Detroit, 1986; *The Cambridge Guide to World Theatre* edited by Martin Banham, Cambridge, 1988; **articles**—in *Theatre Crafts* (New York), November/December 1974, November/December 1975, March/April 1979, August/September 1982; *Lighting Dimensions* (New York), June 1977; *Diversion* (New York), June 1982; *Christian Science Monitor* (Boston), 12 July 1982; *Popular Computing* (New York), August 1983.

*

Lighting design is a most difficult art to verbalize on. I am afraid the work must speak for itself. I am first, last, and always a designer, not a speaker or writer. Thanks to our technology, I believe theatre design in this country, particularly on Broadway, is the best in the world, and still improving.

—Tharon Musser

\*     \*     \*

Tharon Musser is not only the most prolific lighting designer in American theatre history, she is also a pioneer. Since her first professional job as a designer off-Broadway in 1949, her work has brought respect to the lighting designer as a theatre professional. While helping to open a field previously closed to women, she has pioneered the practice of the lighting designer being part of a collaborative artistic team, working from the beginning of a production with the scenic designer, costume designer, and director. Finally, she has, almost singlehandedly, brought modern technology to the Broadway stage by initiating computerized lighting control.

At the American Shakespeare Festival, Musser has designed lighting for more than twenty-five productions, including *Much Ado About Nothing, A Midsummer Night's Dream, The Merry Wives of Windsor, Romeo and Juliet, Antony and Cleopatra, Twelfth Night, The Tempest, As You Like It, Macbeth, Henry V, Comedy of Errors, King Lear, Richard III, Hamlet, The Taming of the Shrew, Julius Caesar* and *The Merchant of Venice.* Her versatility is exemplified by her very different work on Broadway with musicals such as *Hallelujah, Baby!, Applause, The Boy Friend, Follies, A Little Night Music, Mack and Mabel, Good News, The Wiz, Pacific Overtures, The Act, 42nd Street, Ballroom,* and *A Chorus Line.* Moreover, Musser is just as comfortable with contemporary plays as she is with Shakespeare and musical theatre. She designed the lighting for *Any Wednesday, A Delicate Balance, California Suite, Travesties, The Sunshine Boys, The Prisoner of Second Avenue, Chapter Two, Whose Life Is It Anyway?,* and *Same Time, Next Year.*

Musser's talent lies in her ability to paint with color and light, using the stage like a canvas in order to create subtleties of atmosphere and mood. Although she sees each production as an individual entity, one can see some telltale "brush-marks" in her work. For example, she prefers many lamps with a great many cues (e.g., more than 260 lighting cues in *Ballroom*); she experiments with new kinds of lamps and equipment to achieve special effects; she is well known for her preference for a "no-color green" gel and for her fast moving changes of lighting, which are now accomplished through computerized lighting panels. These computerized controls used in the majority of productions today, as a result of her innovation, permit faster, smoother changes of lights; they allow the technicians to run the production from in front of the stage, where they can see what is happening, rather than as before, from a black box off to the side backstage where they could hear but not see; and they make it possible for one or two technicians to run a show, where as previously it took many more.

Musser constantly experiments with new equipment and new methods of using lights in the theatre. In *Ballroom,* for example, she utilized new three-and-one-half-inch units with 750-watt lamps (rather than the approved 500-watt lamps) to replace the standard six-inch lamps for which she did not have room. She also used color wheels and an old-fashioned mirror ball to transform the ballroom into a place of magic. In *Dreamgirls,* Musser exploited all the techniques and technologies of lighting design to create a quickly moving world of show business with lights everywhere; the lighting helps to shift the constantly changing locations of the musical's fast-paced action.

—John E. Hirsch

# MYKKANEN, (August) Martti

Finnish illustrator and graphic designer

**Born:** Iisalmi, 15 November 1926. **Education:** Studied at the Central School of Design Arts, Helsinki, 1946-51, and as an exchange artist, in Basel, Switzerland, 1952. **Family:** Married Raija Liisa Vuorela in 1954 (divorced, 1986); children: Raili and Riitta. **Career:** Graphic artist, working with the Cooperative Chain, Helsinki, 1946-52; illustrator, *Uusi Kuvalehti* weekly magazine, Helsinki, 1953-54; freelance graphic designer, working for Gummerus, Tammi, WSOY, Lahti Art Museum, Talja Traffic Safety Association, *OKO Bankers* magazine, *Look at Finland* magazine, and others, in Helsinki, from 1955. **Member:** Alliance Graphique Internationale, 1966. **Exhibitions:** *Martti Mykkanen: Posters of the 1950s and 1960s,* Lahti Art Museum, Finland, 1989. **Collections:** Stedelijk Museum, Amsterdam; Royal Ontario Museum, Toronto; Poster Museum, Warsaw; Lahti Art Museum. **Honors:** First Prize, Book Cover Competition, Helsinki, 1957, 1958, 1959; Ulkomainos Oy Scholarship, Helsinki, 1966; City of Helsinki Scholarship, 1970; Gold Medal, Travel Poster Competition, Catania, 1971; Goldene Reisekutsche Award, Darmstadt, 1973; State Industrial Design Award, Helsinki, 1979; Björn Landström Award, Helsinki, 1986; Czech Peace Council Award, Brno, 1988. **Address:** Mannerheimintie 146 A 32, 00270 Helsinki, Finland.

## Works

*The Lamb* (F. Mauriac) book cover, for WSOY, 1955.
*The Winter* (F. Griese) book cover, for WSOY, 1955.
*Small Gods* (R. Wright) book cover, for WSOY, 1955.
*Alberte Is Alone* (C. Sandel) book cover, for Gummerus, 1955.
*The Red Room* (A. Strindberg) book cover, for Gummerus, 1957.
*Story of the Seven Hanged* (L. Andrejev) book cover, for Gummerus, 1957.
*Starving Artist* (F. Kafka) book cover, for Gummerus, 1959.
*Beggar's Novel* (B. Brecht) book cover, for Tammi, 1959.
*Love of the Old Prince* (F. Dostojevski) book cover, for Gummerus, 1960.
*Too Late, Water Swallow* (A. Paton) book cover, for WSOY, 1963.
*Ulysses* (J. Joyce) book cover, for Tammi, 1963.
Poster, for the Finnish Heart Disease Association, 1967.
*Remember the Danger When Driving Fast* poster, for Talja Traffic Safety Association, 1967.
*Gallery of the Street* poster, for Ulkomainos Oy, 1969.
*Design '81* poster, for the Helsinki Design Congress, 1981.
*5th Poster Biennale* poster, for Lahti Art Museum, 1982.
*Finnish Graphic Planning* poster, for Association of Graphic Artists, 1983.
*Finnish Graphic Design in Oslo* poster, for Graphic Designers Association, 1986.
*Martti Mykkanen: Graphic Design* poster, for Lahti Art Museum, 1989.

**Publications**

**On MYKKANEN: books**—*Poster Design* by Tom Eckersley, London, 1954; *Posters of Protest and Revolution* by Maurice Rickards, Milan, 1970; *History of the Poster* by Josef and Shizuko Müller-Brockman, Zürich, 1971; *Den Massproducerade Bilden* by Lena Johannesson, Stockholm, 1978; *Who's Who in Graphic Art* edited by Walter Amstutz, Dubendorf, 1982; *The Modern Poster* by Stuart Wrede, Barcelona, 1988; *Martti Mykkanen: Posters of the 1950s and 1960s,* exhibition catalogue with text by Riitta Niskanen, Lahti, 1989; **articles**—"Martti Mykkanen—Finland" by Ludwig Ebenhoh in *Gebrauchsgraphik* (Munich), no. 11, 1957; "From Pure Art to Poster War" by Osmo Pasanen in *Form Function Finland* (Helsinki), no. 1/2, 1980; "The Poster—A Mini-Scandal" by Ullamaria Pallasmaa in *Look at Finland* (Helsinki), no. 1, 1983.

# NAGAI, Kazumasa

Japanese graphic designer

**Born:** Osaka, 20 April 1929. **Education:** Studied sculpture, at Tokyo National University of Fine Arts and Music, 1949-51. **Family:** Married Setsuko Sakuma in 1978; son: Kazufumi. **Career:** Worked as a graphic designer for Daiwa Spinning Company, Osaka, 1951-60; founder-designer, from 1960, president, 1975-86, and representative director, from 1986, of the Nippon Design Center, Tokyo; has designed for Asahi Breweries, Sapporo Winter Olympics, Suruga Bank, *Space Design* magazine, Toyama Museum of Modern Art, Takashimaya Department Stores, Tenri Religious Organization, and others. **Member:** Tokyo Designer's Space; president, Japan Graphic Designers Association; Art Directors Club of Tokyo; Alliance Graphique Internationale. **Exhibitions:** Museum of Modern Art, Warsaw, 1968; Tokyo Designer's Space, 1976, 1978, 1981, 1984, 1992; Ikeda Museum of 20th Century Art, Ito, 1980; Université du Québec a Montréal, Canada, 1985; Israel Museum, Jerusalem, 1986; Machida City Museum of Graphic Art, 1988; Himeji City Museum of Art, 1988; *Kazumasa Nagai & Nippon Design Center Exhibition,* Art Directors Gallery, New York, 1990; Museum of Modern Art, Toyama, 1990; Ginza Matsuya Design Gallery, Tokyo, 1991; Brno Design Centre Gallery, Czechoslovakia, 1992; Ginza Graphic Gallery, 1994. **Collections:** Himeji City Museum of Art, Japan; Museum of Modern Art, Toyama; National Museum of Art, Tokyo; Ikeda 20th Century Museum, Ito City; Poster Museum, Warsaw; Metropolitan Museum of Art, New York; Museum of Modern Art, New York; Kunstindustrimuseet, Copenhagen; Victoria and Albert Museum, London; Musée de la Publicité, Paris; Kunstgewerbemuseum, Zurich; Staatliches Museum für Angewandte Kunst, Munich; Australian National Gallery, Canberra; Israel Museum, Jerusalem. **Honors:** Tokyo Art Directors Club Award, 1962, 1983; Warsaw Poster Biennale Medals, 1966, 1968; Japanese Advertising Artists Club Prize, 1966; Mainichi Design Prize, 1966, 1983, and Mainichi Art Award, 1994, Tokyo; Asahi Advertising Prize, Tokyo, 1966; National Museum of Modern Art Prize, Tokyo, 1968; Yamana Prize, Tokyo, 1980; Japan Graphic Design Exhibition Prize, New York, 1981, 1984; Membership Award, 1983, and Award of Excellence, 1992, Tokyo Art Directors Club; Brno Graphic Design Biennale Award, 1984, 1988; Japanese Ministry of Art Prize, 1988; Educational Minister's Art Encouragement Prize of Fine Arts, Tokyo, 1992; Grand Prize, Moscow International Poster Triennial, 1992; First Prize, International Poster Biennial, Mexico City, 1992; Second Prize, 11th International Biennial of Humour and Satire in the Arts, Gabrovo, 1993; Academy Honorary Award, 14th International Poster Biennial, Warsaw, 1994. **Address:** c/o Nippon Design Center, Chuo Daiwa Building, 1-13-13 Ginza, Chuo-ku, Tokyo 104, Japan.

## Works

*Stiny* beer poster, for Asahi Breweries, Ltd., 1965.
*Growth* poster, for Time-Life science book series, 1966.
*Expo '75* poster, for the Okinawa International Ocean Exposition Organizing Committee, 1972.
*GQ* print magazine poster, for GQ Publishing Company, 1974.
*Wallpaper* poster, for Kawakichi Company, 1974.
Posters, for Adonis Printing Company, 1976.
*Kazumasa Nagai* exhibition poster, for Mikimoto Hall, Tokyo, 1978.
*The World of Kazumasa Nagai* exhibition poster for Ikeda Museum of 20th Century Art, Ito City, 1980.
*Kazumasa Nagai* touring exhibition poster, for the Gallery Nurihiko, Tokyo, 1982.
*Contemporary Japanese Posters* exhibition poster, for the Museum of Modern Art, Toyama, 1982.
*Shuzo Takiguchi and His Favorite Postwar Arts* exhibition poster, for the Museum of Modern Art, Toyama, 1982.
*Tradition et Nouvelles Techniques: 12 Graphistes Japonais* exhibition poster, for the French Ministry of Culture, 1984.
*Georges Rouault's Prints* exhibition poster, for the Museum of Modern Art, Toyama, 1984.
*Hiroshima Appeals '87* poster, for the Hiroshima International Cultural Foundation/Japan Graphic Designers Association, 1987.
*4—G.D., Posters and Marks* exhibition poster for the Four Graphic Designers Exhibition Executive Committee, Tokyo, 1987.
*Japan* posters, for the Four Graphic Designers Exhibition Executive Committee, Tokyo, 1987.
*Japan* posters, for the JAGDA Japan Graphic Designers Association, 1988.
*Images Internationales pour les Droits de l 'Homme et du Citoyen* poster, for the French Revolution Bicentenary Mission, Paris, 1988.
*Europalia 1989: Japan in Belgium* poster, 1989.
*Kazumasa Nagai Exhibition* poster, for Ginza Matsuya Design Gallery, Tokyo, 1991.
*I'm Here* posters, for Peace Campaign, 1992-93.
*Kazumasa Nagai Design Life* poster, for Rikuyo-sha Publishing, Inc., Japan, 1994.
Symbol designs include—11th Olympic Winter Games, 1966; Expo '75-International Ocean Exposition, 1973; Tokyo Electric Power Co., Ltd., 1987; Ibaraki Prefecture, 1991; Niigata Prefecture, 1992.

## Publications

**By NAGAI: books**—*Art Directions,* Tokyo, 1968; (with others) *On Contemporary Design,* Tokyo, 1968; (with others) *Twelve Graphic Designers,* Tokyo, 1968; (with others) *Brief History of*

**Kazumasa Nagai: I'm Here, for Japan Graphic Designers Association, 1992**

*Japanese Design,* Tokyo, 1970; (with Hideo Mukai and Yusuke Kaji) *Graphic Design in the World,* Tokyo, 1974; *Posters by Kazumasa Nagai,* Tokyo, 1976; (with Seiichiro Arai, Yusuke Kaji and Ikko Tanaka) *Japan's Art Direction,* Tokyo, 1977; (with others) *Ads Change, Change Ads,* Tokyo, 1979; *The World of Kazumasa Nagai,* Tokyo, 1985; *Kazumasa Nagai,* Tokyo, 1993; *Kazumasa Nagai Design Life,* Tokyo, 1994.

**On NAGAI: books**—*An International Survey of Press Advertising* edited by Kurt Weidemann, Stuttgart and London, 1966; *An International Survey of Packaging* by Wim Crouwel and Kurt Weidemann, London, 1968; *History of the Poster* by Josef and Shizuko Müller-Brockmann, Zürich, 1971; *Ten Print Artists* by Shozo Kawai, Tokyo, 1976; *Graphic Designers* by Seiichiro Arai, Tokyo, 1981; *Who's Who in Graphic Art* edited by Walter Amstutz. Dubendorf, 1982.

\*

Over the past several years, I have been striving to bring out my own personal, individual consciousness in my design work. I have been doing this because stereotyped advertising and designs are ineffective in this age of wave after wave of information. Although there seem to be certain effective styles that have been established for use in mass communication media, I can never simply repeat such styles.

What I have gained confidence in, however, is something very similar to "personal communication," or, so to speak, the transmitting of ideas to specific individuals. In the ultimate analysis, this is like talking to oneself.

Can I be allowed to have such an idea, however? Most probably, I can't. This is because each poster design—which is usually printed in a volume of several thousand—is viewed by many people. Although I consider poster art the best form of expression that I can trust, on close examination, however, it's impossible to expect every one of the scores of thousands of people who look at a poster to get so much out of it that that poster would be remembered or that everyone would get an identical feeling and effect from seeing that poster. Any such expectation would be merely a fruitless delusion.

A design produced from such a delusive expectation would have to be composed of the most common elements, and such a design would surely quickly disappear into the overflowing sea of information without leaving a trace. Instead of entertaining such false expectations, the artist would do better to express himself to the very best of his ability by aiming at only a few select individuals, perhaps a couple of dozen people who will definitely gain a strong impression from his poster design. In this way, the artist will be sure to effect at least some communication.

I'm afraid the world—especially Japan—has been working too hard for economic success. Most corporations have been seeking material wealth by making profits their major goal, for the just cause that they might eventually offer such material richness to all. Advertising and design, too, have been playing a strong role as a detached force at the commercial warfront for corporate purposes. As a result, we have to realize that something valuable has gone down the drain. An alarm bell has begun to peal its warning that as companies race faster and faster in search of profits, all humanity may be ruined. The environment and culture in which corporations are located deserve more serious consideration. We must discover the way in which our spirit and human mind can peacefully exist in

today's society, where materialism has achieved a dominant place. The money Japan has spent on culture in this sense, compared with that of other advanced countries, is so petty and infinitesimal that we should feel ashamed.

Some Japanese corporations are well aware that their future existence may not be permitted without attempts to improve the local environment, culture, and the arts. And, it is true that some of them have recently begun concrete activities for such community purposes. Still, most corporations are not aware of the importance of returning some portion of their business profits to society.

Concrete, coordinated, cultural and artistic activities for corporate image-building are badly needed both in Japan and around the world. That, I think, is becoming an important role for today's graphic designers. I hope to take a leading part in this activity...

In my recent works with the theme of representational animals, I seek the meaning of living by delving into life, which is universal and common to man and animals. Each animal is a symbol as a mirror of my mind. Types or shapes are definitely not being solely pursued. Before, I made evolved abstract works and expressed the mystery of the universe. They were diffused in a way and related to my converged works now as inside is to outside or front is to back. In terms of the universe, both have a sense of life in common and are based on the idea of continuing to coexist.

—Kazumasa Nagai

\*    \*    \*

The ability to skillfully combine abstract expression and realistic demands has been a characteristic feature of Kazumasa Nagai's work. Nagai states that it is easier to express his inner self with abstraction, but that no doubt has something to do with the fact that he studied sculpture as a student. Nagai's graphic expression is not something which presses one urgently; rather, it persuades quietly. At the same time, however, his modeling shows firmness. In early works, he pursued form, but in recent years, he has added the techniques of color and collage, and his works have gained a certain liveliness.

Nagai has, on the one hand, for quite some time directed a business as president of a design production company, while on the other, he also practices art, particularly printmaking. In addition, he is in a position of leadership in the Japan Graphic Designers Association.

—Masaaki Tanaka

# NAKAMURA, Makoto
Japanese graphic designer

**Born:** Iwate, 9 May 1936. **Education:** Studied design, at the University of Arts, Tokyo, 1944-48. **Family:** Married Shoko Nakamura in 1953; son: Seiichi. **Career:** Staff designer, 1948-83, and advertising and design manager, from 1983, at Shiseido Cosmetics Company Tokyo. **Member:** Art Directors Club of Tokyo; Art Directors Club of New York. **Exhibitions:** *Mona Lisa Smile Exhibition,* Tokyo, 1972; *International Posters,* Musée des Arts Décoratifs, Paris, 1972; Warsaw Poster Biennale, 1978, *Makoto Nakamura: Posters,* Art Directors Club of New York, 1983. **Collections:** Musée des Arts Décoratifs, Paris; Museum of Modern Art, New York. **Honors:** Japan Advertising Art Association Award, Tokyo; Tokyo Art Directors Club Award; Ministry of International Trade and Industry Awards, Tokyo; Dentsu Advertising Art Award, Tokyo; Warsaw Poster Biennale Award; Kinugasa Award, Tokyo; Yamana Award, Tokyo. **Address:** 1403 Hongo House, 1-28-7 Hongo, Bunkyo-ku, Tokyo, Japan.

## Publications

By NAKAMURA: books—*One Hundred Smiles of Mona Lisa,* Tokyo, 1971.

On NAKAMURA: books—*Art Directors Club Yearbook,* Tokyo, 1980; *Ten Poster Artists of the World* by *Idea* magazine editors, Tokyo, 1982; *Makoto Nakamura: Poster Works,* exhibition folder, with text by Kazumasa Nagai, New York, 1983.

*

I like to create a cheerful and happy picture through graphic design in advertising. I hope that the advertisements will be enjoyed by the consumers who view them and that they will have a positive influence on their lives. I hope my work contributes to the culture of everyday life. Further, I wish to express the beauty of Japanese women in pictures through advertising.

—Makoto Nakamura

\*      \*      \*

Makoto Nakamura came to maturity within the enterprise of Shiseido, which has had a tradition ever since its founding as one of the most prominent advertisers in Japan and at which many designers are directly employed because the company does not rely on agencies for its design.

Not surprisingly, therefore, Nakamura is not the type of designer who possesses a strong individuality; rather, as art director and as head of the department of design in that company, he exhibits a well-rounded personality. He often collaborates with photographers and his skillful layouts of those photographs always have great freshness.

—Masaaki Tanaka

# NAPIER, John
British stage and film designer

**Born:** London, 1 March 1944. **Education:** Studied at Hornsey College of Art, London, 1961-62, and at Central School of Arts and Crafts, London, 1962-66. **Family:** Married Andreane Neofitou; children: two; married Donna King; children: two. **Career:** Freelance stage designer, working with the Phoenix Theatre, Leicester, 1967-68, London West End theatres, from 1968, the National Theatre, London, from 1973, and the Royal Shakespeare Company in London and Stratford-upon-Avon, from 1974. **Member:** British Society of Theatre Designers; associate member, Royal Shakespeare Company, London. **Exhibitions:** *British Theatre Design 83-87,*

Riverside Studios, Hammersmith, London, 1988. **Honors:** Society of West End Theatres Award, London, 1977, 1978, 1980; Antoinette Perry (Tony) Award, New York, 1981, 1982, 1987, 1995. **Address:** c/o McNaughton Lowe Representation, 200 Fulham Road, London SW10 9PN, England.

## Works

Stage designs include—(London, unless noted) *A Penny for a Song,* Phoenix Theatre, Leicester, 1967; *Fortune and Men's Eyes,* 1968; *The Ruling Class,* 1969; *The Fun War,* 1969; *Muzeeka,* 1969; *Cancer,* 1970; *Isabel's a Jezebel,* 1970; *Mister,* 1971; *The Foursome,* 1971; *The Lovers of Viorne,* 1971; *Lear,* 1971; *Jump,* 1972; *Sam, Sam,* 1972; *Big Wolf* 1972; *The Devils,* Sadlers Wells Theatre, 1973; *Equus,* Old Vic, 1973; *The Party,* Old Vic, 1973; *Knuckle,* 1974; *King John,* Shakespeare Memorial Theatre, Stratford, 1974; *Richard III,* Shakespeare Memorial Theatre, 1974; *Cymbeline,* Shakespeare Memorial Theatre, 1974; *MacBeth,* Shakespeare Memorial Theatre, 1974; *Richard II,* Shakespeare Memorial Theatre, 1974; *Hedda Gabler,* 1975; *A Midsummer Night's Dream,* Royal Shakespeare Company, 1977; *As You Like It,* Royal Shakespeare Company, 1977; *Twelfth Night,* Royal Shakespeare Company, 1978; *Three Sisters,* Royal Shakespeare Company, 1978; *Comedy of Errors,* Royal Shakespeare Company, 1978; *Nicholas Nickleby,* Royal Shakespeare Company, 1980; *Cats,* 1981 (also Winter Garden Theatre, New York, 1982); *Henry IV,* Royal Shakespeare Company, Barbican Theatre, 1982; *Starlight Express,* 1984 (and Broadway, New York, 1987); *Les Miserables,* 1985 (and Broadway, New York, 1987); *Time,* 1986; *Miss Saigon,* 1989; *The Baker's Wife,* 1989; *Siegfried & Roy,* The Mirage, Las Vegas, 1990; (and co-director) *Children of Eden,* 1990; *Trelawny of the Wells,* 1993; *Sunset Boulevard,* 1993, and New York, 1994; *Burning Blue,* 1995.
Film designs include—*Captain EO* (music video), 1987; *Hook* (Spielberg), 1991.

## Publications

By NAPIER: books—(illustrator) *William Shakespeare: Cymbeline,* London, 1976; (photographs and drawings) *Cats: The Book of the Musical,* London and New York, 1981, 1983, 1986; articles—in *The Designer* (London), April 1981.

On NAPIER: books—*Who's Who in the Theatre* edited by Ian Herbert, London, 1977; *British Theatre Design 83-87,* with texts by Timothy O'Brien and David Fingleton, London, 1988; *Contemporary Theatre, Film and Television,* Detroit, 1988; *British Theatre Design* edited by John Goodwin, London, 1989.

\*      \*      \*

John Napier does not see himself as a pictorial or decorative artist working with abstract forms in a studio remote from the theatre. Instead, he seeks intensively cooperative work, much of which evolves on stage during rehearsals. Preferring productions of human-centered action, he reflects the general tendency of recent art towards neo-realism. Napier's realism, however, dispenses with traditional forms of scenic illusion in favor of assemblages of materials and found objects. "I don't care if it's not naturalistic, but I can't believe in artificiality," he has asserted. Moreover, in his drive for fuller audience involvement with a production, he has often altered the interiors of theatres to create forms of environmental staging: for *Equus* (National Theatre, 1973), he sat part of the audience at the rear and sides of a proscenium stage; for *Nicholas Nickleby* (1980) and *Cats* (1981), he joined audience and acting areas by ramps and bridges.

His background and special interests have lead to two distinct types of scenography. One reflects a spare, highly selective side of his sculpture training as well as a minimalist tradition in modern British staging, largely associated with the Royal Court Theatre. In Royal Shakespeare Company productions such as *A Midsummer Night's Dream* (1977), *As You Like It* (1977), *Twelfth Night* (1978), and Chekhov's *Three Sisters* (1978), relatively few scenic elements were carefully composed within a large space. Conversely, productions such as the Royal Shakespeare Company's *Comedy of Errors* (1978), *Nicholas Nickleby,* and *Cats* reflect a more flamboyant part of Napier's talent—his urge to fill the stage with objects and structures, some found, some hammered or chiseled out of unfinished materials.

Here, echoes of pop art and environmental art of the 1960s combine with his sculptural feel for space and matter, as well as his attraction to tangible reality, no matter how unusually organized. For Shakespeare's *Henry IV,* the initial production at the Royal Shakespeare Company's new Barbican Theatre in 1982, for example, he created mobile sculptures in the form of four huge towers on wheels; these seemingly random artifacts of the fifteenth century evoked an entire age with great vitality. In another example, for the New York production of *Cats* (1982), he broke through the roof of the Winter Garden Theatre to erect an inclined track for the spectacular, rocket-like heavenly ascension of one of the characters at the climax of the musical's action.

—Jarka M. Burian

# NELSON, George

American architect and industrial designer

**Born:** Hartford, Connecticut, 29 May 1908. **Education:** Studied at Yale University, New Haven, Connecticut, BA, 1928, BFA, 1931; Catholic University of America, Washington, D.C., 1932; American Academy in Rome, 1932-34. **Career:** Freelance architect and designer, in partnership with William Hamby, New York, 1936-41; president, George Nelson Associates industrial design firm, New York, from 1946; design director, Herman Miller Furniture Company, Zeeland, Michigan, from 1946; partner, Nelson and Chadwick architects, New York, from 1953. Instructor in design, Yale University, New Haven, Connecticut, 1931-32, Columbia University, New York, 1941-44; design consultant, University of Georgia, Athens, 1952-55, Boston Museum School of Fine Arts, 1968-69; visiting critic in architecture, Harvard University, Cambridge, Massachusetts, 1972-73; visiting professor, Pratt Institute, Brooklyn, New York, 1975-77. Associate editor, 1935-43, co-managing editor, 1943-44, and consultant, 1944-49, *Architectural Forum,* New York; head of *Fortune-Forum* experimental department, Time Incorporated, New York, 1944-45; editor, *Interiors* magazine, New York, 1948-75; editor-in-chief, *Design Journal,* New York, 1968-73. **Member:** Member, Conseil Superieur de la Creation Esthetique Industrielle, Paris, and New York State Council on Architecture, 1968-75; board

member, Industrial Designers Society of America, 1969-76, and Aspen Design Conference, Colorado, from 1965; committee member, Centre de Creation Industrielle, Paris, 1970. **Exhibition:** *Nelson/Eames/Girard/Probst: Design at Herman Miller,* Walker Art Center, Minneapolis, 1975. **Collections:** Museum of Modern Art, New York; Brooklyn Museum, New York; Philadelphia Museum of Art; Musee des Arts Decoratifs, Montreal. **Honors:** American Institute of Architects Industrial Design Medal, 1964, and Medal of Honor, 1979; Industrial Designers Society of America Award, 1974, 1981; American Society of Interior Designers Elsie de Wolfe Award, 1975. DFA: Parsons School of Design, New York, 1979, Minneapolis College of Art and Design, 1980. Fellow, American Institute of Architects, 1963, Industrial Designers Society of America, 1968; Honorary Royal Designer for Industry, Royal Society of Arts, London, 1973. **Died:** New York City, 5 March 1986.

## Works

*Storagewall* cupboard and shelving system (with Henry Wright), for Herman Miller, 1944.
*Basic Cabinet* storage system series, for Herman Miller, 1947.
Herman Miller showrooms, in Chicago, 1948, New York, 1953, 1966, and Washington, D.C., 1964.
Wall clock with brass and birch housing, for Howard Miller Clock Company, 1949.
*Bubble lamp,* for Howard Miller Clock Company, 1952.
*Florence Ware* table service in melamine, for Prolon, 1955.
*Kangaroo* upholstered club chair with steel legs, for Herman Miller, 1956.
*Omni System furniture,* for Structural Products, 1956.
*Marshmallow Sofa* in steel with leather-covered foam upholstery, for Herman Miller, 1956.
Fire alarm unit, for Acme Fire Alarm Company, 1958.
*Design Today in America and Europe* touring exhibition design, for the Government of India, 1958.
Swag-legged chair with fiberglass shell, for Herman Miller, 1958.
Loeb Student Center interiors in La Guardia Place, for New York University, 1959.
Herman Miller factory, Zeeland, Michigan, 1962-66.
*U.S.—Us Show* touring exhibition design, for Herman Miller Company, 1963.
*Industrial Design USA* touring exhibition design, for the United States Information Agency, 1967.
*A02 Action Office* furniture system (with Robert Probst), for Herman Miller, 1968.
Rosenthal Studio showrooms in New York, for Rosenthal Porcelain, 1968.
*The First Two Hundred Years* touring exhibition design, for the American Bicentennial Administration, 1974-76.
*Design Since 1945* exhibition design, for Philadelphia Museum of Art, 1983.

(for a complete list of Nelson's buildings and architectural projects, see *Contemporary Architects*)

## Publications

**By NELSON books**—*Industrial Architecture of Albert Kahn Inc.,* New York, 1939; *Tomorrow's House,* with Henry Wright, New

York, 1946; (editor) *Living Spaces,* New York, 1952; (editor) *Chairs,* New York, 1953; (editor) *Display,* New York, 1953; *Storage,* New York, 1954; *Problems of Design,* New York, 1957, Tokyo, 1960; *How To See. Visual Adventures in a World God Never Made,* Boston, 1978; *George Nelson on Design,* New York, 1979.

**On NELSON: books**—*Public Interiors* by Misha Black, London, 1960; *Art and Design in Home Living* by F. M. Obst, New York and London, 1963; *Design in America* edited by Ralph Caplan, New York, 1969; *Interior Design: An Introduction to Architectural Interiors* by Arnold Friedmann, John F. Pile and Forrest Wilson, New York and Amsterdam, 1970, 1976; *The Modern Chair: Classics in Production* by Clement Meadmore, London, 1974; *In Good Shape: Style and Design in Industrial Products Since 1960* by Stephen Bayley, London, 1979; *Industrial Design* by John Heskett, London, 1980; *Contemporary Furniture* by Klaus-Jurgen Sembach, Stuttgart and London, 1982; *Mid- Century: Furniture of the 1950s* by Cara Greenberg, London, 1985; *Modern Furniture Classics* by Miriam Stimpson, London, 1987; *Office Furniture* by Lance Knobel, London, 1987; *New American Design* by Hugh Aldersley-Williams, New York, 1988; *The American Design Adventure 1940-1975* by Arthur J. Pulos, London and Cambridge, Massachusetts, 1988.

*

During my undergraduate years, a chance exposure to an exhibit of student drawings created a strong desire to become an architect. It took some years to discover that what had attracted me was architecture as expression rather than technique. I enjoyed these years enormously and even more, the two subsequent years at the American Academy in Rome, which provided an almost explosive expansion of awareness.

Returning to New York at the bottom of the Depression provided a very different experience, and I had prepared for unemployment by writing a series of articles on the leading modern architects of Europe. These were published and led to a job with *Architectural Forum,* which again provided a series of invaluable experiences. During this period an association with William Hamby brought me back into architectural work, culminating in a townhouse for Sherman Fairchild, which drastically revised the traditional plan by splitting the house into two elements with a court and glassed-in ramp in between. The house was finished in 1941, when the war broke out, terminating architectural activity for a number of years.

Work at *Architectural Forum* led to a book assignment, *Tomorrow's House* (with Henry Wright), and this in turn triggered the creation of the *Storagewall,* a device which quickly became a standard element in dwellings and offices. Publications of this project came to the attention of Herman Miller, a Michigan furniture manufacturer, and an association developed which continued for many years. An office was opened in 1946, and in subsequent years a very broad range of work—furniture design, graphics, packaging, corporate identity, exhibitions, commercial interiors, products and architecture—was carried out.

Since 1946, many changes have taken place. There were no schools for industrial design at the beginning; now a large network turns out hundreds of graduates each year. The typical client has changed radically, from a hands-on manufacturer to managers more concerned with marketing, promotion, and the bottom line than the product. In the society itself, the direction can perhaps be best described as a lack of direction, accompanied by steadily reduced

standards of living, greatly reduced literacy, and a general decline in morale. At the same time, this period has been one of great creative activity in science, notably cosmology, paleontology, molecular biology, and subatomic physics.

This paradoxical coexistence of increasing dehumanization and alienation, characteristic of a technological society in its later stages, and vigorous work and brilliant accomplishment in a limited number of disciplines is, of course, the mark of a society in a state of radical, massive transformation.

It is thus possible to say, not for the first time in our short and turbulent history, that we are living in the best of times and the worst. If humanity survives the present series of crises, a great leap towards maturity is a possibility.

—George Nelson

\*    \*    \*

In the infancy of the industrial design profession, George Nelson came from an education as an architect, as did Eliot Noyes and Charles Eames, to become one of the most important design theorists and practitioners. During the prewar years in Europe, Nelson's interviews with modern European architects marked an early consummation of his skills at analytical thought and expository writing. Curiosity about the future implications of a designed world led him to investigate further the growth of American architecture and design in his work on the editorial staff of *Architectural Forum* and later in two books: *The Industrial Architecture of Albert Kahn,* and, with Henry Wright, *Tomorrow's House.*

Nelson's accomplishments in both the theory and practice of design reflect an enduring curiosity about process. He continually asked why (or, more often, why not), and then sought answers. This procedure can be traced through the successes of his career. Why do we need more verbiage on the history of architecture when there is so much happening today in Europe?—which led to an editorial career. Why can't walls be used as more than partitions?—which led to his storagewall concept. Why is design necessary to modern society?—which led to his continuing series of essays on such topics as "Design as Communication," "Obsolescence," "The Future of Packaging," and "A New Profession?"

Nelson worked in association with some of the leaders of contemporary industrial design, including Charles Eames and Alexander Girard at Herman Miller and Buckminster Fuller. He likewise collaborated with other designers in the search for the ultimate "Seating Tool" and with the British design group Pentagram. From inside the design profession, he focused a critical eye on the role of design as it contended with function, technology, and social values. He illuminated through insightful, often humorous prose the responsibilities of the designer first to comprehend and then possibly adjust the modern world. In this activity, he emphasized process rather than dwelling on discreet objects, which led him to such definitions as "good design is the manifestation of the capacity of the human spirit to transcend its limitations." A predictor of future trends, Nelson foresaw in the 1950s the breaking down of arbitrary lines between art and design disciplines; he saw that industry and the "real world" would have an impact on education in the 1960s; and he saw the office revolution affecting society as a whole in the 1970s and 1980s. This thinking profoundly influenced the first and subsequent generations of industrial designers to examine and reexamine their profession and its goals. At the same time, Nelson debunked the myth of industrial design as magical process by showing that designers are people.

—Sarah Bodine

# NELSON, Louis
American industrial designer

**Born:** New York, New York, 8 October 1936. **Education:** Pratt Institute, B.I.D., 1958, M.I.D., 1964. **Family:** Married Sandra Balestracci, 1970 (divorced, 1979); married the singer Judy Collins, 1996. **Military Service:** U.S. Army, 1958-62. **Career:** Designer, Corning Glass Works, New York, 1964-68; designer, became co-director and executive vice-president, Robert P. Gersin Associates, 1968-80; founder and president, Louis Nelson Associates, Designers and Planners, New York, from 1980. Advisory board, International Design Conference in Aspen, WORLDesign Foundation, and American Crafts Museum; chair, Rowena Reed Kostellow Fund, Pratt Institute, and Awards Committee, National Alumni Council; spokesperson, U.S. Committee for UNICEF. **Member:** Industrial Designers Society of America; American Institute of Graphic Artists; Society for Environmental Graphic Design; Association of Professional Design Firms. **Honors:** Recipient of awards from Art Directors Club of Los Angeles, Clio, International Association of Business Communicators, *Industrial Design* Annual Review, Printing Industries Award, AIGA Award, Domus, American National Standards Institute, and others. **Addresses:** (office) Louis Nelson Associates Inc., 80 University Place, New York, New York 10003, U.S.A.; (agent) R. Starr Collins, Collins Communications, 32 Owasco Street, Auburn, New York 13021, U.S.A.

## Works

Restaurant at the Statue of Liberty National Monument, New York, for E. Hill Group, 1990.
Coca-Cola Bottling Museum master plan, for Benwood Foundation, Chattanooga, Tennessee, 1992.
Annual reports and communication design, for Central Park Conservancy, New York, from 1994.
Mural wall, for Korean War Veterans Memorial, Washington, D.C., 1995.
Skywalk exhibit and attraction, for Prudential Tower, Boston, Massachusetts, 1995.
"Re-Life" of IAB Building, John F. Kennedy International Airport, Port Authority of New York/New Jersey, in progress.

**Louis Nelson: Korean War Veteran's Memorial. Courtesy of Louis Nelson Associates Inc.**

Communication design and wayfinding system, for New York City Transit, in progress.

## Publications

**On NELSON: articles**—*Inland Architect* (Chicago), May 1978, January-February 1983; *Architectural Record* (New York), August 1978; *Progressive Architecture* (New York), November 1983; "Eye Opener" in *Interior Design* (New York), November 1984.

\*

In the third grade I made covers for my book reports. The teacher liked them and put them on the bulletin board. At home, I wanted to make beautiful things around me—to change the clutter of knick-knacks that I grew up with. Much later, beyond my black and white stage, I told someone I get a great deal of joy seeing people smile when they touch my work or walk through my spaces.

Today, I tell my staff, and myself, "make it beautiful, make it reach the heart of the people, make it original."

Make it absolutely desirable to touch, to pick up, to own—to possess. Designers give this quality to an object or a place. Understanding abstract relationships *and* human needs are at the center of this ability. Technology and ergonomics serve these goals. Make it beautiful, Louis.

Make it mean something to people emotionally, physically, psychically, practically. Learn about people and what they need. Understand the clues behind the actions, words, and gestures. See into their hearts and guts and minds. Make it reach the people.

Give it its own personality so that nothing else is like it. So much around us in these times are warmed over ideas belonging to something else. Through repetition, they belong to no one. Pride of authorship leaves with homogenization of design; transformed by fear of individuality. Personality is what we remember—what we relate to, respond to, desire, want and smile with. I want people to remember what I design, use it, desire it, laugh with it and possess it. Look at most of today's automobiles, toasters, trains, planes, houses, brief cases, packaged goods, and just about anything else that's around. We remember a personality. "Make it original, world."

—Louis Nelson

\*    \*    \*

Louis Nelson strives for three criteria in all his diverse design practice: make it beautiful; make it reach the heart; and make it original. These are uncommon goals in an age when "usability" has become the pennant designers wave as the core attribute they bring to a product. Yet Nelson's goals encompass usability and much, much more.

When Louis Nelson asserts, "make it beautiful," he speaks not about beauty for beauty's sake, but of beauty as an issue of function. He speaks not of beauty as an intuitive question or cosmetic adjustment, a matter of putting a pretty face on an engineering solution, but of beauty as a matter of abstract relationships that can be identified and understood.

Nelson believes that beauty is the one unique element industrial designers bring to the product development process. "If it's beauti-

ful, people will pick it up and that's half the game," he explains. "Being useful can be beautiful."

The foundation of Nelson's philosophy was laid at Pratt Institute by Professor Rowena Reed Kostellow, FIDSA. Nelson has seasoned that education with graduate work outside the industrial design field in the areas of philosophy and psychology, studies that have expanded his interest in and understanding about people. In the process of these studies, it became important to him to make a design that people would need on many levels. "If I can make it beautiful and somehow fill a need and create a sense of enjoyment and reward for the user, then I feel good," he explains. "A design must have heart."

Make it original? In a world beleaguered by copycatting and "me too"-ism, perhaps the most fundamental contribution a designer can make is to offer the consumer something that truly is "new and improved," not with added features and techno-wizardry, but with a real understanding of needs, wants, and opportunities.

Nelson has applied this philosophy throughout his career, a career that has ranged over the full spectrum of industries and on projects that have ranged from museum exhibits to skis. In fact, if Nelson had a defining characteristic it would be a need for diversity to fill his thirst for learning. "I breathe and live off the variety of my projects. It helps me grow," he explains. He is not afraid of spreading out beyond a niche and defines himself not solely in terms of design. Contrast these five projects: the packaging for No Nonsense Panty Hose; the wine exhibit at the California Museum of Science and Industry; the Head skis; the Korean War Memorial's mural; and, most recently, co-chairing UNICEF with his wife, Judy Collins. Few designers would care to act on such a huge stage.

His Head ski redesign program provided the world with two important departures: from metal to plastic and from the "any color so long as it's black" approach to a rainbow of colors. In fact, that rainbow had been carefully worked out across all the models when the engineers discovered that the ski model forecast to be the line's biggest seller would be purple. Convinced that men would reject that model because of the color, engineering lobbied heavily with marketing even after the skis were on the market. Six months later—before sales results had come in—the engineers succeeded in talking marketing into a switch to blue. The change had already been made when the sales results revealed a very different picture: the market loved the colors, all the colors, especially the purple. Every industrial designer has such frustrating stories to share.

Few, however, can share a story with the dramatic emotional appeal of the Korean War Memorial's wall mural. Chosen in a nationwide search for a muralist, Nelson was key to selecting the material (granite) and the method (blast-etching) as well as the proportion, shape, and height of the wall. But perhaps his most noteworthy contribution lay in his concept of letting actual photos taken of soldiers in the Korean War tell the story. He sought to praise the spirit of service, the willingness to sacrifice, and the dedication to the cause of freedom embodied by all participants in the conflict. "It's not a memorial to war but a memorial to those who served in the war, who served their nation."

To achieve the effect of personal contact between the faces on the wall and the people viewing it, Nelson's team sought full-face images, culling through 12,000 to select the several thousand that would span the 41 granite slabs and 164 feet of mural. They then used state-of-the-art techniques on the Macintosh to retouch, size, and position the images to match Nelson's master plan, and the Cold Spring Granite Company in Cold Spring, Minnesota, then used the latest advances in blast etching to photo-etch the images on the granite. The effect has received the highest praise of all—large crowds of Korean War veterans and others visit every day, in all weather.

—Kristina Goodrich

# NEUBURG, Hans

Swiss industrial, display, and graphic designer

**Born:** Grulich, Czechoslovakia, 20 March 1904; emigrated to Switzerland in 1910, naturalized, 1954. **Education:** Elementarschule, Hamburg, 1909-10, and at schools in Zürich, 1910-18; studied at the Art Institut Orell Füssli, Zürich, 1919-22. **Family:** Married Stefi Kovacic in 1934. **Career:** Copywriter and text editor, Max Dalang design agency, Zürich, 1928-29; freelance publicity specialist, working with Max Bill, Anton Stankowski, Herbert Matter, Heiri Steiner and others, Zürich, 1930-31; propaganda chief, for AWZ, Basel, 1931-32; advertising manager, Jean Haecky Import, Basel, 1932-36; freelance advertising and graphic designer, Zürich, from 1936: designed for Leibig, Gebruder Sulzer, Von Roll, Von Moos, Bern Hyspa Exhibition, International Red Cross, Basel Musterrnesse, and others. Editor, *Industrie-Werbung* magazine, Basel, 1933-37; picture editor, *Actualis* daily, Zürich, 1941; founder-editor, *Chamaleon* magazine, Zürich, 1946; sports journalist, *Die Tat* and *Weltwoche,* Zürich, 1950; editor, *Camera* magazine, Lucerne, 1952-53; art critic, *Weltwoche, Werk, Neue Zurcher Zeitung* and *Tagenanzeiger* periodicals, Zürich, 1958, and *Zürcher Woche,* 1962; founder-editor, with Richard Paul Lohse, Josef Muller-Brockmann and Carlo Vivarelli, *Neue Grafik* magazine, Olten, 1958; picture editor and layout artist, *Woche* magazine, Olten, 1963. Director, Arts and Crafts Museum, Winterthur, 1962-64. Instructor, Hochschule fiir Gestaltung, Ulm, from 1963; instructor in abstract art, Migros Klubschule, Zürich. **Member:** Ortsgruppe president from 1959, and central president from 1960, Verband Schweizer Grafiker, Zürich; vice-president, ICOGRADA International Council of Graphic Design Associations, 1963. **Exhibition:** *107 Grafici dell'AGI,* Castello Sforzesco, Milan, 1974. **Honors:** Extraordinary member, Schweizerischer Werkbund, 1962; honorary president, Verband Schweizerischer Grafiker; member, Alliance Graphique Internationale, Paris. **Died:** Zürich, 1983.

## Publications

By NEUBURG: books—*Moderne Werbe- und Gebrauchsgraphik,* Ravensburg, 1960; *Rund um den Buchdruck,* Zürich, 1962; (editor) *Richard Paul Lohse: 60 Geburtstag,* Teufen, 1962; *Fritz Krebs,* Zürich, 1973.

On NEUBURG: books—*The New Graphic Design* by Karl Gerstner and Markus Kutter, Teufen and London, 1959; *Who's Who in Graphic Art* edited by Walter Amstutz, Zürich, 1962, Dubendorf, 1982; *Hans Neuburg,* with texts by Max Bill, Anton Stankowski and others, Teufen, 1964; *Das Plakat* by Anton Sailer, Munich, 1965; *Signet, Signal, Symbol: Handbook of International Signs* by Walter and Marion Diethlem, Zürich, 1970; *History of the Poster* by Josef and Shizuko Müller Brockmann, Zürich, 1971; *107 Grafici dell'AGI,* exhibition catalogue with texts by Renzo Zorzi

and Franco Grignani, Venice, 1974; *Les Annees 60* by Anne Bony, Paris, 1983; *A History of Graphic Design* by Philip B. Meggs, New York and London, 1983.

# NEUMEISTER, Alexander

German industrial designer

**Born:** Berlin, 17 December 1941. **Education:** Educated at Saint Theresa's Academy, Boise, Idaho, 1955-56, and at schools in Germany, 1957-62; studied industrial design, at the Hochschule für Gestaltung, Ulm, 1963-67, and at Tokyo University of Arts, 1968-69. **Family:** Married Gudrun Heinle in 1969, daughters: Sarah and Laura. **Career:** Freelance designer and head of Neumeister Design, Munich, from 1969; partner, with Angela Carvalho, in NCS Design Rio industrial design firm, Rio de Janeiro, from 1988; designed medical equipment, transport and data communication systems for AEG, BMW, Deutsche Aerospace/Dornier, German Railways, Heidelberger Druckmaschine, Hitachi/Japan, Loewe, Mannesmann, Siemens, Thyssen Henschel, and others. Lecturer in industrial design, Fachhochschule, Munich, 1975-80. Group coordinator for design in developing countries, VDID German Association of Industrial Designers, 1975-87; vice-president, ICSID International Council of Societies of Industrial Design, 1985-87; advisory board, Helsinki University of Arts, from 1992. **Honors:** Carozzeria Bertone Sports Car Design Prize, Turin, 1968; Table 80 Design Prize, Hamburg, 1971; Gesika Office Furniture Design Prize, Hannover, 1973; Brunel Design Award, 1988; Design Team of the Year Award, 1992; numerous Stuttgart Design Center and Hannover Gute Industrieform awards. **Address:** Neumeister Design, von Goebel Platz 8, 80638 Munich, Germany.

## Works

*Maglev Transrapid TR05, TR06,* and *TR07* magnetic levitation trains, for Thyssen Henschel, 1978, 1982, 1988.
*ICE* intercity experimental train, for German Railways, 1985.
*Medilas 30* medical laser, for MBB, 1987.
City trolleybus, for VOV, 1988-90.
*VideoCom* video-conference unit, for MBB and Hitachi, 1988, 1993.
*DIS* mobile diagnosis computer, for BMW, 1989.
*Lithotripter-Compact* medical diagnostic equipment, for Dornier Medical Division, 1989.
Aircraft seating, for Recaro, 1989.
Passenger transfer train, for AEG-Magnetbahn, 1989-90.
*HST 350* design study for next generation Shinkansen train, 1992-94.
*ICE/ICT,* next generation of high speed trains, for German Railways, 1995.

## Publications

By NEUMEISTER: books—(with Gudrun Neumeister) *Design Promotion: Facts and Arguments,* Munich, 1981; (with Gudrun Neumeister) *Cultural Identity and Design,* Ulm, 1989; articles—in *Form* (Opladen), no. 71, 1975, no. 83, 1978, no. 99, 1982; *Design*

**Alexander Neumeister: Next generation of Japanese high speed trains project for Hitachi, Japan**

*News Japan* (Tokyo), no. 144, 1981, no. 135, 1982; *Design Quarterly* (Tokyo), no. 2, 1982; also contributor to *Axis* and *md.*

**On NEUMEISTER: articles**—in *Domus* (Milan), no. 598, 1979, no. 616, 1981; *Industrial Design* (New York), September 1979; *Design News Japan* (Tokyo), no. 1, 1980; *Technique and Design in USSR* (Moscow), no. 3, 1983.

\*

Right from the beginning of my professional career, I have chosen to specialize in the design of investment goods, namely transportation systems, medical equipment, and electronics products, as I am deeply suspicious of the still popular version of the "genial designer" who designs a flower vase today and an airplane tomorrow and whose intuition leads him to the perfect answer despite vast differences in technical complexity and the required special know-how.

With the kind of products I am working on, development is a constant team effort, with the designer contributing his special know-how on human factors, ergonomics, and aesthetics. I have found it to be absolutely necessary that, within such a team, the designer be able to speak the language of his counterpart—meaning that in my case I need to have a sound knowledge of engineering and of electronics as well. Only in this way can technical possibilities be exploited to the fullest and innovative solutions rising from teamwork be realized.

It is not the breathtaking design model presented to management by the designer which constitutes the quality of a design or of a designer as such, but what remains of it when the final prototype has gone through testing. As a designer, I am in the unique position of influencing various stages of a development, of being able to blend all factors of influence, technical restraints, and components with their specific limitations into a three-dimensional object and to work it out, down to the details. This three-dimensional puzzle, especially when it is a complex project such as a train, for instance, is what has always fascinated me about design and what will probably continue to do so for a long time.

—Alexander Neumeister

# NILSSON, Barbro

Swedish textile designer

---

**Born:** Barbro Lundberg, in Malmo, 18 July 1899. **Education:** Educated in Lidingo, 1910-13; studied textile design under Johanna Brunsson and Alma Jakobsson, at Brunssons Vavskola, Stockholm, 1913-17, at the Tekniska Skolan, Stockholm, 1917-20, and at the Hogre Konstindustrielle Skolan, Stockholm, 1920-24. **Family:** Married sculptor Rober Nilsson in 1928; son: Pal-Nils. **Career:** Independent textile designer, Stockholm, 1924-42; art director, Marta Maas-Fietterstrom textile workshops, Bastad, from 1942. Instructor, Johanna Brunnstroms Vavskolan, Stockholm, 1919-41, Kunstindustri Skolan, Kunstindustri Dagskolan, and Kunstindustri Aftonskolan, Stockholm, 1934-45; director and chief instructor, with Maria Nordenfelt, of the Craft and Design Seminarium, Göteborg, 1924-25; also visiting instructor, at the Konstfacskolan, Stockholm, and the Konsthantverksolan, Copenhagen. **Exhibition:** *Scandinavian Modern Design 1880-1980,* Cooper-Hewitt Museum, New York, 1982. **Collections:** Nationamuseum, Stockholm; Nordisk Museum, Oslo; Dansk Kunstindustrimuseum, Copenhagen. **Honors:** Litteris et Artibus Medal, Stockholm, 1948; Prince Eugene Medal, Stockholm, 1954; Lengetz Prize, Stockholm, 1969. **Died:** Stockholm, 11 October 1983.

## Works

*Tunes at the Marketplace* tapestry hanging (with Sven Erixson), for the Concert Hall, Göteborg, 1935-39.

*Göteborg Harbour* tapestry (with Sven Erixson), for Swedish American lines ship *M/S Stockolm,* 1938.

*The Snails* rya rug, 1943.

*Harlequins Returning Home* tapestry (with Endre Nemes), 1943.

*Berry-Pattern* rya rug, 1946.

*The Falursquare* rya rug, 1952.

*Tree of Life* flossa rug, for the Storkyrkan, Stockholm, 1955.

*Tribute to Boras Textile Crafts* tapestry (with Olle Nyman), for Boras Town Hall, 1956-57.

*Danish Peasant Woman* tapestry (with William Scharff), for the Folketinget, Copenhagen, 1957-58.

*Gustaf Vasa* tapestry (with Sixten Lundbom), for Vasteras Town Hall, 1960-61.

Series of ten tapestries (with Robert Nilsson), for the Marcus Church, Stockholm, 1961.

*Violets* rya rug, for the Svenska Handelsbanken, Stockholm, 1961.

*Equestrians' Battle* tapestry hanging (with Olle Nyman), for the Svenska Handelsbanken, Stockholm, 1961-62.

*Pomona* tapestry hanging (with Olle Nyman), for the Skandinavska Banken, Stockholm, 1964-65.

Series of five tapestries, for the Gustaf Adolf Church, Helsingborg, 1965.

*Portokalli* rya rug, for the Hotel Anglais, Stockholm, 1966.

Series of seven tapestries, for the Southern Energy Company, Malmo, 1966.

*Wine Master* tapestry hanging (with Olle Nyman), 1969.

## Publications

**On NILSSON: books**—*Contemporary Swedish Design: A Survey in Pictures* by Arthur Hald and Sven Erik Skawonius, Stockholm, 1951; *Scandinavian Design* by Ulf Hard at Segerstad, Stockholm and London, 1961; *Svensk Form* edited by Ake Stavenlow and Ake H. Huldt, Stockholm, 1961; *Marta Maas-Fjetterstrom och Vav-Verkstaden i Bastad* by Tyra Lundgren, Stockholm, 1968; *Design in Sweden* edited by Lennart Lindkvist, Stockholm, 1972; *En Bok om Barbro Nilsson* by Viggo Sten Moller, Stockholm, 1977; *Scandinavian Modern Design 1880-1980* edited by David Revere McFadden, New York, 1982; *Tryckta Tyger fran 30-tal till 80-tal* by Inez Svensson, Stockholm, 1984; *Design in Sweden* edited by Monica Boman, Stockholm, 1985.

\*    \*    \*

Barbro Nilsson possessed all of the characteristics of a great master. Her craftsmanship was impressive, grounded in clarity of self; she knew and could do so much that she allowed herself to let go; she recognized her position in the history of the textile crafts, and thus she was humble; her work was simple, playful, with the sure rhythm of dancing patterns on the surface. And moreover, she had humor. When last I met her, she received me lying in bed after a difficult eye operation. Eighty-four years of age, she was beautiful in a way that expressed itself in her shining eyes and extended into her white hair, which was like a crown around her being. As soon as she was well, she assembled a new weave. Her voice was like that of a young woman, melodic and laughing, carefully avoiding anything pretentious.

Why have I described Nilsson so carefully? Because her work as a pioneer of the Swedish textile crafts was so integrated with her personality. Nilsson was an unusually powerful and active woman. She was gifted with a rich imagination which apparently never ran dry. Her energy allowed her to work on her personal creations as well as to direct Sweden's most prestigious textile mill, AB Marta MaasFjetterstrom, and for several years, to retain the position of principal instructor in the textile subjects at the Academy for Arts and Crafts in Stockholm.

Her combination of humility and confidence made it possible for her to learn not only from the tradition of indigenous Swedish textiles but also from ancient Coptic fabrics. She had the ability to cooperate, and she quickly uncovered the essential concept embedded in several artists' designs. And yet, she always remained herself, a formidable artist untouched by surrounding trends.

Her most lasting contribution to Swedish textile tradition was probably her production of rugs, exquisite works of art as well as useful items. It was not at all easy for the young, gifted artist suddenly to take over and become responsible for the legendary Märta Maas-Fjetterstrom textile mill, to maintain its tradition of many unique and strongly established patterns, and simultaneously, to introduce new concepts into the mill's work. But Nilsson succeeded and apparently without strenuous effort. Her patterns (The Woodpecker, The Snails, Seaweed, Berries) adhere to a fine tradition, they are rhythmic and very decorative, like all indigenous patterns, and they are often created in an unpretentious way around a small detail from nature; and yet, they are highly expressive of a strong personality, of a unique sense of color and a confident knowledge of form. Nilsson could place a light red and a turquoise next to each other and yet achieve a sense of harmony; she could let a rug consist of zig-zag patterns and small medallion shapes—all of different sizes and yet render it so unbound by time as to be used for decades (Seaweed). She always sought out nature as her inspiration, avoided reproducing it but rather created abstractions—interpreted nature through her medium.

One could say so many more wonderful things about her—not the least about her work as a pedagogue. While she was an instructor at the Academy for Arts and Crafts, her importance for the generation of women who were the genesis of the movement bringing Swedish textile crafts to its present level of worldwide recognition cannot be overestimated. Here, the unique artist changed into a humorous and attentive helper towards the young, aspiring talents. One cannot perceive her students as less accomplished copies of her; rather one knows they are Nilsson's students because of their knowledge of earlier textile traditions, their feeling for quality, and their confidence in their own crafts—this is what she succeeded in conveying to them.

—Gertrud Gustafsson

# NISHIZAWA, Takeshi

Japanese industrial and environmental designer

**Born:** Nagano Prefecture, Japan, 1936. **Education:** Graduated from Tokyo National University of Fine Arts & Music, Tokyo, Japan, 1959; Hochschule für Gestaltung, Ulm, Germany, Diploma in Industrial Design, 1964. **Career:** Began work at GK Industrial Design Institute, 1959; president, GK Sekkei, from 1995. Faculty, Keio University, 1967-80, and Tokyo Art University, 1979-93; Board of directors, Urban Design Center Foundation, and Japanese Society for Science of Design; jury member, Ministry of Industry and Trade's G-Mark Prize Committee, and Ministry of Construction's Scenic City Design Awards. **Member:** Urban Design Consultants Association, Japan; Traffic Planning Association; Urban Event Planning Congress. **Honors:** SDA (Space Design Award), Ministry of Industry and Trade (MITI) Grand Prix, Shinjuku Signage, Tokyo, 1991; Ministry of Construction Award (Minister's Prize), Matsumoto Street Design, Matsumoto, 1993; Ministry of Construction Award (Grand Prize), Ginza Street Design, Tokyo, 1993. **Address:** GK Sekkei Incorporated, Yamatane Building, 1-11-22, Minami-Ikebukuro, Toshima-ku, Tokyo 171, Japan.

## Works

Master plan, for Nishi Izu Town, Shizuoka Prefecture, 1985.
Urban environmental design, for Makuhari New Urban Center, 1988.
*Pager* watch design, for NTT, Japan, 1989.
Environmental design, for Forest Country Club, Chiba Prefecture, 1989.
Station Plaza redevelopment plan and environmental design, for Toka Ichiba Station Plaza, Chiba Prefecture, 1989.
Temporary architecture design, for Yokohama Exotic Showcase '89, Yokohama, 1989.
Environmental design, for West Shinjuku Area, Tokyo, 1991.
Street design, for Harumi Street, Ginza, Tokyo, 1992.
Environmental design, for Matsumoto Castle Area, Matsumoto, 1993.
Station design, for Chiba Express Railway Station, Chiba Prefecture, 1995.

## Publications

**By NISHIZAWA: books**—*Environmental Design for People and Urban Facilities,* Kajima Institute, Japan, 1979; Street Furniture, Kajima Institute, Japan, 1983.

*

I have been working at GK Sekkei for more than 30 years. I first began as an industrial designer designing products such as motorcycles and pianos. From there, I worked on street furniture, which coincided with Osaka's EXPO '70. Since that time, I have been involved with street furniture as well as environmental design.

There are several creative designers who have greatly influenced the way I think about design, the most important being: the late Professor Hans Gugelot and his assistant professor at the time, Professor Herbert Lindinger, both of whom I studied under while I was at Ulm; and the co-founder and Chairman of GK Sekkei, Kenji Ekuan.

From Ulm in general and Professors Gugelot and Lindinger in particular, I learned that the meaning of design lies in the interrelationship of man, design, and society. We thought about a project from the viewpoint of design, science, and technology, not simply form and function. At the same time, when it came to a product's formal aspects of design, semantics and morphology were always considered with strong emphasis placed on simplicity.

At GK, Mr. Ekuan is a major force, especially regarding the philosophy of design. We started from the beginning (1957) to think about the open spaces between buildings, the all-too-often forgotten areas of design here in Japan. We conceived of these spaces in such a way that would necessitate a "total design" approach. In other words, we were not simply landscape designers or furniture designers or any one thing. Our concept was to treat the entire space of the project at hand as a designed environment. Thus, if we needed benches, street lamps, signs, traffic signals, or anything else to make the design successful, we would design it. This is how we arrived at the process we refer to as Environmental Design. Throughout the years, we have advanced on a path that made us think in terms of product design, no matter the scale of the project.

When I think about my future direction in the design world, I think about the progression of the project-types that I have been involved in. I have noticed how they have moved from basically industrial design (which were more or less objects) to street furniture (which took the surrounding site into consideration) to environmental design (which was a comprehensive process) all the way through to urban environmental design (in which the day-to-day activities of society are directly involved). Moreover, there has been a parallel progression from commercial concerns to more public issues and social concerns.

The identity of cities in the future will depend more and more not on the individual design of buildings, but how a city's urban space can be a function of culture. It is this aspect of urban environmental design that I will be struggling with in the coming years.

—Takeshi Nishizawa

*    *    *

It was only relatively late that town planners in Japan came to recognize the vital role played by public open spaces in towns, and their functional and aesthetic qualities.

**Takeshi Nishizawa: NTT Pager Watch, 1989**

Whereas in European culture, for example, the presence of certain institutions such as the church in the center of the village led at an early date to the development of rituals of public life and thus to a village square on which they could take place, life in the Japanese tradition remained almost entirely focused upon the family unit.

As a result, and despite the fact that public open space was in any case in far too short supply, in the structures of the new conurbations even more of it was surrendered to the motor car, and with even less regard for other considerations than was the case elsewhere.

In the last few years a process of rethinking has patently been getting under way in this respect. Although a number of planners and architects have been involved in this, the fact that it is taking place appears in no small measure to be thanks to the efforts of Takeshi Nishizawa and his colleagues, and on the broadest level to GK designers.

For almost two decades now, during which he has been engaged in projects of the greatest diversity, Nishizawa has been extremely persistent in his pursuit, not only as a designer but also as a teacher and competition judge and in activities that impinge upon politics, of a vision of a new type of urban environment.

His plans for the Ginza or Matsumoto, which have deservedly been awarded a number of notable prizes, are more than simply arrangements of beautiful street furniture.

It is no doubt the interdisciplinary approach, his ability to think first in term of structures and functional relationships and only afterwards in terms of the forms through which these can suitably be expressed, that makes these projects appear to possess a certain timelessness rather than being exponents of transient fashion, and thus renders them convincing in the long term.

Nishizawa is well aware that urban redesign is first and foremost concerned with creating a new type of meaningfulness, with a return to involving the whole population and not only motorists, and with a new balance between conflicting interests. It is therefore only logical and consistent that Nishizawa seeks to collaborate not only with planners but also with sociologists and psychologists.

As a designer he knows the advantages of exploiting the systematic nature of things, whether for reasons of economy or simply in order to give things a common line. Despite this, he is never in any danger of falling into mere uniformity.

Nishizawa is not first and foremost concerned with the spectacular, but rather with what is apposite in any given case. He tends to prefer restraint and unobtrusiveness, and that is a good thing. One way in which he achieves these qualities, surprisingly, is through his striving after lightness and dematerialization. His enthusiasm for rarefied and filigree designs often leads to very elegant and unusual conceptions.

The extent to which he is also successful in capturing the specific character of each particular place or spot, its genius loci, can ultimately only be judged by those who are directly affected. For outside observers, the urban design he inserts into any given architectural environment always appear to be in harmony with their surroundings.

In any case, his plans are extraordinarily emphatic and significative, right down to the smallest details of design. It may well be the case that they also contribute to an enhanced sense of identification with the development on the part of the local population.

Much of this also applies to his exhibition projects, such as Yokohoma Showcase, which is irresistible in its vivacity, freshness, and delight in experiment.

—Herbert Lindinger

## NOORDA, Bob

Dutch graphic, display, and industrial designer

**Born:** Amsterdam, 15 July 1927. **Education:** Studied at the Instituut voor Kunstnijverheidsonderwijs, Amsterdam, 1944-47. **Career:** Worked as a layout artist on Dutch government military publications, in Jakarta, Indonesia, 1947-50; freelance designer, working in Amsterdam, 1950-52, and in Milan, from 1952; art director, for Pirelli Company, Milan, from 1961; co-founder and senior vice-president, Unimark International design and marketing corporation, Milan, from 1965; has designed for Montecatini, Farmitalia, Remington Rand Italia, Alfa Romeo, Philips, Agip, Mitsubishi, Spear and Jackson, StellaArtois, Upim, Chiari e Forti, Feltrinelli, Mondadori, Total, Shiseido, Olivetti, and others. Commission member, International Council of Societies of Industrial Design (ICSID), 1968-70; general secretary, 1969-70, and national president, from 1979, ADI Associazione Disegno Industriale, Milan; scientific committee member, Istituto Superiore per il Disegno Grafico, Urbino, from 1975. **Exhibitions:** Milan Triennale, 1957; *Manifesti Italiani,* Lugano, 1959; Composing Room, New York, 1960; *107 Grafici dell'AGI,* Castello Sforzersco, Milan, 1974; *Design e design,* Palazzo delle Stelline, Milan, 1979 (toured). **Honors:** Gold Medal, Rimini, 1973; Compasso d'Oro Awards, Milan, and Gold Medal, 12th Milan Triennale. **Addresses:** (office) Via Santa Maria Fulcorina 20, 20123 Milan; (home) Via Leopardi 28, 20123 Milan, Italy.

### Publications

On NOORDA: books—*Packaging: An International Survey of Package Design* edited by Walter Herdeg, Zürich, 1959; *Who's Who in Graphic Art* edited by Walter Amstutz, Zürich, 1962, Dubendorf, 1982; *An International Survey of Packaging* by Wim Crouwel and Kurt Weidemann, London, 1968; *Mongrafie des Plakats* by Herbert Schindler, Munich, 1972; *Arcigraphia: Architectural and Environmental Graphics* edited by Herdeg, Zürich, 1978; *Modern Furniture* by John F. Pile, New York and Toronto, 1979; *Atlante del Design Italiano 1940/1980* by Alfonso Grassi and

Anty Pansera, Milan, 1980; *The Conran Directory of Design* edited by Stephen Bayley, London, 1985; *Italian Modern: A Design Heritage* by Giovanni Albera and Nicolas Monti, New York, 1989.

\*    \*    \*

In the 1950s Bob Noorda appeared in Milan, where he worked for some of the Italian companies most known for their enlightened patronage of design, such as Pirelli and Montecatini. His most outstanding work for this latter company was the design of the graphics for the pavilion at the Milan Samples Fair in 1963. There, he indicated his abilities to handle a range of solutions, which carefully differentiated the various purposes within an overall concept while maintaining a family likeness. For Pirelli, perhaps his most remembered work is the 1956 advertisement for the Cinturato tire, with its startling graphic adaption of the pattern of the tread and its bold typography.

All Noorda's work of the early period combined clear and bold layout with highly imaginative imagery; the results were both rational and effective. With the Milan Metropolitana subway system, however, imagery had scarcely a role to play. There, he organized all the graphics to convey the appropriate message directly and unambiguously but always with deceptively easy elegance, with no labored effect that might have arisen from the deep preparation for the work. Everything was subject to his own rigorous tests within a logical appreciation of what a passenger would expect. The lettering style was the result of an investigation into legibility under the conditions that would prevail on the system, while the positioning of station names on the platforms resulted from a study of the visual restrictions upon a passenger seated in one of the coaches, so that no one might miss or mistake a station. Similar considerations affected the disposition of the exit signs both from the platform and from the underground concourses to the various streets, as well as traffic in the other direction, particularly in the street-level indications of stations and entrances. It is a measure of Noorda's integration into the culture of Milan that his achievements with the Metropolitana were seen as an expression of the best that could be done by that culture, as, in fact, an addition to and an extension of it.

Probably no other work by Noorda has risen quite to the level reached with the graphics for the Metropolitana, but other works have demonstrated the imaginative qualities he has been able to bring to the design of posters, advertisements, exhibition stands, and pavilions. Often, his approach has been to reduce an image to its essential graphic quality, enhanced by a dramatic viewpoint. This has meant, frequently, distancing himself from any naive representation and seizing, rather, upon the indexical signs existentially linked to an object, transforming such signs into magic symbols. He achieved this most effectively in the Pirelli Cinturato tire advertisement, in which the tread pattern was rendered in stark black-and-white patterning.

—Toni del Renzio

## NORELL, Norman

American fashion designer

**Born:** Norman David Levinson, in Noblesville, Indiana, 20 April 1900. **Education:** Studied illustration, at Parsons School of Fine and Applied Arts, New York, 1919, and figure drawing and fashion design, at the Pratt Institute, Brooklyn, New York, 1920-22. **Career:** Worked as a costume designer for Paramount Pictures at Astoria Studio, Long Island, New York, 1922-23; stage costume designer, for Brooks Costume Company, Charles Armour dress manufacturer, and for burlesque, vaudeville, and revues, in New York, 1924-28; designer, Hattie Carnegie custom-order dresses, New York, 1928-40; founder-designer and partner, with wholesale manufacturer Anthony Traina, of Traina-Norell Company, New York, 1941-60; director, Norman Norell fashion company, New York, 1960-72. Instructor, Parsons School of Design, New York. **Member:** President, Council of Fashion Designers of America. **Exhibitions:** *The Art of Fashion,* Metropolitan Museum of Art, New York, 1957; *Fashion: An Anthology,* Victoria and Albert Museum, London, 1971; *Norman Norell: Retrospective,* Metropolitan Museum of Art, New York, 1972. **Honors:** Coty American Fashion Critics Award, 1943, 1951, 1956, 1966, and Hall of Fame Award, 1958; *Sunday Times* International Fashion Award, London, 1963; City of New York Bronze Medallion, 1972. DFA: Pratt Institute, Brooklyn, New York, 1962. **Died:** New York City, 25 October 1972.

## Publications

**By NORELL: articles**—in the *New York Times,* 15 October 1972.

**On NORELL: books**—*Fashion Is Our Business,* by Beryl Epstein, New York, 1945; *The Wheels of Fashion* by Phyllis Levin, New York, 1965; *The Beautiful People* by Marilyn Bender, New York, 1967; *Fashion: An Anthology by Cecil Beaton,* exhibition catalogue compiled by Madeleine Ginsburg, London, 1971; *American Fashion: The Life and Lines of Adrian, Mainbocher, McCardell, Norell, Trigére* edited by Sara Tomerlin Lee, New York, 1975, London, 1976; *In Fashion: Dress in the Twentieth Century* by Prudence Glynn, New York, 1978; *Fairchild's Who's Who in Fashion* edited by Ann Stegemeyer, New York, 1980; *McDowell's Directory of Twentieth Century Fashion* by Colin McDowell, London, 1984; *The Encyclopaedia of Fashion from 1840 to the 1980s* by Georgina O'Hara, London, 1986.

\*    \*    \*

Norman Norell, known as "the dean of American fashion," was the one American designer regarded as an equal by French couturiers. He selected basic American elements and pared them down to their essentials, producing a concise, recognizable style. His success with Traina-Norell during World War II encouraged other American designers to disavow the myth of American fashion inferiority.

Starting with the sailor's middy, the shirtdress, the chemise, and the blazer, Norell brought out their clean lines with substantial fabrics and careful tailoring. For forty years, he reinterpreted these well-chosen classics in new lengths, new proportions, and in different fabrics, with crisper or softer tailoring, depending upon fashion's prevailing mood.

The son of an Indiana haberdasher, Norell designed daytime cardigans, blazers, and shirts in the functional, classic spirit of American menswear. For evening, his theatrical costuming experience surfaced in vivid lace; bouffant, Southern-Belle organdies with candy-box bows; and the famous, sequined, "mermaid" sheath. The sailor's

middy blouse of his childhood inspired at least one nautical design in each Norell collection. His chemise dress, accessorized with simple pumps, plain hose, and neat hairdo, was his idealized version of the 1920s, a fashion period he admired.

As a teacher at Parsons School of Design, he taught from his own experience that a designer should be able to do everything, just in case the need should arise. A perfectionist, Norell oversaw every aspect of production, from the choosing of fabrics through the making of duplicate samples to the inspection of final details.

A master of the constructed look, he was at the fashion forefront and self-avowedly at the top of his form during the 1960s, when his clothes were frequently copied. This bothered him mainly because cheap copies were bound to be poorly made. When his 1960 culotte suit (preceding even European couture in showing divided garments for ladies' daytime wear) was copied, he offered the pattern to the press so that at least the cheap knockoff would be properly made.

Called the Rolls-Royces of fashion, his clothes were expensive because one jacket could take a week to tailor. Norell believed in uncompromising quality, wanting women to appreciate the practicality of looking great in a few perfect pieces they could wear for years, rather than buying lots of cheap, throw-away clothes. Wearing simple blazers and cardigans over skirts or trousers, whether they were tailored in wool or paved with sequins, Norell's customer could count on the same nonchalant luxury for day and night, never having to think twice about being well-dressed.

The Metropolitan Museum's twenty-five-year retrospective of his clothes opened, sadly, the week before his death but proved beyond any doubt that there is such a thing as American style and that, at its best, it is great.

—Sandra Michels Adams

# NOYES, Eliot (Fette)
American architect and industrial designer

**Born:** Boston, Massachusetts, 12 August 1910. **Education:** Phillips Academy, Andover, Massachusetts, 1926-28; Harvard College, Cambridge, Massachusetts, BA, 1932; studied architecture, Harvard University, Cambridge, Massachusetts, M. Arch., 1938. **Military Service:** United States Air Force, 1942-45, Major. **Family:** Married Mary Duncan Weed in 1938; children: Mary, Eliot, Frederick, and Margaret. **Career:** Architect, University of Chicago's Iranian archaeological expedition, 1935-37; draftsman, in the office of Coolidge, Shepley, Bulfinch and Abbot, in Boston, 1938, and in the office of Walter Gropius and Marcel Breuer, in Cambridge, Massachusetts, 1939-40; director of the department of industrial design, Museum of Modern Art, New York, 1940-42, 1945-46; design director, at Norman Bel Geddes and Company, New York, 1946-47; in private architectural and design practice as Eliot Noyes and Associates, New Canaan, Connecticut, 1947-77; design consultant to IBM, 1956-77, Mobil Oil, 1964-77, Westinghouse Electric, 1960-76, Pan American World Airways, 1969-72, and Massachusetts Institute of Technology, 1972-77. Exhibition curator and associate professor of architecture, Yale University, New Haven, Connecticut, 1948-53. President, Aspen Design Conference, Colorado, 1965-70. **Exhibitions:** *Design Since 1945,* Philadelphia Museum of Art, 1983. **Honors:** Eugene Dodd Medal, 1935; Alpha Rho Chi Medal, 1938; AIA Medal, 1938; *Progressive Architecture* Design Award,

New York, 1954; *Architectural Record* Award, New York, 1956, 1957, 1959, 1974; American Institute of Architects Honor Award and Centennial Medal, 1957; Industrial Arts Medal, 1965; *House and Home* Award, New York, 1957; United States Department of Housing Merit Award, 1968; American Society of Landscape Architects Award, 1970; Society of Industrial Artists and Designers Medal, London, 1971; AIA/Connecticut Society of Architects Honor Award, 1975; *Industrial Design* Award, New York, 1975. DFA, Carnegie Mellon University, Pittsburgh, 1969. Fellow, American Institute of Architects, Industrial Designers Society of America, and Royal Society of Arts, London. Associate, National Academy of Design. **Died:** New Canaan, Connecticut, 18 July 1977.

## Works

*IBM Model A Electric* typewriter, for International Business Machines, 1947.
*Wonder Home* exhibit, for the General Electric Corporation, 1954.
*IBM Selectric* typewriter for International Business Machines, 1961.
IBM American Branch Offices, for International Business Machines, 1961-72.
*IBM 1440* data processing system for International Business Machines, 1962 (with W. Furcani and J. Stinger).
*300/Marine Diesel* powerboat, for Cummins Engine Company, 1963.
*Time Capsule Pavilion* at the New York World's Fair, for Westinghouse Electric, 1964.
IBM Aerospace Building in Los Angeles, for International Business Machines, 1964-65.
Gasoline Service Station prototypes, for Mobil Oil, 1965 (55 built).
Showroom interior in New York, for the Xerox Corporation, 1965.
Showroom and Sales Office in Toronto, for General Fireproofing Company, 1967.
United Nations Pavilion at *Expo 67,* Montreal, 1967.
IBM Pavilion at San Antonio *Hemisfair,* for International Business Machines, 1968.
Sales and Service Building prototypes, for Cummins Engine Company, 1969.
Refinery Administration Building in Joliet, Illinois, for Mobil Oil, 1970.
Portuguese Headquarters Building in Lisbon, for Mobil Oil, 1971.
Passenger Terminal interiors at Kennedy Airport, New York, for Pan American World Airways, 1971.
IBM Headquarters lobby interiors in Armonk, New York, for International Business Machines, 1972.

(for a full list of Noyes' buildings and architectural projects, see *Contemporary Architects*)

## Publications

**By NOYES: books**—*Organic Design and Home Furnishing,* New York, 1941; *Symposium on the Esthetics of Automobile Design,* New York, 1950.

**On NOYES: books**—*Inside Today's Home* by Ray and Sarah Faulkner, New York, 1954, 1975; *Design Coordination and Corporate Image* by F. H. K. Henrion and Alan Parkin, London and New York, 1967; *Design in America* by Ralph Caplan, New York, 1969; *The Corporate Search for Visual Identity* by Ben Rosen, New York,

1970; *Interior Design: An Introduction to Architectural Interiors* by Arnold Friedmann, John F. Pile, and Forrest Wilson, New York and Amsterdam, 1970, 1976; *In Good Shape: Style and Design in Industrial Products Since 1960* by Stephen Bayley, London, 1979; *Industrial Design* by John Hesken, London, 1980; *Design Since 1945* edited by Kathryn Hiesinger and George Marcus, Philadelphia and London, 1983; *Design Source Book* by Penny Sparke and others, London, 1986; *The American Design Adventure 1940-1975* by Arthur J. Pulos, London and Cambridge, Massachusetts, 1988; *New American Design* by Hugh Aldersley-Williams, New York, 1988.

\*       \*       \*

Once called "an industrial designer with a conspicuous conscience," Eliot Noyes, when he was Director of Industrial Design at the Museum of Modern Art, wrote: "A design ... is a harmonious organization of the parts within the whole, according to structure, material and purpose. Within this definition there can be no vain ornamentation or superfluity, but the part of beauty is nonetheless great in ideal choice of material, in visual refinement and in the rational elegance of things intended for use."

This philosophy enunciated in 1941 was confirmed and influenced by Bauhaus theories through Noyes' association with Walter Gropius and Marcel Breuer, with whom he had studied and worked as draftsman.

Noyes ascertained that it was the designer's responsibility to define the real character of a company for which he designed and then to express this character, not merely as "corporate identity" in a superficial sense, but throughout the corporation's entire entity: architecture, interiors, graphics, advertising, and products. Believing that good design was good business, Noyes insisted that the entire company had to be considered. He turned down prospective clients who would not be committed to ongoing assignments. Although he consulted with outside experts when necessary, Noyes reserved all final design decisions for himself. The team approach he used in his office was influenced by both Gropius's working methods and by the Olivetti Company's organization.

Noyes' methods are evident in the history of a product for the Cummins Engine Company. When the company decided to go into the small boat field in 1963 with the 300/Marine Diesel, Noyes was commissioned as a designer. Company engineers submitted working drawings for the new diesel, and Noyes had a model made in his office. He realized that the engine must continue the reputation for quality and reliability that Cummins had gained in its large engines for trucks. He deduced the basic requirements of the small boat engine to be: 1) comparability in size and weight with spark-ignition engines of similar power and usage; 2) elimination of exterior tubing where possible to avoid danger of breakage, 3) accessibility for easy maintenance within the confinement of small boats. Confronted with drawings and model, Noyes decided that repositioning of some basic parts of the engine was necessary. Changes were made in consultation with staff engineers. Even the heavy lead logo, bolted to the housing, was eliminated. The metal housing was refined, and the result was a handsome design which solved all requirements of the assignment and fulfilled his own belief that "good design, whether of a building, an office machine, or of a company's operating statement derives from the nature of the problem; when the design problems have been solved, the end products will have in common a clarity and appropriateness of form."

The scope of Noyes' work is vast. He practiced both design and architecture throughout his career, considering both in the same terms. He designed exhibitions, computers, houses, and railroad vehicles. He was president of the International Design Conference from 1965 to 1970, taught at Yale for several years, and acted as design consultant to the president of M.I.T., as well as to IBM, Mobil, and Westinghouse.

—Nina Bremer

# NURMESNIEMI, Antti (Aarre)

Finnish interior, exhibition, graphic, and industrial designer

**Born:** Hameenlinna, 30 August 1927. **Education:** Studied interior design, at the Institute of Industrial Arts, Helsinki, 1947-50. **Military Service:** Served in the Finnish Army, 1950-51, Ensign. **Family:** Married the designer Vuokko Eskolin in 1953. **Career:** Worked as a furniture designer, Stockmann design office, Helsinki, 1949-50; interior designer, Viljo Revell architectural office, Helsinki, 1951-56, and Giovanni Romano architectural office, Milan, 1954-55; freelance designer, establishing Studio Nurmesniemi, Helsinki, from 1956 (principals include Björn Selenius and Jorma Valkama). Instructor in interior and furniture design, Institute of Industrial Arts, Helsinki, 1962-68; visiting lecturer, Industrial Art Institute, Tokyo, 1965, Kingston Polytechnic, London, 1974, and Tokyo Designers College, 1978. President, SIO Finnish Association of Interior Designers, 1960-63, and Ornamo Association of Finnish Designers, 1977-82; chairman, Institute of Industrial Arts, Helsinki, 1968-73, and Museum of Applied Art, Helsinki, from 1975; board member, 1979-1983, president, 1989-1992, and senator, from 1993, ICSID International Council of Societies of Industrial Design; chairman of editorial staff, History of Industrial Art in Finland, from 1988. **Member:** Board member, Centenary Foundation of Finnish Design, Helsinki, 1975; council member, European Foundation for Science, Art and Culture, Paris, from 1982; Cultural Commission of Finland, European Conference on Security and Co-operation, 1985; State Environment Science Committee, Finnish Academy, 1986-90; chairman, Cultural Committee, 70th Anniversary of Finnish Independence, 1987. **Exhibitions:** Artek Showroom, Helsinki, 1957, 1964; Kunstnernes Hus, Oslo, 1960; Hameenlinna Museum of Art, 1967; Kluuvin Gallery, Helsinki, 1971; Norden Hus, Reykjavik, 1975 (toured); Het Meesterteken, Oirschot, 1976; Carelia Studio, Milan, 1980; Malmö Museum, Sweden, 1983 (with wife, Vuokko Eskolin-Nurmesniemi); Historical Museum of Gothenburgs, Sweden, 1984 (with Eskolin-Nurmesniemi); Artek Gallery, Helsinki, 1985; Historical Museum of Lahti, Finland, 1987; National Design Festival, Osaka, Japan, 1991 (with Eskolin-Nurmesniemi); *To Reflect and to Design,* Helsinki City Art Museum, 1992; *Antti Nurmesniemi: Design in Finnish,* toured Scandinavian countries, 1994-95; *Classic Makers,* Design Forum Finland, Helsinki, 1995. **Collections:** Finnish Museum of Applied Art, Helsinki; Museum of Modern Art, New York; Metropolitan Museum of Art, New York; Philadelphia Museum of Art; Röhsska Konstslöjdmuseet, Göteborg; Malmö Museum; Stedelijk Museum, Amsterdam; Royal Scottish Museum, Edinburgh; Die Neue Sammlung, Munich; Norske Kunstindustrimuseum, Oslo; Seibu Museum of Art, Tokyo. **Honors:** Lighting competition award, Helsinki, 1948; Finnish Society of Crafts and Design Award, Helsinki, 1955; Helsinki City Art and Literature Award, 1957; Silver Medal, 1957, 1976, Grand Prize, 1960, 1964, and First Prize, 1963, Milan Triennale; Lunning Prize,

Copenhagen, 1959; Pro Finlandia Medal, 1960; Merivaara Furniture Prize, Helsinki, 1967; Interdesign Competition Award of Honor, 1968; Finnish State Design Award, 1976, 1979; Finnish Artist-Professorship Award, 1978; Society of Industrial Artists and Designers Medal, London, 1981; SIO Best Interior Award, Helsinki, 1984; Honorary Royal Designer for Industry, Royal Society of Arts London, 1986; State Professorship, Helsinki, 1988; honorary member, La Academia Mexicana de Diseno, 1990; Japan Design Foundation Award, Osaka, 1991 (with wife, Vuokko Eskolin-Nurmesniemi); honorary doctorate, Kingston University, London, 1994. **Address:** Studio Nurmesniemi Ky, Hopeasalmentie 27, 00570 Helsinki, Finland.

## Works

Hallapyora Restaurant interiors, Hameenlinna, 1958.
KOP Finnish National Bank branch office interiors, in Lahti, Turku, Jyvaskyla, and other sites, from 1960.
Olavinlinna Fortress interiors, furniture, and visual communications system, 1962-75.
Amer-Yhtma head office interiors, Hyryla, 1964-65, 1978.
Vuokko shops interiors, Helsinki, from 1965.
Kanta-Hame Savings Bank interiors, Hameenlinna, 1966-67, 1976.
*001 Chaise Longue* in fiberglass, foam rubber and steel, for Vuokko Oy, 1967.
Railway carriage interiors, for the President of Finland and the State Council, 1968-70.
IBM managing director's office interiors, Helsinki, 1970.
Finnjet Car Ferry interiors and visual communications system, 1975-76.
Jet Hamburger Restaurant interiors, Helsinki, 1976.
Helsinki Rail Station restoration, from 1980.
Oulu City Main Library interiors, 1981.
Helsinki Metro Rolling stock, 1983, 1995 (with Börje Rajalin).
Monetary Chamber interior, National Museum of Finland, 1984.
Government Guest House, Helsinki, 1984.
*006 Chair* in lacquered birch, for Vuokko Oy, 1986.
Finnish Embassy interior, New Delhi, India, 1987.
Guest house interior, Porvoo, Finland, for Neste Oy, 1989.
Interior restoration of Lahti City Hall, 1989.
Interior restoration of Hämeenlinna City Hall, 1989.
Product designs, for Martela Oy, Helsinki, 1995.
Experimental steel constructions and electric pylons, for IVO International Ltd., Finland, 1994 (with Björn Selenius and Jorma Valkama).

## Publications

**By NURMESNIEMI: books**—*Ornakotijirja/Small House Book,* Helsinki, 1960.

**On NURMESNIEMI: books**—*A Treasury of Scandinavian Design* edited by Erik Zahle, New York, 1961; *Modern Scandinavian Furniture* by Ulf Hård af Segerstad, Copenhagen, 1963, London, 1964; *34 Scandinavian Designers* by Svend Erik Moller, Copenhagen, 1967; *Modern Finnish Design* by Ulf Hård af Segerstad, London, 1969; *Scandinavian Design: Objects of a Life Style* by Eileene Harrison Beer, New York and Toronto, 1975; *History of Modern Furniture* by Karl Mang, Stuttgart, 1978, London, 1979;

*Scandinavian Modern Design 1880-1980* edited by David Revere McFadden, New York and London, 1982; *Design Since 1945* edited by Kathryn Hiesinger and George Marcus, Philadelphia and London, 1983; *The Conran Directory of Design* edited by Stephen Bayley, London, 1985; *Design Source Book* by Penny Sparke and others, London, 1986; *The Lunning Prize,* Stockholm, 1986; *Finnish Industrial Design* edited by Tuula Pontasuo, Helsinki, 1987; *Sourcebook of Modern Furniture* by Jerryll Habegger and Joseph H. Osman, New York, 1989; *Antti Nurmesniemi: To Reflect and to Design,* exhibition catalogue, Helsinki, 1992; *The Dictionary of 20th Century Design* by John Pile, 1994.

*

My "official" degree is in interior design, but during my professional activity, I have worked in very many areas of design. Perhaps this variety stems from the quality of design education at the turn of the 1940s-1950s in Finland: I was exposed to broad-minded teachers, teaching programs that ignored professional borders, and an atmosphere of creativity. In the background, of course, there is my own will, too, to look at the events of the world from the greatest possible number of angles. And not only to look, but to work and create.

I could not operate in my profession without being in close contact with photography, film making, and freehand drawing. I have never liked professional limits because they are not, in my opinion, conducive to creative work or design activity. From my point of view, professional limits would mean nonprofessionalism.

Before starting my design education, I was building gliders and working as a carpenter, too, so I learned to know the nature of wood. I also was an apprentice in a metal shop and an aeroplane factory; there, I learned to know the hardness of metal. In addition, during my studies, I was an assistant to a scenographer in a film studio, and I learned to love the atmosphere of making films. I believe that all this has helped me enormously when planning spaces, objects, structures, exhibitions, and practical and visual environments.

—Antti Nurmesniemi

*    *    *

**Antti Nurmesniemi: Bar chair from guest house of Neste Company, 1988**

Antti Nurmesniemi's design lies closer to that of the rest of Europe than to the work of any other Finnish interior designer. It may be that his year in Italy influenced him out of proportion to his time there; certainly some of his early work, for instance the display at the 1960 Triennale, has a refinement and spatial clarity reminiscent not only of contemporary Italian work but even seeming to hark back to the sparseness and controlled simplicity of Rietveld and De Stijl. Nevertheless, he has always been able to combine this with typical Finnish toughness; for instance, the Hälläpyörä restaurant of the same period sets this elegance firmly and successfully into the native tradition of strongly used, natural materials.

Likewise, the enamelled and cast-iron cooking utensils he designed in the 1960s show the same ability to impart to traditional shapes a greater simplicity and almost classical refinement than is found in the work of many of his contemporaries. This quality is particularly noticeable in his chair design. The chair in the *Triennale* exhibition, a steel frame with the seat and back covered in leather, exploits the structural potential of the material to its utmost. In the same way, his lounge chair of 1979, in steel tube and canvas, although it may be inspired by Le Corbusier and Marcel Breuer, shows again Nurmesniemi's ability to propose a minimal statement.

By contrast, he is equally successful when using traditional materials in traditional ways, but with the same refined simplicity. His garden seat, designed as a self-assembly kit in 1982, eschews advanced timber technology and reverts to simple, straightforward joinery. Strongly reminiscent of some of Saarinen's furniture of eighty years before, it nevertheless shares with other work the sensitivity to the nature and potential of the material that characterises all that he does.

Although Nurmesniemi in no sense would consider himself the founder of a school, his influence on younger designers has been considerable, not only through his work but by his continuous involvement in national and international design associations and competition juries and by his teaching and lecturing in Finland, Britain, Japan, and many other countries. History may well show that Nurmesniemi, the quiet man of Finnish design, will prove to be a major if indirect influence.

—Gordon Steele

# O'BRIEN, Timothy (Brian)

British stage and exhibition designer

**Born:** Of British parents, in Shillong, Assam, India, 8 March 1929. **Education:** Educated at Wellington College, Crowthome, Berkshire, 1942-47; Corpus Christi College, Cambridge, MA, 1952; studied stage design under Donald Oenslager, at Yale University, New Haven, Connecticut, 1952-53. **Military Service:** Served in the British Army Intelligence Corps, Austria, 1948-49, Sergeant. **Career:** Design Assistant, BBC Television, London, 1954-55; designer, Associated Rediffusion Television, London, 1955-56; head of design, ABC Television, London, 1956-66; associate designer, Royal Shakespeare Company, Stratford-upon-Avon, Warwickshire, from 1966; designer, National Theatre, London, 1974-77; worked in collaboration with designer Tazeena Firth, from 1961. Lecturer, Royal College of Art, London 1966-67. Chairman, Society of British Theatre Designers, London, from 1984. **Exhibition:** *British Theatre Design '83-87,* Riverside Studios, London, 1988. **Collections:** Victoria and Albert Museum, London; Theatre Museum, Göteborg. **Honors:** Gold Medal, Prague Quadriennale, 1975. **Address:** 33 Lansdowne Gardens, London SW8 2EQ, England.

## Publications

**By O'BRIEN: books**—(with David Fingleton) *British Theatre Design '83-87,* London, 1988.

\*

The aim is to create a world, its people and their circumstances, in the service of a production and its ideas. The best result is the illumination of life, provoking thought and arousing strong feelings. A designer in the theatre needs good collaborators, since he works in a social art. In particular, his relationship with his director and the script or score is all-important. Design may come easily, even the design of beautiful things, but it has to be relevant. The work has to be understood and its ideas clearly grasped, if they are to be clearly expressed. Design has first to persuade the freshly-arrived audience to clear their minds.

Good design is contemporary in that it seeks to remove stale associations. But contemporary design is no good if fashion obscures content. An audience in the theatre is never free of the artificiality of its surroundings. But the designs are a concrete reality and must arrive at the right degree of abstraction or the figurative. Preconception is dangerous, as the designs should evolve with the production; and when the work is on stage, the opening design statement, however effective, should permit of development and during the performance accumulate effects altogether larger than the means employed. Things connect. Borkman stands, self-impris-

oned in his upstairs room. A hidden door in a faded tapestry of a nymph and her shepherd opens to admit the woman he loved and then forsook when he married her sister for worldly advantage. The audience shivers afresh at the consequences.

—Timothy O'Brien

*See* FIRTH, Tazeena

# O'CONCHUBHAIR, Gearóid

Irish furniture and industrial designer

**Born:** Cloghan, Offaly County, Ireland, 16 October 1959. **Education:** St. Patrick's College, Maynooth; studied industrial design at the National College of Art and Design and National Institute of Higher Education, Limerick, 1982, B.S., 1982. **Career:** Industrial and product designer at ATW, Buncrana, County Donegal, designing off road vehicles, 1982-83; designer, Design ID, Limerick, producing portable computer design, for CPT, GEA Swedish Electrics Co., furniture design, for Shannon Development, digital viscometer design, for Brookfield Instruments, Shannon, 1984-86; freelance designer for Telecom Éireann; established partnership with Richard Lyons and formed Ómós Furniture Design, Heartwell, Kill, County Kildare, 1986. Lecturer, Department of Industrial Design, National College of Art and Design, from 1986. **Member:** Society of Designers of Ireland; assessment panel for design, National Council of Educational Awards. **Exhibitions:** Design Yard Prototype Gallery, 1993-96; Crafts Council Royal Dublin Society Craft Fair, 1993, 1994; Cologne Furniture Fair, 1995. **Honors:** SDI Young Designer of the Year, 1981; Educational Building Society Furniture Prize, 1993, 1994. **Address:** Department of Industrial Design, National College of Art and Design, 100 Thomas Street, Dublin 8, Ireland.

## Works

*Anu* steel frame chair with ash seat and back, 1993.
*Lug* and *Imbolg* steel frame four legged chairs with interwoven black elastic webbing seats, office chair for Dublin Corporation Planning Office, 1995.
Mobile Betting Kiosks, for the Irish Racing Board, 1995.
Table and chairs for the set of *The Black Box,* arts programme, Radió Teilifís Éireann, 1995.
Other designs include—*Gevnu* steel frame chair with central wooden spine; *Danu* chair with continuous back and rear legs in thin vertical strips of ash; *Sirona* steel frame reclining lounge chair, inverted V frame legs, and split central panels; *Oghma* chair steel frame seat, four wooden legs, and continuous press molded

**Gearóid O'Conchubhair:** *Anu* steel frame chair with ash back and seat, 1993

wooden back; *Eiru* steel frame dining chair with molded wooden back; *Naoise* steel frame adjustable reclining lounge chair; *Gleas* portable three-legged stacking chair with adjustable height, for National Symphony Orchestra; *Artio* three legged steel frame chair with inverted V construction.

*     *     *

Gearóid O'Conchubhair is one of the few furniture designers working in Ireland to design domestic furniture for small-scale industrial manufacture. Most furniture designers in Ireland design for craft methods of production or are furniture makers in the craft tradition producing one-off pieces. This is due to the high costs involved in setting up batch production, competition from cheaper imports, and the limited demand for designer furniture in a small economy. O'Conchubhair has overcome some of the design and manufacturing problems by using steel and molded beech or ash which are suited to machine methods of production. He has responded aesthetically to the challenge of designing furniture with these materials by exploiting their potential to create new forms and a highly individual design style. However high production costs and the innate conservatism of the consumer has meant that many designers have not gone beyond the prototype stage.

His approach to design is structural, creating a thin steel framework to support the wooden, upholstered, or molded elements. O'Conchubhair came to furniture design from an industrial and product design background. He has an expert understanding of structure, materials, and ergonomics as well as design. The structure of O'Conchubhair's chairs and table designs reflect this background and the fact that he was greatly influenced by his father, who was a cabinet maker and—significantly—a wheelwright. Other influences include the Spanish architect and designer Santiago Calatrava. Both share an engineering and architectonic approach to design.

The structure of his furniture is exposed and the construction of the chair becomes a feature of the object which can be easily read. The symmetrical chair backs and seats are ergonomically molded for correct and comfortable posture and the skeletal structures are left unadorned. A key element in the structure of the chairs is the tension produced by the steel frame. This tension holds the thin strips of timber together to form the chair back or seat and keeps them in position. This is done in the same way as the spokes of a wheel are held in place. There are few if any joints in the construction and glue is rarely used. It is the steel frame that also provides the strength and this is further emphasized in the design by using an inverted V structure for the legs.

Materials are chosen for their flexibility and all are easily available in Ireland. Steel, ash, oak, and beech are the most important ingredients. The ash tree is native to Ireland and produces soft timber that is both pliable and supple. There is a tradition of making furniture from ash and because of its pliability it is used in making the *camán* or stick used in hurling (the national sport of Ireland). Beech is in plentiful supply and is particularly well suited to press molding the contours of chair backs and seats.

The chairs are called after figures from ancient Irish mythology, *Anu* (the goddess of goddesses), *Imbolg* (metal workers), and *Lug* (god of light). Apart from the names chosen for the designs there is little in his work which could be specifically associated with Irish design, which usually means craft design. By combining timber and the materials of industry with an understanding of the processes of manufacture, structure, and ergonomics, O'Conchubhair has succeeded in creating a new departure in furniture design.

—Paul Caffrey

# ODERMATT, Siegfried
## Swiss typography and graphic designer

**Born:** Neuheim, Zug, 13 September 1926. **Education:** Educated at schools in Neuheim, 1933-42; studied at the Kunstgewerbeschule, Zürich, 1942-44; self-taught in design, from 1944. **Career:** Worked in the Georg Vetter industrial design studio, Zürich, 1944-45; freelance designer, in collaboration with Hans Falk, Zürich, 1946-48; designer, in the Paul Zurrer advertising agency, Wadenswil, 1948-50; freelance designer, establishing Siegfried Odermatt studio, Zürich, 1950-68; partner, with Rosmarie Tissi, in Odermatt and Tissi design studio, Zürich, from 1968; designed for City Druck AG, BP Benzin und Petroleum, Grammo Studio, Apotheke Sammet, Schelling Wellpappen, Univac, Mettler and Company, Union Safe Company, Kimo, Reinhard, and others. **Member:** Alliance Graphique Internationale, Paris; International Center for Typographic Arts, New York. **Exhibitions:** Visual Graphic Gallery, New York, 1966; ICTA Knauer Expo, Stuttgart, 1967; ICTA German Section, Wuppertal, 1968; Stadtische Berufschule, HofSaale, 1972. **Honors:** Typomundus Award 1965, 1970; Type Directors Club Award, New York, 1966; 4th Calendar Competition Award, West Germany, 1972. **Address:** Odermatt and Tissi, Schipfe 45, 8001 Zürich, Switzerland.

## Works

Promotional brochures and leaflets, for Neuenburger Versicherung insurance company, 1960.
Advertisements and brochures, for Univac Computers, 1963-70.
Advertisements, for E. Lutz and Company blockmakers, 1964.
Logotype, advertisements, and promotional brochures, for the Union Safe Company, 1966-75.
*Help Prevent Fire* poster, for Beratungsstelle für Brantverhutung, Bern, 1968.
Trademark logotype, for Mettler and Company Textiles, 1969.
*Antiqua Classica* typeface, 1971, *Sonora, Marabu,* and *Sinalog* typefaces, 1972, and *Mindanao* typeface, 1975, for Englersatz AG.
Advertisements, for Crypto, 1977-78.
Brochures, for BBC Brown Boverie et Cie, 1978-83.
*It's Time for Prime* poster, for Prime Computer AG, 1980.
Trademark logotype, for Kupferschmid Papers, 1980.
*Economical Development in Germany 1950-2000* exhibition poster, for Wirtschaft Woche, Düsseldorf, 1982.

## Publications

**On ODERMATT/TISSI: books—***An International Survey of Packaging* by Wim Crouwel and Kurt Weidemann, London, 1968; *Signet, Signal, Symbol* by Walter Diethelm, Zürich, 1970; *International Trademark Design* by Peter Wildbur, London, 1979; *Architectural Signing and Graphics* by John Follis and Dave Hammer, New York and London, 1979; *Who's Who in Graphic Art* edited by

633

Walter Amstutz, Zürich, 1982; *A History of Graphic Design* by Philip B. Meggs, London and New York, 1983.

*See* TISSI, Rosmarie

\*

We have deliberately kept our team small in order to keep a limited field of graphic design under close personal control. To both of us, graphic design is a vehicle of communication. We generally limit ourselves to the media of typography, photography, and technical drawing. What we stress in our work is a conceptual idea which we try to develop in our design. Thus, we use our media in the manner of elements, assembling them into an informative whole. Generally, we arrive at the solutions of our design problems by means of what could be called a dialectical process. That is, we try to analyze the given content of the intended message into segments which can be translated into the various media we use and then form a synthesis accordingly.

Although we both work in the same manner, we often arrive at startlingly different solutions. Although our manner of work may seem rather intellectual, intuition inevitably plays a distinctive role. As we complement each other in this often argumentative process, many of our works cannot be fairly attributed to either one of us; they are the product of a team. However, many years of collaboration have led us to a rather intimate knowledge of our "graphic brains."

Generally speaking, we tend to use simple, distinctive patterns of design and thus often arrive at signal-type solutions which can easily be remembered and individually recognized. Our main differences are congenial. While Rosmarie Tissi has a more playful approach to graphic problems, Siegfried Odermatt prefers the disciplined mental probing. Our work, however, has developed in the same direction and thus bears the marks of a common style.

—Siegfried Odermatt and Rosmarie Tissi

# OENSLAGER, Donald

American stage designer

**Born:** Harrisburg, Pennsylvania, 7 March 1902. **Education:** Studied at Phillips Exeter Academy, New Hampshire, 1919-20; Harvard University, Cambridge, Massachusetts, BA, 1923; also studied in Europe on Sachs travel grant, 1923-24. **Military Service:** Served in the United States Air Force, 1942-45, Major. **Family:** Married Mary Osborne Polak in 1937. **Career:** Stage designer, working in New York and in New Haven, Connecticut, 1925-75; consultant to the American Pavilion Theatre at the Brussels World's Fair, 1958, Montreal Cultural Center, 1961, Broadmoor International Center, 1961, Philharmonic Hall of the Lincoln Center, New York, 1962, 1969, New York State Theatre, 1964, Scott Theatre at Fort Worth Performing Arts Center, 1965, John F. Kennedy Center for Performing Arts, Washington, D.C., 1969, Meeting Center of Albany South Mall Project, 1969, and others. Instructor in scenic design, Middlebury College, Vermont, 1925; instructor and professor, 1925-71, and professor emeritus, 1971-75, Yale University, New Haven, Connecticut; professor of theatre, City University of New York, 1971-72. **Member:** Honorary Member, American Federation of

Arts; Royal Society of Arts, London; Master Drawing Association, Association Internationale de Bibliophile; Master Drawing Society; Municipal Art Society of New York; New York Mayor La Guardia's Art Committee of One Hundred, 1934; President's Advisory Committee on the Arts, 1960-62; vice-president, 1962-69, and board member, American National Theatre and Academy; United States National Commission for UNESCO, 1963-68; Art Commission of New York, 1965-75. **Exhibitions:** *Donald Oenslager: A Retrospective Exhibition,* Detroit Institute of Arts, 1956; *Russian Stage and Costume Designs from the Lobanov-Rostovsky, Oenslager, and Riabov Collections,* Metropolitan Museum of Art, New York, 1967 (toured); *Changing Concepts in Stage Design from the Donald Oenslager Collection,* Finch College, New York, 1971; *Four Centuries of Scenic Invention from the Donald Oenslager Collection,* International Exhibitions Foundation, Washington D.C., 1974 (toured). **Collections:** Metropolitan Museum of Art, New York; Museum of Modern Art, New York; Museum of the City of New York; Museum of Fine Arts, Boston; Detroit Institute of Arts. **Honors:** American School of Design Scroll of Honor Award, 1939; Bronze Star, 1945; Pennsylvania Ambassador Award, 1950; DFA, Colorado College, 1953; Antoinette Perry Award, New York, 1959; Ford Foundation Grant, 1960. **Died:** Bedford, New York, 21 June 1975.

## Works

Stage productions include—*Sooner or Later,* 1925; *Morals,* 1925; *A Bit o' Love,* 1925; *Pinwheel,* 1927; *Good News,* 1927; *Anna,* 1928; *L'Histoire du Soldat,* 1928; *The New Moon,* 1928; *Follow Thru'* (also co-director), 1929; *Girl Crazy,* 1930; *Overture,* 1930; *The Winter's Tale,* 1931; *Free for All,* 1931; *Singin' the Blues,* 1931; *East Wind,* 1931; *The Emperor Jones,* 1931; *Whistling in the Dark,* 1932; *Adam Had Two Sons,* 1932; *A Thousand Summers,* 1932; *Forsaking All Others,* 1933; *Keeper of the Keys,* 1933; *Jezebel,* 1933; *Uncle Tom's Cabin,* 1933; *Salome,* 1934; *The Lady from the Sea,* 1934; *Dance with Your Gods,* 1934; *Divided by Three,* 1934; *Tristan and Isolde,* 1934; *Anything Goes,* 1934; *Gold-Eagle Guy,* 1934; *Rosenkavalier,* 1934; *The Farmer Takes a Wife,* 1934; *Something Gay,* 1935; *First Lady,* 1935; *Tapestry in Gray,* 1935; *Stage Door,* 1936; *Ten Million Ghosts,* 1936; *Sweet River,* 1936; *Red, Hot and Blue!,* 1936; *200 Were Chosen,* 1936; *Johnny Johnson,* 1936; *Russet Mantle,* 1936; *Matrimony Pfd.,* 1936; *You Can't Take It With You,* 1936; *Miss Quis,* 1937; *Robin Landing,* 1937; *Edna, His Wife,* 1937; *Otello,* 1937; *Of Mice and Men,* 1937; *A Doll's House,* 1937; *I'd Rather Be Right,* 1937; *The Circle,* 1938; *The Fabulous Invalid,* 1938; *Amelia Goes to the Ball,* 1938; *I Am My Youth,* 1938; *Spring Thaw,* 1938; *The Good,* 1938; *A Woman's a Fool to Be Clever,* 1938; *From Vienna,* 1939; *The American Way,* 1939; *Off to Buffalo,* 1939; *Skylark,* 1939; *The Man Who Came to Dinner,* 1939; *Margin for Error,* 1939; *I Know What I Like,* 1939; *Young Couple Wanted,* 1939; *My Dear Children,* 1940; *Beverly Hills,* 1940; *Retreat to Pleasure,* 1940; *The Old Foolishness,* 1940; *My Sister Eileen,* 1940; *The Lady Who Came to Stay,* 1941; *Mr. Big,* 1941; *Claudia,* 1941; *The Doctor's Dilemma,* 1941; *Theatre,* 1941; *Spring Again,* 1941; *Pie in the Sky,* 1941; *The Flowers of Virtue,* 1942; *Hairpin Harmony,* 1943; *Pygmalion,* 1945; *Born Yesterday,* 1946; *Three to Make Ready,* 1946; *On Whitman Avenue,* 1946; *Loco,* 1946; *La Traviata,* 1946; *Present Laughter,* 1946; *The Abduction from the Seraglio,* 1946; *Park Avenue,* 1946; *The*

*Fatal Weakness,* 1946; *Years Ago,* 1946; *Land's End,* 1946; *Lovely Me,* 1946; *The Eagle Has Two Heads,* 1947; *Message for Margaret,* 1947; *Portrait in Black,* 1947; *Fidelio,* 1947; *How I Wonder,* 1947; *Eastward in Eden,* 1947; *Angel in the Wings,* 1947; *The Men We Marry,* 1948; *Cosi Fan Tutte,* 1948; *Life with Mother,* 1948; *Goodbye, My Fancy,* 1948; *Town House,* 1948; *The Leading Lady,* 1948; *The Smile of the World,* 1949; *At War with the Army,* 1949; *The Father,* 1949; *The Rat Race,* 1949; *The Velvet Glove,* 1949; *The Liar,* 1950; *Springboard to Nowhere,* 1950; *The Live Wire,* 1950; *Second Threshold,* 1951; *The Small Hours,* 1951; *Peer Gynt,* 1951; *The Constant Wife,* 1951; *Paris '90,* 1952; *Candida,* 1952; *To Be Continued,* 1952; *La Bohème,* 1952; *Horses in Midstream,* 1953; *Dido and Aeneas,* 1953; *Sabrina Fair,* 1953; *Escapade,* 1953; *Madam Will You Walk,* 1953; *The Prescott Proposals,* 1953; *Coriolanus,* 1954; *Dear Charles,* 1954; *The Wooden Dish,* 1955; *Janus,* 1955; *A Roomful of Roses,* 1955; *Major Barbara,* 1956; *The Ballad of Baby Doe,* 1956; *Four Winds,* 1957; *Mary Stuart,* 1957; *Nature's Way,* 1957; *A Shadow of My Enemy,* 1957; *The Girls in 509,* 1958; *The Pleasure of His Company,* 1958; *The Man in the Dog Suit,* 1958; *The Marriage-Go-Round,* 1958; *J. B.,* 1958; *A Majority of One,* 1959; *The Mikado,* 1959; *The Pink Jungle,* 1959; *The Highest Tree,* 1959; *Orpheus and Eurydice,* 1959; *Dear Liar,* 1960; *Orfeo,* 1960; *The Prisoner,* 1960; *A Far Country,* 1961; *A Call on Kuprin,* 1961; *Blood, Sweat and Stanley Poole,* 1961; *The Wings of the Dove,* 1961; *First Love,* 1961; *Venus at Large,* 1962; *The Irregular Verb to Love,* 1963; *A Case of Libel,* 1963; *One by One,* 1964; *Madame Butterfly,* 1964; *Lady From Colorado,* 1964; *Carmen,* 1966; *The Italian Lady from Algiers,* 1966; *Tosca,* 1966; *Love in E Flat,* 1966; *Der Rosenkavalier,* 1967; *Antigone,* 1967; *The Merry Widow,* 1967; *Don Pasquale,* 1963; *Spofford,* 1967; *Avanti!,* 1968; *The Mikado,* 1968; *Don Carlos,* 1968; *The Wrong Way Light Bulb,* 1969.

## Publications

**By OENSLAGER: books**—*Scenery Then and Now,* New York, 1936; *Theatre of Bali* (booklet), 1940; *Four Centuries of Theatre Design: Drawings from the Donald Oenslager Collection,* New Haven, Connecticut, 1964; (editor) *Four Centuries of Scenic Invention: Drawings from the Collection of Donald Oenslager,* New York, 1974; *Stage Design: Four Centuries of Scenic Invention,* New York and London, 1975; *The Theatre of Donald Oenslager,* Middletown, Connecticut, 1978.

**On OENSLAGER: books**—*Donald Oenslager: Stage Designer and Teacher: A Retrospective Exhibition,* catalogue, Detroit, Michigan, 1956; *Russian Stage and Costume Designs for the Ballet, Opera, and Theatre: A Loan Exhibition from the Lobanov-Rostovsky, Oenslager and Riabov Collections,* catalogue, Washington, D.C., 1967; *Changing Concepts in Stage Design: Drawings from the Donald Oenslager Collection,* New York, 1971.

\* \* \*

Donald Oenslager came to the theatre through study in playwriting with Professor George Pierce Baker at Harvard; thus he always placed his theatrical design work at the service of the script. Time in Europe in 1921 introduced him to the work of Gordon Craig, Adolphe Appia, and many other decorative or impressionistic symbolists, and these influences inhabited his design approach throughout his career. He was also greatly influenced by the work of Robert Edmond Jones, with whom he apprenticed on his return to the United States and for whom he always had the greatest respect. Another powerful factor in his life was his acceptance of a design post at Yale University after Baker was invited to open a professional school of dramatic art there in 1925. As a teacher of young designers, Oenslager always perceived his role as that of the Renaissance master working with talented apprentices, and he always saw his own professional designs on Broadway within the great, historic continuum of artists, craftsmen, and designers to royalty from medieval times to the present. As the only major Broadway designer until the 1960s who was also a teacher, his immense influence on his students always created a sense of professionalism, a sense of respect for the play to be designed, and a sense of theatrical vision that harkened back to the visual dreams of Gordon Craig and the poetic outlook of Robert Edmond Jones.

The essence of Oenslager's teaching lay in his call for student designers to probe a play and the culture within which it was written to find underlying principles of structure and rhythm that could then be embodied in a contemporary stylistic approach for a particular theatre and audience. He did not relate to the concept of the stage setting as a projector of social or intellectual ideas, nor to the concept of the setting as a junk-art collage. He was a person of taste and a certain elegance who preferred these qualities in his designs, and the designs that he admired the most in his personal historical collection were those that presented a striking and evocative beauty. Even among his own designs, the ones he remembered with the most pleasure were those with a Baroque elegance and decorative flamboyance.

—Douglas A. Russell

# OHL, Herbert (Karl)

German architect and furniture and industrial designer

**Born:** Mannheim, 26 August 1926. **Education:** Studied painting and graphics, Akademie der Bildenden Kunste, Karlsruhe, 1947-50; studied architecture under Egon Eiermann, Technische Hochschule, Karlsruhe, Dip.Ing., 1952; studied architecture, Politecnico, Milan, Dott.Arch., 1969. **Career:** Assistant architect to Egon Eiermann, Karlsruhe, 1952-54; chief architect, University Clinics, Saarland, Germany, 1954-56; architect, Institute of Industrialized Building, Ulm School of Design (Hochschule für Gestaltung), Germany, 1959-68; partner, with Gino Valle, in Architects Studio Ohl-Valle, Milan, 1965-68; founder/principal, Ohl Design, Frankfurt and Darmstadt, Germany, Milan and Genova, Italy, from 1968, and Ohl-Design-USA, Chicago, from 1989; has designed for Arflex, Braun AG, Brionvega, Canadian Plywood Association, Correcta Werke AG, Danzer KG, Elements Minvielle, Esso, Fantoni, Farbwerke Höchst AG, Fiat, Hoechst AG, Korrekta-Werke, Krupp, La Rinascente, Lübke International, Max Braun, Metzeler AG, Minvielle, Renus AG, Rosenthal, United Nations Industrial Development Organization, Wilkhahn, Ziegler-Faun, and others. Professor, 1956-68, rector and prorector, 1964-68, Ulm School of Design; professor and director of transportation design,

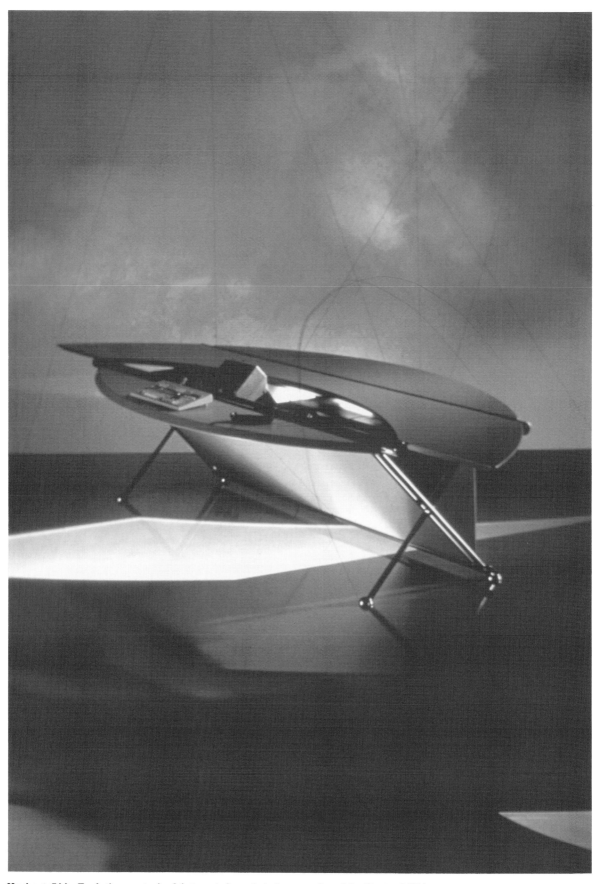

**Herbert Ohl:** *Evolution* motorized integrated workstation, produced by Fantoni SPA

College of Design, Pforzheim, Germany, 1984-91; professor of design, University of Illinois at Chicago, from 1988. Visiting professor, Columbia University, New York, 1960-63, Harvard University, Cambridge, Massachusetts, 1960, Carnegie-Mellon University, Pittsburgh, Pennsylvania, 1960-61, Princeton University, Princeton, New Jersey, 1960, University of California at Los Angeles, 1964, Texas A&M University, College Station, 1964-65, Instituto Nacional de Technologia Industrial, Buenos Aires, 1966, Scola Superior di Disenho, Rio de Janeiro, 1978, National Institute of Design, Ahmedabad, India, 1985, and University of Applied Arts, Vienna, 1986. **Member:** Member, Scientific Committee, International Research Center "Pio Manzu," Verucchio, Italy, from 1968; director, German Design Council, Germany, 1974-84; board member, International Council of Industrial Design Societies, Brussels, Belgium, 1975-79. **Exhibitions:** Ulm School of Design, Munich, 1965; *International Home Furniture Fair,* Milan, 1972-92; *International Office Furniture Fair,* Milan, 1972-92; *German Federal Design Awards International Travel Exhibition,* toured, 1978-80; *International Office Furniture Fair,* Cologne, 1978-92; *Italian Furniture Design Exhibition,* Milan, 1984; *International Furniture Fair,* Cologne, 1984-92; *International Automobile Exhibition,* Frankfurt, 1985-91; *Ulm School of Design International Travel Exhibition,* toured Europe and Japan, 1986-88; *AAA Auto Exhibition,* Berlin, 1988; *Neocon-International Office Furniture Fair,* Chicago, 1990-92; *Italian Furniture Design Exhibition,* Paris, 1991; *German Design International Travel Exhibition,* 1992. **Collections:** Museum of Modern Art, New York; Cooper-Hewitt Museum, New York. **Honors:** Gold Medal, Rimini, 1968; United Nations Low-Cost Housing Prize, New York, 1969; Bundesministerium Integra Building Prize, Bonn, 1973; Gute Form Prize, Darmstadt, 1983; German Federal Design Awards; G-Mark, Japan Design Award; Good Industry Form, Hannover Fair; German Design Selection, House Industry Form; Singapore Furniture Design Award; EIMU—Design Awards of the International Office Furniture Fair, Milan. **Address:** Frankensteiner 86, Darmstadt, Germany.

## Works

Exhibition design and concept at the Milan Triennale, for the Hochschule für Gestaltung, Ulm, 1960.
*Multipli* furniture system, for Fantoni, 1965-73.
German pavilion displays at *Expo 67,* Montreal, for the Bundesministerium, Bonn, 1967.
*OSI 1/2/3, BCCF Basic Concept* car, and *Auto-Bisensi-Trinic* car, for Fiat, 1973-83.
Seating system, for O-Linie, 1974-79.
Design diagnosis and evaluation system, for the German Rat fur Formgebung, Darmstadt, 1974-83.
*Evolution* workstation, for Fantoni, 1995.

## Publications

**By OHL: books**—*Wandverkleidungen aus Hostalit Z Polyfaltplatten,* Frankfurt, 1964; *Die Adequate Wohnform, Stadtebauder Zukunff,* Düsseldorf, 1969; *Centro di tempo libero,* Verucchio, Italy, 1970; *Tempo libero e potere dell'audiovisivo,* Verucchio, 1971; *Flexibles Wohnen,* Bad Godesberg, West Germany, 1972.

**On OHL: books**—*Talk About Design* by James Pilditch, London,

1976; *Design e Forme Nuove nell'Arredamento Italiano* by Paolo Portoghesi and Marino Marini, Rome, 1978.

\*

Even if the designer works in a rational and resolutely functional manner, his designs will show a surprising and distinctive expression and sometimes will even touch on other realms, such as those of beauty or truth. Transcending the rational detachment of product analysis, this expression produces an emotionally direct and spontaneous relation between user and product. Thus it is that while design responds to material imperatives, it may nonetheless minister to the spiritual needs of people.

—Herbert Ohl

\* \* \*

Herbert Ohl is as well-known for his teaching at the Hochschule für Gestaltung in Ulm as he is for his precise and elegant solutions to architectural and industrial design problems. It was during his directorship at Ulm (1964-68) that he also worked with the renowned Italian architect Gino Valle, one of that roster of building architects who expresses a common sense in the face of a general rush toward the outlandishly exceptional. Ohl, who had already made a name for himself as head of Ulm's industrial building department, was much influenced by his contact with Valle's work based on a methodology of design more than on a vocabulary of forms. This experience happily tied in with Ohl's formative studies under the equally-renowned architect Egon Eiermann (in whose office Ohl had subsequently worked), a person whose widely publicized support of rationalism had caused him to be placed in the same critical category as Mies van der Rohe, Walter Gropius, and the Bauhaus. At this time, the early 1950s, Eiermann was executing industrial buildings for Ciba pharmaceuticals, the State silk factories, and technical structures for university complexes, including the Technical School in Karlsruhe where Ohl had met him.

Ohl's subsequent work both in architectural and industrial fields bears Eiermann's stamp and displays a plastic power and elegance unique in Germany. In his designs for low-cost housing, prefabricated building systems, adaptable hospital facilities, modular packaged furniture, seating systems, and radical new conceptions for automobiles, Ohl focuses on the realization of a "catalogue" of required elements, a catalogue that includes modules of human activity as well as modules of form. These compositional elements related to the framework of their environment. The results, however, are relatively independent of programmatic limits and recognize the need to relate human functions to architectural and product design—without which they have little reason to exist. His inheritance of rationalist common sense gives his works a remarkable degree of technical and visual durability.

—George Walsh

# OKADA, Tomoji
Japanese industrial designer

**Born:** Tokyo, 21 November 1936. **Education:** Educated at Tokyo Metropolitan Technical High School, until 1955; studied at Nihon

University, Tokyo, 1958-61, and at Kuwazawa Design School, Tokyo, 1961-62; studied under Jay Doblin at Illinois Institute of Technology, Chicago, MS, 1968. **Family:** Married Kaoru Kayatama in 1968; children: Sanae and Takuya. **Career:** Worked as a mechanical engineer, Nihon Camera, Tokyo, 1960-65; design researcher, at the Trade Center, Chicago, 1965-67; chief industrial designer, Nikon Camera, Tokyo, 1967-70; industrial design manager, 1970-75, technical support manager, 1975-78, audio products manager, 1978-82, automation manufacturing manager, 1982-83, and vice-president for automation, from 1983, at General Electric, Tokyo. Instructor, Kuwazawa Design School, Tokyo, 1968, and Nihon University, Tokyo, 1970. **Honors:** Japan External Trade Organization Award, 1962; Mainichi Industrial Design Award, Tokyo, 1962; Japanese Government Study Grant, 1965. **Address:** 40-29 Todoroki, 2-chome, Setagaya-ku, Tokyo 158, Japan.

### Publications

By OKADA: books—*Still Camera,* thesis, Chicago, 1968; articles—*Industrial Art News* (Tokyo), August 1963, September 1968; *Japan Design House* (Tokyo), August 1968; *Machine Design* (Tokyo), July 1975.

On OKADA: articles—*Industrial Design* (Tokyo), November 1980.

\*       \*       \*

Tomoji Okada creates the impression of being very much his own man.

After graduating in mechanical engineering from Nihon University, he went to work for the world-famous camera maker Nikon, then took a leave of absence to study at the Kuwazawa Design School. He intended to return to Nikon to establish an industrial design department. While at Kuwazawa, however, he heard a lecture by Jay Doblin and was so impressed that he decided to go to America to study with Doblin at the Illinois Institute of Technology (IIT), in Chicago. After receiving an M.S. at IIT, he returned to Nikon, established the promised design section, then resigned and became manager of industrial design at General Electric Japan. Now, he is Vice-President of General Electric Industrial Automation. In the meantime, he has also lectured on industrial design.

In Japan, there are two kinds of designers: those who are specialists and those who are generalists. Okada seems to rise above such either/or designations. A good description of him might be that he is "a unique management executive and an original industrial designer."

Okada is now in charge of the General Electric Industrial Automation computer-aided design department, established in January 1983. He was entirely responsible for its creation—from finding the staff and implementing the systems, to finding a plant to house the operation. In creating the department, he applied the methodology of industrial design. In fact, he later commented that the total process (identifying problems, searching for solutions, evaluation, and implementation) was surprisingly similar to the design process.

Okada is also active as an international businessman. He often faces "tense situations, whether to persuade or to be persuaded by others," and again, he considers that the stages of the design process are effectively applicable. For example, he points out that the final evaluation of a business proposal (like a design proposal)

should be avoided while it is still an abstract concept. And he points out that, in general, the ability to grasp the substance of any business problem can be developed through the application of precepts learned in design work.

Given his example, one would have to agree. One would also have to add that Okada's success has something to do with his character, because success at his kind of work also demands a great deal of creativity.

Design methodology, then, has become second-nature to Okada. He says: "I may be an exceptional case in Japan, but I think that it is desirable that designers go into other fields of work. Instead of having social contacts only among themselves, they should go out to breathe the air of the outside world. The time has now come for such a change."

Because few in Japan share his background, Okada is sure to become the leading proponent of what he preaches.

—Kunio Sano

## OLDHAM, Todd

American fashion designer

**Born:** Corpus Christi, Texas, in 1961. **Education:** Self taught in design. **Career:** Worked in alterations, Ralph Lauren Polo Store, Dallas, Texas, 1980; showed first collection, Dallas, 1981; partner and designer, L-7 company, including Times 7 diffusion line, New York, from 1988; founder and designer, Todd Oldham, New York, from 1989; introduced line of handbags, 1991; produced Todd Oldham patterns for *Vogue Patterns,* from 1992; introduced footwear line, 1993; creative consultant, Escada, Munich, Germany, from 1994. **Honors:** Perry Ellis Award for Fashion Talent, Council of Fashion Designers of America, 1992. **Addresses:** (office) 120 Wooster St. #3FL-SF, New York, New York 10012-5200, U.S.A.; (store) 123 Wooster St., New York, New York 10012, U.S.A.; (store) 7386 Beverly Blvd., Los Angeles, California 90036, U.S.A; (store) 160 8th Street, South Beach, Miami, Florida 33139, U.S.A.

### Publications

On OLDHAM: articles—*New York Times,* 11 April 1991, 6 April 1995; *Newsweek* (New York), 29 April 1991, 12 June 1995; *Rolling Stone* (San Francisco), 14 May 1992; *Paper* (New York), September 1994; *The Advocate,* 18 October 1994; *Avenue* (New York), March 1995; *Philadelphia Inquirer* 6 April 1995; *International Herald Tribune,* 2 November 1995.

\*       \*       \*

Todd Oldham is to fashion design as Andy Warhol was to art and Keith Haring was to graphic design. He creates an essential belief system, an orbit, and an aura about himself as much as he creates artifacts. A home-grown American shaman and phenomenon who always thanks his "Granny" in show credits, Oldham succeeds half as Tom Sawyer, half as Leonardo. He is the winsome maverick who never offends, but always titillates and beguiles. Rising among the American fashion designers of the late 1980s, after moving to New York in 1988, Oldham was initially one among many talented new-

**Todd Oldham:** *Double Face Satin Kate Jacket,* **Spring Collection, 1996. Photo: Dan Lecca courtesy of Todd Oldham**

comers, though he had already established his workshops in Texas in the early 1980s. His work was distinguished by a funky, ingenious and ingenuous, "outsider" art sense of whimsy and surprise. He is always colorful, figuratively if not literally. Fashion's propensity to sameness and to the jaded *Weltschmerz* of the New York design sensibility was suddenly confronted with buttons of Schiaparelli-esque eccentricity, unabashed good-humor drag queens on the runway, and madly "bad-taste" conglomerations of colors and materials. His aesthetic is patchwork and pastiche; he is cued into popular culture, both the grass roots populist kind and in the 1990s media sense, cleverly converting the abject into the art object. His Wooster Street store in New York could at first be confused for a Middle-American thrift shop. While a master of madcap prints, Oldham has also collaborated with artists Ruben Toledo and Kenny Scharf on designs.

Oldham is distinctive, but always regarded as a bellwether. In 1996, amidst declarations of the return of color, Oldham's multicolored shifts were repeatedly singled out for high color, abstract pattern, and bold design. Color and surface embellishment are the chief traits of Oldham's work: he is little concerned with the silhouette and conventionally keeps to basic shapes allowing—like Schiaparelli—all of his creativity to be exercised on the rich surface. In 1992, Macy's in New York advertised Oldham's madras-simulating grid skirt in sequins to be worn with his white cotton blouse with gigantic and cartoonish ladybugs. In the same year, he showed on the runway a beaded leopard skirt, leopard beret and blouse, with a tufted vest and a quilted, tuft-printed coat on top, a trompel'oeil mix of the Princess and the Pea and "Wild Kingdom" that is unforgettable.

Named in 1994 as consultant to Escada, Oldham's immediate impact has been to introduce unabashed color and decorative delight to a wardrobe otherwise somewhat staid. Beginning with his "Times 7" line, Oldham has always produced buttons, accessories, and ornamentation to great success, allowing not only his pastiche, but the client's creative participation. When Oldham received the Council of Fashion Designers of America's Perry Ellis Award for Fashion Talent for 1991, the program notes observed, "Just 30-years-old and with no formal training as a designer, Oldham has turned his three-year-old company into a fun house of design. Seemingly as happy-go-lucky as his clothes, Oldham clearly believes in mixing business with pleasure." Oldham's business-with-pleasure mix of the respectful with the impertinent has an irresistible appeal in an era when clothing must go from workplace to home to social occasion.

Oldham is eclectic and zany. Woody Hochswender, reviewing Oldham's fall 1991 collection in the *New York Times,* called it "a whirlwind round-the-world tour—by plane, flying carpet and Greyhound." All of these vehicles are part of Oldham's ardent vagabondage. In 1991, his Byzantine and Guell-Park mosaics made from Lamontage synthetic-fiber felting were a small art history of elite monuments. The bus route is more likely for Oldham's Genie dress (1991) with cut-out midriff and sides articulated in gold braid and plastic stones in which he invokes Orientalism, but most specifically remembers the "I Dream of Jeannie" television series. His museums of good and bad taste have incorporated both the Mona Lisa onto a skirt and Kitsch horse paintings onto sequined jackets. In 1995-96, a serape print became a pants suit and evening dresses were based on mechanics' coveralls.

Yet Oldham is more than *enfant terrible.* In 1995, Roy Campbell wrote in the *Philadelphia Inquirer,* "Oldham is the glam-king of cartoony couture, one-minute-of-fame fashions that are perfect in

circles shaped by MTV but have little relevance beyond that. His shows in past seasons were video-bite circus spectacles with female impersonators and gag-heavy clothes." But Campbell's assessment of the fall 1995 collection was that Oldham "had no drag queens, few gags, and plenty of wearable design." In 1995, Suzy Menkes reported in the *International Herald Tribune* that Oldham "overcame the excesses of Halloween and the pre-show hype [and] staged a strong show that enlivened the season...." Like Warhol and Haring, Oldham has come to command an important economic empire as well as a social and aesthetic orbit. He imparts, as he always has, a seriousness of purpose to the work and canniness to its ambitions, even as he avoids the dull or the aggressive. A sweet innocence obtains at the core of the imagination that is as compelling in its Texas drawl and outrageous pastiche as one artist's sheepishness or another's struggle to donate his graphics to the subway system. Appraising Oldham's career and status in 1995, Amy M. Spindler claimed in the *New York Times* that she saw the "overwhelmingly, uncompromisingly creative mind" of earlier work a little tempered by commerce, maturity, fragrances, and designerjeans license. She concluded, "Mr. Oldham has grown up ... efficiently setting up for richer, wider horizons." Thus, the American frontier for the native spirit.

In a telling series of images, Oldham undressed partially or wholly for photographs, first for the downtown New York *Paper,* shirtless with cowboy hat, then for the uptown and up-scale New York magazine *Avenue,* then naked for an article entitled "The Natural," and then ostensibly naked with actress Kathy Najimy in anti-fur advertising in 1995-96 for PETA, one of the designer's favorite causes. Consciously or unconsciously, Oldham is the all-American boy, the genuine talent of frankness, genius, and mischief. Huckleberry Finn makes clothes and inexorably they are great clothes.

—Richard Martin

# OTT + STEIN
German graphic design firm

**Founded** in 1978 by Nicolaus Ott (**Born:** in Göttingen, 5 December 1947. **Education:** Apprenticeship with Zeichner in Atelier Fehrecke, Göttingen; studied at the Hochschule der Künste, Berlin, 1969-74. **Family:** Married Angelika Weilert, 1974; children: Moritz.) and Bernard Stein (**Born:** Berlin, 18 October 1949. **Education:** Studied at the Hochschule der Künste, Berlin, 1972-77. **Family:** Married Eva Heinemeyer, 1990; children: Robert, Linda, Hanna, Luise.); co-lecturers, 1980-82, and co-guest professors, 1988, Hochschule der Künste, Berlin. **Member:** Internationales Design Zentrum, Berlin. **Exhibitions:** Internationales Design Zentrum, Berlin, 1983, 1991; Schumacher Gebler, Munich, 1985; Hochschule für Gestaltung, Offenbach, 1987; Hubert Riedel, Berlin, 1989; Museum für Kunst und Gewerbe, Hamburg, 1992; Deutsches Plakat Museum, Essen, 1994. **Collections:** Deutsches Plakat Museum, Essen; Museum für Kunst und Gewerbe, Hamburg; Museum of Modern Art, New York; Museum für Gestaltung, Zürich; Deutsches Historisches Museum, Berlin; Brandenburgische Kunstsammlungen, Cottbus. **Honors:** Awards include: "Das vorbildliche Plakt," Berlin; "Die 100 besten Plakate," Berlin; "Typography Germany," Munich; Poster Biennale, Lahti; Plakat

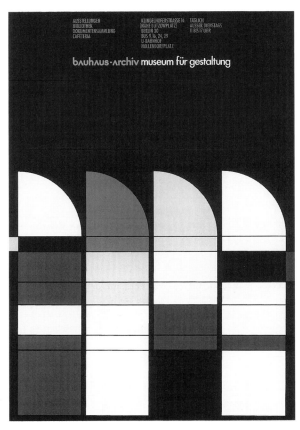

Bernard Stein and Nicholas Ott: *Bauhaus-Archiv Museum für Gestaltung* poster, 1985

Triennale, Essen. **Address:** Bundesplatz 17, 10715 Berlin, Germany.

**Works**

Television logo design, for Sender Freies, Berlin, 1979-81.
Posters and catalogues, for Internationales Design Zentrum, Berlin, from 1980.
Signet and identity, for Architekturgalerie Aedes, Berlin, from 1980.
Signet, for daad-galerie, Berlin, from 1980.
Signet and corporate identity, for Berliner Kammeroper, 1981-1990.
Signet, posters, and catalogues for major exhibitions, for Zeitgeist Gesellschaft, from 1981.
Poster and catalogues, for Bauhaus-Archiv, Berlin, from 1981.
Signet and poster series, for Staatliche Museen Preußischer Kulturbesitz, Berlin, 1983-1994.
Book covers, for Transit Buchverlag, Berlin, 1984-1989.
Signet, for Museum für Kunst und Gewerbe, Hamburg, from 1985.
Signet and poster series, for Stiftung Preußischer Kulturbesitz, Berlin, from 1986.
Signet, identity, and posters, for Schiller Theater, Berlin, from 1991.
Exhibition graphics, for Kunstbibliothek, Berlin, from 1993.
Signet, corporate identity, and poster series, for Kunstsammlungen zu Weimar, from 1993.
Signet, identity, and image posters, for Deutsches Historisches Museum, Berlin, from 1994.

**Publications**

**On OTT + STEIN: books**—*Typography Now* by Rick Poynor and Edward Booth-Clibborn, London, 1991; *Vom Wort zum Bild und zurück* by Ulf Erdmann Ziefler, Germany, 1992; **articles**—*Form* (Germany), no. 112, 1985; *Domus* (Milan), no. 686, 1987; *Forum Typographie* (Germany), no. 4, 1987; *Blueprint* (London), no. 54, 1989; *Idea* (Tokyo), no. 219, 1990; *Neue Werbung* (Germany), no. 6, 1991; *Süddeutsche Zeitung* (Germany), no. 67, 1992; *Der Tagesspiegel* (Germany), no. 14227, 1992; *Der Alltag* (Switzerland), no. 60, 1992; *Novum Gebrauchsgrafik* (Munich), no. 8, 1992; *Creation* (Japan), no. 17, 1993; *Affiche* (Netherlands), no. 7, 1993; *Linea Grafica* (Italy), no. 289, 1994; *Diseño* (Chile), no. 25, 1994.

\*   \*   \*

In the eighties there came a great surge toward new developments in graphic design from Japan, the United States (above all, California), Holland, and England. All of these impulses were quickly taken up in Germany, yet very little that was really new or remarkable evolved. In these parts, the successes of photomontage posters from the seventies were still reverberating and slowly dying. in their place came works—at first timid steps that gave only a hint of the impressive developments to come—which employed a different graphic language and could eventually take their place beside the major international breakthroughs since 1980: the posters of Nicolaus Ott and Bernard Stein.

These two graduates of the Berlin Art College combine illustrative esprit, conceptional clarity, and constructive versatility in their significant designs. In subtle graphic facets, a comprehensive body of work has been created piece by piece which embraces the entire field of print media, above all signets, books and catalogs, as well as the special area of the poster.

Many of Ott + Stein's posters are dominated by rich typographic images. Here the distance from historic functionalism is most clearly seen, as well as the relevancy of the contemporary message. These typographic images are developed through the combining of contrast-rich, dissimilar letter forms, through the resolution of the letters into their individual parts (such as curves, diagonals, verticals, and horizontals), together with lines and blocks of type which melt into illustrations. Or parts of alphabets may be used that look like music notations or express the language of music. All of these design elements are the expression of an enlightened manipulation of language and typography after their renewal through experimental and visual poesy.

In spite of the richness of forms in the Ott + Stein oeuvre, their ideas are always simple and trenchantly visualized. Some posters gain their effect solely from the way that type, pictorial element, and spacing are organized, by the way they relate in the compositions. Superficial visual jokes are never to be found in these posters. Joining this high level of typographic imagination is a writing-like form of expression which is, however, far from any attempt at calligraphic curlicues. These works display a joy in improvisation, with the higher goal of developing a new, expressive art of our times.

Pictorial elements are brief and to the point. This is seldom a single illustrative dictum, but always a signet-like reduction. Through cropping, photos or art works are lifted from their rectangular format and integrated into the poster construction.

The work of Nicolaus Ott and Bernard Stein is characterized by designing intelligence and a multiplicity of forms. It is marked by a style that is never repeated into stereotypes, but individually interpreted in relation to each assignment. The great repertoire of design variations shows a knowledge of history, without which conscious and relevant work would be unthinkable today.

For all their asymmetrical variety, all of these works designed in sensitive duet radiate a mastery of the craft. A body of work complete in content and form that in this era of wild gesturing is becoming more and more rare. (Reprinted from *Novum* (Munich), August 1992.)

—Friedrich Friedl

# P-Q

## PALMQVIST, Sven

Swedish glass designer

**Born:** Lenhovda, Smaland, 4 September 1906. **Education:** Studied at Orrefors Glass Engraving School, Sweden, 1928-30; Tekniska Skolan, Stockholm, 1931-33; Kungliga Konsthogskolan, Stockholm, 1934-36; under Paul Connet, at the Academie Ranson, Paris, 1937-39; also studied in Germany and Czechoslovakia, 1934, and in Italy, Denmark, Holland, Belgium, and the United States, 1937-39. **Military Service:** Served in the Swedish Home Guard, 1939-45. **Family:** Married Gertrud Brolin in 1942 (died, 1969); children: Jonas, Petter, Maria, and Andreas. **Career:** Designer, working with Simon Gate and Edward Hald, at Orrefors Glassworks, Sweden, 1928-72; retired to Valdemarsvik and Orrefors, 1972-81, and to Paris, 1981-84. **Exhibitions:** *Swedish Arts and Crafts,* New York World's Fair, 1939; *Orrefors 1917-42,* Nationalmuseum, Stockholm, 1942; German Crafts Fair, Munich, 1955; Milan Triennale, 1957; *Sven Palmqvist,* at the Venice Biennale, 1976; *Nordisk Industridesign,* Kunstindustrimuseet, Oslo, 1976; Royal Academy of Art, Stockholm, 1982; *Scandinavian Modern Design 1880-1980,* Cooper-Hewitt Museum, New York, 1982; *Design Since 1945,* Philadelphia Museum of Art, 1983; *Scandinavia: Ceramics and Glass in the Twentieth Century,* Victoria and Albert Museum, London, 1989. **Collections:** Philadelphia Museum of Art; Victoria and Albert Museum, London. **Honors:** Schwedisches Schaffen Heute Design Prize, Zurich, 1949; German Crafts Fair Award, Munich, 1955; Grand Prize, Milan Triennale, 1957; State of California Gold Medals, 1953-61; Gold Medal, Liubliana Biennale, 1964; American Institute of Interior Designers Award, New York, 1967; Wasa Order, Stockholm, 1977; Prince Eugen Medal Stockholm, 1977. **Died:** Paris, 6 February 1984.

### Works

*Fasett* vase in blue tinted glass with cut decoration, for Orrefors, 1941.
*Kantara* bowl in white semi-opaque glass, for Orrefors, 1944.
*Kraka* glassware series, for Orrefors, 1944-50.
*Ravenna* glassware series in blue with stained red and blue interior pattern, for Orrefors, 1948-53.
*Girl with Spring Flowers* vase in blue tinted glass with cut decoration, for Orrefors, 1949.
Christening font, for Vantors Church, 1959.
Glass wall, for the International Telecommunications Building, Geneva, 1961.
Glass wall, for the Swedish Broadcasting and Television Corporation, Stockholm, 1961.
Monumental glass decorations, for the Government Building of Dubai, 1981.

Glass sculpture, for the Hospital of Saint Sigfrid, Vaxjo, 1981.
Ceiling decoration, for the Government Assembly Hall, Rosenbad, Stockholm, 1981.

### Publications

**On PALMQVIST: books**—*Orrefors 1917-1942,* exhibition catalogue edited by Elisa Hald-Steenberg, Stockholm, 1942; *Modernt Svenskt Glas* edited by Gregor Paulsson, Stockholm, 1943; *Orrefors* by Carl Hernmarck, Stockholm, 1951; *The Beauty of Modern Glass* by R. Stennett-Willson, London and New York, 1958; *Modern Glass* by Ada Polak, London, 1962; *Svenskt Glas* by Elisa Steenberg, Stockholm, 1964; *Scandinavian Design: Objects of a Life Style* by Eileene Harrison Beer, New York and Toronto, 1975; *International Modern Glass* by Geoffrey Beard, London, 1976; *Sven Palmqvist, Orrefors,* exhibition folder by Dag Widman, Stockholm, 1982; *Design Since 1945* edited by Kathryn Hiesinger and George Marcus, Philadelphia and London, 1983; *Design in Sweden* edited by Monica Boman, Stockholm, 1985; *Twentieth Century Design: Glass* by Frederick Cooke, London, 1986; *Scandinavia: Ceramics and Glass in the Twentieth Century* by Jennifer Hawkins Opie, London, 1989.

\*

During my work as a glass designer, I have found that no material is closer to the light. With glass you can sculpt with light, paint with the spectral colours through the aid of the sun. Glass will express so much more than other materials, it will never be affected—it is eternal, unchangeable. The air bubble born in the heat of a sudden improvisation, locked up forever in the crystal block—a moment of eternity in the wide space of the universe.

—Sven Palmqvist (1983)

## PANTON, Verner

Danish architectural, interior, textile, furniture, and industrial designer

**Born:** Gamtofte, 13 February 1926. **Education:** Studied at the Technical School, Odense 1944-47; Royal Academy of Fine Arts, Copenhagen, 1947-51; also study travels in Holland, Germany, France and Italy, 1953-55. **Military Service:** Served in the Danish Army, 1947. **Family:** Married Marianne Pherson in 1964; daughter: Carin. **Career:** Worked with the architect Arne Jacobsen, Copenhagen, 1950-52; freelance architect and designer, working in

**Verner Panton:** *Pantoflex* **chair of laminated wood and steel tube for VS Vereinigte Spezialmöbelfabriken, 1994**

Denmark, 1955-62, in France, 1962, and in Switzerland, from 1963; designed for Bayer, Spiegel publishing, Gruner and Jahr, Fritz Hansen, Herman Miller, Cassina, Thonet, Louis Poulsen, Unika-Vaev, Mira-X, and others. Visiting professor of industrial design, Hochschule für Gestaltung, Offenbach, 1984. **Member:** Medlem Akademisk Arkitektforening, Denmark; Danske Arkitekters Landsforbund; Industrielle Designere, Denmark; Schweizerischer Werkbund; Fellow of the Royal Society of Arts, London. **Exhibitions:** Dansk Köbestävne, Fredericia, 1958; Bauzentrum, Hamburg, 1961; Musée des Arts Décoratifs, Paris, 1969; Galerie Interieur, Kortrijk, 1978; International Furniture Fair, Brussels, 1987, Copenhagen, 1988, 1989, Cologne, 1995; Bella Center, Copenhagen, 1988; Danish Design Center, Copenhagen, 1991; Scandinavian Furniture Fair, Copenhagen, 1992; Centre Georges Pompidou, Paris, 1992; Schweizer Möbelmesse International, Berne, 1993; Haag, Stockholm, 1993; Museum für Angewandte Kunst, Cologne, 1994. **Collections:** Kunstgewerbemuseum, Cologne; Kunstindustrimuseet, Copenhagen; Musée des Arts Décoratifs, Montreal; Museum des Deutschen Werkbundes, Munich; Museum of Modern Art, New York; Philadelphia Museum of Art, Philadelphia; Design Center Stuttgart; Arkitekturmuseum, Frankfurt; Vitra Design Museum, Weil am Rhein; Centre Georges Pompidou. **Honors:** International Design Award, New York, 1963, 1968, 1981; Rosenthal Studio

Prize, Selb, 1966; Poul Henningsen Prize, Copenhagen, 1967; Eurodomus Award, Milan, 1968; Osterreichisches Bauzentrum Medal, Vienna, 1968; Ehrenpreis, International Furnishing Salon Award, Vienna, 1969; Gute Form Prize, Bonn, 1972, 1986; Möbelprisen, Copenhagen, 1978; Design Center Awards, Stuttgart, 1981, 1982, 1984, 1985, 1986; Sadolin Colour Prize, Copenhagen, 1986; Danish Design Council Annual Award, 1991; IF-Prize, Japan, 1992; Norwegian Design Award, Norway, 1992. **Address:** Kohlenberggasse 21, CH-4051 Basel, Switzerland.

## Works

*Bachelor Chair* in tubular steel and leather, for Fritz Hansen, 1955.
*Cone Chair* in upholstered steel, for Plus Linje, 1957.
Cardboard House, Denmark, 1957.
*Komigen* Inn, Denmark, 1958.
*Topan Lamp* in aluminum, for Louis Poulsen, 1959.
Spherical house, Denmark, 1960.
Plastic house, Denmark, 1960.
Interior designs, for Astoria Hotel, Trondheim, Norway, 1960.
*Geometri* wool carpet, for Unika Vaev, 1961.
*Wire Chair* in upholstered steel wire, for Plus Linje, 1961.
*S-Chair* in laminated wood, for Thonet, 1966.
*Panton Chair* in plastic, for Herman Miller, 1967.
*Visiona O + II* exhibition ships, for Bayer, Cologne, Germany, 1968-70.
Interior designs, for Spiegel Publishing House, Denmark, 1969.
*Living Tower* upholstered furniture, for Herman Miller, 1969.
*Panthella* lamps series in plastic and metal, for Louis Poulsen, 1970.
Interior designs, for Varna Restaurant, Denmark, 1971.
*1·2·3* furniture system in upholstered tubular steel, for Fritz Hansen, 1973.
Interior designs, for Junior Casino, Denmark, 1973.
Interior designs, for Gruner & Jahr Publishing House, Hamburg, 1974.
*Emmenthaler* upholstered furniture, for Cassina, 1979.
Interior designs, for Circus Building, Copenhagen, 1984.
*Pantheon* upholstered sofa, for Erik Jorgensen, 1986.
Bowl in crumpled silver, for Georg Jensen, 1988.
Cone chair in leather, for Polythema, Denmark, 1994.
Cone chair in acrylic, for Polythema, 1994.
*Z-chair* in steel tube with upholstery, for Polythema, 1994.
*Shogun* upholstered chair, for Erik Jørgensen, Denmark, 1994.
*Tatami* chair in laminated wood, for Kohseki Co., Japan, 1995.
*Pantoflex* chair in laminated wood and steel tube, for VS, Denmark, 1995.

## Publications

**By PANTON: books**—*Verner Panton,* Copenhagen, 1986; **articles**—"Form und Material" in *Epoca* (Germany), no. 10, 1969; "Wohnen am Wendepunkt" in *Trautes Heim, Glück allein,* Germany, 1979; "Das Wohlegefühl erhöhen" in *Proceedings from the IFI Congress* (Vienna), May 1980.

**On PANTON: books**—*Brugskunst: Mobler Textiler, Lamper* by Birgit and Christian Enevoldsen, Copenhagen, 1958; *New Furniture* edited by Gerd Hatje, nos. 5, 6, 7, 9, 10, Stuttgart and London, 1960-71; *Nordisk Nyttokonst/Scandinavian Design* by Ulf Hård af Segerstad,

Stockholm and London, 1961; *Modern Scandinavian Furniture* by Ulf Hård af Segerstad, Copenhagen, 1963, London, 1964; *World Furniture* edited by Helena Hayward, London, 1965, 1981; *The Modern Chair: 1850 to Today* by Gilbert Frey, London and Niedertaufen, 1970; *Danish Design* edited by Svend Erik Møller, Copenhagen, 1974; *The Modern Chair: Classics in Production* by Clement Meadmore, London, 1974; *Die Geschichte des Design in Deutschland von 1970 bis Heute* by Gert Selle, Cologne, 1978; *History of Modern Furniture* by Karl Mang, Stuttgart, 1978, London, 1979; *The Contemporary Decorative Arts from 1940 to the Present Day* by Philippe Garner, London, 1980; *Les Années '50* by Anne Bony, Paris, 1982; *Contemporary Furniture* by Klaus-Jürgen Sembach, Stuttgart and London, 1982; *Les Années '60* by Anne Bony, Paris, 1983; *Design Since 1945* edited by Kathryn Hiesinger and George Marcus, Philadelphia and London, 1983; *Mid-Century: Furniture of the 1950s* by Cara Greenberg, London, 1984; *Twentieth Century Design: Furniture* by Penny Sparke, London, 1986; *Weiss ist Farbe* by Kronos Titan, Germany, 1987; *Modern Furniture Classics* by Miriam Stimpson, London, 1987; *Contemporary Masterworks,* Chicago, 1991; *What Modern Was: Design, 1935-65,* Montreal, 1991; *Histoire du Design 1940-1990* by Raymond Guidot, Paris, 1994.

\*

The reason you can sit for years in a saddle without getting back problems lies not only in the saddle, but also in the movements of the horse.

Erwin Morscher, professor of orthopedics, and I have often talked about "the sitting problem." To the orthopedist, this is the problem of chronic backaches and load-damages. These sufferings are some of the most frequent causes impairing the working capabilities.

Research in Western countries has shown that approximately 80 percent of all people, at least once, suffer so severely from back pains that they have to consult a doctor.

"Life is movement and movement is life" became the thesis for our basic idea.

A discus stays healthy through movement. This caused us to develop dynamis chairs. Chairs on which human beings sit dynamically.

For instance, we have created chairs which move when you sit on them and breathe, so that sitting still is impossible.

It is nonsensical to teach children to sit still on a chair.

A chair should roll, rock, or gyrate—and, preferably, vibrate. It must be dynamic—and allow you to sit comfortably.

—Verner Panton

# PAPANEK, Victor

American product designer

**Born:** Vienna, Austria, 22 November 1925; emigrated to the United States in 1939, naturalized, 1946. **Education:** Studied industrial design, at Cooper Union, New York, 1942-50; also studied at Frank Lloyd Wright's Taliesin and Taliesin West, 1949, Massachusetts Institute of Technology, 1954-55, Chicago Institute of General Semantics, 1956, and studied anthropology at other universities, 1950-57. **Military Service:** Served in the camouflage unit of the United States Army, in Alaska and the Aleutian Islands, 1944-45. **Career:** Independent product development designer, from 1964, acting as design consultant to Volvo A/B, Dartington Industries, Planet Prod-

ucts, World Health Organization, Midwest Applied Science Corporation, and others. Instructor, Ontario College of Art, University of Toronto, 1954-59; associate professor of art and design, State University of New York at Buffalo, 1959-62; associate professor and head of product design department, North Carolina State College, Raleigh, 1962-64; associate professor, 1964-68, professor and chairman of environmental and industrial design department, 1968-70, Purdue University, West Lafayette, Indiana; professor, 1970-71, and dean of the school of design, 1971-72, California Institute of the Arts, Valencia; professor and chairman of the design department, Kansas City Art Institute, 1976-81; J. L. Constant professor of design, School of Architecture and Urban Design, University of Kansas, Lawrence, from 1981; also visiting professor and lecturer at Rhode Island School of Design, Providence, 1959, Penland School of Crafts, North Carolina, 1963-67, Kunstakademiets Arkitektskole, Copenhagen, 1972-73, Manchester Polytechnic, 1973-75, Carleton University, Ottawa, 1975-76, and others. Developing Countries Working Group Member, ICSID International Council of Societies of Industrial Design, from 1973; founder-member, Developing Countries Design Information Group, from 1973. **Member:** Industrielle Designere Denmark, 1972; U.S. Federal Design Council, 1977; Industrial Design Institute of Australia, 1978; Design and Craft Societies of Croatia and Slovenia, 1986; Industrial Designers of America, 1988; Design Society of Thailand, 1989; Design Association of Indonesia, 1989. **Exhibitions:** *Visionary Architecture,* Museum of Modern Art, New York, 1962; *Do-It-Yourself Design,* International Design Centre, West Berlin, 1973; *Papanek: Work and Theories,* Galerij Grada, Zagreb, 1974. **Collections:** Centre Georges Pompidou, Paris. **Honors:** Gold Medal, Indianapolis Art Directors Club, 1968; UNESCO Design Award, 1963; ICSID/Philips Design Award, 1978; Kyoto Honours Award, 1981; Dartington/Watershed Speaker Award, 1982; August St. Gaudens Medal, Cooper Union, New York, 1987; National Endowment for the Arts Distinguished Designer Fellowship, Washington, D.C., 1988; IKEA Leading Designer Award, IKEA Foundation, Amsterdam, 1989; Lewis Mumford Award, Architects, Designers, and Planners for Social Responsibility, Atlanta, 1995. Honorary Doctorate: Marycrest College, Davenport, Iowa, 1983; University of Zagreb, 1986. Fellow, Creative Leadership Council 1962, Creative Education Foundation, 1962, Chartered Society of Designers, 1974; honorary fellow, American Scandinavian Foundation, 1966, Industrial Designers Society of Mexico, 1975; honorary member, Society of Designers Ireland, 1992, Graphic Designers Austria, 1992. **Addresses:** 2714 University Drive, Lawrence, Kansas 66049, U.S.A.; School of Architecture and Urban Design, 417 Marvin Hall, University of Kansas, Lawrence, Kansas 66045-2250, U.S.A.

## Works

Candle-heat powered tin can radio, for the United Nations in Bali and Indonesia, 1958.

Exercise environment for children with cerebral palsy, 1967 (with Finnish student team).

24-pod midrange hi-fi speaker clusters, for Altec-Lansing Corporation, 1970-74.

Exercise bicycles for handicapped children, for Ritter Surgical Supplies, St. Louis, 1970-88.

Work enrichment scheme components for foreign guest-workers, for Volvo A/B, Goteborg, 1972 75 (as member of design team).

**Victor Papanek: Brass desk lamps, for Planet Products Pty., Australia**

Do-it-yourself play environment in mixed media, for the American Cerebral Palsy Association, 1973.

Auto-diagnostic medical equipment for developing countries, for the World Health Organization, from 1975.

Medical lamps and task lighting in aluminium, steel, and brass, for Planet Products, Australia, 1978.

*Bata-Koya* (Talking Teacher) cassette tape player, for the governments of Tanzania and Nigeria, 1979.

High-altitude geodesic tents in canvas, plastic and aluminium, for Trans-World Expedition Gear, Berkeley, 1979.

Solar-powered refrigerator with lithium bromide coolant, for the World Health Organization, 1982.

Custom-designed surgical scalpels in steel, for Ritter Surgical Supplies, St. Louis, 1982.

Mobile and adjustable exhibition structures in wood, metal, glass and plastics, for Koch-Multivac Corporation, Kansas City, 1982.

High-performance emergency flashlights in plastic and metal, for Croatia Corporation, Zagreb, 1984.

Exercise environment for multi-handicapped children, for New York Presbyterian Hospital, 1985.

Modular electric heating carpet in wool, cotton, or plastic fibres, for Yamasaki Company, Osaka, 1986.

Musicians' ergonomic chairs in hardwood and steel, for Pro Musica Company, San Diego, 1987.

Biological "grown" packaging, for a Japanese company, 1993-1995.

Development of a specialized 35mm camera, for a Japanese corporation, from 1993.

Development of a movable elevator for the handicapped, funded by an American elevator firm, from 1995.

## Publications

**By PAPANEK: books**—*Creative Engineering,* Hamilton, 1961; *Miljon och Miljonerna,* Stockholm, 1970; *Design for the Real World: Human Ecology and Social Change,* New York, 1971, London, 1972, 1985, Chicago, 1985; (with Jim Hennessey) *Nomadic Furniture 1,* New York, 1972 (also see below); *Big Character Poster No. 1: Work Chart for Designers,* Copenhagen, 1973; (with Hennessey) *Nomadic Furniture 2,* New York, 1974 (also see below); (with Hennessey) *How Things Don't Work,* New York, 1977; *L'Arredamento Mobile 1 e 2,* Milan, 1978; *Design for Human Scale,* New York, 1983; *Viewing the World Whole,* Lawrence, 1983; *Nomadic Furniture 1 and 2,* Zagreb, 1983; (with others) *Design and Society,* London, 1984; (with others) *Kansas Communities,* Lawrence, 1986; (with others) *The Other Side of Design,* Amsterdam, 1988; *The Green Imperative: Ethics and Ecology in Architecture and Design,* London, 1995, published as *The Green Imperative: Natural Design for the Real World,* New York, 1995; **articles**—contributor to *Democratic Design,* Stockholm, 1995.

**On PAPANEK: books**—*The Conran Directory of Design* edited by Stephen Bayley, London, 1985; *Design Source Book* by Penny Sparke and others, London, 1986; *New American Design* by Hugh Aldersley-Williams, New York, 1988; *Design for Society* by Nigel Whiteley, London, 1994.

*

As a working designer who is also involved in teaching graduate students, I feel that product design must address itself primarily to the question of sustainability of life on this planet.

As a profession, Industrial Designers, Product Designers, and Architects still tend to work primarily to bolster their own egos and for profit in the marketplace. I feel that the professions of design and architecture need to reinvent themselves in order to be of service to the people and to preserve harmony and balance in the environment.

It is now a quarter of a century since my first book appeared, *Design for the Real World: Human Ecology and Social Change.* It was the first book to establish a dialectic between design and architecture on one hand, and ecology and social responsibility on the other. During these last twenty-five years some designers and architects have devoted themselves to Green Design, especially in the Nordic Countries, the Netherlands, Austria, Germany, Australia, and Japan. Yet the majority still works with irreplaceable resources and dangerous or toxic substances.

Yet all of us are in the wonderful position of watching the birth of an entirely new aesthetic. If we assemble together design for long-life products, design for disassembly (to comply with laws in several countries that require the original manufacturer to take the goods back for remanufacture or recycling), and add to this such ideas as design-for-sharing (for objects or appliances infrequently used), and the use of non-compound materials in any part of a product or structure—then we must realize that out of all this will arise an entirely new way in which things will look, work, and be needed by people.

In the beginning was the chipped stone tool. From this, design developed to work and be embellished. We have now gone through a brief period during which marketing and advertising switched peoples' needs into wants and then twisted them into desires. Through out all history the design of shelters and tools has been directed by their use, their aesthetics, and the needs and desires of the public. Styles, fads, fashions, and trends have been invented. The only limits were what we were capable of making. Now these limits no longer exist—we can make almost anything. It is at this point that Ecology and Ethics will shape totally unpredictable forms and dwellings that are no longer dictated by fashion.

This ethic will also address the needs of the elderly, the handicapped and retarded, children, babies, and the poor.

The problems of people in the developing world must be met by designers helping the local talent that by now exists in the third world to form their own goals. This will mean: appropriate scale, local autonomy, independence from international and multinational corporations, decentralization, the use of alternative energy, and research into appropriate technology on village levels. These points are explored in my latest book, *The Green Imperative: Ecology and Ethics in Design and Architecture.*

—Victor Papanek

*    *    *

Born in Vienna, Victor Papanek came to New York at the age of fourteen. He studied industrial design at Cooper Union, engineering at the Massachusetts Institute of Technology, and architecture with Frank Lloyd Wright, whom he considers a major influence on his ideas.

While working briefly for Raymond Loewy and, later, Helena Rubenstein, he became critical of advertising and contacted the United Nations, which appointed him a design expert to help developing countries. During this period, he also began his career in teaching. During his years at Purdue University, 1965-70, he started writing his first major book, *Design for the Real World,* which

647

brought much recognition and controversy, since it attacked the very premises of American design—conspicuous consumption and planned obsolescence.

This book established Papanek as a design critic at a time when most designers were more concerned with enhancing their images than defining an ideology for responsible design. *Design for the Real World* became a primer of many design students around the world and remains popular today. In the mid-1970s, while he was teaching widely in the United States and abroad, he co-authored with Jim Hennessey three additional books, *Nomadic Furniture, Nomadic Furniture II,* and *How Things Don't Work.* These "how-to-do-it" books were a necessary extension of his first book, since at that time most manufacturers were insensitive to the needs of an increasingly mobile society. Since moving to the University of Kansas, he has published *Design for Human Scale* and *Viewing the Whole World.*

Some of his commissions include architectural concepts for the dock area of Bristol England and the design of the Greenshade Studio C Lamp which is manufactured in Australia. The lamp utilizes a double parabolic shade to reduce heat and to maximize light from a less powerful bulb.

—Al Gowan

# PARISI, Ico

Italian architect, painter, and stage and industrial designer

**Born:** Palermo, Sicily, 23 September 1916. **Education:** Studied building construction in Como, 1931-35; studied architecture under Alberto Sartoris, at the Instituto Atheneum, Lausanne, Dip.Arch., 1950. **Military Service:** Served in the Italian Army, 1940-43, Major. **Family:** Married Luisa Aiani in 1947. **Career:** Worked in the studio of architect Giuseppe Terragni, Como, 1935-36; stage designer, Como, 1939; freelance designer and visual artist, and founder with Luisa Parisi, of Studio La Ruota, Como, from 1945; has designed for Artecasa, Bonacina, Cassina, A. Colombo, Mobili Italiana Moderni, and others. **Member:** Art Club di Milano, 1952; ADI Associazione Disegno Industriale, Milan, 1956. **Exhibitions:** Villa Olmo, Como, 1937, 1957, 1979; Fondazione La Masa, Venice, 1943; Galerie Germain, Paris, 1974; IN/ARCH, Rome, 1974, 1988; Serre Ratti, Como, 1977; Palazzo delle Prigioni, Venice, 1978, Galleria La Colonna, Como, 1978, 1982; Centro Proposte, Salerno, 1979; Galleria d'Arte Moderna, Rome, 1979; Museum of Art, Slonenj Gradec, 1979; Scuola Caprin, Trieste, 1980; Musee d'Ixelles, Brussels, 1980; Palazzo dei Diamanti, Ferrara, 1980, 1981; Galleria La Boite, Salerno, 1981; Italian Cultural Institute, 1984; Centre Culturel ADF, Lille, 1984; Galleria La Chiocciola, Padua, 1985; Museo Di Cerro Laveno, Varese, 1986; PAC, Milano, 1986; Stildo-mus, Roma, 1987; Milan Triennale, 1989; Artelago, Monate, Varese, 1990; Galleria Civica di Modena, 1990, 1994; Pinacoteca Civica di Como, 1991; Galleria R. Lietti, Como, 1992, 1994; Bobadilla, Dalmine, Bergamo, 1992; Show Room Cappellini, Carugo, Como, 1993; Magazzini Cappellini, Milano, 1994; S. Pietro in Atrio, Como, 1995. **Collections:** Archivi di Ico Parisi, Pinacoteca Civica di Como. **Honors:** Film Prize, Como, 1937; Silver Medal, Milan Triennale, 1954; Compasso d'Oro Award, 1955; Color and Form exhibition medals, Como, 1957; Lurago d'Erba Gold Medal, 1959; Knight of Mark Twain Award, Kirkwood, 1971; Premio Marco Aurelio, Rome, 1974; Abbondino d'Oro, 1993. **Address:** Archivi di Ico Parisi, Pinacoteca Civica di Como, Via Diaz 84, 22100 Como, Italy.

Ico Parisi: *Zoo Mobile,* 1990

## Works

Roll-top desk in rosewood, for Artecasa, 1951.
*Unio* wall unit with interchangeable cabinets and shelves, for MIM Mobili Italiani Moderni, 1952.
Chintz-upholstered armchair and table, for A. Colombo, 1953.
Armchair in metal and plywood, for Cassina, 1955.
Chair in cane with slung leather seat, for Bonacina, 1959.
*Contenitoriumani* human womb-environment, 1968.
*Ipotesi per una Casa Esistenziale* dwelling project, 1973.
*Operazione Arcevia* existential community project, 1976.

## Publications

**By PARISI: books**—*Padiglione Soggiorno,* Como, 1954, Milan, 1955; *Biblioteca al Parco,* Milan, 1955; *Immagine per una Industria,* Como, 1969; *Ipotesi per una Casa Esistenziale,* Rome, 1974; *Operazione Arcevia,* Como, 1975; *Utopia Realizzabile,* Milan, 1978, *Architecture en Papier,* exhibition catalogue, Paris, 1984; *Foto a Memoria,* Como, 1991; *La Biblioteca del Parco Sempione a Milano,* Milano, 1994.

**On PARISI: books**—*Cute Mobel—Schone Raume* edited by Mia Seeger, Stuttgart, 1953; *Art in European Architecture* by P. Damaz, New York, 1956; *Catalogo Bolaffi dell' Architettura Italiana 1963-1966* edited by Pier Carlo Santini and G. L. Marini, Turin, 1966; *Design e Forme Nuove nell'Arredamento Italiano* edited by Paolo Portoghesi and Marino Marini, Rome, 1978; *Ico Parisi: Operazione Arcevia,* exhibition catalogue by G. de Marchis, Rome, 1979; *Ico Parisi,* exhibition catalogue by Pierre Restany, Brussels, 1980; *Contemporary Furniture* edited by Klaus-Jurgen Sembach, Stuttgart and London, 1982; *Mid-Century: Furniture of the 1950s* by Cara Greenberg, London, 1984; *Ico Parisi: L'Officina del Possibile* by F. Gualdoni, Milan, 1986: *Como nel Disegno* exhibition catalogue by L. Caramel, Como, 1987; *L'Art en Europe 1945-1953,* exhibition catalogue by F. Guichon, Sain-Etienne, 1987; *Il Design del Mobile Italiano dal 1946 ad oggi* by Anty Pansera, Milano, 1990; *Ico Parisi & Architetture,* exhibition catalogue by F. Gualdoni, A. Sartoris, and W. Guadagnini, Modena, 1990; *Linee Parallele* by A. Sartoris, Lugano, 1992; *Il Mobile Italiano degli Anni '40 e '50* by M. G. Battistini, P. Deggiovanni, and F. Gualdoni, Modena, 1994; *Ico Parisi & Disegni,* exhibition catalogue by P. Deggiovanni, Modena, 1994.

*

A creative crisis in the current situation—with regard to industrial design—has led to an aesthetic levelling of the objects produced. My analysis sees the following as the decisive causes:

The obligation of almost all designers to concentrate on forms dictated more by fashion than the functional requirements, repetitive even in the most difficult conditions, doing formal violence to the object.

The growing numbers of points of production for the same ranges of products. This results in deliberate imitation of designs, with consequent commercial confusion between one product and another.

The readiness to follow the lead of the consumerist population that believes in the new object and will put up with the formal variations imposed by producers. This forces industries to change the form of the same model ever more frequently to make sure that it will be exchanged, a phenomenon that does not allow an object to be usefully improved aesthetically, economically, or commercially. Such improvement can occur only if the model has a period of steady production.

To my mind, what is needed is a more severe professional approach by the designer, who can then defend us from industrial speculations so as to revalue his creativity, personality, and professionalism.

—Ico Parisi

*     *     *

Ico Parisi and his wife Luisa have been responsible for a long line of designs, chiefly furniture, which have been remarkable for the exploration of the formal and structural possibilities of different sorts of material, including plywood, metal, marble, glass, basketware, cane, leather, and plastic. Typical of their approach is the 1954 villa with its extraordinary front elevation of two overlapping facades or the 1950 Egg easychair, a sort of half-shell supported by splayed legs. All of their work is informed by a masterful sense of geometry, which they call upon to articulate their unconventional proposals. One calls to mind such notions as a free-standing, outdoor fireplace, surmounted by a metal hood and accompanied by a log basket utilising a frame formed of a double

spiral of cane, or the table in rosewood on a white marble base; in the latter, the table top and its support are made of an up-turned cone, with sides curving in to meet the flat, marble circle of the base. The arrangement of cane circles for the 1959 chair for Bonacina further exemplifies this imaginative geometry, as do also the curves of a 1954 lamp.

These geometric forms are always so consonant with the natural structure of the materials they use that it is difficult to pinpoint the exact source of their originality, yet their work is always individual and unmistakable without ever being perverse or eccentric. In a certain sense, they continue within a rationalist scheme of designing without reducing their designs to functionalism pure and simple, and their geometry contributes an elegance of form and concept, becoming thus expressive means.

One can understand how Ico Parisi reacted to the architectural and design situation in the early 1970s when what he came to call the "survival necessities" were given a subordinate role in the making of design decisions and given only the limited attention strictly required to make things work. Other and deeper considerations of human needs were to be dominant. "This project, on which I have been working for two years, does not mean to resolve nowadays architectural problems but rather propose a living space free from all possible bonds. Man and his existential problems are here the subject," he wrote in 1974. In a sense, he suggests that it is human problems that the designer addresses and not any problem of design as such. Certainly, he does not imagine that there are unique solutions to "design problems." In some ways, his position relates to the attitudes of the Memphis designers in the 1980s but with a quite different outcome.

—Toni del Renzio

# PAUL, Art
American graphic and exhibition designer

**Born:** Arthur Paul in Chicago, Illinois, 18 January 1925. **Education:** Studied at the Art Institute of Chicago, 1940-43; Institute of Design, Illinois Institute of Technology, Chicago, 1946-50. **Military Service:** Served in the United States Army Air Force, 1943-46, Master Sergeant. **Family:** Married Beatrice Miller in 1950 (divorced, 1971); children: William, Fredric, and Nina; married Suzanne Seed in 1975. **Career:** Freelance illustrator and designer, Chicago, 1950-54; art director, *Playboy* magazine, Chicago, 1954-82; vice-president and art director, Playboy Enterprises, Chicago, 1962-82; freelance designer and president of Art Paul Design, Chicago, from 1982. Guest instructor, Illustrators Workshop, Tarrytown, New York, 1978; lecturer on design, Chicago. Alumni association board member, Illinois Institute of Technology, Chicago, 1978-79; trustee, Museum of Contemporary Art, Chicago; advisory board member, Moraine Valley College, Illinois, 1980, and University of Illinois School of Art and Design, 1981; trustee, Illinois Summer School of the Arts, 1989-1995. **Member:** Chicago Society of Communicating Arts, 1960; Chicago 27 Designers, 1976; Alliance Graphique Internationale, 1978. **Exhibitions:** Etc. Gallery, Chicago, 1949; Gallery 500D, Chicago, 1957; University of Illinois Chicago, 1965; *Beyond Illustration: The Art of Playboy,* Milan, 1971 (toured); *The Art of Playboy: The First 25 Years,* Cultural Center, Chicago, 1978 (toured); Alumni Exhibition, Rymer

Gallery, Art Institute of Chicago. **Collections:** Art Institute of Chicago. **Honors:** Artists Guild of Chicago Award, 1962; Norfolk Art Directors Club Award, 1962; St. Louis Art Directors Club Medal, 1963; Society of Typographic Arts Special Award, Chicago, 1964; Philadelphia Art Directors Club Creative Achievement Award, 1964, and Polycube Award, 1975; Dallas Art Directors Club Award, 1964; Boston Art Directors Club Award, 1964; City of Milan Gold Medal, 1971; *Art Direction* Magazine Award, 1975; Midwest Commercial Association of Direct Marketing Prize, 1979; New York Art Directors Club Gold Medal, 1980; Illinois Institute of Technology Professional Achievement Award, 1983; Art Directors Hall of Fame Award, 1986. Honorary Member: Artists Guild of Chicago, 1965, and Society of Publication Designers, 1980. **Address:** 175 East Delaware Place, Suite 7511, Chicago, Illinois 60611, U.S.A.

## Works

Playboy Bunny logo, for Playboy Enterprises, 1953.
*Playboy* magazine design and layout, for Playboy Enterprises, 1953-79.
Corporate identity program, for Playboy Enterprises, 1953-82.
Television commercial advertisements, for Playboy Enterprises, 1965-82.
*Beyond Illustration: The Art of Playboy* travelling exhibition layouts, for Playboy Enterprises, 1971.
Poster, for the Chicago International Film Festival, 1980.
Logotype symbol, for Golda's hot dog stands, Chicago, 1986.
Also designer of posters including—Shoshin Society exhibition, for Hiroshima Museum; *Once Upon a Time* series, for Simpson Papers; Chicago Film Festival posters.

## Publications

**By PAUL: books**—*Beyond Illustration: The Art of Playboy,* exhibition catalogue, Chicago, 1971; *The Art of Playboy: The First 25 Years,* exhibition catalogue with preface by Ted Hearne, Chicago, 1978.

**On PAUL: books**—*Playboy Illustration,* exhibition catalogue, Edmonton, 1976; *Beyond Illustration,* exhibition catalogue, Madison, 1978; *Who's Who in Graphic Art* edited by Walter Amstutz, Dubendorf, 198; *Playboy Art Exhibit,* exhibition catalogue, Lafayette, 1983; *The Art of Playboy,* with text by Ray Bradbury, Chicago, 1985; *Visual Identity in Chicago,* Japan, 1991.

\*

For most of my career I haven't needed, or wanted, to work with computers. But to my surprise, in January of 1996, I was the recipient of a Macintosh® computer, a birthday gift from my family. To further my surprise, I found I enjoyed doing drawings on the machine, working with the Adobe Illustrator® program.

I haven't in the least changed my mind, though, about the computer's lack of romance. For me the PC keyboard seems too many steps removed from the designer's hand. I am still in love with holding a pencil that is plotting out an idea on paper. I still enjoy crumpling up a piece of paper with a bad idea on it and chucking it into a waste basket far across the room. It could be

mistaken for some creative dance, but for me hands-on-design is a more total experience. In my more serene moments when fantasies predominate, I envision a bolt of lightning momentarily disconnecting all designing computers long enough for us all once more to hear the scratchings of ideas on paper. I think I'm a romantic. I will continue to dream on....

Yet, though I doubt if I'd miss my machine a great deal if I were to stop using it, I more fully understand its usefulness. And I marvel at the capabilities of computers and often admire what other designers have accomplished using them.

My philosophy about design has not changed over the years. I'm convinced good design is good communication. What disturbs me about some current design trends is that they promote a tolerance for obscurity. I like the energy and attractiveness of many recent designs but I'm critical of those that are hard-to-read, ugly, and chaotic for the sake of having a "contemporary look." I've always believed that it's the function of designers to turn chaos into comprehension. But then again, agreeing with a premise about design even though the finished product doesn't work has been classic designer behavior for decades. It's something like admiring a raincoat that really doesn't keep you dry.

A few years ago I decided to devote most of my time to seriously developing my personal art work. It's been a rewarding experience, allowing me to use my design instincts in my art free from the help or hindrance of another concerned party. So I've pretty much changed my focus and to some degree my studio set-up.

—Art Paul

\*      \*      \*

Art Paul has been credited with leading the "Illustration Liberation Movement." This distinction came from a propitious set of circumstances beginning when Paul, a rebellious art student, found himself questioning the notion of a difference between high and low art. Such nonprejudicial instincts allied him, perhaps unconsciously at first, with the democratic and experimental approach of Bauhaus teaching. His obstinacy about seeing a hierarchy in art was reinforced on his return from World War II when he attended the Institute of Design in Chicago, which had become a modern mecca of graphic design, and especially the Bauhaus philosophy, with the influx of such Bauhaus teachers as Moholy-Nagy.

Uncharacteristically, in a volatile and changeable profession, Paul's notoriety has come from one client—*Playboy* magazine. Hired by publisher/editor Hugh Hefner when the magazine was founded and then given free rein, Paul fashioned a highly original and nonconformist view of men's entertainment in magazine format. This freedom allowed him to indulge his "grand plan" for what a magazine should be in the bland commercialism of the 1950s. This plan viewed the raw material of illustration, an area in which Paul had freelanced prior to his employment at *Playboy,* as important in its own right, as editorial art, to provoke the reader and to establish a mood for the story. At first, unable to persuade painters to work for him in this capacity, he created his own constructions and collages to enliven the magazine's visuals as well as to convince artists that this was a respectable exercise in originality. His insertion of die cuts and pop-ups between pages, techniques previously employed in children's books, made illustration kinetic. In this, he broke the lock that the grid had held on modern layout and humanized the look of the page. This highly conceptual approach may seem uncharacteristic for a magazine that has a reputation of appealing to

**Art Paul:** *War Kills The Sun* poster

men's prurient interests, but it meshed with Hefner's desire for a mix of urbanity and liveliness.

The debonair image carried over to Paul's design of a corporate logo for *Playboy,* the now internationally recognized rabbit symbol, introduced in 1953. The stylized rabbit head with its dignified profile and formal bow tie is set slightly out of kilter by the roguish slant of the ears. It could be compared to the suave and sophisticated, yet somewhat foppish gentleman who graces the pages of *The New Yorker.* In contrast, except for the first issue, the rabbit has been seen on every cover of *Playboy* and has graced hundreds of products of the Playboy corporation. This seemingly ageless corporate logo epitomized the daring, exciting, and risky venture of Playboy, on both a practical and conceptual level.

As the founding art director of *Playboy,* Art Paul not only supported new talent and reversed the tendency to conformity in mass magazines, but he also added credibility and legitimacy to a men's magazine and the taboo content within. Both were avant garde but in different ways—Art Paul's work was legitimate art whereby *Playboy's* intentions were purely risqué.

—Sarah Bodine

# PAWLOSKI, Andrzej

Polish exhibition, stage, film, graphic, and industrial designer

**Born:** Wadowice, 20 July 1925. **Education:** High school and unofficial "underground" school, in Tarnow, 1937-42; studied at the Jagiellonian University, Kraków, 1942-45, and at the Academy of Fine Arts, Kraków, 1945-50. **Military Service:** Served in the Polish Home Army, Kraków, 1942-54. **Family:** Married Wanda Grochowalska in 1950; children; Maciej, Marcin, and Marek. **Career:** Independent painter, sculptor, and designer, in Kraków, from 1950; kinetic artist, working with the Cricot 2 theatre company, Kraków, 1956-57; design specialist for the Prozamet industrial building company, Krakow, from 1960; consultant to the Kraków Metal Products Company, 1963; research consultant on car ergonomics, for the Bielsko-Biala factory, 1978-80. Assistant professor of interior design, 1948-54, dean, 1954-63 and from 1981, chairman of the industrial design department, 1963-71, senate member, from 1963, chairman of industrial form department, 1964-66, chairman of the product design and visual communications department, 1966-68, chairman of the design methodology department, from 1968, professor of industrial design from 1971, and president of the senate committee on publishing, 1978-80, Academy of Fine Arts, Kraków. Chairman, 1965-69, vice chairman, 1973-75, and board member, 1975-79, Association of Industrial Designers, Warsaw; executive vice-president, 1967-69, executive board member, 1969-71, and congress coordinator, 1975, 1979, ICSID International Council of Societies of Industrial Design. **Member:** Union of Polish Graphic Artists, 1953; Association of Industrial Designers, Warsaw, 1965; Union of Polish Artist-Photographers, Warsaw, 1979. **Exhibitions:** Cricot 2 Theatre, Kraków, 1957; KM-PIK Gallery, Warsaw, 1957; Gallery Krzystofory, Kraków, 1964, 1988; National Museum, Kraków-Peiskowa Skala, 1966; BWA Gallery, Lublin, 1966; Art Gallery of Zakopane, 1966; BWA Galleries of Koszalin, Radawica, and Slupsk, 1973; Desa Gallery, Kraków, 1974; Omamy Gallery, Kraków, 1978; Form Gallery, Warsaw, 1980. **Honors:** Silver Cross of Merit, Kraków, 1952; Polish Ministry of Art and Culture Award,

1963, 1964, 1966, 1970, 1977; Polish Industrial Design Award, 1966; Polish Knight's Cross, 1969; Order of Polonia Restituta, 1970; Knight's Cross of Honour, 1976; City of Kraków Cultural Award, 1976; Gold Medal for Services to Kraków, 1977; Polish Teachers Union Medal, 1977. **Address:** 18-Stycznia 60/11, 30 045 Kraków, Poland.

## Works

*Young Plastic Arts* exhibition layouts, for the BWA Gallery, Kraków, 1956.

Telephone apparatus, for the Telecommunications Company, Radom, 1959.

Automatic loading, wire-cutting, and moulding machines, for the Prozamet Company, Kraków, 1960.

*West* sewing machine, for Polna Przemysl, 1961.

*Art in Kraków 1350-1550* exhibition layouts, for the Jagiellonian University, Kraków, 1964.

Lightweight roofing structure in polyester resin, for Stockznia-Ustka, 1972.

*500 Years of Printing in Kraków* exhibition layouts, for the MN Gallery, Kraków, 1974.

*Fiat 126* ergonomic car seating, for the Bielsko-Biala Factory, 1979.

*Fiat KL1000* ergonomic car seating, for the Bielsko-Biala Factory, 1980.

*The History of Jewish Culture* exhibition layouts, for the Historical Museum, Kraków, 1980.

## Publications

**By PAWLOWSKI: books**—*Initiation: On Art, Design, and Design Teaching* edited by Janusz Krupinski, Warsaw, 1987; **articles**—in *Zycie Literackie* (Kraków), no. 49, 1961; *Architektura* (Warsaw), no. 11, 1968; *Polska* (Warsaw), no. 6, 1970; *Suggestions* (Warsaw), no. 1, 1970, no. 2, 1970; *ZPAP Bulletin* (Warsaw), no. 1, 1973; *Wiadomosci IWP* (Warsaw), no. 3/4, 1974, no. 3/4, 1975; *Technicheskaya Estetika* (Moscow), no. 7, 1975; *Projekt* (Warsaw); no. 4, 1987.

**On PAWLOWSKI: books**—*Design for the Real World* by Victor Papanek, New York, 1971; *To See and to Understand,* exhibition catalogue, Warsaw, 1975; *Andrezej Pawlowski,* exhibition catalogue by Mieczyslaw Porebski, Kraków, 1988.

*

During the last dozen or so years in Poland, numerous terms were coined for the field that now can be spoken of as: industrial pattern design, designing industrial forms, graphic arts of industrial forms, industrial artistic design, industrial design, artistic construction, esthetics of industrial production, industrial art, product design, form-making, or industrial form design.

There is no other field that released such an outburst of language fancy and imagination. However, it may be that there are some reasons for it. Perhaps there are different branches within the field of design. But so far, these differences have not been determined, and any attempts to do that have been drowned in the ocean which is proudly called "art integration."

The main reason for such a state is that design is always considered an artistic activity. The means of activity cannot be substituted for the ends of it. A disregard of this basic rule has become a common sin of many graphic artists/designers.

As soon as industrial design developed, there appeared an ardent debate on the question: "Who am I? A graphic artist or an engineer?" A question of this type explains in itself the situation that exists in this field. One cannot ask an Egyptian: "Are you English or Spanish?"

In design, we have to do with such factors as economic, constructive, technological, aesthetic, and utilitarian. These factors are examined during the process of design by teams of experts. It is obvious that the economist (E) examines the constructive (k), technological (t), aesthetic-graphic (p), and utilitarian (u) factors mainly from the economic point of view:

E- k. t. p. u ——————— e

The constructor (K) examines the above factors with regard to the construction:

K- e. t. p. u ——————— k

The technologist (T) examines these factors from the technological point of view:

T- e. k. p. u ——————— t

While the graphic designer (P) examines them from the point of view of his profession and interests, i.e. of graphic arts:

P- e. k. t. u ——————— p

A question arises: who in the design team is to determine the utilitarian qualities of the product? Is it possible that these qualities are less essential than the other ones? Or, is the determining of the utilitarian qualities so simple that it can be done by any of the above mentioned experts?

The industrial designer (U) examines the economic, constructive, technological, and graphic factors from the utilitarian point of view:

U- e. k. t. p ——————— u

The design of the utilitarian form of industrial products is a separate profession which requires expert knowledge and qualifications. The emancipation of this profession is necessary for actual realization of social needs.

To state that the utilitarian aspect of the product can be handled while the graphic and visual factors are examined introduces illusion and mystification, which lead to the domination of the graphic form over the function of the product. It is in the interest of industrial design that all the adjoining fields develop harmoniously, visual design, craftsmanship, and art industry included. Also, a modern graphic art can and should be expected to give many valuable inspirations if it is independent and progressive.

However, we should not attempt to identify industrial design with graphic arts and vice versa. Only the neophytes who have not experienced well the taste of either field can presume that both fields are the same. Let us not mix salt with sugar merely because they look alike. Putting an equation mark between these two professions will doom one of them to failure. (*Excerpted from a paper delivered in 1972 during the Conference of Artists and Designers Union of Poland and the U S. S. R., in Moscow.*)

—Andrzej Pawlowski

\*     \*     \*

Andrzej Pawlowski's philosophical views are rooted in the rationalism of European science and in an intellectual orientation in arts. His strict, analytical mind is turned toward tomorrow. His personality was shaped not by the past but by expectations and anticipations of new events and new insoluble questions.

The idea of an active attitude toward life, as preached by the Greek philosophers, directed Pawlowski to Descartes, Kant, Marx, and finally, to the Polish thinker Tadeusz Kotarbifiski, the author of praxeology, i.e., the theory of effective action. This philosophy, with its main features of rationalism, realism, and activism, accorded with his own world view. He has also relied on his sound judgment of reality. This attitude, which he might have inherited from his peasant ancestors, has allowed him to confront, under specific Polish conditions, an ideal, theoretical model with life itself. He was reinforced in this attitude by the experiences of his youth, first his activity in the resistance movement, an underground education in agriculture, then his employment in a metallurgic plant.

Unlike most other people in the art world, Pawlowski has had regular contact with centers of science and has participated in scholarly councils, e.g., in the Ergonomic Committee of the Polish Academy of Sciences. He is also a member of the Committee on Scientology and of the editorial office of the journal *Designing and Systems* at the same Academy.

His simultaneous participation in scientific research and art has sometimes confused his critics. Once I asked him myself about his opinion on this association of two functions. His answer was: "I am trying to objectivize the creative process, but only in designing. I do not favor rationalization of artistic creativity, in spite of such tendencies existing in art. It is a coincidence that I work in both designing and art. For example, the concept of form naturally shaped is the result of my interest in praxeology and precisely in the principle of minimalization which I still consider very inspiring but unexploited either by designers or by artists."

Pawlowski has strongly emphasized the distinctiveness of design as a creative discipline and its independence of fine arts and applied arts. Hence, his reluctance to consider himself an artist and to misuse this word. However, the dilemma—art or design—becomes pointless in front of works by such creators as Gropius, Itten, Albers, Lissitzky, Eames, Aalto, Ekuan, or Sottsass. Pawlowski's work also shows a unity of artistic and scientific elements.

The division into art and design was not accepted in the past. The Greek term *techne* comprises technics, art, and science. The Latin term *ars* referred to both—to technical and what is today called "artistic" production. A Polish philosopher, Wladyslaw Tatarkiewicz, emphasized that the ancient Greeks and Romans "had not intended to separate technics from arts nor arts from science. There was a deeper thought or instinct involved in their association, i.e., that their essence is the same and that all the three branches—technics, arts, and science—are nothing other than skillful production: *ars est systema praeceptorum.*"

That explains why Pawlowski's work is as indivisible as is Eames's heritage. His *Kineform,* which open up the secrets of motion and light, and the biomorphic *Manekiny,* his museum exhibits, and his designs humanizing man's work and raising his purposeful effort to the level of creativity are all based on the same mental attitude and confidence in logic and the cognitive potentialities of intellect. It is surprising that current times, so strongly marked by scepticism, have not undermined that attitude in Pawlowski's mind.

—Szymon Bojko

# PEDROZA, Gustavo

Argentinian graphic designer

**Born:** La Rioja, Argentina, 6 May 1947. **Education:** Studied at the College of Architecture and Urban Studies, University of Buenos Aires; studied design in Geneva, Switzerland, and Paris, France, 1969-71; studied on scholarship, Center for the Study of Mass Communications and Technological Arts, Buenos Aires, 1973. **Career:** Worked in association with Rubén Fontana, 1976-82; established own design studio, from 1983; professor, Architecture Department, University of Buenos Aires, 1984-1985; director of the Department of Visual Communication, Argentinian Post Office, 1993. **Member:** Asociacion de Disefiadores Graficos de Buenos Aires. **Exhibitions:** *Comunicación visual, trabajos de Juan Carlos Distéfano, Rubén Fontana y Gustavo Pedroza,* Galería Atica, Buenos Aires, 1979; *Gustavo Pedroza, Deseño y Comunicación,* Centro de Arte y Comunicación Buenos Aires, 1992. **Collections:** Centro de Arte y Comunicación, Buenos Aires. **Honors:** First Prize, Subterráneos de Buenos Aires, 1987; Bronze Medal, International Buchkunst Ausstelung, Leipzig, 1989; Grand Prize, The Etiquette of Good Design, Center for the Arts and Communication, 1991; Prize Konex, Buenos Aires, 1992. **Address:** Peru 984, 3 F, 1068 Buenos Aires, Argentina.

**Works**

*Metrópolis y Nuevas Condiciones de Vida* poster, for Sociedad Central de Arquitectos, 1983.
*Tercera Muestra* poster, 1985.
Symbol, for Centro Audiológico, 1985.
Logotype, for Zavalía, 1985.
Logotype, for Documenta, 1986.
Logotype, for Fundación Otológica, 1986.
*Contrastes visuales* poster, for Salas Nacionales de Exposición, 1986.
*Anticuerpo* poster, 1987.
Logotype, for DSG arte, 1987.
*Encuentro Internacional de Fondos y Organismos de Financiamiento de la Cultura* poster, for Fondo Nacional de las Artes, 1987.
*Wladimiro Acosta* exhibition poster, for Facultad de Arquitectura y Urbanismo, 1987.
*Pinturas de Dante Saganías* poster, 1988.
*De la A a la Z* poster, 1988.
Poster, visual identification system, and manuals, for Subterráneos de Buenos Aires y Premetro, 1988-1991.
Logotype, for Palais de Glace, 1990.
*El Diseño es el Objeto* poster, for Sociedad Central de Arquitectos, 1991.

**SUBTERRANEOS de Buenos Aires**

**PREMETRO**

Gustavo Pedroza: visual identification system for Buenos Aires subway and tramway, Suterráneos de Buenos Aires, 1987-1992

*I Congreso Nacional de Bibliotecas y Bibliotecarios* poster and symbol, for Comisión Nacional Protectora de Bibliotecas Populares, 1992.
*Ediciones Zavalía* poster, 1992.
Logotype, for Cybertech, 1992.


## Publications

**By PEDROZA: articles**—"Of Codes and Contexts" in *The Clarin* (Buenos Aires), 22 April 1988; "Typographic Space" in *The Clarin* (Buenos Aires), 31 August 1990; "Symmetry and Asymmetry" in *The Clarin* (Buenos Aires) 10 May 1991.

**On PEDROZA: books**—*Graphis Diagram 1,* Zurich, 1988; *Graphic Design, World Views* edited by Jorge Frascara, Tokyo, 1990; *World Trademarks and Logotypes III* edited by Takenobu Igarashi, Tokyo, 1991; **articles**—*Novum Gebrauchsgraphik* (Munich), August 1985, November 1988; *Idea* (Tokyo), no. 196, 1986, no. 218, 1990, and no. 238, May 1993; *Neue Werbung* (Berlin), April 1991; *Diseño* (Hergar, Chile), no. 24, March/April 1994; *Graphis* (Zurich) no. 297, May 1995.

*

A few reflections on design and communication:

Thinking about design is modified according to changing paradigms. This means that the basic principles of vision are not sufficient to understand the communication process. The congruence between the code, the source, and the receiver of a message, whether verbal or visual, exists within a context.

The communication process depends on socio-cultural codes, that as such, are modified according to history, place, and the specific group of receivers. In the process of transmitting a message, the designer acts as an active mediator, involving his intelligence and his sensitivity, his reason and his intuition. It is precisely through this role as an active mediator that his social responsibility and, at another level, the distinctive features of his language are defined.

The proper framework of the communication process does not imply any pre-determined visual syntax, any closed system of graphic signifiers, any stylistic stereotype. *(Excerpted from "Gustavo Pedroza" in* Idea *(Tokyo) no. 218, January 1990.)*

—Gustavo Pedroza


# PENTAGRAM DESIGN

British architectural, interior, graphic, and product design partnership

**Founded** by Theo Crosby, Alan Fletcher, Colin Forbes, Kenneth Grange, and Mervyn Kurlansky, in London, 1972; subsequently joined by partners John McConnell, 1974, David Hillman, 1978, Peter Harrison, 1979, Kit Hinrichs, Linda Hinrichs, and Neil Shakery in 1986, Etan Manasse, 1987, and Woody Pirtle, 1988. Established offices in New York, 1978, and San Francisco, 1986. **Career:** Major designs include corporate identities for Lloyd's of London, Neiman Marcus, Reuters, Lucas Industries, and Solaglas; alphabets for Arup Associates, IBM Europe, Cunard, Nissan, and Rank Xerox;

promotional graphics for American Express, British Olivetti, Chase Manhattan Bank, Pirelli, Polaroid Corporation, and Roche; industrial designs for British Rail, General Electric, Ideal-Standard, Kenwood, Kodak, Parker, Platignum, Shiseido, Wilkinson Sword, and others. **Collections:** Museum of Modern Art, New York; Stedelijk Museum, Amsterdam; Centre Georges Pompidou, Paris; Musée de la Publicité, Paris; Victoria and Albert Museum, London. **Addresses:** 11 Needham Road, London W11, England; 212 Fifth Avenue, New York, New York 10110, U.S.A.; 620 Davies Street, San Francisco, California 94111, U.S.A.


## Works

High-speed train, for British Rail, 1976 (Grange).
Unilever House interiors, London, for Unilever, 1979-83 (Crosby).
Company identity and book-jacket designs, for Faber and Faber, from 1981 (McConnell).
*IRM: Information and Resource Management* magazine design, for Ericsson Information Systems, 1983-85 (Hillman).
*AIGA Teapot* poster, for the American Institute of Graphic Arts, 1985 (Pirtle).
*Yesterday's Tomorrows* exhibition layouts, for the Smithsonian Institution, Washington, D.C., 1986 (Manasse).
*100 Years of the Motor-Car* poster, for Daimler-Benz, 1985 (Fletcher).
Near Eastern Gallery interiors, for the Metropolitan Museum of Art, New York, 1986 (Manasse).
*Vegetables* book design, for Chronicle Books, 1986 (K. Hinrichs).
Identity, signage, and promotional materials, for the Museum of Modern Art, New York, from 1987 (Kurlansky).
Corporate logotype, for Toray, 1987 (Forbes).
*Children's Hospital at Stanford Capital* campaign brochure, for Lucile Salter Packard, 1987 (L. Hinrichs).
*Fannie Mae: Fifty Years of Opening Doors...* book design, for Fannie Mae, 1988 (Harrison).
*UCLA Summer Sessions* poster, for the University of California at Los Angeles, 1989 (Pirtle).


## Publications

**By PENTAGRAM: books**—*Pentagram: The Work of Five Designers,* London, 1972; *Living by Design,* London, 1978; *Ideas on Design,* London and Boston, 1986.

**On PENTAGRAM: books**—*The Conran Directory of Design* edited by Stephen Bayley, London, 1985; *An Introduction to Design and Culture in the Twentieth Century* by Penny Sparke, London, 1986; *The Design Source Book* by Sparke and others, London, 1986; **articles**—*Design* (London), June 1972, February 1978, January 1988; *Die Verpackung* (Zürich), September 1972; *Cree* (Paris), May 1974; *Idea* (Tokyo), September 1974; *Novum Gebrauchsgraphik* (Munich), March 1976, February 1977, January 1981; *Graphic Design* (Tokyo), September 1984; *Graphis* (Zürich), January/February 1986; *Print* (New York), January/February 1989.

*       *       *

Pentagram came about through the amalgamation of Crosby/Fletcher/Forbes (of which Mervyn Kurlansky had become a partner) and Kenneth Grange's industrial design practice. Pentagram was a more interesting solution to the name problem than a string of surnames. Inevitably, some of the members' individual reputations and clients have stuck with them. Therefore, developments under Pentagram have continued in trends they had already initiated. Nevertheless, there is a quality about the work they do that is now recognizably Pentagram's without in any way being just a set of exercises in a house style. This quality stems from a sort of commitment everyone at Pentagram, not just the senior partners, feels about design. They live *to* and *by* design.

This sense of a "life-style" is reinforced by another aspect of Pentagram's activity, one which has been criticized both for being self-indulgent and self-seeking! This is their publishing program, which has issued the *Pentagram Papers* and the book *Living by Design* which, to be sure, are overwhelmingly full of the works of the group. Linked to this is the impresario-like role they have assumed in presenting the work of photographers such as Enzo Ragazzini and Bruce Davidson.

Another aspect of the partnership's work has been the design of exhibitions, in which area Theo Crosby has tended to be dominant. Indeed, it was his British section at the 1964 Milan Triennale that brought together the relationships that were to be the basis for Pentagram. Some of the outstanding achievements of Pentagram in this field have been *British Genius* (1977), a tented exhibition in Battersea Park, *The Environment Game* (1973), and the British Industry Pavilion at the 1967 Montreal World's Fair.

Given the nature of Pentagram and the interests and commitment of its partners and members, it is not at all surprising to discover that *Living by Design* should characterize the practice of design under headings which, while not particularly unconventional, do demonstrate an intellectually rigorous analysis and an attention to aspects often ignored. Thus, under the main heading "Environment Design," conservation is identified as "Grooming white elephants." Perhaps the sometimes sharp wit and the often gentle irony are as much the consequence of Pentagram's lifestyle as contributory factors to it.

—Toni del Renzio

# PERSSON, Sigurd

Swedish industrial designer

**Born:** Helsingborg, 22 November 1914. **Education:** Studied handicrafts with his father, F. S. Persson, Helsingborg, 1928-37; Akademie fur Angewandte Kunst, Munich, 1937-39; Konstfackskolan, Stockholm, 1939-42. **Family:** Married Iris Flodell in 1942; sons: Stefan and Jesper. **Career:** Freelance industrial designer, gold- and silversmith, Stockholm, from 1942; founded own industrial design office, Stockholm, 1949; designer, Kosta Glassworks, 1968-82; independent glass designer, Transjo Glass Studio, from 1984; designed for Silver och Stal, Kockums Jernverk, Kooperativa Forbundet, Norplasta, Alghults Glasbruk, AB Kronborsten, Ary Stalmobler, Sunnex, Sporrongs, Ron-Produkter, Uno Berg HAB, and others. Also independent sculptor, founding Galleri Sigurd Persson, Helsingborg, 1970, and Argentum Gallery, Stockholm, 1976. **Member:** Swedish State Advisory Group on Culture, 1963-68; KUS Commission into the Education of Artists and Designers, 1967-77. **Exhibitions:** Waldenstrom Art Dealers' Gallery, Stockholm, 1950;

Nordenfjeldske Museum, Trondheim, 1957; Konstindustrimuseet, Oslo, 1959; *68 Rings,* Liberty's, London, 1961; *Sigurd Persson Design,* Malmö Museum, Sweden, 1961; *7 x 7,* Nordiska Kompaniet, Stockholm, 1963; *Stakar,* Hantverket, Stockholm, 1963; *The Eloquent Jewels of Sigurd Persson,* Georg Jensen Inc., New York, 1964; *Sigurd Persson Design,* toured Sweden, 1966-68; *Kosta Glas och Silver,* Galleri Sigurd Persson, Helsingborg, 1972; *New Jewellery by Sigurd Persson,* Nordiska Kompaniet, Stockholm, 1974; *Glass,* Ilums Bolighus, Copenhagen, 1975; *Guld, Silver och Gammal Vals,* Helsingborg, 1977; *Sigurd Persson Shuffles and Deals,* Hoganas Museum, Sweden, 1984; *Sigurd Persson in Retrospect,* Vikingsberg Museum, Helsingborg, 1985; *Sigurd Persson's Golden Wedding with Silver,* Helsingborg and Stockholm, 1987; *Glass,* Galleri Argo, Stockholm, 1989; *Sigurd Persson in Retrospect,* Waldemarsudde, Stockholm, 1994; *77 Rings,* Stockholm, 1994. **Collections:** Nordiska Museet, Stockholm; Nationalmuseum, Stockholm; Röhsska Konstslöjdmuseet, Göteborg; Helsingborgs Museum; Nordenfjeldske Konstindustrimuseum, Trondheim; Konstindustrimuseet, Oslo; Neue Sammlung, Munich; Kestner Gesellschaft, Hannover; Victoria and Albert Museum, London; Museum of Modern Art, New York; Philadelphia Museum of Art. **Honors:** Diploma of Honor, 1951; Silver Medal, 1954, 1957, 1960, Milan Triennale; Gold Ring of Honor, Germany, 1955; Gregor Paulsson Prize, Stockholm, 1958; SAS Cutlery Prize, Stockholm, 1959; Gold Medal and Diplomas, Liubliana Biennale, 1964, 1966; Honorary Member, Worshipful Company of Goldsmiths, London, 1965; Helsingborgs Kulturpris, 1965, 1994; Swedish State Life Stipend, 1967; St. Eligius Prize, Stockholm, 1969; Sydsvenska Dagbladet Kulturpris, 1972; Excellent Swedish Design Prize, 1979, 1985, 1986, 1989, 1995; Prince Eugen Medal, Stockholm, 1980; Helsingborg Medal, 1983; *Vi* Magazine Design Prize, 1985; Titular Professor, Stockholm, 1985; Honorary Royal Designer for Industry, Royal Society of Arts, London, 1987; Fellow of the Royal Society of Arts, 1994. **Address:** Djurgårdsslätten 78, S-115 21 Stockholm, Sweden.

**Works**

Soup tureen in stainless steel, for Silver och Stal, 1950.
*Servus* cutlery in stainless steel, for Kooperativa Forbundet, 1953-55.
Saucepans in enamelled cast iron, for Kockums Jernverk, 1954.
*Servus Svart* cutlery in stainless steel with nylon handles, for Kooperativa Forbundet, 1957-66.
*Jet-line* cutlery in stainless steel, for SAS Scandinavian Airlines System, produced by Kooperativa Forbundet, 1959.
Dinner service, coffee-and tea-set in melamine, for SAS Scandinavian Airlines System, produced by Norplasta, 1959.
Easy chair in steel with velvet upholstery, for Ary Stalmobler, 1964.
Restaurant glasses, for Sara-Bolaget, produced by Alhults Glasbruk, 1965.
Electric cooker, for Kockums Jernverk, 1966.
Armchair in tubular steel and plywood with leather upholstery, for Ary Stalmobler, 1968.
Compressed air nozzle in plastic, for Sunnex, 1974.
*Charlotte* frying pans in cast iron with stainless steel lids, for Ron-Produkter, 1979.
*Colombina* coffee pot in stainless steel, for Hackman, 1979.
Pots in cast iron with stainless steel lids, for Ron-Produkter, 1982.

Dustpan and brush in plastic and aluminium, for AB Kronborsten, 1985.

Works in brass, for Uno Berg HAB, Kallinge, from 1994.

Plates and vases in stainless steel, for Silver och Stal, Vingåkes, 1994.

## Publications

**By PERSSON: books**—(editor) *Modern Swedish Silver,* Stockholm, 1951; *Sigurd Persson Silver,* Stockholm, 1979; *Sigurd Persson Smycken,* Stockholm; *Sigurd Persson Skulptur,* Stockholm, 1983; *Sigurd Persson Design,* Stockholm, 1986; *Sigurd Persson Glas,* Stockholm, 1988.

**On PERSSON: books**—*Contemporary Swedish Design: A Survey in Pictures* by Arthur Hald and Sven Erik Skawonius, Stockholm, 1951; *Swedish Silver* by Erik Andren, Stockholm, 1960; *A Treasury of Scandinavian Design* edited by Erik Zahle, New York, 1961; *Design in Sweden* edited by Lennart Lindkvist, Stockholm, 1972; *Scandinavian Design: Objects of a Life Style* by Eileene Harrison Beer, New York and Toronto, 1975; *Contemporary Furniture* edited by Klaus-Jurgen Sembach, Stuttgart and London, 1982; *Scandinavian Modern Design 1880-1980* edited by David Revere McFadden, New York and London, 1982; *Design Since 1945* edited by Kathryn Hiesinger and George Marcus, Philadelphia and London, 1983; *Design in Sweden* edited by Monica Boman, Stockholm, 1985; *Twentieth-Century Jewelry* by Barbara Cartlidge, New York, 1985; *Faces of Swedish Design,* exhibition catalogue edited by Monica Boman, Stockholm, 1988; *Sigurd Persson—En Mästare I Form* by Dag Widman, Stockholm, 1994; **articles**—*Jewel* (Tokyo), no. 9, 1994; *Euroworld* (Stockholm), no. 4, 1994; "Design Sigurd Persson" by Lars Fimmerstad in *Gold and Silver* (Stuttgart), no. 2, 1995; "80 Jahre Sigurd Persson" by Widar Halén in *Kunsthåndverk* (Oslo), no. 56, 1995.

\*

Designing for industry is taking part in teamwork. The technicians have their points of view, the economists theirs, and the designer his or hers. Each one must take the others into consideration. I like to say that a designed object is the result of a compromise. But that doesn't mean it is bad! Bad designing is when an object looks like something that it is not. You can imagine a bowl which looks heavy but which weighs hardly anything. There is no congruity between what the bowl seems to be and what it really is.

In every well-designed object, it is not just the function that is described in the form. Something else is there, too—we might call it an expression of the times. A Baroque chair, of course, expresses something more than that it is an object to sit on. There is something which is specifically for the seventeenth century. You had to sit straight-backed and stiffly. For various reasons, people liked the pompous, and the chair shows it. You had a role to play, and it placed special expectations on you—all that is in the chair. We perhaps imagine today that our chairs are only functional, but that is quite wrong. The expression of the times is there in just as great a degree. We just can't see it as clearly since it is so close to us.

—Sigurd Persson

\*     \*     \*

**Sigurd Persson: stainless steel plates for Silver & Slåe, Vingåker, Sweden, 1988. Photo by Sune Sundahl, courtesy of Sigurd Persson**

In the 1920s, Sigurd Persson began a traditional silversmithing education under the tutelage of his father, Fritiof Persson. Continuing to work in his medium, he is today perhaps the finest metalsmith in Sweden. His career virtually matches the profile of the growth and development of the interdependence between craft and industry which has transpired in Sweden, as in all Scandinavian countries, over the past fifty to sixty years.

Early in his career, Persson was interested in reviving techniques and processes which had fallen into disuse; these included enamelling, granulation, and niello. Philosophically, he was deeply influenced by the pioneers of the modern movement, which was officially encouraged by the Swedish Society for Industrial Design. Throughout his career he has held the personal convictions that through good craft, good taste is instilled in people and that individuals are capable of exercising independent judgment as to what constitutes work of merit. Through such belief in the designer's responsibility to the buyer, he adheres to the fundamentally moralistic tenets of modern Scandinavian design.

Aesthetically, Persson works as a sculptor, in the round, producing powerful, tectonic forms. Even his small-scale articles, such as rings or bracelets, at times attain monumentality. As a whole, his formally elegant jewelry is unusually extroverted and dramatic for Scandinavia, which has many practitioners more concerned with understatement.

In his strictly functional design, he works with economy and restraint. This can be seen in his 1958 prize-winning cutlery for the Scandinavian Airlines System, as well as in the tableware he later designed to go with it. More recently, he has designed pots and pans in stainless steel for the company Silver and Steel. In the 1970s, Persson worked as a freelance designer for the glass company Kosta-Boda, creating simple glass forms in bright, primary colors with sparse decorations in the form of signs. For this same company, he collaborated with the graphic designer Lisa Bauer in creating the engraved crystal bowl *Wild Strawberries*.

He has designed, or rather redesigned, the badges for the Swedish Army uniforms. Understandably, here he was required to draw heavily on traditional symbolism, but nonetheless, he succeeded in executing them in spirited, modernistic imagery.

Persson's handcrafted silverwork, both jewelry and vessels, has been a vital source of inspiration to American craftsmen in the period since World War II, especially from the 1960s onward, when the craft of metalsmithing was being revitalized in the art departments of colleges and universities across the United States.

—Barbara Young

# PERSSON-MELIN, Signe

Swedish ceramics and glass designer

**Born:** Signe Persson, in Tomelilla, 19 June 1925. **Education:** Trained with potter Nathalie Krebs, in Saxbo, Denmark, 1946-47; School of Handicrafts, Copenhagen, 1947-48; with Robert Nilsson, National College of Art, Craft and Design, Stockholm, 1948-50. **Family:** Married the designer John Melin in 1955; children: three sons. **Career:** Independent ceramics designer, establishing own studio in Malmö, from 1951; designer, for Kosta-Boda glassworks, 1967-77, for Boda Nova, from 1970, and for Rorstrand, from 1980. Professor, National College of Art, Craft and Design, Stockholm, 1985-95. **Exhibitions:** Galerie Moderne, Stockholm, 1953; *Design from Scandinavia,* toured the United States, 1954; *H55,* Helsingborg, 1955; *Hanverkets, 60-tal,* Nationalmuseum, Stockholm, 1968; *Design in Scandinavia,* National Gallery of Victoria, Melbourne, 1968 (toured); *Adventure in Swedish Class,* toured Australia, 1975; *Scandinavian Modern Design 1880-1980,* Cooper-Hewitt Museum, New York, 1982 (toured); *Contemporary Swedish Design,* Nationalmuseum, Stockholm, 1983 (toured); *The Lunning Prize,* Nationalmuseum, Stockholm 1986; *Faces of Swedish Design,* IBM Gallery, New York, 1988 (toured); *Scandinavia: Ceramics and Glass in the Twentieth Century,* Victoria and Albert Museum, London, 1989. **Collections:** Nationalmuseum, Stockholm; Malmö Museum, Sweden; Röhsska Konstslöjdmuseet, Göteborg; Kunstindustrimuseum, Copenhagen; Victoria and Albert Museum, London; Museum of Modern Art, New York, **Honors:** T-Centralen Station Design Prize, Stockholm, 1956 (with Anders Osterlin); Lunning Prize, 1958; Gregor Paulsen Statuette, Stockholm, 1973; Excellent Swedish Design, 1981, 1994; SDS Culture Prize, Stockholm, 1989; Design Plus/Ambiente Frankfurt, 1994. **Address:** Melin Design AB, Vikingagat 81F, 217 74 Malmö, Sweden.

## Works

Ceramic murals, for T-Centralen underground station, Stockholm, 1956 (with Anders Osterlin).
*Ruben* glassware, for Kosta Boda, 1966.

*Original* souffle dish in ovenproof glass and cork, for Boda Nova, 1970.
*Nova* tableware in ovenproof stoneware, for Boda Nova, 1970-86.
Ice bucket in cork with metal lining, for Boda Nova, 1971.
*Hot* teapot and cups in ovenproof glass, for Boda Nova, 1974.
*Corkline* serving cutlery in stainless steel and cork, for Boda Nova, 1974.
*Facette* tableware in ovenproof glass, for Boda Nova, 1980.
*Primeur* tableware in feldspar porcelain, for Rorstrand, 1980.
*Gourmet* cutlery in stainless steel, for Boda Nova, 1981 (with John Melin).
*A la Carte* tableware in feldspar porcelain, for Rorstrand, 1981.
*Chess* tableware in feldspar porcelain, for Boda Nova, 1985.
*Tradition* tableware in ovenproof stoneware, for Hoganas, 1989.
*Signum* tableware, cutlery in stainless steel, and glassware, for Boda Nova, 1994.

## Publications

**On PERSSON-MELIN: books**—*Svensk Form/Forma Sueca* by Ake Stavenlow and Ake H. Huldt, Stockholm, 1961; *Konsthantverk, Konstindustri, Design* by Dag Widman, Stockholm, 1975; *Glasboken: Historia, Teknik och Form* by Carl F. Hermelin and Elsebeth Welander, Boras, 1980; *Scandinavian Modern Design 1880-1980* edited by David Revere McFadden, New York, 1982; *Generationers arbete pa Boda Glasbruk* edited by Boda Glassworks, Jonkoping, 1982; *Form och Tradition i Sverige* by Birgitta Walz, Stockholm, 1982; *Contemporary Swedish Design,* exhibition catalogue by Monica Boman, Lennart Lindkvist, and others, Stockholm, 1983; *The Lunning Prize,* exhibition catalogue edited by Helena Dahlback Lutteman and Marianne Uggla, Stockholm, 1986; *Made in Sweden: Art, Handicrafts, Design* by Anja Notini, London, 1987; *Faces of Swedish Design,* exhibition catalogue edited by Monica Boman, Stockholm, 1988; *Scandinavia: Ceramics and Glass in the Twentieth Century* by Jennifer Hawkins Opie, London, 1989.

*      *      *

Signe Persson-Melin has tried and mastered a great variety of materials ranging from clay and glass to cork, steel, fibrous cement, and iron netting. She is an ingenious and highly original designer. She has gained assurance from a firm, practical training with no deviations, and also—presumably—from the early encouragement she received from her father, Erik Sigfrid Persson, a master builder with an original turn of mind. Like his daughter, he was unusually fond of experimentation and devoid of inhibition in his manner of working.

This is not to say that Signe is afraid of traditions. She dares to follow them as well. She says that pottery, stoneware, means the most to her. Clay is the material she loves best. This is the material she returns to after all her excursions elsewhere. And she is more interested in clay than in glazes. If she glazes the clay body, it is only to lend even more sensual prominence to the naked parts of the clay itself. She has always been quite actively concerned with design as such, but in her heart of hearts she is a craftsperson—a potter ("I don't feel like a designer"). Sometimes she has dug the clay with her own hands, beaten it, soaked it, screened it....

Signe Persson-Melin grew up in Skane, Sweden's southernmost province, a region of rich soil and groaning tables. To her, food is

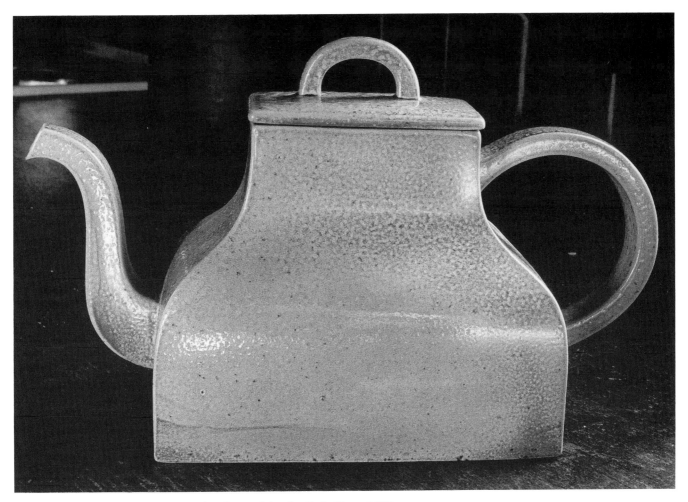

**Signe Persson-Melin: Teapot in sea-glazed porcelain, for Boda Nova, 1985**

very much of a piece with craftsmanship, art, and civilization. Everything she makes, even unique pieces, can be used—be it teapots, salad bowls, or the walls of subway stations. Such is the way her mind works. Everything must be durable, useful, humane, easy to look after, suitable for children. Above all it must not be mean or petty-minded.

But then, of course, she received some of her training in Denmark, Scandinavia's land of Goshen. She studied first with Nathalie Krebs, the Grand Old Lady of Pottery, and then at the School of Handicraft in Copenhagen.

In 1956, together with the artist Anders Österlin, she won a competition for decorating some of the walls of the new Central Station on Stockholm's subway line. Her battle honors include a number of other major decorative commissions, such as the big wall of the Folkets Hus convention hall in Stockholm, an assignment she shared with Anders Liljefors.

By collaborating with her husband John Melin, a graphic designer and advertising man, she began working with, and thinking in terms of, materials other than clay. First came the "Ruben" glass designed for Kosta Boda and named after an old master blower at the glassworks. It has the individuality and charm of hand-blown glass. When Boda Nova launched its program for the set table, Signe Persson-Melin was an obvious candidate for the design group. It was she who introduced cork as a natural material for table settings. Nobody had designed with it in such a way before. Now Signe showed that cork and flameproof glass make an excellent combina-

tion which is both beautiful and practical. Food can be put straight onto the table, where it simmers and keeps warm. And its delicious colors can be viewed through the glass.

The absolutely plain stoneware service with the gentle backward-turned "rolled" brims, which she produced for Boda Nova over ten years ago, is already a classic. Signe Persson-Melin also sets her table with knives, kitchen utensils, and other flatware having handles of pottery, steel, or cork. All these various tablelaying items display an unmistakable family likeness.

Boda Nova's first stoneware service later acquired a younger cousin, "Chess." It is made of porcelain and is a little slimmer and lighter in shape. The bowls and serving dishes are ovenproof. The "checkered" glaze has been allowed to spread unevenly.

Signe Persson-Melin's admirable capacity for alternating between different expressions of design and materials can be seen from another contribution to the set table: the "A la Carte" and "Primeur" services designed for Rorstrand. They are more brittle and "classy" in character than the tableware designed for Boda Nova. "A la Carte," in feldspar porcelain, comes in all white or else white with a brown, pink, or blue stripe. "Primeur" is exactly the same in shape but has a very fine color decoration in pale blue or gold.

"These services are rather on the smart side," says Signe, "and completely different from the others I have designed. But it's fun working with different kinds of assignments, and on such completely different terms."

During her decade as professor of ceramics and glass at the National College of Art and Design, Signe devoted much of her creative energy to improving the quality of teaching and the workshops. A new, highly advanced glassblowing shop was completed in 1987. When it was inaugurated, a large glass workshop was held to which glass artists were invited from the United States and Europe. "I wanted to open the school to the world," said Signe Persson-Melin. In 1995 she returned to the potter's wheel in her studio at home, to work on the "teapot in my head."

—Carin Sjölander

# PESCE, Gaetano

Italian architectural, interior, industrial, and graphic designer

**Born:** La Spezia, 8 November 1939. **Education:** Studied architecture, at the University of Venice, 1959-65; Institute of Industrial Design, Venice, 1961-65. **Family:** Married Francesca Lucco in 1969; children: Tata and Tato. **Career:** Independent artist and filmmaker, working with programmed, kinetic, and serial art, and co-founder of Gruppo N art group, in Padua, 1959-67; freelance designer, in Padua, 1962-67, and in Venice, from 1968; designed for Cassina, Bracciodiferro, Bernini, C & B Italia, Expansion, Knoll, Parisotto, Venini, Vittel, and others. Professor of architectural planning, University of Strasbourg, from 1975; visiting professor and lecturer, Ohio State University, Columbus, 1974, Cooper Union, New York, 1975, 1979, 1980, 1983, 1985, 1986, Pratt Institute, New York, 1979, 1980, 1984, Ecole des Beaux-Arts, Nancy, 1981, University of Technology, Compiegne, 1981, Yale University, New Haven, Connecticut, 1983, Universities of Quebec and Montreal, 1984, Polytechnic of Hong Kong, 1985, Domus Academy, Milan, 1986, 1987, University of Sao Paulo, 1987, and at conferences and symposiums throughout the world. **Exhibitions:** Galleria Bevilacqua La Masa, Venice, 1961; Hochschule für Gestaltung, Ulm, 1964; Finnish Design Centre, Helsinki, 1964; Keski Suomen Museum, Jyväskylä, 1965; Galleria Il Canale, Venice, 1966; Galleria La Carabaga, Genoa, 1966; Galleria La Chiocciola, Padua, 1966; Linea Sud Gallery, Naples, 1967; Atelier d'Urbanisme at Architecture, Paris, 1969; *Italy: A New Domestic Landscape,* Museum of Modern Art, New York, 1972; Galleria Luca Palazzoli, Milan, 1974; *Le futur est peut-être passé?,* Musée des Arts Décoratifs, Paris, 1975; Art Net Gallery, Architectural Association, London, 1978; *Difference Means Life,* JDC Gallery, Tokyo, 1978; *Skyscraper in Manhattan,* Goodwin Gallery, Museum of Modern Art, New York, 1979; Carnegie-Mellon University, Pittsburgh, 1980; Centro de Arte y Communicacion, Buenos Aires, 1981; Yale University, New Haven, Connecticut, 1983; *Les pionniers du meuble,* Theo Jacob Gallery, Bern and Geneva, 1983; Museum of Decorative Arts, Montreal, 1984; *Design since 1945,* Philadelphia Museum of Art, 1984; *Architecture et design de Gaetano Pesce,* Musée des Arts Décoratifs, Montreal, 1984; *Art-Architecture,* Harvard University, Cambridge, Massachusetts, 1985; University of Architecture, Hong Kong, 1985; *Gaetano Pesce 1975-1985,* Musée d'Art Moderne, Strasbourg, 1986; Galerie Leptien 3, Frankfurt, 1988; Deutsches Architekturmuseum, Frankfurt, 1988; Max Protetch Gallery, New York, 1989; Sapporo Brewery, Tokyo, 1989; *Produire industriellement la différence,* University of Quebec, Montreal, 1989; *Gaetano Pesce: Multi-disciplinary Work,* Tel Aviv Museum of Art,

1991; *Good Living Show* (with Istituto Nazionale per il Commercio Estero and Taisei Corporation), Tokyo, 1991; *Child's Play: Furniture for Children,* Peter Joseph Gallery, New York, 1992; *Gaetano Pesce, Cinq Techniques pour le Verre/Expérience au C.I.R.V.A.,* Centre de la Vieille Charité, Marseille, 1992 (works later exhibited in New York, Milan, Paris, Tokyo, and other cities); *Gaetano Pesce La Maison Hubin,* Galeries de Beyrie, Paris, 1993; *Face for Design,* Chicago Athenaeum, Museum of Architecture and Design, Chicago, 1994; retrospective, Museo d'Arte Moderna e Contemporanea, Trento and Rovereto, Italy, 1995; *Subjects and Objects: The Chrysler Award for Innovation in Design,* San Francisco Museum of Modern Art, 1995; retrospective, Centre Georges Pompidou/Musée d'Art Moderne, Paris, 1996. **Collections:** Museum of Modern Art, New York; Metropolitan Museum of Art, New York; San Francisco Museum of Modern Art; Denver Museum of Art, Colorado; Centre Georges Pompidou, Paris; Musée des Arts Décoratifs, Paris; Musée des Arts Décoratifs, Montreal; Centre Canadien d'Architecture, Montreal; Keski Suomen Museum, Helsinki; Museo d'Arte Moderna, Turin; Tel Aviv Museum of Art, Israel; Victoria and Albert Museum, London; Vitra Museum of Design, Basel, Switzerland. **Honors:** Locarno Film Festival Award, 1968; Tokyo Lighting Design Competition Award, 1973; Parc de la Villette Award, Paris, 1982; Office Furniture Competition Award, Paris, 1983; Commandeur dans l'Ordre des Arts et des Lettres, Ministère del la Culture, de la Communication et des Grands Travaux, Paris, 1991; Chrysler Award nomination, 1993; named to Best of Category in Environments list, *I.D.* magazine, 1995; Editors Award for decorative accessories, International Contemporary Furniture Fair, 1995; Compasso d'Oro, Associazione per il Disegno Industriale, Milan, 1995; **Addresses:** San Toma 2775, Venice, Italy; 67 Boulevard Brune, 75014 Paris, France; 158 Crosby Street #2B, New York, New York 10012, U.S.A.

## Works

Bracket and table lamps, for New York Form, 1964.

*Spazio quadridimensionale* architectural sculpture shaped by the wind, 1965.

*Carlotta* furnishing fabric, for Cassina, 1967.

*Yeti* armchair prototype, for Cassina, 1968.

*Up* self-inflating chairs series in polyurethane foam and synthetic jersey, for C & B Italia, 1969.

*Moloch* lamp, for Bracciodiferro, 1970.

*Habitat for Two People* environment, for the Museum of Modern Art, New York, 1971.

*Underground City in the Age of Great Contaminations* environment, for *Italy: A New Domestic Landscape* exhibition, Museum of Modern Art, New York, 1972.

*O Sole Mio* clock lamp, for Progetti, 1972-92.

*Golgotha* series of tables and chairs, and *Il Guanto* clothes hanger, for Bracciodiferro, 1974.

*Sit-Down* upholstered seating group in polyurethane foam and dacron, for Cassina, 1975.

*Tramonto a New York* upholstered three-seat sofa in plywood, polyurethane foam, and dacron, *Sansone I* table, and *Dalila I, II, III* chairs in hard polyurethane with coloured epoxy finish, for Cassina, 1980-83.

*Luigi o mi amate voi?* screen, stand for objects, and folding tables, for G. B. Bernini, 1982.

*Cannaregio* asymmetrical sofa units in plywood with polyurethane foam padding, for Cassina, 1983.

*Prospect Park* chair in urethane, for Cassina, 1983-89.

*Garden* chair in rubber, for Knoll International, 1984.

*Greene Street* chair in steel and polyester, for Edition Vitra, 1984-87.

*Les Ateliers* sideboard/cupboards in beechwood with lacquer finish, for Cassina, 1985.

*Children's House* fragmentary architecture, La Villette, Paris, 1985.

*Unequal Suite* furniture collection, including I *Feltri* armchairs in felt and resin with quilted upholstery, *Cannaregio* sofa, *Sansone II* tables, and *Les Ateliers* cabinet, for Cassina, 1987.

*Nuovi prodotti* showroom, for Cassina, 1987.

*People* fabric, for Cassina, 1987.

*Pluralist Tower* non-homogeneous architecture, Saõ Paolo, Brazil, 1987-89.

Table in rubber, silicone and metal, for Basia Rossignol, 1988.

"Edible architecture," including *Strawberry Bed, Modern Times Bread,* and *Dolcetti Ebraïci di Venezia,* for Steelcase Design Partnership, New York, 1989.

Windows, for Toyosashi, Tokyo, 1990.

Interactive gallery space, doors, and letterhead, for Gallery Mourmans, Knokke-Le-Zoute, Belgium, 1992.

*Organic Building* ecologically-conscious urban building with vertical garden, Osaka, Japan, 1990-93.

*543 Broadway* series of chairs and stools, Bernini S.p.A., 1993.

*Vesuvio* coffeepot, for Zani & Zani, 1993.

Flexible interior layout, logo, and signage design, for *Dujardin* children's store, Brussels, Belgium, 1994.

Virtual office, including tables, lamps, fixtures, flooring, and textiles, for Chiat/Day Inc., New York, 1994.

*Il Bicchiere* resin vases, for the Caffé Florian in celebration of the Centennial of the Venice Biennale, Venice, 1995.

**Publications**

**By PESCE: articles**—in *Keski-Suomen* (Jyväskylä), June 1965; *Mobilia* (Snekkersten), no. 173, 1969; *L'Architecture d'Aujourd'hui* (Paris), no. 155, 1971; *Crée* (Paris), no. 18, 1972, no. 24, 1973, no. 9, 1977; *Space Design* (Tokyo), no. 6, 1972, no. 8, 1973; *Japan Interior Design* (Tokyo), no. 159, 1972; *Casabella* (Milan), no. 375, 1973, no. 378, 1973, no. 383, 1973; *Opus International* (Paris), no. 47, 1973; *Industrial Design* (New York), September/October 1981; *Modo,* no. 161, December 1994/January 1995; *Domus* (Milan), no. 768, February 1995.

**On PESCE: books**—*Modern Chairs 1918-1970,* exhibition catalogue by Carol Hogben, Dennis Young, and Reyner Banham, London, 1970; *Italy: The New Domestic Landscape* edited by Emilio Ambasz, New York and Florence, 1972; *Gaetano Pesce: The Future Is Perhaps Past,* exhibition catalogue with texts by Francois Barre, Alessandro Mendini, and others, Paris and Florence, 1974; *The Modern Chair: Classics in Production* by Clement Meadmore, London, 1974; *Le future est peut-être passé?,* exhibition catalogue, Paris and Florence, 1975; *Design e Forme Nuove nell'Arredamento Italiano* edited by Paolo Portoghesi and Marino Marini, Rome,

Gaetano Pesce, *Feltri* chair, 1987

1978; *Contemporary Furniture* edited by Klaus-Jurgen Sembach, Stuttgart and London, 1982; *The Hot House: Italian New Wave Design* by Andrea Branzi, London and Cambridge, Massachusetts, 1984; *Gaetano Pesce,* Strasbourg, 1986; *Modern Furniture Classics* by Miriam Stimpson, London, 1987; *Italian Design: 1870 to the Present* by Penny Sparke, London and New York, 1988; *Italian Modern: A Design Heritage* by Giovanni Albera and Nicolas Monti, New York, 1989; *Gaetano Pesce: Architecture, Design, Art* by France Vanlaethem, London, Munich, Milan, and New York, 1989; *Gaetano Pesce, Cinq Techniques pour le Verre/Expérience au C.I.R.V.A.,* Marseille, 1992; **articles**—"Western Designers in Japan" by Hiroshiba Watanabe in *Design Quarterly,* no. 161, Summer 1994; "Chiat Daydream" by Keith Seward in *Artforum,* January 1995; *W.I.N.D.* (Tokyo), no. 29, Winter 1995; "Creation of the Virtual Office" by Michael Kaplan in *Graphis,* no. 295, January/February 1995; "Gaetano Pesce, l'Invention utile" by Brigitte Fitoussi in *L'Architecture d'Aujourd'hui* (Paris), February 1995; "Climbing the Walls" by William Bryant Logan in *Garden Design,* February/March 1995; "Gaetano Pesce, an Advertising Agency in New York" by Federica Zanco in *Domus* (Milan), no. 769, March 1995; "Gaetano Pesce: A Fabulist in Plastic" by Adele Freedman in *Globe and Mail* (Toronto), 17 June 1995; *Interview* (New York), July 1995; "Gaetano Pesce per La Biennale di Venezia" in *Domus* (Milan), no. 773, July/August 1995.

*    *    *

Gaetano Pesce studied both architecture and industrial design in Venice. He is best known for the radical furniture and interior spaces he creates, designed for a specific audience.

In 1969, Pesce designed the *Up 1* chair, a polyurethane foam shape covered with stretch nylon and wool jersey. It came compressed in a package and expanded to the correct size and shape when opened. The design of the *Up 1* chair places Pesce's design work in the mainstream of Italian design. During the 1960s Italian designers rejected the concepts of functionalism, finding its theories of mass production and concern for aesthetic value too limiting. They worked instead for a more personal market, utilizing new technologies and concepts of design. The *Up 1* chair was one of the first in a series of original furniture designs.

Pesce worked in close association with the manufacturer, which allowed him to develop his more expressive styles. This also gave him the capacity to produce one of a kind or small quantities of objects such as furniture and lamps. The *Sit Down* series of sofas and chairs are of foam polyurethane padding injected into tufted dacron over a plywood base. Because of this process the shapes vary from one chair or sofa to another. The *Golgotha* chair appears soft, as if fabric somehow magically was formed into a chair-like shape, and would collapse if any weight were put on it. However, the chair is formed of fiberglass cloth and resin and quite rigid, capable of supporting a person. Because each seat is individually contoured by someone sitting in them before they dry completely, the chairs are each a distinct form. Colors vary, shapes are not specific, and surfaces which seem soft are hard. Amorphic shapes are created utilizing the latest technology. His designs challenge the viewer. They are not for everyone, but for a small, more personal market.

For an exhibit *Italy, a New Domestic Landscape,* held at the Museum of Modern Art in New York City, Pesce created an Archeological Environment. This is a subterranean habitation from the period of the great contaminations of 2000 A.D. Not only has Pesce created a site, but one which exits years in the future, discovered by civilization of a much later date. Though the furnishings made of wood and fabric have

disintegrated, the stone structure, which used the square and the rectangle as fundamental forms, remained. Discovery of this space with its enigmatic meanings poses many questions for contemporary designers which Pesce raises in an essay accompanying the exhibit. Though based on this specific site, Pesce raises questions about the purpose of space and its design, both interior and exterior, and how it effects man's behavior. These are the same questions a designer in contemporary society considers during the design process.

In a later design for a skyscraper formed of expanded polyurethane foam blocks which are exactly alike on five sides but vary on the sixth, Pesce creates a 'soft' or modern architecture. It is a building of the future, of contemporary building materials.

Questions are raised by many of Pesce's designs. Questions about historical references in design, the codes which govern lives, and what the future holds. He challenges the purpose of the designer and architect. He challenges the methodology of the designer and architect. He challenges accepted concepts of good design. Pesce writes of design, and is involved in design proceedings. He was molded by the Italian post war design practices which turned away from the functionalism of the Bauhaus, reaching towards an individualized design based on the needs of the individual rather than mass marketing.

—Nancy House

# FRANCESCO + ALDO PICCALUGA, INC.

Canadian interior design and architecture firm

**Founded** by brothers Francesco and Aldo Piccaluga (**Born:** Genoa, Italy, in 1932 and 1936, respectively. **Education:** Studied architecture and design, University of Rome.), 1962. **Career:** Designers (mainly of furniture and interiors), Beirut, Lebanon, 1962-1968; architectural, interior, and product designers, Toronto, Ontario, Canada, from 1968. Visiting instructors and lecturers, University of Toronto, University of Waterloo, Technical University of Nova Scotia, Ohio State University, University of Texas at Arlington, University of Maryland, Ontario College of Art, International Design Conference Banff Session, 1987, Designers Walk, Toronto, Harbourfront, Toronto, 1995, Corcoran Museum of Art, Washington, 1995. **Exhibitions:** Faculty of Architecture, University of Toronto; University of Waterloo; Carlton University; University of Montreal; McGill University; Laval University; Technical University of Nova Scotia; University of Manitoba; *Le Nouveau Nouveau Monde,* Maison de L'Architecture, Paris (toured); *Cleto Munari Collection,* Design Exchange, Toronto, 1995. **Collections:** Museum of Modern Art, New York; Cleto Munari Collection, Vicenza. **Honors:** "Commended Design," *London Daily Mirror* International Furniture Design Competition, 1963. **Address:** 512 King St. East, Suite 102, Toronto, Ontario M5A 1M1, Canada.

## Works

*PICCA* folding chair, for Colautti, Udine, Italy, 1968.
Exhibition design, The Swiss Chapel of Monte Tamaro by Mario Botta and Enzo Cucchi, Italian Cultural Institute of Toronto, Toronto (toured Untied States).

Interior design, Cuban Ambassador's Residence, Beirut.

Interior Design Consultants, for Ministry of Defence and Chief of Staff Headquarters, Beirut (with André Wogenscky, Architect, Paris).

Interior Planning & Design Consultants, Hotel Philadelphia, Aman, Jordan.

Collaborative Planning Consultants, for Commercial-Residential Complex, for St. Charles City Centre, Beirut (with André Wogenscky, Architect, Paris).

Product designs include—furniture, building components, and vacuum cleaners.

Architectural designs include—Defa/Glidden Chemical Plant Addition and Showroom, near Beirut, Lebanon, 1965; Bissat Vacation House, near Tyr, Lebanon, 1968; Condominium Apartment, for Beydoun family, Beirut, 1968; CN Tower Revolving Restaurant and Ground Floor Bars and Restaurant, for Toronto Metro Centre, 1976-1978; Wolf Advertising Ltd., Buffalo, New York, 1978; De Berardinis Hair Salon, Toronto, 1978; The Cut Above, Hairdressing Salon, Toronto, 1980; La Fenice Restaurant and Bar, Toronto, c. 1985; Lowe, Marschalk, Goodgoll Advertising Ltd., Toronto, 1988; Low-cost Apartment House, Toronto, 1991; Galvan House, Toronto, 1992; Le Gavroche Gourmand, Toronto; Fashion Clothing Boutique, Toronto; Fashion Eyewear Boutique, for Karir Opticians, Toronto and North York; Fashion Eyewear Boutique, for First Canadian Optical, Toronto; Quo-Vadis restaurant, Beirut; La Grotte Aux Pigeons restaurant, Beirut; Remtulla & Associates Ltd., advertising agency, Toronto; IBM Ltd. Product Centres, Toronto, Montreal, Ottawa, and London, Ontario; Ferleo Showroom, Toronto; Transformation of existing structures at John and Adelaide St. West rental housing complex, Toronto; dwelling transformation, Goodgoll Residence, Toronto; Remtulla House, Richmond-Hill, Ontario; Marotta/Accarrino House, Toronto; Moscow Narodny Bank, Beirut; world headquarters, for The Arab Bank Ltd., Beirut (with Dar-el-Handasah Consulting Engineers); Barclays Bank Ltd., Middle-East branch; Compagnie Francaise de Crédit et de Banque, Beirut; The Eastern Bank Ltd. (London, England Charter), Middle-East branch, Beirut; Company Pavilion Commercial Fair, for Citrus Corporation Leipzig, Germany; St. Rita Catholic Church and Elementary School, Beirut; Natalori House, Brunico (Bolzano), Italy; Condominium Apartment, for Mouitahed family, Beirut; Farmers Co-operative Housing, southern Lebanon.

**Publications**

**On PICCALUGA: books**—*Neue Möbel,* 9th edition, Stuttgart, 1969; *National Housing Design Competition,* Ottawa, 1979; *Neue Läden* by Karl and Evan Mang, Stuttgart, 1981; *Worldwide Interiors,* Tokyo, 1987; *Sight Lines* by Adele Freedman, Toronto, 1990; **articles**—*Domus* (Milan), November 1963, August 1965, May 1967, July 1968, December 1972, October 1973, August 1976, October 1977, December 1978, September 1981; *Architecture* (Brussels), January 1965; *House and Garden* (New York), December 1966; *L'Architecture d'Aujourd'hui* (Paris), May 1967, October 1988; *MD Moebel Interior Design* (Leinfelden-Echterdingen, Germany), September 1968, November 1968, February 1970, September 1972, May 1973, August 1977; *Abitare* (Milan), October 1968, October 1972, April 1985; *Design* (London), November 1968; *Canadian Interiors* (Toronto), February 1969, May 1969, February 1970, December 1970, December 1971, February 1972, November

1972, December 1972, May 1974, November 1974, October 1977, December 1977, January 1978, March 1978, June 1987; *La Maison de Marie-Claire* (Paris), December 1969, August 1971; *Industrial Design* (New York), March 1973; *Canadian Architect* (Toronto), January 1975, March 1976, July 1977, November 1977, January 1978; *Interiors* (New York), January 1978, April 1988, October 1991; *Progressive Architecture* (Stamford, Connecticut), September 1978, September 1980, June 1991; *Interni* (Milan), December 1978; *Section A* (Montreal, Quebec, Canada), vol. 2, no. 5/6, 1985, vol. 3, no. 4, 1986; *Intramuros* (Paris), October 1987; *Interior Design* (New York), March 1988; *Azure* (Toronto), February 1986, October 1989, May/June 1995; *Design Journal* (Seoul, Korea), October 1990, August 1991; *Pronto* (Tokyo and New York), vol. 8, no.4, 1991; *A+U Architecture and Urbanism* (Tokyo), September 1992; *Case Da Abitare,* Winter 1995; *Insite* (Toronto), November 1995.

# PINELES, Cipe

American graphic designer

**Born:** Slovita, Austria-Hungary (now Poland), 23 June 1910; emigrated to the United States in 1923. **Education:** Bay Ridge High School, Brooklyn, New York, 1924-27; Pratt Institute, Brooklyn, New York, 1927-31; Louis Comfort Tiffany Foundation, New York, 1930, 1931. **Family:** Married the designer William Golden in 1941 (died, 1959); children: Thomas; married the designer Will Burtin in 1961 (died 1972); children: Carol. **Career:** Designer, in the Contempora industrial design studio, New York, 1931-33; assistant to art director Mehemed Fehmy Agha, *Vogue* magazine, New York, 1933-36; associate editor and art director, British *Vogue,* London, 1936-38; art director, *Glamour,* New York, 1943-45, *Overseas Woman,* Paris, 1945-46, *Seventeen,* New York, 1947-50, *Charm,* New York, 1950-58, and *Mademoiselle,* New York, 1958-59; freelance designer from 1959, working mainly for Will Burtin design studio, New York, 1961-72; graphics consultant and designer, Lincoln Center for the Performing Arts, New York, 1965-72; director of publication design, Parsons School of Design, New York, from 1970. Instructor, Parsons School of Design, New York, from 1963; Andrew Mellon Professor, Cooper Union, New York, 1977. **Member:** American Institute of Graphic Arts, New York; Alliance Graphique Internationale, Paris; visiting committee, Harvard University, Cambridge, Massachusetts, from 1978. **Honors:** Art Directors Hall of Fame Award, New York, 1975; Society of Publication Designers Award of Excellence, New York, 1978. **Address:** 40 East 10th Street, New York, New York 10013, U.S.A.

**Publications**

**By PINELES: books**—(editor) *Bread,* New York, 1973, as *Parsons Bread Book,* New York, 1974; (editor) *Cheap Eats,* New York, 1976; (editor) *Parsons T-Shirt Book,* New York, 1979.

**On PINELES: books**—*Magazine USA,* exhibition catalogue, New York 1965; **articles**—in *Studio News* (New York), March 1950;

*Print* (New York), September 1955; *AIGA Journal* (New York), January 1959; *New York Times,* 28 November 1975.

\*

As a designer as well as a teacher of graphic design, my approach to solving a problem has remained the same since my years of basic training—that is, to understand the objective of the message, be it an annual report for Lincoln Center, a school catalogue for Parsons, or a book on bread; to know the audience I am addressing; and to limit my scheme to the time allowed. My intention is to make the type very readable and good-looking; to involve illustrators, artists, and photographers of exceptional quality, preferably the ones who have not handled such assignments before; to seek for the most direct and simple solutions to complicated problems; and to pay constant attention to every detail of the job from its inception to its coming off the press to the packing of the final product. I was pleased to hear from one of my students that he chose Parsons over other schools because the application forms came to him in a red envelope.

—Cipe Pineles

\*       \*       \*

The role of art director is most enigmatic in the graphic arts. As an auteur, driving the creative process, the art director employs the diverse talents of artists, photographers, typographers, and graphic designers in service to a unitary vision. Though that vision is legitimately credited to the art director, for it to be successful, it must be a cooperative effort, synonymous with the content of the publication.

Cipe Pineles learned this lesson well as her apprenticeship was taken under the inestimable Dr. M. F. Agha at *Vogue* magazine, where she worked from 1933-36. More than anyone, Agha established the art director as the editor's partner in the formation of style and the control of visual communication. Under Agha, Pineles learned to focus on the big picture, foregoing a craftsman's preoccupation with the details and forging an expansive idea that was consonant with editorial purpose. Pineles got her first opportunity to test her newly acquired skills in 1938 when she was hired to art direct *Glamour*, another Condé Nast publication aimed at young women. Although this job provided her with a strong sense of her own priorities and the ability to experiment, it wasn't until after the war in 1947, when she was hired to art direct *Seventeen*, that Pineles made her important contribution to magazine design.

During the years at *Glamour*, she married William Golden, then working at *House and Garden*, who pushed her to envision layout, and especially typography, as a sort of adventure, to be sensitive to the way the final outcome is conditioned by opportunities inherent to each component. Design was never considered to be just problem solving but an expression of the copy.

At *Seventeen*, Pineles instituted a new approach to the illustration of fiction. The artwork she commissioned from the likes of Ben Shahn, Robert Gwathmey, and Raphael Soyer was not meant to grace the page as decoration but to successfully interpret the copy as a narrative in its own right. She encouraged artists to consider their work as integral to the overall effect of editorial content. Further, she bought only reproduction rights to the art, returning the original after publication.

In 1950, Pineles moved with editor Helen Valentine to *Charm*, a fledgling publication aimed at the new breed of female, the working woman. To be one is to know one, and Pineles eagerly embarked on an impassioned eight-year stint at *Charm*, parlaying her staunch views about respect for the readership through illustration as art, fashion photography as practical reality for the everyday woman, and layout as reflective of the aspirations and goals of women in the work force.

Her second marriage to Will Burtin, a proponent of Swiss Modernist typography, challenged further her goals of expressive clarity and effective communication, and, subsequently, she joined Burtin's studio as a freelance designer. Her dedicated approach to graphic design bred of these influences became most apparent in her work as consultant and graphic designer for the Lincoln Center for the Performing Arts and as Director of Publications for Parsons School of Design. Also, as a teacher at Parsons since 1963, she has focused on content, pointing to the basic communication need as the ultimate problem, demanding that students discard complicated concepts that might obfuscate the message. She stresses designing from the inside out, consideration of the copy as the inspirational catalyst for visual efficacy. Being natural and comfortable with the medium means avoiding a style that will distinguish the graphic component from its context. Hers is an integrated approach to art direction that reinforces the notion of the art director, learned from Agha and carried on by Pineles as the vortex of imaginative design.

Not the least of Pineles's accomplishments was her example as the first woman to be elected a member of the Art Director's Club of New York and, ostensibly, the first woman art director to head an educational program. She is a model for all women in the profession aspiring to enter positions long dominated by men. Not a feminist per se, nor are there indications of this in her designs, she nonetheless exhibits an expansive tolerance and extraordinary openness to contributions and experiences of a collaborative process. It just may be that her anomaly within the history of the profession was a contributive factor to the freedom she was afforded. No matter; once gained, she fiercely holds to this freedom and continues to instill it in others.

—Sarah Bodine

# PININFARINA

Italian Automobile design firm

**Founded** by Battista "Pinin" Farina (1893-1966) in Turin, 1930; early automotive body designs included six and eight cylinder Alfa Romeos, the Hispano Suiza Coupé, the Lancia Dilambda, Astura, Aprilia, and Cisitalia, and the Fiat Ardita; new works established at Grugliasco, near Turin, 1965; son Sergio (Pinin) Farina (born 1926) became president, from 1966; founded Design and Research Centre aerodynamic body-styling department, 1966; founded Computation Automatic Design Centre for automated calculation and drafting, 1967; opened aerodynamic wind-test tunnel, 1972; company reorganized as Pininfarina S.p.A., 1979; established independent design studio, Pininfarina Studi e Ricerche S.p.A., 1981; began automotive assembly, 1981, with the Fiat Campagnola and Spider Europa and the Alfa Romeo 33 Giardinetta; established Pininfarina Extra S.r.l. company to com-

**Pininfarina: Ferrari F355 Spider, 1995**

pete in other areas of industrial design; established PNA Services, Inc., engineering company, 1988; established United States liaison office, 1988; established Pininfarina Deutschland GmbH in Germany, 1991. Pininfarina has designed cars for Nash, 1952-54, Alfa Romeo and Lancia, from 1953, Fiat, 1954-74, Ferrari and Peugeot from 1955, Cadillac, from 1958, BMC, 1958-68, Nissan, 1965-66, Rolls-Royce, 1975, Jaguar, 1978, and Honda, 1984; also designed wristwatches for Orfina and sunglasses for Ratti Industria Ottica, 1981 82. **Exhibitions:** *Bolide Design,* Musée du Louvre, Paris, 1970; *Car Body Styling Prototypes,* Tokyo, 1977 (toured); *Carrozzeria Italiana,* Palazzino della Promotrice delle Belle Arti, Turin, 1978 (toured); *Die Nutzlichen Kunste,* Messegelande am Funkturm, West Berlin, 1981; *Italian Re-Evolution,* La Jolla Museum of Art, California 1982; *Dal Cucchiaio all Citta,* Milan, 1983. **Collections:** Museo Alfa Romeo, Arese; Museo dell'Automobile, Turin; Museo dei Trasporti, Lucerne; Museo dell'Automobile, Le Mans; Museum of Modern Art, New York. **Honors:** Best in Show, Tokyo Motor Show, *AutoWeek* magazine, 1995; Golden Marker Trophy, *Car Styling* magazine, Japan, 1995-96. **Addresses:** Industrie Pininfarina S.p.A., Casella Postale 295, 10100 Turin, Italy.

**Works**

*Cisitalia GT* 2-seater sports coupe, for Cisitalia, 1947.
*Lancia Aurelia B20* 2-door coupe, for Lancia, 1951.
*Alfa Romeo Giulietta* spider sports car, for Alfa Romeo, 1954.
*Peugeot 403 Prototipo* 4-door saloon, for Peugeot, 1955.
*Alfa Romeo 6 C 3500 CM,* for Alfa Romeo, 1960.
*Giulietta SS Spider Speciale Aerodinamico,* for Alfa Romeo, 1961.
*Ferrari 250 GT* berlinetta, for Ferrari, 1961.
*Fiat 124 Sport* spider, for Fiat, 1966.
*Alfa Romeo 1600* spider duetto, for Alfa Romeo, 1966.
*Ferrari GTB 4 (Daytona)* 2-seater berlinetta, for Ferrari, 1968.
*Ferrari GT4 BB* 2-seater berlinetta, for Ferrari, 1971.
*Rolls-Royce Camargue* 4-seater coupe, for Rolls-Royce, 1974.
*Ferrari 308 GTB* 2-seater coupe, for Ferrari, 1975.
*Lancia Gamma* 4-door/4-seater saloon, for Lancia, 1976.
*Peugeot 205* saloon, for Peugeot, 1983.
*Ferrari Testarossa* 2-seater berlinetta, for Ferrari, 1984.
*Cadillac Allante* 2-seater convertible, for Cadillac, 1986.
*Alfa Romeo 164* 4-seater sedan, for Alfa Romeo, 1987.
*Ferrari F40* 2-seater berlinetta, for Ferrari 1987.
*Peugeot 405* 4-seater sedan, for Peugeot, 1987.

*ETR 500* high-speed train, for Ferrovie dello Stato, Italy, 1987.

*Pininfarina/Lancia HIT* 2-door/2-seater sports coupe, for Lancia, 1988.

*Ferrari 456 GT,* for Ferrari, 1992.

*Ethos, Ethos 2, Ethos 3,* and *Ethos 3 EV (Electric Vehicle)* ecologically-friendly automobile prototypes, in collaboration with Hydro Aluminium, General Electric Plastics, Goodyear, Orbital Engine Company, BBS, and PPG, 1992-1995.

*Coupé Fiat,* for Fiat, 1993.

*Peugeot 306 Cabriolet,* for Peugeot, 1993.

*Alfa Romeo Spider,* for Alfa Romeo, 1994.

*Alfa Romeo GTV,* for Alfa Romeo, 1994.

*Bentley Azure,* for Bentley, 1995.

*Ferrari F50,* for Ferrari, 1995.

*Argento Vivo* spider with aluminium alloy frame and aluminium and resin body, for Honda, 1995.

**Publications**

**By PININFARINA: books**—*Cara Automobile,* Turin, 1968; *Nato per l'Automobile,* Turin, 1968; *La Vaporiera,* Turin, 1970; *Ricerca Teorico Sperimentale di una Forma Aerodinamica Ideale* (report), Turin, 1979; *Il lessico della Carrozzeria,* Turin, 1979; *Pininfarina Cinquantanni,* with texts by Sergio Pininfarina and Renzo Carli, Turin, 1980; *Pininfarina Figurini,* Turin, 1983; *La Galleria del Vento,* Turin, 1984; *Filosofia e Progetto,* Turin, 1985; *Ingegneria del Prodotto e della Produzione,* Turin, 1987; *Il Processo Produttivo,* Turin, 1989.

**On PININFARINA: books**—*L'Esthetique Industrielle* by Denis Huisman and Georges Patrix, Paris, 1961; *Le Ferrari Pininfarina* by Bernabo and Cornil, Milan, 1966; *Transport Design* by Corin Hughes-Stanton, London and New York, 1967; *The Library of Motoring: The Designers* by L. J. K. Setright, London, 1976; *Pininfarina: Master Coachbuilder/Architect of Cars* by Michael Frostick, 2 vols., London, 1977-78; *Carrozzeria Italiana,* exhibition catalogue by A. T. Anselmi, Milan, 1978; *Pininfarina 1930-1980: Prestige and Tradition* by Didier Merlin, Lausanne, 1980; *Pininfarina* by A. Alfieri, Turin, 1982; *Le Ferrari di Pininfarina* by Tito Anselmi, Turin, 1988; *Ferrari e Pininfarina* by Gianni Rogliatti, Turin, 1988.

*

Aspects of my activity include studies of new shapes carried out from experience in the aerodynamic field; studies in the field of passive and active safety; researches for the utilization of new materials in automobiles.

The philosophy of my life and work is inspired by that of my father. In our work, we are seeking a purity of line, harmony of proportions, but above all functionalism. We avoid ostentation. A handle is not valuable because it is gold; it is, if it works well and is made of light material. A car is an extraordinary object, and to design one means living a double experience: for the exterior, so that it has an attractive and aggressive enough personality to act as the main standard-bearer for sales promotion; for the interior, which must confirm the potential buyer's impression that the car is a good buy and make him feel that the vehicle has been made to measure for him—especially if he is going to be using it for several hours a day. Few objects have influenced our way of life and even the landscape

around us more than the car. And we designers have an extremely important task: to introduce a little order into the chaos which surrounds us and to make everyday life a little easier and more pleasant.

—Sergio Pininfarina

*     *     *

In the work of Sergio Pininfarina, we see the development in the industrial sense of the great craft tradition of coachwork design of which his father was one of the great protagonists; Giovan Battista was a pioneer in the very idea of automobile coachwork design, introducing into the field a formal conception with strong reference to the arts as traditionally understood. Pininfarina's cars have for years been synonymous with sculpture, modelled on a precise formal idea, artistic expression in themselves.

Into this tradition Sergio has brought the idea of more advanced technology as a means of bringing the product up to date formally and functionally; he has thus moved on from the creation of form-automobiles that sprang from a craftsman's skill in design and modelling to vehicles planned to give maximum performance on the basis of precise scientific criteria.

The Pininfarina wind tunnel, the first in Italy, made it possible to give rigorous tests to the formal ideas the designer's mind produced; there has now been added to it one of the first Italian computer-aided design centers, with which it has been possible not only to automate the traditional procedures of design but also to study automobile design in terms of every phase in the process of production. Pininfarina thus represents the most progressive phase of modernization and "industrialization" in a long tradition at once artisanal and artistic.

However, the highly advanced technology is not used exclusively for formal ends but also to make effective progress in the quality of the product. The cabs for agricultural factors, for instance, are studied in the light of the conditions in which the driver works; advanced materials and technology are employed to give the vehicle biotechnological features that will ensure the comfort and safety of the driver.

Thus, Pininfarina does not confine himself to the use of existing technology but tries to evolve technical knowledge through his own scientific research. One result of this effort is the experimental vehicle produced in collaboration with the Italian National Centre for Research to test the theory of a car whose form is designed exclusively to reduce wind resistance while still retaining the seating capacity of a current massproduced interior. The vehicle thus produced enables fuel consumption to be reduced by as much as fifteen percent. With this type of experiment, Pininfarina contributes to research that aims to apply design to the solution of general problems as well as to the traditional role of generating ideas for new forms and functions.

—Stefano Casciani

# PINTORI, Giovanni

Italian display, graphic, and industrial designer

**Born:** Tresnuraghes, Sardinia, 14 July 1912. **Education:** Studied design, at the Istituto Superiore per le Industrie Artistiche, Monza,

1930-36. **Career:** Worked as a typist, in Sardinia, 1927-29; graphic designer, 1936-50, and head of publicity, 1950-67, at Olivetti Company, Milan; freelance designer, establishing own studio in Milan, from 1968; designed for magazines *Stile, Industria,* and *Fortune.* **Member:** Alliance Graphique Internationale, Paris. **Exhibitions:** *Giovanni Pintori: Graphic Designs,* Museum of Modern Art, New York, 1952; *Olivetti Design,* Musèe du Louvre, Paris, 1954; *Alliance Graphique Internationale,* Paris, 1955, London, 1956, Lausanne, 1957, and Milan, 1961; *Giovanni Pintori,* Tokyo, 1967. **Honors:** Palma d'Oro Award, Milan, 1950; Grand Prize, Milan Triennale, 1957. **Address:** Via Baracchini 10, Milan, Italy.

## Works

Studio 42 and Studio 44 advertising campaign, for Olivetti, 1937-39 (with I. Sinisgalli).
*The Rose and the Inkwell* poster, for Olivetti, 1939.
*The Bands That Fly* poster, for Olivetti, 1939.
*Abacus* poster, for Olivetti, 1947.
*Numbers in Relief* poster, for Olivetti, 1947.
*Numbers* poster, for Olivetti, 1949.
*Lettera 22: The Boat* poster, for Olivetti, 1955.
*Lexikon: The Ball* poster, for Olivetti, 1955.
*Tetractys: The Arrows* poster, for Olivetti, 1956.
*Divisumma: Boat from America* poster, for Olivetti, 1957.
*Graphika* electric typewriter, for Olivetti, 1957.
*Electrosumma 22* poster, for Olivetti, 1958.
*Olivetti 1908-958* book jacket, for Olivetti, 1958.
*Summa Prima 20* posters, for Olivetti, 1960.
*Raphael* electric typewriter, for Olivetti, 1961.
Showroom interiors in Milan, for Olivetti 1963.
*Three-colour ribbons* posters series, for Olivetti, 1965.

## Publications

**On PINTORI: books**—*Posters: 50 Artists and Designers* edited by W.H. Allner, New York, 1952; *Olivetti 1908-1958,* with texts by Adriano Olivetti, Libero Bigiaretti, and Franco Forlini, Turin, 1958; *The New Graphic Design* by Karl Gerstner and Markus Kuttner, Teufen and London, 1959; *Lettering Today* edited by John Brinkman, London, 1964; *History of the Poster* by Josef and Shizuko Muller-Brockmann, Zürich, 1971; *Graphic Designers in Europe 2* edited by Henri Hillebrand, London, 1972; *Design Process Olivetti 1908-83,* with text by Renzo Zorzi, Milan, 1983.

*       *       *

Giovanni Pintori has been in the forefront of Italian graphic design for nearly fifty years, during which time he contributed much to the distinctive graphic style that has characterized Olivetti publicity material almost from the beginning. Perhaps to him was due their awareness of contemporary art and the adoption of its techniques and effects for advertising, a strategy by which was asserted the modernity of the whole Olivetti enterprise.

Already in the late 1930s and early 1940s, Pintori had designed advertisements for Olivetti that took as their point of departure the business machine itself, typewriter or calculator, sleek and modern-looking, usually represented in the final advertisement by a cut-out photograph. The advertisement's written message was kept to a minimum. Often only the name of the firm or, sometimes, the name of the model were used. To this was added some image derived from an aspect of the machine's purpose, function, or mechanism. This simple "formula" was capable of infinite, sophisticated variation, which Pintori investigated without loss of invention over the years and to which he brought his enthusiasm for the achievements of modern art, particularly juxtapositions of style, technique, and content. In one of those early advertisements, the typewriter is shown on a pale ground within a shape derived from curved brackets, and this in turn is on a night sky where the stars have been replaced by letters and numbers of differing type styles and sizes. Another shows an overhead view of the typewriter against a ground painted like a sky, while curved and folded sheets of paper elegantly float around the machine. In yet another variation of this theme with the paper more in scrolls, the typewriter has been reduced to a row of keys. Extending this direction even further was the famous 1956 poster with the array of coloured digits freely and densely scattered all over a black ground.

In many of these images, however, there was, further, a sensitivity to letter-forms and to the characteristics of the different typefaces, to, in fact, the distinguishing features between fonts and letters and, therefore, to the unifying elements within fonts. This kind of sensibility underlay such enterprises as the skillful design made of the letters of the name "Olivetti," starting with the large, white, capital "O" and so on.

The developments in Pintori's work, for all the consistency and coherency displayed, reflect his continuing interest and involvement in the innovations of contemporary art. Because of his appreciation of contemporary painting, in his work one can read the gradual displacement in the 1950s of, for example, surrealism (which had supplied much of the impetus towards unlikely associations) by a more turbulent and all-over effect, as in the scattering of coloured digits. Later still, newer trends led him to a rediscovery of his own past, from which he was able to launch himself anew.

—Toni del Renzio

# PIRI, Markku

Finnish textile, fashion, and industrial designer

**Born:** Kauhava, 23 January 1955. **Education:** Studied at Parsons School of Design, New York, 1973; fashion and textiles, University of Industrial Arts, Helsinki, 1975-79. **Career:** Printed textile designer, Marimekko Oy, Helsinki, 1979-81; senior designer, China Seas Inc., textile and housewares company, New York, 1981-82; independent textile, housewares and menswear designer, working with ITC, Finlayson, Petritex, Imperial Wallcoverings, Osaka Nishikawa, Burlington Industries, Spring Mills, Reko, Wakabayashi, and others, from 1983; founder, Markku Piri Inc., New York, from 1983, and Markku Piri Oy, Helsinki, from 1986. Also stage costume designer, for Jorma Uotinen, Arja Saijonmaa Cabaret, the Swedish Cullberg Ballet, and Brooklyn Academy of Music, 1978-86. Guest Instructor in Printed Textiles, Parsons School of Design, New York, 1982; also visiting lecturer, at colleges and professional institutes, in Europe, Canada, Japan, and the United States, from 1981. **Exhibitions:** Kluuvi Gallery, Helsinki, 1981, 1986; Gallery Bronda, Helsinki 1984; Piri Atelje, Helsinki, 1988; Galeria Alfa 38, Lisbon, 1989; Galleria 25, Helsinki, 1989. **Collections:** Museum

of Applied Arts, Helsinki; Art Collection of the City of Helsinki.
**Honors:** Scholarship, Parsons School of Design, New York, 1973;
Hoover Foundation Grant, 1978, 1981, 1982; Finnish Culture Foundation Grant, 1980, 1984; Design Award, *Jugend Gestaltet* exhibition, Munich, 1981; Ornamo Finnish Association of Designers Grant, 1981, 1983; City of Helsinki Grant, 1981, 1986; Design Award, Republic of Finland, 1986; Central Organization for the Arts Grant, Helsinki, 1988. **Addresses:** Markku Piri Oy, Nervanderinkatu 7 C, 00100 Helsinki, Finland; Markku Piri Inc., 496 La Guardia Place, Suite 403, New York, New York 10012, U.S.A.

## Works

Printed interior fabrics collection, for Marimekko, 1980-81.
Home furnishing fabrics collection, for ITC-Corporation, 1982.
First collection of household textiles and printed interior fabrics, for Finlayson, 1983.
Second collection of household textiles and printed interior fabrics, for Finlayson, 1984.
Wallcoverings and coordinated fabrics, for Imperial Wallcoverings, 1985.
Summer 1987 menswear collection, for Petritex and Finnwear, 1986.
Bed linen, pyjamas, towels, and blankets collection, for Osaka Nishikawa, 1988.
Three collections of household textiles and interior fabrics, for Finlayson, 1988.
First printed silk scarves collection, for Wakabayashi, 1988.
First men's shoes collection, for Reko/Rentto, 1988 (with Janne Renvall).
Second printed silk scarves collection, for Wakabayashi, 1989.
Menswear collection, for Petritex, 1989 (with Janne Renvall).
Second men's shoes collection, for Reko/Rentto, 1989 (with Janne Renvall).
First jacquard terry towels and bathrobes collection, for Egeria, 1989.

## Publications

**By PIRI: books**—*Vousi/Year,* Helsinki, 1988; **articles**—"New York Art Deco" in *Muoto* (Helsinki), no. 2, 1984; "Essay on Kyoto, Japan" in *Suomen Kuvalehti* (Helsinki), no. 50, 1985; "Clothing for the Future" in *Image* (Helsinki), no. 2, 1986; "Helsinki: Summer Streets and City Planning" in *Suomen Kuvalehti* (Helsinki), no. 30, 1987; "First Collection of Piri Men's Shoes" in *Design Forum* (Helsinki), September 1989.

**On PIRI: books**—*Finnland Gestaltet,* exhibition catalogue by T. Periainen, S. Heikkila, and others, Espoo, 1981; **articles**—"Markku Piri at Kluuvi Gallery" by L. Maunula in *Helsingin Sanomat* (Helsinki), 18 October 1981; "Markku Piri's Recent Work" by L. Uusiniitty in *Suomen Kuvalehti* (Helsinki), no. 49, 1983; "New Piri Shirts" by J. Kuikka in *Suomen Kuvalehti* (Helsinki), no. 18, 1984; "I Think That's The Year" in *Design in Finland* (Helsinki), 1986; "Piri Autumn 86 Menswear Collection" by C. Enbom in *Hufvudstadsbladet* (Helsinki), 27 January 1986; "Ecoute Optique" by K. Kalin in *Muoto* (Helsinki), no. 2, 1986; "Markku Piri Exhibition and Book" by C. Enbom in *Helsingin Sanomat* (Helsinki), 16 November 1988; "Markku Piri: 10 Years" by H. Rantala in *Suomen*

*Kuvalehti* (Helsinki), no. 30, 1989; "Ten Spiritual Years" by K. Valtonen in *Design in Finland* (Helsinki), 1990.

\*

If there weren't colours, I would go mad. With colours, I happily do so. Colour is the basis for my work. I react to colour very emotionally, and to all of my work with passion. Yet, creating colour harmonies and atmospheres is also a rational process.

I am intrigued by patterns, ornaments. The Japanese textile culture has had a great influence on the way that I create textile collections, coordinated collections, or combine shapes and materials. Harmonious wholes can be composed with contrasting rhythms, seemingly clashing colours. I consider my jacquard woven terry towels to be graphic art, soft, mass-produced for the consumers....

The border between fine and applied art can be thin: original paintings can be reproduced with impeccable technique.

The elements of the vulgar and the elegant overlap. I would rather take the risk, as long as my designs convey a sense of life (if not speed), sensuality, and ... fun.

—Markku Piri

\*     \*     \*

Markku Piri has always made well-considered and conscious choices. Although obstacles may force him to consider alternative routes, his determined aim remains constant and his final direction proceeds with sure strides. Following his schooling under an inspiring arts teacher and a year as an exchange student in the United States, Piri's course became clear. It was in his first year at the University of Industrial Arts in the mid 1970s that he resolved to work for the textile firm of Marimekko. He became an unsalaried summer apprentice so that he could pursue a relatively independent line. Then, following an urge to travel in Japan, he wrote a convincing grant application that yielded the desired result.

His professional career also began at Marimekko—a firm large enough to encompass the entire production process through all its stages, yet remaining positive in its attitude to design and experiment. There, Piri was exposed to an exceptional market within the Finnish context, but Marimekko was also directed outwards and internationally. It was a direction eagerly taken by the young designer. After two years, he saw it was time to test his abilities in a wider environment, and went to New York to become head designer at China Seas Inc. He had already created collections for licensed manufacture in Japan whilst at Marimekko, and now continued this activity for the new enterprise. Although still under thirty, Piri had a worldwide network of contacts. In 1983, Markku Piri Inc. was founded, while Markku Piri Oy, the Finnish equivalent, was created three years later.

A significant part of Piri's design production has been an innumerable series of furnishing textiles for a variety of firms in different countries. A survey of his creations over the years reveals a marvellously rich panoply of colour, pattern, character, and design configuration—but a common and unifying thread indicates that the same person is behind them all. This indefinable factor may be characterized as style, honesty, sensitivity, or simply an assured artistic sense.

Early on in Piri's American travels, he realized that most things can be done in many ways in a multicultural society not constrained by such narrow customs as Finland's. He made himself open to the challenge of vigorous competition, difficult and unusual commissions, and learned the necessity of communicating his own opinion. But it was in Japan that he perceived the high value placed on quality. Visiting Kyoto to meet kimono master Moriguchi—a man regarded as a living national treasure—Piri observed how timeless techniques produced divinely beautiful prints. There was also the fascination of Kabuki theatre costume where the richness and multiplicity of up to thirteen fabric layers shone through one another. This coordination of different patterns within a unified whole where clearly demarcated areas of strong graphic pattern harmonize with stripes and squares has become characteristic of Piri's own textile designs.

A remarkable feature of all Piri's activities is his openness and enthusiasm for new forms of expression. He has a keen sense of visual effect, and endeavours to carry his own style—via photography, layout, presentation, and display—throughout production up to the final point of sale. Having created the costumes for several theatre publications, Piri often presents his clothing and textile collections in the form of a multivisual performance.

Clothing was a logical development from textile design. Piri's menswear has a uniquely personal feel constructed from the basis of a unified colour scale. The clothes have a lightness and an elegance that follows neither temporal fashion nor tradition.

Being an artist who uses industry as his main means of expression, Piri nonetheless has a definite leaning toward the unique artwork in writing and painting. In 1988 he held his first exhibition of paintings comprising a series of gouache and serigraph portraits of friends. With seismographic sensitivity, Piri registered essential relationships and rendered them in sparkling crystal colours accented by dark masses and sweeping line. These painted rhythms were later redeveloped in the creation of patterns for fabrics. Concurrent with his painting exhibitions, Piri also published an autobiographical novel drawn from his diary kept during a year of illness, in which he sharply analyses the world around him. Of all his work, Piri believes his exhibitions and book are the most important so far.

Markku Piri has produced a body of work impressive both in range and quality. At his recent exhibition, however, he declared no inclination to review his past work, preferring instead to present what was yet to come. Attention was focused on the latest additions to his repertoire—a range of men's shoes and a collection of silk scarves printed in Japan. Markku Piri continues to strengthen his position as Finland's most international designer.

—Carla Enbom

# PLATNER, Warren

American architect and interior, product, landscape, graphic, and furniture designer

**Born:** Baltimore, Maryland, 18 June 1919. **Education:** Cornell University, Ithaca, New York, B.Arch., 1941. **Family:** Married Joan Payne in 1945, children: Bronson, Joan, Sharon, and Madeleine. **Career:** Worked in the architectural and design offices of Raymond Loewy and Eero Saarinen and Associates, 1945-50; freelance architect and designer, in practice as Warren Platner Associates, New Haven, Connecticut, from 1965; total design concepts have included office headquarters, shopping centers, restaurants, hotels, showrooms, libraries, schools, ferryships, performing arts centers, and others; designed products for Knoll International, Lehigh-Leopold, C. I. Designs, American Standard, Georg Jensen, Steelcase Partnership, and others. **Exhibitions:** *Knoll au Musée,* Musée des Arts Décoratifs, Paris, 1972; *Design Since 1945,* Philadelphia Museum of Art, 1983. **Collections:** Philadelphia Museum of Art. **Honors:** Rome Prize in Architecture, and fellow, American Academy in Rome, 1955; Advanced Research Fulbright Award in Architecture, 1955; Graham Foundation Award for Advanced Studies in the Fine Arts, 1962; New York Designers Lighting Forum Award, 1975; Fellow of the American Institute of Architects; Presidents Fellow, Rhode Island School of Design. **Address:** Warren Platner Associates, 18 Mitchell Drive, New Haven, Connecticut O6511-2595, U.S.A.

## Works

CBS Building restaurant interiors and equipment, New York, 1964.
Lounge chairs and tables with steel-rod supports, for Knoll, 1965.
Executive furniture, for the Ford Foundation Building, New York, 1967.
Design Center interiors, for Georg Jensen Inc., New York, 1968.
Executive furniture range, for Knoll, 1969.
Prospect Center faculty club building, for Princeton University, New Jersey, 1970.
Kent Memorial Library, Suffield, Connecticut, 1972.
Interiors and furnishings, for the Mortgage Guarantee Investment Corporation, Milwaukee, Wisconsin, 1973.
Showroom in the Chicago Merchandise Mart, for Steelcase Partnership, 1974.
American Restaurant interiors, Kansas City, Missouri, 1974.
Windows on the World top-floor restaurant, for the World Trade Center, New York, 1975.
Shopping mall interiors and consulting architects, for Water Tower Place, Chicago, 1977.
Sea Containers Corporation world headquarters building, London, 1982.

## Publications

**By PLATNER: articles**—*Industrial Design* (New York), June 1969.

**On PLATNER: books**—*Inside Today's Home* by Ray and Sarah Faulkner, New York, 1954, 1975; *Knoll au Musée,* exhibition catalogue by Christine Rae, Paris, 1972; *Modern Furniture* by John F. Pile, New York and Toronto, 1979; *Interior Spaces Designed by Architects* edited by Charles K. Hoyt, New York and London, 1981; *Knoll Design* by Eric Larrabee and Massimo Vignelli, New York, 1981; *Contemporary Furniture* edited by Klaus-Jurgen Sembach, Stuttgart and London, 1982; *Interior Design: The New Freedom* by Barbaralee Diamonstein, New York, 1982; *Warren Platner, Architect and Interior Designer: A Bibliography* by Mary A Vance, Monticello, Illinois, 1982; *Design Since 1945* edited by Kathryn Hiesinger and George Marcus, Philadelphia and London, 1983; *Furniture by Architects* by Marc Emery, New York, 1983; *Modern Furniture Classics* by Miriam Stimpson, London, 1987; *The American Design Adventure 1940-1975* by Arthur J. Pulos, London and Cambridge, Massachusetts, 1988.

\*     \*     \*

**Warren Platner: Sea Containers House, London, 1982**

Warren Platner, trained in architecture, found his true metier as an interior designer. His attitude toward building is that one must not relegate the "people space" to the status of afterthought, that is what's left after the building "package" and its internal systems have been organized. He has assumed the humanistic posture which requires that a building grow organically, from the inside out, reflecting the uses to which the space will be put and the feelings it ought to inspire. Kent Memorial Library and the Prospect Center at Princeton, similar glass-enclosed pavilions, are typical of Platner's ability to use architecture as a bridge between internal space and the surrounding landscape .

Platner's work is distinguished by the comprehensiveness of his approach and the virtuosity of his attention to detail. Not content simply to design the architectural space and its fixtures, lighting, and surface finishes, he frequently, as with Mortgage Guarantee Investment Corporation, creates original furniture, designs the art work, and selects even the small, ornamental accessories (vases, lamps, ashtrays, etc.). In fact, his acceptance of a project is sometimes contingent on a client's willingness to support this level of involvement.

Commissioned in 1974 to create a restaurant of unprecedented opulence atop the 107-story World Trade Center in New York, Platner evinced the full-blooded response that characterizes his best efforts and dramatically illustrates the richness of his visual imagination. The well-known result, Windows on the World, was conceived as an "entertainment" wherein the element of dining would be but a part of the total experience. In the textural richness deployed throughout this remarkable restaurant—tasselled silk wall coverings, faceted mirrors, marble edging, brass railing, gilding, glazing, stenciling, and floral patterning—Platner takes issue with the arid value-system of the International Style. Although, strictly speaking, not a post-modernist, Platner exhibits in his project an impatience with the modern movement's disdain for purely ornamental detailing. At Windows on the World, he has indulged in what he unapologetically calls "interior decorating," albeit with an architect's discipline, to achieve a rich, almost "period" ambience. Without actually using devices such as carved moldings, for instance, he has panelled walls in overlapping layers of material to achieve a similar effect, creating what Olga Gueft of *Interiors* magazine called "subliminal associations of traditional grandeur without the prototype."

Speaking of his chair designs for Knoll International, Platner says, "I felt there was room for the kind of decorative, gentle, graceful kind of design that appeared in a period style like Louis XV.... It is important that if you design a chair you produce something that enhances the person in it." A noble ambition in an ignoble age; this assessment could well be applied to the entire body of Platner's work.

—Kenneth Gaulin

# PLUMB, William Lansing

American industrial designer

**Born:** Malone, New York, 13 July 1932. **Education:** Studied at Cornell University, Ithaca, New York, BFA, 1954; attended Politecnico, Milan, 1957-59. **Military Service:** Served in the United States Navy, in Korea, 1954-57. **Family:** Married Catherine Olden in 1973; children: Abigail and Christian. **Career:** Freelance designer, working with Gio Ponti and Gianfranco Frattini, in Milan, 1957-59; design consultant to La Rinascente stores, Milan, 1957-59; senior designer in the office of Eliot Noyes, New Canaan, Connecticut, 1959-63; founder and president, Plumb Design Group, New York, 1963-88; principal, Plumb Pearson Inc. design firm, New York, from 1988; designed for Savin, Dictaphone, Thermo Electric, Bussman/McGraw Edison, Apple Computer, American Telephone and Telegraph, Corning Glass, Citibank, Matsushita Electric Company, Du Pont, Sharp, and others. Editorial board member, *Industrial Design* magazine, New York, from 1978. Lecturer, Rhode Island School of Design, Providence, and Philadelphia College of Art. **Exhibitions:** Museum of Modern Art, New York; Philadelphia Museum of Art; Smithsonian Institution, Washington, D.C.; Whitney Museum, New York; American Crafts Museum, New York; Brooklyn Museum, New York; Gallery 91, New York. **Collections:** Museum of Modern Art, New York. **Honors:** *Industrial Design* Magazine Award, New York; Gute Form Prize, Hannover; American Institute of Graphic Arts Award, New York; Communication Arts Magazine Award, Palo Alto; IEA Focus Award, New York; Fellow, Industrial Designers Society of America and American Academy in Rome; Prix de Rome, 1985. **Address:** Plumb Pearson Inc., 57 East 11th Street, New York, New York 10003, U.S.A.

## Works

*IBM Model D* typewriter, for International Business Machines (IBM), 1960 (with Eliot Noyes).
*IBM Selectric I/O* typewriter, for IBM, 1961 (with Eliot Noyes).
*IBM 214* dictating machine, for IBM, 1963 (with Eliot Noyes).
Corporate identity and design program, for the Savin Corporation.
Corporate identity and design program, for the Thermo Electric Company.
Office interiors, graphics, and Buss bus mobile sales training units, for Bussman Division of McGraw Edison.
*Stereo Spread* portable radio, for J. C. Penney.
*World Timer* quartz alarm clock, for Copal of Japan.
*Pillminder* programmable electronic pillbox, for Greenwich Electronic Time.
*PXL-6* word-processing printer, for AM International.
*Centor* transcutaneous nerve stimulator, for IPCO Hospital Supply Corporation.
Portable AM/FM stereo radio/cassette player, for Sharp, 1987.

## Publications

**On PLUMB: books**—*International Design Yearbook 1988/89* edited by Arata Isozaki, London, 1988; **articles**—*Industrial Design* (New York), September 1972.

# PLUNKETT, Walter

American film and stage costume designer

**Born:** Oakland, California, 5 June 1902. **Education:** Studied at the University of California, Berkeley. **Career:** Vaudeville and stock actor, designing first stage costumes for touring vaudeville chorus, 1923-26; head of wardrobe department, 1926-30, 1932-35, and film costume designer, 1936-39, FBO Studios (later RKO), Hollywood; freelance film costume designer, Hollywood, 1939-47; designer, Metro-Goldwyn-Mayer film studios, Hollywood, 1947-66; also designed for the Metropolitan Opera and Broadway stage shows, New York. **Exhibition:** *Romantic and Glamorous Hollywood Costume Design,* Metropolitan Museum of Art, New York, 1974. **Honors:** Academy Award, 1951. **Died:** 8 March 1982.

## Works

Film productions include—*Ain't Love Funny?* (Andrews), 1926; *One Minute to Play* (Wood), 1926; *Red Hot Hoofs* (DeLacy), 1926; *A Regular Scout* (Kirkland), 1926; *Boy Rider* (L. King), 1927; *Clancy's Kosher Wedding* (Gillstrom), 1927; *The Gingham Girl* (Kirkland), 1927; *Her Summer Hero* (Dugan), 1927; *Legionnaires in Paris* (Gillstrom), 1927; *Lightning Lariats* (DeLacy), 1927; *The Magic Garden* (Meehan), 1927; *Shanghaied* (R. Ince), 1927; *Hard Boiled Haggerty* (Brabin), 1927; *The Bandit's Son* (Fox), 1927; *Sinners in Love* (Melford), 1928; *Bantam Cowboy* (L. King), 1928; *Captain Careless* (Storm), 1928; *Chicago After Midnight* (R. Ince), 1928; *Circus Kid* (Seitz), 1928; *Headin' for Danger* (Bradbury), 1928; *Hey Rube* (Seitz), 1928; *Hit of the Show* (R. Ince), 1928; *Phantom of the Range* (Dugan), 1928; *Sally of the Scandals* (Shores), 1928; *Son of the Golden West* (Forde), 1928; *Tropic Madness* (Vignola), 1928; *Wallflowers* (Meehan), 1928; *When the Law Rides* (DeLacy), 1928; *Wizard of the Saddle* (Clark), 1928; *Stolen Love* (Shores), 1928; *Stocks and Blondes* (Murphy), 1928; *The Red Sword* (Vignola), 1929; *Love in the Desert* (Melford), 1929; *Air Legion* (Glennon), 1929; *Amazing Vagabond* (Fox), 1929; *The Big Diamond Robbery* (Forde), 1929; *Come and Get It* (Fox), 1929; *Dance Hall* (M. Brown), 1929; *Delightful Rogue* (Shores), 1929; *Freckled Rascal* (L. King), 1929; *Gun Law* (DeLacy), 1929; *Half Marriage* (Cowen), 1929; *Hardboiled* (R. Ince), 1929; *The Jazz Age* (Shores), 1929; *Laughing at Death* (Fox), 1929; *The Little Savage* (L. King), 1929; *Night Parade* (St. Clair), 1929; *Outlawed* (Fogwell), 1929; *The Pride of Pawnee* (DeLacy), 1929; *Seven Keys to Baldpate* (Barker), 1929; *Street Girl* (Ruggles), 1929; *Syncopation* (Glennon), 1929; *Tanned Legs* (Neilan), 1929; *Vagabond Lover* (Neilan), 1929; *The Very Idea* (Rosson), 1929; *Voice of the Storm* (Shores), 1929; *Queen Kelly* (Von Stroheim), 1929; *The Woman I Love* (Melford), 1929; *The Case of Sergeant Grischa* (Brenon), 1930; *The Cuckoos* (Sloane), 1930; *Dixiana* (Reed), 1930; *The Fall Guy* (Pearce), 1930; *Half Shot at Sunrise* (Sloane), 1930; *Lawful Larceny* (Sherman), 1930; *Leathernecking* (Cline), 1930; *Love Comes Along* (Julian), 1930; *Midnight Mystery* (Seitz), 1930; *Second Wife* (Mack), 1930; *Cimarron* (Ruggles), 1931; *Night after Night* (Mayo), 1932; *The Conquerors* (Wellman), 1932; *The Phantom of Crestwood* (Ruben), 1932; *Secrets of the French Police* (Sutherland), 1932; *The Past of Mary Holmes* (Thompson), 1933; *Double Harness* (Cromwell), 1933; *Morning Glory* (Sherman), 1933; *The Right to Romance* (Santell), 1933;

*Ace of Aces* (Ruben), 1933; *Aggie Appleby, Maker of Men* (Sandrich), 1933; *Ann Vickers* (Cromwell), 1933; *Blind Adventure* (Schoedsack), 1933; *Chance at Heaven* (Seiter), 1933; *Christopher Strong* (Arzner), 1933; *Cross Fire* (Brower), 1933; *Emergency Call* (Cahn), 1933; *The Great Jasper* (Ruben), 1933; *Lucky Devils* (R. Ince), 1933; *Melody Cruise* (Sandrich), 1933; *Midshipman Jack* (Cabanne), 1933; *No Marriage Ties* (Ruben), 1933; *No Other Woman* (Ruben), 1933; *One Man's Journey* (Robertson), 1933; *Professional Sweetheart* (Seiter), 1933; *Rafter Romance* (Seiter), 1933; *Scarlet River* (Brower), 1933; *The Silver Cord* (Cromwell), 1933; *Sweepings* (Cromwell), 1933; *Tomorrow at Eight* (Enright), 1933; *Little Women* (Cukor), 1933; *Flying Down to Rio* (Freeland), 1933; *The Little Minister* (Wallace), 1934; *Spitfire* (Cromwell), 1935; *Finishing School* (Tuchock and Nicholls), 1934; *Sing and Like It* (Seiter), 1934; *Where Sinners Meet* (Ruben), 1934; *Stingaree* (Wellman), 1934; *The Life of Vergie Winters* (Santell), 1934; *Bachelor Bait* (Stevens), 1934; *Cockeyed Cavaliers* (Sandrich), 1934; *Strictly Dynamite* (Nugent), 1934; *The Age of Innocence* (Moeller), 1934; *The Fountain* (Cromwell), 1934; *His Greatest Gamble* (Robertson), 1934; *We're Rich Again* (Seiter), 1934; *Down to Their Last Yacht* (Sloane), 1934; *The Gay Divorcee* (Sandrich), 1934; *Anne of Green Gables* (Nicholls), 1934; *Kentucky Kernels* (Stevens), 1934; *The Silver Streak* (Atkins), 1934; *Wednesday's Child* (Robertson), 1934; *By Your Leave* (Corrigan), 1934; *Dangerous Corner* (Rosen), 1934; *Lightning Strikes Twice* (Holmes), 1934; *The Crime Doctor* (Robertson), 1934; *Gridiron Flash* (Tyron), 1934; *A Hat, a Coat, and a Glove* (Miner), 1934; *Keep 'em Rolling* (Archainbaud), 1934; *Long Lost Father* (Schoedsack), 1934; *Man of Two Worlds* (Ruben), 1934; *Meanest Gal in Town* (Roberts), 1934; *Of Human Bondage* (Cromwell), 1934; *Romance in Manhattan* (Roberts), 1934; *Success at Any Price* (Ruben), 1934; *Their Big Moment* (Cruze), 1934; *This Man is Mine* (Cromwell), 1934; *Woman in the Dark* (Rosen), 1934; *Mary of Scotland* (Ford), 1935; *Hooray for Love* (W. Lang), 1935; *The Informer* (Ford), 1935; *The Arizonian* (C. Vidor), 1935; *Jalna* (Cromwell), 1935; *Alice Adams* (Stevens), 1935; *Hot Tip* (McCarey and Gleason), 1935; *Freckles* (Killy and Hamilton), 1935; *His Family Tree* (C. Vidor), 1935; *The Three Musketeers* (Lee), 1935; *The Rainmakers* (Cuiol), 1935; *To Beat the Band* (Stoloff), 1935; *Hi, Gaucho* (Atkins), 1935; *The Return of Peter Grimm* (Nicholls), 1935; *Annie Oakley* (Stevens), 1935; *Another Face* (Cabanne), 1935; *Captain Hurricane* (Robertson), 1935; *Chasing Yesterday* (Nicholls), 1935; *A Dog of Flanders* (Sloman), 1935; *Enchanted April* (Beaumont), 1935; *Grand Old Girl* (Robertson), 1935; *Murder on a Honeymoon* (Corrigan), 1935; *Seven Keys to Baldpate* (Hamilton and Killy), 1935; *Strangers All* (C. Vidor), 1935; *Sylvia Scarlett* (Cukor), 1935; *Village Tale* (Cromwell), 1935; *The Plough and the Stars* (Ford), 1936; *The Soldier and the Lady* (Nicholls), 1936; *Chatterbox* (Nicholls), 1936; *Quality Street* (Stevens), 1937; *The Woman I Love* (Litvak), 1937; *Nothing Sacred* (Wellman), 1937; *The Adventures of Tom Sawyer* (Taurog), 1937; *Allegheny Uprising* (Seiter), 1939; *Stagecoach* (Ford), 1939; *The Story of Vernon and Irene Castle* (Potter), 1939; *Gone With the Wind* (Fleming), 1939; *The Hunchback of Notre Dame* (Dieterle), 1939; *Abe Lincoln in Illinois* (Cromwell), 1939; *Virgil in the Night* (Stevens), 1939; *The Corsican Brothers* (Ratoff), 1941; *Lydia* (Duvivier), 1941; *Ladies in Retirement* (C. Vidor), 1941; *Sundown* (Hathaway), 1941; *Go West, Young Lady* (Strayer), 1941; *Lady for a Night* (Jason), 1941; *To Be or Not to Be* (Lubitsch), 1942; *Commandos Strike at Dawn* (Farrow), 1943; *In Old Okla-* homa (Rogell), 1943; *The Heat's On* (Ratoff), 1943; *Knickerbocker Holiday* (H. Brown), 1943; *Can't Help Singing* (Ryan), 1944; *A Song to Remember* (C. Vidor), 1944; *Along Came Jones* (Heisler), 1945; *Song of Love* (C. Brown), 1946; *Because of Him* (Wallace), 1946; *My Brother Talks to Horses* (Zinemann), 1947; *Duel in the Sun* (K. Vidor), 1947; *Sea of Grass* (Kazan), 1947; *Summer Holiday* (Mamoulian), 1947; *Green Dolphin Street* (Seville), 1947; *Fiest* (Thorpe), 1947; *The Three Musketeers* (Sidney), 1948; *The Kissing Bandit* (Benedek), 1948; *Little Women* (LeRoy), 1948; *The Secret Garden* (Wilcox), 1949; *Madame Bovary* (LeRoy), 1949; *That Forsyte Woman* (Bennett), 1949; *Adam's Rib* (Cukor), 1949; *Ambush* (Wood), 1949; *Black Hand* (Thorpe), 1949; *The Outriders* (Rowland), 1949; *Stars in My Crown* (Tourneur), 1950; *Annie Get Your Gun* (Sidney), 1950; *Devil's Doorway* (A. Mann), 1950; *Father of the Bride* (Minnelli), 1950; *The Happy Years* (Wellman), 1950; *Summer Stock* (Walters), 1950; *Toast of New Orleans* (Taurog), 1950; *King Solomon's Mines* (Bennett and Marton), 1950; *The Miniver Story* (Potter), 1950; *Two Weeks With Love* (Rowlands), 1950; *The Magnificent Yankee* (J. Sturges), 1950; *Payment on Demand* (Benhardt), 1950; *Vengeance Valley* (Thorpe), 1950; *Soldiers Three* (Garnett), 1950; *Mr. Imperium* (Hartman), 1950; *Kind Lady* (J. Sturges), 1951; *Man with a Cloak* (Markle), 1951; *Show Boat* (Sidney), 1951; *The Law and the Lady* (Knopf), 1951; *Across the Wide Missouri* (Wellman), 1951; *Westward the Women* (Wellman), 1951; *Singin' in the Rain* (Kelly and Donen), 1951; *Carbine Williams* (Thorpe), 1952; *Plymouth Adventure* (C. Brown), 1952; *The Prisoner of Zenda* (Thorpe), 1952; *Million Dollar Mermaid* (LeRoy), 1952; *Young Bess* (Sidney), 1953; *Scandal at Scourie* (Negulesco), 1953; *Ride, Vaquero* (Farrow), 1953; *The Actress* (Cukor), 1953; *All the Brothers Were Valiant* (Thorpe), 1953; *Kiss Me Kate* (Sidney), 1953; *Seven Brides for Seven Brothers* (Donen), 1954; *The Student Prince* (Thorpe), 1954; *Valley of the Kings* (Pirosh), 1954; *Athen* (Thorpe), 1954; *Deep in My Heart* (Doenen), 1954; *Jupiter's Darling* (Sidney), 1954; *The Glass Slipper* (Walters), 1954; *Many Rivers to Cross* (Rowland), 1954; *Moonfleet* (F. Lang), 1955; *The Scarlet Coat* (J. Sturges), 1955; *The King's Thief* (Leonard), 1955; *Diane* (Miller), 1955; *Forbidden Planet* (Wilcox), 1955; *Tribute to a Bad Man* (Wise), 1955; *Lust for Life* (Minnelli), 1956; *The Wings of Eagles* (Ford), 1956; *The Fastest Gun Alive* (Rouse), 1956; *Gun Glory* (Rowlands), 1957; *Raintree County* (Dymytryk), 1957; *The Brothers Karamazov* (Brooks), 1957; *Merry Andrew* (Kidd), 1957; *The Sheepman* (Marshall), 1958; *The Law and Jake Wade* (J. Sturges), 1958; *Some Came Running* (Minnelli), 1958; *Home from the Hill* (Minnelli), 1959; *Pollyanna* (Swift), 1960; *Bells Are Ringing* (Minnelli), 1960; *Cimarron* (A. Mann), 1960; *Pocketful of Miracles* (Capra), 1961; *The Four Horsemen of the Apocalypse* (Minnelli), 1961; *Two Weeks in Another Town* (Minnelli), 1962; *How the West Was Won* (Ford, Marshall and Hathaway), 1963; *Marriage on the Rocks* (Donohue), 1965; *Seven Women* (Ford), 1966.

**Publications**

**By PLUNKETT: articles**—in *The Velvet Light Trap* (Madison), Spring 1978.

**On PLUNKETT: books**—*Romantic and Glamorous Hollywood Costume Design,* exhibition catalogue by Diana Vreeland, New York, 1974; *Hollywood Costume Design* by David Chierichettie, London,

1976; *Costume Design in the Movies* by Elizabeth Leese, New York, 1976; *In a Glamorous Fashion: The Fabulous Years of Hollywood Costume Design* by W. Robert LaVine, Boston and London, 1981.

\*   \*   \*

Walter Plunkett lacked the knack of high couture. He could not compete in the world of super-rich chic with Paris-trained Adrian or Travis Banton. Instead, Plunkett excelled in designing glorious garments of days gone by. With the fervor of a dedicated archeologist, Plunkett worked to make his name virtually synonymous with the "period" picture.

Originally an actor, Plunkett prepared as if trained by Stanislavski. Endowing his costumes with presence and character, even the humblest handmaid, as seen in *Little Women* (1948), was seamed with integrity. Plunkett worked especially well with Katharine Hepburn at RKO because both artists aimed for veracity in character and era. Because Plunkett's dresses were assuredly accurate even in basic construction, Hepburn rehearsed in costume to achieve proper movement. She insisted on learning how to maneuver hoops and how to turn her head naturally in stiffly starched ruffs in order to insure that costume and characterization became one. Plunkett also was responsible for the Fred Astaire-Ginger Rogers look. Their dance attire, integral to their "carefree" image, depended on Plunkett's elegant lines which inhibited and released certain areas of mobility. Astaire, of course, insisted on comfort and optimum freedom; Rogers preferred glamour and gimmicks to catch the eye.

For David Selznick's *Gone With the Wind* (1939), Plunkett chronicled the fall and rebirth of the South through Scarlett O'Hara's well-researched wardrobe, which marked her passage from selfish innocence to hardened maturity. For example, the famous "dining room curtains" dress, ornamented with jaunty tassels and a smart, one-shoulder cape, illustrated Scarlett's spunky calculation in the face of adversity. As one of the first technicolor movies, *Gone With the Wind* dazzled with picture-postcard color. Plunkett had already worked within the limited range of the two-color process at RKO, but now he filled the screen with sapphire, dusty rose, antique blue, claret red, and infinite shades of green. Still remembered today, the gowns of this film reflected an emerging post-depression fashion trend. However, World War II aborted the cinch waist and wide, fabric-consuming skirt symbolic of prosperity and the romantic ideal of womanhood; only after the war were they resurrected as Dior's postwar "New Look."

Plunkett's later pictures echoed some interesting modern trends. His *American in Paris* (1951) sequence depicted the artist's ball of abstract blacks and whites, more like the flamboyant visions of Adrian than traditional Plunkett. They splashed the screen abstractly as if flung from Jackson Pollock's paint brush.

Throughout the 1950s, Plunkett continued his successful "period" creations. At the same time, he began to mimic the very popular culture that he and other designers had created. His mannerish garb for Judy Garland's *Summer Stock* (1950), for example, recalls Travis Baton's collaborations with Marlene Dietrich. Plunkett's greatest homage to the silver screen however was *Singin' in the Rain* (1952). Exaggerated American motifs paid glorious tribute to those brash Hollywood musicals of his earlier days in the business.

—Edith C. Lee

# POLIDORI, Gianni

Italian painter and stage and film designer

**Born:** Giovanni Polidori in Rome, 7 November 1923. **Education:** Studied painting, under Renato Guttuso, 1941-43, Vittorio Grassi, 1945-46, and Corrado Cagli, 1947-49, in Rome; studied stage design, at the Accademia di Belle Arti, Rome, 1945-46; studied film design, at the Centro Sperimentale di Cinematografia, Rome, 1947-48. **Military Service:** Served as photographer, in the Italian Air Force, 1943, and the military information service, 1944-45. **Family:** Married Marisa D'Andrea in 1950; children: Silva and Carlotta. **Career:** Professional designer for stage and film, from 1946, and for television, from 1959; worked on films of Alessandro Blasetti, Jean Renoir, King Vidor, Luchina Visconti, Michelangelo Antonioni, Alberto Lattuada, Vittorio Gassman, Franco Rossi, Eduardo De Filippo, Nanni Loy, Terence Young, Elio Petri, and others, and on stage productions of Gianfranco De Bosio, Aurel Milloss, Giancarlo Sbragia, Luigi Squarzina, Marco Sciaccaluga, and others. Instructor, Centro Sperimentale di Scenografia, Rome, 1967-68, Accademia Nazionale d'Arte Dramatica, Rome, 1969-71; associate professor of scenography, Universita degli Studi, Bologna, 1971-86. Technical director, Teatro di Genova, Genoa, 1980-82; planning consultant, Carlo Felice Theatre, Genoa, and the Teatro Cavour, Imperia, 1982-83; founder, with Emanuele Luzzati, of the Politecnico G. Byron school of scenography and visual communications, Genoa, 1983. **Exhibitions:** Galleria Schneider, Rome, 1956; Galleria La Medusa, Rome, 1958; Galleria Passeggiata di Ripetta, Rome, 1960; Galleria Il Fiore, Florence, 1965; Galleria La Sferna, Modena, 1965; Grafica dei Greci, Rome, 1980; Studio Firma, Genoa, 1983; Galleria Ellequadro, Genoa, 1988. **Honors:** Premio San Genesio, Milan, 1957. **Address:** Via L. Montaldo 55/35, 16137 Genoa, Italy.

## Works

Film productions include—*Due Moglie sono Troppe,* 1949; *Bellissima,* 1951; *La Signora senza Camellie,* 1952; *La Carrozza d'Oro,* 1952; *Il Cappotto,* 1952; *I Vinti,* 1952; *Amore in Citta,* 1953; *Siamo Donne,* 1953; *Il Sole negli Occhi,* 1953; *Il Seduttore,* 1954; *Guerra e Pace,* 1955; *Le Amiche,* 1955; *Kean,* 1956; *Un Ettaro di Cielo,* 1957; *Il Mondo di Notte,* 1960; *Maciste contro il Vampiro,* 1961; *Il Mondo di Notte 2,* 1960; *I Moschettieri del Mare,* 1961; *Le Quattro Giornate di Napoli,* 1962; *Violenza Segreta,* 1962; *Liola,* 1963; *Una Rosa per Tutti,* 1965; *Spara Forte... Piu Forte: Non Capisco,* 1966; *L' Avventuriero,* 1966; *Come, Quando, Perche...,* 1968; *Riusciranno I Nostri Eroi a Ritrovare il Loro Amico Misteriosamente Scomparso in Africa?,* 1968; *Il Commissario Pepe,* 1969; *Rosolino Paterno Soldato,* 1969; *La Supertestimone,* 1970; *Detenuto in Attesta di Guidizia,* 1971; *La Proprieta non e piu un Furto,* 1973; *Il Mio Nome e Nessuno,* 1973.

Stage productions include—*Woyzeck,* Teatro Eliseo, Rome, 1946; *All My Sons,* Teatro Quirino, Rome, 1948; *Death of a Salesman,* Teatro Eliseo, Rome, 1951; *The Power and the Glory,* San Miniato, 1955; *Anne Frank,* Teatro Eliseo, Rome, 1957; *I Demoni,* Teatro Duse, Genoa, 1957; *Hin und Zuruck,* Teatro Massimo, Palermo, 1959; *The Miracle Worker,* Teatro Odeon, Milan, 1960; *Le Diable et le Bon Dieu,* Teatro Duse, Genoa, 1962; *Hamlet,* Teatro Romano, Verona, 1963; *Johnny Spielt Auf,* Teatro della Pergola, Florence, 1964; *Seeschlacht,* Teatro della Pergola, Florence, 1964;

*Troilus and Cressida,* Teatro Duse, Genoa, 1964; *The Iceman Cometh,* Politeana Genovese, Genoa, 1965; *Julius Caesar,* Music Hall, Kansas City, 1965; *Se Questo e' un Uomo,* Teatro della Pergola, Florence, 1968; *Don Carlos,* Teatro Romano, Verona, 1969; *Caligola,* Teatro Carignato, Turin, 1970; *Il Visio Assurdo,* Teatro Verdi, Padua, 1974; *Our Town,* Teatro Verdi, Padua, 1975; *Lucia di Lammermoor,* Arena, Verona, 1976; *Minnie la Candida,* Piccolo Teatro, Milan, 1980; *Volki I Ovcy,* Teatro Duse, Genoa, 1980; *She Stoops to Conquer,* Teatro Duse, Genoa, 1981; *The Twin Rivals,* Teatro Duse, Genoa, 1982; *Bertoldo,* Teatro Dehon, Bologna, 1983; *Gli Accidenti di Constantinopoli,* Parco di Nervi, Genoa, 1984; *Otello,* Teatro Romano, Verona, 1985; *Affabulazione,* Teatro Manzoni, Pistoia, 1986; *Trois Poemes de Mallarme,* Villa Imperiale, Genoa, 1987; *Dario Fo: Two Farces,* Teatro del Fioldrammatici, Milan, 1988; *Front Page,* Teatro del Giglio, Lucca, 1988.

**Publications**

**On POLIDORI: books**—*Das Buhnebild* by Ottmar Schubert, Munich, 1956; *Scenografia* by Guido Frette, Milan, 1956; *Dizionario del Cinema Italiano 1945-1969* by Gianni Rondolino, Turin, 1969; *Le Decor de Film* by Leon Barsacq, Paris, 1970, as *Caligari's Cabinet and Other Grand Illusions,* Boston, 1976; *Scenografia in Italia Oggi* by Roberto Rebora, Milan, 1974; *Stage Design Throughout the World 1970-1975* by Rene Hainaux and Nicole Leclercq, Brussels and London, 1976; *I'Illusione Alternativa* by Franco Mancini, Turin, 1980.

*

Nowadays you can put on a play without scenery, without a theatre, without actors. Not without an audience. In the final analysis, it is the public that has determined the ways in which a play can be produced. It always has been that way, at every period in our civilization. Today, however, we are trying—at the moment of our creative activity—to orient, to pilot, and sometimes to record both our attitudes and our use (sometimes actually the philological use) of the techniques and materials in an area of research organized so as to accept, by absorbing them, the faculties and intentions of human nature and of life., The play can probably never be produced—never again—according to the rules of the original understanding, of tradition. The almost obsessional search for new and "unpublished" theatrical fields, the evocation of the single gesture/ symbol, of the impossible pure sound, of a new total protagonist, the actor-spectator, are simple confirmation of this endeavour.

The designer of scenery is no longer a decorator, an architect, a painter. For at least the past fifty years, he has been simply a person who is irremediably compromised, the clearest victim in the "new world of active vision and presence"; he is no longer the *grandemagosololuiautorizzato,* the one great self-authorized wizard, of the stage. He is, perhaps, just an anthropologist who studies and records the science of motivations. From A to Z.

—Gianni Polidori

*    *    *

Polidori's training in design was a concerted effort, embracing several disciplines: painting, theatre, and film. As a young man,

during World War II, he studied painting with the famous artists Renato Guttuso, and Vittorio Grassi, and later, after the war, with Corrado Cagli. No less auspicious was his schooling in stage design from 1945 to 1946 at the Accademia di Belle Arti, located in Rome. Soon after, he enrolled in the prestigious Centro Sperimentale di Cinematografia, also in Rome, completing the film design program in 1948. His design work in all of these fields has been distinctive, and has led to a long, illustrious career. Additionally, in 1959 he expanded his training in design by working in television.

In film, Polidori's work is well known because he has designed for such international film directors as Michelangelo Antonioni, Alessandro Blasetti, Vittorio Gassman, Alberto Lattuada, Franco Rossi, King Vidor, and Luchino Visconti. Starting out as an assistant designer to Chiari for *La Carozzo d'oro (The Golden Coach)* (1952), Polidori soon made his mark on the international film community by designing Visconti's neorealistic film, *Bellissima* (1952). This film concerns a stage mother who shuttles her daughter to audition after audition. Polidori provided sets that went from "beauty parlor to ballet and to sound stages," according to the New York Times review. Afterwards, he worked on Lattuada's production of Gogol's *Il Cappotto (The Overcoat)* (1953). His work with Antonioni in *I vinti (The Vanquished)* (1953), *La Signora senza Camellie* (1953), and *Le Amiche (The Girl Friends)* (1955), was equally impressive. León Barsacq, in *Le Decor de Film,* calls his settings "simple and incisive, a style that perfectly suited Antonioni's films." Polidori continued his designs for film into the 1960s with such works as *Il mondo di notte 2* (1960), and *Liola* (1963); and into the 1970s with *La proprieta 'non e' piu' un furto* (1971), and the "spaghetti western," *Il mio nome e' nessuno* (released in the U.S. as *My Name Is Nobody*) (1973). The latter, produced by Sergio Leone and starring Henry Fonda, was shot on location in New Mexico, Colorado, and Spain.

Polidori's stage designs have spanned five decades and range from drama and opera to ballet. He has variously functioned as set, lighting, and costumer designer, and has worked with well-known Italian stage directors such as Giancarlo Sbragia, Luigi Squarzino, and Luchino Visconti, among others. His first professional design was for Buchner's *Woyzeck* (1946), and showed a natural talent for correlating the visual elements of the set with the text in a simple manner. This production was followed by *L'Uomo e il fucile* (1947), and Arthur Miller's *All My Sons* (1947). In 1950, he married Misa D'Andrea, a costumer with whom he had worked on Ibsen's *The Master Builder* and *Enemy of the People* (both 1950).

Polidori has designed many American and British plays that were produced in Italy: Miller's *Death of a Salesman* (1951, in Italy with the Mirelli-Stoppa Company), in which he used Jo Mielziner's original backdrop, and *The Diary of Anne Frank* (1957), for which he created the split-scene attic set against a backdrop of a devastated Rotterdam. Other designs include Archibald MacLeish's *J.B.* (1958), M. V. Gazo's *Hatful of Rain* (1956), John Van Druten's *I Am A Camera* (1957), O'Neill's *The Iceman Cometh* (1965), John Osborne's *Look Back in Anger* (1957), Thornton Wilder's *Our Town* (1975), and Ben Hecht's and Charles McArthur's *The Front Page* (1988). Polidori's success at capturing an American ambience within the designs has been noted by various critics.

He has also designed plays for contemporary Italian playwrights, including *Affabulazione* (1986) by Pier Paolo Pasolini and *Two Farces* (1988) by Dario Fo. Equally adept at designing for the classical theatre, Polidori has applied his craft to such standard works as Moliere's *The Bourgeois Gentleman* (1953), Shakespeare's *Measure for Measure* (1957), *Hamlet* (1963), and *Julius Caesar* (presented at the Kansas City Music Hall in Missouri, 1965), and finally Goldsmith's *She Stoops to Conquer* (1981). Also, he has designed the ballets *Il Capello a tre punte* and *Scarlattiana* (1954), both choreographed by T. Wallmann.

Polidori's technique for design begins with an analysis of the text, from which the design derives its form. As a result of his classical training, his style is distinctive, relying upon strong composition and sufficient detail. He has, however, worked on a wide range of productions, designing abstract as well as realistic sets. His style, therefore, is best described as eclectic. Further, perhaps because of his involvement with film design, he has sometimes employed projections and lighting effects in his productions similar to those of Czechoslovakian scenographer, Josef Svoboda. One example was in his production of *Il Vizio Assurdo* (1974) by Diego Fabbri, produced at the Teatro Verdi in Padua. For this production, he created a set that was a constructivist arrangement of steps, platforms, and back panels on which vast projections appeared.

His illustrious designing career encompasses a multitude of other activities such as theatre consulting, exhibiting his paintings, and teaching. He has consulted on the laboratory theatre at the Nazionale d'Arte Drammatica Art in Rome, the Carlo Felice Theatre in Genoa, and the Teatro Cavour in Imperia, to name only a few examples. His paintings have been shown at major galleries, primarily in Italy. And, he has taught scenography at the Centro Sperimentale di Cinematographia in Rome in 1967-68, and taught as Associate Professor of Scenography at the Universitá degli Studi in Bologna 1971 to 1986. Dedicated to teaching, in 1983 he and Emmanuele Luzzati founded the Polytechnico 'G. Byron' Scuol di Communicazione visiva e scenografia in Genoa.

Philosophizing on the role of the scenographer in the theatre, Polidori's definition goes well beyond that of merely a decorator or architect. He sees the scenographer as an anthropologist, specifically, a person who is engaged in the study of human motivation and how it relates to the "new world of active vision and presence." To Polidori, the scenographer of today must have a thorough understanding of this world, and infuse it into the design.

—Tom Mikotowiez


# POND, Edward (Charles)
British painter, textile, graphic, and industrial designer

**Born:** London, 12 March 1929. **Education:** Royal Liberty School, Romford, Essex, until 1946; studied textiles and lithography, at Southeast Essex Technical College, Dagenham, NDD, 1955; Royal College of Art, London, Des. RCA, 1958. **Military Service:** Served in the British Army Parachute Regiment, 1947-49. **Family:** Married Grace Sparks in 1954; children: Christopher, Rebecca, and Hannah. **Career:** Design director, at Bernard Wardle (Everflex), North Wales, 1958-62, Bernard Wardle Fabrics, Derbyshire, 1962-65, and at The Wallpaper Manufacturers, London, 1965-76; founder-chairman of Edward Pond Associates design firm, London, from 1976; has designed for Crown Wallpapers, Heals Fabrics, Tomkinson Carpets, Edinburgh Weavers, Ford Motor Company, Antiference Limited, Reed Paper Group, Marley Tiles, and others. Also director of Polycell Products, London, 1968-71, Polypops Products, London, 1969-71, Paperchase Products, London, 1969-82, and Panache, London, 1972-76. President, Chartered Society of De-

signers, London, 1981-83. **Exhibitions:** Portmeirion, North Wales, 1960; Scott-Howard, London, 1987; Bournemouth College of Art, Hampshire, 1988; Medway College of Art, Kent, 1988. **Collections:** Victoria and Albert Museum, London; Whitworth Art Gallery, Manchester. **Honors:** Royal College of Art Silver Medal, London, 1958; Design Council Award, London, 1959; Public Arts Development Trust Prize, London, 1988; Packaging Association of America Award, 1988; fellow, Chartered Society of Designers, London, and Royal Society of Arts, London. **Address:** Edward Pond Associates, 9 Alfred Place, London WC1E 7EB, England.


## Works

Printed swimsuit fabric, for Clutsom and Kemp, 1958.
*Harlequin* range of textiles and wallcoverings, for Bernard Wardle, 1958-59.
*Piazza* printed PVC fabric, for Bernard Wardle, 1960.
*Scene Collection* range of wallcoverings, for Crown Wallpapers, 1966.
*Britannia* printed metal serving tray, for Polypops Products, 1969.
Irish tweed suiting fabrics, for Foxford Woollens, 1977.
Wool upholstery fabrics, for Yorkshire Tweed, 1978.
Cosmetic products and packaging, for Boots the Chemist, from 1983.
Screenprinted fabric wall panels at Heathrow, for the British Airports Authority, 1984.
Network Southeast murals and line brand insignia, for the British Railways Board, 1987-88.
Mural panels in melamine laminate, for British Rail/Public Arts Development Trust, 1988.
*Armada 400* ceramic mural, for the City of Plymouth, 1988.


## Publications

**By POND: books**—*Anti-Rationalists,* London, 1960; *A. H. Mackmurdo: His Life and Work,* thesis, London, 1962; *Historic Wallpapers in the Whitworth Gallery,* Manchester, 1972; **articles**—in *The Designer* (London), July/August 1975, December 1982; *The Times* (London), 3 July 1980, 1 June 1981, 12 June 1981.

**On POND: books**—*Designers in Britain 5* edited by Herbert Spencer, London, 1957; *Did Britain Make It? British Design in Context 1946-86* edited by Penny Sparke, London, 1986; **articles**—in the *Financial Times* (London), 22 August 1975; *Greenville News* (South Carolina), 12 April 1978; *The Designer* (London), June 1978, May 1981.

*

Colour, pattern, and texture are the ingredients of what we wear, use, and live with. They are the basic component parts used by designers who design for products as diverse as furnishings, carpets, wallpapers, bed linen, gift wrap, and so on. As such, they are subject for commercial success to the vagaries of fashion—not fashion in the simple, dress sense, but the changes in the design scene which move with the Zeit Geist.

My interest as stylist, producer, coordinator, or what you will, has been to define marketing objectives for design collections, to brief designers, to find designs, and to make it all work. One example of this is the Zambezi Collection (1982), for a manufacturer printing in Zimbabwe: a range of all-cotton furnishing fabrics with a distinct local look—but not ethnic—yet all designed in England. On the same basis, I have produced design collections on special themes for Japan, the United States, South Africa, and Australia.

The best designers are always part of a collection, and collections are at their best when planned. In this way, the best individual characteristics of designers can be used to advantage, as in casting the actors in a play. Viable design statements can be formulated to set trends and influence design worldwide. Good examples are the Palladio Wallpaper Collections, no longer in production, which set out to interpret trends in painting, as large-scale, and sometimes very large-scale, wallcoverings. For twenty years, from 1955-75, these collections moved through tachism, Op art, Pop art, "new" art nouveau, decorative romanticism, and a few styles that never quite "made it." Palladio, along with Heals Fabrics, were without doubt the greatest incentives to the creative ingenuity of British designers during this period, and I was fortunate enough to be involved with both.

It is these design/marketing concepts which interest me in particular. Other specific examples of commercial successes are Harlequin for Bernard Wardle (1958), and the Scene Collection for Crown Wallcoverings (1966).

For some years, my design involvement has been in the coordination of wide ranges of domestic products and now includes the incorporation of packaging, graphics, and promotional materials.

—Edward Pond

\*    \*    \*

In a business where designers often take a low profile, Edward Pond is a colourful personality with an eighteenth-century ebullience and a determination to succeed. His reputation as a designer derives from his combination of ability to interpret modern style and a strong sense for what will actually sell. On leaving art school, he was quickly promoted to chief designer with Bernard Wardle, a company committed to 1950s contemporary taste. Then invited to design textiles for Heals, the London furniture store, he benefited from their policy of promoting young talent (a tactic that was helping British textile designers to achieve an international reputation). Inevitably, London design of the 1960s made a deep impact on his work. This period looked very closely at stylistic revivals, particularly art nouveau, which became the score for many of his patterns. Pond followed through on this interest with the publication of his thesis on the late nineteenth-century designer A. H. Mackmurdo.

Some of his most innovative work was for Palladio Wallpaper, a company whose design policy set out to interpret trends in fine art, and the designs he produced there remain a case study of style throughout the period, including as they do a range from Op- and Pop- inspired patterns, to a more decorative romanticism. Style was not, however, his only concern, and Pond has worked closely with the developments in technology affecting post-war textiles. For the Reed Paper group, he worked on experimental uses for non-woven fabric; for Northern Bedding, the development of coated fabrics for mass-produced upholstered fabrics; for Bernard Wardle, stretch covers.

Since he set up Edward Pond Associates in 1976, his design interests have widened to include packaging, graphics, and design consultancy. Some examples of his company's projects include the

1982 Zambezi collection of cotton furnishing fabrics, designed with a local feel for a manufacturer printing in Zimbabwe, and the design of toiletries, packaging, logo, and graphics for the major retailer and manufacturer Boots the Chemists.

—Catherine McDermott

## PONNELLE, Jean-Pierre

French film and stage designer

**Born:** Paris, 19 February 1932. **Education:** Studied philosophy and art history, at the Sorbonne, Paris, 1949-52. **Military Service:** Served in the French Army, in Algeria, 1959-61. **Family:** Married Margit Saad in 1957; son: Pierre-Dominicq. **Career:** Freelance designer from 1952, and stage director from 1961: designed productions for the Hannover Opera, New York Metropolitan Opera, Vienna State Opera, Munich State Opera, Dusseldorf Schauspielhaus, Zurich Opera, Covent Garden Opera, San Francisco Opera, Chicago Lyric Opera, and for the Salzburg and Bayreuth Festivals. **Died:** Munich, West Germany, 11 August 1988.

### Works

Major stage productions include—*Boulevard Solitude,* Hannover Opera, 1952; *Il Barbiere di Siviglia,* Salzburg Festival, 1968; *Pelleas et Melisande,* Munich State Opera, 1978; *Contes d'Hoffmann,* Salzburg Festival, 1980-82; *Don Giovanni,* Lyric Opera, Chicago, 1980; *Tristan und Isolde,* Bayreuth Festival, 1981; *Lear,* San Francisco Opera, 1981; *I Pagliacci,* Houston Opera, 1982; *Idomeneo,* Metropolitan Opera, New York, 1982; *Mitridate,* Zurich Opera, 1983; *Liebesverbot,* Munich State Opera, 1983; *Parsifal, Cosi Fan Tutte,* Paris Opera, 1983; *Parsifal,* Cologne Opera, 1983; *Idomeneo,* Salzburg Festival, 1983; *Fidelio,* Berlin Opera, 1984; *Nozze di Figaro,* Paris Opera, 1984; *Aida,* Royal Opera House, London, 1984; *Clemenza di Tito,* Metropolitan Opera, New York, 1984; *Cavalliera/Pagliacci,* Vienna State Opera, 1984. Films include-*Carmina Burana, Nozze di Figaro, n Barbniere di Siviglia, Clemenza di Tito, Madama Butterfly, Incoronazione di Poppea, Ritorno d'Ulisse in Patria, Orfeo, Tristan und Isolde, La Cenerentola, Rigoletto.*

### Publications

**On PONNELLE: books**—*Who's Who in Opera* edited by Maria F. Rich, New York, 1976; *Who's Who in Arts and Literature* edited by Karl Strute and Theodor Doelken, Zurich, 1982; *The Cambridge Guide to World Theatre* edited by Martin Banham, Cambridge, 1988.

\*    \*    \*

Ponnelle began his career in theatrical design, but he soon came to realize that in opera he could give the production his own, personal stamp only if he also acted as the stage director. His first great international success was as the director-designer of *Il Barbiere de Siviglia* at Salzburg in 1968, and this reputation was solidified by his 1973 Munich production of *Pelléas et Melisande,* a masterpiece of poetry and symbolism, a feast for both eye and ear. Though most critics have felt that he was at his best with the great, romantic, Italian operas by Rossini, Verdi, and Donizetti, he also achieved success with Mozart.

Ponnelle's approach was to put aside the history of an opera's production and the writings on how it should be interpreted and to look at the story and listen to the music as if they had never been read or heard before. Then, he slowly and carefully developed a personal interpretation that he hoped would make the audience also hear and see the opera as if for the first time. Sometimes, this meant shifting emphases or even scenes, a practice which frequently created sharp controversy, but his end result was always theatrically effective. For Mozart's *Idomeneo,* he took the design of one of the large, Mannerist stone masks of a god from the Tivoli Gardens outside Rome, enlarged it to tremendous size, and placed it on stage to brood over the mythological events transpiring on the stage below, as if it embodied the power of the Greek god Poseidon. He designed the costumes in a mixture of eighteenth-century and Greek fashions, thus reflecting both the nature of the Greek story and the eighteenth-century character of the music.

Always Ponnelle looked for the visual metaphor that would make an opera visually vivid and theatrically pleasurable. He was very aware that opera operates on an audience as much visually as aurally, and he was determined that in his productions there would be no separation between the two. Therefore, once he worked out the setting and costumes for an opera, he directed the stage movement to enhance in every way the visual metaphor of the production. Despite critics' objections to Ponnelle's approach, his visual production was always at the service of the composer and his music. Thus, Ponnelle's greatest influence on the contemporary opera scene was to make the visual production match and equal the musical component in the appreciation of the audience.

—Douglas A. Russell

# PONTI, Gio(vanni)

Italian architect, interior, exhibition, and industrial designer

**Born:** Milan, 18 November 1891. **Education:** Studied architecture, at the Politecnico, Milan, Dip. Arch., 1921. **Military Service:** Italian Army, 1916-18. **Family:** Married Giulia Vimercati in 1921; four children. **Career:** Worked in the architectural studio of Mino Fiocchi and Emilio Lancia, Milan, 1921; designer and product renovator at the Richard Ginori factory, in Milan and Florence, 1923-30; partner, with Emilio Lancia, in Studio Ponti e Lancia architectural firm, Milan, 1927-33; partner, with Antonio Fornaroli and Eugenio Soncini, in Studio Ponti/Fornaroli/Soncini architectural firm, Milan 1933-45; partner, with Fornaroli and Alberto Rosselli, in Studio Ponti/Fornaroli/Rosselli architectural firm, Milan, 1952-76; designed for La Pavoni, La Visa, Argenteria Krupp, Fraser, Greco, Cassina, Edison, Singer, Gallieni, Marazza, Ideal Standard Nordiska Kompaniet, La Luma, Christofle, Rima, Colombi, Arreduluce, Knoll, and others. Founder, 1928, and editor, 1928-41, 1948-79, of *Domus* magazine, Milan; director, *Stile* magazine, Milan, 1941-47. Executive director of the Monza Biennale, subsequently the Milan Triennale, 1933-79; general supervisor of the Italia 61 exhibition in Turin, 1961, and of the Eurodomus exhibitions in Genoa and other

Italian cities, 1966-69. Professor of architecture, Politecnico, Milan, 1936-61; president, Collegio Lombardo degli Architetti, Milan, 1957-60, and the International Museum of Modern Architecture, Milan, 1961.**Member:** Corresponding member, Royal Institute of British Architects; Accademia di San Luca, Rome. **Exhibitions:** Florence, 1937; Galleria Gianferrari, Milan, 1939, 1951; Galleria dell'Obelisco, Rome, 1950; Institute of Contemporary Art, Boston, 1954 (toured); Galleria La Bussola, Turin, 1955; AB Ferdinand Lundquist, Goteborg, 1956; Galleria del Sole, Milan, 1956; Christofle, Paris, 1957; Liberty's, London, 1957; Galleria del Disegno, Milan, 1959; University of California at Los Angeles, 1966 (toured); Galleria de Nieubourg, Milan, 1967; Galleria Toselli, Milan, 1978; Centro Internazionale di Brera, Milan, 1982; University of Padua, 1989. **Honors:** War Cross and Military Medal, Italian Army, 1918; University of Padua English Building Prize, 1934; Art Prize, Accademia d'Italia, 1945; Compasso d'Oro Award, Milan, 1956; Academie d'Architecture Gold Medal, Paris, 1968. Honorary doctorate, Royal College of Art, London, 1958; honorary associate, American Institute of Architects. **Died:** Milan, September 1979.

## Works

*Grotesque* tableware in white porcelain with blue and gold decoration, for Richard Ginori/Doccia, 1923-35.
*The Classic Conversation* bowls, vases, and lamps, in porcelain, for Richard Ginori/ Doccia, 1924-28.
*Orfeo* costumes and scenery, for Teatro alla Scala, Milan, 1949.
Self-illuminating furniture, for the Casa Cremaschi, Milan, 1949.
Espresso coffee machines, for La Pavoni, 1949.
*Leggera* wooden chair with woven rush seat, for Cassina, 1951.
Tables and upholstered chairs, for the Singer Company of New York, 1952.
*Distex* armchair, for Cassina, 1953.
Sanitary fittings, for Ideal Standard, 1953.
*Superleggera* wooden chair with woven rush seat, for Cassina, 1955.
Cutlery and silverwares, for Christofle, 1955, 1958.
Desk in metal, for Rima, 1955.
Pirelli skyscraper building, Milan, 1956 (with Nervi, Danuso, Fornaroii, Roselli, Valtolina and dell'Orto).
*Italia 61* exhibition layouts, Turin, 1961 (with Nervi).
Pavilion at the Milan Fair for Montecatini, 1962.
*Armchair 1215* in walnut with rattan seat, for Knoll International, 1964.
De Bijenkorf shopping center, Eindhoven, 1967 (with Boosten, Negri, and Gast).
Lamps in plastic, for Guzzini, 1968.
Cathedral of Taranto, Italy, 1971.
Denver Museum of Modern Art, Colorado, 1972 (with Sudler and Cronenwett).

(for a complete list of Ponti's buildings and architectural projects, see *Contemporary Architects*)

## Publications

**By PONTI: books**—*La Casa all'Italiana,* Milan, 1933; (with Leonardo Sinisgalli) *Italiani,* Milan, 1937; *Il Coro,* Milan, 1944; *Cifre Parlan I,* Milan, 1944; *Politica dell'Architectura,* Milan, 1944;

*Ideario,* Milan, 1945; *L'Architectura e un Cristallo,* Milan, 1945; *Verso la Casa Esatta,* Milan, 1945; *Ringrazio Iddio che le Cosi non vanno a Mode Mio,* Milan, 1946; *Paradiso Perduto,* Milan, 1956; *Amata l'Architettura,* Genoa, 1957, as *In Praise of Architecture,* New York 1960; *Milano Oggi,* Milan, 1957; *Nuvole sono Immagini,* Milan, 1968.

**On PONTI: books**—*Mobili Tipici Moderni* by G. C. Palanti, Milan, 1933; *Espressione di Giovanni Ponti* by James S. Plaut, Milan, 1954; *Forme Nuove in Italia* by Agnoldomenico Pica, Milan and Rome, 1957; *Ponti: Summing Up* by Mario Labo, Milan, 1958; *World Furniture* edited by Helena Hayward, London, 1965, 1981; *The Modern Chair: 1850 to Today* by Gilbert Frey, London and Niederteufen, 1970; *Design e Forme Nuove nell'Arredamento Italiano* edited by Paolo Portoghesi and Marino Marini, Rome, 1978; *Atlante del Design Italiano 1940/1980* by Alfonso Grassi and Anty Pansera, Milan, 1980; *Gio Ponti alla Manifatura di Doccia* by Paolo Portoghesi and Anty Pansera, Milan, 1982; *Mid-Century: Furniture of the 1950s* by Cara Greenberg, London, 1984; *The Hot House: Italian New Wave Design* by Andrea Branzi, London, 1984; *Modern Furniture Classics* by Miriam Stimpson, London, 1987; *Italian Design: 1870 to the Present* by Penny Sparke, London and New York, 1988; *Italian Modern: A Design Heritage* by Giovanni Albera and Nicolas Monti, New York, 1989; *Gio Ponti Designer: Padova 1936-1941* by Mario Universo, Padua, 1989.

\*     \*     \*

It is impossible to assess Gio Ponti's contribution as a design professional independent from the journal *Domus,* which is devoted to architecture, interiors, industrial design, and art—all of which he himself cherished. However, he did consider himself first and foremost an architect: "I think [about architecture] at night, and work [on architecture] during the day." It is important to note that the original title of his major book was *Amare L'Architeura* [*Love Architecture*], a more definitive command than the English translation, *In Praise of Architecture.*

Graduated in 1921 from Milan's prestigious Politecnico School of Architecture and somewhat stifled by unsuccessful participation in several architectural competitions, Ponti turned to other forms of cultural expression; he developed what would become a life-long interest in painting and concurrently produced ceramic and porcelain designs for one of the largest Italian manufacturers. Appointed a director of the Second Biennial Exposition of Decorative Arts at Monza, and reappointed to succeeding expositions, he eventually helped to expand the fair and move it to Milan in 1933 as the Fifth Triennial Exhibition of Modern Art and Modern Architecture (thereafter, "Ponti's Trienniale"). Ponti continued with the sixth and seventh Triennials, thereby establishing the groundwork for exhibitions that are still held regularly, enjoy an international reputation, and contribute to Italian prominence in design.

Ponti's first architectural commission (1926) was for a house, outside of Paris, for the President of Christofle, a firm for which he eventually designed some tableware. His architectural designs in these early years expressed the neoclassical overtones which were the mode of the day in Italy—a "modern" style which would eventually be dubbed "fascist" as a political system attempted to clothe itself in contemporary dress.

Ponti's first major commission (1936) was for the first of two buildings (the other was commissioned in 1951) for the expansion of the facilities for the Montecatini company, Italy's major chemi-

cal concern. Its design marked a change from the earlier work but still presented a rather formal, stone facade perforated with individual window units in a regular, somewhat scale-less manner, presenting a design problem which Ponti did not completely resolve until twenty years later. The building appeared as if it could be expanded laterally and/or vertically ad infinitum; it had no definite limits. At this same time, he began teaching at his former school.

Four years later, architectural work waned in Italy, as in the rest of the world, when war intervened, but the desire for housing after the war and the obvious need to rebuild facilities destroyed in the conflict presented major opportunities for many architects, Ponti among them. In the early 1950s, Ponti also became involved in the design of the interiors of several Italian steamships, including some for the ill-fated *Andria Doria.* Industrial design products, including an espresso coffee maker with the sleek lines and chrome of a modern automobile, sewing machines, and, of course, furniture, including the now classic La Leggera chair—a simple study in wood with a rush seat—rounded out the oeuvre of this multi-faceted person.

Ponti's unrealized proposal for the Italian Brazilian Center in Sao Paulo (1953) narrowed his search for a definitive form. An attempt was made here to limit the facade and the shape of the building and to define it as a complete entity. In a similar manner, his designs for Ideal Standard's sanitary fixtures remolded the basic shape and derived their final form from a purely functional aesthetic. "I am not a tailor, I am an architect. I am not interested in the fashionable novelty," he stated.

In the Pirelli office building, the search and experimentation culminated. This thirty-two story office tower for a rubber manufacturing firm is perched atop a plaza on an irregularly shaped plot. The plaza itself houses a parking facility for 2,000 cars and provides separation of visitor and employee entrances as well as the necessary service access facilities, all planned around a careful analysis of the functional requirements of circulation and traffic flow. The floors above are supported by a unique structural system designed in collaboration with the masterful Italian engineer Pier Luigi Nervi; concrete fingers thrusting upward carry the floors and roof.

However successful the functional and structural organization, in the visual form of the building lies Ponti's innovation. In the hands of lesser designers, this form might have again been an endless rectangular prism, but as it is, in plane it tapers at its ends, clearly suggesting that no further extension is possible, and in elevation the tapers form solids to bracket the bands of glass windows. The whole is capped by a broad, sheltering, cantilevered roof—a "hat"—which terminates the vertical extension. Ponti had achieved his forma finita.

Ponti's designs in the 1960s took a different tack, apparently an exploration of the enclosure as a "screen"; these experiments led to less successful solutions. From a high-rise apartment in Milan to a department store in Holland to the cathedral in Toronto to the Denver Art Museum, exterior walls take on the role of irregularly perforated masks, often disguising completely the role of the space beyond. Somewhat Middle-Eastern in form and character, they clearly denied the structural and functional role of the volumes they enclosed. Ponti's search for form had perhaps become a psychedelic experience: "Imagination is the ecstasy of a vision."

From its founding in 1928 (with the exception of the wartime period 1941-47) until his death in 1979, Ponti was the editor and motivating source from behind the successful and highly influential magazine *Domus.* He was quick to detect (and in some cases helped to establish) trends and directions in art, architecture, and design.

Just as in his office and at school, talented young artists and designers received his support and encouragement; through pages rich in color and line, they were welcomed into homes, offices, and schools throughout the world. A large portion of Ponti's energies were directed toward helping, influencing, and stimulating others. The late Charles Eames once commented on Ponti's "willingness and need to be completely involved in anything he does. His masteries of skill are those that seem to come automatically to the special few who have the capacity for really caring."

—William Victor Kriebel

# PORSCHE, Ferdinand (Alexander)
German/Austrian automobile and product designer

**Born:** Stuttgart, Germany, 11 December 1935. **Education:** Apprenticed in engineering, at the Bosch Company, Stuttgart; studied at the Hochschule für Gestaltung, Ulm; apprenticed in engineering and design studios, Porsche AG, Stuttgart-Zuffenhausen. **Family:** Married Brigitte Porsche in 1960; children: Ferdinand, Kai, and Mark-Philipp. **Career:** Head of design, 1961-72, and vice-president, 1969-72, of Porsche AG, Stuttgart-Zuffenhausen; founder and director of Porsche Design, in Stuttgart, 1972-75, and in Zell am See, Austria, from 1975; has designed for Yashica, Puch, Roemer, Carrera, British Broadcasting Corporation, and others. **Collections:** Kunstgewerbemuseum, Zurich; Museum of Modern Art, New York. **Honors:** International Automobile Industry Trophy, 1968; Austrian Design Prize, 1979, 1980. **Address:** Porsche Design, Flugplatzstrasse 29, A-5700 Zell am See, Austria.

## Works

*Porche 804 Formula I* racing car, for Porsche AG, 1961.
*Porsche 904* racing/sports car, for Porsche AG, 1963.
*Porsche 911* and *Targa* version sports limousine, for Porsche AG, 1963.
*Contax* camera, for Yashica, 1974.
*Cobra* motorcycle, for Steyr-Puch, 1976.
Motorcycle helmet, for Roemer, 1976.
*Model 911* sunglasses with interchangeable lenses, for Carrera, 1977.
Experimental racing bicycle, for Steyr-Puch/America, 1977.
*Servogor 281* and *Servogor 460* electronic plotting instruments, for the British Broadcasting Corporation, 1978-80.
*AMK* alternative motorcycle project, for *Motorrad* magazine, 1979.

## Publications

**On PORSCHE: books**—*The Porsche Story* by Julius Joseph Weitmann, New York, 1968, 1985; *Automobile Design: Great Designers and Their Work* edited by Ronald Barker and Anthony Harding, Newton Abbot, 1970; *Deutsche Autos 1945-1975* by Werner Oswald, Stuttgart, 1976; *The Library of Motoring: The Designers* by I. J. K. Setright, London, 1976; *Das grosse Buch der Porsche-Typen* by Lothar Boschen and Jurgen Barth, Stuttgart, 1977, as *The Porsche Book*, Cambridge, 1978, 1983; *In Good Shape: Style in Industrial Products Since 1960* by Stephen Bayley, London, 1979; *Industrial Design* by John Heskett, London, 1980; *Porsche*

*Past and Present* by Denis Jenkinson, London, 1983; *Porsche* by Anders Ditlev Clausager, New York, 1983; *Les Années 60* by Anne Bony, Paris, 1983; *The Conran Directory of Design* edited by Stephen Bayley, London, 1985; *Porsche: Portrait of a Legend* by Ingo Seiff, London, 1985, 1989; *Design Source Book* by Penny Sparke and others, London, 1986.

*See* PORSCHE DESIGN

\*

Product design, intended to maintain its appeal beyond today and tomorrow, must follow a number of essential maxims, without which any design becomes mere formalism, and creativity, a useless formula. The problem is to achieve the right balance between principal objectives that seem to compete with each other—e.g., "economy" as opposed to "beauty"—without giving in to a one-sided, intolerant design philosophy.

Correct product design means several things: domination of the whole product over its individual parts; functional styling from the inside, instead of external styling of an article following completion; realism in detecting what is possible, concentration on an assessable future instead of utopian speculation; development of new technologies and products to meet market potentials, and, last but not least, a genuine team spirit to accumulate the knowledge of specialists. Our primary objective is to improve the quality of human life by allowing design and function to complement, not to obstruct, each other, and by concentrating equally on aesthetic, technical, and practical function.

Typical of our approach is the development of our alternative motorcycle concept (AMK) as the result of a competition with such designers as Hans A. Muth and Giorgetto Giugiaro for the *Motorrad* magazine in Germany. It was conceived for a society with limited traffic space and limited energy resources.

The vehicle of the future is a motorcycle—but a rather special motorcycle, with its chassis, engine, and wheels enclosed in aerodynamic body panels for the rider's greater comfort and safety. My vehicle is based on the Yamaha SR 500 motorcycle. The glass-reinforced, plastic body panels that were added to the standard motorcycle help to keep a rider clean without the need for special protective clothing. The body panels also allow the owner to clean the machine with a hose without fear of soaking exposed mechanical parts. For safety, the leg supports—or fairings, as they are called—have built-in knee protectors and are designed to throw a rider clear of the handlebars in the event of a crash. Beneath all this futuristic body work, the Porsche design incorporates convenience features that lift motorcycle riding out of the limited realm of enthusiasts and into the reach of people who desire basic transportation. The bike has an automatic transmission, a car-like pedal-brake, adjustable handlebars and seat, and built-in hand-warmers.

—Ferdinand Alexander Porsche

# PORSCHE DESIGN
Austrian product, industrial, and furniture design company

**Founded** by Ferdinand Alexander Porsche (born 1935) in Stuttgart, Germany, 1972; offices moved to Zell am See in Salzburg, Austria, from 1975; principals in 1996 included Siegfried Ebner, Simon Fraser, Andreas Hentschel, Gerlinde Krempl, Bernd Meyerspeer, F. A. Porsche, Thomas Rudolph, Dirk Schmauser, Detlef Schmidt, Christian Schwamkrug, Jörg Tragatschnig, and Heidi Zauner. **Collections:** Museum of Modern Art, New York; Neue Sammlung, Munich. **Honors:** Compasso d'Oro Award nomination, Center for Design, Milan, 1982; Gute Industrieform Prize, 1989; Award for good industrial design, Industrieforum, Hannover, Design Center, Stuttgart, and Haus Industrieform, Essen, 1994. **Addresses:** (design) Porsche Design Ges.m.b.H., Flugplatzstrasse 29, A-5700 Zell am See, Austria; (marketing) Porsche Design Management, Ges.m.b.H. & Co. KG, Südtiroler Platz 11, A-5020 Salzburg, Austria.

### Works

*Integral CP4* motorcycle helmet, for Kiwi, Switzerland, 1976.
Electric measuring and testing equipment, for BBC-Mettra-Watt/Görz, Germany and Austria, from 1978.
*Compass, Chrono 02, Diver's,* and *Ultra Sportiva* watches, for IWC, Switzerland, from 1978.
Standard telephone, for NEC, Japan, 1981.
*Titanium* line of pens, for Faber-Castell, Germany, 1981.
*Kandido* adjustable table lamp, for Luci S.p.A, Italy, 1982.
Adjustable lounge chair and office furniture, for Poltrona Frau, Italy, 1982.
*Sintheto* system of wall, table, and floor lamps, for Luci, 1984.
"Main-frame" personal computer, for Time Ltd., Australia, 1984.
*IP 84 S* adjustable lounge chair, for Interprofil, Germany, 1984.
Compact headphones, for Yamaha, Japan, 1984.
*Contax T* 35mm compact camera, for Yashica, Japan, 1984.
Compact electric razor, for Payer Elektroproducte Ges.m.b.H, Austria, 1985.
*Mikado* display and exhibition lighting system, for Artemide Litech, Italy, 1985.
*Soft Line* pens, for Faber-Castell, 1987.
*Supernova* washing machine, for Eudora, Austria, 1989.
Telephone, for the German Federal Postal Administration, 1989.
Television set, for Grundig, Germany, 1989.
Bathroom furniture and accessories system, for Laufen, Switzerland, 1989.
*Jazz* halogen table lamp, for Paf, Italy, 1989.
*Luci e Ombre* pots and pans, for Barazzoni, Italy, 1989.
*Espressomachine* espresso maker, for Barazzoni, 1990.
Rechargeable razor, for Payer, Austria, 1990.
*Convex* interior door, for Tre Più, Italy, 1990.
Bathroom mixers (water fixtures), for M & Z, Switzerland, 1990.
*Möve* lighting system, for Artemide, 1991.
*Record* answering machine, for Zettler/Deutsche Telekom, Germany, 1992.
Bathroom furniture, for Das Bad GmbH, Austria, 1993.
*E 72-911* television set, for Grundig AG, Fürth, 1993.
Auto-telephone, for Peiker acustic, 1993.
Automobile antenna for CB, radio, and television, for Sirtel, Italy, 1993.
Steering wheel and aluminum wheel, for Votex GmbH, Germany, 1993.
*World-Time* and *Titan Automatic* watches, for Porsche Design/IWC, 1993.
*The Style* sunglasses, for Carrera/Porsche Design, 1993.
Ultra-low floor tram, for SGP, Vienna, developed, 1993, operational, 1995.
*Scooter* motorbike, for Hero, India, 1994.
*ECX-1* camera, for Samsung, Korea, 1994.

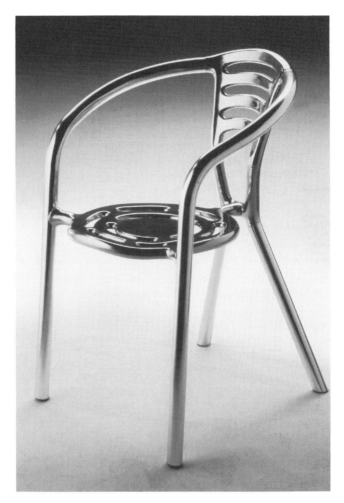

**Porsche Design:** *BOULEVARD* **bistro-chair for Ycami, Italy, 1994**

*Lavotop "S"* bathroom accessories, for Das Bad, 1994.
*Handyman* electronic personal organizer, for Peiker acustic, Germany, 1994.
*2001* house door, for Weru, Germany, 1994.
*Boulevard* bistro chair and *Tubo* table in aluminum, for Ycami, Italy, 1994.
*F O.9* sports sunglasses, for Carrera/Porsche Design Products, 1995.
*Cordless Telephone,* for Samsung Electronics, 1996.
*ULF,* a new Vienna Street Car (TRAM), 1997.
Porsche Design has also developed a proposal for a Computer Aided Taxi System (CATS), a line of smoking accessories, including *Piezo* and *Softline* lighters and *The Pipe,* and leather goods, including an attaché case, belt, and currency binder.

*See* PORSCHE, Ferdinand

# POWELL, Anthony
British film, stage, and interior designer

**Born:** Chorlton-cum-Hardy, Lancashire, 2 June 1935. **Education:** Educated at William Hulme's Grammar School, Manchester, 1940-

46, and Saint Andrew's College, Dublin, 1946-53; studied under Norah Waugh, Margaret Woodward, Ruth Keating, and Alan Davie, at the Central School of Art and Design, London, 1955-58. **Military Service:** Served in the Royal Corps of Signals, British Army on the Rhine, 1953-55. **Career:** Costume designer, Oxford Playhouse, 1958-60; freelance stage designer, from 1960, film designer, from 1968, and interior designer, from 1978. Assistant to Cecil Beaton and Oliver Messel for galas and theatrical events in London, 1958; consultant, to Sabre Sportswear, Jantzen Swimwear, and others, London, 1960-69; lecturer in theatre design, Central School of Art and Design, London, 1958-71. **Exhibitions:** *Pirates,* National Maritime Museum, London, 1992-95. **Collections:** Victoria and Albert Museum, London; Los Angeles County Museum, California; American Museum of the Moving Image, New York. **Honors:** Royal Society of Arts Travel Scholarship, London, 1958; Antoinette Perry (Tony) Award, New York, 1963; Academy Award, Hollywood, 1972, 1979, 1981; Los Angeles Drama Critics Award, 1979, 1993; British Academy Award, 1979; Cesar Award, France, 1987; Dramalogue Critics Award, 1993; Ovations Award, Los Angeles, 1994. **Address:** c/o The London Company, 17 Wilton Place, Knightsbridge, London SW1X 8RL, England.

**Works**

Stage productions include—*Rinaldo,* Sadlers Wells, London, 1960 (and for Komisches Oper, East Berlin, Handel Festival, Halle, East Germany, and the Leipzig Opera House); *School for Scandal,* Haymarket Theatre, London, 1961 (toured the United States); *Women Beware Women,* Royal Shakespeare Company, Arts Theatre, London, 1961; *Comedy of Errors,* Royal Shakespeare Company, Stratford-upon-Avon and London, 1962 (and world tour); *La Belle Helene,* Sadlers Wells, 1962; *Capriccio,* Glyndebourne Opera, Sussex, 1963; *Il Seraglio,* Sadlers Wells, 1963; *Martin's Lie,* American television, 1965; *The Rivals,* Haymarket Theatre, London, 1966; *Fish Out of Water,* London, 1971; *Private Lives,* Queen's Theatre, London, 1972 (toured the United States); *Ring Around the Moon,* Ahmansan Theatre, Los Angeles, 1975; *Amadeus,* Theatre Marigny, Paris, 1982; *Lettice and Louage,* Ethel Barrymore Theatre, New York, 1990; *Hay Fever,* Albery Theatre, London, 1992; *Trelawny of the Wells,* Royal National Theatre, London, 1992; *Sunset Boulevard,* London and Los Angeles, 1993, New York, 1994, Toronto and Frankfurt, 1995.

**Anthony Powell: Costume for Raj Sinjh in Stephen Spielberg's *Indiana Jones and the Temple of Doom,* 1984. Photo: Keith Hamshere**

Film costume designs include—*Royal Hunt of the Sun,* 1968; *Joe Egg,* 1969; *A Town Called Bastard,* 1970; *Nicholas and Alexandra,* 1971; *Travels with My Aunt,* 1972; *Papillon* (Schaffner), 1973; *That Lucky Touch* (Miles), 1974; *Buffalo Bill and the Indians* (Altman), 1975; *Sorcerer* (Friedkin), 1976; *Death on the Nile* (Guillermin), 1977; *Tess* (Polanski), 1978-79; *Priest of Love* (Miles), 1980; *Evil under the Sun* (Hamilton), 1981; *Indiana Jones and the Temple of Doom* (Spielberg), 1983; *Pirates* (Polanski), 1984-85; *Ishtar* (May), 1985-86; *Frantic* (Polanski), 1987; *Indiana Jones and the Last Crusade* (Spielberg), 1988; *Hook* (Spielberg), 1990-91.

## Publications

**By POWELL: books—** (illustrator) *William Shakespeare: The Comedy of Errors,* London, 1969.

**On POWELL: books—***Designing and Making Stage Costumes,* London, 1964; *International Film and Television Yearbook 1979-80* edited by Peter Noble, London, 1979; **articles—***Women's Wear Daily* (New York), 1979; *Denver Post,* 4 March 1982; *Los Angeles Times,* 12 March 1982; *New York Times,* 12 May 1983; interview by John Calhoun in *Theatre Crafts International,* February 1995.

\*

As I see it, the job of the designer in theatre, cinema, or television is essentially an interpretive one—to give visual expression or emphasis to the intentions of the writer/composer, the director, and the performer. This demands not only creative and imaginative ability but a sympathetic understanding of others' points of view in order to achieve a cohesive whole, whilst still being able to make a positive statement of one's own. A talent for designing is, in itself, only fifty percent of the job.

—Anthony Powell

# PREDOCK, Antoine

American architect

**Born:** Lebanon, Missouri, 24 June 1936. **Education:** Attended University of New Mexico, 1957-61; Columbia University, B.Arch., 1962, postgraduate fellow, 1963. **Family:** Married Jennifer Rebecca Masley, November 2, 1964 (divorced 1979); children: Hadrian, Jason. **Career:** Designer, M. Pei & Partners, New York City, 1962-64; designer, with Gerald McCue Associates, San Francisco, California, 1964-67; founder and principal, Antoine Predock, Architect, Albuquerque, New Mexico, from 1967. Kea Distinguished Professor, at the University of Maryland, 1981-82; visiting professor, Arizona State University, Tempe, 1982-84, Southern California Institute of Architecture, 1984, 1990, Harvard University, 1987, and Clemson University, 1988; visiting critic, University of California, Los Angeles, 1989-91; Robert Mills Distinguished Professor, Clemson University, 1995; frequent lecturer at universities and conferences throughout the world; frequent member of juries and award panels. **Member:** Fellow, American Institute of Architects. **Exhibitions:** *Des Architectures de Terre,* Centre Georges

Pompidou, Paris, France, 1981; *The Making of an Architect,* National Academy of Design, New York, 1981; *Annual Exhibition,* American Academy in Rome, 1985; *The Inhabited Landscape,* Urban Center, New York, 1987; *Frammenti d'Italia,* Graham Gallery, Albuquerque, 1987; *Recent Works,* Harvard University Graduate School of Design, 1987; ADPSR Benefit Exhibit, Max Protetch Gallery, New York, 1988; *Unbuilt Architecture of the 80's,* Cooper-Hewitt Museum, New York, 1988; Gallery for Architecture, Los Angeles, CA, 1988; *California Lifeguard Towers,* Kirsten Kiser, Santa Monica, 1988; *Art in Architecture,* Gensler & Associates, Los Angeles, 1988; *Architecture in Perspective III,* American Society of Architectural Perspectivists, Pacific Design Center, Los Angeles, 1988; *Architects' Art,* Gallery of Functional Art, Santa Monica, California, 1989; *Playspaces,* Des Moines Art Center, Iowa, 1989; Biennal '89 Architecture, Buenos Aires, 1989; *Venice Art Walk,* Venice, California, 1989, 1991; Salon International de L'Architecture, Paris, 1990; *Architects & Sketchbooks,* Getty Center, Los Angeles, 1990; Nelson Fine Arts Center, Project in Architects, Planners, and Designers for Socially Responsible Environment USA/USSR Exhibit, New York and Moscow, 1990; *Living Space: Contemporary Western Architecture,* Contemporary Art Museum, Colorado Springs, Colorado, 1990; Seville World Expo '92, 1991; Third Belgrade Triennial of World Architecture, Belgrade, Yugoslavia, 1991; Centre Canadien d'Architecture, Montreal, 1992; *Six New Mexico Houses,* University Art Museum, University of New Mexico, 1992; *Contemporary Architectural Freehand Drawing,* GA Gallery, Tokyo, Japan, 1992; *Angel Art,* Pacific Design Center, Los Angeles, 1993; The Foundation of SCI-Arc, Los Angeles, California, 1993; One Person Exhibition, University of Wyoming Art Museum, Laramie, Wyoming, 1993; Massachusetts Institute of Technology, Cambridge, Massachusetts, 1995. **Honors:** William Kinne Fellows Memorial Traveling Fellowship, Columbia University, 1962-63; Western Home Award, *Sunset* Magazine/American Institute of Architects, 1969-70, 1980-81, 1985-1986, 1986-87; Record House Award, *Architectural Record,* 1970, 1972, 1977, 1982, 1986, 1990, 1994; Design Awards, New Mexico Society of Architects, 1970, 1977, 1979, 1981, 1983, 1986, 1987; Awards for Excellence, Western Mountain AIA, 1971, 1973, 1978, 1983, 1984, 1985, 1986, 1987, 1989, 1990; Albuquerque Conservation Association Award, 1982, 1983, 1986, 1987; Design Award, *Progressive Architecture,* 1984, 1985, 1990; Rome Prize Fellow, American Academy in Rome, 1985; National Honor Award, AIA, 1987, 1990; Distinguished Alumni Award, University of New Mexico, 1989; Gran Premio Internacional de la Biennal Internacional de Arquitectura de Buenos Aires, 1989; Honor Award, AIA and American Library Association, 1990; Design Award, *Interiors* Magazine, 1990, 1994; Honor Award, California Council AIA, 1990; Firm Award, Western Mountain Region, 1990; Honor Award, Los Angeles Chapter AIA, 1990, 1991, 1993, 1994; Domino's 30 Award, 1990, 1991; named to *Architectural Digest* 100 Architects, 1991; Nissan International Fellow, Aspen Design Conference, 1991; Zimmerman Award, University of New Mexico, 1991; Chicago Architecture Award, 1992; National Contractor's Award, Excellence in Construction, 1992; Award, Albuquerque Chapter AIA, 1992; 25 Year Award of Excellence, Albuquerque Chapter AIA, 1993; Awards of Excellence, Albuquerque Chapter AIA, 1993; Design for Excellence for Energy Efficient Design, Southern California Edison, 1993; Honor and Merit Award, Western Mountain Region, 1993, 1995; Design Award, New Mexico AIA, 1994; Portland Concrete Building Award, 1994; Design Award, NCMA AIA, 1994; Merit Award, Los Angeles Chapter AIA, 1995; Design Ovation Award, ASID, 1995. **Addresses:**

Antoine Predock: Arizona State University Fine Arts Building. Photo: Timothy Hursley

300 12th St. N.W., Albuquerque, New Mexico 87102, U.S.A.; 1136 Abbot Kinney Boulevard, Venice, California 90291, U.S.A.

**Works**

La Luz Project, 100 Townhouses, Corporate Office, and 500-acre Master Plan, Albuquerque, New Mexico, 1967-1974.

Twenty Single-Family Residences, New Mexico, 1970-1987.

Mesa de Sol, 200-Unit Townhouse Community, Santa Barbara, California, 1971.

Four Branch Banking Offices, First National Bank, Albuquerque, 1971-73.

The Citadel, 223-Unit Apartment Complex, Albuquerque, 1973.

University of New Mexico Student Union Addition and Renovation, Albuquerque, 1977.

Cochiti Lake Visitor Center, U.S. Corp. of Engineers, Cochiti, New Mexico, 1977.

Museum of Albuquerque, 1979.

A. Montoya Elementary School, Tijeras, New Mexico, 1979.

Student Union, New Mexico Tech, Socorro, New Mexico, 1979.

Corbett Student Center, New Mexico State University, Las Cruces, 1978.

Health & Social Services Department Field Office, Las Vegas, New Mexico, 1978.

KOAT-TV Broadcast Facility, Albuquerque, 1980.

Museum of New Mexico, Fine Arts Museum Renovation and Expansion, Santa Fe 1980 (with Edward Larrabee Barnes, FAIA).

Restaurant, Taos Ski Valley, Taos, New Mexico, 1980.

Miramonte Lodge, Trinidad, Colorado, 1981.

Rio Grande Nature Center Master Plan & Visitor Center, Albuquerque, 1982.

United Blood Services Office Building and Blood Bank, Albuquerque, 1982.

St. Bernard Condominiums, Taos Ski Valley, Taos, 1982.

Desert Highlands New Community, Townhouses, and Commons, Scottsdale, Arizona, 1982.

Tejon Ranch Master Plan, Tejon Pass, California, 1984.

The Beach Apartments, Albuquerque, 1985.

New Mexico Heart Clinic, Albuquerque, 1985.

Marine Science Museum, National Design Competition, Charleston, South Carolina, 1986.

Nelson Fine Arts Center, Arizona State University, Tempe, 1986.

American Heritage Center and Art Museum, University of Wyoming, Laramie, 1987.

Las Vegas Central Library and Museum, Las Vegas, Nevada, 1987.

Los Alamos Library and Cultural Center, Los Alamos, New Mexico, 1987.

Hispanic Cultural Center Master Plan, Albuquerque, 1987.

Mandell Weiss Forum, University of California, San Diego, 1987.

Classroom/Laboratory/Administration Building, California Polytechnic University, Pomona, 1987.

Fuller Residence, Desert Highlands, Arizona, 1987.

Turtle Creek House, Dallas, Texas, 1988.

Winandy Residence, Desert Highlands, 1988.

Hotel Santa Fe, Euro Disney, Paris, France, 1988.

Disney Resort Hotel, Orlando, Florida, 1988.

Housing, Auditorium, Office Building, University of California, Los Angeles, 1988.

United States Pavilion World Expo 1992, National Design Competition, Seville, Spain, 1989.

Thousand Oaks Government Center and Civic Auditorium, Thousand Oaks, California, 1989.

Venice Residence, Venice, California, 1989.

Rosenthal Residence, Manhattan Beach, California, 1989.

Zuber Residence, Paradise Valley, Arizona, 1989.

Arizona State University Campus Sector Plan, Tempe, Arizona, 1989.

Institute of American Indian Arts Museum, Santa Fe, 1989.

Music Facility, University of California, Santa Cruz, 1990.

Social Science & Humanities Building, University of California, Davis, 1990.

Palm Bay Hotel, Convention Center, Casino, and Master Planning, International Design Competition, Agadir, Morocco, 1990.

Arizona Science Center, Phoenix, 1991.

Museum of Science & Industry, Tampa, Florida, 1991.

St. John the Divine South Transept International Design Competition, New York, 1991.

Rangers Ballpark National Design Competition, Texas, 1991.

Central Bookstore/Parking Structure, University of New Mexico, Albuquerque, 1992.

Clark County Government Center, National Design Competition, Las Vegas, Nevada, 1992.

Institute of American Indian Arts, Art Park, Santa Fe, 1992.

Rio Grande Nature Center Addition, Albuquerque, New Mexico, 1992.

Student Affairs & Administrative Services Building, University of California, Santa Barbara, 1993.

Stanford Center For Integrated Systems Extension, Stanford University, California, 1993.

The New Mexico Hispanic Cultural Center, Albuquerque, New Mexico, 1993.

Chemistry and Nanotechnology Building, Rice University, Houston, Texas, 1994.

Spencer Theater for the Performing Arts, Ruidoso, New Mexico, 1994.

## Publications

By PREDOCK: books—*Italian Sketchbooks,* 1985; *Architectural Journeys,* New York, 1995.

On PREDOCK: books—*A View of Contemporary World Architects,* Japan, 1977; *Modern Houses in America,* Tokyo, 1978; *Solar Houses: 48 Energy Saving Designs* by Louis Gropp, New York, 1978; *Houses of the West* by Elisabeth Kendall Thompson, New York, 1979; *Low-Rise Housing in America: The Suburban Scene,* Tokyo, 1980; *The Making of an Architect: 1881-1981,* New York, 1981; *Santa Fe Style* by Christine Mather and Sharon Woods, New York, 1986; *The Inhabited Landscape,* exhibition catalogue, New York, 1987; *The Desert Southwest* by Nora Burba and Paula Panich, 1987; *Playspaces: Architecture for Children,* exhibition catalogue, Des Moines, Iowa, 1989; *Sourcebook of Contemporary North American Architecture from Postwar to Post Modern* by Sylvia Hart Wright, New York, 1989; *The Potential House: Three Centuries of American Dwelling* by Henry Plummer, Tokyo, 1989; *American Architecture of the 1980s,* Washington, D.C., 1990; *100 Contemporary Architects* by Bill Lacy, New York, 1991; *Modern Landscape Architecture: Redefining the Garden* by Jory Johnson and Felice Frankel, New York, 1991; *Epic Space: Towards the Roots of Western Architecture* by Anthony C. Antoniades, New York, 1992; *The American House: Design for Living,* Washington, D.C., 1992; *Contemporary American Architects* by Philip Jodidio, 1993; *Architecture in the 20th Century* by Udo Kultermann, New York, 1993; *Antoine Predock, Architect* by Brad Collins and Juliette Robbins, New York, 1994; *Museum Builders* edited by James Steele, London, 1994; *Museums for the New Century* by Josep M. Montaner, New York, 1995; *The New American House* by Oscar Riera Ojeda, New York, 1995; articles—*Architectural Record* (New York), May 1970, May 1972, September 1976, May 1979, May 1985, March 1986, April, 1986, July 1986, November 1986, May 1987, June 1987, July 1987, October 1987, January 1988, April 1988, October 1988, April 1990, August 1990, October 1990, December 1990, March 1991, July 1991, August 1991, October 1991, May 1992, June 1992, September 1992, February 1993, April 1993, April 1994; *Architecture d'Aujourd'hui* (Paris), September 1971, June 1990, October 1990; *Interiors* (New York), March 1972, January 1991, January 1995; *Progressive Architecture* (New York), March 1974, August 1974, November 1978, January 1984, March 1984, December 1984, January 1985, February 1986, November 1986, December 1987, January 1988, May 1988, June 1989, January 1990, October 1990, December 1990, April 1991, August 1991, January 1993, March 1994, April 1994, December 1994, July 1995; *Architectural Digest* (Los Angeles), May 1979, October 1986, February 1987, August 1987, April 1988, November 1990, December 1990, March 1992, September 1992, March 1994, March 1995; *Architecture* (New York), March 1984, May 1984, December 1984, January 1986, February 1986, October 1986, May 1987, July 1987, December 1987, April 1988, July 1988, March 1989, January 1990, August 1991, September 1991, December 1991, March 1992, April 1992, May 1992, July 1992, August 1992, September 1992, April 1993, June 1993, April 1994, March 1995, April 1995; *Time* (New York), 14 April 1988, 15 July 1991, 29 July 1991; *Rolling Stone* (New York), 17 September 1992; *Form & Function,* September 1993; *House Beautiful* (New York), September 1993; *World Architecture* (London), July 1995.

*

In his work, Antoine Predock, Architect, makes choices which come from the spirit and from an understanding of the actual world around him, both in terms of the present and the past. He responds to the forces of a place—to geology, culture, myth, and ritual—and evokes these qualities in his buildings. In the office we explore the connections between the earth and the sky as in the Turtle Creek House, which has a ramp that aims toward the sky, establishing a trajectory that one follows on ascent. Our buildings in the desert are dug into the site, often suggesting an analogous landscape. The American Heritage Center in Wyoming is an abstraction of land forms in the area—an "archival mountain" in the landscape, with a village, the art museum, at its base. Our built work, for over almost three decades, expresses these initial physical and spiritual impulses.

—Antoine Predock, Architect

\*   \*   \*

It seems to me that Antoine Predock's early buildings all "grow out" of the Southwest ground, out of the desert: scrub, cacti, boulders. "Grow" may convey a misleading impression, since there is nothing folksy-organic about them. On the contrary, his buildings rise sharply, abruptly from the jumble of the site and are complex, both geometrically and spatially. Yet they are firmly earthed in the Arizona-New Mexico soil.

Even if he was given his architectural training in the East and is now building in Europe and on the West Coast, that early earthing in the Rocky Mountain foothills has allowed him a particular vision of how a building should constitute itself on the site. It allows him to operate with a certain freedom in places which may not seem amenable to his approach. In Paris (albeit for Eurodisney), he was able to represent the West in a series of condensed, narrative images: the drive-in cinema screen as a hoarding works well with the formalized use of neon and the anecdotal incidents (the car-carcases, the 'caged' cactus) and are enhanced by the allusive colors of the building. On the South California coast he has managed, in a deceptively simple house, to play the wide-open against the occluded and to temper the inevitable coarseness of an in-situ concrete skeleton with sharp metal detailing and a mirror surface.

Such a knowing use of material surface separates Predock from many of his contemporaries. He may sometimes overplay his hand with reflective glass, but his use of it is quite unlike the common mirror-glass facings of corporate headquarters. On the contrary, he is alone, I think, of his contemporaries to use such a surface *architecturally,* playing reflectivity against translucency, as he does in the Mandell Weiss Center in San Diego.

In all that Predock has been his own man; he is not one to join movements or tendencies. Nor has he been much affected by all the talk which goes by the name of theory. On the other hand he has been articulate and explicit about what he is doing in his architecture. In the Turtle Creek house in Dallas (sited ideally for its bird-watcher owners), the visitor, who approaches down a cul-de-sac, is greeted by well-planted rising limestone terraces that are crowned by a discreetly slit concrete wall. You enter through a sharply outlined artificial cave in those terraces and find yourself facing the garden, and see before you the thin steel bridge rising into the trees—announcing the client's passion for birdwatching: what will also strike you at once is the flow of the interior volume through a number of ingeniously contrived (but quite natural-seeming) level changes to either side. As you walk through the house these levels also reveal themselves to be inflections of the way in which the house is used both for everyday living and for entertaining.

His interpretation of the program and of the site through a representation, even a narrative, is always formally innovative and occasionally quite startling. This is achieved—it seems to me—while maintaining a continuity between exterior and interior that is very unusual in the architecture of this decade. In spite of the power and elaboration of the forms he devises, Predock never neglects surface. While the materiality of his buildings is not finicky or showy it seems always both considered and apposite. In all these ways, Predock may be unique among his contemporaries—who have much to learn from him.

—Joseph Rykwert

# PREMSELA, Benno

Dutch interior, exhibition, and industrial designer

**Born:** Amsterdam, 4 May 1920. **Education:** Studied interior design under A. Bodon at the Nieuwe Kunstschool, Amsterdam, 1937-41. **Career:** Worked as a display designer with Martin Visser, at De Bijenkorf department store, Amsterdam, 1949-51; textile designer, in the studio of Bueno Mesquita, Florence, 1951-53; freelance designer, Amsterdam, from 1953, collaborating with architect Jan Vonk, from 1956; partner in Buro Premsela Vonk, 1963-72, design studio Premsela Vonk, 1972-73, and Premsela Vonk BV architectural firm, from 1973. Head of window display, De Bijenkorf, 1956-63, and consultant to Van Besouw NV, from 1967, Vescon BV, from 1972, and Gerns + Gahler, from 1975. Board member, from 1953, and chairman, 1964-71, Nederlandse Vereiniging tot Integratie van Homosexualiteit COC, Amsterdam; chairman, Gerrit Rietveld Institute, Amsterdam, 1972-80; governor, Kroller-Muller Foundation, Otterlo, 1975; chairman, Amsterdam Council for the Arts, 1980. Advisory committee for the Applied Arts, Amsterdam, 1961-67; visual art and architecture section of the Council for the Arts, Amsterdam, 1964-70; committee for exhibitions abroad, Amsterdam, 1965-81; member, Council for Industrial Design, Amsterdam, 1969-75; advisory board for the Museum Fodor, Amsterdam, 1979-80; acquisitions committee of the Stedelijk Museum, Amsterdam, 1980. **Exhibitions:** *Benno Premsela—onder anderen,* Stedelijk Museum, 1981; *Design Since 1945,* Philadelphia Museum of Art, 1983. **Collections:** Stedelijk Museum; Israel Museum, Jerusalem. **Honors:** Bergoss Carpet Competition Prize, 1956; Knight of the Order of the Oranje Nassau. **Address:** Herengracht 569, 1017 CD Amsterdam, Netherlands.

## Works

Furniture ranges, for Spectrum Company, Bergeyk, 1956-62.
Carpet designs, for Koninklijk Fabrieken Bergoss, from 1956.
*Pioneers of Today* exhibition layouts, for De Bijenkorf, 1961.
*Creative Thinking in Plastics* exhibition layouts, for the Centre for Industrial Design, Amsterdam, 1967.
*Sieraad 1900-1972* exhibition layouts, for the Zonnehof, Amsterdam, 1972.
*Malton* and *Lungi* wall-coverings, for Vescom BV, Deurne, 1973.

Design standardization programme, for the Amro Bank, Amsterdam, 1974.
*Rice Grain* and *Venezuela* textiles, for Aupin BV, Deventer, 1975-76.
*Tetuan* and *Volkswagen* upholstery fabrics, for Gerns + Gahler, 1978-79.
Exhibition stand at the Utrecht Spring Fair, for Pulsar Time Europe, 1981.

## Publications

By PREMSELA: books—(with Cas Oorthuys) *Fotopocket Florence,* Amsterdam, 1953.

On PREMSELA: books—*Window Display 2* edited by Walter Herdeg, Zürich, 1961; *An International Survey of Press Advertising* edited by Kurt Weidemann, Stuttgart and London, 1966; *International Window Display* edited by Karl Kaspar, Stuttgart and London, 1966; *Benno Premsela—onder Anderen,* exhibition catalogue with texts by Martin Visser, Jan Vonk, and others, Amsterdam, 1981; *Design Since 1945* edited by Kathryn Hiesinger and George Marcus, Philadelphia and London, 1983.

*

My training has been dominated by the Bauhaus ideas. My great teacher was the architect Bodon, who taught me awareness of the points of departure. "Form follows function" was the motto, and although that statement is not suitable (there is always more than one solution to a single problem), I was attracted by the unassuming aspect and the sober tone. That's another thing by which I have always tried to be guided, and it is best expressed in the industrial products for which I am responsible. There is an obvious reason for that. Industries often view only their own products as unique and important. Their products end up in an environment where they naturally meet other products. Because of this, I think that sobriety is one of the most important characteristics an industrial designer can develop. Longevity is also important. Being an industrial designer myself, I don't know who is going to arrange different products together. Therefore, in such situations I opt for reticence in the visual information. Leaving room for others—I think you can probably see that in everything I do.

In regards to interiors as a whole, we are not concerned with displaying our fabulous designs to the world; that's not our object. We believe that our work is to render services, and that's why you'll see more of the client than of us in our work. We consider that a compliment. The more restricting factors there are, the more interesting it all becomes. My departure from Bijenkorf had something to do with that. I had so much freedom there that the excitement wore off. In interior architecture and, certainly in the industrial sector, the restrictions are so compelling that the challenge is tremendous. I think that sharpens creativity. I must also add that working together with people is one of the things I enjoy most of all—I haven't been collaborating with Jan Vonk the past 25 years for nothing. The tensions that arise from collaboration, and, in turn, the possibilities they offer, are an inspiration to me. Besides, I consider coordinating and guiding a group of designers just as creative as designing in my own right.

—Benno Premsela

# PRESTINI, James

American industrial and wood designer

**Born:** Waterford, Connecticut, 13 January 1908. **Education:** Studied mechanics at Yale University, New Haven, Connecticut, BS, 1930; Yale School of Education, 1932; University of Stockholm, 1938; Institute of Design, Chicago, 1939; also studied sculpture in Italy, 1953-56. **Career:** Development engineer, Sargeant Lock and Hardware Manufacturing Company, New Haven, Connecticut, 1930-31; research engineer, Armour Institute, Illinois Institute of Technology, Chicago, 1943-53; consultant, Midwest Research Institute, Kansas City, 1946, Museum of Modern Art, New York, 1946-51, Albright Art Gallery, Buffalo, 1947, Institute of Contemporary Art, Washington, D.C., 1948-49, Knoll International, Zurich, 1953-54, American Craftsmens Council, New York, 1957, University of California Department of Architecture, Berkeley, 1958-65, West German Government, Bonn, 1962, Indian National Institute of Design, Ahmedabad, 1962-63, United States Office of Science and Technology, Washington D.C., 1964, University of Washington College of Architecture, Seattle, 1964, University of California School of Architecture, Los Angeles, 1965, University of New Mexico Department of Architecture, Albuquerque, 1966, University of Idaho Department of Architecture, Moscow, 1967, California Institute of the Arts, Valencia, 1967, University of Waterloo School of Architecture, Ontario, 1971, Fulbright-Hayes Program, Washington, D.C., 1972, Institute of International Education, 1973, and others. Instructor in mathematics, Lake Forest Academy, Illinois, 1933-42; instructor, North Texas State College, Denton, 1942; instructor in design, Institute of Design, Chicago, 1939-46, 1952-53; lecturer, 1956-62, professor of design, 1962-75, and professor emeritus, from 1975, University of California, Berkeley; research professor, Bauhaus-Archiv, West Berlin, 1977. **Exhibitions:** Lake Forest Academy, Illinois, 1934-42, 1983; Currier Gallery of Art, Manchester, New Hampshire, 1938; Toledo Museum of Art, Ohio, 1938; Butler Art Institute, Youngstown, Ohio, 1940; Dallas Museum of Fine Arts, 1940; Milwaukee Art Institute, 1940; Seattle Art Museum, Washington, 1940; Smithsonian Institution, Washington, D.C. 1940; Dayton Art Institute, Ohio, 1941; Cincinnati Art Museum, Ohio, 1944; Institute of Contemporary Art, Washington, D.C., 1949; University of California, Berkeley, 1957, 1971, 1975; Ahmedabad Museum India, 1963; San Francisco Museum of Art, 1969; Arts Club of Chicago, 1975. **Collections:** Cooper-Hewitt Museum, New York; Museum of Modern Art, New York; Metropolitan Museum of Art, New York; Boston Museum of Fine Arts; Philadelphia Museum of Art; Art Institute of Chicago; San Francisco Museum of Modern Art; Smithsonian Institution, Washington, D.C.; Musée des Arts Décoratifs, Montreal; Bauhaus-Archiv, West Berlin. **Honors:** Los Angeles County Fair Crafts Prize, 1951, 1952; Honour Award, Milan Triennale, 1954, 1973; Furniture Award, Cantu, 1955; U.S. Department of State Citation, 1958; Graham Foundation Award, Chicago, 1962; Ford Foundation Fellowship, 1962-63; American Steel Institute Award, 1971, 1973; Guggenheim Fellowship, New York, 1972-73; R. S. Reynolds Award, American Institute of Architects, 1972; University of California Berkeley Award, 1975; German Academic Exchange Fellowship, 1977; National Woodturning Conference Award, 1985; Lake Forest Academy Hall of Fame Award, 1987. **Address:** Survived by his library, the Creators Equity Foundation Library, 2324 Blake Street, Berkeley, California 94704, U.S.A. **Died:** Berkeley, California, 26 July 1993.

**Publications**

**By PRESTINI: books**—*James Prestini, 1938-1988,* 2 vols., Berkeley, California, 1990; **articles**—in *The Frontier* (Chicago), March 1948; *Armour Research Foundation Report* (Chicago), September 1948, October 1949, April 1950, January 1953; *Congressional Record* (Washington, D.C.), no. 51, 1950; *Technical Cooperation Administration Report* (Chicago), December 1950, December 1951; *Industrial Design* (New York), May 1964; *Bauhaus-Archiv* (West Berlin), September 1977; "Woodturning 1990" in *Woodturning* (East Sussex, England), no. 1, Autumn 1990.

**On PRESTINI: books**—*Prestini's Art in Wood* by Edgar Kaufmann Jr., Lake Forest, 1950; *Prize Designs for Modern Furniture,* exhibition catalogue by Edgar Kaufmann Jr., New York, 1950; *Chairs* by George Nelson, New York, 1953; *Shaping America's Products* by Don Wallance, New York, 1956; *Twentieth Century Design from the Museum of Modern Art,* exhibition catalogue by Arthur Drexler and Greta Daniel, New York, 1959; *Creative Design in Wood* by Dona A. Meilach, New York, 1968; *Man the Designer* by Helen Marie Evans, New York, 1973; *Innovative Furniture in America from 1800 to the Present* by David A. Hanks, New York, 1981; *Design Since 1945* edited by Kathryn Hiesinger and George Marcus, Philadelphia and London, 1983; *The Art of Turned Wood Bowls* by Edward Jacobson, New York, 1985; *Woodturning: The Modern Movement* by David Ellsworth, New York, 1986; *The American Design Adventure 1940-1975* by Arthur J. Pulos, London and Cambridge, Massachusetts, 1988; **articles**—"James Prestini: An Appreciation" by David Ellsworth in *Woodturning* (East Sussex, England), no. 4, Summer 1991.

\*

To create a humanistic future environment is the chief problem confronting the artist in a technological age. If the art of the future—and particularly its sculpture—is to fulfill man aesthetically, rather than overwhelm him with hollow technical feats, it must express the most humane significance of the new technologies which, precisely because they are so new, complex, and imperfectly understood, have led to confusion and demoralization, instead of enrichment, of the modern environment. One reaction to this problem has been a revival of Luddism—the machine-breaking protest of the early Industrial Revolution. Yet history would indicate that it is the responsibility of the artist to make technology humane, as the heroic nineteenth-century engineers did, rather than to destroy or ignore the life-enhancing potentialities of applied science. Thus, a humane art of the future inevitably must incorporate the technologies of the future, just as the finest art of the past expressed the most advanced technologies of its own time and place. Furthermore, this new art—in the highest sense a socially responsible public art—must be at the scale of the future. To paraphrase a famous statement of Mies van der Rohe: technology reaches its real fulfillment when it transcends itself in becoming art.

—James Prestini

\*     \*     \*

James Prestini was born in Waterford, Connecticut, the son of a skilled stone-carver who had emigrated from Italy. The younger

Prestini chose mechanical engineering as his profession and after earning the B.S. degree in that field at Yale University in 1930, worked as a development engineer for a lock and hardware firm.

Prestini soon turned to teaching by accepting a position at Lake Forest Academy, a preparatory school in suburban Chicago. There, from 1933 to 1942, he taught mathematics and, in addition, served as supervisor of the school's workshop, where he began experimenting with lathe-turned wooden bowls. He also became interested in the student-oriented design pedagogy of Laszlo Moholy-Nagy through reading *The New Vision.* His interest in design was quickened by his close observation of the construction of the nearby Winnetka, Illinois, Crow Island School, designed by Eliel Saarinen and his son Eero (in association with Perkins and Will) and completed in 1939. The innovative wooden furniture for the school was designed by the Saarinens (in association with Carleton Washburne).

The interests in design, in design education, and in wood-turning which Prestini had acquired, converged into his activity as a maker of lathe-turned wooden bowls: he decided to use manual work as a resource to teach himself design. His idea was that he would make an object, draw it, think about it, and then make it again, so that the process, rather than the product, would be important. As he once explained, he was "not interested in turning a good looking bowl," but rather in what one must learn in order to turn a bowl. He added that he felt "reverence not for wood, but for work."

There was no category into which Prestini's bowls might readily fit. They are not craft work, if that term is used to mean the revival of vestigial skills or practices peculiar to a locality, and in any case, the production of lathe-turned, wooden kitchen utensils (except for rolling pins) ceased during the nineteenth century. Rather, Prestini created a new category. Many of the bowls seem to be made for use, but function is nearly always suggested rather than literal. Thus, even a 1939 mahogany salad set, consisting of a tray, a large bowl, and six smaller bowls, was made with such precision that the bowls may be placed so that they touch each other while just fitting within the raised lip of the tray; it was donated to the Metropolitan Museum of Art in 1975, and then reluctantly, because Prestini considered it "to be one of my very best designs."

Prestini began to exhibit his bowls in 1934, first at Lake Forest Academy, then more widely. Because of their light weight, their shell-like, thin walls, and their finish of clear lacquer, which preserved the natural, unstained appearance of the grain of the woods from which they were made (usually cherry, walnut, birch, or mahogany), the bowls were widely acclaimed. They were exhibited in many parts of the United States, and museums began collecting them in 1940. Henry van de Velde, one of the pioneer architects and designers of the modern movement, owned one of Prestini's bowls and assured him, in a letter of 1950, of "the admiration with which an object of such pure and infinite beauty and one made with such perfect execution is held by one of the old pioneers of 'pure forms'.... I have rarely been able to touch an object that has awakened in me a more intense and deep pleasure." At about the same time Edgar Kaufmann, Jr., wrote about Prestini's bowls and other objects in *Prestini's Art in Wood,* describing "the serenity, refinement and purity of his turned forms."

Today Prestini's bowls and other wooden objects are seen in numerous public and private collections in the United States and Western Europe, and many have been widely published. As one result, Prestini's work has had an influence on factory-produced items, such as salad bowls. He also influenced the revival of the craft of wood-turning, which began about 1960. Prestini remained aloof from the newer generation of wood turners, whose interests only partially coincided with his, because wood turning had been only a means to an end for Prestini, and thus only a part-time activity.

During the summer of 1938, Prestini worked with Carl Malmsten as an apprentice furniture designer and craftsman at the University of Stockholm. The following year, he was a part-time student at Moholy-Nagy's School of Design in Chicago, and shortly after enrolling he was asked to become a part-time member of the faculty. In 1942 he taught at North Texas State College in Denton, but he returned to Chicago the following year to resume teaching at the School of Design in Chicago (renamed the research engineer at the Armour Research Foundation of the Illinois Institute of Technology.

The exercises in wood which Prestini encountered in the foundation course at the School of Design in Chicago led to a series of "design experiments" in which qualities of wood not revealed by the use of the lathe were explored. These experiments resulted in pieces such as spirals and wood springs in which the resilience of wood was exploited. At the same time there were abstract, asymmetrical forms which exploited the visual qualities of grain in ways not possible when using the lathe.

Prestini left Chicago in 1953 to go to Italy, where he organized the manufacture of furniture in Milan for Knoll International and conducted a survey of the Italian furniture industry for Knoll, while also finding time to study sculpture. He returned to the United States in 1956 to teach design in the Architecture Department of the University of California in Berkeley, from which he retired as Professor of Design twenty-one years later.

Prestini's research on production methods for low-cost furniture included work as part of a team on a project funded by a grant to the Armour Research Foundation from the Museum of Modern Art. The team's research was the basis for its entry in the Museum of Modern Art's 1949 *International Competition for Lowcost Furniture Design,* in which it won a prize for the best research report. The team's entry was a one-piece chair made of resin-impregnated wood fiber. It was suggested by a series of drawings made in the early 1940s by Ludwig Mies van der Rohe as studies for a conchoidal-form chair (suggested by the conch shell). Although only a prototype of the Armour Research team project was produced, it has had a great influence on mass-produced furniture, especially one-piece, molded, thermoplastic chairs.

In his nickel-plated steel sculpture, begun in 1967, Prestini initially used structural steel elements, such as I-beams and cylindrical pipes, which were fused together, coated with nickel, and finally polished, using industrial methods, to the point of transparency. Gradually, more and more of the work was taken over by assistants, enabling Prestini to abandon the I-beams and other structural elements for the freedom of working with solid plate and to confine his own role to the making of wooden models to guide his assistants. The high degree of polish of Prestini's metal sculpture results in surfaces so reflective they seem to be a microcosm of the surroundings.

Prestini's greatest achievement was his demonstration that there need be no barriers between technology and art or between art and utilitarian objects.

—Lloyd C. Engelbrecht

# PUCCI, Emilio

Italian fashion designer

**Born:** Marchese Emilio Pucci di Barsento, in Naples, 20 November 1914. **Education:** Liceo Galileo, Florence, until 1933; studied at the University of Milan, 1933-35; University of Georgia, Athens, 1935-36; Reed College, Portland, Oregon, MA, 1937; University of Florence, Ph.D., 1941. **Military Service:** Bomber pilot in the Italian Air Force, 1938-42. **Family:** Married Cristina Nannini di Casabianca in 1959; children: Laudomia and Alessandro. **Career:** First designed women's skiwear for *Harper's Bazaar* photographer Toni Frissell, 1947; freelance fashion designer, establishing studio in Florence, from 1949; president of Emilio Pucci S.r.l., Florence, and Emilio Pucci Limited, New York, from 1950; also designed clothing and accessories for Qantas Airlines, Formfit Rogers, Parker Pen Company, Ford Motor Company, Dandolo e Primi, Akerman, Grasset et Pittion Rosenthal, and others. City Councillor, Florence, from 1964; proprietor of the Castelli di Cerreto, Granaiolo, and Coiano wine-producing estates. President of National Association of Shoe Stylists, Shoe Fair Consulting Group, Associazione Proprieta Edilizia, Societa San Giovanni Battista, Antico Setifico Fiorentino, Societa Fiorentina Corse Cavalli, and Societa San Giovanni di Dio Cinqecento Fiorentino. Also Olympic skier, 1934. **Member:** Parliament for the Florence Liberal Party, 1963-72, and head of the Liberal Group of Palazzo Vecchio, 1963-80; board member of SINA Hotels and Finanziaria Banca Popolare di Novara. **Exhibitions:** *Fashion: An Anthology,* Victoria and Albert Museum, London, 1971; *40 Years of Italian Fashion,* Trump Tower, New York, 1983. **Honors:** Neiman-Marcus Fashion Award, 1954, 1967; *Sports Illustrated* Designers Award, 1955, 1961; *Sunday Times* Fashion Award, London, 1963; Association of Industrial Design Award, Milan, 1968; Drexel University Annual Award, Philadelphia, 1975; Italy-Austria Award, 1977; Knighthood, Rome, 1982; Medaille de la Ville de Paris, 1985; Council of Fashion Designers of America Award, 1990. **Died:** Florence, Italy, 29 November 1992.

## Publications

**On PUCCI: books—***Vogue's Book of Houses, Gardens, People,* with text by Valentine Lawford, New York and London, 1968; *Fashion: An Anthology by Cecil Beaton,* exhibition catalogue compiled by Madeleine Ginsburg, London, 1971; *A History of Fashion* by J. Anderson Black and Madge Garland, London, 1975, 1980; *In Fashion: Dress in the Twentieth Century* by Prudence Glynn, London, 1978; *I Mass-Moda: Fatti e Personnaggi dell'Italian Look* by Adriana Mulassano, Florence, 1979; *Magic Names of Fashion* by Ernestine Carter, London, 1980; *The Collector's Book of Twentieth Century Fashion* by Frances Kennett, New York and London, 1983; *40 Years of Italian Fashion,* exhibition catalogue edited by B. G. Aragno, Rome, 1983; *McDowell's Directory of Twentieth Century Fashion* by Colin McDowell, London, 1984; *The Encyclopaedia of Fashion from 1840 to the 1980s* by Georgina O'Hara, London, 1986; *Pucci: A Renaissance in Fashion* by Shirley Kennedy, New York, 1991; **articles—**"Emilio Pucci" in *Current Biography* (New York), February 1961; "If You Knew Pucci" by F. Schiff in *Interview* (New York), September 1974; "Founding Father of the Signature Print" in *The Times* (London), 1 September 1976; "Pucci" by Jody Shields in *Vogue* (New York), May 1990; "Mai come adesso è Pucci" by Anna Gloria Porti in *Vogue* (Milan), September 1990;

"Pucci Superstar" in *Elle,* October 1990; "The New Pucci Coup: Psychedelic Swirls Back" by Lucie Young in *Metropolitan Home* (London), December/January 1990-91; "Emilio Pucci Dead at 78" in *Women's Wear Daily* (New York), 1 December 1992; "Prince of Prints" in *People,* 14 December 1992.

*     *     *

Emilio Pucci created the post-War Italian sensibility for, and business of, sportswear. Even as other aristocratic Italians established fashion businesses based in fine textiles, tailoring, and high style, Pucci was discovered—by photographer Toni Frissell of *Harper's Bazaar* in the December 1948 issue—as a designer of skiwear who expanded hand-painted and wildly patterned silks to the larger rubric of resortwear for which Pucci was briefly known in America as Emilio of Capri after his 1949 boutique of that name. Both sea and ski established Pucci's bright colors and fostered the body-skimming silk's (and later, nylon's) easy association with sensuality in modern life. The epoch that established casual modes and a strong, athletic woman in the 1950s relished the vivid free-style swirls and botanicals of Pucci's design. Manufacturing with White Stag and Formfit Rogers fostered Pucci's reputation in America. He won the Neiman Marcus Award in 1954 and was a long-time close friend to Stanley Marcus; Pucci was especially popular in Texas for his casual style and colors fit for the desert sun. The designer also ingratiated himself with American audiences and clients by remembering that he had studied in the United States in the 1930s. Commercially, Pucci had many personal assets: he was a marchese, a noble; he was a handsome former athlete; and he was a man of the world, including America.

In particular, Pucci's grandiose, supple, and aqueous patterns affected the position of colorful abstract art of the 1950s and 1960s. Borrowing from marine landscape, but with a pronounced effort to abstracting or obscuring the referent, Pucci created clothing that met not only the new sportswear ethic, but the novelty of art both high and decorative in the 1950s and 1960s. Sleek clothing could be esteemed as "modern"; clothing that resembled the visual arts could likewise seem a sunny, optimistic "modern" as well. In retrospect, these associations are patently fallacious, but chic women of the 1960s seized on their "Puccis" as modestly priced aspirations to modern art. *Harper's Bazaar*, in particular, affiliated Pucci again and again with modern art. For example, a Saul Leiter photograph published as a two-page spread in May 1962 places Pucci outfits among Alex Katz cutouts with copy that read, "Making their way through big wooden cutouts, neat, nifty, well-shaped clothes for the sun."

Even the splashiest prints for dresses, beach and leisure pajamas, and the ubiquitous scarves could seem like the Art Nouveau interest of cultivated tastes of the 1960s. Before they collected Tiffany lamps, they collected their Puccis in like kaleidoscopes, effulgent in color, perhaps ultimately vulgar in taste, but seemingly of the best that good taste and art could imagine in the 1960s. Even if Pucci's Op fell short of Art and his big patterns were not quite Pop Art, Pucci projected the sentiment of the new. As Shirley Kennedy described in her book *Pucci: A Renaissance in Fashion,* "Women who purchased Puccis wanted to look sexy, colorful, rich, young, and *in.* And that is exactly how Pucci made them feel."

One sign of artistic disposition may have been the designer's repeated signatures on the works, especially the scarves. Never quite a logo, always rather more like an artist's signature in the fine arts, Pucci's name ("Emilio") added to the work promoted its affinity, however specious, to art.

The standard Pucci dress was a colorful silk jersey print with a simple tie at the waist. Yet Pucci was also able to evoke Renaissance and Fortuny worlds with pajama pants, high-waisted dresses for entertaining in the hip and hippie 1960s, caftans and other Middle Eastern influences reinforced by decorative motives, and the simple slacks, tops, and loose dresses derived from beachwear. Most importantly, Pucci created bodysuits and leggings in the 1960s that extended the presumptuous patterns to a full-body tattoo of adornment. Women of the 1960s could wear Pucci head to toe and even carry Pucci handbags, accessories, and Pucci sunglasses.

Helen Gurley Brown, in her preface to Shirley Kennedy's book, describes vividly her acquaintance with Pucci dresses in the 1960s, declaring that they were so simply, amply, and flatteringly cut that many women felt at ease in these dresses, often baring considerable skin and functioning as summertime play dresses. Yet Brown points out that for all the silhouette and easy style revealed, the prints themselves camouflaged. The French-curve-like shapes and the nearly edible, pleasantly psychedelic colors overwhelmed any personal deficiency in the wearer. Though Pucci was first recognized for skiwear, he became for the 1950s through the 1970s the designer of summer's vibrant symbols. Moreover, his silk with a natural stretch not only flattered many women, but also travelled and packed beautifully, making Pucci a preferred designer for the first jet set, a taste reified in the designer's work in creating flight attendant uniforms for Braniff Airlines in the high-flying days when Harding Lawrence was CEO. Marylin Bender in *The Beautiful People* (1967) recorded the famous design episode: "Pucci devised the stewardesses's 'air strip' to dramatize the airline's flights from cities in the northern United States to the heart of South America, a schedule that involves rapid temperature changes. Printed leotards to match above-the-knee shifts ... gave the passengers something to talk about."

An intense revival of interest in Pucci, prompted by America again but this time chiefly by *Vogue* under Editor Anna Wintour, just before the designer's death spread like wildfire among young women who had not been old enough in the 1960s to wear Pucci the first time around. Pucci's family, most notably daughter Laudomia, who were running the business by then carefully meted a reasonable number of Pucci pieces to fulfill some of the demand, but made clear the company's policy to keep the Pucci style special and elite, even if they were to be knocked off by many copyists in the early 1990s. Perhaps it was the fulfillment of a temperament for clothing as art that had made Emilio Pucci oblivious to his many imitators and later prompted his family to preserve the Pucci art and leave the wider terrain to mere copyists.

—Richard Martin

# PULOS, Arthur J.

American industrial designer

**Born:** Vandergrift, Pennsylvania, 3 February 1917. **Education:** Studied under Alexander Kostellow, Peter Muller-Munk, and F. Clayter, at the Carnegie Institute of Technology, Pittsburgh, BA, 1939; studied under Victoria Avakian, Fred Cuthbert, and Robert Motherwell, at the University of Oregon, Eugene, MFA, 1942. **Military Service:** Served in the United States Air Force, 1944-46;

First Lieutenant. **Family:** Married Elizabeth Jane McQueen in 1944; children: Cristofer, Maria, and Demetra. **Career:** President, Pulos Design Associates product design firm, Syracuse, New York, 1958-88. Associate professor of design, 1946-55, University of Illinois, Urbana; chairman, 1955-82, and professor emeritus, from 1982, Department of Design, Syracuse University, New York. Trustee, American Craftsman's Council, 1955-57; president, chairman of the board, and fellow, Industrial Designers Society of America, 1973-77; policy panel member, National Endowment for the Arts, 1979-81; president, ICSID International Council of Societies of Industrial Design, Brussels, 1980-84. **Collections:** Museum of Modern Art, New York; Newark Museum of Fine Art, New Jersey; Walker Art Center, Minneapolis; Detroit Institute of Arts; University of Wisconsin, Madison. **Honors:** Associate Artists of Pittsburgh Award, 1939, 1940, 1942, 1947; Wichita Art Association Award, 1947, 1950; Ford Foundation Fellowship, 1952-53; Detroit Institute of Arts Award, 1953; Brooklyn Museum of Art Award, 1953; Art Institute of Chicago Award, 1954; Syracuse University Chancellor's Citation, 1982; National Endowment for the Arts Distinguished Design Fellowship, 1984; World Design Award, New York, 1988. **Address:** 3 The Orchard, Fayetteville, New York 13066, U.S.A.

## Publications

**By PULOS: books—***Contact: Selling Design Services,* Ottawa, 1975; *Opportunities in Industrial Design,* Skokie, 1978; *American Design Ethic: A History of Industrial Design to 1940,* Cambridge, Massachusetts, 1983; *The American Design Adventure 1940-1975,* London and Cambridge, Massachusetts, 1988.

**On PULOS: books—***Design in America* by Ralph Caplan, New York, 1969.

\*

I have always had a deep interest in all forms of human expression. I respect and am stimulated by music, dance, theatre, literature, the plastic arts, and architecture. At the same time, I do not consider myself to be so much an artist as a designer. The difference between the two lies in the fact that the artist is properly committed to self-expression, answerable only to inner compulsion. The designer, on the other hand, is dedicated to human service. He is sensitive to the needs and desires of others and the quality of the man-made environment that serves them. He is pained by any discordances between human beings and the products that have been built or manufactured for them and strives to establish a state of environmental harmony. In this sense, the designer serves as the humane conscience of industry. Still, as a designer, I realize that there is aesthetic quality trapped in my work that will be released after its utility has been consumed, as has been the case for all of man's artifacts in the past.

For more than forty years, my philosophy has been heated in the fire of daily practices of design, shaped against the anvil of university teaching, and tempered by a generation of questioning young minds. It has become clearer to me that industrial design is one of the new generalist professions that reaches beyond the narrow specializations of the past to realize that technics, aesthetics, and humanics are vested in every man-made object and must be brought into sensible balance.

I realize that profound changes are underway on this globe as both developed and underdeveloped nations learn how to tame threatening social and technological forces. I am aware that a new morality of things is emerging by which the tyranny of runaway production may be tempered by a democracy of products and product services that is sympathetically matched to the needs of the people.

—Arthur Pulos

\*    \*    \*

Since the industrial revolution, nineteenth- and twentieth-century European theorists, such as William Morris and Walter Gropius, have struggled with the relationship of hand versus industrial production. Arthur Pulos is the first American to put into perspective the alliance between crafts and industrial designs in United States history. From his 1952 study of Colonial silversmithing in New England, he concluded that Colonial smiths were not so much craftsmen as the first industrialists, who used the most advanced tools and processes available to them to meet their client's needs. The industrial design profession grew out of this attitude. Pulos defines design in the United States as the imaginative development of manufactured products to meet both the physical needs and psychological desires of the consumer in a democratic society.

Pulos was a member of the generation—trained as both craftsmen and designers—who pioneered in industrial design as a profession. As a silversmith in the 1940s and 1950s, he hand-produced silver holloware, flatware, and jewelry, influenced by the *moderne* style, which had been introduced into the United States by earlier twentieth-century European emigre silversmiths, such as Peter Muller Munk. The fine finish of his silverwork, which did not show signs of the hand that made it, allied it with the industrial design esthetic. Pulos continued to work in both worlds throughout his post-war career, when he taught both designs and crafts, first at the University of Illinois and later at Syracuse University. At first, these courses were justified primarily as occupational therapy for returning veterans, but as demand for consumer goods grew, crafts made the shift from therapy and recreation to a profession.

Pulos realized that the few pieces he could make by hand were inadequate to growing demand. However, breaking into American industry as a craftsman/designer was almost impossible, as industry discouraged new designs because of the high cost of start-up. Therefore, in the late 1950s Pulos established his own design firm. With this move, he proved that the craftsman and industrial designer are not far apart in the creation of technically sound, appropriate, and useful objects, the major difference being that the craftsman is oriented toward material and process while the designer is oriented toward product. For industry, he has designed diagnostic instruments for Welch Allyn, portable power tools for Rockwell Manufacturing, and dictation machines for Dictaphone.

Pulos advocated industrial design as a profession, free from the dominance of architecture. He felt that industrial designers should apply craftwork to manufactured goods for a mass market. His ongoing research into the roots of the industrial design profession in the United States has resulted in the first history of American industrial design to 1940. In *American Design Ethic,* published in 1983, he champions the growth and development of design in America for its democratic approach and ability to synthesize esthetics and function in designed objects.

—Sarah Bodine

# PUOTILA, Ritva
Finnish textile and glass designer

**Born:** Ritva Soilikki Sairanen, in Viipuri, 7 June 1935. **Education:** Studied at the Institute of Applied Arts, Helsinki, 1954-59. **Family:** Married Pauli Kalevi Puotila in 1955; children: Jukka, Antti, and Mikko. **Career:** Freelance textile designer, from 1959: established own studio in Helsinki, 1960, working for Dansk International Design Ltd., from 1961, Oy Tampella Ab, 1961-86, Dembo Ab, 1967-75, Made In Ab, 1976-87, Oy Partek Ab, 1977-78, Gefjun Ab, 1978-87, Neste Oy, 1979, United Nations International Trade Center, Geneva, 1988; founder-designer, Woodnotes Oy design firm, Helsinki, and Studio Ritva Puotila unique textiles workshop, Helsinki, from 1987; also experimental glass designer, for Hadeland of Norway, from 1987. Consultant to Friends of Finnish Handicraft, from 1959, and Finnish Handicrafts Association, 1989. **Exhibitions:** Museum of Applied Arts, Copenhagen, 1962; touring exhibition of 20 cities in the United States, 1963; Friends of Finnish Handicrafts, Helsinki, 1965; *The Art of Finnish Rya Rugs,* Musée d'Art Moderne, Paris, 1972 (toured); Galleria LaLoche, Paris, 1974; City Library, Espoo, 1976; Gallery Otso, Espoo, 1986; Artek Oy, Helsinki, 1987; *Finn Form,* Museum of Applied Arts, Helsinki, 1987, 1989, 1991; Lammhults Paviljongen, Stockholm, 1988; *New Forms from Finland,* Royal Museum of Scotland, Edinburgh, 1988; Nordisk Möbelgallerie, Oslo, 1989; Galleria 25, Helsinki, 1989; *Perspektive på papir,* Norway, 1989 (touring exhibition); *Language of Wood,* toured United States and Canada, 1989-90; *Nuevas Formas de Finlandia,* Barcelona, Spain, 1989; (with Eva Renvall and Mirja Tissari) *Triangel,* Röhsska Muséet, Gothenburg, Sweden, 1990; Design Center, Malmö, 1990; *Ryijy Textiles Finlandais,* Institut Finlandais, Paris, 1991; *Configura,* Erfurt, Germany, 1991; *Expo '92 World's Fair,* Finnish Pavilion, Seville, Spain, 1992; *RYIJY-RUGS,* Castlegar Art Gallerie, Toronto, Canada, and Nordik Heritage Museum, Seattle, Washington, U.S.A., 1993; Design Forum, Helsinki, 1993; *Nordiska Profiler,* toured Scandinavian countries, 1994; *Ten to Ten,* Västerås Konst Museum, Västerås, Sweden, 1994; Reykjavik, Iceland, 1994; *Classic Makers,* Design Forum, Helsinki, 1995; *Design Finlandais,* Musée d'Art Moderne et d'Art Contemporain, Nices, France, 1995; *Tekstilkunst,* Kunsthallen, Odense, Denmark, 1995; *Finnish Design: Textiles, Crafts, and Furniture,* Finnish Institute, Manchester and London, 1995. **Collections:** Museum of Applied Arts, Helsinki; Museum of Applied Arts, Copenhagen; Victoria and Albert Museum, London; City of Espoo, Finland; Glass Museum, Norway; Röhsska Muséet, Gothenburg; Västerås Konst Museum, Västerås, Sweden; Nationalmusuem, Stockholm; Finnish State Collections. **Honors:** Ryijy rug design prizes, Friends of Finnish Handicraft and Neovius Ltd., 1959-63; First Prize, Villayhtymä Oy Fabric Competition Helsinki, 1960; Gold Medal, Milan Triennale, 1960; First Prize for table textiles, Dansk International Designs, 1961; subsidy, Finnish Culture Fund, 1967, 1986, 1991; State Award for Crafts and Design, Finland, 1981; subsidy, City of Espoo, 1986; Paper Textiles Prize, Finn Form 87, Helsinki, 1987; three-year artists stipend, Finland, 1987; Oscar Award for paper textiles, French National Association of Interior Architects, Paris, 1987; subsidy, Finnish-Swedish Culture Fund, 1990; honourable mention, Pro Finnish Design competition, 1990; subsidy, Finnish Foundation for Visual Art, New York City, 1992; subsidy, Alfred Kordelin Foundation, 1993; Work of the Week, Ministry of Trade and Industry, Finland, 1994. **Addresses:** Hiiralankaari 25 C, 02160 Espoo, Finland; Studio Ritva Puotila Oy, Tallberginkatu 1 B, 00180 Helsinki, Finland.

**Works**

Carpet designs, for Finnrya Oy, 1959-80.
Zeus ryjiy-rug, for the Milan Triennale, made by Friends of Finnish Handicrafts, 1960.
Woollen fashion fabrics, for Villayhtyma Oy, 1960.
Linen and cotton household textiles, for Tampella Oy, 1961-86.
Linen table textile collection, for Dansk International Design, 1963.
Colour scale of enamel household wares, for Dansk International Design, 1964.
Unique textile piece, for Hasselby Castle, Stockholm, 1964.
Unique art textiles, for Kansallis-Osake-Pankki, Helsinki, 1974, 1982, 1992.
Unique linen textile piece, for the City of Espoo, 1975.
Fashion fabric collections, for Made In Ab, 1976-81.
Unique textile piece, for Essen Town Hall, West Germany, 1980.
Unique art textile, for Postipankki Ltd., Kuopio, Finland, 1983.
Unique textile piece, for Neste Company, in Moscow, 1986.
Paper textile collection, for Woodnotes Oy, 1987.
Experimental glass pieces, for Hadeland Glasverk, 1987.
Unique art textile, for the Social Insurance Institution in Finland, Helsinki, 1988.
Unique art textile, for Bank of Finland, Helsinki, 1994.
Unique art textile, for Mäntyniemi (the residence of the President), Helsinki, 1995.

**Publications**

**On PUOTILA: books**—*Tapisseries finlandaises,* exhibition catalogue with text by Jacques Lassaigne, Paris, 1972; *Finnish Industrial Design* by Tua Pontasuo, Helsinki, 1987; **articles**—"Way Out Colors" in the *San Francisco Examiner,* October 1963; "Varikas loyto Suomesta" in *Suomen Kuvalehti* (Helsinki), 1963; "Designer Inspired by Dreams in Color" in the *New York Times,* 22 October 1963; "Ritva Puotila" in *Graphis* (Zurich), no. 111, 1964; "Weaving with Paper and String" in *Design in Finland* (Helsinki), 1988; "Papier und Baumwolle" in *MD Moebel Interior Design* (Hamburg), July 1989; "Papier pa gulvet" in *Textil Forum* (Oslo), no. 6, 1989.

\*   \*   \*

We are sitting on Ritva Puotila's cozily unpretentious porch, where sunlight filters through a white woven linen and paper curtain and the floor is covered with cream and white paper carpets. Grandchildren play around, and we drink tea from glasses she has designed. Conversation ranges over several subjects, and we talk about the designer's responsibility in improving the human environment and the role of textile materials as an essential part of people's lives.

Ritva Puotila regards being able to make a handtowel suitable for all as more significant than concentrating on the creation of artworks for museums. She talks of cooperation with weavers and glassblowers, which must be based on mutual respect. She speaks of the advantage of having her own studio where she can make her own decisions, experiment, develop, and renew her ideas, and where, in all phases of the work, she can stick to her own line—since this is the reason the client has chosen her to design his products. We talk about travel and impressions of foreign lands, which at home are transformed by her own experience and nature's influences,

Ritva Puotila: Black and Nature combinations, Woodnotes Carpets

finally to become something that is genuinely her own. In Finland there is still a pureness and space that opens up all possibilities. On the subject of textile craft traditions, which in Finland has become banal and tired, we discuss how it is no longer possible to produce the fine qualities of a hundred years ago. But in this connection, one cannot but note that Ritva Puotila herself has contributed to a development based both on tradition and a widening of the textile concept.

From the beginning, Ritva Puotila was drawn towards an artistic career. At school she devoted herself seriously to oil painting, and would have liked to become a painter. At home, however, it was regarded important to learn a profession first, so she chose to study at the department of decorative painting and scenography of the Institute of Applied Arts in Helsinki. Finland in the 1950s showed a positive and open attitude towards design, and students participated in a lot of competitions in all fields of design both in and outside school. It was a prize in textile design that influenced Ritva Puotila's future direction. Just one year after leaving school, in 1960, she was awarded a gold medal at the Milan Triennale for a rya rug designed for the Friends of Finnish Handicraft. The rich collection of rya weavings she has designed since include compositions ranging from the strong and assured to the most tenderly delicate. It is in these works that Puotila has been able to most closely approach painting.

In 1961 Ted Nierenberger arrived in Scandinavia looking for designers he could recruit to his firm Dansk Design. At the Friends of Finnish Handicraft, he picked out six rugs, and asked to meet the artists who had designed them. All six were by Ritva Puotila. This was the start of a collaboration that has lasted up to the present day. Primarily she has designed collections for the table, but has also had extensive commissions as colour coordinator. For a long time the Finnish company Tampella had produced textiles for sale in the United States; Puotila worked out a broad colour chart that in its freshness differed totally from the colour ranges to which the American market had been accustomed. Tampella's export figures rose impressively. For Made In AB, where she created textiles for fashion garments, Puotila noticed how indistinct were differences between seasonal collections and how superficial were the attempts of innovation—ultimately, there was never any real innovation. She demonstrated that true designing meant giving the product new qualities instead of merely modifying the look.

In her own studio, Ritva Puotila has not only continued to develop and re-create her design, but she has also experimented with different techniques and materials. Her paper products are a result of such experimentation, something that has come about as a result of her own initiative and not from a client's commission.

As raw material she uses natural Finnish products, beautiful and strong. When Tampella began spinning paper and the first table mats were ready, they were called *Pine Weaves* because of their direct use of the Finnish forest. Puotila's paper textiles are beautiful and durable. The limited range of black, white, and natural colour creates calm and harmonious surfaces in a rhythmic texture. The smoothness of the surface gives a feeling of cleanness, and the material is non-allergenic. The product combines the practical with the aesthetic. Technical problems are invariably resolved in an artistically acceptable manner, which is a constant feature of her work.

In 1987, Hadeland's glass factory of Norway invited designers from different fields to create a glass collection. Ritva Puotila was assigned to design unique pieces, large sculptural vases, and production tablewares. The simple glasses are decorated with a raspberry motif and the bottoms of smooth plates are ribbed. Fine colour stripes appear in the delicate facets of the vases. Even in glass Ritva Puotila shows an acute sensitivity for the possibilities of the material.

—Carla Enbom

# PUTMAN, Andrée

French interior and furniture designer

**Born:** Andrée Christine Aynard, in Paris, 23 December 1925. **Education:** Educated at the College d'Hulst Paris; studied piano under Francis Poulenc, at the Conservatoire, Paris; mainly self-taught in design, from 1960. **Family:** Married Jacques Putman (divorced); children: Cyrille and Olivia. **Career:** Worked as a journalist for *Femina* magazine, Paris, 1950-52; design columnist, *Elle* magazine, Paris, 1952-58; interiors editor, *L'Oeil* magazine, Paris, 1960-64; stylist, Prisunic stores, Paris, 1958-67; designer, with Arnodin and Denise Maime Fayolle's M.A.F.I.A. publicity agency, Paris, 1968-71; founder-member, with Didier Grumbach, of Createurs et Industriels fashion and furniture designers' group, and director of Createurs store, Paris, 1971-76; founder-manager, of Ecart S.A. furniture and interior design company, Paris, from 1978, and Ecart International, Paris, from 1983; has produced classic furniture re-editions of designs by Eileen Gray, Mariano Fortuny, Jean-Michel Frank, Robert Mallet-Stevens, Michel Dufet, and others, and inte-

riors for Thierry Mugler, Karl Lagerfeld, Mendes S.A., Tan Giudicelli, Chanel, and others. **Exhibitions:** *Design Francais 1960-1990,* Centre Georges Pompidou, Paris, 1988; *Andrée Putman,* Chalon Sur Saône Exhibition Space, France, 1993; *Hommage to Richard Hamilton,* FNAC Etoile, 1993; *Baccarat Designs by A. Putman,* Ecart, New York, 1994; Monnaie de Paris, Paris, 1995. **Honors:** *Interior Design* Hall of Fame Award, New York, 1987; Prix Europeen d'Architecture d'Interieur, 1991; Grand Prix Europeen d'Architecture d'Interieur, 1991; Design Achievement Award, American Society of Interior Designers, 1992; Crystal Star Award for Design Excellence, Nesbitt College of Design Arts, Drexel University, U.S.A., 1992; Oscar du Design, 1993; Grand Officer des Arts et des Lettres, France. **Address:** Ecart International, 111 Rue Saint Antoine, 75004 Paris, France.

## Works (with Ecart)

Thierry Mugler boutique, Place des Victoires, Paris, 1979-80.
Yves Saint Laurent boutiques (15), in the United States, 1980-84.
Karl Lagerfeld boutiques and showrooms, in Paris, New York, Melbourne, and Toronto, 1980-85.
Morgans Hotel interiors, New York, 1984.
Palladium nightclub interiors, New York, 1984 (with Arata Isozaki).
Museum of Contemporary Art conversion, Bordeaux, 1984.
Azzedine Alaia showroom, Paris, 1985.
Jack Lang office interiors, Ministry of Culture, Paris, 1985.
World headquarters interiors in New York, brand image, advertising, exhibits, and boutiques, for Ebel, 1986-91.
Saint James Club Hotel interiors, Paris, 1987.
*Ferrari* exhibition layouts, for the Cartier Foundation, Paris, 1987.
Restaurant design, for Museum of Modern Art, Bordeaux, France, 1988-90.
Corporate re-design programme, for Balenciaga, from 1989.
IM Wasserturm Hotel, Koln, 1990.
Le Lac Hotel, near Tokyo, Japan, 1990.
Rights of Man Foundation headquarters in the Grande Arche de la Defense, Paris, from 1990.
Exhibition design for 10th Anniversary of the Via, Musée des Arts Decoratifs, Paris, 1990.
Interior design of children's boutiques, for Cacharel, 1991-92.
*In Black and White* exhibition design, for Wexner Center for the Arts, Ohio, 1992.
Orchid Club House, Kobe, Japan, 1992.
New head office, for Channel Seven/Arte, European television channel, 1992.
Restaurant and VIP room, for French pavilion at Seville Universal Exhibition, 1992.
Management offices, 1992, and club design, 1994, for Guildo Pastor Center, Monaco.
*Le Cafe Francais,* for Museum of Modern Art, New York, 1992.
*A Tribute to Richard Hamilton* exhibition design, for Hitachi/FNAC, Paris, 1993.
Exhibition areas, for Cartier Foundation, 1993.
Headquarters, for Air France, 1993.
*La Rue Est a Nous* concept, for Tati Shops, 1993.
Reception lounge, for Cognacs Louis Royer, Jarnac, 1993.
Interior design for the *Concorde* airplane, for Air France, 1993.
Design for George Rech boutiques and corners, 1993-94.
Design concept, for Bally Boutiques, 1993-94.
Brand image, for Phillips, 1994.

Andree Putman: Hotel Morgans, New York City. Photo: Deidi von Schaewen

Sheraton hotel, Paris-Roissy, 1994.
Tuileries Garden Cafe, Paris, 1994.
Brand image, for Baccarat, 1994.

## Publications

By PUTMAN: articles—*Passion* (Paris), 15 April 1982; *F. Magazine* (Paris), June 1983.

On PUTMAN: books—*French Style* by Suzane Slesin and Stafford Cliff, New York and London, 1982; *Les Annees 60* by Anne Bony Paris, 1983; *Design Francais 1960-1990: Trois Decennies,* exhibition catalogue by Margo Rouard and Francoise Jollant Kneebone, Paris, 1988; *International Design Yearbook 1988/89* edited by Arata Isozaki, London, 1988; *Andrée Putman* by Sophie Tasma Anargyros, London and New York, 1993; articles—*Metropolitan Home* (New York) April 1984; *Vogue* (New York), September 1984; *Decoration Internationale* (Paris), March 1985, May 1985, September 1985, September 1986; *House and Garden* (New York), October 1985, April 1986; *Maison Francaise* (Paris), April 1986, December 1986, January 1987, December 1987, September 1988; *Interiors* (New York), June 1986, December 1987; *House and Garden* (London), November 1986; *Interior Design* (New York), February 1987; *Domus* (Milan), November 1987; *Progressive Architecture* (New York), March 1988; *Harpers* (London), August 1994; *Vogue* (France), September 1995.

*

I have often been asked to explain what Ecart actually is. Perhaps an inventory of all the adjectives already used by critics might reveal, in the depth of its contradictions, an explanation or definition of our approach. There have been numerous descriptions of Ecart, some of them going so far as to include in the same breath, or even to marry, austere and playful, subdued and theatrical, downscale and luxurious. How is anyone to make sense of all this?

I no longer see in our work the aesthetic protest of the early days; it has now become more clear: it was an attempt to change things a little bit, to make them come closer to real life. Perhaps more than serenity, we have sought after a certain dream devoid of any arrogance or certitudes, dreams able to reconcile seriousness and play, the plain and the magical, the rich and the poor; work in which nostalgia now exists only on the conceptual level, work in which there is no fear of an error of taste. One gets the clear impression that in order to find life again we have had to endure blank pages, emptiness and silence.

Today I understand that Ecart means being off the beaten track and swimming against the current. So then what does one do with such a lovely name, that has trace as its anagram, when support and appreciation have been achieved?

Just as work of precision born of obsession and marked by care, appears more relaxed than accurate as time passes, more improvised than obsessive, the notion that arises later is linked more to pleasure than to effort. That is perhaps one of the effects of timelessness.

—Andrée Putman

# QUANT, Mary

British fashion, housewares, and product designer

**Born:** London, 11 February 1934. **Education:** Schools in England, until 1951; studied art and design, at Goldsmith's College of Art, University of London, 1952-55. **Family:** Married Alexander Plunket Greene in 1957 (died, 1990); son: Orlando. **Career:** Fashion designer, London, from 1955; established Bazaar fashion clothing shop and Alexander's Restaurant, in Chelsea, London, 1955, and Bazaar shop, in Knightsbridge, London, 1957; founder-director, Mary Quant Ginger Group wholesale clothing design and manufacturing firm, and Mary Quant Limited, London, 1963; cosmetics line introduced, 1966; Mary Quant Japan franchise shops, throughout Japan, 1983; has designed for J. C. Penney, Puritan Fashions, Alligator Rainwear, Kangol, Dupont Europe, Dorma, Berg River Textiles, Model Toys, Staffordshire Potteries, Polaroid, Templeton Carpets, K. Shoes, Radici Sud, Pollyanna Childrenswear, and others; also director of Mary Quant Wine Shippers, London, 1974-78. **Member:** Design Council, London, from 1971; British/US Bicentennial Commission, 1973-76; Advisory Council of the Victoria and Albert Museum, London, 1976-78. **Exhibitions:** *Fashion: An Anthology,* Victoria and Albert Museum, London, 1971; *Mary Quant's London,* London Museum, 1973; *Eye for Industry,* Victoria and Albert Museum, London, 1986. **Honors:** Woman of the Year Award, London, 1963; *Sunday Times* Design Award, London, 1963; Maison Blanche Rex Award, 1964; Piavola d'Oro Award, Italy, 1966; Chartered Society of Designers Medal, London, 1966; Officer, Order of the British Empire, 1966; Fellow, Chartered Society of Designers, London, 1967; Royal Designer for Industry, Royal Society of Arts, London, 1969; British Fashion Council Hall of Fame Award, 1990; Senior Fellow, Royal College of Art, London, 1991. **Address:** 3 Ives Street, London SW3 2NE, England.

## Works

Fashion collections, for J. C. Penney, 1962.
Dress collections, for Puritan Fashions, 1964.
Mary Quant hosiery, for the Nylon Hosiery Company, 1965.
Berets and hats, for Kangol, 1967.
Bedwear and curtains, for Dorma, 1972.
Axminster carpets, for Templetons, 1978.
Mary Quant shoes, for K Shoes/Mocci Shoes, 1982.
Mary Quant wallcoverings, for Worley, 1984.
Mary Quant rainwear, for Fultons, 1985.
Mary Quant clothing, for Great Universal Stores/Kays, 1987.

## Publications

**By QUANT: books**—*Quant by Quant,* London, 1966, Bath, 1974; *Colour by Quant,* with Felicity Greene, London, 1984; *Quant on Make-Up,* with Vicci Bentley, London, 1986; **articles**—"A Personal Design for Living" in *The Listener* (London), 19 December 1974; "Things I Wish I'd Known at 19" in the *Sunday Express Magazine* (London), 21 June 1982.

**On QUANT: books**—*The Fashion Makers* by Leonard Halliday, London, 1966; *The Beautiful People* by Marylin Bender, New York, 1967; *Fashion: An Anthology by Cecil Beaton,* exhibition catalogue compiled by Madeleine Ginsburg, London, 1971; *Mary Quant's London,* exhibition catalogue by Brian Morris and Ernestine Carter, London, 1973; *The World of Fashion: People, Places, Resources* by Eleanor Lambert, London and New York, 1976; *Fashion in the 60s* by Barbara Bernard, London and New York, 1978; *Magic Names of Fashion* by Ernestine Carter, London, 1980; *The Collector's Book of Twentieth Century Fashion* by Frances Kennett, London and New York, 1983; *Les Années 60* by Anne Bony, Paris, 1983; *McDowell's Directory of Twentieth Century Fashion* by Colin McDowell, London, 1984; *The Conran Directory of Design* edited by Stephen Bayley, London, 1985; *The Encyclopaedia of Fashion from 1840 to the 1980s* by Georgina O'Hara, London, 1986; *Eye for Industry: Royal Designers for Industry 1936-1986* by Fiona MacCarthy and Patrick Nuttgens, London, 1986; *Pop Design: Modernism to Mod,* exhibition catalogue by Nigel Whiteley, London, 1987; *Radical Rags: Fashions of the Sixties* by Joel Lobenthal, New York, 1990; **articles**—"British Couple Kooky Styles" in *Life* (New York), 5 December 1960; "Brash New Breed of British Designers" in *Life* (New York), 8 October 1963; "Mary, Mary, Quite Contrary, How Does Your Money Grow?" by John Davis in *The Observer* (London), 19 August 1973; "The Middle Age of Mary Quant" by Wilfred De'Ath in the *Illustrated London News,* February 1974; "How Does Her Empire Grow?" by H. Kingsley in the *Sunday Telegraph Magazine* (London), 29 March 1981; "Interview with Mary Quant" by Jan Jackson in the *Leicester Mercury* (England), 12 November 1984; "Mary's Quantum Leap into the Eighties" by Shirley Lowe in *The Sunday Times Magazine* (London), 10 August 1986; "Mary Quant" by Percy Savage in *Art and Design* (London), September 1986; "Minis to the Masses" by Deborah Orr in *New Statesman & Society* (London), 10 October 1990; "Uppers and Downers: British Entrepreneurs of the Past 25 Years" in *Management Today* (London), 9 October 1991.

\*   \*   \*

Mary Quant, born into a musical Welsh family, knew from her earliest days that she wanted to design clothes and early manifested her individuality by attending—and leaving—thirteen schools. But her parents insisted on a conventional education, and she finally completed her studies at the Goldsmith's College, London; as recompense for this compliance, she was allowed to attend evening classes in the cutting and construction of clothes. She was only twenty-one when, in 1955, she opened her first shop, Bazaar, in London's artist-quarter, Chelsea. This instantaneous success was followed by a sister shop of the same name in the prestigiously fashionable Knightsbridge.

In 1957 she married Alexander Plunket Greene, son of a famous musical family, and together they went to America where they caused a sensation and were quickly signed by J. C. Penney to design clothes and underwear for the wholesale market. The following year, Quant was nominated "Woman of the Year," won the Sunday *Times* International Award, and founded her Ginger Group, whose aim was to make prototypes for the wholesale market to copy and sell to the retail.

In 1964, she made an agreement with Puritan Fashions of New York to design dresses for the American wholesale market and another to design for the worldwide Butterick Paper Patterns. A born innovator, Quant was the first to explore the possibilities of P.V.C. and the first designer of tights for the Nylon Hosiery Company, soon followed by a collection of swimwear. In 1966, she began to produce a range of cosmetics (since taken over by Max Factor) which have a global distribution and have been particularly successful in Japan. The same year she was given the Order of the British Empire, won the Piavola d'Oro award of Italy, and published her autobiography, *Quant by Quant.*

In 1969, Quant was elected Royal Designer for Industry, but activities did not prevent her bearing a son, Orlando, in 1970. Nineteen seventy-three saw a special exhibition of Mary Quant's London at the London Museum, and during the next eighteen months,

Quant was the pivot of two important promotional campaigns, one for the International Wool Secretariat and the other for I.C.I.'s new dress fabric, Crimpelene. In these and the ensuing years, Quant continued to widen her range to include toys, dolls, sunglasses, pottery mugs for Staffordshire, carpets for Axminster, berets, scarves, uniforms for stewardesses, and household goods.

Nineteen eighty-three saw "Mary Quant at Home" launched in the United States. Under this program, a dozen carefully chosen firms agreed to manufacture their products in correlated colours chosen by Quant, so that any one item of household furnishings could be selected with the certain knowledge that all other household necessities—wallpapers, soft furnishings, carpets, china, etc.—can be obtained in matching colours but in a wide range of designs.

In the 1980s, Quant had sixteen licences, including one for wine, and continues from strength to strength. Just the name Quant conjures up her individual flair for design to anyone with any knowledge of fashion.

—Madge Garland

# RAACKE, Peter
German sculptor and interior and industrial designer

**Born:** Hanau, 27 September 1928. **Education:** Studied metal and glass design under Elisabeth Teskow at the Ecole des Beaux-Arts, Paris, 1942; studied metal and enamelwork, at the Staatliche Zeichenakademie, Hanau, 1942-48; studied metal and glass design, at the Werkschule, Cologne, 1950. **Military Service:** Served in the German Army, 1944-45. **Family:** Married Ingrid Kauffmann in 1952; children: Gordian, Dominic, Katarina, and Roman. **Career:** Freelance furnishing and household appliance designer, working in Saarbrucken and Kassel, 1953-58, in Ulm, 1963-68, and in Hamburg, from 1968; designed for Faltmobel Ellen Raacke, Hessische Metallwerke, ITT Business Systems, Dunlop, Rasch, and others. Assistant instructor in metal construction, State Technical Art School, Darmstadt, 1951-53; instructor in metal design, State Technical Art School, Saarbrucken, 1953-58; head of production design course, State Technical Art School, Kassel, 1958-61; instructor in product design, University of Design, Ulm, 1963-66; professor of industrial design, Hochschule für Bildende Kunste, Hamburg, from 1968. Founder and co-editor, of *Szene* magazine, Hamburg; founder-member, Vereinigung Deutscher Industrie Designer. **Exhibitions:** *Gold und Silber,* Gewerbemuseum, Nuremberg, 1971; *1. Detuscher Designertag,* Karlsruhe, 1977; *Design Since 1945,* Philadelphia Museum of Art, 1983. **Collections:** Musée des Arts Decoratifs, Paris; Museum of Modern Art, New York; Philadelphia Museum of Art. **Honors:** Gold Medal, Milan Triennale, 1964; National German Industry Award, 1971, 1974; Gute Form Prize, Darmstadt, 1973. **Address:** Innocentiastrasse 44, 22 Hamburg 13, Germany.

## Works

*Mono* range of cutlery and kitchen equipment, for Hessische Metallwerke, from 1958.
*Papp* cardboard furniture, for Faltmobel Ellen Raacke, 1967.
*Voko* office furniture range.
*Dunlopillo* beds in foam construction, for Dunlop.
Telephones and electronic equipment, for ITT Business Systems.

## Publications

**On RAACKE: books**—*Stahlmobel* by Gustav Hassenpflug, Düsseldorf, 1960; *The Modern Chair: 1850 to Today* by Gilbert Frey, London and Niederteufen, 1970; *Contemporary Furniture* edited by Klaus-Jurgen Sembach, Stuttgart and London, 1982; *Design Since 1945* edited by Kathryn Hiesinger and George Marcus, Philadelphia and London, 1983.

# RABANNE, Paco
Spanish fashion designer

**Born:** Francisco Rabaneva-Cuervo, in San Sebastian, 18 February 1934; emigrated to France in 1939. **Education:** Educated at the College of Morlaix, France, 1940-45, and the Lycee de Sables d'Olonne, France, 1945-50; studied architecture, at the Ecole Nationale Superieure des Beaux-Arts, Paris, 1952-64. **Career:** Designer of accessories for the fashion houses of Cristobal Balenciaga, Hubert de Givenchy, Christian Dior, and Jacques Griffe, Yves Saint Laurent, and others, in Paris, 1960-64; freelance fashion designer, working in plastics, paper, and metal, from 1965; established Paco Rabanne fashion house, Paris, 1967, offering collections for women, ready-to-wear collections for men, from the early 1980s, and ready-to-wear collections for women, from 1990; established Maison Paco Rabanne furnishings company, Paris, 1981, offering furniture, tableware, and linens; offered scents for men and women, including *Calandre,* 1969, *Paco Rabanne pour Homme,* 1973, *Metal,* 1979, *La Nuit,* 1985, *Sport,* 1986, *Ténéré,* 1988, *XS,* 1993; offered skin care line for men, *Soin pour Homme,* 1984; opened retail shop for full line of goods at 7 rue de Cherche Midi, Paris, 1990. Also film costume designer, from 1964. Founder of Groupe Verseau modern aesthetics group, Paris, 1966, and Theatre Panique group, Paris, 1967. **Exhibitions:** *International Exhibition,* Pavillon Français, Montreal; *International Conference of American Architects,* 1966; *Body Covering Exhibition,* Museum of Contemporary Crafts, New York, 1968; Osaka Fair, Japan, 1970; Royal exhibition, Seville, Spain, 1992; *Exposition Paco Rabanne,* Musée de la Mode, Marseille, France, 1995. **Honors:** Sculpture Prize, Paris Biennale, 1963; Tibere d'Or Fashion Award, Capri, 1967; Beaute-Industrie Award, Institut d'Esthetique Industrielle, Paris, 1969; International Oscar Award for perfume, New York, 1974; L'Aiguille d'Or Award, Paris, 1977; Hommage de la Mode prize, International Fashion Festival, 1985; Officer of the Order of Isabelle the Catholic, Spain, 1989; Chevalier of the Legion of Honour, France, 1989; Dé d'Or, 1990. **Address:** Paco Rabanne Couture, 6 Boulevard du Parc, 92523 Neuilly sur Seine, France.

## Publications

**By RABANNE: books**—*Trajectory,* Paris, 1991; *The End of Times,* Paris, 1994; **articles**—*Maison Francaise* (Paris), May 1983.

**On RABANNE: books**—*Design Through Discovery* by Marjorie Elliott Bevlin, New York, 1977; *In Vogue: Sixty Years of Celebrities and Fashion* edited by Georgina Howell, London, 1975, 1978, New York, 1976; *The World of Fashion: People, Places, Resources* by Eleanor Lambert, New York and London, 1976; *Quest for the Best* by Stanley Marcus, New York, 1979; *The Collector's Book of Twen-*

**Paco Rabanne: Couture fall/winter 1995. Photo by Guy Marineau, courtesy of Paco Rabanne**

*tieth Century Fashion* by Frances Kennett, London and New York, 1983; *Les Annees 60* by Anne Bony Paris, 1983; *McDowell's Directory of Twentieth Century Fashion* by Colin McDowell, London, 1984; *The Encyclopaedia of Fashion from 1840 to the 1980s* by Georgina O'Hara, London, 1986.

\* \* \*

The clothes produced by Paco Rabanne in the 1960s brought a new meaning to the word "couture," as he replaced traditional textiles with plastic, aluminum, and paper, while hand and machine sewing gave way to welding and moulding. Rabanne's creations could be termed "wearable sculptures," for the materials and methods used to produce them had closer similarities to developments in contemporary sculpture and kinetic art than to those used in fashion at the time. His first designs, made of plastic and feathers, were in fact shown in a Paris art gallery as Pop sculptures.

The image he created was shockingly futuristic but serious in intent. To Rabanne, fashion is a reflection of the world in which it is created. If his designs of the 1960s still appear to be bizarre, sci-fi fantasies today, they must, at the same time, be recognized as products of their age. They helped to draw attention to the potential of new fabrics, such as synthetics, and to the widest colour ranges which were becoming available to the world of fashion. The fluorescent and neon effects new to sculpture were suddenly shown to have potential for dressing; with them, came new methods of construction. Welding and boning are now accepted methods for uniting plastic fabrics which have since become so popular, particularly for rainwear. This gave scope for the introduction of new, freer shapes which, for Rabanne, indicate the future of developments in clothing.

It was probably Rabanne's architectural training that impelled him to design clothes which were built up of individual elements such as plastic and metal discs. These discs produced a vogue for huge, bright, plastic earrings which became a commercial fashion in the late 1960s. Ever since, plastic has had a considerable role to play in modern jewelry design. Rabanne's work in the 1960s helped plastics and synthetics to become respected in their own right, rather than being treated as shoddy alternatives to other materials. He also opened up the scope for experiment with more traditional fabrics such as leather and fur.

Rabanne has brought a fresh approach to fashion by showing that there is much to be learned by looking beyond established methods and techniques. The fact that he has continued to widen his interests into the last decade of the twentieth century emphasizes that his view of fashion is broad and that this is no respecter of seasonal changes of style.

—Hazel Clark

# RAMBOW, Gunter

German graphic designer

**Born:** Neustrelitz, 2 March 1938. **Education:** Studied glass painting at the Staatliche Glasfachschule, Hadamar, 1954-58; studied graphics under Hans Hillmann, at the Hochschule für Bildende Künste, Kassel, 1958-64. **Career:** Founder-partner, with Gerhard Lienemeyer, Rambow + Lienemeyer graphic design studio, Kassel, 1960-64, Stuttgart, 1964-67, and Frankfurt, 1967-73; partner, with Lienemeyer and Michael Van de Sand, Rambow/Lienemeyer/Van de Sand studio, Frankfurt, 1972-88; partner, Rambow/Rambow/Van de Sand studio, Frankfurt, 1988-92; partner, Rambow Van de Sand studio, Frankfurt, from 1992; also founder, with Gerhard Lienemeyer, Kohlkunst Verlag publishing company, Frankfurt, 1967. Professor of graphic design, Gesamthochschule, Kassel, 1974-87; professor of visual communications, University of Kassel, 1987-91; professor of visual communications, from 1991, and deputy vice-chancellor, from 1992, Staatliche Hochschule für Bildende Künste, Karlsruhe. **Exhibitions:** *Plakate von Rambow, Lienemeyer, Van de Sand,* Deutsches Plakatmuseum, Essen, 1983; *Rambow, Lienemeyer, Van de Sand,* Wilanow Poster Museum, Warsaw, 1984; *Posters from Rambow, Lienemeyer, Van de Sand,* Galerie Bruno Oldani, Oslo, 1985; *Rambow, Lienemeyer, Van de Sand: Affiches,* 7 Allee Georges Braque, Paris, 1985; *Posters from Lenica, Hillmann, Rambow,* New York Gallery, New York, 1986; *Rambow à la Bibliotheque,* Bibliotheque Nationale, Paris, 1988; *Rambow: Plakate 1960-1988,* Museum Wiesbaden, 1988-92; *Plakatwerke von Rambow,* Akademie der Künste der DDR, Berlin, 1989; *Plakate von Gunter Rambow,* Kunstmuseum, Breda, Netherlands, 1992; *Rambow, work in progress,* Hochschule für Grafik + Buchkunst, Leipzig, 1993. **Collections:** Deutsches Plakatmuseum, Essen; Staatliche Kunstsammlungen, Kassel; Akademie der Künste, Berlin; Preussische Kunstbibliothek, Berlin; Museum Wiesbaden; Stedelijk Museum, Amsterdam; Bibliotheque Nationale, Paris; Musée de l'Affiche, Paris; Wilanow Poster Museum, Warsaw; Library of Congress, Washington, D.C.; Museum of Modern Art, New York; Kunstmuseum, Lahti, Finland; Ruki Matsumoto, Tokyo. **Honors:** Named to 10 best poster list, Bund Deutscher Gebrauchsgrafiker, West Germany, 1960-66; 49 national poster prizes, West Germany, 1960-83; First Prize, Bund Deutscher Gebrauchsgrafiker and ICTA, West Germany, 1967; Bronze Medal, 1968, and Gold Medal, 1980, Warsaw Poster Biennale; Colorado Poster Exhibition Prize, Fort Collins, 1979, 1983; UNESCO Prize, Best European Theater Poster, Florenz, 1979; Silver Medal, 1980, and Prix Toulouse Lautrec and Gold Medal, 1983, Triennial Essen; Special Prize, Graphic Design, Germany, 1981; Bund Deutscher Graphic Designer, Berlin, 1981; Gold Medal, 1982, and Critics' Prize, 1986, Brno Graphic Design Biennale; Grand Prize, 1985, and Gold Medal, 1991, Lahti Poster Biennale; Political Poster Prize, Mons, 1988; Gold Medal, International Poster Biennial, Chaumont, 1990; Gold Medal, German Designers Club, 1992; Infinity Award, International Center of Photography, 1992; Special Prizes, Design Zentrum Nordrhein Westfalen, Essen, 1995; Distinctive Merit Award, Art Directors Club of New York, 1995. **Address:** Kronberger Strasse 32, D-60323 Frankfurt am Main, Germany.

## Works

*Charlie Chaplin, Goldrausch* poster, for Atlas Film, Duisburg, 1962.
*Onkel Onkel* poster, for the Theater der Altstadt, Stuttgart, 1967.
*Stop* poster, for *Egoist* magazine, 1968.
*It's Time to Fly to Hanoi* poster, for Kohlkunstverlag, 1968.
*Hand and Book* poster series, for S. Fischer Verlag, Frankfurt, 1976-79.
*Antigone* poster series, for the Schauspiel, Frankfurt, 1978.
*Othello* poster, for the Schauspiel, Frankfurt, 1978.

21. Juni

FRANKFURTER BÜCHERNACHT

Gunter Rambow: Frankfurter Büchernacht

*Zum Raum wird ier die Zeit...* poster series, for Galerie Rene Block, Berlin, 1981.
*P.E.N. im Exil* poster, for the Deutsche Bibliothek, Frankfurt, 1983.
*Schauspiel im Fruhling* poster, for the Schauspiel, Frankfurt, 1985.
*Nachtlicht* poster, for Hessischer Rundfunk, 1987.
*Nur Wissen schafft keine Kunst* poster, for the University of Kassel, 1988.
*Sudafrikanisches Roulette* poster, for the Staatstheater, Stuttgart, 1988.

## Publications

By RAMBOW: books—*König Immerlustik,* Frankfurt, 1968; *Doris,* Frankfurt, 1970; *Der Glöckner von Notre Dame und die Madonna der sieben Monde,* Frankfurt, 1976; *Das sind eben Bilder der Strasse,* Frankfurt, 1979; *Ein Plakat ist eine Fläche, die ins Auge springt,* Frankfurt, 1979; *Traumstoff,* Frankfurt, 1986; (co-author) *Visuelle Kommunikation,* Berlin, 1989; *Fernsehdesign Modell hessen 3,* Berline, 1991.

On RAMBOW: books—*German Advertising Art* edited by Eberhard Hölscher, Munich, 1967; *The Poster: An Illustrated History from 1860* by Harold F. Hutchinson, London and Toronto, 1968; *Who's Who in Graphic Art* edited by Walter Amstutz,

Dubendorf, 1982; *A History of Graphic Design* by Philip B. Meggs, London and New York, 1983; *Top Graphic Design* by F. H. K. Henrion, Zürich, 1983; *Rambow: Plakate 1960-1988,* exhibition catalogue edited by Volker Rattemeyer, Wiesbaden, 1988; *Kommentare zur Gesellschaft, Plakate von Gunter Rambow* edited by Akademie der Künste der DDR, Berlin, 1990; *The 100 Best Posters from Europe and the United States 1945-1990* edited by Milton Glaser, Tokyo, 1995; articles—*High Quality,* no. 13, 1989; *Idea* (Tokyo), no. 221, 1990; *Graphis* (Zürich), no. 269, 1990.

## RAMS, Dieter

German industrial designer

Born: Wiesbaden, 20 May 1932. Education: Studied architecture and interior design, at the School of Art, Wiesbaden, 1947-48, 1951-53; apprenticed as a carpenter, in Kelkheim, 1948-51. Family: Married Ingeborg Kracht in 1967. Career: Worked in the Otto Appel architecture office, Frankfurt, 1953-55; architect and interior designer, 1955-56, product designer, 1956-60, director of design, 1960-80, and board member, from 1980, at Braun AG, Frankfurt; furniture designer for Otto Zapf (now Wiese Vitsoe), Frankfurt, from 1957. Professor, Hochschule für Bildende Kunste, Hamburg, from 1981. President, German Design Council, Frankfurt, 1987. Exhibitions: *Modern Chairs,* Whitechapel Art Gallery, London, 1971; International Design Centre, West Berlin, 1980 (toured); *Design Since 1945,* Philadelphia Museum of Art, 1983. Collections: Museum of Modern Art, New York. Honors: Interplast Design Award, London, 1961, 1963; Gold Medal, Milan Triennale, 1964; Gold Medal, Liubliana Design Biennale, 1964; Honorary Royal Designer for Industry, Royal Society of Arts, London, 1968; Gold Medal, Vienna Furnishing Salon, 1969; Gute Form Award, Vienna, 1969, 1970, 1973; Society of Industrial Artists and Designers Medal, London, 1978. Address: Braun Aktiengesellschaft, Frankfurter Strasse 145, 6242 Kronberg (Taunus), Germany.

## Works

*Phonosuper SK4* stereo unit, for Braun AG, 1956.
*Hl/H2D* heater-ventilators, for Braun AG, 1959.
*606* shelving system, for Wiese Vitsoe, 1960.
*D 40* slide projector, for Braun AG, 1961.
*T 1000* multiband radio, for Braun AG, 1962.
*620* lounge chair program, for Wiese Vitsoe, 1962.
*Audio 1/2* stereo unit, for Braun AG, 1962.
*Studio 1000* stereo systems, for Braun AG, 1965.
*T2* cylindrical table lighter, for Braun AG, 1968.
*HLD 4* hair dryer, for Braun AG, 1970.
*TG 1000/1020* tape recorder, for Braun AG, 1970.
*Audio 308* stereo units, for Braun AG, 1973.
*Control ET 44* pocket calculator, for Braun AG, 1978.
*Atelier P1, T1, A1,* and *C1* hi-fi components, for Braun AG, 1980.

## Publications

By RAMS: articles—*Management* (Tokyo), March 1974; *Form* (Seeheim), January 1976; *Werk und Archithese* (Stuttgart), April

1977; *Format* (Karlsruhe), May 1977; *The Designer* (London), September 1978; *Design Age* (Tokyo), November 1979; *Werk und Zeit* (Berlin), April 1979.

**On RAMS: books**—*Zeitgemasse Form* by Joann Klockner and others, Munich, 1967; *One Hundred Great Product Designs* by Jay Doblin, New York, 1970; *Made in Germany* by Hans Wichmann, Munich, 1970; *In Good Shape: Style in Industrial Products Since 1960* by Stephen Bayley, London, 1979; *Contemporary Furniture* edited by Klaus-Jurgen Sembach, Stuttgart and London, 1982; *A History of Industrial Design* by Edward Lucie-Smith, London, 1983; *Design Since 1945* edited by Kathryn Hiesinger and George Marcus, Philadelphia and London, 1983; *The Conran Directory of Design* edited by Bayley, London, 1985; *Design Source Book* by Penny Sparke and others, London, 1986.

\*

I think that a good designer must always be an avant-gardist. Always one step ahead of the times. He should—and he must—question everything generally thought to be obvious. He must have an intuition for people's changing attitudes, for the reality in which they live, for their dreams, their desires, their worries, their needs, their living habits. He must also be able to realistically assess the opportunities and the bounds of technology.

—Dieter Rams

\*    \*    \*

As head designer for one company for almost three decades, Dieter Rams would seem less independent than his peers. At Braun, however, he has attained the respect and trust of management and has built a team which can work with unusual freedom. Moreover, Rams has a reputation for drawing engineers to the furthest limits of their possibilities.

In Rams's admiration for Japanese lacquer ware is seen a reflection of his own design concerns—simple yet sleek, stackable yet individually complete, comfortable yet visually stimulating, seamlessly joined yet easily dismantled. Continuity in design development and product families, where several products are interconnected, supplementing and complementing each other, are the hallmarks of the Rams design approach. In both Braun products and Vitsoe furniture, Rams has focused on creating complete systems, which are both functional and combinable. His audio components, with tape deck, stereo turntable, and television capable of being either stacked vertically or aligned horizontally, exemplify this flexibility and ingenuity. Portability in television sets, radios, record players, hair dryers, clocks, and shavers is a highly developed mode in the Braun line, thanks to another aspect of the Rams philosophy. Not only do the designs make efficient use of material and technology, but they are also sensitive to user needs—such as frequent travel, frequent moves from one living space to another, and a faster pace of life. His solutions are streamlined, lightweight, durable everyday objects. In a tribute to the appropriateness of his designs, all the Vitsoe furniture systems, including shelving, stacking units, and wall paneling, which have come on the market since 1958, are still available today.

Rams believes that design should not intrude or be visually aggressive. His product design, therefore, while similar in clarity of expression, precise relationships of volumes and shapes, and

minimalist skin to modern twentieth-century architecture, such as that of Bruno Taut or Erich Mendelsohn, is concerned with the potential of material, engineering, and contemporary technology in its application to user need.

Rams first considers utility, next, practicality, and third, aesthetics. This pragmatic approach, along with the actual products which rely on a simple range of neutrals—black, white, and gray—and basic geometric volumes such as cubes, cylinders, and spheres, has given presence and success to his designs. Rams has brought a high level of design to a large number of people and has influenced the democratization of present-day material culture.

—Sarah Bodine

# RAND, Paul
American graphic designer

**Born:** New York City, 15 August 1914. **Education:** Studied at the Pratt Institute, Brooklyn, New York, 1930-32; Parsons School of Design, New York, 1932; under George Grosz, at the Art Students League, New York, 1939. **Family:** Married Marion Swannie Hall in 1975; children: Catherine. **Career:** Assistant designer in the studio of George Switzer, New York, 1932-35; art director of *Esquire* and *Apparel Arts* magazines, New York, 1937-41; creative director, William H. Weintraub advertising agency, New York, 1941-54; freelance designer, New York, from 1955; consultant to IBM, Cummins Engine Company, and Westinghouse Electric Corporation, from 1956. Instructor in graphic design, Cooper Union, New York, 1938-42, and Pratt Institute, Brooklyn, New York, 1946; professor of graphic design, 1956-1991, professor emeritus, from 1991, Yale University School of Art, New Haven, Connecticut; instructor, Yale Summer Program, Brissago, Switzerland, from 1977. **Exhibitions:** *Advance Guard of Advertising Artists,* Katharine Kuh Gallery, New York, 1941; Composing Room, New York, 1947; Philadelphia Museum of Art, 1948; Boston Museum School of Fine Arts, 1951; University of Florida, Gainesville, 1958; American Institute of Graphic Arts, New York, 1958; Art Directors Club of Tokyo, 1958; School of the Visual Arts, New York, 1964; Carnegie Institute, Pittsburgh, 1964; Temple University, Philadelphia, 1968; Louisiana Arts and Science Center, Baton Rouge, 1969; Virginia Museum of Fine Arts, Richmond, 1970 (toured); *107 Grafici dell'AGI,* Castello Sforzesco, Milan, 1974 (toured); Wichita State University, Kansas, 1977; Pratt Manhattan Center, New York, 1977; Philadelphia College of Art, 1979; Reinhold Brown Gallery, New York, 1982; William Paterson College, Wayne, New Jersey, 1982; Dai Nippon Ginza Gallery, Tokyo, 1992. **Collections:** Museum of Modern Art, New York; Smithsonian Institution, Washington, D.C.; Library of Congress, Washington, D.C.; Kunstgewerbemuseum, Zurich. **Honors:** Philadelphia College of Art Citation, 1962; American Institute of Graphic Arts Medal, 1966; New York Art Directors Club Hall of Fame Award, 1972; honorary Royal Designer for Industry, Royal Society of Arts, London, 1973; Florence Prize for Visual Communication, 1987; Connecticut Art Directors Club Hall of Fame Award, 1995. Honorary professor, Tama University, Tokyo, 1958; honorary master of arts, Yale University; honorary doctorate, Philadelphia College of Art, Parsons School of Design, University of Hartford, and Kutztown University. **Address:** 87 Goodhill Road, Weston, Connecticut 06883, U.S.A.

## Works

Posters, for the 75th anniversary of the University of California at Los Angeles, 1995.
Poster, for Earth Day 1995.

## Publications

**By RAND: books**—*Thoughts on Design,* New York, 1946, 1970, London, 1970; *The Trademarks of Paul Rand,* New York, 1960; *Design and the Play Instinct,* New York, 1965; *Paul Rand: A Designer's Art,* New Haven and London, 1985; *Design Form and Chaos,* New Haven, Connecticut, 1993; *Design: From Lascaux to Brooklyn,* New Haven, 1996.

**On RAND: books**—*Posters: 50 Artists and Designers* edited by Walter Allner, New York, 1952; *Paul Rand: His Work from 1946-58* by Yusaku Kamekura and others, New York and Tokyo, 1959; *The New Graphic Design* by Karl Gerstner and Markus Kutter, Teufen and London, 1959; *An International Survey of Packaging* by Wim Crouwel and Kurt Weidemann, London, 1968; *Design in America* by Ralph Caplan, New York, 1969; *The Corporate Search for Visual Identity* by Ben Rosen, New York and London, 1970; *Communication by Design: A Study in Corporate Identity* by Gerald Woods and others, London, 1972; *In Good Shape: Style in Industrial Products since 1960* by Stephen Bayley, London, 1979; *Who's Who in Graphic Art* edited by Walter Amstutz, Dubendorf, 1982; *Advertising: Reflections of a Century* by Bryan Holme, London, 1982; *The Conran Directory of Design* edited by Stephen Bayley, London, 1985; *The American Design Adventure 1940-1975* by Arthur J. Pulos, London and Cambridge, Massachusetts, 1988; *New American Design* by Hugh Aldersley-Williams, New York, 1988.

\*

The computer has been a boon to the field of communications in general, and a bane to the field of design. The future is a large question mark.

Machines do not contribute to creativity, only people do. This simple fact is not understandable to most people.

—Paul Rand

\*       \*       \*

When Paul Rand began his career, graphic communication was dominated by traditional narrative illustration, and page design often consisted of a symmetrical arrangement of isolated elements: picture, headline, trademark, and others. Seeing the space instead as a visual unit, Rand pushed the separate elements into a dynamic equilibrium and played an important role in introducing the visual language of cubism, constructivism, de Stijl, and the Bauhaus into American design. Also, he further contributed by forging his modernist approach into a graphic design style that was highly personal and uniquely American. From European modern art, Rand learned the use of color, texture, collage, montage, gesture, and visual contrasts as expressive means. His work reflects his understanding of the communicative power of abstract and pictographic symbols,

**Paul Rand: From exhibition at Dai Nippon Ginza Gallery, Tokyo, 1992**

and many of Rand's designs have a disarming simplicity that grows from his ability to comprehend the essence of the subject matter, then project it to the viewer with an economy of means. Always interested in the totality of graphic design, he seeks the strongest possible unity of the visual form with content, which, for him, is conceptual expression rather than narrative matter.

The work that Rand did for IBM, beginning with the 1956 trademark, had a seminal influence upon the evolution of corporate graphic communications. The logo is composed of capital initials developed from a geometric, slabserif typeface, City Medium. Rand applied this to packaging and corporate literature with a consistency that established a strong and memorable image. The 1958 annual report that Rand designed for IBM set the tone and approach for this type of publication for many years. Photographic closeups of electronic circuitry, products, and employees in work environments have simple, elegant design qualities that project an image of an efficient, technologically advanced corporation. Lucid and restrained typography is achieved through the use of wide outer margins and quiet, relatively small headings that depend on weight and placement rather than large size for their contrast with the text.

In other circumstances, Rand has not hesitated to use humor and whimsy as design approaches. He recognizes that the "play instinct," both for the designer searching for a viable solution and for the spectator decoding and responding to the communication, is a vital aspect of effective visual communications.

—Philip B. Meggs

# RASMUSSEN, Jorgen

Danish architect and industrial and graphic designer

**Born:** Odense, 26 April 1931. **Education:** Studied architecture, Royal Danish Academy of Fine Arts, Copenhagen, 1950-55. **Family:** Married Hanne Ringsted in 1957 (divorced, 1972); children: Soren, Maja, Sophie, and Pauline. **Career:** Freelance architect and designer, establishing studio with his twin brother Ib Rasmussen, in Vedbaek, from 1957; designed for Knoll International, Herman Miller, Kevi, Louis Poulsen, and others. Instructor in architecture, Royal Academy of Fine Arts, Copenhagen, 1960-75; Guest Professor, University of Trondheim, 1961; guest lecturer, at Boston University School of Architecture, 1988. **Exhibitions:** *Knoll au Musée,* Musée des Arts Decoratifs, Paris, 1972; *Scandinavian Modern Design 1880-1980,* Cooper-Hewitt Museum, New York, 1982; *New Design for Old,* Boilerhouse/Victoria and Albert Museum, London, 1986. **Collections:** Museum of Applied Arts, Copenhagen. **Honors:** Neuhausen Competition Prize, Copenhagen, 1957; Gold Medal, Royal Academy of Fine Arts, Copenhagen, 1959; ID Danish Design Council Prize, Copenhagen, 1969; Traeprisen Architecture Prize, Copenhagen, 1974; Gute Form Prize, West Germany, 1978; Goed Industriele Ontwerp Prize, Netherlands, 1987. **Address:** Vedbaek Station, 2950 Vedbaek, Denmark.

## Works

Square lamp, for Louis Poulsen, 1960.
Office chairs, for Kevi, 1960-89.
Logos, for Kevi, 1964.
Double-wheel furniture castors, for Kevi, 1967-89.
The Rasmussen Chairs, for Knoll International, 1968.
Kitchen, for Grona Garden exhibition, Sweden 1968.
Tables and filing systems, for Kevi, 1970-75.
Old Man's Wicker Chair, for *New Design for Old* exhibition, Boilerhouse, London, 1986.
Simple seating in laminated wood, for Herman Miller, 1989.

## Publications

**By RASMUSSEN: books**—*Gamle Teglvaerker,* Copenhagen, 1968; **articles**—"Streetscape and its Furniture" in *Havne og Stadsingenioren* (Copenhagen), no. 3, 1989.

**On RASMUSSEN: books**—*Dansk Brugskunst og Design* edited by Landsforeningen DB+D, Copenhagen, 1972; *Knoll au Musée,* exhibition catalogue with text by Christine Rae, Paris, 1972; *50 Designers* by Marc Lavrillier, Novara, 1978; *Knoll Design* edited by Eric Larrabee and Massimo Vignelli, New York, 1979; *Scandinavian Modern Design 1880-1980* edited by David Revere McFadden, New York, 1982; *New Design for Old,* exhibition catalogue with

text by Helen Hamlyn, Eric Midwinter, and others, London, 1986; **articles**—*Mobilia* (Snekkersten), vol. 134, 1966, and vol. 194, 1971.

\*

I was educated as an architect but have always worked in several fields of design, from town and landscape planning to housing and industrial design.

In the mid-1950s, one of my house clients asked me to redesign a whole programme of office chairs, and I have continued working on it for Kevi A/S ever since. Around 1968, I designed "The Rasmussen Chair" for Knoll International, and for it I designed a new double-wheel castor. It was not only functionally perfect, but it also had a neat geometrical appearance. These castors are now produced all over the world in a quantity of 12 million a year, and copy versions must number around 300 million annually.

Although my work is only a small detail of the whole, it has been a pleasure to have contributed to a higher standard of design worldwide. The drive for good design is, for me, the same as the urge to go on living. I assume that somewhere hidden is a better way of doing things. I am a bit afraid of many recent designs and the approach of some designers to their work. I think design should be timeless and functional—not haute couture or art-for-art's sake. Form is not the aim of our work, but an end result.

—Jorgen Rasmussen

# REID, John (Robson)

British architect and exhibition and industrial designer

**Born:** Northampton, 1 December 1925. **Education:** Educated at Wellingborough School, Northamptonshire, until 1941; studied architecture at the Regent Polytechnic, London, Dip. Arch., 1950. **Military Service:** Served in the Green Howards, British Army, 1944-47, Captain. **Family:** Married Sylvia Payne in 1948; children: three. **Career:** Freelance architect and designer, in partnership with Sylvia Reid, London, from 1951; consultant to Thorn Lighting, Rotaflex lighting, Stag Furniture, British Rail, the Post Office, and the United Nations Industrial Development Organization. Dean of art and design, Middlesex Polytechnic, London, 1975-78. Advisory committee member to Central School of Arts and Crafts, London, Leeds College of Art and Design, Newcastle School of Art and Design, and Carleton University, Ottawa; governor, Hornsey College of Art, London. President, Society of Industrial Artists and Designers, London, 1965-66, and of International Council of Societies of Industrial Design (ICSID), 1969-71; vice-president, Illuminating Engineering Society, London, 1969-71; chairman, National Inspection Council for Electrical Installations, London, 1972-73; pageantmaster to the Lord Mayors of London, from 1972. **Honors:** Design Council Awards, London; Milan Triennale Medals; Fellow, Chartered Institution of Building Services, London. **Address:** Arnoside House, 5 The Green, Old Southgate, London N14 7EG, England.

## Works

*The Champion pub* interiors, Wells Street, London, 1955.
Modular storage units in veneered teak, for Stag Furniture, 1960.

Dining chairs in steel and afromosia with leather upholstery, for Stag, 1962.

*Fineline* bedroom furniture range in birch and metal, for Stag, 1966.

Hooper Beach House, Anglesea, Victoria, 1972.

Westminster Arts Theatre office additions, London, 1973.

West Lodge Park Hotel extension, Hadley Wood, 1974.

*The Pyramid* pub, Pin Green, Stevenage, Hertfordshire, 1975.

## Publications

**By REID: books**—*International Code of Professional Conduct,* London, 1969; *A Guide to Conditions of Contract for Industrial Design,* London, 1971; *Design in India, Pakistan, Egypt, and Turkey,* London, 1978.

**On REID: books**—*Public Interiors* by Misha Black, London, 1960; *Looking at Furniture* by Gordon Russell, London, 1964; *Furniture in Britain Today* by Dennis and Barbara Young, London, 1964; *Industrial Design and the Community* by Ken Baynes, London, 1967; *Twentieth Century Furniture* by Philippe Garner, London, 1980.

*       *       *

It was Paul Rickley (now Lord Rickley), then director of the Design Council in 1971, who brought John Reid together with me; each of us heading then the two international design associations. Him as President of the International Council of Societies of Industrial Design, and me as President of the International Council of Graphic Design Associations. My favourable reaction to him as a man confirmed my admiration of his talent as a designer. Competence, professionalism, and imagination. In post-war Britain these qualities were badly needed and were somewhat in short supply. It is no wonder that such a large organisation like Thorn Lighting engaged him as their Design Consultant to design their light fittings and industrial products. Other organisations like Telecom, Savoy Hotel, the New Barbican Art Centre, etc., also employed him to carry out major architectural interior designs. His work eventually expanded over a variety of products as well as architectural and furniture designs, each actively benefiting the other with Reid's typical touch. This touch could be described as an excellent feel for the right type of material to be used for a product and a good sense of space, making the best of limitations by which a location is handicapped. Since his approach to a problem begins with the fundamental research of an assignment and the solution is not only pleasing but inventive, his achievements have a permanency which is not often to be found. The complex theoretical problems are well researched prior to the start of any work, and this is one of the reasons why Reid's skills are so much in demand in countries like India, Pakistan, and Egypt, as well as in Japan, the United States, and many other locations around the world.

—John Halas

# RHODES, Zandra (Lindsey)

British fashion and textile designer

**Born:** Chatham, Kent, 19 September 1940. **Education:** Studied textile design and printmaking, at Medway College of Art, Chatham,

1959-61; textile design, at the Royal College of Art, London, Des. RCA, 1964. **Career:** Established textile design and printing studio, with Alexander McIntyre, London, 1965, and dressmaking firm, with Sylvia Ayton, London, 1966; partner and designer, Fulham Clothes Shop, London, 1967-68; freelance fashion designer, London, 1968-75; director, Zandra Rhodes UK Limited, and Zandra Rhodes Shops Limited, from 1975; launched ready-to-wear collections, in Australia, 1979, and in Britain, 1984; has also designed bedlinens and household textiles. **Exhibitions:** Oriel Gallery, Cardiff, 1978; Texas Gallery, Houston, 1981; Otis Parsons Institute, Los Angeles, 1981; La Jolla Museum of Art, San Diego, 1982; Barbican Centre, London, 1982; School of the Art Institute of Chicago, 1982; Parsons School of Design, New York, 1982; *Zandra Rhodes: A Retrospective with Artworks,* Art Museum of Santa Cruz, California, 1983; El Paso Museum of Art, Texas, 1984. **Collections:** Victoria and Albert Museum, London; City Museum, Stoke on Trent; Bath Museum of Costume, Avon; Royal Pavilion Museum, Brighton; City Art Galley, Leeds; Metropolitan Museum of Art, New York; Chicago Historical Society; La Jolla Museum of Art, California; Smithsonian Institution, Washington, D.C.; Royal Ontario Museum, Toronto. **Honors:** English Fashion Designer of the Year Award, London, 1972; Moore College of Art Award, Philadelphia, 1978; City of Philadelphia Award, 1978; Emmy Award, New York, 1984. DFA, International Fine Arts College of Miami, 1977; Royal Designer for Industry, Royal Society of Arts, London, 1977. **Address:** 87 Richford Street, Hammersmith, London W6 7HJ, England.

## Works

Bedlinens, for Wamsutta USA, 1976.

Interior patterns, for CVP Designs, 1977.

Carpets and rugs, for Regal Rugs, 1977.

Headscarves, for Baar and Beard Incorporated, 1978.

Kitchen textiles and accessories, for Sari Fabrics, 1979.

Printed silk dresses and blouses, for Jack Mulqueen, 1980.

Jeans and T-shirts, for Falmers, 1981.

Knitted silk lingeries, for Courtaulds, 1981.

Cashmere knitwear, for Lyle and Scott, 1982.

ZR perfume, for Fabergé Incorporated, 1984.

*Designs on Legs* hosiery, for Jambetex, 1984.

Shoes, for Pentland Industries, 1984.

Bedlinens, for Monitor Designs, 1985.

## Publications

**By Rhodes: books**—(with Anne Knight) *The Art of Zandra Rhodes,* London, 1984, New York, 1985; **articles**—(with Anne Whitehouse) "A Life in the Day of Zandra Rhodes" in *The Sunday Times Magazine* (London), 24 January 1982; "My Country, Right or Wrong" in the *Sunday Telegraph Magazine* (London), 10 May 1987.

**On RHODES: books**—*Fashion: An Anthology by Cecil Beaton,* exhibition catalogue compiled by Madeleine Ginsburg, London, 1971; *20th Century Fashion: A Scrapbook* by Ernestine Carter, London, 1975; *Zandra Rhodes: A Retrospective with Artworks,* exhibition catalogue, Santa Cruz, 1983; *McDowell's Directory of Twentieth Century Fashion* by Colin McDowell, London, 1984; *Couture: The Great Designers* by Caroline Rennolds Milbank,

London, 1985; *Eye for Industry: Royal Designers for Industry 1936-1986* by Fiona MacCarthy and Patrick Nuttgens, London, 1986; *The Encyclopaedia of Fashion from 1840 to the 1980s* by Georgina O'Hara, London, 1986; *Design Source Book* by Penny Sparke and others, London, 1986; *Radical Rags: Fashions of the Sixties* by Joel Loebenthal, New York, 1990; *Modern Fashion in Detail* by Valerie Mendes and Claire Wilcox, London, 1991; *Women of Fashion* by Valerie Steele, New York, 1991; **articles**—"Zandra's Fantasies" in *Viva* (New York), February 1974; "On the Rhodes" by Lois Perschetz in *Women's Wear Daily* (New York), 26 April 1974; "All Rhodes Lead to Zandra" by Julie Kavanagh in *Women's Wear Daily* (New York), 31 December 1975; "Zandra Rhodes" by Christina Walkley in *Costume* (London), 1976; "British New Style" in Vogue (London), 15 March 1976; "The Zandra Rhodes Dossier" by Georgina Howell in *Vogue* (London), July 1978; "Zandra Rhodes: A Profile" by Joan Bakewell in the *Illustrated London News,* October 1978; "Schooldays" in *Vogue* (London), October 1981; "Zandra Rhodes at Home" in *Connoisseur* (London), December 1981; "Zandra, the Non-stop Rhodes Show" by Antonia Williams in *Vogue* (London), August 1982; "At Long Last Friends: Dress Designer Zandra Rhodes and Her Sister Beverly" by James Fallon in *The Sunday Times Magazine* (London), 8 May 1983; "Zandra Rhodes" in *Art and Design* (London), February 1985; "We'll take the High Rhodes" in *You* magazine of the *Mail on Sunday* (London), 28 February 1988; "The Fashion Fatigue of Zandra Rhodes" in *Design Week* (London), 11 March 1988; "Ware-ability" by Nonie Niesseward in *Connoisseur,* June 1988; "Zandra Rhodes" in *Pins and Needles* (London), July 1988; "The Correspondent Questionnaire: Zandra Rhodes" in *The Correspondent Magazine* (London), 21 October 1990; "Zandra Rhodes Couture" by Claire B. Schaeffer in *Threads* (Newtown, Connecticut), June/July 1990; "The London Home of Zandra Rhodes" by Alan O'Kelly in *House Beautiful* (London), November 1990.

*

I am a person driven by extreme ambition with the desire to make an original contribution to society. My individual statement is made mainly by my prints and the way in which they are transformed into dresses. I believe in the excitement of dressing up and making a woman feel beautiful. Every woman has something wonderful about her, no matter what her size. I enjoy finding the key to each individual in order to enhance her looks.

I am an artist working through the medium of my prints and dresses. I produce specially designed screen prints that set the theme and express my own particular handwriting. The inspiration in these prints comes mainly from artist friends, travel, and landscape, and from my life and where it leads me.

I like to work in the print room with a variety of fabrics: e.g., chiffon, felt, velvet, taffeta, and suede, my arms elbow-deep in dye until I am satisfied by the design and colour. This is where and when I am happiest in my work.

I love to specialise in making evening dresses, but I also like to cover the full spectrum of a woman's daily wardrobe, enabling her to feel "special" at any hour of the day or night.

I do not like to copy the past—my work must represent the present. Retrospective influences are used but not copied.

—Zandra Rhodes

*     *     *

Imaginative, rhythmic, mysterious—one might use these words to describe the art of Zandra Rhodes. Looming out of the late 1960s, she emerged in our world like a painter of dreams, her fantasy illuminating new escape routes from a confused, dizzy world of drugs and nostalgia. Rhodes put fashion with poetic vision into a new dimension. Her colors flow rhythmically through a room and over the wearer's body. Her patterns and prints defy criticism, as lipsticks, teardrops, and teddy bears cover organdy, while cacti and the colors of the New Mexico desert decorate chiffon. Two timeless designs are the T-shaped printed chiffon gown belted in satin, and the Ukranian festival dress with its gathered sleeves and full pleated skirt.

Whereas others of the 1960s English movement died in 1971, when Yves Saint Laurent opened Rive Gauche and Paris once again took the crown of fashion, Rhodes continued to grow. She has developed a personal look through painting fabrics and originating garments that sometimes test the limits of the three-dimensional. A tireless worker, she has labored long to create a vocabulary of intensely personal forms that speak softly of intimacy and nature. As a designer, she has broken new ground, not only by introducing fantasy and a delicate and lyrical content into her designs, but by daring to experiment with new techniques of finishings and application of materials.

Because of the unique and fantastic quality of Rhodes' designs, her clothes do not date. She is one of the most original designers of the late 20th century.

—Andrea Arsenault

# RICHARDSON, Deane

American industrial designer

**Born:** Goldfield, Iowa, 26 January 1930. **Education:** Attended City College of New York, 1955, and the University of Michigan, 1957; Pratt Institute, New York, B.I.D., 1956. **Family:** Married Sandra Nelson Longyear; children: Mark William, Christine Rai, Derek Kendall. **Career:** Industrial designer, Sundberg-Ferrar, Detroit, Michigan, 1956-58; co-founder and principal, from 1959, president, 1965-70, chairman, 1975-85, co-chairman, 1986-88, chairman emeritus, from 1989, RichardsonSmith Inc. (merged with Fitch of London, England, 1988; changed all regional offices names to Fitch, from 1994), Columbus, and later Worthington, Ohio. Chairman, WORLDesign ICSID Congress, 1985; advisory committee, WORLDesign foundation, 1989; lecturer at universities and design conferences throughout the world. **Member:** Fellow, Industrial Designers Society of America; executive board, from 1987, and president, from 1991, International Council of Societies of Industrial Design (ICSID). **Honors:** Alumni Award, Pratt Institute, New York, 1976; Personal Recognition Award, Industrial Designers Society of America, 1985; many other design awards. **Addresses:** (home) 860 Old Woods Rd., Worthington, Ohio 43235, U.S.A.; (office) Fitch Inc., 10350 Olentangy River Rd., PO Box 360, Worthington, OH 43085, Ohio, U.S.A.

## Works

Product design strategy, for Xerox, from 1981 (with RichardsonSmith Inc. and Xerox staff).

**Deane Richardson: part of the core elements of a "living" corporate identity system, which is flexible, communicative, iterative, and creative, for Too Corporation. Fitch/IDEX joint authorship**

Evergreen product design strategy, for NCR, 1980s (with RichardsonSmith Inc. and NCR Design Director Pierre Crease).

Corporate identity program, for .TOO (formerly Izumiya), Tokyo, Japan, 1993.

Design program, for GoldStar Industrial Power Tools, Seoul, Korea, 1994.

Also helped to develop design strategies for Crown Forklift Trucks, New Bremen, Ohio; Mitsubishi Electric cellular telephones, Ofuna and Yokohama, Japan; Bank One; Texas Instruments; Mazda; Toyota Forklift Trucks; Mitsui Insurance; and others.

*

Being a co-founder of RichardsonSmith and currently very active in Fitch, I feel my work has enabled our profession to move forward in three areas.

1. Multi-discipline Teams: To address more challenging needs in products (safety, performance, globalism) we created teams consisting of behavioral psychologists, cognitive psychologists, engineers, market researchers, planners, linguists, etc. to improve the level of input and our design results. An integral part of this process is the use of "war rooms" or dedicated project spaces, now called *design spaces* at Fitch, to encourage and integrate the work and interactions of these multi-disciplined teams. Another part of this work was "working on walls," push pin walls, so that all ideas, research, etc. were fully exposed, encouraging interaction.

2. Product Design Strategy: Design was moving toward a more strategic role in defining the direction of a few companies in the 1970s. U.S. corporations were decentralizing operations and reducing costs to meet the off-shore competition, which often resulted in fragmented product design efforts and a lack of a cohesive plan. Our work in this area required new and rational thinking about the longer term role of design.

3. Design Partnerships between Corporate Design Staffs and Design Consultants: The search for methods and processes in which the consultants and corporate designs may cooperate rather than compete on programs was an important step. RichardsonSmith (later Fitch) is well known for its openness and sharing of information with clients and our profession.

The foundation of the industrial design profession is now well established. As a profession, we are ready to be of service in ways we have not been able to serve before. Segments of our profession are focused on how design can be employed to help improve humanity (the disabled and aging, safety, ecology) rather than on business success alone. We have more knowledge and tools to design for the situation or the event rather than simply the object. Designers have not been empowered to set priorities in the past, but some designers will be so in the future and those designers will take greater responsibility for their actions. There is an awesome future if we pick up the ball. How well we run with it remains to be seen.

—Deane Richardson

*     *     *

Deane Richardson is a man who builds relationships. The ultimate salesperson, he never asks for a sale. He never needs to. By the time the contract is ready, his firm is the only option because he has created a sense of integrity, involvement, credibility, trust, openness, interest, and respect through years of personal contact.

This style particularly suits him to business in the Pacific Rim countries, where executives are uncomfortable with what they characterize as the "hard and fast" business styles of the Americans and British. Deane didn't visit Japan, Korea, and Taiwan a few times, schmooze a little, and expect clients. He has invested the past eight years, spending six months out of the year living in the Orient.

This soft approach to representing a firm has been made possible by the far-sighted funding support of the firm that is now called Fitch Inc. Deane Richardson has been under no pressure to produce; rather, he has taken the time to attend, listen, and make presentations at conferences, observing how each country's people lives, works, and plays, and understanding the cultural and historic underpinnings of each society first hand. In fact, he has often been asked by Japanese business executives, why, after the deal is done, he's still there. His answer? "When you needed to strengthen your economy with exports, you didn't hold focus groups, you never asked a question. You took your cameras and you visited your target markets and you observed, photographed, listened. I am here to return the favor."

Having secured a design program, Deane remains personally involved in the design process. Because when a Japanese or Korean company signs with Fitch, they are signing with Deane. They are responding to his fundamental belief in an atmosphere of respect that encourages sharing and joining—a key to the success of RichardsonSmith from its very founding in 1959. Outwardly expressed as a philosophical commitment to multidisciplinary team building, this theme explains why Deane has always sought to mix things up, creating a dynamic, volatile environment that offers the team members a variety of experiences.

The roots of this Pacific Rim presence lie in a decision made in 1982, after more than 20 years building a design firm that was well-respected in the eastern and mideastern parts of the United States. Deane, his partner, Dave Smith, IDSA, and the RichardsonSmith team made a decision in 1982 that has reshaped the entire U.S. industrial design community. In a particularly prophetic move, they decided to focus on growing into an international design office, leapfrogging the national scene. They didn't measure their growth in more dollars or a bigger staff, although making a profit was necessary to support the effort. The real measure of their growth would be found in an expanded scope of work, involvement, and presence. And one of the first steps down that path was the firm's decision to support Deane's role as chair of the first international industrial design congress held in the United States on behalf of the International Council of Societies of Industrial Design (ICSID).

Deane had wanted to find a way to play a more active role in the Industrial Designers Society of America (IDSA) when its then-President Robert G. Smith, FIDSA, asked him to consider the position. It was perfect. It fit his style, letting Deane work on a project with a concrete deliverable, and it provided his firm with a platform from which to launch its internationalization effort. For the next three years, Deane invested his relationship-building talent on behalf of IDSA and the 1985 international congress that came to be known as WORLDESIGN 85/ICSID USA.

With 2,300 attendees, this congress was one of the most successful (by every measure, both financial and otherwise) ever held for industrial designers. At the end, RichardsonSmith had invested $140,000 to participate, exhibit, send 40-some attendees, and support Deane's innumerable expenses on behalf of organizing and talking-up the event. In the process, Deane had created a network of leaders and personal contacts. Perhaps most importantly, however, he had placed the U.S. industrial design community on the international map, winning the respect of its peers.

Within two years of WORLDESIGN 85, Deane had been elected to a position on the ICSID Board of Directors that culminated in the presidency. For eight years, Deane helped build this international body from a position of financial disarray with insufficient staff and resources to a growing, financially stable, and influential body.

Hand in hand with his ICSID work, Deane worked with his partner and the RichardsonSmith team to expand its international reach and diversify its business into retail design. A merger made the most sense, and by the early 1990s the agreement with Fitch, a publicly traded design firm headquartered in London, had been concluded. With Fitch's strong European reputation as a springboard for building that client base, as well as a natural inclination of respect and interest, it was only natural for Deane to focus on giving his firm a strong presence in the Pacific Rim. That he had such impressive ICSID and IDSA credentials—including the prestigious IDSA Personal Recognition Award and leadership in ICSID—could only help. These earned him instant respect and the entrée through boardroom doors other U.S. designers hadn't even begun knocking on yet.

With 36 years and more in his professional career, Deane has seen dramatic changes in the way the design field operates, particularly on the international scene. He recalls a time when access to out-of-state clients was unworkable. It was a time early in the "Jet Age" when few people flew and the air routes and schedules allowed little flexibility. RichardsonSmith solved the problem by buying its own plane. "All the design firms had the same problem, even the firms located in big cities like Chicago. The only difference was, at RichardsonSmith, we did something about it." As flight schedules proliferated, it sold its now-superfluous private plane.

Today, the very fact that planes fly direct from Detroit to Japan has changed the character of the firm's client base by eliminating the stopover in San Francisco and Los Angeles. "You tend to do business wherever the plane touches down. That was a natural opportunity to make a client contact that's no longer there." Even in the past two years, the way design is accomplished has changed as international communication online has gone from unreliable to integral. "I can work 24 hours a day now." It is a measure of his dynamism and the pleasure he takes both in design and in people, that Deane has embraced this brave new world of round-the-clock access and made it his own.

The firm that Deane Richardson and Dave Smith founded in 1959 has grown from its sylvan design offices in Worthington, Ohio, into one of the world's most prestigious design firms. Fitch is today listed among the ten firms that have won the most awards in the IDSA/*Business Week* Industrial Design Excellence Awards program. This unparalleled record of achievement was made possible by their commitment to building teams, sharing credit, and maintaining an atmosphere in which the finest designers can contribute their best efforts. And by Deane's understanding that you don't sell design, you build relationships.

—Kristina Goodrich

# RISOM, Jens

American furniture and product designer

**Born:** Copenhagen, Denmark, 8 May 1916; emigrated to the United States in 1939, naturalized, 1944. **Education:** Educated at Krebs's School, Copenhagen, until 1928, and St. Anne Vester School, Copenhagen, 1929-32; studied at Niels Brock's Business School,

Copenhagen, 1932-34; studied furniture and interior design, at the School of Arts and Crafts, Copenhagen, 1935-38; apprenticed as interior and furnishings designer, in the Ernst Kuhn architectural office, Copenhagen, 1937-38. **Military Service:** Served in the United States Third Army, in Europe, 1943-45. **Family:** Married Iben Haderup in 1939 (died, 1977); children: Helen, Peggy, Thomas, and Sven; married Henny Panduro in 1979. **Career:** Design director and furnishing textiles designer, at Dan Cooper Incorporated, New York, 1939-41; freelance furniture, interior, and textile designer, New York, 1941-43; founder and chief executive, Jens Risom design, New York, 1946-73, and of Design Control, New Canaan, Connecticut, from 1973; has designed for Knoll International, Georg Jensen Incorporated, Howe Furniture, Library Furniture, Gaylord Brothers, and others. Trustee, Rhode Island School of Design, Providence, 1970-76. **Exhibitions:** *Jens Risom, 1941-1994*, H. Pelham Curtis Gallery, New Canaan Library, Connecticut, 1995. **Collections:** Brooklyn Museum of Art, New York; Cooper-Hewitt Museum, New York; Museum of Decorative Arts, Montreal. **Honors:** Lifetime Achievement Award for furniture design and quality, Brooklyn Museum of Art, 1994. **Address:** 103 Chichester Road, New Canaan, Connecticut 06840. U.S.A.

## Works

*Model Home* interiors and furniture in the Rockefeller Center, New York, for *Collier's* magazine, 1940 (with Edward Durell Stone). Easy chair in wood with webbing seat and tables, for Knoll Associates, 1941.

**Jens Risom: U440 low armchair, for Risom Design Inc., 1960**

*600 Line* range of cabinets and furniture in cherrywood, for Knoll Associates, 1942.

Knoll Associates showroom interiors, Madison Avenue, New York, 1947.

*Risom/Burr* range of folding-leg tables in tubular steel with oak or walnut tops, for Howe Furniture Corporation, 1977 (with Alan Burr).

## Publications

**On RISOM: books**—*Design in America* by Ralph Caplan, New York, 1969; *Modern Furniture* by John F. Pile, New York and Toronto, 1979; *Knoll Design* by Eric Larrabee and Massimo Vignelli, New York, 1981; *Contemporary Furniture* edited by Klaus-Jurgen Sembach, Stuttgart and London, 1982; *Mid-Century: Furniture of the 1950s* by Cara Greenberg, London, 1984; *The American Design Adventure 1940-1975* by Arthur J. Pulos, London and Cambridge, Massachusetts, 1988.

*

Three questions are often asked:
1. Is furniture FUNCTIONAL or DECORATIVE?
2. What does CONTEMPORARY mean?
3. What is GOOD DESIGN?

My answers will be personal ones—but I do feel rather strongly about them.

1. Furniture is primarily functional. A chair has to be comfortable and support one's body for whatever purpose it is to be used. Secondarily, it has to look attractive and express the designer's ideas and taste.

2. Contemporary means that the design is created in our time for today's people, environments, habits, and activities, all quite different from what they were some 200 years ago. Keep in mind that the antiques we all admire were once contemporary, and undoubtedly were questioned as ours are today.

3. Design is a creative effort to successfully solve one or more problems; "good design," therefore, is a "good" solution which must satisfy the many requirements. It must have an attractive appearance and its detailing, materials, execution, and craftsmanship have to be of a high standard whether the product is mass-produced, or made by hand.

An uncomfortable chair, a cabinet or a table which does not fulfill its function, or a poorly made piece which does not stand up under normal, or even excessive use cannot, in my opinion, be considered "good design."

Furniture is not sculpture, nor is a design created only for visual appearance. It is meant to be used, enjoyed, and respected.

—Jens Risom

*   *   *

Jens Risom, son of a well-respected Danish architect, determined in his youth to create modern furniture appropriate to both residential and commercial modern architecture. In Scandinavia, since the Stockholm Workshops exhibition of 1930, modern furniture has been accepted as the norm, so Risom's decision was not radical except perhaps in its architectural orientation. After completing business school, he took his degree from the School of Arts and Crafts in Copenhagen, where he came under the influence of Kaare Klint. Klint reinforced Risom's aim to consider furniture as part of the architectural space, rather than as an isolated sculptural entity, and Klint's teachings led him to seek simplicity and fitness to purpose above any particular style.

In 1939, Risom came to the United States, intending to study or work for a year. Here, he found virtually no interest either in training modern designers or in manufacturing modern furniture. American markets preferred Grand Rapids imitation of older styles, and what the market demanded, the schools and manufacturers supplied. Nevertheless, Risom, armed with introductions to influential people at the Museum of Modern Art in New York, soon met architects and others who encouraged him, and he decided to remain in the United States. Briefly, he worked with textile designer Dan Cooper, for whom he was head of studio, producing designs for printed fabrics and arranging displays of home-like settings with his own furniture designs. In 1940, *Colliers* magazine commissioned Edward D. Stone to design a model home in Rockefeller Center, and Risom was placed in charge of interiors throughout.

This was his first chance to introduce his modern, residential furniture to a broad public. By the next year, he was designing for private clients, for Hans Knoll, a young entrepreneur friend, and for Georg Jensen.

In 1946 Risom formed his own company, in which he remained always the sole designer. From the start, Risom explored production of his designs in components, so his furniture could be individualized either for space requirements or for the specific tastes and needs of individual users. Selling mostly through architects and interior planners, his furniture presented an assortment of options available within any line of furniture.

Risom sought to accommodate his designs to the changing styles of life at home and in the work place. By the early 1960s, he concentrated mostly upon furniture for the office, targeting middle- and upper-level executives as his users. He found that they no longer occupied positions as in the past, no longer required static, throne-like chairs nor heavy desks behind which to barricade themselves. Risom realized that office size, being at a premium, is usually smaller than it used to be, and that the democratic open-planning now standard in most offices must be taken into account when designing furniture. Sofas, low tables, and comfortable chairs, which occur in groupings to accommodate conferences, make office and home more alike.

Among leaders in modern furniture design after World War II, the Herman Miller Company and Knoll International were most radically innovative. Both displayed consistently high quality, and Knoll's designers were particularly identified with avant-garde, Bauhaus, metal, and molded furniture. By contrast, Risom designs of finely crafted woods appealed to a more conservative taste. With the widespread acceptance of modern spaces, particularly in offices and institutions, Risom designs mingle with authentic Chippendale and Bauhaus modern.

—Nina Bremer

# ROBBINS, Carrie

American stage designer

**Born:** Carrie Mae Fishbein, in Baltimore, Maryland, 7 February 1943. **Education:** Studied at Pennsylvania State University, Uni-

PRELIMINARY SKETCHES OF
COSTUMES DESIGNED FOR
"THE MADWOMAN OF CHAILLOT."
WILLIAMSTOWN THEATRE FESTIVAL,
SUMMER 1993

Photo:
MS. KATHERINE HELMOND AS
"THE MADWOMAN"

**Carrie Robbins: collage of sketches for "The Madwoman of Chaillot" costumes designed for Williamstown Summer Theater, 1993**

versity Park, BA, BS, 1964; Yale University School of Drama, New Haven, Connecticut, MFA, 1967. **Family:** Married Richard D. Robbins, M.D., in 1969. **Career:** Freelance stage, costume, and scenic designer, New York, from 1967, and restaurant uniform de-

signer, from 1987; has designed productions for the New York Shakespeare Festival, Lincoln Center Repertory Theatre, Chelsea Theatre Center, Vivian Beaumont Theatre, Martin Beck Theatre, and uniforms for the Rockefeller Center Rainbow Room, Aurora

Grill, Empress Court of Las Vegas, and others; tap-dance choreographer and performer, New York City, from 1990. Instructor in costume design, 1971-84, and master teacher, from 1984, at New York University; visiting lecturer, University of Illinois, Urbana, 1977-78. Steering committee member, League of Professional Theatre Training Programs, and United States Institute of Theatre Technology Costume Commission. **Exhibitions:** Central Falls Gallery, New York, 1980. **Honors:** Drama Desk Award, New York, 1971, 1973; Antoinette Perry (Tony) Award nominations, for *Grease,* 1972, and for *Over Here,* 1974; Maharam Award, New York, 1975; Surface Design Award, Fashion Institute of Technology, New York, 1980; Silver Medal, 1981, and Diplome d'Honneur, 1990, Novi Sad Theatre Design Triennale; Dramalogue Critics' Choice Award, Los Angeles, 1982. **Address:** Carrie Robbins Designage Incorporated, 11 West 30th Street, 15th floor, New York, New York 10001, U.S.A.

## Works

Stage productions include—*Bells are Ringing,* Schwab Auditorium, University Park, Pennsylvania, 1962; *Leda Had a Little Swan,* Cort Theatre, New York, 1968; *Inner Journey* Forum Theatre, New York, 1969; *The Year Boston Won the Pennant,* Forum Theatre, 1969; *The Time of Your Life,* Vivian Beaumont Theatre, New York, 1969; *The Good Woman of Setzuan,* Vivian Beaumont Theatre, 1970; *Look to the Lilies,* Lunt-Fontanne Theatre, New York, 1970; *An Enemy of the People,* Vivian Beaumont Theatre, 1971; *Narrow Road to the Deep North,* Vivian Beaumont Theatre, 1972; *The Crucible,* Vivian Beaumont Theatre, 1972; *Grease,* Eden Theatre, New York, 1972; *The Hostage,* Good Shepherd-Faith Church, New York, 1972; *Sunset,* Chelsea Theatre Center, New York, 1972; *The Beggar's Opera,* Chelsea Theatre Center, 1972; *The Secret Affairs of Mildred Wild,* Ambassador Theatre, New York, 1972; *Let Me Hear You Smile,* Biltmore Theatre, New York, 1973; *The Plough and the Stars,* Vivian Beaumont Theatre, 1973; *Molly,* Alvin Theatre, New York, 1973; *The Iceman Cometh,* Circle in the Square, New York, 1973; *The Beggar's Opera,* Billy Rose Theatre, New York, 1973; *Over Here,* Shubert Theatre, New York, 1974; *Merry Wives of Windsor,* New York Shakespeare Festival, 1974; *Yentl, the Yeshiva Boy,* Chelsea Theatre Center, 1974; *Polly,* Chelsea Theatre Center, 1975; *The Boss,* Chelsea Theatre Center, 1976; *Rebel Women,* New York Shakespeare Festival, 1976; *The Misanthrope,* New York Shakespeare Festival, 1977; *The Creditors,* Public Theatre, New York, 1977; *The Stronger,* Public Theatre, 1977; *Happy End,* Martin Beck Theatre, New York, 1977; (sets and costumes) *Old Man Joseph and His Family,* Chelsea Westside Theatre, New York, 1978; *Fearless Frank,* Princess Theatre, New York, 1980; *Frankenstein,* Palace Theatre, New York, 1981; *El Bravo,* Entermedia Theatre, New York 1981; *The First,* Martin Beck Theatre, 1981; *Agnes of God,* Music Box Theatre, New York, 1983; *The Boys of Winter,* Biltmore Theatre, 1985; *The Octette Bridge Club,* Music Box Theatre, 1985; *Twelfth Night,* Alaska Repertory Theatre, Anchorage, 1986; *Raggedy Ann,* 41st Street Theatre, New York, 1986-87; *Rag Dolly,* 41st Street Theatre, 1986-87; *The Eggthea,* 41st Street Theatre, 1986-87; *The Mass,* Boston Opera Company, 1989; *Sweet Bird of Youth,* Scottsdale, Arizona, and Los Angeles; *Golden Boy,* 1992; *Anna Karenina,* Circle-in-the-Square Theatre, New York, 1993; *Madwoman of Chaillot,* Williamston Summer Festival, 1994; *The Shadow Box,* Circle-in-the-Square Theatre, 1994-95.

Costume designer, for *Saturday Night Live* television series, 1985-86.

Costume designer, for *In the Spirit* (film), 1988-89.

Costume designer and choreographer, *Fellini Parade* New Years Eve galas, Busby Berkeley-style *Living Birthday Cake,* and *Rainbow Acapella Quartet,* for Rockefeller Center Rainbow Room, from 1990.

Uniform designer, for The New Windows on the World restaurant, New York, 1996.

Publications:

**By ROBBINS: articles**—*Theatre Crafts* (New York), September 1967, January/February 1974, November/December 1977, January 1981.

**On ROBBINS: books**—*Encyclopedia of Collectibles,* Alexandria, Virginia, 1980; *Fabric Painting and Dyeing for the Theatre* by Deborah Dryden, New York, 1981; *Costume Design* by Barbara and Cletus Anderson, New York, 1983; *Costume Design: Techniques of Modern Masters* by Lynn Pecktal, New York, 1993; articles—*Theatre Design and Technology*(New York), Winter 1987; *Manhattan Inc.* (New York), December 1987; *New York Magazine,* 8 February 1988; *GQ* (New York), March 1988; *Theatre Crafts* (New York), November 1988, September 1992; *National Forum: The Phi Kappa Phi Journal,* Summer 1990.

\*

My work has expanded from the narrow world of costume design alone to the broader and more challenging arena of producing. Theatrical events staged for the Rainbow Room as well as my own fascination with the art of rhythm tap dance have allowed me to combine design with various entertainment forms that I had previously just dressed. I've also had the opportunity to edit video, and to move from live performers to filmed performers to traditional animation to computer animation and circle back to live performers. This experimental blending of drawing and performance continues to intrigue me. I'm delighted and grateful to be able to continue to grow and explore, and am especially challenged by what the computer can offer to designers willing to suffer the learning curve.

—Carrie Robbins

\*     \*     \*

Carrie Robbins' distinctive style results directly from her rich and obsessive personal vision of period and modern costumes in all their complexity and detail. She has listed "fighting insomnia and workaholism" as forms of recreation, and these personal characteristics become very significant in helping to explain her distinctive personal style. She admits to being obsessed with visions of the complex parts and details of her costumes when she is designing a production and often sketches ideas and costume details in the middle of the night. The results on stage are rich and overpowering in their visual complexity. For a production of *The Little Foxes* for the American Conservatory Theatre of San Francisco, Robbins created wonderfully rich and detailed costumes in which as much time and thought had been placed on the subtle heading on Regina Giddon's gowns as upon the individual costume silhouettes. For the San Francisco Opera's *Samson et Dalila,* she evoked an overpoweringly sumptuous Mesopotamian world that reminded one of the great de Mille Biblical epics or Griffith's *Intolerance.* To create these complex visual worlds on stage, Robbins calls upon the costume technicians who work on her productions to use every technique of construction, decoration, and texturing in present use, as well as to experiment with many new techniques.

Unlike some costume designers for whom the costume sketch is a mere suggestion or initial plan for costume shop construction, Robbins' sketches are masterpieces of rich complexity in color, line, and texture, with full attention to all costume detail. In an age when the impressionistic simplicity of a Gordon Craig or a Robert Edmond Jones is no longer in vogue and there is a fond nostalgia for the rich complexities of the Victorian Age, Robbins' richly complex style is most appealing to opera and theatre audiences throughout the major theatres in the United States. She takes her inspiration for sketching techniques from the graphic artists and painters of the later nineteenth century—people such as Gustave Moreau, Edward Burne-Jones, Dante Gabriel Rosetti, and Gustave Dore. But her rich, personal style is in every way an expression and fulfillment of her individual vision.

—Douglas A. Russell

# ROBERTSON, M(alcolm) Clark

American textile and furniture designer

**Born:** Texas, 17 September 1955. **Education:** Studied at Texas Christian University, Fort Worth, 1974-76; studied textile and interior design, at the University of Kansas, Lawrence, BFA, 1979; attended Kansas City Art Institute, Missouri, 1979. **Career:** Worked as a textile colorist, at Brewster Finishing and Design, New York, 1979; design consultant, China Seas Incorporated, New York, 1980-82; freelance textile and home furnishings designer, New York, from 1983. Teaching assistant, Navosota High School, Texas, 1974, and University of Kansas, Lawrence, 1979; guest lecturer at the Fashion Institute of Technology, New York, 1982-83, Rhode Island School of Design, Providence, 1983, and Cooper-Hewitt Museum, New York, 1983; instructor in textile design, Parsons School of Design, New York, from 1983. **Exhibitions:** Handcrafters Gallery, Fort Worth, Texas, 1976; Kerby Gallery, Austin, Texas, 1976; World Trade Center, Dallas, 1976; Brilezyay Gallery, Omaha, 1977; Pacific Basin School of Textile Arts, Berkeley, 1979; China Seas Showroom, New York, 1981; World Trade Center, New York, 1982; Ophelia Gallery, Miami, 1982; Roscoe Resource Council, New York, 1982; *Contemporary Continuous Pattern Design,* Cooper-Hewitt Museum, 1983; *Textiles for the Eighties,* Rhode Island School of Design, Providence, 1984. **Collections:** Cooper-Hewitt Museum. **Address:** 474 Broadway, 2nd floor, New York, New York 10013, U.S.A.

**Publications**

**On ROBERTSON: books—***Textiles for the Eighties,* exhibition catalogue with text by Sheila Hicks and Maria Tulokas, Providence, 1984.

*      *      *

The textile designer M. Clark Robertson applies pigment to cashmere and silk alike through a combination of processes which include hand-painting, photo-silkscreening, and resist techniques. The results are alluring pastiches of socially poignant imagery on fabric.

His textiles are not created solely for ornamentation, for although they are undoubtedly decorative, they are much more. Robertson's designs contain elements of dissonance and sarcasm. Whether considering Vietnam, androgyny, or the haunting possibility of suicide, a curious sense of lightheartedly delivered unrest pervades his work.

*Twin Borders,* a piece of silk chameuse which appeared in the 1983 exhibit *Contemporary Continuous Pattern* at the Cooper-Hewitt Museum, contains scattered, floating images of contemporary as well as historical figures—male, female, solitary, coupled, black, and white. In this, as in much of his work, color and texture act as a sugarcoating, to camouflage some very serious questions Robertson raises about racism, sexuality, and the human condition.

Robertson, however, does not confine himself solely to textile design. He designs tables that are stylistically considered contemporary Pop and that resemble pieces of Lego. He works with marble, glass, and formica, modeling his pieces after anything but the conventional table—the ancient Chinese clog and inverted table being just two examples.

His most recent endeavors extend to the arena of fine art, where his approach is much like that of his textile designs, but he transfers his work to canvas as a way of asking whether his work will hold up in yet one more medium. Will his message read the same when stretched on canvas, mounted on the wall as a painting?

Regardless of his medium, Robertson's sensitivity to color and texture and his dedication to incorporating meaning into the work he produces remain constant. Eschewing formalism, he produces work that is chaotic, unsettling, and laden with questions. His designs challenge tradition by asking, why can't an object do more than serve its immediate function? Can an object be aesthetically pleasing and conceptually challenging at the same time?

While Robertson's work, in part, denies convention, his expressions of discontent and confusion are skillfully couched in finely blended colors and sensuous surfaces, making both his inquiries and his assertions extremely palatable.

—Dierdre Kerr

# ROBSJOHN-GIBBINGS, Terrence Harold

American furniture and interior designer

**Born:** London, England, in 1905; emigrated to the United States in 1930, naturalized, 1945. **Education:** Apprenticed as an architectural draughtsman, London, then studied architecture, at the University of Liverpool, and London University, BS. **Career:** Head designer, at Ashby Tad Limited, London, 1925-26; art director, British International Pictures film company, Elstree, Essex, 1927; worked for Charles Duveen (Charles of London) antiques and furniture firm, London, 1928-29, and in New York, 1930-35; established Robsjohn-Gibbings Limited interior design firm, New York, 1936-64; sole designer, for Widdicombe Furniture, Grand Rapids, Michigan, 1943-56, and for Saridas company, Athens, Greece, from 1960. **Exhibitions:** Sotheby Parke-Bernet, New York, 1980, 1981;

*High Style: 20th Century American Design,* Whitney Museum, New York, 1985. **Honors:** Waters Award, New York, 1950; Elsie de Wolfe Award, New York, 1962. **Died:** Athens, Greece, 20 October 1976.

## Works

Console table in carved gilt-wood and nickel-plate steel, for Peterson Studios, 1937.

Armchairs in carved oak with loose seat cushions, for Peterson Studios, 1937.

Dining-table in French walnut, for Schmieg-Hungate and Kotzean, 1937.

Large stool in walnut with splayed supports and loose cushion, for Peterson Studios, 1937.

Upholstered sofa in carved Canadian birch, for Peterson Studios, 1937.

Palm-tree pedestal end table in harewood and American walnut, for Peterson Studios, 1937.

Writing table in bleached oak, for Peterson Studios, 1937.

Side chair in wood and leather, for Tifal Limited, 1939.

Wall-backed settee with butterfly table, for Widdicombe Furniture, 1948.

Sectional upholstered sofa, for Widdicombe Furniture, 1949.

Coffee table in walnut and brass with glass top, for Widdicombe Furniture, 1950.

*Bathroom of 1960,* for *Look* magazine, New York, 1951.

## Publications

**By ROBSJOHN-GIBBINGS: books**—*Furniture Today,* New York, n.d.; *Goodbye Mr. Chippendale,* New York, 1944; *Mona Lisa's Mustache: A Dissection of Modern Art,* New York, 1947; *Homes of the Brave,* New York, 1954; (with C. W. Pullin) *Furniture of Classical Greece,* New York, 1963.

**On ROBSJOHN-GIBBINGS: books**—*Neo-Classical Art Moderne Furniture Designed by T. H. Robsjohn-Gibbings,* catalogue, New York, 1980; *Architecture and Interior Design* by Victoria Kloss Ball, New York, 1980; *Mid-Century: Furniture of the 1950s* by Cara Greenberg, London, 1984; *High Style: 20th Century American Design,* exhibition catalogue by David Gebhard, Esther McCoy, and others, New York, 1985; *The American Design Adventure 1940-1975* by Arthur J. Pulos, London and Cambridge, Massachusetts, 1988.

*       *       *

There is a tendency among contemporary critics to spurn reproduction of period furniture, but without the work of T.H. Robsjohn-Gibbings, we could not know the power of the furniture of ancient Greece. Styles as varied as art nouveau and English neoclassic have incorporated, sometimes consciously and more often self-consciously, the dramatic arc of the shoulder-high cresting rail that characterizes the distinctive Greek chair form, the klismos. Designers as disparate as Thomas Hope in early nineteenth-century England and Ole Wanscher in mid twentieth-century Denmark have executed ponderous (as in the case of Hope) and sensitive (Wanscher) adaptations of the Greek model. Before Robsjohn-Gibbings com-

pleted his project, however, time had assured that our only practical contact with the source would be through its interpretations.

Those who have been privileged to see pieces from this collection have been witness to more than impeccable scholarship. Robsjohn-Gibbings' reproductions—so finely executed as to qualify as recreations—have an immediate emotional and aesthetic impact, which can be summed up only by the word "presence." One is struck first of all by the unexpectedly large scale. (Robsjohn-Gibbings extrapolated the measurements from vase drawings and existing fragments; his accuracy was proven when a recreated klini, or chaise with a klismoid back, fit exactly into the impressions left by a similar, original couch at the Sanctuary of Artemis, near Athens.) The next impression is awe at the daring of those ancient artisans whose chairs defied the natural grain and strength of wood as they balanced on the sweeping curves of the out-thrust legs. The diphroi, or stools, exhibit less structural hubris, but with the chairs and the rectangular, three-legged tables, or trapezai, they seem, like genius, to have sprung fully formed from the brow of Zeus. Each object is characterized by a unity so complete that it could serve as the Platonic ideal for its genre.

Excellent though they are, Robsjohn-Gibbings' own designs now appear dated. Although one appreciates them intellectually as among the best of their type, they no longer hold general appeal. But in his patient recreation of the furnishings used four to six hundred years before Christ, Robsjohn-Gibbings established his reputation and made an unequalled contribution to design.

—Reed Benhamou

# ROCH, Ernst

Canadian graphic and environmental designer

**Born:** Of Austrian parents in Osijek, Croatia, 8 December 1928; emigrated to Canada in 1953, naturalized, 1973. **Education:** Educated in Osijek, 1935-44, and in Graz, 1948-53; studied graphic design under professors Peter R. Oberhuber, Otto Brunner, and Rudolf Szyszkowitz, at the Meisterschule fur angewandte Kunst, Graz, 1948-53. **Family:** Married Helene Salchenegger in 1952 (divorced, 1977); children: Ursula, Uli, and Barbara. **Career:** Assistant to professor Hans Wagula, 1953; designer, with Rapid Grip and Batten, Montreal, 1953-54, and with Y and M Studio, Montreal, 1954-59; design director, James Valkus office, Montreal, 1960; founder-principal of Roch Design, Montreal, 1960-65, Design Collaborative, Montreal 1965-77, and of Roch Design, Montreal, from 1977; co-founder of Signum Press, Montreal, from 1973. Postage Stamp Design Advisory Committee, Canadian Post Office, Ottawa, 1975-80; advisory board member, International Institute for Information Design, Vienna, 1988. Lecturer, School of the Museum of Fine Arts, Montreal, 1956-58; guest lecturer, McGill University, Montreal, and Nova Scotia College of Art and Design, Halifax, 1967-77; visiting lecturer, Ohio State University, Columbus, 1980. **Exhibitions:** Goethe Institut, Montreal, 1963, 1977; Goethe Institute, Toronto, 1964; Museum of Fine Arts, Montreal, 1970; Museum of Fine Art, Belgrade, 1973; Museum of Art and Design, Zagreb, 1973; Landesmuseum, Oldenburg, 1974; Hochschule für Bildende Kunste, Braunschweig, 1974; National Library, Ottawa, 1977 (toured Canada). **Collections:** National Library, Ottawa; Museum of Modern Art, New York; Library of Congress, Wash-

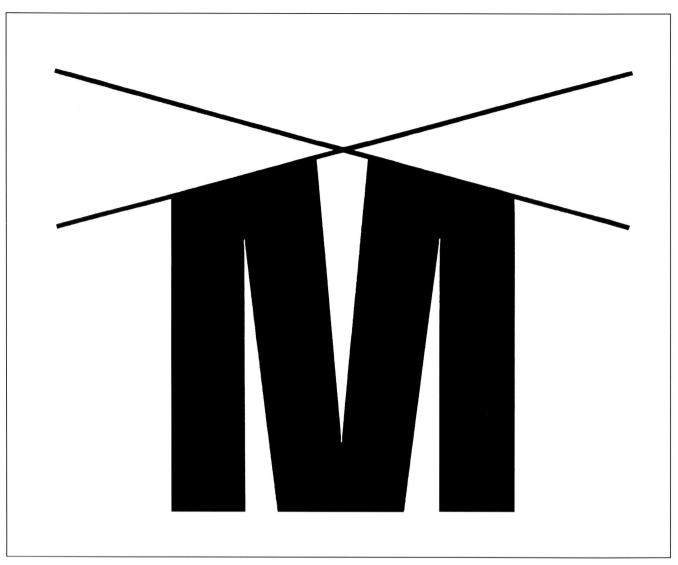

**Ernst Roch: Trademark for Marquesa Knitwear**

ington, D.C.; National Poster Museum, Warsaw. **Honors:** Numerous awards from the American Institute of Graphic Arts, Lahti Poster Biennale, Leipzig Book Fair, Brno Graphic Biennale, and Warsaw Poster Biennale; honorary doctorate, Nova Scotia College of Art and Design, 1988. **Address:** P.O. Box 1056, Station B, Montreal, Quebec H3B 3K5, Canada.

**Works**

*Queen Elizabeth II* set of 5 postage stamps, for the Government of Canada, 1962.

Trademark and visual identity program, for Standard Desk Limited, 1962-66.

Trademark and visual identity program, for Kruger Pulp and Paper Company, 1963-64.

Symbol and visual identity program, for William S. Merrell Company, 1963-64.

Symbol and visual identity program, for the New Brunswick Telephone Company, 1964-66.

Symbol, signage, and visual identity program, for the National Arts Center, Ottawa, 1965-68.

*Sir Oliver Mowat* commemorative postage stamp, for the Government of Canada, 1967.

Visual identity program, for Imasco Limited, from 1970.

*The Visual Image of the Munich Olympic Games* exhibition design and organization, for the Museum of Fine Arts, Montreal, and the Art Gallery of Ontario, Toronto, 1972.

Canadian passport and citizenship certificate, for the Government of Canada, 1974 (project).

Official poster of the 1976 Montreal Olympic Games, for the Organizing Committee of the Olympic Games, 1974.

*Quebec Canada* poster and annual report, for Imasco Limited, 1979.

Symbol and visual identity program, for the Federal Business Development Bank of Montreal, 1980-82.

*AGI Posters* exhibition design and organization, for the Alliance Graphique Internationale, in Montreal, 1982.

*Early Canadian Locomotives* set of 16 commemorative postage stamps, for the Canada Post Corporation, 1983-86.

*Paper Zoo* paper folding kit, published by Signum Press, 1974, and the Museum of Modern Art, New York, 1976-87.
*Arts of the Eskimo: Prints* book design, for Signum Press/Oxford University Press/Barre Publishing Company, 1974.
*Canadian Mushrooms* set of 4 commemorative postage stamps, for the Canada Post Corporation, 1989.

## Publications

**By ROCH: books**— (editor) *Farmer's Year,* Montreal, 1973; (editor) *Arts of the Eskimo: Prints,* Montreal, 1974; (editor) *Paper Zoo,* booklet, Montreal, 1974.

**On ROCH: books**—*Who's Who in Graphic Art* edited by Walter Amstutz, Zürich, 1962, Dubendorf, 1982; *Trademarks and Symbols of the World* by Yusaku Kamekura, Tokyo and New York, 1965; *Signet, Signal, Symbol* by Walter Diethelm, Zürich, 1970; *Die Heraldik der Wirtschaft* by Leonard Herman, Dusseldorf, 1971; *Symbols and Trademarks of the World,* vol. 2, edited by Franco Maria Ricci, Milan, 1973; *107 Grafici dell'AGI,* with texts by Renzo Zorzi and Franco Grignani Venice, 1974, Toronto, 1975; *Graphic Design by Rolf Harder and Ernst Roch* by Allan Harrison and Hans Neuburg, Montreal, 1977; *International Trademark Design* by Peter Wildbur, London, 1979; *World Trademarks and Logotypes II* by Takenobu Igarashi, Tokyo, 1987; *Typography Today* by Helmut Schmid, Tokyo, 1980; *Contemporary Graphic Designers,* vol. 3, edited by Maurice Horn, Detroit, 1988; *AGI Annals* by F.H.K. Henrion, Tokyo, 1989; *Trademarks and Symbols by AGI Members* by Jan Rajlich, Brno, 1989; *World Graphic Design Now 4: Corporate Identity* edited by Kazumasa Nagai and Motoo Nakanishi, Tokyo, 1989; *Graphic Design and Designers* by A. and I. Livingston, London, 1992; *Canadian Trademarks* by Gérard Bochud, Montreal, 1995; **articles**—*HQ* (Munich), June 1986, March 1994.

\*　　\*　　\*

Ernst Roch is recognized as a pioneer of Canadian "international" or "new" graphic design, with its emphasis on rational thinking and formal clarity. This functionalist approach, a product of his Austrian training, which he adapted and applied to the Canadian situation, has retained its élan and humanistic integrity through three decades of work in this country. With wit and sensitivity, Roch has helped shape the visual environment of his adopted homeland by producing a number of influential and memorable designs for government and industry. From symbols and postage stamps to books and posters, his clean, incisive style has left its mark.

Roch's work begins with a thorough and many-faceted investigation of the client's requirements. His designs, which are always based on a painstaking and systematic analysis, are planned and rendered with imagination and a joyful sense of experimentation. This disciplined, methodical approach produces work of enduring symbolic power. Though immediate, accurate communication is his prime concern, the work evinces a purity and universality approaching the timeless. Through the conscientious organization of form, striking aesthetic values emerge in Roch's award-winning designs, the purpose of which, according to one writer, is "to say the most with the least."

—Anne McLean

# ROCHE, Kevin
## American architect

**Born:** Ireland, 14 June 1922; emigrated to the United States, 1948. **Education:** Studied architecture, University College, Dublin, until 1945; apprenticed in the offices of Michael Scott in Dublin and Maxwell Fry in London; studied with Mies van der Rohe at the Illinois Institute of Technology. **Career:** Staff member, United Nations Headquarters Planning Office, New York, 1949; architect, 1950-54, principal design associate, 1954-66, Saarinen, Saarinen and Associates (later Eero Saarinen and Associates), Bloomfield Hills, Michigan; co-founder and principal, with John Dinkeloo (died 1981), of Kevin Roche John Dinkeloo and Associates, from 1966; subsequent partners include Philip Kinsella and James Owens. **Member:** President, American Academy of Arts and Letters; Academie d'Architecture; Academia Nazionale Di San Luca; Royal Institute of British Architects; Academician, National Academy of Design; Fellow, American Academy of Arts and Letters; Fellow, American Academy of Arts and Sciences. **Honors:** New York Chapter American Institute of Architects Award, 1964; Brunner Award, American Institute of Art and Letters, 1965; Brandeis University Creative Arts Award in Architecture, 1967; Medal of Honor, New York Chapter of the A.I.A., 1968; Albert S. Bard First Honor Award, City Club of New York, 1968, 1977, 1979, 1990; California Governor's Award for Excellence in Design, 1968; New York State Award, 1968; Total Design Award, American Society of Interior Designers, 1976; Gold Medal, Academie d'Architecture Grand, 1977; Pritzker Architecture Prize, 1982; R. S. Reynolds Memorial Award, 1985; The Brendan Gill Prize of the Municipal Art Society of New York, 1989; Gold Medal Award for Architecture, American Academy and Institute of Arts and Letters, 1990; Classical America's Arthur Ross Award, 1992; A.I.A. Gold Medal Award, 1993; Honorary Fellow, Royal Institute of the Architects of Ireland. **Address:** (office) Kevin Roche John Dinkeloo and Associates, 20 Davis Street, Hamden, Connecticut 06517, U.S.A.

## Works

Women's Resident Colleges, University of Pennsylvania, Philadelphia, Pennsylvania, 1963.
IBM Pavilion, New York World's Fair, New York, New York, 1964.
Components Plant, Darlington, England, 1966.
Richard C. Lee High School, New Haven, Connecticut, 1967.
Master plan, The Metropolitan Museum of Art, New York, New York, 1967-1995 (including the following wings and galleries: The Sackler Wing, The Robert Lehman Pavilion, The American Wing, Lila Acheson Wallace Galleries of Egyptian Art, The Michael C. Rockefeller Primitive Art Wing, The Astor Court, The Andre Meyer Galleries, The John C. & Charlotte C. Weber Galleries of the Art of Ancient China, The Arts of Japan, The Lila Acheson Wallace Wing for Twentieth Century Art, The European Sculpture and Decorative Arts Wing, The Florence & Herbert Irvin Galleries for the Arts of South & Southeast Asia, Bookshop, and Douglas Dillon Galleries for Chinese Painting).
Ford Foundation Headquarters, New York, New York, 1968.
A Small Orangery, 1968.
The Oakland Museum, Oakland, California, 1969.
Rochester Institute of Technology, Administration, Student Union and Physical Education Buildings, Rochester, New York, 1969.

**Kevin Roche: American Wing of the Metropolitan Museum of Art. Photo courtesy of Kevin Roche John Dinkeloo and Associates**

Knights of Columbus Headquarters, New Haven, Connecticut, 1969.

Aetna Life and Casualty Company Computer Headquarters, Hartford, Connecticut, 1969.

Federal Reserve Bank of New York, New York, New York, 1969.

United Nations Plazas I and II, Apartment/Hotel, and Office Building Complex, New York, New York, 1969-79.

IBM Computer Technology Museum, Armonk, New York, 1969.

United States Post Office, Columbus, Indiana, 1970.

Richardson-Vicks, Inc. Headquarters, Wilton, Connecticut, 1970.

Worcester County National Bank, Worcester, Massachusetts, 1970.

Cummins Engine Company Sub-Assembly Plant, Columbus, Indiana, 1970.

A Project for the Philadelphia Bicentennial, Philadelphia, Pennsylvania, 1971.

Royal Bank of Canada Office Complex Proposal, Toronto, Canada, 1971.

Power Center for the Performing Arts, University of Michigan, Ann Arbor, Michigan, 1971.

Irwin Union Bank and Trust Company, Columbus, Indiana, 1972.

New Haven Veterans Memorial Coliseum, New Haven, Connecticut, 1972.

Headquarters for Indiana & Michigan Power Company and People's Bank, Fort Wayne, Indiana, 1972.

World Headquarters for Fiat, Turin, Italy, 1972.

Denver Center for the Performing Arts, Denver, Colorado, 1972.

Creative Arts Center, Wesleyan University, Middletown, Connecticut, 1973.

Kentucky Power Company Headquarters, Ashland, Kentucky, 1973.

College Life Insurance Company of America Headquarters, Indianapolis, Indiana, 1974.

Fine Arts Center, University of Massachusetts, Amherst, Massachusetts, 1974.

John Deere and Company Headquarters West Office Building, Moline, Illinois, 1975.

Visual Arts and Communication Building, Texas Christian University, Fort Worth, Texas, 1976.

IBM Corporation Thomas J. Watson Research Center Addition, Yorktown Heights, New York, 1976.

Union Carbide Corporation World Headquarters, Danbury, Connecticut, 1976.

Cummins Engine Company Corporate Headquarters, Columbus, Indiana, 1977.

Bell Telephone Laboratories Expansion, Holmdel, New Jersey, 1977.

General Foods Corporation Headquarters, Rye, New York, 1977.

Entrance Lobby and Cafeteria of General Foods, North Street, White Plains, New York, 1977.

Exxon Corporation Headquarters, Fairfield, Connecticut, 1977.

Study of IBM Headquarters, Armonk, New York, 1977.

John Deere Financial Services Headquarters, Moline, Illinois, 1978.

Conoco Inc. Petroleum Headquarters, Houston, Texas, 1979.

Florida Residence, Hobe Sound, Florida, 1979.

Central Park Zoo, New York, New York, 1980.

John Deere Education Center, Moline, Illinois, 1980.

Deutsche Bank AG Headquarters, New York, New York, 1980.

Study of Highrise Downtown Houston, Main Street Project, Houston, Texas, 1981.

Highrise Competition Houston, Houston, Texas, 1981.

IBM Corporation Thomas J. Watson Research Center/Second Addition, Yorktown Heights, New York, 1981.

Block One Development, Denver, Colorado, 1981.

Ravinia Headquarters Complex, including Northern Telecom Headquarters, M.C.I. Headquarters, and Holiday Inn Headquarters, Ravinia Office Park, Atlanta, Georgia, 1981.

Bouygues World Headquarters, Paris, France, 1983.

J. P. Morgan & Company Headquarters, New York, New York, 1983.

Abby Aldrich Rockefeller Folk Art Center, Colonial Williamsburg, Virginia, 1983.

Competition for an Office Building in Dallas, Dallas, Texas, 1984.

IBM Hudson Hills Research Laboratory, New Castle, New York, 1984.

UNICEF Headquarters, New York, New York, 1984.

Leo Burnett Company Headquarters, Chicago, Illinois, 1985.

DeWitt Wallace Museum of Fine Arts, Colonial Williamsburg, Virginia, 1985.

The Jewish Museum, New York, New York, 1985.

750 Seventh Avenue, New York, New York, 1986.

Corning Inc. Corporate Headquarters, Corning, New York, 1986.

American Museum of Natural History, New York, New York, 1986.

Winthrop R. Rockefeller Archaeological Museum, Carter's Grove, Virginia, 1987.

Merck and Company Headquarters, Readington, New Jersey, 1987.

Napa Valley Residence, Napa Valley, California, 1987.

Project for the Marriott Corporation Headquarters, Germantown, Maryland, 1987.

New Jersey Residence, Peapack-Gladstone, New Jersey, 1988.

1000 Westchester Avenue, Harrison, New York, 1988.

300 East Pratt Street, Baltimore, Maryland, 1988.

New York Exchanges Headquarters, New York, New York, 1989.

Dai Ichi-Seimei Headquarters/Norinchukin Bank Headquarters, Tokyo, Japan, 1989.

SAUR/Bouygues, Paris, France, 1989.

NationsBank Plaza, Atlanta, Georgia, 1989.

One North Wacker, Chicago, Illinois, 1989.

Metropolitano Office Building, Madrid, Spain, 1990.

Pontiac Marina Hotel and Office Building, Singapore, 1990.

Borland International, Inc. Headquarters, Scotts Valley, California, 1990.

Eczacibasi Group Corporate Headquarters and Office Buildings, Istanbul, Turkey, 1991.

International Trade Center, Dusseldorf, Germany, 1992.

A Living Memorial to the Holocaust/Museum of Jewish Heritage, New York, New York, 1993.

Headquarters for Tanjong and Binariang/Ampang Tower, Kuala Lumpur, Malaysia, 1993.

Visitors Center, Columbus, Indiana, 1993.

Tata Cummins Private Limited, Jamshedpur, India, 1994.

Cummins Engine Company APEX Manufacturing Facility, Columbus, Indiana, 1994.

DBS Development, Beijing, China, 1994.

Hyundai Kangnam Office Building, Seoul, Korea, 1995.

## Publications

**On ROCHE: books**—*Conversations with Architects* by John Wesley Cook, New York, 1973; *Kevin Roche John Dinkeloo and Associates 1962-1975,* Fribourg, Switzerland, 1975, New York, 1977; *Global Architecture* (Tokyo), no. 4, 1977, nos. 9, 12, 14, 22, 29; (bibliography) *Kevin Roche* by Lamia Doumato, Monticello, Illinois, 1979; (interviews) *Kevin Roche* edited by Francesco Dal Co., New York, Milan, 1985; *Kevin Roche John Dinkeloo and Associates* by Robert A. Kuhner, Monticello, Illinois, 1986; **articles**—"Creating the Unexpected, Kevin Roche Walks Off with Architecture's Biggest Prize" in *Time* (New York), 26 April 1982; "An Architect Who Puts 9-to-5 Workers in 'Family Rooms'" by Andrea Oppenheimer Dean in *Smithsonian* (Washington, D.C.), August 1982; "Kevin Roche," special edition of *Architecture and Urbanism,* August 1987; "Born Again, Kevin Roche, Architecture's Last Puritan, Turns Populist" by Walter McQuade in *Connoisseur* (New York), February 1988; "Kevin Roche: Seven Headquarters," special edition of *Office Age,* 1990.

*

The perception of architecture might be compared to the fable of the perception of an elephant by three blind men.

The casual viewer sees architecture as part of the background, part of the cultural heritage, part of the usable context of day-to-day life, a place to live, a place to eat, a place to work, a place to worship and the appreciation of it is only incidental to the use. The patron sees it as a need fulfilled, an expression of importance, a monument, an opportunity for immortality for one whose abilities have been channeled into the creation of wealth or the organizing of armies or the imposition of will. The historian may see it as the product of some of the forces which actually form it but really considers it as an art and in doing so allows only for those forces which form art.

The responsible architect must see it as all of these things, as well as a release of artistic energies and a commitment to serve. It is important for us as architects to realize that we serve society and that we provide the background and sometimes the central feature almost all human activities. The patron should likewise recognize that the responsibility that is implicit in the role of patron is ultimately that of serving. In our gradually emerging, participatory society, everyone as a small unit in a greater whole finally has some influence over what is built. Recognizing this, each individual in society needs to become educated in the art of architecture to heighten expectations. In that regard, the role of the critic becomes very important; it becomes one of monitoring and contributing ideas and reporting on progress and growth so that all can learn and continue to seek ways to build the most appropriate and stimulating environments. When these conditions are realized, there is then the possibility for significant architecture.

In this context the battle of styles is of less interest to us. What is more important is a method of design that tries to understand the forces at work and to accommodate the needed activity in the very best way. We bring to that a humanist point of view and an understanding of the state of technology and the economic circumstances under which buildings are built, always tempered of course by an artistic impulse ... and a respect for reason.

The process is almost self-sustaining, which while it can be rigidly organized, can also be organized in such a sophisticated way as to appear almost disorganized. The process sometimes takes over and we find that we are working alongside something that in fact is working itself out. One moves forward, not always just relentlessly pursuing a design idea to its end but often allowing it to grow and develop and exchange back and forth between a multitude of different probes, other ideas, responses, and attitudes. In this process we are sometimes guiding, sometimes being guided by events, sometimes forming, sometimes watching the solution being formed again by various pressures and circumstances that emerge, but never taking quick refuge in easy answers.

There are many advantages to this procedure, not the least of which is that we are relieved of those initial pressures of over-anxiety "to create." A concept becomes an evolving experience, rather than a pre-imagined or pre-imposed vision; and we are both entertained and stimulated to find ourselves in the land of new discovery with each step. This method of design is a relaxed and more accommodating approach so that the end result is never one of trying to fit in something after the fact because there is no "after the fact."

Architecture is often considered to be the kind of building that is on the postcard sent home. But there is more than that in the lived-in city—a city that can vary from being disciplined, either by fiat or by modesty of means, or can display an exuberance inspired by a new freedom in the arts or a resurgence of prosperity. Despite the originating forces, successive generations fit into and adapt neighborhoods to reflect their emerging values. The sensitive architect tries to understand this feeling of context within a historical process of change and seeks to add to it in a way which enriches the existing as well as fulfills the immediate purpose of each patron for whom building is almost always an undertaking of immense effort and importance and which we, as architects, fervently hope is also an undertaking of great joy.

—Kevin Roche (November 1992)

\*       \*       \*

Kevin Roche, who completed his architectural studies at the University College in Dublin, joined Eero Saarinen's office in Bloomfield Hills, Michigan, in 1950, after having worked with various architects in Dublin, London, New York, and Chicago. When Saarinen died in 1961, Roche, who had been Saarinen's Principal Design Associate, took over his friend's practice together with two other associates, and became its head in 1981.

While most of the better known architects in the post World War II era became famous in part by creating buildings that were unmistakable expressions of their own architectural preferences, Roche (like Saarinen before him) seemed to approach every architectural commission in ways that responded to its own special requirements. Since no two buildings ever had the same site, or the same program, or the same budget, or the same environmental conditions, neighbors, historic references, or, in all likelihood, the same clients, his own buildings rarely looked alike.

Each of his buildings, he seemed to feel, should respond to the many and varied factors that shaped it. And so each of his buildings had to be, in effect, a new invention, with all the basic ingredients reexamined and reevaluated and often redesigned to respond to entirely new and different sets of circumstances.

The result of this approach has been a series of remarkably innovative designs: the 1968 Ford Foundation Headquarters, in New York City, with its interior garden-atrium, is an amazing urban office building hardly improved upon since. The Oakland, California, Museum, done in the following year—an underground building with a public park on top—was an equally innovative contribution to urban design. In both cases, the unusual structure was a response to certain specific needs: in the case of the Ford Foundation Buildings, the need to create a humanist alternative to the typical, urban office block; in the case of the Oakland Museum, the need to create a large downtown public building without robbing the city of a beautiful public park.

Roche has designed a large number of corporate headquarters (and other building types) in the United States, in Europe, and in Asia, and each of those designs was the result of a thoughtful investigation of the needs of those who would be using those buildings. In one case, Kevin Roche interviewed more than 180 people who would be working in a new corporate headquarters and attempted to involve them as much in the creation of the ultimate design as he was himself.

As a result, these corporate headquarters are extraordinarily varied in their ultimate form. In one case, the available site was a flat and not very interesting stretch of land between highways; and so he created a colorful landscape of lakes and islands and turned the offices into a village of buildings raised on stilts, and connected by pedestrian bridges and walkways shaded by deep overhangs. The resulting complex of three-story structures on stilts looks very much like a modern version of the Japanese Shinden-zukuri—"an oasis that time forgot in a part of Texas subject to both extreme heat and torrential rains," as a Japanese critic put it. At a time when the term "corporate headquarters" conjures up a vision of a big, tall, curtain-walled box containing hundreds of little boxes (or offices), this complex outside Houston suggests an entirely new approach to designing a truly delightful workplace.

Kevin Roche's other designs of corporate workplaces are equally thoughtful and innovative and very different from one another. Each is clearly shaped by a different set of requirements. In one case, he created a complex in which the center was, in fact, a 2850-car, four-story parking garage, surrounded by 15 polygonal satellite structures (or pods) containing offices and supporting facilities for 3200 employees on five levels. The building was constructed on 675 acres of land in Danbury, Connecticut, and most of the employees arrived by car, hence the central point of arrival. The polygonal configuration of the satellites gave most of those inside a different view of the landscape, and a desk close to a window.

Most of Kevin Roche's buildings have three characteristics in common: the first is their sensitivity to the landscape, both without and within, both existing and introduced by the architect. Even when located in the midst of cities, Roche's buildings are likely to be full of references to nature—to trees, plants, rocks, pools and streams, to sun and rain. Even when the sites do not offer much in the way of natural resources, he has usually created an exterior and interior landscape that adds greatly to the quality of living and working within the building.

The second characteristic that Roche's buildings share is their concern with detail. Most of the time, the detailing of walls, windows, doors, and all the rest will be "modern," though hardly ever predictably so. But sometimes the detailing will be shaped by surroundings and other specific concerns, to the point even of copying a neo-Gothic facade when adding to an earlier, neo-Gothic museum. Much more often, however, his detailing will be shaped by the materials, the culture, and the traditions of the place and the program; and he will make the details of his buildings speak to their users as eloquently as the plans themselves.

The third special quality of Roche's work probably comes from his great interest in the other arts: he has long persuaded his clients to invite painters, sculptors, and other artists to contribute to the shaping of their (and his) buildings. This special concern has given most of his buildings a special quality that sets them far apart from more routine contemporary architecture in the United States and else-where.

It is easy to admire Roche's preoccupation with program, with site, with human needs and issues, and with other common concerns that govern the design of buildings. But more than anything else it is Roche's intense preoccupation with the art of architecture that gives his buildings a quality not often found in our time. His numerous university structures, his work for the Central Park Zoo in New York, his work for sophisticated clients like IBM and the Cummins Engine Company: all these are not merely innovative and thoughtful and often flawlessly detailed. They are works of art, at a time when our landscapes and townscapes are not especially well endowed in that regard.

—Peter Blake

# ROSSELLI, Alberto

Italian architect and product and industrial designer

**Born:** Palermo, Sicily, 21 June 1921. **Education:** Studied engineering, 1938-39, and architecture, 1945-47, at the Politecnico, Milan, Dip. Arch., 1947. **Career:** Freelance designer, Milan, 1950-76; partner, with Gio Ponti and Antonio Fornaroli, in the Ponti-Fornaroli-Rosselli architectural and design studio, Milan, 1952-76; design consultant to Arflex, Saponiti, and Fiat-Orlandi. Founder-director, *Stile Industria* magazine, Milan, 1953-63; also contributor to *Design, Domus,* and *Architecture d'Aujourd'hui,* from 1952. Professor of industrial design, Politecnico, Milan, 1963-76. **Member:** Founder-member and president, 1956, and council member, 1967-68, of the ADI Associazione Disegno Industriale, Milan; vice-president, ICSID International Council of Societies of Industrial Design, 1961-63. **Exhibitions:** *Modern Chairs,* Whitechapel Art Gallery, London, 1970; *Italy: The New Domestic Landscape,* Museum of Modern Art, New York, 1972; *28/78 Architettura,* Palazzo delle Stelline, Milan, 1979; *Design Since 1945,* Philadelphia Museum of Art, 1983. **Collections:** Philadelphia Museum of Art. **Honors:** Gold Medals, Milan Triennale, 1954, 1957, 1960; Compasso d'Oro Award, Milan, 1957. **Died:** Milan, 1976.

## Works

Desk with tubular steel frame and glass top, for Vis, 1950.
Desk in moulded wood laminate with glass top, for RIV, 1953.
Chair in laminated bentwood with moulded plywood seat and back, for Cassina, 1954.
Cupboards in laminated wood, for Lips Vago, 1960.
*Corriere della Sera* office building, Milan, 1960-65.
*Brasilia* coffee machine, for Pavone, 1962.
Associazione Industriale Lombardi headquarters building, Milan, 1963-64.
Tables and trolleys in ABS plastic, for Kartell, 1968.
*Jumbo* furniture range in plastic, for Saponiti, 1970.
Pullman car interiors, for the Dutch Railways, 1970.
Modular container furniture in plastic with castors, for Kartell, 1972.
*Mobile House,* for Carrozzerie Boneschi Orlandi, 1972.
Open-space office systems, for Facomet, 1973.
*Pack 1* collapsible chair in polyfoam with dacron and sailcloth upholstery, for Bonacina, 1975.

## Publications

**By ROSSELLI: books**—*Los Spazio Aperto: Ricerca e Progettazione tra Design e Architettura,* Milan, 1974; *Alberto Rosselli: Stile Industria,* edited by Giovanni Klaus Koenig, Parma, 1981.

**On ROSSELLI: books**—*Mobili Tipo* by Robert Aloi, Milan, 1956; *Mercati e Negozi* by Robert Aloi, Milan, 1959; *Il Disegno Industriale e la sua Estetica* by Gillo Dorfles, Bologna, 1963; *Design Italiano: I Mobili* edited by Enrichetta Ritter, Milan and Rome, 1968; *Modern Chairs 1918-1970,* exhibition catalogue with texts by Carol Hogben and others, London, 1970; *Il Design in Italia 1945-1972* by Paolo Fossati, Turin, 1972; *Italy: The New Domestic Landscape* edited by Emilio Ambasz, New York and Florence, 1972; *History of Modern Furniture* by Karl Mang, Stuttgart, 1978, London, 1979; *Atlante del Design Italiano 1940/1980* by Alfonso Grassi and Anty Pansera, Milan, 1980; *Contemporary Furniture* edited by Klaus-Jurgen Sembach, Stuttgart and London, 1982; *Design Since 1945* edited by Kathryn Hiesinger and George Marcus, Philadelphia and London, 1983; *The Hot House: Italian New Wave Design* by Andrea Branzi, London, 1984; *Italian Design: 1870 to the Present* by Penny Sparke, London and New York, 1988.

# ROTH, Ann

American stage and film costume designer

**Education:** Educated at Carnegie-Mellon University, Pittsburgh. **Career:** Freelance stage costume designer, from 1958, and film costume designer, from 1964; designed for the Playhouse Theatre, Circle in the Square, Entermedia Theatre, Helen Hayes Theatre, Majestic Theatre, Imperial Theatre, John Golden Theatre, Music Box Theatre, all in New York, and for other theatres. **Honors:** British Academy Award, 1976; Antionette Perry (Tony) Award nominations, 1979, 1985, 1987; Emmy Award nomination, 1986. **Address:** c/o United Scenic Artists Union, Local 829, AFL-CIO, 575 Eighth Avenue, New York 10018, U.S.A.

## Works

Stage costume designs (New York, unless noted) include—*Maybe Tuesday*, 1958; *Edward II*, 1958; *Make a Million*, 1958; *The Disenchanted*, 1958; *A Desert Incident*, 1959; *The Cool World*, 1960; *Gay Divorce*, 1960; *Ernest in Love*, 1960; *Face of a Hero*, 1960; *The Pleasure of His Company*, Rochester, NY, 1961 (toured); *A Far Country*, 1961; *Purlie Victorious*, 1961; *Look: We've Come Through*, 1961; (sets only) *We Comrades Three*, 1962; *This Side of Paradise*, 1962; *Isle of Children*, 1962; *Venus at Large*, 1962; *A Portrait of the Artist as a Young Man*, 1962; *The Barroom Monks*, 1962; *Natural Affection*, 1963; *Hey You, Light Man!*, 1963; *Children from Their Games*, 1963; *A Case of Libel*, 1963; *In the Summer House*, 1964; *The Last Analysis*, 1964; *Slow Dance on a Killing Ground*, 1964; *I Had a Ball*, 1964; *The Odd Couple*, 1965; *Romeo and Juliet*, 1965; *The Impossible Years*, 1965; *The Wayward Stork*, 1966; *The Star-Spangled Girl*, 1966; *The Deer Park*, 1967; *The Beard*, 1967; *Something Different*, 1967; *Happiness Is Just a Little Thing Called a Rolls Royce*, 1968; *Play It Again, Sam*, 1969; *My Daughter, Your Son*, 1969; *Tiny Alice*, 1969; *The Three Sisters*, 1969; *Gantry*, 1970; *Purlie*, 1970; *What the Butler Saw*, 1970; *The Engagement Baby*, 1970; *Father's Day*, 1971; *Prettybelle*, Boston, 1971; *Fun City*, 1972; *Rosebloom*, 1972; *Twelfth Night*, 1972; *Children! Children!*, 1972; *6 Rms Riv Vu*, 1972; *Enemies*, 1972; *Purlie* (revival), 1972; *The Merchant of Venice*, 1973; *Seesaw*, 1973; *The Women*, 1973; *The Royal Family*, 1975; *The Heiress*, 1976; *The Importance of Being Earnest*, 1977; *Do You Turn Somersaults?*, 1978; *The Best Little Whorehouse in Texas*, 1978; *The Crucifer of Blood*, 1978; *First Monday in October*, 1978; *They're Playing Our Song*, 1979; *Strangers*, 1979; *Lunch Hour*, 1980; *Gardenia*, 1982; *Kaufman at Large* 1982; *Present Laughter*, 1982; *The Misanthrope*, 1983; *Yankee Wives*, Old Globe Theatre, San Diego, 1983; *Open Admissions*, 1984; *Hurlyburly*, Goodman Theatre, Chicago, 1984; *Design for Living*, 1984; *Biloxi Blues*, Ahmanson Theatre, Los Angeles, 1984; *Arms and the Man*, 1985; *Juno's Swans*, 1985; *The Odd Couple*, 1985; *Sing' in the Rain*, 1985; *Social Security*, 1986; *The House of Blue Leaves*, 1986-87; *Light Up the Sky*, 1986; *Woman in Mind*, 1988; *O Pioneers!*, Huntington Theatre Company, Boston, Massachusetts, 1989-90; *Elliot Loves*, 1990; *Square One*, 1990; *Road to Nirvana*, 1991; *Any Given Day*, 1993. Film costume designs include—*The World of Henry Orient* (G.R. Hill), 1964; *A Fine Madness* (Kershner), 1966; *Up the Down Staircase* (Mulligan), 1966; *Pretty Poison* (Black), 1968; *Sweet November* (R. Miller), 1968; *Midnight Cowboy* (Schlesinger), 1969; *The Owl and the Pussycat* (Ross), 1970; *The People Next Door* (Greene), 1970; *Klute* (Pakula), 1971; *The Pursuit of Happiness* (Mulligan), 1971; *They Might Be Giants* (Harvey) 1971; *The Valachi Papers* (Young), 1972; *Day of the Locust* (Schlesinger), 1975; *The Silence* (for TV), 1975; *The Rivalry* (for TV), 1975; *Murder By Death* (Moore), 1976; *Burnt Offering*, 1976; *Independence*, 1976; *The Goodbye Girl*, 1977; *California Suite* (Ross), 1978; *Coming Home*, 1978; *Nunzio*, 1979; *Promises in the Dark*, 1979; *Strangers: The Story of a Mother and Daughter* (for TV), 1979; *Hair* (Forman), 1979; *The Island* (Ritchie), 1980; *Dressed to Kill*, 1980; *Nine to Five*, 1980; *Honky Tonk Freeway* (Schlesinger), 1981; *Only When I Laugh* (G. Jordan), 1981; *Rollover* (Pakula), 1981; *The World According to Garp* (Hill), 1982; *The Man Who Loved Women*, 1983; *Silkwood*, 1983; *The Survivors*, 1983; *Places in the Heart*, 1984; *A Good Sport* (for TV), 1984; *Sweet Dreams*, 1985; *The Slugger's Wife*,

1985; *Maxie*, 1985; *Jagged Edge*, 1985; (consultant) *Roanoak* (for TV), 1986; *Heartburn*, 1986; *The Morning After*, 1986; *The House of Blue Leaves* (for TV), 1987; *Biloxi Blues*, 1988; *Funny Farm*, 1988; *The Unbearable Lightness of Being*, 1988; *Stars and Bars*, 1988; *Working Girls*, 1988; (with Neil Spisak) *The January Man*, 1989; *Her Alibi*, 1989; *Family Business*, 1989; *Everybody Wins*, 1990; (with Spisak) *Q & A*, 1990; (with Bridget Kelly) *Pacific Heights*, 1990; *Postcards from the Edge*, 1990; *The Bonfire of the Vanities*, 1990; *O Pioneers!* (for TV), 1991; (with Gary Jones) *Consenting Adults*, 1992; (with Jones) *Mambo Kings*, 1992; *School Ties*, 1992; (with Jones) *A Stranger among Us*, 1992; *Dennis the Menace*, 1993; *Dave*, 1993.

## Publications

**On ROTH: books**—*Contemporary Theatre, Film, and Television*, vols. 4 and 12, Detroit and London, 1987, 1991; **articles**—*Herald-Examiner* (Los Angeles), 7 February 1974; *Interview* (New York), March 1986.

\*        \*        \*

Ann Roth was associated with a group of brilliant, Carnegie-Mellon University students, who were fascinated by the richness, elegance, and style to be found in certain classic and modern plays. In working with this group (two of whom, William Ball and Ellis Rabb, have become major figures in preserving this tradition in their own productions), Roth also developed a taste for elegant theatricality. She has been little interested in the theatre of rags and distressed clothing and has usually been associated with productions that placed an emphasis on elegance and sophistication.

Even her Shakespearean productions have been noted for their elegant sophistication, rather than for weight, painted texture, or larger-than-life formality. For example, when she designed the costumes for Rabb's production of *The Merchant of Venice* in modern dress, the emphasis was on Via Veneto elegance and sophisticated charm. The same gentle worldliness was apparent in her designs for *Twelfth Night*. Similar precepts guided her designs for the revivals of *The Heiress* and *The Importance of Being Earnest*. Even in such a famous musical as *The Best Little Whorehouse in Texas*, which dealt with the nether side of society, the costumes for the brothel girls came across with their own flashy elegance. Much of the same is true for her best-remembered films. There was a kind of sleazy grace to *Midnight Cowboy* and a west-coast chic in *California Suite*.

Thus, her inspiration comes from elegant designers of the past, such as Rex Whistler, Adrian, Cecil Beaton, and Edith Head rather than from the Brechtian designers who have proliferated in the past two decades. Roth's costumes enhance the characters in a play or film so that an audience sees what normally might be mundane or even ugly with a certain patina of glamour.

—Douglas A. Russell

# ROWLANDS, Martyn (Omar)

British industrial designer

**Born:** Penarth, Glamorgan, Wales, 27 July 1923. **Education:** Educated at Eltham College, London, 1931-40; studied at the Central

School of Arts and Crafts, London, 1946-49. **Military Service:** Served as an engine fitter in the Royal Air Force, in India and Burma, 1941-46. **Family:** Married Ann Patricia Black in 1951 (died, 1974); children: Ceinwen, Glyn, and Dylan; married in 1978 (divorced, 1986). **Career:** Designer, for Bakelite plastics company, London, 1950-54; head of design, Ekco Plastics, Southend-on-Sea, Essex, 1954-59; founder-director of MRDC Martyn Rowlands Design Consultants, London and Essex, from 1959; has designed for Rantan and Company, Standard Telephones and Cables, Thermos, British Airways, Boots Company, IMI/Opella, Fisons Pharmaceuticals, and others. President, Society of Industrial Artists and Designers, London, 1974-75. **Collections:** Victoria and Albert Museum, London. **Honors:** Design Council Award, London, 1958, 1961, 1966, 1969, 1971; fellow, Chartered Society of Designers, London, 1960; fellow, Plastics and Rubber Institute, London, 1973. **Addresses:** MRDC Limited, Parndon Mill, Harlow, Essex CM20 2HP, England; (home) 90 D Hemnall Street, Epping, Essex CM16 4LX, England.

## Works

Moulded baby bath and stand, for Ekco Plastics, 1957.
Moulded watering can in nestable parts, for Ekco Plastics, 1958.
Chemical toilet in high-density polythene, for Ekco Plastics, 1960.
Children's tablewares in melamine, for Rantan and Company, 1960.
*Trimphone* and *Deltaline* lightweight telephones, for STC Standard Telephones and Cables, 1964.
*Intal* drug inhaler, for Fisons Pharmaceuticals, 1967.
*500 Series* domestic water taps in moulded plastic, for IMI/Opella, 1969.
Boots Preview Screen in plastic, for The Boots Company, 1970.
Airline meals servicewares in disposable plastics, for British European Airways, 1972.
*Thermos* vacuum flask jug in plastic, for Thermos, 1973.
Nursery products range in polypropylene, for The Boots Company, 1979.
Kitchen mixer tap monobloc in moulded plastics, for IMI/Opella, 1980.

## Publications

By ROWLANDS: articles—*The Designer* (London), September 1971, November 1975, May 1979; *Plastics Today* (London), May 1976.

On ROWLANDS: books—*The Business of Product Design* by James Pilditch and Douglas Scott, London, 1965; *All Things Bright and Beautiful: Design in Britain, 1830 to Today* by Fiona MacCarthy, London, 1972; *Les Annees 60* by Anne Bony, Paris, 1983.

*

I feel one can only design well if one fully understands the materials and the manufacturing techniques to be used in the product you are designing. I have specialised in design for the plastics industry, and the technology for this industry is developing very fast and provides exciting design opportunities to completely rethink the product. My views are perhaps best illustrated by part of an article in the ICI house journal *Plastics Today,* and I quote from this:

First and foremost, the designer must know and understand exactly why he is undertaking a particular design brief. This is, indeed, one of his most important activities before even beginning to consider visual concepts. A remarkably wide range of influences affect industrial design, and that is especially so where plastics are concerned due to the interrelation between designer, toolmaker, processor and, frequently, the assembler of component parts. For example, when considering a design for the first time, one must analyse its function and decide what material or materials should be used to make it. If it is to be a redesign of an existing article, either as a simple substitute or as an improvement, one naturally considers carefully what materials were used before and why, and whether the use of new material is relevant and what the implications of such a change will be. Today that new material is likely to be one of the wide range of plastics. But caution is necessary. Many of the past failures of products made from plastics can be attributed to a simple desire to make them in plastics—whether the material is suitable for the job or not. Nor does the problem end with manufacture; it continues into use in service and, probably, some kind of maintenance during the life of the product. These latter considerations may be termed the "system" in which the product is used, and it is just as important to study that system as it is to consider the design of the product itself.

If one is designing a product intended to be disposable—say, cutlery for use in a cafeteria—it is obviously important to understand why such a product is wanted in the first place. Probably, the principal reason put forward is that it is uneconomic to have people doing the washing-up, or there may have been problems of loss of valuable cutlery and inexpensive substitutes are required. Note that here the system of usage is to be changed: items are to be used once only. Hence the problem that arises is one of disposal of a quantity of plastics material—either by destruction or by recycling in a sane and sensible manner. As an aside, it may be mentioned that one must make sure that the system is changed in practice; otherwise, there will be accusations of inadequate design should the product be used in the old manner.

Almost every design product has influences on it other than simple aesthetics of the product itself. There are hosts of reasons for the designer to make a critical analysis of the product—from whether it gives "value for money", is "safe" to use, and is ergonomically satisfactory, to its visual attractiveness and its sales appeal. While not wishing to play down these important matters, I feel it is worthwhile to isolate one other that is particularly important in any discussion on design in plastics. It is what in the past may have been described as "validity of the craftsmanship": having decided to use a material—in the present instance, plastics—are the forms chosen relevant to the material and to the process of manufacture? Most people would recognise these attributes in a piece of pottery, or carved wood, or even in blown glass. The touch of the hand and intellect can be seen—at first hand, as it were. The casual movement of the thumb that presses the soft clay form of a handle onto a jug is easy to appreciate. The precise, logical cutting of steel to make a mould for plastics that will later form millions of moulded products is not so easy to discern. It is there, for all that.

One cannot judge the success of a design on just one facet of its make-up. The overall success comes from a skilful blending of them all. Whilst it is important to appreciate these subtle factors, they would certainly be meaningless if the product did not work. Too much "craft" and no "art" is as bad as the other way round.

Consideration for the environment and natural resources are becoming much more important influences on how the product is

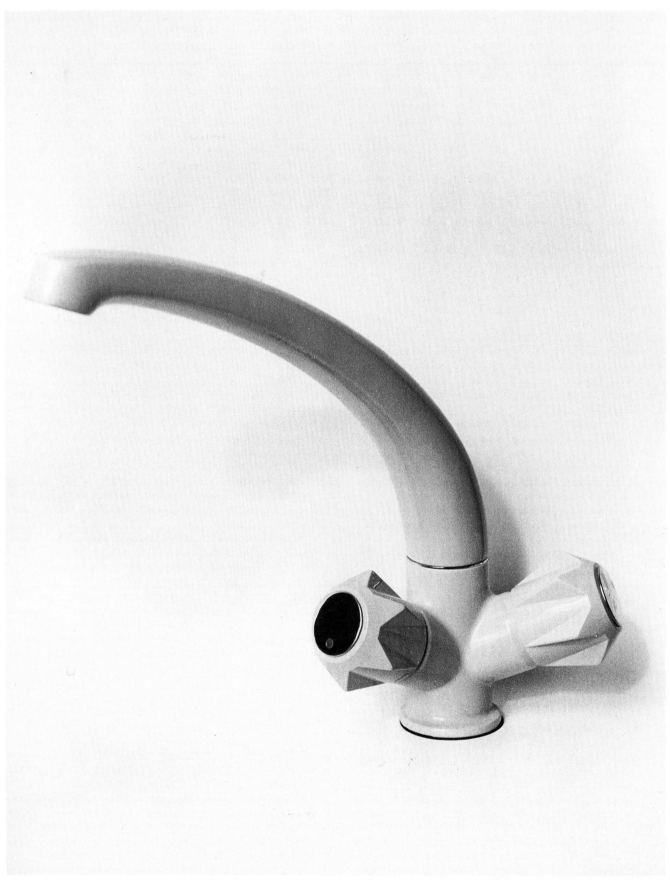

**Martyn Rowlands: Monobloc kitchen water tap, for IMI Opella, 1988**

designed. Once-used packaging and products have to be designed to be recycled. This might imply the use of just one polymer in a package, cap, and bottle, for example, but certainly the marking of the item with its polymer group. A secondary use for packaging is also sometimes of consideration. Designers can influence fundamentally the impact on the environment the products they design will have and therefore need to approach every new project with this in mind.

—Martyn Rowlands

*     *     *

In the 1940s, Martyn Rowlands studied in the first industrial design course at the Central School of Arts and Crafts in London and was attracted to the brand-new field of plastics. His first job was with Bakelite; after that, he headed the design department at Ekco Plastics. Subsequently, he founded his own firm.

Rowlands believes that the manufacturing process is the root of good design. While his career has seen many new polymers being invented, he has insisted on learning all the processes involved, and he will not design something which he does not know how to make himself. To him, the designer must have total control of a product, be able to prevent technicians from messing up his creation, and not be helpless where the quality of the final achievement is concerned. Thus, Rowlands is very much in the craft tradition, and his approach would have been applauded by William Morris, albeit that his materials and machinery are completely different. How interesting it is that one of the exponents of the new art of designing plastics should approach his work in the traditional manner.

His style is one of great simplicity, with few decorative flourishes. Plastic can be moulded into forms as ornate as anyone could wish, so it is not the medium which restricts Rowland's style, but his own design philosophy, which contains a firm measure of functionalism. He admires the Bauhaus products, which have been an influence, to which he has added a belief in the honest simplicity of the good craftsman as applied to industrial processes.

—Diana de Marly

# RUDER, Emil

Swiss typographer and exhibition and graphic designer

**Born:** Zurich, 20 March 1914. **Education:** Apprenticed as a type-compositor, Zurich, 1929-33; studied graphics, in Paris, 1938-39; lettering and book design under Alfred Willimann and Walter Kaech, at the Kunstgewerbeschule, Zurich, 1941-42. **Family:** Married I. S. Schwartz in 1950; children: Martin and Daniel. **Career:** Freelance poster, book, and typographic designer, in Bäsel, 1942-70; postage stamp design advisor to the Swiss Post Office, 1961. Instructor in typography, 1942-47, head of arts and crafts, 1947-65, and director, 1965-70, at the Allgemeine Gewerbeschule, Bäsel; director of the Kunstgewerbemuseum, Bäsel, 1965-70. Contributor to the periodicals *Schweizerische Lehrerzeitung, Typographische Monatsblatter, Werk, Form, und Technik,* and *Der Druckspiegel.* **Member:** Bäsel group chairman, 1948, central committee member, 1956, and vice-chairman, 1966, of the Schweizerischer Werkbund; Swiss regional delegate, ATYPI (Association Typographique

Internationale), 1959; member of the Federal Commission for Fine Arts, Bäsel, 1961; founder-member, International Center for Typographic Arts, New York, 1962. **Exhibitions:** *Der Mensch und die Dinge,* Bäsel, 1955; *Die Gute Form,* Bäsel, 1956; *Typographie,* Kunstgewerbemuseum, Bäsel, 1960; *Schweizerische Landesausstellung* Lausanne, 1964. **Collection:** Kunstgewerbemuseum, Bäsel. **Died:** Bäsel, 13 March 1970.

**Publications**

**By RUDER: book**—*Typographie,* Teufen, 1967, New York, 1981; **articles**—in *Typographische Monatsblatter* (St. Gallen), no.2, 1952, nos. 2 and 5, 1958, no. 4, 1959, no. 6, 1959, no. 1, 1961; *Graphis* (Zurich), no. 85, 1959, no. 146, 1969: *Neue Graphik* (Zurich), no. 2, 1959.

**On RUDER: books**—*The New Graphic Design* by Karl Gerstner and Markus Kutter, Teufen and London, 1959; *Who's Who in Graphic Art* edited by Walter Amstutz, Zurich, 1962; *Buchgestaltung* by Albert Kapr, Dresden, 1963; *The Art of Written Forms* by Donald M. Anderson, New York, 1969; *Typography Today* by Helmut Schmid, Tokyo, 1980.

*     *     *

Emil Ruder understood typography in the classical sense, as a serving art, as the shaping of given contents and meanings, as a means that finds completeness in its unobtrusiveness. As he put it, "Es ist unser Beruf, der Sprache Form zu geben, ihr Dauer zu verleihen und sie in die Zukunft hinüberzuretten. Oft sind wir uns gar nicht bewusst, dass wir diese Aufgabe nur Mittels der Form bewaltigen können." As teacher and, later, as director at the Gewerbeschule in Bäsel, Ruder's imprint on Swiss-style typography is fundamental to the apprentice of typography and, as contributor to the Swiss professional magazine *TM (Typografische Monatsblatter),* to the profession in general. Ruder's works are not monuments. Rather, they speak a clear, meditative form-language in which form and counterform, printed and unprinted, each have their important parts in the message. One of his purest typographic works is a political poster, in which the message is grouped and arranged in such a way that connected text-groups form rhythmical flow from top to bottom.

While his earlier period was dominated by a typography of order, his later period was ruled by organic and natural arrangement of texts. While the typography of order was the purification of the typography of the 1920s and early 1930s, his organic typography arose with the typeface Univers. In the Univers special issue of *TM* in 1961, Ruder reduced the text per page to a readable amount and created a typography of lightness and elegance, which made Swiss-Zurich-style typography look heavy and dated. Ruder's familiarity with Univers since its creation enabled him to bring out the beauty of proportion in the letters by the beauty of proportion in his typography.

Ruder was an ardent believer in the educative value of good typography and honestly styled everyday goods as contributions to the improvement of our environment. His lasting impetus to good typography is the design manual *Typographie.* Here, Ruder tells and shows us that the difference between good and anemic design is often just the difference of a small detail. Further, as he points out, "Contemporary typography is not based primarily on the flash of inspiration and striking idea. It is based on the grasp of the essential underlying laws of form on thinking in connected wholes, so that it avoids, on the one hand, turgid rigidity and monotony and, on the other, unmotivated arbitrary interpretation."

—Helmut Schmid

# RUGGERI, Cinzia

Italian fashion and industrial designer

**Born:** Milan, 1 February 1945. **Education:** Studied design, at the Accademia delle Arti Applicati, Milan, 1963-65. **Career:** Freelance designer, Milan, from 1966. **Exhibitions:** Galleria del Prisma, Milan, 1963; Venice Biennale, 1981; *Italian Re-Evolution,* La Jolla Museum of Contemporary Art, California, 1982; *Per un Vestire Organico,* Palazzo Fortuny, Venice, 1983; *Italia: The Genius of Fashion,* Fashion Institute of Technology New York, 1985; *Dopo Gondrand: Cinzia Ruggeri/Denis Santachiara,* Il Luogo di Corrado Levi, Milan, 1986; *Extra Vacanze di Cinzia Ruggeri,* Galleria Tucci Russo, Turin, 1986; *Internationale Mobel Messe,* Cologne, 1987; *Fashion and Surrealism,* Fashion Institute of Technology, New York, 1987 (toured); *Pianeta Italia,* Kaufhof Stores, Cologne, 1988; *Salon del Mobile,* Milan, 1988; *Verona Neo Eclettismo,* 1994. **Collections:** Museo della Moda, Parma. **Honors:** Fil d'Or Award, Confederation Internationale du Lin, 1981, 1982, 1983. **Address:** Via Crocefisso 21, 20122 Milan, Italy.

## Publications

**By RUGGERI: articles**—in *Casa Vogue* (Milan), April, 1980.

**On RUGGERI: books**—*Vestire Italiano* by Paola Amendola, Rome, 1983; *The Hot House: Italian New Wave Design* by Andrea Branzi, London, 1984; *Il Genio Antipatico* by Pia Soli, Milan, 1984; *La Materia dell'Invenzione* by Ezio Manzini, Milan, 1986; *Fashion and Surrealism* by Richard Martin, New York and London, 1987; *Pranzo alle 8* by Pia Soli, Milan, 1988; *Fashion Illustrators of Europe* by Isao Yajima, Tokyo, 1989.

*       *       *

Cinzia Ruggeri's work belongs to the tendency in Italian design towards "transdisciplinary" activity, in which designers of industrial products, fashion designers, scenic artists, and interior decorators exchange their experiences with each other and collaborate in the creation of new typologies of objects.

The artistic avant-gardes of the twentieth century have certainly been the decisive influence on this kind of attitude to design; the inspiration of Cinzia Ruggeri's frocks is, in fact, strictly abstract in character, with forms and patterns of geometrical types; cubism, futurism, constructivism, and the Bauhaus School are the historical precedents for this kind of work, and it is from the same avant-gardes that Ruggeri gets her interest in the "theatrical" appearance of fashion design; her frocks are often introduced in actual performances, with light and music playing essential parts.

Her interest in sophisticated techniques has led her to introduce directly into her models elements that react so as to change the look of the dress under the influence of light or temperature. She therefore makes great use of liquid crystals, which enable her to create from a single model a number of variants of colour and pattern with each change of temperature. In her own words, "The frock is a changeable and ephemeral entity; the same model worn by different people will give out different messages." This statement makes clear her anthropological view of fashion as connected with the problems of individual expression of whoever "is being dressed." In this sense, her professional practice influences (and is influenced by) the theories that make up the "neo-modern" ideologies of design. These theories find, in makeup and in the decoration of objects as well as of buildings and of the body, the possibility of a recovery of formal qualities in design but also of a real quality of existence.

In the 1980s Ruggeri often used contemporary fabrics to which she adhered appliqués in various, often animal, themes. Early on in her career Ruggeri made it known that she would not wear animal fur, and one 1981 ensemble featured a jacket made of synthetic fur, the back of which was covered with an applique of three pigs. This applique also appeared on the wool trousers and the crepe de chine blouse. A dress cut in a traditional style was printed with huge blossoms and three-dimensional lizards. In the early 1990s, Ruggeri incorporated photography, anthropology, geology, and ecology into her designs by creating textiles with photographs of grass, stones, and marble as part of the pattern.

Ruggeri has also challenged herself by designing ballets and theatrical productions, as well as furniture and interiors.

—Stefano Casciani

# RUSSELL, (Sydney) Gordon

British furniture designer

**Born:** Gricklewood, London, 20 May 1892. **Education:** London and Repton, Derbyshire, until 1904; Chipping Campden, Gloucestershire, 1904-07. **Military Service:** British Army Worcester Regiment, 1914-19, also served as Special Police Officer, London, 1939-45. **Family:** Married Constance Elizabeth Jane Vere (Toni) Denning in 1921; children: Michael, Robert, Kate, and Olive. **Career:** Worked as a purser on the *S.S. Veronese,* to the River Plate, 1908; furniture restorer and manager in his father's antique business, Broadway, Worcestershire, 1908-14; partner, Russell and Sons furniture makers, Broadway, Worcestershire, 1919-46; founder-director, 1926-66, and chairman, 1967-77, of Gordon Russell Limited furniture makers, Chipping Campden, Gloucestershire; founder-director, Gordon Russell design studio, Kingcombe, Gloucestershire, 1960-80. **Member:** Assessor, 1938-53, and council member, 1961-68, National Council for Diplomas in Art and Design, London; chairman, Board of Trade Utility Furniture Design Panel, London, 1943-47; council member, Royal Society of Arts, London, 1947-49, 1951-55; director, 1947-59, and life member, 1960-80, Council of Industrial Design, London; arts panel member, Arts Council of Great Britain, London, 1948-53; fine arts committee member, British Council, London, 1948-58; council member, Royal College of Art, London, 1948-51, 1952-63; executive committee member, Festival of Britain, London, 1951; design panel member, British Railways Board, London, 1956-66; president, Design and Industries Association, London, 1959-62; member, Crafts Advisory Council,

London, 1971-74. **Exhibitions:** *Utility Furniture and Fashion 1941-1951,* Geffrye Museum, London, 1974; *Thirties: British Art and Design Before the War,* Hayward Gallery, London, 1979. **Honors:** Military Cross, 1918; Gold and Silver Medals, *Exposition des Arts Decoratifs,* Paris, 1925; Society of Industrial Artists and Designers Medal, London, 1959; Royal Society of Arts Medal, London, 1962. Honorary doctorates: Birmingham University, 1960; University of York, 1969. Royal Designer for Industry, 1940, and Master of the Faculty, 1947-49, Royal Society of Arts, London; fellow, Society of Industrial Artists, London, 1945; honorary designer, Royal College of Art, London, 1952; honorary associate, Institute of Landscape Architects, London, 1955; fellow, Royal Institute of British Architects, 1965. Commander, Order of the British Empire, 1947; Knight Bachelor, Britain, 1955; Officer of the Order of the Vasa, Stockholm, 1954; Commander, Norwegian Royal Order of Saint Olav, Oslo, 1957. **Died:** Chipping Campden, Gloucestershire, 7 October 1980.

## Publications

**By RUSSELL: books**—*Furniture Making: 12 Cards for Wall Display,* London, 1947; *Things We See: Furniture,* London, 1947, 1953; *The Story of Furniture,* London, 1947, 1967; *How to Buy Furniture,* London and Glasgow, 1951; *How To Furnish Your Home,* with Alan Jarvis, London, 1953; *Looking at Furniture,* London, 1964; *Designer's Trade: Autobiography of Gordon Russell,* London, 1968.

**ON RUSSELL: books**—*Modern English Furniture* by J. C. Rogers, London and New York, 1930; *A Survey of British Industrial Arts* by Henry G. Dowling, Benfleet, 1935; *British Achievement in Design* edited by Noel Carrington and Muriel Harris, London, 1946; *British Furniture Today* by Erno Goldfinger, London, 1951; *World Furniture* edited by Helena Hayward, London, 1965, 1981; *Utility Furniture and Fashion 1941-1951,* exhibition catalogue by Jeffrey Daniels and others, London, 1974; *Industrial Design in Britain* by Noel Carrington, London, 1976; *In Good Shape: Style in Industrial Products 1900-1960* by Stephen Bayley, London, 1979; *Gordon Russell* by Ken and Kate Baynes, London, 1981; *The Conran Directory of Design* edited by Stephen Bayley, London, 1985; *Eye for Industry: Royal Designers For Industry 1936-1986,* exhibition catalogue by Fiona MacCarthy and Patrick Nuttgens, London, 1986; *Twentieth Century Design: Furniture* by Penny Sparke, London, 1986.

\*      \*      \*

When Sidney Russell moved in 1904 from Derbyshire to Broadway, Worcestershire, to take over the Lygon Arms Hotel, he sent his boys to the grammar school at neighbouring Chipping Campden. It was not surprising that Gordon, the eldest, should there acquire an interest in craftsmanship because it was at Campden that C.R. Ashbee had set up his Guild of Craftworkers, which he had first formed in the East End of London and later persuaded to migrate (150 men, women, and children) to the Cotswolds to be closer to nature. On leaving school, Gordon was drafted into the workshop which his father had set up to repair antique furniture. It had been discovered that antiques were a profitable sideline to sell to the guests of the hotel, especially to the Americans who flocked to this attractive Cotswold village.

Russell served with distinction in the First World War. In the trenches, before he was seriously wounded, he often dreamed of the furniture he would design if and when he returned. Following demobilisation, he returned to find a warehouse full of old furniture waiting to be repaired. However, having set up a workshop for himself, he started designing what he felt was more appropriate for his own generation. He also found that the younger craftsmen were eager to work with him. But when his newly designed pieces were set alongside the antiques in the showroom window at Broadway, they met with derision due to the current craze for "period style and reproductions." Gordon's reaction was to publish a booklet, "Honesty and the Crafts," in which he questioned the workmanship of things simply because they were old and claimed that the practice engendered an "army of swindlers faking what a deluded public demanded."

He found Suppon in a body called "Design and Industries," itself a secession from the Arts and Crafts Movement but differing in that its members accepted machine production. To Gordon, the machine was just a special tool, more powerful than a chisel or saw, but a tool the nature of which the designer must have constantly in mind. He never lost his respect for fine, individual craftsmanship, but his mission was to design for his own age. Not until 1929, ten years after the war, was he able to offer a dining room suite, planned for continuous production. Its reception gave him courage to open his showrooms in the West End of London where his work could be shown in company with the best contemporary textiles, pottery, or glass. Here his wife Toni, whom he married in 1921, proved an invaluable help.

In the early 1930s the great American slump caused a serious setback because trade with America had been an important factor in Russell's business. Frank Murphy, an ex-Post Office engineer, was making radio sets to satisfy demand for the "wireless." He was dissatisfied with the cabinets then on offer from the trade, which had persuaded itself that this new invention must be disguised behind a mass of fretwork. Murphy, having seen some of Russell's furniture, approached him for a design.

For months, the radio engineers hammered out their problem with Russell and his younger architect-brother. Murphy found their cabinet logical and seemly as a solution, but when he offered it to a sales conference it was greeted as unsalable and nicknamed by one wit as "Pentonville". However, Murphy stood by his convictions and the set became a public favourite. Its sales outstripped the capacity of the Broadway workshops, thereby necessitating installation of a separate factory in West London for its production. This model was only the first of a series for Murphy Radio.

Thenceforward, until World War II, Gordon Russell enterprises prospered. He was able to recruit a team of young designers, including several architects and, as buyer for the shops, Nicholas Pevsner, a refugee from Nazism who later became known as a brilliant scholar of European architecture. The war's shortage of timber meant difficulties at Russell's workshops, but in 1942, the Board of Trade asked Russell to field a team which could design and make the simplest furniture to replace that lost in bombed-out homes. The result, known as the Utility line, though hardly to the taste of the trade, was serviceable and soundly made. It remained in use for several years after the war and may have done much to wean the public from the reproduction vogue and to prepare the way for the revolutionary designs that appeared at the Festival of Britain in 1951.

Gordon Russell's role by this time became largely that of a public servant. As director of the Design Council, with its showrooms and changing exhibitions, he was able to influence all the trades producing durable consumer goods. One of the original Royal Designers for Industry, he was also honoured with knighthood. Nevertheless, he retained his habit of walking around daily to keep in touch personally with his staff, just as he had done with his workers at Broadway—a habit, as he used to tell me, he had formed in the trenches.

After leaving the Design Council post in 1959, he was still in demand as a consultant by the government for many years. On one such mission, he made an extended tour of India. There, he advised its new government on setting up an institution to maintain the vitality of crafts, for Russell still maintained his respect for handicrafts and likewise secured them government support in Britain. When he finally retired to the home he had built for himself at Campden, he was able to resume what had been his first love, working with his own hands, which he now devoted to masonry, garden design, and carving fine letters in stone.

—Noel Carrington

# RUUHINEN, Erkki (Antero)
Finnish advertising, graphic, and typographic designer

**Born:** Toivakka, 3 September 1943. **Education:** Studied graphic design, at the School for Advertising Design, Helsinki, 1964-66. **Career:** Designer and art director in the agencies Mainosyhtymä Oy, 1966-68, SEK Advertising, 1968-75, and Anderson and Lembke Oy, 1975-85, in Helsinki; founder and managing director, Erkki Ruuhinen Design, Helsinki, from 1983; has designed for The Pohjola Insurance Group, IBM Finland, Kesko Corporation, Finnish Sugar Corporation, KOP Bank, Ilmarinen Pension Insurance Company, Valio Dairies, and others. Chairman, Finnish Society of Graphic Artists, 1970-71. **Member:** Grafia, Finnish Society of Graphic Artists; Finnish Marketing Association; Type Directors Club, New York; Society of Scribes, New York. **Exhibitions:** *International Poster Exhibition,* London, 1967; *Posters of the Year,* Helsinki, 1967-95; *UNICEF Help the Children Posters,* Paris, 1969; *Typomundus 2,* Munich, 1970; *International Poster Biennale,* Warsaw, 1970, 1972, 1974, 1976; *International Graphics Biennale,* Brno, 1970, 1974, 1978; *Filmexpo,* Ottawa, 1972; *International Poster Biennale,* Lahti, 1975, 1977, 1979, 1981; *Creativity Awards,* New York, 1978, 1979, 1980, 1982; *Erkki Ruuhinen: Graphics,* Lahti, 1979; *Clio Awards,* New York, 1979, 1981, 1983; *Calligraphy Today,* New York, 1980, 1981. **Collections:** Lahti Poster Museum, Finland; Stedelijk Museum, Amsterdam; International Poster Museum, Warsaw; Musée d'Affiche, Paris; Poster Museum of Musashino Art University, Tokyo. **Honors:** Finnish State Award for Craftsmanship, 1969; Best Poster of the Year Award, Helsinki, 1968, 1969, 1970, 1971, 1972, 1973, 1976, 1978, 1979, 1980, 1981, 1982, 1983, 1984, 1985; Silver Medal, Poster Biennale, Brno, 1970, 1974; Gold Medal, Rizzoli Advertising Competition, New York, 1972; Film Expo Awards (5), Ottawa, 1972; Gold, silver, and bronze medal, 1975, and silver medal, 1977, 1979, Poster Biennial, Lahti; *Communication Arts* Award, Palo Alto, 1978; New Clio Award, New York, 1979, 1980, 1982, 1983; Type Directors Club Awards, New York, 1982, 1983, 1984, 1985; Graphic Designers of the Year in Finland, 1985; Special Platinum Award for Top of the Year, Advertising and Graphic Design Competition, Helsinki, 1986; Finnish State Prize for Applied Arts, 1989; The Bank Card of the Year in Europe, Frankfurt, 1992. **Addresses:** Riskutie 28, 00950 Helsinki,

Finland; Erkki Ruuhinen Design, Riskutie 26, 00950 Helsinki, Finland.

## Works

Film posters, for Jörn Donner Productions, 1967-95.
Corporate identity program, for The Pohjola Group Insurance Company, 1977-83.
Annual reports, for IBM Finland, 1983-89.
Posters, for Kuopio Dance and Music Festival, 1984-85.
Posters, for Pori Jazz Festival, 1985-87.
Corporate identity program and posters, for Printing House Koteva, 1985-95.
Annual reports, for Enso-Gutzeit Oy, 1986-90.
Annual reports, for Valio Dairies, 1986-90.
Corporate identity program, for the Amos Anderson Art Gallery, Helsinki, 1987.
Corporate identity program, for the Helsinki Stock Exchange, 1987.
Corporate identity program, for Libris Printing Company, 1988.
Corporate identity program, for Heureka Finnish Science Center, 1988.
Posters, for Imatra Big Band Festival, 1988-89.
Corporate identity program, for Enso-Gutzeit forestry industry group, 1989.
Corporate identity program, 1989, and annual reports, 1989-94, for Ilmarinen Pension Insurance Company.
Corporate identity program, for Tampere Civic Center, 1989.
Corporate identity program, for Turva Insurance Company, 1989.
Posters, for Absolut Vodka, 1990.
Annual report, for KOP Bank, 1990.
Corporate identity program, for Kesko Corporation, 1989-94 (including K-Shops, K-Market Stores, K-Supermarket Stores, and K-Citymarket Stores, 1993-94), and annual reports, for Kesko Corporation, 1990-92.
Corporate identity program, 1990-91, and annual reports, 1991-93, for Labsystems.
Corporate identity program, for Finn Coop Pellervo, 1991.
Corporate identity program, for Orion Diagnostica, 1990-1995.

## Publications

**By RUUHINEN: books**—*Erkki Ruuhinen Design,* Helsinki, 1987.

**On RUUHINEN: books**—*Who's Who in Graphic Art* edited by Walter Amstutz, Dubendorf, 1982; *Finnish Industrial Design* edited by Tua Pontasuo, Helsinki, 1987; **articles**—*Graphis* (Zürich); *Graphis Photo* (Zürich); *Poster Publicity* (London); *Idea* (Tokyo); *Communication Arts* (Palo Alto); *Upper and Lower Case* (New York); *Novum Gebrauchsgraphik* (Munich); and others.

\*    \*    \*

Erkki Ruuhinen has been instrumental in developing modern Finnish graphic design. As well as running his own design studio, he works tirelessly to improve professional advertising standards in Finland by lecturing, writing articles, and serving on professional bodies and award panels. Almost everywhere you look there are examples of his work—work that has achieved widespread domestic and international recognition. Recently he was elected the first

# ERKKI RUUHINEN DESIGN

**Erkki Ruuhinen: logo samples**

Graphic Artist of the Year in Finland and was also awarded a state artist's prize for his contribution to the graphic arts. In addition, out of the 130 awards he has received, over half have been international. What is so remarkable for someone from such a small country is that these awards have come from all areas—posters, advertisement campaigns, corporate design programs, direct mail, packaging, typography, calligraphy, and even copy.

An early interest in letters, logos, and signs led Ruuhinen into the study of graphics, calligraphy, and typography as well as a thorough investigation of the relationship between colour, space, and composition. Because he firmly believes that designers should be able to understand their clients' background to provide effective design services, he also started business and marketing studies. After qualifying as a graphic artist, Ruuhinen worked through the late 1960s and 1970s in two of Finland's leading advertising agencies. The first was SEK, which had a reputation for outstanding creativity. Ruuhinen worked on a variety of consumer accounts there before switching to the business-to-business sector and the newly opened Finnish branch of the Swedish Anderson and Lembke chain. In all, he spent eight years there, becoming a board member and helping Anderson and Lembke establish itself as one of the pioneers of business-to-business in Scandinavia and the rest of

Europe by combining in-depth strategic planning with exceptional creativity.

During this period, Ruuhinen continued to carry out special graphic design commissions—posters, logos, trademarks, etc.— and played with the idea of setting up his own graphic design company. The final impetus came from one of Ruuhinen's prime sources of inspiration, Herb Lubalin. While in Helsinki to judge the Finnish advertising awards, Lubalin asked why Ruuhinen had not yet set up on his own and predicted he would do so within five years. Only two years later and Erkki Ruuhinen Design was opening its doors. To date, the company has carried out corporate design programs and projects for many of Finland's leading concerns and institutions including Enso-Gutzeit, the KOP Bank, Postipankki, the former Finnish Sugar Corporation, and Labsystems. Nevertheless, Ruuhinen is not simply concerned with the giants; just as many small, newly begun companies turn to him for their design needs.

Over the years, Ruuhinen has become increasingly interested in the basic elements of art—space, form, colour, and composition. He believes there are examples of internationally oriented thinking and tradition to be found in Finnish architecture and design, the best known practitioners being the architect Alvar Aalto and the glass designers Tapio Wirkkala and Timo Sarpaneva. Representative through their work in the United States are the architects Eliel and Eero Saarinen; via their teaching at the Cranbrook Academy of arts, they spread the Finnish design gospel and exerted a significant influence on the development of American design in the early decades of this century.

Ruuhinen has also studied the teachings of the Bauhaus movement as well as the Russian avant garde, and admires their influence on the subsequent development of art, design, and architecture. As a consequence, he has come to believe that the development of graphic design is tied to the "traditional movements" in modern art. He illustrates this by pointing out that Josef Albers' work on the use of colour can still help open the eyes not only of painters, architects, and textile designers, but also of graphic artists. In a similar vein, he cites the work of Paul Klee, Wassily Kandinsky, Marcel Breuer, Mies van der Rohe, and other Bauhaus designers and students. Recognition of influences is very important to Ruuhinen, since he holds that "we are all only messengers on the long road of art, irrespective of which areas of arts or design we work in. Indeed, the part we play in the overall development of art depends on how significant future generations regard our contribution." Certainly Ruuhinen's work reflects his interest—clear, unadorned designs with bold use of colour, but with an originality all their own.

—Richard Hayhurst

# RYKIEL, Sonia

French fashion, interior, and accessories designer

**Born:** Sonia Flis, in Paris, 25 May 1930. **Education:** Attended a girls' school, Neuilly-sur-Seine, until 1949; mainly self-taught in design. **Family:** Married Sam Rykiel in 1953; children: Nathalie and Jean-Philippe. **Career:** Worked as a stylist, at the Boutique Laura, Paris, 1962-68; founder and president, Sonia Rykiel fashion company, Paris, from 1967; household linens boutique opened, Paris, 1975; Sonia Rykiel Enfant boutique opened, Paris, 1987; cosmetics line launched, Japan, 1987; Rykiel Homme boutique opened, Paris, 1989; Inscription Rykiel collection launched, 1989; new flagship boutique opened, Paris, 1990; menswear collection introduced, 1990; footwear collection launched, 1992; bath line launched, 1994; fragrances include *7ème Sens,* 1978, and *Sonia Rykiel,* 1993. Vice-president, Chambre Syndical du Pret-a-Porter des Couturiers et des Createurs de Mode, Paris, from 1973. Contributor to *Femme* magazine, Paris, from 1983. **Exhibitions:** *Woman of the Year 2000,* Forum des Halles, Paris, 1979; *Tables en Fetes,* International Centre of Tableware, Paris, 1979; *Sonia Rykiel, 20 Ans de la Mode* (retrospective), Galeries Lafayette, Paris, and Seibo Shibuya department store, Tokyo, 1987; retrospective, the Orangerie, Palais du Luxembourg, 1993. **Honors:** Oscar de la Mode, Paris, 1985; New York Fashion Group Award, 1986; Chicago Historical Society's Award for Design Excellence, 1994; Chevalier de la Legion d'Honneur; Chevalier des Arts et des Lettres; Officier de l'Ordre des Arts et des Lettres, 1993. **Address:** 175 Boulevard Saint-Germain, 75006 Paris, France.

## Works

Shopping bag designs, for Galeries Lafayette, Bloomingdale's, Macy's, and Seibu, 1979.

Tablewares and menu designs, for Lutetia and Terminus Saint-Lazare Hotels, Paris, 1979.
Notebooks, diaries and stationery accessories, for Galeries Lafayette, Paris, 1980.
Hotel de Crillon interior renovations, Paris, 1982.
Books illustrated include—*Collette et la Mode,* 1991.

## Publications

**By RYKIEL: books**—*Et Je la Voudrais Nue,* Paris, 1979, Tokyo, 1981; *Rykiel,* Paris, 1985; *Célébrations,* Paris, 1988; *La collection,* Paris, 1989, Tokyo, 1989; *Collection Terminée, Collection Interminable,* Paris, 1993; *Tatiana Acacia,* Paris, 1993.

**On RYKIEL: books**—*A History of Fashion* by J. Anderson Black and Madge Garland, London, 1975, 1980; *In Fashion: Dress in the Twentieth Century* by Prudence Glynn, London, 1978; *25 Ans de Marie-Claire de 1954 a 1979,* compiled by Françoise Mohrt, Paris, 1979; *The Fashionable Mind: Reflections on Fashion, 1970-1981* by Kennedy Fraser, New York, 1981; *The Collector's Book of Twentieth Century Fashion* by Frances Kennett, London and New York, 1983; *McDowell's Directory of Twentieth Century Fashion* by Colin McDowell, London, 1984; *Rykiel* by Madeleine Chapsal, Hélène Cixous, and Sonia Rykiel, Paris, 1985; *Couture: The Great Designers* by Caroline Rennolds Milbank, New York, 1985; *The Encyclopaedia of Fashion from 1840 to the 1980s* by Georgina O'Hara, London, 1986; **articles**—"Sonia Rykiel, ambigue, célèbre et solitaire" in *Elle* (Paris), 25 October 1976; "Sonia Rykiel sa vie, de fil" by Françoise Tournier in *Elle* (Paris), 17 June 1985; "Autour de l'album Rykiel" by Sonia Schoonejans in *Vogue* (Paris), August 1985; "Sonia Rykiel—Winning at Life" by Suzy Menkes in the *International Herald Tribune* (Neuilly, France), 18 October 1988; "Sonia Rykiel, les 20 ans de la dame en noir" by Christiane Sacase in *Biba,* November 1988; "Mes rendez-vous" by Hélène de Turckheim in *Madame Figaro* (Paris), 11 February 1989; "Les vingt ans de Sonia Rykiel by Madeleine Chapsal in *Elle* (Paris), 20 February 1989; "Touch of the Grande Dame" by Roger Tredre in *The Independent* on Sunday (London), 25 February 1990; "Sonia Rykiel" in *Current Biography* (New York), May 1990; "En visite chez Sonia Rykiel" by Dominique Nolin in *Marie-France* (Paris), March 1991; "Sonia Rykiel: une femme d'atmosphere" by Sylvie Raulet in *Vogue* (Japan), March 1991; "Rapping with Rykiel" by Heidi Lender in *Women's Wear Daily* (New York), 18 November 1991; "Sonia Rykiel, la compil" by Barbara Schwarm in *L'Officiel* (Paris), June 1993; "Sex, Sweaters and Sonia Rykiel" by Godfrey Deeny and Heidi Lender in *Women's Wear Daily* (New York), 7 July 1993; "Rykiel in Retrospect: The Unfinished Work of a Designer" by Suzy Menkes in the *International Herald Tribune* (Neuilly, France), 13 July 1993; "Capital Elle" by Ian Webb in *The Times Magazine,* 1994; "The Leading Lady of the Left Bank" by Jean Bond Rafferty in *Town & Country* (New York), December 1994; "Rykiel Sips Tea, Seeks N.Y. Store" by Janet Ozzard in *Women's Wear Daily* (New York), 28 December 1994; "Lacroix and Rykiel: Classics" by Anne-Marie Schiro in *The New York Times,* 18 March 1995.

*

I say that I am mad, that I wanted to create a space between them and myself.

**Sonia Rykiel: From autumn/winter collection, 1995**

They, the other women, all those who were not me, my skeleton, my silhouette. That I wanted to put a distance between what they were and the desire I had to be different, contrary, hallowed, other.

I am certain that I did not want to build an eyrie for these strangers but a special appearance for myself, a deviation from a system that I knew well and that was that uniform, the envelope in which I drowned myself, rolled myself, lost myself.

I thought that I could hide myself inside the dress, but I soon knew that it was I who shaped it, gave it life, supported it.

As a spectator, I witnessed my transformation and that of this dress which became invisible, transparent, while my body assumed increasing importance. At the same time, I worked on this dress. It had become a profession.

I made it fold, obey. I treated it like an infant, seduced it like a mistress, padded it sometimes to make it larger, to give it volume, or I undid it simply to understand.

I turned it inside out to see if it would resist me. It accepted the ideal on one condition, that from then on we would say that the wrong side is as good as the right side.

I even went further. I affirmed that the other side of the garment, that which touches the skin, the wrong side, was much more beautiful because it was emphasized by the seams (now visible) like the beams of a house or the columns of a cathedral.

I gave it symbolic value.

"You have put your sweater on inside out, you'll certainly get a present."

A present, like the wrong side, is a celebration, it is living twice for a few moments, the second living being inside the packet. I remember a very beautiful phrase of Tonino Guerra: "Every time I make up a parcel, I rediscover myself inside."

Every time I make a garment, I rediscover myself inside it. I give it my form, my strength, my soul. I condition it, I show it, I gauge it. Standing in front of the mirror, I judge it, hate it, and adore it. (*Excerpted from* Et Je la Voudrais Nue, *1979.*)

—Sonia Rykiel

\*　　\*　　\*

Although she has never had any formal training in fashion design, Sonia Rykiel has succeeded in creating classic, comfortable clothes which cater more to the wearer than to the vagaries of fashion.

Rykiel has a practical and realistic approach; she designs as a woman for women. Her long, soft lines are not only visually attractive, but free from clutter; they accentuate the natural movement of the body. This is achieved by the use of knitted wools and fabrics such as crepe, which drape naturally. Her concentration on layers means that her garments can be mixed and matched according to the wishes of the individual. While her vertical lines have a timeless quality, her emphasis on coordination is essentially modern.

It is Rykiel's belief that women should not have to spend too much time selecting what they will wear. Her own dissatisfaction with what was available as ready-to-wear led her to become a designer. By creating garments for herself, she found that she was appealing to other women. Her original style is reminiscent of the early 1920s with its calf-length skirts, broad hip sashes, and tiny hats.

In the 1970s Rykiel incorporated words into her designs. "MODE" was emblazoned across the stomach of one dress, and other words used included "PLAISIR," "ARTIST," and "READY." Appearing most frequently, however, was the word "RYKIEL." In the early 1980s Rykiel started producing at least two casual lines a year using a cotton velour fabric. In each new season Rykiel designs at least one dress in addition to pullovers, jackets, trousers, and cardigans. Many of these designs have reverse seams, a Rykiel trademark. In the early 1990s Rykiel turned to designing outerwear, including voluminous fake fur coats.

It is not Rykiel's intention to seduce her customer with novelty. She finds the visual arts, literature, and music more inspiring to her than the ever-changing world of fashion. Colour enlivens her creations, and she will spend up to two months selecting the most suitable combinations for a collection. Like a painter, she instinctively knows where to place a vibrant band of bright colour in order to create maximum impact. The use of limited colourways, usually consisting of a basic tone plus a contrast, gives a visual cohesion to her multi-layered creations. She is a subtle innovator whose work is consciously relaxed and understated. Her clothes wrap themselves around the body, leaving it unrestricted. Knitwear has been stimulated by her utilisation of the soft, natural qualities of wool. An understanding of what women demand from their clothes has enabled Rykiel to eschew fashion and produce some of the most classic designs of the late 20th century.

—Hazel Clark

# SACCO, Bruno
German industrial designer

**Born:** Udine, Italy, 11 November 1933. **Education:** Studied in Tarvisio and Udine, Italy; studied mechanical engineering under Professors Segre and Savonuzzi, Polytechnic University, Turin. **Family:** Married Annemarie Ibe in 1959; children: Marina. **Career:** Designer, 1958-70, head of Bodywork Design and Dimensional Concept Department, 1970-74, senior engineer, 1974-75, manager, Design Department, 1975-87, senior vice president, from 1987, Daimler-Benz, Germany. **Honors:** Honorary member, Academia Mexicana de Diseno, Mexico, 1981; awarded title "Grande Ufficiale dell' Ordine al Merito della Repubblica Italiana," 1991; Cover Award, *Auto & Design* magazine, Turin, Italy, 1993; L'automobile più bella del mondo, *Automobilia* magazine, Milan, 1993; Premio Mexico 1994, Patronato Nacional de las Asociaciones de Diseno A.C. Mexico, 1994. **Address:** Mercedes-Benz AG, HPC G 280, 71059 Sindelfingen, Germany.

## Works

Automobile designs, with Mercedes-Benz, include: Grand Mercedes 600; 230SL; W126 S-class, 1979, and SEC, 1981, and 190, 1982; mid-series, 1984; 300/500 SL, 1989; W140 S-class, 1991, and S-class coupé, 1992; C-class, 1993; E-class, 1995; SLK, 1996.
Automobile prototypes and studies with Mercedes-Benz include: ESV project; F100, 1989; C112, 1991; EXT, 1992; coupé study, 1993; Vision A, 1993; Micro Concept Car MCC, 1994; SLK "Silver" study, 1994; SLK "Blue" study, 1994; AAV Design Concept, 1996.

## Publications

**On SACCO: articles—**"Bruno Sacco, Mercedes-Benz Chief Stylist" by Leon Mandel in *Motor Trend* (Los Angeles), October 1978; "Bruno Sacco, Adding a Turinese Touch to Mercedes-Benz's Teutonic Shapes" by Ron Wakefield in *Road & Track* (Newport Beach, California), September 1979; "Sacco explains" by Steve Cropley in *Car* (London), January 1983; "Bruno Sacco and the 190" by Jean Lindamood in *Car & Driver* (New York), November 1983; "Der Stylist von Mercedes" by Holger Schnitgerhans in *Manager Magazin* (Hamburg, Germany), October 1985; "La Filosofia Mercedes dei Design" by Sergio Favia del Core in *Motor* (Rome), June 1986; "Corte d'Identità" by Marcello Minerbi in *Auto Capital* (Milan), October 1986; "Sacco, Bringing Out Pure Shapes" by Fulvio Cinti in *Auto & Design* (Turin), April 1987; "Bruno Sacco's Stern-Stunde" by Wolfgang Stockklausner in *Esquire* (Munich) April 1989; "Bruno Sacco" by Robert Cumberford in *Automobile* (Ann Arbor, Michi-

gan), July 1989; "Super Coupe" by Kostas Metaxas in *Vive la Vie* (North Fitzroy, Victoria, Australia), no. 17, 1990; "Style Counsel" by Angus MacKenzie in *Wheels* (Sydney, Australia), July 1990; "¿Quién diseña los automóviles Daimler-Benz?" by D.I. Alejandro Lazo Margain in *TOP* (Mexico City), Winter 1990/1991; "Family Man" by Steve Cropley in *Sunday Times Magazine Quality Cars* (London), 1991; "Driving Force" by Phil Patton in *Connoisseur* (New York), August 1991; "Ein Sacco für Mercedes" by Hans Werner in *Stern Magazin* (Hamburg), 29 August 1991; "Im Zeichan des Sterns" by Ruedi Arnold in *Das Magazin* (Berner Zeitung, Zürich) 10 April 1992; "Bruno Sacco" by Jürg Altweeg in *Frankfurter Allgemeine Magazin* (Frankfurt am Main), 5 March 1993; "Maestro Mercedes" by Alfred Prokesch in *Kurier, Motor* (Wien, Austria), 13 September 1993; "Mercedes ist ein Mann" by Helmut Rebholz in *Forbes* (Munich), October 1994; "Profile & Interview, Bruno Sacco" by Hans-Karl Lange in *Car Graphic* (Tokyo), September 1995; "Ich glaube fest an das Automobil" in *Automobil Produktion* (Landsberg, Germany) September 1995; "Bruno Sacco, Head of Design, Daimler-Benz" by Alan E. McPhee in *Carguide* (Oakville, Ontario, Canada), December 1995.

*

Considering the tremendous complexity of our present cars, design must be viewed as interdisciplinary teamwork.

As an active member in this process, I do not consider myself as a design manager, but as a conductor of a very efficient, symphonic Orchestra, the Mercedes-Benz Design-Team.

I do not just see design as the aesthetic mantling of a technological concept, but as an element of this concept. Technology and design should interpenetrate. Design themes and ideas develop on the basis of technological requirements. But, conversely, new design objectives also necessitate new technological solutions.

I am convinced that a car can only find long-term acceptance in the market if it not only fulfills its technical purpose but also possesses symbolic properties and expression.

The customer, too, would like to express something about his personality. He wants to publicly communicate himself to others, and what could be more public that the professed preference for a particular automobile.

Vice versa, a particular automobile can be developed if this development is based on a discernible company philosophy. Such a philosophy has emerged from a process of historically evolved interplay between product and company, customers and general public, and thus forms the basis of the Mercedes corporate identity.

The growing international uniformity of cars in the world's markets is striking. Less trained eyes can hardly see differences between individual makes anymore. So it is our job as designers to counter this trend and to preserve and continue cultural individuality.

**Bruno Sacco:** *Mercedes-Benz SLK,* 1996

The symbolic force and expressive substance of a car shape will represent ever weightier sales arguments, since the increasing technical and functional similarity of cars is an irreversible process.

Design today has become for me the most important element of product differentiation. The designer must be able to think beyond the current state of things. He should have a feel for embryonic developments. I consciously say "feel" because academic theory provides only very scant help.

In 1980 we developed for ourselves a design philosophy which encompasses the following:

It is essential to see the individual models as members of a single family of forms.

All models series in production at any one time are distinguished by a clear degree of commonality of form—the so-called horizontal homogeneity.

In this way, each model is clearly recognizable as part of the Mercedes product family and a distinctive company identity becomes established in the public consciousness.

At the same time, however, all cars should develop continuously, from their preceding model generations. We call this vertical affinity.

However, nothing should be so absolute that it does not permit new interpretations in the course of time.

With creativity, courage, and fantasy, solutions are carried through to meet the goals that have been set.

—Bruno Sacco

## SAGERT, Horst
German painter, medalist, and stage designer

**Born:** Dramburg, 13 October 1934. **Education:** Educated in Hagenow, Mecklenburg, until 1953; studied under Heinrich Kilger at the Kunstschule, Berlin-Weissensee, Dip., 1958. **Family:** Married Eva Stengel in 1963; children: Anna. **Career:** Freelance stage designer, East Berlin, from 1958; designed for the Deutsches Theater, Deutsches Staatsoper, Berliner Ensemble, Freie Volksbuhne of West Berlin, the Zürich Schauspielhaus, and the Buhnen der Stadt Koln. **Exhibitions:** Zentrum für Kunstausstellungen der DDR, East Berlin, 1979; Galerie Oben, Karl-Marx-Stadt, 1983. **Collections:** Staatliche Museen, East Berlin; Staatliche Kunstsammlungen, Dresden. **Honors:** Quadriennale Prize, 1971, and Gold Medal, 1979, Prague; Critics Prize, Venice Biennale, 1971. **Address:** Knaackstrasse 45, 1058 Berlin, Germany.

## Works

Stage productions include—*Der Drache,* Deutsches Theater, Berlin, 1965; *Oedipus Tyrann,* Deutsches Theater, 1967; *Horizons,* Arbeiter Theater Schwedt, 1968; *Turandot oder der Kongress der Weisswascher,* Zürich Schauspielhaus, 1969 (also director); *Dona Rosita bleibt ledig oder die Sprache der Blumen,* Deutsches Theater, 1970 (also director); *Die Komodie von Konig Bamba,* Deutsches Theater, 1972 (also director); *A Midsummer Night's Dream,* Cologne, 1976; *Medea,* Deutsches Theater, 1977 (also director); *The Taming of the Shrew,* West Berlin, 1981.

## Publications

By SAGERT: books—*Die Krahe und die Taube: Ein Todeszauber in der Art der Kinderspiele,* Karl-Marx-Stadt, 1983.

On SAGERT: books—*Horst Sagert: Buhnenbilder und Figurinen zu Jewgeni Schwarz Der Drache* by Lothar Lang, Leipzig, 1971; *Stage Design Throughout the World Since 1960* edited by Rene Hainaux and Yves Bonnat, Brussels, 1972, London, 1973; *Gebrauchsgraphik in der DDR* by Hellmut Rademacher, Dresden, 1975; *Horst Sagert: Buhnenbilder und Bilder,* exhibition catalogue by Ursula Riemann-Reyher and others, Berlin, 1979; *Horst Sagert— Bilder, Buhnenbilder, und Medaillen,* exhibition catalogue, Karl-Marx-Stadt, 1983.

\*     \*     \*

The number of Horst Sagert's works for the stage is not large, for he has often taken long breaks during which he has worked as a painter, graphic artist, and medalist. An international breakthrough in his career, however, resulted from his designs for Benno Besson's 1965 production of *Der Drache* at the Deutsches Theater in Berlin. Here, the essential elements of Sagert's approach came together in a synthesis of great originality.

Sagert's art is influenced on the one hand by the socio-critical impulses of Brechtian theater, but on the other hand, it is close to surrealism and Russian constructivism. His work employs suggestions of so-called naive painting (recalling Friedrich Schroder-Sonnenstern) but also of modern graphic script. The works of his teacher in Berlin, Heinrich Kilger, had a strong influence on Sagert's development. In method too, Sagert is linked to the achievements of the Brechtian stage, particularly (as in the work of Caspar Neher and Karl von Appen) to the importance attributed to design. What is new in Sagert's work is that he has regained an integrated idea of space. Also new are the magically-fantastic element and the eminent subtlety of his draftsmanship, including the handling of script, which functions as a particularly attractive graphic system and makes explicit the literary connection of Sagert's work. From an artistic point of view, Sagert's theater design was a starting point for the total theatrical work of art which the stage designer controls now as director, now as scriptwriter. With drama, to which music is added, he approaches idea opera in the German romantic sense where integration of the arts is presented in a poetic theatrical cosmos.

This artist's obsession for detail—present in his designs on paper and also finding its way through paint room and costume workshop to the stage—is free from naturalistic representation. The precision of detail contributes to the high style of the whole. There

results a single, theatrical, poetic world which does not close its eyes to the real world but includes its freedom. At one time, when the quotation stage of the Brechtian school was popular and often devolved on dogmatism and formalism, Sagert again called attention to the totality of the stage space. From the description of apparent social totalities, he achieved new opportunities in spatial relations on the stage. The result was a coherence that revealed itself precisely in its denseness and in its fragility.

—Friedrich Dieckmann

# SAINT LAURENT, Yves (Henri Donat Mathieu)

French fashion designer

Born: Oran, Algeria, 1 August 1936. Education: The Lycée d'Oran, until 1953; studied at the École de la Chambre, Syndicale de la Couture, Paris, 1954. Career: Independent clothing stylist, Paris, 1953-54; designer and partner, 1954-57, and chief designer, 1957-60, Christian Dior fashion house, Paris; founder and managing director of Société Yves Saint Laurent fashion firm, Paris, from 1962; Rive Gauche ready-to-wear line introduced, 1966; menswear line introduced, 1974; fragrances include *Y* (1965), *Rive Gauche, Opium, Paris*; firm purchased by Elf-Sanofi SA, 1993. Also stage designer, from 1959, and film costume designer, from 1962. Exhibitions: *Fashion: An Anthology,* Victoria and Albert Museum, London, 1971; *Franzosisches Kunsthandwerk Heute,* Overstolzenhaus, Cologne, 1981; *Yves Saint Laurent,* Metropolitan Museum of Art, New York, 1983; *Yves Saint Laurent et le Theatre,* Musée des Arts de la Mode, Paris, 1986; *Yves Saint Laurent: 28 Ans de Creation,* Musée des Arts de la Mode, Paris, 1986; retrospective, Art Gallery of New South Wales, Sydney, Australia, 1987. Honors: International Wool Secretariat Prize, 1954; Neiman-Marcus Fashion Oscar, Dallas, 1958; *Harper's Bazaar* Award, New York, 1966; Council of Fashion Designers of America Award, 1981. Knighthood of the Legion of Honour, Palais de l'Elysée, Paris, 1985; Honorary Degree and Gold Medal for Assistance to Scientific Research, 1987. Addresses: (office) 5 Avenue Marceau, 75016 Paris; (home) 55 rue de Babylone, 75007 Paris, France.

## Publications

By SAINT LAURENT: books—(illustrator) *La Vilaine Lulu,* Paris, 1967; (with others) *Yves Saint Laurent,* New York and London, 1984; *Yves Saint Laurent par Yves Saint Laurent,* Paris, 1986.

On SAINT LAURENT: books—*The Fashionable Savages* by John Fairchild, New York, 1965; *Fashion: An Anthology by Cecil Beaton,* exhibition catalogue compiled by Madeleine Ginsburg, London, 1971; *Couture: An Illustrated History of the Great Paris Designers and Their Creations* edited by Ruth Lynam, New York, 1972; *In Vogue: Sixty Years of Celebrities and Fashion* edited by Georgina Howell, London, 1975, 1978, New York, 1976; *Living for Design: The Yves Saint Laurent Story* by Axel Madsen, New York, 1979; *Magic Names of Fashion* by Ernestine Carter, London, 1980; *McDowell's Directory of Twentieth Century Fashion* by Colin

McDowell, London, 1984; *Couture: The Great Designers* by Caroline Rennolds Milbank, New York, 1985; *Yves Saint Laurent et le Theatre,* with preface by Edmonde Charles-Roux, Paris, 1986; *The Encyclopaedia of Fashion from 1840 to the 1980s* by Georgina O'Hara, London, 1986; *Yves Saint Laurent, Retrospectives,* exhibition catalogue, Sydney, New South Wales, 1987; *W, The Designing Life* edited by Lois Perschetz, New York, 1987; *Yves Saint Laurent: Images of Design,* exhibition catalogue, New York, 1988; *Sultans of Style: 30 Years of Fashion and Passion 1960-1990* by Georgina Howell, London, 1990; *Yves Saint Laurent* by Laurence Benaïm, Paris, 1993; *Orientalism: Visions of the East in Western Dress,* exhibition catalogue by Richard Martin and Harold Koda, New York, 1994; **articles**—"YSL Models Rive Gauche for Men in His Marrakesh Home" in *Vogue* (London), 1 October 1969; "Yves Saint Laurent: His Very Special World" in *McCall's* (New York), January 1970; "Mary Russell Interviews Saint Laurent" in *Vogue* (New York), 1 November 1972; "Yves Saint Laurent Talks to Bianca Jagger" in *Interview* (New York), January 1973; "Les années 20 revues dans les années 70 chez Yves Saint Laurent" by P. Julian in *Connaissance des Arts* (Paris), December 1973; "Yves Saint Laurent Lives" by John Heilpern and Yves Saint Laurent in *The Observer Magazine* (London), 5 June 1977; "Designers of Influence: Yves Saint Laurent, the Great Educator" in *Vogue* (London), June 1978; "Bravo: 20 Years of Saint Laurent" in *Vogue* (London), April 1982; "A Salute to Yves Saint Laurent" in the *New York Times Magazine,* 4 December 1983; "The Truth in Fiction" by Holly Brubach in *The Atlantic Monthly* (Boston), May 1984; "Yves Saint Laurent" by Percy Savage in *Art and Design* (London), August 1985; "Yves Saint Laurent der Modezeichner" by P. Berge in *Du* (Zurich), No. 10, 1986; "Un équilibre définitif: Saint Laurent *Rive Gauche*" in *Vogue* (Paris), February 1986; "All About Yves" by Barbara Griggs in *The Observer* (London), 25 May 1986; "Yves" by Patrick Mauries in *Vogue* (Paris), June 1986; "Le triomphe de Saint Laurent" in *L'Officiel* (Paris), June 1986; "Saint Laurent: sanctifié il entre au musée" by Colombe Pringle in *Elle* (Paris), June 1986; "Saint Laurent: Life as a Legend" by Christa Worthington in *Women's Wear Daily* (New York), 18 July 1986; "Yves Only" in *Vogue* (London), September 1987; "Prince Charmant, Bernard Sanz: L'homme de Saint Laurent" in *Profession Textile* (Paris), 27 May 1988; "Saint Laurent pour toujours" in *Profession Textile* (Paris), 30 September 1988; "Saint Laurent par Duras" by Marguerite Duras in *Elle* (Paris), 31 October 1988; "The Business of Chic" by Nina Hyde and Albert Allart in *National Geographic* (Washington, D.C.), July 1989; "The Secrets of Saint Laurent" by Georgina Howell in *The Sunday Times Magazine* (London), 2 July 1989; "Best Couturier: Yves Saint Laurent" by Georgina Howell in *The Sunday Times Magazine,* 16 July 1989; "The Many Faces of Yves: The Designer of the Half Century" by Diane Rafferty and others in *Connoisseur,* February 1990; "Yves of the Revolution" by Suzy Menkes in the *Sunday Express Magazine* (London), 22 April 1990; "All About Yves" by Stephanie Germain in *Paris Passion* (Paris), October 1990; "Unveiling Saint Laurent" by Michael Roberts and André Leon Talley in *Interview* (New York), June 1991; "Thirty Years at Fashion's Cutting Edge" by Liz Smith in *The Times* (London), 27 January 1992; "Yves Saint Laurent, King of Couture" in *Elle* (New York), February 1992; "Fanfare in a Minor Key" by Holly Brubach in *The New Yorker,* 24 February 1992; "The Saint" by Lesley White in *Vogue* (London), November 1994; "The Impresario's Last Act" by Jane Kramer in *The New Yorker,* 21 November 1994; "Yves Saint Laurent's Shocking New Color: Black" by Anne-Marie Schiro in the *New York Times,* 22 March 1995; "YSL Plays Safe While Valentino Shines at Night" by Suzy Menkes in the *International Herald Tribune* (Paris), 22 March 1995; "Saint Laurent: A Fitting End" in *Women's Wear Daily,* 22 March 1995.

\* \* \*

The name of Yves Saint Laurent must, deservedly, be one of the best known within and outside the world of fashion today. It is often difficult to recall how many of our "basics" first came from his pen. He has helped to create a fundamental, functional, women's wardrobe consisting of jacket, trousers, and suit, styles which he constantly updates in his own collections. Always aware of what is happening about him, he produces garments which reflect the feelings of their time. By introducing Pop art to fashion and opening his Rive Gauche ready-to-wear boutique in 1966, he anticipated the breakdown of social barriers and the emergence of young, liberated styles. Masterminded by his financial partner Pierre Berger, Rive Gauche set the trend for boutique shopping. Like his great influence, Chanel, Saint Laurent believes that clothes should be easy and pleasant to wear. The apparent simplicity of his work is, however, deceptive. While his Trapeze line may have become the standard maternity dress and his Mondrian shift was immediately copied, nothing ever hung as well, or was as well cut, as the originals.

Despite his successes in couture, ready-to-wear, theatre, and film by the later 1960s, he never lost touch with the world at large, His 1968 collection featuring fur duffle coats, fringed buckskins under fox coats, and plaited headbands showed sympathy, in couture terms, with the student demonstrations and anti-Vietnam marches. Likewise his maxi-skirts of 1969 indicated a hippie influence and prefigured the ethnic looks of the 1970s. Saint Laurent had introduced a number of themes, such as his Carmen and Dr. Zhivago looks, in the 1960s, ahead of their time. They returned to make their impact in the 1970s. Having established his reputation and his practical attitude to dressing, he was able to indulge in the fantasy revealed in his love of ethnic costume. In 1970, he returned to Russia for inspiration, then to China, India, Morocco, Japan, and back to Spain in 1976 for his Carmen ready-to-wear collection and his Rich Peasant couture look. The splendour of Diaghilev's Ballets Russes provided the pattern for the sumptuous gold, the brilliant colours, and the full, swirling skirts shown in 1979. Call it escapism if you like, but the 1970s saw Saint Laurent bring gaiety into fashion.

In the 1980s and early 1990s, the small company Yves Saint Laurent founded in 1961 has become a huge conglomerate, listed in the Paris stock market. In May of 1993, Yves Saint Laurent Group merged with Elf Sanofi.

Throughout his career to date, Yves Saint Laurent has been at various times practical, revolutionary, and sensational. His ideas are never static; they capture the feeling of the moment.

—Hazel Clark

# SAKASHITA, Kiyoshi

Japanese industrial designer

**Born:** Osaka, 23 March 1933. **Education:** Studied industrial design, at Tokyo Art University, 1953-57. **Family:** Married Eiko Tani in 1958; children: Shiu. **Career:** Staff designer, 1957-60, home appliances design manager, 1960-63, New York research and marketing manager, 1963-66, audio and tape systems manager, 1966-73, corporate design manager, from 1973, corporate director and international member, from 1981, and corporate adviser, from 1995, Sharp Corporation, Osaka, Japan. Board member, Japan Industrial Designers' Association, Tokyo, from 1975, and Japan Package Design Association, Tokyo, from 1979; adviser, Japan Industrial Design Promotion Organization, Tokyo, from 1980, and Japan Design Foundation, Osaka, from 1981. **Collections:** Museum of Modem Art, New York. **Honors:** Three Good Design Prizes, MITI, Japan, 1992; *What Camcorder* magazine best innovation prize, 1993; *Camcorder User* magazine best innovation, 1993; *Discover* magazine award for technological innovation, 1993; *Popular Science* magazine audio-video grand award, 1993; *Popular Mechanics* magazine design and engineering award, 1994. **Address:** Corporate Design Center, Sharp Corporation, 22-22 Nagaike-cho, Abeno-ku, Osaka 545, Japan.

**Works** (as design supervisor)

*18C-D13E* color television, for Sharp, 1983.
*VC-180* video cassette recorder, for Sharp, 1983.
*VP-1000* video disc player, for Sharp, 1983.

*SA-V500* stereo receiver, for Sharp, 1983.
*RT-V500* stereo cassette deck, for Sharp 1983.
*RP-V500* stereo record player, for Sharp, 1983.
*CP-V500* speaker system, for Sharp, 1983.
*SJ-26K3A* fridge/freezer, for Sharp, 1983.
*ES-320C* washing machine, for Sharp, 1983.
*EC-553* vacuum cleaner, for Sharp, 1983.
*SS-209* electric razor, for Sharp, 1983.
*OK-263V* kerosene fan heater, for Sharp, 1983.
*WD-800* word processor, for Sharp, 1983.
*EI-8152* electronic calculator, for Sharp, 1983.
*PA-7050* electronic graph, for Sharp, 1983.
*SF-755* plain paper copier, for Sharp, 1983.
*X68000* personal workstation, for Sharp, 1986.
*PA-5000* electronic organizer, for Sharp, 1987.
*SJ-38WB* dual-swing door refrigerator, for Sharp, 1989.
*VL-HL1* Hi-8 LCD ViewCam, for Sharp, 1992.
*PI-3000* all-in-one personal information tool, for Sharp, 1993.

**Publications**

**By SAKASHITA: articles—***Design Quarterly* (Tokyo), no. 1, 1980, no. 3, 1981, no. 2, 1983.

**Kiyoshi Sakashita:** *VL-HL100* **Hi-8 LCD ViewCam, for Sharp Corporation, 1995**

**On SAKASHITA books**—*Structure of Dexterity: Industrial Design Works in Japan,* Tokyo, 1983; *World Design Today,* Tokyo, 1983; *Eighty Years of Sincerity and Creativity* by Sharp Corporation, Tokyo, 1992.

\* \* \*

Kiyoshi Sakashita is a corporate director and the general manager of the Design Center of the Sharp Corporation of Japan. His company has been a leader in the design of electrical home appliances and office automation equipment. Besides being notable for his own work in these fields, many of his colleagues admit that it is Sakashita's vitality that provides the driving force for their own work.

Sakashita is a product of the industrial design milieu of postwar Japan. His logic is clear-cut; his attitudes about abstracting future themes from the present are persuasive; and he is one of those speakers who can mobilize a large audience. But his accomplishment is more than simply having been a product of his time.

The revolution in electronics caused by microcomputers has been remarkable, and that revolution has, to a great extent, changed the consciousness of consumers. Some years ago the Sharp Corporation was in the forefront of helping to effect this change: it created a "new life merchandizing strategy" before it occurred to anyone else, impressing the public with its vision of a new lifestyle. As the person responsible for the design section of the Sharp Corporation, Sakashita has since been concerned as well with creating an "integrated style" in personal computers, electronic appliances, and office equipment—concerned, that is, not just with the design of individual products but with the design of complete systems—and, further, with the entire design image of his company. He seems to be intent on creating a corporate style that will permeate to all employees.

Sakashita is a sophisticated international businessman, the sort of person who grasps the realities of commerce, yet he has also been concerned about the role of design in modern society. He has been outspoken about the obligations of corporations to respond to the needs of users through enlightened industrial design. Though ideas and methods will obviously vary from one designer to another, Sakashita believes that linking consumer needs to effective product design is a reasonable, worthwhile goal.

The core of his design philosophy, as he expresses it, is the "humanization of scientific technology—that is, humanware design." This principle is shared by his co-workers, but it is Sakashita to whom they look for inspiration and direction.

—Kunio Sano

# SALADINO, John F.

American interior, furniture, and textile designer

**Born:** Kansas City, Missouri, 23 July 1939. **Education:** Educated at Rockhurst Preparatory High School, Kansas City, until 1957; studied fine arts, at Notre Dame University, Indiana, BFA, 1960; painting and sculpture under Josef Albers at Yale University, New Haven, Connecticut, MFA, 1963; studied in the studio of architect Piero Sartogo, Rome, 1968-69. **Family:** Married Virginia Hendrick in 1969; children: John. **Career:** Freelance interior designer, as

John F. Saladino Incorporated, New York, from 1972. Board member, Parsons School of Design, New York, and Formica Corporation, New York. **Honors:** Illuminating Engineering Society Award, New York, 1976; *Interiors* Magazine Designer of the Year Award, New York, 1980; Daphne Award, New York, 1982; American Society of Designers Distinction Award, New England, 1982; Chicago Design Sources Committee Award, 1982; Euster Merchandise Mart Award, 1982. **Address:** 305 East 63rd Street, New York, New York 10021, U.S.A.

**Works**

Thonet showroom interiors at the Decorative Arts Center, New York, 1980.
*Sectioned Column* table, for Saladino Incorporated, 1981.
Chaus showroom interiors, New York, 1981.
*Pavilion* sofa, for Saladino Incorporated, 1981.
*Papyrus* chair, for Saladino Incorporated, 1981.
Almay office interiors, New York, 1981.
*Corolla* chair, for Saladino Incorporated, 1982.
*Model 404-29* tripod end table, for Saladino Incorporated, 1986.
Chase Manhattan Bank office interiors, New York, 1987.
*Amphora* table lamp, for Saladino Incorporated, 1987.
*The Arch* chair, for Saladino Incorporated, 1988.
*The Tuscan* end table, for Saladino Incorporated, 1988.
NutraSweet headquarters interiors, Deerfield, Illinois, 1988.
*Horseshoe* chair, for Saladino Incorporated, 1988.

**Publications**

**By SALADINO: articles**—*Interior Design* (New York), April 1982.

**On SALADINO: books**—*Living Spaces* edited by Franco Magnani, Milan, 1977, New York and London, 1978; *Hi-Tech: The Industrial Style and Resource Book for the Home* by Joan Kron and Suzanne Slesin, New York, 1978, London, 1979; *Interior Views* by Erica Brown, London, 1980; *Interior Design: The New Freedom* by Barbaralee Diamonstein, New York, 1982; *Designers' Workplaces* by Beverly Russel, New York, 1983; *Modern Furniture Classics* by Miriam Stimpson, London, 1987; *International Design Yearbook 1988/89* edited by Arata Isozaki, London, 1988.

\* \* \*

"Juxtapositions" might be the single-word title of a book by John Saladino, in which he would start, of course, with the old and the new, the grand and the humble, and move into the more subtle areas of shadow and light, solid and void, even of architecture versus interior design. For Saladino is constantly pushing the frontier of interior design further toward the fine arts, toward architecture, as well as toward the refinement of space itself.

Color is one of the designer's most important contributions to interiors in the 1980s. Colors such as mauve, aqua, and terra cotta are all tones that the designer has pointed out he was using considerably earlier than postmodernist architects. But again, juxtaposition is part of the context here, because Saladino will take the lightest and prettiest of hues and counter it with, say, a round, natural, plywood surface. Walls of scratch-coat plaster will be a background for an exquisitely lacquered cabinet. Saladino achieves an effect of piquant and slightly perverse luxury through the use of such devices, as well as through his multifarious references to the classical past. He believes that a cultural context is absolutely necessary for successful design and considers himself as having "one foot in Europe, the other in America." A year spent in Rome made an enormous impression on him, imbuing in him a lasting love for weathered or even corroded surfaces, as well as adding the fondness for fragmentation and fractured perspective that makes his work unique.

"Miniature theater" is another term he has used to describe his effects. Indeed, there is a set-like quality to many of his rooms, especially in their exploitation of dramatically enlarged, classical fragments, their characteristically dynamic lighting, and perhaps most important, the sense that there is something going on *beyond* the room. A scrim-like shade across a window, or a trellis running across a length of a room to suggest a mysterious additional space beyond—these are among the visual aids Saladino uses in his work. He feels that his work manifests an essentially existential attitude toward design, for he believes in hesitancy and incompletion, at least in an intellectual sense. To a selective eye, however, his rooms look very complete. Complete and assured, occupying a fascinating space between two sensibilities in contemporary design, the reductionist and the enriching, and explaining them both well.

—Peter Carlsen

# SALOVAARA, (Aki Heikki) Juhani

Finnish industrial designer

**Born:** Kokkola, 16 March 1943. **Education:** Educated at Kokkola High School, until 1961; studied at the Institute of Industrial Design, Helsinki, Dip., 1967. **Career:** Designer, Upo Oy household apparatus, Helsinki, 1967, N. V. Philips, Eindhoven, Netherlands, 1968, and Wallac Oy, Turku, Finland, 1970; managing director, Ergonomiadesign Oy, Turku, from 1973; has designed for Martela, Nokia, Sohlberg, Treston, Tunturi, and others. Instructor in interior design, 1979-80, and instructor in industrial design, from 1983, University of Applied Arts, Helsinki. Committee Member, 1971-73, Board Member, 1973-76, Hungarian Interdesign Congress Coordinator, 1979, and Deputy Chairman of Helsinki Design Integration Congress, 1981, ICSID International Council of Societies of Industrial Design; Foreign Affairs Committee Member, 1972-77, Chief of Cooperative Projects with Berlin Design Council, 1977-79, Scandinavian Cooperation Chief, 1980-83, Chairman of TKO Industrial Designers Section Board, 1988-89, and First Deputy Chairman, 1988-89, Ornamo Association of Finnish Designers; Scientific-Technical Committee Member, Academy of Finland, 1977-80; chairman of the board, Jobat Oy, Turku, from 1982; Finnish Design Council, 1983-84; editorial board, *Design in Finland,* Helsinki, from 1985. **Exhibitions:** *Finnland Gestaltet,* Museum for Kunst und Gewerbe, Hamburg, 1981 (toured). **Collections:** Museum of Applied Arts, Helsinki; Museum of Modern Art, New York. **Honors:** Institute of Applied Arts Scholarship, Helsinki, 1967; Keski-Pohjanmaa County Cultural Foundation Scholarship, 1967; *Kaunis Koti* magazine design grant, 1972; Finnish State Industrial Art Prize, 1973, 1975; Internationales Design Zentrum Prize, West Berlin, 1974; Finnish Cultural Foundation Design Grant, 1977; Gute Industrieform Recognition Award, 1981, 1983; Ergodesign Award, Montreux, 1984; Finnish Design Council Honorary Diploma, 1985; Finnish State Artist's Grant, 1985; Saab-Valmet Ergonomics Prize, 1988. **Address:** Tervaskuja 72, 1110 Naantali, Finland.

## Publications

**By SALOVAARA: books—**(editor with others) *Playthings,* Helsinki, 1976; (with Y. Kukkapuro and A. Sotamaa) *Preliminary Study on the Needs and Conditions of Work Environment Planning,* Helsinki, 1977; (with others) *Playthings for Play,* Helsinki and West Berlin, 1979; (with others) *Ergonomy of Hairdressing* (report), Helsinki, 1985; *Working Station of Haircare* (report), Helsinki, 1986.

**On SALOVAARA: books—***Finnland Gestaltet,* exhibition catalogue by Tapio Periainen, Simo Heikkila and others, Espoo, 1981.

# SAMBONET, Roberto

Italian painter, architectural, graphic, display, and industrial designer

**Born:** Vercelli, 20 October 1924. **Education:** Studied architecture, at the Politecnico, Milan, 1942-45; self-taught in art and design. **Career:** Independent painter, furnishing, and textile designer, working with Pietro Maria Bardi at the Museu de Arte, Sao Paulo, 1948-53, and with Alvar Aalto in Finland, 1953; freelance designer, working in Vercelli and Milan, from 1953; designed for La Rinascente, Tiffany, Einaudi, Alfieri e Lacroix, Carlo Bestetti, Il Milione Gallery, Baccarat, Bing & Grondahl, Richard Ginori, Pirelli, Olivetti, Pinacoteca di Brera, Lomdardia Region, Banca CRT, TOBU Department Store, Tokyo, Costa Cruise Line, and others. Art director, *Zodiac* magazine, Milan, 1957-66. **Member:** Technical Committee, Milan Triennale, 1960; Alliance Graphique Internationale. **Exhibitions:** Galleria Cardazzo, Venice, 1948; Museu de Arte, Sao Paulo, 1949, 1974; Museu de Arte Moderna, Rio de Janeiro, 1949; Il Milione Gallery, Milan, 1950, 1952, 1969; Artek Gallery, Helsinki, 1956, 1976; Biblioteca Comunale, Milan, 1957; Il Disegno Gallery, Milan, 1960; Palazzo dei Centori, Vercelli, 1962; Profili Gallery, Milan, 1963; Pater Gallery, Milan, 1966; *Italian Design,* Hallmark Gallery, New York, 1969; *Italy: The New Domestic Landscape,* Museum of Modern Art, New York, 1972; *Design Italiano degli anni '50,* Centrokappa, Milan, 1977; Casa del Mantegna, Mantua, 1978; *Design Since 1945,* Philadelphia Museum of Art, 1983; *Italia: Disegno,* Museo Rufino Tamayo, Mexico City, 1986; *Progetto, Percorsi, Propo, ste,* International School of Design, Bologna, 1991; *Roberto Sambonet: Architetti, Architetture, Designers, Design,* Baleri Italia, Milan, 1992; *The Chicago International Biennale,* Chicago, 1993; *Art & Tabac,* Scuderie di Palazzo Rispoli, Rome, 1993; *XXXII Biennale d'Arte Città di Milano,* Permanente, Milan, 1993; *Roberto Sambonet: Il Disegno del Mediterraneo,* Istituto Europeo di Design, Milan, 1994; *Masterworks: Italian Design 1960-1994,* Denver Art Museum, Colorado, 1994; *Italian Metamorphosis,* Guggenheim Museum, New York, 1995; *La Sindrome di Leonardo,* Palazzina di caccia di Stupinigi, Turin, 1994; *Spring Design,* Barcelona, 1995. **Collections:** Design Archive, University of Parma;

**Roberto Sambonet:** *Apollo* **C-shaped die-cast aluminum handle with mechanism incorporated thus avoiding the washer, for RDS, Kleis Division, Padua, 1993**

Museu de Arte, Sao Paulo; Museum of Modern Art, New York; Philadelphia Museum of Art; Denver Art Museum, Colorado. **Honors:** Compasso d'Oro Award, 1956, 1970, 1979, and Compasso d'Oro Award for Career, 1995, Milan; Grand Prize, Milan Triennale, 1960; Art Directors Club Prize, Milan, 1977. **Died:** 1 November 1995.

**Works**

*Pesciera* fish dish with bivalve lid in stainless steel, for Sambonet S.p.A., 1957.
*Center Line* stackable cooking pans in stainless steel, for Sambonet S.p.A., 1965-71.
*Caviar* glass dessert cup and ice container, for Compagnie des Cristalleries de Baccarat, Paris, 1971.
Stackable picnic cutlery in stainless steel, for Sambonet S.p.A., 1971.
*TIR Series* glass tumblers, for Baccarat, 1971.
*Center Line Pan* double-function frying pan and griddle with detachable handle in stainless steel, for Sambonet S.p.A., 1972.
*Empilage* stackable glass tumblers, for Baccarat, 1972.
*845 Flatware* cutlery in stainless steel, for Sambonet S.p.A., 1973.

*Menage* cruet-set in stainless steel, crystal, and wood, for Sambonet S.p.A., 1975-76.
*Prehistoire* hemispheric glass vases, for Baccarat, 1975-77.
Glass corner vases, for Baccarat, 1975-77.
*Cailloux* crystal stones, for Baccarat, 1975-77.
*Quadreglie* square stackable oven pans with detachable handles in stainless steel, for Sambonet S.p.A., 1977.
*Angular Vases* in crystal, for Baccarat, 1978.
*Table System* in porcelain, for Richard Ginori and Settimo Fiorentino, 1979.
*Cubic* triangular vases in traditional Murano color aquamarine crystal, for Seguso, Murano, 1979.
*Demi* coaxial vases with semicircular base, for Seguso, 1979.
*Marine Beast Collection* crystal table sculptures of a tuna fish tail and a shark fin, for Baccarat, 1987.
*Minimal* aluminum ashtrays, one striped and one checkered, for Marzorati & Ronchetti, Cantù, 1992.
*Table for Collections* coffee table with crystal top supported by steel or wood hemispheres, model by Giovanni Sacchi, Milan, 1993.
*Stackable Oval Glasses,* wooden model by Giovanni Sacchi, Milan, 1993.
*Apollo* C-shaped aluminum handle, for RDS, Kleis Division, Padua, 1993.

*Tobacco Mixture* two-bowl pipe to blend sweet and strong tobacco, plaster model by Giovanni Sacchi, Milan, 1993.

## Publications

**By SAMBONET: books**—(with Paolo Fossati) *Il Disegno come Doppio: 61 Disegni 1956-1972,* Milan, 1974; *L'Arte in Tavola* edited by *Il Sole/24 Ore* magazine, Milan, 1988; (with Pietro Maria Bardi) *Dialogo Presocratico* edited by Vanni Scheiwiller, Milan, 1995.

**On SAMBONET: books**—*Sambonet: 22 Cause + 1,* exhibition catalogue by E. Villa, Milan, 1952; *Forme Nuove in Italia* by Agnoldomenico Pica, Milan and Rome, 1957; *Il Disegno Industriale e la sua Estetica* by Gillo Dorfles, Bologna, 1963; *Il Disegno Industriale* by Gillo Dorfles, Milan, 1967; *Forme Disegnate da Roberto Sambonet per la Sambonet S.p.A.* by Pier Carlo Santini, Milan, 1970; *Baccarat: Nuove Forme di Art Design di Roberto Sambonet* by R. Guiducci, Milan, 1972; *Roberto Sambonet: Ricerca e Strutture '49-74,* exhibition catalogue by P. M. Bardi and Fossati, Sao Paulo, 1974; *Il Design Italiano negli anni '50,* Milan, 1979; *Album Progetto Mangiare* by Mario Bellini, Milan, 1980; *Atlante del Design Italiano 1940-1980* by Alfonso Grassi and Anty Pansera, Milan, 1980; *Roberto Sambonet: design grafica pittura '74-'79,* exhibition catalogue edited by Mazzotta, Milan, 1980; *Italian Re-Evolution* by P. Sartogo, La Jolla, California, 1982; *Il Disegno Industriale Italiano 1928-1981* by Enzo Fratelli, Turin, 1983; *Roberto Sambonet: Ritratti '43-'83,* exhibition catalogue by G. Schildt and A. C. Quintavalle, Helsinki, 1985; *L'Italia del Design* by Alfonso Grassi and Anty Pansera, Casale Monferrato, 1986; *La Rinascente 1917-1969* by F. Amatori, Milan, 1986; *Descendants of Leonardo da Vinci: The Italian Design* by Bruno Munari, M. Bellini, and A. Branzi, Tokyo, 1986; *World Graphic Design Now* by Katsuo Kimura and Shin Matsunaga, Tokyo, 1988; *Ritratto com conoscenza, Roberto Sambonet: ritratti '86-'91* by C. Gian Ferrari, Milan, 1991; *Milanesi illustri ed illustrati: 50 designi di Roberto Sambonet,* exhibition catalogue by Davide Campari, Milan, 1991; *Design Roberto Sambonet* by A. C. Quintavalle, Milan, 1993; *The Italian Metamorphosis, 1943-1968,* exhibition catalogue, New York, 1994; *Azienda come cultura La Rinascente* by R. Francesconi, Milan, 1994; *La Sindrome di Leonardo Art e Design in Italia 1940-1975,* exhibition catalogue by E. Biffi Gentili and U. Allemandi, Turin, 1995.

\*

Despite the increasing number of international schools of design and graphics in this post-industrial and service-oriented second half of the twentieth-century, we can see a progressive decadence in contemporary design, both that of its own period and that inherited from the great cultural movements of the second and third decades of the century. The political world, the world of contractors and managers, the great masses, and consumerism generally are, with a few exceptions (Adriano Olivetti, for example), more and more hostile to what is needed for evolution and innovation. The above give no thought to such extraordinary, unique achievements in the history of mankind such as we can see in space travel, especially in the United States and the Soviet Union. After more than 30 years of idealistic and polemical activity in work that was often unpaid, such as my contributions to public bodies, museums, and to the *Milan Triennale,* I now feel that I must devote as much time as

possible to "research" in the expectation that the decadence will end and a recovery will set in. After my objectivist designs of the 1950s, 1960s, and 1970s—not, I hope, formalistic but rather poetic in intention—I feel an increasing need for contact with social reality and the requirements of collective life, which can be developed in the studio and in town planning.

—Roberto Sambonet

# SANDBERG, Willem (Jacob Henri Berend)
Dutch graphic and exhibition designer

**Born:** Amersfoort, 24 October 1897. **Education:** Educated in Assen, until 1917; studied at the Amsterdam Art Academy, 1919-20; independent pictorial studies in Vienna, Berlin, and Dessau, 1927; psychology student and assistant to F. Roels, Utrecht, 1930-35. **Military Service:** Served as coastguard in the Dutch Army, in Assen and Breda, 1917-19. **Family:** Married C. A. Frankamp in 1920 (divorced, 1929); children: Helga; married Alida Augustin Swaneveld in 1937 (died, 1974). **Career:** Worked as a typesetter for a printing company, Heidelberg, 1921; founder and director of the Madaznan spiritual healing centre, in Paris and Amsterdam, 1923-26; freelance professional graphic designer, Amsterdam, from 1927; chief graphic and publications designer for the Stedelijk Museum Amsterdam, 1945-62; also designed for Ploegsma Publishing Company, State Insurance Bank, Economic Information Service, Dutch Post Office, Nijgh en Van Ditmar publishers, and others. Curator of modern art, 1937-41, and director, 1945-62, Stedelijk Museum; Amsterdam director, Fodor and Willet Museums, Amsterdam, 1949-62; organizer and planner of the Historical Museum, Amsterdam, from 1938 (opened, 1962). Co-editor, *Open Oog* magazine, Amsterdam, from 1946; founder and co-editor, *Form* magazine, Amsterdam. Chairman, Architecture and Related Arts Exhibition Council, Amsterdam, 1945-48; vice-chairman, Dutch Arts Council, Amsterdam, 1948-60, Jerusalem, 1964-68, 1971-72. Erasmus Lecturer, Harvard University, Cambridge, Massachusetts, 1969-70. **Exhibitions:** Steendrukkerij De Jong, Hilversum, 1958; Gemeentemuseum, The Hague, 1965; Musée des Arts Decoratifs Paris, 1973; *107 Grafici dell'AGI,* Castello Sforzesco, Milan, 1974. **Honors:** Werkman Prize, Amsterdam, 1959; Gold Medal, City of Amsterdam, 1962; Dutch Award for Art and Architecture, 1968; Progressiven Deutschen Kunsthandler Prize, Cologne, 1973; Erasmus Prize, Amsterdam, 1975. Honorary Doctorate: University of Buffalo, New York, 1962. Honorary member, American Institute of Graphic Arts, 1962; honorary fellow, Israel Museum, Jerusalem, 1975. **Died:** Amsterdam, April 1984.

## Works

*Duitse Kunst na 1945* exhibition catalogue, for the Stedelijk Museum, Amsterdam, 1954.
*Vijf Amerikanen in Europa* exhibition catalogue, for the Stedelijk Museum, Amsterdam, 1955.
*Museumjournaal* magazine designs, for the Stedelijk Museum, Amsterdam, 1956-63.
*Vitality in Art* exhibition catalogue, for the Palazzo Grassi, Venice, 1959.

*Art Since 1950* exhibition catalogue, for the Seattle World's Fair, 1962.

*De Collectie Sandberg* book design, for Uitgeverij Meulenhoff, Amsterdam, 1962.

Logotype symbol, for the Israel Museum, Jerusalem, 1965.

*Heart for Harvard* poster, for Harvard University, 1970.

*Le Corbusier: Vers un Architecture* book design, for Stichting de Roos, Utrecht, 1971.

*Wilhelm Wagenfeld* exhibition poster and catalogue, for the Kunstgewerbemuseum, Cologne, 1973.

*Cobra and Contrast* exhibition poster and catalogue, for the Detroit Institute of Arts, 1974.

*Paribas* poster, for the Banque de Paris et des Pays-Bas, 1977.


## Publications

**By SANDBERG: books** — *Kwadrattbladen: Nu-midden in de XXe euw,* Hilversum, 1959; *Sleutelwoorden/Keywords: Piet Zwart,* The Hague, 1965; *Nu 2,* Hilversum, 1968; *Experimenta Typographica 1943-1968,* Nijmegen, 1969.

**On SANDBERG: books**—*Advertising Direction* edited by Edward M. Gottschall and Arthur Hawkins, New York, 1959; *Typography* by Aaron Bums, New York, 1961; *De Collectie Sandberg,* with introduction by Gerrit Kouwenaar, Amsterdam, 1962; *Design Co-ordination and Corporate Image* by F. H. K. Henrion and Alan Parkin, London and New York, 1967; *Sandberg Designe,* exhibition catalogue with introduction by Edy de Wilde, Paris, 1973; *Sandberg: A Documentary* compiled by Ad Petersen and Pieter Brattinga, Amsterdam, 1975; *Typography: Design and Practice* by John Lewis, London, 1978; *A History of Graphic Design* by Philip B. Meggs, New York and London, 1983.

\*　　\*　　\*

While studying psychology in Vienna during the late 1920s, Sandberg became interested in the system of pictorial statistics, called Isotype, which Otto Neurath was developing there. Returning to Amsterdam, he was commissioned by the Stedelijk Museum to prepare pictorial statistics for an exhibition, *Work for the Disabled,* in 1928. From his first contact with the museum developed the relationship that was to dominate his life—he was appointed curator in 1937 and director in September 1945. A major exhibition of the work of van Gogh in 1945 was followed by a major retrospective of the work of H. N. Werkman, the printer-painter who was shot by the Germans a few days before the liberation of Groningen but whose influences can be traced in many of Sandberg's robust typographic designs.

Sandberg's catalogue and poster designs have had a far-reaching effect on European and American museum publications and publicity. He made extensive use of bold typography, often incorporating large wooden type, torn paper shapes, and interesting paper textures. The use of coarse wrapping papers and other similar cheap materials give many of his catalogues an unusual, tactile quality.

His innovative use of materials and colour is also evident in *Experimente Typographica,* the series of eighteen booklets of experimental typography which he produced during the war. His output of typographic works, especially given his heavy national and international commitments as director of a major museum, is remarkable both for its quantity and for the standard he maintained.

—Mafalda Spencer

# SANDER, Jil
German fashion designer

**Born:** Heidemarie Jiline Sander in Wesselburen, 1943. **Education:** Graduated, Krefeld School of Textiles, near Düsseldorf, 1963; exhange student, University of Los Angeles, 1963-1964. **Career:** Fashion journalist, *McCall's,* Los Angeles, *Constanze,* Hamburg, and, also director of promotions, *Petra,* Hamburg, 1964-1968; freelance clothing designer, 1968-1973; opened first Jil Sander boutique, Hamburg, 1968; founded Jil Sander Moden, Hamburg, 1969; showed first women's collection, 1973; founded Jil Sander GmbH, 1978; introduced fragrance and cosmetics line, 1979; introduced Jil Sander furs, 1982; introduced leather and eyewear collections, 1984; converted Jil Sander GmbH to public corporation, Jil Sander AG, 1989; opened Paris boutique 1993; showed first menswear collection, 1993. **Honors:** Fil d'Or Award, 1980, 1981, 1982, 1983, 1984, 1985; city of Munich Fashion Award, 1983; Vif-Journal Selberne Eule, 1983; Fédération Française du Prêt à Porter Feminin Award, 1985; Aguja de Oro Award, Madrid, 1986; Forum Preis, 1989. **Address:** Osterfeldstrasse 32-34, 2000 Hamburg 54, Germany.


## Publications

**On SANDER: articles**—"Soft und Sander" by Margit J. Mayer in *Deutsch Vogue* (Munich), January 1990; "Less Is More Luxurious" by Edward Gomez in *Time* (New York), 25 June 1990; "Jil Sander" by Melissa Drier in *Mirabella* (New York), June 1991; "Jil Sander: Ganz Privat" by Margit J. Mayer in *Marie Claire* (German), August 1991; "A Walk with Jil Sander: by Margit J. Mayer in *W* (New York), 30 September-7 October 1991; "A Vision of Strength: Jil Sander" by David Livingston in *Globe and Mail* (Toronto), 2 January 1992; "The Selling of Jil Sander" by Annetta Miller in *Newsweek* (New York) 16 November 1992; "Minimalist No More" by Eve Schaenen in *Harper's Bazaar* (New York), March 1993; "The Glorious Haunting of Jil Sander" by Hal Rubenstein in *Interview* (New York), September 1993; "Pure Style: Jil Sander Talks About Clothes with Soul, Fashion with Morals and Stars with Taste" by Ruth La Ferla in *Elle* (New York), 8 March 1995; "Jil Sander: Coming on Strong" in *Women's Wear Daily* (New York), 8 March 1995; "Luminous Design from Jil Sander" by Amy M. Spindler in *New York Times,* 8 March 1995; "Jil Power" by Janet Ozzard in *Women's Wear Daily* (New York), 17 May 1995.


# SANT'ANGELO, Giorgio
American fashion designer

**Born:** Count Giorgio Imperiale de Sant'Angelo, in Florence, Italy, 5 May 1933; emigrated to the United States, 1962. **Education:** Studied architecture in Buenos Aires, industrial design in Barcelona, and fine arts at the Sorbonne, Paris. **Career:** Worked as a cartoonist for Walt Disney Studios, Hollywood, California, 1962-63; fashion stylist, and furnishings and textile designer, for Cohn-Hall-Marx and Marcus Brothers fabric firms, and for E. I. Du Pont, 1963-67; independent fashion designer, establishing Sant-Angelo ready-to-wear, New York, from 1967, and Sant'Angelo Incorporated, New York, 1968; designed for Marjer, Gabar, Ed Rosenthal Neckwear, Eagle Clothing, Charles of the Ritz, Wamsutta, Lane Furniture, Regal Rugs, and others. **Honors:** Coty American Fashion Critics' Winnie Award, New York, 1968, 1970; Inspiration Home Furnishings Award, New York, 1978; Knitted Textile Association Designer Award, New York, 1982; Fashion Designers of America Award, New York, 1988. **Died:** New York City, 29 August 1989.

## Publications

**On SANT'ANGELO: books**—*The World of Fashion: People, Places, Resources* by Eleanor Lambert, New York and London, 1976; *The Fashion Makers* by Bernardine Morris, New York, 1978; *Fairchild's Who's Who in Fashion* edited by Anne Stegemeyer, New York, 1980; *McDowell's Directory of Twentieth Century Fashion* by Colin McDowell, London, 1984; *The Encyclopedia of Fashion from 1840 to the 1980s* by Georgina O'Hara, London, 1986.

\*     \*     \*

Giorgio Sant'Angelo began with startling color contrasts. Early in his career, concentrating on Lycra spandex stretch fabric for jackets and trousers, he created a molded look. In 1981, he looked to metallic effects, as were seen in his gold lurex trouser suit and a suede jacket appliquéd with metal shapes after Miro. His strong color was still evident in a red matte jersey evening gown with bright gold shoulder and bow. Metal beads were applied to pullovers in tones of bronze and green brass. He aimed for striking effects.

Sant'Angelo was born in Italy but spent much of his boyhood in Argentina and Brazil, where his family owned estates. In South America, his grandparents taught him to notice color and shape before he was sent back to Europe to take a degree in architecture and industrial design. He then began to design furniture and, eventually, clothes for the people who sat in his chairs. He never saw himself as a dress designer but rather as someone who applied his talents to a universal range. Thus, he produced womenswear, menswear, children's clothes, swimwear, furniture, and rugs.

Acknowledging that his dramatic creations are not the clothes for every woman and that they require a lot of self-confidence to wear, he maintained that he was not trying to design for everybody. His customers included the singer Lena Horne and the socialite Bianca Jagger—striking individuals who want to look different. Sant'Angelo rarely planned far ahead or sought to establish a design policy. He preferred the excitement of not knowing where he would move next. He would often use the same pattern in a dress and a rug, and which range might dominate in any one year was a matter of chance.

—Diana de Marly

# SAPPER, Richard

German industrial designer

**Born:** Munich, 30 May 1932. **Education:** Studied philosophy, anatomy, graphics, engineering, and economics, at the University of Munich, 1952-56. **Family:** Married Dorit Polz in 1963; children:

Carola, Mathias, and Cornelia. **Career:** Designer, Mercedes-Benz car styling department, Stuttgart, 1956-57; freelance designer, working in the studio of Alberto Rosselli and Gio Ponti, Milan, 1957-59, and in the studio of Marco Zanuso, Milan, 1959-75; established own design studio in Stuttgart, from 1970; design consultant to Fiat car company and Pirelli tire company, 1970-76, and to IBM Corporation, from 1980; has designed for Lorenz, Kartell, Gavina, Brionvega, Terraillon, Italora, Artemide, B & B Italia, Unifor, Batavus, Knoll, Alessi, and others. Founder, with Gae Aulenti, Urban Transport systems study group, Milan, 1972. Professor of industrial design, at the Stuttgart Academy of Fine Arts and the Vienna Hochschule für Angewandte Kunst, from 1986. **Member:** Associazione per il Disegno Industriale. **Exhibitions:** Milan Triennale, 1968, 1979, 1986; *Italy: The New Domestic Landscape,* Museum of Modern Art, New York, 1972; *Italienische Moebel,* Stadtmuseum, Cologne, 1980; *Design Since 1945,* Philadelphia Museum of Art, 1983; *Richard Sapper: 40 Design Projects 1958-1988,* Sala Vincon, Barcelona, 1988. **Collections:** Museum of Modern Art, New York; Philadelphia Museum of Art. **Honors:** Compasso d'Oro Award, Milan 1960, 1962, 1964, 1967, 1979, 1986; Gold Medal, Liubliana Industrial Design Biennale, 1966, 1973; Gute Form Prize, West Germany, 1969, 1983; Premio SMAU, Milan, 1969, 1981, 1986; Honorary Royal Designer for Industry, Royal Society of Arts, London, 1988. **Addresses:** Via Vignino 2, 6926 Montagnola, Ticino, Switzerland; Loewenstrasse 96, 7000 Stuttgart 70, Germany.

## Works

*Static* electronic table-clock, for Lorenz, 1960.
*Doney 14* television set, for Brionvega, 1962 (with Zanuso).
*K-1340* children's chair in polyethylene, for Kartell, 1963 (with Zanuso).
*Lambda* chair in sheet metal, for Gavina, 1963 (with Zanuso).
*Algol* portable television set, for Brionvega, 1965 (with Zanuso).
*Italtel Grillo* telephone, for Brionvega, 1965 (with Zanuso).
*TS502* portable radio, for Brionvega, 1965 (with Zanuso).
*Black 12* portable television set, for Brionvega, 1969 (with Zanuso).
*Tantalo* electric table-clock, for Artemide, 1971.
*Genia* bookshelf system, for B & B Italia, 1971-72.
*Tizio* table lamp, for Artemide, 1972.
*Misura* office furniture system, for Unifor, 1974.
Bicycle in sheet metal, for Batavus, 1976.
*Cafetière* coffee-maker in stainless steel, for Alessi, 1979.
*Sappercollection* office chairs, for Knoll International, 1979.
*Bollitore* Whistling kettle in stainless steel, for Alessi, 1983.
*System 25* office chair, for Comforto, 1984.
*Nena* folding armchair, for B & B Italia, 1984.
*PC Convertible* laptop computer, for IBM, 1986.
*From 9 to 5* office furniture system, for Castelli, 1986.
*Argo* tracklighting system, for Artemide, 1988.
*Uri Uri* watch, for Alessi, 1988.

## Publications

**By SAPPER: articles**—*Design* (London), September 1980.

**On SAPPER: books**—*Italy: The New Domestic Landscape* by Emilio Ambasz, New York and Florence, 1972; *Design e Forme*

*Nuove nell'Arredamento Italiano* edited by Paolo Portoghesi and Marino Marini, Rome, 1978; *Atlante del Design Italiano 1940/1980* by Alfonso Grassi and Anty Pansera, Milan, 1980; *Knoll Design* by Eric Larrabee and Massimo Vignelli, New York, 1981; *Design Since 1945* edited by Kathryn Hiesinger and George Marcus, Philadelphia and London, 1983; *The Conran Directory of Design* edited by Stephen Bayley, London, 1985; *Les Carnets du Design,* Paris, 1986; *Modern Furniture Classics* by Miriam Stimpson, London, 1987; *Italian Design: 1870 to the Present* by Penny Sparke, London and New York, 1988; *Richard Sapper: 40 Progetti di Design 1958-1988,* exhibition catalogue with preface by Roberto Sambonet, Milan, 1988; *Italian Modern: A Design Heritage* by Giovanni Albera and Nicolas Monti, New York, 1989; *80s Style: Designs of the Decade* by Albrecht Bangert and Karl Michael Armer, New York, 1990; *Conran Design Guides: Kitchenware* by Jeremy Myerson and Sylvia Katz, London, 1990.

# SARPANEVA, Timo (Tapani)

Finnish painter, sculptor, exhibition, graphic, textile, and industrial designer

**Born:** Helsinki, 31 October 1926. **Education:** Studied graphics, at the Central School of Industrial Design, Helsinki, 1941-48; influenced by interior designer Arttu Brummer. **Family:** Married Ann-Mari(Pi) Holmberg in 1954 (divorced, 1970); children: Tom and Markus; lived with Marjatta Svennevig, from 1971; children: Johanna and Aleksei. **Career:** Freelance designer, from 1950; artistic director, Porin Puuvilla cotton mill, Pori, 1955-66, and AB Kinnasand textile mill, Kinnasand, 1964-72; designed for A. Ahlstrom glass company, Iittala, from 1950, Villayhtyma woollen rugs, 1960-62, Rosenlew cast iron, 1961-70, Primo building equipment, from 1963, Rosenlew paper, 1964-70, Opa stainless steel, and Rosenthal porcelain and cutlery, from 1970. Instructor in textile printing and design, Central School of Industrial Design, Helsinki, 1953-57. **Exhibitions:** *Fins Glas,* Stedelijk Museum, Amsterdam, 1972 (toured); *Nordisk Industridesign,* Kunstindustrmuseet, Oslo, 1976; *Form und Struktur,* Museum fur Angewandte Kunst, Vienna, 1980 (toured); *Scandinavian Modern Design 1880-1980,* Cooper-Hewitt Museum, New York, 1982; *Design Since 1945,* Philadelphia Museum of Att, 1983; *Timo Sarpaneva: Glaszeit,* Museum fur Angewandte Kunst, Dortmund, 1985; *The Lunning Prize,* Nationalmuseum, Stockholm, 1986; *Scandinavia: Ceramics and Glass in the Twentieth Century,* Victoria and Albert Museum London, 1989. **Collections:** Museum of Applied Arts Helsinki; Nationalmuseum, Stockholm; Det Danske Kunstindustrimuseum, Copenhagen; Nordenfjeldske Kunstindustrimuseum, Trondheim; Stedelijk Museum, Amsterdam; Kunstmuseum, Dusseldorf; Victoria and Albert Museum, London; Museum of Modern Art, New York; National Gallery, of Victoria, Melbourne. **Honors:** Gold and Silver Medals, Milan Triennale, 1954, 1957; *House Beautiful* Award, New York, 1954; Museum of Contemporary Crafts Prize, New York, 1956; Lunning Prize, Copenhagen and New York, 1956; International Design Award, New York, 1963, 1969; Honorary Royal Designer for Industry, Royal Society of Arts, London, 1963; Eurostar Packaging Award, The Hague, 1965; honorary doctorate, Royal College of Art, London, 1967; honorary professor, Helsinki, 1976; Gold Medal, Faenza Ceramics Competition, 1976. **Address:** Via Navegna 7, Minusio, Locamo, Switzerland.

## Works

*Lansett 11* sculpture in clear and opaque white glass, for Iittala Glass, 1952.
*Orkidea* sculpture in clear glass, for Iittala Glass, 1954.
*Nukkuva Lintu* sculpture in steam-blown clear and blue glass, for Iittala Glass, 1957.
Stacking bottles in red, blue, or clear glass, for Iittala Glass, 1959.
Covered cooking pot in cast iron and wood, for Rosenlew, 1959.
*Purkaus* sculpture in mould-blown and cast clear glass, for Iittala Glass, 1964.
*Festivo* candlesticks in textured and moulded clear glass, for Iittala Glass, 1967.
*Bolero* printed cotton fabric, for Tampella, 1968.
*Satula* glassware, for Iittala Glass, 1969.
Covered casserole dish in stainless steel, for Opa, 1970.
Cooking platter and pot in stainless steel, for Opa, 1970.
*Jurmo* series of glasswares in blue and white glass, for Iittala Glass, 1972.
*Suomi* table service in porcelain and stainless steel, for Rosenthal, 1974.
*Arkipelago* drinking glasses and candleholders in mould-blown clear glass, for Iittala Glass, 1978.
*Koh-I-Noor* sculpture-vase in cast and cut clear glass, for Iittala Glass, 1982.
*Claritas* sculptures in free-blown clear glass, for Iittala Glass, 1983-86.
*Lancett-35, 11* sculpture in clear glass and granite, for Iittala Glass, 1985.

## Publications

**By SARPANEVA: books**—(co-editor) *Finnish Decorative Art 1950-54,* Helsinki, 1955; (editor, with Jukka Pellinen) *History of the Cotton Mill Porin Puuvilla,* Helsinki 1957; (editor, with E. Bruun and E. Kruskopf) *Finnish Design 1875-1975,* Helsinki, 1975.

**On SARPANEVA: books**—*Finnish Designers of Today* by Oili Maki, Helsinki, 1954; *Packaging: An International Survey of Package Design* edited by Walter Herdeg, Zurich, 1959; *A Treasury of Scandinavian Design* edited by Erik Zahle, New York, 1961; *Modern Glass* by Ada Polak, London, 1962; *34 Scandinavian Designers* by Svend Erik Moller, Copenhagen, 1967; *Modern Finnish Design* by Ulf Hard af Segerstad, New York, 1969; *Fins Glas,* exhibition catalogue by Hugh Wakefield, Amsterdam, 1972; *Scandinavian Design: Objects of a Life Style* by Eileene Harrison Beer, New York, and Toronto, 1975; *Industrial Design* by John Heskett, London, 1980; *Design Since 1945* edited by Kathryn Hiesinger and George Marcus, Philadelphia and London, 1983; *Timo Sarpaneva,* with text by Kaj Kalin, Helsinki, 1986; *The Lunning Prize,* exhibition catalogue edited by Helena Dahlback Lutteman and Marianne Uggla, Stockholm, 1986; *Scandinavia: Ceramics and Glass in the Twentieth Century* by Jennifer Hawkins Opie, London, 1989.

\*			\*			\*

Like many of his generation, Timo Sarpaneva has worked in a wide range of media and styles, yet his versatility and excellence are almost unparalleled. His success in these fields has brought him numerous awards, exhibitions, and commissions. Sarpaneva's inventiveness and experimentation have acquired for him a reputation for artistic creativity and independence.

In the mid-twentieth century, the debate continued over the production of functional, mass produced objects for the general public versus catering to the artistic preferences of the elite. It is generally acknowledged that of all the Scandinavian countries, Finnish design at mid-century was generally more inclined to be of service to the upper classes. Many of Sarpaneva's early glass designs, such as his 1953 vase in the collection of the Metropolitan Museum of Art in New York, exhibit just such a sophisticated elegance and delicacy. His 1964 vase in the Iittala Museum shows a technique he developed in the later 1950s and 1960s for making "sculptured" glass. The glass is formed in wood molds that are permitted to burn during blowing, giving the finished glass strong patterns and varying textures. Sarpaneva's works from this period show a much greater concern for developing visually interesting, "natural" forms, and some of his latest works have become even more intricate and complex by combining multiple media and processes.

However, Sarpaneva has also made significant contributions to functional, applied art. He has designed extremely popular lines of Scandinavian metal cookware and tableware, glassware, ceramic wares, printed cloths, and textiles and industrial packaging. The range of his widely varying forms and textures is clearly shown by comparing his 1961 Rosenlew cooking pot, with its simplified lines and removable, sculptured handle, with his gleaming, stainless steel cookware manufactured by Opa in 1970. The ease with which Sarpaneva moves from glass to cast iron to stainless steel reflects his underlying concern to show the usefulness and beauty of all the materials he chooses to work with.

He is an artist who has the remarkable ability to pull selectively from historic repertoires and then combine these past ideas with new design inspirations. Often, however, he is totally original. Sarpaneva's works have evolved from purely traditional modes of Scandinavian design to express his adventuresome, artistic nature.

—Virginia A. Rose

# SAWKA, Jan

Polish and American painter, sculptor, and multi-media, graphic, and stage designer

**Born:** Zabrze, Poland, 10 December 1946; emigrated to the United States in 1977, naturalized, 1989; regained Polish citizenship after the collapse of Communism. **Education:** Studied architecture, at the Polytechnic Institute, Wroclaw, 1964-72; Fine Arts Academy, Wroclaw, 1967-72. **Family:** Married Hanna Maletz in 1974; daughter: Hanna. **Career:** Freelance artist and graphic designer, from 1970; artistic director, Bam Gallery, Warsaw, and F.A.M.A. Summer Art Festival on the Baltic coast, 1973-74; has designed for the Wroclaw Jazz Festival, Bam Art Center, *New York Times,* Harold Clurman Theatre, Samuel Beckett Theatre, Jean Cocteau Repertory Theatre, and others. **Exhibitions:** Wilanow Museum, Warsaw, 1976, 1980; Galerie Noire, Paris, 1977; Pulchri Studio, The Hague, 1977; Centre Georges Pompidou, Paris, 1978; Ankrum Gallery, Los New York, 1982; Deutsch Gallery, New York 1983, 1985; Di Laurenti Gallery, New York 1988; Dorsky Gallery, New York, 1989; State University of New York, New Paltz, 1989; Arvada Arts Center, Denver, Colorado, 1990; Nicolaysen Museum of Art,

Casper, Wyoming, 1990; *Prints and Posters,* Graphic Art Biennale, Brno, 1990; International Poster Biennale, Fort Collins, Colorado, 1991; *Banners,* Dorsky Gallery, and Wilanow Museum, Warsaw, 1991; *The Returns,* National Museum, Warsaw, and National Museum, Krakow, 1991, National Museum, Gdansk, and Museum of Science and Art, Prague, 1992; *Work in Progress,* Creation Gallery, G8, Tokyo, 1992; *Jan Sawka: Mixed Media Paintings,* Queens Museum of Art, New York, 1992; *My Europe,* International Art Pavilion, Universal Expo, Seville, Spain, 1992; National Museum, Wroclaw, 1992; *Banner Installation,* Art Tower Mito, Mito, Japan, 1993; *The World of Jan Sawka,* Atrium Gallery, University of Connecticut, Storrs, 1993; *Print Retrospective,* Striped House Museum, Tokyo, Japan, 1994, and Pecsi Galeria, Pecs, Hungary, 1995. **Collections:** Museum of Modern Art, New York; Library of Congress, Washington, D.C.; Centre Georges Pompidou, Paris; Musée des Arts Decoratifs, Paris; Musée de l'Affiche, Paris; National Museums of Krakow, Gdansk, Poznan, Warsaw, and Wroclaw, Poland; Wilanow Museum, Warsaw; Deutsches Plakatmuseum, Essen; Die Neue Sammlung, Munich; Stedelijk Museum, Amsterdam; Art Museum, Lahti, Finland; Arts and Science Museum, Prague, Czech Republic; Museum of Decorative Art, Copenhagen; Museum of Modern Art, Toyama, Japan; Tokyo Museum of Modern Art; Israel Museum, Jerusalem. **Honors:** Best Young Artist Award, Katowice Poster Biennale, 1974; Ministry of Culture Special Award, Warsaw, 1974; International Painting Festival Award, Cagnessur-Mer, 1975; Warsaw Poster Biennale Award, 1978; Lahti Poster Biennale Award, 1980; Silver Medal, International Graphic Art Biennale, Brno, 1990; named Artist Laureate, International Poster Biennale, Fort Collins, Colorado, 1991; Best Book of the Year, Warsaw, 1991; Japanese Cultural Agency Award, Tokyo, 1994. **Address:** 54 Old Rte. 213, High Falls, New York 12440, U.S.A.

## Works

*A Conversation* installation, for the Deutsch Gallery, New York, 1983.

*A Book of Fiction,* 25 prints, for Clarkson N. Potter Incorporated, 1986.

*Krapp's Last Tape* installation, for the Samuel Beckett Theatre, New York, 1986.

*The Shoemakers* (Witkacy) set design, for the Cocteau Theatre, New York, 1987.

*The Trial* (Kafka) set design, for the Cocteau Theatre, New York, 1987.

*Macbeth* (Shakespeare) set design, for the Cocteau Theatre, New York, 1989.

*Grateful Dead* touring concert stage sets, for The Grateful Dead band, 1989.

*The Room* installation, for the Dorsky Gallery New York, 1989.

Set and poster for *Waiting for Godot* (Beckett), for Apple Blossom Production, Poughkeepsie, New York, 1990.

*Dead Set* book design, for Viking-Penguin, 1990.

*The Sphere* installation, combining paintings, prints, and projections with music by composer Ed Summerlin, for MASC Art Center, Poughkeepsie, New York, 1990.

Sets and installations for Handel's *Messiah,* presented to the Pope at St. Peter's Square, the Vatican, 1992.

*The Eyes* installation, combining painted banners and kinetic projections with music by composer Adam Makowicz, produced by Tadashi Suzuki, for Art Tower Mito, Mito, Japan, 1993 (travelled to Germany and Italy).

Concert sets, for Steve Winwood and Traffic rock band, U.S. Summer Tour, 1994.

*Creation* set and installation, for theatrical productions, England, 1995 (with John Russell Brown).

*The Tower of Light,* 100-meter obelisk with kinetic projections and music composed by Ed Summerlin, produced in collaboration with Japanese companies Chiyoda, Sumitomo, Nippon Glass, and Sharp, for presentation to the ruler of the United Arab Emirates, Abu Dhabi, 1996.

## Publications

**On SAWKA: books**—*Contemporary Polish Posters in Full Color* edited by Joseph S. Czestochowski, New York, 1979; *Polish Posters 1970-1980* by Zdzislaw Schubert, Warsaw, 1982; *Who's Who in Graphic Art* edited by Walter Amstutz, Dubendorf, 1982; *Visual Design Exhibition,* catalogue by Giovanni Brunazzi, Aosta, 1988; *A Selected Retrospective,* exhibition catalogue with texts by James Beck, Elena G. Millie, and Niel C. Trager, New York, 1989; *A Selected Retrospective,* exhibition catalogue with text by Stanley Cuba, Arvada, Colorado, 1990; *The Returns,* exhibition catalogue with texts by Marek Rostworowski and James Beck, Krakow, 1991; *My Europe,* exhibition catalogue with text by Rostworowski, Seville, 1992; **articles**—*Cree* (Paris), October 1974, November 1976; *Projekt* (Warsaw), no. 4, 1974, no. 4, 1975, no. 4, 1976, no. 3, 1979; *Art and Artists* (London), June 1976; *Idea* (Tokyo), July 1977, March 1982, February 1993, December 1995; *Novum* (Munich), June 1978; *Artnews* (New York), September 1983, October 1984; *New York Times,* 4 March 1985; "Jan Sawka: Human Histories" by Ruth Eisenberg in *Arts Magazine* (New York), March 1985; "Jan Sawka Makes an Elegiac Impression in Print" by Charles Solomon in *Los Angeles Times,* 1 December 1986; *Backstage* (New York), March 1989; "Jan Sawka" by Pierre Souchaud in *Artension #35* (Paris), October 1991; "Jan Sawka" by Shoji Katagish in *Creation* (Tokyo), no. 13, 1992; *Affiche* (Amsterdam), October 1995; *Print* (New York), 1995.

*

I'm sure I know why and what I paint. It's something like a feeling of warmness in your head: a half-ready answer is waiting. But when I must put it down, my God, it's not so easy.

From the very beginning, from childhood, something was wrong with me (oversensitivity, the family physician stated). Books and reading interested me first. As far as I can remember drawing was somehow regarded as natural, not respected at all—like eating or playing with toys. My parents' house was overwhelmed by books and discussions during those dark, Stalin years. Little groups of friends gathered over the bridge table, not so much to play but mostly to talk.

Up to the last moment before entering higher education, I was unsure what to choose—philology at the university or fine arts at the academy. But the "oldies" decided to push me toward some "practical" career—architecture, engineering. And that *was* the beginning of my way to the current painting. Nothing fitted me properly, the frustrations built up; now I understand it was very positive, this sneaky, manytimes-forced way.

Disillusioned by technical training in architecture, I began desperately to add something more to this boring existence. The relatively lively cultural life of city students lured me quickly. Jazz,

"nightlife," cabarets, theatre—I lived for it, waiting nervously every day at the drawing rooms of school. Troubles built; I hardly managed to pass all the exams. Finally, after two years, without resigning from my engineering school, I joined the Fine Arts Academy, trying to cope with two problems. But my "off-duty" activity didn't cease; it even grew. Although extremely hectic, it was a far more exciting life. The next event, which shaped my entire life, was not designed by me but by the "Reds." Nineteen sixty-eight: student riots, Zionists, Revisionists, tanks rumbling down Prague streets. It was a time of extreme tensions and simple "yes" or "no."

After the amnesty was granted by the government to all (almost all) unruly students, I tried to rebuild. But the amnesty was mainly on paper. Practically, I was eliminated. However, some brave people fought back, and by 1969 I had a carefully constructed, multi-media study program, which protected me from being pushed out of the schools but gave me a mad schedule. Staying at the architecture faculty, I studied mostly design, while I worked also at the history of art institute as a junior researcher in my free time, restoring churches, etc. To keep "them" happy, I worked around the clock.

My "post-school" activities had grown serious. By the early 1970s, I was among those who had rejected the "Socialist way" and tried to pursue "free culture" (read: "counter-Red establishment"). My real companions were theatre, poetry, cabaret, the visual arts—and I did anything that was needed. Thank God, it paid well, not in money but in far more important bonuses: I travelled abroad, all over Western Europe. You don't understand how hungry somebody can be to see the normal, civilized life of the Western world. During this time, I worked on those hard-to-formulate, private tensions—my private world.

Now, how do I say *what* I paint? Maybe it sounds megalomaniacal, but I try to discuss the world I see and feel. I try to care about the composition, shape, color, the so-called "form," of course. I try to execute painting in the best possible way—no easy tricks, no airbrushes, no copying from slides—all hand, pure hand.

But, most importantly, I try to communicate with all, concerned and unconcerned. I have no idea which trend of art I represent. Nothing interests me less. Of course, I'm sensitive to many currents of modern art, but I try to understand art as a whole. I love Old Masters but try to put their work into a larger context, not to separate their canvases from literature, music, society. I listen to music during my work. I read. I try to know a little of everything. They did the same, I think. You cannot close yourself in a personal shell. Or maybe you can. I can't. (*Adapted from an interview published in* Arts Magazine *(New York), May 1983.*)

Since my last entry in this publication, in 1990, dramatic changes occurred in my life and work. Once a leading artist of the Polish Poster school, today I do very little in graphic design. In the 1980s I established myself in the galleries of New York City as a painter and printmaker. The 1990s further reinforced my position as an installation artist, only sporadically active as a graphic designer. Starting in 1990 I have had a series of museum shows of my works all over the world.

I started to develop two new and important new venues in my work: sculpture and multi-media experiments. It all started with the 1989 concert sets for the Grateful Dead. From there I went to the new and highly experimental projects. The art created directly by me, on canvas or paper, is being transformed to the kinetic images projected on the screens or directly on the walls by computer synchronized projectors supported by light and original pieces of art. I designed the series of concepts for such theatrical or music pieces with the entire "visual space" created by me.

**Jan Sawka: Four views of "The Tower of Light," 1994-95**

The concept for Handel's *Messiah* was followed by my production of the Visual Theatre spectacle at the Art Tower Mito, in Mito, Japan, in 1993. It was the first time I collaborated with California-based projections and light designer Marc I. Rosenthal, with whom I am working on almost all new projects of such nature. After the first successful production I designed projection-based concert sets for Steve Winwood and Traffic in 1994.

Later that year I went to Tokyo to concentrate on the development of sculptures, multi-media works, and projects for architecture. I was awarded a special grant by the Japanese Cultural Agency to stay in Tokyo and experiment. The results were fantastic! I was teamed with the best architects, designers, and electronic engineers Japan has today. The series of large sculptures emerged in concepts which will soon be realized, but the most important project born in Tokyo was the Tower of Light. The giant monument as well as the live screen for kinetic images was prepared for presentation to the ruler of the United Arab Emirates. In designing and preparing the proposal for the tower I got formidable help from leading Japanese corporations like Chiyoda, Sumitomo, Nippon Glass, and Sharp, besides the architectural offices and planners.

Sometimes I must pinch myself when flying to Tokyo or Abu Dhabi again.... It feels like a magic trip for an artist who began his career as an underground graphic artist in Krakow, Poland. Years ago, when my father was pushing me to study architecture before turning to painting, I hated him. But he insisted, saying: "The true artists must know architecture—it could come in handy one day, you never know." God bless my father.

To put it the simplest way, I see design, architecture, and art as one potent mixture of ideas, rules, and challenges. Not only to create the new space and color and images for people, but also to use this magic mix to work with the musicians, actors, writers, dancers, and all creative types on building THE CULTURE, regardless of religions, borders, systems....

—Jan Sawka

*     *     *

Perhaps Jan Sawka is a visionary of our times. In 1980, he designed a poster titled "Car of the Year" which won first prize at the *Eighth International Poster Biennale* in Warsaw. It pictured a new-style, Russian tank rolling down a city street. On December 13, of the next year, tanks did indeed roll in Poland as a show of strength behind the government-imposed martial law. Sometime before that fateful day, Sawka had also been requested by the leaders of Solidarnosc, the powerful Polish union, to design the official Solidarnosc poster which would express, among other things, the hopes of the Polish people. The design for the poster showed the sun of Solidarnosc shining down forever on the hopes and dreams of a colorful landscape of the Polish people below. The original artwork for the poster was secretly transported into Poland and proudly displayed in the headquarters of Solidarnosc until it was destroyed by the Polish government. The poster, however, could not be suppressed; nor could Solidarnosc, which contributed to the toppling of the Communist regime in Poland.

As a student, Sawka had participated in the political underground, but being a talented and gifted artist, he was rescued from any serious repercussions. He was a student of design and the fine arts at the time of his emergence into the Polish poster movement. Realizing that acceptance into the Polish poster school would have to be step-by-step up the already established ladder, he set out designing posters according to his own rules, artistic expertise, and

available technique. His first poster was a linoleum cut for a student musical group; after that, he was asked to design other posters for various music clubs and student groups. By the time of his diploma show for graduation, Sawka had thirty posters to exhibit, as well as his paintings, prints, and drawings.

Later, Sawka moved to Krakow, which he considered the cultural center of Poland. There he was asked to be art director for the renowned Polish avant-garde theater, STU. Although he received no salary, he was given a free hand to design whatever he chose.

In his student days, he had studied all aspects of design in order to understand all the processes and fine art of culture. By understanding the varied aspects of culture, Sawka believes that he can then better understand the relationships and complexities of mankind. He attempts to express this in his work.

As an artist who developed during the 1960s, Sawka reveals the influence of the psychedelic in both his compositions and in his use of colors. While his designs are always—without exception—powerful, they are also satirical, symbolic, humorous, bursting with energy, and imaginatively created. The colors he uses are combined in an explosive melange. The lasting and overall effect is one of total honesty. Sawka converses in his language—art—succinctly, truthfully, and creatively. He does not compromise his ideas or designs for expediency. His images cause one to confront oneself, to examine one's thinking, one's way of life, one's hopes and dreams.

A versatile artist, Sawka paints, draws, and designs what he sees and what he believes in. His graphics reveal his insights into every phase of life—culture, politics, society, history, etc. He considers the poster a personal statement about the problem or subject. When designing a poster, he uses the medium he is working on at the time. If he is working on a print, the poster will look like a print; if a painting, the poster will look like a painting. Having studied architecture, his work naturally includes many architectural elements. He displays talent in every medium: etching, engraving, stencil, linocut, drypoint, etc. From miniatures to wall-size works, he works on masonite, paper, plywood, etc., using gouache, crayon, felt-tip, ball point, and acrylic—in any combination.

While in the United States, Sawka has become recognized not only for his expertise as a painter, but also as an illustrator. He has made more than 200 illustrations for the op-ed pages of the *New York Times* and the Boston *Globe*. These assignments have helped Sawka to understand the United States. Before he could execute the commission, he had to understand the current political or social situation he was to interpret. He has a knack for reducing each complex assignment to its simplest common denominator. His social comments on "the system" are artfully and delightfully drawn.

Freedom, as one can imagine, is very important to this designer, and he has expressed this through his graphics. His designs warrant more than one look, for although the exuberance is apparent, the real meaning, which is often biting, is sometimes concealed, often in narratives in the form of the comic strip, revealing the message which has been interwoven through the design.

Sawka's first major international award was won in 1975 in Cagnes-sur-Mer for a painting. The painting consisted of 216 smaller pictures that give the illusion of being prints and drawings. In New York City in the 1980s, he again turned his creativity to painting. Sawka's achievements and zest serve as an inspiration to other young designers throughout the world. As Sawka himself has said of his life so far in this country: "I am successful, I do what I want, I shall stay my old self, I, Jan Sawka."

—Elena Millie

The exhibition by Jan Sawka in the Queens Museum of Art offers a total panorama of the artist's long-range objectives. Standing as a telling event on the basis of the depth of his artistic invention, it documents his emergence as a painter of pictures from the time he arrived in America in 1979. After all, given the restriction under the totalitarian governments in his native Poland in the recent past, fine artists were never at liberty to take up one or another medium merely out of desire, gift, or interest. Sawka, who was oriented toward the creation of posters, graphics, and stage designs, carved out a prominent position at a very young age. Still, he was not free to paint, despite his yearnings to work with the brush and with tubes of color. So when he came to America, leaving restrictions behind, he was finally able to explore the potential of pure painting to the fullest extent. Thus as he moved from images that are more or less dependent upon his graphic habits to a more painterly statement—where he could move naturally from one extreme to another—we are permitted to follow his process toward pictorial independence.

To designate Sawka as a complex man and a complex creator is an understatement. Yet, approaching his pictures requires forays into both aspects, that is to say the artist and the man, although the two are of course inseparable.

At the very core of one aspect of his essence is an intense connection, affection, passion, and high hopes for his Poland, which has endured, despite more than its share of crash landings. Occupation at the hands of two cruel invaders was coupled with economic and ecological calamities. Behind all of these hardships stands the strength of a people and its tradition which is also Sawka's strength. What I am trying to say, even if it sounds incurably romantic and from another historical moment, is that Jan Sawka is a patriot. His Poland is not its armies or national ambitions for new borders but a land of struggling intellectuals, poets, writers, dramatists, composers, and fellow fine artists, all on or close to the financial edge but creatively churning. Although essentially he has been absent from Europe for a long time, by commitment and personality, by temperament and vision, Jan has retained a close bond with the uncompromising artistic spirits back home.

His aspirations for Poland's future are in step with his concerns for the neighboring countries once again locked within a historical vise between Germany and Russia. Jan retains a curious and unrivaled intermingling of cosmopolitan realpolitik and a land-based wholesomeness. A large dose of fantasy combined with an healthy, inherent optimism conditions his thinking towards basic human conditions. Memory may be mixed with desire but it takes place within a claustrophobic interior room or within the confines of a phone booth: obituaries fade away into shadows of recollections on the pavement.

The point is that Jan Sawka is a very smart fellow. His lively thoughts accelerate like a Ferrari Testa Rossa on the Utah Flats, there being very little affecting our modern society that he does not ponder. He is an avid reader on all subjects, from biographies of world class automobile moguls to avant garde theater. Jan has a flair for rigorous analysis of current trends, political in-fighting, papal strategies vis-a-vis the Ukraine, artistic maneuverings of the establishment toward Arte Povera, and even the latest video from the Grateful Dead.

Another side of Jan Sawka thinks in images, in segments and snippets, jagged Tuscan horizons and green fields in the New York Catskills. That is, the painter slides through his world of printmaking, for he has never stopped etching and he is still a master of the poster: in these mediums his visions are elaborate and even grandi-ose. Even in his most ambitious projects—filling a stadium full of his banners or lighting a vast, columned piazza with an unprecedented performance of light and color imaginings—the artist and the social individual coalesce.

It is a relatively easy matter for a critic to describe his paintings, since they are quite suitable to narrative explication, being graphic, clear, blunt statements in a modern context. More difficult is pinning down the synthesis between the individual and the artist, each aspect reinforcing the other. The Queens exhibition is the most effective manifestation of Sawka's passionate pictures executed in America. To further complicate the equation, however, he is very much an American too, operating in the distinguished tradition that has offered constantly renewed strength to the United States as a nation and to its newly arrived as well. His American experience, which is the overt subject of the Queens exhibition, then, is the final factor in the process of cross-stimulations that have given rise to a unique statement. (*Adapted from "Jan Sawka in Queens" in the exhibition catalogue* Jan Sawka: Mixed Media Paintings *by James Beck.*)

—James Beck

# SCARPA, Carlo (Alberto)

Italian architect and interior, exhibition, and industrial designer

**Born:** Venice, 2 June 1906. **Education:** Studied architecture, at the Accademia di Belle Arti, Venice, Dip. Arch., 1926; student and assistant to Guido Ginelli, at the Institute of Architecture, University of Venice, 1926-27. **Family:** Married Onorina Lazzari in 1934; son: Tobia. **Career:** Assistant to the architect Vincenzo Rinaldi, Venice, 1922-24; freelance architect, designer and graphic artist, in Venice, 1927-62, in Asolo, 1962-72, and in Vicenza, 1972-78; artistic consultant to Murano Cappellin and Company Glassworks, Venice, 1972-30, and to Venini Glassworks, Venice, 1933-47; design consultant to the Venice Biennale, from 1941, and to Cassina and B & B Italia furniture companies, 1969. Assistant teacher, 1926-29, 1932-33, professor, 1933-76, and director, 1970-78, at the Istituto Universitario di Architettura, Venice; head of design course, Istituto Artistico Industriale, Venice, 1945-47; head of visual studies, Istituto Superiore di Disegno Industriale, Venice, 1960-61. **Member:** British Institute of Design, 1970; Pierre Chareau Foundation, Paris, 1975 (honorary); Accademia Olimpica, Vicenza, 1974; Academician, Accademia di San Luca, Rome, 1976. **Exhibitions:** *Carlo Scarpa,* at the Milan Triennale, 1960; *Museum Architecture,* Museum of Modern Art, New York, 1966; Royal Institute of British Architects, London, 1972; Accademia Olimpica, Vicenza, 1974; Institut de l'Environnement Paris, 1975; Palazzo delle Stelline, Milan, 1978; Galeria l.D., Madrid, 1978; Accademia di San Luca, Rome, 1979; Istituto Statale di Architettura, Reggio Calabria, 1981; Museo Castelvecchio, Verona, 1982; Italian Cultural Institute, Paris, 1983; Galleria dell'Accademia, Venice, 1984. **Honors:** Diploma of Honour, 1934, and Grand Jury Prize, 1960, Milan Triennale; Olivetti National Award, Turin, 1956; Ministry of Public Information Medal, Rome, 1962; In/Arch National Award, Rome, 1962; Regional Architecture Award, Verona, 1964; President's Architecture Prize, Rome, 1967; Accademia dei Lincei Prize, 1971; D. Arch., Istituto Universitario di Architettura, Venice, 1978. **Died:** Sendai, Japan, 28 November 1978.

## Works

Onion-shaped decanter in smoked glass, for Cappellin and Company, 1927.

Sfriso silverware shop interiors, Campo San Toma, Venice, 1932.

Drinking glasses in double-layered black and green glass, for Venini, 1936.

Oval bottle in textured red and black glass, for Venini, 1940.

11 Cavallino modern art gallery interiors, Riva degli Schiavoni, Venice, 1942.

Dish in azure and violet glass with mauve circular decoration, for Venini, 1940.

*Giovanni Bellini* exhibition layouts, Palazzo Ducale, Venice, 1948.

Public telephones in Venice, for the Twelve Company, 1950.

*Piet Mondrian* exhibition layouts, Valle Giulia, Rome, 1956.

Olivetti shop interiors, St. Mark's Square, Venice, 1957.

Gavina shop (now Simon shop) interiors, via Altabella, Bologna, 1961.

Doge table in steel and glass, 1968.

*Florentine Frescoes* exhibition layouts, Hayward Gallery, London, 1969.

*Orseolo* writing table in treated wood and black lacquer, 1973.

*Le Corbusier* exhibition layouts, Querini-Stampalia, Venice, 1973.

*Toledo* range of beds in turned wood with leather headboards, 1975.

Logotype sign, for the Banca Popolare of Verona, 1977.

Cutlery set in gold and silver, for Cleto Munari, 1977-78.

(for a complete list of Scarpa's buildings and architectural projects, see *Contemporary Architects*)

## Publications

**By SCARPA: books**—(editor) *Memoriae Causa,* Verona, 1977; **articles**—in *Modo* (Milan), January/February, 1979.

**On SCARPA: books**—*Carlo Scarpa: Architetto Poeta* by Sergio Los, Venice, 1967; *Carlo Scarpa: Architetto Poeta,* exhibition catalogue by Sherban Cantacuzino, London, 1974; *Carlo Scarpa,* exhibition catalogue by Neri Pozza, Vicenza, 1974; *Carlo Scarpa,* exhibition catalogue by Luciana Miotto-Muret, Paris, 1975; *Carlo Scarpa* by Neri Poza, Padua, 1978; *Carlo Scarpa per Bemini* edited by G. Scarpa, Venice, 1979; *Carlo Scarpa: Venezia 1906—Sendai 1978—I Sette Foglie Giapponese* edited by G. Scarpa, Venice, 1979; *Carlo Scarpa a Castelvecchio,* exhibition catalogue edited by L. Magnagnato, Milan, 1982; *Carlo Scarpa* by M. A. Crippa, Milan, 1984; *Carlo Scarpa 1906-1978* edited by Francesco Dal Co and Giuseppe Mazzariol, Milan, 1984; *Carlo Scarpa: Theory, Design, Projects* by Maria Antonietta Crippa, Milan, 1984, Cambridge, Massachusetts, 1986.

# SCARPA, Tobia

Italian architect, furniture, and product designer

**Born:** Venice, 1 March 1935; son of the architect Carlo Scarpa. **Education:** Studied architecture at the Instituto Universitario di Architettura, Venice, Dip. Arch., 1957. **Family:** Married the designer Afra Bianchini. **Career:** Designer, at the Venini Glassworks, Murano, Venice, 1958-61; freelance designer, in partnership with Afra Scarpa, in Montebelluna, from 1960; designed for C & B, Stildomus, Maxalto, B & B Italia, Unifor, Flos, Cassina, Knoll, Gavina, and others. Lecturer, School of Industrial Design, Venice. **Exhibitions:** Milan Triennale, 1960, 1964, 1968; *Selection 66,* Museum für Angewandte Kunst, Vienna, 1966; *Italian Furniture Design,* Furniture Salon, Tokyo, 1968; *Modern Chairs,* Whitechapel Art Gallery, London, 1970; *One Hundred Modern Chairs,* National Gallery of Victoria, Melbourne, 1974; *Design and Design,* Palazzo delle Stelline, Milan, 1979 (toured); *Design Since 1945,* Philadelphia Museum of Art, 1983. **Collections:** Museum of Modern Art, New York; Philadelphia Museum of Art. **Honors:** Compasso d'Oro Award, Milan, 1970; American Society of Interior Designers Award, New York, 1979. **Address:** Corso Manzini 10, Montebelluna, Treviso, Italy.

## Works

*Pigreco* armchair in molded plywood with leather or cloth seat, produced by Santabona, Gavina, and Knoll, 1959-60.

*Bastiano* 2- or 3-seat sofa in wood, steel, and leather, produced by Gavina and Knoll, 1961.

*Seky-Han* fluorescent floor lamp in wood and metal, produced by Flos, 1963.

*Nibai* extending table in wood and metal, for Gavina, 1963.

*915* and *923* sofas in metal with polyfoam and leather upholstery, produced by Cassina, 1964.

*Torcello* container system of furniture, produced by Stildomus, 1964.

*Coronado* armchair, divan, and pouf in tubular steel with foam and leather upholstery, produced by C & B Italia and B & B Italia, 1966.

*Ciprera* armchair in polyurethane foam with reinforced polyester covering, produced by Cassina, 1968.

*Soriana* armchair, divan, and pouf in metal, polyfoam, polyester, and dacron, produced by Cassina, 1969.

*Pozzetto* armchair in pre-formed resin, produced by C & B Italia and B & B Italia, 1970.

*TL 59* Circular table in aluminum and glass, produced by Roberto Poggi, 1972.

*Crispino* and *Bordo* ceramic tableware, produced by Galvani, 1973.

*Mix* upholstered swivel office chair, produced by Unifor, 1975.

*Artona* range of furniture, produced by Maxalto, 1975-79.

*Miro* modular storage furniture units, produced by Molteni & Cie, 1981.

*Abatina* table lamp, produced by Flos, 1981.

*Serenda* armchairs in wood with upholstered seats, produced by Stildomus, 1983.

## Publications

**On SCARPA: books**—*Modern Furniture* by Ella Moody, London, 1966; *Design Italiano: I Mobili* edited by Enrichetta Ritter, Milan and Rome, 1968; *Modern Chairs 1918-1970,* exhibition catalogue with text by Carol Hogben and others, London, 1970; *The Modern Chair: Classics in Production* by Clement Meadmore, London, 1974; *One Hundred Modern Chairs,* exhibition catalogue by Terence Lane, Melbourne, 1974; *Knoll Design* by Larrabee and Massimo Vignelli, New York, 1981; *Contemporary Furniture* edited by Klaus-Jurgen Sembach, Stuttgart and London, 1982; *Design Since 1945* edited by Kathryn Hiesinger and George Marcus, Philadelphia and London, 1983; *Afra and Tobia Scarpa, Architetti e Designers* by Antonio Piva, Milan, 1985; *Modern Furniture Classics* by Miriam Stimpson, London, 1987; *Designed by Architects in the 1980s* by Juli Capella and Quim Larrea, London, 1988; *Italian Modern: A Design Heritage* by Giovanni Albera and Nicolas Monti, New York, 1989.

\*    \*    \*

After Tobia Scarpa graduated with an architectural degree in Venice, he went to work as a designer at the Murano glass works. Two years later, in 1958, he started to work for Paolo Venini, also in glass design. In 1960, he opened his own office in collaboration with his wife, Afra.

It was about this time that the first of many successful furniture designs, Bastiano, was conceived. Architecturally detailed in matte finished rosewood, the cushions crisply finished in fine leather, the seating units would soon become classic in the furniture world.

There followed a succession of innovative designs from this team. Nuvola, a cocoon hanging light in spun fiberglass over a metal frame, and Fantasma Piccolo, a floor-mounted version; Coronado, an upholstered armchair and sofa; Juker, a spun-aluminum table lamp with a tilting shade that creates a "personality" for an otherwise inanimate object; Fior di Loto and Nictea, mushroom-like hanging lamps in polished metal; Ciprea, an upholstered polyurethane foam design that simultaneously conveys the character of a stuffed Victorian chair and a front seat from a modern automobile; and Foglio, an incredibly simple, wall-mounted light fixture which conveys the notion of a metal bracelet encircling the lamps and screening them from direct view. They also produced some unique uses of precast concrete, as in the Maglieria factory, where long, x-shaped (cross-section) beams are interspaced with roof glazing panels to provide natural daylighting for the interior, and in the C+B Furniture factory, where vertical and horizontal elements are interlocked like a gigantic children's puzzle.

A favorite design is Soriana, armless seating in tufted fabric or leather over multi-density polyurethane foam and dacron fiberfill, the marshmallow-like forms girdled by a chrome-plated, spring-steel, external skeleton which holds the forms in shape and provides the necessary finishing detail. The chair was the winner of the 1970 Compasso d'Oro and, together with a leather-covered, molded-plywood and wood chair, called simply *925,* is included in the permanent design collection of the Museum of Modern Art in New York.

Possibly reflecting his training at the glass works, Biagio, a table lamp made from two pieces of hollowed-out, white marble, somewhat resembles a space-age or sports (or perhaps religious) headdress. Recently, Bollo and Papillona halogen wall and floor lighting fixtures appeared.

Most recently, the pair has produced the *Master* range of modular office furniture components, which can also function as individual pieces. Finely detailed in leather-edged woods on a painted aluminum structure, the inherent design and precision manufacturing (one-tenth millimeter tolerance) destine this line to become another classic.

—William Victor Kriebel

# SCHEICHENBAUER, Mario

Italian architectural and industrial designer

**Born:** Milan, 31 May 1931. **Education:** Studied architecture, at the Politecnico, Milan, 1957. **Career:** Freelance designer, specializing in plastics and solar-energized structures, Milan, from 1954; designed for Societa RPD, Montedison, Marini e Sordelli, ENI, Milani Resine, and others. President, Associazione Progamma ERG, Milan. **Member:** Associazione degli Architetti di Milano. **Exhibitions:** Battersea College of Technology, London, 1970; Guildford School of Art, Surrey, 1973; Faculty of Architecture, University of Bucharest, 1974; Faculty of Architecture, University of Sofia, 1975; University of Moscow, 1981. **Address:** Via Vincenzo Bellini 11, 20122 Milan, Italy.

## Works

*Ogamma* system plastic roofed buildings, in Lugano and Varese, for Societa RPD, 1965.
*Montenapo* upholstered armchair in molded white plywood, for Zanotta, 1967.
Monoblock bathroom units, for Societa RPD, 1968.
Beach cabins in GF-UP plastics, for Brianza Plastica, 1969.
Experimental plastic-construction building, for Montedison, 1972.
Beach cabins in ABS plastic, for Marini e Sordelli, 1972.
City car in ABS plastic, for Marini e Sordelli, 1973.
Experimental thermoplastic building materials, for ENI, 1973-78.
Prefabricated buildings in thermoplastics, for ENI, 1977.
Extruded plastic flooring, for Milani Resine, 1980.
Thermoplastic solar panels, for Milani Resine, 1981.

## Publications

**By SCHEICHENBAUER: books**—*A. Campanini, Architetto,* Milan, 1968; *Il Poliestere Rinforzato,* Milan, 1972; *La Termoformatura,* Milan, 1979; (translator) *Il Libro della Casa Solare,* Rome, 1980; *Sintesi dei Corsi sull'Energia Solare,* Milan, 1981; *Bilancio Energetico dell' Abitazione,* Milan, 1982.

**On SCHEICHENBAUER: books**—*Catalogo Bolaffi dell'Architettura Italiana 1963-66* edited by Pier Carlo Santini and Giuseppe Luigi Marini, Turin, 1966; *Design Italiano: I Mobili* edited by Enrichetta Ritter, Milan and Rome, 1968; *Idee per la Casa/ Modern Interiors* by Franco Magnani, Milan and London, 1969; *Design e Forme Nuove nell'Arredamento Italiano* by Paolo Portoghesi and Marino Marini, Rome, 1978; *Storia e Cronaca della Triennale* by Anty Pansera, Milan, 1978; *Da Cosa Nasce Cosa* by Bruno Munari, Bari, 1981.

\*

New ideas spring from new problems or new ways of solving them. Industrial design and planning have to tackle (and translate the answers into form-language) the problems connected with industrial production (including products for the building industry), the problems derived from the new awareness of energy and ecology, and the new means available for solving these problems (new materials such as plastics, new technologies such as pressings, programming, and marketing).

—Mario Scheichenbauer

# SCHLEGER, Hans

British corporate, exhibition, and graphic designer

**Born:** Kempen, Germany, 29 December 1898; settled in Britain in 1932, naturalized, 1938. **Education:** Studied painting and drawing, at the Kunstgewerbescule, Berlin, 1918-21. **Military Service:** Served in the German Army, 1916-18. **Family:** Married Pat Maycock in 1956; daughters: Maria and Lalli. **Career:** Publicity manager and film set designer for Karl Hagenbeck, Berlin, 1921-24; magazine layout artist and freelance advertising designer, establishing own Madison Avenue studio under the name "Zero," New York, 1924-29; designer, in the German branch office of W. S. Crawford advertising agency, Berlin, 1929-32; freelance designer, London, 1932-76; founder-director, Hans Schleger and Associates design studio, London, 1953-76; designed corporate images for MacFisheries, Associated Electrical Industries, Imperial Chemical Industries, Fisons, Jaeger, Finmar Furniture, Grant's Whiskey, British Sugar, British Rail, Edinburgh International Festival, Manchester Polytechnic, and others. Visiting lecturer at the Chelsea School of Art, London, Royal College of Art, London, and at the Regional College of Art, Manchester; visiting associate professor, Institute of Design, Chicago, 1950-51. **Member:** Alliance Graphique Internationale, Paris; Designers and Art Directors Association, London. **Exhibitions:** Lund Humphries, London, 1934; Institute of Design, Chicago, 1951; Manchester Polytechnic, 1977; North Staffordshire Polytechnic, 1978. **Collections:** Victoria and Albert Museum, London; London Transport Museum; British Railway Museum, York; Imperial War Museum, London; National Gallery of Australia, Canberra. **Honors:** Royal Designer for Industry, Royal Society of Arts, London, 1959; Fellow, Society of Industrial Artists and Designers, London. **Died:** London, 18 September 1976.

## Works

*Plain or Fancy* newspaper advertisements, for Weber and Heilbroner, 1927-29.

Bus stop designs, for London Transport, 1935.

*The Highway Code* exhibition layout and poster, for the Ministry of Transport, London, 1937.

*These Men Use Shell* poster, for Shell Oil Company, 1938.

Trade mark, for the Coal Utilisation Council, 1947.

*Hands at Your Service* posters, for London Passenger Transport Board, 1947.

*With Gin This Is It* promotional poster, for Martini Vermouth, 1949.

Logo and corporate identity programme, for MacFisheries, 1952-59.

Trade mark, for Finmar, 1953.

*Terylene: Handle and Drape* press advertisements, for Imperial Chemical Industries, 1954.

Symbol, for the Design Centre, London, 1955.

*Standfast* triangular whiskey bottle, for W. Grant and Sons, 1956.

*Stop for Super Shell and Go* poster, for Shell Oil Company, 1958.

Fisons Pest Control manuals and advertisements, for Fisons, 1959-64.

Corporate identity programme, for the British Sugar Corporation, 1961-75.

Hardback book symbol, for Allen Lane/The Penguin Press, 1966.

Unified design programme, for the Edinburgh International Festival, 1966-75.

## Publications

**By SCHLEGER: books**—(with others) *The Practice of Design,* London, 1946; **articles**—in *Arts and Industry* (London), March, 1949; *Advertising Review* (London), nos. 1-4, 1954-55, no. 8, 1956, no. 18, 1958; *Idea* (Tokyo), no. 43, 1960.

**On SCHLEGER: books**—*Line Drawing for Reproduction* by Ashley Havinden, London, 1933, 1941; *Lettering Today* edited by C. G. Holme, London and New York, 1937, 1948; *The New Graphic Design* by Karl Gerstner and Markus Kutter, Teufen and London, 1959; *Who's Who in Graphic Art* edited by Walter Amstutz, Zurich, 1962; *Graphic Design in Britain* edited by Frederick Lambert, London, 1967; *An International Survey of Packaging* by Wim Crouwel and Kurt Weidemann, London, 1968; *107 Grafici dell'AGI,* with texts by Renzo Zorzi and Franco Grignani, Venice, 1974; *Archigraphia: Architectural Graphics* edited by Walter Herdeg, Zurich, 1978; *Thirties: British Art and Design Before the War,* exhibition catalogue with texts by Ian Jeffrey and others, London, 1979; *Eye for Industry: Royal Designers for Industry 1936-1986* by Fiona MacCarthy and Patrick Nuttgens, London, 1986.

\* \* \*

Hans Schleger's German background and his early experience in the United States seem very much present in his British work and may partly account for its assurance and easy grasp of modernist principles. He embodied the foreign influences that fostered a native belated British modernism, and his work played a leading role in the development from "commercial art" of the prewar period to "graphic design" proper, as it emerged in the 1950s and 1960s. In Schleger's case, the passage is from the artist Zero to the design practice Hans Schleger and Associates. It is a development that can be seen also, for example, in the career of F. H. K. Henrion, another of the pioneer graphic designers in Britain and also an emigré.

Schleger first became known in Britain for his posters and work in press advertising. At this stage, he was already a sophisticated artist; his early work, often employing montage, shows the tendency towards simplification and integration of text and image that characterizes his postwar work in graphic design. This process reaches a culmination in the trade symbols that he designed. Here, as in his earlier drawing, especially from the years in New York, the forms are subtle and not at all tempted by crude geometry.

The postwar work in corporate identity, in which Schleger was among the early leaders in Britain, shows the breadth of his talents. His trademarks take their place in the design of a whole range of items. Schleger showed a special interest in package design, as is clear from the Finmar work and also in his whiskey bottle for Grant's. It seems typical of his approach that he found a fresh form for the bottle itself and dispensed with the traditional label. (The client retained the bottle's form, but applied a label, not of Schleger's design.)

Apart from the inevitably ephemeral products of this graphic design work, standing as more lasting testimony to Schleger's talent is the book *The Practice of Design* (1946), a compilation of essays predominantly by members of the Design Research Unit; it includes a short written contribution by Schleger on "designing this book." The volume is still a distinguished object (reminiscent of the best American work of the period) and must have stood out sharply from the normal level of book production in postwar Britain.

As his published statements suggest, Schleger became interested in the human aspects of design (which figure largely in work of the scale he came to tackle) as much as in the purely visual or formal problems. Aware of the need to fuse both aspects of a task satisfactorily, he approached the project, as well as its visual forms, in a way that can properly be described as elegant, sensitive, and refined.

—Robin Kinross

# SCHMIDT, Douglas W.

American stage designer

**Born:** Cincinnati, Ohio, 4 October 1942. **Education:** Educated at High Mowing School, Wilton, New Hampshire, until 1960; studied at the School of Fine and Applied Arts, Boston University, 1961-64. **Career:** Designer and stage manager, Monmouth Repertory Theatre, Maine, 1961; assistant to designer Ming Cho Lee, in New York, 1964-67; designer, Playhouse in the Park, Cincinnati, Ohio, 1964-68; freelance stage designer, New York, from 1965, and television designer, from 1974; resident designer, Lincoln Center Repertory Theatre, New York, 1969-73; designer, Old Globe Theatre, San Diego, California, 1985-92; also designed for the Juilliard Opera Theatre, Juilliard Dance Company, New York Shakespeare Festival, East Side Playhouse, 41st Street Theatre, Ethel Barrymore Theatre, and others. Lecturer, New York Center for Field Studies. Board member, Studio and Forum of Stage Design, New York. **Member:** American Society of Interior Designers; United Scenic Artists Local Union 829; Society of Motion Picture and TV Art Directors. **Honors:** Joseph Maharam Award, New York, 1972, 1977; New York Drama Desk Award, 1973, 1974 (2); Obie Award, *Village Voice* magazine, New York, 1977. **Address:** 245 West 52d Street, New York, New York 10019, U.S.A.

## Works

Stage productions (New York, unless noted) include—(and stage manager) *The Importance of Being Earnest,* Monmouth Repertory Theatre, Monmouth, Maine, 1961; *The Devil's Disciple,* Monmouth Repertory Theatre, 1961; *Othello,* Monmouth Repertory Theatre, 1961; *Androcles and the Lion,* Monmouth Repertory Theatre, 1961; *Ghosts,* Playhouse in the Park, Cincinnati, 1965; *The Collection,* Playhouse in the Park, 1965; *The Lover,* Playhouse in the Park, 1965; *Major Barbara,* Playhouse in the Park, 1965; *The Summer of the Seventeenth Doll,* Playhouse in the Park, 1965; *She Stoops to Conquer,* Playhouse in the Park, 1965; *The Glass Menagerie,* Playhouse in the Park, 1965; *Caesar and Cleopatra,* Center Stage Theatre, Baltimore, Maryland, 1965; *La Bohème,* 1965; *Man and Superman,* Playhouse in the Park, 1966; *Benito Cereno,* Playhouse in the Park, 1966; *The*

*American Dream,* Playhouse in the Park, 1966; *Charley's Aunt,* Playhouse in the Park, 1966; *Eh?,* Playhouse in the Park, 1966; *The Skin of Our Teeth,* Playhouse in the Park, 1966; *The Ox Cart,* York, 1966-67; *The Marriage of Figaro,* 1967; *The Mines of Sulphur,* 1967; *A Clearing in the Woods,* 1967; *The Importance of Being Earnest,* Playhouse in the Park, 1967; *To Bury a Cousin,* 1967; *The Cavern,* Playhouse in the Park, 1967; *King John,* 1967; *Anatol,* Playhouse in the Park, 1967; *Father Uxbridge Wants to Marry,* 1967; *The Entertainer,* Theatre of the Living Arts, Philadelphia, Pennsylvania, 1967; *The Great White Hope,* Arena Stage, Washington, D.C., 1967; *Silent Night, Lonely Night,* 1967; *Tonantzintla,* 1968; *Misalliance,* 1968; *The Memorandum,* 1968; *Camino Real,* 1968; *The Madwoman of Chaillot,* Playhouse in the Park, 1968; *Huui-Huui,* 1968; *Twelfth Night,* 1969; *Geese,* 1969; *The Time of Your Life,* 1969; *The Good Woman of Setzuan,* 1970; *Operation Sidewinder,* 1970; (double-bill, also designed costumes) *Landscape* and *Silence,* 1970; *The Disintegration of James Cherry,* 1970; *Paris is Out!,* 1970; *Playboy of the Western World,* 1971; *Landscape,* 1971; *Silence,* 1971; *An Enemy of the People,* 1971; *Antigone,* 1971; *Play Strindberg,* 1971; *The Merry Wives of Windsor,* Stratford, Connecticut, 1971; *Pictures in the Hallway,* 1971; *Mary Stuart,* 1971; *People are Living There,* 1971; *The Wedding of Iphigenia,* 1971; *Iphigenia in Concert,* 1971; *The Losers,* 1971; *Huckleberry Finn,* 1971; *Narrow Road to the Deep North,* 1972; *The Love Suicide at Schofield Barracks,* 1972; *Grease,* 1972-79 (toured United States, Australia, and Britain); *Twelfth Night,* 1972; *The Country Girl,* 1972; *The School for Scandal,* 1972 (toured); *The Hostage,* 1972 (toured); *Women Beware Women,* 1972 (toured); *Lower Depths,* 1972 (toured); *Enemies,* 1972; *Happy Days,* 1972; *Act Without Words 1,* 1972; *Krapp's Last Tape,* 1972; *Not I,* 1972; *Macbeth,* Stratford, Connecticut, 1973; *The Plough and the Stars,* 1973; *A Streetcar Named Desire,* 1973; *A Breeze from the Gulf,* 1973; *Veronica's Room,* 1973; *The Three Sisters,* 1973; *Measure for Measure,* 1973; *An American Millionaire,* 1974; *Fame,* 1974; *Kid Champion,* 1974; *Who's Who in Hell,* 1974; *Over Here!,* 1974; *The Three Sisters,* 1975; *Our Late Night,* 1975; *The Robber Bridegroom,* 1975; *Edward II,* 1975; *The Time of Your Life,* 1975; *Angel Street,* 1975; *Truckload,* 1975; *Threepenny Opera,* 1976; *Let My People Come,* 1976; *Herzl,* 1976; *The Crazy Locomotive,* 1977; *Agamemnon,* 1977; *Sunset,* Los Angeles, 1977; *Stages,* 1978; *Runaways,* 1978; *They're Playing Our Song,* 1979-82 (toured United States and European cities); *The Most Happy Fella,* 1979; *Romantic Comedy,* 1979; *Frankenstein,* 1981; *The Death of von Richtofen as Witnessed from Earth,* 1982; *The Skin of Our Teeth,* 1983; *Porgy and Bess,* 1983; *Chaplin,* 1983; *Detective Story,* 1984; *Black Comedy,* 1984; *Scapino,* 1984; *The Loves of Don Perlimpin,* 1984; *Dancing in the End Zone,* 1985; *Palladium Club Phase 1,* 1985; *Smile,* 1986; *Legends!,* (toured United States), 1986; *The Incredibly Famous Willy Rivers,* Old Globe Theatre, San Diego, California, 1987-88; *A Midsummer Night's Dream,* Los Angeles Music Center Opera, California, 1987; *There's One in Every Marriage,* Old Globe Theatre, 1987-88; *The Comedy of Errors,* Old Globe Theatre, 1987-88; *White Linen,* Old Globe Theatre, 1988; *Truffles in the Soup,* Seattle Repertory, Washington, 1988; *Elvis: A Rockin' Remembrance,* Beacon Theatre, New York, 1989; *Nick and Nora,* Marriott Marquis Theatre, New York, 1991.

Television set designs for PBS include—"Antigone," *Playhouse New York,* 1972; "Enemies," *Theatre in America,* 1974; "The Most Happy Fella," *Great Performances,* 1980; "Wings," *Ameri-*

_can Playhouse,_ 1983; "The Skin of Our Teeth," _American Playhouse,_ 1983; (special effects) "The San Francisco Ballet in Cinderella," _Great Performances: Dance in America,_ 1985; (art direction) "Painting Churches," _American Playhouse,_ 1986; "The Rise and Rise of Daniel Rocket," _American Playhouse,_ 1986.

## Publications

**On SCHMIDT: books**—_Who's Who in the Theatre,_ vol. 17, London and Detroit, 1981; _Contemporary Theatre, Film, and Television,_ Detroit, 1986, 1992.

\*     \*     \*

Since the beginning of the twentieth-century, when set designers were elevated to the level of creative artists, it has been assumed that a good designer would have a distinctive style. Douglas Schmidt, by his own admission, is eclectic. Yet, he is one of the most successful Broadway designers. Basically, he is a theatricalist in the nineteenth-century tradition. His sets are large, often pictorial, with their own theatrical quality, moving elements, multiple units, and special effects. It is because of his fascination with theatricality and "presentationism" that he is drawn to nineteenth-century opera, for which he has designed _Aida_ and _Samson and Delilah,_ among many others. Although he assisted Ming Cho Lee in the early 1960s at the New York Shakespeare Festival, and his early work shows Lee's influence, Schmidt's real influence comes from his teachers at Boston University, Raymond Sovey and Horace Armistead, both traditional Broadway designers from the pre-World War II era. As a result, his design proclaims itself as such, rather than as naturalistic illusion or subtle thematic statement.

Almost inadvertently, then, Schmidt has become the quintessential designer of the 1980s. This is because American theatre now lacks distinguished play-writing and outstanding actors and has come to be dominated by spectacle. Design is the innovative aspect of current theatre, and Schmidt is in the forefront. He thrives on unabashed theatricality, slickness, invention, and spectacle. In this, he is like fellow designers Robin Wagner and John Lee Beatty. It is significant that in the past decade, opera has become a focal point for innovation in design and directing.

Besides the flying airplane in _The Death of von Richtofen as Witnessed from Earth,_ Schmidt's mechanisms have included audience seating sections moving on air casters (_Agamemnon,_ 1977), interlocking steel pieces of a backdrop (_Macbeth,_ 1973), a revolving garden that allowed the audience to view each scene from a different angle (_Enemies,_ 1972), moving walls (_Threepenny Opera,_ 1976, and _Stages,_ 1978), multiple sets for which the changes became a spectacle in itself (_They're Playing Our Song,_ 1979), and a treadmill (_Over Here!_ 1974). He has stated that scenery should play the part of an actor and be as entertaining as the play itself. Interestingly, he is an admirer of the work of avant-garde director Richard Foreman, for whom he has designed two shows on Broadway. Foreman's work contains moving sets or set pieces which are as important as the performers, and Schmidt considers Foreman not only a significant director but a major designer as well.

The high point of Schmidt's career to date was the ill-fated _Frankenstein._ Despite the show's critical and box-office failure, it was one of the most spectacular productions on Broadway in the twentieth-century. Eight gothic sets moved on and off the stage to con-

clude in a cataclysmic scene in which the laboratory was reduced to rubble. The curtain descended on the scene only to rise within five seconds on a totally bare stage. The show was a potpourri of scenographic tricks and spectacle reminiscent of nineteenth-century staging.

Schmidt's sets do not evolve from artistic theory. They make no subtle statements. Rather, they delight in their own presentation and serve the needs of the play.

—Arnold Aronson

# SCHMOLLER, Hans (Peter)
British typographer and book designer

**Born:** Berlin, Germany, 9 April 1916; emigrated in 1938, naturalized British citizen, 1946. **Education:** Kaiser-Friedrich-Schule, Berlin-Charlottenburg, until 1933; apprenticed as a compositor in a printing firm, Berlin, 1933-37; part-time studies in calligraphy and lettering, Hohere Graphische Fachschule, Berlin, 1935-36. **Family:** Married Dorothee Wachsmuth in 1947 (died, 1948); children: Monica; married Tatyana Kent in 1950; children: Sebastian. **Career:** Assistant manager, Morija Printing Works, Lesotho, 1938-46; assistant to Oliver Simon, Curwen Press, London, 1947-49; typographer, 1949-56, head of production, 1956-76, director, 1960-76, and consultant, 1976-80, Penguin Books publishers, Harmondsworth, Middlesex. Chief examiner in typography, City and Guilds Institute, London, 1956-57; **Member:** President, Double Crown Club, London, 1968-69; council member, Royal Society of Arts, London, 1979-85. **Exhibitions:** _British Book Design,_ National Book League, London, from 1951; _Penguin Production and Design,_ Monotype Corporation, London, 1951; _Eye for Industry,_ Victoria and Albert Museum, London, 1986. **Honors:** Gold Medal, Leipzig Book Fair, 1971; Francis Minns Award, London, 1974. Royal Designer for Industry, Royal Society of Arts, London, 1976. Corresponding member, Bund Deutscher Buchkunstler, 1965. **Died:** London, 25 September 1985.

## Works

_Painting in Britain 1530 to 1790_ (E. K. Waterhouse) book design, for Penguin Books, 1953.
_The Art and Architecture of India_ (B. Rowland) book design, for Penguin Books, 1953.
_Silas Marner_ (G. Eliot) book design, for The Limited Editions Club, New York, 1953.
_Gargantua and Pantagruel_ (F. Rabelais) book design for Penguin Books, 1955.
_The Penguin Story 1935-1956_ (W. E. Williams) book design, for Penguin Books, 1956.
_The Fairy Tales of Charles Perrault_ book design, for Penguin Books, 1957.
_The Twelve Caesars_ (Suetonius/R. Graves) book design, for Penguin Books, 1957.
_The Story of an African Farm_ (O. Schreiner) book design, for the Limited Editions Club, New York, 1961.
_C. A. Mace: A Symposium_ book design, for Methuen and Company, and Penguin Books, 1962.

*Without Prejudice: One Hundred Letters from Frederick William Rolfe to John Lane* book design, for Allen Lane, 1963.
*Concerning Architecture: Essays Presented to Nikolaus Pevsner* book design, for Allen Lane/The Penguin Press, 1968.
*The Complete Pelican Shakespeare* book design, for Penguin Books Incorporated and Allen Lane/The Penguin Press, 1969.
*Camden's Britannia: Surrey and Sussex* book design, for Hutchinson and Company, 1977.

## Publications

**By SCHMOLLER: books**—(editor) *Giovanni Mardersteig: Die Officina Bodoni 1923-77,* Hamburg, 1979, Verona, 1980; *Mr. Gladstone's Washi,* Newtown, 1983; **articles**—in *Penrose Annual* (London), no. 52, 1958; *Der Druckspiegel* (Stuttgart), no. 6, 1959; *The Book Collector* (London), no. 2, 1982;

**On SCHMOLLER: books**—*Who's Who in Graphic Art* edited by Walter Amstutz, Zurich, 1962, Dubendorf, 1982; *Eye for Industry: Royal Designers for Industry 1936-1986,* exhibition catalogue by Fiona MacCarthy and Patrick Nuttgens, London, 1986.

*   *   *

Hans Schmoller seems to have been perfectly suited for his job at Penguin Books. Knowing about typography in an absolutely practical way from his apprenticeship in Berlin and his work in Africa, then at the Curwen Press, he could deal confidently with printers. He also brought with him a background of German culture, with its craft traditions in book production better maintained than those in Britain. He thus shared many of the same assumptions as his predecessor at Penguin, Jan Tschichold. Meticulous care for the smallest details (of letter spacing or word division, for example) is a chief characteristic of this approach. Success in these things depends on the quality of layouts and specifications. Schmoller's directions to printers are notable for their precision but also for knowing what can and what cannot be exactly instructed—the "voice" of these instructions is an understanding one. Outside of the special field of mass-produced paperbacks—in the design of cased or hardback books—Schmoller's concern for the book as a working object becomes fully evident. Because of careful choice of materials and vigilant attention to presswork and finishing processes, the final products of Schmoller's typography have a physical distinction unusual among British books. His typographic manner, most obvious in display work, shows his allegiances—perhaps "neo-classical" (though averting its glance from late-nineteenth-century excess), but willing to work with new techniques. One might place his work in the tradition to which C. E. Poeschel or Jakob Hegner belong.

A particular strength of Schmoller's work has been its treatment of editorially complex text matter. This is evident in the Penguin reference books and in editions of texts with annotations. The design of *The Complete Pelican Shakespeare* (1969) may be his most successfully achieved single work. The edition provides consistently satisfactory settings of the different verse and prose forms, along with related notes on each page, and welds these pages, with supplementary editorial matter, into a visually coherent, useable, and attractive book. Schmoller's writings on the history of printing and typography followed from his design work. They have been confined to occasional articles

and to translating and editing. His subjects have included the history of paperbacks, patterned papers, and the work of other typographers. His writing shows qualities that correspond to his typography: a relish for detail and for clarification of complexity, along with humane presentation.

—Robin Kinross

# SCHUITEMA, (Geert) Paul (Hendrikus)
Dutch painter, photographer, and exhibition, furniture, and graphic designer

**Born:** Groningen, 27 February 1897. **Education:** Educated in the Hague and Rotterdam, until 1914; studied painting and drawing, at the Akademie van Beeldende Kunsten en technische Wetenschappen, Rotterdam, 1915-17, 1919-20. **Military:** Served in the Dutch Army, 1917-18. **Family:** Married Elly van Dobben in 1936. **Career:** Independent painter, establishing studio with his brother E. B. W. Schuitema, in Rotterdam, 1922-25; graphic and industrial designer from 1925, photographer and filmmaker from 1928, working in Rotterdam, 1925-36, The Hague, 1936-39, and in Wassenaar, 1940-73; head of publicity, NC Mij. van Berkel's Patent company, Rotterdam, 1927-31; founder and director of the steel furniture co-operative workshops, Rotterdam, 1930-31; co-founder, Nederlandische Werkgemeenschap voor Film productie, Wassenaar, 1945; typographic designer, *Cement* magazine, for Verkoopassociatie Enci-Cemij NV, Wassenaar, 1948-67; also designed for C. Chevalier printing company, Boel and Van Eesteren, I. J. van Ettinger, Philip Dekker, Philips, Eternit, Algemeene Kunstzijde Unie, Dutch Posts and Telecommunications, and others. Chief editor, *De Fakkel* magazine, Rotterdam, 1926; contributor to *Filmliga* magazine, Rotterdam, 1932-33, and *De 8 en Opbouw* magazine, Rotterdam, 1933-36. Instructor in publicity design, Akademie van Beeldende Kunsten, The Hague, 1930-62; guest professor, West of England College of Art, Bristol, 1966. **Member:** Chairman, Centrale van Bonden van Leerligen en Oud-Leerligen van Kunstscholen Nederland, Rotterdam, 1926; secretary, Opbouw group, Rotterdam, 1928-34; advisory council member, Nederland-Nieuwe Russland association, Rotterdam, 1932-33; cultural advisory commission member, Nederlandse Bioskoopbond, Wassenaar, 1946. **Exhibitions:** C. Chevalier print showroom, Rotterdam, 1935; Stedelijk Museum, Amsterdam, 1965; Kunstgewerbemuseum, Zurich, 1967. **Honors:** Dutch Royal State Subsidy, 1923-25; Award of Honour, Concours du Meilleur Siege in Aluminium, Paris, 1933; Dutch Ministry of Culture Stipend, 1970. Honorary member, Gebonden Kunsten Federatie, The Hague, 1963. **Died:** Wassenaar, 25 October 1973.

## Publications

**By SCHUITEMA: book**—*Syst-o-Colour,* 2 vols., The Hague, 1966; **articles**—in *i 10* (Leiden), no. 16, 1928; *Schoonheid en Opvoeding* (Amsterdam), January 1929; *Links Rechten* (Rotterdam), February 1933; *De Reclame* (Amsterdam), November 1933; *Neue Grafik* (St. Gallen), December 1961.

**On SCHUITEMA: books**—*Die Neue Typografie* by Jan Tschichold, Berlin, 1928; *Foto-Auge* by Franz Roh and Jan

Tschichold, Stuttgart, 1929; *Eine Stunde Druckgestaltung* by Jan Tschichold, Stuttgart, 1930; *Pismo a Fotografie v Reklame* by Z. Rossmann, Brno, 1938; *The New Graphic Design* by Karl Gerstner and Markus Kutter, Teufen and London, 1959; *Functional Graphic Design in the 20s* by Eckhard Neumann, New York, 1967; *A History of the Dutch Poster 1890-1960* by Dick Dooijes and Pieter Brattinga, Amsterdam, 1968; *Pioneers of Modern Typography* by Herbert Spencer, London, 1969; *Paul Schuitema 1897-1973,* dissertation by Flip Bool, Amsterdam, 1974; *Fotografie in Nederland 1920-1940,* exhibition catalogue by Flip Bool and Kees Broos, The Hague, 1979.

*       *       *

Paul Schuitema, with G. Kiljan and Piet Zwart, formed a trinity of Dutch modernist designers, practising (to different degrees) across the whole field of design but now regarded principally as graphic designers. Zwart's pre-World War II graphic work, notable for its inventiveness, has come to overshadow that of the other two (and Kiljan is still almost unknown outside The Netherlands). In comparison with Zwart's, Schuitema's work is more direct and plainer. His work of the late 1920s and early 1930s, for Berkel and for the printers Chevalier (two of his major clients), shows all the qualities of the nieuwe zakelijkheid of that moment; it belongs to the specifically Dutch variety of functionalism evident also in the work of contemporaneous architects in the groups around the publication *De 8 en Opbouw* (for which Schuitema did some graphic work). By contrast, the German and Central European modernists—Tschichold, above all, of course—followed a path of increasing sophistication, particularly in employing the more refined sanserif typefaces (such as Futura), as they became available. The Dutch seemed to prefer the slightly crude, older sanserifs, perhaps for their very lack of sophistication.

Schuitema's production of these years exhibits an air of great confidence and assurance. In the case of the work for Berkel, one may attribute some of this to what must have been the privileged status accorded to Schuitema by the firm. Concerned as he was with all aspects of design, including that of their weighing and meat-cutting machines, his role prefigures the emergence of the "consultant designer." (Peter Behrens at AEG, in the early years of the century, would be the progenitor for this kind of designer.)

Schuitema was a committed socialist and took part, for example, in the workers' photography movements in The Netherlands in the 1930s. For books and magazines of the left, he designed covers that embody both the formal and social principles of modernism: formal and social revolutions are implied as inseparable. The spirit of this work was well evoked by Schuitema years later in his text "New Typographical Design in 1930," published in 1961 with extensive reproduction of the Berkel jobs: "The form was not predetermined but was the outcome of an attitude to life. And life itself took on form when it was given a new meaning..." By the same token, the impetus and confidence of the modern movement would desert it as the late 1930s wore on. Schuitema began to teach graphic design and to practice less, but he remained a lively presence. As a younger designer reported of him in 1966, following his teaching visit at the West of England College of Art, he was "instantly recognizable as a colleague, not a monument."

—Robin Kinross

# SCHULTES, Herbert H.

German industrial designer

**Born:** Freiburg, Germany, in 1938. **Education:** Studied engineering and design, Munich. **Career:** assistant head of design, 1961-67, head of design, from 1985, Siemens AG, Munich; co-founder, Schlagheck Schultes Design, from 1967. Founder of industrial design course, Advanced Technical College, Munich 1967-68; lecturer in industrial design, Kölner Werkschulen, 1967-68; art consultant for furniture industries. **Member:** Board member, Industrie Forum Design, Hannover; board member, Internationales Design Zentrum, Berlin; chairman of the board and founder, Design Zentrum, Munich. **Collections:** Chicago Anthenaeum, Museum of Architecture and Design, Chicago, Illinois; Museum of Modern Art, New York; Die Neue Sammlung, Staatliches Museum für angewandte Kunst, Munich. **Honors:** Stipendiat des Kulturkreises der Deutschen Industrie, 1960; Auswahl 92, Design Center Stuttgart; (with Siemens) named "Design Team '95"; several iF Industrie Forum Design Hannover awards. **Address:** (office) Siemens AG, Postfach 80 17 60, 81617 Munich, Germany.

## Works

Pocket camera, for Agfa-Gevaert, 1975.
*Filmkamera Movexoom,* for Agfa-Gevaert, 1975.
*Camera Optima,* for Agfa-Gevaert, 1976.
Ski bindings, for Marker, 1978.
Ski bindings, for Ess, 1980.
Surfboards and sailings, for HiFly, 1982.
Rain boots, for Elefanten-Schuh, 1983.
*Dekospot* halogen lamp, for Osram, 1984.
Ski boots, for Dynafit, 1985.
*Olymp* lamp, for ClassiCon, 1985.
*Orion* lamp, for ClassiCon, 1989.
*Orbis* lamp, for ClassiCon, 1992.
*System 25* kitchen, for bulthaup, 1992.
Siemens Logo and art direction for Siemens Corporate Design Manual, Siemens AG, 1989-1992.
Third-generation ICE train, for Deutsche Bahn AG, 1995 (with others).

## Publications

**By SCHULTES: books**—*Hans Wichmann: Industrial Design,* Munich, 1985; articles—"Das Verschwinden der Dinge—Herausforderung des Design" in *Design Zentrum München: Neue Technologien und Design,* Munich, 1993; "Das Telefon—die Grenzen des Design" in *Design Zentrum München: Akustik—eine Aufgabe des Design,* Munich 1993; "Farbe ist Leben" in *Design Zentrum München: Farbgebung—eine Aufgabe des Design,* Munich, 1994; "So einfach ist das Einfache nicht" in *md: moebel interior design,* December 1994; "Einfach Gebrauchsgüter" in Internationales Forum für Gestaltung Ulm, Giessen, 1995.

**On SCHULTES: books**—*Siemens Design,* exhibition catalogue, Munich; articles—"Party mit Design" by Peter Wingert in *Feinschmecker,* May 1987; "Warum muß Design elitär sein, Herr Schultes?" by Michael Freitag in *Frankfurter Allgemeine Magazin,* no. 375, 1987; "Design im Großkonzern" by Uta Brandes in

**Herbert Schultes:** *ORBIS* **lamp, for ClassiCon GmbH, Munich**

*Hochparterre,* May 1990; "Klasse trotz Masse" by Hans Ottomann in *Mensch & Büro,* February 1992; interview in *CITIZEN OF-FICE—Ideen und Notizen zu einer neuen Bürowelt* by Uta Brandes, Göttingen.

*       *       *

Herbert H. Schultes started his career along a classical path, training as an engineer in precision toolmaking. This conventional vocational education, however, masked another career goal: to be a film director. With the benefit of hindsight, one could see it as a natural development that, during an internship at Siemens, he ended up in the design department and suddenly discovered his passion for design.

And he's remained true to this love, with his whole heart—for, although his approach has remained faithful to the traditions of Bauhaus and the Ulmer School, he's never designed "from the head." He does this whether he's working as the head designer of the international company Siemens, which produces a broad range of the products, all high-tech, or as the co-founder of the Studio Schlagheck Schultes Design, which chalked up successes in every area of the market, designing everything from sports equipment to buttons, film cameras to furniture and plant machinery.

Herbert H. Schultes' special talent is his eye for future developments in design, for coming trends. Certainly, he doesn't pursue this in the manner of so many people, who predict the future on the basis of trend studies or forecasts based on the continuation of existing data; rather, he seems to have a kind of antennae for the future, an ability the Bavarians call "G'spür," which we might more conventionally term "intuition" or a gut feeling. Schultes has another quality that is no less important to success in the field of design: a sense of what is actually possible, an eye to reality.

The task of a head designer in a mammoth company such as Siemens consists in large measure of developing a design concept, implementing this in all of the company's branches and partner firms, and realizing it with the help of design teams. A head designer's job is, to a great degree, design management. True, he establishes the general direction of the company's design—he develops the company's design signature, and ensures that the creative potential of his designers is both activated an used to best effect—but there's little room, in all of this, for his own independent design work.

For any true designer, this is a regrettable omission; and this holds for Herbert H. Schultes, as well. Therefore, in order to avoid both such an omission and the accompanying risk that his own creativity could wither, he's never stopped pursuing his own private design work. In his efforts to "keep his hand in" he has produced, as "Sunday morning designs," so to speak, a range of products that have nothing to do with his work at Siemens, such as lighting units and furniture.

As a committed professional designer, Schultes, in addition to all of his own practical design work, has always made a conscious effort to promote thinking about design and raise the general consciousness of design and the need for good design. From the beginning of his career, therefore, he's been actively involved in design teaching and working with young designers. He also serves on the boards of a number of leading German design institutions.

Furthermore, he has always done everything in his power, with the help of his professional connections, to promote dialogue among international designers and continue the search for new design avenues, to prevent stagnation or dogmatism in the field of design.

In Hungary, the saying goes that if you wake up a true gypsy musician in the middle of the night, he'll grab his violin and start to play. Herbert H. Schultes is a designer in this sense; a 24-hour designer, a designer through and through, a designer to the tips of his fingers and the very marrow of his bones.

—Dr. Julius Lengert

# SERAFINOWICZ, Leokadia

Polish stage designer

**Born:** Janow, 23 February 1915. **Education:** Studied fine arts, at Copernicus University, Torun. **Career:** Artistic director and general manager, of the Marcinek Theatre, Poznan, 1960-75. **Honors:** Gold Medal, Prague Quadriennale of Scenography, 1971. **Address:** Lipowa 13/2, 62-041 Puszczykowo, K-Poznan, Poland.

## Works

Stage productions (Poznan, unless noted) include—*Ball at Professor Baczynski's,* 1961; *Little Tiger,* 1963; *Nightingale,* 1965; *Bath,* 1967; *Misterium Buffo,* Plovdiv, 1968; *Kathy Who Lost Her Geese,* 1969; *Hobby-Horse,* 1969; *Wanda,* 1970; *Tigrisorul,* Timisoara, 1970; *Hefajstos,* Lublin, 1974; *Ojczyzna,* 1974; *Wkole,* 1974; *Pani Koch,* 1975; *Janosik,* 1975; *Petrushka's Theatre,* 1976.

## Publications

**On SERAFINOWICZ: books**—*Contemporary Polish Stage Design* by Zenobiusz Strzelecki, Warsaw, 1983.

*       *       *

The puppet theatre is, above all, a theatre of the plastic arts. The practitioner of such an art plays a very important role in it, the more so if, like Leokadia Serafinowicz, she happens to be the director as well as the general manager of a theatre. A repertoire for children as well as for adults offered her great creative possibilities for ambitions in both directions, and the theatre which she led belonged to a narrow elite of the very best in Poland. In part, this is also due to the services of artistic director Wojciech Wieczorkiewicz and artist Jan Berdyszek, thanks to whom the Theatre Marcinek has a decidedly artistic and modern face.

There, folklorism makes its appearance. This tendency within Polish scenography, so rich and alive in Poland, consists of analogies to folk art and its sculpture, painting, and architecture. Serafinowicz, however, does not copy or imitate. Rather, she only follows the principles of facture and material. She usually utilizes wood, straw, and linen cloth as, for example, in *Kasis, co gaski zgubila* [*Kathy Who Lost Her Geese*], *Lajkonik* [*Hobby-Horse*], and *Wanda.* The latter spectacle—in which the puppets are roughly chiseled wood blocks and the set, just cloth strips—participates in the creation of a monumental Polish theatre.

Serafinowicz's devices are very rich. In *Teatr Pietrushki* [*Petrushka's Theatre*], she alludes to the Russian folk theatre. In *Tygrysek* [*Little Tiger*], the live actor wears a metal mesh mask with a design of colored sponge. In *Balwanowa bajka* [*Snowman's Tale*], the figures are of styrofoam and the birds, formed into expressive designs, are wire. Finally, in *Bath* some of the puppets are made of feathers and others from rags (as if to delineate characteristics of the play's two worlds simply by means of facture). One also encounters experiments in the area of stage space. There may be a screen (as is usual in a puppet theatre) or none at all (in other words, no mystification). Or sometimes, a center stage (as in *Nightingale*) is used, while at other times, the whole theatre becomes a stage.

One should also take into account Serafinowicz's work as a director in productions such as Witkiewicz's *Matwa* [*The Cuttlefish*] and *Szalona lokomotywa* [*The Crazy Locomotive*], Wyspianski's *Wesele* [*Wedding*], and Milobedzka's *Siala baba mak* [*She Sowed Poppies*]. As a director, her love for a new poetic, synthetic, and metaphoric theatrical form finds expression. Indeed, she leaves much room for the spectator's imagination.

—Zenobiusz Strzelecki

# SPENCER FRANCEY PETERS

Canadian graphic design firm

**Founded** as Fifty Fingers, Toronto, 1975; became the Spencer Francey Group, 1977; merged with the Toronto-based office of Michael Peters Design to become Spencer Francey Peters, 1990; partners include Peter Francey, Clark Spencer, Paul Hodgson, Gary Ludwig, Jeannette Hanna, and Robynne Budish. Clients include Apple Canada, Bank of Nova Scotia, Canada Post Corporation, Compaq Canada, E. D. Smith & Sons Ltd., Four Seasons/Regent Hotels & Resorts, Horizon Foods, Imperial Oil Limited, Kaufman Footwear Co., Nortel, Ontario Hydro, Random House Canada, Rogers Cantel, Second Cup Coffee Co., Southern California Healthcare Network, and Teknion Furniture Systems Inc. **Honors:** Design Effectiveness Awards, 1992, 1994, 1995; ZGRAF, Zagreb, Yugoslavia; Ovation Award of Excellence, IABC Gold Quill Awards; Silver Medal, New York Art Director's Show. **Address:** 250 The Esplanade, Toronto, Ontario, M5A 1J2, Canada.

\*　　\*　　\*

Spencer Francey Peters (SFP) is a Toronto-based graphic design firm that specializes in corporate communications and package design. SFP embraced the computer-age, pioneering the design of electronic templates to help large corporations integrate desktop publishing into their organizations.

Originally founded in 1975 under the name Fifty Fingers, the Spencer Francey Group merged with the Toronto office of Michael Peters Design becoming Spencer Francey Peters in 1990. Paul Hodgson, Gary Ludwig, Jeanette Hanna, and Robynne Budish have joined founding partners Clark Spencer and Peter Francey. The firm is organized in three divisions: Brands Design for packaging and brand identity, Systems Design for electronic design management, and Communications Design for the more traditional corporate design projects.

SFP started using computers as soon as they became available in the mid 1980s. SFP was quick to identify both the computers's benefits

and its drawbacks. While the technology of the computer empowers individual employees to publish professional-looking documents, it restricts a company's ability to ensure consistently formatted output. In 1988, SFP launched a new service called eMerge Electronic Design Management. The service examines a company's total paper output—brochures, newsletters, and correspondence—and develops a system of templates for the staff to use. The system helps the corporation to maintain a consistent look by guiding the user through every step, from choosing the format to coordinating mailing. Major clients for the program include Apple Canada and Imperial Oil.

In 1992, the Second Cup, an Ontario-based chain of specialty coffee stores, hired SFP to improve its image from an American fast-food outlet to an old-style European café. Their existing coffee bag was indistinguishable from grocery-store packaging, depicting a steaming mug against a background of beans. SFP specified ecological tan craft paper and created a worldly design featuring the new logo, a graphic rendition of a steaming cup and saucer. Passport stamps from coffee-producing countries enhance the cachet of the package. The new corporate identity and packaging coupled with sophisticated interiors positioned the Second Cup for success in the café-crazed 1990s.

In exhibit design, SFP created a playful ergonomic testing stage for the furniture company Teknion Furniture Systems. Designed in 1995 for the International Interior Design Exposition in Toronto, the booth included iconic elements, such as a gigantic tape-measure seat and an oversize out-of-focus eye chart, to humorously educate the public on the importance of well-being in the work-place.

SFP has been successful in all areas of corporate communications. They have designed annual reports and glossy brochures. The company has designed packaging for a variety of products from work boots to software. SFP has also explored exhibition design, and new areas of digital design.

—Elizabeth Crawford and Rachel Gotlieb

# SHAKESPEAR, Raul (Lorenzo)

Argentinian graphic designer

**Born:** Buenos Aires, 7 July 1947. **Education:** Studied at Raggio Polytechnic School, Buenos Aires, 1960-65. **Family:** Married Silvia Paez in 1971; children: Victoria and Andres. **Career:** Freelance graphic designer and art director, Buenos Aires, 1965-72; designer, in the Guillermo Gonzalez Ruiz and Ronald Shakespear design studio, Buenos Aires, 1972-73; co-director, with Ronald Shakespear, of Shakespear Brothers Design Team, Buenos Aires, from 1973. Permanent graphic design contributor, *Summa* magazine, Buenos Aires. **Member:** Centro de Arte y Comunicacion, Buenos Aires; Asociacion Disenadores Graficos; Centro de Investigacion del Disegno Industrial y Grafico, Buenos Aires. **Exhibitions:** Galeria Espanola, Buenos Aires, 1977; Teatro Municipal General San Martin, Buenos Aires, 1980; Centro de Arte y Comunicacion, Buenos Aires, 1981; *Dal Cucchiaio al Citta,* Centro Kappa, Milan, 1983. **Collections:** Museo de Arte Moderno, Mar del Plata. **Address:** Shakespear Studio, Juan Jose Diaz 594, San Isidro, 1642 Buenos Aires, Argentina.

*See* SHAKESPEAR, Ronald

# SHAKESPEAR, Ronald

Argentinean graphic designer

**Born:** Rosario, Sante Fe Province, 18 September 1941. **Education:** Studied at Raggio Polytechnic School, Buenos Aires, 1954-58. **Military Service:** Served in the Argentine Army, 1962. **Family:** Married Elena Peyron in 1968; children: Lorenzo, Barbara, Juan, Maria, and Sofia. **Career:** Freelance graphic designer and art director, Buenos Aires, 1960-67; partner, with Guillermo Gonzales Ruiz, in Ruiz and Shakespear design studio, Buenos Aires, 1967-73; co-director, with Raul Shakespear, of Shakespear Brothers Design Team, Buenos Aires, from 1973. Permanent graphic design contributor, *Summa* magazine, Buenos Aires. Committee member of the Centro de Arte y Comunicacion, Buenos Aires. **Member:** Asociacion Disenadores Graficos, Buenos Aires; Centro de Investigacion del Disegno Industrial y Grafico, Buenos Aires. **Exhibitions:** Galeria Española, Buenos Aires, 1977; Teatro Municipal General San Martin, Buenos Aires, 1980; Centro de Arte y Comunicacion, 1981; *Dal Cucchiaio al Citta,* Centro Kappa, Milan, 1983. **Collections:** Museo de Arte Moderno, Mar del Plata. **Address:** Shakespear Studio, Juan Jose Diaz 594, San Isidro, 1642 Buenos Aires, Argentina.

## Works

Sign system and unified identity programme, for the City of Buenos Aires, 1971-73 (with Ruiz and Shakespear).
Symbol and logotype, for Corp women's clothing firm, 1973 (with Shakespear Studio).
Symbol and logotype, for Argemac toolmakers, 1975 (with Shakespear Studio).
Super-graphics environmental design, for Marby building and metallurgy company, 1975 (with Shakespear Studio).
Symbol, logotype, and signage, for Harrod's, Buenos Aires, 1975 (with Shakespear Studio).
Newspaper advertisements, for Fate tyre company, 1975-77 (with Shakespear Studio).
Symbol and logotype, for Cafetal coffee makers and importers, Buenos Aires, 1976 (with Shakespear Studio).
Symbol and logotype, for Vega men's clothing, Buenos Aires, 1976 (with Shakespear Studio).
Total signage system and visual identity, for Buenos Aires hospitals, from 1980 (with Shakespear Studio).

## Publications

**By SHAKESPEAR: books**—*Ronald and Raul Shakespear: 20 Years of Design in Argentina,* Buenos Aires, 1976; *Trademarks: Shakespear Studio,* Buenos Aires, 1981.

**On SHAKESPEAR: books**—*Illustration: Aspects and Directions* by Bob Gill and John Lewis, London, 1964; *Archigraphia: Architectural Graphics* edited by Walter Herdeg, Zürich, 1978; *Top Symbols of the World* edited by Franco Maria Ricci, Milan, 1979; *The Shakespear Brothers* by Jorge Glusberg, Buenos Aires, 1980; *Who's Who in Graphic Art* edited by Walter Amstutz, Dubendorf, 1982.

*See* SHAKESPEAR, Raul

*       *       *

The visual style of the work of Ronald and Raul Shakespear is rooted in the work of Josef Müller-Brockman, Armin Hofmann, and Herb Lubalin. The almost typographical character of the Shakespears' images (e.g., Sports Centre, Buenos Aires), the interaction between figure and ground which are equal in their abstract and expressive power, and the monumentality of their conceptions cause the designs to overflow their initial informational objective. This monumentality—deriving not only from size but also from proportion—creates vitality, energy, and optimism in its environments and communicates these qualities to their inhabitants (e.g., Maternity Hospital, Buenos Aires). In signage, where this level of communication is normally and willfully reduced or neglected, the Shakespears' approach is especially praiseworthy. In addition to informing the public, their approach to graphic communication also forms the environment.

Simplicity, abstractness, and monumentality appear in Ronald Shakespear's early work, continues during his association with Guillermo Gonzalez Ruiz, and develops to its present maturity in the Shakespears' own studio. In their design conception, form follows function, a non-reductionist function that recognizes, along with the primary objective of a given project, the general and specific requirements of the human environment. In the Shakespears' hands, graphic design becomes architecture, art, and cityscape.

Although many designers have been influenced by the Shakespears' work of the 1960s and 1970s, this influence might initially have been attributed to those designers who had previously influenced the Shakespears. But their recent work is not only qualitatively comparable to the best produced anywhere (as Ronald's has been since 1963), but it has also ceased to follow any other designer; Josef Müller-Brockman, Armin Hofmann, Herbert Lubalin, Alan Fletcher, Romuio Maccio, and Juan Carlos DiStefano, among others, no longer look at us through the Shakespears' works. The high quality of the Shakespears' corporate identity work is unquestionable, but their historical significance derives from their signage projects.

The work of the Shakespears represents a fourth stage in the evolution of graphic design, a profession where the first stage was craft-oriented, the second was artistic/intuitive, and the third, in an attempt to control reality, was rational/reductionist. In this fourth stage, the Shakespears integrate freedom and control, function and expression, performance and pleasure, as a consequence of their understanding of the complexity of communication problems, along with their ability to deal with them. This ability makes their studio one of the most exciting working studios around.

—Jorge Frascara

# SHAMASK, Ronaldus

Dutch fashion designer

**Born:** Amsterdam, 24 November 1945. **Education:** Trained as an architect; self-taught in design, from 1960. **Career:** Window display artist, in Melbourne, Australia, 1963-66; fashion illustrator, working for *The Times* and *Observer* newspapers, London, 1967-68; freelance stage set and costume designer for ballet, opera, and for Company of Man multimedia artists' group, in Buffalo, New York, 1968-71; freelance interior and clothing designer, New York, 1971-77; founder-partner, with Murray Moss, of Moss Shamask fashion company, New York, 1978-90; opened Moss boutique on Madison Avenue, New York, 1979, closed, 1986; introduced first menswear collection, 1985; showed new collection under his own name, and formed new company, SUSA (Shamask USA), 1990. **Exhibitions:** *Intimate Architecture: Contemporary Clothing Design,* Massachusetts Institute of Technology, Cambridge, 1982; *Infra-Apparel,* Metropolitan Museum of Art, New York, 1993. **Collections:** Smithsonian Institution, Washington, D.C. **Honors:** Coty Fashion Award, New York, 1981; Council of Fashion Designers of America Award, 1987; Confederation Internationale du Lin Fil d'Or Award, 1982, 1987, 1989; Woolmark Award, 1989. **Address:** c/o Revlon, 625 Madison Avenue, New York 10022, USA.

### Publications

**By SHAMASK: articles**—"Commentary" in *Details* (New York), April 1989.

**On SHAMASK: books**—*Intimate Architecture: Contemporary Clothing Design,* exhibition catalogue, Cambridge, Massachusetts, 1982; *McDowell's Directory of Twentieth Century Fashion* by Colin McDowell, London, 1984; *Fashion: The Inside Story* by Barbaralee Diamonstein, New York, 1985; *New York Fashion: The Evolution of American Style* by Caroline Rennolds Milbank, New York, 1989; **articles**—in *Daily News* (New York), March 1979, September 1979; *New York Times* 1 March 1979, 8 February 1981, 16 August 1981; *Gentleman's Quarterly* (New York), November 1979; *San Francisco Chronicle,* 6 December 1979; *Women's Wear Daily* (New York), 3 November 1980, 26 April 1982; *People Weekly* (Chicago), 24 August 1981; *Vogue* (New York), June 1982; "Ronaldus Shamask" by Marina Sturdza in *Fashion 85* (New York), 1984; "Designer, Client: The Modern Equation" by Paul Sinclaire in *Vogue* (New York), November 1987; "Who's That Shamasked Man?" by Bart Boehlert in *New York,* 8 February 1988; "Cultural Influences" by Robert Parola in the *Daily News Record,* 3 October 1988; "Three US Designers, Less or More in the Mainstream" by Anne-Marie Schiro in the *New York Times,* 4 November 1988; "Ronaldus Shamask Enjoying a Sense of Pleasure" by Lawrence Chua in *Women's Wear Daily: Best of New York,* March 1989; "Designing Men" in *GQ* (New York), July 1989; "The Two Mr. Shamasks" by Vincent Boucher in *Seven Days* (New York), 7 March 1990; "The Word to Men: Hang Looser" in *People Weekly* (Chicago), Spring 1990; "The Look of the Nineties: Four Designers Lead the Way" by Stephen Fenichell in *Connoisseur* (New York), March 1991.

\*     \*     \*

In late 1970s and early 1980s, something of a cult grew up around the clothes of Ronaldus Shamask. His grave and hieratic presentations made it clear that he sees a fashion show as a theatrical event, in the way many Japanese designers also conceive of these presentations. Music by Philip Glass and severe minimalist backgrounds are all suggestive of Shamask's sensibilities. But of course, it is by his clothes that a fashion designer must be judged, and as far as Shamask is concerned, the verdict is essentially—or will be, in the course of time—that what he really creates are wearable works of art. Contemplative, austere, yet luxurious in their very denial of overt pattern, and highly refined, they attract a woman who has a connoisseur's eye for fabric and quality and who is not afraid of the abstraction of Shamask's shapes.

Shamask dresses an elite—the largely self-appointed elite comprising the devotees of high style. Certainly, his work is part of a way of life that is bound up with living in Manhattan; his clothes are meant to be worn in lofts, to downtown openings, are meant to signal to other members of what might be called the esthetic establishment their wearers' good standing in its ranks. Which is not to be negative; every city in its prime, or during one of the many bloomings it may undergo, has its definers of esoteric style. What Charles James was to 1940s New York, Shamask was to the late 1970s and early 1980s—a quintessence of the stern discipline which is always at the heart of high style, whether it be the strict and complicated construction of a James creation or the seemingly effortless silhouette of a Shamask.

In the 1990s, Shamask has focused on menswear, creating logical, tailored clothing with an emphasis on a precise fit. Although he does not have a profound commercial impact, he continues to engage an elite group of devoted admirers.

—Peter Carlsen

# SHARAFF, Irene

American stage and film costume designer

**Born:** Boston, Massachusetts, in 1910. **Education:** Studied at the School of Fine and Applied Arts, New York, the Art Students League, New York, and at the Academie de la Grande Chaumiere, Paris. **Career:** Assistant to stage designer Aline Bernstein, at the Civic Repertory Theatre Company, 1928-30; freelance stage costume designer, working for New York Broadway shows, Ballet Russe de Monte Carlo, New York City Ballet, Joffrey Ballet, Royal Ballet, and others, from 1932; film costume designer, mainly for Metro-Goldwyn-Mayer (MGM), in Hollywood, California, from 1942. **Exhibitions:** *Romantic and Glamorous Hollywood Design,* Metropolitan Museum of Art, New York, 1974. **Honors:** Academy Award, 1951, 1956, 1961, 1963, 1966. **Address:** c/o Gloria Safier, 677 Madison Avenue, New York, New York 10021, U.S.A.

### Works

Stage productions (New York, unless noted) include—*Alice in Wonderland* (also sets), 1932; *As Thousands Cheer,* 1933; *Life Begins at 8:40,* 1934; *The Great Waltz,* 1934; *Crime and Punishment,* 1935 (also sets); *Parade,* 1935; *Jubilee,* 1935; *Rosmersholm,* 1935 (also sets); *Idiot's Delight,* 1936; *On Your Toes,* 1936; *White Horse Inn,* 1936; *Virginia, I'd Rather Be Right,* 1937; *The Boys from Syracuse,* 1938; *The American Way,* 1939; *Gay New Orleans,* 1939; *Streets of Paris,* 1939; *Boys and Girls Together,* 1940; *All in Fun,* 1940; *Lady in the Dark,* 1941; *The Land Is Bright,* 1941; *Sunny River,* 1941; *Banjo Eyes,* 1941; *By Jupiter,* 1942; *Star and Carter,* 1942; *Count Me In,* 1942; *Billion Dollar Baby,* 1945; *The Would-Be Gentleman,* 1946; *GI Hamlet,* 1946; *Bonanza Bound,* 1948; *Montserrat,* 1949; *Dance Me a Song,* 1950; *Mike Todd's Peep-Show,* 1950; *The King and I,* 1951; *A Tree Grows in Brooklyn,* 1951; *Of Thee I Sing,* 1952; *Me and Juliet,* 1953; *The King and I,* London, 1953; *On Your Toes,* 1954; *By the Beautiful Sea,* 1954; *Shangri-La,* 1956; *Candide,* 1956; *Happy Hunting,* 1956; *West Side Story,* 1957; *Small War on*

*Murray Hill,* 1957; *Flower Drum Song,* 1958; *Juno,* 1959; *Do Re Mi,* 1960; *Jenny,* 1963; *The Girl Came to Supper,* 1963; *The Boys from Syracuse,* London, 1963; *Funny Girl,* 1964; *The King and I,* 1964 (revival); *Sweet charity,* 1965; *Hallelujah, Baby!,* 1967; *Irene,* 1972.

Film productions include—*Girl Crazy* (Taurog), 1943; *I Dood It* (Minnelli), 1943; *Madame Curie* (LeRoy), 1943; *Broadway Rhythm* (Del Ruth), 1943; *Meet Me in St. Louis* (Minnelli), 1944; *Bathing Beauty* (Sidney), 1944; *Yolanda and the Thief* (Minnelli), 1945; *The Best Years of Our Lives* (Wyler), 1946; *The Dark Mirror* (Siodmak), 1946; *Ziegfeld Follies* (Minnelli), 1946; *The Bishop's Wife* (Kosta), 1947; *The Secret Life of Walter Mitty* (McLeod), 1947; *A Song Is Born* (Hawks), 1947; *Every Girl Should Be Married* (Hartman), 1948; *An American in Paris* (Minnelli), 1951; *Call Me Madam* (W. Lang), 1953; *A Star Is Born* (Cukor), 1954; *Brigadoon* (Minnelli), 1954; *Guys and Dolls* (Mankiewicz), 1955; *The King and I* (W. Lang), 1956; *Porgy and Bess* (Preminger), 1959; *Can-Can* (W. Lang), 1960; *Flower Drum Song* (Koster), 1961; *West Side Story* (Wise and Robbins), 1961; *Cleopatra* (Mankiewicz), 1963; *The Sandpiper* (Minnelli), 1965; *Who's Afraid of Virginia Woolf?* (Nichols), 1966; *The Taming of the Shrew* (Zefffirelli), 1967; *Funny Girl* (Ross), 1968; *Hello Dolly* (Kelly), 1969; *Justine* (Cukor), 1969; *The Great White Hope* (Ritt), 1970; *The Way We Were* (Pollack), 1974; *Mommie Dearest* (Perry), 1981.

**Publications**

By SHARAFF: books—*Broadway and Hollywood: Costumes Designed by Irene Sharaff,* New York, 1976; **articles**—*Metropolitan Museum of Art Bulletin* (New York), November 1967.

On SHARAFF: books—*Romantic and Glamorous Hollywood Design,* exhibition catalogue by Diana Vreeland, New York, 1974; *Hollywood Costume Design* by David Chierichetti, London, 1976; *In a Glamorous Fashion: The Fabulous Years of Hollywood Costume Design* by W. Robert La Vine, Boston and London, 1981; *McDowell's Directory of Twentieth Century Fashion* by Colin McDowell, London, 1984; *International Dictionary of Films and Filmmakers,* Chicago and London, 1987, 1991.

\*   \*   \*

Making motion pictures often demands more from an artist than the duties suggested by an official title. Had "costume designer" Irene Sharaff merely sketched pretty dresses for stunning starlets, prestigious Metro-Goldwyn-Mayer studios would have slammed shut the pages of her drawing pad. But Sharaff's talents included a strong intellect, a fine eye, intuitive insights, an ingenious ability for original adaption, and an integrating mind that united all into workable designs.

Sharaff succeeded quickly as a New York stage designer. She showed a clever use of color in her costumes for Irving Berlin's "Easter Parade" from the play *As Thousands Cheer* (1933). For this stage revue, various shades of browns, tans, and other neutrals mimicked the pages of the *New York Times* rotogravure. Sharaff's designs for *Alice in Wonderland* (1932) won acclaim as reconstructions of the original Tenniel illustrations. These successes caught the attention of MGM filmmakers who hoped to translate Sharaff's theatrical skills into money-making Hollywood ventures. Specifi-

cally, they sought a suitable designer to deal with the new technicolor process. Irene Sharaff did not disappoint them after she joined the staff in 1942.

MGM designated Sharaff's skills to the Freed unit, which made some of the world's most memorable musicals. Almost immediately, Sharaff's touch turned projects into screen gold. *Meet Me in St. Louis* (1944), for instance, was a nostalgic valentine of lace, swiss dots, and ruffles. But the *American in Paris* (1951) ballet sequence proved to be Sharaff's finest hour because it utilized a multitude of her varied talents. For this ballet, Sharaff based her visuals on a number of famous French painters. Paying homage to the impressionists and several post-impressionists, she translated the colors and techniques of individual artists to set design and costume, even as she facilitated Gene Kelly's dances with garments constructed specifically for movement. Even the fabrics flowed with harmonizing rhythms.

Sharaff's career displayed considerable variety. *The King and I* (1956) sparkled with exotic ethnic dress. *Can-Can* (1960) offered an imaginative "Adam and Eve" ballet complete with guise from animal to insect. In 1961, *West Side Story* glorified the uniforms of working-class New York toughs. A few years later, *The Sandpiper* (1965) peopled the beaches of Big Sur with contemporary bohemians. Sharaff often dressed Elisabeth Taylor, be it as Egyptian queen (*Cleopatra,* 1963), a brilliant but testy Renaissance jewel (*Taming of the Shrew,* 1967), or an overweight, aging slob (*Who's Afraid of Virginia Woolf?,* 1966).

Whatever her script, Sharaff's quality continued. She translated her visions from stage to screen, using all the artistries of the world as inspiration. Understanding the natures of film, the stage, and ballet, she recognized their similarities and differences. She splashed her knowledge with just the right colors and elevated each creation to optimum advantage. Sharaff took the superficial show out of show business and replaced it with the depth of fine art.

—Edith Cortland Lee

# SIMPSON, Adele

American fashion designer

**Born:** Adele Smithline, in New York City, 28 December 1904. **Education:** Studied dressmaking, at the Pratt Institute of Design, Brooklyn, New York, 1921-22. **Family:** Married textile manufacturer Wesley William Simpson in 1930 (died); children: Jeffrey and Joan. **Career:** Assistant designer, 1922, then head dress designer, 1923-26, at Ben Gershel's ready-to-wear fashion house, New York; chief designer, William Bass, New York, 1927-28; designer of Adele Simpson fashions, at Mary Lee Fashions, New York, 1929-49; president and director of Adele Simpson Inc. (bought out Mary Lee Fashions), New York, from 1949. **Member:** The New York Couture Group; treasurer and board member, Fashion Group, New York; co-founder and board member, Fashion Designers of America. **Collections:** Brooklyn Museum, New York; Metropolitan Museum of Art, New York; Dallas Public Library, Texas. **Honors:** Neiman-Marcus Award, 1946; Coty American Fashion Critics Winnie Award, New York, 1947. **Died:** 1995.

## Publications

**On SIMPSON: books**—*Celebrity Register,* New York, 1963; *Current Biography Yearbook 1970* edited by Charles Moritz, New York, 1970; *Living Christian Science: Fourteen Lives* by Marcy Babbitt, Englewood Cliffs, New Jersey, 1975; *The Fashion Makers* by Barbara Walz and Bernadine Morris, New York, 1978; *Fairchild's Who's Who in Fashion* edited by Ann Stegemeyer, New York, 1980; *The Fashion Encyclopedia* by Catherine Houck, New York, 1982; *Les Annees 60* by Anne Bony, Paris, 1983; *McDowell's Directory of Twentieth Century Fashion* by Colin McDowell, London, 1984; *The Encyclopaedia of Fashion from 1840 to the 1980s* by Georgina O'Hara, London, 1986; *Fairchild's Dictionary of Fashion* by Charlotte Mankey Calasibetta, New York, 1988; *New York Fashion: The Evolution of American Style* by Caroline Rennolds Milbank, New York, 1989; **articles**—"First Lady Selects Spring Wardrobe" in the *New York Times,* 25 March 1966; "Mrs. Johnson to Wear Slim Tunic for Easter" in the *New York Times,* 9 April 1966; "Mrs. Nixon's One Midiskirt: She Bought It 'Just For Fun'" by Bernadine Morris in the *New York Times,* 14 March 1970; "Beene's Surprise: Not Only Elegance, But Humor As Well" by Bernadine Morris in the *New York Times,* 1 November 1973; "Cheerful Designs For Winter Sun" by Bernadine Morris in the *New York Times,* 27 August 1975; "Joyful Fashions with a Folkloric Flavor" by Bernadine Morris in the *New York Times,* 6 November 1976; "Adele Simpson" by Marielle Bancou in *American Fabrics and Fashions* (New York), Fall 1978; "Designers Softly Changing the Way Women Will Dress" by Bernadine Morris in the *New York Times,* 23 April 1977; "Fashion: Serious About Summer" by Bernadine Morris in the *New York Times,* 18 January 1978; "Simsoniana on Display" by Linda Anster in the *New York Times,* 15 November 1978; "For Resort Wear: Trousers Are Shorter and Waistlines Easier" by Bernadine Morris in the *New York Times,* 19 August 1978; "Long Reach of the Reagan Style" by Bernadine Morris in the *New York Times,* 24 February 1981; "4 Designers Present Easy-to-Wear Clothes" by Bernadine Morris in the *New York Times,* 29 October 1982; "7th Ave. Winner: Coat Dresses, Suits" by Bernadine Morris in the *New York Times,* 1 March 1983; "Short Gowns Shine for Night" by Bernadine Morris in the *New York Times,* 17 May 1983; "Klein's Spring Look: Fluid and Flattering" by Bernadine Morris in the *New York Times,* 7 November 1984; "Perry Ellis Returns to Sportswear Look" by Bernadine Morris in the *New York Times,* 6 November 1985.

* * *

Adele Simpson was for several decades a fixture in the the world of fashion and the clothing industry. Never a designer to startle by bizarre innovations, she used her awareness of new ideas to design wearable clothes. Her travels and collecting of historic and native costumes and fabrics added a richness to her clothing, especially in the use of fabrics, which were selected not only for their surface decoration but considered as well in construction and design. Her designs were more often created directly on the model than from sketches. Simpson also, with a touch of lightheartedness, removed longstanding fashion prejudices, for instance those against cotton and boots for evening wear. Critics, when speaking of her contributions to the field of clothing design, always mention wearability, richness, and appropriateness for the active woman. Designing for the ready-to-wear market, mostly in the higher-priced lines, she maintained high standards in all aspects of her work, which was always conservative with flair, feminine, and carefully constructed.

Her work was consistently acclaimed for the thoughtful coordination of the complete costume from underwear out, an idea most commonplace in the 1980s and 1990s, but not as much so when Simpson entered the design field. The long history of her success gives reason for her influence on fashion and clothing design. She removed pretense and replaces it with good design sense and wearability. Simpson's designs were appreciated and worn in public by first ladies Pat Nixon and Rosalynn Carter, among others.

A designer who never took the fashion world by surprise, she consistently produced clothes that quietly and tastefully expressed the quality of carefully chosen materials structured through good design and that considered the needs of the person who wore them.

—Harlan Sifford

# SMITH, Jack Martin

American film designer

**Education:** Studied architecture, University of Southern California, Los Angeles. **Career:** Worked as sketch artist, then designer, at Metro-Goldwyn-Mayer film studios, Hollywood, California, 1938-53; designer, 1953-61, and supervising art director, 1961-75, at 20th Century-Fox film studios, Hollywood; worked on films of Robert Aldrich, George Cukor, Stanley Donen, Victor Fleming, Walter Lang, Mervyn LeRoy, Rouben Mamoulian, Joseph Mankiewicz, Vincente Minnelli, Nicholas Ray, and others. **Honors:** Academy Award, 1963, 1966, 1969. **Address:** c/o Twentieth Century-Fox Film Corporation, Post Office Box 900, Beverly Hills, California 90213, U.S.A.

## Works

Films include—*The Wizard of Oz* (Fleming), 1939; *Meet Me in St. Louis* (Minnelli), 1944; *Yolanda and the Thief* (Minnelli), 1945; *Holiday in Mexico* (Sidney), 1946; *Ziegfeld Follies* (Minnelli), 1946; *The Pirate* (Minnelli), 1948; *Summer Holiday* (Mamoulian), 1948; *Easter Parade* (Walters), 1948; *Words and Music* (Taurog), 1948; *Madame Bovary* (Minnelli), 1949; *On The Town* (Kelly and Donen), 1949; *Nancy Goes to Rio* (Leonard), 1950; *Summer Stock* (Walters), 1950; *Royal Wedding* (Donen), 1951; *Show Boat* (Sidney) 1951; *An American in Paris* (Minnelli), 1951; *The Belle of New York* (Walters), 1952; *Million Dollar Mermaid* (LeRoy), 1952; *I Love Melvin* (Weis), 1953; *Dangerous When Wet* (Walters), 1953; *Easy to Love* (Walters), 1953; *Valley of the Kings* (Pirosh), 1954; *White Feather* (Webb), 1955; *Soldier of Fortune* (Dymytryk), 1955; *Seven Cities of Gold* (Webb), 1955; *Carousel* (H. King), 1956; *The Man in the Gray Flannel Suit* (Johnson), 1956; *Bigger Than Life* (Ray), 1956; *Bandido* (Fleischer), 1956; *Teenage Rebel* (Goulding), 1956; *Boy on a Dolphin* (Negulesco), 1957; *An Affair to Remember* (McCarey), 1957; *Peyton Place* (Robson), 1957; *The Barbarian and the Geisha* (Huston), 1958; *Woman Obsessed* (Hathaway), 1959; *The Best of Everything* (Negulesco), 1959; *Can-Can* (W. Lang), 1960; *North to Alaska* (Hathaway), 1960; *All Hands on Deck* (Taurog), 1961; *The Comancheros* (Curtiz), 1961; *Marines, Let's Go* (Walsh), 1961; *Pirates of Tortuga* (Webb), 1961; *Return to Peyton Place* (J. Ferrer), 1961; *Sanctuary* (Richardson), 1961; *The Second Time Around*

(V. Sherman), 1961; *Snow White and the Three Stooges* (W. Lang), 1961; *Voyage to the Bottom of the Sea* (Allen), 1961; *Wild in the Country* (Dunne), 1961; *Bachelor Flat* (Tashlin), 1962; *Five Weeks in a Balloon* (Allen), 1962; *Hemingway's Adventures of a Young Man* (Ritt), 1962; *Mr. Hobbs Takes a Vacation* (Koster), 1962; *State Fair* (J. Ferrer), 1962; *Tender Is the Night* (H. King), 1962; *Cleopatra* (Mankiewicz), 1963; *Move Over, Darling* (Gordon), 1963; *The Stripper* (Schaffner), 1963; *Take Her, She's Mine* (Koster), 1963; *Fate Is the Hunter* (Nelson), 1964; *Goodbye Charlie* (Minnelli), 1964; *The Pleasure Seekers* (Negulesco), 1964; *Rio Concho* (Douglas), 1964; *Shock Treatment* (Sanders), 1964; *What a Way to Go* (Lee Thompson), 1964; *The Agony and the Ecstasy* (Reed), 1965; *Dear Brigitte* (Koster), 1965; *Do Not Disturb* (Levy), 1965; *John Goldfarb, Please Come Home* (Lee Thompson), 1965; *Morituri* (Wicki), 1965; *The Reward* (Bourguignon), 1965; *Von Ryan's Express* (Robson), 1965; *Batman* (Martinson), 1966; *Fantastic Voyage* (Fleischer), 1966; *I Deal in Danger* (Grauman), 1966; *Our Man Flint* (Daniel Mann), 1966; *Smoky* (G. Sherman), 1966; *Stagecoach* (Douglas), 1966; *Way....Way Out* (Douglas), 1966; *Caprice* (Tashlin), 1967; *Doctor Dolittle* (Fleischer), 1967; *A Guide for the Married Man* (Kelly), 1967; *Hombre* (Ritt), 1967; *In Like Flint* (Douglas), 1967; *Tony Rome* (Douglas), 1967; *The St. Valentine's Day Massacre* (Corman), 1967; *Valley of the Dolls* (Robson), 1967; *The Flim-Flam Man* (Kershner), 1967; *Bandolero* (McLaglen), 1968; *The Boston Strangler* (Fleischer), 1968; *The Detective* (Douglas), 1968; *Planet of the Apes* (Schaffner), 1968; *Pretty Poison* (Black), 1968; *The Sweet Ride* (Hart), 1968; *The Secret Life of an American Wife* (Axelrod), 1968; *Butch Cassidy and the Sundance Kid* (Hill), 1969; *Che* (Fleischer), 1969; *Hello, Dolly* (Kelly), 1969; *Justine* (Cukor), 1969; *Daughter of the Mind* (Grauman—for TV), 1969; *Beneath the Planet of the Apes* (Post), 1970; *Beyond the Valley of the Dolls* (Meyer), 1970; *Cover Me, Babe* (Black), 1970; *M\*A\*S\*H* (Altman), 1970; *Move* (Rosenberg), 1970; *Myra Breckinridge* (Sarne), 1970; *Tora-Tora-Tora* (Fleischer, Masuda, and Fukasaku), 1970; *The Challenge* (Smithee—for TV), 1970; *Tribes* (Sargent—for TV), 1970; *Escape from the Planet of the Apes* (Taylor), 1971; *Powderkeg* (Hayes—for TV), 1971; *Fireball Forward* (Chomsky-for TV), 1972; *The Culpepper Cattle Company* (Richards), 1972; *Emperor of the North Pole* (Aldrich), 1973; *Rhinoceros* (Horgan), 1974; *The Reincarnation of Peter Proud* (Lee Thompson), 1975; *Bug* (Szwarc), 1975; *Strange New World* (Butler—for TV), 1975; *The Great Scout and Cathouse Thursday* (Taylor), 1976.

**Publications**

**By SMITH: articles**—in *Film Comment* (New York), May/June 1978.

**On SMITH: books**—*Le Decor de Film* by Leon Barsacq, Paris, 1970, as *Caligari's Cabinet and other Grand Illusions,* Boston, 1976; *Don't Say Yes Until I Finish Talking* by Mel Gussow, New York, 1971; *The World of Entertainment: Hollywood's Greatest Musicals* by Hugh Fordin, New York, 1975; *Dance in the Hollywood Musical* by Jerome Delamater, Ann Arbor, 1981; *International Dictionary of Films and Filmmakers,* Chicago and London, 1987, 1991.

\*    \*    \*

Jack Martin Smith's training in architecture at the University of Southern California prepared him well for his film design career, which had its high point in the fifteen-year period he spent at MGM designing the popular musicals produced by Arthur Freed. At MGM, Smith had the good fortune to work with the director Vincente Minnelli who was also visually oriented because of his own background as a stage designer. For Minnelli's fable-like *Yolanda and the Thief,* Smith drew upon the eighteenth-century paintings of Tiepolo; a dream sequence in the same film was patterned after Salvador Dali paintings. Elsewhere, Smith's film designs were inspired by baroque and rococo art, as was, apparently, the curvilinear ballroom furniture in Minnelli's famous *An American in Paris* (1951).

Smith's greatest talent as a designer is his technical finesse. His skill has saved film producers thousands of dollars, since they were able to film in his settings on the studios' back lots in lieu of costly on-location shooting. Smith's recreations of reality are many. At MGM, Smith designed film sets resembling turn-of-the-century Kensington Avenue for *Meet Me in St. Louis,* the top of the Empire State Building for *On the Town,* Fifth Avenue for *Easter Parade* (1948), and a full-scale paddle-wheeler for *Show Boat* (1951). Smith continued this trend at 20th Century-Fox, where he rebuilt a small Maine town for *Peyton Place* (1957) and first century B.C. Rome and Egypt for *Cleopatra.*

Just as Smith's architectural training helped him to accurately reproduce real and historical settings, it also allowed him to devise technical tricks which add to a film's visual impact. For example, he surrounded Esther Williams with blue, yellow, and red smoke in *Million Dollar Mermaid* (1952) by placing smoke pots in the swimming tank, and for this effect, he designed the necessary adjunct— an air evacuation system. For *Royal Wedding* (1951), Smith conceived the famous room in which Fred Astaire appears to be dancing on the walls and ceiling. To achieve this strange and convincing illusion, Smith put the room inside a revolving barrel and affixed the light sources, camera, and camera operator to the set.

Smith's career has illustrated a combination of skills. His sets at MGM, especially, exhibit a flair for design and a knowledge of art and historical sources. He was also gifted with the technical talent to fashion any trick or illusion that a director could desire.

—Lois Miklas

# SMITH, Oliver (Lemuel)

American stage and film designer

**Born:** Wawpawn, Wisconsin, 13 February 1918. **Education:** Pennsylvania State University, University Park, BA, 1939. **Career:** Freelance stage designer, New York, from 1941, and film designer from 1953; co-director, with Lucia Chase, of the American Ballet Theatre, New York, 1948-51; has designed for the Metropolitan Opera, Cuevas International Ballet, Biltmore Theatre, Adelphi Theatre, Playhouse Theatre, Belasco Theatre, Booth Theatre, New York City Center, and others; also designed interiors for the Waldorf-Astoria Ballroom, New York, 1962. Master instructor in scene design, School of the Arts, New York, from 1972. **Member:** National Council for the Arts, Washington, D.C., 1965-70. **Honors:** Donaldson Award, New York, 1946, 1947, 1949, 1953; New York Drama Critics Award, 1956, 1957, 1959, 1960, 1964; Antoinette

Perry (Tony) Award, New York, 1957, 1958, 1960, 1961, 1964, 1965; Sam S. Shubert Theatre Award, New York, 1960; Pennsylvania State University Distinguished Alumnus Award, 1962; Handel Medallion, New York, 1975. **Address:** 70 Willow Street, Brooklyn, New York 11201, U.S.A.

## Works

Stage productions (New York, unless noted) include—*Saratoga* (ballet for Leonid Massine), 1941; *Rodeo* (ballet for Agnes DeMille), 1942; *Rosalinda*, 1942; *Fancy Free* (ballet for Jerome Robbins), 1944; *The New Moon*, 1944; *The Perfect Marriage*, 1944; *Rhapsody*, 1944; *On the Town* (also co-produced), 1944; *Billion Dollar Baby* (also co-produced), 1945; *On Stage* (ballet for Michael Kidd), 1945; *Twilight Bar*, 1946; *No Exit* (also co-produced), 1946; *Beggar's Holiday*, 1946; *Brigadoon*, 1947; *High Button Shoes*, 1947; *The Medium* (opera), 1947; *Topaz*, 1947; *Look, Ma, I'm Dancin'!*, 1948; *Me and Molly*, 1948; *Fall River Legend* (ballet for Agnes DeMille), 1948; *Along Fifth Avenue*, 1949; *Miss Liberty*, 1949; *No Exit*, 1949; *Bless You All*, 1949; *Gentlemen Prefer Blondes* (also co-produced), 1949; *Paint Your Wagon*, 1951; *Pal Joey*, 1952; *Carnival in Flanders*, 1953; *At Home with Ethel Waters*, 1953; *In the Summerhouse*, 1953; *The Burning Glass*, 1954; *On Your Toes*, 1954; *Will Success Spoil Rock Hunter?*, 1955; *Mr. Wonderful*, 1956; *My Fair Lady*, 1956; *Auntie Mame*, 1956; *The Amazing Adele*, 1956; *Candide*, 1956; *A Clearing in the Woods* (also co-produced), 1957; *Eugenia*, 1957; *Visit to a Small Planet*, 1957; *The Saturday-Night Kid* (also co-produced), 1957; *Carousel* (revival), 1957; *The Carefree Heart*, 1957; *West Side Story*, 1957; *Jamaica*, 1957; *Time Remembered*, 1957; *Nude with Violin*, 1957; *La Traviata*, Metropolitan Opera, 1957; *Present Laughter*, 1958; *Winesburg, Ohio*, 1958; *My Fair Lady*, London, 1958; *Say Darling*, 1958; *Flower Drum Song*, 1958; *West Side Story*, London, 1958; *Juno* (also co-produced), 1959; *Destry Rides Again*, 1959; *Chéri*, 1959; *Take Me Along*, 1959; *The Sound of Music*, 1959; *Five Finger Exercise*, 1959; *Juniper and the Pagans*, 1959; *Goodbye, Charlie*, 1959; *Flower Drum Song*, London, 1960; *A Taste of Honey*, 1960; *Becket*, 1960; *The Unsinkable Molly Brown*, 1960; *Under the Yum-Yum Tree*, 1960; *Camelot*, 1961; *Martha*, Metropolitan Opera, 1961; *Show Girl* (also co-produced), 1961; *Mary, Mary*, 1961; *The Sound of Music*, London, 1961; *The Night of the Iguana*, 1961; *Sail Away*, 1961; *The Gay Life*, 1961; *Oh Dad, Poor Dad, Mama's Hung You in the Closet and I'm Feelin' So Sad*, London, 1961; *Daughter of Silence*, 1961; *Romulus*, 1962; *Sail Away*, London, 1962; *Come on Strong*, 1962; *Lord Pengo*, 1962; *Tiger, Tiger, Burning Bright* (also co-produced), 1962; *Natural Affection* (also co-produced), 1963; *Children from Their Games*, 1963; *On the Town* (also co-produced), London, 1963; *The Time of the Barracudas*, 1963; *110 in the Shade*, 1963; *Barefoot in the Park*, 1963; *The Girl Who Came to Supper*, 1963; *The Chinese Prime Minister*, 1964; *Hello, Dolly!* (also national and international companies and Australian production), 1964; *Dylan*, 1964; *In the Summerhouse* (revival), 1964; *Beckman Place*, 1964; *Ben Franklin in Paris*, 1964; *I Was Dancing*, 1964; *Luv*, 1964; *Bajour*, 1964; *Slow Dance on a Killing Ground*, 1964; *Poor Richard*, 1964; *Kelly*, 1965; *Baker Street*, 1965; *The Odd Couple*, 1965; *The Great Waltz*, 1965; *On a Clear Day You Can See Forever*, 1965; *Hot September*, 1965; *Cactus Flower*, 1965; *Barefoot in the Park*, London, 1965; *Hello, Dolly!*, London, 1965; *The Best Laid Plans*,

1966; *This Winter's Hobby*, 1966; *Show Boat*, 1966; *I Do! I Do!*, 1966; *The Star-Spangled Girl*, 1966; *The Odd Couple*, London, 1966; *110 in the Shade*, London, 1967; *Cactus Flower*, London, 1967; *Illya Darling*, 1967; *A Certain Young Man* (co-produced), 1967; *Swan Lake* (ballet re-created by David Blair), 1967; *Stephen D* (also co-produced), 1967; *Niggerlovers* (also co-produced), 1967; *Song of the Grasshopper*, 1967; *How Now, Dow Jones*, 1967; *Darling of the Day*, 1968; *Plaza Suite*, 1968; *Weekend*, 1968; *The Exercise* (also co-produced), 1968; *I Do! I Do!*, London, 1968; *Collision Course* (also co-produced) 1968; *Dear World*, 1969; *But Seriously...*, 1969; *Come Summer*, 1969; *Adaptation and Next* (also co-produced), 1969; *A Patriot for Me*, 1969; *Indians* (also co-produced), 1969; *Jimmy*, 1969; *Last of the Red Hot Lovers*, 1969; *Alice in Wonderland* (also co-produced), 1970; *Lovely Ladies, Kind Gentlemen*, 1970; *Four on a Garden*, 1971; *Prettybelle* (tour), 1971; *Candide* (tour), 1971; *Lost in the Stars*, 1972; *The Little Black Book*, 1972; *Leonard Bernstein's Mass*, 1972; *The Time of Your Life*, Washington, D.C., 1972; *Doctor Selavy's Magic Theatre* (also co-produced), 1972; *The Mother of Us All* (also co-produced) 1972; *Tricks*, 1973; *The Women*, 1973; *Gigi*, 1973; *Alice in Wonderland* (also co-produced), 1974; *Endgame* (also co-produced), 1974; *Perfect Pitch* (also co-produced), Washington, D.C., 1974; *Present Laughter* (tour), 1975; *Don't Call Back*, 1975; *Hello, Dolly!*, 1975; *The Royal Family*, 1975; *Contredances* (ballet for Glenn Tetley), 1979; *Carmelina*, 1979; *Summer Hotel*, 1980.

Film designs include—*Band Wagon* (Minnelli), 1953; *Oklahoma* (Zinnemann), 1955; *Guys and Dolls* (Mankiewicz), 1955; *Porgy and Bess* (Preminger), 1959; *Sound of Music* (Wise), 1965.

## Publications

By SMITH: **articles**—in *Dance Magazine* (New York), March 1967; *Harper's Bazaar* (New York), September 1971.

On SMITH: **books**—*The Biographical Encyclopaedia and Who's Who of the American Theatre* edited by Walter Rigdon, New York, 1966; *Le Decor de Film* by Leon Barsacq, Paris, 1970, as *Caligari's Cabinet and Other Grand Illusions*, Boston, 1976; *Who's Who in the Theatre 17* edited by Ian Herbert, Detroit, 1981.

\*     \*     \*

Oliver Smith's beginnings in design were through the ballet, an association which he keeps to this day. For American Ballet Theatre, he designed classic works such as *Swan Lake, Giselle*, and *Sleeping Beauty*, but his main function, early on, was to design new works. As a result, he was actively involved in helping to create American ballet, which had previously been predominantly European in style. The sets for *Rodeo, Fancy Free*, and *Fall River Legend*, which are still used today, exemplify Smith's artistic contribution.

Smith's theory of design focuses on the dialectic between "painterly" and "sculptural" settings—that is, between two-dimensional backdrops, which are derived from the easel painting tradition, and three-dimensional "plastic" or architectural elements. His settings use either one of these forms or, more often, an admixture to create designs that range from romantic realism to abstraction. Examples of his predominantly sculptural settings for the theater include the designs for *Dylan, Indians*, and *Night of the Iguana*, while many of

763

his other designs, although including "sculptural" elements, make use of the "painterly" approach. The backcloths of the ballets *Rodeo* and *Fancy Free* and the backdrops for the musical comedies *Hello, Dolly!* and *Baker Street* indicate the latter approach.

Smith believes that, in general, musicals should visually entertain the audience through bright, lively, attractive colors and forms, which should change rapidly and beautifully. "The design is not something to be looked at just as a static thing in itself.... It's really part of the choreography," he has stated.

This concept is evident in DeMille's ballet *Fall River Legend,* for which the setting is intrinsic to the dance movement. Through the reassembly of the main house unit, the dancers create a gallows, a church, and variations on the house. The dancers even revolve the unit 360 degrees in full view of the audience. In other examples, the colorful sets for *Hello, Dolly!* moved rapidly, but gracefully, from the feed store to the millinery shop to the Harmonia Gardens Restaurant, while in *West Side Story,* the scenes dissolved one into the other in front of the audience, yet unobtrusively. There is no doubt to anyone who has seen these productions that the sets were choreographed into the shows to become intrinsic to the presentation. Smith elevates decor to a level equal to music and dance, thereby creating harmonious combinations.

Through all of his work, however, runs a concept which he often states to his students: that a setting should be simple, free from unnecessary details and fussiness. Smith continues to influence new generations of designers through his teaching, and, ultimately, through the example of his work which is ubiquitous in many revivals, as well as showing that he continues to design.

—Tom Mikotowicz

# SNYDER, Jerome

American muralist, illustrator, and graphic designer

**Born:** New York City, 20 April 1916. **Education:** New York City schools; mainly self-taught in art and design. **Military Service:** United States Army, in Europe, 1942-46, Captain. **Family:** Married Gertrude Goodrich; sons: Rowan and Todd. **Career:** Muralist, working for the Federal Art Project, New York, 1939-41; freelance artist and graphic designer, New York, 1946-76; art director and associate editor, 1954-60, special projects director and consultant from 1960, *Sports Illustrated* magazine, New York; art director, *Scientific American* magazine, New York, from 1961. **Honors:** National Mural Competition Honour Award, San Francisco, 1940; United Nations Poster Prize, New York, 1946; Art Directors Gold Medal, New York, 1956, and Merit Award, 1960; also numerous awards from the New York Art Directors Club and the Society of Illustrators. **Died:** New York City, 2 May 1976.

## Works

"A Politician's Map of the Farm Problem" layout, for *Fortune,* New York, March, 1954.
*Mozart* record sleeve series, for the Haydn Society, Boston, 1958-59.
Boxed programme promotional kit, for CBS Radio, New York, 1959.
*The Lives and Times of Peter Cooper* (M. Gurko) book design, for Crowell, New York, 1959.

*Days to Remember* (W. Lipkind) book design, for Obolensky, New York, 1960.
*A Day in Ancient Rome* (G. Kirtland) book design, for Harcourt Brace, New York, 1961.
*Umbrellas, Hats and Wheels* (A. Rand) book design, for Harcourt Brace, New York, 1961.
*One Day in Elizabethan England* (G. Kirtland) book design, for Harcourt Brace, New York 1962.
*Scientists and Scoundrels* (R. Silverberg) book design, for Crowell, New York, 1965.
*Why the Sun Was Late* (B. Elkin) book design, for Parents' Magazine Press, New York, 1966.

## Publications

**By SNYDER: books**—(with Milton Glaser) *The Underground Gourmet,* New York, 1967; **articles**—in *Graphis* (Zurich), no. 126, 1966, no. 133, 1967, no. 142, 1969, no. 143, 1969, no. 161, 1972, no. 163, 1972, no. 174, 1974, no. 177, 1975, no. 179, 1975, no. 182, 1975; *Print* (New York), January 1969; *American Artist* (New York), October/December 1970.

**On SNYDER: books**—*Posters: 50 Artists and Designers* edited by W. H. Allner, New York, 1952; *Illustration: Aspects and Directions* by Bob Gill and John Lewis, London, 1964; *Graphis Record Covers* edited by Walter Allner, Zurich, 1974; *The Language of Graphics* by Edward Booth-Clibborn and Daniele Baroni, London, 1980.

*       *       *

Well-known for his extensive, diversified talents, self-taught Jerome Snyder established himself as an important, innovative graphic artist and illustrator. Born in New York City, Snyder embodied all the dynamic qualities of that city: respect, intelligence, wit, and determination.

Before World War II, he painted murals for the WPA Federal Art Project, then served in the United States Army for four years as a captain in an infantry unit in Europe. After teaching art for two years at the Army University in Biarritz, France, Snyder returned to the United States to enter the commercial art field and teach, influence, and inspire students at such institutions as Parsons School of Design, Cooper Union, New York's Workshop School of Advertising and Editorial Art, Pratt Institute, and Yale University.

Intelligence and humor characterize Snyder's works, including the intricate and whimsical line drawings for which he was especially known. Reminiscent of the work of such artists as Joan Miro and Paul Klee, these renderings, despite intricately detailed patterns, paradoxically create a certain simplicity, as seen on the record covers for Boston's Haydn Society. His drawings are embellished with a brocade of lines, spirals, and circles, and yet they are not lost in this complexity, partly because colors create decorative patterns. His intelligent playfulness is particularly well exemplified in his witty Mark Cross Christmas catalogue cover depicting Santa Claus at each month of the year.

Snyder correlated the complexity of his art with the complexity of postwar man and society. However, he believed that form should be enhanced, not dominated, by this complexity.

As an art director and writer, Snyder combined his knowledge with practical artistic experience. In 1954, as the first art director of *Sports Illustrated,* Snyder designed the magazine's graphic format, then went on to become art director for *Scientific American* in 1961. As a writer, Snyder wrote intelligent, informative articles for such magazines as *Graphis*; however, he is more widely known as the co-author of the popular *Underground Gourmet.* Written with designer Milton Glaser, the book's goal was to inform the public of inexpensive but good New York restaurants.

—Eumie Imm

# SOLOVIEV, Yuri

Russian industrial designer

**Born:** Kostroma, 12 January 1920. **Education:** Studied design, Poligraphic Institute, Moscow, 1938-43. **Family:** Married Ksenia Moskalenko in 1945; children: Ksenia. **Career:** Professional industrial, transport, and furniture designer, Moscow, from 1945. Founder-director and chief designer of the Architectural and Art Bureau, Ministry for Transport Industry, Moscow, 1946-56; director and chief engineer, Central Design Bureau of the Ministry for Shipbuilding, Moscow, 1956-59; expert on design, State Committee for Science and Technology of the USSR, Moscow, 1959-62; founder-director, USSR Research Institute of Industrial Design (VNIITE), Moscow, 1962-87; director and editor-in-chief, *Tekhnicheskaya Estetika* magazine, Moscow, from 1964. Organizer, ICSID Interdesign Seminar, Minsk, 1971; vice-president, 1969 and 1976, president, 1977-80, and senate member, from 1981, International Council of Societies of Industrial Design (ICSID); president, Society of Soviet Designers, Moscow, from 1987. People's Deputy, Soviet Parliament, Moscow, 1989. **Honors:** Best Design Project Prize, USSR Council of Ministers, 1980; DDR State Prize for Outstanding Merit in Design, Berlin, 1980; Design Development Prize, Mexico City, 1987; International World Design Prize, Washington, D.C., 1988; International Design Award, Japan Design Foundation, Tokyo, 1989. **Address:** Society of Soviet Designers, Arbatskaya Square 1/2, Moscow 121019, Russia.

## Works

All-metal passenger rail carriage, for the Kalinin Coach Plant, 1946 (with Y. Somov, G. Lebedev, and I. Kulakov).
Noiseless tram, for the Riga Factory, 1950.
City trolleybus, for the Uritsky Factory, 1951.
Moskva-Rostov fleet diesel-electric passenger flagship, 1951 (with G. Botcharov).
Convertible wardrobe/desk/bed furniture set, 1953 (with S. Logginiva).
Combined desk/bookcase/bed furniture set, 1953 (with S. Logginiva).
MKS-1 collapsible motor boat, 1953.
MK-3 motor boat, 1954.
*Tissa* motor boat, 1956.
*Lenin* atomic-powered icebreaker ship, 1956.
*Festival* motor boat, 1957.
Plastic motor boat for mass-production, 1958.
Official sea yacht, 1959.

## Publications

**By SOLOVIEV: books—***Industry's Requirements from the Projects of Artists and Designers,* VNIITE report, Moscow, 1964; *Mutual Influences of the Arts and Sciences in the Context of Contemporary Scientific and Technological Thought,* UNESCO symposium paper, Paris, 1968; (editor) *Methodologies of Design,* Moscow, 1983; **articles—**"On Combined Furniture" in *Wood and Timber Products Industry Journal* (Moscow), no. 8, 1954; "The International Design Conference in Aspen" in *Man: Problem Solver,* Chicago, 1961; "On a Variety of Domestic Goods" in *Tekhnicheskaya Estetika* (Moscow), no. 6, 1966; "Yuri Soloviev: Russian Industrial Designer" in *Communication Arts* (Palo Alto), September 1961; "All-Union Industrial Design Conference" in *Journal of the Industrial Design Society of America* (Great Falls, New York), no. 1, 1971; "Organization as Design" in *Industrial Design* (New York), no. 4, 1971; "Soviet Design of the Last Ten Years" in *Tekhnicheskaya Estehka,* no. 5, 1972; "Industrial Design in the USSR" in *Design Industrie* (Paris), no. 110, 1973; (with K. M. Yakuolevas-Matenkis) "On Neglected Methods of Protecting the Environment" in *Tekhnicheskaya Estetika,* no. 9, 1974; "Design Problems in the Creation of the Urban Environment" in *Tekhnicheskaya Estetika,* no. 9, 1978; "Evolution of Industrial Design in Developed Countries" in *UNIDO-ICSID India 79: Design for Development,* Ahmedabad, 1979; "Soviet Design: Progress and Problems" in *Tekhnicheskaya Estetika,* no. 4, 1982.

**On SOLOVIEV: books—***Industrial Design* by John Heskett, London, 1980; **articles—**"Russian Institute Pushes Product Planning" by H. Rausch in *Product Engineering* (New York), 1 January 1968; "That Was the Beginning" by S. Sylvestrova in *Design Issues* (Chicago), Spring 1986.

*

People are lazy by nature, and life is constantly creating difficulties which they have to overcome. With this in mind, I try to design for convenience. In the majority of cases, people would like to get more for what they are prepared to pay. I believe this is a natural human characteristic, and therefore try to design things to be easily produced. All people, consciously or unconsciously, like beautiful things; hence I make this a prime consideration in my design.

In practice, I prefer designing complex objects (passenger ships, for example), where all objects in one spatial interior are designed to help each other to better fulfill their function, and together require less space and render better service whilst affording aesthetic pleasure.

Our world is full of unnecessary or superfluous things. To produce them, we waste a lot of manpower, material, and time. I think that the designer's task is to reduce to the minimum the number of such items, to help regain a feeling of delight from contact with nature, whilst utilizing the comfort provided by scientific and technical advances to enrich our lives.

On the whole, I consider that the designer has a great responsibility in society. His professional duty is to present those proposals and solutions that would safeguard ecology and preserve national resources.

—Yuri Soloviev

*   *   *

In 1945 among the most critical problems facing the Soviet Union was restoration of the nation's severely war-damaged transportation system. When the Minister of Transport Machine Building, V. M. Malyshev, selected the Kalinin Railway Coach Company to replace old wooden passenger coaches with ones that would provide maximum comfort with minimum materials, the company in turn assigned Yuri Soloviev, a 25-year-old graduate from the Polytechnic Institute Moscow and a Doctor of Science, to head up the project. The result was a coach that borrowed heavily from aircraft technology to build a product that in competition with another proposal made by the original coach builder was judged superior and was approved for production. Soloviev and his associates had gone beyond technological problems to propose a concept that was not only attractive but also considered ergonomic factors that were often simply passed over in the past. Forty years later the same design with minor modifications was still in service in the Soviet Union as well as the German Democratic Republic.

As a result of this demonstration—that technical, aesthetic, and ergonomic considerations could be put into balance—the Architectural-Artistic Bureau was set up in 1946 within the ministry with Soloviev as director. At the time designers were called "craftsmen" because the term "designer" was considered to be seditious. Soloviev put together a team of fellow designers and technicians that began to concentrate on products to be mass-produced rather than custom-built, employing principles of comfort, economy, appearance, and production logic that are now standard practice for professional industrial designers. In short order, their assignments also included river passenger ships, excursion launches, city trolley buses, as well as furniture and interior design for the nation's atomic-powered icebreaker. These transportation projects were further expanded into other areas to include the design of interiors, furniture, and appliances for comfortable one-family flats. To assist him Soloviev called upon students from Moscow's schools of architecture, art, and engineering, thus setting the basis for industrial design education in the Soviet Union.

In 1959 the State Committee for Science and Technology invited Yuri Soloviev to propose a plan for the expansion of design to a national scale. In the course of developing his proposal, Lord Paul Reilly, Director of the British Design Council, and Raymond Loewy, a major American industrial designer, were invited to visit the Soviet Union and share their experiences with him as well as others. As a result of his proposal in 1962, the government established the USSR Research Institute of Industrial Design, VNIITE, with Soloviev as director. In 1965 the first All-Union Exhibition of Industrial Design was organized, followed by the first All-Union conference on industrial design, organized by VNIITE, with participation of designers from socialist countries. VNIITE grew into a statewide system of research laboratories and applied studios for industrial design practice, with some twelve branch offices of VNIITE across the various republics as well as 1500 design studios in industries across the country.

After the Soviet Union and the United States signed a Cultural Exchange Agreement, also in 1962, the American government sent three design exhibitions to the Soviet Union over the next six years, the first one on graphics, the second on tools and machines, and a third on industrial design. In 1967, while serving as a specialist with the last exhibition in Leningrad, the author was invited to visit VNIITE in Moscow to lecture on industrial design practice and education in the United States. Later that year, on the initiative of Soloviev with support of UNESCO, the Soviets conducted an international seminar in Tbilisi on the subject of Art and Technology. In 1969 VNIITE became a member of the International Council of Societies of Industrial Design and, in 1975, under his leadership, the biannual Congress of ICSID was staged in Moscow, with the title, "Design for Man and Society." Soloviev was elected President of ICSID for the 1978-79 term and subsequently became Senator of that organization.

Soloviev was the pioneer in organizing and holding international working seminars on design that are unique to ICSID. Called "Interdesigns," they bring together a team of foreign specialists to work with the host country team on a design problem of global interest. In 1971, Yuri Soloviev organized the first one in Minsk on the subject of baking bread and has since staged others, more than any other country, on subjects as diverse as the design of a self-sufficient small town and watchmaking. Over the years Soloviev has served as a jury member for a number of international design competitions. He has been honored for his accomplishments by the German Democratic Republic and the Mexican Academy of Design, as well as receiving the WORLDESIGN Award from the Industrial Designers Society of America.

In 1988 Yuri Soloviev left his position at VNIITE to become founding member and the first President of the Society of Soviet Designers, the only voluntary self-governing creative organization that amalgamates professional designers in the Soviet Union. Its some 2000 members are free to take on private contracts for design service to government agencies and industries. Its purpose, as stated in its charter, is "to promote designer's creative activity in aesthetic and functional perfecting of the subject area in order to improve labor, living, and leisure conditions of the Soviet people."

—Arthur J. Pulos

# SOPRANI, Luciano

Italian fashion designer

**Born:** Reggiolo, Reggio Calabria, 12 April 1946. **Education:** Educated in Guastalla, until 1959; studied at agricultural college, Guastalla, 1960-65; self-taught in design. **Career:** Assistant stylist, 1967-70, and designer, 1970-74, at Achille Maramotti's Max Mara fashion company, in Reggio Emilia and Milan; freelance fashion designer, working for Dorian, Helyett, Pims, Gruppo Finanziario Tessile, and others, in Reggio Emilia and Milan, 1975-81; founder and director of Luciano Soprani SRI fashion company, Milan, from 1981; designed collections for Basile and Gucci. **Exhibitions:** *Florida Salute to Basile,* Jordan Marsh Store, Miami, 1981. **Collections:** Museo della Moda, Parma. **Honors:** Fil d'Or Award, Festival du Lin, 1981, 1982, 1983. **Address:** Via Santo Spirito 24, 20121 Milan, Italy.

## Publications

**On SOPRANI: books**—*I Mass-Moda: Fatti e Personaggi dell'Italian Look* by Adriana Mulassano, Florence, 1979; *Leaders in Fashion* by Maria Vittoria Alfonsi, Bologna, 1983; *The Fashion Year* by Brenda Polan, London, 1983; *McDowell's Directory of*

*Twentieth Century Fashion* by Colin McDowell, London, 1984; *The Encyclopedia of Fashion from 1840 to the 1980s* by Georgina O'Hara, London, ]986.

\*

I was born into a big peasant family, a truly patriarchal family like the ones Bertolucci describes in *Novecento*. All the branches of the tree, all the generations were together, from grandparents to grandchildren. In the golden years, there were 24 of us around the table. The house no longer exists, but Reggiolo, a little village near Reggio Emilia, is still there with its medieval castle in the middle, its air of by-gone revolutions, its cooperatives, its workers' associations, and the socialist playing cards with the priest. And on Sundays, only Sunday best will do, while on feast days, new clothes are worn. Respect for oneself and for others forgo signs of exhibitionism. I owe my love for music to my grandfather, who was a keen Verdi fan, and my love for drawing to my grandmother, who used to buy me exercise books and pencils and would stand for hours and watch me sketching figures, heads, hats, and clothes.

But after I had completed secondary school at Guastalla, I had to go to agricultural school and get a diploma. I worked in this sector for a few months but was fixated on fashion. I don't know why. Maybe I had inherited this passion from my mother who adored beautiful lingerie and nice clothes. I remember some brocades, some wools, some lovely soft silks, and then I remember going to the dressmaker with my mother. Because my mother was against it, I had to learn fashion design by myself, copying clothes from magazines. Once, twice, three times. Changing, inventing, adding, and taking away. And then, after a letter to Achille Maramotti, the owner of Max Mara, I went to Reggio Emilia with a folder full of sketches. I answered his questions very shyly, and the next day at nine o'clock in the morning I was on the job. He had hired me. This was in March, 1967. I was nineteen years old. Month after month I did nothing but study, take part in the fittings, and learn the secrets of designing and cutting. And within two years, I had designed seven Max Mara collections out of fourteen.

I stayed with Max Mara until 1974. I liked it there, and I also learned a lot. I took my time and let things mature, which is a typical country habit I learned from my grandfather. Then I gradually took off on my own. Two years of freelance consulting, then new experiences. I wanted to find out who I was, what I was doing, and what I could do. I divided my time between Milan and Reggio Emilia until 1978, when I made my final move to Milan, for that was where my future was. In fact, Pims' was my first complete adventure and it included an education from the point of view of image and press relations. I then met Gigi Monti and Basile, who represented tradition, reliability, and international fashion styles. I prepared a spring/summer 1980 collection, and it was a great success. This led, in 1981, to the beginning of the Luciano Soprani signature. And it is slowly but surely being completed. Shoes, accessories, spectacles, everything was present but leather which is going to be presented next season with a well-balanced, refined touch. And in the winter of 1985, the men's line I had been working on for some time was released. I still think I have something to say.

I am fascinated by the seasons, by the birth of animals, by the passing of time. Everything that is real, natural, and precise. Definite outlines, no uncertainties. It's my peasant origin. I want wool to be wool and cotton to be cotton. I neither mix fibers nor exasperate them. You must be able to recognize them, they must be known. And I love the colours of the earth, the grays, whites, and neutral shades. They are reassuring. They are the other side of my undeniable love of the 1920s, Art Deco, the Bloomsbury group, and Vita Sackville-West. And I like travelling to South America, the Far East, and India, but I also like coming home.

—Luciano Soprani

\*       \*       \*

In 1981, Luciano Soprani, designer of high-style ready-to-wear fashions, presented the first collection under his own label. The collection assured Soprani a distinct place in recent Italian design circles, including as it did so many outstanding outfits. There were wonderful coats with fur shoulders, coats and capes in tweeds, plaids, flannels, and loden. There was his individualistic use of the layered look, with kneepants and finely tailored jackets in variations of the safari and blouson under outer layers of coat or cape. There were the poncho layerings with quietly patterned plaids and tweeds intermixed with Soprani's characteristic duck print and black and white or browns and grays. There was the so-called "choir girl look" and the "preppie" tuxedo blouse worn with short skirt. There were short, blousy pants in satins of stripes and solids.

In 1982, Soprani was busy with his vivacious, yellow and red, draped and wrapped gabardine jackets, his leather and brown tweed jackets under olive and marine-green, short, hooded coats, and his blouses with puffy sleeves worn with sleeveless jackets of leather and tweed. Among the designs he created for Basile during that same year is his combination of sable jacket under brown hooded and sleeveless blouson. It was also for Basile that Soprani came up with a stunning, all white sports outfit composed of wool challis shirt and wide-wale corduroy pants worn with undyed wool vest, wool hopsack jacket, and cozy leg warmers.

In 1983 Soprani was in a more romantic mood in his linen dresses, but continuing the layered look in his light wool gabardine jacket with pants and in his suede jacket over floral and bayadere prints for Basile. Also for the Basile collection, Soprani came up with a line of tailored clothes and sportswear which begins with the essentials of the Basile style and locates new variations for an updated feeling. For example, he adds new pocket treatments and one-inch cuffs to the characteristically loose-fitting Basile trousers, widens the cut of blousons and jackets, and enlarges collars on topcoats. This collection is a fine representation of Soprani's place in the Milanese style of the comfortable, loose, and easy-layered feel which maintains a body-consciousness in the silhouettes by draping or fitting over the form. The result is a subtle sense of the sensuous shape underneath.

—Barbara Cavaliere

# SØRENSEN, Johnny

Danish architect, interior, and furniture designer

**Born:** Helsingor, 3 February 1944. **Education:** Studied furniture design, School of Arts and Crafts (Kunsthandvaerkskolan), Copenhagen, Dip., 1967. **Family:** Married Lis Ostergard Berthelsen. **Career:** Freelance furniture designer, establishing design firm with Rud Thygesen, in Copenhagen, from 1967; has designed for Mogens Kold, Domus Danica, Erik Boisen, Per Jorgensen, Textil Lassen,

**Johnny Sørensen: seating**

Magnus Olesen, Zon International, and others. **Exhibitions:** Den Permanente, Copenhagen, 1972; Danske Kunstindustrimuseum, Copenhagen, 1976; Museum of Contemporary Crafts, Chicago, 1977; Royal Danish Embassy, Washington, D.C., 1978, Stockholm, 1980, and London, 1980, 1986; Oslo Museum of Applied Art, Norway, 1981; Nordenfjeldske Museum of Applied Art, Trondheim, Norway, 1981; *Scandinavian Modern Design 1880-1980,* Cooper-Hewitt Museum, New York, 1982 (toured); Maison du Danemark, Paris, 1982; Galerie Helan, Stockholm, 1983; Grieghallen, Bergen, Norway, 1986; *Denmark in Britain: Design and Architecture,* Business Design Centre, London, 1989; Galleria Designs, Vancouver, Canada, 1991; Axishouse, Tokyo, 1992; Grand Palais, Paris, 1993; Casaidea, Rome, 1995. **Collections:** Nordenfjeldske Kunstindustrimuseum, Trondheim; Museum of Decorative Art, Copenhagen; Olso Museum of Applied Art; Art Gallery and Museums and the Royal Pavilion, Brighton, England; Victoria and Albert Museum, London; Museum of Modern Art, New York; Staatliches Museum für angewandte Kunst, Munich. **Honors:** First Prize, Society of Cabinetmakers Exhibition, Copenhagen, 1966, 1969; Central Bank Jubilee Award, Copenhagen, 1969, 1975; Danish Furniture Fair prize, 1971; Alex Foss Industrifond Award, Copenhagen, 1976; honorary award, Danish Furniture Manufacturers Association, 1978; Danish Furniture Prize, 1978; Institute of Business Designers medal, 1978; "G-Prize," Japan, 1989; Best of Show, Design Foundation, U.S.A., 1989; Oscars Snai, France, 1991; Bruno Mathssons Prize, 1992; Design Prize Schweiz, 1993; MMi-Prize, Denmark, 1994. **Address:** Grønnegade 3, 1107 Copenhagen K., Denmark.

**Works** (with Rud Thygesen)

Upholstered furniture, for Skippers Møbler, 1967.
*King's Furniture* chairs and side table, originally presented to King Frederik IX, made by Find Christensen and Willum Larsen, 1969; range extended to include conference tables, loveseats, and many other pieces, for Botium, from 1981.
Varnished lounge furniture on wheels, for Magnus Olesen A/S, 1969.
*HG70* shelf system, for HG Møbler, Ålborg, 1970.
*Greyhound 1971* chairs and lounges, for Mogens Kold, 1971.
Tubular steel chair with canvas, for Mogens Kold, 1971.
Stacking chair and trolley, for Magnus Olesen, 1972.
Laminated easy chair and table, for Magnus Olesen, 1972.

*MO 5131* furniture range, for Magnus Olesen, 1974.

Stand, for Textil Lassen, 1974.

Salt and pepper mills and nut crackers, for PP Linie, Randers, 1974.

Aluminum salt and pepper grinders, for PP Linie, 1974.

*Uni-Set* textiles, for Centertex, 1974.

Conference table and stacking conference chair, for Magnus Olesen, 1975.

Cantilevered beech armchair with webbed seat and back, for Magnus Olesen, 1975.

Chess set and board of maple and bubinga, for PP Linie, 1975.

*EB 82* shelf system and table range, for Erik Boisen A/S, 1977.

*MO 5931* high-backed nursing home chair and *MO 4574* conference chair, for Magnus Olesen, 1978.

*8000* range of furniture, including chairs, tables, loveseats, and others, for Magnus Olesen, from 1980.

Cafe chair and table in laminated beech, for Magnus Olesen, 1982.

*MO 4554* stacking chair, for Magnus Olesen, 1982.

Desk with drawer unit, for Erik Boisen, 1982-86.

Laminated stacking chair with webbing, for Magnus Olesen, 1985.

Mobile lounge chair, for Magnus Olesen, 1986.

*EB* beech counter, desk, shelving, and divider systems, for Erik Boisen, from 1986.

*Dark Horse* tubular steel range, including tables, chairs, and clothes tree, for Botium, 1988, 1990.

*Swinger* modular sofa, for Magnus Olesen, 1988.

*Brass Band* café chair of galvanized tubular steel and brass, for Botium, 1990.

## Publications

**On SØRENSEN/THYGESEN: books**—*Rud Thygesen and Johnny Sørensen: Industry and Design* by Henrik Sten Møller, London, 1976; *Scandinavian Modern Design 1880-1980* edited by David Revere McFadden, New York, 1982; *International Design Yearbook 1985/86* edited by Robert A. M. Stern, London, 1985; *Objects One: An Account of Danish Arts and Crafts 1985/86* edited by the Objects Group, Copenhagen, 1986; *International Design Yearbook 1987/88* edited by Philippe Starck, London, 1987; *Magnus Olesen 1937-1987: A Danish Furniture Factory* by Frederik Sieck, Copenhagen, 1987; *Denmark in Britain: Design and Architecture,* exhibition catalogue with texts by Per Bernsen and others, Copenhagen, 1989; *9006 Days of Design* by Mike Rømer, Copenhagen, 1991; films—*Danish Designers Rud Thygesen and Johnny Sørensen,* Ministry of Education, 1977.

*See* THYGESEN, Rud

# SOTTSASS, Ettore, Jr.

Italian architect, interior, exhibition, and industrial designer

**Born:** Of Italian parents, in Innsbruck, Austria, 14 September 1917. **Education:** Educated in Trento and Turin, until 1934; studied architecture, at the Politecnico, Turin, Dip.Arch., 1939. **Military Service:** Served in the Italian Army, in Montenegro and Sargiaccato, 1942-45. **Family:** Married Femanda Pivano in 1949; lived with Eulalia Grau, 1970-75, and with Barbara Radice, from 1976. **Career:** Worked as a writer, associating with designer Luigi Spazzapan, in Turin, 1937-40, and with Giuseppe Pagano's group of architects, Turin, 1945; freelance architect and designer, Milan, from 1945; worked in studio of designer George Nelson, New York, 1956; design consultant, Olivetti company, Turin, from 1958; founder-member, Global Tools group, Milan, 1975, and Studio Alchymia design group, Milan, 1979; founded Sottsass Associati architectural design partnership, Milan, 1980, and Memphis design co-op, Milan, 1981; co-founder, with Christopher Radl and Ambrogio Borsani, Italiana di Communicazione publicity agency, from 1986. **Exhibitions:** Milan Triennale, from 1954; *Italy: The New Domestic Landscape,* Museum of Modern Art, New York, 1972; Internationales Design Zentrum, West Berlin, 1976 (toured); Centre de Creation Industrielle, Paris, 1976; Cooper-Hewitt Museum, New York, 1976, 1991; *Design Process Olivetti 1908-78,* University of California, Los Angeles, 1979; *Italian Re-Evolution,* La Jolla Museum of Art, California, 1982; *Design Since 1945,* Philadelphia Museum of Art, 1983; *Ettore Sottsass, Jr.: De l'objet fini à la fin de l'objet,* Centre Georges Pompidou, 1987, 1991; Salone del Mobile, Milan, 1989; *Mobili Italiani 1961-1991: Le Vaire Età dei linguaggi,* Milan, 1991; Jay Gonney Modern Art, New York, 1995. **Collections:** Philadelphia Museum of Art; Museum of Modern Art, New York. **Honors:** Compasso d'Oro Award, Milan, 1959; Honorary Doctorate, Royal College of Art, London, 1968. **Address:** Via Manzoni 14, 20121 Milan, Italy.

## Works

*Oggetti per la Casa* exhibition layouts, at the Milan Triennale, 1947.

Side table in marble and brass alloy, for Italia Disegno, 1956.

*Italian Glass* exhibition layouts, at the Milan Triennale, 1957.

*Elea 9003* electronic computer, for Olivetti, 1959.

*Prime Materials* exhibition layouts, at *Italia '61,* Turin, 1961.

*Tekne 3* electric typewriter, for Olivetti, 1962 (with Hans von Klier).

*Praxis 48* electric typewriter, for Olivetti, 1964 (with Hans von Klier).

*Lucrezia* bench with tip-up seat in walnut and white lacquer, for Poltronova, 1964-65.

*Asteroide* lamp in two-coloured perspex and aluminum, for Poltronova, 1968.

Olivetti display stand, at *La Macchina della Informazione,* Turin, 1968.

*Nefertiti* desk in plywood with white and green striped laminate, for Poltronova, 1968.

*Lettera 36* portable electric typewriter, for Olivetti, 1969.

*Valentine* portable typewriter in red ABS plastic housing, for Olivetti, 1970 (with Perry King).

*Mickey Mouse* table in ABS plastic, and chair with stain-proof upholstery, for BBB Bonacina, 1971.

*Synthesis 45* office furniture system, for Olivetti, 1971-73.

*Flying Carpet* armchair with carpet footrest, for Bedding Brevetti, 1974-75.

Sign system and graphics programme, for Fiumicino Airport, Rome, 1977.

*Consolle* table in plastic laminate, for Croff Centro Casa, 1978-79.

*Beverly* sideboard in root-wood and plastic laminate, produced by Memphis for Renzo Brugola 1981.

*Treetops* floor lamp, for Memphis, 1981.

*Tahiti* and *Ashoka* table lamps, for Memphis, 1981.

*Park Lane* circular coffee table in fiberglass and marble, produced by Memphis for Up & Up, 1983.
*Bay* table lamp, for Memphis, 1983.
*Tigris, Nilo,* and *Euphrates* vases, for Memphis, 1983.
*Schizzo, Rete,* and *Lettraset* fabrics, for Memphis, 1983.
*Hyatt* and *Mimosa* side tables, for Memphis, 1984.
*Diva* table lamp, for Memphis, 1984.
*Palm Spring* and *Holebid* tables, for Memphis, 1984.
*Freemont* and *Tartar* consoles, and *Ivory* table, for Memphis, 1985.
*Indivia, Lettuce,* and *Rucola* plates, for Memphis, 1985.
*Max* bookcase and *Donald* table, for Memphis, 1987.

(for a list of Sottsass' buildings and architectural projects, see *Contemporary Architects*)

**Publications**

**By SOTTSASS: books**—*Europe e America,* exhibition catalogue, Turin, 1946; *Arte Astratta e Concreta,* exhibition catalogue, Rome, 1948; *Ceramiche dell'tenebre,* exhibition catalogue, Milan, 1963; *Miljo for en Ny Planet,* exhibition catalogue, Stockholm, 1969; *De l'Objet Fini a la Fin de l'Objet,* exhibition catalogue, Paris, 1977; *Esercizio Formale,* Crusinallo, 1979; *Esercizio Formale II,* Milan, 1980; (with others) *Alcantara,* Milan, 1983; *Memphis Milano 1986: The Firm,* Milan, 1986; *Design Metaphors,* Milan, 1987; (with others) *Sottsass Associati,* New York, 1988; *Sottsass Ceramics,* London, 1995; **articles**—(foreword) *80s Style: Designs of the Decade* by Albrecht Bangert and Karl Michael Armer, New York, 1990; (foreword) *Fornasetti: Designer of Dreams* by Patrick Mauries, Boston, 1991; (foreword) *Ron Arad Associates: One Off Three* by Volker Abus, London, 1993; (foreword) *George Nelson: The Design of Modern Design* by Stanley Abercrombie, Cambridge, Massachusetts, 1995.

**On SOTTSASS: books**—*Forme Nuove in Italia* by Agnoldomenico Pica, Milan and Rome, 1957; *Design Italiano: I Mobili* edited by Enrichetta Ritter, Milan and Rome, 1968; *Italy: The New Domestic Landscape* by Emilio Ambasz, New York and Florence, 1972; *Il Design in Italia 1945-72* by Paolo Fossati, Turin, 1972; *Sottsass's Scrapbook* edited by Frederica Di Castro, Milan, 1976; *Il Design di Ettore Sottsass,* thesis by Milena Fornari, University of Turin, 1978; *Ettore Sottsass,* exhibition catalogue by Izzika Gaon, Jerusalem, 1978; *Ettore Sottsass Jr.: Ipotesi di Controdesign,* thesis by Simona Riva, University of Parma, 1978; *History of Modern Furniture* by Karl Mang, Stuttgart, 1978, London, 1979; *Atlante del Design Italiano 1940/l980* by Alfonso Grassi and Anty Pansera, Milan, 1980; *Memphis: The New International Style* by Barbara Radice, Milan, 1981; *Ettore Sottsass Jr.* by Penny Sparke, London, 1982; *Design Process Olivetti 1908-83,* with text by Renzo Zorzi, Milan, 1983; *Ettore Sottsass Jr.,* thesis by Philippe Thome, University of Geneva, 1984; *Ettore Sottsass: Mobili e Qualche Arredamento* edited by Guia Sambonet, Milan, 1985; *Memphis: Research, Experience, Results, Failures and Success of New Design* by Radice, New York, 1985; *Ettore Sottsass: Design Metaphors* edited by Radice, Milan, 1987; *Sottsass Associates* by Radice, Milan and New York, 1988; *Designed by Architects in the 1980s* by Juli Capella and Quim Larrea, London, 1988; *Italian Modern: A Design Heritage* by Giovanni Albera and Nicolas Monti, New York, 1989; *80s Style: Designs of the Decade* by Albrecht Bangert and Karl Michael Armer, New York, 1990; *Memphis or*

*Milan 1981-88,* exhibition catalogue, Karlsruhe, Germany, 1990; *Ettore Sottsass* by Jan Burney, London, 1991; *Ettore Sottsass: A Critical Biography* by Radice, New York, 1993; *Ettore Sottsass: Designer, Artist, Architect* by Hans Höger, Tübingen, 1993; **articles**—*New York Times,* 23 April 1992; *Design Week* (London), 22 October 1993; *Architecture d'Aujourd Hui* (Paris) April 1994; *Connaissance des Arts* (Paris), May 1994; *ID,* May-June 1994; *Oeil: Magazine International d'Art* (Paris) June 1994; *Architectural Record* (New York), July 1994; *Architectural Design* (London), no. 108, 1994.

\*　　\*　　\*

As a leading philosophical figure who continues to put out numerous design ideas and products, Ettore Sottsass Jr. has a profound influence in Italy. In fact, his influence has been particularly dramatic after becoming involved with the Memphis group. In his deliberate veering away from "serious" design to a vocabulary that is anarchic, colorful, and witty, Sottsass is attempting to return a sense of life and adventure to furniture design. When asked what he thought were the key properties of good design, Sottsass was quoted as saying that "This is a question that supposes a Platonic view of the situation. That is, that somewhere, somehow, there is a place where GOOD DESIGN is deposited. The problem, then, is to come as close as possible to that 'good design.' On the contrary, my idea when I design is to keep as near as possible to the anthropological state of things, which, in turn, is to be as near as possible to the need a society has for an image of itself."

Sottsass further suggests that the only design that is not valid for contemporary conditions is that which attempts to be timeless, to offer a permanent solution to a given problem—certainly the moral and metaphysical mission of the Bauhaus and of modernism in general. Thus, Sottsass must be seen as a rebel against the tradition of the pure and the functional and as a seeker after a richer and more poignant relationship between the consumer and the artifact.

Another important component of Sottsass' recent output has been its conscious historicism. For Memphis, the result has been a surrealistic kaleidoscope of many cultures and period styles. Art Deco interacts with freeform shapes of the 1950s, with Egyptian, neo-Classical, and with elements that can only be described as kitsch. This too is consistent with Sottsass' world view that brings together many civilizations and ideologies. It is a tribute to the extraordinary synthesizing talent of the man that what has emerged is not a chaotic mish-mash of non-style, but a smooth, glamorous, highly knowing hybrid *style*. One suspects that if it becomes the most characteristic style of the 1980s, Sottsass would be well satisfied. Certainly, it is the hitherto most colorful marriage between high design and consumer culture, the ultimate consummation of the former's 20-year flirtation with popular culture and the ironic coda to the twentieth-century's search for an appropriate style suited to industrial society.

—Peter Carlsen

# SPACE DESIGN GROUP
American architectural, interior, and graphic design firm

**Founded** by Marvin B. Affrime (born 1925), in New York City, 1958; executives have included Marvin B. Affrime, Frank R. Failla,

Leonard F. Pepi, Gerard L. Krush, Jules I. Lasky, Connie Mack Locklin, George Como, and Richard Rockstuhl. **Career:** Designed for Johns-Manville Corporation, IBM, International Paper Company, National Westminster Bank, Eastman Kodak, Air France, Lippincott & Margulies, McCann-Erickson, and others. **Honors:** *Interior Design* 100 Giants Award, 1981; Hall of Fame Award, 1986; numerous Fifth Avenue Association awards, New York. **Address:** The Space Design Group, 8 West 40th Street, New York, New York 10018, U.S.A.

## Works

Benton and Bowles headquarters, New York, 1969.
Philadelphia National Bank public facility, 1971, and offices, 1977.
Touche Ross and Company headquarters, New York, 1971.
Johns-Manville computer center and offices, and headquarters, 1971-77.
Clarendon Bank and Trust Company headquarters, Virginia, 1976.
All-Steel showrooms, New York, 1978.
Philadelphia National Corporation headquarters, 1979.
IBM data processing headquarters, White Plains, New York, 1979.
Sterling Sound graphic image program, New York, 1980.
Morgan Finnegan Pine Foley & Lee law offices, New York, 1980.
The Itkins graphic image program, New York, 1982.
International Paper Company headquarters and public plaza, New York, 1982-83, 1988.
Hotel Riverparc graphic image program, Miami, 1983.
First American Bank of Virginia headquarters, Fairfax, 1983.
Porchester Partners offices and public lobby, Pittsburgh, 1983.
National Westminster Bank North American headquarters, New York, 1983.
BBDO Worldwide headquarters, New York, 1987.
First American Metro Corporation headquarters, Virginia, 1989-90.

## Publications

On SPACE DESIGN GROUP: books—*Lighting and Its Design* by Leslie Larson, New York, 1964; *Shops and Showrooms* by Karl Kaspar, New York, 1967; *Interiors Book of Offices* edited by Jon F. Pile, New York, 1969, 1976; *The Office Book,* New York, 1982; *Corporate Design,* New York, 1983.

\*      \*      \*

The list of clients of The Space Design Group includes some of the most prestigious corporations in the United States. Although the most significant contribution to interior design has been made by the firm's superior corporate offices, clients have included firms in banking, travel, and advertising.

The firm's founding president, Marvin B. Affrime, is the key person in the organization. Several of his associates, however, have been with him from the firm's inception—and some even in a prior venture. If measured by its influence and quantity of work, the firm is lean in size. Several key associates, together with Affrime, function as a team. The firm is well organized yet consciously avoids the internal corporate structure that is the norm for large design firms. Every project is so thoroughly researched that Affrime often

surprises his clients with the knowledge and understanding that he acquires in the course of his interviews and subsequent research.

One cannot characterize the resulting work in a particular aesthetic category. Every project seems to be elegant, beautiful, and unique in some way, yet totally functional. A recent project, the executive offices for the International Paper Company, was given the almost unheard-of coverage of 28 pages in the magazine *Interior Design.* More than any other interior design firm, the Space Design Group has achieved its goal of creating buildings from the inside outward. Two of the firm's most renowned projects are the interiors of the Johns-Manville World Headquarters in Denver, Colorado, and of the First American Bank of Virginia Headquarters in Fairfax, Virginia. In both cases, the firm worked closely with the architects and essentially determined the shape of the buildings with them. Both projects were exceptionally successful because their programs originated in the people-oriented research upon which Affrime insists.

In a recent article on Affrime, the magazine *Contract* referred to him and his firm as being at the pinnacle of design. It is an opinion widely shared by critics and design professionals alike.

—Arnold Friedmann

# SPENCE, Basil (Urwin)

British architect and interior, exhibition, and furniture designer

**Born:** Of British parents, in Bombay, India, 13 August 1907. **Education:** George Watson's College, Edinburgh, 1920-25; Heriot Watt University School of Architecture, Edinburgh, 1925-29; Bartlett School of Architecture, University College, London, 1929-30. **Military Service:** British Army, 1939-45, Major. **Family:** Married Mary Joan Ferris in 1934; children: Milton and Gillian. **Career:** Assistant in the office of architect Edward Lutyens, London, 1929-30; architect, working with William Kininmonth, in the office of Rowland, Anderson, and Paul, Edinburgh, 1931-33; partner, Rowland, Anderson, and Paul, Edinburgh, 1934-37; in private architectural and design practice, Edinburgh, 1937-39, and as Basil Spence and Partners, Edinburgh, 1946-63; partnership divided into Sir Basil Spence, London, 1964-76, Spence, Glover, and Furguson, Edinburgh, 1964-74, and Spence, Bonnington, and Collins, London, 1964-70; Sir Basil Spence International (later The Sir Basil Spence Partnership), London, established 1974. Adviser to the Board of Trade for the British Industries Fair, London, 1947, 1948, and 1949; planning consultant to the universities of Edinburgh, Southampton, and Nottingham, and to Basildon, New Town, and Hoffman Wood. Professor of Architecture, University of Leeds, 1955-56; professor of architecture, Royal Academy, London, 1961-68. **Member:** Council member, 1952, vice-president, 1954-55, honorary secretary, 1956, and president, 1958-60, Royal Institute of British Architects; Fine Art Commission, London, 1956-70; treasurer, Royal Academy, London, 1962-64. **Exhibitions:** *Eye for Industry,* Victoria and Albert Museum, London, 1986. **Honors:** Fellow, Royal Institute of British Architects, 1947; Festival of Britain Award, London, 1951; Coventry Cathedral Competition Prize, 1951; Saltire Society Award, 1952; Associate of the Royal Scottish Academy, 1952; Associate, 1953, and Academician, 1960, Royal Academy of Art, London; Royal Designer for Industry, Royal Society of Arts, London, 1960; Knighted, 1960; Royal Institute of

British Architects Bronze Medal, 1962; Order of Merit, London, 1962; Honorary Fellow, Royal College of Art, London, 1962, and American Institute of Architects, 1963; City of Coventry Merit Award, 1970; Honorary Member, Accademia di San Luca, Rome, 1973; Academie d'Architecture Gold Medal, Paris, 1974. Honorary Doctorate, University of Leicester, 1963, University of Manitoba, 1963, University of Southampton, 1965. **Died:** Eye, Suffolk, 19 November 1976.

## Works

*Britain Can Make It* exhibition layouts, Victoria and Albert Museum, London, 1946.
*Enterprise Scotland* exhibition layouts, Edinburgh, 1947.
*Scottish Industries* Exhibition layouts, Glasgow, 1949.
*Allegro* chair, produced by H. Morris, 1949.
*Heavy Industries* exhibition layouts, at the Festival of Britain, South Bank, London, 1951.
Sea and Ships pavilion, at the Festival of Britain, South Bank, London, 1951.
British pavilion, at Expo 67, Montreal, 1967.
Cathedral of Saint Michael, Coventry, 1962.
British Embassy Chancery Building, Rome, 1971.

(for a complete list of Spence's buildings and architectural projects, see *Contemporary Architects*)

## Publications

**By SPENCE: books**—(with others) *Exhibition Design,* London, 1950; *The Cathedral of St. Michael, Coventry,* London, 1962; *Phoenix at Coventry: The Building of a Cathedral,* London, 1962, 1964; (with Henk Snoek) *Out of the Ashes: A Progress Through Coventry Cathedral,* London, 1963; (with others) *The Idea of a New University: An Experiment in Sussex,* London, 1964; *New Buildings in Old Cities,* Southampton, 1973.

**On SPENCE: books**—*British Furniture Today* by Erno Goldfinger, London, 1951; *Design in British Industry: A Mid-Century Survey* by Michael Farr, Cambridge, 1955; *Furniture in Britain Today* by Dennis and Barbara Young, London, 1964; *Case di Abitazione by Giampiero Aloi,* Milan, 1971; *A Century of Chair Design* edited by Frank Russell, London, 1980; *A Broken Wave: The Rebuilding of England 1940-1980* by Lionel Esher, London, 1981; *Contemporary Furniture* edited by Klaus Jurgen Sembach, Stuttgart and London, 1982; *Eye for Industry: Royal Designers for Industry 1936-1986* by Fiona MacCarthy and Patrick Nuttgens, London, 1986.

# SPENCER, Herbert

British painter, photographer, and graphic designer

**Born:** London, 22 June 1924. **Family:** Married Marianne Mols in 1954; children: Mafalda. **Career:** Freelance designer, London, from 1945; editor of *Typographica* magazine, London, 1949-67, and of the *Penrose Annual,* London, 1964-73; advisor to the Post Office Stamp Design Committee, London, 1968-94, and to the British

Telecom Design Committee, 1981-83; design consultant to W. H. Smith Limited, from 1973, Tate Gallery, London, 1981-91, and British Rail, 1984-86; also consultant designer to the Westminster Press newspapers, Lund Humphries printers, University of Leeds, University of East Anglia, Imperial War Museum, and the Royal Institute of British Architects. Director, Lund Humphries publishers, London, 1970-88. Lecturer, Central School of Arts and Crafts, London, 1949-55; senior research fellow, 1966-78, and professor of graphic arts, 1978-85, Royal College of Art, London; master of the faculty of Royal Designers for Industry, Royal Society of Arts, London 1979-81; governor, Bath Academy of Art, Corsham, 1982-83. International president, Alliance Graphique Internationale, 1971-74; vice-president, Royal Society of Arts, London, 1979-81. **Exhibitions:** Zwemmer Gallery, London, 1953; *107 Grafici dell'AGI,* Castello Sforzesco, Milan, 1974; *Eye for Industry,* Victoria and Albert Museum, London, 1986; Bleddfa Trust, Wales, 1986. **Collections:** Victoria and Albert Museum, London. **Honors:** Fellow, Society of Industrial Artists, London, 1947; Royal Designer for Industry, Royal Society of Arts, London, 1965; doctorate, 1970, and honorary fellow, 1985, Royal College of Art, London. **Address:** 75 Deodar Road, Putney, London SW15 2NU, England.

## Works

Catalogue layout and cover design, for Common Ground Limited, 1951.
Letterhead and stationery design, for Chamberlin Powell & Bon, 1954.
Letterhead and symbol, for Lund Humphries, London, 1964.
Train timetable re-design, for British Railways, 1961-62.
Logotype symbol, for Span Developments, 1965.
*5 Young Artists* exhibition catalogue design, for the British Council, 1966.
*Recent British Painting* exhibition catalogue design, for the Peter Stuyvesant Foundation, 1967.
Annual Report layout and cover design, for Bovis Holdings, 1969.
Logotype symbol, for Hamish Hamilton publishers, London, 1971.
*Vordemberge-Gildewart* exhibition catalogue design, for Annely Juda Fine Art, London, 1974.

## Publications

**By SPENCER: books**—*Design in Business Printing,* London, 1952; *Designers in Britain,* no. 4 and no. 5, London, 1954, 1957; *London's Canal,* London, 1961; *Printers and Designers,* London, 1963; *The Visible Word,* London and New York, 1969; *Pioneers of Modern Typography,* London, 1969, New York, 1970, London and Cambridge, Massachusetts, 1983; *Words, Words, Words,* London and Cologne, 1972; (with Colin Forbes) *New Alphabets A to Z,* London and New York, 1973, Paris, 1974; (with Mafalda Spencer) *The Book of Numbers,* London, 1977; *The Liberated Page,* London, 1987.

**On SPENCER: books**—*Graphic Design Britain* edited by Frederick Lambert, London, 1967; *107 Grafici dell'AGI,* with texts by Renzo Zorzi and Franco Grignani, Venice, 1974; *The Thames and Hudson Manual of Typography* by Ruari McLean, London, 1980; *Who's Who in Graphic Art* edited by Walter Amstutz,

**Vordemberge-Gildewart**

BERLIN

AMSTERDAM

HANOVER

ULM

PARIS

ZURICH

Herbert Spencer: Exhibition catalogue cover, for Annely Juda
Fine Art, London, 1974

Dubendorf, 1982; *Eye for Industry: Royal Designers for Industry
1936-1986* by Fiona McCarthy and Patrick Nuttgens, London,
1986; *Typographers on Type* by Ruari McLean, London, 1995.

\*

No matter how great the author's wisdom or how vital the message or how remarkable the printer's skill, unread print is merely a
lot of paper and a little ink. The true economics of printing must be
measured by how much is read and understood and not by how
much is produced. (*Reprinted from* The Visible Word, 1969.)

—Herbert Spencer

\*   \*   \*

Herbert Spencer's first jobs as a freelance designer show him
applying the lessons of Jan Tschichold's new typography, and his
book, *Design in Business Printing,* echoes Tschichold's
*Typographische Gestaltung* in both form and content. Spencer's
modernism, here as throughout his work, is not doctrinal and has
been expressed in forms that are accessible to a wide selection of
designers, printers, and print-buyers. His cumulative achievement
has been to diffuse, through a number of channels, reformed and
enlightened practice.

A leading theme of his first book was concern for non-book
("business") printing, and Spencer has acted as an encouraging sponsor to the generation of graphic designers who emerged in the 1950s

and 1960s. His journal *Typographica* was important for its publication of work by foreign designers, of both earlier and contemporary
generations. (The work of the prewar Continental modernists was
brought together in *Pioneers of Modern Typography.*) If historical
articles came to predominate in *Typographica*—from around the
time when Spencer became editor of *Penrose Annual*—the journal
had served, in a critical period, as a forum for discussion and had let
fresh (foreign) air into the rather stuffy British situation. The two
exhibitions *Purpose and Pleasure* (1952) and *Typography in Britain today* (1963), organized at Lund Humphries under Spencer's
direction and published in *Typographica,* were significant focussing
events in British graphic design.

The attempt to find empirically tested grounds for practice,
at which he had hinted in *Design in Business Printing,* was taken
up in the research conducted under Spencer's direction at the
Royal College of Art. Perhaps for the first time, experimental
research in this field was directed by a designer, and the published results (though inevitably limited) have had a corresponding pertinence for practising designers. *The Visible Word* was an
early, widely distributed product of this work; it provided a
well-ordered presentation of the results of previous research
and of current issues of legibility. Spencer has since gone on
within the Royal College of Art to introduce more critical, infor-
mation-oriented approaches to graphic design.

Spencer's own design work has been firmly rooted in typography and book design, though it extended to graphic design of all
kinds. It is an achievement of consistent quality.

—Robin Kinross

## SPOHN, Jurgen

German illustrator and graphic designer

**Born:** Leipzig, 10 June 1934. **Education:** Studied under Hans
Leistikow at the Hochschule für Bildende Kunste, Kassel, 1956-
61. **Career:** Freelance designer, in Berlin, from 1961; designed for
Taschenbucher/Harenberg, Siegbert Mohn Verlag, Bertelsmann
Verlag, Verlag Beltz & Gelberg, Thienemann Verlag, Neuer Finken
Verlag, Otto Maier Verlag, Bibliophilen Taschenbucher, Nishi Nura,
Running Press, and others. Professor of visual communications,
Technische Universitat, Berlin, 1961-72; professor of graphic de-
sign, Hochschule der Kunste, Berlin, from 1972. **Exhibitions:** Haus
am Lutzowplatz, Berlin, 1967, 1969; Galerie Saucke, Hamburg,
1969; Neuer Berliner Kunstverein, Berlin, 1972; Theater Foyer,
Munster, 1973; Kunstamt, Berlin-Zehlendorf, 1976; Martinihalle,
Emmerich, 1976; Berliner Festspiele Galerie, Berlin, 1983; Goethe
Institute, Madrid, 1985; Berliner Bank City Service, Berlin, 1987.
**Collections:** Kunstbibliothek, Berlin; Museum of Modem Art,
New York; Koniglijke Academie voor Kunst en Vormgeving, Den
Bosch. **Honors:** Poster Prize, *Expo 67,* Montreal, 1967; Graphik
Design Deutschland Poster Prize, 1968; Golden Apple Award, 1969,
and Plakette Award, 1987, Bratislava Biennale of Illustration;
Bronze Medal, 1970, and Albatross-Prize, 1972, 1980, Brno
Graphic Biennale; Silver Medal, Leipzig Book Fair, 1971; Deutscher
Jugendliteraturpreis, 1981; German Post Office Stamp Design Prize,
1983; Graphics Prize, Bologna Children's Book Fair, 1986. **Ad-
dress:** Tapiauer Allee 21, 1000 Berlin 19, Germany.

## Works

*Der Spielbaum* book design, for Siegbert Mohn Verlag, 1966.
*Eledil & Krokofant* book design, for Siegbert Mohn Verlag, 1967.
*Der Mini-Mini-Dusenzwerg* book design, for Bertelsmann Verlag, 1971.
*Nanu* book design, for Verlag Beltz & Gelberg, 1975.
*Der Papperlapapp-Apparat* book design, for Annette Betz Verlag, 1978.
*Herzlich grusst...* book design, for Taschenbucher/Harenberg, 1982.
*Vom Kochen* book design, for Taschenbucher/Harenberg, 1983.
*Oh, Manhattan* book design, for Taschenbucher/Harenberg, 1983.
*10 Jahre BRD in den Vereinten Nationen* postage stamp, for the German Post Office, 1983.
*Augenreise duch die Provence* book design, for Taschenbucher/ Harenberg, 1984.
*Nocturno Veneziano* book design, for Taschenbucher/Harenberg, 1984.
*London Life* book design, for Taschenbucher/Harenberg, 1985.
*Das Schnepfenkofferchen* book design, for Thienemann Verlag, 1985.
*Circus Quatsch* book design, for Neuer Finken Verlag, 1987.
*Moritz kann* book design, for Otto Maier Verlag, 1987.
*Drauf & Dran* book design, for Carlsen Verlag, 1988.
*Flausensausen* book design, for Verlag Ravensburger, 1989.
*Villen und Landhauser in Berlin* book design, for Verlag Nicolai, 1989.

## Publications

**On SPOHN: books**—*German Advertising Art* edited by Eberhard Holscher, Munich, 1967; *Plakate der Kasseler Schule,* Kassel, 1979; *Kurschner's Graphiker Handbuch,* West Berlin, 1967; *Modern Publicity,* annual, London, 1980; *Who's Who in Graphic Art* edited by Walter Amstutz, Dubendorf, 1982.

\*

Graphic design is whatever you use it for. It can consist of pretty pictures (delicious), it can serve commercial purposes, or it can try to make life and circumstances different from what they used to be. This choice is what expresses your personality. If you are lucky enough, you will find a creative metaphor that puts you in touch with people. I try to stimulate imagination and, because of this adventure, I "can't help" but be a graphic designer.

—Jurgen Spohn

# STAECK, Klaus

German illustrator and graphic designer

**Born:** Pulsnitz, near Dresden, 28 February 1938. **Education:** Educated at schools in Biterfeld, Halle/Saale, 1944-56; studied law, at the universities of Heidelberg, Hamburg, and West Berlin, Dip., 1969. **Family:** Married Ingeborg Karst in 1982. **Career:** Independent artist, book, and graphic designer, Heidelberg, from 1964; founder of Edition Tangente (now Edition Staeck) press, Heidelberg, 1965; founder and co-editor, with Peter Knorr and Siegfried

Mehnert, of *Tangente-Report* magazine, Heidelberg, 1965. Founder, Politischer Arbeitskreises student association, Heidelberg, 1961; candidate, Social Democratic Party (SPD), West Germany, 1967; chairman, lawyer, and graphics editor, Freie Hochschule für Kreativitat und Interdisziplinare Forschung, Dusseldorf, 1973. Art tutor, Studenthochhausen, Klausenpfad, Heidelberg, 1967-69; guest professor, Gesamthochschule, Kassel, 1971, and at the Gesamthochschule, University of Essen, 1981-82; professor, Kunstakademie, Dusseldorf, 1986-88. **Exhibitions:** Viola Gallery, Prague, 1965; Kunsthalle, Dusseldorf, 1973; Van Abbemuseum, Eindhoven 1975; Kunstverein, Frankfurt, 1978 (toured); Wilhelm Lehmbruck Museum, Duisburg, 1979; Henie-Onstad Kunstsenter, Oslo, 1983; Konsthall, Malmo, 1985; Kunsthalle, Darmstadt, 1986. **Collections:** Kunstverein, Heidelberg; Kunstverein, Dusseldorf; Kunsthalle, Cologne; Kaiser-Wilhelm Museum, Krefeld; Kunstmuseum, Basel; Museum des 20. Jahrhunderts, Vienna; Van Abbemuseum; Mahnsche Galerie, Brno; Kulturhuset, Stockholm; Poster Museum, Warsaw. **Honors:** Pratt Center Prize, New York, 1968; Zille Prize, Berlin, 1970; Verkehrsburo Prize, Graphic Biennale, Vienna, 1972; Forderpreis, Intergrafik Biennale, Beriin, 1976; Kritikerpreis, West Berlin, 1979; Gold Medal, Gridziadz Photomontage Biennale, Poland, 1979; Lahti Poster Biennale Prize, Finland, 1979. **Address:** Ingrimstrasse 3, Postfach 102063, 6900 Heidelberg, Germany.

## Works

*Konsumgedenktage '68* calendar, for Edition Tangente, 1967.
*NPD/SIEG/HEIL* object-book, for Edition Tangente, 1969.
*Pornografie* book design, for Anabas Verlag, 1971.
*Plakate abreissen verboten* book design, for Steidl Verlag, 1972.
*Die Reichen mussen noch reicher werden* book design, for Rowohlt Verlag, 1973.
*Gedichte/Collagen* (Boll/Staeck) book design, for Lamuv-Verlag, 1975.
*Die Kunst findet nicht im Saale statt* book design, for Rowohlt Verlag, 1976.
*Der Bonner Bildersturm* book design, for Steidl Verlag, 1976.
*Worte des Statthalters Kohl* book design, for Steidl Verlag, 1976.
*Eine Zensur findet gelegentlich statt* book design, for Steidl Verlag, 1977.
*Briefe zur Verteidigung der Republik* book design, for Rowohlt Verlag, 1977.
*Brief zur Verteidigung der burgerlichen Freiheit* book design, for Rowohlt Verlag, 1978.
*Einschlagige Worte des kandidaten Strauss* book design, for Steidl Verlag, 1979.
*Die Gedanken sind frei* book design, for Eulenspiegel-Verlag, 1981.
*Verteidigt die Republik* book design, for Steidl Verlag, 1983.

## Publications

**By STAECK: books**—*Intermedia 69,* exhibition catalogue, Heidelberg, 1969; (editor) *Befragun der Dokumenta,* Gottingen, 1972; *Der Fall Staeck,* Gottingen, 1975; *Staeck's Umwelt,* Gottingen, 1984.

**On STAECK: books**—*Kunst und Politik,* exhibition catalogue by Robert Kudielka and others, Karlsruhe, 1970; *Mail Art* by Jean-

Marc Poinsot, Paris, 1971; *Deutsche Kunst der 60er Jahre* by Jurgen Morschel, Munich, 1972; *Demonstrative Fotografie,* exhibition catalogue by Hans Gercke, Heidelberg, 1974; *Klaus Staeck: Ruckblick in Sachen Kunst und Politik,* exhibition catalogue by Dieter Adelmann and others, Frankfurt, 1978; *Images de la Revolte 1965-1975,* exhibition catalogue by Steef Davidson, Paris, 1982.

# STANKOWSKI, Anton

German painter, advertising, and graphic designer

**Born:** Gelsenkirchen, 18 June 1906. **Education:** Apprenticed as a church painter and decorator, Düsseldorf, 1921-26; studied painting under Max Burchartz, at the Folkwangschule, Essen, 1927-29. **Military Service:** Served in the German Army, 1940-45; prisoner of war, 1945-48. **Family:** Married Else Hetzler in 1933 (died, 1980). **Career:** Freelance graphic designer, working in Zürich, 1929-37; photographer and typographer at the Max Dalang agency, Zürich, 1929-37; freelance painter and designer, working in Stuttgart, from 1937; head of typography, *Stuttgarter Illustrierte* magazine, Stuttgart, 1949-51; freelance advertising and graphic designer, Stuttgart, 1951-70; partner, with Karl Duschek and O. S. Rechenauer, in Stankowski + Partner design studio, Stuttgart, from 1970; chairman of the Organizing Committee's panel for visual design, 20th Olympic Games, Munich, 1969-72. Guest instructor in visual communications, Hochschule für Gestaltung, Ulm, 1964. **Member:** Member, Deutscher Werkbund, 1953; member, 1956, German president, 1962-75, Alliance Graphique Internationale, Paris; Deutscher Künstlerbund, 1975; Verband Bildender Kunstler; Bund Deutscher Graphiker. **Exhibitions:** *Anton Stankowski,* London College of Printing, 1958; *Dokumentation der Grafik und Malerei,* Landesgewerbeamt, Stuttgart, 1962 (toured); *Documentation of Graphic Art Works of Anton Stankowski,* 1962 (toured the United States and Canada); Reuchlinhaus, Pforzheim, 1962; London College of Printing, 1968; Rosenthal AG, Selb, 1971; Stadtische Galerie Die Fahre, Saulgau, 1973; *Funktionelle Grafik und Seriegrafien,* Kunstgewerbemuseum, Zürich, 1973; *Malerei,* Club 44, La Chaux-de-Fonds, 1973; Galerie Schloss Remseck, Neckarrems, 1974, 1979; Kunstbibliothek, Berlin, 1976; *Signale und Zeichen,* Staatliche Musseen, Berlin, 1976; *Painting and visual information,* Goethe-House, New York, 1976; *Bilder und Zeichnungen,* Galerie Springer, Berlin, 1976; *Funktionelles Grafik-Design 1927-1977,* Design-Center, Stuttgart, Design-Center of Belgie, Brussels, 1977; *Fotografien,* Kunsthalle, Tübingen, 1979; *Photogalerie,* Kunsthaus, Zürich, 1979; *Malerei und Grafik,* Salon Sztuki, Lodz, 1980 (toured); Galerie Teufel, Cologne, 1980; *Fotografien,* Fachhochschule, Würzburg, 1980; Institut für Technische Form, Darmstadt, 1982; *Fotografie,* Galerie Zur Stockeregg, Zürich, 1983; *Fotografie von 1927-1939,* Galeria Balucka, Lodz and Warsaw, 1983; Deutsches Plakatmuseum, Essen, 1983; *14 Bladen Lijnen,* Print Gallery Pieter Brattinga, Amsterdam, 1984; Kunsthaus, Zürich, 1984; *Fotografie,* PPS. Galerie Grundlach, Hamburg, 1985; *Retrospecktive,* Orangerie, Kassel, 1986; Neues Rathaus, Leonberg, 1987; Städtisches Galerie Altes Theater, Ravensburg, 1988; Wilhelm-Hack-Museum, Ludwigshafen, 1988; exhibitions of life's work as commemoration of 85th birthday at Staatsgalerie, Stuttgart, Städtische Galerie, Stuttgart, Ulmer Museum, Ulm, and Institut für Auslandsbeziehungen (toured), 1991; Graf und Schelble, Basel, 1991; Kunsthaus am Moritzplatz, Berlin, 1992; Galerie am Fischmarkt,

Erfurt, 1993. **Collections:** Galerie Schloss Remseck, Neckarrems; Kunstgewerbemuseum, Zürich; Staatsgalerie, Stuttgart; Museum of Modern Art, New York. **Honors:** Bavarian Advertising Association Medal, Munich, 1958, 1959; named professor, Baden-Württemberg, 1976; Villa Massimo Prize, Rome, 1982; Anton Stankowski Foundation and Prize established, Zürich, Stuttgart, and Gelsenkirchen, 1985; Molfenter Prize, Stuttgart, 1991; Bundesverdienstkreuzes am Bande, 1991. **Address:** Menzelstrasse 92, 7000 Stuttgart 1, West Germany.

## Works

*Antikrieg* photomontage, 1927.
30 variations of mannequins, 1933.
*Wann kommen sie wieder?* poster, 1950.
Trademark, for SEL, 1954.
Advertising and graphics, for Pausa AG, 1954-74.
Advertising and graphics, for Süddeutscher Rundfunk, 1955.
Advertising and graphics, for Standard Elektrik, 1955-65.
Graphic programmes and publicity, for IBM, 1956-66.
Advertising and promotional graphics, for Viessmann, 1960-83.
Designs for the children's book, *Gucken,* 1968.
Unified graphics programme, for the 1972 Olympic Games, Munich, 1970-72.
Visual identity programme and graphics, for the Deutsche Bank, 1972-80.
Malerei in der Arkitektur, Stadthaus, Bonn, 1974.
*System einer Farbharmonie,* series of 28 pictures, 1975.
Logo and graphics programme, for the Stadthaus, Bonn, 1976.
Graphics programme and signage, for the Klinik, Göttingen, 1976.
Emblem and graphics programme, for the Savag Insurance Company, from 1978.
Visual identity programme, for the 11th Olympic Congress in Baden-Baden, 1978.
Photographs for the publication *Zahlen,* for Württembergischen Hypo, 1993 (with Heike Rambow).

## Publications

**By STANKOWSKI: books**—*Spiel und Gleichnis 1958,* print portfolio, Stuttgart, 1958; *Funktion und ihre Darstellung in der Werbegrafik,* Teufen, 1960; (with Dr. Fink) *Augenblick,* Stuttgart, 1968; *Gipfel,* print portfolio, Stuttgart, 1968; (with O. S. Rechenauer) *Augenblick: Ein Bildesbuch vom Sehen und Drücken,* Düsseldorf, 1969; (with O. S. Rechenauer) *Firmenimage,* Düsseldorf, 1969; (with Joachim Stankowski and Eugen Gomringer) *Kunst und Umwelt, Band 1: Der Pfeil—Spiel, Gleichnis, Kommunikation,* Starnberg, 1972; *Anton Stankowski: 6 Seriegrafien von 1931-1972,* graphics portfolio, Stuttgart, 1973; *Magnet Multiple,* book/object, Stuttgart, 1973; (with Günther Wirth and Eugen Gomringer) *Konkretes von Anton Stankowski,* Stuttgart, 1974; *Signet Bilder,* print portfolio, Stuttgart, 1974; *Bildpläne,* with forward by F. Seitz, Stuttgart, 1979; (with Eugen Gomringer) *Gucken,* children's book, Stuttgart, 1979; (with Peter von Kornatzki and Dr. Günther Thiem) *Gestaltungsfibel 1929-1937,* Heidelberg, 1991; (with Günther Wirth) *FormFinden,* Stuttgart, 1991.

**On STANKOWSKI: books**—*Layout: Complete Introduction to the Fundamentals of Layout* by Franz Herman Wills, Düsseldorf,

**Anton Stankowski:** *Erkundungen* **poster, 1985**

ential typographer of his time, he emerged as the forerunner and precursor of the New Photography and the Zürich school of Concrete Art. In postwar Stuttgart, he worked under exacting circumstances as a designer of trademarks, logos, sign systems, and advertising, as well as continuing his highly original studies in painting—but most importantly he became chief editor responsible for the typographic and visual layout of the outstanding picture magazine *Stuttgarter Illustrierte.*

His first important comprehensive graphic information production was the design of publicity materials for the provisions company Hill AG in Hattingen-an-der-Ruhr. From corporate signature to company stationery, packaging, posters, advertising, and other announcements, Stankowski gave visual definition to every aspect of this retail business's identity. It was at the time not so much a company identity as a real family characterisation—a unity of all visual programming. He went on to develop this precise and definitive treatment of design systems in work for Standard Elektrik, Pausa AG, International Business Machines, the Savag Insurance Company, the Deutsche Bank, and others. During the 1950s and 1960s, Stankowski began working with the Graphics Atelier on architectural information systems, colour concepts, and laminated reliefs in buildings throughout Germany. In numerous retrospective exhibitions from 1970, a unity of these apparently disparate paths of free and applied art emerges more clearly. It is now seen that the varied ideals he inherited from the Bauhaus, Russian constructivism, and De Stijl have, for half a century, in no way compromised this unity.

—George Walsh

## STARCK, Philippe (Patrick)

French architect and interior, exhibition, and industrial designer

**Born:** Paris, 18 January 1949. **Education:** Studied in the Institution Notre-Dame de Saint Croix, Neuilly-sur-Seine, until 1966; attended the Ecole Nissim de Camondo, Paris, 1966-68. **Family:** Married Brigitte Laurent in 1977 (died 1992); children: Ara. **Career:** Designer, from 1968. Founder-director, with Lino Ventura, Perce-Neige inflatable dwellings company, Paris, 1969-70; Art Director, Pierre Cardin fashion house, Paris, 1971-72, Chalet du Lac nightclub, Paris, 1973-74, and Centre Ville restaurant, Paris, 1974; Founder-director, Starck Product design company, in Montfort l'Amaury, France, from 1979; designed for Alessi, Baleri (furniture), Beneteau (boats), Dorothee Bis, Casatec, Creeks Fashion Shop, Daum (vases), Jean Claude Decaux (urban furniture), Disform (furniture), Driade (furniture), Habitat, Idée (furniture), Kansai Yamamoto, Kartell, Owo, Rateri (furniture), Sasaki, Vuitton (luggage), Thomson Consumer Electronics, from 1993, and others; Artistic Director, XO furniture company, Paris, from 1984, and Centre Culturel des Arts Plastiques, Paris, from 1986. Instructor, Domus Academy, Milan, from 1986, and École des Arts Decoratifs, Paris, from 1987. **Exhibitions:** *Art et Industrie,* Musée des Monuments Francais, Paris, 1985; *Nouveaux Plaisirs d'Architecture,* Centre Georges Pompidou, Paris, 1985; Kyoto Museum of Art, Japan, 1985; Seibu Museum of Art, Tokyo, 1985; Kadewe, West Berlin, 1986; *Neocone 18,* Chicago, 1986; Maison Descartes, Amsterdam, 1987; *Starck Mobilier,* Marseille 1987; *Les Cent*

1957, 1960, New York and London, 1965; *The New Graphic Design* by Karl Gerstner and Markus Kutter, Teufen and London, 1959; *Moderne Werbe- und Gebrauchs-Graphik* by Hans Neuburg; *An International Survey of Press Advertising* edited by Kurt Weidemann, Stuttgart and London, 1966; *Design Coordination and Corporate Image* by F. H. K. Henrion and Alan Parkin, London and New York, 1967; *Signale and Zeichen: Funktionelle Grafik 1927-1976—Anton Stankowski,* exhibition catalogue by Eckhart Berckenhagen and Manfred Kroplein, Düsseldorf, 1976; *Anton Stankowski: Das Gesamtwerk 1925-82,* with text by Stephan Wiese and others, Stuttgart, 1983; *A History of Graphic Design* by Philip B. Meggs, New York and London, 1983; *Typogramme* by H. Heissenbüttel, Leonberg, 1985; *Eigenformen* by Harald A. Held, Dauchingen, 1991.

*          *          *

Famed as a pioneer of modern advertising and graphic design, Anton Stankowski has engaged in all aspects of visual communications for half a century. After his formative studies under Max Burchartz at Essen's Folkwangschule, Stankowski spent the 1930s in Zürich where he soon established himself as a leader of experimental photography and constructive art. Already the most influ-

*Chaises,* Boulogne, 1987; *Nouvelles Tendances,* Centre Georges Pompidou, 1987; *L'Art de Vivre,* Cooper-Hewitt Museum, New York, 1989; *Les Années VIA,* Musée des Arts Décoratifs, Paris, 1990; *Mobili Italiani 1961-1991,* Salone del Mobile, Milan, 1991; *Commodes Comme Mode,* Salone Internazionale, Milan, 1995. **Collections:** Musée des Arts Décoratifs, Paris. **Honors:** Oscar du Luminaire, Paris, 1980; Carte Blanche Award, VIA, 1982; Creator of the Year, Paris, 1985; Chevalier des Arts et des Lettres, France, 1985; three furniture prizes, *Neocone 18,* Chicago, 1986; Delta de Plata Award, Barcelona, 1986; Chair Fair Award, New York, 1986; Platinum Circle Award, Chicago, 1987; *Design 87* Award, Tokyo, 1987; Grand Prix National de la Creation Industrielle, Paris, 1988; awards for hotels in the United States, 1990, 1991, 1992. **Addresses:** Starck-Ubix, 3 rue de la Roquette, 75011 Paris, France; Starck Product, 4 rue de Dion, 78 490 Montfort L'Amaury, France.

## Works

*Francesca Spanish Chair,* 1968.
La Main Bleue nightclub interiors, Paris, 1976.
Les Bains-Douches nightclub interiors, Paris, 1978.
*Ed Archer, Miss Dorn,* and *Pratfall* three-legged chairs, 1981.
President's Office and Apartment interiors, Elysee Palace, Paris, 1982.
Starck Club interiors, Dallas, Texas, 1982.
*Tippy Jackson* folding table, 1982.
Lecture Room interiors, La Villette Museum of Sciences, Paris, 1984.
Le Café Costés interiors, Paris, 1984.
Furniture collection, for 3 Suisses, Paris, 1984.
*Café Costés* chair, 1985.
*Titos Apostos* table, 1985.
Printemps department store interiors, Paris, 1986.
Cutlery, for Sasaki, 1986.
Manin Restaurant interiors, Tokyo, 1986.
Lemoult House interiors, Paris, 1987.
La Cigale interiors, Paris, 1987.
Restaurants Castel interiors, Paris, Dijon, and Nice, 1987.
Artistic direction, *International Design Yearbook,* 1987.
Royalton Hotel interiors, New York, 1988.
Arango Restaurants interiors, Madrid and Barcelona, 1988.
Laguiole Cutlery Factory interiors, France, 1988.
Naninant Apartment Block interiors, Tokyo, 1988.
*Ara* table lamp, for Flos, 1988.
Crystal, for Daum, 1988.
Design and decoration, for Hotel Royalton, New York, 1988.
*Lucifair* phallic sconce, for Flos, 1989.
Clock, for Spirale, 1989.
Toothbrush, for Fluocaril, 1989.
*Bob Dubois* wooden dining chair, for Aleph, 1989.
Domestic goods, for Alessi, 1990.
Asahi Beer Headquarters Building interiors, Tokyo, 1990.
Design and decoration, for Paramount Hotel, New York, 1990.
Teatriz Restaurant interiors, Madrid, 1990.
Plastic bottle, for Vittel, 1991.
*Super Glob* plastic chair, for Kartell, 1991.
*Royalton* chair, for Driade, 1991.
Light fixtures, for Flos, 1993.
*Delano Hotel* renovation, Miami, Florida, 1995.
*Excalibur* toilet brush, 1995.

## Publications

**By STARCK: articles**—"Café Costés" in *Passion* (Paris), February 1985; "Philippe Starck: The World's Hottest Designer Interviewed" in *Blueprint* (London), November 1985.

**On STARCK: books**—*Le Mobilier Francais* edited by Sophie Anagyros, Paris, 1980; *Le Mobilier Francais 1965-1979* edited by Gilles de Bure, Paris, 1983; *Nouvelles Tendances: Les Avant-Gardes de la Fin du XXe Siècle,* Paris, 1986; *International Design Yearbook 1988/89* edited by Arata Isozaki, London, 1988; *Starck* by Christine Colin, Liege, 1988; *Les Années VIA,* exhibition catalogue, Paris, 1990; *Philippe Starck* by Olivier Boissière, Cologne, 1991; *Au Bonheur des Formes, le Design Français 1945-1992* by François Mathey, Paris, 1992; *Architecture of Philippe Starck* by Franco Bertoni, London, 1994; **articles**—"Starck" by de Bure and O. Fillion in *Architecture Crée* (Paris), February/March 1982; "Les Habits neufs de l'Elysee" by M. Champenois in *Le Monde* (Paris), November 1983; "Temps, les sharks de Starck" by C. Colin in *L'Evenement du Jeudi* (Paris), 8 November 1984; "Starck Contrasts" in *Progressive Architecture* (New York), September 1985; "Designing Furniture in the Fast Lane" by C. Smart in *Christian Science Monitor* (Boston), 24 December 1985; "Starck Treatment" in *Homes and Gardens* (London), April 1986; "Starck and Stardom" by H. Aldersley-Williams in *Industrial Design* (New York), May/June 1987; "Paris" by I. Grant in *Interior Design* (New York), March 1988; *Domus* (Milan), no. 736, March 1992, no. 740, July/August 1992, no. 751, July/August 1993, no. 758, March 1994, no. 764, October 1994; *Abitare,* no. 306, April 1992, no. 309, July/August 1992; "Starck Lite, Starck Brite" by Marilyn Zelinsky in *Interiors* (New York), no. 152, August 1993; "Starck Staring" by Charles Hall in *Art Review* (London), no. 45, September 1993; *Novum Gebrauchsgraphik* (Munich), no. 64, October 1993; "Philippe Starck: faire du produit un ami" by Brigitte Fitoussi in *L'Architecture d'Aujourd'hui* (Paris), no. 291, February 1994; "Home Delivery!" by Jean Bond Rafferty in *Harper's Bazaar,* 9 July 1994; *Architectural Review,* November 1994.

\*     \*     \*

To be immortalized, a designer must in some way represent a specific cultural epoch. His work must capture the elusive spirit, the style, the very character of a significant portion of society. In this regard, Philippe Starck is a likely candidate as the designer to represent the latter part of this century, for those who see it as the fin-de-siecle of the 20th century. Changes have occurred—in the way we live and the way we see ourselves—without which an understanding of Starck's work would be impossible. Television, the cult of celebrity, the invasiveness of popular music, music videos, punk and new wave fashions, performance, the nightclub as cutting-edge experience, the action movie, the jet set as cultural heroes, science fiction and cyberspace, designer water, the illusionist, the dealmaker, the spectacle, the crowd, Las Vegas, and a surreal urbanity of universal objects: all of these are part of the melting pot of impressions that not only apply to contemporary lifestyle but to the very industries that capitalize on it, and thus to the ultimate success of Starck's designs.

The roots of Starck's vocabulary are "French," despite his international cult status. The last great French style was Art Deco, synonymous with a period of fast times, ecstatic surfaces, streamlined attitudes, style, and fashion, a modern elegance, a self-confident bravado, a *joi-de-vivre*. Today we have Art Starck, with a teardrop juicer (Juicy Salif, 1990), a restaurant complex that looks like a green bow of an ocean liner (Nani Nani, Tokyo, 1989), a private residence that resembles a pyramid (Maison Lemoult, Paris, 1987), chairs, tables, and assorted furniture that call to mind the legs, backs, and details of past work ranging from Eileen Gray to the great *ebenistes* like Ruhlmann. This is Starck's Deco, animated Deco that roots itself in the rational engineering and glamour of the French with an international flair for the cosmopolitan culture of fiction and the movies. Starck takes these now codified elements of Art Deco and gives them context in our society, gives them a narrative and a personality as performers in a theatrical environment.

Starck will be barely 50 when the century turns over; he will be in mid-career, yet for many of his generation he will be past his prime, past when he could connect with the ever-younger world that now embraces him. As of today, Starck has a hold on them with his interiors, the public places of orchestrated spectacle: the Café Costés (Paris, 1984) with its cinematic staircase and clock that dominates the visual proscenium; the gangsteresque Restaurant Manin (Tokyo 1987) with its black granite, velvet, and mahogany—a corporate speakeasy; the restaurant/office complex Nani Nani (Tokyo 1989); and the Asahi restaurant/bar/hall (Tokyo 1990), with its surreal appendages that seem right out of erotic science fiction. Then there are the two New York projects: the Hotel Royalton (1988) and the Paramount (1990), where a respect for the glamour of Old New York combines with a little cheek, a little subversive undermining of the visual vocabulary in favor of camp and sarcasm. All these projects have come within a short time, within a quick spurt of celebrity that thrust Starck into the spotlight like a rock star with a hit song.

Early on, Starck's personal roots suggested the signs of a different path taken. His father was in aerodynamics, the inventive sort, instilling the Citroen spirit in Philippe. Art school was but a transition on the way to building his own inflatable houses, then working for Pierre Cardin, then on what would be two influential Paris nightclubs at the height of the punk movement (great timing); out of this, a hero of the nouvelle vague emerges. He goes on to do a club in his own name—the Starck Club in Dallas, Texas—and the cult of the bavard, the bad boy of design, is forged. His working style is consistent with his image—fast, prolific, forever on the go, borrowing images and sources, working on every type of project from bottled water to architecture. Starck is an unlikely amalgam of technological ingenuity and aesthetic foolishness. He is very much of his generation: a skeptic with know-how, somewhat disillusioned but nevertheless willing to play out the existential moment.

—Sarah Bodine and Michael Dunas

# STAROWIEYSKI, Franciszek (von Biberstein)

Polish illustrator, muralist, and graphic designer

**Born:** Krakow, 8 July 1930; pseudonym, Jan Byk. **Education:** Studied painting and graphics under Wojciech Weiss and Adam Mareczynski at the School of Arts and Crafts, Krakow, 1949-52, and under Michael Bylina at the Academy of Art, Warsaw, 1952-55. **Career:** Freelance designer, Warsaw, from 1958; worked for the Kosciuszko Foundation, New York, from 1974. Visiting professor, Hochschule der Kunste, East Berlin, 1980. **Member:** Polish Artists Association, Warsaw; Alliance Graphique Internationale, Paris. **Exhibitions:** *107 Grafici dell'AGI,* Castello Sforzesco, Milan, 1974. **Honors:** Polish State Graphics Prize, Warsaw, 1953; Film Poster Prize, Warsaw Poster Biennale, 1970; Graphics Prize, Bienal de Sao Paulo, 1973; Film Poster Prize, Cannes, 1974; Annual Key Art Award, Los Angeles, 1978. **Address:** Bernardynska 23, m.75, 02-804 Warsaw, Poland.

## Works

Books illustrated include—*Varciavski slad* by L. Kruczkowski, Warsaw, 1955; *Taszent Niasto chleba* by A. Niewievow, Warsaw, 1956; *Karnawal* by S. Dygat, Warsaw, 1968; *Dziecko Przez Prysniesione* by A. Kijowski, Warsaw, 1968; *Chwila ulotna* by D. Vivant de Non, Warsaw, 1969; *Nagrobek czlekoksztaltny* by W. Sadurski, Warsaw, 1970; *Niebo Piekto* by E. Biatous, Warsaw, 1976; *Czarny Pajak,* Warsaw, 1976.

## Publications

**By STAROWIEYSKI: books**—*Plakat Polski: slownik artystow plastykow,* Warsaw, 1972; *Affiches et dessins,* exhibition catalogue, Quimper, 1979; films—*Bykowi chwala,* 1971.

**On STAROWIEYSKI: books**—*Polnische Plakatkunst* by Jozef Mroszczak, Vienna and Dusseldorf, 1962; *Who's Who in Graphic Art* edited by Walter Amstutz, Zürich, 1962, Dubendorf, 1982; *Plakat Polski* by Jerzy Wasniewski, Warsaw, 1968; *Polski Plakat Filmowy 1947-1967* by Zdzislaw Schubert, Poznan Warsaw, 1969; *A Concise History of Posters* by John Barnicoat, London, 1972; *Polish Poster Art Today* by Szymon Bojko, Warsaw, 1972; *Contemporary Polish Posters in Full Color* edited by Joseph S. Czestochowski, New York, 1979; *The Polish Poster 1970-1978,* with introduction by Schubert, Warsaw, 1979; *Polish Graphic Artists: Franek Starowieyski,* Warsaw, 1981; *A History of Graphic Design* by Philip B. Meggs, New York and London, 1983.

*         *         *

Franciszek Starowieyski.
Or Franek von Byk.
1768.
Maybe 1882.
A myth. A legend.
It seems impossible in the rigid, Communist, police-state of Poland to have an individual such as Starowieyski moving around freely.

A flamboyant, handsome man dressed with the nonchalance of a Parisian bohemian of the 1910s—with a whiff of Bavarian baron from the nineteenth-century—"Franek von Byk" sits over the cafe table reeling off his new fairytales about his adventures, aristocratic titles, his castles on the Loire, the princesses begging for his favors, purchases of antique swords and china, and so on and on. You know he's not a prince, his collection is a bit smaller than Elizabeth II's, his Maserati turns out to be a battered Fiat, and his castle is located on the top floor of an old Warsaw apartment building. But you love his stories. They overwhelm you, and everything seems true in his mouth. Moreover, his pose is an integral part of his creativity.

He lives in his own world, half Kafkaesque, half Borgesian, or from another angle, the naive world of turn-of-the-century tales about princes, castles, hunting, Monte Carlo casinos, and grand prix races. The entire picture is richly colored by the Renaissance flavor of an old master born 400 years too late. O.K., you say, but why do the Commies tolerate such an animal in a golden cage—this first-rate example of the enemy of the proletariat, self-advertising himself wildly? It is only thanks to an even wilder and more obvious talent and vision that he has.

By western standards, the Polish poster can, in general, hardly be treated as an applied art. It is too freewheeling and non-commercial. Starowieyski's work is even further apart, insofar as personal freedom, style, and total lack of limits are concerned. Since his beginnings, he has set his own standards. He is unbeatable, impossible to copy with any success. He competes against himself, goes his own ways and, in the end, he's the sole representative of the curious style he has created.

The conclusion after some 25 years of Starowieyski's activity is that he is creating one gigantic poster, a mosaic of hundreds and thousands of pieces of the same vision. The "movie" continues, despite all his shifts, meanders, ups, and downs. It's one world—or one hell, as you like—the same formula. Yet, his amazing fantasy creates new mini-worlds in the general galaxy of Starowieyski's mind. Confronted by hundreds of his works from many years, we drown helplessly in his dreamy, illusory, crazy, out-of-time ocean, made by Starowieyski or von Byk, now or a hundred years ago, who knows?

Many lesser artists try to base their work on surreal and Old Master schemes. Almost all end fatally, producing kitschy, cheap copies of something nobody can copy or follow. Starowieyski walks his high rope in a risky manner. But he doesn't fall, thanks to his masterful skills in drawing and painting, deep understanding of traditional techniques and the rules of anatomy, knowledge of calligraphy, and enormous control over color, shadow, shape, and composition. He even gets better, which is another mystery of the *enfant terrible* Franciszek Starowieyski.

A twin brother of von Byk.

Born, Florence, 1741; re-born, Bavaria, 1820; actually living in Warsaw, 1980s.

—Jan Sawka

# STEINER, Henry

American graphic designer

**Born:** Hans Steiner, in Vienna, Austria, 13 February 1934; emigrated to the United States in 1939, naturalized 1945. **Education:** Studied under William Baziotes, Doug Kingman, and Robert Motherwell, at Hunter College, New York, BFA, 1955; studied under Josef Albers, Armin Hoffman, and Paul Rand, at Yale University, New Haven, Connecticut, MFA, 1957; Sorbonne University, Paris, 1958-59. **Military Service:** Served in the United States National Guard, New York and New Haven, 1952-58. **Family:** Married Leela Singh in 1963; children: Karl and Kurt. **Career:** Design assistant, at Brownjohn, Chermayeff, and Geismar, New York, 1957; designer, with Irving Miller Incorporated, New York, 1958; art director, Societé Nationale Industrielle Publicitaire, Paris, 1959-60; design director, *Asia Magazine,* Hong Kong, 1961-63;

managing director, Graphic Communication Ltd. (later Steiner&Co.), Hong Kong, from 1964. Lecturer, Hong Kong University, from 1965. Chairman of the design advisory committee, Hong Kong Polytechnic, from 1973; founder, The Communication School, Hong Kong, 1985; vice-president, American Chamber of Commerce in Hong Kong, 1986-88; president, Alliance Graphique Internationale, from 1993. **Member:** American Institute of Graphic Arts; Alliance Graphique Internationale; Art Directors Club of New York. **Exhibitions:** *Four Hong Kong Designers,* Hong Kong Arts Centre, 1988; *Alliance Graphique Internationale Posters Show,* Blois, France, 1990; *XIV Biennale of Graphic Design Posters Show,* Brno, 1990; *Graphic Design Today,* National Museum of Modern Art, Tokyo, Japan, 1990; *The Poster in Asia,* Contemporary Masters, Hong Kong, 1992; *Private Pursuits and Public Problems,* London, 1993; Ginza Graphic Gallery, Tokyo, 1993; *70 Affiches pour le droit à la dignité des prisonniers ordinaires,* Paris, 1993; AGI Corporate Image Design Exhibition, Beijing, 1995. **Honors:** Typomundus 20 Award of Excellence, 1966; Asian Advertising Congress Creative Award, 1969, 1971, 1972, 1974; Mead Library Award of Excellence, 1969, 1970, 1973, 1974, 1975, 1977, 1981, 1983; Hong Kong Governor's Award, 1970; Brno Graphic Biennale Medal, 1972; Warsaw Poster Biennale Award, 1972, 1976; The *Times* Financial Advertising Award, London, 1974; *Communication Arts* Award of Excellence, Palo Alto, 1974, 1975, 1976, 1977, 1978, 1980, 1982; Worldstar Packaging Award, 1974; Hong Kong Designers Association Award, 1975, 1976, 1977, 1978, 1979, 1980; Merit Awards, New York Art Directors Club, 1976-90; Tehran Biennale Asian Graphics Award, 1978; Society of Typographic Arts Award of Excellence, New York, 1978, 1979, 1980; Type Directors Club of New York Award, 1979, 1981, 1987; fellow, Chartered Society of Designers, London, 1982; Bronze Medal, Book Art Biennale, Brno, 1984; TTF Paper Gold Award, Hong Kong, 1988; Association of Accredited Advertising Agents Award, Hong Kong, 1988; honorary member, New Zealand Society of Designers, 1989; Designer of the Year, Hong Kong Artists' Guild, 1990; Sponsor's Award, 33rd All-Japan Poster Exhibition, 1991; Award of Excellence, Best of International Self-Promotion, United States, 1993. **Address:** Steiner&Co., 28C Conduit Road, Hong Kong.

## Works

Corporate identity program and advertising, for *Asia Magazine,* Hong Kong, 1960-63.

Hotel corporate identity program, for the Hong Kong Hilton, 1963.

Department store corporate identity, for the Lane Crawford Company, 1964.

Ocean Terminal architectural graphics, for Hong Kong & Kowloon Wharf, 1967.

Annual reports, for the Hong Kong Bank, 1956-84.

Corporate identity program, for The Hong Kong Land Company, 1969.

Amoy Peanut Oil package design, for the Amoy Canning Corporation, 1972.

Connaught Centre architectural graphics, for The Hong Kong Land Company, 1973.

Corporate identity program, for Duty Free Shoppers International, 1974.

Banknote designs, for the Standard Chartered Bank, 1976, 83.

Corporate identity program, for The Hong Kong Telephone Company, 1978.

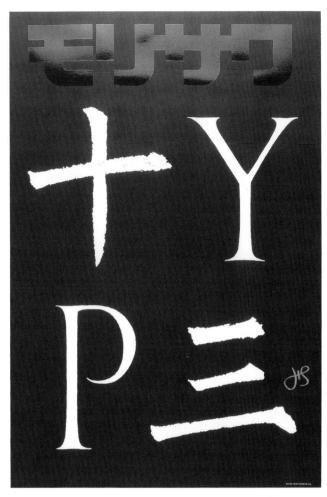

Henry Steiner: design which synthesizes examples from stone inscriptions of both Latin and Chinese writing systems into the word T Y P E. "It exemplifies my continuing interest in the contrast and fusion of iconography from East and West."— Henry Steiner (1991)

*Idea* magazine cover design, for Seibundo Shinkosha Publishing Company, 1980, 1991.

Logo and cover designs, for *Asiaweek* magazine, 1980-82.

Corporate identity program, for the Dairy Barm Company, 1982.

Four commemorative gold coins, for the Singapore Mint, 1982.

Corporate identity program, for the Hong Kong Bank, 1983.

Logo and magazine redesign, for the *Far Eastern Economic Review,* 1984, 1989.

Bond Centre architectural graphics, for First Pacific Davies (HK) Limited, 1988.

Supermarket corporate identity program, for the Wellcome Company, 1988.

Ssangyong Corporation corporate identity program, for DesignFocus Incorporated, Korea, 1989.

Corporate identity program for Ankor Group, distributor of Saab, Inveco, and Opel Cars in Hong Kong and China, 1993.

Corporate identity program, for CITIC Pacific, 1993.

"Post-Colonial" banknote design, for Standard Chartered Bank, Hong Kong, 1993.

*KreditAsia* corporate identity program, for PT KreditAsia, Indonesia, 1994.

*Millenia* office and hotel complex identity, for Pontiac Marina Ltd., Singapore, 1994.

Corporate identity program, for Gold Peak Industries (Holdings) Ltd., Hong Kong, 1995.

## Publications

**By STEINER: books**—(with Ken Haas) *Cross-Cultural Design,* New York and London, 1995; **articles**—in *Typographica* (London), no. 13, 1966; *Icographic* (London), no. 8, 1974; *Design Intercourse* (Hong Kong), March 1988; *Monthly Design* (Seoul), August 1988; *The English Journal* (Tokyo), December 1988; *Design Exchange* (Hong Kong), nos. 5, 6, 7, 8, 1989-91; "Ozmosis" in *Design Down Under 2* edited by Ray Bennett, Australia, 1991; "An Introduction to the Pacific Rim" in *Pacific Rim Design* edited by Wei Yew, Canada, 1991.

**On STEINER: books**—*Penrose Annual* edited by John Anstey, London, 1964; *Hong Kong Album,* compiled by P. C. Lee, Hong Kong, 1965; *Graphic Design of the World,* by Hideyuki Oka, Tokyo, 1974; *Form and Communication* by Walter Diethelm, Zürich, 1975; *Who's Who in Graphic Art* edited by Walter Amstutz, Dubendorf, 1982; *World Trademark and Logotypes* by Takenobu Igarashi, Tokyo, 1983, 1987; *High Tech Trademarks* by John Mendenhall, New York, 1985; *World Graphic Design Now,* vols. 1, 3, 4, and 5, Tokyo, 1987-89; *Graphis Posters* edited by Walter Herdeg, Zürich, 1988; *Shopping Bags and Wrapping Paper* edited by Seiko Okuda, Tokyo, 1988; *Photographic Art,* Hong Kong, 1989; *Business Cards 1* and 2 by Takenobu Igarashi, Tokyo, 1989, 1994; *First Choice* by Ken Cato, Tokyo, 1989; *Designers' Self Image* by Joshua Marcus, New York, 1991; *Pacific Rim Design* by Wei Yew, Canada, 1991; *New Decomas* by Motoo Nakanishi, Tokyo, 1993; *Logoword* by Paul Ibou, Belgium, 1995.

*

I can recall nothing from Vienna, but in New York there were wonderfully drawn comic books; they taught me to read English and today I see in them the influence of Ukiyo-e prints. Then there were playful subway posters and package designs by Paul Rand (his graphics led me to try my first cigar—an El Producto!), the wit and elegance of Henry Wolf's *Esquire* covers, and the tightly organized titles of Saul Bass (more exciting than the films appended to them). Overseas, there were confirmations of what I was learning: the Lettera-perfect typographic authority of Basel's illuminated shop signs; the modesty, utter correctness and clarity of the *Guides Michelin;* the endlessly varied and subtle match boxes of Tokyo.

Gabor Peterdi, my print-making teacher at Hunter and Yale, showed me how, in a multi-color print, no single block should be self-contained; each had to be incomplete and interdependent. Josef Albers taught me how to get the most effect with the least means: take one square out of a checkerboard pattern and you get a cross. Both the figure and the ground have to work. (When we criticized designs at school we spoke not of how good they looked but how they *worked.*) From Rand himself, I learned the value of analysis and the need for a clearly stated idea before beginning to sketch. He also taught me that contrast, visual and psychological, is the life-blood of a successful design.

The remarkable thing about my working life is that most of it has been spent in Hong Kong—the place you come out when you dig straight down from New York. At first, my work disseminated the attitudes then current in New York and New Haven. Later, I decided to embrace the "exotic" visual vocabulary of Asia. By analyzing and respecting it, I have been able to restore to what have seemed quaint Oriental visual cliches a dignity and conviction which has influenced a younger generation of indigenous designers.

When I first came to Hong Kong, printing was primitive and the range of typefaces (Roman and Chinese) restricted. This brought out a talent for improvisation and a preference for the challenge of working with a limited technical palette. The best of Asian art, it seems to me, has always involved lavish effort and frugal means.

My exposure to the twin vulgarities of developing world commercialism and socialist realism has reinforced a distaste for cute conventions and received, undigested styles. As much as feasible, I avoid a patronizing tone in my work. I try to bring to bear on a project the full experience of my matured self. The struggle begun in the fifties for recognition of graphic design as a profession is over: we are no longer commercial artists. Ironically, we are now in danger of becoming stuffy, making pronouncements about "market positioning," and losing sight of the basic quality which is the charm of our work—the enhancement of the quotidian.

We are here to make ordinary objects extraordinary—pleasant, useful, witty, and sometimes inspiring. Using our powers of observation and working with economy and improvisation, we battle the enemies: mediocrity, cynicism, neglect.

What matters is to send through our craft modest messages which others will receive as saying: somebody cared about this.

My book *Cross-Cultural Design* (with Ken Haas) was published in 1995 and summarizes some of the work I have done in Asia for over thirty years. Today, I find a renewed challenge in the branding of corporations, starting with my own, which was re-named Steiner&Co. in February of 1995. As current President of AGI, I am aware of the massive schism between traditional graphic practitioners (or "designosaurs") and the young turks (or "cyberpunks"). This discord has its roots largely in electronic technology and sociology. I would like to think that classic standards (albeit reinterpreted) will eventually prevail and am encouraged, for example, by the work of Adobe Systems in reviving and spreading professional, historically grounded typography through the computer. In the meantime, I continue to work in Hong Kong, in exile, awaiting with interest my second, Chinese, *Anschluss*.

—Henry Steiner

\*       \*       \*

One of the distinctions of the career of Henry Steiner is the many years he has worked in a culture foreign to his European-American training. Hong Kong is not totally Asiatic, being an outpost of the West and a focal point for a great deal of the international trade and communications in the Pacific Basin; however, Hong Kong's proximity to the Asian mainland and to the various island cultures that ring the continent have had a notable impact on Steiner's work. He has plumbed the symbology of the Orient but not allowed it to dominate. Nor has he embraced the ubiquitous international style with the fervor of many of the contemporary designers of the countries of modern Asia. Steiner's way is eclectic, picking out useful cultural emblems to enrich his work. The thought process is

no doubt the accepted designer approach, but Steiner has the overlay of the East-West interplay to his advantage.

For all of this, a most significant feature of Steiner's work is his use of the natural ingredients of a situation. He likes to create his pictures without the traditional pen-and-pencil, two-dimensional art work. For example, the cover of an annual report for a textile company is a photograph of the back of a model who wears a jacket on which are stitched the words which otherwise might have been set in type. Charts and graphs in the report are photographs of stitchery on contrasting pieces of fabric. For the Hong Kong and Shanghai Hotel annual report, Steiner had chefs at each of the group's hotels create pastry models of the hotels, then used photographs of these in the publication. Steiner designs photographs of a chalk drawing (a handsome illustration) on a brick wall, baggage and identification tags on a businessman's briefcase, toys, hand tools, anything that falls naturally into the situation. He sees richness in the world around him and makes use of all of it.

—Jerry Steimle

# STEPHENSEN, Magnus (Laessoe)
Danish architectural and industrial designer

**Born:** Copenhagen, 12 October 1903. **Education:** Studied at the Royal Academy of Fine Arts, Copenhagen, 1925-30. **Family:** Married Else Widding in 1939; children: Karl, Jens, Snorre, and Hannes. **Career:** Freelance architect and industrial designer, from 1930; designed for Kaj Bojesen, Georg Jensen, Royal Copenhagen Porcelain, Fritz Hansen, Ernst Dahl, and others. **Exhibitions:** *Nordisk Industridesign,* Kunstindustrimuseet, Oslo, 1976; Statens Kunstfond, Copenhagen, 1978; *Scandinavian Modern Design 1880-1980,* Cooper-Hewitt Museum, New York, 1982; *Design Since 1945,* Philadelphia Museum of Art, 1983. **Collections:** Louisiana Museum, Humlebaek; Kunstindustrimuseum, Copenhagen; Kunstindustrimuseet; Nordenfjeldske Kunstindustrumuseum, Trondheim; Vesterlandske Museet, Bergen; Röhsska Konstslöjdmuseet, Goteborg; Staatliches Museum, Munich; Museum für Angewandte Kunst, Munich; Kunstgewerbemuseum, Zürich; Victoria and Albert Museum, London; Metropolitan Museum of Art, New York; Museum of Modern Art, New York. **Honors:** Eckersberg Medal, Copenhagen, 1948; Gold Medal, 1952, and Grand Prize, 1954, Milan Triennale; honorary member, IDD Industrielle Designere Danmark, 1971. **Address:** Hellebopark 37, 3000 Helsingor, Denmark.

**Works**

*Dan* chair, for Fritz Hansen, 1931.
Chair in elm wood and leather, for Villadsen, c.1935.
Child's high chair, for Kaj Bojesen, 1938.
*Bregner* carpet, for Ernst Dahl's Tapetfabrik, 1943.
Coffee service in silver, for Kaj Bojesen, 1949.
*Shades* glassware, for Holmegaards Glassworks, 1950.
Covered marmalade pot in silver and cane, for Georg Jensen, 1951.
Coffee service in stainless steel, for Georg Jensen, 1952.
Teapot and covered water-jug in stainless steel, for Georg Jensen, 1953.

Teapot in sterling silver and ivory, for Georg Jensen, 1953.
Casserole dish and lid in silver, for Georg Jensen, 1954.
*Tuja* cutlery in stainless steel, for Georg Jensen, 1955.
Fondue dish and trivet in silver, for Georg Jensen, 1956.
*Patella* ceramic tablewares, for Royal Copenhagen Porcelain, 1957.
Ice bucket in stainless steel, for Georg Jensen, 1959.
*Prunella* china tableware, for Royal Copenhagen Porcelain, 1960.
*Timiana* china tableware, for Royal Copenhagen Porcelain, 1960.
*Fregat* cutlery in silver, for Georg Jensen, 1961.


## Publications

**By STEPHENSEN: books**—(with Snorre Stephensen) *Brugsting fra Japan,* Copenhagen, 1969.

**On STEPHENSEN: books**—*Moderne Danske Kunsthandvaerk* by Mogens Koch, Copenhagen, 1948; *Esempi de Decorazione Moderna de Tutto il Mondo* by Roberto Aloi, Milan, 1951; *Dansk Mobelkunst* by Viggo Sten Moller and Svend Erik Moller, Copenhagen, 1951; *Modern Danish Silver* by Esbjorn Hiort, Copenhagen, New York, and London, 1954; *Fifty Years of Danish Silver in the Georg Jensen Tradition* by Edgar J. Kaufmann Jr. and others, Copenhagen, 1956; *Made in Denmark* by Arne Karlsen and Anker Tiedmann, Copenhagen and New York, 1960; *A Treasury of Scandinavian Design* edited by Erik Zahle, New York, 1961; *Contemporary Danish Design* edited by Arne Karlsen and others, Copenhagen, 1966; *Mobilia: Georg Jensen 1866-1966* by Svend Erik Moller, Copenhagen, 1966; *Dansk Kunstindustri 1900-1950* by Viggo Sten Moller, Copenhagen, 1970; *Scandinavian Design: Objects of a Life Style* by Eileene Harrison Beer, New York and Toronto, 1975; *Magnus Stephensen: Arbejder 1930-1978,* exhibition catalogue by Hiort, Copenhagen, 1978; *History of Modern Furniture* by Karl Mang, Stuttgart, 1978, London, 1979; *Scandinavian Modern Design 1880-1980* edited by David Revere McFadden, New York, 1982; *Design Since 1945* edited by Kathryn Hiesinger and George Marcus, Philadelphia and London, 1983.

*       *       *

Magnus Stephensen is dually notable for his architectural achievements and his work in metal and ceramics. Each field, though, exhibits stylistic concerns of particular importance to this designer. In the 1940s, Stephensen was constructing low-income housing blocks in Denmark, such as his row houses at Husum (1948), which clearly illustrate his preference for structurally visible horizontals and verticals, economical materials, and open, repetitive floor plans. His silver designs for Kay Bojesen also show this pure, simple emphasis on line and on tangible volumes and spaces, and his restrained teapots of the late 1930s allow the viewer, and the user, to concentrate on the inherent beauty of the material and the ease with which they fulfill their function.

Stephensen's ardent interest in the Oriental arts is also reflected in his forms. His architecture often contains the same accent on projecting horizontal and vertical members that is characteristic of Japanese architecture. Many of his silver works have handles wrapped in bamboo, and his design shapes are often reminiscent of Japanese and Chinese ceramic forms. He worked at the Royal Copenhagen porcelain factory following a period in which it produced works of an extreme Oriental flavor, and undoubtedly the

impact of this work, along with his subsequent research and travels in the Far East, accounts for the Oriental character of his works.

His later works for Georg Jensen, including his 1951 serving bucket and salad set, show greater individuality. His technical excellence and important stature in the Scandinavian design world increasingly led to a freedom that aided him in producing works which could be recognized at first sight as his alone, not merely the work of one designer among many in a workshop. These later works were distinguished by more pronounced curves and more clearly defined edges, for instance. Like other important Scandinavian designers of the 1930s, 1940s, and 1950s, Stephensen helped to mend the gap between the forces of straightforward functionalism and those of artistic elegance. In his works, the two ideas went hand in hand.

—Virginia A. Rose


# STERN, Robert A. M.
American architect

**Born:** New York City, 23 May 1939. **Education:** Columbia University, New York, B.A., 1960; Yale University, New Haven, Connecticut, M.Arch., 1965. **Family:** Married Lynn Solinger in 1966 (divorced, 1978); children: Nicholas. **Career:** Worked for the Perkins and Will Partnership, Washington, D.C., 1964; program director, Architectural League of New York, 1965-66; designer, Office of Richard Meier, New York, 1966; consultant to Philip Johnson for *Eye on New York* television documentary, CBS-TV, 1966-67; member, Mayor Lindsay's Task Force on Urban Design, 1966-67; consultant, Small Parks Program, New York, 1966-70; urban designer and assistant for design policy to Assistant Administrator Samuel Ratensky, Housing and Development Administration, New York, 1967-70; partner, Robert A. M. Stern and John S. Hagmann, architects, New York, 1969-77; principal. Robert A. M. Stern Architects, New York, from 1977. Lecturer, 1970-72, assistant professor, 1973-77, associate professor, 1977-82, professor, from 1982, and director of the Temple Hoyne Buell Center for the Study of American Architecture, from 1984, Columbia University, New York; William Henry Bishop Visiting Professor, Yale University, 1978. Vice-president, Cunningham Dance Foundation, 1969-73; Mayor's Panel of Architects, New York, from 1975; editorial consultant, Architectural History Foundation, New York, 1979-83. Exhibition organizer for *40 under 40,* American Federation of the Arts travelling exhibition, 1966; *Another Chance for Cities,* Whitney Museum, New York, and tour, 1970-71; *Some Younger New York Architects,* Columbia University and Boston Architectural Center, 1971-72; *Ornament in the 20th Century,* Cooper-Hewitt Museum, New York, Fall 1978; *Trends in Contemporary Architecture New Gallery of Contemporary Art,* Cleveland, 1978. **Member:** Trustee, American Federation of the Arts, from 1967; board of directors, Yale Arts Association, 1968-72; architecture committee, Whitney Museum, New York, 1970-76; president, 1973-77, and executive committee member from 1977, Architectural League of New York; visiting fellow, 1974-76, Architectural Education Program advisor, 1974-77, and trustee, from 1983, Institute for Architecture and Urban Studies, New York; board member, Society of Architectural Historians, New York, 1975-78; director, New York Chapter, American Institute of Architects, 1976-78; board member, Preservation League of New York, from 1984. **Exhibitions:** *Roosevelt Island Competition,* Architectural League of New York, 1975; North Carolina School of Design, Raleigh, 1976; Biennale, Venice, 1976; *Palaces for the People,* Cooper-Hewitt Museum, New York, 1977; *Drawing Toward a More Modern Architecture,* Drawing Center and Cooper-Hewitt Museum, New York, 1977; *Art and Contemporary Architecture,* David Findlay Galleries, New York, 1977; Art Net, London, 1977; Architectural Club, Miami, 1978; *Celebration of Water,* Cooper-Hewitt Museum, New York, 1978; *Transformations in Modern Architecture,* Museum of Modem Art, New York, 1979; *City Segments,* Walker Art Center, Minneapolis, 1980; *Speaking a New Classicism,* Smith College, Northampton, Massachusetts, 1981; *Collaboration: Artists and Architects,* Architectural League of New York, 1981; *Post-Modernism Comes to England,* Architectural Design Gallery, London, 1981; Young Hoffman Gallery, Chicago, 1981; Neuberger Museum, State University of New York at Purchase, 1982; *Ornamentalism,* Hudson River Museum, Yonkers, New York, 1983 (travelled to the Fendrick Gallery, Washington, D.C., and University of Texas, Austin); *A Tribute to Contemporary Architecture,* University Place Gallery, Cambridge, Massachusetts, 1984; *Ideas/Ideal/Deal/Real,* University of Maryland, College Park, 1985. **Collections:** Tehran Museum of Contemporary Art. **Honors:** Award of Honor, New York Society of Architects, 1974; First Prize, Roosevelt Island Housing Competition, New York, 1975; Certificate of Honor, New York State Association of Architects, 1975; Certificate of Merit, New York State Association of Architects/American Institute of Architects, 1976; Award of Merit, *House and Home*/AIA, 1977; Residential Design Award, AIA, New York Chapter, 1977; First Honor Award, Homes for Better Living, *Housing,* 1978; Lumen Award, New York Section, Illuminating Engineering Society/International Association of Lighting Designers, 1978, 1982, 1983; National Honor Award, American Institute of Architects, 1980, 1985; Distinguished Architecture Award, 1982, 1984 (2), 1985, and Medal of Honor, 1984, American Institute of Architects, New York Chapter; *Interiors* Award, New York, 1982, 1985; *Builder Magazine* Award, New York, 1984; First Honor Award, American Institute of Architects, Westchester/Mid-Hudson Chapter, 1984; Award of Excellence, *Architectural Record,* New York, 1984; fellow, American Institute of Architects, 1984. **Address:** Robert A. M. Stern Architects, 211 West 61st Street, New York, New York 10023, U.S.A.

## Publications

By STERN: *40 Under 40: Young Talent in Architecture,* exhibition catalogue, New York, 1966; *New Directions in American Architecture,* New York, 1969, 1977; *George Howe: Toward a Modern American Architecture,* New Haven, Connecticut, 1975; (introduction) *The PSFS Building* (booklet), Philadelphia, 1976; (foreword, with Wilder Green) *200 Years of American Architectural Drawing* by David Gebhard and Deborah Nevins, New York, 1977; (with others) *Europa/America: Architetture Urbane Alternative Suburbane,* Biennale exhibition catalogue, Venice, 1978; (commentary) *Philip Johnson: Collected Writings,* New York, 1979; (with Deborah Nevins) *The Artist's Eye: American Architectural Drawings, 1779-1979,* New York, 1979; (editor, with John Montague Massengale) *The Anglo-American Suburb,* London, 1981; (with Thomas P. Catalano) *Raymond Hood,* New York, 1982; (with Clay Lancaster and Robert Hefner) *East Hampton's Heritage,* New York, 1982; (with Gregory Gilmartin and John M. Massengale) *New York*

*1900: Metropolitan Architecture and Urbanism, 1890-1915,* New York, 1983; (with Gilmartin and Thomas Mellins) *New York 1930: Architecture and Urbanism between the Two World Wars,* New York, 1987; (with Thomas Mellins and Raymond Gastil) *Pride of Place: Building the American Dream,* New York, Boston, 1986; *Modern Classicism,* London, 1988; *Robert A. M. Stern: Selected Works,* London, New York, 1991; *Robert A. M. Stern: Buildings and Projects, 1987-1992* edited by Elizabeth Kraft, introduction by Vincent Scully, New York, 1992; articles-"PSFS: Beaux Arts Theory and Rational Expressionism" in *Journal of the Society of Architectural Historians* (Philadelphia), May 1962; "Relevance of the Decade 1929-1939" in *Journal of the Society of Architectural Historians* (Philadelphia), March 1965; "Paul Rudolph: The First Twenty-Five Years" in *Kokusai Kenchiku* (Tokyo), May 1965; (editor) *Perspecta* (New Haven, Connecticut), no. 9/10, 1965; "Constitution Plaza One Year After" in *Progressive Architecture* (New York), December 1965; "A Static Gallery" in *Progressive Architecture* (New York), April 1966; "Random Shots at USA 65" in *Progressive Architecture* (New York), May 1966; "Stompin' at the Savoye" in *Architectural Forum* (New York), May 1973; "Tape Recorder Chats" in *Architectural Record* (New York), May 1973; "Raymond Hood" in *Progressive Architecture* (New York), July 1974; "Yale 1950-1965" in *Oppositions* (New York), October 1974; "Toward an Architecture of Symbolic Assemblage" in *Progressive Architecture* (New York), April 1975; (editor) "White and Gray," special issue of *Architecture + Urbanism* (Tokyo), April 1975; "A Serious Discussion of an Apparently Whimsical House" in *Architectural Record* (New York), July 1975; "Park Avenue Is Almost All Right (Maybe)" in *Architectural Record* (New York), February 1976; "Letter to the Editor" in *Oppositions* (New York), Winter 1976; "Robert Stern on Jim Stirling" in *Design Quarterly 100* (Minneapolis), Spring 1976; "Gray Architecture: Quelques Variations Post-Modernistes Autour de l'Orthodoxie" in *L'Architecture d'Aujourdhui* (Paris), August/Septemher 1976; (guest editor) "40 Under 40 + 1O," special issue of *Architecture + Urbanism* (Tokyo), January 1977; "At the Edge of Modernism" in *Architectural Design* (London), April 1977; "Forum: The Beaux Arts Exhibition" in *Oppositions* (New York), Spring 1977; "Letter to the Editor" in *Contract Interiors* (New York), July 1977; (with George Baird and Charles Jencks) "Further Thoughts on Millbank" in *Architectural Design* (London), July/August 1977; "Report: New York Notebook" in *Architecture + Urbanism* (Tokyo), August 1977; "The Evolution of Philip Johnson's Glass House, 1947-48" in *Oppositions* (New York), Fall 1977; "Something Borrowed, Something New" in *Horizon* (New York), December 1977; "After the Modern Movement" in *The Japan Architect* (Tokyo), December 1977; "Venturi and Rauch: Learning to Love Them" in *Architectural Monographs* (London), vol. 1, 1978; "New Directions in Modern American Architecture: Postscript" in *Architectural Association Quarterly* (London), no. 2/3, 1978; "The Suburban Alternative: Coping with the Middle City" in *Architectural Record* (New York), August 1978; "How to Redesign New York" in *Art News* (New York), November 1978; "Models for Reality: Some Observations" in *Great Models* (student publication, North Carolina State University School of Design, Raleigh), no. 27, 1978; (with Frances Halsband, R. M. Kliment, and Richard B. Oliver) "Drawing from Models" in *Journal of Architectural Education* (Washington, D.C.), September 1978; "Doubles of Post-Modern" in *Harvard Architecture Review* (Cambridge, Massachusetts), vol. 1, 1979; "With Rhetoric: The New York Apartment House" in *Via* (Philadelphia), vol. 4, 1980; "Interview: Robert A. M. Stern" by Jay Murphy in *Dimen-*

*sions* (Lincoln, Nebraska), vol. 2, no. 1, 1981; "Behind the Facades," interview by Charles Gandee in *Architectural Record* (New York), March 1981; "An Interview with Robert A. M. Stern" in *Crit* (Washington, D.C.), Spring 1981; "Robert Stern on Modern Architecture" in *Architect and Builder* (Cape Town, South Africa), April 1982; "Duplications of Post-Modernism" in *Arquitectura* (Madrid), September/October 1982; "The Temple of Love and Other Musings," interview in *Historic Preservation* (Washington, D.C.), September/October 1982; "Robert Stern and Michael Graves," interview by Katherine Dolgy, in *Fifth Column* (Montreal), Fall 1983; recordings—*The Presence of the Past,* tape cassette and slides, London, 1980; films—*Pride of Place: Suburbs: Arcadia for Everyone,* and *The Garden and the Grid,* Films for the Humanities, Princeton, New Jersey, 1986.

**On STERN: books**—*The Roosevelt Island Competition,* exhibition catalogue edited by Barbara Goldstein, New York 1975; *Wohnen im Eigenen Haus* by Gerhard Schwab, Stuttgart 1976; *The Form of Housing,* edited by Sam Davis, New York 1977; *The Language of Post-Modern Architecture* by Charles Jencks, London 1977; *Decorative Art and Modern Interiors 1978,* edited by Maria Schofield, New York 1978; *Post-Modern Classicism* by Charles Jencks, London 1980; *American Architecture Now,* edited by Barbaralee Diamonstein, New York 1980; *Robert A. M. Stern 1965-1980: Toward a Modern Architecture after Modernism,* edited by Peter Arnell and Ted Bickford, New York 1981; *Robert Stern,* edited by David Dunster, with introduction by Vincent Scully, London 1981; *After Modern Architecture* by Paolo Portoghesi, New York 1982; *The Charlottesville Tapes,* edited by Jaquelin Robertson, New York 1985; *Robert A. M. Stern: A Bibliography* by Mary Ellen Huls, Monticello, Illinois, 1987; **articles**—"Lang Residence: Where Are We Now, Vincent Scully?" by Charles Moore in *Progressive Architecture* (New York), April 1975; "Residence for an Academical Couple, Washington, Connecticut, 1973-74" in *Architecture + Urbanism* (Tokyo), April 1975; "The Work of Robert A. M. Stern and John S. Hagmann" in *Architecture + Urbanism* (Tokyo), October 1975; "Stern Dimensions" in *Progressive Architecture* (New York), June 1976; "Les Cendres de Jefferson" by Manfredo Tafuri and "Robert Stern/John Hagmann" in *L'Architecture d'Aujourd'hui* (Paris), August/September 1976; "Architecture: Letting Go with Color" in *House and Garden* (New York), September 1976; "Stern Star Estrella: La Obra de Robert A.M. Stern" in *Arquitecturas Bis* (Barcelona), September 1976; "40 under 40: Robert A. M. Stern" in *Architecture + Urbanism* (Tokyo), January 1977; "Grand Allusions" by Suzanne Stephens in *Progressive Architecture* (New York), February 1977; "The Stern View" by Jane Holtz Kay in *Building Design* (London), 11 February 1977; "Robert A. M. Stern's Two Houses" by Paul Goldberger in *Architecture + Urbanism* (Tokyo), September 1977; "The Re-emergence of Color as a Design Tool" by Nory Miller in *AIA Journal* (Washington, D.C.), October 1978; "Designs for Living" by Douglas Davis in *Newsweek* (New York), 6 November 1978; "U.S. Architects: Doing Their Own Thing" by Robert Hughes in *Time* (New York), 8 January 1979; "The Doubles of Post-Modern" in *Harvard Architecture Review* (Cambridge, Massachusetts), Spring 1980; "Robert A. M. Stern Projects" in *Controspazio* (Bari, Italy), April/June 1981; "Five Projects of Robert A. M. Stern" in *Architecture + Urbanism* (Tokyo), June 1981; "Robert A. M. Stern-From *Perspecta* to Post-Modern" in *Architectural Design* (London), vol. 51, no. 12, 1981; "The Maturing of Robert Stern" by Paul Goldberger in the *New York Times,* 4 April 1982; "Robert A. M, Stern" in *Architecture South Africa* (Cape

Town), May/June 1982; "Three Interiors by Robert Stern" in *Architectural Review* (London), July 1982; "The Residential Works of Robert A. M. Stern", special issue of *Architecture + Urbanism* (Tokyo), July 1982; "Decoration Is Not a Crime" in *Connaissance des Arts* (Paris), May 1983; "Architecture: Robert A. M. Stern" by Vincent Scully in *Architectural Digest* (Los Angeles), June 1984; "The Trend-Setting Traditionalism of Architect Robert A. M. Stern" by Carol Vogel in *New York Times Sunday Magazine,* 13 January 1985.

\*        \*        \*

Robert Stern combines a significant and prestigious architectural practice with an interwoven and quite prolific writing career. Stern's earliest journalistic contributions include the editorship of issue 9/10 of *Perspecta: The Yale Architectural Journal,* which included selections from one of the twentieth century's most significant writings on architecture, "Complexity and Contradiction in Architecture," the then soon-to-be-published theories of architect Robert Venturi. In 1969 Stern authored *New Directions in American Architecture,* presenting seven American "third generation modern architects" as successors to first generation (Le Corbusier, Frank Lloyd Wright) and second generation post-war architects. Both literary contributions were timely and well received, establishing Stern as an authority on American architecture. Subsequently, Stern has delivered a Public Television series on American architecture entitled "Pride of Place," and published a multi-volume series on New York architecture.

Stern originally founded his architectural practice in 1969 with partner John S. Hagmann; it later became the office of Robert A. M. Stern in 1977. He concentrated largely on residential commissions for wealthy clients in New York and New England. These early commissions are influenced heavily by the Shingle style of architecture indigenous to the Northeast coastline and also owe much to the emerging "post-modernist" movement in architecture instigated in part by Venturi's "Complexity and Contradiction in Architecture" and played out by architects such as Michael Graves and Charles Moore, among others. Stern was to become one of the chief proponents of Post-Modernism along with Graves and architectural trendsetter Philip Johnson, with whom Stern had collaborated on several writing and exhibit projects in New York.

The epitome of Stern's early work is the Lang Residence in Connecticut. The house is a series of modernist boxes and intersecting planes with applied decoration that in the architect's words are a "witty recollection of older modes of architectural expression. Is this a neo-Palladian Regency Art Deco farmhouse?" This applied ornament, along with a plan that owes much to Robert Venturi's seminal earlier house for his mother in Chestnut Hill, Pennsylvania, make an elegant statement and set the tone for much of Stern's architecture. Such commissions have continued to the present and the office is an acknowledged expert for large residential projects, appearing regularly in style-setting magazines such as *Architectural Digest.* In 1994, the office of Robert A. M. Stern was also hired to design the first in a series of "American Homes" for *Life* magazine—surely a milestone to be recognized by such an American cultural barometer as *Life.*

Stern's office has also received many corporate and institutional architectural projects. The most significant of these are from the Walt Disney Companies, for whom Stern has become an active participant in the development of projects. Stern himself has designed hotels, visitor centers, and offices for Disney in Paris, Florida, and California, where he was responsible for the charming Disney Feature Animation Building in Burbank, complete with Mickey Mouse's hat (albeit at a very large scale) from "The Sorcerer's Apprentice" in *Fantasia.*

As with many architects during the 1980s and 1990s, Stern's involvement spread to decorative arts commissions. This has included custom furniture for the Walt Disney Company and for the William Gates Science Center at Stanford University. Commercially available pieces have been produced for Swid Powell (china and silverware), Acme (jewelry), Atelier Martex (bed and bath furnishings), and others (carpet and fabric designs). Notably the silverware for Swid Powell is based on the iconography of the columns found in Minoan palaces and Gothic cathedrals. Swid Powell also produced Stern's designs for flatware to be used in the Rainbow Room atop New York's Rockefeller Center, no doubt further asserting Stern's New York standing, respect, and influence. His lavish bath and bed textiles for Atelier Martex are wonderful interpretations of Pompeii and Newport, bringing evocative images of historical architecture and landscape to the intimate rooms of homes.

Stern's contributions within the architectural profession as a designer and critic are well established and respected; what elevates his significance as an architect and designer is his ability to have these contributions permeate into the public realm and for them to gain widespread acceptance in magazines such as *Life* and through products such as Martex linens. This is a unique achievement for an architect.

—Peter Exley

# STEVENS, Brooks

American industrial and product designer

**Born:** Milwaukee, Wisconsin, 7 June 1911. **Education:** Studied architecture at Cornell University, 1929-33. **Family:** Married Alice Kopmeier in 1937; children: David, William Clifford (Steve), Sandra Alice, and Kipp. **Career:** Intern, Eschweiler & Eschweiler Architects, Milwaukee, 1930-32; package designer, Jewett and Sherman, Milwaukee, 1932-33; opened design studio, with funding from his father, 1934; design consultant, Outboard Marine Corporation, 1938; firm became Brooks Stevens Design Associates, Mequon, Wisconsin; worked for more than 600 clients in his career; retired from active designing, 1980. Instructor, Milwaukee Institute of Art & Design, Wisconsin, 1983-95; lecturer on design at universities and conferences throughout the world. Appointed director, Road America, 1978; appointed trustee, Milwaukee Institute of Art & Design, 1980. **Member:** Founding member (1944), Society of Industrial Designers; founding member, Sports Car Club of America; Academy of Fellows, Industrial Designers Society of America; Society of Automotive Engineers; Société des Ingénieurs de l'Automobile, Paris; Institut de l'Esthetique Industrielle, Paris. **Exhibitions:** Layton School of the Arts, Milwaukee, 1949; Haggerty Museum of Art, Marquette University, 1979; Milwaukee Institute of Art & Design, 1985; *Transportation,* for founding of Brooks Steven Gallery of Industrial Design, Milwaukee Institute of Art & Design, 1992; *Imagineering,* Brooks Steven Gallery of Industrial Design, 1993; *Designs on Wisconsin,* State of Wisconsin Department of Administration, 1994; *60 Formative Years of Industrial*

*Design,* Brooks Steven Gallery of Industrial Design, 1994. **Collections:** Brooks Stevens Design Center, Milwaukee Institute of Art & Design; Brooks Stevens Automotive Museum, Mequon, Wisconsin. **Honors:** Outstanding Contribution, 2nd Annual International Motorsports Show, New York, 1953; Award of Merit, Los Angeles Industrial Fair and Congress, 1964; award for "distinguished advancement of industrial design," IDSA, 1965; Gimbels Fashion Forum Award, 1972; Design in Steel Citation, American Iron and Steel Institute, 1973; honorary doctorate, Milwaukee School of Engineering, 1979, and Milwaukee Institute of Art & Design, 1985; elected to Automotive Hall of Fame, 1985; Vocational Recognition Award, Rotary Club of Milwaukee, 1986; Lifetime Achievement Award, IDSA Wisconsin Chapter, 1988; William Goldsmith Award, IDSA Midwest District, 1991; Congressional Honor, United States Senate, 1991; Citation for contribution to education, National Association of Schools of Art & Design, 1991; Personal Recognition Award, IDSA, 1993.

**Address:** For information contact Public Relations Director, Milwaukee Institute of Art & Design, 273 East Erie Street, Milwaukee, Wisconsin 53202, U.S.A. **Died:** Milwaukee, 4 January 1995.

## Works

Styling of enclosures, handles, knobs, logos, for Cutler Hammer, 1933.
Styling and design of outboard motors in fiberglass and aluminum, from 6 horsepower to V8 350 horsepower, for Evinrude and Johnson (later Outboard Marine Corp.), 1934-80.
Styling of radiator grill, hood, teardrop gas tank, and fenders for farm tractor, for Allis-Chalmers, 1936.
Styling, for *Barton* washing machine and *Hamilton* dryer, 1937-38.
*Steam-0-Matic* steam iron in cast aluminum, 1938
Cab-over-engine streamlined trucks and tractor trailers, for General American Company, Chicago, 1938.
*FWD Snowmobile,* for Four Wheel Drive Truck Company for Lend Lease Program to Russia, 1939.
Playground equipment, including rocket swings and elephant slides, for New York World's Fair Children's World, 1939.
Single chassis, front wheel drive mobile office and mobile home, for Johnson Wax Co., 1939.
*Jeep* all metal station wagon, truck, and jeepster, for Willys Motors, 1942.
Sterneverdt recreational castle building, for new office headquarters, Miller Brewing Co., 1942.
Complete packaging, labeling, and glass bottle design, trucks, and mobile museum, for Miller Brewing Co., 1942-78.
*Ben Hur* freezers and refrigerators, 1945.
Milwaukee Road *Twin Cities,* and Olympian *Hiawatha,* railroad train design motif with Skytop observation car, long dome car, sleeperettes, coach, parlor car, diner, club cars and compartment cars, 1946.
*Globe* runabouts with first "sweep styled" sheer line and downswept transoms, 1946.
*Wagoneer* station wagon, for Willys-Overland, 1948.
Streamlining of bicycles, velocipedes, tricycles, and toy automobiles, for Cleveland Welding Co., Junior Toy Corp., and Binghampton Mfg. Co., 1949.
Streamlined motorcycle concepts, for Harley-Davidson, 1949.
Gas engines, for Briggs & Stratton, 1950-80.

Aluminumware, percolators, and first colored cookware, for Mirro, 1950-78.

Machine tools, milling machines, first machining center, office building, and plant architecture, for Kearney & Trecker, 1953.

First sliding roof station wagon, town car, convertible sedan, and retractable top coupe, for Olin Aluminum, 1954.

Excalibur J Car, 1954.

First enclosed bridge deck cruisers, for Chris-Craft, 1954.

Styling of original rotary mowers, including creation of Lawn-Boy green color, for Lawn-Boy, 1954-80

*Lark Runabout* boat with two bucket seats, individual wraparound windshields, stainless steel tailfins with running lights and retractable ski-toe lines, for Evinrude, 1956.

Appliances, barbecues, and first mobile entertainment centers, for Hotpoint Corp., Chicago, 1956.

*Fisherman* round fiberglass boat with twin 15 H.P. outboards, throttle steering, depth finder instruments, radar screen, fish finder, and radial passenger seating for safe fishing, for Evinrude, 1957.

*Rocket* tricycle, for Junior Toy Co., 1957.

*Station Wagon of the Sea* enclosed boat with seating for six people, and convertible sliding cabin roof for open cockpit fishing, water skiing and picnicking, for Evinrude, 1958.

Excavating equipment and 100 ton cranes with first panoramic vision cabs, for Bucyrus-Erie, 1958.

Redesign of *Oscar Mayer Wienermobile* (mobile billboard), using Plexiglas and adding a bun for the hot dog, 1958-88.

*Showboat* pontoon boat, with deckside cooking grille and passenger "head" in pilot house, for Evinrude, 1959.

*Helibout* runabout, powered by 75 H.P. Evinrude outboard convertible to helicopter rotor blade for flights from lake to lake and lake to shore, for Evinrude, 1960.

*Jeep* station wagons and *Jeep* trucks, for Aero Willys do Brazil, 1960-75.

Full line automobile design, for Studebaker, 1960-64.

*Housefloat* modular pontoon houseboat from single cabin to three cabin capacity, for Evinrude, 1961.

*Jetstream* runabout with dual speed hull, for Evinrude, 1962.

*Lakester* dunebuggy with 50 H.P. outboard motor, convertible to passenger boat hull for water use, for Evinrude, 1963.

Lawn and garden equipment, rotary mowers, and first four cylinder, water-cooled garden tractors, for Gutbrod-Werke, Germany, 1963-80.

First fixed pontoon Wankel powered air boat for high speed running, for Evinrude, 1964.

*Balloon-about* ascension hot air balloon powered by Evinrude 7.5 H.P. motor for air and water travel, for Evinrude, 1965.

*Excalibur SSK* contemporary classic sports car, for SS Automobile Corp., 1964.

Coupe De Ville roof styling, for Studebaker *Hawk,* 1964.

*Sceptre* sedan styling, with front half vinyl roof design, transverse headlight and taillight, and wrap-around bumpers and body side rub rails, for Studebaker, 1964.

*411-412 Series* front-engine, water-cooled automobile lines, for Volkswagen, Wolfsburg, Germany, 1966-70.

First dragster bicycle and magnesium wheel concept, for Sears, Roebuck, 1970.

First visual identity and multiple identity 100-300 ton metal stamping presses, for Niagara Machine & Tool Works, Buffalo, New York, 1974.

Frame styling for bicycles, for Iverson, 1975.

Back hoe and excavating equipment with Panoramic cab enclosure, for J. C. Bamford, Uttoxeter, England, 1975.

*Free Spirit* bicycle design and the first introduction of the magnesium wheel to the bicycle and motorcycle industry, for Sears Roebuck, 1975.

## Publications

**On STEVENS: books—***Formica and Design: From the Counter Top to High Art* edited by Susan Grant Lewin, New York, 1991; **articles—**"A Designer of Our Time" by Thomas David in *Innovation,* Winter 1995; *IDSA Newsletter* (Great Falls, Virginia), February 1995; "Flair, Fun & Form" by Paul G. Hayes in *Wisconsin* (Milwaukee), 6 December 1992.

*       *       *

Brooks Stevens was a remarkable man. One of the founding fathers of the profession of industrial design, Brooks overcame childhood polio to become one of the country's most prolific and gifted designers. He was instrumental in shaping design and the professional practice of industrial design. Brooks took great pride in his association with SID (Society of Industrial Designers), and then IDSA (The Industrial Designers Society of America), and SAE (Society of Automotive Engineers). At the time of his death he was the sole surviving Charter Fellow of the SID he had helped to found in 1944. He became a member of the Academy of Fellows of the IDSA in 1988, the highest professional recognition; received the only Wisconsin IDSA Chapter's Lifetime Achievement Award ever given; received the William Goldsmith Award for his humanitarian efforts in 1991; and in 1993 received IDSA's Personal Recognition Award recognizing his personal contributions to design.

After a childhood of intense effort banishing the crippling effects of polio, Brooks began his study of architecture at Cornell. This was at the height of the Depression, and luckily for us, he took his father's advice and put his design talents to good use in the emerging field of industrial design. Brooks was a master story teller and his tales of life as a fledgling designer in the 1930s were always highly entertaining. He would recount with laughter, "I'd have to fight my way in to talk to anybody in the early days, and then not only justify myself but my profession as well."

During the 1930s his work ranged from the design of industrial equipment and machinery, to packaging, graphics, and corporate identity, as well as to a great many consumer products. He used his talent and ability to bring safety, style, and what we now call human factors to an amazing variety of products in this prewar era. He designed the first motor home, called then a "living room on wheels," for Johnson Wax. He brought such dramatic styling to the design of Allis Chalmers tractors that farmers drove them to church on Sunday. He began a whole industry with his 1939 design of the first snowmobile made by the Four Wheel Drive Truck Co. for Lend Lease in Russia. Then there were his wonderfully whimsical designs of the children's playground for the 1939 New York World's Fair. Stevens took a noisy, crude, and dangerous mechanical device and gave us the first modern outboard motor for Evinrude in 1934. During this period he put the now famous "window" in the front of the first gas clothes dryer. "From just looking at it, a big white enameled box, nobody could tell what the thing was," he once said. "I put a glass panel in the front, filled it full of argyle socks, and sales took off."

**Brooks Stevens:** *Jeepster,* 1948

From his solid base established in the decade of the 1930s, Stevens was able to explore new avenues for design. He gave us the wide mouth peanut butter jar, the flowing lines of Harley Davidson motorcycles, and steam irons that didn't burn our fingers. He developed color applications for household appliances for the Mirro Co., defined another industry with his rotary lawn mower, and stole the show at the annual New York Boat Show for many years with his inventive designs for boats and motors. He formed the classic sweeping lines of the Chris Craft deck cruisers, developed corporate identity and graphic design for Miller Brewing, still in use after 45 years, and for Oscar-Mayer he redesigned the famous and much loved Weinermobile. Soon he had an international client list with work for GuteBrod in Germany, Willis do Brazil, and Alfa Romeo in Italy. Brooks took great pride in his designs for the small utility vehicles and ground maintenance vehicles for the 1972 Munich Olympics. The sheer volume of his work is staggering. The Stevens Archives at the Milwaukee Institute of Art & Design has more than 50,000 pieces of original art period photographs and sketches that document thousands of his designs.

Brooks designed from a very personal perspective. As he said "I loved peanut butter and jelly sandwiches, but couldn't get the last of the peanut butter out of the jar. So I made the mouth as wide as the whole jar and designed a big cap." Such was his motivation for this ground breaking approach to consumer packaging. The brilliant green color still in use on Lawn Boy products was an attempt by Brooks to bring some sense of enjoyment to an otherwise tedious task, mowing the lawn. His toy designs always stressed what he termed "play value." All of this was many years ago before the concepts of "human factors", or "user friendly" were heard. These are common concepts today, yet Brooks was using them and advocating their implementation in every day products as early as 1940.

Automobiles were a big part of Brooks life. Everyone would recognize his landmark styling exercise, the Excalibur. This two seat sports car was designed in the early 1960s and manufactured by his two eldest sons, David and Steve, until 1987. Brooks loved to joke, "at one time they were America's 5th largest automobile manufacturer—and there was no 6th". Not many people know that he was responsible for the design of the first all-metal station wagon for jeep, the Wagoneer. Redesigned in 1960 and 1980, Wagoneers are still in production. Brooks almost singlehandedly started today's craze for the sport utility vehicle with the revolutionary jeep Cherokee. He was retained by Volkswagen AG of Germany to design the

VW 411 and 412 series. He loved to tell of his meetings with VW's highest staff, "after walking along a mile long plant we would pass through ten-foot-high carved oak doors into a meeting room big enough to land an airplane in. I thought I was in Valhalla."

Brooks had very serious open heart surgery in 1978. He lost the sight of one eye to cataracts, and was confined to a wheel chair as a consequence of his polio. His energy wasn't blunted, however, as he passed the leadership of his office to his youngest son Kipp in 1980. This allowed Brooks to begin a new career as an educator. From 1982 until his death on January 4th 1995, he taught three days a week at the Milwaukee Institute of Art & Design. He shared his passion for design, and his wealth of experience with a whole new generation of young designers. As a reflection of his dedication to education, Brooks and his wife Alice served as honorary co-chairs of MIAD's capitol campaign, which raised over $9.5 million for the Institute's new facility. MIAD's Design Division is named in honor of Alice and Brooks.

Brooks was a brilliant, prolific, and influential designer, gave selflessly of his time to others, served with SID to form the very basis for professional industrial design practice, and he was treasured friend.

—Thomas M. David

# STEVENS, Richard (William)

British industrial designer

**Born:** Dorking, Surrey, 1 October 1924. **Education:** Educated at the County Grammar School, Dorking, 1935-40; studied physics at Regent Street Polytechnic, London, BS, 1946. **Family:** Married Anne Clara Hammond in 1947; children: Paul and Nicole. **Career:** Technician, at Siemens Lamps and Supplies Limited, London, 1942-53; designer, for Metropolitan Vickers, London, 1953-54; designer, then chief of design, Atlas Lighting, London, 1954-63; industrial design manager, Standard Telephones and Cables, London, 1963-69; design manager, Post Office Telecommunications (now British Telecom), London, 1969-83; founder, Richard Stevens Design Associates, London, from 1987. Index committee member, Council of Industrial Design, London, 1960-62; president, Society of Industrial Artists and Designers, London, 1972-73; treasurer and executive board member, International Council of Societies of Industrial Design (ICSID), 1973-77; governor, Croydon College of Design and Technology, Surrey, 1975-79. **Exhibitions:** Eye for Industry, Victoria and Albert Museum, London, 1986. **Honors:** Gold Medal, Milan Triennale, 1957; three Design Centre Awards, London, 1959-60; fellow, Chartered Society of Designers, London, 1960; Royal Designer for Industry, Royal Society of Arts, London, 1973; fellow, Chartered Institution of Building Services, London, 1977. **Address:** Hazel Cottage, Ewood Lane, Newdigate, Dorking, Surrey R5 5AR, England.

## Works

Injection-molded acrylic plastic street light units, for Atlas Lighting, 1955.
Fluorescent road lanterns in opal plastic and aluminum, for Thorn Electrical Industries, 1957.

Hermetically-sealed sodium road lantern in injection-molded plastic, for Thorn, 1957.
Decorative domestic lighting units, for Atlas, 1958.
Street light units with integrated support column, for Atlas, 1959.
Radio receiver units, for Ferguson Radio, 1961.
Programmable laboratory power supply unit, for Standard Telephones and Cables, 1972.
Young Scientist of the Year Award trophy, 1976.

## Publications

**By STEVENS: articles**—*Transactions of the Illuminating Engineering Society* (London), no. 18, 1953, no. 25, 1960; *The Designer* (London), September 1971, April 1973, December 1978; *Institute of Electrical Engineers Journal* (London), November 1974.

**On STEVENS: books**—*Designers in Britain,* vols. 5-7, 1957-71; *Industrial Design and the Community* by Ken Baynes, London, 1967; *British Design Since 1880* by Fiona MacCarthy, London, 1982; *Eye for Industry: Royal Designers for Industry* by MacCarthy and Patrick Nuttgens, London, 1986.

*

Product designers share common ground with engineers and artists. Engineers assume, wrongly, that the missing element provided by those with an arts background is concern primarily for visual aspects—aesthetics. In fact, the difference (and only difference) between an industrial designer and an engineering designer is that the latter aims to be wholly objective in his approach, whereas the former is entirely happy dealing with those aspects of design that may be regarded as subjective—including (but not only) aesthetics. The value of an arts training is that it gives one confidence in making decisions based on subjective judgements. In truth, much engineering is also based on subjective assessment, but it is deprecated by engineers who regard it as a weakness. Much effort is expanded in reducing the subjective element, so that all decisions may become wholly objective. The engineer would like this to apply to the industrial design contribution and cannot understand why this is not possible or desirable.

A facility for making subjective judgements—intuitive thinking—is also conducive to creativity and, although it is not an attribute of which industrial designers have a monopoly, it is perhaps an asset they may have in greater measure. Now, subjective judgements depend in the end on dogmatic assumptions—deeply held convictions on matters that are essentially irrational and not necessarily shared with others, although those who do share them are strongly drawn together, as in religion or politics. It is important for designers to be aware of their own dogmas, especially if they wish to be wholly professional in designing for others whose convictions they may not share.

My personal dogma—reinforced by Robert Pirsig in his book *Zen and the Art of Motorcycle Maintenance*—is that judgement on whether or not a design solution is acceptable depends on the degree to which it may be recognized as having a measure of quality, not only in an objective sense (nor subjective either) but in that special sense of a value recognizable yet undefinable, where the total value is greater than the sum of the components, as was so well described by Pirsig. A satisfying design is one in which one may perceive this special kind of quality in the solution of the complex problems inherent in the design task.

—Richard Stevens

\*     \*     \*

Richard Stevens took his degree in physics and then moved into design, a subject that he learned through application. He believes the big difference between an engineer and an industrial designer is that the former has to be very objective, whereas the latter has to have a good understanding of the subjective. An engineer can say a bridge must look this way or it will fall down; a designer can modify a creation to please the customer. Stevens says the good professional designer should be able to satisfy a customer whose tastes he does not condone himself. There is no room for the ego in this approach. Stevens strongly disapproves of the designer who wants to put his own stamp on everything and who wants every product to shout his own name. That is bad design, for it is not putting the job before the personality. Stevens' modest approach is very British, but he admits that the United States has had an influence on him through the designer Walter Dorwin Teague and Robert Pirsig's book *Zen and the Art of Motorcycle Maintenance.* Pirsig's book emphasizes the importance of quality in everything, though the West does not need to borrow from Japan when it already has the Protestant work ethic.

Although Stevens' prizes have been for lighting, now that Post Office Telecommunications has been separated from the Post Office and has become British Telecom, he has also designed telephones and associated equipment to create that variety of telephones on offer as part of their new look. Push-button models, one-piece earpiece-and-dialling instruments, and new tone types all came from Stevens' department. Above all, his style is one of simplicity. His telephone stands are smoothed at the edges to prevent accidents. Such consideration shows a careful approach, producing a product that will perform safely in addition to working properly and looking nice. A good creation, to Stevens, is one that can be used almost without being noticed. It should do its job and no more, and Stevens tries to do his best without attracting more attention than the job deserves.

—Diana de Marly

# STONE, (Alan) Reynolds

British painter, illustrator, calligrapher, typographer, and graphic designer

**Born:** Eton, Buckinghamshire, 13 March 1909. **Education:** Durnsford School, Furbeck, and Eton School, Buckinghamshire, 1919-26; studied history, at Magdalen College, Cambridge University, 1926-30. **Military Service:** Photo-interpreter, Royal Air Force, 1941-45. **Family:** Married Janet Woods in 1938; children: Emma, Phillida, Edward, and Humphrey. **Career:** Apprentice type compositor under Walter Lewis, at the Cambridge University Press, 1930-32; type compositor, Barnicott and Pearce printers, Taunton, Somerset, 1932-34; freelance typographer and book designer from 1934, and calligrapher from

1939, working in Codicote, Hertfordshire, 1934-51; contributor to the *Times Literary Supplement* weekly, London. **Exhibitions:** Aldeburgh Festival, Suffolk, 1958; Art Council Gallery, London, 1959 (toured); Agnew's Gallery, London, 1965, 1969; Abbot Hall Art Gallery, Kendal, 1972; New Grafton Gallery, London, 1972, 1975, 1978; Fitzwilliam Museum, Cambridge, 1978; St. Paul's School Library, London, 1981; Dorset County Museum, Dorchester, 1981; *Eye for Industry,* Victoria and Albert Museum, London, 1986. **Honors:** Commander, Order of the British Empire, 1953; Royal Designer for Industry, 1956; Fellow, Royal Society of Arts, London, 1964. **Died:** Dorchester, Dorset, 23 June 1979.

## Works

*Nonesuch Shakespeare Anthology* chapter headings for the Nonesuch Press, 1935.
Heraldic arms, for Cambridge University, 1946.
Three pence victory commemoration postage stamp, for the General Post Office London, 1946.
Heraldic device, for the British Council, London, 1946.
Heraldic device, for the Rampant Lions Press, 1947.
Clock device, for *The Times* newspaper, London, 1948-51.
Logotype device, for Dolcis Shoes, 1951.
*Minerva* typeface, for the Linotype Corporation, 1954.
Heraldic device, for the Oxford University Press, 1955.
Engraved design of the £5 banknote, for the Royal Mint, London, 1961.
Logotype device, for Blackwell's Bookshop, Oxford, 1963.
Janet alphabet and typefount, privately produced, 1965.

## Publications

**By STONE: books—***A Book of Lettering,* London, 1935; *Wood Engravings of Thomas Bewick,* London, 1953; *The Wood Engravings of Gwen Raverat,* London, 1959; (with Philip Beddingham and Will Carter) *Concerning Book Labels,* London, 1963; *Reynolds Stone: Engravings,* London, 1977.

**On STONE: books—***Reynolds Stone: His Early Development as an Engraver on Wood* by J. W. Goodison, London, 1947; *Reynolds Stone* by Myfanwy Piper, London, 1951; *Graphic Design* by John Lewis and John Brinkley, London, 1954; *Modern Book Design* by Ruari McLean, London, 1958; *Reynolds Stone: An Exhibition of Engravings and Designs,* catalogue with introduction by Kenneth Clark, London, 1959; *Calligraphy Today* by Heather Child, London, 1963, 1976; *Schriftkunst* by Albert Kapr, Dresden, 1971; *Paintings and Drawings by Reynolds Stone,* exhibition catalogue with introduction by M. E. Burkett, Kendal, 1972; *Reynolds Stone 1909-1979,* exhibition catalogue by J. W. Goodison and Ruari McLean, Dorchester, 1979; *Eye for Industry: Royal Designers for Industry 1936-1986,* exhibition catalogue by Fiona MacCarthy and Patrick Nuttgens, London, 1986.

\*     \*     \*

English craftsman and designer Reynolds Stone was an uncomplicated man. He produced a large volume of work based on letterforms and nature, with great precision and skill.

Stone's early career centered on lettering and wood engraving. In the wood engraving process lines are incised across the end grain of a piece. The result is a high contrast black and white image. Stone learned this craft as an apprentice at the Cambridge University Press. He became acquainted with the work of Stanley Morison, who called for a revival of the pure classic lettering style of the Renaissance, and its passion for precise geometric forms with additive flourishes which surround the letterforms. The revival Morison called for is evident in Stone's work based on the 26 letters of the Roman alphabet. The simple, pure letters are crafted with precision and demonstrate sensitivity to the correct proportions between the height and width and the intersection of curved and straight sections. Stone adds flourishes which enhance the basic letter form, and often decorates spaces surrounding the letters, but never the letter itself. Sometimes the form was planned and drawn out on the wood. At other times, Stone followed the lead of the chisel, letting the flourishes emerge from the wood.

Early in his career, Stone also began collecting the books of Thomas Bewick, an 18th century wood engraver, known for his accurate representations of nature. Knowledge of these illustrations reinforced Stone's reverence for nature. Love of nature is evident in his illustrations where he shows idyllic landscapes with perfect forms and textures. His bookplates combine letter forms with these natural shapes in a decorative manner. The influence of Bewick's nature illustrations, and Monson's love of the classic Roman letter forms, is seen in Stone's work. Though he is known primarily as a wood engraver, Stone also practiced the art of stone cutting and watercolor painting.

Books illustrated by Stone range from *The Shakespeare Anthology* for Nonesuch Press, to *Omoo,* by Herman Melville, for Hentage Press. Stone designed bookplates for various members of the British Royal Family; the Five Pound note for the Bank of England; stamps for the Post Office; and logotypes for Bally Shoes, the London Library Label, and Dolcis. He created devices for the University Presses of Oxford and Cambridge. He carved Winston Churchill's memorial stone in Westminster Abbey. This is but a partial listing of his oeuvre. But Stone never appeared interested in developing a following or cult. He never made a statement of belief. Though he lectured at the Royal College of Art, he did not find joy in public speaking. He was rarely involved with commercial design problems such as designing books. He was not an experimental artist. He was an artist who sought to perfect his craft.

Stone collected hand letter presses, some in working order, and used these to print small editions of a book or pamphlet, such as the 125 copies of Kenneth Clark's *The Other Side of the Alde* in 1968. He used the typeface Janet for the first time on this 16 page booklet. This was a typeface he designed and retained for private use. It worked well with his wood engraved illustrations. Minerva was the name of the type he designed for the Linotype Company in 1953. This was used for article headings and the *New Statesman* until discontinued in 1970.

Reynolds Stone died in 1979. He left behind a large volume of work. He was a quiet man, who produced a quiet art. His work, deceptively simple with its black and white forms based on twenty-six letters of the Roman alphabet and nature, is beautiful in its precision and grace.

—Nancy House

# STOPPINO, Giotto

Italian industrial designer

**Born:** Luigi Stoppino, in Vigevano, Pavia, 30 April 1926. **Education:** Studied architecture, at the University of Milan, 1945-50, and at the University of Venice, 1955-57. **Family:** Married Deda Boccalini in 1965. **Career:** Partner, in Stoppino/Gregotti/Meneghetti design firm, in Novara, 1952-63, and Milan, 1964-68; independent designer, Milan, from 1968; has designed for Poltrona Frau, Arteluce, Kartell, Bernini, Acerbis International, Zanotta, Rexite, Porro, and others. Visiting lecturer in architectural history, at the Italian Studies Centre of the University of Oregon, Pavia, 1963-69. President, Associazione Disegno Industriale, Milan, 1982-84, and ICSID Congress, Milan, 1983. **Exhibitions:** Galleria Arte Borgogna, Milan, 1983; Pentagono Arredamenti, Lugano, 1984; *Design Furniture from Italy,* Tokyo, 1984. **Collections:** Staatliches Museum fur Angewandte Kunst, Munich; Victoria and Albert Museum, London; Museum of Contemporary Art, Chicago; Museum of Modern Art, New York; City Hall, Shanghai. **Honors:** Grand Prize, Milan Triennale, 1964; First Prize, Trieste Concorso, 1968; Compasso d'Oro Award, Milan, 1979; Bio 9 Gold Medal, Liubliana, 1981; Business Designers Product Design Award, New York, 1981. **Address:** Via Argelati 30/A, 20143 Milan, Italy.

## Works

*Cavour* chair series in upholstered heartwood, produced by S.I.M., 1955, and by Poltrona Frau, 1988 (with Gregotti and Meneghetti).
*537 Table Lamp* in turned aluminum, for Arteluce, 1967.
Set of three nesting tables in ABS plastic, for Kartell, 1968.
*Maia* furniture range in tubular steel and wood, for Bernini, 1969.
Mobile serving table in injection-moulded ABS plastic, for Kartell, 1970.
*Tic-Tac* table lamp in injection-moulded plastic, for Kartell, 1970.
Magazine rack with integral handle in injection-moulded ABS plastic, for Kartell, 1971.
*Jot Chair* in metal and leather, for Acerbis International, 1976.
*Sheraton Program* cupboards in metal and lacquered wood, for Acerbis International, 1977.
*Brooklyn Bookcase* in steel rod with suspended shelves, for Acerbis International, 1977.
*Hilton System* modular furniture in enamelled wood and plastic, for Acerbis International, 1978.
*Liuba Chair* in plywood, steel rod, and beechwood, for Zanotta, 1979.
*Biblio* cassette racks in injection-moulded ABS plastic for Rexite, 1981.
*Menhir Tables* in disc-welded steel, for Acerbis International, 1983.
*Soffio di Vento* adjustable storage and shelving system, for Acerbis International, 1986.
*Elba Series* sofa and armchair in steel and elasticated polyurethane with leather or fabric upholstery, for Rossi di Albizzate, 1987.
*Mugello Table* in leather-clad aluminum with crystal top, for Acerbis International, 1987.
*Amadeus* sideboard/cupboard with hinge-column supports, for Porro, 1987.
*Arlette* chaise lounge in tubular steel and padded leather upholstery, for Living, 1988.

## Publications

By STOPPINO: books—(with others) *Italienisches Mobel,* Milan, 1980; (with others) *La Sedia Italiano,* Rome, 1983.

On STOPPINO: books—*Mercati e Negozi* by Robert Aloi, Milan, 1959; *Design Italiano: I Mobili* edited by Enrichetta Ritter, Milan and Rome, 1968; *Plastics as Design Form* by T. R. Newman, New York, 1972; *Design e Forme Nuove nell'Arredamento Italiano* edited by Paolo Portoghesi and Marino Marini, Rome, 1978; *Atlante del Design Italiano 1940/1980* by Alfonso Grassi and Anty Pansera, Milan, 1980; *Contemporary Furniture* edited by Klaus-Jurgen Sembach, Stuttgart and London, 1982; *Mobel aus Italien* by E. J. Auer and F. Burkhardt, Milan, 1983; *Giotto Stoppino: d'all'Architettura al Design* by Daniele Baroni and Gillo Dorfles, Milan, 1983; *The Hot House: Italian New Wave Design* by Andrea Branzi, London, 1984; *The Conran Directory of Design* edited by Stephen Bayley, London, 1985; *Italian Design: 1870 to the Present* by Penny Sparke, London and New York, 1988; *Designed by Architects in the 1980s* by Juli Capella and Quim Larrea, London, 1988; *Italian Modern: A Design Heritage* by Giovanni Albera and Nicolas Monti, New York, 1989.

\*   \*   \*

My activities began in 1951 with my participation in the ninth Milan *Triennale* and continued over the next eighteen years with the formation of a professional studio with my partners Gregotti and Meneghetti. We turned out some significant work, particularly in the architectural field. But I shall not be talking of architecture here; rather, of my work as a designer.

An important date is the year 1968, which marks the start of my independent activities and of my collaboration with the firm of Kartell, with the stackable, plastic coffee tables which won a prize at the year's Trieste *Concorso* as objects for distribution by department stores.

The application of plastics technology to furniture was then still quite new. Research into these materials was based at that time on the need to produce materials for low-cost housing, so as make them available to consumers at every social level. The interest of design in this sector depended on the specific characteristics of the plastic materials (I mean in particular ABS plastic and other analogous materials moulded by the injection technique). These considerations could be summed up in four essential points:

(1) Form, understood as an aesthetic expression.

(2) Structure, in the sense of the rigidity of the moulded object in relation to its shape.

(3) The conception of the useful function in relation to the purpose of the object.

(4) The color intrinsic to the actual material of the product.

The expressive possibilities of an object made from a plastic material were moreover closely linked to the limitations imposed by logic and by the economy of the injection press and to the weight-cost of the finished product.

Taking all these factors into account, planning in the field of plastic materials meant to me following what was almost the paradigmatic line of design research. From that time until 1974, my work on design with Kartell had a look of continuing collaboration in the study of a number of products, some of which are still in production. Of course, during that period, many other items of furniture designed in Italy used a great variety of materials, from wood to glass and metal, sometimes in combination with synthetic materials.

The success of Italian furniture design from the 1950s on has been due to three essential factors. In the first place, there was the development of a number of concerns created with the explicit purpose of studying products with designers involved throughout and of applying the latest technologies that emerge from the evolution of the use of the materials. These included Arflex, Kartell, Artemide, Poltronova, Zanotta, Anonima Castelli. Similarly important was the evolution of concerns which have a tradition of high-class work in wood but which are nonetheless ready to consider new ideas; these include Poggi, Cassina, and Bernini.

The success of Italian furniture design on an international level was to be crowned by the great 1972 show, *Italy: The New Domestic Landscape,* at the Museum of Modern Art in New York. It is interesting to note that of the 153 products exhibited there, sixty-nine were carried out entirely in plastic materials and twenty-two in plastics to such an extent as to be decisive for the object's appearance.

After the New York exhibition, and especially after the oil crisis in 1973, we saw a rethinking of the use of plastic materials both for economic reasons and on ecological grounds from the point of view of the materials' degradability. I must add, however, that the products studied most carefully, those in which there is the most coherent relationship between object and material, still retain their place on the international market. At present, the tendency is to use every kind of material available from industrial production, taking care, of course, to use the right material in the right place.

The second factor was the establishment of design as an independent discipline, with a precise structure, quite separate from architectural research. One might even say that the chronic difficulties have directed Italian creativity towards the field of design, not only in the sector of furniture but also in the other sectors, as can be seen from the products of firms such as Olivetti, Brionvega, Solari, and Necchi, and above all, the motor industry.

The third factor, which must not be underestimated, is the existence of an uncommon number of specialized journals, which have helped to propagate the image of new products and, in some cases, to emphasize the significance of the new profession of design, understood as a process that can be integrated with the complex processes of industrial production. Here, too, the list is quite long extending from the traditional *Domus, Casabella,* and *Architettura* through new titles such as *Abitare, Interni, Casa Vogue, Ottagono* and *Rassegna,* up to the more recent *Modo* and *Gran Bazar.* During the time of the economic boom, the idea began to spread of furnishing houses following models in the magazines, thus obliging the furniture manufacturers to turn out adequate products.

Another decisive date in this survey is the year 1976, when I began to collaborate with the Acerbis International company. I worked closely with Lodovico Acerbis, aiming to give the firm a new image. This business was founded more than 100 years ago, in 1870, as a workshop for craft woodwork; it has gone through remarkable changes in the course of three generations to reach its present industrial form, which aims to apply the most advanced design to the production of furniture. There were essentially three points that encouraged involvement in this industry:

(1) The relationship between technology and design. One might say that creativity in design is always closely related to technology. Living in continual contact with the actual production of the firm, we tried to make as much use as possible of the potentialities of our own machinery, and only when that was not possible did we turn to

materials produced by other industries. The unifying factor of these apparently disparate elements was, and still is, design, understood as research, perfected through successive stages by a considerable number of tests and prototypes in a process of development that sometimes lasts as much as two years for a single product.

(2) Synthetic ductility. In order to appeal to the greatest number of potential users, we have naturally made a study of furniture that can be assembled in very different ways. New methods of assembly allow the furniture to be put together in the shortest possible time without using screws or other traditional means of fixing.

(3) Wood and synthetic lacquers. With wood continuing to be the main material used in production, we tried to enhance its quality with extremely accurate work, or, in certain cases, with lacquers, using polyesters. This brought out the relationship with established tradition, going back to the ancient Chinese lacquers. In design research, color has always been a primary problem. The world around us is filled with colors, and not at random; nature expresses itself with an infinite palette of chromatic tones, and the rainbow which appears only in special atmospheric conditions, is like a revelation of the colors of the universe arranged in a geometrical form.

(4) The last aspect to which we gave special importance was the application of sources of artificial light to furniture. It is generally recognized that social relationships in homes generally flower in the evening, and consequently we wanted our pieces of furniture to have a life of their own on those occasions, too, to create special effects and a characteristic atmosphere. This research resulted in such items of furniture as Brooklyn, Sheraton, Hilton, Madison, Axton, and Solemio, which have not only been widely taken up by the market but have also won remarkable recognition, winning, for instance, the Compasso d'Oro prize in 1979, the gold medal at Ljubljana in 1981, and the Product Design Award in New York in the same year, as well as being on permanent exhibition at the Victoria and Albert Museum in London.

But it is not those prizes of which I am most proud; what matters to me most of all is that by constant research, by work that always aimed at maintaining the characteristics of innovation and beauty at the highest level, I have made a small contribution to the efforts to improve the quality of life.

—Giotto Stoppino

# STUDIO PER
Spanish architectural, industrial, and graphic design firm

**Founded** by Pep Bonet (born 1941), Cristian Cirici (born 1941), Lluis Clotet (born 1941), and Oscar Tusquets (born 1941), in Barcelona, 1965; also established BD Ediciones de Diseno furniture and interior products firm, Barcelona, 1972. **Career:** Designed for Feria de Barcelona, Profitos, Bazan, Zanotta, Polinax, Alessi, Cleto Munari, Matteo Grassi, Casas, Quartett, Artespana, Carlos Jane, Ceramicas Bidasoa, Escofet, Aleph, and others. **Exhibitions:** *Arquitectura de Studio Per,* Colegio de Arquitectos, Lerida, 1971; *Arquitectura y Lagrimas,* Sala Vincon, Barcelona, 1975; *Transformations in Modern Architecture,* Museum of Modern Art, New York, 1979; *The House As Image,* Louisiana Museum, Humlebaek, 1981; *Ten Buildings,* Institute of Contemporary Arts, London, 1983; *Contemporary Spanish Architecture,* Architectural League of New

York, 1986; *Documenta,* Kassel, 1987. **Collections:** Centre Georges Pompidou, Paris; Museum of Modern Art, New York. **Honors:** Premio FAD, Barcelona, 1965, 1970, 1972, 1978, 1979, 1987; Premio Azulejo de Deo, Barcelona, 1970; Delta de Oro Industrial Design Prize, Barcelona, 1974, 1979, 1980, 1986; Creu de Sant Jordi Award of Catalunya, 1987. **Address:** Caspe 151, 08013 Barcelona, Spain.

## Works

Books designed (by Clotet and Tusquets) include—*Neutral Corner,* Barcelona, 1965; *Arquitectura Gotica Catalana,* Barcelona, 1968; *Arquitectura y Lagrimas,* exhibition catalogue, Barcelona, 1975.
*Girafa* standard lamp, for Polinax, 1967.
*Miro Otro* exhibition layouts, for the Centro Joan Miro, Barcelona, 1968-69.
Factory building and interiors at Polinya, Barcelona, for Profitos, 1973.
Transparent bookcase and shelving, for BD Ediciones de Diseno, 1973.
*Portrait of Mae West as a Living Room* exhibit, for the Salvador Dali Museum, Figueras, 1974.
*La Balsa* restaurant interiors, Barcelona, 1978-79.
*Catalano* armchair and coffee-table, for BD Ediciones de Diseno, 1979.
*Hipostila* bookcase, for BD Ediciones de Diseno, 1980.
*Oronda* teapot, for Alessi, 1980-83.
*Serpent* fruit bowl, for Cleto Munari, 1983.
*Varius* armchair, for Casas, 1984.
*Aluda* table, 1985, and *Gaulino* chairs, 1986-87, for Casas.
*Metalastica* chair, for BD Ediciones de Diseno, 1986-87.
*Sofanco* seating, for Escofet, 1988.
*Astrolabio* table, for Aleph, 1988.
*Nipon* ceramic jug, for Bidaso, 1988.

(for complete lists of Studio Per buildings and architectural projects, see *Contemporary Architects*)

## Publications

**On PER: books**—*El Studio Per o los Confines de la Arquitectura Actual* by J. Muntanola, Barcelona, 1976; *Contemporary Furniture* edited by Klaus-Jurgen Sembach, Stuttgart and London, 1982; *Clotet, Tusquets* by Claudia Mann, Barcelona, 1983; *Spanish Contemporary Architecture* by E. Bru and J. L. Mateo, Barcelona, 1984; *Industrial Design* by Hans Wichmann, Munich, 1985; *Encyclopedia of 20th-Century Architecture* edited by David Mackay and Vittorio Magnago Lampugnani, New York, 1986.

# STUMPF, William (Eugene)
American industrial, furniture, and environmental designer

**Born:** St. Louis, Missouri, 1 March 1936. **Education:** Studied at the School of the Art Institute of Chicago, 1954-56, and the University of Chicago, 1954-57; studied industrial design, University of Illinois, Urbana, BFA, 1959; studied environmental design, University of Wisconsin, Madison, MS, 1968. **Military Service:** Served in the United States Naval Reserve, 1955-60. **Family:** Married

Sharon Rose Ford in 1957; children: Carol, Jon, and Erich. **Career:** Designer, Peter Muller-Munk Associates, Pittsburgh, 1959-62; Manager of Advanced Industrial Design, Franklin Division, Studebaker Industries, Minneapolis, 1962-67; Vice-President, Herman Miller Research Corporation, Ann Arbor, Michigan, 1970-72; Design Consultant, Herman Miller Inc., Zeeland, Michigan, from 1972; Director, William Stumpf and Associates, in Madison, Wisconsin 1972-76, Winona, Minnesota, 1976-85, and Minneapolis, from 1985. Also design consultant work for General Mills, 1966, American Telephone and Telegraph, 1969, and Knape and Vogt, 1988. Assistant professor of environmental design, University of Wisconsin, Madison, 1968-69; assistant professor of product design, Institute of Design, Illinois Institute of Technology, Chicago, 1969-70; professor, Minneapolis College of Art and Design, 1982-83, 1983-84; visiting lecturer, Minneapolis College of Art and Design, 1970, Aquinas College, Grand Rapids, Michigan, 1972, 1973, 1974, University of Minnesota, Minneapolis, 1973, Kansas City Art Institute, 1974, Rhode Island School of Design, Providence, 1974, University of Illinois, Urbana, 1974, University of Wisconsin, Madison, 1975, University of Cincinnati, 1975-76, Cranbrook Academy of Art, Bloomfield Hills, Michigan, 1983, Taliesin East, Spring Green, Wisconsin, 1985-86, Rochester Institute of Technology, Royal College of Art, London, and Glasgow School of Art, Scotland. Lecturer and design consultant, Zeeland Planning Commission, Michigan, 1970-72; lecturer, Interior Design Congress '86, Kortrijk, Belgium, 1986, *Design in America* seminar, United States Information Agency, Belgrade, Yugoslavia, 1986, IDCA Congress, Amsterdam, 1987, Hobart Design Triennial, Australia, 1991; juror, National Endowment for the Arts, 1987, 1988, and IDEA, 1991; co-chair and board member, Aspen Design Conference, 1992. **Member:** Industrial Designers Society of America (IDSA); Human Factors Society; Design Management Institute. **Exhibitions:** *Design in Michigan 1967/1977,* Cranbrook Academy of Art, Bloomfield Hills, Michigan, 1978 (toured); *Please Be Seated,* University of Minnesota, St. Paul, 1984; *A Serious Chair,* Walker Art Center, Minneapolis, 1984 (toured); *The Art of Design,* University of Wisconsin, Milwaukee, 1988 (traveled to Chicago, 1989); *Equa Chair and Ethospace,* Henry Ford Museum, Dearborn, Michigan, 1991; *William Stumpf, Design Exhibition,* I-Space Gallery, University of Illinois, Chicago, 1995. **Collections:** Henry Ford Museum, Dearborn, Michigan; Museum of Modern Art, New York. **Honors:** Motorola Design Scholarship, 1958; University of Illinois Award in Design, 1959; Alcoa Design Award, 1959; American Society of Industrial Design Award, 1959, 1976; University of Wisconsin Fellowship, 1967; Design Michigan Award, 1977; Designer of the 1970s Award, 1979, Annual Design Award, 1984, 1985, and Top Designers in America selection, 1993, *ID* magazine; Certificate of Merit, Art Directors Club of Los Angeles, 1984; Design Excellence Award, IDSA, 1985; IBD Gold Award, 1984, 1985; Design Center Stuttgart Award, 1987; Product of the Decade selection, *Time* magazine, 1990; Nissan Award and Fellowship, Aspen Conference, 1991. **Address:** William Stumpf and Associates Inc., 128 North Third Street, Minneapolis, Minnesota 55401, U.S.A.

## Works

Harlem Preparatory School interiors, Harlem, New York, 1968.
*Ergon* office chair, for Herman Miller, 1976.
*Equa* chair, for Herman Miller, 1984 (with Don Chadwick).
*Ethospace* office system, for Herman Miller, 1986 (with Jack Kelley).
*Ergon 2* chair, for Herman Miller, 1988.
*Aeron* chair, for Herman Miller, 1994 (with Don Chadwick).
*SARAH* chair, table, bookcase, and accessories for the transgenerational, for Herman Miller, 1996.

## Publications

**By STUMPF: books**—*Leisure: A Study of Man and the Environment,* Chicago, 1970; *Environmental Quality,* Madison, Wisconsin, 1970; *The High School: The Process and the Place,* New York 1971; (with Michael Wodka) *Products: A Design Premise,* Cambridge, Massachusetts, 1972; (with the Walker Art Center) *Design Quarterly 104: Julia Child's Kitchen—A Design Anatomy,* Cambridge Massachusetts, 1984; **articles**—"Conference: Environmental Bases for Design" in *Office Design* (New York), March 1969; "The Junkyard Backlash" in *Design* (London), April 1977; "Home Sweet Office" in *Ideas* (Zeeland, Michigan), 1978; "Design/Big Wheels" in *Parenting* (New York), May 1987; "The Crisis of Comfort" in *Arts* (Minneapolis), June 1987; "Reflections on the Urban Street" in *Inform* (Minneapolis), May 1989.

**On STUMPF: books**—*Design in Michigan 1967/1977* by Katherine McCoy, Detroit, 1978; *Design Quarterly 126: A Serious Chair,* exhibition catalogue, 1984; **articles**—"Mobile Housing" in *Look* (New York), February 1960; "Supermarket School" in *Progressive Architecture* (New York), February 1971; "The Resources General Store" by R. Weinstock in *Educational Facilities Newsletter* (New York), March 1971; "Design Aid" in *International Design Magazine,* January/February 1984; "The Perfect Chair" by M. Mittelbach in *Republic* (New York), February 1986; "Looking Good Is Not Enough" by K. Anderson in *Time* (New York), 24 March 1986; "Designing Serendipity" by C. Kent in *Metropolis* (New York), November 1986; "Antidote to Ho-Hum Designs—A Sense of Playfulness" in *Design News* (Newton, Massachusetts), 3 November 1986; "Ethos Office System by Bill Stumpf for Herman Miller" in *Abitare* (Milan), April 1987; "Nine to Five and After" by G. Hollington in *Blueprint* (London), April 1987; "Furniture Designer Refuses to Sit on Laurels" by A. Patterson in *The Arizona Republic* (Phoenix), 31 May 1987; "Civil Liberties" by P. Donner in *IQ* (London), May 1988; "Chairs That Work" by K. Lanpher in the *Chicago Tribune,* 19 June 1988; "Industrial Ingenuity Takes On An Identity" by D. Wascoe in the *Minneapolis Star and Tribune,* 31 June 1988; "Memories at Play" in *AM: Architecture Minnesota,* September/October 1990; "Aeron Story" in *Blueprint* (London), 1994; films—*Redesign of the Police Car,* KTCA-TV, Minneapolis, 1992; *Portrait Series: William Stumpf,* KTCA-TV, 1992.

\*

Working from a design perspective that has always involved a deep love affair with things that are animated versus things that are static such as structures and buildings, I view my work as a challenge to temper the machine to mankind. I see industrial design as a discipline compatible with the domestic realm of the home, as a benign but pro-active force towards a clean environment, and as a primary extension of man's toolmaking ability and culture. I see my work as neither a subset of architecture, the so-called mother of the arts, nor a puppet of economics and marketing. I see it essentially

**William Stumpf:** *Sarah,* **reclining chair and accessories designed to accomodate the needs and limitations of the elderly, for Herman Miller**

as an extension of toolmaking, an art, and a craft. Industrial design has yet to find its legitimate place in the world.

I see man's fundamental need to play vested in his ability to make and manipulate machines and tools; the pursuit of the frivolous as well as the profound is critical to both pleasure and survival. The best of industrial design provides an admixture of play and physicality in objects; the best of my work, I hope, is comfortable, playful, accessible, and resistant to arbitrary obsolescence.

Like Blanche DuBois in *A Streetcar Named Desire,* I have always depended on the kindness of strangers. In an increasingly impersonal global and industrial milieu, it is precisely the quality of this kindness on which we all depend. Industrial design is, in my opinion, an activity devoted to being kind to strangers. By strangers, I mean us.

—William Stumpf

\*     \*     \*

A number of years ago I walked into Herman Miller's New York showroom and was impressed not so much by the furniture, with which I was familiar, as by the weight and breadth of the books and magazines scattered around the place. I was familiar with most of those too, but I had never encountered their like in furniture showrooms,

where what is grandly called "literature" is merely a device for what is prosaically called "accessorizing product." Books are chosen for this purpose irrespective of content, since their only function is to show a bookshelf in use. Periodicals are intended to provide "context," which means that, if the product is office furniture, a copy of *Forbes* or *The Wall Street Journal* is unsubtly laid on a credenza for effect. Otherwise, the only magazines on display are the trades.

The publications in this showroom were different. These were books to be read—books, as E. M. Forster said, that *had* to be read, for it was the only way of finding out what was in them. Who in a furniture company, I wondered, read books like this? Who, in a furniture company, even knew there *were* books like this? Where had they come from, and why?

They had come, I was told, from a reading list provided by a designer named Bill Stumpf. No product of his had yet made its way into the Herman Miller line, but his thinking had. And Stumpf's thinking is his principal contribution to his clients and to industrial design.

Not that there is anything theoretical about Stumpf's design approach. Or anything bookish about his thinking, which is less evocative of academe than of general stores, barber shops, garages, and baseball clubhouses—places where real work gets done.

Which is not a bad way to describe the William Stumpf Associates office: it is a place where real work gets done. One can tell a lot from the ambience of a design office. Some look corporate, like their clients. Others look cautiously arty, as if to say they are *in* business but not of it. One in Toronto that I particularly like has its kitchen front and center in the belief that, at work as at home, it is the most productive gathering place. There are design offices with no entrances as such at all, their front doors opening directly onto drafting tables in a self-conscious insistence that this is a no-nonsense operation. Stumpf's office is dominated by the shop, which gives the premises the ambience of a small-run manufacturing business. This is no coincidence, for making things, rather than making statements, is what the office is engaged in.

A design office so blatantly involved in the work process is appropriately concerned with products for the workplace, and that is where Stumpf has had his strongest influence. The design of the *Ergon* chair, which appeared in 1976, began with a serious study both of contemporary office work and of the kind of support the human body requires while sitting. *Ergon,* introduced in 1976, was a contract chair designed to support a variety of bodies, housing a variety of minds, performing various levels of work in offices. It was an effective interpretation for end users of what Stumpf had learned from human factors experts, physiologists, orthopedists, and other specialists.

Through such projects Bill Stumpf has become known as "research oriented," which is technically accurate, I suppose, but misleading. The frame-and-tile office system called *Ethospace* is a case in point. As densely researched as any office furniture product on the market, it nevertheless reflects at every point the proclivities of the designer himself. "Given a choice, wouldn't anyone rather have a window?" Stumpf asked rhetorically, before incorporating the sense of that choice into the product. Even the best panel systems available at the time communicated a temporary feeling. Was there a way to combine the physicality, the *presence* of a room with the openness, flexibility, and economy of a partitioned space?

As it turned out, there wasn't. That is, there wasn't any *one* way. But by introducing a combination of features—e.g., walls that are thick and strong but light—Stumpf was able to address the problem humanely. The result is a product that introduced to the open office the feeling of interior solidity that had heretofore been the exclusive province of rooms with dry walls.

Among Stumpf's current interests is a series of products for the elderly and the disabled. Here again, the research is deep and broad, but at every point subordinate to common sense. The actor John Barrymore once portrayed a man with a severe limp. An admirer asked how he had trained himself to limp so authentically. "I didn't," Barrymore retorted. "I trained myself to think like a man who limps. Then I tried as hard as I could to walk normally."

Some end users are disabled by genetics or accident or age. Many more of us are disabled by the built environment. The process of designing for them is the same for Bill Stumpf. He identifies first with the user's humanity, *then* with his or her problems.

Then he tries as hard as he can to walk normally.

—Ralph Caplan

# SUGIURA, Kohei

Japanese exhibition, book, poster, and graphic designer

**Born:** Tokyo, 8 September 1932. **Education:** Studied at the University of Arts and Architecture, Tokyo, Dip., 1955. **Family:**

Married Fumiko Hasegawa in 1957 (died, 1982). **Career:** Freelance book, magazine, poster, logotype, and graphic designer, Tokyo, from 1955, and exhibition designer and organizer, from 1966; art director of Tokyo magazines, *Space Design,* 1966-70, *Toshi Jutaku,* 1967-70, *Ginka,* from 1968, *Yu,* 1971-80, *Asian Culture,* from 1972, and *Episteme,* 1975-79. Guest professor, Hochschule für Gestaltung, Ulm, 1964-65, 1966-67; assistant professor, Zokei University, Tokyo, 1968-70; professor, from 1989, and chief professor of the graduate school, from 1993, Kobe University, Kobe, Japan. **Exhibitions:** *The World of Kohei Sugiura,* Hong Kong, 1986. **Collections:** Museum of Modern Art, New York. **Honors:** Mainichi Design and Industry Prize, Tokyo, 1961; Kodansha Publishing and Cultural Award, Tokyo, 1970; Gold Medal, Leipzig Book Fair, 1978, 1982; Japanese Ministry of Education Prize, 1982. **Address:** 3-3-10-507 Shibuya, Shibuya-ku, Tokyo, Japan.

## Works

*Fluorescent Chrysanthemum* exhibition layout and catalogue, for the Institute of Contemporary Arts, London, 1969.
*Mandala—Now You See, Now You Don't* exhibition layouts, for the Seibu Museum of Art, Tokyo, 1980.
*The Mysterious World of Asian Masks* exhibition layouts and posters, for the Seibu Museum of Art, Tokyo, 1981.
*Asian Cosmology* touring exhibition layouts, for La Foret Museum, Tokyo, and the Kyoto Shinbun Museum, Kyoto, 1982.
Stamps, for Bhutan, 1983-86.
*Fluid Dynamics* laser disc design and editing, Tokyo, 1989.
Japanese stamp commemorating Nagoya Design Exposition, 1989.
Posters, for National Museum of Japanese Folk and History, 1989-1995.
*Dai Nikko* laser disc design and editing, Tokyo, 1990.
Stage design for Buddhist chant performance, National Theatre, Tokyo, 1990, 1991.
Stage and poster design and planning, for Harmonic Choir concert, Tokyo, 1991.
Posters, for ASEAN Cultural Centre, Japan Foundation, 1991.
Posters, for annual concert of Esashi Oiwake, 1991-93.
Posters, for Tateyama Museum, Toyama Prefecture, from 1991.
*Floral Cosmology—Traditions in Dyeing, Weaving, and Ornaments in Asia* exhibition design, for La Foret Museum, Tokyo, 1992 (toured).
Book designs include—(with K. Kawata) *The Map,* Tokyo, 1965; *Zen Uchu-si, Summa Cosmologica,* Tokyo, 1973-78; (with Y. Ishimoto) *Denshingonin Ryokai Mandala,* Tokyo, 1978; (with I. Narahara) *Seven Photographs from Ikko,* Tokyo, 1978; (with K. Kato) *Mandala, nishi-Tibet no Nukkyo Bijutso,* Tokyo, 1980; (with I. Narahara) *Portici di Luche—Piazza San Marco,* Tokyo, 1981; (with H. Tomiyama) *Chinese Peking Opera,* Tokyo, 1981; *Ajia no Uchukan—Kosumosu Mandala,* Tokyo, 1982; *139 Sheets of Tibetan Mandalas of the Sakya Sect,* Tokyo, 1983; (with H. Suga) *Bali—Devassphere, Ashrassphere, Fatassphere,* Tokyo, 1983; *Heibonsha Encyclopaedia,* Tokyo, 1983; *Daijirin,* Tokyo, 1989, 1995; *Collected Works of Leibniz,* Tokyo, 1989-95; *Dai Nikko* (photography), Tokyo, 1990.

## Publications

**By SUGIURA: books**—(with others) *Visual Communication,* Tokyo, 1976; *Venus Urania Pandemos,* exhibition catalogue, Tokyo,

**Kohei Sugiura: exhibition poster for** *Traditions and New Techniques,* **(illustration by Fujio Watanabe, design collaboration by Akihiko Tanimura), 1984**

1982; (and designer, with others) *Mandala no Sekai,* Tokyo, 1983; (and designer, with others) *Moji no Uchu,* Tokyo, 1985; (and designer, with others) *Rittai de Miru Hoshi no Hon,* Tokyo, 1986; (and designer, with others) *Ajia no Uchukan,* Tokyo, 1991; (and designer) *Nihon no Katachi, Ajia no Katachi,* Tokyo, 1994; (and designer, with others) *Enso no Geijutsu Kogaku,* Tokyo, 1995; (and designer, with others) *Moji no Shukusai,* Tokyo, 1995.

**On SUGIURA: books**—*Typography Today* edited by Helmut Schmid, Tokyo, 1981; **articles**—in *Graphic Design* (Tokyo), no. 34, 1969; *Typography* (Tokyo), January 1974; *Design* (Tokyo), November 1977; *Idea* (Tokyo), September 1979; *Creation* (Tokyo), no. 3, 1990, no. 20, 1994.

\*   \*   \*

Kohei Sugiura is an architect of information design. He has given contemporary editorial design new life and new meaning by creating faces of contents rather than make-up. His information starts on the cover, as a magazine is observed at first glance by letting the pages run through the fingers. His covers—extracts of ideas, quotations, and illustrative materials—are two-dimensional with a three-dimensional effect. His interest in time and space makes him positively accept the baptism of the reflecting medium (TV), since a book "is not a thing which sticks to the congealing moment to become a still life, but a thing which structurizes and vectorizes the surroundings to become a dynamic element." Sugiura has invented what might be called "talking typography," which has revolutionized editorial design in Japan. Since the advent of his covers for the magazine *Space Design* in 1966, Sugiura has created many epochal works which shock at first sight but which unfold themselves as having been clearly and conceptually planned and executed. His use of type-size contrasts, for example, are not just the result of his design considerations but his invitation to the reader to enjoy multiple reading distances in order to contact the surface and smell of the paper. The smell of the paper is recently almost always a smell of printing ink. In his book design for *Summa Cosmographica,* the pages are of entirely solid black ink, with text and material in stardust-like white. Here, he even designed the book edge: bent to the left, the Andromeda nebula appears; bent to the right, a constellation table is visible. Sugiura uses the four-color printing process to its limit. His black color, as used on the covers for the magazine *Yu,* is the precise accumulation of three process-colors. "Colors are in black. Black contains all the spectrum in it," he points out.

Sugiura has recently added a new material to visual art—air. In his book design for *Age of Human Dolls,* a seven-millimeter hole is punched through the whole book, symbolizing "a breathing duct for the prana of the cosmos."

—Helmut Schmid

# SUMITA, Yoichi

Japanese industrial designer

**Born:** Ishikawa Prefecture, 22 April 1924. **Education:** Studied at the Ishikawa Prefectural Industrial School, 1937-42; studied under Teizo Hano and Matsugoro Hirokawa, at the University of Arts, Tokyo, 1942-47. **Military Service:** Served in the Second Army for Reserve Officers, at Kurume Military Academy, 1945, Sergeant-Major. **Family:** Married Waka Iwai in 1951; children: Masaaki and Kazuya. **Career:** Designer, for the Technology Institute of the Ministry of Trade and Industry, Tokyo, 1947-52, Tokyo Electric Company, 1952-56, and Yao Electric Company, Kanagawa, 1956-63; freelance designer, working at the Toyoguchi Design Institute, Tokyo, 1963-77; independent designer, working mainly with the Telecommunication Institute and the Japan Telecommunication and Telephone Corporation, Tokyo, from 1977. Professor of design, Tokyo University of Arts, from 1977; visiting lecturer, at Iwate University, Morioka, from 1979, Kyushu Arts and Technology College, Fukuoka, from 1981, and Kanazawa Arts and Design College, from 1982. Director, 1967-81, and director-general, from 1982, Japan Industrial Designers Association, Tokyo; industrial design secretary, Japan Human Engineering Academy, Tokyo; trustee, Japan Design Academy, Tokyo, from 1977. **Exhibitions:** Tokyo University of Arts, 1977. **Collections:** Postage and Telecommunications Museum, Tokyo. **Honors:** Vanzato Prize, 1942; Japan Electrical Industries Prize, Tokyo, 1975. **Address:** 6-23-12 Okusawa, Seata ya-ku, Tokyo 158, Japan.

## Works

*Zuiko Pearlcorder* micro-cassette tape recorder, for Olympus Optical Company, 1968.
*Gastrocamera GT-6* medical camera, for Olympus Optical Company, 1970.
*BH Series* microscope, for Olympus Optical Company, 1975.
*Xenon* 16mm sound projector, for Hokushin Electric Company, 1975.
Car telephone, for Japan Telecommunication and Telephone, 1976.
*Mini* push-button telephone, for Japan Telecommunication and Telephone, 1976.
*Mini-Type* push-button telephone, for Japan Telecommunication and Telephone, 1978.
*Loll* paper holder, for Pultex Japan Limited, 1989.

## Publications

**By SUMITA: books**—*Complete Collection of Industrial Design,* vols. 2-6, Tokyo, 1982-84; **articles**—in *Design News* (Tokyo), no. 6, January 1950, no. 1, 1951, no. 64, 1976; *Industrial Design* (Tokyo), no. 12, 1959, no. 112, 1981; *Modern Living* (Tokyo), no. 3, 1967; *Journal of the Japan Industrial Designers Association* (Tokyo), no. 5, 1972; *Mainichi Shimbun* (Tokyo), 14 January 1975; *Den Den Kensetsu* (Tokyo), no. 94, 1978.

**On SUMITA: articles**—in *Design News* (Tokyo), no. 10, 1955; *Living Design* (Tokyo), no. 6, 1955, no. 4, 1958; *Japan Illuminating Engineering Society Bulletin* (Tokyo), no. 3, 1956; *Industrial Design* (Tokyo), Summer 1961.

\*

I was fortunate to have been employed by the Industrial Arts Institute of the Ministry of International Trade and Industry (MITI) in 1947 when Japan was lacking in basic human needs and when there were few openings for graduates from industrial design school. The Institute, established in 1928, was a national institute to make studies of design of local industries and to promote production of merchandise to be exported. It played a great part in the promotion of industrial design in Japan before modern concepts were introduced.

My assignment during the early period of this employment decided my future course. In the third year, I was given the theme of the container with a spout for serving liquid, such as water or soybean sauce, and was supposed to design safeguards against the overflow of liquid when pouring. In the near absence of reference materials, I devised experimental instruments, tested some samples, and expressed the data numerically. This outcome, published in 1950, was well received and led me into the world of industrial design even before Japan had received modern ideas in this field.

Based on my initial experiences, I came to conclude that objects of everyday life should be beautiful in shape, as well as easy and pleasant to use for a long time. By identifying what the product should be like and grasping the needs of consumers correctly, designers can offer better products—which, in turn, will bring greater social recognition to designers.

Japan's present material affluence could never have been imagined three decades ago. However, the present situation leads to uniformity of individual lives because of mass-production, whereas man at present has reached the stage of seeking self-realization and individuality. Designers now should search for ways of satisfying the diversified desires of the future, when no one can foresee how to cope with the various possibilities that the advancement of technology may bring about.

Means for identifying the needs of people and for grasping the new lifestyle in the bud and mechanisms for mobilizing those involved in the work are essential problems today. I would like to do my best to make both the ideals and the practical role of designers effective in the problem-solving process.

—Yoichi Sumita

\*       \*       \*

The consistency found in Yoichi Sumita's work derives from his "research and design" approach. In the 1950s, he tackled research on the functions of containers with spouts. He took as his main problem how to prevent liquid in the container from running out, and he studied this by developing methodology and methods for testing. Significantly, his study was accomplished right before the modern concept of industrial design was introduced to Japan. Later, he was employed by a maker of illumination and lighting apparatuses, and he drew public attention with his non-symmetric fluorescent desk stands. He then moved to a firm that made electrical appliances for the home, and here he devoted himself more to organizational work and management.

In 1963, he became a freelance designer at the Toyoguchi Design Institute, where his major work was the development of telephones for the Japan Telecommunication and Telephone Corporation. Here again, he displayed his "research and design" approach to its full extent. His basics are "observation of product sample in use," in which human engineering is adopted, and "knowing the usefulness of something to hold by holding it yourself." His logical and verifiable method, which he put to use in designing public utilities is of epoch-making importance, for the Japanese in general tend to be sentimental, emotional, and conceptual even when making things.

He believes that design is "the making of high-quality products," and that "the making of long-lived products takes long prepara-

tion." At present committed to bettering the design of public utilities/facilities, he is making approaches to governmental offices, so that government workers might be well aware of the importance of design. Sumita also teaches at the Tokyo University of Arts and has been Director General of the Japan Industrial Designers Association since 1981.

—Kunio Sano

## SVENSSON, Inez (Gudrun Linnea)
Swedish textile and ceramics designer

**Born:** Mariestad, 28 March 1932. **Education:** Studied fashion and textile design, Anders Beckman's School, Stockholm, 1951-53, School of the Art Institute of Chicago, 1956. **Career:** Worked under Astrid Sampe, Nordiska Kompaniet textile design studio, Stockholm, 1954; textile designer, Stobo-Textil company, Stockholm, 1954-55; head of design, Boras Wäfveri cotton mills, Sweden, 1957-67; founder-director, with Gunila Axen, Britt-Marie Christoffersson, Carl Johan De Geer, Susanne Grundell, Lotte Hagerman, Birgitta Hahn, Tom Hedqvist, Ingela Hakansson, and Tage Moller, of Tio-Gruppen (Group of Ten) textile design company, Stockholm, from 1970; also freelance designer, for Ikea, from 1964, for Boras, from 1967, and for Rorstrand, from 1988. Fashion illustrator and reporter, for *Dagens Nyheter, Vi, Expressen, Form,* and others, Stockholm, from 1961; co-founder and director, with Carl Butler, of Svensson and Butler cook-shop and restaurant, Stockholm, from 1968; product development expert, United Nations Industrial Design Organization (UNIDO), Pakistan, 1974-75. **Member:** Board Member, National Association of Swedish Handicraft Societies, 1984-88; Statens Konstmuseet, Stockholm, from 1989. **Exhibitions:** *H55 International Design Exhibition,* Halsingborg, Sweden, 1955; *Design in Scandinavia,* toured the United States, 1955; *Scandinavian Modern Design 1880-1980,* Cooper-Hewitt Museum, New York, 1982; *Contemporary Swedish Design,* Nationalmuseum, Stockholm, 1983; *Design in Sweden,* Swedish Institute, Paris, 1987 (toured); *Tio-Gruppen: retrospective,* Stockholm Cultural Centre, 1987. **Collections:** Nationalmuseum, Stockholm; Röhsska Konstslöjdmuseet, Göteborg; Staatliches Museum fur Angewandte Kunst, Munich. **Honor:** SIDA Swedish Aid Grant, Stockholm, 1978. **Address:** Vikingagatan 13, 11342 Stockholm, Sweden.

### Works

*Kally* fabric, for Stobo-Textil, 1954.
*Strix* and *Strax* fabrics, for Ikea, 1971.
*Cuba* fabric, for Tio-Gruppen, 1972.
*Pensel* fabric, for Boras, 1977.
*Banana Split* fabric, for Tio-Gruppen, 1979.
*Amadeus* and *Zero* fabrics, for Boras, 1983.
*Ultra* fabric, for Tio-Gruppen, 1983.
*Ratsch* printed cotton, for Boras, 1983.
*MM* fabric, for Boras, 1985.
*Tam-Tam* fabric, for Tio-Gruppen, 1986.
*Havanna* fabric, for Tio-Gruppen, 1986.
*Break-Dish* ceramic plates, for Rorstrand, 1988.
*A Taste of Lemon* ceramic plates, for Rorstrand, 1988.

*Trumf* and *Trix* fabrics, for Boras, 1988.
*Sang* printed cotton, for Boras, 1988.


**Publications**

**By SVENSSON: books**—*Tryckta Tyger, fran 30-tal till 80-tall,*
Stockholm, 1984; (with others) *Den Svenska Formen,* Stockholm,
1985; *Formgivarnas Stickbok,* Stockholm, 1986.


**On SVENSSON: books**—*Forma Sueca* by Ake Stavenow and
Ake H. Huldt, Göteborg, 1961; *Svensk Textilkonstl Swedish Textile
Art* by Edna Martin and Beate Sydhoff, Stockholm, 1980; *Form
och Tradition i Sverige* edited by Birgitta Walz, Stockholm, 1982;
*Scandinavian Modern Design 1880-1980* edited by David Revere
McFadden, New York, 1982; *Contemporary Swedish Design,* exhi-
bition catalogue by Monica Boman, Lennart Lindkvist, and others,
Stockholm, 1983.


\*


I nearly always work with geometrical patterns with delicate
shifts of nuance. Early functionalism is one of my sources of inspiration. I hate patterns that float out into nothingness. Patterns
must be tangible, and sound like music—jazz or pop.

Design should always be about searching for quality. Printed
textile is a sort of mass-produced art. I believe in the old slogan
from 1919: "More Beautiful Things for Everyday Life."

But it is easier said than done: design has become a tool of industry, instead of industry being a tool for the designer. It takes a lot of
fighting.

—Inez Svensson

\*      \*      \*


The patterns are like visualized jazz on the white or black surfaces of the cotton fabrics. The air is filled with impertinent signals,
whirring and roaring. The shapes spin and streak like comets,
amoeba-like and futuristic. We are clattering and chattering into
tomorrow. Such is The Group of Ten's latest collection, *Mega-
phone,* an obvious descendent of such early 20th-century avant-
garde figures as Kandinsky and Mayakovsky.

How can multiprint sold here by the yard be as concentrated and
expressive as art pictures? Perhaps the pattern units are a work of
art in some sort of way. The Group of Ten have broken the bounds
of the "permissible" in most things they have undertaken. Their
patterns have migrated to streets and squares, three-piece suites,
kitchen tables, sheets and pillow cases and walls. Both skinny
teenage legs and adult corporations have been made much more fun
to look at. In all modesty, The Group of Ten have fulfilled the
dreams of the avant-garde pioneers of this century. They have
taken art to the masses. To understand how this was possible, one
has to think back into the 1960s. The new Swedish School of Arts,
Crafts and Design in Stockholm (built in 1958) had a printed fabrics
department. Young students acquired a new opportunity of self-
expression: hand printing, using silk-screen frames. (Until then,
only woven pictures had been considered presentable.)

The School also had a printer, Richard Kunzl, who knew most of
what there was to know about dyes, recipes, and printing techniques. He would never allow himself to be put off by difficulties;

every problem had a solution. If it had not been for Kunzl, The
Group of Ten would probably never have existed. He has backed
them up over the years with information and advice. For although
The Group of Ten's fabrics are woven industrially at Boras Wäfveri,
craft knowledge is an essential foundation. And although their products may seem avant-garde, they have a source of inspiration in the
exuberance of Swedish folk art.

But there are many reasons why the ten became what they became. Inez Svensson, one of the members of the group, was employed in the mid-sixties as Art Director at Boras Wäfveri. She
managed to convince the management that they needed a "free
pattern quota." The patterns in this collection were allowed to be
bigger and bolder than the rest of the product range, most of which
consisted of turgid, run-of-the-mill floral designs. The new fabrics
appeared on department store counters like cheerful, cheeky exclamation marks. Fresh, bright colours, clear, sweeping, humorous
patterns. They felt like a present and a release. This is what one's
own home could be made to look like, as opposed to itsy-bitsy
conservatism and a colour scheme as romantic as brown Windsor
soup. Some of the patterns became best-sellers: Gunila Axen's
*Cloud* fabric (1966) and Brigitta Hahn's *Poppy* (1968), for example.
But the collection was still dependent on seasonal sales. A pattern
had just about three months in which to gain the consumers' approval, otherwise it would disappear from the collection, no matter
how good it was. In addition, many pattern designers saw their
ideas being corrupted by industry. Colour schemes were changed,
and outlines lost their sharpness. The artists were mentioned by
name, but they were not always willing to be associated with the
end product. Suppose the artist could also take charge of production, deciding independently what the color schemes were to be and
how long the patterns were to remain in production?

Inez Svensson had an idea—a group of ten pattern designers who
were capable of working together and of turning out patterns that
would really catch on. She was as good as her word. It took a few
years, but by 1970 she had mobilized ten pattern designers: Gunila
Axen, Britt-Marie Christoffersson, Carl Johan De Geer, Susanne
Grundell, Lotta Hågerman, Brigitta Hahn, Tom Hedqvist, Ingela
Håkansson, Tage Möller, and Inez Svensson. Together they printed
a poster in English, offering their services: "We are ten Swedish
designers working with textiles, paper and plastic. Swedish textile
manufacturing is in a state of crisis. This concerns us too. We feel
isolated and we want to reach out. If you're interested in good
Swedish design, please get in touch with us whether you are passing through Sweden or not...."

Many people did get in touch, in the belief that the fabrics shown
in the poster were commercially available. But some of them did
not even exist as yet. It was time to start production, and Boras
Wäfveri undertook to print the fabrics—ten fabrics altogether.
(Finlayson had previously backed out. "Nobody could possibly
want to buy such eccentric fabrics!")

In 1973 the group opened a shop of its own in Gamla Brogatan,
Stockholm. But its biggest successes were scored outside Sweden.
Henri Deconinch, head of Boras Wäfveri's European office, has
always been full of encouragement. The group's exhibitions have
been given jubilant receptions in Paris and Italy. One French fashion designer, France Andre Vie, has brought out three collections
using fabrics produced by The Ten.

Now at last the group is beginning to receive the attention it
deserves in Sweden as well. Boras Wäfveri displays their fabrics at
international trade fairs. Nordiska Kompaniet has recently added a
number of their fabrics to its range, and in Stockholm itself the

group's patterned garments are beginning to be seen on the streets, mostly in the younger age group. A glance back at the 1970s will suffice to show what pioneers the group have really been, not only through their patterns but also through their attitude to interior design. In museums and galleries all over the country, they have put on impudent and unconventional exhibitions. They have upholstered furniture and produced interiors of a kind which Italy has only come to match in very recent years. They have provided collective, hand-printed decorations for eighteen dining rooms and restrooms at the National Prison and Probation Administration and the National Administration of Shipping and Navigation in Norrkoping. They have produced magnificent pictures in a kind of patchwork technique (skarvsöm), in which the basic patterns acquire completely different qualities of expression. They have displayed unique pictures at art galleries, and they have produced joint collections for Ikea (a hypermarket chain dealing in furniture and furnishings) and the Duro wallpaper factory.

Their versatility is unrivalled in the textile design profession. They have a knack of doing what one least expects, boldly and cheerfully. Their shop window displays in Gamla Brogatan are a thing apart. They paint furniture like dainty suites and they devise gismos and combinations way ahead of the commercial trend setters. *Festival, Space,* and *Jazz* are pattern names which say a great deal about the way they work. They have loyally supported one another, sharing proceeds and outgoings, ups and downs. They are a strong team and each individual member is good at his or her particular expertise. Separately they would never have made it. They always start by working out the general concept, what they want to achieve in a new collection, what different types of patterns it should contain so that the recipients can get as much out of it as possible. A recent pattern collection begins with four large, expressionist patterns with two striped fabrics in between, "like a sort of glue." The first manifestation, the second basic collection, the third (entitled *Marine*), the fourth (in black and white) and the fifth (entitled *Jamaica*) included many patterns which are still being manufactured. This if anything shows that patterns are capable of surviving more than one season, and that we consumers are not always on the lookout for something new—we can stick to old friends as well. The Ten are at the thin end of the wedge for commercialism. Living proof that things can be done differently.

—Kerstin Wickman

# SVOBODA, Josef

Czechoslovak stage, film, and exhibition designer

**Born:** Caslav, 10 May 1920. **Education:** Educated at a gymnasium, Caslav, until 1938; studied carpentry and cabinetmaking with his father, Caslav, 1935-37; studied philosophy, at Charles University, Prague, 1939; studied carpentry, at a vocational school, Prague, 1940-41; studied interior design, at the Industrial and Technical School, Prague, 1941-43; studied architecture, at the School of Fine and Applied Arts, Prague, Dip. Arch., 1950. **Family:** Married Libuse Hrubesova in 1948. **Career:** Amateur stage designer, Prague, 1941-45; founder-member and designer, 1945, technical director and chief designer, 1946-48, at the Grand Opera of the Fifth of May, Prague; technical supervisor and deputy designer, 1948-50, chief designer and technical director, from 1950, at the Smetana

Theatre and National Theatre, Prague; artistic director, Laterna Magica experimental studio of the National Theatre, Prague, from 1973. Founder-member, New Group of theatre writers and artists, Prague, 1943-45; general secretary, International Organization of Scenographers and Theatre Technicians, from 1971. Instructor in scenography, Theatre Academy, Prague, 1952-58; professor, Academy of Fine and Industrial Arts, Prague, from 1969. **Exhibitions:** National Theatre, Prague, 1961; Theatre Institute, Prague, 1966, 1969. **Honors:** Czech State Prize, Prague, 1954; Industrial Design Award and Gold Medals, World's Fair, Brussels, 1958; Scenography Award, Bienal of Sao Paulo, 1961; Merited Artist of the CSSR, Prague, 1966; National Artist of the CSSR, Prague, 1968; Sikkens Prize, Amsterdam, 1969; Honorary Royal Academician, London, 1969. **Address:** Filmarska 535/17, 15200 Prague, Czechoslovakia.

## Works

Stage productions include—*Empedokles,* Smetana Museum, Prague, 1943; *The Bride,* Smetana Museum, 1943; *The Fox Trap,* Municipal Chamber Theatre, Prague, 1944; *Manon Lescaut,* Municipal Theatre, Teplice, 1946; *Tales of Hoffman,* Grand Opera, Prague, 1946; *Andre and the Dragon,* Horacka Theatre, Jihlava, 1946; *The Bartered Bride,* Grand Opera of 5 May, 1946; *Insect Comedy,* National Theatre, Prague, 1946; *Aida,* Grand Opera of 5 May, 1947; *The Mayor of Stilmond,* Theatre of 5 May, Prague, 1947; *The Purge,* Satire Theatre, Prague, 1947; *The Little Foxes,* National Theatre, Prague, 1948; *El Amor Brujo,* Grand Opera of 5 May, 1948; *The Rogue's Ballad,* Grand Opera of 5 May, 1948; *Marysa,* National Theatre, Prague, 1948; *The Czech Manager,* Smetana Theatre, Prague, 1949; *The Flaming Border,* Tyl Theatre, Prague, 1949; *The Bride of Chod,* Tyl Theatre, 1949; *The 11th Commandment,* State Film Theatre, Prague, 1950; *Der Freischutz,* Smetana Theatre, 1952; *The Robber,* Tyl Theatre, 1954; *A High Summer Sky,* Tyl Theatre, 1955; *Janosik,* State Opera, Dresden, 1956; *The Entertainer,* Tyl Theatre, 1957; *Rusalka,* Teatro La Fenice, Venice, 1958; *The Flying Dutchman,* Smetana Theatre, 1959; *The Seagull,* Tyl Theatre, 1960; *Intoleranza 1960,* Teatro La Fenice, Venice, 1961; *The Story of a Right Man,* National Theatre, Prague, 1961; *Julietta,* National Theatre, Prague, 1963; *La Sonnambula,* The National Ballet, Amsterdam, 1964; *The Whirlpool,* National Theatre, Prague, 1964; *Hamlet,* Belgian National Theatre, Brussels, 1965; *Atomtod,* Teatro La Scala, Milan, 1965; *The Makropulos Affair,* National Theatre, Prague, 1965; *The Storm,* National Theatre, London, 1966; *The Three Sisters,* National Theatre, London, 1967; *Delibor,* National Theatre, Prague, 1967; *One-Ended Rope,* Theatre Behind the Gate, Prague, 1967; *Faust,* State Theatre, Wiesbaden, West Germany, 1968; *The Soldiers,* State Opera, Munich, 1969; *The Fiery Angel,* Municipal Theatre, Frankfurt, 1969; *Pélleas ei Mélisande,* Royal Opera House/Covent Garden, London, 1969; *The Clown,* Municipal Theatre, Düsseldorf, 1970; *Waiting for Godot,* State Theatre, Salzburg, 1970; *Idomeneo,* State Opera, Vienna, 1971; *Tannhäuser,* Royal Opera House/Covent Garden, London, 1973; *Tristan and Isolde,* Bayreuth, 1974; *The Ring,* Royal Opera House/Covent Garden, London, 1974-76; *Die Soldaten,* Hamburg, 1976; *The Queen of Spades,* Prague, 1976; *The Magic Circus,* Prague, 1977; *Idomeneo,* Prague, 1982; *Hamlet,* Prague, 1982; *Antigone,* Zurich, 1983; *Saint Joan at the Stake,* Zurich, 1983; *Six Characters in Search of an Author,* Louvain, 1984; *Break of Noon,* Louvain, 1984; *The Sea Gull,*

Prague, 1986; *Ghetto,* Oslo, 1986; *Nabucco,* Zurich, 1986; *Odysseus,* Prague, 1987; *Vivisection,* Prague, 1987; *Ring Cycle,* Orange, France, 1988; *Faust,* Milan, 1989; *Minotaur,* Prague, 1989.

## Publications

**By SVOBODA: articles**—in *Informacni Zpravy Scenograficke Laboratore* (Prague), September 1958; *Divadlo* (Prague), no. 1, 1964, no. 5, 1966, no. 8, 1967, no. 2, 1968; *Opera* (New York), August 1967; *Acta Scenographia* (Prague), January 1969.

**On SVOBODA: books**—*Le Theatre en Tchecoslovaquie: Scenographie* edited by Vladimir Jindra, Prague, 1962; *Josef Svoboda,* exhibition catalogue by Denis Bablet, Prague, 1966; *Laterna Magica* edited by Jiri Hrbas, Prague, 1968; *The Art of Stage Lighting* by Frederick Bentham, London, 1968, 1980; *Josef Svoboda* by Denis Bablet, Turin and Lausanne, 1970; *The Scenography of Josef Svoboda* by Jarka Burian, Middletown, 1971, 1974; *Teatr Josefa Svobody* by V. Berjozkin, Moscow, 1973.

\*     \*     \*

Josef Svoboda's creativity may be viewed as an evolution of the major non-realistic movements in Western theatre of the last century. Without having studied their work, he is the heir of Adolphe Appia and Gordon Craig; his work also reflects many aspects of futurism, constructivism, and the Bauhaus approach, and he drew from the work of his own countrymen, especially E. F. Burian, Frantisek Troster, and Alfred Radok. He has, however, gone beyond the work of these partial prototypes to create new archetypes in scenography for the twentieth century.

Svoboda prefers the term "scenographer" to "scene designer" because the latter has traditionally been associated with easel painting and decoration, whereas the scenographer is concerned with many other means of bringing a script and production concept to life on stage. A scenographer is primarily concerned with spatial relations not only on stage but also in relation to total theatre space. Moreover, a scenographer relies not only on painted decor but on sound and lighting, including projections; not only on static scenery but its expressive movement. Science and technology are not alien mysteries to a scenographer, but sources of enriched stage performance.

For Svoboda, the total stage environment does not merely establish a passive "place" for the dramatic action but provides a dynamic element of the total theatrical creation, an element capable of expressing (in its own "language") the meanings of the play with a force equal to the spoken or mimed parts of the action. In short, scenography becomes another actor in the total performance, and, like the actor, the scenography must be capable of transformation during the performance in response to the flow of the action, whether materially by kinetics or insubstantially by lighting, projections, sound, or other special means.

Svoboda most often seeks a relatively abstract, architectonic, and metaphoric expression for his scenography. He does not reject realism as a valid method for certain works, but he prefers to eliminate literal detail and fanciful decoration in favour of highly selective, figurative, and dramatically functional forms. His creative process involves a search for the scenographic "system" that will most fully convey a play's meanings as interpreted by the mutual delib-

erations of director and designer. The system may be a fundamentally architectonic configuration of plastic forms, or it may be based on combinations of technical instruments and special materials. Whatever the system, it will probably involve contemporary materials and instruments, and it will certainly reflect a contemporary sensibility rather than reproduce or echo past traditions. The ultimate goal is the achievement of a scenographic instrument that offers the greatest opportunities for the expression of the central production concept.

A few of Svoboda's key productions illustrate the range of his scenography. Smetana's opera *Dalibor* (Prague, 1967) involved two huge towers on separate turntables plus specially designed, high-intensity lighting instruments to create curtains of light. F. Hrubin's *A Sunday in August* (Prague, 1958) also made use of these lighting instruments in conjunction with frontal and rear projectors casting light and images onto a specially arranged series of scrims and opaque screens. Wagner's *Ring* at Covent Garden (1974-76) had as its central scenographic component a square platform capable of rising, sinking, rotating, and tilting; its mirrored undersurface reflected action below stage while the top surface contained sections of stairs that automatically adjusted their position depending on the angle of the platform. In this production, Svoboda also made use of filmed laser projections in conjunction with scene changes.

Literally miles of strung cords filled much of the stage for *Tristan and Isolde* (Bayreuth, 1974) to create an effect of three-dimensional color as the cords received pointillistic, front-and-rear-projected images from a battery of high-powered instruments. Similar, originally created and projected color images were used in *Tannhäuser* (Covent Garden, 1973) in conjunction with suspended panels and mirrors above a series of inflated forms at stage level to create the erotic Venusberg scene. For Alois Zimmerman's opera *Die Soldaten* (Hamburg, 1976), Svoboda used the series of multi-tiered stage lifts of the theatre to create simultaneous performing areas in multiple planes and elevations. On more than one occasion, most notably for a Prague *Don Giovanni* (1969), Svoboda built on stage a background that was a mirror-like reproduction of the auditorium of the theatre. For this *Giovanni,* it heightened the significance of the theatre building itself (the site of the opera's premiere) and added to the essential theatricality of the performance.

Svoboda's protean creativity continued to explore the parameters of scenography in the 1980s. Several productions exhibited his talents in no-proscenium spaces: Orff's *Antigone* and Honegger's *Saint Joan at the Stake,* both in 1983 in Zurich's Congress Palace, Joshua Sobol's *Ghetto* in a complete arena staging in Oslo, 1986, and Verdi's *Nabucco* in 1986 in Zurich's Hallenstadion. Other productions employed highly poetic projections in conjunction with architectonic forms in studio productions: Pirandello's *Six Characters in Search of the Author* and Claudel's *Break of Noon,* both in Louvain, 1984.

Of special interest is Svoboda's multi-media production of *Odysseus,* a highly expressive combination of live choreography, complex projections of documentary, live, and animated material, and multi-track stereophonic sound. The whole production is the product of the Laterna Magika team, now part of the National Theatre and headed by Svoboda. Since its opening in Prague's Cultural Palace in 1987 it has also played in Munster, GFR, and plans are being made to tour other parts of Europe.

In the summer of 1988 Svoboda designed his third Wagner *Ring* cycle, this time in the spacious antique Roman theatre in Orange, France. The scenography was based on a huge geodesic quarter globe lined with perforated material to take projections but also allow sight of the sculpturesque Roman scenic wall behind it. Laterally movable platform elements beneath the globe reflected the concave shape of the Orange auditorium itself.

Currently Svoboda is closely collaborating on productions with two other internationally celebrated theatre artists: with Georgio Strehler he is working on a production of Goethe's *Faust* in Milan; and after teaming with Friedrich Durrenmatt on the premiere of the latter's *Achterloo* (1988) in West Germany, he premiered Durrenmatt's new work, *Minotaur,* presented in Prague.

—Jarka M. Burian

# SWIERZY, Waldemar

Polish graphic designer

**Born:** Katowice, 9 September 1931. **Education:** Studied graphics, at the Academy of Fine Arts, Krakow, 1947-51. **Family:** Married Magdalena Karaskiewicz in 1981; children: Dorota. **Career:** Freelance poster and graphics designer, Warsaw, from 1952. Assistant, 1965-67, lecturer, 1967-88, and professor, from 1988, Higher School of Fine Arts, Poznan. **Member:** Polish section chairman, Alliance Graphique Internationale, from 1974; president, International Poster Biennale, Warsaw, from 1978. **Exhibitions:** Alexanderplatz, East Berlin, 1959; Polish Cultural Centre, Budapest, 1959; Polish Cultural Centre, Prague, 1959; Biberstrasse Galerie, Vienna, 1960; *Soyuz Chudoznikow,* Moscow, 1965; Bienal of Sao Paulo, 1969; Casa de las Americas, Havana, 1970; Kungliga Biblioteket, Stockholm, 1976; Poliforum Siqueiros, Mexico City, 1980; Oxe Galleri, Copenhagen, 1982; Art Gallery, Pecs, Hungary, 1984; Muzeum Sztuki, Poznan, 1986; Museo d'Aosta, Italy, 1987; Kunstakademie, Kassel, 1990; Creation Gallery, Tokyo, 1991; Festival de Affiche, Chaumont, 1993; Galeria Design BWA, Wroclaw, 1995. **Collections:** Poster Museum, Warsaw; Pushkin Museum, Moscow; Stedelijk Museum, Amsterdam; Galleria d'Arte Moderna, Venice; Museum of Modern Art, New York. **Honors:** Prix Toulouse-Lautrec, Paris, 1959, 1962; Gold Medal, Katowice Poster Biennale, 1965, 1971, 1975; Gold Medal, Bienal of Sao Paulo, 1969; Silver Medal, Warsaw Poster Biennale, 1972, 1976; *Hollywood Reporter* Prize, California, 1975, 1985; Gold Medal, Lahti Poster Biennale, Finland, 1977. **Address:** ul. Piwna 45/47, m 14, 00-265 Warsaw, Poland.

## Works

*Mazowsze* poster, for WAG, Warsaw, 1954.
*Czerwona Oberza* poster, for CWF, Warsaw, 1955.
*Matka Joanna od Aniolow* poster, for CWF, Warsaw, 1961.
*Cyrk* poster, for WAG, Warsaw, 1970.
*Budowniczy Solness* poster, for Teatr Klasyczny, Warsaw, 1971.
*Biesy* poster, for Teatr Stary, Krakow, 1972.
*Tadeusz Brzozowski* poster, for KAW, Poznan, 1974.
*Jimi Hendrix* poster, for KAW, Warsaw, 1974.
*Szepty i krzyki* poster, for CWF, Warsaw, 1974.
*Stanislaw Teisseyre* poster, for CBWA, Warsaw, 1975.
*Charlie Parker* poster, for KAW, Warsaw, 1975.
*Jozef Mroszczak* poster, for Galeria PP, Desa, 1976.
*Jazz Jamboree 76* poster, for PSJ, Warsaw, 1976.

*Psy Wojny* poster, for Polfilm, 1984.
*Count Basie* poster, for Plakat Polski, 1985.
*Majakowski* poster, for Teatr Nowy, Warsaw, 1988.
*Jazz Jamboree 88* poster, for PSJ, Warsaw, 1988.

## Publications

**By SWIERZY: articles**—in *Projekt* (Warsaw), February 1976, February 1977.

**On SWIERZY: books**—*The New Graphic Design* by Karl Gerstner and Markus Kutter, Teufen and London, 1959; *Polnische Plakatkunst* by Jozef Mroszczak, Vienna, 1962; *The Poster: An Illustrated History from 1860* by Harold F. Hutchinson, London and Toronto, 1968; *Polish Poster Art Today* by Szymon Bojko, Warsaw, 1972; *Circus Posters* by Jack Rennert, New York, 1974; *Contemporary Polish Posters in Full Color* edited by Joseph S. Czestochowski, New York, 1979.

*

To hear doesn't necessarily mean to listen, but to see, you are bound to look at something. A poster is not designed for the purpose of a particular exhibition, but rather for the street—the place which is least suited for contemplation. A poster designer cannot depend on the goodwill of a passerby and one's immediate acceptance of the work. Thus, to achieve the desired effect, the artist must employ extreme means to arrest the viewer's attention.

Aggression and impudence are a poster's qualities. A poster must be observed unconsciously, even against one's will. It must attract a whole range of one's sensibilities, and it must also clearly communicate its basic impact in as loud a "voice" as possible.

I speak of the poster designer, for it is the only creative discipline in which I am interested. I began my gamble of missing spectators' attention thirty years ago, and I still find myself overwhelmed by poster design and under its spell.

—Waldemar Swierzy

*       *       *

The phrase "the ultimate poster machine" best characterizes Waldemar Swierzy. Now in his early fifties, Swierzy has produced more than 1,200 posters, or according to some estimates, two thousand. Inflated figures? Real ones. Since the mid 1950s when this incredible locomotive began to gain steam, an unbroken flood of posters has come from his studio to Poland as well as to several Western European countries. He creates all kinds of posters—film, theatrical, political advertising, art, social, music, jazz, holiday, tourist. Anything which demands the publishing of a poster can count on Swierzy's skills and overwhelming versatility.

If someone could assemble all of this amazing mass of paper designed by Swierzy in one place (perhaps Madison Square Garden would not be big enough), one would see the changing panorama of world art styles from the 1950s to today. Early, his work was painterly, typical of the Polish poster school. This was followed by the 1960s Art Deco, Pop art, and psychedelic themes and then by 1970s New Figuration portraits. Although Swierzy's creations show an amazingly wide range, don't think that he simply changes his hand or style like a chameleon. True, Swierzy's posters

**Waldemar Swierzy: Exhibition poster for the Muzeum Sztuki, Poznan, 1986**

differ dramatically if seen from the distance of a decade, but remember, the poster is a short-lived butterfly of the street. It serves a day's, maybe a month's duty only to be destroyed by the next wave of new ones, or the rain, or simply a hostile hand.

Swierzy's magic lies in his sense of our times, in the actuality of his work being created today for tomorrow. The film poster for *The Wedding,* a romantic play by the early twentieth century writer Wyspianski, captures all of the nostalgia, struggle, and craziness of the times, as recreated on the silver screen. Jimi Hendrix's high-flying, psychedelic, and fluorescent poster serves its hero ideally, suggesting the madness of his days, the music, even the dust of Woodstock. Painter Tadeusz Brzozowski's retrospective poster, beautifully painted (yes, painted) by his friend Swierzy relates closely to its subject's style. No other poster artist changes style with such ease, focuses right on target, and almost never misses.

Some of his friends are unhappy that Swierzy never seriously tried to become a "real" painter of oil on canvas. But he rebukes them, saying his joy is not to create pure-art "nonsense" for its own sake but rather to communicate thousands of ideas directly to the public. Like colorful video-recordings, his posters tirelessly show the kaleidoscope of trends, fancies, horrors, and dreams, all of them magically transformed from the simple light in Swierzy's mind to street displays available to all without cost.

—Jan Sawka

# SYLBERT, Richard
American film designer

**Born:** Brooklyn, New York, in 1928. **Education:** Studied at Tyler School of Art, Philadelphia, 1946-50. **Career:** Television art director, New York, 1951-53; freelance film designer, Hollywood, California, 1953-75; head of production, Paramount Pictures, Hollywood, 1975-78; independent film designer, from 1979. **Honors:** Academy Award, 1966. **Address:** c/o Paramount Pictures Corporation, 5555 Melrose Avenue, Hollywood, California 90038-3197, U.S.A.

## Works

Film designs include—*Crowded Paradise* (Pressburger), 1956; *Baby Doll* (Kazan), 1956; *A Face in the Crowd* (Kazan), 1957; *Edge of the City* (Ritt), 1957; *Wind Across the Everglades* (Ray), 1958; *The Fugitive Kind* (Lumet), 1960; *Murder Inc.* (Balaban and Rosenberg), 1960; *Mad Dog Coll* (Balaban), 1961; *Splendor in the Grass* (Kazan), 1961; *The Young Doctors* (Karlson), 1961; *Walk on the Wild Side* (Dymytryk), 1962; *The Manchurian Candidate* (Frankenheimer), 1962; *The Connection* (Clarke), 1962; *Long Day's Journey into Night* (Lumet), 1962; *All the Way Home* (Segal), 1963; *Lilith* (Rossen), 1964; *How to Murder Your Wife* (Quine), 1965; *The Pawnbroker* (Lumet), 1965; *What's New Pussycat?* (Donner), 1965; *Who's Afraid of Virginia Woolf?* (Nichols), 1966; *Grand Prix* (Frankenheimer), 1966; *The Graduate* (Nichols), 1967; *Rosemary's Baby* (Polanski), 1968; *The April Fools* (Rosenberg), 1969; *The Illustrated Man* (Smight), 1969; *Catch-22* (Nichols), 1970; *Carnal Knowledge* (Nichols), 1971; *Fat City* (Huston), 1972; *The Heartbreak Kid* (May), 1972; *The Day of the Dolphin* (Nichols), 1973; *Chinatown* (Polanski), 1974; *The Fortune* (Nichols), 1975; *Shampoo* (Ashby), 1975; *Last Hours Before Morning* (Hardy—for TV), 1975; *Players* (Harvey), 1979; *Reds* (Beatty), 1981; *Partners* (Burrows), 1982; *Frances* (Clifford), 1982; *Breathless* (McBride), 1983; *The Cotton Club* (Coppola), 1984; *Under the Cherry Moon* (Prince), 1986; *Dick Tracy* (Beatty), 1990.

## Publications

**By SYLBERT: articles**—in *Film Heritage* (Dayton, Ohio), Fall 1975; *Film Comment* (New York), January/February 1982; *Stills* (London), May 1985, *American Film* (Washington, D.C.), December 1985.

**On SYLBERT: book**—*International Dictionary of Films and Filmmakers,* Chicago and London, 1987, 1991.

\* \* \*

Sylbert's choices for the lush, wealthy worlds of contemporary Los Angeles in *Shampoo* also ring true as actual locations, although the design program is based mostly on color and pattern. The key characters, especially the women of the story, each have distinctive houses, offices, or bedrooms. The comfortable spaces are characterologically conceived: dark, warm forms are contrasted with bright, cheerier ones and each character-space is identified with socioeconomic details. Moreover, the slightly exaggerated iconography of the design is appropriate to the pop, comic caricatures of the plot.

*Chinatown's* Los Angeles, a dusty one of the 1930s, is a different universe, a drought-stricken world; it would be hard to imagine that this was created by the designer of the Los Angeles in *Shampoo*. Just as the narrative of *Chinatown* is a mystery, the design program wears a disguise which unravels subtly during the story. Again, color and light are programmatically used. At the beginning of the film Sylbert stresses dry, brown desert-tones as the detective becomes involved in the murder-mystery. The screen is eventually sparked by bright, vibrant blues as the major clues appear. This color program is tied to the basic plot, in that the murder-mystery is mixed with a search for control of Los Angeles water supply. As the blue appears, so does the path to the murderer. This design program combines form and iconography with a masterful aesthetic efficiency.

Sylbert's most ambitious historical film is *Reds*. Never departing from his personally selective authenticity, Sylbert boldly juxtaposed a large number of socioeconomic environments in this biopicture of John Reed, the American writer and communist. Oregon, New York, and the Soviet Union—seen in many different aspects—share little, and Sylbert stresses their differences through color, light, and texture, thereby expanding the picture to give it a complicated, episodic scope. The scale of the Russian sequences also enlarges because of the number of people and largeness that history requires. These encyclopedic details of the design are kept in control visually by the camera's close views of the main characters and by the color program, with red dominating, of course, in the Soviet Union sequences.

Interestingly, *Reds'* design program is noteworthy for what it does not use. Sylbert does not imitate the historical period's famous visions whether in filmic or graphic media, whether in realistic or modernist styles. For example, *Reds* does not look like paintings of the Ash Can School or the Constructivists, nor like the films of Griffith or Eisenstein. Just as *Chinatown* does not imitate the noir mystery films on which its story is based, *Reds* evokes but does not mimic; through Sylbert's own view of the past, the film gives a demythologized, artful, realistic vision. He has made an original history picture, offering a personalized, artistic realism like that of the Romantic painters Gericault or Daumier.

Examining the great range in the images of Sylbert's film designs leads me to conclude that he designs more often from his responses to plot than to character. He is looking rationally for a way to design the overall drama to create a holistic design, a film's vision. He sets strict conceptual limits for himself, a tight rule or design program for each film story. He never decorates because he designs within structural definitions, and he has succeeded best with directors who give him visual control or the opportunity for creative collaboration.

—Norman Gambill

# SZAJNA, Jozef

Polish painter, theater director, stage, and graphic designer

**Born:** Rzeszów, 13 March 1922. **Education:** Studied graphics and stage design, at the Academy of Fine Arts, Kraków, diplomas, 1952, 1953; studied in Paris, 1957-58. **Military Service:** Served in Polish resistance; prisoner-of war in concentration camps at Auschwitz and Buchenwald, 1941-45. **Family:** Married Bozena Sierowslawska; children: one son. **Career:** Scenographer, 1955-63, managing director and head of stage design, 1963-66, at the Ludowy Theater, Nowy Huta; freelance designer, working with the Stary Theater, Kraków, the Śląski Theater, Katowice, the Współczesny Theater, Wrocław, the Polish Theater, Warsaw, and others, 1966-71; manager and artistic director of the Studio Theater Gallery (formerly, Klasyczny Theater), Warsaw, 1971-81 (left upon imposition of martial law); freelance designer, painter, and teacher, Warsaw, from 1981. Teacher, Kraków Academy of Fine Arts, 1954-65; head of scenography, 1972-78, and professor, from 1972, at the Academy of Fine Arts, Warsaw. **Exhibitions:** BWA Gallery, Kraków, 1958, 1962, 1966, 1968, 1970, 1974; Pergola Theater, Florence, 1965, 1973; Atelier 212, Belgrade, 1967; Artaud Club, Nice, 1968; Quadriennale of Scenography, Prague, 1967, 1971; Venice Biennale, 1970, 1990; Ernst Museum, Budapest, 1975; Kunstverein, Frankfurt, 1978; Studio Gallery, Warsaw, 1979, 1982, 1987; Institute of Polish Culture, Stockholm, 1979; Biennial of Saõ Paulo, 1979; Polish Cultural Centre, Sofia, 1981; Kunstmuseum, Bochum, 1985; Studio Gallery, Kraków, 1986; Polish Cultural Centre, Paris, 1987; Art Biennial, Saõ Paulo, 1989; Museum of Painting, Lvov, 1989; Palace of the Abbots, 1991; *Szajna Festival,* Santa Cruz de Tenerife, Canary Islands, 1991; National Museum, Gdańsk, 1991; retrospective, Polish Culture Foundation, Art Centre Studio, and Polish Centre of the International Theater Institute, Warsaw, 1992; *Szjana 70 lat,* Centrum Sztuki Studio, Warsaw, 1992. **Collections:** National Museum, Warsaw; Theater Museum, Warsaw; Studio Art Centre, Warsaw; National Museum, Kraków; Museum Sztuki, Lodz; Kunstmuseum, Bochum; Konstmuseet, Göteborg; History of Germany Museum, Bonn; Pushkin Museum, Moscow; Accademia Italia delle Arte e del Lavoro, Salsomaggiore. **Honors:** Artistic Award, Nowa Huta Theater, 1956; Award of Critics, *Cultural Review,* 1957; Order of the Builder, Nowa Huta Theater, 1959; Polish Film Festival Prize, Kraków, 1962; Award, Ministry of Art and Culture, Poland, 1962, 1971; Order of Polonia Restituta Knight's Cross, 1969, City of Kraków Award, 1971; Gold Medal, Prague Quadriennale, 1971; Gold Medal, Warsaw Art Festival, 1972; Exemplar Medal, Munich, 1974; named Merited Cultural Activist, Warsaw, 1975; 30th and 40th Anniversaries of the Polish Republic Medals, 1975, 1984; Letter of Honour, Polish Ministry of Foreign Affairs, 1978; Prime Minister's Award, Warsaw, 1979; Commandor Cross of Poland's Revival Medal, 1979; Award, 1981, and Golden Centaur Prize, 1982, 1987, Accademia Italia delle Arti e del Lavoro, Salsomaggiore Terme; Gold Medal, International Parliament, Salsomaggiore, 1983; Oscar d'Italia, Academia d'Europea-Calvatorme, 1985; Order of the Banner of Labour, 1985; Special Ministry Prize, Warsaw 1988; Commandor Cross with Star, Order of Polonia Restituta, 1992. **Address:** Smulikowskiego 14 m 8, 00-389 Warsaw, Poland.

**Works**

Stage productions include—*Princess Turandot,* Teatr Ludowy, Nowa Huta, 1956; *Of Mice and Men,* Teatr Ludowy, 1956; *Jacobovski and Colonel,* Teatr Ludowy, 1957; *The State of Siege,* Teatr Ludowy, 1958; *Names of Power,* Teatr Ludowy, 1958; *Pantegleize,* 1958; *The Madman and the Nun,* 1959; *In Manor-House,* Teatr Dramatyczny, Warsaw, 1959; *Joy from Regained Scrap-Heap,* Teatr Ludowy, 1960; *Leonce and Lena,* Warsaw, 1962; *Forefathers' Eve,* Teatr Ludowy, 1962; *Clate, Funeral Procession,* Teatr Ludowy, 1962; *Akropolis,* Theater of 13 Rows, Opole, Poland, 1962; *Revizor/The Government Inspector,* Teatr Ludowy, 1963;

Jozef Szajna: *Reminiscenje,* for Biennale Sztuki W Wenecji, 1970

*Don Quixote,* Teatr Ludowy, 1963; *A Midsummer Night's Dream,* Teatr Ludowy, 1963; *Fast among Cannibals,* Teatr Polski, Częstochowa, 1963; *Death on a Pear Tree,* Teatr Ludowy, 1964; *The Empty Field,* Teatr Ludowy, and Florence, 1965; *The Castle,* Teatr Ludowy, 1966; *The Buffo Mystery,* Teatr Ludowy, 1966; *They, New Liberation,* 1967; *Faustus,* Opera Theater, Kraków, 1967; *The Bathhouse,* Stary Teatr, Kraków, 1967, Belgrade, 1968; *Crimson Dust,* Teatr Sląski, Katowice, 1968; *November Affair,* Teatr Sląski, 1969; *Macbeth,* The Playhouse, Sheffield, England, 1970; (also author of screenplay and director) *Faust,* Teatr Polski, Warsaw, 1971; (also author of screenplay and director) *Witkacy,* Teatr Polski, 1972 (toured 1973-77); (also author of screenplay and director) *Replika,* Teatr Studio, Warsaw, 1973 (toured the world, 1973-85); (also author of screenplay and director) *Dante,* Teatr Studio, 1974 (toured the world, 1974-85); (also author of screenplay and director) *Gulgutiera,* Teatr Studio, 1975; (also author of screenplay and director) *Cervantes,* Teatr Studio, 1976 (and Mexico, 1980); (also author of screenplay and director) *Mayakovsky,* Teatr Studio, 1978 (and Finland, 1979); (also author of screenplay and director) *Dante II,* Theater Marina Drziča, Doubruvnik, 1981; (also author of screenplay and director) *Contemporary Dante,* Opernhaus, Essen, Germany, 1985; (also author of screenplay and director) *Replika VII,* Theater Habimah, Tel-Aviv, Israel, 1986; (also author of screenplay and director) *Traces,* Chorzów, 1993.

## Publications

**By SZAJNA: articles**—in *Dialog* (Warsaw), no. 10, 1958. no 1, 1978, no. 7, 1982, no. 7, 1988; *Zycie Literackie* (Kraków), no. 51, 1962, no. 1, 1978, no. 14, 1982, no. 43, 1985, no. 12, 1987; *Wspolczenosc* (Warsaw), no. 22, 1971; *Kierunki* (Warsaw), no. 22, 1972; *Ekran* (Warsaw), no. 19, 1973; *Kultura* (Warsaw), no. 44, 1974, no. 30, 1986; *Fakty* (Warsaw), no. 32, 1977, no. 21, 1980; *Argumenty* (Warsaw), no. 8, 1978; *Scena* (Warsaw), no. 8, 1978, no. 3, 1979; *Literatura* (Warsaw), no. 48, 1979; *Projekt* (Warsaw), no. 2, 1980; *Teatr* (Warsaw), no. 22, 1980, no. 10, 1984, no. 10, 1987; *Tu i Teraz* (Warsaw), no. 11, 1982; *Dialectics and Humanism,* no. 1, 1983.

**On SZAJNA: books**—*Fine Arts in the Polish Theater* by Zenobiusz Strzelecki, Warsaw, 1963; *Jozef Szajna* by Jerzy Madeyski, Kraków, 1970; *Talks with People of the Theater* edited by Andrzej Hausbrandt, Kraków, 1973; *Experimental Theater from Stanislavsky to Today* by J. Roosse-Evans, New York, 1973; *Szajna* by Maria Czanerle, Gdańsk, 1974; *Jozef Szajna: Plastyka, Teatr* by Jerzy Madeyski and Etzbieta Morawiec, Kraków, 1974; *Maske und Kostume* by Stanislaw Kaszynski, Vienna, 1977; *Contemporary Polish Theater* by Witold Filler, Warsaw, 1977; *Word and Image in Jozef Szajna's Theater* by Ewa Wronska, Lodz, 1978; *Familiar Strangers* by Teresa Krzemien, Warsaw, 1978; *Directors of the Polish Theater* by August Grodzicki, Warsaw, 1979; *Talks About the Theater* by Zbigniew Tananicnko, Warsaw, 1981; *Dimmed Lights* by Konstantyn Puzyna, Warsaw, 1982; *Art of the Holocaust* by J. Blatter and S. Milton, London, Sydney, 1982; *Jozef Szajna and His Theater* by Zofia Watrak, Warsaw, 1985; *Sztuka Szajny* by Jerzy Madeyski and Andrzej Zurowski, Warsaw, 1988; *Szajna 70 lat,* exhibition catalogue with text by Zbigniew Taranienko, Warsaw, 1992.

\*

Shaping man's imagination is a duty and not only a privilege of people dealing with art....

Art means reducing the distance between known phenomena and merely suspected ones, between our ignorance and probability; it reaches universal time and meanings that live longer than the present and our today. To show only one side of reality means to tell just a part of the truth, that is, nothing is to be revealed.

Art does not like divisions, it aims at synthesis—hence, the need to find its own language, to determine its own philosophy. A constant dialogue with time, expressed in the play of signs and meanings, means a selection of meanings and elements. A continuous confrontation in an attempt to surprise oneself with new phenomena, to negate oneself. Art is also a risk: of taking responsibility for the situation which we create....

These values I try to convey in my creative work: the structure and relations of facts proceeding beyond illustrative literalism, place, and time....

The actor is often restricted to playing the part of an object. He is absorbed by the artistic reality. He livens an inanimate space and the reverse: he becomes an object of action. Taken out of the background-surrounding, he undergoes simultaneous reification. The barrow leads the man, the man wheels the barrow, the man sets the wheel, the wheel destroys the man.... (*Excerpted from an address given in 1978 in Caracas.*)

—Jozef Szajna

\*      \*      \*

The experience of being a youthful inmate of concentration camps in World War II left an indelible impression on Jozef Szajna; as he repeatedly asserts, he is obsessed by the memory of the camps and man's dehumanization of man. Reflecting that preoccupation, the grotesque has played a constant, major role in his work, as have recurrent symbols of torture, aggression, and deformity, especially since the early 1970s when he began to be responsible for the texts or scenarios of his works as well as for their design. Even before that, however, surrealistic images dominated his idiosyncratic stage settings, even for traditional scripts directed by others, such as Witkiewicz's *In a Small Country House* (Warsaw, 1959), Büchner's *Leonce and Lena* (Warsaw, 1962), Steinbeck's *Of Mice and Men* (Wroclaw, 1962), and Mayakovsky's *The Bathhouse* (Kraków 1967). Although he was trained as a painter, even his relatively traditional scenography showed the influence of constructivist sculpture and architecture.

Szajna's concentration camp experience was vividly embodied in his scenography for a production of Wyspianski's *Akropolis* (Opole 1962), freely adapted and directed by Jerzy Grotowski; the set consisted of stove pipes strung on wires at eccentric angles throughout a central space surrounded by the audience. Even more striking was Szajna's production of *Replika* (Warsaw, 1971) which he has performed in several versions throughout Europe and abroad. It is a "spatio-visual composition" with no text and little traditional action. From a mound of earth littered with battered scraps of western civilization, mutilated survivors emerge to mime actions that metaphorically recapitulate humanity's destructiveness and yet also, its eternal revival. Like many of Szajna's other celebrated, subsequent creations, the work most nearly echoes the tradition of Antonin Artaud, as both men perceive theater as an art of images rather than words. In productions such as *Dante* (1973) or *Mayakovsky* (1978), traditional stage design was rejected in favor of highly subjective groupings of seemingly random objects and artifacts in conjunction with carefully evolved gestures and movements of the performers, who relate themselves organically to the scenic elements and objects. The action may occur in all parts of the theater, not only on a conventional stage. Strange sounds and *musique concrète* become as important as words. The text that remains consists of fragmentary passages that stress vocal dynamics and rhythms or suggestive verbal images as much as rational discourse. When compared to traditional theater or scenography, Szajna's productions may seem haphazard and cryptic, perhaps self-indulgent, but there is no denying the power of their unorthodox, often shocking imagery and their thematic and aesthetic coherence.

—Jarka M. Burian

# T

## TAC INTERIOR ARCHITECTURE AND GRAPHIC COMMUNICATION
### American interior and graphic design firm

The Architects Collaborative (TAC) was founded by Walter Gropius, Norman Fletcher, Jean B. Fletcher, John Harkness, Sarah Pillsbury Harkness, Robert MacMillan, Louis McMillen, and Benjamin Thompson, in Cambridge, Massachusetts, 1945; TAC International established in 1960; TAC Incorporated established in 1964. **Honors:** Boston Arts Festival Award, 1954, 1956, 1959, 1960, 1963, 1964; Parker Medal, Boston Society of Architects, 1961, 1973, 1978; American Institute of Architects Award, 1964, 1966, 1967, 1970, 1971, 1972, 1974, 1976, 1977, 1978, 1979; Prestressed Concrete Institute Award, 1966, 1983; American Society of Landscape Architects Award, 1967; United States Department of Housing and Urban Development Award, 1968; American Concrete Institute Award, 1972, 1984; United States General Services Administration Award, 1973; Johns Manville Competition Prize, Colorado, 1973; Connecticut Society of Architects Award, 1974; Arab Investment Company Competition Prize, 1976; Abu Dhabi Library Competition Prize, 1976; American Institute of Steel Construction Award, 1979; Owens-Corning Energy Conservation Award, 1982; Passive Solar Design Award, 1982; United States Department of Consumer Affairs White House Award, 1983; Concrete Industry Board of New York Prize, 1984. **Addresses:** 46 Brattle Street, Cambridge, Massachusetts 02138; 639 Front Street, San Francisco, California 94111, U.S.A.

### Works

Interior designs include—AIA Headquarters Building, Washington, D.C.; Amathus Resort Hotel, Limassol, Cyprus; Bahrain Chancery, Washington, D.C.; Basrah Sheraton Hotel, Basrah, Iraq; Blue Cross/Blue Shield of Connecticut, Corporate Headquarters, North Haven; Government Service Insurance System Headquarters Building, Manila, Philippines; Hotel Bemardin Resort, Piran, Yugoslavia; Indonesian Embassy Addition, Washington, D.C.; Institute of Public Administration, Riyadh, Saudi Arabia; Kuwait Fund Headquarters, Kuwait City, Kuwait; Lahey Clinic Medical Center, Burlington, Massachusetts; Maine State Office Building, Augusta; New York State Veterans Home, Oxford; Petra Hotel, Petra, Jordan; Shawmut Bank of Boston; Southern Illinois University, Edwardsville; St. Joseph's Hospital, Tampa, Florida; St. Mary's Hospital, Kansas City, Missouri; University of Baghdad, Baghdad, Iraq.
Graphic designs include—signage systems for Charlestown Savings Bank, Boston; Childrens Hospital Medical Center, Boston; Harvard University Athletic Facilities, Cambridge, Massachu-

setts; Institute of Public Administration, Riyadh, Saudi Arabia; Ishtar World Headquarters, Denver; Petra Hotel, Petra, Jordan; University of Baghdad, Baghdad, Iraq; Architectural Graphics for IBM Offices, East Fishkill, New York; Josiah F. Quincy Elementary School, Boston; Kuwait Investment Co., Souk al Manakh, and Souk al Safat, Kuwait City, Kuwait; Smith College Gymnasium, Northampton, Massachusetts; printwork for Adelphi University, Garden City, New York; Amathus Hotel, Limassol, Cyprus; Copley Place, Boston; Government Service Insurance System, Manila, Philippines; Healthcare International, Boston; King Faisal University, Al Hasa Campus, Saudi Arabia; Kuwait Foundation for the Advancement of Sciences, Kuwait City, Kuwait.

### Publications

**By TAC: books**—*Town Plan for the Development of Selb* by Walter Gropius and TAC, Cambridge, Massachusetts, 1970; *A Design Manual for Parking Garages* by Sergio Brizzi and TAC, Cambridge, Massachusetts, 1975; *Streets: A Program to Develop Awareness of the Street Environment,* Boston, 1976; *Building without Barriers* by Sarah P. Harkness and James N. Groom, Jr., New York, 1976.

**On TAC: books**—*The Architects Collaborative 1945-1965* edited by Walter Gropius and others, Teufen, 1966; *The Architects Collaborative 1945-1972,* Barcelona, 1972; *The Architects Collaborative (TAC): A Bibliography of Books and Articles 1945-83* by Edward Teague, Monticello, Illinois, 1984.

*

Our main concern has always been the person and society for which we design. This often complicates the actual design process. It may, for example, dictate offering several alternative office furnishings selections as a choice for a corporate staff, although one uniform selection for everybody would be preferable as a design concept. It also means throwing a brilliant idea overboard if it doesn't fully satisfy the needs of a particular project.

Uncovering those needs involves much probing beyond the surfaces of, for instance, an abstract corporate image, the official design policy of a university, the directions of a hospital administration, or the traditions of another society. One way we at TAC try to isolate the real design is by involving actual users of the building as much as possible in the design process: the patients as well as the nurses, the hotel guests, and the office workers. Although it is time-consuming and often frustrating, this is one of the most rewarding experiences of design.

Another way of making sure that the design solution really fits the client is in-house design reviews by our peers—a rather unique process initiated by Gropius as part of the overall collaborative philosophy at TAC. The design integrity which can easily be the loser in such a review process is maintained by giving the designer the last word.

We try to avoid following designs or fads, unless we are sure our client can shed his interior architecture as easily as last year's car or clothing. This responsibility towards our client is supplemented by our responsibility towards society. Energy-conscious design is one of the constant concerns for all of our projects. We attempt to utilize renewable energy resources and to reduce pollution and dependence on yet untamed nuclear energy without compromising the quality of the indoor environment.

Design is constantly evolving as new psychological, social and technological criteria develop so that the most rewarding project is always the next one.

—TAC Interior Architecture and Graphic Communication

\*   \*   \*

TAC Interior Architecture's reputation and, indeed, its standards of excellence in design are so closely intertwined with those of its parent company, The Architect's Collaborative, that it is difficult to separate the two. In any case, that is perhaps the largest compliment one can pay to interior design: that one cannot tell where architecture left off and interior design began—or possibly the other way around. TAC Interior Architecture carries out work which epitomizes the best of contemporary design. Its handling of space is dramatic—colors are subtle yet bold—and its solutions are functional yet elegant. Work is carried out with emphasis on the collaborative method of teamwork, which was the original concept of the company. The interior design department which also deals with graphic design, can call upon the resources of the parent company and use the company's computer-based design system. The department thus can handle every aspect of interior design from feasibility studies to programming and space planning to producing working drawings and details.

The department has completed many large commissions, including government, municipal, corporate, and medical facilities. The meticulous care that is given to large projects is also given to small ones, such as restaurants and office spaces. Some of the more outstanding projects designed by TAC Interior Architecture include the Hotel Bernardin Resort in Yugoslavia, the Shawmut Bank of Boston, and the AIA Headquarters building in Washington, D.C.

Since 1974 the Interior Architecture and Graphic Communication department has been headed by Klaus E. Muller, whose wide experience included the work of international scope done in several leading firms. If one cannot refer to a particular stylistic expression for TAC Interior Architecture, nevertheless one thread running through all the projects is the unfailing quality in design.

—Arnold Friedmann

# TALLON, Roger

French environmental, graphic, and industrial designer

**Born:** Paris, in 1929. **Education:** Studied electrical engineering, Paris, 1947-50. **Career:** Designer, with Studio Asvas, Paris, 1951-53; freelance designer, working for Dupont Europe, Caterpillar,

General Motors, Thompson Company, and others, in Paris, 1953-62; designer, in collaboration with Jacques Vienot, 1962-63, then director of design research, 1963-73, at Technès design agency, Paris; founder and director of Design Programmes S.A. design agency, Paris, 1973-83; associate, Euro-RSCG design firm, Paris, from 1983; collaborated with Vignelli Associates of New York; consultant to Frigidaire, General Motors, and SNCF French Railways; also designed for Edition Lacloche, Blaupunkt, Salomon Shoes, Lip, Certina, Métro de Mexico, French Post Office, Elf Petroleum, Erco Systems, Testut, Société il Buyss, Eurosit, Cineco, and others. Professor of design, École Nationale Supérieure des Arts Décoratifs, Paris, from 1964. Founder-member and commission member, ICSID International of Societies of Industrial Design, 1964-69; founder-member, Collectif Enseignants-Chercheurs pour l'Environnement, Paris. **Exhibitions:** *l'Objet,* Musée des Arts Décoratifs, Paris, 1968; *Qu'est-ce que le Design?,* Musée des Arts Décoratifs, 1969; *Modern Chairs 1918-1970,* Whitechapel Art Gallery, London, 1970; *Le Design Francais,* Centre de Création Industrielle, Paris, 1971; *Paris,* Centre Georges Pompidou, Paris, 1981; *Design Since 1945,* Philadelphia Museum of Art, 1983; *Design Francais 1960-1990: Trois Décennies,* Centre Georges Pompidou, 1988 (toured); *Roger Tallon: Itinéraires d'un designer industriel,* Centre Georges Pompidou, 1993; *Roger Tallon,* Toronto, Ottawa, and Montreal, Canada, 1994. **Collections:** Centre Georges Pompidou, Paris; Musée des Arts Décoratifs, Paris; Vitra Design Museum, Bâle. **Honors:** Silver Medal, Milan Triennale, 1960; Honorary Royal Designer for Industry, Royal Society of Arts, London, 1973; Grand Prix national de la création industrielle, France, 1985; Commandeur de l'ordre des Arts et Lettres, Paris, 1992. **Address:** 13 Avenue de la Bourdonnais, 75007 Paris, France.

## Works

*Véronique* ciné cameras, for SEM, 1957.
Domestic appliances, for Peugeot, 1957-58.
*Teleavia* television set, for Thompson, 1960.
Typewriter, for Japy, 1960.
*Frigeavia* domestic refrigerator, for Frigidaire, 1964.
Stool in aluminum and polyester foam, for Edition Lacloche, 1965.
Spiral staircase, for Edition Lacloche, 1966-70.
*Bulle Urbaine* city bubble-car, for Technès, 1968.
*Urbatrican* electro-magnetic city hovercraft, for Technès, 1969.
Crystal glasswares, for Daum, 1970.
Tableware and cutlery range, for Sola, 1970.
*Corail* city train, for SNCF, 1970-75.
Lamp, for Erco Systems, 1972-73.
Wrist watches, for Lip, 1973.
Stereophonic record player, for Cineco, 1975.
*TGV Atlantique* high-speed train, for Alsthom and SNCF, 1986.
*Mega TGV* double-decker train, 1991.
Funiculaire de Montmartre coach and station, 1991.
*METEOR* underground fast line, for RATP, 1991.
*VAL208* underground light system, for MATRA, 1992.
Signage system, for Toulouse, Rennes, and Eurotunnel, 1992.
North American high-speed train project designs, Texas and Canada, 1993.
Visual identity, for Finnish Railways, 1993.
*IC 2000* design programme, for Swiss Railways, 1994.
Project leader for *Design Labor* naval design, Bremerhaven, Germany, 1995.

Roger Tallon: Mega TGV (double-decker TGV), 1991

**Publications**

**On TALLON: books**—*L'Esthétique Industrielle* by Denis Huisman and Georges Patrix, Paris, 1961; *Modern Chairs 1918-1970,* exhibition catalogue with texts by Carol Hogben and others, London, 1970; *Le Design Francais,* exhibition catalogue with introduction by Francois Mathey, Paris, 1971; *Twentieth Century Furniture* by Philippe Garner, London, 1980; *Design Since 1945* edited by Kathryn Hiesinger and George Marcus, Philadelphia and London, 1983; *Le Mobilier Francais 1965-1979* by Gilles de Bure, Paris, 1983; *Les Années 60* by Anne Bony, Paris, 1983; *The Conran Directory of Design* edited by Stephen Bayley, London, 1985; *Design Source Book* by Penny Sparke and others, London, 1986; *Design Francais 1960-1990: Trois Decénnies,* exhibition catalogue by Margo Rouard and Françoise Jollant Kneebone, Paris and London, 1990; *Roger Tallon,* exhibition catalogue, Paris, 1993; *Roger Tallon: From TV to TGV,* Paris, 1995.

\*   \*   \*

Roger Tallon is one of the few pioneers of industrial design in both its theoretical and practical aspects of the postwar years in France. French industry was slow to accept the professional designer, and although he was to create products for SEM, Peugeot, Japy, and others, his principal commissions were foreign; his most important work was done as consultant to General Motors for their range of Frigidaire refrigerators, while he also designed for the multinational companies Caterpillar and Dupont. His work of this early period bears the stamp of his close cooperation with Jacques Vienot at the Technès agency, where he designed ciné cameras, milling machines, motorcycles, chairs, tables, lighting equipment, coat-stands, stools, and others. Tallon's favourite subject, however, is private and public transport. In 1968 he designed a small car, the Bulle Urbaine, with universal drive. In 1969, in cooperation with the French Society for Studies and Realization of City Transport, he carried out studies on the underground system in Mexico. In 1970, he constructed a model of a vehicle based on the invention of Maurice Barthelon, namely, the Urbatrican—an electromagnetic hovercraft for communication within cities.

Tallon founded his own design company, Design Programmes S.A., in 1973. During its relatively short period of activity, it won a prominent position among European enterprises of the kind. The bureau completed literally hundreds of programmes for the design of objects and sets of objects, such as office equipment, telephones, watches, furniture—in short, everything in industrial design from trademarks to the overall production policy of a given enterprise. Employing experts representing the mass media, typography, industrial production, the building sector, and the economy, Design

Programmes operated in working groups cooperating, according to need, with specialists of all disciplines. Among the studies carried out in these conditions were those on the Corail train, a recent acquisition to SNCF rolling-stock, the prototype of which was first presented to the French public in March 1975. The daring design, which utilized central corridors with seats on either side, incorporated numerous redesigns for seat profile, air conditioning, lighting systems, signalling, luggage racks, rubbish bins, recreation areas, shops, and bars—all projected in conjunction with a renewal of railway station facilities and equipment.

The starting point for Tallon's works has always been to combine the function of an object with the conveniences of the user. This very concrete premise requires that industrial design differ from industrial aestheticizing, the main objective of which is not the structure nor the construction of an object but its appearance. Tallon was never satisfied with such a role, and has expressed this both as a designer and a teacher.

—George Walsh

# TANAKA, Ikko

Japanese art director and display, corporate identity, and graphic designer

**Born:** Nara City, 13 January 1930. **Education:** Studied at the City College of Fine Arts, Kyoto, 1947-50. **Career:** Textile designer, at Kanebo Ltd., Kyoto, 1950-52; graphic designer, at Sankei Newspaper Co., Ltd., Osaka, 1952-57, and at Light Publicity Limited, Tokyo, 1957-59; co-founder and art director, Nippon Design Centre, Tokyo, 1960-63; founder and director of Tanaka Design Atelier, Tokyo, 1963-76, and of Ikko Tanaka Design Studio, Tokyo, from 1976; co-founder, Off-Design typographic studio, Tokyo, from 1972. Art director, Kobunsha Kappa Books, 1964-72; art director, Takenaka Corporation's *Approach* magazine, from 1965; art director, *Weekly Sankei* magazine, 1969-71; art director, *Stereo Sound* magazine, from 1970; art director, *Fancy Paper,* from 1971; creative director, Seibu department stores, Tokyo, from 1975; graphics art director, Seibu Museum of Art, Tokyo, from 1975; consultant, *Ryuko Tsushin* fashion magazine, Tokyo, from 1976; creative director, Seiyu Stores, Tokyo, from 1978; art director, *Taiyo* magazine, 1983-86; design committee, TOTO Ltd., from 1984; art director, Gallery Ma, Tokyo, from 1985; planning member, Ginza Graphic Gallery, Tokyo, from 1986; advertising design consultant, IBM Japan, from 1986. Founder-member, Tokyo Designers Space, Tokyo, from 1976; trustee, Sezon Museum of Contemporary Art. Lecturer, Kuwazawa Design Institute, Tokyo, 1957-65, and at conferences and universities around the world; frequent member of exhibition and prize juries, from 1967, including Mainichi Design Award, from 1976, and National Calendar Exhibition, from 1979; organizer and planner of numerous exhibitions throughout Japan. **Member:** Alliance Graphique Internationale; Tokyo Art Directors Club; Japan Graphic Designers Association; Tokyo Designers Space; Fashion Foundation. **Exhibitions:** Steendrukkerij De Jong, Hilversum, 1965; International Poster Biennial, Warsaw, 1966, 1968, 1970, 1972, 1974, 1976, 1978, 1980, 1984, 1986; *Graphic Design in Japan,* Amsterdam, 1967; Imahashi Gallery, Osaka, 1970, 1973 (toured), 1974, 1978; Green Collections, Tokyo, 1976, 1979; International Biennale of Graphic Design, Brno, 1976, 1978; Galleria

Grafica, Tokyo, 1977; *Ikko Tanaka Serigraphs,* Ban Gallery, Osaka, and Nakamura Gallery, Kyoto, 1979; *Ikko Tanaka Print Show* and *Ikko Tanaka's Graphic Art,* Asahi Gallery, Kyoto, 1981; *Ikko Tanaka's Masks,* Tokyo Designers Space, Tokyo, 1981; *Ikko Tanaka's Graphic Art,* Art Center, Tokyo, 1982 (toured), and Gallery Haku, Osaka, 1983; *Ikko Tanaka's Posters,* Asahi Gallery, 1984 (toured); *First International Poster Triennial,* Toyama, 1985; *Ikko Tanaka: Design Crossroads,* Seibu Museum of Art, Tokyo, 1987; *Ikko Tanaka at Cooper Union,* Cooper Union, New York, 1987; *Ikko Tanaka L.A.—Graphic Design of Japan,* Japanese American Cultural and Community Center, Los Angeles, 1987; *Ikko Tanaka Design,* Nara Prefectural Museum, Nara, 1988; *Ikko Tanaka Affichiste,* Musée de la Publicité, Paris, 1988; *Japan Print '91,* 1991; *Ikko Tanaka's Posters 1953-1991,* Keihan Gallery of Art and Science, Osaka, 1991; *Japanese Contemporary Poster Exhibition,* Beijing History Museum, Beijing, China, 1992; *Ikko Tanaka Graphic Art 1992-1993,* Gallery Haku, Osaka, 1993; Centro Cultural Arte Contemporaneo, Saõ Paolo, 1995. **Collections:** Museum of Modern Art, New York; Walker Art Center, Minneapolis, Minnesota; Cooper-Hewitt Museum, New York; Parsons School of Design, New York; Musée de la Publicité, Paris; Kunstgewerbemuseum, Zürich; Stedelijk Museum, Netherlands; Warsaw Poster Museum; Israel Museum, Israel; Lahti Poster Museum, Finland; Kyoto Institute of Technology; Nara Prefectural Museum, Japan; Toyama Museum of Modern Art; Sitama Prefectural Museum; Tokyo Setagaya Museum; **Honors:** Mainichi Industrial Design Award, Tokyo, 1954, 1966, 1973; Tokyo Art Directors Club Medal, 1957, 1958, 1959, 1960, 1961, 1963, 1965, 1967, 1968, 1969, 1970, 1973, 1985, 1986; Japan Advertising Artists Club, 1959; International Council of Industrial Editors Award, 1964, 1965, 1969; National PR Magazine Award, 1965, 1982; Japan Sign Design Association Award, 1966, 1967, 1971, 1972, 1973, 1974, 1975, 1976, 1977, 1979 (Grand Prize), 1980, 1981, 1983, 1988; Warsaw Poster Biennale Award, 1968, 1970, 1972, 1984; Osaka Theater Award, 1971; All-Japan Calendar Exhibition Awards, Tokyo, 1973, 1974, 1976, 1978-93; Kodansha Cultural Award, Tokyo, 1973; Japan Display Design Association Award, 1976, 1978, 1979; Commercial Space Design Award, 1978; Japanese Ministry of Education Artists' Award, 1980; Gold Medal, West German International Calendar Exhibition, 1980, 1981, 1985; Yamana Prize, Japan Advertising Awards, 1983; English Publication Contest winner, Japan Institute for Social & Economic Affairs, 1984; CS Design Award, 1984, 1988; Minister of Education Award, Book Binding & Design Contest, 1984; Japan Graphic Design Exhibition Prize, 1984; Second Cultural Prize, Lahti Poster Biennial, 1985; First Prize, International Symbol Mark Competition, 1992; Gold Medal, 1986, Awards, 1989, 1990, 1992, 1993, and Hall of Fame, 1994, Art Directors Club of New York; Washington Art Directors Club Award, 1986; Tokyo Typodirectors Club Award, 1988; Grand Prize, Japan Cultural Design Award, 1991; Best Work, Japan Typography Annual '92, 1992; Art Directors Club International Exhibition Award, 1993; Purple Ribbon Medal, from the Emperor of Japan, 1995. **Address:** 9F Odakyu-Minami Aoyama Bldg., 7-8-1 Minami Aoyama, Minato-ku, Tokyo 107, Japan.

**Works**

Poster series, for the Sankei Kanze Noh Play, from 1954.
Murals, for Japan Pavilion at the New York World Exposition, 1964.

Logotype symbol and medals, for the Tokyo Olympiad, 1964.

*Long Peace* cigarette package, for Japan Tobacco Corp., 1964.

Book design for *Japanese Patterns: Flower, Bird, Wind, & Moon,* 4 volumes, for Tankoshinsha Publishing Co., Ltd., 1968.

Building exterior, for Akasaka Tokyu Hotel, Tokyo, 1969.

Art direction, for movie *The World of Hanae Mori,* 1969.

Japanese Government Pavilion displays, at *Expo 70,* Osaka, 1970.

Corporate identity programme, for Hanae Mori International, Tokyo, 1970.

Announcement cards and medals, for the Winter Olympiad, Sapporo, 1970.

Art direction and design for special issue of *Taiyo* magazine, for Okakyu Family Land, 1974.

Oceanic Cultural Museum displays, at *Ocean Expo 75,* Okinawa, 1975.

*Roots of Contemporary Clothing* exhibition layouts, for the Museum of Modern Art, Kyoto, 1975.

Wall relief, for Odori station of Hokkaido Bank, Sapporo, 1976.

*Issey Miyake in the Museum* exhibition layouts, for the Seibu Museum of Art, Tokyo, 1977.

*Mandala: Photos by Yasuhiro Ishimoto* exhibition layouts, for the Seibu Museum of Art, Tokyo, 1977.

Corporate identity programme, for the Seiyu Store, Tokyo, 1978.

Art direction for environmental planning, for Osaka Namba City, 1978.

Art direction, for *Visual Message* magazine, Goma Publishing Co., 1978.

*The Universe of Tamasaburo* exhibition layouts, for the Seibu Department Store, Tokyo, 1978.

Exhibition art direction, for *Umetsuzure* by Shinya Fujiwara, 1979.

*Japan Style* exhibition layouts, for the Victoria and Albert Museum, London, 1980.

Art direction, for *Best Six* fashion event, 1980-84.

Art direction, for Star Ballet Dancers, Aoyama Tower Hall, Tokyo, 1980.

Art direction, Ballet Art Space, Shinjuku Cultural Center, Tokyo, 1982.

Art direction, for corporate history of Takeda Chemical Industries, Ltd., 1982.

Art direction for first edition of *Tategumi Yokogumi* magazine, for Morisawa & Co., Ltd., 1983.

Graphic design, for National Athletic Meet, Nara, 1984.

Graphic design and art direction, for 2nd International Design Competition, Japan, 1984.

Exhibition art design for *Folk Art of the Edo Period,* for Yurakucho Art Forum, Tokyo, 1986.

Art direction, for Matsuda Showroom, Osaka, 1986.

Art direction, for Ginza Saison Theater, 1987.

Art direction, for Nara Silk Road Exposition, Nara, 1988.

Art direction, for history of the Saison Group, 1991.

Organizer and exhibition producer, Sabie Contemporary Tea Ceremony, Jarajuku Quest, Tokyo, 1992-93

Murals, for 2nd Travellers' Terminal, Tokyo New International Airport, Narita, 1992.

## Publications

**By TANAKA: books**—(with others) *Graphic Japanese Folktale,* Tokyo, 1964; (with others) *Twelve Graphic Designers,* Tokyo, 1968; (with others) *Japanese Patterns,* Tokyo, 1968; (with others) *Modern Design Series: Color Scheme and Design,* Tokyo, 1969; *The Works of Ikko Tanaka,* Tokyo, 1974; *Design and Typography*

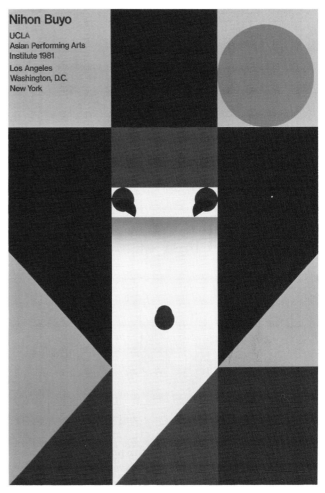

**Ikko Tanaka:** *Nihon Buyo* **(Japanese Dance) Performing Arts Series, University of California, Los Angeles, 1981**

by Ikko Tanaka, Tokyo, 1977; *The Environs of Design: Essays,* Tokyo, 1980; (with others) *Japanese Coloring,* Libro Port Co., Ltd., 1982; (editor) *JAGDA Who's Who,* Tokyo, 1983; *Entrance to Art,* Libro Port Co., Ltd., 1985; *Forefront of Culture—50 People's Views,* Tokyo, 1985; (editor) *Peace Poster,* exhibition catalogue, Tokyo and New York, 1985; *The Design World of Ikko Tanaka,* Tokyo, 1987; *From the Desk of Ikko Tanaka: Essays,* Tokyo, 1990; *Ikko Tanaka—World Graphic Design Series No. 5,* Trans Art Inc., 1993.

**On TANAKA: books**—*The Poster: An Illustrated History from 1860* by Harold F. Hutchinson, London and Toronto, 1968; *Modern Graphics* by Keith Murgatroyd, London, 1969; *Book Jackets and Record Sleeves* edited by Kurt Weidemann, Stuttgart and London, 1969; *History of the Poster* by Josef and Shizuko Müller-Brockmann, Zürich, 1971; *Monografie des Plakats: Entwicklung, Stil, Design* by Herbert Schindler, Munich, 1972; *The Language of Graphics* by Edward Booth-Clibborn and Daniele Baroni, London, 1980; *Who's Who in Graphic Art* edited by Walter Amstutz, Dubendorf, 1982; *Les Années 60* by Anne Bony, Paris, 1983; *Japanese Design* by Penny Sparke, London, 1987.

* * *

Probably the person who had the most influence on Ikko Tanaka as a designer was Yoshio Hakayawa. Recollecting that time around 1952-53, Tanaka has written "When one passes through the Ikomayama tunnel of the Kintetsu train line linking Nara and Osaka, the whole expanse of the Kawachi Plains spreads out before one like an aerial photograph. I stole the scene that appears at the small station which lies at the entrance to the second short tunnel for the 'Poster of the Shusai Group of Yoshio Hayakawa' (1964)."

Another influence was modern jazz. While under the spell of Hayakawa's illustrations, with their delicate sense of color, and of the bold American jazz of the time, Tanaka governed form and meaning by the intellectual manipulation of shape. Eventually, he became aware of the vibrant, lively form and music seen in such forms as the Noh theater, which at first glance appear to be static, and this awareness came to be expressed in his own form and color. The beauty of his work wafts forth and fascinates me, like the karma of nirvana released from a mandala painting.

Tanaka's bold, clear form and sense of coloration are wonderful. In many of his works, each color is painted flatly, without gradation, on top of forms or letters which have been transformed into indeterminate shapes. His works show both the sadness and the brightness of startled surprise which are characteristic of the Kansai area of Japan.

Tanaka is also skilled at writing. His book The *Environs of Design* [*Dezain no shuhen*] is a collection of the essays he has written over the years. The prose has a lustre to it, and the work is an excellent place to learn about Tanaka's erudition.

—Shukuro Habara

# TANAKA, Masaaki

Japanese graphic designer

**Born:** Tokyo, 14 March 1931. **Education:** Studied graphic design, at the National University of Arts, Tokyo, B.A., 1953; independent design education studies in the United States and Europe, 1962-63; research studies at the Illinois Institute of Technology, Chicago, 1981. **Family:** Married Reiko Toyozumi in 1956; children: Eriko. **Career:** Worked as a graphic designer, at Bijutsu-Shuppan Publishing Company, Tokyo, 1953-56; freelance designer and consultant, Tokyo, from 1956. Lecturer, National University of Arts, Tokyo, from 1965; associate professor, 1966-76, and professor, from 1976, Women's College of Art, Tokyo; special lecturer, Sookmyung Women's University, Seoul, 1982. Director, Japanese Society for the Science of Design, Tokyo, from 1964; chairman, Typography Society of Japan, Tokyo, from 1977. **Address:** 1-17-1-110 Ishikawa-cho, Ohta-ku, Tokyo 145, Japan.

## Publications

**By TANAKA: books—**(editor) *Outline of Graphic Design,* 5 vols., Tokyo, 1960; *Design Techniques: Layout,* Tokyo, 1964; (with others) *Design Techniques: Lettering and Typography,* Tokyo, 1965; *Outline of Design Education: Visual Design,* Tokyo, 1967; *Letters and Printing,* Tokyo, 1970; *Graphic Design,* Tokyo, 1971; *Contemporary Graphic Design,* 3 vols., Tokyo, 1971; *Graphic Design of the World: Editorial Design,* Tokyo, 1975; *Introduction to West-*

*ern Alphabet,* Tokyo, 1978; *Japanese Typography Design,* Tokyo, 1978; *Practical Art Education: Visual Communications Design,* Tokyo, 1982.

\*      \*      \*

In 1962-63, Masaaki Tanaka observed the state of affairs throughout the world in institutions of higher education specializing in design and reviewed these institutions in numerous journals. As a result, he became the leading authority on design education in Japan. Moreover, he has a broad knowledge of graphic design itself. In particular, his scholarship on nineteenth-century typography and Bodoni printing is extensive. Particularly illustrative of his erudition is his writing in which he explains the history and structure of European literature, as well as its beauty, to the Japanese in a manner that is both interesting and easy to understand.

As Director of the Society of Japanese Design, Tanaka is a key figure in the management of the society. His balanced judgement and demeanor have been indispensable in the governing of the society, which on occasion becomes one-sided in its viewpoint.

Overall, the basis of Tanaka's research and thought with regard to his design is a common sense combined with a world view. His papers, many of his introductory articles, and his attitude toward life all display democratic common sense as the ideal. This may just be the natural process of thinking for an educator who has researched many European and American schools and who furthermore knows the history of design. His idea of design education is that it is "something which does not go along with the current of the time, but will cultivate a spirit that will discern what is correct for modern production, communication, and environment; in other words, something that will develop critical minds that will learn in order to become the creators of the culture of the future and something that cultivates a sense of the plastic arts which respect individuality." This philosophy may well be a healthy one for a professor to hold.

—Shukuro Habara

# TAN GUIDICELLI

Vietnamese fashion designer

**Born:** Haiphong, 12 November 1934; settled in France, 1955. **Education:** Studied at the Ecole de La Chambre Syndicale de la Couture, Paris, 1956-57. **Career:** Apprentice designer, Christian Dior fashion house, Paris, 1957-59; assistant to Jules Francois Crahay, at Nina Ricci fashion studio, Paris, 1959-61; assistant, studio of Jacques Heim, Paris, 1961-62; freelance fashion designer working for Chloe, Trell, and others, Paris, from 1962; chief stylist for Gunther Sachs of MicMac, Saint-Tropez, 1968-73; founder-director of Tan Guidicelli ready-to-wear fashions, Pans, from 1974; launched perfumes *T-Vert* and *T-Fumé.* **Address:** 45 rue de Babylone, 75007 Paris,

## Publications

**On TAN GUIDICELLI: books—***Fairchild's Dictionary of Fashion* edited by Charlotte Calasibetta, New York, 1975; *The World of*

*Fashion: People, Places, Resources* by Eleanor Lambert, New York and London, 1976; *25 Ans de Marie-Claire de 1954 a 1979* compiled by Francoise Mohrt, Paris, 1979; *Fashion 2001* by Lucille Khornak, London, 1982; *McDowell's Directory of Twentieth Century Fashion* by Colin McDowell, London, 1984.

\*   \*   \*

Many young designers go overboard for an extreme style because restraint is more characteristic of maturity. By declaring that women's clothes are plumage, Tan Guidicelli was saying that fashion is theatre before it is reality. Of course, among wild animals and many primitive tribes, plumage is the monopoly of the males. It was also a male privilege in western society until the rise of the middle classes in the nineteenth century when, under the influence of the puritan ethic, the male handed his plumage to his wife and told her to be his social advertisement. Women did literally wear the plumage during the belle époque, but since then, with more and more women working, they also follow the puritan ethic, and occasions for plumage have decreased. As Jean Muir has pointed out, young designers, suckers for glamour, produce cocktail dresses and teagowns without first asking just how many women still lead that sort of life. Tan Guidicelli appears to be of this fraternity, considering the show more exciting than the real routine. While a number of rich women can still afford plumage, even they simplify the greater part of their wardrobe because they travel so much, if only from resort to resort.

If Tan Guidicelli is to be a successful businessman in addition to a designer, he must learn to create models which can be reproduced for the mass market, where occasions for plumage are limited to wedding days. However, the young usually have to learn the hard way, and too many designers do not appreciate that fashion is ruthless business; it is easier to be a flash in the pan than it is to become a lasting presence. It is one thing to win a royal order and another to retain royal patronage thereafter, as the makers of a recent royal wedding gown have discovered. Tan Guidicelli has lasted for a decade, but how much he has learnt in that time remains to be seen. He can create such good designs when he keeps the look simple, but there have also been some ill-disciplined concoctions. Which will win, purity or extravagance?

—Diana de Marly

# TAPIOVAARA, (Yrjo) Ilmari

Finnish exhibition, film, interior, and industrial designer

**Born:** Helsinki, in 1914. **Education:** Apprenticed with furniture manufacturers in Helsinki, 1933-35; studied interior design, at the Central School of Industrial Design, Helsinki, 1933-37; University of London, 1936-37; apprentice in the studio of architect Le Corbusier, Paris, 1937. **Family:** Married Iris Annikki Hyvarinen in 1939 (died, 1972); children: Timo, Eva and Lassi; married Riitta Kurikka in 1972. **Career:** Art director, Asko Tehtaat Oy furniture manufacturers, Lahti, 1937-40; founder and designer, Keravan Puuteollisuus Oy furniture firm, Kerava, 1949-50; freelance designer, working for Marva Production, Knoll International, Thonet, Edsbyverk, Asko Konsern, Lukkiseppu, Oy Skanno Ab, Laukaan Puu, Hackmann Oy, Stockmann Orno, and others, in Helsinki, from

1951. Head, 1950-52, and chairman of interior design department, 1953-56, at the Central School of Industrial Design, Helsinki; visiting professor, Illinois Institute of Technology, Chicago, and Art Institute of Chicago, 1952-53, and at the University of Technology, Helsinki, from 1965. **Member:** Finnish representative, ICSID International Council of Societies of Industrial Design; Finnish State Commission for Foreign Programmes, Helsinki; chairman, Central Organization of Industrial Design, Helsinki, 1959-68. **Exhibitions:** Milan Triennale, from 1951; *Design in Scandinavia,* Museum of Modern Art, New York, 1954 (toured); *Formes Scandinaves,* Musée des Arts Decoratifs, Paris, 1958; *Finlandia,* Kunstgewerbemuseum, Zurich, 1961 (toured); *Modern Chairs 1918-1970,* Whitechapel Art Gallery, London, 1970; *Scandinavian Modern Design 1880-1980,* Cooper-Hewitt Museum, New York, 1982; *Design Since 1945,* Philadelphia Museum of Art, 1983; *Ilmari Tapiovaara,* Museum of Applied Arts, Helsinki, 1984. **Honors:** Good Design Award, Chicago, 1950; Museum of Modern Art Low Cost Furniture Prize, New York, 1951; Gold Medal, Milan Triennale, 1951, 1954, 1957, 1966; American Interior Design Award, New York, 1963; National Furniture Prize, Milan, 1968; Honorary Royal Designer for Industry, Royal Society of Arts, London, 1969; Furniture Prize, Cantu, 1970. **Address:** Itaranta 6, 02100 Espoo 10, Finland.

## Works

*Domus* stackable wooden chair, for the Domus Accademica hostel, Helsinki, 1946, produced by Wilhelm Schauman, 1946-65.
Olivetti showroom interiors, Helsinki, 1954.
Corvair and Caravelle aircraft interiors, for Finnair, 1957.
Children's furniture range, for Heal's, 1960.
*Kiki* upholstered stackable wooden chairs, for Merivaara, 1960.
*Polar* cutlery in stainless steel, for Hackmann Oy, 1963.

## Publications

**By TAPIOVAARA: books**—(editor) *Finnish Decorative Art: 13th Yearbook,* Helsinki, 1949; **articles**—in *Form Function Finland* (Helsinki), 1983.

**On TAPIOVAARA: books**—*Prize Designs for Modern Furniture* by Edgar Kaufmann, Jr., New York, 1950; *Gute Möbel—Schöne Raume* edited by Mia Seeger, Stuttgart, 1953; *Mohili Tipo* by Robert Aloi, Milan, 1956; *A Treasury of Scandinavian Design* edited by Erik Zahle, New York, 1961; *Scandinavian Domestic Design* edited by Erik Zahle, Copenhagen, 1961, London, 1963; *Modern Finnish Design* by Ulf Hard af Segerstad, London, 1969; *Modern Chairs 1918-1970,* exhibition catalogue with texts by Carol Hogben and others, London, 1970; *Scandinavian Design: Objects of a Life Style* by Eileene Harrison Beer, New York and Toronto, 1975; *History of Modern Furniture* by Karl Mang, Stuttgart, 1978; *One Hundred Great Finnish Designs,* edited by Per Mollerup, Snekkersten, 1979; *Twentieth Century Furniture* by Philippe Garner, London, 1981; *Knoll Design* by Eric Larrabee and Massimo Vignelli, New York, 1981; *Scandinavian Modern Design 1880-1980* edited by David Revere McFadden, New York, 1982; *Contemporary Furniture* edited by Klaus-Jurgen Sembach, Stuttgart, London and New York, 1982; *Design Since 1945* edited by Kathryn Hiesinger and George Marcus, Philadelphia and London, 1983; *Finnish Vision,* with texts by Pekka Suhoncn and others, Helsinki, 1983; *The Conran Directory of Design* edited by Stephen Bayley, London, 1985; *Mid-Century: Furniture of the 1950s* by Cara Greenberg, London, 1985; *Twentieth Century Design: Furniture* by Penny Sparke, London, 1986.

*     *     *

"Being a designer is rather like being a doctor; once you have the professional skill, you can practise wherever you like. If what you do is good, it's good everywhere." These words from Ilmari Tapiovaara sum up his philosophy and his career. The experience of working as a young man with Aalto and Le Corbusier, and later with Mies van der Rohe, fostered his own professionalism; rather than indulging in highflown theory, he has seen the designer's task as making the object right for its job, efficient and economic but with "a sense of dimension and intellectual readiness." His almost accidental involvement after the war with mass-produced furniture for export led him to extend the principle of economic fitness to the economics of packaging; this additional element of design led in its turn to such things as the Domus chair which is packable, stackable, economic in its use of timber technology, and, above all, comfortable to use and good to look at. With 750,000 made between 1946 and 1965 this is a piece of furniture worthy to rank with the best of Aalto, Breuer, and Mies van der Rohe.

Some fifteen years after the Domus chair came another, even more refined use of wood—the Wilhelmina chair of 1959. Perhaps the most elegant of all his designs, it is a superb combination of use and economy. Tapiovaara's ingenuity was in full spate, when simultaneously with the Wilhelmina chair, he produced the Kiki range of stools, chairs, and tables, all based on a simple steel frame with seat and back covered in leather or fabric, widely variable and still capable of easy packing and stacking.

It was about the time of these designs that Tapiovaara, through his work with the International Labour Office, first became concerned with aiding underdeveloped countries by designing ranges of furniture for export using native materials, exploiting and adapting high-quality handcraftsmanship. From projects in Paraguay and Mauritius, his commitment to this service has become worldwide. He believes fervently in the value of international design cooperation, and this is arguably his greatest contribution. His own example of economic design, inspired by sensitivity to materials and to the product in use, is now mainly devoted to the furtherance of international aid, even to "the process of renewal that's going on in the world. The world uses goods up rapidly because it wants a more rational environment. Fortunately, we're moving from excess towards economy and at the same time towards better quality, a higher standard of living." he asserts.

—Gordon Steele

# TATTERSFIELD, Brian

British graphic, interior, and industrial designer

**Born:** Heckmondwike, Yorkshire, 12 April 1936. **Education:** Educated at Heckmondwike Grammar School, until 1953; studied at Batley School of Art, Yorkshire, NDD, 1957; Royal College of Art,

London, ARCA, 1962. **Military Service:** Served in the Royal Air Force, 1957-59. **Family:** Married Mary Wakelin in 1964; children: Jane and Emma. **Career:** Art director, at Young and Rubicam agency, London, 1962-63; designer, at Fletcher/Forbes/Gill design partnership, Geneva, 1963-64; founder-partner, with Marcello Minale, of Minale Tattersfield and Partners design firm, London, from 1964. Visiting lecturer, Royal College of Art, London; governor, Norwich School of Art, Norfolk. **Exhibitions:** Design Centre, London, 1979; *Penguin Books,* Manchester Polytechnic, 1981; Museo d'Arte Contemporanea, Milan, 1983. **Collections:** Poster Museum, Warsaw; Museum of Modern Art, New York; Victoria and Albert Museum, London. **Honors:** Silver Medals, Design and Art Directors Association, London 1972-82; Gold Medal, Art Directors Club of New York, 1977; fellow, Chartered Society of Designers, London. **Address:** Minale Tattersfield and Partners, The Courtyard, 37 Sheen Road, Richmond, Surrey TW9 1AJ, England.

## Works

Corporate identity for Heathrow Express train, 1993.
Corporate identity for Eurostar Train, 1994.
Design of the Hammersmith Underground station, for London Transport, 1994.
Graphic identity, for Royal Armouries Museum, Leeds, 1995.

## Publications

**By TATTERSFIELD: books**—(editor, with Marcello Minale) *Minale Tattersfield,* vols. 1-4, London, 1965-72.

**On TATTERSFIELD/MINALE: books**—*Graphic Design Britain* edited by Frederick Lambert, London, 1967; *Modern Graphics* by Keith Murgatroyd, London, 1969; *European Designers: England, France, Italy* by Idea Publishers, Tokyo, 1970; *Minale Tattersfield Designers* by Marcello Minale, edited by Edward Booth Clibborn, London, 1977; *Minale Tattersfield Designers* by Idea Publishers, Tokyo, 1978; *Penguin Books: The Pictorial Cover 1960-1980,* exhibition catalogue by Evelyne Green, Manchester, 1981; *Who's Who in Graphic Art* edited by Walter Amstutz, Dubendorf, 1982; *Contemporary Furniture* edited by Klaus Jurgen Sembach, Stuttgart and New York, 1982; *Design Source Book* by Penny Sparke and others, London, 1986; *International Design Yearbook 1987/88* edited by Philippe Starck, London, 1987; *Design: The World of Minale Tattersfield* edited by Minale, London, 1987; *The Leader of the Pack: How to Design Successful Packaging* by Minale, London, 1992.

*

I firmly believe that good design should touch the lives of everyone, not only in the form of expensively tasteful objects, but in everyday things like knives and forks, comfortable chairs, cornflake packets.

Too much design concerns itself with nostalgia, or the fantasy of tomorrow, instead of making the realities of today more bearable.

—Brian Tattersfield

*See* MINALE, Marcello

# TAVOULARIS, Dean

American film designer

**Born:** Lowell, Massachusetts, in 1932. **Education:** Studied architecture, at Otis Art Institute, Los Angeles, 1950-54. **Career:** Worked in the animation department, then on live production films, at Walt Disney Studios, Hollywood, California, until 1963; assistant designer, then art director, at Columbia Studios and Warner Studios, Hollywood, from 1964. **Honor:** Academy Award, 1974. **Address:** c/o Academy of Motion Picture Arts and Sciences, 8949 Wilshire Boulevard, Beverly Hills, California 90211, U.S.A.

## Works

Film productions include—*Ship of Fools* (Kramer), 1965; *Inside Daisy Clover* (Mulligan), 1965; *Bonnie and Clyde* (Penn), 1967; *Candy* (Marquand), 1968; *Petulia* (Lester), 1968; *Zabriskie Point* (Antonioni), 1970; *Little Big Man* (Penn), 1970; *The Godfather* (Penn), 1972; *The Conversation* (Coppola), 1974; *The Godfather Part II* (Coppola), 1974; *Farewell, My Lovely* (Richards), 1975; *Apocalypse Now* (Coppola), 1978; *The Brink's Job* (Friedkin), 1978; *One From the Heart* (Coppola), 1982; *The Escape Artist* (Deschanel), 1982; *Hammett* (Wenders), 1982; *The Outsiders* (Coppola), 1983; *Rumble Fish* (Coppola), 1983; *Testament* (Littman), 1983.

## Publications

**By TAVOULARIS: articles**—in *Positif* (Paris), September 1979.

**On TAVOULARIS: books**—*Le Décor de Film* by Leon Barsacq, Paris, 1970, as *Caligari's Cabinet and Other Grand Illusions,* Boston, 1976; *International Dictionary of Films and Filmmakers,* Chicago and London, 1987, 1991.

# TELNACK, John J.

American automobile designer

**Born:** 1 April 1937; also known as "Jack." **Education:** Graduated, Art Center College of Design, 1958. **Career:** Worked at Ford Motor Co., Dearborn, Michigan, from 1958; stylist, A-Ford Studio, 1962, head stylist, Mercury Production Styling, 1964, head stylist, Lincoln and Mercury Production, 1965, chief designer, Ford Motor Co., Australia, 1967, design executive, Falcon and Mustang Ford Motor Co., Dearborn, 1969, design executive, Mustang and Pinto, 1971, design executive, Mustang Maverick and Pinto, 1972, chief designer Engineering, 1973, vice-president design, Ford of Europe, 1974, director international special vehicles and advanced concepts design office, Ford Motor Co., Dearborn, 1976, executive director North America light car and interior design, 1978, executive director North America mid-size and luxury car design and engineering, chief design executive North America design, 1980, vice-president design, 1987-1993, vice-president corporate design, 1993, vice-president design Ford Automotive Operations (Ford's global design chief), from 1994. **Member:** Industrial Designers Society of America. **Honors:** Automotive Industry's Man of the Year, 1989; Honorary Degrees, Pratt Institute, Parsons School of Design, and the Art Center College of Design. **Address:** Ford Motor Co., The American Road, Dearborn, Michigan 48121.

## Works (for Ford Motor Co.)

*Mustang,* 1979.
*T-Bird/Cougar,* 1983.
*Taurus/Sable,* 1986.
*Probe GT,* 1992.
*Mark VIII,* 1993.
*Explorer,* 1994-95.

*

Our company, like a lot of others, has spent a great deal of time, effort, and money in creating successes over the years. And it seems like every time we do it, we find ourselves building a box around that success in an effort to preserve it. I'm not sure from who. The irony is, eventually you discover that what you have in the box is just a "thing"—the product you've built—not the process or the effort that created that success in the first place. It isn't the "thing", the product, that needs to be enshrined and defended, it's the process of creation, the freedom to change, the drive to search and sift and remain open to new ideas that needs to be preserved. It requires the ability to see beyond what has always been done to what can be done and to find new ways of doing it.

The newer the idea the more adjustment it requires. You should have a period of adjustment. The original Taurus was like that. When we first presented it to market research focus groups, it made a lot of people uncomfortable. But, the point is, we had made a breakthrough, and the box—both literally and figuratively—was broken. Of course, as soon as our success became obvious, our competitors stopped making jelly-bean jokes and started copying the new mold. And pretty soon, another box was being built, and a vision was trapped inside it. The disturbing thing is, how many really great visions were lost because everybody was focusing on duplicating the one inside the box? You have to get outside the box—away from the familiar—and into uncharted areas if you're really going to create something significant.

A new idea ought to be a little uncomfortable. It ought to challenge you. It gives the particular function of the vehicle a real and tangible shape that expresses its purpose. If we build a box around a single idea simply because it's been successful, we're not just protecting that sucess—we're walling ourselves off from other ideas or visions that we need to continue in order to grow and prosper.

—Jack Telnack

*   *   *

Ever since he was four years old, Jack Telnack has loved to draw and has loved cars and has loved to draw cars. If he'd grown up in Paris or Rome, he might have become an architect, but as it was he grew up in Detroit, and that really left very little doubt about just what he'd spend his life and his talent doing—designing cars.

"I was very lucky to know what I wanted to do," he admits, adding that, with friends and relatives working at Ford and General Motors, it was a simple thing to find out how the companies worked,

**Jack Telnack:** *INDIGO* **concept vehicle**

how they could use people with drawing talent. At 17, Jack left for the only school that had a focused automotive design program at the time, the Art Center College of Design in Pasadena.

That move began a career that has spanned almost 30 years and has taken him around the globe, to Australia and Europe and back to Detroit, always one step further up the corporate design ladder. In the process, Jack's talent, leadership, and inspiration have put one of his cars in almost every family's driveway at one point or another. And the likeliest car of all to find in those driveways was from the Ford Taurus and Mercury Sable line, introduced in 1986. With it, Ford established the aero-look and changed the character of automotive design for the next decade.

The success of this line and all Jack's cars grows out of his design philosophy. To Louis Sullivan's statement, "Form follows function," Jack adds "Flair." As he explains it, "We're dealing with emotion when we design. The customer doesn't know what they want. The designer has to understand the customer and then add the magic that connects the customer to the product. Flair is very important in automotive design." And a look at the way cars have appealed to people regardless of culture and tradition speaks of something beyond the practical. People all over the world don't flock to auto shows to evaluate transportation, they go to bask in the magic of cars.

Without the flair, they'd get bored and stay home. As it is, they require change every few years. They want something new. The

challenge lies in capturing an idea and the customer's imagination and to do that you have to be very carefully atuned to the world at large, according to Jack. Influences and inspiration can lie anywhere, in culture, in politics, in technology, in lifestyle.

"Designers have a sixth sense, an intuitive understanding of the future, but to use it and keep it honed, designers have to be open and aware of what's going on around them." He points to the fins so common on cars in the 1950s as an expression of the times that spoke to people's mood and perspective on the future. And in the 1990s, Jack believes that the permeating presence of technology offers both opportunities for innovation and new suggestions for form. The Stealth aircraft's form, for instance, have helped to inspire the forms of Ford's "New Edge" look, introduced in the GT90 and winner of a 1996 Bronze Industrial Design Excellence Award.

Jack also believes that designers see the world differently than others, actually reading a landscape, a scene or an object and understanding many levels of information beyond the aesthetic one. So a designer can be said to read the world's visual messages every day. "Designers see light playing on form differently from others," Jack explains. "I'm very aware of the location of the sun wherever I am and how its placement will differ from one hemisphere to the other."

Most modern automotive design is carried out using sophisticated computer-aided design and rapid prototyping equipment. Yet Jack's sensitivity to the complexities of visual communication and the designer's responsibility to the customer keep one traditional step current at Ford: a clay model. Until solid holograms come along, he says, the clay model will be necessary. "We could design a whole car relying only on technology's representations of the car in two-dimensional space, but there's a real danger that such a car would have a two-dimensional look. It doesn't slow our speed to market at all to spend one night milling a clay model. Put it out in the sun, see how it looks from all the angles. That's what the customer sees, after all."

What will the customer see in the coming years? Cars designed with honesty, functionality, and global appeal, according Jack. He believes that, given the power, speed, and scope of global mass communication, the world is now truly one market. "It's not just design for one market any more. Tastes are more similar than dissimilar today. Everyone around the world knows what's hot and wants it, regardless of national and governmental barriers. Good design sells around the world. Design has become a universal language. Like classical music, you don't have to study it to appreciate it."

—Kristina Goodrich

# TER-ARUTUNIAN, Rouben

American stage designer

**Born:** Of Armenian parents, in Tifiis, Russia, 24 July 1920; emigrated to the United States in 1951, naturalized, 1957. **Education:** Educated at schools in Berlin, 1927-38; studied piano, Berlin, from 1939; studied design, at the Reimann Art School, Berlin, 1939-41, film music, at the Musik Hochschule, and art history and theatre arts, at the Friedrich Wilhelm University, Berlin, 1941-43; University of Vienna, 1943-45; studied painting and sculpture, at the Ecole des Beaux-Arts, Academie Julien, and at the Academie de la Grande Chaumiere Paris, 1945-50. **Career:** Designer of stage sets and costumes, and club interiors, for the United States Third Army Special Services, in Heidelberg, 1945-47; jewellery designer for Harry Winston, New York, 1951; sketch artist, Staples and Smith display firm, New York, 1951; staff designer, CBS Television, 1951-53, ABC Television, 1953, and NBC Television, New York, 1954-57; freelance stage, film and television designer, New York, from 1957. **Exhibitions:** Wright/Hepburn/Webster Gallery, New York, 1968; Canyon Road Art Gallery, Santa Fe, New Mexico, 1968; Vincent Astor Gallery, Lincoln Center, New York, 1970. **Collections:** Museum of Modern Art, New York; Houghton Library, Harvard University, Cambridge, Massachusetts; Library and Museum of Performing Arts, Lincoln Center, New York. **Honors:** Emmy Award, New York, 1957; Outer Critics' Circle Award, New York, 1958; Armenian Bicentennial Award, 1976. **Address:** 360 East 55th Street, Apt. 15, New York, New York 10022, U.S.A.

## Works

Set and costume designs include—(New York, unless noted) *King John,* 1956, *Measure For Measure,* 1956, *Othello,* 1957, *Merchant of Venice,* 1957, *Much Ado About Nothing,* 1957, *Twelfth Night,* 1960, *Antony and Cleopatra,* 1960, all at The American Shakespeare Festival, Stratford, Connecticut; *New Girl in Town,* 1957; *Who Was That Lady I Saw You With?,* 1958; *Redhead,* 1959; *Advise and Consent,* 1960; *A Passage to India,* 1962; *Arturo Ui,* 1963; *The Milktrain Doesn't Stop Here Anymore,* 1964; *The Deputy,* 1964; *The Devils,* 1965; *Ivanov,* London, 1965, and New York, 1966; *Medea,* Rome, 1966; *Exit the King,* 1967; *All Over,* 1971; *Leibelei,* 1972, and *Anatol,* 1973, both at Akademie Theater, Vienna; *Good Time Charley,* 1975; *The Lady from the Sea,* 1976; *The Lady from Dubuque,* 1980.

Opera and lyric presentations include—*The Bartered Bride,* Volksoper, Dresden, 1943; *Salome,* Volksoper, Vienna, 1944; *Bluebeard's Castle,* 1952, *L'Heure Espagnole,* 1952, *La Cenerentola,* 1953, and *The Trial,* 1953, all New York City Opera; *Maria Golovin,* World's Fair, Brussels, 1958 (travelled to Teatro all Scala, Milan); *Blood Moon,* San Francisco Opera, 1961; *Orpheus and Euridice,* Staatsoper, Hamburg, 1963; *The Play of Herod,* New York Pro Musica, The Cloisters of the Metropolitan Museum of Art, 1963; *Pelléas et Melisande,* Festival of Two Worlds, Spoleto, Italy, 1966; *The Bassarids,* 1968 (sets only), and *The Devils of Loudun,* 1969, both Santa Fe Opera; *Pelléas et Mélisande,* Teatro alla Scala, Milan, 1973 (travelled to Teatro La Fenice, Venice, 1973, and Teatro all'Opera, Rome, 1974); *Pelléas et Mélisande,* Opéra de Monte Carlo, 1976 (travelled to Teatro Regio, Tunn, 1979); *Dido and Aeneas,* New York City Opera, 1979; *Die Liebe der Danae,* Santa Fe Opera, 1982.

Dance costume designs include—costume designs for soloists of the Berlin State Opera Ballet, 1941; *Getantze Malerei,* Vera Mahlke Ballet Company, Dresden and Berlin, 1942; *Concerto,* Ballet of the Opera Comique, Paris, 1950; *Souvenirs,* 1955, and *Seven Deadly Sins,* 1958, both New York City Ballet; *Fibers,* Paul Taylor Dance Company, 1960; *Samson Agonistes,* Martha Graham Company, 1961; *Pierrot Lunaire,* Glen Tetley Company, 1962; *The Nutcracker,* 1964 (sets only), and *Harlequinade,* 1965, both New York City Ballet; *Ricercare,* American Ballet Theatre, 1966; *Firebird,* Harkness Ballet, 1967; *Requiem Canticle,* New York City Ballet, 1968; *Transitions,* Operhaus, Cologne, 1969; *The Unicorn, the Gorgon, and the Manticore,* Festival of Two Worlds, Spoleto, Italy, 1971; *Chronochromie,* Staatsoper, Hamburg, 1971; *The Song of the Nightingale, Symphony of Psalms,* and special decor for closing night, all for the New York City Ballet, at the Stravinsky Festival, 1972; *Laborintus,* Royal Opera House, London, 1972; *Chopiniana,* New York City Ballet, 1972 (not produced); *Remembrances,* City Center Joffrey Ballet, 1973; *Voluntaries,* Stuttgart Ballet, 1973; *Dybbuk Variations,* and *Coppelia,* both New York City Ballet, 1974; *Pulcinella,* reconstruction of Picasso designs, City Center Joffrey Ballet, 1974; *The Real McCoy,* Eliot Feld Ballet, 1975; *The Mooche,* Alvin Ailey Dance Theater, 1975 (sets only); *Union Jack,* New York City Ballet, 1976; *Vienna Waltzes,* New York City Ballet, 1977 (sets only); *Sphinx,* American Ballet Theatre, 1977 (sets only); *Pierrot Lunaire,* BBC-TV, 1978; *L'Après-Midi d'un faune,* Joffrey Ballet and London Festival Ballet, 1979; *Night Piece,* Maggio Musicale, Florence, 1979; *Robert Schumann's Davidsbündlertänze,* New York City Ballet, 1980; *Souvenir de Florence, Mozartiana* (costumes only), and *Adagio Lamentoso,* for New York City Ballet, at the Tchaikovsky Festival, 1981; *Noah and the Flood,* for the New York City Ballet, at the Stravinsky Centennial Celebration, 1982; *Sphinx,* National Ballet of Canada, 1983; *Romantic Pieces,* San Francisco Ballet, 1983; *Components,* National Ballet of Canada, 1984; *Ballet Imperial,* American Ballet Theatre, Chicago, 1988.

Television designs include—*This Is Show Business* (sets only), 1951; *The Bert Parks Show,* (sets only), 1952; *Toast of the Town* (sets only), 1952; and *Studio One,* 1952-53, all series for CBS-TV; *The Abduction from the Seraglio,* NBC Opera, 1954; *The Magic Flute,* NBC Opera, 1956; *The Taming of the Shrew,* for Hallmark Hall of Fame series, NBC, 1956; *Twelfth Night,* for Hallmark Hall of Fame series, NBC, 1957; *Swing into Spring,* CBS, 1958; *The Tempest,* for Hallmark Hall of Fame series, NBC, 1959; *Maria Colovin,* NBC Opera, 1959; *A Musical Bouquet for Maurice Chevalier* (sets only), CBS, 1960; *Noah and the Flood,* CBS, 1962; *The Art of the Prima Donna,* for Bell Telephone Hour, NBC, 1966; *Marlene Dietrich: I Wish You Love,* BBC and CBS, 1973; *Rachel La Cubana,* NET Opera, 1973; *Other Dances* (sets only), for Dance in America series, NET-TV, 1979.

Film designs include—*The Loved One,* MGM Filmways, (production and costume design), 1964-65; *Such Good Friends* (production design only), Paramount Pictures, 1971.

## Publications

**On TER-ARUTUNIAN: books**—*Stravinsky and the Dance,* New York, 1962; *Stravinsky and the Theatre,* New York, 1963; *Rouben Ter-Arutunian: Theater Designs,* exhibition catalogue with preface by Gian Carlo Menotti, New York, 1970; *From Script to Stage* by Randolph Goodman, New York, 1971; *Stage Design* by Howard Bay, New York, 1974; *Designing and Planning for the Theatre* by Lynn Pektal, New York, 1976; *Stage Design Throughout the World 1970-1975* by Rene Hainaux and Nicole Leclercq, Brussels and London, 1976; *Theatrical Evolution 1776-1976* by Kenneth Spritz, New York, 1976; *Spotlight: Four Centuries of Ballet Costume* by Richard Buckle and others, London, 1981.

\*

I have searched to find a visual complement to drama, poetry, music, and movement by means of organization of the cubic space of the stage and the dressing of the human body—hopefully with simplicity, clarity, and a certain element of mystery.

—Rouben Ter-Arutunian

\*    \*    \*

Although born in Tiflis, Soviet Georgia, internationally famous Rouben Ter-Arutunian is a distinctly American set and costume designer for stage, film, and television. He became enamoured of his future profession at age fifteen while viewing Colonel de Basil's Ballets Russes as the company toured Europe. Due in part to this stimulus, he subsequently studied the humanities at the Universities of Berlin and Vienna and also classical painting at the Ecole des Beaux Arts in Paris. Following World War Two, he worked for the Special Services division of the United States Third Army. Soon after coming to America, Ter-Arutunian began his professional life by designing commercials and soap operas for CBS Television in 1951.

In considering the possibilities for design in the service of dance, Ter-Arutunian came to distinguish four basic approaches: "the classic," which employs a decor-less stage; "the romantic," which uses realistic-illusionistic devices; "the sculptural," which uses three-dimensional scenery; and "the decorative," which derives from the easel-painting tradition. In practice, Ter-Arutunian has designed settings which range from "the decorative" to "the sculptural," combining "romantic" and "classic" principles.

Ter-Arutunian's now-legendary *Nutcracker* for the New York City Ballet, an organization for which he is especially fond of working, exemplifies a primarily "decorative" approach, as do his designs for *Coppelia*. His production for Glenn Tetley's *Ricercare,* which was produced for American Ballet Theater, is an example of "the sculptural," his preferred mode at its best. When the curtain opens, the audience is confronted with a half-moon-shaped object, in which the dancers lay down. It is a symbolic, minimal object which summarizes the meaning of the dance but does not dominate the stage or "crowd" the dancers. Ter-Arutunian believes that plenty of space on stage should be organized around minimal scenery. His concern for the use of space, no doubt, led him to design the permanent stage for the American Shakespeare Festival.

Ter-Arutunian's work on Edward Albee's *All Over* on Broadway illustrates the creative approach which the designer employs. Instead of designing the realistic interior originally specified by the playwright, he decided to begin at the essence of the situation, using only those pieces of furniture which were necessary. Clive Barnes, in the *New York Times,* remarked, "The staging was perfect in its sensibility, Rouben Ter-Arutunian's setting has exactly the same sparse elegance as the play." In the ballet *Vienna Waltzes,* Ter-Arutunian's strength of imagination was evident in his use of mylar-mirrored, crystal chandeliers which were transformed out of the trees of a forest. In the hundreds of designs credited to Ter-Arutunian, the mark of his genius is that he never repeats himself.

—Tom Mikotowicz

# TERRAZAS (de la Pena), Eduardo

Mexican architect and interior, exhibition, and graphic designer

**Born:** Guadalajara, Jalisco, 5 March 1936. **Education:** Studied architecture, at the Universidad Nacional Autonoma de Mexico, Mexico City, 1954-58; Cornell University, Ithaca, New York, M. Arch., 1959; University of Rome, 1959-60; Centre Scientifique et Technique du Bâtiment, Paris, 1961-62. **Career:** Worked as an architect in the offices of Howell, Killick, and Partridge, London, 1961; Candilis, Josic, and Woods, Paris, 1962; Pedro Ramirez Vazquez and Rafael Mijarez, New York, 1963-64; and George Nelson, New York, 1965; founder-director, Eduardo Terrazas y Asociados, Mexico City, from 1966; technical director, INDECO National Institute for Community Development and Housing, Mexico City, 1971, and AURIS Institute for Urban Action and Social Integration, Mexico City, 1972-73; consultant to the City Development Authority, Karachi, and to the Capital Development Authority, Islamabad, 1974. Director of the New Alternatives Institute, Mexico City; co-founder and secretary general, Centro Tepotztlan, Mexico, 1980. Professor of architectural design, Columbia University, New York, 1963-66; visiting lecturer at design institutions and congresses in Mexico, Canada, United States, India, and elsewhere from 1969. **Exhibitions:** Palacio Nacional de Bellas Artes, Mexico City, 1971; Knoll International, Paris, 1973; Museo Nacional de Bellas Artes, Santiago, 1973; Museo Nacional de Arte, La Paz, 1973; Galeria Fundacion Eugenio Mendoza, Caracas, 1974; Benjamin Franklin

Library, Mexico City, 1975 (with Arnaldo Coen); Museo de Alhondiga de Granaditas, Guanajuato, 1975 (with Arnaldo Coen). **Address:** Eduardo Terrazas y Asociados, Cordoba 23N, Mexico 7, D.F., Mexico.

## Works

*Masterpieces of Mexican Art* touring exhibition layouts, in the Soviet Union, Poland, and France, 1961-62.
Mexican Pavilion, at the 1964 World's Fair, New York, 1963-64.
Mexican Pavilion, at the XIV Milan Triennale, 1968.
*Mexico 68* publications and unified identity programme, for the Olympic Games, Mexico City, 1966-69.
*Mexican Image* city-wide exhibition displays, Mexico City, 1969.
Logotype symbol, for the IX World Cup Football Championship, Mexico City, 1969.
Visual identity graphics, for the Secretariat of Press and Propaganda, Mexico City, 1975-76.
*Family Planning* publicity campaign, for the United Nations, 1976.
*Architecture of Public Spaces* urban roads and signage program, for Alternativas XXI Incorporated, Mexico City, 1979.
Macro Plaza urban renewal plan, for the City of Monterrey, 1981.
Logotype, visual identity programme and conference hall design, for the North-South International Cooperation Congress, Cancun, 1981.

## Publications

**On TERRAZAS: books**—*World Architecture One* edited by John Donat, London, 1964; *Art of the Environment* edited by Gyorgy Kepes, New York, 1972; *Spazio e Società* edited by Giancarlo de Carlo, Milan, 1978; *Archighraphia: Architectural and Environmental Graphics* edited by Walter Herdeg, Zurich, 1978; *The Language of Graphics* by Edward Booth-Clibborn and Daniele Baroni, London, 1980.

\*   \*   \*

Eduardo Terrazas is a many-faceted creative planner, architect, painter, and designer whose wide experience and activities have led to important interactions with his own culture in Mexico, as well as with other countries and cultures. His many innovative and seminal programs have influenced the thinking and planning of wide-ranging activities and have reflected the advancing industrialization and the social and cultural life of Mexico.

On the occasion of the opening of the Mexico Metro system, his exhibition *Imagen Mexico* was a spectacular testimony to his graphic imagination. In the poster for it, silkscreened on aluminized paper with a multicolored background of arrows, the letters which make up the title are dropped out so that they make an overall pattern which reveals the aluminum. Thus, the viewer is reflected in the poster and becomes part of the image. This was produced in a single size (12" x 12") and used in multiples of up to four feet square.

At times working independently in his own office, Alternativas XXI, or when working for the Government of Mexico, he has been a true cultural ambassador. For example, he served as the Director of Technical Assistance provided by Mexican Government to the government of Tanzania for the design and construction of its new capital city Dodoman. This project included urban design, an architectural system for schools, and renovation of existing settlements. At home, he has combined his urban and graphic concerns in such projects as the System of Urban Furnishings, Signs, Symbols and Gardens for the orderly circulation system through the streets of Mexico City and the Dialogue North-South for the Cancun Conference.

His disciplines are never separate. Prolific and richly gifted, he is at once theoretician, teacher, and artist in his analytical projects, which have application to his own country as well as to other expanding and developing nations.

—Mildred Constantine

# TESTA, Armando

Italian graphic designer

**Born:** Turin, 23 March 1917. **Education:** Apprenticed to a locksmith, 1928-29, sheet metal worker, 1930, and typesetter, Turin, 1931-33; studied under abstract painter Ezio d'Errico, at the Vigliardi Paravia School of Graphic Arts, Turin, 1932-34. **Military Service:** Served as an aerial photographer in the Italian Air Force, 1940-43. **Family:** Married Lidia de Barberis in 1945; children: Delfina, Marco, and Antonella; married Gemma de Angelis in 1978. **Career:** Founder, designer, and chairman, Armando Testa S.p.A. graphic studio, Turin, 1946; Armando Testa S.p.A. became a full service advertising agency (in association with Lidia and Franco de Barberis), Turin, 1956; clients included Martini & Rossi, Carpano, Pirelli, Borsalino, Fater, Lavazza, Punt e Mes, Antonetto, Euchessina, Simmenthal, San Pellegrino, *Graphicus, Publitransport,* and others. Instructor in graphic design and contemporary art, at the Advanced School of Print Sciences and Arts, Polytechnic Institute, Turin, 1965-75. Monthly columnist, *Giornale dell'Arte,* Turin, May 1983-March 1992. **Exhibitions:** Poster Museum, Warsaw, 1972; *Italian Re-Evolution,* La Jolla Museum of Art, California, 1982; Padiglione d'Arte Contemporanea, Milan, 1984; *Italie d'Aujourd'hui,* Villa Arson, Nice, 1985; Mole Antonelliana, Turin, 1985; Maison Gerbollier, La Salle, 1986; Parsons School of Design, New York, 1987; Niccoli Art Gallery, Parma, 1987; *Reklama 88,* Krasnaja Presnja, Moscow, 1988; Otis Parsons School of Design, Los Angeles, 1988; Lincoln Center Gallery, Fort Collins, Colorado, 1989; Circulo de Bellas Artes, Madrid, 1989; Galleria Target, Turin, 1989; Museo d'Arte Contemporanea all'aperto, Maglione Cananvese, Italy, 1989 (permanent exhibition of paintings on the town's walls); Palazzo della Permanente, Milan, 1989; Museo Nazionale della Montagna; Turin, 1989-90; Colombari Art Gallery, Milan, 1990; Palazzo a Vela, Turin, 1990; Promotrice delle Belle Arti, Turin, 1991; Pécsi Galérie, Pecs, Hungary, 1991; Galleria Bianca Pilat, Milan, 1992; Castello di Rivoli Museum of Contemporary Art, Rivoli, 1993; *Armando Testa—una retrospettiva,* Palazzo Strozzi, Florence, 1993; *Armando Testa: Posters from the Collection,* The Israel Museum, Jerusalem, September, 1993/January, 1994. **Collections:** Poster Museum, Trento; Communications Archives, University of Parma; Kunstmuseum, Munich; Stedelijk Museum, Amsterdam; Poster Museum, Warsaw; Moravian Gallery, Brno; Colorado State University, Fort Collins; Rufino Tamayo Museum, Mexico City; Museum of Modern Art, New York; Musée de l'Affiche, Paris; The Israel Museum, Jerusalem; Olympisches

Museum, Lausanne, Switzerland. **Honors:** ICI Poster Competition Prize, Milan, 1937; Olympic Games Poster Competition Prize, Rome, 1958/1959; Gold Medal, Italian Ministry of Culture, 1958/1959; First Prize, Warsaw International Poster Biennale, 1970 (for the poster Plast 72); Federazione Italiana Pubblicita Medal, Milan, 1974; Torchio d'Oro, Progresso Grafico, Turin, 1980; Special Prize, Associazione Aziende Pubblicitaire Italiene, Milan, 1982 (for contribution to poster creativity); Citizen of the Year, Turin, 1986; Honor Laureate, Colorado State University, Fort Collins, Colorado, 1989; Piemontevip Prize, Biella, 1991; Special Mention, New York Art Directors Club, 1991 and 1992. **Died:** Turin, 20 March 1992.

## Works

*ICI Industria Colori e Inchiostri* poster project, for ICI Printing Inks, Milan, 1937.
*Martini Rooster* poster, for Gallo Martini, 1948.
*Elephant* poster, for Pirelli Tyres, 1954.
*Giochi della XVII Olimpiade* poster, for the 1960 Rome Olympics, 1959.
Globe-and-a-half poster, for Punt e Mes, 1960.
*Caballero and Carmencita* television commercial characters modelled in plaster, for Cafe Paulista, 1965.
*Pippo* television commercial hippopotamus dummy in polyurethane resin, for Lines diapers, 1966-67.
*Plast 72* poster, for the plastics exhibition, Milan, 1969.
*Finger in Water* cover design, for *Graphicus* magazine, 1969.
Trademark, for Perugina Candies, 1971.
*Shadow-figure* poster, for Amnesty International, 1979.
Trademark, for Urama Simmonds mechanical engineering company, 1982.
Poster and trademark, for *Avanti* newspaper, 1983.
*Magia* exhibition poster, for the Municipality of Milan, 1984.
*Torino Ufficio* exhibition poster, for the Annual Office Furniture Show, Turin, 1985.
Trademark and symbol, for Sanlorenzo haute couture, 1987.
Logotype symbol, for the Castello di Rivoli museum of contemporary art, Turin, 1988.
*MACAM* poster, for the Museum of Contemporary Art, Magliano, 1988.
*Giovanna d'Arco* poster, for modern drama about Jeanne d'Arc, 1989.
*Linea 3* billboard poster series, for the new Milan underground train line, 1989.
*Cremazione* poster promoting cremation, for the Municipality of Turin, 1989.
*Visual Design* poster, for an international posters exhibition, La Salle, 1990.
*Il Giornale dell'Arte/The Art Newspaper* posters, for the Italian and English edition of an art journal, 1990.
*Eurographic Press* poster, for an Icograda Congress, 1990.
*9. Festival Cinema Giovani* poster, for an International Movie Festival devoted to young directors, Turin, 1991.
*Pozzo Gros Monti* poster, for a posters exhibition devoted to 100 years of activity of a printing company, 1991.
*Neuroradiologia* trademark and poster, for a Medical Association and Congress, 1991.
*10. Festival Cinema Giovani* poster, for an International Movie Festival devoted to young directors, Turin, 1992.

## Publications

**By TESTA: books**—*Dalla Parte di chi Guarda* (a selection of the articles published on *Giornale dell'Arte*), Turin, 1992; **articles**—in *Serigrafia* (Milan), 1962; *Pagina* (Milan), June 1963; *Parete* (Milan), October 1964; *Graphicus* (Turin), March 1970, March 1985; *Strategia* (Milan), October 1974, February 1986, April 1986; *Campaign Europe* (London), December 1979; *Publirama Italian 1979* (Milan), May 1980; *Pubblicità Domani* (Milan), March 1982; *Campaign* (Milan), November/December 1982; *Il Giornale dell'Arte* (Turin), May 1983, June 1983; *Ricerca e Innovazione* (Milan), 1986; *Epoca* (Milan), June 1987; *Arte e Cronaca* (Bari), September 1988; *Global* (Milan), July 1988; *Quaderni ISIA* (Urbino), no. 1, 1988/89; *Quaderni dell'Archivo Storico GFT* (Turin), December 1989; *Nuova Cucina* (Milan), December 1989; *Portfolio Illustratori e Fotografi* (Milan), June 1990; *Pubblico* (Milan), June 1991; *Tema Celeste* (Siracusa), January 1992; *Italia Oggi* (Milan), 1 February 1992.

**On TESTA: books**—*Packaging: An International Survey Package Design* edited by Walter Herdeg, Zürich, 1959; *Window Display 2* edited by Walter Herdeg, Zürich, 1961; *The Poster: An Illustrated History from 1860* by Harold F. Hutchinson, London and Toronto, 1968; *A History of Graphic Design* by Philip B. Meggs, New York, 1983; *Armando Testa,* exhibition catalogue with texts by Gillo Dorfles and A. C. Quintavalle, Milan, 1984; *Armando Testa: Il Segno e la Pubblicità,* exhibition catalogue with texts by Gillo Dorfles, A. C. Quintavalle, and Omar Calabrese, Turin, 1985; *Armando Testa: 40 Years of Italian Creative Design,* exhibition catalogue with texts by Gillo Dorfles and A. C. Quintavalle, Turin, 1987; *Alle Radici della Comunicazione Visiva Italiana* by Heinz Waibl, Milan, 1988; *Storia della Pubblicità Italiana* by G. P. Ceserani, Bari, 1988; *Armando Testa,* exhibition catalogue by with texts G. Celant, Omar Calabrese, Milton Glaser, and A. C. Quintavalle, Milan, 1993; *Il Dizionario della Pubblicità,* Bologna, 1993; **articles**—"Armando Testa" by Jerry Steimle in *Communication Arts* (Palo Alto, California), January/February 1976; "Testa, the Primitive, the Wild Man of Turin" by E. Durie in *Advertising Age/Europe* (Chicago), 23 October 1978; "Just One More ... The Testa's Ham-Armchair" in *Life* (New York), August 1981; "The Italian Designer Armando Testa" by H.C. Besemer in *Novum* (Munich), April 1982; "Nel Castello di Kafka" by A. C. Quintavalle in *Panorama* (Milan), 19 December 1983; "Arte e Pubblicità" by M. Gandini in *Flash Art* (Milan), January/February 1988; *Juliet Art* (Trieste), no. 47, April 1990; *Playboy* (Bologna), September 1990; "The New Aesthetic Order" by M. Blonsky in *Connoisseur* (New York), September 1991; "Armando Testa Mago dello Spot" by G. Vergani in *La Repubblica* (Milan) 22 March 1992; "Prima lo Stile poi il Marketing" by O. Camerana in *La Repubblica* (Milan) 22 March 1992; "Il Caballero non c'é più" by M. Guisti in *Il Manifesto* (Rome), 22 March 1992; "Armando Testa" by Umberto Allemandi in *Il Giornale dell'Arte* (Turin), April 1992; *Graphicus* (Turin), May 1992; *The Practitioner* (Milan), 4 May 1992; "Elogio di Armando Testa come Pensatore" by G. P. Ceserani in *Strategia* (Milan), May 1992; "Testa: L'Uomo-L'Artista" by Laura Franconi in *Advertiser* (Milan), June 1992; *Graphis* (New York), September/October 1992; *Sette,* 6 May 1993; *La Stampa,* 8 May 1993; *Corriere della Sera,* 10 May 1993; *Arte In,* June 1993; *Print,* November/December 1993.

\*

When people ask me how it all started, I use to say that I was born poor but modern.

I was still in my teens and I already aimed at creating simple, clear, and striking images. Synthesis was the law of my whole life both in my works and in my words. Synthesis is an extraordinary rule; when you follow it, everyone is grateful to you.

The love for graphics and art and the curiosity towards all the newest media in visual communication contributed to the molding of my cultural background. A background that was not built up rationally but which today allows me to look at an image without any preconceived idea about the content or the historical context. I read old works with the same eyes as I read the art of the 1990s: through form, colors, signs.

While in the past poster designers could be recognized through their well defined style, I have never wanted to have an immediately distinguishable graphic sign. I have created posters handling painting, photography, or typographic characters indifferently. But all the same, the synthesis, the use of white backgrounds and primary colors, the centrality of the image, have become my own style.

The advent of TV advertising was for me a new challenge. I had to move from the static image to the dynamic one, to face different visual languages and to research visual elements equally strong in a poster, in an ad, or in a commercial.

During my life the severe marketing rules as well as the necessity to communicate in a simple and attractive way have always been linked to the most avant-garde art experiences.

To be constantly restless; to be avid to know the latest "ism" in art field, the most creative director in Hollywood, the TV show most appreciated by housewives, or the most trendy novelist; to be able to understand the beauty both of a Chinese alphabet letter and a Manhattan street sign: that is what I am expecting of my young creative people today. Curiosity is the first step towards creativity.

—Armando Testa (Turin, 22 January 1992)

\*　　\*　　\*

Armando Testa had an intense interest in the world around him. He was unique in the world of design, where talented people constantly question how things are put together and strive for new and better ways to do things. Gillo Dorfles described Testa in an exhibition catalogue at Parsons School of Design in New York in 1987 as "an accomplished creator of images, an inventor of visual paradoxes and, in sum, the person I would like to call a 'global visualizer' of relationships between man and the world, production and consumption, 'pure' creativity and creativity exercised for a purpose." Testa's voracious appetite for new experiences led him to experiment with painting, photography, architecture, film, and television, among other mediums. He was one of the first to skillfully use photomontage, as can be witnessed in his posters for the XVII Olympics in 1959.

Very little passed by Testa without setting his mind to work. Whatever he saw that he admired, he would have liked to have been the one who did it. Testa would, for example, be just as pleased to do medieval liturgical paintings as his playful, modern posters. In fact, that he would do either or both would satisfy his great motivation to "do it all."

As head of one of Italy's leading advertising agencies, Testa involved himself with the full range of promotion. This took him into all media, which presented him with constant opportunity to do

**Armando Testa: poster *Plast*, 1972**

the same old things in different and unusual ways. But at the same time, it limited his time to do the other-Testa things, works that were expressions of his own personal interests and tastes.

In these things, here again, Testa was Testa, off in his own world, carefully distilling the essence of every situation, applying his own thought processes, and developing unique solutions. One of the most pervasive elements of his work was surrealism, as can be witnessed in the images of and his fur-lined tea cup and the 1954 Pirelli tire that turned into the head of an elephant. Bizarre was better than banal with Testa.

He could play with a single idea in endless variations. His exploration of the uses, some really far-fetched, of the tip of a finger (the pointer finger) have exploited just about every possibility. Testa has put his "fingers" to work in non-commercial serigraphs, personal greeting cards, promotion for his agency, and in advertisements for his clients. Some examples include his bunch of asparagus fingers and, in the poster for il Milanese, the pointing red hand that, when given black glasses, transformed into a face.

Through Testa's eye, the view was just a bit different. Throughout Italy, designers recognize Testa's individuality and divide into camps, for and against. His work does not encourage apathy.

—Jerry Steimle

# THOMASS, Chantal

French fashion designer

**Born:** Chantal Genty, in Malakoff, Seine, 4 September 1947. **Education:** Mainly self-taught in design. **Family:** Married Bruce Thomass in 1967; children: Louise and Robin. **Career:** Worked as a secretary, Paris, 1965-66; freelance clothing designer, selling to Dorothée Bis in Paris, and Le Café des Arts in Saint-Tropez, 1966-68; partner, with Bruce Thomass, in Ter et Bantine fashion company, Paris, 1968-76; founder-director, Société Chantal Thomass fashion firm, Paris, from 1976; introduced lingerie and hosiery collections, 1975; maternity wear, 1981; children's clothing line, 1982; signed partnership with World Company for distribution, licensing, and boutiques in Japan, 1985; second boutique for clothing and household accessories opened, Paris, 1991. **Member:** Chambre Syndicale de la Couture, Paris, from 1981. **Honors:** Chevalier des Arts et Lettres, France. **Addresses:** (office) 100 rue du Cherche-Midi, 75006 Paris; (home) 12 rue Armangaud, 92210 Saint-Cloud, France.

## Publications

**On THOMASS: books**—*Fairchild's Who's Who in Fashion* edited by Anne Stegemeyer, New York, 1980; *Fashion 2001* by Lucille Khornak, London, 1982; *French Style* by Suzanne Slesin and Stafford Cliff, New York and London, 1982; *McDowell's Directory of Twentieth Century Fashion* by Colin McDowell, London, 1984; *The Encyclopaedia of Fashion from 1840 to the 1980s* by Georgina O'Hara, London, 1986; *Women of Fashion: Twentieth-Century Designers* by Valerie Steele, New York, 1991; **articles**—"Les stylistes" in *Elle* (Paris), 23 May 1977; "Chantal Thomass: la renouveau du froufrou" in *Jardin des Modes* (Paris), October 1982; "Chantal Thomass" by Gérard Depardieu in *La Mode en Peinture,* Winter 1982-83; "Chantal Thomass" in *Profession Textile* (Paris), 18 September 1987.

\*   \*   \*

Of this husband-and-wife team, Bruce Thomass was the one with training at the École des Beaux Arts, while Chantal herself was a secretary who grew bored with her job and wanted to do something creative, although she did not know a pattern from a toile. She may be regarded as an instinctive designer rather than one with an intellectual approach. Prettiness is important to her, as is typified by her lingerie, which includes silk petticoats and lashings of lace. She says she designs for the young woman who wants to look young and who is feminine and reasonably romantic, so her concept of woman is very conservative.

There have not been any important attempts in her work to discover a new look; rather, she reinterprets many existing styles, as can be seen in her North African pantaloons, oriental embroidered black taffeta gowns, the hacking habit presented in rose-pink wool, Victorian lace hemlines on embroidered satin dresses, a Scottish kilt and jacket done in huge checks, a 1950s shawl collar on a lambswool coat, and a 1950s siren look in a cerise cotton frock bedecked with too many rows of white beads. Regularly featured in her collections are trousers, such as the 1978 blue pantaloons with T-shirt, the 1979 print trousers with matching long coat, and the clinging cotton jersey overalls, more subtly seductive than reveal-ing. Accordingly, Thomass is a safe designer, who is not trying to overthrow the existing order, but who tries to create attractive versions of current garments.

This traditional path is one that has proved successful for many designers to follow, for what revolutionary designers often forget is that the customers who can afford to buy original creations are usually women in middle age or older. Thus, while Chantal may have young women in mind, her clothes will be bought mainly by their mothers who prefer a traditional approach. A reputation for invention is not all-important in dress design, for a traditional garment presented in a different material or colour from usual will appeal to many. A slight variation can be novelty enough.

In the early 1990s, Thomass had 12 boutiques throughout France, two in Paris. She assures herself a solid place in the fashion world by adapting her youthful designs to the current trend.

—Diana de Marly

# THOMPSON, Bradbury

American graphic designer

**Born:** Topeka, Kansas, 25 March 1911. **Education:** Studied at Washburn University, Topeka, B.A., 1934. **Military Service:** Served as a designer in the United States Office of War Information, 1942-45. **Family:** Married Della Deen Dodge in 1939; children: Leslie, Mark, David and Elizabeth. **Career:** Art director, for Capper Publishers, 1934-38, and for Rogers-Kellogg-Stilson agency, 1938-42; freelance graphic designer and art director, New York, from 1945: consultant to *Art News,* Westvaco Corporation, Pitney-Bowes, Famous Artists Schools, Time-Life Books, McGraw-Hill, Field Enterprises, Cornell University, and others. Visiting critic, Yale School of Art and Architecture, New Haven, Connecticut, from 1956. **Member:** Advisory board member, Parsons School of Design, New York, 1945-55; governing board member, Philadelphia Museum College of Art, 1956-59; board member, Perrot Memorial Library, from 1966; member of the First Federal Design Assembly, 1973, and the University American Arbitration Association, 1976-78; trustee, Washburn University, Topeka, from 1972; former vice-president, Art Directors Club of New York. **Exhibitions:** American Institute of Graphic Arts, New York, 1959, 1975; Washburn University, Topeka, Kansas, 1964; Cornell University, Ithaca, New York, 1969; Harvard University, Cambridge, Massachusetts, 1965; Yale University, New Haven, Connecticut, 1976; Museum of Modern Art, New York, 1977. **Collections:** Museum of Modern Art, New York. **Honors:** New York Art Directors Club Medal, 1945, 1947, 1951, 1955, and Hall of Fame Award, 1973; American Institute of Graphic Arts Award, 1948, and Gold Medal, 1975; National Society of Art Directors Gold T-square Award, 1950; Silver Medal, 1963, and Gold Medal, 1965, Biennial of Sao Paulo. **Address:** Jones Park, Riverside, Connecticut 06878, U.S.A.

## Works

*Westvaco Inspirations* magazine design and layouts, for the West Virginia Pulp and Paper Company, 1938-62.
*Mademoiselle* magazine design and layouts, New York, 1945-49.
*Art News* magazine and annual design and layouts, New York, 1945-72.

*Freedom of the American Road* single-issue magazine design, for Ford Motor Company, 1955.

*Print* magazine cover design, New York, January/February 1962.

*Harvard Business Review* magazine design and layouts, Cambridge, Massachusetts, 1965-67.

*Library of America* book design, for Time-Life Books, New York, 1966.

*Food of the World* book design, for Time-Life Books, New York, 1966.

*The Swing Era* book design, for Time-Life Books, 1970.

*The Washburn Bible* book design, for Washburn University Press, Topeka, 1982-83.

**Publications**

**By THOMPSON: books**—*The Monalphabet,* New York, 1945; *Modern Painting and Typography,* New York, 1947; *Alphabet 26,* New York, 1950.

**On THOMPSON: books**—*Posters: 50 Artists and Designers* edited by W. H. Allner, New York, 1952; *The New Graphic Design* by Karl Gerstner and Markus Kutter, Teufen and London, 1959; *The Design Concept* by Allan Hurlburt, New York, 1981; *Who's Who in Graphic Art* edited by Walter Amstutz, Dubendorf, 1982; *A History of Graphic Design* by Philip B. Meggs, New York and London, 1983; *Typographic Design: Form and Communication* by Rob Carter, Ben Day and Philip Meggs, New York, 1985; *Nine Pioneers in American Graphic Design* by Roger R. Remington and Barbara Hodik, Cambridge, Massachusetts, 1989.

\*   \*   \*

The elegant and quiet work of Bradbury Thompson very much reflects the person. His influence on the printed page carries on a noble and distinguished tradition. The design of a book often tests the abilities and skills of a designer, yet Thompson has made that medium his art form and has created innumerable classics, culminating in the recently completed *Washburn Holy Bible.*

In 1958, the West Virginia Paper and Pulp Company began production of a series of limited edition books based on great American classics. This unique series served the two-fold purpose of demonstrating the quality of Westvaco's papers and of serving as Christmas souvenirs to its customers and friends. Each six-by-nine-and-one-half-inch volume is slip-cased, creating an elegant effect, along with additional touches such as head bands, end sheets, and a colophon. One of the editions of Edgar Allen Poe contains four of his tales, each designed in an unusual and individual way. Thompson carefully integrated type, paper, color, and illustration to achieve an attractive and cohesive balance between the visual and written elements. In the tale of "The Great Balloon Hoax," the entire layout is treated like a newspaper article of the period, with the text, arranged in columns, accompanied by appropriate headlines and line drawings. Color, texture of paper, and illustration add richness to the page and story.

Drama plays a special part in Thompson's creation for Stephen Crane's *Red Badge of Courage,* which displays an unusual but appropriate graphic element—a bullet hole! After much historical research experimentation, Thompson felt this rather violent symbol would serve as an effective device to represent the horrors of war. The effect was attained with a carefully drilled hole through the volume.

Westvaco's edition of Benjamin Franklin's writing is another marvelous example of typographic experimentation. The treatment is appropriate to the subject, and Thompson's use of large type creates a harmonious, overall pattern. Full-page Diderot engravings beautifully complement the opposing text pages to produce highly textual and effective spreads.

The overall mood created in each of the twenty-four volumes is very special. The visual effects do not in any way impede reading but rather enhance the enjoyment and appreciation of these classics. The foreword to each issue contains a concise analysis of the design concept and so invites the reader to observe the mind of the designer.

—D. Ichiyama

## THYGESEN, Rud

Danish architect, interior, and furniture designer

**Born:** Saeby, 15 August 1932. **Education:** Studied at the Business School, 1948-1952, and Handels-school, Copenhagen, 1953-57; School of Arts and Crafts (Kunsthandvaerkskolan), Copenhagen,

**Rud Thygesen: chair**

M.A.A., 1966. **Family:** Married to Lillian Simonsen. **Career:** Freelance furniture designer, establishing design studio with Johnny Sørensen, in Copenhagen, from 1967; has designed for Mogens Kold, Domus Danica, Erik Boisen, Per Jorgensen, Textil Lassen, Magnus Olesen, Zon International, and others. **Exhibitions:** Den Permanente, Copenhagen, 1972; Danske Kunstindustrimuseum, Copenhagen, 1976; Museum of Contemporary Crafts, Chicago, 1977; Royal Danish Embassy, Washington, D.C., 1978, Stockholm, 1980, and London, 1980, 1986; Oslo Museum of Applied Art, Norway, 1981; Nordenfjeldske Museum of Applied Art, Trondheim, Norway, 1981; *Scandinavian Modern Design 1880-1980,* Cooper-Hewitt Museum, New York, 1982 (toured); Maison du Danemark, Paris, 1982; Galerie Helan, Stockholm, 1983; Grieghallen, Bergen, Norway, 1986; *Denmark in Britain: Design and Architecture,* Business Design Centre, London, 1989; Galleria Designs, Vancouver, Canada, 1991; Axishouse, Tokyo, 1992; Grand Palais, Paris, 1993; Casaidea, Rome, 1995. **Collections:** Nordenfjeldske Kunstindustrimuseum, Trondheim; Museum of Decorative Art, Copenhagen; Olso Museum of Applied Art; Art Gallery and Museums and the Royal Pavilion, Brighton, England; Victoria and Albert Museum, London; Museum of Modern Art, New York; Staatliches Museum für angewandte Kunst, Munich. **Honors:** First Prize, Society of Cabinetmakers Exhibition, Copenhagen, 1966, 1969; Central Bank Jubilee Award, Copenhagen, 1969, 1975; Danish Furniture Fair prize, 1971; Alex Foss Industrifond Award, Copenhagen, 1976; honorary award, Danish Furniture Manufacturers Association, 1978; Danish Furniture Prize, 1978; Institute of Business Designers medal, 1978; "G-Prize," Japan, 1989; Best of Show, Design Foundation, U.S.A., 1989; Oscars Snai, France, 1991; Bruno Mathssons Prize, 1992; Design Prize Schweiz, 1993. **Address:** Ostergade 26 C, 1100 Copenhagen K., Denmark.

# TIGERMAN, Stanley

American architect and product designer

**Born:** Chicago, Illinois, 20 September 1930. **Education:** Attended Chicago public schools; attended Massachusetts Institute of Technology, Cambridge, Massachusetts, 1948-1949, Institute of Design, Chicago, Illinois, 1949-1950, and Yale University, New Haven, Connecticut, B.Arch, M.Arch, 1959-1961. **Military Service:** United States Navy, 1950-54. **Family:** Married Margaret McCurry; children: Judson Joel, Tracy Leigh. **Career:** Architectural apprentice with George Fred Keck, Chicago, Illinois, 1949-50; worked in various architectural offices, Chicago, 1954-57; designer, Skidmore, Owings and Merrill, Chicago, 1957-59; draftsman, Paul M. Rudolph, New Haven, Connecticut, 1959-61; chief of design, Harry M. Weese, Chicago, 1961-62; partner, Tigerman & Koglin, Chicago, 1962-64; principal, Stanley Tigerman and Associates, Chicago, 1964-82; partner, Tigerman Fugeman McCurry, 1982-88; partner, Tigerman McCurry Architects, from 1988. Professor, 1965-71, 1980-93, and director, school of architecture, University of Illinois at Chicago; University of Illinois, Chicago, from 1985; lecturer at universities and conferences throughout the world; frequent member of award juries and panels. **Member:** American Institute of Architects (AIA). **Exhibitions:** Chicago Art Institute, 1954-57, 1962-64, 1973, 1977,

1979, 1982, 1984, 1987, 1989; Walker Art Center, Minneapolis, Minnesota, 1965, 1978, 1980, 1981; Art Institute of Chicago, 1965, 1981, 1986, 1988, 1992, 1993, 1994; Ravinia Festival, 1965; Midland Art Center, Michigan, 1965; Evanston Art Center, Illinois, 1969, 1984; Springfield Arts Association, Illinois, 1969; Kansas City Art Research Center, Missouri, 1969, 1976; One Illinois Center, Chicago, 1971; Matrix Show, 1975; University of Chicago, 1975; Cooper Union, 1976, 1981; Harvard University, 1976; Museum of Contemporary Art, Chicago, 1976, 1980; Virginia Polytechnic Institute, Blacksburg, Virginia, 1976; Time-Life Building, Chicago, 1976; Venice Biennale, 1976, 1980; Richard Gray Gallery, 1976; University of Houston, Texas, 1976, 1977; University of California, Berkeley, 1976, 1977; Sao Paulo, Brazil, 1976; Pacific Design Center, Los Angeles, 1977; Telic-Art Research Center, Kansas City, 1977; Drawing Center, New York, 1977; Walter Kelly Gallery, Chicago, 1977; Otis Art Institute, Los Angeles, 1977, 1981, 1982; Graham Foundation for Advanced Studies in the Fine Arts, Chicago, 1978; Louisville Arts Association, Kentucky, 1978; Tehran Museum of Contemporary Art, Iran, 1978; Queens Historical Society, New York, 1978; N.A.M.E. Gallery, Chicago, 1978; Arts Club of Chicago, 1978; Yale University, 1978, 1981; University of North Carolina, Charlotte, 1978; P.S.I., New York, 1979; University of California, Los Angeles, 1979; Museum of Modern Art, New York, 1979; Architectural Association, London, 1979; Academy Von Baukunst, Amsterdam, 1979; Museum of Contemporary Art, La Jolla, California, 1980, 1984; American Academy, Rome, Italy, 1980, 1994; Museum of Finnish Architecture, Helsinki, 1980; Design Center, Aspen, Colorado, 1981; National Academy of Design, New York, 1981; New York Historical Society, 1981; House Pompidou, Beauborg, Paris, 1981; Dallas Museum of Fine Arts, Texas, 1981; Corcoran Gallery of Art, Washington, D.C., 1982; Rosa Esman Gallery, New York, 1982; Rizzoli Gallery, Chicago, 1982; University of Palermo, Italy, 1982; *Pop Architecture,* Deutsches Architeckturmuseum, Frankfort, Germany, 1984; San Francisco Museum of Modern Art, California, 1984; Victoria and Albert Museum, London, 1984; Centre Georges Pompidou, Paris, 1985; National Museum of Modern Art, Kyoto, Japan, 1985; Museum Boymans-Van Beunigen, Rotterdam, Netherlands, 1985; Museum of Science and Industry, Chicago, 1985, 1992; Hamano Institute, Tokyo and Osaka, Japan, 1985; National Building Museum, Washington, D.C., 1986; Cincinnati Art Center, Ohio, 1986; Deutsches Architekturmuseum, 1986, 1988, 1990; Museum of Modern Art, Tokyo, 1986; Gallery of Design, Merchandise Mart, Chicago, 1987; Venice Design Art Gallery, Italy, 1987; IBM Gallery, New York, 1987; Cooper Hewitt Museum, New York, 1987; Art Museum, Phoenix, Arizona, 1988; Bonnzfantenmuseum, Maastricht, Netherlands, 1988; Kunst Halle, West Berlin, West Germany, 1988; Metropolitan Museum of Art, New York, 1988; Museum Porto, Portugal, 1989; Museum of Contemporary Art, Antwerp, Belgium, 1989; Gallery for Architecture, Santa Monica, California, 1989; USIA, Moscow, Russia, 1989; Pavillion de l'Arsenal, Paris, 1989; Fukuoka City, Kiushu, Japan, 1989; Design Center, Washington, D.C., 1990; City Hall, Belgrade, Yugoslavia, 1990; *Interior Design Hall of Fame,* Waldorf Astoria Hotel, New York, 1990; Triennale of World Architecture, Belgrade, Yugoslavia, 1991; Chicago Historical Society, 1991, 1992, 1993, 1994; Los Angeles County Museum of Art, 1992; Athenaeum, Chicago, 1992; Power House Energy Museum, Zion, Illinois, 1992; *Assopiastrelle,* McCormick Place, Chicago, 1992; Guggenheim Museum, New York, 1993; Graham Foundation, Buenos Aires, Argentina, 1993. **Collections:** Tehran Museum of Contemporary Art, Iran; Chicago Art

Institute; Deutsches Architekturmuseum, Frankfurt; Museum of Modern Art, New York. **Honors:** Award of Excellence, *Architectural Record* magazine, New York, 1970, 1978; Award of Merit, AIA, 1970, 1974, 1975; Distinguished Building Award, Chicago AIA, 1971, 1973, 1975 (2), 1977 (2), 1979 (5), 1981, 1985, 1991, 1994 (3); Gold Medal Award of Excellence in Masonry, Metropolitan Chicago Masonry Council, 1974, 1991; Continued Excellence of Design Award, Illinois AIA Annual Award, 1976; Award of Merit, Chicago Lighting Institute, 1976, 1988, 1993; Chicago Art Award, 1978; Honor Award, Chicago AIA, 1978, 1979, 1984 (2); Honor Award, Illinois AIA, 1978; Interior Award, *Architectural Record* magazine, 1979, 1990; Record House Award, *Architectural Record,* 1980, 1987, 1993; Citation and Design Award, *Progressive Architecture* magazine, New York, 1980, 1984; 6th Place Prize, International Competition, Bruhl, Germany, 1980; Honorable Mention, International Competition for Museum, Guernica, Spain, 1981; Distinguished Service Award, Chicago AIA, 1983; Award, Gypsum Drywall Contractors of Northern Illinois, 1983; Honor Award, National AIA, 1984, 1987, 1991 (2), 1992; Grand Prize, *Builder's Magazine* House of the Year, 1985; Yale Arts Award, 1985; Honor Award, Neocon Product Display, 1986, 1988; Distinguished Building Award, AIA, 1986; Young Architect Award, 1986; Interiors Award, Chicago AIA, 1987, 1988 (2), 1991, 1992 (2), 1994; Design Award, Chicago AIA, 1987; Certificate of Merit, Pratt Institute, 1988; Design Award, Art Institute of Chicago, 1988; Citation for Service, ACSA, 1989 (2); Citation, Chicago School of Professional Psychology, 1989; Nomination, National Jewish Book Award, 1989; National Professor of the Year Nomination, 1989; In the Public Interest Award, *Architectural Record,* 1989; Dean of Architecture Award, Merchandise Mart, 1989; Award for Best Temporary Showroom, IDCNY, 1989; "Design 100" Selection, *Metropolitan Home* magazine, 1990; honorary member, Golden Key National Honor Society, 1990; Hall of Fame Award, *Interior Design* magazine, 1990; Merit Award, American Wood Council, 1990; Certificate of Merit, Art Director's Club Award, 1991; Domino's Gold 30 Award for Excellence in Architecture, 1991; Award, Illinois Chapter, National Organization of Minority Architects (NOMA), 1991; 1st Award, American Society of Interior Designers (ASID), 1992, 1994 (2); Illinois Academy of Fine Arts Award, 1992, 1993; Merit Award, Western Red Cedar Lumber Association, 1992; Honorable Mention, *Chicago Tribune* competition for Cabrini Green, 1993; Illinois Energy Award, 1994; Award of Recognition, Chicago Building Congress, 1994. **Address:** Tigerman McCurry Architects, 444 N. Wells St., Chicago, Illinois 60610, U.S.A.

## Works

Chair Design, for Knoll International, 1979-80.
Prototype Decorative Screen, for Rizzoli, 1982.
Prototype Furniture, for Formica Corporation, 1982.
Decorative Objects, for Swid/Powell Designs, 1983.
Herman Miller product designs, 1984.
Exhibition for Architecture Museum, Frankfort, W. Germany, 1984.
Internationalism Exhibition Installation, 1985.
Fabric Design, Hamano Institute, Osaka, Japan, 1985.
Thyboney Exhibit, Merchandise Mart, Chicago, 1986.
Expressways Children's Museum Exhibit, Chicago, 1986.
Exhibition installation, curating, and catalog, for Gulbenkian Foundation, Lisbon, Portugal, 1987.
Calendar Design, 1988.

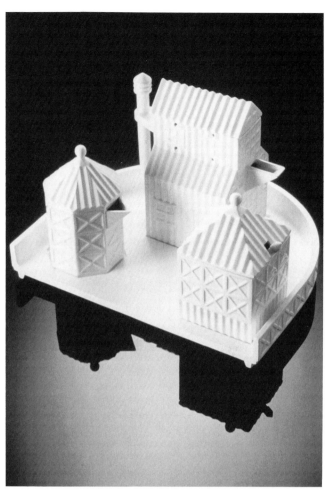

**Stanley Tigerman: tea service for Swid Powell, 1984**

Lighting, for Baldinger Company Project, New York, 1988.
Product Design, for American Standard, 1989.
Product Design, for Canon/Fieldcrest, 1989.
Corporate Headquarters Exhibition Project, for American Standard, New York, New York, 1989.
Art Institute of Chicago Installation for 1992 Exhibition, 1990.
Design of Weathervane, 1991.
Bookend Designs, for Rizzoli, 1991.
Design of Marble Objects, for "Petrafina," 1991.
Arts Club Exhibition for 1992, 1991.
Sets of three act play, for Victory Garden Theater, 1991.
Idiosyncratic lighting for the play *The Creation,* Rockefeller Chapel, 1991.
1993 100th AIC Anniversary Exhibition Installation, 1992.
Power House Graphics, 1992.
*Architextually Speaking* exhibition installation, University of Illinois at Chicago, 1992.
*A Weekend Retreat for Romeo & Juliet* dollhouse, 1992.
Doorknocker, for Markuse Corporation, 1992.
New Line, for Swid Powell, 1992.
New plumbing line, for American Standard, 1992.
Wristwatch designs, for Playboy, 1993.
Lighting design, for Baldinger, New York, 1993.
Exhibition installation, curating, and catalogue, Madrid, Spain, 1993.

Window Display, Richard Gray Gallery, Chicago, 1993.
Watch, for Jack Markuse, U.S.A., 1994.
Sample Box, for *Interior Design* magazine project, New York, 1994.

(for a complete listing of Tigerman's architectural designs, see *Contemporary Architects*)

## Publications

**By TIGERMAN: books**—*Versus: An American Architect's Alternatives,* New York, 1982; (with S. G. Lewin) *The California Condition: A Pregnant Architecture,* exhibition catalogue, La Jolla, California, 1982; *The Architecture of Exile,* New York, 1988; *Stanley Tigerman: Buildings and Projects, 1966-1989* edited by Sarah Mollman Underhill, New York, 1989; (illustrations, with Margaret McCurry) *Dorothy in Dreamland,* New York, 1991; **articles**—"Introduction" in *The Villa of Dionysius,* 1980; "Introduction" in *Chicago Houses* by Janet Bailey, New York, 1981; "Villa with a View" in *Architectural Digest* (Los Angeles), November 1985; "Introduction" in *The Architecture of Rome* by Giovanni Cipriani, New York, 1986; "Introduction" in *The Chicago Tapes,* New York, 1987; "Representation Can Teach Us No More than the Original it Emulates" in *Interiors* (New York), December 1987; "Introduction" in *Bruce Graham,* 1989; "Introduction" in *Gustav Peichl,* 1989; "Exhibition: Chicago Categorized" in *Progressive Architecture* (New York), September 1990; "Has Theory Displaced History as a Generator of Ideas for Use in the Architectural Studio...?" in *Journal of Architectural Education,* September 1992; "Beyond Trinkets and Teapots" in *Architecture* (New York), September 1994; "Introduction" in *Hugh Newell Jacobsen, Architect,* Rockport, Massachusetts, 1994.

**On TIGERMAN: books**—*Chicago on Foot* by Ira Bach, Chicago, 1969; *New Directions in American Architecture* by Robert A. M. Stern, New York, 1969; *Urban Structures for the Future* by Justic Dahinden, London, 1972; *Interior Spaces Designed by Architects* by Barclay Gordon, New York, 1974; *Housing* by John Mascai, New York, 1976; *Chicago Architects* by Stuart Cohen, Chicago, 1976; *Living Barns* by Ernest Burden, Boston, 1977; *Die Architektur in Jahrhundert* by Udo Kultermann, New York, 1977; *A Treasury of Contemporary Houses* by Walter Wagner, New York, 1978; *The Alternative House* by Rita Tatum, 1979; *Global Architecture #6,* Tokyo, 1979; *Chicago's Famous Buildings* edited by Ira Bach, 3d edition Chicago, 1980; *Architecture in the Seventies* by Udo Kultermann, New York, 1980; *Interior Spaces Designed by Architects* by Chas. K. Hoyt, New York, 1981; *Interiors Book of Shops and Restaurants,* New York, 1981; *Gehry, SITE, Tigerman* by Olivier Roissiere, 1981; *New Chicago Architecture* by Maurizio Casari and Vincenzo Pavan, Chicago, 1981; *Architectural Drawing: The Art and the Process* by Gerald Allen and Richard Oliver, New York, 1981; *Free Style Classicism* edited by Charles Jencks, London, 1982; *Chicago Architects Design* by John Zukowsky, New York, 1982; *Designers Workplaces* by Beverly Russell, New York, 1983; *Chicago Furniture 1833-1983: Art, Craft, and Industry* by Sharon Darling, New York, 1984; *Der Revision Der Moderne, Post Moderne Architektur* by Heinrich Klotz, Frankfurt, 1984; *American Architecture Now* by Barbarlee Diamondstein, New York, 1985; (bibliography) *Stanley Tigerman* by Lamia Doumato, Monticello, Illinois, 1986; *The Language of Post Modern Architecture* by Charles Jencks, 5th edition, 1987; *Design Haute* by Victor Fischer, 1988; *Architecture*

*ture and Design, 1970-1990: New Ideas in America* by Beverly Russell, New York, 1989; *Post Modern Design* by Michael Collins and Andreas Papadakis, New York, 1989; *Swid Powell: Objects by Architects,* New York, 1990; *American Architects and the Mechanics of Fame* by Roxanne Kuter Williamson, Austin, Texas, 1991; *Chicago Access* by Richard Saul Wurman, Newport, Connecticut, 1991; *Formica Design* by Susan Grant Levin, New York, 1991; *Behind the Postmodern Facade* by Magali Larson, University of California Press, 1993; *Chicago Architecture and Design 1923-1993* by John Zukowsky, Chicago, 1993; *Architectural Study Drawings* by Daniel M. Berbert, New York, 1993; *Architects House Themselves* by Michael Webs, Princeton, New Jersey, 1994; *The Theory of Architecture* by Paul Alan Johnson, New York, 1994; *A & U Tigerman McCurry Monograph,* 1994.

\*    \*    \*

Stanley Tigerman established his architectural practice during the 1960s in a Chicago that remained under the architectural influence of Mies van der Rohe and corporate modernists, Skidmore, Owings and Merrill (SOM). After a degree from Yale University and stints in the offices of Paul Rudolph, George F. Keck, and SOM, Tigerman might have been expected to continue in the strict modernist tradition; quite the contrary in fact. As Tigerman states, in an interview with clients Swid Powell, "I've always rebelled against authoritarian forces." So it is no surprise that his work is often considered irreverent and Tigerman himself the "bad boy" of Chicago architecture. From early unbuilt projects such as the "Visionary Megastructure" (1965-66), a massive city enclosed within a pyramidal arch recalling the groundbreaking work of the British group "Archigram," to more recent built projects such as the Fukuoka City Mixed Use Apartments in Kishu, Japan, Tigerman challenges expected norms and treats each project as an individual entity; there is no Tigerman "signature building."

All of Tigerman's projects, usually collaborations with his wife and partner Margaret McCurry, are typically sensitive to context and to individual client needs; the 1975 Illinois Regional Library for the Blind and Physically Handicapped has an easily memorized plan to assist blind visitors; the Chicago Anti-Cruelty Society Adoption Center (1977-78) has two-story windows at the entrance that are shaped in the profile of a bassett hound, giving clues to the building's function.

The firm of Tigerman McCurry has an impressive portfolio of built works that covers a diverse range of project types. This portfolio includes private residences throughout the United States and in Berlin and Japan, churches, parking garages, restaurants such as the Hard Rock Cafe in Chicago, showrooms, and exhibits, as well as work for corporate clients such as BEST and Knoll. Imagery is prevalent in all of the firm's work and it is gestures such as the dog ears on the Anti Cruelty Society building or the midwestern barn apparent in the Power House Museum (Zion, Illinois, 1987-90), or in the architect's own weekend retreat in Michigan that make Tigerman's work so visually appealing and endearing. Naturally enough, these are qualities that have enabled Tigerman to work successfully on decorative arts projects in addition to architectural work. Most significantly these have included china for Swid Powell and chairs for Knoll International and Herman Miller. The Teaside tea-set produced for Swid Powell is an arrangement of teapot, water-pot, and milk jug on a tray literally recalling in miniature form the architect's designs for barns and silos at the Michigan retreat. A cookie jar is similarly inspired. A pair of rocking chairs designed (but never commercially produced) for Knoll relate to classical columns and were affectionately referred to (with typical Tigerman whimsy) as "Mama Bear" and "Papa Bear."

Beyond his professional practice, Tigerman has excelled as an educator and has taught at many schools of architecture including Harvard, Yale, and the University of Illinois at Chicago (UIC). He was Director of the School of Architecture at UIC for seven years, introducing a faculty of international repute and elevating the program to one of the most reputable in the United States. Currently, Tigerman is co-founder and director of ARCHEWORKS, a design laboratory and school based in Chicago. This project, conceived with longtime collaborator Eva Maddox, directs students and its curriculum to address design issues appropriate to current relevant social issues.

Tigerman remains a significant and provocative force in American architecture and design through his built and academic work as well as his writings. In part this has much to do with what the *Architectural Record* describes as "a lot of serious and important building in and around Chicago and around the world" and to his being "an explorer and an articulate exponent of alternatives." In Chicago, where America discovered the skyscraper, Stanley Tigerman continues to push the limits of architecture and design.

—Peter Exley

## TISSI, Rosmarie
Swiss typography and graphic designer

**Born:** Scaffhausen, 13 February 1937. **Education:** Studied design, at the Kunstgewerbeschule, Zurich, 1954-55. **Career:** Apprentice, 1955-59, and designer, 1959-68, in Siegfried Odermatt design studio, Zurich; partner, with Siegfried Odermatt, in Odermatt and Tissi design studio, Zurich, from 1968; has designed for City Druck AG, Burlet AG, Baumgartner, AG, Cliche Lutz, Univac, Telelift, Union Safe Company, Mettler and Company, Benz AG, Elektrowatt AG, and others. **Member:** Alliance Graphique Internationale, Paris; International Center for Typographic Arts, New York. **Exhibitions:** Visual Graphic Gallery, New York, 1966; ICTA Knauer Expo, Stuttgart, 1967; ICTA German Section, Wuppertal, 1968; Stadtische Berufsschule, Hof-Saale, 1972. **Honors:** Typomundus Award, New York, 1965, 1970; Type Directors Club Award, New York 1966; 4th Calendar Competition Award, West Germany, 1972. **Address:** Odermatt and Tissi, Schipfe 45, 8001 Zurich, Switzerland.

See ODERMATT, Siegfried

## TOIKKA, Oiva (Kalervo)
Finnish ceramics and glass designer

**Born:** Viipuri, 29 May 1931. **Education:** Studied ceramics, 1953-56, and art education, 1959-60, Institute of Applied Arts, Helsinki. **Career:** Designer, at Oy Wärtsilä AB Arabia ceramics firm, Helsinki, 1956-59, at Marimekko Textiles, Helsinki, 1959, and at Oy Wärtsilä

Nuutajärvi Glass firm, Finland, from 1963; also designed stage sets and costumes for the Finnish National Theatre and National Opera, Helsinki. Instructor, Sodankyla Secondary School, 1960-63, and Institute of Applied Arts, Helsinki, 1961-63. **Exhibitions:** Helsinki, 1956, 1963, 1965, 1972, 1981, 1984, 1987; Stockholm, 1967, 1974, 1985; Malmö, 1967; London, 1968; Amsterdam, 1976, 1986; Finnish Glass Museum, Riihimaki, 1988; Museum of Science and Industry, Los Angeles, 1989. **Collections:** Museum of Applied Arts, Helsinki; City Art Collection, Helsinki; National Museum, Helsinki; Sara Hilden Art Museum, Tampere; Finnish Glass Museum, Riihimaki; Nationalmuseum, Stockholm; Nordenfjeldske Kunstindustrimuseum, Trondheim; Leerdam Museum, Amsterdam; Kunstgewerbemuseum, Hamburg; Museum für Kunstgewerbe, Frankfurt; Victoria and Albert Museum, London; Museum of Modern Art, New York; Corning Glass Museum of Modern Art, Japan. **Honors:** Internationales Kunsthandwerk Diploma, Stuttgart, 1960; Finnish State Scholarship, 1969, 1975; Lunning Prize, 1970; Alfred Kordelin Foundation Scholarship, 1980; Pro Finlandia Medal, 1980; Prize of Honour, World Glass Now, Hokkaido, Japan, 1985. **Address:** c/o Nuutajärvi Glass, 31160 Nuutajärvi, Finland.

### Works

*Kurkkupurkki* pickle jar in grey-brown blown glass, for Nuutajärvi, 1963.
*Kastehelmi* range of decorated tablewares in pressed glass, for Nuutajärvi, 1964.
*Pioni* range of tablewares in pressed glass, for Nuutajärvi, 1967.
*Lollipop* Isle sculpture in coloured glass, for Nuutajärvi, 1969.
*Asimetsa* balloon-sculptures in coloured glass, for Nuutajärvi, 1972.
*Vuosikuutiot* series of nine coloured glass sculptures in clear glass cubes, for Nuutajärvi, 1977.
*Snow Castle* sculpture in opaque white glass, for Nuutajärvi, 1980.

### Publications

**On TOIKKA: books**—*Scandinavian Design: Objects of a Life Style* by Eileene Harrison Beer, New York, 1975; *Finnish Design 1875-1975* by Timo Sarpaneva, Enk Bruun, and Erik Kruskopf, Helsinki, 1975; *Nordisk Kunsthandverk og Design* by Fredrik Wildhagen and others, Oslo, 1981; *Finnland Gestaltet,* exhibition catalogue by Tapio Periainen, Simo Heikkila, and others, Espoo, 1981; *Glas: Unikate Finnische Künstler,* exhibition catalogue by Helmut Ricke, Dusseldorf, 1982; *Scandinavian Modern Design 1880-1980* edited by David Revere McFadden, New York, 1982; *Finnish Vision,* with texts by P. Suhonen, J. Lintinen, and others, Helsinki, 1983; *The Lunning Prize,* exhibition catalogue edited by Helena Dahlback Lutteman and Marianne Uggla, Stockholm, 1986; *Form Finland* edited by Marianne Aav and Kaj Kalin, Helsinki, 1986; *Finnish Industrial Design* edited by Tua Pontasuo, Helsinki, 1987.

\*    \*    \*

Oiva Toikka rose to prominence as a glass designer in the 1960s when his fanciful, eccentrically-shaped, and strikingly colored works appeared as an emphatic break from the sublimely elegant forms and cool tones of the work of the Finnish masters of glass design who had preceded him in the 1950s. Indeed, much has been made of the presence of an "inner relationship with nature" in Finnish design and such a sensibility is discernible in the finest and most well known examples of Finnish glass, especially the work of Timo Saarpeneva and that of Tapio Wirkaala. But a significant, yet less recognized genre of Scandinavian design characterized by a playful sensibility that blends the consciously naive and the ornate has developed parallel to this tendency towards a natural purity. The whimsically themed ceramics of Birger Kapainen in Finland and Bjorn Winblad in Denmark are typical of this style. Oiva Toikka's designs, for the Nuutajarvi glassworks since 1963, partake of what he describes as the "richness" of this lighthearted decorative sensibility but without its thematic or narrative aspects.

Toikka explores techniques rather than themes in his glassmaking. Though much of his work appears as or incorporates mimetic images, such as his ongoing series of birds which has been in production since 1971, he has never set out to copy models from nature. Toikka's mass-produced and hugely successful "Flora" (1970) and "Peony" (1976) tableware incorporate stylized floral imagery that derives from glass making method rather than any attempt at botanical similitude. In all of his works any reference to nature is secondary to the desire to exploit new and different techniques of glass making. This is particularly true of his ongoing series called "Vuosikuutiot" (Year cubes), paper-weight cubes which seem to hold frozen the most extraordinary flowers or delicately grotesque sea creatures which are not intentionally either of these, but instead are simply exquisite evidence of technique.

Toikka's explorations of technique have frequently led to designs that defy conventional notions of beauty. This was recognized early in his career when Ulf Hard af Segerstad commented in a review of Toikka's 1967 exhibition in Stockholm that though it may not have been the most beautiful it was certainly the most exciting exhibition in Sweden in years. Toikka is of the generation that grew up with the modernist ideology of "good design" and who seem to have concluded that perhaps it was a bit overrated. Toikka himself has said that "very beautiful things are boring" and that "everybody makes their own rules for what is beautiful."

Indeed Toikka has been able to make his own rules of beauty even for mass produced objects. His mold-blown vases of the mid 1960s, although smooth and symmetrical, are distinguished by a voluptuous bulbuousness achieved by basing the molds on lathe-turned wood forms; and his pressed glass "Kastehelmi," or "Dewdrop," tableware of the same period recalls 19th century pressed glass and yet appears completely modern at the same time.

Among Toikka's most well known sculptural works in glass is the 1969 "Lollipop Isle," in the collection of the Victoria and Albert Museum in London, which, as its name suggests, appears as a cluster of candy colored lollipop-like forms floating on a glass horizon. Related works from the same time, including his individual "Lollipop" ornamental sculptures and "Pom Pom" vases, which have variously colored glass sprouts "growing" from their rims, are similarly fanciful and realized in what Toikka describes as "sweet" colors. Toikka's "sweet" is sweet as a persimmon is sweet: rich, succulent, even pungent. These elements of whimsical form combined with adventurous color have resulted in works of an unconventional beauty that are both extravagant and naive. These characteristics are consistent throughout his design career and are evident in Toikka's work up to the present time.

—Alan Rosenberg

# TOMASZEWSKI, Henryk

Polish illustrator, stage, and graphic designer

**Born:** Warsaw, 10 June 1914. **Education:** Studied graphics under Mieczyslaw Kotarbinski, at the Academy of Fine Arts, Warsaw, 1934-39. **Career:** Freelance designer, working in Warsaw, from 1945; has designed for PIW, KAW, and Czytelnik publishers, and for the Teatr Ateneum, Teatr Powszechny, Teatr Nowy, and Teatr Narodowy. Head of poster design department, from 1951, and professor of graphic design, from 1955, at the Academy of Fine Arts, Warsaw. **Exhibitions:** *International Poster Exhibition,* Vienna, 1948; Bienal of Saõ Paulo, 1963, 1979; Kongresshaus, Biel-Beinne, 1969; *Vier Polnische Plakatkunstler,* Deutsches Plakatmuseum, Essen, 1971; Wilanow Poster Museum, Warsaw, 1972, 1991; *International Design Biennale,* Wroclaw, 1978; *Das Polnische Plakat von 1892 bis Heute,* Hochschule der Künste, West Berlin, 1980; *Graphic Arts Biennale,* Brno, 1982; Gallery A. and B. Wahl, Warsaw, 1984; *International Poster Biennal,* Warsaw, 1988, 1994; *Affiches de Pologne 1945-1988: Hommage à Henryk Tomaszewski,* Centre de la Gravure et de l'Image Imprimée, La Louviere, Belgium, 1989; *Poolse Affiches 1945-1990,* Hessenhuis, Antwerp, Belgium, 1990; International Poster Triennal, Toyama, Japan, 1991, 1994; Stedelijk Museum, Amsterdam, 1991; Ginza Graphic Gallery, Tokyo, 1992; ifa Galerie Friedrichstrasse, Berlin, 1993; Muzeum Narodowe, Poznan, Poland, 1993; Centre Culturel de Blanc Mesnil, France, 1995; School of Visual Arts Gallery, New York, 1996. **Collections:** National Museum, Warsaw; Deutsches Plakatmuseum, Essen; Stedelijk Museum, Amsterdam; Museum of Applied Arts, Stockholm; Museum of Modern Art, Kamakura; Museu de Arte Moderno, Saõ Paulo; Museum of Modern Art, New York; Museum of Modern Art, Toyama, Japan. **Honors:** Five First Prizes, *International Poster Exhibition,* Vienna, 1948; Polish National Art Prize, 1953; Poster and Illustration Prize, Warsaw, 1955; First Prize, *Polish Posters Exhibition,* Vienna, 1956; Poster of the Month Award, Vienna, 1957; *Przeglad Kulturalny* Satirical Drawing Prize, Warsaw, 1960; Graphics Prize, Bienal of Saõ Paulo 1963; Advertising Poster of the Year Award, Warsaw, 1963, 1965, 1967; Gold Medal, Leipzig Book Fair, 1965; Gold Medal, Warsaw Poster Biennale, 1967, 1970, 1988; honorary Royal Designer for Industry, Royal Society of Arts, London, 1976; Lahti Poster Biennale Prize, 1979; Colorado Poster Exhibition Prize, Fort Collins, 1981; Alfred Jurzykowski Foundation Award, New York, 1984; ICOGRADA Special Prize, International Council of Societies of Graphic Design, 1986; Gold and Silver Medal, 1988, and Bronze Medal, 1994, International Poster Biennal, Warsaw; Bronze Medal, 1991, and Silver Medal, 1994, International Poster Triennal, Toyama. **Address:** Jazgarzewska Street 13, 00-730 Warsaw, Poland.

**Publications**

**By TOMASZEWSKI: books**—*Book of Complaints,* Warsaw, 1961.

**On TOMASZEWSKI: books**—*The Graphic Arts in Poland 1945-1955* by Jan Bialostocki, Warsaw, 1956; *Henryk Tomaszewski* by Barbara Kwiatkowska, Warsaw, 1959; *Buchgestaltung* by Albert Kapr, Dresden, 1963; *Das Plakat* by Anton Sailer, Munich, 1965; *The Poster: An Illustrated History from 1860* by Harold F. Hutchinson, London and Toronto, 1968; *Polski Plakat Filmowy 1947-1967,* exhibition catalogue by Zdzislaw Schubert, Poznan,

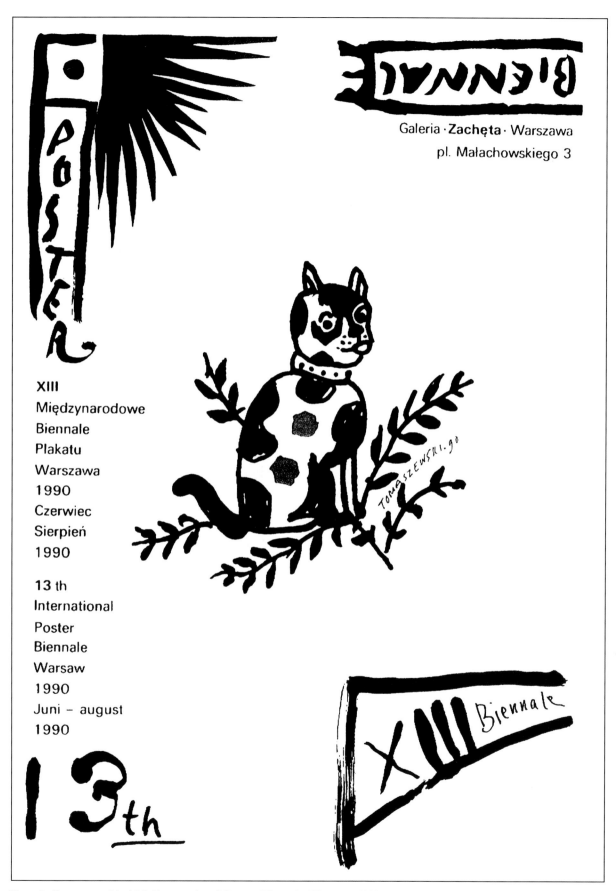

Henryk Tomaszewski: 13th International Poster Biennale Warsaw, 1990

1969; *Polska Sztuka Plakatu* by Szymon Bojko, Warsaw, 1971; *Vier Polnische Plakatkunstler,* exhibition catalogue by H. Schardt, Essen, 1971; *Monografie des Plakats: Entwicklung, Stil, Design* by Herbert Schindler, Munich, 1972; *The Polish Poster 1970-1978,* with introduction by Zdzislaw Schubert, Warsaw, 1979; *The Language of Graphics* by Edward Booth-Clibborn and Daniele Baroni, London, 1980; *Das Polnische Plakat von 1892 bis Heute,* exhibition catalogue by Jan Bialostocki and others, West Berlin, 1980; *Top Graphic Design* by F. H. K. Henrion, Zurich, 1983; *A History of Graphic Design* by Philip B. Meggs, New York and London, 1983; *Les Années 60* by Anne Bony, Paris, 1983; *Henryk Tomaszewski* by Shoji Katagishi, Tokyo, 1992; *100th Anniversary of Polish Poster Art,* exhibition catalogue by David Crowley, Germany and Poland, 1993; *Henryk Tomaszewski, Graphic Artist* by Jan Lenica, Poland, 1994; *The 100 Best Posters from Europe and the United States, 1945-1990* edited by Paul Rand, Tokyo, 1995; **articles**—in *HQ* (Germany), no. 2, 1989; by Shiego Fukuda in *Creation* (Tokyo), no. 6, 1990; by Andrzej Klimowski in *Eye* (London), no. 4, 1991; by Alain le Quernec in *IDEA* (Tokyo), no. 241, 1993; by Maciej Gutowski in *Pokaz* (Poland), 1994; by James Victore in *Print* (New York), October 1995.

* * *

The famed Polish poster school is now almost forty years old. Many scholars and observers have counted its ups and down—its early periods, heroic 1960s, 1970s and crisis, recently more international outlook, and others. In this history, there are many names— from the founders to the recent third or fourth generation. But Henryk Tomaszewski belongs to all of it. One of the founders just after the war, he is still one of the youngest. A paradox? Not at all. In the incredible competition of the small, crowded market of several dozen really top-class designers, he is the towering figure.

More than simply a designer, Tomaszewski is a living legend. Always the front-runner, crisp critic, the joker, he is the clown of a gray, rigid, unhappy country, a diplomat and educator, a great one. His intellectual power mixes with an outstanding sense of humour. He unbeatably selects the important from "decor" or empty ornamentalism. If we are able to remove him from his Warsaw studio and his times, he could easily have been a great conceptual artist of the Soho galleries in the late 1960s. Tomaszewski uses a word, a phrase, a meaning as the basis of creation. His best works are manifestoes of the idea, of the concept—pure intellectual marvels. Removed from the poster frame, his simple, colored-paper cut-outs would rank with the best dadaistic works. Or, in drawings, his lines are nervous, sharp, close to abstract painting. It is almost an impossible task to complete this giant poster-designer's portrait.

When all the bits and pieces are compiled and organized on the white board of his poster space, the effect is stirring. A simple peace dove, a tragic circus clown pedaling a bicycle that is breaking apart, Henry Moore's name formed like his own sculptures, a cheap official slogan, "To work better," transformed into a powerful message, endless magnificent theatrical posters that create their own theater of allusions and concepts—this is Tomaszewski in his prime. And nobody can surpass him in the longevity of his prime. Every discussion among young students who make their first steps in the poster field must focus on "Professor Henryk's" work.

Again and again, the lightning strikes from a blue sky. New work by Tomaszewski, fresh, original, refined, cutting harder. He's a real poet of the poster.

His unique personality and lasting enthusiasm toward his life-long love, the poster, make him a formidable teacher. Even the laziest student is forced to think in Tomaszewski's Warsaw Academy studio. In this demanding training program, wit must work quickly; the simplest and most direct realization of the concept counts most. Everybody dreams of being accepted to his classes. Half of them are foreign students. Even the Japanese are hovering around.

This rare sample of a big artist, this flamboyant, individual and caring teacher, Tomaszewski shapes the past, present, and future well-being of his country's favorite art form—the poster.

—Jan Sawka

## TOMS, Carl
British stage, film, exhibition, interior, and graphic designer

**Born:** Kirkby-in-Ashfield, Nottinghamshire, 29 May 1927. **Education:** Studied at High Oakham School, Mansfield, Nottinghamshire, until 1945; studied at Mansfield College of Art, Nottinghamshire, 1946-49; Royal College of Art, London, 1949-53; Old Vic Theatre School, London, 1954-57. **Career:** Freelance stage designer, working for the Royal Shakespeare Company, Old Vic Theatre, Young Vic, Welsh National Opera, New York State Opera, Edinburgh Festival, Glyndebourne Opera, Chichester Festival, Aldeburgh Festival, and others, from 1957; head of design and associate director, for the Young Vic at the National Theatre, London, from 1970; redesigned and decorated the Theatre Royal, Windsor, 1965, Theatre Royal, Bath, 1982, Garrick Theatre, London, 1986, Cambridge Theatre, London, 1987, and the refurbishment of the Richmond Theatre. Also design consultant, for the investiture of the Prince of Wales, Caernarvon Castle, 1969; film designer, from 1954, and television designer, from 1959. **Exhibitions:** *British Theatre Design '83-87,* Riverside Studios, London, 1988. **Collections:** Theatre Museum, London. **Honors:** Officer, Order of the British Empire, 1969; Antoinette Perry Award, New York, 1974-75; Drama Desk Award, New York, 1975; Society of West End Theatres Design Award, London 1980; Critics Award, Hollywood Dramalogue, 1984; Fellow, Royal Society of Arts, 1987. **Addresses:** (home) The White House, Beaumont, near Wormley, Broxboume, Hertfordshire EN10 7QJ, England; (agent) Rosalind Chatto, Chatto & Linnit Ltd., Prince of Wales Theatre, Coventry Street, London W1V 7FE, England.

### Works

Stage productions include—*Apollo de Bellac,* Royal Court Theatre, 1957; *Beth,* London, 1958; *Something to Hide,* London, 1958; *The Complaisant Lover,* London, 1959, *The Seashell,* Edinburgh Festival, 1959; *No Bed for Bacon,* Bristol, 1959; *The Merry Wives of Windsor,* London, 1959, *La Cenerentola,* Sadler's Wells Theatre, London, 1959; *New Cranks,* Lyric Theatre, London, 1960; *A Midsummer Night's Dream,* Aldeburgh Festival 1960; *The Barber of Seville,* Sadler's Wells Theatre, London, 1960; *Camille,* Old Vic Theatre, London (and world tour), 1961; *Iphigenie en Tauride,* Royal Opera House/Covent Garden, Lon-

**Carl Toms: Stage set for Tom Stoppard's *Rough Crossing*, National Theatre, London, 1984**

don, 1961; *Write Me a Murder,* London, 1962; *A Time to Laugh,* London, 1962; *Who'll Save the Plowboy?,* London, 1963; *The Importance of Being Earnest,* Nottingham, 1963; *Ballet Imperial,* Royal Opera House/Covent Garden, London, 1963; *Our Man in Havana,* Sadler's Wells Theatre, London, 1963; *The Merchant of Venice,* British Council touring production, 1964; *A Midsummer Night's Dream,* British Council touring production, 1964; *A Singular Man,* London, 1965; *Public Mischief,* London, 1965; *The Trojan Women,* Pop Theatre, London, 1966; *The Winter's Tale,* Pop Theatre, London, 1966; *Die Frau ohne Schatten,* Royal Opera House/Covent Garden, London, 1967; *The Burglar,* London, 1967; *Fallen Angels,* London, 1967; *The Tricks of Scapin,* Pop Theatre, London, 1967; *A Midsummer Night's Dream,* Pop Theatre, London, 1967; *The Soldier's Tale,* Pop Theatre, London, 1967; *Edward II,* National Theatre, London, 1968; *Love's Labour's Lost,* National Theatre, London 1968; *The Magistrate,* London (and Chichester Festival Theatre), 1969; *Antony and Cleopatra,* Chichester Festival Theatre, 1969; *Girlfriend,* London, 1970; *Sleuth,* London (also New York and Paris), 1970; *Vivat! Vivat Regina!,* London, 1970 (also Chichester Festival Theatre, 1970, and New York, 1972); *The Alchemist,* Chichester Festival Theatre, 1970; *Cyrano de Bergerac,* National Theatre, London, 1970; *The Rivals,* Chichester Festival Theatre, 1971; *Caesar and Cleopatra,* Chichester Festival Theatre, 1971; *Re-*

*union in Vienna,* Chichester Festival Theatre, 1971 (and London, 1972); *The Beheading,* London, 1972; *Dear Love,* London, 1973; *Section Nine,* London, 1973; *Fanfare for Europe,* Royal Opera House/Covent Garden, London, 1973; *Peter Grimes,* San Francisco Opera, 1973; *Sherlock Holmes,* London (and New York), 1974; *Travesties,* London, 1974 (also New York, 1975, and Vienna, 1976); *Waltz of the Toreadors,* London, 1975; *Die Meistersinger von Nürnberg,* New York City Opera, 1975; *Murderer,* London, 1976; *Thais,* San Francisco Opera, 1976; *Norma,* San Diego Opera, 1976; *La Traviata,* San Diego Opera, 1976; *Long Day's Journey into Night,* Los Angeles, 1977; *Man and Superman,* Malvern Festival (and London), 1977; *The Devil's Disciple,* Los Angeles, 1977 (and New York, 1978); *Travesties,* National Theatre, Vienna, 1977; *The Marriage of Figaro,* New York City Opera, 1977; *The Voice of Ariadne,* New York City Opera, 1977; *The Merry Widow,* San Diego Opera, 1977; *Look After Lulu,* Chichester Festival Theatre (and Haymarket Theatre, London), 1978; *Night and Day,* Phoenix Theatre, London, 1978 (and New York, 1979); *She Stoops to Conquer,* National Theatre, Vienna, 1978; *Betrayal,* National Theatre, Vienna, 1978; *Thais,* Metropolitan Opera, New York, 1978; *Hamlet,* San Diego Opera, 1978; *Stage Struck,* Vaudeville Theatre, London, 1979; *For Services Rendered,* National Theatre London, 1979; *The Guardsman,* National Theatre, Vienna, 1979; *Playbill,* National Theatre,

London, 1980; *The Provok'd Wife,* National Theatre, London, 1980; *Night and Day,* National Theatre, Vienna, 1980; *On the Razzle,* National Theatre, London, 1981; *The Second Mrs. Tanqueray,* National Theatre, London, 1981; *Der Freischutz,* New York City Opera, 1981; *Windy City,* Victoria Palace, London, 1982; *Swan Lake,* Festival Ballet, London, 1982; *Macbeth,* Vienna State Opera, 1982; *Romeo and Juliet,* San Diego Opera, 1982; *The Rehearsal,* Yvonne Arnaud Theatre, Guildford, 1982; *The Real Thing,* Strand Theatre, London, 1982; *A Patriot for Me,* Chichester Festival, 1983; *The Winslow Boy,* Lyric Theatre/ Hammersmith, London, 1983; *Hay Fever,* Queens Theatre, London, 1983 *The Italian Girl in Algiers,* Geneva, 1983; *The Hot House,* Burgtheater, Vienna, 1983; *The Real Thing,* Burgtheater, Vienna, 1983; *Amadeus,* Burgtheater, Vienna, 1984; *The Aspern Papers,* Theatre Royal/Haymarket, London, 1984; *Rough Crossing,* National Theatre, London, 1984; *Faust,* State Opera, Vienna, 1985; *The Dragon's Tail,* Apollo Theatre, London, 1985; *Lucia di Lammermoor,* Cologne Opera, 1985; *Jumpers,* Aldwych Theatre, London, 1985; *Where She Danced,* Yvonne Arnaud Theatre, Guildford, 1985; *The Happiest Days of Your Life,* Royal Shakespeare Company/Barbican, London, 1985; *Wildfire,* Phoenix Theatre, London, 1986; *The Magistrate,* National Theatre, London, 1986; *Blithe Spirit,* Vaudeville Theatre, London, 1986; *Brighton Beach Memoirs,* National Theatre, London, 1986; *Noel and Gertie,* Donmar Warehouse, London, 1986; *Oberon,* Edinburgh Festival, 1986; *Dalliance,* National Theatre, London, 1986; *Fanfare for Elizabeth,* Royal Opera House/Covent Garden, London, 1986, *Six Characters in Search of an Author,* National Theatre, London, 1987; *The Importance of Being Earnest,* Royal Theatre, Copenhagen 1987; *Carry On, Jeeves,* Wyndhams Theatre, London, 1987; *The Importance of Being Earnest,* Royalty Theatre, London, 1987; *Ting Tang Mine,* National Theatre, London, 1987; *The Living Room,* Royalty Theatre, London, 1987; *Hapgood,* Aldwych Theatre, London, 1988; *Rigoletto,* New York State Opera, 1988; *Playbill,* Royalty Theatre, London, 1988; *Richard II,* Phoenix Theatre, London, 1988; *Artist Descending a Staircase,* Duke of York's Theatre, London, 1988; *Richard III,* Phoenix Theatre, London, 1989; *Hapgood,* Doolittle Theatre, Los Angeles, 1989; *Noel and Gertie,* Comedy Theatre, London, 1989; *The Man Who Came to Dinner,* Royal Shakespeare Company/Barbican, London, 1989; *Thark,* Lyric Theatre, Hammersmith, 1989; *Look Look,* Aldwych Theatre, London, 1990; *Private Lives,* Aldwych Theatre, 1990; *The Silver King,* Chichester Festival Theatre, 1990; *Painting Churches,* Nuffield Theatre, Southhampton, (and The Playhouse, London), 1991; *Straight and Narrow,* Wyndhams Theatre, London, 1991; *Making It Better,* Josefstadt Theatre, Vienna, 1991; *Preserving Mr. Panmure,* Chichester Theatre, 1991; *It's Ralph,* Comedy Theatre, London, 1991; *An Ideal Husband,* Globe Theatre, London, 1992; *Arcadia,* Zurich, 1993; *She Stoops to Conquer,* Queens Theatre, London, 1993; *Swan Lake,* English National Ballet, Southampton (and The Festival Hall, London), 1993; *Separate Tables,* Albery Theatre, London, 1993; *Three Tall Women,* Wyndhams Theatre, London, 1994; *Indian Ink,* Aldwych Theatre, London, 1995.

Films include—*Rocket to the Moon,* 1954; *She,* 1965; *The Quiller Memorandum,* 1966; *One Million Years B.C.,* 1967; *Prehistoric Women,* 1967; *Those Fantastic Flying Fools,* 1967; *The Winter's Tale,* 1968, *The Lost Continent,* 1968; *The Vengeance of She,* 1968, *Moon Zero Two,* 1970.

**Publications**

**By TOMS: books**—*The Winter's Tale* (stage designs), London, 1975; *The Tricks of Scapin* (stage designs), London, 1975.

**On TOMS: books**—*Who's Who in Opera* edited by Maria F. Rich, New York, 1976; *Notable Names in the American Theatre,* Clifton, New Jersey, 1976; *Who's Who in the Theatre* edited by Ian Herbert, London, 1977; *International Who's Who in Music and Musicians' Directory* edited by Adrian Gaster, Cambridge, 1977, 1980; *International Film & TV Year Book 1979-80* edited by Peter Noble, London, 1979; *British Theatre Design 1983-87,* with texts by Timothy O'Brien and David Fingleton, London, 1988, *British Theatre Design: The Modern Age* edited by John Goodwin, London, 1989.

\*

I have nothing new to contribute except for my personal objection to the increasing use of the computer in design. It removes, eradicates, personality in the work of the designer.

And I am also rather bored with sets knocked sideways in order to demand attention at the cost of the text.

—Carl Toms (1995)

\*　　\*　　\*

Going to the Old Vic School from the Royal College of Art, Carl Toms singlemindedly dedicated himself to the theatre, and in this has lain his strength. Though susceptible to much that has gone on in contemporary art, he has brought to his theatre designs a sense of style rather than a style to impose. His work has thus been genuinely of the theatre without any slide into Camp theatricality except where, as in *New Cranks,* for example, it was required in an ironic sense which he marvelously satisfied, and reacting creatively to John Cranko's requirements, Toms made his Scarlatti ballet a little gem.

In much the same way, his work for television has been relentlessly tailored to the demands of the medium, so he avoided many of the difficulties that arise when designs are primarily conceived behind the proscenium arch. Indeed, his television *Twelfth Night* is utterly unlike his other Shakespeare productions for the theatre, except, of course, for the evidence of his careful attention to requirements and his respect for the play and the director. However, this is not to say he merely carried out instructions; he is far too imaginative for that.

His first major design was for *Apollo de Bellac* at the Royal Court Theatre in 1957. It immediately announced that an important talent had appeared, but it also put Toms in touch with some of the liveliest minds in stage production. He was able to profit from these contacts, but he was also equal to their demands. This first work had none of the shortcomings that so often mar a young designer's debut though, to be sure, it left room for development, which indeed has been the most outstanding characteristic of his subsequent career.

It is difficult to pick out any one design as the masterpiece. Rather, one recalls so many magical moments in the theatre, particularly at the outset, when his achievement was not always to be taken for granted. Then, the success seemed the more enjoyable, and in this respect, memorable occasions include that Royal Court production of 1957, the ballet *La Reja,* and *The Merry Wives of Windsor* in 1959, and, of course, *New Cranks* the following year.

Finally, in the renewal of a Victorian manor for the Nevills, Toms has taken a new departure, one that has called upon quite different resources. The interiors are theatrical in a way none of the stage sets are, perhaps because Toms is working to an unknown drama, indeed to a drama still to be written or, rather, improvised.

—Toni del Renzio

# TRAUNER, Alexandre
French film and stage designer

**Born:** Sandor Trauner, in Budapest, Hungary, 3 September 1906; emigrated to France, 1929, naturalized, 1944. **Education:** Studied painting, at the School of Fine Arts, Budapest, 1925-29. **Career:** Assistant to film designer Lazare Meerson, Paris, 1929-36; freelance art director, working on films of Rene Clair, Julien Duvivier, Marcel Carné, Jacques Feyder, Marc Allegret, Billy Wilder, Fred Zinnemann, Howard Hawks, Anatole Litvak, Stanley Donen, Joseph Losey, and others, in France and the United States, from 1937; also stage designer, Paris, from 1953. Founder-member, Cinemateque Française, Paris, 1936. **Member:** Académie du Cinema, Paris. **Exhibitions:** Musée National d'Art Moderne, Budapest, 1981; Mucsarnok Gallery, Budapest, 1982; National Gallery, Budapest, 1982; *Hommage à Trauner,* Telluride Film Festival, Colorado, U.S.A., 1985; École des Beaux Arts, Paris, 1986; and exhibitions throughout France, 1987-95. **Collections:** Musée du Cinema, Paris; National Gallery, Budapest. **Honors:** Academy Award for *The Apartment,* 1960; César Awards for *Mr. Klein,* 1978, for *Don Giovanni,* 1979, and for *Subway,* 1982, Paris; Grand Prix National du Cinema, Paris, 1983. **Died:** Omonville la Petite, France, 5 December 1993.

## Works

Film productions include—*Sous les Toits de Paris* (Clair), 1930; *David Golder* (Duvivier), 1930; *Jean de la Lune* (Choux), 1931; *A Nous la Liberte* (Clair), 1931; *Le Million* (Clair), 1931; *L'Affaire est dans le Sac* (P. Prevert), 1932; *Quatorze Juillet* (Clair), 1932; *Danton* (Roubaud), 1932; *Ciboulette* (Autant-Lara), 1933; *Amok* (Ozep), 1933; *L'Hotel du Libre-Exchange* (M. Allegret), 1934; *Sans Famille* (M. Allegret), 1934; *La Kermesse Héroique* (Feyder), 1935; *Gribouille* (M. Allegret), 1937; *La Dame de Malacca* (M. Allegret), 1937; *Drôle de Drame* (Carné), 1937; *Mollenard* (Siodmak), 1937; *Quai des Brumes* (Carné), 1937; *Entrée des Artistes* (M. Allegret), 1938; *Hôtel du Nord* (Carné), 1938; *Le Jour se Léve* (Carné), 1938; *Soyez les Bienvenus* (de Baroncelli), 1940; *Remorques* (Gremillon), 1941; *Le Soleil a Toujours Raison* (Billon), 1941; *Les Visiteurs du Soir* (Carné), 1941; *Lumiére d'Ete* (Gremillon), 1943; *Les Enfants du Paradis* (Carné), 1943; *Les Malheurs de Sophie* (Audry), 1945; *Les Portes de la Nuit* (Carné), 1946; *Reves d'Amour* (Stengel), 1946; *Voyage Surprise* (P. Prevert), 1946; *La Fleur de l'Age* (Carné), 1947; *La Marie du Port* (Carné), 1949; *Maneges; Y.* (Allegret), 1950; *Les Miracles n'ont Lieu qu'une Fois* (Y. Allegret), 1950; *Juliette, ou la Clé des Songes* (Carné), 1951; *The Green Glove* (Mate), 1951; *Othello* (Welles), 1952; *Les Sept Peches Capitaux* (Y. Allegret), 1952; *La Jeune Folle* (Y. Allegret), 1952; *Un Acte d'Amour* (Litvak), 1953; *Land of the Pharaohs* (Hawks), 1954; *Du Rififi chez les Hommes* (Dassin), 1955; *L'Amant de Lady Chatterley* (M. Allegret), 1955; *The Happy Road* (Kelly), 1956; *En Effeuillant la Marguerite* (M. Allegret), 1956; *Love in the Afternoon* (Wilder) 1956; *Witness for the Prosecution* (Wilder), 1957; *The Nun's Story* (Zinnemann), 1958; *Le Secret du Chevalier d'Eon* (Audry) 1959; *Once More with Feeling* (Donen), 1960; *The Apartment* (Wilder), 1960; *Romanoff and Juliet* (Ustinov), 1961; *Paris Blues* (Ritt), 1961; *Aimez-Vous Brahms* (Litvak), 1961; *One, Two, Three* (Wilder), 1961; *Le Couteau dans la Plaie* (Litvak), 1962; *Irma La Douce* (Wilder), 1962; *Behold a Pale Horse* (Zinnemann), 1963; *Kiss Me, Stupid* (Wilder), 1964; *How to Steal a Million* (Wyler), 1966; *The Night of the Generals* (Litvak), 1967; *La Puce a l'Oreille* (Charon), 1967; *Uptight* (Dassin), 1968; *The Private Life of Sherlock Holmes* (Wilder), 1970; *Les Maries de l'An II* (Rappeneau), 1970; *La Promesse de l'Aube* (Dassin), 1971; *L'Impossible Objet* (Frankenheimer), 1972; *Grandeur Nature* (Berlanga), 1972; *The Man Who Would Be King* (Huston), 1972; *La Premiére Fois* (Berri), 1976; *Mr. Klein* (Losey), 1977; *Les Routes du Sud* (Losey), 1977; *Fedora* (Wilder), 1978; *Don Giovanni* (Losey), 1978; *The Fiendish Plot of Dr. Fu Manchu* (Haggard), 1979; *Coup de Torchon* (Tavernier), 1981; *The Trout* (Losey), 1982; *Subway* (Besson), 1985; *Around Midnight* (Tavernier), 1985; *Harem* (Joffé), 1985; *Le Moustachu* (Chaussois), 1986; *La Nuit Bengali* (Klotz), 1987.

## Publications

**On TRAUNER: books**—*Ragionamenh sulla Scenografia* by Baldo Bandini and Glauco Viazzi, Milan, 1945; *Les 1001 Métiers du Cinema* by Pierre Leprohon, Paris, 1947; *La Scenografia del Film* by Mario Verdone, Rome, 1956; *Dictionnaire des Cinéastes* by Georges Sadoul, Paris, 1964; *The Cinema as Art* by Ralph Stephenson and R. Debrix, London, 1965; *Le Décor de Film* by Leon Barsacq, Paris, 1970, as *Caligari's Cabinet and Other Grand Illusions,* Boston, 1976; *The World Encyclopedia of Film* edited by Tim Cawkwell and John M. Smith, London, 1972; *International Dictionary of Films and Filmmakers,* London and Chicago, 1987, 1991; *Alexandre Trauner: Decors du Cinema* by J. P. Berthomé, Paris, 1989.

\*     \*     \*

When I told Alexandre Trauner I was writing this piece about him, he gave a start and said with a slight, malicious frown: "We'll have to do it with humour!" His vast career is mentioned and analysed in all books about production design, but he remained modest and does not talk about his skills. "I work in the shadow of the authors, and it's just as well," he once said. "A designer is a manipulator, he makes believe ... and makes audiences believe. And as a magician, he should not reveal too much of his tricks!"

What kind of tricks did Trauner use, for instance, to build houses, towns, atmospheres, that have become for millions of people throughout the world, *the* houses, *the* towns, *the* atmospheres of Paris, London, or the Pharaohs' Egypt? Even those who don't precisely remember the docks in *Quai des Brumes* or the boulevard in *Children of Paradise* imagine them just as Trauner designed them.

"What makes my job most interesting," said Trauner, "is that there are no two identical films, even though producers would like to repeat indefinitely the same success. Every time I start working

Alexandre Trauner: Film set design for Marcel Carne's *Hotel du Nord,* 1938

on a movie, I try to forget all that I have experienced." He claimed that invention is the one and only acceptable rule. That's trick number one. Another of his tricks I might call friendship. The best of his work was done with people who became his friends: poet and screenwriter Jacques Prévert, directors Billy Wilder, Orson Welles, Joseph Losey, composer Maurice Jaubert, designers Ray and Charles Eames, actors Jean Gabin, Yves Montand, Jack Lemmon, and others.

"Shooting a film is collective work," said Trauner, and that was obviously something he enjoyed. "Each member of the team contributes, everything is important, but what's decisive for me is to have an adventure in common!"

Trauner's sets were immediately recognisable. During World War II, when France was occupied and he worked undercover, everyone in the profession felt his touch and knew that he had designed Grémillon's *Lumière d'été* or Carné's *Les Visiteurs du soir,* for his style was unmistakable. The basic trick was simplicity. He banished the picturesque and loathed the decorative. "It's useless," said he, "to fill the screen with superfluous things. Come to think about it, what a designer refrains from doing is almost more important that what he actually does. He's like a sculptor who eliminates material from the marble block. He cannot show everything; he chooses the significant elements, the unexpected ones, and these must look true, they must sound right."

That is how Trauner achieved the sturdiest, the most meaningful and imaginative of sets. He created the Paris that many people have in their minds, but he believed that movies become interesting when they don't stick to reality. Showing reality is not enough: the picture must be new and surprising. Only then does it become real. "It's a question of point of view, just as painting is a question of vision, and from Far Eastern to European painting, there are many different visions!" claimed Trauner.

Painting, since his beginnings at the Fine Arts School of Budapest, remained essential for him. He was the best known of production designers, the most ignored of painters. Only his close friends, Prévert or Picasso, knew about it, as he was always too modest or careless to do or let do anything about it; yet his set designs turned out to be fascinating pieces of painting. They were made with paint and a brush, just as the sets are made of plaster, wood, and sunlight. They were made by a person whose trick, all said and done, was to have no tricks—only an incisive eye, a keen understanding of people and places, and talent, as they say.

—André Pozner

# TREACY, Philip
## Irish fashion designer

**Born:** Ahacragh, County Galway, Ireland. **Education:** Graduated in fashion design, National College of Art & Design, Dublin, 1988, Royal College of Art, 1990. **Career:** Hat designer for various designers including Karl Lagerfeld, Marc Bohan, Rifat Ozbek, and Gianni Versace; presented his first collection of signature millinery, London Collections, 1993; produces hats for other couture houses and ready-to-wear firms, as well as the Philip Treacy for Right Impression label. **Address:** Philip Treacy Limited, 69 Elizabeth Street, Belgravia, London, England, SW1W 9PJ.

## Publications

**On TREACY: articles—**"Treacy: Another Feature at BG" in *Women's Wear Daily* (New York), 15 November 1991; "Philip Treacy: The Shape of Things to Come" by James Fallon in *Women's Wear Daily* (New York), 6 July 1990; "Hats Off to Philip Treacy—His Fanciful Designs Are Turning Heads" by Mary Killen in *Vogue* (New York), October 1991; "The Big Fat Hat" by Joe McKenna in *Interview* (New York), November 1991; "Style Makers: Philip Treacy" by Martha Ann Overland in *New York Times,* 5 April 1992; "The New Enlightenment" by Hamish Bowles in *Vogue* (New York), March 1993; "London Calling" by Alison Moore in *New York Times Magazine,* 19 December 1993; "Glad Hatter" in *People Weekly* (Chicago), 4 July 1994; "Feather Sculptures From a Mod Hatter" by Suzy Menkes in *International Herald Tribune* (Paris), 26 June 1995.

*          *          *

Ex-Royal College of Art student Philip Treacy was recognized as a talented milliner even before graduating from college where his final show was sponsored by *Harper's and Queen* magazine, London. In the years since leaving college, Irish-born Treacy has moved to the forefront of the fashion world, producing hats for some of the most prestigious couture and ready-to-wear designers, including Karl Lagerfeld at Chanel, Marc Bohan at Hartnell, and Rifat Ozbek. Described as the Rembrandt of millinery by the established hat designer, Shirley Hex, Treacy's monumental creations for the fashion catwalks often receive as much publicity as the outfits for which they are designed.

Treacy's millinery designs reflect his unquestionably vivid imagination, drawing upon diverse subjects such as surrealism, the dance of Martha Graham, as well as religious and historical imagery. Treacy asserts that to create a modern hat does not require space age influences, preferring to plunder the past for inspiration and then make it appear totally new. A floral hat by Philip Treacy is a crash helmet covered in flowers and butterflies, the traditional guardsman's busby is completely transformed in yellow ostrich feathers, a towering turban is created by an intricately wrapped blanket with fringed edging, a large cluster of black coq feathers are tied together with white feathers to form a brim and crown. Treacy's hats, like those of other British milliners, are often described as eccentric. Treacy attributes this eccentricity to the common association of the British with idiosyncracy, but says that he does not set out to create deliberately unusual hats. Using what he describes as "boring" fabrics, Treacy begins working upon these materials with different treatments—feathers, for example, are singed so that they take on the appearance of a very fine gossamer.

An important factor in Treacy's work is his mastery of highly skilled traditional millinery techniques which ensure the correct balance, fit, and proportion for the hat, which he concedes are as much mathematical as aesthetic. It is this artisan approach, with the emphasis on craft and technique, that characterizes much of Treacy's work. Treacy produces hats for nine different companies—three couture houses and six ready-to-wear firms, one of which is the Philip Treacy for Right Impression label designed for his backer. Treacy's ability to work at all levels of the market, from the costly couture creations to the less expensive ready-to-wear field, illustrates his versatility as a designer for whom price barriers are seen as a challenge rather than an obstacle.

While Treacy's use of imagery and visual effects for his millinery creations is a vital element in his success, fashion critic Brenda Polan claims that Treacy's mastery of technique is what singles him out as a great milliner, stating, "The balance of his hats, their swooping and curving, is perfect. A Treacy hat sits naturally upon the head, its proportions complementing those of the body, its horizontal and vertical lines extending and dramatizing the planes of the faces. It is a perfection only an obsessive can achieve."

—Catherine Woram

# TRIGÈRE, Pauline
American fashion designer

**Born** in Paris, France, 4 November 1912; emigrated to the United States in 1937, naturalized, 1942. **Education:** Jules Ferry and Victor Hugo Colleges, Paris, 1923-28. **Family:** Married Lazar Radley in 1929 (separated); children: Jean-Pierre and Philippe. **Career:** Apprenticed as trainee clothing cutter, at Martial et Armand, Place Vendôme, Paris, 1928-29. Assistant cutter and fitter in her father's tailoring business, Paris, 1929-32; freelance fashion designer and clothing cutter, Paris, 1933-36; design assistant to Travis Banton, at Hattie Carnegie fashion house, New York, 1937-42; founder and partner, with her brother Robert, in House of Trigère fashion firm, New York, from 1942. **Member:** Critic and board member, Fashion Institute of Technology, New York. **Honors:** Coty American Fashion Critics' Winnie Award, New York, 1949, 1951, 1959; Hall of Fame Award, 1959; Neiman-Marcus Award, New York, 1950; National Cotton Council of America Award, New York, 1951; Filene Award, 1959; Silver Medal, City of Paris, 1972. **Address:** 498 Seventh Avenue, New York, New York 10018, USA.

## Publications

**On TRIGÈRE: books—***The Fashionable Savages* by John Fairchild, New York, 1965; *The Wheels of Fashion* by Phyllis Lee Levin, New York, 1965; *American Fashion: The Life and Lines of Adrian, Mainbocher, McCardell, Norell, Trigère* edited by Sarah Tomerlin Lee, New York, 1975; *The Fashion Makers* by Bernadine Morris and Barbara Walz, New York, 1978; *Quest for the Best* by Stanley Marcus, New York, 1979; *Fairchild's Who's Who in Fashion* edited by Anne Stegemeyer, New York, 1980; *McDowell's Directory of Twentieth Century Fashion* by Colin McDowell, London, 1984; *Fashion: The Inside Story* by Barbaralee Diamonstein, New York, 1985; *Couture: The Great Designers* by Caroline Rennolds Milbank, New York, 1985; *The Encyclopaedia of Fashion from 1840 to the 1980s* by Georgina O'Hara, London, 1986; *New York and Hollywood Fashion: Costume Designs from the Brooklyn Museum Collection,* New York, 1986; *New York Fashion: The Evolu-*

*tion of American Style* by Caroline Rennolds Milbank, New York, 1989; **articles**—"Designers Who Are Making News" in *American Fabrics and Fashions* (New York), No. 38, 1956; "New York's Queen of Fashion" by J. Alexander in the *Saturday Evening Post* (New York), 8 April 1961; "The Style of Pauline Trigère: Enduring Qualities Enliven Her New York Residence" by Gael Greene and Peter Vitale in *Architectural Digest* (Los Angeles), September 1988; "Vicki Woods Crosses Paths with the Eccentric Pauline Trigère— and Comes Away with an Earful" by Vicki Woods in *Vogue* (New York), October 1989; "Most Elegant Pauline" by James Brady in *Advertising Age* (New York), 21 November 1994.

\*     \*     \*

Pauline Trigère, born into a French tailoring family, began her own clothing business in 1942 out of economic necessity. Practicality in an elegant guise has continued to distinguish her designs for the wives of wealthy American businessmen. She creates flattering, couture-quality clothes, investments her customers can depend upon season after season. Living the same active and social life as her customers, her design approach is based on personal experience.

A master fitter, she designs without toile or paper pattern. With a surgeon's skill, she cuts directly into the final fabric, shaping it on a live model until every detail has been perfected. Her use of bias-cut and princess seaming has resulted in designs such as the one she calls Everybody's Dress, a simple, jersey dress which skims the mature figure gracefully. Cowls and scarves soften necklines. Trigère daytime ensembles allow a busy woman to be completely well-dressed with no bother. Full-cut Greatcoats are chic and warm. Her variations of the cape swing dramatically with the wearer's every gesture. Her showy evening gowns, frequently trimmed with fur, sequins, or feathers, offer imaginative but ladylike elegance beyond fashion's changes. In all, her handling of fabrics is superb, from carefully-matched woolen plaids to spectacularly bold silk prints. Trigère's princess line dress is considered the best of its kind, and the rhinestone bra top she first introduced in 1967 was revived in 1985 and 1992.

Trigère travels with her collections to the prestigious American shops which carry her clothes. She enjoys meeting with salespeople and customers, helping them select fabrics from the swatches which accompany each garment. Her own enthusiastic commentary at her fashion shows includes formulas for efficient elegance, such as the Trigère Plan, a suggested basic wardrobe of one color for simplified traveling. This individualized attention allies Trigère's approach more closely with couture than with ready-to-wear.

Her busy schedule includes teaching, both at the Fashion Institute of Technology and through student visits to her workrooms, where she stresses to would-be designers the necessity of hard work and high standards. She enjoys entertaining in her eclectically elegant city and country homes, amidst her collection of the turtle objects which are her symbols of good luck and longevity. The turtle motif recurs in her perfume packaging, jewelry, and line of serving pieces.

Through many decades of devotion to her work, she has won the respect of fellow designers and the continuing loyalty of her satisfied customers. Trigère brings a woman designer's realistic approach to elegance.

—Sandra Michels Adams

# TROIKE, Gero
German stage and costume designer

**Born:** Gero Brauner, in Schönheide, Erzgebirge, 29 June 1945. **Education:** Educated at the Oberschule, Berlin-Köpenick, 1959-63; geology and mineralogy laboratory assistant, at Humboldt-Universität, Berlin, 1963-64; mainly self-taught in design. **Family:** Married Angela Troike in 1966; children: Anne and Sara. **Career:** Worked for VEB Bero-Kaffee, Berlin, 1964; Saint-Laurentius Cemetery, Berlin-Kopenick, 1965-66; stagehand, set painter and assistant stage designer, working for the Volksbühne, Berlin, 1964-65, 1969-71, 1972-81, for the Maxim Gorki Theatre, Berlin, 1967-69, and for the Komische Oper, Berlin, 1971-72; resident stage set and costume designer, for the Deutsches Theatre, Berlin, from 1981; also independent painter. **Exhibitions:** Galerie am Prater, Berlin, 1976; Galerie im Schloss Kopenick, Berlin, 1977. **Address:** Dahmestrasse 11180 Berlin, Germany.

## Works

Stage designs include—*The Chairs,* Volksbühne, Berlin, 1974; *Die Schlacht,* Volksbühne, Berlin, 1975; *Pauline,* Deutsches Theatre, Berlin, 1976; *The Burger General,* Volksbühne, Berlin, 1977; *Horribilicribifax,* Deutsches Theatre, Berlin, 1978; *Leonce and Lena,* Volksbühne, Berlin, 1978; *King Lear,* Ro-Theater, Amsterdam, 1978; *Midsummer Night's Dream,* Deutsches Theatre, Berlin, 1980; *Maria Stuart,* Deutsches Theatre, Berlin, 1980; *Maria Magdalena,* Kai Theatre, Brussels, 1980; *Dick Hunt,* Municipal Theatre, Dresden, 1981; *The Birds,* Municipal Theatre, Dresden, 1981; *The Sad Story of Frederick the Great,* Deutsches Theatre, Berlin, 1982; *Faust II,* Deutsches Theatre, Berlin, 1983.

## Publications

**By TROIKE: articles**—in *Bauten der Kultur* (Berlin), March 1983.

**On TROIKE: book**—*Malerei und Grafik in der DDR* by Lothar Lang, Leipzig, 1978; **articles**—in *Sibylle* (Berlin), June 1977; *Der Morgen* (Berlin), May 1983.

\*     \*     \*

The stage designer Gero Troike did not attend an arts academy. Rather, he is self-taught and acquired artistic and technical skills by assisting the leading designers of the German Democratic Republic, Reinhart Zimmerman and Pieter Hein. He modelled himself on the Old Masters of Germany, on the Romantic Caspar David Friedrich, and on Otto Dix, but he was stimulated more by the working methods of leading directors Benno Besson, Manfred Karge, Matthias Langhoff, and Alexander Lang than by painterly techniques. Even his interest in the work of designer Karl von Appen was mainly directed toward the style of his methods, its thoroughness and culture. With these major theatre artists, Troike learned to respect responsible collaboration and to understand that genuine teamwork is an integral component of theatrical activity.

In his own designs, Troike aims at symbolic expression via simple, sparse, and very functional effects, whilst his stage spaces create concrete acting opportunities for the players.

In these designs, he introduced specific stage movement recommendations, whereby the conceptual intent of the producer/director and the designer is evidenced in relationships of the stage space to the actors.

Troike uses the period of the play's original production as an artistic inspiration for the creation of his images (Baroque, Shakespearian, classic theatre of Goethe, etc.) and varies his techniques according to the type of play under production. His first major independent production was the design of Georg Hirschfeld's piece *Pauline* at the Deutsches Theater in Berlin. The action of the play takes place in Berlin at the turn of the century, the precise location being an elegant kitchen in which the resolute serving-girl Pauline lives. For this setting, Troike built a kitchen with a tiled floor and everything bright, clean, precise, and well-kept. Every item of lovingly researched period detail, such as little spice cupboards, pots, and ladles, told of the neat habits of its user. With minimal technical outlay, the kitchen was transformed into an old Berlin tavern where Pauline goes dancing once a week—a scene of poetic realism which creates for the actors a space in which they can live.

For Goethe's *Bürgergeneral* at the Berlin Volksbühne, Troike built another kitchen, again neat and bright—and yet of another world. The compact and heavy furniture, the Thunngian landscape of the poet Goethe, and the atmosphere of rural life dominate the scene. Such realistic poetry, which creates its own idyll, makes historical detachment possible. On the other hand, his attempt to illustrate a social pyramid with a triple-staggered stage, for the Baroque writer Gryphius's *Horribilicribifax,* was a failure. The stage design was too heavily "statuesque," precluding any relationship between the actors themselves or between actors and scenic space.

Troike's genius and originality, however, were to surface again in the production of Shakespeare's *A Midsummer Night's Dream,* for which he created a dramatically luminous, red space merely from three simple walls with a single doorway cut into each, the forest setting being conceived as within the characters themselves. The apogee of his creative work has been reached in recent productions of Heinrich Mann's *The Sad Story of Frederick the Great,* for which the stage was covered in tiles and punctuated by economically selected items of furniture to represent Prussian asceticism, and of Goethe's *Faust II,* both for the Berlin Deutsches Theater.

—Ingeborg Pietzsch

# TROXLER, Niklaus

Swiss graphic designer

**Born:** Willisau, 1 May 1947. **Education:** Studied graphics, at the Kunstgewerbeschule, Lucerne, 1968-71. **Family:** Married Ems Baettig in 1973; children: Kathrin, Annik, and Paula. **Career:** Art director, at Hollenstein Creation agency, Pans, 1972-73; freelance graphic designer, establishing Niklaus Troxler Grafik-Studio, Willisau, from 1973; has designed for the Willisau Jazz Festival, Lucerne Little Theatre, Zürich Kunstgewerbemuseum, Circus Knie, Autosalon Geneva, Olma Agriculture Fair, Mostly Mozart Festival, Tokyo, Mad Theater, Berne, City Theater, Lucerne, and others. **Exhibitions:** Galerie Raeber, Lucerne, 1978; Plakat-Galerie Migros, Bern, 1981; Artcurial, Paris, 1981; *Poster Triennale,* Deutsches Plakatmuseum, Essen, 1987, 1990, 1993; Reinhold Brown Gallery, New York, 1987, 1995; *The Big Show: The Modern Poster,* Museum of Modern Art, New York, 1988; Amerika

Haus, Frankfurt, 1992; Gallery Parterre, Berlin, 1993; Ginza Graphic Gallery, Tokyo, 1995. **Collections:** Kunstgewerbemuseum, Zürich; Ginza Graphic Gallery, Tokyo; Museum of Modern Art, New York; Zürich Poster Collection; Museum for Art and Craft, Hamburg; Chaumont Poster Museum, France. **Honors:** Vestag Kulturpreis, Lucerne, 1977; Swiss Poster of the Year Awards, 1977-80, 1982, 1984-93; Swiss Art Directors Club Silver Awards, 1979-93, and Gold Award, 1981, 1982; Innerschweizer Kulturpreis, 1982; Toulouse-Lautrec Gold Medal, Essen, 1987, 1993; First Prize, Chaumont Poster Competition, France, 1992; First Prize, 1993, and honorable mention, 1995, Lahti Poster Biennale, Finland; First Vienna Poster Award, 1994; Bronze Medal, Toyama Poster Triennale, Japan, 1994; Bronze Medal, Tokyo Typodirectors Club, 1995; two honorable mentions, Political Poster Triennale, Mons, Belgium, 1995. **Address:** Bahnhofstrasse 22, 6130 Willisau, Switzerland.

## Works

*McCoy Tyner Sextet* poster, for Jazz in Willisau, 1980.
*Arthur Blythe Quartet* poster, for Jazz in Willisau, 1982.
*Hermeto Pascoal: Brazilian Jazz* poster, for Jazz in Willisau, 1985.
*A Tribute to the Music of Thelonious Monk* poster, for Jazz in Willisau, 1986.
*Funk Night: Willisau* poster, for Jazz in Willisau, 1987.

**Niklaus Troxler: poster for Jazz Festival, Willisau, Switzerland, 1991**

*Maria Joao-Aki Takase:* Concert poster, Jazz in Willisau, 1988.
*Entweder-oder* poster, for the Madtheater, Bern, 1988.
*OLMA: Fair of Eastern Switzerland* poster, for Olma, St. Gallen, 1988, 1992, 1994.
*Wirz ist auf Talentsuche* poster, for Wirz Publicity, Zürich, 1988.
*Luzerner Unwelt- und Besinnungstage* poster, for Forum Neuland, 1988.
*African Echoes* poster, for Jazz in Willisau, 1988.
*Bobby Burri Quartet* poster, for Jazz in Willisau, 1989.
*Anthony Braxton Trio* poster, for Jazz in Willisau, 1989.
*Dead Trees* poster, 1992.
*Stop Violence* poster, 1993.
Murals, for Willisau Sports Center and schools, 1993.
Murals, for Cultural Center, Sursee, 1993.
Murals, for Alfred Escher House, Zürich, 1995.

## Publications

**By TROXLER: books**—*Jazz-Plakate von Niklaus Troxler,* Willisau, 1978.

**On TROXLER: books**—*Graphis Posters,* annuals edited by Walter Herdeg, Zürich, 1975, 1979, 1980, 1982-94; *Jazz in Willisau,* Lucerne, 1978; *Art Directors Club of Switzerland,* annuals, Zürich, 1979, 1980, 1981, 1982, 1983, 1994; *The Dictionary of Visual Language* by Philip Thompson and Peter Davenport, London, 1980; *Romeo und Julia in Willisau,* Zürich, 1982; *Swiss Posters 1970-1980* edited by Idea Publishers, Tokyo, 1982; *The Modern Poster* by Stuart Wrede, New York, 1988; *Who's Who in Graphic Design,* Zürich, 1994; *The 100 Best Posters from Europe and the United States 1945-1990,* Tokyo, 1995; *Niklaus Troxler—Jazz Posters,* exhibition catalogue, Germany.

*

I feel that a poster must have a personal style and convey an artistic message; personal interpretation is all important. Moreover, the design of the poster must be true to the medium, that is to say, it is essential that I create a "poster." The solution is simplicity: I do what I can for myself in my studio. The secret is to concentrate, and to rely on my curiosity, to let myself be carried away by improvisation, trusting that my taste, or sensibilities, won't allow banalities. The message has priority over form, creativeness over aesthetics, and expression over perfect design.

If I succeed, it is because beauty must follow, be it by chance or as a logical result of the basic idea being fundamentally good; if the result appears new and simple, one is left wondering why something so elementary had not been realized.

—Niklaus Troxler

# TSCHERNY, George

American graphic designer

**Born:** Budapest, Hungary, 12 July 1924; emigrated to the United States in 1941, naturalized, 1943. **Education:** Studied at Newark School of Fine and Industrial Arts, New Jersey, 1946-47; Pratt

Institute, Brooklyn, New York, 1947-50. **Military Service:** Served in the United States Army, in Europe, 1943-45, Corporal. **Family:** Married Sonia Katz in 1950; children: Nadia and Carla. **Career:** Staff designer, at Donald Deskey and Associates, New York, 1950-53; associate and head of graphic design, at George Nelson and Associates, New York, 1953-55; founder and president of George Tscherny Incorporated graphic design studio, New York, from 1955; has designed for Johnson and Johnson, Pan American, Public Broadcasting System, Mobil, IBM, Texasgulf, Aluminium Association, Air Canada, General Dynamics, and others. Instructor, at the Pratt Institute, Brooklyn, New York, 1956-57, and the School of Visual Arts, New York, 1956-64; Mellon visiting professor, Cooper Union, New York, 1976. Curriculum consultant, Philadelphia College of Art 1967-68; advisory board member, Pratt Institute, Brooklyn, New York, 1979. President, American Institute of Graphic Arts, 1966-68. **Member:** Alliance Graphique Internationale; American Institute of Graphic Arts. **Exhibitions:** School of Visual Arts, New York, 1959; Landesgewerbeamt, Stuttgart, 1962; Galerie Intergraphis, Munich, 1967; Pratt Institute, Brooklyn, New York, 1972; *107 Grafici dell'AGI,* Castello Sforzesco, Milan, 1974; *Images of un Era: The American Poster 1945-1975,* Corcoran Gallery of Art, Washington, D.C., 1975; *The Modern Poster,* Museum of Modern Art, New York, 1988; *The Masters Series,* Visual Arts Museum, New York, 1992 (toured); *16th International Biennale of Graphic Design,* Brno, 1994; *Poster '95,* Lahti, Finland, 1995. **Collections:** Museum of Modern Art, New York; Cooper-Hewitt Museum, New York; Library of Congress, Washington, D.C.; Kunstgewerbemuseum, Zürich. **Honors:** Silver Medal, Warsaw Poster Biennale, 1976; American Institute of Graphic Arts Gold Medal, 1988; Masters Series Award, Visual Arts Museum, New York, 1992; plus awards from the American Institute of Graphic Arts, New York Art Directors Club, and Type Directors Club. **Address:** George Tscherny, Inc., 238 East 72nd Street, New York, New York 10021, U.S.A.

## Works

Series of advertisements, for Herman Miller Furniture Company, 1953-55.
Theater program designs, for Marcel Marceau, Martha Graham, Benny Goodman, and others, New York, 1954-56.
Appointment calendar designs, for the Museum of Modern Art, New York, 1957-60.
Annual reports and publication designs, for the Ford Foundation, 1958-61.
Subway poster series, for the School of Visual Arts, New York, 1960-62.
*Jose de Rivera* exhibition catalogue, for the American Federation of Arts, 1961.
*Imagination 10: Trains and Railroads* brochure, for Champion Papers, 1967.
*Lark, Chesterfield,* and *L&M* modular cigarette pack designs, for Liggett and Myers Tobacco Company, 1968.
*Oceanography* poster series, for General Dynamics Corporation, 1968.
*Destinations* modular displays, for Pan American Airways, 1971.
Corporate identity program and publications, for W. R. Grace and Company, from 1974.
*Happy Birthday USA* bicentennial poster, for Davis-Delaney-Arrow, 1975.

*Telephone Centenary* commemorative postage stamp, for the U.S. Postal Service, 1976.

Series of exhibition posters, for Goethe House, New York, 1977-80.

Annual reports, for SEI Corporation, from 1981.

*Connections* poster, for the Simpson Paper Company, 1982.

*IBM Yesterday and Today* illustrated book design, for IBM, 1984.

*Swim for Breath* poster, for the Cystic Fibrosis Foundation, 1985.

*1986 Connecticut Special Olympics* poster, 1986.

Logotype, packaging, and advertising, for San Francisco Clothing, 1987.

Appointment calendars, for Sandy-Alexander Incorporated, 1989, 1991.

*Progress in Skin Care* report, for Johnson and Johnson, 1989.

*Pull and Let Go—Design and communication for the W.C.* publication design, for Champion International, 1990.

Corporate identification program, for Interactive Language Teaching Ltd., London, 1991.

*Odd & Even—A study of house numbers* publication design, for Champion International, 1992.

*Graphic Design USA: The Annual of the American Institute of Graphic Arts* jacket design, 1993.

Poster, for the 70th anniversary of the Long Island State Park Commission, 1994.


## Publications

**By TSCHERNY: articles**—in *Communication Arts* (Palo Alto), February 1962; *High Quality* (Munich), no. 4, 1986.

**On TSCHERNY: books**—*Packaging: An International Survey of Package Design* edited by Walter Herdeg, Zürich, 1959; *Who's Who in Graphic Art* edited by Walter Amstutz, Zürich, 1962, Dubendorf, 1982; *The Poster: An Illustrated History from 1860* by Harold F. Hutchinson, London and Toronto, 1968; *107 Grafici dell'AGI,* with texts by Renzo Zorzi and Franco Grignani, Venice, 1974; *The Language of Graphics* by Edward Booth-Clibborn and Daniele Baroni, London, 1980; *A History of Graphic Design* by Philip B. Meggs, New York, 1983; *Thirty Centuries of Graphic Design* by James Craig and Bruce Barton, New York, 1987; *Contemporary Graphic Artists* edited by Maurice Horn, Detroit, 1988; *Annual Report War Stories* edited by Simpson Paper Company, San Francisco, 1988; *First Choice* by Ken Cato, Tokyo, 1989; *AGI Annals* by F.H.K. Henrion, Tokyo, 1989; *Typographic Communications Today* by E. M. Gottshall, Cambridge, Massachusetts, 1989; *Expressive Typography* by K. Elam, New York, 1990; *Graphic Design: New York,* Rockport, Massachusetts, 1992; *Who's Who in Graphic Design,* Zürich, 1994; *The 100 Best Posters from Europe and the United States 1945-1990,* Tokyo, 1995; **articles**—in *Novum Gebrauchsgraphik* (Munich), no. 11, 1961, no. 10, 1975, no. 4, 1988; *Print* (New York), no. 5, 1965; *Graphis* (Zürich), no. 161, 1972, no. 230, 1984; *Communication Arts* (Palo Alto), no. 7, 1966; *Idea* (Tokyo), no. 5, 1969, no. 11, 1978, no. 11, 1983, no. 3, 1991; "The Disarmingly Simple Design of George Tscherny" by S. Heller in *Graphic Design USA: 10* (New York), 1989; *Tategumi Yokogumi/ Morisawa Quarterly* (Tokyo), no. 44, 1995.

*

Although the pioneering phase of the modern design movement took place largely in the 1920s and 1930s, it became a popular and accepted style only in the 1950s and 1960s. Despite having been very much a part of this second phase, I never felt a dogmatic allegiance to the International Style. It was, I suppose, simply not wanting to be too closely identified with any style or movement. Moreover, I had my differences with many of my colleagues during those years: their fascination with manmade, ersatz materials, the sterile "one-typeface" ideology of some, and the typographic gluttony of others. Nor will I miss the typographic acrobatics that followed the introduction of film type. My joys in typography were not derived from squeezing, pulling, and otherwise manipulating type, nor by "killing widows." Still, surprisingly, I share little of the general disillusionment with modernism which has overtaken designers today.

Why then did I not eagerly embrace post-modernism as an alternative? Although, historically, protest movements have tended to be destructive rather than constructive, the novel aspect of postmodernism was that it recycled, in large part, the very past it was repudiating. Here, I must give credit to the fashion designers who aptly called their parallel movement "Retro." Moreover postmodernism chose to celebrate the most trivial and pedestrian aspects of the past; it never rose above its mannerisms. The purported goal of rejecting humanism was never implemented or even honestly pursued. Fortunately, protest movements are shortlived. About the only legacy postmodernism has left us is a refreshing color palette.

I don't know what is next. I do know what I would wish for. I would wish for a truly human and humane period in design. For sure, it will have to be called "Post-Mortem" design. I have already detected beginnings of this human touch in illustrations. We are done with the noodled, air-brushed, embalmed faces that dominated much of illustration in the 1970s. I am looking for an indication that the brush or pencil was held by a human hand.

The big unknown in our future is the computer. Will it be aid or a hindrance? I know it will make me design faster; I am not sure it will make me design better.

—George Tscherny

\*     \*     \*

George Tscherny does not fit the mold of most professional graphic designers. Even though his career began within design offices such as Donald Deskey's and George Nelson's in the 1950s, he has devoted the majority of his career to maintaining a flourishing, small, independent office. He has said that there are no revolutionaries in design today and adds, "In my generation, in school, we were stirred by a still-developing art. We had our idols in such men as Lester Beall, Charles Eames, and Paul Rand."

But in the more than thirty years of Tscherny's career, how has he been innovative in his creative design? He claims that he pursues two opposite directions in design. He sometimes extracts the essence of a subject and presents it simply and dramatically, as in the Triennale poster and the Art Auction publication. Alternatively, he utilizes a more pluralistic, scrapbook technique when that approach seems useful in order to intensify or deepen communication. This method is exemplified in the Champion Papers *Imagination* book on railroads, the poster on nineteenth-century Germany, and the Simpson Paper Company *Connections* poster. With either method, he attempts to avoid being timid or predictable. Tscherny is a keen and intelligent analyst who finds answers to design problems within the natures of the problems themselves. The problem establishes the form, and he uses whatever solution appears appropriate to

George Tscherny: catalog cover for the University of California, Los Angeles, 1995

enhance the content in the simplest, most communicative manner. He feels that "the designer" is the creator of his own visual vocabulary, and the recycled form is a denial of that commitment. His delightful graphic solutions evidence integration, surprises, economy of means, and a special elegance of orchestration.

By reason of its subtle ingenuity, self-possession, and intellectual maturity his work offers an invigoratingly distinctive oasis of achievement. His versatility has kept him independent and vice versa, as his practice has engaged in wide-ranging types of projects, including corporate identity, advertising, posters, displays, stamps, annual reports, displays, and more. Tscherny's work has been influential in that he is consistently producing graphic design that is different and fresh. His work is logical, and he insists on doing nothing more or less than what serves the interests of the "unmistakable design."

Tscherny has said that in his design he attempts to "zig when everyone else zags." He is indeed one of the select few of contemporary graphic designers who have evolved an authentic and unique American style.

—R. Roger Remington

# TSCHICHOLD, Jan

Swiss typographer, lettering, typeface, and book designer

**Born:** Leipzig, Germany, 2 April 1902; emigrated to Switzerland in 1933, naturalized, 1942. **Education:** Studied at the Teacher Training College, Grimma, near Leipzig, 1916-19; private studies in graphics and typography, at the Hall of Culture, Leipzig, 1915-19; studied graphic design under Hermann Delitsch, at the Academy for Graphic Arts and Book Production, Leipzig, 1919-21; under Heinrich Wieynck, at the School of Arts and Crafts, Dresden, 1921. **Family:** Married Edith Kramer in 1926; children: Peter. **Career:** Typographer, at Poeschl und Trepte printing firm, Leipzig, 1922; freelance typographer and graphic designer, working for Fischer und Wittig and Insel-Verlag publishers, in Leipzig, 1923-25, for Phoebus-Palast cinemas in Berlin and Munich, 1926-33, for Verlag Benno Schwabe, Verlag Holbein, and Uhertype, in Basel, 1933-46; design chief, Penguin Books, Harmondsworth, Middlesex, 1947-49; freelance typography and design consultant to German and Swiss publishers, in Basel, from 1950; design consultant to F. Hoffman-La Roche, Basel, 1955-67; retired to Berzona, near Locarno, 1968-74. Assistant in charge of evening classes, under Walter Tiemann, Academy for Graphic Arts and Book Production, Leipzig, 1921-22; instructor, at Paul Renner's German Master Printing School, Munich, 1925-33, and at the Kunstgewerbeschule, Basel, 1933-46. **Exhibitions:** Lund Humphries, London, 1935; *Commercial Typography,* Victoria and Albert Museum, London, 1936; St. Bride Printing Library, London, 1975; Kunstgewerbemuseum, Zurich, 1976; National Library of Scotland, Edinburgh, 1982. **Collections:** Lund Humphries, London; Victoria and Albert Museum, London. **Honors:** Honorary member, Double Crown Club, London, 1949; American Institute of Graphic Arts Gold Medal, New York, 1954; Gutenberg Prize, Leipzig, 1965; Honorary Royal Designer for Industry, Royal Society of Arts, London, 1965; Honorary corresponding member, Akademie der Kunste, West Berlin, 1966. **Died:** Locarno, 11 August 1974.

## Publications

**By TSCHICHOLD: books**—*Die neue Typographie,* Berlin, 1928; (with Franz Roh) *Foto-Auge; 76 Fotos der Zeit,* Stuttgart, 1929, New York, 1973; *Eine Stunde Druckgestaltung,* Stuttgart, 1930; *Das neue Plakat,* 1930; (designer) *Fototek 1: L. Moholy-Nagy—60 Fotos,* Berlin, 1930; *Schriftschreiben für Setzer,* Frankfurt am Main, 1931; *Typographiscle Entwurfstechnik,* Stuttgart, 1932; *Typographische Gestaltung,* Basel, 1935, Copenhagen and Stockholm, 1937, Amsterdam, 1938, as *Asymmetric Typography,* New York, Toronto, and London, 1967; *Der frühe chinesisches Farbendruck,* Basel, 1940, New York and London, 1953; *Geschichte der Schrift in Bildern,* Basel, 1941, London, 1946; *Gute Schriftformen,* Basel, 1941; *Schriftkunde, Schreibungen und Skizzieren für Setzer,* Basel, 1942; *Chinesische Farbendruck der Gegenwart,* Basel, 1944; *Schatzkammer der Schreibkunst,* Basel, 1945; *Im Dienst des Buches,* St. Gallen, Switzerland, New York, and Copenhagen, 1951; *Meisterbuch der Schrift,* Ravensburg, West Germany, 1952, New York, 1966; *Formenwandlungen der Et-Zeichen,* Frankfurt, 1953; (compiler and designer) *Schonste, liehe mich,* Heidelberg, 1957; *Der Chinesische und der Japanesische mehrfarbige Holzfafeldruck, technische,* Basel, 1959; *Erfreuliche Drucksachen durch gute Typography,* Ravensburg, West Germany, 1960; *Zur Typographie der Gegenwart,* Bern, 1960; *Die Bildersammlung der Zehnbarnbushalle,* Erlebach, 1970; *Ausgewählte Aufsätze über Fragen der Gestalt des Buches und der Typographie,* Basel, 1975; *Leben und werk des Typographen Jan Tschichold* (with bibliography), Dresden, 1977.

**On TSCHICHOLD: books**—*Lettering of Today* edited by C. G. Holme, London and New York, 1937, 1949; *Design in British Industry: A Mid-Century Survey* by Michael Farr, Cambridge, 1955; *Modern Graphic Design 2: The Typography of Jan Tschichold,* Cincinnati, 1957; *Modern Book Design* by Ruari McLean, London, 1958; *The New Graphic Design* by Karl Gerstner and Markus Kutter, Teufen and London, 1959; *The Typographic Book 1450-1935* by Stanley Morison and Kenneth Day, London, 1963; *Functional Graphic Design in the 20s* by Eckhard Neumann, New York and London, 1967; *Pioneers of Modern Typography* by Herbert Spencer, London, 1969; *History of the Poster* by Josef and Shizuko Muller-Brockmann, Zurich, 1971; *Jan Tschichold,* exhibition catalogue with foreword by James Mosley, London, 1975; *Jan Tschichold, Typographer* by Ruari McLean, London, 1975; *J. T.: Johannes Tschichold, Iwan Tschichold, Jan Tschichold* edited by Philipp Luidl, Munich, 1976; *The Thames and Hudson Manual of Typography* by Ruari McLean, London, 1980; *Jan Tschichold: Typographer and Type Designer,* exhibition catalogue, Edinburgh, 1982; *Typographic Design; Form and Communication* by Rob Carter, Ben Day, and Philip Meggs, New York, 1985.

\*     \*     \*

The son of a sign-writer, trained in calligraphy and book-production, Jan Tschichold was grounded in a knowledge of production processes. Unlike artist-typographers, he could communicate his intentions precisely. Among other characteristic features of all his mature work (both "new" and "traditional") are sensitivity to physical materials and to letterforms, as well as to the semantic content of text and image; great care in the smallest details of visual placing; and a willingness to experiment within quite severely defined constraints.

By his own testimony, Tschichold experienced a sudden conversion to modernism in 1923, on seeing the exhibition of the Weimar Bauhaus. His achievement was to absorb and refine principles suggested by slightly preceding modernists (Lissitzky and Moholy-Nagy, for example), then to propagate them within the printing trade.

The seriousness with which Tschichold practised typography can be seen in the arguments that surrounded his break with modernism. He explained that he had come to see parallels between the absolutism of his advocacy of a new typography and the totalitarianism of National Socialism; on a lesser plane, he suggested that new typography could not deal adequately with the complexities of book design. However, his mature new typography, such as his work for the Social-Democratic "Bücherkreis" club, or the content and design of *Typographische Gestaltung,* suggests that such an explanation should be questioned. In any case, it is this phase of his work (roughly 1930-35) that has been most influential for younger generations of typographers.

Tschichold turned away from modernism, but he continued to work with the tasks and technologies of the modern world. Penguins were a new kind of book: mass produced paperbacks, cheap, but serious and worthwhile in content. In less than two years of intensive work, Tschichold was able to obtain high standards of text composition from undistinguished printers, as well as lay down new standards for the design of the text and covers of the whole range of books.

Tschichold's historical research and writing ranged widely and often meshed with his practise. He produced notable contributions on Chinese colour printing, on systems of page proportion, and more generally on the history of written and printed letterforms. His writing always had a polemical, rather authoritarian edge. It was typical that he should have supplied his own pseudonymous account of his work, "Jan Tschichold: Praeceptor Typographiae" (reprinted in the posthumous *Leben und Werk* that he planned and designed). Subsequent historians may adjust and expand this account, but the importance of Tschichold's typography will remain undeniable.

—Robin Kinross

# TSYPIN, George

Russian artist and stage and film set designer

**Born:** Kazakhstan, Russia (U.S.S.R.), 1 January 1954; emigrated to the United States, 1979. **Education:** Studied architecture, Moscow Architectural Institute, Moscow, Soviet Union, M.F.A., 1977; studied theater design, New York University, M.F.A., 1984. **Career:** Freelance set designer and artist, from 1984; worked with Peter Sellars, American National Theater, Kennedy Center, Washington, D.C., 1985-86; visiting professor, Tisch School of Arts, New York University. **Exhibitions:** *All That Is Solid Melts into the Air,* Twining Gallery, New York, 1991; Prague Quadriennale, 1991, 1995. **Collections:** Lincoln Center Theater Collection, New York; Theater Museum, Texas. **Honors:** Winner, International Competition, Free and Spontaneous View on Contemporary Theater for New Generations, U.S.S.R., 1978; First Prize, All Soviet Competition of Diploma Prizes, 1979; De Menlil Fellowship Award, 1983; Seldman Award for Excellency in Design, 1986; Helen Hayes Award

nomination, 1987; Bay Area Theater Critics Circle Award, 1989; Obie Award for sustained excellence in set design, 1990; Drama-Logue Critics Award, 1991; *Boston Globe* Award, 1994. **Addresses:** (agent) Helen Merrill, 435 W. 23rd St., #1A, New York, New York 10011, U.S.A.; (office) George Tsypin Design, 25-10 30 Road, #5-O, Astoria, New York 11102, U.S.A.

## Works

Stage set designs include—*The Power and the Glory,* Philadelphia Drama Guild, Philadelphia, Pennsylvania, 1984; *A Seagull,* American National Theater, Kennedy Center, Washington, D.C., 1985; *The Count of Monte Cristo,* American National Theater, 1985; *Suor Angelica,* Opera Company of Philadelphia, 1986; *The Balcony,* American Repertory Theater, Cambridge, Massachusetts, 1986; *Ajax,* American National Theater (toured), 1986; *Idiot's Delight,* American National Theater, 1986; *Measure for Measure,* Arena Stage, Washington, D.C., 1986; *Galileo,* Goodman Theater, Chicago, Illinois, 1986; *Death in Venice,* Opera Company of Philadelphia, 1986; *Zangezi: A Supersaga in Twenty Planes,* Museum of Contemporary Art, Los Angeles, 1986-87; *Don Giovanni,* PepsiCo Summerfare, Purchase, New York, 1987; *Leon and Lena and Lenz,* Guthrie Theater, Minneapolis, Minnesota, 1987; *Electrification of the Soviet Union,* Gyndebourne Opera Festival, Gyndebourne, England, 1987; *Tannhauser,* Lyric Opera, Chicago, 1988; *Landscape of the Body,* Goodman Theater, 1988; *Nothing Sacred,* American Conservatory Theater, San Francisco, 1989; *Cymbeline,* New York Shakespeare Festival, 1989; *The Misanthrope,* La Jolla Playhouse, La Jolla, California, and Goodman Theater, Chicago, 1989; *The Screens,* Guthrie Theater, 1989; *Don Giovanni,* ORF National Television and Maison de la Culture, Vienna and Paris, 1989; *Henry IV, Parts I and II,* Shakespeare Festival, New York, 1991; *Jelly's Last Jam,* Mark Taper Theater, Los Angeles, 1991; *The Death of Klinghoffer,* toured, 1991-92; *Rigoletto,* Canadian Opera Company, Toronto, Ontario, 1992; (with Jessi Norman) *Oedipus Rex,* for World Wide Television, Saito Kinen Festival, Matsumoto, Japan, 1992; *Saint Francis of Assisi,* Bastille Opera, Paris, and Salzburg Festival, Salzburg, 1992; *Peleas ed Melisande,* Netherland Opera, 1993; *Orfeo ed Euridiche,* Vienna Festival and Zürich Opera, 1995; *Mathis der Maler,* Covent Garden, London, 1995; *The Gambler,* La Scala, Milan, 1996; *The Ring Cycle,* Netherland Opera, 1997-99.

Film set designs include—*The Cabinet of Dr. Ramirez* (Sellars), 1989.

## Publications

**On TSYPIN: books**—*American Set Design 2* by Ronn Smith, New York, 1991; **articles**—"Philip Glass and George Tsypin Discuss Their Concept for *Cymbeline*'s Music and Set" in *Theater Week* (New York), 19-25 June 1989; "Did Frank Rich Really Look?" by Nancy Graves in *American Theater* (New York), December 1989; "Permanence" in the *New Yorker,* 14 May 1990; "The Fantasies of Designer George Tsypin" in *American Theater* (New York), December 1990; "Tales from the Crypt" in *Village Voice* (New York), 29 January 1991; "Designs on Design: George Tsypin" in *Theatre Craft* (New York), February 1991; "Russian Roulette" in *WWD* (New York), 27 March 1991; "Deconstructing Make Be-

**George Tsypin: set design for *Oedipus Rex*, Matsumoto Festival, Japan, 1992**

lieve" by Ronn Smith in *Metropolis* (New York), May 1991; "Set Pieces from Set Designer" by Stephen Sherrill in *New York Observer*, 20 May 1991; "George Tsypin" by Arnold Aronson in *Theatre Design and Technology* (New York), Summer 1991; "Medieval Yet Modern: Tsypin's *Rigoletto* Sets Serve Verdi Well" in *Globe and Mail* (Toronto), 24 September 1992.

*

In designing for the theater, especially opera, my role as a set designer is to create a spatial drama that does not illustrate or serve the text and the music, but rather exists on its own as a sort of sculpture or architectural space that develops in time. Therefore, after reading and studying about the piece and listening to the music you ultimately arrive at a place where you are faced with a very formal problem of shape, space, and color that on the surface seems very similar to the problem facing a fine artist. The crucial difference, though, is that by using the same means you conceive an event or series of events involving the actors as well as music and light. And then if these events are strategically well timed you have a good show. That is where your job overlaps with that of the director.

There are two schools of designing for the theater: painterly-illusionistic and sculpturally-constructivist. My work tends to be the latter. In the era of total predominance of television and film, both flat mediums, I believe one has to be very aggressive spatially in theater. It is important not only to violate the space of the stage, but sometimes the auditorium as well.

I try to design sets that are honest structurally. If the set looks good if not better from the back, I consider it a good design. I also believe in the honesty of materials used. One has to strive to use real wood, steel, or glass. When so much that surrounds us is fake, that alone becomes a statement of conviction. And then if you manage to create magic out of that, you have real theater.

—George Tsypin

*    *    *

Avant-garde director-playwright Richard Foreman once expressed the essence of aesthetic distance and Brechtian alienation in breathtakingly simple form in his play *Rhoda in Potatoland*: "Only by being a tourist," says a voice, "can you experience a place." Kazakhstan-born designer George Tsypin, who trained as an architect in the former Soviet Union, is the American theatre's "tourist." Perhaps because of his ability to look at the American landscape with the distance and fascination that only an outsider can have, he has succeeded in tapping into the essence of contemporary society.

843

Just as Jo Mielziner expressed the yearning and romanticism of the country in the 1930s, 1940s, and 1950s, and just as Ming Cho Lee mixed Chinese and European aesthetics to reshape the landscape of American theatre in the 1960s and 1970s, Tsypin has found a visual vocabulary that is the ideal expression of our present culture. He is the most original and daring of that group of designers now identified as imagistic, deconstructivist, or postmodern.

Tsypin moved to New York in 1979 and studied stage design at New York University. His unique vision was apparent even then, and shortly after graduation he began to work with iconoclastic director Peter Sellars at the short-lived American National Theatre at the Kennedy Center. Though his work was clearly informed by his architectural background, Tsypin is perhaps best described as a poet of space, though Tsypin himself has reversed this image and called himself an "architect of the mind."

Because he came to theatre relatively late, and because he was not imbued with an American sensibility, Tsypin seems to have no self-conscious limits or sense of aesthetic propriety in his work. His ideas proceed from the text, not from some theatrical tradition. There is a raw energy in Tsypin's work that ransacks history, draws freely from wide-ranging styles and periods, and bluntly mixes the stunningly beautiful with the harsh and ugly. Furthermore, there is a sense of scale, space, and verticality in his work virtually unmatched in American theatre. Until recently, he has worked extensively with steel—a material capable of sleek beauty and strength, but one also subject to distortion and the decay of rust. A Tsypin setting, such as the John Adams opera *The Death of Klinghoffer* (1992) contains towering images, skeletal scenic pieces, and moving components that recall the Russian Constructivism that is a strong part of his heritage while simultaneously evoking Islamic architecture. There is often a physical danger to his sets—the risk of actors falling through gaps in the floor or tumbling from overhead structures—but there is also an aesthetic danger. His designs can be jarring, ugly, or disconcerting, thus making the audience uncomfortable. Yet visual disjunction is carefully planned.

His most exciting work has come with America's leading directors: Robert Falls, JoAnne Akalaitis, Julie Taymor, and Sellars. In recent years he has moved beyond the confines of the stage, as if even the largest opera houses could no longer contain his visions. Messiaen's *St. Francis of Assisi*, directed by Sellars, was presented against the cliff of the main square in Salzburg, Austria. A skeletal cathedral was built that was as much architecture as design. Skilled artisans and construction machinery were brought in to build the set. Stravinsky's *Oedipus Rex* was staged in a 60,000-seat arena in Japan. And *Symphony for the Earth,* a television production with Seiji Ozawa and the Tokyo Symphony, finally abandoned the idea of live audience in a confined space and instead, through satellite television connections, spanned the whole earth.

Ironically, as the projects grow larger, Tsypin's artwork has gotten smaller. Formerly, he created conceptual models that were really sculptures (usually made of steel) that captured the essence of the work but were not intended as working models for directors or technicians. For them he created meticulously designed mechanical drawings; what many designers consider drudge work is, for Tsypin, a beautiful part of the process. Recently, he has moved to two-dimensional artwork that combines painting and collage. Again, the works are expressionistic—they are not the renderings intended to provide tangible information for the production personnel. They are unique and haunting works of art that embody ideas and are thus, in many senses, truer expressions of the production than a conventional model or rendering. Tsypin is the energetic artist of the American theatre.

—Arnold Aronson

# TYE, Alan

British architect and industrial designer

**Born:** London, 18 September 1933. **Education:** Studied architecture, at Regent Street Polytechnic, London, Dip.Arch., 1960. **Family:** Married Anita Birgitta Goethe in 1966; children: Madeleine, Nicholas, and Kevin. **Career:** Assistant architect, in the office of Arne Jacobsen, Copenhagen, 1960-62; freelance designer, as Alan Tye Design RDI Limited, London and Hertfordshire, from 1962; partnership with Knud Holscher, as Holscher-Tye Architects, London and Copenhagen, from 1964; designed for Adamsez, Allgood, Headway-Syncronol, Apple, Mallinson-Denny, Sissons, Domaine International, and others. Tutor, at the Royal College of Art, London, 1978-83; also visiting lecturer, at the Ceramic Society, London, 1974, and the Royal Institute, London, 1976, 1978. **Member:** Design selection committee member, Council of Industrial Design, London, 1967; assessor, Civic Trust Awards, London, 1968-69; juror, Royal Society of Arts, London, 1980; specialist advisor to the Council for National Academic Awards, London, 1980; architectural awards assessor, Royal Institute of British Architects, London, 1981, 1988; Young Designers in Industry juror, Royal Society of Arts, London, 1986-89; advisor to the Wuxi University Industrial Design School, China, 1987; external degrees examiner, Royal College of Art, London, 1987-89. **Exhibitions:** Design Society, Copenhagen, 1972; Design Centre, London, 1979; *New Design for Old,* Victoria and Albert Museum, London, 1985 (toured); *Eye for Industry,* Victoria and Albert Museum, London, 1986. **Collections:** Victoria and Albert Museum, London; Ringling Museum, Sarasota, Florida. **Honors:** International Bathroom Design Prize, Rome, 1962; Council of Industrial Design Award, London, 1965, 1966; Guild of Architectural Ironmongers Award, London, 1966, 1969, 1971, 1976; British Aluminum Industry Design Award, 1966, and Eros Trophy, 1973; Stainless Steel Development Association Prize, London, 1966; Silver Cup for Exhibition Display, London, 1969; *Observer* Design Award, London, 1969; Ringling Museum Design Award, Sarasota, 1969; Star Design Award and Gold Medal, London, 1970; Building Centre Exceptional Merit Award, London, 1970; *Architects' Journal* Graphic Design Award, London, 1976; Interbuild Gold Lion Award, 1978, Design Award, 1981, and Exhibition Award, 1983, 1985; London and Birmingham Roscoe Design Award, New York, 1988; fellow, 1974, and Royal Designer for Industry, 1986, Royal Society of Arts, London; fellow, Chartered Society of Designers, London, 1975; member, Royal Institute of British Architects, 1965. **Address:** Great West Plantation, Tring, Hertfordshire HP23 6DA, England.

## Works

*Meridian* ceramic sanitary fittings, for Adamsez, from 1965.
*Hedway* signposting system in stainless steel, for Syncronol Industries Limited, from 1970.

*Modric Limbar* hospital rails and handle in aluminum and steel, for G. and S. Allgood Limited, from 1972.

*Modric* cloakroom system in aluminum, for C. and S. Allgood Limited, from 1973.

Computer disc storage furniture in plastic laminate, for Data Efficiency, from 1976.

Barrier rail system in stainless steel, for Marler Haley, 1977.

Office furniture system, for Hille International, 1979.

Intravenous operation workstation in stainless steel and plastic, for Travenol, 1979.

Wood-burning stove in cast iron and brass, for a private client, 1979.

*System 94* anti-vandal sanitary fittings in aluminum, for W. G. Sissons, from 1981.

Cubicle and washroom system in laminated aluminum and steel, for Mallinson-Denny and Brooke Bond Liebig, from 1981.

Mirror storage system in wood, glass and metal, for Finnmirror, 1981.

Security system in thermoplastic mouldings, for Reed International, 1983.

*Vallum* ceiling tile system in perlite, for Themmo-Acoustic Products, from 1983.

Low-voltage light fittings, for Concord, 1984.

Conservatory in wood, glass and cemfil, for Pilkington, 1984.

*Min* table system in brass, glass, wood and cast iron, for Messin Oy, 1985-88.

*Modric Spectra* electrostatic paint colour system, for G. and S. Allgood Limited, from 1986.

*Modric Unilite* hardware in photoluminescent plastic, for G. and S. Allgood Limited, from 1988.

*Sport* changing cubicles in stainless steel and solid laminate, for Bushboard Parker-Celcon, from 1988.

**Publications**

**By TYE: articles**—in *The Architect* (London), March 1976; *Architects' Journal* (London), 1 December 1976; *Architectural Review* (London), May 1978; *The Designer* (London), November 1978.

**On TYE: books**—*Modern Design in Metal* by Richard Stewart, London, 1979; *New Design for Old,* exhibition catalogue with texts by Helen Hamlyn, Eric Midwinter, and others, London, 1986; *Eye for Industry: Royal Designers for Industry 1936-1986* by Fiona MacCarthy and Patrick Nuttgens, London, 1986; *International Design Yearbook 1988-1989* edited by Arata Isozaki, London, 1988; **articles**—in *Architectural Review* (London), October 1976; *House and Garden* (London), March 1977; *MD: Moebel Interior Design* (Leinfelden), March 1977; *RIBA Journal* (London), August 1977, August 1978; *Architecture + Urbanism* (Tokyo), February 1979; *Ville Giardini* (Milan), September 1981; *Building* (London), 16 April 1982; *Building Enquirer* (London), June 1988.

\*

Only 1/200th of the weight of coffee is the oil which gives coffee its lovely smell and taste. Without this, it is just blackish caffeine-water.

Design is like that. It takes very little to make or spoil it, and very few people can honestly provide that special ingredient which makes all the difference.

What is the origin of this quality?

I do not see it coming from value analysis, ease of manufacture, doing what the wholesaler wants, ergonomics, or market research. The answer is so simple that it seems too easy; yet it is easy, and also profound. The following poem from our Christmas card of 1975 explains:

WHY IS THIS SO BEAUTIFUL? IT HAS NO STYLE NO AESTHETICS. IT'S PURPOSEFUL NOT ARTFUL.

Fortunately, the client doesn't have to understand the working of the designer, but just let the right designer get on with it for him.

—Alan Tye

\*       \*       \*

The 1950s in Britain were an exciting time for young architects and designers. The opportunity to build after more than ten years of inactivity, combined with the development of design consciousness fostered by the Council of Industrial Design and given sudden impetus by the 1951 Festival of Britain, stimulated a new and enterprising school of designers. Ready to look anew at accepted solutions, as well as to experiment with and exploit the technological developments of wartime industry, they saw themselves as builders of a new Britain.

Alan Tye, like most students of his generation, was strongly influenced by Scandinavian designers, in his case, by the Danish and, in particular, by Arne Jacobsen, for whom he later worked. He claims also to have been influenced by James Stirling, who was one of his teachers; Stirling's direct and uncompromising attitude may be discernible in Tye's approach, but to it must be added the refinement and visual suavity characteristic of the Danish designers.

Tye's first notable success was the 1965 Meridian range of bathroom fittings for Adamsez. Washbasins, WC's, and the like had seldom if ever been the subject of either ergonomic or aesthetic consideration; most were inefficient or ugly, or both. Tye evolved fittings which were not only easy and comfortable to use, easy to clean and maintain, and simple to manufacture and install, but they also looked good. Thus for the first time, bathroom fittings became a considered part of house furniture.

His outstanding achievement came in the following year. Hitherto, British architects could get an integrated range of building ironmongery (door handles, window catches, locks, letter plates) only by importing from Denmark or Germany, a costly and frequently slow process, and by no means a complete solution. In these circumstances, Paul Shirville, managing director of the ironmongery firm of G & S Allgood and chairman of the newly formed Guild of Architectural Ironmongers, asked Tye to design a fully integrated line. Close cooperation between designer, manufacturer, and merchant from the beginning rapidly resulted in the Modric range, based on a modular grid but by no means purely a cold, mathematical exercise. For instance, the standard door handle, carefully calculated ergonomic design though it may appear to be, evolved from a fat candle carved out until it looked good, fit the grid system, and was easy and comfortable to use. The Modric range completely transformed the British market. It alone stands as an example of Tye's philosophy of design: not visual design for its own sake, but design whose beauty is inherent in its fitness for its purpose.

—Gordon Steele

# U

## ULIBARRI, Ximena

Chilean art director and graphic designer

**Born:** Santiago de Chile, 12 May 1947. **Education:** Studied design, Pontificia Universidad Católica de Chile (P.U.C). **Career:** Art director, Publicidad Universitaria, Design Department, P.U.C., from 1975; professor, School of Design, P.U.C. **Exhibitions:** Instituto Chileno-Norteamericano de Cultura Cinetic Art Exhibition, 1969; *Arte Gráfico Publicitario,* Museo Nacional de Bellas Artes, 1984, 1991; *Arte Gráfico Publicitario,* Instituto Cultural Municipalidad de Las Condes, 1986; Bienal de Diseño Gráfico, Chile, 1992, 1994. **Honors:** First Prize in Luminous Painting and Cinetic Art, Instituto Chileno-Norteamericano de Cultura, 1969; First Prize Poster Category, Concurso de Deportes Marinos, Iquique, 1970; First and Second Prize, Poster Category, and Honour Recognition, Brochures, II Concurso de Gráfica Utilitaria Chilena, 1984; First Great Prize, IV Concurso de Arte Gráfico Publicitario, 1991; Great Prize and Excellence Prize, in Images "Mauricio Amster," 1994. **Address:** Publicidad Universitaria, Avda. Lib. Bernardo O'Higgins 406, 5to. Piso, Santiago de Chile, Chile.

**Works**

Art direction, for Craftmanship Fairs, Cinema, and Theater Festivals, P.U.C., 1975-87.
Art direction, for *Revista Universitaria* magazine, P.U.C., from 1978.
Art direction, for Colecciones Editorial, P.U.C.,1985.

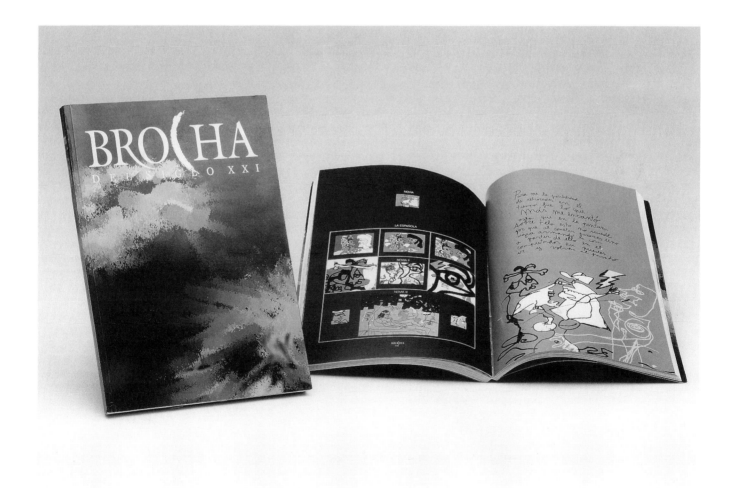

Ximena Ulibarri: *Brocha del Siglo XXI* book design, 1994

Corporate graphic image, for Centro de Extensión, P.U.C., 1986.
Art direction, *170 Años Shell en Chile,* for Shell Chile, 1989.
Art direction, *Explorando el mundo del Arte,* for P.U.C. and Teleduc, 1991.
Art direction, *50 Años de Coca-Cola en Chile,* for Embottelladora Andina S.A., 1991.
Art direction, *La Capacidad de Asombro ante la Vida Cotidiana,* for Unión AFP S.A., 1991.
Art direction, Colección V Centenario, for Cámara Chilena del Libro, 1992.
Annual reports, for Embottelladora Andina S.A., from 1992.
Annual reports, for Empresas Pizzareño S.A., from 1992.
Art direction, *El Hombre y el Mineral,* for Ediciones Despertar, 1993.
Art direction, *Bienaventurados,* for Ediciones Despertar, 1994.
Art direction, *Brocha del Siglo XX,* for Apple-Chile, 1994.
Art direction, *Historia de la Pontificia Universidad Católica de Chile,* for P.U.C., 1994.
Art direction, *La Fiesta: Metamorfosis de lo Cotidiano,* for P.U.C., 1995.
Art direction, *Museo de Artes Decorativas, Casas de Lo Matta,* for Editorial Cal y Canto, 1996.

**Publications**

**On ULIBARRI: books**—*Who's Who in Graphic Design,* Zürich, 1994; **articles**—in *El Mercurio* (Santiago), 1984, 1991, 1992; *Vivienda y Decoración* (Chile), 1991, 1994; *Revista de Publicidad* (Chile), 1991; *Revista Cosas* (Chile), 1991; *Visión Universitaria* (Chile), 1992; *Novum Gebrauchsgraphik* (Munich), August 1992; *Revista Diseño* (Chile), 1992, 1994.

\*

My work and the work of my design team is based on the graphic interpretation of subjects related to the Pontificia Universidad Católica de Chile, for final publication to internal and public areas at the national and international level. I also work with businesses in the design of editorial and corporate graphic images. Besides this, I have created architectural and environmental graphics for events and exhibitions.

Information, articulated through expressions and images, looks for its sense with movement, transparency, volume, and a language that inserts art in design.

Contemporary design has a uniformity that is a result of the universality of computing. Access to typographical sources and software, which suggest the use of certain graphical resources, makes the creation of a cultural or personal identity difficult to achieve, but nevertheless it is possible to gather images coming from several forms of expression, play with them, and apply intervention.

Design mixes the past with present time, creating classics which share space with new lines, colors, and other images, making the design appear new to the contemporary world.

—Ximena Ulibarri

# UNGARO, Emanuel (Matteotti)

French fashion designer

**Born:** Of Italian parents, in Aix-en-Provence, 13 February 1933. **Education:** Educated at the Lycée, Aix-en-Provence, 1943-50. **Family:** Married Laura; children: Cosima. **Career:** Worked in his father's

**Emanuel Ungaro: Silk red dress, autumn/winter Haute Couture collection, 1996**

tailoring business, Aix-en-Provence, 1951-54; stylist, at Maison Camps tailoring company, Paris, 1955-57; designer, Balenciaga fashion house, Paris, 1958-64, and head of design, Balenciaga fashion house, Madrid, 1959-61; designer, Courrèges fashion house, Paris, 1964-65; founded Emanuel Ungaro SARL couture house, Avenue Mac Mahon, Paris, 1965-67, renamed Emanuel Ungaro S.A. upon move to 2 Avenue Montaigne, Paris, from 1967; launched *Ungaro Parallèle* women's ready-to-wear fashion range, 1968, *Ungaro pour l'Homme* menswear range, 1973, *Ungaro Ter* diffusion line, 1978, *Ungaro Solo Donna* diffusion line, 1982, *Diva* women's fragrance, 1983, *Senso* women's fragrance, 1987, 1993, *Ungaro* women's fragrance, 1990, *Ungaro pour l'Homme* men's fragrance, 1991, *Emanuel* bridge line, 1991, *Ungaro pour l'Homme II* men's fragrance, 1992, *Ungaro pour l'Homme III* men's fragrance, 1993; opened boutiques in Paris and New York, from 1968. **Exhibitions:** *Fashion: An Anthology,* Victoria and Albert Museum, London, 1971. **Honors:** Neiman Marcus Award, Dallas, 1969; Prize for Best Couturier, Mexico, 1971; Golden Spinning Wheel Award, Krefeld, Germany, 1971; Golden Thimble Award (Dé d'Or), Paris, 1980, 1981; Best Five Award, *Women's Wear Daily* (Japan), 1981; Mode Wuche award, Munich, 1990; Prix de la Ville de Marseille, 1991; Ad Honorem, Textile University, China, 1995; Colonna Romana prize, Camera Nazionale della Moda Italiana, Rome, 1995. **Address:** 2 Avenue Montaigne, 75008 Paris, France.

## Works

Film costume designs include—Catherine Deneuve in *Le Sauvage* (Rappeneau), 1975; Gena Rowlands in *Gloria* (Casavettes), 1979; Isabelle Huppert in *La Truite* (Losey), 1981; Isabelle Adjani in *Mortelle Randonnée* (Miller), 1982; Anouk Aimée in *Viva la Vie* (Lelouch), 1983; Aimée in *Success Is the Best Revenge* (Skolimowski), 1984; Aimée in *Vinq Ans Déjà* (Lelouch), 1986.

## Publications

**By UNGARO: articles**—in *Balenciaga,* Paris, 1988.

**On UNGARO: books**—*The Fashion Makers* by Leonard Halliday, London, 1966; *Fashion: An Anthology by Cecil Beaton,* exhibition catalogue compiled by Madeleine Ginsburg, London, 1971; *Paris Fashion: The Great Designers and Their Creations* edited by Ruth Lynam, London, 1972; *In Vogue: Sixty Years of Celebrities and Fashion* by Georgina Howell, London, 1975, 1978, New York, 1976; *A History of Fashion* by J. Anderson Black and Madge Garland, London, 1975, 1980; *25 Ans de Marie-Claire de 1954 a 1979,* compiled by Françoise Mohrt, Paris, 1979; *Fashion 2001* by Lucille Khornak, London, 1982; *The Collector's Book of Twentieth Century Fashion* by Frances Kennett, London and New York, 1983; *Les Années 60* by Anne Bony, Paris, 1983; *McDowell's Directory of Twentieth Century Fashion* edited by Colin McDowell, London, 1984; *The Encyclopaedia of Fashion from 1840 to the 1980s* by Georgina O'Hara, London, 1986; *Emanuel Ungaro,* with texts by Federico Fellini, Katia D. Kaupp, Yves Navarre, Hélène de Turckheim, and Alain Weill, and photographs by Richard Avedon, Milan, 1992.

*

Memories from my childhood of Aix-en-Provence: sunshine, pink stone, and fountains. What many people call *joie de vivre.* A privileged place to grow up. Where there is beauty. And gravity too. Aix is a capital city of classical culture. It is also the mountain of Sainte-Victoire, Cézanne: Impressionism is there.

I learned my trade with my father. A feeling for work well done, the perfect garment: this I owe to him. At 22, I enter the House of Balenciaga as a "qualified tailor's assistant." In my six years with this grand *couturier,* I discover perseverance, pride in my job, and a frenzied taste for work; and freedom, too, of the kind qualified by constraint and respect for restrictions. A feeling for clothes worn and lived in, a sense of movement, all this I learn from him. After these six years, I launch out fully armed, or should I say disarmed, as an artist is when he dares to be himself.

Fashion defines itself, and I pave the way for it. The dress designer in me is at one and the same time humble, purposeful, and terribly proud. Pride in colour and treatment of colour. I love whatever sings to me. I love Debussy and jazz, Uccello and Motherwell, Proust and Handke, colours, colour values, every kind of Impressionism. I love the warmth of the South and the rigours of the North. In this, I am fundamentally European, a Westerner, constantly torn between my Mediterranean origins and my aspirations, which are Nordic, Saxon, Germanic. As for music, I was about to forget the School of Vienna. I love dissonances, the superimposition of tones, the interaction of pattern and line.

In reality, every woman creates the dress she wears. A designer worth his salt, who deserves the name of couturier, has to capture her verve and interpret her desires. That's my metier.

—Emanuel Ungaro

\* \* \*

It is not surprising that Emanuel Ungaro's first collection, presented in 1965, acknowledged debts both to Cristobal Balenciaga and to Andre Courrèges, since the Parisian fashion designer had spent six years apprenticed to the widely influential Balenciaga and had worked with Courrèges. From the beginning of his career, Ungaro's has been a combination of the geometric silhouette and minidressed Courrèges look with a more classic and less faddish touch, stressing the feminine and recalling his connections with Balenciaga.

Exemplary of Ungaro's designs of the late 1960s for day and evening wear for women are A-line minidresses with tone-on-tone inserts, Bermuda shorts under shifts or minidresses, jumpers in rabbit fur, and pleated print shirts with long jackets in suedes and wool. He was making wide use of leather and the pantsuit in outfits such as his flared, long, leather jacket teamed with calfskin pants of 1969. Always, Ungaro incorporated a variety of accessories, such as white, knee-length socks and black, patent-leather shoes to help achieve the youthful, freedom-loving mood he desired. He wanted to create outfittings which were "more than a dress" for women of individual personality with a vivacious flair. During this period, Ungaro became known for his quirky combinations of patterns, textures, and colors mingled together and layered in outfits which blend contemporary flavor with clean-lined elegance.

As he moved into the decade of the 1970s, Ungaro slowly but surely tempered the stiffness and toughness of his work from the previous decade, evolving toward a more graceful, feminine tone, using soft fabrics such as crepe, satin, and Qiana and concentrating on a more flowing line and liquid silhouette. For a period during the 1970s, entranced by the man-tailored look which was then coming into vogue, Ungaro designed outfits such as knickers with high boots accompanied by canvas coat and big-brimmed hat. But the characteristic fusion with classic line and individualistic flavor persisted and came to the fore again toward the end of the decade, showing itself in Ungaro's 1977 flared plaid coat superimposed by a soft, large shawl of another plaid.

During the mid 1980s, Ungaro enjoyed a resurgence in acclaim, giving a boost in America to Parisian couture and gaining such significant recognition as to bring him comparisons with Yves Saint Laurent, to whom he is said to be running "a close second." Ungaro's 1983 collection was precisely cut, attuned to the very feminine woman, vibrantly colorful and patterned, and geared for flowing movement and sex appeal. There are daring cocktail dresses, draped and hitched in several places, in cobblestone-patterned silk jacquard. One is worn with a square-cut coat in fuchsia mohair with seaming visible. Among the many jackets are one which is yoked of black, cream, and gray wool and another which is lightly quilted with an asymmetric opening of plum and sea-blue wool. There are ample touches of flamboyance in a number of fox boas and slightly wild hats, and, most dramatically, in the Belle Epoque gown with puffed sleeves and swept-up skirt of diagonal stripes worn with a boa around the neck. Ungaro's mid 1980s work shows him reaching a mature style which has evolved steadily through longtime study and practice into a unique synthesis which lends contemporary vigor to the tradition of Parisian high fashion for women.

—Barbara Cavaliere

# URBANIEC, Maciej (Jerzy)

Polish graphic designer

**Born:** Zwierzyniec, 1 September 1925. **Education:** Studied at the School of Fine Arts, Wroclaw, 1952-54; Academy of Fine Arts, Warsaw, 1954-58. **Military Service:** Served in Polish resistance, Warsaw uprising, 1944. **Family:** Married Maria Kotarbinska in 1952; children: Barbara. **Career:** Freelance poster, advertisement and graphic designer, Warsaw, from 1958. Lecturer, at the School of Fine Arts, Wroclaw; head of the graphics department, at the Academy of Fine Arts, Warsaw. **Member:** Zwiazek Polskich Artystow Plastykow, Warsaw; Alliance Graphique Internationale, Paris. **Exhibitions:** Dom Artysty Plastyka, Warsaw, 1958; WAG Gallery, Szczecin, 1969; Biuro Wystaw Artystycznych, Radom, 1975; Biuro Artystycznych, Poznan, 1975; Galeria Dom Wojska Pokskiego, Warsaw, 1975; Biuro Wystaw Artystycznych, Kielce, 1976. **Collections:** Vilanov Poster Museum, Warsaw; National Museum, Poznan; Centre Georges Pompidou, Paris; Stedelijk Museum, Amsterdam. **Honors:** Tadeusz Trepkowski Prize, Warsaw, 1958; Social Poster of the Year Awards, Warsaw, 1964-82; Five Gold Medals, Katowice Poster Biennale, 1967-78; Silver Medal, Brno Graphics Biennale, 1970, 1974; Bronze Medal, Leipzig Book Fair, 1970, 1982. **Address:** Academicka 3, m.94, 02-038 Warsaw, Poland.

## Publications

**By URBANIEC: articles**—in *Projekt* (Warsaw), no. 3, 1974.

**On URBANIEC: books**—*Polish Poster Art Today* by Szymon Bojko, Warsaw, 1972; *107 Grafici dell'AGI,* with texts by Renzo Zorzi and Franco Grignani, Venice, 1974; *100 Years of Circus Posters* by Jack Renner, New York, 1974; *Glad Konst* by Sten Mollerstrom and Bra Becker, Hoganas, 1975; *Contemporary Polish Posters in Full Color* edited by Joseph S. Czestochowski, New York, 1979; *The Polish Poster 1970-1978,* with introduction by Zdzislaw Schubert, Warsaw, 1979; *The Language of Graphics* by Edward Booth-Clibborn and Daniele Baroni, London, 1980; *Who's Who in Graphic Art* edited by Walter Amstutz, Dubendorf, 1982.

\*

I am a poster designer. My idea is the synthetic expression of thoughts. If I could better express my thoughts in words than in images, I would not make posters but would have become a writer. Forgive my modesty; the older a man is, the shorter his biography because many events lose their significance. I have executed more than 300 posters, which after I have painted them, begin a life of their own, and I am unable to follow their plights.

—Maciej Urbaniec

\*     \*     \*

Let us take two posters and hang them together. The first attacks us with vulgar colors and, even more, with its shocking subject—a circus performer in a somewhat forced, unnatural position with raised, crossed legs. She has the torso of the *Mona Lisa,* Leonardo's famous lady. The top of this poster bears the word "circus." After a moment of confusion, you have to laugh. All those trivial colors

and the obviously cheap trick with the *Mona Lisa* don't offend; rather, they play together so well that we draw some conclusions immediately. One: the artist is winking his eye on the real cheapness of the circus as an art form. Another: He makes a point about his own discipline by suggesting the question "Is a poster truly art?"

The second poster we discuss is a world apart from the previous one. It is a simple composition of letters composed of thick, brutal, raw rope against a clear, glowing red background. The rope letters spell "The Wedding," the title of a play by Stanislaw Wyspianski, famous Polish playwright of the early twentieth century. *The Wedding* is a traumatic, agonizing discussion about the fate of Poland, the struggle for freedom, lost hopes, futile dreams, the faults of national character, lack of ideology. Every Pole remembers this message, keeps it in the corner of his mind, for it is still very accurate almost a century later.

Both of these posters are signed by Maciej Urbaniec, one of the true masters of the Polish school. His approach differs from that of such colleagues as Tomaszewsk or Starowievski whose works are recognizable at a glance because of Urbaniec's craftsmanship. He could paint anything in an almost Renaissance manner. But he sees no point in working in one style on every poster he creates. His major concern is to reach "the target" in the simplest and most powerful way. Every subject is carefully studied by the artist in order to choose the best way to convey the message. Among the techniques he uses are assemblage, collage, tempera painting, and colored-paper cut-outs. Despite this versatility. Urbaniec never overdoes his work and his solutions are always intelligent.

Another important factor is humor in all possible cases. His Mona Lisa's, "Renaissance" madonnas making faces—somewhat too serious looking "icons" that are almost better done than Andrei Rublev's originals—many of his works make us smile, help us to distance ourselves from the not too happy reality of daily life. When matters are serious, he is sharp, strikes to a painful point, no gimmicks, no smoky allusions. In every other situation, he tries to find the optimistic side of the problem, make a little face on you, on himself, and on the subject.

A formidable teacher, Urbaniec is loved by his students. He doesn't act flamboyantly, and the atmosphere in his studio scarcely resembles the master-pupil scheme. The pressure to learn and perform well and think fast is not evident after a short time. He tries to keep a rather low-key, intimate communication with his "chickens." Day after day, the conversation continues on equal terms. Literature, theatre, the movies, art, jokes, everyday happenings, a little gossip—that's it. Meanwhile, a relationship is growing. The student doesn't feel it at the beginning, but he is slowly lured into thinking about the artist and society, about the graphic designer and the variety of art's problems. Slowly, everyone is trapped by Urbaniec's method and comes to know something very important— that after graduating from the Academy, he has a friend, a true guide, defender, and the best advisor in the difficult, fresh years of real professional testing that confront each young artist.

—Jan Sawka

# URBAŃSKI, Leon

Polish typographer and graphic designer

**Born:** Tarnow, 11 September 1926. **Education:** Studied at the High School of Fine Arts, Warsaw, 1946-48; Academy of Fine Arts, Warsaw, 1948-59. **Family:** Married Krystyna Urbański in 1952; children: Jacek, Marek, and Dorota. **Career:** Freelance book and graphic designer, Warsaw, from 1959; art director, Arkady Publishers, Warsaw. Associate professor of graphic arts, Academy of Fine Arts, Warsaw, 1977-82. **Member:** Juror, Leipzig Book Fair, 1977-82; secretary of the executive council, Association of Polish Artists, Warsaw. **Collections:** Plock Scientific Society Collection, Muzeum Ksiazki, Wroclaw; Regional Museum, Sanok; Deutsche Bucherei, Leipzig. **Honors:** Gold Medal, Polish Association of Book Publishers; Leipzig Book Fair Medal, 1959, 1965, and Grand Prize, 1971; teaching award, Academy of Fine Arts, Warsaw, 1978, 1980; Knight of the Order of Polonia Restituta, Warsaw; Merited Activist in Culture, Warsaw. **Address:** ul. Gagarina 33, m.25, 00-595 Warsaw, Poland.

## Publications

**On URBANSKI: books—***Grafika Polska* by Danuta Wroblewska, Warsaw, 1983.

*

I work in a narrow branch of graphic arts. My main interest is the world in every form, from an exclamation to an epic poem, and the ways by which it reaches its audience. I wish for the reception of words to bring enjoyment and to be like the touch of a hand in today's mechanized world. I would like to work for a million people. I hate bibliophiles, rare books, and elitism. I want to do things for everybody. My tastes are somewhat traditional, and I would like to preserve in this crazy desensitized world something that has an old-fashioned name—beauty which can be found in the unique perfume label, in a sound commercial, in the seriousness of a monument, or in the esthetic appearance of a book.

I have to admit that I have never considered my work as art but, rather, as a kind of social service. I am only a designer. It would be possible to classify my work as an art only if the work of the engineer Eiffel or of the technicians who built the American cosmic pendulum could be considered as great art.

Jan Tschichold said that only two in a thousand graphic designers have an ideal sense of proportion, and they become typographers.

How am I different from my colleagues? Most of the time, they already have the shape for their word when they begin. For me, the word form comes much later because I wait for the word to suggest it. Sometimes it comes immediately, but other times, it takes a long time. That is why I am so sensitive to the text. I never work on poorly formulated or bad sounding texts.

The reason that I have never wanted to exhibit my works is that the intention of my design manifests itself best in its natural function: a book, when it is being read; a sign, when it is warning; a diploma, when in the hands of someone who earned it. If they were displayed, all these objects would look dead. If I ever do arrange an exhibit of my work, it will be one in which my prints will be passed from hand to hand or one that will show all stages of my work.

I love my work, and at the same time I hate it. I also love music, and I think that the two of them have something in common.

I am a perfectionist in that I am satisfied only with my own work. When I stand by the type case or when I work on book-binding, I know that I have a full command of my work. The work of others always has less spirit for me.

I regret that in Poland it is not customary to have a private assistant. Although I dream of one, I am aware that he would have a hard time with me.

—Leon Urbański

\*   \*   \*

As much as typography in general is a field for industrious people, Leon Urbański's nature makes it a benedictine task. Being a technical perfectionist forces him to devote to each project more plans of form and arrangement, more studies of coloring than are usually done. Besides that, Urbański is an ambitious man, full of a sense of his own independence. This genetic inheritance from mountaineer ancestors allied with a line of Austro-Hungarian, Galician gentry gives him a strong sense of identity, a strong foundation in the center of an expressive historical culture.

It is difficult to say what is most interesting in Urbański: his own powerful creativity, his penetrating and analytic understanding of plastic and word forms (the twin means of communication), or his didactic passion for opening the talents of others. As a typographer, he does not close himself in specialization. Rather, he responds to contemporary art and technology, he understands literature and music. He is interested in linguistic knowledge. However, as a humanist, he feels the weight of technology on culture.

Working in almost every field of graphic design, he believes, above all else, in the power of the book as the basic means for the transfer of thoughts—independent of time, space, and all adversity of fate. He believes in its culturally creative force. He also sees that its architecture and form are a condensation of the characteristics of the reality which shapes it. All elements of the book ripened between the sixteenth and eighteenth centuries; the sequel consists just of delicate mutations. In letter design, says Urbański, there are no old or new forms, just bad and good ones. The printer's sign will always be supported by that which has already been catalogued. He is, however, interested in the new possibilities of computer technology and electronic recording because these contain different possibilities of expression.

At the Academy of Fine Arts, Urbański was the pupil of professor Andrzej Rudziriski, a good graphic artist and sensitive book artist. From him, he took a classical orientation which he strengthened with his own sense of harmony. In the European milieu, the views of Jan Tschichold and the Swiss typographers were closest to his own, though his outlook was much broader. Urbański's creativity, though contained within the golden canon of the European esthetic of print, introduces into it a certain lightness and romanticism. The best example of these characteristics, as well as the most beautiful connection of the letter with free composition, are to be found in his little volumes of Far Eastern poetry. The lessons learned during his Asian trips showed how consonant his earlier intuitions were with the oriental art of the sign.

Urbański's work as a teacher lasted not quite five years. In such a short time, he was able to accomplish the most difficult thing imaginable in the Department of Graphic Arts of the Academy of Fine Arts: he awoke a great typographical sensitivity in the young people, who were hitherto unconscious of it. He did not so much teach typography, as open students to the essence of the sign and all of its functions and contexts. In general, he directed them to the culture of form. In 1981, at the Leipzig *Internationale*

*Buchkunstausstellung,* his students received the gold medal for their collective work. A year later, his great achievement was a portfolio of typographical exercises with the texts of Czeslaw Milosz. This explains the unprecedented case of such a young teacher being awarded two rector's prizes in such a short span of time.

—Danuta Wróblewska

# VALENTINO
Italian fashion designer

**Born:** Valentino Garavani in Voghera, near Milan, 11 May 1932.
**Education:** Studied French and fashion design, Milan, until 1948; studied at the Chambre Syndicale de Couture, in the École des Beaux-Arts, Paris, 1949-51. **Career:** Assistant designer, in Jean Dessès fashion house, Paris, 1950-55, and in Guy Laroche fashion house, Paris, 1956-58; assistant to Princess Irene Galitzine, 1959; founder and partner, with Giancarlo Giammetti, of Valentino fashion house, Rome, from 1960, and of Valentino Piu interior decor, textile and gift company, Rome, from 1973; showed first ready-to-wear collection, 1962; opened ready-to-wear fashion boutiques in Paris, 1968, Rome, 1972, 1988, Milan, 1979, and in London, 1987; menswear collection introduced, 1972; signature fragrance introduced, 1978; established Rome headquarters in the newly-restored Palazzo Gabnelli, from 1987. Also film costume designer, from 1964. **Exhibitions:** *Fashion: An Anthology,* Victoria and Albert Museum, London, 1971; *Italian Re-Evolution,* La Jolla Museum of Art, California, 1982; Metropolitan Museum of Art, New York, 1982; *40 Years of Italian Fashion,* Trump Tower, New York 1983; *Atelier delle Illusioni,* Castello Sforzesco, Milan, 1985; Royal Academy of Arts, London, 1989; retrospective, Capitoline Museum, Rome, 1991, and New York, 1992. **Honors:** Neiman Marcus Award, 1967, 1988; National Italian American Foundation Award, 1989. **Address:** Piazza Mignanelli 22, 00187 Rome, Italy.

## Publications

**On VALENTINO: books—***Fashion: An Anthology by Cecil Beaton,* exhibition catalogue compiled by Madeleine Ginsburg, London, 1971; *Fashion Merchandizing* by Mary D. Troxell, New York, 1971, 1976; *Fairchild's Dictionary of Fashion* by Charlotte Calasibetta, New York, 1975; *The World of Fashion: People, Places, Resources* by Eleanor Lambert, New York and London, 1976; *Quest for the Best* by Stanley Marcus, New York, 1979; *I Mass Moda: Fatti e Personaggi dell'Italian Look* by Adriana Mulassano, Florence, 1979; *Fashion 2001* by Lucille Khornak, London, 1982; *Italian Re-Evolution: Design in Italian Society in the Eighties,* exhibition catalogue edited by Piero Sartogo, La Jolla, 1982; *Valentino* edited by Franco Mana Ricci, Milan, 1982; *The Collector's Book of Twentieth Century Fashion* by Frances Kennett, London and New York, 1983; *40 Years of Italian Fashion,* exhibition catalogue compiled by B. G. Aragno, Rome, 1983; *Leaders in Fashion: I grandi personaggi della modda* by Maria-Vittoria Alfonsi, Bologna, 1983; *McDowell's Directory of Twentieth Century Fashion* by Colin McDowell, London, 1984; *Il genio antipatico,* exhibition catalogue by Pia Soli, Venice, 1984; *Valentino che Veste di Nuovo* by Marina Cosi, Milan, 1984; *Valentino* by André Leon Talley, Milan, 1984;

*Couture: The Great Designers* by Caroline Rennolds Milbank, New York, 1985; *The Encyclopaedia of Fashion from 1840 to the 1980s* by Georgina O'Hara, London, 1986; *W, The Designing Life* edited by Lois Perchetz, New York, 1987; *The Fashion Conspiracy* by Nicholas Coleridge, London, 1988; *Moda Italia: Creativity and Technology in the Italian Fashion System* by Bonizza Giordani Aragno, Milan, 1988; *Sultans of Style: 30 Years of Fashion and Passion 1960-1990* by Georgina Howell, London, 1990; *Valentino: Thirty Years of Magic,* Rome, 1991; *Orientalism: Visions of the East in Western Dress,* exhibition catalogue by Richard Martin and Harold Koda, New York, 1994; **articles—**"Valentino" in *Current Biography* (New York), November 1973; "Valentino: 25 anni nella moda compiuti" by Marina Pertile in *Vogue* (Milan), September 1984; "Palace Evolution" by Meredith Etherington-Smith and Caroline Clifton-Magg in *Harper's and Queen* (London), June 1989; "Valentino 59-89" by Carlo Ducci and Lele Acquarone in *Vogue* (Milan), September 1989; "Valentino" by Diane Rafferty in *Connoisseur* (New York), August 1990; "Valentino, Take a Bow!" by Mariuccia Casadio in *Interview* (New York), September 1991; "When Valentino Fêtes His Anniversary, There's No Place Like Rome" by Rhoda Koenig in *Vogue* (New York), September 1991; "The Sultan of Style" by Jane Mulvagh in *The European* (London), 1 November 1991; "Our Funny Valentino" by Guy Lesser in *Town and Country* (New York), September 1992; "Hello, Valentino?" by Brooke Shields in *Interview* (New York), September 1992; "Lunch with Mr. Armani, Tea with Mr. Versace, Dinner with Mr. Valentino" by Stephen Schiff in *The New Yorker,* 7 November 1994; "Craft Is in the Details: Artistry is In, Supermodels are Out" by Suzy Menkes in the *International Herald Tribune* (Paris), 24 January 1995; "Valentino: The Sophisticated Lady" in *Women's Wear Daily* (New York), 21 March 1995; "Yves Saint Laurent's Shocking New Color: Black" by Anne-Marie Schiro in the *New York Times,* 22 March 1995; "YSL Plays Safe While Valentino Shines at Night" by Suzy Menkes in the *International Herald Tribune* (Paris), 22 March 1995.

\* \* \*

On the pages of many fashionable magazines, prestigious women of the world have often been featured wearing the feminine, glamorous, and flattering dresses of Valentino. Among them have been Consuelo Crespi, Christina Ford, Gloria Guinness, Audrey Hepburn, and Jacqueline Onassis. The advertisements for various Valentino franchises are exquisitely photographed, often by the French and Japanese, to create a world one imagines to be exclusively of the upper classes.

I often note his dramatic use of floral fabrics, fluidly patterned, occasionally incorporating butterflies, petals, leaves, tropical themes, and some geometrics. Generally, his fabrics are created by such Italian companies as Setanum, Lucchini, Gandini, Taroni, Stucchi, Clerici, and Rainbow. The patterns always complement the feminine lines of the dresses and are often printed in mysterious black with touches, to dramatize, of white or bright colors. I once met a young child wearing a black velveteen Valentino smock with a white pique collar and ribbon trim.

Valentino showed little interest in formal education until he arrived at the Chambre Syndicale in Paris to study cutting and sewing. He left his first position with Jean Dessès to work with Guy Laroche until he returned to Rome, where he opened his first atelier. High fashion, though, was really happening on the runways of the Pitti Palace in Florence. His first collection, introduced there in 1962, was praised and purchased by I. Magnin. At the beginning of the 1970s, he introduced a more accessible ready-to-wear line and opened the first of many boutiques. In the 1980s, there were more than 100 throughout the United States, Europe, and Japan, where he enjoys a flurry over anything he designs.

The Valentino empire comprising couture, ready-to-wear, fashion accessories, lingerie, the home furnishing line Valentino Piu, cosmetics, and the fragrance *Valentino* by Valentino has flourished with the help of nearly three hundred employees as well as the guidance and friendship of partner Giancarlo Giametti.

In the 1990s, Valentino reaches the younger generation with his Oliver line, which is casual but distinctively Valentino. He also has a special eveningwear collection called Valentino Night, which features his couture designs adjusted for a wider audience. In 1991 Valentino celebrated 30 years of designing with a lavish all-night party and a retrospective exhibition in Rome. To his admirers, he represents not only a way of dressing, but a way of life, a life emphasizing opulence and luxury.

—Gillion Skellenger

# VALLIEN, Bertil (Erik)

Swedish glass, ceramics, and metalware designer

**Born:** Stockholm, 17 January 1938. **Education:** Studied under Stig Lindberg, School of Art, Craft and Design, Stockholm, 1957-61; also studied in the United States and Mexico, 1961-63. **Family:** Married Ulrica Hydman in 1963; children: Hampus and Markus. **Career:** Glass designer, since 1963, and Head of Design, 1983-86, Åfors Glasbruk (Kosta Boda Group), Eriksmala; established Rebus Design AB company, working with sandblast sculpture and art glass, Eriksmala, from 1986; also freelance industrial, ceramics and cutlery designer, working for Boda Nova, Gense, Rorstrand, Alfa-Laval, and others. Instructor in Glass Design, University of Stockholm (Konstfackskolan), 1967-83; Pilchuk Glass Center, Washington, 1980-89; artist-in-residence, Rhode Island School of Design, Providence, 1985; also guest lecturer throughout Britain, the United States and Canada, from 1973. **Exhibitions:** Ryder Gallery, Los Angeles, 1963; Bonniers, New York, 1966; George's Gallery, Melbourne, 1968, 1980; Heal's Gallery, London, 1974; Nordiska Kompaniet, Stockholm, 1976; Seibu Gallery, Tokyo, 1980, 1982; David Jones Gallery, Sydney, 1980; Konsthantverkarna, Stockholm, 1980; Gallen Gamla Stan, Stockholm, 1983; Atelier d'Amon, Paris, 1983; Heller Gallery, New York, 1983, 1985, 1987; Norrkoping Museum, Sweden, 1984; Gallery Takanawa-Kai, Tokyo, 1984; Galleri Ikaros, Goteborg, 1985; Galerie Rosenthal, Hamburg, 1986; Collier Gallery, Phoenix, Arizona, 1986; The Works Gallery, Philadelphia, 1987; Gallery Malen, Helsingborg, 1987;

Betsy Rosenfield Gallery, Chicago, 1988; Travers-Sutton Gallery, Seattle, Washington, 1988; Smalands Museum, Vaxo, Denmark, 1988. **Collections:** Nationalmuseum, Stockholm; Rohsska Konstslojdmuseet, Goteborg; Vaxjo Glassmuseum, Sweden; Art Institute of Chicago; Corning Glass Museum, New York; Musée des Arts Décoratifs, Paris; Victoria and Albert Museum, London. **Honors:** Swedish Royal Scholarship, 1961; Young Americans Prize, 1962; Illum Prize, Copenhagen, 1967; Swedish State Major Award for Design, 1970; Most Influential Artist Award, Japan Interior Design magazine, 1981; First Prize for Swedish Design, Nationalmuseum, Stockholm, 1983; Silver Medal, International Art Competition, New York, 1985; Coburger Glass Prize, West Germany, 1985; Formland Prize, Denmark, 1988. **Address:** Åfors Glasbruk, 351 04 Eriksmala, Sweden.

## Works

*Husar* glassware, for Kosta Boda, 1965.
*Spiral* candle-holders, for Dansk Design, 1967.
*Network* decorative blown glass on iron netting, for Kosta Boda, 1977.
*Artist's Collection* range of glass stemware, for Kosta Boda, 1977-89.
*Oktav* glass stemware, for Kosta Boda, 1978.
*Chateau* optically-blown glass stemware, for Kosta Boda, from 1981.
*Oktav* cutlery, for Gense, 1981.
*Ships* sandcast glass sculptures, for Kosta Boda, 1985.
*Next* cutlery, for Boda-Nova, 1986.
*Petit Point* cutlery, for Gense, 1987.
Glass with rubber details, for Kosta Boda, 1987.
*Provence* glassware, for Kosta Boda, 1988.
*Blue Water* decorative glassware, for Kosta Boda, 1988.
*Apostrof* glassware, for Kosta Boda, 1989.
Separator, for Alfa-Laval, 1989.

## Publications

**On VALLIEN: books**—*Glasboken: Historia, Teknik och Form* by Carl F. Hermelin and Elsebeth Welander, Boras, 1980; *Scandinavian Modern Design 1880-1980* edited by David Revere McFadden, New York, 1982; *Form och Tradition i Sverige* edited by Birgitta Walz, Stockholm, 1982; *Bertil Valliens Glass, Sandcasted* by Ulf Thomas Moberg and Ole Terje, Stockholm, 1983; *Contemporary Swedish Design*, exhibition catalogue by Monica Boman, Lennart Lindkvist, and others, Stockholm, 1983; *Den Svenska Formen* by Monica Boman and others, Stockholm, 1985; *Kosta* by Ann Marie Herlitz-Gezelius, Lund, 1987; *Faces of Swedish Design,* exhibition catalogue edited by Monica Boman, Stockholm, 1988; *Bertil Vallien* by Gunnar Lindqvist, Stockholm, 1990.

*       *       *

Bertil Vallien belongs to the generation which received its training at the end of the 1950s, when Swedish design was at its highest point. He studied pottery at the National College of Art and Design in Stockholm under the legendary Kåge disciple, Prof. Stig Lindberg, who died in 1982. Graduating in 1961, Bertil Vallien spent two years in the United States, where he worked as a designer at a small factory. At the same time his duties included practical pottery. Designer or sculptor? That was the question. He opted hand with pottery, and the free Scandinavian style in ceramics was his model.

One profoundly symbolic piece of work which today ranks as the apogee and turning point of a period, is a large earthenware sphere at the National Museum in Stockholm, painted in red lacquer! That was in 1968, the year of rebellion. To Bertil Vallien, who had been teaching at the National College of Art and Design since his return home from America, it was an emancipation from the "Scandinavian Design" which had enclosed him like well-tailored armour plating, obstructing any kind of expansion—the tyranny of good taste.

For almost 20 years now Bertil Vallien has been a designer at the Åfors glassworks, part of the Kosta Boda Group. Services, single pieces and art collections have taken shape in his hands in a never-ceasing flow. There was heavier, more rustic glassware in the 1960s and thinner designs in the 1970s with the highly successful "Octav." Thin-walled octagonal shapes, blown in an iron mold, classic and yet new in design. The serving pieces especially had many exciting new variations of form.

Personal expression has always been a strong point with Bertil Vallien, without being contrived or far-fetched. This is particularly true of his unique and ever-flowing output, not only in glassware. New techniques such as sand-molding glass, netted mold-blowing, and others have given him a firm profile.

As a glassware artist he has always been a rebel and transgressor. Where others utilize the brilliance and reflective power of glass, Vallien creates glass that "eats light," cast in sand molds to have a rough surface and magical, arcane content.

One of the distinguishing qualities of his glassware has been his admirable capacity for getting the glassworkers on his side, and making them active participants in the process. He has always tried to give free rein to their knowledge, and this too is the idea behind the "Artists' Collection." He wanted to be part of the great activity constituted by a glass-works—not so much a conductor as the first violinist. "Glass as a material has difficulty in conveying anything," he says. "It is sufficient unto itself."

Bertil Villien's dilemma is that glass in itself is so beautiful. But he has never hesitated to express profound seriousness even in glass. Using simple and sometimes almost excessively distinct symbols, he can make the decor of his unique glass compositions convey a profounder dimension: the dynamics of the waterfall; the wistful searchings of the flying man; the reindeer as an emblem of nature; the key and the keyhole.

The boats which he cast in glass during the '80s give the impression of having reached a climax. They are small, large, or huge, all of them inscribed with secret symbols. Hovering, floating, inaccessible—uniting all the symbolic ships created by human mythology from the Ship of Dreams to Charon's ferry. It is like peering into the universe and trying to solve its eternal mystery of When and Where: a macro-cosmos within a micro-cosmos. That is where Bertil Vallien is today—a classicist with new forms of expression.

Clay seems to be his most intimate material often in bold combinations. He was the first artist in Sweden to use feathers in sculpture. There is something about Bertil Vallien's interminable flow of creativity that feels like immense, uncomplicated generosity.

And I have still not mentioned his public sculptures, cutlery, or wrought ironwork.

A truly profound and somewhat diffident seriousness combined with an infinite warmth of feeling which also contains a great deal of sensuality and sensuousness, plus a tremendous capacity for giving

of himself—this is how I would like to characterize Bertil Vallien as personality and artist.

—Åke Livstedt

# VANČURA, Jan
Czech stage designer and painter

**Born:** Milevsko, 3 April 1940. **Career:** Glass designer, 1968-1974; freelance art designer, 1974-1986; theatre designer, from 1986. President, United Scenic Artists, from 1993. **Member:** The Union of Czech Creative Artists (Painters); The Union of Czech Creative Artists (Scenography). **Exhibitions:** Prague Quadrennial, Prague, 1979, 1983, 1987, 1991, 1995; Tokyo International Exhibition of Scenography, Tokyo, 1984, Bristol, 1985; 9th Exposition of International Scenography of Costumes for Theatres, Novi Sad, 1990; Exposition of Czech Scenography, Prague, 1991, 1995. **Collections:** National Gallery, Prague; Town Gallery Louny, Litohérioe; Town Gallery Libérec, Olomovc, Prague; Gallery of Central Bohemia, Prague; National Museum, Prague; Memorial of Bohoslav Martino°-Poličus. **Honors:** Silver Medal, 1979, 1983, Gold Medal, 1991, Prague Quadrennial; Silver Medal, Novi Sad, 1990. **Address:** Dobrovskémo 480/8, 46001-Libérec II, Czech Republic.

## Works

Stage designs include—*Tales from the Vienna Woods,* Theatre F. X. Saldy, Libérec, 1974; *The Insect Play,* Theatre F. X. Saldy, Libérec, 1978; *A Poet's Last Love,* Theatre F. X. Saldy, Libérec, 1979; *Der Freischültz,* Theatre F. X. Saldy, Libérec, 1980, 1995; *Musicians,* Theatre F. X. Saldy, Libérec, 1980; *An Opera for Three Asses,* Theatre F. X. Saldy, Libérec, 1981; *La Traviata,* Theatre F. X. Saldy, Libérec, 1982, 1992; *Alína or Prague in a Different Piece of World,* Ústí Nad Labem, 1983; *The Kiss,* Ústí Nad Labem, 1984, Theatre F. X. Saldy, Libérec, 1993, National Theatre, Praha, 1993; *Painted Fairy Tale,* Theatre Prazská-Rokoko, Praha, 1984; *Mignon,* Theatre F. X. Saldy, Libérec, 1984; *The Tragical History of Doctor Faustus,* Theatre F. X. Saldy, Libérec, 1985; *Rodelinda,* State Theatre, Brno, 1985; *Der Vogelhändler,* Ceské Budejovice, 1986; *The Magic Flute,* Theatre F. X. Saldy, Libérec, 1987, *The Flying Dutchman,* Theatre F. X. Saldy, Libérec, 1987; *Little Square,* State Theatre, Brno, 1987; *Indians,* Theatre F. X. Saldy, Libérec, 1987; *Madame Butterfly,* Theatre F. X. Saldy, Libérec, 1987; *Salome,* Theatre F. X. Saldy, Libérec, 1988; *The Marriage of Figaro,* National Theatre, Praha, 1988, 1992, Theatre F. X. Saldy, Libérec, 1994; *Henry IV,* Theatre F. X. Saldy, Libérec, 1988; *The Barber of Seville,* Theatre F. X. Saldy, Libérec, 1988, Zemské Theatre, Brno, 1991; *Orpheus in the Underworld,* Theatre F. X. Saldy, Libérec, 1988, *Manon,* Theatre F. X. Saldy, Libérec, 1989; *Carmen,* State Theatre, Ostrava, 1989; *The North Against the South,* Ceské Budejovice, 1989; *Star Comedy,* Theatre F. X. Saldy, Libérec, 1989; *Asanace,* Theatre F. X. Saldy, Libérec, 1990; *Ludi Mariae,* State Theatre, Brno, 1990; *Spalíček,* Theatre F. X. Saldy, Libérec, 1990; *Strange Afternoon of Dr. Zvonko Burke,* Theatre F. X. Saldy, Libérec, 1990; *Snow White and the Seven Dwarfs,* Theatre F. X. Saldy, Libérec, 1991; *Bat,* Theatre F. X. Saldy, Libérec, 1991; *Don Giovanni,* Theatre F. X.

**Jan Vančura: G.F. Händel's *Rodelinda*, Janáček Opera Brno, 1985**

Saldy, Libérec, 1991, Theatre Josefa Kajetána Tyla, Plzen, 1995; *Coppélia,* Theatre F. X. Saldy, Libérec, 1992; *Czech Year,* Theatre Branou II, Praha, 1993, *Fidelio,* Music Theatre Stadt Görlitz, 1993; *Moon,* Theatre F. X. Saldy, Libérec, 1993; *Whirl,* Labyrint, Praha, 1993; *Paddle and Rose,* Labyrint, Praha, 1993; *Cabbage Soup,* Theatre F. X. Saldy, Libérec, 1993; *Merry Widow,* Theatre F. X. Saldy, Libérec, 1993; *Polish Blood,* Krusnohorské Theatre, Teplice, 1994; *Merchant of Venice,* Theatre F. X. Saldy, Libérec, 1994; *Lantern,* Stredoceské Theatre, Kladno, 1994; *Don Carlos,* Theatre F. X. Saldy, Libérec, 1995; *Undina,* Theatre F. X. Saldy, Libérec, 1995; *Two Nights with Girl,* Theatre F. X. Saldy, Libérec, 1995.

**Publications**

On VANCURA: books—*Czech Scenography of XX Century,* Prague, 1982; *The Mirror of World Theatre,* Prague, 1995; articles—*Interscena* (Prague), February/March 1982, January/February 1983; *Theatre* (Prague) January 1991, February 1991; *TD&T* (New York), January 1991, March 1991, January 1993.

*

Theorists say that I am a resuscitator of painted decoration. I answer that painted decoration replaces three dimension theatre decoration when the budget of my small provincial theatre is low. I often do not have a patient technical staff and satisfying light conditions in the theatre I work for. Painted decoration in my situation is not the aim, but the way of saving something. Theorists judge my becoming famous with the help of this provisional arrangement.

Happy is the theatre designer, whose director of a drama is on the same frequency.

Nowadays there is no chance for a theatre designer to choose a suitable director of a drama unless the designer is not an owner of a theatre.

I admire directors of a drama who have their visual imagination—it is not a typical phenomenon. Despite this fact, we are creatively dependant on them.

I do not have enough power to become a director of a drama. Some theatre designers succeeded in both activities, for example, Ponelle and Zeffirelli.

—Jan Vančura

\*      \*      \*

Born in 1940 in Milevsko, Jan Vančura did not contemplate a career in stage design as a youth, concentrating instead on industrial design and glass making in his formal schooling; in the evenings he studied painting. In 1974 he was invited by stage designer Jaroslav Malina and director Karel Kříž to collaborate on a production of *Tales From the Vienna Woods.* Following that he designed *The Insect Comedy* for Kříž in 1976, and devoted himself from then on to scenography.

As his career began to develop, Vančura found himself more and more attracted to opera, and he began to develop his own unique personal style. Vančura admits that he is a Romantic, but his designs are not lifeless copies of old ideas. Instead, they combine elements of past theatrical design styles with a new and sophisticated vision.

This vision is clearly evident in Vančura's setting for Handel's *Rodelinda* and shows his simultaneous fascination with two things: one, the techniques, materials, and ideas of Baroque and Romantic stagecraft, and two, the ornate and fantastic architecture of the opera houses in his own country and throughout Europe. But his designs—his sensitive re-working of historical stagecraft, his hyperrealistic style of painting, and his ever present incorporation of the proscenium arch—are more than just chances for him to indulge in his dual loves of illusionistic painting and fantasy theatre architecture. His designs are actually dialogues about the function of stage design and the relationship of the design to the environment and its proportion in the theatre. The designs carry on this dialogue in two ways.

First, his designs are intended as statements of fantasy. His designs are a world of the imagination which he and the audience could freely enter into—a world that stood as a buffer between normal human aspirations and the crushing and mundane routine of the socialist ideal which was forcibly imposed on the population following the Soviet invasion of 1968. Second, many of his designs are also intended to engage both the drama and the spectator in a dialogue with a specific theatrical space. His designs are speculations on the magic world of opera and the beautiful opera houses of Central Europe. In 1988 Vančura designed *The Marriage of Figaro* for the National Theatre in Prague. But he also did a special rendering that showed that same setting in the Stavovske Theatre in Prague, which has a special relationship with Mozart. *Don Giovanni* premiered in this theatre in 1787, and Vančura's painting/set rendering is his way of asserting that his design for *The Marriage of Figaro* "belongs" in the Stavovske Theatre. It is his statement about the special symbiotic relationship of the design and the opera and the theatre. In performance, Vančura says, the design and the opera and the theatre derive strength from one another. A new source of energy is created that does not know the bounds of time and space. We are present in the theatre and the time of Mozart, and Mozart is present with us. It is an enchanting and mystical idea that transcends the all too often routine concerns of theatrical production, and, for however brief a time, the reality that was Czechoslovakia under the Communists. This sense of transcendence and dreaming is the key to understanding Vančura's work for the stage. It permeates all of his designs and epitomizes his philosophy: "Theatre, opera, is not a business. It is a dream."

Vančura's work is unique among his contemporaries in Czechoslovakia—perhaps even in the world, and has been so recognized by the many prizes he has won in international design competitions. No designer in our time, with the possible exception of Eugene Berman, has been able to combine a love of period architecture, traditional stagecraft, and superior painting technique with a transforming contemporary imagination and a underlying philosophy that reaffirms our most deeply felt human need for theatre. We need theatre, Vančura's work shows us, because theatre represents our dreams.

—Delbert Unruh

# VAN DEN AKKER, Koos

American fashion designer

**Born:** The Hague, Netherlands, 16 March 1939; emigrated to the United States in 1968, naturalized, 1982. **Education:** Studied at the Royal Academy of Arts, The Hague, 1956-58; L'École Guerre Lavigne, Paris, 1961. **Military Service:** The Royal Dutch Army, 1958-60. **Career:** Worked as an apprentice designer, in the Christian Dior fashion house, Paris, 1963-65; freelance designer, establishing own custom fashion boutique, The Hague, 1965-68; designer, in the Eve Stillman lingerie company, New York, 1969-70; freelance designer, establishing own boutiques on Columbus Avenue, New York, 1971-75, and on Madison Avenue, New York, from 1975; opened shop in Beverly Hills, California, 1978; established separate showrooms on Seventh Avenue, New York, from 1978; introduced diffusion line, Hot House, 1983. Has designed clothing for Bill Cosby, Elizabeth Taylor, Cher, Erica Jong, Barbara Walters, Diahann Carroll, Marilyn Horne, Glenn Close, Ringo Starr, Madonna, George Benson, and others. **Collections:** Kostum Museum, The Hague; Metropolitan Museum of Art, New York. **Honors:** Gold Coast Award, 1978; American Printed Fabrics Council Tommy Award, 1982. **Address:** 550 7th Avenue, 18th Floor, New York, New York 10018, USA.

## Works

Collaged fur coat range, for Ben Kahn Furs, from 1981.
Handbag range, for Meyers Manufacturing, 1986-88.

Couture lingerie collections, for La Lingerie stores, from 1987.
Collaged upholstery furniture ranges, for James II Galleries, from 1988.

## Publications

**On VAN DEN AKKER: books**—*Fashion 2001* by Lucille Khornak, London, 1982; *The Encyclopaedia of Fashion from 1840 to the 1980s* by Georgina O'Hara, London, 1986; **articles**—"Designer Koos van den Akker: Berserk on the Surface" by Martha de Llosa in *American Fabrics and Fashions* (New York), Spring 1980; "The Uncrowned King of Collage" by James A. Revson in *Newsday* (New York), 9 August 1984; "Koos, the Master of Collage" by David Page Coffin in *Threads* (Newtown, Connecticut), December/January 1989-90; "New York Now" in *Women's Wear Daily* (New York), 9 April 1990; "Koos Comes Back" by Chuck Struensee in *Women's Wear Daily* (New York), 23 March 1993.

\*

I paint with fabrics, as a painter paints with paint. Fabrics are where it all starts. I create my own fabrics by collages and combinations.

—Koos van den Akker

# VASSOS, John

American illustrator and graphic, display, interior, and industrial designer

**Born:** Of Greek parents, in Bucharest, Romania, 23 October 1898; emigrated to the United States in 1919, naturalized, 1924. **Education:** Studied at Robert College, Constantinople, 1912-14; Fenway Art School, Boston, 1920; studied with the painter John Singer Sargent, Boston Museum of Fine Arts School, 1921; studied with George Bridgman, John Sloan, Charles Hawthorne and Louis Bouche, Art Student's League, New York, 1921-22; New York School of Design, 1923. **Military Service:** Served with the British Army, in Gallipoli, 1916-18, and with the United States Army intelligence unit, in North Africa, 1942-45, Lieutenant-Colonel. **Family:** Married Ruth Carriere in 1923 (died, 1965). **Career:** Worked as assistant stage designer to Joseph Urban, Boston Opera Company, and promotional graphics designer, Columbia Records, Boston, 1921; freelance commercial illustrator, muralist, and display designer, working for *Harper's Bazaar,* Macy's, Saks Fifth Avenue, Namm's Lord and Taylor, Best and Company, Bonwit Teller Packard, French Lines, and others, New York, from 1923; industrial designer, for Waterman, Remington, Dupont, Savage Arms, Imperial Cutlery, Perey Turnstiles, Egli Lighting, American Telephone and Telegraph Company, and others, New York, from 1926; established New York Display Company design studio, New York, 1924; Design Consultant, RCA Victor Company, New York, 1932-74. Lecturer, Pratt Institute, Brooklyn, Syracuse University, New York, and Vassar College, Poughkeepsie, New York. Founder-President, Industrial Design Institute, New York, 1938-41. **Exhibitions:** New York Public Library; Toledo Public Library, Ohio; New School for Social Research, New York; Riverside Museum, New York; Silvermine Art

Guild, Connecticut, 1977; *Art Deco,* Finch College Museum, New York; *High Style: 20th Century American Design,* Whitney Museum, New York, 1985; *The Machine Age in America 1918-1941,* Brooklyn Museum, 1986. **Collections:** Athens Museum, Greece; Athens Public Library, Greece; Syracuse University, New York; Greek Museum, Washington, D.C. **Honors:** Greek Cross of the Golden Phoenix, 1945; Industrial Designers Institute Award, New York, 1955, 1961, 1968; Paidea Award, Hellenic University Club of New York, 1964; American Society of Neo-Hellenic Studies Award, New York, 1973. Fellow, Silvermine Guild of Artists, Connecticut, 1973. **Died:** Norwalk, Connecticut, 6 December 1985.

## Works

Mural for Rivoli Cinema, New York, c. 1928.
*Sound and Fury* mural for Riviera Cinema, New York, c. 1928.
Lucite fountain pen, for Waterman, 1928.
"Passimeter" turnstile, for Perey Company, 1929.
"Magic Lock" adjustable table and standard lamps, for Egli Company, 1929.
Mural for United Artists Egyptian Theater, Los Angeles, c.1930.
Chromium flatware cutlery, for Wallace Silverware Company, 1930.
Mural for WCAU Radio Station, Philadelphia, 1932.
Electron microscope housing, for RCA, 1934.
Kitchen utensils, for Remington Dupont, 1934.
Plastic radio with horizontal tuning dial, for RCA, 1934.
RCA Victor Special portable phonograph, 1935.
*Eternal Quest of Electronics* mural for RCA office, Washington, D.C., c. 1935.
Mural for Military Electronic Center, Van Nuys, California, c. 1950.
U.S. Pavilion, New Delhi Trade Fair, 1955.
U.S. Pavilion, Karachi Trade Fair, 1955.
Refrigerated 400-cup Coca-Cola dispenser, 1956.
Undersea mural for Condado Beach Hotel, San Juan, Puerto Rico, c. 1958.
Books illustrated include—*Salome* by Oscar Wilde, New York, 1927; *The Ballad of Reading Gaol* by Oscar Wilde, New York, 1928; *The Harlot's House and Other Poems* by Oscar Wilde, New York, 1929; *Elegy in a Country Churchyard* by Thomas Gray, New York, 1931; *Kubla Khan* by Samuel Taylor Coleridge, New York, 1933.

## Publications

**By VASSOS: books**—*Contempo: This American Tempo,* with Ruth Vassos, New York, 1929; *Ultimo: An Imaginative Narration of Life Under the Earth,* with Ruth Vassos, New York, 1930; *Phobia,* New York, 1931; *Humanities,* with Ruth Vassos, New York, 1935; *Contempo, Phobia, and Other Graphic Interpretations,* with foreword by P. K. Thomajan, New York, 1976; **articles**—"Controlled Light" in *Interiors* (New York), February 1948.

**On VASSOS: books**—*American Design Ethic* by Arthur J. Pulos, London, and Cambridge, Massachusetts, 1983; *High Style: 20th Century American Design,* exhibition catalogue by David Gebhard, Esther McCoy, and others, New York, 1985; *An Introduction to Design and Culture in the Twentieth Century* by Penny Sparke, London, 1986; *The Machine Age in America 1918-1941,* exhibition catalogue by Richard Guy Wilson and Dianne H. Pilgrim, New

York, 1986; **articles**—"A Half-century of Design" in *Industrial Design* (New York), June 1971; "John Vassos: Master Designer" in *Fairpress* (Fairfield, Connecticut), 10 October 1973; "Obituary: John Vassos" in the *New York Times,* 10 December 1985.

\* \* \*

By all the accounts of his time and many since, John Vassos is a growing legend of American art and industrial design. He was a handsome Greek, medium in height, a solidly built man always with a sparkle in his eyes. Dynamically eloquent, he tended by sheer logic and tenacity to persuade his audiences to his point of view—corporate executives, engineers, marketing types, educators, and even fellow designers.

Excelling in practically every facet of the arts, he always seemed to find time to involve himself in salvaging local art groups. He also found time to create the Industrial Designer's Institute, the first society of industrial designers to spearhead a legal effort to achieve professional licensing for industrial designers though the organization lost the battle to inspire local zoning boards to choose better design. And always, he found time to provide a plethora of free design services to several Greek Hellenic Societies. He even designed the medals they later awarded him. These are but a partial listing of his myriad activities through the years. Whatever the cause, it always seemed that John Vassos ended up being President and the driving force of the endeavor. Perhaps the deep moral idealism and compassion for his fellow man first became manifest in the underlying themes of his superb *Gouache in Black, White and Shades of Gray.* Whether in advertising art or creating illustrations for his nine books written often with his wife, Ruth Carriere, his theme was always the smallness of man against the soaring, inescapable size of the universe.

In his major work, *Phobia,* all his pent-up compassion for humans were summed up in over twenty Gouache's, "Interpretations", as he called them. Written with Dr. Harry Stack Sullivan, he graphically delineated in his hard-edged style the major phobias of human kind. Not only has the book become an art and medical classic, it more than any other Vassos activity clearly identified the compassion of the innermost man.

By the 1920s and 1930s, he discovered his talent for what was to be industrial design. Without losing interest in past involvements, industrial design for the next sixty years was to become the focal point of his life. Initially he designed with the Art Deco trends—furniture, store windows, the first open-front fastfood operation—and then turned to designing products including a turnstile and dispensers for Coca Cola. Except for the turnstile, which became a classic, these were not noteworthy designs and Vassos reassessed his work. Interestingly, he returned to designing in terms of human needs and product functionalism at a time when his peers were happily embracing "streamlining" on stationary objects.

In the early 1930s, Vassos found the answer to a designer's prayer in his long affiliation with RCA. Here a new vista of involvement occurred; first with corporate management, then with the mechanical functions of product electronics. He adjusted to team management while creating a long list of mechanical and design patents that frequently revolutionized the appearance of the company's many products. Visibly back again and evident in the products and environments he designed was his compassion for how people related to their surroundings. We now call it human factors or ergonomics, or better yet, the "friendly look and feel" of a product. By whatever name we now identify the result, in Vassos's world it was building into a product or environment his compassion for those who must use or work in a man-made world.

Vassos was one of the small handful of founders of United States Industrial Design, who provided corporate-wide product, exhibitions, human factor, graphic, and design education for the corporate executives and sales staffs or their clients. Of this small group Vassos was the only designer who personally originated and developed the concepts, then executed or oversaw the developments to the market levels. Others amassed large staffs and quite often became directors of design, rather than the originators of designs that many were during the infancy of industrial design.

This has been but a glimpse of this remarkable man. Perhaps his own public description of an industrial designer for an educational film tells much: "Leonardo de Vinci was the first industrial designer—he could paint pictures, design tools, guns, fortifications, water systems, air-planes, even clothes for his patrons. The perfect example of the Renaissance Man and the industrial designer." The same could be said for John Vassos.

Finally, the greatest compliment to an individual's professional career and life can come only from his peers. Thus, Raymond Loewy's description of John Vassos to *Industrial Design* editor, Rodger Gillfoyle: "John Vassos is unsung and unsullied." Hopefully to become sung about, he will remain unsullied.

—Raymond Spilman

# VENTURI, Robert Charles

American architect

**Born:** Philadelphia, Pennsylvania, 25 June 1925. **Education:** Episcopal Academy, Philadelphia, graduated 1943; studied under Donald Drew Egbert and Jean Labatut, Princeton University, New Jersey, B.A. 1947, M.F.A., 1950; American Academy, Rome, 1954-56. **Family:** Married the architect Denise Scott Brown in 1967; children: James. **Career:** Worked as a designer for the firms of Oscar Stonorov, Philadelphia, Eero Saarinen, Bloomfield Hills, Michigan, and Louis I. Kahn, Philadelphia, 1950-58; partner, with Paul Cope and H. Mather Lippincott, Venturi, Cope and Lippincott, Philadelphia, 1958-61, and with William Short, Venturi and Short, Philadelphia, 1961-64; partner, with John Rauch, 1964-89, and with Rauch and Denise Scott Brown, 1967-89, Venturi, Rauch and Scott Brown (formerly Venturi and Rauch), Philadelphia; principal, with Scott Brown, Venturi, Scott Brown and Associates, Philadelphia, from 1989. Assistant Professor, then Associate Professor of Architecture, University of Pennsylvania, Philadelphia, 1957-65; State Department lecturer in the U.S.S.R., 1965; architect-in-residence, American Academy in Rome, 1966; Charlotte Shepherd Davenport Professor of Architecture, Yale University, New Haven, Connecticut, 1966-70; visiting critic, Rice University, Houston, Texas, 1969; Walter Gropius Lecturer, Graduate School of Design, Harvard University, Cambridge, Massachusetts, 1982. **Member:** American Institute of Architects; panel of visitors, School of Architecture and Urban Planning, University of California at Los Angeles, 1966-67; trustee, American Academy in Rome, 1969-74; board of advisors, Department of Art and Archaeology, Princeton, New Jersey, 1969-72, and from 1977; board of advisors, School of Architecture and Urban Design, Princeton University, New Jersey, from 1977; board of advisors, Ossabaw Island Project, Savannah, Georgia, from

1977. **Exhibitions:** Gold Medal Awards, Architectural League of New York, 1965; *The Work of Venturi and Rauch,* toured the United States, 1965; *40 under 40,* Architectural League of New York, 1966; *The Work of Venturi and Rauch,* Whitney Museum, New York, 1971; *The Invisible Artist,* Philadelphia Museum of Art, 1974; *The Work of Venturi and Rauch,* Pennsylvania Academy of Fine Arts, Philadelphia, 1975; *Suburban Alternatives: 11 American Projects,* at the Biennale, Venice, 1976; *200 Years of American Architectural Drawing,* Cooper-Hewitt Museum, New York, 1977; *Drawings for a More Modern Architecture,* Drawing Center, New York, and Cooper-Hewitt Museum, New York, 1977; *Architecture 1: An Exhibition,* Leo Castelli Gallery, New York, and Institute of Contemporary Art, Philadelphia, 1977; *Roma Interotta,* Incontri Internazionali d'Arte, Rome, 1977-78; *Palaces for People,* Cooper-Hewitt Museum, New York, 1977; *Presence and Absence,* Galleria d'Arte Moderna, Bologna, Italy, 1977; *The Federal City in Transition,* Barbara Fiedler Gallery, Washington, D.C., 1979; *Venturi and Rauch: Architektur im Alltag Amerikas,* Kunstgewerbemuseum, Zürich, 1979 (toured Switzerland); *Venturi, Rauch and Scott Brown,* Galleria dell'Accademia, Florence, Italy, 1981; *Speaking a New Classicism,* Smith College, Northampton, Massachusetts, 1981 (toured the United States); *Architectural Fantasies,* American Institute of Architects Foundation, Washington, D.C., 1981; *Correspondences: 5 Architects, 5 Sculptors,* Palacio de las Alhajas, Madrid, 1982; *Buildings by Venturi, Rauch and Scott Brown,* Max Protetch Gallery, New York, 1982; *Ornamentalism,* Hudson River Museum, New York, 1983 (travelled to the University of Texas, Austin, and the Fendrick Gallery, Washington, D.C.); *Venturi, Rauch and Scott Brown: A Generation of Architecture,* University of Illinois, Urbana, 1984 (toured the United States); *Robert Venturi: Architect's Furniture,* Syndennan Gallery, Philadelphia, 1985; *250 Years of Drawings by Philadelphia's Architects,* Pennsylvania Academy of the Fine Arts, Philadelphia, 1985; *The Sainsbury Wing: A Presentation of Designs by Venturi, Rauch and Scott Brown,* National Gallery, London, 1987; *Venturi, Scott Brown and Associates: Architecture and Decorative Arts,* Knoll Showroom, Tokyo, then toured Japan, Korea, and Philadelphia, 1991-93. **Honors:** Rome Prize Fellowship, American Academy in Rome; 1954-56; Graham Foundation Grant, 1963; Design Award, *Progressive Architecture,* 1967; First Prize, Yale University Mathematics Building Competition, 1970; Gold Medal, 1972, and Adaptive Re-use Award, 1976, American Institute of Architects, Philadelphia Chapter; Award of Merit, *House and Home*/AIA, 1973; Arnold W. Brunner Memorial Prize in Architecture, National Institute of Arts and Letters, 1973; Creative Arts Award, Brandeis University, Waltham, Massachusetts, 1976; Casebook Award, *Print Magazine,* 1976 (three times); Honor Award, 1977, and Medal, 1978, AIA; Case Studies Award, Urban Design, 1977; Medal of Achievement, Philadelphia Art Alliance, 1978; Citation, National Association of Schools of Art, 1980; Hazlett Memorial Award, Commonwealth of Pennsylvania, 1983; Thomas Jefferson Memorial Foundation Medal, University of Virginia, Charlottesville, 1983; Louis Sullivan Award, International Union of Bricklayers and Allied Craftsmen, 1983; Commandatore of the Order of Merit, Republic of Italy, 1986; Pritzker Architecture Prize, 1991; National Medal of Arts, U.S. Presidential Award, 1992; Benjamin Franklin Medal, Royal Society for the Encouragement of Arts, Manufacture, and Commerce, 1993; fellow, American Institute of Architects; Accademia Nazionale di San Luca, Rome; honorary fellow, Royal Institute of British Architects; honorary fellow, Royal Incorporation of Architects of Scotland. Honorary doctorates from: Oberlin College, Ohio, 1977; Yale University, New Haven, Connecticut, 1979; University of Pennsylvania, Philadelphia, 1980; Princeton University, New Jersey, 1983; New Jersey Institute of Technology, Newark, 1984; Bard College, Annandale-on-Hudson, New York, 1993; University of Rome, 1994. **Address:** Venturi, Scott Brown and Associates, 4236 Main Street, Philadelphia, Pennsylvania 19127, U.S.A.

## Works

Industrial designs include furniture, fabrics, and housewares for clients including: Fabric Workshop, Philadelphia, 1983; Alessi International, Milan, 1983, 1985; Formica Corporation, New York, 1983; Swid Powell, New York, 1984, 1985; Knoll International, New York, 1984; Elective Affinities, Milan, 1985; Arc International, Milan, 1985; Hanssem Corporation, Seoul, Korea, 1990.

(for a complete listing of Venturi's architectural designs see *Contemporary Architects*)

## Publications

**By VENTURI: books**—*Complexity and Contradiction in Architecture,* New York, 1966, Tokyo, 1969, Paris, 1971, Barcelona, 1972; (with Denise Scott Brown) *The Highway,* exhibition catalogue, Philadelphia, 1970; (with Scott Brown) *Aprendiendo de Todas Las Cosas,* Barcelona, 1971; (with Scott Brown and Steven Izenour) *Learning from Las Vegas,* Cambridge, Massachusetts, 1972, 1977; (with Scott Brown) *A View from the Campidoglio: Selected Essays, 1953-84,* New York, 1984; **articles**—"The Campidoglio: A Case Study" in *Architectural Review* (London), May 1953; "Project for a Beach House" in *Architectural Design* (London), November 1960; "Weekend House" in *Progressive Architecture* (New York), April 1961; "A Justification for a Pop Architecture" in *Arts and Architecture* (Los Angeles), April 1965; "Three Projects: Architecture and Landscape, Architecture and Sculpture, Architecture and City Planning" in *Perspecta* (New Haven, Connecticut), no. 11, 1967; "Trois bâtiments pour une ville de l'Ohio" in *L'Architecture d'Aujourd'hui* (Paris), December 1967/January 1968; (with Scott Brown) "A Significance for A & P Parking Lots; or, Learning from Las Vegas" in *Architectural Forum* (New York), March 1968; "A Bill-Ding Board Involving Movies, Relics and Space" in *Architectural Forum* (New York), April 1968; "On Architecture" in *L'Architecture d'Aujourd'hui* (Paris), September 1968; (with Scott Brown) "On Ducks and Decoration" in *Architecture Canada* (Toronto), October 1968; (with Scott Brown) "Venturi versus Gowan" in *Architectural Design* (London), January 1969; (with Scott Brown) "Learning from Lutyens" in *RIBA Journal* (London), August 1969; (with Scott Brown) "The Bicentennial Commemoration 1976" in *Architectural Forum* (New York), October 1969; (with Scott Brown) "Mass Communications on the People Freeway; or, Piranesi Is Too Easy" in *Perspecta* (New Haven, Connecticut), no. 12, 1969; (with Scott Brown) "Co-op City: Learning to Like It" in *Progressive Architecture* (New York), February 1970; (with Scott Brown) "Reply to Pawley-'Leading from the Rear'" in *Architectural Design* (London), July 1970; (with Scott Brown) "Some Houses of III Repute: A Discourse with Apologia on Recent Houses of Venturi and Rauch" in *Perspecta* (New Haven, Connecticut), no. 13/14, 1971; (with Scott Brown) "Ugly and Ordinary Architecture;

or, The Decorated Shed" in *Architectural Forum* (New York), part I, November 1971, part II, December 1971; (with Scott Brown) "Bicentenaire de l'Indépendance Américaine" in *L'Architecture d'Aujourd'hui* (Paris), November 1973; (with Scott Brown) "Functionalism Yes, But..." in *Architecture+ Urbanism* (Tokyo), November 1974; "Plain and Fancy Architecture by Cass Gilbert at Oberlin" in *Apollo* (London), February 1976, expanded version in *Allen Memorial Art Museum Bulletin* (Oberlin, Ohio), no. 2, 1976-77; "A Reaction to Complexity and Contradiction in the Work of Furness" in *Pennsylvania Academy of the Fine Arts Newsletter* (Philadelphia), Spring 1976; "Learning from Aalto" in *Progressive Architecture* (New York), April 1977; "A Definition of Architecture as Shelter with Decoration on It" in *Architecture + Urbanism* (Tokyo), January 1978; "Learning the Right Lessons from the Beaux Arts" in *Architectural Design* (London), January 1979; "Allen Memorial Art Museum, Oberlin" in *Werk/Archithese* (Zürich), January/February 1979; "Interview: Robert Venturi and Denise Scott Brown" in *Harvard Architecture Review,* (Cambridge, Massachusetts), Spring 1980; "Interview with Robert Venturi" in *Modo* (Milan), November 1981; "Il Proprio Vocabolario" in *Gran Bazaar* (Milan), 1982; "RIBA Discourse" in *RIBA Journal* (London), May 1982; "Diversity, Relevance and Representation in Architecture" in *Architectural Record* (New York), June 1982; (with others) "On Aalto" in *Quaderns* (Barcelona), April/ June 1983; "Proposal for the Iraq State Mosque, Baghdad" in *L'Architecture d'Aujourd'hui* (Paris), September 1983; "Eero Saarinen and his Works" in special issue of *Architecture + Urbanism* (Tokyo), April 1984; "From Intervention to Convention in Architecture" in *RSA Journal* (London), January 1988; "Urban Concepts" in *Architectural Design* (London), January/February 1990; "POPular Architecture" in *Architectural Design* (London), March/April 1992; "Learning from Philadelphia" in *Abitare* (Milan), November 1992; "The Sixties Revisited" in *Architecture South Africa* (Cape Town), July/August 1993; "Sweet and Sour" in *Architecture* (New York), May 1994; "Mal Mots: Aphorisms—Sweet and Sour—by an Anti-Hero Architect" in *Grand Street,* Fall 1995.

**On VENTURI: books**—*American Architecture and Urbanism* by Vincent Scully, New York, 1969; *New Directions in American Architecture* by Robert A. M. Stern, New York, 1969; *Will They Ever Finish Bruckner Boulevard?* by Ada Louise Huxtable, New York, 1970; *Architecture for the Arts: The State University of New York College at Purchase,* New York, 1971; *The Work of Venturi and Rauch,* exhibition catalogue by Vincent Scully, New York, 1971; *After the Planners* by Robert Goodman, New York, 1971; *Third Generation: The Changing Meaning of Architecture* by Philip Drew, New York, 1972; *Wasteland: Building the American Dream* by Stephen A. Kurtz, New York, 1973; *Conversations with Architects* by John W. Cook and Heinrich Klotz, New York and London, 1973; *Architettura Radicale* by Paolo Navone and Bruno Orlando, Milan, 1974; *The Shingle Style Today* by Vincent Scully, New York, 1974; *Global Architecture 39: Venturi and Rauch* by Paul Goldberger and Yukio Futagawa, Tokyo, 1976; *Supermannerism: New Attitudes in Post Modern Architecture* by C. Ray Smith, New York, 1977; *New Directions in American Architecture* by Robert A. M. Stern, New York, 1977; *Architectural Monographs 1: Venturi and Rauch* edited by David Dunster, London, 1978; (bibliography) *Robert Charles Venturi* by Lamia Doumato, Monticello, Illinois, 1978; *Transformations in Modern Architecture* by Arthur Drexler, New York, 1979; *Venturi and Rauch: Architektur im Alltag Amerikas,* exhibition catalogue by Stanislaus von Moos, Zürich, 1979; *Origini* *ed eclisse del movimento moderno* by Cesare De Seta, Bari, Italy, 1980; *Venturi, Rauch and Scott Brown* edited by Gianni Pettena and Maurizio Vogliazzo, Milan, 1981; *Poetica y Arquitectura* by Josep Muntanola, Barcelona, 1981; (bibliography) *Venturi, Rauch and Scott Brown,* Monticello, Illinois, 1982; *Immagini del Post-Moderno* edited by Claudio Aldegheri and Maurizio Sabini, Venice, 1983; *Venturi, Rauch and Scott Brown: A Generation of Architecture,* exhibition catalogue by Rosemarie Haag Bletter, Urbana, Illinois, 1984; *Venturi, Rauch and Scott Brown: Buildings and Projects* by Stanislaus von Moos, New York, 1987; *Venturi, Scott Brown e Associati* by Carolina Vaccaro and Frederic Schwartz, Bologna, 1991.

\*   \*   \*

In 1965 Robert Venturi published his first book, *Complexity and Contradiction*, an architectural manifesto vhich rejected the austere modernist aesthetic, and advocated, in its place, an architecture with the capacity to embrace the ordinary. Since its publication, *Complexity and Contradiction* has exerted remarkable influence on the practice of architecture, and has been instrumental, noted Stanislaus von Moos in his essay "The Challenge of the Status Quo," in changing the modernist conception of the profession. Following *Complexity and Contradiction,* it was no longer appropriate to consider an architect the chief agent of social change. Rather, as von Moos observed, "the question became how to design while allowing for the existence of such [social] problems." This is the task, with his wife and partner Denise Scott Brown, that Robert Venturi has undertaken.

One of their early collaborations was another book, *Learning from Las Vegas,* a spatial analysis of the Las Vegas strip. Arguing that commercial districts have long been ignored by American architects, the authors proposed an architectural sensibility vested in a sympathetic analysis of these neglected spaces. Because of its linear arrangement, and its unique concentration of signage and improbable architecture, Las Vegas provided an ideal setting for their research. Paralleling the Pop movements in painting and other branches of the arts, Scott Brown and Venturi marked the everyday as the stuff of architecture.

This fascination with pop culture is manifest in their work of the period. In Venturi's 1967 entry for the National Football Hall of Fame competition, a shed-like building is fronted by a gigantic billboard. The quality of the interior, however, is inspired by a renaissance depiction of a church. This is the curious and provocative nature of Venturi's work: while advancing the ordinary, it simultaneously supposes familiarity with the canonical works of art and architecture. Venturi's buildings, then, are characterized by a "literary" reading, dependent on an informed audience, where the dialogue between parts comes to represent the whole.

An earlier Venturi building, the Guild House of 1961, has become a landmark in the development of the post-modern sensibility. Built in Philadelphia as elderly housing for a Quaker community, the mid-rise Guild House typifies Venturi's conflation of the high/low aspects of architecture. Constructed on a modest budget, the guild house is clad primarily in brick, and utilizes standard windows and components. Confirming society's obsession with signs, the words "GUILD HOUSE" are written in overscaled-text above the entrance. There are, however, incursions on these plain devices throughout the building. A large granite column, in reference, perhaps, to the stone columns of classicism, divides the entrance. The ground floor of the front facade is clad in white tile to differentiate it from both the street and the remainder of the building behind,

while the symmetrical composition is topped by a large, golden reproduction of a television antenna.

The vocabulary of Venturi's work has since expanded to include increasingly explicit references to the architecture of the past. Classically inspired columns make appearances in his work, as do pointed, Gothic arches, and other more recent stylistic innovations. Nonetheless, these references are not made without a sense of irony. In the Allen Memorial Art Museum addition of 1977, a round column is clad in wood and made to resemble an Ionic column, while masking its connection to the ground. In other words, an element that is typically understood as massive and fixed becomes light, and appears to float. The humor in this depends, of course, on familiarity with the conventions of architecture, and because of this, risks becoming little more than an inside joke, and at its worst, elitist.

Venturi's 1991 scheme for the Seattle Art Museum, for example, deployed a series of alternating round and pointed arches on the building's long, primary facade. Without really addressing the issue of how the building meets the ground, the arches seem an exercise in architectural variety. In "Going Global," Kay Larson of *New York* magazine voiced no objections to the museum's "thesaurus of references." Instead, she found the building perfectly suited to the postmodern ideal of "a museum based not on 'hero' objects but on a collaborative level of quality in which things work together because none screams its moral superiority."

While Venturi and Scott Brovn are often cited as the progenitors of post-modernism, they resist labeling themselves. Unlike many of their contemporaries, Venturi and Scott Brown's preoccupation is not with the formal qualities of architectural per se, but with the critical and communicative properties of that form. As Herbert Muschamp wrote in "American Gothic," for *The New Republic,* Venturi and Scott Brown's work "tells who we are by showing us what others like."

—David P. Johnson

# VERSACE, Gianni

Italian fashion designer

**Born:** Reggio Calabria, Italy, 2 December 1946. **Education:** Studied architecture, at a technical school, Reggio Calabria, 1964-67; mainly self-taught in fashion design. **Career:** Worked as a fashion buyer in Paris and London, for his mother's dressmaking studio, Reggio Calabria, 1968-72; freelance fashion designer, working for Callaghan, Complice, and Genny companies, Milan, 1972-77; established Gianni Versace fashion company, Milan, 1978; first womenswear collection, 1978, menswear collection, 1979, and first fragrance, 1981; home furnishings collection launched, 1993. Also stage costume designer, for La Scala Opera and Bejart Ballet, from 1982. **Exhibitions:** Galleria Rizzardi, Milan, 1982; Studio La Città, Verona, 1983; *Italian Fashion,* Civic Museum, Osaka, 1983; Galerie Focus, Munich, 1983; *It's Design,* Padiglione d'Arte Contemporanea, Milan, 1983; *40 Years of Italian Fashion,* Trump Tower, New York, 1983; *Gianni Versace: dialogues de mode,* Palais Galliera, Paris, 1986; retrospective, Fashion Institute of Technology, New York, 1992-93. **Collections:** Museo Civico, Parma; Rijksmuseum, Amsterdam; Metropolitan Museum of Art, New York. **Honors:** Occhio d'Oro Award, Milan, 1982, 1984, 1990, 1991; Revlon Golden Eye Award, Milan, 1982; Cutty Sark Award, Philadelphia, 1983,

1988; Council of Fashion Designers of America International Award, 1993. **Address:** Via Gesu, 20121 Milan, Italy.

## Publications

**By VERSACE: books**—(with Omar Calabrese) *Vanitas: lo stile dei semsi,* Rome, 1991; (with Omar Calbrese) *Versace Signatures,* Rome, 1992; *Designs: Gianni Versace,* Milan, 1994; *The Man Without Tie,* Milan, 1994; *Men Without Ties,* New York, 1995; **articles**—in *Vogue* (New York), November 1983.

**On VERSACE: books**—*A History of Fashion* by J. Anderson Black and Madge Garland, London, 1975, 1980; *I Mass-Moda: Fatti e Personaggi dell'Italian Look* by Adriana Mulassano, Florence, 1979; *The Collector's Book of Twentieth Century Fashion* by Frances Kennett, London and New York, 1983; *Leaders in Fashion: I grandi personaggi della moda* by Maria-Vittoria Alfonso, Bologna, 1983; *40 Years of Italian Fashion,* exhibition catalogue compiled by B. G. Aragno, Rome, 1983; *McDowell's Directory of Twentieth Century Fashion* by Colin McDowell, London, 1984; *The Italian Look Reflected* by Silvia Giacomondi, Milan, 1984; *Il genio antipatico,* exhibition catalogue by Pia Soli, Venice, 1984; *The Encyclopaedia of Fashion from 1840 to the 1980s* by Georgina O'Hara, London, 1986; *Gianni Versace: dialogues de mode,* exhibition catalogue, Milan, 1986; *Versace Teatro* by Mario Pasi, Milan, 1987; *The Fashion Conspiracy* by Nicholas Coleridge, London, 1988; *Gianni Versace: l'abito per pensare* by Nicoletta Bocca and Chiara Buss, Milan, 1989; *Infra-Apparel* by Richard Martin and Harold Koda, New York, 1993; *Orientalism: Visions of the East in Western Dress,* exhibition catalogue by Richard Martin and Harold Koda, New York, 1994; **articles**—"Gianni Versace: Disciplined Negligence" by Peter Carlsen in *Gentleman's Quarterly* (New York), August 1979; "The Palace of Versace" by Jane Withers in *The Face* (London), December 1984; "Gianni Versace: ordito e trama" by Helen Simpson in *Vogue* (Milan), October 1985; "A Dialog with Gianni Versace" by Christopher Petkanas in *Women's Wear Daily* (New York), 22 October 1986; "Gianni Versace: l'immigrato eccellente" by Silvia Del Pozo in *L'Uomo Vogue* (Milan), October 1987; "The Satanic Versace" by Kathy Phillips in *You* magazine of the *Mail on Sunday* (London), 19 March 1989; "Sailing to Byzantium: A Fashion Odyssey, 1990-91" by Richard Martin in *Textile and Text,* 14 February 1991; "Chic or Cruel? Gianni Versace's Styles Take a Cue from the World of S & M..." by James Servin in the *New York Times,* 1 November 1992; "The Once and Future Versace" by Bernadine Morris in the *New York Times,* 8 November 1992; "Gianni Versace" in *Current Biography* (New York), April 1993; "Lunch with Mr. Armani, Tea with Mr. Versace, Dinner with Mr. Valentino" by Stephen Schiff in *The New Yorker,* 7 November 1994; "Versace's Castle in the Sand" by Charles Gandee in *Vogue* (New York), December 1994; "Book Preview [*L'Uomo Senza Cravatta*]" in *L'Uomo Vogue,* November 1994; "Milan: Versace/Istante" in *Daily News Record* (New York), 18 January 1995; "Versace's Pastiche Amid Couture Upheaval" by Suzy Menkes in the *International Herald Tribune* (Paris), 23 January 1995; "Versace: Clean and Mean for Fall" by Amy M. Spindler in the *New York Times,* 8 March 1995; "Gianni Versace: The Right Stuff" in *Women's Wear Daily* (New York), 8 March 1995; "Gianni's American Dream" by Barry Van Lenten in *Women's Wear Daily,* 10 April 1995.

\*   \*   \*

In many ways, Gianni Versace is the most visionary of the current generation of designers dominating Italian fashion. Yet his style is deceptively calm, smooth, and undemonstrative. Both in terms of his work and his personality, Versace is low-keyed. It is only the closer look that yields the critical detail, which that year pushes clothing a little further in the direction one assumes he would wish to see it. He is more of a historicist, however, than a revivalist. Versace is intrigued by a particular school of painting, rather than, say, the look affected by French socialites of 1930. In a fashion world where so much is simply an endless cycle of repeated ideas about past clothing history, Versace is more interested in using the broader context of the past, its furniture, its architecture, to suggest a new way of dressing for the present. This is not to say that Versace is merely an essayist in nostalgia; it is simply to say that as a romantic, he is naturally attracted to a lush and visionary view of clothing, rather than a purely architectural or utilitarian one. At his most successful, such as in his experiments with neo-Grecian tunic dresses, he achieves a superbly limpid and supple elegance which can truly be called timeless, with none of the rather fatigued overtones that epithet can have.

Versace at his most inspired suggests a realistic futurism, a pleasant Arcadia equally as remote from the morbid vampire fantasies of Claude Montana as it is from the slowly fossilizing, beaded visions of the older French couturiers. On a more meaningful level, however, that is to say in the day-to-day chronology of changing fashion, Versace generates consistently, more than any other designer, those small and telling gestures that, by expanding a line here or contracting one there, change the course of style. His widening of the hips and narrowing of the calf on his men's trousers had a great impact on the silhoutte of men's clothing of the 1980s, for instance, just as the aforementioned tunic dresses had on women's clothing.

—Peter Carlsen

# VIAU, Jean Pierre
Canadian interior and furniture designer

**Born:** 1959. **Education:** Studied environmental design, Université du Québec, Montréal, 1982. **Career:** Interior and furniture designer, from 1982; founder and partner, with Jacques Biladeau, Carré III design firm, 1984; founder, Jeann Pierre Viau Design, Montréal, from 1993. **Exhibitions:** Virtu, Toronto, 1985; Virtu, Montréal, 1986; *50 Années de Luminaire,* Montréal, 1987; *Salon des Artists Décorateurs 87,* Paris, 1987; *Salon International du Design d'Intérieur de Montréal,* 1992; *Interior 92,* Salon de Design d'Intérieur, Courtrai, Belgium, 1992. **Honors:** Bourse Designer de Montréal, Commission d'Initiative de Développement Économique de Montréal (CIDEM) and Salon International de Design d'Intérieur de Montréal (SIDIM), 1992; Mention en Design Commercial, CIDEM and SIDIM, 1995. **Address:** Jean Pierre Viau Design, 55 Mont Royal West, #801, Montréal, Québec H2T 2S6, Canada.

## Works

Sculpture, for Mikado restaurant, Montréal, 1988 (with TDI Design). Furniture consultant, for Citi bar, Boston, Massachusetts, U.S.A., 1988.

Interior and furniture design, for Klik exposition stand, Montréal, 1988.

Interior and furniture design, for Clinique Vétérinaire Laurier, 1988.

Interior design, for Keyuk exposition stand, 1988.

Sculpture, for Beverly Hills Café, Montréal, 1988.

Interior and furniture design, for By American office and show-room, Montréal, 1989.

Interior design, for Robert Krief showroom, Montréal, 1989.

Interior and furniture design, for Val de L'Anse private residence, 1989.

Interior and furniture design, for Citrus restaurant, Montréal, 1989.

Furniture design, for F.O.O.D. boutique, Montréal, 1989 (with J. Rousseau architects).

Interior and furniture design, for Kyoze boutiques, Montréal, 1990, 1991, 1992.

Interior and furniture design, for Lucas restaurant, New York, 1990.

Interior and furniture design, for Pizzedelic restaurants in Laval, St. Laurent, St. Catherine, and Laurier, 1990-93.

Interior and furniture design, for Quartier Latin building, Montréal, 1990 (with G.G.D. architects).

Interior and furniture design, for Orbite hair salon, Montréal, 1990.

Interior and furniture design, for Condominium St.-Paul, Montréal, 1990.

Furniture consultant, for Bar L'Oeuf, Montréal, 1990 (with J. Rousseau architects).

Architectural design, for Résidence Alepin, Montréal, 1990.

Interior and furniture design, for Tonic hair salon, Montréal, 1990.

Interior design, for Résidence Bellevue, Montréal, 1990 (with Paulin Larivière architects).

Furniture design, for S.S.Q. executive offices, Montréal, 1990 (with Gauthier Guité Daoust architects).

Interior and furniture design, for Bronx bar, Montréal, 1991.

Furniture design, for Visitation park, Montréal, 1991 (with Gauthier Guité Daoust architects).

Furniture design, for Giovanni agency, Montréal, 1991.

Interior and furniture design, for Michel Tétreault art gallery, Montréal, 1992.

Interior and furniture design, for Hilary Radley showroom, Montréal, 1992.

Interior and furniture design, for Cafétéria restaurant, Montréal, 1992.

Interior and furniture design, for Bruzze restaurant, Ottawa, 1993.

Interior and furniture design, for Palais de la Civilisation, Montréal, 1993.

Interior and furniture design, for Publix restaurant, Montréal, 1993.

Interior and furniture design, for Globe restaurant, Montréal, 1993.

Furniture design, for Casino de Montréal, 1993.

Interior and furniture design, for Kyoze boutique, Montréal, 1993.

Interior and furniture design, for La Baignoire boutiques, Montréal, Vancouver, and Toronto, 1993.

**Publications**

**On VIAU: books**—*Guide Design Montréal,* Montréal, 1990; **articles**—*Section A* (Montréal), vol. 2, no. 5, 1985; *Interiors* (New York), April 1988; *World Spaces* (Japan), no. 11, 1989; *Design Issues* (New York), no. 4, 1989; *Les Plaisirs de la Table* (Montréal), vol. 5, no. 2, 1990; *Contract Magazine* (Toronto), April 1990; *Canadian Architect* (Toronto), May 1990, September 1991; *La Presse* (Montréal), September 1990, October 1992; *Design Jour-nal* (Korea), October 1990; *MTL* (Montréal), October 1990; *Le Devoir* (Montréal), January 1991, April 1995; *Clin d'Oeil* (Montréal), May 1991, September 1992; *Arquitectura Viva* (Spain), August 1991; *Flare* (Toronto), August 1991; *The Gazette* (Montréal), November 1991, May 1993; *Max* (Paris), February 1992; *Design Québec* (Montréal), June 1992; *Elle Québec* (Montréal), June 1992; *Modern Salon* (New York), July 1992; *Contract Design* (New York), August 1992, April 1994; *Azure* (Toronto), September 1992, June 1994; *International Contract* (Toronto), March 1993; *Mirror* (Montréal), March 1993; *Contract* (New York), March 1993; *Voir,* June, 1993; *Chez Soi* (Montréal), September 1993; *Fame* (Toronto), September 1993; *Interior Design* (New York), April 1994; *Wind* (Tokyo), April 1994; *Décormag* (Montréal), November 1994.

# VIEMEISTER, Tucker
## American industrial designer

**Born:** Dayton, Ohio, 14 August 1948. **Education:** Attended Shimer College, Mt. Carroll, Illinois, 1966-68, and Shimer-in-Oxford, England, 1967; studied industrial design, Pratt Institute, New York, B.I.D., 1974. **Career:** Junior designer in father's industrial and graphic design business, Vie Design Studios, Inc., Yellow Springs, Ohio, 1969; youth department supervisor and in-house photographer, YMCA, Berkeley, California, 1970-71; owner and designer, Ohio Silver jewelry store, Yellow Springs, Ohio, 1971-73; instructor, Industrial Design Workshop '74, Santarem, Portugal, 1974; designer, Wyman & Cannon Co., New York, 1974-77; technical and production director, business manager, and partner, Ted Muehling, Brooklyn, New York, 1977-79; vice-president, Smart Design Inc. (originally Davin Stowell Associates), New York, from 1979. Editor, IDSA/New York newsletter, 1984; Pratt Institute Advisory Committee, 1987; teacher, Les Ateliers, Ecole Nationale Supérieure de Creation Industrielle, Paris, France, 1988; co-curator, *The Fine Art of American Industrial Design,* National Arts Club, New York, 1988; trustee, Rowena Reed Kostellow Fund, Pratt Institute, Brooklyn New York, 1989; team teacher, interdisciplinary workshop, Cal Arts, Venice, California, and University of Cincinnati, Ohio, 1991; president of co-op board, 74 Fifth Avenue Owners' Corp., New York, New York, 1992; senior critic, Yale University, New Haven, Connecticut, 1994. **Member:** Industrial Designers Society of America; American Institute of Graphic Artists; American Center for Design. **Exhibitions:** *Three Generations of Viemeisters,* Henderson Gallery, Yellow Springs, Ohio, 1985; *Design in America,* United States Information Agency, Eastern Europe, 1986; *Forma Finlandia: Plastics for Tomorrow,* Neste Oy, Helsinki, Finland, Design Center, London, England, RAI, Amsterdam, Holland, and IDCNY, New York, 1987; *Pride of Place Setting,* Parsons School of Design, New York, 1988; *100 Years of Design Excellence,* Bloomingdale's, New York, 1988; *The Fine Art of American Industrial Design,* National Arts Club, New York, 1988; *Design 89,* Science Place, Dallas, Texas, 1989; *Good Offices,* Museum of Art, Fort Lauderdale, Florida, 1989; *Mondo Materialis,* Steelcase Design Partnership, Murray Feldman Gallery, Los Angeles, California, and Cooper-Hewitt Museum, New York, 1990; *The Idea is Mightier than the Tool,* Windows on Broad, University of the Arts, Philadelphia, Pennsylvania, 1990; *Cranbrook Design: The New Discourse,* Steelcase Design Partnership, New York, 1991; *Platinum Jewelry Exhibition,* Creator House, Seibu, Tokyo, Japan, 1992;

*Designs aus Amerika,* Ambiente, Frankfurt, Germany, 1994; *Strengthening the Dollar,* New American Money, for the *New York Times,* Artists Space, New York, 1994; *New Acquisitions,* Museum of Modern Art, New York, 1995; *Mutant Materials,* Museum of Modern Art, New York, 1995; *Faculty Works on Paper,* Art & Architecture gallery, Yale University, New Haven, Connecticut, 1995. **Collections:** Museum of Modern Art, New York; Cooper-Hewitt Museum, New York; Design Center Stuttgart, Germany; Staatliches Museum for Angewandte Kunst, Munich, Germany; Grand Rapids Art Museum, Michigan. **Honors:** Selected to *ID* magazine Annual Design Review, 1983, 1985 (2), 1986, 1989 (3), 1990, 1991; Presidential Design Achievement Award, 1984; IDEA Commendation, Industrial Design Excellence Awards, 1986; "Best Use of Symbol," Architectural League Chair Fair, 1986; Best Concept, *ID* magazine Annual Design Review, 1986; First prize, Forma Finlandia International Design, 1987; Silver IDEA Award, 1990, 1992, and Gold IDEA Award, 1992, IDSA; Design 100, *Metropolitan Home* magazine, 1992; International Designpreis des Landes Baden-Württemberg, 1993; Design Leadership Award, *Inc.* magazine, 1993; Forma Finlandia 3 Selection, Helsinki, Finland, 1993; Tylenol/Arthritis Foundation Design Award, 1993; America's Hottest 40, *ID* magazine, 1995. **Address:** Smart Design Inc., 137 Varick St., New York, New York 10013, U.S.A.

## Works

Architectural signage system for the Washington, D.C., mall, for Wyman & Cannan Co., 1976.

SSM aviator sunglasses, for Corning, 1985.

*Pool* chair, 1986 (with Lisa Krohn and Steven Holt).

*Phonebook* telephone answering machine, 1987 (with Lisa Krohn).

*Sardine* light made from a spring and paper shade, 1989 (with Lisa Krohn).

Exhibition design, for *The Fine Art of American Industrial Design,* National Arts Club, New York, 1989.

*Good Grips* kitchen utensils with oversized rubber handles, for Oxo, 1991.

*Metropolitan* "soft shape" toaster, for Black & Decker, 1992.

*Home Phone,* for Cicena, 1994.

*Joe Boxer* watches, for Timex, 1995.

## Publications

**By VIEMEISTER: books**—(editor) *Product Design 6,* Glen Cove, New York, 1994; **articles**—"Design 87" in *Perspectives* (Great Falls, Virginia), November 1987; "They Say, 'It's None of Your Business'" in *Innovations* (McLean, Virginia), Fall 1988; "Head Designers: There's More to Designing Glasses than Meets the Eye" in *Paper* (New York), October 1988; "Letter from Aspen: The State of Things?" in *Blueprint* (London), November 1988; "Lippincott Takes Two Tuckers for a Ride" *Perspectives* (Great Falls, Virginia), November 1988; (with Ann DeForest) "Waste Not, Want Not" in *ID* (New York), November/December 1989; (with Sarah Verdone) "Design Carnival in Nagoya" in *ID* (New York), January/February 1990; (with Sarah Verdone) "An Emerging Landscape Full of Log Cabins" in *Blueprint* (London), February 1990; "Doing Nothing" in *Design* (London), January 1992; "How I See It: Seize the Moment" in *Innovations* (McLean, Virginia), Spring 1992; (with David Hales) "Letter to Detroit: Let's Talk Transpor-

tation" in *ID* (New York), May/June 1992; "On Doing Nothing" in *Rethinking Design* (Cohoes, New York), November 1992; "Psycho, Ergo and Eco" in *Graphis Design* (Zürich), 1994; "What Comes After World Domination?" in *Communication Arts* (Palo Alto, California), May/June 1994; "Believe It or Else?" in *Great Packaging Design,* New York, 1994; "Degenerate Design?" in *Design Statements* (Chicago), Spring 1994; (with Rie Norregaard) "Strengthening the Dollar" in *New York Times Magazine* (New York), 30 October 1994; "Toward Utopia" in *Innovations* (McLean, Virginia), Summer 1995.

**On VIEMEISTER: books**—*American Design Classics* by Nada Westerman and Joan Wessel, New York, 1985; *The International Design Yearbook* by Emilio Ambasz, New York, 1986; *Product Design 2* by Sandra Edwards, New York, 1987; *High Touch* by Robert Janjigian, New York, 1987; *The International Design Yearbook* by Arata Isozaki, New York, 1988; *New American Design* by Hugh Aldersey-Williams, New York, 1988; *397 Chairs* by Arthur Danto, New York, 1988; *Product Design 3* by Joe Dolce, New York, 1988; *Horn of Plenty* by Gosse Oosterhof, Amsterdam, 1989; *80s Style: Design of the Decade* by Abrecht Babgert and Karl Armer, New York, 1990; *The Meaning of Modern Design* by Peter Dormer, New York, 1990; *International Lighting Design* by V. Lorenzo Porcelli, Rockport, Massachusetts, 1991; *World Design* by Hugh Aldersey-Williams, New York, 1992; *Industrial Design: Reflection of a Century* by Jocelyn de Noblet, Paris, 1993; *Urgent Images* by Edward Booth-Clibborn, London, 1994; *Mutant Materials in Contemporary Design,* exhibition catalogue by Paola Antonelli, New York, 1995; **articles**—"Graphic Design of the National Zoo" by Jean Coyne in *Communication Arts* (Palo Alto, California), 1976; "No More Milling Around the Mall" by Rose DeNeve in *Print* (New York), November/December 1977; "From Concept to Consumer" by Mark Matousek in *Metropolis* (New York), January/February 1984; "Overseas Frequency, New York" by Steven Holt in *Axis* (Tokyo), Autumn 1986; "Smart in Manhattan" by Hugh Aldersey-Williams in *Designweek* (London), 23 January 1987; "Design with Everything" by Steven Holt in *Blueprint* (London), March 1987; "Designer Phonebook" by Hugh Aldersey-Williams in *New York* (New York), 28 September 1987; "Industrial Design: Romancing the Commonplace" by Arlene Hirst in *Metropolitan Home* (New York), January 1988; "Bringing Grace to the Quotidian" by Hugh Aldersey-Williams in *World & I* (Washington, D.C.) March 1988; "Tucker Viemeister" by Akiko Moriyama in *Nikkei Design* (Tokyo), June 1988; "Form+Function: Designers Assert Role as Artists" by Stephen MacDonald in *Wall Street Journal* (New York), 8 November 1988; "Good-bye to the Eighties" by Susan Szenasy in *Metropolis* (New York), October 1989; "Grading Education—The *ID* Debate" by Chee Pearlman in *ID* (New York), September/October 1990; "V.P. Brains" by Setsuko Kiuchi in *Gap* (Tokyo), October 1990; "Maverick Design" by Douglas Davis in *Village Voice* (New York), 23 October 1990; "Snips 'n Snails: That's What Design Is Made Of" by Steven Holt in *Metropolitan Home* (New York), November 1990; "Smart Moves" by Nicholas Backlund in *ID* (New York), November 1990; "Profile: Design and Stuff" by Lisa Krohn in *Blueprint* (London), April 1991; "My Job—Tucker Viemeister" by Marion Hancock in *Design* (London), August 1991; "Viemeister has 'Good Grips' on Reality" by Gerald Levitch in *Globe and Mail* (Toronto, Canada), 5 December 1991; "P Scott Makela is Wired" by Michael Rock in *EYE* (London), Spring 1994; "What Works for One Works for All" by Bruce Nussbaum in *Business Week* (New York), 20 April 1992; "Consideran a México campo

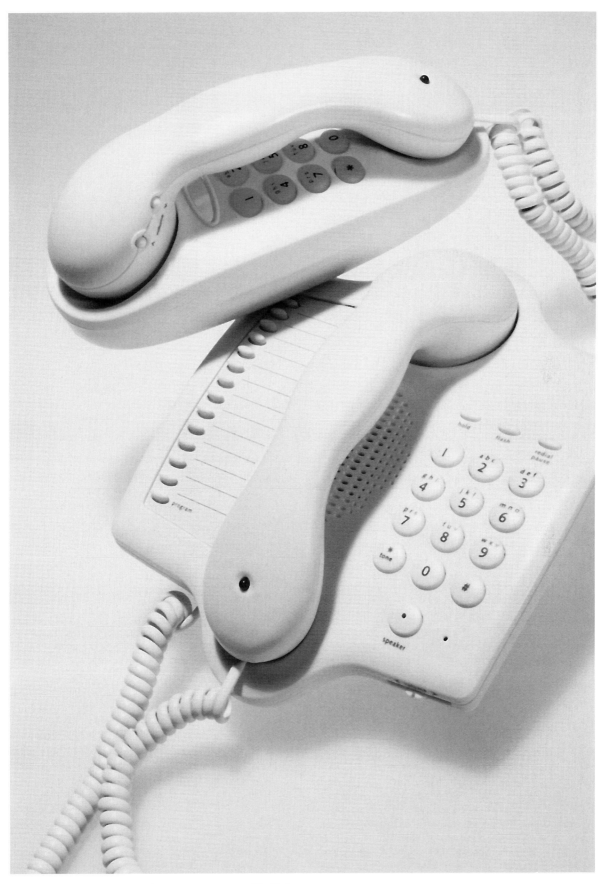

**Tucker Viemeister:** *Home Phones.* Photo: Peter Medilek

virgen en diseño" by Juan Carlos Martinez in *El Norte* (Monterrey, Mexico), 26 April 1994; "Defining Design, Over to You" by Gaynor Williams in *Design* (London), May 1994; "Coffee Klatsch, Henry Myerberg/Smart Design" by Mayer Rus in *Interior Design* (New York), June 1994; "From Cars to Phones, US Companies Begin to Export Their Stylish Looks" by Milan Ruzucka in *Journal of Commerce* (New York), 10 June 1994; "America's Hottest 40" by Peter Hall in *ID* (New York), January-February 1995; "Narcissism in Print" by Akiko Busch in *Metropolis* (New York), June 1995; "Survey" by Susan Szenasy and Laura Riley in *Metropolis* (New York), September 1995.

\*

Everyone designs. Design is what separates man from animals. All humans exploit their intuition and ingenuity to improve their lives. Professional designers—with our training, experience, and talent—help people design.

We live in an age of great change—more sweeping than the Industrial Revolution, more dominating than the Egyptian Empire, even more dynamic than the Renaissance. More than any other time in human history, more aspects of people's lives are in flux. Technology, jobs, neighborhoods, families, medicine—everything is changing. There is more change happening to everyone now than happened to any other life form since that big meteor landed on the dinosaurs.

Our opportunities for designing utopia are slipping away. Soon instead of working to improve the quality of our lives, all our energy will be consumed by basic survival, and our time will be spent protecting our lives. People once divided between have's and have-not's are now further separated between know's and dunno's. Human desires dominate the balance of Nature. This fragmentation of our society, the explosion of technology, and the collapse of the natural environment is demanding a new and improved designer.

I have a vision of a future that is fair, that puts the trust back in technology, that makes commerce sustainable and collaborative, that fosters family and community, with a voluntary simplicity that puts the beauty back in life. That will happen when design becomes an integral part of all activities. Design will be invisible. It won't be special. Design will be natural.

—Tucker Viemeister

\*   \*   \*

Design is the very air Tucker Viemeister, IDSA, breathes. It is the glass through which he views experience, and it is the means he would use to gain a more beautiful and socially just world. Shaped in his childhood, his belief in design's power to effect change has made of Tucker one of the most successful industrial designers of his time.

On the professional and business level, Tucker succeeds in the design of paradigm-setting products, working in a team with other members of the firm he helped to form, Smart Design Inc. Known for its execution of thoroughly considered ergonomics, superbly detailed aesthetics, and appropriate application of new technologies, Smart has earned a position of respect in the profession as a serious business partner. But, just because the work's outcome is serious—a matter of millions of dollars of investment and implicit risk—doesn't mean the process must be laden with gravity. Tucker always has fun in the process.

Tucker's professional leadership emerges most clearly when you look at his record of contributing to the ideas and discourse of his profession. Perhaps the most quoted industrial designer of the past ten years, Tucker has broadened the discussion of design through political activism, participating in President-elect Bill Clinton's Roundtable on Design in 1993, as well as through his writings for various design journals. He has been invited to jury prestigious competitions and speak at local, national, and international conferences, and most recently he took on the challenge of redesigning how the Industrial Designers Society of America holds a conference. The resulting structural innovations broke the invisible barriers that inhibit networking and gave registrants the opportunity to think about the future, how design can improve it and survive in it.

There is nothing "comfortable" or "conformable" about Tucker Viemeister. But, then, the process of achieving innovation and stimulating thought probably requires a degree of irreverence and cockiness. The net effect Tucker has had on his profession is compelling.

Tucker goes beyond the business implications of design—to which he is as committed as any designer—to celebrate the small and large ways it shapes, and can improve, everyday life. This broad view, that everything in life, from nature to culture, society to politics, has been—will he, nill he—designed, is not unique to Tucker. But he is perhaps the only industrial designer with the effrontery to have argued that what the United States needs is another designer as president.

—Kristina Goodrich

# VIGNEAULT, Nelson

Canadian photographer and graphic designer

**Born:** Sept-Iles, Quebec, 16 November 1951. **Education:** Studied graphic communication, Laval University, Quebec, BACC, 1976; independent photography and design studies, Quebec, 1976-77; studied photography, at the Banff Centre, Alberta, 1978-79; photography, graphics, and painting, at Rochester Institute of Technology, New York, M.F.A., 1981. **Career:** Freelance photographer and graphic designer, Calgary, Alberta, from 1981; vice-president, Paperworks Press, Calgary. Instructor, at Rochester Institute of Technology, New York, 1981, Banff Centre, Alberta, 1981-82, and at the Visual Art Centre, Montreal, 1983. **Exhibitions:** *Nelson Vigneault: Laser Scan Photos,* Peter Whyte Gallery, Banff, 1981; *Solos de Imagem: Visao Americana,* Museu da Imagem e do Som, Brasilia, 1982 (toured); *Bundesfotoschau 83,* Wurzburg, 1983; *Alternative Scans,* Stephens College, Missouri, 1983. **Honors:** Printing Industries of America Prize, 1981; American Institute of Graphic Arts Excellence Award, 1981; Western Canadian Art Association Award, 1982, 1983; Toronto Art Directors Silver Award, 1982; International Society of Performing Art Administrators Award of Excellence, New York, 1982. **Address:** 2943 19th Street N.E., Calgary, Alberta T2E 7A2, Canada.

## Works

Book designs include—*1981 Techmila: 150 Years of Celebration* by Tom Grotta, Rochester, New York, 1981; *William Townsend in Alberta* by Karyn Elizabeth Allen, Calgary, Alberta, 1982; *A*

*Delicate Wilderness* by Edward Cavell, Banff, Alberta, 1983; *Legacy in Ice* by Edward Cavell, Banff, Alberta, 1983; *Calgary: Places and People* by Harry Palmer, Calgary, Alberta, 1983; *Barbara Astman* by Karen Allen, Calgary, Alberta, 1983; *Inese Bir-stins and Anne Pixley* by Lorne Falk, Banff, Alberta, 1983.

**Publications**

On VIGNEAULT: book—*Creative Source,* 4th edition, Toronto, 1983; articles—"News" in *Graphic Arts Buyer* (New York), March/ April 1981.

*

My special area of interest is the production of graphic work for the fine arts community. Because most people experience works of art through printed documentation and not through contact with original works, the designer/graphic artist is charged with the responsibility of defining an appropriate translation of a work of art or capturing the essential nature of a field of artistic endeavor.

The goal is not to reproduce the works of art, as this cannot be done, but to provide access to that interpretation which is most consistent with the intentions of the artist, or at least to suggest that many interpretations are possible and to provoke the viewer to seek out the original work. The point is that the viewer must not be fooled into imagining that experiencing the design is an adequate substitute for experiencing the original art. The emotional impact of the design should trigger or reinforce the emotional essence of the art. The designer must have a well-developed visual, technical, and critical sensibility in order to evolve a visual concept that will translate this essence to the intended viewer.

—Nelson Vigneault

# VIGNELLI, Lella (Elena)

Italian furniture, interior, graphic, and product designer

Born: Lella Valle, in Udine, in 1936. Education: Attended Massachusetts Institute of Technology, School of Architecture, Cambridge, 1955-58; University of Venice, School of Architecture, D. Arch., 1962. Family: Married Massimo Vignelli in 1957; children: Luca and Valentina. Career: Designer in the interiors department, Skidmore, Owings, and Merrill architectural firm, Chicago, 1959-60; founder and principal, Lella and Massimo Vignelli Office of Design and Architecture, Milan, 1960-64; head of interiors department, Unimark International, Milan and New York (1966), 1965-71; executive vice-president and co-founder, Vignelli Associates, New York, from 1971; president and co-founder, Vignelli Designs, New York, specializing in furniture and product design, from 1978. Board member, Artemide U.S.A., New York, from 1980; board member, New York City Landmarks Preservation Foundation. Member: Ordine Degli Architetti, Milan, 1962; Decorators Club of New York, 1982; Industrial Designers Society of America; American Institute of Graphic Arts; International Furnishings and Design Association. Exhibitions: *Italy: The New Domestic Landscape,* Museum of Modern Art, New York, 1972; *Knoll au Musée,* Musée des Arts Décoratifs, Paris, 1972; *107 Grafici dell'AGI,* Castello

Sforzesco, Milan, 1974; *design: Vignelli,* Boston Architectural Center, 1976, Kansas City Art Institute, Missouri, 1978, and Art Center College of Design, Pasadena, 1979; *Design & design,* Associazione Disegno Industriale, Milan and Venice, 1979; Padiglione d'Arte Moderna, Milan, 1980; *The Work of Lella and Massimo Vignelli,* Parsons School of Design, New York, 1980; *Vignelli,* Padiglione d'Arte Contemporanea, Milan, 1980; *Design Since 1945,* Philadelphia Museum of Art, 1983; *The Twentieth Century Poster,* Walker Art Center, Minneapolis, 1984; *New Design for Old,* Boilerhouse/Victoria and Albert Museum, London, 1986; *Lella and Massimo Vignelli, Recent Works,* Ontario Art Gallery, Toronto, 1987; *Vignelli in Miami,* Luminaire, Inc., Miami, Florida, 1987; *The Modern Poster,* Museum of Modern Art, New York, 1988; *Graphic Design in America,* Walker Art Center, Minneapolis, 1989-90 (toured); *Design USA,* United States Information Agency sponsored tour of the Soviet Union, 1989-1991; *Design: Vignelli,* Academy of the Arts of the U.S.S.R., 1989 (toured ten European cities, 1989-93, ending at the Musée des Arts Décoratifs, Paris). Collections: Museum of Modern Art, New York; Cooper-Hewitt Museum, New York; Metropolitan Museum of Art, New York; Philadelphia Museum of Art; Musée des Arts Décoratifs, Montreal; Israel Museum, Jerusalem; Die Neue Sammlung, Munich; Museum für Kunst und Gewerbe, Hamburg; Vitra Museum, Weil Am Rhein. Honors: American Institute of Architects Industrial Arts Medal, 1973; Honorary Member, Women in Design, New York, 1981; *Interiors* Magazine Special Award, New York, 1982; Gold Medal, American Institute of Graphic Arts, 1983; Excellence Award, Industrial Designers Society of America, 1983, 1985; Citation of Distinguished Contributions, National Associated Schools of Art and Design, 1983; Edwin F. Guth Memorial Award of Distinction, Illuminating Engineering Society of North America, 1983; Award of Design Excellence, Presidential Design Awards, National Endowment for the Arts, Washington, D.C., 1984; *Interior Design* Hall of Fame, 1988; Collab Award for Excellence in Design, Philadelphia Museum of Art, 1988; Gold Medal for Design, National Arts Club, 1991; Fellowship of Excellence, Interior Product Designers, 1992; honorary doctorates, from Parsons School of Design, New York, Corcoran School of Art, Washington D. C., Pratt Institute, Rhode Island School of Design, and Università di Venezia. Vignelli Associates has also received numerous other awards for graphic design and interior design excellence. Address: Vignelli Associates, 475 Tenth Avenue, New York, New York 10018, U.S.A.

# VIGNELLI, Massimo

Italian graphic, corporate, book, exhibition, interior, furniture, and product designer

Born: Milan, 10 January 1931. Education: Studied at the Brera Academy of Art, Milan, 1948-50, at the Politecnico, Milan, 1950-53, and at the School of Architecture, University of Venice, 1953-57. Family: Married Lella Elena Valle in 1957; children: Luca and Valentina. Career: Founder and principal, of Lella and Massimo Vignelli Office of Design and Architecture, Milan, 1960-64; design director and co-founder, Unimark International, New York, 1965-71; president and co-founder, Vignelli Associates, New York, from 1971; chairman and co-founder, Vignelli Designs, New York, from

1978. President, American Institute of Graphic Arts, New York, 1976-77; trustee, Institute for Architecture and Urban Studies, New York, from 1978. **Member:** American Institute of Graphic Arts; Industrial Designers Society of America; Architectural League of New York; Alliance Graphique Internationale. **Exhibitions:** *Italy: The New Domestic Landscape,* Museum of Modern Art, New York, 1972; *Knoll au Musée,* Musée des Arts Décoratifs, Paris, 1972; *107 Grafici dell'AGI,* Castello Sforzesco, Milan, 1974; *design: Vignelli,* Boston Architectural Center, 1976, Kansas City Art Institute, Missouri, 1978, and Art Center College of Design, Pasadena, 1979; *Design & design,* Associazione Disegno Industriale, Milan and Venice, 1979; Padiglione d'Arte Moderna, Milan, 1980; *The Work of Lella and Massimo Vignelli,* Parsons School of Design, New York, 1980; *Vignelli,* Padiglione d'Arte Contemporanea, Milan, 1980; *Design Since 1945,* Philadelphia Museum of Art, 1983; *The Twentieth Century Poster,* Walker Art Center, Minneapolis, 1984; *New Design for Old,* Boilerhouse/Victoria and Albert Museum, London, 1986; *Massimo Vignelli,* Cooper Union, New York, 1986; *Lella and Massimo Vignelli, Recent Works,* Ontario Art Gallery, Toronto, 1987; *Vignelli in Miami,* Luminaire, Inc., Miami, Florida, 1987; *The Modern Poster,* Museum of Modern Art, New York, 1988; *Graphic Design in America,* Walker Art Center, Minneapolis, 1989-90 (toured); *Design USA,* United States Information Agency sponsored tour of the Soviet Union, 1989-1991; *design: Vignelli,* Academy of the Arts of the U.S.S.R., 1989 (toured ten European cities, 1989-93, ending at the Musée des Arts Décoratifs, Paris). **Collections:** Museum of Modern Art, New York; Cooper-Hewitt Museum, New York; Metropolitan Museum of Art, New York; Philadelphia Museum of Art; Musée des Arts Décoratifs, Montreal; Israel Museum, Jerusalem; Die Neue Sammlung, Munich; Museum für Kunst und Gewerbe, Hamburg; Vitra Museum, Weil Am Rhein. **Honors:** Towle Silversmiths Fellowship, 1957; Moholy-Nagy Fellowship, Chicago Institute of Design, 1958; Compasso d'Oro, Italian Association for Industrial Design, 1964; Gran Premio Triennale di Milano, 1964; American Institute of Architects Industrial Arts Medal, 1973; New York Art Directors Club Hall of Fame Award, 1982; Gold Medal, American Institute of Graphic Arts, 1983; Excellence Award, Industrial Designers Society of America, 1983, 1985; Citation of Distinguished Contributions, National Associated Schools of Art and Design, 1983; Edwin F. Guth Memorial Award of Distinction, Illuminating Engineering Society of North America, 1983; Award of Design Excellence, Presidential Design Awards, National Endowment for the Arts, Washington, D.C., 1984; Collab Award for Excellence in Design, Philadelphia Museum of Art, 1988; *Interior Design* Hall of Fame, 1988; Gold Medal for Design, National Arts Club, 1991; Fellowship of Excellence, Interior Product Designers, 1992; honorary doctorates, from Parsons School of Design, New York, Corcoran School of Art, Washington D. C., Pratt Institute, Rhode Island School of Design, and Università di Venezia. Vignelli Associates has also received numerous other awards for graphic design and interior design excellence. **Address:** Vignelli Associates, 475 Tenth Avenue, New York 10018, U.S.A.

## Works

Posters and graphics, for the Venice Biennale, 1962, 1964.
Stacking dinner and tableware ranges in ceramic and melamine, for Heller, 1964.
Corporate identity program, for Knoll International, 1966.
Logotype symbol, for American Airlines, 1967.

*Nuts and Bolts* series of toiletry containers in glass and plastic laminates, for Colton/Gillette, 1970.
Cocktail bar accessories in stainless steel, for Sanlorenzo, 1971.
Lotogype symbol and identity, for Bloomingdale's Department Store, 1972.
Gallery and office interiors, for the Minneapolis Institute of Fine Arts, 1974.
Cookwares in ovenproof glass, for Heller, 1975.
St. Peter's Church interiors, New York, 1975.
Corporate identity program, for Lancia automobiles, 1978.
Corporate identity program, for Ciga Hotels, 1979.
Publications program, for the United States National Parks Administration, 1983-85.
The work of Vignelli Associates has included—corporate identity programs for clients including American Airlines, Ford Motor Company, JC Penney, Solomon R. Guggenheim Museum, and Xerox Corporation; graphic programs for clients including Champion International, IBM Corporation, Museum of Modern Art, New York, and Ritz-Carlton Hotels; architectural graphics for clients including AT&T Building (with John Burgee Architects with Philip Johnson), Citicorp (with Stubbins Associates), Credit Lyonnais Corporate Offices (with Skidmore, Owings, and Merrill Architects), and Price Waterhouse Corporate Headquarters (with ISI/Interiorspace International); publication design for clients including Abbeville Press, Pantheon Books, Penguin Books, Rizzoli, Rockport Publishers, *American Heritage, The Herald, Industrial Design,* and *Nation's Business*; packaging design for clients including Anne Klein, Barney's, Gillette, IBM Corporation, Saks Fifth Avenue, CIBA GEIGY AG, and Fassati Wines; interior design of showrooms, stores, and office for clients including Artemide, Inc., Guggenheim Foundation, Venice, Knoll-Gavina, New York, Olivetti, Milan, Steelcase Design Partnership, New York, and the United States Postal Service; exhibition, museum, and trade show design for clients including the American Institute of Graphic Arts, FIAT/LANCIA, Panasonic, Pirelli, Sara Lee Corporation, and Xerox Corporation; and furniture and product design for Acerbis International, Arteluce, Corning Glass Works, Formica Corporation, Knoll International, Poltronova, San Lorenzo, and Steuben.

## Publications

**By VIGNELLI: books**—*Graphic Design for Nonprofit Organizations,* New York, 1980; (with Eric Larrabee) *Knoll Design,* New York, 1981; **articles**—in *Journal of Graphic Design* (New York), November 1982; *Upper and Lower Case* (New York), December 1982.

**On VIGNELLI: books**—*An International Survey of Packing* by Wim Crouwel and Kurt Weideman, London, 1968; *Knoll au Musée,* exhibition catalogue by Christine Rae, Paris, 1972; *107 Grafici dell'AGI,* with texts by Renzo Zorzi and Franco Grignani, Venice, 1974; *Design: Vignelli* by Emilio Ambasz, New York, 1980; *The Language of Graphics* by Edward Booth-Clibborn and Daniele Baroni, London, 1980; *Who's Who in Graphic Art* edited by Walter Amstutz, Dubendorf, 1982; *Design Since 1945* edited by Kathyrn Hiesinger and George Marcus, Philadelphia and London, 1983; *The Twentieth Century Poster: Design of the Avant-Garde* by Dawn Ades, New York, 1984; *The Conran Directory of Design* edited by Stephen Bayley, London, 1985; *New Design for Old,* exhibition

**Lella and Massimo Vignelli: furniture designs, 1964-1979**

catalogue with texts by Helen Hamlyn, Eric Midwinter, and others, London, 1986; *New American Design* by Hugh Aldersley-Williams, New York, 1988.

*See* VIGNELLI, Lella

\*

Our design philosophy is based on discipline—intended as methodology and attitude; appropriateness—intended as the search for the specific; and ambiguity—intended as a plurality of meaning.

We believe in improving the visual quality of our environment and in the commitment to achieve this goal; in design dignity and its influence on people; and in timelessness and change, in consistency and contradiction, and in classicism and friendliness. We love to affect design and affects others by design. We love to create and to transform until projects, objects, and ideas become "things."

—Massimo and Lella Vignelli

\*     \*     \*

Massimo and Lella Vignelli are total designers whose work enhances our physical and emotional environment with a subtle combination of mind and eye. Their design work is varied and ubiquitous, including furniture, glassware, and silverware, exhibitions, showrooms and stores, interiors, books, and other publications, posters, transportation graphics, and corporate identity programs. Theirs is a multi-layered bond, personal and professional.

If their "style" is to be defined, it is one of erudition and elegance: a Euclidian approach articulating geometry in two- and three-dimensional form. They carry their stylistic momentum into contemporary lives, absorbing the history of art, architecture, and design, while elaborating it significantly. The aesthetic import is of first consideration, whether for a poster, a book, a chair, or an interior. They do not disregard functional requirements but always eschew the austere and the merely decorative.

No rigid formula keeps down their quest for solutions, often now with flashes of randomness; however focused and refined, their designs are rendered with an emotional elan, a simplicity born of abstracting from complexities and redundancies. Theirs has been a gradual metamorphosis away from a formal visual language which sometimes played with the past. With perceptual shifts and ambiguities, their work titillates our vision with a careful selection of particular values. The balancing of myriad intangibles and unconscious mental force produces a judgmental act which adds up to tangible works of art. One of their strong points is their ability to break even their own rules, so that "style" evolves, bringing in new principles that bring in transformations.

In graphics, Massimo Vignelli's most distinctive successes are achieved through brilliant use of typography and the grid. With his masterful use of the grid as structures, he has altered the look of both the single page and full publications while emphasizing the legibility of the message. He has made lettering itself a means of expression by using contrasts of scale, type size and weight, color, texture, and spacing to create powerful patterns with emotional value. Close coordination of image and typography carries the message with potent force. Derived from the Swiss, the Vignelli devotion to the grid produces results which are clear and ordered; the design principles are applied vigorously, effectively, but never slavishly.

These two extraordinary, talented people have pooled their innermost resources to endow our visual world with tangible and unmistakable character. Theirs has been a great journey of discovery wherein people and process are of utmost concern.

—Mildred Constantine

# VIONNET, Madeleine (Marie Valentine)

French fashion designer

**Born:** Chilleurs-aux-Bois, Loiret, 22 June 1876. **Education:** Studied at the Ecole Communale, Chilleurs-aux-Bois, until 1888. **Family:** Married in 1893 (divorced, 1894); children: one (died); married Dmitri Netchvolodov in 1925 (divorced, 1955). **Career:** Apprenticed to a dressmaker, Aubervillers, 1888-93; dressmaker, in House of Vincent fashion company, Paris, 1893-95; cutter, then head of workshops, at Kate Reilly fashion house, London, 1895-1900; saleswoman, at Bechoff fashion company, Paris, 1900-01; head of studios, under Marie Gerber, at Callot Soeurs fashion house, Paris, 1901-05; designer, in Robert Doucet fashion house, Paris, 1905-11; founder and director of Maison Vionnete fashion house in the Rue de Rivoli, Paris, 1912-14, 1919-22, and in the Avenue Montaigne, 1922-39; retired 1940. **Exhibitions:** *Exposition International des Arts Decoratifs,* Paris, 1925; *Grands Countries Parisiens 1910-1939,* Musée Carnavet, Paris, 1965; *Fashion: An Anthology,* Victoria and Albert Museum, London, 1971; *The Tens, Twenties, and Thirties,* Metropolitan Museum of Art, New York, 1974; *Art and Fashion 1900-1939,* Victoria and Albert Museum, London, 1975. **Collections:** Centre de Documention du Costume, Paris; Metropolitan Museum of Art, New York; Victoria and Albert Museum, London. **Honors:** Chevalier de la Legion d'Honneur, France. **Died:** Paris, 2 March 1975.

## Publications

**On VIONNET: books**—*Dressmakers of France* by Mary Brooks Picken and Dora Miller, New York, 1956; *Paris a la Mode* by Celia Bertin, Paris and London, 1956; *Kings of Fashion* by Anny Latour, Stuttgart, 1956, London, 1958; *The World in Vogue 1893-1963*

edited by Bryan Holme and others, New York and London, 1963; *Grands Countries Parisiens 1910-1039,* exhibition catalogue edited by Madeleine Delpierre and Henriette Vanier, Paris, 1965; *Fashion: An Anthology by Cecil Beaton,* exhibition catalogue complied by Madeleine Ginsburg, London, 1971; *Couture,* edited by Ruth Lynam, New York, 1972; *In Vogue: Sixty Years of Celebrities and Fashion* edited by Georgina Howell, London, 1975, 1978, New York, 1976; *A History of Fashion* by J. Anderson and Madge Garland, London, 1975, 1980; *The World of Fashion: People, Places, Resources* by Eleanor Lambert, London and New York, 1976; *Inventive Paris Fashions 1909-1939* by Diana Vreeland, New York and London, 1977; *Magic Names of Fashion* by Ernestine Carter, London, 1980; *Fairchild's Who's Who in Fashion* edited by Anne Stegemeyer, New York, 1980; *McDowell's Directory of Twentieth Century Fashion* by Colin McDowell, London, 1984; *The Encyclopaedia of Fashion from 1840 to the 1980s* by Georgina O'Hara, London, 1986.

\*     \*     \*

Madeleine Vionnet said that she designed not fashions but harmonies. As a talented young designer in Paris at the turn of the century, she was influenced by avant-garde notions of physical freedom and the romantic classicism popularly expressed by dancer Isadora Duncan. By 1907, a skilled modiste for the prestigious House of Doucet, she boldly insisted that models remove the black cotton underdress then worn for the sake of modesty. She wanted the clothes to be shown as customers would wear them. Her first collection for Doucet consisted of dishabille, the loose "tea gowns" accepted for at-home wear, at that time the only kind of garment a lady would wear without corseting. But in a radical attempt at dress reform not appreciated by Doucet's conservative clients, Vionnet intended her designs for street wear. With the support of friends and demimondaines who favored emancipated dress, Vionnet opened her own couture house in Paris in 1912 and developed her unique contribution to garment technology, the bias-cut. Working with the actual fabric custom-woven two yards longer than usual, she turned it diagonal to the straight grain and draped it on a small-scale, wooden mannequin. Exploiting the fabric's natural elasticity, her mathematically precise cuts and intricate seams molded the fabric to the female form like a second skin. Surface embellishment was totally integrated with design, always serving to amplify line and motion. Technique had been wedded to philosophy. As Vionnet said, "The dress must accompany its wearer, and when a woman smiles, the dress must smile with her."

While Vionnet worked to create gowns of individual beauty and timeless proportions, her designs nevertheless kept pace with changes in fashion, expressing what she called "harmonic variations on a given theme." Asymmetrical handkerchief-prints fluttered gracefully from her silk dresses of the 1920s. She offered classically-draped gowns popular in the early 1930s and molten satin evening sheaths, which became archetypal movie-star glamour, in the mid-1930s. At the decade's end, her interpretation of the Victorian revival was accomplished not with stiff crinolines but with knowing manipulation of crisp taffeta. What mattered to Vionnet most was not fashion but the behavior of the fabric and its enhancement of the body beneath it.

By the time World War II caused her to close her business, her clientele included the royal and social aristocracy of Europe. After retirement, she served as a frequent consultant to the French couture industry. While her intricate designs were difficult to copy, the bias-cut had become the basic garment construction method of the 1930s. Vionnet's singular technique has come into standard usage by contemporary designers creating comfortable, body-conscious clothes.

—Sandra Michels Adams

# VON APPEN, Karl

German painter and stage designer

**Born:** Düsseldorf, 12 May 1900. **Education:** Studied at schools in Krefeld, Hamburg, and Frankfurt, 1906-15; apprenticed as a chemigraph, Frankfurt, 1915-18; apprentice scene painter, under Ludwig Aievert, at the Schauspielhaus, Frankfurt, 1918-22; studied painting and graphics under F.K. Delavilla, at the Kunstgewerbeschule, Frankfurt, and under Max Beckmann, at the Stadelsches Institut, Frankfurt, 1922-24. **Family:** Married Manja Behrens. **Career:** Worked as a stage decor designer, at the Kunstlertheater für Rhein und Main, Frankfurt, 1924-27; independent painter and graphic artist, Berlin, 1927-30; stage designer, at the Stadttheater, Würzburg, 1930; freelance designer and painter, working in Dresden, from 1930; joined Communist Party and forbidden to work, 1935-40; scene painter, at the Staatstheater, Dresden, 1940-41; arrested as a resistance group member and imprisoned at camp in Niederroden, near Frankfurt, 1941-45; head of design 1945-54, and art director, 1947-49, at the Staatstheater, Dresden; chief stage designer, for the Berliner Ensemble, Berlin, 1954-81; worked with producers Heinz Arnold, Bertolt Brecht, Benno Besson, Erich Engel, Manfred Karge, Matthias Langhoff, Joachim Tenschert, and others. **Member:** State Professor of the DDR, 1960; Member of the Akadamie der Kunste, Berlin, 1961; DDR Order of Marx, 1975; Honorary President, Organization Internationale des Scenographes et des Techniciens du Theatre. **Exhibitions:** East Berlin, 1975, 1982; Leipzig, 1976; Warsaw, 1976; Bratislava, 1978; Prague, 1978; Stockholm, 1978; Venice, 1980; Dresden, 1983. **Collections:** Graphic collections of the State Galleries of Berlin and Dresden. **Honors:** DDR National Prize, German Democratic Republic, 1956, 1969; DDR National Order of Merit, 1965; Gold Medal, Prague Quadriennale, 1967. **Died:** East Berlin, 21 August 1981.

## Works

Stage productions include—for the Schauspielhaus, Frankfurt— *Herzog Blaubarts Burg,* 1922; *Der holzgeschnitzte Prinz,* 1922; for the Staatstheater, Dresden—*Die Zauberflöte,* 1946; *Die Flut,* 1947; *Die Kluge,* 1947; *Salome,* 1947; *Rusalka,* 1948; *Cosi fan tutte,* 1948; *Fidelio,* 1948; *Antigonae,* 1950; *Des Simplicius Simplicissimus Jugend,* 1950; *Carmen,* 1951; *Die Brücke des Lebens,* 1952; *Die der Danae,* 1952; for the Berliner Ensemble, East Berlin—*Katzgraben,* 1953; *Der kaukasische Kreidekreis,* 1954; *Winterschlacht,* 1955; *Pauken und Trompeten,* 1955; *The Playboy of the Western World,* 1956; *Furcht und Elend des Brittischen Reiches,* 1957; *Der gute Mensch von Sezuan,* 1957; *Optimistische Tragödie,* 1958; *Der aufhatsame Aufstieg des Arturo Ui,* 1959; *Die Dreigroschenoper,* 1960; *Frau Flinz,* 1961; *Die Tage der Commune,* 1962; *Coriolanus,* 1964; *Der Brotladen,* 1967; *Die heilige Jonna der Schlachthofe,* 1968; *Turamdot order*

*der Kongress der Weisswascher,* 1973; *Der Unbedeutende,* 1976; for the Deutsches Theater, East Berlin—*Wallenstein,* 1959; *Die Sommerfrische,* 1974; in Halle—*Polly order Die Bataile am Bluewater Creek,* 1965.

## Publications

**By VON APPEN: book**—*Karl Von Appen, Altes und Neues: Bilder und Text* edited by Friedrich Dieckmann, Berlin, 1975.

**On VON APPEN: books**—*The Theatre of Bertolt Brecht* by John Willett, London, 1969, 1967, 1977; *Bertolt Brecht: Der Brotladen* by Manfred Karge and Matthias Langhoff, Frankfurt, 1967; *Notate Arbeit des Berliner Ensembles 1956-1966* by Manfred Wekwerth, Berlin and Weimar, 1967; *Buhnenbildarbeit in der Deutschen Demokratische Republik* edited by Friedrich Dieckmann, Berlin, 1971; *Karl Von Appens Buhnenbilder am Ensemble* by Friedrich Dieckmann, Berlin, 1971, 1973; *Monografie des Plakats: Entwicklung, Stil, Design* by Herbert Schindler, Munich, 1972; *Gebrauchsgraphik in der DDR* by Helmut Rademacher, Dresden, 1975; *Die Schauspiel-theater der DDR und das Erbe 1970-1974* edited by Manfred Nossig, 1976; *Streifzuge: Aufsatze und Kritiken* by Friedrich Dieckmann, Berlin, Weimar, 1977.

\*    \*    \*

Most of Karl von Appen's work prior to 1945 was destroyed by the Nazi terror and the war. The paintings from this period reveal the artist's sympathy with the Neue Sachlichkeit, a number of his graphic works exhibiting a pungent socio-critical accent. In the designs, a strong sense of color liberated from the confines of illusionism makes itself felt.

His post-1945 Dresden stage work is marked by a spirit of penetrating honesty with a sure sense of spatial and colour effect to give the director appropriate possibilities of action. The meeting with Brecht in 1953 had a decisive influence on von Appen and soon led to a close relationship with the Berliner Ensemble. With Brecht, von Appen discovered the theoretical and materially practicable bases for those efforts which had only begun to be effective in his previous work in Dresden. Von Appen adapted the achievements of epic theatre to his own artistic temperament—a temperament of quiet, painterly ingenuity, which the Brechtian stage used as a means of individualising the scenic element. The solution of integrated illusion or "symbol scene" pursued by Brecht and Caspar Neher in the 1920s and early 1930s was adapted by von Appen according to changes in the social situation, a method by which the empty space acted both as a dividing and unifying element. The method was described and praised by Brecht in "Chinese Painting."

Von Appen also gave adequate expression to the dialectical realism of the later Brecht, who regarded von Appen's stage sketches for *Katzgraben* as having, for the first time in the theatre, revealed the face of the working class. In von Appen's subsequent work, there was a physiognomic certainty not previously seen in the realm of stage design. By means of the stage movement and layout drawings, the designer influences the work of the director; this preferred instrument of the epic theatre was exactingly adapted by von Appen to the demands of the piece and used as a starting point for his work on the decor and costumes. The objectively distanced perusal of historical stage settings plays a large role in Von Appen's productions of classical pieces. Among his most famous productions are the *Caucasian Chalk Circle* (1954), *Kettle Drums and Trumpets* (1955), *The Good Woman of Sezuan* (1957), *Optimistic Tragedy* (1958), *The Incredible Rise of Arturo Ui* (1959), and *The Three-penny Opera* (1960).

—Friedrich Dieckmann

# VOSSOUGHI, Sohrab

American product and industrial designer

**Born:** Tehran, Iran, 14 December 1956. **Education:** Studied Industrial Design, San Jose State University, B.S., 1979. **Career:** designer, Hewlett-Packard, 1979-1982; independent consultant, 1982-1984; president and founder, ZIBA Design, Inc., Portland, Oregon, from 1984. **Member:** Industrial Designers Society of America (IDSA), World Economic Forum, Human Factors, Corporate Design Management. **Exhibitions:** IDSA Exhibition, 1985, 1986, 1988, 1989, 1990, 1991, 1993, 1994; IDSA Northwest Design Invitational, 1990, 1992, 1994; ZIBA Design Exhibit, Tokyo, Japan, 1991, 1993; Design Zentrum, Nordrhein Westfalen e.V. Germany, 1993, 1994; Tidex Exhibit, Taipei World Trade Center, 1994; iF Industrie Forum Design Hannover, Germany, 1994. **Collections:** Museum of Modem Art, New York; Museum of London, England; Design Center Stuttgart; State of Baden-Württemberg, Germany. **Honors:** (all with ZIBA Design Inc.) Designer's Choice Awards, *Industrial Design* magazine, 1984, 1985, 1988, 1989 (4); Silver Award, 1985, 1986, 1988 (2), 1989 (2), 1990 (2), 1991 (2), 1993 (4), 1994, 1995 (2), Bronze Award, 1988, 1989, 1993, 1994, 1995 (2), and Gold Award, 1989, 1991, 1993 (2), 1994, Industrial Design Excellence Awards (IDEA), IDSA; Best of Category Award, 1988 (2), 1994, Gold Award, 1990, Bronze Award, 1990 (5), 1992 (3), Silver Award, 1992 (2), Award of Merit, 1994 (2), Technical Achievement Award, 1994 (4), Northwest Design Invitational, IDSA; Best Consumer Product, 1989, 1991, *Business Week* magazine, 1989; Designer's Choice Awards, *International Design* magazine, Annual Design Review, 1990 (3), 1991 (3), 1992 (3), 1993 (1); Best of 1991 Design, *Time* magazine, 1991; First Place in Test and Measurement, 1992, and First Place in Computer/Business Equipment, 1995, Excellence in Design Awards, *Appliance Manufacturer* magazine; International Design Prize, Design Center Stuttgart, 1993; High Design Quality Red Dot Award, 1993 (4), 1994, *Design Innovations* Competition, Design Zentrum, Nordrhein Westfalen e.V. Germany; iF Seal for Good Industrial Design (7), iF Industrie Forum Design Hannover, Hannover Fair, Germany, 1994; GOOD DESIGN Award (2), Chicago Athenaeum, Museum of Architecture and Design, Illinois, 1994. **Address:** ZIBA Design, 305 NW 21st Avenue Portland, Oregon 97209, U.S.A.

## Works

*The Cleret,* for Hanco, 1989.
*Drake Willock System 1000 Dialysis Machine,* for Althin CD Medical, 1991.
*Biojector,* for Bioject Inc., 1993.
*Flat Panel Display,* for Hewlett-Packard Company, 1994.
*Natural Keyboard,* for Microsoft, 1995.

## Publications

**By VOSSOUGHI: articles**—(with Steve McCallion) "Industrial Design Made Easy: Three Steps to Communicating Value" in *Design Management Journal,* Spring 1994.

**On VOSSOUGHI and ZIBA DESIGN: articles**—"Dialysis, Gently," by Dori Jones Yang in *Business Week* (New York), 17 June 1991; "The Best Design in America" in *ID Annual Design Review* (MacLean, Virginia), 1992; "The Best Entrepreneurs" in *Business Week,* 11 January 1993; "A Shot in the Arm for Sales" by Yang in *Business Week,* 7 June 1993; "Global Leader Joins the Pack" in *Design,* April 1994; "Creating A 'Desk Sculpture'" by Yang in *Business Week,* 6 June 1994; "Form + Function" by John Pierson in *Wall Street Journal* (New York), 6 June 1994; "Good Design Can't Do It All" by Yang in *Business Week,* 5 June 1995.

\*

*Origins*

People are at the center of everything ZIBA creates. Our designs are used by people. Our designs are manufactured by people. Our designs are created by people.

We strive to make our product designs human. To accomplish this, we combine information and art to create products that are useful.

Our design approach is based on a unique tool kit. Our most important tools include: Passion; Respect; Excellence; Responsibility.

Passion is the drive to create something truly innovative. Our product development team is constantly challenging itself. We believe innovation is found just beyond the point where most people give up. For us, design is more than a profession. Design is an opportunity and a privilege.

Respect is a key value for ZIBA. Respect for customer needs and wants. Respect for every member of our team. Respect for the environment. Respect gives us the ability to listen and care. Respect allows us to keep learning.

Excellence is a moving finish line. We never lose sight of it. And we never stop trying to reach it. Excellence is a powerful source of motivation for ZIBA. The longer it is pursued, the more important it becomes.

Responsibility comes with opportunity. At ZIBA, we have a special responsibility to our clients and their customers. We have a broader responsibility to society and the environment. We also have a responsibility to ourselves to reach our full potential as individuals.

*Relevance*

Relevance is a responsibility. Our work is relevant to the extent that it improves life. Products create value through use. Our objective is to create products that people will use and benefit from.

Every product is a human experience that will be released over the life of that product. We rely on informed creativity to realize the potential of every design opportunity. Every product can be summarized in terms of information. Information about customers' needs. Information about competing products. Information about manufacturing methods. Using information, we approach product designs in their appropriate market and cultural context. Without context, design loses much of its value.

Sohrab Vossoughi: Natural Keyboard, for Microsoft, 1995. Photo: Michael Jones

Sohrab Vossoughi: Flat Panel Display, for Hewlett-Packard Company, 1994. Photo: Michael Jones

*Ambitions*

The ambition of our work is product design that is relevant without being trendy. Our ambition is to create products based on simple, enduring ideas. Good design is timeless. It is based on values rather than fashion.

Advancement is an important part of our vision. From products that are "earth-friendly" to products that are designed "for everyone," our work is meant to set new limits and eliminate boundaries.

Our vision is to create products that are forward-looking and socially responsible. The ambition of our work is the creation of designs that reflect the interdependence of our society, our environment, and our economy.

—ZIBA Design Inc.

\*     \*     \*

What is design? Sohrab Vossoughi, IDSA, explains it this way: "To make the complex simple. To reinvent the obvious. To solve problems. To apply nonlinear thinking to everything. Crossing the street requires design thinking." So basic and universal is design, that Sohrab applies its principles on the most unexpected situations. In fact, today Sohrab's firm, ZIBA Design, is being asked by clients to apply design thinking to solve problems whose eventual outcome may be a process, a product, or a strategy.

Sohrab didn't set out with this view of design and such wide-ranging projects. He set out to create a family whose goal was to have fun by following the passion to create. In a little over ten years, that family has grown to more than 43 people, earning a huge number of awards and many, many happy clients. The key to that success lies very much, not only in his firm's excellent design work, but in Sohrab's core values. These he has articulated for his firm to help everyone remember the cornerstone of the company.

First of all, Sohrab values long-term thinking. He doesn't look at a project as an isolated event but as part of building a continuous relationship. Business is not about making a dollar today, but about doing well in ten years. Money is the by-product of quality work; if you give people the freedom to do their best, the financial reward will follow.

In his value system, relationships take precedence over monetary issues. He prides himself on never having laid off or fired anyone, always taking the time to find them another job if ZIBA didn't work out for them. "We don't just hire based on skills," he says, "we hire mostly based on attitude and personality. That's because teamwork isn't about brainstorming together occasionally, it's about pulling for each other all the time. If that means that we all have to work around the clock to help one person achieve a goal, then that's what we do."

Sohrab believes in humility. "The better you are, the more humble you have to be. We've done very well in Asia as a result," he explains.

And, finally, Sohrab believes in having fun. "It's got to be fun. But fun is in the way you think about the project. Challenge is fun to me. Sometimes it may be frustrating, yes. But the net effect is satisfying. And satisfaction is fun. I won't let anything go out of ZIBA if we're not satisfied with it, even if the client is. We work until we've done the thing right by our standards. Then we are having fun."

So when have you done it right? According to Sohrab, when you've asked questions about why things "have" to be the way they are, tested the validity of the assumptions and found new answers, then you're getting there. For example, much of the trend toward putting color back in products was born at ZIBA Design in the mid 1980s when they asked, "why does exercise equipment have to be black?" While the query may seem like a superficial styling focus, in fact it demonstrated an interest in finding a better way to appeal to the emotional, social, and cultural context of fitness equipment. Perhaps if equipment looked more charming and inviting, less intimidating and impersonal, people would want to use it more often.

Today Sohrab believes that design is moving up the corporate food chain, where its real value is being put to work creating business strategies. More and more, ZIBA is defining what a company should be making, defining products that people want and need and find useful. "Styling doesn't sell," he points out. "You have to meet users needs, but give them something more, too. You have to give them value."

The danger here is, of course, "feature creep," the tendency to add features rather than really understanding what the user needs and wants. "To succeed at creating value, design has to be total. It has to understand and respond to the entire business picture, including the fact that people respond at a basic level to how much a product costs." This sort of thinking about a product, not from its dimensional point of view, but from the point of view of the user and the context of its use, has led Sohrab to form an in-house research group at ZIBA.

Sohrab also believes that industrial designers must accept social responsibility on behalf of its customers—the product's users. "Many designers are building in visual obsolescence. Look at Braun. There's a company with a classic, timeless aesthetic. The timelessness of a product is our social responsibility."

Sohrab has come a long way in the past 12 years. A few years ago, there was a need for another ZIBA designer to have a drafting table, so Sohrab sadly gave his up. Was he no longer a designer? Was he now a different person? A manager? With the help of a good friend, Sohrab realized he was still a designer, only his medium had changed.

—Kristina Goodrich

# VUORI, Pekka (Vaino Johannes)

Finnish illustrator and graphic designer

**Born:** Kiikka, 12 November 1935. **Education:** Studied graphic design, Institute of Industrial Arts, Helsinki, 1953-56. **Family:** Married Marjatta Nupponen in 1963; children: Joonas and Julia. **Career:** Worked as a magazine and newspaper layout artist, Helsinki, 1959-73; freelance illustrator and graphic designer, working for *Lipas, Suomen Kuvalehti, Helsingin Sanomat, Form Function Finland,* and the publishers Kirjasieppo, SKS, WSOY, Tammi, and Kustannuskiila, in Helsinki, since 1973. **Exhibitions:** Pinx Gallery, 1963, 1964; SKS Gallery, Helsinki, 1978; Vellamo Gallery, Helsinki, 1982; AKK Gallery, Helsinki, 1985, 1986, 1987; Rotunda Gallery, Helsinki, 1988; Ruka Art Gallery, Finland, 1989; Voipaala Art Centre, Valkeakoski, Finland, 1993; Design Forum, Helsinki, 1995. **Honors:** Church Film Award, Helsinki, 1969 (with Seppo Saves); Rudolf Koivu Awards, Helsinki, 1972, 1978, 1982; Finnish State Award for Applied Arts, 1972, 1983; Well Done

Pekka Vuori: *Italian Problems* (Helsingin Sanomat) newspaper illustration, 1993

Book Award, Tokyo, 1985; GRAFIA Graphic Artist of the Year Award, Helsinki, 1987; Finnish State Literature Award, 1988; Honorary Diploma, IBBY, 1988; Two Honorary Diplomas, Leipzig Book Fair, 1989; Björn Landström award, 1989; Pier Paolo Vergerio Honorary Diploma, 1989; Finnish State Grants, 1978, 1986, 1990 (five-year grant); Second Prize, Mikkeli Illustrations Triennial Exhibition, 1993. **Address:** Vyökatu 10 B 22, FIN-00160 Helsinki, Finland.

## Works

*Kapalamak/Folk Tales* book illustrations, for Kirjasieppo, 1977.
*Helsingin Sanomat* newspaper illustrations, from 1978.
*Form Function Finland* magazine design, from 1980.
*Jättiläiset/The Giant* book illustrations, for SKS, 1981.
*Kotimainen Krokotiili* (Jukka Parkkinen) book illustrations, for WSOY, 1981.
*Sysdämeni Laulu/The Song of My Heart* (Aleksis Kivi) book illustrations, for SKS, 1984.
*Lintukotolaiset/Folk Tales* book illustrations, for SKS, 1985.

*Into, Parrakas Vauva/Into, Bearded Baby,* Otava, 1985.
*Treasures of the Orthodox Church Museum* book design, for Kustannuskiila, 1985.
*Viktor Barsokevitsch: Photos 1893-1927* book design, for Kustannuskiila, 1987.
*Kadonneet Alushameet/The Lost Petticoats,* Otava, 1987.
*Joe-Setä/Uncle Joe* (Veikko Huovinen) book illustrations, for WSOY, 1988.
*Suomalasia Nykykirjailijoita/Contemporary Finnish Writers* (Pekka Tarkka) book illustrations, for Tammi, 1989.
*Suuri Juorukirja/The Big Book of Rumours* (Ilari Lindholm) book illustrations, for Pikku-idis, 1993.

## Publications

**By VUORI: books**—*Otto Ja Ville,* Helsinki, 1972; *Into Parakas Vauva,* with text by K. Helakisa, Helsinki, 1985; *Kadonneet Alushameet,* Helsinki, 1987; *Ei Housut Lainissa Parane,* Helsinki 1989; *Hullu Hajusuola,* Otava, 1991; *Romuluksen Raketti-Ja Paket-Timatkat,* Otava, 1992.

VYCHODIL CONTEMPORARY DESIGNERS

**On VUORI: books**—*Parhaat Pilapiirtajat,* Helsinki, 1979; *Finnish Industrial Design* edited by Tua Potasuo, Helsinki, 1987; *Finnish Illustrators of Children's Books,* Helsinki, 1989; **articles**—"Graphic Artist of the Year" in *Form Function Finland* (Helsinki), no. 1, 1987.

*    *    *

As an illustrator and graphic artist, Pekka Vuori's varied output and use of line put him in the front rank of Finns in his field. Vuori skillfully combines numerous talents. His all-round ability and creativity are shown by the fact that he has written and illustrated several much-admired and award-winning children's books, illustrated works on children's culture and folk traditions in the 1970s and 1980s, designed books and jackets for publishers from the 1960s, and created the layout of many major illustrated works and historical books over a period of three decades.

Vuori also illustrated and designed the visual aspects of many Finnish newspapers and periodicals, including *Lipas* magazine (published for children by the Savings Bank), the prestigious *Suomen Kuvalehti,* and served Finland's leading daily newspaper, *Helsingin Sanomat,* as an illustrator under the signature "Pekka" from 1978. Since 1980, he has been responsible for the look of the high-class *Form Function Finland* magazine, which deals with the arts and industrial design and is distributed internationally. During the late 1960s, Vuori also made short films and animated movies.

The fine arts have been strongly represented in Pekka Vuori's output since he painted his first canvas in oils at the age of twelve. More recently, he has concentrated on drawings and serigraphy. As well as participation in survey shows of illustrators in Finland and abroad, exhibitions of Vuori's paintings, drawing and illustrations have presented in Helsinki since 1963.

Pekka Vuori has worked on many children's projects for the Manerheim League for Child Welfare and several banks, and was the first Finn to make a UNICEF card. Among his books of fairy tales are *Into, the Bearded Baby* (1985) and *The Lost Petticoats* (1987). The latter was also published in Japanese, Danish, and Italian.

He has illustrated about twenty-five different books. One of these was a collection of folk tales entitled *Jättiläiset (The Giants),* a large edition of which was published in Japanese. Among his recent illustration work are Veikko Houvinen's stories of Stalin, *Uncle Joe* (1988), and Pekka Tarkka's *Modern Finnish Writers* (1989).

Vuori's work in designing illustrated volumes and historical books has received recognition. To date, the eighteen such works he has designed have been the recipients of numerous Book of the Year diplomas, awarded annually by the Finnish Book Design Selection Committee.

—Jukka Sorjo-Smeds

# VYCHODIL, Ladislav

Czechoslovak stage designer

---

**Born:** Hacky, 28 February 1920. **Education:** Attended secondary school in Olomouc, 1931-38; studied geometric drawing and design under Oldrich Blazicek, Cyril Bouda, and A. Pokorny, at the Uni-

versity of Architecture, Prague, 1938-39, 1945. **Family:** Married Vera Krausova in 1944; children: Ivana, Daniela, and Ladislav. **Career:** Chief stage designer, the Slovak National Theatre, Bratislava, from 1945; head of the scenography department, 1952-83; professor, University of Theatre Arts, Bratislava, from 1983. Columnist, *Slovak National Theatre Bulletin* (Bratislava), 1946-67. **Exhibitions:** Bratislava, 1965; Biennial of Sao Paulo, 1965; Paris, 1966; Brighton, Sussex, 1967; Sofia, 1967; Budapest, 1968; Vienna, 1969; Santa Barbara, California, 1974; Berlin, 1975; Venice, 1976, Bratislava, 1990. **Collections:** Slovak National Gallery, Bratislava; Smetana Museum, Prague; Toneel Museum, Amsterdam; University of Texas, Austin; National Museum, Prague; Moravian Museum, Brno. **Honors:** Czechoslovak State Prize, Prague, 1951, 1960; Gold Medal, Biennial of Sao Paulo, 1965; Merited Artist, Prague, 1966; National Artist, Prague, 1975; Order of Work, Prague, 1980. **Address:** Prokopa Velkeho 15, 811 04 Bratislava, Slovakia.

## Works

Stage productions include (for the Slovak National Theatre)—*Tartuffe,* 1946; *Ivan the Terrible,* 1947; *Boris Godunov,* 1954; *Optimistic Tragedy,* 1957; *Galileo,* 1959; *A View from the Bridge,* 1959; *Atlantida,* 1961; *Twelfth Night,* 1962; *Hamlet,* 1963; *The Play of Love and Death,* 1964; (for theatres abroad) *Schweik in World War II,* Theater an der Wien, Vienna, 1972; *Schlaues Fuechslein,* Leipzig opera House, Leipzig, 1973; *The Process,* Stockholm, 1976; *The Strange Case of Dr. Jekyll and Mr. Hyde,* Repertory Theatre, San Diego, 1986; *Romeo and Juliet,* National Theatre, Prague, 1994.

## Publications

**By VYCHODIL: books**—*Ladislav Vychodil: Complete Works,* exhibition catalogue, Slovak National Gallery, Bratislava, 1990; **articles**—in *Acta Scenographica* (Prague), no. 9, 1961; *Theatre Design and Technology* (Charlottesville), no. 10, 1974.

**On VYCHODIL: books**—*Ladislav Vychodil* by Miroslav Kouril, Bratislava, 1963; *Sucasna Slovenska Scenografia* by Ladislav Lajcha, Bratislava, 1977; *Ladislav Vychodil* by Ladislav Lajcha, Bratislava, 1980; *The Cambridge Guide to World Theatre* edited by Martin Banham, Cambridge, 1988.

*

During my fifty-year career, I have designed approximately 350 sets for both drama and opera. In my opinion, scenography is a space discipline, not one related to painting. Despite this, I think it would be a pity to exclude painting and colour from scenography. However, I do not use them in their primary form—I use colour as light and painting as material.

When a scenographer works in theatre, he must belong to the team of stage director-author-dramaturgist-scenographer-actor. Each scenographer works in a certain dependence on this team, and this is one of the differences from being an "independent" artist. A scenographer must take the influence of these disciplines into account, as well as that of light, theatre technology, and others. Scenography can be compared to the background of a figural painting. Let's use the famous Rembrandt work *Return*

**Ladislav Vychodil: set design for *Atlantida*, Bratislava, 1961. Photo by Jozef Novy, courtesy of L. Vychodil**

*of the Prodigal Son* for comparison. We shall have the image of scenography if we take out the figures. How does this "stage" look: As to space, the background is not too well articulated; the artist has taken into account that the quality of space will enter the picture along with the figures. As to colour, the "stage" (background) is neutral. The costumes are in most attractive colours. As to light, it falls on the furniture and on the figures (now absent). Without the figures, the pictures is incomplete; the figures are necessary to provide the picture as a whole. The

"stage" (background) is made in such a way that the figures (actors) dominate the pictures. The costuming is achieved similarly. It is realized as a background that underlines and emphasizes the actor's face, which is the carrier of the action.

Scenography is a discipline developing in space and time (similar to theatre). This means that it should not contain constant, invariable elements. Its nature should change as time passes. The scenographer should not be limited to one kind of acting (e.g. drama). Even a tragedy begins as a conversational play, and there are some comic elements as well. Scenography must take these facts and requirements into account, and it must change according to them.

—Ladislav Vychodil

\*          \*          \*

Ladislav Vychodil's scenography falls between two main devices—scene painting and architecture—of stage design as an indicator of place. For him, the question of architectonic space is central, but color as produced by lighting (rather than paint), on varying materials, textures, and forms is also highly significant. With regard to style, Vychodil inclines toward the lyrical and emotive, but with restraint, economy, and grace rather than force or distortion. The logical extension of this tendency is a suppression of traditional stage decor and increased emphasis on properties and related scenographic elements. Vychodil is also conservative with regard to reliance on technical innovations, which he de-emphasizes as primary sources of striking effects.

Vychodil's career evolved in several places. In the early postwar years, he showed the influence of his mentor, Frantisek Tröster. Then, a preoccupation with architectonic, abstract forms, often against an indefinite, darkened background was exemplified by *Tartuffe* (1946) and Tolstoy's *Ivan the Terrible* (1947). In the early 1950s, when socialist realism dominated east European arts, Vychodil turned to more traditional techniques of scene painting and realistic detail, as in *Boris Gudonov* (1954). In the late 1950s, as if in reaction to such literalness, Vychodil's works suggested an effort to sweep the stage clean of both the illusion of actuality and conventional decor. The emphasis was on economy, function, and the actor (Vishnevsky's *Optimistic Tragedy,* 1957). Vychodil also

began to make increasing use of the cyclorama and special lighting, including projections, to convey both mood and information (Brecht's *Galileo* and Miller's *A View From the Bridge,* both 1959). In the 1960s, his settings once again became more expressive and emotive, made so chiefly by more complex patterns of suspended elements in layers and by more complex lighting effects on textured surfaces (*Twelfth Night,* 1962; *Hamlet,* 1963).

In the 1960s, Vychodil also began to work with Alfred Radok, co-inventor of the Laterna Magika form of blending live and filmed action for the stage. They did not employ this technique per se but its poetic essence: the juxtaposition of seemingly disparate elements to present ironic, metaphoric insights about reality. Traditional scenography was subordinated to a collage of actors and carefully chosen properties, furniture, and other "signs" that took on various functions and meanings. By far the most striking example of this approach occurred in Rolland's *The Play of Love and Death* (1964), for which Vychodil created a setting that had no basis in the text: a metaphoric, rough-hewn bull ring in which French aristocrats played out their destinies during Revolution. Vychodil's subsequent work has consisted of variations and refinements of these last phases, with consistent attention to textured, layered backgrounds that establish the quality or mood of a piece and to an often ironic interplay of actors and scenic objects.

Vychodil has increasingly worked in Scandinavia and North America. Especially noteworthy has been his scenography based on simultaneous settings for *Crime and Punishment* (Stockholm, 1984), *Romeo and Juliet* (Oslo, 1985), and *Dr. Jekyll and Mr. Hyde* (San Diego, 1986).

—Jarka M. Burian

# WAGENFELD, Wilhelm

German metalsmith, glass, ceramic, and industrial designer

**Born:** Bremen, 15 April 1900. **Education:** Apprenticed as a draughtsman, in Koch und Bergfeld silverware factory, Bremen, 1915-18; studied design at the Kunstgewerbeschule, Bremen, 1916-18; attended Staatliche Zeichenakademie, Hanau, 1919-22; studied privately in Bremen and Worpswede, 1922-23; studied metalwork under Laszlo Moholy-Nagy, at the Staatliche Bauhaus, Weimar, 1923-25. **Military Service:** Served in the German Army, 1942-45. **Career:** Designer, Schott & Gen. glass-works, Jena, 1931-39, Fürstenberg china works, Fürstenberg, 1934, and Rosenthal porcelain factory, Selb, 1938; and in the Thuringer Wald glass-works, 1930-32; artistic director, Vereinigte Lausitzer Glaswerke, Weisswasser, 1935-48; design consultant, Württembergische Metalware factory, Geisslingen, 1949-77, Rosenthal porcelain factory, Selb, 1952-53, Peill & Putzler glass-works, Düren, 1952-58, Braun AG, Frankfurt, 1954-55, Johannes Buchsteiner plastic works, Gingen, 1955-58, Ogro metalware factory, Velbert, 1955-66, Lindner GmbH, 1955-70, and others; freelance designer, Stuttgart, 1954-78. Assistant metalwork instructor, 1926-28, and head of metalwork classes, 1928-30, Staatliche Bauhochschule, Weimar; instructor, Staatliche Kunstschule, Berlin-Schöneberg, 1931-35; instructor in standardization, Institut für Bauwesen, Leibniz Akademie, West Berlin, 1947-49; professor of industrial design, Hochschule für Bildenden Künste, West Berlin, 1948-49; referee, Landesgewerbeamt, Stuttgart, 1949-51. **Exhibitions:** Neue Sammlung, Munich, 1939, 1961; Kunstmuseum, Gorlitz, 1939; Kunstgewerbemuseum, Breslau, 1940; Kunstdienst, Berlin, 1940; Kunstmuseum, Bautzen, 1940; Kunsthalle, Mannheim, 1941, 1957; Museum für Kunst und Gewerbe, Hamburg, 1941, 1990; Milan Triennale, 1957; Kunstgewerbe-Museum, Zürich, 1960; Stedelijk Museum, Amsterdam, 1961; Akademie der Künste, West Berlin, 1962; Landesgewerbeamt, Stuttgart, 1965; Landesmuseum, Oldenburg, 1965; Kunstkreis, Hameln, 1965; Deutsches Goldschmiedehaus, Hanau, 1966; Kunstgewerbemuseum, Cologne, 1973 (toured); Musée des Arts Décoratifs, Paris, 1975; Württembergisches Landesmuseum, Stuttgart, 1980; Bremer Landesmuseum, 1987-88 (toured); Bauhaus Dessau, 1990; Palazzo Serra Gerace, Genoa, 1990; Securitas Galerie, Bremen, 1991 (toured); Museum Hanau, 1993; Glasmuseum, Wertheim, 1994; Institut für Neue Technische Form, Darmstadt, 1994; Galerie im Buntentor, Bremen, 1995; Stadtmuseum, Jena, 1995. **Collections:** Philadelphia Museum of Art; Cooper-Hewitt Museum, New York; Metropolitan Museum of Art, New York; Museum of Modern Art, New York; Musée des Arts Décoratifs, Paris; Wilhelm Wagenfeld Foundation, Bremen (and every other museum for design and applied art in Germany); Victoria and Albert Museum, London; Stedelijk Museum, Amsterdam; Museum für Gestaltung, Zürich; Museum Bellerive, Zürich. **Honors:** Grand Prize, Paris Exposition, 1937; Bronze Medal, 1937, Grand Prize, 1940, 1957, Milan Triennale; Berliner Kunstpreis, West Berlin, 1968; Heinrich Tessenow Medal, Technische Universität, Hannover, 1968; Gute Form Prize, Bonn, 1969. Honorary Member, Staatliche Akademie der Künste, Stuttgart, 1962; Honorary Senator, Technische Universität, Stuttgart, 1964; Extraordinary Member, Akademie der Künste, West Berlin, 1965; Guest of Honor, Villa Massimo, Rome, 1968. **Died:** Stuttgart, 28 May 1990; survived by the Wilhelm Wagenfeld Foundation, Buntentorsteinweg 112, 28201 Bremen, Germany.

## Works

*Bauhaus* table lamp in nickel-plated metal or clear glass and opaque globe, 1924, reproduced by Tecnolumen, Bremen, 1980.
Metalwares and lamps, for Walter and Wagner, 1926-30.
Tea service in clear glass, for Schott & Gen., 1932.
*Oberweimar* table service in glass, for Vereinigte Lausitzer Glaswerke, 1935.
*Kubus* refrigerator storage wares in pressed glass, for Vereinigte Lausitzer Glaswerke, 1938.
Vases in tourmaline-colored crystal, for Württembergische Metallwarenfabrik, 1949.
*Form 3000* cutlery in stainless steel, for Württembergische Metallwarenfabrik, 1952.
*Bremen* pendant lamp, for Peill and Putzler, 1953-54.
Portable radio, for Braun AG, 1954.
*Atlanta* cutlery, for Württembergische Metallwarenfabrik, 1954-55.
Tablewares in melamine, produced by Johannes Buchsteiner, for Lufthansa German Airlines, 1955.
Hotel service in silverplate, for Württembergische Metallwarenfabrik, 1956-58.
Mirror-light in porcelain and opalescent glass, for Lindner, 1958.
*Osiris* pendant lamp, for Peill und Putzler, 1958.
Wine lasses, for Württembergische Metallwarenfabrik, 1962.
Vases in china, for Fürstenberg, 1972-73.

## Publications

**By WAGENFELD: books**—*Wesen und Gestalt der Dinge um Uns,* Potsdam, 1948; *Deutsche Institut für Industrielle Standardform: Zur Diskussion gestellt,* Stuttgart, 1950.

**On WAGENFELD: books**—*Wilhelm Wagenfeld,* exhibition catalogue by O. Eberle, Munich, 1939; *Die Gute Industrieform,* exhibition catalogue by Hans Eckstein and Robert Gutmann, Hamburg, 1955; *Wilhelm Wagenfeld: Ein Künstler in der Industrie,* exhibition catalogue by Siegfried Asche, Mannheim, 1957; *Industrieware von Wilhelm Wagenfeld 1930-1960,* exhibition catalogue edited by Hans

Wilhelm Wagenfeld: *Kubus* pressed glass storage wares, for Vereinigte Lausitzer Glaswerke, 1938. Photo: Joachim Fliegner. ©1995 Wilhelm Wagenfeld Stiftung, Bremen, Germany

Fischli and Willy Rotzler, Zürich, 1960; *Wagenfeld: Ontwerpen en Fabriek Werken voor Dagelijks Gebruiek,* exhibition catalogue by Willem Sandberg, Amsterdam, 1961; *Wilhelm Wagenfeld: 30 Jahre Künstlerische Mitarbeit in der Industrie,* exhibition catalogue by Hans Eckstein, Munich, 1961; *Wilhelm Wagenfeld: Zusammenarbeit mit Fabriken 1930-1962,* exhibition catalogue by Herta Elisabeth Killy, Hans Scharoun, and Johanna Hofmann, West Berlin, 1962; *Moderne Deutsche Industrieform* by Heinz Spielmann, Hamburg, 1962; *Wilhelm Wagenfeld: Vom Bauhaus in die Industrie,* exhibition catalogue by Eduard Leuze and J. A. Thuma, Stuttgart, 1965; *Crafts of the Weimar Bauhaus 1919-1924,* by Walther Scheidig, Leipzig, 1966, London, 1967; *Wilhelm Wagenfeld: 50 jahre mitarbeit in fabriken,* exhibition catalogue edited by Carl Wolfgang Schümann, Cologne, 1973; *International Modern Glass* by Geoffrey Beard, London, 1976; *Classics of Modern Design,* exhibition catalogue by Barnard Gay, London, 1977; *In Good Shape: Style in Industrial Products 1900-1960* by Stephen Bayley, London, 1979; *Schone Form, Gute Ware: Wilhelm Wagenfeld,* exhibition catalogue edited by Claus Zoege von Manteuffel, Stuttgart, 1980; *Design Since 1945* edited by Kathryn Hiesinger and George Marcus, Philadel-

phia and London, 1983; *The Conran Directory of Design* edited by Stephen Bayley, London, 1985; *Twentieth Century Design: Glass* by Frederick Cooke, London, 1986; *Design-Geschichte in Deutschland* by Gert Selle, Cologne, 1987; *Täglich in der Hand: Industrieformen von Vilhelm Wagenfeld aus sechs Jahrzehnten* edited by Beate Manske and Gudrun Scholz, Lilienthal, 1987; *Design im 20. Jahrhundert,* exhibition catalogue edited by Gabriele Lueg, Cologne, 1989; *Bauhaus 1919* by Magdalena Droste, Berlin, 1990; *Wilhelm Wagenfeld,* exhibition catalogue, Dessau, 1990; *Il design di Wilhelm Wagenfeld 1990-1990,* exhibition catalogue edited by Giacomo Ferrigno, Genoa, 1990; *Wilhelm Wagenfeld,* exhibition catalogue, Hanau, 1993; *Wilhelm Wagenfeld und die moderne Glasindustrie* by Walter Scheiffele, Hatje, 1994; *Wilhelm Wagenfeld: gestern, heute, morgen—Lebenskultur im Alltag,* exhibition catalogue edited by Wilhelm Wagenfeld Foundation, Bremen, 1995.

\*     \*     \*

A pioneer of industrial design, Wilhelm Wagenfeld belongs also among its most important representatives since the 1920s. His particular achievements lie in metal and glass work. With a consistency hardly matched by any other Bauhaus graduate, he converted into fact the Bauhaus slogan "Art and technology—a new unity." His *Bauhaus* lamp of 1924 suited contemporary taste as much as it embodied the spirit of the early Bauhaus, whilst Wagenfeld himself described Moholy-Nagy as his most important teacher there.

From his earliest activities at the Weimar Bauhochschule, Wagenfeld consistently worked with industry. It is not the single product which is characteristic of his work but the long-term collaboration with a few firms and the renovation of whole production processes. Wagenfeld's products were consistently successful, frequently being marketed for decades after their original design. His intense preoccupation with manufacturing processes often led him to new and unusual design solutions: his first discovery was of modern and practical forms for hollow and compressed glass (tea and coffee services, baking dishes, and the Kubus storagewares). The glass products of the Vereinigte Lausitzer Glaswerke gained an international reputation through his designs. The diamond shape introduced by Wagenfeld soon developed into a mark of quality. Among the designers introduced to the factory by Wagenfeld were Heinz Loffelhardt, Hermann Gretsch, Walter Dexel, Josef Hoffmann, and Wolfgang von Wesin.

In the postwar period, the chief accent was on metalwork for the Württembergische Metallwarenfabrik. This firm's production was also marked for decades by Wagenfeld's stamp. Their shapes developing out of the material itself, his Cromagan utensils are characterized by simplicity, beauty of form, and superb fitness to their purposes. Wagenfeld's long-standing design work for industry rested on an ethos that vetoed any expression of the artist's individuality in the product design. His belief in the moral strength of a well-designed form marked his professional attitude throughout.

—Magdalena Droste

# WAGNER, Robin (Samuel Anton)

American stage designer

**Born:** San Francisco, California, 31 August 1933. **Education:** Balboa High School, San Francisco, until 1952; studied at the California School of Fine Arts, San Francisco, 1952-54. **Family:** Married Joyce Marie Workman in 1959 (divorced); children: Kurt, Leslie, and Christie. **Career:** Freelance stage set designer, working in San Francisco, 1953-59, and in New York, from 1959; also film designer, from 1970. **Member:** Theatre Advisory Council Member, New York; board member, Corporate Fund for Theatre; steering committee member, League of Professional Theatre Training Programs; member, United Scenic Artists. **Honors:** Drama Desk Award, New York, 1971, 1978; Joseph Maharam Award, New York, 1973, 1975, 1981; Lumen Award, New York, 1975; Outer Circle Critics Award, New York, 1978; Antoinette Perry "Tony" Award, New York, 1978. **Address:** 890 Broadway, 6th floor, New York, New York 10003, U.S.A.

## Works

Stage productions include: for the Golden Gate Opera Workshop, San Francisco—*Don Pasquale,* 1953; *Amahl and the Night Visitors,* 1953; *Zanetto,* 1953; for the Theatre Arts Colony, San Francisco—*Tea and Sympathy,* 1954; for the Encore, San Francisco—*The Immoralist* and *Dark of the Moon;* for the Actors Workshop, San Francisco—*Waiting for Godot,* 1957; *The Miser,* 1958; *The Ticklish Acrobat,* 1958; *The Plaster Bambino,* 1959; for the San Francisco Ballet Company—*The Filling Station,* 1958; all in New York unless indicated—*And the Wind Blows,* 1959; *The Prodigal,* 1960; *Between Two Thieves,* 1960; *Borak,* 1960; *A Worm in Horseradish,* 1961; *Entertain a Ghost,* 1962; *The Days and Nights of Beebee Fenstermaker,* 1962; *The Playboy of the Western World* (for the Irish Players), 1962; *Cages,* 1963; *In White America,* 1963; *The Burning,* 1963; *The White Rose and the Red,* 1964; *Dark of the Moon* (for the Arena Stage, Washington, D.C.), 1964; *Galileo* (for the Arena Stage, Washington, D.C.), 1964; *A View from the Bridge,* 1965; *An Evening's Frost,* 1965; *The Condemned of Altona,* 1966; *Galileo,* 1967; *The Trial of Lee Harvey Oswald,* 1967; *A Certain Young Man,* 1967; *Love Match* (in Los Angeles), 1967; *Hair,* 1968; *Lovers and Other Strangers,* 1968; *The Cuban Thing,* 1968; *The Great White Hope,* 1968; *Promises, Promises,* 1968; *Hair* (at the Shaftesbury Theatre, London), 1968; *The Watering Place,* 1969; *My Daughter, Your Son,* 1969; *Promises, Promises* (in London), 1969; *Gantry,* 1970; *Mahagonny,* 1970; *The Engagement Baby,* 1970; *Lenny,* 1971; *Jesus Christ Superstar,* 1971; *Inner City,* 1971; *Sugar,* 1971; *Lysistrata,* 1972; *Seesaw,* 1973; *Full Circle,* 1973; *Mack and Mabel,* 1974; *Sergeant Pepper's Lonely Hearts Club Band on the Road,* 1974; *A Chorus Line,* 1975; *The Red Devil Battery Sign* (in Boston), 1975; *Les Troyen* (for the Vienna State Opera), 1976; *Hamlet Connotations* (for the American Ballet Theatre), 1976; *West Side Story* (for the Hamburg State Opera), 1977; *On the Twentieth Century,* 1978; *Ballroom,* 1978; *Comin' Uptown,* 1979; *Swing,* 1980; *42nd Street,* 1980; *One Night Stand,* 1980; *Semmelweiss,* 1981; *Dreamgirls,* 1981; *Barber of Seville* (for the Metropolitan Opera), 1982; *Mahalia,* 1982; *Rolling Stones Concert* (Madison Square Garden), 1982; *Merlin,* 1983; *Three Dances* (for Eliot Field Ballet), 1983; *Jewels* (for New York City Ballet), 1983; *Song and Dance,* 1985; *Teddy and Alice,* 1986; *Chess* (London production), 1987; *Chess* (New York production), 1988; *Jerome Robbins Broadway,* 1989.

## Publications

**On WAGNER: books**—*The Biographical Encyclopaedia and Who's Who of the American Theatre* edited by Walter Rigdon, New York, 1966; *Who's Who in the Theatre* edited by Ian Herbert, Detroit, 1981; *Contemporary Theatre, Film and Television* edited by Monica M. O'Donnell, Detroit, 1986; *The Cambridge Guide to World Theatre* edited by Martin Banham, Cambridge, 1988.

\* \* \*

Since he designed *Hair,* the breakthrough musical that altered the look of American theatre in the late 1960s, Robin Wagner's personal style of large-scale, fast-moving, automated scenery has set a standard for contemporary design in America. During the 1970s Wagner designed the scenery for *Lenny, Jesus Christ Superstar, Sugar, Seesaw, Mack and Mabel, A Chorus Line, On the Twentieth Century* and *Ballroom;* since 1980, he has designed the musicals *42nd Street* and *Dreamgirls.* These have won him all of the major theatre design awards. In addition to his work on Broadway, Wagner has designed scenery for the Vienna State Opera, the Hamburg State Opera, the American Ballet Theatre, the Arena Stage in Washington, D.C., and the American Shakespeare Festival in Stratford, Connecticut, as well as for television, film, and rock group tours.

Robin Wagner's structural, sometimes minimal, technologically exciting, visually simulating, and kinetic work will be remembered as the classic scenic design of the 1970s and 1980s. He is not a set designer in the old-fashioned sense of the term. He is not painterly; he does not design traditional box sets or painted drops. His work cannot be called delicate or decorative. He does not sketch pretty pictures for the scene shop, but rather, builds models of good scale, models that work, models that show how the scenery works.

The most memorable facet of Wagner's scenery is that it moves. Automation plays a key role in all of his designs, which are in constant motion—movement that is full of surprises. No one who saw *Jesus Christ Superstar* can forget the floor slowly rising in the back as though it were hinged at the footlights, then bodies beginning to crawl, and finally the floor continuing to rise almost straight upwards. And what about the excitement of the train speeding across the night sky in *On the Twentieth Century* and then, three-dimensionally, the train with its headlight gleaming, heading down the track right towards the audience? And in *Dreamgirls,* constantly moving light towers created different spaces as they pivoted and moved back and forth across the stage.

The second memorable aspect of Wagner's scenery is its scale: the larger structural scenery in *Lenny,* the tall light towers in *Dreamgirls,* the cavernous spaces in *A Chorus Line* and in *Ballroom.* Also, he seems to work well with lighting designers, and his scenery allows for the theatricality of light. His sets are filled with lights—not the lighting designer's lamps hung from rails or at the sides of the stage, nor foot-lights, nor follow spots, but lights that are part of the scenery, lights that can be seen from the audience, lights that are part of the action of the show. The train lights in *On the Twentieth Century* not only lit the stage, they were part of the moving scenery. The theatrical lights of *A Chorus Line* and *Dreamgirls* similarly served a dual purpose. The lights surrounding the Stardust Ballroom created the space and mood of *Ballroom.*

Finally, Wagner's scenery has substance; it never consists of painted canvas flats. There is wood and metal and weight. The act "curtain" in *On the Twentieth Century,* made of contemporary materials such as formica-covered plywood, weighed 6,000 pounds.

—John E. Hirsch

# WALLANCE, Don

American industrial designer

**Born:** New York City, 26 September 1909. **Education:** Studied at New York University, B.A., 1930; Design Laboratory, New York, 1935-39. **Military Service:** Served as a technologist in the United States Army, Washington, D.C., 1942-43, 1945, and in the United States Air Force, Alaska, 1943-44, Staff Sergeant. **Family:** Married Shula R. Cohen in 1941 (died 1979); children: Gregory and David. **Career:** Design and technical director, National Youth Administration, New Orleans, 1940-41; freelance designer, working in Washington, D.C., 1946-50, and in Croton-on-Hudson, New York, from 1950. Visiting lecturer, University of Illinois, Urbana-Champaign, 1964, and Rhode Island School of Design, Providence, 1980. **Exhibitions:** *A Designer's Case History of a Product,* Aspen Design Conference, Colorado, 1955; *Design Since 1945,* Philadelphia Museum of Art, 1983. **Collections:** Museum of Modern Art, New York; Philadelphia Mu-

seum of Art; Musee des Arts Decoratifs, Montreal; Centre de Creation Industrielle, Centre Georges Pompidou, Paris. **Honors:** Museum of Modern Art Research Grant, New York, 1948; Golden Form Award, Utrecht, 1954. **Address:** 56 Mount Airy Road, Croton-on-Hudson, New York 10520, U.S.A.

## Works

*Design 1* cutlery in stainless steel, for H. E. Lauffer Company, 1954, now produced by Towle Manufacturing Company.
*Design 2* cutlery in stainless steel, for H. E. Lauffer Company, 1957, now produced by Towle Manufacturing Company.
*ALCOA Forecast Collection* of cooking and serving wares in aluminum, for the Aluminum Corporation of America, 1962.
Hospital furniture in steel and plastics, for the Hard Manufacturing Company, 1965.
Auditorium seating in steel and upholstered polyurethane foam, for the Philharmonic Hall of the Lincoln Center, New York, produced by the American Seating Corporation, 1965.
*Palisander* cutlery in stainless steel and rosewood, for H. E. Lauffer Company, 1969, now produced by Towle Manufacturing Company.
*Magnum* cutlery in stainless steel, for H. E. Lauffer Company, 1970, now produced by Towle Manufacturing Company.
*Design 10* cutlery in coloured plastics, for H. E. Lauffer Company, 1971, now produced by Towle Manufacturing Company.

## Publications

**By WALLANCE: books**—*Shaping America's Products,* New York, 1956.

**On WALLANCE: books**—*Industrial Design* by John Heskett, London, 1980; *Design Since 1945* edited by Kathryn Hiesinger and George Marcus, Philadelphia and London, 1983; *American Design Classics* by Joan Wessel and Nadia Westerman, New York, 1985; *The American Design Adventure* by Arthur J. Pulos, London and Cambridge, Massachusetts, 1988; *Dictionary of Twentieth Century Design* by John Pile, New York, 1989; *Design in Plastics* by Douglas Cleminshaw, New York, 1990.

*

As the practise of industrial design has become more comprehensive, it has involved such diverse functions as ergonomics, product planning, product engineering, market analysis, and, most recently, computer-aided design. But the essential core of the design process remains the creation of forms that have an esthetic vitality which is communicable to other people. Design in this sense is the function of a designer who has creative skill, inner conviction, technical competence, and esthetic sensibility and who is attuned to the needs and aspirations of his fellow human beings.

I work as an industrially oriented craftsman, concerned with every detail of a project from initial concept to technical specifications and, wherever possible, I fabricate my own product models.

—Don Wallance

*   *   *

After World War II, the mandate for American industrial designers was to fulfill the promise of the good life in the manufacture of better designed consumer goods. This mandate entailed styling that was simple, elegant and modern, coupled with advances in technology and industrial materials that facilitated mass production and distribution. Of the many pioneers who emerged during this period of frenetic design activity, Don Wallance is credited with establishing stainless steel flatware as a suitable replacement for silver as the conventional domestic service.

The shift from silver to steel was rapid and effective. At first, silver-plating alloys, like those designed by Garth and Ada-Louise Huxtable, were being accepted in restaurants, as was crude stainless steel in the home. However, for the most part, it was perceived only as a temporary substitute until fine silver could be purchased. But, with the application of stamping and embossing techniques, this sheet metal flatware acquired an intricacy of decoration that challenged silver for a permanent place on the table. Working with this technology, Russel Wright had simplified designs, producing the first American expression of minimal, reductive, yet organically pleasing, stainless steel flatware.

In Don Wallance's designs of the 1950s, there was a radical break in the evolution of flatware. Forging, the traditional method of producing fine sterling silver flatware was found applicable to the mass production of stainless steel. Wallance, who staunchly defended and proselytized for the retention of a craftsman's esthetic in industrial methods, saw forging as a method for maintaining the sculptural solidity and dimensional feel that was prized in classic handforged silver. His designs that employed deep forging procedures came closest to replicating the clean, fluid lines, the satin finish, and the fully rounded bowls that respected the material's nature. The absence of superficial styling was more than compensated for by the harmony of form that rendered the designs the epitome of classic modernism.

Wallance's dedication in forcing a craftsman's esthetic onto the field of industrial design extended beyond flatware into other consumer products, as well as various educational activities. Most notable in this regard was Wallance's seminal "Study of Design and Craftsmanship in Today's Products," sponsored jointly by the Walker Art Center in Minneapolis, and the American Craftsmen's Council in New York, and later developed into a traveling exhibition, and the book *Shaping America's Products* (1956). In his study, Wallance examined large-scale manufacturers like Bell Laboratories, Corning Glass, small-scale industry like Herman Miller and Lauffer as well as independent craftsmen-designers in pottery and jewelry with an eye on the contribution that the human instinct for workmanship can and must make while utilizing the full benefit of mechanization. As a pathbreaking effort to establish the relationship between craftsmanship and industry and its confluence in the modern industrial design, Wallance's study stands as the earliest treatment of the ethic and esthetic of the design process since the Arts and Crafts Movement.

—Sarah Bodine

# WALTON, Tony

English stage and film set and costume and graphic designer

**Born:** Walton-on-Thames, Surrey, England, 24 October 1934. **Education:** Radley College, Oxford, City of Oxford School of Technology, Art and Commerce, and Slade School of Fine Art, London. **Military Service:** Royal Air Force, 1952-54. **Career:** Assistant designer and designer, Peter Haddon's Company, Wimbeldon Theatre, England, 1955-1956; designer of caricatures and illustrations, for *Harpers* (New York), 1955-57, *Vogue* (New York), 1956-57, *Theatre Arts* (New York), 1956-57, *The Reporter* (New York), 1956-57, *Playbill* (New York), 1957-58, *The Observer* (London), 1958, and others; designer of posters, album covers, and book and magazine covers and illustrations, from 1957; freelance set and costume designer, for the stage, from 1957, and for films, from 1964. Instructor of design for directors, Actors Studio, New School of Social Research, New York; Board of Directors, Theatre Hall of Fame; Board of Directors, American Museum of the Moving Image; Advisory Board, Bay Street Theatre, Sag Harbor, Maine, Musical Theatre Works, and Spectrum Stage. **Member:** United Scenic Artists; Costume Designers Guild, California; Academy of Motion Picture Arts and Sciences. **Exhibitions:** New York Circulating Library of Paintings, New York, 1957; Wright-Hepburn Gallery, London, 1967, 1968; Wright-Hepburn, Webster Gallery, New York, 1968; The Gallery at Water Mill Museum, New York, 1986; American Museum of the Moving Image, Astoria, New York, 1989-90; Hurlbutt Gallery, Greenwich, Connecticut, 1991-92. **Collections:** American Museum of the Moving Image, Astoria, New York; Museum of the City of New York; James Tobin Collection, McNay Museum, San Antonio, Texas. **Honors:** The Scotsman Medallion (for book jacket of the year), 1964; Whitbread Anglo-American Theatre Award, 1964-65; Drama Desk Award, 1972, 1985-86, 1991-92; Antoinette Perry "Tony" Award, 1972-73, 1985-86, 1991-92; Silver Award, Designers & Art Directors Association, London, 1975; All American Press Award, 1979; Academy Award, 1980; Best Broadway Poster Award, *New York Daily News,* 1981; Bay Area Theatre Critics Circle Award, 1985; American Theatre Wing Design Award, 1985-86, 1994; Primetime Emmy Award, 1985-85; Clio Award, 1987; Lion of the Performing Arts Award, New York Public Library, 1987; Outer Critics Circle Award, 1988-89; Best of Broadway Award, Art Deco Society, 1989, 1992; inducted into Theatre Hall of Fame, 1991; Special Recognition Award for Achievement in Theatre, New England Theatre Conference, 1992; Lifetime Achievement Award, Guild Hall of Easthampton, 1992; Joan Cullman Award, Lincoln Center, 1992; New York Municipal Art Society Award, 1993; elected to Interior Design Hall of Fame, 1993; 20th Annual Carbonell Award, Florida, 1995; Lucille Lortel Award (Best of Off Broadway), 1996. **Address:** (agent) Paul Martino, International Creative Management, 40 West 57th Street, New York, New York 10019, U.S.A.

## Works

Stage designs (in New York) include—*Conversation Piece,* Barbizon Plaza Theatre, 1957; *Valmouth,* York Theatre, 1960; *Once There Was a Russian,* Music Box Theatre, 1961; *A Funny Thing Happened on the Way to the Forum,* Alvin Theatre, 1962; *Golden Boy,* Majestic Theatre, 1964; *The Rehearsal,* Booth Theatre, 1964; *The Apple Tree,* Shubert Theatre, 1966; *Pippin,* Imperial Theatre, 1972 (also television production design, cable and video, 1981); *Uncle Vanya,* Circle in the Square, 1973; *Shelter,* Golden Theatre, 1973; *The Good Doctor,* O'Neill Theatre, 1973; *Bette Midler's Clams on the Half Shell Revue,* Minskoff Theatre, 1975; *Chicago,* 46th Street Theatre, 1975; *Streamers,* Newhouse, Lincoln Center, 1977; *The Act,* Majestic Theatre, 1977; *Drinks Before*

*Dinner,* Newman Theatre, 1978; *A Day in Hollywood/A Night in the Ukraine,* Golden and Royale Theatre, 1980; *Sophisticated Ladies,* Lunt-Fontanne Theatre, 1981; *Woman of the Year,* Palace Theatre, 1981; *Little Me,* O'Neill Theatre, 1982; *The Real Thing,* Plymouth Theatre, 1984; *Hurlyburly,* Promenade and Barrymore, 1984; *Leader of the Pack,* Ambassador Theatre, 1985; *I'm Not Rappaport,* American Place and Booth, 1985; *Social Security,* Barrymore Theatre, 1986; *House of Blue Leaves,* Newhouse, Beaumont, and Plymouth, 1986; *The Front Page,* Beaumont, Lincoln Center, 1987; *Anything Goes,* Beaumont, Lincoln Center, 1987; *Linda Ronstadt's Canciones De Mi Padre,* City Center and Minskoff, 1988 (also television production design, P.B.S., 1989); *Waiting for Godot,* Newhouse, Lincoln Center, 1989; *Lend Me a Tenor,* Royale Theatre, 1989; *Jerome Robbin's Broadway* "Comedy Tonight" sequence from *A Funny Thing Happened on the Way to the Forum,* Imperial Theatre, 1989; *Grand Hotel,* Martin Beck Theatre, 1990; *Square One,* 2nd Stage Theatre, 1990; *Elliot Loves,* Promenade Theatre, 1990; *Six Designers of Separation,* Newhouse, Beaumont, Lincoln Center, 1990; *The Will Rogers Follies,* Palace Theatre, 1991; *Conversations with My Father,* Royale Theatre, 1992; *Death and the Maiden,* Brooks Atkinson, 1992; *Four Baboons Adoring the Sun,* Beaumont, Lincoln Center, 1992; *Guys and Dolls,* Martin Beck Theatre, 1992; *Tommy Tune Tonight,* Gershwin Theatre, 1992; *She Loves Me,* Roundabout Theatre and Brooks Atkinson, 1993; *A Grand Night for Singing,* Roundabout Theatre, 1993; *Laughter on the 23rd Floor,* Richard Rogers Theatre, 1993; *Picnic,* Roundabout Theatre, 1994; *A Christmas Carol,* Madison Square Garden Theatre, 1994-1995; *Company,* Roundabout Theatre, 1995; *Moonlight,* Laura Pels/ Roundabout, 1995; *A Fair Country,* Newhouse, Lincoln Center, 1996; *A Funny Thing Happened on the Way to the Forum,* St. James Theatre, 1996.

Opera designs include—*The Love of Three Oranges,* Sadlers Wells Opera, London, 1963, and Coliseum, 1966; *The Rape of Lucretia,* Edinburgh Festival, 1963 (toured); *Otello,* Spoleto Festival, Italy, 1965; *Midsummer Marriage,* Covent Garden Opera, London, 1968; *The Cunning Little Vixen,* Sante Fe Opera Festival, 1975; *Tosca,* San Francisco Opera, 1992, and Lyric Opera of Chicago, 1993.

Ballet designs include—*Harp Concerto,* San Francisco Ballet, 1973; *Mother Blues,* San Francisco Ballet, 1974; *The Tempest,* San Francisco Ballet, 1980; *Stravinsky Piano Pieces,* San Francisco Ballet, 1982; *To The Beatles,* San Francisco Ballet, 1982; *King Lear,* San Francisco Ballet, 1985; *Hearts,* San Francisco Ballet, 1986; *Peter and the Wolf,* American Ballet Theatre, New York, 1992; *Who Cares,* Pacific Northwest Ballet, Seattle, 1992; *Jewels,* Miami City, Ballet, Florida, 1995.

Film designs include—(costumes and visual consultant) *Mary Poppins,* 1964; (production and costumes) *A Funny Thing Happened on the Way to the Forum,* 1966; (production, with Syd Cain, and costumes) *Fahrenheit 451,* 1966; (production and costumes) *Petulia,* 1968; (production and costumes) *The Sea Gull,* 1968; (production) *The Boy Friend,* 1971; (production and costumes) *Murder on the Orient Express,* 1974; (production and costumes) *Equus,* 1977; (production and costumes) *The Wiz,* 1978; (design consultant and fantasy designer) *All That Jazz,* 1979; (production and costumes) *Just Tell Me What You Want,* 1980; (production and costumes) *Deathtrap,* 1981; (production) *Prince of the City,* 1981; (production and costumes) *Star 80,* 1983; (production and costumes) *The Goodbye People,* 1984; (production) *Death of a*

*Salesman,* 1986 (also television production design, C.B.S., 1986); (production) *Heartburn,* 1986; (production and costumes) *The Glass Menagerie,* 1987; (production) *Regarding Henry,* 1991.

Poster designs (for Broadway) include—*Pippin,* Imperial Theatre, 1972; *Uncle Vanya,* Circle in the Square, 1973; *Shelter,* Golden Theatre, 1973; *Chicago,* 46th Street Theatre, 1975; *Barnum,* St. James Theatre, 1980; *Sophisticated Ladies,* Lunt-Fontanne Theatre, 1981; *Woman of the Year,* Palace Theatre, 1981; *Little Me,* Eugene O'Neill Theatre, 1982; *Leader of the Pack,* Ambassador Theatre, 1985; *I'm Not Rappaport,* American Place and Booth Theatre, 1985; *A Grand Night for Singing,* Roundabout Theatre, 1993; *She Loves Me,* Roundabout Theatre and Brooks Atkinson Theatre, 1993.

## Publications

**By WALTON: books**—*Wonders* edited by May Gimble and Jonathan Cott, New York, 1980; **articles**—"Of Munchkins, Winkies, and the Emerald City" in *American Cinematographer* vol. 59, no. 11, November 1978; "Hal Prince" in *Double Exposure—Take Two* by Roddy McDowall, New York, 1989; in *Calman at the Movies* by Mel Calman, London, 1990; in *Broadway Day and Night,* New York, 1992; "Twiggy Lawson" in *Double Exposure—Take Four* by Roddy McDowall, New York, 1993.

**On WALTON: books**—*T. H. White—A Biography* by Sylvia Townsend Warner, London, 1967; *The White/Garnett Letters* edited by David Garnett, New York, 1968; *America at Last: the American Journals of T. H. White* by T. H. White, New York, 1968; *Stage Lighting* by Richard Pilbrow, New York, 1970, 1979, 1991; *Contemporary Stage Design* edited by Elizabeth B. Burdick, Peggy C. Hansen, and Brenda Zanger, New York, 1975; *Designing and Painting for the Theatre* by Lynn Pectal, New York, 1975; *Murder Ink: The Mystery Reader's Companion* by Dilys Winn, New York, 1977; *The Wiz Scrapbook* by Richard J. Anobile, MCA Publishing, 1978; *Let There Be Neon* by Rudi Stern, New York, 1979; *The Art of the Broadway Poster* by Michael Patrick Hearn, New York, 1980; *The Magic of Neon* by Michael Webb, Salt Lake City, Utah, 1983; *Adventures in the Screen Trade* by William Goldman, New York, 1983; *Broadway Musicals* by Martin Gottfried, New York, 1984; *Take 1—New York on Film,* catalogue by Ellin Burke, New York, 1986; *Theatre in America* by Mary C. Henderson, New York, 1986; *Costume Design on Broadway* by Bobbi Owen, New York, 1987; *The New Let There Be Neon* by Rudi Stern, New York, 1988; *Broadway Ballyhoo* by Mary C. Henderson, New York, 1989; *Double Exposure—Take Two* by Roddy McDowall, New York, 1989; *Razzle Dazzle* by Kevin Boyd Grubb, New York, 1989; *Tony Walton: Designs for Stage and Screen,* exhibition brochure, American Museum of the Moving Image, New York, 1989; *No Tricks in My Pocket* by Stewart Stern, Grove Press, 1989; *All His Jazz* by Martin Gottfried, New York, 1990; *Scenic Design on Broadway* by Bobbi Owen, New York, 1991; *More Broadway Musicals (since 1980)* by Martin Gottfried, New York, 1991; *Art Deco Interiors* by Patricia Bayer, London, 1992; *Art Deco Architecture* by Patricia Bayer, New York, 1992; *By Design: Interviews with Film Production Designers* by Vincent LoBrutto, New York, 1992; *The Music of Disney: A Legacy in Song* by David J. Fisher, Buena Vista, 1992; *Broadway Stories* by Marty Bell, Limelight Editions, 1993; *Cambridge Guide to American Theatre* edited by Don Wilmeth and Tice

**Tony Walton: Set design model for** *A Funny Thing Happened on the Way to the Forum,* **1996**

L. Miller, Cambridge, 1993; *Four Baboons Adoring the Sun and Other Plays* by John Guare, New York, 1993; *Costume Design* by Lynn Pecktal, Backstage Books, 1993; *Teamwork in Der Traumfabrik* by Lars-Olav Bier and Gerhard Midding, Berlin, 1993; *Making Movies* by Sidney Lumet, New York, 1995; *Designed in the USA,* exhibition catalogue by Arnold Aronson, New York, 1995; *Designing and Drawing for the Theatre* by Lynn Pecktal, New York, 1995; *Stage Lighting Design* by Richard Pilbrow, New York, 1996; *Surfaces* by Judie Juracek, New York, 1996; **articles**—"Creative Artists in the Theatre" by Elizabeth Coranthiel in *Theatre World,* June 1963; "Tony Walton: Theatrical Jack of All Trades" by Neal Weaver in *After Dark,* April 1969; "The Designer Talks: Tony Walton in Conversation" by Michael Billington in *Plays and Players,* February 1970; "A Diversity of Designs by Production Designer Tony Walton" by Sidney Lumet in *Lithopinion,* summer 1971; "Twiggy and the Boyfriend" by Leslie Wilkinson in *Photoplay,* March 1972; "Dressed to Kill ... on the Orient Express" by Antonia Williams in *British Vogue,* 15 September 1974; "The Most Glamourous Movie in Years: *Murder on the Orient Express*" by Leo

Lerman in *Vogue,* December 1974; "Tony Walton Designs in Black Vinyl and Neon" by Patricia MacKay in *Theatre Crafts,* October 1975; "The Admirable Showman" by Martin Fox in *Print,* September/October 1975; "Sidney Lumet on *The Wiz*" by Dan Yakir in *Film Comment,* November/December 1978; "Tony Walton: The Wizard Behind the Sets and Costumes of *The Wiz*" by Joseph Curley in *Millimeter,* November 1978; "Tony Walton: Designing *The Wiz*" by Judith McNally in *Film and Video, Monthly Filmmakers,* December 1978; "The Wonderful World of Wizardry (*The Wiz*)" by Jonathan Moor in *G.Q.,* November 1978; "The Golden Road to a Grand New Oz (*The Wiz*)" by James Watters in *Life,* October 1978; "The Wiz of *The Wiz*" by John Duka in *New York,* 16 October 1978; "*The Wiz* Is a Wow Again" by Patricia MacKay in *Theatre Crafts,* October 1980; "Two Views of the San Francisco Ballet, Part 1: A Brave New Tempest" by Janice Ross in *Dance,* May 1980; "Tony Walton—The Invisible Crowd Pleaser" by Norman Nadel in *Horizon,* April 1981; "New Life for Neon" by Michael Webb in *Lighting Dimensions,* May/June 1982; "Prop Masters" by Martin Fox in *Print,* September/October 1982; "A Celluloid

*Deathtrap*—Tony Walton Designs the Film" by Ronn Smith in *Theatre Crafts,* April 1982; "Tony Walton: Movie Magic by Design" by Mason Wiley in *G.Q.,* November 1983; "It's the Real Thing" by Ellen Levine in *Theatre Crafts,* May 1984; "Design: The Set's the Thing" by Marilyn Bethany in *New York,* 23 July 1984; "Design: No Set Style" by Suzanne Stephens in *House & Garden,* May 1985; "Inside *Heartburn*" by Georgia A. Brown in *American Film,* March 1986; "Tony Walton at the Beaumont" by Gary M. Stern in *Theatre Crafts,* March 1987; "Partners by Design" by Ron Jenkins in *American Theatre,* February 1989; "Design for Living: Tony Walton" by Simi Horwitz in *Theatre Crafts,* March 1989; "Setting the Stage" by Kenny Mann in *House in the Hamptons—International,* August 1989; "The Lively Arts: The World of Tony Walton" by Lawrence Chua in *W.,* 18 September, 1989; "Six Degrees of Selective Reduction" by Michael Sommers in *Theatre Crafts,* October 1990; "The Fine Art of a Set Designer" by Jon Istel in *Diversion,* March 1990; "Moving in Place" by Carol Stevens in *Print,* March/April 1990; "*Grand Hotel*: Deluxe Design for a Major Musical" by Michael Sommers in *Theatre Crafts,* January 1990; "The Last American Musical?" by Martin Gottfried in *Theatre Week,* 8 July 1991; "Details, Details, Details" by Karl G. Ruling in *Theatre Crafts,* August/September 1991; "*The Will Rogers Follies*: A Ziegfeld Follies for 1991" by Robert Sandla in *Theatre Crafts,* August/September 1991; "*Guys & Dolls* & Other Hot Tickets" by William A. Henry III in *Time,* 25 May 1992; "Theatre Scenery: *Guys & Dolls*" by Robert Sandla in *T.C.I.,* August/September 1992; "Who's Here: Tony Walton Scenic Designer" by Marion ·Wolberg Weiss in *Dan's Papers,* 23 July 1993; "Astoria-eine Studiogeschtchte" by Gerhard Middling in *Film Bulletin,* November 1993; "The Brilliance of New York" by John Simon in *New York,* 21-28 December 1993; "A Toast to Tony Walton" by Alan Wallach in *Theatre Week,* 9 August 1993; "Designer Sketchbook: She Loves Me" by David Barbour in *T.C.I,* August/September 1993; "1993 Hall of Fame" by M. R. in *Interior Design,* December 1993; "Spectacle on 33rd Street" by Peter Kaminsky in *New York,* 28 November 1994; "Designer Sketchbook: Christmas Carol" by Robert Sandla in *T.C.I,* January 1995; "Two Scenes for Tony Walton" by Jennifer Allen in *Architectural Digest,* November 1995; "Walton's World Part 1" by Eric Grode in *Show Music,* Spring 1995; "Walton's World Part 2" by Eric Grode in *Show Music,* Summer 1995; "Designer Sketchbook: Company" by Robert Sandla in *T.C.I,* January 1996; "Echoes in the Moonlight" by Sean Abbott in *American Theatre,* January 1996.

*

Young designers are often concerned about creating a "signature" style so that their work will have some defining characteristic for people to remember. This is probably the last thing one should be concerned with. One's short-comings—in art and craft—will ultimately result in some sort of "signature" whether one likes it or not.

For me it is preferable to try and start out as a blank slate—completely available to the special nature of the piece. I hope to let the piece itself—via the director's approach to it—dictate the design.

In attempting to serve the piece itself, without reference to previous experience, one might—at best—produce a design that is not reminiscent of any other production and that—ideally—belongs solely to the work at hand.

Starting completely afresh with each project—and, if possible, moving as far away from the character of other recent designs I have done—becomes a big part of the pleasure of the process for me.

—Tony Walton

# WARM, Hermann
German painter and stage and film designer

**Born:** Berlin, 5 May 1889. **Education:** Studied design, at the Kunstgewerbeschule, Berlin, 1905-07; trained in stage design at the Szenograph, Berlin, 1908-09, and at the Schauspielhaus, Dusseldorf, 1910-11. **Career:** Independent painter, associating with Der Sturm expressionist artists, Berlin; film set designer, under contract to Vitaskop, then working for Union, Decla-Bioskop, Greenbaum film company, and others, Berlin, 1912-60; freelance architect and set designer, in Hungary, France, and Britain, 1924-33, and in Switzerland, 1941-44; collaborated with designers Walter Rohrig, Walter Reimann, Otto Hunte, Carl Kirmse, Ernst Meivers, Erich Czernowski, Rudolf Bamberger, Gustav Knauer, Franz Schroedter, Ferdinand Ballen, Mathieu Osterman, Bruno Morden, Robert Herlth, Kurt Herlth, Alfons Windau, Erik Grave, Paul Markwitz and Fritz Maurischat, in Berlin and Munich, from 1919. **Died:** Berlin, 1976.

**Works**

Film productions include—*Der Shylock von Krakau* (Wilhelm), 1913; *Menschen und Masken* (Piel), 1913; *Der Letzte Tag* (Mack), 1913; *Wo ist Colletti?* (Mack), 1913; *Der Konig* (Mack), 1913; *Die Blaue Maus* (Mack), 1913; *Der Andere* (Mack), 1913; *Die Geschichte der Stillen Muhle* (Oswald), 1914; *Pauline* (Etievant), 1914; *Der Hund von Baskerville* (Oswald), 1914; *Der Spion* (Schmidt-Hasler), 1914; *Die Beiden Rivalen* (Etievant), 1914; *Die Millionen-Mine* (Piel), 1914; *Totentanz* (Rippert), 1919; *Der Volontar* (Neuss), 1919; *Die Pest von Florenz* (Rippert), 1919; *Der Tunnel* (Meinert and Wauer), 1919; *Die Spinnen* (Lang), 1920; *Das Kabinett von Dr. Caligari* (Wiene), 1920; *Die Toteninsel* (Froelich), 1920; *Masken* (Wauer), 1920; *Das Blut der Ahmen* (Gerhardt), 1920; *Das Haupt des Juarez* (Guter), 1920; *Der Richter von Zalamea* (Berger), 1920; *Kamfende Herzen* (Lang), 1920; *Der Mude Tod* (Lang), 1921; *Der Ewige Flug* (Wendhausen), 1921; *Die Fliegenden Briganten* (Felmy), 1921; *Die Jagd nach dem Tode* (Gerhardt), 1921; *Schloss Vogelod* (Murnau), 1921; *Zirkus des Lebens* (Guter), 1921; *Phantom* (Murnau), 1922; *Das Spiel der Konigin* (Berger), 1923; *Der Kaufmann von Venedig* (Flener), 1923; *Quarantine* (Mack), 1923; *Grafin Donelli* (Pabst), 1924; *Rosenmontag* (Meinert), 1924; *Konigsliebschen* (Schall), 1924; *Madels von Heute* (Friesler), 1925; *Die Rote Maus* (Meinert), 1925; *Soll Man Heiraten?* (Noa), 1925; *Das Susse Madel* (Noa), 1926; *Student von Prag* (Galeen), 1926; *Fraulein Josette, meine Frau* (Ravel), 1926; *Die Frau ohne Namen* (Jacoby), 1926; *Die Flucht in die Nacht* (Palermi), 1926; *Die Frauen von Folies Bergeres* (Obal), 1926; *Die Insel der Verbotenen Kusse* (Jacoby), 1926; *Liebe* (Czinner), 1926; *Parkettsessel 47* (Ravel), 1926; *Die Liebe Jeanne Ney* (Pabst), 1927; *Die Jagd nach der Braut* (Jacoby), 1927; *Colonialskandal* (Jacoby), 1927;

*Millionenraub im Rivieraexpress* (Delmont), 1927; *La Passion de Jeanne d'Arc* (Dreyer), 1928; *Eine Nacht in London* (Pick), 1928; *Priscillas fahrt ins Gluck* (Asquith), 1928; *Die Weissen Rosen von Ravensberg* (Meinert), 1929; *Masken* (Meinert), 1929; *Fundvogel* (Hoffmann-Harnisch), 1929; *Das Erlebnis einer Nacht* (Brignone), 1929; *Freiheit in Fess* (Wolff), 1929; *Vertauschte Gesichter* (Randolf), 1929; *Dreyfus* (Oswald), 1930; *Es Kommt alle Tage vor ...* (Natge), 1930; *Der Mann, der den Mord Beging* (Bernhardt), 1931; *Der Herr Finanzdirektor* (Friedmann-Frederich), 1931; *Vampyr* (Dreyer), 1932; *Friederike* (Friedmann-Frederich), 1932; *Gehetzte Menschen* (Feher), 1932; *Hochzeit am Wolfgangsee* (Behrendt), 1933; *Wenn am Sonntagabend die Dorfmusik Spielt* (Schundler), 1933; *Peer Gynt* (Wendhausen), 1934; *Wenn ich Konig War* (Hubler-Kahla), 1934; *Musik im Blut* (Waschneck), 1934; *Peter, Paul und Nanette* (Engels), 1934; *Pappi* (Rabenalt), 1934; *Zigeunerblut* (Klein), 1934; *Der Student von Prag* (Robison), 1935; *Mazurka* (Forst), 1935; *Ich Liebe alle Frauen* (Lamac), 1935; *Krach im Interhaus* (Harlan), 1935; *Ein Hochzeitstraum* (Engel), 1936; *Madchenjahre einer Konigin* (Engel), 1936; *Die Nacht mit Kaiser* (Engel), 1936; *Gefahrliches Spiel* (Engel), 1937; *Ein Volksfeind* (Steinhoff), 1937; *Die Warschauer Zitadelle* (Butch), 1937; *Jugend* (Harlan), 1938; *Verwehte Spuren* (Harlan), 1938; *Das Unsterbliche Herz* (Harlan), 1939; *Die Geierwally* (Steinhoff), 1940; *Le Corbeau* (Clouzot), 1943; *Wozzeck* (Klaten), 1947; *Morituri* (York), 1948; *Vors uns Leigt das Leben* (Rittau), 1948; *Tragodie einer Leidenschaft* (Meisal), 1949; *Konigskinder* (Kautner), 1950; *Sehnsuchte des Herzens* (Martin), 1950; *Das Ewige Spiel* (Cap), 1951; *Herz der Welt* (Braun), 1952; *Cuba Cabana* (Buch), 1952; *Die Privatsekretarin* (Martin), 1953; *Hokuspokus* (Hoffmann), 1953; *Der Raub des Sabinerinnen* (Hoffmann), 1954; *Verrat an Deutschland* (Harlan), 1955; *Hannusse Hanussen* (Fischer), 1955; *Konigswalzer* (Tourjansky), 1955; *Dany, Bitte Schreiben Sie* (von Borsody), 1956; *Helden* (Wirth), 1959; *Die Nackte und der Satan* (Trivas), 1959; *Die Wahrheit uber Rosemarie* (Jugert), 1959; *Die Botschafterin* (Braun), 1960.

## Publications

**By WARM: articles**—in *Filmkunst* (Vienna), no. 43, 1965; *Film* (Hannover), July 1965; *Kosmorama* (Copenhagen), October 1965.

**On WARM: books**—*Ragionamenti sulla Scenografia* by Baldo Bandini and Glauco Viazzi, Milan, 1945; *From Caligari to Hitler: A Psychological History of the German Cinema* by Siegfried Kracauer, Princeton, 1947; *La Scenografia del Film* by Mario Verdone, Rome, 1956; *Murnau* by Lotte H. Eisner, Paris, 1964, London 1973; *The Haunted Screen: Expressionism in the Cinema* by Lotte H. Eisner, Berkeley, 1969, 1973; *Film in the Third Reich* by David Stewart Hull, Los Angeles, 1969; *Le Decor de Film* by Leon Barsacq, Paris, 1970, as *Caligari's Cabinet and Other Grand Illusions,* Boston, 1976; *Schopferische Filmarchitektur* by Walter Kaul, West Berlin, 1971; *The German Cinema* by Roger Manvell and Heinrich Fraenkel, London, 1971; *Caligari's Children: The Film as Tale of Terror* by S. S. Prawe, New York, and Oxford, 1980; *German Expressionist Film* by John D. Barton, Boston, 1982; *International Dictionary of Films and Filmmakers,* Chicago and London, 1987, 1991.

\*    \*    \*

Hermann Warm had been designing films for several years when the script of *The Cabinet of Dr. Caligari* was handed to him in 1919. He called in Walter Reimann and Walter Rohrig, fellow designers who were also employed by Decla-Bioscop Studios. Together they decided upon an expressionistic mode and made rough sketches of the film setting. The designers' methodical approach was unusual in early film; *Caligari* is one of the first films in which the visual program was completely planned in advance by the designers.

*The Cabinet of Dr. Caligari* jolted critics and audiences at that time because of its unreal appearance and lack of illusionistic space. Warm articulated the concept underlying this style when he said, "The cinema image must become an engraving." Warm's statement recognizes the fact that film is a two-dimensional art form and explains, in part, why the designers looked to expressionist painting for inspiration.

Warm organized the art direction of Fritz Lang's *Destiny,* just as he had done for *The Cabinet of Dr. Caligari.* The film has several parts: Rohrig designed the prologue and epilogue; Robert Herlth, the Chinese segment; and Warm, the Venetian and Arabian segments. Warm's work in this film is not expressionistic. The glow of torchlight against the cloaked rlgures of Renaissance Venice are reminiscent of Max Reinhardt's Deutsches Theatre productions, which were quite popular in Berlin from 1907 to 1919.

One of the most successful of the many films based on romantic literature is Hennck Galeen's *Student of Prague* of 1926. Warm's sets are faithful to the early nineteenth-century period of the story. His use of looming shadows and hazy light filtering through windows imbues the film with a romantic aura. Warm's sets appear to have been based on paintings by the German romantic painter Caspar David Friedrich.

Warm's greatest accomplishment after *The Cabinet of Dr. Caligari* was his setting for *The Passion of Joan of Arc.* For Danish director Carl Dreyer, Warm and theatrical designer Jean Hugo reproduced an entire medieval town. Although they based their construction on medieval painting, the town is somewhat abstract, with smooth, neutral walls. The set was not shot in its entirety but used as a backdrop to the close-ups of the characters' faces and the silhouetted implements of torture that are seen in the famous montage at the end of the film.

Warm's long and varied career as an art director indicates not only his technical skills but also his ability to carry out research on historical periods and his adaptability to various material and directors.

—Lois Miklas

# WATANABE, Tokuji

Japanese industrial designer

**Born:** Nagoya, 8 May 1934. **Education:** Studied at Aichi Prefectural College of Education, Okazaki City, B.A., 1960. **Family:** Married Mioko Futamura in 1957; children: Osamu, Makoto, and Yoko. **Career:** Freelance industrial designer, establishing UNI Design Office, in Nagoya, from 1960. Instructor in art, Tempaku Junior High School, Nagoya, 1960-63; lecturer in design, Miye University, Tsu City, 1973-77, Ministry of Trade and Industry Design Administration Section, Tokyo, 1975, and Aichi Prefecture College of Arts, Nagakute-machi, 1975-76. Executive director, Central Japan Designers' Association, from 1970; director general, Miye Prefecture Designers and Craftsmens Association, 1977-79; advisor on design development and promotion, Japan Industrial Design Promotion Society, Tokyo, 1976; Design Promotion Council member, Miye Prefecture, 1980-82; City Landscape Council member, Nagoya, 1980-83; Town Scenery Review Committee member, Aichi Prefecture, 1982. **Member:** Japan Industrial Designers Association; Miye Local Industry Design Promotion Council; Central Japan Designers Association; Miye Designers and Craftsmen's Association. **Exhibitions:** Yamagiwa Showroom, Nagoya, 1981. **Collections:** Die Neue Sammlung, Munich. **Honor:** Kunii Kitaro Industrial Design Prize, 1981. **Address:** UNI Design, 1-341 Kameiri, Tashiro-cho, Chicakasu-ku, Nagoya 464, Japan.

## Publications

**By WATANABE: books**—*Scissors ABC,* Seki City, 1980; **articles**—*Design News* (Tokyo), January 1973, January 1980; *Chunichi Shimbun* (Nagoya), November 1977; *Industrial Design* (Tokyo), November 1979; Chibu Designers *Research Report* (Anjo City), April 1980.

**On WATANABE: books**—*Japanese Design* by Penny Sparke, London, 1987; **articles**—*Interior* (Tokyo), June 1981.

                                        *

The 1980s and 1990s may be the decades when drastic solutions must be found for the problems raised during the 1960s and 1970s: resources, food, nationalism, big business, controlled society, and human alienation. Moreover, in the daily life of people, changes are taking place in the value system, as is suggested by the phrases "from quantity to quality" and "from material to heart."

Although Japanese product design now holds a high international reputation as a result of improvements in tools and home appliances during the last three decades, if you turn your eyes to products for public use, such as tableware for school lunch, trains, and other public transportation facilities, furniture used in hospitals and other public facilities, they reveal an imbalance in design, if design is defined as "activity to satisfy the material and spiritual desires of man to live a cozy humane life." This fact indicates that designers have forgotten their role in society; they are too much concerned about desirable relations between products and consumers.

The mainstream of our present lifestyle consists of a consumerism created when energy and other resources were obtained cheaply. This lifestyle must be totally revamped in the 1980s. Now, desirable relations among products, consumers, and nature must be demanded of designers. When the meaning of making things and of marketing and consuming products is questioned, then the meaning of creating must also be questioned. Courage, mental toughness, and insight must be the minimum requirements for qualified designers in the coming age.

—Tokuji Watanabe

                        *      *      *

Tokuji Watanabe is best known as a designer of scissors—produced under the Allex brand and notable for the beauty of their forms. The scissors were first put on the market in 1973, and at that time such high quality, small-size scissors were not available in Japan. In the last ten years more than five million of these scissors have been produced. They have achieved an international reputation, and are now the world's best seller.

The Allex scissors are made of pressed stainless plate. Soft plastic rings are inserted within the finger holes. Polishing the finger holes to make them smooth is usually the most difficult part of making ordinary scissors: the plastic rings in the Allex scissors solved the problem—and the rings, done in a variety of shades, create an agreeable and colorful accent.

The success of Watanabe's scissors demonstrated several "lessons." Watanabe showed that, for local industries, it made more sense—that is, produced a better result—to work with an "indigenous product" than to attempt to produce what one imagined would have international appeal. Ironically, he also showed that a traditional product, produced by a local industry, could achieve international fame if it were well designed. And it occurred not only to other designers but also to other manufacturers that the simplest products can be well designed and that such well-designed products have great commercial appeal.

Watanabe has always said that designers should be good members of society if they wish to be good designers. If the role of the industrial designer is defined as "creative activity to produce materials and an environment that will satisfy man's natural and spiritual desires to live a humane life," then the actual circumstances in Japan seem to be very far from the ideal. Moreover, designers have tended to be too much involved in just one sector of society; they know very little about society as a whole. Watanabe has tried to be what he preaches: he has spoken out on many occasions about the world's limited resources, the energy crisis, pollution, and environmental problems, and, as a designer, he has advocated good design for public amenities.

Watanabe strives to achieve quality in both his life and his art: it fact, it could be said that he attempts to design his life and to make design a reflection of his larger concerns.

—Kunio Sano

# WEALLEANS, Jon
British architect and interior and furniture designer

**Born:** Yorkshire, 10 February 1946. **Education:** Studied at the Architectural Association School, London, 1966-67; Royal College of Art, London, M.A., 1970. **Family:** Married Jane Hill in 1970. **Career:** Designer, in the Building Partnership, Manchester and London, 1969-70, and with Foster associates, London, 1970-71; freelance designer, London, 1971-85; creative director, Crighton Limited design group, London, from 1985; interior design consultant to Rock Townsend Architects, London, 1973-78. Unit staff lecturer, Architectural Association School, London, 1982-83; senior lecturer in three-dimensional design, Kingston Polytechnic, Surrey, from 1983. **Addresses:** 9 Grange Walk, London SEI; Crighton Limited, 10 New Oxford Street, London WC1A 1EE, England.

## Works

Bank of England headquarters interiors, Leeds, Yorkshire, 1969-70.
IBM Building interiors, Havant, Hampshire, 1971.
Roscoes Restaurant interiors, Soho, London, 1973.
Furniture, for Luna BV, Milan, 1973-78.

## Publications

**On WEALLEANS: book**—*The Contemporary Decorative Arts from 1940 to the Present Day* by Philippe Garner, London, 1980; *Twentieth Century Furniture* by Philippe Garner, London, 1981; *Restaurants: Architektur and Ambiente* by Egon Schirmbeck, New York, 1982; *Fireplaces* by Nicholas Hills, London, 1983; *Street Style* by Catherine McDermott, London, 1988.

*

It is a fact—and important to me—that I do not have a particular style or hallmark other than an emphasis on detail design and the establishment of whether or not a (potential) client *needs* an architect and then whether or not I am the correct choice. I don't normally work with lavish budgets and, indeed, I am not uninterested in small-scale projects or budgets.

My criteria for accepting a commission are the same as those of Eliot Noyes: potential clients should be in agreement with my design philosophy; they should allow adequate time for each project; and the programme and the budget should be in scale with one another.

—Jon Wealleans

\*      \*      \*

Jon Wealleans describes himself as an eclectic designer without a strong sense of personal style, but with however, a clear philosophy behind his design work. He believes that the designer should adapt his talents to the requirements of individual commissions, with the result that his work has been diverse. He is careful to take only briefs demanding innovative work, not pastiches, and only clients with sufficient finances and time to produce good work. This policy, which ensures that both client and designer have decided on the right person, has lost work for him but gained him a great deal of respect. The question of pastiche is critical because he is inspired by design individualists such as Charles Rennie Mackintosh, Frank Lloyd Wright, Ettore Sottsass, and Robert Stern. It's a mixture explained by Wealleans' background as one of a group of talented designers who graduated from the Royal College of Art in the 1960s, and who contributed to a feeling of excitement in British design during that period. His list of design inspirations is a classic 1960s amalgam of avant-grade Italian radicalism, images from popular culture, and stylistic motifs from previously unfashionable art nouveau designers. Not surprisingly, some of his work from this early period reflects a pop design ethic.

His most important designs include the famous Mr. Freedom boutique in Kensington Church Street (1969) and, in the early 1970s, a house for a member of the rock group Led Zeppelin. Designed as a backdrop for the musician's collection of Art Deco, this interior features pink and cream colour, decorative inlays,

etched glass, and painted troupe l'oeil perspectives. More recently, in the design of the IBM interior at Edinburgh, he has adapted Mackintosh's work to a modern idiom. Wealleans's style of creatively transforming the work of other designers can be best seen in his own flat, featured in *Abitare* in May 1983. Using a standard Arts and Crafts formula of black floor and cream walls, doors, and curtains, he then added Liberty, Breuer, OKM, and his own furniture designs. The effect is comfortable, stylish, and very impressive. Wealleans is also developing as a serious design commentator, appearing on television programmes and in design magazines.

—Catherine McDermott

# WECKSTRÖM, Björn (Ragnar)

Finnish sculptor, jewellery, glass, and metalwork designer

**Born:** Helsinki, 8 February 1935. **Education:** Studied at the Finnish Goldsmith School, Helsinki, Dip., 1956. **Family:** Married Britta Berg in 1957 (divorced, 1983); married Lelia Viljanen in 1989; children: Joachim and Cecilia. **Career:** Freelance professional goldsmith and jewellery designer, Helsinki, 1956-67; designer, for Hopeakontu Oy, Helsinki, 1957, and for Lapponia Jewellery Oy, Helsinki, from 1963; also glass designer for Wartsila-Nuutajarvi Glassworks, from 1967. Established own gallery in Helsinki, from 1958, and in Stockholm, from 1989; concentrated on sculpture in Agnano, Italy, from 1981. Lecturer, throughout the world, from 1978; jury member, from 1983. **Member:** Finnish Sculptors' Association; ORNAMO. **Exhibitions:** Röhsska Könstslöjdmuseet, Göteborg, 1967; Finland House, London, 1969; Amos Anderson Art Museum, Helsinki, 1973; David Jones Gallery, Sydney, 1975; Galerie der Greef, Brussels, 1977; Waino Aaltonen Museum, Turku, Finland, 1978; Sculpture Galleria, Palm Beach, Florida, 1978; Mikimoto Gallery, Tokyo, 1979; Boardwalk Gallery, Houston, 1979; Vestlandske Kunstindustrimuseum, Bergen, 1982; Kunstmuseum, Cologne, 1984; Stadtpart, Dortmund, 1985; Goldsmith's Hall, London, 1986; National Museum, Utrecht, 1987; *30th Anniversary Exhibition,* Galerie Björn Weckström, Helsinki, 1988; Galerie Schindler, Zermatt, 1988; Tammisaari Museum, Tammisaari, 1989; Ekenas Museum, Finland, 1989; Charlottenborg, Copenhagen, 1990; Museum of Applied Arts, Helsinki, 1990; The Cathedral Crypt, Helsinki, 1995. **Collections:** Museum for Arts and Crafts, Helsinki; Finnish Glass Museum, Riihimäki; Victoria and Albert Museum, London; Royal Scottish Museum, Edinburgh; Röhsska Könstslöjdmuseet, Göteborg; Vestlandske Kunstindustrimuseum, Bergen. **Honors:** Medal, Milan Triennale, 1960; 2nd Prize, Finnish Goldsmiths' Association, 1962; Purchase Prize, Norstaal Contest, Oslo, 1964; Grand Prix, International Jewellery Contest, Rio de Janeiro, 1965; Finnish Goldsmith's Medal of Honour, 1967; Lunning Prize, 1968; Pro Finlandia Medal, 1971; Illum Prize, 1972; Honorary Professor, Helsinki, 1986. **Addresses:** Marjaranta 12, 002260 Esbo, Finland; Via Settembrini 18, Agnano, Pisa, Italy.

## Works

Wall relief, for Rettig Strengborg, Turku, 1986.
Commission, for Fazer Headquarters, Helsinki, 1989.

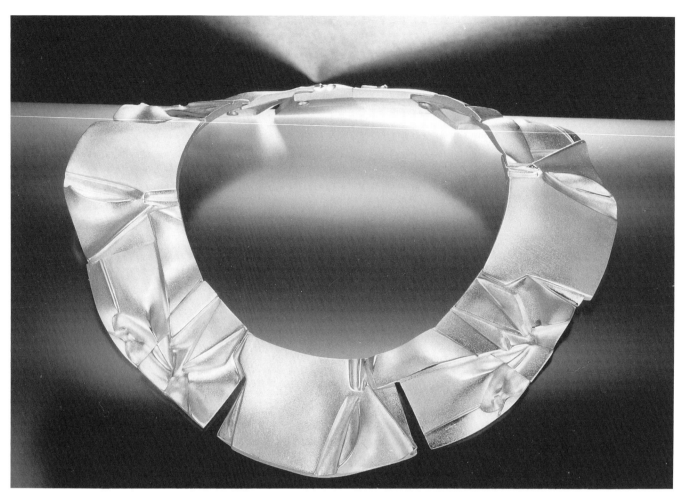

Björn Weckström: *Poema* sterling silver necklace, manufactured by Lapponia Jewelry Oy, Helsinki, Finland, 1994

Monument in honor of Fazer's 100th Anniversary, 1991. Commission, for YLE Headquarters, Helsinki, 1993.

**Publications**

**On WECKSTRÖM: books**—*Finnish Design 1875-1975* by Timo Sarpaneva, Erik Bruun, and Erik Kruskopt, Helsinki, 1975; *Finland Creates* edited by Jack Fields and David Moore, Jyvaskyla, 1977; *Björn Weckström,* with texts by Christer Kihlman and Marika Hausen, Helsinki, 1980; *Glas: Unikate finnische kunstler,* exhibition catalogue by Helmut Ricke, Dusseldorf, 1982; *The Lunning Prize,* exhibition catalogue edited by Helena Dahlback Lutteman and Marianne Uggla, Stockholm, 1986; **articles**—"New Line of Jewellery for Lapponia Oy, Finland" in *Aurum* (Geneva), summer 1987.

# WEGNER, Hans J(orgensen)

Danish architectural, interior, and furniture designer

**Born:** Tønder, Jutland, 2 April 1914. **Education:** Educated in Tønder until 1926; apprenticed as a cabinet-maker, Tønder, 1927-

31; studied at the Danish Institute of Technology, Copenhagen, 1936; studied furniture design under O. Moelgaard Nielsen, at the School of Arts and Crafts, Copenhagen, 1936-38. **Family:** Married Inga Helbo in 1940. **Career:** Furniture designer, working in the office of architects Flemming Lassen and Erik Moller, Århus, 1939, and in the office of Erik Moller and Arne Jacobsen, Århus, 1940-43; freelance interior and furniture designer in Århus, 1943-46, and in Copenhagen, from 1946; has designed for Johannes Hansens Møbelsnedkeri, Fritz Hansen, Tarm Stoleog Mobelfabrik, RY-Mobler, Carl Hansen, Andreas Tuck, AP Stolen, Getama, PP Møbler, Fredericia Stolefabrik, Erik Jorgensen, and others. Assistant to Palle Suenson, 1946-48, instructor in design, 1946-53, at the School of Arts and Crafts, Copenhagen. **Exhibitions:** Cabinetmakers Guild Exhibitions, Copenhagen, 1938-67; *The Arts of Denmark,* toured the United States, 1960; *Modern Chairs 1918-1970,* Whitechapel Art Gallery, London, 1972; *Scandinavian Modern Design 1880-1980,* Cooper-Hewitt Museum, New York, 1982; *Design Since 1945,* Philadelphia Museum of Art, 1983; Osaka Industrial Design Institute, Japan, 1988; Selvini, Milan, Italy, 1988; Nordiska Galleriet, Stockholm, 1988; Kunstindustrimuseet, Copenhagen, 1989; Arkitektskolen, Århus, Denmark, 1990; National Museum of Scotland, Edinburgh, 1990; *Mostra Internazionale dell'arredamento,* Monza, Italy, 1992; Business Design Center, London, 1994; Living Design

Center, OZONE Building, Tokyo, 1995; Dean Clough Galleries, Halifax, England, 1995. **Collections:** Museum of Modern Art, New York; Metropolitan Museum of Modern of Art, New York; Philadelphia Museum of Art; Victoria & Albert Museum, London; Die Neue Sammlung, Munich; Röhsska Konstslöjdmuseet, Göteborg; Nordenfjeldske Museum, Trondheim; Nationalmuseum, Stockholm; Kunstindustrimuseet, Oslo; Kunstindustrimuseet, Copenhagen; Vitra Design Museum, Weil am Rhein; Louisiana, Humlebaek; National Gallery, Melbourne; Sønderjyllands Kunstmuseum, Tønder. **Honors:** Lunning Prize, 1951; Grand Prix, 1951, Gold Medal, 1954, Silver Medal, 1957, Diploma, 1973, Milan Triennale; Eckersberg Medal, 1956; Danish Trade Fair Medal, 1956; Cabinetmakers Guild Prize, Copenhagen, 1959, 1965; Citation of Merit, Pratt Institute, New York, 1959; honorary Royal Designer for Industry, Royal Society of Arts, London, 1959; American Institute of Decorators Award, 1961; Prince Eugen Medal, Stockholm, 1961; American Institute of Interior Designers Prize, 1967, and Citation of Merit, 1968; Danish Furniture manufacturers Prize, 1980; C.F. Hansen Medal, 1982; Knight of the Dannebrog, 1984; IDD Industrial Design Prize, Copenhagen, 1987; Hæderslegat Nationalbankens Jubilæumsfond, 1989; Legat fra Ole Haslunds Kunstfond, 1989. **Address:** Tinglevej 17, 2820 Gentofte, Denmark.

## Works

*Rocking Chair J 16* in beech with woven cord seat, for Tarm Stoleog Mobelfabrik, 1944.

*Chinese Chair PP 66* in ash with woven string seat, for PP Møbler, 1944.

*Chinese Chair FH 4283* in cherrywood with leather cushion, for Fritz Hansen, 1944.

*Peter's Chair* and *Peter's Table*, for Johannes Hansen Møbelsnedkeri, 1944.

*Peacock Chair JH 550* in ash, oak and woven cord, for Johannes Hansen, 1947.

*Lounge Chair PP 105,* for PP Møbler, 1947.

*Folding Chair JH 512* in oak and woven cane, for Johannes Hansen, 1949.

*Classic Chair JH 501* in oak and woven cane, for Johannes Hansen, 1949.

*Shell Chair* prototype, 1949.

*Wishbone Chair CH 24* in oak with woven string seat, for Carl Hansen and Son, 1950.

*Flag Haliyard Chair* upholstered steel-frame chair, for Getama, 1950.

*Chair CH 229* and *Easy Chair CH 25,* for Carl Hansen Ogsøn, 1951.

*Cowhorn Chair JH 505,* for Johannes Hansen, 1952.

*Valet Chair PP 250* in pine and teak, for PP Møbler, 1953.

*Swivel Chair JH 502* in tubular steel and teak with leather seat and wheels, for Johannes Hansen, 1955.

*Easy Chair JH 40* in tubular steel with leather upholstery, for Johannes Hansen, 1958.

*Airport Chair FS 401,* for Fredericia Stolefabrik, 1958.

*Armchair JH 518* in teak and wickerwork, for Johannes Hansen, 1961.

*Chair CH 36,* for Carl Hansen Ogsøn, 1962.

*Conference Chair JH 513,* for Johannes Hansen, 1962.

*Three-legged Shell Chair* prototype, 1963.

*Easy Chair CH 44* in oak and beech with woven cord seat, for Carl Hansen and son, 1965.

*Chair JH 701* in steel and maple with leather upholstery, for Johannes Hansen, 1965.

*Bull Chair EJ 100* in chrome steel with leather upholstery, for Erick Jorgensen, 1968.

*Chair PP 201* in ash with woven string seat, for PP Møbler, 1969.

*Armchair PP 63,* for PP Møbler, 1975.

*Easy Chair GE 460,* for Getama, 1975.

*Chair PP 112* in ash with woven string seat, for PP Møbler, 1978.

*Rocking Chair PP 124* in ash with rope seat and back, for PP Møbler, 1983.

*Easy Chair PP 130* in laminated ash with woven seat and back, for PP Møbler, 1986.

*Easy Chair JH 477* and *JH 478* in laminated ash with upholstered back and seat, for Johannes Hansen, 1986.

*Table GE 126, Chair GE 155,* and *Armchair GE 156,* for Getama, 1986.

*Chair PP 58* and *Armchair PP 68,* for PP Møbler, 1987.

*Chair FS 881, Armchair FS 882,* and *Easy Chair 883,* for Fredericia Stolefabrik, 1988.

*The V-Chair 51/3, Chair 58/3, Rocking Chair PP 124,* and *Coffee Tables PP 14, 16,* and *20,* all for PP Møbler, 1988.

*Sofas FS 402, 403,* and *404,* for Fredericia Stolefabrik, 1989.

*Coffee Table PP 12, The Chinese Chair PP 56,* and *Table PP 75/200,* for PP Møbler, 1989.

*Easy Chair PP 114* and *Armchair PP 240,* for PP Møbler, 1990.

*Table PP 70/130,* for PP Møbler, 1991.

*Armchair PP 93* and *PP 193,* for PP Møbler, 1993.

## Publications

**On WEGNER: books**—*Dansk Mobelkunst* by Viggo Sten Moller and Svend Erik Moller, Copenhagen, 1951; *Danish Chairs* edited by Nanna and Jorgen Ditzel, Copenhagen, 1954; *Modern Danish Furniture* by Esbjorn Hiort, Copenhagen, New York, and London, 1956; *Made in Denmark* by Arne Karlsen and Anker Tiedemann, Copenhagen, 1960; *A Treasury of Scandinavian Design* edited by Erik Zahle, New York, 1961; *Scandinavian Domestic Design* edited by Erik Zahle, Copenhagen, 1961, London, 1963; *Wegner: En Dansk Mobel-kunstner* by Johann Moller-Nielsen, Copenhagen, 1965; *Contemporary Danish Design* edited by Arne Karlsen and others, Copenhagen, 1966; *34 Scandinavian Designers* by Svend Erik Moller, Copenhagen, 1967; *Modern Chairs 1918-1970,* exhibition catalogue with texts by Carol Hogben and others, London, 1970; *The Modern Chair: Classics in Production* by Clement Meadmore, London, 1974; *Scandinavian Design: Object of a Life Style* by Eileen Harrison Beer, New York and Toronto, 1975; *History of Modern Furniture* by Karl Mang, Stuttgart, 1978, London, 1979; *Tema med Variationer: Hans J. Wegner's Mobler* by Henrik Sten Moller, Tønder, 1979; *Twentieth Century Furniture* by Philippe Garner, London, 1980; *A Century of Chair Design* edited by Frank Russell, London, 1981; *Knoll Design* by Eric Larrabee and Massimo Vignelli, New York, 1981; *Contemporary Classics: Furniture by the Masters* by Charles D. Gandy and Susan Zimmerman-Stidham, New York, 1981; *Contemporary Furniture* edited by Klaus-Jurgen Sembach, Stuttgart and London, 1982; *Design Since 1945* edited by Kathryn Hiesinger and George Marcus, Philadelphia and London,

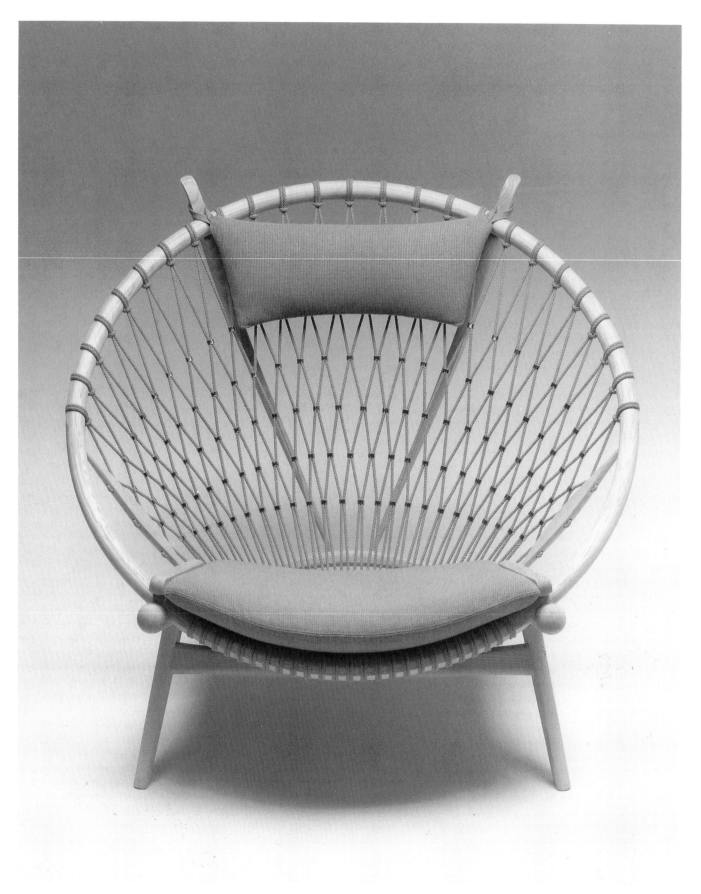

**Hans J. Wegner:** *PP 130* easy chair in laminated ash and woven cord, for P P Mobler, 1986

1983; *Industrial Design: Unikate Serienzeugnisse* by Hans Wichmann, Munich, 1985; *Mid-Century: Furniture of the 1950s* by Cara Greenberg, London, 1985; *Modern Furniture Classics* by Miriam Stimpson, London, 1987.

\* \* \*

Hans Wegner exemplifies the prolific designer, one comparable to an author who produces best-sellers year after year. And yet, to parallel Wegner's output, this would have to be a novelist who also turns out histories, biographies, and even an occasional volume of verse. Over the years, Wegner has produced an extensive line of furnishings: storage systems and storage pieces; wood-framed and fully upholstered seating; lamps and wallpapers; tables of every type; pieces for the home and, more recently, for public spaces; and, of course, chairs. His approach is literally that of the artist-craftsman, with prototypes developed in his basement workshop and tested in the home he designed for himself outside Copenhagen before being given over to the firm that produces his work.

Again indicative of his mastery of many genres is the fact that although he appears to prefer wood to other materials, he is also willing to experiment with metals, as he did in the steel-framed "hammock" chair which is innovatively upholstered with 230 meters of flag cord anchored with an obvious knot at one end.

It is not for his versatility that Wegner is celebrated, however. It is for his wood chairs—his poetry. As counterpoint to his other designs, which are united more by a general level of craft and utility than by stylistic similarities, Wegner's wood chairs have consistently explored subtle sculptural relationships. Their origins are frequently Oriental—the back rails often wrapping into the front uprights—and occasionally traditional, as in the examples of the Boston rockers and Windsor-like Peacock. Seats frequently appear to float on their supporting rails and both joints and combinations of woods and materials break from the expected.

Wegner exhibits the poet's ability to interpret and reinterpret a theme, to make statements which are complete without being final. Moreover, his chairs are beyond the mainstream. Their complexity prevents their being readily copied. Thus they avoid being cheapened by imitations (as happened to other Danish designs in the 1950s, for example, as they were insensitively transformed into "Danish modern" by American manufacturers).

—Reed Benhamou

# WEINGART, Wolfgang

German graphic and typographic designer

**Born:** 1941. **Education:** Apprenticed as a hand-typesetter, Basel; mainly self-taught in design. **Career:** Freelance designer and teacher, in Basel, from 1968. Founder of *TM/Communication and Typographic Process,* in collaboration with *Typographische Monatsblätter,* St. Gallen. Instructor, School of Design, Basel, from 1968; also visiting lecturer throughout Europe and the United States, from 1972; instructor, Yale Summer Program in Graphic Design, Brissago, Switzerland. **Member:** Alliance Graphique

Internationale. **Exhibitions:** Woods-Gerry Gallery, Rhode Island School of Design, 1973; *The Twentieth Century Poster: Design of the Avant Garde,* Walker Art Center, Minneapolis, 1984; *WortZeichen/SchriftFelder/BildRäume,* Institut für Neue Technische Form, Darmstadt, 1990. **Collections:** Museum of Modern Art, New York; Walker Art Center, Minneapolis; Plakatsammlung Museum für Gestaltung, Zürich. **Honors:** Numerous poster and graphics prizes from the Swiss Department of Cultural Affairs. **Address:** Postfach 2235, CH 4001 Basel, Switzerland.

## Works

*Typographische Monatsblätter* magazine covers, St. Gallen, 1972-73, 1976.
*Kunstkredit* posters in B2 format, 1977-83.
*Idea* no. 12 magazine cover, Tokyo, 1979.
*Projekte/Projects* book jacket design, for Verlag Arthur Niggli, 1979.
*Didacta* booklets and folders, 1980-81.
*Didacta* poster in B2 format, 1981.
*Schreibkunst* poster in B2 format, 1981.
*The Swiss Poster* book jacket design, for Birkhauser Verlag, 1983.
*The Swiss Poster* promotion poster in B2 format, 1983.

## Publications

**By WEINGART: books**—*How Can One Make Swiss Typography,* Basel, 1972, London, 1987; *Projects: Typographic Research at the Basel School of Design,* Niederteufen, 1979; **articles**—*Druckspiegel* (Stuttgart), no. 7, 1963, no. 3, 1966; *Form und Technik* (Stuttgart), no. 1, 1965; regular contributor, *Typographische Monatsblätter* (St. Gallen), from 1968; *Design Quarterly* (Minneapolis), no. 130, 1985; *Octavo* (London), no. 4, 1987.

**On WEINGART: books**—*Top Graphic Design* by F. H. K. Henrion, Zürich, 1983; *The Twentieth Century Poster: Design of the Avant-Garde* by Dawn Ades, New York, 1984; *Basic Typography* by Ruedi Ruegg, Zürich, 1989; *20th Century Type* by Lewis Blackwell, London, 1992; **articles**—in *Typographische Monatsblätter* (St. Gallen), January 1970, November 1970, October 1973, December 1976; *Idea* (Tokyo), no. 1, 1978; *Graphis* (Zürich), no. 227, 1983; *Emigre* (Berkeley, California), no. 14, 1990; *High Quality* (Heidelberg), no. 16, 1990; *Design Report* (Frankfurt), no. 16, 1991; *Eye* (London), no. 4, 1991.

\*

Today's graphics look *almost* the same globally: an unreadable chaos.

—Wolfgang Weingart

\* \* \*

The use of sans serif typography, rigid adherence to a grid system, asymmetrical balance, and flush left/ragged right type settings characterized the universal and harmonious typographic style that

**Wolfgang Weingart: Exhibition poster for Herbert Bayer at the Gewerbe Museum, Basel, Switzerland, 1982**

emerged from Switzerland and found advocates throughout the world. Just as this approach started to harden into a formula, Weingart began to teach at Basel and to challenge prevailing concepts of typographic design. Wide letterspacing of type, the swelling of typography through photographic overexposure, and the mixing of type sizes and weights in the same design (or even in the same word) were explored in an effort to revitalize and invigorate typography. Rather than use traditional means to indicate paragraphs, such as indenting the first line or separating paragraphs with a space, Weingart inverted new devices to serve this function. For example, he placed paragraphs throughout the page in one advertisement, using arrows and numbers to direct the reader through the information. In another project, paragraphs had stepped geometric shapes and were locked together like a puzzle. Numerals informed the reader of their reading order.

As Weingart's design innovations from the early 1970s (including step-rules, size and weight contrasts, letterspaced type, and fine rules moving through the space to link elements together) were widely emulated during the late 1970s, Weingart moved on to create collage-like compositions by layering film positives of images and type. This innovative technique enabled Weingart to juxtapose and overlay complex visual information. During this period, Weingart delighted in contrasts. Type images, moiré and halftone patterns, torn collage elements, and linear patterns are densely layered and stacked into rich, tonal graphic expressions.

—Philip B. Meggs

# WEITZ, John

American fashion and industrial designer

**Born:** Berlin, Germany, 25 May 1923; emigrated to Britain in 1934, then to the United states in 1940, naturalized, 1943. **Education:** Attended Hall School, and St. Paul's School, London, 1935-39; apprenticed to fashion designer Edward Molyneux, Paris, 1939-40. **Military Service:** Served in the United Stated Army, 1943-46, Captain. **Family:** Married actress Susan Kohner in 1964; children: Robert, Karen, Paul, and Christopher. **Career:** Designer of women's sportswear, working with several companies in London and New York, until 1954; founder-designer and chairman of John Weitz Incorporated men's fashion designs, New York, from 1954. Professional race car driver, 1954-64. Board member, Allen-Stevenson School, New York, Phoenix House, New York, William J. Donovan Foundation, Council of Fashion Designers of America, Veterans of the OSS, New York, American Council on Germany; council member, Museum of the City of New York. **Member:** Old Pauline Club, London; Union Club, New York; The Century Association, New York; The Pilgrims, New York; Special Forces Club, London; Vintage Sports Car Club of America; Sports Car Club of America. **Exhibitions:** *Manhattan Faces,* Museum of the City of New York, 1984; *Berlin Summer,* Berlin, 1989. **Collections:** Smithsonian Institution, Washington, D.C.; Crawford Auto-Aviation Museum, Cleveland, Ohio. **Honors:** *Sports Illustrated* Award, 1959; *NBC Today* Award, 1960; Philadelphia Museum of Art Award, 1960; Caswell-Massey Awards, 1963-66; *Harper's Bazaar* Medallion,

1966; Moscow Diploma, 1967; International Best Dressed List Hall of Fame Award, 1971; Coty American Fashion Critics Award, 1974; Cartier Design Award, 1981; Mayor's Liberty Medal, New York, 1986; Cutty Sark Career Achievement Award, 1986; First Class Order of Merit, West Germany, 1988; Dallas Menswear Mart Award, 1990; President's Award, Fashion Institute of Technology, 1990; Ellis Island Medal of Honor, 1992; Commander, Order of Merit, Federal Republic of Germany, 1995. **Address:** 600 Madison Avenue, New York 10022, U.S.A.

## Publications

**By WEITZ: books**—*Sports Clothes and Cars,* New York, 1959; *The Value of Nothing,* New York and London, 1970; *Man in Charge,* New York, 1974; *Friends in High Places,* New York, 1982; *Hitler's Diplomat,* New York and London, 1992, Tokyo, 1995.

**On WEITZ: books**—*Dress Optional* by Bennett-England, London, 1967; *The Fashion Makers* by Vecchio and Riley, New York, 1968; *The Beautiful People* by Marilyn Bender, New York, 1968; *Esquire's Encyclopedia of Men's Fashions,* New York, 1973; *Mature Man's Guide to Style* by Gale, New York, 1980; *Fairchild's Who's Who in Fashion* edited by Anne Stegemeyer, New York, 1980; *Inside the Fashion Business* by Jarrow, Judelle, and Goerreiro, New York, 1981; *McDowell's Directory of Twentieth Century Fashion* by Colin McDowell, London, 1984.

*

Obviously, form follows function and fashion follows form. Therefore, I have always tried to think of function first, be it technical, physical, or emotional.

—John Weitz

* * *

Although born in Germany, John Weitz, the son of a well-to-do textile manufacturer, was educated in England in the late 1930s (safe from the Nazis). The combination of an English education and an apprenticeship with the famous couturier Edward Molyneaux, whose classic style was legendary, developed in Weitz a taste for the classically tailored.

His early work as a designer in America was in women's sportswear—a relatively new field after World War II. Weitz innovatively introduced men's tailored sportswear to American women, thereby setting a style for the rest of the fashion world. His "second career" as a menswear designer in the 1960s and 1970s brought him even greater success. While most designers were experimenting in the men's market with outlandish colors and fabrics and extreme cuts, Weitz made an important name for himself with conservatively designed clothing, such as navy blue flannel blazers, oxford cloth tailored shirts, and classically "English" ties—a style once called Ivy League, but now called Preppy—in the moderate price range that non-Preppy young men could afford.

As much a businessman as he is a designer, he was one of the first American designers to put his signature on the exterior of the menswear he designed. With the success of the John Weitz

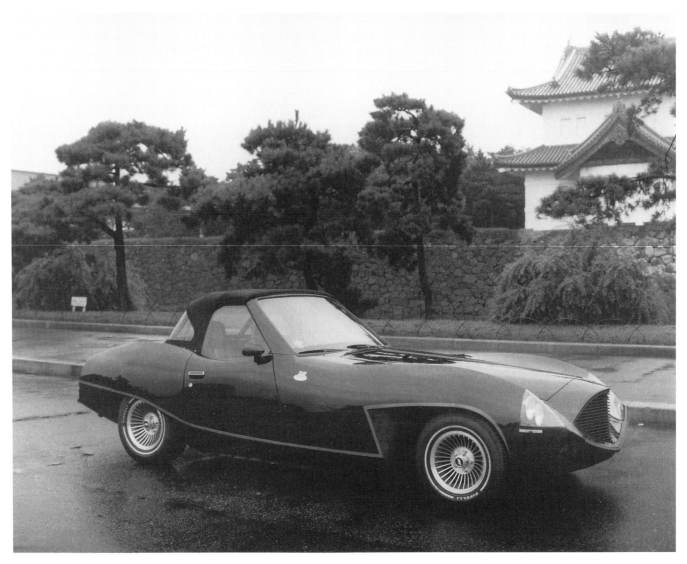

John Weitz: *X600* aluminum bodied sportscar, 1980

signature, he licensed his name to manufacturers of many different kinds of products, ranging from traditional clothing for men, women, and boys, to accessories such as scarves, gloves, and handbags and to non-clothing articles like cigar boxes and ice buckets.

Though Weitz has won many awards for his designs, including the Coty, which is the grand prix of American fashion awards, one of his most prestigious awards is the 1981 Cartier Design Award for an all-aluminum sports car dubbed the X-600 and nicknamed the Weitzmobile. Weitz believes that a man should wear his car as he would wear his clothes; the X-600 fits the well dressed man in the same manner that his classically tailored clothes should fit. Although Weitz designs only a very small percentage of the clothing (and other articles) produced under his name, he supervises most of the licensed articles, so he can veto those things which do not conform to his taste.

—John E. Hirsch

## WELCH, Robert (Radford)
British silversmith and product designer

**Born:** Hereford, 21 May 1929. **Education:** Educated at Hanley Castle Grammar School, Worcestershire, 1941-46; studied under Victor Moody, Malvern School of Art, Worcestershire, 1946-47, 1949: studied under C. J. Shiner and R. Baxendale, Birmingham College of Art, 1950-52; studied under Robert Gooden, Royal College of Art, London, 1952-55. **Military Service:** Served as a wireless operator in the Royal Air Force, 1947-49. **Family:** Married Patricia Marguerite Hinksman in 1959; children: Alice, Alan, and Leonard. **Career:** Independent silversmith and metalware designer, with workshop in Chipping Campden, Gloucestershire, from 1955; design consultant, J. and J. Wiggin Old Hall Tableware, Bloxwich, from 1955; opened Robert Welch Studio Shop in Chipping Campden, from 1969, and in Warwick, from 1991; visiting designer, Yamazaki Kinzoku Kogyo Co. Ltd., Japan, 1979. Lecturer, Central School of Art and Design, London, 1956-59, and Royal College of Art, London, 1960-71. **Exhibitions:** Foyles Art Gallery, London, 1956; Heal and Sons, London, 1964; Skjalm Petersen Shop, 1967, 1992; Leeds Art Gallery, Yorkshire, 1969; Rohsska Museum, Göteborg, Sweden, 1969; Crafts Advisory Committee, Waterloo Place Gallery, London, 1974; *Treasures of London,* Smithsonian Institution, Washington, D.C., 1976; *Design Since 1945,* Philadelphia Museum of Art, 1983; *Eye for Industry,* Victoria and Albert Museum, London, 1986; *Finely Taught, Finely Wrought,* Birmingham Museum and Art Gallery, 1987; *British Goldsmiths of Today,* Goldsmiths' Hall, London, 1992; *20th-century Silver,* Crafts Council Gallery, Islington, London, 1993; *Robert Welch Designer-Silversmith: A Retrospective Exhibition, 1955-1995,* Cheltenham Art Gallery and Museum, 1995 (toured, 1995-96). **Collections:** Victoria and Albert Museum, London; Worshipful Company of Goldsmiths, London; Birmingham Museum; Leeds Museum, Yorkshire; Bergen Museum, Norway; Museum of Decorative Art, Denmark; Stedelijk Museum, Amsterdam; Museum of Modern Art, New York; Philadelphia Museum of Art. **Honors:** Charlotte Jacob Prize, 1950; Charles Foye Scholarship, Birmingham College of Art, 1951; Prize and Medal, Royal College of Art, 1955; Design Centre Award, London, 1958, 1963, 1964, 1965, 1984; Silver Medal, Milan Triennale, 1958; fellow, Chartered Society of Designers, London, 1962; Royal Designer for Industry, Royal Society of Arts, London, 1965; Design Award, *The Observer,* London, 1969; honorary fellow, Royal College of Art, London, 1972; Silver Medal, Jerusalem Art Book Biennale, 1975; Member, Order of the British Empire, 1980; Liveryman, Worshipful Company of Goldsmiths, London, 1982. **Address:** The Mill, Chipping Campden, Gloucestershire GL55 6DU, England.

## Works

Toast rack in stainless steel, for Old Hall Tableware, 1956.
*Campden* cutlery in stainless steel, 1956 (with David Mellor).
*Campden* coffee set, for Old Hall Tableware, 1957.
*Permutit* water softener, for Permutit Company Ltd., 1957.
Nutcracker in stainless steel, for Old Hall Tableware, 1958.
*S. S. Oriana* dishes and stainless steel tableware cutlery, for Old Hall Tableware, 1958-60.
*Lynton* washbasin, for Doulton Sanitary Potteries Ltd., 1960.
*Alveston* or *R.W. No. 1* cutlery and tea service in stainless steel, for Old Hall Tableware, 1961.
*Bistro* cutlery in stainless steel with rosewood handles, for Old Hall Tableware, from 1961.
*Moonbeam* alarm clock, for Westclox Ltd., 1961.
*Astoria* wall clock, for Westclox Ltd., 1962.
*Merlin* electric alarm clock, for Westclox Ltd., 1963.
*Chantry* knife sharpener, for Harrison Fisher Ltd., 1964.
Hacksaw, for Footprint Tools Ltd., 1964.
Range of silverware, including coffee set, condiments set, and candlesticks, for Heal's, from 1964.
Pepper grinder in cast iron with wood knob, for Campden Designs Ltd., 1964.
Long toast rack in silver, for Old Hall Tableware, 1965.
*Range Flexi* flexible lamps, for Lumitron Ltd., 1966-91.
*Concord* kitchen scissors, for Harrison Fisher/Taylor's Eye Witness, Sheffield, from 1968.
*J.B.* tea and coffee set, commissioned by J. B. Priestley, 1968-74.
Oval lidded casserole/roaster in cast iron, for Victor Cast Ware, Telford, 1970-71.

Cast iron cookware, commissioned by H. E. Lauffer Inc., manufactured by Qualcast (Wolverhampton Ltd.), 1970-71.
Kitchen tool range, for Prestige Ltd., from 1971.
*Albany* bathroom fittings, for Adie & Nephew Ltd., 1976 (later for Celmac Ltd.).
*Kitchen Devil* knives, for Taylor's Eye Witness, 1979.
Altar cross and candlesticks in silver-plate, for Canterbury Cathedral, 1979.
*Regalia* cutlery, for Yamazaki Tableware Inc., New York, 1979-80.
Candelabra, for Victoria and Albert Museum, London, 1980.
*Yamazaki Serving Collection* in stainless steel, including icebucket and cover, for Yamazaki Kinzoku Kogyu Company Ltd., Japan, 1981.
*Beach* cutlery in stainless steel, for Yamazaki Tableware Inc., 1982.
Six candelabra in silver, for the British Museum, London, 1983.
*Premier* cutlery, made by Harrison Fisher Ltd., Sheffield, for Courtier Ltd., 1984.
Chalice in sterling silver, for Malvern Priory Church, 1986.
*Merit* cutlery in stainless steel, for Courtier Ltd., 1988 (and Ginkgo Inc., Illinois, from 1989).
*November* uplighter, for Chad Lighting Ltd., Birmingham, 1990.
Chalice in sterling silver, for Worcester College, Oxford, 1991.
*Galerie Cuisine* stainless steel steamer/stockpot, sauciere pan, and kettle, for Cuisine Cookware Inc., New York, 1991.
*Sparta* and *Dryad* table lamps, for Chad Lighting, 1991.
*BDK Tableware* stainless steel serving range and candlesticks, for BDK, Walsall, 1992.
Two coffee sets in silver, commissioned by the Silver Trust for use at No. 10 Downing Street, London, 1993.
*Ammonite* cutlery in stainless steel, for Ginkgo Inc., 1994.
Coffee pot in sterling silver, commissioned by Cheltenham Art Gallery and Museum, 1995.

## Publications

**By WELCH: books**—*The Design and Production of Stainless Steel* (thesis), Royal College of Art, London, 1955; *Robert Welch: Design in a Cotswold Workshop,* London, 1973; *Hand and Machine,* London, 1986.

**On WELCH: books**—*Modern Jewelry: An International Survey 1890-1964* by Graham Hughes, London, 1963, 1964; *Modern Silver Throughout the World 1880-1967* by Graham Hughes, London, Toronto, 1967; *Industrial Design and the Community* by Ken Baynes, London, 1967; *All Things Bright and Beautiful: Design in Britain 1830 to the Present Day* by Fiona MacCarthy, London, 1972; *The Contemporary Decorative Arts from 1940 to the Present Day* by Philippe Garner, London, 1980; *A History of Industrial Design* by Edward Lucie-Smith, Oxford, 1983; *Design since 1945* edited by Kathryn Hiesinger and George Marcus, Philadelphia, 1983; *Eye for Industry: Royal Designers for Industry 1936-1986* by Fiona MacCarthy and Patrick Nuttgens, London, 1986; *Robert Welch Designer-Silversmith: A Retrospective Exhibition, 1955-1995,* exhibition catalogue with texts by Margot Coatts and Jeremy Myerson, Cheltenham, 1995.

*

For the first two years of my training I studied drawing, painting, and silversmithing. Product design came much later in my career. In

**Robert Welch: stainless steel kitchen tools designed for Prestige P.L.C., 1971 (still in production, 1995). Photo by David Grant, courtesy of Robert Welch**

fact, not until my last year at the Royal College of Art, in 1955, did I consider the possibility of designing for industrial production. From the beginning of my workshop in 1955 to the present day, I continue to pursue two roles—silversmith and product designer. I believe that this dual development is mutually beneficial to both pursuits, especially so in the area of product design, as the silversmithing craft really has no limitations on the objects that can be made, and the finished result is a complete entity in its own right.

—Robert Welch

\*    \*    \*

Of particular interest in Robert Welch's career is his successful combination of silversmithing with designing for industry. He was one of the group of Royal Group of Art-trained silversmiths who revived the craft in the late 1950s and early 1960s. Like David Mellor and others, he set up an independent workshop on leaving the college in the mid-1950s and, like them, benefitted from the boom in sales of individually made goods after World War II.

Welch's most successful designs for silver demonstrate his particular attention to craftsmanship and materials, legacies of the Arts and Crafts movement. His ability to achieve impressive results from apparently simple elements gives many of his designs their classic quality. Some more elaborate pieces, such as his silver candelabrum of 1970 for Goldsmiths' Hall and the cigar box with radial ribs of 1974, show interest in surface texture and decoration, often achieved after experimentation with unorthodox techniques.

Welch initially turned towards industrial design as a result of the influence of Scandinavian domestic products in stainless steel; these had been developed during the war by Sigurd Persson and by designers for Gense and Georg Jensen. Welch's study of this work led to his early design consultancy for J. & J. Wiggin (marketing under the name of "Old Hall"), the only manufacturers of stainless steel domestic products in Britain at the time. Through this association, he pioneered the introduction of stainless steel in Britain for domestic wares. Welch sees himself as having also been "nudged" towards industrial design by two other factors: the difficulty of surviving on special commissions for silver during the 1960s and the prevalent early 1960s ideology favoring the combination of a craft with designing for production.

In his early craft and industrial work, including the Alveston range of cutlery, the then-current preoccupation with organic forms was evident. But the influence of Scandinavian design as well as the contemporary sculpture of Hepworth and Moore was quickly modified by his preference for symmetry. A retention of flowing elements, however, can be seen in some of Welch's more recent cutlery, designed for Yamazaki of Japan.

Welch's proficiency in his designs for stainless steel and cast-iron is clear. His Bistro range of 1966 was the first stainless steel cutlery with laminated wood handles. In his cast-iron cookware for Lauffer, his attention to the problems of manufacturers is demonstrated by the ease with which the flash can be removed from the ribs and the pieces hung from the handles for enameling.

—Karen Moon

# WHEELER, Lyle

American film designer

**Born:** Woburn, Massachusetts, 2 February 1905. **Education:** Studied at the University of California, Los Angeles, 1923-26. **Career:** Worked as a magazine illustrator and industrial designer, Los Angeles, 1927-35; film designer, Los Angeles, from 1936; art director for David O. Selznick, Los Angeles, 1938-42, and for Metro Goldwyn Mayer Studios, 1945-47; supervising art director, at 20th Century-Fox film studios, Hollywood, 1947-60; freelance production designer, working for Columbia studios and others, 1961-75. **Honors:** Academy Awards, Hollywood, 1939, 1946, 1953, 1956, 1959. **Died:** Los Angeles, California, 10 January 1990.

## Works

Film designs include—*The Garden of Allah* (Boleslawsky), 1936; *A Star is Born* (Wellman), 1937; *The Prisoner of Zenda* (Cromwell), 1937; *Nothing Sacred* (Wellman), 1938; *The Young in Heart* (Wallace), 1938; *The Adventures of Tom Sawyer* (Taurog), 1938; *Gone With the Wind* (Fleming), 1939; *Made for Each Other* (Cromwell), 1939; *Intermezzo* (Ratoff), 1939; *Rebecca* (Hitchcock), 1940; *That Hamilton Woman* (A. Korda), 1941; *Keeper of the Flame* (Cukor), 1942; *The Jungle Book* (Z. Korda), 1942; *Cairo* (Van Dyke), 1942; *Bataan* (Garnett), 1943; *Laura* (Preminger), 1944; *Dragon Seed* (Conway and Bucquet), 1944; *Thirty Seconds Over Tokyo* (LeRoy), 1944; *Winged Victory* (Cukor), 1944; *Wing and a Prayer* (Hathaway), 1944; *Hangover Square* (Brahm), 1945; *Leave Her to Heaven* (Stahle), 1945; *A Tree Grows in Brooklyn* (Kazan), 1945; *The Dolly Sisters* (Cummings), 1945; *The House on 92nd Street* (Hathaway), 1945; *Fallen Angel* (Preminger), 1945; *Anna and the King of Siam* (Cromwell), 1946; *Cluny Brown* (Lubitsch), 1946; *My Darling Clementine* (Ford), 1946; *Centennial Summer* (Preminger), 1946; *Wake Up and Dream* (Bacon), 1946; *Dragonwyck* (Mankiewicz), 1946; *Daisy Kenyon* (Preminger), 1947; *Forever Amber* (Preminger), 1947; *The Foxes of Harrow* (Stahl), 1947; *Gentlemen's Agreement* (Kazan), 1947; *Kiss of Death* (Hathaway), 1947; *Nightmare Alley* (Goulding), 1947; *Call Northside 777* (Hathaway), 1948; *The Art Director* (documentary), 1948; *That Lady in Ermine* (Lubitsch), 1948; *Unfaithfully Yours* (P. Sturges),

1948; *The Iron Curtain* (Wellman), 1948; *Cry of the City* (Stodmak), 1948; *Give My Regards to Broadway* (Bacon), 1948; *The Snake Pit* (Litvak), 1948; *Street With No Name* (Keighley), 1948; *Thieves Highway* (Dassin), 1949; *Twelve O'Clock High* (H. King), 1949; *Mother is a Freshman* (Bacon), 1949; *Slattery's Hurricane* (De Toth), 1949; *I Was a Male War Bride* (Hawks), 1948; *House of Strangers* (Mankiewicz), 1949; *The Fan* (Preminger), 1949; *A Letter to Three Wives* (Mankiewicz), 1949; *Dancing in the Dark* (Reis), 1949; *Down to the Sea in Ships* (Hathaway), 1949; *Panic in the Streets* (Kazan), 1940; *Cheaper by the Dozen* (W. Lang), 1950; *All About Eve* (Mankiewicz), 1950; *Broken Arrow* (Daves), 1950; *American Guerilla in the Philippines* (F. Lang), 1950; *Two Flags West* (Wise), 1950; *When Willie Comes Marching Home* (Ford), 1950; *No Way Out* (Mankiewicz), 1950; *Where the Sidewalk Ends* (Preminger), 1950; *Fourteen Hours* (Hathaway), 1950; *Bird of Paradise* (Davies), 1951; *The House on Telegraph Hill* (Wise), 1951; *David and Bathsheba* (H. King), 1951; *Halls of Montezuma* (Milestone), 1951; *Fixed Bayonets* (Fuller), 1951; *Rawhide* (Hathaway), 1951; *The Guy Who Came Back* (Newman), 1951; *Golden Girl* (Bacon), 1951; *The Frogmen* (Bacon), 1951; *The Day the Earth Stood Still* (Wise), 1951; *Call Me Mister* (Bacon), 1951; *Anne of the Indies* (Tourneur), 1951; *People Will Talk* (Mankiewicz), 1951; *Love Nest* (Newman), 1951; *The Thirteenth Letter* (Preminger), 1951; *The Desert Fox* (Hathaway), 1951; *Deadline: USA* (Brooks), 1952; *My Cousin Rachel* (Koster), 1952; *Viva Zapata* (Kazan), 1952; *The President's Lady* (Levin), 1952; *The Snows of Kilimanjaro* (H. King), 1952; *Five Fingers* (Mankiewicz), 1952; *Monkey Business* (Hawks), 1952; *Return of the Texan* (Daves), 1952; *The Model and the Marriage Broker* (Cukor), 1952; *Red Skies of Montana* (Newman), 1952; *Diplomatic Courier* (Hathaway), 1952; *My Pal Gus* (Parrish), 1952; *Pony Soldier* (Newman), 1952; *Something for the Birds* (Wise), 1952; *The Robe* (Koster), 1953; *Call Me Madam* (W. Lang), 1953; *Titanic* (Negulesco), 1953; *Gentlemen Prefer Blondes* (Hawks), 1953; *The Farmer Takes A Wife* (Levin), 1953; *Man in the Attic* (Fregonese), 1953; *Treasure of the Golden Condor* (Daves), 1953; *Dangerous Crossing* (Newman), 1953; *How to Marry a Millionaire* (Negulesco), 1953; *Pickup on South Street* (Fuller), 1953; *White Witch Doctor* (Hathaway), 1953; *The I Don't Care Girl* (Bacon), 1953; *Niagara* (Hathaway), 1953; *King of the Khyber Rifles* (H. King), 1953; *River of No Return* (Preminger), 1954; *Three Coins in the Fountain* (Preminger), 1954; *Garden of Evil* (Hathaway) 1954; *The Egyptian* (Curtiz), 1954; *Desiree* (Koster), 1954; *Hell and High Water* (Fuller), 1954; *The Siege at Red River* (Mate), 1954; *Demetrius and the Gladiators* (Daves), 1954; *There's No Business Like Show Business* (W. Lang), 1954; *Love is a Many-Splendored Thing* (H. King), 1955; *The Racers* (Hathaway), 1955; *The Girl in the Red Velvet Swing* (Fleischer), 1955; *Daddy Long Legs* (Negulasco), 1955; *The Seven Year Itch* (Wilder), 1955; *Violent Saturday* (Fleischer), 1955; *House of Bamboo* (Fuller), 1955; *The Tall Men* (Walsh), 1955; *The Left Hand of God* (Dymytryk), 1955; *Bus Stop* (Logan), 1956; *Teenage Rebel* (Goulding), 1956; *The King and I* (W.Lang), 1956; *The Bottom of the Bottle* (Hathaway), 1956; *Carousel* (H. King), 1956; *The Lieutenant Wore Skirts* (Tashlin), 1956; *The Man in the Gray Flannel Suit* (Johnson), 1956; *The Revolt of Mamie Stover* (Walsh), 1956; *Bigger Than Life* (Ray), 1956; *The Lazy Wagon* (Daves), 1956; *The Girl Can't Help It* (Tashlin), 1956; *Between Heaven and Hell* (Fleischer), 1956; *The Sun Also Rises* (H. King), 1957; *A Hatful of Rain* (Zinnemann), 1957; *Peyton Place* (Robson),

1957; *An Affair to Remember* (McCarey), 1957; *Stopover Tokyo* (Breen), 1957; *The Three Faces of Eve* (Johnson), 1957; *Kiss Them for Me* (Donen), 1957; *No Down Payment* (Ritt), 1957; *South Pacific* (Logan), 1958; *A Certain Smile* (Negulesco), 1958; *The Young Lions* (Dymytryk), 1958; *From Hell to Texas* (Hathaway), 1958; *Ten North Frederick* (Dunne), 1958; *The Bravados* (H. King), 1958; *The Long Hot Summer* (Ritt), 1958; *The Hunters* (D. Powell), 1958; *The Barbarian and the Geisha* (Huston), 1958; *These Thousand Hills* (Fleischer), 1958; *The Fiend Who Walked the West* (Doughlas), 1958; *Rally 'round the Flag Boys* (McCarey), 1958; *Compulsion* (Fleischer), 1959; *Blue Denim* (Dunne), 1959; *Journey to the Center of the Earth* (Levin), 1959; *A Farewell to Arms* (C. Vidor), 1959; *The Diary of Anne Frank* (Stevens), 1959; *The Sound and the Fury* (Ritt), 1959; *Woman Obsessed* (Hathaway), 1959; *Hound Dog Man* (Siegel), 1959; *The Man Who Understood Women* (Johnson), 1959; *The Story on Page One* (Odets), 1959; *From the Terrace* (Robson), 1960; *Wild River* (Kazan), 1960; *Wake Me When It's Over* (LeRoy), 1960; *Seven Thieves* (Hathaway), 1960; *Can-Can* (W.Lang), 1960; *Advise and Consent* (Preminger), 1962; *The Cardinal* (Preminger), 1963; *The Best Man* (Schaffner), 1964; *In Harm's Way* (Preminger), 1965; *The Big Mouth* (Lewis), 1967; *The Swimmer* (Perry), 1969; *Tell Me That You Love Me, Julie Moon* (Preminger), 1970; *The Love Machine* (Haley), 1971; *Doctor's Wives* (Schaefer), 1971; *Bless the Beasts and the Children* (Kramer), 1972; *Stand Up and Be Counted* (Cooper), 1972; *Posse* (K. Douglas), 1975.

## Publications

**By WHEELER: articles**—in *Film Comment* (New York), May 1978.

**On WHEELER: books**—*Le Décor de Film* by Leon Barsacq, Paris, 1970, as *Caligari's Cabinet and Other Grand Illusions,* Boston, 1976; *The World Encyclopedia of Film,* edited by Tim Cawkwell and John M. Smith, London, 1972; *The International Film Encyclopedia* by Ephraim Katz, New York and London, 1980; *International Dictionary of Films and Film-makers,* Chicago and London, 1987, 1991.

*         *         *

Lyle Wheeler began his career in art direction on a high note, precociously winning an Academy award for *Gone With the Wind* (1939). His role was to execute the sets which were painstakingly sketched by William Cameron Menzies, the production designer. Wheeler's talent for creating historically accurate sets is not only evident in this epic but is also seen in his later films, such as *That Hamilton Woman* (1941, with Vincent Korda), about the lives of Lord Nelson and Lady Hamilton, and *The Robe.*

Wheeler's black-and-white films are characterized by a sharp, clean look. In the contemporary psychological thrillers *Rebecca* (1940, directed by Alfred Hitchcock) and *Laura* (1944, directed by Otto Preminger), the sharp shadows cast on and around the characters became more overbearing during tense moments. Though Wheeler's black-and-white films are much admired, he regretted that some of them could not have been made in color. The Academy Award-winning *Anna and the King of Siam* (1946) was made in black-and-white because of a painter's strike. To compensate for

the lack of color, Wheeler built the sets of plaster treated to appear in varying values. The result is a black-and-white film so vivid that it almost convinces the audience that it was shot in color.

Wheeler's color films are as beautiful as his black-and-white. He was able to design the "Anna and the King" story in bold, stunning colors when he worked on the musical version, *The King and I.* Wheeler even made the unusual decision to shoot one of the *noir* films, *Leave Her to Heaven* (1947), in color. Instead of the dark, rain-soaked streets typical of that genre, this tale of deception is set effectively against bright country lawns and sunny skies.

From 1945 to 1960, Wheeler was supervising art director at 20th Century-Fox. As such, he oversaw the visual aspects of each film from its inception, as he worked with the writer, scouted locations with the art director assigned to each film, and approved all sketches.

During his career as an art director, Wheeler was in on the ground floor of many advances in film technology. He experimented with Technicolor as early as 1936 when he worked on *The Garden of Allah* with producer David O. Selznick. He led 20th Century-Fox through the transition from black-and-white to color production and from the standard shot-size to Cinema Scope.

—Lois Miklas

# WHITLOCK, Albert

British film effects artist and designer

**Born:** London in 1915; emigrated to the United States in 1954. **Education:** Mainly self-taught in scenic design and matte painting, from 1934. **Career:** Worked at a variety of jobs in the British film industry, 1934-40; title designer and backdrop artist, 1935-54; Walt Disney Studios, Hollywood, California, 1954-61; freelance film designer and matte artist, Hollywood, 1961-63; contract designer, Universal Studios, Hollywood, from 1963. **Member:** Former board member, Academy of Motion Picture Arts and Sciences, Beverly Hills, California; associate member, American Society of Cinematographers. **Honors:** Academy Award, Hollywood, 1974, 1975. **Address:** Department of Special Effects, Universal International Films, 100 Universal City Plaza, North Hollywood, California 99608, U.S.A.

## Works

Film productions include—*The Man Who Knew Too Much* (Hitchcock), 1955; *Greyfriars Bobby* (Chaffey), 1961; *The Birds* (Hitchcock), 1963; *Captain Newman MD* (Miller), 1963; *I'd Rather Be Rich* (Smight), 1964; *Marnie* (Hitchcock), 1964; *Island of the Blue Dolphins* (Clark), 1964; *Mirage* (Dmytryk), 1965; *Shenandoah* (McLaglen), 1965; *Ship of Fools* (Kramer), 1965; *That Funny Feeling* (Thorpe), 1965; *The War Lord* (Schaffner), 1965; *Beau Geste* (Hayes), 1966; *Blindfold* (Dunne), 1966; *Munster, Go Home* (Bellamy), 1966; *The Rare Breed* (McLaglen), 1966; *Torn Curtain* (Hitchcock), 1966; *The King's Pirate* (Weis), 1967; *The Reluctant Astronaut* (Montague), 1967; *Rough Night in Jericho* (Laven), 1967; *Tobruk* (Hiller), 1967; *Thoroughly Modern Millie* (Hill), 1967; *The War Wagon* (Kennedy), 1967; *The Ballad of Josie* (McLaglen), 1968; *Counterpoint* (Nelson), 1968; *The Shakiest Gun in the West* (Rafkin),

1968; *The Learning Tree* (Parks), 1969; *Topaz* (Hitchcock), 1969; *Catch-22* (Nichols), 1970; *The Forbin Project* (Sargent), 1970; *Skullduggery* (Douglas and Wilson), 1970; *Diamonds Are Forever* (Hamilton), 1971; *Short Walk to Daylight* (Shear—for TV), 1972; *The Sting* (Hill), 1973; *The Questor Tapes* (Colla—for TV), 1974; *Killdozer* (London—for TV), 1974; *Earthquake* (Robson), 1974; *Day of the Locust* (Schlesinger), 1975; *The Hindenburg* (Wise), 1975; *The Man Who Would Be King* (Huston), 1975; *Bound for Glory* (Ashby), 1976; *The Car* (Silverstein), 1977; *MacArthur* (Sargent), 1977; *High Anxiety* (Brooks), 1977; *Airport '77* (Jameson), 1977; *Exorcist II: The Heretic* (Boorman), 1977; *Dracula* (Badham), 1979; *The Prisoner of Zenda* (Quine), 1979; *The Wiz* (Lumet), 1979; *Cheech and Chong's Next Movie* (Chong), 1980; *The Blues Brothers* (Landis), 1980; *Ghost Story* (Irvin), 1981; *Heartbeeps* (Arkush), 1981; *History of the World, Part I* (Brooks), 1981; *Missing* (Costa Garvas), 1982; *The Thing* (Carpenter), 1982; *Cat People* (Schrader), 1982; *The Best Little Whorehouse in Texas* (Higgins), 1982; *Psycho II* (Franklin), 1983; *The Lonely Guy* (Hiller), 1984; *Dune* (Lynch), 1984; *Greystoke: The Legend of Tarzan* (Hudson), 1984; *Red Sonja* (Fleischer), 1985; *Clue* (Lynn), 1985.

## Publications

**By WHITLOCK: articles**—in *Filmmakers' Newsletter* (Ward Hill), October 1974; *American Cinematographer* (Los Angeles), November 1974, November 1978; *Super-8 Filmmaker* (San Francisco), May 1977; *Cinefantastique* (New York), February 1982; *Cahiers du Cinema* (Paris), June 1982.

**On WHITLOCK: books**—*The Saga of Special Effects* by Ron Fry and Pamela Fourson, Englewood Cliffs, 1977; **articles**—in *Variety* (New York), 20 April 1977; *New Times* (New York), 29 May 1978; *New York Times Magazines,* May 1980; *Starburst* (London), no. 56, 1983; *American Cinematographer* (Los Angeles), January 1986.

*

Artificially created backgrounds—painted or filmed—have been exploited to the full in movies other than cartoons. This is due to the fact that movie-makers today tend to concentrate on big films that make vast sums, so in contrast to earlier times, long, experienced careers do not develop. Spielberg and Lucas are, of course, the obvious exceptions. They endure.

Nevertheless, matte painting will also endure, as it is without doubt the cost-saving technique in movie visuals. With little cost, one can construct a scene and, with good preparation, matte or black out part of it later to replace the matte area with another subject. This description perhaps oversimplifies the technique, but faced with this simple premise, a designer has the world, in the movie sense, at his disposal. A process using painting or photography can be used to show movement in clouds, water, etc. *Bound for Glory* had a three-dimensional dust storm integrated into the painted area. *The Learning Tree* had a sequence of matte shots with a tornado forming and then moving away over the scene.

Such work can be done by applying the work to the original negative (the method I favor) or when copying the original film. The latter is most often done on a larger negative, Vista Vision of 65mm film, so as to recoup definition lost during copying or duplicating. As with illustrations, the reduction of size improves the quality.

Narrative generally deals with characters in stationary positions, and their environs are our domain. However, chases will always occur, and movement is necessary, but in these cases, the matte technique can work for all movies. Hitchcock summarized it to me: "You plan the master scene with the needed image and design the sequence around it." As always with Hitchcock, the problem well stated is half solved. His summary is in itself design.

—Albert Whitlock

\*     \*     \*

The space and science fiction films of the late 1970s and 1980s have focused attention on special effects artists in Hollywood. Generally, these effects are obvious ones, involving other planets, prehistoric times, fantastic robots, inorganic creatures. These kind of effects do not interest Albert Whitlock, whose idea of a great effect is one that the public does not recognize as one. Whitlock's art furthers the illusion that what is seen on the screen is "real" and causes the thrill that often accompanies such illusions. Whitlock is an artist of the natural world, creating images of things that cannot be filmed realistically because of their violent nature, such as an earthquake or a dust-storm (*Bound for Glory,* 1976) or because of their cost to build, such as an entire castle (*Dracula* and *The Prisoner of Zenda,* both 1979) or a mountaintop city (*The Man Who Would Be King,* 1975).

Whitlock's art makes movies cheaper to produce. His is a world of matte paintings, models,and filming at different speeds. In his emphasis on illusionism, Whitlock can be seen as part of an artistic tradition going back to the Italian Renaissance and the invention of perspective to make two-dimensional pictures appear to be windows on the world. The impact of the Renaissance appears in his painting because he is more interested in the study of phenomena and the effects of light than in objects themselves.

In the late 1950s, Whitlock was influenced by working under Peter Ellenshaw Sr., an effects supervisor for Disney studios. He has been associated with Universal since 1963 and has worked with a number of art directors, including Robert Boyle (*The Birds,* 1963). Though his work may go unrecognized because it is so convincing, Whitlock's artistry with special effects is important in understanding three concepts: the collaboration necessary in movie-making, the need to use effects for budgetary reasons, and the fact that film is a two-dimensional illusionistic medium.

—Floyd W. Martin

# WIERCHOWICZ, Zofia

Polish stage designer

**Born:** Deblin, Lublin Province, 30 December 1924. **Education:** Studied design, at the Higher School of Fine Arts, Warsaw, 1948-54. **Career:** Resident stage designer, at the Teatr Ziemi Mazowieckiej, Warsaw, 1955-56, and at the Jaracz Theatre, Olsztyn, 1956-58; freelance designer, working for the Teatr Beltycki, Koszalin, Teatr Powzechny, Warsaw, Opera House of Poznan, Boguslawski Theatre, Kalisz, Teatr Polski, Poznan, and the Chamber Opera, Warsaw, 1959-78. **Exhibitions:** Artists' Union, Warsaw, 1975; Zapiecek Gallery, Warsaw, 1978; *Contemporary Stage Design,* Berlin, 1978. **Collections:** Wielki Theatre Museum, Warsaw; Centre of Polish Stage Design, Gdansk; National Museum, Warsaw. **Honors:** Gold Medal, Novi Sad Triennale, 1969; Gold Medal, Prague Quadriennale, 1971. **Died:** Warsaw, 8 January 1978.

## Works

Stage productions include—*Much Ado About Nothing,* Teatr Ziemi Mazowieckiej, Warsaw, 1956; *Twelfth Night,* Teatr Baltycki, Koszalin, 1957; *Hamlet,* Teatr Baltycki, 1960; *Romeo and Juliet,* Teatr Baltycki, 1962; *War and Peace,* Teatr Powszechny, Warsaw, 1963; *Henry VI,* Teatr Bydgoszcz, 1964; *The Apothecary,* Chamber Opera, Warsaw, 1965; *Polish Amphitryon,* Chamber Opera, 1965; *Charlatan,* Opera, Warsaw, 1965; *Prince Igor,* Wroclaw Opera, 1966; *Othello,* Teatr Polski, Szczecin, 1966; *Richard III,* Teatr Polski, 1966; *La Bohème,* Warsaw Opera, 1967; *Tannahauser,* Poznan Opera, 1968; *The Queen of Spades,* Poznan Opera, and in Oslo, Norway, 1969; *Tristan and Isolde,* Poznan Opera, 1968; *Salomea's Silver Dream,* Boguslawski Theatre, Kalisz, 1969; *Apollo the Lawgiver,* Chamber Opera, Warsaw, 1969; *Knovanshtchina,* Poznan Opera, 1969; *Henry VI,* Teatr Polski Szczecin, 1969; *Romeo and Juliet* ballet, Teatr Wielki, Warsaw, 1970; *La Traviata,* Teatr Wielki, 1971; *L'Incoronazione di Poppea,* Teatr Wielki, 1971, Yugoslavia, 1976; *Waiting for Godot,* Teatr Ateneum, Warsaw, 1971; *Othello,* Novi Sad, Yugoslavakia, 1972; *Spartacus,* Wroclaw Opera, 1972; (and director) *The Tempest,* Boguslawski Theatre, Kalisz, 1972; (and director) *Timon of Athens,* Theatre in Grudziadz, 1975; *Dusk,* Jewish Theatre, Warsaw, 1976; *Don Giovanni,* Teatr Wielki, 1976; (and director) *Richard III,* Teatr Ziemi Pomorskiej, Grudziadsz, 1976; *King Roger,* Krakow Opera, 1976; (and director) *Comedy of Errors,* Teatr Ziemi Mazowieckiej, 1976; *La Nozze di Figaro,* Krakow Opera, 1978; *Narciso,* Teatr Wielki, 1978.

## Publications

**By WIERCHOWICZ: articles**—in *Poland* (Warsaw), September, 1970.

**On WIERCHOWICZ: books**—*Polish Stage Design* by Zenobiusz Strzelecki, Warsaw, 1963; *Trends in Contemporary Stage Design* by Zenobiusz Strzelecki, Warsaw, 1970; *Zofia Wierchowicz,* exhibition catalogue by A. Oseka, Warsaw, 1978; *Contemporary Polish Stage Design* by Zenobiusz Strzelecki, Warsaw, 1983.

*       *       *

Zofia Wierchowicz was primarily interested in two types of theatre: Shakespearean and musical, although many different types of drama interested her, as long as they were worthwhile. She designed sets and costumes for fourteen Shakepearean plays, and many plays by other authors, including Polish ones, which she placed in settings similar to those which she had designed for the Elizabethan theatre. Toward the end of her short life, she began directing, precisely and only Shakespearean dramas. For the two types of theatre that preoccupied her, she created two different plastic conceptions: for one, functional constructions—stark, wooden, blackened—and costumes, often leather, also blackened;

for the other, painted decorations and costumes, sparkling with colors.

Those Shakepearean sets which are most characteristic of Wierchowicz are not reconstructions of the Globe's stage. Rather, they feature a podium supported by posts (an equivalent of the Elizabethan balcony), the height of two stories, which at the stage's central axis connects with the level of the floor by means of a staircase. This arrangement could be adapted to the needs of a particular dramatic scene by the addition of arcades, doors, or other functional forms, whereas the lower level could be given bars or metal doors fastened to the posts which support the podium (as in *Othello*). Sometimes the wood construction was covered by rusted iron sheets (*Richard III*); sometimes the stage was covered with dirt, forming something akin to a trough hollowed out in the earth for *Hamlet*; this also could be Caliban's territory in *The Tempest,* while Prospero and Ariel act on the podium.

In her early work, costumes are the skins of animals which are born "armed." Helmets, cuirasses, whole armours forming an integral part of the "body" are fused with man from birth—such is his fate: to kill, and because of that, he was endowed with "fangs and claws." In a later period of the artist's life, the tragedy of Shakespearean characters was moved more into the interior; it exists in the soul and seems to tear apart Hamlet, Richard, Othello. Towards the end of her life, she felt the need to enliven her dead world of sets and costumes and undertook directing. Among others, she produced *Timon of Athens,* in which, on the universe of the stage, out of the whole world, only a clump of earth remains—a tragic vision of humanity's, or her own, fate.

Her operatic scenography encompassed a wide range from Monteverdi to Wagner, from nineteenth century verists to smaller musical forms, often of Polish or little-known composers. In it appears the Polish tendency toward painted scenography, for which she utilized the experiences of new plastic directions—among others, "action painting." This offered, both in the sets as well as (more interestingly) in the costumes, a richness of factures and colors. (The costumes were often painted, not dyed one hue; colors were "entered," utilizing the so-called "degrade" method.) A kind of equivalent for the sublime music and poetics resulted.

Wierchowicz, like many Polish scenographers, also attempted painting. Disquieting birds in flight were a common motif. A solemn artist, seriously and responsibly practicing her profession, she was honored for many of her scenographies at national theatrical festivals.

—Zenobiusz Strzelecki

# WIESE, Bruno K(arl)
German graphic designer

**Born:** Berlin, 7 April 1922. **Education:** Studied under O. H. W. Hadank at the Staatliche Hochschule für Bildende Kunste, Berlin, 1945-49. **Military Service:** Served as a military cartographer in the German Army, 1942-45. **Family:** Married Ruth Kern in 1954; children: Carola. **Career:** Assistant designer in the graphics studio of O. H. W. Hadank, Hamburg, 1949-54; freelance designer, establishing own graphic design studio, Hamburg, from 1954; designed for the United Nations Postal Administration, German Post Office, D. Stempel AG, Kristinus Cigarette Company, Kieler Woche, Stall-

**B. K. Wiese: proposed logo for Berlin 2000 candidate XXVIIth Olympic Games**

ing-Filmsatz AG, Zanders Feinpapiere AG, S. Fischer Verlag, German Aerospace Research Establishment (DLR), Museum of Contemporary History, Bonn, DC & A Strategic Design Consultants, Seoul, and others. Instructor in communications design, 1978-80, and Professor, 19801-88, at the Fachhochschule, Kiel. **Exhibitions:** *B. K. Wiese: Visual Design,* Kiel, 1987, Fachbereich Gestaltung, Hamburg, 1987-88, and German Poster Museum, Essen, 1988. **Honors:** Henkell Packaging Competition Prize, Wiesbaden, 1970; Kieler Woche Poster Prize, Kiel, 1970; German Aerospace Research Establishment Prize, 1975; United Nations Stamp Prize, 1977; Kieler Woche Visual Programme Prize, Kiel, 1982; Industrial Designers Society of America Prize, 1983; Toulouse-Lautrec Silver Medal, Essen, 1983; Logo Contest Prize, German Ministry of Justice, 1984; City of Hamburg Arts and Crafts Award, 1987; International Poster Competition Prize, Deutsche Bank AG, 1988. **Member:** Alliance Graphique Internationale; Deutscher Werkbund; Bund Deutscher Graphiker. **Address:** Allhornweg 7, D-22359 Hamburg, Germany.

## Works

*Henkell-Sekt* packaging, for Sektkellerei Henkell, 1966.
Logotype symbol, for Stalling-Filmsatz AG, 1972.

*Lotus* cigarette packaging and promotional graphics, for Kristinus, 1973.
*Combat Racism* postage stamp, for the UN Postal Administration, 1977.
*Neujahrsblatt* New Year card, for D. Stempel AG, 1979.
*United Nations Peace-Keeping Operations* postage stamp, for the UN Postal Administration, 1980.
*100 Jahre Kieler Woche* posters and visual identity, Kiel, 1982.
*Kammer Jazz Ensemble* poster, for the Kiel Jazz Ensemble, 1986.
*Es geht um gute Werbe-Nasen* promotional design, for Zanders Feinpapiere AG, 1986.
*Gute Designer braucht das Land* exhibition poster, for the Fachhochschule, Kiel, 1987.
Postage stamps, for the Deutsche Bundespost, including *Europe, Census,* and *Architecture of the 20th Century,* 1987, *25 Years of Third World Developmental Aid,* 1988, and *European Parliament Elections,* 1989 and 1994.
Corporate identity, for Museum of Contemporary History, Bonn, 1989-91.
Logo design, for second German Spacelab Mission D2, 1990.
Calendar design, for DC & A Strategic Design Consultants, Seoul, 1995.

## Publications

**By WIESE: articles**—in *Graphis* (Zürich), no. 199, 1978; *Form* (Seeheim), no. 92, 1980; *Der Druckspiegel* (Heusenstamm), no. 5, 1989.

**On WIESE: books**—*An International Survey of Packaging* by Wim Crouwel and Kurt Weidemann, London, 1968; *Top Symbols and Trademarks of the World* edited by Franco Maria Ricci, Milan, 1973, 1978; *Who's Who in Graphic Art* edited by Walter Amstutz, Dubendorf, 1982; *World Trademarks and Logotypes* edited by Takenobu Igarashi, Tokyo, no. I, 1983, no. II, 1987, and no. III, 1989, *B. K Wiese: Visual Design,* exhibition catalogue with texts by Harald Kohne and Fritz Seitz, Kiel, 1987; *International Typography Almanac,* Tokyo, 1991; *Graphis Posters 90 and 91* edited by B. Martin Pedersen, Zürich, 1992; *Paper Design* by Nancy Williams, London, 1993; *3-D Greeting Cards* edited by Igarashi, Tokyo, 1993; *Graphis Ephemera I* edited by Pedersen, Zürich, 1995; articles—*IDEA* (Tokyo), no. 150, 1978-79, no. 180, 1983; *Novum* (Munich), no. 11, 1988, no. 3, 1989, no. 11, 1991; *Form* (Leverkusen), no. 128, 1989; *PAGE* (Hamburg), no. 11, 1992.

*

If one starts from the position that communications design is to be understood as the intellectual and material mastery of a given problem, there are two stages in the solution of such a problem. First, there is the conceptual phase, both non-material and material; via discovery of ideas and visual trials, this leads to the decision. Second comes the realization phase, with the formulation of a prototype and the development of a working copy for presentation and reproduction. Therefore, the intellectual phase of the problem-solving process lies at the beginning. At this point, the designer has to analyze the informative and psychological content of the message in a thought process which is already broadly directed toward the investigation of the content of items, which can lead to a meaningful visualization.

As a result of the synthesis of this investigation, the solution will rest on what is discovered as the particularity of an important "special aspect" of the content. This process will logically penetrate and encircle the problem in order to produce a convincing image-idea that—in the ideal case—is neither inter-changeable nor repeatable. Simply stated, the solution is immanent to the content of the message; it needs to be sought out, to be set free. After possible modification of the result at that stage with regard to its use or to the sociological structure of the group at which it is aimed, the second phase begins. In this phase of objectivization, the material concept is worked out and the coding of the message is achieved. Insofar as it is not specified, the medium must then be chosen. This choice of a vehicle for conveying the message depends upon an analysis of the general and particular possibilities of the medium and tests of its adaptability with respect to the previously discovered image-idea.

The repertoire of symbols from which the image is formulated—that is, the visual language—must be suited to the understanding of the groups at which it is aimed. Those individuals must be able to decode it. Only then can communication take place.

The concrete work-up of the image then follows by a process that takes into account a special catalogue of criteria which will not be discussed here. In a number of stages, the weight and correlation of iconic and typographic signs will be tested, selected, and cor-

rected. Finally, a decision is taken, and the conceptual stage is complete. The non-material and material conceptual stages described above can be seen as creativity operating systematically. Such a process does not, as one might assume, exclude intuition. Indeed, it leads directly to it—particularly in the stage of thought process. Originality and innovation have their roots here. Plagiarism, even unconscious, will hardly ever be found in this kind of search for ideas. Creativity—in relation to communication design—comes possibly in the use of the intellect, in the presence of artistic sensibility, and through specific experience.

The realization of the concept, the final visual formulation of the prototype, should demonstrate a logical correspondence to the facts of the case, adequacy and precision in the repertoire of signs, perfect organizations of the surface through form and colour, and, not last, originality and power of conviction in the visualized message.

—Bruno K. Wiese

# WIRKKALA, Tapio (Veli Ilmaari)

Finnish sculptor and industrial designer

**Born:** Hanko, 2 June 1915. **Education:** Studied sculpture, at the Institute of Industrial Arts, Helsinki, 1933-36. **Military Service:** Served in the Finnish Army, in Karelia, 1940-45, Lieutenant. **Family:** Married Rut Bryk in 1945; children: Sami and Maaria. **Career:** Glass designer, for Karhula-Iitala, 1946-85; founder and director of Tapio Wirkkala Design Studio, Helsinki, from 1955: designed for Soinneek Venini, Hackmann, Airam, Rosenthal, and others. Artistic director, Institute of Industrial Arts, Helsinki, 1951-54; Exhibition designer, for various exhibitions, from 1951-1972; Chairman, Finnish Government Industrial Arts Commission, Helsinki, 1968-73. **Exhibitions:** Kunstnernes Hus, Oslo, 1952; Symbol of the Jablonec glass exhibition, Czechoslovakia, 1965; Goldsmith's Hall, London, 1972; Stedelijk Museum, Amsterdam, 1976: *Six Masters of Glass,* Venice, Biennale, 1976; *Europäische Keramik,* Museum für Kunst und Gewerbe, Hamburg, 1979 (toured); Museum of Architecture, Moscow, 1981 (toured); Museo de Arte Moderno, Mexico City 1982; *Scandinavian Modern Design 1880-1980,* Cooper-Hewitt Museum, New York, 1982; *Design Since 1945,* Philadelphia Museum of Art, 1983; Musée des Arts Décoratifs, Paris, 1983; IBM Gallery of Science and Art, New York, 1985; *The Lunning Prize,* Nationalmuseum, Stockholm, 1986; *Scandinavia: Ceramics and Glass in the Twentieth Century,* Victoria and Albert Museum, London, 1989. **Collections:** National Gallery of Victoria, Melbourne; The Newark Museum, New Jersey; Royal Ontario Museum, Ontario; Greenfield Village & Henry Ford Museum, Dearborn, Michigan; Renwick Gallery, The National Collection of Fine Arts, Smithsonian Institution, Washington, D.C.; Finnish Glass Museum, Riihimaki; Nationalmuseum, Stockholm; Nordenfjeldske Kunstindustrimuseet, Trondheim; Kunstindustrimuseum, Copenhagen; Die Neue Sammlung, Munich; Staatliche Kunstsammlung, Dresden; Sledelijk Museum, Amsterdam; Kunstgewerbemuseum, Zurich; Museum of Modern Art, Tokyo; Victoria and Albert Museum, London; Museum of Modern Art, New York; Metropolitan Museum of Art, New York; Philadelphia Museum of Art; The Corning Museum of Glass, Corning. **Honors:** Bank of Finland Banknote Prize, 1947; Grand Prize, 1951, 1954, 1960, Gold Medal, 1960, Silver Medal, 1963, Milan Triennale;

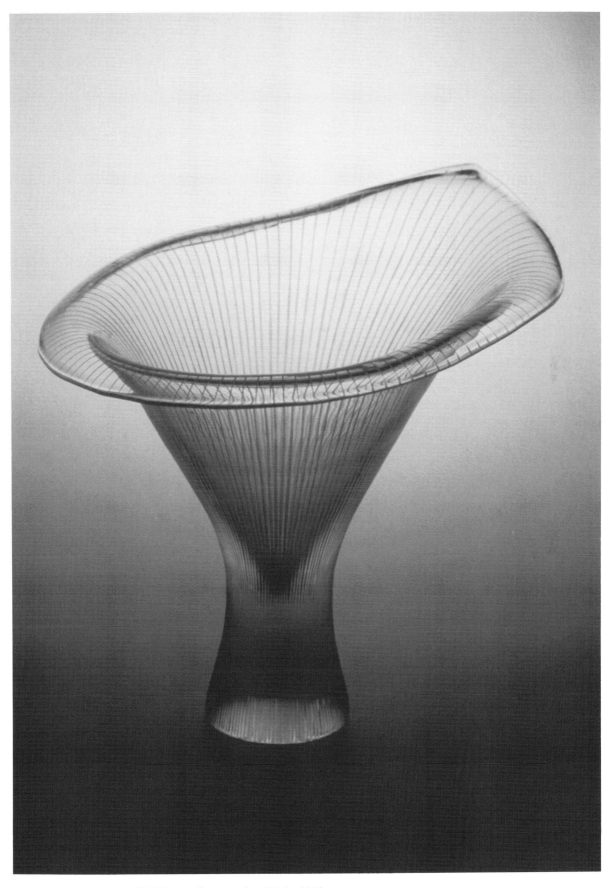

**Tapio Wirkkala:** *Kantarelli (Chantarelle)* vase, for Iittala, 1946

Lunning Prize, 1951; *House Beautiful* Award, New York, 1951; Olympic Games Stamps Prize, Helsinki, 1952; Department Store Competition Prize, Brussels World's Fair, 1957; Society of Industrial Artists "Medal of the Year," London, 1958; Museum of Contemporary Crafts Silver Cutlery Prize, New York, 1960; Badische Anilin- und Sodafabrik Prize, 1962; Domus Golden Obelisk Award, Milan, 1963; International Ceramics Gold Medal, Faenza, 1963, 1966, 1967, 1973; Premio Internazionale, Vicenza Ceramics Competition, 1963, 1966, 1967; Finnish Cultural Foundation honorary award, 1968; Creative Work Medal, Finnish Composers's International Copyright Bureau, 1980; Prince Eugene Medal, Stockholm, 1980; Silver Medal, Académie de l'Architecture, France, 1983. Honorary Royal Designer of Industry, Royal Society of Arts, London, 1964; honorary doctorate, Royal College of Art, London, 1971; honorary associate, Worshipful Company of Goldsmiths, London, 1971; honorary academician, Helsinki, 1972; honorary member, Diseñadores Industriales Instituto Politecnico Nacional, Mexico, 1982; honorary academician, Academia Mexicana de Diseño, 1982. Knight of the Order of the White Rose, Finland. **Died:** Helsinki, 19 May 1985.

## Works

*Kantarelli* vases in clear blown and cut glass, for Iitala, 1946.
*Jaavuori* vase in clear mould-blown glass, for Iitala, 1950.
*Jaapal* vase in clear mould-blown glass, for Iitala, 1950.
*Platter* in laminated birch, for Soinneek Kni, 1951.
*Tuonen Virta* vase in clear glass with vertical cut lines, for Iitala, 1951.
*Tokio* vase in clear mould-blown glass with bubble insert, for Iitala, 1954.
*Paaderin jaa* sculpture in clear mould-blown glass, for Iitala, 1960.
*Wirkkala* hanging lamps, for Airam and Idman, 1960.
*Composition* cutlery in stainless steel, for Rosenthal, 1963.
*Puukko* hunting knife in stainless steel, brass and polyamide, for Hackmann, 1963.
*Ultima Thule* sculpture, 300 X 900 cm laminated birch, for Montreal World Fair, 1967.
*Finlandia* vodka bottles in clear mould-blown glass, for Iitala, from 1969.
*Bolla* vase in decorated glass, for Venini, 1970.
*Composito* stainless steel knife, 1972.
*Kartano* drinking glasses in clear glass, for Iitala, 1978.
*Primavera* drinking glasses in clear glass, for Iitala, 1978-79.
*Viva* jugs and tumblers in clear mould-blown glass for Iitala, 1978-79.
*Pallas* vase in clear moulded glass with rib and bubble decoration, for Iitala, 1983.
*Kelo* jugs and tumblers in clear textured glass, for Iitala, 1984.

## Publications

By WIRKKALA: books—(editor) *Finnish Decorative Art: 13th Yearbook,* Helsinki, 1941; articles—in *Domus* (Milan), July/August 1981.

On WIRKKALA: books—*Finnish Designers of Today* by Oili Maki, Helsinki, 1954; *The Beauty of Modern Glass* by R. Stennett-Willson, London and New York, 1958; *Introduction to Twentieth*

*Century Design* by Arthur Drexler and Greta Daniel, New York, 1959; *A Treasury of Scandinavian Design* edited by Erik Zahle, New York, 1961; *Modern Glass* by Ada Polak, London, 1962; *Modern Scandinavian Furniture* by Ulf Hard af Segerstad, Copenhagen, 1963, London, 1964; *34 Scandinavian Designers* by Svend Erik Moller, Copenhagen, 1967; *Modern Finnish Design* by Ulf Hard af Segerstad, London, 1969; *New Design in Wood* by Donald J. Willcox, London and New York, 1970; *Finnish Design: Facts and Fancy* by Donald J. Willcox, New York, 1973; *Finnish Design 1875-1975* by Timo Sarpaneva and others, Helsinki, 1975; *Scandinavian Design: Objects of a Life Style* by Eileene Harrison Beer, New York and Toronto, 1975; *International Modern Glass* by Geoffrey Beard, London, 1976; *Europäische Keramik seit 1950,* exhibition catalogue edited by Heinz Spielmann and Hans Thiemann, Hamburg, 1979; *Tapio Wirkkala,* Helsinki, 1981; *Scandinavian Modern Design 1880-1980* edited by David Revere McFadden, New York and London, 1982; *Design Since 1945* edited by Kathryn Hiesinger and George Marcus, Philadelphia and London, 1983; *Les Annees 60* by Anne Bony, Paris, 1983; *The Conran Directory of Design* edited by Stephen Bayley, London, 1985; *Twentieth Century Design: Glass* by Frederick Cooke, London, 1986; *The Lunning Prize,* exhibition catalogue edited by Helena Dahlback Lutteman and Marianne Uggla, Stockholm, 1986; *Scandinavia: Ceramics and Glass in the Twentieth Century* by Jennifer Hawkins Opie, London, 1989.

*       *       *

Tapio Wirkkala entered the Scandinavian design scene in the postwar era when functionalism had become "organic"—less severe and dogmatic than it had been in the 1930s. He was a product of an age in Scandinavia when the ideal came to be commonly held that ordinary people had a right to a comfortable home that was both functional and esthetically pleasing. Although developing his designs through craft techniques, he sought to work with industry to bring these designs to a large public. His 1951 laminated-wood serving pieces were some of the first examples of this type of collaboration. While exploring laminated wood for sculptural purposes, he arrived at leaf-shaped, functional trays and platters, which were then produced at Soinne et Kni in Helsinki. He also ventured into more mundane household items, such as oddly shaped light bulbs which transformed the bulb into its own fixture.

Wirkkala created his award-winning design for the Finnish exhibition at the 1951 Milan Triennale in the beginning of an era when the outside world became aware of "Scandinavian Modern" as a style. Although each country in Scandinavia had contributed at varying rates and quantities to this style, its general character became known as primarily functionalist, with simple geometric lines and exposed materials and construction. Such recognition meant a large export market to an influential and affluent public; in turn, this meant growing opportunities for Scandinavian designers within industry. Along with other new designers, such as Arne Jacobsen and Henning Koppel in Denmark, Wirkkala was hired by industry to design products in wood, glass, silver, and ceramic.

In both his production lines and one-of-a-kind ware, Wirkkala was perhaps best known for his art glass, a Finnish industry dating back to the seventeenth century. Influenced by art nouveau and by natural forms, Wirkkala investigated both the integral structure of the material and its optical qualities. For example, he used layers of color to refract light, curved upper surfaces, and interior lines to resemble melting ice, or rippled effects to connote liquid in the bottom of a goblet. Control over the metamorphosis of an abstract idea to create a product from modern material with modern production methods is the essence of Wirkkala's contribution to design. This subtle understanding of material and technique has made many of his products classics of Finnish modern design.

—Sarah Bodine

# WOLF, Henry
American painter, photographer, and graphic designer

**Born:** Vienna, Austria, 23 May 1925; emigrated to the United States in 1941, naturalized, 1943. **Education:** Educated at the Lycee Hoche, Versailles, France, 1938-41; studied at the School of Industrial Art, New York, 1941-42, and at the New School for Social Research, New York, 1947-50. **Military Service:** Served in the United States Army 32nd Division, 1943-46, Sergeant. **Family:** Married Renate Vogel in 1951 (divorced, 1956); married Macha Gagarine in 1960 (divorced, 1960). **Career:** Graphic designer, working in New York, from 1946; designer, at Arnold Studios, New York, 1946-47; art director, at Geer duBois and Company, New York, 1947-51, United States Department of State, 1951-52, *Esquire* magazine, New York, 1952-58, *Harper's Bazaar* magazine, New York, 1958-61, and *Show* magazine, New York, 1961-64, Jack Tinker and Partners, 1964-65, and at The Center for Advanced Practice, McCann Erickson advertising agency, New York, 1964-66; executive vice-president and creative director, Trahey/Wolf Advertising, New York, 1966-71 (clients included Charles of the Ritz, Ogden, Elizabeth Arden, Danskin, Olivetti, Union Carbide, and other); president of Henry Wolf Productions, New York, from 1971; freelance art director and photographer, from 1974, creating catalogs for Saks Fifth Avenue, I. Magnin, Bloomingdales, Van Cleef & Arpels, RCA, BF Goodrich, and others, advertisements for Xerox, IBM, Revlon, GTE, Olivetti, and others, and editorial photographs for *Esquire, Town & Country, New York, Bazaar, Domus,* and others; also creator of television commercials. Instructor, Parsons School of Design, from 1954, Cooper Union, New York, 1955-64, and the School of Visual Arts, New York, 1964-74; visiting professor, Cooper Union, 1976. Vice-president, International Design Conference, Aspen, Colorado, 1968; member, President's Commission for Propaganda, 1969; president, American Institute of Graphic Arts, New York, 1970-72; executive board member, 1973-75, and president, 1989-91, Art Directors Club of New York; vice-president, Architectural League of New York, 1974. **Member:** American Institute of Graphic Arts; Alliance Graphique Internationale; Art Directors Club of New York; The Century Association. **Honors:** Art Directors Club of New York Gold Medal, 1956, 1957, 1959, 1961, 1963, and Hall of Fame Award, 1981; Benjamin Franklin Fellow, Royal Society of Arts and Sciences, London, 1970; American Institute of Graphic of Arts Gold Medal, 1976; Herb Lubalin Award, Society of Publication Designers, 1989; Honorary Royal Designer for Industry, London, 1990; Honorary Doctorate, Corcoran Gallery, Washington, D.C., 1992. **Address:** Henry Wolf Productions Incorporated, 167 East 73rd Street, New York, New York 10021. U.S.A.

## Publications

**By WOLF: books**—(with text by Gerald Silk) *Automobile and Culture,* New York, 1987; *Visual Thinking: Methods for Making Images Memorable,* New York, 1988; **articles**—in *Graphics* (Zürich), no. 149, 1970; *American Photographer* (New York), February 1983.

**On WOLF: books**—*Who's Who in Graphic Art* edited by Walter Amstutz, Zürich, 1962, Dubendorf, 1982; *Designers in the USA: Volume 1* edited by Henri Hillbrand, London, 1971; *Art Without Boundaries 1950-1970* edited by Gerald Woods and others, London, 1972; *The Language of Graphics* by Edward Booth-Clibborn and Daniele Baroni, London, 1980; *The Design Concept* by Allen Hurlburt, New York, 1981; *Great Magazine Covers* by Pat Kerry, New York, 1983; *The Art of Persuasion* by Robert Sobieszek, New York, 1987.

*

A designer is a problem-solver. I have no philosophy about it, except to do the best possible design and still get published. No philosophy could span all the assignments I have undertaken. We are not artists who gratify their own obsessions but professionals who help clients with their visual problems.

—Henry Wolf

\*     \*     \*

Wherever this multi-talented, creative professional in graphic design, art direction, photography, and publication design puts his creative energy, excellence results. Henry Wolf emerged as a force in the magazine publishing business in the 1940s. Extending earlier traditions established by Dr. M. F. Agha at Condé Nast, William Golden, and Paul Rand, Wolf has been influenced particularly by Alexey Brodovitch and his work at *Harper's Bazaar.* Wolf has said of Brodovitch, "The man was the most informative and self-contradictory person I have ever met, and yet in his own strange way, the most stimulating." During the heyday of the magazine publishing business, Wolf consistently designed and produced magazines of unmatched quality. Beginning in 1953, his work at *Esquire* showed the blending of an artistic eye with the pragmatics of the editorial/journalistic milieu. After 1958, he brought *Harper's Bazaar* to a point of high refinement with his special vision as it was directed toward the fashion world. In 1961, as art director of *Show* magazine, he began a new arts-oriented magazine from scratch. Its photography, layouts, covers, editorial stance, and overall fresh, innovative look stand in combination, to this day, as a benchmark in magazine design. In spite of its short life span, *Show* was well ahead of its time in both form and content.

Wolf has been innovative in the way in which he has blended several disciplines together in a particularly unique way. He is a graphic designer with a controlled method and a working knowledge of the pragmatics of structure, economics, etc. As an art director, he widens an eye for the editorial and an understanding of the communication requirements of mass media. Above all, he has shown in his photography a concern for the message and for the appropriate visual way to achieve the goal of this medium. Wolf's photographic vision is strongly perceptual, reminding one of the paintings of

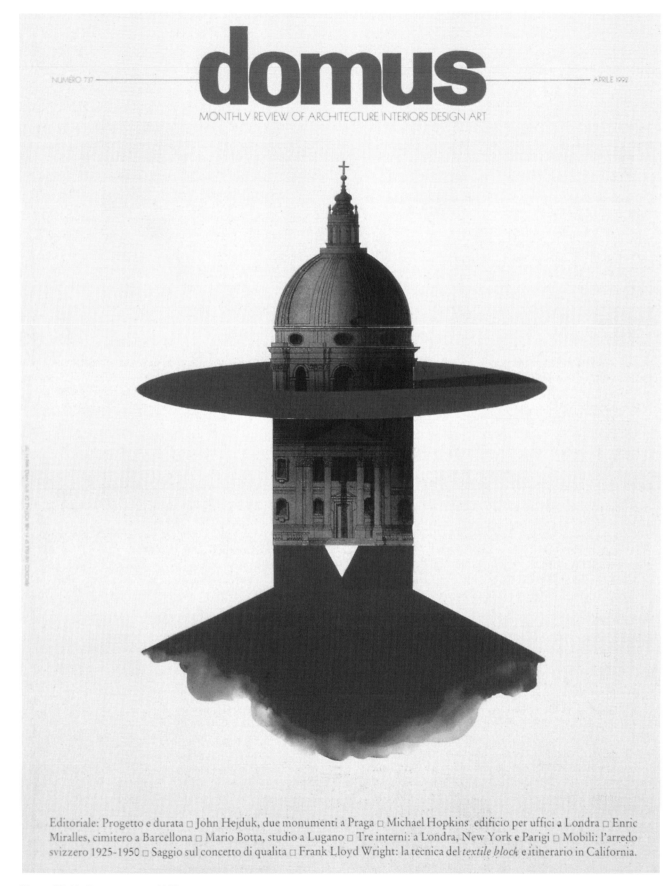

**Henry Wolf:** *Domus* **cover, 1992**

René Magritte with playfulness and ambiguity in the arrangement of elements. His work is simple and direct but maintains a human touch.

His career has shown him to be a prolific producer in whatever field he is working. His total creative energies, as directed toward *Show,* for example, pushed the boundaries of photography, layout, typography, and editorial art to new heights of quality. Wolf has been very influential in stimulating directions in photography, graphic design, and magazine publishing. The products of his career have greatly improved our collective visual environment and continue as a testament to what is possible by a very talented, sensitive man with great vision and skill.

—R. Roger Remington

# WOLFF, Ann

Swedish artist, painter, sculptor, and glass designer

**Born:** Ann Schaefer, in Lubeck, Germany, 26 February 1937; adopted mother's family name Wolff in 1985. **Education:** Studied drawing, Meisterschule für Mode, Hamburg, 1953-54; visual communications, under Thomas Maldonado, Hochschule für Gestaltung, Ulm, 1956-59. **Family:** Married Swedish glass designer Goran Warff in 1960 (divorced, 1972); children: Hanna and Amanda; lives with artist Dirk Bimberg, from 1973; children: Lina. **Career:** Designer, Pukebergs Glassworks, Nybro, 1960-64, and Kosta Boda, 1964-78; independent glass artist, establishing own studio in Transjö, Kosta, from 1978, and in Berlin, from 1990; founder, with Wike Adolfsson, of Stenhytta glass studio, Transjö, 1978-1983; founder-director, with Jan Erik Ritzmann, Sven Åke Carlsson, and Dirk Bimberg, of Transjö Kulturarbetare i Glas glass studio, Transjö, 1982-84; also painter, sculptor and graphic artist, from 1982. Guest instructor, at California College of Arts and Crafts, Fullerton University, Vanderbilt University, Penland School of Crafts, in the United States, 1976; guest professor, Pilchuck Glass Center, Stanwood, Washington, 1977, 1979, 1984, 1986; professor of cognitive design, Hochschule für Bildende Künste, Hamburg, from 1993; also visiting teacher at other schools in Europe, Japan and the United States, from 1974. **Exhibitions:** Varbergs Museum, Sweden, 1966, 1985; Norrkopings Museum, Sweden, 1967; Galerie Wulff, Helsinki, 1968; Galerie Doktor Glas, Stockholm, 1976, 1979, 1984, 1987; Galerie SM, Frankfurt, 1978; Seibu Store, Tokyo, 1978; Galerie der Kunsthandwerker, Hamburg, 1979; Yamaha Gallery, Kyoto, 1980; Essener Galerie, Essen, 1981; Galerie Mors Mössa, Göteborg, 1981, 1984; Heller Gallery, New York, 1982, 1987; Ivor Kurland Glass Art Gallery, Los Angeles, 1983, 1987; Holsten Galleries, Palm Beach, Florida, 1983, 1986; Gallerie Lietzow, West Berlin, 1984; Galerie Gamla Stan, Stockholm, 1985; Galerie Artichoque, Velp, Holland, 1985; Galerie Belle, Västeras, 1985; Galerie Nylla Nyborg, Borgholm, Sweden, 1985; Kilkenny Art Gallery, Ireland, 1985; Maurice, Littleton Gallery, Washington, D.C., 1985; Gotlans Fornsal, Visby, 1986; Galleri F 15 Moss, Norway, 1987; Galerie Kaplanen, Visby, 1987; Landesmuseum Schloß Gottorf, Schleswig, 1987; Galerie Heidi Schneider, Horgen, Switzerland, 1987; Växjö Konstnärscentrum, Sweden, 1988; Stockholm Art Fair, 1988; Karlshamm Museum, Sweden, 1988; Galerie Gottschalk Betz, Frankfurt, 1988; Galerie Clara Scemini, Chicago Art Fair, 1989; Mejeriet, Alskog, Gotland, 1989, 1993; Grafiska Sällskapet,

Stockholm, 1989; Konstmuseum, Visby, 1990; Musée-Château d'Annecy, France, 1990; Noahs Art Space, Tokyo, 1992; Arts Decouverts, Palais Royal, Paris, 1992; Musée Palais Bénedictine, Fecamp, France, 1993; Gamla Riksbanken, Vänersborg, Sweden, 1994; Chicago Art Fair, Chicago, 1994; Heller Gallery, Palm Beach, 1995; Gösta Werner Museum, Simrishamm, 1995. **Collections:** Nationalmuseum, Stockholm; Rohsska Konstslodmuseet, Goteborg; Danske Kunstindustrimuseet, Copenhagen; Museum für Kunst und Gewerb, Hamburg; Stedelijk Museum, Amsterdam; Musee of Glass, New York; Metropolitan Museum of Art, New York. **Honors:** Lunning Prize, for Scandinavia, 1968; Coburger Glass Prize, Germany, 1977; First and Third Prize, Central Swiss Glass Prize, 1980; Award Honor, *Internationale Glaskunst 81,* Kassel, 1981; Glassprize, World's Crafts Exhibition, Bratislava, 1984; Gold Medal, Bayerischer Staatspreis, München, 1988. **Address:** Transjö, 360 52 Kosta, Sweden.

## Works

Household and tableware series, for Pukebergs Glassworks, 1960-64.

Children's toys in wood, for Boda, 1964.

Chair in wood, for Stockaryds Stofabrik, 1973.

Household and tableware series *Party, Garden, Grape, Brava, Krinolin, Snowball,* and others, for Kosta Boda, 1964-78.

*Litet Fro* relief in metal, for Djurangsskola, Kalmar, 1969.

*Kontrapunkt* relief in wood, for the Volvo diningroom, Goteberg, 1971.

*Flanores Dag* relief in metal, for the Restaurant Flanor, Gavle, 1971.

Staircase reliefs, for Stena Lines transit hall, Goteberg, 1971.

Staircase reliefs in metal and glass, for Umea Karhus, 1971.

*Pladsk* relief in metal for Norrkoping Swimming Hall, 1971.

*Livets Tra* reliefs in etched glass and iron, for Dalsjofors Old People's Home, 1972.

*Vitliv, Bla och Scenen* three reliefs in wood and glass, for the Scandinavska Enskilda Banken, Goteborg, 1973.

*Hurlig ar orden* relief in metal, for the Hogbyskola, Jarfalla, 1975.

*Hyttorgel* sculptures in glass, for the Lansstyrelsen, Växjö, 1976.

Glass wall, for Nybro Kommunhus, 1981. Panels and relief in glass, for the Kontorshus VBB, Växjö, 1982.

*Gaster hos Verkligheten* wall in stained glass, for the Lansstyrelsen, Kalmar, 1983.

*Vid Floden* five panels in stained glass, for Trelleborg Library, 1983.

*Tragard full av Liv* sculpture in stained glass, for Laholms Library, 1984.

*Ganymedes,* Kowzerthall, Växjö, 1991.

*Ödestugu,* Altarfönster, 1992.

*Kopf* glass sculpture, 1995.

## Publications

**By WOLFF: articles**—"Selbstmord eines Glashauses/Suicide of a Glasshouse" in *Neues Glas/New Glass* (Düsseldorf), February 1990.

**On WOLFF: books**—*I Glasrike* by Bertil Palmqvist, Lund, 1979; *Ann Warff,* exhibition catalogue with texts by Helga Hilschenz and Barbro Werkmaster, Malmo, 1982; *Geschichte des Studioglases* by Christian Sellner, Frankfurt, 1984; *Ann Wolff: Fornsalens*

**Ann Wolff:** *Bildschale,* 1994

*Bildtenshall,* exhibition catalogue by Mailis Stensman, Visby, 1986; *A Signal Had to Be Given,* exhibition catalogue by Verena Tafel, Transjö, 1986; *Scandinavia: Ceramics and Glass in the Twentieth Century* by Jennifer Hawkins Opie, London, 1989; *Qui n'est plus engagé dans quoi ou le reflet du reflectuer ddans la fenêtre/Who Is No Longer Involved with What or the Reflection of the Reflector in the Window?,* exhibition catalogue by Klaus Zerhusen, Annecy, France, 1990; **articles**—"Glass Windows designed by Ann Warff" by K. Moriyama in *Japan Interior Design* (Tokyo), no. 214, 1977; "Work by Ann Warff" by K. Moriyama in *Japan Interior Design* (Tokyo), no. 234, 1978; "Svenskt Glas" by Michael Taylor in *Glass studio* (New York), January/February 1978; "Kvinnobilder i glas" by Mailis Stensman in *Form 75* (Stockholm), no. 6, 1979; "Woman Designer from Sweden—Ann Warff" by K. Moriyama in *GraphicDesign* (Tokyo), no. 73, 1979; "Der Große Aufbruch EuroPaische Glaskunst seit 1945" by J. Schou-Christensen in *Neues Glas* (Düsseldorf), January 1980; "Das Pilchuck Glass Center" by Klaus Moje in *Neues Glas* (Düsseldorf), January 1980; "Ann Warff" by Ruby Bernstein and Caryl Hansen in *Glass Art Society,* no. 5, 1980; *Form 77* (Stockholm), no. 5, 1981; *Form 78* (Stockholm) no. 4, 1982; *Horizon* (New York), 25 July 1982; "Ann Warff" by Sylvie Girard in *La Revue de la Céramique et du Verre,* no. 10, 1983; *American Craft* (New York), February 1983; *Form 80* (Stockholm), no. 1, 1983; "Discoveries and Changes: New Works by Ann Wolff" by Verena Tafel in *Neues Glas* (Düsseldorf), April 1986; "In Search of Truth" by Kuroki Rika in *Glassworks* (Japan), November 1993.

# WOUDHUYSEN, Lewis

British architectural, exhibition, graphic, and industrial designer

**Born:** the Netherlands, 15 September 1912; emigrated to Britain in 1940, naturalized. **Education:** Studied architecture in Delft, 1930-34, graphic design in Amsterdam, 1936-37, and book design in Leipzig, 1938. **Career:** Art director, working for J. Walter Thompson agency, and for Adprint, London, 1949-53; freelance designer from 1953, establishing Woudhuysen Consultant Designers, London, from 1955; designed for the Clydesdale Bank, Department of Health and Social Security, Manpower Services Commission, Shenley Trust, EMI Laboratories, William Mallinson and Sons, Courtaulds, Plessey, Arbuthnot Factors, Acme Signs and Displays, Advance Electronics Bass Charrington, Bertorelli, British Petroleum, Cape Building Products, Castrol, General Post Office, Lambert Chemical Company, Rootes Limited, Scottish Brewers, Twinlock, United

Linen Services, and others. **Member:** Fellow, Society of Industrial Artists and Designers, London; associate, Designer and Art Directors Association, London; Institute of Packaging, London. **Died:** London, 12 November 1985.

## Publications

**By WOUDHUYSEN: articles**—in *The Designer* (London), November 1970, December 1975.

**On WOUDHUYSEN: books**—*Designers in Britain* edited by Herbert Spencer, London, 1954, 1957; *The Silent Salesman: Packaging That Sells* by James Pilditch, London, 1961; *Design Coordination and Corporate Image* by F.H.K. Henrion and Alan Parkin, London and New York, 1967; *An International Survey of Packaging* by Wim Crouwel and Kurt Weidemann, London, 1968; *All Things Bright and Beautiful: Design in Britain 1830 to Today* by Fiona MacCarthy, London, 1972.

*       *       *

Lewis Woudhuysen studied architecture at Delft and graphics at Amsterdam and Leipzig. At the outbreak of World War Two, he escaped by rowing a boat to England. There, he became art director for J. Walter Thompson and, in 1949, for Adprint. In 1955, he founded his own Woudhuysen Design Group, which covered corporate identity programmes, marketing, public relations schemes, product innovation, product consultancy, design packaging, brand images, beer labels, advanced instrumentation design research, and modular systems.

Woudhuysen was a down-to-earth designer. Believing that design is a job, he had little time for high-flown concepts. As he saw it, the first duty is to make an object which is fit for its purpose. One should listen to what the customer wants and then advise him on the best way to achieve his goal. Thinking that some designers overrate their own importance, Woudhuysen preferred to believe that the designer creates part of the ordinary furniture of life, not some romantic monument to his own importance. To Woudhuysen, the commercial requirement was the dominating concern, but he would allow moral consideration to enter if, say, an order came from South Africa when it was under apartheid; that he would refuse, despite knowing the language. Woudhuysen's practicality has been recognised by his awards, including four from the Design Council, for his products do what is required of them.

—Diana de Marly

## WRIGHT, Russel

American stage, interior, and industrial designer

**Born:** Lebanon, Ohio, 3 April 1904. **Education:** Studied under Frank Duveneck, at Cincinnati Academy of Art, Ohio, 1921-22, and under Leo Lentell and Kenneth Hayes Miller, at the Art Students League, New York, 1922; studied law and theater, at Princeton University, New Jersey, 1922-24; Columbus University School of Architecture, New York, 1923; New York University School of Architecture, 1938-39. **Family:** Married Mary Small Einstein in 1927 (died, 1952); daughter: Eve. **Career:** Stage, set, and costume designer, working with Norman Bel Geddes, New York, 1925-26; stage manager, at the Theater Guild, Neighborhood Playhouse, and the Group Theater, New York, 1926-30; freelance stage prop, furnishing, and product designer, establishing own workshops in New York, from 1930; established Russel Wright Associates designer furniture firm, New York, 1943-67: designed for Sears Roebuck, Colgate Aircraft Corporation, Acme Fluorescent, Amplex Corporation, Steubenville Pottery, Sterling China, Paden City Pottery, Edwin M. Knowles Pottery, American Cyanamid, Ideal Toy Company, John Hull Cutlery, Imperial Glass, Century Metalcraft, Duraware Corporation, General Electric, Simtex Mills, and others. Consultant, United States Technical Aid Missions to Cambodia, Vietnam and Taiwan, 1956-60; crafts consultant to the Government of Japan, 1957-58, and to the Government of Barbados, 1970. President, Society of Industrial Designers of America, 1952-53; director, Summer in the Parks Program, Washington, D.C., 1968, and Nature Center of the Nature Conservatory, Manitoga, New York, 1975-76. **Exhibitions:** *Russel Wright, American Designer,* Hudson River Museum, Yonkers, New York, 1983; *Design Since 1945,* Philadelphia Museum of Art, 1983; *High Style: 20th Century American Design,* Whitney Museum, New York, 1985; *The Machine Age in America 1918-1941,* Brooklyn Museum, New York, 1986. **Collections:** Museum of Modern Art, New York; Metropolitan Museum of Art, New York; Cooper-Hewitt Museum, New York; Arents Research Library, Syracuse University, New York. **Honors:** Tiffany Sculpture Competition Prize, 1921; Museum of Modern Art Good Design Award, New York, 1950, 1952, 1953; Home Furnishings League Trailblazer Award, New York, 1951; Society of Industrial Designers Medal, New York; Beautification Committee Citation, Washington, D.C., 1968. **Died:** New York City, 21 December 1976.

## Works

*Modern Living/American Modern* upholstered furniture, for Conant Ball Company, 1935.
*American Modern* ceramic dinnerware, for Steubenville Pottery, 1937-39.
*American Way* furniture range, for Monitor Company, and Sprague and Carleton Company, 1940.
*Knockdown* furniture range, for Sears Roebuck, 1942.
Alcohol stove and coffee-maker, for Silex Corporation, 1942.
*Meladur* melamine plastic dinnerware, for American Cyanamid and General American Transportation, 1945-49.
Cutlery range in stainless steel and plastic, for Englishtown Cutlery, 1946.
*American Modern* table linen range, for Lecock and Company, 1946-48.
*Stove-to-Table* aluminum serving wares, for the Aluminum Goods Manufacturing Corporation, 1946-48.
Swivel lamp, for Amplex Corporation, 1949.
*Flair* tumblers in clear, colored, and seed glass, for Imperial Glass, 1949.
*Easier Living* wooden furniture range, for Staton Furniture Company, 1950.
*Samsonite* folding metal chairs and tables, for Shwayder Corporation, 1950.
*American Modern* stainless steel cutlery, for John Hull Cutlery, 1951.

*Broil Quick* electric cooking appliance, for Peerless Electric, 1955.

*Idealware* polyethylene plastic dinnerware, for Ideal Toy Company, 1955.

*Esquire Collection* ceramic dinnerware, for Edwin M. Knowles Pottery, 1956.

Electro-thermal serving trays, for Cornwall Corporation, 1958-61.

*Big Top Peanut Butter* jar and label, for Procter and Gamble, 1959.

Trays, buckets, and colanders in plastic, for Duraware Corporation, 1964-65.

## Publications

**By WRIGHT: books**—*Home Furnishings at the Fair,* booklet, New York, 1939; (with Mary Wright) *A Guide to Easier Living,* New York, 1951; **articles**—in *American Home* (New York), January 1934; *Arts and Decoration* (New York), February 1935; *Architectural Forum* (New York), October 1937, September 1942; *House and Garden* (New York), April 1938; *Country Life* (New York), May 1938; *Design* (New York), March 1941; *Interiors* (New York), June 1943, December 1951, April 1955, August 1956; *Better Homes and Gardens* (New York), September 1944, February 1945; *Woman's Home Companion* (New York), September 1956.

**On WRIGHT: books**—*A History of American Furniture* edited by N. I. Bienenstock, East Stroudsburg, 1936; *The Story of Modern Applied Art* by Rudolph Rosenthal and Helena Ratzka, New York, 1948; *The Consultant Designer in American Industry,* thesis by Jerry Streichler, New York University, 1963; *Depression Modern: The 30s Style in America* by Martin Greif, New York, 1975; *The Streamlined Decade* by Donald Bush, New York, 1975; *Twentieth Century Limited: Industrial Design in America 1925-39* by Jeffrey Meikle, Philadelphia, 1979; *Industrial Design* by John Heskett, London, 1980; *Russel Wright, American Designer,* exhibition catalogue by James Hennessey, Cambridge, Massachusetts, 1983; *Design Since 1945* edited by Kathryn Hiesinger and George Marcus, Philadelphia and London, 1983; *High Style: 20th Century American Design,* exhibition catalogue by David Gebhard, Esther McCoy, and others, New York, 1985; *Mid-Century: Furniture of the 1950s* by Cara Greenberg, London, 1985; *The Machine Age in America 1918-1941* by Richard Guy Wilson and Dianne H. Pilgrim, New York, 1986; *The American Design Adventure 1940-1975* by Arthur J. Pulos, London and Cambridge, Massachusetts, 1988.

\* \* \*

As a student at Princeton in the 1920s, Russel Wright was strongly enough influenced by the work of Norman Bel Geddes to leave school and enter the design field. He began by designing theater sets and costumes with his mentor. By the early 1930s, his interest in the design of theatrical environments had expanded into the domestic arena. Here, Wright distinguished himself as a breed apart from his noteworthy peers, among whom it was fashionable to design consumer products only to assure their commercial desirability, by placing a premium on style and modernity.

Wright revealed a strong commitment to improving daily life for American families. He devoted the remainder of his life to developing an American national style based on modern, functional simplicity brought into line with the needs, materials, and technology of the twentieth century. He rejected many aspects of the austere formalism of European modernists, recognizing early a need for a

more humanistic approach to the domestic landscape. Wright subscribed to a philosophy, recurrent since the mid-nineteenth century, that improvement of environments in which people live and work improves the quality of those people's lives.

Wright's recognition of the designer's role as both a mirror and arbiter of taste yielded great commercial success for his products. His *American Modern* furniture of 1935 was widely accepted and brought "blonde," solid-wood furniture into the mainstream as it paved the way for the Scandinavian Modern taste of several decades later. As late as 1976, in the design of his own house and grounds, Dragon Rock, north of New York City, he still sought to prove that contemporary design could be as liveable, romantic, and sentimental as traditional design.

Wright's analysis of living spaces (he defined living areas for specific activities such as relaxing, eating, cleaning, and others) changed the way middle-class Americans perceived their needs and defined their priorities. For example, his experiments with spun aluminum and informal dinnerware pioneered the stove-to-table concept of serving meals and were influential by virtue of altered function in redefining the needs for dining space. The culmination of this drive for improvement of daily life was the 1950 *Guide to Easier Living,* co-authored by his wife, Mary Einstein Wright. In the book, the Wrights outlined their philosophy for socially based design. In so doing, they described a generation of Americans.

—Ken Carls

## WURMAN, Richard Saul

American graphic designer

**Born:** 26 March 1935. **Education:** University of Pennsylvania, 1953-59, B.Arch, M.Arch. **Family:** Married the novelist Gloria Nagy; children: four. **Career:** Archeological surveyor, Tikal, Guatemala, 1958; assistant, Office of Louis I. Kahn, 1960-62; project director, North Carolina Film Board, 1962-64; partner and designer, Murphy Levy Wurman Architecture & Urban Planning, 1964-76; founder and director, GEE! Group for Environmental Education, from 1968; deputy director, Housing and Community Development, City of Philadelphia, 1977; founded ACCESS Press Ltd., 1981 (sold to HarperCollins, 1991); partner, with Frank O. Gehry, The Furniture Brothers (Tables by the Slice), 1984; founder and creator, TED Conferences (Technology Entertainment Design), from 1984; founder, TUB, The Understanding Business, 1987 (sold to HarperCollins, 1991); creator, SMART Yellow Pages, for Pacific Bell Directory, 1987; founded TIPS (The Initial Press Syndicate), Newport, 1995; chairman and creative director, MEDICAL Conference, Charleston, South Carolina, 1995, and TEDSELL Conference, Monterey, California, 1996. Faculty member, North Carolina State, Raleigh, 1962-64, 1977, Washington University, St. Louis, 1965, Princeton University, 1965-67, Cambridge University, Cambridge, England, 1967-68, Cornell University, New York City Program, 1968-70, City College of New York, 1968-79, University of California Los Angeles, 1976, University of Southern California, 1976; Dean and full professor, School of Environmental Design, California State Polytechnic University, Pomona, 1978-79; chairman of Interior Architecture, Otis Parsons, Los Angeles, 1979-84; visiting scholar, Department of Architecture & Planning, Massachusetts Institute of Technology, from 1993; visiting professor,

**Richard Saul Wurman: Neighborhood layout from *Tokyo Access* guidebook**

Rhode Island School of Design 1995. Consultant, Office of Charles and Ray Eames, 1976-77, AIA Research Corporation, 1976, 1978, Advance Research Agency Defense Department, 1977-80, American Association of Retired Person, 1990, Knight Ridder, 1990, News Corporation, 1990; *TV Guide,* 1990. **Member:** Fellow, American Institute of Architects; Alliance Graphique Internationale; fellow, World Economic Forum; board of directors, 1970-80, and advisor, from 1981, International Design Conference in Aspen; board of directors, 1978-83, International Design Education Foundation; vice-

president, 1985-90, American Institute of Graphic Artists. **Exhibitions:** *City/2: Half the City Belongs to You,* Philadelphia Museum of Art, 1971; *MLW;* Philadelphia Art Alliance, 1971; *Making the City Observable,* Walker Art Center, Minneapolis (traveled to 20 cities), 1971-74; *The Design Necessity,* Washington, D.C. (traveled), 1973; *Energy Conscious Design,* AIA Research Corporation, Philadelphia, 1976; *America 200,* Philadelphia Art Alliance, 1976; *200 Years—Images of Los Angeles,* Pershing Square Museum of Science and Industry, Los Angeles, 1981; *10—A Retrospective of* *the Work of Richard Saul Wurman,* AXIS Design Gallery, Tokyo, Japan, 1991. **Honors:** T.P. Chandler Fellowship, University of Pennsylvania, 1958-59; Arthur Spayd Brookes Gold Medal, 1959; AIA Medal, 1959; Guggenheim Fellowship, 1969; National Endowment for the Arts Grants, 1970, 1973, 1974, 1976; Kevin Lynch Award, Massachusetts Institute of Technology (M.I.T.), 1991; Fellow, World Economic Forum, Davos, Switzerland, 1994; honorary doctorate, University of the Arts, Philadelphia, 1994, and Art Center College of Design, Pasadena, California, 1995. **Address:** The Orchard, 180 Narragansett Avenue, Newport, Rhode Island 02840, U.S.A.

## Publications

**By WURMAN: books**—(editor and designer, with Eugene Feldman) *Notebooks & Drawings* by Louis I. Kahn, New York, Philadelphia, 1962; *Cities: A Comparison of Form and Scale,* 1963, Philadelphia, 1974; *Various Dwellings Described in a Comparative Manner....,* Philadelphia, 1964; *Man Made Philadelphia: A Guide to Its Physical and Cultural Environment,* Cambridge, Massachusetts, 1972; *The Nature of Recreation,* Cambridge, Massachusetts, 1972; *Making the City Observable,* Minneapolis, 1971; (travel guide) *Los Angeles,* Newport, Rhode Island, 1980, 1982, 1984, 1987, 1991, 1993; (sports guide) *Football Access,* Newport, 1982; (travel guide) *Hawaii,* Newport, 1982, 1984, 1989, 1992; (travel guide) *San Francisco,* Newport, 1982, 1984, 1987, 1991, 1993; (travel guide) *New York City,* Newport, 1983, 1985, 1989, 1991, 1993; (sports guide) *Olympic Access,* Newport, 1984; (sports guide) *Baseball Access,* Newport, 1984; *Dog Access,* Newport, 1984; (travel guide) *Washington, D.C.,* Newport, 1984, 1990, 1993; (travel guide) *Tokyo,* Newport, 1984; (travel guide) *New Orleans,* Newport, 1984, 1993; (travel guide) *Las Vegas,* Newport, 1985; *Medical Access,* Newport, 1985; *What Will Be Has Always Been: The Words of Louis I. Kahn,* New York, 1986; (travel guide) *London,* Newport, 1987, 1991, 1993; (travel guide) *Paris,* Newport, 1987, 1990, 1992; (travel guide) *Rome,* Newport, 1987, 1991, 1993; (sports guide) *Summer Games,* Newport, 1988, 1992; (sports guide) *Winter Games,* Newport, 1988; *Information Anxiety,* New York, 1989, Japan, London, 1990, Italy, 1991, Brazil, 1992; *Wall Street Journal Guide to Understanding Money & Markets,* New York, 1989; *Polaroid Access,* Newport, 1989; (atlas and directory) *USAtlas,* Newport, 1990, 1991, 1992; *Follow the Yellow Brick Road,* New York, 1991, as *Instruction Anxiety,* Tokyo, 1993; *ON TIME Airline Guide to North America,* East/West Network, 1991; (travel guide) *Boston,* Newport, 1991, 1993; (travel guide) *Chicago,* Newport, 1991, 1993; (travel guide) *Barcelona,* Newport, 1992; (travel guide) *San Diego,* Newport, 1992; (travel guide) *California Wine Country,* Newport, 1992; (travel guide) *Florence/Venice/Milan,* Newport, 1992; *Fortune Guide to Investing in the 90's,* New York, 1993; *N: The Newport, Rhode Island Guide,* Newport, 1995; *C: The Urban Atlas: 20 American Cities,* Cambridge, Massachusetts, 1996.

**On WURMAN: articles**—"Non-author" in *New Statesman* (London), 12 July 1968; "Richard Wurman and His City Resuscitation Kit" in *Philadelphia Magazine,* January 1969; "Banking Boutique" in *Progressive Architecture* (New York), August 1969; "Forms as a Kit of Parts" in *Progressive Architecture* (New York), April 1970; "Opening Your Eyes" in *Time,* May 1970; "City/2" in *Today Magazine: Philadelphia Inquirer,* 13 June 1971; "Richard Saul Wurman" in *Metropolitan* (New York), December 1971; "Sand Castles for

Keeps" in *Look* (New York), 1 June 1971; "We the People/The City's Friends" in *Discovery Magazine,* 1972; "The Invisible City" in *Architectural Forum* (New York), May 1972; "Yellow Pages for City Learning/ABC's" in *Saturday Review* (Canada), 19 August 1972; "Turn on to the City" in *Parade,* 10 September 1972; "Man-Made Philadelphia" in *Today,* 17 September 1972; "Understanding Cities" in *Time,* 16 October 1972; "New Guidebooks to Cities: Why None for LA?" in *Los Angeles Times,* 17 November 1972; "Links for Learning Network Wraparound" in *Harper's* (New York), May 1974; "Richard Wurman" in *Metropolitan* (New York), June 1974; "Richard Saul Wurman and GEE! Group" in *Idea* (Tokyo), 1974; "Rick Wurman: The Originators" in *Architectural Design* (New York), December 1975; "An Interview with the Commissioner of Curiosity and Imagination of the City of Could Be" in *AIA Journal* (New York), 1976; "Seeing a City Function in a Fabulous Way" in *Los Angeles Times,* 1977; "Richard Saul Wurman" in *Graphis* (Zürich), January/February 1983; *Communication Arts* (Palo Alto, California), January/February 1983, January/February 1988; "The PT Barnum of Design" in *Christian Science Monitor* (Boston), 1983; "Access Reinvents the Guidebook" in *Time,* 18 June 1984; "Traveling Companions" in *Vis A Vis,* September 1987; "The Data Doctor" in *Continental Magazine,* July 1988; "Information Overload" in *Los Angeles Times Magazine,* January 1989; *AXIS* (Japan), Spring 1989; "ACCESS GUIDE to Richard Saul Wurman" in *Electric Word,* July/August 1990; "Information's Architect" in *Print* (New York), October 1990; *HQ* (Germany), no. 20, 1991; *Design* (London), July 1992; "TED3 Report" in *AXIS* (Japan), Summer 1992; "The Father of TED" in *Design World,* Summer 1992; "TED4 Report" in *AXIS* (Japan), Summer 1993; *Brutus* (Japan), 15 January 1994; "Richard Saul Wurman's War Against Stupidity" in *Graphis* (Zürich), January/February 1994; "In the Service of Learning" in *Electronic Learning,* January 1994; "The Wizard of TED" in *Successful Meetings,* February 1994; "Richard Saul Wurman Gets What He Deserves" by Janet Abrams in *ID Magazine* (New York), March/April 1994; "TED5: Technology Entertainment Design" by Patrick Coyne in *Communication Arts* (Palo Alto), May/June 1994; "TED5: TED Celebrates a Decade of Convergence" by Larry Keeley in *ID Magazine* (New York), May 1994; "Richard Saul Wurman" in *Graphis* (Zürich), January 1995; "Life Among the Cyberfolk" by John Leo in *U.S. News and World Report,* 20 March 1995; "TED6: It's Alive" by Larry Keeley in *ID Magazine* (New York), May/June 1995; "TED6" by Stephanie Steyer-Coyne in *Communication Arts* (Palo Alto), July 1995.

\*       \*       \*

Richard Saul Wurman is unique among designers: educated as an architect (at the University of Pennsylvania), he has for decades pursued his own, personal vision of a career in what, when he began, was called "graphic design." It is now called that less and less, as a broad range of practitioners invent and explore appropriate and viable ways of communicating new, unfamiliar, often extremely dense and complex information to a wide range of audiences. Wurman was one of the first to do this, to think about the very nature of the specific information needing to be communicated, its meaning, its structure, the relationship and hierarchy of its components; and at least as important, what the information means to the people who will use it, how they will use it, and in what context. In this practice, which has extended over three decades, Wurman has turned many routine structures literally upside down in his indefatigable search for the right way to make information accessible and understandable, to make information—that which informs—out of mere data.

This profession, or practice, doesn't even have a name to keep pace with the stunning growth of data and our desperate need for people of insight and intelligence to organize it, to distill it, to structure it. Wurman calls himself and those with whom he feels a sense of shared endeavor "information architects." The phrase is understandable for Wurman, given his education and early career; other practitioners describe themselves as "information designers" or "information engineers"; some still retain the use of "graphic designers," which more and more seems to emphasize surface over content. Wurman's pursuit of understanding and his efforts to define and explore a new profession combining elements of several existing disciplines with new pursuits demanded by the democratization of technology is collaborative and inclusive. As he has found avenues for his own ideas he has opened up opportunities for other designers who share his point of view and commitment. It is important to realize that Wurman's strength is as much as impresario as thinker and designer.

Wurman has always combined insatiable curiosity with superhuman energy; add to this combination what he himself calls the advantage of needing to satisfy his own "dumbness": "I do these things so that I can understand them," he has often said. For "dumb" one should really read "rational," "logical," even "obvious." In a series of projects—courses, exhibitions, books, and conferences, and with a list of collaborators and associates that spans not only design, architecture, and planning, but business, medicine, social science, history, and statistics as well—Wurman has fashioned a unique career out of making usable connections between both disparate things and ideas and like things that have simply never been presented in usable form before.

A class project in 1962 at the University of North Carolina is an example of the latter. Students made clay models of a wide range of cities, ancient and modern, at a constant scale, and on panels of uniform size. Beijing and Paris require 12 panels each; Manhattan six; Amsterdam and Bern, one. For the first time, it is possible to compare not only city form but also city size. An understanding of the true meaning of comparison, and the context necessary for it to be meaningful, runs through Wurman's work: in *American Atlas* (1966), twenty American cities are compared and analyzed at a single scale and uniform statistical module. *U.S. Atlas,* first published in 1989, is the only road atlas structured the way people drive: each page is a days drive—250 miles x 250 miles, with a one-hour/50-mile grid. Time and distance are integrated: no longer is the driver tyrannized by political divisions irrelevant to his needs and experience—in this atlas as in life, Massachusetts is not adjacent to Maryland.

In 1981, with the publication of *LA Access,* Wurman singlehandedly reinvented the guidebook. Wurman's insight was that, if you are in an unfamiliar city and you know where you are, you want to know what's nearby—shops, culture, restaurants—at that moment. So, Wurman's Access guidebooks were organized geographically rather than by category. If, for example, you are at the corner of rue St. André des Arts and rue des Grands-Augustins in the St. Germain district of Paris, you can immediately ascertain that within a block radius are eight cafés and restaurants (from * to ***, and from $ to $$$$), two hotels, and nine points of interest. Although guides to architecture featuring walking and driving tours have long been organized by proximity, the Access books were the first coherent set of general purpose guides which addressed the immediate needs of a tourist at a particular place and time. Color-coded text clearly differentiated between the different categories of resources; biased to an intelligent and cultured audience, the books were written with charm and wit, and with a keen appreciation of history and architecture and an eye for the unusual and fascinating. The series grew to more than 30 titles by the time Wurman sold Access Press in 1991; since that time, the quality of the writing, the cartography, and the production values, have all markedly deteriorated.

With TUB (The Understanding Business), a sibling venture to Access Press sold at the same time, Wurman rationally reorganized, branded, and redesigned the San Francisco Smart yellow pages. The TED (Technology Entertainment Design) Conferences were begun by Wurman in 1984 and continue with annual meetings planned in Monterey, California.

Wurman moved to a huge Newport, Rhode Island "cottage" in 1993, where he directs a small staff in a warren of dormer-windowed low-ceilinged rooms on the third floor, working on his current wide-ranging projects: books, conferences, and exhibitions, including MEDICAL, a branch of TED, held in Charleston, South Carolina, in October 1995; *Information Architects,* jointly published by Graphis Press and Wurman in January 1996; and a conference about selling the transactional future, The $ Conference, held in Monterey in February 1996. He has also published his first two guidebooks in a new format under the imprint of TIPS (The Initial Press Syndicate) on Newport and Charleston.

—Joel Katz

# WYMAN, Lance

American graphic designer

**Born:** Newark, New Jersey, 2 July 1937. **Education:** Educated in public schools, Kearny, New Jersey, 1943-55; studied advertising, Fairleigh Dickinson College, Rutherford, New Jersey, 1955-56; studied design, Pratt Institute, Brooklyn, New York, BA, 1960. **Military Service:** Served in the United States Army Reserve, 1960-61, in the Michigan National Guard, 1961-63, and in the New York National Guard, 1963-66, Staff Sergeant. **Family:** Married Neila Cohalan in 1966; daughter: Stacey. **Career:** Designer, at General Motors Corporation, Detroit, 1960-61, William M. Schmidt Associates, Detroit, 1961-63, and with George Nelson and Company, New York, 1963-66; graphic design director, Summer Olympic Games, Mexico City, 1966-71; designer, Mexico City, 1966-71; founder/president, Wyman and Cannan Limited, New York, 1971-79; principal, Lance Wyman Limited, New York, from 1979. Instructor, Parsons School of Design, New York, from 1973; lecturer, University of Cincinnati, Ohio, 1990, and at universities throughout the United States and Mexico; also contributor of visual identity systems to community organizations and public activities, New York City, from 1972. **Member:** American Institute for Graphic Arts; Society for Environmental Graphic Design (board member, from 1989). **Exhibitions:** *Trademarks USA,* National Design Center, Chicago, 1964; *World Poster Art,* Museum of Modern Art, New York, 1968; *Graphics of the Mexican Olympics,* American Institute of Graphic Arts, New York, 1968; *L'Espace Collectif,* Centre de Creation Industrielle, Paris, 1970; *Mexican Stamps by Lance Wyman,* Smithsonian Institution, Washington, D.C., 1971; *Work by Lance Wyman and Bill Cannan,* Pratt Institute, Brooklyn,

**Lance Wyman: directional icons designed for the Museum of Natural History, New York, 1992**

New York, 1973; *Wyman and Cannan Company,* Kutztown State College, Pennsylvania, 1976; *Environmental Design,* American Institute of Graphic Arts, New York, 1978; *Abecedarian Art,* Camino Real Gallery, Mexico City, 1979; *Lance Wyman,* La Chinche Gallery, Mexico City, 1981; *Artists Against Nuclear Madness,* Parsons Exhibit Center, New York, 1982; **Collections:** Museum of Modern Art, New York; Cooper-Hewitt Museum, New York; Smithsonian Institution, Washington, D. C.; Poster Museum, Warsaw. **Honors:** Gold Plaque, Milan Triennale, 1968; Pratt Institute Achievement Award, New York, 1968; Gold Medal, Ministry of Education, Mexico, 1969; *Creativity* Magazine Prize, Mexico City, 1979; Honorary Professor, University of Guadalajara, Mexico, 1979; New York Art Directors Club Silver Medal, 1981; *Time* Magazine Best of the Year Award, New York, 1982; Académico de Honor, Mexican Academy of Design, 1986; fellow, Society for Environmental Graphic Design, 1992; Honor Award and Merit Award, Society for Environmental Graphic Design, 1993. **Address:** Lance Wyman Ltd., 118 W. 80th St., New York, New York 10024, U.S.A.

**Works**

Olympic graphics and signage program, for the Mexican Olympics Committee, 1966-68.

Graphics program, for the Camino Real Hotel, Mexico City, 1968.

Graphics program, for the Mexico City Metro System, 1969.

World Cup of Soccer poster, Mexico City, 1971.

*Dr. Martin Luther King Jr.* postage stamps, for Mexican government, 1971.

Four postage stamps to commemorate 1972 Munich and Sapporo Olympics, for United States Postal Service, 1972.

Maps and signage, for the Washington Metro System, 1974.

Graphics system, for the National Zoo, Washington D.C., 1975.

Graphic signage, for Jeddah International Airport, Saudi Arabia, 1978.

Architectural signage system, for Capitol Hill, Washington, D.C., 1979.

Graphic masterplan including zoo symbol, pedestrian and vehicular signing, and printed materials, for Minnesota Zoo, Minneapolis, Minnesota, 1981.

Central de Abasto graphics system, for the new market, Mexico City, 1982.

Signage and graphics masterplan, for Museum of Contemporary Art, Monterrey, Mexico, 1992.

Signage and graphics masterplan, for American Museum of Natural History, New York, 1992.

Corporate identity and graphic programs for clients including—Caleta Hotel, Mexico; Fambé Department Stores, Mexico; de Todo Stores, Mexico; HYLSA Steel Corp., Mexico; IMCE, Mexico; Leona Textiles, Mexico; NYLMEX Synthetic Fibers, Mexico; Odin Car Rentals, Mexico; Penóles Mining, Mexico; Titan Cartons, Mexico; Volkswagen Rent, Mexico; WCVB-TV, Boston; Oxford Development Group Ltd., Edmonton, Alberta, Canada; Syntex Corporation, Palo Alto, California; El Presidente Chapultepec Hotel, Mexico City.

Designer of signage and graphic systems, usually for publicly accessible spaces, for clients including—Toronto Dominion Square, Calgary, Alberta; Washington Mall, Smithsonian Institution, Washington, D.C.; Royal Saudi Air Force, Jeddah; Washington Convention Center, Washington, D.C.; First Canadian Centre,

Calgary; Jurica, Queretaro, Mexico; Manufacturers Hanover Plaza, New York; Hilton Hotel, Orlando, Florida; Irving Trust, New York; Lafayette Centre, Washington, D.C.; (visual identification for Child Survival program) UNICEF, United Nations, New York; The News Building, New York; (elevated pedestrian bridge system) Calgary +15, Calgary; Calgary Parking Commission; Shearson/American Express, New York; Methodist Hospital, Houston, Texas; Exchange Place Centre, Jersey City, New Jersey; USTA National Tennis Center, Flushing Meadows, New York; Prudential Center, Newark, New Jersey; Merrill Lynch, New York; West Concourse, Rockefeller Center, New York; Edmonton Pedway System, Alberta; Paine Webber-Lincoln Harbor, Weehawken, New Jersey; San Antonio Pictograms, San Antonio, Texas; Tampa Stadium, Tampa, Florida; Newark International Airport, Newark, New Jersey; Pan Am Building, New York; Toronto Underground, Ontario; Toronto Transit Commission; Papalote, The Children's Museum, Mexico City; New York City Subway; San Antonio Public Library, Texas; Mercer Cemetery, Trenton, New Jersey; City of Trenton, New Jersey.

## Publications

**By WYMAN: articles**—"Subway Signage" in *Subways,* New York, 1977; "Bodies in Motion: New Directions in Transportation Graphics" in *SEGD Messages* (Cambridge, Massachusetts), vol. 3, no. 1, Spring 1989; "Urban Legibility and Signs: Finding Our Way Around" in *The Wheel Extended* (Tokyo), vol. 19, no. 4, 1990; "Bridge Fest '90/University Village" in *GDEA Proceedings,* 1991; "A Multicultural View from Mexico City" in *Dimension* (Cambridge), vol. 1, no. 1, 1994; "Multicultural Environmental Graphic Design" in *Designing and Planning Environmental Graphics,* New York, 1994.

**On WYMAN: books**—*World and Image* by Mildred Constantine and Alan M. Fern, New York, 1968; *Signet, Signal, Symbol* by Walter Diethelm, Zürich, 1972; *World Sports Posters,* Warsaw, 1972; *Urban Spaces* by David Kenneth Specter, New York, 1974; *Public Transportation Systems* edited by the Institute of Business Administration, Tokyo, 1976; *The Federal Design Response,* American Institute of Graphic Arts, 1977; *Architectural Signing and Graphics* by John Follis and Dave Hammer, New York, 1979; *Visual Puns in Design* by Eli Kince, New York, 1982; *Signage,* New York, 1982; *Maps,* New York, 1982; *Design Systems for Corporations,* Tokyo, 1983; *A History of Graphic Design* by Philip Meggs, New York, 1983; *American Corporate Identity,* New York, 1986; *Marcas Simbolos y Logos en Mexico 2,* Mexico City, 1987; *Tipografica,* Buenos Aires, 1987; *Trademarks & Symbols of the World 2,* Tokyo, 1989; *Environmental Graphic Design USA/East,* Tokyo, 1989; *Sign Design,* New York, 1991; *International Logos & Trademarks: The 80s,* New York, 1991; *Museum and Art Gallery Graphics,* Edmonton, Alberta, 1991; *Animal Symbols 2,* Belgium, 1993; *Graphically Bold,* Carson, California, 1993; *Signs and Spaces,* Rockport, Massachusetts, 1994; *City Signs: Innovative Urban Graphics,* New York, 1994; **articles**—*American Philatelist* (Phoenix), September 1968, June 1969, November 1969, May 1970; *Graphis* (Zürich), December 1968; *Expansion* (Mexico City), 17 June 1970; *Design Quarterly* (Minneapolis), 1971; *Print Casebooks* (Washington, D.C.), no. 1, 1975, no. 6, 1984; *Urban Design* (New York), Summer 1977, Fall 1977, Winter 1977; *Smithsonian* (Washington, D.C.), December 1977; interview in *The School of Visual Arts Guide to Careers,* New York, 1987; *Identity* (Cincinnati, Ohio), Spring 1992, Fall 1993, January/February 1994; *I.D.* (New York), November 1993.

*

In looking back over my career as a graphic designer, I find that my work has ranged from postage stamps to a ten-ton architectural sign. However, my most significant designing has probably been that of graphic symbols in the form of trademarks, logos, and pictograms. I have designed or directed the design of some 300 graphic symbols, ranging from complete systems, such as the forty symbols that identified the sporting and cultural events of the Mexican Olympic Games, to the symbol that identifies our West 80th Street Block Association here in New York. I love designing symbols and figuring out interesting ways of using them, not only for international projects such as airports and Olympic Games, where graphic symbols bridge multi-language gaps, but in general. Graphic symbols can add a different kind of order and personality to a subway system, a zoo, or a city market place, where most people speak the same language.

Of course, I use words, too. I've designed more than thirty typefaces for making words, but my heart is with graphic symbols. They are one of our most ancient forms of communication, and we are still learning how to design and use them. If a picture is worth a thousand words, then a symbol, such as the Red Cross, for example, is certainly worth a thousand pictures. Sometimes the simple, direct expression of a graphic symbol works better than anything else to identify a corporation or an institution, to mark a trail at the zoo, or to give directions. The directional arrow, probably our most used graphic symbol, can tell us which way to go without saying a word. Einstein once said that "everything should be made as simple as possible, but not simpler." I think this is good advice for a graphic designer.

—Lance Wyman

\*       \*       \*

The graphic communications system designed by Lance Wyman for the XIX Olympiad is a bellwether project in the evolution of graphic design. Wishing to create an image that could evoke the spirit of the host nation, Mexico, Wyman made extensive study of Mexican folk art and Aztec relics, which led him to two motifs: repeated multiple lines to form patterns and bright color. Using them, Wyman developed an alphabet composed of five bands or ribbons to be used for the logo, "MEXICO 68," and all titling on brochures, signage, and others. To accommodate a multilingual audience, Wyman used pictographs and color-coding to communicate with visitors from nations around the world. A set of twenty sports pictographs communicated nonverbally through images of the equipment while an additional twenty pictographs symbolized cultural events. Color coding and pictographs conveyed information on tickets. A pictographic clock, for example, communicated the time for an event to all visitors regardless of their language.

Because the XIX Olympiad was held in facilities located in and around one of the world's largest cities, rather than in a specially constructed facility, Wyman created an environmental signage system using modular components. A rainbow of colors was used on the official maps, and color bands were painted onto the curbs of the corresponding streets. The design system of pictographs and color-coding was so effective that the *New York Times* observed that a visitor to the Mexico Olympics could "be illiterate in all languages as long as you are not colorblind." The complex exterior environmental system developed by Wyman and Murdoch was composed of modular and interchangeable parts, which included directional signs, clocks, mailboxes, telephones, and maps. Thirty informational kiosks, placed at strategic locations throughout Mexico City, were covered with the sports pictographs printed in bright, vibrant colors. In addition to providing information to thousands of visitors from all over the world, the totality of Wyman's design system for the XIX Olympiad provided a joyous, celebratory aspect that commemorated the Olympic games and provided a source of national pride for Mexico, an emerging nation that was striving toward a more progressive and prominent role in the community of nations. Since his return to New York, Wyman has applied his knowledge and experience to visual identification and systems design for numerous clients.

—Philip B. Meggs

# YABU, George

Canadian interior, furniture, and textile designer

**Born:** Toronto, Ontario, 30 July 1953. **Education:** Studied interior design at Ryerson Polytechnic Institute (now Ryerson Polytechnic University), B.A., 1976. **Career:** Co-founder, with Glenn Pushelberg, Yabu Pushelberg interior design firm, from 1980. **Member:** Association of Registered Interior Designers of Ontario (ARIDO); American Society of Interior Designers (ASID); National Association of Japanese Canadians (NAJC). **Collections:** Royal Ontario Museum, Toronto. **Honors:** Corporate Design award, ARIDO, 1987, 1988, 1990; Corporate/Retail Design award, ARIDO, 1987; Corporate/Retail Design award, ICSC International, 1987; Retail/Mixed Use Design award, ARIDO, 1987, 1988; Retail Design, ID International, 1987; Retail Design award, Institute of Store Planners, 1987; Retail Design award, ARIDO, 1987, 1988, 1990; Hospitality Design award, ARIDO, 1987, 1990; Design Principal of the Year, ARIDO, 1987, 1990, 1993; Hospitality Design award, *Interiors* magazine, 1988; Hospitality Design award, East Meets West (USA), 1988; Furniture Design award, ARIDO, 1988; Award of Exellence, *Contract* magazine, 1990; Toronto Arts Award, Arts Foundation of Toronto, 1990; Best of the Best International award, ASID, 1991; Retail/Mixed Use Design award, *Interiors* magazine, 1991; Award of Excellence, Art Directors Club of Toronto, 1992; Entertainment Design award, *Architectural Record* magazine, 1993; Entertainment Design award, *Interiors* magazine, 1994; Design Distinction award, IIDA, 1995; Design Distinction Award, *I.D.* magazine annual design review, 1995. **Address:** Yabu Pushelberg, 55 Booth Avenue, Toronto, Ontario, Canada, M4M 2M3.

## Works

Interior design, for Club Monaco Shops, North America, 1985-1991.

Interior design, for Leone Department Store, Vancouver, Canada, 1986.

Interior design, for Capezio Stores, Canada, 1986.

Interior design, for Cineplex Odeon, Canada, 1987.

Interior design, for Terrelonge Design Offices and Studio, Toronto, 1987.

Interior design, for Celadon Stores, Toronto, 1988.

Interior design, for Le Chateau Stores, Canada, 1988.

Interior design, for Les Cours Mont Royal Shopping Centre, Montreal, 1988.

Interior design, for Sunrise Department Store, Hsin Chiu, Taiwan, 1988.

Interior design, for Park Plaza Hotel, Toronto, 1988.

Interior design, for Stilife Nightclub, Toronto, 1988.

Interior design, for Issey Miyake, Toronto, 1989.

Interior design, for Alfred Sung, Toronto, 1991.

Interior design, for Sunrise Department Store, Taipei, Taiwan, 1992.

Interior design, for ATT Department Stores, Taipei, Taiwan, 1992-93.

*Beehive* and *Faces* carpets, for Tai Ping Carpets, Hong Kong, 1993.

*Virso* tables for ICF/Nienkämper, Toronto and New York, 1993.

Louis chairs and chesterfields, for Louis Furniture, Toronto, 1993.

Interior design, for Sukhothai Restaurant, Toronto, 1993.

Interior design, for Galerie des Beaux Arts, Pei Tao, Taiwan, 1993.

Interior design, for Royton Hotel, Sapporo, Japan, 1993.

Interior design, for Sotto Voce Wine Bar, Toronto, 1993.

Interior design, for The Princess of Wales Theatre, Toronto, 1993.

Interior design, for Matsuya Department Store, Fukuoka, Japan, 1994.

Interior design, for Tennoji Railway Terminal, Osaka, Japan, 1995.

Interior design, for Corporate Headquarters, *South China Morning Post* newspaper, Hong Kong, 1995.

Interior design, for Corporate Headquarters, OTP Bank, Budapest Hungary, 1995.

Interior design, for Plaza Escada, Vancouver, 1995.

Interior design, for Dai Myou Bashi restaurant, Toronto, 1995.

Interior design, for Canoe Restaurant, Toronto, 1995.

Interior design, for The First Lifestyle Store, Osaka, Japan, 1995.

Interior design, for Ciaopanic Lifestyle Store, Osaka, 1995.

Interior design, for Ivory Lounge, Toronto, 1995.

Interior design, for Bellair Café, Toronto, 1995.

Interior design, for Corporate Design Group studio and offices, Northern Telecom, Ottawa, 1995.

Interior design, for Japan Foundation Cultural Centre, Toronto, 1995.

Interior design, for Iceberg Store and Shop-in-Shops, Europe, Asia, North America, from 1995.

## Publications

**On YABU: articles**—*Globe and Mail* (Toronto), June 1985, September 1990, December 1993, May 1993, March 1995; *Canadian Interiors,* December 1985, May/June 1987, September 1987, September 1988, November/December 1988, November/December 1990, May/June 1991; *Visual Merchandising & Design,* August 1986, April 1989, November 1990, December 1993; *Interior Design* (New York), November 1986, July 1987, January 1988, March 1989, June 1991, December 1993; *Contract* (New York), January/February 1987, November/December 1988, June/July 1990, December/January 1991, February/March 1991; *Canadian Architect* (Don Mills), April 1987, July 1995; *Toronto Life Fashion* (Toronto) Spring 1987; *International Design* (New York), July/August 1987, May/June 1988, September 1995; *Worldwide Interiors,* January 1987; *Sun* (Vancouver), May 1987; *Intramuros,* September 1987; *Star* (Toronto), October 1987, April 1993, May 1993, December 1993; *Interiors* (New York), January 1988, December 1988, April 1989, June 1991, December 1992, January 1994; *Toronto,* May 1988, October 1990; *House and Home,* May/June 1988; *Interna-*

Yabu Pushelberg: interior of main hall looking toward design studio. Photo: David Whittaker

tional Design (New York), September 1988; International Lighting Review, Autumn 1988; Retail Merchandising, October 1988; Azure, November/December 1988; Nikkei Architecture (Tokyo), March 1989; Fusion Planning, Spring 1989; International Design Network, Spring 1989; Rotunda, Spring 1990; Flare (Long Beach), March 1990; En Route, August 1990; World of International Design, Autumn 1990, Autumn 1991, July 1995; Design Journal, November/December 1990; Canadian Hotel and Restuarant, May 1991; Pronto, June 1991; Pace, June 1991; Progressive Architec-

ture (New York), October 1991; Chatelaine, December 1993; International Contract, December 1993; Lighting Design (New York), December 1993; Architectural Record (New York), September 1993; City and Country Home, June 1993; In-Site (London), September 1993; NOW, May 1993; Shotenkenshiku (Japan) January, 1994; Interior (United Kingdom), January 1994; Canadian House and Home, June 1995, August 1995.

*

As with many other northern cultures, Canadians have the reputation of being diffident and introspective, suspicious of artifice and ostentation. Like most cliches, this one has a strong element of truth in it. It seems to be in our natures to strip down ourselves, other people, and situations, to reveal them for what they really are. I believe this same impulse permeates the Canadian design aesthetic, leading us to expose the true nature of forms and materials, paring away superfluous details and clutter and letting the essence of the object and of the medium carry the weight of the design.

To the more established cultures of Europe and Asia, this rather earnest approach simply betrays North America's lack of an established culture. Obviously, it coincides with the major design movement of this century, which I believe has helped Canadian design gain momentum and coherence in the second half of the century. Without a rooted, centuries-old indigenous culture to access, Canadians are forced to look elsewhere to express something that is truly their own—to do otherwise would be to trivialize both the design process and the end result. Canadian designers choose to focus on materials and processes for their inspiration.

To that extent, I would have to say that my work is part of the Canadian design aesthetic, although I have never wanted to imitate a particular style, or to form or follow specific design doctrines. The most important thing about fads and trends is to understand them well enough so that you can stay away from them. Instead, I try to approach each project and client with a clean slate, and to explore and discover design solutions that are the most appropriate in that situation.

Introspective tendencies and the impulse to seek consensus are equally part of the Canadian character. I find in my own work that this expresses itself through a particular sensitivity to ambience, and to the psychological importance of interiors to the user and the client. I have always felt that it is crucial to build a creative consensus, to satisfy the needs of the client and user of the facility as well as my own creative impulses.

I have always tried to push the possibilities of proportion and scale, colour, light, texture, and the manipulation of space to create impressions of mystery, sanctuary, serenity, and comfort. With regard to the latter, the impression of luxury is in the design details, not necessarily in the materials themselves. What continues to interest me is experimenting with new applications for 'off-the-shelf' catalogue lighting, hardware, and industrial products, and using simple, prosaic materials like particle board, etc., in fresh and unusual applications.

To be a Canadian designer, living in a culture less than two hundred years old, is not to be provincial. In fact, the opposite is true: we are freed from convention, and not stifled by the feeling that all of the answers have already been discovered. We are free to look inward, to our own sources of inspiration, and at the same time to look beyond our local environment, to travel, research new materials, network with other designers, manufacturers and architects, striving continually to relearn and rethink our purpose.

—George Yabu

\*    \*    \*

Founded by George Yabu and Glenn Pushelberg in 1980, the Toronto-based interior design firm Yabu Pushelberg raised the profile of design in Canada, winning numerous international awards for large and small retail projects, restaurants, and nightclubs.

Yabu and Pushelberg met while studying interior design at Ryerson Polytechnic Institute in Toronto. Four years after graduating, they chose to open their own consultancy. Yabu heads the design team and Pushelberg supervises marketing and client relations.

The firm made its first international impact with its 1986 design for the nightclub Stilife. Yabu Pushelberg transformed the club's potential setback—its location in the basement of a former warehouse—into an asset by emphasizing architectural details that would enhance the impression of a descent into the underworld. Yabu Pushelberg left much of the existing pipes and raw concrete exposed. Undulating metal-chain partitions created a sinister yet seductive gateway onto the dance floor. Cone-shaped, sheet-metal sinks, and cubicles with porthole mirrors, made the bathrooms equally important social spaces. Stilife ignited a fever for nightclubs in Toronto and revived the city's derelict garment district.

Yabu Pushelberg's first interior design work for commercial shopping malls began in 1987 with its retrofit design of Les Cours Mont-Royal in Montréal. Converting the turn-of-the century four-level hotel, Yabu Pushelberg eschewed cookie-cutter sameness in its design. Instead, irregularly-shaped balconies and a custom-patterned terrazzo floor created sculptural intimacy and complexity.

Yabu Pushelberg broadened its markets to include Asia in 1989. Commissioned to design the high-end Sunrise Department Store in Taiwan, Yabu Pushelberg's challenge was to create a retail environment that combined sophisticated North American store planning with sensitivity to Chinese culture. Yabu Pushelberg created a 250,000-square-foot masterpiece of custom design. In Taiwan, where materials are expensive but labour is cheap, Yabu Pushelberg made innovative use of low-cost materials through extensive sculptural detailing. For example, from ubiquitous bathroom tiles, Yabu Pushelberg created spectacular floor and wall designs featuring ancient Chinese-inspired patterns. Yabu Pushelberg trained local craftsman in the faux-finish art of polished plaster, starting a trend in Taiwan. Sculptural details included steel shirt buttons for drawer pulls in the men's shirt and tie department, as well as reversed basketball nets as stools in the sporting goods area.

Their most important recent project is the Princess of Wales Theatre completed in 1993 for entertainment mogul David Mirvish. Yabu Pushelberg's design holds its own alongside commissioned murals by Frank Stella and within the architectural framework of Lett/Smith Architects. Venetian cut glass, Minoan-like tile mosaics, and sprinkler heads concealed in flower-shaped ceiling recesses all contribute to a sense of theatricality in the building's lobby.

Yabu Pushelberg is distinctive for their preference for custom design over catalogue specification. The firm is renowned for marrying the Old World arts and crafts trades with contemporary styling. Masters with materials and lighting, they obscure the boundaries of spaces with curved walls and translucent partitions.

Over the years, Yabu Pushelberg's designs have evolved from experimental punk, to conspicuous opulence, to the ecological, post-recessionary restraint of the 1990s. Whatever Yabu Pushelberg's phase the adjectives—theatrical, sculptural, eclectic, colourful, curvaceous, handcrafted—always hold true of the company's work.

—Elizabeth Crawford and Rachel Gotlieb

# YAMAMOTO, Kansai

Japanese fashion designer

**Born:** Yokohama in 1944. **Education:** Studied civil engineering, at Yokohama High School, 1959-62; studied English literature at Nippon

University, Tokyo, 1962-65. **Career:** Worked as an assistant designer, in Hisashi Hosono Studio, Tokyo, 1966-70; freelance designer, establishing his own fashion company, Yamamoto Kansai Company, Ltd., Tokyo, from 1971; first Paris showing, 1975; opened Kansai Boutique, Paris, 1977; produces ready-to-wear men's clothing, bags, household linens, and stationery. **Exhibitions:** *Fashion: An Anthology,* Victoria and Albert Museum, London, 1971. **Collections:** Victoria and Albert Museum, London. **Awards:** Soen Prize, Bunka College of Fashion, 1967; Fashion Editors Award, Tokyo, 1977. **Address:** 4-3-15 Jungumae, Shibuya-ku, Tokyo 150, Japan.

## Publications

**On YAMAMOTO: books**—*Fashion: An Anthology by Cecil Beaton,* exhibition catalogue compiled by Madeleine Ginsburg, London, 1971; *The World of Fashion: People, Places, Resources* by Eleanor Lambert, New York and London, 1976; *In Vogue: Sixty Years of Celebrities and Fashion* edited by Georgina Howell, New York, 1976; *Fashion 2001* by Lucille Khornak, London and New York, 1982; *McDowell's Directory of Twentieth Century Fashion* by Colin McDowell, London, 1984; *New Fashion Japan* by Leonard Koren, Tokyo, New York, and San Francisco, 1984; *The Encyclopaedia of Fashion from 1840 to the 1980s* by Georgina O'Hara, London, 1986; *Japanese Design* by Penny Sparke, London, 1987; *Advancing Towards the Future,* Tokyo, 1988; **articles**—"Kansai Confidence" by Bobbie Queen in *Women's Wear Daily* (New York), 28 January 1985; "Future Shock, with the Brilliant Innovators of Japanese Fashion" by Maggie Steber in *Connoisseur,* September 1986; "Zen and the Art of the Real Shirt" by Charlotte DuCann in *The Independent* (London), 29 June 1989; "Au vrai chic wendersein" by Frédéric Strauss in *Cahiers du Cinema* (Paris), December 1989; "Sailing to Byzantium: A Fashion Odyssey, 1990-1991" by Richard Martin in *Textile and Text,* 14 February 1991.

*       *       *

The fashion press has commented that some of Kansai Yamamoto's creations have the appeal of collector's items, due to his exquisite attention to detailed decoration. These views, expressed in 1981, harken back to his first English collection of 1971, which was based on Japanese Kabuki costume. The clothes did not sell but were widely talked about because of their rich colours and fabrics. He has built on that experience to produce clothes which combine Japanese and Western influences, function and fantasy. Not hard to find is the inspiration for an embroidered dragon motif or for the huge mohair sweater with the simple moon-and mountain motif seen in Paris in summer 1977. However, sources of his designs are by no means always Japanese. His layered, oversize look of 1974 was perhaps as much Peruvian as Oriental. In 1976, he introduced white and brightly coloured miniskirts, some with small front panels, which had a distinctly Egyptian flavour.

The particular quality that unifies his designs is an adventurous approach to colour and surface effects. Quite simple shapes have become canvases for brightly abstract and complex naturalistic designs. His love of beading, appliqué, embroidery, and rich fabrics has made his garments expensive, but these clothes have produced ideas which have been adapted for ready-to-wear, printed T-shirts, and separates. For him, the T-shirt dress is an ideally simple, sensible garment, which reflects his concern with the functional role of clothing. Despite their often dazzling surfaces, his clothes are created to be easy to wear.

His space-age suits show that his thoughts are on the future. Theatrical in appearance, with their large, pointed shoulders and often metal like surfaces, these suits show an awareness of a need for future change in clothing concepts. While his backless, transparent, plastic rainsuits shown in 1977 might have been dismissed as pure fantasy at the time, the future may reveal the innovative power of such garments. He proved himself one of the exciting Japanese designers of the 1970s.

In the 1980s, Yamamoto remained an intriguing presence in the fashion world. His embrace of Japanese popular culture did not create a sensation in the West, but to select admirers his work is joyously original, often theatrical, but still wearable. Yamamoto said in 1985 that his designs are not for those who are interested in "chicness," but for those who want to create bold visual "exclamations."

—Hazel Clark

# YAMAMOTO, Yohji

Japanese fashion designer

**Born:** Yokohama, Japan, 1943. **Education:** Graduated in law, Keio University, 1966; studied fashion, Fashion Culture Institute, Tokyo, 1966-1969; won scholarship to study in Paris, 1969. **Career:** Worked in haute couture industry, Paris, 1970-71; established own company, Y's, offering moderately priced women's wear, Tokyo, 1972; added men's line to Y's offerings, 1977; showed first couture collection in Tokyo, 1981, and in Paris, 1982; established Yohji Yamamoto Incorporated, 1984; markets clothing through his own retail outlets in Japan and abroad. **Honors:** Soen and Endu prizes, Tokyo, 1969; Fashion Editors Club Award, Tokyo, 1982 and 1991; Mainichi Grand Prize, 1986. **Address:** San Shin Building 1, 1-22-11 Higashi Shibuya-ku, Tokyo, Japan.

## Publications

**On YAMAMOTO: books**—*A New Wave in Fashion: 3 Japanese Designers,* exhibition catalogue, Phoenix, Arizona, 1983; *New Fashion Japan* by Leonard Koren, Tokyo, 1984; *Scenes from the Fashionable World* by Kennedy Fraser, New York, 1987; *Japanese Design* by Penny Sparke, London, 1987; *The Fashion Conspiracy* by Nicholas Coleridge, London, 1988; **articles**—"In Pursuit of Excellence" in *i-D* (London), May 1987; "Yohji Yamamoto: Fashion Designer" in *Blueprint* (London), February 1987; "Mr. Yamamoto Comes Back to Town" in *Blueprint* (London), December 1987; "Yohji Yamamoto: La Vie d'Artiste" in *Elle* (Paris), 19 September 1988; "A Life in the Day of Yohji Yamamoto" by Georgina Montagu in *Sunday Times Magazine* (London), 26 February 1989; "Yohji by Knight; Photography at Work" by Kathryn Flett in *The Face* (London), April 1989; "Le Long Voyage a la Recontre de Yohji Yamamoto" by Ainree Deslaudieres in *L'Officiel* (Paris), May 1989; "Yohji Yamamoto: Les femmes et moi" in *Vogue* (Paris), November 1989; "Go Yohji, Go!" by Deyan Sudjic in *Sunday Times Magazine* (London), 2 December 1990; "The Paris Collections: The Ideas of March: Yohji Yamamoto" in *Women's Wear Daily* (New York), 17 March

1995; "In Paris, Outsiders are Officially In" by Amy M. Spindler in *New York Times,* 16 October 1995; "Cyber-SoHo and Free Shirts: A Golden Week for Hubbub" by Jonathan Napack in *New York Observer,* 30 October 1995; films—*Notebook on Cities and Clothes* by Wim Wenders, 1991.

# YANAGI, Sori

Japanese industrial designer

**Born:** Tokyo, 29 June 1915. **Education:** Studied oil painting at the National University of Arts, Tokyo, 1936-40; apprenticed as a designer, in the office of architect Junzo Sakakura, Tokyo 1940-42. **Family:** Married Fumiko Nakanishi in 1981; children: Shinichi, Mariko, Muneaki, and Michiko. **Career:** Assistant to designer Charlotte Perriand, Tokyo, 1942; designer, working for various agencies, Tokyo, from 1946; founder and director of Yanagi Industrial Design Office, Tokyo, from 1952; designed for Matsumura Ceramics, Tendo Mokko (wooden furniture), Kotobuki (metal and plastic furniture), Mitsui-seiki (automobiles), Shussai Potteries, Tajimi Ceramic Institute, Kyoto-Gojozaka Kilns, Yamaya Glass, Hakusan-toki, Akita-mokko (bent wood furniture), Aoki Ceramics Japan, and others. Director, Japan Folk Crafts Museum, Tokyo, from 1977. Lecturer, Women's College of Art, Tokyo, 1953-54; professor, Kanazawa University of Arts and Crafts, from 1954; visiting professor, Staatliche Werkkunstschule, Kassel, Germany, 1961-62. **Member:** Founding member, Japan Industrial Designers Association; Japan Committee on International Design, Tokyo, 1953; executive committee member, World Design Conference, Tokyo, 1960. **Exhibitions:** Matsuya Department Store, Tokyo, 1956; *Documenta,* Kassel, 1964; Padigilione d'Arte Moderna, Milan, 1980; Italian Cultural Center, Tokyo, 1983. **Collections:** Musée du Louvre, Paris; Stedelijk Museum, Amsterdam; Metropolitan Museum of Art, New York; Museum of Modern Art, New York. **Honors:** Japanese Industrial Design Competition Prize, Tokyo, 1951; Gold Medal, Milan Triennale, 1957; Honorary Member, Accademia Tiberina, Rome, 1978; Honorary Member, Finnish Designers Association, Helsinki, 1981; Order of the Purple Ribbon, Tokyo, 1981. **Address:** Yanagi Design Office, 8 Honshio-cho, Shinjuku-ku, Tokyo 160, Japan.

## Works

Stacking ashtray in ironstone china, for Matsumura China Company, 1950.
Record player and radio, for Nihon-Columbia, Tokyo, 1952.
*Speed* kettle, for Nikkei Aluminum, Tokyo, 1953.
Stacking stool in fiberglass, for Kotobuki Company, 1954.
*Orient* three-wheeled car, for Mitsu-seiki Company, 1956.
*Butterfly Stool* in plywood and steel, for Tendo Mokko Company, 1956.
Teapot in porcelain with bamboo handle, for Tajimi Ceramic Institute, 1956.
Soy-sauce container, for Tajimi Ceramic Institute, 1956.
Teapot in black ironglaze with rattan handle, for Kyoto-Gojozaka Kiln, 1958.
Pitcher in stainless steel, for Uehan Shoji Company, 1958.
Casserole in black ironglaze, for Shussai Kiln, 1960.

Torch, for Eighteenth Olympic Games, Tokyo, 1964.
Stacking chair in polypropylene and tubular steel, for Kotobuki Company, 1965.
Water jug in clear glass, for Yamaya Glass Company, 1967.
Stacking chairs and tables in molded beech, for Akita-mokko Company, 1967.
Torch, for the Winter Olympics, Sapporo, 1972.
Sales kiosk with hood shutter, for the Yokohama Subway, 1973.
Small teapot in porcelain, for Hakusan-toki Company, 1975.
Armchair in solid beech, for Tendo-mokko Company, 1978.
Sound-absorbing screen-panel, for the Tomei super highway, Tokyo, 1980.
Stainless tableware, for Sato Shoji, 1980-90.
Porcelain dinnerware, for Ceramic Japan Company, 1988.
Valves and tap handles, for Kitz Ltd., 1990-95.
Tomei Ashigara Suspension Bridge, 1992.
Kan-etsue Tunnel mouth design, 1993.
Tokyo Bay trans-bay highway tollgate, 1995.

## Publications

**By YANAGI: books**—*Sori Yanagi: Design,* with introduction by Charlotte Perriand, Tokyo, 1983.

**On YANAGI: books**—*New Furniture 6* edited by Gerd Hatje, Stuttgart and London, 1962; *Il Disegno Industriale e la sua Estetica* by Gillo Dorfles, Bologna, 1963; *The Modern Chair, 1860 to Today* by Guilbert Frey, London and Niederteufen, 1970; *Design no Otoshi Ana: Symposium — 20 seiki no yoshiki, katachi to kokoro 1930-75,* Tokyo, 1975; *Contemporary Furniture* edited by Klaus Jurgen Sembach, Stuttgart and London, 1982; *Contemporary Vessels: How to Pour,* exhibition catalogue, Tokyo, 1982; *Japanese Design* by Penny Sparke, London, 1987; *Japanese Design: A Survey Since 1950* edited by Kathryn Heisinger and Felice Fischer, Philadelphia, 1994; *Design no "Kentoshi" no koro: Show no Design, Pioneahen,* Tokyo, 1995; **articles**—"Decor: Era of the Machine-made and Decoration" in *Space Design* (Tokyo), April 1977; *Design,* March 1978; *Industrial Design,* no. 123, August 1983; *Design no Genba,* October 1988; *Nikkei Design,* April 1990; *New Furniture,* June 1991; *JSSD,* vol. 1, 1993; "Interview with Yanagi Sori" in *Serai,* January 1995; "Is Design Evolving?" in *BRUTUS,* 1 June 1995.

\*

The most important factor in "design" must be one's mind. In the real sense of the word, "design" does not exist without creation. That is the reason something lacking creativity is mere imitation and cannot be called true design. Creative design does not concern itself with superficial alterations in outward appearance. Rather, it works out original means of reforming the inner structure. The beauty of design cannot be achieved by mere cosmetic change. It must exude from within. Whether a design results in success or not, its quality hinges upon the process by which it is made. Here, the workshop has a central role. Basic concepts and beautiful forms do not come from the drawing board alone.

Scientific technique is helpful for creating design images and undoubtedly contributes to developing fresh artistic presentations. But needless to say, each scientific technique has its own characteristics and respectively has its own limits. Therefore, scientific techniques can go against the design's intrinsic nature, depending on

Sori Yanagi: *Butterfly* stool, 1954

Sound designs are found in a sound society. Such a society can be defined as one that is held together by the principle of *gemeinschaft*. When people are unified in such a common spirit, designs that attempt to deceive the public will probably not be produced. With the depleting of the earth's limited resources, a more acute problem by the day, the curtain will be coming down hard and fast upon designs that merely fuel the fires of economic growth and promote high stock turnover and consumerism. For the survival of civilization, man will have to turn back, re-examine his roots, and reflect deeply on the course he is to take. As for design, the problem is similar. The time has come for us to take a step back and think over the ultimate question: What is design?

—Sori Yanagi

\*     \*     \*

Sori Yanagi is an internationally-known designer who has established his own context in industrial design in Japan. A designer of products, particularly domestic products, he has been strongly influenced by Walter Gropius and the Bauhaus philosophy; he also inherited purely modern design concepts from Charlotte Perriand.

His father, Soetsu Yanagi, was the first advocate in Japan of applying artistic concepts to individual items used in the average home; his interest was in utensils, the instruments of daily life. His concept—"what is useful is beautiful"—was not so different in its artistic philosophy from that which informs Western functionalism; as well, it reflects traditional Japanese views on the making of goods and Japanese aesthetics and ethics.

Growing up in such an environment, Yanagi absorbed his father's principles, but he established his own unique, modern individuality when still quite young. As early as the 1950s, Yanagi was already his own man, and his works from then until now are glorious. They are all handmade, and each work has a presence and beauty of form that is appropriate to the modern world but that revitalizes the essence of traditional Japanese forms.

Industrial society in Japan enjoyed its greatest growth in the 1960s. There were, of course, many positive results, but such rapid growth also revealed and created new problems. Industrialists placed the highest priority on economy and on efficiency in production—and design itself was too often judged according to such criteria. Yanagi has been openly critical of such attitudes. He believes that designers should be autonomous, that they should resist becoming the servants of materialism or of the worst aspects of modern industrialism. Among his targets have been showy designs, the bastardization of arts, the intrusion of government in setting design policies in developing countries, the degradation of design techniques by commercialism, and the countless products churned out by industries obviously oblivious to the ways in which people actually live.

His attitude is best expressed in his own words:

"Design is a culture of mankind as a whole. As design finds itself moving with vigorous momentum through the changing and merging of various regional cultures toward an everlasting unit and a future world culture, the timing will no doubt come when the authenticity of an integrated human culture can be established. At present, however, amid the confusion caused in the transition from the age of handicrafts to the age of the machine, and with the many contradictions that emerge suddenly with the advance of modernization, it is not yet possible."

how it is utilized. It must also be remembered that scientific knowledge can work as a brake upon design creativity.

So-called market research is little help in the production of a good design. In fact, for the creative designer, it is an inhibiting factor. Market research consists of the analysis of past data, whereas the primary mission of the designer whose aim is creative work, lies in bringing forth something superior to anything that has existed in the past. On the other hand, the cooperation of the flexible-minded, forward-looking, skilled techniques is vital. Success or failure in producing a good design depends in large upon finding such well-qualified associates and also upon the way in which they are allowed to contribute to the work. Another person who must share with the designer the credit for a good design is the business executive who is able to recognize a good design and who commissions a qualified designer to create it. Well designed products are born under the patronage of the business executive who regards his products with a genuine pride and love. The "productmanship" of such a person is equivalent to the craftsmanship which goes into the creation of handmade articles.

The articles which sell well today are not necessarily well designed, and conversely, well designed articles do not necessarily sell well. For today's designer, it is not enough to work merely with the aim of creating good designs. He must also take into consideration what is likely to sell. That means he must discover the point at which good design and salability come together. The majority of today's designs bow subserviently to current tastes. But true design consists in challenging the prevailing fashion.

At the heart of folk crafts, it is possible for us to see the fundamental circumstances of human existence. Their purity enables us to drink at the fountain-head of beauty. Such folk crafts make us consider the meaning of modernization. Tradition exists in the cause of creation. Good design without tradition and creation is inconceivable.

What is needed, in Yanagi's view, is that designers must stand their ground: they must coolly contemplate the alternative, then resolve to become the leaders, not the blind followers, of industrial progress—and never consider compromise until that brave new world he describes has come to pass.

—Kunio Sano

# YANEFF, Chris

Canadian advertising executive and graphic designer

**Born:** Toronto, Ontario, 18 May 1933. **Education:** Attended Central Technical School; studied graphic design, Ontario College of Art, Toronto; studied advertising and marketing at the University of Toronto. **Family:** Married Kathleen Anna (died); children: Gregory Mark, Martha Jane. **Career:** Art director, *The Financial Post,* Toronto, 1949-56; president and owner, Chris Yaneff Ltd., from 1956; director, Yaneff Gallery, from 1975. Former graphic designer, Stratford Shakespearean Festival, Stratford, Ontario; former associate professor of visual arts, York University, Toronto; advisor, George Brown College, and Georgian College. **Member:** Past president, Graphic Designers of Canada; past director and treasurer, Royal College of Art; Professional Art Dealers Association. **Address:** 12295 Highway 50, Bolton, Ontario L7E 1M2, Canada.

## Publications

**By YANEFF: books**—*Trademarks by Chris Yaneff Ltd.,* Toronto, 1974.

**On YANEFF: articles**—"Chris Yaneff/Fred Gotthans" by Winnie Czulinski in *Studio Magazine* (Canada), July-August 1989.

\*      \*      \*

Chris Yaneff Limited is a graphic design firm specializing in corporate trademark design. Established in 1956, the firm's client list includes many of the largest corporations in Canada.

Chris Yaneff was born in Toronto. He studied graphic design at the Ontario College of Art and advertising and marketing at the University of Toronto. In 1949 he joined MacLean Hunter Publishers as art director of the *Financial Post.* He founded Chris Yaneff Ltd. in 1956. Fred Gotthans was born in Mannheim, Germany. He apprenticed in Germany before coming to Canada and working for the *Financial Post,* where he met Yaneff. He joined Chris Yaneff Ltd. as creative director in 1959.

Within the partnership the outgoing Yaneff handles marketing and client relations while Gotthans carries out the graphic design. The firm also specializes in public relations and advertising. One of Yaneff's first clients was Commodore Business Machines, a tiny typewriter shop in Toronto. He designed a logo for them in return for a small fee and a used typewriter. The company went on to produce the first mass-market personal computer, each one with Yaneff's stylized "C" symbol.

In 1960 the firm created a design familiar to most Canadians: the Windsor Salt box. Gotthans used the recently released type face Helvetica with a bold pattern of blue and gold circles on a white field. The clean, modern rectangular package is still seen on grocery store shelves today.

Trained in Europe, Gotthans adheres to the Swiss style of graphic design, a grid-based system with narrow columns of text and a preference for sans serif typefaces. Building on this system, the firm has developed strong criteria for trademark design. For Chris Yaneff Ltd., a symbol must work equally well in black-and-white and in color, and look good ten feet away and reduced to the size of your fingernail.

Conklin Shows, the production company responsible for the Canadian National Exhibition, Canada's largest fair, hired Chris Yaneff Ltd. in 1959 to design a symbol. Yaneff and Gotthans came up with a stylized clown's face which became instantly recognizable and now, 30 years later, stands alone without the Conklin name.

The firm of Chris Yaneff Limited has designed symbols for some of Canada's largest companies including: Rogers Broadcasting, Canada Trust, Sheridan Nurseries, Crown Life, New Brunswick Hydro, Monarch Industries, Maple Leaf Mills, and Hunt Windows & Doors.

—Elizabeth Crawford

# YANG, Jay

American textile and furnishing designer

**Born:** Hsin-Chu, Taiwan, in 1946; emigrated to the United States in 1967, naturalized, 1977. **Education:** Studied under Neil Welliver, at the University of Pennsylvania, Philadelphia, M.F.A., 1970. **Family:** Married Myra Hines in 1973. **Career:** Illustrator, New York, 1970-73; freelance textile and home furnishings designer, New York, from 1973; founder and president of Jay Yang Designs Limited, New York, from 1975. **Honors:** Paritex Design Award, Paris, 1980; Editeurs-Createurs Design Award, Paris, 1982. **Address:** Jay Yang Designs Limited, 41 Madison Avenue, New York, New York 10010, U.S.A.

## Works

Victoria and Albert: Rowena glazed chintz fabric, for Anstoetz, 1985.
Victoria and Albert: Ivanhoe glazed chintz fabric, for Anstoetz, 1985.
Victoria and Albert: Chatterley glazed chintz fabric, for Anstoetz, 1985.
Victoria and Albert: Lancelot glazed chintz fabric, for Anstoetz, 1985.
Victoria and Albert: Camelot glazed chintz fabric, for Anstoetz, 1985.
Victoria and Albert; Fairlawn glazed chintz fabric, for Anstoetz, 1986.
Victoria and Albert: Hampton Court glazed chintz fabric, for Anstoetz, 1986.
Victoria and Albert: Abington glazed chintz fabric, for Anstoetz, 1986.
Victoria and Albert: Chelsea glazed chintz fabric, for Anstoetz, 1986.

Victoria and Albert: Sandringham glazed chintz fabric, for Anstoetz, 1986.

Victoria and Albert: Kensington glazed chintz fabric, for Anstoetz, 1986.

Versailles Collection: Fontain Bleau glazed chintz fabric, for Chanee, 1987.

Versailles Collection: Marie Antoinette glazed chintz fabric, for Chanee, 1987.

Versailles Collection: Pompadour glazed chintz fabric, for Chanee, 1987.

Versailles Collection: Josephine glazed chintz fabric, for Chanee, 1987.

Versailles Collection: Orangerie glazed chintz fabric, for Chanee, 1987.

Versailles Collection: Strie glazed chintz fabric, for Chanee, 1987.

Books illustrated include—*The Pai-Pai Pig* by Joy Anderson, New York, 1967; *Hai-Yin, The Dragon Girl* by Joy Anderson, New York, 1970; *Tales That People Tell in China,* New York, 1971; *The Wooden Cat Man* by Flishman, Boston, 1972.

\*

If I have, indeed, made a contribution in the field since I started designing fabrics in 1973, much of the credit goes to the American consumer in whose innate good taste I strongly believe. In fact, I have always "designed up" to the consumer, not down. During my first few years as a novice designer in the United States, I worked with exclusive fabric houses which sold only to decorators who, in turn, reached a very limited, and generally affluent, audience. My fabric designs sold very well, but I was not satisfied. My goal was—and is—to bring a "decorator look" to a broad consumer market and give the customers who buy at department stores and open retail outlets an opportunity to buy fine fabric designs, whether on upholstery and drapery materials or on sheets, pillows, table linens, etc. Creative Designs. In fresh palettes. That's exactly what I've striven to do since I opened my own business in 1975. My contribution? I hope I've helped to raise the general level of design in the American home.

My philosophy of design might be called "historical eclecticism." "Historical," because I believe that tradition is the basis for renewal and that radical innovation can come only from those steeped in tradition. "Eclecticism" because my designs are a synthesis of different times and places. My belief is that if the proportions are right, diverse styles from past and present can live together esthetically. My own country house started as a small farmhouse to which different generations of people have added, wing by wing. I'm adding on, too, blending the old parts of the house with the new in happy harmony that's all the richer because of the "time blocks" that reach back into the past, bespeak the present, and move forward to the future.

—Jay Yang

\*    \*    \*

First achieving prominence through his Orient Express Collection, Jay Yang helped place P. Kaufman's firmly in the volume design market in the mid-1970s. He demonstrated considerable energy by freelancing at the same time for Clarence House and Brunschwig et Fils. His designs often included unusual features, such as more than a dozen colors per pattern and patterns that were uneven and off-center.

The founding of his own company, Jay Yang Designs, allowed him to broaden his base. He licensed designs for soft goods, fine china for International China, and, most recently, furniture for Bernhardt. His furniture, like all his work, embodies his dictum that design is a trade, not an art. The furniture is basically functional, incorporating the classic simplicity of Chinese lines, with the minimum of detailing that gives it an Art Deco look. His Chinese touch has also been employed in designing a commemorative collection of fabrics for England's Brighton Pavilion, which houses the best in Chinoiserie interior design and objets d'art. His historical sensitivity was sought out by the Louvre's Musée des Arts Décoratifs, for which he designed a collection based on eighteenth- and nineteenth-century documents. Through his converting company, Fabriyaz, he has also been responsible for bringing Givenchy designs to the American market.

An important part of the Yang philosophy is his belief in "designing up" to consumer taste, rather than down to it. He would like his own company to be a medium through which "good, clean design" can be made available to everyone. He has never underestimated the public's ability to appreciate the unusual and unexpected in design. For instance, his 1976 Imari design for P. Kaufman displayed random, uncentered patterns, with both geometric and floral motifs. His willingness to take chances and to explore the unusual has been a part of his success. His decorator fabrics have been lapped up by the consumer, and his designs helped Wamsutta to become the maker of the world's best-selling sheets.

While his designs have won recognition for their individuality and sheer beauty, he has still remained true to historical traditions. His acquisitive eye for the beautiful has enabled him to draw ideas from many sources. His designs for the Musée des Arts Décoratifs, which have been introduced at fine stores around the country, demonstrate his understanding of forms and colors suitable for contemporary American living, while keeping the charm and spirit of the classic French motifs. Yet, his interest in history and his own Taiwanese background have not rendered him incapable of the odd surprise. In the "Made in USA" collection, he departed from the "oriental floral" pigeonhole to celebrate his new homeland by featuring American and contemporary materials. Designs such as Apple Pie, Yankee Doodle Dandy, and Pop Corn employed American folk art geometrics, ikats, contemporary solids and prints, and applique and patchwork looks. His designs are tailored to the environment, and prove that he is sensitive to the society that has matured his talent.

While Yang's designs are numerous, he strictly confines himself to the interior design market and rejects chances to broaden his scope, feeling that to become a designer of too many things is to dilute one's talent. Similarly, even though schooled in the fine arts, he shuns the artist's label. He sees himself as a tradesman and is very involved in the running of his two companies.

He produced a tenth anniversary collection in 1984 consisting of his most successful lines, updated to suit contemporary trends and tastes, and some new ones. He posits that something good will always be so and that one should be careful in just how he tries to improve it.

—Augustine Hope

## YOH, Shoei (Hamura)

Japanese architect, interior, and industrial designer

**Born:** Of Chinese parents in Kumanoto, Japan, 7 March 1940; naturalized Japanese citizen, 1975. **Education:** Studied economics, Keio Gijuku University, Tokyo, BA, 1962; studied design,

Wittenberg University, Springfield, Ohio, 1962-63. **Family:** Married Kimiko Nakakita in 1966; children: Masaki, Kaori, and Motoki. **Career:** Project designer, for International Design Associates, Tokyo, 1964-67, and for NIC, Fukuoka, 1967-69; freelance architect, interior, and furniture designer, establishing Shoei Yoh + Architects, Fukuoka, from 1970. Chairman, Kyushu Design Committee, Fukuoka, 1974-76; visiting professor of architecture, Graduate School of Architecture, Planning, and Preservation, Columbia University, New York, 1992; lecturer, Architecture Department, Kyushu University, 1992-94. **Exhibitions:** *Glass Chair WXYZ,* Tokyo Designers Space, 1978; *Transformation from Space to Space,* Japan Design Commission, Tokyo, 1980; *Light Architecture,* Tokyo Designers Space, 1982; *Forms in Wood,* Japan Design Committee, Tokyo, 1985; *Interface Design,* Gallery MA, Tokyo, 1987; *Aquarchitecture,* Japan Design Committee, Tokyo, 1991. **Collections:** International Art Museum, Osaka. **Honors:** Lighting Design Competition Silver Award, Tokyo, 1973; Japan Interior Designers Association Award, 1979; Japan Institute of Architects Award, 1983; Mainichi Design Award, Tokyo, 1983; Architectural Excellence Award, Kumamoto City, 1984; Commercial Space Design Award, Tokyo, 1984; Commercial Environment Design Award, Tokyo 1985, 1986; Architectural Culture Award, Kita Kyushu City, 1987; Architectural Institute of Japan Award, 1989; Gold Medal, International Association for Sports and Leisure Facilities, Köln, Germany, 1993; Benedictus Award finalist, American Institute of Architects, Washington, D.C., 1994. **Address:** 1-12-30 Heiwa, Minami-ku, Fukuoka-shi 815, Japan.

## Works

Free-form microwave-powered lamps, 1976.
*Ingot* coffee shop in the form of a glass prism, Tokyo, 1977.
Kinoshita Clinic in structural plastic, Fukuoka City, 1979.
Stainless steel house with latticed lights, 1981.
*WXYZ* chairs in photobonded glass, 1982.
Egami Clinic building in aluminium, 1982.
Laforet Museum of Art, Akasaka, 1982-86.
Pavilion shopping centre, Kumamoto City, 1983.
Aluminium house with sundial, 1984.
House with illuminated cross-of-light structure, 1985.
Music atelier, Kumamoto Prefecture, 1986.
Aspecta outdoor theatre, Mount Aso, Kumamoto Prefecture, 1987.
Bus Station building in glass, Oguni, 1987.
Forestry Centre, Oguni, 1987.
Oguni Dome gymnasium in wooden structure, Oguni, 1987.
Saibu Gas Museum, Tokyo, 1989.
Pyramid of Sea ferry terminal, 1990.
Wakita Hitecs office, 1990.
Matshshita Clinic, 1990.
*Glass House between Sea and Sky,* 1991.
Karatsu Golf Club, 1991.
Arashiyama Golf Club, 1991.
*Prospecta '92* observatory tower, Toyama, 1992.
*Galaxy* gymnasium, Toyama, 1992.
*Glass Station* gas station, 1993.
Kanada Children training house, 1994.
Naiju community center and nursery school, 1994.
Six cubes in light, 1994.
Oguni Rinpokan community center, 1995.
Uchino community center for seniors and children, 1995.

## Publications

**By YOH: articles**—in *Japan Architect* (Tokyo), no. 209, 1974, no. 210, 1974, no. 246, 1977, no. 252, 1978, no. 263, 1980, no. 267, 1981, no. 300, 1982, no. 302, 1982; *Space Design* (Tokyo), February 1980.

**On YOH: books**—*Decorative Art and Modern Interiors,* 5 vols., London, 1975-79; *Transformations in Modern Architecture* by Arthur Drexler, New York, 1979; **articles**—in *Domus* (Milan), no. 506, 1972, no. 584, 1978, no. 586, 1978, no. 588, 1978, no. 608, 1980, no. 625, 1982, no. 640, 1983; *Global Architecture* (Tokyo), no. 4, 1978, no. 14, 1983; *Architecture d'Aujourd'hui* (Paris), September 1980; *Architectural Review* (London), April 1981; *AIA Journal* (Washington, D.C.), August 1982; *Progressive Architecture* (New York), May 1983.

*

Simple form, materials, and details express my belief that unconscious design is the best, which makes me feel free from all of the restrictions such as gravity and the process of evolution. Design is the creation of an object in a form that has never existed in the past. The new form is derived from an evaluation which goes far back to the root of the process of development of our time. The technology for men to control nature is really only the means to borrow a part of nature temporarily. It has nothing to do with conquering or taming nature.

My designs begin with the recognition of mutual relationships among men, technology, and nature. Unlike Icarus in the Greek myth, the Solar Challenger could cross the straits of Dover using solar energy, by borrowing 15,000 solar batteries from NASA. It was not the sun but man who was challenged. Dedicated to our great designers, my *WXYZ* glass chairs, which are photo-bonded through ultra-violet rays while standing in the sunlight, will be found someday fallen into hundreds of pieces of glass shining in the morning sun.

Professor Teijiro Muramatsu of Tokyo University speaks of my work as the handmade architecture of a highly industrial technology. He points out the importance of enthusiasm in enterprising, technological achievement by making things with the highest quality of industrial materials available in our time, just as the old carpenters used to select and handle wood. After all, the ceramic tile cladding on the United states space shuttle was attached piece by piece with hands! Advanced technology has always been tested by hands through many trials and failure. I see nothing but beauty in making an effort to make these experiments possible.

—Shoei Yoh

*   *   *

When Shoei Yoh received the prestigious Japan Architects Association Award for 1983, it was given in recognition of his achievements in building design, but in his case, architecture is simply one aspect of a remarkably coherent design oeuvre. "High-tech" inadequately describes his approach, which is characterized, rather, by an overriding concern for minimalism—in both the sense of primary geometric forms and the sense of minimal physical substance. Matter is seemingly stretched to its limits in order to enfold the greatest volume of space.

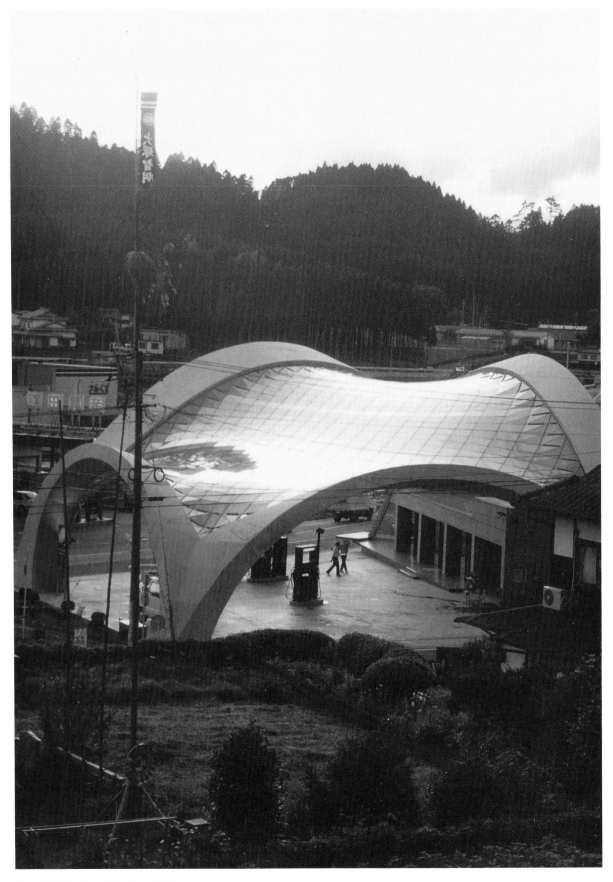

**Shoei Yoh: Glass Station, 1993**

A transparent or translucent membrane enveloping a pristine volume has consistently been his solution to problems at quite different scales, from lamps to entire buildings. Structure is reduced to the most slender members possible. His works thus have both delicacy (of membrane) and boldness (of form), a combination that distinguishes him from most of the so-called avant-garde architects and designers in Japan. He has quite obviously been influenced by traditional Japanese elements such as the shoji screens, but that influence has perhaps been filtered through the Western sensibility of designers such as Eames. Yoh's works are surreal objects in the interior and exterior landscape. These poetic and scrupulously detailed works have earned him a unique place among contemporary Japanese designers.

—Hiroshi Watanabe

# YOKOO, Tadanori

Japanese painter, printmaker, and graphic designer

**Born:** Nishiwaki City, Hyogo Prefecture, 17 June 1936. **Education:** Educated at Nishiwaki High School until 1954. **Family:** Married Yasue Tani in 1958; children: Ei and Mimi. **Career:** Worked as a block copy artist, Seibundo Printing company, Kakogawa City, 1954-56; graphic artist, Kobe Shimbu-sha newspaper company, Kobe, 1956-59; designer, National Advertisement Laboratory, Osaka, 1959-60, and Nippon Design Center, Tokyo, 1960-64; co-founder and director, with Akira Uno and Chunao Harada, of Studio Illfil graphic design firm, Tokyo, 1964-65; freelance designer, Tokyo, from 1965; founder and partner, with Masamichi Oikawa, of The End Studio graphic design firm, Tokyo, 1968-71; in private design practice as Tadanori Yokoo Design Studio, Tokyo, from 1971; has designed books for Shinshokan, Kodansha, Gakugeishorin, Chikunmashobo, Kawadeshobo, Bungeishunju, Shobunsha, Tokyo Ongakusa, Shiya-soshosha, Hirakawa Shuppansha, and others. **Exhibitions:** Matsuya Department Store, Tokyo 1965; Nantenshi Gallery, Tokyo, 1966, 1984, 1994; Museum of Modern Art, New York, 1972; Museum für Kunst und Gewerbe, Hamburg, 1973, 1982; Stedelijk Museum, Amsterdam, 1974; Okayama Museum, Japan, 1980; Otani Memorial Art Museum, Nishinomiya City, 1983; Musée de la Publicité, Paris, 1983; Otis Parsons Gallery, Los Angeles, 1984; Palazzo Bianco, Genoa, 1985; Falcone Theatre, Genoa, 1985; Kunstlerhaus Bathanien, West Berlin, 1985; Laforet Museum, Harajyuku, Tokyo, 1985; Japanese American Cultural Center, Los Angeles, 1985; Nishimura Gallery, Tokyo, 1985; Roberta English Gallery, San Francisco, 1986; Roy Boyd Gallery, Los Angeles, 1986; *Tokyo: Form and Spirit,* Walker Art Center, Minneapolis, 1986; *Trends in Contemporary Art in Japan,* Museum of Modern Art, Toyama, 1986; *Avant-Garde Art of Japan 1910-1970,* Centre Georges Pompidou, Paris, 1986; *Neo-Roman Baroque,* Seibu Museum of Art, Tokyo, 1987; *Tadanori Yokoo Design,* Carnegie-Mellon University, Pittsburgh, 1987; Galerie Silvia Menzel, West Berlin, 1988; *Art Kites,* toured Japan and the world, 1988; *Total Graph-T.Y.,* Shibuya Seibu, Tokyo, 1989; Miyagi Prefectural Museum of Art, 1990; Museum of Modern Art, Tokoshima, 1990; *Tadanori Yokoo's Prints: From the Maiden Works to the Latest,* Seed Hall, Shibuya, Tokyo, 1990; *Tadanori Yokoo Exhibition: The Laws of the Heavens,* Kirin Plaza, Osaka, 1991; *Tears, Waterfall,* Sagacho Exhibit Space, Tokyo, 1991; *Pregnancy Announcement,* Nantenshi Gallery, Tokyo, 1991; *Electric Brain Cosmos by Tadanori Yokoo,* Seibu Department Store, Ikebukuro, Tokyo, 1993; *Tadanori Yokoo: The Shocking Sixties and Today,* Kakogawa Cultural Center, 1993; *Tadanori Yokoo and Mark Costabi Collaboration,* Azabu Museum of Arts and Crafts, Tokyo, 1993; *Tadanori Yokoo: Multiple Crimes,* Namba City Gallery, Osaka, 1993; *Tadanori Yokoo: A Childhood Retrospective of the Early Showa Era,* Yayoi Museum of Art, Tokyo, 1994; *Tadanori Yokoo Spiritual Pop 1994 with Love,* Laforet Museum, Harajuku, Tokyo, 1994; *Cinema in Painting by Tadanori Yokoo,* Park Tower, Tokyo, 1994; *60s by Tadanori Yokoo,* Kirin Plaza, Osaka, 1995; Contemporary Art Center, New Orleans, Louisiana, 1995; *Tadanori Yokoo: Poster and Bookcover,* Ehisu Mitsukoshi, Tokyo, 1995; *Tadanori Yokoo: A Boy's Romance of the Early Showa Era,* Navio Hankyu Museum, Osaka, 1995; *Photosophia: Digital Technamations by Tadanori Yokoo,* Tokyo Metropolitan Museum of Photography, Tokyo, 1995. **Collections:** Museum of Modern Art, New York; Museum of Fine Art, Boston; Walker Art Center, Minneapolis; Library of Congress, Washington, D.C.; Stedelijk Museum, Amsterdam; Musée de la Publicité, Paris; Museum für Kunst und Gewerbe, Hamburg; Museum of Modern Art, Vienna; Kunstgewerbemuseum, Zürich; Poster Museum, Warsaw; Israel Museum, Jerusalem; Konstindustrimuseet, Copenhagen; Metropolitan Art Museum, Tokyo; National Museum of Modern Art, Tokyo; National Library, Tokyo; Municipal Museum of Art, Kyoto; Museum of Industrial Encouragement, Toyama; Ohara Museum of Art, Okayama. **Honors:** Japan Advertising Artist Club Prize, 1957; Tokyo Art Directors Club Prize, 1961, 1962, 1971, 1973, 1974, 1975, 1980; Grant Print Prize, Paris Biennale, 1969; UNESCO Prize, 1972, and Gold Medal, 1974, Warsaw Poster Biennale; Brno Graphic Biennale Prize, 1972, 1974, 1984; Hyogo Museum of Modern Art Prize, 1974; Mainichi Design Prize, Tokyo, 1974; Hollywood Reporter Key Art Prize, 1976; Kodansha Cultural Award, Tokyo, 1978; Lahti Poster Biennale Prize, 1979; Hyogo Prefecture Cultural Award, 1987; honorary award, 4th Asian Art Biennial, Bangladesh, 1989. **Address:** 4-19-7 Seijo, Setagaya-ku, Tokyo 157, Japan.

## Works

*A la Maison de M. Civecawa* poster, for the Garmera Company, 1965.

*Tadanori Yokoo: Persona* exhibition poster, for the Matsuya Department Store, Tokyo, 1965.

*The City and Design* book promotion poster, for Kajima Institute Publishing Company, 1965.

*Koshimaki-Osen* poster, for the Jyokyo Gekijyo Troupe, 1966.

*A Ballad Dedicated to a Small Finger Cutting Ceremony* book promotion poster, for Yakuza Shobo Publishing, 1966.

*Tenjo Sajiki* poster, for Shuji Terayama and the Tenjo Sajiki Troupe, 1967.

*Word and Image* exhibition poster, for the Museum of Modern Art, New York, 1968.

*Chinzei Yumihari-Zuki* poster, for the National Theater, Tokyo, 1969.

*Punishment by Roses* (Y. Mishima) book illustrations, for Shuei-Sha Publishing Company, 1970.

Pavilion design at *Expo 70,* Osaka, for Japan Textiles, 1970.

*Wonderland* poster, for Shimojima seaside resort, 1971.

*The Beatles* poster, for Apple Records and Toshiba Records, 1972.

*Santana Amigos* record sleeve, for CBS Sony, 1974.

**Tadanori Yokoo: "Japanese Culture: The Fifty Postwar Years," 1995**

*Suntry* campaign posters, for the Suntry Brewery, 1978.
Chiyonofuji sumo wrestling sash/belt, for Kokonoe-Beya, 1981.
*Bow Wow Wow* publicity poster, for RCA Records, 1982.
*Tadanori Yokoo* exhibition poster, for the Musée de la Publicité, Paris, 1984.
*Issey Miyake: Body Works* exhibition poster, for the Victoria and Albert Museum, London, 1985.
*JASRAC* poster, for the Japanese Society for the Rights of Authors, Composers, and Publishers, 1988.
*Yamatotakeru* poster, for the Tokyo Electric Company, 1989.

## Publications

**By YOKOO: books**—*The 170cm Blues,* Tokyo, 1968; *Tadanori Yokoo's Posthumous Works,* Tokyo, 1968; *The Complete Tadanori Yokoo,* Tokyo, 1970, as *Tadanori Yokoo,* Woodbury, New York, 1977; *An Escape to Incompletion,* Tokyo, 1970; *Contemporary Prints—Tadanori Yokoo,* Tokyo, 1971; *Push,* Tokyo, 1972; *Groping in the Dark,* Tokyo, 1973; *Yearning for Millennium,* Tokyo, 1974; *Why I am Here,* Tokyo, 1976; *To India,* Tokyo, 1977; *Tadanori Yokoo's Collage Design,* Tokyo, 1977; *A Dove Flying from the Ark,* Tokyo, 1977; *My Zen Apprenticeship,* Tokyo, 1978; *100 Posters of Tadanori Yokoo,* Tokyo and New York, 1978; *Haragyate,* Tokyo, 1978; *YFO Revolution,* Tokyo, 1979; *My Dream Diary,* Tokyo, 1979; *A Child of Aquarius,* Tokyo, 1979; *Gleaming Woman,* Tokyo, 1980; *Cosmic Meditation,* Tokyo, 1980; *Yesterday I Was, Today I Am,* Tokyo, 1980; *Get Up 8:00am, Fine,* Tokyo, 1980; *Bigeiko,* Tokyo, 1981; *Paintings, Prints and Drawing by Tadanori Yokoo,* Tokyo, 1981; *Tadanori Yokoo,* Kobe, Japan, 1982.

**On YOKOO: books**—*Modern Graphics* by Keith Murgatroyd, London, 1969; *Graphics Record Covers* edited by Walter Herdeg, Zürich, 1974; *Japan: Tradition und Gegenwart* by Jurgen Harten, Joseph Love, and others, Dusseldorf, 1974; *Art in Japan today* edited by S. Takashima and others, Tokyo, 1974; *Album Cover Album: The Book of Record Jackets* edited by Storm Thorgerson and Roger Dean, Limpsfield, 1979; *The Language of Graphics* by Edward Booth-Clibborn and Daniele Baroni, London, 1980; *Album Cover Album 2* by Roger Dean and David Howells, New York, 1982; *A History of Graphic Design* by Philip B. Meggs, New York and London, 1983; *Les Années 60* by Anne Bony, Paris, 1983; *The Twentieth Century Poster: Design of the Avant-Garde* by Dawn Ades, New York, 1984; *Japanese Design* by Penny Sparke, London, 1987; *Tadanori Yokoo: Japanese Contemporary Artists Series Vol. I,* Tokyo, 1990.

\*

It is my principle not to have a definite style for my work. I always rely on my instincts. What scares me most is creating images with ideology. I do not know where I came from or where I am going. I do not even know who I am. How could I possibly adopt one style as my own?

—Tadanori Yokoo

\*　　\*　　\*

Since the 1960s, Tadanori Yokoo has been an advertising designer, poster artist, printmaker, architect, actor, and author, and in Japan he achieved the kind of celebrity usually accorded rock musicians and film stars. It is his work as a poster artist, however, that brought him to international attention.

The great poster artist A. M. Cassandre likened the poster-maker to the telegraph operator whose sole duty is to transmit a client's message. Yokoo has exemplified the reverse. The poster in his hands became a vehicle for personal opinion, social and political commentary, and personal revelation.

As a student and young designer, Yokoo was both fascinated by and resentful of the increasing influence of the West on Japanese life and on the growing internationalism of its art and design. In 1965, he was commissioned to produce for Tatsumi Hijikata's modern dance company. Hijikata shared Yokoo's concern for restoring an indigenous imagery and sensibility to Japanese design. The result was a startling poster filled with rising suns, Hiroshige-like ocean waves, a mixture of Japanese and English text, deliberately obscure phrases, and unabashed eroticism.

This eclectic, audacious poster struck a responsive chord with the Tokyo intellectual community, and Yokoo was soon commissioned to design posters for exhibitions, publications, and the theatre, and given the same freedom of expression. Yokoo's client themselves unknowingly became allies in his subversion of the traditional well-made poster. It is precisely the personal nature of his work and its notoriety that attracts them. Although their messages might become lost or incidental, a Yokoo poster is never ignored. Yokoo's work is saved from its own iconoclasm and self-indulgence by the over-all creative intelligence, brilliance of execution, and underlying seriousness of purpose.

Yokoo was commissioned to design the Textile Pavilion for *Expo 70* in Osaka. This project also became an opportunity for Yokoo's comment. In its finished state, the building still appeared to be under construction—even the scaffolding remained intact. Yokoo's explanation: "The precise moment when the building can first be said to have been complete will be the moment when the act of living there is denied us and it has become a ruin. Therefore, the fact that I turned the significance of what would be the ultimate fate of the building into the very building itself can be considered as representing my attitude towards architecture and my creative work."

—Mildred Constantine

# ZACCAI, Gianfranco
Italian industrial and product designer

**Born:** Trieste, Italy, 29 May 1947. **Education:** Syracuse University, B.I.D.; Boston Architectural Center, B.Arch. **Career:** Director of Corporate Design, Instrumentation Laboratory, Inc.; co-founder, president, and director of design, Design Continuum, Boston, Massachusetts, and San Francisco, California, and Design Continuum Italia, Milan, Italy, from 1983. **Member:** Industrial Designers Society of America (ISDA); Association Disegno Industriale (ADI). **Exhibitions:** *Design USA,* United States Information Agency sponsored tour of the Soviet Union, 1989-1991; Ketonah Gallery, 1990; *Good Design 1994,* Chicago Athenaeum, Illinois, 1994; *Mutant Materials in Contemporary Design,* Museum of Modern Art, New York, 1994. **Honors:** (all with Design Continuum Inc.) IDEA Recognition of Design Achievement, IDSA, 1982, 1983 (2), 1985, 1988; Excellence in Design Award, 1982 (2), 1983, 1986, Designer's Choice Award, 1990 (2), 1994, and Gold Award, 1992, *ID* Magazine Annual Design Review; Merit Award, Art Directors Club of Boston, 1983, 1984, 1986; iF Award for Good Design, Hannover Fair West Germany, 1984; New York Publishers' Award for Magazine Design, 1985; Massachusetts Achievement Award for Promotional Campaign, 1986; Compasso d'Oro for Instrument Design, ADI, 1987; GEP Award, General Electric Plastics, Italy, 1987; Smau Industrial Design Award, Office Products, 1988, 1990; Gutes Design Blutgas, 1989; IDEA Designs of the Decade, IDSA, 1990; Merit Award, 1990 (2), Bronze Award, 1991, Creative Club of Boston; Gold Medal, 1992, 1993, 1995, Silver Medal, 1992 (2), 1995 (3), and Bronze Medal, 1991, 1992, 1993 (2), 1995 (4), IDEA Competition, IDSA; Presidential Design Award, 1992; Design and Engineering Award, *Innovations '92* Consumer Electronics Show, 1992 (3); Small Business of the Year Award Finalist, Greater Boston Chamber of Commerce, 1993; Special Theme Prize, Shinanogawa Technolopolis International Design Competition '94, 1994; Interior Design Competition Award, *Restaurants & Institutions* magazine, 1994; Excellence in Design Competition Award, *Appliance Manufacturer* magazine, 1994; American Product Excellence (APEX) Award, Management Roundtable, 1995; Gold Award, New Products for Mature Markets Design Competition, American Society on Aging, 1995; Award, Appliance Manufacturer Excellence in Design Competition, 1995. **Address:** Design Continuum Inc., 1220 Washington St., West Newton, Massachusetts 02165, U.S.A.

**Works**

*The Pump* sneaker, for Reebok International Ltd.
*Metaform Personal Hygiene System,* for Herman Miller, Inc.

*Automated Coagulation Laboratory,* for Instrumentation Laboratory Inc.

**Publications**

**By ZACCAI: articles**—"Equipment" in *ID* (New York), July/August 1986; "Bringing Convenience to the Whole Family" in *Innovation* (MacLean, Virginia), Winter 1990; "How to Make Client/Consultant Relationship More Like a Basketball Game than a Relay Race" in *Design Management Journal,* Spring 1991; "The New DFM: Design for Marketability" in *World Class Design to Manufacture* (England), vol. 1, no. 6, 1994.

**On ZACCAI: books**—*New American Design* by Hugh Aldersey Williams, New York, 1988; *Good Design 1994,* exhibition catalogue, Chicago, 1994; *Design as a Strategic Tool for Economic Development,* Coyoacan, Mexico, 1994; **articles**—"Ease and Economy in the Lab" by Paul Angiolillo in *Business Week,* 11 April 1988; "Source of Success" by Beth Wolfensberger in *New England Business* (Boston), March 1991; "Design That Sells and Sells and..." by Brian Dumane in *Fortune* (New York), 11 March 1991; "Global Design Is Here, But..." by James Braham in *Machine Design* (Tokyo), 26 March 1993; "Hot Products" by Bruce Nussbaum in *Business Week* (New York), 7 June 1993.

\*

In my work, I try to focus as much as possible on designing the "Experience of the User." By this I mean trying not to design one dimensionally, focusing simply on one of the sensory perceptions, but rather designing for the total experience, which is created through all points of contact between the object and its intended user. This means going beyond the visual qualities which historically have been the main focus of design, and even beyond "functional" qualities which have been the extended focus of design since the Bauhaus integration of form following function.

At this point, I believe that designing for kinesthetic perception of objects and spaces which are dynamic in nature is extremely important. This means that the design of sounds, textures, and transitory experiences is essential. The design of products which are more culturally sensitive and based on cultural traditions is an additional area of interest, along with designs which are sensitive to ecological issues, sustainable development, and an aging population. These are realities which I feel all designers should be aware of and integrate in their design processes.

—Gianfranco Zaccai

\*    \*    \*

Gianfranco Zaccai: *Automated Coagulation Laboratory* (two views), for Instrumentation Laboratory

To understand Gianfranco Zaccai and the reputation he has built for himself, you need to understand his childhood. At age ten, he and his family emigrated to the United States from Italy. He had to adapt culturally, learn a new language and a new social system, all without losing his sense of the Italian in him.

His early life in Italy had left an indelible impression, spent as it was among family and friends involved in architecture and the arts. Merging business and home life, his father and mother brought the emphasis on quality, preparation, and presentation of their photography studio to the home. Meals weren't just tasty and nutritious, they were visual feasts. Clothes didn't just keep up with fads, they hung well and lasted because they were well-made of quality fabrics.

In every detail Gian's parents demonstrated that design is not something that looks good or works well, but both, simultaneously. "Design is not a result, but a process," Gian explains. "Sometimes that process has no concrete, visible product as its outcome, and usually the solution is much more than its physical representation."

Gian chose to focus on the medical industry when he began as an industrial designer because it seemed a way to contribute to the quality of life, given the "unfriendly" state of medical equipment at the time. He found an industry driven entirely by the engineering perspective, which required him to draw on both his ability to bridge cultures and his respect for function as key to design success. It also taught him the importance of effective communication. "You can't assume the excellence of your design solution will be self-evident. The odds are it will need cogent articulation that facilitates people's ability to understand why and how you arrived at the solution."

But working closely with people who at least get the greater possibilities of design in all its personae, *including* engineering, does help and, fortunately, Instrumentation Laboratory Inc. did have one such personality in Jerry Zindler, the head of mechanical engineering. Within a few years, the two had partnered to form Design Continuum.

Among the first design firms to be led by both industrial design and engineering, Design Continuum offered Gian one advantage over working internally for a company. While he had been able to make his design group a part of the product development process at Instrumentation Laboratory, he had been unable to overcome the professional compartmentalizing that continued to undermine teamwork by encouraging contention.

When they formed Design Continuum, Gian and his partner broke away from departments as the basic organizational unit, creating instead product development groups made up of several disciplines. Each group was responsible for the totality of the products assigned to them. Now another profession's failure was no longer a source of snickers and glee, but rather a direct threat to each group member's own performance evaluation. "If you realize that your performance depends on every aspect of a product's development, you make sure the others in the group have a chance to do their best," Gian explains. And so his designers and engineers must bridge barriers, respecting each other's knowledge and learning each other's language.

Almost from the firm's beginning, Gian was able to pursue his concern for improving the patients' and the user's total experience with medical products. He achieved this by engaging in in-depth market and user research, a focus that has been formalized in the past six years. "I've always been interested in the phenomenon of individual and cultural diversity. It has a clear relevance to design.

You can't design for the world market without understanding it," he remarks. With growing offices in Milan, San Francisco, and Boston, and clients around the world, Gian has demonstrated the power of professional and cultural diversity as a fuel for the design process first hand.

—Kristina Goodrich

# ZANUSO, Marco

Italian architect and exhibition, interior, and industrial designer

**Born:** Milan, 14 May 1916. **Education:** Studied architecture, at the Politecnico, Milan, Dip. Arch., 1939. **Military Service:** Served in the Italian Navy, 1940-45, Lieutenant. **Family:** Married Marialisa Pedroni in 1944; children: Federica, Lorenza, and Susanna. **Career:** Freelance architect and designer, Milan, from 1945; designed for Olivetti, Necchi, Edgards, IBM, Arflex, Elam, Brionvega, Moretti e Bianchi, Gavina, Bonacina, Techniform, Kartell, Lumenform, Zanotta, Mim Mobilli, Anic, Lanerissi, Fiat, Poggi, Borletti, Siemens, Fusital, Villeroy e Boch, and others. Editor, *Casabella* magazine, Milan, from 1947; councilor, 1956-60, building commission member, 1961-63, and planning commission member from 1961, City of Milan; president, ADI Associazione Disegno Industriale, Milan, 1957-59, 1966-74; council member, Milan Triennale, from 1977; regional councilor, IN/ARCH building institute, Milan, from 1977. Professor of industrial design, from 1965, professor of the development of materials, 1966-68, Athens commission member, 1980-82, president of the planning and production department, from 1981, president of the council of address, from 1982, at the Politecnico, Milan. **Exhibitions:** *Marco Zanuso,* Spoleto Festival of Two Worlds, 1967; *Italy: The New Domestic Landscape,* Museum of Modern Art, New York, 1972; *Design Since 1945,* Philadelphia Museum of Art, 1983. **Collections:** Museum of Modern Art, New York; Philadelphia Museum of Art. **Honors:** Cross of Valour for service in World War Two; Grand Prize, 1948, 1954, Gold Medal, 1951, 1954, 1957, 1964, Silver Medal, 1960, Milan Triennale; Compasso d'Oro Award, Milan, 1956, 1962, 1964, 1979; Villa Olmo Silver Medal, Como, 1957; La Casa Abitata Gold Award, Florence, 1965; Interplas Award, London, 1965; Bio 2 Biennale Gold Award, Liubliana, 1966; Estetica Sperimentale Gold Medal, Rimini, 1966; Industrial Design Gold Medal, Yverdon, 1969; Associazione Italiana per Edilizia Industrializzata Prize, Milan, 1971; Bolaffi Prize, Turin, 1972. **Address:** Via Laveno 6, 20148 Milan, Italy.

## Works

*MOMA* armchair, for Moretti e Bianchi, 1949.
*Lady* armchair, for Arflex, 1951.
*Sleep-o-matic* sofa bed, for Arflex, 1954.
*1100/2* sewing machine, for Borletti, 1956.
*Carosello* coffee-maker, for Girmi/Subalpina, 1958.
*Lambda* chair in sheet steel, for Gavina, 1958-62.
*Doney 14* television set, for Brionvega, 1962 (with Richard Sapper).
*K-1340* children's chair in polyethylene, for Kartell, 1963 (with Richard Sapper).
*Lambda* chair in sheet metal, for Gavina, 1963 (with Richard Sapper).

*Springtime* armchair, sofa and table, for Arflex, 1964.
*Algol* portable television set, for Brionvega, 1965 (with Richard Sapper).
*Italtel Grillo* telephone, for Brionvega, 1965 (with Richard Sapper).
*TS502* portable radio, for Brionvega, 1965 (with Richard Sapper).
*Grillo* television, for Auso/Siemens, 1966.
*Black 12* portable television set, for Brionvega, 1969 (with Richard Sapper).
*Marcuso* table, for Zanotta, 1969.
*ST/201* black television set, for Brionvega, 1970.
*575* sewing machine, for Necchi, 1972.
*Ariante* ventilator fan with slatted plastic housing, for Vortice, 1974.
*Eta Beta* table, for Zonotta, 1978.
*SD 60* upholstered chair, for Poggi, 1979.
Medical pacemaker programmer, for Sorin Biomedica, 1981.
*Monobloc* bathroom unit, for Villeroy e Boch, 1982.
*Caraffa* teapot, for Cleto Munari, 1983.
*Due Z* cutlery and hardware, for Fusital, 1985.
*Laveno* table, for Zanotta, 1986.

(for a list of Zanoso's building and architectural projects, see *Contemporary Architects*)

## Publications

**By ZANUSO: books**—*La Macchina per Cucire,* exhibition catalogue, Milan, 1962; *Elemtni di Tecnologia dei Materiali come Introduzione allo Studio del Designs,* Milan, 1967; (with Pierluigi Nicolin) *La Progettazione e L'Organiozzazione degli Ambiente di Lavoro,* Milan, 1974; **articles**—in *Domus* (Milan), no 197, 1944, no. 1, 1988; *Stile Industria* (Milan), no. 21, 1959, no. 2, 1962; *Rivista Ideal Standard* (Milan), no. 59, 1961; *Abitare* (Milan), no. 10, 1962; *La Repubblica* (Milan), no. 18, 1979.

**On ZANUSO: books**—*Prize Design for Modern Furniture* by Edgar Kaufmann, Jr., New York, 1950; *Gute Mödel: Schöne Räume* edited by Mia Seeger, Stuttgart, 1953; *Mobili Tipo* by Robert Aloi, Milan, 1956; *Design for Modern Living* by Gred and Ursula Hatje, Munich, 1961, London, 1962; *Il Nuovo Arredamento* by Morris Alfieri, Venice, 1964; *The Modern Chair: 1850 to Today* by Gilbert Frey, London and Neiderteaufen, 1970; *Zanuso* edited by Trevor Wilson, Melbourne, 1971; *Marco Zanuso: Designer* by Gillo Dorfles, Rome, 1971; *Italy: The New Domestic Landscape* by Emilio Ambasz, New York and Florence, 1972; *Il Design in Italia 1945-1972* by Paolo Fossati, Turin, 1972; *Design e Forme Nuove nell'Arredamento Italiano* edited by Paolo Portoghesi and Marino Marini, Rome, 1978; *History of Modern Furniture* by Karl Mang, Stuttgart, 1978, London, 1979; *Atlante del Design Italiano 1940/1980* by Alfonso Grassi and Anty Pansera, Milan, 1980; *Industrial Design* by John Heskett, London, 1980; *Il Design Italiano degli Anni '50* edited by Andrea Branzi and Michele De Lucchi, Milan, 1981; *Contemporary Furniture* edited by Klaus-Jurgen Sembach, Stuttgart and London, 1982; *Design Since 1945* edited by Kathryn Hiesinger and George Marcus, Philadelphia and London, 1983; *Design Process Olivetti 1908-1983,* with text by Renzi Zorzi, Milan, 1983; *Mid-Century: Furniture of the 1950s* by Cara Greenberg, 1984; *Twentieth Century Design: Furniture* by Penny Sparke, London, 1986; *Modern Furniture Classics* by Miriam Stimpson, London, 1987; *Italian Design: 1980 to the present* by Penny Sparke,

London and New York, 1988; *Design by Architects in the 1980s* by Juli Capella and Quim Larrea, London, 1988.

\*     \*     \*

In his introduction to the 1972 Museum of Modern Art's *Italy: The New Domestic Landscape,* Emilio Ambasz noted three prevalent attitudes in post-war design: conformation, reformation, and contestation. Marco Zanuso represents the last. He understood contemporary design as a continual inquiry into culture, questioning Italy's inability to move on from the "morality" of Rationalist architecture, the sentimentalism of the Arts and Crafts approach, as well as the decorativeness of the lingering Art Nouveau style. He held, on the other hand, a determination to engage the new industrialized society from within, challenging established social patterns with a new technological aesthetic.

Zanuso started with industrial materials and techniques as the basis of his domestic program. Foam-rubber padding, polyethylene structuring, sheet-metal stamping, aluminum die-casting were used in disarmingly simple yet memorably sophisticated products, from furniture to electronics, that retained the Italian tradition of sensuousness and craftsmanship with a respectful synthesis of art and technology.

Zanuso's influence was pervasive in architecture, exhibition design, interior, and industrial design, as well as through the design journals he edited—*Domus,* from 1947 to 1949, and *Casabella,* from 1952 to 1956—which became the advocates of an industrial aesthetic. It was at the 1951 Milan Triennale that Zanuso had made his mark, proving the potential of independent design allied with industry with his *Lady* armchair, a cooperation with the technicians at Pirelli which culminated in the establishment of the furniture company Arflex. The chair looked much like an automobile seat, and employed much of the same materials and processes of car-seat assembly, including foam-rubber, then a new material, that was fully integrated into the structure of the seat, arms, and back. The specific purpose of this experiment was to produce furnishings on a small scale, like the traditional Italian workshop system, yet employ industrial methods. This pioneering effort to link designers with industry fostered innovative relationships between Zanuso's office, which toward the end of the 1950s also included Richard Sapper as co-designer, and some of the leading post-war consumer manufacturers—Pirelli, Arflex, Olivetti, Necchi, Brionvega, and Fiat.

In the 1960s, Zanuso, often with the collaboration of Sapper, created objects that while bordering on the idolization of industrial processes never acquired the stigma of mere consumer fashion. Among the best known of these are the 1961 elementary-school chair, the first injection-molded polyethylene carcass, whose lightweight rigidity schooled children in the revolutionary duality that a chair is really a stackable plaything; the reductivist TV sets designed for Brionvega, especially the "Doney," the first completely transistorized TV designed in Europe, where the screen is set in a skin-tight plastic bezel, and sits on a table like a minimal sculpture; the Grillo "Cricket" telephone for Sit-Siemens, with built-in dial inside a contoured carapace, a forerunner to the hinged shell of the contemporary cellular phone.

Marco Zanuso has consistently believed that the design process must be identified with the entire range of decision-making activities, ultimately, now, an interface with the cybernetics of modern culture. "The role of the designer in society," he writes in his essay on "Design and Society" in the Philadelphia Museum of Art's *Design Since 1945* catalog, "is not to translate the accumulation of specialized research or to optimize the economic and manufacturing functions into concrete reality, but rather to convey, through the creative process, a suggestion, an idea capable of synthesizing those elements and judging and expressing the present historical and social context, which has always led design to be considered the meaningful embodiment of the society that generates it."

—Sarah Bodine and Michael Dunas

# ZAPF, Hermann

German calligrapher and lettering, typeface and book designer

**Born:** Nuremberg, 8 November 1918. **Education:** Studied as apprentice retoucher in a printing firm, Nuremberg, 1934-38; also private studies in lettering, from manuals of Edward Johnston and Rudolf Koch, 1935-37; studied at Paul Koch's Haus zum Fursteneck type workshop, Frankfurt, 1938. **Military Service:** Served in a geographic unit of the German Army, 1941-45. **Career:** Type director, at D. Stempel typefoundry, Frankfurt, 1947-56; design consultant, at Mergenthaler Linotype Company, Brooklyn, New York, and Frankfurt, 1957-74; consultant to Hallmark International, Kansas City, Missouri, 1966-73; vice-president, Design Processing International, New York, 1977-1987; Chairman, Zapf, Burns & Company, New York, 1987-1991. Instructor in lettering, Werkkunstschule, Offenbach, 1947-50; professor of graphic design, Carnegie Institute of Technology, Pittsburgh, 1960; instructor in typography, Technische Hochschule, Darmstadt, 1972-82; professor of typographic computer programs. Rochester Institute of Technology, New York, 1977-87; also visiting lecturer at colleges throughout the United States, Japan, and Europe. **Exhibitions:** Cooper Union, New York, 1951 (with Fritz Kredel); Book Club of California, San Francisco, 1963, 1961, 1972, 1977; University of California, Los Angeles, 1957; Carnegie Institute of Technology, Pittsburgh, 1960 (toured); Bibliotheque Albert I, Brussels, 1962 (toured); Stadtbibliothek, Nuremberg, 1963 (with Rudolf Koch); Gutenberg Museum, Mainz, 1964, 1974; Hallmark Incorporated, Kansas City, 1967 (toured); Rijksmuseum Meermanno-Westreenianum, The Hague, 1968; Musée de Nice, France, 1969; University of Texas, Austin, 1970; Museo Civico, Saluzzo, 1972; Institute fuer Neue Technische Form, Darmstadt, 1973; Museo Bodoniano, Parma, 1975; University of Kentucky, Lexington, 1976; Stanford University, California, 1960; Rochester Institute of Technology, New York, 1980; National Museum, Tokyo, 1982 (toured), and others. **Collections:** Pierpont Morgan Library, New York; Newberry Library, Chicago; Harvard University, Cambridge, Massachusetts; San Francisco Public Library; Bibliothèque Royale, Brussels; Klingspor Museum, Offenbach; Gutenberg Museum, Mainz. **Honors:** Silver medal, Belgian Ministry of Information, 1962; Brno Graphics Biennale Typography Prize, 1966; Type Directors Club Gold Medal, New York, 1967; Goudy Award, Rochester Institute of Technology, New York 1969; Silver medal, Leipzig Book Fair, 1971; Gutenberg Prize, Mainz, 1974; Museo Bodoniano Gold Medal, Parma, 1975; Merck Award, Darmstadt, 1978; National Composition Award 1986; Robert H. Middleton Award, 1987. Honorary citizen, State of Texas, 1970; Honorary Royal Designer for Industry, Royal Society of Arts, London, 1985. Honorary Member: Type Directors Club of New York; Society of Typographic Arts, Chicago; Association of Stanford University Librar-

ies; Double Crown, London; Society of Scribes and Illuminators, London; Societé Typographique de France; Grafiska Institutet, Stockholm; Society of Typographic Designers, Toronto; The Typophiles, New York; Art Directors Club Of Kansas City; Society for Calligraphy, Los Angeles; Washington Calligraphers Guild; Typographers International Association, Washington, D.C; Estonian Calligraphers Union, Tallin; Alpha Beta Club, Hong Kong; Bund Deutscher Buchkunstler; The Aleuin Society, Vancouver; Society of Scribes, New York; Friends of Calligraphy, San Francisco; Monterey Calligraphers Guild; Society of Printers, Boston; The Gondy International Center, Rochester; Zeta Chapter, Gamma Epsilon Tau, Rochester; Wynkyn de Worde Society, London. **Address:** Seitersweg 35, 64287 Darmstadt, Germany.

## Works

Typeface designs include—*Gilgengart*, 1938-41; *Alkor*, 1989-40; *Novalis*, 1946-47; *Melior*, 1948-49; *Virtuosa*, 1948-49; *Palatino*, 1948-50; *Festival Figures*, 1948-50; *Primavera Ornaments*, 1948-50; *Michelangelo Titling*, 1949-50; *Zodiac Signs*, 1950; *Sistina titling*, 1950; *Saphir*, 1950; *Linotype Janson*, 1951; *Kompakt*, 1952; *Linotype Aldus*, 1952-53; *Optima*, 1952-58; *Attika Greek*, 1953; *Artemis Greek*, 1953; *Phidias Greek*, 1953; *Heraklit Greek*, 1953; *Frederika Greek*, 1953; *Linotype Mergenthaler*, 1953; *Alahram Arabic*, 1954; *Magnus San Serif*, 1956-58; *Trajanus Cyrillic*, 1957; *Linofilm Venture*, 1960-67; *Hunt Roman*, 1961-63; *Hallmark Jeannette Script*, 1966-67; *Hallmark Firenze*, 1967-68; *Hallmark Textura*, 1968-69; *Linofilm Medici*, 1969; *Orion*, 1974; *ITC Zapf Book*, 1976; *Comenius*, 1976; *Digiset Marconi*, 1976; *Zapf International*, 1977; *Digiset Edison*, 1978; *ITC Zapf Chancery*, 1979; *AMS Euler*, 1983; *Aurelia*, 1984; *Pan-Nigerian*, 1985; *Zapf Renaissance Roman*, 1985; *URW Roman*, 1985; *Sans Serif*, 1985; *AT&T Garamond*, 1988.

## Publications

**By ZAPF: books**—*William Morris: Sein Leben und Werk*, Lubeck 1949; *Das Blumen-ABC*, Frankfurt, 1949; *Feder und Stichel*, Frankfurt, 1950, 1952, as *Pen and Graver*, New York, 1952; *Manuale Typographicum*, Frankfurt, 1954, 1968, New York, 1968; *About Alphabets*, Frankfurt and New York, 1960, Cambridge, Massachusetts, 1970; *Typographische Variationen*, Frankfurt, 1963, New York, 1964, New Rochelle, 1980; *Hunt Roman: The Birth of a Type*, Pittsburgh, 1965; *Orbis typographicus*, Prairie Village, Kansas, 1980; *Hermann Zapf: Hora Fugit—Carpe Diem*, Darmstadt and Hamburg, 1984; *Hermann Zapf and His Design Philosophy*, Chicago, 1987; *ABC-XYZapf*, Frankfurt and London, 1989; *L'Opera di Hermann Zapf*, Verona, 1991; *Poetry through Typography*, New York, 1993; *The Design Philosophy of Hermann Zapf* (Japanese), Tokyo, 1995.

**On ZAPF: books**—*Modern Lettering and Calligraphy* edited by Rathbone Holme and Kathleen Frost, London and New York, 1954; *Modern Book Design* by Ruari McLean, London, 1958; *Hermann Zapf: Calligrapher, Type-Designer and Typographer*, exhibition catalogue by Noel Martin Cincinnati, 1960; *Who's Who in Graphic Art* edited by Walter Amstutz, Zurich, 1962, Dubendorf, 1982; *Calligraphie et Typographie de Hermann Zapf*, exhibition cata-

**Hermann Zapf:** *Time Flies—Seize the Day, Horace* **three-dimensional letters cut in aluminum, 1984**

logue, Brussels, 1962; *Buchgestaltung* by Albert Kapr, Dresden, 1963; *Design With Type* by Carl Dair, London and Toronto, 1967; *Herman Zapf: Kalligrafie, Drukletters en Typografische Verzorging,* exhibition catalogue by C. Reedijk, The Hague, 1968; *The Salesman's Herald, Book 39: Dedicated to the Work of Herman Zapf* by Edward Russell and David Brown, Stamford, Connecticut, 1978; *The Thames and Hudson Manual of Typography* by Ruari McLean, London, 1980; *A History of Graphic Design* by Philip B. Meggs, New York and London, 1983; *Les Annes 60* by Anne Bony, Paris, 1983; *Typographic Design: form and Communication* by Rob Carter, Ben Day, and Philip B. Meggs, New York, 1985; *Eye for Industry: Royal Designers for Industry 1936-1986* by Fiona MacCarthy and Patrick Nuttgens, London, 1986.

*

We don't create heroic things to earn fame. No scratches we put on the globe; perhaps with our gentle art, we add a few little dabs of joy into life, in a nicely written praise of the Lord, written with the complete engagement of our heart.

Calligraphy is a peaceful and noble art, done by well-educated human beings who do their work with full commitment, with intense concentration. For we want to put into our letters a little of our own feelings, of our personality and mood. Letters should have grace and beauty in themselves.

We see everywhere a growing interest in calligraphy. In the future, people will work fewer hours a day and hopefully, some may use their free time to do something creative with their hands.

A few more facts about us. No calligrapher is polluting rivers with his ink or is poisoning the air we breathe. Calligraphy makes no noise. We don't fight with arms nor with our pens, but we want to convince sometimes with a handwritten message of special importance in which we believe.

Of course, we know we are not the navel of the world; merely, we like to make nice things with our given talent. And we have a burden of responsibility, the heritage of the great masters of the past, the tradition of the scribes of the Middle Ages, of the royal and imperial ancestors in Europe and Asia. Calligraphy is still a royal activity.

—Hermann Zapf

*    *    *

As a typographer and type-designer, Hermann Zapf is probably most significant for his reintroduction of calligraphic detail and difference into the shapes and spacing of roman type design. More precisely, he has translated many of the qualities of Fraktur type—variety in the swell of the letter stroke, attention to the balance of curved and straight elements in each letter, and fluidity and vigor in

938

line quality—into the more restricted forms of the Latin alphabet. Zapf's first type design was a Fraktur, Gilgengart, but his roman types, especially Palatino and Optima, display in their graceful swell and their slightly squared-off curves a mixture of past and present proportions that has led the way to late-twentieth-century re-evaluation of the appropriateness of the serif type for virtually all aspects of typography, display as well as text.

Both Zapf's roman and serif faces emphasize varied letter widths, a fact that represents an innovative stance in the postwar period, which tended to be dominated by redesigns of the nineteenth-century grotesque sans serifs, which were characterized by, to quote Zapf, "a thoroughgoing equalization of all the letter-widths, rendering them to a certain degree uniform." Zapf's variety in both line quality and letter shape allowed a more active interaction between the paper and the printed letter, while large counters, the open letter spacing required by varied letter widths, and generous leading produced a distinctive German page, spacious and quiet, which has continued to typify German books and has influenced book design throughout the world.

Zapf also designed a Cyrillic face and an Arabic type, as well as display faces and a redrawing of Nicholas Kis's Janson type. He has continued to produce relevant designs for each of the new developments in the rapidly changing technology of the twentieth-century, designing for lead, for phototype (faces for International Typeface Corporation include Zapf Book and Zapf International), and now digital type design. He is working closely with the mathematician Donald Knuth on the Metafont program, which will allow computer generation of new letterforms, and their first face, for use in mathematical publications, is named Euler. That Zapf works for a maximum of technical efficiency while maintaining as much non-technical variety as possible reflects his understanding of the value of innovation and of the human capacity to pay attention and to learn from distinctive detail, not uniformity.

—Frances Butler

# ZEFFIRELLI, (Gian)Franco (Corsi)

Italian stage and film director and designer

**Born:** Florence, 12 February 1923. **Education:** Educated at schools in Florence until 1939; studied painting, at the Accademia di Belle Arti, Florence, 1939-40; studied architecture, at the University of Florence, 1941-46. **Career:** Worked as a radio and stage actor, appearing with the Morelli Stoppa Company, Florence and Rome, 1946-47; film actor and designer, working with Luchino Visconti, Michelangelo Antonioni, and Vittorio de Sica, Rome, 1947-53; freelance stage director and designer, mainly of operas and Shakespearian plays, from 1951; film director and designer from 1957; contract director to Paramount Pictures, 1967-71. **Member:** Directors Guild of America. **Honors:** Academy Award nomination, 1968. **Address:** Via DueMaceli 1, 00180 Rome, Italy.

## Works

Stage productions include—*A Streetcar Named Desire,* Morelli Stoppa Company, Rome, 1949; *Troilus and Cressida,* Morelli Stoppa Company, 1949; *Three Sisters,* Morelli Stoppa Com-

pany, 1951; *La Cenerentola,* La Scala, Milan, 1953; *Lucia di Lammermoor,* Covent Garden, London, 1959; *Cavalliera Rusticana,* Covent Garden, London, 1959; *Romeo and Juliet,* Old Vic, London, 1960; *Othello,* Royal Shakespeare Company, Stratford-upon-Avon, 1961; *Falstaff,* Covent Garden, 1961; *L'Elisir d'Amore,* Glyndebourne Opera, Sussex, 1961; *Don Giovanni,* Covent Garden, 1962; *Alcina,* Covent Garden, 1962; *Romeo and Juliet,* City Center, New York, 1962; *The Lady of the Camellias,* Winter Gardens, New York, 1963; *Who's Afraid of Virginia Woolf?,* Festival de Teatro, Venice, 1963; *After the Fall,* Rome, 1964; *Hamlet,* Old Vic, London, 1964; *Tosca,* Covent Garden, 1964; *Rigoletto,* Covent Garden, 1964; *Much Ado About Nothing,* Old Vic, London, 1965; *Norma,* Paris Opera, 1965; *The She Wolf,* Aldwych Theatre, London, 1969; *Don Giovanni,* Staatsoper, Vienna, 1972; *Otello,* Metropolitan Opera, New York, 1972; *Un Ballo in Maschera,* La Scala, Milan, 1972; *Pagliacci,* Covent Garden, 1973; *Saturday, Sunday, Monday,* Old Vic, London, 1973; *Antony and Cleopatra,* Metropolitan Opera, New York, 1973; *Otello,* La Scala, Milan, 1976; *Lorenzaccio,* Comedie Francaise, Paris, 1976; *Filumena,* Lyric Theatre, London, 1977; *Carmen,* Staatsoper, Vienna, 1978; *Turandot,* Metropolitan Opera, New York, 1987.

Films include—*Giorni de Distruzione* (for TV), 1966; *Taming of the Shrew,* 1967; *Romeo and Juliet,* 1968; *Beethoven's Fidelio* (for TV), 1970; *Beethoven's Missa Solemnis* (for TV), 1970; *Brother Sun, Sister Moon,* 1973; *Jesus of Nazareth* (for TV), 1977; *The Champ,* 1979; *Endless Love,* 1981; *La Traviata,* 1982; *I Pagliaci* (for TV), 1984; *Otello,* 1986; *Young Toscanini* (unreleased), 1988; *Hamlet* (1991).

## Publications

**By ZEFFIRELLI: books**—*Jesus,* Paris and Montreal, 1978: *Zeffirelli: An Autobiography,* London, 1986; **articles**—in *Films and Filming* (London), April 1973, August 1979; *Filmmakers Newsletter* (Ward Hill), September 1973.

**On ZEFFIRELLI: books**—*The Biographical Encyclopedia and Who's Who of the American Theatre* edited by Walter Rigdon, New York, 1966; *The World Encyclopedia of Film* edited by Tim Cawkwell and John M. Smith, London, 1972; *The Oxford Companion to Film* edited by Lis-Anne Bawden, London and New York, 1976; *Stage Design Throughout the World 1970-1975* by Rene Hainaux and Nicole Leclercq, Brussels and London, 1976; *The International Film Encyclopedia* by Ephraim Katz, New York and London, 1980; *International Dictionary of Films and Filmmakers,* Chicago and London, 1984; *The Cambridge Guide to World Theatre* edited by Martin Banham, Cambridge and New York, 1988.

\*       \*       \*

The important influences on the work of Franco Zeffirelli, aside from the cinematic style of his early mentor Lunchino Visconti, have been the great artists of Italy's past from the Renaissance through the nineteenth century. From his early work as an actor, Zeffirelli gained a sense of a performance in action against a rich visual setting, and from his early apprenticeship in films, he learned the importance of the visual envelope that surrounds the actor. He soon began to practice his craft in the theatres and opera houses of Italy, and after his work for the Old Vic, he fully established his mature style of rich, romantic, opulent productions. For example, in his production of *Romeo and Juliet,* he made the audience feel as if it were enveloped within the dust, light, color-atmosphere, and texture of Renaissance Verona. The same elements were at work when he filmed the production, and they were fully operative in the films *The Taming of the Shrew* and *Brother Sun, Sister Moon.* During the 1960s and 1970s, Zeffirelli's work came to be synonymous with richness and romantic opulence, and audiences looked forward to becoming a part of past times and faraway places as they watched the tapestry of his vision unroll upon the stage. Zeffirelli is not an innovator but a conservator, a designer who takes the best from the great artists of Italy's past and recreates their esthetic for modern audiences. He projects no political or social values in his work, no innovative artistic ideals from the contemporary art world. He is a director-designer wedded to presenting a unified visual and aural vision of past times for modern audiences, hoping to make them appreciate with a new awareness the values of Baroque, Renaissance, and Romantic art as a basis for theatrical production. When one attends a Zeffirelli film or a Zeffirelli production of an opera or play, one has the sense that the artist at work on the stage is a direct inheritor of the vision of Titian, Rubens, or Guardi.

—Douglas A. Russell

## ZEISEL, Eva

American ceramic, furniture, and product designer

**Born:** Eva Polanyi Stricker, in Budapest, Hungary, in 1906; emigrated to the United States in 1938, naturalized, 1944. **Education:** Studied painting under Vaszari, at the Royal Academy of Fine Arts, Budapest, 1923-25; apprenticed at Karapnscik's pottery, Budapest, 1924-25. **Family:** Married Hans Zeisel in 1938; children: Jean and John. **Career:** Ceramics designer, at Kilspester Earthenware Factory, Budapest, 1926-27, Hansa Kunstkeramik, Hamburg, 1927, Schramberger Majolika Fabrik, Schramberg, 1928-30, Christian Carstens Kommerzial, Berlin, 1930-32; freelance designer and art director, working for the Lomanossova Porcelain Factory, Dulevo Porcelain Factory and the China and Glass Industry of the U.S.S.R., Leningrad, 1932-37; freelance designer, in New York and Chicago, from 1938; designed for Bay Ridge Specialty Company, Castleton China Company, Red Wing Pottery, Riverside Ceramic Company, Hall China Company, Rosenthal Porcelain, General Mills Company, Sears Roebuck, Loza Gina, Federal Glass Company, Mancioli, Noritake, Nikkon Toki, Zsolnay Factory, and others. Instructor in industrial design, Pratt Institute, Brooklyn, New York, 1939-55; professor, Rhode Island School of Design, Providence, 1954-55; guest lecturer, Royal College of Art, London, 1987-89. **Exhibitions:** Museum of Modern Art, New York, 1946; Walker Art Center, Minneapolis, 1947; Akron Art Institute, Ohio, 1947; Florida Gulf Coast Art Center, Clearwater, 1950; Brooklyn Museum, New York, 1957, 1984; Art Institute of Chicago, 1985; Flint Institute of Art, Michigan, 1985; New Jersey State Museum, Trenton, 1985; St. Louis Art Museum, Missouri, 1985; Everson Museum of Art, Syracuse, New York, 1986; Musée des Arts Décoratifs, Montreal, 1986; Museum of Decorative Arts, Budapest, 1987; Museum fur Angewandte Kunst, Vienna, 1987; Konstindustrumuseum, Helsinki, 1987; Museum of Decorative Arts, Amersfoort, 1988; Stadtmuseum, Schramberg, 1988; Staatsmuseum, Karlsruhe, 1989; Keramik Mu-

seum, Metleach, 1989. **Collections:** Museum of Modern Art, New York; Victoria and Albert Museum, London. **Honors:** Hungarian Exhibition Honor Award, Philadelphia, 1926; National Endowment for the Arts Senior Grant, Washington, D.C., 1982; Hungarian Order of the Star, Budapest, 1984; Honorary Doctorate, Royal College of Art, London, 1988. **Address:** 5825 South Dorchester Avenue, Chicago, Illinois 60637, U.S.A.

## Works

Pitcher in earthenware, for Schramberger Majolika Fabrik, 1929-30.

Tea service in yellow and red glazed porcelain, for Dulevo Porcelain Factory, 1934-36.

Tea service in black, yellow and orange underglazed porcelain, for Dulevo Porcelain Factory, 1934-36.

*Diamond Design* tea service in black and red underglazed porcelain, for Dulevo Porcelain Factory, 1934-36.

*Museum* dinner service in clear glazed porcelain, for Castleton China Company, 1942-43.

*Town and Country* earthenware dinner service, for Red Wing Pottery, 1945.

*Hallcraft Tomorrow's Classic* white glazed earthenware dinner sevice, for Hall China Company, 1949-50.

Chair in tubular steel, for Chicago Metalcraft/Richards Morgenthau and Company, 1950-51.

Stoneware dinner sevice, for Western Stoneware Company, 1952.

*Hallcraft Century* white glazed earthenware dinner service, for Hall China Company, 1955.

*Form Eva* white glazed porcelain dinner service, for Rosenthal Glasund Porzellan, 1957-58.

Lidded casserole, teapot and creamer in white and blue glazed porcelain, for Noritake, 1963.

Lidded bottle in porcelain, for Zsolnay Porcelain Factory, 1983.

Vase in porcelain, for Zsolnay Porcelain Factory, 1983.

Set of majolica bowls, for the Staatliche Mojolika Manufadtur, 1989.

## Publications

**By ZEISEL: articles**—in *Die Schaulade* (Bamberg), February 1932; *Legkaia Industriia* (Moscow), 4 April 1936; *China, Glass and Lamps* (New York), June 1940, June 1941, May 1942; *Interiors* (New York), November 1941, July 1946; *Ceramic Age* (Olmsted), July 1942; *Crockery and Glass Journal* (New York), September/February 1958; *Everyday Art Quarterly* (Minneapolis), Fall 1946.

**On Zeisel: books**—*Modern China: New Designs by Eva Zeisel,* exhibition catalogue, New York, 1946; *The Art of Interior Design* by Victoria Kloss Ball, New York, 1960; *World Ceramics* edited by Robert J. Charleston, London, 1968, 1981; *One hundred Great Product Designs Since 1945* edited by Kathryn Hiesinger and George Marcus, Philadelphia and London, 1983; *Eva Zeisel: Designer for Industry* by Martin Eidelberg and others, Montreal and Chicago, 1984; *The American Design Adventure 1940-1975* by Arthur J. Pulos, London and Cambridge, Massachusetts, 1988.

*

My ideas on contemporary design? Too much has been written, too much forbidden; too many principles have inhibited too much playfulness and have introduced too many idiosyncracies into the gentle endeavor of making beautiful and practical things, which can also be produced by our contemporary method production. To design such things is a comfortable activity, one that has been enjoyed since time immemorial. But this activity flourished in a tacit atmosphere, a tolerant one, a joyful one—giving pleasure to the maker and his audience. The less said, the less written, the more pleasurable, the more practical will be our surroundings. Let's forget the word "functional" and the form-language for which it now stands.

—Eva Zeisel

\*    \*    \*

For forty years, from the late 1920s to the late 1960s, Eva Zeisel held a position at the top of her profession as china and glassware designer for industry. The list of factories that employed her includes the most prestigious and most prolific in the business—Schramberg and Rosenthal in Germany, Dulevo in the U.S.S.R., Universal, Red Wing, Castleton, and Hallcraft in the United States.

Although an intellectual working in Austria and Germany in the late 1920s and early 1930s, Zeisel did not join any academic group, such as the Bauhaus, as she preferred to work from inside industry rather than impose a set of values and standards from the outside. Her conviction that good design should be based on communication with an audience, as well as usefulness and esthetics, differentiated her attitude from the strictly functionalist philosophy of modernism.

Throughout her career, Zeisel continued as an independent designer, applying her talents to the problems at hand and seeking solutions which communicated with her audience. In an era inspired by machine iconography, Zeisel formulated a design philosophy based on familiar and friendly associations for the greatest number of people. For example, she examined the associations of lines and shapes with form and line in nature, with human proportions or reminiscences of classic forms, or with the order of geometry. Small deviations from these she felt could make the viewer uncomfortable.

During the postwar era in the United States, when a premium was placed on design of consumer goods for the home, Zeisel designed a broad range of wares. The most elegant of these, and the one that drew the most acclaim, was a dinnerware set designed in collaboration with New York's Museum of Modern Art (MOMA) and Castleton China. This unusual circumstance was a result of the MOMA design department's orientation, under the direction of Eliot Noyes, both to raise quality and bring good design to the American public. The first contemporary, translucent, porcelain dinnerware produced in the United States for a general audience, the Museum White line competed with those of traditional European porcelain manufacturers such as Rosenthal. Its design relied on the company's technical proficiency for its thick-to-thin development from foot to rim and its blemish-free, shiny white glaze.

Throughout her career, Zeisel's designs have shown influences from the shapes and decoration of her native Hungary's traditional, handmade peasant pottery. Although drawn to both classic design and geometry, she brought an inventive playfulness to her work, which distinguished it from the stark geometry of her European contemporaries. Zeisel used the possibilities of industrial production to create complex relationships of shapes in families of ceramic forms. She sought to synthesize humanistic functionalism in timely designs, which were both pleasant to touch and easy to use.

As a teacher at the Pratt Institute for many years, Zeisel endorsed a design approach that drew on human resources and communication through objects. She relished making things for the pleasurable use of others, and those pursuits made her designs classics of their time.

—Sarah Bodine

## ZIMMERMANN, Reinhart

German stage designer

**Born:** Erfurt, 1 March 1936. **Education:** Trained as a stage set painter, at the Stadtische Buhnen, Erfurt, 1952-54, and as set designer, at the Landestheater, Halle ander Saalel, 1954-57. **Family:** Married Nadeshda Denisowa in 1973; children: Sophie-Marija. **Career:** Assistant to designer Rudolf Heinrich, 1957-61; resident designer, 1961-63, and head of stage design, from 1963, Komische Oper, East Berlin. **Member:** Chairman, DDR section, Organisation Internationale des Scenographes et des Techniciens de Theatre. **Exhibitions:** Prague Quadriennale of Scenography, 1967, 1971, 1976, 1979, 1983. **Collections:** Markisches Museum, Berlin. **Honors:** *Berliner Zeitung* Critics' Prize, 1976; DDR National Prize, Berlin, 1976. **Address:** Kustrinerstrasse 65, 1125 Berlin, German Democratic Republic.

### Works

Stage designs include—(at the Komische Oper, Berlin, unless noted) *Cosi fan Tutte,* 1962; *Der fliegende Hollander,* Opernhaus, Leipzig, 1962 (travelled to Bolschoi Theater, Moscow, 1963); *Boris Godunow,* Opernhaus, Leipzig, 1964; *Jenufa,* Konigliche Oper, 1964, Stockholm, 1972, Opera de Paris, 1980; *Lohengrin,* Opernhaus, Leipzig, 1965; *Heimkehr des Odysseus,* 1966; *Don Giovanni,* 1966; *Der junge Lord,* 1968; *Simone Boccanegra,* Konigliches Theater, Copenhagen, 1968; *Salome,* Theater der Freien Hnsestadt, Bremen, West Germany, 1968; *Aida,* 1969, Holland Festival, Amsterdam, 1973; *Falstaff,* Norske Opera, Oslo, 1969, Holland Festival, Amsterdam, 1972; *Porgy and Bess,* 1969; *Der tolle Tag,* Deutsches Theater, Berlin, 1970; *Hoffmanns Erzähhungen,* for GDR television, Berlin, 1970, Norske Opera, Oslo, 1974; *Eugen Onegin,* Konigliches Theater, Copenhagen, 1971; *Don Quichotte,* 1971; *Romeo and Juliet,* 1972; *Hary Janos,* 1973; *Die Wahlverwandtschaften,* DEFA film studio, East Berlin, 1973; *Figaros Hochzeit,* 1975; *Lulu,* 1975, complete version, 1980; *Aufstieg und Fall der Stadt Mahagonny,* 1977; *Erdgeist und Büchse der Pandora,* Schauspielhaus, Graz, Austria, 1977; *Madame Butterfly,* 1978 (travelled to the Welsh National Opera, Cardiff); *Nachtasyl,* Schauspielhaus, Graz, Austria, 1978; *Fidelio,* English National Opera, London, 1980; *Peter Grimes,* 1981; *La Bohème,* 1982; *Lear,* 1983.

### Publications

**By ZIMMERMANN: articles**—in *Jahrbuch der Komische Oper,* Berlin, 1968, 1969; *Walter Felsenstein Inszeniert Mozart: Die Hochzeit des Figaro,* Berlin, 1981.

**On ZIMMERMANN: articles**—in *Opernwelt Jahrbuch,* Berlin, 1970.

\*

Just as the actors, singers, dancers, words, music, gestures, costumes, and lighting all are parts, stage design is a part, but only a part, of the complete artistic performance. To achieve a unified whole, it is necessary to have the creative cooperation of many people, all of whom must want the same thing, namely, to make the work comprehensible to the public. The director and stage designer, as equal authorities in charge of the production, must devote themselves to this task.

The director should be able to envision the finished product, while the stage designer must be able to comprehend clearly the thought of the director. Both should attempt to develop their ideas out of the work itself and to test the results again and again in the work. They should be able to recognize and understand what the author—or composer—was trying to achieve, to comprehend his times and state of existence, and to know where they now find themselves and what is happening around them. Only then can a unification of a faithfulness to the work and contemporaneity occur and be successfully transmitted to the audience.

—Reinhart Zimmermann

\*   \*   \*

For two decades, Reinhart Zimmermann has been counted among Germany's leading stage designers in the field of musical theatre. He was decisively influenced by his work as assistant to the important stage designer Rudolf Heinrich. One finds traces of this collaboration chiefly in Zimmermann's fundamentally intellectual and aesthetic attitude. A hallmark of his work is the opulent balance between fantasy and energy of form, stemming from a basic dramaturgic analysis. In his best works, which arise mainly from his collaboration with leading producers, such as Walter Felsenstein (*Don Giovanni, Hary Janos, The Marriage of Figaro*), Joachim Herz (*The Young Lord, Lulu, Peter Grimes*), Gotz Fredrich (Siegried Matthus's *The Last Shot, The Return of Odysseus,* Massenet's *Don Quixote*), and Harry Kupfer (*Moses and Aaron* in Dresden, *La Bohème,* and Reimann's *Lear*), Zimmermann's creative energy and ability are clearly evident, making specific and cohesive connections with the work. The most creative principle in Zimmermann's design work is to assist the expression of a production's spirit and essence. His works are functionally and aesthetically integrated into the total artistic performance. Zimmermann is concerned with strong synthetic effect, based on a meaningful dovetailing of production, musical interpretation, performance, and decor. As a designer, he does not strive for any symbolic encoding of the scene but for clarity of staging which effectively speeds the action for a precisely registered social atmosphere and interpretive accent.

—Wolfgang Lange

# ZIPPRODT, Patricia

American stage and film costume designer

**Born:** Evanston, Illinois, in 1925. **Education:** Studied at Wellesley College, Massachusetts, BA, 1946; School of the Art Institute of Chicago, 1946-49; Art Students League, New York, 1950-52; Fashion Institute of Technology, New York, 1952-53. **Career:** Worked as an assistant to stage designers Rouben Ter-Arutunian, William and Jean Eckart, Boris Aronson, Robert Fletcher, and Irene Sharaff, New York, 1953-57; freelance costume designer, New York, from 1957; artistic advisor to the Ballet Hispanico, New York, from 1975. Professor of theatre design, University of Utah, Salt Lake City; visiting lecturer, instructor, and artist at colleges and universities throughout the United States; also founding member, National Theatre for the Deaf. **Exhibitions:** Wright Hepburn Gallery, London, 1966; Capricorn Gallery, New York, 1968; Museum of the City of New York, 1972; University of California, San Diego, 1974; *International Stage Design,* Toneel Museum, Amsterdam, 1975; *American Stage Design,* Lincoln Center, New York, 1975 (toured); *American Ballet Theatre,* New York, 1976-78 (toured); *Sleeping Beauty* sketches, Lincoln Center, New York, 1994; *Paints, Props and Process,* Castle Gallery, New Rochelle, 1994. **Collections:** Museum of the City of New York. **Honors:** Antoinette Perry "Tony" Award, New York, 1964, 1966, 1986; Drama Desk Award, New York, 1968, 1972, 1978, 1990; Emmy Television Award, New York, 1969; Wellesley College Alumnae Achievement Award, 1971; New England Theatre Conference Award of Excellence, 1973; Fashion Institute of Technology Ritter Award, New York, 1977; Joseph P. Maharam Award, New York, 1969, 1981, 1983, 1990; Southeastern Theatre Conference Career Award, 1985; Inducted, Theatre Hall of Fame, 1992; Jane Cooke Runyon Award, Bradford College, 1994. **Address:** 29 King Street, New York, New York 10014, U.S.A.

## Works

Stage productions (New York, unless noted) include—*The Potting Shed,* 1957; *A Visit to a Small Planet,* 1957; *The Virtuous Island,* 1957; *The Apollo of Bellac,* 1957; *Miss Lonely-hearts,* 1957; *The Rope Dancers,* 1957; *The Crucible,* 1958; *Back to Methuselah,* 1958; *The Night Circus,* 1958; *Our Town,* 1958; *The Gang's All Here,* 1959; *The Balcony,* 1960; *Camino Real,* 1960; *Period of Adjustment,* 1960; *The Blacks,* 1961; *The Garden of Sweets,* 1961; *Laurette,* 1961; *Sunday in New York,* 1961; *Madame Aphrodite,* 1961; *Ah Dad, Poor Dad, Mama's Hung You in the Closet and I'm Feelin' So Sad,* 1962; *A Man's a Man,* 1962; *The Matchmaker,* 1962; *Step on a Crack,* 1962; *The Dragon,* 1963; *She Loves Me,* 1963; *Morning Sun,* 1963; *Next Time I'll Sing to You,* 1963; *Too Much Johnson,* 1964; *Fiddler on the Roof,* 1964; *The Tragical Historie of Dr. Faustus,* 1964; *Anya,* 1965; *Pousse-Café,* 1966; *Cabaret,* 1966; *The Little Foxes,* 1967; *Fiddler on the Roof* (London), 1967; *Plaza Suite,* 1968; *Zorba,* 1968; *Gianni Schicchi* (opera), 1969; *The Tale of Kasane,* 1969; *Blueprints,* 1969; *1776,* 1969; *Georgy,* 1970; *Scratch,* 1971; *Pippin,* 1972, *The Mother of Us All* (opera), 1972; *Waiting for Godot* (Minneapolis, Minnesota), 1973; *Pippin* (London), 1973; *Dear Nobody,* 1974; *Mack and Mabel,* 1974; *All God's Chillun Got Wings,* 1975; *Chicago,* 1975; *Poor Murderer,* 1976; *Four Saints in Three Acts,* National Theatre of the Deaf, 1976; *Tannhauser,* 1977; *Naughty Marietta,* 1978; *Stages,* 1978; *King of Hearts,* 1978; *Swing,* 1979; *One Night Stand,* 1980; *Kingdoms,* 1981; *Fools,* 1981; *Whodunnit,* 1982; *Alice in Wonderland,* 1982; *Don Juan,* Tyrone Guthrie Theatre, Minneapolis, 1982; *Sunset,* 1983; *Brighton Beach Memoirs,* 1983; *The Glass Menagerie,* 1983; *Accidental Death of an Anarchist,* 1984; *Anna Christie,* Central Theatre Institute, Beijing, 1984; *Sunday in the Park with George,*

1984; *Sweet Charity,* 1985-86; *Big Deal,* 1986; *Cabaret* (revival), 1987; *Macbeth,* 1988; *Cat on a Hot Tin Roof,* 1989; *Dangerous Games,* 1989; *Fiddler on the Roof* (revival), 1990; *Shogun: The Musical,* 1990; *The Crucible,* 1991; *The Master Builder,* 1992; *Little Hotel on the Side,* 1992; *My Favorite Year,* 1992; *My Fair Lady,* 1993; *School for Scandal,* Shakespeare Company, Washington D.C., 1994.

Ballets include—*Les Noces,* American Ballet, Theatre, 1965; *La Sonnambula,* National Ballet, 1965; *Watermill,* New York City Ballet, 1972; *Dumbarton Oaks,* New York City Ballet, 1973; *Dybbuk Variations,* New York City Ballet, 1974; *The Leaves Are Fading,* American Ballet Theatre, 1975; *Tres Cantos,* Ballet Hispanico, 1976; *Caprichos,* Ballet Hispanico, 1976; *Estuary,* American Ballet Theatre, 1983; *Llamada,* Ballet Hispanico, 1983; *Tito on Tambales,* Ballet Hispanico, 1984; *Beads of Memory,* Houston Ballet, 1985; *Cada Noche ... Tango,* Ballet Hispanico, 1988; *Inez de Castro,* Ballet Hispanico, 1988; *Sondheim Suite,* Pacific North West Ballet, 1989; *Coppelia,* American Ballet Theatre, 1990; *The Sleeping Beauty,* New York City Ballet, 1991; *Who Cares,* Pacific Northwest Ballet, 1992.

Films and television specials include—*The Graduate,* 1967; *The Last of the Mobile Hotshots,* 1969; *Anne Bancroft Special,* 1970; *1776,* 1972; *June Moon,* 1973; *The Glass Menagerie* (with Katherine Hepburn), 1973; *Pippin,* 1981; *Alice in Wonderland,* 1983; *Sunday in the Park with George,* 1986.

Operas include—*La Boheme,* Boston Opera, 1962; *Madame Butterfly,* Boston Opera, 1962; *Hippolyte E Arcie,* Boston Opera, 1966; *Katerina Ismailova,* New York City Opera, 1967; *The Flaming Angel,* New York City Opera, 1968; *The Rise and Fall of the City of Mahagony,* Boston Opera, 1972; *The Mother of Us All* (revival), Guggenheim Museum, 1973; *Lord Byron,* Julliard Opera, 1973; *Tannhauser,* Metropolitan Opera, 1977; *Naughty Marietta,* New York City Opera, 1978; *The Barber of Seville,* Metropolitan Opera, 1982; *The Loves of Don Perlimplin,* San Francisco Opera, 1984; *Fall of the House of Usher,* American Repertory Theater, 1988, Maggiore Festivale Musicale, Italy, 1992.

**Publications**

**By ZIPPRODT: articles**—in *Contemporary Stage Design USA,* New York, 1974; *Theatre Crafts* (New York), 1971, 1973, 1974, 1977, 1987, 1991, 1994.

**On ZIPPRODT: books**—*Contemporary Theatre, Film and Television 2,* Detroit, 1986; *The Cambridge Guide to World Theatre* edited by Martin Banham, Cambridge and New York, 1988; *Costume Design: Techniques of Modern Masters* by Lynn Pecktad, 1993; **articles**— *Vogue,* 1985, 1986; *Theater Week,* 1987; *Elle,* 1987; *New York Times Magazine,* 1987; *DNR,* 1990; *Dance,* 1991; *People,* 1991; "A Costume Designer's Process" in *Fiberarts* by Whitney Blausen, 1991; *TDF* by Stuart Little, 1993; and frequently mentioned in the Sunday edition *New York Times.*

\*     \*     \*

Patricia Zipprodt might be considered a director's designer because she epitomizes the ideal, so often preached in conservatories and schools of design, that the costume designer should subordinate personal design preferences or stylistic approaches to those of the play and the director. She is thus unlike Robert Edmond Jones, Leon Bakst, and Gordon Craig, who are known for developing personal styles and personal philosophic approaches to theatrical design.

When the work of Jean Genet was very little known in this country, she designed the original New York production of *The Balcony* and *The Blacks* and created such distinctive costumes that they have come to be accepted as the "right" way to interpret the intertwined, mirror-reflecting realities of this absurdist. When Zipprodt worked on the musical *Pippin,* she faced, with the director and the choreographer, the seemingly insoluble problem of creating breastplates and armor for an extremely active chorus. Not to be deterred, she worked with one of the costume profession's finest craftsmen on a new form of completely flexible, rubber latex to make armor that broke new ground for costuming. In this case, the new product dictated the nature of her designs rather than the reverse.

When she worked on the original production of *Fiddler on the Roof* for Broadway, she let the nature of the material, the background stories behind the libretto, and the music lead her to a collaboration with the director, choreographer, librettist, and composer to produce a completely cohesive visual whole in which the costumes presented the Russian texture and ethnic Jewish flavor that seemed absolutely appropriate. Other examples as well would demostrate that Zipprodt never appears to have a distinctive, personal style because she always subordinates herself to explorations and decisions made in consultation. Her artistic position is clear: Costume design today is a collaborative art.

—Douglas A. Russell

# ZWART, Piet

Dutch photographer and architect and interior and graphic designer

**Born:** Zaandijk, 28 May 1885. **Education:** Studied at the Rijksschool voor Kunstnijverheid, Amsterdam, 1902-07; Technische Hogeschool, Delft, 1913-14. **Military Service:** Served in the Dutch Army, 1908, 1914-17. **Family:** Married Nel Cleyndert; children: four. **Career:** Furniture and interior designer from 1911, photographer and designer from 1919, and typographer from 1921, working in Leeuwarden, 1909-13, in Voorburg, 1913-26, and in Wasenaar, 1927-77; assistant in the office of architect Jan Wils, Voorburg, 1919-21, and in the office of H.P. Berlage, The Hague, 1921-27; designed for Dutch Posts and Telecommunications, Lagafabriek flooring, Nederlandsche Kabelfabriek, Bruynzeel Company, Kristal Unie, Scheveningen Radio, Trio Printers, and others. Instructor in drawing and art history, at the Industrie en Huishoudschool voor Meisjes, Leeuwarden, 1909-19; instructor in design and ornament, Academie voor Beeldende Kunsten en Technische Wetenschappen, Rotterdam, 1919-23; visiting instructor, Technische Hogeschool, Delft, 1929, and at the Staatliche Bauhaus, Dessau, 1931. Architecture correspondent, *Het Vaderland* newspaper, Amsterdam, 1925-28; president, De 8 en Opbouw architects' group, Amsterdam, 1931-37. **Exhibitions:** Drukkerij Trio, The Hague, 1933; Stedelijk Museum, Amsterdam, 1961; Haags Gemeentemuseum, The Hague, 1968, 1973 (toured), 1985; Wassenaarse Galerie-Bibliotheek, Wassenaar, 1974; Ex Libris, New York, 1980. **Collections:** Piet Zwart Archive,

Prentenkabinet, Leiden University; Haags Gemeentemuseum, The Hague; Stedelijk Museum, Amsterdam; Museum Folkwang, Essen; Kestner-Gesellschaft, Hannover. **Honors:** Quellinus Typography Prize, 1959; David Roell Prize, 1964. Honorary Royal Designer for Industry, Royal Society of Arts, London, 1966. **Died:** Leidschendam, 24 September 1977.

## Works

Books designed—*De Absolute Film* by Ter Braaks, Rotterdam, 1931; *De Techniek van de Kunstfilm* by Mannus Franken and Joris Ivens, Rotterdam, 1931; *Wij Slaven van Suriname* by Anton de Kok, Rotterdam, 1934; and other books in the series *Monografien over Filmkunst,* for W.L. & J. Brusse Publishers, Rotterdam, 1931-34; also numerous publications for Nederlandsche Kabelfabriek, Delft; the Dutch PTT, The Hague; Bruynzeel Company, Zaandam; Drukkerij Trio, The Hague; Nijgh & Van Ditmar, Rotterdam; De 8 en Opbouw, Amsterdam.

## Publications

**By ZWART: books**—*Filmreclame,* Rotterdam, 1933; *Documents in the Visual Arts, Vol. 1: Piet Zwart,* with text by F. Muller and P.E. Althaus, Teufen, 1966; *Piet Zwart: 12 Fotografien,* portfolio, with an introduction by Kees Broos, Cologne, 1974.

**On ZWART: books**—*Die Neue Typografie* by Jan Tschichold, Berlin, 1928; *Eine Stunde Druckgestaltung* by Jan Tschichold, Stuttgart, 1930; *The New Graphic Design* by Karl Gerstner and Markus Kutter, Teufen and London, 1959; *Piet Zwart: Typotekt,* exhibition catalogue designed by Otto Treumann and Wim Crouwel, Amsterdam, 1961; *Sleutelwoorden/Keywords: Piet Zwart* edited by Jurrian Schrofer and Will Sandberg, The Hague, 1965; *Piet Zwart* by Fridolin Muller, New York, 1966; *Piet Zwart en PTT,* exhibition catalogue by Karst Zwart, The Hague, 1968; *Pioneers of Modern Typography* by Herbert Spencer, London, 1969; *A History of Visual Communication* by Josef Muller-Brockmann, New York, 1971; *Piet Zwart,* exhibition catalogue by Kees Broos, The Hague, 1973; *Fotografie in Nederland 1920-1940,* exhibition catalogue by Flip Bool and Kees Broos, The Hague, 1979; *Tubular Steel Furniture* edited by Barbie Campbell-Cole and Tim Benton, London, 1979; *Piet Zwart: Typotekt,* exhibition catalogue with introduction by Arthur Cohen, New York, 1980; *Retrospective Fotografie: Piet Zwart* by Kees Broos, Dusseldorf, 1981; *Piet Zwart 1885-1977* by Kees Broos, Amsterdam, 1982; *The Twentieth-Century Poster: Design of the Avant-Garde* by Dawn Ades, New York, 1984; *Typographic Design: Form and Communication* by Rob Carter, Ben Day, and Philip Meggs, New York, 1985.

\* \* \*

Before joining Jan Wils, a member of the de Stijl group, as an assistant in 1919 at the age of 34, Piet Zwart had already carried out a few minor furniture designs in the style of Berlage, Dijsselhof, and Bazel. The influence of de Stijl can clearly be seen in the first typographical design (a letterhead for Wils) which he executed at that time. In 1921, Zwart became assistant to the famous Dutch architect, H.P. Berlage, with whom he collaborated on the construction of a Christian Science church and on early designs for a municipal museum, both in the Hague. While working in Berlage's office, Zwart produced his first advertisement designs (for a firm of flooring manufacturers in the Hague) and carried out his first commissions for industrial design. About this time, too, he designed a brochure for Fortoliefabriek in Utrecht. Berlage then introduced Zwart to one of his relatives who was manager of the Nederlandsche Kabelfabriek (NKF) at Delft, and by 1925, at the age of forty, Zwart had begun to devote the greater part of his time to typography. During the next few years, he produced many hundreds of designs for advertisements and catalogues for the Nederlandsche Kabelfabriek. These designs, like the earlier Wils letterhead, make use of heavy rules and strong contrasts.

Zwart had an extraordinary ability to organise layout so that essential information could be grasped by the reader with a minimum of effort. He made increasingly effective use of imaginative photography (after 1938, his own), and this became a major interest for him. Photography plays an important part in much of the graphic design, including stamps he executed for the Dutch post office from 1928 onwards.

Zwart's designs for Nederlandsche Kabelfabrick catalogues and booklets and for the Dutch post office are full of vigorous and imaginative surprises. His colours are those of de Stijl—primary blue, yellow, and red—but Zwart's clever use of words, his ingenious manipulation of type and printer's rules, his dramatic use of strong-contrast photographs and of negative reproductions, the dexterity with which he superimposed photographs in one strong colour over other photographs in other colours, his use of transparent materials, of cut-out shapes and cleverfolds, and indeed, the whole uninhibited, pioneering enthusiasm of his attack suddenly charged the printed page with a new power, a new tension and gave it, in effect, a new dimension.

—Herbert Spencer

# NATIONALITY INDEX

## Algerian
Abdelkader Farrah

## American
Adolfo
Mehemed Fehmy Agha
Anni Albers
Theoni Aldredge
Walter Heinz Allner
Boris Aronson
Associated Space Design
Scott Barrie
James Basevi
Saul Bass
Howard Bay
Herbert Bayer
Geoffrey Beene
Ward Bennett
Lucian Bernhard
Harry Bertoia
Betanova
Michael Bierut
Joseph Binder
Robert I. Blaich
Bill Blass
Robert Boyle
Peter Bradford
Marcel Breuer
Alexey Brodovitch
Robert Brunner
Aaron Burns
Stephen Burrows
Will Burtin
Frances Butler
Ben Carré
David Carson
Don Chadwick
Ivan Chermayeff
Serge Chermayeff
Chermayeff & Geismar Associates
Seymour Chwast
David Colley
Muriel Cooper
Morison S. Cousins
Louis Danziger
Richard Day
Rudolph de Harak
Donald Deskey
Niels Diffrient
Jay Doblin
Louis Dorfsman
Henry Dreyfuss
Raoul Pène du Bois
Joseph D'Urso
Charles Eames
Ray Eames
Perry Ellis
Emigre
Environetics Group
Gene Federico

Perry Ferguson
Edward Fields
Jules Fisher
Gregory Fossella
Arnold Friedmann
frogdesign Inc.
S. Neil Fujita
Richard Buckminster Fuller
James Fulton
James Galanos
Frank Gehry
Thomas H. Geismar
Steff Geissbuhler
Rudi Gernreich
Robert Gersin
Bob Gill
Alexander Girard
Milton Glaser
Mordecai Gorelik
Michael Graves
J. Malcolm Grear
April Greiman
Maija Grotell
GVO Inc.
Halston
William J. Hannon
Cathy Hardwick
Edith Head
Dale Hennesy
Helena Hernmarck
Catherine Hipp
Gerald P. Hirshberg
Harry Horner
Ann Hould-Ward
Allen Hurlburt
ISD
Robert Israel
George Jenkins
Norma Kamali
Donna Karan/Louis Dell'Olio
Gyorgy Kepes
Chip Kidd
Mark-Lee Kirk
Anne Klein
Calvin Klein
Vincent G. Kling
Florence Klotz
Florence Knoll
Boris Kroll
Walter Landor
Anya Larkin
Jack Lenor Larsen
Ralph Lauren
Michael Lax
Eugene Lee
Harold Eliot Leeds
Boris Leven
Ross Littell
Raymond Loewy
George Lois

947

William Ivey Long
Santo Loquasto
Eugene Lourié
Herbert Lubalin
Gerald Luss
Ronald L. MacNeil
Mainbocher
Michael Manwaring
Noel Martin
John Massey
Katherine McCoy
Michael McCoy
Mary McFadden
Richard Alan Meier
Jo Mielziner
Ludwig Mies van der Rohe
James Miho
Tomoko Miho
Gene Moore
Tharon Musser
George Nelson
Louis Nelson
Norman Norell
Eliot Noyes
Donald Oenslager
Todd Oldham
Victor Papanek
Art Paul
Cipe Pineles
Warren Platner
William Lansing Plumb
Walter Plunkett
Antoine Predock
James Prestini
Arthur J. Pulos
Paul Rand
Deane Richardson
Jens Risom
Carrie Robbins
M. Clark Robertson
Terrence Harold Robsjohn-Gibbings
Kevin Roche
Ann Roth
John F. Saladino
Giorgio Sant'Angelo
Douglas W. Schmidt
Irene Sharaff
Adele Simpson
Jack Martin Smith
Oliver Smith
Jerome Snyder
Space Design Group
Henry Steiner
Robert A. M. Stern
Brooks Stevens
William Stumpf
Richard Sylbert
TAC Interior Architecture and Graphic Communication
Dean Tavoularis

John J. Telnack
Rouben Ter-Arutunian
Bradbury Thompson
Stanley Tigerman
Pauline Trigére
George Tscherny
Koos van den Akker
John Vassos
Robert Charles Venturi
Tucker Viemeister
Sohrab Vossoughi
Robin Wagner
Don Wallance
John Weitz
Lyle Wheeler
Henry Wolf
Russel Wright
Richard Saul Wurman
Lance Wyman
Jay Yang
Eva Zeisel
Patricia Zipprodt

## Argentinian
Emilio Ambasz
Guillermo Gonzalez Ruiz
Gustavo Pedroza
Raul Shakespear
Ronald Shakespear

## Austrian
Carl Auböck
Hans Hollein
Karl Mang
Porsche Design

## Belgian
Jean-Michel Folon

## British
Ken Adam
Alan Aldridge
Bruce Archer
Laura Ashley
Brian Asquith
John Bates
Edward Bawden
Misha Black
John Box
John Bury
Henry Thomas Cadbury-Brown
Edward Carrick
Matthew Carter
Hugh Casson
Chamberlin Powell and Bon
Susan Collier/Sarah Campbell
Terence Conran
Theo Crosby
Lucienne Day

Robin Day
Willy Maks De Majo
Duffy-Eley-Giffone-Worthington
Tom Eckersley
Tazeena Firth
Alan Fletcher
Colin Forbes
Gina Fratini
Anthony Froshaug
Margaret Furse
Roger Furse
Abram Games
James Gardner
Kenneth Garland
Bill Gibb
Ernö Goldfinger
Kenneth Grange
Milner Gray
Ashley Havinden
Desmond Heeley
F. H. K. Henrion
Jocelyn Herbert
Robert Heritage
David Hicks
George Him
Hipgnosis
James Holland
Alec Issigonis
Sally Jacobs
Jock Kinneir
Andrzej Klimowski
Peter Kneebone
Ralph Koltai
Vincent Korda
Mervyn Kurlansky
Bernard Leach
Dennis Lennon
Jan Le Witt
Ian Logan
Peter Lord
Leonard Manasseh
Enid Marx
David Mellor
Francis Meynell
Marcello Minale
Tanya Moiseiwitsch
Alex Moulton
Jean Muir
John Napier
Timothy O'Brien
Pentagram Design
Edward Pond
Anthony Powell
Mary Quant
John Reid
Zandra Rhodes
Martyn Rowlands
Gordon Russell
Hans Schleger
Hans Schmoller

Basil Spence
Herbert Spencer
Richard Stevens
Reynolds Stone
Brian Tattersfield
Carl Toms
Alan Tye
Tony Walton
Jon Wealleans
Robert Welch
Albert Whitlock
Lewis Woudhuysen

## Canadian
Paul Rodney Arthur
Lida Baday
Douglas Cameron Ball
Jonathan Crinion
Donna Cummings
Tom Deacon
Louis Fishauf
Allan Robb Fleming
John Fluevog
Peter Fox
Francesco + Aldo Piccaluga, Inc.
Claude Gidman
Rolf Harder
Diti Katona
Kerr Keller Design Inc.
Burton Kramer
Thomas Lamb
Michael Levine
Marshall Cummings & Associates
Marian Marshall
Bruce Douglas Mau
Ernst Roch
Spencer Francey Peters
Jean Pierre Viau
Nelson Vigneault
George Yabu
Chris Yaneff

## Chilean
Ximena Ulibarri

## Chinese-American
Ming Cho Lee

## Columbian
David Consuegra

## Cuban
Félix Beltrán

## Czechoslovak
Wilfried Minks
Josef Svoboda
Jan Vančura
Ladislav Vychodil

## Danish

Lis Ahlmann
Acton Bjørn
Erik Herlow
Knud Holscher
Arne Jacobsen
Finn Juhl
Poul Kjaerholm
Henning Koppel
Erik Magnussen
Grethe Meyer
Børge Mogensen
Verner Panton
Jorgen Rasmussen
Johnny Sørensen
Magnus Stephensen
Rud Thygesen
Hans J. Wegner

## Dominican

Oscar de la Renta

## Dutch

Pieter Brattinga
Wim Crouwel
Jan de Fouw
Bob Noorda
Benno Premsela
Willem Sandberg
Paul Schuitema
Ronaldus Shamask
Piet Zwart

## Finnish

Alvar Aalto
Eero Aarnio
Erik Bruun
Rut Bryk
Vuokko Eskolin-Nurmesniemi
Kaj Franck
Simo Heikkila
Dora Jung
Markku Kosonen
Yrjo Kukkapuro
Irma Kukkasjärvi
Maija Lavonen
Perttu Mentula
Marjatta Metsovaara
Martti Mykkanen
Antti Nurmesniemi
Markku Piri
Ritva Puotila
Erkki Ruuhinen
Juhani Salovaara
Timo Sarpaneva
Ilmari Tapiovaara
Oiva Toikka
Pekka Vuori
Björn Weckström
Tapio Wirkkala

## French

Agnes B.
Pierre Balmain
Marc Bohan
Jean Cacharel
Pierre Cardin
Jean Carlu
Gabrielle Chanel
Pierre Charbonnier
Roman Cieslewicz
Paul Colin
André Courrèges
Lucien Coutaud
Jean D'Eaubonne
Jean-Charles de Castelbajac
Hubert de Givenchy
Jean-Claude de Luca
Erté
André François
Jean-Paul Gaultier
Grapus
Madame Grès
Emmanuelle Khanh
Ted Lapidus
Jean Larcher
Jan Lenica
Alain Le Quernec
Robert Massin
Claude Montana
Olivier Mourgue
Thierry Mugler
Jean-Pierre Ponnelle
Andrée Putman
Sonia Rykiel
Yves Saint Laurent
Philippe Starck
Roger Tallon
Chantal Thomass
Alexandre Trauner
Emanuel Ungaro
Madeleine Vionnet

## German

Otl Aicher
Hans Theodor Baumann
Karl Oskar Blase
Gui Bonsiepe
Marianne Brandt
Rido Busse
Karl Duschek
Heinz Edelmann
Hartmut Esslinger
Jochen Finke
Richard Fischer
Willy Fleckhaus
Achim Freyer
Friedrich Friedl
Albrecht Zeppo Graf Goertz
Hein Heckroth
Pieter Hein

Karl-Ernst Herrmann
Hans Hillmann
Wolfgang Joop
Herbert W. Kapitzki
Albert Kapr
Leo Kerz
Günther Kieser
Werner Klemke
Karl Lagerfeld
Olaf Leu
Holger Matthies
Ingo Maurer
Almir Mavignier
Rolf Felix Müller
Alexander Neumeister
Herbert Ohl
Ott + Stein
Ferdinand Porsche
Peter Raacke
Gunter Rambow
Dieter Rams
Bruno Sacco
Horst Sagert
Jil Sander
Richard Sapper
Herbert H. Schultes
Jurgen Spohn
Klaus Staeck
Anton Stankowski
Gero Troike
Karl von Appen
Wilhelm Wagenfeld
Hermann Warm
Wolfgang Weingart
Bruno K. Wiese
Hermann Zapf
Reinhart Zimmermann

## Hungarian
György Kemény

## Irish
Sybil Connolly
Paul Costelloe
Arthur Gibney
Eileen Gray
Denis Handy
Paul Hogan
Gearóid O'Conchubhair
Philip Treacy

## Italian
Franco Albini
Walter Albini
Giorgio Armani
Sergio Asti
Gae Aulenti
Carlo Bartoli
Basile
Melchiorre Bega

Mario Bellini
Laura Biagiotti
Cini Boeri
Antonio Boggeri
Rodolfo Bonetto
Bruno Bozzetto
Brioni
Eugenio Carmi
Anna Castelli Ferrieri
Achille Castiglioni
Livio Castiglioni
Pier Giacomo Castiglioni
Pierluigi Cerri
Paolo Chessa
Joe Colombo
Giulio Confalonieri
Enrico Coveri
Michele De Lucchi
Danilo Donati
Rinaldo Donzelli
Fendi
Gianfranco Ferré
Elio Fiorucci
Gianfranco Frattini
A. G. Fronzoni
Piero Gherardi
Dante Giacosa
Giorgetto Giugiaro
Vittorio Gregotti
Franco Grignani
Giancarlo Iliprandi
Pino Lancetti
Ugo La Pietra
Emanuele Luzzati
Vico Magistretti
Tomas Maldonado
Mariuccia Mandelli
Angelo Mangiarotti
Giovanni Mardersteig
Enzo Mari
Ottavio Missoni
Rosita Missoni
Carlo Mollino
Bruno Munari
Ico Parisi
Gaetano Pesce
Pininfarina
Giovanni Pintori
Gianni Polidori
Gio Ponti
Emilio Pucci
Alberto Rosselli
Cinzia Ruggeri
Roberto Sambonet
Carlo Scarpa
Tobia Scarpa
Mario Scheichenbauer
Luciano Soprani
Ettore Sottsass Jr.
Giotto Stoppino

Armando Testa
Valentino
Gianni Versace
Lella Vignelli
Massimo Vignelli
Gianfranco Zaccai
Marco Zanuso
Franco Zeffirelli

**Japanese**
Junichi Arai
Kiyoshi Awazu
Kenji Ekuan
Shigeo Fukuda
GK Graphics
Yoshio Hayakawa
Takenobu Igarashi
Fujiwo Ishimoto
Shima Ito
Yusaku Kamekura
Toshihiro Katayama
Mitsuo Katsui
Kenzo
Kazuo Kimura
Iwataro Koike
Tom Matano
Minoru Matsuba
Takaaki Matsumoto
Masa Minagawa
Issey Miyake
Hanae Mori
Kazumasa Nagai
Makoto Nakamura
Takeshi Nishizawa
Tomoji Okada
Kiyoshi Sakashita
Kohei Sugiura
Yoichi Sumita
Ikko Tanaka
Masaaki Tanaka
Tokuji Watanabe
Kansai Yamamoto
Yohji Yamamoto
Sori Yanagi
Shoei Yoh
Tadanori Yokoo

**Mexican**
Eduardo Terrazas

**Nigerian**
Haig David-West

**Norwegian**
Tias Eckhoff

**Polish**
Bogusław Balicki
Roman Duszek

Mieczyslaw Górowski
Jerzy Gurawski
Hubert Hilscher
Tadeusz Kantor
Krzysztof Lenk
Jan Młodozeniec
Jozef Mroszczak
Marcin Mroszczak
Andrzej Pawloski
Jan Sawka
Leokadia Serafinowicz
Franciszek Starowieyski
Waldemar Swierzy
Jozef Szajna
Henryk Tomaszewski
Maciej Urbaniec
Leon Urbański
Zofia Wierchowicz

**Polish-American**
Anton Grot

**Russian**
Sonia Delaunay
Yuri Soloviev
George Tsypin

**Spanish**
Cristobal Balenciaga
Javier Mariscal
Paco Rabanne
Studio Per

**Swedish**
Tom Ahlström
Åke Axelsson
Maria Benktzon
Prince Sigvard Bernadotte
Karin Björquist
Jonas Bohlin
Torun Vivianna Bülow-Hübe
Gunnar Cyrén
Ingrid Dessau
Hans Ehrich
Age Faith-Ell
Sven Fristedt
Elisabet Hasselberg-Olsson
Erik Höglund
Johan Huldt
Ulrica Hydman-Vallien
Sven-Eric Juhlin
Börge Lindau
Bo Lindekrantz
Vicke Lindstrand
Carl Malmsten
Bruno Mathsson
Rune Monö
Barbro Nilsson
Sven Palmqvist

Sigurd Persson
Signe Persson-Melin
Inez Svensson
Bertil Vallien
Ann Wolff

## Swiss
Walter Ballmer
Max Bill
Max Caflisch
Hermann Eidenbenz
Hans Erni
Adrian Frutiger
Karl Gerstner
Ernst and Ursula Hiestand
Hans Peter Hoch
Armin Hofmann
Max Huber
Herbert Leupin
Hans-Rudolf Lutz
Herbert Matter
Bruno Monguzzi
Josef Müller-Brockmann
Hans Neuburg
Siegfried Odermatt
Emil Ruder
Rosmarie Tissi
Niklaus Troxler
Jan Tschichold

## Vietnamese
Tan Guidicelli

# DESIGN FIELD INDEX

## Advertising
Ward Bennett
Karl Oskar Blase
Bruno Bozzetto
Herbert Leupin
Erkki Ruuhinen
Anton Stankowski
Chris Yaneff

## Architect
Alvar Aalto
Franco Albini
Emilio Ambasz
Sergio Asti
Carl Auböck
Gae Aulenti
Carlo Bartoli
Herbert Bayer
Melchiorre Bega
Harry Bertoia
Max Bill
Misha Black
Cini Boeri
Jonas Bohlin
Marcel Breuer
Henry Thomas Cadbury-Brown
Hugh Casson
Anna Castelli Ferrieri
Achille Castiglioni
Livio Castiglioni
Pierluigi Cerri
Chamberlin Powell and Bon
Ivan Chermayeff
Serge Chermayeff
Chermayeff & Geismar Associates
Paolo Chessa
Joe Colombo
Terence Conran
Theo Crosby
Duffy-Eley-Giffone-Worthington
Joseph D'Urso
Charles Eames
Environetics Group
A. G. Fronzoni
Richard Buckminster Fuller
Frank Gehry
Thomas H. Geismar
Arthur Gibney
Ernö Goldfinger
Guillermo Gonzalez Ruiz
Michael Graves
Eileen Gray
Vittorio Gregotti
Franco Grignani
Jerzy Gurawski
Denis Handy
Erik Herlow
Knud Holscher
Arne Jacobsen
Finn Juhl

Gyorgy Kepes
Poul Kjaerholm
Vincent G. Kling
Florence Knoll
Thomas Lamb
Ugo La Pietra
Harold Eliot Leeds
Dennis Lennon
Peter Lord
Vico Magistretti
Leonard Manasseh
Karl Mang
Angelo Mangiarotti
Richard Alan Meier
Perttu Mentula
Grethe Meyer
Ludwig Mies van der Rohe
Carlo Mollino
George Nelson
Eliot Noyes
Herbert Ohl
Verner Panton
Ico Parisi
Pentagram Design
Gaetano Pesce
Francesco + Aldo Piccaluga, Inc.
Warren Platner
Gio Ponti
Antoine Predock
Jorgen Rasmussen
John Reid
Kevin Roche
Alberto Rosselli
Roberto Sambonet
Carlo Scarpa
Tobia Scarpa
Mario Scheichenbauer
Johnny Sørensen
Ettore Sottsass Jr.
Space Design Group
Basil Spence
Philippe Starck
Magnus Stephensen
Robert A. M. Stern
Studio Per
Eduardo Terrazas
Rud Thygesen
Stanley Tigerman
Alan Tye
Robert Charles Venturi
Jon Wealleans
Hans J. Wegner
Lewis Woudhuysen
Shoei Yoh
Marco Zanuso
Piet Zwart

## Art director
Mehemed Fehmy Agha
Antonio Boggeri

Richard Day
Ray Eames
Gianfranco Frattini
Alexander Girard
Hans Hollein
Ikko Tanaka
Ximena Ulibarri

**Book**
Alan Aldridge
Edward Bawden
Karl Oskar Blase
Max Caflisch
Pierluigi Cerri
Seymour Chwast
Muriel Cooper
Willy Fleckhaus
Allan Robb Fleming
Alan Fletcher
Yoshio Hayakawa
Hans Hillmann
Hubert Hilscher
Hans Peter Hoch
Albert Kapr
Chip Kidd
Giovanni Mardersteig
Francis Meynell
Hans Schmoller
Kohei Sugiura
Jan Tschichold
Massimo Vignelli
Hermann Zapf

**Ceramics**
Karin Björquist
Rut Bryk
Torun Vivianna Bülow-Hübe
Sybil Connolly
Tias Eckhoff
Hans Erni
Kaj Franck
Maija Grotell
Ulrica Hydman-Vallien
Fujiwo Ishimoto
Arne Jacobsen
Poul Kjaerholm
Henning Koppel
Bernard Leach
Vicke Lindstrand
Erik Magnussen
Grethe Meyer
Signe Persson-Melin
Inez Svensson
Oiva Toikka
Bertil Vallien
Wilhelm Wagenfeld
Eva Zeisel

**Corporate**
Erik Bruun

Chermayeff & Geismar Associates
Rinaldo Donzelli
Karl Duschek
Gregory Fossella
GK Graphics
Gottschalk and Ash
Paul Hogan
Takenobu Igarashi
Walter Landor
Javier Mariscal
Hans Schleger
Ikko Tanaka
Massimo Vignelli

**Costume**
Theoni Aldredge
Gabrielle Chanel
Danilo Donati
Achim Freyer
Margaret Furse
Edith Head
Pieter Hein
Ann Hould-Ward
Robert Israel
Sally Jacobs
Florence Klotz
Eugene Lee
William Ivey Long
Mainbocher
Hanae Mori
Walter Plunkett
Ann Roth
Gero Troike
Tony Walton
Patricia Zipprodt

**Design planner**
Robert I. Blaich
Jay Doblin

**Display**
Walter Ballmer
Betanova
Karl Oskar Blase
Jean Carlu
Yoshio Hayakawa
Max Huber
Gene Moore
Hans Neuburg
Bob Noorda
Giovanni Pintori
Roberto Sambonet
Ikko Tanaka
John Vassos

**Environmental**
Kiyoshi Awazu
Gottschalk and Ash
April Greiman

Takenobu Igarashi
Toshihiro Katayama
Kerr Keller Design Inc.
Walter Landor
Leonard Manasseh
Takeshi Nishizawa
Ernst Roch
William Stumpf
Roger Tallon

**Exhibition**
Alvar Aalto
Franco Albini
Emilio Ambasz
Sergio Asti
Gae Aulenti
Walter Ballmer
Betanova
Max Bill
Misha Black
Pieter Brattinga
Erik Bruun
Will Burtin
Henry Thomas Cadbury-Brown
Hugh Casson
Achille Castiglioni
Pier Giacomo Castiglioni
Pierluigi Cerri
Ivan Chermayeff
Serge Chermayeff
Chermayeff & Geismar Associates
Paolo Chessa
Joe Colombo
Theo Crosby
Wim Crouwel
Michele De Lucchi
Charles Eames
Ray Eames
Vuokko Eskolin-Nurmesniemi
Tazeena Firth
Gregory Fossella
Gianfranco Frattini
Friedrich Friedl
James Gardner
Thomas H. Geismar
Milton Glaser
Ernö Goldfinger
Guillermo Gonzalez Ruiz
Milner Gray
Vittorio Gregotti
Simo Heikkila
Erik Herlow
Ernst and Ursula Hiestand
George Him
Hans Peter Hoch
Hans Hollein
Toshihiro Katayama
Gyorgy Kepes
Leo Kerz
Günther Kieser

Yrjo Kukkapuro
Ugo La Pietra
Michael Lax
Karl Mang
Angelo Mangiarotti
Noel Martin
Carlo Mollino
Bruno Monguzzi
Gene Moore
Jozef Mroszczak
Bruno Munari
Antti Nurmesniemi
Timothy O'Brien
Art Paul
Andrzej Pawloski
Gio Ponti
Benno Premsela
John Reid
Emil Ruder
Willem Sandberg
Timo Sarpaneva
Carlo Scarpa
Hans Schleger
Paul Schuitema
Ettore Sottsass Jr.
Basil Spence
Philippe Starck
Kohei Sugiura
Josef Svoboda
Ilmari Tapiovaara
Eduardo Terrazas
Carl Toms
Massimo Vignelli
Lewis Woudhuysen
Marco Zanuso

**Fashion**
Adolfo
Agnes B.
Walter Albini
Giorgio Armani
Laura Ashley
Carl Auböck
Lida Baday
Cristobal Balenciaga
Pierre Balmain
Scott Barrie
Basile
John Bates
Geoffrey Beene
Ward Bennett
Laura Biagiotti
Bill Blass
Marc Bohan
Brioni
Stephen Burrows
Jean Cacharel
Pierre Cardin
Gabrielle Chanel
Sybil Connolly

Paul Costelloe
André Courrèges
Enrico Coveri
Jean-Charles de Castelbajac
Hubert de Givenchy
Oscar de la Renta
Jean-Claude De Luca
Perry Ellis
Erté
Vuokko Eskolin-Nurmesniemi
Fendi
Gianfranco Ferré
Elio Fiorucci
John Fluevog
Peter Fox
Gina Fratini
James Galanos
Jean-Paul Gaultier
Rudi Gernreich
Bill Gibb
Madame Grès
Halston
Cathy Hardwick
Catherine Hipp
Wolfgang Joop
Norma Kamali
Donna Karan/Louis Dell'Olio
Kenzo
Emmanuelle Khanh
Anne Klein
Calvin Klein
Karl Lagerfeld
Pino Lancetti
Ted Lapidus
Ralph Lauren
Mainbocher
Mariuccia Mandelli
Javier Mariscal
Mary McFadden
Marjatta Metsovaara
Ottavio Missoni
Rosita Missoni
Issey Miyake
Claude Montana
Hanae Mori
Thierry Mugler
Jean Muir
Norman Norell
Todd Oldham
Markku Piri
Emilio Pucci
Mary Quant
Paco Rabanne
Zandra Rhodes
Cinzia Ruggeri
Sonia Rykiel
Yves Saint Laurent
Jil Sander
Giorgio Sant'Angelo
Ronaldus Shamask

Adele Simpson
Luciano Soprani
Tan Guidicelli
Chantal Thomass
Philip Treacy
Pauline Trigére
Emanuel Ungaro
Valentino
Koos van den Akker
Gianni Versace
Madeleine Vionnet
John Weitz
Kansai Yamamoto
Yohji Yamamoto

## Film
Ken Adam
Kiyoshi Awazu
James Basevi
Howard Bay
John Box
Robert Boyle
Bruno Bozzetto
Ben Carré
Edward Carrick
Pierre Charbonnier
Richard Day
Jean D'Eaubonne
Danilo Donati
Raoul Pène du Bois
Charles Eames
Ray Eames
Heinz Edelmann
Erté
Perry Ferguson
Achim Freyer
Roger Furse
Piero Gherardi
Mordecai Gorelik
Anton Grot
Hein Heckroth
Dale Hennesy
Jocelyn Herbert
Harry Horner
George Jenkins
Gyorgy Kepes
Leo Kerz
Mark-Lee Kirk
Andrzej Klimowski
Vincent Korda
Eugene Lee
Jan Lenica
Boris Leven
Santo Loquasto
Eugene Lourié
Emanuele Luzzati
John Napier
Andrzej Pawloski
Gianni Polidori

Jean-Pierre Ponnelle
Anthony Powell
Ann Roth
Irene Sharaff
Jack Martin Smith
Oliver Smith
Josef Svoboda
Richard Sylbert
Ilmari Tapiovaara
Dean Tavoularis
Carl Toms
Alexandre Trauner
George Tsypin
Tony Walton
Hermann Warm
Lyle Wheeler
Albert Whitlock
Franco Zeffirelli

## Furniture
Alvar Aalto
Franco Albini
Åke Axelsson
Melchiorre Bega
Ward Bennett
Harry Bertoia
Cini Boeri
Jonas Bohlin
Rodolfo Bonetto
Anna Castelli Ferrieri
Pier Giacomo Castiglioni
Don Chadwick
Serge Chermayeff
Joe Colombo
Jonathan Crinion
Robin Day
Tom Deacon
Jean-Charles de Castelbajac
Niels Diffrient
Duffy-Eley-Giffone-Worthington
Charles Eames
Ray Eames
Tias Eckhoff
Kaj Franck
frogdesign Inc.
Frank Gehry
Ernö Goldfinger
Michael Graves
Eileen Gray
Simo Heikkila
Robert Heritage
David Hicks
Johan Huldt
Arne Jacobsen
Kerr Keller Design Inc.
Poul Kjaerholm
Florence Knoll
Yrjo Kukkapuro
Thomas Lamb
Ugo La Pietra

Dennis Lennon
Börge Lindau
Bo Lindekrantz
Ross Littell
Erik Magnussen
Carl Malmsten
Karl Mang
Enzo Mari
Bruno Mathsson
Grethe Meyer
Ludwig Mies van der Rohe
Børge Mogensen
Gearóid O'Conchubhair
Herbert Ohl
Verner Panton
Warren Platner
Porsche Design
Andrée Putman
Jens Risom
M. Clark Robertson
Terrence Harold Robsjohn-Gibbings
Gordon Russell
John F. Saladino
Tobia Scarpa
Paul Schuitema
Johnny Sørensen
Basil Spence
William Stumpf
Rud Thygesen
Jean Pierre Viau
Lella Vignelli
Massimo Vignelli
Jon Wealleans
Hans J. Wegner
George Yabu
Jay Yang
Eva Zeisel

## Garden
Frances Butler

## Glass
Alvar Aalto
Torun Vivianna Bülow-Hübe
Sybil Connolly
Gunnar Cyrén
Kaj Franck
Maija Grotell
Erik Höglund
Ulrica Hydman-Vallien
Henning Koppel
Vicke Lindstrand
Erik Magnussen
Sven Palmqvist
Signe Persson-Melin
Ritva Puotila
Oiva Toikka
Bertil Vallien
Wilhelm Wagenfeld
Björn Weckström
Ann Wolff

**Graphic**

Mehemed Fehmy Agha
Otl Aicher
Anni Albers
Alan Aldridge
Walter Heinz Allner
Emilio Ambasz
Paul Rodney Arthur
Kiyoshi Awazu
Bogusław Balicki
Walter Ballmer
Saul Bass
Herbert Bayer
Félix Beltrán
Lucian Bernhard
Harry Bertoia
Betanova
Michael Bierut
Joseph Binder
Antonio Boggeri
Peter Bradford
Pieter Brattinga
Alexey Brodovitch
Erik Bruun
Aaron Burns
Will Burtin
Frances Butler
Jean Carlu
Eugenio Carmi
David Carson
Pierluigi Cerri
Chamberlin Powell and Bon
Ivan Chermayeff
Chermayeff & Geismar Associates
Seymour Chwast
Roman Cieslewicz
Paul Colin
David Colley
Giulio Confalonieri
Terence Conran
David Consuegra
Muriel Cooper
Wim Crouwel
Haig David-West
Jan de Fouw
Rudolph de Harak
Michele De Lucchi
Willy Maks De Majo
Rinaldo Donzelli
Louis Dorfsman
Karl Duschek
Roman Duszek
Tom Eckersley
Heinz Edelmann
Hermann Eidenbenz
Emigre
Hans Erni
Erté
Gene Federico
Louis Fishauf

Willy Fleckhaus
Allan Robb Fleming
Alan Fletcher
Jean-Michel Folon
Colin Forbes
André François
Achim Freyer
Friedrich Friedl
frogdesign Inc.
A. G. Fronzoni
Anthony Froshaug
Adrian Frutiger
S. Neil Fujita
Shigeo Fukuda
Abram Games
Kenneth Garland
Thomas H. Geismar
Steff Geissbuhler
Robert Gersin
Karl Gerstner
Bob Gill
GK Graphics
Milton Glaser
Guillermo Gonzalez Ruiz
Mieczyslaw Górowski
Gottschalk and Ash
Grapus
Milner Gray
J. Malcolm Grear
April Greiman
Franco Grignani
Rolf Harder
Ashley Havinden
Yoshio Hayakawa
F. H. K. Henrion
Ernst and Ursula Hiestand
Hans Hillmann
Hubert Hilscher
George Him
Hipgnosis
Hans Peter Hoch
Armin Hofmann
James Holland
Knud Holscher
Max Huber
Allen Hurlburt
Takenobu Igarashi
Giancarlo Iliprandi
Yusaku Kamekura
Tadeusz Kantor
Herbert W. Kapitzki
Toshihiro Katayama
Diti Katona
Mitsuo Katsui
György Kemény
Gyorgy Kepes
Leo Kerz
Chip Kidd
Günther Kieser
Jock Kinneir

Werner Klemke
Andrzej Klimowski
Peter Kneebone
Burton Kramer
Mervyn Kurlansky
Walter Landor
Jean Larcher
Jan Lenica
Krzysztof Lenk
Alain Le Quernec
Olaf Leu
Herbert Leupin
Jan Le Witt
Ian Logan
George Lois
Herbert Lubalin
Hans-Rudolf Lutz
Emanuele Luzzati
Michael Manwaring
Enzo Mari
Javier Mariscal
Noel Martin
Enid Marx
John Massey
Robert Massin
Takaaki Matsumoto
Herbert Matter
Holger Matthies
Bruce Douglas Mau
Almir Mavignier
Katherine McCoy
Perttu Mentula
James Miho
Tomoko Miho
Marcello Minale
Jan Młodozeniec
Bruno Monguzzi
Rune Monö
Jozef Mroszczak
Marcin Mroszczak
Josef Müller-Brockmann
Rolf Felix Müller
Bruno Munari
Martti Mykkanen
Kazumasa Nagai
Makoto Nakamura
Hans Neuburg
Bob Noorda
Antti Nurmesniemi
Siegfried Odermatt
Ott + Stein
Art Paul
Andrzej Pawloski
Gustavo Pedroza
Pentagram Design
Gaetano Pesce
Cipe Pineles
Giovanni Pintori
Warren Platner
Edward Pond

Gunter Rambow
Paul Rand
Jorgen Rasmussen
Ernst Roch
Emil Ruder
Erkki Ruuhinen
Roberto Sambonet
Willem Sandberg
Timo Sarpaneva
Jan Sawka
Hans Schleger
Paul Schuitema
Raul Shakespear
Ronald Shakespear
Jerome Snyder
Space Design Group
Spencer Francey Peters
Herbert Spencer
Jurgen Spohn
Klaus Staeck
Anton Stankowski
Franciszek Starowieyski
Henry Steiner
Reynolds Stone
Studio Per
Kohei Sugiura
Waldemar Swierzy
Jozef Szajna
TAC Interior Architecture and Graphic Communication
Roger Tallon
Ikko Tanaka
Masaaki Tanaka
Brian Tattersfield
Eduardo Terrazas
Armando Testa
Bradbury Thompson
Rosmarie Tissi
Henryk Tomaszewski
Carl Toms
Niklaus Troxler
George Tscherny
Ximena Ulibarri
Maciej Urbaniec
Leon Urbański
John Vassos
Nelson Vigneault
Lella Vignelli
Massimo Vignelli
Pekka Vuori
Tony Walton
Wolfgang Weingart
Bruno K. Wiese
Henry Wolf
Lewis Woudhuysen
Richard Saul Wurman
Lance Wyman
Chris Yaneff
Tadanori Yokoo
Piet Zwart

**Illustrator**

Alan Aldridge
Lucian Bernhard
Jean Carlu
Edward Carrick
Ivan Chermayeff
Seymour Chwast
Roman Cieslewicz
Paul Colin
David Consuegra
Hans Erni
Erté
Jean-Michel Folon
André François
Roger Furse
Milton Glaser
Yoshio Hayakawa
Hans Hillmann
George Him
Chip Kidd
Werner Klemke
Andrzej Klimowski
Peter Kneebone
Herbert Leupin
Jan Le Witt
Emanuele Luzzati
Enzo Mari
Enid Marx
Jan Młodozeniec
Jozef Mroszczak
Marcin Mroszczak
Rolf Felix Müller
Martti Mykkanen
Jerome Snyder
Jurgen Spohn
Klaus Staeck
Franciszek Starowieyski
Reynolds Stone
Henryk Tomaszewski
John Vassos
Pekka Vuori

**Industrial**

Eero Aarnio
Tom Ahlström
Emilio Ambasz
Bruce Archer
Brian Asquith
Sergio Asti
Carl Auböck
Gae Aulenti
Douglas Cameron Ball
Carlo Bartoli
Hans Theodor Baumann
Mario Bellini
Maria Benktzon
Prince Sigvard Bernadotte
Max Bill
Acton Bjørn
Misha Black

Marianne Brandt
Marcel Breuer
Robert Brunner
Rido Busse
Eugenio Carmi
Anna Castelli Ferrieri
Achille Castiglioni
Livio Castiglioni
Pierluigi Cerri
Joe Colombo
Giulio Confalonieri
Terence Conran
Morison S. Cousins
Jonathan Crinion
Theo Crosby
Wim Crouwel
Robin Day
Michele De Lucchi
Willy Maks De Majo
Donald Deskey
Niels Diffrient
Jay Doblin
Rinaldo Donzelli
Henry Dreyfuss
Joseph D'Urso
Hans Ehrich
Kenji Ekuan
Hartmut Esslinger
Richard Fischer
Gregory Fossella
Gianfranco Frattini
frogdesign Inc.
James Fulton
Robert Gersin
Dante Giacosa
Claude Gidman
Alexander Girard
Giorgetto Giugiaro
Albrecht Zeppo Graf Goertz
Mieczyslaw Górowski
Kenneth Grange
Milner Gray
Vittorio Gregotti
Franco Grignani
GVO Inc.
William J. Hannon
F. H. K. Henrion
Erik Herlow
Gerald P. Hirshberg
James Holland
Knud Holscher
Max Huber
Johan Huldt
Giancarlo Iliprandi
Alec Issigonis
Shima Ito
Finn Juhl
Sven-Eric Juhlin
Herbert W. Kapitzki
Kerr Keller Design Inc.

Günther Kieser
Kazuo Kimura
Iwataro Koike
Thomas Lamb
Walter Landor
Michael Lax
Raymond Loewy
Vico Magistretti
Erik Magnussen
Tomas Maldonado
Angelo Mangiarotti
Enzo Mari
Javier Mariscal
Tom Matano
Minoru Matsuba
Ingo Maurer
Katherine McCoy
Michael McCoy
Richard Alan Meier
David Mellor
Perttu Mentula
Grethe Meyer
Masa Minagawa
Marcello Minale
Carlo Mollino
Rune Monö
Alex Moulton
Olivier Mourgue
Bruno Munari
George Nelson
Louis Nelson
Hans Neuburg
Alexander Neumeister
Takeshi Nishizawa
Bob Noorda
Eliot Noyes
Antti Nurmesniemi
Gearóid O'Conchubhair
Herbert Ohl
Tomoji Okada
Verner Panton
Ico Parisi
Andrzej Pawloski
Sigurd Persson
Gaetano Pesce
Pininfarina
Giovanni Pintori
Markku Piri
William Lansing Plumb
Edward Pond
Gio Ponti
Ferdinand Porsche
Porsche Design
Benno Premsela
James Prestini
Arthur J. Pulos
Peter Raacke
Dieter Rams
Jorgen Rasmussen
John Reid

Deane Richardson
Alberto Rosselli
Martyn Rowlands
Cinzia Ruggeri
Bruno Sacco
Kiyoshi Sakashita
Juhani Salovaara
Roberto Sambonet
Richard Sapper
Timo Sarpaneva
Carlo Scarpa
Mario Scheichenbauer
Herbert H. Schultes
Yuri Soloviev
Ettore Sottsass Jr.
Philippe Starck
Magnus Stephensen
Brooks Stevens
Richard Stevens
Giotto Stoppino
Studio Per
William Stumpf
Yoichi Sumita
Roger Tallon
Ilmari Tapiovaara
Brian Tattersfield
John J. Telnack
Alan Tye
John Vassos
Tucker Viemeister
Sohrab Vossoughi
Wilhelm Wagenfeld
Don Wallance
Tokuji Watanabe
John Weitz
Tapio Wirkkala
Lewis Woudhuysen
Russel Wright
Sori Yanagi
Shoei Yoh
Gianfranco Zaccai
Marco Zanuso

**Interior**
Eero Aarnio
Associated Space Design
Gae Aulenti
Åke Axelsson
Herbert Bayer
Melchiorre Bega
Ward Bennett
Lucian Bernhard
Jonas Bohlin
Rodolfo Bonetto
Marcel Breuer
Henry Thomas Cadbury-Brown
Hugh Casson
Pier Giacomo Castiglioni
Pierluigi Cerri
Chamberlin Powell and Bon

Serge Chermayeff
Paolo Chessa
Joe Colombo
Sybil Connolly
Terence Conran
Theo Crosby
Donna Cummings
Robin Day
Jean-Charles de Castelbajac
Michele De Lucchi
Donald Deskey
Duffy-Eley-Giffone-Worthington
Joseph D'Urso
Charles Eames
Ray Eames
Environetics Group
Gregory Fossella
Kaj Franck
Gianfranco Frattini
Arnold Friedmann
A. G. Fronzoni
Arthur Gibney
Alexander Girard
Milton Glaser
Ernö Goldfinger
Michael Graves
Eileen Gray
Vittorio Gregotti
Denis Handy
Cathy Hardwick
Simo Heikkila
David Hicks
Ernst and Ursula Hiestand
Hans Hollein
ISD
Shima Ito
Arne Jacobsen
Vincent G. Kling
Florence Knoll
Yrjo Kukkapuro
Harold Eliot Leeds
Dennis Lennon
Börge Lindau
Bo Lindekrantz
Peter Lord
Gerald Luss
Vico Magistretti
Carl Malmsten
Leonard Manasseh
Karl Mang
Angelo Mangiarotti
Marian Marshall
Marshall Cummings & Associates
Bruno Mathsson
Perttu Mentula
Ludwig Mies van der Rohe
Marcello Minale
Carlo Mollino
Rune Monö
Antti Nurmesniemi

Verner Panton
Pentagram Design
Gaetano Pesce
Francesco + Aldo Piccaluga, Inc.
Warren Platner
Gio Ponti
Anthony Powell
Benno Premsela
Andrée Putman
Peter Raacke
Terrence Harold Robsjohn-Gibbings
Sonia Rykiel
John F. Saladino
Carlo Scarpa
Johnny Sørensen
Ettore Sottsass Jr.
Space Design Group
Basil Spence
Philippe Starck
TAC Interior Architecture and Graphic Communication
Ilmari Tapiovaara
Brian Tattersfield
Eduardo Terrazas
Rud Thygesen
Carl Toms
John Vassos
Jean Pierre Viau
Lella Vignelli
Massimo Vignelli
Jon Wealleans
Hans J. Wegner
Russel Wright
George Yabu
Shoei Yoh
Marco Zanuso
Piet Zwart

**Jewelry**
Ward Bennett
Harry Bertoia
Torun Vivianna Bülow-Hübe
Björn Weckström

**Landscape**
Warren Platner

**Lighting**
Ingo Maurer

**Metalware**
Tias Eckhoff
Henning Koppel
Horst Sagert
Bertil Vallien
Wilhelm Wagenfeld
Björn Weckström

**Multimedia**
Jan Sawka

**Mural**
Edward Bawden
Lucien Coutaud
Hans Erni
Jerome Snyder
Franciszek Starowieyski

**Packaging**
Walter Ballmer
Karl Oskar Blase
Roman Cieslewicz
Donald Deskey
Alan Fletcher
GK Graphics
Gottschalk and Ash
Ian Logan

**Painter**
Walter Heinz Allner
Boris Aronson
Bogusław Balicki
Edward Bawden
Lucian Bernhard
Max Bill
Joseph Binder
Marianne Brandt
Eugenio Carmi
Ben Carré
Pierre Charbonnier
Paul Colin
Lucien Coutaud
Jean D'Eaubonne
Sonia Delaunay
Hans Erni
Jean-Michel Folon
Achim Freyer
Roger Furse
Karl Gerstner
Franco Grignani
Ashley Havinden
Hein Heckroth
Dale Hennesy
Ulrica Hydman-Vallien
Tadeusz Kantor
Gyorgy Kepes
Werner Klemke
Henning Koppel
Vincent Korda
Ming Cho Lee
Herbert Leupin
Boris Leven
Jan Le Witt
John Massey
Almir Mavignier
Bruno Munari
Ico Parisi
Gianni Polidori
Edward Pond
Horst Sagert

Roberto Sambonet
Timo Sarpaneva
Jan Sawka
Paul Schuitema
Herbert Spencer
Anton Stankowski
Reynolds Stone
Jozef Szajna
Jan Vančura
Karl von Appen
Hermann Warm
Henry Wolf
Ann Wolff
Tadanori Yokoo

**Photographer**
Mehemed Fehmy Agha
Herbert Bayer
Antonio Boggeri
Alexey Brodovitch
David Colley
Franco Grignani
Gyorgy Kepes
Herbert Matter
Holger Matthies
Carlo Mollino
Gene Moore
Marcin Mroszczak
Bruno Munari
Paul Schuitema
Herbert Spencer
Nelson Vigneault
Henry Wolf
Piet Zwart

**Poster**
Alan Aldridge
Bogusław Balicki
Sonia Delaunay
Willy Fleckhaus
Mieczyslaw Górowski
April Greiman
Günther Kieser
Ott + Stein
Kohei Sugiura

**Product**
Tom Ahlström
Laura Ashley
Brian Asquith
Herbert Bayer
Cini Boeri
Rodolfo Bonetto
Gui Bonsiepe
Robert Brunner
Morison S. Cousins
Vuokko Eskolin-Nurmesniemi
Richard Fischer
frogdesign Inc.

A. G. Fronzoni
Claude Gidman
Kenneth Grange
Maija Grotell
Robert Heritage
Hans Hollein
Knud Holscher
Takenobu Igarashi
Shima Ito
Takaaki Matsumoto
Ingo Maurer
Victor Papanek
Pentagram Design
Warren Platner
Ferdinand Porsche
Porsche Design
Mary Quant
Jens Risom
Alberto Rosselli
Tobia Scarpa
Brooks Stevens
Stanley Tigerman
Lella Vignelli
Massimo Vignelli
Sohrab Vossoughi
Robert Welch
Gianfranco Zaccai
Eva Zeisel

## Researcher
Ronald L. MacNeil

## Sculptor
Boris Aronson
Ward Bennett
Harry Bertoia
Max Bill
Eugenio Carmi
Hans Erni
Erté
Armin Hofmann
Erik Höglund
Ulrica Hydman-Vallien
Henning Koppel
Bruno Munari
Peter Raacke
Timo Sarpaneva
Jan Sawka
Björn Weckström
Tapio Wirkkala
Ann Wolff

## Signage
Paul Rodney Arthur
GK Graphics
Peter Kneebone

## Silversmith
Brian Asquith

Torun Vivianna Bülow-Hübe
Gunnar Cyrén
Robert Welch

## Special effects
James Basevi

## Stage
Boris Aronson
Gae Aulenti
Kiyoshi Awazu
Howard Bay
Max Bill
Jonas Bohlin
John Bury
Edward Carrick
Hugh Casson
Pierre Charbonnier
Paul Colin
Lucien Coutaud
Sonia Delaunay
Danilo Donati
Henry Dreyfuss
Raoul Pène du Bois
Hans Erni
Erté
Abdelkader Farrah
Jochen Finke
Tazeena Firth
Jules Fisher
Jean-Michel Folon
Achim Freyer
Roger Furse
Piero Gherardi
Mordecai Gorelik
Jerzy Gurawski
Hein Heckroth
Desmond Heeley
Pieter Hein
Jocelyn Herbert
Karl-Ernst Herrmann
Armin Hofmann
Harry Horner
Robert Israel
Sally Jacobs
George Jenkins
Tadeusz Kantor
Leo Kerz
Günther Kieser
Andrzej Klimowski
Ralph Koltai
Eugene Lee
Ming Cho Lee
Jan Lenica
Dennis Lennon
Michael Levine
Jan Le Witt
Santo Loquasto
Emanuele Luzzati

Jo Mielziner
Wilfried Minks
Tanya Moiseiwitsch
Gene Moore
Marcin Mroszczak
Tharon Musser
John Napier
Timothy O'Brien
Donald Oenslager
Ico Parisi
Andrzej Pawloski
Gianni Polidori
Jean-Pierre Ponnelle
Anthony Powell
Carrie Robbins
Ann Roth
Horst Sagert
Jan Sawka
Douglas W. Schmidt
Leokadia Serafinowicz
Irene Sharaff
Oliver Smith
Josef Svoboda
Jozef Szajna
Rouben Ter-Arutunian
Henryk Tomaszewski
Carl Toms
Alexandre Trauner
Gero Troike
George Tsypin
Jan Vančura
Karl von Appen
Ladislav Vychodil
Robin Wagner
Tony Walton
Hermann Warm
Zofia Wierchowicz
Russel Wright
Franco Zeffirelli
Reinhart Zimmermann

## Textile
Lis Ahlmann
Anni Albers
Junichi Arai
Laura Ashley
Edward Bawden
Ward Bennett
Frances Butler
Susan Collier/Sarah Campbell
Sybil Connolly
Lucien Coutaud
Lucienne Day
Sonia Delaunay
Ingrid Dessau
Vuokko Eskolin-Nurmesniemi
Age Faith-Ell
Edward Fields
Kaj Franck

Sven Fristedt
Eileen Gray
Elisabet Hasselberg-Olsson
Ashley Havinden
Helena Hernmarck
Ulrica Hydman-Vallien
Fujiwo Ishimoto
Arne Jacobsen
Dora Jung
Florence Knoll
Boris Kroll
Irma Kukkasjärvi
Anya Larkin
Jack Lenor Larsen
Maija Lavonen
Ross Littell
Carl Malmsten
Enzo Mari
Javier Mariscal
Enid Marx
Marjatta Metsovaara
Børge Mogensen
Hanae Mori
Barbro Nilsson
Verner Panton
Markku Piri
Edward Pond
Ritva Puotila
Zandra Rhodes
M. Clark Robertson
John F. Saladino
Timo Sarpaneva
Inez Svensson
George Yabu
Jay Yang

## Typography
Mehemed Fehmy Agha
Edward Bawden
Lucian Bernhard
Joseph Binder
Karl Oskar Blase
Aaron Burns
Will Burtin
Max Caflisch
Matthew Carter
David Colley
Louis Danziger
Jan de Fouw
Hermann Eidenbenz
Emigre
Allan Robb Fleming
Alan Fletcher
Colin Forbes
Anthony Froshaug
Adrian Frutiger
Karl Gerstner
Ashley Havinden
Max Huber

Giancarlo Iliprandi
Albert Kapr
Werner Klemke
Jean Larcher
Herbert Lubalin
Hans-Rudolf Lutz
Giovanni Mardersteig
Francis Meynell
Siegfried Odermatt
Emil Ruder
Erkki Ruuhinen
Hans Schmoller
Reynolds Stone
Rosmarie Tissi
Jan Tschichold
Leon Urbański
Wolfgang Weingart
Tadanori Yokoo
Hermann Zapf

## Woodcrafts

Markku Kosonen
James Prestini

# NOTES ON
# ADVISERS and CONTRIBUTORS

**AAV, Mariane.** Essayist. Principal curator, Museum of Applied Arts, Helsinki. Author of several catalogues on twentieth-century Finnish craft and design. **Essay:** Kukkasjarvi.

**ADAMS, Sandra Michels.** Essayist. Instructor in history of costume, School of the Art Institute of Chicago; clothing designer, in the collaboration of Dress Code; and freelance costume specialist (exhibit consultant, lecturer, and teacher), all from 1982. Display designer and fashion coordinator, Marshall Field and Company, Oak Park, Illinois, 1976-79; assistant to the curator of costumes, Chicago Historical Society, 1979-82. **Essays:** Balenciaga; Galanos; Norell; Trigère; Vionnet.

**ALEXANDER, James M.** Essayist. Professor of industrial design, from 1947, and head of Industrial Design Department, 1948-76, University of Cincinnati, Ohio; also freelance architect and designer. Detailer, designer, and planner, Raymond Loewy Associates, New York, 1942, 1946-47; director, Design Research Collaborative, University of Cincinnati, 1964-75. Author of numerous articles in professional journals. **Essay:** Loewy.

**ARONSON, Arnold.** Advisor and essayist. Chair, Theatre Division, Columbia University. Author, *American Set Design* and *The Theory of Environmental Scenography;* former editor, *Theatre Design & Technology* magazine. **Essays:** Hould-Ward; Israel; E. Lee; Ivey Long; Loquasto; Schmidt; Tyspin.

**ARSENAULT, Andrea.** Essayist. Fashion instruction, School of the Art Institute of Chicago; also freelance fashion designer. **Essays:** Ashley; de Castelbajac; Rhodes.

**ASHWIN, Clive.** Essayist. Dean of the Faculty of Education and Performing Arts, Middlesex Polytechnic. Editor of *Art Education: Documents and Policies,* 1975; author of *Drawing and Education in German-Speaking Europe 1800-1900,* 1975; *Encyclopedia of Drawing,* 1982; and *History of Graphic Design and Communication: A Source Book,* 1983. **Essays:** Eckersley; Havinden.

**AUBÖCK, Carl.** Essayist and entrant. See his own entry. **Essay:** Ekuan.

**BAKKILA, Christopher Matthew.** Essayist. Graduated, Columbia University, B.Arch., University of Michigan, M.Arch. Works at Albert Kahn Collaborative, Detroit, Michigan. **Essays:** Ishimoto; Kukkapuro.

**BARNICOAT, John.** Essayist. Principal, Chelsea School of Art, London, since 1980. Senior tutor in painting, Royal College of Art, London, 1976-80. Author of *Concise History of Posters,* 1972. **Essays:** Aldridge; Brattinga; Carlu; Chwast; Colin; Edelmann; Fletcher; Games; Glaser; Müller-Brockmann.

**BECK, James.** Essayist. Professor of art history, Columbia University, New York. **Essay:** Sawka.

**BENHAMOU, Reed.** Essayist. Professor of interior design, Purdue University, West Lafayette, Indiana, from 1978; member of editorial board, *Journal of Interior Design Education and Research,* from 1979. **Essays:** Deskey; Kjaerholm; Jacobsen; Mourgue; Robsjohn-Gibbings; Wegner.

**BLAICH, Robert.** Essayist and entrant. See his own entry. **Essay:** Chadwick.

**BLAKE, Peter.** Essayist. Architect, FAIA, Branford, Connecticut. **Essay:** Roche.

**BLAUENSTEINER, Charlotte.** Essayist. Secretary general, Osterreichisches Institute fur Formgebung, Vienna, from 1958. **Essay:** Auböck.

**BODINE, Sarah.** Essayist. Freelance writer, lecturer, and curator; formerly editor, *Documents of American Design;* contributor to *AIGA Journal, Design Book Review, Industrial Design and American Ceramics.* Exhibition coordinator, Andrew Dickson White Museum of Art, Cornell University, Ithaca, New York, 1970-71, and Leonard Hutton Gallery, New York, 1971-73; craft editor, Watson Guptill Publications, 1973-76; senior editor, Whitney Library of Design, 1973-79; columnist with Michael Dunas, *Metropolis.* **Essays:** Agha; Agnes B.; Ambasz; Grotell; Leach; Maldonado; Nelson; Paul; Pineles; Pulos; Rams; (with Michael Dunas) Starck; Wallance; Wirkkala; (with Michael Dunas) Zanuso; Zeisel.

**BOIGON, Brian.** Essayist. Art director, Art Gallery of Ontario, Toronto. Assistant professor, University of Toronto; author, *Speed Reading Tokyo;* and founding-editor, Culture Lab Book Series. Currently working on new content development for Internet Television. **Essay:** Mau.

**BOJKO, Szymon.** Essayist. Freelance art and design critic, Warsaw. Board member, responsible for design education, state Council of Industrial Design, Warsaw, 1960-67; editorial board member, *Projekt,* 1969-74; editor, *Polish Art Review,* Warsaw, 1971-72; also formerly visiting lecturer in visual communication, School of Design, Lodz, Poland. Author of *Art of the Polish Poster,* 1972; *New Graphic Design in Revolutionary Russia,* 1972; *The Polish Poster,* 1973; co-author of *Mass Culture,* 1976; editor of *Art as Environment,* 1972; also contributor to many art and design journals in Poland and abroad. **Essays:** Balicki; Danziger; Duszek; Folon; Gorowski; Kamekura; Kemeny; Lenk Mentula; Pawlowski; Telingater; Zamecznik.

**BOMAN, Monica.** Essayist. Freelance editor and writer, Stockholm. Editor, *Form,* 1973-76; also worked for the HSB Housing cooperative, and the Swedish National Board for Consumer Politics. Editor of *Design in Sweden,* 1985; *Design Art,* 1988. **Essay:** Axelsson.

**BREMER, Nina.** Essayist. Instructor, University of Bridgeport, Connecticut, from 1979. Formerly instructor, Lehman College, Bronx, New York, and Hunter College, New York; Freelance lecturer for Museum of Modern Art, New York, for Knoll International, for United Nations groups, and for other museums. **Essays:** Breuer; Chermayeff and Geismar Associates; Federico; Noyes; Risom.

**BURIAN, Jarka M.** Essayist. Professor, Department of Theatre, State University of New York at Albany, from 1955. Formerly producer and artistic director, Albany Arena Theatre. Author of *Americke Drama a Divadelnictvi* ("American Drama and

Theatre"), 1966; *The Scenography of Josef Svoboda,* 1971; *Svoboda: Wagner,* 1983. **Essays:** Bury; Farrah; Herbert; Koltai; Napier; O'Brien/Firth; Svoboda; Szajna; Vychodil.

**BUTLER, Frances.** Essayist and entrant. See her own entry. **Essays:** Manwaring; Mardersteig; Zapf.

**BYRNE, Elizabeth Douthitt.** Essayist. Librarian and head of the Environmental Design Library, University of California at Berkeley, from 1984. Head of the Art Library, University of Louisville, Kentucky, 1979-71; assistant head of fine arts, Detroit Public Library, 1972-76; head of the Design, Architecture, Art, and Planning Library, University of Cincinnati, Ohio, 1978-84. Co-author of *Great Cooks of the Western World,* 1977. **Essays:** Butler; Colombo; de la Renta.

**CAFFREY, Paul.** Essayist. Educated in New Zealand, Ireland, and England. Formerly curator of Castletown House, County Kildare, Ireland; lecturer in the faculty of History of Art and Design, National College of Art and Design, Dublin. Special interests include industrial design, architectural, and interior design history; has written on aspects of eighteenth-century art, design, and architecture. **Essays:** Connolly; Gibney; Handy; Hogan; O'Conchubhair.

**CAPLAN, Ralph.** Essayist. Freelance writer and communication design consultant, New York. Editor in chief, *Industrial Design,* 1958-62. Author of *Design in America,* 1969; *The Design Necessity,* 1972; *The Design of Herman Miller,* 1976; *Chair,* 1978; and *By Design,* 1982. **Essay:** Stumpf.

**CARLS, Ken.** Essayist. Professor of graphic design, University of Illinois at Urbana-Champaign, from 1978. **Essays:** Monguzzi; Wright.

**CARLSEN, Peter.** Essayist. Freelance writer and commentator on design, fashion, and the visual arts, New York City, for *New York Magazine, New York, Architectural Digest, Gentlemen's Quarterly, Art News,* and others. Author of *Manstyle* (compendium of men's fashion), 1978; and *Design Quarterly* (monograph on Joseph Paul D'Urso), 1984. **Essays:** Ellis; Ferré; Hipp; Saladino; Shamask; Sottsass; Versace.

**CARRINGTON, Noel** (died, 1989). Essayist. Retired former editor and art consultant to Penguin Books, Roxe Publications, and others. Member, Design Council, London, 1948-55. Author of design, 1935; *Design in the Home,* 1938; *The Shape of Things,* 1939; *Colour in the Home,* 1947; *Industrial Design in Britain,* 1976; co-author of *The Face of the Land,* 1930; *Popular English Art,* 1944; *Life in the English Village,* 1949; and others. **Essays:** Meynell; Russell.

**CASCIANI, Stefano.** Essayist. Freelance writer on art and design, Milan. **Essays:** Bonetto; Pininfarina; Ruggeri.

**CAVALIERE, Barbara.** Essayist. Freelance writer on art and design, New York City. Associate editor, *Womanart* magazine (New York), 1976-78; contributing editor, *Arts Magazine* (New York), 1976-83. Fellowship in art criticism, National Endowment for the Arts, 1979-80. Author of exhibition catalogues for

*Abstract Expressionism: The Formative Years* (Ithaca, New York), 1978; *William Baziotes: A Retrospective* (Newport Beach, California), 1978; *Stamos: Paintings 1958-60* (New York), 1981; *Theodoros Stamos: On the Horizon of Mind and Coast* (Aachen, West Germany), 1984. Contributor to *Flash Art, Soho Weekly News, High Performance,* and other magazines; to *Contemporary Artists,* edited by Muriel Emmanuel and others, 1983; and to *Academic American Encyclopedia.* **Essays:** Albers; Armani; Basile; Bill; Blass; Cardin; de Givenchy; Donati; du Bois; Fiorucci; Fuller; Hardwick; Head; Mandelli; McFadden; Montana; Mugler; Soprani; Ungaro.

**CLARK, Hazel.** Essayist. Assistant registrar for art and design, Council for National Academic Awards. Research assistant in design history, Brighton Polytechnic, 1978-82; lecturer in design, fashion, and textile history, Brighton Polytechnic and Ravensbourne College of Art, Kent, 1981-83. Founder-committee member, Textile Society, from 1982. **Essays:** Bohan; Collier/Campbell; Courrèges; Ertè; Karan; Kenzo; Khanh; Lauren; Miyake; Mori; Rabanne; Rykiel; Saint Laurent; K. Yamamoto.

**COHEN, Howard E.** Advisor. Educated at University of Manitoba, Winnipeg, B.Arch.; president, Design Exchange, Toronto, Canada, from 1991.

**CONSTANTINE, Mildred.** Essayist. Independent consultant on art, architecture, and design to museums, universities, and industry. Assistant to the director, secretary of traveling exhibitions, and editorial assistant on the *Art Bulletin and Parnassus,* College Art Association, New York, 1930-37; curator, Department of Architecture and Design and special assistant to the director, Museum of Modern Art, New York, 1948-71. Author or editor of *Art Nouveau,* 1959; *Sign Language,* 1961; *Lettering by Modern Artists,* 1963; *The Object Transformed,* 1963; *World and Image,* 1967; *Wall Hangings,* 1969; *Beyond Craft: The Art Fabric,* 1973; *Soviet Film Posters,* 1974; *Tina Modotti: A Fragile Life,* 1975, 1978; and *The Art Fabric: Mainstream, 1981.* **Essays:** Delaunay; Dreyfuss; Hurlburt; Larsen; Mavignier; Terrazas; Vignelli; Yokoo.

**CONWAY, Hazel.** Essayist. Principal lecturer in design history, Leicester Polytechnic, from 1980. Open University course tutor in history of architecture and design, 1975-76; chairman, Design History Publications Sub-Committee of the Association of Art Historians, 1978-81. Author of *Ernest Race* 1982. **Essay:** Eileen Gray.

**COULSON, Anthony J.** Essayist. Liaison librarian (Arts), Open University Library, from 1970. Author of *A Bibliography of Design in Britain, 1851-1970;* and of project, literature, and library guides for Open University published courses. **Essays:** Archer; Bawden; Black; Milner Gray.

**CRAWFORD, Elizabeth.** Essayist. Graduate of the industrial design program, Ontario College of Art, Toronto. Worked extensively on the Design Exchange Encyclopedia of Canadian Design, a multimedia reference to Canadian design. Freelance industrial designer and teaches at Humber College. **Essays:** Baday; Fluevog; Fox; Marshall Cummings; Yabu; Yaneff; (with

Rachel Gotlieb): Crinion; Deacon; Gidman; Levine; Spencer Francey Peters.

**CURRIER, Catherine L.** Essayist. Graduate student in art history (special program in history of design), University of Cincinnati, Ohio. Editor, Providence College art journal *Interface,* 1983. **Essay:** Crouwel.

**DAHLBACK LUTTEMAN, Helena.** Essayist. Keeper of the Department of Applied Art, at the National Museum, Stockholm. Author of Svendkt *Porslin/Svensk Keramix,* 1980; *Majolika fran Urbino,* 1981; *Svenskt Silver,* 1989. **Essays:** Björquist; Bülow-Hübe; Cyrén; Höglund.

**DAVID, Tom.** Essayist. Endowed Stevens Design Chair, Milwaukee Institute of Art and Design, Wisconsin; FIDSA; has held many positions in IDSA, including Educators Committee and Conference chair, Midwest district vice-president. **Essay:** Stevens.

**DAVID-WEST, Haig.** Essayist and entrant. See his own entry. **Essay:** Betanova.

**DAVIES, Carainn Childers.** Advisor. Executive officer, Society of Designers in Ireland, from 1975; freelance administrative consultant, principally to the design industry, from 1972; clients have included the Irish Footwear Fashion Institute, the Irish Fashion Institute, the Design Department of the Irish Export Board, the Crafts Council of Ireland, and the Society of Designers in Ireland. Founder member and director, Institute for Design and Disability, from 1991; member IFI Ireland 1997 Congress organizing committee, the Biennial International Congress of the Federation of Interior Architects.

**DAVIS, Mary W.** Advisor. Executive director, American Center for Design, Chicago, from 1993.

**Del RENZO, Toni.** Essayist. Director and professor, British Studies Centre of the Institute of American Universities, from 1982. Principal lecturer in charge of the Department of History of Art/Design and Complementary Studies, Canterbury College of Art, 1975-80; has also taught at the Camberwell School of Arts and Crafts, Bath Academy of Art, and Chelsa School of Art, London. Author of numerous articles on art and design in *Architectural Design, Architectural Review, Art and Artists, Art International, Che Fare, Horizon, Interior Design, Studio International, Art Monthly,* and others. **Essays:** Franco Albini; Bega; Bertoia; Cadbury-Brown; Carmi; Livio Castiglioni; Chamberlin, Powell and Bon; Chessa; Confalonieri; Frattini; Fronzoni; Gill; Giugiaro; Gregotti; Heckroth; Huber; Lennon, Mangiarotti; Noorda; Parisi; Pentagram; Pintori; Toms.

**De MARLY, Diana.** Essayist. Regular guest lecturer, Department of History of Dress, Courtauld Institute of Art, University of London, from 1970. Lecturer, London College of Fashion, 1971-73, and Croydon College of Art, 1973-75; Susette Taylor Research Fellow, Lady Margaret Hall, University of Oxford, 1977-78; guest of the German Academic Exchange. Author of *The History of Haute Couture 1850-1950,* 1980; *Charles Frederick Worth: A Biography,* 1980; and *Costume on the Stage; Reform Movements in Relation to Artistic Theory,*

*1600-1940,* 1982. **Essays:** Adolfo; Asquith; Balmain; Barrie; Bates; Beene; Burrows; Chadwick; Chanel; Conran; de Luca; Duffy-Eley-Giffone-Worthington; Grès; Halston; Issigonis; Kamali; Kneebone; Lagerfeld; Lancetti; Lord; Mainbocher; Manasseh; Muir; Rowlands; Sant'Angelo; R. Stevens; Tan Guidicelli; Thomass; Woudhuysen.

**D'EMILIA, Florence.** Essayist. Writer on visual and performing arts and design; established D'Emilia Public Relations, New York, New York, relocated Cleveland, Ohio; has served on boards of arts, educational, and social service organizations; has taught public relations and business writing courses. **Essay:** Cousins.

**DIECKMANN, Friedrich.** Essayist. Writer, East Berlin. Dramaturge, Berliner Ensemble, 1972-76. Author of *Karl von Appens Bühnenbilder am Berliner Ensemble* 1971; *Streifzüge* 1972, and *Theaterbilder* 1979; editor of *Bühnenbilder der D D R,* 1978. **Essays:** Sagert; von Appen.

**DROSTE, M.** Essayist. Research assistant Bauhaus Archiv, Berlin, from 1980. Author of exhibition catalogues for *Klee and Kandinsky* Stuttgart, 1979; *George Muche: Das kinsterlische Werk, 1912-1927* Berlin, 1980; and *Herbert Bayer: Das kunsterlische Werk, 1912-1938* Berlin, 1981. **Essays:** Bayer; Blase; Kapitzki; Wagenfeld.

**DUNAS, Michael.** Essayist. Freelance writer, lecturer, and curator in the field of design, art, and craft. Has published with Dover Publications, Watson-Guptill Publications, and the Whitney Library of Design; contributor, *AIGA Journal Design Book Review* among others; columnist with Sarah Bodine, *Metropolis.* **Essays** (with Sarah Bodine): Starck; Zanuso.

**EKUAN, Kenji.** Advisor and entrant. See his own entry.

**ENBOM, Carla.** Essayist. Freelance writer on design and applied arts, Stockholm. **Essays:** Piri; Puotila.

**ENGELBRECHT, Lloyd C.** Essayist. Professor of history of design, Art History Department, University of Cincinnati, Ohio, and curator of the Design Archives, and Rare Books Department, University of Cincinnati Libraries. Professor, Bradley University, Peoria, Illinois, 1970-73; Indiana State University, Terre Haute, 1973-77; and Wichita State University, Kansas, 1977-78. Author, with June F. Englebrecht, of *Henry C. Trost: Architect of the Southwest,* 1981. **Essays:** Aalto; S. Chermayeff; Eames; Kepes; Martin; Prestini.

**EXLEY, Peter J.** Essayist. Graduate, University of Pennsylvania; worked for Venturi, Scott Brown and Associates and Skidmore, Owings & Merrill; past-chair, AIA Chicago's design committee, former director, AIA Chicago; founded Peter J. Exley Architect, from 1994. Instructor, School of the Art Institute of Chicago; contributor, *Inland Architect* and *Focus.* **Essays:** Meier; Stern; Tigerman.

**FITZGERALD, Alison.** Essayist. Graduated in History of Art, University College Dublin, M.A. Instructor, National College of Art and Design, Dublin, and University College Dublin. **Essay:** de Fouw.

**FRASCARA, Jorge.** Essayist. Professor, from 1977, and chairman, from 1981, Department of Art and Design University of Alberta, Edmonton; associate editor, *Icographic,* from 1982. Vice-president, International Council of Graphic Design Associations, 1979-81; member, National Council, Society of Graphic Designers of Canada, 1979-81. Author of *Introduction to Aesthetix Evaluation,* 1969; *Drawing as a Teaching Aid,* 1972; and *Art in General Education,* 1973. **Essays:** Frutiger; Ruiz; Shakespear.

**FRIENDMANN, Arnold.** Essayist and entrant. See his own entry. **Essays:** Associated Space Design; D'Urso; Environetics Group; ISD (Interior Space Design); Leeds; Luss; Space Design Group; TAC Interior Architecture and Graphic Communication.

**GAMBILL, Norman.** Essayist. Head of the Art Department, South Dakota State University, Brookings, from 1984. Professor, Department of Art and Design, University of Illinois at Urbana-Champaign, 1966-83; also previously guest curator, International Museum of Photography at George Eastman House, Rochester, New York; and consultant, Learning Museum Program, Indianapolis Museum of Art, Indiana. **Essays:** Horner; Leven; Sylbert.

**GARLAND, Madge** (died, 1990). Essayist. Freelance writer on fashion, architecture, design, and travel, London. Formerly, fashion editor, English *Vogue;* professor of fashion design, Royal College of Art, London. Author of *The Changing Face of Beauty* 1957; *The Changing Face of Childhood* 1963; *The Indecisive Decade* 1968; *The Changing Form of Fashion* 1970; *The Small Garden in the City* 1974; *A History of Fashion* with J. Anderson Black, 1975, 1980; and others. Contributor to *Apollo, Country Life, Harpers, The Saturday Book* and others. **Essays:** Fratini; Quant.

**GAUDET, Larry.** Essayist. Writer and consulting iconoclast. Lives in Toronto. **Essay:** Katona.

**GAULIN, Kenneth.** Essayist. Design writer and consultant, Boston. Former sales representative, Knoll International; consultant-designer, Haffenreffer Museum, Brown University, Bristol, Rhode Island, and Education Development Center, Newton, Massachusetts; technical director, New York University Medical Center. **Essays:** Aulenti; Diffrient; Knoll; Platner.

**GOODRICH, Kristina.** Essayist. Senior director of communication and chapter development, Industrial Designers Society of America, Great Falls, Virginia, from 1981. Editor of the association's quarterly journal, *Innovation,* and organizer of the Industrial Design Excellence Awards program. **Essays:** frogdesign; GVO; Hirshberg; Matano; K. McCoy; L. Nelson; Richardson; Telnack; Viemeister; Vossoughi; Zaccai.

**GOTLIEB, Rachel.** Essayist. Curator of design, Gallery 76, Ontario College of Art, 1987-89; curator, Design Exchange, Toronto, from 1990; creator, *Pop in Orbit: Design from the Space Age* exhibition, Design Exchange, 1995/96. Contributor to *Globe and Mail* (Toronto), *Azure,* and *Ontario Craft.* **Essays:** Fishauf; Lamb; (with Elizabeth Crawford) Crinion; Deacon; Gidman; Levine; Spencer Francey Peters.

**GOWAN, Al.** Essayist. Design historian, and novelist. Coordinator, Graduate Design Program, Massachusetts College of Art. Contributor to *Print,* and other design periodicals. **Essays:** Beltràn; Burns; Carter; Cooper; Hannon; MacNeil; Papanek.

**GREAPENTROG, Grant.** Essayist. Professor, Design Department, Drexel University, Philadelphia, from 1979. College department, Appleton-Century-Crofts, 1964-71, and Harcourt Brace Jovanovich, 1971-79. **Essays:** Fields; Moore.

**GREEN, Nancye.** Advisor. Partner, Donovan and Green, New York, from 1974. Past president, American Institute of Graphic Arts; board member and past president, International Design Conference in Aspen; board member, Hallmark Cards, Inc. Recipient of funds from National Endowment for the Arts, HEW, Ford Foundation, and others; former consultant to the NEA, helping to develop the template for the Architects-in-the-Schools Program.

**GUSTAFSSON, Gertrud.** Essayist. Editor, *Paletten* (Goteborg, Sweden), from 1981; correspondent, *Form* (Stockholm), from 1980. **Essay:** Nilsson.

**HABARA, Shukuro.** Essayist. Design editor, *SD (Space Design)* (art and architecture journal), from 1975; lecturer, Tama University of Fine Arts. Editor-in-chief, *Design* (Tokyo), 1962-68; professor, Tokyo University of Arts, 1968-74. Co-author of *Introduction to Modern Art,* 1970; *The Origin of Design: The Philosophy and Background of Braun & Co. Design,* 1978; and *The Secret of a Musician—Dedication to Glenn Gould,* 1978. **Essays:** Awazu; Katayama; Ikko Tanaka; Masaaki Tanaka.

**HALAS, John.** Essayist. Co-producer and director of more than 2,000 animated and live-action films. Founder and creative director, Halas and Batchelor Animation, 1940-81. Founder and creative director, Educational Film Centre; president and chairman of the Research and Development Commission, ASIFA (International Animated Film Association); president, British Federation of Film Societies. Graphic design correspondent, *Novun Gebrauchsgraphik.* Author of *How to Cartoon,* with Bo Privett, 1959; *Design in Motion,* 1962; *Film and TV Graphics,* with Walter Herdeg, 1968; *The Technique of Film Animation,* with Roger Manvell, 1969; *Art in Movement,* with Roger Manvell, 1970; *Computer Animation,* 1974; *Visual Scripting,* 1975; *The Great Movie Cartoon Parade,* with David Rider, 1976; *Film Animation: A Simplified Approach,* 1976; *Full Length Animated Feature Film,* with Bruno Edera, 1977; *Timing for Animation,* with Harold Whitaker, 1981; *Graphics in Motion,* 1981. **Essays:** Adam; Bozzetto; Casson; de Majo; Gardner; Henrion; Le Witt and Him; Korda; Lenica; Luzzati; Reid.

**HÅRD af SEGERSTAD, Ulf.** Essayist. Art and design critic, *Svenska Dagbladet,* Stockholm. Editor, *Form,* Stockholm, 1957-60; design consultant to Philips, Sweden, 1964-67; vice president, International Council of Societies of Industrial Design, 1967-71; visiting professor, University of Minnesota, 1975, and, Danish Royal Academy of Fine Arts, 1979. Author of *Bild-komposition,* 1952; *Scandinavian Design,* 1961; *Modern*

*Scandinavian Furniture,* 1963; *Modern Svensk Texilkonst,* 1963; *Design in Finland,* 1968; *Keramik* 1976. **Essay:** Mono.

**HAYHURST, Richard.** Essayist. Freelance writer, London. Director of the Hayhurst, Conington and Cripps advertising agency. Copywriter, at AC-Mainos, Helsinki, 1984-87; marketing and communications manager, Labsystems, Helsinki, 1987-89. **Essay:** Ruuhinen.

**HELLER, Steven.** Essayist. Senior art director, *New York Times;* editor, AIGA Journal of Graphic Design; director of design education conference, How We Learn What We Learn, School of Visual Arts, 1977; director, School of Visual Arts' *Modernism & Eclectism: A History of American Graphic Design;* author, co-author, and editor of over 50 books, most on the history and practice of graphic design, illustration, and satiric art; contributing editor to numerous design magazines. **Essay:** Bierut.

**HIESINGER, Kathryn B.** Advisor. Curator, European Decorative Arts, Philadelphia Museum of Art, Pennsylvania. Exhibition and catalogue organizer, *Design Since 1945, Art Nouveau in Munich,* and *Japanese Design: A Survey Since 1950;* co-author, *Landmarks of Twentieth Century Design.*

**HIRSCH, John E.** Essayist. Instructor, Department of English, New York University, from 1980; also theatrical costume designer and director. Writer of theatrical reviews and feature articles, *The Villager* (New York), 1977-80. **Essays:** Klotz; Musser; Wagner; Weitz.

**HOPE, Augustine.** Essayist. Editor, *Encyclopedia of Light and Color* for Color Association of the United States. Formerly, associate editor, *American Fabrics and Fashions* (New York); and editor, *Cherwell Magazine* (United Kingdom). **Essay:** Yang.

**HOUSE, Nancy.** Essayist. Freelance writer on art and design, Marblehead, Massachusetts. **Essays:** Aicher; Forbes; Hillmann; Massin; Pesce; Stone.

**HUBBARD, Edmund.** Advisor. Educated, Westminster School and Cambridge Queen's College, M.Arch. Projects manager, Contemporary Art Society, 1992-96; established Projects, an arts project management service, from 1996.

**ICHIYAMA, D.** Essayist. Professor, Visual Communications Design, Purdue University, West Lafayette, Indiana, from 1980. **Essays:** Gerstner; Hofmann; Leupin; Matter; Thompson.

**INKO-DOKUBO, Alaboigoni.** Essayist. Film producer and editor, 1977-78, and head of Film Centre, from 1978, directorate of information and public relations, Port Harcourt, Nigeria; culture and art columnist for various Nigeria newspapers, from 1977; chairman, Seiyefa Publishing Company, Port Harcourt, Nigeria. Author of *Rivers of My Passion* 1982; *Go to the Ants* 1982; and *Songs of the Eagle* 1982. **Essay:** David-West.

**JACOBSON, Lee.** Essayist. Studied architecture and urban planning at M.I.T. Principal, Vandenberg & Co. (communications consulting firm), Toronto; business and design columnist, *Globe and Mail* (Toronto). **Essay:** Kerr/Keller.

**JENNINGS, Jan.** Essayist. Visiting professor, College of Design, Iowa State University, Ames; principal, Jennings, Gottfriend (check design consultants), Ames, Iowa. Planner, Tulsa Metropolitan Area Planning Commission, Oklahoma, 1969-73; director, Tulsa Historic Preservation Office, Oklahoma, 1977-79; formerly instructor at several universities in interior design housing, planning, and urban design. Author, with Herbert Gottfried, of *American Vernacular: A Design Handbook* 1984. **Essay:** Magistretti.

**JOHNSON, David.** Essayist. Graduated, Harvard University, B.A., University of Michigan, M.Arch., 1992. Working as an intern architect, Ann Arbor, Michigan. **Essays:** Graves; Venturi.

**KATAYAMA, Toshihiro.** Essayist and entrant. See his own entry. **Essay:** T. Miho.

**KATZ, Joel.** Essayist. Principal, Joel Katz Design Associates (an information and graphic design firm), Philadelphia, Pennsylvania; clients have included Philadelphia's Center City District, Wharton School, Pennsylvania Physician Healthcare Plan, International Paediatric Nephrology Association, Elcom Technologies, and Unisys; lecturer and past-teacher, Yale, Rhode Island School of Design, Philadelphia College of Art, and others; contributor, *Messages AIGA Journal of Graphic Design* and *Visible Language;* co-author, *Aspen Visible* (Cambridge) and *The Nature of Recreation* (Cambridge); author, *And I Said No Lord* (Athens, Georgia), 1996. **Essay:** Wurman.

**KERR, Deirdre.** Essayist. Pseudonym of an assistant editor at *Harpers' Bazaar* and freelance writer for *Gentlemen's Quarterly.* Formerly, intern, Costume Institute, Metropolitan Museum of Art, New York, and apprentice to fashion designer Yeohlee Teng. **Essays:** Larkin, Robertson.

**KINROSS, Robin.** Essayist. Freelance typographer and writer. Lecturer, Department of Typography, University of Reading, Berkshire, 1977-82. **Essays:** Froshaug; Garland; Kinneir; Schmoller; Spencer; Tshichold.

**KLOS, Sheila.** Essayist. Librarian and head of the Architecture and Allied Arts Library, University of Oregon; book review coordinator, *Art Documentation,* from 1988. Associate curator of slides and photographers, Brown University, 1977-83; serials librarian, Cleveland Museum of Art, 1983-85. Co-editor, *Historical Bibliography of Art Museum Serials,* 1987. **Essay:** Munari.

**KODA, Harold.** Essayist. Curator of the Edward C. Blum Design Laboratory, Fashion Institute of Technology, New York. Author of *Jocks and Nerds,* 1989; *The Historical Mode,* 1989. **Essay:** Matsumoto.

**KRAMER, Burton.** Essayist and entrant. See his own entry. **Essays:** (update) Beltrán.

**KRIEBEL, Marjorie.** Essayist. Professor of design, Drexel University, Philadelphia, from 1975; also registered architect, Philadelphia. Member board of directors, National Council for Interior Design Qualifications, from 1982. **Essay:** Friedmann.

**KRIEBEL, William Victor.** Essayist. Instructor, Department of Interiors and Graphic Studies, College of Design Arts, Drexel University, Philadelphia; also a registered architect in independent private practice. **Essays:** Bellini; A. Castiglioni; P. G. Castiglioni; De Lucchi; Hollein; Mari; Ponti; C. Scarpa; T. Scarpa.

**KUNKEL, Paul.** Essayist. Freelance writer based in New York, specializing in design. **Essay:** Brunner.

**LANGE, Wolfgang.** Essayist. Writer on theatre, East Berlin. **Essay:** Zimmermann.

**LARGE, Michael.** Essayist. Coordinator of the graphic design program, Sheridan College. Involved with inter-institutional curriculum development in design. Taught at several colleges and universities in Canada and the U.K., and worked as a designer and consultant in both countries. His Ph.D. thesis, *Graphic Design and Corporate Identity* (Concordia University, Montreal, 1989), examined organizational and cultural factors in identity design. Contributor to journals in Canada, the U.K. and the U.S.A., include articles about visual identity case histories, reviews and conference papers concerning educational and design issues. **Essays:** Arthur; Emigre; Greiman.

**LEE, Edith Cortland.** Essayist. Freelance writer and consultant on film and video, Chicago. **Essays:** Carrick; Richard Day; Ferguson; Margaret Furse; Roger Furse; Hipgnosis; Kirk; Plunkett; Sharaff.

**LENGERT, Julius.** Essayist. Studied literature, American Studies, philosophy, and cultural anthropology. Earned Ph.D. Former editor with *Euromed* (medical magazine), literature and article department, *Playboy* (Germany); freelance consultant of applied philosophy to architects, designers, and companies, Munich, Germany. **Essay:** Schultes.

**LINDGREN, Maud.** Essayist. Freelance writer and public relations consultant, Stockholm. **Essay:** Huldt.

**LINDINGER, Herbert.** Essayist. Director, Industrial Design Department, Universität Hannover, Germany. **Essay:** Nishizawa.

**LINDKVIST, Lennart.** Essayist. Retired director and board member, Foreningen Svensk Form, Stockholm. Editor-in-chief, *Form* magazine, 1963-73. Editor, *Design in Sweden,* 1977. **Essays:** Ahlström and Ehrich; Benktzon and Juhlin.

**LIVSTEDT, Ake.** Essayist. Freelance art critic and lecturer, Stockholm. Curator, National Museum, Stockholm, 1971-77. **Essay:** Vallien.

**LUNDAHL, Gunilla.** Essayist. Freelance architecture and design critic, Stockholm. Editor, *Nordisk Funktionalism,* 1980; *Recent Developments in Swedish Architecture,* 1983; *Memory of a Landscape,* 1984; *Swedish Textile Art,* 1987. **Essays:** Bohlin; Dessau.

**MARTIN, Floyd W.** Essayist. Professor of art history, University of Arkansas, Little Rock, from 1982. Visiting lecturer in art history, University of Illinois at Urbana-Champaign, 1981-82. **Essays:** Box; Boyle; Gherardi; Grot; Whitlock.

**MARTIN, Richard.** Essayist. Curator, The Costume Institute, Metropolitan Museum of Art, New York; adjunct professor, art history and archaeology, Columbia University; adjunct professor, Art, New York University; formerly editor, *Arts Magazine,* 1974-88; taught for twenty years, Fashion Institute of Technology, formerly executive director, Shirley Goodman Resource Center and Educational Foundation for the Fashion Industries. Author of books, including *Fashion and Surrealism; The New Urban Landscape;* and *Contemporary Fashion;* co-author of many exhibition catalogues, including *Splash!: A History of Swimwear; The Historical Mode: Fashion and Art in the 1980s; Flair: Fashion Collected by Tina Chow; Infra-Apparel; Orientalism: Visions of the East in Western Dress;* and *Haute Couture.* **Essays:** Brioni; Cacharel; Coveri; Gehry; Gibb; Joop; Lapidus; Oldham; Pucci.

**MAUNULA, Leena.** Essayist. Architecture and design critic of *Helsingin Sanomat,* Helsinki, from 1968. **Essay:** Lavonen.

**McDERMOTT, Catherine.** Essayist. Senior lecturer in history of design, Kingston Polytechnic, Kingston upon Thames, Surrey. Chairman, Design History Society, 1981-84. **Essays:** Crosby; Lucienne Day; Franck; Goldfinger; Juhl; Marx; Mathsson; Minale/Tattersfield; Pond; Wealleans.

**McLEAN, Anne.** Essayist. Freelance writer on design. **Essay:** Roch.

**MEGGS, Phillip B.** Essayist. Professor, from 1965, and chairman, from 1974, Department of Communication Arts and Design, Virginia Commonwealth University, Richmond. Senior designer, Reynolds Metals Company, 1965-66; art director, A. H. Robins Company, 1966-68. Author of *A History of Graphic Design,* 1983, and *Typographic Design,* with Robert C. Carter and Ben Day, 1984. **Essays:** Bass; Binder; Brodovich; Cieslewicz; Lubalin; Odermatt/Tissi; Rand; Weingart; Wyman.

**MENARD, Gloria.** Essayist. Principal of Gloria Menard and Associates communications consultants, Montreal; contributing editor, *MacLean's.* Formerly manager of internal communications, for Alcan Aluminum Limited, and editor of *Alcan News.* **Essays:** Harder.

**MERZDORF, Russell.** Essayist. Professor, Department of Creative Arts, Purdue University, West Lafayette, Indiana. **Essays:** Colley.

**MIKLAS, Lois Irene.** Essayist. Intern, 1982-83, and assistant to the program coordinator, 1983-84, Children's Museum, Indianapolis, Indiana; also participant-interpreter, Canner Prairie Pioneer Settlement, Noblesville, Indiana. **Essays:** Carré; Jenkins; Lourié; Jack Martin Smith; Warm; Wheeler.

**MIKOTOWICZ, Tom.** Essayist. Assistant professor of theatre, University of Maine. Associate editor, *Theatre Design and Technology,* 1985-89. **Essays:** Aronson; Fisher; Mong Cho Lee; Polidori; Oliver Smith; Ter-Arutunian.

**MILLIE, Elena.** Essayist. Curator, Poster Collection, Library of Congress, Washington D.C., from 1970. **Essays:** Allner; Sawka.

**MOON, Karen.** Essayist. Design assistant (visual effects) with BBC Television, London, 1974-78 (1975-78, solely on Open University productions); lecturer, History of Art and Design Department, Kingston Polytechnic, Kingston upon Thames, Surrey, 1978-79. **Essays:** Grange; Welch.

**MYERSON, Jeremy.** Essayist. London-based writer on design and author of a number of books, including *Conran Design Guides* and *Design Renaissance*. Visiting professor in contemporary design, De Montfort University. **Essays:** Holscher; Kurlansky; Maurer; Michael McCoy.

**NEUMANN, Eckhard.** Design promotion manager, Rat fur Formgebung (German Design Council), Darmstadt, from 1975. Formerly, advertising manager, Swissair-Germany; creative director for an advertising agency; and manager of communication design for Braun AG, Kronberg; also teacher at several design schools. Founder and co-editor of the annual *Werbung in Deutschland,* from 1964; author of *Functional Graphic Design in the 20s,* 1967; editor of *Bauhaus and Bauhaus People,* 1970. **Essay:** Friedl.

**PAATERO, Kristina.** Essayist. Researcher at the Museum of Finnish Architecture in Helsinki. Assistant editor, *Form Function Finlandy* magazine, 1980-88. Co-author, *The Things Around Us,* 1981; *Arabia,* 1987. **Essay:** Kosonen.

**PACEY, Philip.** Essayist. Art librarian, Preston Polytechnic, Lancashire, from 1975. **Essay:** Logan.

**PALLASMAA, Juhani.** Essayist. Freelance writer and architect, Helsinki. Exhibitions curator, 1968-72, and director, 1983-83, Museum of Finnish Architecture, Helsinki; rector, Institute of Industrial Arts, Helsinki, 1970-72; associate professor, Haile Selassie University, Addis Ababa, 1972-74; state artist and professor, Helsinki, 1983-88. Editor, *Alvar Aalto,* 1977; *Tapio Wirkkala,* 1977; *Alvar Aalto: Furniture,* 1984; *Phenomenon Marimekko,* 1986; *Hvittrask: The Home as a Work of Art,* 1987; *The Language of Wood,* 1987. **Essay:** Bryk.

**PERIAINEN, Tapio.** Essayist. Managing director of the Finnish Society of Crafts and Design. Architect in private practice, Helsinki, 1955-75; research assistant at the Academy of Finland's Council for Social Sciences, 1965-68; advisor to the Mannerheim League for Child Welfare, 1969-71, and head of the Children's Environmental Project, 1972-75. Author of *Nature, Man, Architecture,* 1969; *Goals for Housing Policy,* 1971; and *Recommendations for Playgrounds,* 1972. **Essay:** Eskolin-Nurmesniemi.

**PIETZSCH, Ingeborg.** Essayist. Editor and theatre critic, *Theatre der Zeity,* East Berlin, from 1967. Author of *Werkstatt Theatre* 1975, and *Gardenbengespräche,* 1982. **Essays:** Finke; Hein; Troike.

**PISCIOTTA, Henry.** Essayist. Head of Fine Arts and Special

Collections, Carnegie Mellon University Libraries, from 1982. Doctoral student, Department of Art and Architecture, University of Pittsburgh, from 1994. **Essay:** Hicks.

**POZNER, André.** Essayist. Writer and journalist, Chécy, France. **Essay:** Trauner.

**PULOS, Arthur J.** Essayist and entrant. See his own entry. **Essays:** Blaich; Soloviev.

**REMINGTON, R. Roger.** Essayist. Professor of graphic design, Rochester Institute of Technology, New York. Author of *Nine Pioneers in American Graphic Design,* 1989. **Essays:** Tscherny; Wolf.

**RIDDELL, Richard V.** Essayist. Professor, University of California, San Diego, from 1978; freelance scene and lighting designer, from 1976. Contributing editor, *Theatre Crafts,* 1980. Author of articles on German theatre for *Theatre Crafts,* and other publications. **Essays:** Freyer; Herrmann; Minks.

**ROSENBERG, Alan.** Essayist. Graduated, Fashion Institute of Technology; associate of applied science degree in fashion design, Hunter College of the City University of New York; B.A. in art history, Fashion Institute Technology; M.A. degree in museum studies in applied arts. Director of the Metropolitan Historic Structures Association, for three years, and research fellow in the Costume Institute, Metropolitan Museum of Art. **Essay:** Toikka.

**ROSE, Virginia.** Essayist. Instructor of art and architectural history, Beirut University College, Lebanon, from 1983. **Essays:** Sarpaneva; Stephensen.

**RUSSAC, Patricia A.** Essayist. Freelance writer on art and design. **Essays:** Bernadotte, Fossella, Grear, Landor.

**RUSSELL, Douglas A.** Essayist. Professor of drama, Stanford University, California, from 1961; trainer and educational consultant to the American Conservatory Theatre of San Francisco, from 1973. Director of costume, Oregon Shakespeare Festival, Ashland, 1948-61; also formerly costume designer for the Missouri Repertory Theatre, for The Old Globe in San Diego, California, and for the Berkeley, California, Shakespeare Festival. Vice-commissioner of costume, 1978-82, and board member, United States Institute of Theatre Technology. Author of *Stage Costume Design,* 1973; *Theatrical Style: A Visual Approach to the Theatre,* 1976, *Period Style for the Theatre,* 1980; *An Anthology of Austrian Drama,* 1982; and *Costume History and Style,* 1983. **Essays:** Aldredge; Bay; Gorelik; Heeley; Jacobs; Kerz; Moiseiwitsch; Oenslager; Ponnelle; Robbins; Roth; Zeffirelli; Zipprodt.

**RYKWERT, Joseph.** Essayist. Paul Philippe Cret Professor of Architecture, University of Pennsylvania. **Essay:** Predock.

**SANO, Kunio.** Essayist. Director, Joint Design System, since 1972; lecturer, Kuwazawa Design School, from 1977. Information and Planning Committee chairman, Japan Industrial Designers Association, from 1983; editorial committee member, from 1970, and chairman, 1978-79, *Industrial Design* (Tokyo). Author of *Maker, User and Designer*, 1975, and "Image and Industrial Design," monthly column in *Industrial Engineering* (Tokyo), 1977; editor of *The Futurology of Rice*, 1977, and *The Structure of Dexterity* (Japan Industrial Designers Association thirtieth-anniversary commemorative publication), 1983. **Essays:** Ito; Kimura; Koike; Matsuba; Minagawa; Okada; Sakashita; Sumita; Watanabe; Yanagi.

**SAWKA, Jan.** Entrant and essayist. See his own entry. **Essays:** Fukuda; Hilscher; Kantor; Klimowski; Le Quernec; Matthies; Młodozeniec; Jozef Mroszczak; Marcin Mroszczak; Starowieyski; Swierzy; Tomaszewski; Urbaniec.

**SCHEINMAN, Pamela.** Essayist. Adjunct professor, Department of Fine Arts, Montclair Stage College, New Jersey. Publications editor, Philadelphia Museum of Art, 1975; crafts instructor, Tyler School of Art, Elkins Park, Pennsylvania, 1976-79; Mexico City correspondent, *Craft International*, 1984-85. Contributor to *Threads, Surface Design, Craft International*, and *America Craft*. **Essay:** Hernmarck.

**SCHMID, Helmut.** Essayist. Typographer, designer, and art director, living in Japan. Editor and designer of *Typography Today* 1980, and special issue on Japanese typography, *Typografische Monatsblattery* (St. Gallen, Switzerland), 1973. **Essays:** Ruder; Sugiura.

**SCHÖNBERGER, Angela.** Advisor. Studied history of art, archaeology, and psychology, Munich and Berlin, Ph.D., 1978. Director, Internationales Design Zentrum Berlin, from 1985. Member of various juries and selection committees of national and international design institutions; published numerous books and catalogues on design, including *Designinitiative Sanssouci: Wachstumsimpulse für die neuen Bundesländer,* Berlin, 1994.

**SCHWARTZ, Robert T.** Advisor. Executive director and chief operating officer, Industrial Designers Society of America and its affiliated Worldesign Foundation, from 1990; former head of corporate industrial design and architecture, American Red Cross, 1976-88; former director of Science and Technology Programs, Health Industry Manufacturers Association, 1988-90; testified before Congress to establish a Design Council in the Department of Commerce; official state delegate for Maryland and Virginia during National Arts Advocacy day on Capitol Hill; recipient of five patents and numerous grants, and awards.

**SHARMAN, Lydia Ferrabee.** Essayist. Associate professor, teaching the history and theory of design and the design art seminar in the Department of Design Art, Faculty of Fine Arts, Concordia University. Designer, London, New York, and Montreal; contributor, European and North American design journals, mainly on Canadian design; author, *The Amazing Book of Shapes,* Dorling Kindersley: London, England, 1994. Lithographs, etchings, and embossments have been exhibited in London and Montreal and are in collections in England and Canada. **Essays:** Ball; Gersin.

**SHAW, Paul.** Essayist. Freelance calligrapher, letterer, and designer. Instructor, School of Visual Arts, New York; New

York Institute of Technology Metro Campus; and Long Island University, Brooklyn, New York. Contributor, *Calligraphy Quarterly,* 1978-81, and *Printing News.* Author of articles on calligraphy and printing for *Scripsit, A.B. Bookman's Weekly, Fine Print,* and others. **Essays:** Bernhard; Larcher.

**SIFFORD, Harlan.** Essayist. Art librarian, University of Iowa City, from 1962. Professor of Art, Furman University, Greenville, South Carolina, 1953-54, and Shorter College, Rome, Georgia, 1954-60. Author of *The Alcock Collection of Silver Plate in the University of Iowa Museum of Art,* 1978, and of silver catalogues for *The Owen and Leone Elliot Collection; Selected Works,* Iowa City, 1964, and *The Owen and Leone Elliot Collection,* Iowa City, 1969. **Essays:** Erni; Gernreich; Girard; Anne Klein; Simpson.

**SJÖLANDER, Carin.** Essayist. Staff journalist, Degens Nyheter Newspaper, Stockholm. Formerly, art critic, *Sydsvenska Dagbladety* newspaper, Malmo, 1965-71; editorial staff member, *Form,* Stockholm, 1970-72. **Essay:** Persson-Melin.

**SKELLENGER, Gillion.** Essayist. Freelance wallpaper and fabric designer, Chicago; instructor in Fashion Department, the Art Institute of Chicago, from 1977. **Essays:** Walter Albini; Biagiotti; Fendi; Missoni; Valentino.

**SOLURI, Michael Robert.** Essayist. Professor in photography, Rochester Institute of Technology, Rochester, New York, from 1979; also freelance photographer. **Essays:** Dorfsman, Lois.

**SORJO-SMEDS, Jukka.** Essayist. Copywriter, T:m; Mainosideointi Leena Serlachius advertising agency, Helsinki. Author, *Odours of the Wind* 1983. **Essay:** Vuori.

**SPENCER, Herbert.** Entrant and essayist. See his own entry. **Essay:** Zwart.

**SPENCER, Mafalda.** Essayist. Typographic designer and lecturer on design history, London. Author of *The Book of Numbers* with Herbert Spencer, 1974. **Essay:** Sandberg.

**SPILMAN, Raymond.** Essayist. Director, Raymond Spilman Industrial Design, Connecticut. Staff designer, General Motors, Detroit, 1935-40; product designer in office of Walter Dorwin Teague, New York, 1940-42; director and product designer, at Johnson-Cushing-Nevell, New York, 1942-46. Chairman, president, and director, American Society of Industrial Designer, 1950-62; director, Inter Society Color Council, 1970-72, 1978-78. **Essay:** Vassos.

**STEELE, Gordon.** Essayist. Open University tutor and lecturer on art, architecture, and design history. Education secretary to the Building Centre Trust, 1965-74. Author of articles, mainly on architecture in the Nordic countries and on housing there in Britain, for architectural journals in Britain and Netherlands. **Essays:** Aarnio; Metsovaara; Nurmesniemi; Tapiovaara; Tye.

**STEIMLE, Jerry.** Essayist. Freelance writer, Palo Alto, California. Author of articles for *Communication Arts* (Palo Alto,

California) and Graphis (Zürich). **Essays:** François; Henry Steiner; Testa.

**STRANGER, Ivar.** Essayist. Keeper, West Northway Museum of Applied Art, Bergen, from 1988. Assistant keeper, National Gallery, Oslo, 1981-82; curator, Vest-Agder County Museum, Kristiansand, 1982-88. Author of *Norwegian Studio Ceramics 1890-1914,* 1981. **Essay:** Eckhoff.

**STRZELECKI, Zenobiusz.** Essayist. Specialist in theatrical set and costume design, Warsaw. Author of *Wspolczesna Scenografia Polska/Contemporary Polish Stage Design,* 1983. **Essays:** Gurawski; Serafinowicz; Wierchowicz.

**SUDICK, Barbara.** Essayist. Designer-partner, Nightswander-Sudick design firm, New Haven, Connecticut. Instructor in graphic design, University of New Haven, 1982; University of Hartford, 1982-83. **Essays:** Geissbuhler; James Miho.

**TANAKA, Masaaki.** Essayist and entrant. See his own entry. **Essays:** Hayakawa; Igarashi; Nagai; Nakamura.

**TAYLOR, Benjamin de Brie.** Essayist. Professor, from 1973, and director, 1973-75, Institute of Design, Illinois Institute of Technology, Chicago. Instructor, Pratt Institute, Brooklyn, New York, 1960-68; dean, Parsons School of Design, New York, 1968-70; dean, Herron School of Art, Indiana University, Indianapolis, 1970-73. Author of *Design Lessons from Nature,* 1974. **Essay:** Doblin.

**TOUSSAINT, Jacques.** Essayist. Educated at Institut des Études Économiques et Commerciales and L'École Nationale Supérieure des Beaux Arts. Consultant for Bernini, Carate and Matteo Grassi, Mariano Comense; established, Atelier, a furniture editing company, from 1985; art director, Arbos Company (a producer of objects in recycled paper), from 1994. **Essays:** Bartoli; Castelli Ferrieri; Littell.

**TRIGGS, Teal Ann.** Essayist. Designer, University of Texas Press, Austin, from 1983. **Essays:** Calvin Klein; Massey.

**TULOKAS, Maria.** Essayist. Head of the Textile Design Department, Rhode Island School of Design, Providence. Author of *Fabrics for the 80s,* 1985. **Essay:** Arai.

**UMAÑA, Camilo.** Essayist. Graphic designer, Bogotá, Columbia. **Essay:** Consuegra.

**UNRUH, Delbert.** Essayist. Professor of theatre and film and Director of the University Theatre, University of Kansas, Lawrence. Author of numerous articles on Eastern European design theory in the journal *Theatre Design and Technology* and

of *Towards a New Theatre: The Lectures of Robert Edmond Jones* Limelight Editions, New York, 1992. **Essay:** Vančura.

**VOTOLATO, G.** Essayist. Head of Art History Department, Buckinghamshire College, High Wycombe, from 1980. **Essay:** Basevi.

**WALSH, George.** Essayist. Freelance art and design critic and writer, Chicago. **Essays:** Grapus; Ohl; Stankowski; Tallon.

**WATANABE, Hiroshi.** Essayist. Architect and writer, Tokyo. Member of Kenchiku Keikaku Kobo (Architectural Planning Workshop), Tokyo. Author of *The Japanese Conception of Space.* **Essay:** Yoh.

**WEISS, David W.** Essayist. Professor of drama, from 1954, and Chairman, 1966-75 and 1978-83, Department of Drama, University of Virginia, Charlottesville. Member, board of directors, United States Institute of Theatre Technology, 1966-67, and American Theatre Association, 1976-79; president, Southeastern Theatre Conference, 1972-73. **Essay:** Mielziner.

**WIDMAN, Dag.** Essayist. Director, Prins Eugens Waldemarsudde Art Gallery, Stockholm. Director of Svensk Form (society of industrial design), Stockholm, 1963-65; keeper of the Applied Art and Design Department, at the Nationalmuseum, Stockholm, 1966-80. Author of *Cezanne,* 1957; *Stig Lindberg,* 1962; *Konsthantverk, Konstindustri, Design 1895-1975,* 1975. **Essay:** Hasselberg-Olsson.

**WRÓBLEWSKA, Danuta.** Essayist. Writer on art and design, and advisor on contemporary arts to the Archdiocese Museum, Warsaw. Staff member, *Projekt* (art design magazine), Warsaw, 1956-83. Author of books on Polish graphic art and weaving. **Essay:** Urbański.

**WURMAN, Richard Saul.** Essayist and entrant. See his own entry. **Essay:** Bradford.

**WYLIE, Liz.** Essayist. Lecturer in art history, University of Saskatchewan, Sasktoon. Instructor, York University, Toronto, 1980-81, and Brock University, St. Catherine's, Ontario, 1981-82; editorial assistant, *Artmagazine,* Toronto, 1980-81. Author of reviews and articles for *Artscanada,* Toronto, *Arts Magazine,* New York, *Artmagazine,* Toronto, *The Journal of Canadian Art History,* Montreal, *Photo-Communique,* Toronto, *Vanguard,* Vancouver, and others. **Essays:** Fleming; Gottschalk and Ash International.

**YOUNG, Barbara.** Essayist. Head, Art Department, California Polytechnic State University, San Luis Obispo, from 1983. Senior lecturer, Sheffield City Polytechnic, England, 1980-83. **Essays:** Brandt; Robin Day; Koppel; Mellor; Persson.